# The Top 6000 Companies in Yorkshire and Humberside

**Companies with assets exceeding £3,000,000**

John D Blackburn
Editor

dp

First Edition

Spring 2019

ISBN-13: 978-1-912736-19-5

ISBN-10: 1-912736-19-5



Printed in 8pt Nimbus Sans L

Designed by URW++ Design and Development GmbH

Dellam Publishing Limited

2 Heath Drive, Sutton, Surrey, SM2 5RP

Fax: 020 8770 7478 email: enquiries@dellam.com

SAN: 0177881 EAN/GLN: 5030670177882

# Table of Contents

# Acknowledgements

This is a long and detailed publication containing thousands of facts and figures. It is only to be expected, despite continuous and repeated editing and checking, that errors may occur. In such cases, once we are aware of any, we publish a correction on our website.

**Readers are encouraged to check regularly at www.dellam.com/books for any corrections and updates.**

Although we take extreme care to ensure accuracy and being up-to-date, we cannot accept responsibility for any errors or omissions.

Contains public sector information licensed under Open Government Licence v3.0. from The Charity Commission (England and Wales) and The Charity Commission for Northern Ireland. © Crown Copyright and database right (2018).

Contains information from the Scottish Charity Register supplied by the Office of the Scottish Charity Regulator and licensed under the Open Government Licence v.2.0. © Crown Copyright and database right (2018).

Contains OS data © Crown copyright and database right (2018)

Contains Royal Mail data © Royal Mail copyright and database right (2018)

Contains National Statistics data © Crown copyright and database right (2018)

Contains Office for National Statistics © Crown copyright and database right (2018)

Maps based on those produced by the Office for National Statistics Geography GIS & Mapping Unit (2012 and 2018).

Contains HM Land Registry data © Crown copyright and database right (2018).

Contains Parliamentary information licensed under the Open Parliament Licence v3.0.

House of Commons Library Briefing Papers licensed under the Open Parliament Licence v3.0.

Contains Food Standards Agency data © Crown copyright and database right (2018).

Contains Eurostat data, 1995-2018, copyright European Commission by the Decision of 12 December 2011.

Maps based on produced by ONS Geography GIS & Mapping Unit.

Contains Companies House data supplied under section 47 and 50 of the Copyright, Designs and Patents Act 1988 and Schedule 1 of the Database Regulations (SI 1997/3032).

We appreciate your interest in our publications, and your comments and suggestions are always welcome. Please contact us at enquiries@dellam.com.

Scotland
Northern Ireland
North East (England)
North West (England)
Yorkshire and The Humber
East Midlands (England)
West Midlands (England)
Wales
East of England
See London Inset
South East (England)
South West (England)

Scotland
North East (England)
North West (England)
Yorkshire and The Humber
Wales
West Midlands (England)
East Midlands (England)
East of England
London
South East (England)
South West (England)

# Introduction

This study looks at all companies registered in Yorkshire and Humberside and where their total assets are more than £3,000,000.

The region has a population of 5.5 million in 2017 with the UK being 66 million.

There are seven cities in the region: Bradford, Hull, Leeds, Ripon, Sheffield, Wakefield and York; the largest towns being Barnsley, Doncaster, Grimsby, Halifax, Harrogate, Huddersfield and Scunthorpe.

The aim of this study is to provide an overview of the key movers and shakers in the Yorkshire and Humberside corporate sector. Only key data has been isolated, particularly the company's net worth and total assets, but also its full name, date incorporated, registered office, activities, shareholders, directors (with date of birth, occupation and nationality) and number of employees.

Two indicators of size are used: net worth and total assets. These are preferable to turnover which is influenced by profit margins and whether the companies are capital or labour intensive.

A short summary of the corporate sector in Yorkshire and Humberside:

The region did rely on large-scale heavy industry, manufacturing, textiles and agriculture but is now moving to more diverse markets. Manufacturing currently accounts for just under a fifth of the region's economy. It has a higher percentage of companies in distribution, hospitality, manufacturing and public administration than in other regions whilst there is a smaller proportion in banking, finance and insurance. It is strong in food and drink, basic metals and metal products. It also performs well in medicinal and pharmaceutical products, organic chemicals and general industrial machinery, which are the region's top three exporting sectors.

There were 419,000 businesses in 2017 (UK 5,695,000). The number of new businesses in 2017 was 22,600 (up 11% on 2016) and the number that ceased trading was 23,935 (up 12% on 2016). Manufacturing jobs in 2018 was 9.9% of all jobs and public sector jobs was 17.7%.

Total regional output (GVA) in 2017 was £112 billion (UK £1,748 billion) and total output (GVA) per head was £20,678 (UK £26,621).

Cumulative economic growth from 2010 to 2016 was 12% in UK whereas the weakest growth was this region at 7% with the North East at 4%. Between 1998 and 2016, slowest total growth over this 18-year period was this region (29%), the North East and the West Midlands (both 30%); London in comparison was 71%.

The unemployment rate May-July 2018 was 4.4%.

The region's investment in R&D is one of the lowest in the UK at 1.14% of GDP against UK average of 1.67%.

Standard cataloguing guidelines for company names in the profile section have been used, but there will be occurrences when the name may not be strictly alphabetical. A certain licence was adopted where it was felt that strictly alphabetical could lead to improper cataloguing. Some company names have been shortened in the league tables for aesthetic reasons.

John D Blackburn
Editor

*This page is intentionally left blank*

# Total Assets League Table

| Company | Value |
|---|---|
| Aviva Life & Pensions UK Limited | £311,367,991,296 |
| WMT Global Holdings LLP | £57,082,150,912 |
| CYBG PLC | £43,456,000,000 |
| Accord Mortgages Limited | £19,933,483,008 |
| UK Asset Resolution Limited | £19,812,999,168 |
| Asda Group Limited | £16,451,699,712 |
| Broadstreet Great Wilson Europe Limited | £14,449,500,160 |
| Aptiv Global Investments UK LLP | £13,120,447,488 |
| Bradford & Bingley PLC | £11,857,000,448 |
| Aptiv Luxembourg Holdings (UK) Limited | £10,558,920,704 |
| Asda Stores Limited | £10,425,100,288 |
| Aviva Life Holdings UK Limited | £10,043,778,048 |
| Kelda Eurobond Co Limited | £9,855,200,256 |
| Asda Holdings UK Limited | £9,804,635,136 |
| Wm Morrison Supermarkets P L C | £9,667,000,320 |
| The Mortgage Business PLC | £9,653,497,856 |
| Barmston Developments Limited | £9,379,686,400 |
| Kelda Finance (No.1) Limited | £9,222,899,712 |
| Yorkshire Water Services Limited | £9,004,600,320 |
| U K Insurance Limited | £8,940,399,616 |
| Wal-Mart Stores (UK) Limited | £8,857,400,320 |
| Gordons LLP | £8,831,439,872 |
| Aptiv International Holdings UK Two LLP | £7,905,390,080 |
| Arris International PLC | £7,624,257,024 |
| Orvet UK | £6,602,298,880 |
| Aviva Erfa 15 UK Limited | £6,540,103,168 |
| Aptiv Financial Investment Services (UK) Limited | £6,520,739,328 |
| Aptiv International Holdings (UK) LLP | £5,012,650,496 |
| Persimmon Public Limited Company | £4,756,800,000 |
| Aptiv Asia Pacific Holdings (UK) LLP | £4,729,740,288 |
| McLagan Investments Limited | £4,518,543,872 |
| Persimmon Homes Limited | £4,504,612,864 |
| Safeway Stores Limited | £4,403,999,744 |
| HBOS Covered Bonds LLP | £4,215,993,088 |
| Safeway Limited | £3,827,000,064 |
| Wm Morrison Supermarkets Holdings Limited | £3,560,000,000 |
| Drax Group PLC | £3,517,600,000 |
| Aptiv International Financial Services (UK) LLP | £3,501,495,040 |
| Froneri Limited | £3,390,711,040 |
| Mortgage Express | £3,366,981,888 |
| Dart Group PLC | £3,125,600,000 |
| Drax Corporate Limited | £3,076,291,072 |
| Northern Gas Networks Limited | £2,988,598,016 |
| Provident Financial PLC | £2,965,900,032 |
| Northern Gas Networks Holdings Limited | £2,949,750,016 |
| Northern Foods Limited | £2,824,233,984 |
| Yorkshire Building Society Covered Bonds LLP | £2,584,763,904 |
| Teva Acquisition Limited | £2,490,702,080 |
| Drax Power Limited | £2,427,275,008 |
| Aptiv Latin America Holdings (UK) LLP | £2,333,206,528 |
| Jet2.Com Limited | £2,224,199,936 |
| Croda Investments No 3 Limited | £2,201,199,104 |
| Froneri International Limited | £1,859,410,432 |
| Vanquis Bank Limited | £1,855,100,032 |
| Stores Group Limited | £1,850,067,968 |
| Persimmon Finance Limited | £1,847,659,008 |
| Drax Group Holdings Limited | £1,774,241,024 |
| Leeds Building Society Covered Bonds LLP | £1,761,878,016 |
| Abbot Group Limited | £1,673,629,696 |
| Siccar Point Energy Limited | £1,668,652,672 |
| Siccar Point Energy (Holdings) Limited | £1,665,017,472 |
| Drax Smart Generation Holdco Limited | £1,653,528,960 |
| Croda International Public Limited Company | £1,648,700,032 |
| Yorkshire Water Services Finance Limited | £1,646,716,032 |
| Clydesdale Covered Bonds No.2 LLP | £1,599,218,944 |
| Zenith Automotive Holdings Limited | £1,511,522,944 |
| Norton Healthcare Limited | £1,498,274,944 |
| Boparan Holdings Limited | £1,451,399,936 |
| KCA Deutag Alpha Limited | £1,400,145,152 |
| AGS Airports Limited | £1,398,000,000 |
| AGS Airports Holdings Limited | £1,398,000,000 |
| Charles Church Developments Limited | £1,394,449,024 |
| Arla Foods Limited | £1,381,943,040 |
| Siccar Point Energy E & P Limited | £1,348,219,392 |
| Jet2holidays Limited | £1,345,900,032 |
| International Personal Finance PLC | £1,342,599,936 |
| Persimmon Holdings Limited | £1,328,592,000 |
| McCain UK H1 Limited | £1,301,148,032 |
| Simon Bidco Limited | £1,285,280,000 |
| McCain UK H2 Limited | £1,283,360,000 |
| Ardagh Holdings (UK) Limited | £1,200,614,016 |
| Aptiv European Holdings (UK) Limited | £1,149,200,768 |
| KCAD Holdings I Limited | £1,129,836,800 |
| Northgate PLC | £1,118,932,992 |
| Aptiv Financial Holdings (UK) LLP | £1,104,040,448 |
| Principal Hotels Topco 1 Limited | £1,092,055,040 |
| Yorkshire Bank Home Loans Limited | £1,080,285,056 |
| Northgate (Europe) Limited | £1,062,262,016 |
| Airport Holdings NDH1 Limited | £1,049,000,000 |
| Kelda Group Limited | £1,011,601,024 |
| Metis Bidco Limited | £981,692,992 |
| Kelda Finance (No.2) Limited | £977,777,024 |
| Stericycle International Holdings Limited | £970,721,152 |
| Zeus Bidco Limited | £940,974,016 |
| Shree Investment PLC | £934,681,024 |
| Northern Gas Networks Finance PLC | £923,840,000 |
| Arris Global Ltd. | £912,290,112 |
| British Steel Holdings Limited | £897,830,976 |
| Aviva Equity Release UK Limited | £885,800,000 |
| Boparan Finance PLC | £874,718,016 |
| Total Lindsey Oil Refinery Limited | £872,945,984 |
| Fenner International Limited | £861,675,008 |
| Indivior UK Limited | £848,174,016 |
| Lowell Portfolio I Ltd | £825,873,984 |
| KCAD Holdings II Limited | £799,920,000 |
| Northgate Vehicle Hire Limited | £794,702,976 |
| Cyan Bidco Limited | £791,876,992 |
| Langley Holdings PLC | £791,284,864 |
| Farmers Boy Limited | £782,220,992 |
| Yorkshire Water Services Holdings Limited | £778,318,976 |
| Arla Foods UK Holding Limited | £776,121,024 |
| Jet2 Transport Services Limited | £775,041,984 |
| DFS Furniture PLC | £774,200,000 |
| 2 Sisters Food Group Limited | £773,107,968 |
| T.J.Smith and Nephew,Limited | £770,148,992 |
| Fleetcor UK Acquisition Limited | £740,777,984 |
| Optimisation Investments Limited | £728,412,992 |
| British Steel Limited | £724,134,016 |
| KCA Deutag Alpha II Limited | £722,623,808 |
| Ardagh Glass Limited | £720,115,008 |
| Rome Investco Ltd | £716,057,984 |
| Fenner Group Holdings Limited | £711,100,032 |
| DFS Furniture Holdings PLC | £703,000,000 |
| Delphi Automotive Operations UK Limited | £702,000,000 |
| Millennium Inorganic Chemicals Overseas Holdings | £698,991,872 |
| IPF Financing Limited | £691,630,208 |
| KCA Deutag UK Finance PLC | £673,424,512 |
| NHP Securities No. 3 Limited | £672,915,008 |
| Arrow Enterprise Computing Solutions Limited | £670,864,000 |
| Valad Diversified LLP | £660,131,328 |
| BH Acquisitions Limited | £657,078,016 |
| Cranswick PLC | £651,299,968 |
| Provident Personal Credit Limited | £650,200,000 |
| Titan Global Finance PLC | £644,104,512 |
| Premier Farnell Limited | £643,708,032 |
| Simon Midco Limited | £640,769,024 |
| Arla Foods UK PLC | £637,915,008 |
| James Fisher and Sons Public Limited Company | £618,600,000 |
| Crown Acquisition Topco Limited | £611,483,008 |
| Actavis Holdings UK II Limited | £603,851,008 |
| Crown Acquisition Midco 2 Limited | £603,542,976 |
| Polypipe Group PLC | £602,800,000 |
| Aptiv Holdfi (UK) Limited | £594,188,480 |
| Linpac Packaging Limited | £591,017,984 |

| Company | Value |
|---|---|
| Dart Leasing & Finance Limited | £589,579,136 |
| Libra Careco Limited | £586,443,200 |
| Neerock Limited | £581,259,008 |
| Northgate (CB) Limited | £567,025,024 |
| Teva UK Limited | £561,601,984 |
| Linpac Group Holdings Limited | £559,849,024 |
| Drax Finco PLC | £554,318,016 |
| BAA Lynton Limited | £552,683,008 |
| Amber Homeloans Limited | £548,196,992 |
| Head UK Ltd | £541,217,600 |
| Keepmoat Limited | £538,776,000 |
| Polypipe Limited | £537,100,032 |
| Croda Overseas Holdings Limited | £536,140,160 |
| Hallmark Cards PLC | £533,958,016 |
| International Personal Finance Investments Ltd | £533,035,008 |
| HC-ONE Oval Limited | £532,830,016 |
| Cristal Pigment UK Limited | £528,820,000 |
| Castle 1 Limited | £527,662,016 |
| Young's Seafood Limited | £526,859,008 |
| Atlantic Acquisition Holdings UK Limited | £525,318,016 |
| Marshalls Group Limited | £524,132,000 |
| Hain Frozen Foods UK Limited | £518,023,008 |
| Zeus Finco Limited | £516,009,984 |
| Croda Europe Limited | £513,164,992 |
| Convenience Foods Limited | £512,590,016 |
| Gestamp Tallent Limited | £511,540,000 |
| CCL Syrinx (UK) Limited | £511,204,416 |
| Zeus Midco Limited | £507,048,992 |
| Keystone Midco Limited | £504,443,008 |
| Keystone JVCO Limited | £503,755,008 |
| SPH 2011 Limited | £503,477,792 |
| Siccar Point Energy Finance Limited | £492,055,744 |
| CCL Industries (U.K.) Limited | £483,079,008 |
| Crown Acquisition Bidco Limited | £471,912,992 |
| Croda Investments No 2 Limited | £470,505,952 |
| InOne Holdings Limited | £465,952,000 |
| The Hain Daniels Group Limited | £455,222,880 |
| Keepmoat Homes Limited | £452,708,000 |
| Incommunities Group Limited | £452,579,008 |
| Ever 2010 Limited | £450,774,016 |
| Drax Smart Supply Holdco Limited | £449,884,992 |
| Tunstall Healthcare Group Limited | £448,660,992 |
| Abbot Holdings Limited | £448,204,992 |
| Wm Morrison Produce Limited | £448,190,016 |
| Non-Standard Finance PLC | £447,908,000 |
| Aviva Life Services UK Limited | £447,574,016 |
| Card Factory PLC | £446,500,000 |
| VP PLC | £440,038,016 |
| Premier Farnell UK Limited | £439,047,008 |
| Actavis UK Group Limited | £439,019,008 |
| Nufarm UK Limited | £438,000,992 |
| DB Cargo (UK) Limited | £437,000,000 |
| Marshalls Mono Limited | £436,910,016 |
| Ackers P Investment Company Limited | £433,584,000 |
| Millennium Inorganic Chemicals UK Holdings Ltd | £432,994,464 |
| Drax Smart Sourcing Holdco Limited | £432,537,760 |
| JCT600 Limited | £431,950,016 |
| CCL Syrinx (UK Holding) Limited | £431,160,672 |
| GD Global Holdings UK II Limited | £425,850,304 |
| Haven Power Limited | £424,048,992 |
| Libra Careco CH2 Propco Limited | £422,870,016 |
| JLA Debtco Limited | £418,547,008 |
| Provident Financial Management Services Limited | £417,500,000 |
| Manheim Global Management UK Limited | £416,267,008 |
| Marshalls PLC | £415,446,016 |
| Ballyvesey Holdings Limited | £413,624,768 |
| AGS Airports Investments Limited | £411,000,000 |
| Engie Power Limited | £406,560,000 |
| The Burwood House Group Limited | £403,814,016 |
| Cranswick Country Foods PLC | £401,519,008 |
| Tunstall Group Limited | £399,606,016 |
| Zaic - A Limited | £394,169,632 |
| Farnell Holding Limited | £387,835,008 |
| IPF Financial Services Limited | £380,622,848 |
| Stericycle International, Ltd. | £379,075,008 |
| Tunstall Group Holdings Limited | £378,345,984 |
| Tunstall Group Acquisition Limited | £377,736,992 |
| Shepherd Building Group Limited | £377,500,000 |
| Gym Topco Limited | £374,880,992 |
| CF Bidco Limited | £371,140,992 |
| NHP Limited | £370,082,240 |
| Brenntag UK Holding Limited | £368,656,000 |
| Croda Investments Limited | £366,340,000 |
| Centrica Offshore UK Limited | £366,168,000 |
| GHD Group Holdings Limited | £360,796,992 |
| PPDI Assetco Limited | £359,000,704 |
| Dechra Limited | £355,960,992 |
| Hadrian Bidco 2 Limited | £354,865,984 |
| Wavin Limited | £353,940,992 |
| Lion/Gloria Bidco Limited | £353,334,016 |
| Portakabin Limited | £351,055,008 |
| Cardale PFI Investments Limited | £350,339,904 |
| Hadrian Bidco Limited | £348,416,992 |
| PPDI Finance Limited | £346,520,192 |
| Stadium Parkgate (Holdings) Limited | £337,031,200 |
| Evans Management Limited | £336,796,864 |
| Nobia Holdings UK Limited | £335,708,992 |
| Communisis Limited | £327,335,008 |
| KCOM Holdings Limited | £326,521,984 |
| DFS Trading Limited | £326,100,000 |
| NG Bailey Group Limited | £314,800,000 |
| Broadland Properties Limited | £313,428,000 |
| Principal Hotels Topco 3 Limited | £312,675,008 |
| Zenith Vehicle Contracts Limited | £312,025,984 |
| Histon Sweet Spreads Limited | £311,652,000 |
| Glid Wind Farms Topco Limited | £309,873,984 |
| Principal Hayley Limited | £308,863,008 |
| Cristal Inorganic Chemicals UK Limited | £305,355,008 |
| Principal Hotel Company Limited | £303,343,008 |
| Libra Careco Investments 1 Limited | £302,528,736 |
| TMD Friction Holdings (UK) Ltd | £301,074,112 |
| M.K.M. Building Supplies (Group) Limited | £299,198,016 |
| TGH Acquisitions Limited | £299,102,016 |
| TGH Investments Limited | £298,462,016 |
| Eneco UK Limited | £298,342,528 |
| K & A Merger Limited | £297,492,992 |
| Ithaca Petroleum Limited | £295,589,824 |
| North Yorkshire Mortgages Limited | £293,478,016 |
| Crown Acquisition Midco Limited | £291,612,000 |
| Interactive Investor Services Limited | £289,913,984 |
| Beverley House Investments Limited | £287,383,008 |
| Linpac Finance Limited | £286,167,008 |
| KCOM Group Public Limited Company | £286,041,984 |
| R & R Ice Cream UK Limited | £285,327,008 |
| Renew Holdings PLC. | £284,444,000 |
| Tunstall Healthcare (UK) Limited | £280,566,016 |
| Connells Limited | £280,401,984 |
| Element UK Topco Limited | £279,800,000 |
| Element UK Midco Limited | £279,800,000 |
| Masco Corporation Limited | £277,832,000 |
| Clayton Dewandre Holdings Limited | £272,478,688 |
| Saltend Cogeneration Company Limited | £269,847,008 |
| Riviera Acquisitions Limited | £269,595,904 |
| New R & R Ice Cream Limited | £268,284,784 |
| Pure Gym Limited | £267,035,008 |
| HBOS Investment Fund Managers Limited | £264,628,992 |
| International Procurement and Logistics Limited | £260,690,000 |
| Halifax General Insurance Services Limited | £260,447,008 |
| Together Housing Finance PLC | £258,434,000 |
| Manheim Holdings Limited | £258,188,000 |
| Leeds Bradford Airport Limited | £258,012,000 |
| SSP Topco Limited | £257,456,000 |
| Dalmore Capital (Issuer 1) Limited | £255,219,216 |
| Northern Foods Grocery Group Limited | £254,975,008 |

| Company | Turnover |
|---|---|
| Riviera Topco Limited | £254,074,176 |
| Severfield PLC | £253,707,008 |
| Ulixes Limited | £252,112,992 |
| Dalmore Capital (Para 1) Limited | £249,147,152 |
| Acis Group Limited | £248,668,992 |
| Motors Insurance Company Limited | £246,604,000 |
| McCain Foods (G.B.) Limited | £246,008,992 |
| Scientific Games International Holdings Ltd | £243,448,992 |
| Bannatyne Fitness Limited | £242,144,992 |
| PIB Group Limited | £240,946,000 |
| Siccar Point Energy U.K. Limited | £239,940,480 |
| Ideal Homes Holdings Limited | £239,766,000 |
| Zenith Remarketing Limited | £236,410,000 |
| BBRG Finance (UK) Ltd. | £235,947,072 |
| Turner & Townsend Limited | £235,692,000 |
| Ideal Boilers Limited | £235,566,000 |
| Gardner Denver Holdings Limited | £234,855,392 |
| SigmaKalon (BC) UK Limited | £233,300,000 |
| Centrica Storage Limited | £233,000,000 |
| Turner & Townsend Partners LLP | £232,791,008 |
| The West Retail Group Limited | £230,448,112 |
| Yara UK Limited | £225,638,000 |
| Decidebloom Limited | £224,798,000 |
| LBIA Holding Limited | £224,772,992 |
| R & R PIK Limited | £224,768,656 |
| SSP Midco 2 Limited | £224,683,008 |
| DVV Investco Limited | £224,646,000 |
| KCA Deutag Drilling Group Limited | £224,063,008 |
| Callcredit Limited | £222,332,000 |
| Outwood Grange Academies Trust | £221,362,000 |
| Gardner Denver Industries Ltd | £220,029,664 |
| Wavin UK (Holdings) Limited | £220,024,000 |
| Grattan Public Limited Company | £219,515,008 |
| SigmaKalon UK Holding Limited | £218,700,000 |
| Hermes Parcelnet Limited | £218,484,000 |
| Tunstall Holdings Limited | £216,888,000 |
| Delta Academies Trust | £215,894,000 |
| Depuy International Limited | £214,067,008 |
| BOS (Shared Appreciation Mortgages) No. 4 PLC | £213,753,504 |
| GHD BondCo PLC | £213,357,280 |
| Halifax Financial Services (Holdings) Limited | £210,926,000 |
| Ideal Standard Holdings (BC) UK Ltd | £209,936,000 |
| DB Cargo (UK) Holdings Limited | £207,000,000 |
| Sulzer (UK) Holdings Limited | £206,959,008 |
| McJunkin Red Man UK Ltd | £206,370,944 |
| UKIOSH Ltd. | £205,976,640 |
| Rome Holdco Ltd | £205,564,000 |
| Tunstall Group Finance Limited | £205,084,992 |
| Saria Limited | £204,424,336 |
| Diamond Holdco 7 Limited | £203,200,000 |
| Opus Energy Limited | £201,091,008 |
| Actavis Holdings UK Ltd. | £200,594,000 |
| SSP Limited | £199,524,000 |
| Asda Financial Services Limited | £199,371,008 |
| Kelda Finance (No.3) PLC | £199,023,008 |
| Communisis UK Limited | £198,235,008 |
| Arla Foods Cheese Company Limited | £197,992,992 |
| BBRG Production (UK) Ltd. | £197,856,000 |
| Diamond Holdco 2 Limited | £197,300,000 |
| EWH Holdco Limited | £196,611,008 |
| Pipe Holdings PLC | £196,124,992 |
| Energy Works (Hull) Limited | £195,052,000 |
| SSP Bidco Limited | £194,844,000 |
| Barrett Steel Limited | £194,532,000 |
| PPG Architectural Coatings UK Limited | £193,640,992 |
| Libra Careco CH3 Propco Limited | £193,359,008 |
| Stericycle International Holdings Canada Limited | £193,212,992 |
| Nisa Retail Limited | £193,080,000 |
| Leeds Diocesan Board of Finance | £192,356,992 |
| Redruth Holdings Limited | £191,944,320 |
| TCS Holdings Limited | £191,937,152 |
| M.K.M. BS (Holdings) 3 Limited | £191,589,088 |

| Company | Turnover |
|---|---|
| Ideal Standard (UK) Limited | £191,520,992 |
| SSP Midco 1 Limited | £191,496,992 |
| Univar UK Limited | £190,382,000 |
| Knaresborough Investments Limited | £189,714,000 |
| Ruby Acquisitions Limited | £187,855,008 |
| Bridon-Bekaert Ropes Group (UK) Ltd | £186,019,248 |
| Proactis Holdings PLC | £185,496,000 |
| Andrew Marr International Limited | £184,164,992 |
| Keadby Generation Limited | £183,900,000 |
| Wren Kitchens Limited | £183,475,712 |
| Principal Hayley Group Limited | £183,435,008 |
| Kinetic Worldwide Limited | £183,257,792 |
| Clipper Logistics PLC | £183,248,000 |
| Lowell Finance Holdings Limited | £182,963,008 |
| De Vere Limited | £181,735,008 |
| IHS Lothian Corporate Holdings Limited | £180,534,000 |
| Jemella Limited | £180,370,000 |
| Emis Group PLC | £179,879,008 |
| Brenntag UK Limited | £179,372,992 |
| Poundstretcher Limited | £179,085,936 |
| NHP Securities No. 1 Limited | £179,075,328 |
| Marshall Holdings Limited | £178,856,992 |
| Manheim Limited | £178,246,000 |
| Non-Standard Finance Subsidiary III Limited | £176,291,008 |
| BBRG Operations (UK) Ltd. | £176,279,408 |
| BBRG (Subsidiary) Ltd | £176,279,408 |
| BBRG (Purchaser) Ltd | £176,279,408 |
| Dunhills (Pontefract) P L C | £176,239,808 |
| Cranswick Convenience Foods Limited | £175,806,000 |
| Cap Hpi Limited | £175,327,008 |
| Lighthouse UkCo 6 (Treasury) Limited | £175,070,000 |
| UK Fisheries Limited | £174,440,224 |
| IPF International Limited | £173,278,000 |
| Gym Bidco Limited | £172,098,000 |
| Island Wharf (300) Limited | £171,656,992 |
| Teva UK Holdings Limited | £170,868,000 |
| William Jackson Food Group Limited | £170,280,992 |
| HPI Limited | £168,931,008 |
| AAK (UK) Limited | £168,078,000 |
| Project Aqua Bidco Limited | £166,758,000 |
| Conquest Bidco Limited | £166,508,000 |
| Pegler Yorkshire Group Limited | £165,936,992 |
| Lion/Gloria Midco 2 Limited | £165,412,992 |
| Arco Limited | £164,059,008 |
| Castlecrafts Limited | £163,714,000 |
| ASD Limited | £162,987,008 |
| Lion/Gloria Midco Limited | £162,912,000 |
| Apollo Support Services Group Limited | £162,647,008 |
| LA 2012 Limited | £162,075,008 |
| Linpac Senior Holdings Limited | £161,852,576 |
| HC-ONE Limited | £161,444,000 |
| Scientific Games International Limited | £160,915,008 |
| GD Aria Holdings #2 Limited | £160,359,152 |
| Persimmon Shared Equity Limited | £160,288,992 |
| Carclo PLC | £160,087,008 |
| Kalon Investment Company Limited | £160,000,000 |
| BBRG Holding (UK) Ltd | £159,747,552 |
| Bettys & Taylors Group Ltd | £159,559,008 |
| Hayley Conference Centres Acquisitions Limited | £159,500,992 |
| Leasedrive Limited | £159,344,992 |
| C H Jones Limited | £159,168,992 |
| Persimmon Developments (No 5) Limited | £158,756,992 |
| NG Bailey Limited | £158,464,992 |
| White Rose (Leeds) Limited | £157,780,880 |
| MMCG Holdings Limited | £157,572,000 |
| Commercial Development Projects Limited | £156,766,000 |
| Redmayne-Bentley LLP | £156,738,624 |
| Bond Street Real Estate Holdings Limited | £156,491,296 |
| Callcredit Information Group Limited | £156,140,000 |
| KCH (Holdings) Limited | £155,716,992 |
| Bridon Holdings Limited | £155,476,000 |
| Total Downstream UK PLC | £155,406,000 |

| Company | Value | Company | Value |
|---|---|---|---|
| SPX International Limited | £155,188,000 | Drifford Group Limited | £127,326,000 |
| High Point Estates Ltd. | £154,814,688 | Harron Group Limited | £127,229,000 |
| Project Aqua Topco Limited | £154,470,000 | Encon Limited | £127,196,000 |
| ADP Primary Care Services Limited | £153,772,928 | Encon Insulation Limited | £124,362,000 |
| AFI Topco Limited | £152,560,992 | Vetpartners UK Holdings Ltd. | £124,149,576 |
| Allamhouse Limited | £152,432,848 | IPN Topco Limited | £124,108,288 |
| Gands (U.K.) | £152,284,992 | Optimisation Developments Limited | £123,627,000 |
| Animalcare Group PLC | £151,272,992 | TPP Finance Limited | £123,303,680 |
| Highstone Estates (Kidderminster) Limited | £151,183,040 | Rushbond PLC | £123,159,008 |
| TMD Friction UK Limited | £150,936,000 | Guardian Industries U.K. Limited | £122,736,000 |
| M.K.M. Building Supplies (Holdings) Limited | £150,307,008 | Lynn Wind Farm Limited | £122,575,000 |
| Fuel Card Services Limited | £150,231,008 | Hire Station Limited | £122,384,000 |
| ADP Primary Care Acquisitions Limited | £149,346,352 | JCT600 (Properties) Limited | £122,349,000 |
| Element UK Bidco Limited | £149,200,000 | Armitage Shanks Ltd | £121,669,000 |
| Cavaghan & Gray Limited | £148,972,000 | State Bidco Limited | £121,658,000 |
| Lion/Gloria Midco 3 Limited | £148,374,000 | Tandem 1987 Limited | £121,148,240 |
| Lion/Gloria Holdco Limited | £148,279,008 | Strata Homes Limited | £121,086,000 |
| York St John University | £148,270,000 | Strata Homes Holdings Limited | £121,086,000 |
| Island Wharf (100) Limited | £146,724,000 | Tollbar Multi Academy Trust | £120,580,000 |
| Stadium Retail (Holdings) Limited | £146,593,472 | Wesco Aircraft Europe, Ltd | £120,411,000 |
| Diamond Resorts (Europe) Limited | £145,904,992 | John Cotton Group Limited | £120,162,000 |
| First West Yorkshire Limited | £144,775,008 | Freemans Public Limited Company | £119,725,000 |
| Student Loans Company Limited | £144,728,992 | Fairbriar Real Estate Limited | £119,147,808 |
| Nippon Gohsei UK Ltd. | £144,577,264 | Thornton & Ross Limited | £119,136,000 |
| President Energy PLC | £144,096,416 | Skipton Business Finance Limited | £118,995,400 |
| Park Leisure Group Limited | £142,045,456 | Engie Gas Limited | £118,549,000 |
| Serviced Dispense Equipment Limited | £141,040,992 | Park Leisure 2000 Limited | £118,243,992 |
| London Security PLC. | £140,763,008 | Bandwood Limited | £117,940,000 |
| Northern Foods Finance Limited | £140,612,000 | Speedboat Holdco Limited | £117,827,000 |
| Northgate (CB 2) Limited | £140,232,992 | Beaumont House Properties Limited | £117,787,000 |
| De Vere Venues Properties Limited | £140,028,992 | Skipton Group Holdings Limited | £117,420,000 |
| Lanes Group PLC | £140,026,576 | J.R. Rix & Sons Limited | £117,239,224 |
| Yorkshire Housing Finance PLC | £140,003,008 | Masco UK Window Group Limited | £117,109,000 |
| Arris International IP Ltd | £139,804,160 | Speedboat Acquisitionco Limited | £116,901,000 |
| Hestview Limited | £139,688,000 | Thorpe Park Holdings Limited | £116,716,000 |
| Allied Glass Containers Limited | £139,652,992 | Nufarm Crop Products UK Limited | £116,646,000 |
| Ardagh Glass (UK) Limited | £137,658,000 | TCS Properties Limited | £116,425,048 |
| Caddick Group PLC | £137,480,000 | Gardner Denver International Ltd | £116,281,200 |
| IPF Holdings Limited | £137,332,000 | Southgate - Dan at Spyglass Hill - Bidco Limited | £115,435,000 |
| Gym Midco Limited | £135,944,992 | Howarth Timber Group Limited | £115,232,000 |
| Gym Midco 2 Limited | £135,944,992 | Group Auto Union UK and Ireland Limited | £115,125,920 |
| Redcentric PLC | £135,599,008 | Hesco Group Limited | £114,990,744 |
| Borgwarner Limited | £134,960,000 | The Gorse Academies Trust | £114,599,000 |
| Q-Park Limited | £134,887,312 | The Education Alliance | £114,375,000 |
| Automotive Chassis Products UK Limited | £134,648,992 | Keystone Topco Limited | £113,879,000 |
| Serviced Dispense Equipment (Holdings) Limited | £133,512,000 | Bristan Group Limited | £113,149,904 |
| Evans Property Holdings Limited | £133,427,616 | Lowell Group Limited | £113,017,000 |
| TCS Freehold Investments Limited | £132,934,352 | Lowell Funding Limited | £112,839,000 |
| BOS (Shared Appreciation Mortgages) No. 2 PLC | £132,797,056 | Dr. Oetker (UK) Limited | £112,662,000 |
| Aptiv Financial Services (UK) Limited | £132,638,200 | DC3 (Issuer) Limited | £112,382,664 |
| Dixondale Limited | £132,260,952 | DC3 (Assetco) Limited | £112,382,664 |
| Borgwarner Holdings Limited | £132,127,000 | CYB Intermediaries Limited | £111,651,000 |
| Strata Homes Yorkshire Limited | £132,049,000 | SNF (UK) Limited | £111,250,928 |
| Interactive Investor Holdings Limited | £131,677,000 | Element14 Finance UK Limited | £110,437,592 |
| Kexgill Limited | £131,030,448 | Lowell Acquisitions Limited | £109,965,000 |
| Park Lane Properties (Leeds) Limited | £130,795,376 | TPPH (Leeds) Limited | £109,793,800 |
| GD Aria Holdings Limited | £130,660,352 | Freemans Grattan Holdings Limited | £109,669,000 |
| Wykeland Group Limited | £130,508,288 | FC Beamish Bidco Ltd | £109,660,432 |
| Ardagh Metal Packaging UK Limited | £130,476,000 | Power4all Limited | £108,909,000 |
| Diamond Resorts (Holdings) Limited | £129,410,000 | IPN Bidco Limited | £108,688,256 |
| Covance Laboratories Limited | £129,157,000 | David Brown Group Limited | £108,347,000 |
| Centrica Storage Holdings Limited | £128,684,000 | The Fuelcard Company UK Limited | £107,867,000 |
| SRCL Limited | £128,540,000 | Egton Medical Information Systems Limited | £107,616,688 |
| Severfield (UK) Limited | £128,283,000 | Gardner Denver Ltd | £106,573,000 |
| Daniels Chilled Foods Limited | £128,186,000 | Hornbeam Park Developments Limited | £106,295,744 |
| De Vere 2 Limited | £128,146,000 | Camphill Village Trust Limited (The) | £106,047,000 |
| Sportswift Limited | £128,105,000 | Quad Bidco Limited | £105,987,000 |
| PFI Para (Holdings) Limited | £127,941,920 | KCA European Holdings Limited | £105,903,000 |
| Skirfare Investments Limited | £127,618,672 | Dewhirst Group Limited | £105,796,000 |
| Redcentric Solutions Limited | £127,581,000 | Southgate - Dan at Spyglass Hill - Propco 2 Limited | £105,573,624 |
| Harron Homes Limited | £127,580,000 | M. K. M. Building Supplies Limited | £105,353,000 |
| Swift Acquisitions Limited | £127,491,768 | Stadium (Newport) Limited | £105,287,552 |

| Company | Turnover |
|---|---|
| Deborah Services (Holdings) Limited | £105,279,000 |
| Sedalcol UK Limited | £105,026,800 |
| Sulzer Pumps (UK) Limited | £104,992,000 |
| Pipe Holdings 2 Limited | £104,700,000 |
| J.Pullan & Sons Limited | £104,425,352 |
| YM Group Limited | £104,400,000 |
| Hoyer Container Rental UK Limited | £104,213,136 |
| Pure Leisure Group Limited | £104,165,000 |
| American Standard (U.K.) Co. | £103,517,000 |
| Willerby Group Limited | £103,438,000 |
| Actavo (UK) Limited | £103,309,000 |
| Opus Energy (Corporate) Limited | £103,078,000 |
| Pace Distribution (Overseas) Limited | £102,970,624 |
| Keystone Bidco Limited | £102,818,000 |
| Keystone Financing PLC | £102,332,000 |
| Univar Limited | £102,042,000 |
| Leo Group Limited | £101,921,592 |
| JLA Limited | £101,281,000 |
| Winsfield Limited | £100,829,000 |
| Scarborough International Properties Limited | £100,551,000 |
| Omya UK Limited | £100,472,000 |
| Thorpe Park Developments Limited | £100,346,288 |
| The Consortium Academy Trust | £100,264,216 |
| Instore Limited | £100,035,008 |
| Hillreed Homes Limited | £99,785,576 |
| BSN Medical UK Holding Limited | £99,295,736 |
| Drive Devilbiss Healthcare Limited | £99,211,000 |
| Hull Citycare (Investments) Limited | £99,105,784 |
| Safeway (Overseas) Limited | £98,877,000 |
| Pipe Holdings 1 PLC | £98,832,000 |
| Libra Careco Investments 2 Limited | £98,782,400 |
| Halifax Share Dealing Limited | £98,558,000 |
| ICR Integrity (Group) Limited | £98,230,856 |
| Modern Market Retailing Limited | £98,012,312 |
| Bramall Properties Limited | £97,769,744 |
| Seatruck Ferries Holding Ltd | £97,762,592 |
| M.K.M. BS (Holdings) 1 Limited | £97,570,120 |
| M.K.M. BS (Holdings) 2 Limited | £97,465,120 |
| AFI-Uplift Limited | £97,450,000 |
| DFS Furniture Company Limited | £96,700,000 |
| Community Ventures (Leeds) Limited | £96,534,992 |
| Cephalon (UK) Limited | £96,363,000 |
| McLean & Appleton (Holdings) Limited | £96,254,000 |
| Community Ventures Company (No 1) Limited | £96,138,136 |
| Cox Automotive UK Limited | £95,578,000 |
| Rever Offshore International Limited | £95,533,000 |
| York Diocesan Board of Finance Limited (The) | £95,518,000 |
| Fairbriar Real Estate Developments Limited | £95,344,480 |
| GH Brighton Limited | £95,144,008 |
| Non-Standard Finance Subsidiary II Limited | £95,067,208 |
| Project Light Topco Limited | £94,798,840 |
| Norwich and Peterborough (LBS) Limited | £94,722,000 |
| Middlewood Locks Residential Limited | £94,698,736 |
| Liberty2803 Limited | £94,697,000 |
| Augean PLC | £94,590,000 |
| CPP Worldwide Holdings Limited | £94,434,000 |
| Clariant Services UK Ltd | £94,367,000 |
| IPN Midco 1 Limited | £94,099,240 |
| Labelon Group Limited | £94,078,400 |
| SNF Oil and Gas Ltd | £94,014,376 |
| Eggborough Power Limited | £94,000,000 |
| Arran Isle Limited | £94,000,000 |
| Amalgamated Construction Ltd | £93,960,000 |
| Fenner International Australia Limited | £93,709,000 |
| IPN Midco 2 Limited | £93,670,928 |
| Hull Citycare Limited | £92,735,560 |
| GH Plymouth Grove Limited | £92,489,056 |
| JLA Clean Limited | £92,268,000 |
| Waddington Limited | £92,016,000 |
| AETC Limited | £91,967,000 |
| Can-Pack UK Limited | £91,805,152 |
| Blythmore Limited | £91,203,000 |
| The Constellation Trust | £90,739,000 |
| Allam Marine Limited | £90,522,888 |
| Husqvarna UK Limited | £89,893,000 |
| Boston Mayflower Finance PLC | £89,555,784 |
| Pluss-Staufer Limited | £89,537,000 |
| Principle Global Limited | £89,483,064 |
| JLA Total Care Limited | £89,434,000 |
| Global Autocare Limited | £89,336,800 |
| JCT600 (South Yorkshire) Limited | £89,069,000 |
| Contract Natural Gas Limited | £89,012,048 |
| Morses Club PLC | £88,911,000 |
| Redruth Holdings 2 Limited | £88,805,920 |
| Turner & Townsend Holdings Limited | £88,145,000 |
| Aptiv (UK) Holdings Limited | £87,951,000 |
| Hallmark Cards (Holdings) Limited | £87,926,000 |
| DFDS Logistics Limited | £87,908,800 |
| SSP Holdings Limited | £87,847,000 |
| Universal Parking Limited | £87,768,552 |
| NHP Securities No. 2 Limited | £87,624,400 |
| The Dining Club Group Limited | £87,564,000 |
| State Interco Limited | £87,541,000 |
| Wellesley Holdco Limited | £87,507,800 |
| Adler & Allan Group Limited | £87,356,000 |
| ATC Properties Limited | £87,292,816 |
| Kloeckner Metals UK Holdings Limited | £87,190,000 |
| British Smaller Companies VCT PLC | £86,873,000 |
| JCT600 Vehicle Leasing Solutions Limited | £86,817,000 |
| Country Style Foods Limited | £86,695,392 |
| Bonmarche Limited | £86,599,000 |
| CNG (Group) Limited | £86,344,368 |
| Clugston Group Limited | £86,212,000 |
| Minster Law Limited | £85,410,000 |
| Persimmon Finance (No.2) Limited | £85,156,000 |
| Forza Foods Limited | £85,124,000 |
| DVV Properties 2 Limited | £85,029,000 |
| Trimble Solutions (UK) Ltd | £84,654,480 |
| Dr. Reddy's Laboratories (EU) Limited | £84,630,296 |
| Meridian Healthcare Limited | £84,519,000 |
| WYG PLC | £84,425,000 |
| Chicago Midco Limited | £83,873,224 |
| Guardian Industries UK Holding Limited | £83,650,000 |
| WGL Bidco Limited | £83,466,000 |
| Lakeland Limited | £83,440,000 |
| Aalberts Industries U.K. Ltd. | £83,396,000 |
| Solway Foods Limited | £83,345,000 |
| Ardagh MP Holdings UK Limited | £83,242,000 |
| LZN Limited | £83,167,712 |
| Symington's Limited | £83,131,000 |
| Spire Bidco Hotels Limited | £83,090,000 |
| Bettys & Taylors of Harrogate Ltd | £82,559,000 |
| Brandon Hire Limited | £82,352,000 |
| Element UK Holdco Limited | £81,900,000 |
| Cobalt Project Investments Limited | £81,794,192 |
| Engie Supply Holding UK Limited | £81,534,000 |
| Dixons Academies Charitable Trust Ltd | £81,480,000 |
| 600 Group Public Limited Company (The) | £81,121,672 |
| Witherslack Group (Holdings) Limited | £81,108,952 |
| The Enquire Learning Trust | £80,694,464 |
| Swift Group Limited | £80,527,048 |
| Turner & Townsend Group Limited | £80,440,000 |
| Young's Seafood International Holdings Limited | £80,273,000 |
| UCLH Investors (Holdings) Limited | £80,227,696 |
| UK Greetings Limited | £80,218,000 |
| J.N. Bentley Limited | £79,753,416 |
| Fives UK Holding Limited | £79,697,720 |
| Broomco (3554) Limited | £79,372,840 |
| Project Rock Equityco Limited | £79,369,000 |
| Trinity Exploration & Production PLC | £78,960,608 |
| Arran Isle Holdings Limited | £78,700,000 |
| Inhoco 3498 Limited | £78,679,000 |
| WYG Group Limited | £78,676,000 |
| James Fisher Marine Services Limited | £78,675,328 |

| Company | Value |
|---|---|
| Fowler Welch Limited | £78,655,000 |
| Deepocean 1 UK Limited | £78,220,000 |
| Southgate - Dan at Spyglass Hill - Propco 1 Limited | £77,815,856 |
| 4D Pharma PLC | £77,738,000 |
| CarnaudMetalbox Engineering Limited | £77,520,000 |
| MRC Transmark Holdings UK Limited | £77,447,384 |
| Vantage Motor Group Limited | £76,638,000 |
| Bridon International Ltd. | £76,623,000 |
| Care & Recreation Holdings Limited | £76,508,272 |
| Thomas Topco Limited | £76,342,000 |
| Rathbone Kear Limited | £76,311,000 |
| Drifford Limited | £75,502,304 |
| Kirkgate Group Limited | £75,487,000 |
| Camira Holdings Limited | £75,375,512 |
| ICR (Investment 1) Limited | £75,326,472 |
| Senator Homes Limited | £75,256,000 |
| Lenzing Fibers Grimsby Limited | £74,945,000 |
| De Vere Wokefield Property Limited | £74,900,000 |
| ABI (UK) Limited | £74,885,000 |
| Cardale Infrastructure Investments Limited | £74,881,496 |
| BF Propco (No.12) Limited | £74,845,920 |
| ICR (Investment 2) Limited | £74,709,280 |
| Axis Topco Limited | £74,573,520 |
| Coral Project Investments (Issuer) Limited | £74,512,208 |
| Coolsilk Property & Investment Limited | £74,251,992 |
| USI Mayfair Ltd. | £73,844,064 |
| Pavers Holdings Limited | £73,603,000 |
| Chicago Bidco Limited | £73,376,832 |
| Coral Project Investments (Assetco) Limited | £73,223,288 |
| Baird Group (Holdings) Limited | £73,093,000 |
| ISG Boiler Holdings Limited | £72,959,000 |
| Premier Technical Services Group PLC | £72,842,264 |
| SRH 2011 Limited | £72,383,272 |
| Impact Fork Trucks Limited | £72,072,312 |
| Plasmor Limited | £72,021,832 |
| Clariant Production UK Ltd | £72,015,000 |
| Broomco (3555) Limited | £71,820,904 |
| Colne Topco Limited | £71,750,328 |
| Health Management (Carlisle) Holdings Limited | £71,691,000 |
| Health Management (Carlisle) Limited | £71,689,000 |
| Omega PLC | £71,615,000 |
| Camira Group Holdings Limited | £71,541,760 |
| Bonmarche Holdings PLC | £71,234,000 |
| Merrion House Limited Liability Partnership | £71,154,184 |
| Rockliffe Hall Limited | £71,100,000 |
| Danesmoor Limited | £71,081,336 |
| The Freedom Group of Companies Ltd. | £70,844,000 |
| BSN Medical Distribution Ltd. | £70,633,856 |
| Nilerace Limited | £70,569,888 |
| MS International PLC | £70,141,000 |
| Project Light Midco Limited | £70,127,064 |
| State Debtco Limited | £69,906,000 |
| CCL Label Limited | £69,546,000 |
| Project Magnum (Bidco) Limited | £69,316,000 |
| The Phoenix Partnership (Leeds) Ltd | £69,271,392 |
| Braveshire Limited | £69,102,480 |
| Interface Europe Ltd. | £69,083,000 |
| Gleadell Agriculture Limited | £68,907,000 |
| Metamark Group Holdings Limited | £68,789,000 |
| The Reed Boardall Group Limited | £68,733,088 |
| B & B Pickard (Leeds) Limited | £68,571,768 |
| Richmond Foods Limited | £68,350,000 |
| David Brown Gear Systems Limited | £68,331,000 |
| J. Marr (Seafoods) Limited | £68,251,000 |
| Sovereign Health Care | £68,236,264 |
| Eneco Moy Limited | £68,200,504 |
| Pelsis Holding (UK) Limited | £67,949,376 |
| Stadium Retail Group Limited | £67,777,608 |
| Hexadex Limited | £67,620,000 |
| Refood UK Limited | £67,601,232 |
| James Cropper Public Limited Company | £67,509,000 |
| Total System Services Processing Europe Limited | £67,058,000 |

| Company | Value |
|---|---|
| Allied Glass Group Limited | £66,921,000 |
| F and N One Limited | £66,821,088 |
| BMB Clothing Limited | £66,732,000 |
| Witherslack Group Limited | £66,685,040 |
| ABI Midco Limited | £66,619,000 |
| Hickson Investments Limited. | £66,603,000 |
| Speedboat LNCO Limited | £66,573,000 |
| Warrington Garages Limited | £66,355,116 |
| LRUK (Retail) Limited | £66,034,000 |
| PWS Distributors Limited | £66,023,188 |
| J.S.R. Farms Limited | £65,738,000 |
| Mamas & Papas (Holdings) Limited | £65,633,000 |
| Speedboat Midco Limited | £65,200,000 |
| Contis Group Limited | £64,578,788 |
| S Harrison Group Limited | £64,116,000 |
| Magenta Prime Limited | £63,914,000 |
| Danesmoor Holdings Limited | £63,852,992 |
| The Auckland Project | £63,791,912 |
| Stadium Retail Investments (2003) Limited | £63,514,468 |
| Aviva Pension Trustees UK Limited | £63,494,000 |
| British Smaller Companies VCT2 PLC | £63,406,000 |
| S.D. Taylor Limited | £63,347,000 |
| Wykeland Properties Limited | £63,119,288 |
| ICR Integrity (Holdings) Limited | £62,776,164 |
| Kingspan Metl-Con Limited | £62,542,728 |
| Tampnet UK Limited | £62,346,236 |
| Broker Network Holdings Limited | £62,182,184 |
| Northcoast Seafoods Limited | £62,163,272 |
| Aptiv Global Holdings (UK) Limited | £62,102,276 |
| Hull City Tigers Limited | £61,959,872 |
| Berens & Company Limited | £61,920,392 |
| Exceed Academies Trust | £61,678,000 |
| LNT Group Limited | £61,668,848 |
| Persimmon Harts Limited | £61,604,000 |
| Newly Weds Foods Acquisition Limited | £61,465,000 |
| F.W. Farnsworth Limited | £61,223,000 |
| Den Hartogh Dry Bulk Logistics Limited | £61,055,752 |
| Evans Regeneration Investments Limited | £61,051,840 |
| Cawingredients Limited | £60,866,140 |
| W.Boyes & Co.,Limited | £60,780,804 |
| Cristal Investments UK Limited | £60,621,300 |
| Tracsis PLC | £60,389,000 |
| Camira Fabrics Limited | £60,373,840 |
| CPPGroup PLC | £60,175,000 |
| Hudson Contract Services Limited | £60,145,200 |
| JCT600 (Rawdon) Limited | £60,102,000 |
| Jotun Paints (Europe) Limited | £60,081,000 |
| Team 17 Holdings Limited | £60,019,000 |
| Hull Collaborative Academy Trust | £59,877,336 |
| Acorn Mobility Services Ltd. | £59,685,564 |
| Vinter Estates Limited | £59,651,364 |
| Reward Finance Group Limited | £59,632,000 |
| UKOS Investments Limited | £59,630,088 |
| Uris Group Limited | £59,545,000 |
| Porth Investments Limited | £59,397,000 |
| Crossroads Truck & Bus Limited | £58,691,000 |
| Genus Pharmaceuticals Limited | £58,685,000 |
| Fender Care Marine Ltd | £58,681,588 |
| Shepherd Industries Limited | £58,633,000 |
| Newincco 1072 Limited | £58,600,000 |
| Coolsilk Limited | £58,496,148 |
| Thomas Bidco Limited | £58,475,000 |
| Auden McKenzie Holdings Limited | £58,363,072 |
| Dean Clough Limited | £58,263,872 |
| Shaman Investments Limited | £58,017,644 |
| Anatis UK Limited | £57,852,392 |
| Broker Network Partner Holdings Limited | £57,810,000 |
| UK General Insurance Group Limited | £57,652,652 |
| Really Useful Products Ltd | £57,637,776 |
| Denso Marston Ltd | £57,599,000 |
| Cilantro Acquisitions Limited | £57,587,000 |
| Clugston Construction Limited | £57,284,892 |

| Company | Value |
|---|---|
| Carclo Overseas Holdings Limited | £57,233,328 |
| Jackson's Bakery Limited | £57,065,000 |
| Abbey Multi Academy Trust | £56,888,000 |
| OSI International Holdings Limited | £56,770,000 |
| Ashcourt Contracts Limited | £56,252,908 |
| Hesley Holdings Limited | £56,175,568 |
| Hall Construction Services Limited | £55,951,588 |
| Cephalon Limited | £55,934,000 |
| Project Rock Bidco Limited | £55,889,000 |
| Scroll Bidco Limited | £55,752,984 |
| Econ Engineering Limited | £55,709,648 |
| Beverley House (9000) Limited | £55,708,000 |
| Angus International Safety Group Limited | £55,362,000 |
| National Tube Stockholders Limited | £55,347,908 |
| Hartley Investment Trust Limited | £55,267,000 |
| Kelling Property Limited | £55,245,000 |
| C.A. Group (Holdings) Limited | £55,144,112 |
| ABI Bidco Limited | £55,116,000 |
| DFDS Seaways PLC | £55,035,020 |
| The Brigshaw Learning Partnership | £54,981,000 |
| Axis Bidco Limited | £54,893,912 |
| Humber Education Trust | £54,871,888 |
| Ascribe Limited | £54,758,744 |
| York Racecourse Knavesmire LLP | £54,728,000 |
| PFI 2005 Limited | £54,720,000 |
| Leeds Commercial Limited | £54,472,020 |
| Marsh & Parsons (Holdings) Limited | £54,292,000 |
| Durham & Tees Community Ventures Limited | £54,216,976 |
| Pavers Limited | £54,086,000 |
| 123 Leeds Limited | £54,064,892 |
| Euro-Pro Europe Limited | £53,987,292 |
| Multisol Limited | £53,984,000 |
| Fives Landis Limited | £53,962,000 |
| Montracon Limited | £53,875,076 |
| Hickson International Limited | £53,776,000 |
| Cashel Limited | £53,765,000 |
| Dalmore Highway Investment Holdings Limited | £53,695,584 |
| TSP Projects Limited | £53,687,000 |
| Mitrefinch Holdings Limited | £53,473,184 |
| Leeds Cares | £53,431,000 |
| Hoyer Petrolog UK Limited | £53,259,184 |
| FMG Support (FIM) Ltd | £53,101,000 |
| Cromwell European Holdings Limited | £53,084,368 |
| Henderson Insurance Brokers Limited | £53,080,428 |
| Contis Financial Services Limited | £52,986,408 |
| The Potter Group (Holdings) Limited | £52,915,188 |
| Donaldson UK Holding Limited | £52,894,000 |
| Uris Topco Limited | £52,830,000 |
| Turner & Townsend International Limited | £52,734,000 |
| Holf Investments Limited | £52,697,452 |
| Rosti Automotive Pickering Ltd. | £52,551,000 |
| Singleton Birch Limited | £52,426,000 |
| Gartland Whalley and Barker Limited | £52,420,532 |
| Decorative Panels Holdings Limited | £52,168,356 |
| Carlton Court Investments Limited | £52,106,000 |
| Magnet Limited | £52,031,000 |
| Vivimed Labs UK Limited | £51,978,000 |
| Marshall Construction (West Yorkshire) Limited | £51,951,216 |
| Q-Park Real Estate UK I Limited | £51,939,968 |
| 600 UK Limited | £51,912,000 |
| Equine and Livestock Insurance Company Limited | £51,904,000 |
| L. Batley Holdings Limited | £51,873,928 |
| Lowell Holdings Ltd | £51,743,000 |
| KVH Industries UK Limited | £51,689,388 |
| James Fisher Holdings UK Limited | £51,661,944 |
| Tenet Group Limited | £51,504,028 |
| President Energy Holding UK Limited | £51,181,176 |
| Woodhead Investments & Development Services Ltd | £51,137,208 |
| Fastnet Holdings Limited | £51,013,000 |
| Q-Park UK Limited | £51,000,000 |
| WGL Midco Limited | £50,888,000 |
| Birdsall Estates Company Limited | £50,853,388 |
| Turner & Townsend Project Management Limited | £50,771,000 |
| Optare Group Ltd | £50,716,000 |
| De Vere Cotswold Water Park Limited | £50,655,000 |
| Bayford & Co Ltd | £50,616,000 |
| Packo Inox Limited | £50,562,288 |
| Hamsard 3466 Limited | £50,445,044 |
| Arch Chemicals UK Holdings Limited | £50,424,000 |
| Third Energy UK Gas Limited | £50,261,000 |
| Cyden Homes Limited | £50,137,760 |
| WGL Holdco Limited | £49,934,000 |
| Reuse Glass UK Limited | £49,851,392 |
| WYG Environment Planning Transport Limited | £49,606,000 |
| Coral PFI Holdings 2003 Limited | £49,410,000 |
| Caddick Developments Limited | £49,394,000 |
| Ithaca Gamma Limited | £49,386,344 |
| Trinity Multi Academy Trust | £49,299,000 |
| Omega Proteins Limited | £49,215,280 |
| Spinko Limited | £49,098,048 |
| Moorgarth Group Limited | £49,093,000 |
| Origin Group Holdco Limited | £49,017,368 |
| Surfachem Limited | £48,918,872 |
| Prospect Estates Limited | £48,912,764 |
| MRC Transmark Limited | £48,901,844 |
| W.E.Rawson Limited | £48,833,896 |
| International Fibres Group (Holdings) Limited | £48,752,000 |
| Aptiv Services UK Limited | £48,752,000 |
| United Healthcare Developments Limited | £48,652,680 |
| Ian Mosey Limited | £48,573,188 |
| Cider of Sweden Ltd | £48,552,928 |
| Willerby Limited | £48,543,000 |
| Emerald Group Holdings Limited | £48,496,000 |
| Walker Modular Limited | £48,472,956 |
| Bridge Leisure Parks (Holdings) Limited | £48,426,020 |
| Newly Weds Foods Limited | £48,375,000 |
| Severfield (Design & Build) Limited | £48,360,000 |
| ICR Integrity Limited | £48,354,312 |
| Vanilla Group Limited | £48,204,000 |
| James Cropper Speciality Papers Limited | £48,188,000 |
| Adare SEC Holdings Limited | £48,122,000 |
| Trackwork Limited | £48,096,000 |
| GB-Bio Limited | £48,060,360 |
| INEOS Compounds Aycliffe Limited | £47,999,000 |
| Yorkshire Cancer Research | £47,987,416 |
| Yesss (A) Electrical Ltd | £47,879,000 |
| The Hesley Group Limited | £47,874,436 |
| Hesco Bastion Limited | £47,801,896 |
| Kaye Aluminium (Holdings) Limited | £47,727,748 |
| Leeds Trinity University | £47,676,596 |
| Llandudno Retail Park Limited | £47,636,512 |
| Portakabin (Site Accommodation) Limited | £47,563,000 |
| David Wood Baking Limited | £47,488,092 |
| David Wood Baking UK Limited | £47,488,092 |
| Aker Offshore Partner Limited | £47,478,000 |
| Arla Foods (Westbury) Limited | £47,422,000 |
| Wakefield City Academies Trust | £47,336,000 |
| Premier Modular Limited | £47,222,000 |
| Carlisle Brass Limited | £47,148,000 |
| Team Industrial Services (UK) Limited | £47,113,000 |
| Cilantro Parent Limited | £47,000,000 |
| Cilantro Midco Limited | £47,000,000 |
| Power Topco Limited | £46,958,000 |
| Allied Glass Holdings Limited | £46,849,000 |
| Arbor Forest Products Limited | £46,812,000 |
| Standard Wool UK (Holdings) Limited | £46,660,424 |
| Damartex UK Limited | £46,514,000 |
| Inspired Pet Nutrition Limited | £46,454,408 |
| Multisol Group Limited | £46,309,000 |
| S.G. Petch Limited | £46,303,224 |
| Dean & Wood Limited | £46,237,000 |
| Gweco 511 Limited | £46,217,224 |
| Tissue Regenix Group PLC | £46,171,000 |
| Student Accommodation Provision Three LLP | £46,114,016 |

| Company | Value |
|---|---|
| Hever Castle Limited | £46,064,356 |
| Transdev PLC | £46,053,000 |
| Project Light Bidco Limited | £45,849,384 |
| BJSS Limited | £45,809,000 |
| Project Light Cleanco Limited | £45,624,840 |
| Northern Commercials (Mirfield) Limited | £45,624,000 |
| Sir Robert Ogden Estates Ltd | £45,566,088 |
| Red Kite Learning Trust | £45,551,000 |
| Mabey Hire Limited | £45,521,832 |
| Drax Fuel Supply Limited | £45,458,000 |
| Aalberts Industries Limited | £45,360,000 |
| Onward Investment Limited | £45,220,292 |
| Reed Boardall Cold Storage Limited | £45,186,116 |
| Car Care Plan Limited | £44,982,000 |
| Shorewood Leisure Group Limited | £44,953,364 |
| Contis Card Solutions Limited | £44,930,600 |
| Crossroads Group Limited | £44,869,000 |
| H.P.A.S. Limited | £44,841,000 |
| Hamsard 3465 Limited | £44,824,152 |
| BOS (Shared Appreciation Mortgages) No. 3 PLC | £44,785,860 |
| Kirkella Limited | £44,730,424 |
| Stroma Group Limited | £44,713,036 |
| Trackwork Group Limited | £44,615,000 |
| ATC Developments (Leeds) Limited | £44,584,184 |
| The Retreat York | £44,551,456 |
| UFP (UK) Limited | £44,503,432 |
| Nippon Gases UK Limited | £44,414,000 |
| Genus Pharmaceuticals Holdings Limited | £44,398,000 |
| BPG Acquisitions Limited | £44,398,000 |
| Buy It Direct Ltd | £44,358,000 |
| Dunlop Oil & Marine Limited | £44,321,000 |
| Auto-Trail V.R. Limited | £44,286,888 |
| Opus Gas Supply Limited | £44,057,000 |
| Origin Group Finance Limited | £43,966,280 |
| Terberg DTS (UK) Limited | £43,877,000 |
| Bradford Diocesan Academies Trust | £43,854,000 |
| Pacific Shelf 1809 Limited | £43,853,000 |
| Kemira Chemicals (UK) Limited | £43,831,000 |
| Leeds United Football Club Limited | £43,740,748 |
| INEOS Compounds Holdings Limited | £43,656,452 |
| A-Fax Holdings Limited | £43,644,056 |
| Varnish Topco Limited | £43,533,000 |
| EPTA George Barker Ltd | £43,515,160 |
| The Joseph Rowntree Reform Trust Limited | £43,390,568 |
| Celdis Limited | £43,362,000 |
| BB Investments | £43,333,332 |
| Esplanade Group (Scarborough) International Ltd | £43,262,268 |
| Punch Graphix Limited | £43,236,164 |
| De Vere Tortworth Court Limited | £43,208,000 |
| Strawson Group Investments Limited | £43,045,000 |
| Beverley Funerals Limited | £43,028,960 |
| Ascribe Holdings Limited | £42,957,680 |
| Fellowes Ltd | £42,890,304 |
| Furmanite Limited | £42,851,000 |
| ABI (UK) Group Limited | £42,680,000 |
| A. Schulman Gainsborough Ltd | £42,659,000 |
| FMG Support Group Limited | £42,659,000 |
| Stadium Retail Investments (2004) Limited | £42,654,360 |
| Arch UK Biocides Limited | £42,653,000 |
| Johnstone's Paints Limited | £42,605,000 |
| Walter Lilly & Co. Limited | £42,538,000 |
| Crerar Hotel Group Limited | £42,490,916 |
| CPM Group Limited | £42,393,000 |
| Reward Capital Limited | £42,365,000 |
| Enserve Group Limited | £42,300,000 |
| Cohen & Wilks International (Holdings) Limited | £42,264,636 |
| Accord Multi Academy Trust | £42,252,000 |
| Caddick Construction Limited | £42,247,000 |
| Kautex Textron (UK) Limited | £42,202,000 |
| Jemella Group Limited | £42,189,000 |
| Tereos UK & Ireland Ltd | £42,158,000 |
| International Seafoods Limited | £42,126,000 |
| Donaldson Filter Components Limited | £42,103,000 |
| P. & B. Foods Holdings Limited | £42,091,252 |
| Eneco Burn of Whilk Limited | £42,060,384 |
| Scarborough Partnership Limited | £42,013,000 |
| Lancaster Royal Grammar School | £41,996,000 |
| One Call Insurance Services Limited | £41,951,292 |
| Regenco (Winchburgh) Limited | £41,884,600 |
| Mardix Holdings Ltd | £41,829,688 |
| SEW-Eurodrive Limited | £41,829,144 |
| Rema Tip Top Holdings UK Limited | £41,746,372 |
| Roxor Group Limited | £41,633,000 |
| SFS Group Fastening Technology Limited | £41,601,092 |
| Tower Centre Hoddesdon Limited | £41,362,000 |
| Chaucer Foods Limited | £41,306,432 |
| Redhall Group PLC | £41,298,000 |
| C.A. Group Limited | £41,254,328 |
| Pickards (Leeds) Limited | £41,242,272 |
| Agfa Graphics Limited | £41,229,000 |
| UoE Deaconess Limited | £41,080,680 |
| AFI Midco Limited | £41,061,000 |
| Camira Group Ltd | £40,953,956 |
| Element 14 Limited | £40,948,000 |
| Stork Beta Limited | £40,867,000 |
| Countrywide Care Homes Limited | £40,858,000 |
| Distrupol Limited | £40,779,000 |
| Stolzle Flaconnage Limited | £40,760,280 |
| Horncastle Group PLC | £40,743,404 |
| Oxbow Coal Limited | £40,720,300 |
| S.Daniels Limited | £40,644,000 |
| Dovecote Park Limited | £40,589,000 |
| Glentrool Land and Estates Limited | £40,509,160 |
| Pathfinder Multi Academy Trust | £40,449,000 |
| KVH Media Group Limited | £40,388,000 |
| Northern Gas Networks Operations Limited | £40,364,000 |
| Pharmacy2u Limited | £40,305,000 |
| Yorwaste Limited | £40,264,952 |
| York Mailing Group Limited | £40,232,544 |
| Hull Citycare (Fundco 1) Limited | £40,124,664 |
| Findpath Limited | £40,093,216 |
| GHSR LLP | £40,047,832 |
| Knightwood Trust Farms Limited | £40,028,000 |
| Extra Detail Limited | £39,991,000 |
| Adler & Allan Limited | £39,970,000 |
| Four Pillars Hotels Limited | £39,966,000 |
| Simply Biz Limited | £39,963,884 |
| Bridge Leisure Parks Limited | £39,916,536 |
| GBUK Group Limited | £39,912,000 |
| Blackshaw Holdings Limited | £39,819,392 |
| Gear4music (Holdings) PLC | £39,731,000 |
| Weir Valves & Controls UK Limited | £39,610,000 |
| Wastecare Group Limited | £39,589,716 |
| Standard Wool (UK) Limited | £39,450,252 |
| H.I.Weldrick Limited | £39,377,784 |
| Humdinger Limited | £39,320,280 |
| Paw Topco Limited | £39,269,000 |
| BSN Medical Limited | £39,263,000 |
| Wykeland Beverley Limited | £39,145,688 |
| Fender Care Limited | £39,129,128 |
| Yorkshire Agricultural Society | £39,047,912 |
| Highgrove Group PLC | £39,043,712 |
| CPP Group Limited | £38,881,000 |
| PIB Risk Services Limited | £38,819,148 |
| Sulzer Chemtech (UK) Limited | £38,804,000 |
| Lazarus Properties Limited | £38,625,656 |
| Bridon Limited | £38,618,000 |
| Cycene Limited | £38,569,000 |
| Piksel Limited | £38,562,784 |
| R.N. Wooler & Co (Holdings) Limited | £38,549,788 |
| Thomas Midco Limited | £38,543,000 |
| Somlie Limited | £38,534,744 |
| West Coast Capital Investments Limited | £38,520,380 |
| Curtis Wool Direct Holdings Limited | £38,481,192 |

| Company | Turnover |
|---|---|
| Gear4music Limited | £38,425,000 |
| Howarth Timber & Building Supplies Limited | £38,387,000 |
| Cockburn Multi Academy Trust | £38,368,000 |
| Aptiv Holdings (UK) Limited | £38,337,140 |
| Swaledale Investments Limited | £38,302,780 |
| M.B. Goodwin (Skipsea) Limited | £38,195,488 |
| Belzona International Limited | £38,011,936 |
| Strawson Group Developments Limited | £38,001,176 |
| Sheds for Logistics Limited | £37,989,000 |
| Fullers Foods International PLC | £37,817,912 |
| Anord Mardix (UK) Limited | £37,739,444 |
| Flintbrook Limited | £37,713,000 |
| The Simplybiz Group PLC | £37,662,000 |
| Continental Wine & Food Limited | £37,602,080 |
| Contract Vehicles Limited | £37,597,000 |
| Friends Provident Charitable Foundation | £37,590,652 |
| Skills for Care Ltd | £37,581,128 |
| City Health Care Partnership CIC | £37,558,512 |
| Nexus Vehicle Management Ltd. | £37,461,516 |
| Inoveight Limited | £37,433,000 |
| Gilkes Hydro Investments Limited | £37,429,784 |
| Construction Marine Limited | £37,419,172 |
| Estates U.K. Limited | £37,416,088 |
| Hickson Limited | £37,152,000 |
| De Vere Wokefield Estate Limited | £37,150,000 |
| Aston Properties (Leeds) Limited | £37,137,264 |
| Student Accommodation Provision LLP | £37,136,236 |
| Verdant Leisure 2 Limited | £37,121,000 |
| Kingspan Access Floors Limited | £36,959,488 |
| Timec 1444 Limited | £36,957,308 |
| Wilkinson Building Co.(Leeds) Limited | £36,872,400 |
| Wright Leisure Limited | £36,703,392 |
| Samsung C & T ECUK Limited | £36,701,696 |
| Dr Reddy's Laboratories (UK) Limited | £36,693,180 |
| Trilogy (Leamington Spa) Limited | £36,630,000 |
| L.N.T. Construction Limited | £36,608,320 |
| Belzona Polymerics Limited | £36,607,104 |
| Applied Composites Group Ltd | £36,541,000 |
| DVV Holdco Limited | £36,534,000 |
| Scarborough Development Group Limited | £36,478,592 |
| Cherry Valley Farms Limited | £36,448,360 |
| James Fisher Fender Care Limited | £36,385,148 |
| Covance Clinical Research Unit Limited | £36,261,000 |
| Onward Holdings Limited | £36,181,512 |
| Dale Farm (GB) Limited | £36,175,000 |
| McManus Group Holdings Limited | £36,173,720 |
| Fastnet Fish Limited | £36,129,000 |
| McCain Finance (GB) Limited | £36,118,000 |
| The Fuel Card Group Limited | £36,027,000 |
| Doorway Holdings Limited | £36,020,000 |
| URM (UK) Limited | £35,891,136 |
| Pilgrim Food Holdings Limited | £35,791,296 |
| R.H. Smith & Sons (Wigmakers) Limited | £35,659,572 |
| Evans Dakota Hotels Limited | £35,645,308 |
| Sentamu Academy Learning Trust | £35,567,000 |
| Hambleton Holdings Limited | £35,550,408 |
| S. Harrison Developments Limited | £35,544,000 |
| Timothy Taylor & Co.,Limited | £35,537,816 |
| South Bank Multi Academy Trust | £35,510,000 |
| Low Wood Hotel (1958) Limited | £35,472,832 |
| Hope Learning Trust, York | £35,433,000 |
| Computer Services Consultants (U.K.) Limited | £35,418,812 |
| Specialist People Services Group Limited | £35,416,824 |
| Lakeside 1 Limited | £35,286,000 |
| Ebuyer (UK) Limited | £35,278,404 |
| SMS Towage Limited | £35,185,588 |
| I.G. Industries Holdings Limited | £35,140,952 |
| J.F. and E. Hadwin Limited | £35,101,696 |
| Deep Sea Electronics Limited | £35,025,928 |
| Great Rail Journeys Partnership Limited | £34,993,000 |
| The Rodillian Multi Academy Trust | £34,993,000 |
| Sewell Ventures Limited | £34,992,000 |
| Lakeland Leisure Estates Limited | £34,969,364 |
| Brigdale Limited | £34,936,000 |
| Siena Holdco Limited | £34,933,000 |
| Siena Bidco Limited | £34,933,000 |
| Altra Industrial Motion UK Holding Limited | £34,881,520 |
| Ultima Furniture Systems Limited | £34,836,156 |
| Camborne Holdings Limited | £34,767,500 |
| Axis Midco Limited | £34,729,816 |
| East Riding Holdings Company | £34,702,680 |
| County Properties (Northern) Limited | £34,685,616 |
| I.G. Industries Public Limited Company | £34,680,196 |
| SSP Sirius Solutions Limited | £34,647,000 |
| Ping Europe Limited | £34,633,984 |
| Stonecroft Holdings Limited | £34,595,000 |
| Driver Hire Group Services Limited | £34,522,716 |
| Bishopdyke Enterprises Limited | £34,473,540 |
| F M G Support (Ho) Limited | £34,444,000 |
| Generator Power Limited | £34,435,704 |
| Rural & Commercial Holdings Limited | £34,431,952 |
| Gatenbysanderson Midco Limited | £34,396,256 |
| Ripon Farm Services Limited | £34,324,872 |
| Ecco Safety Group (UK) Limited | £34,315,408 |
| Beckfoot Trust | £34,297,000 |
| Sidhil Group Limited | £34,290,000 |
| Optare PLC | £34,286,000 |
| Chippindale Plant Limited | £34,284,416 |
| Mary Randall Vickers & Co Limited | £34,264,360 |
| SIL Holdings Limited | £34,232,000 |
| Scruton & Co.,(Builders) Limited | £34,174,472 |
| Winterquay Limited | £34,159,640 |
| Superbreak Mini-Holidays Limited | £34,089,096 |
| Gott Agri Synergy Limited | £33,995,704 |
| EMIH Limited | £33,972,392 |
| ABI Beta Limited | £33,967,000 |
| Leo Sawrij Limited | £33,937,492 |
| Zyro Limited | £33,901,000 |
| DC Projects (Rotherham) Limited | £33,875,544 |
| Heywood Williams Components Limited | £33,840,000 |
| Blue3 (Staffs) Limited | £33,833,000 |
| Caterers Choice Limited | £33,824,092 |
| Circuit Launderette Services Ltd. | £33,806,000 |
| Curtis Wool Direct Limited | £33,756,576 |
| Castle Crown Properties Limited | £33,731,720 |
| Peter Stevens Estates Limited | £33,727,936 |
| J. Marr & Son Limited | £33,708,872 |
| Gatenbysanderson Holdings Limited | £33,596,064 |
| Methodist Chapel Aid Limited | £33,576,836 |
| Frank Marshall Estates Limited | £33,574,296 |
| Yesss (B) Electrical Ltd | £33,529,000 |
| Dalmore Capital (Issuer 2) Limited | £33,510,446 |
| Carclo Holding Limited | £33,496,088 |
| R.T. Consultants Limited | £33,365,464 |
| Airea Floor Coverings Limited | £33,335,000 |
| Yorkshire and Humber Co-operative Learning Trust | £33,312,000 |
| Wakefield Grammar School Foundation | £33,296,932 |
| Rever Offshore North Star Limited | £33,201,140 |
| Rail Express Systems Limited | £33,145,000 |
| Eleven Arches | £33,142,104 |
| IP Assist Services Limited | £33,105,178 |
| Fire Protection Holdings Limited | £33,008,000 |
| Sharp Business Systems UK PLC | £32,822,000 |
| Corrboard UK Limited | £32,787,916 |
| Aketon Limited | £32,782,760 |
| Teva Laboratories UK Limited | £32,736,420 |
| James Fisher (Aberdeen) Limited | £32,731,682 |
| Whitby Seafoods Limited | £32,663,260 |
| Y H Residential Limited | £32,620,000 |
| Finlay Beverages Limited | £32,561,000 |
| Blackshaw Properties (2014) Limited | £32,486,092 |
| Beauchamp Real Estate Holdings Limited | £32,463,970 |
| Leigh Holdings Limited | £32,454,968 |
| BPG Midco Limited | £32,395,000 |

| | |
|---|---|
| Moortown Group Limited | £32,377,078 |
| Aviva Wrap UK Limited | £32,310,000 |
| Cobalt Project Investments (Issuer) Limited | £32,270,988 |
| Augean South Limited | £32,266,000 |
| Rudding Park Limited | £32,252,504 |
| Koso Kent Introl Limited | £32,175,000 |
| Bridge Leisure Parks (Finance) Limited | £32,137,076 |
| Pindar Scarborough Ltd | £32,081,462 |
| DFDS Pension Limited | £32,053,000 |
| Stadium Welton Limited | £31,995,820 |
| Wescott Homes Limited | £31,964,172 |
| Hunt Group Limited | £31,947,550 |
| Pontefract Academies Trust | £31,935,000 |
| St Anne's Community Services | £31,932,000 |
| TSYS Card Tech Limited | £31,903,000 |
| Sweco UK Holding Limited | £31,880,000 |
| Moolmoor (Waverley) Limited | £31,842,000 |
| All Steels Trading Limited | £31,838,166 |
| Airedale International Air Conditioning Limited | £31,837,000 |
| FMG Support (RRRM) Ltd | £31,823,000 |
| Atkinson Holdings Limited | £31,803,580 |
| ADL PLC | £31,783,940 |
| Pace Overseas Distribution Limited | £31,677,176 |
| Burgess Group PLC | £31,667,256 |
| VTL Group (Holdings) Limited | £31,666,000 |
| Complete Business Solutions Group Holdings Ltd | £31,663,916 |
| Great Rail Journeys Limited | £31,626,000 |
| Stroma Holdings Limited | £31,600,000 |
| Flower of May Holiday Parks Limited | £31,583,248 |
| J.E.Hartley Limited | £31,581,656 |
| Cielivestock Limited | £31,567,284 |
| Cotterhill Limited | £31,499,112 |
| Scarborough Overseas Holdings Limited | £31,460,972 |
| Tekmar Limited | £31,411,000 |
| ESCO EMEA Holdings (UK) Limited | £31,401,000 |
| Decisionmetrics Limited | £31,383,000 |
| Cox Motor Group Limited | £31,382,536 |
| Tissue Regenix Limited | £31,343,000 |
| Secanim Limited | £31,335,372 |
| Bosideng UK Limited | £31,313,828 |
| Emerald Publishing Limited | £31,308,000 |
| Sheard Properties Limited | £31,255,004 |
| ALS Laboratories (UK) Limited | £31,245,000 |
| West Ella Estates Limited | £31,180,200 |
| Hallborough Properties Limited | £31,175,850 |
| Coletta Holdings Limited | £31,140,912 |
| Eleonora Sport Limited | £31,122,922 |
| Complete Business Solutions Group Limited | £31,094,758 |
| Yorkshire Causeway Schools Trust | £31,047,660 |
| Angus Holdings Safety Group Limited | £31,045,000 |
| GMI Construction Group PLC | £31,016,254 |
| Clifton Properties (Yorkshire) Limited | £30,976,644 |
| R.J. & A.E. Godfrey | £30,923,104 |
| IPF Digital Group Limited | £30,895,244 |
| Engie Fabricom UK Limited | £30,868,000 |
| Mill Garages North East Limited | £30,837,000 |
| Cobco 867 Limited | £30,822,640 |
| Car Care Plan (Holdings) Limited | £30,757,000 |
| Yorkcare Limited | £30,700,164 |
| Project Tulip Topco Limited | £30,666,716 |
| Simpson Millar LLP | £30,666,224 |
| Towngate PLC | £30,583,000 |
| Style Group Holdings Limited | £30,555,000 |
| Christeyns UK Ltd | £30,519,140 |
| Great Rail Journeys Holdings Limited | £30,205,000 |
| Poster Publicity Holdings Ltd | £30,176,492 |
| Batley Multi Academy Trust | £30,167,000 |
| Masternaut Limited | £30,164,000 |
| Esteem Systems Limited | £30,160,000 |
| C Spencer Limited | £30,131,000 |
| Turner & Townsend Cost Management Limited | £30,128,000 |
| St Peter's School, York | £30,031,820 |
| SGS Packaging Europe Limited | £29,994,000 |
| GH Runwell Limited | £29,948,010 |
| EOF Holdings Limited | £29,886,888 |
| Rollfold Holdings Limited | £29,881,000 |
| LRUK (Holdings) Limited | £29,838,000 |
| Spencer Engineering Group Limited | £29,785,000 |
| Hartshorne Motor Services Limited | £29,713,000 |
| Hartshorne Group Limited | £29,690,000 |
| Strawson Management Limited | £29,667,000 |
| Rosti Automotive Larkhall Ltd. | £29,650,000 |
| Keigar Homes Limited | £29,528,278 |
| JCT600 (Yorkshire) Ltd | £29,522,000 |
| Access Hire Nationwide Limited | £29,503,238 |
| YTC Limited | £29,499,316 |
| Silgan Closures UK Limited | £29,489,000 |
| Cupa-Burton Group Limited | £29,487,428 |
| Lawton Yarns Limited | £29,405,960 |
| Standeven Holdings Ltd | £29,342,384 |
| Metaldyne International (UK) Ltd | £29,304,598 |
| Bawtry Carbon International Limited | £29,300,920 |
| New Kadampa Tradition - Kadampa Buddhist Union | £29,285,740 |
| Myers Group 1959 Ltd | £29,267,576 |
| Myers Group Holdings Ltd | £29,267,572 |
| Corporate Travel Management (North) Limited | £29,248,764 |
| Liberty Merchant Bar PLC | £29,232,000 |
| Rixonway Kitchens Limited | £29,201,846 |
| Dyneley Holdings Limited | £29,196,000 |
| Gilbert Gilkes & Gordon Limited | £29,166,000 |
| F R Evans (Leeds) Limited | £29,138,350 |
| Crimson Project Investments (Issuer) Limited | £29,098,004 |
| Central North Sea Fibre Telecommunications Co Ltd | £29,087,098 |
| York Conservation Trust Limited | £29,086,666 |
| Hungate (York) Regeneration Limited | £29,066,000 |
| Benjn.R.Vickers & Sons,Limited | £29,050,784 |
| Town Centre Car Parks Limited | £29,039,584 |
| The MFG Academies Trust | £29,024,000 |
| Shepley Engineers Limited | £29,014,000 |
| Fambo UK Limited | £28,978,000 |
| Dalmore Capital (Para 2) Limited | £28,967,392 |
| Scientific Laboratory Supplies Group Ltd | £28,936,802 |
| Firsdell Ltd | £28,900,000 |
| Ligentia Group Holdings Limited | £28,898,000 |
| John H. Whitaker (Holdings) Limited | £28,863,348 |
| Cranage Hall Properties Limited | £28,860,000 |
| Transdev Blazefield Limited | £28,859,000 |
| Motorhog Holdings Limited | £28,846,332 |
| Victoria Plum Limited | £28,805,000 |
| Modine UK Dollar Limited | £28,726,482 |
| Esteem Holdings Limited | £28,722,000 |
| Fortlands Limited | £28,647,706 |
| Lake District Holdings Limited | £28,619,136 |
| High Street TV Holdings Limited | £28,534,000 |
| NG Bailey IT Services Limited | £28,524,000 |
| McLean & Appleton Limited | £28,507,228 |
| Feversham Education Trust | £28,504,000 |
| Provecta Car Plan Limited | £28,488,000 |
| Willow Properties (Yorkshire) Limited | £28,414,364 |
| Beal Securities Limited | £28,381,898 |
| VPG Systems UK Limited | £28,364,256 |
| Technical Fibre Products Limited | £28,362,000 |
| Encon Investments Limited | £28,337,000 |
| M.C.I. Developments Limited | £28,304,000 |
| D J Cox Limited | £28,240,468 |
| Software Box Limited | £28,239,000 |
| Marrtree Investments Limited | £28,236,368 |
| Komori U.K. Limited | £28,190,000 |
| Tekmar Holdings Limited | £28,179,000 |
| S J Bargh Group Limited | £28,153,784 |
| EHIF (Denmark) Limited | £28,147,366 |
| Diamond Power Specialty Limited | £28,130,000 |
| Land Energy Girvan Limited | £28,103,104 |
| Crown Chicken Limited | £28,061,000 |

| Company | Value |
|---|---|
| Jack Lunn (Properties) Limited | £28,038,936 |
| D.M.Keith Limited | £27,996,794 |
| Younger Homes (Northern) Limited | £27,970,892 |
| Isaac Timmins Limited | £27,926,976 |
| Daifuku Logan Ltd | £27,907,000 |
| CPP Holdings Limited | £27,879,000 |
| WYG Engineering Limited | £27,840,000 |
| SHG (Care Villages) Limited | £27,833,068 |
| AMT Vehicle Rental Limited | £27,766,232 |
| Swift Property (East Yorkshire) Limited | £27,733,940 |
| Beal Developments Limited | £27,731,016 |
| RX Systems Limited | £27,622,706 |
| Holgates Holdings Limited | £27,605,936 |
| Owens-Corning Veil U.K. Ltd. | £27,604,000 |
| YJL Limited | £27,597,000 |
| Newbegin Holdings Limited | £27,554,964 |
| Carclo Technical Plastics Limited | £27,493,020 |
| Lagonda Selsdon Propco Limited | £27,487,000 |
| Valli Forecourts Limited | £27,465,824 |
| Venture Business Parks Limited | £27,460,056 |
| Habasit (UK) Limited | £27,454,000 |
| Yorkwold Pigpro Limited | £27,434,216 |
| Sedbergh School | £27,403,000 |
| Baird Group Limited | £27,402,000 |
| Glasson Grain Limited | £27,394,434 |
| Stowe Family Law Finance Limited | £27,384,440 |
| Mott MacDonald Bentley Ltd | £27,362,158 |
| Scotfield Group Limited | £27,355,116 |
| The Broker Network Limited | £27,321,000 |
| NL Commercials Holdings Limited | £27,305,426 |
| Stowe Family Law Holdings Limited | £27,304,150 |
| Mamas & Papas Limited | £27,253,000 |
| Langley Aviation Limited | £27,159,438 |
| Associated Waste Management Limited | £27,129,756 |
| The Education Village Academy Trust | £27,073,000 |
| Seagold Limited | £27,044,544 |
| Q-Park Securities Limited | £26,951,274 |
| Prism UK Medical Limited | £26,944,140 |
| RFS (Ripon) Limited | £26,941,930 |
| Leeds Group PLC | £26,941,000 |
| HRP Limited | £26,911,000 |
| The Kerfoot Group Limited | £26,899,852 |
| Scantech Offshore Limited | £26,878,544 |
| High Street TV (Group) Limited | £26,878,000 |
| Cavalier Marketing Limited | £26,834,770 |
| Bondshold Limited | £26,814,928 |
| Prism Medical Healthcare Limited | £26,800,188 |
| Lake District Estates Company Limited | £26,777,914 |
| Bericap U.K. Limited. | £26,701,420 |
| DB Cargo International Limited | £26,656,000 |
| Northern Ambition Academies Trust | £26,628,000 |
| Billing Aquadrome Limited | £26,608,974 |
| GBA Group Limited | £26,581,736 |
| Pelagia (UK) Limited | £26,545,000 |
| Bradford College Education Trust | £26,506,000 |
| Rever Offshore UK Limited | £26,505,000 |
| Nu-Oval Acquisitions 2 Limited | £26,500,000 |
| Amco Group Holdings Limited | £26,500,000 |
| Venn Academy Trust | £26,482,032 |
| Emballator (UK) Limited | £26,469,628 |
| Brand Partnership (Holdings) Limited | £26,467,000 |
| Ithaca Epsilon Limited | £26,451,092 |
| Huddersfield Town Association Football Club Limited | £26,443,560 |
| Q Underwriting Services Limited | £26,374,618 |
| Arla Foods UK Property Company Limited | £26,352,000 |
| Elsham Wold Estates Limited | £26,342,422 |
| Covance Limited | £26,250,000 |
| Foundation for Credit Counselling | £26,239,000 |
| NG Bailey Facilities Services Limited | £26,239,000 |
| Holgates (Caravan Parks) Limited | £26,230,654 |
| Con Mech Group Limited | £26,221,920 |
| Hocomm Limited | £26,200,000 |
| Wykeland Limited | £26,197,308 |
| Homecare Insurance Limited | £26,177,744 |
| Harpin Limited | £26,176,280 |
| Windermere Educational Trust Limited | £26,166,776 |
| Image Data Group Limited | £26,130,586 |
| Q-Park Real Estate Holding UK Limited | £26,104,000 |
| Silver Cross (UK) Limited | £26,060,000 |
| Br1dge Estates Limited | £25,969,792 |
| Abraham Moon Holdings Limited | £25,967,658 |
| Abraham Moon & Sons Limited | £25,967,656 |
| Ring Automotive Limited | £25,940,000 |
| Shirestone Estates Limited | £25,900,550 |
| Stirling Investment Properties LLP | £25,892,592 |
| EP Realisations Limited | £25,892,000 |
| Rosti Automotive Stamford Bridge Ltd. | £25,892,000 |
| Yorkshire Air Ambulance Limited | £25,889,802 |
| FMG Finance Limited | £25,840,000 |
| Five Star Fish Limited | £25,834,000 |
| Kelling Midco Limited | £25,814,216 |
| Autohorn Group Limited | £25,802,016 |
| ABI Alpha Limited | £25,754,000 |
| Share Multi Academy Trust | £25,720,000 |
| Yorkare Homes Limited | £25,719,032 |
| Cavaghan & Gray Group Limited | £25,709,000 |
| Mill Nurseries Limited | £25,703,300 |
| Provimi Limited | £25,682,012 |
| Froneri South Africa Holdings Limited | £25,641,210 |
| York University Energy Supply Company Limited | £25,546,398 |
| James Fisher Everard Limited | £25,525,968 |
| Novus Finance Ltd | £25,518,256 |
| Mark H Poskitt Limited | £25,512,144 |
| Havwoods Global Holdings Limited | £25,491,988 |
| Inspired Pet Nutrition Holdings Limited | £25,455,386 |
| Crimson Project Investments Limited | £25,382,160 |
| T L Dallas Group Limited | £25,373,560 |
| Moores Furniture Group Limited | £25,269,000 |
| Hallriver Holdings Limited | £25,253,352 |
| High Street TV Bidco Limited | £25,245,712 |
| Richardsons Westgarth Limited | £25,226,000 |
| Swift Holdings (UK) Limited | £25,215,926 |
| Adva Optical Networking Limited | £25,211,000 |
| Hartley Property Trust Limited | £25,112,952 |
| Bradford Academy Trust | £25,112,000 |
| P. & B. (Foods) Limited | £25,103,768 |
| Marshall Group Services Limited | £25,075,788 |
| Central European Aggregates Limited | £25,057,604 |
| Be Fuelcards Ltd | £25,034,744 |
| ECG Holdings (UK) Limited | £25,032,388 |
| Century Health (Nottingham) Limited | £25,027,772 |
| Community Foundation for Leeds | £24,979,000 |
| Dewhirst Sportswear Limited | £24,971,532 |
| Devonshire Club (Holdings) Limited | £24,948,000 |
| Willerby Group Property Limited | £24,912,000 |
| Verdant Leisure Limited | £24,896,000 |
| Caring 4 Croydon Limited | £24,892,668 |
| Burrows Motor Company Limited | £24,860,000 |
| Vetpartners Group Finance Limited | £24,834,974 |
| Airedale Chemical Company Limited | £24,819,348 |
| A-Safe HQ Ltd | £24,774,996 |
| Holdco 123 Limited | £24,770,296 |
| Frear Investments Limited | £24,756,392 |
| Ultimate Packaging Limited | £24,737,268 |
| Haas TCM Group of The UK Limited | £24,733,000 |
| R.N. Wooler & Company Limited | £24,726,868 |
| Rotherham Group Realisations Limited | £24,690,000 |
| DC Projects (Amber Valley) Limited | £24,648,136 |
| Thistle Insurance Services Limited | £24,635,000 |
| Mibelle Ltd | £24,631,000 |
| Roberts, Mart (Holdings) Co. Ltd. | £24,570,988 |
| J.E.G Hire Limited | £24,521,016 |
| York Mailing (Holdings) Ltd | £24,510,442 |
| Dalby Offshore Services Limited | £24,475,796 |

| Company | Turnover |
|---|---|
| Elite Office Furniture (UK) Ltd. | £24,452,628 |
| Koppers UK Holding Limited | £24,441,362 |
| Motor Depot Limited | £24,426,590 |
| J. Marr Limited | £24,425,396 |
| Park Leisure 2000 (Northumberland) Limited | £24,423,690 |
| Horwood House Properties Limited | £24,398,000 |
| York Mailing Limited | £24,381,672 |
| Dantex Group Limited | £24,330,000 |
| Chesterfield Poultry Limited | £24,273,272 |
| Crosslee PLC | £24,261,000 |
| Queen Ethelburga's College Limited | £24,223,672 |
| Ian Mosey (Livestock) Limited | £24,203,228 |
| Vinewood Limited | £24,150,636 |
| John Good & Sons Limited | £24,148,000 |
| Citygate Developments No.1 Limited | £24,100,688 |
| Simpson (York) Holdings Limited | £24,098,904 |
| Crown Properties (Scarborough) Limited | £24,074,540 |
| Catfoss Renewables Ltd | £24,056,644 |
| Martin House | £24,030,822 |
| Winander Group Holdings Limited | £24,012,318 |
| Ebac Holdings Limited | £23,954,116 |
| Ultra Finishing Limited | £23,916,000 |
| Silgan Closures UK Holdings Limited | £23,894,000 |
| Link Up Mitaka Limited | £23,888,000 |
| Areopagus Limited | £23,887,084 |
| Tilsatec Limited | £23,887,000 |
| Queens Staith Leisure Limited | £23,884,086 |
| Whitworth Chemists Limited | £23,874,412 |
| Wortlea Estates (Leeds) Limited | £23,860,962 |
| Gardner Denver Group Services Limited | £23,823,616 |
| Windsor Engineering (Hull) Limited | £23,807,120 |
| Iceland Seafood Barraclough Ltd | £23,803,130 |
| Jos.Richardson & Son,Limited | £23,784,202 |
| Nickle Holdings Limited | £23,754,636 |
| Autohorn Fleet Services Limited | £23,727,102 |
| M.F. Strawson Limited | £23,718,104 |
| Ebac Limited | £23,696,664 |
| Walker Morris LLP | £23,690,000 |
| Eltherington Group Limited | £23,686,984 |
| Northamptonshire Leisure Estates Limited | £23,685,732 |
| The Bay Learning Trust | £23,622,000 |
| Moxon (Farms) Limited | £23,582,688 |
| Crosslee Holdings Limited | £23,576,000 |
| Multisol Europe Limited | £23,566,464 |
| Interface UK Manufacturing Limited | £23,545,000 |
| Acropolis Corporate Limited | £23,504,694 |
| DLG Legal Services Limited | £23,490,580 |
| Avacta Group PLC | £23,453,000 |
| Status International (UK) Ltd | £23,357,990 |
| Westex (Carpets) Limited | £23,355,000 |
| Apollo 11 Investments | £23,353,708 |
| Forward Investment Group LLP | £23,332,292 |
| C & D Foods (UK) Unlimited | £23,328,000 |
| Brenntag Inorganic Chemicals Limited | £23,307,000 |
| S & J Industries Limited | £23,298,780 |
| Keyland Developments Limited | £23,295,000 |
| Fradley Park Developments Limited | £23,266,396 |
| Minsthorpe Academy Trust | £23,202,000 |
| Leisure Resorts Limited | £23,200,224 |
| Towngate Estates Limited | £23,184,000 |
| Horizon Academy Trust | £23,183,594 |
| Farmhouse Fare Limited | £23,172,000 |
| Teddy Clark Group Limited | £23,164,940 |
| Newport Buildings LLP | £23,144,372 |
| Kirklees Stadium Development Limited | £23,128,936 |
| XL Joinery Limited | £23,120,752 |
| Seabrook Crisps Holdings Limited | £23,113,000 |
| TCS (Merrion House JVCO1) Limited | £23,078,492 |
| Cardinal Limited | £23,069,344 |
| TCS (Milngavie) Limited | £23,044,088 |
| LPD (Holdings) Limited | £23,032,200 |
| Kelda Non-Reg Holdco Limited | £23,010,000 |
| Koppers UK Limited | £22,985,516 |
| Principle Systems Limited | £22,976,020 |
| Peter Ward Homes Limited | £22,971,718 |
| Havwoods Limited | £22,962,686 |
| Aptar UK Limited | £22,952,000 |
| Advanced Alloy Services Limited | £22,941,786 |
| Ideal Carehomes Limited | £22,937,280 |
| Lawcris Panel Products Limited | £22,911,604 |
| Northern Star Academies Trust | £22,902,000 |
| Empowering Minds Academy Trust | £22,840,560 |
| The Wilf Ward Family Trust | £22,808,056 |
| Ligentia UK Limited | £22,806,000 |
| Monocon International Refractories Limited | £22,804,108 |
| Strainstall Group Limited | £22,776,506 |
| Seabrook Crisps Limited | £22,770,000 |
| Reliance RG Limited | £22,761,320 |
| Airedale Chemical Holdings Limited | £22,757,900 |
| Thomas Bell & Sons Limited | £22,737,012 |
| The Boutique Workplace Company Limited | £22,727,000 |
| Card Protection Plan Limited | £22,721,984 |
| Colne Investments 2 Holdco Limited | £22,712,956 |
| Ashcourt Properties Limited | £22,694,464 |
| Torrent Trackside Limited | £22,689,000 |
| Yorkshire House Development One Limited | £22,661,618 |
| Teconnex Limited | £22,644,000 |
| Strawson Holdings Limited | £22,640,000 |
| Al. Murad D.I.Y. Limited | £22,633,194 |
| Arrow Commercial Centre (Huddersfield) Limited | £22,588,456 |
| Q-Park Real Estate UK II Limited | £22,553,400 |
| Seatruck Panorama Ltd | £22,550,480 |
| Teddy Clark Limited | £22,517,372 |
| SGS Packaging Europe Holdings Limited | £22,511,284 |
| Scarborough Thorpe Park Holdings Limited | £22,500,000 |
| Joe Browns Ltd | £22,491,886 |
| Airea PLC | £22,489,000 |
| The Grammar School at Leeds | £22,472,000 |
| The Harratts Group Limited | £22,443,074 |
| Willerby Wold Piggeries Limited | £22,415,580 |
| Barkers (Northallerton) Limited | £22,383,788 |
| George Allinson (Transport) Limited | £22,334,648 |
| Halifax Loans Limited | £22,287,000 |
| Goldenfry Limited | £22,281,904 |
| Kelda Water Services Limited | £22,260,000 |
| Russell's (Kirbymoorside) Limited | £22,251,052 |
| The Right Fuelcard Company Limited | £22,248,164 |
| BW Integrated Systems UK Limited | £22,238,028 |
| Pickards (Commercial) Limited | £22,219,832 |
| Createcity Limited | £22,212,944 |
| Cromwell European Management Services Limited | £22,192,710 |
| Rosehill Polymers Group Limited | £22,187,772 |
| Sandal Motors (Bayern) Limited | £22,176,564 |
| Burton Roofing Merchants Limited | £22,097,224 |
| The Rose Learning Trust | £22,075,048 |
| Wolds Learning Partnership | £22,064,938 |
| Catfoss Finance Limited | £22,056,808 |
| Diamond Resorts Financial Services Limited | £22,040,228 |
| Clytha Holdings Limited | £22,035,164 |
| Leeds Cricket Football and Athletic Company Limited | £22,028,116 |
| Sirdar Holdings Limited | £22,003,000 |
| Coordination Group Publications Ltd | £21,993,424 |
| W.D.Sellers and Sons Limited | £21,972,444 |
| HGF Limited | £21,967,000 |
| UK General Insurance Limited | £21,930,604 |
| Integra Insurance Solutions Limited | £21,860,000 |
| Deeside Power (UK) Limited | £21,852,000 |
| WYG Management Services Limited | £21,849,000 |
| Seatruck Pennant Ltd | £21,841,716 |
| Prestigious Textiles Limited | £21,841,024 |
| Hugh Rice Holdings Limited | £21,837,544 |
| Hisense UK Limited | £21,817,208 |
| Billerudkorsnas Beetham Ltd | £21,797,196 |
| Karro Food Frozen Limited | £21,787,000 |

| | |
|---|---|
| Amnack Limited | £21,782,600 |
| Hoerbiger UK Limited | £21,749,298 |
| Waterton Academy Trust | £21,744,848 |
| BOS (Shared Appreciation Mortgages) No. 1 PLC | £21,729,268 |
| Curo Transatlantic Limited | £21,695,000 |
| Furness Academies Trust | £21,663,000 |
| L Jackson & Co Limited | £21,661,828 |
| Maria Mallaband Limited | £21,589,596 |
| John Wade (Holdings) Limited | £21,569,942 |
| Firth Steels Limited | £21,548,312 |
| Thebigword Group Limited | £21,526,000 |
| Impala Estates Limited | £21,522,600 |
| Turkey Mill Investments Limited | £21,518,080 |
| Kober Limited | £21,515,000 |
| Premium Restaurants Limited | £21,480,392 |
| Amerdale Investments LLP | £21,441,484 |
| Fairfax Plant Hire Limited | £21,441,112 |
| Wilson & Co. (Motor Sales) Limited | £21,434,108 |
| The Lettershop Limited | £21,391,344 |
| Thomas Broadbent & Sons,Limited | £21,376,194 |
| Paynes Dairies Limited | £21,368,500 |
| Jessgrove Limited | £21,343,628 |
| Streejaane | £21,316,900 |
| Dale Power Solutions Limited | £21,286,000 |
| Simpson (York) Limited | £21,269,120 |
| Munchkin UK Trading Company Ltd | £21,267,034 |
| Microcourt Limited | £21,245,448 |
| Hemingways (Furnishers) Limited | £21,237,252 |
| Rofin-Sinar UK Ltd. | £21,237,000 |
| Kingstown Works Limited | £21,234,084 |
| F. Smales & Son (Fish Merchants) Limited | £21,229,200 |
| The Zurbaran Trust | £21,224,660 |
| Sweco UK Limited | £21,198,000 |
| Bonus Electrical Group Limited | £21,170,524 |
| Europa Crown Limited | £21,161,000 |
| Varnish Bidco Limited | £21,158,000 |
| Univar Specialty Consumables Limited | £21,154,000 |
| Redhead Freight Limited | £21,135,844 |
| The Snaith School Academy Trust | £21,135,268 |
| Space4 Limited | £21,130,000 |
| Ripon Select Foods Limited | £21,114,132 |
| Brother Bidco Limited | £21,105,822 |
| Thorpe Underwood Services Limited | £21,104,746 |
| Uris Central Administration Limited | £21,001,000 |
| Shepherd Construction Limited | £20,989,000 |
| Bradford Hide Company Limited | £20,972,912 |
| Straight Manufacturing Limited | £20,969,000 |
| Old Innserve Limited | £20,957,000 |
| Banner Contracts (Halnaby) Limited | £20,927,932 |
| Edwin Woodhouse & Co. (Investments) Limited | £20,927,376 |
| NIC Services Group Limited | £20,897,418 |
| Belle Vue Girls' School | £20,896,596 |
| Arla Foods Ingredients UK Limited | £20,893,000 |
| H. Dawson Sons and Company (Wool) Limited | £20,891,972 |
| Eminox Limited | £20,876,000 |
| Vale of Mowbray Limited | £20,835,672 |
| Dyson Properties Limited | £20,820,920 |
| Skipton Properties Limited | £20,746,972 |
| Varnish Intermediate Holdco Limited | £20,725,000 |
| North Lincs Property Limited | £20,700,908 |
| Team 17 Digital Limited | £20,683,972 |
| Pelican Engineering Co. Limited | £20,671,300 |
| James Fisher Nuclear Holdings Limited | £20,624,048 |
| Reliance Precision Limited | £20,619,516 |
| Castleford Academy Trust | £20,605,000 |
| JZ Flowers International Limited | £20,573,284 |
| RMS Group Holdings Limited | £20,548,840 |
| Ringways Garages (Leeds) Limited | £20,519,340 |
| Wykeland Properties (Holdings) Limited | £20,498,096 |
| Clarke Telecom Limited | £20,485,000 |
| Orion Developments Limited | £20,479,736 |
| Pyramid Display Materials Limited | £20,451,652 |
| Arboretum Devon (RLH) Limited | £20,440,832 |
| Simon Gibson Transport Limited | £20,426,252 |
| Olam Food Ingredients UK Limited | £20,421,000 |
| TSC Engineering Limited | £20,394,076 |
| Samuel Grant (Holdings) Ltd | £20,389,220 |
| The Priestley Academy Trust | £20,369,740 |
| Thai Leisure Group Limited | £20,342,756 |
| Leeds Plywood & Doors Limited | £20,328,650 |
| Rural Concepts Construction Limited | £20,325,900 |
| Vetpartners Group Limited | £20,250,000 |
| Onward Fishing Company Limited | £20,216,628 |
| Alfred Bagnall and Sons Limited | £20,209,920 |
| Audio-Technica Limited | £20,201,568 |
| Bootham School | £20,186,580 |
| Kingston Equity & Finance Limited | £20,176,028 |
| Scarborough China Holdings Limited | £20,171,924 |
| Hesley Care & Education Limited | £20,159,432 |
| Newlincs Development Limited | £20,158,892 |
| Sewell Construction Limited | £20,152,884 |
| PD & MS Holdings Limited | £20,147,000 |
| Sarval (Hartshill) Limited | £20,119,218 |
| Stroma Developments Limited | £20,115,224 |
| JMCD Investments Limited | £20,108,916 |
| Replay Associates Limited | £20,093,328 |
| Towndoor Limited | £20,073,072 |
| Phoenix Oil & Marine Limited | £20,066,000 |
| ACM Global Central Laboratory Operations Ltd | £20,051,550 |
| York Sports Village LLP | £20,051,398 |
| Heathfield Holdings Limited | £20,050,068 |
| Killgerm Group Limited | £20,044,574 |
| Yorkshire Ventures (Estates) Limited | £20,039,540 |
| G S M Automotive Limited | £20,025,992 |
| Wild Life Group Limited | £20,010,396 |
| Rural Concepts (Libya) Limited | £20,000,000 |
| B - Sporting Limited | £19,957,704 |
| Roberts,Mart & Co.Limited | £19,920,552 |
| Wayland Farms Limited | £19,898,000 |
| Maramar (Holdings) Limited | £19,891,792 |
| Airedale Catering Equipment Limited | £19,881,000 |
| Tekmar Energy Limited | £19,866,000 |
| Ghyll Royd Properties Ltd | £19,857,868 |
| James Fisher MFE Limited | £19,832,776 |
| Seatruck Ferries Ltd | £19,808,392 |
| Facultatieve Technologies Limited | £19,797,892 |
| Tompkins UK Limited | £19,790,000 |
| Merewood Group Limited | £19,776,000 |
| James Fisher Subtech Group Limited | £19,753,288 |
| Enhance Academy Trust | £19,751,000 |
| Image Colourprint Limited | £19,749,644 |
| T L Dallas & Co Limited | £19,719,796 |
| Torque Logistics Limited | £19,717,000 |
| RSR Limited | £19,709,656 |
| Wensleydale Dairy Products Limited | £19,702,678 |
| Gatenbysanderson Limited | £19,690,180 |
| Peacock & Binnington | £19,682,708 |
| Peacock & Binnington Holdings Limited | £19,677,984 |
| Dugdale Limited | £19,669,692 |
| Cleveland Bridge UK Limited | £19,660,000 |
| Brandon Hire Group Limited | £19,651,000 |
| John Hudson Trailers Ltd | £19,632,368 |
| James Robinson Fibres Limited | £19,599,088 |
| Lincoln & York Limited | £19,566,230 |
| Univar Europe Limited | £19,565,000 |
| Leisure Parks Limited | £19,558,336 |
| Northern Powerhouse Developments Limited | £19,548,508 |
| National Floorcoverings Limited | £19,545,408 |
| Sandal Motors (Huddersfield) Limited | £19,528,562 |
| Polynt Composites UK Limited | £19,497,000 |
| Harrogate Spring Water Limited | £19,496,768 |
| Venice Bidco 1 Limited | £19,495,000 |
| Mamas & Papas (Retail) Limited | £19,428,000 |
| Westward Care Limited | £19,425,154 |

| Company | Value |
|---|---|
| Lido Leisure Parks Limited | £19,417,146 |
| Style Group UK Limited | £19,416,000 |
| Senior Architectural Systems Limited | £19,397,584 |
| Adler & Allan Holdings Limited | £19,392,000 |
| GSM Automotive Holdings Limited | £19,381,160 |
| SDG (Rhyl) Limited | £19,360,060 |
| Turner & Price Limited | £19,347,670 |
| V.H.E. Construction PLC | £19,332,000 |
| Vale of Mowbray Holdings Limited | £19,328,004 |
| Ebor Academy Trust | £19,319,000 |
| Powell (UK) Limited | £19,313,000 |
| Providence Holdings Limited | £19,299,356 |
| Icelolly Bidco Limited | £19,288,480 |
| Pegler Holdings Limited | £19,285,000 |
| Burmatex Limited | £19,261,000 |
| St Paul's Street (Investments) Limited | £19,248,686 |
| Glendon Estates | £19,246,400 |
| Calrec Audio Limited | £19,231,496 |
| FEL Group Limited | £19,218,502 |
| Numecent Holdings Ltd | £19,175,376 |
| Crop Health and Protection Limited | £19,168,354 |
| Ebac Group Limited | £19,141,164 |
| Crofton Academy | £19,138,986 |
| T.F. & J.H. Braime (Holdings) P.L.C. | £19,132,000 |
| Warrendale Farms Limited | £19,096,464 |
| Thomas Mawer Limited | £19,092,290 |
| Strategic Team Group Limited | £19,079,550 |
| Brother Topco Limited | £19,062,032 |
| Altra Industrial Motion UK Limited | £19,050,000 |
| Lexia Solutions Group Limited | £19,031,000 |
| Technical Absorbents Limited | £19,025,000 |
| Park Lane Properties (Holdings) Limited | £19,017,952 |
| J.H. Fenner & Co. Limited | £18,995,000 |
| GH Braintree Limited | £18,965,940 |
| Cox Automotive Retail Solutions Limited | £18,965,000 |
| HS Products Ltd | £18,944,188 |
| Ashcourt Farms Limited | £18,944,180 |
| Eden Rock Estates Limited | £18,921,228 |
| The Ground Group Limited | £18,911,886 |
| Prefere Resins UK Limited | £18,908,000 |
| Lambson Building Products Limited | £18,868,860 |
| CPP International Holdings Limited | £18,803,000 |
| L.Nettleton & Son Limited | £18,787,322 |
| Nurture Academies Trust | £18,768,384 |
| James Cropper Converting Limited | £18,765,000 |
| D. S. Estates Limited | £18,751,736 |
| Videcon Holdings Limited | £18,742,280 |
| CRH Fencing & Security Group (UK) Ltd | £18,732,000 |
| Citynet Insurance Brokers Limited | £18,728,236 |
| Cubic Holdings Limited | £18,720,168 |
| Driver Hire Investments Group Limited | £18,666,760 |
| Vida Healthcare Limited | £18,654,348 |
| P.D.R. Construction Limited | £18,647,044 |
| Asda Southbank Limited | £18,644,568 |
| J Maguire Holdings Limited | £18,642,422 |
| Arch Chemicals UK Finance | £18,638,000 |
| S.J.Bargh Limited | £18,628,768 |
| I'anson Bros Limited | £18,625,000 |
| Amberbeach Ltd. | £18,618,216 |
| The Inspire Holding Company Limited | £18,613,634 |
| White Rose Property Investments No.2 Limited | £18,602,762 |
| Filtronic PLC | £18,600,000 |
| Leodis Academies Trust | £18,596,000 |
| Coopland & Son (Scarborough) Limited | £18,574,510 |
| Riverside Motors (Doncaster) Limited | £18,572,256 |
| Graypen Limited | £18,572,252 |
| Westcourt Properties Limited | £18,564,062 |
| Schultz Bidco Limited | £18,554,000 |
| Surgical Innovations Group PLC | £18,539,000 |
| Holme Styes Holdings Limited | £18,515,172 |
| Yorkshire Sculpture Park | £18,510,892 |
| Idexx Laboratories Limited | £18,509,580 |
| Trenton (Hull) Limited | £18,494,908 |
| Pickering Vale (RLH) Limited | £18,489,496 |
| Hemingways Marketing Services Limited | £18,481,944 |
| Moolmoor Investments Limited | £18,468,000 |
| Donaldson Filtration (GB) Limited | £18,457,000 |
| Green Flag Limited | £18,438,000 |
| Metamark (UK) Limited | £18,418,000 |
| Styrene Packaging & Insulation Limited | £18,410,504 |
| The Elizabethan Academy Trust | £18,400,954 |
| Sand Le Mere Caravan Park Limited | £18,399,456 |
| Thornton Meat Company Limited | £18,396,880 |
| The Queen Katherine School Multi Academy Trust | £18,388,988 |
| TCS Leasehold Investments Limited | £18,371,990 |
| A.W. (Europe) Limited | £18,344,730 |
| Harvard Group Holdings Limited | £18,338,000 |
| De Vere Grand Connaught Rooms Limited | £18,329,000 |
| Sun Branding Solutions Ltd | £18,314,132 |
| PTSG Access and Safety Limited | £18,311,144 |
| Emovis Operations Leeds Ltd | £18,305,036 |
| Competition Line (U.K.) Limited | £18,303,044 |
| Durham & Tees Community Ventures Fundco (No.3) | £18,273,004 |
| GH Lanchester Road Limited | £18,261,228 |
| St. Leonard's Hospice York | £18,252,448 |
| S. Sheard & Son Limited | £18,247,364 |
| Ashcourt Properties (Newland) Limited | £18,242,176 |
| Portbond Limited | £18,228,068 |
| IFG Drake Limited | £18,221,000 |
| Bradshaws Driffield (Holdings) Limited | £18,210,434 |
| Transwaste Recycling and Aggregates Limited | £18,189,920 |
| Giacom Holdings Limited | £18,178,912 |
| H.M. Pigs Limited | £18,148,660 |
| Elmet Investments | £18,146,906 |
| John Shaw and Son Limited | £18,144,092 |
| Alfred Hymas Limited | £18,142,768 |
| Harewood House Trust Limited | £18,137,920 |
| Image Digital Print Limited | £18,137,752 |
| OE Electrics Limited | £18,108,280 |
| CB Imports Limited | £18,102,000 |
| J. & J. Ward Limited | £18,072,598 |
| Moolmoor Holdings Limited | £18,071,000 |
| Aghoco 1085 Limited | £18,070,000 |
| Uptownleeds Limited | £18,066,364 |
| AW Flow Holdings Limited | £17,979,284 |
| Clariant Oil Services UK Ltd | £17,972,000 |
| Hollingsworth & Vose Air Filtration Limited | £17,971,000 |
| YM Chantry Limited | £17,957,262 |
| Paragon Property Investments Limited | £17,940,832 |
| Farnell Electronic Components Limited | £17,929,000 |
| Sunny Day Capital Limited | £17,923,000 |
| Dantex Graphics Limited | £17,903,000 |
| E.B.Bradshaw & Sons,Limited | £17,897,612 |
| Sarval Limited | £17,894,198 |
| William Sinclair & Sons (Stationers) Limited | £17,873,256 |
| Ginetta Cars Limited | £17,868,628 |
| Aegeus Industries Limited | £17,830,000 |
| Commercial Legal Limited | £17,823,404 |
| Impact Development Training International Limited | £17,808,576 |
| Forward Investment Pannal LLP | £17,801,648 |
| Victory Leisure Homes Limited | £17,778,096 |
| Harold Hinchliffe Limited | £17,753,664 |
| Z.Hinchliffe & Sons Limited | £17,753,418 |
| Binks (Holdings) Limited | £17,748,254 |
| Cohen & Wilks International Limited | £17,741,052 |
| Peter Duffy Limited | £17,738,488 |
| Cancede Limited | £17,723,000 |
| Bridon-Bekaert Ropes Group Ltd | £17,723,000 |
| Dale Erskine Power Solutions Limited | £17,713,000 |
| C & D Foods (Driffield) Unlimited | £17,692,000 |
| Bramhope Property and Investments Limited | £17,686,522 |
| Bartlett Group (Holdings) Limited | £17,683,000 |
| Advance Learning Partnership | £17,655,814 |
| Brand Partnership Group Limited | £17,641,000 |

| Company | Amount |
|---|---|
| Emsley Crane Hire Limited | £17,623,108 |
| Emsley Brothers Limited | £17,623,108 |
| North Carr Collaborative Academy Trust | £17,527,096 |
| BOS Personal Lending Limited | £17,514,000 |
| Rider Holdings Limited | £17,510,000 |
| Airedale Catering Equipment Group Limited | £17,505,000 |
| Harrogate Water Brands Limited | £17,489,630 |
| Countrywide Belmont Limited | £17,485,080 |
| OSI Food Solutions UK Limited | £17,471,000 |
| Modus Seabed Intervention Limited | £17,462,000 |
| Flamingo Land Resort Limited | £17,446,090 |
| Pye Motors,Limited | £17,435,020 |
| Pro-Pak Foods Limited | £17,415,384 |
| Healing Multi Academy Trust | £17,398,000 |
| Dransfield Novelty Company Limited | £17,384,638 |
| D. Noble Limited | £17,339,764 |
| Hanson Plywood (Holdings) Ltd | £17,334,348 |
| Hanson Plywood Limited | £17,334,192 |
| B.W.Industries Ltd | £17,316,454 |
| Hungerhill Academy Trust | £17,295,344 |
| Wastecare Limited | £17,259,588 |
| James Dawson & Son,Limited | £17,255,000 |
| Sunny Day Trading | £17,243,936 |
| Gaunts Limited | £17,237,912 |
| Lunesdale Learning Trust | £17,229,258 |
| Scarborough Property (UK) Limited | £17,229,000 |
| Vcep Limited | £17,225,744 |
| Warrens Group Limited | £17,211,688 |
| Beaumont Morgan Developments Limited | £17,208,296 |
| Provenance Hospitality Holdings Limited | £17,201,760 |
| John H King (Developments) Limited | £17,186,332 |
| Alphabet BC Limited | £17,164,964 |
| Reeds Rains Limited | £17,147,000 |
| East Riding Sacks Limited | £17,122,012 |
| Roando Investments Limited | £17,120,802 |
| Fullers Foods Holdings Limited | £17,109,132 |
| Cars 2 Limited | £17,076,940 |
| Techrete (U.K.) Limited | £17,066,628 |
| J Marr (Property) Limited | £17,059,528 |
| Crossco (1317) Limited | £17,050,328 |
| Bentley & Bentley Limited | £17,021,272 |
| Guyson (Holdings) Limited | £17,016,700 |
| Tenet Limited | £17,008,892 |
| Parkside Flexibles (Europe) Limited | £17,008,298 |
| White Rose Residential Sales Limited | £17,002,094 |
| Crosthwaite Hotels (Westmorland) Limited | £16,991,574 |
| South Westmorland Multi Academy Trust | £16,987,976 |
| Marr Management Limited | £16,985,716 |
| RMSpumptools Limited | £16,978,528 |
| G.B. Terminals Limited | £16,957,776 |
| P.P. Group Holdings Limited | £16,883,732 |
| Esseco UK Limited | £16,868,916 |
| Caygill Holdings Limited | £16,830,668 |
| Huskisson Shipping Limited | £16,800,772 |
| Superbreak Mini Holidays Group Limited | £16,794,000 |
| Grantley Hall Group Limited | £16,788,204 |
| Scarborough Holdings (UK) Limited | £16,787,000 |
| Intechnology PLC | £16,785,000 |
| The Lapwing Estate Limited | £16,775,153 |
| The Hayfield School | £16,761,000 |
| Lowell Financial Ltd | £16,754,000 |
| D & M Middleton Limited | £16,753,870 |
| Lambert Automation Limited | £16,747,762 |
| Nimbus Building Products Limited | £16,738,498 |
| Hall Cross Academy Trust | £16,732,000 |
| Spellman & Walker Group Limited | £16,719,959 |
| Atlas Leisure Homes Limited | £16,718,174 |
| Royds Properties Ltd | £16,716,515 |
| Salendine Nook Academy Trust | £16,712,000 |
| Innserve Limited | £16,704,074 |
| Spooner Industries Limited | £16,699,000 |
| Kexgill (Cottingham) 2 Limited | £16,698,422 |
| Exlabesa Extrusions (Doncaster) Limited | £16,690,285 |
| Rainheath Limited | £16,679,847 |
| Leeds Bronze Engineering Limited | £16,672,000 |
| Acropolis Investments Limited | £16,656,775 |
| Z & D Property Investments Limited | £16,649,207 |
| Kirkby 2017 Limited | £16,648,575 |
| Arena Group Holdings Limited | £16,645,678 |
| Gweco 510 Limited | £16,644,015 |
| Limestone Farming Company Limited | £16,622,000 |
| F & G Commercials (Huddersfield) Ltd | £16,620,336 |
| Young Herts Limited | £16,610,764 |
| Nortech Foods Limited | £16,607,925 |
| Hummersknott Academy Trust | £16,601,000 |
| Berkeley de Veer Limited | £16,596,233 |
| London Wiper Company Limited | £16,580,775 |
| Kongsberg Actuation Systems Limited | £16,568,000 |
| FTL Seals Technology Limited | £16,563,235 |
| Callcredit Marketing Limited | £16,560,000 |
| Penmoor UK Ltd | £16,559,593 |
| J.H. Bacon Limited | £16,558,602 |
| Primekings Holding Limited | £16,538,000 |
| Rhodar Limited | £16,530,000 |
| Salzgitter Mannesmann UK Limited | £16,528,853 |
| Mysing Capital Limited | £16,516,282 |
| Lhasa Limited | £16,515,000 |
| Bannatyne Hotels Limited | £16,511,102 |
| G.B.Turnbull Limited | £16,504,861 |
| Leisure World Group Limited | £16,499,221 |
| MV Ingredients Limited | £16,493,000 |
| Cranswick Gourmet Pastry Company Limited | £16,481,000 |
| Goodwin Development Trust | £16,475,000 |
| Xiros Limited | £16,471,479 |
| Oakmere Homes (Northwest) Ltd | £16,467,149 |
| Natures Crops International Limited | £16,466,757 |
| Farmstar Limited | £16,458,039 |
| T. Quality Limited | £16,453,471 |
| Hardroad Limited | £16,448,573 |
| Proactis Limited | £16,445,681 |
| Filtronic Wireless Ltd | £16,443,319 |
| Kingston Restaurants Limited | £16,441,485 |
| G.F.Smith & Son (London),Limited | £16,438,245 |
| Jemmtec Limited | £16,416,664 |
| Tamar (Selby) Limited | £16,411,788 |
| Lifterz Holdings Limited | £16,410,596 |
| Lingfield Education Trust | £16,401,000 |
| Grosvenor PFI Holdings Limited | £16,388,580 |
| Park Lane Healthcare Limited | £16,387,404 |
| Kings Solutions Group Limited | £16,367,000 |
| AHR Management Services LLP | £16,359,465 |
| Drighlington Fibres Limited | £16,359,000 |
| Elsham Linc Limited | £16,355,370 |
| Asda Supermarkets Limited | £16,340,000 |
| Newquip Limited | £16,334,907 |
| Denaro Partners LLP | £16,299,361 |
| Tenetconnect Limited | £16,290,184 |
| G2M Capital Limited | £16,287,647 |
| Scriven Park Estates Limited | £16,281,995 |
| De Smet Rosedowns Limited | £16,280,000 |
| Leeds City Football Club Limited | £16,273,257 |
| I'anson Bros. (Holdings) Limited | £16,260,000 |
| Narbourne Limited | £16,259,516 |
| Pelican Engineering Company (Sales), Limited | £16,256,447 |
| Klinger Limited | £16,253,460 |
| John Horsfall & Sons (Greetland),Limited | £16,252,473 |
| Omnivale Limited | £16,248,000 |
| Wilkin Chapman LLP | £16,247,229 |
| D.G. Taylor Commercial Vehicles Limited | £16,216,689 |
| Sweco Services UK Limited | £16,209,000 |
| Denaro (UK) Limited | £16,208,622 |
| Myers Building Supplies Ltd | £16,201,076 |
| Donbac Limited | £16,169,669 |
| Corrosioneering Group Limited | £16,169,497 |

| Company | Value |
|---|---|
| Woodlands Home & Garden Group Limited | £16,155,704 |
| Duchy Homes (Holdings) Limited | £16,139,335 |
| Countrywide Care Homes (3) Limited | £16,138,033 |
| Duchy Homes Limited | £16,137,645 |
| Production Park Ltd | £16,122,188 |
| Aflex Hose Limited | £16,118,271 |
| Lakeland Arts | £16,093,805 |
| Mack & Lawler Builders Limited | £16,069,941 |
| BBB Services Limited | £16,060,391 |
| Dewhirst Overseas Limited | £16,058,204 |
| Harrison Spinks Beds Ltd | £16,026,563 |
| H. B. Projects Limited | £16,024,207 |
| Ryburn Valley High School | £16,007,129 |
| The Wordsworth Trust | £15,989,000 |
| Community of The Resurrection (The) | £15,969,000 |
| The Brooksbank School Sports College | £15,964,080 |
| Arizonaco Limited | £15,954,986 |
| RDG Midas Holdings (NI) Limited | £15,952,000 |
| Wartsila Valves Limited | £15,951,707 |
| The Academy @ Ridgewood Trust | £15,921,000 |
| Hull Citycare (Fundco 3) Limited | £15,918,468 |
| Springfir Estates Limited | £15,912,141 |
| Carillion Powerlines Limited | £15,912,000 |
| Opera North Limited | £15,910,666 |
| Delta Caravans Holdings Limited | £15,895,966 |
| YPP Holdings Limited | £15,885,434 |
| Abel & Cole Limited | £15,861,000 |
| Harrison & Clough,Limited | £15,851,211 |
| Manthorpe Building Products Limited | £15,847,099 |
| Standeven Properties Limited | £15,820,355 |
| Wykeland Treasury Management Limited | £15,811,371 |
| Roche Healthcare Limited | £15,806,044 |
| Lewis Civil Engineering Limited | £15,790,000 |
| Notman Enterprise Limited | £15,743,477 |
| Samara Properties Limited | £15,739,478 |
| Powar Developments Limited | £15,710,050 |
| Britcom International Limited | £15,709,928 |
| Lifterz Limited | £15,678,441 |
| Weir Drilling Services Limited | £15,677,000 |
| Rix Petroleum (Hull) Limited | £15,674,897 |
| John Dobson & Son (Carlton) Limited | £15,674,872 |
| Golden Fry Foods Limited | £15,665,043 |
| Colin Appleyard Limited | £15,650,636 |
| Talasey Ltd | £15,637,078 |
| Czajka Properties Limited | £15,611,584 |
| Northern Ballet Limited | £15,609,313 |
| TCCP (Clarence Dock) Limited | £15,597,927 |
| Dalmore Capital (Corsham 1) Limited | £15,588,716 |
| Bekaert Bradford UK Limited | £15,575,388 |
| Alco Valves Group Limited | £15,566,812 |
| Endless LLP | £15,561,000 |
| P V H Holdings Limited | £15,532,225 |
| Envirovent Limited | £15,519,591 |
| ACS Stainless Limited | £15,518,241 |
| Abzorb Group Ltd | £15,504,257 |
| Hillcroft Ltd | £15,501,591 |
| R N Wooler & Co (Developments) Limited | £15,478,157 |
| Rouse Homes Limited | £15,465,962 |
| Britcon (UK) Limited | £15,462,231 |
| SPX Flow Technology Limited | £15,459,000 |
| Rawdon Asset Finance Limited | £15,451,812 |
| Animalcare Ltd | £15,445,000 |
| Hull Truck Theatre Company Limited | £15,434,528 |
| Mosaic Group Limited | £15,431,028 |
| Burlington Care Holdings Limited | £15,417,607 |
| Welfare Hire Nationwide Limited | £15,408,192 |
| Drive Devilbiss Sidhil Limited | £15,407,000 |
| Coletta and Tyson Limited | £15,400,093 |
| The Mast Academy Trust | £15,388,000 |
| Kelkay Limited | £15,376,045 |
| SEA Holdings (UK) Limited | £15,367,506 |
| A.W. Lumb (Midlands) Limited | £15,350,104 |
| Hugh Steeper Limited | £15,346,287 |
| Neill & Brown Global Logistics Group Limited | £15,329,693 |
| Abacus Direct Manufacturing Group Limited | £15,324,764 |
| Cassellie Limited | £15,320,947 |
| Sherborne Upholstery Limited | £15,311,740 |
| HMCA/S PLC | £15,311,429 |
| Mech-Tool Holdings Limited | £15,303,754 |
| Abstract Securities Limited | £15,302,403 |
| Spencer Properties (UK) Limited | £15,287,685 |
| Videcon Ltd | £15,287,209 |
| W Denis (Holdings) PLC | £15,285,091 |
| Three Oceans Fish Company Limited | £15,265,449 |
| The Fresh Olive Company Ltd. | £15,261,112 |
| W.S.Chapman & Sons Limited | £15,258,661 |
| Provenance Inns Limited | £15,235,845 |
| Belgrade Insulations Limited | £15,234,166 |
| Lambert Engineering Limited | £15,227,867 |
| Dewhirst Properties Limited | £15,226,755 |
| Tullo Wind Farm Limited | £15,216,790 |
| Scientific Laboratory Supplies Limited | £15,213,655 |
| Brook Crompton UK Limited | £15,199,604 |
| Paneltex Limited | £15,196,796 |
| Joseph Camm Farms Limited | £15,188,856 |
| Sanipex Limited | £15,182,837 |
| Decorative Panels Furniture Limited | £15,174,810 |
| Elland Steel Structures (UK) Limited | £15,173,802 |
| Steeper Group Holdings Limited | £15,154,591 |
| KCOM International Limited | £15,150,002 |
| William Birch & Sons Limited | £15,143,503 |
| Mech-Tool Engineering Limited | £15,136,529 |
| Collett Holdings Limited | £15,135,713 |
| ESCO (UK) Holdings Limited | £15,135,000 |
| Tolsa UK Limited | £15,134,000 |
| Home Shopping Personal Finance Limited | £15,134,000 |
| Swinton Park Limited | £15,132,712 |
| Icon Aerospace Technology Ltd | £15,102,000 |
| Conservatory Outlet Group Limited | £15,094,346 |
| Civic PFI Investments Limited | £15,092,564 |
| Polypearl Management Ltd | £15,079,195 |
| LPT Trading Ltd | £15,070,979 |
| Weidmann Whiteley Limited | £15,068,064 |
| London Property Investments Ltd | £15,061,746 |
| Persimmon Developments (Didcot) Limited | £15,060,762 |
| Garlock (Great Britain) Limited | £15,057,989 |
| Rastrick High School Academy Trust | £15,050,000 |
| LS UK Fire Group Ltd | £15,036,000 |
| William Lamb (Holdings) Limited | £15,032,545 |
| Optimum4 Limited | £15,030,000 |
| Waco UK Holdings Limited | £15,024,000 |
| Dawn Developments Limited | £15,022,132 |
| A.W.Lumb & Co.Limited | £15,020,063 |
| High Grove Beds Limited | £15,015,159 |
| The Saville Group Limited | £14,998,991 |
| Birch Valley Holdings Limited | £14,997,736 |
| NHP Management Limited | £14,994,578 |
| Bulk Logistics Group Ltd | £14,976,294 |
| Getech Group PLC | £14,965,000 |
| Forth Bridges Business Park Developments Limited | £14,964,136 |
| Q-Park Real Estate UK III Limited | £14,955,732 |
| Leeds College of Music | £14,938,000 |
| Browallia Holdings Limited | £14,930,074 |
| Q-Park (Taunton) Limited | £14,923,229 |
| Ashdale UK Limited | £14,907,057 |
| Radicon Transmission UK Limited | £14,899,201 |
| Expect Distribution Limited | £14,897,299 |
| Scarborough Property Developments Limited | £14,889,419 |
| Stored Value Solutions UK Limited | £14,857,000 |
| VTL Precision (Huddersfield) Limited | £14,843,000 |
| Hunters Property PLC | £14,833,000 |
| Dugdale Compounds Limited | £14,796,207 |
| Zenith International Freight Limited | £14,747,042 |
| CB Imports Group Limited | £14,737,000 |

| Company | Amount |
|---|---|
| Ian Mosey (Feed) Limited | £14,733,397 |
| Quarmby Holdings Limited | £14,729,808 |
| Solina UK Trading Limited | £14,723,000 |
| Family Fund Trust for Severely Disabled Children | £14,720,000 |
| MRC Flangefitt Limited | £14,705,335 |
| WFH Propco 1 Limited | £14,678,707 |
| Scattergood & Johnson Limited | £14,676,210 |
| D.B. Ramsden & Company Limited | £14,676,026 |
| Mixer Bidco Limited | £14,673,000 |
| Tudhoe Learning Trust | £14,660,907 |
| Normanby Estate Company Limited (The) | £14,659,411 |
| Rossett School | £14,659,000 |
| Park Leisure 2000 (Cornwall) Limited | £14,655,632 |
| King James I Academy, Bishop Auckland Limited | £14,652,000 |
| The Rugby Football League Limited | £14,642,323 |
| Doncaster Bus Station Limited | £14,642,287 |
| Kexgill (Liverpool) Limited | £14,638,567 |
| South Craven Academy Trust | £14,636,000 |
| Festino (Finance) Limited | £14,596,897 |
| Financial Funding Limited | £14,594,277 |
| Viewstone Limited | £14,582,462 |
| CCL Stressing International Limited | £14,577,359 |
| Nu-Swift International Limited | £14,552,840 |
| Leman International Transport Limited | £14,544,463 |
| Garth Pig Practice Limited | £14,541,293 |
| British Mohair Holdings Limited | £14,539,707 |
| Strategic Team Maintenance.Co. Limited | £14,536,613 |
| H B Raylor & Company Limited | £14,527,726 |
| South Parade Properties Limited | £14,522,014 |
| Sheffield Housing Company Limited | £14,488,862 |
| Multiflight Limited | £14,469,956 |
| Hunters Property Group Limited | £14,462,978 |
| Exelby Services Limited | £14,453,305 |
| North York Moors Historical Railway Trust Limited | £14,445,776 |
| Witt & Son UK Holdings Limited | £14,443,477 |
| Lambson Limited | £14,441,156 |
| GVS Filter Technology UK Ltd | £14,432,078 |
| West & N Yorks Chamber of Commerce and Industry | £14,418,096 |
| H C Slingsby P L C | £14,417,000 |
| Prahi Limited | £14,415,687 |
| Read Motor Group Limited | £14,415,330 |
| Hague Computer Supplies Limited | £14,411,105 |
| Globesign Limited | £14,407,290 |
| Decorative Panels Components Limited | £14,404,349 |
| Blencathra Hydro Limited | £14,401,901 |
| Impex Parts Limited | £14,392,870 |
| G.W.Proudfoot Limited | £14,391,309 |
| Hartford Holdings Limited | £14,385,548 |
| A.M. Packaging Limited | £14,384,299 |
| Cliffe Hill Second Investments Limited | £14,377,501 |
| RBM Agricultural Limited | £14,363,864 |
| Lamba Trading Co. Limited | £14,359,649 |
| Kingstown Holdings Limited | £14,353,263 |
| Sigma GRP Limited | £14,340,839 |
| Tajj Limited | £14,319,546 |
| Kudos Shower Products Limited | £14,292,851 |
| Carnaby Caravans Limited | £14,281,634 |
| Bright Steels Limited | £14,279,443 |
| Yearsleydale LLP | £14,273,472 |
| Rema Tip Top Automotive UK Limited | £14,259,143 |
| Sea Holdings Limited | £14,241,488 |
| Toiletry Sales Group Limited | £14,239,072 |
| Sandsfield Gravel Company Limited | £14,237,423 |
| Phoenox Textiles Limited | £14,225,304 |
| Grays Wharf Limited | £14,220,576 |
| Pitcliffe Properties Limited | £14,211,161 |
| Haas Group International SCM Limited | £14,203,000 |
| Robimatic Limited | £14,201,000 |
| Royal Armouries (International) Limited | £14,201,000 |
| Siddall & Hilton Products Limited | £14,192,000 |
| Aston Student Lets LLP | £14,183,403 |
| Exponent International Limited | £14,179,486 |

| Company | Amount |
|---|---|
| Seven Technologies Group Limited | £14,179,140 |
| CPP European Holdings Limited | £14,170,000 |
| Thompson Commercials Limited | £14,157,114 |
| R.S. Cockerill (York) Limited | £14,150,297 |
| TCS (Whitehall Plaza) Limited | £14,150,001 |
| Alton Cars Limited | £14,143,826 |
| Links Investment Holdings Limited | £14,129,000 |
| The Goodall Group Limited | £14,122,672 |
| Printcraft Limited | £14,119,000 |
| Humberside Farmers Limited | £14,111,197 |
| Krone UK Ltd | £14,104,531 |
| Thurston Holdings Limited | £14,101,056 |
| Hymers College Trustee Limited | £14,094,210 |
| Lindam Limited | £14,078,833 |
| Hull Citycare (Fundco 4) Limited | £14,063,685 |
| Peaspring Limited | £14,056,951 |
| Brook Taverner Limited | £14,056,792 |
| Shorewood Parks Limited | £14,052,623 |
| Bussey & Armstrong Projects Limited | £14,045,539 |
| Anglia Metal Limited | £14,042,583 |
| Hull Truck Enterprises Limited | £14,026,008 |
| Thebigword Interpreting Services Limited | £14,014,000 |
| Warrens Emerald Biogas Ltd | £14,008,520 |
| Langdale Owners PLC | £13,996,474 |
| Dalian Properties Limited | £13,981,339 |
| R.Caudwell (Produce) Limited | £13,978,393 |
| Vida Grange Limited | £13,971,124 |
| Diagmed Healthcare Limited | £13,946,107 |
| Augean Treatment Limited | £13,922,000 |
| Martins Bidco Limited | £13,891,000 |
| Lancaster Girls' Grammar School | £13,890,000 |
| Chartford Developments Limited | £13,875,027 |
| Arena Group Limited | £13,868,894 |
| Glusburn Holdings Limited | £13,864,061 |
| Thompson Property Ltd | £13,863,441 |
| J Rotherham (Holdings) Limited | £13,856,126 |
| Vivimed Labs Europe Ltd | £13,855,000 |
| Acer Healthcare Operations Limited | £13,850,152 |
| Hill House School Limited | £13,849,135 |
| Mileta Sports Limited | £13,843,307 |
| Engie Gas Shipper Limited | £13,839,000 |
| Fairbriar Developments (Salford) Limited | £13,838,468 |
| Kluman and Balter Limited | £13,826,543 |
| Bramall & Ogden Limited | £13,801,472 |
| Glen Mhor Estates Limited | £13,793,589 |
| Plant Impact Limited | £13,787,000 |
| Gamebore Cartridge Co. Limited | £13,767,753 |
| A.E.Spink Limited | £13,764,359 |
| Coachman Group Limited | £13,757,135 |
| Finsbury (Instruments) Limited | £13,749,000 |
| Mysing Care Limited | £13,747,631 |
| High Point Residential Limited | £13,721,190 |
| Kirklees Community Association | £13,720,258 |
| Van Centre (West Yorkshire) Limited | £13,713,685 |
| The North Halifax Grammar School Academy Trust | £13,678,000 |
| Augean North Limited | £13,653,000 |
| Bedfords Limited | £13,651,978 |
| The University of Chicago Booth School of Business | £13,638,635 |
| Triton Construction Holdings Limited | £13,598,400 |
| James H.Heal and Company Limited | £13,598,299 |
| Nu-Oval Acquisitions 1 Limited | £13,598,000 |
| McDonald King Limited | £13,590,029 |
| Ramscove Limited | £13,581,667 |
| Promised Land Developments Limited | £13,573,696 |
| Bartoline Limited | £13,571,753 |
| Personal Touch Financial Services Limited | £13,562,463 |
| Mainprize Offshore Ltd | £13,539,133 |
| Lymington Holdings Limited | £13,536,788 |
| Bluebird UK Topco Limited | £13,536,000 |
| Humankind Charity | £13,527,386 |
| Illuminating Investments Limited | £13,524,670 |
| Yorkshire Initiatives Limited | £13,516,789 |

| Company | Amount |
|---|---|
| The Storey Group Limited | £13,510,884 |
| Finestline Limited | £13,480,709 |
| Benson Park Limited | £13,476,000 |
| Kolorcraft Limited | £13,469,792 |
| Wakefield Shirt Company Limited (The) | £13,469,791 |
| East Coast Construction (N.E.) Ltd | £13,464,739 |
| Elland Steel Structures Limited | £13,462,442 |
| ABI (UK) Holdings Limited | £13,422,000 |
| Archbold Holdings Limited | £13,410,161 |
| Peover Eye Investments Limited | £13,407,615 |
| Wakefield and District Health and Community Support | £13,404,025 |
| Middle Caves Ltd | £13,399,682 |
| Harris Construction Management Limited | £13,396,922 |
| Interface Administration Services Limited | £13,394,000 |
| Chapter of The Order of The Holy Paraclete | £13,378,181 |
| CD (UK) Limited | £13,375,443 |
| Decorative Panels Lamination Limited | £13,370,861 |
| Wilkes Properties (Wakefield) Limited | £13,367,784 |
| Hawthorn Timber Limited | £13,361,529 |
| Lorica Insurance Brokers Limited | £13,358,540 |
| Booth Industries Limited | £13,349,000 |
| Edwin Woodhouse & Co. Limited | £13,344,132 |
| Windermere Lake Cruises Limited | £13,335,218 |
| A-Fax Limited | £13,323,953 |
| Windward Phase 2 Limited | £13,323,559 |
| PC Specialist Limited | £13,316,483 |
| ACM Global Central Laboratory Limited | £13,310,193 |
| Carmel Education Trust | £13,294,000 |
| Regenco Properties LLP | £13,292,072 |
| Logistik Holdings Limited | £13,288,749 |
| Kirkwood Hospice | £13,277,806 |
| Craven Cattle Marts Limited | £13,260,178 |
| James Hare,Limited | £13,253,238 |
| Dilbag Cloth House Limited | £13,238,610 |
| Mayflower Specialist School Academy Trust | £13,236,913 |
| Broady Flow Control Limited | £13,235,734 |
| Sweet Squared Limited | £13,231,162 |
| Ideal Carehomes (Number One) Limited | £13,229,600 |
| Quality Hydraulic Power Limited | £13,217,522 |
| Abbeyfield Ilkley Society Limited (The) | £13,210,962 |
| Yorparks Limited | £13,209,664 |
| Taskmaster Resources Limited | £13,193,411 |
| Prosperity Noor Ltd | £13,169,473 |
| Waxman Group Limited | £13,167,000 |
| ERM Regulatory Services Limited | £13,163,512 |
| Keyingham Power Limited | £13,161,256 |
| T P Jordeson & Company Limited | £13,142,707 |
| Blackrow Corporation Limited | £13,119,816 |
| Nexus Vehicle Holdings Limited | £13,119,099 |
| JTE Holdco Limited | £13,105,231 |
| Hargreaves Group (GB) Limited | £13,104,702 |
| Paragon Quality Foods Ltd | £13,099,159 |
| J.T.Ellis and Company Limited | £13,094,966 |
| High Seat Limited | £13,094,334 |
| Heritage Commercial Finance Limited | £13,092,778 |
| Landmark Wholesale Limited | £13,090,641 |
| Sheffield United (Hotel) Limited | £13,085,297 |
| Clyde Bergemann Materials Handling Limited | £13,071,000 |
| Chaucer Foods UK Limited | £13,066,000 |
| Avenue Lets Limited | £13,062,826 |
| Dove House Hospice Limited | £13,038,327 |
| Witton Castle Country Park Limited | £13,035,293 |
| The Great North Air Ambulance Service | £13,020,887 |
| Seal It Services Limited | £13,019,669 |
| GSM Group Holdco Limited | £13,016,105 |
| Parkmount Estate Company (Allerton) Limited | £13,007,789 |
| Carnaby Caravans Group Limited | £13,002,500 |
| Stonegrave Aggregates Limited | £12,979,007 |
| Horsforth Mill Limited | £12,970,818 |
| Premium Leasing Limited | £12,959,146 |
| ACWA Services Limited | £12,957,808 |
| Neargoal Limited | £12,950,972 |
| Orion Homes Limited | £12,947,815 |
| Steers Group Limited | £12,936,885 |
| Eurotrail UK Limited | £12,936,870 |
| Lupfaw 365 Limited | £12,934,147 |
| Chapel Allerton Investments LLP | £12,931,494 |
| G R Potter Plant Hire Limited | £12,927,739 |
| Condor Aviation Limited Liability Partnership | £12,921,388 |
| Grandlane Limited | £12,920,167 |
| Jeffrey Walton Jewellery Limited | £12,903,697 |
| L & K Group PLC | £12,902,260 |
| Amos Nelson,Limited | £12,893,315 |
| Sirdar Group Limited | £12,887,000 |
| Intercontinental Brands (Icb) Limited | £12,876,102 |
| Rockar 2016 Limited | £12,854,000 |
| Windermere Aquatic Limited | £12,844,775 |
| Vicarage Estate Company,Limited (The) | £12,843,943 |
| Kolorcraft Holdings Limited | £12,842,918 |
| Thomas Fawcett & Sons,Limited | £12,834,715 |
| Burlington Slate Limited | £12,833,722 |
| Surfachem Group Limited | £12,830,437 |
| Tickhill Engineering Company Limited | £12,829,847 |
| G.B. Agencies Limited | £12,823,125 |
| Reward Invoice Finance Limited | £12,822,000 |
| Fast Freeze International Limited | £12,805,888 |
| York Bioanalytical Solutions Limited | £12,786,844 |
| Crossco (1318) Limited | £12,785,712 |
| TOG 24 Limited | £12,784,605 |
| The Bowes Museum | £12,768,553 |
| Neal Investments Limited | £12,765,337 |
| Olicana Properties Limited | £12,755,480 |
| The Right Car (UK) Ltd | £12,748,076 |
| Interbulk (UK) Holdings Limited | £12,743,677 |
| Holetch Holdings Limited | £12,743,605 |
| Oughtred & Harrison (Facilities) Ltd. | £12,741,410 |
| Nizh Yug (UK) LLP | £12,731,267 |
| William Lamb Group Limited | £12,731,188 |
| The Monobuoy Company Ltd. | £12,727,001 |
| Alexanders Prestige Group Limited | £12,722,405 |
| Thurston Group Limited | £12,721,272 |
| Platinum Stairlifts Limited | £12,717,056 |
| Doncaster Children's Services Trust Limited | £12,695,512 |
| Roman Limited | £12,695,148 |
| Interaction and Communication Academy Trust Ltd | £12,690,226 |
| Oilgear European Holdings Limited | £12,682,128 |
| Cattle (Holderness) Limited | £12,681,107 |
| Trinity Fire and Security Systems Ltd | £12,679,837 |
| Hutton Wandesley Estate LLP | £12,668,781 |
| Pelsis Limited | £12,654,000 |
| Barnard Castle School | £12,651,875 |
| Bankside Patterson Limited | £12,649,863 |
| Durham & Tees Community Ventures Fundco (No.2) | £12,648,089 |
| Stoneferry Estates Limited | £12,629,015 |
| Indian Queens Power Limited | £12,623,000 |
| JBA Group Limited | £12,621,534 |
| WNF Group Limited | £12,619,406 |
| Logical Personnel Solutions Limited | £12,613,042 |
| Fairfax Securities Limited | £12,612,400 |
| Oxley Group Limited | £12,609,647 |
| Yorkshire Wildlife Trust | £12,608,122 |
| Ledden Developments Limited | £12,603,061 |
| Wool Growers (Great Britain) Limited | £12,594,000 |
| Calder Group (Dewsbury) Limited | £12,590,954 |
| Yorkshire Design Services Limited | £12,572,297 |
| Sargent Electrical Services Limited | £12,567,135 |
| Winder Power Limited | £12,564,834 |
| High Seat Holdings Limited | £12,559,411 |
| DB Cargo Components Limited | £12,555,000 |
| Care Holdings Limited | £12,543,189 |
| Cromwell Investment Management Services Limited | £12,541,688 |
| High Point Estates (Darlington) Limited | £12,538,468 |
| Lincs. Electrical Wholesalers Limited | £12,536,188 |
| Private Medicare Limited | £12,527,216 |

| Company | Amount |
|---|---|
| Motorhog Limited | £12,520,971 |
| Wilson Power Solutions Group Limited | £12,520,474 |
| J. Marr (Fishing) Limited | £12,519,450 |
| Needlers Limited | £12,487,227 |
| Winder Power Holdings Limited | £12,482,617 |
| Kingston Carton Company Limited (The) | £12,475,833 |
| Durham & Tees Community Ventures Fundco (No.4) | £12,470,140 |
| Pegler Limited | £12,466,000 |
| C.A. (Evenwood) Limited | £12,463,219 |
| Redline Specialist Cars Limited | £12,463,215 |
| Redline Holdings Limited | £12,463,215 |
| All Property Management Ltd | £12,460,267 |
| Plasmor (Halton) Limited | £12,453,471 |
| Dent Steel Services (Yorkshire) Limited | £12,449,064 |
| Whittaker's Jewellers Limited | £12,448,789 |
| Akari Care Limited | £12,447,203 |
| St. Gemma's Hospice | £12,446,028 |
| Smith Bros.(Caerconan) Wholesale Limited | £12,442,139 |
| Idexx UK Acquisition Limited | £12,441,462 |
| Hurst Group (Northern) Limited | £12,428,000 |
| Brighouse High School Academy Trust | £12,424,000 |
| Park Homes (UK) Limited | £12,422,386 |
| Newlay Concrete Limited | £12,422,077 |
| Oakhurst Court Holdings Limited | £12,421,883 |
| L'Arche | £12,410,055 |
| Jerry Green Dog Rescue | £12,406,064 |
| J.C. Lister Farms Limited | £12,402,999 |
| Potter Family Holdings Limited | £12,401,705 |
| Unipol Student Homes | £12,387,303 |
| Hathaway Roofing Limited | £12,385,601 |
| GH Stanley Limited | £12,385,079 |
| Dormeuil Manufacturing Limited | £12,384,076 |
| Piccadilly Motors Limited | £12,382,484 |
| GH Newco 1 Limited | £12,374,185 |
| Hartshorne Crossroads Group Contracts Limited | £12,371,000 |
| Pure Collection Limited | £12,358,425 |
| Northern Life Care Limited | £12,343,750 |
| Giggleswick School | £12,335,618 |
| Kings Security Systems Limited | £12,329,000 |
| M.Brittain (York) Limited | £12,321,306 |
| Moorlands Learning Trust | £12,316,000 |
| Charles F Stead (Holdings) Limited | £12,313,319 |
| Builders Supply (North West) Limited | £12,306,700 |
| Eltherington Industries Limited | £12,303,513 |
| H. Mitton Limited | £12,295,626 |
| Geo. Houlton & Sons (Holdings) Limited | £12,295,495 |
| Seabrook Group Limited | £12,284,000 |
| Bemis Elsham Limited | £12,283,000 |
| Impact Education Multi Academy Trust | £12,283,000 |
| Millers Oils Limited | £12,280,125 |
| RW Refrigeration Wholesale Limited | £12,279,000 |
| John H.Whitaker (Tankers) Limited | £12,275,578 |
| Drivecheck Limited | £12,274,751 |
| Plum Bidco Limited | £12,271,020 |
| Almit Group Limited | £12,266,704 |
| Geo Houlton & Sons Limited | £12,217,081 |
| Seymour (Civil Engineering Contractors) Ltd. | £12,200,000 |
| Reliance Garage (Ryedale) Limited | £12,197,267 |
| Bunton Plant Hire Limited | £12,191,872 |
| B.C.A. Group Ltd | £12,189,318 |
| Derek Parnaby Cyclones International Limited | £12,179,378 |
| Fender Care Marine Services Group Limited | £12,178,921 |
| J Rotherham Masonry Ltd | £12,172,358 |
| GBUK Enteral Limited | £12,149,000 |
| Moorgarth Living Limited | £12,148,000 |
| Metcalfe Farms (Haulage) Limited | £12,141,026 |
| A. Andrews & Sons (Marbles & Tiles) Limited | £12,138,115 |
| Countrywide Care Homes (2) Limited | £12,129,572 |
| H & P Freightways Limited | £12,119,847 |
| UK Ambulances Ltd | £12,105,635 |
| Talbot House Limited | £12,097,344 |
| We Are Vista Limited | £12,095,238 |
| Richard Alan Engineering Company Limited | £12,085,506 |
| T S Bloor & Sons Limited | £12,076,491 |
| Mondi Scunthorpe Limited | £12,075,195 |
| Today's Wholesale Services Limited | £12,075,000 |
| Kepwick Estate Limited | £12,071,774 |
| Lambert Engineering Group Limited | £12,068,040 |
| Sigma Retail Solutions Limited | £12,064,608 |
| LNT Care Developments Limited | £12,062,556 |
| NYT (Holdings) Limited | £12,042,025 |
| Paw Structures Limited | £12,039,000 |
| Naylors Finance Limited | £12,038,025 |
| Vectair Aviation (1995) Limited | £12,037,494 |
| Icando UK Limited | £12,033,146 |
| Forza AW Limited | £12,033,000 |
| A J Access Platforms Limited | £12,030,000 |
| Blackrow Engineering Co. Limited | £12,026,690 |
| Promenade Car Parks Limited | £12,022,440 |
| Andrew Hillas Properties Limited | £12,021,830 |
| Toiletry Sales Limited | £12,016,796 |
| Trinity Ten Limited | £12,013,802 |
| FMG Support Ltd | £12,011,000 |
| Kexgill (Middlesbrough) Limited | £12,010,203 |
| LBBC Limited | £12,008,905 |
| UK Thermos Limited | £12,006,162 |
| Broadley (Group) Limited | £12,004,231 |
| Dalmore Intermediate Limited | £12,000,002 |
| A.W.Hainsworth & Sons Limited | £11,997,163 |
| A.W. Hainsworth Holdings Limited | £11,997,163 |
| Sheridan Fabrications Limited | £11,988,873 |
| Wrapid Investments Limited | £11,987,472 |
| Ganton School | £11,985,359 |
| Roubaix Bidco Limited | £11,984,778 |
| DFDS Seaways Newcastle Limited | £11,977,824 |
| Optident Limited | £11,970,613 |
| Collins (Seafoods) Limited | £11,950,874 |
| ISP Holdings (U.K.) Ltd. | £11,944,000 |
| J & E Importers & Distributors Green Jem Mfg | £11,941,527 |
| Westpoint Group Trading Limited | £11,931,653 |
| Together Roof Energy SPV Limited | £11,927,074 |
| Community Foundation for Calderdale | £11,927,057 |
| The Family of Learning Trust | £11,917,373 |
| 4urban (Harrogate) Limited | £11,909,900 |
| Viamaster Transport Limited | £11,902,423 |
| York Museums and Gallery Trust | £11,896,002 |
| The Black Sheep Brewery PLC | £11,888,239 |
| Ossett Brewery Group Holdings Limited | £11,878,732 |
| Barwick Bathroom Distribution LLP | £11,872,946 |
| Gilpin Lodge Country House Hotel Limited | £11,868,375 |
| 4x4 Accessories & Tyres Limited | £11,853,743 |
| Horizon Platforms Limited | £11,850,270 |
| Bremsen Technik (UK) Limited | £11,849,014 |
| Stage One Group Limited | £11,837,488 |
| Security Window Shutters Limited | £11,836,527 |
| B & F Potatoes Limited | £11,831,452 |
| Amerdale Ventures LLP | £11,825,851 |
| Sheetfed Holdings Limited | £11,822,634 |
| DEU Estates Properties Limited | £11,819,769 |
| XTR Holding Limited | £11,812,812 |
| Leisure Infrastructure Investors Limited | £11,800,813 |
| Reynolds 2000 Limited | £11,799,712 |
| Langleys Solicitors LLP | £11,780,967 |
| Real Life Options | £11,770,000 |
| On Line Group Limited | £11,768,164 |
| Brewery Wharf (Leeds) Limited | £11,767,099 |
| Giffen Group Limited | £11,764,000 |
| Twentyfour28 Limited | £11,757,364 |
| Garthwest Limited | £11,755,816 |
| Clariant Plastics & Coatings (UK) Ltd | £11,754,000 |
| Wardbright Properties Limited | £11,748,217 |
| Agriargo UK Limited | £11,746,000 |
| Visit Yorkshire Holdings Ltd | £11,745,838 |
| John Hebb (Motor Engineers) Limited | £11,739,629 |

| Company | Value | Company | Value |
|---|---|---|---|
| Itch Propco Limited | £11,696,306 | Sunny Day Property Limited | £11,299,793 |
| Ctrack Europe Holdings Ltd | £11,684,398 | Hair Tools Limited | £11,294,763 |
| Tate Fuel Oils Limited | £11,681,780 | Phoenix Whirlpools Limited | £11,287,708 |
| The Coniston Hotel Limited | £11,673,084 | Hird (UK) Ltd | £11,285,611 |
| Purex International Limited | £11,668,132 | Karl Hanover Properties Limited | £11,285,597 |
| Gilbert Thompson (Leeds) Limited | £11,655,981 | Aura DC Limited | £11,281,323 |
| Home Products Group Limited | £11,646,765 | Thos. Bentley & Son Limited | £11,280,448 |
| Transit 2017 Limited | £11,631,073 | Leger Education Trust | £11,280,000 |
| Wilfred Scruton Limited | £11,628,653 | Moda Living Limited | £11,279,698 |
| The Lingholm Estate Limited | £11,620,631 | CSC (World) Limited | £11,269,660 |
| DP Publicity Limited | £11,607,975 | Tomrods Limited | £11,269,069 |
| Grand Principal Birmingham Limited | £11,593,000 | Smith Brothers (Contracting) Limited | £11,268,540 |
| Intouch Advance Limited | £11,585,966 | Icelolly Topco Limited | £11,246,801 |
| Longley Holdings Limited | £11,581,313 | Sam Turner and Sons Limited | £11,242,189 |
| Ashton Agricultural and General Limited | £11,579,314 | J & E Marshall Finance Limited | £11,241,074 |
| Winander Leisure Limited | £11,578,051 | Lake House Investments Limited | £11,234,444 |
| Bartlett & Company Limited | £11,570,000 | Czajka Group Holdings Limited | £11,231,666 |
| Home Marketing Group Ltd | £11,569,538 | Harris CM Limited | £11,227,076 |
| Home Marketing Limited | £11,569,537 | Argrain Holdings Limited | £11,222,746 |
| Cathedral Church of England Academy Trust | £11,554,000 | John Good Shipping Limited | £11,222,000 |
| Ridge Medical Limited | £11,549,248 | Gamston Aviation Limited | £11,219,322 |
| Camira Transport Fabrics Limited | £11,539,930 | Coachman Caravan Company Limited | £11,217,928 |
| CRG Holdings Ltd | £11,518,456 | St Aidan's Church of England Academy Limited | £11,216,000 |
| J.A.Jewitt | £11,516,055 | Grainsby Farms Limited | £11,215,108 |
| Yorkshire Plywood Limited | £11,514,519 | Ay & Y. Patel (Dewsbury) Limited | £11,210,200 |
| HSH Cold Stores Limited | £11,514,369 | Specialist Coatings Limited | £11,207,234 |
| Cellhire (Holdings) Limited | £11,512,957 | YBS Holdings Limited | £11,205,948 |
| Astonish Holdings Limited | £11,511,288 | Pure Leisure Estates Limited | £11,205,250 |
| The London Oil Refining Co. Limited | £11,511,164 | The Ames Companies UK Ltd. | £11,202,576 |
| Three60 Energy Limited | £11,510,150 | Karro Food Group Limited | £11,200,000 |
| Cellhire PLC | £11,502,957 | Sealord (Europe) Limited | £11,197,848 |
| Cellhire Group Limited | £11,502,957 | Kaye's Hotels Limited | £11,197,836 |
| Leeds and London Holdings Limited | £11,502,159 | Bradbury Group Limited | £11,197,548 |
| Corporate Document Services Limited | £11,499,721 | Morco Products Limited | £11,196,964 |
| Profile Security Services Limited | £11,497,011 | DSS Group Limited | £11,187,691 |
| Taste Marketing Ltd | £11,495,000 | Rever Offshore ROV Limited | £11,184,796 |
| UK Thermos Holdings Limited | £11,493,671 | Verulam Holdings Limited | £11,182,000 |
| The Wilberforce Trust | £11,492,402 | Hull Trains Company Limited | £11,179,000 |
| G. & M. Westgarth Limited | £11,462,633 | Conservatory Outlet Limited | £11,177,190 |
| Wilton Developments Limited | £11,462,232 | Edwin Woodhouse Properties Limited | £11,176,233 |
| Ukar Corporate Services Limited | £11,462,000 | Fairbriar Residential Developments Limited | £11,156,770 |
| William Thompson (York) Limited | £11,454,597 | The Square Chapel Trust | £11,151,071 |
| Communisis BBF Ltd | £11,453,795 | North Yorkshire Timber Company Limited | £11,146,615 |
| Horsforth School | £11,451,000 | First Actuarial LLP | £11,129,273 |
| Ansell Microgard Limited | £11,450,000 | Newross Impex Limited | £11,126,621 |
| Dunns (Long Sutton) Limited | £11,449,457 | AWLC Limited | £11,126,166 |
| L.& W.Wilson (Endmoor) Limited | £11,448,025 | Watershed Packaging Limited | £11,122,858 |
| Mobili Office Limited | £11,447,704 | Heavy Duty Parts Limited | £11,121,196 |
| Zetland Estates Limited | £11,445,721 | Kirklees Neighbourhood Housing Limited | £11,117,000 |
| Wrapid Group Limited | £11,443,563 | Seismic Image Processing Limited | £11,113,156 |
| Triesse Limited | £11,440,638 | Eco-Power Environmental Limited | £11,108,231 |
| Hi-Level Enterprises Limited | £11,438,746 | Low Street Properties Limited | £11,092,812 |
| Gablesea Limited | £11,434,994 | Berry Investment Holdings Limited | £11,090,000 |
| Lebus Upholstery Limited | £11,432,992 | Marshall (Building Contractors) Ltd | £11,083,207 |
| Rolf C. Hagen (U.K.) Limited | £11,429,122 | Bradbury Investments Limited | £11,076,230 |
| Ideal Building Systems Limited | £11,414,167 | Cardale Asset Management Limited | £11,074,268 |
| Tennants of Yorkshire Antique & Fine Art Auctioneers | £11,412,870 | EFS Group Limited | £11,070,000 |
| Febi (UK) Limited | £11,406,003 | Faculty of Queen Ethelburga's Limited | £11,068,648 |
| Barnby C H Limited | £11,399,031 | Yorkshire Building Services Limited | £11,068,338 |
| Flannery Construction Limited | £11,389,500 | Kexgill (Bradford) Limited | £11,065,836 |
| W.T.Johnson & Sons (Huddersfield) Limited | £11,385,716 | GWE Biogas Ltd | £11,058,325 |
| Guyson International Limited | £11,385,532 | Sing Kee Group Limited | £11,057,223 |
| Poster Publicity Group Limited | £11,381,576 | St Andrew's Hospice Limited | £11,055,795 |
| Hider Food Imports Limited | £11,366,635 | Dam Structures Limited | £11,041,158 |
| Hider Group Holdings Limited | £11,366,635 | Harder Bros. Limited | £11,039,431 |
| Ferno (UK) Limited | £11,357,673 | Linfit Investments Limited | £11,027,361 |
| Andrew James UK Ltd | £11,346,492 | Fibrelite Composites Limited | £11,022,731 |
| Mitrefinch Limited | £11,340,335 | Lawton Yarns (Holdings) Limited | £11,012,100 |
| Shepley Spring Limited | £11,338,697 | Rhino Enterprises Limited | £11,006,632 |
| Dalmore Capital (Carlisle 1) Limited | £11,334,521 | Planas Properties Limited | £11,006,546 |
| John Roberts Holdings Limited | £11,313,177 | MCE Concept Limited | £11,001,584 |
| White Horse Machinery Limited | £11,300,949 | Scarborough (UK) Limited | £10,995,026 |

| Company | Amount |
|---|---|
| Goliath Footwear Limited | £10,990,135 |
| Zenith International Freight Holdings Ltd | £10,986,947 |
| Profile Security Group Ltd | £10,985,373 |
| NHP Operations (York) Limited | £10,984,877 |
| Clarion Solicitors Limited | £10,966,457 |
| Sandburn York Limited | £10,959,043 |
| Cleckheaton Properties Limited | £10,957,610 |
| Rudding Park Estate Limited | £10,945,925 |
| Parkacre Enterprises Limited | £10,942,910 |
| City Fusion Limited | £10,942,605 |
| Chippindale Foods Limited | £10,942,273 |
| P.Holmes Properties Limited | £10,937,436 |
| JM Packaging Limited | £10,930,004 |
| The Swan Hotel (Newby Bridge) Limited | £10,922,865 |
| The Swan Hotel (Newby Bridge) Holdings Limited | £10,922,865 |
| Park Leisure Marketing Limited | £10,921,698 |
| Castleton Group Limited | £10,911,922 |
| Sheffield United Group Limited | £10,911,900 |
| Kirkbie Kendal School Academy Trust | £10,896,320 |
| Vetpartners Practices Limited | £10,890,583 |
| Hadrian (Residential) Limited | £10,889,535 |
| Morris & Co. (Handlers) Limited | £10,878,698 |
| Stangs Limited | £10,870,868 |
| Living Care Pharmacy Group Limited | £10,870,453 |
| Ward Bros. (Steel) Limited | £10,867,774 |
| Harrogate Ladies' College Limited | £10,854,767 |
| Evans (Ashford) Limited | £10,827,894 |
| Kuwait Petroleum International Lubricants (UK) Ltd | £10,827,000 |
| Interiors UK Limited | £10,818,129 |
| The Continuum Group Limited | £10,816,183 |
| Charco Ninety-Nine Limited | £10,815,000 |
| Maltgrade Limited | £10,811,841 |
| W.Clifford Watts Limited | £10,809,248 |
| Apollo 1 Investments | £10,804,547 |
| Yorkshire & Lincolnshire Developments Limited | £10,801,026 |
| Kexgill (Nottingham) Limited | £10,794,570 |
| Wooltex U.K. Limited | £10,794,270 |
| Moorgarth Retail Limited | £10,794,000 |
| Hydrema (U.K.) Limited | £10,793,207 |
| Acumen Waste Services Limited | £10,780,715 |
| Silver Cross Nurseries Limited | £10,777,000 |
| Laudale Estate LLP | £10,767,788 |
| DC Projects (Wolverhampton) Limited | £10,758,986 |
| W. Denis (Insurance Brokers) PLC | £10,754,158 |
| VTL Precision (Bradley) Limited | £10,754,000 |
| A.One Feed Supplements Limited | £10,752,965 |
| Investments in Education Limited | £10,751,566 |
| The Columbo Group Limited | £10,746,395 |
| Highcrest Retail Brands Limited | £10,745,225 |
| Hull Citycare (Fundco 6) Limited | £10,744,770 |
| Brooklands Business Estates Limited | £10,739,471 |
| The Glendower Group Limited | £10,735,516 |
| Juratek Limited | £10,734,957 |
| Acorn Web Offset Limited | £10,733,886 |
| R. Bunton Limited | £10,732,973 |
| John Sylvester Engineering Company Limited | £10,716,795 |
| Montpelier Professional Limited | £10,701,604 |
| D. D. Porter Limited | £10,692,574 |
| Clicklink Logistics Limited | £10,690,000 |
| James Stockdale Limited | £10,682,791 |
| B.W. Industries (Group) Limited | £10,672,721 |
| Hobson and Porter Limited | £10,670,172 |
| TWR Developments Limited | £10,666,259 |
| Brecks Holdings Limited | £10,662,934 |
| JRRT (Properties) Limited | £10,660,518 |
| HC-ONE Beamish Limited | £10,645,000 |
| TD Holdings Ltd | £10,644,750 |
| ISS Labour Group Limited | £10,631,938 |
| Wax Lyrical Limited | £10,630,000 |
| Dalmore Capital Limited | £10,621,863 |
| Holdgrove Limited | £10,616,000 |
| Moventas Gears UK Limited | £10,612,001 |

| Company | Amount |
|---|---|
| Future Forwarding (Group) Limited | £10,603,054 |
| Hodson Family Investments Limited | £10,602,043 |
| Brookfield Property (Holdings) Ltd | £10,597,530 |
| IPF Development (2003) Limited | £10,590,000 |
| Dellstrong Limited | £10,586,897 |
| Humber Fishing Limited | £10,582,922 |
| Fourth Argyll Limited | £10,580,138 |
| Orion Commercial Properties Limited | £10,578,338 |
| Rhomberg Sersa UK Limited | £10,577,179 |
| Isle Education Trust | £10,576,000 |
| Maru International Limited | £10,568,979 |
| Mach Recruitment Limited | £10,568,476 |
| AKV Group Ltd | £10,566,855 |
| Holliday International Limited | £10,561,000 |
| Newsmith Stainless Limited | £10,559,840 |
| Narang Group Ltd | £10,552,641 |
| Natures Aid Ltd | £10,550,804 |
| Preston Road Neighbourhood Development Co Ltd | £10,550,054 |
| Search Group Holdings Limited | £10,547,393 |
| Kitching Plant Hire Ltd | £10,545,089 |
| Amazone Limited | £10,539,722 |
| Arch Chemicals Limited | £10,539,000 |
| Liberty Guard (U.K.) Limited | £10,531,724 |
| Hydram Engineering Limited | £10,529,852 |
| Business & Enterprise Finance Ltd. | £10,529,806 |
| Romero Insurance Brokers Limited | £10,529,661 |
| 600 Group (Overseas) Limited (The) | £10,526,000 |
| Caravan Guard Limited | £10,512,736 |
| Stage One Creative Services Limited | £10,505,640 |
| Bayram Timber Limited | £10,492,940 |
| Channon Holdings Limited | £10,491,141 |
| Contractsure Limited | £10,490,174 |
| Eddisons Commercial (Holdings) Limited | £10,489,082 |
| PFF Packaging Limited | £10,488,791 |
| Rack Systems (Engineering) Ltd. | £10,485,893 |
| Quarters Developments Limited | £10,485,311 |
| Mantis Holdings Ltd | £10,482,000 |
| Thames Ambulance Service Limited | £10,469,663 |
| Propharma Group MIS Holdings Limited | £10,462,714 |
| F B Taylor (Holdings) Limited | £10,459,824 |
| Education PFI Investments Limited | £10,457,146 |
| W.P.Brown Limited | £10,455,018 |
| Leeds Theatre Trust Limited | £10,454,614 |
| Jennings Roofing Limited | £10,453,955 |
| Wetherby Steeplechase Committee,Limited | £10,453,694 |
| Hi-Wire Limited | £10,451,624 |
| Charles F.Stead & Company,Limited | £10,442,861 |
| Sewell Retail Limited | £10,418,000 |
| LEBC Group Limited | £10,416,084 |
| Frickley Holdings.Limited | £10,410,980 |
| Foremans Properties Limited | £10,410,496 |
| G - Tuft Limited | £10,410,156 |
| Caddick (JPC Developments) Limited | £10,409,250 |
| Copernus Limited | £10,408,615 |
| Caddick (City One) Limited | £10,396,719 |
| Richard Preston & Son Limited | £10,394,385 |
| The Brecks Company Limited | £10,391,438 |
| Chameleon Technology (UK) Limited | £10,389,502 |
| Waddington & Ledger Group Limited | £10,386,547 |
| Queen Margaret's School, York Limited | £10,384,000 |
| Livwell Limited | £10,378,000 |
| Wilson Power Solutions Limited | £10,373,076 |
| Dhoot Transmission (UK) Limited | £10,371,649 |
| Narang Wholesalers Limited | £10,358,287 |
| Redhead Holdings Limited | £10,350,670 |
| Cardinal Shopfitting + Systems Limited | £10,347,988 |
| Ossett Holdings Limited | £10,342,975 |
| J.A. Jewitt (Meat) Limited | £10,331,672 |
| Mone Brothers Group Ltd | £10,327,567 |
| Pryers Solicitors LLP | £10,324,270 |
| Ontrac Limited | £10,322,958 |
| Total Recycling Services Limited | £10,322,000 |

| Company | Value |
|---|---|
| Res-Q Outsourcing Solutions Limited | £10,314,955 |
| Depho Estates Limited | £10,314,646 |
| Holker Holdings Limited | £10,308,650 |
| Infra Safety Services Labour Limited | £10,306,807 |
| Boarcross Limited | £10,296,976 |
| Kingspan Hot Water Systems Limited | £10,295,490 |
| J.Townend & Sons (Hull) Limited | £10,289,166 |
| Saint Leonard's Property Company Limited | £10,276,689 |
| W. H. Strawson (Notts.) Limited | £10,272,617 |
| Risedale Estates Limited | £10,270,579 |
| Bleu Properties Ltd | £10,269,798 |
| The Cadman Housing Project Ltd | £10,263,143 |
| Forteq (UK) Limited | £10,260,605 |
| Just Trays Limited | £10,259,000 |
| United Reformed Church (Yorkshire Province) Trust | £10,248,710 |
| Rhino Enterprises Properties Limited | £10,246,801 |
| Barton Park Estates Limited | £10,242,474 |
| Marsylka Manufacturing Co.Limited | £10,241,097 |
| Kexgill (Preston) Limited | £10,239,568 |
| Britannia Construction Limited | £10,233,000 |
| Delifresh Limited | £10,230,132 |
| Bender UK Limited | £10,225,942 |
| Crafter's Companion Limited | £10,221,818 |
| The Burton Constable Foundation | £10,216,752 |
| Martin Williams (Hull) Limited | £10,197,229 |
| Zeina Foods Limited | £10,196,569 |
| Thornsett Vale Limited | £10,186,243 |
| RMS Europe Group Limited | £10,177,256 |
| Locala Community Partnerships C.I.C. | £10,175,000 |
| Solway Foods Holdings Limited | £10,174,000 |
| Dent Steel Holdings Limited | £10,167,203 |
| Scarborough Partnership Properties Limited | £10,166,303 |
| Lancaster University Energy Services Ltd | £10,163,059 |
| Catterick Caravan & Camping Centre Limited | £10,158,976 |
| Fisher Outdoor Leisure Holdings Limited | £10,158,000 |
| Hamsard 3225 Limited | £10,140,569 |
| P D Bannister Haulage Limited | £10,129,471 |
| Cirteq Limited | £10,115,584 |
| Rayrigg Estates Ltd | £10,113,785 |
| Service Timber Limited | £10,107,561 |
| Gawith Hoggarth & Co.,Limited | £10,106,349 |
| W. H. Strawson (Farms) Limited | £10,094,875 |
| Yorkshire Premier Meat Limited | £10,088,754 |
| Richard Wellock & Sons Limited | £10,084,591 |
| Third Energy Services Limited | £10,075,000 |
| K A Anderson (Metal Recyclers) Limited | £10,068,004 |
| Certex Lifting Limited | £10,067,886 |
| Bostonair Group Limited | £10,064,500 |
| Anlaby Office Cleaning Services Limited | £10,063,727 |
| Simon Bailes Limited | £10,062,287 |
| Contract Experts Limited | £10,059,955 |
| Amsgro Limited | £10,059,322 |
| Atlantic Fresh Limited | £10,048,314 |
| Marshall Brothers Finance Co Limited | £10,042,562 |
| Ascribe Group Limited | £10,040,000 |
| Spectrum Yarns Limited | £10,032,694 |
| The Feel Good Group Limited | £10,025,705 |
| Strawson Investments Limited | £10,025,000 |
| H & C Whitehead (Holdings) Limited | £10,016,459 |
| Navigo Health and Social Care CIC | £10,013,655 |
| Jack Lunn (Holdings) Limited | £10,008,020 |
| Sandtoft Developments Limited | £10,004,758 |
| Crown Acquisition Consumer Limited | £10,000,000 |
| Marshall Wooldridge Group Holdings Limited | £10,000,000 |
| Troy Foods Limited | £9,997,575 |
| Tanks and Vessels Industries Limited | £9,980,119 |
| TM Advances Limited | £9,973,595 |
| ASD Westok Limited | £9,972,000 |
| Bracken Limited | £9,969,940 |
| Mitton Mechanical Services Limited | £9,968,003 |
| Hugh Rice Limited | £9,960,503 |
| Interchange and Consort Hotels Limited | £9,942,964 |
| Bayfields Z Limited | £9,937,946 |
| Homecare (Holdings) Limited | £9,936,510 |
| Key Growing Limited | £9,921,987 |
| Cod Beck Blenders Limited | £9,919,414 |
| Greif Flexibles UK Limited | £9,911,659 |
| Bailey Leasing Limited | £9,906,000 |
| Charlesworth Family Group Limited | £9,898,166 |
| Braegate Produce Limited | £9,894,269 |
| JT Holdings (UK) Limited | £9,894,000 |
| JSJ Partnership Limited | £9,881,800 |
| Prospect Business Centres Limited | £9,873,365 |
| Precious Holdings (Wakefield) Limited | £9,865,710 |
| Owens-Corning Britinvest Limited | £9,858,000 |
| Samuel Grant Group Limited | £9,849,391 |
| MAS Management Services Ltd | £9,846,246 |
| Hallmark Cards Property Company Limited | £9,833,000 |
| Eneco Sevor Limited | £9,831,945 |
| The Union Discount Company of London Limited | £9,823,346 |
| Ashleighsigns Limited | £9,821,650 |
| Leeds and Bradford Boiler Company Limited (The) | £9,816,651 |
| Torque Retail Services Limited | £9,811,000 |
| Neoss Limited | £9,810,743 |
| Epil Carlisle Limited | £9,807,257 |
| Etrickbank Limited | £9,806,578 |
| Highfield Caravans Limited | £9,798,393 |
| Abirose Limited | £9,779,000 |
| Stephenson Group Ltd | £9,778,523 |
| Luxury Fibres Limited | £9,774,231 |
| Hull Citycare (Fundco 5) Limited | £9,768,501 |
| Cragwood International Limited | £9,766,283 |
| Whitaker Fibres Limited | £9,763,839 |
| Harder Bros (Holdings) Limited | £9,763,687 |
| Farmhouse Potato Bakers Limited | £9,761,861 |
| IRISNDT UK Holdings Limited | £9,754,032 |
| St Mary's Academy Trust | £9,752,173 |
| CSC (Holdings) Limited | £9,750,335 |
| I.C.S. (UK) Limited | £9,743,381 |
| Blackburns Waste Disposal Limited | £9,738,907 |
| Park Valley Huddersfield Limited | £9,738,320 |
| Mitchell's Brewery Limited | £9,737,000 |
| Termrim Construction Limited | £9,730,742 |
| H Walton Limited | £9,729,111 |
| Navartis Limited | £9,719,215 |
| Red Circle Investments Limited | £9,715,563 |
| Russell Armer Group Limited | £9,707,496 |
| H.H Services Limited | £9,689,649 |
| Tony Rampton Trust | £9,687,264 |
| J3 Business Park Doncaster LLP | £9,685,991 |
| Longley Concrete Ltd | £9,680,275 |
| Hallite Seals International Limited | £9,676,000 |
| Principle Healthcare International Limited | £9,670,585 |
| Trojan Plastics Limited | £9,668,100 |
| The Dewsbury Learning Trust | £9,660,680 |
| Thornhill Community Academy Trust | £9,660,000 |
| Harmony Bridge Limited | £9,656,671 |
| Elevate Multi Academy Trust | £9,653,428 |
| Star Brands Limited | £9,633,871 |
| Almara Residential Limited | £9,632,550 |
| TGH Finance Limited | £9,628,000 |
| G2M Unilets Limited | £9,627,463 |
| ICIEA Limited | £9,626,000 |
| Y.E.S. (Your Event Solutions) Limited | £9,622,847 |
| Broom House Investments Limited | £9,620,780 |
| R. Kendall Limited | £9,620,688 |
| Niko (Int) Limited | £9,616,000 |
| Recruitex Limited | £9,611,688 |
| G.W. Sissons and Son Limited | £9,608,780 |
| 4B Braime Components Limited | £9,605,028 |
| Zenith Ef Limited | £9,600,000 |
| The Label Makers Limited | £9,598,212 |
| LNT Properties Limited Liability Partnership | £9,594,800 |
| Planet Overseas Holdings Limited | £9,584,000 |

| | |
|---|---|
| Lesjofors Springs (UK) Limited | £9,578,142 |
| Raysul Holdings Limited | £9,573,999 |
| Pipes UK (Holdings) Limited | £9,568,424 |
| Beatty Topco Limited | £9,568,373 |
| Catford & Longford Limited | £9,565,344 |
| Triton Construction Limited | £9,560,418 |
| Lightwater Holdings Limited | £9,558,352 |
| TWS Property Limited | £9,550,827 |
| Arville Holdings Limited | £9,548,216 |
| Riddochhill Developments Limited | £9,547,524 |
| Advice Champion.co.uk Limited | £9,545,193 |
| William F.Moore (Warplands) Limited | £9,540,275 |
| Total Foodservice Solutions Limited | £9,533,898 |
| College Holdings 2012 Ltd | £9,530,667 |
| Dormot Limited | £9,525,573 |
| TEI Limited | £9,521,521 |
| Jacuzzi Spa and Bath Limited | £9,521,383 |
| Select Alloys & Materials Limited | £9,519,941 |
| King James's School | £9,491,000 |
| TGC (2015) Limited | £9,489,863 |
| Ness Hall Ltd | £9,488,306 |
| Bulmer & Lumb Group Limited | £9,484,025 |
| First 4 Lawyers Limited | £9,482,214 |
| P.P. Plasma Limited | £9,480,616 |
| Yorkshire Collaborative Academy Trust | £9,472,000 |
| Integra Buildings Limited | £9,463,415 |
| Bee Health Limited | £9,460,570 |
| Westcourt Group Limited | £9,457,894 |
| Heart Research UK | £9,454,175 |
| Emacrow Limited | £9,452,108 |
| GC Motors Limited | £9,451,021 |
| Talbert Limited | £9,436,813 |
| Aquaspersions Limited | £9,434,733 |
| Cornelius Beverage Technologies Limited | £9,433,000 |
| Edward P Wright (Holdings) Limited | £9,432,605 |
| Northern Paper Board Limited | £9,423,499 |
| Conroy Brook (Developments) Limited | £9,414,668 |
| Beverley Grammar School | £9,397,089 |
| PPB Ltd | £9,397,063 |
| Saint Catherines Hospice Trust | £9,393,320 |
| Hermes European Logistics Limited | £9,388,465 |
| Malton Foods Limited | £9,387,252 |
| Cromar Building Products Limited | £9,384,502 |
| VBP Group Limited | £9,382,823 |
| Hassan Group Limited | £9,380,766 |
| Biker Group Limited | £9,377,360 |
| William Smith (Wakefield) Limited | £9,373,015 |
| Bemrose Booth Paragon Limited | £9,372,000 |
| Biowise Limited | £9,355,694 |
| Newitt & Co (Properties) Limited | £9,354,781 |
| Sirdar Properties Limited | £9,354,572 |
| Park Lane Healthcare (Croston Park) Limited | £9,348,508 |
| Martech (UK) Ltd | £9,339,998 |
| Marcrist International Limited | £9,336,575 |
| Charles Birch Limited | £9,330,364 |
| York Forty-Four Limited | £9,327,214 |
| Sissons of Sherburn Holdings Limited | £9,318,750 |
| Maria Mallaband 16 Limited | £9,311,598 |
| Joseph E.Swiers,Limited | £9,303,319 |
| Millennium Insurance Brokers Limited | £9,300,000 |
| Coriant UK Limited | £9,292,609 |
| CNIM Clugston (Avonmouth) Limited | £9,290,450 |
| Eshton Ltd | £9,288,616 |
| C.K.Batchelor Limited | £9,288,510 |
| Switch2 Energy Limited | £9,288,291 |
| Andrew Lumley Limited | £9,274,820 |
| Premier Vanguard Limited | £9,270,862 |
| Cromwell Capital Ventures UK Limited | £9,269,515 |
| Urmi Capital Limited | £9,266,426 |
| Holt Doctors Limited | £9,258,548 |
| Bemis Packaging UK Ltd | £9,254,000 |
| Bhullar Bros.Limited | £9,250,804 |
| LGK Farms LLP | £9,245,114 |
| Dreamplayer Limited | £9,244,000 |
| Dreamphoto Limited | £9,242,000 |
| Albert Hill Commercials Limited | £9,236,276 |
| Reed Boardall Transport Limited | £9,232,017 |
| East Transportation Holdings Limited | £9,231,951 |
| Russell Armer Limited | £9,231,119 |
| Connection Flooring Limited | £9,220,939 |
| Minstergate Limited | £9,219,303 |
| C F Abraham Limited | £9,216,807 |
| The Hull & East Yorkshire Medical Research Centre | £9,214,629 |
| Latitude Digital Marketing Limited | £9,214,000 |
| Hornsea Leisure Limited | £9,212,426 |
| J.H. Fenner & Co.(Advanced Engineered Products) | £9,205,000 |
| Hambleton Steel Group Ltd | £9,198,661 |
| Dressadmire Limited | £9,198,000 |
| The Asda Foundation | £9,187,907 |
| Mobus Fabrics Limited | £9,182,448 |
| Advanced Plastics Limited | £9,178,498 |
| Yorkshire Sheeting Group Limited | £9,177,583 |
| Winston (UK) Limited | £9,158,025 |
| Kirk Sandall Academy Trust | £9,147,666 |
| C.F.Struthers Limited | £9,145,919 |
| Inchem Finance Limited | £9,140,764 |
| IUKH Limited | £9,140,600 |
| FMG Group Holdings Limited | £9,140,000 |
| Howarth Timber Engineered Solutions Limited | £9,133,000 |
| Oakmere Homes (Longtown) Ltd | £9,110,162 |
| S.T.L. Trading Company Limited | £9,109,631 |
| Lockers Trawlers Limited | £9,104,109 |
| Wm Morrison Growers Limited | £9,102,000 |
| Rotherham Sand and Gravel Company Limited (The) | £9,099,646 |
| Lowdham Outdoor Leisure Limited | £9,090,144 |
| Bewley's Tea and Coffee UK (Roastery) Limited | £9,084,000 |
| Lightwater Quarries Limited | £9,082,318 |
| G.R. Electrical Services Limited | £9,073,570 |
| Century Construction Limited | £9,067,115 |
| Bossdean Properties Limited | £9,065,578 |
| M. J. McCarthy (Holdings) Limited | £9,060,164 |
| YRG Group Limited | £9,059,953 |
| Concept Recruitment Group Limited | £9,055,847 |
| Collaborative Learning Trust | £9,052,000 |
| John Brooke & Sons Ltd | £9,051,380 |
| SmarDTV (UK) Limited | £9,049,656 |
| Pitts Wilson Limited | £9,049,172 |
| Atkinson Group (Yorkshire) Limited | £9,045,001 |
| WSG Property (Holdings) Limited | £9,044,837 |
| Boost Drinks Limited | £9,042,268 |
| Jones & Egan Estates Limited | £9,039,471 |
| Casterton Leisure Limited | £9,029,864 |
| Key Electrical Contractors & Storefitters Limited | £9,025,106 |
| Carver Engineering Holdings Limited | £9,023,925 |
| Energy Services (Business Power) Ltd | £9,019,670 |
| Lane Rental Services Limited | £9,010,363 |
| Together Roof Energy Limited | £9,010,120 |
| Advance HE | £9,010,000 |
| Appleyard Lees IP LLP | £9,008,981 |
| Monocon Overseas Limited | £9,008,282 |
| OPM (Labels & Packaging) Group Limited | £9,004,478 |
| Crompton Lamps Limited | £9,002,155 |
| Keelham Farm Shop Limited | £9,001,236 |
| John Pawson (Holdings) Limited | £8,996,731 |
| Exemplary Group PLC | £8,993,956 |
| Hacs Holdings Limited | £8,992,585 |
| Bayford & Co. (Developments) Limited | £8,991,345 |
| DFDS Logistics Services Limited | £8,984,952 |
| Elvaston Investments Limited | £8,980,586 |
| Newby Foods Limited | £8,980,258 |
| Hunprenco (Precision Engineers) Limited | £8,977,302 |
| The Big Bale Company (North) Limited | £8,970,258 |
| Apollo Holdco Limited | £8,966,000 |
| G & H Building Services Ltd. | £8,948,401 |

| Company | Value |
|---|---|
| Neil Hudgell Limited | £8,943,898 |
| Centre at Three Ways | £8,937,723 |
| Healthcare House Limited | £8,932,716 |
| Yorkcourt Paragon Limited | £8,932,128 |
| The Kingswood Parks Development Company Limited | £8,926,311 |
| Pick Fisk Limited | £8,926,074 |
| Jeremy Benn Associates Limited | £8,918,719 |
| Cardinal Project Management Limited | £8,918,508 |
| ESP Systex Holdings Limited | £8,913,763 |
| Byworth Boiler Hire Limited | £8,909,464 |
| PFM Packaging Machinery Limited | £8,909,439 |
| 2 Plan Group Limited | £8,902,219 |
| First York Limited | £8,897,000 |
| G-Tuft (2015) Limited | £8,894,229 |
| Insituform Technologies Limited | £8,893,646 |
| HLD (Manchester) Limited | £8,891,788 |
| One Fortress Limited | £8,889,610 |
| Herbert Walkers Limited | £8,889,204 |
| J. Jeffery (Builder) Limited | £8,884,784 |
| Eppleton Quarry Products Limited | £8,883,238 |
| Bramstone Limited | £8,879,825 |
| North Bay Leisure Limited | £8,879,146 |
| Alexanders Prestige Limited | £8,873,615 |
| Optima Legal Services Limited | £8,873,000 |
| Sia Fibral Limited | £8,869,000 |
| London Ebor Developments PLC | £8,868,088 |
| J.R. Williams & Sons Limited | £8,860,664 |
| High Crane Limited | £8,858,034 |
| Star Brands (Holdings) Limited | £8,857,692 |
| Shulmans LLP | £8,851,474 |
| Yes Car Credit (Holdings) Limited | £8,847,000 |
| Cox 22 Limited | £8,839,662 |
| Murton Feeds Limited | £8,836,661 |
| Kendal Caravans Limited | £8,836,437 |
| Provfin Limited | £8,834,000 |
| Arlington Automotive NE Limited | £8,830,000 |
| Leeds and London Group Ltd | £8,828,489 |
| Douglas James Limited | £8,828,094 |
| Bradman-Lake Limited | £8,819,751 |
| Bridgewood Trust Limited | £8,818,329 |
| Watergate Developments Limited | £8,815,089 |
| Shipton Estates Limited | £8,815,018 |
| Nationwide Window Cleaning Limited | £8,803,095 |
| J. & C. Joel Limited | £8,797,836 |
| I-Trust Education | £8,797,322 |
| Christopher Pickering Primary School | £8,784,198 |
| Scarborough College Limited | £8,784,149 |
| The Mosaic Tile Company Limited | £8,763,970 |
| Produmax Limited | £8,762,699 |
| Oxley Developments Company Limited | £8,761,511 |
| Hidrostal (GB) Limited | £8,759,691 |
| R. McDowell Haulage and Distribution Limited | £8,758,004 |
| Opus Energy Group Limited | £8,751,000 |
| Broadacres Services Limited | £8,747,940 |
| Ortus Secured Finance III Limited | £8,735,002 |
| Marpak Extrusions Limited | £8,719,237 |
| C.G. Kendall Limited | £8,712,120 |
| Sheppee International Limited | £8,705,707 |
| Browntree Properties Limited | £8,697,666 |
| New Daffodil Limited | £8,696,000 |
| Dual Seal Glass Ltd. | £8,694,570 |
| National Flexible Limited | £8,688,595 |
| Dusrolbake Limited | £8,685,288 |
| Red Embedded Consulting Limited | £8,682,779 |
| Shepherd Development Company Limited | £8,672,000 |
| Vossloh Cogifer UK Limited | £8,670,083 |
| Fenwick Brothers Limited | £8,669,131 |
| York University Development Company Limited | £8,654,048 |
| Sangwin Holdings Limited | £8,648,869 |
| Shaw & Rhodes Holdings Limited | £8,648,749 |
| Acre Products Limited | £8,645,450 |
| Belle Vue Mills Limited | £8,642,864 |

| Company | Value |
|---|---|
| Ebac Industrial Products Limited | £8,636,351 |
| Swanland Education Trust | £8,633,242 |
| Walkers Holdings One Limited | £8,632,256 |
| George Walker Transport Limited | £8,632,252 |
| West Moor Holdings Limited | £8,630,989 |
| Go Green Limited | £8,630,826 |
| Bawtry Farms Limited | £8,629,964 |
| Apollo Endosurgery UK Ltd | £8,624,000 |
| Scunthorpe United Football Club Limited | £8,620,104 |
| Three Sixty Water Limited | £8,619,000 |
| J.W. Crowther & Son Limited | £8,615,637 |
| EYG Holdings Limited | £8,615,601 |
| Dalesview Developments Limited | £8,615,577 |
| Schenck Process UK Holding Limited | £8,609,000 |
| Aberdeen Enterprise Finance Limited | £8,608,109 |
| Oakapple Homes (Scarborough) Limited | £8,608,046 |
| Hensall Mechanical Services Limited | £8,601,649 |
| MTS Nationwide Limited | £8,585,317 |
| Saur Services (Glasgow) Limited | £8,585,000 |
| Hobson Farming Limited | £8,584,353 |
| C & K Wood (U.K.) Limited | £8,581,554 |
| Nafferton Wold Farms Limited | £8,578,304 |
| F1rst Actuarial PLC | £8,577,406 |
| Skipton Investments Limited | £8,571,000 |
| Mount St John Sporting LLP | £8,566,312 |
| Thomas Owen Care Limited | £8,553,783 |
| Orvec International Limited | £8,552,193 |
| Shouksmith Properties Limited | £8,543,958 |
| Wrigleys Solicitors LLP | £8,518,083 |
| E P E International Limited | £8,517,135 |
| Bridge Street Pentecostal Church | £8,514,140 |
| Techbuyer Limited | £8,512,439 |
| Holf Technologies Limited | £8,510,865 |
| Filtermech Plant Sales Limited | £8,510,836 |
| MCP Environmental Limited | £8,510,657 |
| Crest Roofing Limited | £8,508,032 |
| Temple Way Properties Limited | £8,503,374 |
| PCS Property Solutions Limited | £8,500,021 |
| Mobili Office Design International LLP | £8,498,451 |
| Yorkshire Grown Produce Limited | £8,498,147 |
| (Aq) Limited | £8,496,552 |
| Longwood Engineering Company (Holdings) Limited | £8,495,572 |
| Holmfirth Dyers Holdings Limited | £8,494,353 |
| Hull Cartridge Company Limited | £8,493,687 |
| Techbuyer Group Holdings Limited | £8,492,877 |
| Rhodar Demolition Limited | £8,489,000 |
| Tasker Investments Limited | £8,484,931 |
| Translift Freight Limited | £8,482,747 |
| Futurama Signs Holdings Limited | £8,478,167 |
| Mulgrave Property Group Limited | £8,470,761 |
| Holt Family (Holdings) Limited | £8,467,867 |
| The Bridge Properties & Investments Limited | £8,467,346 |
| Hes Humber Bulk Terminal Limited | £8,467,012 |
| United Autosports Limited | £8,462,466 |
| GO2 Foods Limited | £8,456,783 |
| Oakdale Homes Limited | £8,445,888 |
| CR Estates Limited | £8,444,143 |
| SP & PL Holdings Limited | £8,442,080 |
| Hillcrest Garages (Sowerby Bridge) Limited | £8,434,588 |
| Kexgill (Salford) Limited | £8,434,064 |
| Tydd St Giles Lodge Developments Limited | £8,429,567 |
| Loop Customer Management Limited | £8,416,000 |
| Hospitaller Order of Saint John of God | £8,411,000 |
| Brooklands Property Holdings Limited | £8,406,865 |
| Impact Development Training Ltd. | £8,406,503 |
| C L Medicall Aid Limited | £8,405,868 |
| J.E.C. Investment Company Limited | £8,405,775 |
| T.H.Hobson Limited | £8,393,925 |
| Chas. Long & Son (Aggregates) Limited | £8,387,234 |
| Electrix International Limited | £8,385,830 |
| William G. Search Limited | £8,385,818 |
| Brook Group (Holdings) Limited | £8,384,873 |

| Company | Amount |
|---|---|
| Labelon UK Limited | £8,381,103 |
| Whinlatter Energy Limited | £8,379,922 |
| Surgeforward Limited | £8,375,853 |
| Solvgrin Limited | £8,368,349 |
| Burg-Wachter UK Limited | £8,360,632 |
| Rolawn Limited | £8,359,799 |
| Bulloughs Cleaning Services Limited | £8,355,123 |
| Stainforth Construction LLP | £8,350,218 |
| Bring Cargo Limited | £8,350,098 |
| Waiting for Anya Limited | £8,349,580 |
| Rabbit (Holdings) Limited | £8,346,261 |
| J.Stell & Sons,Limited | £8,343,368 |
| Ormsborough Limited | £8,340,984 |
| Robinson Group (Holdings) Limited | £8,340,191 |
| Fenton Packaging Limited | £8,333,665 |
| Monread Lodge Nursing Home Limited | £8,331,274 |
| The Valley Printing Company, Limited | £8,330,000 |
| Inclusion Housing Community Interest Company | £8,327,506 |
| Tekjur Limited | £8,325,059 |
| Nat Flex Group Limited | £8,320,385 |
| Pipeline Engineering & Supply Co. Limited | £8,317,000 |
| Medical Imaging UK Limited | £8,310,889 |
| Delta Caravans International Limited | £8,306,896 |
| Shorts Industries Limited | £8,306,000 |
| Ward Recycling Limited | £8,298,018 |
| Yorktest Group Limited | £8,297,554 |
| Mulberry Homes Yorkshire Limited | £8,294,768 |
| Horbury Bridge (Holdings) Limited | £8,289,623 |
| Elm Bank (Northumberland) Limited | £8,287,380 |
| Longthorp (Kilpin) Limited | £8,284,226 |
| Provenance Hotels Limited | £8,281,924 |
| Johnsons of Whixley Limited | £8,280,900 |
| Hunters Franchising Limited | £8,272,745 |
| Spectrum Community Health C.I.C. | £8,265,916 |
| Stell Cardboard Tubes Limited | £8,263,559 |
| Trust Care Ltd | £8,263,396 |
| Roberts, Mart (Properties) Ltd. | £8,257,779 |
| Hatfields V Limited | £8,253,861 |
| Holbeck Ghyll Hotel LLP | £8,253,351 |
| Belgrave (North West) Limited | £8,250,138 |
| Ortho-Care (U.K.) Limited | £8,244,353 |
| BFWG Charitable Foundation | £8,242,840 |
| Desk Top Publishing Micro Systems Limited | £8,239,714 |
| Middleton Hall Limited | £8,237,301 |
| JJC Hire Limited | £8,236,143 |
| Bannatyne Fitness (2) Limited | £8,231,819 |
| Assent Building Control Limited | £8,227,262 |
| Procter Bros. Limited | £8,224,126 |
| John Edward Crowther (Holdings) PLC | £8,221,775 |
| Walter Thompson (Contractors) Limited | £8,218,894 |
| Riverside Healthcare Limited | £8,214,113 |
| Sterne Properties Limited | £8,212,129 |
| Holmfirth Dyers Limited | £8,208,684 |
| John Laithwaite Investments Limited | £8,206,637 |
| Stoneferry Limited | £8,203,779 |
| Ypsomed Limited | £8,202,953 |
| M.K.M. Building Supplies (Hull) Limited | £8,202,603 |
| Collett & Sons Limited | £8,199,873 |
| Cleethorpes Properties Limited | £8,194,487 |
| PBS Holdings Limited | £8,189,537 |
| Healthsource (Bromley) Limited | £8,187,948 |
| Congregational Memorial Hall Trust (1978) Limited | £8,180,509 |
| F.C. Stubbings & Sons Limited | £8,180,507 |
| Cutwel Limited | £8,172,209 |
| Regroup (UK) Limited | £8,171,819 |
| Hindle Group Limited | £8,165,647 |
| West Park Estates Limited | £8,163,670 |
| Teescraft Engineering Limited | £8,163,295 |
| C2 Investment Limited | £8,161,580 |
| Hiatt Hardware (UK) Limited | £8,160,066 |
| Mardon Holdings Limited | £8,159,258 |
| Codecrest Limited | £8,148,503 |
| Technimark Limited | £8,146,804 |
| Martindale Group Limited | £8,144,795 |
| The Clarke Chapman Group Limited | £8,144,587 |
| Direct Trade (Yorkshire) Limited | £8,143,643 |
| Yorkshire Halal Meat Supplier Limited | £8,140,659 |
| Johnny's Entertainments (Tyneside) Limited | £8,138,466 |
| Cleaning and Paper Disposables Limited | £8,135,249 |
| The Harris Partnership Limited | £8,125,658 |
| Navartis Holdings Limited | £8,110,066 |
| Smoothwall Limited | £8,108,781 |
| Nightjar Sustainable Power Limited | £8,106,106 |
| Specialist Power Engineering Contracts Limited | £8,105,933 |
| Fred Walter & Sons Limited | £8,104,276 |
| Town Head Farm Products Limited | £8,098,609 |
| GMI Holdings Limited | £8,097,364 |
| Ossett Brewery Pub Company Limited | £8,097,317 |
| The Fuel Trading Company Ltd | £8,096,272 |
| The Boulevard Academy Trust | £8,094,563 |
| Driver Hire Investments Limited | £8,093,015 |
| Polyframe Halifax Limited | £8,092,000 |
| Beaumont ABS Ltd | £8,088,268 |
| BTL Group Limited | £8,086,211 |
| Croft Carehomes Limited | £8,085,563 |
| Schosween 6 Limited | £8,077,556 |
| Global Shipping Services Estates Limited | £8,077,475 |
| Premier Housing (Bradford) Ltd | £8,069,797 |
| Peter Gradon Meat and Poultry Marketing Limited | £8,066,950 |
| M.B. & J. Goodwin Limited | £8,058,624 |
| Power Link Machine (UK) Co Limited | £8,058,320 |
| Clive Brook Limited | £8,050,639 |
| The Harris Group Limited | £8,047,732 |
| BH Energygap LLP | £8,045,942 |
| Grosvenor House Group Holdings Limited | £8,041,852 |
| Harold Newsome Limited | £8,037,933 |
| Mailway Packaging Solutions Limited | £8,035,364 |
| St. Catherines Developments Limited | £8,031,653 |
| Urquhart-Dykes & Lord LLP | £8,029,631 |
| Welcom Software Holdings Limited | £8,026,696 |
| Damac Group Limited | £8,023,029 |
| John King Chains Limited | £8,019,393 |
| Mount St John Equestrian LLP | £8,013,592 |
| Farnsworth Investments Limited | £8,011,000 |
| Clugston Distribution Services Limited | £8,010,413 |
| LEBC Holdings Limited | £8,004,615 |
| High Point Estates (Birstall) Limited | £8,000,337 |
| Hambleton Steel Limited | £7,999,759 |
| Seamore Court Freehold Limited | £7,992,165 |
| Grosvenor Funding Solutions Limited | £7,989,280 |
| Central Land Holdings Ltd | £7,986,600 |
| Bonus Accessories Limited | £7,984,577 |
| CPD Direct Limited | £7,984,005 |
| IQRA Academy Education Trust | £7,983,665 |
| Quirkco Investments Limited | £7,982,103 |
| Yorvik Homes Limited | £7,978,971 |
| P Waddington Limited | £7,976,666 |
| National Coal Mining Museum for England Trust Ltd | £7,975,573 |
| Screen Yorkshire Limited | £7,964,434 |
| Chemfix Products Limited | £7,953,865 |
| Neville Tucker (Group) Limited | £7,952,282 |
| NCA Group Limited | £7,952,000 |
| Angloco Limited | £7,949,193 |
| Job Earnshaw & Bros.Limited | £7,944,610 |
| Eltham Properties Limited | £7,944,296 |
| Moore Building Enterprises Limited | £7,944,132 |
| Ian Firth Holdings Limited | £7,941,722 |
| Academy Leisure Limited | £7,941,605 |
| Pinion Services Limited | £7,939,451 |
| Tenet Business Solutions Limited | £7,922,442 |
| West Yorkshire Spinners Limited | £7,920,797 |
| Elmwood Property Investments Limited | £7,919,345 |
| Rhodes Asset Management Limited | £7,916,497 |
| Furmanite 1986 | £7,915,000 |

| Company | Value |
|---|---|
| Verder Limited | £7,911,800 |
| Tucker Mechanical and Electrical Building Services | £7,908,002 |
| Pure Technology Group Limited | £7,907,969 |
| C.K. Foods (Processing) Limited | £7,900,821 |
| W.E. Jameson and Son Limited | £7,898,114 |
| Victorguard Care PLC | £7,893,992 |
| Gemco Service Limited | £7,889,650 |
| Amco Group Limited | £7,887,219 |
| Gould Tech Solutions Limited | £7,887,000 |
| Wykeland Investments Limited | £7,886,980 |
| Entertainment Alliance (Holdings) Limited | £7,882,731 |
| Entertainment Alliance (UK) Limited | £7,882,731 |
| Mansfield, Pollard & Co. Limited | £7,875,562 |
| LPG Homeheat Limited | £7,874,440 |
| Tower Hill Investments Limited | £7,861,867 |
| Aureus Leisure Limited | £7,859,524 |
| Communisis Data Intelligence Limited | £7,859,001 |
| Walk Investments Limited | £7,851,716 |
| Durham Box Company Limited | £7,850,847 |
| Rosenbauer UK Limited | £7,845,870 |
| Victor Investments & Securities Ltd | £7,844,233 |
| Sewell Education (York) Limited | £7,844,031 |
| Sewell Education (York) Holdings Limited | £7,844,031 |
| Neill & Brown (Shipping) Limited | £7,841,667 |
| Leeds Grand Theatre and Opera House Limited | £7,839,015 |
| Kentmere Limited | £7,835,726 |
| Coal Contractors Limited | £7,834,127 |
| WYG International Projects Limited | £7,832,000 |
| Roseville Care Homes Limited | £7,831,545 |
| Bar 24 Limited | £7,830,906 |
| Chalemere Limited | £7,818,538 |
| Weetwood Hall Limited | £7,818,058 |
| Mytum & Selby Waste Recycling Limited | £7,809,105 |
| CCL Holdings Limited | £7,808,000 |
| Simply Biz Services Limited | £7,805,623 |
| Wilkes Vending Services Limited | £7,798,800 |
| Kexgill (Stockton) Limited | £7,798,080 |
| Consultant Services Group Limited | £7,797,526 |
| Mager Homes Limited | £7,796,762 |
| Automobile Association Personal Finance Limited | £7,795,000 |
| Associated Utility Supplies Limited | £7,790,420 |
| Ceramica Impex Limited | £7,787,237 |
| TFP (Wakefield) Limited | £7,781,263 |
| Zubrance Limited | £7,781,000 |
| Mardon Public Limited Company | £7,780,109 |
| West Yorkshire Fellmongers Limited | £7,776,726 |
| D. Stoker Group Limited | £7,775,774 |
| Church Property Holdings Limited | £7,774,106 |
| Tenetconnect Services Limited | £7,771,862 |
| Salts Estates Limited | £7,770,405 |
| Abram Pulman & Sons Limited | £7,765,058 |
| Lupton Fawcett LLP | £7,764,388 |
| Sunny Day Property Holdings Limited | £7,760,491 |
| Actavo Building Solutions (UK) Limited | £7,759,275 |
| Westway Veterinary Centres Limited | £7,757,779 |
| Corrocoat Limited | £7,755,506 |
| Evans Homes Limited | £7,754,500 |
| Super League (Europe) Limited | £7,750,949 |
| Strachan Holdings Limited | £7,747,093 |
| Sharpsmart Limited | £7,746,783 |
| Teleware Public Limited Company | £7,746,000 |
| Deliver Net Limited | £7,744,923 |
| Fern Hill Holdings Limited | £7,743,659 |
| Darren Smith Builders Limited | £7,731,458 |
| BKS Holdings Limited | £7,728,051 |
| Uriah Woodhead & Son Limited | £7,727,050 |
| TEF Transport Limited | £7,718,015 |
| S.Ross & Co.Limited | £7,714,117 |
| Aston Hall Hotel Limited | £7,713,244 |
| Jubilee Milling Limited | £7,705,935 |
| Yorkshare Limited | £7,700,000 |
| LPG Direct Limited | £7,693,182 |
| CIP (Mill Road Development) LLP | £7,688,000 |
| Wirquin Ltd | £7,686,000 |
| Earthoil Plantations Limited | £7,683,000 |
| Immingham Industrial Estates Limited | £7,681,638 |
| Joda Holdings Limited | £7,681,555 |
| Haddow Group Limited | £7,676,344 |
| Ye Olde Oak Foods Limited | £7,676,213 |
| Kirncroft Engineering Limited | £7,674,754 |
| Abbey Glen Limited | £7,674,632 |
| Morrey Oils Limited | £7,673,684 |
| Carver Engineering Services Limited | £7,671,341 |
| Optibiotix Health PLC | £7,669,203 |
| Logicor (CH) Limited | £7,666,812 |
| Bawtry Investments Limited | £7,665,761 |
| J D Engineering (Northern) Limited | £7,661,311 |
| Evans Residential Holdings Limited | £7,660,413 |
| Matrix International Limited | £7,660,000 |
| Wynperg Investments Limited | £7,659,981 |
| Caspian Group Limited | £7,658,355 |
| Ascot Road Watford Limited | £7,654,000 |
| Eddisons Commercial Limited | £7,652,497 |
| Woodgreen Construction Limited | £7,651,792 |
| Fairfield Developments (Doncaster) Limited | £7,650,907 |
| Heck! Food Limited | £7,641,158 |
| Waxman Energy Limited | £7,637,407 |
| Sewell Facilities Management Limited | £7,629,664 |
| Wrapid Manufacturing Limited | £7,629,174 |
| Thomas Wright/Thorite Group Limited | £7,626,275 |
| Sanderson Contracts Limited | £7,624,837 |
| Eureka! The National Children's Museum. | £7,620,380 |
| Teddy Clark (Holdings) Limited | £7,616,522 |
| West Park Group Limited | £7,607,608 |
| Spellman & Walker Direct Limited | £7,601,286 |
| GM Legato Limited | £7,598,709 |
| Ithaca Energy Developments UK Limited | £7,596,044 |
| Thomas of York Limited | £7,593,923 |
| Arise Virtual Solutions Limited | £7,589,816 |
| H. Wicks (Lindal) Limited | £7,584,210 |
| Advanced Diesel Engineering Limited | £7,577,304 |
| Imexpart Limited | £7,574,660 |
| Manor Coating Systems (Holdings) Limited | £7,573,066 |
| Ellis Patents Holdings Limited | £7,572,219 |
| Grantside Limited | £7,570,232 |
| Duynie Limited | £7,568,990 |
| Control4 EMEA Ltd | £7,566,526 |
| Alvercroft Limited | £7,563,896 |
| Just Teachers Limited | £7,560,216 |
| Humberside Engineering Training Association Ltd | £7,559,012 |
| TEV Holdings Limited | £7,551,275 |
| BDS (Yorkshire) Limited | £7,550,966 |
| Harrison Farms (Kilham) Limited | £7,549,482 |
| Calverts Carpets Limited | £7,548,000 |
| Extract Technology Limited | £7,547,920 |
| Davis Tate Ltd | £7,546,000 |
| Channon and Company Limited | £7,544,441 |
| DAM Investments and Properties Limited | £7,542,690 |
| York Archaeological Trust for Excavation & Research | £7,535,628 |
| Arrow Film Converters Limited | £7,532,842 |
| Cook & Lucas Frozen (Holdings) Limited | £7,531,154 |
| Forward Investment LLP | £7,525,917 |
| Moventas Wind UK Limited | £7,525,001 |
| Cubico (UK) Limited | £7,524,152 |
| Continental Sports Limited | £7,507,731 |
| Luxihomes Limited | £7,496,106 |
| Scarborough Holding Company Limited | £7,495,494 |
| Dutch Imports & Daughters Limited | £7,495,020 |
| Ulster Yarns Limited | £7,488,578 |
| North Killingholme Storage Limited | £7,484,063 |
| Broadland Renewable Energy Limited | £7,478,567 |
| The Darlington Farmers Auction Mart Co Ltd | £7,475,696 |
| Thirsk Farmers Auction Mart Company Limited | £7,472,398 |
| Al-Murad Management Ltd | £7,470,014 |

| Company | Value |
|---|---|
| MHLL Limited | £7,463,930 |
| New Equipment Holdings Limited | £7,459,879 |
| Birstall 140 Limited | £7,458,636 |
| Easypay Services Limited | £7,455,299 |
| The Ice Co Storage & Logistics Limited | £7,454,797 |
| Bulmer & Lumb Holdings Limited | £7,453,764 |
| Wabco Automotive U.K. Limited | £7,451,000 |
| Grimsby Fish Dock Enterprises Limited | £7,446,493 |
| DRC Contract Services Ltd | £7,445,000 |
| Kexgill (Durham) Limited | £7,444,808 |
| E & S Environmental Services Limited | £7,444,000 |
| Braun & Co. Limited | £7,435,812 |
| Thompson Homes (Yorkshire) Ltd. | £7,435,295 |
| Bradonwood Limited | £7,432,206 |
| Ideal Building Systems Holdings Limited | £7,430,316 |
| FLD Limited | £7,429,280 |
| Total Hardware Limited | £7,425,876 |
| Mumtaz Food Products Limited | £7,425,491 |
| Matrix Chemie Holdings Limited | £7,425,346 |
| Matrix Chemie Limited | £7,425,278 |
| J.K.B.Megginson & Sons Limited | £7,417,607 |
| Mansfield Pollard (Holdings) Limited | £7,416,787 |
| Midas Paper Converters Limited | £7,408,378 |
| Sargents Properties Limited | £7,407,376 |
| J P Wild Limited | £7,406,808 |
| Rose Roofing Limited | £7,406,485 |
| K. Fresh Ltd | £7,406,139 |
| Kino & Co. Limited | £7,400,904 |
| Harratts of Wakefield Limited | £7,398,006 |
| Mulard Renewables Limited | £7,395,972 |
| Edward P. Wright Ltd. | £7,393,920 |
| Surgical Innovations Limited | £7,391,000 |
| Lubna Foods Limited | £7,388,081 |
| Alfred Brown (Worsted Mills) Limited | £7,383,857 |
| Future Cleaning Services Limited | £7,383,016 |
| Argrain Limited | £7,376,489 |
| Catholic Care (Diocese of Leeds) | £7,373,479 |
| W.B. Ritchie Farms Limited | £7,369,583 |
| Priestley Homes Limited | £7,361,378 |
| Park Lane Healthcare (Magnolia House) Limited | £7,360,041 |
| Grosvenor Facilities Management Limited | £7,355,590 |
| Candelisa Limited | £7,354,347 |
| Indomito Properties LLP | £7,352,491 |
| RFPG Holdings Limited | £7,350,758 |
| Property Renaissance Limited | £7,350,510 |
| J M Construction (Leeds) Limited | £7,349,994 |
| KTH Engineering Group Limited | £7,348,757 |
| Bradford Trident Limited | £7,344,935 |
| Marble Building Products (Yorkshire) Limited | £7,343,267 |
| GBUK Ltd | £7,339,000 |
| Imerys Fused Minerals Hull Limited | £7,332,000 |
| Bessacarr Properties Limited | £7,331,104 |
| Northgate Lighting Limited | £7,327,151 |
| William Smith Group 1832 Limited | £7,326,137 |
| Knightwood Holdings (2011) Limited | £7,325,000 |
| Michael Wheatley Management Limited | £7,322,615 |
| G.H.Brooks & Co.(Harrogate) Limited | £7,320,532 |
| Sanderson Weatherall Group Limited | £7,312,636 |
| Victor Manufacturing Limited | £7,312,146 |
| Westdale Group Limited | £7,306,822 |
| Mark Anglin Associates Limited | £7,305,398 |
| QWP Limited | £7,301,590 |
| Parkhouse Lakeland LLP | £7,300,251 |
| W. S. Westin Group Limited | £7,299,867 |
| Kingstown Furniture Limited | £7,298,008 |
| M. Kettlewell (Melmerby) Limited | £7,295,883 |
| Twiflex Limited | £7,295,000 |
| West Riding Masonic Charities Limited | £7,289,974 |
| Abacus Direct Limited | £7,282,809 |
| Wm.Allison & Sons Limited | £7,276,834 |
| Quintor (UK) Limited Liability Partnership | £7,273,434 |
| Brandon Group Limited | £7,271,373 |
| Green Flag Group Limited | £7,269,389 |
| Quay Propco Limited | £7,266,498 |
| Norman Jackson (Farmers) Limited | £7,263,844 |
| Audley Court Hollins Hall Limited | £7,255,681 |
| C P Group of Companies Limited | £7,254,812 |
| Riding Properties Limited | £7,254,600 |
| Rockar 2 Limited | £7,253,450 |
| York & District Investment Company Limited | £7,250,515 |
| Alfa Site Services Limited | £7,242,923 |
| Nationwide Structures Limited | £7,238,779 |
| The Franklyn Group Limited | £7,226,316 |
| E. Houseman & Son Limited | £7,225,148 |
| Doncaster Central Development Trust CIC | £7,219,111 |
| Everard Group Limited | £7,218,611 |
| Ivy Farm Limited | £7,215,347 |
| Humber Properties Limited | £7,213,677 |
| Stafford Mills Holdings Limited | £7,208,849 |
| Keston Boilers Limited | £7,206,000 |
| Stiller Warehousing & Distribution Limited | £7,204,536 |
| Samuel Grant (Leeds) Limited | £7,189,171 |
| Llandudno Bay Hotel & Spa Limited | £7,188,976 |
| Specialist Cars of Malton Limited | £7,188,080 |
| Talpole Limited | £7,187,587 |
| Nagra Properties Limited | £7,187,409 |
| Univer Manufacturing Company Ltd | £7,179,782 |
| Leeds Design Innovation Centre Ltd | £7,179,359 |
| York Civic Trust | £7,175,404 |
| John Rannoch Limited | £7,174,000 |
| Stevro (Holdings) Limited | £7,169,592 |
| T Soanes & Son (Potatoes) Ltd | £7,167,140 |
| The Leeds Library | £7,164,296 |
| Wellbridge Properties Limited | £7,161,178 |
| Collett Logistics Limited | £7,157,548 |
| W.S. Bayston & Son Limited | £7,156,713 |
| Wandahome (South Cave) Limited | £7,155,596 |
| Pacific Lifestyle Limited | £7,154,893 |
| Maria Mallaband 7 Limited | £7,153,771 |
| 24 Seven Communications Limited | £7,152,069 |
| R.J. Howard Engineers Limited | £7,151,239 |
| Newby Manor Estates Limited | £7,140,896 |
| Express Bi Folding Doors Limited | £7,137,476 |
| John Laithwaite Partners LLP | £7,135,912 |
| Calderys UK Ltd | £7,134,768 |
| SLS Group Limited | £7,132,289 |
| Eurocentral Hotels Limited | £7,130,856 |
| Primeur Limited | £7,130,508 |
| Rackham Housefloors Limited | £7,130,419 |
| Sabrina Health Care Limited | £7,129,353 |
| Yorkshire Prosperity Limited | £7,125,829 |
| N. Peal (Retail) Limited | £7,119,010 |
| Edmund Optics Ltd. | £7,113,301 |
| R.Smith (Windermere) Limited | £7,112,623 |
| Abbot Investments (North Africa) Limited | £7,110,889 |
| Tenetlime Limited | £7,109,083 |
| Extrudakerb (Maltby Engineering) Limited | £7,108,184 |
| Cumbria Wildlife Trust Limited | £7,107,688 |
| K.M. Holmes (Bradford) Limited | £7,103,112 |
| John Roberts Ventures Limited | £7,103,004 |
| Service Metals (Midlands) Limited | £7,101,123 |
| Lookrich Ltd | £7,098,417 |
| Gregory Property Group Limited | £7,098,403 |
| Kingsoak Limited | £7,094,380 |
| Oakland Farms Limited | £7,089,447 |
| West Retford Hotel Limited | £7,079,026 |
| Talk Direct (Leeds) Ltd | £7,075,408 |
| Durham & Tees Community Ventures Fundco (No.1) | £7,072,157 |
| Whymar Limited | £7,070,277 |
| Amvale Medical Transport Limited | £7,070,172 |
| AMT2 Limited | £7,070,172 |
| Richard Maxwell Limited | £7,065,031 |
| Etas Limited | £7,062,110 |
| Hazel Products UK Limited | £7,059,598 |

| Company | Amount |
|---|---|
| Shepherd Homes Limited | £7,059,000 |
| GM Legato Property Limited | £7,057,761 |
| NCI Vehicle Rescue PLC | £7,056,217 |
| The Irongate Group Limited | £7,051,268 |
| Aire Valley Properties Limited | £7,050,554 |
| Armstrong Priestley Holdings Limited | £7,050,515 |
| Waterside Colours Limited | £7,049,195 |
| J R Firby Ltd | £7,047,908 |
| LTT Vending Ltd | £7,044,693 |
| C. K. Properties (UK) Limited | £7,043,956 |
| Ravensfield Properties Limited | £7,036,497 |
| Parkin International Engineering Services Limited | £7,033,755 |
| P. I. Bioscience Limited | £7,030,000 |
| WMK Securities LLP | £7,028,678 |
| Bahson Colour Print Limited | £7,023,557 |
| Rothay Garden Hotel Limited | £7,017,113 |
| 2 Plan Wealth Management Limited | £7,012,711 |
| Setbray Properties (1997) Limited | £7,010,128 |
| K Rouse Civil Engineers Limited | £7,006,178 |
| Power Health Products Limited | £7,005,117 |
| R M Solar Limited | £7,004,510 |
| Julian Roche Associates Limited | £7,001,895 |
| Pamant Limited | £7,000,258 |
| Morris Family Investments Ltd | £7,000,084 |
| ANB Advanced Solutions Limited | £6,994,252 |
| Burton Agnes Stud Company Limited (The) | £6,993,302 |
| Hugh Rice (Whitefriargate) Limited | £6,982,234 |
| Ovalhouse Limited | £6,979,794 |
| W W Hotels Limited | £6,975,428 |
| Sewell Investments Limited | £6,967,884 |
| Hi Resolution (Production) Limited | £6,966,081 |
| Augean Property Limited | £6,964,000 |
| Woodham Academy | £6,962,000 |
| Context World Limited | £6,959,775 |
| Bradleys Jewellers Limited | £6,956,417 |
| Rollings Investments Limited | £6,954,009 |
| John Dickinson Transport Limited | £6,952,823 |
| Sissons Limited | £6,948,688 |
| The George A. Moore Foundation | £6,943,880 |
| Eden Holdings (UK) Limited | £6,937,941 |
| Stickyeyes Limited | £6,937,000 |
| Maria Mallaband (6) Limited | £6,931,560 |
| Joshua Ellis and Company,Limited | £6,929,004 |
| Overseas Trading Limited | £6,927,554 |
| Fradley Properties Ltd | £6,925,966 |
| Olympus Print Group Limited | £6,923,480 |
| Q. R. I. Ltd | £6,920,941 |
| Leeds Jewish Welfare Board | £6,919,244 |
| Polyframe Norwich Ltd | £6,919,000 |
| JCCO 387 Limited | £6,918,258 |
| Parker & Parker Limited | £6,917,421 |
| Whitakers Chocolates Limited | £6,914,470 |
| Daniel Gath Homes Limited | £6,913,615 |
| Riby Grange Farming Company Limited | £6,900,235 |
| Bronte Academy Trust | £6,899,262 |
| Brocklesby Limited | £6,899,110 |
| Morris & Son (Leeds) Limited | £6,898,652 |
| Mrs. J. C. Altham & Sons (Morecambe) Limited | £6,897,950 |
| Sanderson Weatherall LLP | £6,891,882 |
| Team (Impression) Limited | £6,890,558 |
| Team (Impression) Holdings PLC | £6,890,558 |
| Woodgreen Construction Holdings Limited | £6,888,955 |
| Evolution Schools Learning Trust | £6,884,000 |
| ACL Estates Limited | £6,883,089 |
| Paragon Foodservice Limited | £6,882,275 |
| San Pedro Properties Limited | £6,881,247 |
| Redbrick Yorkshire Limited | £6,879,325 |
| John Veitch Limited | £6,876,713 |
| Blackwood Hall Ltd | £6,875,361 |
| Arncliffe Homes Limited | £6,873,447 |
| Inspiring Futures Academy Trust | £6,869,202 |
| Butterfield Signs Limited | £6,868,311 |

| Company | Amount |
|---|---|
| B.R.T. Supplies Limited | £6,867,991 |
| Taniya Properties Ltd | £6,866,502 |
| T.L.G. Properties Limited | £6,853,620 |
| Ralph Ellerker (1795) Limited | £6,852,614 |
| APC (GB) Limited | £6,851,825 |
| M.N.S. Textiles Limited | £6,850,807 |
| Daresbury Park Developments Limited | £6,845,533 |
| Metal Drum Company Limited (The) | £6,842,350 |
| Confection By Design Limited | £6,842,000 |
| Thirsk Racecourse Limited | £6,840,445 |
| Eimskip UK Limited | £6,833,338 |
| Steadplan Group Limited | £6,832,957 |
| LMM Holdings Limited | £6,827,562 |
| A. Dyson & Son (Patterns) Limited | £6,826,248 |
| Kwiktuf Holdings Limited | £6,826,050 |
| EPMS Group Limited | £6,824,816 |
| Wolds Investments Limited | £6,823,630 |
| J.A. Richardson (Electrical) Limited | £6,821,206 |
| Boxford Holdings Limited | £6,819,343 |
| Kexby Investments Limited | £6,818,139 |
| Place2invest Ltd | £6,816,634 |
| Elmwood Design Limited | £6,811,926 |
| Healan Ingredients Limited | £6,801,903 |
| Dakin Industries Limited | £6,800,247 |
| M H & J Park and Son Limited | £6,795,207 |
| Arville Textiles Limited | £6,792,275 |
| Matisa (U.K.) Limited | £6,790,409 |
| Benenden Wellbeing Limited | £6,790,000 |
| Skelton Limited | £6,786,900 |
| Peak Oil Products (Northern) Limited | £6,785,770 |
| Tracsis Traffic Data Limited | £6,785,000 |
| Strata Homes Midlands Limited | £6,783,000 |
| Osprey Limited | £6,780,147 |
| Pear Tree Projects Limited | £6,779,746 |
| R.N.Smith Holdings Limited | £6,777,683 |
| F.T.Everard & Sons Limited | £6,777,676 |
| York Science Park Limited | £6,774,824 |
| Ticket Arena Limited | £6,773,197 |
| The Christian Trust | £6,772,846 |
| United Anodisers Limited | £6,772,735 |
| York123 Limited | £6,770,524 |
| Fridlington Farms Limited | £6,768,004 |
| E K Holdings Limited | £6,763,358 |
| E K Motor Factors Limited | £6,763,258 |
| Weightlifter Bodies Limited | £6,760,288 |
| Halbert Limited | £6,760,236 |
| Naught One Ltd | £6,758,679 |
| Pattinson 3 Limited | £6,754,343 |
| National Coaching Foundation (The) | £6,747,385 |
| Purple Bricks Company Limited | £6,736,512 |
| Pagani UK Limited | £6,736,359 |
| JVL Homewares (UK) Limited | £6,732,930 |
| Hawes & Co Limited | £6,731,000 |
| Michael Wheatley Finance Limited | £6,730,185 |
| Yarm Estates Limited | £6,726,748 |
| Peter Ramsey & Sons Limited | £6,723,840 |
| Nidec SR Drives Ltd. | £6,723,260 |
| 8point8 Support Limited | £6,723,066 |
| Keighley Fleece Mills Company Limited | £6,721,422 |
| Christians Against Poverty | £6,721,000 |
| Hannibal Holdings Limited | £6,720,000 |
| Advanced Couplings Limited | £6,718,171 |
| Cromwell Polythene Limited | £6,716,504 |
| The Kej LLP | £6,713,246 |
| Kingstown Associates Limited | £6,711,871 |
| Hartley Property Trust (1991) Limited | £6,710,658 |
| Harpers Environmental Limited | £6,710,298 |
| Normanton Laminating Services Limited | £6,710,266 |
| Trupart Limited | £6,704,825 |
| Inhoco 2082 Limited | £6,704,825 |
| Redmayne Capital Limited | £6,703,000 |
| Pet Brands Limited | £6,702,825 |

| Company | Value |
|---|---|
| Pure Retirement Limited | £6,701,000 |
| South Coast Catering Limited | £6,698,000 |
| Shedden Farms Limited | £6,696,635 |
| Arctic Waters Limited | £6,696,613 |
| Specialist Surfacing Limited | £6,689,308 |
| Leach Colour Limited | £6,688,141 |
| House of Townend Limited | £6,687,892 |
| Cullingworth LLP | £6,686,769 |
| Robinson Contract Services Limited | £6,686,764 |
| County Turf Limited | £6,686,297 |
| Saferoad UK Ltd | £6,685,925 |
| Laurence Kirkby (Farms) Limited | £6,679,599 |
| West Tower Property Limited | £6,679,127 |
| Jacksons Transport (West Riding) Limited | £6,678,589 |
| Dufton Plumbing & Heating Supplies Limited | £6,674,416 |
| W. P. Holdings Limited | £6,671,719 |
| Strong Life Care Limited | £6,664,062 |
| Fope Limited | £6,663,000 |
| Future Forwarding Company Limited | £6,658,975 |
| West Tower Country House Limited | £6,655,521 |
| Yarrows Aggregates Limited | £6,654,394 |
| Callcredit Data Solutions Limited | £6,652,000 |
| Sundown Pets Garden Limited | £6,651,747 |
| Havelok Limited | £6,648,812 |
| PAS Holding Company Ltd | £6,644,989 |
| Heatseam Limited | £6,643,113 |
| Batteryback PLC | £6,642,090 |
| NTEX Limited | £6,641,742 |
| SWL Holdings Limited | £6,640,821 |
| Surefreight (International) Limited | £6,638,041 |
| Armstrong-Priestley Limited | £6,636,966 |
| Ernest Cooper Limited | £6,631,030 |
| Steel Beams and Columns Limited | £6,629,005 |
| Yorkshire Farmhouse Eggs Limited | £6,621,763 |
| Luscombe Motors Limited | £6,620,787 |
| Gees Haulage Limited | £6,619,141 |
| Gico Limited | £6,615,675 |
| Pettra Limited | £6,614,345 |
| Barwick of Bradford Limited | £6,611,644 |
| Newby Manor Investments Limited | £6,611,178 |
| Giovanni Tomasso Limited | £6,610,512 |
| GES Recycling Ltd. | £6,610,437 |
| West Park Inns Limited | £6,600,398 |
| Luxury Fabrics Limited | £6,599,472 |
| W.McClure Limited | £6,597,411 |
| C.S.L. Industrial Limited | £6,597,145 |
| Apex Hydraulics Limited | £6,596,953 |
| Patrington Haven Leisure Park Limited | £6,596,699 |
| Nynet Limited | £6,595,646 |
| Shine: Support and Help in Education | £6,592,991 |
| Highfield Awarding Body for Compliance Limited | £6,591,566 |
| Made Television Ltd. | £6,587,992 |
| Orean Personal Care Limited | £6,587,196 |
| R Safety Products Holdings Limited | £6,583,839 |
| Melbourne Street Properties Limited | £6,580,539 |
| M. Higgins Limited | £6,579,923 |
| Flatfish Limited | £6,579,251 |
| Henry Williams Limited | £6,575,311 |
| Tall Oaks Academy Trust Ltd | £6,570,000 |
| W. Nutt & Son Limited | £6,555,392 |
| Donelec Group Limited | £6,553,706 |
| Formula Films Limited | £6,552,452 |
| Hodgson Sealants (Holdings) Limited | £6,547,002 |
| Federation of Mowden Schools Academy Trust | £6,547,000 |
| Access 13 Limited | £6,543,659 |
| EFS Property Holdings Limited | £6,542,999 |
| Healthtrak (UK) Limited | £6,541,531 |
| Malik Halls Limited | £6,535,921 |
| Unison Limited | £6,534,455 |
| Chadwick Lawrence LLP | £6,533,457 |
| B.W. Industries (Holdings) Limited | £6,532,192 |
| On Line Design & Engineering Limited | £6,530,757 |
| Londyne Limited | £6,530,349 |
| Jimmy Corrigan's Limited | £6,527,887 |
| Specialised Orthotic Services Limited | £6,523,001 |
| Jacksons Building Components Limited | £6,522,837 |
| Dryband One Limited | £6,520,188 |
| Procter (Bordley) Limited | £6,513,314 |
| Bay Properties Letting Company Limited | £6,512,755 |
| Danby Holdings Limited | £6,512,332 |
| High Point Estates (Gateshead) Limited | £6,509,340 |
| Head Office Interiors Limited | £6,508,200 |
| Bonus Electrical Limited | £6,501,499 |
| ACS Stainless Steel Fixings Limited | £6,493,566 |
| Vida Hall Limited | £6,491,547 |
| Boxer Properties (Bradford) Limited | £6,488,382 |
| NVELOPE Rainscreen Systems Limited | £6,488,198 |
| British American Railway Services Limited | £6,471,127 |
| Gettheworldmoving Ltd | £6,465,605 |
| Easysoft Limited | £6,465,506 |
| Giles Foods Limited | £6,464,000 |
| Northern Touch Limited | £6,459,714 |
| Abacus Direct Properties Limited | £6,459,212 |
| T L B Properties Limited | £6,458,832 |
| John L. Brierley Limited | £6,456,603 |
| Learning Accord Multi Academy Trust | £6,449,308 |
| Bell Elliot Leisure Limited | £6,443,571 |
| A. Rhodes (Haulage) Limited | £6,441,149 |
| Regal Food Products Group PLC | £6,437,918 |
| Bibby Transmissions Limited | £6,435,000 |
| Project Kahn Ltd | £6,434,416 |
| J.N. Bentley Properties Limited | £6,432,696 |
| The Bishop Konstant Catholic Academy Trust | £6,431,106 |
| Info Supplier Limited | £6,431,000 |
| Castle Hall Academy Trust | £6,431,000 |
| Repchoice Limited | £6,429,127 |
| Transforming Lives for Good (TLG) Ltd | £6,428,286 |
| Merritt & Fryers Limited | £6,427,277 |
| Virtual College Limited | £6,425,079 |
| Takahe Holdings Ltd | £6,424,423 |
| Cambridge Glasshouse Company Limited | £6,422,699 |
| Alphamore Corporation Ltd | £6,422,254 |
| Total Oynx Limited | £6,421,439 |
| Spring Cottage Academy | £6,420,685 |
| Freedom Refreshments Limited | £6,419,540 |
| Torne Valley Limited | £6,419,472 |
| York Heritage (The Hall Thornton Le Dale) Limited | £6,416,227 |
| Just Lettings Limited | £6,414,418 |
| F A S 2000 Limited | £6,409,000 |
| Scothern Construction Limited | £6,407,802 |
| Stamp Jackson & Procter Limited | £6,406,011 |
| That Company Called If Limited | £6,405,384 |
| Hollin Hall Holdings Limited | £6,400,033 |
| Gaynor Sports Limited | £6,399,801 |
| ERS Transition Limited | £6,398,649 |
| Wakefield Hospice | £6,395,988 |
| Rema Tip Top Industry UK Limited | £6,395,498 |
| Robert Rook Estates Limited | £6,386,894 |
| AJS 22 Ltd | £6,385,859 |
| Century Homes Limited | £6,385,543 |
| Donisthorpe Hall | £6,384,996 |
| Wemmergill Moor Limited | £6,382,962 |
| Harold Newsome Holdings Limited | £6,379,583 |
| Harrogate14 Limited | £6,376,814 |
| Motorsure Limited | £6,373,772 |
| Northern Energy Supplies Limited | £6,370,661 |
| Leeds Welding Company Limited (The) | £6,369,190 |
| Thermac (Hire) Limited | £6,369,000 |
| Overgate Hospice | £6,364,767 |
| Brighter Futures Academy Trust | £6,361,151 |
| MTW Architectural Limited | £6,359,153 |
| Kepwick Farms Limited | £6,358,572 |
| Pointer Holdings Limited | £6,358,180 |
| P & B Kennedy Holdings Limited | £6,356,910 |

| Company | Turnover |
|---|---|
| Gradebatch Limited | £6,356,758 |
| F B Taylor (Cable Contractors) Limited | £6,355,368 |
| York Area Quaker Meeting in Britain | £6,352,690 |
| Ice Fresh Seafood Limited | £6,348,604 |
| Dalekim Developments Limited | £6,346,927 |
| Leeds University Union | £6,342,411 |
| Better Fish Limited | £6,340,903 |
| Murphy (Yorkshire) Ltd | £6,339,133 |
| Bower Green Limited | £6,338,209 |
| HCF Poultry Limited | £6,337,507 |
| Caddick (Mill Harbour) Limited | £6,337,193 |
| Neil Price Limited | £6,335,094 |
| Rhal Farms Limited | £6,331,266 |
| IF Cardboard Creations Limited | £6,328,084 |
| Dennis Williams Limited | £6,319,750 |
| Capernwray Missionary Fellowship of Torchbearers | £6,319,417 |
| Paragon Creative Limited | £6,316,103 |
| Wetherells Contracts Limited | £6,314,174 |
| M.B.E. Glazing Systems Limited | £6,314,125 |
| Architectural Steel Limited | £6,313,418 |
| Crows Nest Camp Limited | £6,313,383 |
| Scan-Thors (U.K.) Limited | £6,311,498 |
| Titan Cement U.K. Limited | £6,310,740 |
| Psona Limited | £6,308,850 |
| Cat Tech (Europe) Limited | £6,307,947 |
| Strainstall UK Limited | £6,307,703 |
| Parrs Point Limited | £6,307,373 |
| Drinkwater's Mushrooms Limited | £6,307,143 |
| Land Acquisitions Limited | £6,306,726 |
| SKB2016 Limited | £6,301,403 |
| Waste Services Group Limited | £6,298,529 |
| One Stop Business Finance Limited | £6,297,749 |
| TGH Capital Limited | £6,297,431 |
| Winterton Community Academy | £6,296,931 |
| Eido Limited | £6,295,456 |
| Aquarm (Hull) Limited | £6,293,300 |
| Gale and Phillipson Investment Services Ltd | £6,292,617 |
| Rufforth Park Limited | £6,291,053 |
| Stock Redler Limited | £6,290,000 |
| Moda Living (Angel Gardens) Limited | £6,289,261 |
| J.H. McCloy & Co Limited | £6,288,351 |
| Frontica Business Solutions Limited | £6,288,000 |
| Bermar Building Company Limited | £6,285,043 |
| Specialist Ceiling Services Holdings Limited | £6,279,840 |
| Everlast (Group) Limited | £6,277,057 |
| Turnberry Holiday Park Limited | £6,274,469 |
| Whaleys (Bradford) Limited | £6,273,664 |
| Triangle Motor Co. Limited | £6,271,105 |
| Hensall Group Limited | £6,270,466 |
| Hexon Limited | £6,268,956 |
| GEV Holdings Limited | £6,268,332 |
| Warden Farming Company Limited | £6,267,300 |
| Bluestone Leasing Limited | £6,266,584 |
| Pecan Deluxe Candy (Europe) Limited | £6,265,502 |
| IQ Power Holdings Limited | £6,265,000 |
| Chinnaraja Estates Limited | £6,262,404 |
| Revis Transport Limited | £6,257,121 |
| Malik Real Estate Limited | £6,257,083 |
| Techmotion Limited | £6,255,134 |
| Warners Fishmerchants Limited | £6,253,958 |
| Aysgarth School Trust Limited | £6,251,172 |
| The Inn at Grasmere Limited | £6,251,122 |
| F. Peter Robinson Limited | £6,250,694 |
| Sukho Limited | £6,249,959 |
| Academic Appointments 2017 Limited | £6,243,434 |
| DFDS Seaways Irish Sea Holding Ltd | £6,242,159 |
| Rishworth School | £6,240,405 |
| R and A Hotels Group Ltd | £6,237,904 |
| Blacks Visual Merchandising Limited | £6,237,552 |
| Arrow Industrial Group Limited | £6,234,213 |
| Huntcliff Academy Trust | £6,233,588 |
| Advertising Principles Holdings Limited | £6,232,214 |
| H.A. Lambert (Farmers) Limited | £6,225,982 |
| Ribblesdale Motors Limited | £6,225,803 |
| Clays of Addingham Limited | £6,225,383 |
| Joda Freight Limited | £6,221,817 |
| Waxman Holdings Limited | £6,221,062 |
| New Month Limited | £6,219,822 |
| The Calls' Riverside Property Company Limited | £6,218,767 |
| Springfield Solutions Limited | £6,218,166 |
| Brianplant (Humberside) Limited | £6,216,076 |
| Togel Contractors Limited | £6,214,073 |
| Holmesterne Farm Co. Limited | £6,213,938 |
| The Just Partnership Limited | £6,209,919 |
| Enact Conveyancing Limited | £6,209,000 |
| Langlands Nurseries Limited | £6,208,712 |
| Shiny Sky Limited | £6,208,078 |
| Johnston and Jeff Limited | £6,205,282 |
| Thomson Limited | £6,204,113 |
| Sayers Road Tanker Rentals Limited | £6,204,066 |
| R.O.Arnold,Limited | £6,203,053 |
| K Hewitt Holdings Limited | £6,199,472 |
| SDG (Newport) Limited | £6,199,011 |
| On Line People Limited | £6,196,157 |
| Prestige Recruitment Specialists Limited | £6,193,814 |
| Ebco (Holdings) Limited | £6,190,259 |
| Virtual College Holdings Limited | £6,190,192 |
| Johnsons Wellfield Ltd | £6,188,132 |
| Longwood Engineering Company Limited | £6,187,718 |
| Lindley (Holdings) Limited | £6,186,159 |
| Armthorpe Academy Trust | £6,186,000 |
| Eastman Staples Limited | £6,183,430 |
| Kadmous Holdings (UK) Limited. | £6,183,145 |
| Origin Packaging Limited | £6,181,596 |
| Larkham Leisure Limited | £6,181,064 |
| Allsop Holdings Limited | £6,179,257 |
| Kingstown Associates (Holdings) Limited | £6,176,275 |
| Kirwin Brothers Ltd. | £6,175,269 |
| Gazelle Travel Limited | £6,173,293 |
| Torsion Group Holdings Limited | £6,172,372 |
| Hull & Humber Chamber of Commerce Industry | £6,171,418 |
| Anord Mardix Critical Power Services Limited | £6,163,623 |
| Munford Haulage Limited | £6,163,288 |
| Lights4fun Limited | £6,162,224 |
| Larchwell Limited | £6,162,024 |
| Hapimag Resorts & Residences (UK) Limited | £6,161,000 |
| Quest 4 Limited | £6,159,772 |
| Whetley Mills Limited | £6,159,364 |
| XP School Trust Limited | £6,152,000 |
| Bibis Restaurants Limited | £6,151,203 |
| Evans Ashford Investments Limited | £6,148,712 |
| Stramongate Properties Limited | £6,147,928 |
| Batley Academy Trust | £6,144,359 |
| Avacta Life Sciences Limited | £6,143,788 |
| Tocketts Mill Limited | £6,143,131 |
| The Real Yorkshire Pudding Co Limited | £6,142,472 |
| R.E. and R. Duffield and Sons Limited | £6,142,128 |
| Precis (1638) Limited | £6,139,629 |
| K. Hewitt and Co. Limited | £6,139,007 |
| Adapted Vehicle Hire Limited | £6,133,799 |
| Loscoe Investments Ltd | £6,132,237 |
| OC317233 LLP | £6,130,549 |
| Cramscene Limited | £6,130,488 |
| DB Cargo Maintenance Limited | £6,127,000 |
| Cheque Exchange Limited | £6,126,000 |
| Sovereign Reserve Limited | £6,123,735 |
| RF Racing Limited | £6,120,565 |
| D Sales (U.K.) Limited | £6,118,134 |
| David Frost Estate Agents Limited | £6,114,000 |
| LSS Waste Management Limited | £6,113,851 |
| C.K. (Fast Food Suppliers) Limited | £6,112,846 |
| Waxman International Limited | £6,112,058 |
| Eldred (1982) Holdings Limited | £6,111,096 |
| Low Moor Properties Limited | £6,108,042 |

| | |
|---|---|
| Eldercliff Limited | £6,107,408 |
| The Propaganda Agency Limited | £6,106,919 |
| Wauldby Associates Limited | £6,105,789 |
| Ramsdens Solicitors LLP | £6,103,136 |
| Hexagon Properties Limited | £6,102,216 |
| West Coast Railway Company Ltd | £6,100,849 |
| Pipes & Tubes (2010) Limited | £6,099,530 |
| Harpin Parkin Aviation Limited | £6,087,185 |
| Shaws (Huddersfield) Limited | £6,083,441 |
| TEV Limited | £6,080,708 |
| Pure Data Solutions Limited | £6,077,301 |
| P. W. Greenhalgh Holdings Limited | £6,076,860 |
| Britt Broadbent Limited | £6,075,474 |
| Trans-European Port Services (G.B.) Limited | £6,073,000 |
| Thimbleby Farms Limited | £6,072,814 |
| F.T. Construction Group (Holdings) Ltd. | £6,069,442 |
| Echem Limited | £6,066,739 |
| Rossendale Transport Limited | £6,062,221 |
| Bellow Properties Limited | £6,059,304 |
| GBA (Holdings) Limited | £6,058,541 |
| Cerros Properties Limited | £6,056,470 |
| Pengems Limited | £6,051,949 |
| Brian Mager Limited | £6,050,239 |
| Finley Structures Ltd | £6,042,917 |
| Lidget LLP | £6,042,062 |
| L.F.C. Horkstow Limited | £6,041,359 |
| Rollfields Limited | £6,038,251 |
| Premier People Solutions Limited | £6,036,372 |
| Inspired Learning Multi Academy Trust | £6,034,157 |
| Snugpak Limited | £6,032,697 |
| Lundie Farming Limited | £6,031,971 |
| Grand-Riverland & Co. Limited | £6,030,480 |
| Marshall Quarry Products Limited | £6,028,407 |
| J.A.Godfrey & Sons,Limited | £6,024,350 |
| Plasmor (Sabey Kirby) Limited | £6,023,699 |
| Futurama Limited | £6,023,623 |
| Brecks Farm Limited | £6,020,584 |
| J.Long & Sons (Haulage) Limited | £6,017,895 |
| Newlands Community Association (Trading) Limited | £6,015,645 |
| 4B Elevator Components Limited | £6,009,338 |
| Tradepark Limited | £6,002,306 |
| Mena Residential Limited | £6,000,678 |
| Athena PTS Holdings Limited | £6,000,120 |
| CYB Investments Limited | £6,000,000 |
| Carus Green Limited | £5,998,833 |
| Saferoad VRS Ltd | £5,996,440 |
| Sherwood Restaurants Ltd | £5,993,591 |
| Castle Industrial Supplies Ltd | £5,993,190 |
| Dukeries Homes Limited | £5,990,898 |
| Interactive Projects & Design Limited | £5,989,634 |
| James Chambers (Timber Merchants) Limited | £5,986,053 |
| Makins Limited | £5,984,891 |
| Webevents Limited | £5,977,661 |
| Richard Craven (Keighley) Limited | £5,977,307 |
| Anthony Hodges Consulting Limited | £5,976,207 |
| YPS Valves Limited | £5,975,981 |
| Springfield Healthcare (The Grange) Limited | £5,974,054 |
| G M Stephenson Ltd | £5,972,901 |
| Wood Auto Supplies Limited | £5,972,761 |
| Don Valley Engineering Holdings Limited | £5,972,140 |
| Keepflying LLP | £5,972,016 |
| Premier Communications Ltd | £5,962,435 |
| Age Partnership Limited | £5,960,000 |
| Principles Communications Limited | £5,959,616 |
| Newlands Community Association | £5,958,119 |
| M.F. Strawson (Maidenwell) Limited | £5,954,116 |
| Quest Solutions (UK) Ltd | £5,954,081 |
| Havercroft Construction Limited | £5,952,474 |
| Deehurst Limited | £5,948,578 |
| Ian Firth Hardware Limited | £5,945,352 |
| Boparan Foods Limited | £5,944,000 |
| Absolutely Cultured Limited | £5,943,800 |
| John Hornby Skewes and Company Limited | £5,940,197 |
| Edward Fisher & Co. Limited | £5,939,764 |
| Barton Park Homes Limited | £5,938,509 |
| Stuncroft Limited | £5,937,721 |
| Iconx Ltd | £5,932,440 |
| Kingasia Foods Limited | £5,930,015 |
| White Rose Finance Company Limited | £5,927,005 |
| L.S. Transmission Consultancy Limited | £5,924,797 |
| Swarco Traffic Limited | £5,921,731 |
| Smiles for Miles Limited | £5,917,767 |
| Turbine Efficiency Group Limited | £5,917,165 |
| Carafax Limited | £5,916,370 |
| Sellers International Limited | £5,912,552 |
| L. Harrison (Properties) Limited | £5,907,462 |
| Giroscope Limited | £5,905,291 |
| Compair Holdings Limited | £5,903,883 |
| Provident Print Limited | £5,903,000 |
| C F Struthers (Holdings) Limited | £5,902,560 |
| Dalmore Capital (Rochdale 2) Limited | £5,901,293 |
| Langdale Close Properties Limited | £5,900,451 |
| New Century Foods Limited | £5,890,012 |
| Bennett Potatoes Limited | £5,889,750 |
| Askern UK Limited | £5,889,012 |
| Moortown Plant Limited | £5,888,806 |
| Encounter Production Limited | £5,888,802 |
| PVM Investments Limited | £5,888,400 |
| Calder Properties Limited | £5,886,934 |
| RSP Investments Limited | £5,886,000 |
| Olicana Holdings Limited | £5,880,294 |
| Ellis Patents Limited | £5,879,154 |
| Schofield Sweeney LLP | £5,877,847 |
| Silentbloc UK Limited | £5,876,000 |
| Core Telecom Limited | £5,874,960 |
| Alliance Office Systems Limited | £5,874,788 |
| Sullivan Student Properties Limited | £5,873,082 |
| Ingenuity Digital Holdings Limited | £5,872,834 |
| Luminar Partnership Limited | £5,872,231 |
| The Tile Company Limited | £5,869,507 |
| Luxury Yarns International Limited | £5,865,919 |
| Dennis Barnfield Limited | £5,862,578 |
| Yorkshire Sheeting and Insulation Services Limited | £5,862,577 |
| Modav Limited | £5,861,486 |
| Weardale Motor Services Limited | £5,861,025 |
| Groundwork North East | £5,859,213 |
| Belem Investments Limited | £5,859,161 |
| Kendal Nutricare Ltd | £5,858,630 |
| European Integrated Carriers Limited | £5,848,963 |
| East Transportation Limited | £5,848,791 |
| Trevor Iles Limited | £5,847,279 |
| Cundall Manor Limited | £5,843,724 |
| Bonds Foundry Company Limited | £5,842,745 |
| City & Provincial (Equity Partners 3) Limited | £5,841,187 |
| Richard Carter,Limited | £5,840,720 |
| Stollers Furniture World Limited | £5,840,065 |
| Des Winks Cars Limited | £5,839,662 |
| G.B. Terminals (Northern) Limited | £5,838,892 |
| Westgate Motors Limited | £5,837,368 |
| Target Components Limited | £5,835,749 |
| Frank Marshall & Sons Ltd | £5,834,777 |
| Total Energy Gas Supplies Limited | £5,831,533 |
| Mosaic Print Management Holdco Limited | £5,829,002 |
| Outwood Investments Limited | £5,827,377 |
| CG Estates Limited | £5,826,814 |
| Simba Smoby Toys (UK) Limited | £5,821,030 |
| Von Roll UK Limited | £5,815,000 |
| GBA Transport Limited | £5,813,150 |
| Waxman Ceramics Limited | £5,809,067 |
| City of Bradford Y.M.C.A. | £5,807,779 |
| R.Yates & Sons Limited | £5,805,021 |
| Beal (UK) Limited | £5,802,973 |
| Everlast Waterproofing Limited | £5,799,906 |
| Doncaster Culture and Leisure Trust | £5,794,054 |

| Company | Amount |
|---|---|
| Tech Search Associates Limited | £5,791,441 |
| Solis Film Limited | £5,788,603 |
| P.V. Dobson and Sons (Motors) Limited | £5,788,301 |
| Lambert Engineering Holdings Limited | £5,784,532 |
| Thomas Fattorini Limited | £5,777,249 |
| Procters Coaches (North Yorkshire No3) Limited | £5,776,423 |
| Exceed Learning Partnership | £5,774,491 |
| Copley Motors Limited | £5,773,797 |
| Yorkcloud Limited | £5,773,469 |
| Autobrokers Limited | £5,773,195 |
| SCS Building Solutions Limited | £5,772,282 |
| J.P. Distribution Ltd. | £5,762,155 |
| Leeds Church Institute (Incorporated) | £5,760,635 |
| Adrian Johnson Limited | £5,759,839 |
| Pebbles Care Limited | £5,758,576 |
| Blackrow Holdings Limited | £5,754,610 |
| A.W. Lumb (Northern) Limited | £5,752,989 |
| Marton Mills Company Limited | £5,752,328 |
| Graypen Holdings Limited | £5,747,106 |
| Yorkshire Packaging Systems Limited | £5,743,710 |
| CTS (Shopfitting) Limited | £5,743,038 |
| Primepak Foods Limited | £5,742,509 |
| Standeven Builders (Yorkshire) Limited | £5,742,098 |
| Ulrome Seaside Caravan Company Limited | £5,740,489 |
| Filtronic Broadband Limited | £5,738,191 |
| CCL Computers Limited | £5,736,449 |
| The Peel Entertainment Group Limited | £5,732,585 |
| Coachman Holdings Limited | £5,731,257 |
| Cromwell Poland Retail LLP | £5,729,394 |
| T W Logistics Limited | £5,728,179 |
| Lucas Properties Limited | £5,726,689 |
| Hanover Developments (Wakefield) Limited | £5,716,483 |
| J.Wild (Confectioners) Limited | £5,715,947 |
| Doncaster Rotherham and District Motor Trades Group | £5,710,999 |
| Darlington Homes Limited | £5,710,022 |
| S S Components Limited | £5,710,000 |
| Trackwork Moll Limited | £5,707,411 |
| UKDN Waterflow (LG) Limited | £5,705,707 |
| Real Time Communications Limited | £5,705,416 |
| Stem Learning Limited | £5,703,000 |
| Fussey Piling Ltd | £5,702,040 |
| C.W.Fields & Son Limited | £5,700,134 |
| RPP Group Holdings Limited | £5,699,722 |
| Express Group Limited | £5,699,665 |
| G S M Group Limited | £5,697,935 |
| Bradford Girls' Grammar School Trust | £5,693,690 |
| Niko Extrusions Limited | £5,690,069 |
| Kapil Care Homes Limited | £5,688,672 |
| Acumen Credit Insurance Brokers Limited | £5,684,891 |
| Welcom Digital Limited | £5,682,894 |
| Edgar F Shepherd Ltd | £5,681,888 |
| The Widd Group Limited | £5,676,439 |
| Belle Vue Property Limited | £5,673,635 |
| Cornucopia Investments Limited | £5,673,495 |
| SIP Properties LLP | £5,670,025 |
| RMS Trent Ports Limited | £5,666,097 |
| CMG Lancaster Limited | £5,660,518 |
| Pacy and Wheatley Limited | £5,658,471 |
| Darley Properties Limited | £5,656,353 |
| MMS Ship Repair and Dry Dock Co. Ltd | £5,653,586 |
| Fired Up Corporation Limited | £5,652,104 |
| Moorgarth Property Investments Limited | £5,648,000 |
| Philip Myers Web (Neston) Limited | £5,642,577 |
| Ctrack UK Limited | £5,639,728 |
| A.F. Connell Limited | £5,639,244 |
| TAG Industries Limited | £5,638,996 |
| DLA Design Group of Companies Limited | £5,637,928 |
| Busysky Limited | £5,636,773 |
| Makin Developments Wakefield Ltd | £5,631,460 |
| Waddington and Ledger Limited | £5,622,490 |
| Andrew Atkinson Livestock Limited | £5,620,823 |
| Hazlewood Holdings Limited | £5,620,017 |
| Leck Construction Limited | £5,617,852 |
| Leeds Rugby Limited | £5,617,816 |
| Dadibhais (Bradford) Limited | £5,613,929 |
| Procters Coaches (North Yorkshire) Limited | £5,611,037 |
| The Haulage (Holdings) Organisation Limited | £5,610,373 |
| Donaldson's Vets Limited | £5,610,296 |
| Reece Safety Products Ltd | £5,610,113 |
| Holker Estates Co. Limited | £5,605,504 |
| P.P.S. Electrical Limited | £5,605,000 |
| JPT Group Limited | £5,602,600 |
| Finespark (Horsham) Limited | £5,602,188 |
| Kwiktuf Limited | £5,601,992 |
| Cartonplast (UK) Limited | £5,600,874 |
| Gateways Educational Trust Limited | £5,595,886 |
| West Park Properties Limited | £5,590,729 |
| Cravenhurst Properties Limited | £5,587,000 |
| Dortek Limited | £5,584,639 |
| Evangelical Fellowship of Congregational Churches | £5,584,069 |
| East Yorkshire Concrete Products Limited | £5,583,160 |
| Ian Blowers Jewellers Limited | £5,581,317 |
| Bagel Nash Group Limited | £5,576,422 |
| The Manny Cussins Foundation | £5,574,237 |
| Hospice of St. Mary of Furness | £5,573,820 |
| Cronkhill Properties Limited | £5,573,718 |
| Delta Engineering Group Limited | £5,569,844 |
| Malik Halls 2 Ltd | £5,567,914 |
| Lantern Debt Recovery Services Limited | £5,567,328 |
| Torpoint Limited | £5,566,241 |
| Trepko (UK) Limited | £5,563,531 |
| NMT Limited | £5,563,253 |
| Ozziefields Limited | £5,562,656 |
| (Aq) Networks Limited | £5,558,332 |
| Morley Glass & Glazing Limited | £5,557,359 |
| Renewable Heat Generation Limited | £5,557,232 |
| Osprey Green Power Limited | £5,554,619 |
| M.K.M. Building Supplies (Durham) Limited | £5,553,433 |
| Park Lane Homes Limited | £5,550,535 |
| RPP Limited | £5,547,792 |
| Calder Textiles Limited | £5,545,751 |
| Print-Leeds Limited | £5,545,437 |
| Yamato Scale Dataweigh (UK) Ltd. | £5,545,190 |
| James Mortimer,Limited | £5,543,088 |
| F.S.H. (Group) Limited | £5,541,053 |
| Dadibhais Holdings Limited | £5,540,435 |
| OHES Environmental Limited | £5,539,000 |
| P & J Properties (Yorkshire) Limited | £5,538,937 |
| W. & J. Williams (Haulage) Limited | £5,538,504 |
| Linpac Packaging China Holdings Limited | £5,538,000 |
| Oakstone Developments Limited | £5,537,364 |
| Oceanic Seafoods Limited | £5,535,861 |
| UK Ambulances 2 Ltd | £5,533,585 |
| Richmond Management (Northern) Limited | £5,530,216 |
| Community Links (Northern) Ltd | £5,527,404 |
| Wykeland (Humberside) Limited | £5,527,186 |
| SWC Trade Frames Limited | £5,527,089 |
| King Cole Limited | £5,525,568 |
| Caval Limited | £5,524,719 |
| Queens Hotel (Llandudno) Limited | £5,523,962 |
| William S. Graham Limited | £5,522,348 |
| J Denham Metals Ltd | £5,520,155 |
| Nova Contracting Ltd | £5,517,528 |
| Portland of Bawtry Limited | £5,516,072 |
| ACAD Holdings Limited | £5,511,112 |
| Rodgers Plant Hire Ltd. | £5,509,230 |
| P.P. Profiles (West Yorkshire) Limited | £5,507,883 |
| Jackie Hobson Investments | £5,505,791 |
| McCarthy Caravans Limited | £5,504,455 |
| Vodecca Properties Limited | £5,502,458 |
| C R & C L Donaldson Ltd | £5,502,456 |
| British Bung Manufacturing Company Limited (The) | £5,496,195 |
| Stirling Properties (Leeds No.4) LLP | £5,494,491 |
| Electricity Distribution Services Limited | £5,493,416 |

| | | | |
|---|---|---|---|
| Sabre Rail Services Limited | £5,492,826 | JNP Estate Agents Limited | £5,352,000 |
| Lindsey Lodge Limited | £5,491,938 | Living Care Health Limited | £5,351,610 |
| RSM Lining Supplies Global Ltd | £5,488,917 | EPMS Supplies Limited | £5,351,028 |
| Stoneferry Marfleet Limited | £5,481,082 | YTM Group Limited | £5,349,570 |
| Melrose Pigs Limited | £5,480,470 | Byworth Boilers Ltd | £5,348,961 |
| T.Freemantle Limited | £5,476,993 | Chiorino U.K. Limited | £5,347,593 |
| Holden Grange Care Group Limited | £5,475,938 | Melrose Textile Co.,Limited | £5,345,463 |
| Checkmate Fire Solutions Limited | £5,475,015 | The Candlelighters Trust | £5,343,180 |
| Primus Alliance Nottingham Limited | £5,465,345 | CB Farms LLP | £5,338,835 |
| Read Hyundai Limited | £5,460,393 | Silverback Developments Limited | £5,338,422 |
| Powell Engineering UK Limited | £5,459,230 | Citu (Low Fold) LLP | £5,338,028 |
| Milford Limited | £5,457,512 | Koti Industrial & Technical Brushes Limited | £5,336,888 |
| David Gee Associates Limited | £5,455,909 | Harrogate District Hospice Care | £5,332,411 |
| Riverside Hull Limited | £5,455,122 | CO2Sense C.I.C. | £5,331,176 |
| D L Rogers & Sons Limited | £5,453,144 | Chrislind Services Limited | £5,329,715 |
| Bond House Systems Limited | £5,452,921 | Ventura Telecom Holdings Limited | £5,329,086 |
| Halifax Rack & Screw Cutting Co. Limited | £5,447,958 | Yorkshire Feedstuffs Limited | £5,325,380 |
| That Good Night Limited | £5,444,446 | Northwood Tissue (Lancaster) Limited | £5,323,686 |
| Iconx Holdings Limited | £5,440,492 | Lakehill Estates Limited | £5,320,840 |
| Goball Limited | £5,440,203 | OSI Food Solutions UK Holdings Limited | £5,319,000 |
| Concorde BGW Limited | £5,439,512 | B & T S Builders Merchants Ltd | £5,316,292 |
| Ashford Cladding Systems Limited | £5,438,059 | Sia Abrasives (G.B.) Ltd | £5,316,000 |
| Paul Davies Limited | £5,436,672 | Royd House Investments Limited | £5,308,440 |
| Castlewood Securities Limited | £5,433,000 | PFF Packaging (North East) Limited | £5,306,425 |
| Wilfreda Luxury Coaches Limited | £5,430,460 | Foot Forward Property Investments Ltd | £5,306,276 |
| John Winter & Company Limited | £5,428,392 | Keyo Agricultural Services Ltd | £5,305,672 |
| Redhall Marine Limited | £5,428,000 | T M Enterprises Limited | £5,297,913 |
| GM Stephenson Farm and Commercial LLP | £5,427,241 | Carlac Limited | £5,296,316 |
| Allied Protek Engineering Solutions Limited | £5,423,163 | B M Howarth Limited | £5,292,370 |
| Fenton Finance Limited | £5,420,254 | The Icon Consultancy Ltd | £5,290,676 |
| Wot-a-Pullet Limited | £5,416,626 | Primex Plastics Limited | £5,290,423 |
| Akebar Park Leisure Limited | £5,416,280 | Broadland Energy (Laudale) Limited | £5,280,493 |
| Moody Direct Limited | £5,413,713 | S.H. Somerscales Limited | £5,278,844 |
| Employee Pulsecheck Limited | £5,413,382 | Hunter Holdings Limited | £5,278,731 |
| ADGM Limited | £5,412,344 | Logopak International Limited | £5,277,132 |
| Hull University Union Limited | £5,412,320 | Hurst Stores and Interiors Limited | £5,276,000 |
| A.T.G. Turnbull Limited | £5,411,669 | Aldby Field Nurseries Limited | £5,274,263 |
| ESCO Hydra (UK) Limited | £5,411,000 | Willerby Manor Hotels Limited | £5,274,239 |
| Mazuma Mobile Limited | £5,410,619 | Vallectric Limited | £5,272,812 |
| Bioganix Ltd | £5,405,564 | Hystat Systems Limited | £5,269,435 |
| Monks Cross Property Ltd | £5,405,451 | Waxman Fibres Limited | £5,268,064 |
| RP Net Media Ltd | £5,400,555 | A-Fax Properties Limited | £5,266,469 |
| Caddick (Scarborough) Limited | £5,400,279 | Eagerlux Limited | £5,265,837 |
| High Point Estates (Bury) Limited | £5,400,192 | Tompkins Investments Limited | £5,263,681 |
| Scarborough Management Limited | £5,395,960 | Lingard Bell Limited | £5,261,470 |
| Elite Systems (GB) Limited | £5,395,832 | D & P Haulage Limited | £5,260,794 |
| Wold Farms Limited | £5,395,000 | Hull Culture and Leisure Limited | £5,259,000 |
| Birch Close Trading Ltd | £5,394,377 | Wortley Developments Limited | £5,256,751 |
| Bidco (Impex) Limited | £5,394,000 | HPC Laser Holdings Limited | £5,255,009 |
| Dunelm Optical Co. Limited | £5,392,817 | GHG-AFCO (Luton) Limited | £5,254,108 |
| Tradeway (Shipping) Limited | £5,389,989 | H.S. Wood (Textiles) Limited | £5,253,400 |
| Peter Ramsey & Sons (Denholme) Timber Limited | £5,389,892 | Commercial Vehicle Auctions Limited | £5,251,277 |
| BBR Graphic Sales Limited | £5,389,642 | Tom Willoughby Limited | £5,250,783 |
| York Against Cancer | £5,387,619 | Advanced Processing Limited | £5,250,506 |
| Help for Health | £5,386,331 | Bull Brand Limited | £5,250,433 |
| Arundel Kerr Produce Limited | £5,383,169 | Eastburn Farms Limited | £5,244,107 |
| Sumo UK Ltd. | £5,383,055 | Williamsons Solicitors Limited | £5,242,581 |
| Yorkshire and Humberside Co-operative Academies | £5,381,000 | Eaglesure Limited | £5,242,539 |
| Hallmark Group Products Limited | £5,380,724 | Ligentia Group Limited | £5,240,281 |
| Q Electronics Limited | £5,377,699 | Arrow Industrial Holdings Limited | £5,237,206 |
| Kanika Limited | £5,376,860 | Patrick Construction Group Limited | £5,233,985 |
| Navenio Limited | £5,375,406 | Webasto Thermo & Comfort UK Ltd | £5,233,000 |
| Andy Thornton Limited | £5,374,938 | Nikolas Shaw Limited | £5,232,817 |
| Brighton Holdings Limited | £5,374,234 | Willow Developments (Howden) Ltd | £5,229,335 |
| Flannery Civil Engineering Limited | £5,374,224 | Ermine Farms Limited | £5,225,387 |
| Morris and Son (Holdings) Limited | £5,373,693 | Yorkshire Stone Co. (Bradford) Limited | £5,224,551 |
| Croft Properties (Harrogate) Limited | £5,370,855 | Chris Bowker Limited | £5,215,038 |
| Brass Agency Limited | £5,360,478 | Trevella Caravan Company Limited | £5,211,304 |
| AKV Cladding Products Ltd | £5,357,911 | Tower Corporation Limited | £5,211,001 |
| Numecent Limited | £5,355,629 | Furness Park LLP | £5,209,486 |
| AJ Foam Ltd | £5,353,871 | Pitcliffe (Holdings) Limited | £5,207,167 |
| Hallmark Panels Limited | £5,352,781 | Simpson and Webb Limited | £5,202,814 |

| Company | Value | Company | Value |
|---|---|---|---|
| Braavos Investments Limited | £5,202,630 | End of Term Limited | £5,080,363 |
| Dickinson Properties UK Limited | £5,201,517 | BW Skip Hire Limited | £5,079,198 |
| Landteam Property Investments Limited | £5,195,989 | Crest Brick Slate & Tile Limited | £5,077,572 |
| B.B. Farms Limited | £5,195,503 | T R M Marketing Limited | £5,077,515 |
| Staunch Limited | £5,195,142 | ATB Morley Limited | £5,075,220 |
| W B White Foundry Limited | £5,193,225 | Ctrack Limited | £5,073,358 |
| Bridge 3 LLP | £5,187,669 | J.S. Miller Distribution Limited | £5,071,590 |
| Alan Dick Communications Limited | £5,185,088 | NYOS (York) Limited | £5,070,907 |
| Abstract (Bristol) Limited | £5,182,700 | Blacks Solicitors LLP | £5,070,366 |
| Hemplow Limited | £5,181,878 | Imperial Automotive Limited | £5,068,302 |
| Fibreline Limited | £5,180,823 | More (UK) Limited | £5,065,389 |
| Jack Tighe Limited | £5,179,608 | West Yorkshire Van Rental Limited | £5,059,488 |
| GDS Holdings Limited | £5,177,760 | Bliss Films Limited | £5,059,022 |
| Cater-Kwik Limited | £5,177,370 | Cobalt Project Investments (Taycare) Limited | £5,057,994 |
| Graycliffe Homes Limited | £5,174,695 | Peagar Ltd | £5,056,063 |
| Central Insulations Limited | £5,172,256 | Corkel Limited | £5,055,635 |
| Permoid Industries Limited | £5,170,345 | The Yorkshire Provender Ltd | £5,055,000 |
| Woodhead Brothers Farms Ltd | £5,170,012 | Eshton Oakfield Ltd | £5,054,957 |
| Victoria Farm Garden Centre Ltd | £5,169,935 | DCSW Ltd | £5,053,295 |
| Renovotec Ltd | £5,164,731 | T & G Automotive Ltd | £5,052,207 |
| Oxbow Sulphur & Fertiliser (UK) Limited | £5,158,945 | My Lockup Limited | £5,051,809 |
| Lightwater Leisure Limited | £5,156,456 | Harrison Thompson and Company Limited | £5,049,391 |
| Cardale Park Properties Ltd | £5,155,151 | St. Laurence Education Trust | £5,047,000 |
| Proma Construction Management Limited | £5,155,063 | Mark Proudfoot Investments Ltd | £5,046,326 |
| Sagars Accountants Ltd | £5,153,313 | A. & J. Fabtech Limited | £5,045,801 |
| Trycare Limited | £5,152,590 | Orphans in Need | £5,045,423 |
| Royds Estates Limited | £5,149,735 | Keighley and Worth Valley Railway Preservation Society | £5,042,886 |
| Drydens Limited | £5,148,437 | Linley & Simpson Limited | £5,042,058 |
| Stroma Building Control Limited | £5,148,377 | Advanced Forwarding Limited | £5,037,819 |
| Burbank Produce Limited | £5,147,000 | Ashtree Vision & Safety Limited | £5,037,179 |
| H.B. Food Services Ltd | £5,146,580 | Computype Europe Limited | £5,036,292 |
| Stroma Certification Limited | £5,142,614 | Lovel Capital Projects Limited | £5,035,984 |
| Deltawaite Limited | £5,140,750 | W Eves & Co (Service Stations) Limited | £5,034,086 |
| Stearsby Hagg Property Company Limited | £5,140,430 | Dowse Haulage Limited | £5,033,034 |
| Urban Development Projects (2) Ltd | £5,139,914 | Omega Signs Limited | £5,029,319 |
| Automint Limited | £5,134,686 | Pigment Productions Limited | £5,029,288 |
| Verage Limited | £5,134,038 | Middleton Lodge Events Limited | £5,027,341 |
| Lesley, Stephen & Co. Limited | £5,132,339 | Futurama Signs Limited | £5,027,124 |
| Hayden Daniel Properties Limited | £5,130,653 | Abbey House (Cumbria) Limited | £5,025,931 |
| Maritime Bunkering Limited | £5,130,201 | SJS (Norton) Limited | £5,025,915 |
| The Matson Ground Estate Company Limited | £5,129,592 | The Clifford Street Venture LLP | £5,025,688 |
| Metallink Fluid Power Systems Limited | £5,127,709 | IFGL Monocon Holdings Limited | £5,025,000 |
| Audasi Holdings Limited | £5,127,109 | Brandon Medical Company Limited | £5,024,649 |
| Silver Sands Leisure Park Ltd | £5,127,095 | IRISNDT Limited | £5,021,775 |
| Northminster Holdings Limited | £5,124,340 | Charminster Estates Limited | £5,020,091 |
| Sovereign Build Limited | £5,124,315 | Brooke Edgley Specialist Technical Services Limited | £5,019,918 |
| Glassflake Limited | £5,122,974 | Jito Trading Limited | £5,019,721 |
| Falcon Electrical Wholesalers Limited | £5,118,889 | Industrial Pallet and Transport Services Limited | £5,019,548 |
| Universal A.V. Services Limited | £5,117,309 | Oakmere Homes (Lancaster) Limited | £5,017,910 |
| Trinity Developments Leeds Ltd | £5,115,757 | AMS No-Dig Limited | £5,017,649 |
| Clerical Medical Investment Fund Managers Limited | £5,114,000 | Springfield Care Services Limited | £5,017,371 |
| The Reed Group Ltd | £5,113,227 | Nationwide Bearing Company Ltd. | £5,015,974 |
| Richardsons Limited | £5,108,687 | DBS Clothing Limited | £5,014,169 |
| Fish Administration Limited | £5,108,011 | M1 Engineering Holdings Limited | £5,012,289 |
| Richardsons (Holdings) Limited | £5,107,250 | Family Dies Limited | £5,009,251 |
| R H Leonard Limited | £5,105,254 | Sapphire Technologies Limited | £5,007,000 |
| Agrimin Limited | £5,103,089 | GKF Group Limited | £5,004,129 |
| Global Components (UK) Ltd | £5,100,980 | G. Williams & Co. (Grain) Limited | £5,003,070 |
| The Health Factor Limited | £5,100,000 | LDK Investments Ltd | £5,002,604 |
| Ison Harrison Limited | £5,097,276 | Brass Agency Group Limited | £5,002,369 |
| Lister Horsfall Limited | £5,096,727 | Distribution Cable Jointing Ltd | £5,001,937 |
| Murton Grange Limited | £5,095,666 | Colenso Holdings Limited | £5,001,160 |
| Penman MW Limited | £5,094,460 | Steve Ltd | £5,000,104 |
| Hartford Trading Limited | £5,093,362 | Ebus Ltd | £5,000,000 |
| ROK Associates Limited | £5,092,193 | Barwick Investments (Leeds) Limited | £4,999,587 |
| Omco UK Limited | £5,087,586 | Rainbow Schools Trust | £4,996,443 |
| The Conservation Volunteers | £5,086,000 | K P H (Plant Hire) Limited | £4,994,515 |
| Zain Holdings Limited | £5,085,718 | Kenneth Hall (Builder) Limited | £4,994,060 |
| Chris Variava Limited | £5,085,041 | Rocal Insulating Panels Ltd. | £4,992,961 |
| Autoelectro Limited | £5,084,531 | Champagne Warehouse Ltd | £4,992,298 |
| ADW Enterprises Limited | £5,084,407 | Craig's Motorcycles Limited | £4,991,389 |
| Old Clee Primary Academy | £5,081,918 | Agercon Limited | £4,989,956 |

| Company | Value |
|---|---|
| Major Recruitment Limited | £4,988,759 |
| S.B.S. (Cumbria) Limited | £4,984,907 |
| Blue Sky Resorts Limited | £4,981,899 |
| Apelson Appliances UK Ltd | £4,979,329 |
| Alt Berg Holdings Limited | £4,978,485 |
| Renovotec Investments Limited | £4,975,395 |
| Sonic Megastore Limited | £4,970,332 |
| KTS Wire Limited | £4,970,160 |
| Marine Services (Grimsby) Limited | £4,968,947 |
| Carlac Group Limited | £4,967,024 |
| Sam Longthorp Limited | £4,966,755 |
| WV Associates Limited | £4,963,336 |
| Multiflight Charter Services LLP | £4,961,073 |
| Burg-Wachter UK (Holdings) Limited | £4,960,191 |
| Greens Desserts UK Ltd | £4,960,122 |
| Sing Ko Limited | £4,959,659 |
| Howard Civil Engineering Limited | £4,958,773 |
| Mysing Investments 3 Limited | £4,957,509 |
| Greentech Limited | £4,955,878 |
| Be Fuelcards Holdings Limited | £4,953,985 |
| H.S.G. (Packing Cases) Limited | £4,953,959 |
| Hanson Family Holdings Limited | £4,950,831 |
| Roundbrand Limited | £4,950,763 |
| Emic Group Limited | £4,949,573 |
| Gregory Projects Limited | £4,948,035 |
| Cleeve Primary School | £4,947,934 |
| Hird Limited | £4,947,827 |
| Thrunscoe Primary and Nursery Academy | £4,947,708 |
| Hamilton (Building Contractors) Ltd. | £4,944,660 |
| T.& R. Theakston Limited | £4,944,000 |
| De Vere Selsdon Estate Limited | £4,944,000 |
| Crime & Fire Defence Systems Limited | £4,943,487 |
| Lune Holdings Limited | £4,943,288 |
| Fredrickson International Limited | £4,942,000 |
| M.Woodhouse Transport (Lancaster) Limited | £4,941,494 |
| Venice Newco 1 Limited | £4,939,000 |
| Dishforth UK Limited | £4,937,534 |
| R.E. Thornber Limited | £4,936,168 |
| Tom Chambers Limited | £4,935,232 |
| Entertainment and Leisure Insurance Services Limited | £4,935,194 |
| Robin Mills Properties Limited | £4,934,258 |
| Harte Woodworking Limited | £4,933,464 |
| Burlington Care Limited | £4,931,882 |
| Ali-A Entertainment Ltd | £4,929,662 |
| Kirklees Active Leisure | £4,928,029 |
| Cambridge Park Academy Limited | £4,926,848 |
| A.E. Burt and Company Limited | £4,926,801 |
| Brunswick Court Development (Leeds) Limited | £4,923,833 |
| Grants Pro-Agri Limited | £4,922,790 |
| Colt Industrial Services Limited | £4,921,000 |
| Shared Vision Learning Trust | £4,921,000 |
| Manor Coating Systems Limited | £4,919,538 |
| Crescent Estates (Ilkley) Limited | £4,918,741 |
| Jet Aire (DC) Limited | £4,918,243 |
| Elvaston Properties Limited | £4,917,576 |
| Geoplan Spatial Intelligence Limited | £4,917,325 |
| Inglis and Son (Jewellers) Limited | £4,916,198 |
| G Brocklehurst Transport Limited | £4,916,048 |
| M. H. Industrial Limited | £4,913,717 |
| The John Strutt Conservation Foundation | £4,910,639 |
| Stevro Limited | £4,908,710 |
| Majestic Polymers Limited | £4,906,682 |
| JA Hotels Limited | £4,902,313 |
| Shallowdale Limited | £4,902,009 |
| Eville & Jones (UK) Limited | £4,900,053 |
| G3 Remarketing Limited | £4,897,975 |
| Alf Kitching Limited | £4,895,082 |
| Harper & Wilkes Limited | £4,894,800 |
| GCD Limited | £4,894,054 |
| Northern Installations CP LLP | £4,892,649 |
| Sutcliffe Group Limited | £4,891,216 |
| Turner & Townsend Europe Limited | £4,891,000 |
| Withernsea Primary Academy Trust | £4,889,908 |
| Lone Star Estates (1) Limited | £4,889,776 |
| Sycamore Lighting Limited | £4,888,625 |
| Burley Developments Group Limited | £4,887,572 |
| Thornber Chicks Limited | £4,886,439 |
| Claritas Solutions Limited | £4,886,192 |
| Portakabin (Refurbished) Limited | £4,883,000 |
| The Lerrix Tankship Limited | £4,880,827 |
| Cat Tech International Limited | £4,877,814 |
| Connection Seating Limited | £4,871,366 |
| Hanson Logistics Limited | £4,869,916 |
| Neasden Primary School | £4,869,875 |
| Affordable Cars (Yorkshire) Limited | £4,869,357 |
| Kexgill (Construction) Limited | £4,866,866 |
| Subsea Innovation Limited | £4,863,847 |
| Wothersome Limited | £4,863,381 |
| Matwest Ltd | £4,854,022 |
| Triesse Group Limited | £4,852,541 |
| Madison Hosiery Limited | £4,849,931 |
| List Group PLC | £4,849,657 |
| Mysing Investments 4 Limited | £4,845,257 |
| Warmafloor (GB) Limited | £4,842,000 |
| East Midlands Instrument Company Limited | £4,841,448 |
| Gem Environmental Building Services Limited | £4,839,994 |
| DLA Architecture Limited | £4,839,809 |
| Pegasus World Ltd | £4,839,671 |
| Scarborough Flower Fund Homes | £4,839,660 |
| G. Nowell Limited | £4,839,493 |
| The Fisherman Limited | £4,838,050 |
| Van-Line Limited | £4,837,369 |
| Bower Roebuck & Co.,Limited | £4,837,043 |
| The Federation of Abbey Schools Academy Trust | £4,837,000 |
| Highgrove Property Developments Limited | £4,834,297 |
| Mysing Investments 2 Limited | £4,833,832 |
| Money4yourmotors.Com Limited | £4,832,000 |
| H H Construction (Groundwork Contractors) Limited | £4,830,673 |
| Saur (UK) Limited | £4,829,000 |
| J M McGill Ltd. | £4,828,577 |
| Storth Limited | £4,828,378 |
| Westfield Farms Limited | £4,827,856 |
| Caldex Limited | £4,825,457 |
| Longbeach Leisure Limited | £4,823,726 |
| F D Bird & Sons Limited | £4,820,027 |
| Leeds Real Estate Ltd | £4,816,001 |
| Leisure Park Management Limited | £4,815,431 |
| Castle Residential Properties Limited | £4,814,799 |
| St Leger Homes of Doncaster Limited | £4,813,000 |
| The Westmorland County Agricultural Society Ltd | £4,812,532 |
| Supagard Limited | £4,812,167 |
| BSC Filters Limited | £4,811,120 |
| Ackworth Service Station Ltd | £4,806,082 |
| John Roe (Hull) Limited | £4,803,830 |
| Dura Beds Ltd | £4,801,927 |
| Specialist Trailer Hire Limited | £4,799,053 |
| HRP Holdings Limited | £4,799,000 |
| Fairhurst Stone Merchants Limited | £4,798,925 |
| Wm.Grant (Paull) Limited | £4,793,296 |
| Beckside Developments Limited | £4,793,030 |
| A.M. Warkup Limited | £4,792,934 |
| Air Berlin Holding Limited | £4,790,351 |
| Wilton Cobley Limited | £4,790,152 |
| Liveco Limited | £4,789,303 |
| Herbert Fletcher Transport Limited | £4,788,854 |
| Wharfedale Homes Limited | £4,787,084 |
| Nordika Design Limited | £4,783,916 |
| BCA Leisure Ltd | £4,781,919 |
| Northern LPG Supplies Limited | £4,780,151 |
| Stephen B Wells Limited | £4,779,523 |
| G.W. Axup & Co Limited | £4,777,443 |
| Evansis Ltd | £4,777,345 |
| Pinheiros Corporation Limited | £4,774,671 |
| Square Peg Properties Limited | £4,774,451 |

| Company | Amount |
|---|---|
| B.Allsop Limited | £4,773,974 |
| Bradford Flower Fund Homes | £4,772,264 |
| Mitton Aftercare Limited | £4,770,649 |
| AJH Pump Supply & Repair Limited | £4,770,184 |
| J S Alton & Son Limited | £4,770,167 |
| William's Den Limited | £4,767,591 |
| RMS Goole Limited | £4,764,497 |
| Finishchoice Limited | £4,760,060 |
| Air Handling Systems Limited | £4,758,956 |
| Vellco Limited | £4,758,357 |
| Link Scheme Holdings Ltd | £4,757,372 |
| Global Shipping Services Group Limited | £4,755,545 |
| Derek Lewis Limited | £4,751,815 |
| NSA (Ventures) Limited | £4,751,579 |
| Pennine Camphill Community Limited (The) | £4,750,787 |
| Eco Modular Buildings Ltd | £4,746,178 |
| Redline Worldwide Limited | £4,745,741 |
| Emacrow Holdings Limited | £4,743,674 |
| Boulton & Cooper Limited | £4,740,179 |
| Brighouse Estate Co (Contractors) Ltd | £4,739,163 |
| Specma Samwon Ltd | £4,735,587 |
| T Soanes & Son (Poultry) Ltd | £4,734,096 |
| N.R. Burnett (Holdings) Limited | £4,731,743 |
| Aspire-Igen Group Ltd | £4,731,132 |
| Europa Caravans Ltd | £4,730,704 |
| WJ Drennan Limited | £4,729,509 |
| Turnbull (Corn Sales) Limited | £4,727,308 |
| Pland Stainless Limited | £4,726,155 |
| Urban I (Blonk Street) Ltd | £4,724,677 |
| Simon Cook Holdings Limited | £4,719,224 |
| E Handcock Limited | £4,719,172 |
| Crossgreen Investments Limited | £4,717,427 |
| Delahope Limited | £4,716,574 |
| SUSD Asset Management (Holdings) Limited | £4,714,152 |
| Urban Development Projects Ltd | £4,713,378 |
| Blue Star Fibres Company Limited | £4,711,000 |
| WB White Foundry (Holdings) Limited | £4,710,018 |
| L & O Investments (U.K.) | £4,710,000 |
| Holbeck Homes Limited | £4,708,138 |
| Heights (U.K.) Limited | £4,707,268 |
| Hainsworth Sterne & Co. Limited | £4,704,600 |
| Say Scaffolding Limited | £4,703,848 |
| The A1 Steam Locomotive Trust | £4,702,708 |
| Yarborough Academy | £4,700,732 |
| Andrew Jackson Solicitors LLP | £4,699,770 |
| Pasuda Buildings Limited | £4,699,633 |
| GFEA Limited | £4,699,000 |
| Corinthian Brands (CBL) Limited | £4,696,398 |
| Scarborough Enterprises (UK) Limited | £4,696,147 |
| W F & L Limited | £4,694,817 |
| Calder Conferences Limited | £4,694,494 |
| D. E. Ford Holdings Limited | £4,690,000 |
| M.K. Consultants (U.K.) Limited | £4,689,423 |
| Riva Paoletti Limited | £4,688,811 |
| Diamond Resorts (Group Holdings) PLC | £4,688,000 |
| Cameron Integrated Services Limited | £4,684,755 |
| Walney Island South End Caravan Site Limited | £4,684,419 |
| Pasuda (Hire) Limited | £4,684,255 |
| The Neil Martin Group Limited | £4,684,237 |
| CPPGroup Services Limited | £4,684,000 |
| Extremis Production Limited | £4,683,904 |
| St James Securities Limited | £4,680,957 |
| Horus Limited | £4,680,584 |
| Alfred Bagnall & Sons (Administration) Limited | £4,676,708 |
| Bullseye Superfactors Ltd | £4,675,806 |
| Parkinson - Spencer Refractories Limited | £4,675,428 |
| Lincolnshire House Association | £4,674,409 |
| Darntonb3 Limited | £4,672,629 |
| Stoneledge Plant and Transport Limited | £4,670,844 |
| ICH Limited | £4,669,889 |
| Gatsby Property Limited | £4,668,372 |
| Pittstop (Ripon) Limited | £4,668,289 |
| Walker Distribution (Hull) Limited | £4,667,805 |
| Firsure Limited | £4,666,987 |
| Pneumatic & Electrical Systems Limited | £4,665,656 |
| Centurion Europe Limited | £4,665,562 |
| Optima International Limited | £4,665,349 |
| Yorkshire Caravans of Bawtry Limited | £4,661,866 |
| Morecambe Metals Limited | £4,660,710 |
| Foregale Limited | £4,658,731 |
| I & S Properties Limited | £4,656,348 |
| Allure Developments Limited | £4,654,690 |
| M.K.M. Leisure Limited | £4,651,936 |
| Bremsen Technik Holdings Ltd | £4,651,900 |
| GH North Yorkshire Limited | £4,651,365 |
| Bishopton Veterinary Group LLP | £4,650,683 |
| Running Deep Limited | £4,649,796 |
| J.S.R. Genetics Limited | £4,649,000 |
| Abaxis UK Limited | £4,648,750 |
| Technical Control Systems Limited | £4,647,000 |
| The Bishop Wheeler Catholic Academy Trust | £4,644,000 |
| Oilgear Towler Limited | £4,643,851 |
| GSD Riverside Limited | £4,642,542 |
| Belaris Ltd. | £4,642,465 |
| Moorhead Excavations Limited | £4,640,867 |
| Communisis Chorleys Ltd | £4,639,000 |
| Impact (UK) Limited | £4,638,381 |
| The Davy Group Limited | £4,637,018 |
| Falcon Sportswear Limited | £4,636,836 |
| GW Hire Limited | £4,636,280 |
| Alatas UK Limited | £4,635,745 |
| The Greetland Academy Trust | £4,633,266 |
| Kysor Europe Limited | £4,632,085 |
| Bright Screw Company Limited (The) | £4,628,772 |
| Galtec Solutions Limited | £4,628,185 |
| Mainport Engineering (1990) Limited | £4,626,641 |
| MMCD Investments Limited | £4,625,559 |
| TG-F Investments (No. 1) Limited | £4,623,372 |
| G. & A. Thursby Limited | £4,616,059 |
| Double-Ten Limited | £4,615,297 |
| ALM Manufacturing Limited | £4,615,228 |
| Gladwin Bros. (Farms) Limited | £4,614,505 |
| York Pullman Bus Company Limited | £4,614,234 |
| W. & A.C. Rose (Farms) Limited | £4,613,875 |
| Manners Farms Limited | £4,613,461 |
| Lund Court Farm Limited | £4,612,136 |
| Evans Homes No.2 Limited | £4,610,907 |
| TG-F Investments (No. 2) Limited | £4,610,492 |
| Headland Plant Limited | £4,607,843 |
| Prospect House (Malpas) Limited | £4,606,448 |
| MBI Walsden Care Limited | £4,605,765 |
| Ghyll Royd Nursing Home Limited | £4,605,741 |
| Dakin-Flathers Limited | £4,605,679 |
| Dalquinto Limited | £4,603,280 |
| Planet Platforms (Holdings) Limited | £4,601,497 |
| Eurotek Foundry Products Limited | £4,601,235 |
| Ashlea Landscaping Holdings Limited | £4,598,283 |
| Serius Group Limited | £4,593,879 |
| Horndean Ltd | £4,593,790 |
| Holgates Silver Ridge Ltd | £4,592,917 |
| The Southfield Grange Trust | £4,592,327 |
| Creativerace Limited | £4,591,329 |
| NK Chemicals Europe Limited | £4,590,832 |
| G.A. Robson and Son Ltd | £4,589,836 |
| C.R. Reynolds Limited | £4,589,327 |
| Holmefield Farm Services Limited | £4,589,170 |
| Molescroft Farms Limited | £4,586,125 |
| Landplan Properties Limited | £4,585,163 |
| Balltec Limited | £4,585,102 |
| Fuel Proof Limited | £4,584,321 |
| Venturian Property Development Limited | £4,583,906 |
| Prem Sehmi Holdings Limited | £4,583,863 |
| Phoenix Building Systems Limited | £4,582,551 |
| Sandmoor Properties Limited | £4,582,230 |

| Company | Value |
|---|---|
| Dream Property Holdco Limited | £4,578,714 |
| Centurion Europe Holdings Limited | £4,577,252 |
| Worthington Homes Limited | £4,577,214 |
| Clugston Estates Limited | £4,576,244 |
| Townson Tractors Limited | £4,572,060 |
| Keep Your Trap Shut Limited | £4,568,500 |
| Lebus Furniture Limited | £4,566,293 |
| Foxton Farmers Limited | £4,566,206 |
| Hilldene Holdings Limited | £4,565,218 |
| Unicolour Limited | £4,560,577 |
| Chambers Parking Limited | £4,558,839 |
| Airedale Springs Limited | £4,558,096 |
| Technical Arc Ltd | £4,557,624 |
| Harratts Limited | £4,556,297 |
| Yorkwold (Overseas) Limited | £4,556,288 |
| Aggregates R Us Ltd | £4,554,829 |
| Hewitson Limited | £4,553,179 |
| Grimsby & Cleethorpes Area Doorstep | £4,550,084 |
| Northern Cladding Limited | £4,544,325 |
| A Dawson and Company (Estates) Limited | £4,541,688 |
| S.A.R. Recycling Ltd | £4,541,330 |
| Scarborough Rugby Union Football Club Limited | £4,540,572 |
| Peter Strawson Limited | £4,536,550 |
| Doncaster Property Trading Limited | £4,535,216 |
| Brooksbank Valves Limited | £4,534,791 |
| Strong Developments Limited | £4,532,970 |
| Turner & Townsend Consulting Limited | £4,532,000 |
| Thompson Green & Co. Limited | £4,531,460 |
| Oakvine Limited | £4,524,440 |
| Braime Pressings Limited | £4,523,016 |
| Carrington House Yorkshire Limited | £4,523,014 |
| Parkhead Investments Limited | £4,522,850 |
| Refreshment Systems Limited | £4,521,722 |
| Further Instructions Ltd | £4,520,987 |
| Polyseam Limited | £4,520,086 |
| Oakwood Veterinary Practice Limited | £4,514,570 |
| Team 17 Software Limited | £4,513,053 |
| Applelec Sign Components (UK) Ltd. | £4,512,838 |
| J.H. Clissold & Son Ltd. | £4,512,059 |
| Stercap Limited | £4,509,624 |
| The Comedian's Guide To Survival Limited | £4,509,436 |
| Capitol Park Leeds PLC | £4,509,062 |
| Manor Farm Feeds Limited | £4,508,056 |
| Feversham Arms Limited | £4,507,774 |
| Horridge Limited | £4,506,226 |
| Lunchbox Theatrical Productions Limited | £4,505,508 |
| C.T. Hayton Limited | £4,505,277 |
| Triple T Engineering Limited | £4,503,872 |
| Hall & Associates (Marketing) Ltd | £4,502,436 |
| Sellmor Farming Limited | £4,500,691 |
| Ballards Removals Holdings Limited | £4,500,531 |
| Bootham Crescent Holdings Limited | £4,500,000 |
| Rushbond Retail Limited | £4,498,241 |
| David Hopkinson Limited | £4,497,895 |
| Ventia Limited | £4,497,422 |
| H.E.C. Contracting Limited | £4,495,920 |
| Becker UK Limited | £4,494,265 |
| W E Barton Limited | £4,494,224 |
| Potato Manufacturing Science Limited | £4,492,915 |
| Crystal Investment Holdings Limited | £4,491,451 |
| Market Town Taverns Limited | £4,491,026 |
| Marshall Wooldridge Limited | £4,489,747 |
| Kexgill (Hull) Limited | £4,489,505 |
| Pitts Wilson Holdings Limited | £4,489,435 |
| Ascentis | £4,489,271 |
| Justmerc Limited | £4,488,915 |
| Mowden Controls Limited | £4,488,043 |
| Mabanes Properties Limited | £4,487,918 |
| Ashridge Contractors Limited | £4,483,426 |
| Rhinox Group Ltd | £4,480,592 |
| Templer Management Limited | £4,480,307 |
| Blacks Industries Limited | £4,480,072 |
| Financial Systems & Consultancy Ltd. | £4,479,994 |
| Stoneacre Property Investments Ltd | £4,478,092 |
| B.Danby & Co,Limited | £4,477,745 |
| Larsen Road Limited | £4,476,407 |
| Doncaster Deaf Trust | £4,476,000 |
| Harrowells Limited | £4,474,978 |
| One in a Million Free School | £4,470,556 |
| Atlantic Bay Hotel (Woolacombe) Limited | £4,469,756 |
| Hair Burst Limited | £4,469,557 |
| Cube (Yorkshire) Ltd | £4,465,357 |
| Turner & Townsend Contract Services Limited | £4,464,000 |
| Hill Giftware Limited | £4,463,803 |
| Croft Care Trust | £4,463,154 |
| Hopkins Properties Limited | £4,462,459 |
| Whitaker and Leach Limited | £4,460,693 |
| Emersons Green Limited | £4,460,000 |
| PDS Design & Build Limited | £4,458,734 |
| Retsco Limited | £4,458,163 |
| Lodestone Projects Limited | £4,457,065 |
| BHJ UK Food Limited | £4,455,242 |
| Anabas (UK 2) Limited | £4,455,062 |
| Hoyer UK Limited | £4,454,536 |
| Calder Valley Holdings Limited | £4,453,019 |
| Allsigns International Limited | £4,451,281 |
| Oakwood Kitchen Design Consultants Limited | £4,451,192 |
| Tarnhelm Securities Limited | £4,448,438 |
| Scheme Underwriting (U.K.) Limited | £4,447,546 |
| Doncast Limited | £4,446,337 |
| Frog Education Limited | £4,445,981 |
| Caddick (Rose Wharf) Limited | £4,445,119 |
| Main Line Bearing Co. Limited | £4,444,966 |
| Chamber Acorn Fund (Humber) Ltd | £4,441,418 |
| York City Football Club Limited | £4,441,410 |
| Vascular Perspectives Limited | £4,440,302 |
| Haztec International Ltd | £4,439,099 |
| JSJ Finance Limited | £4,438,561 |
| Shaw Timber Limited | £4,434,503 |
| Easilift Loading Systems Limited | £4,433,633 |
| Global George Limited | £4,433,000 |
| M. & B. Commercial Properties Limited | £4,430,949 |
| Proaktive Ltd | £4,428,039 |
| Red Hall (Bury) Limited | £4,426,807 |
| Golam Properties Limited | £4,425,909 |
| MBR Acres Limited | £4,425,833 |
| JM Developments (Guiseley) Limited | £4,423,536 |
| Eastbay Limited | £4,423,231 |
| Business Lines Limited | £4,421,151 |
| KM School Limited | £4,419,731 |
| Hindle Gears Limited | £4,419,129 |
| Premo Fabrications Limited | £4,417,726 |
| Avocet Trust | £4,415,039 |
| ESCO (UK) Limited | £4,412,000 |
| Ravenheat Manufacturing Limited | £4,409,816 |
| The Access Panel Company Ltd | £4,409,667 |
| Klinger Holdings Limited | £4,408,476 |
| Blessed Peter Snow Catholic Academy Trust | £4,407,000 |
| Howarth Timber (Windows & Doors) Limited | £4,406,000 |
| Power Plastics Limited | £4,402,411 |
| Warmest Welcome Limited | £4,400,892 |
| Kokoon Holdings Limited | £4,400,010 |
| Kenworth Limited | £4,398,416 |
| Stainless Band Limited | £4,397,619 |
| Wiseton Developments Limited | £4,393,150 |
| Sheppee Holdings Ltd | £4,390,725 |
| John Jordan Limited | £4,388,892 |
| Stadium (Bradford) Limited | £4,388,861 |
| Health Innovations (UK) Limited | £4,387,863 |
| Gawith Hoggarth Tobacco Trading Limited | £4,386,670 |
| Retford Wallcoverings Limited | £4,384,442 |
| John Betts Quality Used Cars Limited | £4,384,260 |
| Metcalfe Farming Limited | £4,383,954 |
| Banks Lyon Jewellers Limited | £4,382,537 |

| Company | Value | Company | Value |
|---|---|---|---|
| Place2live Ltd | £4,381,720 | KSDL Land Limited | £4,284,844 |
| John Bull (Confectioners) Limited | £4,381,691 | Pugh & Company Limited | £4,284,749 |
| Baddow Properties Limited | £4,380,969 | Furness Mortgage Services Limited | £4,281,793 |
| United Fresh Consortium Limited | £4,378,339 | Advanced Supply Chain (Logistics) Ltd | £4,280,181 |
| DB Orthodontics Limited | £4,378,261 | Buckley Jewellery Limited | £4,276,263 |
| Morgan Travel Limited | £4,374,846 | Handler Hire Ltd | £4,274,199 |
| Oakwell Securities Limited | £4,370,158 | Mount School (York) (The) | £4,270,175 |
| X-Force UK Ltd | £4,369,224 | M & D Foundations & Building Services Limited | £4,268,973 |
| Praesto Consulting UK Ltd | £4,367,052 | K.M. Norris Limited | £4,267,922 |
| Price Express Transport Limited | £4,365,993 | Authentix Limited | £4,267,147 |
| Thomas B. Ramsden & Co. (Bradford) Limited | £4,365,354 | Michael Barugh Steel Stockholding Limited | £4,265,885 |
| Higgins Agriculture Limited | £4,363,908 | S D C Enterprises Limited | £4,265,172 |
| THS Industrial Textiles Limited | £4,363,876 | Tracsis Retail and Operations Limited | £4,264,184 |
| Wandahome (Knottingley) Limited | £4,361,437 | Mirabelle Partners Limited | £4,263,848 |
| SNG Commercial (Holdings) Limited | £4,361,371 | Read Hyundai Lincoln Limited | £4,263,671 |
| Manningham Concrete Limited | £4,359,946 | Acklam's Coaches Limited | £4,260,012 |
| The Partnership Investment Fund Limited | £4,359,853 | Atherton Godfrey LLP | £4,259,681 |
| Crossway Scaffolding (Elland) Limited | £4,358,293 | H. & C. Whitehead Limited | £4,258,964 |
| B & K Systems Limited | £4,356,281 | Responsible Life Limited | £4,257,952 |
| Groupe Samat UK Limited | £4,352,138 | A-Safe UK Ltd | £4,257,951 |
| Allam Developments Limited | £4,350,540 | Dominion Print Ltd | £4,256,850 |
| Universal Group Holdings Limited | £4,349,495 | Boge Compressors Limited | £4,255,917 |
| Northern Eye UK Limited | £4,348,676 | Roger Miles Plant Sales Ltd. | £4,255,735 |
| MSS Developments Limited | £4,346,895 | A.B.G. Limited | £4,250,626 |
| Neill & Brown Limited | £4,346,795 | Orange Mountain Bikes Limited | £4,249,007 |
| Bentley Yorkshire Limited | £4,346,732 | Q Medical Technologies Ltd | £4,247,232 |
| Vallectric (Holdings) Limited | £4,345,767 | Crowle Wharf Engineers Limited | £4,246,109 |
| Principle Healthcare Limited | £4,341,947 | Icelolly Marketing Limited | £4,245,141 |
| Illingworth & Gregory Limited | £4,339,997 | KMA Properties Limited | £4,244,621 |
| Cash Converters Yorkshire Limited | £4,339,962 | Modular Plantrooms Limited | £4,243,223 |
| Mena Commercial Limited | £4,339,879 | UKGlobal Holdings Limited | £4,242,768 |
| John Wade (Haulage) Limited | £4,337,429 | Yamuna Renewables Limited | £4,241,193 |
| McIlroy Estates Limited | £4,336,971 | Airco Refrigeration and Airconditioning Limited | £4,239,913 |
| Turnbull (Potato Sales) Limited | £4,335,659 | Henton & Co LLP | £4,238,511 |
| Heselden Investments Limited | £4,333,466 | Wm Sugden & Sons Limited | £4,235,324 |
| Hurst Plastics Limited | £4,330,000 | Everik Limited | £4,233,981 |
| Premium Motorhomes Limited | £4,329,253 | A.& E.Baines Limited | £4,232,033 |
| The Crown Hotel (Bawtry) Limited | £4,327,851 | F.T.L. Holdings Limited | £4,232,000 |
| Woodland Healthcare Limited | £4,327,788 | Gill Insulation Nottinghamshire Limited | £4,231,828 |
| Spafield Properties Limited | £4,326,117 | Allied Properties (Hull) Limited | £4,228,639 |
| YP Real Estate Limited | £4,325,744 | Extron Electronics UK Limited | £4,228,000 |
| Killgerm Chemicals Limited | £4,325,529 | Zarafa Height Solutions Limited | £4,227,918 |
| S.A.Mossop (Farms) Limited | £4,325,011 | Bon Coeur Fine Wines Limited | £4,226,339 |
| SDG (Preston) Limited | £4,322,810 | T.W.Falkingham Limited | £4,226,152 |
| C C Properties (Yorkshire) Ltd | £4,320,186 | J H Dixon & Son LLP | £4,225,964 |
| Fredshaw & Co Limited | £4,318,959 | Third Energy Trading Limited | £4,225,000 |
| Old HK Limited | £4,318,494 | Network Mapping Limited | £4,223,842 |
| PTM Holdings Limited | £4,316,526 | HEM Holdings Limited | £4,223,290 |
| Dante Capital Limited | £4,315,927 | Fussey Holdings Limited | £4,219,902 |
| Potters Farm Production LLP | £4,315,273 | AFI Bidco Limited | £4,219,000 |
| Serenity Parks Limited | £4,315,054 | Nutec Holdings Limited | £4,217,717 |
| Minster Veterinary Practice Ltd | £4,309,224 | Roadridge Limited | £4,216,641 |
| Coaching Inns (North) Limited | £4,309,044 | Inventry Limited | £4,214,776 |
| Consort Furniture Limited | £4,307,978 | Mark Royston Contracting Limited | £4,214,375 |
| Ant Hire Solutions LLP | £4,307,808 | Batchelors of Ripon Limited | £4,212,107 |
| East Riding Builders & Estate Development Co Ltd | £4,304,615 | Splicegroup Europe Limited | £4,210,750 |
| Marrtree Residential Ltd | £4,302,117 | Nidd Transport Limited | £4,210,511 |
| Kirkminster Engineering Limited | £4,301,421 | L S S Properties (Leeds) Limited | £4,210,357 |
| Effective Security Services Limited | £4,300,405 | Plowman Brothers Limited | £4,208,166 |
| Lion Estate and Investment Company Limited | £4,299,093 | Fruugo.Com Ltd | £4,207,140 |
| Dakota Pharma Limited | £4,299,038 | Mena Developments Limted Limited | £4,204,611 |
| Mister Capital Holdings Limited | £4,297,983 | Dukeries Healthcare Limited | £4,203,954 |
| TYK Limited | £4,296,220 | 121 Mountco 074 Limited | £4,203,688 |
| Owens Developments Ltd | £4,295,975 | Gill Demolitions Limited | £4,200,375 |
| Jenkar Shipping Limited | £4,294,948 | Dalmore Group Limited | £4,200,100 |
| CCL Stressing Systems Limited | £4,294,300 | Riverside Eastern Limited | £4,197,234 |
| Resdev Limited | £4,292,717 | Rory Kemp Limited | £4,195,179 |
| Whitston Group Limited | £4,291,239 | Frazer Estates Limited | £4,194,749 |
| DKB Crop Protection Limited | £4,289,687 | Vapour Cloud Limited | £4,193,161 |
| Yorkshire Property Finance Ltd | £4,289,035 | 56 George Street Limited | £4,190,888 |
| CB Solutions U.K. Ltd | £4,288,776 | Parkway Entertainment Company Limited | £4,190,562 |
| Xander 97 Limited | £4,288,115 | M6 Truck Services Limited | £4,190,038 |

| Company | Amount |
|---|---|
| Benson Turner Limited | £4,189,652 |
| Wiltel Limited | £4,189,114 |
| Tate Properties Limited | £4,188,416 |
| NSS Properties Limited | £4,185,827 |
| Trinity McQueen Limited | £4,183,603 |
| Double Two Limited | £4,183,193 |
| C.E.A.Towne (Ship Riggers) Limited | £4,182,719 |
| Explorer (UK) Limited | £4,182,042 |
| Varlink Limited | £4,180,519 |
| Transition Glass Products Limited | £4,178,820 |
| Blenheim House Properties (Bradford) Limited | £4,178,389 |
| Staff Finders (Yorkshire) Limited | £4,175,663 |
| Allerton Steel Limited | £4,175,511 |
| Chase Petroleum Limited | £4,171,618 |
| Partners in Care Limited | £4,171,081 |
| EFS Chalfont Limited | £4,169,402 |
| Al Halal Supermarket Limited | £4,168,865 |
| Viking Fishing Limited | £4,168,858 |
| P.J. Edwards & Co. (UK) Ltd. | £4,167,958 |
| Bendrigg Trust | £4,166,322 |
| L.W. Safety Limited | £4,164,852 |
| Pennock & Ivory Limited | £4,164,143 |
| Buxton Pickles Ltd. | £4,163,372 |
| Keith Rennie Machinery Limited | £4,160,979 |
| Stephen A. Sims (Cars) Limited | £4,159,949 |
| Ryedale Printing Works Limited | £4,157,213 |
| J.G. Bellerby (Farms) Limited | £4,157,126 |
| Project FF & E Limited | £4,155,122 |
| Middlegate (Europe) Limited | £4,148,515 |
| Tebway Limited | £4,148,219 |
| Yorkshire Period Hotels Limited | £4,147,099 |
| Central Properties (Leeds) Limited | £4,144,391 |
| R.P.M. Industrial Services Limited | £4,143,300 |
| Hyco Manufacturing Limited | £4,142,395 |
| SFS Developments Limited | £4,141,658 |
| Watson Pallets Limited | £4,140,847 |
| Hollings Limited | £4,140,444 |
| Kahn Landmark Limited | £4,135,737 |
| Igen Trust | £4,134,763 |
| Harrogate Steel Trading Ltd | £4,131,983 |
| Lindhurst 2013 Limited | £4,131,567 |
| Punch Bowl Investments Limited | £4,131,045 |
| Redhall Networks Limited | £4,131,000 |
| Laminated Products Limited | £4,130,630 |
| Kirens International Limited | £4,127,790 |
| Magneco Metrel U.K. Limited | £4,127,699 |
| Spellman & Walker Limited | £4,127,192 |
| Communisis One Ltd | £4,127,000 |
| FJG Property LLP | £4,126,964 |
| Pendle Sportswear Limited | £4,124,566 |
| Craven Educational Trust | £4,124,144 |
| Flixborough Wharf Limited | £4,122,827 |
| Lee Gibson Properties Ltd | £4,121,361 |
| B & K Universal Limited | £4,120,777 |
| BBP Investments Limited | £4,120,081 |
| Savoy Tyres Limited | £4,115,287 |
| Rogerthorpe Manor Hotel Limited | £4,114,757 |
| Orvec Holdings Limited | £4,111,922 |
| Ashcourt (Durham) Limited | £4,111,159 |
| KVH Media Group International Limited | £4,107,000 |
| James E. Smith (Northern) Limited | £4,106,465 |
| Manor Estate Properties (UK) Limited | £4,102,503 |
| Foresight North East Lincolnshire Ltd. | £4,102,212 |
| Dalmore Capital (Rochdale) Limited | £4,101,317 |
| Huddersfield Fine Worsteds Limited | £4,100,423 |
| Raiseprint Limited | £4,096,926 |
| Redhouse Projects Limited | £4,093,192 |
| First Subsea Limited | £4,092,604 |
| Iles (York) Limited | £4,091,395 |
| Priory Primary School | £4,091,109 |
| M. and B. Barker Limited | £4,089,131 |
| Ogden Waller Developments LLP | £4,088,160 |
| Rodgers of York Ltd. | £4,085,801 |
| Kirkdale Industrial Training Services Limited | £4,084,137 |
| Huggate Church Farm Properties Limited | £4,083,233 |
| Innserve Technical Solutions Limited | £4,082,223 |
| Acorn Assessors Limited | £4,080,459 |
| East Yorkshire Aluminium & Glass Limited | £4,079,143 |
| AC Hobson LLP | £4,078,145 |
| Romero Catholic Education Trust | £4,078,000 |
| Robert D. Webster Limited | £4,077,063 |
| LJV Investments Limited | £4,076,534 |
| Sissons Depot Limited | £4,075,166 |
| Straight Limited | £4,074,000 |
| Closepatch Limited | £4,073,907 |
| Friends of The Lake District | £4,073,324 |
| Lowwood Products Company Limited (The) | £4,072,652 |
| The Creative Art House | £4,070,694 |
| Venturian Property Holdings Limited | £4,068,649 |
| James H. Tennant Limited | £4,067,608 |
| Foster Farms Limited | £4,065,612 |
| C T Glass Holdings Limited | £4,064,789 |
| D.T. Industries Limited | £4,064,433 |
| Lakeland Motor Museum Limited | £4,063,822 |
| PSP Architectural Ltd | £4,063,337 |
| Tudorshore Limited | £4,062,978 |
| Road Traffic Solutions Limited | £4,061,396 |
| Redhouse Holdings Limited | £4,059,024 |
| Creditscale Limited | £4,058,559 |
| Ecovert Group Limited | £4,058,000 |
| Derek Lambert Polythene Limited | £4,057,778 |
| Black Swan (Yorkshire) Limited | £4,056,220 |
| Tees & Durham (Lift) Investments Limited | £4,056,162 |
| Garrards (Huddersfield) Limited | £4,054,810 |
| Long Folly Limited | £4,052,178 |
| Metanoia Film Limited | £4,052,151 |
| Blackhall Engineering Limited | £4,052,089 |
| Buy-Investment-Properties Limited | £4,051,231 |
| Hireport Limited | £4,050,478 |
| Consultant Cleaners Limited | £4,050,103 |
| IETG Limited | £4,049,103 |
| Hebden Bridge Community Association Ltd | £4,046,872 |
| WJS Properties 2 Limited | £4,046,000 |
| Deepsleep Beds UK Ltd | £4,038,588 |
| Corkel Holdings Limited | £4,037,846 |
| Gilbran (Management) Limited | £4,037,463 |
| E.W.G.A. Limited | £4,036,547 |
| Roberts Graphics Limited | £4,036,411 |
| Alan Wood Partnership Limited | £4,036,357 |
| Birchgrove Estates Limited | £4,035,769 |
| Micron Hydraulics Holdings Limited | £4,035,326 |
| The Forget Me Not Children's Hospice Limited | £4,034,792 |
| Castleford Rugby League Football Club Limited (The) | £4,033,585 |
| Amanda Hobson Limited | £4,033,178 |
| Padgetts (Batley) Limited | £4,032,587 |
| J.B.Schofield & Sons Limited | £4,031,223 |
| Taodail Hydro Limited | £4,030,892 |
| Future Forwarding (Holdings) Limited | £4,028,835 |
| Meritec Limited | £4,027,530 |
| E.F.C. Consultancy Limited | £4,025,118 |
| Salamander Fabrications Limited | £4,022,339 |
| Musgrave & Sagar Limited | £4,021,930 |
| Treadwell Developments Limited | £4,021,274 |
| DSA Chemicals Limited | £4,021,233 |
| GGR Holdings Limited | £4,020,387 |
| Geofabrics Limited | £4,020,186 |
| Orangechart Limited | £4,018,000 |
| Ambitemp (M & E) Limited | £4,017,622 |
| Dart Cubicles LLP | £4,017,420 |
| Kudos International Limited | £4,014,714 |
| STC Research Foundation | £4,012,396 |
| Peel Street Developments Limited | £4,011,677 |
| W.E. Foers & Son Limited | £4,009,069 |
| Todds Highway Maintenance Limited | £4,008,790 |

| | | | |
|---|---|---|---|
| S.A.R. Metals Limited | £4,007,714 | Rumford Tankers Limited | £3,912,882 |
| Royds Community Association | £4,006,476 | Primary Care Commissioning CIC | £3,912,403 |
| Direct Investments (Yorkshire) Limited | £4,004,743 | Surcoat Group Limited | £3,912,132 |
| Leading Labels Retail Limited | £4,004,717 | A.E. Morris Limited | £3,911,099 |
| Leading Labels Ltd | £4,004,716 | Eastmist Limited | £3,910,512 |
| CE Holdings Limited | £4,000,000 | Agenda Management Services Limited | £3,908,406 |
| Cyan Blue Core Limited | £4,000,000 | Valley Vets Ltd. | £3,908,383 |
| Eaton Smith LLP | £3,999,898 | Clare Hill (Huddersfield) LLP | £3,906,892 |
| J.H. Mewburn Limited | £3,999,742 | Dempsey Dyer Limited | £3,906,217 |
| Youngmight Limited | £3,998,986 | Springfield Healthcare (Grove House) Limited | £3,904,995 |
| JPI (Holdings) Limited | £3,998,161 | Tudor International Freight Limited | £3,904,835 |
| Hindle Gears Holdings Limited | £3,997,931 | Z.A. Akram Limited | £3,901,342 |
| Mount Vale Venture LLP | £3,997,149 | M S A Engineering Systems Limited | £3,900,566 |
| P & A Food Management Services Limited | £3,995,927 | AK (SPV) Limited | £3,900,100 |
| D & MA Sunderland & Son Limited | £3,993,593 | WDS Component Parts Limited | £3,899,184 |
| Sharp Holdings Limited | £3,992,934 | Complete IT Systems Limited | £3,898,793 |
| Hartwell Manufacturing Ltd | £3,991,324 | Abracs 2013 Limited | £3,898,020 |
| Jabe Foods Limited | £3,990,820 | Speedclad Limited | £3,897,494 |
| Darlington & District Hospice Movement | £3,986,437 | Naylor Wintersgill Limited | £3,890,385 |
| Vacation Club Partnerships Limited | £3,986,417 | Oriental Merchant (Europe) Limited | £3,888,687 |
| John Horsfall & Sons Limited | £3,986,142 | HACS Construction Limited | £3,888,216 |
| Brent Scaffold Boards Limited | £3,985,348 | KCA Deutag (Land Rig) Limited | £3,885,840 |
| Wavemaster (TGOF) Limited | £3,983,680 | Label Worx Limited | £3,884,578 |
| Aspire-Igen Ltd | £3,983,632 | K T Hydraulics Limited | £3,882,359 |
| Delta Salvage Limited | £3,982,089 | Heathvine Properties Limited | £3,881,423 |
| Triesse Holdings Limited | £3,980,460 | W.Swinbank & Sons Limited | £3,881,166 |
| Callauto Limited | £3,978,954 | Sykes House Farm Limited | £3,880,318 |
| Peter Ambrose (Castleford) Limited | £3,978,406 | Live Yorkshire Limited | £3,880,318 |
| Hassan (Holdings) Ltd | £3,977,473 | Superior Developments Limited | £3,879,741 |
| Deco-Pak Limited | £3,976,673 | Freshwater Biological Association (The) | £3,878,414 |
| JTR and RB Land Developments LLP | £3,976,540 | MM Band Services Limited | £3,877,371 |
| Concorde Technology Group Limited | £3,975,395 | Forest Homes Limited | £3,876,429 |
| Technikraft Limited | £3,974,807 | Concorde Excel Holdings Limited | £3,874,174 |
| Weavers Properties Limited | £3,971,355 | Savant Limited | £3,873,696 |
| Perio News Limited | £3,970,407 | J.B. Components Limited | £3,871,059 |
| WTJ Insurance Brokers Limited | £3,970,125 | Securi-Plex Limited | £3,869,715 |
| JMS of Doncaster Limited | £3,969,161 | Folding Sliding Doors Limited | £3,867,671 |
| B Batch Shopfitters Limited | £3,968,504 | George Walker Transport Manchester Limited | £3,866,937 |
| Steel Supplies Limited | £3,966,133 | Durham & Tees Community Ventures Primary Care | £3,866,079 |
| GSP Distribution Limited | £3,963,639 | Teleware Group PLC | £3,863,000 |
| Leading Solvent Supplies Limited | £3,962,650 | Controlled Building Measures (Holdings) Limited | £3,862,796 |
| CGP Estates Limited | £3,961,021 | Anglo Indian Exports Limited | £3,861,654 |
| Quintor (Homes) Limited | £3,958,950 | Wm Morrison Bananas Limited | £3,860,000 |
| Rowanway Limited | £3,956,956 | Outform EMEA Limited | £3,857,686 |
| A V Ogden Holdings Limited | £3,956,171 | Nortonthorpe Industrial Park Limited | £3,856,785 |
| Fellside Property Rentals Limited | £3,955,431 | Boston Holdings Limited | £3,853,834 |
| Elitebliss Limited | £3,954,799 | N.L. Durdy & Son Limited | £3,853,418 |
| Kirkleavington Property Company Limited | £3,953,699 | Alan Wood Holdings Limited | £3,852,753 |
| Vetuk Limited | £3,952,552 | JLM Global Foods Limited | £3,851,580 |
| George Fordy Properties Limited | £3,952,424 | Strata Holdings Limited | £3,849,671 |
| Tyto Finance Limited | £3,946,870 | Whole Crop Marketing Limited | £3,847,304 |
| Clarks UK Limited | £3,945,909 | Hire It Plant Limited | £3,847,297 |
| G.P. Atkin Limited | £3,944,670 | Epax Pharma UK Ltd | £3,847,000 |
| Elvington Holdings Limited | £3,944,619 | Inner Space Stations Limited | £3,845,064 |
| RCS Limited | £3,944,378 | Stockton Drilling Limited | £3,844,684 |
| Medicare Chemists Limited | £3,943,095 | Residue Limited | £3,844,579 |
| Castlehouse Construction Ltd | £3,942,378 | JBC Industrial Services Limited | £3,843,369 |
| CI Estates Limited | £3,938,636 | Redstart Renewables Limited | £3,842,365 |
| J Cooper Properties Limited | £3,931,393 | Imagexps Limited | £3,842,347 |
| EC Surfacing Ltd | £3,931,040 | Rodgers Group Limited | £3,841,600 |
| Wolds Engineering Services Limited | £3,926,955 | ECSC Group PLC | £3,841,000 |
| Highacre Builders Limited | £3,926,873 | Erivan Holdings Limited | £3,840,017 |
| Panacea Finance Solutions Limited | £3,926,703 | Broomgrove Developments Limited | £3,839,277 |
| Yesss (C) Electrical Ltd | £3,926,000 | Sewell Education (Hull) Limited | £3,838,948 |
| YCE Catering Equipment Limited | £3,924,993 | I A P Investments Ltd | £3,836,826 |
| Stirling Properties (Leeds No.2) LLP | £3,921,048 | Dalestead Limited | £3,832,406 |
| Keysterne Limited | £3,919,797 | Mayfair Curzon Properties Limited | £3,831,544 |
| Living Care Group Limited | £3,919,208 | The Collegiate Formation Limited | £3,826,120 |
| Goldmart Limited | £3,918,669 | Clarke Meats Limited | £3,825,909 |
| Drury Engineering Services Limited | £3,915,645 | J.H.Shouksmith & Sons Limited | £3,821,416 |
| Butt & Hobbs Limited | £3,914,678 | Rosti UK Ltd. | £3,816,000 |
| Modgate Limited | £3,914,037 | Pentamon Limited | £3,814,085 |

| Company | Value |
|---|---|
| Kingfisher (Lubrication) Limited | £3,811,854 |
| Cobalt Project Investments (Hull) Limited | £3,811,053 |
| Wilbraham Securities LLP | £3,811,011 |
| Fleetcor Fuel Cards Europe Limited | £3,809,000 |
| Yorplace Limited | £3,808,853 |
| Office Interiors Wholesale Limited | £3,807,753 |
| Yorpower Limited | £3,807,573 |
| Radical Services Limited | £3,807,321 |
| High Hedley Hope Farm Limited | £3,806,399 |
| Leeds Golf Leisure LLP | £3,805,653 |
| Bridgewood (UK) Limited | £3,804,344 |
| The St.Quinton LLP | £3,801,530 |
| Positive Location Properties Limited | £3,799,260 |
| Baydale Control Systems Limited | £3,798,632 |
| Oak Electrical Limited | £3,798,241 |
| Risby Homes Limited | £3,797,043 |
| Parkhouse Lakeland Estate Limited | £3,796,162 |
| Malton Road Developments Limited | £3,791,196 |
| Tri-Pack Plastics Limited | £3,790,524 |
| Harlen Ltd | £3,789,602 |
| Hargreaves Enterprises Ltd | £3,788,370 |
| P.K.A. Company Limited | £3,785,731 |
| Hamsard Five Thousand and Eighteen Limited | £3,784,978 |
| Burnley & Pendle Travel Limited | £3,784,000 |
| Hindu Cultural Society of Bradford | £3,780,339 |
| Lakeland Fashion Limited | £3,780,324 |
| J L Services & Son Limited | £3,778,529 |
| Til-Ex Limited | £3,776,357 |
| Riverhead Commercial Services Limited | £3,774,662 |
| Impact Property Services Limited | £3,773,833 |
| J. & E. Medcalf Limited | £3,772,442 |
| H B Tunnelling Limited | £3,771,455 |
| Hanbeck Properties Limited | £3,769,748 |
| Collard Cole Limited | £3,768,471 |
| Wilby (Group) Limited | £3,768,314 |
| East Riding Securities Limited | £3,767,630 |
| Arkoni Limited | £3,766,670 |
| Quest Consumables Limited | £3,765,156 |
| IT @ Spectrum Limited | £3,764,226 |
| Hird & Partners LLP | £3,763,581 |
| Humberston Park Special School | £3,762,086 |
| Chatsworth Windows Limited | £3,758,010 |
| Aventador Consultancy Limited | £3,757,865 |
| Stockbridge Technology Centre Limited | £3,757,252 |
| Direct Auto Finance Insurance Services Limited | £3,757,000 |
| Saftronics Limited | £3,756,820 |
| Lilys of London Limited | £3,755,235 |
| Hydramotion Limited | £3,755,198 |
| Armthorpe Falconry Limited | £3,755,045 |
| Wetherby Shade Card Company Limited | £3,754,946 |
| Dalesauna Limited | £3,751,466 |
| PR Books Limited | £3,751,292 |
| Yorhold Limited | £3,750,007 |
| Global Holdings Limited | £3,750,003 |
| KCA Deutag Enterprises Limited | £3,749,780 |
| Grafitec Holdings Limited | £3,749,713 |
| Krimpterm Limited | £3,749,429 |
| Cromwell Holdings Europe Limited | £3,747,686 |
| Hector, Lamont, Florence Associates Limited | £3,746,566 |
| Strand Paper Northern Limited | £3,746,470 |
| CLS Civil Engineering Limited | £3,744,569 |
| Wilby Limited | £3,744,081 |
| Avant Worldwide Ltd | £3,738,933 |
| Park Lane Homes Developments Limited | £3,738,700 |
| Shaw Pallet Limited | £3,738,659 |
| Hillas Group Limited | £3,738,193 |
| Low Grange Quarry Limited | £3,735,079 |
| Dennis Distribution LLP | £3,734,981 |
| Nobleoak Limited | £3,732,759 |
| Letts Properties Limited | £3,732,392 |
| J. and H. Property Management Limited | £3,732,163 |
| Oakapple Commercial Limited | £3,731,493 |
| Easington Caravan Sites Limited | £3,730,713 |
| Peter Fowler (Electrical) Limited | £3,730,710 |
| Furniture Choice Limited | £3,728,189 |
| York House Investment Company Ltd | £3,727,366 |
| Damac (Transporters) Limited | £3,725,166 |
| The Walshford Inn Limited | £3,724,859 |
| Bark and Bite Ltd | £3,724,696 |
| Willowbank Holiday Park Limited | £3,723,613 |
| Crossways Commercial Estates Limited | £3,723,000 |
| Cromwell Management Holdings Limited | £3,721,862 |
| Bruntons Aero Products Limited | £3,721,803 |
| Yarwood Leather Limited | £3,719,826 |
| Ninehundred Communications Group Limited | £3,719,733 |
| Athena Civil Engineering Ltd | £3,717,597 |
| Mechanical Facilities Services Limited | £3,717,567 |
| Rapid EPS Limited | £3,716,806 |
| Dickinsons (Plumbing & Heating Contractors) Limited | £3,715,748 |
| Kirklees Theatre Trust | £3,715,460 |
| Yorkshire Botanicals Limited | £3,714,776 |
| Europa Wools Limited | £3,714,700 |
| A.D.D. Express Ltd | £3,713,700 |
| DB Systel UK Limited | £3,713,000 |
| Calvesten Limited | £3,712,592 |
| Imbue Property Ltd | £3,712,231 |
| Southfield Health Care Limited | £3,711,725 |
| Newitt & Co Limited | £3,709,940 |
| Orkla Foods UK PLC | £3,709,095 |
| Doorstep of Hull | £3,708,807 |
| RC Marsden Properties Limited | £3,707,617 |
| Ashtree Partners LLP | £3,707,331 |
| Ardent Limited | £3,707,229 |
| MMM Medical Equipment UK Limited | £3,707,085 |
| Northern Crop Driers Limited | £3,705,864 |
| TRS Tyres Ltd | £3,705,203 |
| Cityblock Lettings Limited | £3,701,855 |
| Scout Cragg Holiday Park Limited | £3,701,204 |
| G & R Properties (Yorkshire) Limited | £3,700,744 |
| JT Group (UK) Limited | £3,700,000 |
| North Sea Ventilation Limited | £3,699,885 |
| Southgate Lighting Limited | £3,698,735 |
| Trade Furniture Company Ltd | £3,697,477 |
| Power Body Nutrition Ltd | £3,695,002 |
| Group-14 Ltd | £3,694,205 |
| H. Peel & Sons Limited | £3,694,119 |
| Wickframe Limited | £3,693,858 |
| DGP Intelsius Limited | £3,693,131 |
| Karman Ltd | £3,691,680 |
| Hawkesworth Appliance Testing Limited | £3,690,901 |
| MMCG Limited | £3,690,782 |
| Eddison & Wanless Limited | £3,690,601 |
| JMC Developments (Hunslet) Limited | £3,687,777 |
| C & H Antiques Limited | £3,686,798 |
| Tony Cook Limited | £3,682,592 |
| Hoveden Builders Limited | £3,682,517 |
| Sensio Limited | £3,682,411 |
| International Pipeline Products Limited | £3,682,287 |
| Premier Traffic Management Limited | £3,682,012 |
| Prorun Limited | £3,681,824 |
| Prasco UK Limited | £3,679,725 |
| Bradford City Football Club Limited | £3,674,872 |
| Queensway Properties Limited | £3,674,828 |
| Argyle Square Properties Limited | £3,674,128 |
| M. Gallagher (Civil Engineering) Limited | £3,669,975 |
| Cobalt Project Investments (Hull - Sewell) Limited | £3,669,589 |
| USG-Gledco Ltd | £3,666,937 |
| Stratex Warehouse Ltd | £3,665,653 |
| English Lakes Hotels Limited | £3,664,076 |
| Henry Lax Limited | £3,664,009 |
| Law Distribution Limited | £3,661,581 |
| Playdale Playgrounds Limited | £3,661,032 |
| The City of Leeds YMCA | £3,660,365 |
| Hever Castle Golf Club Limited | £3,660,010 |

| Company | Value |
|---|---|
| P. Barker Properties Limited | £3,659,307 |
| Marble 4 Life Ltd | £3,654,830 |
| Tricogen Laboratories Limited | £3,653,428 |
| Thirsk Investments Limited | £3,652,662 |
| Steffco Limited | £3,652,363 |
| Fortis Foods Limited | £3,652,139 |
| Meller Flow Trans Limited | £3,651,184 |
| Kass Bathroom Products Limited | £3,650,768 |
| Lindley Junior School | £3,649,776 |
| Reflecting Roadstuds Limited | £3,648,784 |
| Knightwood Developments Limited | £3,648,000 |
| Edwards Excavations Limited | £3,645,263 |
| The Hunslet Club | £3,643,380 |
| Tate of Leeds Limited. | £3,643,078 |
| Madala Limited | £3,642,684 |
| Explosive Developments Limited | £3,642,384 |
| George W. Barker Limited | £3,640,579 |
| Tower Estates (York) Limited | £3,640,393 |
| Sanmet Limited | £3,640,337 |
| Compass Broker Networks Limited | £3,638,700 |
| Hidrostal Limited | £3,636,337 |
| G. Collinson (Construction) Limited | £3,635,950 |
| Parkside Property (Yorkshire) Limited | £3,635,146 |
| Keighley and Worth Valley Light Railway Limited | £3,633,069 |
| Aztek International Freight Limited | £3,632,614 |
| Pall Mall Developments Limited | £3,631,345 |
| C.H. Scholey & Sons Limited | £3,629,938 |
| Multi-Tech Engineering (UK) Limited | £3,629,821 |
| Jack Pennington Limited | £3,628,983 |
| J.G.Swiers (Helperby) Limited | £3,625,007 |
| Grosvenor House Papers Limited | £3,624,968 |
| Gainsborough Industrial Controls Limited | £3,624,219 |
| Gordon Harrison Limited | £3,624,108 |
| Cohen Cramer Limited | £3,623,129 |
| Rural Insurance Group Limited | £3,622,563 |
| Broadland Energy (Donich) Limited | £3,620,777 |
| Egg Homes Limited | £3,620,492 |
| Devonshire Square Properties Limited | £3,620,160 |
| Transwaste Services Limited | £3,619,830 |
| Jeff Skinner Skip Hire Limited | £3,619,425 |
| Park Property (World) Ltd | £3,618,756 |
| Strachan Furniture Makers Limited | £3,618,102 |
| John Edward Crowther Limited | £3,617,580 |
| Vickers Laboratories Limited | £3,616,620 |
| Glen Avon Growers Limited | £3,615,388 |
| Dunlop Conveyor Belting Investments Limited | £3,614,000 |
| Alfred Bagnall & Sons (North) Limited | £3,613,654 |
| Shand Engineering Limited | £3,612,644 |
| Doran Scott Williams & Co Ltd | £3,610,900 |
| Gedore U.K. Ltd | £3,609,554 |
| SDS International Ltd. | £3,607,991 |
| Kennedy Travel (Yorkshire) Limited | £3,607,680 |
| James C Brett (Yarn Merchants) Ltd | £3,606,747 |
| Steamtown Railway Museum Limited | £3,605,789 |
| Havwoods Australia Limited | £3,605,070 |
| Cashmere Fibres International Limited | £3,604,690 |
| Dacre, Son & Hartley Limited | £3,603,702 |
| Coast and Vale Community Action | £3,603,644 |
| Shouksmith Holdings Limited | £3,601,372 |
| One Brewery Wharf Limited | £3,600,020 |
| Wire Estates Limited | £3,599,251 |
| Earthmill Holdings Limited | £3,597,330 |
| SDG (Boston) Limited | £3,596,947 |
| Batchelors Motor Group Limited | £3,596,532 |
| Barry Robinson Leisure Limited | £3,596,278 |
| Jungle Products Limited | £3,594,969 |
| Temeridge Limited | £3,594,795 |
| E-Factor Group Ltd | £3,594,487 |
| Tasca Tankers Limited | £3,594,465 |
| Proton (Southern) Limited | £3,594,407 |
| Ace Group (Engineering) Limited | £3,592,715 |
| Wellvend Limited | £3,592,303 |

| Company | Value |
|---|---|
| Keyland (Midpoint) Limited | £3,592,000 |
| S.W. Durham Training Limited | £3,590,411 |
| Grimsby Operations Limited | £3,589,960 |
| Don Valley Engineering Company Limited | £3,588,712 |
| Kankku (Holdings) Limited | £3,587,770 |
| M.A. Estates Limited | £3,586,827 |
| 2 Sister Food Services Limited | £3,586,000 |
| Transdek U.K. Limited | £3,585,193 |
| Metalcraft Europe Limited | £3,585,118 |
| Optimum Medical Solutions Limited | £3,584,528 |
| Audit Partnership Limited | £3,581,571 |
| D & J Estate Limited | £3,580,721 |
| CV Anderson Ltd | £3,579,758 |
| Marrtree Developments Ltd | £3,579,177 |
| Ghyllside School | £3,579,040 |
| Goodprofit Limited | £3,578,008 |
| Epax Pharma UK Holdings Unlimited | £3,578,000 |
| Molekula Limited | £3,577,469 |
| W. Cropper Limited | £3,577,196 |
| Hayton & Lamb Limited | £3,576,732 |
| Total Value Headhunting LLP | £3,576,053 |
| Zuka Ltd. | £3,574,604 |
| Alternative Windows (Leeds) Limited | £3,573,588 |
| Broughton Laboratories Limited | £3,571,395 |
| White Rose (Caravan Park) Limited | £3,570,382 |
| Bannatyne Properties Limited | £3,570,154 |
| Redfern Developments and Investments Limited | £3,570,028 |
| John T. Fall Limited | £3,569,902 |
| Hitha Limited | £3,569,546 |
| PBS Construction (North East) Limited | £3,568,982 |
| Lashlake Property Limited | £3,568,852 |
| Excel Laminating Limited | £3,568,432 |
| Jordan & Company (Hull) Limited | £3,566,318 |
| Pontefract Park Race Company Limited (The) | £3,566,210 |
| Industrial Textiles & Plastics Ltd | £3,564,281 |
| Cater-Kwik Group Limited | £3,562,797 |
| Dathan Tool & Gauge Co Limited | £3,561,795 |
| Select Legal Systems Limited | £3,561,619 |
| Claire Whitaker Limited | £3,560,849 |
| Fussey Engineering Limited | £3,559,868 |
| Newroc Ltd | £3,559,408 |
| Foundation | £3,559,000 |
| Checkmate Holdings Ltd | £3,558,572 |
| Taplanes Limited | £3,558,250 |
| Hydrastore Limited | £3,557,458 |
| Kirklees PFI Limited | £3,556,793 |
| Call Lane Social Leeds Limited | £3,556,623 |
| Linkway Distribution Services Limited | £3,553,048 |
| Bee Jay Scaffolding Limited | £3,552,814 |
| Bonus Securities Limited | £3,552,180 |
| Sterling Capitol PLC | £3,550,808 |
| H.R. Fell and Sons Limited | £3,549,643 |
| Emerald Investments (GB) Limited | £3,549,150 |
| SSL Healthcare Ltd | £3,548,177 |
| Ultimate (Commercial Interiors) Limited | £3,546,235 |
| Mill Mount Properties Limited | £3,546,000 |
| Nunns of Grimsby Limited | £3,545,180 |
| Shepherd Group Properties Limited | £3,543,000 |
| Pneumatic & Electrical Holdings Limited | £3,542,987 |
| Patchett Developments Limited | £3,541,569 |
| Metroplan Limited | £3,541,544 |
| YCR Distribution Limited | £3,540,951 |
| MLC Investments Limited | £3,540,502 |
| Podrigo Ltd | £3,540,134 |
| Holmfirth Properties Limited | £3,538,861 |
| Richard Baldwin Motorhomes LLP | £3,538,647 |
| MWS Group Ltd | £3,536,769 |
| Evans Easyspace (Chester) Limited | £3,534,662 |
| Methodist Holiday Hotels Limited | £3,531,981 |
| Duchy Homes (Humshaugh) Limited | £3,531,879 |
| Boldarch Limited | £3,528,707 |
| York Bioanalytical (Holdings) Limited | £3,528,036 |

| Company | Amount |
|---|---|
| Caldex Holdings Limited | £3,527,225 |
| Paramount Retail Group Holdings Limited | £3,525,001 |
| B C (Roofing Contractors) Limited | £3,524,781 |
| Old Earth School | £3,523,845 |
| Cirrus Laminations Limited | £3,522,401 |
| LMB Mechanical Services Limited | £3,520,634 |
| PLS Civil Engineering Limited | £3,519,202 |
| Fuel Express Limited | £3,517,770 |
| Resource Management Solutions (North East) Ltd | £3,517,428 |
| Overdale Trailer Park (Skipton) Limited | £3,516,148 |
| Dinsdale Farming Limited | £3,515,235 |
| Amvale Limited | £3,513,444 |
| Belmont-Birklands School Trust Limited | £3,513,191 |
| V Wilkins & Sons Limited | £3,508,883 |
| Dortech Architectural Systems Limited | £3,507,812 |
| Bhullar Limited | £3,507,003 |
| Sullivan Homes Limited | £3,506,058 |
| United Transmission Services Limited | £3,505,165 |
| Yates Media Ltd | £3,505,070 |
| The Aire and Ouse Farms Limited | £3,504,778 |
| Inspire 2 Independence (I2i) Ltd | £3,504,633 |
| Bennett-Ings (Developments) Limited | £3,504,618 |
| Prospect House Leeds Limited | £3,504,561 |
| Viking Arms Limited | £3,500,791 |
| Barden Biomass Holdings Limited | £3,500,002 |
| On Board Leisure (Holdings) Limited | £3,500,000 |
| S & A Builders Merchants Limited | £3,499,354 |
| Greendown Trust | £3,498,571 |
| Southridge Estates Limited | £3,498,556 |
| Vogue Leisure Limited | £3,498,505 |
| Weldtite Products Limited | £3,495,843 |
| Stewart Lawton Limited | £3,495,585 |
| Wannops Farms Ltd | £3,495,135 |
| Tocketts Mill Leisure Limited | £3,494,093 |
| Arena Capital MP Limited | £3,492,463 |
| Landown Limited | £3,492,423 |
| Filltex Limited | £3,491,807 |
| Comnet Europe Limited | £3,490,897 |
| Asset Finance UK Limited | £3,489,102 |
| Calvary Chapel York | £3,488,124 |
| Therapy in Praxis Limited | £3,487,553 |
| White House Livestock & Energy Limited | £3,487,498 |
| Meads Trust.Limited | £3,485,527 |
| Holbeach Buildings LLP | £3,484,381 |
| Bolton Brow Primary Academy | £3,483,563 |
| Swinton Technology Limited | £3,482,106 |
| Concepta PLC | £3,481,351 |
| York Holdings Limited | £3,479,796 |
| A.Watkinson Limited | £3,479,462 |
| Dunsville Primary Academy Trust | £3,478,569 |
| Wetherby Stone Products Limited | £3,478,117 |
| Teal & Mackrill Limited | £3,475,634 |
| Support Warehouse Limited | £3,471,015 |
| Kettlewell Fuels Limited | £3,466,520 |
| BPC Yorkshire Limited | £3,465,155 |
| Northallerton Auctions Limited | £3,463,569 |
| Daropeant Properties Limited | £3,461,967 |
| MBI Hawthorn Care Limited | £3,460,833 |
| Naburn Leisure Limited | £3,459,328 |
| Townham Limited | £3,459,263 |
| Watsons BS (Holdings) Limited | £3,459,023 |
| Neil Price Construction Services Limited | £3,458,963 |
| St George's Crypt | £3,458,703 |
| Apttus EMEA Limited | £3,458,631 |
| Harris Properties (Manchester) Limited | £3,458,624 |
| Webster Properties (Skipton) Limited | £3,457,989 |
| Stanwell Technic Ltd. | £3,457,458 |
| River Street Limited | £3,456,222 |
| The Dragonfly Agency Limited | £3,454,997 |
| Cornbrook Group Ltd | £3,454,845 |
| Hanover Properties Limited | £3,454,798 |
| David O'Meara Racing Ltd | £3,451,716 |

| Company | Amount |
|---|---|
| IETG Holdings Limited | £3,451,281 |
| Keystream Limited | £3,451,256 |
| 4L's Products Limited | £3,450,515 |
| Opera North Productions Limited | £3,450,309 |
| Homes for Students Limited | £3,449,362 |
| Selkirk Mechanical Handling Limited | £3,449,140 |
| Newman Properties Limited | £3,447,965 |
| Bosworth Estates Limited | £3,446,413 |
| Skanwear Clothing Company Ltd | £3,445,170 |
| Hodson Properties Limited | £3,444,628 |
| Ipsosolo Limited | £3,442,301 |
| Greentek Solutions Ltd | £3,440,521 |
| Rollits Limited Liability Partnership | £3,439,320 |
| PMW Quarries Limited | £3,439,106 |
| Machenair Limited | £3,437,308 |
| Paramount Wholesale Ltd | £3,436,105 |
| Caterleisure Services Limited | £3,435,542 |
| Sharma Investments Limited | £3,435,021 |
| Millwood Investments Limited | £3,434,627 |
| Gibson Pharmacy Limited | £3,433,925 |
| Woolrow Farm Limited | £3,433,367 |
| Lincolnshire Employment Accommodation Project | £3,433,141 |
| Camira Yarns Limited | £3,432,334 |
| Untha UK Limited | £3,430,101 |
| Mold Systems Limited | £3,429,692 |
| Harold Sergeant and Sons Limited | £3,429,349 |
| Adams and Green Limited | £3,428,568 |
| Oakwood Homeloans Limited | £3,428,287 |
| Zarafa Group Limited | £3,427,392 |
| Sweepcharm Limited | £3,427,257 |
| William Hepworth (Huddersfield) Limited | £3,427,031 |
| Mermaid Panels Limited | £3,426,202 |
| Hultafors Group UK Limited | £3,424,593 |
| 123 Retail Limited | £3,423,922 |
| Savers Wholesale Ltd | £3,421,983 |
| Wakefield Acoustics Limited | £3,421,705 |
| Metcalfe Bros Limited | £3,421,109 |
| Specialist Glass Products Limited | £3,420,968 |
| Gravers Care Home Ltd | £3,420,668 |
| Partline Limited | £3,418,526 |
| T G L (UK) Limited | £3,417,897 |
| Knightsbridge Furniture Productions Limited | £3,417,668 |
| Northern Divers (Holdings) Limited | £3,417,157 |
| Eridor Investments Limited | £3,415,185 |
| Ace Gas Limited | £3,414,933 |
| Ryedale Garages (1946) Limited | £3,413,895 |
| Banks Lane Investments Limited | £3,409,703 |
| Derwent Dale Limited | £3,409,138 |
| Glasshouses123 Limited | £3,406,748 |
| Lishman Sidwell Campbell & Price Limited | £3,405,902 |
| Crombie Freehold Limited | £3,405,795 |
| Farsley Transport Limited | £3,405,063 |
| Sands Care Holdings Limited | £3,404,521 |
| The Woodlands Academy Scarborough | £3,402,586 |
| Edmondsons (Freightliners) Limited | £3,398,734 |
| Premier Equine International Limited | £3,397,804 |
| C B T Clinics Limited | £3,397,226 |
| Katell Limited | £3,396,543 |
| Richard Sullivan Consulting Ltd | £3,394,544 |
| Sutcliffe Play Limited | £3,394,136 |
| Monster Group (UK) Limited | £3,391,308 |
| Regent House Estates Limited | £3,389,993 |
| D and K Chapman Limited | £3,389,389 |
| Halifax Investment Services Limited | £3,388,000 |
| Sound Leisure Limited | £3,387,335 |
| Masons Textiles Limited | £3,386,634 |
| Iceco Limited | £3,384,869 |
| NSF Health Sciences Ltd. | £3,383,283 |
| Idigital Investments Ltd | £3,381,763 |
| Almit Properties Limited | £3,380,901 |
| Keighley & District Travel Limited | £3,375,000 |
| The Holbeck Charitable Trust | £3,375,000 |

| Company | Value |
|---|---|
| Plant Theatre Ltd | £3,374,575 |
| Whitelock Developments Limited | £3,373,178 |
| D & L S Developments Limited | £3,372,825 |
| Fablink Tank Systems Limited | £3,372,168 |
| Ferdinand Properties Limited | £3,367,765 |
| Prious Limited | £3,366,920 |
| Peppers Marquees Limited | £3,360,755 |
| Bootyman Printers Limited | £3,358,806 |
| Bright Beginnings Childcare Centre Leeds | £3,349,777 |
| Bellutex Limited | £3,348,223 |
| Boston Healthcare Limited | £3,345,252 |
| Hartford Properties Limited | £3,345,106 |
| W.A. Howarth (Aphrodites Lodge) Limited | £3,344,594 |
| Agercon Holdings Limited | £3,342,894 |
| Felldale Retail Limited | £3,342,778 |
| Wakefield88 Limited | £3,342,600 |
| Rayner Marketing (Holdings) Limited | £3,342,065 |
| Pugh Holdings Limited | £3,341,626 |
| AE Cook Holdings Limited | £3,340,917 |
| Cammax Limited | £3,340,530 |
| Harrison Electrical Limited | £3,337,921 |
| Kingston Research Limited | £3,337,794 |
| Europipes (UK) Limited | £3,337,732 |
| AMS Bobcat Limited | £3,336,351 |
| Cityblock Holdings Limited | £3,335,509 |
| Specialised Car Covers Limited | £3,334,431 |
| Caswick Limited | £3,333,316 |
| R.E. Dickie Limited | £3,332,941 |
| M Rugs Limited | £3,331,937 |
| Help-Link UK Limited | £3,331,000 |
| High Croft Care Limited | £3,329,588 |
| Hird Rail Services Limited | £3,328,667 |
| Dick Garner & Sons Limited | £3,327,835 |
| DG Asset Enterprise Ltd | £3,327,346 |
| J. M. Holling Limited | £3,326,978 |
| White Cross Rubber Products Limited | £3,326,903 |
| Tayrol Limited | £3,326,819 |
| Oakwood Solicitors Limited | £3,326,741 |
| A & C Wood Limited | £3,326,451 |
| Habico Limited | £3,321,312 |
| Esvagt UK Limited | £3,320,000 |
| Vacform Group (Yorkshire) Limited | £3,317,902 |
| Isotek (Holdings) Limited | £3,316,826 |
| Decision First Limited | £3,316,170 |
| Lightbrook Limited | £3,315,266 |
| The Broadway (SPV) Limited | £3,314,677 |
| A & K Hosiery Limited | £3,312,785 |
| Carr Mount Estate Limited | £3,312,729 |
| Westfield War Memorial Village - Lancaster | £3,310,989 |
| Darlington Arena Limited | £3,310,839 |
| Fearnley Rhodes Limited | £3,309,254 |
| Answer Digital Limited | £3,309,004 |
| Chartford Arthington Limited | £3,307,622 |
| Prospero Growth Limited | £3,307,131 |
| Rradar (Holdings) Limited | £3,307,098 |
| Alt Berg Limited | £3,301,337 |
| Investment in Media Limited | £3,300,162 |
| PPG Performance Coatings UK Limited | £3,297,161 |
| Normanton Golf Club Limited | £3,297,147 |
| NL Commercials Management Ltd | £3,295,819 |
| Wortley Construction Limited | £3,295,564 |
| Therma Q Limited | £3,295,306 |
| Triple A Lets Limited | £3,292,363 |
| Clarks Vehicle Conversions Limited | £3,292,349 |
| Lassic Properties Limited | £3,292,085 |
| Eureka Display Limited | £3,290,531 |
| MacKay Transport & Storage Limited | £3,290,481 |
| Oakesway Limited | £3,289,298 |
| Great Grimsby Seafood Village Ltd | £3,288,822 |
| Walkers Nurseries Limited | £3,287,793 |
| Toiletry Sales Holdings Limited | £3,287,486 |
| Canley Food Packers Ltd | £3,287,177 |

| Company | Value |
|---|---|
| SSG Insight Limited | £3,286,338 |
| F. Machin & Sons Limited | £3,286,054 |
| Redmed Limited | £3,285,859 |
| R.M. English & Son Limited | £3,285,200 |
| Proma Boatman Limited | £3,284,421 |
| Humber Grain Limited | £3,282,863 |
| TRU Property Investments Limited | £3,282,760 |
| McCann Limited | £3,280,928 |
| Shaks Specialist Cars Ltd | £3,280,172 |
| Turner Commercial Developments Ltd | £3,278,848 |
| Ravens Ing Properties Limited | £3,278,420 |
| Astorbush Limited | £3,277,375 |
| Causey Hill Caravan Park Limited | £3,276,803 |
| M.S. Design International Limited | £3,276,151 |
| Dalkeith Laboratories Limited | £3,276,042 |
| Kaver Limited | £3,275,567 |
| HD1 Developments Limited | £3,272,814 |
| Infact UK Limited | £3,272,297 |
| Mitchell Farrar Group LLP | £3,272,051 |
| Kings Hall Leisure Limited | £3,270,965 |
| Street Clothes Limited | £3,270,248 |
| D.J. Prescott (Builders) Limited | £3,269,550 |
| Isberg Limited | £3,266,775 |
| G R Finance Limited | £3,266,348 |
| Bussey and Armstrong Limited | £3,266,250 |
| City Portfolio Limited | £3,266,242 |
| Blowers Jewellers Holdings Limited | £3,265,101 |
| Property Investments (Yorkshire) Limited | £3,264,421 |
| Buckley Properties (Leeds) Limited | £3,264,350 |
| City Red (Holdings) Limited | £3,264,141 |
| Flexiglobal (UK) Limited | £3,263,830 |
| Pollybell Farms Limited | £3,263,255 |
| Rawson Brook Group Holdings Limited | £3,262,731 |
| Snainton Golf Centre Limited | £3,262,061 |
| Citispace Properties Limited | £3,261,657 |
| Archway Engineering (U.K.) Limited | £3,261,376 |
| C.T. Transport (Castleford) Partnership LLP | £3,260,996 |
| The Finest Flats Company Limited | £3,260,788 |
| Fine Motor Cars Ltd | £3,260,012 |
| Diamondcut Limited | £3,259,689 |
| Jonro Properties Limited | £3,258,794 |
| The Calverley Reservoir Sales Company Limited | £3,256,976 |
| S Jackson & Sons Holdings Limited | £3,256,839 |
| Fast Trade Venture Limited | £3,251,659 |
| Techwax Limited | £3,251,541 |
| Roclad Systems Limited | £3,251,512 |
| Jam Homes Ltd | £3,248,947 |
| Secondtour Limited | £3,247,478 |
| TMPC Unlimited | £3,247,132 |
| Early Excellence Limited | £3,246,803 |
| Tadcaster Pub Company Limited | £3,244,937 |
| Hedley Hydraulics Limited | £3,244,609 |
| Crosshall Developments (Leeds) Limited | £3,241,461 |
| Ground-Guards Ltd | £3,240,552 |
| J. Pidgeon & Son Limited | £3,238,835 |
| Aclet Property Management & Services Limited | £3,238,724 |
| Birkett Bogmats Limited | £3,236,132 |
| Weybourne Estates Limited | £3,235,418 |
| Yorkshire Grain Limited | £3,234,188 |
| Northern Racing College | £3,232,424 |
| Lectra UK Limited | £3,231,251 |
| Project Development International Limited | £3,231,000 |
| Redhall Jex Limited | £3,230,000 |
| Lindley Church of England Infant School | £3,228,684 |
| Beech Hill Residential Investments Limited | £3,227,252 |
| Technowash Limited | £3,227,231 |
| Map Ventilation Limited | £3,226,428 |
| Airedale House Limited | £3,224,687 |
| D.G. Payne Limited | £3,223,186 |
| HK Timbers Limited | £3,221,939 |
| Sweeting Brothers (Land Drainage) Limited | £3,221,864 |
| Tillbrook Products UK Ltd | £3,221,295 |

| Company | Value |
|---|---|
| Cloth Fair Point Capital Limited | £3,221,124 |
| Hendersons of Selby Limited | £3,221,085 |
| Tuby Leisure Ltd | £3,221,076 |
| C.N. Trading Limited | £3,220,861 |
| Shaw Moisture Meters (U.K.) Limited | £3,217,755 |
| Lambton Clothing Company Partnership LLP | £3,217,038 |
| Energy Containment Concepts Limited | £3,215,379 |
| Ray Owen Waste Disposal Limited | £3,214,959 |
| Shine Childcare Limited | £3,214,316 |
| Marl International Limited | £3,213,808 |
| S B & A Clark Farming Limited | £3,213,790 |
| Integrated Polymer Systems (U.K.) Limited | £3,213,183 |
| Guy Bentley Limited | £3,212,999 |
| Sedbergh Hotel Enterprises Limited | £3,211,025 |
| Aqmen Holdings Limited | £3,210,751 |
| Kingfisher UPVC Windows & Doors Limited | £3,209,343 |
| Myrtle Grange Renewables Limited | £3,209,013 |
| R G Bassett & Sons Limited | £3,208,403 |
| A.Schofield (Pontefract) Limited | £3,208,079 |
| Croda Distillates Limited | £3,208,000 |
| Ronald Coates (Farms) Limited | £3,207,621 |
| Bates & Co. (Huddersfield) Limited | £3,207,482 |
| The Blues Kitchen Brixton Limited | £3,205,787 |
| Fenton Packaging (Leeds) Limited | £3,203,371 |
| The Axholme Academy | £3,202,787 |
| Lighthouse School | £3,202,463 |
| Addplant Limited | £3,201,331 |
| Tailormade Design Limited | £3,200,175 |
| Jonathan Potts Limited | £3,198,993 |
| Stocks Group Limited | £3,198,890 |
| Lissett Residentials Limited | £3,198,331 |
| Swanbridge Veterinary Group Limited | £3,197,791 |
| Rolco 188 Limited | £3,194,373 |
| Moorview Care Limited | £3,193,197 |
| EMHEDA Limited | £3,191,626 |
| Salthaugh Grange Farm Limited | £3,190,976 |
| Regenco Borrower Limited | £3,190,719 |
| Access Property Finance Limited | £3,190,147 |
| Replan (U.K.) Limited | £3,188,120 |
| William Thompson Group Holdings Ltd | £3,187,146 |
| The Kendal Brewery Arts Centre Trust Limited | £3,185,556 |
| Willoughby (891) Limited | £3,184,428 |
| QX Limited | £3,184,384 |
| Country Publications Limited | £3,184,314 |
| Acrastyle Limited | £3,183,253 |
| Lily Lolo Limited | £3,182,162 |
| O.& C.Holdsworth Limited | £3,181,949 |
| Continuity Promotions Limited | £3,179,899 |
| Red Roofs Nursery Limited | £3,179,791 |
| Keystone Healthcare Holdings Limited | £3,179,007 |
| T.Manners & Sons Limited | £3,178,039 |
| Triline (2014) Limited | £3,176,688 |
| Autocar Logistics (Irl) Limited | £3,175,202 |
| M.H. Whittaker & Son Limited | £3,175,060 |
| J. Brown Fabrics Limited | £3,174,579 |
| Richmond Properties (UK) Limited | £3,172,454 |
| Wilf Noble Building Supplies Limited | £3,171,716 |
| Ashwell Academy | £3,170,259 |
| Nordic Fashions One Limited | £3,170,169 |
| Brian Yates (Interiors) Limited | £3,169,776 |
| D. Harrison Limited | £3,169,542 |
| Berrygate Hill Nurseries Limited | £3,166,782 |
| I.R. Sarjantson Limited | £3,166,674 |
| Durest Beds Ltd | £3,163,497 |
| Emerald Care Holdings Yorkshire Limited | £3,158,800 |
| Holme Lane Haulage Limited | £3,158,619 |
| Grand Construction Products Limited | £3,157,493 |
| Graham Developments (Property Holdings) Ltd | £3,156,885 |
| Medetcrown Limited | £3,156,812 |
| Clive Soanes (Broilers) Ltd. | £3,156,680 |
| Bat 2 Limited | £3,156,082 |
| Keighley Laboratories,Limited | £3,154,733 |
| J.Jackson Limited | £3,152,644 |
| St Hybald's Academy Trust | £3,152,142 |
| SCD Group Limited | £3,150,242 |
| Canons Garth LLP | £3,149,078 |
| Dennis Winter (Leven) Limited | £3,149,011 |
| The Towel Rail Limited | £3,148,214 |
| Oriium Consulting Ltd | £3,147,998 |
| EPTA Service UK Limited | £3,147,902 |
| Orcina Limited | £3,146,393 |
| Scho62 Investments Limited | £3,143,178 |
| Sangwin Plant Hire Limited | £3,143,003 |
| Harrogate Investments Limited | £3,140,457 |
| Whiteghyll Limited | £3,139,814 |
| Sunflower Medical Limited | £3,135,698 |
| Hull Community Church | £3,135,624 |
| Morton Michel Holdings Limited | £3,135,000 |
| Vision Supplies Limited | £3,134,665 |
| S.M.K. Textiles Limited | £3,134,391 |
| Platinum Print Limited | £3,134,310 |
| J & S Brooksbank LLP | £3,133,814 |
| Willis of Skipton Limited | £3,133,318 |
| Stonegate Precision Tooling Limited | £3,128,785 |
| Dawngreen Limited | £3,128,500 |
| Electric Support Limited | £3,127,488 |
| Newclose Properties Limited | £3,127,167 |
| Kastronix Limited | £3,126,226 |
| H. H. James & Son Limited | £3,125,142 |
| Tetley's Motor Services Limited | £3,125,087 |
| Link Distribution (UK) Limited | £3,122,971 |
| Michael Nichol-Smith Limited | £3,121,033 |
| Shepherd Group Built Environment Limited | £3,119,000 |
| Adina Developments Ltd | £3,116,600 |
| S B Homes Ltd. | £3,116,249 |
| Northern Marquees Limited | £3,115,892 |
| Willow Grove Properties Limited | £3,115,421 |
| Stan Weston LLP | £3,115,356 |
| Caird Peckfield Limited | £3,113,163 |
| Ripon Race Company Limited (The) | £3,111,966 |
| Zeffirellis Limited | £3,111,297 |
| Airkool Contracts Limited | £3,107,437 |
| Parkrowe Estates Limited | £3,105,474 |
| Oakgate Group Limited | £3,105,026 |
| Marshall Wooldridge Holdings Limited | £3,102,582 |
| Megaplant Limited | £3,102,043 |
| Novaglaze Limited | £3,101,780 |
| Ashfield (Hull) Limited | £3,101,062 |
| P and E Yorkshire Ltd | £3,100,468 |
| Craftsman Tools Limited | £3,099,983 |
| Hull Super League Limited | £3,098,975 |
| Calvadon Limited | £3,098,384 |
| Ral Holdings Limited | £3,098,116 |
| On-Site Property Solutions Limited | £3,097,256 |
| Aghoco 1419 Limited | £3,096,384 |
| Custom Fittings Limited | £3,092,957 |
| 47A Limited | £3,091,950 |
| Oriel Printing Co. Limited | £3,091,622 |
| M Hillas (Properties) Limited | £3,091,541 |
| M. B. Locking Logistics Group Limited | £3,090,044 |
| Norman Jackson (Flixborough) Limited | £3,089,938 |
| Cascade Homes Ltd | £3,089,884 |
| Northern Pump Suppliers Limited | £3,088,538 |
| Wallum Farms (North) Limited | £3,087,965 |
| Jaines & Son (Grimsby) Limited | £3,085,898 |
| Provu Holdings Limited | £3,083,614 |
| Track Record Holdings Limited | £3,083,519 |
| Bolster Moor Farm Shop Limited | £3,080,511 |
| Clark Care Estates Limited | £3,079,726 |
| Aluminium Bronze Valves Limited | £3,079,058 |
| Fender Steel Limited | £3,078,503 |
| Bellbrooke LLP | £3,078,138 |
| Rawson Fillings Limited | £3,077,627 |
| Huntington Primary Academy | £3,077,196 |

| | |
|---|---|
| Invalesco Limited | £3,076,716 |
| Simon Holmes Limited | £3,075,675 |
| A B Print Group Limited | £3,073,488 |
| Towsure Products Limited | £3,069,355 |
| YLC Holdings Limited | £3,068,486 |
| One Commercial Limited | £3,067,776 |
| Professional Response Limited | £3,067,759 |
| Artesian Spas UK Limited | £3,067,741 |
| John Street Developments Limited | £3,066,674 |
| Hutton Wandesley Farms Company Limited | £3,065,828 |
| Rainbow Equine Hospital Limited | £3,064,245 |
| Beckenreid Limited | £3,062,570 |
| Cairngorm Ski Services Limited | £3,057,767 |
| Prospect Business Centres (Old Jewry) Limited | £3,057,513 |
| OPH Property Holdings Limited | £3,056,443 |
| Britto Psychiatry Limited | £3,056,103 |
| Haricovert Limited | £3,054,394 |
| Wilton Cobley (Holdings) Limited | £3,053,056 |
| KWH (Hull) Limited | £3,052,168 |
| J.V.Sleightholme Limited | £3,051,799 |
| Cogri Group Limited | £3,050,348 |
| Global Shipping Services Limited | £3,049,771 |
| Paramount Retail Group Holdco Limited | £3,048,877 |
| Wyreside Leisure Limited | £3,046,807 |
| GDS Technologies Limited | £3,046,197 |
| Progarm Limited | £3,045,843 |
| David M Brockbank LLP | £3,045,831 |
| T P Dibdin Limited | £3,045,058 |
| Las Metals Limited | £3,043,605 |
| Yorkshire Baptist Association (Incorporated) (The) | £3,041,014 |
| One Commercial (Claims) Limited | £3,040,889 |
| Sty.Com Limited | £3,039,501 |
| West Building Supplies Limited | £3,037,383 |
| Highbury Homes (Yorkshire) Limited | £3,035,748 |
| CID Products LLP | £3,034,558 |
| Nutclough Mill Limited | £3,032,835 |
| Cave Developments Limited | £3,030,890 |
| People Apps Limited | £3,030,754 |
| Perago Limited | £3,030,627 |
| Padgett Brothers (A To Z) Limited | £3,030,363 |
| Broad Carr Investments Limited | £3,029,972 |
| Bear Leisure Limited | £3,028,817 |
| Anhul Management Limited | £3,026,211 |
| Lowson & Co. Limited | £3,025,426 |
| HSL Manufacturing Limited | £3,022,990 |
| J & L (North East) Limited | £3,022,631 |
| Alta Enterprises Limited | £3,022,022 |
| Brathay Trust | £3,022,000 |
| United Anodisers Holdings Limited | £3,021,263 |
| Mailing & Marketing Solutions Ltd | £3,020,458 |
| Cyrus Developments Limited | £3,018,791 |
| DCMK Limited | £3,018,750 |
| EHLP Holdings Limited | £3,017,832 |
| The Leeds Jewish Free School | £3,015,103 |
| BC Bantams Limited | £3,014,919 |
| Cleves Cross Learning Trust | £3,014,084 |
| Principle Spira Limited | £3,012,591 |
| SB Wakefield Limited | £3,012,160 |
| Servemet (N.W.) Limited | £3,011,878 |
| Wetherby Group of Companies Limited | £3,010,759 |
| The Miles Partnership Limited | £3,010,748 |
| Smarts of York Limited | £3,010,347 |
| BBP Group Limited | £3,010,100 |
| Leader Limited | £3,007,682 |
| A Kahn Design Limited | £3,007,146 |
| SHFT Properties Ltd | £3,004,954 |
| Combined Selection Group Ltd | £3,003,851 |
| The Craggs Country Business Park LLP | £3,001,132 |
| Jaskaran S Deu Properties Limited | £3,000,870 |
| Kubler Holdings Limited | £3,000,001 |

*This page is intentionally left blank*

# Age of Companies

**1800s** [28]

Bower Roebuck & Co.,Limited
British Mohair Holdings Limited
Thomas Broadbent & Sons,Limited
John Brooke & Sons Ltd
Browallia Holdings Limited
Bruntons Aero Products Limited
James Cropper PLC
James Dawson & Son,Limited
De Smet Rosedowns Limited
Finlay Beverages Limited
Gaunts Limited
William S. Graham Limited
Hull & Humber Chamber of Commerce Industry & Shipping
Keighley Fleece Mills Co Ltd
Leeds Cricket Football and Athletic Co Ltd
Leeds and Bradford Boiler Co Ltd
London Security PLC.
J. Marr (Fishing) Limited
Methodist Chapel Aid Limited
Morco Products Limited
Northgate PLC
Abram Pulman & Sons Limited
Ripon Race Co Ltd
Roberts,Mart & Co.Limited
Scarborough College Limited
Singleton Birch Limited
West and North Yorkshire Chamber of Commerce and Industry
Edwin Woodhouse & Co. (Investments) Ltd

**1900-1909** [33]

Bekaert Bradford UK Limited
Billerudkorsnas Beetham Ltd
W.Boyes & Co.,Limited
Richard Carter,Limited
Crerar Hotel Group Limited
B.Danby & Co,Limited
J.T.Ellis and Co Ltd
Joshua Ellis and Co Ltd
John Good & Sons Limited
James Hare,Limited
Z.Hinchliffe & Sons Limited
John Horsfall & Sons (Greetland),Limited
Howarth Timber Group Limited
Ideal Standard (UK) Limited
Kentmere Limited
Kingspan Access Floors Limited
L & K Group PLC
LRUK (Holdings) Limited
Leeds Group PLC
Longwood Engineering Co Ltd
J. Marr Limited
Middleton Hall Limited
Musgrave & Sagar Limited
Onward Fishing Co Ltd
Richardsons Westgarth Limited
Shaws (Huddersfield) Limited
T.J.Smith and Nephew,Limited
Sovereign Health Care
Charles F.Stead & Co Ltd
Stephenson Group Ltd
Thirsk Farmers Auction Mart Co Ltd
Valley Printing Company, Limited
Vivimed Labs Europe Ltd

**1910-1919** [42]

600 UK Limited
Abbey Glen Limited
Aire and Ouse Farms Limited
Arco Limited
Ardagh Glass (UK) Limited
Arran Isle Holdings Limited
Alfred Bagnall and Sons Limited
Bartoline Limited
Bibby Transmissions Limited
William Birch & Sons Limited
Bright Steels Limited
Cavaghan & Gray Limited
Communisis BBF Ltd
Croda Distillates Limited
Diamond Power Specialty Limited
Dunhills (Pontefract) P L C
Job Earnshaw & Bros.Limited
Eimskip UK Limited
Thomas Fattorini Limited
Thomas Fawcett & Sons,Limited
Kingston Carton Co Ltd
Kino & Co. Limited
LRUK (Retail) Limited
Leeds Church Institute (Incorporated)
T.Manners & Sons Limited
Mansfield, Pollard & Co. Limited
Melbourne Street Properties Limited
Millers Oils Limited
Northallerton Auctions Limited
Oxbow Coal Limited
Pontefract Park Race Co Ltd
Procter Bros. Limited
Provident Personal Credit Limited
Scunthorpe United Football Club Limited
J.H.Shouksmith & Sons Limited
Teal & Mackrill Limited
Univar Limited
Benjn.R.Vickers & Sons,Limited
Waddington and Ledger Limited
Westfield War Memorial Village - Lancaster
John H. Whitaker (Holdings) Limited
Woodlands Home & Garden Group Limited

**1920-1929** [75]

600 Group PLC
Airedale House Limited
R.O.Arnold,Limited
BFWG Charitable Foundation
Benson Turner Limited
Birdsall Estates Co Ltd
E.B.Bradshaw & Sons,Limited
Braime Pressings Limited
Bridon Limited
John L. Brierley Limited
Camira Yarns Limited
Carclo PLC
Castleford Rugby League Football Club Ltd
Clayton Dewandre Holdings Limited
Cox 22 Limited
Craven Cattle Marts Limited
Cristal Pigment UK Limited
Croda Europe Limited
Croda International PLC
Darlington Farmers Auction Mart Co Ltd
East Riding Securities Limited
Eastman Staples Limited
F.T.Everard & Sons Limited
James Fisher and Sons PLC
Gardner Denver Industries Ltd
Gilbert Gilkes & Gordon Limited
Samuel Grant Group Limited
A.W.Hainsworth & Sons Limited
Harrogate Ladies' College Limited
Gawith Hoggarth & Co.,Limited
Howarth Timber & Building Supplies Ltd
Keighley Laboratories,Limited
Koppers UK Limited
Lettershop Limited
Lion Estate and Investment Co Ltd
Lister Horsfall Limited
MHLL Limited
Mabanes Properties Limited
J. Marr (Seafoods) Limited
Matson Ground Estate Co Ltd
McLean & Appleton Limited
Abraham Moon & Sons Limited
James Mortimer,Limited
Amos Nelson,Limited
Normanby Estate Co Ltd
Parkinson - Spencer Refractories Limited
Pelican Engineering Co. Limited
J.Pullan & Sons Limited
Pye Motors,Limited
Reliance Precision Limited
Russell's (Kirbymoorside) Limited
Safeway (Overseas) Limited
Scattergood & Johnson Limited
Shepherd Construction Limited
SigmaKalon UK Holding Limited
A.E.Spink Limited
Hugh Steeper Limited
Timothy Taylor & Co.,Limited
Team Industrial Services (UK) Limited
Thirsk Racecourse Limited
William Thompson (York) Limited
Thornton & Ross Limited
Isaac Timmins Limited
Total Downstream UK PLC
J.Townend & Sons (Hull) Limited
Vicarage Estate Co Ltd
Waddington Limited
Wetherby Steeplechase Committee,Limited
Wetherells Contracts Limited
John H.Whitaker (Tankers) Limited
Windermere Aquatic Limited
Thomas Wright/Thorite Group Limited
Yes Car Credit (Holdings) Limited
York Diocesan Board of Finance Limited
Yorkshire Baptist Association (Incorporated)

**1930-1939** [82]

Adler & Allan Limited
A. Andrews & Sons (Marbles & Tiles) Ltd
Anglo Indian Exports Limited
Archbold Holdings Limited
NG Bailey Limited
Berens & Co Ltd
Bosworth Estates Limited
W.P.Brown Limited
Clugston Estates Limited
Clugston Group Limited
Community of The Resurrection
John Cotton Group Limited
John Edward Crowther Limited
Dakin-Flathers Limited
H. Dawson Sons and Company (Wool) Ltd
Delahope Limited
Denso Marston Ltd
Equine and Livestock Insurance Co Ltd
F.W. Farnsworth Limited
Fenner Group Holdings Limited
Forteq (UK) Limited
Freemans PLC
Freshwater Biological Association
Giffen Group Limited
Glendon Estates
Grattan PLC

Hallite Seals International Limited
Hanson Plywood Limited
Harrison Spinks Beds Ltd
Hemingways (Furnishers) Limited
Hickson Limited
O.& C.Holdsworth Limited
Holetch Holdings Limited
Geo. Houlton & Sons (Holdings) Limited
Icon Aerospace Technology Ltd
Ideal Boilers Limited
Ideal Homes Holdings Limited
Instore Limited
Interface Europe Ltd.
C H Jones Limited
Lake District Estates Co Ltd
Walter Lilly & Co. Limited
Limestone Farming Co Ltd
Manor Coating Systems Limited
Marrtree Developments Ltd
Marton Mills Co Ltd
Meads Trust.Limited
Merritt & Fryers Limited
Neill & Brown Limited
Harold Newsome Limited
Northern Foods Grocery Group Limited
Nu-Swift International Limited
Onward Holdings Limited
Packo Inox Limited
Peacock & Binnington
Polynt Composites UK Limited
Provident Financial Management Services Ltd
RMS Trent Ports Limited
John Rannoch Limited
Rawson Fillings Limited
W.E.Rawson Limited
Redhall Group PLC
Reflecting Roadstuds Limited
Richardsons Limited
S.Ross & Co.Limited
Rotherham Sand and Gravel Co Ltd
The Joseph Rowntree Reform Trust Ltd
A.Schofield (Pontefract) Limited
Shipton Estates Limited
William Smith (Wakefield) Limited
Smith Bros.(Caerconan) Wholesale Limited
J.Stell & Sons,Limited
C.F.Struthers Limited
Teva UK Limited
Thistle Insurance Services Limited
Translift Freight Limited
Uriah Woodhead & Son Limited
W. S. Westin Group Limited
Whaleys (Bradford) Limited
H. & C. Whitehead Limited
J.Wild (Confectioners) Limited
R.Yates & Sons Limited

**1940-1949** [108]

Airedale Springs Limited
Arla Foods UK Property Co Ltd
Asda Stores Limited
Barkers (Northallerton) Limited
Bartlett & Co Ltd
Berrygate Hill Nurseries Limited
Billing Aquadrome Limited
Bridon International Ltd.
Bright Screw Co Ltd
Brook Taverner Limited
Burgess Group PLC
Bussey and Armstrong Limited
Butterfield Signs Limited
Carclo Overseas Holdings Limited
CarnaudMetalbox Engineering Limited
James Chambers (Timber Merchants) Ltd
Chippindale Plant Limited
Con Mech Group Limited
Coopland & Son (Scarborough) Limited
Cornelius Beverage Technologies Limited
Crosthwaite Hotels (Westmorland) Limited
John Edward Crowther (Holdings) PLC
S.Daniels Limited
Davy Group Limited
A Dawson and Company (Estates) Limited
Dean & Wood Limited
Dewhirst Sportswear Limited
Don Valley Engineering Co Ltd
Dransfield Novelty Co Ltd
East Riding Builders & Estate Development Co Ltd
Ecco Safety Group (UK) Limited
R.M. English & Son Limited
Erivan Holdings Limited
Ermine Farms Limited
Farnell Electronic Components Limited
Fenton Packaging (Leeds) Limited
Dick Garner & Sons Limited
Gestamp Tallent Limited
Wm.Grant (Paull) Limited
HRP Holdings Limited
Hargreaves Enterprises Ltd
Hartley Property Trust Limited
James H.Heal and Co Ltd
Hemingways Marketing Services Limited
Hindle Group Limited
Huggate Church Farm Properties Limited
I'anson Bros Limited
IFG Drake Limited
International Fibres Group (Holdings) Ltd
JCT600 Limited
Jaines & Son (Grimsby) Limited
Johnsons Wellfield Ltd
Lashlake Property Limited
Leck Construction Limited
Leeds Welding Co Ltd
Longley Concrete Ltd
Luxury Fabrics Limited
Manheim Limited
Marsylka Manufacturing Co.Limited
Methodist Holiday Hotels Limited
William F.Moore (Warplands) Limited
Wm Morrison Supermarkets P L C
Myers Group 1959 Ltd
Newly Weds Foods Limited
Northern Foods Limited
Omya UK Limited
Oxley Developments Co Ltd
PPG Architectural Coatings UK Limited
Pegler Yorkshire Group Limited
J. Pidgeon & Son Limited
Plasmor (Sabey Kirby) Limited
H B Raylor & Co Ltd
Ribblesdale Motors Limited
Jos.Richardson & Son,Limited
James Robinson Fibres Limited
Rodgers of York Ltd.
Ryedale Garages (1946) Limited
Scruton & Co.,(Builders) Limited
Seabrook Crisps Limited
William G. Search Limited
Secanim Limited
Shepherd Homes Limited
H C Slingsby P L C
Sutcliffe Play Limited
T. Quality Limited
Walter Thompson (Contractors) Limited
Gilbert Thompson (Leeds) Limited
Thompson Green & Co. Limited
Triangle Motor Co. Limited
Tricogen Laboratories Limited
Sam Turner and Sons Limited
Twiflex Limited
Victor Manufacturing Limited
P Waddington Limited
Wakefield Shirt Co Ltd
Herbert Walkers Limited
W.Clifford Watts Limited
Wavin Limited
Waxman Holdings Limited
Wellbridge Properties Limited
West Riding Masonic Charities Limited
Wilfreda Luxury Coaches Limited
Willerby Limited
Windward Phase 2 Limited
Ye Olde Oak Foods Limited
York Conservation Trust Limited
York Heritage (The Hall Thornton Le Dale) Ltd
Yorkshire Wildlife Trust

**1950-1959** [168]

600 Group (Overseas) Limited
Abbot Group Limited
Airea PLC
Wm.Allison & Sons Limited
Arbor Forest Products Limited
Ardagh Glass Limited
Arville Textiles Limited
Askern UK Limited
Authentix Limited
A.& E.Baines Limited
Bankside Patterson Limited
S.J.Bargh Limited
Bellow Properties Limited
Belzona International Limited
Bettys & Taylors Group Ltd
Bettys & Taylors of Harrogate Ltd
Bradford Flower Fund Homes
T.F. & J.H. Braime (Holdings) P.L.C.
Braun & Co. Limited
Broadland Properties Limited
Brooke Edgley Specialist Technical Services Ltd
Brooklands Property Holdings Limited
Alfred Brown (Worsted Mills) Limited
Burmatex Limited
Camphill Village Trust Limited
Castlecrafts Limited
Cattle (Holderness) Limited
W.S.Chapman & Sons Limited
Cherry Valley Farms Limited
Coal Contractors Limited
R.S. Cockerill (York) Limited
College Holdings 2012 Ltd
Corporate Travel Management (North) Ltd
Craftsman Tools Limited
Crossroads Truck & Bus Limited
D. S. Estates Limited
T L Dallas & Co Limited
R.E. Dickie Limited
John Dobson & Son (Carlton) Limited
Double Two Limited
Drive Devilbiss Sidhil Limited
N.L. Durdy & Son Limited
Dyson Properties Limited
Econ Engineering Limited

Eltham Properties Limited
Etrickbank Limited
Facultatieve Technologies Limited
T.W.Falkingham Limited
J.H. Fenner & Co. (Advanced Engineered Products) Ltd
J.H. Fenner & Co. Limited
Fenner International Limited
Fenwick Brothers Limited
James Fisher Everard Limited
Foxton Farmers Limited
Fredshaw & Co Limited
Fridlington Farms Limited
Futurama Signs Limited
Gleadell Agriculture Limited
J.A.Godfrey & Sons,Limited
R.J. & A.E. Godfrey
Group-14 Ltd
Harris Properties (Manchester) Limited
Harrison & Clough,Limited
D. Harrison Limited
J.E.Hartley Limited
Hickson International Limited
T.H.Hobson Limited
Holgates (Caravan Parks) Limited
P.Holmes Properties Limited
Alfred Hymas Limited
Iles (York) Limited
Inglis and Son (Jewellers) Limited
J.E.C. Investment Co Ltd
J.Jackson Limited
H. H. James & Son Limited
J.A.Jewitt
W.T.Johnson & Sons (Huddersfield) Ltd
Johnsons of Whixley Limited
Johnstone's Paints Limited
KVH Media Group International Limited
Kingfisher (Lubrication) Limited
Laurence Kirkby (Farms) Limited
Knightsbridge Furniture Productions Ltd
LS UK Fire Group Ltd
H.A. Lambert (Farmers) Limited
Leeds Commercial Limited
Lindley (Holdings) Limited
London Property Investments Ltd
Longthorp (Kilpin) Limited
Low Moor Properties Limited
Low Wood Hotel (1958) Limited
Lowdham Outdoor Leisure Limited
Lowwood Products Co Ltd
Brian Mager Limited
Manners Farms Limited
Marshalls Group Limited
Marshalls Mono Limited
Mitton Mechanical Services Limited
S.A.Mossop (Farms) Limited
National Floorcoverings Limited
W. Nutt & Son Limited
Oilgear Towler Limited
Orkla Foods UK PLC
Osprey Limited
Owens-Corning Veil U.K. Ltd.
Parker & Parker Limited
Phoenox Textiles Limited
Pitcliffe Properties Limited
Plasmor Limited
Playdale Playgrounds Limited
Mark H Poskitt Limited
Poundstretcher Limited
G.W.Proudfoot Limited
Quirkco Investments Limited
Riby Grange Farming Co Ltd
Ringways Garages (Leeds) Limited
J.R. Rix & Sons Limited
Rix Petroleum (Hull) Limited
F. Peter Robinson Limited
Robert Rook Estates Limited
SGS Packaging Europe Limited
SPX International Limited
Saria Limited
Sarval Limited
C.H. Scholey & Sons Limited
Scout Cragg Holiday Park Limited
Wilfred Scruton Limited
W.D.Sellers and Sons Limited
Sewell Construction Limited
Sherborne Upholstery Limited
William Sinclair & Sons (Stationers) Ltd
J.V.Sleightholme Limited
G.F.Smith & Son (London),Limited
R.Smith (Windermere) Limited
Spafield Properties Limited
Spooner Industries Limited
James Stockdale Limited
M.F. Strawson Limited
F.C. Stubbings & Sons Limited
Wm Sugden & Sons Limited
S.D. Taylor Limited
Teva Laboratories UK Limited
Thompson Commercials Limited
Thornber Chicks Limited
Total Lindsey Oil Refinery Limited
Tower Estates (York) Limited
C.E.A.Towne (Ship Riggers) Limited
Trans-European Port Services (G.B.) Ltd
Trevella Caravan Co Ltd
Tunstall Group Limited
G.B.Turnbull Limited
VP PLC
VTL Precision (Bradley) Limited
Vallectric Limited
Wakefield and District Health and Community Support Ltd
Fred Walter & Sons Limited
Wandahome (Knottingley) Limited
A.Watkinson Limited
H.I.Weldrick Limited
Wetherby Shade Card Co Ltd
White Rose Finance Co Ltd
Wilkinson Building Co.(Leeds) Limited
Dennis Williams Limited
Wool Growers (Great Britain) Limited
YJL Limited
York & District Investment Co Ltd
York Civic Trust
Yorkshire Stone Co. (Bradford) Limited

**1960-1969** [261]

4B Elevator Components Limited
Abbeyfield Ilkley Society Limited
C F Abraham Limited
Acrastyle Limited
Acropolis Corporate Limited
George Allinson (Transport) Limited
B.Allsop Limited
Mrs. J. C. Altham & Sons (Morecambe) Ltd
Alvercroft Limited
Anord Mardix (UK) Limited
Aysgarth School Trust Limited
BHJ UK Food Limited
M. and B. Barker Limited
Dennis Barnfield Limited
Bartlett Group (Holdings) Limited
Beal Developments Limited
Belmont-Birklands School Trust Limited
Bemis Packaging UK Ltd
Thos. Bentley & Son Limited
Better Fish Limited
Beverley House (9000) Limited
Bhullar Bros.Limited
Blackhall Engineering Limited
Blenheim House Properties (Bradford) Ltd
Bramall & Ogden Limited
Brandon Group Limited
Brenntag Inorganic Chemicals Limited
G.H.Brooks & Co.(Harrogate) Limited
Buckley Properties (Leeds) Limited
Burton Agnes Stud Co Ltd
Joseph Camm Farms Limited
Car Care Plan Limited
Carlac Limited
R.Caudwell (Produce) Limited
Central Land Holdings Ltd
Christeyns UK Ltd
Cliffe Hill Second Investments Limited
Clugston Construction Limited
Communisis Chorleys Ltd
Consultant Services Group Limited
Continental Sports Limited
Continental Wine & Food Limited
Contract Vehicles Limited
Ernest Cooper Limited
Cravenhurst Properties Limited
Croft Properties (Harrogate) Limited
Crowle Wharf Engineers Limited
Crows Nest Camp Limited
J.W. Crowther & Son Limited
Cumbria Wildlife Trust Limited
Cyden Homes Limited
DFDS Pension Limited
Dale Power Solutions Limited
Dalesauna Limited
Damartex UK Limited
Dantex Graphics Limited
Dathan Tool & Gauge Co Limited
Dawn Developments Limited
Decorative Panels Holdings Limited
W. Denis (Insurance Brokers) PLC
Distrupol Limited
Dusrolbake Limited
E K Motor Factors Limited
EPTA George Barker Ltd
Easington Caravan Sites Limited
Eastbay Limited
Eastburn Farms Limited
Bell Elliot Leisure Limited
Eltherington Group Limited
Everik Limited
Farnell Holding Limited
Fellowes Ltd
C.W.Fields & Son Limited
Fisherman Limited
Fullers Foods International PLC
Gardner Denver International Ltd
Garthwest Limited
Gateways Educational Trust Limited
Gill Demolitions Limited
Global Shipping Services Estates Limited
Golden Fry Foods Limited
Grainsby Farms Limited
Graypen Limited
HBOS Investment Fund Managers Limited
HRP Limited
Kenneth Hall (Builder) Limited
Hanson Family Holdings Limited
Hanson Logistics Limited

Harder Bros. Limited
Hartshorne Motor Services Limited
Hawthorn Timber Limited
Hider Food Imports Limited
Higgins Agriculture Limited
High Seat Limited
Highfield Caravans Limited
Hill House School Limited
Harold Hinchliffe Limited
Holbeck Homes Limited
Holker Estates Co. Limited
Horncastle Group PLC
House of Townend Limited
Humberside Farmers Limited
Hutton Wandesley Farms Co Ltd
IPF International Limited
International Personal Finance Investments Ltd
JCT600 (Yorkshire) Ltd
JCT600 Vehicle Leasing Solutions Limited
Norman Jackson (Flixborough) Limited
W.E. Jameson and Son Limited
J. Jeffery (Builder) Limited
Johnston and Jeff Limited
Jordan & Company (Hull) Limited
Jotun Paints (Europe) Limited
Keighley and Worth Valley Light Railway Ltd
D.M.Keith Limited
Kemira Chemicals (UK) Limited
Rory Kemp Limited
Kings Hall Leisure Limited
Kingsoak Limited
Kirkleavington Property Co Ltd
Kysor Europe Limited
LTT Vending Ltd
Label Makers Limited
Lakeland Limited
Lamba Trading Co. Limited
Lambson Building Products Limited
Landmark Wholesale Limited
Lapwing Estate Limited
Leeds Theatre Trust Limited
R H Leonard Limited
Lilys of London Limited
Linpac Group Holdings Limited
Linpac Packaging Limited
J.Long & Sons (Haulage) Limited
Sam Longthorp Limited
A.W.Lumb & Co.Limited
Jack Lunn (Properties) Limited
MS International PLC
MSS Developments Limited
Mack & Lawler Builders Limited
Manningham Concrete Limited
Marshall (Building Contractors) Ltd
Matisa (U.K.) Limited
McCain Foods (G.B.) Limited
W.McClure Limited
J. & E. Medcalf Limited
J.K.B.Megginson & Sons Limited
Melrose Textile Co.,Limited
Metal Drum Co Ltd
Molescroft Farms Limited
Montracon Limited
Wm Morrison Produce Limited
Motorhog Limited
Mowden Controls Limited
Multisol Limited
L.Nettleton & Son Limited
Newsmith Stainless Limited
D. Noble Limited
Northern Ballet Limited
Northern Energy Supplies Limited
Norton Healthcare Limited
Sir Robert Ogden Estates Ltd
A V Ogden Holdings Limited
Olicana Properties Limited
Optima International Limited
Overdale Trailer Park (Skipton) Limited
Oxley Group Limited
Padgetts (Batley) Limited
Parkmount Estate Company (Allerton) Ltd
Portakabin Limited
D. D. Porter Limited
Premier Farnell Limited
Premier Farnell UK Limited
Richard Preston & Son Limited
Produmax Limited
Provident Financial PLC
R & R Ice Cream UK Limited
Thomas B. Ramsden & Co. (Bradford) Ltd
D.B. Ramsden & Co Ltd
Rema Tip Top Automotive UK Limited
Renew Holdings PLC.
J.A. Richardson (Electrical) Limited
Riding Properties Limited
Rodgers Plant Hire Ltd.
Rollings Investments Limited
Russell Armer Limited
S.W. Durham Training Limited
SEW-Eurodrive Limited
Safeway Stores Limited
Salamander Fabrications Limited
Sandsfield Gravel Co Ltd
Sangwin Plant Hire Limited
Sarval (Hartshill) Limited
Scarborough Flower Fund Homes
J.B.Schofield & Sons Limited
Harold Sergeant and Sons Limited
Shedden Farms Limited
Shepherd Building Group Limited
Shepherd Development Co Ltd
Shepherd Group Properties Limited
Sia Abrasives (G.B.) Ltd
Simpson (York) Limited
John Hornby Skewes and Co Ltd
William Smith Group 1832 Limited
R.N.Smith Holdings Limited
Solina UK Trading Limited
Spellman & Walker Limited
Springfir Estates Limited
St. Catherines Developments Limited
Standard Wool (UK) Limited
Steamtown Railway Museum Limited
D. Stoker Group Limited
W. H. Strawson (Farms) Limited
W. H. Strawson (Notts.) Limited
Peter Strawson Limited
Sun Branding Solutions Ltd
J.G.Swiers (Helperby) Limited
Joseph E.Swiers,Limited
Swift Group Limited
W.Swinbank & Sons Limited
Sykes House Farm Limited
John Sylvester Engineering Co Ltd
Technical Control Systems Limited
Thomas of York Limited
R.E. Thornber Limited
Tickhill Engineering Co Ltd
Jack Tighe Limited
Towngate PLC
Treadwell Developments Limited
A.T.G. Turnbull Limited
Ulrome Seaside Caravan Co Ltd
Vacform Group (Yorkshire) Limited
Viking Arms Limited
Vogue Leisure Limited
Wabco Automotive U.K. Limited
Warden Farming Co Ltd
Weardale Motor Services Limited
Weir Valves & Controls UK Limited
Whitakers Chocolates Limited
H. Wicks (Lindal) Limited
Wilkes Properties (Wakefield) Limited
Wilkes Vending Services Limited
Willerby Manor Hotels Limited
Willerby Wold Piggeries Limited
Tom Willoughby Limited
Wiltel Limited
Wilton Cobley Limited
Windermere Educational Trust Limited
Windermere Lake Cruises Limited
John Winter & Co Ltd
Dennis Winter (Leven) Limited
Wood Auto Supplies Limited
Woodhead Investments & Development Services Ltd
Edwin Woodhouse & Co. Limited
Edwin Woodhouse Properties Limited
M.Woodhouse Transport (Lancaster) Ltd
Wortlea Estates (Leeds) Limited
Wykeland Limited
Yarwood Leather Limited
York Forty-Four Limited
Yorkshire Caravans of Bawtry Limited

**1970-1979** [426]

4B Braime Components Limited
A B Print Group Limited
A. & J. Fabtech Limited
A.One Feed Supplements Limited
ASD Limited
Acre Products Limited
Aflex Hose Limited
Agercon Limited
Agrimin Limited
Airedale Chemical Co Ltd
Airedale International Air Conditioning Ltd
Richard Alan Engineering Co Ltd
Alton Cars Limited
Amalgamated Construction Ltd
American Standard (U.K.) Co.
Animalcare Group PLC
Colin Appleyard Limited
Aptar UK Limited
Aquaspersions Limited
Arch Chemicals Limited
L'Arche
Argrain Limited
Armstrong-Priestley Limited
Asda Group Limited
Ashleighsigns Limited
Audio-Technica Limited
B & K Universal Limited
B.W.Industries Ltd
J.H. Bacon Limited
Alfred Bagnall & Sons (Administration) Ltd
Alfred Bagnall & Sons (North) Limited
George W. Barker Limited
C.K.Batchelor Limited
Bayford & Co. (Developments) Limited
Belgrade Insulations Limited
Thomas Bell & Sons Limited
Bendrigg Trust
J.N. Bentley Limited
Bermar Building Co Ltd

John Betts Quality Used Cars Limited
Bewley's Tea and Coffee UK (Roastery) Ltd
Charles Birch Limited
Bonus Electrical Group Limited
Bonus Electrical Limited
Booth Industries Limited
Brandon Hire Limited
Brecks Farm Limited
Bring Cargo Limited
Bristan Group Limited
Britannia Construction Limited
British Bung Manufacturing Co Ltd
M.Brittain (York) Limited
Britt Broadbent Limited
Brooksbank Valves Limited
Broom House Investments Limited
Builders Supply (North West) Limited
John Bull (Confectioners) Limited
R. Bunton Limited
A.E. Burt and Co Ltd
Byworth Boiler Hire Limited
CPM Group Limited
Caddick Construction Limited
Cairngorm Ski Services Limited
Calderys UK Ltd
Callauto Limited
Camborne Holdings Limited
Car Care Plan (Holdings) Limited
Carnaby Caravans Limited
Cavaghan & Gray Group Limited
Celdis Limited
Tom Chambers Limited
Chapter of The Order of The Holy Paraclete (The) Unlimited
Chiorino U.K. Limited
Chrislind Services Limited
Charles Church Developments Limited
City Fusion Limited
Clariant Oil Services UK Ltd
Clays of Addingham Limited
Cleethorpes Properties Limited
J.H. Clissold & Son Ltd.
Cohen & Wilks International Limited
Collett Logistics Limited
Commercial Development Projects Limited
Commercial Vehicle Auctions Limited
Communisis One Ltd
Communisis UK Limited
Congregational Memorial Hall Trust (1978) Ltd
Conservation Volunteers
Consultant Cleaners Limited
Tony Cook Limited
Copley Motors Limited
Coriant UK Limited
Corrocoat Limited
Corrosioneering Group Limited
County Properties (Northern) Limited
Covance Laboratories Limited
Cramscene Limited
Cranswick PLC
Richard Craven (Keighley) Limited
Creativerace Limited
Crescent Estates (Ilkley) Limited
W. Cropper Limited
Cundall Manor Limited
Czajka Properties Limited
D.T. Industries Limited
DB Orthodontics Limited
DFDS Seaways Newcastle Limited
DFS Furniture Co Ltd
Damac (Transporters) Limited
Dart Group PLC
Paul Davies Limited
De Vere Limited
Deep Sea Electronics Limited
Dempsey Dyer Limited
Dent Steel Services (Yorkshire) Limited
Dewhirst Group Limited
P.V. Dobson and Sons (Motors) Limited
Donaldson Filter Components Limited
Dormeuil Manufacturing Limited
R.E. and R. Duffield and Sons Limited
Peter Duffy Limited
Dunelm Optical Co. Limited
A. Dyson & Son (Patterns) Limited
Easilift Loading Systems Limited
East Yorkshire Aluminium & Glass Limited
Ebac Limited
Edmondsons (Freightliners) Limited
Ralph Ellerker (1795) Limited
Ellis Patents Limited
Elvington Holdings Limited
Eminox Limited
Emsley Crane Hire Limited
Encon Insulation Limited
Engie Fabricom UK Limited
English Lakes Hotels Limited
Eridor Investments Limited
Eurotrail UK Limited
Exelby Services Limited
Extrudakerb (Maltby Engineering) Limited
Falcon Sportswear Limited
John T. Fall Limited
Farmers Boy Limited
H.R. Fell and Sons Limited
Ferno (UK) Limited
Festino (Finance) Limited
Filtronic Wireless Ltd
Finsbury (Instruments) Limited
Flannery Civil Engineering Limited
Flatfish Limited
Herbert Fletcher Transport Limited
Four Pillars Hotels Limited
Fowler Welch Limited
Fradley Properties Ltd
Frickley Holdings.Limited
Future Forwarding Co Ltd
Gablesea Limited
Gamebore Cartridge Co. Limited
Gamston Aviation Limited
Garlock (Great Britain) Limited
Gartland Whalley and Barker Limited
Gladwin Bros. (Farms) Limited
Glasson Grain Limited
M.B. Goodwin (Skipsea) Limited
M.B. & J. Goodwin Limited
Green Flag Limited
Group Auto Union UK and Ireland Limited
H.S.G. (Packing Cases) Limited
HMCA/S PLC
Hainsworth Sterne & Co. Limited
Hambleton Holdings Limited
Harratts Group Limited
Gordon Harrison Limited
Harrogate Investments Limited
Harte Woodworking Limited
Hartford Trading Limited
Hartwell Manufacturing Ltd
Havwoods Limited
Hayden Daniel Properties Limited
C.T. Hayton Limited
Headland Plant Limited
John Hebb (Motor Engineers) Limited
Hedley Hydraulics Limited
William Hepworth (Huddersfield) Limited
Heritage Commercial Finance Limited
Hestview Limited
Hidrostal Limited
M. Higgins Limited
Hillreed Homes Limited
Hobson and Porter Limited
Hodson Properties Limited
K.M. Holmes (Bradford) Limited
Holmfirth Properties Limited
David Hopkinson Limited
Hoveden Builders Limited
R.J. Howard Engineers Limited
Howarth Timber (Windows & Doors) Limited
Hoyer Petrolog UK Limited
John Hudson Trailers Ltd
Hull Truck Theatre Co Ltd
Humberside Engineering Training Association Ltd
Hunprenco (Precision Engineers) Limited
Hurst Stores and Interiors Limited
Husqvarna UK Limited
Hystat Systems Limited
Illingworth & Gregory Limited
Immingham Industrial Estates Limited
Interchange and Consort Hotels Limited
J.S.R. Farms Limited
JLA Limited
JRRT (Properties) Limited
Jenkar Shipping Limited
Jessgrove Limited
J.A. Jewitt (Meat) Limited
J. & C. Joel Limited
Johnny's Entertainments (Tyneside) Ltd
Jonro Properties Limited
K P H (Plant Hire) Limited
KCA Deutag Drilling Group Limited
Keigar Homes Limited
Kennedy Travel (Yorkshire) Limited
M. Kettlewell (Melmerby) Limited
Kexgill Limited
Killgerm Group Limited
Kings Security Systems Limited
Kingstown Furniture Limited
Kirkdale Industrial Training Services Ltd
Kirncroft Engineering Limited
Klinger Limited
Kolorcraft Limited
L.F.C. Horkstow Limited
L.W. Safety Limited
Lambert Engineering Limited
Langley Holdings PLC
Henry Lax Limited
Leeds Grand Theatre and Opera House Ltd
Derek Lewis Limited
Lightwater Leisure Limited
Lightwater Quarries Limited
Linpac Finance Limited
Lishman Sidwell Campbell & Price Limited
List Group PLC
J.C. Lister Farms Limited
Lorica Insurance Brokers Limited
Lowson & Co. Limited
Lubna Foods Limited
A.W. Lumb (Midlands) Limited
M. & B. Commercial Properties Limited
M6 Truck Services Limited
F. Machin & Sons Limited
Main Line Bearing Co. Limited
Mainprize Offshore Ltd
Marl International Limited

Marshall Construction (West Yorkshire) Ltd
Marshall Group Services Limited
Marshall Holdings Limited
Marshall Wooldridge Limited
Thomas Mawer Limited
McCann Limited
McIlroy Estates Limited
Megaplant Limited
Metroplan Limited
Mileta Sports Limited
Milford Limited
Mitrefinch Limited
Modgate Limited
Mondi Scunthorpe Limited
Monocon International Refractories Ltd
The George A. Moore Foundation
Moores Furniture Group Limited
Morris & Co. (Handlers) Limited
Ian Mosey Limited
Moxon (Farms) Limited
Myers Building Supplies Ltd
NTEX Limited
Naylors Finance Limited
Neill & Brown (Shipping) Limited
Nisa Retail Limited
Normanton Laminating Services Limited
K.M. Norris Limited
North Killingholme Storage Limited
North York Moors Historical Railway Trust Ltd
North Yorkshire Timber Co Ltd
Northern Commercials (Mirfield) Limited
Northern Crop Driers Limited
Northern Divers (Holdings) Limited
Northgate Vehicle Hire Limited
OPM (Labels & Packaging) Group Limited
OSI Food Solutions UK Limited
Oakland Farms Limited
Oriel Printing Co. Limited
Orion Developments Limited
Orion Homes Limited
Orvec International Limited
P. & B. (Foods) Limited
P.P. Profiles (West Yorkshire) Limited
PPB Ltd
Pamant Limited
Parkin International Engineering Services Ltd
Derek Parnaby Cyclones International Ltd
Pavers Limited
D.G. Payne Limited
Peak Oil Products (Northern) Limited
Pegler Limited
Pengems Limited
Penmoor UK Ltd
Pennine Camphill Community Limited
Jack Pennington Limited
Ping Europe Limited
Polypipe Limited
Potter Group (Holdings) Limited
Power Health Products Limited
Precious Holdings (Wakefield) Limited
Price Express Transport Limited
Procter (Bordley) Limited
Provimi Limited
Quarmby Holdings Limited
Quest Consumables Limited
R.P.M. Industrial Services Limited
Rainheath Limited
Tony Rampton Trust
Peter Ramsey & Sons (Denholme) Timber Ltd
Redhall Jex Limited
Redhead Freight Limited
Reed Boardall Cold Storage Limited
Reliance Garage (Ryedale) Limited
Rema Tip Top Industry UK Limited
Resdev Limited
Rhal Farms Limited
Rhodar Limited
A. Rhodes (Haulage) Limited
Ripon Select Foods Limited
Rixonway Kitchens Limited
Barry Robinson Leisure Limited
Julian Roche Associates Limited
Ronald Coates (Farms) Limited
Ryedale Printing Works Limited
Safeway Limited
Sandal Motors (Bayern) Limited
I.R. Sarjantson Limited
Savoy Tyres Limited
Leo Sawrij Limited
Sellers International Limited
Seymour (Civil Engineering Contractors) Ltd.
Shallowdale Limited
Shand Engineering Limited
Nikolas Shaw Limited
Shaw Pallet Limited
Shaw Timber Limited
John Shaw and Son Limited
S. Sheard & Son Limited
G.W. Sissons and Son Limited
F. Smales & Son (Fish Merchants) Ltd
R.H. Smith & Sons (Wigmakers) Limited
Snugpak Limited
Solvgrin Limited
S.H. Somerscales Limited
Sound Leisure Limited
Spectrum Yarns Limited
Springfield Solutions Limited
St Anne's Community Services
St. Leonard's Hospice York
Stadium Welton Limited
Standeven Builders (Yorkshire) Limited
Stonegrave Aggregates Limited
Stoneledge Plant and Transport Limited
Street Clothes Limited
Sweeting Brothers (Land Drainage) Ltd
T M Enterprises Limited
TEF Transport Limited
TRU Property Investments Limited
Tanks and Vessels Industries Limited
Taplanes Limited
Tate Fuel Oils Limited
F B Taylor (Cable Contractors) Limited
D.G. Taylor Commercial Vehicles Limited
Teconnex Limited
Temple Way Properties Limited
Termrim Construction Limited
Third Energy UK Gas Limited
Thomson Limited
Thurston Group Limited
Tomrods Limited
Torne Valley Limited
Torrent Trackside Limited
Towsure Products Limited
Trackwork Limited
Trevor Iles Limited
Tri-Pack Plastics Limited
Triesse Limited
Tunstall Healthcare (UK) Limited
Turnbull (Corn Sales) Limited
Turnbull (Potato Sales) Limited
U K Insurance Limited
Unison Limited
Univar Europe Limited
Univar Specialty Consumables Limited
V.H.E. Construction PLC
Chris Variava Limited
Viamaster Transport Limited
Vickers Laboratories Limited
Von Roll UK Limited
George Walker Transport Limited
Walney Island South End Caravan Site Ltd
Jeffrey Walton Jewellery Limited
Ward Bros. (Steel) Limited
Waxman International Limited
Robert D. Webster Limited
Weightlifter Bodies Limited
West Ella Estates Limited
Wetherby Stone Products Limited
Whitaker Fibres Limited
White Rose (Caravan Park) Limited
M.H. Whittaker & Son Limited
J.R. Williams & Sons Limited
L.& W.Wilson (Endmoor) Limited
H.S. Wood (Textiles) Limited
Wortley Construction Limited
Wykeland (Humberside) Limited
Wykeland Investments Limited
Wykeland Properties Limited
YCR Distribution Limited
YPS Valves Limited
York Archaeological Trust for Excavation and Research Ltd
Yorkshire Packaging Systems Limited
Yorkshire Sheeting and Insulation Services Ltd
Yorkwold Pigpro Limited

**1980-1989** [709]

123 Leeds Limited
A-Fax Limited
A.B.G. Limited
A.M. Packaging Limited
A.W. (Europe) Limited
AAK (UK) Limited
ACS Stainless Steel Fixings Limited
ACWA Services Limited
AJS 22 Ltd
ALS Laboratories (UK) Limited
ATC Properties Limited
Accord Mortgages Limited
Ackers P Investment Co Ltd
Acorn Web Offset Limited
Acumen Credit Insurance Brokers Limited
Addplant Limited
Advanced Couplings Limited
Airedale Catering Equipment Limited
Aker Offshore Partner Limited
Alatas UK Limited
Allied Properties (Hull) Limited
Alta Enterprises Limited
Amazone Limited
Amvale Limited
Angloco Limited
Animalcare Ltd
Apex Hydraulics Limited
Arena Group Limited
Areopagus Limited
Arkoni Limited
Arla Foods Limited
Arlington Automotive NE Limited
Arris Global Ltd.
Arrow Commercial Centre (Huddersfield) Ltd
Ascribe Limited
Ashford Cladding Systems Limited
Ashtree Vision & Safety Limited

Astorbush Limited
Automint Limited
Automobile Association Personal Finance Ltd
Automotive Chassis Products UK Limited
Aviva Life Holdings UK Limited
Aviva Life Services UK Limited
Aviva Pension Trustees UK Limited
G.W. Axup & Co Limited
B - Sporting Limited
B.B. Farms Limited
B.C.A. Group Ltd
B.R.T. Supplies Limited
BSC Filters Limited
BTL Group Limited
Simon Bailes Limited
NG Bailey Group Limited
NG Bailey IT Services Limited
Barwick of Bradford Limited
R G Bassett & Sons Limited
B Batch Shopfitters Limited
Batchelors of Ripon Limited
Bates & Co. (Huddersfield) Limited
L. Batley Holdings Limited
W.S. Bayston & Son Limited
Be Fuelcards Ltd
Becker UK Limited
Bee Jay Scaffolding Limited
Bidco (Impex) Limited
Big Bale Company (North) Limited
Blackrow Engineering Co. Limited
T S Bloor & Sons Limited
Boarcross Limited
Bonus Accessories Limited
Bootham School
Borgwarner Holdings Limited
Borgwarner Limited
Chris Bowker Limited
Boxer Properties (Bradford) Limited
Boxford Holdings Limited
Bradford Hide Co Ltd
Bradshaws Driffield (Holdings) Limited
Brass Agency Limited
Braveshire Limited
Brianplant (Humberside) Limited
Bridgewood Trust Limited
Brigdale Limited
Britcom International Limited
G Brocklehurst Transport Limited
J. Brown Fabrics Limited
David Brown Group Limited
Buckley Jewellery Limited
Bulloughs Cleaning Services Limited
Burg-Wachter UK Limited
Burlington Slate Limited
N.R. Burnett (Holdings) Limited
Burnley & Pendle Travel Limited
Burton Roofing Merchants Limited
Burwood House Group Limited
Business & Enterprise Finance Ltd.
Business Lines Limited
Busysky Limited
C.A. Group Limited
CCL Industries (U.K.) Limited
CPP Holdings Limited
CYB Investments Limited
Caddick Group PLC
Caird Peckfield Limited
Calder Properties Limited
Calder Textiles Limited
Caldex Limited
Calrec Audio Limited
Calvadon Limited
Camira Fabrics Limited
Carafax Limited
Card Protection Plan Limited
Cardinal Shopfitting + Systems Limited
Carlisle Brass Limited
Casterton Leisure Limited
Caswick Limited
Caterers Choice Limited
Caterleisure Services Limited
Catford & Longford Limited
Catholic Care (Diocese of Leeds)
Cavalier Marketing Limited
Cellhire PLC
Central Insulations Limited
Centurion Europe Limited
Century Homes Limited
Ceramica Impex Limited
Charco Ninety-Nine Limited
Chaucer Foods UK Limited
Chippindale Foods Limited
Cleaning and Paper Disposables Limited
Clifton Properties (Yorkshire) Limited
Closepatch Limited
Dean Clough Limited
Coachman Caravan Co Ltd
Cod Beck Blenders Limited
Codecrest Limited
Cogri Group Limited
Collins (Seafoods) Limited
Colt Industrial Services Limited
Community Links (Northern) Ltd
Competition Line (U.K.) Limited
Computer Services Consultants (U.K.) Ltd
Computype Europe Limited
Concorde Technology Group Limited
A.F. Connell Limited
Consort Furniture Limited
Construction Marine Limited
Continuity Promotions Limited
Continuum Group Limited
Contract Experts Limited
Convenience Foods Limited
Cragwood International Limited
Cranswick Convenience Foods Limited
Cranswick Country Foods PLC
Cromwell Polythene Limited
Crosslee PLC
Curtis Wool Direct Limited
Custom Fittings Limited
DB Cargo Maintenance Limited
DFDS Logistics Services Limited
DFDS Seaways PLC
DFS Trading Limited
DLA Architecture Limited
T L Dallas Group Limited
Darlington & District Hospice Movement
Daropeant Properties Limited
De Vere 2 Limited
Deehurst Limited
Den Hartogh Dry Bulk Logistics Limited
Diamond Resorts (Europe) Limited
Diamond Resorts Financial Services Ltd
Dixondale Limited
Dixons Academies Charitable Trust Ltd
Donbac Limited
Doncast Limited
Doncaster Rotherham and District Motor
Trades Group Training Association Ltd
Doorstep of Hull
Dortek Limited
Dove House Hospice Limited
Dr Reddy's Laboratories (UK) Limited
Dr. Reddy's Laboratories (EU) Limited
Drinkwater's Mushrooms Limited
Driver Hire Group Services Limited
Dufton Plumbing & Heating Supplies Ltd
Durham Box Co Ltd
EP Realisations Limited
ESCO (UK) Limited
Eagerlux Limited
East Riding Holdings Company
East Riding Sacks Limited
Eddison & Wanless Limited
P.J. Edwards & Co. (UK) Ltd.
Egton Medical Information Systems Ltd
Eldred (1982) Holdings Limited
Electrix International Limited
Elland Steel Structures Limited
Elmwood Design Limited
Elvaston Investments Limited
Entertainment and Leisure Insurance
Services Ltd
Esseco UK Limited
Esteem Systems Limited
Eureka! The National Children's Museum.
Europa Wools Limited
European Integrated Carriers Limited
Europipes (UK) Limited
Expect Distribution Limited
Explosive Developments Limited
Express Group Limited
F A S 2000 Limited
F.T.L. Holdings Limited
Fairfax Plant Hire Limited
Fairfax Securities Limited
Farmhouse Potato Bakers Limited
Farmstar Limited
Fastnet Fish Limited
Fastnet Holdings Limited
Fender Care Limited
Fender Steel Limited
Fenton Packaging Limited
Fibreline Limited
Fibrelite Composites Limited
Filtermech Plant Sales Limited
Findpath Limited
First West Yorkshire Limited
First York Limited
Firsure Limited
Ian Firth Hardware Limited
Firth Steels Limited
Edward Fisher & Co. Limited
Flannery Construction Limited
Fleetcor Fuel Cards Europe Limited
Flixborough Wharf Limited
Flower of May Holiday Parks Limited
W.E. Foers & Son Limited
Foregale Limited
Foundation
Fuel Card Services Limited
Furmanite 1986
Fussey Piling Ltd
G.B. Agencies Limited
G.R. Electrical Services Limited
GMI Construction Group PLC
Gainsborough Industrial Controls Limited
Gardner Denver Group Services Limited
Gazelle Travel Limited
Gedore U.K. Ltd
Genus Pharmaceuticals Limited
Geoplan Spatial Intelligence Limited
Gill Insulation Nottinghamshire Limited
Gilpin Lodge Country House Hotel Limited
Giroscope Limited

Glassflake Limited
Glendower Group Limited
Golam Properties Limited
Goldenfry Limited
Goldmart Limited
John Good Shipping Limited
Gould Tech Solutions Limited
Grants Pro-Agri Limited
Graycliffe Homes Limited
Greendown Trust
Gregory Property Group Limited
Groupe Samat UK Limited
Guyson International Limited
H.H Services Limited
HSL Manufacturing Limited
Haddow Group Limited
J.F. and E. Hadwin Limited
Rolf C. Hagen (U.K.) Limited
Hague Computer Supplies Limited
Halifax Financial Services (Holdings) Ltd
Halifax Loans Limited
Hall & Associates (Marketing) Ltd
Hall Construction Services Limited
Hallborough Properties Limited
Hallmark Cards (Holdings) Limited
Hallmark Cards Property Co Ltd
Hapimag Resorts & Residences (UK) Ltd
Harewood House Trust Limited
Harpers Environmental Limited
Harratts Limited
Harris Partnership Limited
Harrogate District Hospice Care
Hartley Investment Trust Limited
Hartley Property Trust (1991) Limited
Hatfields V Limited
Havercroft Construction Limited
Hayton & Lamb Limited
Heights (U.K.) Limited
Henderson Insurance Brokers Limited
Hes Humber Bulk Terminal Limited
Hever Castle Limited
K. Hewitt and Co. Limited
Hi-Level Enterprises Limited
Hickson Investments Limited.
High Point Estates Ltd.
Hillcrest Garages (Sowerby Bridge) Ltd
Hird Limited
Hireport Limited
Hoerbiger UK Limited
Holker Holdings Limited
Holme Lane Haulage Limited
Holmesterne Farm Co. Limited
Holmfirth Dyers Limited
Hospice of St. Mary of Furness
Geo Houlton & Sons Limited
E. Houseman & Son Limited
Huddersfield Town Association Football Club Ltd
Hull Cartridge Co Ltd
Hultafors Group UK Limited
Humankind Charity
Hunt Group Limited
Hydramotion Limited
Hydrastore Limited
Hydrema (U.K.) Limited
I.G. Industries PLC
IPF Holdings Limited
IT @ Spectrum Limited
Iceland Seafood Barraclough Ltd
Idexx Laboratories Limited
Image Colourprint Limited
Image Data Group Limited
Image Digital Print Limited
Imagexps Limited
Imexpart Limited
Inchem Finance Limited
Industrial Textiles & Plastics Ltd
Insituform Technologies Limited
Interactive Investor Services Limited
International Pipeline Products Limited
Isberg Limited
J.P. Distribution Ltd.
JBC Industrial Services Limited
JCT600 (Properties) Limited
JCT600 (Rawdon) Limited
JCT600 (South Yorkshire) Limited
Jennings Roofing Limited
Jet2 Transport Services Limited
T P Jordeson & Co Ltd
Jubilee Milling Limited
Juratek Limited
K T Hydraulics Limited
KCOM Group PLC
Kadmous Holdings (UK) Limited.
Kapil Care Homes Limited
Kautex Textron (UK) Limited
Keepmoat Homes Limited
Keepmoat Limited
Keighley & District Travel Limited
Kelda Group Limited
Kelda Water Services Limited
Kendal Caravans Limited
Kenworth Limited
Kerfoot Group Limited
Kettlewell Fuels Limited
Kexgill (Liverpool) Limited
Key Growing Limited
Keyland Developments Limited
Kinetic Worldwide Limited
John King Chains Limited
Kingston Equity & Finance Limited
Kingstown Holdings Limited
Kirklees Theatre Trust
Kirkwood Hospice
Kirwin Brothers Ltd.
Komori U.K. Limited
Kuwait Petroleum International Lubricants (UK) Ltd
Labelon UK Limited
Lake District Holdings Limited
William Lamb (Holdings) Limited
Derek Lambert Polythene Limited
Laminated Products Limited
Lancaster University Energy Services Ltd
Larchwell Limited
Lawcris Panel Products Limited
Leasedrive Limited
Lectra UK Limited
Leeds Bradford Airport Limited
Leeds Design Innovation Centre Ltd
Leeds Plywood & Doors Limited
Leeds and London Holdings Limited
Lewis Civil Engineering Limited
Lhasa Limited
Liberty Merchant Bar PLC
Lightwater Holdings Limited
Lincolnshire House Association
Lincs. Electrical Wholesalers Limited
Lindam Limited
Lindsey Lodge Limited
Link Up Mitaka Limited
Lissett Residentials Limited
Lockers Trawlers Limited
Logopak International Limited
London Ebor Developments PLC
London Wiper Co Ltd
Longley Holdings Limited
A.W. Lumb (Northern) Limited
Lund Court Farm Limited
Jack Lunn (Holdings) Limited
Luxihomes Limited
M.S. Design International Limited
MMS Ship Repair and Dry Dock Co. Ltd
MRC Flangefitt Limited
MacKay Transport & Storage Limited
Machenair Limited
Mager Homes Limited
Maria Mallaband Limited
Mamas & Papas (Retail) Limited
Manthorpe Building Products Limited
Map Ventilation Limited
Marble Building Products (Yorkshire) Ltd
Mardon PLC
Andrew Marr International Limited
Martin House
Maru International Limited
Masco Corporation Limited
J.H. McCloy & Co Limited
R. McDowell Haulage and Distribution Ltd
McLagan Investments Limited
McLean & Appleton (Holdings) Limited
Medetcrown Limited
Merewood Group Limited
Meridian Healthcare Limited
Mermaid Panels Limited
J.H. Mewburn Limited
Millennium Inorganic Chemicals Overseas Holdings
Millennium Insurance Brokers Limited
Mitchell's Brewery Limited
Modus Seabed Intervention Limited
Moorhead Excavations Limited
Morrey Oils Limited
A.E. Morris Limited
Mortgage Business PLC
Mortgage Express
Mount School (York)
My Lockup Limited
National Coaching Foundation
National Coal Mining Museum for England Trust Ltd
National Tube Stockholders Limited
Neill & Brown Global Logistics Group Ltd
New Daffodil Limited
New Equipment Holdings Limited
Newby Manor Estates Limited
Newman Properties Limited
Newross Impex Limited
Nidd Transport Limited
Nidec SR Drives Ltd.
Niko Extrusions Limited
Ninehundred Communications Group Limited
Normanton Golf Club Limited
Nortech Foods Limited
North Yorkshire Mortgages Limited
Northern LPG Supplies Limited
Northern Life Care Limited
Northern Pump Suppliers Limited
Northern Racing College
Nunns of Grimsby Limited
Oakstone Developments Limited
Oakwell Securities Limited
Oakwood Kitchen Design Consultants Ltd
Office Interiors Wholesale Limited
On Line Design & Engineering Limited
Opera North Limited

Optare Group Ltd
Optident Limited
Orange Mountain Bikes Limited
Orcina Limited
Orion Commercial Properties Limited
Ortho-Care (U.K.) Limited
Oughtred & Harrison (Facilities) Ltd.
Ovalhouse Limited
Overgate Hospice
Thomas Owen Care Limited
Oxbow Sulphur & Fertiliser (UK) Limited
PBS Construction (North East) Limited
PFM Packaging Machinery Limited
PWS Distributors Limited
Pacific Lifestyle Limited
Padgett Brothers (A To Z) Limited
Riva Paoletti Limited
Park Lane Healthcare (Croston Park) Ltd
Parkway Entertainment Co Ltd
Parrs Point Limited
Ay & Y. Patel (Dewsbury) Limited
Patrington Haven Leisure Park Limited
Pelican Engineering Company (Sales), Ltd
Pelsis Limited
Peppers Marquees Limited
Perio News Limited
Persimmon Harts Limited
Persimmon PLC
Persimmon Shared Equity Limited
Planet Overseas Holdings Limited
Plasmor (Halton) Limited
Positive Location Properties Limited
Potato Manufacturing Science Limited
Jonathan Potts Limited
Premier Vanguard Limited
D.J. Prescott (Builders) Limited
Prestigious Textiles Limited
Principle Systems Limited
Principles Communications Limited
Private Medicare Limited
Profile Security Services Limited
Prospect House Leeds Limited
Provfin Limited
Provident Print Limited
Psona Limited
Pyramid Display Materials Limited
Q-Park Limited
Quality Hydraulic Power Limited
Queen Margaret's School, York Limited
Quest 4 Limited
RCS Limited
RMSpumptools Limited
ROK Associates Limited
Rack Systems (Engineering) Ltd.
Rackham Housefloors Limited
Ravenheat Manufacturing Limited
Rayner Marketing (Holdings) Limited
Raysul Holdings Limited
Redhall Marine Limited
Reed Boardall Transport Limited
Refreshment Systems Limited
Keith Rennie Machinery Limited
Repchoice Limited
Replan (U.K.) Limited
Revis Transport Limited
C.R. Reynolds Limited
Hugh Rice Limited
Rider Holdings Limited
Ripon Farm Services Limited
Risedale Estates Limited
Riverside Eastern Limited
Riverside Motors (Doncaster) Limited
Roadridge Limited
Robimatic Limited
Rodgers Group Limited
Roman Limited
W. & A.C. Rose (Farms) Limited
Rose Roofing Limited
Rossendale Transport Limited
Rothay Garden Hotel Limited
J Rotherham Masonry Ltd
Roundbrand Limited
Royds Properties Ltd
Rudding Park Limited
Rufforth Park Limited
Rural Insurance Group Limited
Rushbond PLC
SFS Group Fastening Technology Limited
SNF (UK) Limited
SNF Oil and Gas Ltd
Sabre Rail Services Limited
Saftronics Limited
Saint Catherines Hospice Trust
Salts Estates Limited
Salzgitter Mannesmann UK Limited
Sand Le Mere Caravan Park Limited
Sandburn York Limited
Sanmet Limited
Saur (UK) Limited
Savant Limited
Saville Group Limited
Scheme Underwriting (U.K.) Limited
Scientific Games International Limited
Scotfield Group Limited
Scothern Construction Limited
Securi-Plex Limited
Security Window Shutters Limited
Servemet (N.W.) Limited
Service Metals (Midlands) Limited
Service Timber Limited
Severfield PLC
Sewell Retail Limited
Sharp Business Systems UK PLC
Shorts Industries Limited
Sia Fibral Limited
Siccar Point Energy E & P Limited
Skipton Properties Limited
SmarDTV (UK) Limited
Darren Smith Builders Limited
Clive Soanes (Broilers) Ltd.
Software Box Limited
Solway Foods Limited
South Parade Properties Limited
C Spencer Limited
Square Chapel Trust
St Paul's Street (Investments) Limited
Steel Beams and Columns Limited
Stores Group Limited
Straight Manufacturing Limited
Stramongate Properties Limited
Strand Paper Northern Limited
Strata Homes Limited
Strata Homes Yorkshire Limited
Strawson Holdings Limited
Student Loans Co Ltd
Styrene Packaging & Insulation Limited
Sulzer Pumps (UK) Limited
Sundown Pets Garden Limited
Supagard Limited
Superbreak Mini-Holidays Limited
Surfachem Limited
Surgical Innovations Group PLC
Sutcliffe Group Limited
Swarco Traffic Limited
Sweco UK Holding Limited
Switch2 Energy Limited
T & G Automotive Ltd
TCS Holdings Limited
TRS Tyres Ltd
TYK Limited
Tajj Limited
Tarnhelm Securities Limited
Tate of Leeds Limited.
Tayrol Limited
Tebway Limited
Technical Fibre Products Limited
Technikraft Limited
Techrete (U.K.) Limited
Teescraft Engineering Limited
Tenetconnect Services Limited
James H. Tennant Limited
Tennants of Yorkshire Antique and Fine Art Auctioneers Ltd
Thermac (Hire) Limited
Thorpe Underwood Services Limited
G. & A. Thursby Limited
Til-Ex Limited
Titan Cement U.K. Limited
Togel Contractors Limited
Toiletry Sales Limited
Towndoor Limited
Townson Tractors Limited
Tradeway (Shipping) Limited
Trenton (Hull) Limited
Triple T Engineering Limited
Trojan Plastics Limited
Trupart Limited
Tudorshore Limited
Turner & Townsend International Limited
Turner & Townsend Project Management Ltd
Ultima Furniture Systems Limited
Ultimate Packaging Limited
Ultra Finishing Limited
Unicolour Limited
United Reformed Church (Yorkshire Province) Trust Ltd
United Transmission Services Limited
Univer Manufacturing Co Ltd
John Veitch Limited
Victor Investments & Securities Ltd
Viewstone Limited
Vinewood Limited
W. P. Holdings Limited
WV Associates Limited
WYG Engineering Limited
WYG PLC
John Wade (Haulage) Limited
Wakefield Acoustics Limited
Wakefield Hospice
Peter Ward Homes Limited
Wardbright Properties Limited
Warners Fishmerchants Limited
Warrens Group Limited
Warrington Garages Limited
Wastecare Limited
Wax Lyrical Limited
Webasto Thermo & Comfort UK Ltd
Weidmann Whiteley Limited
Weir Drilling Services Limited
Wellvend Limited
Wesco Aircraft Europe, Ltd
West Yorkshire Fellmongers Limited
West Yorkshire Van Rental Limited
Westex (Carpets) Limited
Westgate Motors Limited
Claire Whitaker Limited

Whitby Seafoods Limited
White Cross Rubber Products Limited
W B White Foundry Limited
Wickframe Limited
Henry Williams Limited
Willis of Skipton Limited
Windsor Engineering (Hull) Limited
Des Winks Cars Limited
Wirquin Ltd
Alan Wood Partnership Limited
Woodhead Brothers Farms Ltd
R.N. Wooler & Co Ltd
Wortley Developments Limited
Edward P. Wright Ltd.
Wykeland Group Limited
Xiros Limited
YCE Catering Equipment Limited
YTM Group Limited
Brian Yates (Interiors) Limited
York Holdings Limited
Yorkcare Limited
Yorkcloud Limited
Yorkshare Limited
Yorkshire Agricultural Society
Yorkshire Bank Home Loans Limited
Yorkshire Cancer Research
Yorkshire Design Services Limited
Yorkshire Plywood Limited
Yorkshire Water Services Limited
Yorparks Limited
Younger Homes (Northern) Limited
Zenith Vehicle Contracts Limited

**1990-1994** [429]

2 Sisters Food Group Limited
A & K Hosiery Limited
A1 Steam Locomotive Trust
ADL PLC
AMS No-Dig Limited
Abbot Holdings Limited
Academy Leisure Limited
Acorn Mobility Services Ltd.
Acumen Waste Services Limited
Advanced Alloy Services Limited
Advanced Plastics Limited
Z.A. Akram Limited
Allam Marine Limited
Alliance Office Systems Limited
Allure Developments Limited
Alt Berg Limited
Alternative Windows (Leeds) Limited
Amber Homeloans Limited
Aptiv Services UK Limited
Archway Engineering (U.K.) Limited
Ardagh Metal Packaging UK Limited
Arncliffe Homes Limited
Asda Southbank Limited
Ashridge Contractors Limited
Autoelectro Limited
Avocet Trust
B & F Potatoes Limited
BB Investments
BJSS Limited
Banner Contracts (Halnaby) Limited
Barrett Steel Limited
Bedfords Limited
Beech Hill Residential Investments Ltd
Bemis Elsham Limited
Bennett-Ings (Developments) Limited
Bentley & Bentley Limited
Bericap U.K. Limited.
Beverley House Investments Limited
Bibis Restaurants Limited
Biker Group Limited
Black Sheep Brewery PLC
Bluestone Leasing Limited
Bootyman Printers Limited
Bracken Limited
Bradbury Group Limited
Bramall Properties Limited
Brandon Medical Co Ltd
Brathay Trust
Brecks Co Ltd
Brent Scaffold Boards Limited
Brighton Holdings Limited
Britcon (UK) Limited
Broker Network Limited
Joe Browns Ltd
Burton Constable Foundation
C & D Foods (Driffield) Unlimited
CCL Holdings Limited
CD (UK) Limited
CRH Fencing & Security Group (UK) Ltd
Caddick Developments Limited
Callcredit Marketing Limited
Calvesten Limited
Caspian Group Limited
Cellhire (Holdings) Limited
Cheque Exchange Limited
Christian Trust
Circuit Launderette Services Ltd.
City of Bradford Y.M.C.A.
Clerical Medical Investment Fund Managers Ltd
Clyde Bergemann Materials Handling Ltd
Clytha Holdings Limited
Collard Cole Limited
Collegiate Formation Limited
G. Collinson (Construction) Limited
Communisis Limited
Community Foundation for Calderdale
Concorde BGW Limited
Contract Natural Gas Limited
Corporate Document Services Limited
Country Style Foods Limited
Covance Clinical Research Unit Limited
Covance Limited
Cox Automotive Retail Solutions Limited
Createcity Limited
Crest Roofing Limited
Croft Care Trust
Cromwell Management Holdings Limited
Crosslee Holdings Limited
DB Cargo (UK) Limited
DSA Chemicals Limited
Dadibhais (Bradford) Limited
Danesmoor Limited
Darlington Homes Limited
Dawngreen Limited
Decidebloom Limited
Deepocean 1 UK Limited
Desk Top Publishing Micro Systems Ltd
Dewhirst Properties Limited
Diamond Resorts (Group Holdings) PLC
Dickinsons (Plumbing & Heating Contractors) Ltd
Dilbag Cloth House Limited
Dortech Architectural Systems Limited
Double-Ten Limited
Drivecheck Limited
Dryband One Limited
EFS Chalfont Limited
EFS Group Limited
Eaglesure Limited
Easysoft Limited
Edwards Excavations Limited
Element 14 Limited
Elite Systems (GB) Limited
Engie Supply Holding UK Limited
Europa Crown Limited
Eurotek Foundry Products Limited
Evangelical Fellowship of Congregational Churches Trust Corporation Ltd
Ever 2010 Limited
F & G Commercials (Huddersfield) Ltd
FMG Support (FIM) Ltd
FMG Support (RRRM) Ltd
Farnsworth Investments Limited
Febi (UK) Limited
Filtronic PLC
Financial Systems & Consultancy Ltd.
Finespark (Horsham) Limited
Finishchoice Limited
First Subsea Limited
Flintbrook Limited
Fortlands Limited
Foundation for Credit Counselling
Fourth Argyll Limited
Peter Fowler (Electrical) Limited
Fredrickson International Limited
Freedom Group of Companies Ltd.
David Frost Estate Agents Limited
Furmanite Limited
Furness Mortgage Services Limited
G.B. Terminals Limited
GBA (Holdings) Limited
GKF Group Limited
GVS Filter Technology UK Ltd
Gands (U.K.)
Geofabrics Limited
Getech Group PLC
Ginetta Cars Limited
Global Holdings Limited
Gradebatch Limited
Grafitec Holdings Limited
Samuel Grant (Leeds) Limited
Grantside Limited
Green Flag Group Limited
Grimsby & Cleethorpes Area Doorstep
Grimsby Fish Dock Enterprises Limited
Grosvenor House Papers Limited
Groundwork North East
H & P Freightways Limited
H.P.A.S. Limited
HACS Construction Limited
Habico Limited
Halifax General Insurance Services Ltd
Halifax Investment Services Limited
Hanover Developments (Wakefield) Limited
Harpin Limited
L. Harrison (Properties) Limited
Harrison Electrical Limited
Harrison Thompson and Co Ltd
Health Management (Carlisle) Limited
Heavy Duty Parts Limited
Hensall Mechanical Services Limited
Hesco Bastion Limited
Hesley Group Limited
Hever Castle Golf Club Limited
Hexadex Limited
Hexagon Properties Limited
Heywood Williams Components Limited
Highacre Builders Limited
Hillcroft Ltd
Homecare Insurance Limited
Hoyer Container Rental UK Limited

Hoyer UK Limited
Hurst Group (Northern) Limited
Hyco Manufacturing Limited
Hydram Engineering Limited
ICH Limited
IRISNDT Limited
Ideal Building Systems Limited
Imerys Fused Minerals Hull Limited
Impact Development Training Ltd.
Impact Fork Trucks Limited
Indian Queens Power Limited
Inspired Pet Nutrition Limited
Integrated Polymer Systems (U.K.) Ltd
Intercontinental Brands (Icb) Limited
Irongate Group Limited
J & E Importers & Distributors Green Jem Mfg Associates Co Ltd
JLA Total Care Limited
Jacksons Transport (West Riding) Limited
Jet2.Com Limited
KCOM International Limited
KM School Limited
Kalon Investment Co Ltd
Kaye's Hotels Limited
Keadby Generation Limited
Keyo Agricultural Services Ltd
Killgerm Chemicals Limited
John H King (Developments) Limited
Kingasia Foods Limited
Kingfisher UPVC Windows & Doors Limited
Kirklees Community Association
Kirklees Stadium Development Limited
Klinger Holdings Limited
Kluman and Balter Limited
Koti Industrial & Technical Brushes Ltd
L.N.T. Construction Limited
Lakeland Leisure Estates Limited
William Lamb Group Limited
Lambson Limited
Land Acquisitions Limited
Landown Limited
Landplan Properties Limited
Lane Rental Services Limited
Law Distribution Limited
Stewart Lawton Limited
Leading Labels Ltd
Leading Solvent Supplies Limited
Leeds Jewish Welfare Board
Leisure Park Management Limited
Lesjofors Springs (UK) Limited
Lightbrook Limited
Lincoln & York Limited
Lincolnshire Employment Accommodation Project Ltd
London Oil Refining Co. Limited
Longbeach Leisure Limited
M S A Engineering Systems Limited
M. B. Locking Logistics Group Limited
M.B.E. Glazing Systems Limited
MTS Nationwide Limited
Madison Hosiery Limited
Magneco Metrel U.K. Limited
Magnet Limited
Mainport Engineering (1990) Limited
Maltgrade Limited
Masco UK Window Group Limited
Masons Textiles Limited
McDonald King Limited
Medicare Chemists Limited
Metamark (UK) Limited
Middlegate (Europe) Limited
Mobus Fabrics Limited
Motors Insurance Co Ltd
Multiflight Limited
Al. Murad D.I.Y. Limited
Myers Group Holdings Ltd
NCA Group Limited
NHP Limited
Nationwide Bearing Co Ltd.
Natures Aid Ltd
Neargoal Limited
Neerock Limited
New Kadampa Tradition - International Kadampa Buddhist Union
Newby Manor Investments Limited
Nobleoak Limited
Northern Cladding Limited
Norwich and Peterborough (LBS) Limited
G. Nowell Limited
Nufarm UK Limited
Nutec Holdings Limited
OE Electrics Limited
OSI Food Solutions UK Holdings Limited
Oakdale Homes Limited
Olam Food Ingredients UK Limited
Olympus Print Group Limited
Omega PLC
Omega Signs Limited
P V H Holdings Limited
P.D.R. Construction Limited
P.P.S. Electrical Limited
PFF Packaging Limited
PIB Risk Services Limited
Paneltex Limited
Paramount Retail Group Holdings Limited
Park Lane Homes Limited
Pasuda (Hire) Limited
Pasuda Buildings Limited
Peacock & Binnington Holdings Limited
Pear Tree Projects Limited
Pecan Deluxe Candy (Europe) Limited
H. Peel & Sons Limited
Pelagia (UK) Limited
Permoid Industries Limited
S.G. Petch Limited
Piccadilly Motors Limited
Pitcliffe (Holdings) Limited
Pittstop (Ripon) Limited
Pollybell Farms Limited
Polyseam Limited
Portakabin (Refurbished) Limited
Portland of Bawtry Limited
Premier Modular Limited
Primeur Limited
Principle Spira Limited
Prious Limited
Queen Ethelburga's College Limited
Queens Staith Leisure Limited
Queensway Properties Limited
Quintor (Homes) Limited
R.T. Consultants Limited
RMS Goole Limited
Rail Express Systems Limited
Ramscove Limited
Real Life Options
Redfern Developments and Investments Ltd
Redhouse Projects Limited
Reeds Rains Limited
Rhino Enterprises Limited
Richmond Foods Limited
Risby Homes Limited
Roberts Graphics Limited
Rocal Insulating Panels Ltd.
Roche Healthcare Limited
Roclad Systems Limited
Rosti Automotive Larkhall Ltd.
Royal Armouries (International) Limited
Royds Community Association
Royds Estates Limited
Rumford Tankers Limited
S & J Industries Limited
S.B.S. (Cumbria) Limited
SCS Building Solutions Limited
SDS International Ltd.
SPX Flow Technology Limited
Sandtoft Developments Limited
Scan-Thors (U.K.) Limited
Scientific Laboratory Supplies Limited
Sealord (Europe) Limited
Select Legal Systems Limited
Severfield (UK) Limited
Sewell Facilities Management Limited
Shaw Moisture Meters (U.K.) Limited
Shepley Engineers Limited
Sheppee International Limited
Shorewood Leisure Group Limited
Silgan Closures UK Limited
Simpson (York) Holdings Limited
Simpson and Webb Limited
Stephen A. Sims (Cars) Limited
Solway Foods Holdings Limited
South Coast Catering Limited
Southfield Health Care Limited
Southgate Lighting Limited
Specialised Orthotic Services Limited
Specialist Coatings Limited
Splicegroup Europe Limited
St Andrew's Hospice Limited
St. Gemma's Hospice
Stangs Limited
Stanwell Technic Ltd.
Status International (UK) Ltd
Steers Group Limited
Stollers Furniture World Limited
Stolzle Flaconnage Limited
Stoneferry Estates Limited
Storey Group Limited
Strachan Furniture Makers Limited
Straight Limited
M.F. Strawson (Maidenwell) Limited
Sulzer Chemtech (UK) Limited
Superbreak Mini Holidays Group Limited
Surgical Innovations Limited
Sweco Services UK Limited
Sweco UK Limited
Symington's Limited
TCS Properties Limited
Tasca Tankers Limited
Team 17 Digital Limited
Technical Absorbents Limited
Techwax Limited
Tenetconnect Limited
Three Oceans Fish Co Ltd
Torpoint Limited
Torque Logistics Limited
Torque Retail Services Limited
Towel Rail Limited
Transdev Blazefield Limited
Transdev PLC
Trepko (UK) Limited
Tudor International Freight Limited
Turner & Price Limited
Turner & Townsend Contract Services Ltd
UFP (UK) Limited
Universal A.V. Services Limited
Uris Group Limited

Vanilla Group Limited
Vanquis Bank Limited
Verdant Leisure Limited
Wartsila Valves Limited
Watershed Packaging Limited
Waxman Ceramics Limited
Waxman Fibres Limited
Weetwood Hall Limited
Weldtite Products Limited
Wensleydale Dairy Products Limited
West Coast Capital Investments Limited
Westcourt Group Limited
Westcourt Properties Limited
Westward Care Limited
Wharfedale Homes Limited
White Horse Machinery Limited
White Rose (Leeds) Limited
Whiteghyll Limited
Wilby Limited
W. & J. Williams (Haulage) Limited
Willow Grove Properties Limited
Wilson Power Solutions Limited
Witt & Son UK Holdings Limited
Woodgreen Construction Limited
Woodland Healthcare Limited
Wykeland Properties (Holdings) Limited
Wynperg Investments Limited
Yamato Scale Dataweigh (UK) Ltd.
Yorhold Limited
York Science Park Limited
York University Development Co Ltd
York University Energy Supply Co Ltd
Yorkshire Building Services Limited
Yorkshire Grown Produce Limited
Yorvik Homes Limited
Yorwaste Limited
Zarafa Height Solutions Limited

**1995** [106]

Altra Industrial Motion UK Limited
Aspire-Igen Group Ltd
Autohorn Fleet Services Limited
BOS (Shared Appreciation Mortgages) No. 1 PLC
Ballyvesey Holdings Limited
Boge Compressors Limited
Bond House Systems Limited
British Smaller Companies VCT PLC
Brooklands Business Estates Limited
Bullseye Superfactors Ltd
Cadman Housing Project Ltd
Candlelighters Trust
Carclo Technical Plastics Limited
Castlewood Securities Limited
Charminster Estates Limited
Cirteq Limited
City of Leeds YMCA
Clariant Services UK Ltd
Clipper Logistics PLC
Complete Business Solutions Group Ltd
Cromwell European Management Services Ltd
Cromwell Investment Management Services Ltd
Crossway Scaffolding (Elland) Limited
DB Cargo (UK) Holdings Limited
Dacre, Son & Hartley Limited
Daifuku Logan Ltd
Dalestead Limited
Daniels Chilled Foods Limited
Dewhirst Overseas Limited
T P Dibdin Limited
Direct Investments (Yorkshire) Limited
Dreamphoto Limited
Dreamplayer Limited
Dressadmire Limited
Dual Seal Glass Ltd.
EFS Property Holdings Limited
East Transportation Limited
Emerald Publishing Limited
Explorer (UK) Limited
Falcon Electrical Wholesalers Limited
Fast Freeze International Limited
Fender Care Marine Ltd
Fern Hill Holdings Limited
Gardner Denver Ltd
Gear4music Limited
Grammar School at Leeds
Grand-Riverland & Co. Limited
Grosvenor Facilities Management Limited
H.E.C. Contracting Limited
Hair Tools Limited
Hallmark Panels Limited
Hambleton Steel Limited
Harron Homes Limited
Heart Research UK
Holme Styes Holdings Limited
Hurst Plastics Limited
Huskisson Shipping Limited
J M Construction (Leeds) Limited
P & B Kennedy Holdings Limited
Kexgill (Hull) Limited
Kingswood Parks Development Co Ltd
M. K. M. Building Supplies Limited
MLC Investments Limited
Manor Farm Feeds Limited
Martech (UK) Ltd
McCain Finance (GB) Limited
Millennium Inorganic Chemicals UK Holdings Ltd
Monread Lodge Nursing Home Limited
Moore Building Enterprises Limited
NHP Securities No. 1 Limited
Narang Wholesalers Limited
Nortonthorpe Industrial Park Limited
Oak Electrical Limited
Oakgate Group Limited
Omco UK Limited
Park Lane Properties (Leeds) Limited
Partline Limited
Piksel Limited
Pluss-Staufer Limited
Provecta Car Plan Limited
RBM Agricultural Limited
Radical Services Limited
Richmond Management (Northern) Limited
J Rotherham (Holdings) Limited
Rotherham Group Realisations Limited
Sheridan Fabrications Limited
Specialist Surfacing Limited
Subsea Innovation Limited
T.L.G. Properties Limited
TSP Projects Limited
Target Components Limited
Thornsett Vale Limited
USG-Gledco Ltd
VBP Group Limited
Vale of Mowbray Limited
Vectair Aviation (1995) Limited
Videcon Ltd
Virtual College Limited
WYG Environment Planning Transport Ltd
Warmafloor (GB) Limited
Waxman Energy Limited
West Coast Railway Co Ltd
Willerby Group Property Limited
Winander Group Holdings Limited
Zubrance Limited
Zyro Limited

**1996** [156]

AETC Limited
ALM Manufacturing Limited
Ace Group (Engineering) Limited
Allam Developments Limited
Amnack Limited
Ardagh MP Holdings UK Limited
Ashcourt Properties Limited
Aspire-Igen Ltd
Aviva Equity Release UK Limited
Aviva Life & Pensions UK Limited
BCA Leisure Ltd
BOS (Shared Appreciation Mortgages) No. 2 PLC
BW Skip Hire Limited
Bahson Colour Print Limited
Bannatyne Fitness Limited
Bannatyne Hotels Limited
P D Bannister Haulage Limited
Bay Properties Letting Co Ltd
Belzona Polymerics Limited
Bender UK Limited
Jeremy Benn Associates Limited
Blackburns Waste Disposal Limited
Boparan Foods Limited
CCL Computers Limited
Cameron Integrated Services Limited
Capitol Park Leeds PLC
Care & Recreation Holdings Limited
Centrica Storage Limited
Cephalon (UK) Limited
Chaucer Foods Limited
Claritas Solutions Limited
Connells Limited
Conroy Brook (Developments) Limited
Cox Automotive UK Limited
Creditscale Limited
Cromar Building Products Limited
Cutwel Limited
DB Cargo International Limited
Dovecote Park Limited
East Midlands Instrument Co Ltd
Ecovert Group Limited
Eddisons Commercial Limited
Elitebliss Limited
Enserve Group Limited
F.S.H. (Group) Limited
F.T. Construction Group (Holdings) Ltd.
Faculty of Queen Ethelburga's Limited
Fairfield Developments (Doncaster) Ltd
Family Fund Trust for Families with Severely Disabled Children
Farsley Transport Limited
Fired Up Corporation Limited
T.Freemantle Limited
M. Gallagher (Civil Engineering) Ltd
Grandlane Limited
Great Rail Journeys Limited
H.M. Pigs Limited
Halifax Share Dealing Limited
Hamilton (Building Contractors) Ltd.
Harratts of Wakefield Limited
Heatseam Limited
Hendersons of Selby Limited
High Crane Limited
Andrew Hillas Properties Limited

Hird Rail Services Limited
Hollings Limited
Hornbeam Park Developments Limited
Horus Limited
I'anson Bros. (Holdings) Limited
IF Cardboard Creations Limited
InOne Holdings Limited
Industrial Pallet and Transport Services Ltd
Interactive Investor Holdings Limited
John Jordan Limited
Jungle Products Limited
Kingspan Metl-Con Limited
Knightwood Trust Farms Limited
Koppers UK Holding Limited
L & O Investments (U.K.)
Lambert Engineering Holdings Limited
Langdale Owners PLC
Leeds Rugby Limited
Ligentia UK Limited
MMM Medical Equipment UK Limited
Maritime Bunkering Limited
Marshall Quarry Products Limited
Meritec Limited
Metallink Fluid Power Systems Limited
Mobili Office Limited
Modav Limited
Morris & Son (Leeds) Limited
NHP Management Limited
NHP Securities No. 2 Limited
NHP Securities No. 3 Limited
Nafferton Wold Farms Limited
OSI International Holdings Limited
Orvet UK
PTSG Access and Safety Limited
Pace Distribution (Overseas) Limited
Paragon Quality Foods Ltd
Patchett Developments Limited
Platinum Stairlifts Limited
Poster Publicity Holdings Ltd
Neil Price Limited
Proactis Limited
Professional Response Limited
Promenade Car Parks Limited
Propaganda Agency Limited
Prorun Limited
Prospect Estates Limited
Prospect House (Malpas) Limited
Real Yorkshire Pudding Co Limited
Redhall Networks Limited
Riverhead Commercial Services Limited
John Roberts Holdings Limited
K Rouse Civil Engineers Limited
SRCL Limited
SSP Sirius Solutions Limited
Saltend Cogeneration Co Ltd
Sapphire Technologies Limited
A. Schulman Gainsborough Ltd
Sea Holdings Limited
Seagold Limited
Selkirk Mechanical Handling Limited
Sheard Properties Limited
Shepley Spring Limited
Stage One Creative Services Limited
Steffco Limited
Stiller Warehousing & Distribution Ltd
Sumo UK Ltd.
Super League (Europe) Limited
Surfachem Group Limited
Swan Hotel (Newby Bridge) Limited
T W Logistics Limited
Taskmaster Resources Limited
Thimbleby Farms Limited
Todds Highway Maintenance Limited
Tolsa UK Limited
Tower Corporation Limited
Triesse Holdings Limited
Trycare Limited
Turner & Townsend Consulting Limited
Turner & Townsend Group Limited
Vacation Club Partnerships Limited
Verder Limited
Victorguard Care PLC
Vodecca Properties Limited
WYG International Projects Limited
Wastecare Group Limited
We Are Vista Limited
West Park Properties Limited
G. & M. Westgarth Limited
Westmorland County Agricultural Society Ltd
G. Williams & Co. (Grain) Limited
Winterquay Limited
Yorkshire Feedstuffs Limited
Youngmight Limited

**1997** [142]

2 Sister Food Services Limited
APC (GB) Limited
Advanced Diesel Engineering Limited
Advanced Processing Limited
Airco Refrigeration and Airconditioning Ltd
Aqua-Therm (Hull) Limited
Astonish Holdings Limited
G.P. Atkin Limited
Autobrokers Limited
BAA Lynton Limited
BOS (Shared Appreciation Mortgages) No. 3 PLC
BOS (Shared Appreciation Mortgages) No. 4 PLC
BOS Personal Lending Limited
Banks Lane Investments Limited
W E Barton Limited
Bawtry Farms Limited
J.G. Bellerby (Farms) Limited
Boldarch Limited
Bower Green Limited
Brocklesby Limited
C & H Antiques Limited
CSC (Holdings) Limited
Caddick (Rose Wharf) Limited
Chalemere Limited
Channon and Co Ltd
Clariant Production UK Ltd
Coast and Vale Community Action
Coniston Hotel Limited
Connection Seating Limited
Creative Art House
Croda Overseas Holdings Limited
Dalian Properties Limited
Deltawaite Limited
Depuy International Limited
Dukeries Healthcare Limited
Dunlop Oil & Marine Limited
Early Excellence Limited
Ebac Group Limited
Elite Office Furniture (UK) Ltd.
Elvaston Properties Limited
Encon Investments Limited
Encon Limited
Etas Limited
Excel Laminating Limited
FEL Group Limited
Filtronic Broadband Limited
Fuel Card Group Limited
Fuel Express Limited
GMI Holdings Limited
Daniel Gath Homes Limited
David Gee Associates Limited
Generator Power Limited
Gilbran (Management) Limited
Giles Foods Limited
Glen Avon Growers Limited
Global Autocare Limited
Global Shipping Services Group Limited
Hallmark Cards PLC
Hathaway Roofing Limited
Hire Station Limited
Hobson Farming Limited
Holliday International Limited
Home Shopping Personal Finance Limited
Homecare (Holdings) Limited
Horridge Limited
Hudson Contract Services Limited
I & S Properties Limited
Icon Consultancy Ltd
Integra Buildings Limited
Isotek (Holdings) Limited
JZ Flowers International Limited
Norman Jackson (Farmers) Limited
Jet Aire (DC) Limited
Joda Freight Limited
KCOM Holdings Limited
Kingston Restaurants Limited
Alf Kitching Limited
Lazarus Properties Limited
Leader Limited
M.K. Consultants (U.K.) Limited
M1 Engineering Holdings Limited
MRC Transmark Limited
Manor Estate Properties (UK) Limited
Metaldyne International (UK) Ltd
Mill Nurseries Limited
Monocon Overseas Limited
Morecambe Metals Limited
Murton Grange Limited
NSF Health Sciences Ltd.
National Flexible Limited
Nordika Design Limited
Northern Touch Limited
Omnivale Limited
Park Homes (UK) Limited
Park Leisure 2000 Limited
Personal Touch Financial Services Ltd
Pick Fisk Limited
Pipeline Engineering & Supply Co. Ltd
Pitts Wilson Limited
Planas Properties Limited
Primex Plastics Limited
RW Refrigeration Wholesale Limited
Raiseprint Limited
Redline Specialist Cars Limited
Regent House Estates Limited
Richardsons (Holdings) Limited
W.B. Ritchie Farms Limited
Rofin-Sinar UK Ltd.
Romero Insurance Brokers Limited
S B Homes Ltd.
S S Components Limited
SCD Group Limited
Sagars Accountants Ltd
Sargent Electrical Services Limited
Seismic Image Processing Limited
Setbray Properties (1997) Limited
Sewell Education (Hull) Limited
Siddall & Hilton Products Limited
Silentbloc UK Limited

St. Laurence Education Trust
Strawson Management Limited
Sullivan Homes Limited
Sulzer (UK) Holdings Limited
Surgeforward Limited
Sweepcharm Limited
T G L (UK) Limited
Tate Properties Limited
Tenet Business Solutions Limited
Tetley's Motor Services Limited
Transdek U.K. Limited
Trinity Fire and Security Systems Ltd
Turkey Mill Investments Limited
UK Greetings Limited
USI Mayfair Ltd.
Unipol Student Homes
VTL Precision (Huddersfield) Limited
John Wade (Holdings) Limited
Walkers Nurseries Limited
Waxman Group Limited
West Yorkshire Spinners Limited
Wordsworth Trust
YRG Group Limited

**1998** [128]

(Aq) Limited
ABI (UK) Limited
AFI-Uplift Limited
Aalberts Industries U.K. Ltd.
Acis Group Limited
Acorn Assessors Limited
Actavis Holdings UK II Limited
Adva Optical Networking Limited
Airkool Contracts Limited
Alco Valves Group Limited
Answer Digital Limited
Applelec Sign Components (UK) Ltd.
Arla Foods UK PLC
Associated Utility Supplies Limited
Atkinson Holdings Limited
Augean North Limited
Auto-Trail V.R. Limited
B & K Systems Limited
BBR Graphic Sales Limited
BDS (Yorkshire) Limited
Baddow Properties Limited
Blacks Visual Merchandising Limited
Bootham Crescent Holdings Limited
Boparan Holdings Limited
Bradbury Investments Limited
Brewery Wharf (Leeds) Limited
C.S.L. Industrial Limited
CB Imports Limited
CTS (Shopfitting) Limited
Calls' Riverside Property Co Ltd
Capernwray Missionary Fellowship of Torchbearers
Cardinal Project Management Limited
Confection By Design Limited
Crest Brick Slate & Tile Limited
Croft Carehomes Limited
D & J Estate Limited
DGP Intelsius Limited
DLA Design Group of Companies Limited
Direct Trade (Yorkshire) Limited
E K Holdings Limited
EMIH Limited
Edmund Optics Ltd.
Emballator (UK) Limited
Emerald Group Holdings Limited
Estates U.K. Limited
F M G Support (Ho) Limited
FTL Seals Technology Limited
Futurama Limited
G & H Building Services Ltd.
G S M Group Limited
GDS Technologies Limited
Gemco Service Limited
Genus Pharmaceuticals Holdings Limited
H. B. Projects Limited
HD1 Developments Limited
Haas Group International SCM Limited
Hanson Plywood (Holdings) Ltd
S. Harrison Developments Limited
Health Management (Carlisle) Holdings Ltd
Help-Link UK Limited
Hi-Wire Limited
Anthony Hodges Consulting Limited
Gawith Hoggarth Tobacco Trading Limited
Holf Technologies Limited
Hull Super League Limited
I.C.S. (UK) Limited
Impex Parts Limited
J.B. Components Limited
JM Packaging Limited
A Kahn Design Limited
Keston Boilers Limited
King Cole Limited
Kolorcraft Holdings Limited
LSS Waste Management Limited
Leeds Bronze Engineering Limited
Linfit Investments Limited
M.A. Estates Limited
M.K.M. Building Supplies (Hull) Limited
Makins Limited
Market Town Taverns Limited
Matrix International Limited
Monobuoy Co Ltd.
Morley Glass & Glazing Limited
NK Chemicals Europe Limited
NMT Limited
North Lincs Property Limited
Northern Gas Networks Operations Limited
Northern Paper Board Limited
Optimum4 Limited
P & A Food Management Services Limited
PDS Design & Build Limited
Park Property (World) Ltd
Paynes Dairies Limited
Precis (1638) Limited
Pro-Pak Foods Limited
Property Investments (Yorkshire) Limited
Property Renaissance Limited
Renovotec Ltd
Reuse Glass UK Limited
Running Deep Limited
Rural Concepts Construction Limited
SFS Developments Limited
Saur Services (Glasgow) Limited
Scantech Offshore Limited
Specialist Trailer Hire Limited
Sportswift Limited
Strata Holdings Limited
D & MA Sunderland & Son Limited
Superior Developments Limited
Sycamore Lighting Limited
T R M Marketing Limited
TCS Freehold Investments Limited
TCS Leasehold Investments Limited
Terberg DTS (UK) Limited
Thames Ambulance Service Limited
Thurston Holdings Limited
Transforming Lives for Good (TLG) Ltd
Turner & Townsend Europe Limited
West Park Estates Limited
Widd Group Limited
Willowbank Holiday Park Limited
Wilson & Co. (Motor Sales) Limited
Witherslack Group Limited
Wrapid Manufacturing Limited
York Mailing Limited
Yorkshire Sculpture Park
Young's Seafood International Holdings Ltd
Zuka Ltd.

**1999** [156]

ACM Global Central Laboratory Limited
AMS Bobcat Limited
AMT Vehicle Rental Limited
Aclet Property Management & Services Ltd
Allied Glass Containers Limited
Allsigns International Limited
Altra Industrial Motion UK Holding Ltd
Peter Ambrose (Castleford) Limited
Ardagh Holdings (UK) Limited
Arena Group Holdings Limited
Arundel Kerr Produce Limited
Andrew Atkinson Livestock Limited
Augean Property Limited
Baydale Control Systems Limited
Beal (UK) Limited
Guy Bentley Limited
F D Bird & Sons Limited
Ian Blowers Jewellers Limited
Blythmore Limited
Bowes Museum
Burrows Motor Co Ltd
Bussey & Armstrong Projects Limited
C.K. (Fast Food Suppliers) Limited
CGP Estates Limited
Calder Conferences Limited
Calverts Carpets Limited
Cammax Limited
Cashmere Fibres International Limited
Century Health (Nottingham) Limited
Clarke Meats Limited
Clarks Vehicle Conversions Limited
Cleveland Bridge UK Limited
Coletta Holdings Limited
Coletta and Tyson Limited
Complete Business Solutions Group Holdings Ltd
Coordination Group Publications Ltd
County Turf Limited
Crime & Fire Defence Systems Limited
Cronkhill Properties Limited
Crown Properties (Scarborough) Limited
Cubic Holdings Limited
Dalkeith Laboratories Limited
Dalquinto Limited
Damac Group Limited
De Vere Tortworth Court Limited
Dellstrong Limited
Direct Auto Finance Insurance Services Ltd
Donisthorpe Hall
Doran Scott Williams & Co Ltd
Echem Limited
Eggborough Power Limited
Eido Limited
Elmwood Property Investments Limited
Emacrow Holdings Limited
Emacrow Limited
Engie Gas Limited
Engie Gas Shipper Limited
Evans Homes Limited
FLD Limited

FMG Support Ltd
Fire Protection Holdings Limited
Foremans Properties Limited
Freemans Grattan Holdings Limited
Gem Environmental Building Services Ltd
Greif Flexibles UK Limited
Grimsby Operations Limited
Habasit (UK) Limited
Hamsard Five Thousand and Eighteen Ltd
Hermes Parcelnet Limited
High Point Estates (Bury) Limited
High Point Estates (Darlington) Limited
High Point Estates (Gateshead) Limited
Hill Giftware Limited
J. M. Holling Limited
Simon Holmes Limited
Hull Trains Co Ltd
ISP Holdings (U.K.) Ltd.
J. and H. Property Management Limited
JNP Estate Agents Limited
Douglas James Limited
Adrian Johnson Limited
Keyland (Midpoint) Limited
Kirkella Limited
Kudos Shower Products Limited
Landteam Property Investments Limited
Lanes Group PLC
Leach Colour Limited
Linley & Simpson Limited
Loop Customer Management Limited
M & D Foundations & Building Services Ltd
Marcrist International Limited
M. J. McCarthy (Holdings) Limited
J.S. Miller Distribution Limited
Modern Market Retailing Limited
Mott MacDonald Bentley Ltd
Newlincs Development Limited
Nexus Vehicle Management Ltd.
Old HK Limited
Omega Proteins Limited
P.K.A. Co Ltd
Park Leisure Marketing Limited
Peel Entertainment Group Limited
Pharmacy2u Limited
Place2live Ltd
Platinum Print Limited
Powell Engineering UK Limited
Q Electronics Limited
Q. R. I. Ltd
RSR Limited
Really Useful Products Ltd
Retford Wallcoverings Limited
Reynolds 2000 Limited
Rhomberg Sersa UK Limited
Right Car (UK) Ltd
Riverside Hull Limited
John Roe (Hull) Limited
Rugby Football League Limited
SLS Group Limited
Sanderson Contracts Limited
Skills for Care Ltd
Smith Brothers (Contracting) Limited
Snainton Golf Centre Limited
Space4 Limited
Specialist Cars of Malton Limited
Stadium (Newport) Limited
Steel Supplies Limited
Stored Value Solutions UK Limited
Strategic Team Maintenance.Co. Limited
Sunny Day Trading
T L B Properties Limited
Talbot House Limited
Talpole Limited
Tenet Limited
Therapy in Praxis Limited
Thompson Homes (Yorkshire) Ltd.
Tile Co Ltd
Tocketts Mill Limited
Total Energy Gas Supplies Limited
Tracsis Traffic Data Limited
Transwaste Recycling and Aggregates Ltd
Transwaste Services Limited
Trimble Solutions (UK) Ltd
Tucker Mechanical and Electrical Building Services Ltd
Tunstall Holdings Limited
Wal-Mart Stores (UK) Limited
Welcom Digital Limited
West Moor Holdings Limited
Whitworth Chemists Limited
Wolds Engineering Services Limited
XL Joinery Limited
YTC Limited
Yara UK Limited
York Bioanalytical Solutions Limited
Young's Seafood Limited
Zenith International Freight Limited
Zetland Estates Limited

**2000** [186]

ATB Morley Limited
Abaxis UK Limited
Abel & Cole Limited
Abstract Securities Limited
Access Panel Co Ltd
Actavo (UK) Limited
Air Handling Systems Limited
Airea Floor Coverings Limited
Al Halal Supermarket Limited
Alphamore Corporation Ltd
Mark Anglin Associates Limited
Arch Chemicals UK Holdings Limited
Architectural Steel Limited
Arrow Enterprise Computing Solutions Ltd
Asda Holdings UK Limited
Ashton Agricultural and General Limited
Associated Waste Management Limited
Augean Treatment Limited
B & T S Builders Merchants Ltd
BMB Clothing Limited
BSN Medical Limited
Bailey Leasing Limited
Barton Park Homes Limited
Michael Barugh Steel Stockholding Ltd
Barwick Investments (Leeds) Limited
Bayram Timber Limited
Belem Investments Limited
Belle Vue Property Limited
Blackshaw Holdings Limited
Bonds Foundry Co Ltd
Bossdean Properties Limited
Bradford & Bingley PLC
Bradford Trident Limited
Brand Partnership (Holdings) Limited
British Smaller Companies VCT2 PLC
Broady Flow Control Limited
Brook Group (Holdings) Limited
Bull Brand Limited
C.A. (Evenwood) Limited
CB Solutions U.K. Ltd
CCL Stressing Systems Limited
CYB Intermediaries Limited
Caddick (Scarborough) Limited
Callcredit Limited
Caravan Guard Limited
Cartonplast (UK) Limited
Central North Sea Fibre Telecommunications Co Ltd
Champagne Warehouse Ltd
Citynet Insurance Brokers Limited
Clarke Chapman Group Limited
Cotterhill Limited
D J Cox Limited
DP Publicity Limited
Daresbury Park Developments Limited
De Vere Cotswold Water Park Limited
Deliver Net Limited
Delta Caravans International Limited
Delta Salvage Limited
Diamondcut Limited
Donaldson Filtration (GB) Limited
Doncaster Deaf Trust
Dugdale Limited
Dunns (Long Sutton) Limited
ECG Holdings (UK) Limited
ECSC Group PLC
ESCO Hydra (UK) Limited
Ebuyer (UK) Limited
Evans (Ashford) Limited
W Eves & Co (Service Stations) Limited
Finley Structures Ltd
Frog Education Limited
Fuel Proof Limited
GBA Transport Limited
GH North Yorkshire Limited
Garrards (Huddersfield) Limited
Go Green Limited
Peter Gradon Meat and Poultry Marketing Ltd
HPI Limited
Harrogate Spring Water Limited
Hi Resolution (Production) Limited
Albert Hill Commercials Limited
M Hillas (Properties) Limited
Hollingsworth & Vose Air Filtration Ltd
Home Marketing Limited
Hull & East Yorkshire Medical Research Centre
Hull City Tigers Limited
Hunters Property Group Limited
I.G. Industries Holdings Limited
ISG Boiler Holdings Limited
Idexx UK Acquisition Limited
Impact Development Training International Ltd
Inhoco 2082 Limited
Intechnology PLC
Interbulk (UK) Holdings Limited
J.S.R. Genetics Limited
William Jackson Food Group Limited
Jackson's Bakery Limited
Jemella Limited
K. Fresh Ltd
Kahn Landmark Limited
Kendal Brewery Arts Centre Trust Limited
LEBC Group Limited
LEBC Holdings Limited
Langley Aviation Limited
M. H. Industrial Limited
Marine Services (Grimsby) Limited
Marpak Extrusions Limited
Mech-Tool Engineering Limited
Meller Flow Trans Limited
H. Mitton Limited
Moody Direct Limited
Moortown Plant Limited
Moorview Care Limited

Nationwide Structures Limited
Neoss Limited
Wilf Noble Building Supplies Limited
Northcoast Seafoods Limited
Northern Foods Finance Limited
Owens-Corning Britinvest Limited
Peaspring Limited
Persimmon Finance Limited
Persimmon Holdings Limited
Persimmon Homes Limited
Phoenix Oil & Marine Limited
Phoenix Partnership (Leeds) Ltd
Pland Stainless Limited
G R Potter Plant Hire Limited
Premier Housing (Bradford) Ltd
Premier Traffic Management Limited
Prestige Recruitment Specialists Limited
Preston Road Neighbourhood Development Co Ltd
Primepak Foods Limited
Procters Coaches (North Yorkshire) Ltd
Profile Security Group Ltd
Pugh & Co Ltd
Redhead Holdings Limited
Redhouse Holdings Limited
Redmayne Capital Limited
Redmed Limited
Resource Management Solutions (North East) Ltd
Robinson Group (Holdings) Limited
D L Rogers & Sons Limited
San Pedro Properties Limited
Sedbergh School
Select Alloys & Materials Limited
Senior Architectural Systems Limited
Severfield (Design & Build) Limited
Sheffield United Group Limited
Shine: Support and Help in Education
Skelton Limited
Skipton Group Holdings Limited
Smiles for Miles Limited
Specialist Power Engineering Contracts Ltd
Steve Ltd
Strainstall Group Limited
Strainstall UK Limited
Sty.Com Limited
Style Group UK Limited
Richard Sullivan Consulting Ltd
Support Warehouse Limited
Swinton Park Limited
Technowash Limited
Tenet Group Limited
Thompson Property Ltd
Tilsatec Limited
Troy Foods Limited
UK Thermos Limited
URM (UK) Limited
Ulster Yarns Limited
Ultimate (Commercial Interiors) Limited
United Healthcare Developments Limited
Univar UK Limited
Vossloh Cogifer UK Limited
WNF Group Limited
Walshford Inn Limited
Wandahome (South Cave) Limited
Webevents Limited
West Tower Country House Limited
Westfield Farms Limited
Wiseton Developments Limited
R N Wooler & Co (Developments) Limited
Wooltex U.K. Limited
Yorkshire Air Ambulance Limited
Yorkshire Farmhouse Eggs Limited
Yorkshire Period Hotels Limited
Zeina Foods Limited

**2001** [184]

(Aq) Networks Limited
Abacus Direct Limited
All Steels Trading Limited
Anlaby Office Cleaning Services Limited
Apollo Holdco Limited
Asda Supermarkets Limited
Audley Court Hollins Hall Limited
Bar 24 Limited
P. Barker Properties Limited
Biowise Limited
Birchgrove Estates Limited
Boost Drinks Limited
Bremsen Technik (UK) Limited
Broadley (Group) Limited
Brook Crompton UK Limited
Bulmer & Lumb Group Limited
Burbank Produce Limited
Buxton Pickles Ltd.
Buy It Direct Ltd
C.N. Trading Limited
C2 Investment Limited
CCL Label Limited
Caddick (JPC Developments) Limited
Cambridge Glasshouse Co Ltd
Cascade Homes Ltd
Cashel Limited
Catfoss Finance Limited
Central Properties (Leeds) Limited
Centrica Offshore UK Limited
Chemfix Products Limited
Teddy Clark Limited
Coachman Holdings Limited
Contractsure Limited
Cromwell Capital Ventures UK Limited
Curo Transatlantic Limited
DEU Estates Properties Limited
Decorative Panels Components Limited
Decorative Panels Lamination Limited
Dr. Oetker (UK) Limited
Drighlington Fibres Limited
Drive Devilbiss Healthcare Limited
Drury Engineering Services Limited
Dura Beds Ltd
Dyneley Holdings Limited
Eden Holdings (UK) Limited
Engie Power Limited
Eppleton Quarry Products Limited
Eshton Ltd
Eureka Display Limited
Exlabesa Extrusions (Doncaster) Limited
Exponent International Limited
Farmhouse Fare Limited
Finest Flats Co Ltd
Fish Administration Limited
Folding Sliding Doors Limited
George Fordy Properties Limited
Foresight North East Lincolnshire Ltd.
Franklyn Group Limited
Friends Provident Charitable Foundation
G S M Automotive Limited
G2M Unilets Limited
GHG-AFCO (Luton) Limited
Ghyll Royd Nursing Home Limited
Goodall Group Limited
Gregory Projects Limited
Guardian Industries U.K. Limited
H.B. Food Services Ltd
Hallmark Group Products Limited
Harris Group Limited
S Harrison Group Limited
Haztec International Ltd
Head UK Ltd
Healthsource (Bromley) Limited
Healthtrak (UK) Limited
Heathvine Properties Limited
Henton & Co LLP
High Point Estates (Birstall) Limited
High Point Residential Limited
Highbury Homes (Yorkshire) Limited
Highstone Estates (Kidderminster) Ltd
Holdgrove Limited
B M Howarth Limited
Humdinger Limited
Hungate (York) Regeneration Limited
Iconx Ltd
Imperial Automotive Limited
Incommunities Group Limited
Inoveight Limited
Intouch Advance Limited
JMS of Doncaster Limited
Just Lettings Limited
KCA European Holdings Limited
Katell Limited
Kelkay Limited
Kexgill (Middlesbrough) Limited
Kexgill (Nottingham) Limited
Kexgill (Preston) Limited
Kirkgate Group Limited
Kirklees Active Leisure
Knaresborough Investments Limited
L.S. Transmission Consultancy Limited
Lagonda Selsdon Propco Limited
Lambert Engineering Group Limited
Ledden Developments Limited
Leo Group Limited
Lighthouse UkCo 6 (Treasury) Limited
Lynn Wind Farm Limited
Microcourt Limited
Midas Paper Converters Limited
More (UK) Limited
Morgan Travel Limited
Mosaic Tile Co Ltd
Motor Depot Limited
Motorhog Holdings Limited
NSA (Ventures) Limited
New Century Foods Limited
Newitt & Co (Properties) Limited
Newlands Community Association
Nippon Gohsei UK Ltd.
Nobia Holdings UK Limited
OHES Environmental Limited
Oriental Merchant (Europe) Limited
Ray Owen Waste Disposal Limited
PVM Investments Limited
Park Lane Properties (Holdings) Limited
Park Leisure 2000 (Northumberland) Ltd
Partners in Care Limited
Phoenix Whirlpools Limited
Pilgrim Food Holdings Limited
Pinion Services Limited
Porth Investments Limited
Power Plastics Limited
Principle Healthcare Limited
Print-Leeds Limited
Proaktive Ltd
Q-Park UK Limited
Rayrigg Estates Ltd
Real Time Communications Limited
Retreat York

Rhodar Demolition Limited
Richmond Properties (UK) Limited
Rowanway Limited
S D C Enterprises Limited
SIL Holdings Limited
SSG Insight Limited
SSP Limited
SWL Holdings Limited
Sayers Road Tanker Rentals Limited
Senator Homes Limited
Sharpsmart Limited
Skipton Business Finance Limited
Smoothwall Limited
Spinko Limited
Standeven Properties Limited
Star Brands Limited
Stercap Limited
Stockbridge Technology Centre Limited
Stockton Drilling Limited
Stonecroft Holdings Limited
Strata Homes Midlands Limited
Strawson Investments Limited
Stroma Building Control Limited
Swinton Technology Limited
TMD Friction UK Limited
Tamar (Selby) Limited
Team (Impression) Limited
Thorpe Park Developments Limited
Tracsis Retail and Operations Limited
United Anodisers Limited
Universal Parking Limited
VTL Group (Holdings) Limited
Vellco Limited
Victoria Plum Limited
Vision Supplies Limited
WTJ Insurance Brokers Limited
Wakefield Grammar School Foundation
J. & J. Ward Limited
Waste Services Group Limited
Richard Wellock & Sons Limited
West Building Supplies Limited
Wilberforce Trust
C & K Wood (U.K.) Limited
Yorkcourt Paragon Limited
Yorkshire & Lincolnshire Developments Ltd

**2002** [156]

24 Seven Communications Limited
4x4 Accessories & Tyres Limited
ASD Westok Limited
Aalberts Industries Limited
Ackworth Service Station Ltd
Allied Glass Holdings Limited
Amvale Medical Transport Limited
K A Anderson (Metal Recyclers) Limited
Arla Foods Cheese Co Ltd
Arrow Industrial Group Limited
Artesian Spas UK Limited
Asda Financial Services Limited
Aviva Wrap UK Limited
Aztek International Freight Limited
BSN Medical Distribution Ltd.
Banks Lyon Jewellers Limited
Benson Park Limited
Bonus Securities Limited
Bradonwood Limited
Britto Psychiatry Limited
Broadacres Services Limited
Broadstreet Great Wilson Europe Limited
Browntree Properties Limited
CLS Civil Engineering Limited
CPP European Holdings Limited
CPP International Holdings Limited
Canley Food Packers Ltd
Carclo Holding Limited
Cat Tech (Europe) Limited
Cater-Kwik Limited
Centrica Storage Holdings Limited
Chesterfield Poultry Limited
Citispace Properties Limited
Cityblock Holdings Limited
Cityblock Lettings Limited
Community Foundation for Leeds
Compair Holdings Limited
Condor Aviation Limited Liability Partnership
Contis Card Solutions Limited
Cromwell Holdings Europe Limited
Curtis Wool Direct Holdings Limited
DKB Crop Protection Limited
Davis Tate Ltd
Dechra Limited
Delifresh Limited
Doncaster Culture and Leisure Trust
E.F.C. Consultancy Limited
Ebco (Holdings) Limited
Eltherington Industries Limited
J R Firby Ltd
Fives UK Holding Limited
Frazer Estates Limited
Fussey Engineering Limited
GCD Limited
GGR Holdings Limited
Gatenbysanderson Limited
Simon Gibson Transport Limited
Glusburn Holdings Limited
Goodwin Development Trust
Great North Air Ambulance Service
Greentech Limited
Ground Group Limited
HK Timbers Limited
E Handcock Limited
Harron Group Limited
Help for Health
Hexon Limited
High Grove Beds Limited
Holf Investments Limited
Holmefield Farm Services Limited
IP Assist Services Limited
IPF Financial Services Limited
Island Wharf (100) Limited
Island Wharf (300) Limited
Jet2holidays Limited
Kexgill (Durham) Limited
Kexgill (Stockton) Limited
Keysterne Limited
Kingspan Hot Water Systems Limited
Kirklees Neighbourhood Housing Limited
Liberty Guard (U.K.) Limited
Linkway Distribution Services Limited
Lowell Financial Ltd
M.K.M. Leisure Limited
J Marr (Property) Limited
J M McGill Ltd.
Medical Imaging UK Limited
Micron Hydraulics Holdings Limited
Roger Miles Plant Sales Ltd.
Minstergate Limited
Mirabelle Partners Limited
Mytum & Selby Waste Recycling Limited
NHP Operations (York) Limited
NVELOPE Rainscreen Systems Limited
Nagra Properties Limited
Newclose Properties Limited
Newitt & Co Limited
Newlands Community Association (Trading) Ltd
Newly Weds Foods Acquisition Limited
Northern Marquees Limited
Opus Energy Group Limited
Opus Energy Limited
Overseas Trading Limited
Paragon Creative Limited
Paw Structures Limited
Pennock & Ivory Limited
Pinheiros Corporation Limited
Pneumatic & Electrical Systems Limited
Poster Publicity Group Limited
Premier Equine International Limited
Pure Collection Limited
Q-Park Securities Limited
RF Racing Limited
Peter Ramsey & Sons Limited
Reece Safety Products Ltd
Regroup (UK) Limited
Rolawn Limited
Rushbond Retail Limited
S.M.K. Textiles Limited
SMS Towage Limited
Schofield Sweeney LLP
Scientific Games International Holdings Ltd
Screen Yorkshire Limited
Seabrook Crisps Holdings Limited
Seal It Services Limited
SigmaKalon (BC) UK Limited
Silver Cross (UK) Limited
Simply Biz Limited
Simply Biz Services Limited
Specialist Ceiling Services Holdings Ltd
Staff Finders (Yorkshire) Limited
Stocks Group Limited
Storth Limited
Sunflower Medical Limited
Teva UK Holdings Limited
Tullo Wind Farm Limited
UK General Insurance Limited
Union Discount Company of London Limited
Untha UK Limited
VPG Systems UK Limited
Valli Forecourts Limited
Wannops Farms Ltd
Ward Recycling Limited
A.M. Warkup Limited
Warrendale Farms Limited
Weybourne Estates Limited
Whetley Mills Limited
Whymar Limited
R.N. Wooler & Co (Holdings) Limited
Wykeland Treasury Management Limited
Y H Residential Limited
Y.E.S. (Your Event Solutions) Limited
Yarrows Aggregates Limited
York Museums and Gallery Trust
York St John University
Zeffirellis Limited

**2003** [207]

ABI (UK) Holdings Limited
Ace Gas Limited
Advance HE
Agenda Management Services Limited
Aire Valley Properties Limited
Aketon Limited
Amsgro Limited
Anabas (UK 2) Limited
Ansell Microgard Limited
Arch UK Biocides Limited

Argyle Square Properties Limited
Arla Foods UK Holding Limited
Armitage Shanks Ltd
Arrow Film Converters Limited
Aston Properties (Leeds) Limited
Augean South Limited
Avacta Group PLC
BBB Services Limited
Barton Park Estates Limited
Bayford & Co Ltd
Bemrose Booth Paragon Limited
Blackrow Holdings Limited
Boston Holdings Limited
David M Brockbank LLP
CCL Stressing International Limited
CSC (World) Limited
Calder Group (Dewsbury) Limited
Callcredit Information Group Limited
Cardale Asset Management Limited
Cephalon Limited
Checkmate Fire Solutions Limited
Christians Against Poverty
City Red (Holdings) Limited
Commercial Legal Limited
Coral PFI Holdings 2003 Limited
Cornbrook Group Ltd
James Cropper Converting Limited
James Cropper Speciality Papers Limited
Crown Chicken Limited
Crown Hotel (Bawtry) Limited
Ctrack Limited
Cyrus Developments Limited
D & P Haulage Limited
DC Projects (Amber Valley) Limited
DFDS Seaways Irish Sea Holding Ltd
Dale Farm (GB) Limited
Dalesview Developments Limited
Danby Holdings Limited
De Vere Selsdon Estate Limited
Deborah Services (Holdings) Limited
Delta Caravans Holdings Limited
W Denis (Holdings) PLC
Diagmed Healthcare Limited
Distribution Cable Jointing Ltd
Donaldson UK Holding Limited
Doncaster Bus Station Limited
Donelec Group Limited
Dowse Haulage Limited
Drax Power Limited
Dutch Imports & Daughters Limited
E P E International Limited
E.W.G.A. Limited
EHIF (Denmark) Limited
ESCO (UK) Holdings Limited
Earthoil Plantations Limited
East Yorkshire Concrete Products Limited
Eastmist Limited
Ebac Industrial Products Limited
Electricity Distribution Services Ltd
Emsley Brothers Limited
Enact Conveyancing Limited
Feversham Arms Limited
Filltex Limited
Friends of The Lake District
Frontica Business Solutions Limited
G & R Properties (Yorkshire) Limited
G.B. Terminals (Northern) Limited
Goliath Footwear Limited
Grays Wharf Limited
Great Rail Journeys Partnership Limited
HBOS Covered Bonds LLP
HSH Cold Stores Limited
Harris Construction Management Limited
Harrison Farms (Kilham) Limited
Heathfield Holdings Limited
Hemplow Limited
Hocomm Limited
Hopkins Properties Limited
Howard Civil Engineering Limited
Hull Citycare Limited
Humber Properties Limited
ICIEA Limited
IPF Development (2003) Limited
IPF Financing Limited
IRISNDT UK Holdings Limited
Infact UK Limited
Interactive Projects & Design Limited
J & L (North East) Limited
JLM Global Foods Limited
Jemella Group Limited
Kwiktuf Limited
LNT Group Limited
LZN Limited
Lakehill Estates Limited
Las Metals Limited
Leeds City Football Club Limited
Leisure Parks Limited
Lerrix Tankship Limited
Chas. Long & Son (Aggregates) Limited
Longwood Engineering Company (Holdings) Ltd
Low Grange Quarry Limited
Lowell Portfolio I Ltd
MM Band Services Limited
Mamas & Papas (Holdings) Limited
Mamas & Papas Limited
Marshall Wooldridge Holdings Limited
Matrix Chemie Limited
Middle Caves Ltd
Minster Law Limited
Mitton Aftercare Limited
Moorgarth Group Limited
Morris and Son (Holdings) Limited
Mosaic Group Limited
Multisol Group Limited
Ness Hall Ltd
Newby Foods Limited
Newroc Ltd
Nimbus Building Products Limited
Oakapple Homes (Scarborough) Limited
Oakmere Homes (Northwest) Ltd
Old Innserve Limited
One Call Insurance Services Limited
P & J Properties (Yorkshire) Limited
P. I. Bioscience Limited
PC Specialist Limited
PR Books Limited
Park Lane Homes Developments Limited
Pebbles Care Limited
Pegler Holdings Limited
Perago Limited
Phoenix Building Systems Limited
Principal Hayley Group Limited
Prism UK Medical Limited
Project Development International Ltd
Project Kahn Ltd
Q-Park (Taunton) Limited
QX Limited
Quest Solutions (UK) Ltd
RX Systems Limited
Red Roofs Nursery Limited
Retsco Limited
Rever Offshore UK Limited
Riverside Healthcare Limited
Robinson Contract Services Limited
Rolco 188 Limited
Roseville Care Homes Limited
Rudding Park Estate Limited
Sanderson Weatherall Group Limited
Scarborough China Holdings Limited
Serius Group Limited
Serviced Dispense Equipment (Holdings) Ltd
Serviced Dispense Equipment Limited
Seven Technologies Group Limited
Sewell Investments Limited
Silgan Closures UK Holdings Limited
T Soanes & Son (Potatoes) Ltd
Specialist Glass Products Limited
Specma Samwon Ltd
Spencer Properties (UK) Limited
Springfield Care Services Limited
Stadium Retail Investments (2003) Ltd
Sterne Properties Limited
Peter Stevens Estates Limited
Stickyeyes Limited
Stock Redler Limited
Stuncroft Limited
Sukho Limited
Surefreight (International) Limited
Swift Holdings (UK) Limited
TEV Limited
TSC Engineering Limited
Teleware PLC
Tenetlime Limited
T.& R. Theakston Limited
Thornton Meat Co Ltd
Total Value Headhunting LLP
Town Head Farm Products Limited
Transition Glass Products Limited
Urban I (Blonk Street) Ltd
Valley Vets Ltd.
Vantage Motor Group Limited
Vascular Perspectives Limited
Verage Limited
Victoria Farm Garden Centre Ltd
Vinter Estates Limited
WYG Management Services Limited
H Walton Limited
Watson Pallets Limited
Wemmergill Moor Limited
Wescott Homes Limited
Willerby Group Limited
Martin Williams (Hull) Limited
Winsfield Limited
York City Football Club Limited
Yorkare Homes Limited
Yorkshire Halal Meat Supplier Limited
Yorkshire Water Services Finance Limited

**2004** [211]

ABI (UK) Group Limited
ACL Estates Limited
Abbot Investments (North Africa) Limited
Actavis Holdings UK Ltd.
Age Partnership Limited
Allsop Holdings Limited
Arch Chemicals UK Finance
Ascribe Holdings Limited
Ashdale UK Limited
Assent Building Control Limited
Asset Finance UK Limited
Augean PLC
BF Propco (No.12) Limited
BW Integrated Systems UK Limited
Balltec Limited
Bellbrooke LLP

Bioganix Ltd
Blacks Solicitors LLP
Bleu Properties Ltd
Blue Sky Resorts Limited
Bradford City Football Club Limited
Brenntag UK Limited
Broker Network Holdings Limited
Broomco (3554) Limited
Broomco (3555) Limited
C & D Foods (UK) Unlimited
C P Group of Companies Limited
C. K. Properties (UK) Limited
Cardale Park Properties Ltd
Carlac Group Limited
Castle Residential Properties Limited
Cave Developments Limited
Central European Aggregates Limited
Cerros Properties Limited
Certex Lifting Limited
Chamber Acorn Fund (Humber) Ltd
Church Property Holdings Limited
City & Provincial (Equity Partners 3) Ltd
Cleckheaton Properties Limited
Columbo Group Limited
Community Ventures (Leeds) Limited
Community Ventures Company (No 1) Ltd
Corkel Limited
Country Publications Limited
DC Projects (Wolverhampton) Limited
DFDS Logistics Limited
Dam Structures Limited
Decisionmetrics Limited
Deco-Pak Limited
Depho Estates Limited
Diamond Resorts (Holdings) Limited
Dominion Print Ltd
Drax Fuel Supply Limited
Driver Hire Investments Limited
Durham & Tees Community Ventures Fundco (No.1) Ltd
Durham & Tees Community Ventures Limited
E & S Environmental Services Limited
East Coast Construction (N.E.) Ltd
Esteem Holdings Limited
Evans Easyspace (Chester) Limited
F1rst Actuarial PLC
Fender Care Marine Services Group Ltd
James Fisher Marine Services Limited
James Fisher Nuclear Holdings Limited
Future Cleaning Services Limited
GBUK Ltd
GC Motors Limited
GH Braintree Limited
Galtec Solutions Limited
Global Components (UK) Ltd
Globesign Limited
Graham Developments (Property Holdings) Ltd
HC-ONE Beamish Limited
HCF Poultry Limited
HS Products Ltd
Halifax Rack & Screw Cutting Co. Limited
Handler Hire Ltd
Heck! Food Limited
Hesley Care & Education Limited
Hewitson Limited
Highgrove Group PLC
Highgrove Property Developments Limited
Clare Hill (Huddersfield) LLP
Horndean Ltd
John Horsfall & Sons Limited
W.A. Howarth (Aphrodites Lodge) Limited
Huddersfield Fine Worsteds Limited
Hull Citycare (Fundco 1) Limited
Hull Citycare (Investments) Limited
Hull Truck Enterprises Limited
Hymers College Trustee Limited
Indomito Properties LLP
Info Supplier Limited
Inner Space Stations Limited
Inspire 2 Independence (I2i) Ltd
Interiors UK Limited
International Procurement and Logistics Ltd
Ithaca Petroleum Limited
Jacksons Building Components Limited
Just Trays Limited
Kaye Aluminium (Holdings) Limited
Kej LLP
Kexgill (Construction) Limited
Kexgill (Salford) Limited
Key Electrical Contractors & Storefitters Ltd
Keyingham Power Limited
Kirens International Limited
Kloeckner Metals UK Holdings Limited
L S S Properties (Leeds) Limited
LA 2012 Limited
LNT Properties Limited Liability Partnership
Labelon Group Limited
Langdale Close Properties Limited
Langlands Nurseries Limited
Lexia Solutions Group Limited
Libra Careco Investments 1 Limited
Libra Careco Investments 2 Limited
Libra Careco Limited
Liveco Limited
Lowell Holdings Ltd
Lunchbox Theatrical Productions Limited
M.N.S. Textiles Limited
Majestic Polymers Limited
Marble 4 Life Ltd
Marshalls PLC
McCarthy Caravans Limited
Montpelier Professional Limited
Multisol Europe Limited
Philip Myers Web (Neston) Limited
NCI Vehicle Rescue PLC
NIC Services Group Limited
NYT (Holdings) Limited
Narbourne Limited
Natures Crops International Limited
Naught One Ltd
Niko (Int) Limited
Nilerace Limited
North Bay Leisure Limited
Northern Gas Networks Holdings Limited
Northern Gas Networks Limited
Nufarm Crop Products UK Limited
Oakwood Homeloans Limited
One Brewery Wharf Limited
Opus Energy (Corporate) Limited
Ossett Brewery Pub Co Ltd
PBS Holdings Limited
Pacy and Wheatley Limited
Park Leisure 2000 (Cornwall) Limited
Parkrowe Estates Limited
Partnership Investment Fund Limited
Pipe Holdings PLC
President Energy PLC
Principle Healthcare International Ltd
Promised Land Developments Limited
Proton (Southern) Limited
Providence Holdings Limited
Pugh Holdings Limited
Pure Leisure Group Limited
Purex International Limited
RMS Europe Group Limited
Replay Associates Limited
Ring Automotive Limited
Road Traffic Solutions Limited
S.T.L. Trading Co Ltd
SB Wakefield Limited
SSP Holdings Limited
STC Research Foundation
Say Scaffolding Limited
J L Services & Son Limited
Sewell Education (York) Holdings Limited
Sewell Education (York) Limited
Shaks Specialist Cars Ltd
Shaw & Rhodes Holdings Limited
Shine Childcare Limited
Shiny Sky Limited
Sing Kee Group Limited
Skipton Investments Limited
T Soanes & Son (Poultry) Ltd
Stadium Parkgate (Holdings) Limited
Stadium Retail (Holdings) Limited
Stadium Retail Investments (2004) Ltd
Standard Wool UK (Holdings) Limited
Star Brands (Holdings) Limited
Stem Learning Limited
Stericycle International, Ltd.
Stirling Investment Properties LLP
Stroma Developments Limited
TEI Limited
Talasey Ltd
Teleware Group PLC
Teva Acquisition Limited
Total Foodservice Solutions Limited
Total Hardware Limited
Towngate Estates Limited
Tracsis PLC
Trade Furniture Co Ltd
Triple A Lets Limited
UK Fisheries Limited
Urquhart-Dykes & Lord LLP
Vale of Mowbray Holdings Limited
Van Centre (West Yorkshire) Limited
W W Hotels Limited
Watergate Developments Limited
Weavers Properties Limited
Stephen B Wells Limited
West Retail Group Limited
Whitston Group Limited
Whittaker's Jewellers Limited
Winston (UK) Limited
Wot-a-Pullet Limited
Yorkwold (Overseas) Limited

**2005** [198]

4L's Products Limited
A-Safe HQ Ltd
A.D.D. Express Ltd
ANB Advanced Solutions Limited
Access 13 Limited
Adapted Vehicle Hire Limited
Al-Murad Management Ltd
Alexanders Prestige Limited
Aluminium Bronze Valves Limited
Amerdale Investments LLP
Apollo Support Services Group Limited
Ardent Limited
Atlantic Fresh Limited
Audit Partnership Limited
BSN Medical UK Holding Limited
NG Bailey Facilities Services Limited
Bandwood Limited

Barwick Bathroom Distribution LLP
Belaris Ltd.
Belgrave (North West) Limited
Bessacarr Properties Limited
Bhullar Limited
Blackwood Hall Ltd
Bon Coeur Fine Wines Limited
Bradford Academy Trust
Bradleys Jewellers Limited
Burg-Wachter UK (Holdings) Limited
Butt & Hobbs Limited
C.K. Foods (Processing) Limited
CO2Sense C.I.C.
Camira Group Ltd
Carver Engineering Services Limited
Chadwick Lawrence LLP
Chambers Parking Limited
Chase Petroleum Limited
Cirrus Laminations Limited
Clariant Plastics & Coatings (UK) Ltd
Clugston Distribution Services Limited
Cobalt Project Investments (Hull) Ltd
Conservatory Outlet Limited
Core Telecom Limited
Crompton Lamps Limited
Crossroads Group Limited
Crossways Commercial Estates Limited
D Sales (U.K.) Limited
DB Cargo Components Limited
Dakota Pharma Limited
De Vere Venues Properties Limited
Dickinson Properties UK Limited
Drax Corporate Limited
Drax Group PLC
Dunlop Conveyor Belting Investments Ltd
Durham & Tees Community Ventures Fundco (No.2) Ltd
Durham & Tees Community Ventures Fundco (No.3) Ltd
Duynie Limited
East Transportation Holdings Limited
Easypay Services Limited
Effective Security Services Limited
Elsham Linc Limited
Endless LLP
Energy Containment Concepts Limited
Esvagt UK Limited
Everlast Waterproofing Limited
Extron Electronics UK Limited
Fambo UK Limited
James Fisher (Aberdeen) Limited
James Fisher Fender Care Limited
Fisher Outdoor Leisure Holdings Limited
Fives Landis Limited
Forget Me Not Children's Hospice Limited
Formula Films Limited
Furniture Choice Limited
GH Brighton Limited
GH Plymouth Grove Limited
Gale and Phillipson Investment Services Ltd
Giggleswick School
Global George Limited
Global Shipping Services Limited
Goodprofit Limited
Gravers Care Home Ltd
Great Rail Journeys Holdings Limited
P. W. Greenhalgh Holdings Limited
Grosvenor House Group Holdings Limited
Hacs Holdings Limited
Hawkesworth Appliance Testing Limited
Hayley Conference Centres Acquisitions Ltd
Hodgson Sealants (Holdings) Limited
Holbeach Buildings LLP
Hunters Franchising Limited
IETG Limited
IFGL Monocon Holdings Limited
Ice Fresh Seafood Limited
Icelolly Marketing Limited
Impact Property Services Limited
Andrew James UK Ltd
Joda Holdings Limited
Just Teachers Limited
KCA Deutag (Land Rig) Limited
Kanika Limited
Kass Bathroom Products Limited
Kastronix Limited
Kirkminster Engineering Limited
Knightwood Developments Limited
Koso Kent Introl Limited
Lebus Furniture Limited
Lebus Upholstery Limited
Leeds Library
Libra Careco CH2 Propco Limited
Libra Careco CH3 Propco Limited
Lily Lolo Limited
Lupton Fawcett LLP
M.K.M. Building Supplies (Holdings) Ltd
MRC Transmark Holdings UK Limited
MTW Architectural Limited
Malton Foods Limited
Marr Management Limited
RC Marsden Properties Limited
The Neil Martin Group Limited
Mibelle Ltd
Robin Mills Properties Limited
Millwood Investments Limited
Modine UK Dollar Limited
Abraham Moon Holdings Limited
Needlers Limited
Newquip Limited
Northamptonshire Leisure Estates Limited
Northern Eye UK Limited
Northern Gas Networks Finance PLC
Oakapple Commercial Limited
Olicana Holdings Limited
One Commercial (Claims) Limited
PFI 2005 Limited
PPG Performance Coatings UK Limited
Park Lane Healthcare (Magnolia House) Ltd
Park Lane Healthcare Limited
Parkacre Enterprises Limited
Parkhouse Lakeland Estate Limited
Parkside Flexibles (Europe) Limited
Pipe Holdings 1 PLC
Pipe Holdings 2 Limited
Plant Impact Limited
Powell (UK) Limited
Prasco UK Limited
Prospect Business Centres Limited
Punch Graphix Limited
Purple Bricks Co Ltd
Q Medical Technologies Ltd
Ramsdens Solicitors LLP
Rathbone Kear Limited
Read Hyundai Limited
Roberts, Mart (Holdings) Co. Ltd.
Roberts, Mart (Properties) Ltd.
Rollfields Limited
Rouse Homes Limited
Mark Royston Contracting Limited
Russell Armer Group Limited
SGS Packaging Europe Holdings Limited
SJS (Norton) Limited
SUSD Asset Management (Holdings) Limited
Salthaugh Grange Farm Limited
Seatruck Ferries Holding Ltd
Seatruck Ferries Ltd
Seatruck Panorama Ltd
Seatruck Pennant Ltd
Shorewood Parks Limited
Simpson Millar LLP
Southridge Estates Limited
Spellman & Walker Direct Limited
Spellman & Walker Group Limited
St Leger Homes of Doncaster Limited
St.Quinton LLP
Stirling Properties (Leeds No.2) LLP
Style Group Holdings Limited
Taste Marketing Ltd
Techbuyer Limited
Thebigword Group Limited
Andy Thornton Limited
Toiletry Sales Holdings Limited
Town Centre Car Parks Limited
Triton Construction Limited
Tunstall Group Acquisition Limited
Tunstall Group Finance Limited
Tunstall Group Holdings Limited
Tydd St Giles Lodge Developments Limited
University of Chicago Booth School of Business
Van-Line Limited
Varlink Limited
Waco UK Holdings Limited
Ogden Waller Developments LLP
Wavin UK (Holdings) Limited
Welcom Software Holdings Limited
West Retford Hotel Limited
H & C Whitehead (Holdings) Limited
J P Wild Limited
Wilton Developments Limited
Winder Power Limited
Wrapid Group Limited
York Bioanalytical (Holdings) Limited

**2006** [188]

121 Mountco 074 Limited
2 Plan Group Limited
2 Plan Wealth Management Limited
ACAD Holdings Limited
AJ Foam Ltd
ATC Developments (Leeds) Limited
Aegeus Industries Limited
Agfa Graphics Limited
Amerdale Ventures LLP
BBP Group Limited
BBP Investments Limited
Bawtry Carbon International Limited
Beaumont House Properties Limited
Blue Star Fibres Co Ltd
Brand Partnership Group Limited
Brenntag UK Holding Limited
Bridge Street Pentecostal Church
J & S Brooksbank LLP
Broughton Laboratories Limited
C.A. Group (Holdings) Limited
Callcredit Data Solutions Limited
Caring 4 Croydon Limited
Cars 2 Limited
Catterick Caravan & Camping Centre Ltd
Causey Hill Caravan Park Limited
Centurion Europe Holdings Limited
Chapel Allerton Investments LLP
Cider of Sweden Ltd
Citygate Developments No.1 Limited
Clarks UK Limited

Concept Recruitment Group Limited
Crafter's Companion Limited
Cranage Hall Properties Limited
DC Projects (Rotherham) Limited
Dantex Group Limited
John Dickinson Transport Limited
Dishforth UK Limited
Drifford Limited
Eden Rock Estates Limited
Eldercliff Limited
Electric Support Limited
Elm Bank (Northumberland) Limited
F R Evans (Leeds) Limited
Evans Ashford Investments Limited
Evans Homes No.2 Limited
Evans Property Holdings Limited
Evans Regeneration Investments Limited
Evans Residential Holdings Limited
Extract Technology Limited
FJG Property LLP
Feel Good Group Limited
Fenton Finance Limited
Fleetcor UK Acquisition Limited
Forth Bridges Business Park Developments Ltd
Forward Investment LLP
Forza AW Limited
Fradley Park Developments Limited
Freedom Refreshments Limited
Froneri International Limited
Fuelcard Company UK Limited
G R Finance Limited
GB-Bio Limited
GH Runwell Limited
Gordons LLP
Great Grimsby Seafood Village Ltd
Haas TCM Group of The UK Limited
Hain Daniels Group Limited
Hain Frozen Foods UK Limited
Haven Power Limited
Hazlewood Holdings Limited
Healthcare House Limited
Hidrostal (GB) Limited
High Croft Care Limited
Horbury Bridge (Holdings) Limited
Horwood House Properties Limited
IPF Digital Group Limited
IQ Power Holdings Limited
Impala Estates Limited
Innserve Technical Solutions Limited
International Personal Finance PLC
Ithaca Epsilon Limited
Ithaca Gamma Limited
JA Hotels Limited
JT Group (UK) Limited
John Street Developments Limited
Kexgill (Bradford) Limited
Kingstown Works Limited
LBIA Holding Limited
LMB Mechanical Services Limited
LMM Holdings Limited
Lakeland Motor Museum Limited
Lambert Automation Limited
Leading Labels Retail Limited
Lenzing Fibers Grimsby Limited
Lifterz Limited
Linpac Packaging China Holdings Limited
Llandudno Retail Park Limited
Logical Personnel Solutions Limited
Malik Real Estate Limited
Mardix Holdings Ltd
Matwest Ltd
Richard Maxwell Limited
Mazuma Mobile Limited
Metcalfe Bros Limited
Metcalfe Farms (Haulage) Limited
Middleton Lodge Events Limited
Minster Veterinary Practice Ltd
Mister Capital Holdings Limited
Modular Plantrooms Limited
Multi-Tech Engineering (UK) Limited
NSS Properties Limited
Naburn Leisure Limited
Navartis Limited
Northgate (Europe) Limited
Northgate Lighting Limited
Novaglaze Limited
OC317233 LLP
Optibiotix Health PLC
Optima Legal Services Limited
Orvec Holdings Limited
Pace Overseas Distribution Limited
Pall Mall Developments Limited
M H & J Park and Son Limited
N. Peal (Retail) Limited
Pegasus World Ltd
Pentamon Limited
Persimmon Finance (No.2) Limited
Pigment Productions Limited
Plowman Brothers Limited
Portakabin (Site Accommodation) Limited
Premier People Solutions Limited
Premier Technical Services Group PLC
Premium Restaurants Limited
Principle Global Limited
Proactis Holdings PLC
Production Park Ltd
Pure Leisure Estates Limited
Quintor (UK) Limited Liability Partnership
R M Solar Limited
Rhodes Asset Management Limited
Hugh Rice (Whitefriargate) Limited
Riddochhill Developments Limited
Rishworth School
Roando Investments Limited
Rockliffe Hall Limited
Rollfold Holdings Limited
Ruby Acquisitions Limited
Saferoad UK Ltd
Saferoad VRS Ltd
Sanipex Limited
Seabrook Group Limited
Jeff Skinner Skip Hire Limited
Stadium (Bradford) Limited
Charles F Stead (Holdings) Limited
G M Stephenson Ltd
Stirling Properties (Leeds No.4) LLP
Strachan Holdings Limited
Swan Hotel (Newby Bridge) Holdings Ltd
Sweet Squared Limited
TMPC Unlimited
TSYS Card Tech Limited
Talk Direct (Leeds) Ltd
Temeridge Limited
Third Energy Services Limited
Third Energy Trading Limited
Tissue Regenix Group PLC
Tissue Regenix Limited
Total System Services Processing Europe Ltd
Tower Hill Investments Limited
Turner Commercial Developments Ltd
Tyto Finance Limited
United Anodisers Holdings Limited
Uptownleeds Limited
Vallectric (Holdings) Limited
Venice Bidco 1 Limited
Venice Newco 1 Limited
Ventura Telecom Holdings Limited
Walk Investments Limited
Walker Modular Limited
Warmest Welcome Limited
White Rose Property Investments No.2 Ltd
Winander Leisure Limited
Worthington Homes Limited
Wrigleys Solicitors LLP
YBS Holdings Limited
York Mailing (Holdings) Ltd
Yorkshire Building Society Covered Bonds LLP
Zarafa Group Limited

**2007** [184]

Access Hire Nationwide Limited
Acklam's Coaches Limited
Acropolis Investments Limited
Adler & Allan Holdings Limited
Air Berlin Holding Limited
Airport Holdings NDH1 Limited
Aldby Field Nurseries Limited
Arise Virtual Solutions Limited
Arla Foods (Westbury) Limited
Arrow Industrial Holdings Limited
Audasi Holdings Limited
B.W. Industries (Holdings) Limited
BPC Yorkshire Limited
BPG Acquisitions Limited
BPG Midco Limited
Barmston Developments Limited
Black Swan (Yorkshire) Limited
Blacks Industries Limited
Bradman-Lake Limited
Clive Brook Limited
Burlington Care Limited
Buy-Investment-Properties Limited
CB Imports Group Limited
CE Holdings Limited
Caldex Holdings Limited
Camira Transport Fabrics Limited
Can-Pack UK Limited
Cash Converters Yorkshire Limited
Castle 1 Limited
Caygill Holdings Limited
Cellhire Group Limited
City Health Care Partnership CIC
City Portfolio Limited
Teddy Clark (Holdings) Limited
Coaching Inns (North) Limited
Cobco 867 Limited
Complete IT Systems Limited
Conquest Bidco Limited
Contis Financial Services Limited
Cristal Inorganic Chemicals UK Limited
Dalby Offshore Services Limited
De Vere Wokefield Property Limited
Delta Engineering Group Limited
Dent Steel Holdings Limited
Dhoot Transmission (UK) Limited
WJ Drennan Limited
Driver Hire Investments Group Limited
E-Factor Group Ltd
EHLP Holdings Limited
EYG Holdings Limited
Eaton Smith LLP
Elland Steel Structures (UK) Limited
Elsham Wold Estates Limited

Emersons Green Limited
Envirovent Limited
Evans Management Limited
Express Bi Folding Doors Limited
Fast Trade Venture Limited
Ferdinand Properties Limited
Foster Farms Limited
Furness Park LLP
GH Lanchester Road Limited
GH Stanley Limited
GHD Group Holdings Limited
Gettheworldmoving Ltd
Gico Limited
Grosvenor PFI Holdings Limited
Hadrian Bidco 2 Limited
Hadrian Bidco Limited
Harrogate Water Brands Limited
Health Innovations (UK) Limited
Heselden Investments Limited
Hindu Cultural Society of Bradford
Holgates Holdings Limited
Horizon Platforms Limited
Ideal Building Systems Holdings Limited
Ideal Standard Holdings (BC) UK Ltd
Inclusion Housing CIC
Infra Safety Services Labour Limited
Investments in Education Limited
J D Engineering (Northern) Limited
JBA Group Limited
JJC Hire Limited
JSJ Finance Limited
JTR and RB Land Developments LLP
KCA Deutag Alpha Limited
KCH (Holdings) Limited
Karman Ltd
Kelda Eurobond Co Limited
Kelda Non-Reg Holdco Limited
Keystream Limited
Kirklees PFI Limited
Kongsberg Actuation Systems Limited
Kudos International Limited
Lakeside 1 Limited
Larkham Leisure Limited
Leeds Trinity University
Leeds United Football Club Limited
Lights4fun Limited
Link Distribution (UK) Limited
Luxury Fibres Limited
MAS Management Services Ltd
MWS Group Ltd
Mach Recruitment Limited
Malik Halls 2 Ltd
Malik Halls Limited
Maramar (Holdings) Limited
Mardon Holdings Limited
Monster Group (UK) Limited
Motorsure Limited
Network Mapping Limited
Newport Buildings LLP
Nexus Vehicle Holdings Limited
Nu-Oval Acquisitions 1 Limited
Nu-Oval Acquisitions 2 Limited
Numecent Limited
Nynet Limited
Oakmere Homes (Longtown) Ltd
Oilgear European Holdings Limited
Oriium Consulting Ltd
P.P. Plasma Limited
PSP Architectural Ltd
Peel Street Developments Limited
Persimmon Developments (Didcot) Limited
Persimmon Developments (No 5) Limited
Planet Platforms (Holdings) Limited
Polypipe Group PLC
Power4all Limited
Praesto Consulting UK Ltd
Neil Price Construction Services Ltd
Principal Hayley Limited
Pure Data Solutions Limited
RMS Group Holdings Limited
RSM Lining Supplies Global Ltd
Redbrick Yorkshire Limited
Regenco (Winchburgh) Limited
Rhino Enterprises Properties Limited
Ridge Medical Limited
River Street Limited
Rosehill Polymers Group Limited
S.A.R. Recycling Ltd
Sabrina Health Care Limited
Schenck Process UK Holding Limited
Seamore Court Freehold Limited
Sensio Limited
Sheffield United (Hotel) Limited
Shouksmith Holdings Limited
Shouksmith Properties Limited
Sigma Retail Solutions Limited
Sirdar Holdings Limited
St Aidan's Church of England Academy Ltd
Stainless Band Limited
Sterling Capitol PLC
Stoneferry Marfleet Limited
Strategic Team Group Limited
Stroma Certification Limited
TCCP (Clarence Dock) Limited
TCS (Milngavie) Limited
TOG 24 Limited
Tadcaster Pub Co Ltd
Team (Impression) Holdings PLC
Tekmar Energy Limited
Thebigword Interpreting Services Limited
William Thompson Group Holdings Ltd
Titan Global Finance PLC
Tompkins UK Limited
Trust Care Ltd
Turner & Townsend Cost Management Ltd
UKDN Waterflow (LG) Limited
UKOS Investments Limited
Ulixes Limited
United Fresh Consortium Limited
Uris Central Administration Limited
Urmi Capital Limited
Venture Business Parks Limited
WJS Properties 2 Limited
Walker Distribution (Hull) Limited
Whitelock Developments Limited
Witton Castle Country Park Limited
Edward P Wright (Holdings) Limited
York Pullman Bus Co Ltd
York Racecourse Knavesmire LLP
Yorkshire Provender Ltd
Young Herts Limited

**2008** [179]

A-Fax Properties Limited
Aberdeen Enterprise Finance Limited
Aggregates R Us Ltd
Agriargo UK Limited
Alfa Site Services Limited
Almit Group Limited
Almit Properties Limited
J S Alton & Son Limited
Amco Group Holdings Limited
Amco Group Limited
Ascribe Group Limited
Asda Foundation
Autocar Logistics (Irl) Limited
Avacta Life Sciences Limited
Aviva Erfa 15 UK Limited
B C (Roofing Contractors) Limited
Baird Group Limited
Barnard Castle School
Bawtry Investments Limited
Bee Health Limited
Bennett Potatoes Limited
Bradford College Education Trust
Bright Beginnings Childcare Centre Leeds
British American Railway Services Ltd
Brookfield Property (Holdings) Ltd
David Brown Gear Systems Limited
CPP Group Limited
Calverley Reservoir Sales Co Ltd
Candelisa Limited
Cardinal Limited
Carr Mount Estate Limited
Castleton Group Limited
Caval Limited
Cawingredients Limited
Cobalt Project Investments (Taycare) Ltd
Comnet Europe Limited
Concepta PLC
Concorde Excel Holdings Limited
Constellation Trust
Contis Group Limited
Control4 EMEA Ltd
Craig's Motorcycles Limited
Crombie Freehold Limited
Cube (Yorkshire) Ltd
Cupa-Burton Group Limited
Czajka Group Holdings Limited
Dadibhais Holdings Limited
Darntonb3 Limited
Decorative Panels Furniture Limited
C R & C L Donaldson Ltd
Doncaster Central Development Trust CIC
Drydens Limited
Eddisons Commercial (Holdings) Limited
Emis Group PLC
Employee Pulsecheck Limited
Eneco UK Limited
F and N One Limited
FMG Support Group Limited
First 4 Lawyers Limited
Ian Firth Holdings Limited
Flexiglobal (UK) Limited
Fruugo.Com Ltd
GWE Biogas Ltd
Gardner Denver Holdings Limited
Gees Haulage Limited
Glid Wind Farms Topco Limited
H H Construction (Groundwork Contractors) Ltd
A.W. Hainsworth Holdings Limited
Hargreaves Group (GB) Limited
Harlen Ltd
Harris CM Limited
Hebden Bridge Community Association Ltd
Hermes European Logistics Limited
Hesley Holdings Limited
High Street TV (Group) Limited
Highfield Awarding Body for Compliance Ltd
Hitha Limited
Holbeck Ghyll Hotel LLP
Hornsea Leisure Limited
Hunslet Club
Igen Trust
Inhoco 3498 Limited

Inspired Pet Nutrition Holdings Limited
Integra Insurance Solutions Limited
Ison Harrison Limited
JSJ Partnership Limited
KCA Deutag Alpha II Limited
KCA Deutag Enterprises Limited
KTS Wire Limited
KVH Media Group Limited
Keelham Farm Shop Limited
Keepflying LLP
Kingstown Associates Limited
LPD (Holdings) Limited
Label Worx Limited
Lantern Debt Recovery Services Limited
Larsen Road Limited
Leeds Building Society Covered Bonds Limited Liability Partnership
Leigh Holdings Limited
Lidget LLP
Ligentia Group Limited
Live Yorkshire Limited
Livwell Limited
Lowell Acquisitions Limited
Lowell Funding Limited
Lowell Group Limited
Luxury Yarns International Limited
Major Recruitment Limited
Mechanical Facilities Services Limited
Metalcraft Europe Limited
Mill Garages North East Limited
Moorgarth Property Investments Limited
Mumtaz Food Products Limited
New Month Limited
Newlay Concrete Limited
Nova Contracting Ltd
Novus Finance Ltd
Numecent Holdings Ltd
Ontrac Limited
Optare PLC
Optimisation Developments Limited
Optimisation Investments Limited
Optimum Medical Solutions Limited
Orean Personal Care Limited
PTM Holdings Limited
Pet Brands Limited
Plant Theatre Ltd
Powar Developments Limited
Pryers Solicitors LLP
Pure Gym Limited
Red Embedded Consulting Limited
Reed Boardall Group Limited
Refood UK Limited
Regenco Borrower Limited
Regenco Properties LLP
Rema Tip Top Holdings UK Limited
Rosenbauer UK Limited
SSP Bidco Limited
SSP Midco 1 Limited
Saint Leonard's Property Co Ltd
Sandal Motors (Huddersfield) Limited
Sands Care Holdings Limited
Sangwin Holdings Limited
Scarborough Partnership Properties Ltd
Scroll Bidco Limited
Search Group Holdings Limited
Sentamu Academy Learning Trust
Sheppee Holdings Ltd
Sherwood Restaurants Ltd
Speedclad Limited
Stevro Limited
Strawson Group Developments Limited
Strawson Group Investments Limited
Sunny Day Property Holdings Limited
Sunny Day Property Limited
TGH Acquisitions Limited
TGH Finance Limited
TGH Investments Limited
TWR Developments Limited
Tasker Investments Limited
Techmotion Limited
Ticket Arena Limited
Tocketts Mill Leisure Limited
Trackwork Group Limited
Tunstall Healthcare Group Limited
Turner & Townsend Limited
WYG Group Limited
Walker Morris LLP
Wallum Farms (North) Limited
Wayland Farms Limited
Wetherby Group of Companies Limited
Whitaker and Leach Limited
WB White Foundry (Holdings) Limited
Whole Crop Marketing Limited
Wilbraham Securities LLP
Wild Life Group Limited
David Wood Baking Limited
David Wood Baking UK Limited
Yearsleydale LLP

**2009** [174]

4urban (Harrogate) Limited
ACM Global Central Laboratory Operations Ltd
ADP Primary Care Acquisitions Limited
ADP Primary Care Services Limited
AJH Pump Supply & Repair Limited
Actavo Building Solutions (UK) Limited
Advanced Forwarding Limited
Allamhouse Limited
Allerton Steel Limited
Ambitemp (M & E) Limited
Anatis UK Limited
Aptiv (UK) Holdings Limited
Aptiv International Holdings (UK) LLP
Aptiv International Holdings UK Two LLP
Arran Isle Limited
Ascentis
Ashcourt Contracts Limited
Atlas Leisure Homes Limited
Bark and Bite Ltd
Bat 2 Limited
Batteryback PLC
Belle Vue Mills Limited
Blackrow Corporation Limited
Bridge 3 LLP
Bridge Leisure Parks (Finance) Limited
Bridge Leisure Parks (Holdings) Limited
Bridge Leisure Parks Limited
Bridgewood (UK) Limited
Burley Developments Group Limited
C L Medicall Aid Limited
CB Farms LLP
Cancede Limited
Care Holdings Limited
Cassellie Limited
Castlehouse Construction Ltd
Chartford Arthington Limited
Combined Selection Group Ltd
Controlled Building Measures (Holdings) Ltd
Jimmy Corrigan's Limited
D & M Middleton Limited
Dalmore Capital Limited
De Vere Grand Connaught Rooms Limited
Deepsleep Beds UK Ltd
J Denham Metals Ltd
Durest Beds Ltd
Durham & Tees Community Ventures Fundco (No.4) Ltd
EC Surfacing Ltd
Eshton Oakfield Ltd
Europa Caravans Ltd
Evansis Ltd
Fablink Tank Systems Limited
Family Dies Limited
First Actuarial LLP
Flamingo Land Resort Limited
Fresh Olive Co Ltd.
Fuel Trading Co Ltd
Furness Academies Trust
Future Forwarding (Holdings) Limited
G3 Remarketing Limited
H B Tunnelling Limited
Health Factor Limited
Hiatt Hardware (UK) Limited
High Seat Holdings Limited
Highcrest Retail Brands Limited
Holt Doctors Limited
Neil Hudgell Limited
Hull Citycare (Fundco 3) Limited
Ice Co Storage & Logistics Limited
Iceco Limited
Investment in Media Limited
Ipsosolo Limited
Ithaca Energy Developments UK Limited
J.E.G Hire Limited
Jemmtec Limited
KMA Properties Limited
Kingston Research Limited
Krone UK Ltd
LPG Homeheat Limited
Lake House Investments Limited
Land Energy Girvan Limited
Latitude Digital Marketing Limited
Leman International Transport Limited
Linpac Senior Holdings Limited
Lucas Properties Limited
Luscombe Motors Limited
MCE Concept Limited
Mabey Hire Limited
J Maguire Holdings Limited
McJunkin Red Man UK Ltd
Metcalfe Farming Limited
Mitchell Farrar Group LLP
Mold Systems Limited
Molekula Limited
Morses Club PLC
Ian Mosey (Feed) Limited
Ian Mosey (Livestock) Limited
Mulberry Homes Yorkshire Limited
Munchkin UK Trading Co Ltd
NYOS (York) Limited
Narang Group Ltd
Nationwide Window Cleaning Limited
David O'Meara Racing Ltd
OPH Property Holdings Limited
Oakwood Solicitors Limited
Oceanic Seafoods Limited
Opus Gas Supply Limited
Origin Packaging Limited
Outwood Grange Academies Trust
PFF Packaging (North East) Limited
PMW Quarries Limited
Paragon Property Investments Limited
Patrick Construction Group Limited
Pattinson 3 Limited
Pelsis Holding (UK) Limited

Pickering Vale (RLH) Limited
Pneumatic & Electrical Holdings Limited
Portbond Limited
Power Body Nutrition Ltd
Premo Fabrications Limited
Primary Care Commissioning CIC
Printcraft Limited
Proma Construction Management Limited
Provenance Inns Limited
Rapid EPS Limited
Rawdon Asset Finance Limited
Read Motor Group Limited
Redmayne-Bentley LLP
Regal Food Products Group PLC
Reliance RG Limited
G.A. Robson and Son Ltd
Rogerthorpe Manor Hotel Limited
Rollits Limited Liability Partnership
Sanderson Weatherall LLP
Scarborough (UK) Limited
Scarborough Holdings (UK) Limited
Scarborough Property Developments Ltd
Sedalcol UK Limited
Shaman Investments Limited
Shepherd Industries Limited
Shulmans LLP
Sigma GRP Limited
Silver Cross Nurseries Limited
Simba Smoby Toys (UK) Limited
James E. Smith (Northern) Limited
Sonic Megastore Limited
St Peter's School, York
Stafford Mills Holdings Limited
Strong Developments Limited
C F Struthers (Holdings) Limited
Surcoat Group Limited
THS Industrial Textiles Limited
Tailormade Design Limited
F B Taylor (Holdings) Limited
Technimark Limited
Total Recycling Services Limited
Trilogy (Leamington Spa) Limited
Trinity Multi Academy Trust
UK General Insurance Group Limited
United Autosports Limited
Urban Development Projects Ltd
Ventia Limited
Victory Leisure Homes Limited
WDS Component Parts Limited
George Walker Transport Manchester Ltd
Warrens Emerald Biogas Ltd
Watsons BS (Holdings) Limited
Wilkin Chapman LLP
Williamsons Solicitors Limited
Wren Kitchens Limited
York Against Cancer
York Area Quaker Meeting of The Religious Society of Friends (Quakers) in Britain
Yorkshire Grain Limited
Yorkshire Water Services Holdings Ltd
Yorpower Limited

**January-June 2010** [96]

AW Flow Holdings Limited
Allied Glass Group Limited
Anhul Management Limited
Arville Holdings Limited
Ashlea Landscaping Holdings Limited
Aureus Leisure Limited
Richard Baldwin Motorhomes LLP
Be Fuelcards Holdings Limited
Beal Securities Limited
Beauchamp Real Estate Holdings Limited
Bellutex Limited
CF Bidco Limited
CPP Worldwide Holdings Limited
CPPGroup PLC
Carus Green Limited
Castle Industrial Supplies Ltd
Clarion Solicitors Limited
Clydesdale Covered Bonds No.2 LLP
Copernus Limited
Ctrack UK Limited
DFS Furniture Holdings PLC
DFS Furniture PLC
Dewsbury Learning Trust
Diamond Holdco 2 Limited
Diamond Holdco 7 Limited
Don Valley Engineering Holdings Limited
ESP Systex Holdings Limited
Eneco Moy Limited
Energy Services (Business Power) Ltd
Esplanade Group (Scarborough) International Ltd
Extra Detail Limited
Fairbriar Residential Developments Ltd
Five Star Fish Limited
Forza Foods Limited
Fussey Holdings Limited
GBUK Enteral Limited
GFEA Limited
Gaynor Sports Limited
Hartshorne Group Limited
Havwoods Australia Limited
Head Office Interiors Limited
Hilldene Holdings Limited
Hospitaller Order of Saint John of God
Indivior UK Limited
Innserve Limited
JLA Clean Limited
JLA Debtco Limited
Keighley and Worth Valley Railway Preservation Society Ltd
LBBC Limited
LPG Direct Limited
Leeds University Union
Leisure Infrastructure Investors Limited
Living Care Group Limited
MMCG Limited
Made Television Ltd.
Mailway Packaging Solutions Limited
Maria Mallaband (6) Limited
J. Marr & Son Limited
Multiflight Charter Services LLP
Michael Nichol-Smith Limited
Northgate (CB) Limited
Oakhurst Court Holdings Limited
Parkhouse Lakeland LLP
Pipes & Tubes (2010) Limited
Power Link Machine (UK) Co Limited
Project FF & E Limited
Pure Retirement Limited
RPP Limited
Responsible Life Limited
Rever Offshore International Limited
SDG (Boston) Limited
SDG (Newport) Limited
SDG (Preston) Limited
SDG (Rhyl) Limited
Scarborough Development Group Limited
Scarborough Partnership Limited
Scarborough Rugby Union Football Club Ltd
Sharma Investments Limited
Edgar F Shepherd Ltd
Skanwear Clothing Co Ltd
Sovereign Reserve Limited
Specialised Car Covers Limited
Spectrum Community Health C.I.C.
Spire Bidco Hotels Limited
Staunch Limited
Strong Life Care Limited
Student Accommodation Provision LLP
Sunny Day Capital Limited
Swanbridge Veterinary Group Limited
Templer Management Limited
Tower Centre Hoddesdon Limited
Trinity Ten Limited
UK Thermos Holdings Limited
Westway Veterinary Centres Limited
Ypsomed Limited
Zenith Ef Limited

**July-December 2010** [92]

8point8 Support Limited
Abbey House (Cumbria) Limited
Arla Foods Ingredients UK Limited
Armthorpe Falconry Limited
Ashfield (Hull) Limited
Athena Civil Engineering Ltd
Baird Group (Holdings) Limited
Bliss Films Limited
Bond Street Real Estate Holdings Limited
Bondshold Limited
Bosideng UK Limited
Brandon Hire Group Limited
Bridon Holdings Limited
Broadland Renewable Energy Limited
Byworth Boilers Ltd
CNG (Group) Limited
Calvary Chapel York
Chameleon Technology (UK) Limited
Cilantro Acquisitions Limited
Cilantro Midco Limited
Cilantro Parent Limited
S B & A Clark Farming Limited
Corinthian Brands (CBL) Limited
Cullingworth LLP
DAM Investments and Properties Limited
De Vere Wokefield Estate Limited
Delta Academies Trust
Eco Modular Buildings Ltd
Eville & Jones (UK) Limited
Fenner International Australia Limited
Ghyll Royd Properties Ltd
Gibson Pharmacy Limited
Gorse Academies Trust
Greetland Academy Trust
Hamsard 3225 Limited
Hartford Holdings Limited
Healing Multi Academy Trust
Hensall Group Limited
Holgates Silver Ridge Ltd
Hull Citycare (Fundco 4) Limited
Interface Administration Services Ltd
Interface UK Manufacturing Limited
Inventry Limited
KTH Engineering Group Limited
Kober Limited
John Laithwaite Investments Limited
Lancaster Girls' Grammar School
Lancaster Royal Grammar School
Lesley, Stephen & Co. Limited
Lunesdale Learning Trust
MV Ingredients Limited
Maria Mallaband 7 Limited
Mansfield Pollard (Holdings) Limited

Mobili Office Design International LLP
Munford Haulage Limited
Navigo Health and Social Care CIC
Naylor Wintersgill Limited
New R & R Ice Cream Limited
Northern Installations CP LLP
Onward Investment Limited
P. & B. Foods Holdings Limited
Podrigo Ltd
Premier Communications Ltd
Premium Leasing Limited
Project Magnum (Bidco) Limited
Queen Katherine School Multi Academy Trust
Radicon Transmission UK Limited
Rainbow Schools Trust
Recruitex Limited
Red Hall (Bury) Limited
Reward Finance Group Limited
S.A.R. Metals Limited
SSL Healthcare Ltd
Sellmor Farming Limited
Stainforth Construction LLP
Streejaane
The John Strutt Conservation Foundation
TM Advances Limited
Team 17 Software Limited
Technical Arc Ltd
Tees & Durham (Lift) Investments Limited
Tompkins Investments Limited
Triesse Group Limited
UK Asset Resolution Limited
Vida Hall Limited
WMK Securities LLP
Wakefield City Academies Trust
Wauldby Associates Limited
Michael Wheatley Management Limited
Witherslack Group (Holdings) Limited
York Sports Village LLP
Yorkshire Prosperity Limited

**January-June 2011** [133]

A J Access Platforms Limited
ADGM Limited
AKV Cladding Products Ltd
Abirose Limited
Accord Multi Academy Trust
Anord Mardix Critical Power Services Ltd
Aptiv Holdfi (UK) Limited
Ascot Road Watford Limited
BC Bantams Limited
BH Acquisitions Limited
Bagel Nash Group Limited
Bannatyne Fitness (2) Limited
Bannatyne Properties Limited
Batley Academy Trust
Bay Learning Trust
Beaumont Morgan Developments Limited
Bentley Yorkshire Limited
Beverley Grammar School
Boparan Finance PLC
Boston Healthcare Limited
Brighouse High School Academy Trust
Bunton Plant Hire Limited
Carrington House Yorkshire Limited
Castleford Academy Trust
Centre at Three Ways
Clarke Telecom Limited
Consortium Academy Trust
Context World Limited
Countrywide Care Homes Limited
Craggs Country Business Park LLP
Crofton Academy
Cycene Limited
DRC Contract Services Ltd
Darlington Arena Limited
Dormot Limited
Dragonfly Agency Limited
Ebac Holdings Limited
Education Alliance
Eneco Sevor Limited
Epax Pharma UK Holdings Unlimited
Epax Pharma UK Ltd
Evolution Schools Learning Trust
Firsdell Ltd
Fullers Foods Holdings Limited
Further Instructions Ltd
Gweco 510 Limited
Gweco 511 Limited
Hardroad Limited
Hartford Properties Limited
Haulage (Holdings) Organisation Limited
Hayfield School
Hazel Products UK Limited
Hesco Group Limited
Hope Learning Trust, York
Humberston Park Special School
Hummersknott Academy Trust
I-Trust Education
ICR Integrity Limited
Ideal Carehomes (Number One) Limited
Ingenuity Digital Holdings Limited
JM Developments (Guiseley) Limited
L Jackson & Co Limited
KCAD Holdings I Limited
KCAD Holdings II Limited
Kaver Limited
Kepwick Estate Limited
Kepwick Farms Limited
King James I Academy, Bishop Auckland Ltd
Kirkbie Kendal School Academy Trust
Kitching Plant Hire Ltd
Knightwood Holdings (2011) Limited
LGK Farms LLP
Langleys Solicitors LLP
Leeds College of Music
Leeds Golf Leisure LLP
Leeds Jewish Free School
Lighthouse School
Locala Community Partnerships C.I.C.
Luminar Partnership Limited
M.C.I. Developments Limited
MFG Academies Trust
Metis Bidco Limited
Minsthorpe Academy Trust
Moorlands Learning Trust
Nat Flex Group Limited
Newincco 1072 Limited
North Halifax Grammar School Academy Trust
Northern Ambition Academies Trust
Northern Star Academies Trust
Northminster Holdings Limited
Notman Enterprise Limited
Nutclough Mill Limited
P and E Yorkshire Ltd
Pathfinder Multi Academy Trust
Pendle Sportswear Limited
Pindar Scarborough Ltd
Pitts Wilson Holdings Limited
Red Kite Learning Trust
Right Fuelcard Co Ltd
Rossett School
SPH 2011 Limited
SRH 2011 Limited
Scarborough Holding Co Ltd
Scarborough Management Limited
Scarborough Overseas Holdings Limited
Shared Vision Learning Trust
Sheffield Housing Co Ltd
South Craven Academy Trust
South Westmorland Multi Academy Trust
Specialist People Services Group Limited
St James Securities Limited
Stericycle International Holdings Ltd
Sullivan Student Properties Limited
Swanland Education Trust
Taniya Properties Ltd
Together Roof Energy Limited
Trackwork Moll Limited
Trinity Exploration & Production PLC
Vivimed Labs UK Limited
W F & L Limited
Waddington & Ledger Group Limited
Wavemaster (TGOF) Limited
Wilf Ward Family Trust
A & C Wood Limited
Wright Leisure Limited
Wyreside Leisure Limited
X-Force UK Ltd
Yesss (A) Electrical Ltd
Yesss (B) Electrical Ltd
Yorkshire Causeway Schools Trust
Yorkshire Property Finance Ltd
Zaic - A Limited
Zenith Remarketing Limited

**July-December 2011** [116]

ABI Alpha Limited
ABI Beta Limited
Abbey Multi Academy Trust
Academy @ Ridgewood Trust
Adams and Green Limited
Advice Champion.co.uk Limited
Akari Care Limited
Ali-A Entertainment Ltd
Aptiv Holdings (UK) Limited
Arctic Waters Limited
Argrain Holdings Limited
Arizonaco Limited
Aston Hall Hotel Limited
Axholme Academy
BH Energygap LLP
Batley Multi Academy Trust
Bolton Brow Primary Academy
Bostonair Group Limited
Boulton & Cooper Limited
Brooksbank School Sports College
CID Products LLP
Cambridge Park Academy Limited
Carmel Education Trust
Castle Hall Academy Trust
Cat Tech International Limited
Cathedral Church of England Academy Trust (Wakefield)
Collaborative Learning Trust
Countrywide Care Homes (2) Limited
Cranswick Gourmet Pastry Co Ltd
Cristal Investments UK Limited
Ctrack Europe Holdings Ltd
Denaro (UK) Limited
Alan Dick Communications Limited
Donaldson's Vets Limited
Drax Smart Generation Holdco Limited
Drax Smart Sourcing Holdco Limited
Duchy Homes Limited

EPMS Supplies Limited
Education PFI Investments Limited
Education Village Academy Trust
Emerald Care Holdings Yorkshire Limited
Energy Works (Hull) Limited
Fairbriar Developments (Salford) Limited
Family of Learning Trust
Federation of Abbey Schools Academy Trust
Feversham Education Trust
GD Aria Holdings Limited
GHSR LLP
GSP Distribution Limited
Gear4music (Holdings) PLC
Goball Limited
Guyson (Holdings) Limited
HC-ONE Limited
Harper & Wilkes Limited
Hindle Gears Limited
Hird (UK) Ltd
AC Hobson LLP
Holt Family (Holdings) Limited
Horsforth School
Hull Citycare (Fundco 5) Limited
Humber Grain Limited
International Seafoods Limited
Isle Education Trust
Jabe Foods Limited
Just Partnership Limited
Kings Solutions Group Limited
Krimpterm Limited
John Laithwaite Partners LLP
Leger Education Trust
Leodis Academies Trust
Liberty2803 Limited
Lindley Junior School
Lodestone Projects Limited
Marsh & Parsons (Holdings) Limited
Masternaut Limited
Mayfair Curzon Properties Limited
Melrose Pigs Limited
Morton Michel Holdings Limited
Mount St John Sporting LLP
Nizh Yug (UK) LLP
Old Earth School
Orphans in Need
President Energy Holding UK Limited
Rastrick High School Academy Trust
Read Hyundai Lincoln Limited
Rever Offshore ROV Limited
Romero Catholic Education Trust
Salendine Nook Academy Trust
Scarborough Enterprises (UK) Limited
Scarborough Property (UK) Limited
Share Multi Academy Trust
Silver Sands Leisure Park Ltd
Skirfare Investments Limited
Southfield Grange Trust
St George's Crypt
Stage One Group Limited
Stericycle International Holdings Canada Ltd
Stoneferry Limited
Stonegate Precision Tooling Limited
TFP (Wakefield) Limited
Tekmar Holdings Limited
Tekmar Limited
Tillbrook Products UK Ltd
Today's Wholesale Services Limited
Together Roof Energy SPV Limited
Total Oynx Limited
Turbine Efficiency Group Limited
UKIOSH Ltd.
UoE Deaconess Limited
Urban Development Projects (2) Ltd
Verdant Leisure 2 Limited
Webster Properties (Skipton) Limited
Wilby (Group) Limited
Yesss (C) Electrical Ltd
York Mailing Group Limited
Zurbaran Trust

**January-March 2012** [63]

Advance Learning Partnership
Advertising Principles Holdings Limited
Aghoco 1085 Limited
Almara Residential Limited
Anglia Metal Limited
Auckland Project
Barnby C H Limited
Belle Vue Girls' School
Bluebird UK Topco Limited
Bonmarche Limited
Bradford Girls' Grammar School Trust
Civic PFI Investments Limited
Connection Flooring Limited
Crosshall Developments (Leeds) Limited
Dale Erskine Power Solutions Limited
Dennis Distribution LLP
Drifford Group Limited
EOF Holdings Limited
Element14 Finance UK Limited
Elizabethan Academy Trust
Ellis Patents Holdings Limited
Emerald Investments (GB) Limited
Enhance Academy Trust
Fairhurst Stone Merchants Limited
G - Tuft Limited
GH Newco 1 Limited
Hall Cross Academy Trust
Hanover Properties Limited
Histon Sweet Spreads Limited
Holbeck Charitable Trust
Hull Community Church
Hungerhill Academy Trust
Huntcliff Academy Trust
K & A Merger Limited
Lawton Yarns (Holdings) Limited
Lawton Yarns Limited
Leisure World Group Limited
Lowell Finance Holdings Limited
Marrtree Residential Ltd
Harold Newsome Holdings Limited
Northgate (CB 2) Limited
On Line People Limited
One in a Million Free School
Pipes UK (Holdings) Limited
Place2invest Ltd
Prem Sehmi Holdings Limited
RFPG Holdings Limited
RPP Group Holdings Limited
Rever Offshore North Star Limited
Rodillian Multi Academy Trust
Sandmoor Properties Limited
Secondtour Limited
Sheetfed Holdings Limited
St Hybald's Academy Trust
St Mary's Academy Trust
Stoneacre Property Investments Ltd
Swaledale Investments Limited
Swift Acquisitions Limited
Swift Property (East Yorkshire) Limited
Tech Search Associates Limited
WSG Property (Holdings) Limited
Welfare Hire Nationwide Limited
Woodgreen Construction Holdings Limited

**April-June 2012** [46]

CV Anderson Ltd
Apttus EMEA Limited
Armthorpe Academy Trust
Bramhope Property and Investments Ltd
Brighouse Estate Co (Contractors) Ltd
Cap Hpi Limited
Cardale Infrastructure Investments Ltd
Cubico (UK) Limited
Dalmore Capital (Issuer 1) Limited
Dalmore Capital (Issuer 2) Limited
Dalmore Capital (Para 1) Limited
Dart Cubicles LLP
Decision First Limited
Denaro Partners LLP
Dinsdale Farming Limited
Enquire Learning Trust
Fearnley Rhodes Limited
Federation of Mowden Schools Academy Trust
D. E. Ford Holdings Limited
GD Aria Holdings #2 Limited
Grosvenor Funding Solutions Limited
Havelok Limited
Hollin Hall Holdings Limited
Howarth Timber Engineered Solutions Ltd
Kelda Finance (No.1) Limited
Kelda Finance (No.2) Limited
Leeds Real Estate Ltd
Lingfield Education Trust
Marrtree Investments Limited
Frank Marshall Estates Limited
Moortown Group Limited
Nordic Fashions One Limited
Prahi Limited
Schosween 6 Limited
Speedboat Acquisitionco Limited
Speedboat Holdco Limited
Speedboat LNCO Limited
Speedboat Midco Limited
Springfield Healthcare (The Grange) Ltd
Thornhill Community Academy Trust
Thrunscoe Primary and Nursery Academy
Tollbar Multi Academy Trust
Giovanni Tomasso Limited
UCLH Investors (Holdings) Limited
White House Livestock & Energy Limited
Yarborough Academy

**July-September 2012** [42]

Aptiv Financial Investment Services (UK) Ltd
Beckfoot Trust
Beckside Developments Limited
Boulevard Academy Trust
Brighter Futures Academy Trust
C.T. Transport (Castleford) Partnership LLP
Calder Valley Holdings Limited
D and K Chapman Limited
DG Asset Enterprise Ltd
Dalmore Capital (Para 2) Limited
Danesmoor Holdings Limited
Fellside Property Rentals Limited
Fope Limited
GES Recycling Ltd.
Ghyllside School
Healan Ingredients Limited
Hisense UK Limited
King James's School
Lakeland Arts
Logicor (CH) Limited
Lovel Capital Projects Limited

North Sea Ventilation Limited
People Apps Limited
B & B Pickard (Leeds) Limited
Pickards (Commercial) Limited
Pickards (Leeds) Limited
Premium Motorhomes Limited
John Roberts Ventures Limited
Samsung C & T ECUK Limited
Sewell Ventures Limited
GM Stephenson Farm and Commercial LLP
Thai Leisure Group Limited
Turnberry Holiday Park Limited
Uris Topco Limited
WFH Propco 1 Limited
West Park Inns Limited
West Tower Property Limited
Wilson Power Solutions Group Limited
Winterton Community Academy
Woodham Academy
Yarm Estates Limited
Yates Media Ltd

**October-December 2012** [62]

AK (SPV) Limited
Abacus Direct Manufacturing Group Ltd
Airedale Catering Equipment Group Ltd
Alt Berg Holdings Limited
Ant Hire Solutions LLP
Apelson Appliances UK Ltd
Aptiv Financial Holdings (UK) LLP
Aptiv Global Holdings (UK) Limited
Aptiv International Financial Services (UK) LLP
Ashtree Partners LLP
Aston Student Lets LLP
Auden McKenzie Holdings Limited
Batchelors Motor Group Limited
Benenden Wellbeing Limited
Beverley Funerals Limited
Bishop Konstant Catholic Academy Trust
Bradford Diocesan Academies Trust
Croda Investments Limited
Croda Investments No 2 Limited
DLG Legal Services Limited
Delphi Automotive Operations UK Limited
Dunsville Primary Academy Trust
Egg Homes Limited
Greentek Solutions Ltd
Ground-Guards Ltd
Guardian Industries UK Holding Limited
Hartshorne Crossroads Group Contracts Ltd
Humber Fishing Limited
Invalesco Limited
Jacuzzi Spa and Bath Limited
Karro Food Group Limited
Kelda Finance (No.3) PLC
Kirk Sandall Academy Trust
Lambton Clothing Company Partnership LLP
Lion/Gloria Bidco Limited
Lion/Gloria Holdco Limited
Lion/Gloria Midco 2 Limited
Lion/Gloria Midco 3 Limited
Lion/Gloria Midco Limited
Low Street Properties Limited
McCain UK H1 Limited
McCain UK H2 Limited
Northwood Tissue (Lancaster) Limited
On Line Group Limited
Orangechart Limited
PCS Property Solutions Limited
PFI Para (Holdings) Limited
Priestley Homes Limited
Redcentric Solutions Limited
Renewable Heat Generation Limited
TMD Friction Holdings (UK) Ltd
TWS Property Limited
That Company Called If Limited
Together Housing Finance PLC
Toiletry Sales Group Limited
Tradepark Limited
Tudhoe Learning Trust
UK Ambulances 2 Ltd
UK Ambulances Ltd
Viking Fishing Limited
Winder Power Holdings Limited
Yorkshire Premier Meat Limited

**January-March 2013** [51]

47A Limited
AFI Bidco Limited
AFI Midco Limited
Abracs 2013 Limited
Airedale Chemical Holdings Limited
Allied Protek Engineering Solutions Ltd
Angus Holdings Safety Group Limited
Angus International Safety Group Limited
Ashwell Academy
Bishop Wheeler Catholic Academy Trust
Blue3 (Staffs) Limited
Braegate Produce Limited
Channon Holdings Limited
Cromwell Poland Retail LLP
DBS Clothing Limited
Dakin Industries Limited
Entertainment Alliance (Holdings) Ltd
Everlast (Group) Limited
Grand Construction Products Limited
HPC Laser Holdings Limited
Hassan (Holdings) Ltd
Hector, Lamont, Florence Associates Ltd
High Hedley Hope Farm Limited
Amanda Hobson Limited
Horizon Academy Trust
J3 Business Park Doncaster LLP
JVL Homewares (UK) Limited
LPT Trading Ltd
Lupfaw 365 Limited
Mount St John Equestrian LLP
North Carr Collaborative Academy Trust
Old Clee Primary Academy
On Board Leisure (Holdings) Limited
PD & MS Holdings Limited
Pontefract Academies Trust
Redcentric PLC
Renovotec Investments Limited
Riviera Acquisitions Limited
Riviera Topco Limited
Rome Holdco Ltd
Rome Investco Ltd
Student Accommodation Provision Three LLP
TG-F Investments (No. 1) Limited
TG-F Investments (No. 2) Limited
Tall Oaks Academy Trust Ltd
Thomas Bidco Limited
Thomas Midco Limited
Thomas Topco Limited
Trinity McQueen Limited
Woodlands Academy Scarborough
XP School Trust Limited

**April-June 2013** [52]

AFI Topco Limited
Agercon Holdings Limited
Apollo 1 Investments
Apollo 11 Investments
J.N. Bentley Properties Limited
Blowers Jewellers Holdings Limited
Bramstone Limited
James C Brett (Yarn Merchants) Ltd
Caddick (Mill Harbour) Limited
Countrywide Belmont Limited
Countrywide Care Homes (3) Limited
Crossco (1317) Limited
Crossco (1318) Limited
The Manny Cussins Foundation
Dalekim Developments Limited
Dalmore Capital (Carlisle 1) Limited
Dalmore Capital (Corsham 1) Limited
Dalmore Capital (Rochdale) Limited
Dukeries Homes Limited
Durham & Tees Community Ventures Primary Care Ltd
Earthmill Holdings Limited
Euro-Pro Europe Limited
Future Forwarding (Group) Limited
Lee Gibson Properties Ltd
Gym Bidco Limited
Gym Midco 2 Limited
Gym Midco Limited
Gym Topco Limited
Jackie Hobson Investments
Hull Collaborative Academy Trust
Hull University Union Limited
Impact Education Multi Academy Trust
KVH Industries UK Limited
Laudale Estate LLP
Living Care Health Limited
M.K.M. Building Supplies (Durham) Ltd
Frank Marshall & Sons Ltd
Marshall Brothers Finance Co Limited
J & E Marshall Finance Limited
Mixer Bidco Limited
Moventas Gears UK Limited
Moventas Wind UK Limited
Outwood Investments Limited
Progarm Limited
R & R PIK Limited
Residue Limited
SIP Properties LLP
Shepherd Group Built Environment Limited
TCS (Merrion House JVCO1) Limited
Ukar Corporate Services Limited
Valad Diversified LLP
Wykeland Beverley Limited

**July-September 2013** [46]

Arris International IP Ltd
Bonmarche Holdings PLC
Cobalt Project Investments (Issuer) Ltd
Cobalt Project Investments Limited
Cohen & Wilks International (Holdings) Ltd
Cohen Cramer Limited
Cornucopia Investments Limited
DB Systel UK Limited
Dugdale Compounds Limited
ESCO EMEA Holdings (UK) Limited
Eco-Power Environmental Limited
Emovis Operations Leeds Ltd
Gatsby Property Limited
Jerry Green Dog Rescue
Haricovert Limited
Hawes & Co Limited
Humber Education Trust
INEOS Compounds Aycliffe Limited

INEOS Compounds Holdings Limited
IQRA Academy Education Trust
Icando UK Limited
Icelolly Bidco Limited
Icelolly Topco Limited
Lingholm Estate Limited
Merrion House Limited Liability Partnership
Wm Morrison Bananas Limited
Neasden Primary School
Owens Developments Ltd
Panacea Finance Solutions Limited
Parkside Property (Yorkshire) Limited
Pavers Holdings Limited
John Pawson (Holdings) Limited
Prefere Resins UK Limited
Priory Primary School
Project Aqua Bidco Limited
Project Aqua Topco Limited
Q-Park Real Estate Holding UK Limited
Q-Park Real Estate UK I Limited
Q-Park Real Estate UK II Limited
Q-Park Real Estate UK III Limited
R Safety Products Holdings Limited
Spencer Engineering Group Limited
Spring Cottage Academy
TAG Industries Limited
West Park Group Limited
Wold Farms Limited

**October-December 2013** [54]

Affordable Cars (Yorkshire) Limited
Aptiv Global Investments UK LLP
Aventador Consultancy Limited
Bremsen Technik Holdings Ltd
Broadland Energy (Donich) Limited
Broadland Energy (Laudale) Limited
Carver Engineering Holdings Limited
Chatsworth Windows Limited
Chinnaraja Estates Limited
Citu (Low Fold) LLP
Cleeve Primary School
Cleves Cross Learning Trust
Coolsilk Limited
Coolsilk Property & Investment Limited
Corrboard UK Limited
Crimson Project Investments (Issuer) Ltd
Crimson Project Investments Limited
DVV Holdco Limited
DVV Investco Limited
Dante Capital Limited
Darley Properties Limited
Doncaster Children's Services Trust Ltd
Ebor Academy Trust
Eneco Burn of Whilk Limited
Eurocentral Hotels Limited
Extremis Production Limited
Finestline Limited
Home Products Group Limited
ISS Labour Group Limited
Illuminating Investments Limited
LJV Investments Limited
Leeds Diocesan Board of Finance
Lindhurst 2013 Limited
Llandudno Bay Hotel & Spa Limited
Lundie Farming Limited
MBI Walsden Care Limited
Manor Coating Systems (Holdings) Limited
Mulard Renewables Limited
Origin Group Finance Limited
Origin Group Holdco Limited
PPDI Assetco Limited
PPDI Finance Limited
Primekings Holding Limited
Propharma Group MIS Holdings Limited
Quad Bidco Limited
Rainbow Equine Hospital Limited
Rhinox Group Ltd
Rose Learning Trust
Shirestone Estates Limited
Sirdar Properties Limited
Timec 1444 Limited
Vapour Cloud Limited
Wothersome Limited
YP Real Estate Limited

**January-March 2014** [72]

4D Pharma PLC
Akebar Park Leisure Limited
Ashcourt Farms Limited
Berkeley de Veer Limited
Carillion Powerlines Limited
Castle Crown Properties Limited
Cloth Fair Point Capital Limited
Comedian's Guide To Survival Limited
Conservatory Outlet Group Limited
Crown Acquisition Bidco Limited
Crown Acquisition Midco 2 Limited
Crown Acquisition Midco Limited
Crown Acquisition Topco Limited
Deeside Power (UK) Limited
Devonshire Square Properties Limited
Doorway Holdings Limited
Eleonora Sport Limited
Fairbriar Real Estate Developments Ltd
Fairbriar Real Estate Limited
GHD BondCo PLC
GSM Automotive Holdings Limited
GSM Group Holdco Limited
Samuel Grant (Holdings) Ltd
Hair Burst Limited
Hutton Wandesley Estate LLP
ICR (Investment 1) Limited
ICR (Investment 2) Limited
ICR Integrity (Group) Limited
ICR Integrity (Holdings) Limited
Imbue Property Ltd
Impact (UK) Limited
Inn at Grasmere Limited
Inspire Holding Co Ltd
Itch Propco Limited
JMCD Investments Limited
JT Holdings (UK) Limited
JTE Holdco Limited
Kankku (Holdings) Limited
Keep Your Trap Shut Limited
Lido Leisure Parks Limited
Logistik Holdings Limited
M Rugs Limited
MMCD Investments Limited
Maria Mallaband 16 Limited
Manheim Holdings Limited
Mech-Tool Holdings Limited
Miles Partnership Limited
Mosaic Print Management Holdco Limited
Murton Feeds Limited
Prism Medical Healthcare Limited
Procters Coaches (North Yorkshire No3) Ltd
Q Underwriting Services Limited
Quay Propco Limited
Redstart Renewables Limited
Sargents Properties Limited
Shree Investment PLC
Snaith School Academy Trust
Stell Cardboard Tubes Limited
Stroma Group Limited
Stroma Holdings Limited
TGH Capital Limited
TPP Finance Limited
TPPH (Leeds) Limited
That Good Night Limited
Triline (2014) Limited
Neville Tucker (Group) Limited
Varnish Bidco Limited
Varnish Topco Limited
Wakefield88 Limited
Westpoint Group Trading Limited
V Wilkins & Sons Limited
York House Investment Co Ltd

**April-June 2014** [70]

Absolutely Cultured Limited
Adler & Allan Group Limited
Apollo Endosurgery UK Ltd
Aptiv Latin America Holdings (UK) LLP
Birkett Bogmats Limited
Blessed Peter Snow Catholic Academy Trust
Call Lane Social Leeds Limited
Card Factory PLC
Carlton Court Investments Limited
Communisis Data Intelligence Limited
Craven Educational Trust
EPTA Service UK Limited
Eleven Arches
Entertainment Alliance (UK) Limited
Evans Dakota Hotels Limited
Exemplary Group PLC
Felldale Retail Limited
James Fisher MFE Limited
Futurama Signs Holdings Limited
Gatenbysanderson Holdings Limited
Gatenbysanderson Midco Limited
HGF Limited
Hadrian (Residential) Limited
Hird & Partners LLP
Hire It Plant Limited
IUKH Limited
KCA Deutag UK Finance PLC
Kelling Midco Limited
Kelling Property Limited
Kexby Investments Limited
Keystone Bidco Limited
Keystone Financing PLC
Keystone JVCO Limited
Keystone Midco Limited
Keystone Topco Limited
LNT Care Developments Limited
Lindley Church of England Infant School
Lookrich Ltd
MBI Hawthorn Care Limited
MMCG Holdings Limited
Moda Living (Angel Gardens) Limited
Monks Cross Property Ltd
Navartis Holdings Limited
Nightjar Sustainable Power Limited
Oakmere Homes (Lancaster) Limited
Ortus Secured Finance III Limited
Osprey Green Power Limited
PLS Civil Engineering Limited
Pagani UK Limited
Polyframe Norwich Ltd
Provenance Hospitality Holdings Limited
Provenance Hotels Limited
Punch Bowl Investments Limited
Rabbit (Holdings) Limited
Ryburn Valley High School
Siccar Point Energy (Holdings) Limited

Siccar Point Energy Finance Limited
Siccar Point Energy Limited
Somlie Limited
Sovereign Build Limited
Tampnet UK Limited
Therma Q Limited
Thirsk Investments Limited
Vida Grange Limited
Vida Healthcare Limited
Michael Wheatley Finance Limited
Wolds Investments Limited
Xander 97 Limited
Yorkshire Initiatives Limited
Yorplace Limited

**July-September 2014** [41]

56 George Street Limited
AGS Airports Holdings Limited
AGS Airports Investments Limited
AGS Airports Limited
Ballards Removals Holdings Limited
Binks (Holdings) Limited
Blackshaw Properties (2014) Limited
Bolster Moor Farm Shop Limited
Boston Mayflower Finance PLC
Braavos Investments Limited
CPPGroup Services Limited
Catfoss Renewables Ltd
Colne Topco Limited
Crossgreen Investments Limited
Crystal Investment Holdings Limited
Cyan Bidco Limited
Dalmore Capital (Rochdale 2) Limited
Financial Funding Limited
Harrowells Limited
Havwoods Global Holdings Limited
Idigital Investments Ltd
Karro Food Frozen Limited
Keystone Healthcare Holdings Limited
Mailing & Marketing Solutions Ltd
Moda Living Limited
Mysing Capital Limited
Nickle Holdings Limited
Non-Standard Finance PLC
One Stop Business Finance Limited
Opera North Productions Limited
Ozziefields Limited
Prospect Business Centres (Old Jewry) Ltd
Prospero Growth Limited
Scarborough International Properties Ltd
Stadium Retail Group Limited
Standeven Holdings Ltd
Stork Beta Limited
Strata Homes Holdings Limited
Waterton Academy Trust
White Rose Residential Sales Limited
Yorkshire Housing Finance PLC

**October-December 2014** [55]

AHR Management Services LLP
Aptiv Financial Services (UK) Limited
Ashcourt Properties (Newland) Limited
Atlantic Acquisition Holdings UK Limited
BBRG Finance (UK) Ltd.
BBRG Operations (UK) Ltd.
BBRG Production (UK) Ltd.
Bridge Properties & Investments Limited
Bridon-Bekaert Ropes Group (UK) Ltd
Bridon-Bekaert Ropes Group Ltd
Broad Carr Investments Limited
C C Properties (Yorkshire) Ltd
Caddick (City One) Limited
Colne Investments 2 Holdco Limited
FMG Finance Limited
FMG Group Holdings Limited
GD Global Holdings UK II Limited
GEV Holdings Limited
Ganton School
Hodson Family Investments Limited
IHS Lothian Corporate Holdings Limited
JPI (Holdings) Limited
S Jackson & Sons Holdings Limited
Jam Homes Ltd
Justmerc Limited
Makin Developments Wakefield Ltd
Mysing Investments 2 Limited
Mysing Investments 3 Limited
Mysing Investments 4 Limited
Neal Investments Limited
One Commercial Limited
P.P. Group Holdings Limited
Peover Eye Investments Limited
Pettra Limited
Christopher Pickering Primary School
Principal Hotel Co Ltd
Principal Hotels Topco 1 Limited
Principal Hotels Topco 3 Limited
QWP Limited
Res-Q Outsourcing Solutions Limited
Rural & Commercial Holdings Limited
SHFT Properties Ltd
SHG (Care Villages) Limited
SNG Commercial (Holdings) Limited
SP & PL Holdings Limited
SSP Midco 2 Limited
Sheds for Logistics Limited
Siena Bidco Limited
Siena Holdco Limited
Silverback Developments Limited
Tereos UK & Ireland Ltd
Trinity Developments Leeds Ltd
Wellesley Holdco Limited
Wire Estates Limited
Yorkshire and Humberside Co-operative Academies Trust

**January 2015** [19]

Ashcourt (Durham) Limited
Blues Kitchen Brixton Limited
Boutique Workplace Co Ltd
Cromwell European Holdings Limited
J H Dixon & Son LLP
Fine Motor Cars Ltd
Fortis Foods Limited
GSD Riverside Limited
Kendal Nutricare Ltd
Leeds and London Group Ltd
Money4yourmotors.Com Limited
Oakvine Limited
On-Site Property Solutions Limited
RFS (Ripon) Limited
Ravens Ing Properties Limited
Stevro (Holdings) Limited
TGC (2015) Limited
Townham Limited
Stan Weston LLP

**February 2015** [23]

Bayfields Z Limited
Birch Valley Holdings Limited
Bishopdyke Enterprises Limited
British Steel Limited
Clifford Street Venture LLP
James Fisher Subtech Group Limited
Froneri South Africa Holdings Limited
GBUK Group Limited
Horsforth Mill Limited
Hull Culture and Leisure Limited
Hunters Property PLC
IPN Bidco Limited
IPN Midco 1 Limited
IPN Midco 2 Limited
IPN Topco Limited
Ivy Farm Limited
Lune Holdings Limited
Reward Capital Limited
Reward Invoice Finance Limited
SSP Topco Limited
Videcon Holdings Limited
Willow Properties (Yorkshire) Limited
Wrapid Investments Limited

**March 2015** [23]

ADW Enterprises Limited
Aptiv European Holdings (UK) Limited
C B T Clinics Limited
Camira Group Holdings Limited
Cardale PFI Investments Limited
Devonshire Club (Holdings) Limited
Foot Forward Property Investments Ltd
Forward Investment Group LLP
Forward Investment Pannal LLP
G-Tuft (2015) Limited
Garth Pig Practice Limited
Hider Group Holdings Limited
High Street TV Bidco Limited
High Street TV Holdings Limited
Huntington Primary Academy
Lakeland Fashion Limited
Ossett Holdings Limited
R and A Hotels Group Ltd
Redline Worldwide Limited
Rradar (Holdings) Limited
Sing Ko Limited
Sirdar Group Limited
Withernsea Primary Academy Trust

**April 2015** [14]

AKV Group Ltd
Arris International PLC
Bear Leisure Limited
Brother Bidco Limited
Camira Holdings Limited
GBA Group Limited
GM Legato Limited
Hallriver Holdings Limited
Lingard Bell Limited
Pure Technology Group Limited
Hugh Rice Holdings Limited
Sidhil Group Limited
William's Den Limited
Yorkshire Botanicals Limited

**May 2015** [9]

Actavis UK Group Limited
Brother Topco Limited
CYBG PLC
Emic Group Limited
Matrix Chemie Holdings Limited
Mayflower Specialist School Academy Trust
Mill Mount Properties Limited
Plum Bidco Limited
State Bidco Limited

**June 2015** [12]
AMT2 Limited
Arboretum Devon (RLH) Limited
Aura DC Limited
Autohorn Group Limited
Canons Garth LLP
Carnaby Caravans Group Limited
Gilkes Hydro Investments Limited
Morris Family Investments Ltd
Pacific Shelf 1809 Limited
Simplybiz Group PLC
Taodail Hydro Limited
Venn Academy Trust

**July 2015** [20]
ACS Stainless Limited
DVV Properties 2 Limited
Dining Club Group Limited
Grantley Hall Group Limited
Greens Desserts UK Ltd
Harvard Group Holdings Limited
K Hewitt Holdings Limited
Inspired Learning Multi Academy Trust
Madala Limited
Mysing Care Limited
NL Commercials Holdings Limited
Non-Standard Finance Subsidiary II Ltd
PAS Holding Co Ltd
Rural Concepts (Libya) Limited
Simon Bidco Limited
State Debtco Limited
State Interco Limited
Steadplan Group Limited
Yorkshire Collaborative Academy Trust
Yorkshire House Development One Limited

**August 2015** [16]
Amberbeach Ltd.
Aptiv Asia Pacific Holdings (UK) LLP
Charlesworth Family Group Limited
GW Hire Limited
Hannibal Holdings Limited
Jones & Egan Estates Limited
Ormsborough Limited
Queens Hotel (Llandudno) Limited
Scarborough Thorpe Park Holdings Limited
Simon Midco Limited
Sissons of Sherburn Holdings Limited
Thorpe Park Holdings Limited
Vetpartners Group Finance Limited
Vetpartners UK Holdings Ltd.
YM Group Limited
Z & D Property Investments Limited

**September 2015** [23]
Adina Developments Ltd
Beaumont ABS Ltd
Blencathra Hydro Limited
Brass Agency Group Limited
Kingstown Associates (Holdings) Limited
MCP Environmental Limited
McManus Group Holdings Limited
Mount Vale Venture LLP
Myrtle Grange Renewables Limited
Oakesway Limited
Paramount Wholesale Ltd
Peagar Ltd
Polypearl Management Ltd
Red Circle Investments Limited
Sissons Depot Limited
Sissons Limited
Turner & Townsend Holdings Limited
Turner & Townsend Partners LLP
Venturian Property Development Limited
Venturian Property Holdings Limited
WMT Global Holdings LLP
Willow Developments (Howden) Ltd
Alan Wood Holdings Limited

**October 2015** [13]
CPD Direct Limited
Home Marketing Group Ltd
Homes for Students Limited
Mantis Holdings Ltd
Murphy (Yorkshire) Ltd
Navenio Limited
Non-Standard Finance Subsidiary III Ltd
Redline Holdings Limited
Rosti Automotive Pickering Ltd.
Rosti Automotive Stamford Bridge Ltd.
Rosti UK Ltd.
Vcep Limited
Whinlatter Energy Limited

**November 2015** [28]
Access Property Finance Limited
Appleyard Lees IP LLP
Avant Worldwide Ltd
Axis Bidco Limited
Axis Midco Limited
Axis Topco Limited
Beatty Topco Limited
Br1dge Estates Limited
Brecks Holdings Limited
Broadway (SPV) Limited
Bulmer & Lumb Holdings Limited
CMG Lancaster Limited
Cox Motor Group Limited
DCSW Ltd
Drax Group Holdings Limited
EPMS Group Limited
EWH Holdco Limited
James Fisher Holdings UK Limited
GO2 Foods Limited
Hindle Gears Holdings Limited
Manheim Global Management UK Limited
Martindale Group Limited
Paramount Retail Group Holdco Limited
S & A Builders Merchants Limited
Siccar Point Energy U.K. Limited
Universal Group Holdings Limited
Vetuk Limited
Yorkshire Ventures (Estates) Limited

**December 2015** [23]
Aptiv Luxembourg Holdings (UK) Limited
BBRG (Subsidiary) Ltd
BBRG Holding (UK) Ltd
Broomgrove Developments Limited
Cielivestock Limited
Croda Investments No 3 Limited
Crop Health and Protection Limited
Crown Acquisition Consumer Limited
HLD (Manchester) Limited
JCCO 387 Limited
Martins Bidco Limited
Metanoia Film Limited
Wm Morrison Growers Limited
PIB Group Limited
Quarters Developments Limited
RDG Midas Holdings (NI) Limited
RSP Investments Limited
Schultz Bidco Limited
Sharp Holdings Limited
Square Peg Properties Limited
TCS (Whitehall Plaza) Limited
Three Sixty Water Limited
XTR Holding Limited

**January 2016** [16]
Avenue Lets Limited
Cockburn Multi Academy Trust
Dalmore Group Limited
Dalmore Intermediate Limited
Forest Homes Limited
LDK Investments Ltd
NL Commercials Management Ltd
Nippon Gases UK Limited
Northern Powerhouse Developments Limited
Paragon Foodservice Limited
Project Rock Bidco Limited
Project Rock Equityco Limited
Rawson Brook Group Holdings Limited
Rockar 2016 Limited
SWC Trade Frames Limited
TD Holdings Ltd

**February 2016** [19]
All Property Management Ltd
BBRG (Purchaser) Ltd
BKS Holdings Limited
C T Glass Holdings Limited
D & L S Developments Limited
Doncaster Property Trading Limited
End of Term Limited
GM Legato Property Limited
Gott Agri Synergy Limited
Karl Hanover Properties Limited
Hillas Group Limited
Holden Grange Care Group Limited
Jito Trading Limited
KWH (Hull) Limited
Potter Family Holdings Limited
Potters Farm Production LLP
Triton Construction Holdings Limited
Vetpartners Group Limited
Yamuna Renewables Limited

**March 2016** [32]
Armstrong Priestley Holdings Limited
S J Bargh Group Limited
Birstall 140 Limited
Bulk Logistics Group Ltd
CRG Holdings Ltd
Cater-Kwik Group Limited
J Cooper Properties Limited
DSS Group Limited
Jaskaran S Deu Properties Limited
ERM Regulatory Services Limited
Ebus Ltd
Exceed Academies Trust
G2M Capital Limited
Giacom Holdings Limited
Glen Mhor Estates Limited
Hanbeck Properties Limited
Hassan Group Limited
Kubler Holdings Limited
Nurture Academies Trust
Power Topco Limited
Redruth Holdings Limited
Reed Group Ltd
SKB2016 Limited

Scho62 Investments Limited
Solis Film Limited
South Bank Multi Academy Trust
Tekjur Limited
UKGlobal Holdings Limited
Vetpartners Practices Limited
Waiting for Anya Limited
Wilton Cobley (Holdings) Limited
YLC Holdings Limited

**April 2016** [15]

Abacus Direct Properties Limited
Aqmen Holdings Limited
Athena PTS Holdings Limited
Clicklink Logistics Limited
Compass Broker Networks Limited
AE Cook Holdings Limited
Cyan Blue Core Limited
DCMK Limited
Elmet Investments
Froneri Limited
Kwiktuf Holdings Limited
Samara Properties Limited
Savers Wholesale Ltd
Track Record Holdings Limited
YPP Holdings Limited

**May 2016** [18]

ABI Bidco Limited
ABI Midco Limited
Aghoco 1419 Limited
Applied Composites Group Ltd
British Steel Holdings Limited
Bronte Academy Trust
YM Chantry Limited
Halbert Limited
Harpin Parkin Aviation Limited
Loscoe Investments Ltd
Paw Topco Limited
Project Tulip Topco Limited
RP Net Media Ltd
Rockar 2 Limited
Talbert Limited
Tuby Leisure Ltd
Virtual College Holdings Limited
Willoughby (891) Limited

**June 2016** [20]

Abstract (Bristol) Limited
Acer Healthcare Operations Limited
Advanced Supply Chain (Logistics) Ltd
Alexanders Prestige Group Limited
Bishopton Veterinary Group LLP
Teddy Clark Group Limited
HC-ONE Oval Limited
Interaction and Communication Academy Trust Ltd
Lifterz Holdings Limited
Living Care Pharmacy Group Limited
Long Folly Limited
Polyframe Halifax Limited
Project Light Bidco Limited
Project Light Cleanco Limited
Project Light Midco Limited
Project Light Topco Limited
Roubaix Bidco Limited
Scientific Laboratory Supplies Group Ltd
York123 Limited
Zain Holdings Limited

**July 2016** [21]

Atkinson Group (Yorkshire) Limited
Birch Close Trading Ltd
Brigshaw Learning Partnership
Broker Network Partner Holdings Limited
Chartford Developments Limited
Collett & Sons Limited
Collett Holdings Limited
Corkel Holdings Limited
Hull Citycare (Fundco 6) Limited
Hunter Holdings Limited
Kexgill (Cottingham) 2 Limited
Learning Accord Multi Academy Trust
Marshall Wooldridge Group Holdings Ltd
Moorgarth Living Limited
Moorgarth Retail Limited
Newbegin Holdings Limited
Proma Boatman Limited
Prosperity Noor Ltd
Tandem 1987 Limited
Team 17 Holdings Limited
Verulam Holdings Limited

**August 2016** [10]

Century Construction Limited
Cook & Lucas Frozen (Holdings) Limited
Simon Cook Holdings Limited
Everard Group Limited
Graypen Holdings Limited
Holmfirth Dyers Holdings Limited
Ossett Brewery Group Holdings Limited
Park Valley Huddersfield Limited
Serenity Parks Limited
Yorkshire Sheeting Group Limited

**September 2016** [19]

B.W. Industries (Group) Limited
Coachman Group Limited
Dalmore Highway Investment Holdings Ltd
Derwent Dale Limited
Epil Carlisle Limited
Holdco 123 Limited
C.G. Kendall Limited
R. Kendall Limited
Mast Academy Trust
Mitrefinch Holdings Limited
Moolmoor Holdings Limited
Moolmoor Investments Limited
Techbuyer Group Holdings Limited
Three60 Energy Limited
Visit Yorkshire Holdings Ltd
Waterside Colours Limited
Westdale Group Limited
Yorkshire and The Humber Co-operative Learning Trust
Zeus Bidco Limited

**October 2016** [16]

Checkmate Holdings Ltd
Duchy Homes (Humshaugh) Limited
EMHEDA Limited
Glasshouses123 Limited
Harrogate14 Limited
I A P Investments Ltd
IETG Holdings Limited
Iconx Holdings Limited
KSDL Land Limited
Kokoon Holdings Limited
Middlewood Locks Residential Limited
Penman MW Limited
Priestley Academy Trust
Roxor Group Limited
Smarts of York Limited
Zenith International Freight Holdings Ltd

**November 2016** [10]

Atlantic Bay Hotel (Woolacombe) Limited
Chicago Bidco Limited
Chicago Midco Limited
Cobalt Project Investments (Hull - Sewell) Ltd
GDS Holdings Limited
Leeds Cares
Londyne Limited
Mark Proudfoot Investments Ltd
Takahe Holdings Ltd
Woolrow Farm Limited

**December 2016** [19]

123 Retail Limited
A-Safe UK Ltd
CCL Syrinx (UK) Limited
CIP (Mill Road Development) LLP
FC Beamish Bidco Ltd
Grand Principal Birmingham Limited
Ideal Carehomes Limited
Andrew Jackson Solicitors LLP
Lassic Properties Limited
Leisure Resorts Limited
Link Scheme Holdings Ltd
Lone Star Estates (1) Limited
Southgate - Dan at Spyglass Hill - Bidco Ltd
Stearsby Hagg Property Co Ltd
Stowe Family Law Finance Limited
Stowe Family Law Holdings Limited
Stratex Warehouse Ltd
Varnish Intermediate Holdco Limited
Wolds Learning Partnership

**January 2017** [16]

AWLC Limited
Burlington Care Holdings Limited
Andrew Lumley Limited
Lymington Holdings Limited
Malton Road Developments Limited
Mena Commercial Limited
Mena Developments Limted Limited
Mena Residential Limited
Mone Brothers Group Ltd
Moolmoor (Waverley) Limited
Oakwood Veterinary Practice Limited
SEA Holdings (UK) Limited
Steeper Group Holdings Limited
Zenith Automotive Holdings Limited
Zeus Finco Limited
Zeus Midco Limited

**February 2017** [28]

Atherton Godfrey LLP
Berry Investment Holdings Limited
Brunswick Court Development (Leeds) Ltd
CG Estates Limited
CI Estates Limited
CR Estates Limited
Clark Care Estates Limited
Dream Property Holdco Limited
Hambleton Steel Group Ltd
Harder Bros (Holdings) Limited
Harmony Bridge Limited
JMC Developments (Hunslet) Limited
M.K.M. BS (Holdings) 1 Limited
M.K.M. BS (Holdings) 2 Limited
M.K.M. BS (Holdings) 3 Limited
M.K.M. Building Supplies (Group) Limited
Magenta Prime Limited
Metamark Group Holdings Limited
Mulgrave Property Group Limited
One Fortress Limited
Outform EMEA Limited
Park Leisure Group Limited
Ravensfield Properties Limited
Sedbergh Hotel Enterprises Limited
Southgate - Dan at Spyglass Hill - Propco 1 Ltd
Southgate - Dan at Spyglass Hill - Propco 2 Ltd
Stamp Jackson & Procter Limited
TEV Holdings Limited

**March 2017** [24]

A-Fax Holdings Limited
Academic Appointments 2017 Limited
CNIM Clugston (Avonmouth) Limited
Coral Project Investments (Assetco) Ltd
Coral Project Investments (Issuer) Ltd
Dart Leasing & Finance Limited
Drax Finco PLC
Drax Smart Supply Holdco Limited
Element UK Bidco Limited
Element UK Holdco Limited
Element UK Midco Limited
Element UK Topco Limited
Empowering Minds Academy Trust
Exceed Learning Partnership
Glentrool Land and Estates Limited
HEM Holdings Limited
Inspiring Futures Academy Trust
JPT Group Limited
Letts Properties Limited
Ligentia Group Holdings Limited
Redruth Holdings 2 Limited
Scriven Park Estates Limited
Springfield Healthcare (Grove House) Ltd
Mary Randall Vickers & Co Limited

**April 2017** [9]

DC3 (Assetco) Limited
DC3 (Issuer) Limited
Harrogate Steel Trading Ltd
Kirkby 2017 Limited
MBR Acres Limited
Provu Holdings Limited
Royd House Investments Limited
Torsion Group Holdings Limited
Walkers Holdings One Limited

**May 2017**

Abzorb Group Ltd
Barden Biomass Holdings Limited
ERS Transition Limited
Ral Holdings Limited

**June 2017** [14]

Adare SEC Holdings Limited
Alphabet BC Limited
Ames Companies UK Ltd.
CCL Syrinx (UK Holding) Limited
Duchy Homes (Holdings) Limited
Elevate Multi Academy Trust
Frear Investments Limited
Wm Morrison Supermarkets Holdings Ltd
Pointer Holdings Limited
Transit 2017 Limited
WGL Bidco Limited
WGL Holdco Limited
WGL Midco Limited
Yorktest Group Limited

**July 2017** [5]

Colenso Holdings Limited
Hamsard 3465 Limited
Hamsard 3466 Limited
Links Investment Holdings Limited
Parkhead Investments Limited

**August 2017**

Primus Alliance Nottingham Limited
Twentyfour28 Limited

**October 2017**

Encounter Production Limited

**November 2017**

Beckenreid Limited

**December 2017**

Arena Capital MP Limited

*This page is intentionally left blank*

# Company Profiles

**(Aq) Limited**
*Incorporated:* 9 November 1998 *Employees:* 76
*Net Worth:* £4,686,043 *Total Assets:* £8,496,552
*Registered Office:* 13-15 Hunslet Road, Leeds, LS10 1JQ
*Activities:* Other telecommunications activities
*Major Shareholder:* Adam Jason Beaumont
*Officers:* Stephen Mark Neale, Secretary/Solicitor; Dr Adam Jason Beaumont [1972] Director

**(Aq) Networks Limited**
*Incorporated:* 11 July 2001
*Net Worth:* £5,041,785 *Total Assets:* £5,558,332
*Registered Office:* 13-15 Hunslet Road, Leeds, LS10 1JQ
*Activities:* Other telecommunications activities
*Major Shareholder:* Adam Jason Beaumont
*Officers:* Stephen Mark Neale, Secretary; Dr Adam Jason Beaumont [1972] Director

**121 Mountco 074 Limited**
*Incorporated:* 5 May 2006
*Net Worth:* £1,662,223 *Total Assets:* £4,203,688
*Registered Office:* 2 South Park Road, Harrogate, N Yorks, HG1 5QU
*Activities:* Construction of commercial buildings
*Major Shareholder:* Alan Burke
*Officers:* Philip Ashworth, Secretary; Alan Burke [1952] Director/Developer

**123 Leeds Limited**
*Incorporated:* 19 December 1984 *Employees:* 806
*Net Worth Deficit:* £2,321,397 *Total Assets:* £54,064,892
*Registered Office:* 1 Bridgewater Place, Water Lane, Leeds, LS11 5RU
*Activities:* Dispensing chemist in specialised stores
*Officers:* Graeme Ramsay Murdoch, Secretary/Accountant; Stewart Mein [1971] Director/Chartered Accountant; David Charles Moulsdale [1968] Director/Optician; June Moulsdale [1964] Director/Dispensing Optician

**123 Retail Limited**
*Incorporated:* 21 December 2016
*Net Worth:* £220,943 *Total Assets:* £3,423,922
*Registered Office:* 34 Roundhay Road, Leeds, LS7 1AB
*Activities:* Other letting and operating of own or leased real estate
*Major Shareholder:* Stephen Andrew Buck
*Officers:* Stephen Andrew Buck [1958] Director/Business Owner

**2 Plan Group Limited**
*Incorporated:* 4 July 2006
*Net Worth Deficit:* £17,362,444 *Total Assets:* £8,902,219
*Registered Office:* 3rd Floor, Bridgewater Place, Water Lane, Leeds, LS11 5BZ
*Activities:* Activities of head offices
*Parent:* Openwork Independent Solutions Limited
*Officers:* Peter Davis [1960] Director; Nicolas Keith Hewitt [1970] Director; Michael David George Morrow [1968] Director; Christopher Mark Smallwood [1963] Director; Mark Smith [1969] Director; Michael Anthony Williams [1982] Director

**2 Plan Wealth Management Limited**
*Incorporated:* 14 November 2006
*Net Worth:* £3,745,573 *Total Assets:* £7,012,711
*Registered Office:* 3rd Floor, Bridgewater Place, Water Lane, Leeds, LS11 5BZ
*Activities:* Financial intermediation not elsewhere classified
*Parent:* 2 Plan Group Limited
*Officers:* Nicolas Keith Hewitt [1970] Director; Christopher Mark Smallwood [1963] Director

**2 Sister Food Services Limited**
*Incorporated:* 28 November 1997
*Net Worth:* £3,234,000 *Total Assets:* £3,586,000
*Registered Office:* Trinity Park House, Trinity Business Park, Fox Way, Wakefield, W Yorks, WF2 8EE
*Activities:* Wholesale of meat and meat products
*Parent:* Boparan Holdings Limited
*Officers:* Ranjit Singh Boparan [1966] Director/Secretary; Baljinder Kaur Boparan [1968] Director; Ronald Klaas Otto Kers [1969] Director/Group CEO [Dutch]; Craig Ashley Tomkinson [1982] Director/Group CFO

**2 Sisters Food Group Limited**
*Incorporated:* 15 June 1993 *Employees:* 5,835
*Net Worth Deficit:* £39,694,000 *Total Assets:* £773,107,968
*Registered Office:* Trinity Park House, Trinity Business Park, Fox Way, Wakefield, W Yorks, WF2 8EE
*Activities:* Processing and preserving of poultry meat
*Parent:* Boparan Holdings Limited
*Officers:* Ranjit Singh Boparan [1966] Director; Baljinder Kaur Boparan [1968] Director/Manager; Ronald Klaas Otto Kers [1969] Director/Group CEO [Dutch]; Andrew Ronald McInnes [1972] Managing Director; Craig Ashley Tomkinson [1982] Director/Group CFO

**24 Seven Communications Limited**
*Incorporated:* 25 June 2002 *Employees:* 13
*Net Worth:* £2,979,566 *Total Assets:* £7,152,069
*Registered Office:* Novis & Co Chartered Accountants, 1 Victoria Court, Bank Square, Morley, Leeds, LS27 9SE
*Activities:* Other telecommunications activities
*Major Shareholder:* David Anthony Samuel
*Officers:* Lyndsay Jayne Samuel, Secretary; David Anthony Samuel [1975] Director; Lyndsay Jayne Samuel [1978] Director

**47A Limited**
*Incorporated:* 15 March 2013
*Net Worth:* £108,508 *Total Assets:* £3,091,950
*Registered Office:* 33 Summervale, Holmfirth, W Yorks, HD9 7AG
*Activities:* Other letting and operating of own or leased real estate
*Major Shareholder:* Gregory Cross
*Officers:* Gregory Cross [1970] Director

**4B Braime Components Limited**
*Incorporated:* 28 May 1974 *Employees:* 25
*Previous:* Braime Elevator Components Limited
*Net Worth:* £4,799,009 *Total Assets:* £9,605,028
*Registered Office:* Hunslet Road, Leeds, LS10 1JZ
*Activities:* Manufacture of lifting and handling equipment
*Shareholders:* T.F. & J.H. Braime (Holdings) P.L.C; T.F & J.H Braime (Holdings) P.L.C
*Officers:* Cielo Malaluan Bicol Cartwright, Secretary; Alan Quentin Braime [1981] Commercial Director; Carl Oliver Braime [1979] Sales Director; Oliver Nicholas Anderson Braime [1950] Sales Director; Cielo Bicol Cartwright [1963] Finance Director; Robert Fieldsend [1958] Director/Engineer

**4B Elevator Components Limited**
*Incorporated:* 20 June 1962 *Employees:* 37
*Net Worth:* £3,031,439 *Total Assets:* £6,009,338
*Registered Office:* Hunslet Road, Leeds, LS10 1JZ
*Activities:* Manufacture of lifting and handling equipment
*Shareholders:* T.F. & J.H. Braime (Holdings) P.L.C; TF & JH Braime (Holdings) PLC
*Officers:* Cielo Malaluan Bicol Cartwright, Secretary; Alan Quentin Braime [1981] Commercial Director; Carl Oliver Braime [1979] Sales Director; Oliver Nicholas Anderson Braime [1950] Sales Director; Cielo Bicol Cartwright [1963] Finance Director; Jonathan Norman Wheat [1965] Director/Engineer

**4D Pharma PLC**
*Incorporated:* 10 January 2014 *Employees:* 93
*Net Worth:* £69,786,000 *Total Assets:* £77,738,000
*Registered Office:* 4D Pharma PLC, 9 Bond Court, Leeds, LS1 2JZ
*Activities:* Other research and experimental development on natural sciences and engineering
*Officers:* Laurence Smith Dale, Secretary; Dr. Edgardo Baracchini [1959] Director [American]; Thomas Engelen [1958] Director [Dutch]; Axel Gaston Glasmacher [1960] Director/Consultant [German]; David Robert Norwood [1968] Director; Duncan Joseph Peyton [1970] Director; Alexander James Stevenson [1971] Director

**4L's Products Limited**
*Incorporated:* 4 February 2005 *Employees:* 16
*Net Worth:* £900,755 *Total Assets:* £3,450,515
*Registered Office:* 4L's Products Ltd, Coulman Street, Thorne, Doncaster, S Yorks, DN8 5JS
*Activities:* Operation of warehousing and storage facilities for land transport activities
*Officers:* Colette Porter, Secretary; Peter Holling [1965] Director; Colette Melanie Porter [1975] Finance Director

**4urban (Harrogate) Limited**
*Incorporated:* 20 August 2009
*Net Worth:* £895,400 *Total Assets:* £11,909,900
*Registered Office:* 30 Victoria Avenue, Harrogate, N Yorks, HG1 5PR
*Activities:* Development of building projects
*Parent:* 4 Urban (Holdings) Limited
*Officers:* Suzannah Clare Allard [1968] Director; Rebecca Helen Bletcher [1969] Director/Property Developer; Elizabeth Bramall [1944] Director; Terence George Bramall [1942] Director

**4x4 Accessories & Tyres Limited**
*Incorporated:* 14 August 2002 *Employees:* 40
*Net Worth:* £7,161,393 *Total Assets:* £11,853,743
*Registered Office:* Meridian Park, Leeming Bar Industrial Estate, Leeming Bar, N Yorks, DL7 9UN
*Activities:* Wholesale trade of motor vehicle parts and accessories
*Shareholder:* Timothy Snowden
*Officers:* Ian Christopher Robinson [1963] Finance Director; Timothy Snowden [1973] Director

**56 George Street Limited**
*Incorporated:* 24 September 2014
*Net Worth:* £637,149 *Total Assets:* £4,190,888
*Registered Office:* 137 Scalby Road, Scarborough, N Yorks, YO12 6TB
*Activities:* Other letting and operating of own or leased real estate
*Officers:* Barry Peter Swiers, Secretary; Peter John Guthrie [1971] Director; Richard Guthrie [1972] Director

**600 Group (Overseas) Limited (The)**
*Incorporated:* 20 February 1958
*Net Worth Deficit:* £381,000 *Total Assets:* £10,526,000
*Registered Office:* 1 Union Works, Union Street, Heckmondwike, W Yorks, WF16 0HL
*Activities:* Activities of head offices
*Parent:* The 600 Group PLC
*Officers:* Neil Richard Carrick [1961] Finance Director; Paul Rich Dupee [1943] Director/Chief Executive [American]

**600 Group Public Limited Company (The)**
*Incorporated:* 26 March 1924 *Employees:* 217
*Net Worth:* £45,033,352 *Total Assets:* £81,121,672
*Registered Office:* 1 Union Works, Union Street, Heckmondwike, W Yorks, WF16 0HL
*Activities:* Manufacture of other machine tools
*Officers:* Neil Richard Carrick, Secretary; Neil Richard Carrick [1961] Finance Director; Paul Rich Dupee [1943] Director/Investor [American]; Stephen Eugene Fiamma [1953] Director [American]; Stephen John Rutherford [1951] Director; Derek Zissman [1944] Director/Chartered Accountant

**600 UK Limited**
*Incorporated:* 30 September 1916 *Employees:* 89
*Net Worth:* £12,333,000 *Total Assets:* £51,912,000
*Registered Office:* 1 Union Works, Union Street, Heckmondwike, W Yorks, WF16 0HL
*Activities:* Manufacture of other machine tools
*Parent:* The 600 Group PLC
*Officers:* Andrew Donald Tearne, Secretary; Neil Richard Carrick [1961] Finance Director; Paul Rich Dupee [1943] Director/Chairman [American]

**8point8 Support Limited**
*Incorporated:* 8 September 2010 *Employees:* 157
*Net Worth:* £2,363,590 *Total Assets:* £6,723,066
*Registered Office:* Unit 12 Yorkshire Way, Armthorpe, Doncaster, S Yorks, DN3 3FE
*Activities:* Wireless telecommunications activities
*Shareholders:* Martin Debnam; Karl Martin Hampson
*Officers:* Martin Debnam [1970] Director; Karl Martin Hampson [1975] Director; Duncan Sam Storer [1975] Commercial Director

**A & K Hosiery Limited**
*Incorporated:* 3 February 1994 *Employees:* 7
*Net Worth:* £2,791,426 *Total Assets:* £3,312,785
*Registered Office:* Valentine Trade Park, 104 Gelderd Road, Leeds, LS12 6BY
*Activities:* Wholesale of clothing and footwear
*Shareholders:* Andrew Valentine Morris; Kim Morris
*Officers:* Kim Deborah Morris, Secretary; Andrew Valentine Morris [1962] Director; Simon Andrew Morris [1990] Director

**A B Print Group Limited**
*Incorporated:* 17 February 1970 *Employees:* 51
*Net Worth:* £2,008,110 *Total Assets:* £3,073,488
*Registered Office:* 1 Grange Valley Road, Batley, W Yorks, WF17 6GH
*Activities:* Printing n.e.c.
*Officers:* Dianne Morley, Company Secretary; Alan Goodall [1973] Sales Director; James Edward Kemp [1972] Production Director; Richard Walmsley [1965] Director; Alan Williamson [1965] Director/Company Secretary

**A J Access Platforms Limited**
*Incorporated:* 27 April 2011 *Employees:* 15
*Net Worth:* £2,605,000 *Total Assets:* £12,030,000
*Registered Office:* 2nd Floor, West Wing, Diamond House, Diamond Business Park, Thornes Moor Road, Wakefield, W Yorks, WF2 8PT
*Activities:* Repair of machinery
*Parent:* AJ Access Holdings Limited
*Officers:* Steven James Woodhams, Secretary; David Anthony McNicholas [1972] Director; David Cyril Shipman [1959] Director; Steven James Woodhams [1979] Director/Chartered Accountant

**A-Fax Holdings Limited**
*Incorporated:* 6 March 2017 *Employees:* 291
*Net Worth:* £10,468,072 *Total Assets:* £43,644,056
*Registered Office:* Habergham Works, Ainley Industrial Estate, Elland, W Yorks, HX5 9JP
*Activities:* Manufacture of plastics in primary forms
*Shareholders:* James Richard Smith; Luke Thomas Smith
*Officers:* James Richard Smith [1978] Director; Luke Thomas Smith [1980] Director

**A-Fax Limited**
*Incorporated:* 5 December 1983
*Net Worth Deficit:* £239,418 *Total Assets:* £13,323,953
*Registered Office:* Habergham Works, Ainley Industrial Estate, Elland, W Yorks, HX5 9JP
*Activities:* Manufacture of plastics in primary forms
*Officers:* James Richard Smith [1978] Director; Luke Thomas Smith [1980] Director

**A-Fax Properties Limited**
*Incorporated:* 19 September 2008
*Net Worth:* £3,188,441 *Total Assets:* £5,266,469
*Registered Office:* Habergham Works, Ainley Industrial Estate, Elland, W Yorks, HX5 9JP
*Activities:* Other letting and operating of own or leased real estate
*Parent:* A-Fax Limited
*Officers:* James Richard Smith [1978] Director; Luke Thomas Smith [1980] Director

**A-Safe HQ Ltd**
*Incorporated:* 30 March 2005 *Employees:* 154
*Previous:* A-Safe (UK) Limited
*Net Worth:* £16,315,273 *Total Assets:* £24,774,996
*Registered Office:* Habergham Works, Ainley Industrial Estate, Elland, W Yorks, HX5 9JP
*Activities:* Manufacture of other plastic products
*Parent:* A-Fax Limited
*Officers:* James Richard Smith [1978] Director; Luke Thomas Smith [1980] Director

**A-Safe UK Ltd**
*Incorporated:* 17 December 2016 *Employees:* 28
*Net Worth:* £2,252,879 *Total Assets:* £4,257,951
*Registered Office:* Habergham Works, Ainley Industrial Estate, Elland, W Yorks, HX5 9JP
*Activities:* Manufacture of other plastic products
*Parent:* A-Safe HQ Ltd
*Officers:* James Richard Smith [1978] Managing Director; Luke Thomas Smith [1980] Managing Director

**A. & J. Fabtech Limited**
*Incorporated:* 6 March 1975 *Employees:* 70
*Net Worth:* £1,159,979 *Total Assets:* £5,045,801
*Registered Office:* 700 Bretton Way, Bretton Park Industrial Estate, Dewsbury, W Yorks, WF12 9BS
*Activities:* Manufacture of metal structures and parts of structures
*Officers:* Amanda Falsey, Secretary; Amanda Falsey [1974] Director/Chartered Accountant; Alan David Wright [1947] Director/Retired; Mark Alan Wright [1972] Managing Director

**A.B.G. Limited**
*Incorporated:* 5 July 1988 *Employees:* 65
*Net Worth:* £1,601,682 *Total Assets:* £4,250,626
*Registered Office:* E7, Meltham Mills Road, Meltham, Holmfirth, W Yorks, HD9 4DS
*Activities:* Other specialised construction activities n.e.c.
*Shareholder:* Alan Bamforth
*Officers:* Alan Bamforth, Secretary; Alan Bamforth [1956] Director; Elizabeth Ann Bamforth [1959] Export Director; Peter William Van Ruiten [1960] Director/Operations

**A.D.D. Express Ltd**
*Incorporated:* 6 July 2005 *Employees:* 49
*Net Worth:* £974,537 *Total Assets:* £3,713,700
*Registered Office:* Unit H2, Premier Way, Lowfields Business Park, Elland, Halifax, W Yorks, HX5 9HF
*Activities:* Freight transport by road
*Major Shareholder:* David Fairbrother
*Officers:* Mark Anthony Dunne [1974] Operations Director; David Fairbrother [1966] Director; Darrell Richard Sharp [1967] Director; Alyson Elizabeth Squire [1963] Director

**A.M. Packaging Limited**
*Incorporated:* 30 October 1980 *Employees:* 154
*Net Worth:* £4,960,136 *Total Assets:* £14,384,299
*Registered Office:* Amp Rose, Somerby Way, Gainsborough, Lincs, DN21 1QT
*Activities:* Manufacture of machinery for food, beverage and tobacco processing
*Major Shareholder:* Alan Mann
*Officers:* Paul Vernon Mann, Secretary; Alan Mann [1946] Director/Chairman; Andrew Howard Mann [1969] Sales Director; David Alan Francis Mann [1977] Production Director; Paul Vernon Mann [1967] Managing Director

**A.One Feed Supplements Limited**
*Incorporated:* 17 April 1975 *Employees:* 55
*Net Worth:* £4,770,099 *Total Assets:* £10,752,965
*Registered Office:* Office, North Hill, Dishforth Airfield, Thirsk, N Yorks, YO7 3DH
*Activities:* Manufacture of prepared feeds for farm animals
*Parent:* Devenish Nutrition Limited
*Officers:* Peter Francis Wallace, Secretary; Owen Brennan [1960] Director [Irish]; Richard Kennedy [1965] Director [Irish]; Donal MacAteer [1968] Director [Irish]; Patrick Anthony McLaughlin [1966] Director [Irish]; Peter Francis Wallace [1957] Director/Accountant [Irish]

**A.W. (Europe) Limited**
*Incorporated:* 12 September 1980 *Employees:* 39
*Net Worth:* £1,718,670 *Total Assets:* £18,344,730
*Registered Office:* 2nd Floor East, F Mill, Dean Clough Mills, Halifax, W Yorks, HX3 5AX
*Activities:* Manufacture of woven or tufted carpets and rugs
*Officers:* Erik Lucien Judith Deporte [1960] Managing Director [Belgian]; Stephen John Kaye [1971] Retail Sales Director; Simon Lee Lewyckyj [1974] Commercial Director; Gavin Pugh [1977] Managing Director; Michel Georges Van Waeyenberge [1963] Director/Chief Financial Officer [Belgian]

**The A1 Steam Locomotive Trust**
*Incorporated:* 12 August 1991
*Net Worth:* £4,449,751 *Total Assets:* £4,702,708
*Registered Office:* Darlington Locomotive Works, Hopetown Lane, Darlington, Co Durham, DL3 6RQ
*Activities:* Manufacture of railway locomotives and rolling stock
*Officers:* Mark Colin Allatt [1965] Director/Public Relations Manager; Paul Andrew Bruce [1961] Director/Railway Consultant; Graeme Bunker [1974] Director; David Andrew Elliott [1951] Director/Consulting Engineer; Graham Philip Langer [1961] Director/Farmer; Huw Jonathan Parker [1962] Operations Director; James Christopher Walker [1943] Director/Retired

**AAK (UK) Limited**
*Incorporated:* 14 September 1981 *Employees:* 407
*Net Worth:* £30,666,000 *Total Assets:* £168,078,000
*Registered Office:* King George Dock, Kingston upon Hull, HU9 5PX
*Activities:* Manufacture of oils and fats
*Parent:* AAK AB
*Officers:* Damian Peter Taylor, Secretary; Timothy Andrew Stephenson [1961] Finance Director; Damian Peter Taylor [1969] Finance Director

**Aalberts Industries Limited**
*Incorporated:* 30 January 2002
*Net Worth:* £45,360,000 *Total Assets:* £45,360,000
*Registered Office:* Belmont Works, St Catherines Avenue, Doncaster, S Yorks, DN4 8DF
*Activities:* Activities of head offices
*Parent:* Aalberts Industries UK Limited
*Officers:* Kevin Michael Parker, Secretary; Craig Malloy [1970] Finance Director; Weibe Arnold Pelsma [1963] Director [Dutch]

**Aalberts Industries U.K. Ltd.**
*Incorporated:* 13 July 1998
*Net Worth:* £71,398,000 *Total Assets:* £83,396,000
*Registered Office:* Belmont Works, St Catherines Avenue, Doncaster, S Yorks, DN4 8DF
*Activities:* Activities of head offices
*Parent:* Aalberts Industries N.V.
*Officers:* Kevin Michael Parker, Secretary; John Eijgendaal [1964] Finance Director [Dutch]; Craig Malloy [1970] Finance Director; Wiebe Arnold Pelsma [1963] Director [Dutch]

**Abacus Direct Limited**
*Incorporated:* 29 November 2001 *Employees:* 48
*Net Worth:* £3,826,490 *Total Assets:* £7,282,809
*Registered Office:* Abacus House, Jubilee Court, Copgrove, Harrogate, N Yorks, HG3 3TB
*Activities:* Wholesale of hardware, plumbing and heating equipment and supplies
*Parent:* Abacus Direct Manufacturing Group Limited
*Officers:* Stephen Paul Bradbury [1952] Director; Ian David Pattison [1965] Director

**Abacus Direct Manufacturing Group Limited**
*Incorporated:* 19 December 2012 *Employees:* 79
*Net Worth:* £6,152,261 *Total Assets:* £15,324,764
*Registered Office:* Abacus House, Jubilee Court, Copgrove, Harrogate, N Yorks, HG3 3TB
*Activities:* Activities of other holding companies n.e.c.
*Shareholders:* Ian David Pattison; Stephen Paul Bradbury
*Officers:* Stephen Paul Bradbury [1952] Director; Ian David Pattison [1965] Director

**Abacus Direct Properties Limited**
*Incorporated:* 20 April 2016
*Net Worth:* £342,648 *Total Assets:* £6,459,212
*Registered Office:* Abacus House, Jubilee Court, Copgrove, Harrogate, N Yorks, HG3 3TB
*Activities:* Other letting and operating of own or leased real estate
*Parent:* Abacus Direct Maunfacturing Group Limited
*Officers:* Stephen Bradbury [1952] Director; Ian David Pattison [1965] Director

**Abaxis UK Limited**
*Incorporated:* 8 March 2000 *Employees:* 32
*Net Worth:* £1,691,104 *Total Assets:* £4,648,750
*Registered Office:* Chessingham Park, Common Road, Dunnington, York, YO19 5SE
*Activities:* Other professional, scientific and technical activities n.e.c.
*Officers:* Jamie Andrew Brannan [1972] Director/Senior Vice President and Cluster Lead; Brian Renn [1977] Managing Director [American]

**Abbey Glen Limited**
*Incorporated:* 30 September 1919 *Employees:* 205
*Net Worth:* £4,039,091 *Total Assets:* £7,674,632
*Registered Office:* 451 Bentley Road, Doncaster, S Yorks, DN5 9TJ
*Activities:* Washing and (dry-)cleaning of textile and fur products
*Shareholder:* Timothy Youle Sempers
*Officers:* David Vincent Horsfield, Secretary/Accountant; Paul Michael Hogan [1977] Director; David Vincent Horsfield [1974] Director/Accountant; Sophie Elizabeth Sempers [1992] Director; Thomas David Youle Sempers [1995] Director/Economist; Timothy Youle Sempers [1965] Director; Tracy Elizabeth Sempers [1964] Director; Benjamin James West [1979] Director

**Abbey House (Cumbria) Limited**
*Incorporated:* 25 August 2010
*Net Worth Deficit:* £237,325 *Total Assets:* £5,025,931
*Registered Office:* c/o Abbey House Hotel, Abbey Road, Barrow in Furness, Cumbria, LA13 0PA
*Activities:* Hotels and similar accommodation
*Officers:* Brian Gerard Conroy [1971] Director; Neil Hopkins-Coman [1962] Director/Chartered Accountant; Timothy Anthony Kilroe [1964] Director [Irish]

**Abbey Multi Academy Trust**
*Incorporated:* 14 July 2011 *Employees:* 493
*Net Worth:* £49,281,000 *Total Assets:* £56,888,000
*Registered Office:* Abbey Grange Church of England Academy, Butcher Hill, Leeds, LS16 5EA
*Activities:* Primary education
*Officers:* Frances Baker [1983] Director/Barrister; Colin Ronald Blair [1955] Director of Estates Services; Peter Jonathan Laurence [1953] Development Director; Theresa Mary Mason [1953] Director/Independent Consultant; Gefrin Price [1972] Director; Steve Simkins [1971] Director/Actuary; Reverend Judith Smith [1974] Director/Minister of Religion; Michael Dean Stratton [1975] Director/Shopping Centre Manager; Paul Gwynn Whitman [1973] Director/Training Consultant

**Abbeyfield Ilkley Society Limited (The)**
*Incorporated:* 15 August 1968
*Net Worth:* £11,691,347 *Total Assets:* £13,210,962
*Registered Office:* Grove House, 12 Riddings Road, Ilkley, W Yorks, LS29 9BF
*Activities:* Renting and operating of Housing Association real estate
*Officers:* Amanda Louise Ashby [1964] Director/Solicitor; David Roger Binns [1948] Director; Stephen Robert Davidson [1950] Director; Frances Jane Johnson [1942] Director/Retired; Dale Smith [1940] Director/Paint Manufacturer

**Abbot Group Limited**
*Incorporated:* 17 March 1959 *Employees:* 1
*Net Worth:* £114,763,920 *Total Assets:* £1,673,629,696
*Registered Office:* 1 Park Row, Leeds, LS1 5AB
*Activities:* Extraction of crude petroleum
*Parent:* KCA Deutag Alpha Limited
*Officers:* Anthony Joseph Byrne [1976] Director/General Counsel; Neil Porteous Gilchrist [1967] Director/Chief Financial Officer; Norrie Andrew McKay [1959] Director/Chief Executive Officer; Gary Neil Paver [1967] Director/SVP - Finance

**Abbot Holdings Limited**
*Incorporated:* 30 January 1992
*Net Worth:* £448,204,992 *Total Assets:* £448,204,992
*Registered Office:* 1 Park Row, Leeds, LS1 5AB
*Activities:* Other business support service activities n.e.c.
*Parent:* Abbot Group Limited
*Officers:* Anthony Joseph Byrne [1976] Director/General Counsel; Neil Porteous Gilchrist [1967] Director/Chief Financial Officer; Gary Neil Paver [1967] Director/Senior Vice President Finance

**Abbot Investments (North Africa) Limited**
*Incorporated:* 29 September 2004
*Net Worth Deficit:* £190,146,112 *Total Assets:* £7,110,889
*Registered Office:* 1 Park Row, Leeds, LS1 5AB
*Activities:* Other business support service activities n.e.c.
*Parent:* Abbot Group Limited
*Officers:* Anthony Joseph Byrne [1976] Director/General Counsel; Neil Porteous Gilchrist [1967] Director/Chief Financial Officer; Gary Neil Paver [1967] Director/Senior Vice President Finance

**Abel & Cole Limited**
*Incorporated:* 15 February 2000 *Employees:* 495
*Net Worth:* £2,308,000 *Total Assets:* £15,861,000
*Registered Office:* The Riverside Building, Livingstone Road, Hessle, E Yorks, HU13 0DZ
*Activities:* Other retail sale not in stores, stalls or markets
*Parent:* William Jackson Food Group Limited
*Officers:* Gary Martin Urmston, Secretary; Damian Thomas Paul Dixon [1966] Director; Sarah Jayne Doyle [1974] Director; Emma Healey [1984] Marketing Director; Ben Reardon [1974] Director; Hannah Jane Shipton [1977] Sales & Customer Director; Norman Graeme Scott Soutar [1960] Director; Tim John Taylor [1979] Director/Accountant; Gary Martin Urmston [1967] Director

**Aberdeen Enterprise Finance Limited**
*Incorporated:* 1 August 2008 *Employees:* 6
*Net Worth:* £1,469,963 *Total Assets:* £8,608,109
*Registered Office:* Regent House, 11 Regent Street, Pocklington, York, YO42 2QN
*Activities:* Credit granting by non-deposit taking finance houses and other specialist consumer credit grantors
*Officers:* Michael Backhouse [1956] Director; Terence Irvine [1947] Director

**ABI (UK) Group Limited**
*Incorporated:* 30 December 2004
*Net Worth:* £19,538,000 *Total Assets:* £42,680,000
*Registered Office:* Swinemoor Lane, Beverley, E Yorks, HU17 0LJ
*Activities:* Activities of head offices
*Parent:* ABI Beta Limited
*Officers:* Richard James Jones, Secretary; Melvin Graham Copper [1952] Director; Dean Andrew Hague [1969] Sales Director; Richard James Jones [1971] Finance Director

**ABI (UK) Holdings Limited**
*Incorporated:* 9 September 2003
*Net Worth:* £930,000 *Total Assets:* £13,422,000
*Registered Office:* Swinemoor Lane, Beverley, E Yorks, HU17 0LJ
*Activities:* Activities of head offices
*Parent:* ABI (UK) Group Limited
*Officers:* Richard James Jones, Secretary; Melvin Graham Copper [1952] Director; Richard James Jones [1971] Finance Director

**ABI (UK) Limited**
*Incorporated:* 27 April 1998 *Employees:* 456
*Net Worth:* £61,751,000 *Total Assets:* £74,885,000
*Registered Office:* Swinemoor Lane, Beverley, E Yorks, HU17 0LJ
*Activities:* Other manufacturing n.e.c.
*Parent:* ABI Bidco Limited
*Officers:* Richard James Jones, Secretary; Paul Alan Clackstone [1968] Director; Melvin Graham Copper [1952] Director; Dean Andrew Hague [1969] Sales Director; Richard James Jones [1971] Finance Director

**ABI Alpha Limited**
*Incorporated:* 18 August 2011
*Net Worth:* £365,000 *Total Assets:* £25,754,000
*Registered Office:* Swinemoor Lane, Beverley, E Yorks, HU17 0LJ
*Activities:* Activities of head offices
*Parent:* ABI Bidco Limited
*Officers:* Richard James Jones, Secretary; Paul Alan Clackstone [1968] Director; Melvin Graham Copper [1952] Director; Dean Andrew Hague [1969] Director; Richard James Jones [1971] Director

**ABI Beta Limited**
*Incorporated:* 18 August 2011
*Net Worth:* £3,075,000 *Total Assets:* £33,967,000
*Registered Office:* Swinemoor Lane, Beverley, E Yorks, HU17 0LJ
*Activities:* Activities of head offices
*Parent:* ABI Alpha Limited
*Officers:* Richard James Jones, Secretary; Paul Alan Clackstone [1968] Director; Melvin Graham Copper [1952] Director; Dean Andrew Hague [1969] Director; Richard James Jones [1971] Director

**ABI Bidco Limited**
*Incorporated:* 5 May 2016
*Net Worth Deficit:* £1,537,000 *Total Assets:* £55,116,000
*Registered Office:* Swinemoor Lane, Beverley, E Yorks, HU17 0LJ
*Activities:* Activities of head offices
*Parent:* ABI Midco Limited
*Officers:* Thomas Robert Biddle [1980] Director/Private Equity Investor; Paul Alan Clackstone [1968] Director; Melvin Graham Copper [1952] Director; Dean Andrew Hague [1969] Director; Mathew James Edward Hutchinson [1972] Director/Private Equity Investor; Richard James Jones [1971] Director

**ABI Midco Limited**
*Incorporated:* 5 May 2016 *Employees:* 456
*Net Worth:* £2,936,000 *Total Assets:* £66,619,000
*Registered Office:* Swinemoor Lane, Beverley, E Yorks, HU17 0LJ
*Activities:* Activities of head offices
*Parent:* CBPE Capital LLP
*Officers:* Thomas Robert Biddle [1980] Director/Private Equity Investor; Paul Alan Clackstone [1968] Director; Melvin Graham Copper [1952] Director; Dean Andrew Hague [1969] Director; Mathew James Edward Hutchinson [1972] Director/Private Equity Investor; Richard James Jones [1971] Director

**Abirose Limited**
*Incorporated:* 20 January 2011
*Net Worth Deficit:* £64,865,000 *Total Assets:* £9,779,000
*Registered Office:* 3 Whitehall Quay, Leeds, LS1 4BF
*Activities:* Other letting and operating of own or leased real estate
*Parent:* Cygnet Park LLP
*Officers:* Darren William Forshaw [1972] Director/Chartered Accountant; Garry Wilson [1967] Director

**Abracs 2013 Limited**
*Incorporated:* 25 March 2013
*Net Worth:* £983,553 *Total Assets:* £3,898,020
*Registered Office:* Abracs House, Unit 3 George Cayley Drive, York, YO30 4XE
*Activities:* Activities of head offices
*Officers:* Robin Neil Womersley, Secretary; David Hartley [1956] Director/Chairman; Robert Christopher Jeffery [1979] Director; Robin Neil Womersley [1971] Finance Director

**C F Abraham Limited**
*Incorporated:* 7 January 1960 *Employees:* 4
*Net Worth:* £5,661,390 *Total Assets:* £9,216,807
*Registered Office:* Hall Garth, Carperby, Leyburn, N Yorks, DL8 4DQ
*Activities:* Maintenance and repair of motor vehicles
*Officers:* Roger Fenwick Abraham, Secretary; Andrew James Abraham [1970] Director/Engineer; Anthony Fell Poad Abraham [1943] Director; Charles Thomas Fenwick Abraham [1974] Director/Solicitor; Roger Fenwick Abraham [1945] Director/Electrical Engineer

**Absolutely Cultured Limited**
*Incorporated:* 27 June 2014 *Employees:* 69
*Previous:* Hull UK City of Culture 2017 Limited
*Net Worth:* £2,404,033 *Total Assets:* £5,943,800
*Registered Office:* Pacific Exchange, 40 High Street, Hull, HU1 1PS
*Activities:* Performing arts
*Officers:* Georgia Faye Allenby [1992] Director/Property Developer; Sameera Anwar West [1975] Director/Solicitor; Councillor Stephen Brady [1945] Director/Leader of Hull City Council; Professor Peter Glenn Burgess [1961] Director/Deputy Vice-Chancellor; Lee Anne Corner [1954] Director; Susan Sheila Fisher [1964] Director of Development; Neil Robert Hodgkinson [1960] Director/Media Editor; Matthew Scott Jukes [1971] Director/Local Authority Chief Executive; Stephen John Liddle [1957] Director/Educational Consultant; Dr Tapan Kumar Mahapatra [1955] Director/Consultant Surgeon; Benedict Peter Norman [1972] Director/Manager; Karen Ann Ama Okra [1961] Director

**Abstract (Bristol) Limited**
*Incorporated:* 7 June 2016
*Net Worth:* £862,359 *Total Assets:* £5,182,700
*Registered Office:* Queens House, 34 Wellington Street, Leeds, LS1 2DE
*Activities:* Buying and selling of own real estate
*Parent:* Abstract Securities Limited
*Officers:* Stephanie Miles, Secretary; Mark Lewis Glatman [1956] Director; Christopher John McPherson [1963] Director/Chartered Surveyor

**Abstract Securities Limited**
*Incorporated:* 14 March 2000 *Employees:* 13
*Net Worth:* £8,859,228 *Total Assets:* £15,302,403
*Registered Office:* Queens House, 34 Wellington Street, Leeds, LS1 2DE
*Activities:* Management of real estate on a fee or contract basis
*Shareholders:* Mark Lewis Glatman; John Alexander Charles Kirkland; John Nigel Kirkland
*Officers:* Stephanie Miles, Secretary; Mark Lewis Glatman [1956] Director; John Alexander Charles Kirkland [1980] Director; John Nigel Kirkland [1938] Director; Christopher John McPherson [1963] Development Director; Stephanie Miles [1972] Director/Accountant

**Abzorb Group Ltd**
*Incorporated:* 19 May 2017
*Net Worth:* £8,562,041 *Total Assets:* £15,504,257
*Registered Office:* c/o Abzorb Group Ltd, Armytage Road, Brighouse, W Yorks, HD6 1QF
*Activities:* Other telecommunications activities
*Major Shareholder:* Steven Andrew Beeby
*Officers:* Steven Andrew Beeby [1969] Director

**ACAD Holdings Limited**
*Incorporated:* 17 January 2006
*Net Worth:* £5,392,994 *Total Assets:* £5,511,112
*Registered Office:* Beckwith Health Club, Central House, Otley Road, Harrogate, N Yorks, HG3 1UF
*Activities:* Activities of other holding companies n.e.c.
*Parent:* ACAD Ltd
*Officers:* Mark Simon Silver [1960] Director; Tina Louise Silver [1966] Director

**Academic Appointments 2017 Limited**
*Incorporated:* 16 March 2017
*Net Worth:* £1,058,069 *Total Assets:* £6,243,434
*Registered Office:* Templar House, 4225 Park Approach, Leeds, LS15 8GB
*Activities:* Activities of other holding companies n.e.c.
*Parent:* Solingen Private Equity Partners LLP
*Officers:* Paul Aaron Betts [1975] Director; Maureen Janet Parkin [1960] Director; Peter Anthony Riley [1976] Director; Robin Neil Womersley [1971] Director

**The Academy @ Ridgewood Trust**
*Incorporated:* 3 October 2011 *Employees:* 152
*Net Worth:* £12,497,000 *Total Assets:* £15,921,000
*Registered Office:* Ridgewood School, Barnsley Road, Scawsby, Doncaster, S Yorks, DN5 7UB
*Activities:* General secondary education
*Officers:* Dominic Carlin [1989] Director/Teacher; Stuart Cameron Cousins [1955] Director/Educational Consultant; Margaret Helen Dunn [1965] Director/Headteacher; David Andrew Grace [1962] Director/Health and Safety Advisor; Adrian Hayes [1976] Director/Junior School Headteacher; Keith Arthur Mears [1940] Director/Specialist Teaching Assistant; Mandy Elizabeth Oxer [1958] Director; Galit Judith Sharpe [1973] Director/Retail Area Manager; Pamela Jane Ullyott [1964] Director/Solicitor

**Academy Leisure Limited**
*Incorporated:* 8 April 1993 *Employees:* 2
*Net Worth:* £7,061,653 *Total Assets:* £7,941,605
*Registered Office:* Beckwith Health Club, Central House, Otley Road, Harrogate, N Yorks, HG3 1UF
*Activities:* Buying and selling of own real estate
*Parent:* Acad Holdings Limited
*Officers:* Mark Simon Silver [1960] Director; Tina Louise Silver [1966] Director

**Access 13 Limited**
*Incorporated:* 19 October 2005
*Net Worth:* £1,241,818 *Total Assets:* £6,543,659
*Registered Office:* Calls Wharf, 2 The Calls, Leeds, LS2 7JU
*Activities:* Activities of head offices
*Shareholder:* Julian Mark Kynaston
*Officers:* Bruce Stewart Cameron [1969] Director/Chartered Accountant; Craig William Harrold [1971] Accounts Director; Julian Aaron Horberry [1970] Director; Julian Mark Kynaston [1967] Director; Laura Kynaston [1981] Director/Business Strategist; Richard James McMurrough [1968] Accounts Director

**Access Hire Nationwide Limited**
*Incorporated:* 30 July 2007 *Employees:* 35
*Net Worth:* £11,634,049 *Total Assets:* £29,503,238
*Registered Office:* Unit F, Trident Park, Rosie Road, Normanton, W Yorks, WF6 1ZB
*Activities:* Renting and leasing of trucks and other heavy vehicles
*Parent:* Kelling Midco Limited
*Officers:* Jonathan Simon Battersby, Secretary; Jonathan Simon Battersby [1964] Finance Director; Danny Cooper [1960] Sales Director; John Brad Wood [1976] Managing Director

**The Access Panel Company Ltd**
*Incorporated:* 30 May 2000
*Net Worth:* £1,722,537 *Total Assets:* £4,409,667
*Registered Office:* Unit 5 Atkinsons Way, Foxhills Industrial Estate, Scunthorpe, N Lincs, DN15 8QJ
*Activities:* Manufacture of other fabricated metal products n.e.c.
*Major Shareholder:* Simon Jonathan Crabtree
*Officers:* Simon Jonathan Crabtree [1966] Sales Director

**Access Property Finance Limited**
*Incorporated:* 3 November 2015
*Net Worth:* £27,386 *Total Assets:* £3,190,147
*Registered Office:* 4 Brewery Place, Leeds, LS10 1NE
*Activities:* Other credit granting n.e.c.
*Parent:* Access Commercial Finance Limited
*Officers:* Paul Cooper [1972] Director/Solicitor; Nicholas Robert King [1973] Director

**Accord Mortgages Limited**
*Incorporated:* 11 June 1987
*Net Worth:* £340,607,008 *Total Assets:* £19,933,483,008
*Registered Office:* Yorkshire House, Yorkshire Drive, Bradford, W Yorks, BD5 8LJ
*Activities:* Activities of mortgage finance companies
*Officers:* Deborah Colley, Secretary; Charles Peter Canning [1963] Director; Jeremy Michael Duncombe [1969] Director of Intermediary Distribution; Paul Howley [1967] Director/Manager; Rob Andrew Purdy [1972] Director/Accountant; Richard Stephen Wells [1963] Director/General Manager - Risk; Mr Stephen White [1971] Chief Operating Officer & Executive Director

**Accord Multi Academy Trust**
*Incorporated:* 6 January 2011 *Employees:* 473
*Previous:* Ossett Academy and Sixth Form College
*Net Worth:* £37,866,000 *Total Assets:* £42,252,000
*Registered Office:* Ossett Academy & Sixth Form College, Storrs Hill Road, Ossett, W Yorks, WF5 0DG
*Activities:* General secondary education
*Officers:* Nicholas Paul Adams [1968] Director/Sales and Marketing Consultant; Rosalyn Sarah Collins [1978] Director/Head of Sales/Commercial; Lynne Cramphorn [1961] Director/Retired; Richard Thomas Arthur Dennett [1961] Director/Solicitor; David Dickinson [1965] Director/Chief Executive Officer; Michael Jeremy Dyson [1960] Director/Retired; John Leam [1949] Director/Educational Leadership Consultant; Maureen Ann Mathers [1974] Director/Credit Manager; Sonya Helen Strafford [1967] Director/Police Officer

**Ace Gas Limited**
*Incorporated:* 23 April 2003
*Net Worth:* £1,429,502 *Total Assets:* £3,414,933
*Registered Office:* Blackbrook Way, Greetland, Halifax, W Yorks, HX4 8ED
*Activities:* Wholesale of petroleum and petroleum products
*Officers:* Stuart Pierce, Secretary; Annette Michelle Crawshaw [1971] Director; Richard Shaun Pierce [1968] Director/Coal & Gas Merchant; Stuart Andrew Pierce [1969] Director

**Ace Group (Engineering) Limited**
*Incorporated:* 15 February 1996
*Previous:* Advanced Compressor Engineering Ltd.
*Net Worth:* £505,710 *Total Assets:* £3,592,715
*Registered Office:* Unit 1 Bradley Junction Industrial Estate, Huddersfield, W Yorks, HD2 1UR
*Activities:* Repair of machinery
*Shareholders:* Mark Edward John Peacock; Denise Peacock
*Officers:* Mark Edward John Peacock, Secretary/Director; Richard Andrew Coar [1968] Operation Director; Denise Peacock [1963] Director; Mark Edward John Peacock [1962] Director; Martin Paul Wardle [1963] Service Director

**Acer Healthcare Operations Limited**
*Incorporated:* 23 June 2016 *Employees:* 436
*Net Worth Deficit:* £1,098,969 *Total Assets:* £13,850,152
*Registered Office:* Westcourt, Gelderd Road, Leeds, LS12 6DB
*Activities:* Residential nursing care facilities
*Parent:* Maria Mallaband Care Group Limited
*Officers:* Christopher Ball [1968] Director; Philip John Burgan [1951] Director; Peter Gervais Fagan [1957] Director; Jason Lock [1972] Director

**Acis Group Limited**
*Incorporated:* 6 July 1998 *Employees:* 209
*Net Worth:* £36,019,000 *Total Assets:* £248,668,992
*Registered Office:* ACIS House, Bridge Street, Gainsborough, Lincs, DN21 1GG
*Activities:* Renting and operating of Housing Association real estate
*Officers:* Catherine Alice Kelly, Secretary; Carole Anne Hodson [1960] Director/Project Manager; Michael Kay [1961] Group Director of Property; Bruce Kerr [1958] Director/Consultant; Denise Maguire [1962] Director/Retired Lawyer; Ronan O'Hara [1971] Director/Chartered Surveyor; Paul Satchwell [1979] Finance Director; Kathryn Lois Smart [1971] Director/Accountant; Graham Charles Ward [1960] Director of Own Consultancy Business; Nigel Robert Whitaker [1961] Director/Procurement Consultant

**Ackers P Investment Company Limited**
*Incorporated:* 18 February 1982 *Employees:* 2,651
*Net Worth:* £77,610,000 *Total Assets:* £433,584,000
*Registered Office:* c/o VP PLC, Beckwith Knowle, Otley Road, Harrogate, N Yorks, HG3 1UD
*Activities:* Activities of head offices
*Officers:* Nicholas Hugh Barlow, Secretary; Nicholas Hugh Barlow [1973] Director/Solicitor; Simon John Kinna [1958] Director/Chartered Accountant; Jeremy Frederic George Pilkington [1951] Director

**Acklam's Coaches Limited**
*Incorporated:* 25 June 2007 *Employees:* 71
*Net Worth:* £1,433,978 *Total Assets:* £4,260,012
*Registered Office:* Barmston Close, Swinemoor Lane, Beverley, E Yorks, HU17 0LA
*Activities:* Other urban, suburban or metropolitan passenger land transport (not underground, metro or similar)
*Parent:* Acklams Properties Limited
*Officers:* Josephine Acklam, Secretary; Alan Acklam [1978] Director; Paul Acklam [1949] Director

**Ackworth Service Station Ltd**
*Incorporated:* 6 February 2002 *Employees:* 43
*Net Worth:* £2,907,969 *Total Assets:* £4,806,082
*Registered Office:* 35 Warren Street, Savile Town, Dewsbury, W Yorks, WF12 9LX
*Activities:* Retail sale of automotive fuel in specialised stores
*Shareholders:* Haroon Valli; Yunus Valli; Farook Valli
*Officers:* Farook Valli, Secretary/Director; Farook Valli [1968] Director/Petrol Station Retailer; Haroon Valli [1966] Director; Yunus Valli [1972] Director

**ACL Estates Limited**
*Incorporated:* 10 May 2004
*Net Worth Deficit:* £595,366 *Total Assets:* £6,883,089
*Registered Office:* c/o Ground Floor, St Paul's House, 23 Park Square, Leeds, LS1 2ND
*Activities:* Development of building projects
*Officers:* Dominik Ceavash Karimi, Secretary; Ali-Reza Reza Golesorkhi [1963] Director [Iranian]

**Aclet Property Management & Services Limited**
*Incorporated:* 24 November 1999 *Employees:* 3
*Net Worth Deficit:* £1,025,468 *Total Assets:* £3,238,724
*Registered Office:* Sherwood, 4 Watling Road, Bishop Auckland, Co Durham, DL14 6RP
*Activities:* Buying and selling of own real estate
*Major Shareholder:* Leslie Wood
*Officers:* Diane Wood, Secretary; Diane Wood [1955] Director/Administrator; Harry Wood [1984] Director/Property Consultant; Leslie Wood [1952] Director/Housing Consultant

**ACM Global Central Laboratory Limited**
*Incorporated:* 20 July 1999 *Employees:* 161
*Net Worth:* £10,087,352 *Total Assets:* £13,310,193
*Registered Office:* 23 Hospital Fields Road, York, YO10 4DZ
*Activities:* Other professional, scientific and technical activities n.e.c.
*Officers:* John Vincent Foley [1960] Director/Executive VP Strategy & Business Development [American]

**ACM Global Central Laboratory Operations Limited**
*Incorporated:* 4 February 2009 *Employees:* 161
*Net Worth:* £7,056,280 *Total Assets:* £20,051,550
*Registered Office:* 23 Hospital Fields Road, York, YO10 4DZ
*Activities:* Non-trading company
*Officers:* John Vincent Foley [1960] Director/Executive VP Strategy & Business Development [American]

**Acorn Assessors Limited**
*Incorporated:* 24 April 1998 *Employees:* 35
*Net Worth:* £3,542,059 *Total Assets:* £4,080,459
*Registered Office:* Acorn House, Acorn Business Park, Clay Pit Lane, Roecliffe, York, YO51 9LS
*Activities:* Risk and damage evaluation
*Major Shareholder:* Pamela Jane Townsend
*Officers:* Richard Henry Thomlinson, Secretary; Pamela Jane Townsend [1961] Director

**Acorn Mobility Services Ltd.**
*Incorporated:* 21 March 1991 *Employees:* 1,485
*Net Worth:* £17,524,536 *Total Assets:* £59,685,564
*Registered Office:* Telecom House, Millennium Business Park, Station Road, Steeton, Bradford, W Yorks, BD20 6RB
*Activities:* Other manufacturing n.e.c.
*Major Shareholder:* John Stewart Jakes
*Officers:* Patrick Francis Bethell [1988] Global Systems Director [Bahamian]; John Stewart Jakes [1956] Director/Chairman; Michael Jonathan Oldham [1951] Director/Accountant; Joanne Amanda Richardson [1976] Director/Chartered Accountant; Nicholas Wilson [1973] Director/Operations Manager

**Acorn Web Offset Limited**
*Incorporated:* 8 June 1987 *Employees:* 119
*Net Worth:* £7,232,790 *Total Assets:* £10,733,886
*Registered Office:* Loscoe Close, Normanton Industrial Estate, Normanton, W Yorks, WF6 1TW
*Activities:* Printing n.e.c.
*Parent:* Investment in Media Limited
*Officers:* Nicholas Robert Alexander [1968] Director; Matthew Robert Carry [1977] Sales Director; Claire Rennison [1978] Finance Director; Mark Graham Roberts [1970] Managing Director

**Acrastyle Limited**
*Incorporated:* 27 June 1962 *Employees:* 64
*Net Worth Deficit:* £449,205 *Total Assets:* £3,183,253
*Registered Office:* Acrastyle Limited, North Lonsdale Road, Ulverston, Cumbria, LA12 9DP
*Activities:* Manufacture of electricity distribution and control apparatus
*Parent:* Acrastyle Switchgear Limited
*Officers:* William Samuel Wilson, Secretary/Financial Controller; Oliver Guy Blackaby [1962] Director/Consultant; Ashish Jalan [1964] Director [Indian]; Sushil Jalan [1938] Director/Business Executive [Indian]; Ashok Kumar Vishwakarma [1968] Managing Director [Indian]; Peter John Woolrich [1948] Director

**Acre Products Limited**
*Incorporated:* 26 October 1973 *Employees:* 7
*Net Worth:* £7,380,983 *Total Assets:* £8,645,450
*Registered Office:* Dalton Lane, Keighley, W Yorks, BD21 4JH
*Activities:* Development of building projects
*Shareholders:* Robert Simon Smallwood; Andrew Charles Smallwood; David Mark Smallwood
*Officers:* Andrew Charles Smallwood, Secretary; Andrew Charles Smallwood [1961] Director/Purchasing; David Mark Smallwood [1967] Managing Director; Robert Simon Smallwood [1963] Director/Sales

**Acropolis Corporate Limited**
*Incorporated:* 26 July 1961 *Employees:* 329
*Previous:* Acropolis Hotels Limited
*Net Worth:* £8,397,882 *Total Assets:* £23,504,694
*Registered Office:* 18a Chevet Lane, Sandal, Wakefield, W Yorks, WF2 6HL
*Activities:* Security dealing on own account
*Major Shareholder:* George Costa Demetriou
*Officers:* Zoe Georgiou, Secretary; George Costa Demetriou [1938] Director; Maritza George Demetriou [1966] Director; Kevin Francis Henry [1955] Director

**Acropolis Investments Limited**
*Incorporated:* 11 January 2007 *Employees:* 329
*Net Worth:* £11,107,911 *Total Assets:* £16,656,775
*Registered Office:* 18a Chevet Lane, Sandal, Wakefield, W Yorks, WF2 6HL
*Activities:* Activities of head offices
*Major Shareholder:* George Costa Demetriou
*Officers:* Zoe Georgiou, Secretary; George Costa Demetriou [1938] Director; Maritza George Demetriou [1966] Director; Kevin Francis Henry [1955] Director

**ACS Stainless Limited**
*Incorporated:* 17 July 2015 *Employees:* 60
*Net Worth:* £11,479,087 *Total Assets:* £15,518,241
*Registered Office:* 1 Cross Green Approach, Leeds, LS9 0SG
*Activities:* Other manufacturing n.e.c.
*Major Shareholder:* Michael Joseph Flannery
*Officers:* Brigid Mary Flannery [1948] Director; David Anthony Flannery [1970] Director; Michael Joseph Flannery [1944] Director; Clare Louise Riddington [1975] Director; Paul Antony Riddington [1976] Director

**ACS Stainless Steel Fixings Limited**
*Incorporated:* 5 September 1984 *Employees:* 60
*Net Worth:* £3,158,668 *Total Assets:* £6,493,566
*Registered Office:* 1 Cross Green Approach, Leeds, LS9 0SG
*Activities:* Manufacture of other fabricated metal products n.e.c.
*Parent:* ACS Stainless Limited
*Officers:* Richard Seadon, Secretary; Brigid Mary Flannery [1948] Director; David Anthony Flannery [1970] Director; Michael Joseph Flannery [1944] Director; Clare Louise Riddington [1975] Director; Paul Antony Riddington [1976] Director/IT Consultant

**Actavis Holdings UK II Limited**
*Incorporated:* 28 April 1998
*Net Worth:* £316,351,008 *Total Assets:* £603,851,008
*Registered Office:* Ridings Point, Whistler Drive, Castleford, W Yorks, WF10 5HX
*Activities:* Manufacture of pharmaceutical preparations
*Parent:* Actavis Holdings UK Ltd
*Officers:* Dean Michael Cooper [1972] Director/Chartered Accountant; Kim Innes [1968] Director/General Manager

**Actavis Holdings UK Ltd.**
*Incorporated:* 3 February 2004
*Net Worth:* £200,594,000 *Total Assets:* £200,594,000
*Registered Office:* Ridings Point, Whistler Drive, Castleford, W Yorks, WF10 5HX
*Activities:* Combined office administrative service activities
*Parent:* Actavis UK Group Limited
*Officers:* Dean Michael Cooper [1972] Director/Chartered Accountant; Kim Innes [1968] Director/General Manager

**Actavis UK Group Limited**
*Incorporated:* 21 May 2015
*Net Worth:* £30,169,000 *Total Assets:* £439,019,008
*Registered Office:* Ridings Point, Whistler Drive, Castleford, W Yorks, WF10 5HX
*Activities:* Activities of head offices
*Parent:* Teva Pharmaceutical Industries Limited
*Officers:* Dean Michael Cooper [1972] Director/Chartered Accountant; Kim Innes [1968] Director/General Manager

**Actavo (UK) Limited**
*Incorporated:* 13 June 2000 *Employees:* 1,742
*Previous:* Deborah Services Limited
*Net Worth:* £20,148,000 *Total Assets:* £103,309,000
*Registered Office:* Unit C, Cedar Court Office Park, Denby Dale Road, Calder Grove, Wakefield, W Yorks, WF4 3QZ
*Activities:* Installation of industrial machinery and equipment
*Parent:* Deborah Services (Holdings) Limited
*Officers:* Barry O'Donnell, Secretary; Brian Kelly [1977] Director [Irish]; Sean Lucey [1962] Director [Irish]; Stuart McDonald [1987] Director

**Actavo Building Solutions (UK) Limited**
*Incorporated:* 28 August 2009 *Employees:* 59
*Previous:* Roan Building Solutions Limited
*Net Worth Deficit:* £3,808,245 *Total Assets:* £7,759,275
*Registered Office:* 30 Freightliner Road, Brighton Street Industrial Estate, Hull, HU3 4UW
*Activities:* Other specialised construction activities n.e.c.
*Parent:* Siteserv Management Limited
*Officers:* Barry O'Donnell, Secretary; Brian Kelly [1977] Director [Irish]; Sean Lucey [1962] Director [Irish]; Stuart McDonald [1987] Director

**Acumen Credit Insurance Brokers Limited**
*Incorporated:* 29 January 1988 *Employees:* 38
*Previous:* The John Reynolds Group Limited
*Net Worth:* £4,504,450 *Total Assets:* £5,684,891
*Registered Office:* Trueman House, Capitol Park, Tingley, Leeds, LS27 0TS
*Activities:* Non-life insurance
*Officers:* Stephen Farrow [1974] Director; Joseph Edgar Henderson [1951] Director; Peter Robert Hodgson [1966] Director/Insurance Broker; Jane Elizabeth Kielty- O'Gara [1976] Managing Director; Paul David Martin [1972] Director/Insurance Broker

**Acumen Waste Services Limited**
*Incorporated:* 6 April 1994 *Employees:* 79
*Net Worth:* £6,662,872 *Total Assets:* £10,780,715
*Registered Office:* Acumen House, Headlands Lane, Knottingley, W Yorks, WF11 0LA
*Activities:* Collection of non-hazardous waste
*Major Shareholder:* Jonathan Stephen Morris
*Officers:* Kristian David Sutton, Secretary; Andrew Crossley [1976] Director; Leon Kirk [1965] Managing Director; Kristian David Sutton [1980] Financial Director

**ACWA Services Limited**
*Incorporated:* 3 June 1986 *Employees:* 27
*Net Worth Deficit:* £2,534,222 *Total Assets:* £12,957,808
*Registered Office:* ACWA House, Unit 9 Acorn Business Park, Skipton, N Yorks, BD23 2UE
*Activities:* Water collection, treatment and supply
*Parent:* Consolidated Contractors International (UK) Ltd
*Officers:* David Clegg, Secretary; Peter Brewer [1968] Director/General Manager; Yasser Adeeb Khalil Burgan [1964] Director/Assistant Vice President - CCC [Jordanian]; The Hon Stephen John Byers [1953] Director/Member of Parliament; Naji Mohammed El Moheb [1954] Director [Lebanese]; Akl Jamal [1949] Director/Vice President-Estimation [Canadian]; Wail Said Khouri [1961] Director/Chairman/Area Manager [Belizean]

**Adams and Green Limited**
*Incorporated:* 15 November 2011 *Employees:* 11
*Net Worth:* £1,323,737 *Total Assets:* £3,428,568
*Registered Office:* Brocklesby House, Crosslands Lane, North Cave, Brough, N Humbers, HU15 2PG
*Activities:* Manufacture of prepared feeds for farm animals
*Shareholder:* Robert Paul Brocklesby
*Officers:* Paul Nigel Brocklesby [1954] Director; Robert Paul Brocklesby [1973] Director

**Adapted Vehicle Hire Limited**
*Incorporated:* 14 February 2005 *Employees:* 33
*Net Worth:* £4,101,485 *Total Assets:* £6,133,799
*Registered Office:* Nexus House, 2 Owlcotes Court, 141 Richardshaw Lane, Stanningley, Pudsey, W Yorks, LS28 6AA
*Activities:* Renting and leasing of cars and light motor vehicles
*Parent:* Nexus Vehicle Holdings Limited
*Officers:* Ian Cherry, Secretary; David Martin Brennan [1966] Director/Chief Executive; Ian Cherry [1970] Finance Director; John Christian Ellis [1977] Director

**Adare SEC Holdings Limited**
*Incorporated:* 20 June 2017 *Employees:* 513
*Net Worth Deficit:* £10,870,000 *Total Assets:* £48,122,000
*Registered Office:* Park Mill, Wakefield Road, Clayton West, Huddersfield, W Yorks, HD8 9QQ
*Activities:* Activities of other holding companies n.e.c.
*Parent:* Endless LLP
*Officers:* Neil Gaydon [1960] Director/Chairman; Rachael Rebecca Nevins [1967] Director/Chief Financial Officer; James Christopher Michael Woolley [1977] Director/Private Equity Partner

**Addplant Limited**
*Incorporated:* 23 October 1984 *Employees:* 32
*Net Worth:* £2,383,035 *Total Assets:* £3,201,331
*Registered Office:* Grovehill, Beverley, E Yorks, HU17 0JN
*Activities:* Renting and leasing of construction and civil engineering machinery and equipment
*Major Shareholder:* Peter Michael Barrett
*Officers:* Wendy Marie Conquest, Secretary; Allason Rosemary Barrett [1954] Director/Retired; Christopher Edward Barrett [1983] Director; Peter Michael Barrett [1950] Director/Manager

**ADGM Limited**
*Incorporated:* 18 January 2011 *Employees:* 210
*Net Worth:* £1,742,214 *Total Assets:* £5,412,344
*Registered Office:* Bleak House, High Street, Honely, Holmfirth, W Yorks, HD9 6AW
*Activities:* Activities of head offices
*Shareholder:* David Malcolm Jackson
*Officers:* Ian Swire, Secretary; Linda Jane Instone [1962] Director; Richard Ralph Instone [1960] Director; David Malcolm Jackson [1947] Director; Lynn Jackson [1949] Director [Australian]; Ian Swire [1963] Director; Jill Rebecca Swire [1961] Director; Mark Turner [1957] Director

**Adina Developments Ltd**
*Incorporated:* 23 September 2015
*Net Worth Deficit:* £194,275 *Total Assets:* £3,116,600
*Registered Office:* Hall Farm Barns, 11 Hillam Hall View, Hillam, N Yorks, LS25 5NR
*Activities:* Construction of domestic buildings
*Officers:* Paul Hesp [1963] Director; Mark Simon Webber [1964] Director [Australian]; Ian Charles Wotton [1962] Director

**ADL PLC**
*Incorporated:* 26 January 1990 *Employees:* 642
*Net Worth:* £20,369,562 *Total Assets:* £31,783,940
*Registered Office:* Woodlands of Woolley Residential Home, Woolley Low Moor Lane, Woolley, Wakefield, W Yorks, WF4 2LN
*Activities:* Activities of head offices
*Officers:* William Jeremy Davies, Secretary; William Jeremy Davies [1947] Director; Pearl Lorraine Jackson [1958] Director; Sir William Henry Weston Wells [1940] Director

**Adler & Allan Group Limited**
*Incorporated:* 18 June 2014 *Employees:* 509
*Net Worth Deficit:* £24,631,000 *Total Assets:* £87,356,000
*Registered Office:* 80 Station Parade, Harrogate, N Yorks, HG1 1HQ
*Activities:* Activities of head offices
*Parent:* LDC III LP
*Officers:* Dale Brent Alderson [1979] Director; Robert Leonard Contreras [1962] Director; Michael James Dunn [1965] Director; Robin Clive Powell [1965] Director; Ruth Spratt [1973] Director; Michael Derek Willink [1964] Director

**Adler & Allan Holdings Limited**
*Incorporated:* 18 April 2007
*Net Worth Deficit:* £15,527,000 *Total Assets:* £19,392,000
*Registered Office:* 80 Station Parade, Harrogate, N Yorks, HG1 1HQ
*Activities:* Activities of head offices
*Parent:* Adler & Allan Group Limited
*Officers:* Robert Leonard Contreras [1962] Director; Michael James Dunn [1965] Director; Ruth Spratt [1973] Director; Michael Derek Willink [1964] Director

**Adler & Allan Limited**
*Incorporated:* 14 September 1936 *Employees:* 401
*Net Worth:* £30,439,000 *Total Assets:* £39,970,000
*Registered Office:* 80 Station Parade, Harrogate, N Yorks, HG1 1HQ
*Activities:* Agents involved in the sale of fuels, ores, metals and industrial chemicals
*Parent:* Adler & Allan Holdings Limited
*Officers:* Robert Leonard Contreras [1962] Director; Michael James Dunn [1965] Director; Ruth Spratt [1973] Director; Michael Derek Willink [1964] Director

**ADP Primary Care Acquisitions Limited**
*Incorporated:* 18 September 2009 *Employees:* 2
*Net Worth:* £18,232,116 *Total Assets:* £149,346,352
*Registered Office:* 1 Park Row, Leeds, LS1 5AB
*Activities:* Other business support service activities n.e.c.
*Parent:* ADP Primary Care Services Limited
*Officers:* Jean Michel Claude Bonnavion [1971] Director/Investment Professional [French]; Louis Goodman Elson [1962] Director/Managing Partner, Palamon Capital Partners [American]

**ADP Primary Care Services Limited**
*Incorporated:* 18 September 2009 *Employees:* 2
*Net Worth:* £17,624,862 *Total Assets:* £153,772,928
*Registered Office:* 1 Park Row, Leeds, LS1 5AB
*Activities:* Dental practice activities
*Officers:* Jean Michel Claude Bonnavion [1971] Director/Investment Professional [French]; Louis Goodman Elson [1962] Director/Managing Partner, Palamon Capital Partners [American]

**Adva Optical Networking Limited**
*Incorporated:* 1 July 1998 *Employees:* 113
*Net Worth:* £13,830,000 *Total Assets:* £25,211,000
*Registered Office:* Advantage House, Tribune Way, Clifton Moor, York, YO30 4RY
*Activities:* Manufacture of computers and peripheral equipment
*Parent:* Adva Optical Networking SE
*Officers:* Ian Blackburn, Secretary; Maurice Baarslag [1970] Director [Dutch]; Kristen Louise Clovis [1981] Director; Ulrich Dopfer [1973] Director [German]

**Advance HE**
*Incorporated:* 14 October 2003 *Employees:* 93
*Previous:* The Higher Education Academy
*Net Worth:* £2,555,000 *Total Assets:* £9,010,000
*Registered Office:* Advance HE York Science Park, Innovation Way, York, YO10 5BR
*Activities:* Educational support services
*Officers:* Hannah Louise Purkis, Secretary; Nicola Jane Arnold [1969] Director of Finance; Professor Rebecca Mary Bunting [1955] Director/Deputy Vice Chancellor; Nigel Martyn Carrington [1956] Director/Vice Chancellor; Amatey Victor Doku [1995] Director/Vice President; Professor Helen Elisabeth Higson [1960] Director/University Professor; Professor Janice Margaret Kay [1956] Director/Senior Deputy Vice Chancellor; Professor Geoffrey Mark Layer [1955] Director/Vice Chancellor; Stephen Andrew Marston [1961] Director/Vice Chancellor; Professor Helen Mary O'Sullivan-Heritage [1966] Director/University Leader/Academic; Helen Samantha Parrett [1969] Director/Group Principal and CEO; Saad Mahmood Qureshi [1987] Director/UK Dean; Professor Colin Bryan Riordan [1959] Director/Vice Chancellor; Christoper Mark Sayers [1960] Director/Chairman; Professor Nigel Anthony Seaton [1970] Director/Vice Chancellor; Professor Eunice Angela Simmons [1961] Director/Academic Manager; Rose Wangen-Jones [1964] Director/Chief Executive [British/American]

**Advance Learning Partnership**
*Incorporated:* 30 January 2012 *Employees:* 186
*Previous:* Parkside Academy
*Net Worth:* £12,757,199 *Total Assets:* £17,655,814
*Registered Office:* Advance Learning Partnership, Whitworth Road, Whitworth Lane, Spennymoor, Co Durham, DL16 7LN
*Activities:* General secondary education
*Officers:* Claire Oates, Secretary; Ellen Beveridge [1973] Director/Headteacher; Linda Ann Davies [1958] Director/Headteacher; John Deller [1952] Director; Steve Leech [1974] Director/Lecturer; Marie Roe [1978] Director; Linda Christine Thompson [1954] Director/Retired

**Advanced Alloy Services Limited**
*Incorporated:* 3 March 1993 *Employees:* 28
*Net Worth:* £16,368,525 *Total Assets:* £22,941,786
*Registered Office:* 65 Market Place, Market Weighton, York, YO43 3AN
*Activities:* Recovery of sorted materials
*Major Shareholder:* Alan Fisher
*Officers:* Doreen Ashton, Secretary; Alan Fisher [1948] Director/Metal Trader; Stephen Hall [1977] Director

**Advanced Couplings Limited**
*Incorporated:* 23 August 1988 *Employees:* 21
*Net Worth:* £4,198,147 *Total Assets:* £6,718,171
*Registered Office:* Unit 3a Riverside Business Park, Royd Ings Avenue, Keighley, W Yorks, BD21 4AF
*Activities:* Manufacture of other fabricated metal products n.e.c.
*Officers:* Winifred Anne Henry, Secretary; Shaun Henry [1965] Director/Sales Engineer; Victoria Jane Henry [1969] Director; James Keith Kendrick [1988] Director/Design Engineer; Peter Roman Wasylyk [1967] Director/Accountant

**Advanced Diesel Engineering Limited**
*Incorporated:* 13 August 1997 *Employees:* 86
*Net Worth:* £3,352,728 *Total Assets:* £7,577,304
*Registered Office:* Unit 14 Langthwaite Grange Ind Est, South Kirkby, Pontefract, W Yorks, WF9 3AP
*Activities:* Other business support service activities n.e.c.
*Shareholders:* Darren Robson; Lee Robson
*Officers:* Darren Robson, Secretary; Philip David Billingsley [1961] Director; Darren Robson [1971] Director; Lee Robson [1969] Director

**Advanced Forwarding Limited**
*Incorporated:* 29 April 2009 *Employees:* 16
*Net Worth:* £2,056,194 *Total Assets:* £5,037,819
*Registered Office:* 606 Building, Wharfedale Road, Euroway Industrial Estate, Bradford, W Yorks, BD4 6SG
*Activities:* Freight transport by road
*Shareholders:* Mohsin Pervez Chohan; David Glyn Rogan; Michael David Danby; Advanced Supply Chain Group Limited
*Officers:* Mohsin Pervez Chohan [1958] Director; Michael David Danby [1960] Director; Rory James Watts [1970] Operations Director, ASC International [Irish]; Claire Webb [1973] Director/Chief Financial Officer

**Advanced Plastics Limited**
*Incorporated:* 23 October 1992 *Employees:* 187
*Net Worth:* £4,903,724 *Total Assets:* £9,178,498
*Registered Office:* Advanced Plastics, Bergen Way, Hull, HU7 0YQ
*Activities:* Manufacture of other plastic products
*Parent:* Merrimex Limited
*Officers:* Robert John Anderson, Secretary; Robert John Anderson [1964] Director; Christopher James Pearson [1969] Director

**Advanced Processing Limited**
*Incorporated:* 15 May 1997
*Net Worth:* £3,131,103 *Total Assets:* £5,250,506
*Registered Office:* 606 Building, Wharfedale Road, Euroway Trading Estate, Bradford, W Yorks, BD4 6SG
*Activities:* Freight transport by road
*Shareholders:* David Glyn Rogan; Michael David Danby; Mohsin Pervez Chohan; Advanced Supply Chain Group Limited
*Officers:* Michael David Danby, Secretary; Mohsin Pervez Chohan [1958] Director/Businessman; Michael David Danby [1960] Director; Claire Webb [1973] Director/Chief Financial Officer

**Advanced Supply Chain (Logistics) Ltd**
*Incorporated:* 3 June 2016 *Employees:* 105
*Net Worth:* £511,656 *Total Assets:* £4,280,181
*Registered Office:* 606 Building, Wharfedale Road, Euroway Industrial Estate, Bradford, W Yorks, BD4 6SG
*Activities:* Freight transport by road
*Shareholders:* David Glyn Rogan; Michael David Danby; Mohsin Pervez Chohan; Advanced Supply Chain Group Limited
*Officers:* Michael David Danby [1960] Director; Claire Webb [1973] Director/Chief Financial Officer

**Advertising Principles Holdings Limited**
*Incorporated:* 9 February 2012 *Employees:* 3
*Net Worth Deficit:* £54,314 *Total Assets:* £6,232,214
*Registered Office:* White Rose House, Otley Road, Headingley, Leeds, LS6 2AD
*Activities:* Activities of head offices
*Officers:* Mark Curtis [1962] Director; Christopher Goodwin [1955] Director; Bernard May [1956] Director

**Advice Champion.co.uk Limited**
*Incorporated:* 11 October 2011 *Employees:* 6
*Net Worth:* £1,431,678 *Total Assets:* £9,545,193
*Registered Office:* No 2 The Bourse, Leeds, LS1 5DE
*Activities:* Activities of financial services holding companies
*Parent:* Mike Edge Holdings Ltd
*Officers:* Gabriel Marie Joseph Crayford, Secretary; Alistair Alexander Callander [1974] Director; Michael Robert Edge [1955] Director; Robert Calvin Morse [1966] Director; Stuart Duncan Phillips [1977] Director; David James Wicks [1950] Director/Marketing Consultant; Nigel Brinley Yeo [1967] Director/Financial Adviser

**ADW Enterprises Limited**
*Incorporated:* 26 March 2015 *Employees:* 1
*Net Worth:* £470,163 *Total Assets:* £5,084,407
*Registered Office:* 2a Acomb Court, Front Street, Acomb, York, YO24 3BJ
*Activities:* Buying and selling of own real estate
*Officers:* Nicola Whitwam, Secretary; Andrew David Whitwam [1970] Director

**Aegeus Industries Limited**
*Incorporated:* 8 February 2006 *Employees:* 203
*Net Worth:* £8,243,000 *Total Assets:* £17,830,000
*Registered Office:* Moorland Engineering Works, Lower Railway Road, Ilkley, W Yorks, LS29 8JB
*Activities:* Other manufacturing n.e.c.
*Shareholder:* Richard Douglas Michael John Summers
*Officers:* Michael Jonathan Brook [1961] Director; Stephen Richard Clarke [1961] Director; Brian John Lawrence [1942] Director; Richard Anton Summers [1972] Director; Richard Douglas Michael John Summers [1944] Director/Engineer

**AETC Limited**
*Incorporated:* 29 May 1996 *Employees:* 404
*Net Worth:* £19,693,000 *Total Assets:* £91,967,000
*Registered Office:* Victoria Avenue, Yeadon, Leeds, LS19 7AW
*Activities:* Manufacture of metal structures and parts of structures
*Parent:* Berkshire Hathaway Inc.
*Officers:* Paul Edelstyn, Secretary; Janet Freeman-Massey, Secretary; Stephane Frederique Michel Martin, Secretary; Anna Marie Armagno [1981] Director [American]; Roger Paul Becker [1953] Director/Vice President - Taxes [American]; Ruth Ann Beyer [1955] Director/Lawyer [American]; Shawn Rene Hagel [1965] Director [American]; Patrick James McIlroy [1972] Managing Director; Dean Alan Wheeler [1962] Director/President [American]

**Affordable Cars (Yorkshire) Limited**
*Incorporated:* 3 October 2013
*Net Worth:* £213,727 *Total Assets:* £4,869,357
*Registered Office:* A19 Crockley Hill, York, YO19 4SJ
*Activities:* Sale of used cars and light motor vehicles
*Officers:* Jasbir Singh Dhesi [1963] Director; Sukpaul Singh Dhesi [1986] Director; Tajinderbir Singh Dhesi [1968] Director

**AFI Bidco Limited**
*Incorporated:* 11 February 2013 *Employees:* 7
*Net Worth Deficit:* £5,357,000 *Total Assets:* £4,219,000
*Registered Office:* Second Floor, West Wing, Diamond House, Diamond Business Park, Thornes Moor Road, Wakefield, W Yorks, WF2 8PT
*Activities:* Activities of head offices
*Parent:* AFI Topco Limited
*Officers:* Steven James Woodhams, Secretary; Oliver John Tudor Jones [1976] Director; David Anthony McNicholas [1972] Director; Kajen Mohanadas [1982] Director/Investment Executive; Nicholas John Selley [1968] Director; David Cyril Shipman [1959] Director/Chairman; David Richard Wardrop [1977] Investment Director; Steven James Woodhams [1979] Director

**AFI Midco Limited**
*Incorporated:* 11 February 2013 *Employees:* 7
*Net Worth Deficit:* £38,201,000 *Total Assets:* £41,061,000
*Registered Office:* Second Floor, West Wing, Diamond House, Diamond Business Park, Thornes Moor Road, Wakefield, W Yorks, WF2 8PT
*Activities:* Activities of head offices
*Parent:* AFI Topco Limited
*Officers:* Steven James Woodhams, Secretary; Oliver John Tudor Jones [1976] Director; David Anthony McNicholas [1972] Director; Kajen Mohanadas [1982] Director/Investment Executive; Nicholas John Selley [1968] Director; David Cyril Shipman [1959] Director/Chairman; David Richard Wardrop [1977] Investment Director; Steven James Woodhams [1979] Director

**AFI Topco Limited**
*Incorporated:* 4 April 2013 *Employees:* 625
*Net Worth Deficit:* £28,745,000 *Total Assets:* £152,560,992
*Registered Office:* Second Floor, West Wing, Diamond House, Diamond Business Park, Thornes Moor Road, Wakefield, W Yorks, WF2 8PT
*Activities:* Activities of head offices
*Officers:* Steven James Woodhams, Secretary; Oliver John Tudor Jones [1976] Director; John May [1955] Director; David Anthony McNicholas [1972] Director; Kajen Mohanadas [1982] Director/Investment Executive; Nicholas John Selley [1968] Director; David Cyril Shipman [1959] Director/Chairman; David Richard Wardrop [1977] Investment Director; Steven James Woodhams [1979] Director

**AFI-Uplift Limited**
*Incorporated:* 2 April 1998 *Employees:* 542
*Net Worth:* £17,281,000 *Total Assets:* £97,450,000
*Registered Office:* 2nd Floor, West Wing, Diamond House, Diamond Business Park, Thornes Moor Road, Wakefield, W Yorks, WF2 8PT
*Activities:* Renting and leasing of other machinery, equipment and tangible goods n.e.c.
*Parent:* AFI Holdings Limited
*Officers:* Steve Woodhams, Secretary; Geoffrey Gibson [1956] Director; Nicholas Higgins [1968] Director; Christopher Jowett [1976] Director; David Anthony McNicholas [1972] Director; Richard David Saunders [1967] Director; Nicholas John Selley [1968] Director; David Cyril Shipman [1959] Director; Carlo Vinci [1962] Director; Peter Wajner [1975] Director; Steve Williams [1979] Director; Steve Woodhams [1979] Director

**Aflex Hose Limited**
*Incorporated:* 21 December 1972 *Employees:* 255
*Net Worth:* £14,337,945 *Total Assets:* £16,118,271
*Registered Office:* Spring Bank Mill Industrial Estate, Watson Mill Lane, Sowerby Bridge, W Yorks, HX6 3BW
*Activities:* Manufacture of plastic plates, sheets, tubes and profiles
*Parent:* Spirax-Sarco Investments Limited
*Officers:* Peter Millen, Secretary; Sean Coyne [1969] Director; Susan Mary Godzicz [1956] Director; Jeremy Robert Hudson [1970] Director; Christopher Andrew Magor [1961] Director; Peter Millen [1978] Director; James Lawrence Whalen IV [1956] Director [American]

**Age Partnership Limited**
*Incorporated:* 21 October 2004 *Employees:* 485
*Net Worth:* £2,304,000 *Total Assets:* £5,960,000
*Registered Office:* 2200 Century Way, Thorpe Park, Leeds, LS15 8ZB
*Activities:* Financial intermediation not elsewhere classified
*Parent:* Age Partnership Group Limited
*Officers:* Jonathan Paul Simpson, Secretary; Daniel Baines [1979] Sales Director; Timothy John Loy [1965] Director/Chartered Accountant; James Patrick Mitchell [1957] Director/Solicitor; Christopher Gage Neave [1962] Director/Consultant; Jonathan Paul Simpson [1976] Finance Director; Andrew Robin Thirkill [1959] Director/Marketing; Simon Warhurst [1979] Operations Director; David Paul Wing [1962] Risk & Compliance Director; Justin John Wysocki [1983] Director

**Agenda Management Services Limited**
*Incorporated:* 15 January 2003 *Employees:* 165
*Net Worth:* £3,060,932 *Total Assets:* £3,908,406
*Registered Office:* 4th Floor, Fairfax House, Merrion Street, Leeds, LS2 8BX
*Activities:* Other business support service activities n.e.c.
*Officers:* Philip Holden, Secretary/Director; Philip Holden [1965] Director; Christopher William Jones [1953] Director/Solicitor; Timothy James Pope [1955] Director

**Agercon Holdings Limited**
*Incorporated:* 20 May 2013
*Net Worth:* £464,473 *Total Assets:* £3,342,894
*Registered Office:* 373 Beverley Road, Hull, HU5 1LA
*Activities:* Buying and selling of own real estate
*Major Shareholder:* Peter Anthony Chaplin
*Officers:* Peter Anthony Chaplin [1956] Director

**Agercon Limited**
*Incorporated:* 7 April 1972 *Employees:* 17
*Net Worth:* £1,351,915 *Total Assets:* £4,989,956
*Registered Office:* The Gables, Molescroft Road, Beverley, N Humbers, HU17 7DU
*Activities:* Other letting and operating of own or leased real estate
*Officers:* Norah Marie Louise Taylor, Secretary; Peter Anthony Chaplin [1956] Director/Property Investor

**Agfa Graphics Limited**
*Incorporated:* 8 November 2006 *Employees:* 100
*Net Worth:* £25,369,000 *Total Assets:* £41,229,000
*Registered Office:* Coal Road, Leeds, LS14 2AL
*Activities:* Treatment and coating of metals
*Parent:* Agfa NV
*Officers:* Anthony John Akroyd, Secretary; Anthony John Akroyd [1966] Director/Accountant; Graham Philip Cooper [1958] Director/Production Manager

**Aggregates R Us Ltd**
*Incorporated:* 22 April 2008 *Employees:* 39
*Net Worth:* £1,158,296 *Total Assets:* £4,554,829
*Registered Office:* Unit 10 Hayfield Business Park, Field Lane, Auckley, Doncaster, S Yorks, DN9 3FL
*Activities:* Wholesale of other intermediate products
*Shareholder:* Mark Russell Robinson
*Officers:* Mark Russell Robinson [1968] Managing Director; Paul Robert Shepherd [1962] Operations Director

**Aghoco 1085 Limited**
*Incorporated:* 28 February 2012 *Employees:* 6
*Net Worth Deficit:* £5,957,000 *Total Assets:* £18,070,000
*Registered Office:* 12b Beechburn Industrial Estate, Prospect Road, Crook, Co Durham, DL15 8RA
*Activities:* Management consultancy activities other than financial management
*Parent:* Pedes Investments Limited
*Officers:* Ian Ralph Bailey [1963] Managing Director; Clinton Wayne George Edy [1962] Director; Jonathan Hammond [1975] Finance Director; Hiroaki Kobayashi [1963] Director [Japanese]; Eijiro Nireki [1971] Director [Japanese]; Hitoshi Suyama [1961] Director [Japanese]

**Aghoco 1419 Limited**
*Incorporated:* 31 May 2016
*Net Worth:* £3,096,384 *Total Assets:* £3,096,384
*Registered Office:* 5th Floor, Central Square, Wellington Street, Leeds, LS1 4DL
*Activities:* Activities of other holding companies n.e.c.
*Major Shareholder:* Stephen Mark Feldman
*Officers:* Dr Stephen Mark Feldman [1962] Director

**Agriargo UK Limited**
*Incorporated:* 24 November 2008 *Employees:* 21
*Net Worth Deficit:* £829,000 *Total Assets:* £11,746,000
*Registered Office:* Unit D3, Harworth Industrial Estate, Bryans Close, Harworth, Doncaster, S Yorks, DN11 8RY
*Activities:* Wholesale of agricultural machinery, equipment and supplies
*Major Shareholder:* Tiago Bonomo
*Officers:* Tiago Bonomo [1984] Director/President [Italian]; Adrian John Winnett [1967] Managing Director

**Agrimin Limited**
*Incorporated:* 18 April 1978 *Employees:* 55
*Net Worth:* £2,605,878 *Total Assets:* £5,103,089
*Registered Office:* No 1 Arlanda Way, Humberside Airport, Kirmington, Ulceby, N Lincs, DN39 6YH
*Activities:* Support activities for animal production (other than farm animal boarding)
*Shareholders:* Josephine Lucie Bennison; Lucinda Helen Jackson; Jo-Ann Clare McCulloch
*Officers:* Robin Arthur Jackson, Secretary; Mark Adrian Armstrong [1964] Sales Director; Doctor James John Bennison [1960] Technical Director; Robin Arthur Jackson [1961] Director; James Forbes McCulloch [1961] Director/Marketing Specialist; Edwin Thomas William Torr [1960] Director

**AGS Airports Holdings Limited**
*Incorporated:* 30 September 2014 *Employees:* 994
*Net Worth:* £198,000,000 *Total Assets:* £1,398,000,000
*Registered Office:* 1 Park Row, Leeds, LS1 5AB
*Activities:* Activities of head offices
*Shareholders:* Faero UK Holding Limited; Macquarie Infrastructure and Real Assets (Europe) Limited
*Officers:* Juan Carlos Bullon Aleman [1972] Director/Lawyer [Spanish]; Ignacio Aitor Garcia Bilbao [1970] Director/Financier [Spanish]; Martyn Booth [1950] Director/Banker; John Kevin Bruen [1972] Director [Irish]; Simon Boyd Geere [1968] Director/Banker; Gonzalo Velasco Zabalza [1979] Director [Spanish]

**AGS Airports Investments Limited**
*Incorporated:* 24 September 2014
*Net Worth:* £99,000,000 *Total Assets:* £411,000,000
*Registered Office:* 1 Park Row, Leeds, LS1 5AB
*Activities:* Activities of head offices
*Parent:* AGS Airports Holdings Limited
*Officers:* Juan Carlos Bullon Aleman [1972] Director/Lawyer [Spanish]; Ignacio Aitor Garcia Bilbao [1970] Director/Financier [Spanish]; Martyn Booth [1950] Director/Banker; John Kevin Bruen [1972] Director [Irish]; Simon Boyd Geere [1968] Director/Banker; Gonzalo Velasco Zabalza [1979] Director [Spanish]

**AGS Airports Limited**
*Incorporated:* 3 September 2014 *Employees:* 994
*Net Worth:* £199,000,000 *Total Assets:* £1,398,000,000
*Registered Office:* 1 Park Row, Leeds, LS1 5AB
*Activities:* Activities of head offices
*Parent:* AGS Airports Investments Limited
*Officers:* Juan Carlos Bullon Aleman [1972] Director/Lawyer [Spanish]; Ignacio Aitor Garcia Bilbao [1970] Director/Financier [Spanish]; Martyn Booth [1950] Director/Banker; John Kevin Bruen [1972] Director [Irish]; Simon Boyd Geere [1968] Director/Banker; Sir Peter James Mason [1946] Director/Engineer; Gonzalo Velasco Zabalza [1979] Director [Spanish]

**AHR Management Services LLP**
*Incorporated:* 6 November 2014 *Employees:* 344
*Net Worth:* £7,317,295 *Total Assets:* £16,359,465
*Registered Office:* Norwich Union House, High Street, Huddersfield, W Yorks, HD1 2LF
*Officers:* Robert Alwynne Charles Grayson [1961] Member; Samantha Jane Grayson [1967] Member; Anthony Michael Langan [1965] Member; Michael Barry Walters [1967] Member; Martin Wright [1958] Member; Karle Burford [1967] LLP Member; David Da Sousa [1976] LLP Member; Andrew France [1974] LLP Member; Bryan Robert Hamilton [1958] LLP Member; Wai-Lun Ho [1971] LLP Member; Allan Hunt [1970] LLP Member; Martin Hyams [1968] LLP Member; Michal Kus [1974] LLP Member; Dominic Manfredi [1971] LLP Member; Gary Charles Overton [1969] LLP Member

**Air Berlin Holding Limited**
*Incorporated:* 24 January 2007
*Net Worth:* £1,381,579 *Total Assets:* £4,790,351
*Registered Office:* First Floor, East Bridge Mills, Stramongate, Kendal, Cumbria, LA9 4UB
*Activities:* Service activities incidental to air transportation
*Parent:* Air Berlin PLC
*Officers:* Michael Lucht [1961] Director/Businessman [German]

**Air Handling Systems Limited**
*Incorporated:* 25 February 2000 *Employees:* 91
*Net Worth:* £1,493,419 *Total Assets:* £4,758,956
*Registered Office:* 3-5 Furnace Industrial Estate, Shildon, Co Durham, DL4 1QB
*Activities:* Other manufacturing n.e.c.
*Major Shareholder:* Leonard George Johnson
*Officers:* Leonard George Johnson, Secretary; Robert Wesley Campbell [1969] Technical Director; Wayne Hodgson [1969] Operations Director; Lee Hartley Johnson [1974] Finance Director; Leonard George Johnson [1951] Managing Director; Richard Matthew Taylor [1981] Sales Director

**Airco Refrigeration and Airconditioning Limited**
*Incorporated:* 13 August 1997 *Employees:* 96
*Net Worth:* £808,567 *Total Assets:* £4,239,913
*Registered Office:* Airco House, Goulton Street, Hull, HU3 4DL
*Activities:* Plumbing, heat and air-conditioning installation
*Major Shareholder:* Neil Fisher
*Officers:* Andrew Patrick Hirst, Secretary; Neil Fisher [1965] Director/Refrigeration Engineer; Christopher Arthur Goodwin [1967] Engineer/Director; Nicholas Daglish Oxtoby [1978] Director/Engineer; Richard Tuplin [1976] Director

**The Aire and Ouse Farms Limited**
*Incorporated:* 20 September 1915 *Employees:* 8
*Net Worth:* £3,228,893 *Total Assets:* £3,504,778
*Registered Office:* Gresham House, 5-7 St Pauls Street, Leeds, LS1 2JG
*Activities:* Growing of cereals (except rice), leguminous crops and oil seeds
*Shareholders:* Ian Johnstone Stephen; Sagars Trustees LLP
*Officers:* Christopher Winston Jones [1959] Director/Chartered Accountant; Ian Johnstone Stephen [1942] Director/Solicitor

**Aire Valley Properties Limited**
*Incorporated:* 28 November 2003
*Net Worth:* £3,895,878 *Total Assets:* £7,050,554
*Registered Office:* 20-22 Bridge End, Leeds, LS1 4DJ
*Activities:* Other letting and operating of own or leased real estate
*Officers:* Charles Alexander Moran [1996] Director/Property; Patricia Moran [1938] Director/Housewife

**Airea Floor Coverings Limited**
*Incorporated:* 18 April 2000
*Net Worth Deficit:* £2,365,000 *Total Assets:* £33,335,000
*Registered Office:* Victoria Mills, The Green, Ossett, W Yorks, WF5 0AN
*Activities:* Activities of production holding companies
*Parent:* Airea PLC
*Officers:* Paul Stevenson, Secretary; Neil Rylance [1956] Director; Paul Stevenson [1978] Director/Accountant

**Airea PLC**
*Incorporated:* 8 December 1953 *Employees:* 192
*Net Worth:* £15,319,000 *Total Assets:* £22,489,000
*Registered Office:* Victoria Mills, The Green Ossett, Wakefield, W Yorks, WF5 0AN
*Activities:* Activities of head offices
*Officers:* Paul Stevenson, Secretary; Neil Rylance [1956] Director/Chief Executive Officer; Paul Stevenson [1978] Director/Accountant; Martin Toogood [1946] Director

**Airedale Catering Equipment Group Limited**
*Incorporated:* 30 October 2012 *Employees:* 280
*Net Worth:* £2,429,000 *Total Assets:* £17,505,000
*Registered Office:* Airedale House, Victoria Road, Eccleshill, Bradford, W Yorks, BD2 2BN
*Activities:* Activities of head offices
*Shareholders:* Robert Howard Bywell; Rockpool Investment Nominee Limited
*Officers:* Andrew Wyatt Bristow [1962] Director; Robert Howard Bywell [1973] Director; Michael Gordge [1963] Director; Ian Richard Sisson [1958] Director; Paul Woodford [1971] Director

**Airedale Catering Equipment Limited**
*Incorporated:* 14 May 1985 *Employees:* 106
*Net Worth:* £9,227,000 *Total Assets:* £19,881,000
*Registered Office:* Airedale House, Victoria Road, Eccleshill, Bradford, W Yorks, BD2 2BN
*Activities:* Installation of industrial machinery and equipment
*Parent:* Airedale Catering Equipment Group Ltd
*Officers:* Robert Howard Bywell [1973] Commercial Director; Michael Gordge [1963] Contracts Director; Ian Richard Sisson [1958] Sales Director; Paul Woodford [1971] Director

**Airedale Chemical Company Limited**
*Incorporated:* 4 December 1973 *Employees:* 121
*Net Worth:* £6,480,642 *Total Assets:* £24,819,348
*Registered Office:* Airedale Mills, Skipton Road, Cross Hills, Keighley, W Yorks, BD20 7BX
*Activities:* Manufacture of other inorganic basic chemicals
*Parent:* Airedale Chemical Holdings
*Officers:* Craig Thomson, Secretary; Christopher John Chadwick [1983] Sales Director; Daniel Fox [1976] Operations Director; Brenda Malvina Hall [1929] Director/Retired; Anthony Joseph Mark Howell [1964] Procurement Director; Martin Leighton [1964] Commercial Director; Daniel George Marr [1983] Marketing Director; Craig Thomson [1974] Director/Accountant; Robert Mark Wolff [1968] Sales Director

**Airedale Chemical Holdings Limited**
*Incorporated:* 21 January 2013 *Employees:* 136
*Net Worth:* £2,374,289 *Total Assets:* £22,757,900
*Registered Office:* Airedale Mills, Skipton Road, Crosshills, Keighley, W Yorks, BD20 7BX
*Activities:* Manufacture of other inorganic basic chemicals
*Officers:* Chris John Chadwick [1983] Sales Director; David Michael Chadwick [1959] Director/Dyestuff Merchant; John Whitney Chadwick [1959] Director/Dyestuff Merchant; Craig Thomson [1974] Director/Accountant

**Airedale House Limited**
*Incorporated:* 24 November 1925 *Employees:* 7
*Net Worth:* £984,146 *Total Assets:* £3,224,687
*Registered Office:* 421 Kirkstall Road, Leeds, LS4 2HA
*Activities:* Renting and operating of Housing Association real estate
*Shareholders:* Martyn Ernest Duffield; Martyn Ernest Duffield
*Officers:* Adam James Duffield [1985] Director; Martyn Ernest Duffield [1954] Director; Simon Christopher Duffield [1988] Director

**Airedale International Air Conditioning Limited**
*Incorporated:* 7 June 1974 *Employees:* 455
*Net Worth:* £12,371,000 *Total Assets:* £31,837,000
*Registered Office:* Rawdon Factory, Leeds Road, Rawdon, Leeds, LS19 6JY
*Activities:* Other manufacturing n.e.c.
*Parent:* Modine Manufacturing Company
*Officers:* Simon Andrew Thorburn, Secretary; Anthony Cole [1963] Director; Steven Joyce [1965] HR Director; Scott Miller [1964] Director/Company Vice President [American]

**Airedale Springs Limited**
*Incorporated:* 7 June 1945 *Employees:* 32
*Net Worth:* £4,209,244 *Total Assets:* £4,558,096
*Registered Office:* The Spring Works, Bridgehouse Lane, Haworth, Keighley, W Yorks, BD22 8PA
*Activities:* Manufacture of wire products, chain and springs
*Shareholder:* Michael Henry Parkinson
*Officers:* Malcolm Sean Parkinson, Secretary; Susan Rachel Brook [1967] Commercial Director; Steven John Hart [1975] Production Director; Malcolm Sean Parkinson [1967] Commercial Director; Michael Henry Parkinson [1935] Director; Timothy Michael Parkinson [1959] Director/Chairman

**Airkool Contracts Limited**
*Incorporated:* 22 April 1998 *Employees:* 36
*Net Worth:* £2,322,040 *Total Assets:* £3,107,437
*Registered Office:* Strickland Street, Hull, HU3 4AD
*Activities:* Plumbing, heat and air-conditioning installation
*Parent:* Airkool Holdings Limited
*Officers:* Wayne Andrew Dawson, Secretary; Richard Peter Dawson [1973] Director; Wayne Andrew Dawson [1977] Director

**Airport Holdings NDH1 Limited**
*Incorporated:* 24 October 2007
*Net Worth Deficit:* £425,000,000 *Total Assets:* £1,049,000,000
*Registered Office:* 1 Park Row, Leeds, LS1 5AB
*Activities:* Activities of head offices
*Parent:* AGS Airports Limited
*Officers:* Ignacio Aitor Garcia Bilbao [1970] Director/Financier [Spanish]; John Kevin Bruen [1972] Director [Irish]; Simon Boyd Geere [1968] Director/Banker; Derek Rodger Provan [1966] Director/Chief Executive Officer; Gonzalo Velasco Zabalza [1979] Director [Spanish]

**AJ Foam Ltd**
*Incorporated:* 30 May 2006 *Employees:* 34
*Net Worth:* £3,430,151 *Total Assets:* £5,353,871
*Registered Office:* Unit B, HLB Business Park, Grange Road, Soothill, Batley, W Yorks, WF17 6LN
*Activities:* Manufacture of mattresses
*Shareholder:* Jabar Shahzad Khan
*Officers:* Khalid Suleman Pandor, Secretary; Jabar Shazad Khan [1977] Director

**AJH Pump Supply & Repair Limited**
*Incorporated:* 6 May 2009 *Employees:* 13
*Net Worth:* £3,304,741 *Total Assets:* £4,770,184
*Registered Office:* Mazars House, Gelderd Road, Gildersome, Leeds, LS27 7JN
*Activities:* Repair of other equipment
*Officers:* Steve Garner [1970] Director/Sales; Andrew John Hyett [1964] Director/Pump Distributor; Deborah Ann Hyett [1964] Director/Accounts

**AJS 22 Ltd**
*Incorporated:* 21 October 1988 *Employees:* 4
*Net Worth:* £6,075,429 *Total Assets:* £6,385,859
*Registered Office:* The Annexe, 9 Regent Parade, Harrogate, N Yorks, HG1 5AN
*Activities:* Other letting and operating of own or leased real estate
*Shareholders:* Alan Stephenson; Ann Stephenson
*Officers:* Alan Stephenson, Secretary/Chairman; Sally Ann Basterfield [1979] Director; Alan Stephenson [1950] Director/Chairman; Ann Stephenson [1950] Director; Jane Elizabeth Stephenson-Smith [1981] Director

**AK (SPV) Limited**
*Incorporated:* 23 October 2012 *Employees:* 2
*Net Worth:* £3,900,100 *Total Assets:* £3,900,100
*Registered Office:* 84 Albion Street, Leeds, LS1 6AG
*Activities:* Activities of other holding companies n.e.c.
*Parent:* Project Light Bidco Limited
*Officers:* Oliver James Lightowlers [1972] Director/Chartered Accountant

**Akari Care Limited**
*Incorporated:* 11 August 2011 *Employees:* 1,833
*Net Worth Deficit:* £14,103,818 *Total Assets:* £12,447,203
*Registered Office:* 84 Albion Street, Leeds, LS1 6AG
*Activities:* Residential care activities for the elderly and disabled
*Parent:* Akari Care Group Limited
*Officers:* Oliver James Lightowlers [1972] Director/Chartered Accountant

**Akebar Park Leisure Limited**
*Incorporated:* 25 March 2014 *Employees:* 38
*Net Worth:* £1,424,074 *Total Assets:* £5,416,280
*Registered Office:* Akebar Park, Wensleydale, Leyburn, N Yorks, DL8 5LY
*Activities:* Recreational vehicle parks, trailer parks and camping grounds
*Shareholders:* Giles Dominic Procter Ellwood; Judith Mary Ellwood
*Officers:* Giles Dominic Procter Ellwood [1966] Director; Judith Mary Hodgson [1958] Director

**Aker Offshore Partner Limited**
*Incorporated:* 3 December 1980
*Net Worth:* £26,414,000 *Total Assets:* £47,478,000
*Registered Office:* 1 Park Row, Leeds, LS1 5AB
*Activities:* Manufacture of other general-purpose machinery n.e.c.
*Parent:* Aker Solutions ASA
*Officers:* Sian Lloyd Rees [1960] Director/UK Country Manager & SVP CM EMEA; Douglas Leslie Roger [1978] Director; Craig Charles Wiggins [1968] Director

**Aketon Limited**
*Incorporated:* 26 March 2003 *Employees:* 381
*Net Worth:* £13,134,762 *Total Assets:* £32,782,760
*Registered Office:* Rudding Park Hotel, Rudding Park, Follifoot, Harrogate, N Yorks, HG3 1JH
*Activities:* Activities of other holding companies n.e.c.
*Major Shareholder:* Simon Peter Mackaness
*Officers:* Graham Molyneux, Secretary; Peter John Banks [1968] Director; Judith Mary Mackaness [1946] Director; Nicholas John Mackaness [1984] Director; Simon Peter Mackaness [1949] Director/Chartered Accountant

**Z.A. Akram Limited**
*Incorporated:* 26 February 1992
*Net Worth:* £3,492,981 *Total Assets:* £3,901,342
*Registered Office:* 2 Thorne Road, Huddersfield, W Yorks, HD1 3JJ
*Activities:* Dispensing chemist in specialised stores
*Shareholders:* Zulfkar Akram; Fakrhun Nisa Akram
*Officers:* Fakhrun Nisa Akram, Secretary; Fakhrun Nisa Akram [1962] Director/Pharmacy Assistant; Zulfkar Akram [1954] Director

**AKV Cladding Products Ltd**
*Incorporated:* 27 June 2011 *Employees:* 66
*Net Worth:* £1,459,082 *Total Assets:* £5,357,911
*Registered Office:* Unit 3 Hackworth Industrial Park, Shildon, Co Durham, DL4 1HF
*Activities:* Other manufacturing n.e.c.
*Parent:* AKV Group Limited
*Officers:* Karl James Everitt [1984] Director; Kevin Everitt [1958] Director; Lee Hammond [1978] Director; Mark Jones [1979] Production Director; Andrew Sneddon [1988] Operations Director

**AKV Group Ltd**
*Incorporated:* 14 April 2015 *Employees:* 66
*Net Worth:* £4,390,168 *Total Assets:* £10,566,855
*Registered Office:* The Old Forge Site, Hackworth Industrial Park, Byerley Road, Shildon, Co Durham, DL4 1HF
*Activities:* Activities of production holding companies
*Officers:* Karl James Everitt [1984] Director; Kevin Michael Everitt [1958] Director; Lee Hammond [1978] Director

**Al Halal Supermarket Limited**
*Incorporated:* 9 August 2000 *Employees:* 72
*Net Worth:* £2,397,446 *Total Assets:* £4,168,865
*Registered Office:* Al Halal Supermarket, Woodhead Road, Bradford, W Yorks, BD7 1PD
*Activities:* Other retail sale in non-specialised stores
*Officers:* Pervez Alam [1956] Director/Businessman

**Al-Murad Management Ltd**
*Incorporated:* 15 March 2005
*Net Worth:* £2,544,965 *Total Assets:* £7,470,014
*Registered Office:* Howley Park Road Estate, Morley, Leeds, LS27 0QN
*Activities:* Other professional, scientific and technical activities n.e.c.
*Officers:* Irfan Patel, Secretary/Purchases; Irfan Patel [1979] Director/Purchases; Ismail Patel [1981] Director/Purchases; Mohammed Patel [1981] Director/Sales; Rizwan Patel [1986] Director/Sales

**Richard Alan Engineering Company Limited**
*Incorporated:* 25 February 1970 *Employees:* 133
*Net Worth:* £4,786,131 *Total Assets:* £12,085,506
*Registered Office:* Shaw Cross Business Park, Owl Lane, Dewsbury, W Yorks, WF12 7RD
*Activities:* Manufacture of metal structures and parts of structures
*Parent:* Richard Alan Holdings Ltd
*Officers:* Stuart Deakes, Secretary; Benjamin David Hancock [1991] Director; Robert Paul Johnson [1957] Director/Engineer; Tracey Jayne Johnson [1964] Director/Business Manager

**Alatas UK Limited**
*Incorporated:* 18 November 1988 *Employees:* 43
*Net Worth:* £2,610,237 *Total Assets:* £4,635,745
*Registered Office:* Unit B, Olympic Park, Low Moor, Bradford, BD12 0LP
*Activities:* Repair and maintenance of ships and boats
*Officers:* Richard De'ath [1980] Director; Alexander George Sparrow [1986] Director; Timothy Roger Sparrow [1958] Director

**Alco Valves Group Limited**
*Incorporated:* 9 November 1998 *Employees:* 113
*Net Worth:* £2,281,626 *Total Assets:* £15,566,812
*Registered Office:* Alco Valves Group Limited, Gooder Lane, Brighouse, W Yorks, HD6 1HB
*Activities:* Manufacture of other fabricated metal products n.e.c.
*Shareholders:* Graco BVBA; Graco Inc.
*Officers:* Karen Park Gallivan, Secretary; Karen Park Gallivan [1956] Director/Vice President, General Counsel & Secretary [American]; Mark William Sheahan [1964] Director/Finance and Accounting [American]

**Aldby Field Nurseries Limited**
*Incorporated:* 5 January 2007 *Employees:* 36
*Net Worth:* £2,181,844 *Total Assets:* £5,274,263
*Registered Office:* Aldby Field Farm, Sand Hutton, York, YO41 1LG
*Activities:* Growing of vegetables and melons, roots and tubers
*Shareholders:* Paul Coulter; Helen Louise Coulter
*Officers:* Helen Louise Coulter, Secretary; Helen Louise Coulter [1964] Director/Nurseryman; Paul Coulter [1960] Director/Nurseryman

**Alexanders Prestige Group Limited**
*Incorporated:* 16 June 2016 *Employees:* 61
*Net Worth:* £1,826,346 *Total Assets:* £12,722,405
*Registered Office:* Alexander House, Bar Lane, Roecliffe, Boroughbridge, N Yorks, YO51 9LS
*Activities:* Sale of used cars and light motor vehicles
*Shareholders:* Alexander Brimelow; Andrew Mark North
*Officers:* Alexander James Brimelow [1978] Director; Irfan Khalid [1979] Director; Andrew Mark North [1978] Director

**Alexanders Prestige Limited**
*Incorporated:* 7 July 2005 *Employees:* 54
*Net Worth:* £1,128,953 *Total Assets:* £8,873,615
*Registered Office:* Alexander House, Bar Lane, Roecliffe, Boroughbridge, N Yorks, YO51 9LS
*Activities:* Sale of used cars and light motor vehicles
*Shareholders:* Alex James Brimelow; Andrew Mark North
*Officers:* Alexander James Brimelow, Secretary; Alexander James Brimelow [1978] Managing Director; Andrew Mark North [1978] Managing Director

**Alfa Site Services Limited**
*Incorporated:* 29 May 2008 *Employees:* 6
*Net Worth:* £3,345,791 *Total Assets:* £7,242,923
*Registered Office:* 48 Outgate, Ealand, Scunthorpe, N Lincs, DN17 4JD
*Activities:* Construction of commercial buildings
*Major Shareholder:* Stephen Noel Berdett
*Officers:* Stephen Noel Burdett, Secretary; Stephen Noel Burdett [1968] Director/Groundworks; Wendy Burdett [1971] Director/Administrator

**Ali-A Entertainment Ltd**
*Incorporated:* 4 October 2011 *Employees:* 1
*Net Worth:* £4,349,922 *Total Assets:* £4,929,662
*Registered Office:* The Lindens, 3 Willingham Road, Lea, Gainsborough, Lincs, DN21 5EH
*Activities:* Other business support service activities n.e.c.
*Major Shareholder:* Alastair James Aiken
*Officers:* Alastair James Aiken [1993] Director/Media Consultant

**All Property Management Ltd**
*Incorporated:* 26 February 2016 *Employees:* 10
*Net Worth:* £5,260,276 *Total Assets:* £12,460,267
*Registered Office:* 1 Commercial Court, Briggate, Leeds, LS1 6ER
*Activities:* Other letting and operating of own or leased real estate
*Shareholders:* Michael Rothwell; Terence George Kernachan
*Officers:* Ian Ellis, Secretary; Ian Ellis [1971] Director/Chartered Accountant; Darren John Rothwell [1966] Director; Michael Rothwell [1968] Director

**All Steels Trading Limited**
*Incorporated:* 5 November 2001 *Employees:* 11
*Net Worth:* £8,272,199 *Total Assets:* £31,838,166
*Registered Office:* Vulcan House, York Road, Thirsk, N Yorks, YO7 3BT
*Activities:* Wholesale of metals and metal ores
*Parent:* All Steels Trading Holdings Ltd
*Officers:* Kim Heidi McDougall [1963] Communications Director; Laurence John McDougall [1964] Director; Matthew John Rhodes [1988] Finance Director

**Allam Developments Limited**
*Incorporated:* 15 March 1996
*Net Worth:* £4,100,751 *Total Assets:* £4,350,540
*Registered Office:* Wyke Way, Melton West Business Park, Melton, Hull, HU14 3BQ
*Activities:* Development of building projects
*Parent:* Allamhouse Limited
*Officers:* Ehab Allam, Secretary; Assem Allam [1939] Director; Ehab Allam [1971] Director

**Allam Marine Limited**
*Incorporated:* 21 April 1992 *Employees:* 37
*Net Worth:* £58,759,696 *Total Assets:* £90,522,888
*Registered Office:* Wyke Way, Melton West Business Park, Melton, Hull, HU14 3BQ
*Activities:* Manufacture of engines and turbines, except aircraft, vehicle and cycle engines
*Parent:* Allamhouse Limited
*Officers:* Ehab Allam, Secretary; Dr Assem Allam [1939] Director; Ehab Allam [1971] Director

**Allamhouse Limited**
*Incorporated:* 14 October 2009 *Employees:* 453
*Net Worth:* £63,683,184 *Total Assets:* £152,432,848
*Registered Office:* Wyke Way, Melton West Business Park, Melton, Hull, HU14 3BQ
*Activities:* Activities of head offices
*Shareholders:* Assem Allam; Fatima Allam
*Officers:* Dr Assem Allam [1939] Director; Ehab Allam [1971] Director

**Allerton Steel Limited**
*Incorporated:* 24 March 2009 *Employees:* 132
*Net Worth:* £2,443,591 *Total Assets:* £4,175,511
*Registered Office:* 20 Leases Road, Leeming Bar, Northallerton, N Yorks, DL7 9AW
*Activities:* Manufacture of metal structures and parts of structures
*Officers:* Giles Francis John Penn, Company Secretary; Andrew Robert Gatenby [1974] Director; John Gatenby [1946] Director; Giles Francis John Penn [1967] Managing Director

**Alliance Office Systems Limited**
*Incorporated:* 14 January 1994 *Employees:* 42
*Net Worth:* £3,969,543 *Total Assets:* £5,874,788
*Registered Office:* Victoria Works, Holmfield Industrial Estate, Holmfield, Halifax, W Yorks, HX2 9TN
*Activities:* Manufacture of office and shop furniture
*Major Shareholder:* Michael Tyszyk
*Officers:* Michael Tyszyk, Secretary/Director; Andrew Paul Brown [1974] Financial Director; Kylie Jane Tyszyk [1987] Director; Michael Tyszyk [1959] Director

**Allied Glass Containers Limited**
*Incorporated:* 22 September 1999 *Employees:* 613
*Net Worth:* £59,396,000 *Total Assets:* £139,652,992
*Registered Office:* 69 South Accommodation Road, Leeds, LS10 1NQ
*Activities:* Manufacture of hollow glass
*Officers:* James Stewart McLean, Secretary; Jonathan Mark Culley [1977] Business Development Director; Alan Stephen Henderson [1974] Managing Director; Michael John Hogley [1986] NPD Director; Neil Anthony Maskrey [1967] Finance Director; Philip Morris [1966] Sales Director; John Steven Naughton [1975] Director; Richard Summers [1971] Operations Director

**Allied Glass Group Limited**
*Incorporated:* 19 May 2010
*Net Worth:* £1,837,000 *Total Assets:* £66,921,000
*Registered Office:* 69 South Accommodation Road, Leeds, LS10 1NQ
*Activities:* Manufacture of hollow glass
*Officers:* James Stewart McLean, Secretary; Alan Stephen Henderson [1974] Director; Neil Anthony Maskrey [1967] Finance Director; Philip Morris [1966] Director; John Steven Naughton [1975] Director; Richard Summers [1971] Director

**Allied Glass Holdings Limited**
*Incorporated:* 22 October 2002
*Net Worth:* £5,680,000 *Total Assets:* £46,849,000
*Registered Office:* 69 South Accommodation Road, Leeds, LS10 1NQ
*Activities:* Other business support service activities n.e.c.
*Officers:* James Stewart McLean, Secretary; Alan Stephen Henderson [1974] Director; Neil Anthony Maskrey [1967] Finance Director; Philip Morris [1966] Director; Richard Summers [1971] Director

**Allied Properties (Hull) Limited**
*Incorporated:* 15 November 1988 *Employees:* 5
*Net Worth:* £2,713,321 *Total Assets:* £4,228,639
*Registered Office:* 198 Willerby Road, Hull, HU5 5JW
*Activities:* Buying and selling of own real estate
*Shareholder:* Andrew Kenneth Wheeldon
*Officers:* Andrew Kenneth Wheeldon, Secretary; Andrew Slee [1953] Director/Property Developer; Linda Georgina Slee [1952] Director/Property Developer; Amanda Louise Wheeldon [1967] Director/Property Developer; Andrew Kenneth Wheeldon [1962] Director/Property Developer

**Allied Protek Engineering Solutions Limited**
*Incorporated:* 10 January 2013 *Employees:* 70
*Net Worth:* £1,066,576 *Total Assets:* £5,423,163
*Registered Office:* Allied Protek Building, Armstrong Street, Grimsby, N E Lincs, DN31 1XD
*Activities:* Manufacture of metal structures and parts of structures
*Major Shareholder:* Paul Andrew Wilson
*Officers:* Carrie Pickerden, Secretary; John Bracken [1952] Director; Paul Wilson [1962] Director/Engineer

**George Allinson (Transport) Limited**
*Incorporated:* 21 August 1969 *Employees:* 117
*Net Worth:* £18,915,820 *Total Assets:* £22,334,648
*Registered Office:* Faverdale North, Faverdale Industrial Estate, Darlington, Co Durham, DL3 0PH
*Activities:* Sale of other motor vehicles
*Major Shareholder:* David Allinson
*Officers:* David Joseph Jackson, Secretary; David Allinson [1948] Managing Director; Denise Allinson [1959] Director; George William Allinson [1955] Director; Irene Allinson [1949] Director

**Wm.Allison & Sons Limited**
*Incorporated:* 19 May 1954 *Employees:* 52
*Net Worth:* £4,227,288 *Total Assets:* £7,276,834
*Registered Office:* 7 South Church Road, Bishop Auckland, Co Durham, DL14 7LB
*Activities:* Mixed farming
*Major Shareholder:* Michael Nixon Allison
*Officers:* Paul Richard Allison, Secretary/Director; Michael Nixon Allison [1939] Director; Paul Richard Allison [1965] Director

**Allsigns International Limited**
*Incorporated:* 24 June 1999
*Net Worth:* £2,297,774 *Total Assets:* £4,451,281
*Registered Office:* Brunel Industrial Estate, Blyth Road, Harworth, Doncaster, S Yorks, DN11 8LA
*Activities:* Other manufacturing n.e.c.
*Major Shareholder:* Stuart David Turner
*Officers:* David Eric Kiggin, Secretary; Stuart David Turner [1961] Director

**Allsop Holdings Limited**
*Incorporated:* 20 May 2004 *Employees:* 139
*Net Worth:* £3,290,274 *Total Assets:* £6,179,257
*Registered Office:* Hope Bank Works, New Mill Road, Honley, Huddersfield, W Yorks, HD9 6QG
*Activities:* Other manufacturing n.e.c.
*Major Shareholder:* Paul Anthony Goodwin
*Officers:* Ian Johnson, Secretary; Paul Goodwin [1961] Director

**B.Allsop Limited**
*Incorporated:* 19 February 1964 *Employees:* 139
*Net Worth:* £1,802,028 *Total Assets:* £4,773,974
*Registered Office:* Hope Bank Works, New Mill Road, Honley, Holmfirth, Huddersfield, W Yorks, HD9 6QG
*Activities:* Manufacture of other fabricated metal products n.e.c.
*Parent:* Allsop Holdings Ltd
*Officers:* Ian Johnson, Secretary; Paul Goodwin [1961] Managing Director; Ian Johnson [1976] Director/Accountant; Stephane Patrick Paul Lericolais [1973] Director/Engineer [French]; Robert Machon [1972] Sales Director; Robert Lyndon Tyas [1969] Director/Engineer

**Allure Developments Limited**
*Incorporated:* 23 August 1990 *Employees:* 7
*Previous:* A.K.V. (Cladding Fabrications) Limited
*Net Worth:* £3,031,498 *Total Assets:* £4,654,690
*Registered Office:* Hackworth Industrial Park, Byerley Road, Shildon, Co Durham, DL4 1HF
*Activities:* Other manufacturing n.e.c.
*Parent:* AKV Holdings Limited
*Officers:* Kevin Michael Everitt, Secretary; Karl James Everitt [1984] Director; Kevin Michael Everitt [1958] Director/Company Secretary

**ALM Manufacturing Limited**
*Incorporated:* 11 June 1996 *Employees:* 24
*Net Worth:* £984,673 *Total Assets:* £4,615,228
*Registered Office:* Grimbald Crag Close, St James Business Park, Knaresborough, N Yorks, HG5 8PJ
*Activities:* Other manufacturing n.e.c.
*Parent:* ALM Group Limited
*Officers:* Theresa Ann Adcock, Secretary/Manufacturer; Paul Richard Adcock [1945] Director/Manufacturer; Theresa Ann Adcock [1948] Director/Manufacturer

**Almara Residential Limited**
*Incorporated:* 4 January 2012
*Net Worth:* £1,508,796 *Total Assets:* £9,632,550
*Registered Office:* Sanderson House, Station Road, Horsforth, Leeds, LS18 5NT
*Activities:* Development of building projects
*Parent:* Atkinson Holdings Limited
*Officers:* Katharine Elizabeth Riall [1973] Director; Patrick Guy Riall [1972] Director

**Almit Group Limited**
*Incorporated:* 28 July 2008 *Employees:* 121
*Net Worth:* £5,124,689 *Total Assets:* £12,266,704
*Registered Office:* Faverdale Industrial Estate, Darlington, Co Durham, DL3 0PP
*Activities:* Activities of head offices
*Shareholders:* Allan Mitchell; Irene Mitchell
*Officers:* Irene Mitchell, Secretary/Director; Allan David Mitchell [1970] Director; Dr Allan Mitchell [1941] Director; Irene Mitchell [1941] Director; Mark Mitchell [1980] Director; Stephen Mitchell [1974] Director

**Almit Properties Limited**
*Incorporated:* 9 July 2008
*Net Worth Deficit:* £441,147 *Total Assets:* £3,380,901
*Registered Office:* Faverdale Industrial Estate, Darlington, Co Durham, DL3 0PP
*Activities:* Other letting and operating of own or leased real estate
*Shareholders:* Allan Mitchell; Irene Mitchell
*Officers:* Irene Mitchell, Secretary/Director; Dr Allan Mitchell [1941] Director; Allan David Mitchell [1970] Director; Irene Mitchell [1941] Director; Mark Mitchell [1980] Director; Stephen Mitchell [1974] Director

**Alphabet BC Limited**
*Incorporated:* 16 June 2017 *Employees:* 34
*Net Worth Deficit:* £254,607 *Total Assets:* £17,164,964
*Registered Office:* 4 Navigation Court, Calder Park, Wakefield, W Yorks, WF2 7BJ
*Activities:* Other professional, scientific and technical activities n.e.c.
*Parent:* Alpina Partners (ScotGP) LP
*Officers:* Richard Charles Batte [1961] Director; Sebastian Canzler [1973] Director/Investment Advisor [German]; John Michael Dilley [1964] Director

**Alphamore Corporation Ltd**
*Incorporated:* 17 April 2000 *Employees:* 28
*Net Worth:* £4,779,077 *Total Assets:* £6,422,254
*Registered Office:* 5 Methley Road, Castleford, W Yorks, WF10 1LX
*Activities:* Activities of other holding companies n.e.c.
*Major Shareholder:* Peter John Ambrose
*Officers:* Kathryn Joan Ambrose, Secretary; Caroline Lucy Ambrose [1984] Director; Patrick Joseph Hamar Ambrose [1988] Director; Peter John Ambrose [1949] Director

**ALS Laboratories (UK) Limited**
*Incorporated:* 5 June 1989 *Employees:* 680
*Previous:* Eclipse Scientific Limited
*Net Worth:* £21,432,000 *Total Assets:* £31,245,000
*Registered Office:* Sands Mill, Huddersfield Road, Mirfield, W Yorks, WF14 9DQ
*Activities:* Technical testing and analysis
*Parent:* ALS Testing Services (UK) Limited
*Officers:* John Raymond Crabtree, Secretary; Matthew Graham Masters [1973] Director

**Alt Berg Holdings Limited**
*Incorporated:* 23 October 2012 *Employees:* 1
*Net Worth:* £4,784,334 *Total Assets:* £4,978,485
*Registered Office:* 14-15 Harelands Courtyard Offices, Moor Road, Melsonby, Richmond, N Yorks, DL10 5NY
*Activities:* Activities of other holding companies n.e.c.
*Major Shareholder:* Michael Joseph Sheehan
*Officers:* Angela Sheehan [1945] Director; Michael Joseph Sheehan [1947] Director

**Alt Berg Limited**
*Incorporated:* 28 November 1990 *Employees:* 20
*Net Worth:* £2,173,539 *Total Assets:* £3,301,337
*Registered Office:* Unit 2b Racecourse Road, Gallowfields Industrial Estate, Richmond, N Yorks, DL10 4XB
*Activities:* Manufacture of footwear
*Parent:* Alt Berg Holdings Limited
*Officers:* Angela Sheehan, Secretary/Director; Joseph Sheehan [1989] Director; Tara May Sheehan [1971] Director

**Alta Enterprises Limited**
*Incorporated:* 19 May 1983 *Employees:* 1
*Net Worth:* £1,180,248 *Total Assets:* £3,022,022
*Registered Office:* Victoria Court, 91 Huddersfield Road, Holmfirth, W Yorks, HD9 3JA
*Activities:* Buying and selling of own real estate
*Officers:* Robert Anthony Betts, Secretary; Christopher Betts [1985] Director/General Manager; David Richard Betts [1950] Director; Robert Anthony Betts [1953] Director/Retired; Susan Gledhill [1954] Director/Manager

**Alternative Windows (Leeds) Limited**
*Incorporated:* 1 October 1992 *Employees:* 82
*Net Worth:* £1,504,787 *Total Assets:* £3,573,588
*Registered Office:* Sycamore House, Knowsthorpe Lane, Cross Green Industrial Estate, Leeds, LS9 0PJ
*Activities:* Other manufacturing n.e.c.
*Shareholders:* Darren Andrew Barraclough; Nigel Mark Fletcher
*Officers:* Gillian Shields, Secretary; Darren Andrew Barraclough [1962] Director; Nigel Mark Fletcher [1963] Director

**Mrs. J. C. Altham & Sons (Morecambe) Limited**
*Incorporated:* 25 March 1965 *Employees:* 103
*Net Worth:* £3,404,348 *Total Assets:* £6,897,950
*Registered Office:* Mrs J C Altham & Sons (Morecambe) Ltd, Northgate, White Lund Industrial Estate, Morecambe, Lancs, LA3 3AY
*Activities:* Production of meat and poultry meat products
*Parent:* Altham Catering Butchers Ltd
*Officers:* Maria Valerie Altham, Secretary; James Carr Altham [1974] Director; Maria Valerie Altham [1950] Director; Richard Charles Altham [1977] Director

**J S Alton & Son Limited**
*Incorporated:* 14 January 2008 *Employees:* 27
*Net Worth:* £3,728,902 *Total Assets:* £4,770,167
*Registered Office:* North Tanfield Farm, North Tanfield, Ripon, N Yorks, HG4 5JT
*Activities:* Raising of swine and pigs
*Shareholders:* James Howard Christopher Alton; The JSA Settlement
*Officers:* James Howard Christopher Alton, Secretary; James Howard Christopher Alton [1978] Director/Farmer; Nicola Louise Alton [1978] Director/Farmer

**Alton Cars Limited**
*Incorporated:* 27 December 1979 *Employees:* 280
*Previous:* Alton Cars Leeds Ltd
*Net Worth:* £4,806,273 *Total Assets:* £14,143,826
*Registered Office:* Alton Cars, Cross Green Approach, Cross Green Industrial Estate, Leeds, LS9 0SG
*Activities:* Other manufacturing n.e.c.
*Shareholders:* Anthony John Parish; Diane Julie Parish
*Officers:* Diane Julie Parish, Secretary; Paul Blundell [1971] Group HR Director; Sophie Jane Braithwaite [1968] Finance Director; Graham Connell [1967] Group Bodyshop Director; Roland Arthur Davis [1955] Director/Works Manager; Neilson Anthony Jones [1972] Group Commercial Director; Julian Paul Milner [1966] Group Managing Director; Anthony John Parish [1954] Director/Group Company Chairman; Diane Julie Parish [1959] Director/PA; Mathew John Parish [1987] Director; Tracy Ann Parish [1985] Director

**Altra Industrial Motion UK Holding Limited**
*Incorporated:* 16 December 1999
*Previous:* Warner Electric UK Group Limited
*Net Worth:* £24,510,908 *Total Assets:* £34,881,520
*Registered Office:* Cannon Way, Dewsbury, W Yorks, WF13 1EH
*Activities:* Activities of head offices
*Officers:* Richard Ian Laws, Secretary; Glenn Deegan [1966] Director/VP, Legal & HR, General Counsel [American]; Todd Patriacca [1969] Director/VP Finance/Corporate Controller [American]

**Altra Industrial Motion UK Limited**
*Incorporated:* 27 December 1995
*Previous:* The Hay Hall Group Limited
*Net Worth:* £18,947,000 *Total Assets:* £19,050,000
*Registered Office:* Cannon Way, Dewsbury, W Yorks, WF13 1EH
*Activities:* Activities of head offices
*Parent:* Altra Industrial Motion UK Holding Limited
*Officers:* Richard Ian Laws, Secretary; Glenn Deegan [1966] Director/VP, Legal & HR, General Counsel [American]; Todd Patriacca [1969] Director/VP Finance/Corporate Controller [American]

**Aluminium Bronze Valves Limited**
*Incorporated:* 13 December 2005 *Employees:* 2
*Net Worth:* £2,572,124 *Total Assets:* £3,079,058
*Registered Office:* Unit 4 The Crossings Business Park, Riperian Way, Crosshills, Keighley, W Yorks, BD20 7BW
*Activities:* Activities of head offices
*Shareholders:* Jonathan Edward Brooksbank; Robert James Brooksbank
*Officers:* Miranda Diane Whitehead, Secretary; Jonathan Edward Brooksbank [1965] Director; Robert James Brooksbank [1966] Director

**Alvercroft Limited**
*Incorporated:* 23 April 1964
*Net Worth:* £2,788,316 *Total Assets:* £7,563,896
*Registered Office:* 2 West Parade Road, Scarborough, N Yorks, YO12 5ED
*Activities:* Other letting and operating of own or leased real estate
*Parent:* The Goodall Group Limited
*Officers:* Joan Margaret Goodall, Secretary; James Rawling Goodall [1980] Director; Joan Margaret Goodall [1941] Director

**Amalgamated Construction Ltd**
*Incorporated:* 2 December 1970 *Employees:* 1,025
*Net Worth:* £13,236,000 *Total Assets:* £93,960,000
*Registered Office:* 3175 Century Way, Thorpe Park, Leeds, LS15 8ZB
*Activities:* Construction of other civil engineering projects n.e.c.
*Parent:* Amco Group Limited
*Officers:* John Henry Booth [1971] Commercial Director; Andries Petrus Liebenberg [1967] Rail Director [South African]; Paul Scott [1964] Director/Engineer; Daniel Warren Toffolo [1968] Director/Chartered Accountant

**Amazone Limited**
*Incorporated:* 26 November 1982 *Employees:* 29
*Net Worth:* £3,527,004 *Total Assets:* £10,539,722
*Registered Office:* Orchard Farm, Hurst Lane, Auckley, Doncaster, S Yorks, DN9 3NW
*Activities:* Wholesale of other machinery and equipment
*Shareholder:* Amazonen-Werke H Dreyer GmbH & Co KG
*Officers:* Ludger Braunsmann, Secretary; Simon Charles Brown [1999] Managing Director; Andreas Hemeyer [1962] Managing Director [German]

**Amber Homeloans Limited**
*Incorporated:* 19 May 1993
*Net Worth:* £369,000 *Total Assets:* £548,196,992
*Registered Office:* The Bailey, Skipton, N Yorks, BD23 1DN
*Activities:* Activities of mortgage finance companies
*Parent:* Skipton Building Society
*Officers:* John Joseph Gibson, Secretary; Ian Geoffrey Moore [1968] Director of Specialist Lending; Andrew Walter Nelson [1964] Director/Accountant; Henry Varney [1972] Director/General Manager

**Amberbeach Ltd.**
*Incorporated:* 21 August 2015
*Net Worth:* £8,501,000 *Total Assets:* £18,618,216
*Registered Office:* Hatfields, Calder Island Way, Denby Dale Road, Wakefield, W Yorks, WF2 7AW
*Activities:* Management consultancy activities other than financial management
*Major Shareholder:* Gareth Sinclair Williams
*Officers:* Gareth Sinclair Williams [1964] Director

**Ambitemp (M & E) Limited**
*Incorporated:* 11 March 2009 *Employees:* 15
*Net Worth:* £1,509,291 *Total Assets:* £4,017,622
*Registered Office:* Heritage Exchange, Wellington Mills, Wellington Street, Huddersfield, W Yorks, HD3 3HR
*Activities:* Other business support service activities n.e.c.
*Major Shareholder:* Wayne Anthony Jones
*Officers:* Wayne Anthony Jones [1973] Director; Mark Philip Robinson [1973] Director

**Peter Ambrose (Castleford) Limited**
*Incorporated:* 26 October 1999 *Employees:* 28
*Net Worth:* £2,120,968 *Total Assets:* £3,978,406
*Registered Office:* 5 Methley Road, Castleford, W Yorks, WF10 1LX
*Activities:* Sale of new cars and light motor vehicles
*Parent:* Alphamore Corporation Ltd
*Officers:* Kathryn Joan Ambrose, Secretary; Peter John Ambrose [1949] Director/Manager

**Amco Group Holdings Limited**
*Incorporated:* 24 November 2008
*Net Worth:* £22,999,602 *Total Assets:* £26,500,000
*Registered Office:* 3175 Century Way, Thorpe Park, Leeds, LS15 8ZB
*Activities:* Activities of head offices
*Parent:* Renew Holdings PLC
*Officers:* Andries Petrus Liebenberg [1967] Director [South African]; Paul Scott [1964] Director/Engineer; Daniel Warren Toffolo [1968] Director/Chartered Accountant

**Amco Group Limited**
*Incorporated:* 17 January 2008 *Employees:* 3
*Net Worth:* £2,987,350 *Total Assets:* £7,887,219
*Registered Office:* 3175 Century Way, Thorpe Park, Leeds, LS15 8ZB
*Activities:* Activities of head offices
*Parent:* Amco Group Holdings Limited
*Officers:* Andries Petrus Liebenberg [1967] Director [South African]; Paul Scott [1964] Director/Engineer; Daniel Warren Toffolo [1968] Director/Chartered Accountant

**Amerdale Investments LLP**
*Incorporated:* 2 June 2005
*Net Worth:* £5,634,742 *Total Assets:* £21,441,484
*Registered Office:* The Coach House, Arncliffe, Skipton, N Yorks, BD23 5QD
*Officers:* Joanne Haigh [1957] Member; David Richard Hood [1948] Member

**Amerdale Ventures LLP**
*Incorporated:* 12 December 2006
*Net Worth:* £11,823,177 *Total Assets:* £11,825,851
*Registered Office:* The Coach House, Arncliffe, Skipton, N Yorks, BD23 5QD
*Officers:* Peter Allport [1955] Member; James Richard Elliott Andrew [1967] Member; Isobel Boissier [1967] Member; James Stanley Caldwell [1944] Member; Roger William Carey [1944] Member; Anthony Danaher [1955] Member; Dominic John Dinan [1966] Member; Robert Evans [1952] Member; Mark Edward Hancock [1965] Member; David Richard Hood [1948] Member; Nigel Justin Kempner [1956] Member; Adam Charles Kerr [1966] Member; Iain Cameron MacDonald [1974] Member; Christopher Michael Manning [1964] Member; Mark Nicholas Lewis Morgan [1962] Member; Andrew Richard Mullins [1964] Member; Geoffrey William Phillips [1961] Member; Mark Ridehalgh [1967] Member; Sir Malcolm Conrad Walker [1946] Member; Paul Ashley Williams [1962] Member

**American Standard (U.K.) Co.**
*Incorporated:* 25 July 1977
*Net Worth:* £100,874,000 *Total Assets:* £103,517,000
*Registered Office:* The Bathroom Works, National Avenue, Hull, HU5 4JJ
*Activities:* Activities of production holding companies
*Parent:* Ideal Standard Holdings (BC) UK Ltd
*Officers:* Joanne Caroline Elwell, Secretary; David Barber [1965] Finance Director; Jonathan Peter Edge [1971] Director

**The Ames Companies UK Ltd.**
*Incorporated:* 9 June 2017 *Employees:* 46
*Net Worth Deficit:* £454,432 *Total Assets:* £11,202,576
*Registered Office:* The Old Airfield, Heck and Pollington Lane, Pollington, E Yorks, DN14 0BA
*Activities:* Non-trading company
*Parent:* Griffon Corporation
*Officers:* Anthony Neil Harker [1969] Director; Brian Gerard Harris [1969] Director/SVP, CFO [American]; Simon Andrew Hupfeld [1976] Director/Chief Executive Officer [Australian]; Dale Elizabeth McGrath [1961] Director/Chief Financial Operator [Australian/American]; Robert Francis Mehmel [1962] Director/Business Executive [American]

**Amnack Limited**
*Incorporated:* 27 February 1996 *Employees:* 110
*Net Worth:* £1,221,980 *Total Assets:* £21,782,600
*Registered Office:* Millfield Industrial Estate, Arksey Lane, Bentley, Doncaster, S Yorks, DN5 0SJ
*Activities:* Manufacture of other electronic and electric wires and cables
*Officers:* Terence Guest [1957] Director; Christopher Cyril Mallinson [1947] Director/General Manager; Neil Mallinson [1971] Managing Director; Valentin Parisi [1964] Director/Accountant [French]

**AMS Bobcat Limited**
*Incorporated:* 29 March 1999 *Employees:* 20
*Net Worth:* £2,289,848 *Total Assets:* £3,336,351
*Registered Office:* A M S Bobcat Ltd, Brigg Road, Scunthorpe, N Lincs, DN16 1AP
*Activities:* Agents involved in the sale of machinery, industrial equipment, ships and aircraft
*Major Shareholder:* George William Aitkenhead
*Officers:* George William Aitkenhead [1956] Director; Steven McIntosh [1967] Director

**AMS No-Dig Limited**
*Incorporated:* 3 April 1992 *Employees:* 44
*Net Worth:* £3,150,562 *Total Assets:* £5,017,649
*Registered Office:* AMS No-Dig Ltd, Brigg Road, Scunthorpe, N Lincs, DN16 1AP
*Activities:* Construction of utility projects for fluids
*Major Shareholder:* George William Aitkenhead
*Officers:* Beverley Elizabeth Aitkenhead [1965] Director; George William Aitkenhead [1956] Director; Peter Charles Guilliatt [1963] Operations Director

**Amsgro Limited**
*Incorporated:* 3 June 2003 *Employees:* 7
*Net Worth:* £1,577,069 *Total Assets:* £10,059,322
*Registered Office:* Alpha House, 96 City Road, Bradford, W Yorks, BD8 8ES
*Activities:* Other manufacturing n.e.c.
*Parent:* Alpha Instrumatics Holding Company Limited
*Officers:* Bernard Mark McDonald, Secretary; Himanshu Suryakant Patel [1961] Director; Suryakant Patel [1932] Director/Businessman

**AMT Vehicle Rental Limited**
*Incorporated:* 16 February 1999 *Employees:* 142
*Net Worth:* £2,779,652 *Total Assets:* £27,766,232
*Registered Office:* Amt House, 174 Armley Road, Leeds, LS12 2QH
*Activities:* Financial leasing
*Parent:* AMT Global Investments Limited
*Officers:* Gina Maria McGawley, Secretary; Neil McGawley [1963] Director/Leasing Broker

**AMT2 Limited**
*Incorporated:* 19 June 2015 *Employees:* 481
*Net Worth:* £3,393,192 *Total Assets:* £7,070,172
*Registered Office:* Unit 1 C/D Birkdale Road, South Park Industrial Estate, Scunthorpe, N Lincs, DN17 2AU
*Activities:* Activities of other holding companies n.e.c.
*Shareholder:* Michael John Godfrey
*Officers:* Michael John Godfrey [1957] Director

**Amvale Limited**
*Incorporated:* 13 June 1985 *Employees:* 33
*Net Worth:* £2,118,464 *Total Assets:* £3,513,444
*Registered Office:* Unit 1 C/D Birkdale Road, South Park Industrial Estate, Scunthorpe, N Lincs, DN17 2AU
*Activities:* Renting and leasing of cars and light motor vehicles
*Shareholders:* Amvale Holdings Limited; Amvale Holdings Limited
*Officers:* Jemma Louise Godfrey, Secretary; Shay Fowler [1971] Director/Transport Manager; Michael John Godfrey [1957] Director/Motor Trader

**Amvale Medical Transport Limited**
*Incorporated:* 2 August 2002 *Employees:* 481
*Net Worth:* £3,393,192 *Total Assets:* £7,070,172
*Registered Office:* Unit 1 C/D South Park Industrial Estate, Birkdale Road, Scunthorpe, N Lincs, DN17 2AU
*Activities:* Other business support service activities n.e.c.
*Shareholders:* AMT2 Limited; AMT2 Limited
*Officers:* Jemma Louise Godfrey, Secretary; Michael John Godfrey [1957] Director

**Anabas (UK 2) Limited**
*Incorporated:* 18 February 2003 *Employees:* 344
*Net Worth:* £1,018,582 *Total Assets:* £4,455,062
*Registered Office:* 2 Pioneer Court, Darlington, Co Durham, DL1 4WD
*Activities:* Other business support service activities n.e.c.
*Major Shareholder:* Mark Patrick Cooper
*Officers:* Mark Patrick Cooper [1967] Director; Alistair Craig [1971] Managing Director

**Anatis UK Limited**
*Incorporated:* 13 April 2009
*Net Worth:* £32,267,118 *Total Assets:* £57,852,392
*Registered Office:* Cherry Valley House, Laceby Business Park, Grimsby Road, Laceby, N E Lincs, DN37 7DP
*Activities:* Activities of production holding companies
*Officers:* Katharine Mary Butler, Secretary; Peimin Liang [1974] Director/Businessman [Chinese]; Jiantong Liu [1968] Director/Businessman [Chinese]; Liang Shi [1983] Director/Businessman [Chinese]; Dr Xinjian Yan [1958] Managing Director [Chinese]

**ANB Advanced Solutions Limited**
*Incorporated:* 22 November 2005 *Employees:* 49
*Net Worth:* £2,538,476 *Total Assets:* £6,994,252
*Registered Office:* c/o Roche Audio Visual, Ainleys Industrial Estate, Elland, W Yorks, HX5 9JP
*Activities:* Activities of head offices
*Shareholders:* Elizabeth Bate; Anthony Norman Bate
*Officers:* Elizabeth Bate, Secretary; Anthony Norman Bate [1963] Managing Director; Elizabeth Bate [1963] Director

**K A Anderson (Metal Recyclers) Limited**
*Incorporated:* 21 October 2002 *Employees:* 37
*Net Worth:* £8,096,225 *Total Assets:* £10,068,004
*Registered Office:* Dallamires Way South, Dallamires Lane Industrial Estate, Ripon, N Yorks, HG4 1TN
*Activities:* Recovery of sorted materials
*Shareholders:* Keith Arthur Anderson; Joan Anderson
*Officers:* Keith Arthur Anderson, Secretary; James Philip Anderson [1977] Director/Metal Recycle; Joan Anderson [1952] Director/Metal Recycler; Keith Anderson [1973] Director/Metal Recycler; Keith Arthur Anderson [1945] Director/Metal Recycler

**CV Anderson Ltd**
*Incorporated:* 5 April 2012 *Employees:* 2
*Net Worth:* £3,578,564 *Total Assets:* £3,579,758
*Registered Office:* Adwalton House, Bruntcliffe Avenue, Morley, Leeds, LS27 0LL
*Activities:* Other business support service activities n.e.c.
*Shareholders:* Clive Vernon Anderson; Heather Mary Anderson
*Officers:* Clive Vernon Anderson [1958] Director

**A. Andrews & Sons (Marbles & Tiles) Limited**
*Incorporated:* 5 June 1936 *Employees:* 132
*Net Worth:* £7,188,118 *Total Assets:* £12,138,115
*Registered Office:* 324-330 Meanwood Road, Leeds, LS7 2JE
*Activities:* Floor and wall covering
*Parent:* A Andrews Trustee Limited
*Officers:* Rodney Christopher Horton, Secretary; David Matthew Clough [1972] Director; Rodney Christopher Horton [1953] Finance Director; Michael Wilson [1958] Contracts Director

**Anglia Metal Limited**
*Incorporated:* 21 February 2012 *Employees:* 33
*Net Worth:* £495,350 *Total Assets:* £14,042,583
*Registered Office:* Good Hope Close, Normanton Industrial Estate, Normanton, W Yorks, WF6 1TR
*Activities:* Cold drawing of wire
*Major Shareholder:* Giulio Properzi
*Officers:* Dimitri Cordublas [1979] Director/Businessman [Italian]; Giulio Properzi [1942] Director/Businessman [Italian]

**Mark Anglin Associates Limited**
*Incorporated:* 27 July 2000 *Employees:* 2
*Net Worth:* £1,352,246 *Total Assets:* £7,305,398
*Registered Office:* Kirby Farm, Tetney Road, Humberston, Grimsby, N E Lincs, DN36 4JN
*Activities:* Other letting and operating of own or leased real estate
*Officers:* Mark Terence Anglin [1966] Director

**Anglo Indian Exports Limited**
*Incorporated:* 18 September 1937 *Employees:* 4
*Net Worth:* £3,401,978 *Total Assets:* £3,861,654
*Registered Office:* Holly Park Mills, Calverley, Pudsey, W Yorks, LS28 5QS
*Activities:* Other business support service activities n.e.c.
*Shareholders:* Lesley Thompson; Elliott Yaffe; Graham Albert Yaffe
*Officers:* Graham Albert Yaffe, Secretary; Elliott Yaffe [1928] Director; Graham Albert Yaffe [1959] Director/Company Secretary

**Angloco Limited**
*Incorporated:* 14 November 1985 *Employees:* 70
*Net Worth:* £4,213,869 *Total Assets:* £7,949,193
*Registered Office:* Station Road, Batley, W Yorks, WF17 5TA
*Activities:* Manufacture of motor vehicles
*Officers:* David Thomas Bramfitt [1959] Service Director; Julie Christine Brown [1937] Director; Nicholas Brown [1968] Director; William Robert Alistair Brown [1974] Director; William Thompson Brown [1936] Chairman/Managing Director; Christopher Michael Childs [1956] Finance Director; Vanessa Jane Stanford [1966] Director

**Angus Holdings Safety Group Limited**
*Incorporated:* 12 March 2013 *Employees:* 8
*Net Worth Deficit:* £14,223,000 *Total Assets:* £31,045,000
*Registered Office:* Station Road, High Bentham, Lancaster, LA2 7NA
*Activities:* Activities of production holding companies
*Parent:* Angus International Safety Group Limited
*Officers:* Charles Delle-Case [1971] Director [French]; Lynda Michelle Guest [1962] Director; Christopher John Thomas [1955] Non-Executive Director Chairman; Paul Williams [1964] Director

**Angus International Safety Group Limited**
*Incorporated:* 12 March 2013 *Employees:* 324
*Net Worth Deficit:* £14,308,000 *Total Assets:* £55,362,000
*Registered Office:* Station Road, High Bentham, Lancaster, LA2 7NA
*Activities:* Activities of production holding companies
*Shareholder:* LDC II LP
*Officers:* Nicholas John Barker [1970] Director; Charles Delle-Case [1971] Director [French]; Lynda Michelle Guest [1962] Director; Christopher Peter Handy [1965] Investment Director; Christopher Milburn [1966] Director; Christopher John Thomas [1955] Non-Executive Director Chairman; Paul Williams [1964] Director

**Anhul Management Limited**
*Incorporated:* 22 February 2010
*Net Worth:* £1 *Total Assets:* £3,026,211
*Registered Office:* 25 Queens Square Business Park, Huddersfield Road, Honley, Holmfirth, W Yorks, HD9 6QZ
*Activities:* Dormant company
*Major Shareholder:* Andrew David Hulme
*Officers:* Andrew David Hulme [1952] Managing Director; Anne Burnett Hulme [1953] Director

**Animalcare Group PLC**
*Incorporated:* 14 June 1972
*Net Worth:* £148,472,992 *Total Assets:* £151,272,992
*Registered Office:* Unit 7, 10 Great North Way, York Business Park, Nether Poppleton, York, YO26 6RB
*Activities:* Activities of distribution holding companies
*Officers:* Christopher Brewster, Secretary; Jan Marcel Mattieu Maria Boone [1971] Non-Executive Director Chairman [Belgian]; Christopher James Brewster [1976] Director/Chief Financial Officer; Christiaan Andre Cardon [1968] Director/Chief Executive Officer [Belgian]; Marc Coucke [1965] Director [Belgian]; James Scott Lambert [1958] Director; Edwin Thomas William Torr [1960] Director; Lord Arthur Francis Nicholas Wills Hill Marquess of Downshire [1959] Director; Jennifer Ann Julia Winter [1960] Director

**Animalcare Ltd**
*Incorporated:* 10 June 1980 *Employees:* 62
*Net Worth:* £9,898,000 *Total Assets:* £15,445,000
*Registered Office:* Unit 7, 10 Great North Way, York Business Park, Nether Poppleton, York, YO26 6RB
*Activities:* Wholesale of pharmaceutical goods
*Parent:* Animalcare Group PLC
*Officers:* Christopher Brewster, Secretary; Christopher James Brewster [1976] Director/UK Country Manager; Lord Arthur Francis Nicholas Wills Marquess of Downshire [1959] Director; Jennifer Ann Julia Winter [1960] Director

**Anlaby Office Cleaning Services Limited**
*Incorporated:* 13 February 2001
*Net Worth:* £1,973,742 *Total Assets:* £10,063,727
*Registered Office:* 27a Lidget Hill, Pudsey, Leeds, LS28 7LG
*Activities:* Other business support service activities n.e.c.
*Shareholders:* Arthur Patrick John Gallagher; Lesley Barbara Gallagher
*Officers:* Lesley Barbara Gallagher, Secretary; Arthur Patrick John Gallagher [1958] Director/Manager

**Anord Mardix (UK) Limited**
*Incorporated:* 7 January 1966 *Employees:* 467
*Previous:* Mardix Limited
*Net Worth:* £15,772,283 *Total Assets:* £37,739,444
*Registered Office:* Castle Mills, Aynam Road, Kendal, Cumbria, LA9 7DE
*Activities:* Manufacture of other electrical equipment
*Parent:* Mardix Holdings Ltd
*Officers:* Kevin Yamashita, Secretary; Jeffrey Mark Drazan [1958] Director [American]; Kevin Finegan [1960] Director [Irish]; David Andrew Gardner [1969] Director; Timothy Heston [1979] Director [American]; Shreyas Kataria [1991] Director [Indian]; Anthony Nordon [1946] Director [Irish]; James Peacock [1971] Director; Kevin Yamashita [1975] Director [American]

**Anord Mardix Critical Power Services Limited**
*Incorporated:* 27 April 2011
*Previous:* Anord Mardix Critical Power Systems Limited
*Net Worth:* £1,426,303 *Total Assets:* £6,163,623
*Registered Office:* Castle Mills, Aynam Road, Kendal, Cumbria, LA9 7DE
*Activities:* Repair of electrical equipment
*Parent:* Mardix Holdings Ltd
*Officers:* Kevin Yamashita, Secretary; Jeffrey Mark Drazan [1958] Director [American]; Kevin Finegan [1960] Director [Irish]; David Andrew Gardner [1969] Director; Timothy Heston [1979] Director [American]; Shreyas Kataria [1991] Director [Indian]; Anthony Nordon [1946] Director [Irish]; James Peacock [1971] Director; Kevin Yamashita [1975] Director [American]

**Ansell Microgard Limited**
*Incorporated:* 13 November 2003 *Employees:* 23
*Previous:* Microgard Limited
*Net Worth:* £7,457,000 *Total Assets:* £11,450,000
*Registered Office:* 9 Saltmarsh Court, Priory Park East, Hull, HU4 7DZ
*Activities:* Manufacture of workwear
*Parent:* Ansell (U.K.) Limited
*Officers:* Paul Bryce [1979] Director; John Rikard Froberg [1974] Director [Swedish]

**Answer Digital Limited**
*Incorporated:* 23 October 1998 *Employees:* 40
*Previous:* Answer Consulting Limited
*Net Worth:* £1,429,161 *Total Assets:* £3,309,004
*Registered Office:* Union Mills, 9 Dewsbury Road, Leeds, LS11 5DD
*Activities:* Business and domestic software development
*Shareholders:* Catherine Monica Parlett; Kenneth Gary Parlett
*Officers:* Kenneth Gary Parlett, Secretary; Catherine Monica Parlett [1964] Director; Kenneth Gary Parlett [1961] Director

**Ant Hire Solutions LLP**
*Incorporated:* 18 October 2012 *Employees:* 34
*Net Worth:* £3,254,085 *Total Assets:* £4,307,808
*Registered Office:* Unit 4 Queen Street, Stourton, Leeds, LS10 1SL
*Officers:* Alistair Nigel Thompson [1943] Member; Doreen Mary Thompson [1944] Member; Julia Lindsey Thompson [1968] Member; Nigel Adrian Thompson [1967] Member

**APC (GB) Limited**
*Incorporated:* 17 April 1997 *Employees:* 21
*Net Worth:* £4,862,030 *Total Assets:* £6,851,825
*Registered Office:* Ings Road, Doncaster, S Yorks, DN5 9TL
*Activities:* Other manufacturing n.e.c.
*Shareholder:* Saria Limited
*Officers:* Generald Michael Frankl [1965] Director [American]; Alberto Gibert Perez [1963] Director [Spanish]; Louis Edward Russell [1956] Director [American]; Andrew Richard Smith [1962] Director

**Apelson Appliances UK Ltd**
*Incorporated:* 23 October 2012 *Employees:* 33
*Net Worth:* £411,934 *Total Assets:* £4,979,329
*Registered Office:* Unit 3 Normandy Landings, Pope Street, Castleford, W Yorks, WF6 2AG
*Activities:* Manufacture of electric motors, generators and transformers
*Major Shareholder:* Juan Jose Morales Del Pino
*Officers:* Anthony Peter Rex, Secretary; Juan Jose Morales Del Pino [1963] Director [Spanish]

**Apex Hydraulics Limited**
*Incorporated:* 24 April 1987 *Employees:* 29
*Net Worth:* £5,705,084 *Total Assets:* £6,596,953
*Registered Office:* Tenter Fields, Thornhill Road Business Park, Dewsbury, W Yorks, WF12 9QT
*Activities:* Machining
*Shareholder:* Maureen Oldroyd
*Officers:* Maureen Oldroyd, Secretary; James Russell Oldroyd [1973] Director; Jason Oldroyd [1971] Director; Jonathan Peter Oldroyd [1970] Director; Maureen Oldroyd [1947] Director

**Apollo 1 Investments**
*Incorporated:* 17 June 2013
*Net Worth Deficit:* £53,925 *Total Assets:* £10,804,547
*Registered Office:* Progeny House, 46 Park Place, Leeds, LS1 2RY
*Activities:* Security dealing on own account
*Shareholders:* Andrea Shelley; Eleanor Marie Kernighan
*Officers:* Eleanor Marie Kernighan [1974] Director; Andrea Shelley [1961] Director

**Apollo 11 Investments**
*Incorporated:* 17 June 2013
*Net Worth Deficit:* £116,668 *Total Assets:* £23,353,708
*Registered Office:* Progeny House, 46 Park Place, Leeds, LS1 2RY
*Activities:* Security dealing on own account
*Shareholders:* Eleanor Marie Kernighan; Andrea Shelley
*Officers:* Eleanor Marie Kernighan [1974] Director; Andrea Shelley [1961] Director

**Apollo Endosurgery UK Ltd**
*Incorporated:* 16 April 2014 *Employees:* 31
*Net Worth:* £959,000 *Total Assets:* £8,624,000
*Registered Office:* Unit 10 St James Business Park, Grimbald Crag Court, Knaresborough, N Yorks, HG5 8QB
*Activities:* Wholesale of pharmaceutical goods
*Parent:* Apollo Endosurgery, Inc.
*Officers:* Stefanie LEA Cavanaugh, Secretary; Stefanie LEA Cavanaugh [1964] Director/Accountant [American]; Dennis McWilliams [1971] Director/Chief Executive Officer [American]; Brian Szymczak [1972] Director [American]; Jane Wright [1969] Director/Accountant

**Apollo Holdco Limited**
*Incorporated:* 16 July 2001
*Net Worth:* £8,702,000 *Total Assets:* £8,966,000
*Registered Office:* The Waterfront, Lakeside Boulevard, Doncaster, S Yorks, DN4 5PL
*Activities:* Other specialised construction activities n.e.c.
*Parent:* Apollo Support Services Group Limited
*Officers:* Mark Richard Priest [1966] Director; James Michael Douglas Thomson [1966] Director

**Apollo Support Services Group Limited**
*Incorporated:* 8 November 2005
*Net Worth:* £162,626,000 *Total Assets:* £162,647,008
*Registered Office:* The Waterfront, Lakeside Boulevard, Doncaster, S Yorks, DN4 5PL
*Activities:* Combined facilities support activities
*Parent:* Conquest Bidco Limited
*Officers:* Mark Richard Priest [1966] Director; James Michael Douglas Thomson [1966] Director

**Applelec Sign Components (UK) Ltd.**
*Incorporated:* 12 November 1998 *Employees:* 80
*Net Worth:* £2,825,282 *Total Assets:* £4,512,838
*Registered Office:* Unit 1 Wharfedale Business Park, Shetcliffe Lane, Bradford, W Yorks, BD4 9RW
*Activities:* Other manufacturing n.e.c.
*Shareholders:* Ian Mark Drinkwater; Paul Jeremy Stothers; Vertical Corporation Ltd
*Officers:* Ian Mark Drinkwater, Secretary; Ian Mark Drinkwater [1967] Director/Engineer; Paul Jeremy Stothers [1966] Director/Engineer

**Appleyard Lees IP LLP**
*Incorporated:* 12 November 2015
*Net Worth:* £7,190,645 *Total Assets:* £9,008,981
*Registered Office:* 15 Clare Road, Halifax, W Yorks, HX1 2HY
*Officers:* Paul Laurence Brandon [1966] Member; Anthony Paul Brierley [1965] Member; Dr David Moy [1968] Member; Ian Michael Robinson [1967] Member; Robert Alan Smithson [1979] Member; Richard Waddington [1969] Member; Dr David Patrick Walsh [1965] Member; Simon Timothy Nicholas Bradbury [1977] LLP Member; Richard Anthony Bray [1980] LLP Member; David James Clark [1977] LLP Member; Robert William Cumming [1979] LLP Member; Robert Ean Davies [1970] LLP Member; Doctor Jennifer Sarah Delaney [1977] LLP Member; Dr Barbara Fleck [1975] LLP Member; Julia Gwilt [1975] LLP Member; Kate Hickinson [1973] LLP Member; Graham Pierssene Johnson [1978] LLP Member; Stephen William Lister [1955] LLP Member

**Colin Appleyard Limited**
*Incorporated:* 29 March 1976 *Employees:* 146
*Net Worth:* £6,794,796 *Total Assets:* £15,650,636
*Registered Office:* Head Office, Cornmill Garage, Halifax Road, Keighley, W Yorks, BD21 1AH
*Activities:* Sale of new cars and light motor vehicles
*Shareholders:* Peggy Appleyard; Judith Carol Parker; Robin Michael Appleyard
*Officers:* Peggy Appleyard, Secretary; Peggy Appleyard [1939] Director/Secretary; Robin Michael Appleyard [1964] Director/Sales Manager; Antony Dodsworth [1971] Director/Accountant; Judith Carol Parker [1961] Director/Work Shop Manager

**Applied Composites Group Ltd**
*Incorporated:* 20 May 2016 *Employees:* 577
*Net Worth Deficit:* £163,000 *Total Assets:* £36,541,000
*Registered Office:* Victoria Works, Thrumpton Lane, Retford, Notts, DN22 6HH
*Activities:* Activities of production holding companies
*Shareholder:* LDC (Managers) Limited
*Officers:* Robert John Jozef Apollo [1985] Director; Christopher Martin Coulton [1979] Director; Craig Andrew Harris [1969] Director/Chief Executive; David James Ring [1962] Director

**Aptar UK Limited**
*Incorporated:* 24 January 1979 *Employees:* 99
*Net Worth:* £10,313,849 *Total Assets:* £22,952,000
*Registered Office:* 5 Bruntcliffe Avenue, Leeds 27 Industrial Estate, Leeds, LS27 0LL
*Activities:* Manufacture of plastic packing goods
*Parent:* Aptargroup Inc.
*Officers:* Mark William Newell, Secretary; John Ryan Kenny [1972] Director/Vice President, Business Development and Strategy [American]; Daniel Stephan Madl [1983] Director of Operations [German]; Peter Michael Shaw [1970] Sales Director; Hedi Jallel Tlili [1974] Director/European President [French]

**Aptiv (UK) Holdings Limited**
*Incorporated:* 20 May 2009
*Previous:* Delphi (UK) Holdings Limited
*Net Worth:* £82,569,000 *Total Assets:* £87,951,000
*Registered Office:* 1 Park Row, Leeds, LS1 5AB
*Activities:* Activities of head offices
*Shareholders:* Delphi Global Investments LLP; Delphi Luxembourg Limited
*Officers:* Sean Patrick Corcoran [1958] Director/Assistant General Counsel [American]; Gavin Stewart Gray [1969] Director/Chartered Accountant

**Aptiv Asia Pacific Holdings (UK) LLP**
*Incorporated:* 20 August 2015
*Previous:* Delphi Automotive Luxembourg LLP
*Net Worth:* £1,567,890,816 *Total Assets:* £4,729,740,288
*Registered Office:* 1 Park Row, Leeds, LS1 5AB

**Aptiv European Holdings (UK) Limited**
*Incorporated:* 9 March 2015
*Previous:* Delphi European Holdings Limited
*Net Worth:* £60,390,764 *Total Assets:* £1,149,200,768
*Registered Office:* 1 Park Row, Leeds, LS1 5AB
*Activities:* Other professional, scientific and technical activities n.e.c.
*Shareholders:* Delphi Luxembourg Limited; Delphi Global Investments LLP
*Officers:* Sean Patrick Corcoran [1958] Director/Assistant General Counsel [American]; Gavin Stewart Gray [1969] Director/Chartered Accountant; David Matthew Sherbin [1959] Director/General Counsel [American]

**Aptiv Financial Holdings (UK) LLP**
*Incorporated:* 25 October 2012
*Previous:* Delphi Financial Holdings LLP
*Net Worth:* £1,104,040,448 *Total Assets:* £1,104,040,448
*Registered Office:* 1 Park Row, Leeds, LS1 5AB

**Aptiv Financial Investment Services (UK) Limited**
*Incorporated:* 30 August 2012
*Previous:* Delphi UK Investments Limited
*Net Worth:* £5,821,513,216 *Total Assets:* £6,520,739,328
*Registered Office:* 1 Park Row, Leeds, LS1 5AB
*Activities:* Activities of head offices
*Shareholder:* Aptiv Global Investments UK LLP
*Officers:* Sean Patrick Corcoran [1958] Director/Assistant General Counsel [American]; Brett McMillan [1984] Director, Capital Markets & Hedging [American]; David Matthew Sherbin [1959] Director/General Counsel [American]

**Aptiv Financial Services (UK) Limited**
*Incorporated:* 11 December 2014
*Previous:* Delphi Financial Services Limited
*Net Worth:* £132,638,200 *Total Assets:* £132,638,200
*Registered Office:* 1 Park Row, Leeds, LS1 5AB
*Activities:* Other professional, scientific and technical activities n.e.c.
*Parent:* Aptiv Financial Holdings (UK) LLP
*Officers:* Sean Patrick Corcoran [1958] Director/Assistant General Counsel [American]; Brett McMillan [1984] Director, Capital Markets & Hedging [American]; David Matthew Sherbin [1959] Director [American]

**Aptiv Global Holdings (UK) Limited**
*Incorporated:* 23 October 2012
*Previous:* Delphi Global Holdings Limited
*Net Worth:* £62,102,276 *Total Assets:* £62,102,276
*Registered Office:* 1 Park Row, Leeds, LS1 5AB
*Activities:* Other professional, scientific and technical activities n.e.c.
*Parent:* Delphi International Holdings LLP
*Officers:* Sean Patrick Corcoran [1958] Director/Assistant General Counsel [American]; Brett McMillan [1984] Director, Capital Markets & Hedging [American]; David Matthew Sherbin [1959] Director [American]

**Aptiv Global Investments UK LLP**
*Incorporated:* 21 November 2013
*Previous:* Delphi Global Investments LLP
*Net Worth:* £9,323,008,000 *Total Assets:* £13,120,447,488
*Registered Office:* 1 Park Row, Leeds, LS1 5AB

**Aptiv Holdfi (UK) Limited**
*Incorporated:* 30 June 2011
*Previous:* Delphi Holdfi UK Limited
*Net Worth Deficit:* £47,535,076 *Total Assets:* £594,188,480
*Registered Office:* 1 Park Row, Leeds, LS1 5AB
*Activities:* Other professional, scientific and technical activities n.e.c.
*Parent:* Aptiv International Holdings (UK) LLP
*Officers:* Sean Patrick Corcoran [1958] Director/Assistant General Counsel [American]; Brett McMillan [1984] Director, Capital Markets & Hedging [American]; David Matthew Sherbin [1959] Director/General Counsel [American]

**Aptiv Holdings (UK) Limited**
*Incorporated:* 4 August 2011
*Previous:* Delphi Automotive Holdings Limited
*Net Worth:* £16,960,648 *Total Assets:* £38,337,140
*Registered Office:* 1 Park Row, Leeds, LS1 5AB
*Activities:* Activities of head offices
*Parent:* Aptiv PLC
*Officers:* Sean Patrick Corcoran [1958] Director/Assistant General Counsel [American]; Gavin Stewart Gray [1969] Director/Chartered Accountant; David Matthew Sherbin [1959] Director/General Counsel [American]

**Aptiv International Financial Services (UK) LLP**
*Incorporated:* 2 November 2012
*Previous:* Delphi UK Financial Services LLP
*Net Worth:* £3,501,495,040 *Total Assets:* £3,501,495,040
*Registered Office:* 1 Park Row, Leeds, LS1 5AB

**Aptiv International Holdings (UK) LLP**
*Incorporated:* 19 August 2009
*Previous:* Delphi Automotive LLP
*Net Worth:* £3,681,668,352 *Total Assets:* £5,012,650,496
*Registered Office:* 1 Park Row, Leeds, LS1 5AB

**Aptiv International Holdings UK Two LLP**
*Incorporated:* 30 September 2009
*Previous:* Delphi International Holdings LLP
*Net Worth:* £7,275,933,696 *Total Assets:* £7,905,390,080
*Registered Office:* 1 Park Row, Leeds, LS1 5AB

**Aptiv Latin America Holdings (UK) LLP**
*Incorporated:* 24 April 2014
*Previous:* Delphi Latin America Holdings LLP
*Net Worth:* £2,015,214,848 *Total Assets:* £2,333,206,528
*Registered Office:* 1 Park Row, Leeds, LS1 5AB

**Aptiv Luxembourg Holdings (UK) Limited**
*Incorporated:* 16 December 2015
*Previous:* Delphi Luxembourg Limited
*Net Worth:* £10,558,920,704 *Total Assets:* £10,558,920,704
*Registered Office:* 1 Park Row, Leeds, LS1 5AB
*Activities:* Other professional, scientific and technical activities n.e.c.
*Parent:* Aptiv Global Investments UK LLP
*Officers:* Sean Patrick Corcoran [1958] Director/Assistant General Counsel [American]; Gavin Stewart Gray [1969] Director/Chartered Accountant; David Matthew Sherbin [1959] Director/General Counsel [American]

**Aptiv Services UK Limited**
*Incorporated:* 8 October 1993 *Employees:* 78
*Previous:* Delphi Automotive Systems UK Limited
*Net Worth:* £9,231,000 *Total Assets:* £48,752,000
*Registered Office:* 1 Park Row, Leeds, LS1 5AB
*Activities:* Manufacture of other parts and accessories for motor vehicles
*Parent:* Aptiv (UK) Holdings Limited
*Officers:* Sean Patrick Corcoran [1958] Director/Assistant General Counsel [American]; Gavin Stewart Gray [1969] Director/Chartered Accountant

**Apttus EMEA Limited**
*Incorporated:* 16 May 2012 *Employees:* 58
*Net Worth:* £2,240,360 *Total Assets:* £3,458,631
*Registered Office:* Framework House, 1-3 Church Lane, Snaith, Goole, E Yorks, DN14 9HN
*Activities:* Other information technology service activities
*Parent:* Apttus Corporation
*Officers:* Neehar Giri [1961] Director [American]

**Aqmen Holdings Limited**
*Incorporated:* 28 April 2016
*Net Worth:* £1,671,862 *Total Assets:* £3,210,751
*Registered Office:* Rossington's Business Park, West Carr Road, Retford, Notts, DN22 7SW
*Activities:* Activities of head offices
*Parent:* PIB Group Limited
*Officers:* Ryan Christopher Brown [1973] Director/CFO - Insurance; Brendan James McManus [1959] Director/CEO - Insurance

**Aqua-Therm (Hull) Limited**
*Incorporated:* 2 October 1997 *Employees:* 35
*Net Worth:* £2,656,289 *Total Assets:* £6,293,300
*Registered Office:* Westmoreland House, Westmoreland Street, Hull, HU2 0DJ
*Activities:* Plumbing, heat and air-conditioning installation
*Major Shareholder:* Malcolm Charles Walker
*Officers:* Lee Davies, Secretary; Lee Davies [1972] Financial Director; George William Griffin [1956] Production Director; Malcolm Charles Walker [1948] Director/Plumber; Shane Malcolm Walker [1972] Director

**Aquaspersions Limited**
*Incorporated:* 17 April 1974 *Employees:* 38
*Net Worth:* £5,009,874 *Total Assets:* £9,434,733
*Registered Office:* Beacon Hill Road, Halifax, W Yorks, HX3 6AQ
*Activities:* Manufacture of other chemical products n.e.c.
*Shareholder:* Michael Richardson
*Officers:* Agnes Richardson, Secretary; Agnes Richardson [1939] Director/Company Secretary; Geoffrey Richardson [1935] Director; Michael Richardson [1959] Director

**Arbor Forest Products Limited**
*Incorporated:* 13 November 1951 *Employees:* 161
*Net Worth:* £27,845,000 *Total Assets:* £46,812,000
*Registered Office:* The Lincoln Castle, Lincoln Castle Way, New Holland, Barrow upon Humber, N Lincs, DN19 7RX
*Activities:* Sawmilling and planing of wood
*Officers:* Julie Ann Howarth, Secretary; Andrew Peter Howarth [1955] Director/Timber Merchant; Deborah Jane Howarth [1958] Director; Julie Ann Howarth [1960] Director; Nicholas David Howarth [1957] Director/Timber Merchant; Jason Ostler [1971] Managing Director; Philip Adam Yell [1959] Director/Operations Manager

**Arboretum Devon (RLH) Limited**
*Incorporated:* 12 June 2015 *Employees:* 1
*Net Worth:* £6,496,208 *Total Assets:* £20,440,832
*Registered Office:* Pickering Showground, Malton Road, Pickering, N Yorks, YO18 8EA
*Activities:* Holiday centres and villages
*Major Shareholder:* Jason Lee Bruton
*Officers:* Jason Bruton, Secretary; Jason Bruton [1968] Director

**Arch Chemicals Limited**
*Incorporated:* 24 February 1978
*Net Worth:* £5,158,000 *Total Assets:* £10,539,000
*Registered Office:* Wheldon Road, Castleford, W Yorks, WF10 2JT
*Activities:* Manufacture of other inorganic basic chemicals
*Officers:* Nicholas Thomas Carter, Secretary; Nicholas Thomas Carter [1981] Director/Financial Accountant; Anthony William Kelly [1963] Director; Christian Wichert [1974] Director/Global Executive [German]

**Arch Chemicals UK Finance**
*Incorporated:* 31 March 2004
*Net Worth:* £15,823,000 *Total Assets:* £18,638,000
*Registered Office:* Wheldon Road, Castleford, W Yorks, WF10 2JT
*Activities:* Financial intermediation not elsewhere classified
*Officers:* Nichols Thomas Carter, Secretary; Nicholas Thomas Carter [1981] Director/Financial Accountant; Anthony William Kelly [1963] Director

**Arch Chemicals UK Holdings Limited**
*Incorporated:* 3 May 2000
*Net Worth:* £50,424,000 *Total Assets:* £50,424,000
*Registered Office:* Wheldon Road, Castleford, W Yorks, WF10 2JT
*Activities:* Activities of head offices
*Officers:* Bradley Generald Luria, Secretary; Nicholas Thomas Carter [1981] Director/Financial Accountant; Alexander Henry Hoy [1966] Director; Anthony William Kelly [1963] Director

**Arch UK Biocides Limited**
*Incorporated:* 8 December 2003 *Employees:* 80
*Net Worth:* £28,066,000 *Total Assets:* £42,653,000
*Registered Office:* Wheldon Road, Castleford, W Yorks, WF10 2JT
*Activities:* Manufacture of soap and detergents
*Officers:* Nicholas Thomas Carter, Secretary; Nicholas Thomas Carter [1981] Director/Financial Accountant; Alexander Henry Hoy [1966] Director; Anthony William Kelly [1963] Director; Franklin Delano Kicklighter [1958] Director/General Manager [American]; Jordan Todorov Petkov [1966] Global Head R&D Consumer Care CPI Director; Astrid Schnidrig [1968] Director/SVP BU Head Coating & Composites [Swiss]; Peter Jozef Van Aken [1968] Director/Head of Material Protection Europe [Belgian]

**Archbold Holdings Limited**
*Incorporated:* 3 February 1937 *Employees:* 174
*Net Worth:* £4,973,864 *Total Assets:* £13,410,161
*Registered Office:* Albert Road, Morley, Leeds, LS27 8TT
*Activities:* Other letting and operating of own or leased real estate
*Shareholder:* David Stuart Archbold
*Officers:* Julie Holmes, Secretary; Benedicte Isabelle Catherine Archbold [1978] Director; David Stuart Archbold [1941] Director/Chairman; Xavier Marc Archbold [1974] Director; Yannis Christophe Archbold [1976] Non-Executive Director; Brian George David Ashford [1946] Director; Martin Holmes [1965] Director; Alan Maher [1968] Director; Dominique Claire Katrina Pitman [1982] Director

**L'Arche**
*Incorporated:* 18 May 1972 *Employees:* 298
*Net Worth:* £11,050,042 *Total Assets:* £12,410,055
*Registered Office:* 10 Briggate, Silsden, Keighley, W Yorks, BD20 9JT
*Activities:* Residential care activities for learning difficulties, mental health and substance abuse
*Officers:* John Francis Sargent, Secretary; Catherine Mary Baines [1941] Director/Retired; Roland Clark [1954] Director/Retired; Dr Carole Glasson [1955] Director/Dr; Isobel Watson Gray [1953] Director/Retired; Aedan Michael Mary MacGreevy [1964] Director/Retired; Benedict Robert Kirwan Moorhead [1958] Director/Lawyer; John Paul O'Brien [1961] Director/Accountant; Bernadette Elizabeth Ann Rijnenberg [1956] Director/Retired; Marie Roberts [1960] Director/Management Consultant; Peter James Whalley [1947] Director/Chartered Accountant; Susan Margaret Williams [1955] Director/Counsellor

**Architectural Steel Limited**
*Incorporated:* 4 January 2000 *Employees:* 73
*Net Worth:* £4,168,176 *Total Assets:* £6,313,418
*Registered Office:* Oakley House, 1 Hungerford Road, Huddersfield, W Yorks, HD3 3AL
*Activities:* Manufacture of basic iron and steel and of ferro-alloys
*Major Shareholder:* Kenneth Lamont Hodge
*Officers:* Victoria Hodge, Secretary; Kenneth Hodge [1971] Director; Jared Mann [1973] Director; Heidi Maria Elizabeth Riley [1959] Director

**Archway Engineering (U.K.) Limited**
*Incorporated:* 12 April 1991 *Employees:* 37
*Net Worth:* £2,575,656 *Total Assets:* £3,261,376
*Registered Office:* Ainleys Industrial Estate, Elland, W Yorks, HX5 9JP
*Activities:* Manufacture of other machine tools
*Major Shareholder:* Robin Graeme Arak
*Officers:* Dr Robin Graeme Arak [1956] Director/Company Chairman; Rudolf Arak [1931] Technical Director; Ian Ashley Jackson [1971] Managing Director

**Arco Limited**
*Incorporated:* 6 February 1914 *Employees:* 1,667
*Net Worth:* £68,579,000 *Total Assets:* £164,059,008
*Registered Office:* P O Box 21, Waverley Street, Hull, HU1 2SJ
*Activities:* Wholesale of clothing and footwear
*Shareholders:* Tom Martin; Stephen Martin
*Officers:* Charles Eugene Shackleton Strickland, Secretary; Kevin Appleton [1960] Director; David Evison [1964] Director; Simon Paul Harrison [1967] Director; Nicholas Alexander Cyril Hildyard [1954] Director; Susan Jones [1960] Director; Bryan James Ian Lawrie [1973] Director; Alexandra Gabrielle Martin [1962] Director; Richard Martin [1972] Director; Stephen Martin [1939] Director; Tom Martin [1936] Director; Helen Jane Wright [1976] Director

**Arctic Waters Limited**
*Incorporated:* 13 September 2011 *Employees:* 4
*Net Worth Deficit:* £43,103 *Total Assets:* £6,696,613
*Registered Office:* 127 Cleethorpe Road, Grimsby, N E Lincs, DN31 3EW
*Activities:* Wholesale of other food, including fish, crustaceans and molluscs
*Major Shareholder:* Igor Smirnov
*Officers:* Andrew Liam Jackson, Secretary; Andrew Liam Jackson [1973] Director

**Ardagh Glass (UK) Limited**
*Incorporated:* 13 December 1919
*Net Worth:* £127,105,000 *Total Assets:* £137,658,000
*Registered Office:* Headlands Lane, Knottingley, W Yorks, WF11 0HP
*Activities:* Activities of head offices
*Parent:* Ardagh Holdings (UK) Limited
*Officers:* Keith Jeffrey Swindell, Secretary; Johannes Gorter [1959] Director/Chief Executive [Dutch]; John Passant [1952] Director; Mark Rozmus [1962] Regional Operations Director; Keith Jeffrey Swindell [1959] Director/Accountant

**Ardagh Glass Limited**
*Incorporated:* 20 June 1956 *Employees:* 1,389
*Net Worth:* £204,988,000 *Total Assets:* £720,115,008
*Registered Office:* Headlands Lane, Knottingley, W Yorks, WF11 0HP
*Activities:* Manufacture of hollow glass
*Parent:* Ardagh Glass (UK) Limited
*Officers:* Keith Jeffrey Swindell, Secretary; Michael Morrison Dick [1968] Director/Business Development Manager; Johannes Gorter [1959] Director/Chief Executive [Dutch]; David John Matthews [1964] Director/Chief Financial Officer; John Passant [1952] Director; Alex Robertson [1960] Director/Chief Commercial Officer; Mark Rozmus [1962] Regional Operations Director; Keith Jeffrey Swindell [1959] Director/Accountant; Johannes Charles Elisabeth Marie Vissers [1960] Director/Chief Human Resources Officer [Dutch]

**Ardagh Holdings (UK) Limited**
*Incorporated:* 5 January 1999 *Employees:* 6
*Net Worth:* £466,396,000 *Total Assets:* £1,200,614,016
*Registered Office:* c/o Ardagh Glass Limited, Headlands Lane, Knottingley, W Yorks, WF11 0HP
*Activities:* Other business support service activities n.e.c.
*Parent:* Ardagh Packaging Holdings Limited
*Officers:* Keith Jeffrey Swindell, Secretary; Michael Leonard [1974] Director/Tax Accountant [Irish]; David John Matthews [1964] Director/Chief Financial Officer; John Passant [1952] Director; Mark Rozmus [1962] Regional Operations Director; John Sheehan [1966] Investor Relations Director [Irish]; Keith Jeffrey Swindell [1959] Director/Accountant

**Ardagh Metal Packaging UK Limited**
*Incorporated:* 29 October 1990 *Employees:* 397
*Net Worth:* £51,814,000 *Total Assets:* £130,476,000
*Registered Office:* Headlands Lane, Knottingley, W Yorks, WF11 0HP
*Activities:* Manufacture of light metal packaging
*Parent:* Ardagh MP Holdings UK Limited
*Officers:* Keith Jeffrey Swindell, Secretary; Michael Morrison Dick [1968] Director/Business Development Manager; David John Matthews [1964] Director/Chief Financial Officer; John Passant [1952] Director; Mark Rozmus [1962] Director; Keith Jeffrey Swindell [1959] Director; Johannes Charles Elisabeth Marie Vissers [1960] Director [Dutch]

**Ardagh MP Holdings UK Limited**
*Incorporated:* 18 October 1996
*Net Worth Deficit:* £3,877,000 *Total Assets:* £83,242,000
*Registered Office:* Headlands Lane, Knottingley, W Yorks, WF11 0HP
*Activities:* Activities of financial services holding companies
*Parent:* Ardagh Holdings (UK) Limited
*Officers:* Keith Jeffrey Swindell, Secretary; Johannes Gorter [1959] Director [Dutch]; John Passant [1952] Director; Mark Rozmus [1962] Director; Keith Jeffrey Swindell [1959] Director; Johannes Charles Elisabeth Marie Vissers [1960] Director [Dutch]

**Ardent Limited**
*Incorporated:* 6 December 2005 *Employees:* 30
*Net Worth:* £2,661,989 *Total Assets:* £3,707,229
*Registered Office:* Unit 3 Becklands Close, Bar Lane, Roecliffe, Boroughbridge, N Yorks, YO51 9NR
*Activities:* Agents specialised in the sale of other particular products
*Major Shareholder:* Neil Kenneth Crowther
*Officers:* Daniel Michael Brunt [1979] Director; Neil Kenneth Crowther [1962] Director/Mechanical Engineer; Alison Hunter [1968] Director

**Arena Capital MP Limited**
*Incorporated:* 5 December 2017
*Net Worth Deficit:* £7,168 *Total Assets:* £3,492,463
*Registered Office:* Unit 14 Follifoot Ridge Business Park, Pannal Road, Follifoot, Harrogate, N Yorks, HG3 1DP
*Activities:* Production of electricity
*Parent:* Arena Capital Partners Limited
*Officers:* Barry Vincent Corcoran [1977] Director [Irish]; Thomas Alan Costello [1975] Director [Irish]; Ian Greer [1977] Director [Irish]

**Arena Group Holdings Limited**
*Incorporated:* 18 March 1999 *Employees:* 198
*Net Worth:* £10,937,714 *Total Assets:* £16,645,678
*Registered Office:* Armitage House, Thorpe Lower Lane, Robin Hood, Wakefield, W Yorks, WF3 3BQ
*Activities:* Activities of head offices
*Major Shareholder:* Adrian John Fitzpatrick
*Officers:* Adrian John Fitzpatrick, Secretary; Adrian John Fitzpatrick [1964] Director; Claire Teresa Fitzpatrick [1962] Director/Credit Controller; Gary John Putson [1977] Director

**Arena Group Limited**
*Incorporated:* 23 September 1987 *Employees:* 157
*Net Worth:* £8,231,308 *Total Assets:* £13,868,894
*Registered Office:* Armitage House, Thorpe Lower Lane, Robin Hood, Wakefield, W Yorks, WF3 3BQ
*Activities:* Photocopying, document preparation and other specialised office support activities
*Officers:* Adrian John Fitzpatrick, Secretary; Adrian John Fitzpatrick [1964] Director; Gary John Putson [1977] Director

**Areopagus Limited**
*Incorporated:* 28 February 1980 *Employees:* 133
*Net Worth:* £14,917,483 *Total Assets:* £23,887,084
*Registered Office:* Brackenholme Business Park, Brackenholme, Selby, N Yorks, YO8 6EL
*Activities:* Non-trading company
*Officers:* Karen Patricia Marshall, Secretary; Joseph William Richardson [1978] Managing Director

**Argrain Holdings Limited**
*Incorporated:* 9 September 2011 *Employees:* 25
*Net Worth:* £6,370,863 *Total Assets:* £11,222,746
*Registered Office:* Mill Farm, Raskelf, York, YO61 3LB
*Activities:* Post-harvest crop activities
*Shareholders:* Derek Padgett; MT David Padgett
*Officers:* David Padgett [1964] Director/Grain Merchant; Derek Padgett [1935] Director/Grain Merchant

**Argrain Limited**
*Incorporated:* 15 August 1975 *Employees:* 25
*Net Worth:* £2,408,155 *Total Assets:* £7,376,489
*Registered Office:* Mill Farm, Raskelf, York, YO61 3LB
*Activities:* Post-harvest crop activities
*Shareholders:* David Padgett; Derek Padgett
*Officers:* Julia Padgett, Secretary; David Padgett [1964] Director/Grain Merchant; Derek Padgett [1935] Director/Grain Merchant

**Argyle Square Properties Limited**
*Incorporated:* 9 September 2003 *Employees:* 3
*Net Worth:* £142,422 *Total Assets:* £3,674,128
*Registered Office:* The Barn, Cobshaw Farm, Langthorne, Bedale, N Yorks, DL8 1PJ
*Activities:* Development of building projects
*Officers:* Jason Living, Secretary; Bernard Courtney Living [1936] Director/Chartered Surveyor; Jason Living [1966] Director/Chartered Surveyor; Joanna Kirsty Living [1968] Director/Property Investor

**Arise Virtual Solutions Limited**
*Incorporated:* 13 September 2007 *Employees:* 10
*Net Worth:* £501,312 *Total Assets:* £7,589,816
*Registered Office:* 1 Park Row, Leeds, LS1 5AB
*Activities:* Other telecommunications activities
*Officers:* Lisa Ross Carstarphen [1965] Director/Senior Vice President and General Counsel [American]; Scott Etheridge [1971] Director; Keir Greenwood [1973] Director/Vice President, Operations; John Anthony Meyer Jr [1956] Director/Chief Executive Officer [American]

**Arizonaco Limited**
*Incorporated:* 4 August 2011
*Net Worth:* £15,920,618 *Total Assets:* £15,954,986
*Registered Office:* Shire House, Humboldt Street, Bradford, W Yorks, BD1 5HQ
*Activities:* Other service activities n.e.c.
*Parent:* Corporate Travel Management (UK) Limited
*Officers:* Stephen John Fleming, Secretary; Deborah Ann Carling [1963] Director/CEO CTM Travel Europe; Stephen John Fleming [1968] Director/Global CFO [Australian]; Jamie Michael Pherous [1968] Managing Director [Australian]

**Arkoni Limited**
*Incorporated:* 18 November 1987 *Employees:* 52
*Net Worth:* £2,766,701 *Total Assets:* £3,766,670
*Registered Office:* Horley Green House, Horley Green Road, Halifax, W Yorks, HX3 6AS
*Activities:* Manufacture of other fabricated metal products n.e.c.
*Shareholders:* Mark Prentice; Julie Prentice
*Officers:* Julie Prentice, Secretary; Mark Prentice [1961] Director/Engineer; Quincy Prentice [1963] Director/Sheet Metal Worker; Martin Quarmby [1958] Director

**Arla Foods (Westbury) Limited**
*Incorporated:* 31 May 2007 *Employees:* 4
*Net Worth:* £24,917,000 *Total Assets:* £47,422,000
*Registered Office:* 4 Savannah Way, Leeds Valley Park, Leeds, LS10 1AB
*Activities:* Wholesale of dairy products, eggs and edible oils and fats
*Parent:* Arla Foods Limited
*Officers:* Kingsley Ajerio [1962] Director; Afshin Amirahmadi [1969] Director; Ivar Andreas Vatne [1978] Director [Norwegian]

**Arla Foods Cheese Company Limited**
*Incorporated:* 29 May 2002
*Net Worth:* £33,945,000 *Total Assets:* £197,992,992
*Registered Office:* Arla House, Savannah Way, Leeds Valley Park, Leeds, LS10 1AB
*Activities:* Other business support service activities n.e.c.
*Parent:* Arla Foods Limited
*Officers:* Kingsley Ajerio [1962] Director; Afshin Amirahmadi [1969] Director; John Steven Phillips [1962] Trustee Director; Ivar Andreas Vatne [1978] Director [Norwegian]

**Arla Foods Ingredients UK Limited**
*Incorporated:* 12 October 2010
*Net Worth:* £15,048,000 *Total Assets:* £20,893,000
*Registered Office:* Arla House, 4 Savannah Way, Leeds Valley Park, Leeds, LS10 1AB
*Activities:* Manufacture of other milk products
*Parent:* Arla Foods Limited
*Officers:* Afshin Amirahmadi [1969] Director; Henrik Hojen Andersen [1960] Director/Chief Executive [Danish]; Klaus Kristiansen [1966] Finance Director [Danish]; Jesper Nielsen [1976] Director/Senior Manager Finance [Danish]; Ivar Andreas Vatne [1978] Director [Norwegian]

**Arla Foods Limited**
*Incorporated:* 30 June 1987 *Employees:* 3,493
*Net Worth:* £299,448,992 *Total Assets:* £1,381,943,040
*Registered Office:* Arla House, 4 Savannah Way, Leeds Valley Park, Leeds, LS10 1AB
*Activities:* Liquid milk and cream production
*Parent:* Arla Foods UK PLC
*Officers:* Lucy Kate Williams, Secretary; Kingsley Ajerio [1962] Director; Afshin Amirahmadi [1969] Director; Peter Gioertz-Carlsen [1973] Director/Executive Vice President [Danish]; Pauline Louise Hogg [1975] Director; Kent Krarup Skovsager [1970] Director [Danish]; Ivar Andreas Vatne [1978] Director [Norwegian]

**Arla Foods UK Holding Limited**
*Incorporated:* 7 February 2003 *Employees:* 7
*Net Worth:* £585,678,016 *Total Assets:* £776,121,024
*Registered Office:* Arla House, 4 Savannah Way, Leeds Valley Park, Leeds, LS10 1AB
*Activities:* Activities of head offices
*Parent:* Arla Foods International A/S
*Officers:* Kingsley Ajerio [1962] Director; Afshin Amirahmadi [1969] Director; Peter Gioertz-Carlsen [1973] Director/Executive Vice President [Danish]; Pauline Louise Hogg [1975] Director; Kent Krarup Skovsager [1970] Director [Danish]; Ivar Andreas Vatne [1978] Director [Norwegian]

**Arla Foods UK PLC**
*Incorporated:* 2 January 1998 *Employees:* 3
*Net Worth:* £465,193,984 *Total Assets:* £637,915,008
*Registered Office:* Arla House, 4 Savannah Way, Leeds Valley Park, Leeds, LS10 1AB
*Activities:* Liquid milk and cream production
*Parent:* Arla Foods UK Holding Limited
*Officers:* Lucy Kate Williams, Secretary; Kingsley Ajerio [1962] Director; Afshin Amirahmadi [1969] Director; Peter Gioertz-Carlsen [1973] Director/Executive Vice President [Danish]; Pauline Louise Hogg [1975] Director; Kent Krarup Skovsager [1970] Director [Danish]; Ivar Andreas Vatne [1978] Director [Norwegian]

**Arla Foods UK Property Company Limited**
*Incorporated:* 21 September 1949 *Employees:* 3
*Net Worth:* £24,164,000 *Total Assets:* £26,352,000
*Registered Office:* Arla House, 4 Savannah Way, Leeds Valley Park, Leeds, LS10 1AB
*Activities:* Activities of head offices
*Parent:* Arla Foods UK PLC
*Officers:* Kingsley Ajerio [1962] Director; Afshin Amirahmadi [1969] Director; Ivar Andreas Vatne [1978] Director [Norwegian]

**Arlington Automotive NE Limited**
*Incorporated:* 6 March 1984 *Employees:* 103
*Previous:* DPE Automotive Limited
*Net Worth:* £4,071,000 *Total Assets:* £8,830,000
*Registered Office:* Arlington Automotive NE Limited, Gurney Way, Aycliffe Business Park, Newton Aycliffe, Co Durham, DL5 6UJ
*Activities:* Manufacture of metal structures and parts of structures
*Parent:* Arlington Automotive Holdings Limited
*Officers:* Peter William Coates [1971] Director/Engineer; Mark Franckel [1962] Director; Simon George Greenhalgh [1972] Director/Chief Financial Officer; Kevin Morley [1950] Director

**Armitage Shanks Ltd**
*Incorporated:* 12 August 2003 *Employees:* 469
*Previous:* Ideal Standard Manufacturing (UK) Limited
*Net Worth:* £8,106,000 *Total Assets:* £121,669,000
*Registered Office:* National Avenue, Hull, HU5 4HS
*Activities:* Manufacture of other plastic products
*Parent:* Ideal Standard (UK) Limited
*Officers:* Joanne Caroline Elwell, Secretary; David Barber [1965] Finance Director; Jonathan Peter Edge [1971] Director; Joanne Caroline Elwell [1965] Director/Accountant

**Armstrong Priestley Holdings Limited**
*Incorporated:* 8 March 2016 *Employees:* 83
*Net Worth:* £1,807,906 *Total Assets:* £7,050,515
*Registered Office:* 77 Holbeck Lane, Leeds, LS11 9UL
*Activities:* Activities of other holding companies n.e.c.
*Officers:* Peter Armstrong [1945] Managing Director; Terence Christopher Bennett [1963] Sales Director; Steven John Brailey [1968] Joint Managing Director; Anne-Marie Cable [1968] Financial Director and Joint Managing Director; Barry Alan Ebbs [1971] Director; Karen Susan Taylor [1965] Director

**Armstrong-Priestley Limited**
*Incorporated:* 24 March 1976 *Employees:* 83
*Net Worth:* £3,119,570 *Total Assets:* £6,636,966
*Registered Office:* Seventy Seven, Holbeck Lane, Leeds, LS11 9UL
*Activities:* Other construction installation
*Parent:* Armstrong Priestley Holdings Limited
*Officers:* Peter Armstrong [1945] Director; Terence Christopher Bennett [1963] Sales Director; Steven John Brailey [1968] Operations Director; Anne-Marie Cable [1968] Finance Director; Barry Alan Ebbs [1971] Director/Senior Project Engineer; Karen Susan Taylor [1965] Director/General Manager

**Armthorpe Academy Trust**
*Incorporated:* 16 May 2012 *Employees:* 89
*Net Worth:* £5,140,000 *Total Assets:* £6,186,000
*Registered Office:* Armthorpe Academy, Mere Lane, Armthorpe, Doncaster, S Yorks, DN3 2DA
*Activities:* General secondary education
*Officers:* Ann Nicholson, Secretary; Louise Bisby [1971] Director/Teacher; Andrew Steven Cope [1958] Director; John Thomas Gillis [1946] Director/Retired; Lynne Piper [1963] Director/Teaching Assistant; Sally Shearman [1959] Director; Martin John Shevill [1955] Director/Educational Consultant & CEO Consilium Academies; Tracey Starbuck [1968] Director

**Armthorpe Falconry Limited**
*Incorporated:* 7 July 2010
*Net Worth:* £3,151,981 *Total Assets:* £3,755,045
*Registered Office:* B Close, West Moor Lane, Doncaster, S Yorks, DN3 3EA
*Activities:* Raising of other animals
*Shareholders:* Shirley Close; Bryn Close
*Officers:* Bryn Albert Close [1953] Director; Shirley Close [1958] Director/Secretarial

**Arncliffe Homes Limited**
*Incorporated:* 19 June 1991 *Employees:* 16
*Net Worth:* £1,183,743 *Total Assets:* £6,873,447
*Registered Office:* Arncliffe House, Bramley Grange, Skeltons Lane, Thorner, Leeds, LS14 3DW
*Activities:* Construction of domestic buildings
*Officers:* Michael James Stafford, Secretary; Lee James Stafford [1978] Director; Michael James Stafford [1949] Director; Robert Grant Stafford [1980] Director; Helen Margaret Whitelock [1953] Director

**R.O.Arnold,Limited**
*Incorporated:* 17 July 1923
*Net Worth:* £3,980,565 *Total Assets:* £6,203,053
*Registered Office:* Fireplace Works, Wheatley Hall Road, Doncaster, S Yorks, DN2 4NY
*Activities:* Wholesale of hardware, plumbing and heating equipment and supplies
*Shareholders:* Cynthia Gaylor; Nutley Goring Holdings Limited
*Officers:* Cynitha Gaylor, Secretary; Gary Baker [1966] Director/Bathrooms Manager; Cynthia Gaylor [1947] Director/Chairman; David Richard Gaylor [1967] Director; LEA Walters [1977] Director

**Arran Isle Holdings Limited**
*Incorporated:* 29 April 1910 *Employees:* 33
*Net Worth:* £25,600,000 *Total Assets:* £78,700,000
*Registered Office:* Premier Way, Lowfields Business Park, Elland, W Yorks, HX5 9HF
*Activities:* Other manufacturing n.e.c.
*Parent:* Arran Isle Limited
*Officers:* Rachel Helen Balbi, Secretary; Robert George Anthony Barr [1956] Director [Irish]; Richard Karcher [1953] Director [American]; Robert Michael McTighe [1953] Director; Michael James Russell Richards [1964] Director; Martin Wardhaugh [1960] Director; Mark Steven Wild [1960] Director/Accountant

**Arran Isle Limited**
*Incorporated:* 15 October 2009 *Employees:* 1,060
*Net Worth:* £26,800,000 *Total Assets:* £94,000,000
*Registered Office:* Brindley House, Premier Way, Lowfields Business Park, Elland, W Yorks, HX5 9HF
*Activities:* Activities of head offices
*Officers:* Mark Steven Wild, Secretary; Robert George Anthony Barr [1956] Director [Irish]; Richard Karcher [1953] Director [American]; Robert Michael McTighe [1953] Director; Michael James Russell Richards [1964] Director; Martin Wardhaugh [1960] Director; Mark Steven Wild [1960] Director

**Arris Global Ltd.**
*Incorporated:* 20 October 1982 *Employees:* 318
*Previous:* Pace Limited
*Net Worth:* £431,802,496 *Total Assets:* £912,290,112
*Registered Office:* Victoria Road, Saltaire, W Yorks, BD18 3LF
*Activities:* Wireless telecommunications activities
*Parent:* Arris International PLC
*Officers:* Stephen McCaffery [1966] Director/Senior Vice President; David Bernard Potts [1957] Director/Executive Vice President [American]; Anthony Emilien Zuyderhoff [1971] Director [American]

**Arris International IP Ltd**
*Incorporated:* 28 August 2013 *Employees:* 2
*Previous:* Pace International Finance Limited
*Net Worth:* £60,326,652 *Total Assets:* £139,804,160
*Registered Office:* Victoria Road, Saltaire, W Yorks, BD18 3LF
*Activities:* Financial management
*Parent:* Arris Global Ltd.
*Officers:* David Bernard Potts [1957] Director/Businessman [American]; Anthony Emilien Zuyderhoff [1971] Director [American]

**Arris International PLC**
*Incorporated:* 20 April 2015 *Employees:* 7,188
*Net Worth:* £3,168,567,040 *Total Assets:* £7,624,257,024
*Registered Office:* Victoria Road, Saltaire, W Yorks, BD18 3LF
*Activities:* Wired telecommunications activities
*Officers:* Patrick W Macken, Secretary; Andrew McGregor Barron [1965] Director/Businessman; John Timothy Bryan [1961] Director [American]; James Alan Chiddix [1945] Director [American]; Andrew Todd Heller [1955] Director [American]; Dr. Jeong Hun Kim [1960] Director/Company Founder [American]; Bruce McClelland [1967] Director/Chief Executive Officer [Canadian]; Barton Shigemura [1959] Director [American]; Robert Stanzione [1948] Director/Executive Chairman [American]; Doreen Toben [1949] Director [American]; Debora Jane Wilson [1957] Director [American]; David Woodle [1955] Director/CEO and Chairman [American]

**Arrow Commercial Centre (Huddersfield) Limited**
*Incorporated:* 17 December 1987 *Employees:* 84
*Net Worth:* £6,136,296 *Total Assets:* £22,588,456
*Registered Office:* Grove Garage, Guy Edge, Linthwaite, Huddersfield, W Yorks, HD7 5TQ
*Activities:* Sale of new cars and light motor vehicles
*Shareholders:* Robert Edwin Hill; Christopher Taylor
*Officers:* James Richard Hill [1980] Director/Rental Sales; Robert Edwin Hill [1953] Managing Director

**Arrow Enterprise Computing Solutions Limited**
*Incorporated:* 16 March 2000 *Employees:* 490
*Net Worth:* £21,441,000 *Total Assets:* £670,864,000
*Registered Office:* Nidderdale House, Beckwith Knowle, Otley Road, Harrogate, N Yorks, HG3 1SA
*Activities:* Other information technology service activities
*Parent:* Arrow Electronics Inc
*Officers:* Kieran David Cooper, Secretary; Kieran David Cooper [1969] Director; Paul Hayhurst [1962] Operations Director; Mark McHale [1965] Sales Director; Christopher David Stansbury [1965] Director [American]; Gregory Paul Tarpinian [1962] Director/Senior Vice President Legal Affairs [American]

**Arrow Film Converters Limited**
*Incorporated:* 22 January 2003 *Employees:* 40
*Net Worth:* £977,770 *Total Assets:* £7,532,842
*Registered Office:* Unit 3 Speedwell Road, Whitwood, Castleford, W Yorks, WF10 5PY
*Activities:* Packaging activities
*Major Shareholder:* John Thomas Graham
*Officers:* John Graham [1962] Sales Director

**Arrow Industrial Group Limited**
*Incorporated:* 5 April 2002 *Employees:* 80
*Net Worth:* £3,895,798 *Total Assets:* £6,234,213
*Registered Office:* 930 Hedon Road, Hull, HU9 5QN
*Activities:* Other building completion and finishing
*Major Shareholder:* Mark Edward Thistlethwayte
*Officers:* David Christopher Harbord [1961] Director; Neil Beaumont Oliver [1953] Director; Mark Edward Thistlethwayte [1964] Director

**Arrow Industrial Holdings Limited**
*Incorporated:* 24 October 2007 *Employees:* 3
*Net Worth:* £89,184 *Total Assets:* £5,237,206
*Registered Office:* 930 Hedon Road, Hull, HU9 5QN
*Activities:* Activities of head offices
*Parent:* Portchester Equity Limited
*Officers:* David Christopher Harbord [1961] Director; Neil Beaumont Oliver [1953] Director; Mark Edward Thistlewaite [1964] Director/Investment Manager

**Artesian Spas UK Limited**
*Incorporated:* 14 October 2002 *Employees:* 14
*Net Worth:* £2,863,229 *Total Assets:* £3,067,741
*Registered Office:* Artesian House, Silk Road, Quest Park, Doncaster, S Yorks, DN2 4LT
*Activities:* Other retail sale not in stores, stalls or markets
*Parent:* Artesian Spas Ltd
*Officers:* Victoria Ruth Wrigglesworth, Secretary; Gareth James McKerchar [1981] Director; Simon John Wrigglesworth [1982] Director; Victoria Ruth Wrigglesworth [1985] Director/Accountant

**Arundel Kerr Produce Limited**
*Incorporated:* 3 November 1999 *Employees:* 27
*Net Worth:* £837,191 *Total Assets:* £5,383,169
*Registered Office:* Pegasus House, Pegasus Road, Elsham Wolds Industrial Estate, Elsham, Brigg, N Lincs, DN20 0SQ
*Activities:* Processing and preserving of potatoes
*Shareholders:* Bruce William Kerr; Richard David Arundel
*Officers:* Emma Arundel, Secretary; Richard David Arundel [1969] Produce Marketing Director; Bruce William Kerr [1970] Director/Farmer; Benjamin Ralph Mordue [1972] Director/Potato Storage and Grading

**Arville Holdings Limited**
*Incorporated:* 11 April 2010 *Employees:* 106
*Net Worth:* £7,802,692 *Total Assets:* £9,548,216
*Registered Office:* Arville House, Sandbeck Way, Wetherby, W Yorks, LS22 7DQ
*Activities:* Activities of production holding companies
*Shareholder:* Robin Alexander Fairbairn Wight
*Officers:* Declan John Salter [1959] Director; Andrew Doveton Stewart [1966] Director/Management Consultant; James William Fairbairn Wight [1966] Managing Director

**Arville Textiles Limited**
*Incorporated:* 4 April 1951 *Employees:* 64
*Net Worth:* £5,460,316 *Total Assets:* £6,792,275
*Registered Office:* Arville House, Sandbeck Way, Wetherby, W Yorks, LS22 7DQ
*Activities:* Weaving of textiles
*Parent:* Arville Holdings Limited
*Officers:* Andrew Doveton Stewart [1966] Director; James William Fairbairn Wight [1966] Managing Director

**Ascentis**
*Incorporated:* 23 January 2009 *Employees:* 126
*Net Worth:* £3,734,715 *Total Assets:* £4,489,271
*Registered Office:* Office 4 Lancaster Business Park, Mannin Way, Caton Road, Lancaster, LA1 3SW
*Activities:* Technical and vocational secondary education
*Officers:* Fiona Victoria Lugiano, Secretary; Alison Bolton [1964] Director/Admissions Manager; Stephen Carlisle [1957] Director/College Principal; Rosemarie Davies [1952] Director/Head of Higher Education Programmes; Robin Hedley Newton-Syms [1958] Executive Director; Paul James Ernest Rowe [1971] Director of Partnerships; Ruth Tomlinson [1976] Director/Programme Area Leader; Anthony Joseph Turjansky [1955] Director/University Manager; Philip Charles Wilkinson [1956] Director/Chief Executive

**Ascot Road Watford Limited**
*Incorporated:* 31 January 2011
*Net Worth Deficit:* £609,000 *Total Assets:* £7,654,000
*Registered Office:* Hilmore House, Gain Lane, Bradford, W Yorks, BD3 7DL
*Activities:* Development of building projects
*Parent:* Optimisation Developments Limited
*Officers:* Jonathan James Burke, Secretary; Jonathan James Burke [1966] Director; Joanna Louise Goff [1978] Finance Director

**Ascribe Group Limited**
*Incorporated:* 15 October 2008
*Net Worth:* £3,650,000 *Total Assets:* £10,040,000
*Registered Office:* Rawdon House, Green Lane, Yeadon, Leeds, LS19 7BY
*Activities:* Other information technology service activities
*Parent:* Emis Group PLC
*Officers:* Christine Benson, Secretary; Dean Anthony Barber [1977] Director/Group Financial Controller; Peter John Southby [1973] Director/Financial Controller

**Ascribe Holdings Limited**
*Incorporated:* 12 August 2004
*Net Worth:* £12,375,537 *Total Assets:* £42,957,680
*Registered Office:* Rawdon House, Green Lane, Yeadon, Leeds, LS19 7BY
*Activities:* Other information technology service activities
*Parent:* Scroll Bidco Limited
*Officers:* Christine Benson, Secretary; Dean Anthony Barber [1977] Director/Group Financial Controller; Peter John Southby [1973] Director/Financial Controller

**Ascribe Limited**
*Incorporated:* 14 June 1989 *Employees:* 249
*Net Worth:* £2,731,523 *Total Assets:* £54,758,744
*Registered Office:* Rawdon House, Green Lane, Yeadon, Leeds, LS19 7BY
*Activities:* Business and domestic software development
*Parent:* Ascribe Holdings Limited
*Officers:* Christine Benson, Secretary; Peter John Southby [1973] Director/Financial Controller; Ian Taylor [1967] Director; Andrew John Thorburn [1962] Director

**ASD Limited**
*Incorporated:* 25 May 1978 *Employees:* 694
*Net Worth:* £13,721,000 *Total Assets:* £162,987,008
*Registered Office:* Valley Farm Road, Stourton, Leeds, LS10 1SD
*Activities:* Wholesale of metals and metal ores
*Parent:* Kloeckner Metal UK Holdings Limited
*Officers:* David Gross [1977] Finance Director [American]; George Clinton Jones [1956] Director; Barrie Clive Salter [1970] Director

**ASD Westok Limited**
*Incorporated:* 15 July 2002 *Employees:* 78
*Net Worth:* £7,468,000 *Total Assets:* £9,972,000
*Registered Office:* Valley Farm Road, Stourton, Leeds, LS10 1SD
*Activities:* Manufacture of metal structures and parts of structures
*Officers:* George Clinton Jones [1956] Director; Barrie Clive Salter [1970] Director

**Asda Financial Services Limited**
*Incorporated:* 15 October 2002 *Employees:* 5
*Net Worth:* £199,330,000 *Total Assets:* £199,371,008
*Registered Office:* Asda House, Southbank, Great Wilson Street, Leeds, LS11 5AD
*Activities:* Non-trading company
*Parent:* Asda Group Limited
*Officers:* Alexander Simpson, Secretary; Roger Michael Burnley [1966] Director; Robert Gerard McWilliam [1969] Director; Andrew Murray [1963] Director [American]; Alexander Simpson [1973] Director; Hayley Marie Tatum [1969] Director

**The Asda Foundation**
*Incorporated:* 22 January 2008
*Net Worth:* £8,988,600 *Total Assets:* £9,187,907
*Registered Office:* Asda Stores, Great Wilson Street, South Bank, Leeds, LS11 5AD
*Activities:* Other business support service activities n.e.c.
*Officers:* Emily Georgina Elizabeth Harrison, Secretary; John Giles Cookman [1945] Director/Retired; Jane Suzanne Earnshaw [1969] Senior Director Reward; Carolyn Heaney [1968] Director/Consultant; Jason Martin [1969] Director/VP (Holding) Supermarkets; Eliesabeth Anne Massey [1968] Director/Vice President Ambient; Andrew Murray [1963] Director/Chief Customer Officer [American]; Annmarie Rocks [1970] Director/Foundation Co-ordinator; Alison Margaret Seabrooke [1963] Director/Chief Executive

**Asda Group Limited**
*Incorporated:* 27 October 1978 *Employees:* 155,941
*Net Worth:* £8,719,500,288 *Total Assets:* £16,451,699,712
*Registered Office:* Asda House, South Bank, Great Wilson Street, Leeds, LS11 5AD
*Activities:* Activities of head offices
*Parent:* Asda Holdings UK Limited
*Officers:* Alexander Simpson, Secretary; Roger Michael Burnley [1966] Director; Anthony Stuart Hemmerdinger [1969] Director; Nicholas Jones [1972] Director; Robert Gerard McWilliam [1969] Director; Andrew Murray [1963] Director [American]; Alexander Simpson [1973] Director; Hayley Marie Tatum [1969] Director

**Asda Holdings UK Limited**
*Incorporated:* 3 February 2000 *Employees:* 4
*Previous:* Wal-Mart LN (UK) Limited
*Net Worth:* £9,745,283,072 *Total Assets:* £9,804,635,136
*Registered Office:* Asda Stores Ltd, Asda House, Great Wilson Street, Leeds, LS11 5AD
*Activities:* Non-trading company
*Parent:* Wal-Mart Stores (UK) Limited
*Officers:* Richard Mayfield [1968] Director; John Caraway McDowell [1964] Director [American]

**Asda Southbank Limited**
*Incorporated:* 6 February 1992 *Employees:* 3
*Net Worth:* £18,380,458 *Total Assets:* £18,644,568
*Registered Office:* Asda House, Southbank, Great Wilson Street, Leeds, LS11 5AD
*Activities:* Other service activities n.e.c.
*Parent:* Asda Group Limited
*Officers:* Alexander Simpson, Secretary; Roger Michael Burnley [1966] Director; Robert Gerard McWilliam [1969] Director; Alexander Simpson [1973] Director; Alexander Simpson [1973] Director

**Asda Stores Limited**
*Incorporated:* 19 February 1949 *Employees:* 151,756
*Net Worth:* £5,198,300,160 *Total Assets:* £10,425,100,288
*Registered Office:* Asda House, South Bank, Great Wilson Street, Leeds, LS11 5AD
*Activities:* Other retail sale in non-specialised stores
*Parent:* Asda Group Limited
*Officers:* Alexander Simpson, Secretary; Roger Michael Burnley [1966] Director; Robert Gerard McWilliam [1969] Director; Alexander Simpson [1973] Director

**Asda Supermarkets Limited**
*Incorporated:* 19 January 2001 *Employees:* 3
*Net Worth:* £2,440,000 *Total Assets:* £16,340,000
*Registered Office:* Asda Stores, Asda House, Southbank, Great Wilson Street, Leeds, LS11 5AD
*Activities:* Non-trading company
*Parent:* Asda Stores Limited
*Officers:* Alexander Simpson, Secretary; Roger Michael Burnley [1966] Director; Robert Gerard McWilliam [1969] Director; Alexander Simpson [1973] Director

**Ashcourt (Durham) Limited**
*Incorporated:* 2 January 2015
*Net Worth Deficit:* £1,801,811 *Total Assets:* £4,111,159
*Registered Office:* Ashcourt Group, Foster Street, Hull, HU8 8BT
*Activities:* Development of building projects
*Parent:* Ashcourt Properties Limited
*Officers:* Daphne Mary Boak [1953] Director; Alistair James Kyle Bousfield [1988] Director; Kurt James Nicholas Bousfield [1983] Director; Robert James Nelson Bousfield [1946] Director

**Ashcourt Contracts Limited**
*Incorporated:* 24 March 2009 *Employees:* 43
*Net Worth:* £11,458,868 *Total Assets:* £56,252,908
*Registered Office:* Ashcourt Group, Foster Street, Hull, HU8 8BT
*Activities:* Other specialised construction activities n.e.c.
*Major Shareholder:* Kurt James Nicholas Bousfield
*Officers:* Kurt James Nicholas Bousfield [1983] Director; Leigh Jon Churchill [1974] Finance Director

**Ashcourt Farms Limited**
*Incorporated:* 7 March 2014
*Net Worth:* £1,197,434 *Total Assets:* £18,944,180
*Registered Office:* Ashcourt Group, Foster Street, Hull, HU8 8BT
*Activities:* Mixed farming
*Parent:* Ashcourt Properties Limited
*Officers:* Daphne Mary Boak [1953] Director; Alistair James Kyle Bousfield [1988] Director; Kurt James Nicholas Bousfield [1983] Director; Robert James Nelson Bousfield [1946] Director

**Ashcourt Properties (Newland) Limited**
*Incorporated:* 8 December 2014
*Net Worth:* £1,507,890 *Total Assets:* £18,242,176
*Registered Office:* Ashcourt Group, Foster Street, Hull, HU8 8BT
*Activities:* Development of building projects
*Parent:* Ashcourt Properties Limited
*Officers:* Robert James Nelson Bousfield, Secretary; Daphne Mary Boak [1953] Director; Alistair James Kyle Bousfield [1988] Director; Kurt James Nicholas Bousfield [1983] Director; Robert James Nelson Bousfield [1946] Director

**Ashcourt Properties Limited**
*Incorporated:* 15 January 1996 *Employees:* 18
*Net Worth:* £16,650,965 *Total Assets:* £22,694,464
*Registered Office:* Ashcourt Group, Foster Street, Hull, HU8 8BT
*Activities:* Management of real estate on a fee or contract basis
*Shareholders:* Alistair James Kyle Bousfield; Kurt James Nicholas Bousfield
*Officers:* Robert James Nelson Bousfield, Secretary/Property Manager; Daphne Mary Boak [1953] Director; Alistair James Kyle Bousefield [1988] Director; Kurt James Nicholas Bousfield [1983] Director; Robert James Nelson Bousfield [1946] Director/Property Manager

**Ashdale UK Limited**
*Incorporated:* 23 April 2004 *Employees:* 124
*Net Worth:* £2,977,240 *Total Assets:* £14,907,057
*Registered Office:* Dower Hotel & Spa, 48 Bond End, Knaresborough, Harrogate, N Yorks, HG5 9AL
*Activities:* Hotels and similar accommodation
*Shareholders:* Ian Lawrence Hanson; Martin Gregory Michael Wicks; Joanne Emma Wicks
*Officers:* Ian Lawrence Hanson, Secretary/Lawyer; Ian Lawrence Hanson [1964] Director/Lawyer; Martin Gregory Michael Wicks [1963] Director/Hotelier

**Ashfield (Hull) Limited**
*Incorporated:* 7 October 2010 *Employees:* 5
*Net Worth:* £350,275 *Total Assets:* £3,101,062
*Registered Office:* 103 Princes Avenue, Hull, HU5 3QP
*Activities:* Other letting and operating of own or leased real estate
*Shareholders:* Michael David Barton; Carol Marion Barton; Louise Mukerjea; David Morris Barton
*Officers:* Louise Mukerjea, Secretary; Michael David Barton [1968] Director; Louise Mukerjea [1971] Director/Property Investor

**Ashford Cladding Systems Limited**
*Incorporated:* 21 September 1988 *Employees:* 44
*Net Worth:* £2,093,162 *Total Assets:* £5,438,059
*Registered Office:* National House, 325 National Avenue, Hull, HU5 4JB
*Activities:* Roofing activities
*Major Shareholder:* Ashley John Hackford
*Officers:* Ashley John Hackford [1962] Director; David Orr [1965] Contracts Director; Christopher John Walmsley [1971] Managing Director

**Ashlea Landscaping Holdings Limited**
*Incorporated:* 8 February 2010 *Employees:* 83
*Net Worth:* £764,936 *Total Assets:* £4,598,283
*Registered Office:* Scotland Road, Carnforth, Lancs, LA5 9RE
*Activities:* Activities of head offices
*Officers:* David Philip Carney [1969] Director; Michael Shaun Carney [1966] Managing Director; Wayne Dand [1970] Contracts Director; Richard David Ford [1965] Operations Director; Peter Jeffreys [1954] Finance Director; Gavin Knowles [1975] Commercial Director; Colin Harvey Morgan [1973] Director; Stuart George Simpson [1968] Director; Bruce James Tyrer [1965] Projects Director

**Ashleighsigns Limited**
*Incorporated:* 11 August 1977 *Employees:* 158
*Net Worth:* £7,121,448 *Total Assets:* £9,821,650
*Registered Office:* Ashleigh House, Beckbridge Road, Normanton Industrial Estate, Normanton, W Yorks, WF6 1TE
*Activities:* Other construction installation
*Officers:* Avril Elizabeth Sadler, Secretary; Andrew Stephen Bedford [1963] Director; Antony Warren Sadler [1962] Managing Director; Avril Elizabeth Sadler [1962] Director; Andrew John Wilson [1969] Director

**Ashridge Contractors Limited**
*Incorporated:* 11 August 1994 *Employees:* 47
*Net Worth:* £2,034,265 *Total Assets:* £4,483,426
*Registered Office:* Ashridge House, Upton Street, Hull, HU8 7DA
*Activities:* Construction of other civil engineering projects n.e.c.
*Shareholders:* Barry James Thomas; Deena Thomas
*Officers:* Deena Thomas, Secretary; Barry James Thomas [1958] Director/Quantity Surveyor

**Ashton Agricultural and General Limited**
*Incorporated:* 9 August 2000 *Employees:* 5
*Net Worth:* £3,747,522 *Total Assets:* £11,579,314
*Registered Office:* Ashlack Hall, Grizebeck, Kirkby in Furness, Cumbria, LA17 7XN
*Activities:* Raising of other animals
*Parent:* Leinster Asset Management Ltd
*Officers:* Michael William Barton [1957] Director; Mark Fitzpatrick Keegan [1948] Director; Thomas Patrick Keegan [1990] Director

**Ashtree Partners LLP**
*Incorporated:* 17 December 2012
*Net Worth:* £3,567,478 *Total Assets:* £3,707,331
*Registered Office:* Sanderson House, Station Road, Horsforth, Leeds, LS18 5NT
*Officers:* Barbara Mary Precious [1943] Member; David Edwin Precious [1940] Member; Katy Davey [1970] LLP Member; Claire Tara Precious [1968] LLP Member; David Precious [1991] LLP Member; Sophie Camilla Precious [1990] LLP Member

**Ashtree Vision & Safety Limited**
*Incorporated:* 27 August 1982 *Employees:* 26
*Net Worth:* £4,564,605 *Total Assets:* £5,037,179
*Registered Office:* Ashtree Works, Brownroyd Street, Bradford, W Yorks, BD8 9AF
*Activities:* Other manufacturing n.e.c.
*Shareholder:* Alan Roper
*Officers:* Janet Roper, Secretary; Alan Roper [1941] Director; Janet Roper [1945] Director; John Alan Roper [1965] Sales Director; Lucille Kirsty Smith [1969] Director/Office Manageress

**Ashwell Academy**
*Incorporated:* 25 February 2013 *Employees:* 30
*Net Worth:* £2,394,958 *Total Assets:* £3,170,259
*Registered Office:* Ashwell Academy, Snowdon Way, Bransholme, Kingston upon Hull, HU7 5DS
*Activities:* General secondary education
*Officers:* Janet Adamson [1957] Director/Retired Headteacher; Dawn Broadbent [1965] Director; Stephen Cook [1948] Director/Retired Secondary Headteacher/College Principal; Eunice Evans [1951] Director/Co-ordinator of Governor Service; Jane Harris [1958] Director/Retired Teacher; Samantha Marshall [1986] Director/Teacher; Patricia Scott [1948] Director/Retired; Deborah Wrapson [1955] Director/Retired

**Askern UK Limited**
*Incorporated:* 18 April 1956 *Employees:* 78
*Net Worth:* £1,884,157 *Total Assets:* £5,889,012
*Registered Office:* 28 Lidgate Crescent, Langthwaite Business Park, South Kirkby, Pontefract, W Yorks, WF9 3NR
*Activities:* Manufacture of other products of wood; manufacture of articles of cork, straw and plaiting materials
*Parent:* Askern Holdings Limited
*Officers:* Robert Black [1967] Director/Production Manager; Carl Dodd [1957] Director/Certified Chartered Accountant; Duncan Murray [1952] Director; Anthony Thomas Veater [1956] Director/General Manager

**Aspire-Igen Group Ltd**
*Incorporated:* 20 March 1995 *Employees:* 254
*Previous:* Aspire-I Limited
*Net Worth:* £1,801,192 *Total Assets:* £4,731,132
*Registered Office:* The Opportunity Centre, 21-27 Cheapside, Bradford, BD1 4HR
*Activities:* Educational support services
*Officers:* Caroline Harrison, Secretary; John Malcolm Charles Cole [1944] Director/Retired School Teacher; Lucci Damone [1957] Director/Lawyer; Caroline Harrison [1963] Managing Director/Chartered Accountant; Ian Malcolm Hartley [1949] Director/Financial Executive; Dr Barrie Hopson [1943] Director; Yasmin Akhtar Khan [1971] Director/Manager; Michele Sutton [1949] Director

**Aspire-Igen Ltd**
*Incorporated:* 8 January 1996 *Employees:* 149
*Previous:* Igen Limited
*Net Worth:* £2,172,681 *Total Assets:* £3,983,632
*Registered Office:* The Opportunity Centre, 33 Eastgate, Leeds, LS2 7RD
*Activities:* Other education n.e.c.
*Officers:* John Cole [1944] Director; Lucci Damone [1957] Director/Lawyer; Caroline Harrison [1963] Director/Chartered Accountant; Ian Malcolm Hartley [1949] Director/Chartered Accountant; Dr Barrie Hopson [1943] Director; Yasmin Akhtar Khan [1971] Director; Michele Sutton [1949] Director/Consultant

**Assent Building Control Limited**
*Incorporated:* 13 December 2004 *Employees:* 34
*Net Worth:* £3,615,071 *Total Assets:* £8,227,262
*Registered Office:* 4 Navigation Court, Calder Park, Wakefield, W Yorks, WF2 7BJ
*Activities:* Other engineering activities
*Parent:* Assent Holdings Limited
*Officers:* Richard Charles Batte, Secretary/Building Surveyor; Richard Charles Batte [1961] Director/Building Surveyor; John Michael Dilley [1964] Director/Building Surveyor

**Asset Finance UK Limited**
*Incorporated:* 1 July 2004 *Employees:* 1
*Net Worth:* £970,134 *Total Assets:* £3,489,102
*Registered Office:* Ground Floor, Mayesbrook House, Lawnswood Business Park, Redverse Close, Leeds, LS16 6QY
*Activities:* Sale of new cars and light motor vehicles
*Officers:* Nigel Roderick McKenzie [1968] Director

**Associated Utility Supplies Limited**
*Incorporated:* 13 January 1998 *Employees:* 68
*Net Worth:* £4,069,870 *Total Assets:* £7,790,420
*Registered Office:* Riverside House, Colliers Way, Clayton West, Huddersfield, W Yorks, HD8 9TR
*Activities:* Other retail sale not in stores, stalls or markets
*Major Shareholder:* Simon Timothy Gibson
*Officers:* Kim Gibson, Secretary; Kim Rachel Gibson [1963] Director/Administrator; Simon Timothy Gibson [1961] Director/Sales Manager

**Associated Waste Management Limited**
*Incorporated:* 18 October 2000 *Employees:* 258
*Net Worth:* £1,720,703 *Total Assets:* £27,129,756
*Registered Office:* St Bernard's Mill, Gelderd Road, Gildersome, Morley, Leeds, LS27 7NA
*Activities:* Collection of non-hazardous waste
*Parent:* DM Topco Limited
*Officers:* Brian McCabe [1972] Director [Irish]; Eamon Waters [1960] Director [Irish]

**Aston Hall Hotel Limited**
*Incorporated:* 26 October 2011 *Employees:* 71
*Net Worth:* £2,960,558 *Total Assets:* £7,713,244
*Registered Office:* 19 The Square, Retford, Notts, DN22 6DQ
*Activities:* Hotels and similar accommodation
*Major Shareholder:* Andrew John Lavin
*Officers:* Andrew John Lavin [1967] Director

**Aston Properties (Leeds) Limited**
*Incorporated:* 28 February 2003
*Net Worth:* £18,355,208 *Total Assets:* £37,137,264
*Registered Office:* 10 Ash Road, Headingley, Leeds, LS6 3JF
*Activities:* Other letting and operating of own or leased real estate
*Shareholders:* Richard William Aston; Nichola Suzanne Aston
*Officers:* Nichola Suzanne Aston, Secretary; Nicola Suzanne Aston [1970] Director; Richard William Aston [1964] Director

**Aston Student Lets LLP**
*Incorporated:* 30 November 2012 *Employees:* 3
*Net Worth:* £11,420,645 *Total Assets:* £14,183,403
*Registered Office:* 10 Ash Road, Headingley, Leeds, LS6 3JF
*Officers:* Nicola Suzanne Aston [1970] Member; Richard William Aston [1964] Member

**Astonish Holdings Limited**
*Incorporated:* 20 August 1997 *Employees:* 72
*Net Worth:* £8,686,991 *Total Assets:* £11,511,288
*Registered Office:* Astonish House, Unit 1 Premier Point, Staithgate Lane, Bradford, W Yorks, BD6 1DW
*Activities:* Manufacture of cleaning and polishing preparations
*Major Shareholder:* Howard William Moss
*Officers:* Howard William Moss [1974] Managing Director

**Astorbush Limited**
*Incorporated:* 22 August 1984 *Employees:* 4
*Net Worth:* £1,612,442 *Total Assets:* £3,277,375
*Registered Office:* Churchill House, 29 Mill Hill, Pontefract, W Yorks, WF8 4HY
*Activities:* Other letting and operating of own or leased real estate
*Shareholders:* Andrew Martin Waller; Jonathan Spence
*Officers:* Sheila Mary Metcalfe, Secretary; Joanne Kathryn Denton [1972] Director; Sheila Mary Metcalfe [1949] Director/Secretary; Jonathan Spence [1969] Director; Andrew Martin Waller [1971] Director

**ATB Morley Limited**
*Incorporated:* 19 July 2000
*Net Worth:* £5,075,220 *Total Assets:* £5,075,220
*Registered Office:* Troy Works, Ruskin Street, Stanningley, Pudsey, W Yorks, LS28 6QA
*Activities:* Manufacture of engines and turbines, except aircraft, vehicle and cycle engines
*Parent:* ATB Austria Antriebstechnik AG
*Officers:* Stephen Kolowiecki [1958] Director; Ian David Lomax [1958] Managing Director; Peter Jack Ramsden [1959] Technical Director

**ATC Developments (Leeds) Limited**
*Incorporated:* 30 June 2006 *Employees:* 3
*Net Worth:* £33,741,896 *Total Assets:* £44,584,184
*Registered Office:* 7 Cottage Road, Headingley, Leeds, LS6 4DD
*Activities:* Other letting and operating of own or leased real estate
*Officers:* Julie Alison Cooper, Secretary; David John Barrass [1964] Director; Christopher David Ure [1962] Director; Gillian Susan Ure [1963] Director

**ATC Properties Limited**
*Incorporated:* 5 October 1989 *Employees:* 11
*Net Worth:* £45,653,096 *Total Assets:* £87,292,816
*Registered Office:* 7 Cottage Road, Headingley, Leeds, LS6 4DD
*Activities:* Buying and selling of own real estate
*Officers:* Julie Alison Cooper, Secretary; David John Barrass [1964] Director/Surveyor; Christopher David Ure [1962] Director; Gillian Susan Ure [1963] Director

**Athena Civil Engineering Ltd**
*Incorporated:* 20 August 2010 *Employees:* 10
*Net Worth:* £581,195 *Total Assets:* £3,717,597
*Registered Office:* Belfast Yard, Gelderd Road, Birstall, Batley, W Yorks, WF17 9PY
*Activities:* Construction of other civil engineering projects n.e.c.
*Parent:* Athena (UK) Limited
*Officers:* Marie Joan Staves, Secretary; Jonathan Peter Hotham [1985] Director; James Michael Marshall [1982] Director

**Athena PTS Holdings Limited**
*Incorporated:* 27 April 2016
*Net Worth:* £6,000,120 *Total Assets:* £6,000,120
*Registered Office:* Kendal House, Murley Moss Business Village, Oxenholme Road, Kendal, Cumbria, LA9 7RL
*Activities:* Activities of other holding companies n.e.c.
*Officers:* Keith James Bennett [1970] Director; David Shawcross [1982] Director; Mark Skeels [1963] Director; Neil Malcolm Smith [1980] Director

**Atherton Godfrey LLP**
*Incorporated:* 14 February 2017 *Employees:* 122
*Net Worth:* £2,243,575 *Total Assets:* £4,259,681
*Registered Office:* 8 Hall Gate, Doncaster, S Yorks, DN1 3LU
*Officers:* Donald John Bird [1956] Member; John Edward McQuater [1958] Member; Sarah Louise Naylor [1983] Member; Diane Parker [1967] Member; Kellymarie Homar [1985] LLP Member; Janet Lee [1955] LLP Member; Gillian Ward [1974] LLP Member

**G.P. Atkin Limited**
*Incorporated:* 14 May 1997 *Employees:* 1
*Net Worth:* £3,595,671 *Total Assets:* £3,944,670
*Registered Office:* 34 Middle Street South, Driffield, E Yorks, YO25 6PS
*Activities:* Development of building projects
*Major Shareholder:* Paul Butler
*Officers:* Samantha Louise Pallister, Secretary; Gregory Peter Atkin [1954] Director/Builder

**Atkinson Group (Yorkshire) Limited**
*Incorporated:* 8 July 2016
*Net Worth:* £1 *Total Assets:* £9,045,001
*Registered Office:* Sanderson House, 22 Station Road, Horsforth, Leeds, LS18 5NT
*Activities:* Activities of other holding companies n.e.c.
*Officers:* Katharine Elizabeth Riall [1973] Director; Patrick Guy Riall [1972] Director

**Atkinson Holdings Limited**
*Incorporated:* 1 June 1998
*Net Worth:* £30,906,614 *Total Assets:* £31,803,580
*Registered Office:* Sanderson House, Station Road, Horsforth, Leeds, LS18 5NT
*Activities:* Activities of other holding companies n.e.c.
*Shareholder:* Atkinson Group Yorkshire Limited
*Officers:* Katharine Elizabeth Riall, Secretary; Katharine Elizabeth Riall [1973] Director; Patrick Guy Riall [1972] Director

**Andrew Atkinson Livestock Limited**
*Incorporated:* 1 April 1999 *Employees:* 13
*Net Worth:* £622,248 *Total Assets:* £5,620,823
*Registered Office:* Croft House Farm, Long Lane, Felliscliffe, Harrogate, N Yorks, HG3 2LU
*Activities:* Agents selling agricultural raw materials, livestock, textile raw materials and semi-finished goods
*Shareholders:* Jillian Rebecca Barbara Elizabeth Atkinson; Andrew Atkinson
*Officers:* Jillian Rebecca Barbara Elizabeth Atkinson, Secretary; Andrew Atkinson [1969] Director/Livestock Dealer

**Atlantic Acquisition Holdings UK Limited**
*Incorporated:* 24 November 2014 *Employees:* 8
*Net Worth:* £405,652,992 *Total Assets:* £525,318,016
*Registered Office:* National Avenue, Hull, HU5 4JB
*Activities:* Activities of head offices
*Parent:* Atlantic SFDT
*Officers:* Pierre-Louis Francois [1956] Director/Chief Executive Officer [French]; Philippe Redon [1961] Director/Chief Financial Officer [French]

**Atlantic Bay Hotel (Woolacombe) Limited**
*Incorporated:* 25 November 2016
*Net Worth Deficit:* £1,213,014 *Total Assets:* £4,469,756
*Registered Office:* D2 Riorges Link, Lowfields Business Park, Elland, W Yorks, HX5 9DG
*Activities:* Buying and selling of own real estate
*Parent:* Northern Powerhouse Developments Limited
*Officers:* Gavin Lee Woodhouse [1978] Director/Property Developer

**Atlantic Fresh Limited**
*Incorporated:* 14 December 2005 *Employees:* 24
*Net Worth:* £5,537,304 *Total Assets:* £10,048,314
*Registered Office:* Grimsby Fish Market, Wharncliffe Road, Grimsby, S Humbers, DN31 3QJ
*Activities:* Wholesale of other food, including fish, crustaceans and molluscs
*Shareholders:* Orn Eyfjord Jonsson; Magnus Gudmundsson
*Officers:* Orn Eyfjord Jonsson, Secretary/Fish Importer [Icelander]; Magnus Gudmundsson [1966] Director [Icelander]; Orn Eyfjord Jonsson [1977] Director [Icelander]

**Atlas Leisure Homes Limited**
*Incorporated:* 24 April 2009 *Employees:* 257
*Net Worth:* £10,098,195 *Total Assets:* £16,718,174
*Registered Office:* Atlas Leisure Homes Limited, Wiltshire Road, Hull, HU4 6PD
*Activities:* Other manufacturing n.e.c.
*Parent:* Atlas Saturn Holdco Limited
*Officers:* Michael Arthur Durrant, Secretary; Colin Drew Jeffrey [1958] Operations Director; Steven Jon McGawn [1974] Commercial Director; Philip Spark [1961] Sales & Marketing Director

**The Auckland Project**
*Incorporated:* 1 February 2012 *Employees:* 104
*Previous:* The Auckland Castle Trust
*Net Worth:* £62,629,276 *Total Assets:* £63,791,912
*Registered Office:* Vinovium House, Saddler Street, Bishop Auckland, Co Durham, DL14 7BH
*Activities:* Operation of historical sites and buildings and similar visitor attractions
*Officers:* Nicholas John Eldred, Secretary; Robert Hilton Bigley [1959] Director/Chartered Accountant; Jane Elizabeth Bonnar Dean [1955] Director of Hospitality and Catering; Dr Malcolm Austin Rogers [1948] Director/Retired; Nicholas Timothy Turner [1961] Director/Investment Manager; Daniel Richard Wolfe [1972] Director of Communications and Development

**Audasi Holdings Limited**
*Incorporated:* 19 April 2007 *Employees:* 152
*Net Worth:* £1,737,700 *Total Assets:* £5,127,109
*Registered Office:* 31 The Square, Dringhouses, York, YO24 1UR
*Activities:* Other business support service activities n.e.c.
*Major Shareholder:* Adrian Charles Barraclough
*Officers:* Audrey Weber, Secretary; Adrian Charles Barraclough [1965] Director; Audrey Weber [1955] Commercial Director

**Auden McKenzie Holdings Limited**
*Incorporated:* 17 October 2012
*Net Worth:* £328,239 *Total Assets:* £58,363,072
*Registered Office:* Ridings Point, Whistler Drive, Castleford, W Yorks, WF10 5HX
*Activities:* Activities of other holding companies n.e.c.
*Parent:* Chilcott UK Ltd
*Officers:* Dean Michael Cooper [1972] Director/Chartered Accountant; Kim Innes [1968] Director/General Manager

**Audio-Technica Limited**
*Incorporated:* 22 August 1978 *Employees:* 92
*Net Worth:* £13,318,163 *Total Assets:* £20,201,568
*Registered Office:* Technica House, Unit 5 Millennium Way, Leeds, LS11 5AL
*Activities:* Agents specialised in the sale of other particular products
*Parent:* Audio-Technica Europe Holding BV
*Officers:* Adrian John Rooke, Secretary; Philip James Cajka [1955] Director/Business Executive [American]; Shinji Horibe [1970] Director/Business Executive [Japanese]; Kazuo Matsushita [1948] Director [Japanese]; Robert Morgan-Males [1968] European Marketing Director; Kotaro Narihara [1977] Director [Japanese]; Adrian John Rooke [1969] Director

**Audit Partnership Limited**
*Incorporated:* 9 February 2005 *Employees:* 157
*Net Worth:* £2,505,624 *Total Assets:* £3,581,571
*Registered Office:* Moorside Business Park, Moorside, Tockwith, York, YO26 7QG
*Activities:* Accounting and auditing activities
*Parent:* H5 Group Ltd
*Officers:* Philippa Lucy Cook, Secretary; James Frederick Cook [1971] Director/Businessman; Philippa Lucy Cook [1976] Director

**Audley Court Hollins Hall Limited**
*Incorporated:* 2 July 2001 *Employees:* 4
*Net Worth:* £4,546,636 *Total Assets:* £7,255,681
*Registered Office:* Hollins Hall, Killinghall, Harrogate, N Yorks, HG3 2GP
*Activities:* Buying and selling of own real estate
*Parent:* Lawgra (No 1088) Limited
*Officers:* William Esplen, Secretary/Chartered Accountant; John Simon Esplen [1970] Director/Solicitor; William Esplen [1947] Director/Chartered Accountant; Malcolm Nicholas Sanderson [1959] Director/Property Developer

**Augean North Limited**
*Incorporated:* 20 October 1998
*Net Worth:* £2,985,000 *Total Assets:* £13,653,000
*Registered Office:* 4 Rudgate Court, Walton, Wetherby, W Yorks, LS23 7BF
*Activities:* Collection of non-hazardous waste
*Parent:* Augean PLC
*Officers:* Mark Rupert Maxwell Fryer [1967] Finance Director; John Hugo Rauch [1970] Director/Group Operating Officer; Gene Barry Wilson [1957] Technical Director

**Augean PLC**
*Incorporated:* 6 August 2004 *Employees:* 341
*Net Worth:* £50,105,000 *Total Assets:* £94,590,000
*Registered Office:* 4 Rudgate Court, Walton, Wetherby, W Yorks, LS23 7BF
*Activities:* Activities of head offices
*Shareholder:* Harwood Capital LLP
*Officers:* Angela McGhin, Secretary; Andrew John Bryce [1947] Director; Mark Rupert Maxwell Fryer [1967] Finance Director; John Albert Martin Grant [1945] Director; Roger Steven McDowell [1955] Director; James Robert Meredith [1960] Director; Christopher Harwood Bernard Mills [1952] Director

**Augean Property Limited**
*Incorporated:* 8 October 1999
*Previous:* Colt Holdings Limited
*Net Worth:* £6,216,000 *Total Assets:* £6,964,000
*Registered Office:* 4 Rudgate Court, Walton, Wetherby, W Yorks, LS23 7BF
*Activities:* Other letting and operating of own or leased real estate
*Parent:* Augean PLC
*Officers:* Mark Rupert Maxwell Fryer [1967] Finance Director; John Hugo Rauch [1970] Director/Group Operating Officer

**Augean South Limited**
*Incorporated:* 14 January 2003
*Net Worth:* £22,293,000 *Total Assets:* £32,266,000
*Registered Office:* 4 Rudgate Court, Walton, Wetherby, W Yorks, LS23 7BF
*Activities:* Other business support service activities n.e.c.
*Parent:* Augean PLC
*Officers:* Mark Rupert Maxwell Fryer [1967] Finance Director; John Hugo Rauch [1970] Director/Group Operating Officer; Gene Barry Wilson [1957] Technical Director

**Augean Treatment Limited**
*Incorporated:* 31 August 2000
*Net Worth Deficit:* £31,097,000 *Total Assets:* £13,922,000
*Registered Office:* 4 Rudgate Court, Walton, Wetherby, W Yorks, LS23 7BF
*Activities:* Other business support service activities n.e.c.
*Parent:* Augean PLC
*Officers:* Mark Rupert Maxwell Fryer [1967] Finance Director; John Hugo Rauch [1970] Director/Group Operating Officer; Gene Barry Wilson [1957] Technical Director

**Aura DC Limited**
*Incorporated:* 23 June 2015
*Net Worth Deficit:* £1,167,460 *Total Assets:* £11,281,323
*Registered Office:* 1 Park Row, Leeds, LS1 5AB
*Activities:* Financial intermediation not elsewhere classified
*Parent:* PPDI Assetco Limited
*Officers:* Jennifer McKay, Secretary; David Honeyman [1967] Director/Finance Controller; Peter Kenneth Johnstone [1965] Finance Director; Robert John William Wotherspoon [1967] Director/Chartered Accountant

**Aureus Leisure Limited**
*Incorporated:* 19 March 2010 *Employees:* 11
*Net Worth:* £1,369,404 *Total Assets:* £7,859,524
*Registered Office:* The Hawthorns Holiday Park, Bempton Lane, Bridlington, E Yorks, YO16 6XA
*Activities:* Recreational vehicle parks, trailer parks and camping grounds
*Shareholders:* Ambrose Amos Larkham; Arron Ainsley Larkham; William Henry Larkham
*Officers:* Ambrose Amos Larkham [1971] Director; Arron Ainsley Larkham [1983] Director; William Henry Larkham [1970] Director

**Authentix Limited**
*Incorporated:* 24 September 1959 *Employees:* 37
*Net Worth:* £1,239,673 *Total Assets:* £4,267,147
*Registered Office:* 7 Chessingham Park, Common Road, Dunnington, York, YO19 5SE
*Activities:* Other professional, scientific and technical activities n.e.c.
*Officers:* Mark Lawrence Weintrub, Secretary; Dianna Lynn MacDonald [1958] Director/Chief Financial Officer [American]; Mark Lawrence Weintrub [1961] Director/Chief Administrative Officer & General Counsel [American]

**Auto-Trail V.R. Limited**
*Incorporated:* 24 March 1998 *Employees:* 213
*Net Worth:* £20,526,296 *Total Assets:* £44,286,888
*Registered Office:* Trigano House, Genesis Way, Europarc, Grimsby, N E Lincs, DN37 9TU
*Activities:* Manufacture of caravans
*Shareholders:* Francois Marie Feuillet; Trigano
*Officers:* Shane Guy Devoy, Secretary; Shane Guy Devoy [1964] Finance Director; Jean Paul Fassinotti [1957] Commercial Director [French]; Francois Marie Feuillet [1948] Director [French]; Marie Helene Simone Feuillet [1948] Director [French]; Michel Freiche [1960] Director/Chief Financial Officer [French]; David Gareth Thomas [1959] Joint Managing Director

**Autobrokers Limited**
*Incorporated:* 21 March 1997 *Employees:* 44
*Net Worth:* £1,947,430 *Total Assets:* £5,773,195
*Registered Office:* Hawthorne House, Dark Lane, Birstall, W Yorks, WF17 9LW
*Activities:* Sale of new cars and light motor vehicles
*Officers:* Alexander James Sloane, Secretary; Kevin Sloane [1962] Director/Motor Dealer; Valerie Jayne Sloane [1960] Director

**Autocar Logistics (Irl) Limited**
*Incorporated:* 25 April 2008
*Net Worth:* £1,338,216 *Total Assets:* £3,175,202
*Registered Office:* Westwood Business Park, Belton Road, Sandtoft, Doncaster, S Yorks, DN8 5BF
*Activities:* Freight transport by road
*Shareholders:* Andrea Catherine Ann Crosbie; Thomas Joseph Crosbie
*Officers:* Andrea Crosbie, Secretary/Director [Irish]; Thomas Joseph Crosbie [1974] Director [Irish]

**Autoelectro Limited**
*Incorporated:* 12 November 1993 *Employees:* 46
*Net Worth:* £1,476,713 *Total Assets:* £5,084,531
*Registered Office:* Nirmalec House, 848 Leeds Road, Bradford, W Yorks, BD3 9TU
*Activities:* Manufacture of other parts and accessories for motor vehicles
*Shareholder:* Satnam Singh Bhogal
*Officers:* Gopal Singh Bhogal, Secretary/Accounts Manager; Ekonkar Singh Bhogal [1969] Director/Auto Electrical Engineer; Gopal Singh Bhogal [1973] Director/Accounts Manager; Satnam Singh Bhogal [1964] Director/Manager

**Autohorn Fleet Services Limited**
*Incorporated:* 7 August 1995 *Employees:* 75
*Previous:* Autohorn Limited
*Net Worth:* £2,514,706 *Total Assets:* £23,727,102
*Registered Office:* The Engine Works, Fermetol Trading Estate, Foundry Lane, Leeman Road, York, YO26 4XD
*Activities:* Renting and leasing of cars and light motor vehicles
*Parent:* Autohorn Group Ltd
*Officers:* Frances Mary Baines, Company Secretary; Frances Mary Baines [1968] Director/Company Secretary; Richard James Baines [1968] Managing Director; Scott Jenkins [1974] Director; Fraser Robert MacLean [1976] Director; Lee Ramon Underwood [1974] Managing Director

**Autohorn Group Limited**
*Incorporated:* 25 June 2015 *Employees:* 75
*Net Worth:* £4,226,707 *Total Assets:* £25,802,016
*Registered Office:* The Engine Works, Fermetol Trading Estate, Foundry Lane, Leeman Road, York, YO26 4XD
*Activities:* Renting and leasing of cars and light motor vehicles
*Shareholders:* Richard James Baines; Frances Baines
*Officers:* Frances Baines, Secretary; Frances Mary Baines [1968] Director; Richard James Baines [1968] Director; Lee Ramon Underwood [1974] Director

**Automint Limited**
*Incorporated:* 7 November 1989 *Employees:* 33
*Net Worth:* £3,928,790 *Total Assets:* £5,134,686
*Registered Office:* Unit 7 Fieldhouse Park, Old Fieldhouse Lane, Huddersfield, W Yorks, HD2 1FA
*Activities:* Wholesale of other intermediate products
*Shareholders:* Peter Richard Mattock; Patrick Edward Rawnsley
*Officers:* Sarah Watson, Secretary; Graham William James Boyle [1973] Sales Director; Peter Richard Mattock [1954] Director; Patrick Edward Rawnsley [1964] Director; Marcus John Thornton [1973] Director

**Automobile Association Personal Finance Limited**
*Incorporated:* 24 November 1983
*Net Worth Deficit:* £78,220,000 *Total Assets:* £7,795,000
*Registered Office:* Trinity Road, Halifax, W Yorks, HX1 2RG
*Activities:* Financial intermediation not elsewhere classified
*Parent:* Bank of Scotland PLC
*Officers:* Alyson Elizabeth Mulholland, Secretary; Sara Jayne Bayley [1969] Director; Israel Santos Perez [1972] Director [Spanish]

**Automotive Chassis Products UK Limited**
*Incorporated:* 8 June 1988 *Employees:* 1
*Net Worth:* £134,524,000 *Total Assets:* £134,648,992
*Registered Office:* 1 Skerne Road, Aycliffe Business Park, Newton Aycliffe, Co Durham, DL5 6EP
*Activities:* Forging, pressing, stamping and roll-forming of metal; powder metallurgy
*Shareholders:* Francisco Jose Riberas Mera; Juan Maria Riberas Mera
*Officers:* David Vazquez Pascual, Secretary; Francisco Jose Riberas Mera [1968] Director [Spanish]

**Avacta Group PLC**
*Incorporated:* 29 April 2003 *Employees:* 114
*Net Worth:* £21,413,000 *Total Assets:* £23,453,000
*Registered Office:* Unit 20 Ash Way, Thorp Arch Estate, Wetherby, W Yorks, LS23 7FA
*Activities:* Activities of head offices
*Officers:* Tony Peter Gardiner, Secretary; Dr Eliot Richard Forster [1966] Director; Tony Peter Gardiner [1971] Director; Dr Trevor John Nicholls [1956] Director; Michael John Owen [1951] Director; David Alastair MacLaughlin Smith [1966] Director; Dr Samuel Cameron Williams [1969] Director

**Avacta Life Sciences Limited**
*Incorporated:* 29 May 2008 *Employees:* 64
*Net Worth Deficit:* £20,574,816 *Total Assets:* £6,143,788
*Registered Office:* Unit 20 Ash Way, Thorp Arch Estate, Wetherby, W Yorks, LS23 7FA
*Activities:* Research and experimental development on biotechnology
*Parent:* Avacta Group PLC
*Officers:* Tony Peter Gardiner [1971] Director; David Alastair MacLaughlin Smith [1966] Director

**Avant Worldwide Ltd**
*Incorporated:* 12 November 2015
*Net Worth:* £3,654,811 *Total Assets:* £3,738,933
*Registered Office:* Euroway Trading Estate, Bradford, W Yorks, BD4 6SF
*Activities:* Non-specialised wholesale trade
*Major Shareholder:* Henry Griffin
*Officers:* Henry Griffin [1975] Director

**Aventador Consultancy Limited**
*Incorporated:* 24 October 2013
*Net Worth:* £100,942 *Total Assets:* £3,757,865
*Registered Office:* 28 Dudley Street, Grimsby, N E Lincs, DN31 2AB
*Activities:* Tax consultancy
*Officers:* Peter Charles Matthews [1956] Director

**Avenue Lets Limited**
*Incorporated:* 11 January 2016 *Employees:* 8
*Net Worth Deficit:* £35,297 *Total Assets:* £13,062,826
*Registered Office:* 16 Dudley Street, Grimsby, N E Lincs, DN31 2AB
*Activities:* Real estate agencies
*Major Shareholder:* Jonathan Christopher Lovelle
*Officers:* Jonathan Christopher Lovelle [1974] Director

**Aviva Equity Release UK Limited**
*Incorporated:* 2 December 1996
*Net Worth:* £283,100,000 *Total Assets:* £885,800,000
*Registered Office:* Aviva, Wellington Row, York, YO90 1WR
*Activities:* Financial intermediation not elsewhere classified
*Parent:* Aviva Life & Pensions UK Limited
*Officers:* Stephen James Hayes [1975] Director; Simon Roger Marsden [1973] Director; Martin John Muir [1967] Director/Group Chief Capital Officer; Lindsey Claire Rix [1980] Director; Stuart Edmund Robinson [1972] Director

**Aviva Erfa 15 UK Limited**
*Incorporated:* 28 February 2008
*Previous:* Aviva Investors Group Holdings Limited
*Net Worth:* £464,000 *Total Assets:* £6,540,103,168
*Registered Office:* Aviva, Wellington Row, York, YO90 1WR
*Activities:* Dormant company
*Parent:* Aviva Life & Pensions UK Limited
*Officers:* Karina Jane Bye [1972] Director/Company Secretary; Richard Joseph Priestley [1969] Director/Accountant; Nicholas Mark Rowley [1964] Director

**Aviva Life & Pensions UK Limited**
*Incorporated:* 18 September 1996
*Net Worth:* £6,709,000,192 *Total Assets:* £311,367,991,296
*Registered Office:* Aviva, Wellington Row, York, YO90 1WR
*Activities:* Life insurance
*Parent:* Aviva Life Holdings UK Limited
*Officers:* Andrew David Briggs [1966] Director; Mel Gerard Carvill [1962] Non-Executive Director; Valerie Frances Gooding [1950] Director/Chief Executive; Robert William Albert Howe [1949] Director; John Brendan O'Roarke [1958] Director; Hiteshkumar Rameshchandra Patel [1961] Director; Stephen Paul Trickett [1957] Director; Jason Michael Windsor [1972] Director

**Aviva Life Holdings UK Limited**
*Incorporated:* 12 July 1989
*Net Worth:* £9,643,149,312 *Total Assets:* £10,043,778,048
*Registered Office:* Aviva, Wellington Row, York, YO90 1WR
*Activities:* Activities of head offices
*Parent:* Aviva Group Holdings Limited
*Officers:* Andrew David Briggs [1966] Director; Mel Gerard Carvill [1962] Director; Valerie Frances Gooding [1950] Director/Chief Executive; Robert William Albert Howe [1949] Director; John Brendan O'Roarke [1958] Director; Hiteshkumar Rameshchandra Patel [1961] Director; Stephen Paul Trickett [1957] Director; Jason Michael Windsor [1972] Director

**Aviva Life Services UK Limited**
*Incorporated:* 12 July 1989
*Net Worth:* £101,797,000 *Total Assets:* £447,574,016
*Registered Office:* Aviva, Wellington Row, York, YO90 1WR
*Activities:* Other business support service activities n.e.c.
*Parent:* Aviva Life Holdings UK Limited
*Officers:* Andrew David Briggs [1966] Director; Jason Michael Windsor [1972] Director

**Aviva Pension Trustees UK Limited**
*Incorporated:* 25 July 1989
*Net Worth:* £26,019,000 *Total Assets:* £63,494,000
*Registered Office:* Aviva, Wellington Row, York, YO90 1WR
*Activities:* Financial intermediation not elsewhere classified
*Parent:* Aviva Life & Pensions UK Limited
*Officers:* William Ernest Burnside [1966] Director; Matthew Ross McGill [1975] Director; Stuart Edmund Robinson [1972] Director; Patrick Colm Peter Tiernan [1975] Director/Accountant [Irish]

**Aviva Wrap UK Limited**
*Incorporated:* 26 June 2002
*Net Worth:* £14,707,000 *Total Assets:* £32,310,000
*Registered Office:* Aviva, Wellington Row, York, YO90 1WR
*Activities:* Other business support service activities n.e.c.
*Parent:* Aviva Life Holdings UK Limited
*Officers:* William Ernest Burnside [1966] Director; Matthew Ross McGill [1975] Director; Stuart Edmund Robinson [1972] Director; Patrick Colm Peter Tiernan [1975] Director/Accountant [Irish]

**Avocet Trust**
*Incorporated:* 20 September 1991 *Employees:* 277
*Net Worth:* £2,002,154 *Total Assets:* £4,415,039
*Registered Office:* 60-62 Clarence Street, Hull, HU9 1DN
*Activities:* Residential care activities for learning difficulties, mental health and substance abuse
*Officers:* Sue Baker [1963] Director/Manager; Christopher McDonald Brown [1961] Director; Florence Lesley Irene Cartwright [1992] Director/Support Services Assistant; Lesley Irene Cartwright [1953] Director; Jacqueline Comerford [1956] Director/Retired; Wendy Denise Holmes [1960] Director/Hull FC Lottery Manager; Andrew David Tearle [1960] Director/Deputy Headteacher

**AW Flow Holdings Limited**
*Incorporated:* 15 June 2010
*Net Worth:* £14,457,907 *Total Assets:* £17,979,284
*Registered Office:* D Shed, West Building, 72-74 Humber Enterprise Park, Skua Road, Brough, E Yorks, HU15 1EQ
*Activities:* Dormant company
*Parent:* Wartsila Hamworthy International Limited
*Officers:* Mario Zinno, Secretary; Timo Koponen [1969] Director/Vice President Finance & Control [Finnish]; Robert Stewart Moulds [1970] Managing Director

**AWLC Limited**
*Incorporated:* 8 January 2017 *Employees:* 74
*Net Worth:* £2,531,623 *Total Assets:* £11,126,166
*Registered Office:* Dewsbury Depot, Mill Street East, Dewsbury, W Yorks, WF12 9BD
*Activities:* Non-trading company
*Officers:* Andrew Christoper Roberts, Secretary; Edward John Cureton [1950] Director; Trevor Jones [1952] Director; Martin Donald Keay [1964] Director; Gavin Joseph McEntee [1971] Director; Andrew Christopher Roberts [1973] Finance Director; Michael Denis Smith [1955] Director

**The Axholme Academy**
*Incorporated:* 9 November 2011 *Employees:* 59
*Net Worth:* £2,615,711 *Total Assets:* £3,202,787
*Registered Office:* The Axholme Academy, Wharf Road, Crowle, Scunthorpe, N Lincs, DN17 4HU
*Activities:* General secondary education
*Officers:* Sophie Emma Leggott, Secretary; Dawn Marie Adams Da Costa [1969] Director/Learning Delivery Manager; Christian Burke [1975] Director/Police Officer; Ian Hamilton [1982] Director/Teacher; Natalie Harrision [1977] Director/Senior Administrator; Kate Reich [1974] Director/HR Business; Joseph Pickering Sellars [1959] Director/Headteacher; Nichola Jane Shaw [1972] Director/Self Employed Accountant; Dean Ashley Southam [1972] Director/Policeman; Scott Spence-Hill [1978] Director/Fireman; Karen Wallwork [1974] Managing Director; Georgina Wright [1972] Director/Teaching Assistant

**Axis Bidco Limited**
*Incorporated:* 23 November 2015 *Employees:* 5
*Net Worth Deficit:* £3,139,453 *Total Assets:* £54,893,912
*Registered Office:* Nexus House, Richardshaw Lane, Stanningley, Pudsey, Leeds, LS28 6AA
*Activities:* Activities of other holding companies n.e.c.
*Parent:* Axis Midco Limited
*Officers:* David Martin Brennan [1966] Director; Ian Cherry [1970] Director; John Christian Ellis [1977] Director

**Axis Midco Limited**
*Incorporated:* 23 November 2015
*Net Worth Deficit:* £6,603,575 *Total Assets:* £34,729,816
*Registered Office:* Nexus House, Richardshaw Lane, Stanningley, Pudsey, Leeds, LS28 6AA
*Activities:* Activities of other holding companies n.e.c.
*Parent:* Axis Topco Limited
*Officers:* David Martin Brennan [1966] Director; Ian Cherry [1970] Director; John Christian Ellis [1977] Director

**Axis Topco Limited**
*Incorporated:* 23 November 2015 *Employees:* 139
*Net Worth Deficit:* £6,928,195 *Total Assets:* £74,573,520
*Registered Office:* Nexus House, Richardshaw Lane, Stanningley, Pudsey, Leeds, LS28 6AA
*Activities:* Dormant company
*Parent:* Saturn Bidco Limited
*Officers:* David Martin Brennan [1966] Director; Ian Cherry [1970] Director; John Christian Ellis [1977] Director

**G.W. Axup & Co Limited**
*Incorporated:* 30 November 1987 *Employees:* 10
*Net Worth:* £4,312,071 *Total Assets:* £4,777,443
*Registered Office:* Buttfield Road, Howden, Goole, E Yorks, DN14 7DY
*Activities:* Water collection, treatment and supply
*Shareholders:* David Andrew Axup; Robert George Axup
*Officers:* David Andrew Axup, Secretary; David Andrew Axup [1962] Director; Robert George Axup [1955] Director

**Aysgarth School Trust Limited**
*Incorporated:* 14 February 1967 *Employees:* 66
*Net Worth:* £5,344,300 *Total Assets:* £6,251,172
*Registered Office:* Aysgarth School, Newton-le-Willows, Bedale, N Yorks, DL8 1TF
*Activities:* Pre-primary education
*Officers:* Lucinda Mary Hoskyns-Abrahall, Secretary; James Luke Bourne-Arton [1977] Director/Barrister; Melissa Ann Bowring [1960] Director/Housewife; Robert James Brooksbank [1966] Finance Director; David James Christian Faber [1961] Director/Headmaster; Sarah Guthe [1966] Director/Mother; Bennet Mansel Leigh Hoskyns-Abrahall [1971] Director; Hon William James Kay-Shuttleworth [1979] Director/School Teacher; Alastair Land [1971] Director/Headmaster; Thomas Edmund Justin Nolan [1969] Director/Deputy Head; William James Roe [1969] Director/Retail Executive; Peter John Stuart Thompson [1946] Director/Lawyer; Mark Clouston Wallace [1971] Director/Investment Manager; Christy York [1968] Director/Farmer

**Aztek International Freight Limited**
*Incorporated:* 10 June 2002 *Employees:* 24
*Net Worth:* £316,361 *Total Assets:* £3,632,614
*Registered Office:* Albion House, 64 Vicar Lane, Bradford, W Yorks, BD1 5AH
*Activities:* Operation of warehousing and storage facilities for water transport activities
*Shareholders:* Peter Robert Taylor; Nicholas David Driver
*Officers:* Nicholas David Driver [1957] Director/Freight Forwarder; Peter Robert Taylor [1960] Director/Freight Forwarder

**B & F Potatoes Limited**
*Incorporated:* 10 August 1993 *Employees:* 53
*Net Worth:* £7,164,830 *Total Assets:* £11,831,452
*Registered Office:* Glebe Farm, Butterwick, Malton, N Yorks, YO17 8HF
*Activities:* Wholesale of fruit and vegetables
*Officers:* Olive Ann Bannister, Secretary; John Andrew Bannister [1971] Director/Farmer; Stephen John Bannister [1951] Director/Farmer

**B & K Systems Limited**
*Incorporated:* 1 April 1998 *Employees:* 62
*Net Worth:* £2,491,211 *Total Assets:* £4,356,281
*Registered Office:* 1 College Court, College Road, Gildersome, Leeds, LS27 7WF
*Activities:* Other specialised construction activities n.e.c.
*Parent:* BKS Holdings Ltd
*Officers:* Elizabeth Jack, Secretary; Andrew Charles Cumberland [1959] Director/General Manager; Elizabeth Jack [1982] Financial Director; Adam James Langstaff [1983] Sales Director; Iris Marion Wainwright [1957] Director/Financial Controller; Martin Alec Wainwright [1955] Managing Director

**B & K Universal Limited**
*Incorporated:* 18 September 1972 *Employees:* 34
*Net Worth:* £2,813,948 *Total Assets:* £4,120,777
*Registered Office:* Grimston, Aldbrough, Hull, HU11 4QE
*Activities:* Raising of other animals
*Parent:* BK Star Limited
*Officers:* Cyril Desvignes [1969] Director of European Operations [French]; Andrew Smith [1972] Director/Chief Operating Officer [American]

**B & T S Builders Merchants Ltd**
*Incorporated:* 3 April 2000 *Employees:* 20
*Net Worth:* £4,403,168 *Total Assets:* £5,316,292
*Registered Office:* 30 Leeds Road, Otley, W Yorks, LS21 1BT
*Activities:* Agents involved in the sale of timber and building materials
*Shareholder:* Richard Houldsworth
*Officers:* Sheila Ann Houldsworth, Secretary; Richard Houldsworth [1955] Director/Builder

**B - Sporting Limited**
*Incorporated:* 5 April 1982 *Employees:* 144
*Net Worth:* £9,917,382 *Total Assets:* £19,957,704
*Registered Office:* Lawrence House, James Nicolson Link, York, YO30 4WG
*Activities:* Retail sale of footwear in specialised stores
*Shareholder:* Bruce Ian Bannister
*Officers:* Bruce Ian Bannister, Secretary/Director; Brett William Bannister [1974] Director; Bruce Ian Bannister [1947] Director; Janet Irene Bannister [1947] Director/Secretary; Victoria Corlett Bannister [1972] Director

**B C (Roofing Contractors) Limited**
*Incorporated:* 21 December 2008 *Employees:* 41
*Net Worth:* £1,218,777 *Total Assets:* £3,524,781
*Registered Office:* 31 Northampton Road, Scunthorpe, N Lincs, DN16 1UJ
*Activities:* Roofing activities
*Shareholder:* Ian Catterall
*Officers:* Ian Catterall, Secretary/Director; Ian Catterall [1968] Director; Barry Collen [1938] Director; Steven Collen [1964] Director

**B.B. Farms Limited**
*Incorporated:* 31 December 1984
*Net Worth:* £4,281,156 *Total Assets:* £5,195,503
*Registered Office:* Burn Butts, Cranswick, Driffield, E Yorks, YO25 9JJ
*Activities:* Growing of cereals (except rice), leguminous crops and oil seeds
*Shareholders:* Peter Hutchinson Blacker; Andrew James Blacker
*Officers:* Peter Hutchinson Blacker, Secretary; Andrew James Blacker [1957] Director/Farming; Peter Hutchinson Blacker [1930] Director/Farming

**B.C.A. Group Ltd**
*Incorporated:* 18 June 1981 *Employees:* 150
*Net Worth:* £9,307,791 *Total Assets:* £12,189,318
*Registered Office:* Unit H9, Premier Way, Lowfields Business Park, Elland, W Yorks, HX5 9HF
*Activities:* Activities of other holding companies n.e.c.
*Shareholders:* Teresa Batist; HCW Investments Limited; Wilhelmus Johannus Maria Batist
*Officers:* Teresa Batist, Secretary; Teresa Batist [1962] Director/Secretary; Wilhelmus Johannus Maria Batist [1951] Director [Dutch]; Adam Slater [1962] Director

**B.R.T. Supplies Limited**
*Incorporated:* 2 March 1982 *Employees:* 56
*Net Worth:* £2,619,396 *Total Assets:* £6,867,991
*Registered Office:* 45 Field Lane, Thornes, Wakefield, W Yorks, WF2 7RX
*Activities:* Activities of head offices
*Shareholders:* Leslie Sykes; Jeremy Abraham
*Officers:* Ann Sykes, Secretary; Max Abraham [1937] Director; Ann Sykes [1945] Director; Leslie Sykes [1944] Director

**B.W. Industries (Group) Limited**
*Incorporated:* 5 September 2016 *Employees:* 136
*Net Worth:* £2,691,427 *Total Assets:* £10,672,721
*Registered Office:* Carnaby Industrial Estate, Lancaster Road, Carnaby, Bridlington, N Yorks, YO15 3QY
*Activities:* Activities of head offices
*Officers:* Neil Pilling [1965] Director; Gareth Rounding [1969] Director; Daniel Robert Smith [1987] Director

**B.W. Industries (Holdings) Limited**
*Incorporated:* 6 August 2007
*Net Worth:* £6,532,192 *Total Assets:* £6,532,192
*Registered Office:* Carnaby Industrial Estate, Lancaster Road, Carnaby, Bridlington, E Yorks, YO15 3QY
*Activities:* Activities of head offices
*Officers:* Daniel Smith, Secretary; Neil Pilling [1965] Sales Director; Gareth Rounding [1969] Managing Director; Daniel Robert Smith [1987] Financial Director

**B.W.Industries Ltd**
*Incorporated:* 31 October 1974 *Employees:* 136
*Net Worth:* £10,240,716 *Total Assets:* £17,316,454
*Registered Office:* Lancaster Road, Carnaby Industrial Estate, Bridlington, E Yorks, YO15 3QY
*Activities:* Cold forming or folding
*Parent:* B W Manufacturing Limited
*Officers:* Daniel Robert Smith, Secretary; Neil Pilling [1965] Sales Director; Graham Reiss [1982] Sales Director; Gareth Rounding [1969] Sales Director; Daniel Robert Smith [1987] Financial Director

**BAA Lynton Limited**
*Incorporated:* 4 March 1997
*Net Worth:* £534,924,992 *Total Assets:* £552,683,008
*Registered Office:* 1 Park Row, Leeds, LS1 5AB
*Activities:* Development of building projects
*Parent:* Airport Holdings NDH1 Limited
*Officers:* Ignacio Aitor Garcia Bilbao [1970] Director/Financier [Spanish]; John Kevin Bruen [1972] Director [Irish]; Simon Boyd Geere [1968] Director/Banker; Derek Rodger Provan [1966] Director/Chief Executive Officer; Gonzalo Velasco Zabalza [1979] Director [Spanish]

**J.H. Bacon Limited**
*Incorporated:* 11 March 1974 *Employees:* 9
*Net Worth:* £6,744,229 *Total Assets:* £16,558,602
*Registered Office:* Riby Grove, Riby, Grimsby, N E Lincs, DN37 8NP
*Activities:* Growing of cereals (except rice), leguminous crops and oil seeds
*Shareholders:* James Harold Bacon; Executors of James Harold Bacon
*Officers:* Edwin James Henry Bacon, Secretary; Edwin James Henry Bacon [1972] Director/Farmer; Lesley Mary Bacon [1942] Director

**Baddow Properties Limited**
*Incorporated:* 3 June 1998 *Employees:* 3
*Net Worth:* £3,297,854 *Total Assets:* £4,380,969
*Registered Office:* Moore Stephens, 50-51 Hungate, Pickering, N Yorks, YO18 7DG
*Activities:* Buying and selling of own real estate
*Parent:* Baddow Investments Limited
*Officers:* Derek Winston Shaw, Secretary; Christine Ann Shaw [1946] Director/Property Manager; Derek Winston Shaw [1944] Director/Chartered Surveyor

**Bagel Nash Group Limited**
*Incorporated:* 12 May 2011 *Employees:* 111
*Net Worth Deficit:* £1,725,166 *Total Assets:* £5,576,422
*Registered Office:* 122 North Street, Leeds, LS7 1AF
*Activities:* Unlicenced restaurants and cafes
*Shareholders:* Andrew Micklethwaite; Sara Jayne Micklethwaite
*Officers:* Andrew Micklethwaite [1959] Director; Sara Jayne Micklethwaite [1969] Director; Philip Graham Siddall [1966] Finance Director

**Alfred Bagnall & Sons (Administration) Limited**
*Incorporated:* 11 February 1972 *Employees:* 11
*Net Worth:* £282,051 *Total Assets:* £4,676,708
*Registered Office:* 6 Manor Lane, Shipley, W Yorks, BD18 3RD
*Activities:* Other business support service activities n.e.c.
*Parent:* Alfred Bagnall & Sons Limited
*Officers:* John Charles Kirkham, Secretary; Michael Graham Davenport [1965] Director/Chartered Accountant; Elspeth Helen Jobes [1980] Director/Painting Contractor; John Charles Kirkham [1952] Director/Painting Contractor

**Alfred Bagnall & Sons (North) Limited**
*Incorporated:* 29 February 1972 *Employees:* 62
*Net Worth:* £326,889 *Total Assets:* £3,613,654
*Registered Office:* 6 Manor Lane, Shipley, W Yorks, BD18 3RD
*Activities:* Painting
*Parent:* Alfred Bagnall & Sons Limited
*Officers:* John Charles Kirkham, Secretary; Stephen John Bagnall [1968] Director/Painting Contractor; Joanne Gualda [1968] Director/Painting Contractor; Lindsay Mark Robertshaw [1960] Director/Painting Contractor

**Alfred Bagnall and Sons Limited**
*Incorporated:* 4 August 1911 *Employees:* 620
*Net Worth:* £10,989,348 *Total Assets:* £20,209,920
*Registered Office:* 6 Manor Lane, Shipley, W Yorks, BD18 3RD
*Activities:* Activities of head offices
*Officers:* John Charles Kirkham, Secretary; John Keith Bagnall [1941] Director/Chartered Accountant; Stephen John Bagnall [1968] Director/Painting Contractor; Stephen Bethell [1958] Director/Painting Contractor; Richard John Britten [1974] Director/Painting Contractor; Paul James Curry [1968] Director/Painting Contractor; Michael Graham Davenport [1965] Director/Chartered Accountant; Joanne Gualda [1968] Director/Painting Contractor; Elspeth Helen Jobes [1980] Director/Painting Contractor; John Charles Kirkham [1952] Director/Painting Contractor; Lindsay Mark Robertshaw [1960] Director/Painting Contractor

**Bahson Colour Print Limited**
*Incorporated:* 11 December 1996 *Employees:* 55
*Net Worth:* £2,247,977 *Total Assets:* £7,023,557
*Registered Office:* Maven Hey Reservoir, Farm Court, Ferry Top Lane, Wintersett, Wakefield, W Yorks, WF4 2EB
*Activities:* Printing n.e.c.
*Major Shareholder:* Sukhvinder Jenkinson
*Officers:* Sukhvinder Kaur Jenkinson, Secretary; Ian Paul Jenkinson [1963] Director/Sales in Print; Sukhvinder Kaur Jenkinson [1969] Director/Accountant

**Simon Bailes Limited**
*Incorporated:* 9 February 1988 *Employees:* 97
*Net Worth:* £4,976,793 *Total Assets:* £10,062,287
*Registered Office:* 2-3 Tannery Lane, Northallerton, N Yorks, DL7 8DS
*Activities:* Sale of new cars and light motor vehicles
*Major Shareholder:* Simon Dominic Bailes
*Officers:* Simon Dominic Bailes, Secretary; Simon Dominic Bailes [1952] Director/Dealer Principal; Julie Kirby [1967] Director/Accountant; Tessa Rose Sanderson [1957] Director/Graphic Artist; John Sedgwick [1963] Director

**NG Bailey Facilities Services Limited**
*Incorporated:* 6 June 2005 *Employees:* 748
*Net Worth:* £2,164,000 *Total Assets:* £26,239,000
*Registered Office:* Denton Hall, Ilkley, W Yorks, LS29 0HH
*Activities:* Other specialised construction activities n.e.c.
*Parent:* NG Bailey Limited
*Officers:* Rachel Clare Salmon, Secretary; David Stuart Hurcomb [1964] Director/Engineer & Accountant; Michael Porter [1967] Director/Chief Financial Officer

**NG Bailey Group Limited**
*Incorporated:* 11 April 1980 *Employees:* 2,764
*Net Worth:* £139,000,000 *Total Assets:* £314,800,000
*Registered Office:* Denton Hall, Ilkley, W Yorks, LS29 0HH
*Activities:* Activities of head offices
*Officers:* Rachel Clare Salmon, Secretary; Christopher Edward Bailey [1975] Director; Claire Elizabeth East [1985] Director; Peter Richard Emery [1962] Director; David Stuart Hurcomb [1964] Director/Engineer & Accountant; Whiteman Kevin [1956] Non-Executive Director Chairman; Jane Moriarty [1964] Director [Irish]; Michael Porter [1967] Director/Chief Financial Officer

**NG Bailey IT Services Limited**
*Incorporated:* 24 January 1989 *Employees:* 419
*Net Worth:* £10,427,000 *Total Assets:* £28,524,000
*Registered Office:* Denton Hall, Ilkley, W Yorks, LS29 0HH
*Activities:* Other specialised construction activities n.e.c.
*Parent:* NG Bailey Limited
*Officers:* Rachel Clare Salmon, Secretary; David Stuart Hurcomb [1964] Director/Engineer & Accountant; Michael Porter [1967] Director/Chief Financial Officer

**Bailey Leasing Limited**
*Incorporated:* 5 June 2000 *Employees:* 4
*Net Worth:* £135,000 *Total Assets:* £9,906,000
*Registered Office:* Denton Hall, Ilkley, W Yorks, LS29 0HH
*Activities:* Financial leasing
*Parent:* NG Bailey Group Limited
*Officers:* Rachel Clare Salmon, Secretary; David Stuart Hurcomb [1964] Director/Engineer & Accountant; Michael Porter [1967] Director/Chief Financial Officer

**NG Bailey Limited**
*Incorporated:* 22 July 1938 *Employees:* 1,403
*Net Worth:* £41,451,000 *Total Assets:* £158,464,992
*Registered Office:* Denton Hall, Ilkley, W Yorks, LS29 0HH
*Activities:* Electrical installation
*Parent:* NG Bailey Group Limited
*Officers:* Rachel Clare Salmon, Secretary; David Stuart Hurcomb [1964] Director/Engineer & Accountant; Michael Porter [1967] Director/Chief Financial Officer

**A.& E.Baines Limited**
*Incorporated:* 15 December 1951 *Employees:* 2
*Net Worth:* £2,239,366 *Total Assets:* £4,232,033
*Registered Office:* Crown Chambers, Princes Street, Harrogate, N Yorks, HG1 1NJ
*Activities:* Development of building projects
*Officers:* Linda Christine Baines, Secretary; Colin Baines [1923] Director/Motor Engineer; Derek Alfred Baines [1953] Director/Physiotherapy Manager; Linda Christine Baines [1949] Director/Secretary; Steven Malcolm Baines [1954] Director/Property Portfolio Manager; Generald Charles Firth [1951] Director/Business Systems Analyst; Ann Patricia Lofthouse [1951] Director; Jill O'Boyle [1943] Director/Shop Assistant

**Baird Group (Holdings) Limited**
*Incorporated:* 13 September 2010 *Employees:* 978
*Net Worth Deficit:* £2,458,000 *Total Assets:* £73,093,000
*Registered Office:* Granary Building, 1 Canal Wharf, Leeds, LS11 5BB
*Activities:* Activities of head offices
*Parent:* Al Arafa for Investments and Consultancies SAE
*Officers:* Nicholas Scott, Secretary; Mark Michael Sean Cotter [1963] Director; Hala Hashem [1965] Director/Manager [Egyptian]; Mohamed Talaat Mohamed Khalifa [1982] Director [Egyptian]; Mohamed Ahmed Elsayed Morsy [1978] Director [Egyptian]

**Baird Group Limited**
*Incorporated:* 21 November 2008
*Net Worth:* £16,986,000 *Total Assets:* £27,402,000
*Registered Office:* Granary Building, 1 Canal Wharf, Leeds, LS11 5BB
*Activities:* Activities of head offices
*Shareholders:* Bair Group (Holdings) Ltd; Al Arafa for Investments and Consultancies SAE
*Officers:* Nicholas Scott, Secretary; Mark Michael Sean Cotter [1963] Director; Hala Hashem [1965] Director/Manager [Egyptian]; Mohamed Talaat Mohamed Khalifa [1982] Director [Egyptian]; Mohamed Ahmed Elsayed Morsy [1978] Director [Egyptian]

**Richard Baldwin Motorhomes LLP**
*Incorporated:* 26 May 2010 *Employees:* 16
*Net Worth:* £1,193,287 *Total Assets:* £3,538,647
*Registered Office:* Wakefield Road, Copley, Halifax, W Yorks, HX3 0TP
*Officers:* Richard Baldwin [1963] Member; Gary Michael Morgan [1964] Member

**Ballards Removals Holdings Limited**
*Incorporated:* 26 September 2014
*Net Worth:* £799,089 *Total Assets:* £4,500,531
*Registered Office:* Ballards Business Park, Old London Road, Markham Moor, Retford, Notts, DN22 0TE
*Activities:* Activities of other holding companies n.e.c.
*Shareholder:* Sarah Elizabeth Cooke
*Officers:* Janette Ballard [1960] Director; Joseph Luke Ballard [1985] Director; Matthew Ballard [1981] Director; Richard Peter Ballard [1952] Director; Stephen Paul Cooke [1953] Director

**Balltec Limited**
*Incorporated:* 23 July 2004 *Employees:* 24
*Net Worth:* £3,193,756 *Total Assets:* £4,585,102
*Registered Office:* Unit 2b The Gateway, Morecambe, Lancs, LA3 3PB
*Activities:* Other engineering activities
*Shareholders:* Kenna Invest AS; Robert Emmett
*Officers:* Russell John Benson [1980] Managing Director; Morten Borge [1981] Director/Investment Manager [Norwegian]; Katrine Eide [1971] Director/VP QHSE and Administration [Norwegian]; Dr Marco Andre Teixeira [1966] Technical Director [Canadian]

**Ballyvesey Holdings Limited**
*Incorporated:* 12 June 1995 *Employees:* 2,521
*Net Worth:* £115,001,504 *Total Assets:* £413,624,768
*Registered Office:* c/o Montracon Limited, Carr Hill, Doncaster, S Yorks, DN4 8DE
*Activities:* Financial intermediation not elsewhere classified
*Shareholders:* The HH Montgomery A & M Trust; HH Montgomery Family Trust 2012
*Officers:* Harold Hugh Montgomery, Secretary; Nigel Moutray Anketell [1955] Director; David Nigel Birkmyre [1952] Director; James Alexander Darragh [1968] Director; Colin John Hugh Montgomery [1976] Director; Harold Mark Joseph Montgomery [1983] Director; Harold Hugh Montgomery [1948] Director/Haulage Contractor; Noreen P Montgomery [1949] Director

**Bandwood Limited**
*Incorporated:* 11 April 2005
*Net Worth:* £117,940,000 *Total Assets:* £117,940,000
*Registered Office:* National Avenue, Hull, HU5 4JB
*Activities:* Activities of head offices
*Parent:* Atlantic SFDT
*Officers:* Steven Hairsine, Secretary; Shaun Barry Edwards [1968] Director; Pierre Louis Andre Francois [1956] Director [French]

**Banks Lane Investments Limited**
*Incorporated:* 28 July 1997 *Employees:* 2
*Net Worth:* £295,283 *Total Assets:* £3,409,703
*Registered Office:* Unit 3a Riverside Business Park, Royd Ings Avenue, Keighley, W Yorks, BD21 4AF
*Activities:* Other letting and operating of own or leased real estate
*Officers:* Peter Roman Wasylyk, Secretary; Shaun Henry [1965] Director/Salesman; Peter Roman Wasylyk [1967] Director/Accountant

**Banks Lyon Jewellers Limited**
*Incorporated:* 3 May 2002 *Employees:* 17
*Net Worth:* £3,084,554 *Total Assets:* £4,382,537
*Registered Office:* 36-40 Church Street, Lancaster, LA1 1LH
*Activities:* Other retail sale not in stores, stalls or markets
*Shareholder:* Rodney Banks-Lyon
*Officers:* Rodney Banks-Lyon, Secretary/Retailer; Jasmin Banks-Lyon [1958] Director/Interior Design; Maxine Pascal Banks-Lyon [1988] Director; Rodney Banks-Lyon [1956] Director/Retailer; Alexander Edward Antoni Pecko [1987] Director

**Bankside Patterson Limited**
*Incorporated:* 22 January 1959 *Employees:* 168
*Net Worth:* £4,781,080 *Total Assets:* £12,649,863
*Registered Office:* Catwick Lane, Brandesburton, Driffield, E Yorks, YO25 8RW
*Activities:* Manufacture of other fabricated metal products n.e.c.
*Shareholders:* David Arthur Wineberg; Christopher David Adams
*Officers:* Heather Mackintosh, Secretary; Christopher David Adams [1959] Director/Executive Chairman; Richard Stabler [1970] Finance Director; Neil Keith Taylor [1969] Managing Director; David Arthur Wineberg [1930] Director

**Bannatyne Fitness (2) Limited**
*Incorporated:* 20 June 2011 *Employees:* 60
*Net Worth:* £4,851,537 *Total Assets:* £8,231,819
*Registered Office:* Power House, Haughton Road, Darlington, Co Durham, DL1 1ST
*Activities:* Fitness facilities
*Parent:* The Bannatyne Group PLC
*Officers:* Edwin James, Secretary; Kenneth Peter Campling [1963] Director/Chief Financial Officer; Anthony Craig Elliott [1981] Director; Steven Hancock [1965] National Technical Services Director; Edwin Michael Lewis James [1980] Director/Solicitor; Justin Musgrove [1969] Director

**Bannatyne Fitness Limited**
*Incorporated:* 4 December 1996 *Employees:* 2,777
*Net Worth:* £41,972,000 *Total Assets:* £242,144,992
*Registered Office:* Power House, Haughton Road, Darlington, Co Durham, DL1 1ST
*Activities:* Fitness facilities
*Parent:* The Bannatyne Group PLC
*Officers:* Edwin James, Secretary; Kenneth Peter Campling [1963] Director/Chief Financial Officer; Anthony Craig Elliott [1981] Director; Steven Hancock [1965] National Technical Services Director; Edwin Michael Lewis James [1980] Director/Solicitor; Justin Musgrove [1969] Director

**Bannatyne Hotels Limited**
*Incorporated:* 25 October 1996 *Employees:* 226
*Net Worth:* £6,773,347 *Total Assets:* £16,511,102
*Registered Office:* Power House, Haughton Road, Darlington, Co Durham, DL1 1ST
*Activities:* Hotels and similar accommodation
*Parent:* The Bannatyne Group PLC
*Officers:* Edwin James, Secretary; Kenneth Peter Campling [1963] Director/Chief Financial Officer; Anthony Craig Elliott [1981] Director; Steven Hancock [1965] National Technical Services Director; Edwin Michael Lewis James [1980] Director/Solicitor; Justin Musgrove [1969] Director

**Bannatyne Properties Limited**
*Incorporated:* 20 June 2011 *Employees:* 3
*Net Worth:* £1,933,901 *Total Assets:* £3,570,154
*Registered Office:* Power House, Haughton Road, Darlington, Co Durham, DL1 1ST
*Activities:* Other letting and operating of own or leased real estate
*Major Shareholder:* Duncan Walker Bannatyne
*Officers:* Edwin James, Secretary; Duncan Walker Bannatyne [1949] Director; Hollie Nicole Bannatyne [1985] Director; Abigail Victoria Bannatyne-Elliott [1983] Director

**Banner Contracts (Halnaby) Limited**
*Incorporated:* 24 February 1993 *Employees:* 86
*Net Worth:* £12,494,721 *Total Assets:* £20,927,932
*Registered Office:* The Coach House, Halnaby Hall, Croft on Tees, Darlington, Co Durham, DL2 2TJ
*Activities:* Repair of machinery
*Parent:* Banner Holdings (Halnaby) Limited
*Officers:* Andrew Michael Banner [1981] Director; Jonathan Laurence Banner [1978] Director; Michael Stuart Banner [1953] Executive Director

**P D Bannister Haulage Limited**
*Incorporated:* 3 April 1996 *Employees:* 145
*Net Worth:* £2,239,922 *Total Assets:* £10,129,471
*Registered Office:* West Yorkshire Industrial Estate, Weaverthorpe Road, Bradford, W Yorks, BD4 6SX
*Activities:* Freight transport by road
*Major Shareholder:* David John Bannister
*Officers:* Betty Bannister, Secretary; Betty Bannister [1954] Director/Clerk; David John Bannister [1972] Director/Haulier; Paul Leadbeater [1976] Director

**Bar 24 Limited**
*Incorporated:* 6 September 2001 *Employees:* 22
*Net Worth:* £3,292,838 *Total Assets:* £7,830,906
*Registered Office:* 3 Bradford Row, Doncaster, S Yorks, DN1 3NF
*Activities:* Construction of commercial buildings
*Shareholders:* John Edgar Lloyd Nicholson; Michael Patrick Murray
*Officers:* Michael Patrick Murray [1969] Director; John Edgar Lloyd Nicholson [1962] Director

**Barden Biomass Holdings Limited**
*Incorporated:* 31 May 2017 *Employees:* 2
*Net Worth:* £3,500,002 *Total Assets:* £3,500,002
*Registered Office:* Fleet Farm, Lupton, Carnforth, Lancs, LA6 2PT
*Activities:* Activities of other holding companies n.e.c.
*Shareholders:* Louise Heather Barden; William Thomas Barden
*Officers:* Louise Heather Barden [1979] Director; William Thomas Barden [1983] Director

**S J Bargh Group Limited**
*Incorporated:* 22 March 2016 *Employees:* 461
*Net Worth:* £17,722,360 *Total Assets:* £28,153,784
*Registered Office:* S J Bargh Ltd, Caton Road, Lancaster, LA1 3PE
*Activities:* Freight transport by road
*Shareholders:* Helen Elizabeth Lloyd; Rebecca Mary Towers; Rachel Kenyon Thomas
*Officers:* Tonnia Michelle Park, Secretary; Anthony Raymond Finlayson-Green [1961] Director; Thomas James Lloyd [1972] Director/Farmer; Tonnia Michelle Park [1982] Director/Chartered Accountant; Rachel Kenyon Thomas [1953] Director; Rebecca Mary Towers [1950] Director

**S.J.Bargh Limited**
*Incorporated:* 20 April 1954 *Employees:* 369
*Net Worth:* £11,817,422 *Total Assets:* £18,628,768
*Registered Office:* Head Office, S J Bargh Limited, Caton Road, Lancaster, LA1 3PE
*Activities:* Freight transport by road
*Parent:* S J Bargh Group Limited
*Officers:* Tonnia Michelle Park, Secretary; Anthony Raymond Finlayson-Green [1961] Managing Director; Thomas James Lloyd [1972] Director/Farmer; Tonnia Michelle Park [1982] Director/Chartered Accountant; Rachel Kenyon Thomas [1953] Director; Rebecca Mary Towers [1950] Director

**Bark and Bite Ltd**
*Incorporated:* 29 May 2009 *Employees:* 14
*Net Worth:* £3,245,702 *Total Assets:* £3,724,696
*Registered Office:* 45 Birchfields Rise, Leeds, LS14 2HU
*Activities:* Advertising agencies
*Shareholders:* Christian Charles Edward Knowles-Fitton; Rose Knowles-Fitton
*Officers:* Christian Charles Edward Knowles-Fitton [1975] Director; Rose Knowles-Fitton [1977] Director

**M. and B. Barker Limited**
*Incorporated:* 16 August 1966 *Employees:* 1
*Net Worth:* £3,907,043 *Total Assets:* £4,089,131
*Registered Office:* c/o Bull Brand Limited, 16 Steeton Grove, Steeton, Keighley, W Yorks, BD20 6TT
*Activities:* Other letting and operating of own or leased real estate
*Officers:* Michael Barker, Secretary; Andrew Barker [1960] Director

**George W. Barker Limited**
*Incorporated:* 24 February 1978
*Net Worth:* £2,097,566 *Total Assets:* £3,640,579
*Registered Office:* Manor House Farm, Whitwell Scorton, Richmond, N Yorks, DL10 6AZ
*Activities:* Mixed farming
*Major Shareholder:* Benjamin George William Barker
*Officers:* George William Barker, Secretary; Benjamin George William Barker [1968] Director/Farmer; George William Barker [1940] Director/Farmer

**P. Barker Properties Limited**
*Incorporated:* 6 September 2001 *Employees:* 2
*Net Worth:* £2,592,093 *Total Assets:* £3,659,307
*Registered Office:* Staithes Road, Saltend, Hull, HU12 8DX
*Activities:* Other letting and operating of own or leased real estate
*Shareholders:* Ian Andrew Inman Altass; Andrew John Firth; Diana Firth
*Officers:* Andrew John Firth, Secretary/Director; Ian Andrew Inman Altass [1964] Director; Andrew John Firth [1965] Director

**Barkers (Northallerton) Limited**
*Incorporated:* 1 April 1947 *Employees:* 158
*Net Worth:* £18,974,414 *Total Assets:* £22,383,788
*Registered Office:* 198-202 High Street, Northallerton, N Yorks, DL7 8LP
*Activities:* Other retail sale in non-specialised stores
*Shareholder:* Charles Wilfred Barker
*Officers:* Robert Baker, Secretary; Charles Wilfred Barker [1951] Department Store Director; Guy Charles Barker [1989] Director; Ian David Barker [1969] Director of Retail Store

**Barmston Developments Limited**
*Incorporated:* 2 April 2007
*Net Worth Deficit:* £427,251,008 *Total Assets:* £9,379,686,400
*Registered Office:* 10 South Parade, Leeds, LS1 5QS
*Activities:* Development of building projects
*Shareholders:* Wilton Developments Limited; Clugston Estates Limited
*Officers:* Nicholas John Child [1958] Director; Richard William Dawson [1966] Director/Chartered Accountant; Jason Paul Stowe [1970] Director/Chartered Surveyor; Robert John Vickers [1956] Director/Chief Executive

**Barnard Castle School**
*Incorporated:* 19 May 2008 *Employees:* 200
*Net Worth:* £8,584,007 *Total Assets:* £12,651,875
*Registered Office:* Newgate, Barnard Castle, Co Durham, DL12 8UN
*Activities:* Other education n.e.c.
*Officers:* Suzanne Marie Metcalf, Secretary; Ian Martin Allison [1957] Director/Teacher; Nicholas John Bliss [1959] Director/Lawyer; Ruth Dent [1947] Director; Dr Jonathan Richard Elphick [1970] Director/Consultant Engineer; Alan John Fielder [1948] Director; Norman Peter Hodges [1954] Director/Chartered Builder; John Harvey Hunter [1968] Director/Banker; Paul Anthony Kelsall [1954] Director/Chemist; Robert Iain Moffatt [1961] Director/Chartered Accountant; Peter David Alan Mothersill [1957] Director; Clare Margaret Newman [1967] Director/Sales Account Manager; David Charles Osborne [1970] Director; David Simpson Penny [1960] Director; Erland Robert Rendall [1971] Director/Chartered Surveyor; Cllr George Morland Richardson [1949] Director/Farmer; Donald Frederick Starr [1945] Director/Lecturer; Catherine Jean Sunley [1964] Director; Neil Thorpe [1967] Director/Lecturer; Donna Vinsome [1964] Director/Headmistress

**Barnby C H Limited**
*Incorporated:* 2 February 2012 *Employees:* 462
*Net Worth:* £6,308,497 *Total Assets:* £11,399,031
*Registered Office:* Ye Old Bell, Great North Road, Barnby Moor, Retford, Notts, DN22 8SQ
*Activities:* Activities of head offices
*Major Shareholder:* Allen Paul Levack
*Officers:* Allen Paul Levack [1951] Director/Care Home/Hospital Operator

**Dennis Barnfield Limited**
*Incorporated:* 30 October 1967 *Employees:* 28
*Net Worth:* £3,543,064 *Total Assets:* £5,862,578
*Registered Office:* Lodge Quarry, Carnforth, Lancs, LA5 9DW
*Activities:* Repair of machinery
*Major Shareholder:* Sheila Barnfield
*Officers:* Sheila Barnfield, Secretary; Graham John Barnfield [1956] Director/Area Sales Manager; Sheila Barnfield [1932] Director/Administration; Terence Lindsay Barnfield [1953] Director/Plant Hire & Sales Manager; Malcolm Lewis MacKay [1956] Sales Director

**Barrett Steel Limited**
*Incorporated:* 14 October 1992 *Employees:* 1,078
*Net Worth:* £54,319,000 *Total Assets:* £194,532,000
*Registered Office:* Barrett House, Cutler Heights Lane, Dudley Hill, Bradford, W Yorks, BD4 9HU
*Activities:* Wholesale of metals and metal ores
*Shareholders:* Richard Braithwaite Barrett; James Stephenson Barrett
*Officers:* Marcus Tyldsley, Secretary; James Stephenson Barrett [1955] Director; Richard Braithwaite Barrett [1957] Director/Structural Engineer; Marcus Tyldsley [1980] Director/Chartered Accountant; Andrew Warcup [1965] Director

**Bartlett & Company Limited**
*Incorporated:* 5 December 1940 *Employees:* 89
*Net Worth:* £5,605,000 *Total Assets:* £11,570,000
*Registered Office:* Broadway Hall, Horsforth, Leeds, LS18 4RS
*Activities:* Non-life insurance
*Major Shareholder:* Frederick Michael Bartlett
*Officers:* John Howard Ransome, Secretary; Andrew Bartlett [1979] Director/Insurance Broker; Richard Frederick Bartlett [1980] Director; Michael Joseph Briggs [1963] Director; Ian Andrew Roberts [1970] Director/Insurance Broker; Nicholas John Stubbs [1965] Director/Insurance Broker

**Bartlett Group (Holdings) Limited**
*Incorporated:* 1 January 1969 *Employees:* 103
*Net Worth:* £10,116,000 *Total Assets:* £17,683,000
*Registered Office:* Broadway Hall, Horsforth, Leeds, LS18 4RS
*Activities:* Life insurance
*Major Shareholder:* Frederick Michael Bartlett
*Officers:* John Howard Ransome, Secretary; Andrew Bartlett [1979] Director/Insurance Broker; Frederick Michael Bartlett [1942] Director/Insurance Broker; Richard Bartlett [1980] Director/Accountant; Anthony Richard Sharp [1947] Director/Corporate Financier; Robin Anthony Smith [1943] Director/Solicitor

**Bartoline Limited**
*Incorporated:* 31 May 1912 *Employees:* 95
*Net Worth:* £7,922,240 *Total Assets:* £13,571,753
*Registered Office:* Barmston Close, Beverley, E Yorks, HU17 0LW
*Activities:* Manufacture of other inorganic basic chemicals
*Officers:* Simon Christopher Barton, Secretary; Simon Christopher Barton [1953] Director; Gwynneth Mary Firth [1944] Director; Stuart Ockleton [1964] Director/Operations Manager; Mark Andrew Tingay [1960] Sales Director

**W E Barton Limited**
*Incorporated:* 3 April 1997 *Employees:* 3
*Net Worth:* £2,751,418 *Total Assets:* £4,494,224
*Registered Office:* Hall Farm, Saundby, Retford, Notts, DN22 9ER
*Activities:* Growing of cereals (except rice), leguminous crops and oil seeds
*Shareholders:* Karen Judith Barton; William Edward Barton
*Officers:* Karen Judith Barton, Secretary; Alistair Samuel Barton [1987] Director/Farmer; George William Barton [1984] Director/Farmer; Harry Charles Barton [1985] Director/Farmer

**Barton Park Estates Limited**
*Incorporated:* 26 March 2003 *Employees:* 5
*Net Worth:* £3,815,376 *Total Assets:* £10,242,474
*Registered Office:* Offices G12-G16, City Lab, 4-6 Dalton Square, Lancaster, LA1 1PP
*Activities:* Recreational vehicle parks, trailer parks and camping grounds
*Shareholders:* Charles Howard Barton Jnr; Charles Howard Barton
*Officers:* Anita Louise Barton, Secretary; Anita Louise Barton [1951] Director/Caravan Park Operator; Charles Howard Barton [1948] Director/Caravan Park Operator; Charles Howard Barton Jnr [1987] Director

**Barton Park Homes Limited**
*Incorporated:* 18 February 2000 *Employees:* 2
*Net Worth:* £4,898,249 *Total Assets:* £5,938,509
*Registered Office:* Offices G12-G16, Citylab, 4-6 Dalton Square, Lancaster, LA1 1PP
*Activities:* Other retail sale not in stores, stalls or markets
*Shareholders:* Anita Louise Barton; Charles Howard Barton; Ian John Norman Gee
*Officers:* Anita Louise Barton, Secretary; Anita Louise Barton [1951] Director/Residential Park Home Operator; Charles Howard Barton [1948] Director/Residential Park Home Operator; Charles Barton Jnr [1987] Director/Mobile Home Salesman

**Michael Barugh Steel Stockholding Limited**
*Incorporated:* 16 August 2000 *Employees:* 31
*Net Worth:* £1,889,292 *Total Assets:* £4,265,885
*Registered Office:* English Street, Hull, HU3 2BS
*Activities:* Wholesale of metals and metal ores
*Parent:* M.B.S.S. Limited
*Officers:* Lisa Anne Norrie, Secretary; Mark Donoghue [1974] Director/Steel Stockholders; Jeffrey Duffield [1966] Director/Steel Stockholding; Derek Stuart Grantham [1956] Director/Warehouse Manager; John Milner [1961] Director/Transport Supervisor; Lisa Anne Norrie [1962] Director/Accounts Clerk

**Barwick Bathroom Distribution LLP**
*Incorporated:* 30 November 2005 *Employees:* 96
*Net Worth:* £5,049,963 *Total Assets:* £11,872,946
*Registered Office:* 40 Wharfedale Road, Euroway Industrial Estate, Bradford, W Yorks, BD4 6SG
*Officers:* John Barwick [1953] Member; Michael Gabriel Barwick [1951] Member; Richard Brian Bower [1964] Member

**Barwick Investments (Leeds) Limited**
*Incorporated:* 2 November 2000 *Employees:* 4
*Net Worth:* £4,261,228 *Total Assets:* £4,999,587
*Registered Office:* 7a Potterton Lane, Barwick in Elmet, Leeds, LS15 4DU
*Activities:* Other letting and operating of own or leased real estate
*Parent:* Barwick Investments (Leeds) Holdings Limited
*Officers:* Keith Jones, Secretary/Director; Keith Jones [1951] Director; Susan Jones [1954] Director

**Barwick of Bradford Limited**
*Incorporated:* 8 July 1985 *Employees:* 4
*Net Worth:* £5,507,956 *Total Assets:* £6,611,644
*Registered Office:* 40 Wharfedale Road, Euroway Industrial Estate, Bradford, W Yorks, BD4 6SG
*Activities:* Wholesale of hardware, plumbing and heating equipment and supplies
*Shareholders:* John Barwick; Michael Gabriel Barwick
*Officers:* John Barwick, Secretary/Joint Managing Director; John Barwick [1953] Director/Joint Chairman; Michael Gabriel Barwick [1951] Director/Joint Chairman; Richard Brian Bower [1964] Financial Director; Gary David Campbell [1962] Managing Director

**R G Bassett & Sons Limited**
*Incorporated:* 21 June 1988 *Employees:* 92
*Net Worth:* £1,880,998 *Total Assets:* £3,208,403
*Registered Office:* SJ Bargh, Caton Road, Lancaster, LA1 3PE
*Activities:* Freight transport by road
*Parent:* S J Bargh Group Limited
*Officers:* Tonnia Michelle Park, Secretary; Anthony Raymond Finlayson-Green [1961] Director; Thomas James Lloyd [1972] Director/Farmer; Tonnia Michelle Park [1982] Director/Chartered Accountant; Rachel Kenyon Thomas [1953] Director; Rebecca Mary Towers [1950] Director

**Bat 2 Limited**
*Incorporated:* 8 November 2009 *Employees:* 6
*Net Worth:* £230,900 *Total Assets:* £3,156,082
*Registered Office:* Lake Coast and Dale Leisure, Scotland Road, Carnforth, Lancs, LA5 9RF
*Activities:* Wholesale of other intermediate products
*Shareholders:* Robert John Passey Walters; Batesons Hotels (1958) Limited
*Officers:* David Brunton Bateson [1951] Director; Teresa Maria Bateson [1954] Director; Robert John Passey Walters [1957] Sales Director

**B Batch Shopfitters Limited**
*Incorporated:* 21 November 1988 *Employees:* 49
*Net Worth:* £972,229 *Total Assets:* £3,968,504
*Registered Office:* 2025 Spring Bank West, Hull, HU5 5EP
*Activities:* Joinery installation
*Major Shareholder:* Tristan David Batch
*Officers:* Amanda Jane Batch, Secretary; Amanda Jane Batch [1957] Director/General Assistant; Tristan David Batch [1957] Director/Manager

**C.K.Batchelor Limited**
*Incorporated:* 23 June 1971 *Employees:* 25
*Net Worth:* £8,563,159 *Total Assets:* £9,288,510
*Registered Office:* Cold Bath Place, Harrogate, N Yorks, HG2 0PH
*Activities:* Development of building projects
*Shareholders:* Andrew Charles Batchelor; John Albert Batchelor; David Henry Batchelor
*Officers:* Andrew Charles Bachelor, Secretary; Andrew Charles Bachelor [1967] Director; Mr David Henry Bachelor [1969] Director/Building Manager; John Albert Bachelor [1940] Director/Quantity Surveyor

**Batchelors Motor Group Limited**
*Incorporated:* 27 November 2012 *Employees:* 42
*Previous:* Batchelors of Ripon 2013 Limited
*Net Worth:* £633,221 *Total Assets:* £3,596,532
*Registered Office:* Camphill Close, Dallamires Lane, Ripon, N Yorks, HG4 1TT
*Activities:* Activities of other holding companies n.e.c.
*Shareholders:* Karen Louise Denton; Antony Michael Denton
*Officers:* Antony Michael Denton, Secretary; Antony Michael Denton [1967] Managing Director; Karen Louise Denton [1966] Director

**Batchelors of Ripon Limited**
*Incorporated:* 30 November 1987 *Employees:* 42
*Net Worth:* £1,463,759 *Total Assets:* £4,212,107
*Registered Office:* Camphill Close, Dallamires Lane, Ripon, N Yorks, HG4 1TT
*Activities:* Sale of new cars and light motor vehicles
*Parent:* Batchelors Motor Group Limited
*Officers:* Antony Michael Denton, Secretary; Antony Michael Denton [1967] Managing Director; Karen Louise Denton [1966] Director

**Bates & Co. (Huddersfield) Limited**
*Incorporated:* 6 September 1982 *Employees:* 3
*Net Worth:* £2,687,675 *Total Assets:* £3,207,482
*Registered Office:* Fairfield Mills, Milford Street, Huddersfield, W Yorks, HD1 3DX
*Activities:* Other business support service activities n.e.c.
*Shareholders:* Alistair Duncan Bates; Nigel Gordon Bates; Richard John Fleming Bates
*Officers:* Richard John Fleming Bates [1960] Director

**Batley Academy Trust**
*Incorporated:* 28 January 2011 *Employees:* 94
*Net Worth:* £5,602,272 *Total Assets:* £6,144,359
*Registered Office:* Batley Grammar School, Carlinghow Hill, Batley, W Yorks, WF17 0AD
*Activities:* Primary education
*Officers:* Paul Bevington, Secretary; Roland Clark [1954] Director/Certified Chartered Accountant; Mike Cook [1964] Director/Retired Headteacher; Professor John Anthony Double [1942] Director; Helene Ghosh [1976] Director/Head of HR; Alistair Julian Hartley [1971] Director/Engineer; Amanda Jane Keeton [1967] Director/Project Manager; Jonathan Kidd [1966] Director/Chartered Surveyor; Aldean Marcia Newman-Agar [1970] Director/HR Business Partner; Ebrahim Suleman [1956] Director/Businessman; Oliver Tiplady [1964] Director/Teacher; Brigid Patricia Tullie [1957] Director/Headmistress; Dr Yasmin Zia [1962] Director/Doctor [Pakistani]

**L. Batley Holdings Limited**
*Incorporated:* 13 July 1989 *Employees:* 6
*Net Worth:* £47,539,880 *Total Assets:* £51,873,928
*Registered Office:* Room F2, Boston House, 214 High Street, Boston Spa, Wetherby, W Yorks, LS23 6AD
*Activities:* Activities of head offices
*Parent:* LBH (2012) Limited
*Officers:* Bruce Firth, Secretary; Rupert James Bullock [1966] Director; Simon Timothy Bullock [1962] Director; Bruce Firth [1939] Director; Rita Firth [1940] Director; Sarah Joanne Lawrance [1965] Director

**Batley Multi Academy Trust**
*Incorporated:* 8 August 2011 *Employees:* 214
*Previous:* Batley Girls' High School
*Net Worth:* £27,273,000 *Total Assets:* £30,167,000
*Registered Office:* Windmill Lane, Batley, W Yorks, WF17 0LD
*Activities:* General secondary education
*Officers:* Dr David Alan Brown, Secretary; Nailah Ahmed [1983] Director/Recruitment Manager; Trude Feiweles [1963] Director/Deputy Headteacher; Mandy Anne Marie Kennedy [1962] Director; Ellen Loughhead [1950] Director/Retired; Siraj Ahmed Mayet [1971] Director/Local Authority Officer; Jeremy Leslie Townend [1963] Director/Sessional Tutor

**Batteryback PLC**
*Incorporated:* 13 May 2009 *Employees:* 4
*Net Worth:* £998,920 *Total Assets:* £6,642,090
*Registered Office:* Richmond House, Selby Road, Garforth, Leeds, LS25 1NB
*Activities:* Other business support service activities n.e.c.
*Parent:* Wastecare Group Ltd
*Officers:* Christopher John Gay, Secretary; Peter Timothy Hunt [1955] Director

**Bawtry Carbon International Limited**
*Incorporated:* 4 January 2006 *Employees:* 69
*Net Worth:* £20,700,912 *Total Assets:* £29,300,920
*Registered Office:* High Street, Austerfield, Doncaster, S Yorks, DN10 6QT
*Activities:* Other manufacturing n.e.c.
*Parent:* Coretex Trading Limited
*Officers:* Carl Hammerton, Secretary; Yunjia Lu [1992] Director [Chinese]; Shuze Ren [1993] Director [Swiss]

**Bawtry Farms Limited**
*Incorporated:* 2 October 1997 *Employees:* 2
*Net Worth:* £7,624,585 *Total Assets:* £8,629,964
*Registered Office:* Serlby Hall, Serlby, Bawtry, S Yorks, DN10 6BA
*Activities:* Mixed farming
*Major Shareholder:* Kevin McDonald
*Officers:* Donna McDonald, Secretary; Amie McDonald [1993] Director; Donna Brigitte McDonald [1962] Director/Company Secretary; Kevin McDonald [1933] Managing Director

**Bawtry Investments Limited**
*Incorporated:* 15 October 2008 *Employees:* 4
*Net Worth Deficit:* £264,296 *Total Assets:* £7,665,761
*Registered Office:* High Street, Austerfield, Doncaster, S Yorks, DN10 6QT
*Activities:* Non-trading company
*Parent:* Nicholl Investments PTE Limited
*Officers:* Yunjia Lu [1992] Director [Chinese]; Shuze Ren [1993] Director/Manager [Swiss]

**The Bay Learning Trust**
*Incorporated:* 1 April 2011 *Employees:* 203
*Previous:* Ripley St Thomas Church of England Academy
*Net Worth:* £20,107,000 *Total Assets:* £23,622,000
*Registered Office:* The Lodge, Ripley St Thomas CE Academy, Ashton Road, Lancaster, LA1 4RR
*Activities:* General secondary education
*Officers:* Andrew McKinnell, Secretary; Ben Ardern [1978] Director/CIMA Qualified Accountant; Peter Ballard [1955] Director/Chief Executive; Dawn Elizabeth Cheetham [1963] Director; Professor John David Crewdson [1942] Director; Michael Henry Dudfield [1947] Director/Solicitor; Jacqueline Gloria Garnett [1956] Director/Retired; Nicola Gomersall [1971] Director/Headteacher; Elizabeth Olive Nicholls [1953] Director/Principal; Jane Margaret Watson [1963] Managing Director; Robert Mitchel Webb [1950] Managing Director; Valerie Margaret Wilson [1947] Director/District Councillor

**Bay Properties Letting Company Limited**
*Incorporated:* 22 March 1996 *Employees:* 7
*Net Worth:* £3,537,474 *Total Assets:* £6,512,755
*Registered Office:* 70 Buckingham Road, Morecambe, Lancs, LA3 1BD
*Activities:* Other letting and operating of own or leased real estate
*Major Shareholder:* Bryan Richard Long
*Officers:* Brian Richard Long, Secretary/Property Manager; Brian Richard Long [1962] Director/Property Manager

**Baydale Control Systems Limited**
*Incorporated:* 29 November 1999 *Employees:* 47
*Net Worth:* £2,413,722 *Total Assets:* £3,798,632
*Registered Office:* Unit I6, Morton Park Way, Darlington, Co Durham, DL1 4PH
*Activities:* Electrical installation
*Major Shareholder:* Neil James Pentland
*Officers:* Neil James Pentland, Secretary/Managing Director; Neil James Pentland [1964] Managing Director

**Bayfields Z Limited**
*Incorporated:* 18 February 2015 *Employees:* 40
*Previous:* Bayfields (South) Limited
*Net Worth:* £3,364,999 *Total Assets:* £9,937,946
*Registered Office:* The Fold Home Farm, The Avenue, Esholt, Shipley, W Yorks, BD17 7RH
*Activities:* Retail sale by opticians
*Major Shareholder:* Royston Edward Bayfield
*Officers:* Royston Edward Bayfield [1980] Director

**Bayford & Co Ltd**
*Incorporated:* 10 October 2003 *Employees:* 61
*Net Worth:* £25,046,000 *Total Assets:* £50,616,000
*Registered Office:* Bowcliffe Hall, Bramham, Wetherby, W Yorks, LS23 6LP
*Activities:* Other letting and operating of own or leased real estate
*Major Shareholder:* Jonathan Charles Deacon Turner
*Officers:* Lindsay Elizabeth McPhearson Austin [1977] Director; Christopher Ritchie [1976] Director; Jonathan Charles Deacon Turner [1966] Director

**Bayford & Co. (Developments) Limited**
*Incorporated:* 25 February 1977 *Employees:* 3
*Net Worth:* £3,056,132 *Total Assets:* £8,991,345
*Registered Office:* Bowcliffe Hall, Bramham, Wetherby, W Yorks, LS23 6LP
*Activities:* Other letting and operating of own or leased real estate
*Parent:* Bayford & Co Ltd
*Officers:* John Deacon Turner [1945] Director; Jonathan Charles Deacon Turner [1966] Director

**Bayram Timber Limited**
*Incorporated:* 17 May 2000 *Employees:* 152
*Net Worth:* £3,246,107 *Total Assets:* £10,492,940
*Registered Office:* Gibson Lane, Melton, North Ferriby, E Yorks, HU14 3HF
*Activities:* Sawmilling and planing of wood
*Major Shareholder:* Geoffrey Goodwin
*Officers:* Ian William Jordan, Secretary; Geoffrey Goodwin [1947] Director/Chairman; John Andrew Grace [1958] Managing Director; Christopher John Husband [1962] Commercial Director; Ian William Jordan [1965] Financial Director

**W.S. Bayston & Son Limited**
*Incorporated:* 9 January 1985 *Employees:* 4
*Net Worth:* £6,813,402 *Total Assets:* £7,156,713
*Registered Office:* Coldhill Farm, Coldhill Lane, Aberford, Leeds, LS25 3EE
*Activities:* Growing of cereals (except rice), leguminous crops and oil seeds
*Shareholders:* Richard William Bayston; John Charles Cox; Elizabeth Angela Bayston; Kevin Gamble
*Officers:* Kevin Gamble, Secretary; Richard William Bayston [1965] Director/Farmer

**BB Investments**
*Incorporated:* 28 August 1990 *Employees:* 2
*Net Worth:* £42,310,360 *Total Assets:* £43,333,332
*Registered Office:* Old Mill Lane, Low Road, Hunslet, Leeds, LS10 1RB
*Activities:* Financial intermediation not elsewhere classified
*Parent:* Jacuzzi Luxco S.A.R.L
*Officers:* Anthony Lovallo [1961] Director/Attorney [American]; Kevin Teague [1957] Director/Accountant

**BBB Services Limited**
*Incorporated:* 27 March 2003 *Employees:* 2
*Net Worth Deficit:* £886,323 *Total Assets:* £16,060,391
*Registered Office:* Unit 25 Bloom Lane, Scunthorpe, N Lincs, DN15 9AJ
*Activities:* Manufacture of other parts and accessories for motor vehicles
*Shareholder:* Egidio Brugola
*Officers:* Karl Erik Tommy Andersson [1963] Director/President [Swedish]; Carlo Rosario Arminio [1964] Director [Italian]; Elena Lidia Bestetti [1961] Director [Italian]; Egidio Stefano Brugola [1979] Director [Italian]; Steven David Gidney [1985] Director/Key Account Manager; Sukhvinder Gill [1966] Director/Project Manager; Sven Anders Karlsson [1949] Director [Swedish]; Neal Robert Thomas [1961] Director/Operations Manager; Anna Helena Christina Wennerstrom [1965] Director/Chief Financial Officer [Swedish]

**BBP Group Limited**
*Incorporated:* 22 August 2006
*Net Worth:* £2,120,100 *Total Assets:* £3,010,100
*Registered Office:* B B P House, 14 Keld Close, Barker Business Park, Melmerby, Ripon, N Yorks, HG4 5NB
*Activities:* Other letting and operating of own or leased real estate
*Shareholders:* Brian Wilfred Barker; Hannah Bean Barker
*Officers:* Suzanne Mary Scawthorn, Secretary; Brian Wilfred Barker [1933] Director/Farmer; Hannah Bean Barker [1940] Director/Housewife; John Richard Chapman [1958] Director; Suzanne Mary Scawthorn [1963] Company Secretary/Director; Dennis Alan Walton [1954] Finance Director

**BBP Investments Limited**
*Incorporated:* 25 May 2006
*Net Worth:* £623,851 *Total Assets:* £4,120,081
*Registered Office:* BBP House, 14 Keld Close, Barker Business Park, Melmerby, Ripon, N Yorks, HG4 5NB
*Activities:* Other letting and operating of own or leased real estate
*Parent:* BBP Group Limited
*Officers:* Suzanne Mary Scawthorn, Secretary; Brian Wilfred Barker [1933] Director; Hannah Bean Barker [1940] Director/Housewife; John Richard Chapman [1958] Director; Suzanne Mary Scawthorn [1963] Director; Dennis Alan Walton [1954] Finance Director

**BBR Graphic Sales Limited**
*Incorporated:* 29 December 1998 *Employees:* 6
*Net Worth:* £2,053,724 *Total Assets:* £5,389,642
*Registered Office:* Kings Yard, Low Mill Road, Ossett, W Yorks, WF5 8ND
*Activities:* Other retail sale not in stores, stalls or markets
*Shareholders:* David Blakeley; David Ian Ross
*Officers:* David Blakeley, Secretary/General Contractors; David Blakeley [1944] Director/General Contractor; Phillip James Rawden [1972] Director/Accountant; David Ian Ross [1956] Director/Engineer

**BBRG (Purchaser) Ltd**
*Incorporated:* 24 February 2016
*Net Worth:* £89,930,504 *Total Assets:* £176,279,408
*Registered Office:* Ground Floor, Icon Building, Balby Carr Bank, Doncaster, S Yorks, DN4 5JQ
*Activities:* Activities of head offices
*Parent:* BBRG (Subsidiary) Ltd
*Officers:* Claudia Maria Griffin [1967] Director/Chief Financial Officer [German]

**BBRG (Subsidiary) Ltd**
*Incorporated:* 3 December 2015
*Net Worth:* £78,351,744 *Total Assets:* £176,279,408
*Registered Office:* Ground Floor, Icon Building, Balby Carr Bank, Doncaster, S Yorks, DN4 5JQ
*Activities:* Activities of head offices
*Parent:* BBRG Holding (UK) Ltd
*Officers:* Claudia Maria Griffin [1967] Director/Chief Financial Officer [German]

**BBRG Finance (UK) Ltd.**
*Incorporated:* 3 October 2014 *Employees:* 22
*Net Worth Deficit:* £57,063,436 *Total Assets:* £235,947,072
*Registered Office:* Ground Floor, Icon Building, Balby Carr Bank, Doncaster, S Yorks, DN4 5JQ
*Activities:* Activities of head offices
*Parent:* BBRG Production (UK) Limited
*Officers:* Claudia Maria Griffin [1967] Director/Chief Financial Officer [German]; Brett Simpson [1964] Director/Chief Executive [Australian]

**BBRG Holding (UK) Ltd**
*Incorporated:* 3 December 2015
*Net Worth:* £18,432,680 *Total Assets:* £159,747,552
*Registered Office:* Ground Floor, Icon Building, Balby Carr Bank, Doncaster, S Yorks, DN4 5JQ
*Activities:* Activities of head offices
*Parent:* NV Bekaert
*Officers:* Matthew Taylor [1960] Director/Chief Executive Officer; Curd Vandekerckhove [1965] Director [Belgian]

**BBRG Operations (UK) Ltd.**
*Incorporated:* 5 November 2014 *Employees:* 4
*Net Worth:* £159,698,864 *Total Assets:* £176,279,408
*Registered Office:* Ground Floor, Icon Building, Balby Carr Bank, Doncaster, S Yorks, DN4 5JQ
*Activities:* Activities of head offices
*Parent:* Bridon-Bekaert Ropes Group (UK) Ltd
*Officers:* Claudia Maria Griffin [1967] Director/Chief Financial Officer [German]

**BBRG Production (UK) Ltd.**
*Incorporated:* 5 November 2014
*Net Worth:* £197,856,000 *Total Assets:* £197,856,000
*Registered Office:* Ground Floor, Icon Building, Balby Carr Bank, Doncaster, S Yorks, DN4 5JQ
*Activities:* Activities of head offices
*Parent:* BBRG Operations (UK) Ltd
*Officers:* Claudia Maria Griffin [1967] Director/Chief Financial Officer [German]

**BC Bantams Limited**
*Incorporated:* 9 May 2011
*Net Worth:* £2,728,405 *Total Assets:* £3,014,919
*Registered Office:* Valley Parade Stadium, Valley Parade, Bradford, W Yorks, BD8 7DY
*Activities:* Other sports activities
*Officers:* Alan Keith Biggin, Secretary; Alan Keith Biggin [1949] Director; Stefan Albert Rupp [1969] Director/Chairman [German]

**BCA Leisure Ltd**
*Incorporated:* 1 May 1996 *Employees:* 126
*Net Worth:* £4,085,742 *Total Assets:* £4,781,919
*Registered Office:* Unit H9, Premier Way, Lowfields Business Park, Elland, W Yorks, HX5 9HF
*Activities:* Manufacture of other plastic products
*Parent:* B.C.A. Group Ltd
*Officers:* Teresa Batist, Secretary; Teresa Batist [1962] Director/Company Secretary; Wilhelmus Johannus Maria Batist [1951] Director [Dutch]; Wayne Boyd [1970] Director/Sales & Marketing Manager; Dean Hans [1977] Director/Technical Sales; Martin Price [1961] Director/IT and Purchasing; Adam Slater [1962] Director

**BDS (Yorkshire) Limited**
*Incorporated:* 21 April 1998 *Employees:* 56
*Net Worth:* £1,410,126 *Total Assets:* £7,550,966
*Registered Office:* Unit 55 Kelleythorpe Industrial Estate, Driffield, E Yorks, YO25 9DJ
*Activities:* Other specialised construction activities n.e.c.
*Parent:* Raysul Holdings Limited
*Officers:* William Arthur Sullivan, Secretary; Maan Hamed Salim Al Rawahi [1979] Director [Omani]; Is-Haq Hamed Salim Al-Rawahy [1957] Director; Rebecca Marie Johnson [1991] Director; Nicholas Paul Sullivan [1963] Director

**Be Fuelcards Holdings Limited**
*Incorporated:* 7 June 2010
*Previous:* Jaytee Energy Ltd
*Net Worth:* £3,380 *Total Assets:* £4,953,985
*Registered Office:* Bowcliffe Hall, Bramham, Wetherby, W Yorks, LS23 6LP
*Activities:* Activities of head offices
*Parent:* The Right Fuelcard Company Limited
*Officers:* Paul Simon Althasen [1964] Director; Patrick Bataillard [1964] Director/Executive Vice President Finance [French]; Aurelien Pierre Samuel Briand [1980] Performance Director [French]; Antoine Jacques Alexandre Dumurgier [1973] Director [French]; Jonathan Charles Deacon Turner [1966] Director; Johann Fabrice Martin Vaucanson [1973] Managing Director [French]

**Be Fuelcards Ltd**
*Incorporated:* 2 September 1987 *Employees:* 35
*Net Worth:* £11,707,327 *Total Assets:* £25,034,744
*Registered Office:* Bowcliffe Hall, Bramham, Wetherby, Leeds, LS23 6LP
*Activities:* Wholesale of petroleum and petroleum products
*Parent:* Jaytee Energy Ltd
*Officers:* Paul Simon Althasen [1964] Director; Patrick Bataillard [1964] Director/Executive Vice President Finance [French]; Aurelien Pierre Samuel Briand [1980] Performance Director [French]; Antoine Jacques Alexandre Dumurgier [1973] Director/C O O [French]; Jonathan Charles Deacon Turner [1966] Managing Director; Johann Fabrice Martin Vaucanson [1973] Managing Director [French]

**Beal (UK) Limited**
*Incorporated:* 7 April 1999 *Employees:* 44
*Net Worth:* £5,110,650 *Total Assets:* £5,802,973
*Registered Office:* Sterling Works, Texas Street, Morley, Leeds, LS27 0HG
*Activities:* Wholesale trade of motor vehicle parts and accessories
*Major Shareholder:* Dean Stefan Beal
*Officers:* Nicola Tracey Beal, Secretary; Sir Dean Stefan Beal [1963] Director; Nicola Tracy Beal [1967] Director

**Beal Developments Limited**
*Incorporated:* 17 May 1968 *Employees:* 140
*Net Worth:* £15,908,830 *Total Assets:* £27,731,016
*Registered Office:* Holderness House, Bridgehead Business Park, Hessle, Hull, HU13 0DH
*Activities:* Construction of domestic buildings
*Parent:* Beal Holdings Limited
*Officers:* Gemma Caroline Beal [1980] Director; Richard Luther Beal [1970] Director; Wayne Bowser [1952] Director; John Roland Goodfellow [1954] Director/Builder; Guy Jewitt [1986] Associate Technical Director; Simon William Lunt [1962] Director/Solicitor; Christopher Murphy [1976] Associate Land Director; Susan Pamela Waudby [1953] Sales Director; Jason Aran Williams [1982] Finance Director

**Beal Securities Limited**
*Incorporated:* 4 February 2010 *Employees:* 141
*Net Worth:* £18,353,032 *Total Assets:* £28,381,898
*Registered Office:* Holderness House, Bridgehead Business Park, Hessle, Hull, HU13 0DH
*Activities:* Activities of head offices
*Officers:* Gemma Caroline Beal [1980] Director; John Luther Beal [1939] Director/Builder; Richard Luther Beal [1970] Director/Builder

**Bear Leisure Limited**
*Incorporated:* 24 April 2015
*Net Worth Deficit:* £63,421 *Total Assets:* £3,028,817
*Registered Office:* 1 Mariner Court, Calder Business Park, Wakefield, W Yorks, WF4 3FL
*Activities:* Buying and selling of own real estate
*Shareholders:* Stuart Andrew Lomax; Rachel Jayne Lomax
*Officers:* Gregory Allsopp [1980] Director/Solicitor; Graham Leslie Berks [1954] Director; Paul Richard Halliday [1974] Director

**Beatty Topco Limited**
*Incorporated:* 16 November 2015 *Employees:* 109
*Net Worth Deficit:* £5,377,382 *Total Assets:* £9,568,373
*Registered Office:* 1 Park Row, Leeds, LS1 5AB
*Activities:* Activities of head offices
*Shareholder:* Synova Capital General Partner 4 Limited
*Officers:* Timothy James West Ashlin [1977] Investor Director; Sheena Marion Beckwith [1965] Finance Director; Matthew Chairman [1987] Director/Investment Manager; Stuart James Davidson [1980] Director; Stephen William Duncan [1951] Director; James Ferguson Hall [1958] Director

**Beauchamp Real Estate Holdings Limited**
*Incorporated:* 30 April 2010 *Employees:* 2
*Net Worth:* £19,525,026 *Total Assets:* £32,463,970
*Registered Office:* Cumberland House, Greenside Lane, Bradford, BD8 9TF
*Activities:* Activities of property unit trusts
*Parent:* Praxisifm Trustees (UK) Limited
*Officers:* Claire Marie Cain [1970] Director; Christopher Stephen Smith [1972] Director

**Beaumont ABS Ltd**
*Incorporated:* 10 September 2015 *Employees:* 194
*Net Worth Deficit:* £4,555,651 *Total Assets:* £8,088,268
*Registered Office:* 1 Paragon Avenue, Paragon Business Village, Wakefield, W Yorks, WF1 2UF
*Activities:* Solicitors
*Parent:* Legalzoom UK Holdings Ltd
*Officers:* Piers Chead [1972] Director; Craig John Holt [1978] Director; Helen Linda Leman Torresi [1976] Director; Peter Henry Oey [1970] Director [Australian]; James Peters [1975] Director [American]

**Beaumont House Properties Limited**
*Incorporated:* 18 October 2006 *Employees:* 4
*Net Worth:* £23,108,000 *Total Assets:* £117,787,000
*Registered Office:* The Inspire, Hornbeam Square West, Harrogate, N Yorks, HG2 8PA
*Activities:* Other letting and operating of own or leased real estate
*Parent:* De Vere 2 Limited
*Officers:* James Alexander Burrell [1974] Director/Accountant; Generaldine Josephine Gallagher [1965] Finance Director [Irish]; Gail Susan Hunter [1963] Human Resources Director; Anthony Gerrard Troy [1962] Director [Irish]

**Beaumont Morgan Developments Limited**
*Incorporated:* 3 May 2011 *Employees:* 86
*Net Worth:* £580,023 *Total Assets:* £17,208,296
*Registered Office:* Westcott House, Hesslewood Country Estate, Ferriby Road, Hessle, E Yorks, HU13 0LH
*Activities:* Construction of domestic buildings
*Shareholders:* DMC Estates Limited; Direct Property Investments Ltd
*Officers:* Darren Kingsley McLellan [1972] Director; Kieran Stuart Moore [1975] Director; Gareth Morgan [1984] Director

**Beckenreid Limited**
*Incorporated:* 24 November 2017
*Net Worth:* £1,405,703 *Total Assets:* £3,062,570
*Registered Office:* 34 Lowther Street, Kendal, Cumbria, LA9 4DX
*Activities:* Activities of construction holding companies
*Major Shareholder:* James William Dickinson
*Officers:* James William Dickinson [1986] Director/Electrical Engineer

**Becker UK Limited**
*Incorporated:* 21 December 1982 *Employees:* 24
*Net Worth:* £3,989,599 *Total Assets:* £4,494,265
*Registered Office:* Link 63, Liverpool Street, Hull, HU3 4XS
*Activities:* Manufacture of pumps
*Officers:* Timothy John Shields, Secretary; Dorothee Becker [1966] Director [German]; Neil Hughes [1953] Director

**Beckfoot Trust**
*Incorporated:* 24 July 2012 *Employees:* 1,014
*Previous:* The Beckfoot and Hazelbeck Trust
*Net Worth:* £23,020,000 *Total Assets:* £34,297,000
*Registered Office:* Beckfoot Trust, Wagon Lane, Bingley, W Yorks, BD16 1EE
*Activities:* Pre-primary education
*Officers:* Sadiq Ali [1973] Director/Social Work Consultant and Social Worker; Paul Hill [1961] Director/Local Government Officer; David James Horn [1959] Director/Headteacher and CEO; Michael Joseph Kelly [1952] Director/Retired; Robert Lawrence [1958] Director/Clinical Psychologist; David Maybury [1952] Director/Retired; Susan Claire Pierce [1959] Director/Retired; Paul Speight [1972] Director/Head of Business Development; Charles David Tebbutt [1961] Finance Director; Susan Kim Tollervey [1962] Director/Continuous Improvement Team LEA; John Winkley [1968] Director

**Beckside Developments Limited**
*Incorporated:* 6 August 2012 *Employees:* 9
*Net Worth:* £482,032 *Total Assets:* £4,793,030
*Registered Office:* 1 Amos Drive, West Green, Pocklington, York, YO42 2BS
*Activities:* Development of building projects
*Officers:* Dr Emily Jane Armitage [1976] Director/GP Partner; Dr Alison Diane Atkinson [1962] Director/GP Partner; Dr Mari Ellen Austin [1962] Director/GP Partner; Dr Jane Patricia Brooke [1957] Director/GP Partner; Dr Joseph James Green [1972] Director/GP Partner; Bernadette Mary Judge [1964] Director/Managing Partner; Dr James Horatio William Laing [1963] Director/GP Partner; Dr Timothy Peter Maycock [1971] Director/GP Partner; Dr Nigel David Robinson [1966] Director/GP Partner

**Bedfords Limited**
*Incorporated:* 22 May 1991 *Employees:* 113
*Net Worth:* £7,646,354 *Total Assets:* £13,651,978
*Registered Office:* Bedfords Limited, Pheasant Drive, Gelderd Road Industrial Estate, Birstall, W Yorks, WF17 9LT
*Activities:* Freight transport by road
*Parent:* Bedfords Holdings Limited
*Officers:* David Ian Storey, Secretary; Lee Michael Nichols [1968] Director; David Ian Storey [1953] Director/Chartered Accountant; David Robert Webster [1969] Director

**Bee Health Limited**
*Incorporated:* 22 July 2008 *Employees:* 253
*Net Worth:* £3,294,942 *Total Assets:* £9,460,570
*Registered Office:* 33 George Street, Wakefield, W Yorks, WF1 1LX
*Activities:* Manufacture of other food products n.e.c.
*Shareholder:* Steven Paul Ryan
*Officers:* Janis Richardson Fletcher OBE [1954] Director; Steven Paul Ryan [1958] Director; Neil Smillie [1954] Director

**Bee Jay Scaffolding Limited**
*Incorporated:* 5 January 1988 *Employees:* 85
*Net Worth:* £1,641,122 *Total Assets:* £3,552,814
*Registered Office:* 3 Aireville House, Ross Mills, Rodley Lane, Leeds, LS13 1BJ
*Activities:* Other specialised construction activities n.e.c.
*Major Shareholder:* Barry David Stephenson
*Officers:* Barry David Stephenson, Secretary; Barry David Stephenson [1950] Director; David Daniel Stephenson [1976] Director; Gillian Corrine Stephenson [1950] Director

**Beech Hill Residential Investments Limited**
*Incorporated:* 13 April 1993 *Employees:* 1
*Net Worth:* £1,678,212 *Total Assets:* £3,227,252
*Registered Office:* Unicorn House, 8 Innovation Drive, Newport, Brough, N Humbers, HU15 2FW
*Activities:* Other letting and operating of own or leased real estate
*Major Shareholder:* Andrew Nigel Horncastle
*Officers:* Carole Diane Horncastle, Secretary; Andrew Nigel Horncastle [1959] Director; Carole Diane Horncastle [1957] Director

**Bekaert Bradford UK Limited**
*Incorporated:* 3 December 1907 *Employees:* 110
*Previous:* Cold Drawn Products Limited
*Net Worth:* £8,810,578 *Total Assets:* £15,575,388
*Registered Office:* Park House Road, Low Moor, Bradford, W Yorks, BD12 0PX
*Activities:* Cold drawing of bars
*Parent:* NV Bekaert SA
*Officers:* David Charles Smith, Secretary; Jan Boelens [1965] Director [Belgian]; Serge Piceu [1976] Director [Belgian]; Piet Van Riet [1962] Director [Belgian]

**Belaris Ltd.**
*Incorporated:* 6 December 2005
*Net Worth:* £4,508,197 *Total Assets:* £4,642,465
*Registered Office:* The Picasso Building, Caldervale Road, Wakefield, W Yorks, WF1 5PF
*Activities:* Other business support service activities n.e.c.
*Major Shareholder:* Gert Huegler
*Officers:* Stephanie Maria Beatrice Huegler, Secretary; Beatrice Karla Sophie Huegler [1994] Director/Student [German]; Gert Leopold Huegler [1957] Director/Businessman [German]; Stephanie Maria Beatrice Huegler [1960] Director [German]; Valerie Lena Marie Huegler [1991] Director/Student [German]

**Belem Investments Limited**
*Incorporated:* 27 October 2000
*Net Worth:* £3,139,896 *Total Assets:* £5,859,161
*Registered Office:* 1 Parkview Court, St Pauls Road, Shipley, W Yorks, BD18 3DZ
*Activities:* Other business support service activities n.e.c.
*Shareholder:* Peper Trust
*Officers:* Annemari Nilhagen Holmes, Secretary; Joakim Andrew Holmes [1983] Director/General Manager; Annemari Nilhagen-Holmes [1952] Director/Consultant [Swedish]

**Belgrade Insulations Limited**
*Incorporated:* 17 March 1976 *Employees:* 111
*Net Worth:* £2,009,217 *Total Assets:* £15,234,166
*Registered Office:* Unit T, Gildersome Industrial Estate, Stone Pits Lane, Leeds, LS27 7JZ
*Activities:* Manufacture of other plastic products
*Parent:* Belgrade Trading Limited
*Officers:* Gerard Alexander Fallon [1956] Director; Raja Alexander Khan [1962] Director; Philip Anthony Kirk [1957] Director/Accountant

**Belgrave (North West) Limited**
*Incorporated:* 29 September 2005 *Employees:* 1
*Net Worth Deficit:* £4,231,681 *Total Assets:* £8,250,138
*Registered Office:* Prospect House, 32 Sovereign Street, Leeds, LS1 4BJ
*Activities:* Other letting and operating of own or leased real estate
*Officers:* Collette Sunderland, Secretary; Warren Christopher Hill [1965] Director/Developer

**Thomas Bell & Sons Limited**
*Incorporated:* 30 July 1976 *Employees:* 43
*Net Worth:* £10,489,621 *Total Assets:* £22,737,012
*Registered Office:* Bigby Road, Brigg, N Lincs, DN20 8RA
*Activities:* Agents selling agricultural raw materials, livestock, textile raw materials and semi-finished goods
*Shareholders:* Andrew Martin Major; Andrew Martin Major
*Officers:* Paula Major, Secretary; Matthew Peter Holden Dawson [1978] Director; Andrew Martin Major [1962] Managing Director

**Bellbrooke LLP**
*Incorporated:* 15 August 2004
*Net Worth:* £852,846 *Total Assets:* £3,078,138
*Registered Office:* Club Chambers, Museum Street, York, YO1 7DN
*Officers:* Michael Paul Hammill [1955] Member; Erica Louise Rogers [1966] Member

**Belle Vue Girls' School**
*Incorporated:* 28 February 2012 *Employees:* 204
*Net Worth:* £18,917,636 *Total Assets:* £20,896,596
*Registered Office:* Thorn Lane, Bingley Road, Bradford, BD9 6NA
*Activities:* General secondary education
*Officers:* Barbara Janet Edwards, Secretary; Vivianne Frances Brealey [1968] Director/Communications Manager; Ian Broadbent [1970] Director/Facilities Manager; Mary Copeland [1958] Director/Headteacher

**Belle Vue Mills Limited**
*Incorporated:* 18 December 2009 *Employees:* 3
*Net Worth:* £1,442,263 *Total Assets:* £8,642,864
*Registered Office:* 5 Hawthorn Park, Coal Road, Leeds, LS14 1PQ
*Activities:* Buying and selling of own real estate
*Parent:* Rushbond PLC
*Officers:* Richard Mark Powell, Secretary; Mark Richard Finch [1967] Director/Chartered Surveyor Chartered Town Planner; Jonathan William Maud [1960] Director; Richard Mark Powell [1967] Director/Chartered Accountant

**Belle Vue Property Limited**
*Incorporated:* 24 July 2000
*Net Worth:* £2,381,559 *Total Assets:* £5,673,635
*Registered Office:* 13-15 Netherhall Road, Doncaster, S Yorks, DN1 2PH
*Activities:* Other letting and operating of own or leased real estate
*Shareholders:* Neville Christopher Brown; Carl Colin Osborne
*Officers:* Neville Christopher Brown, Secretary; Neville Christopher Brown [1959] Managing Director; Carl Colin Osborne [1965] Director/Builder

**J.G. Bellerby (Farms) Limited**
*Incorporated:* 27 October 1997 *Employees:* 2
*Net Worth:* £3,728,455 *Total Assets:* £4,157,126
*Registered Office:* Manor Dairy Farm, Crag Lane, Killinghall, Harrogate, N Yorks, HG3 2BD
*Activities:* Raising of dairy cattle
*Shareholders:* John Gordon Bellerby; Caroline Ann Bellerby
*Officers:* Caroline Ann Bellerby, Secretary/Director; Caroline Ann Bellerby [1952] Director

**Bellow Properties Limited**
*Incorporated:* 12 October 1950
*Net Worth:* £4,145,954 *Total Assets:* £6,059,304
*Registered Office:* Wine & Co, 20-22 Bridge End, Leeds, LS1 4DJ
*Activities:* Other letting and operating of own or leased real estate
*Officers:* The Honourable Asha Bellow, Secretary; The Honourable Stephen Jeremy Bellow [1953] Director

**Bellutex Limited**
*Incorporated:* 8 June 2010
*Net Worth:* £746,936 *Total Assets:* £3,348,223
*Registered Office:* 90 Kirkgate, Leeds, LS2 7DJ
*Activities:* Renting and operating of Housing Association real estate
*Major Shareholder:* George Scott Storey
*Officers:* Maureen Hatton, Secretary; George Scot Storey [1964] Director

**Belmont-Birklands School Trust Limited**
*Incorporated:* 17 September 1969 *Employees:* 37
*Net Worth:* £626,347 *Total Assets:* £3,513,191
*Registered Office:* Swarcliffe Hall, Birstwith, Harrogate, N Yorks, HG3 2JG
*Activities:* Primary education
*Officers:* Helen Kernaghan, Secretary; Victoria Jane Dixon Grafton [1970] Director/Sales Administrator; Geoffrey William Lowde [1959] Director/Financial Controller; Kate Emma Louise Standen [1962] Director; Frances Elizabeth Trowell [1963] Director/Solicitor; Timothy Alexander James Waring [1960] Director/Estate Agent; Dr Belinda Jane Whitehead [1963] Director/Research

**Belzona International Limited**
*Incorporated:* 14 April 1954 *Employees:* 221
*Net Worth:* £33,294,172 *Total Assets:* £38,011,936
*Registered Office:* Claro Road, Harrogate, N Yorks, HG1 4DS
*Activities:* Manufacture of paints, varnishes and similar coatings, mastics and sealants
*Parent:* Orbex Ltd
*Officers:* Ronald Campbell [1954] Director; Joel Christopher Longster Svendsen [1970] Director

**Belzona Polymerics Limited**
*Incorporated:* 20 September 1996 *Employees:* 160
*Net Worth:* £33,655,948 *Total Assets:* £36,607,104
*Registered Office:* Belzona Polymerics Ltd, Claro Road, Harrogate, N Yorks, HG1 4DS
*Activities:* Manufacture of other chemical products n.e.c.
*Parent:* Belzona International Ltd
*Officers:* Ronald Campbell [1954] Director; Stephen Conrad Cooper [1967] Director; Jevon Daryl Pugh [1969] Research & Development Director; Neil Andrew Robinson [1972] Director

**Bemis Elsham Limited**
*Incorporated:* 31 March 1992 *Employees:* 94
*Net Worth:* £8,804,000 *Total Assets:* £12,283,000
*Registered Office:* The Flarepath, Elsham Wolds Industrial Estate, Brigg, N Lincs, DN20 0SP
*Activities:* Manufacture of other plastic products
*Officers:* William Francis Austen [1958] Director/Executive [American]; Jerry Scott Krempa [1960] Director/Vice President and Controller - Bemis Company, Inc [American]; Guillaume Bruno Claude Taillandier [1975] Director/Head of Legal [French]; Willem Ludwig Jozef Van Der Smissen [1960] Director/Manager [Belgian]

**Bemis Packaging UK Ltd**
*Incorporated:* 7 March 1969 *Employees:* 17
*Net Worth:* £5,095,000 *Total Assets:* £9,254,000
*Registered Office:* The Flarepath, Elsham Wold Industrial Estate, Brigg, N Lincs, DN20 0SP
*Activities:* Other business support service activities n.e.c.
*Officers:* Willem Jozef Ludwig Van Der Smissen, Secretary; Guillaume Bruno Claude Taillandier [1975] Director/Head of Legal [French]; Willem Ludwig Jozef Van de Smissen [1960] Director/Manager [Belgian]

**Bemrose Booth Paragon Limited**
*Incorporated:* 8 September 2003 *Employees:* 137
*Net Worth:* £944,000 *Total Assets:* £9,372,000
*Registered Office:* Stockholm Road, Sutton Fields, Hull, HU7 0XY
*Activities:* Manufacture of other articles of paper and paperboard n.e.c.
*Officers:* Richard Joseph Cahill, Secretary; Patrick James Crean [1963] Director [Irish]; Laurent Thierry Salmon [1963] Director [French]

**Bender UK Limited**
*Incorporated:* 18 December 1996 *Employees:* 46
*Net Worth:* £9,062,357 *Total Assets:* £10,225,942
*Registered Office:* J L Winder and Co, 125 Ramsden Square, Barrow in Furness, Cumbria, LA14 1XA
*Activities:* Non-specialised wholesale trade
*Officers:* Sabine Bender-Suhr, Secretary [German]; Sabine Bender-Suhr [1965] Director [German]; Gareth Brunton [1973] Director/Engineer; Steven John Mason [1972] Director/Engineer

**Bendrigg Trust**
*Incorporated:* 27 October 1978 *Employees:* 30
*Net Worth:* £3,868,569 *Total Assets:* £4,166,322
*Registered Office:* Bendrigg Lodge, Old Hutton, Kendal, Cumbria, LA8 0NR
*Activities:* Other amusement and recreation activities n.e.c.
*Officers:* Nicholas Peter Liley, Secretary; Peter James Bates [1958] Director/Solicitor; Robert Simon Drummond Hay [1967] Director/Land Agent; Anne Judith Fleck [1962] Director; Donald James Harding [1942] Director/Retired; Tom Walsh Hibbert [1936] Director/Retired; Rachael Hodgson [1952] Director/Retired Headteacher; John Milburn Holmes [1939] Director/Retired; Timothy Richard Lawrence Lowe [1957] Director/Local Government Officer; Brian Andrew McDonough [1953] Director of South Lakeland Housing; Clare Hilary Millington [1963] Director/Teacher; Kim Parry [1965] Finance Director; Anne Judith Rayner [1950] Director/Housewife; Adrian Walter [1959] Director/Retired; Giles Wingate-Saul [1945] Director/Retired

**Benenden Wellbeing Limited**
*Incorporated:* 29 October 2012
*Net Worth:* £1,099,000 *Total Assets:* £6,790,000
*Registered Office:* Benenden Healthcare Society, Holgate Park Drive, York, YO26 4GG
*Activities:* Activities of insurance agents and brokers
*Officers:* Richard Alan Johnston, Secretary; Robert Kenneth Andrews [1963] Director; Helen Chamberlain [1963] Director/Chief Financial Officer; Stella Croot [1967] Director; Helen Louise Smith [1975] Director

**Jeremy Benn Associates Limited**
*Incorporated:* 6 September 1996 *Employees:* 439
*Net Worth:* £4,911,528 *Total Assets:* £8,918,719
*Registered Office:* South Barn, Broughton Hall, Skipton, N Yorks, BD23 3AE
*Activities:* Engineering related scientific and technical consulting activities
*Parent:* JBA Group Ltd
*Officers:* Craig Robson, Secretary; David Graham Henry Bassett [1966] Director/Civil Engineer; Richard George Buck [1965] Director/Consulting Engineer; Alastair George Jervis Dale [1957] Director/Engineering Manager; Gary John Deakin [1960] Director/Engineering Manager; Andrew David Gubbin [1963] Director/Engineering Manager; Rachel Louise Huitson-Little [1980] Director/Hydrologist; Dr Mark Reuben Lawless [1974] Director [Canadian]; Stephen Maslen [1958] Director/Landscape Architect; Marc Graham Pinnell [1970] Director/Engineering Manager

**Bennett Potatoes Limited**
*Incorporated:* 27 August 2008 *Employees:* 67
*Net Worth:* £3,091,613 *Total Assets:* £5,889,750
*Registered Office:* 1 Station Yard, Scawby, Brigg, N Lincs, DN20 9DP
*Activities:* Processing and preserving of potatoes
*Officers:* James Gardiner Orr, Secretary; Ian William Bennett [1964] Director; George Jack Orr [1959] Director; James Gardiner Orr [1968] Director

**Bennett-Ings (Developments) Limited**
*Incorporated:* 2 March 1992 *Employees:* 1
*Net Worth:* £3,344,056 *Total Assets:* £3,504,618
*Registered Office:* The Farm House, Tomlin Well Lane, Bradford, W Yorks, BD10 0FE
*Activities:* Development of building projects
*Officers:* Lyndsay Ruth Lardner, Secretary; Lyndsay Ruth Lardner [1963] Director/Librarian; Carolyne Margaret Wilson [1959] Director/Neonatal Sister; Rosamund Frances Wilson [1953] Director/University Lecturer; Russell Philip Wilson [1955] Director/Housing Manager

**Benson Park Limited**
*Incorporated:* 9 August 2002
*Net Worth:* £13,359,000 *Total Assets:* £13,476,000
*Registered Office:* Crane Court, Hesslewood Office Park, Ferriby Road, Hessle, E Yorks, HU13 0PA
*Activities:* Production of meat and poultry meat products
*Parent:* Cranswick Country Foods PLC
*Officers:* Steven Garrick Glover, Secretary; John Mark Bottomley [1963] Director; James Robert Brisby [1974] Director; Adam Hartley Couch [1968] Director; Jason Peter Key [1972] Operations Director; David Charles Park [1969] Director

**Benson Turner Limited**
*Incorporated:* 24 August 1920 *Employees:* 3
*Net Worth:* £3,848,738 *Total Assets:* £4,189,652
*Registered Office:* Stone Hall Mills, Stone Hall Road, Eccleshill, Bradford, W Yorks, BD2 2EW
*Activities:* Other letting and operating of own or leased real estate
*Shareholder:* Charles Wilfred David Sutcliffe
*Officers:* Charles Peter David Sutcliffe [1961] Director; Charles Wilfred David Sutcliffe [1936] Director

**Bentley & Bentley Limited**
*Incorporated:* 3 June 1993 *Employees:* 116
*Net Worth:* £4,543,582 *Total Assets:* £17,021,272
*Registered Office:* Airedale Business Centre, Millennium Road, Keighley Road, Skipton, N Yorks, BD23 2UB
*Activities:* Sale of new cars and light motor vehicles
*Major Shareholder:* Kevin Philip Bentley
*Officers:* Omer Khan, Secretary; Edward James Bentley [1973] Director; Julie Mary Bentley [1943] Director; Kevin Philip Bentley [1945] Director; Mark Peter Bentley [1969] Director

**Thos. Bentley & Son Limited**
*Incorporated:* 18 March 1965 *Employees:* 89
*Net Worth:* £2,970,700 *Total Assets:* £11,280,448
*Registered Office:* Brookfoot House, Low Lane, Horsforth, Leeds, LS18 5PU
*Activities:* Other letting and operating of own or leased real estate
*Shareholders:* Thomas James MacAulay Bentley; Hannah Victoria Bentley; J M Norris, T J M Bentley & T R Bentley as Trustees of The T R Bentley 1997 Discretionary Settlement
*Officers:* Thomas James MacAulay Bentley [1971] Business Development Director; Thomas Richard Bentley [1943] Chairman & Managing Director; Lisa Flannery [1965] Finance Director

**Guy Bentley Limited**
*Incorporated:* 17 June 1999 *Employees:* 2
*Net Worth:* £2,443,634 *Total Assets:* £3,212,999
*Registered Office:* Bentley Buildings, Windhill, Glaisdale, Whitby, N Yorks, YO21 2QY
*Activities:* Construction of other civil engineering projects n.e.c.
*Shareholders:* Rachel Ann Bentley; Tom David Bentley
*Officers:* Rachel Ann Bentley, Secretary; Rachel Ann Bentley [1964] Director; Tom David Bentley [1964] Director

**J.N. Bentley Limited**
*Incorporated:* 7 December 1972 *Employees:* 1,218
*Net Worth:* £10,747,796 *Total Assets:* £79,753,416
*Registered Office:* Snaygill Industrial Estate, Keighley Road, Skipton, N Yorks, BD23 2QR
*Activities:* Construction of utility projects for fluids
*Parent:* Bentley Holdings Limited
*Officers:* Jonathan David Rhodes, Secretary; David Mark Bentley [1969] Commercial Director; Paul Rogerson Bentley [1967] Managing Director; John Alastair Binns [1960] Commercial Director; Philip Robert Cundill [1977] Commercial Director; James Richard Fitton [1971] Operations Director North; John Matthew Greenwood [1975] Engineering Director; Michael David Haigh [1960] Director; James How Keir Harris [1968] Director; Judith Jeffery [1969] HR Director; Jonathan David Rhodes [1974] Finance and IT Director; Angus James Anderson Ridge [1966] Operations Director; Richard Risdon [1974] Operations Director South; Edwin George Roud [1963] Finance Director; Steven Christopher Tetlow [1966] Bidding & Estimating Director

**J.N. Bentley Properties Limited**
*Incorporated:* 8 April 2013
*Net Worth:* £1,184,271 *Total Assets:* £6,432,696
*Registered Office:* 19 Hornbeam Square South, Hornbeam Park, Harrogate, N Yorks, HG2 8NB
*Activities:* Buying and selling of own real estate
*Officers:* Andrew Robert Davies, Secretary; John Philip Bentley [1968] Managing Director; Martin Matthew Bentley [1971] Director

**Bentley Yorkshire Limited**
*Incorporated:* 20 April 2011 *Employees:* 31
*Net Worth:* £261,955 *Total Assets:* £4,346,732
*Registered Office:* Airedale Business Centre, Millennium Road, Keighley Road, Skipton, N Yorks, BD23 2UB
*Activities:* Sale of other motor vehicles
*Parent:* Bentley & Bentley Limited
*Officers:* Omer Khan, Secretary; Edward James Bentley [1973] Director; Kevin Philip Bentley [1945] Director; Mark Peter Bentley [1969] Director

**Berens & Company Limited**
*Incorporated:* 29 June 1939 *Employees:* 114
*Net Worth:* £50,553,772 *Total Assets:* £61,920,392
*Registered Office:* 62 Albion Street, Leeds, LS1 6AD
*Activities:* Other retail sale of new goods in specialised stores (not commercial art galleries and opticians)
*Parent:* Berens Group Limited
*Officers:* Alyson Moss [1970] Director; Markus Elliot Rosenberg [1972] Director/Jeweller; Debra Tomlinson [1964] Director; Simon Bennett Walton [1967] Director/Jeweller

**Bericap U.K. Limited.**
*Incorporated:* 10 December 1990 *Employees:* 178
*Net Worth:* £14,793,230 *Total Assets:* £26,701,420
*Registered Office:* Oslo Road, Sutton Fields Industrial Estate, Hull, HU7 0YN
*Activities:* Manufacture of plastic packing goods
*Parent:* Bericap Holding GmbH
*Officers:* Jane Elizabeth Kerr, Secretary; Christian Krautkramer [1966] Director [German]; Timothy Bruce Margetts [1966] Director/General Manager; Peter Shearman [1966] Director; Jorg Thiels [1965] Director [German]

**Berkeley de Veer Limited**
*Incorporated:* 23 January 2014 *Employees:* 22
*Net Worth:* £5,041,809 *Total Assets:* £16,596,233
*Registered Office:* Thorp Arch Grange, Walton Road, Thorp Arch, Wetherby, W Yorks, LS23 7BA
*Activities:* Construction of domestic buildings
*Shareholders:* David Ian Newett; Daniel George Newett
*Officers:* Daniel George Newett [1990] Director; David Ian Newett [1959] Director

**Bermar Building Company Limited**
*Incorporated:* 4 May 1972 *Employees:* 51
*Net Worth:* £2,201,312 *Total Assets:* £6,285,043
*Registered Office:* Unit 2 Bull Royd Industrial Estate, Bull Royd Lane, Bradford, BD8 0LH
*Activities:* Development of building projects
*Shareholders:* Steven John Ludkin; Robert Anthony James Moon
*Officers:* Robert Moon, Secretary; Michael Patrick Kelly [1961] Director/Quantity Surveyor; John Steven Ludkin [1947] Director/Builder; Steven John Ludkin [1968] Director/Contracts Manager; Robert Anthony James Moon [1973] Managing Director; Robert Moon [1946] Director/Builder; Stuart Braithwaite Smith [1961] Director/Commercial Manager

**Berry Investment Holdings Limited**
*Incorporated:* 21 February 2017
*Net Worth:* £3,923,000 *Total Assets:* £11,090,000
*Registered Office:* Hexagon House, Grimbald Crag Close, St James Business Park, Knaresborough, N Yorks, HG5 8PJ
*Activities:* Activities of financial services holding companies
*Parent:* Broker Network Partner Holdings Limited
*Officers:* Simon Drew, Secretary; Simon Richard Drew [1969] Director/Accountant; Desmond O' Connor [1971] Director/Insurance Broker; Eric Herbert Richardson [1961] Director/Insurance Broker; Margaret Shearer Craig Richardson [1962] Director/Insurance Broker

**Berrygate Hill Nurseries Limited**
*Incorporated:* 25 February 1949 *Employees:* 30
*Net Worth:* £914,208 *Total Assets:* £3,166,782
*Registered Office:* Berrygate Hill Nurseries Ltd, Hull Road, Keyingham, Hull, HU12 9ST
*Activities:* Plant propagation
*Shareholders:* Peter Andrew Overvoorde; Johannes Overvoorde Discretionary Trust
*Officers:* Rosemary Jane Overvoorde, Secretary; Peter Andrew Overvoorde [1957] Director/Market Gardener; Rosemary Jane Overvoorde [1959] Director/Secretary

**Bessacarr Properties Limited**
*Incorporated:* 26 October 2005 *Employees:* 3
*Net Worth:* £6,163,569 *Total Assets:* £7,331,104
*Registered Office:* M & D House, Brooklands Road, Adwick-le-Street, Doncaster, S Yorks, DN6 7BA
*Activities:* Construction of other civil engineering projects n.e.c.
*Parent:* DSS Group Limited
*Officers:* Andrew Robert Wykes, Secretary; Steven Roy Edgworth [1959] Director; David Drew Wylie [1963] Director/Contract Manager

**Better Fish Limited**
*Incorporated:* 7 October 1963 *Employees:* 225
*Net Worth:* £4,877,891 *Total Assets:* £6,340,903
*Registered Office:* First Floor, Mayesbrook House, Lawnswood Business Park, Redvers Close, Leeds, LS16 6QY
*Activities:* Licenced restaurants
*Parent:* Murphy (Yorkshire) Ltd
*Officers:* Phillip Edward Murphy, Secretary; Janine Elizabeth Murphy [1944] Director; Phillip Edward Murphy [1943] Director

**John Betts Quality Used Cars Limited**
*Incorporated:* 31 August 1976 *Employees:* 3
*Net Worth:* £3,566,750 *Total Assets:* £4,384,260
*Registered Office:* 100 High Ash Drive, Alwoodley, Leeds, LS17 8RE
*Activities:* Development of building projects
*Shareholders:* Emma Jane Betts; Steven Graham Betts
*Officers:* Barbara Annette Betts, Secretary; Barbara Annette Betts [1942] Director/Secretary; Steven Graham Betts [1975] Director/Property Manager; Emma Jayne Taylor-Betts [1978] Accounts Director

**Bettys & Taylors Group Ltd**
*Incorporated:* 30 October 1951 *Employees:* 1,411
*Net Worth:* £118,760,000 *Total Assets:* £159,559,008
*Registered Office:* 1 Parliament Street, Harrogate, N Yorks, HG1 2QU
*Activities:* Manufacture of bread; manufacture of fresh pastry goods and cakes
*Shareholder:* Jonathan Wild
*Officers:* Paul Murray Cogan, Secretary; Paul Murray Cogan [1969] Director; Rachel Elizabeth Louise Fellows [1970] Director; Philip David Hanson [1957] Director; Clare Morrow [1960] Director; Berenice Susan Smith [1962] Director; Lesley Wild [1952] Director; Andrew James Wildsmith [1977] Director

**Bettys & Taylors of Harrogate Ltd**
*Incorporated:* 27 January 1955 *Employees:* 1,334
*Net Worth:* £49,985,000 *Total Assets:* £82,559,000
*Registered Office:* 1 Parliament Street, Harrogate, N Yorks, HG1 2QU
*Activities:* Manufacture of bread; manufacture of fresh pastry goods and cakes
*Parent:* Bettys & Taylors Group Limited
*Officers:* Paul Murray Cogan [1969] Director; Rachel Elizabeth Louise Fellows [1970] Director; Philip David Hanson [1957] Director; Clare Morrow [1960] Director; Berenice Susan Smith [1962] Director; Lesley Wild [1952] Director; Andrew James Wildsmith [1977] Director

**Beverley Funerals Limited**
*Incorporated:* 13 November 2012 *Employees:* 107
*Net Worth:* £15,946,869 *Total Assets:* £43,028,960
*Registered Office:* Suite C, Annie Reed Court, Annie Reed Road, Beverley, N Humbers, HU17 0LF
*Activities:* Funeral and related activities
*Shareholder:* George Anthony David Whittaker
*Officers:* George Anthony David Whittaker, Secretary; Simon John Barrick [1967] Director/Accountant; George Anthony David Whittaker [1969] Director; Keith Andrew Willis [1963] Director/Chartered Accountant

**Beverley Grammar School**
*Incorporated:* 30 June 2011 *Employees:* 113
*Net Worth:* £8,624,818 *Total Assets:* £9,397,089
*Registered Office:* Beverley Grammar School, Queensgate, Beverley, E Yorks, HU17 8NF
*Activities:* General secondary education
*Officers:* Kelly Ann Smith, Secretary; Jonathan William Baker [1961] Director/Vicar; Louise Jane Barrett [1971] Director/Marketing Manager; Gavin John Chappell [1970] Director/Headteacher; Angela Coulbeck [1954] Director; Karen Lesley Harper [1968] Director; Melanie Harrington [1978] Director/Teacher; Peter John Hemsley [1959] Director/Retired; Thomas James Manson [1974] Director; Sally-Ann Louise Pindar [1963] Director/Education Plan Coordinator, Technical Support Officer; Derek James Thorpe [1958] Director; Mark Wilkinson [1963] Director/Teacher

**Beverley House (9000) Limited**
*Incorporated:* 29 August 1963
*Net Worth:* £2,612,000 *Total Assets:* £55,708,000
*Registered Office:* Trinity Park House, Fox Way, Wakefield, W Yorks, WF2 8EE
*Activities:* Activities of head offices
*Parent:* Convenience Foods Limited
*Officers:* Ronald Klaas Otto Kers [1969] Director/Group CEO [Dutch]; Craig Ashley Tomkinson [1982] Director/Group CFO

**Beverley House Investments Limited**
*Incorporated:* 1 March 1990
*Net Worth:* £58,084,000 *Total Assets:* £287,383,008
*Registered Office:* Trinity Park House, Fox Way, Wakefield, W Yorks, WF2 8EE
*Activities:* Financial intermediation not elsewhere classified
*Parent:* Northern Foods Limited
*Officers:* Ronald Klaas Otto Kers [1969] Director/Group CEO [Dutch]; Craig Ashley Tomkinson [1982] Director/Group CFO

**Bewley's Tea and Coffee UK (Roastery) Limited**
*Incorporated:* 27 September 1972 *Employees:* 111
*Previous:* Bewley's Tea and Coffee UK Limited
*Net Worth Deficit:* £82,000 *Total Assets:* £9,084,000
*Registered Office:* Bent Ley Industrial Estate, Bent Ley Road, Meltham, Huddersfield, W Yorks, HD9 4EP
*Activities:* Production of coffee and coffee substitutes
*Major Shareholder:* Patrick Campbell
*Officers:* Michael O'Sullivan, Secretary; John Cahill [1964] Director [Irish]; Michael O'Sullivan [1944] Director [Irish]

**BF Propco (No.12) Limited**
*Incorporated:* 26 October 2004
*Net Worth:* £54,080,060 *Total Assets:* £74,845,920
*Registered Office:* 1 Park Row, Leeds, LS1 5AB
*Activities:* Development of building projects
*Officers:* Horst Bauman [1961] Director [German]; Dr Berhard Christian Paul Engelbrecht [1967] Director [German]

**BFWG Charitable Foundation**
*Incorporated:* 23 May 1925 *Employees:* 1
*Net Worth:* £8,131,011 *Total Assets:* £8,242,840
*Registered Office:* 57 Alma Road, Leeds, LS6 2AH
*Activities:* Post-graduate level higher education
*Parent:* BFWG
*Officers:* Sally Elizabeth Dowell, Secretary; Professor Cynthia Veronica Burek [1948] Director/Associate Lecturer; Dr Carolyn Anne Carr [1958] Director/Associate Professor; Anna Maria Assunta Frost [1955] Director/Administrator; Professor Jane Karen Hart [1962] Director/Professor of Geography; William Samuel Nicholson Tully [1965] Director and Consultant; Rachael Unsworth [1958] Director/Urban Geography Consultant; Alicia Videon [1968] Director/Lawyer [British/Australian]; Patrice Suzanne Wellesley-Cole [1952] Director/Tribunal Judge

**BH Acquisitions Limited**
*Incorporated:* 17 January 2011
*Net Worth Deficit:* £212,794,000 *Total Assets:* £657,078,016
*Registered Office:* Trinity Park House, Fox Way, Wakefield, W Yorks, WF2 8EE
*Activities:* Activities of head offices
*Parent:* Boparan Holdings Limited
*Officers:* Baljinder Kaur Boparan [1968] Director; Ranjit Singh Boparan [1966] Director/Company Secretary; Ronald Klaas Otto Kers [1969] Director/Group CEO [Dutch]; Craig Ashley Tomkinson [1982] Director/Group CFO

**BH Energygap LLP**
*Incorporated:* 13 July 2011 *Employees:* 2
*Net Worth:* £7,660,114 *Total Assets:* £8,045,942
*Registered Office:* Ground Floor, 6 Queen Street, Leeds, LS1 2TW

**BHJ UK Food Limited**
*Incorporated:* 27 July 1966 *Employees:* 10
*Net Worth:* £1,374,576 *Total Assets:* £4,455,242
*Registered Office:* 30 Omega Business Park, Neptune Street, Hull, HU3 2BP
*Activities:* Other food services
*Parent:* LGI Denmark ApS
*Officers:* Paul David Charles Wickenden, Secretary; Keith Binns [1960] Director/Trader; Jon Paul Constable [1974] Sales Director; Christian Oebro Mattesen [1969] Director [Danish]; Torben Matzen [1965] Director [Danish]

**Bhullar Bros.Limited**
*Incorporated:* 22 October 1964
*Net Worth:* £7,674,005 *Total Assets:* £9,250,804
*Registered Office:* 144 Moorhill Road, Salendine Nook, Huddersfield, W Yorks, HD3 3XA
*Activities:* Residents property management
*Officers:* Jatinderjit Singh Bhullar, Secretary; Inderjit Singh Bhullar [1963] Director; Jatinderjit Singh Bhullar [1966] Director; Rajinder Kaur Bhullar [1942] Director/Office Worker [Indian]

**Bhullar Limited**
*Incorporated:* 2 March 2005
*Net Worth:* £1,842,478 *Total Assets:* £3,507,003
*Registered Office:* 144 Moor Hill Road, Huddersfield, W Yorks, HD3 3XA
*Activities:* Activities of head offices
*Shareholder:* Jatinderjit Singh Bhullar
*Officers:* Jatinderjit Singh Bhullar, Secretary; Inderjit Singh Bhullar [1963] Director; Jatinderjit Singh Bhullar [1966] Director; Rajinder Kaur Bhullar [1942] Director [Indian]

**Bibby Transmissions Limited**
*Incorporated:* 16 September 1919 *Employees:* 72
*Net Worth:* £3,219,000 *Total Assets:* £6,435,000
*Registered Office:* Cannon Way, Dewsbury, W Yorks, WF13 1EH
*Activities:* Machining
*Parent:* Altra Industrial Motion UK Limited
*Officers:* Richard Ian Laws, Secretary; Glenn Deegan [1966] Director/VP, Legal & HR, General Counsel [American]; Todd Patriacca [1969] Director/VP Finance/Corporate Controller [American]

**Bibis Restaurants Limited**
*Incorporated:* 9 September 1991 *Employees:* 79
*Net Worth:* £2,063,392 *Total Assets:* £6,151,203
*Registered Office:* Criterion Place, Swinegate, Leeds, LS1 4AG
*Activities:* Licenced restaurants
*Major Shareholder:* Oliver Enrico Esterino Teodarani
*Officers:* Luciana Da Silva Sperandio, Secretary; Oliver Enrico Esterino Teodorani [1952] Director/Restaurateur

**Bidco (Impex) Limited**
*Incorporated:* 9 November 1982 *Employees:* 6
*Net Worth:* £4,181,784 *Total Assets:* £5,394,000
*Registered Office:* First Floor, Mayesbrook House, Lawnswood Business Park, Redvers Close, Leeds, LS16 6QY
*Activities:* Wholesale of other machinery and equipment
*Officers:* Daksha Bhogaita, Secretary; Rameshchandra Amritlal Bhogaita [1952] Director/Businessman

**The Big Bale Company (North) Limited**
*Incorporated:* 14 March 1984 *Employees:* 19
*Net Worth:* £4,072,206 *Total Assets:* £8,970,258
*Registered Office:* Heck Hall Farm, Great Heck, Goole, E Yorks, DN14 0BB
*Activities:* Agents involved in the sale of machinery, industrial equipment, ships and aircraft
*Major Shareholder:* David Brown Eunson Johnson
*Officers:* Elizabeth Ruth Johnson, Secretary; David Brown Eunson Johnson [1951] Director/Raw Materials Manager; Elizabeth Ruth Johnson [1954] Director

**Biker Group Limited**
*Incorporated:* 15 June 1993 *Employees:* 143
*Previous:* Biker Wenwaste Limited
*Net Worth:* £3,293,682 *Total Assets:* £9,377,360
*Registered Office:* Moor Park, Moor Road, Leyburn, N Yorks, DL8 5LA
*Activities:* Construction of domestic buildings
*Major Shareholder:* Antony William Biker
*Officers:* Bruce Shepherd, Secretary; Anthony William Biker [1945] Director/Builder/Plant Operator/Hirer; Benjamin Robert Biker [1978] Director/Quantity Surveyor; Matthew Anthony Biker [1976] Director/Land Agent; Howard Mark Pearson [1968] Financial Director

**Billerudkorsnas Beetham Ltd**
*Incorporated:* 18 March 1901 *Employees:* 152
*Net Worth:* £12,427,426 *Total Assets:* £21,797,196
*Registered Office:* Waterhouse Mills, Beetham, Milnthorpe, Cumbria, LA7 7AR
*Activities:* Manufacture of other articles of paper and paperboard n.e.c.
*Parent:* Billerudkorsnas AB
*Officers:* Sharon Peill, Secretary; Claes Fredrik Wilhelm Engvall [1964] Director/Group Business Control Manager [Swedish]; Hakan Karl Krantz [1962] Mill Director [Swedish]

**Billing Aquadrome Limited**
*Incorporated:* 10 February 1945 *Employees:* 104
*Net Worth:* £19,111,668 *Total Assets:* £26,608,974
*Registered Office:* South Lakeland House, Main A6, Yealand Redmayne, Carnforth, Lancs, LA5 9RN
*Activities:* Other amusement and recreation activities n.e.c.
*Officers:* Paul Rossiter, Secretary; John Charles Morphet [1954] Managing Director; Paul Rossiter [1964] Director/Chartered Accountant; Gordon Alexander Walker [1964] Operations Director; Trevor James White [1952] Director/Marketing Manager

**Binks (Holdings) Limited**
*Incorporated:* 23 September 2014
*Net Worth:* £6,259,620 *Total Assets:* £17,748,254
*Registered Office:* Nook Farm, Haigh Moor Road, West Ardsley, Wakefield, W Yorks, WF3 1EF
*Activities:* Buying and selling of own real estate
*Major Shareholder:* Richard David Binks
*Officers:* Harriet Jane Hunter, Secretary; Hannah Rose-Emma Binks [1986] Director; Pauline Binks [1945] Director; Richard David Binks [1943] Director; Helen Louisa Davies [1975] Director/Solicitor; Harriet Jane Hunter [1978] Director

**Bioganix Ltd**
*Incorporated:* 24 September 2004 *Employees:* 22
*Previous:* Bio Waste Solutions Limited
*Net Worth:* £1,072,629 *Total Assets:* £5,405,564
*Registered Office:* Bonby Lane, Bonby, Brigg, N Lincs, DN20 0PJ
*Activities:* Treatment and disposal of non-hazardous waste
*Shareholders:* Christopher Richard White; Clive Desmond Tyler; Lewis MacRae Dodds
*Officers:* Lewis MacRae Dodds [1965] Director/Farmer; Clive Desmond Tyler [1957] Director; Christopher Richard White [1972] Director

**Biowise Limited**
*Incorporated:* 16 October 2001 *Employees:* 25
*Net Worth:* £2,422,340 *Total Assets:* £9,355,694
*Registered Office:* Biowise Limited, Albion Lane, Willerby, E Yorks, HU10 6TS
*Activities:* Treatment and disposal of non-hazardous waste
*Shareholders:* Wastewise Holdings Limited; James Alexander Charles Landau; Paul Christopher Warrington Landau
*Officers:* James Alexander Charles Landau [1976] Director; Stephen John Wardell [1979] Finance Director; Robert Morris Wilkes [1975] Development & Operations Director

**William Birch & Sons Limited**
*Incorporated:* 28 June 1913 *Employees:* 89
*Net Worth:* £10,240,132 *Total Assets:* £15,143,503
*Registered Office:* 1 Link Road Court, Osbaldwick, York, YO10 3JQ
*Activities:* Construction of commercial buildings
*Parent:* William Birch Holdings Limited
*Officers:* Christopher William Birch [1947] Director; Paul Alfred Goyea [1959] Director; Simon Thomas Potter [1967] Director; Gemma Victoria Shahjahan [1980] Director

**Birch Close Trading Ltd**
*Incorporated:* 27 July 2016 *Employees:* 52
*Net Worth:* £1,014,443 *Total Assets:* £5,394,377
*Registered Office:* Allerton Mills, Allerton Road, Allerton, Bradford, W Yorks, BD15 7QX
*Activities:* Manufacture of other carpets and rugs
*Major Shareholder:* Andrew Peter Murphy
*Officers:* Andrew Peter Murphy [1969] Director

**Charles Birch Limited**
*Incorporated:* 25 February 1974 *Employees:* 65
*Net Worth:* £7,733,639 *Total Assets:* £9,330,364
*Registered Office:* 4 Brown Lane West, Gelderd Road, Leeds, LS12 6BH
*Activities:* Wholesale of clothing and footwear
*Major Shareholder:* Christopher Howard Wilson
*Officers:* Clare Moran, Secretary; David James Barber [1974] Sales Director; Mr Mark Jackson [1964] Director; David Daniel MacDonald [1961] Director; Christopher Howard Wilson [1961] Director/General Manager

**Birch Valley Holdings Limited**
*Incorporated:* 13 February 2015 *Employees:* 152
*Net Worth:* £8,774,733 *Total Assets:* £14,997,736
*Registered Office:* Estate Office, Eastburn Road, Eastburn, Driffield, E Yorks, YO25 9DP
*Activities:* Activities of other holding companies n.e.c.
*Shareholders:* Thomas Alan Taylor Megginson; John Derek Taylor Megginson
*Officers:* Charles Peter Barker [1979] Director/Chartered Accountant; John Derek Taylor Megginson [1944] Director/Farmer; Patricia Megginson [1942] Director/Housewife; Thomas Alan Taylor Megginson [1974] Director

**Birchgrove Estates Limited**
*Incorporated:* 25 October 2001 *Employees:* 6
*Net Worth:* £2,974,985 *Total Assets:* £4,035,769
*Registered Office:* Unit 2 Therm Road, New Cleveland Street, Hull, HU8 7BF
*Activities:* Other letting and operating of own or leased real estate
*Major Shareholder:* Vanessa Birch
*Officers:* Vanessa Birch [1964] Director

**F D Bird & Sons Limited**
*Incorporated:* 8 April 1999 *Employees:* 5
*Net Worth:* £3,028,497 *Total Assets:* £4,820,027
*Registered Office:* The Old Hall, Riston Road, Catwick, Beverley, E Yorks, HU17 5PR
*Activities:* Operation of warehousing and storage facilities for land transport activities
*Shareholders:* John Christopher Bird; Paul Adrian Bird; Mark Desmond Bird
*Officers:* Paul Adrian Bird, Secretary; John Christopher Bird [1965] Director/Farmer; Mark Desmond Bird [1958] Director; Paul Adrian Bird [1956] Director/Farmer

**Birdsall Estates Company Limited**
*Incorporated:* 15 March 1928 *Employees:* 45
*Net Worth:* £41,465,552 *Total Assets:* £50,853,388
*Registered Office:* The Estate Office, Birdsall, Malton, N Yorks, YO17 9NU
*Activities:* Other letting and operating of own or leased real estate
*Major Shareholder:* Michael Charles James Middleton
*Officers:* Lord Michael Charles James Middleton, Secretary; George Charles Nicholas Lane Fox [1963] Director; Lord Michael Charles James Middleton [1948] Director/Farms Manager; Brian Turnbull Julius Stevens [1938] Director/Solicitor; Rt Hon James William Michael Willoughby [1976] Director/Barrister

**Birkett Bogmats Limited**
*Incorporated:* 18 June 2014 *Employees:* 4
*Net Worth:* £1,932,792 *Total Assets:* £3,236,132
*Registered Office:* The Tower, Daltongate Business Centre, Daltongate, Ulverston, Cumbria, LA12 7AJ
*Activities:* Other business support service activities n.e.c.
*Shareholders:* Lee Andrew Watts; Juanita Birkett Watts
*Officers:* Juanita Birkett Watts [1974] Director; Amanda Young [1970] Director

**Birstall 140 Limited**
*Incorporated:* 29 March 2016
*Net Worth Deficit:* £73,916 *Total Assets:* £7,458,636
*Registered Office:* Holden Ing Way, Birstall, Batley, W Yorks, WF17 9AD
*Activities:* Other letting and operating of own or leased real estate
*Shareholders:* Jalil Nicholas Kamaruddin; Ahmad Fadzil Mohamad
*Officers:* Robert Reah, Secretary; Jalil Nicholas Kamaruddin [1966] Director [Malaysian]; Ahmad Fadzil Mohamad [1967] Director [Malaysian]

**The Bishop Konstant Catholic Academy Trust**
*Incorporated:* 15 October 2012 *Employees:* 711
*Net Worth Deficit:* £331,909 *Total Assets:* £6,431,106
*Registered Office:* The Zucchi Suite, The Nostell Estate Yard, Nostell, Wakefield, W Yorks, WF4 1AB
*Activities:* General secondary education
*Officers:* Richard John Atkinson [1974] Director/Chartered Accountant; Father Simon Bradbury [1965] Director/Clergyman; Claire Elizabeth Anne Cade [1976] Director/Headteacher; Lesley Darren [1971] Director/Executive Headteacher; Charles Richard Edmund Gillott [1958] Director/Solicitor; Karen Anne House [1963] Director; Professor John Timothy Leach [1963] Director of The Institute of Childhood & Education; Julie Noble [1959] Deputy Director of Education; Carmen Louise Pearce [1971] Director/Education; Sarah Maria Spencer [1967] Director/Headteacher

**The Bishop Wheeler Catholic Academy Trust**
*Incorporated:* 12 February 2013 *Employees:* 12,533
*Net Worth Deficit:* £454,000 *Total Assets:* £4,644,000
*Registered Office:* The Bishop Wheeler Catholic Academy Trust, Bradford Road, Menston, Ilkley, W Yorks, LS29 6AE
*Activities:* Pre-primary education
*Officers:* Anne Elsie Lillian Tindall, Secretary; Darren Martin Beardsley [1974] Director/Headteacher; Edward Anthony Gerard Diamond [1969] Director/Chartered Accountant [Irish]; Diane Catherine Gaskin [1959] Director/Group Tax Manager; Caroline Mary Elizabeth Hyde [1963] Director & Deputy Director of Education; Robert Lavery [1955] Director/Purchasing Manager; Joseph Anthony McDonnell [1965] Director/Partner; Janet Sheehan [1952] Director/Retired

**Bishopdyke Enterprises Limited**
*Incorporated:* 3 February 2015 *Employees:* 4
*Net Worth Deficit:* £3,320,600 *Total Assets:* £34,473,540
*Registered Office:* 8 Wells Promenade, Ilkley, W Yorks, LS29 9LF
*Activities:* Growing of cereals (except rice), leguminous crops and oil seeds
*Parent:* Glentrool Land and Estates Limited
*Officers:* Katie Pannu, Secretary; Sarah Louise Canelle [1970] Director; Anna Marie Nolan [1972] Director; Jeremy John Nolan [1971] Director; Paul Richard Nolan [1968] Director

**Bishopton Veterinary Group LLP**
*Incorporated:* 28 June 2016 *Employees:* 86
*Net Worth:* £2,877,038 *Total Assets:* £4,650,683
*Registered Office:* Mill Farm, Studley Road, Ripon, N Yorks, HG4 2QR
*Officers:* Philip Gareth Alcock [1980] Member; Duncan Iain Francis Berkshire [1979] Member; Neil Thomas Eastham [1984] Member; Ian Andrew McClive [1978] Member; Mark Spilman [1982] Member; Jonathan Mark Statham [1971] Member; Nigel John Woolfenden [1962] Member

**BJSS Limited**
*Incorporated:* 6 January 1993 *Employees:* 775
*Net Worth:* £30,444,000 *Total Assets:* £45,809,000
*Registered Office:* First Floor, Coronet House, Queen Street, Leeds, LS1 2TW
*Activities:* Business and domestic software development
*Shareholders:* Andrew Vincent; David Mark Hunter
*Officers:* Angela Adele Pickard, Secretary; Stuart Derek Bullock [1969] Director; David Mark Hunter [1962] Technical Director; Angela Adele Pickard [1970] Director; Glynn Peter Robinson [1964] Managing Director; Simon Sear [1972] Director; Andrew Vincent [1956] Managing Director; James Michael Whitehouse [1974] Director

**BKS Holdings Limited**
*Incorporated:* 20 February 2016 *Employees:* 62
*Net Worth:* £833,415 *Total Assets:* £7,728,051
*Registered Office:* 1 College Court, Gildersome, Morley, Leeds, LS27 7WF
*Activities:* Non-trading company
*Officers:* Elizabeth Jack [1982] Director; Adam James Langstaff [1983] Director; Iris Marion Wainwright [1957] Director; Martin Alec Wainwright [1955] Director

**The Black Sheep Brewery PLC**
*Incorporated:* 7 February 1992 *Employees:* 102
*Net Worth:* £5,656,933 *Total Assets:* £11,888,239
*Registered Office:* Wellgarth, Masham, Ripon, N Yorks, HG4 4EN
*Activities:* Manufacture of beer
*Officers:* Stephen John Constable, Secretary; Stephen John Constable [1964] Finance Director; Charlene Lyons [1978] Director/Management Consultant; Paul Richard Nolan [1968] Director; Andrew Peter Slee [1965] Director; Jonathan Francis Theakson [1976] Director; Robert Joseph Theakston [1973] Director

**Black Swan (Yorkshire) Limited**
*Incorporated:* 23 March 2007 *Employees:* 71
*Net Worth Deficit:* £3,868,183 *Total Assets:* £4,056,220
*Registered Office:* Market Place, Helmsley, York, YO62 5BJ
*Activities:* Hotels and similar accommodation
*Parent:* Bayfair Properties Limited
*Officers:* John Allan Jameson [1955] Director/Consultant [Zimbabwean]; Wayne Douglas Parham [1963] Director [Zimbabwean]

**Blackburns Waste Disposal Limited**
*Incorporated:* 10 June 1996
*Net Worth:* £8,761,625 *Total Assets:* £9,738,907
*Registered Office:* West End Mills, Watergate Road, Dewsbury, W Yorks, WF12 9QB
*Activities:* Collection of non-hazardous waste
*Officers:* Karen Louise Hardcastle, Secretary/Administration Director; Colin Blackburn [1931] Director; Ian Mark Blackburn [1960] Director; Martyn Karl Blackburn [1963] Director; Karen Louise Hardcastle [1962] Administration Director

**Blackhall Engineering Limited**
*Incorporated:* 22 April 1965 *Employees:* 54
*Net Worth:* £1,234,747 *Total Assets:* £4,052,089
*Registered Office:* Bradford Road, Brighouse, W Yorks, HD6 4DJ
*Activities:* Manufacture of other fabricated metal products n.e.c.
*Officers:* Alastair James Hilton Blackhall, Secretary; Alastair James Hilton Blackhall [1965] Director; John Lewthwaite [1960] Director

**Blackrow Corporation Limited**
*Incorporated:* 13 October 2009 *Employees:* 145
*Net Worth:* £2,819,731 *Total Assets:* £13,119,816
*Registered Office:* Estate Road 7, South Humberside Industrial Estate, Grimsby, N E Lincs, DN31 2TP
*Activities:* Activities of head offices
*Officers:* Darren Broughton [1961] Director; Neil Ellis [1954] Director/Chartered Accountant; James Patrick Leahy [1955] Director; Christopher Marfleet [1955] Director; Glenn Andrew Ritchie [1961] Director

**Blackrow Engineering Co. Limited**
*Incorporated:* 15 October 1980 *Employees:* 128
*Net Worth:* £4,564,961 *Total Assets:* £12,026,690
*Registered Office:* Estate Road No 7, South Humberside Industrial Estate, Grimsby, N E Lincs, DN31 2TP
*Activities:* Manufacture of metal structures and parts of structures
*Parent:* Blackrow Engineering Co Ltd
*Officers:* Anthony Stuart Booker [1973] Project Director; Darren Broughton [1961] Director/Engineers; Neil Ellis [1954] Director/Chartered Accountant; James Patrick Leahy [1955] Director/Sheetmetal Worker; Christopher Marfleet [1955] Director; Glenn Andrew Ritchie [1961] Director

**Blackrow Holdings Limited**
*Incorporated:* 14 July 2003 *Employees:* 5
*Net Worth:* £1,533,131 *Total Assets:* £5,754,610
*Registered Office:* Blackrow Business Centre, Estate Road 7, South Humberside Industrial Estate, Grimsby, N E Lincs, DN31 2TP
*Activities:* Activities of other holding companies n.e.c.
*Parent:* Blackrow Corporation Limited
*Officers:* Darren Broughton [1961] Director; Neil Ellis [1954] Director/Chartered Accountant; James Patrick Leahy [1955] Director; Christopher Marfleet [1955] Director; Glenn Andrew Ritchie [1961] Director

**Blacks Industries Limited**
*Incorporated:* 13 December 2007 *Employees:* 58
*Net Worth:* £2,004,920 *Total Assets:* £4,480,072
*Registered Office:* Rudgate Walton, Thorp Arch, Wetherby, W Yorks, LS23 7AU
*Activities:* Activities of head offices
*Shareholders:* Jason Mark Greenbaum; Antoni Vilarrubi
*Officers:* Jason Mark Greenbaum [1967] Director; Antoni Vilarrubi [1970] Director

**Blacks Solicitors LLP**
*Incorporated:* 12 October 2004 *Employees:* 175
*Net Worth:* £1,880,575 *Total Assets:* £5,070,366
*Registered Office:* City Point, 29 King Street, Leeds, LS1 2HL
*Officers:* David Christopher Allen [1968] Member; Nicholas Mark Dyson [1974] Member; David Alan Gilman [1962] Member; Paul Andrew Kelly [1979] Member; Paul Lancaster [1975] Member; Lukman Patel [1968] Member; David James Paterson [1980] Member; Ann Elise Robinson [1966] Member

**Blacks Visual Merchandising Limited**
*Incorporated:* 7 September 1998 *Employees:* 58
*Net Worth:* £3,896,222 *Total Assets:* £6,237,552
*Registered Office:* Rudgate Walton, Thorp Arch, Wetherby, W Yorks, LS23 7AU
*Activities:* Other manufacturing n.e.c.
*Shareholders:* Jason Mark Greenbaum; Antoni Vilarrubi
*Officers:* Jason Mark Greenbaum [1967] Director; Antoni Villarrubi [1970] Director

**Blackshaw Holdings Limited**
*Incorporated:* 3 May 2000 *Employees:* 16
*Net Worth:* £4,192,177 *Total Assets:* £39,819,392
*Registered Office:* Clifton House, Birkby Lane, Bailiff Bridge, Brighouse, W Yorks, HD6 4JJ
*Activities:* Other letting and operating of own or leased real estate
*Parent:* Blackshaw Investment Group Ltd
*Officers:* Susan Brooksbank, Secretary; John Stephen Brooksbank [1956] Director/Waste Management

**Blackshaw Properties (2014) Limited**
*Incorporated:* 1 August 2014 *Employees:* 1
*Net Worth:* £5,113,152 *Total Assets:* £32,486,092
*Registered Office:* Clifton House, Birkby Lane, Bailiff Bridge, Brighouse, W Yorks, HD6 4JJ
*Activities:* Activities of head offices
*Parent:* Blackshaw Holdings (2014) Ltd
*Officers:* Susan Brooksbank, Secretary; John Stephen Brooksbank [1956] Director/Property Developer

**Blackwood Hall Ltd**
*Incorporated:* 28 February 2005 *Employees:* 11
*Net Worth:* £4,861,990 *Total Assets:* £6,875,361
*Registered Office:* Blackwood Hall Business Park, North Duffield, Selby, N Yorks, YO8 5DD
*Activities:* Residents property management
*Major Shareholder:* Guy Rhoderic Gordon Mills
*Officers:* Robert Charles Wetherill, Secretary; Paul Fox [1981] Director; Guy Rhoderic Mills [1960] Director; Robert Charles Wetherill [1954] Director/Accountant

**Blencathra Hydro Limited**
*Incorporated:* 3 September 2015
*Net Worth:* £3,208,910 *Total Assets:* £14,401,901
*Registered Office:* Canal Head North, Kendal, Cumbria, LA9 7BZ
*Activities:* Production of electricity
*Parent:* Gilkes Hydro Investments Limited
*Officers:* Robert Henry Moffett Chaplin [1963] Director; Charles William Nepean Crewdson [1964] Director; Carl Peter Crompton [1973] Director

**Blenheim House Properties (Bradford) Limited**
*Incorporated:* 15 September 1960
*Net Worth:* £3,591,692 *Total Assets:* £4,178,389
*Registered Office:* Suit 9a Mercury Quays, Ashley Lane, Shipley, W Yorks, BD17 7DB
*Activities:* Other letting and operating of own or leased real estate
*Parent:* The Harry and Mary Foundation
*Officers:* John Andrew Watson Clough, Secretary; John Andrew Watson Clough [1960] Director/School Master; Mary Clough [1926] Director; David Malcolm Rishworth [1946] Director/Estate Management

**Blessed Peter Snow Catholic Academy Trust**
*Incorporated:* 3 June 2014 *Employees:* 264
*Net Worth:* £2,026,000 *Total Assets:* £4,407,000
*Registered Office:* St John Fisher Catholic Voluntary Academy, Oxford Road, Dewsbury, W Yorks, WF13 4LL
*Activities:* General secondary education
*Officers:* Edwin James Kirkwood [1955] Director/Local Government Officer; Susan Elizabeth McManamin [1960] Director/Headteacher; Anne Carolyn McNally [1968] Director/Headteacher; Reverend Peter Nealon [1941] Director/Catholic Priest; Beverley Peartree [1966] Director/Lecturer; Colette Ann Short [1966] Director/Scholl Business Manager; James Taylor [1974] Director/Acting Headteacher; Felicity Wilson [1958] Director/Advanced Practitioner Nurse in The NHS

**Bleu Properties Ltd**
*Incorporated:* 27 August 2004 *Employees:* 10
*Net Worth:* £1,857,282 *Total Assets:* £10,269,798
*Registered Office:* Suite 1, Buttershaw Works, Buttershaw Lane, Bradford, W Yorks, BD6 2DD
*Activities:* Buying and selling of own real estate
*Officers:* Anthony David Wormald [1961] Director

**Bliss Films Limited**
*Incorporated:* 1 September 2010
*Net Worth:* £710,467 *Total Assets:* £5,059,022
*Registered Office:* Highfield Grange, Bubwith, Selby, N Yorks, YO8 6DP
*Activities:* Motion picture production activities
*Parent:* GSP Studios International Limited
*Officers:* Tobias Angus Giles Mathews, Secretary; Alan Richard Latham [1960] Director

**T S Bloor & Sons Limited**
*Incorporated:* 19 December 1988 *Employees:* 122
*Net Worth:* £9,688,638 *Total Assets:* £12,076,491
*Registered Office:* c/o Karro Food Limited, Norton Grove Industrial Estate, Hugden Way, Norton, Malton, N Yorks, YO17 9NE
*Activities:* Production of meat and poultry meat products
*Parent:* T S Bloor Holdings Limited
*Officers:* Charles David Thomas Bloor [1971] Director; Stephen Paul Ellis [1971] Director; Michael Kamiel Jan Alfons Kestemont [1978] Director [Belgian]; Diane Susan Walker [1972] Director

**Blowers Jewellers Holdings Limited**
*Incorporated:* 15 May 2013
*Net Worth:* £2,321,001 *Total Assets:* £3,265,101
*Registered Office:* Princes House, Wright Street, Hull, HU2 8HX
*Activities:* Dormant company
*Major Shareholder:* Mark Ian Blowers
*Officers:* Mark Ian Blowers [1974] Director

**Ian Blowers Jewellers Limited**
*Incorporated:* 14 May 1999 *Employees:* 9
*Net Worth:* £4,968,804 *Total Assets:* £5,581,317
*Registered Office:* 43 Savile Street, Hull, HU1 3EA
*Activities:* Retail sale of watches and jewellery in specialised stores
*Parent:* Blowers Jewellers Holdings Limited
*Officers:* Ian Harold Blowers [1948] Director/Jeweller; Mark Ian Blowers [1974] Director/Jeweller

**Blue Sky Resorts Limited**
*Incorporated:* 17 March 2004
*Net Worth:* £1,744,267 *Total Assets:* £4,981,899
*Registered Office:* Nostell Priory Holiday Park, Nostell Estate, Doncaster Road, Wakefield, W Yorks, WF4 1QE
*Activities:* Recreational vehicle parks, trailer parks and camping grounds
*Shareholders:* Mark Linden Alston; Jason Spencer Caine
*Officers:* Mark Linden Alston, Secretary/Director; Mark Linden Alston [1964] Director; Jason Spencer Caine [1970] Director

**Blue Star Fibres Company Limited**
*Incorporated:* 29 November 2006 *Employees:* 5
*Net Worth Deficit:* £179,235,008 *Total Assets:* £4,711,000
*Registered Office:* P O Box 24, 1 Moody Lane, corner with Woad Lane, Great Coates, Grimsby, N E Lincs, DN31 2SS
*Activities:* Manufacture of man-made fibres
*Parent:* Bluestar Fibres Investment Company Limited
*Officers:* Michile Ann Riley, Secretary; Dr Zhigang Hao [1978] Director/Chemical Engineer [Chinese]; Michael Koenig [1963] Director/Chief Executive Officer [German]; Michael James Parkington [1969] Director/Engineer

**Blue3 (Staffs) Limited**
*Incorporated:* 14 February 2013
*Net Worth:* £141,000 *Total Assets:* £33,833,000
*Registered Office:* 1 Park Row, Leeds, LS1 5AB
*Activities:* Construction of commercial buildings
*Parent:* Blue3 (Staffs) (Holdings) Limited
*Officers:* Peter Kenneth Johnstone, Secretary; Rory William Christie [1958] Director; John Stephen Gordon [1962] Director

**Bluebird UK Topco Limited**
*Incorporated:* 13 January 2012
*Net Worth:* £773,000 *Total Assets:* £13,536,000
*Registered Office:* Bonmarche Ltd, Jubilee Way, Grange Moor, Wakefield, W Yorks, WF4 4SJ
*Activities:* Activities of head offices
*Parent:* Bonmarche Holdings PLC
*Officers:* Stephen Alexander Alldridge [1966] Finance Director; Helen Connolly [1972] Director

**The Blues Kitchen Brixton Limited**
*Incorporated:* 14 January 2015 *Employees:* 71
*Net Worth:* £317,241 *Total Assets:* £3,205,787
*Registered Office:* BCL House, 2 Pavilion Business Park, Royds Hall Road, Leeds, LS12 6AJ
*Activities:* Public houses and bars
*Shareholders:* Steven Ian Ball; Rizwan Khaleel Shaikh
*Officers:* Steven Ian Ball [1974] Director; Rizwan Khaleel Shaikh [1977] Director

**Bluestone Leasing Limited**
*Incorporated:* 6 July 1990 *Employees:* 41
*Net Worth:* £3,699,193 *Total Assets:* £6,266,584
*Registered Office:* Lakeside House, Navigation Court, Calder Park, Wakefield, W Yorks, WF2 7BJ
*Activities:* Activities auxiliary to financial intermediation n.e.c.
*Parent:* Tyto Finance Limited
*Officers:* Mark Hargreaves, Secretary; Phillip James Bennett [1960] Director; Jonathan Rowland Bourne [1968] Director; Mark Hargreaves [1984] Finance Director; Vineesh Madaan [1971] Managing Director; Stephen Conrad Russell [1968] Director/Technology Leasing

**Blythmore Limited**
*Incorporated:* 31 March 1999 *Employees:* 1
*Net Worth Deficit:* £87,259,000 *Total Assets:* £91,203,000
*Registered Office:* Whitley Lodge, Whitley Bridge, Doncaster, S Yorks, DN14 0HR
*Activities:* Activities of head offices
*Parent:* Tunstall Holdings Limited
*Officers:* Jonathan Paul Furniss, Secretary; Craig Parsons [1970] Director; John Lee Robinson [1958] Director

**BMB Clothing Limited**
*Incorporated:* 13 October 2000 *Employees:* 960
*Net Worth Deficit:* £10,083,000 *Total Assets:* £66,732,000
*Registered Office:* Granary Building, 1 Canal Wharf, Leeds, LS11 5BB
*Activities:* Wholesale of clothing and footwear
*Shareholders:* Al Arafa for Investments and Consultancies SAE; BMB Group Limited; Al Arafa for Investments and Consultancies SAE
*Officers:* Luke Banks [1980] Managing Director; Mark Michael Sean Cotter [1963] Director; Hala Hashem [1965] Director/Manager [Egyptian]; Mohamed Talaat Mohamed Khalifa [1982] Director [Egyptian]; Mohamed Ahmed Elsayed Morsy [1978] Director [Egyptian]; Nicholas Scott [1976] Director/Chief Financial Officer

**Boarcross Limited**
*Incorporated:* 9 January 1984 *Employees:* 3
*Net Worth:* £3,162,448 *Total Assets:* £10,296,976
*Registered Office:* Eastgate Farm, Main Street, Thwing, Driffield, E Yorks, YO25 3DS
*Activities:* Raising of poultry
*Major Shareholder:* Timothy Charles Field
*Officers:* Timothy Charles Field, Secretary; Sara Silvani Field [1965] Director; Timothy Charles Field [1958] Director; Emily Sara Field-Corrigan [1988] Director

**Boge Compressors Limited**
*Incorporated:* 13 January 1995 *Employees:* 32
*Net Worth:* £2,455,300 *Total Assets:* £4,255,917
*Registered Office:* Units 10-12 Park Valley Mills, Meltham Road, Huddersfield, W Yorks, HD4 7BH
*Activities:* Repair of machinery
*Officers:* Ian Paul Svenson, Secretary; Wolf Dietrich Meier-Scheuven [1959] Director [German]

**Boldarch Limited**
*Incorporated:* 20 October 1997
*Net Worth:* £2,052,163 *Total Assets:* £3,528,707
*Registered Office:* 29-31 Hainton Avenue, Grimsby, N E Lincs, DN32 9AS
*Activities:* Other letting and operating of own or leased real estate
*Major Shareholder:* Charles Gordon MacDonald
*Officers:* Charles James Allan MacDonald [1971] Commercial Director; Hamish Gordan Robert MacDonald [1974] Director

**Bolster Moor Farm Shop Limited**
*Incorporated:* 12 September 2014 *Employees:* 90
*Net Worth:* £1,543,562 *Total Assets:* £3,080,511
*Registered Office:* Harden Road Farm, Bolster Moor Road, Golcar, Huddersfield, W Yorks, HD7 4JU
*Activities:* Retail sale of fruit and vegetables in specialised stores
*Shareholders:* Simon John Haigh; Andrew Whitwam
*Officers:* Debbie Joanne Haigh, Secretary; Simon John Haigh [1966] Director/Butcher; Andrew Whitwam [1968] Director/Butcher

**Bolton Brow Primary Academy**
*Incorporated:* 5 August 2011 *Employees:* 38
*Net Worth:* £3,208,680 *Total Assets:* £3,483,563
*Registered Office:* Bolton Brow Primary Academy, Bolton Brow, Sowerby Bridge, Halifax, W Yorks, HX6 2BA
*Activities:* Primary education
*Officers:* Julie Banham, Secretary; Daniel Adam Burns [1972] Director/Headteacher; Bob England [1962] Director/Health and Safety Professional; David French [1976] Director/Financial Controller; Danny Christian Hilton [1969] Director/Self Employed Design Engineer; Melanie Juma [1976] Director/Civil Servant; Lisa Masters [1964] Director/Retail Assistant; Deborah Nixon [1970] Director/Housewife; Gail Oldroyd [1970] Director/Beauty Therapist; Heather Sturmel [1970] Director/Business Administrator; Elliot Taylor [1984] Director/Operational Risk Manager; Julie Wolstenholme [1970] Director/Teaching Assistant; Donna Wood [1971] Director/Supply Teacher

**Bon Coeur Fine Wines Limited**
*Incorporated:* 24 May 2005 *Employees:* 18
*Net Worth:* £690,964 *Total Assets:* £4,226,339
*Registered Office:* Moor Park, Moor Road, Melsonby, Richmond, N Yorks, DL10 5PR
*Activities:* Wholesale of wine, beer, spirits and other alcoholic beverages
*Shareholders:* James Henry Goodhart; Samantha Jane Goodhart
*Officers:* Jonathon Timothy Mann, Secretary; James Henry Goodhart [1970] Director/Wine Merchant; Samantha Jane Goodhart [1967] Director; Jonathon Timothy Mann [1976] Finance Director

**Bond House Systems Limited**
*Incorporated:* 13 October 1995
*Net Worth:* £5,135,607 *Total Assets:* £5,452,921
*Registered Office:* 5 Manor Gates, Bramhope, Leeds, LS16 9HA
*Activities:* Other letting and operating of own or leased real estate
*Major Shareholder:* Ian David Prescott
*Officers:* Ian David Prescott [1963] Director

**Bond Street Real Estate Holdings Limited**
*Incorporated:* 13 August 2010 *Employees:* 2
*Net Worth:* £98,087,008 *Total Assets:* £156,491,296
*Registered Office:* Cumberland House, Greenside Lane, Bradford, BD8 9TF
*Activities:* Other business support service activities n.e.c.
*Parent:* Praxisifm Trustees (UK) Limited
*Officers:* Claire Marie Cain [1970] Director; Christopher Stephen Smith [1972] Director/Trust Manager

**Bonds Foundry Company Limited**
*Incorporated:* 10 April 2000 *Employees:* 90
*Net Worth:* £1,237,148 *Total Assets:* £5,842,745
*Registered Office:* 1 Prospect Road, Crook, Co Durham, DL15 8JL
*Activities:* Casting of steel
*Parent:* Bondshold Limited
*Officers:* Robert Jon Blackett, Secretary/Director; Robert Jon Blackett [1973] Director; Trevor John Machin [1966] Director; Andrew Shaw [1965] Managing Director

**Bondshold Limited**
*Incorporated:* 10 August 2010 *Employees:* 292
*Net Worth:* £11,723,407 *Total Assets:* £26,814,928
*Registered Office:* 1 Prospect Road, Crook, Co Durham, DL15 8JL
*Activities:* Activities of head offices
*Major Shareholder:* Paul Robson Duncan
*Officers:* Robert Jon Blackett, Secretary; Robert Jon Blackett [1973] Director; Melissa Joy Duncan [1968] Director/Head of Communications [American]; Paul Robson Duncan [1948] Director; Andrew Shaw [1965] Director

**Bonmarche Holdings PLC**
*Incorporated:* 5 August 2013 *Employees:* 1,951
*Net Worth:* £28,562,000 *Total Assets:* £71,234,000
*Registered Office:* Jubilee Way, Grange Moor, Wakefield, W Yorks, WF4 4SJ
*Activities:* Activities of head offices
*Shareholder:* BM Holdings S.A.R.L
*Officers:* Caroline Louise Farbridge, Secretary; Stephen Alexander Alldridge [1966] Director/Chartered Accountant; John Coleman [1952] Director/Retailer; Helen Connolly [1972] Director; Mark McClennon [1965] Director; Ishbel McPherson [1960] Director; Sergei Spiridinov [1972] Director

**Bonmarche Limited**
*Incorporated:* 13 January 2012 *Employees:* 1,949
*Net Worth:* £29,396,000 *Total Assets:* £86,599,000
*Registered Office:* Jubilee Way, Grange Moor, Wakefield, W Yorks, WF4 4SJ
*Activities:* Retail sale of clothing in specialised stores
*Parent:* Bluebird UK Holdco Ltd
*Officers:* Caroline Louise Farbridge, Secretary; Stephen Alexander Alldridge [1966] Director/Chartered Accountant; Helen Connolly [1972] Director

**Bonus Accessories Limited**
*Incorporated:* 16 July 1985 *Employees:* 55
*Net Worth:* £4,790,338 *Total Assets:* £7,984,577
*Registered Office:* 18 Plane Tree Croft, Leeds, LS17 8UQ
*Activities:* Retail sale of electrical household appliances in specialised stores
*Parent:* Bonus Electrical Group Ltd
*Officers:* Rodney Jackson, Secretary; Shaun Trevor Eric Boanas [1970] Director; Rodney Jackson [1955] Director/Chartered Accountant; Darren Madden [1966] Director

**Bonus Electrical Group Limited**
*Incorporated:* 23 May 1979 *Employees:* 124
*Net Worth:* £15,182,662 *Total Assets:* £21,170,524
*Registered Office:* 18 Plane Tree Croft, Leeds, LS17 8UQ
*Activities:* Buying and selling of own real estate
*Major Shareholder:* Trevor Samuel Eric Boanas
*Officers:* Rodney Jackson, Secretary; Pamela Boanas [1947] Director; Shaun Trevor Eric Boanas [1970] Director; Trevor Samuel Eric Boanas [1946] Director; Rodney Jackson [1955] Director/Chartered Accountant

**Bonus Electrical Limited**
*Incorporated:* 19 November 1974 *Employees:* 44
*Net Worth:* £2,450,840 *Total Assets:* £6,501,499
*Registered Office:* 18 Plane Tree Croft, Leeds, LS17 8UQ
*Activities:* Wholesale of radio, television goods & electrical household appliances (other than records, tapes, CDs)
*Parent:* Bonus Electrical Group Ltd
*Officers:* Rodney Jackson, Secretary; Shaun Trevor Eric Boanas [1970] Director; Rodney Jackson [1955] Director/Chartered Accountant; Darren Madden [1966] Director

**Bonus Securities Limited**
*Incorporated:* 26 June 2002
*Net Worth:* £107,946 *Total Assets:* £3,552,180
*Registered Office:* 18 Plane Tree Croft, Leeds, LS17 8UQ
*Activities:* Other service activities n.e.c.
*Parent:* Bonus Electrical Group Ltd
*Officers:* Rodney Jackson, Secretary; Shaun Trevor Eric Boanas [1970] Director; Rodney Jackson [1955] Director/Accountant

**Boost Drinks Limited**
*Incorporated:* 27 June 2001 *Employees:* 29
*Net Worth:* £3,759,396 *Total Assets:* £9,042,268
*Registered Office:* 1270 Century Way, Thorpe Park, Leeds, LS15 8ZB
*Activities:* Agents involved in the sale of food, beverages and tobacco
*Shareholders:* Simon Andrew Gray; Alasdair John Gunn; Alison Sarah Gray
*Officers:* Alison Sarah Gray, Secretary; Simon Andrew Gray [1973] Director; Alasdair John Gunn [1958] Director/Sales Executive

**Booth Industries Limited**
*Incorporated:* 26 November 1976 *Employees:* 102
*Net Worth:* £9,465,000 *Total Assets:* £13,349,000
*Registered Office:* Unit 3 Calder Close, Wakefield, W Yorks, WF4 3BA
*Activities:* Manufacture of doors and windows of metal
*Parent:* Redhall Group PLC
*Officers:* Simon Philip Comer, Secretary; Simon Philip Comer [1972] Director; Russell David Haworth [1955] Director

**Bootham Crescent Holdings Limited**
*Incorporated:* 5 June 1998
*Net Worth:* £4,377,571 *Total Assets:* £4,500,000
*Registered Office:* Bootham Crescent, Newborough Street, York, YO30 7AQ
*Activities:* Other business support service activities n.e.c.
*Parent:* York City Football Club Limited
*Officers:* Robert William Charles McGill, Secretary; Jason Alexander McGill [1966] Managing Director; Michael Shannon [1946] Director/Solicitor

**Bootham School**
*Incorporated:* 10 December 1982 *Employees:* 169
*Net Worth:* £11,645,489 *Total Assets:* £20,186,580
*Registered Office:* 51 Bootham, York, YO30 7BU
*Activities:* General secondary education
*Officers:* Gavin Charles Blackstone, Secretary; Dr Robert Alexander Barton [1959] Director/University Academic; Nicholas Burton [1970] Director/Academic; Sharon Hodgson [1950] Director/Community Advocate; Catherine Tria Limb [1959] Director/Retired; David Benedict Pearcy [1968] Director; Donald Andrew Purves [1959] Director/Senior Lecturer HE; Graham Ralph [1952] Director/Retired; Alexander Damian Vincent Raubitschek [1971] Director/Business Owner; Stephen Frederick Sayers [1946] Director/Retired; David Leslie Stanton [1943] Director/Retired; Malcolm Crompton Sterratt [1946] Director/Solicitor; Richard John Vesey [1947] Director/Retired; Heather Caroline Woolley [1965] Director/Teacher

**Bootyman Printers Limited**
*Incorporated:* 22 July 1992 *Employees:* 23
*Net Worth:* £954,419 *Total Assets:* £3,358,806
*Registered Office:* Units 1 & 2 Brighton Street Industrial Estate, Freightliner Road, Hull, HU3 4UW
*Activities:* Printing n.e.c.
*Shareholders:* Northland Private Equity Limited; Sandco 1101 Limited
*Officers:* Andrew Binks [1969] Director; Robert Alan Johnson [1968] Director [Canadian]; Tania Alena MacIver [1971] Director

**Boparan Finance PLC**
*Incorporated:* 6 April 2011
*Net Worth:* £8,862,000 *Total Assets:* £874,718,016
*Registered Office:* Trinity Park House, Trinity Business Park, Fox Way, Wakefield, W Yorks, WF2 8EE
*Activities:* Non-trading company
*Parent:* Boparan Holdings Limited
*Officers:* Craig Ashley Tomkinson, Secretary; Baljinder Kaur Boparan [1968] Director; Ranjit Singh Boparan [1966] Director; Ronald Klaas Otto Kers [1969] Director/Group CEO [Dutch]; Craig Ashley Tomkinson [1982] Director/Group CFO

**Boparan Foods Limited**
*Incorporated:* 22 April 1996
*Net Worth:* £5,657,000 *Total Assets:* £5,944,000
*Registered Office:* Trinity Park House, Trinity Business Park, Fox Way, Wakefield, W Yorks, WF2 8EE
*Activities:* Production of meat and poultry meat products
*Parent:* Boparan Holdings Limited
*Officers:* Ranjit Singh Boparan [1966] Managing Director; Baljinder Kaur Boparan [1968] Director; Ronald Klaas Otto Kers [1969] Director/Group CEO [Dutch]; Craig Ashley Tomkinson [1982] Director/Group CFO

**Boparan Holdings Limited**
*Incorporated:* 5 May 1998 *Employees:* 22,272
*Net Worth Deficit:* £334,000,000 *Total Assets:* £1,451,399,936
*Registered Office:* Trinity Park House, Trinity Business Park, Fox Way, Wakefield, W Yorks, WF2 8EE
*Activities:* Activities of head offices
*Parent:* Boparan Midco Limited
*Officers:* Charles Lamb Allen [1957] Director; Baljinder Kaur Boparan [1968] Director; Ranjit Singh Boparan [1966] Company Secretary/Director; Andrew Graham Cripps [1957] Director; David St John Thomas Gregory [1953] Director; Ronald Klaas Otto Kers [1969] Director/Group CEO [Dutch]; Susan Elizabeth Murray [1957] Director; Dr Ros Catherine Rivaz [1955] Director; Craig Ashley Tomkinson [1982] Director/Group CFO

**Borgwarner Holdings Limited**
*Incorporated:* 17 November 1989 *Employees:* 403
*Net Worth:* £105,468,000 *Total Assets:* £132,127,000
*Registered Office:* Roydsdale Way, Euroway Industrial Estate, Bradford, W Yorks, BD4 6SE
*Activities:* Non-trading company
*Parent:* Borgwarner Inc.
*Officers:* Alan McMaken, Secretary; Dr. Bela Csonka [1968] Director/Plant Manager [Hungarian]; Thomas McGill [1966] Director/Treasurer [American]; Alan McMaken [1970] Tax Director [American]; Charles Polzin [1954] Director/Attorney [American]; Jeremiah Shives [1977] Director/European General Counsel [American]; Matthias Uhrig [1964] Director - Finance [German]

**Borgwarner Limited**
*Incorporated:* 10 February 1989 *Employees:* 403
*Net Worth:* £95,371,000 *Total Assets:* £134,960,000
*Registered Office:* Roydsdale Way, Euroway Industrial Estate, Bradford, W Yorks, BD4 6SE
*Activities:* Manufacture of other parts and accessories for motor vehicles
*Parent:* Borgwarner Inc.
*Officers:* Alan McMaken, Secretary; Dr. Bela Csonka [1968] Director/Plant Manager [Hungarian]; Thomas McGill [1966] Director/Treasurer [American]; Alan McMaken [1970] Tax Director [American]; Charles Polzin [1954] Director/Attorney [American]; Jeremiah Shives [1977] Director/European General Counsel [American]; Matthias Uhrig [1964] Director - Finance [German]

**BOS (Shared Appreciation Mortgages) No. 1 PLC**
*Incorporated:* 5 October 1995
*Net Worth:* £473,510 *Total Assets:* £21,729,268
*Registered Office:* Trinity Road, Halifax, W Yorks, HX1 2RG
*Activities:* Credit granting by non-deposit taking finance houses and other specialist consumer credit grantors
*Parent:* Bank of Scotland PLC
*Officers:* David Dermot Hennessey, Secretary; Emma Louise Lawrence [1982] Director; Janet Turner [1959] Director

**BOS (Shared Appreciation Mortgages) No. 2 PLC**
*Incorporated:* 23 January 1996
*Net Worth:* £1,576,783 *Total Assets:* £132,797,056
*Registered Office:* Trinity Road, Halifax, W Yorks, HX1 2RG
*Activities:* Credit granting by non-deposit taking finance houses and other specialist consumer credit grantors
*Parent:* Bank of Scotland PLC
*Officers:* David Dermot Hennessey, Secretary; Emma Louise Lawrence [1982] Director; Janet Turner [1959] Director

**BOS (Shared Appreciation Mortgages) No. 3 PLC**
*Incorporated:* 12 March 1997
*Net Worth:* £2,266,944 *Total Assets:* £44,785,860
*Registered Office:* Trinity Road, Halifax, W Yorks, HX1 2RG
*Activities:* Credit granting by non-deposit taking finance houses and other specialist consumer credit grantors
*Parent:* Bank of Scotland PLC
*Officers:* David Dermot Hennessey, Secretary; Emma Louise Lawrence [1982] Director; Janet Turner [1959] Director

**BOS (Shared Appreciation Mortgages) No. 4 PLC**
*Incorporated:* 12 March 1997
*Net Worth:* £2,523,438 *Total Assets:* £213,753,504
*Registered Office:* Trinity Road, Halifax, W Yorks, HX1 2RG
*Activities:* Credit granting by non-deposit taking finance houses and other specialist consumer credit grantors
*Parent:* Bank of Scotland PLC
*Officers:* David Dermot Hennessey, Secretary; Emma Louise Lawrence [1982] Director; Janet Turner [1959] Director

**BOS Personal Lending Limited**
*Incorporated:* 8 August 1997
*Previous:* Britannia Personal Lending Limited
*Net Worth:* £12,776,000 *Total Assets:* £17,514,000
*Registered Office:* Trinity Road, Halifax, W Yorks, HX1 2RG
*Activities:* Financial intermediation not elsewhere classified
*Parent:* Bank of Scotland PLC
*Officers:* Alyson Elizabeth Mulholland, Secretary; Paul Andrew Gordon [1967] Managing Director; Israel Santos Perez [1972] Director [Spanish]

**Bosideng UK Limited**
*Incorporated:* 27 October 2010
*Net Worth Deficit:* £1,763,650 *Total Assets:* £31,313,828
*Registered Office:* 1 Victoria Court, Bank Square, Morley, Leeds, LS27 9SE
*Activities:* Wholesale of clothing and footwear
*Officers:* Dekang Gao [1952] None-Executive Director [Chinese]; Yun Kuen Mak [1975] Director [Chinese]; Gaofeng Zhu [1974] Director [Chinese]

**Bossdean Properties Limited**
*Incorporated:* 25 January 2000 *Employees:* 5
*Net Worth:* £5,266,457 *Total Assets:* £9,065,578
*Registered Office:* Suite 2, Morley Carr House, Morley Carr Road, Lowmoor, Bradford, BD12 0RA
*Activities:* Other letting and operating of own or leased real estate
*Parent:* Brunn SA
*Officers:* Richard Anthony Rowe, Secretary; David Francis Craven [1954] Sales Director; John de Jong [1954] Director/Steel Stockholder [Dutch]

**Boston Healthcare Limited**
*Incorporated:* 18 April 2011 *Employees:* 6
*Net Worth:* £1,391,012 *Total Assets:* £3,345,252
*Registered Office:* 6 Navigation Court, Calder Park, Wakefield, W Yorks, WF2 7BJ
*Activities:* Wholesale of pharmaceutical goods
*Shareholders:* Finance Yorkshire Equity GP Limited; Viking Fund Managers Limited
*Officers:* Hamish George Salmond, Secretary; Ian David Brown [1959] Director; Colin Pollock Darroch [1953] Director; Nicholas John Jones [1968] Director; Hamish George Salmond [1957] Director/Accountant; Steven Stocks [1952] Director

**Boston Holdings Limited**
*Incorporated:* 24 January 2003 *Employees:* 2
*Net Worth:* £3,203,725 *Total Assets:* £3,853,834
*Registered Office:* Boston House, High Street, Boston Spa, Wetherby, W Yorks, LS23 6AD
*Activities:* Other letting and operating of own or leased real estate
*Shareholders:* Martin Brendan Spencer; Matthew Timothy Spencer
*Officers:* Andrew Mark Johnson, Secretary; Martin Brendan Spencer [1957] Director; Matthew Timothy Spencer [1960] Director

**Boston Mayflower Finance PLC**
*Incorporated:* 5 August 2014
*Net Worth:* £50,633 *Total Assets:* £89,555,784
*Registered Office:* Westgate Park, Charlton Street, Grimsby, N E Lincs, DN31 1SQ
*Activities:* Other accommodation
*Parent:* Lincolnshire Housing Partnership Limited
*Officers:* Michael James Walters, Secretary; Mark Jonathan Jones [1966] Director of Property; Bridget Elizabeth Lloyd [1962] Director of Customers; Murray Alexander MacDonald [1967] Director/CEO, Social Housing

**Bostonair Group Limited**
*Incorporated:* 25 November 2011 *Employees:* 226
*Net Worth:* £5,093,603 *Total Assets:* £10,064,500
*Registered Office:* Norwood House, Norwood, Beverley, E Yorks, HU17 9ET
*Activities:* Temporary employment agency activities
*Officers:* Mark Neil Parkes [1974] Managing Director; Adam Winston Sumner [1970] Financial Director

**Bosworth Estates Limited**
*Incorporated:* 18 October 1937 *Employees:* 7
*Net Worth:* £2,821,989 *Total Assets:* £3,446,413
*Registered Office:* Gresham House, 5-7 St Pauls Street, Leeds, LS1 2JG
*Activities:* Buying and selling of own real estate
*Officers:* Jane Rosalie Gunner, Secretary; Jane Rosalie Gunner [1959] Director/Company Secretary; Richard Timothy Gunner [1952] Director/Electronics Engineer

**The Boulevard Academy Trust**
*Incorporated:* 9 August 2012 *Employees:* 70
*Net Worth:* £7,779,905 *Total Assets:* £8,094,563
*Registered Office:* 75 Massey Close, Hull, HU3 3QT
*Activities:* General secondary education
*Officers:* Carol-Ann Bernadette Daniel, Secretary; James Andrew Davies [1983] Director/Lecturer; Patricia Dearnaley [1961] Director; Claire Angela Grimwood [1966] Director; Linda Ann Robinson [1953] Director/Governor; Ovidiu Vasile Staicu [1972] Director; Paul Tempest [1952] Director/Retired Teacher

**Boulton & Cooper Limited**
*Incorporated:* 23 August 2011
*Net Worth:* £3,625,266 *Total Assets:* £4,740,179
*Registered Office:* St Michaels House, 1 Market Place, Malton, N Yorks, YO17 7LU
*Activities:* Activities of head offices
*Shareholders:* James Frederick Stephenson; Reginald Edward Foster Stephenson
*Officers:* James Frederick Stephenson [1939] Director; Reginald Edward Foster Stephenson [1967] Director

**The Boutique Workplace Company Limited**
*Incorporated:* 28 January 2015 *Employees:* 63
*Net Worth:* £602,000 *Total Assets:* £22,727,000
*Registered Office:* Central House, 47 St Pauls Street, Leeds, LS1 2TE
*Activities:* Other letting and operating of own or leased real estate
*Shareholders:* Christoffel Wiese; Jacob Wiese; Philip Biden; Gerhardus Liebenberg; Mandy Dix-Peek; Michael Black
*Officers:* Daniel James Smith, Secretary; David Paul Andrew Hall [1970] Operations Director; David Anthony Harrop [1970] Finance Director; Karen Louise Nordier [1967] Finance Director [South African]; Timothy Andrew Vaughan [1965] Managing Director; Daniel Reeves Wheble [1976] Director

**Bower Green Limited**
*Incorporated:* 9 May 1997 *Employees:* 70
*Net Worth:* £2,593,065 *Total Assets:* £6,338,209
*Registered Office:* Dryden Street, Bradford, W Yorks, BD1 5ND
*Activities:* Freight transport by road
*Shareholders:* Alan Mark Pattison; Roger Michael Pattison; Jodie Miles Pattison
*Officers:* Patricia Mary Smith, Secretary; Alan Mark Pattison [1967] Director; Jodie Miles Pattison [1977] Director; Roger Michael Pattison [1965] Director; Patricia Mary Smith [1951] Director

**Bower Roebuck & Co.,Limited**
*Incorporated:* 11 May 1899 *Employees:* 68
*Net Worth:* £3,729,946 *Total Assets:* £4,837,043
*Registered Office:* Glendale Mills, New Mill, Holmfirth, W Yorks, HD9 7EN
*Activities:* Weaving of textiles
*Parent:* Scabal SA
*Officers:* Diane Louise Swift, Secretary; Michael Day [1959] Director; Timothy Roland Hoyle [1960] Managing Director; Stefano Rivera [1965] Director [Belgian]; Diane Louise Swift [1974] Finance Director; Gregor Thissen [1962] Director [German]

**The Bowes Museum**
*Incorporated:* 18 November 1999 *Employees:* 74
*Net Worth:* £11,952,136 *Total Assets:* £12,768,553
*Registered Office:* The Bowes Museum, Newgate, Barnard Castle, Co Durham, DL12 8NP
*Activities:* Museums activities
*Officers:* Prof John Howard Anstee [1943] Director; Keith Bartlett [1961] Director; Mark Blackett-Ord [1950] Director/Lawyer; Adrian Jenkins [1965] Director/Chief Executive; Peter David Alan Mothersill [1957] Director; Janice Blair Murray [1957] Director; Susan Lesley Palmer OBE [1952] Director; Caroline Patricia Peacock [1947] Director; Cllr Tracie Jane Smith [1961] Director

**Chris Bowker Limited**
*Incorporated:* 10 June 1982 *Employees:* 132
*Net Worth:* £1,684,892 *Total Assets:* £5,215,038
*Registered Office:* Whitegate, White Lund, Morecambe, Lancs, LA3 3BS
*Activities:* Electrical installation
*Shareholders:* Richard Bowker; Simon Christopher Bowker; Irene Edith Bowker
*Officers:* Nicola Margaret Little, Company Secretary; Irene Edith Bowker [1944] Director; Richard Bowker [1970] Director/Chairman; Simon Christopher Bowker [1972] Director/Engineer; Nicholas Michael Shield [1961] Director/Electrical Engineer

**Boxer Properties (Bradford) Limited**
*Incorporated:* 19 October 1988 *Employees:* 54
*Previous:* Spectrum Computer Supplies Limited
*Net Worth:* £3,562,019 *Total Assets:* £6,488,382
*Registered Office:* c/o RSM, Fifth Floor, Central Square, 29 Wellington Street, Leeds, LS1 4DL
*Activities:* Other information technology service activities
*Major Shareholder:* Geraldine Ann Marie Burns
*Officers:* Maximilian Buttinger, Secretary; Amanda Louise Buttinger [1978] Director

**Boxford Holdings Limited**
*Incorporated:* 15 February 1983 *Employees:* 29
*Net Worth:* £4,742,319 *Total Assets:* £6,819,343
*Registered Office:* 100 Dewsbury Road, Elland, W Yorks, HX5 9BG
*Activities:* Manufacture of other machine tools
*Shareholders:* Robert Alan Greenway; William Dawsom Currie
*Officers:* Robert Alan Greenway, Secretary; Paul Barraclough [1967] Director; William Dawsom Currie [1943] Director; Robert Alan Greenway [1949] Director; David John Wood [1960] Director/Chartered Accountant

**W.Boyes & Co.,Limited**
*Incorporated:* 18 June 1900 *Employees:* 1,738
*Net Worth:* £47,464,812 *Total Assets:* £60,780,804
*Registered Office:* Havers Hill, Eastfield, Scarborough, N Yorks, YO11 3DT
*Activities:* Other retail sale in non-specialised stores
*Parent:* Boyes Holdings (Scarborough) Limited
*Officers:* Diane Mary Shortland, Secretary; Andrew Peter Boyes [1947] Director; Richard Malcolm Boyes [1975] Director; Timothy John Boyes [1948] Director; Diane Mary Shortland [1969] Director; Robert Van Der Heijden [1965] Director

**BPC Yorkshire Limited**
*Incorporated:* 31 January 2007 *Employees:* 1
*Net Worth Deficit:* £1,011,142 *Total Assets:* £3,465,155
*Registered Office:* 1st Floor, Clifton House, Birkby Lane, Bailiff Bridge, Brighouse, W Yorks, HD6 4JJ
*Activities:* Buying and selling of own real estate
*Officers:* Susan Brooksbank, Secretary; John Stephen Brooksbank [1956] Director/Property Developer

**BPG Acquisitions Limited**
*Incorporated:* 11 June 2007
*Net Worth Deficit:* £8,983,000 *Total Assets:* £44,398,000
*Registered Office:* Unit 8 South Fork Industrial Estate, Dartmouth Way, Leeds, LS11 5JL
*Activities:* Manufacture of other food products n.e.c.
*Parent:* BPG Midco Limited
*Officers:* Henry Strother Colquhoun Breese [1968] Director/Chartered Accountant; Matthew Lee [1976] Director/Chief Commercial Officer; John Power [1962] Director/Chief Executive Officer

**BPG Midco Limited**
*Incorporated:* 11 June 2007
*Net Worth Deficit:* £22,090,000 *Total Assets:* £32,395,000
*Registered Office:* Unit 8 South Fork Industrial Estate, Dartmouth Way, Leeds, LS11 5JL
*Activities:* Manufacture of other food products n.e.c.
*Parent:* BPG Equityco Limited
*Officers:* Henry Strother Colquhoun Breese [1968] Director/Chartered Accountant; Matthew Lee [1976] Director/Chief Commercial Officer; John Power [1962] Director/Chief Executive Officer

**Br1dge Estates Limited**
*Incorporated:* 18 November 2015 *Employees:* 3
*Net Worth:* £13,731,355 *Total Assets:* £25,969,792
*Registered Office:* Clayton House, Midland Road, Leeds, LS10 2RJ
*Activities:* Other letting and operating of own or leased real estate
*Shareholders:* Arthur Brownridge; Kathryn Jane Brownridge
*Officers:* Arthur Brownridge [1963] Director; Kathryn Jane Brownridge [1964] Director

**Braavos Investments Limited**
*Incorporated:* 3 July 2014
*Net Worth Deficit:* £130,492 *Total Assets:* £5,202,630
*Registered Office:* 20 York Place, Leeds, LS1 2EX
*Activities:* Other letting and operating of own or leased real estate
*Shareholders:* Khalsmith Investments Limited; Longbell Limited
*Officers:* David Frank Khalastchi [1991] Director/Property Management; Michael Robert Khalastchi [1989] Director/Management and Property; Timothy John Smith [1987] Director/Management and Property

**Bracken Limited**
*Incorporated:* 27 July 1994 *Employees:* 12
*Net Worth:* £4,381,433 *Total Assets:* £9,969,940
*Registered Office:* The Tannery, 91 Kirkstall Road, Leeds, LS3 1HS
*Activities:* Other letting and operating of own or leased real estate
*Shareholders:* Bracken Developments (Northern) Limited; Bracken Developments (Yorkshire) Limited
*Officers:* John Maurice Clark [1967] Director/Chartered Surveyor; Neil Matthew Clark [1968] Director/Chartered Surveyor; Matthew Fuller [1966] Director/Chartered Surveyor; William Peter Fraser Hardie [1962] Director/Accountant; Denise Catherine Marie McGeachy [1978] Director/Operations Manager

**Bradbury Group Limited**
*Incorporated:* 2 October 1992 *Employees:* 228
*Net Worth:* £2,835,253 *Total Assets:* £11,197,548
*Registered Office:* Plot 6 Atkinsons Way, Foxhills Industrial Estate, Scunthorpe, N Lincs, DN15 8QJ
*Activities:* Manufacture of other fabricated metal products n.e.c.
*Shareholders:* Timothy Michael Strawson; Kerry Elizabeth Strawson
*Officers:* Kerry Elizabeth Strawson, Secretary; William Anthony Morran [1967] Finance Director; Peter Aubrey Noble Jones [1961] Director; Kerry Elizabeth Strawson [1965] Director; Timothy Michael Strawson [1961] Director/Chairman

**Bradbury Investments Limited**
*Incorporated:* 6 August 1998 *Employees:* 4
*Net Worth:* £3,780,043 *Total Assets:* £11,076,230
*Registered Office:* Folly Hall Mills, St Thomas Road, Huddersfield, W Yorks, HD1 3LT
*Activities:* Other letting and operating of own or leased real estate
*Shareholder:* John Patrick Lyttle
*Officers:* Paul Richard Bailey, Secretary/Chartered Town Planner; Paul Richard Bailey [1965] Director/Chartered Town Planner; Sarah Margaret Bailey [1967] Director/Administration; Ann Vivien Lyttle [1957] Director; John Patrick Lyttle [1960] Managing Director

**Bradford & Bingley PLC**
*Incorporated:* 28 February 2000 *Employees:* 175
*Net Worth:* £3,670,700,032 *Total Assets:* £11,857,000,448
*Registered Office:* Croft Road, Crossflatts, Bingley, W Yorks, BD16 2UA
*Activities:* Activities of mortgage finance companies
*Parent:* UK Asset Resolution Limited
*Officers:* John Gornall, Secretary; Ian John Hares [1958] Finance & Investment Director; Susan Carol Langley [1963] Director; Brendan Paul McDonagh [1958] Director [Irish]; Keith Charles William Morgan [1963] Director; Brendan John Russell [1961] Director; John Hartley Tattersall [1952] Director; Holger Randolph Vieten [1969] Director/Head of Banking and Capital Markets [German]

**Bradford Academy Trust**
*Incorporated:* 14 July 2005 *Employees:* 311
*Net Worth:* £22,435,000 *Total Assets:* £25,112,000
*Registered Office:* Teasdale Street, Bradford, W Yorks, BD4 7QJ
*Activities:* Pre-primary education
*Officers:* Andrew Blake, Secretary; Richard Keith Arnold [1953] Director/Retired; Bruce Berry [1946] Director/Consultant; Adrian Farley [1977] Director/Councillor; Nadine Good [1965] Assistant Director - Childrens Services; Helen Theresa Griffin [1952] Director/Schools Advisor; Alan John Jarvis [1948] Director/Retired; Manojkumar Narottam Liladhar Joshi [1952] Director/Healthcare Professional; Jagdeep Paul Singh Kainth [1984] Director/Operations Manager; Ruth Leetham [1964] Director/Parent Governor; Reverend Peter Mayo-Smith [1949] Director/Reverend; Darren Metcalfe [1971] Director/Businessman; Robert Ian Taylor [1968] Director/Minister; Rev Timothy Charles Rank Thomas [1975] Director/Reverend; Steve Walker [1970] Director/Teacher

**Bradford City Football Club Limited**
*Incorporated:* 15 April 2004
*Net Worth:* £1,057,258 *Total Assets:* £3,674,872
*Registered Office:* Northern Commercials Stadium, Valley Parade, Bradford, W Yorks, BD8 7DY
*Activities:* Other sports activities
*Officers:* Alan Keith Biggin, Secretary; Alan Keith Biggin [1949] Director/Chartered Accountant; Stefan Albert Rupp [1969] Director/Chairman [German]

**Bradford College Education Trust**
*Incorporated:* 12 December 2008 *Employees:* 289
*Net Worth:* £22,941,000 *Total Assets:* £26,506,000
*Registered Office:* Bradford College Further Education Corporation, Great Horton Road, Bradford, W Yorks, BD7 1AY
*Activities:* General secondary education
*Officers:* Eve Gregory [1968] Director/Solicitor; Dawn Janice Leak [1967] Director; Christopher James Malish [1977] Director/Accountant

**Bradford Diocesan Academies Trust**
*Incorporated:* 18 October 2012 *Employees:* 1,241
*Net Worth:* £32,707,000 *Total Assets:* £43,854,000
*Registered Office:* 2nd Floor, Jade Building, Albion Mills, Albion Road, Greengates, Bradford, W Yorks, BD10 9TQ
*Activities:* Primary education
*Officers:* Peter Addison Child [1964] Director/Consultant; Nurjahan Ali Arobi [1974] Director/Patient and Public Involvement Manager; Ruby Khalid Bhatti [1970] Director/Solicitor; Roland Clark [1954] Director/Retired; Carol Ann Dewhurst [1981] Director/Executive Officer; Stephen James Emsley [1981] Managing Director; Pauline Mary Hagen [1958] Director/Principal; Bill Henry [1960] Director/Retired; Anthony Peter Hesselwood [1949] Director/Chartered Accountant; Theresa Mary Mason [1953] Director/DofE Consultant Adviser; Denise Averezene Sterling [1957] Director/Occupational Therapist; Catherine Mary Wilson [1966] Director/Solicitor

**Bradford Flower Fund Homes**
*Incorporated:* 31 March 1958
*Net Worth:* £4,720,790 *Total Assets:* £4,772,264
*Registered Office:* Flat 7, Flower Mount, Baildon, Shipley, W Yorks, BD17 6SB
*Activities:* Renting and operating of Housing Association real estate
*Officers:* David Tarren, Secretary; Richard Norman Farrar [1952] Director/Retired; Mark Theodore Gerdes [1954] Director/Retired; Paul Hooper [1952] Director/Retired; Gillian Mary Maddison [1939] Director/Housewife; John Francis Parker [1939] Director/Retired; Stephen Rhodes [1946] Director/Health and Safety Consultant; Stephen Russell Thornton [1956] Director/Independent Consultant; John Phillip Whitaker [1944] Director/Retired; Ian Frank Whitley [1959] Director/Retired; Chris Wood [1956] Director/Retired; Pauline Wood [1936] Director/Retired

**Bradford Girls' Grammar School Trust**
*Incorporated:* 15 February 2012 *Employees:* 187
*Previous:* Bradford Girls' Grammar School Trust
*Net Worth:* £5,183,036 *Total Assets:* £5,693,690
*Registered Office:* c/o Bradford Girls' Grammar School, Squire Lane, Bradford, BD9 6RB
*Activities:* General secondary education
*Officers:* Michelle Taylor, Secretary; Hamayun Arshad [1965] Director/Self Employed Consultant; Kathryn Hazel Brooke [1966] Director/Marketing Manager; Alison Jane Cooper [1953] Director/Business Consultant; Christine Day [1955] Director/Teacher; Joanne Jenkinson [1970] Director/Primary School Principal; Loabnah Naz Khan [1979] Director/Solicitor; Helen Janet Roberts [1966] Finance Director

**Bradford Hide Company Limited**
*Incorporated:* 18 February 1982 *Employees:* 78
*Net Worth:* £15,067,515 *Total Assets:* £20,972,912
*Registered Office:* Dryden Street, Bradford, W Yorks, BD1 5ND
*Activities:* Wholesale of hides, skins and leather
*Officers:* Louise Roscoe, Secretary; John Anthony Woodward [1964] Director

**Bradford Trident Limited**
*Incorporated:* 5 October 2000 *Employees:* 51
*Net Worth:* £6,144,413 *Total Assets:* £7,344,935
*Registered Office:* Park Lane Centre, Park Lane, Bradford, W Yorks, BD5 0LN
*Activities:* Other letting and operating of own or leased real estate
*Officers:* Carlton James Smith, Secretary; Habib Rehman Afsar [1973] Director/Teacher; Mohammed Saeed Afsar [1987] Director/Family Support Worker; Yaqoob Ayoob [1971] Director; Ramenpreet Kaur Haire [1980] Director/Certified Chartered Accountant; Sarah Jane Hinton [1962] Director/Health Visitor; Hawarun Hussain [1974] Director/NHS Health Improvement Partnership Manager; Balaal Hussain Khan [1983] Director/Solicitor; Nasreen Khan [1967] Director/Health Worker; Sadaqat Ali Khan [1981] Director; Shahzada Meer [1957] Director/Telecoms Engineer; Fareeda Mir [1970] Director/NHS Public Health; Talat Sajawal [1979] Director/Family Support Worker; Taj Salam [1966] Director/PCV Driver; Imran Younis [1977] Director

**Bradleys Jewellers Limited**
*Incorporated:* 10 January 2005 *Employees:* 25
*Net Worth:* £5,380,330 *Total Assets:* £6,956,417
*Registered Office:* 6 Prospect Crescent, Harrogate, N Yorks, HG1 1RH
*Activities:* Retail sale of watches and jewellery in specialised stores
*Shareholders:* Peter Bradley (Senior); Janet Therese Bradley
*Officers:* Peter Bradley Senior, Secretary; Janet Therese Bradley [1953] Director/Jeweller; Peter Bradley Senior [1943] Director/Jeweller

**Bradman-Lake Limited**
*Incorporated:* 20 June 2007 *Employees:* 172
*Net Worth:* £718,976 *Total Assets:* £8,819,751
*Registered Office:* Enterprise Way, Retford, Notts, DN22 7HH
*Activities:* Manufacture of plastics and rubber machinery
*Parent:* Bradman-Lake Group Limited
*Officers:* Bernard James Langley [1993] Director; John Marlee [1966] Managing Director

**Bradonwood Limited**
*Incorporated:* 13 December 2002 *Employees:* 4
*Net Worth:* £6,081,136 *Total Assets:* £7,432,206
*Registered Office:* Church View Cottage, Fordon Road, Burton Fleming, Driffield, E Yorks, YO25 3PS
*Activities:* Growing of cereals (except rice), leguminous crops and oil seeds
*Shareholders:* Crispin Richard Blyth; Paula Jean O'Kane
*Officers:* David James Dewar, Secretary; Crispin Richard Blyth [1962] Director/Chartered Accountant; Paula Jean O'Kane [1944] Director

**E.B.Bradshaw & Sons,Limited**
*Incorporated:* 29 June 1927 *Employees:* 66
*Net Worth:* £9,059,593 *Total Assets:* £17,897,612
*Registered Office:* Bell Mills, Driffield, E Yorks, YO25 6XL
*Activities:* Grain milling
*Shareholders:* Patrick Simon Bradshaw; Bradshaws Driffield (Holdings) Limited; Stuart Edward Bradshaw
*Officers:* Robert Mason, Secretary; Ronald Mathieson Hamilton Beston [1933] Director/Chartered Accountant; Patrick Simon Bradshaw [1959] Director/Mill Manager; Stuart Edward Bradshaw [1964] Director/Miller

**Bradshaws Driffield (Holdings) Limited**
*Incorporated:* 27 May 1980 *Employees:* 86
*Net Worth:* £11,146,682 *Total Assets:* £18,210,434
*Registered Office:* Bell Mills, Driffield, E Yorks, YO25 6XL
*Activities:* Retail sale of flowers, plants, seeds, fertilizers, pet animals and pet food in specialised stores
*Shareholders:* Stuart Edward Bradshaw; Patrick Simon Bradshaw
*Officers:* Ronald Mathieson Hamilton Beston, Secretary; Ronald Mathieson Hamilton Beston [1933] Director/Chartered Accountant; Patrick Simon Bradshaw [1959] Director/Mill Manager; Stuart Edward Bradshaw [1964] Director/Miller

**Braegate Produce Limited**
*Incorporated:* 12 March 2013 *Employees:* 82
*Previous:* Ibbotsons Produce Limited
*Net Worth:* £1,471,877 *Total Assets:* £9,894,269
*Registered Office:* Mill Hill, Braegate Lane, Tadcaster, N Yorks, LS24 8EW
*Activities:* Growing of vegetables and melons, roots and tubers
*Parent:* Yorkshire Initiatives Limited
*Officers:* Tony Edwards [1975] Director

**T.F. & J.H. Braime (Holdings) P.L.C.**
*Incorporated:* 4 November 1950 *Employees:* 169
*Net Worth:* £11,324,000 *Total Assets:* £19,132,000
*Registered Office:* Hunslet Road, Leeds, LS10 1JZ
*Activities:* Activities of head offices
*Shareholder:* Oliver Nicholas Anderson Braime
*Officers:* Cielo Malaluan Bicol Cartwright, Secretary; Peter John Osborne Alcock [1936] Director/Engineer; Alan Quentin Braime [1981] Commercial Director; Carl Oliver Braime [1979] Sales Director; Oliver Nicholas Anderson Braime [1950] Director/Chairman; Cielo Bicol Cartwright [1963] Finance Director; Andrew William Walker [1944] Director/Solicitor

**Braime Pressings Limited**
*Incorporated:* 18 July 1923 *Employees:* 72
*Net Worth:* £798,800 *Total Assets:* £4,523,016
*Registered Office:* Hunslet Road, Leeds, LS10 1JZ
*Activities:* Forging, pressing, stamping and roll-forming of metal; powder metallurgy
*Shareholders:* T.F. & J.H. Braime (Holdings) P.L.C; TF & JH Braime (Holdings) PLC
*Officers:* Cielo Malaluan Bicol Cartwright, Secretary; Alan Quentin Braime [1981] Commercial Director; Carl Oliver Braime [1979] Director; Oliver Nicholas Anderson Braime [1950] Sales Director; Cielo Bicol Cartwright [1963] Finance Director

**Bramall & Ogden Limited**
*Incorporated:* 3 September 1969 *Employees:* 3
*Net Worth:* £3,346,491 *Total Assets:* £13,801,472
*Registered Office:* 30 Victoria Avenue, Harrogate, N Yorks, HG1 5PR
*Activities:* Development of building projects
*Parent:* Braymarsh Limited
*Officers:* Rebecca Helen Bletcher, Secretary; Rebecca Helen Bletcher [1969] Director/Engineer; Timothy Rex Bletcher [1970] Director/Property Developer

**Bramall Properties Limited**
*Incorporated:* 24 September 1990 *Employees:* 8
*Net Worth:* £52,148,692 *Total Assets:* £97,769,744
*Registered Office:* 12 Cardale Court, Cardale Park, Beckwith Head Road, Harrogate, N Yorks, HG3 1RY
*Activities:* Buying and selling of own real estate
*Shareholders:* Karen Susanah Bramall Ogden; Anna Bramall; Melanie Jane Foody
*Officers:* Alison Rae Lockwood, Secretary; Anna Bramall [1973] Director; Douglas Charles Antony Bramall [1935] Managing Director; Karen Susanah Bramall Ogden [1964] Director; Melanie Jane Foody [1966] Director; Peter Jones [1956] Director; Alison Rae Lockwood [1969] Director/Chartered Accountant

**Bramhope Property and Investments Limited**
*Incorporated:* 14 May 2012
*Net Worth:* £11,502,524 *Total Assets:* £17,686,522
*Registered Office:* Broad Close, Rossett Green Lane, Harrogate, N Yorks, HG2 9LH
*Activities:* Other letting and operating of own or leased real estate
*Major Shareholder:* Michael David Shotton
*Officers:* Carl Pate, Secretary; Carl Pate [1968] Director; Michael David Shotton [1956] Director

**Bramstone Limited**
*Incorporated:* 8 May 2013 *Employees:* 4
*Net Worth:* £210,397 *Total Assets:* £8,879,825
*Registered Office:* 35 Westgate, Huddersfield, W Yorks, HD1 1PA
*Activities:* Other letting and operating of own or leased real estate
*Parent:* Leigh Holdings Limited
*Officers:* Brian Herbert Leigh-Bramwell [1951] Director; Robert Philip Leigh-Bramwell [1986] Director/Property Surveyor; Jennifer Leigh Mitchell [1948] Director

**Brand Partnership (Holdings) Limited**
*Incorporated:* 17 April 2000
*Net Worth:* £10,933,000 *Total Assets:* £26,467,000
*Registered Office:* Unit 8 South Fork Industrial Estate, Dartmouth Way, Leeds, LS11 5JL
*Activities:* Manufacture of other food products n.e.c.
*Parent:* Brand Partnership Group Limited
*Officers:* Henry Strother Colquhoun Breese [1968] Director/Chartered Accountant; Matthew Lee [1976] Director/Chief Commercial Officer; John Power [1962] Director/Chief Executive Officer

**Brand Partnership Group Limited**
*Incorporated:* 26 April 2006
*Net Worth Deficit:* £980,000 *Total Assets:* £17,641,000
*Registered Office:* Unit 8 South Fork Industrial Estate, Dartmouth Way, Leeds, LS11 5JL
*Activities:* Manufacture of other food products n.e.c.
*Parent:* BPG Acquisitions Limited
*Officers:* Henry Strother Colquhoun Breese [1968] Director/Chartered Accountant; Matthew Lee [1976] Director/Chief Commercial Officer; John Power [1962] Director/Chief Executive Officer

**Brandon Group Limited**
*Incorporated:* 2 September 1964 *Employees:* 60
*Net Worth:* £3,493,274 *Total Assets:* £7,271,373
*Registered Office:* Brandon Medical Company Ltd, Elmfield Road, Morley, Leeds, LS27 0EL
*Activities:* Activities of head offices
*Shareholders:* Graeme Andrew Hall; Adrian Alexander Hall
*Officers:* Mary Hall, Secretary; Adrian Alexander Hall [1969] Director/Engineer; Eric Hall [1932] Director; Graeme Andrew Hall [1962] Engineering Director; Mary Hall [1937] Director/Secretary

**Brandon Hire Group Limited**
*Incorporated:* 23 July 2010
*Net Worth Deficit:* £24,546,000 *Total Assets:* £19,651,000
*Registered Office:* Central House, Beckwith Knowle, Otley Road, Harrogate, N Yorks, HG3 1UD
*Activities:* Activities of head offices
*Parent:* Brandon Hire Group Holdings Limited
*Officers:* Allison Margaret Bainbridge [1960] Director; Neil Andrew Stothard [1958] Director

**Brandon Hire Limited**
*Incorporated:* 19 April 1971 *Employees:* 909
*Net Worth:* £43,873,000 *Total Assets:* £82,352,000
*Registered Office:* Central House, Beckwith Knowle, Otley Road, Harrogate, N Yorks, HG3 1UD
*Activities:* Other engineering activities
*Parent:* Brandon Hire Group Limited
*Officers:* Allison Margaret Bainbridge [1960] Director; Neil Andrew Stothard [1958] Director

**Brandon Medical Company Limited**
*Incorporated:* 15 June 1993 *Employees:* 58
*Net Worth:* £1,714,360 *Total Assets:* £5,024,649
*Registered Office:* Brandon Medical Company Ltd, Elmfield Road, Morley, Leeds, LS27 0EL
*Activities:* Manufacture of medical and dental instruments and supplies
*Officers:* Mary Hall, Secretary; David Alan Anderson [1960] Sales Director; Nigel William Davill [1966] Technical Director; Colin Glass [1943] Director; Adrian Alexander Hall [1969] Director/Engineer; Eric Hall [1932] Director; Graeme Andrew Hall [1962] Director/Engineer; Keith Robert Jackson [1966] Director/Chartered Engineer; Andrew Law [1967] Director/Accountant; Michael Kenneth Rimmer [1967] Operations Director; Professor Jonathan Sackier [1957] Clinical Director

**Brass Agency Group Limited**
*Incorporated:* 17 September 2015 *Employees:* 77
*Net Worth:* £1,164,577 *Total Assets:* £5,002,369
*Registered Office:* Moorfield House, Alma Road, Leeds, LS6 2AH
*Activities:* Activities of other holding companies n.e.c.
*Officers:* Gillian Barclay Ball [1982] Director/Managing Partner; Clifford Cyril John Beer [1966] Director; Paul Mallett [1969] Director/Managing Partner; Paul Martin McGann [1971] Director/Managing Partner; John Alexander Morgan [1959] Director

**Brass Agency Limited**
*Incorporated:* 22 March 1983 *Employees:* 77
*Net Worth:* £1,568,043 *Total Assets:* £5,360,478
*Registered Office:* Moorfield House, Headingley, Leeds, LS6 2AH
*Activities:* Advertising agencies
*Parent:* Brass Agency Group Ltd
*Officers:* Clifford Cyril John Beer, Secretary; Gillian Barclay Ball [1982] Director/Managing Partner; Clifford Cyril John Beer [1966] Director/Accountant; Paul Mallett [1969] Director; Paul Martin McGann [1971] Director; John Alexander Morgan [1959] Joint Managing Director

**Brathay Trust**
*Incorporated:* 30 April 1993 *Employees:* 113
*Net Worth:* £1,927,000 *Total Assets:* £3,022,000
*Registered Office:* Brathay Hall, Ambleside, Cumbria, LA22 0HP
*Activities:* Other education n.e.c.
*Officers:* Heather Tracey Dixon, Secretary; Joanna Hazel Coleman [1981] Director/Marketing & Communications Officer; Charles Cowling [1952] Director/Actuary; Paul Johnson [1956] Managing Director; Katharine Sarah McIntyre [1962] Director; Diane Millward [1968] Director/Head of Operations & Finance; Marc Andrew Pate [1987] Director/Stonemason; Michelle Skeer [1966] Director/Police Officer

**Braun & Co. Limited**
*Incorporated:* 17 February 1951 *Employees:* 15
*Net Worth:* £2,057,371 *Total Assets:* £7,435,812
*Registered Office:* 11b/11c Harrier Road, Humber Bridge Industrial Estate, Barton upon Humber, N Lincs, DN18 5RP
*Activities:* Other manufacturing n.e.c.
*Major Shareholder:* Barry Roy Shepherd
*Officers:* Lucy Marie Lyon, Secretary/Business Development Manager; Susanna Allenby [1961] Director; Lucy Marie Lyon [1981] Director/Manager; Barry Roy Shepherd [1949] Director; James Roy Shepherd [1986] Director/Medical Engineer

**Braveshire Limited**
*Incorporated:* 11 May 1982 *Employees:* 370
*Net Worth:* £43,019,872 *Total Assets:* £69,102,480
*Registered Office:* Castle Bank Mills, Portobello Road, Wakefield, W Yorks, WF1 5PS
*Activities:* Manufacture of non-wovens and articles made from non-wovens, except apparel
*Major Shareholder:* Hector Elsworth Rawson
*Officers:* Andrew Charles Watson, Secretary; Alexander Charles Edward Johnson [1962] Director; Joanna Jones [1964] Director/Marketing Executive; Ann Rawson [1938] Director; Hector Elsworth Rawson [1939] Director; Julia Rawson [1961] Director/Marketing Executive

**The Brecks Company Limited**
*Incorporated:* 1 February 1990 *Employees:* 76
*Net Worth:* £5,875,193 *Total Assets:* £10,391,438
*Registered Office:* Breighton Airfield, Bubwith, Selby, N Yorks, YO8 6DH
*Activities:* Manufacture of breakfast cereals and cereals-based food
*Parent:* Brecks Holdings Limited
*Officers:* James Edward Hirst, Secretary; James Edward Hirst [1967] Director

**Brecks Farm Limited**
*Incorporated:* 20 January 1978 *Employees:* 7
*Net Worth:* £5,058,948 *Total Assets:* £6,020,584
*Registered Office:* Brecks Farm, Swillington, Leeds, LS26 8BY
*Activities:* Raising of swine and pigs
*Shareholders:* Fred Hirst; Jenifer Hirst
*Officers:* Jenifer Hirst, Secretary; Fred Hirst [1936] Director/Farmer; Jenifer Hirst [1941] Director/Farmer

**Brecks Holdings Limited**
*Incorporated:* 19 November 2015 *Employees:* 89
*Net Worth:* £4,593,483 *Total Assets:* £10,662,934
*Registered Office:* Breighton Airfield, Bubwith, Selby, N Yorks, YO8 6DH
*Activities:* Activities of other holding companies n.e.c.
*Shareholders:* Brian Willis; James Edward Hirst
*Officers:* Charles David Hirst [1965] Director/Farmer; James Edward Hirst [1967] Director; Robert Philip Hirst [1970] Director/Farmer

**Bremsen Technik (UK) Limited**
*Incorporated:* 14 December 2001 *Employees:* 30
*Net Worth:* £4,412,140 *Total Assets:* £11,849,014
*Registered Office:* Unit 6 Easton Way, Colburn, Catterick Garrison, N Yorks, DL9 4GA
*Activities:* Wholesale trade of motor vehicle parts and accessories
*Parent:* Bremsen Technik Holdings Ltd
*Officers:* Robin James Anderson, Secretary; Robin James Anderson [1980] Director; Brian Reginald Hall [1959] Director

**Bremsen Technik Holdings Ltd**
*Incorporated:* 25 October 2013
*Net Worth:* £1,210,466 *Total Assets:* £4,651,900
*Registered Office:* Unit 6 Easton Way, Colburn, Catterick Garrison, N Yorks, DL9 4GA
*Activities:* Activities of other holding companies n.e.c.
*Major Shareholder:* Brian Reginald Hall
*Officers:* Jane Louise Hall, Secretary; Robin James Anderson [1980] Director; Brian Reginald Hall [1959] Director

**Brenntag Inorganic Chemicals Limited**
*Incorporated:* 15 September 1967 *Employees:* 3
*Net Worth:* £22,061,000 *Total Assets:* £23,307,000
*Registered Office:* Alpha House, Lawnswood Business Park, Redvers Close, Leeds, LS16 6QY
*Activities:* Activities of head offices
*Parent:* Brenntag UK Holding Ltd
*Officers:* Martin Gratton, Secretary/Group Financial Director; Russel Argo [1973] Managing Director; Martin Gratton [1969] Group Financial Director; Richard Ward [1972] Director/Chief Operating Officer

**Brenntag UK Holding Limited**
*Incorporated:* 11 April 2006 *Employees:* 4
*Net Worth:* £63,008,000 *Total Assets:* £368,656,000
*Registered Office:* Alpha House, Lawnswood Business Park, Redvers Close, Leeds, LS16 6QY
*Activities:* Activities of head offices
*Parent:* Brenntag AG
*Officers:* Martin Gratton, Secretary/Group Financial Director; Russel Argo [1973] Managing Director; Martin Gratton [1969] Group Financial Director; Yves Merolle [1961] Director [French]; Richard Ward [1972] Director/Chief Operating Officer

**Brenntag UK Limited**
*Incorporated:* 18 October 2004 *Employees:* 701
*Net Worth:* £91,228,000 *Total Assets:* £179,372,992
*Registered Office:* Alpha House, Lawnswood Business Park, Redvers Close, Leeds, LS16 6QY
*Activities:* Manufacture of other organic basic chemicals
*Parent:* Brenntag UK Holding Limited
*Officers:* Martin Gratton, Secretary/Group Financial Director; Russel Argo [1973] Managing Director; Martin Gratton [1969] Group Financial Director; Richard Ward [1972] Director/Chief Operating Officer

**Brent Scaffold Boards Limited**
*Incorporated:* 16 November 1992 *Employees:* 28
*Net Worth:* £464,220 *Total Assets:* £3,985,348
*Registered Office:* Breighton Airfield, Breighton, Selby, N Yorks, YO8 6DJ
*Activities:* Other service activities n.e.c.
*Shareholders:* David Anthony Appleby; Maureen Linda Appleby
*Officers:* Maureen Linda Appleby, Secretary; David Anthony Appleby [1954] Director/Company Business Executive; Maureen Linda Appleby [1959] Director/Company Secretary

**James C Brett (Yarn Merchants) Ltd**
*Incorporated:* 13 June 2013 *Employees:* 21
*Net Worth:* £2,143,110 *Total Assets:* £3,606,747
*Registered Office:* Suite 3, Aireside House, Aireside Business Centre, Royd Ings Avenue, Keighley, W Yorks, BD21 4BZ
*Activities:* Wholesale of textiles
*Shareholders:* Jamie Thomas Brett; Edward Gabriel McBrien
*Officers:* James Thomas Brett [1971] Director; James Cameron Brett [1944] Director; Edward Gabriel McBrien [1957] Director

**Brewery Wharf (Leeds) Limited**
*Incorporated:* 5 May 1998 *Employees:* 3
*Net Worth:* £4,270,399 *Total Assets:* £11,767,099
*Registered Office:* 5 Hawthorn Park, Coal Road, Leeds, LS14 1PQ
*Activities:* Buying and selling of own real estate
*Parent:* Rushbond PLC
*Officers:* Richard Mark Powell, Secretary; Mark Richard Finch [1967] Director/Chartered Surveyor Chartered Town Planner; Jonathan William Maud [1960] Director; Richard Mark Powell [1967] Director/Chartered Accountant

**Brianplant (Humberside) Limited**
*Incorporated:* 29 August 1984 *Employees:* 48
*Net Worth:* £3,934,055 *Total Assets:* £6,216,076
*Registered Office:* Estate Road No 2, South Humberside Industrial Estate, Grimsby, N E Lincs, DN31 2TG
*Activities:* Other specialised construction activities n.e.c.
*Shareholders:* Cindy Ann Thornley; Clive Richard Thornley; Cindy Ann Thornley; Clive Richard Thornley
*Officers:* Christine Emmerson, Secretary; Clive Richard Thornley [1957] Director/Civil Engineer; Jean Anne Thornley [1935] Director/Housewife

**Bridge 3 LLP**
*Incorporated:* 21 April 2009
*Net Worth:* £2,214,035 *Total Assets:* £5,187,669
*Registered Office:* Clayton House, Midland Road, Leeds, LS10 2RJ
*Officers:* Emma Brownridge [1989] Member; Harry Brownridge [1995] Member; Jonathan Arthur Brownridge [1991] Member

**Bridge Leisure Parks (Finance) Limited**
*Incorporated:* 10 November 2009 *Employees:* 2
*Net Worth Deficit:* £5,153,081 *Total Assets:* £32,137,076
*Registered Office:* Southfield Lane, Tunstall, Hull, HU12 0JF
*Activities:* Holiday centres and villages
*Parent:* Bridge Leisure Parks (Holdings) Limited
*Officers:* Simon Elliott, Secretary; Simon John Elliott [1969] Director; Andrew Stephen Howe [1968] Director

**Bridge Leisure Parks (Holdings) Limited**
*Incorporated:* 12 November 2009 *Employees:* 4
*Net Worth:* £424,900 *Total Assets:* £48,426,020
*Registered Office:* Southfield Lane, Tunstall, Hull, HU12 0JF
*Activities:* Holiday centres and villages
*Parent:* Bridge Leisure Bidco Limited
*Officers:* Simon Elliott, Secretary; Simon John Elliott [1969] Director; Andrew Stephen Howe [1968] Director; Sandy Alastair William Muirhead [1953] Director; William Skinner [1984] Director

**Bridge Leisure Parks Limited**
*Incorporated:* 10 November 2009 *Employees:* 62
*Net Worth Deficit:* £1,368,782 *Total Assets:* £39,916,536
*Registered Office:* Southfield Lane, Tunstall, Hull, HU12 0JF
*Activities:* Holiday centres and villages
*Parent:* Bridge Leisure Parks (Finance) Limited
*Officers:* Simon Elliott, Secretary; Simon John Elliott [1969] Director; Andrew Stephen Howe [1968] Director; Richard Andrew Hunt [1961] Director; Simon Jamie Williams [1972] Director

**The Bridge Properties & Investments Limited**
*Incorporated:* 27 November 2014 *Employees:* 5
*Net Worth:* £143,380 *Total Assets:* £8,467,346
*Registered Office:* 36 Stonebridgegate, Ripon, N Yorks, HG4 1TP
*Activities:* Other letting and operating of own or leased real estate
*Major Shareholder:* Abubaker Ahmed Abdulla Sheibani
*Officers:* Abubaker Shaibani [1961] Director

**Bridge Street Pentecostal Church**
*Incorporated:* 22 June 2006 *Employees:* 20
*Net Worth:* £8,383,429 *Total Assets:* £8,514,140
*Registered Office:* Bridge Community Church, Rider Street, Leeds, W Yorks, LS9 7BQ
*Activities:* Activities of religious organisations
*Officers:* David Andrew Gooud [1959] Director; Dr George Nicholas Hagan [1966] Director/Construction Project Manager; Craig Cecil Inwood [1975] Director/I T Manager; Alan John Jarvis [1948] Director/Accountant; Ian Philip Jones [1953] Director/Retired; Dr Rebecca Aherina Katundu Lasseko [1968] Director/Medical Doctor; Oneneobari Osarojire Osarollor [1971] Director/School Teacher; Dr Olorunda Rotimi [1968] Director/Hospital Doctor

**Bridgewood (UK) Limited**
*Incorporated:* 21 January 2009 *Employees:* 133
*Net Worth:* £1,150,817 *Total Assets:* £3,804,344
*Registered Office:* Bridge Works, Ferry Lane, Hessle, E Yorks, HU13 0TP
*Activities:* Manufacture of other plastic products
*Parent:* Bridgewood Holdings Limited
*Officers:* Simon William Lunt, Secretary; Richard Clynes [1962] Director; Nabiel Khan [1967] Director

**Bridgewood Trust Limited**
*Incorporated:* 28 March 1988 *Employees:* 164
*Net Worth:* £8,514,552 *Total Assets:* £8,818,329
*Registered Office:* St Pauls House, Armitage Bridge, Huddersfield, W Yorks, HD4 7NR
*Activities:* Residential care activities for learning difficulties, mental health and substance abuse
*Officers:* Dawn June Langford, Secretary; Catherine Rowena Elizabeth Edwards [1958] Director/Retired; Beverley Jane Ireland [1958] Director/Teacher; Malcolm Riley [1940] Director/Retired; Linda Margaret Roberts [1948] Director/Retired; Malcolm Tagg [1954] Managing Director; John Leslie Turner [1950] Director/Hydraulic Engineer; Robert Wray [1964] Director/Garage Proprietor

**Bridon Holdings Limited**
*Incorporated:* 23 August 2010
*Net Worth:* £108,974,000 *Total Assets:* £155,476,000
*Registered Office:* Icon Building Firstpoint, Balby Carr Bank, Doncaster, S Yorks, DN4 5JQ
*Activities:* Activities of head offices
*Parent:* Bridon Limited
*Officers:* Claudia Maria Griffin [1967] Director/Chief Financial Officer [German]; Luc Vankemmelbeke [1971] Director/Executive Vice President [Belgian]

**Bridon International Ltd.**
*Incorporated:* 7 August 1946 *Employees:* 593
*Net Worth Deficit:* £34,904,000 *Total Assets:* £76,623,000
*Registered Office:* Icon Building, First Point, Balby Carr Bank, Doncaster, S Yorks, DN4 5JQ
*Activities:* Manufacture of wire products, chain and springs
*Parent:* Bridon Limited
*Officers:* Claudia Maria Griffin [1967] Director/Chief Financial Officer [German]; Luc Vankemmelbeke [1971] Director/Executive Vice President [Belgian]

**Bridon Limited**
*Incorporated:* 6 June 1924 *Employees:* 2
*Net Worth:* £38,266,000 *Total Assets:* £38,618,000
*Registered Office:* Icon Building, First Point, Balby Carr Bank, Doncaster, S Yorks, DN4 5JQ
*Activities:* Activities of head offices
*Parent:* Bridon-Bekaert Ropes Group
*Officers:* Claudia Maria Griffin [1967] Director/Chief Financial Officer [German]; Luc Vankemmelbeke [1971] Director/Executive Vice President [Belgian]

**Bridon-Bekaert Ropes Group (UK) Ltd**
*Incorporated:* 4 November 2014 *Employees:* 4
*Previous:* Bridge Holdco 1 Ltd.
*Net Worth:* £185,457,056 *Total Assets:* £186,019,248
*Registered Office:* Ground Floor, Icon Building, Balby Carr Bank, Doncaster, S Yorks, DN4 5JQ
*Activities:* Activities of head offices
*Parent:* BBRG (Purchaser) Ltd
*Officers:* Claudia Maria Griffin [1967] Director/Chief Financial Officer [German]

**Bridon-Bekaert Ropes Group Ltd**
*Incorporated:* 3 October 2014
*Previous:* Bridge Bidco Ltd.
*Net Worth Deficit:* £283,542,016 *Total Assets:* £17,723,000
*Registered Office:* Ground Floor, Icon Building, Balby Carr Bank, Doncaster, S Yorks, DN4 5JQ
*Activities:* Activities of head offices
*Parent:* BBRG Finance (UK) Limited
*Officers:* Claudia Maria Griffin [1967] Director/Chief Financial Officer [German]; Luc Vankemmelbeke [1971] Director/Executive Vice President [Belgian]

**John L. Brierley Limited**
*Incorporated:* 24 April 1925 *Employees:* 34
*Net Worth:* £5,830,947 *Total Assets:* £6,456,603
*Registered Office:* Turnbridge Mills, Huddersfield, W Yorks, HD1 6QT
*Activities:* Wholesale of textiles
*Major Shareholder:* Ian Hirst Brierley
*Officers:* Ian Hirst Brierley, Secretary/Director; Ian Hirst Brierley [1966] Director; Sarah Margaret Brierley [1938] Director

**Brigdale Limited**
*Incorporated:* 26 March 1984
*Net Worth:* £14,081,000 *Total Assets:* £34,936,000
*Registered Office:* Woodvale House, Woodvale Road, Brighouse, W Yorks, HD6 4AB
*Activities:* Buying and selling of own real estate
*Officers:* Stephen Phillip Forrest, Secretary; Stephen Phillip Forrest [1966] Director/Chartered Accountant; Stephen David Guy [1949] Director/Consultant; Alan David Smith [1967] Director/Chartered Surveyor; David Smith [1940] Director; Robert Brigg Smith [1969] Director/Chartered Surveyor; Valerie Elaine Smith [1942] Director; John Rufus Wignall [1952] Director/Chartered Surveyor

**Brighouse Estate Co (Contractors) Ltd**
*Incorporated:* 12 April 2012
*Net Worth:* £4,716,971 *Total Assets:* £4,739,163
*Registered Office:* 4a Greengate, Cardale Park, Harrogate, N Yorks, HG3 1GY
*Activities:* Other letting and operating of own or leased real estate
*Officers:* George Henry Ross Marshall [1978] Director; William Ross Marshall [1975] Director

**Brighouse High School Academy Trust**
*Incorporated:* 16 March 2011 *Employees:* 134
*Net Worth:* £10,099,000 *Total Assets:* £12,424,000
*Registered Office:* Brighouse High School, Finkil Street, Brighouse, W Yorks, HD6 2NY
*Activities:* General secondary education
*Officers:* Madeleine Brearley [1943] Director/Retired; Martyn Cooper Bullick [1964] Director/Project Manager; Elizabeth Cresswell [1962] Director/Headteacher; Julie Anne Haslam [1965] Director/Accountant; James Alfred Jones [1952] Director/Nurse Prescriber; Kevin Robert Jones [1969] Director/Retired; Diane Rachel Kirby [1965] Director/PE Technician; Dr Andrew John McElligott [1967] Medical Director; Anne Moffat [1966] Director/Accountant; Fiona Roberts [1973] Director/School Support; Brian Robson [1960] Director/Fire Officer; Karen Rosemary Stepney [1950] Director/Retired; Stephen John Sykes [1950] Director/Retired; John Thompson [1956] Director/Family Support Officer; Sue Thompson [1950] Director/Retired; Rebecca Venus [1983] Director/Teacher

**Bright Beginnings Childcare Centre Leeds**
*Incorporated:* 9 May 2008 *Employees:* 51
*Net Worth:* £362,462 *Total Assets:* £3,349,777
*Registered Office:* The Company Secretariat, 11-75 E C Stoner Building, University of Leeds, Leeds, LS2 9JT
*Activities:* Primary education
*Officers:* Catherine Li Lin Cho, Secretary; Antonia Frezza [1974] HR Director; Linda Jane Mortimer-Pine [1966] Deputy Director of Human Resources; Stewart Martin Ross [1972] Director/Commercial Manager; Tamsin Emily Scott [1996] Director/Sabbatical Officer, Equality & Diversity; Shelley Louise Tyson [1974] Director/Finance Manager; Paul Veevers [1985] Director of Health & Safety Services; Carolyn Walker [1978] Director/Human Resources Manager

**Bright Screw Company Limited (The)**
*Incorporated:* 13 March 1941 *Employees:* 98
*Net Worth:* £1,821,626 *Total Assets:* £4,628,772
*Registered Office:* Boundary Works, Bagley Lane, Rodley, Leeds, LS13 1JB
*Activities:* Manufacture of fasteners and screw machine products
*Major Shareholder:* Nigel Craig Metcalf Brown
*Officers:* Hilary Varley Brown, Director/Company Secretary; Hilary Varley Brown [1959] Director; Nigel Craig Metcalf Brown [1966] Managing Director

**Bright Steels Limited**
*Incorporated:* 24 September 1919 *Employees:* 76
*Net Worth:* £11,021,632 *Total Assets:* £14,279,443
*Registered Office:* Norton Works, Malton, N Yorks, YO17 9BD
*Activities:* Cold drawing of bars
*Shareholder:* Lindsay Paul Chouler
*Officers:* Lindsay Paul Chouler, Secretary/Director; Lindsay Paul Chouler [1953] Director; Marianne Rebecca Chouler Pratt [1981] Director

**Brighter Futures Academy Trust**
*Incorporated:* 10 August 2012 *Employees:* 96
*Net Worth:* £5,644,003 *Total Assets:* £6,361,151
*Registered Office:* Siddal Primary School, Backhold Lane, Siddal, Halifax, W Yorks, HX3 9DL
*Activities:* Primary education
*Shareholders:* Pamela Elizabeth Burton; Michael Anthony Moriarty
*Officers:* Jane Burton, Secretary; Marie Briggs [1972] Director/Children Nursery; Rebecca Denham [1972] Director/Executive Headteacher; Jane Mary George [1957] Director/Programme Manager; Andrea Hughes [1967] Director/Retired; Venetia Louise Knight [1973] Director/Charity Senior Manager; Sarah Lysiak [1976] Director/Self Employed; Sally Moore [1974] Director/Human Resources Manager; Michael Anthony Moriarty [1949] Director/Retired Headteacher

**Brighton Holdings Limited**
*Incorporated:* 28 October 1991 *Employees:* 53
*Net Worth:* £2,167,430 *Total Assets:* £5,374,234
*Registered Office:* 650-652 Leeds Road, Huddersfield, W Yorks, HD2 1UB
*Activities:* Activities of head offices
*Major Shareholder:* Stephen Brighton
*Officers:* Stephen Brighton, Secretary; Stephen Brighton [1963] Managing Director

**The Brigshaw Learning Partnership**
*Incorporated:* 28 July 2016 *Employees:* 441
*Net Worth:* £50,907,000 *Total Assets:* £54,981,000
*Registered Office:* Brigshaw High School, Brigshaw Lane, Allerton Bywater, W Yorks, WF10 2HR
*Activities:* Pre-primary education
*Shareholders:* Martin Dove; Kenneth William Morton
*Officers:* Jo-Anna Jane Barr, Secretary; Rachel Oluwabunmi Bajulaiye [1977] Director; Neil Henry Clephan [1957] Director/Headteacher; Emma Jackson [1980] Director; Anne Marie Lewis [1961] Director/Senior Manager in Further Education; Nick Robert Mitchell [1962] Director/University Lecturer; Kenneth William Morton [1957] Director/Education Consultant; Robert Charlton Stott [1958] Director/Retired Headteacher; Sarah Fiona Titterington [1962] Director/Chartered Librarian

**Bring Cargo Limited**
*Incorporated:* 10 November 1972 *Employees:* 68
*Net Worth Deficit:* £327,683 *Total Assets:* £8,350,098
*Registered Office:* Scandic Terminal, North Moss Lane, Stallingborough, N E Lincs, DN41 8DD
*Activities:* Freight transport by road
*Parent:* Bring Logistics AS
*Officers:* Martin George Blades, Secretary; Martin George Blades [1957] Director/Accountant; Lena Blixt Landgren [1969] Director/Manager Business Development [Swedish]; Jessica Larsson [1984] Director [Swedish]; Per Erik Roth [1975] Director/Management [Swedish]; Robert Tutass [1965] Operating Director

**Bristan Group Limited**
*Incorporated:* 22 June 1977 *Employees:* 324
*Net Worth:* £90,620,352 *Total Assets:* £113,149,904
*Registered Office:* 1 Park Row, Leeds, LS1 5AB
*Activities:* Non-specialised wholesale trade
*Parent:* Masco Corporation Limited
*Officers:* Ken Ellis [1965] Director/Accountant; Darius Padler [1970] Director/Vice President [German]

**Britannia Construction Limited**
*Incorporated:* 22 March 1974 *Employees:* 62
*Net Worth:* £945,000 *Total Assets:* £10,233,000
*Registered Office:* 3175 Century Way, Thorpe Park, Leeds, LS15 8ZB
*Activities:* Construction of commercial buildings
*Parent:* YJL Limited
*Officers:* Andries Petrus Liebenberg [1967] Director [South African]; Paul Scott [1964] Director/Engineer

**Britcom International Limited**
*Incorporated:* 9 February 1981 *Employees:* 78
*Net Worth:* £11,746,090 *Total Assets:* £15,709,928
*Registered Office:* York Road, Market Weighton, E Yorks, YO43 3QX
*Activities:* Sale of other motor vehicles
*Shareholders:* Christopher Urwin; Paul Frederick Mercer
*Officers:* Paul Frederick Mercer [1958] Managing Director; Kenneth Moor [1962] Finance Director; Christopher Urwin [1972] Managing Director

**Britcon (UK) Limited**
*Incorporated:* 26 January 1990 *Employees:* 90
*Net Worth:* £5,491,193 *Total Assets:* £15,462,231
*Registered Office:* 26-30 Midland Road, Scunthorpe, N Lincs, DN16 1DQ
*Activities:* Construction of commercial buildings
*Shareholder:* Derrick Thomas Hunt
*Officers:* Gloria Hunt, Secretary; Paul Clarkson [1966] Construction Director; Nicholas Irwin Evans [1959] Director/Engineering Manager; Derrick Thomas Hunt [1948] Director/Civil Engineer; Gloria Patricia Hunt [1949] Director/Secretary; Shaun Antony Hunt [1970] Director/Contracts Manager; John Whitmore [1961] Director/Senior Estimator

**British American Railway Services Limited**
*Incorporated:* 8 July 2008 *Employees:* 71
*Net Worth Deficit:* £10,718,907 *Total Assets:* £6,471,127
*Registered Office:* Stanhope Station, Station Road, Stanhope, Bishop Auckland, Co Durham, DL13 2YS
*Activities:* Activities of head offices
*Officers:* Edwin Ellis [1954] Director/Manager [American]; Hugh Michael McConville [1961] Director [American]

**British Bung Manufacturing Company Limited (The)**
*Incorporated:* 17 May 1978 *Employees:* 33
*Net Worth:* £4,098,877 *Total Assets:* £5,496,195
*Registered Office:* Lowlands Works, Lowlands Road, Mirfield, W Yorks, WF14 8LY
*Activities:* Manufacture of other products of wood; manufacture of articles of cork, straw and plaiting materials
*Major Shareholder:* Catherine Anne Gledhill
*Officers:* Douglas Richard Taylor, Secretary; Catherine Anne Gledhill [1949] Director/Housewife; David Michael Gledhill [1942] Director/Bung Manufacturer; Edward Charles Gledhill [1986] Director; Michael John Steer [1962] Director

**British Mohair Holdings Limited**
*Incorporated:* 19 October 1893 *Employees:* 1
*Net Worth Deficit:* £1,116,974 *Total Assets:* £14,539,707
*Registered Office:* Old Mills, off Whitehall Grove, Drighlington, Bradford, W Yorks, BD11 1BY
*Activities:* Activities of head offices
*Officers:* Kathryn Anne Davenport, Secretary; Peter Jan Patrik Valentin Gyllenhammar [1953] Director [Swedish]

**British Smaller Companies VCT PLC**
*Incorporated:* 6 December 1995
*Net Worth:* £86,137,000 *Total Assets:* £86,873,000
*Registered Office:* 5th Floor, Valiant Building, 14 South Parade, Leeds, LS1 5QS
*Activities:* Activities of venture and development capital companies
*Officers:* Charles Walter Edward Ralph Buchan [1951] Director; Rupert William Cook [1969] Director; Helen Rachelle Sinclair [1966] Director

**British Smaller Companies VCT2 PLC**
*Incorporated:* 4 October 2000
*Net Worth:* £63,234,000 *Total Assets:* £63,406,000
*Registered Office:* 5th Floor, Valiant Building, 14 South Parade, Leeds, LS1 5QS
*Activities:* Activities of venture and development capital companies
*Officers:* Richard Last [1957] Director; Robert Martin Pettigrew [1944] Director; Peter Charles Waller [1946] Director

**British Steel Holdings Limited**
*Incorporated:* 17 May 2016 *Employees:* 5,395
*Net Worth:* £79,249,000 *Total Assets:* £897,830,976
*Registered Office:* Administration Building, Brigg Road, Scunthorpe, N Lincs, DN16 1BP
*Activities:* Manufacture of basic iron and steel and of ferro-alloys
*Shareholders:* Marc Joseph Meyohas; Nathaniel Jerome Meyohas
*Officers:* Damian Paul Hargreaves, Secretary; Antonius Wilhelmus Marcus Jozef Deelen [1965] Director/Chief Marketing Officer [Dutch]; Daniel Moshe Goldstein [1978] Corporate Director; Samuel Peter Hancock [1980] Director; Roland Junck [1955] Director/Chairman [Luxembourger]; Marc Joseph Meyohas [1971] Director [French]; Generald Reichmann [1976] Director/Chief Financial Officer [Austrian]

**British Steel Limited**
*Incorporated:* 13 February 2015 *Employees:* 4,238
*Net Worth:* £18,892,000 *Total Assets:* £724,134,016
*Registered Office:* Administration Building, Brigg Road, Scunthorpe, N Lincs, DN16 1BP
*Activities:* Manufacture of basic iron and steel and of ferro-alloys
*Parent:* British Steel Holdings Limited
*Officers:* Damian Hargreaves, Secretary; Antonius Wilhelmus Marcus Jozef Deelen [1965] Director/Chief Marketing Officer [Dutch]; Roland Junck [1955] Director [Luxembourger]; Generald Reichmann [1976] Director/Chief Financial Officer [Austrian]

**M.Brittain (York) Limited**
*Incorporated:* 24 May 1972 *Employees:* 93
*Net Worth:* £6,567,877 *Total Assets:* £12,321,306
*Registered Office:* Northgate Lodge, Warthill, York, YO19 5XR
*Activities:* Manufacture of other tanks, reservoirs and containers of metal
*Major Shareholder:* Antony Peter Brittain
*Officers:* Diane Sarah Brittain, Secretary; Antony Peter Brittain [1973] Managing Director

**Britto Psychiatry Limited**
*Incorporated:* 11 July 2002 *Employees:* 2
*Net Worth:* £2,853,959 *Total Assets:* £3,056,103
*Registered Office:* 14 Thornhill Road, Huddersfield, W Yorks, HD3 3DD
*Activities:* Specialists medical practice activities
*Parent:* The Britto Healthcare Group Ltd
*Officers:* Lelia Britto, Secretary; Dr Darryl John Joseph Britto [1959] Director/Psychiatrist; Lelia Generaldine Britto [1970] Director

**Broad Carr Investments Limited**
*Incorporated:* 16 December 2014
*Net Worth:* £28,660 *Total Assets:* £3,029,972
*Registered Office:* The Office, Broad Carr House, Broad Carr Lane, Holywell Green, Halifax, W Yorks, HX4 9BS
*Activities:* Activities of open-ended investment companies
*Major Shareholder:* Anthony Gartland
*Officers:* James Edward Barker [1958] Director; Anthony Gartland [1941] Director/Retired

**Broadacres Services Limited**
*Incorporated:* 24 September 2002
*Net Worth:* £970,190 *Total Assets:* £8,747,940
*Registered Office:* Broadacres House, Mount View, Standard Way Industrial Estate, Northallerton, N Yorks, DL6 2YD
*Activities:* Buying and selling of own real estate
*Parent:* Broadacres Housing Association Ltd
*Officers:* Christopher John Robert Fawcett, Secretary; Jacqui Bateson [1961] Director/Senior Proposition Manager; June Patricia Mulroy [1949] Director/Retired; Peter Anthony Ottowell [1955] Director/Retired; Phil Summers [1960] Director; Martin Warhurst [1974] Director/Chief Executive; Colin Wilkie [1954] Director/Retired

**Thomas Broadbent & Sons,Limited**
*Incorporated:* 15 January 1895 *Employees:* 146
*Net Worth:* £3,238,099 *Total Assets:* £21,376,194
*Registered Office:* Queen Street South, Huddersfield, W Yorks, HD1 3EA
*Activities:* Manufacture of other special-purpose machinery n.e.c.
*Officers:* John Emerson Knapp, Secretary; Alan Ainsworth [1956] Director/Engineer; Simon Andrew Broadbent [1953] Joint Managing Director; Nicholas Hartley Couch [1932] Director; Dr Geoffrey Clive Grimwood [1952] Joint Managing Director; John Emerson Knapp [1952] Director/Accountant; Ian Livesey [1965] Sales Director; Martin James Standring [1964] Director/Engineer; Michael John Thewlis [1962] Commercial Director; Dr Weihong Zhao [1969] Director/Engineer [Chinese]

**Britt Broadbent Limited**
*Incorporated:* 5 April 1976 *Employees:* 1
*Net Worth:* £5,294,124 *Total Assets:* £6,075,474
*Registered Office:* Westfield Farm, Kirk Smeaton, Pontefract, W Yorks, WF8 3LT
*Activities:* Other letting and operating of own or leased real estate
*Shareholders:* Charlotte Samantha Jayne Broadbent; Daphne Sarah Broadbent
*Officers:* Charlotte Samantha Jayne Broadbent, Secretary; Charlotte Samantha Jayne Broadbent [1975] Director/Farmer

**Broadland Energy (Donich) Limited**
*Incorporated:* 5 December 2013 *Employees:* 3
*Net Worth:* £241,213 *Total Assets:* £3,620,777
*Registered Office:* 137 Scalby Road, Scarborough, N Yorks, YO12 6TB
*Activities:* Production of electricity
*Parent:* Broadland Properties Limited
*Officers:* Barry Peter Swiers, Secretary; Richard Guthrie [1972] Director; David Cedric Mosgrove [1980] Director/Estate Factor; Martin Robson [1975] Director

**Broadland Energy (Laudale) Limited**
*Incorporated:* 5 December 2013 *Employees:* 3
*Net Worth:* £1,180,604 *Total Assets:* £5,280,493
*Registered Office:* 137 Scalby Road, Scarborough, N Yorks, YO12 6TB
*Activities:* Production of electricity
*Parent:* Broadland Properties Limited
*Officers:* Barry Peter Swiers, Secretary; Richard Guthrie [1972] Director; David Cedric Mosgrove [1980] Director/Estate Factor; Martin Robson [1975] Director

**Broadland Properties Limited**
*Incorporated:* 28 June 1950 *Employees:* 413
*Net Worth:* £292,118,016 *Total Assets:* £313,428,000
*Registered Office:* 137 Scalby Road, Scarborough, N Yorks, YO12 6TB
*Activities:* Mixed farming
*Officers:* Barry Peter Swiers, Company Secretary; John Guthrie [1936] Director; Peter John Guthrie [1971] Director; Richard Guthrie [1972] Director; James Maxwell Hill [1974] Director/Surveyor; Martin Robson [1975] Director/Accountant; Ronald Graham Urquhart [1957] Director

**Broadland Renewable Energy Limited**
*Incorporated:* 1 July 2010
*Net Worth:* £1,863,473 *Total Assets:* £7,478,567
*Registered Office:* 137 Scalby Road, Scarborough, N Yorks, YO12 6TB
*Activities:* Production of electricity
*Parent:* Broadland Properties Limited
*Officers:* Barry Peter Swiers, Secretary; John Guthrie [1936] Director; Peter John Guthrie [1971] Director; Richard Guthrie [1972] Director; David Cedric Mosgrove [1980] Director/Estate Factor; Martin Robson [1975] Director

**Broadley (Group) Limited**
*Incorporated:* 14 June 2001 *Employees:* 136
*Net Worth:* £1,016,900 *Total Assets:* £12,004,231
*Registered Office:* Broadley Group, Whitehouse Street, Leeds, LS10 1AD
*Activities:* Electrical installation
*Shareholder:* Park Lane Properties (Leeds) Limited
*Officers:* Victoria Louise Binks, Secretary; Naveen Nazir Ahmed [1962] Director; Jonathan Armitage [1969] Director/Company Decorator; Gary Stephen Broadley [1963] Director; Ian Stewart Campbell [1965] Director; Christopher Leonard [1958] Director; Inderpaul Singh Manku [1965] Director

**Broadstreet Great Wilson Europe Limited**
*Incorporated:* 29 August 2002 *Employees:* 155,941
*Net Worth:* £6,293,300,224 *Total Assets:* £14,449,500,160
*Registered Office:* Asda House, Great Wilson Street, Leeds, LS11 5AD
*Activities:* Non-trading company
*Parent:* Walmart, Inc.
*Officers:* Richard Mayfield [1968] Director; John Caraway McDowell [1964] Director [American]

**The Broadway (SPV) Limited**
*Incorporated:* 27 November 2015
*Net Worth:* £2,072,680 *Total Assets:* £3,314,677
*Registered Office:* 20a Queen Street, Lancaster, LA1 1RX
*Activities:* Development of building projects
*Officers:* Gail Stainton, Secretary; James Robert Christopher Davison [1970] Director Fund Manager; Marcus Stewart Paddington Fincham [1975] Director; John Peter Hepworth [1954] Director; Mr Martin James Higginson [1963] Director; Michael Henry Stainton [1964] Director

**Broady Flow Control Limited**
*Incorporated:* 29 March 2000 *Employees:* 73
*Net Worth:* £8,065,695 *Total Assets:* £13,235,734
*Registered Office:* English Street, Hull, HU3 2DU
*Activities:* Manufacture of other fabricated metal products n.e.c.
*Officers:* Anthony Wenman Ellis [1961] Director/Vice President Sales & Marketing; Alison Ruth Robinson [1969] Director; Paul Robinson [1975] Director; Massimiliano Ruggeri [1974] Director/Vice President Manufacturing [Italian]; Salvatore Ruggeri [1949] Chairman and Managing Director [Italian]

**David M Brockbank LLP**
*Incorporated:* 8 April 2003
*Net Worth:* £503,285 *Total Assets:* £3,045,831
*Registered Office:* Staveley Mill Yard, Staveley, Kendal, Cumbria, LA8 9LS
*Officers:* David Murray Brockbank [1955] Member; Annabel Mary Williams [1960] Member; Sarah Charlotte Brockbank [1986] LLP Member; Catherine Lucy Millington [1984] LLP Member

**G Brocklehurst Transport Limited**
*Incorporated:* 14 March 1986 *Employees:* 47
*Net Worth:* £3,355,000 *Total Assets:* £4,916,048
*Registered Office:* Goods Lane, off Railway Street, Dewsbury, W Yorks, WF12 8DZ
*Activities:* Freight transport by road
*Shareholders:* Gordon Brocklehurst; Jean Denise Hoole
*Officers:* Janet Terry, Secretary; Dr Jean Denise Hoole [1955] Director/Secretary; Janet Terry [1963] Finance Director; David Alan Webster [1963] Managing Director

**Brocklesby Limited**
*Incorporated:* 13 March 1997 *Employees:* 45
*Net Worth:* £3,677,218 *Total Assets:* £6,899,110
*Registered Office:* Brocklesby House, Crosslands Lane, North Cave, E Yorks, HU15 2PG
*Activities:* Manufacture of oils and fats
*Shareholder:* Robert Paul Brocklesby
*Officers:* Paul Nigel Brocklesby [1954] Director; Robert Paul Brocklesby [1973] Managing Director

**Broker Network Holdings Limited**
*Incorporated:* 16 February 2004
*Net Worth:* £52,879,888 *Total Assets:* £62,182,184
*Registered Office:* Hexagon House, Grimbald Crag Close, St James Business Park, Knaresborough, N Yorks, HG5 8PJ
*Activities:* Activities of head offices
*Parent:* Towergate Insurance Limited
*Officers:* Dean Clarke, Secretary; Antonios Erotocritou [1971] Director/Deputy CFO [Cypriot]; David Christopher Ross [1969] Director [Irish]

**The Broker Network Limited**
*Incorporated:* 8 March 1994 *Employees:* 162
*Net Worth:* £6,111,000 *Total Assets:* £27,321,000
*Registered Office:* Hexagon House, Grimbald Crag Close, Knaresborough, N Yorks, HG5 8PJ
*Activities:* Other business support service activities n.e.c.
*Parent:* Bravo Investment Holdings 3 Limited
*Officers:* Simon Richard Drew, Secretary; Alexander Douglas Alway [1960] Director; Ian Edward Clark [1960] Director; Simon Richard Drew [1969] Director/Accountant; Desmond Joseph O'Connor [1971] Director/Insurance Broker

**Broker Network Partner Holdings Limited**
*Incorporated:* 13 July 2016 *Employees:* 87
*Net Worth Deficit:* £6,735,000 *Total Assets:* £57,810,000
*Registered Office:* Hexagon House, Grimbald Crag Close, St James Business Park, Knaresborough, N Yorks, HG5 8PJ
*Activities:* Activities of financial services holding companies
*Parent:* Bravo Investment Holdings 3 Limited
*Officers:* Simon Drew, Secretary; Alexander Douglas Alway [1960] Director; Ian Edward Clark [1960] Director/Chairman; Simon Richard Drew [1969] Director/Accountant; Desmond Joseph O'Connor [1971] Director/Insurance Broker

**Bronte Academy Trust**
*Incorporated:* 26 May 2016 *Employees:* 152
*Net Worth:* £5,422,008 *Total Assets:* £6,899,262
*Registered Office:* Tree Tops, Haworth Primary School, Rawdon Road, Haworth, Keighley, W Yorks, BD22 8DW
*Activities:* Primary education
*Officers:* John Anthony Broughton [1950] Director/Solicitor; Sarah-Jayne Cotton [1960] Director/Teacher; Joshua Terence Greaves [1989] Director/Chief Operating Officer; Trevor Olsson [1949] Director/Retired; Kath Waddington [1954] Director/Retired

**Brook Crompton UK Limited**
*Incorporated:* 16 October 2001 *Employees:* 32
*Net Worth:* £11,678,879 *Total Assets:* £15,199,604
*Registered Office:* St Thomas Road, Huddersfield, W Yorks, HD1 3LJ
*Activities:* Manufacture of electric motors, generators and transformers
*Officers:* Tao Li, Secretary; Richard MacIndoe Eason [1966] Director; Barry Scales [1950] Sales Director

**Brook Group (Holdings) Limited**
*Incorporated:* 29 June 2000 *Employees:* 2
*Net Worth:* £6,362,885 *Total Assets:* £8,384,873
*Registered Office:* Two Acres, New Road, Holmfirth, W Yorks, HD9 3XX
*Activities:* Other business support service activities n.e.c.
*Shareholders:* Timothy Nicholas Gledhill; Sarah Louise Gledhill; Robin Matthew Gledhill
*Officers:* Timothy Nicholas Gledhill, Secretary; Sarah Louise Gledhill [1966] Director; Timothy Nicholas Gledhill [1967] Managing Director

**Clive Brook Limited**
*Incorporated:* 19 October 2007 *Employees:* 74
*Net Worth:* £857,742 *Total Assets:* £8,050,639
*Registered Office:* Bank Chambers, Market Street, Huddersfield, W Yorks, HD1 2EW
*Activities:* Sale of new cars and light motor vehicles
*Shareholders:* Clive Rupert John Brook; Tracey Kim Brook
*Officers:* Tracey Kim Brook, Secretary; Clive Rupert John Brook [1963] Director; Tracey Kim Brook [1964] Director

**Brook Taverner Limited**
*Incorporated:* 9 March 1948 *Employees:* 124
*Net Worth:* £10,184,334 *Total Assets:* £14,056,792
*Registered Office:* Prospect Mill, Haincliffe Road, Ingrow, Keighley, W Yorks, BD21 5BU
*Activities:* Wholesale of clothing and footwear
*Parent:* Peaspring Limited
*Officers:* Andrew Philip Booth, Secretary/Chartered Accountant; Andrew Philip Booth [1968] Director/Chartered Accountant; Jo-Anne Booth [1969] Director; John Benjamin Jones [1969] Managing Director; Rachel Jones [1970] Director; Jason Edwin Russell Scott [1970] Director; Rebecca Scott [1970] Director

**John Brooke & Sons Ltd**
*Incorporated:* 21 February 1898 *Employees:* 2
*Net Worth:* £8,255,679 *Total Assets:* £9,051,380
*Registered Office:* Brooke's Mill, Armitage Bridge, Huddersfield, W Yorks, HD4 7NR
*Activities:* Other letting and operating of own or leased real estate
*Shareholder:* The Mark Brooke 2000 Settlement
*Officers:* Charles Donald Saggers, Secretary; Mark Roger Hanbury Brooke [1950] Director; Hannah Theresa Joan Roberts [1975] Director/Consultant; Charles Donald Saggers [1975] Director

**Brooke Edgley Specialist Technical Services Limited**
*Incorporated:* 15 October 1957 *Employees:* 151
*Net Worth:* £2,677,539 *Total Assets:* £5,019,918
*Registered Office:* 13-14 Flemming Court, Castleford, W Yorks, WF10 5HW
*Activities:* Construction of utility projects for fluids
*Parent:* Brooke Edgley (Industrial Chimneys) Ltd
*Officers:* Adam John Coates, Secretary; Sally Ann Bedford [1968] Director; Colin Charles Clinkard [1980] Director; Paul William Teasdale [1967] Director; Roger Peter Teasdale [1967] Director; Mark Ian Watford [1967] Director

**Brookfield Property (Holdings) Ltd**
*Incorporated:* 11 March 2008
*Net Worth:* £5,089,834 *Total Assets:* £10,597,530
*Registered Office:* Suite 7, Victoria Mills Business Park, Mill Street East, Dewsbury, W Yorks, WF12 9AQ
*Activities:* Retail sale of automotive fuel in specialised stores
*Officers:* Aziz Patel, Secretary/Self Employed; Ayub Patel [1960] Director/Self Employed; Aziz Patel [1966] Director/Self Employed; Mehboob Patel [1958] Director/Self Employed; Rashida Patel [1963] Director/Self Employed; Sabiha Patel [1971] Director/Self Employed; Saira Patel [1968] Director/Self Employed; Salim Patel [1967] Director/Self Employed; Shahenaz Patel [1960] Director/Self Employed

**Brooklands Business Estates Limited**
*Incorporated:* 31 January 1995 *Employees:* 3
*Net Worth:* £9,375,295 *Total Assets:* £10,739,471
*Registered Office:* Stable Court, Hesslewood Office Park, Hessle, E Yorks, HU13 0LH
*Activities:* Other letting and operating of own or leased real estate
*Major Shareholder:* Deborah Anne Barbor
*Officers:* Jacquie Whurr, Secretary; Charles Edward Dixon Barbor [1988] Director; Deborah Anne Barbor [1959] Director/Property Management; Peter Dixon Barbor [1940] Director

**Brooklands Property Holdings Limited**
*Incorporated:* 2 May 1957 *Employees:* 7
*Net Worth:* £6,545,590 *Total Assets:* £8,406,865
*Registered Office:* Stable Court, Hesslewood Hall, Ferriby Road, Hessle, E Yorks, HU13 0LH
*Activities:* Other letting and operating of own or leased real estate
*Major Shareholder:* Peter Dixon Barbor
*Officers:* Jacquie Whurr, Secretary; Charles Edward Dixon Barbor [1988] Director; Deborah Anne Barbor [1959] Director; Peter Dixon Barbor [1940] Director

**G.H.Brooks & Co.(Harrogate) Limited**
*Incorporated:* 7 January 1960
*Net Worth:* £4,861,598 *Total Assets:* £7,320,532
*Registered Office:* Hartwith House, Claro Road, Harrogate, N Yorks, HG1 4DS
*Activities:* Agents involved in the sale of timber and building materials
*Major Shareholder:* John Peter Broadwith
*Officers:* Gillian Brown, Secretary; Andrew John Broadwith [1977] Director/Manager; John Peter Broadwith [1946] Director; Judith Broadwith [1946] Director; Gillian Brown [1970] Director; James Dawson [1987] Director

**J & S Brooksbank LLP**
*Incorporated:* 4 December 2006
*Net Worth Deficit:* £294,075 *Total Assets:* £3,133,814
*Registered Office:* 1st Floor, Clifton House, Birkby Lane, Bailiff Bridge, Brighouse, W Yorks, HD6 4JJ

**The Brooksbank School Sports College**
*Incorporated:* 5 September 2011 *Employees:* 282
*Net Worth:* £14,529,429 *Total Assets:* £15,964,080
*Registered Office:* The Brooksbank School, Victoria Road, Elland, W Yorks, HX5 0QG
*Activities:* General secondary education
*Officers:* Marion Helen Bain [1951] Director; Anne Bryant [1939] Director/Retired; Peter Graham Newton [1947] Director/Retired School Teacher

**Brooksbank Valves Limited**
*Incorporated:* 11 March 1971 *Employees:* 51
*Net Worth:* £2,924,305 *Total Assets:* £4,534,791
*Registered Office:* Unit 4 The Crossing Business Park, Riparian Way, Cross Hills, Keighley, W Yorks, BD20 7BW
*Activities:* Manufacture of taps and valves
*Parent:* Aluminium Bronze Valves
*Officers:* Miranda Diane Whitehead, Secretary; Jonathan Edward Brooksbank [1965] Managing Director; Robert James Brooksbank [1966] Director/Chartered Accountant

**Broom House Investments Limited**
*Incorporated:* 10 January 1974 *Employees:* 40
*Net Worth:* £6,716,149 *Total Assets:* £9,620,780
*Registered Office:* Unit 1 River Street, Brighouse, W Yorks, HD6 1LU
*Activities:* Wholesale of wine, beer, spirits and other alcoholic beverages
*Major Shareholder:* Ian James Clay
*Officers:* Ruth Ann Clay, Secretary; Ian James Clay [1953] Director; James Anthony Clay [1984] Director

**Broomco (3554) Limited**
*Incorporated:* 17 September 2004 *Employees:* 581
*Net Worth:* £1,795,599 *Total Assets:* £79,372,840
*Registered Office:* Unit 26 Brighton Street Industrial Estate, Freightliner Road, Hull, HU3 4EN
*Activities:* Activities of head offices
*Shareholders:* Nagatanien Holdings Co Ltd; Innovation Network Corporation of Japan
*Officers:* Paul Frampton, Secretary; Tatsuo Kogure [1984] Director/Investment Officer [Japanese]; Tom Malkoski [1956] Director/Chief Executive Officer [American]; Peter Niklai [1973] Director [Hungarian]; Hiroshi Shimizu [1973] Director/Office Worker [Japanese]; Shuei Shimizu [1963] Director/Chief Strategic Officer [Japanese]

**Broomco (3555) Limited**
*Incorporated:* 17 September 2004
*Net Worth:* £37,371,768 *Total Assets:* £71,820,904
*Registered Office:* Unit 26 Brighton Street Industrial Estate, Freightliner Road, Hull, HU3 4UN
*Activities:* Activities of head offices
*Parent:* Broomco (3554) Limited
*Officers:* Paul Frampton [1970] Director/Accountant; Tom Malkoski [1956] Director/Chief Executive Officer [American]

**Broomgrove Developments Limited**
*Incorporated:* 1 December 2015
*Net Worth:* £496,146 *Total Assets:* £3,839,277
*Registered Office:* The Estate Office, Campsmount Farm, Campsall, Doncaster, S Yorks, DN6 9AP
*Activities:* Management of real estate on a fee or contract basis
*Officers:* Mark Richard Barnes [1967] Director; Richard James Bland [1970] Director; Richard Boothroyd [1955] Director; David Arthur Hodkin [1961] Director; Robert Charles Taylor [1955] Director

**Brother Bidco Limited**
*Incorporated:* 28 April 2015
*Net Worth Deficit:* £3,811,135 *Total Assets:* £21,105,822
*Registered Office:* 1 Park Row, Leeds, LS1 5AB
*Activities:* Other business support service activities n.e.c.
*Parent:* Brother Topco Limited
*Officers:* Andy James [1976] Director; Christopher Paul Lloyd [1958] Director; John McPherson [1953] Director; Iain Wolstenholme [1970] Investment Director

**Brother Topco Limited**
*Incorporated:* 11 May 2015 *Employees:* 70
*Net Worth Deficit:* £7,778,304 *Total Assets:* £19,062,032
*Registered Office:* 1 Park Row, Leeds, LS1 5AB
*Activities:* Other business support service activities n.e.c.
*Major Shareholder:* Christopher Paul Lloyd
*Officers:* John Forrest [1956] Director/Company Chairman; Andy James [1976] Director; Christopher Paul Lloyd [1958] Director; John McPherson [1953] Director; Iain Wolstenholme [1970] Investment Director

**Broughton Laboratories Limited**
*Incorporated:* 8 May 2006 *Employees:* 70
*Net Worth:* £1,854,122 *Total Assets:* £3,571,395
*Registered Office:* c/o Pearson & Associates, Suite E Canal Wharf, Eshton Road, Gargrave, Skipton, N Yorks, BD23 3SE
*Activities:* Other professional, scientific and technical activities n.e.c.
*Parent:* Broughton Ventures Limited
*Officers:* Chris Allen [1975] Director; Dr Paul Moran [1973] Director

**Browallia Holdings Limited**
*Incorporated:* 24 April 1883 *Employees:* 1
*Net Worth:* £9,149,142 *Total Assets:* £14,930,074
*Registered Office:* Old Mills, Moor Top, Drighlington, Bradford, W Yorks, BD11 1BY
*Activities:* Activities of head offices
*Officers:* Kathryn Davenport, Secretary; Peter Jan Patrik Valentin Gyllenhammar [1953] Director [Swedish]

**Alfred Brown (Worsted Mills) Limited**
*Incorporated:* 19 October 1950 *Employees:* 81
*Net Worth:* £6,045,688 *Total Assets:* £7,383,857
*Registered Office:* Empire Mills, Bramley, Leeds, LS13 3HG
*Activities:* Weaving of textiles
*Officers:* Majorie Andrea Brown, Secretary; Sally Alice Dalton, Secretary; Alfred Nigel Brown [1961] Director/Worsted Manufacturer; Alfred Willmot Brown [1933] Director/Worsted Manufacturer; Ian Jonathan Brown [1959] Director/Worsted Manufacturer; Majorie Andrea Brown [1938] Director/Secretary; Joanne Mary Handley [1967] Export Sales Director; Roger David Hugh McArdle [1959] Director/Worsted Manufacturer

**J. Brown Fabrics Limited**
*Incorporated:* 13 April 1983 *Employees:* 27
*Net Worth:* £2,001,133 *Total Assets:* £3,174,579
*Registered Office:* Unit 1 Express Way, Wakefield Europort, Castleford, W Yorks, WF6 2AE
*Activities:* Wholesale of textiles
*Shareholders:* John Brown; Eleanor Brown
*Officers:* Graham David Clark, Secretary; Donna Louise Brown [1978] Director; Eleanor Brown [1956] Director; John Brown [1955] Managing Director; Jonathan Kevin Brown [1982] Director/Sales Representative; Andrew Halls [1963] Sales Director

**David Brown Gear Systems Limited**
*Incorporated:* 19 June 2008 *Employees:* 240
*Net Worth:* £22,901,000 *Total Assets:* £68,331,000
*Registered Office:* Park Works, Park Road, Lockwood, Huddersfield, W Yorks, HD4 5DD
*Activities:* Manufacture of bearings, gears, gearing and driving elements
*Parent:* David Brown Group Limited
*Officers:* Karen Ann Tulley, Secretary; David Armitt [1975] Director; Stewart Robert Macintosh [1979] Director; James Allan McColl [1951] Director

**David Brown Group Limited**
*Incorporated:* 16 October 1989 *Employees:* 28
*Net Worth:* £102,644,000 *Total Assets:* £108,347,000
*Registered Office:* Park Road, Lockwood, Huddersfield, W Yorks, HD4 5DD
*Activities:* Activities of head offices
*Officers:* Karen Ann Tulley, Secretary; David Armitt [1975] Director; Kate Hilary Norman [1977] HR & Comms Director

**W.P.Brown Limited**
*Incorporated:* 16 April 1930 *Employees:* 221
*Net Worth:* £6,089,903 *Total Assets:* £10,455,018
*Registered Office:* 17 Davygate, York, YO1 8QT
*Activities:* Other retail sale in non-specialised stores
*Officers:* Shane Longhorne, Secretary; Nicholas Edward Rhodes Brown [1959] Director; Elizabeth Joy Hudson [1956] Director; Shane Longhorne [1957] Director

**Joe Browns Ltd**
*Incorporated:* 17 September 1990 *Employees:* 95
*Net Worth:* £15,034,071 *Total Assets:* £22,491,886
*Registered Office:* Kandy Works, Brown Lane East, Leeds, LS11 0BT
*Activities:* Wholesale of clothing and footwear
*Shareholders:* Simon Ferguson Brown; GE Capital Bank Limited
*Officers:* Darren Trevor Abbott, Secretary; Darren Trevor Abbott [1962] Director/Accountant; Simon Ferguson Brown [1960] Director

**Browntree Properties Limited**
*Incorporated:* 9 April 2002 *Employees:* 10
*Net Worth:* £4,133,428 *Total Assets:* £8,697,666
*Registered Office:* Legrams Commercial Centre, Legrams Lane, Bradford, W Yorks, BD7 1NH
*Activities:* Buying and selling of own real estate
*Shareholder:* Mozafar Gorji
*Officers:* Rida Gorji, Secretary; Zahra Daneshyar [1967] Director; Mozafar Gorji [1949] Managing Director; Nabil Gorji [1987] Director/Civil Engineer; Rida Gorji [1985] Director/Architect

**Brunswick Court Development (Leeds) Limited**
*Incorporated:* 9 February 2017 *Employees:* 4
*Net Worth:* £1,378,168 *Total Assets:* £4,923,833
*Registered Office:* 6 North Lane, Roundhay, Leeds, LS8 2QJ
*Activities:* Development of building projects
*Parent:* Tonia Investments Limited
*Officers:* Sophie Nina Brown [1977] Director/Business Person; Patrick James Finn [1962] Director/Business Person [Irish]; Chenyi Qian [1971] Director [Chinese]; Geoffrey Gareth Thomas [1975] Director/Chartered Accountant

**Bruntons Aero Products Limited**
*Incorporated:* 7 November 1895 *Employees:* 53
*Net Worth:* £1,798,812 *Total Assets:* £3,721,803
*Registered Office:* P O Box 88, 27 Dewsbury Road, Ossett, W Yorks, WF5 9WS
*Activities:* Manufacture of wire products, chain and springs
*Parent:* Carclo PLC
*Officers:* Richard John Ottaway, Secretary; Alan Hook [1964] Director; Christopher John Malley [1967] Director; Richard John Ottaway [1971] Director/Chartered Accountant

**BSC Filters Limited**
*Incorporated:* 18 May 1989 *Employees:* 69
*Net Worth:* £3,652,728 *Total Assets:* £4,811,120
*Registered Office:* Units 10-11 Sterling Park, York, YO30 4WU
*Activities:* Manufacture of electronic components
*Parent:* Dover Fluids UK Ltd
*Officers:* Martyn Lee [1956] Managing Director; Andrew Arthur Stringer [1961] Sales Director; Russell Toney [1969] Director/Corporate President [American]

**BSN Medical Distribution Ltd.**
*Incorporated:* 26 February 2002 *Employees:* 36
*Net Worth:* £10,953,021 *Total Assets:* £70,633,856
*Registered Office:* Willerby Hill Business Park, Willerby, Hull, HU10 6FE
*Activities:* Operation of warehousing and storage facilities for land transport activities
*Parent:* BSN Medical UK Holding Ltd
*Officers:* David Hall, Secretary; Christian Goeke [1971] Director/Logistics [German]; David Hall [1959] Director/Accountant; Anita Jordan [1966] Director/Finance Controller

**BSN Medical Limited**
*Incorporated:* 6 October 2000 *Employees:* 107
*Net Worth:* £34,691,000 *Total Assets:* £39,263,000
*Registered Office:* Willerby Business Park, Willerby, Hull, HU10 6FE
*Activities:* Retail sale of medical and orthopaedic goods in specialised stores (not incl. hearing aids) n.e.c.
*Parent:* BSN Medical UK Holding Limited
*Officers:* Paul Ralph Richard Goodman [1960] Director/General Manager; David Hall [1959] Director/Accountant; Anita Jordan [1966] Director/Accountant

**BSN Medical UK Holding Limited**
*Incorporated:* 29 December 2005
*Net Worth Deficit:* £18,349,912 *Total Assets:* £99,295,736
*Registered Office:* Willerby Hill Business Park, Beverley Road, Willerby, E Yorks, HU10 6WS
*Activities:* Activities of other holding companies n.e.c.
*Parent:* BSN Medical Netherlands Holding B.V
*Officers:* David Hall, Secretary; Paul Ralph Richard Goodman [1960] Director/Country Manager; David Hall [1959] Director/Accountant; Anita Jordan [1966] Director/Accountant

**BTL Group Limited**
*Incorporated:* 18 January 1985 *Employees:* 119
*Net Worth:* £5,168,024 *Total Assets:* £8,086,211
*Registered Office:* Salts Wharf, Ashley Lane, Shipley, W Yorks, BD17 7DB
*Activities:* Other information technology service activities
*Major Shareholder:* Ian Robert Gomersall
*Officers:* Thomas Audsley Gomersall, Secretary/Consultant; Dr Ian Robert Gomersall [1950] Director; Charles Peabody Hadden Kernan [1963] Director [American]; Andrew John McAnulla [1980] Service Design Director; Allan Keith Myers [1959] Managing Director; Sonya Jane Whitworth [1973] Operations Director

**Buckley Jewellery Limited**
*Incorporated:* 6 February 1989 *Employees:* 44
*Net Worth:* £2,505,645 *Total Assets:* £4,276,263
*Registered Office:* Unit G3, Wyther Lane Industrial Estate, Wyther Green, Leeds, LS5 3AR
*Activities:* Wholesale of watches and jewellery
*Shareholders:* Adrian James Ludbrook Buckley; Rachel Elizabeth Buckley
*Officers:* Mark Jonathan Francis, Secretary; Adrian James Ludbrook Buckley [1962] Director/Jewellery Sales; Christina Verity Lenihan [1980] Director/Jewellery Product Developer; Sir William Eric Peacock [1944] Director

**Buckley Properties (Leeds) Limited**
*Incorporated:* 19 January 1960
*Net Worth:* £3,151,336 *Total Assets:* £3,264,350
*Registered Office:* Town Centre House, The Merrion Centre, Leeds, LS2 8LY
*Activities:* Buying and selling of own real estate
*Shareholder:* Town Centre Securities PLC
*Officers:* Mark John Dilley [1972] Finance Director; Lynda Margaret Shillaw [1965] Group Property Director; Edward Max Ziff [1960] Director

**Builders Supply (North West) Limited**
*Incorporated:* 8 August 1975 *Employees:* 75
*Net Worth:* £7,167,037 *Total Assets:* £12,306,700
*Registered Office:* c/o Border Aggregates, Scotland Road, Carnforth, Lancs, LA5 9JZ
*Activities:* Agents specialised in the sale of other particular products
*Parent:* Hardroad Limited
*Officers:* Carolyn Elizabeth Masters, Secretary; Terry Billington [1944] Director; Thomas William Cross [1932] Director; Andrew Hetherington [1969] Finance Director; Stephen Pelter [1957] Director; Harold Donald Rogerson [1931] Director

**Bulk Logistics Group Ltd**
*Incorporated:* 23 March 2016 *Employees:* 110
*Net Worth Deficit:* £62,687 *Total Assets:* £14,976,294
*Registered Office:* The Garage, Patrick Brompton, Bedale, N Yorks, DL8 1JP
*Activities:* Freight transport by road
*Major Shareholder:* Michael James Ward
*Officers:* Paul William Tolmie [1961] Director; Michael James Ward [1968] Director

**John Bull (Confectioners) Limited**
*Incorporated:* 19 November 1976 *Employees:* 163
*Net Worth:* £1,801,055 *Total Assets:* £4,381,691
*Registered Office:* Lancaster Road, Carnaby, Bridlington, N Yorks, YO15 3QY
*Activities:* Manufacture of sugar confectionery
*Parent:* JBC Holdings Limited
*Officers:* James Nicholas Hodgson, Secretary/Confectioner; James Nicholas Hodgson [1976] Director/Confectioner; Trevor Leonard Hodgson [1945] Director/Confectioner

**Bull Brand Limited**
*Incorporated:* 2 August 2000 *Employees:* 13
*Net Worth:* £4,298,953 *Total Assets:* £5,250,433
*Registered Office:* 16 Steeton Grove, Steeton, Keighley, W Yorks, BD20 6TT
*Activities:* Wholesale of tobacco products
*Shareholder:* Andrew Barker
*Officers:* Alison Janette Barker, Secretary; Alison Janette Barker [1960] Director; Andrew Barker [1960] Director; William Barker [1992] Director

**Bulloughs Cleaning Services Limited**
*Incorporated:* 19 February 1987 *Employees:* 1,575
*Net Worth:* £6,282,534 *Total Assets:* £8,355,123
*Registered Office:* Craven House, Carleton New Road, Skipton, N Yorks, BD23 2DE
*Activities:* General cleaning of buildings
*Shareholders:* Duncan Scott Bullough; Frederick Bullough
*Officers:* Michael Bogg [1963] Director; Duncan Scott Bullough [1965] Managing Director; David Samuel Wellock [1990] Director/Financial Controller

**Bullseye Superfactors Ltd**
*Incorporated:* 22 December 1995 *Employees:* 159
*Net Worth:* £1,936,645 *Total Assets:* £4,675,806
*Registered Office:* Bullseye Distribution Centre, Hunt Lane, Bentley, Doncaster, S Yorks, DN5 9SE
*Activities:* Wholesale trade of motor vehicle parts and accessories
*Shareholders:* Trevor Michael Morris; Linda Morris
*Officers:* Donald Renshaw, Secretary; Kerry Lesley Lock [1978] Human Resources Director; Linda Morris [1950] Director; Trevor Michael Morris [1950] Director; Stacy Edward Phillips [1961] Director; Donald Renshaw [1947] Director/Certified Accountant

**Bulmer & Lumb Group Limited**
*Incorporated:* 6 June 2001 *Employees:* 94
*Net Worth:* £5,151,908 *Total Assets:* £9,484,025
*Registered Office:* Bulmer & Lumb Group Limited, Royds Hall Lane, Buttershaw, Bradford, W Yorks, BD6 2NE
*Activities:* Preparation and spinning of textile fibres
*Parent:* Bulmer & Lumb Holdings Limited
*Officers:* Matthew Ian Whitehead, Secretary; Lee Darvill [1973] Export Sales Director; Paul Hamilton [1969] Group Technical Director; David William Midgley [1968] Managing Director; Matthew Ian Whitehead [1977] Financial Director

**Bulmer & Lumb Holdings Limited**
*Incorporated:* 19 November 2015 *Employees:* 95
*Net Worth:* £2,956,027 *Total Assets:* £7,453,764
*Registered Office:* Royds Hall Lane, Buttershaw, Bradford, W Yorks, BD6 2NE
*Activities:* Activities of head offices
*Major Shareholder:* David William Midgley
*Officers:* Doctor Elizabeth Jane Midgley, Secretary; David William Midgley [1968] Director; Matthew Ian Whitehead [1977] Finance Director

**R. Bunton Limited**
*Incorporated:* 2 January 1979 *Employees:* 78
*Net Worth:* £3,781,851 *Total Assets:* £10,732,973
*Registered Office:* The Sidings, Station Road, Harecroft, Wilsden, Bradford, BD15 0BS
*Activities:* Renting and leasing of construction and civil engineering machinery and equipment
*Parent:* Bunton Plant Hire Limited
*Officers:* Tracey Bunton, Secretary; Andrew Bunton [1967] Director/Manager; Joyce Beryl Bunton [1948] Director/Secretary; Robert Leslie James Bunton [1948] Director/Builder; Robert Hall [1967] Director

**Bunton Plant Hire Limited**
*Incorporated:* 18 January 2011 *Employees:* 73
*Net Worth:* £5,326,377 *Total Assets:* £12,191,872
*Registered Office:* The Sidings, Station Road, Harecroft, Wilsden, Bradford, W Yorks, BD15 0BS
*Activities:* Activities of construction holding companies
*Shareholders:* Robert Leslie James Bunton; Joyce Beryl Bunton; Andrew Robert Bunton
*Officers:* Andrew Bunton [1967] Director/Manager; Joyce Beryl Bunton [1948] Director/Secretary; Robert Leslie James Bunton [1948] Director/Builder

**Burbank Produce Limited**
*Incorporated:* 13 June 2001 *Employees:* 67
*Net Worth:* £1,751,000 *Total Assets:* £5,147,000
*Registered Office:* 2 St James Market, Bradford, W Yorks, BD4 7PW
*Activities:* Other food services
*Shareholders:* Total Produce Limited; Simon Anthony Kershaw
*Officers:* Johnathan Francis Kershaw [1972] Director/Sales; Simon Anthony Kershaw [1963] Director/Fruit Merchant; Francis Gerard McKernan [1962] Managing Director UK & Ireland [Irish]; Mark Christopher Owen [1965] Finance Director; Stephen Mark Webster [1962] Managing Director UK Wholesale Division

**Burg-Wachter UK (Holdings) Limited**
*Incorporated:* 13 October 2005
*Previous:* Burg-Wachter UK Limited
*Net Worth:* £4,960,190 *Total Assets:* £4,960,191
*Registered Office:* Unit 3 Eurocam Technology Park, Chase Way, Bradford, W Yorks, BD5 8HW
*Activities:* Wholesale of hardware, plumbing and heating equipment and supplies
*Officers:* Christopher Markus Luling [1983] Director [German]; Dietmar Adalbert Luling [1955] Director [German]; Harald Alfred Luling [1958] Director [German]

**Burg-Wachter UK Limited**
*Incorporated:* 26 November 1987 *Employees:* 36
*Previous:* Sterling Locks Limited
*Net Worth:* £7,001,016 *Total Assets:* £8,360,632
*Registered Office:* Unit 3 Eurocam Technology Park, Chase Way, Bradford, W Yorks, BD5 8HW
*Activities:* Wholesale of household goods (other than musical instruments) n.e.c
*Officers:* Nina Williams, Secretary; Andrew James Field [1977] Managing Director; Christopher Markus Luling [1983] Director [German]; Dietmar Adalbert Luling [1955] Director [German]; Harald Alfred Luling [1958] Director [German]

**Burgess Group PLC**
*Incorporated:* 22 November 1947 *Employees:* 108
*Net Worth:* £27,561,120 *Total Assets:* £31,667,256
*Registered Office:* P O Box 46, Victory Mill, Thornton-le-Dale, Pickering, N Yorks, YO18 7YB
*Activities:* Manufacture of prepared pet foods
*Parent:* Burgess Group Holdings Limited
*Officers:* Howard John Duddell, Secretary; Margaret Gillian Burgess [1934] Director/Housewife; Thomas Lionel Ashley Burgess [1933] Director; James Philip Godfrey Naylor [1946] Retired Director; Sara Gillian Roberts [1961] Director; Simon Paul Roberts [1957] Director/Surveyor; Thomas Henry Roberts [1988] Director; Nicholas Ian Vermont [1958] Director/Consultant

**Burley Developments Group Limited**
*Incorporated:* 11 December 2009 *Employees:* 3
*Net Worth:* £1,457,178 *Total Assets:* £4,887,572
*Registered Office:* 6 Wells Promenade, Ilkley, W Yorks, LS29 9LF
*Activities:* Development of building projects
*Shareholders:* Michael John Smith; Jennifer Lynne Smith; Fortlands Limited
*Officers:* James Peter Banfi, Secretary; Jennifer Lynne Smith, Secretary; Paul Martin Walker, Secretary; Jennifer Lynne Smith [1962] Director/Administrator; Michael John Smith [1967] Director; Paul Richard Turner [1946] Director

**Burlington Care Holdings Limited**
*Incorporated:* 25 January 2017 *Employees:* 1,070
*Net Worth:* £4,361,838 *Total Assets:* £15,417,607
*Registered Office:* Lancaster House, Lancaster Road, Carnaby, Bridlington, E Yorks, YO15 3QY
*Activities:* Residential nursing care facilities
*Major Shareholder:* Richard Michael Hoggart
*Officers:* Andrew Alan Hoggart [1966] Director/Operations Manager; Richard Michael Hoggart [1974] Director

**Burlington Care Limited**
*Incorporated:* 5 March 2007 *Employees:* 934
*Net Worth:* £2,789,325 *Total Assets:* £4,931,882
*Registered Office:* Lancaster House, Lancaster Road, Carnaby, Bridlington, E Yorks, YO15 3QY
*Activities:* Medical nursing home activities
*Parent:* Burlington Care Holdings Limited
*Officers:* Joanne Fogg [1968] Operations Director; Andrew Alan Hoggart [1966] Director/Operations Manager; Richard Michael Hoggart [1974] Director/Bank Manager

**Burlington Slate Limited**
*Incorporated:* 9 January 1984 *Employees:* 138
*Net Worth:* £5,628,860 *Total Assets:* £12,833,722
*Registered Office:* Cavendish House, Kirkby in Furness, Cumbria, LA17 7UN
*Activities:* Quarrying of ornamental and building stone, limestone, gypsum, chalk and slate
*Shareholders:* Peter Anthony Bostock; RBC Trustees (CI) Ltd
*Officers:* Lucy Georgiana Cavendish [1973] Director/Painter; Lord Richard Hugh Baron Cavendish [1941] Director/Landowner; Michael Gerard Faughy [1958] Managing Director; Allen Joseph Gibb [1966] Director; Right Honourable Grania Mary Lady Cavendish [1947] Director; David Neil Sarti [1965] Director

**Burmatex Limited**
*Incorporated:* 3 January 1958 *Employees:* 125
*Net Worth:* £14,993,000 *Total Assets:* £19,261,000
*Registered Office:* Victoria Mills, Ossett, W Yorks, WF5 0AN
*Activities:* Manufacture of woven or tufted carpets and rugs
*Parent:* Airea PLC
*Officers:* Paul Stevenson, Secretary; Neil Rylance [1956] Director; Paul Stevenson [1978] Director/Accountant

**N.R. Burnett (Holdings) Limited**
*Incorporated:* 16 January 1984 *Employees:* 2
*Net Worth:* £4,568,450 *Total Assets:* £4,731,743
*Registered Office:* 1 Global Business Park, Hamburg Road, Hull, HU7 0AE
*Activities:* Activities of other holding companies n.e.c.
*Shareholders:* Paul Nigel Rodney Burnett; Linda Maureen Burnett; Burnett Discretionary Trust
*Officers:* Paul Nigel Rodney Burnett, Secretary; Hugh Barry Burnett [1938] Director; Paul Nigel Rodney Burnett [1949] Director

**Burnley & Pendle Travel Limited**
*Incorporated:* 13 December 1983 *Employees:* 226
*Net Worth Deficit:* £520,000 *Total Assets:* £3,784,000
*Registered Office:* Prospect Park, Broughton Way, Starbeck, Harrogate, N Yorks, HG2 7NY
*Activities:* Other passenger land transport
*Parent:* Transdev Blazefield Limited
*Officers:* Alex Lloyd Hornby [1981] Managing Director; Gordon Duncan Irvine [1957] Engineering Director; Seth King [1971] Finance Director

**Burrows Motor Company Limited**
*Incorporated:* 1 June 1999 *Employees:* 355
*Net Worth:* £3,047,000 *Total Assets:* £24,860,000
*Registered Office:* Burrows Motor Company, Wheatley Hall Road, Doncaster, S Yorks, DN2 4LT
*Activities:* Sale of new cars and light motor vehicles
*Shareholder:* Steven Richard Burrows
*Officers:* Louise Holmes, Secretary; Steven Richard Burrows [1951] Director; Dean Cooper [1964] Operations Director

**A.E. Burt and Company Limited**
*Incorporated:* 22 September 1977 *Employees:* 23
*Net Worth:* £1,027,684 *Total Assets:* £4,926,801
*Registered Office:* Oakwood House, 80 Eastmount Road, Darlington, Co Durham, DL1 1LA
*Activities:* Other letting and operating of own or leased real estate
*Major Shareholder:* Marion Barbara Todd
*Officers:* Marion Barbara Todd, Secretary; Claire Elizabeth Kerr [1971] Director; Graeme Stuart Kerr [1971] Director; Marion Barbara Todd [1948] Director; Nigel Robert Todd [1975] Director

**Burton Agnes Stud Company Limited (The)**
*Incorporated:* 5 February 1962 *Employees:* 12
*Net Worth:* £3,899,217 *Total Assets:* £6,993,302
*Registered Office:* The Estate Office, Burton Agnes, Driffield, E Yorks, YO25 4NB
*Activities:* Growing of cereals (except rice), leguminous crops and oil seeds
*Officers:* Simon Charles Cunliffe-Lister, Secretary; William Anthony Bethell [1957] Director/Farmer; The Honourable Elizabeth Susan Cunliffe-Lister [1944] Director; Olivia Claire Cunliffe-Lister [1976] Director; Simon Charles Cunliffe-Lister [1977] Director; Owen Edward Tebbs [1932] Director/Solicitor; Nicholas Hugh Tremayne Wrigley [1955] Director

**The Burton Constable Foundation**
*Incorporated:* 23 May 1991 *Employees:* 19
*Net Worth:* £10,124,365 *Total Assets:* £10,216,752
*Registered Office:* Burton Constable Hall, Burton Constable, Skirlaugh, E Yorks, HU11 4LN
*Activities:* Operation of historical sites and buildings and similar visitor attractions
*Officers:* Christopher Mark Day, Secretary; Yvonne Louise Hardman [1978] Director/Museum Curator; Nicholas Alexander Cyril Hildyard [1954] Director; Camilla Jane Nichol [1973] Director/Museum Head; Andrew Charles Travers Procter [1958] Director/Solicitor; Dr Christopher Lloyd Ridgway [1958] Director; James Andrew John Straker [1959] Director/Landowner; Rodrica Conseulo Straker [1963] Director/Land Agent; Robert Arthur Hallifax Sword [1952] Director/Chartered Surveyor

**Burton Roofing Merchants Limited**
*Incorporated:* 11 April 1983 *Employees:* 167
*Net Worth:* £10,866,500 *Total Assets:* £22,097,224
*Registered Office:* Chapman Street, Cleveland Street, Hull, HU8 8AE
*Activities:* Wholesale of wood, construction materials and sanitary equipment
*Officers:* Lee Michael George Hustwait, Secretary; Andrew Cowham [1958] Director/Accountant; Antonio Trincado Fernandez [1972] Director [Spanish]; Javier Fernandez Fernandez [1968] Director [Spanish]; Paul Arthur Hattee [1962] Director; Eamonn David Howley [1960] Director/Branch Manager; Lee Michael George Hustwait [1983] Finance Director; Lee Keates [1968] Director/Sales; Gary McManus [1963] Director/Branch Manager; Eduardo Mera [1971] Managing Director [Spanish]; Mark Purvis [1979] Director; Javier Quindos [1979] Commercial Director [Spanish]

**The Burwood House Group Limited**
*Incorporated:* 12 July 1989
*Net Worth:* £139,560,992 *Total Assets:* £403,814,016
*Registered Office:* Asda House, Southbank, Great Wilson Street, Leeds, LS11 5AD
*Activities:* Development of building projects
*Parent:* McLagan Investments Limited
*Officers:* Alexander Simpson, Secretary; Roger Michael Burnley [1966] Director; Robert Gerard McWilliam [1969] Director; Alexander Simpson [1973] Director

**Business & Enterprise Finance Ltd.**
*Incorporated:* 15 February 1984 *Employees:* 22
*Previous:* Bradford Enterprise Agency Limited
*Net Worth:* £8,448,721 *Total Assets:* £10,529,806
*Registered Office:* Devere House, Vicar Lane, Little Germany, Bradford, W Yorks, BD1 5AH
*Activities:* Other credit granting n.e.c.
*Parent:* West & North Yorkshire Chamber of Commerce
*Officers:* Julian Chima Abenbrook [1967] Director/Lawyer; Andrew Mark Caton [1963] Director; Malcolm John Lynch [1955] Director/Lawyer; Sandra Needham [1955] Director; Stephen John Nicholson [1963] Director; Kim Louise Rebecchi [1966] Director/Self Employed Advisor; Lee Ramon Underwood [1974] Managing Director; Stephen Arthur Waud [1968] Fund Director

**Business Lines Limited**
*Incorporated:* 11 February 1986 *Employees:* 20
*Net Worth:* £3,850,075 *Total Assets:* £4,421,151
*Registered Office:* Unit 9 Kellet Road Industrial Estate, Carnforth, Lancs, LA5 9XP
*Activities:* Wholesale trade of motor vehicle parts and accessories
*Shareholders:* Beryl June Marczynski; Michael Marczynski
*Officers:* Beryl June Marczynski, Secretary; Beryl June Marczynski [1947] Director; Michael Marczynski [1948] Director

**Bussey & Armstrong Projects Limited**
*Incorporated:* 13 September 1999
*Net Worth:* £11,386,949 *Total Assets:* £14,045,539
*Registered Office:* Brinkburn, 147 Brinkburn Road, Darlington, Co Durham, DL3 9LA
*Activities:* Development of building projects
*Major Shareholder:* Anthony John Cooper
*Officers:* Angela Edwina Cooper, Company Secretary; Anthony John Cooper [1950] Director

**Bussey and Armstrong Limited**
*Incorporated:* 11 February 1949 *Employees:* 31
*Net Worth:* £3,021,448 *Total Assets:* £3,266,250
*Registered Office:* Brinkburn, 147 Brinkburn Road, Darlington, Co Durham, DL3 9LA
*Activities:* Development of building projects
*Major Shareholder:* Anthony John Cooper
*Officers:* Angela Edwina Cooper, Secretary; Angela Edwina Cooper [1950] Director; Anthony John Cooper [1950] Director/Builder

**Busysky Limited**
*Incorporated:* 13 October 1988
*Net Worth:* £2,157,861 *Total Assets:* £5,636,773
*Registered Office:* c/o Ground Floor, St Paul's House, 23 Park Square, Leeds, LS1 2ND
*Activities:* Other letting and operating of own or leased real estate
*Major Shareholder:* Rosalie Priestley
*Officers:* Rosalie Priestley, Secretary; Jeremy John Paul Priestley [1964] Director/Accountant; Rosalie Priestley [1959] Director

**Butt & Hobbs Limited**
*Incorporated:* 9 February 2005
*Net Worth:* £1,218,605 *Total Assets:* £3,914,678
*Registered Office:* Taylor House, 55-57 Bradford Road, Dewsbury, Wakefield, W Yorks, WF13 2EG
*Activities:* Wholesale of pharmaceutical goods
*Shareholders:* Zaheer Younis-Butt; Mohammad Saeed Younis; Naheed Younis
*Officers:* Mohammad Saeed Younis, Secretary; Mohammad Saeed Younis [1960] Director; Naheed Younis [1969] Director/Administration; Zaheer Younis Butt [1967] Director/Sales

**Butterfield Signs Limited**
*Incorporated:* 6 May 1946 *Employees:* 142
*Net Worth:* £3,523,051 *Total Assets:* £6,868,311
*Registered Office:* 174 Sunbridge Road, Bradford, BD1 2RZ
*Activities:* Manufacture of other plastic products
*Shareholder:* Edward Andrew Butterfield
*Officers:* Christopher Mark Speak, Secretary; Edward Andrew Butterfield [1959] Director; David Sunderland [1947] Director/Chartered Accountant

**Buxton Pickles Ltd.**
*Incorporated:* 21 June 2001 *Employees:* 17
*Net Worth:* £774,659 *Total Assets:* £4,163,372
*Registered Office:* 112 Bolling Road, Ilkley, W Yorks, LS29 8PN
*Activities:* Wholesale of clothing and footwear
*Major Shareholder:* George Austen Pickles
*Officers:* Nigel David Prance, Secretary; George Austen Pickles [1969] Director; Nigel David Prance [1967] Financial Director

**Buy It Direct Ltd**
*Incorporated:* 2 March 2001 *Employees:* 396
*Net Worth:* £10,522,277 *Total Assets:* £44,358,000
*Registered Office:* Unit A, Trident Business Park, Leeds Road, Huddersfield, W Yorks, HD2 1UA
*Activities:* Retail sale via mail order houses or via Internet
*Major Shareholder:* Nicholas Harvey Glynne
*Officers:* Simon Anthony Barnett [1965] Director; Andrew Field [1971] Commercial Director; Nicholas Harvey Glynne [1966] Managing Director; Matthew James Mitchell [1984] Finance Director; James Rigg [1970] Sales Director

**Buy-Investment-Properties Limited**
*Incorporated:* 18 December 2007 *Employees:* 4
*Net Worth:* £3,620,954 *Total Assets:* £4,051,231
*Registered Office:* Buy Investment Properties Ltd, Vicarage Chambers, 9 Park Square East, Leeds, LS1 2LH
*Activities:* Buying and selling of own real estate
*Shareholders:* Asim Ali; Qasim Ali; Abrar Shah
*Officers:* Asim Ali, Secretary; Asim Ali [1980] Director; Qasim Ali [1981] Director; Abrar Shah [1981] Director

**BW Integrated Systems UK Limited**
*Incorporated:* 4 August 2004 *Employees:* 107
*Previous:* Barry-Wehmiller Container Systems Limited
*Net Worth:* £3,124,645 *Total Assets:* £22,238,028
*Registered Office:* Plumtree Farm Industrial Estate, Bircotes, Doncaster, S Yorks, DN11 8EW
*Activities:* Manufacture of machinery for food, beverage and tobacco processing
*Officers:* Lee Mark Pinder, Secretary; Robert Hall Chapman [1945] Director [American]; Gregory Loran Coonrod [1956] Director [American]; Richard Martin Cranston [1969] Operations Director; Lee Mark Pinder [1967] Director/Accountant; Michael John Redwood [1970] Director

**BW Skip Hire Limited**
*Incorporated:* 9 December 1996 *Employees:* 92
*Net Worth:* £3,766,769 *Total Assets:* £5,079,198
*Registered Office:* 263 Whitehall Road, Leeds, LS12 6ER
*Activities:* Collection of non-hazardous waste
*Major Shareholder:* Roger Woodhead
*Officers:* Adele Woodhead, Secretary; Roger Woodhead [1961] Director

**Byworth Boiler Hire Limited**
*Incorporated:* 12 March 1973 *Employees:* 25
*Net Worth:* £7,915,648 *Total Assets:* £8,909,464
*Registered Office:* Beaconsfield House, Thwaites, Keighley, W Yorks, BD21 4NG
*Activities:* Renting and leasing of other machinery, equipment and tangible goods n.e.c.
*Parent:* Baldwin Holdings Limited
*Officers:* Allan Peter Baldwin [1953] Director/Boiler Manufacturer; Helen Baldwin [1960] Director/Accountant; Michael Anthony Rutter [1962] Sales Director

**Byworth Boilers Ltd**
*Incorporated:* 6 October 2010 *Employees:* 111
*Net Worth:* £1,622,518 *Total Assets:* £5,348,961
*Registered Office:* Parkwood Boiler Works, Parkwood Street, Keighley, W Yorks, BD21 4NW
*Activities:* Manufacture of other general-purpose machinery n.e.c.
*Officers:* Allan Peter Baldwin [1953] Director; Helen Baldwin [1960] Director; Robert Peter Baldwin [1985] Production Director; Gavin John Hindle [1977] Projects Director; Adrian Rhodes [1973] Technical Director; Rachel Elaine Westerman [1981] Finance Director

**C & D Foods (Driffield) Unlimited**
*Incorporated:* 16 January 1992 *Employees:* 100
*Previous:* C & D Foods (Driffield) Ltd
*Net Worth:* £2,680,000 *Total Assets:* £17,692,000
*Registered Office:* Kelleythorpe Industrial Estate, Driffield, E Yorks, YO25 9DJ
*Activities:* Manufacture of prepared pet foods
*Parent:* C & D Foods (UK) Unlimited
*Officers:* Aubrey Mulveen, Secretary; Aubrey Mulveen [1968] Director/Accountant [Irish]; Philip John Reynolds [1964] Managing Director [Irish]

**C & D Foods (UK) Unlimited**
*Incorporated:* 1 June 2004 *Employees:* 160
*Previous:* C & D Foods (UK) Limited
*Net Worth:* £2,116,000 *Total Assets:* £23,328,000
*Registered Office:* Kellythorpe Industrial Estate, Driffield, E Yorks, YO25 9DJ
*Activities:* Activities of head offices
*Officers:* Aubrey Mulveen, Secretary; Aubrey Mulveen [1968] Director/Accountant [Irish]; Philip John Reynolds [1964] Managing Director [Irish]

**C & H Antiques Limited**
*Incorporated:* 17 January 1997 *Employees:* 4
*Net Worth:* £2,606,888 *Total Assets:* £3,686,798
*Registered Office:* 33 George Street, Wakefield, W Yorks, WF1 1LX
*Activities:* Retail sale of antiques including antique books in stores
*Shareholders:* William Edward Cundall; Fiona Balfour Cundall
*Officers:* Fiona Balfour Cundall, Secretary/Marketing Executive; Fiona Balfour Cundall [1963] Director/Marketing Executive; William Edward Cundall [1960] Director/Antique Dealer

**C B T Clinics Limited**
*Incorporated:* 25 March 2015 *Employees:* 24
*Net Worth:* £1,437,716 *Total Assets:* £3,397,226
*Registered Office:* C B T Clinics Limited, Suite 10, Aspire Building, 31 Bootham, York, YO30 7BT
*Activities:* Other service activities n.e.c.
*Parent:* CBTC Bidco Limited
*Officers:* Antony Brown [1966] Director; Patrik Johnson [1980] Director [Swedish]; Mark William Joseph [1968] Director; Edmund Alfred Lazarus [1968] Director

**C C Properties (Yorkshire) Ltd**
*Incorporated:* 1 October 2014
*Net Worth:* £91,936 *Total Assets:* £4,320,186
*Registered Office:* 119-129 Chapeltown Road, Leeds, LS7 3DU
*Activities:* Other letting and operating of own or leased real estate
*Officers:* Mohammed Rashid [1960] Director; Mohammed Zaheer [1976] Director

**C L Medicall Aid Limited**
*Incorporated:* 12 January 2009 *Employees:* 55
*Net Worth:* £3,180,120 *Total Assets:* £8,405,868
*Registered Office:* Unit 1 Carolina Court, Doncaster, S Yorks, DN4 5RA
*Activities:* Other business support service activities n.e.c.
*Major Shareholder:* John Lawrence Radford
*Officers:* Alexandra Maria Sheriff, Secretary; John David Goacher [1964] Finance Director; Dr Sameer Gupta [1972] Director/Chief Medical Officer [Indian]; John Matthew Parker [1976] Managing Director; John Lawrence Radford [1965] Director/Chief Executive Officer; John Steele [1953] Compliance Director

**C P Group of Companies Limited**
*Incorporated:* 29 March 2004
*Net Worth:* £1,055,811 *Total Assets:* £7,254,812
*Registered Office:* 12 Greenhead Road, Huddersfield, W Yorks, HD1 4EN
*Activities:* Activities of head offices
*Major Shareholder:* Anthony John Taylor
*Officers:* Anthony John Taylor [1955] Director/Chairman

**C T Glass Holdings Limited**
*Incorporated:* 3 February 2016 *Employees:* 1
*Net Worth:* £4,000,129 *Total Assets:* £4,064,789
*Registered Office:* c/o 1 Sheepscar Court, Meanwood Road, Leeds, LS7 2BB
*Activities:* Activities of production holding companies
*Major Shareholder:* Gary Thirkell
*Officers:* Gary Thirkell [1967] Director

**C. K. Properties (UK) Limited**
*Incorporated:* 11 February 2004 *Employees:* 1
*Net Worth:* £1,938,112 *Total Assets:* £7,043,956
*Registered Office:* 70 Northumberland Avenue, Hull, HU2 0JB
*Activities:* Renting and operating of Housing Association real estate
*Shareholders:* Abbas Bhamji; Usman Bhamji
*Officers:* Omar Bhamji, Secretary/Director; Abbas Bhamji [1971] Director; Omar Bhamji [1975] Director

**C.A. (Evenwood) Limited**
*Incorporated:* 21 January 2000 *Employees:* 3
*Net Worth:* £12,353,357 *Total Assets:* £12,463,219
*Registered Office:* Evenwood Industrial Estate, Evenwood, Bishop Auckland, Co Durham, DL14 9SF
*Activities:* Other letting and operating of own or leased real estate
*Parent:* C.A. Group (Holdings) Limited
*Officers:* Desmond Joseph Webster, Secretary; Steven William Forster [1968] Director; Martin Kenneth Lowther [1967] Director; Desmond Joseph Webster [1963] Director/Accountant

**C.A. Group (Holdings) Limited**
*Incorporated:* 9 August 2006 *Employees:* 227
*Net Worth:* £22,921,366 *Total Assets:* £55,144,112
*Registered Office:* Evenwood Industrial Estate, Evenwood, Bishop Auckland, Co Durham, DL14 9SF
*Activities:* Roofing activities
*Parent:* C.A. Foundation
*Officers:* Desmond Joseph Webster, Secretary; Neil James Alderson [1976] Director; Steven William Forster [1968] Director; Martin Kenneth Lowther [1967] Director; Peter William Rowe [1961] Director; Desmond Joseph Webster [1963] Managing Director

**C.A. Group Limited**
*Incorporated:* 9 August 1983 *Employees:* 220
*Net Worth:* £10,075,248 *Total Assets:* £41,254,328
*Registered Office:* Evenwood Industrial Estate, Evenwood, Co Durham, DL14 9SF
*Activities:* Roofing activities
*Parent:* C.A. Group (Holdings) Limited
*Officers:* Desmond Joseph Webster, Secretary; Neil James Alderson [1976] Commercial Director; Stuart Iain Brown [1976] Director; Lee Andrew Davies [1974] Technical Director; Steven William Forster [1968] Commercial Director; Martin Kenneth Lowther [1967] Operations Director; Peter William Rowe [1961] Contracts Director; Desmond Joseph Webster [1963] Managing Director

**C.K. (Fast Food Suppliers) Limited**
*Incorporated:* 18 November 1999 *Employees:* 70
*Net Worth:* £3,591,502 *Total Assets:* £6,112,846
*Registered Office:* 70 Northumberland Avenue, Hull, HU2 0JB
*Activities:* Other food services
*Shareholders:* Abbas Bhamji; Omar Bhamji
*Officers:* Abbas Bhamji [1971] Director; Omar Bhamji [1975] Commercial Director

**C.K. Foods (Processing) Limited**
*Incorporated:* 11 January 2005 *Employees:* 45
*Net Worth:* £2,102,485 *Total Assets:* £7,900,821
*Registered Office:* 70 Northumberland Avenue, Hull, HU2 0JB
*Activities:* Manufacture of other food products n.e.c.
*Officers:* Omar Bhamji, Secretary/Operations Director; Abbas Bhamji [1971] Director; Abubaker Bhamji [1977] Commercial Director; Omar Bhamji [1975] Operations Director

**C.N. Trading Limited**
*Incorporated:* 13 April 2001 *Employees:* 6
*Net Worth:* £744,036 *Total Assets:* £3,220,861
*Registered Office:* Calderside Nurseries, Oakville Road, Hebden Bridge, W Yorks, HX7 6NG
*Activities:* Sale of other motor vehicles
*Major Shareholder:* Christopher John Mellin Greenwood
*Officers:* Scott Eric Greenwood, Secretary; Christopher John Mellin Greenwood [1951] Director/Motor & General Trading; Julia Dawn Taylor [1971] Director/Accountant

**C.S.L. Industrial Limited**
*Incorporated:* 20 August 1998 *Employees:* 24
*Net Worth:* £3,744,555 *Total Assets:* £6,597,145
*Registered Office:* Aurillac Way, Hallcroft, Retford, Notts, DN22 7PX
*Activities:* Other professional, scientific and technical activities n.e.c.
*Shareholders:* Clive Raymond Hewgill; Sharon Elaine Hewgill
*Officers:* Sharon Elaine Hewgill, Secretary/Accounts Director; Clive Raymond Hewgill [1957] Managing Director; Sharon Elaine Hewgill [1956] Accounts Director

**C.T. Transport (Castleford) Partnership LLP**
*Incorporated:* 26 September 2012 *Employees:* 13
*Net Worth:* £1,185,637 *Total Assets:* £3,260,996
*Registered Office:* 18 Maple Drive, Pontefract, W Yorks, WF8 3QR
*Officers:* Andrew David Cuttle [1967] Member; Brenda Cuttle [1935] Member

**C2 Investment Limited**
*Incorporated:* 16 October 2001 *Employees:* 116
*Net Worth:* £3,493,298 *Total Assets:* £8,161,580
*Registered Office:* Lancaster Leisure Park, Wyresdale Road, Lancaster, LA1 3LA
*Activities:* Public houses and bars
*Shareholders:* Matthew Scott Jackson; Phillip Anthony Simpson
*Officers:* Raluca Simpson, Secretary; Matthew Scott Jackson [1972] Director; Phillip Anthony Simpson [1971] Director

**Caddick (City One) Limited**
*Incorporated:* 3 October 2014 *Employees:* 4
*Net Worth:* £1,407,416 *Total Assets:* £10,396,719
*Registered Office:* Castlegarth Grange, Scott Lane, Wetherby, W Yorks, LS22 6LH
*Activities:* Buying and selling of own real estate
*Shareholders:* Carl Brewins; Caddick (JPC Developments) Limited
*Officers:* Carl Brewins [1965] Director; John Paul Caddick [1981] Director; Paul Caddick [1950] Director; James Phillip Dyson [1970] Director

**Caddick (JPC Developments) Limited**
*Incorporated:* 9 May 2001 *Employees:* 3
*Previous:* Caddick (Tingley) Limited
*Net Worth Deficit:* £205,151 *Total Assets:* £10,409,250
*Registered Office:* Castlegarth Grange, Scott Lane, Wetherby, W Yorks, LS22 6LH
*Activities:* Activities of other holding companies n.e.c.
*Parent:* Caddick Developments Limited
*Officers:* Paul Andrew Bullers, Secretary; Paul Andrew Bullers [1966] Finance Director; John Paul Caddick [1981] Director; Paul Caddick [1950] Director

**Caddick (Mill Harbour) Limited**
*Incorporated:* 21 June 2013 *Employees:* 2
*Net Worth Deficit:* £649,304 *Total Assets:* £6,337,193
*Registered Office:* Castlegarth Grange, Scott Lane, Wetherby, W Yorks, LS22 6LH
*Activities:* Buying and selling of own real estate
*Parent:* Caddick (JPC Developments) Limited
*Officers:* Paul Andrew Bullers, Secretary; Paul Andrew Bullers [1966] Finance Director; John Paul Caddick [1981] Director; Paul Caddick [1950] Director

**Caddick (Rose Wharf) Limited**
*Incorporated:* 5 August 1997 *Employees:* 4
*Net Worth:* £268,036 *Total Assets:* £4,445,119
*Registered Office:* Castlegarth Grange, Scott Lane, Wetherby, W Yorks, LS22 6LH
*Activities:* Buying and selling of own real estate
*Parent:* Caddick Developments Limited
*Officers:* Paul Andrew Bullers, Secretary; Paul Andrew Bullers [1966] Finance Director; Paul Caddick [1950] Director; James Phillip Dyson [1970] Development Director; Myles Edward Hartley [1969] Director

**Caddick (Scarborough) Limited**
*Incorporated:* 12 June 2000
*Net Worth Deficit:* £3,098,271 *Total Assets:* £5,400,279
*Registered Office:* Castlegarth Grange, Scott Lane, Wetherby, W Yorks, LS22 6LH
*Activities:* Buying and selling of own real estate
*Parent:* Caddick Developments Limited
*Officers:* Paul Andrew Bullers, Secretary; Paul Andrew Bullers [1966] Finance Director; Paul Caddick [1950] Director; James Phillip Dyson [1970] Director; Myles Edward Hartley [1969] Director

**Caddick Construction Limited**
*Incorporated:* 6 July 1979 *Employees:* 108
*Net Worth:* £13,815,000 *Total Assets:* £42,247,000
*Registered Office:* Calder Grange, Knottingley, W Yorks, WF11 8DA
*Activities:* Construction of commercial buildings
*Parent:* Caddick Group PLC
*Officers:* Paul Andrew Bullers, Secretary; Keith Bradley [1958] Purchasing Director; Paul Andrew Bullers [1966] Finance Director; Alexandra Esther Caddick [1952] Director; Paul Caddick [1950] Director; Adrian Christopher Dobson [1960] Director; Andrew Murray [1951] Director; Ian Keith Plowman [1970] Operations Director

**Caddick Developments Limited**
*Incorporated:* 12 January 1990 *Employees:* 16
*Net Worth:* £25,922,000 *Total Assets:* £49,394,000
*Registered Office:* Castlegarth Grange, Scott Lane, Wetherby, W Yorks, LS22 6LH
*Activities:* Buying and selling of own real estate
*Parent:* Caddick Group PLC
*Officers:* Paul Andrew Bullers, Secretary; Paul Andrew Bullers [1966] Finance Director; John Andrew Bywater [1947] Managing Director; Alexandra Esther Caddick [1952] Director; John Paul Caddick [1981] Director/Chartered Surveyor; Paul Caddick [1950] Director; James Phillip Dyson [1970] Director/Chartered Surveyor; Myles Edward Hartley [1969] Director/Chartered Surveyor; Alexandra Victoria Hulme [1977] Retail Director; Lee Michael Savage [1970] Director; Steven Craig Widdowson [1965] Director

**Caddick Group PLC**
*Incorporated:* 17 October 1986 *Employees:* 406
*Net Worth:* £65,225,000 *Total Assets:* £137,480,000
*Registered Office:* Castlegarth Grange, Scott Lane, Wetherby, W Yorks, LS22 6LH
*Activities:* Activities of head offices
*Major Shareholder:* Paul Caddick
*Officers:* Paul Andrew Bullers, Secretary; Paul Andrew Bullers [1966] Finance Director; Alexandra Esther Caddick [1952] Director; Paul Caddick [1950] Director; Peter Graham Hirst [1945] Director/Chartered Accountant

**The Cadman Housing Project Ltd**
*Incorporated:* 26 October 1995 *Employees:* 7
*Net Worth:* £7,385,667 *Total Assets:* £10,263,143
*Registered Office:* Suite 30, The Junction, Charles Street, Horbury, Wakefield, W Yorks, WF4 5FD
*Activities:* Hospital activities
*Shareholders:* Amanda Darlene Amies; Sonia Estcourte Cadman
*Officers:* Amanda Darlene Amies, Company Secretary; Amanda Darlene Amies [1968] Director/Residential Social Landlord; Sonia Estcourte Cadman [1967] Director

**Caird Peckfield Limited**
*Incorporated:* 16 October 1989 *Employees:* 10
*Net Worth:* £1,581,747 *Total Assets:* £3,113,163
*Registered Office:* Peckfield Landfill Site, Ridge Road, Micklefield, Leeds, LS25 4DW
*Activities:* Treatment and disposal of non-hazardous waste
*Parent:* Seneca Global Energy Limited
*Officers:* Alex William Hornshaw [1986] Director

**Cairngorm Ski Services Limited**
*Incorporated:* 30 June 1977 *Employees:* 56
*Net Worth:* £1,357,154 *Total Assets:* £3,057,767
*Registered Office:* 35 Aire Street, Goole, E Yorks, DN14 5QW
*Activities:* Tour operator activities
*Officers:* Diane Mary Southcott, Secretary; Diane Mary Southcott [1949] Director; Phillip Southcott [1948] Director

**Calder Conferences Limited**
*Incorporated:* 27 January 1999
*Net Worth:* £3,929,295 *Total Assets:* £4,694,494
*Registered Office:* Unit 4 Woodside Court, Clayton Wood Rise, Leeds, LS16 6RF
*Activities:* Hotels and similar accommodation
*Parent:* Depho Estates Limited
*Officers:* Deborah Ann Hoban [1959] Director/Functions Manager; James Dean Turner [1969] Commercial Director

**Calder Group (Dewsbury) Limited**
*Incorporated:* 6 March 2003 *Employees:* 221
*Net Worth:* £7,598,939 *Total Assets:* £12,590,954
*Registered Office:* Dewsbury Mills, Thornhill Road, Dewsbury, W Yorks, WF12 9QF
*Activities:* Activities of head offices
*Shareholder:* Derek John Bedford
*Officers:* Carol Lesley Brown, Secretary; Derek John Bedford [1939] Director/Textile Merchant; Gregory Quinton Bedford [1971] Director; Carol Lesley Brown [1968] Director/Bookkeeper; Malcolm Rawson [1939] Director/Textile Merchant

**Calder Properties Limited**
*Incorporated:* 6 February 1984
*Net Worth:* £3,474,179 *Total Assets:* £5,886,934
*Registered Office:* Anchor House, Dewsbury Mills, Thornhill Road, Dewsbury, W Yorks, WF12 9QE
*Activities:* Other letting and operating of own or leased real estate
*Officers:* Carol Lesley Brown, Secretary; David Kevin Bedford [1967] Production Director; Derek John Bedford [1939] Director/Textile Merchant; Gregory Quinton Bedford [1971] Managing Director; Carol Lesley Brown [1968] Director/Bookkeeper; Malcolm Rawson [1939] Director/Textile Merchant; Tracy Jane Wadsworth [1967] Personnel Director

**Calder Textiles Limited**
*Incorporated:* 26 March 1984 *Employees:* 154
*Net Worth:* £2,298,119 *Total Assets:* £5,545,751
*Registered Office:* Anchor House, Dewsbury Mills, Thornhill Road, Dewsbury, W Yorks, WF12 9QE
*Activities:* Preparation and spinning of textile fibres
*Officers:* Carol Lesley Brown, Secretary; David Kevin Bedford [1967] Production Director; Derek John Bedford [1939] Director/Textile Merchant; Gregory Quinton Bedford [1971] Director; Timothy Booth [1965] Director; Stephen Brough [1959] Development Director; Carol Lesley Brown [1968] Director; Mark Mawson [1969] Director; Malcolm Rawson [1939] Director/Textile Merchant; Tracy Jane Wadsworth [1967] Director/Personnel Manager

**Calder Valley Holdings Limited**
*Incorporated:* 30 July 2012
*Net Worth:* £2,611,253 *Total Assets:* £4,453,019
*Registered Office:* Pellon Lane Saw Mills, Pellon Lane, Halifax, W Yorks, HX1 4PX
*Activities:* Activities of other holding companies n.e.c.
*Shareholders:* Robert James Moore; Joseph William Sawrij; Joseph William Sawrij; Robert James Moore
*Officers:* Robert James Moore [1961] Director/Timber Merchant; Joseph William Sawrij [1985] Director

**Calderys UK Ltd**
*Incorporated:* 21 January 1972 *Employees:* 25
*Net Worth Deficit:* £392,771 *Total Assets:* £7,134,768
*Registered Office:* Units H3 & H4, Gildersome Spur, Morley, Leeds, LS27 7JZ
*Activities:* Other manufacturing n.e.c.
*Parent:* Imerys SA
*Officers:* Christopher John Henderson, Secretary; Gerardus Wouter Lodevicus Franciscus Koevoets [1965] Director/Regional Manager [Dutch]; Julie Marie Thiery [1984] Director/Senior Project Lead [French]

**Caldex Holdings Limited**
*Incorporated:* 17 October 2007 *Employees:* 6
*Net Worth:* £691,906 *Total Assets:* £3,527,225
*Registered Office:* Shay Lane, Holmfield, Halifax, W Yorks, HX2 9AP
*Activities:* Other manufacturing n.e.c.
*Shareholders:* Mary Elizabeth Egan; Nigel Waite Pullan
*Officers:* Nigel Waite Pullan, Secretary; Daniel Patrick Egan [1985] Director; Mary Elizabeth Egan [1954] Director; Max James Waite Pullan [1992] Director; Nigel Waite Pullan [1958] Director; Sarah Elizabeth Pullan [1959] Director

**Caldex Limited**
*Incorporated:* 19 February 1985 *Employees:* 16
*Net Worth:* £4,122,651 *Total Assets:* £4,825,457
*Registered Office:* Shay Lane, Holmfield, Halifax, W Yorks, HX2 9AP
*Activities:* Other manufacturing n.e.c.
*Parent:* Caldex Holdings Limited
*Officers:* Nigel Waite Pullan, Secretary; Nigel Waite Pullan [1958] Director

**Call Lane Social Leeds Limited**
*Incorporated:* 3 June 2014 *Employees:* 13
*Net Worth:* £907,179 *Total Assets:* £3,556,623
*Registered Office:* 38 Call Lane, Leeds, LS1 6DT
*Activities:* Public houses and bars
*Shareholders:* Phil Harrison; Melanie Elizabeth Harrison
*Officers:* Melanie Elizabeth Harrison [1976] Director; Philip James Harrison [1976] Director

**Callauto Limited**
*Incorporated:* 18 July 1977 *Employees:* 4
*Net Worth:* £3,705,812 *Total Assets:* £3,978,954
*Registered Office:* 3365 Century Way, Thorpe Park, Leeds, LS15 8ZB
*Activities:* Activities of head offices
*Officers:* Ann Marsh, Secretary; Ann Marsh [1945] Director/Secretary; David Marsh [1946] Director/Builder; Robert David Marsh [1972] Director/Manager; Elizabeth Ann Rispin [1970] Director/Manager

**Callcredit Data Solutions Limited**
*Incorporated:* 20 March 2006 *Employees:* 4
*Previous:* The Trading Floor Limited
*Net Worth:* £6,096,000 *Total Assets:* £6,652,000
*Registered Office:* 1 Park Lane, Leeds, LS3 1EP
*Activities:* Data processing, hosting and related activities
*Parent:* Callcredit Information Group Limited
*Officers:* Colin James Rutter, Secretary; Michael Jon Gordon [1970] Director; Mark Edward Horsey [1968] Director; Robert Kenneth Campbell Munro [1965] Director/Chief Financial Officer; Colin James Rutter [1965] Director

**Callcredit Information Group Limited**
*Incorporated:* 18 November 2003
*Net Worth:* £8,757,000 *Total Assets:* £156,140,000
*Registered Office:* One Park Lane, Leeds, LS3 1EP
*Activities:* Non-trading company
*Parent:* Crown Acquisition Bidco Limited
*Officers:* Colin James Rutter, Secretary; David Gilbert [1969] Director [American]; Michael Jon Gordon [1970] Director; Mark Edward Horsey [1968] Director; Robert Kenneth Campbell Munro [1965] Director/Chief Financial Officer; David Neenan [1965] Director [American/Irish]; Colin James Rutter [1965] Director; Satrajit Saha [1974] Director [Indian]

**Callcredit Limited**
*Incorporated:* 28 March 2000 *Employees:* 700
*Net Worth:* £162,622,000 *Total Assets:* £222,332,000
*Registered Office:* One Park Lane, Leeds, LS3 1EP
*Activities:* Data processing, hosting and related activities
*Parent:* Callcredit Information Group Limited
*Officers:* Colin James Rutter, Secretary; David Gilbert [1969] Director [American]; Michael Jon Gordon [1970] Director; Robert Kenneth Campbell Munro [1965] Director/Chief Financial Officer; David Neenan [1965] Director [American/Irish]; Colin James Rutter [1965] Director/Chief Risk Officer and General Counsel; Satrajit Saha [1974] Director [Indian]

**Callcredit Marketing Limited**
*Incorporated:* 21 July 1992 *Employees:* 184
*Net Worth Deficit:* £7,358,000 *Total Assets:* £16,560,000
*Registered Office:* One Park Lane, Leeds, LS3 1EP
*Activities:* Data processing, hosting and related activities
*Parent:* Callcredit Information Group Limited
*Officers:* Colin James Rutter, Secretary; Michael Jon Gordon [1970] Director; Mark Edward Horsey [1968] Director; Robert Kenneth Campbell Munro [1965] Director/Chief Financial Officer; Colin James Rutter [1965] Director

**The Calls' Riverside Property Company Limited**
*Incorporated:* 8 May 1998 *Employees:* 2
*Net Worth:* £6,111,418 *Total Assets:* £6,218,767
*Registered Office:* Rockley House, Mill Lane, Rockley, Retford, Notts, DN22 0QP
*Activities:* Other letting and operating of own or leased real estate
*Shareholders:* Peter Joseph Rossington; Davina Janet Rossington; Peter Joseph Rossington; Davina Janet Rossington; Peter Joseph Rossington
*Officers:* Davina Janet Rossington, Company Secretary; Oliver Peter Rossington [1984] Director; Peter Joseph Rossington [1949] Director

**Calrec Audio Limited**
*Incorporated:* 6 June 1989 *Employees:* 125
*Net Worth:* £13,221,574 *Total Assets:* £19,231,496
*Registered Office:* Nutclough Mill, Valley Road, Hebden Bridge, W Yorks, HX7 8EZ
*Activities:* Manufacture of other special-purpose machinery n.e.c.
*Parent:* Mixer Bidco Limited
*Officers:* Keith Edwards, Secretary; Nigel Beaumont [1961] Director; Keith Edwards [1965] Finance Director; Henry Goodman [1963] Director

**Calvadon Limited**
*Incorporated:* 29 November 1982
*Net Worth:* £2,544 *Total Assets:* £3,098,384
*Registered Office:* Inglebrook, Micklefield Lane, Rawdon, Leeds, LS19 6BA
*Activities:* Other service activities n.e.c.
*Parent:* Rayner Marketing Holdings Ltd
*Officers:* Debbie Dawn Rayner, Secretary; Simon Peter Rayner [1968] Director

**Calvary Chapel York**
*Incorporated:* 8 October 2010 *Employees:* 5
*Net Worth:* £1,942,082 *Total Assets:* £3,488,124
*Registered Office:* 1 Barbican Road, York, YO10 5AA
*Activities:* Other education n.e.c.
*Officers:* Brian Donald Brodersen [1956] Director/Minister of Religion [American]; David Scott Sylvester [1956] Director/Minister of Religion [American]

**The Calverley Reservoir Sales Company Limited**
*Incorporated:* 30 January 2008 *Employees:* 1
*Net Worth Deficit:* £315,231 *Total Assets:* £3,256,976
*Registered Office:* The Gas Light, Lower Warrengate, Wakefield, W Yorks, WF1 1SA
*Activities:* Buying and selling of own real estate
*Major Shareholder:* David Henry Rock
*Officers:* Alexander Edward Hyett [1962] Director/Property Consultant

**Calverts Carpets Limited**
*Incorporated:* 19 October 1999 *Employees:* 78
*Net Worth:* £5,760,380 *Total Assets:* £7,548,000
*Registered Office:* 29-33 Westgate, Thirsk, N Yorks, YO7 1QR
*Activities:* Retail sale of carpets, rugs, wall and floor coverings in specialised stores
*Major Shareholder:* William Calvert
*Officers:* Suzanne Calvert, Secretary; James William Calvert [1975] Director; Suzanne Calvert [1955] Director; William Mark Calvert [1983] Director; William Calvert [1951] Director

**Calvesten Limited**
*Incorporated:* 24 February 1994 *Employees:* 3
*Net Worth:* £2,626,097 *Total Assets:* £3,712,592
*Registered Office:* c/o Ground Floor, St Paul's House, 23 Park Square, Leeds, LS1 2ND
*Activities:* Other letting and operating of own or leased real estate
*Shareholders:* Granite Trustee Company Ltd (as Trustees for The Calvesten Limited Succession Trust); Diane Catherine Milner (As Trust Protector)
*Officers:* Diane Catherine Milner, Secretary; Diane Catherine Milner [1940] Director; Bridget Catherine Milner-Moore [1970] Director

**Camborne Holdings Limited**
*Incorporated:* 26 July 1974
*Net Worth:* £2,116,749 *Total Assets:* £34,767,500
*Registered Office:* The Watermill, Wheatley Park, Mirfield, W Yorks, WF14 8HE
*Activities:* Other business support service activities n.e.c.
*Parent:* Camira Group Limited
*Officers:* Anthony Stuart Croall, Secretary; Lucy Caroline Bolton [1981] Finance Director; Grant Lindon Russell [1964] Director/Chief Executive

**Cambridge Glasshouse Company Limited**
*Incorporated:* 8 August 2001 *Employees:* 60
*Net Worth:* £3,766,763 *Total Assets:* £6,422,699
*Registered Office:* Wallingfen Park, 236 Main Road, Newport, Brough, E Yorks, HU15 2RH
*Activities:* Other specialised construction activities n.e.c.
*Officers:* Steven Anthony Hinch, Secretary/Director; David Ross Hibbs [1962] Director; Steven Anthony Hinch [1967] Director; John Derrick Holland [1960] Director/Project Engineering

**Cambridge Park Academy Limited**
*Incorporated:* 22 July 2011 *Employees:* 193
*Net Worth:* £2,060,007 *Total Assets:* £4,926,848
*Registered Office:* Cambridge Park Maths & Computing, Cambridge Road, Grimsby, N E Lincs, DN34 5EB
*Activities:* Pre-primary education
*Officers:* Anthony Collins [1962] Director/Semi Retired Carpenter; Mark Eames [1965] Director/Headteacher; Carol Klug [1957] Director/Teacher; Reece Leggett [1993] Director/Lecturer; Vicky McGuire [1974] Director/Teacher; Stephen Andrew Stead [1983] Director/Construction Worker

**Cameron Integrated Services Limited**
*Incorporated:* 31 May 1996
*Net Worth Deficit:* £2,353,144 *Total Assets:* £4,684,755
*Registered Office:* 3 Greengate, Cardale Park, Harrogate, N Yorks, HG3 1GY
*Activities:* Other engineering activities
*Major Shareholder:* Mehdi Kazem Metghalchi
*Officers:* Mehdi Kazem Metghalchi [1945] Director [Iranian]

**Camira Fabrics Limited**
*Incorporated:* 1 February 1988 *Employees:* 262
*Net Worth:* £16,213,720 *Total Assets:* £60,373,840
*Registered Office:* The Watermill, Wheatley Park, Hopton, Mirfield, W Yorks, WF14 8HE
*Activities:* Weaving of textiles
*Parent:* Camborne Holdings Limited
*Officers:* Anthony Stuart Croall, Secretary; Lucy Caroline Bolton [1981] Finance Director; Abigail Lesley Bomford [1980] Creative Director; Nicholas Andrew Brown [1964] Executive Director; Anthony Stuart Croall [1969] Commercial Director; Grant Lindon Russell [1964] Director/Chief Executive; Alan Lloyd Williams [1972] Director/Manufacturing; Mark Terence Young [1967] Group Sales Director

**Camira Group Holdings Limited**
*Incorporated:* 26 March 2015 *Employees:* 693
*Net Worth:* £8,446,963 *Total Assets:* £71,541,760
*Registered Office:* The Watermill, Wheatley Park, Mirfield, W Yorks, WF14 8HE
*Activities:* Activities of head offices
*Shareholder:* Nicholas Andrew Brown
*Officers:* Paul Michael Barnard [1961] Non-Executive Director Chairman; Lucy Caroline Bolton [1981] Finance Director; Abigail Lesley Bomford [1980] Creative Director; Nicholas Andrew Brown [1964] Executive Director; Anthony Stuart Croall [1969] Commercial Director; Edward Jolly [1980] Director/Investment Professional; Grant Lindon Russell [1964] Director; Allen Weaver [1957] Senior Managing Director [American]; Alan Lloyd Williams [1972] Operations Director; Mark Terence Young [1967] Group Sales Director

**Camira Group Ltd**
*Incorporated:* 24 November 2005
*Net Worth:* £606,497 *Total Assets:* £40,953,956
*Registered Office:* The Watermill, Wheatley Park, Mirfield, W Yorks, WF14 8HE
*Activities:* Other business support service activities n.e.c.
*Parent:* Camira Holdings Limited
*Officers:* Anthony Stuart Croall, Secretary; Lucy Caroline Bolton [1981] Finance Director; Abigail Lesley Bomford [1980] Creative Director; Nicholas Andrew Brown [1964] Executive Director; Anthony Stuart Croall [1969] Commercial Director; Grant Lindon Russell [1964] Director/Chief Executive; Alan Lloyd Williams [1972] Director/Manufacturing; Mark Terence Young [1967] Group Sales Director

**Camira Holdings Limited**
*Incorporated:* 1 April 2015
*Net Worth:* £14,941,501 *Total Assets:* £75,375,512
*Registered Office:* The Watermill, Wheatley Park, Mirfield, W Yorks, WF14 8HE
*Activities:* Management consultancy activities other than financial management
*Parent:* Camira Group Holdings Limited
*Officers:* Paul Michael Barnard [1961] Non-Executive Director Chairman; Lucy Caroline Bolton [1981] Finance Director; Abigail Lesley Bomford [1980] Creative Director; Nicholas Andrew Brown [1964] Executive Director; Anthony Stuart Croall [1969] Commercial Director; Edward Jolly [1980] Director/Investment Professional; Grant Lindon Russell [1964] Director; Allen Arthur Weaver [1957] Senior Managing Director [American]; Alan Lloyd Williams [1972] Operations Director; Mark Terence Young [1967] Group Sales Director

**Camira Transport Fabrics Limited**
*Incorporated:* 17 September 2007 *Employees:* 26
*Net Worth:* £2,178,674 *Total Assets:* £11,539,930
*Registered Office:* The Watermill, Wheatley Park, Mirfield, W Yorks, WF14 8HE
*Activities:* Weaving of textiles
*Parent:* Camira Holdsworth Limited
*Officers:* Anthony Stuart Croall, Secretary; Lucy Caroline Bolton [1981] Finance Director; Abigail Lesley Bomford [1980] Creative Director; Nicholas Andrew Brown [1964] Executive Director; Anthony Stuart Croall [1969] Commercial Director; Grant Lindon Russell [1964] Director/Chief Executive; Alan Lloyd Williams [1972] Operations Director; Mark Terence Young [1967] Group Sales Director

**Camira Yarns Limited**
*Incorporated:* 7 February 1923 *Employees:* 96
*Net Worth:* £1,318,431 *Total Assets:* £3,432,334
*Registered Office:* The Watermill, Wheatley Park, Woodbottom, Mirfield, W Yorks, WF14 8HE
*Activities:* Preparation and spinning of textile fibres
*Parent:* Flying Magic Limited
*Officers:* Anthony Stuart Croall, Secretary; Lucy Caroline Bolton [1981] Finance Director; Grant Lindon Russell [1964] Director; Alan Lloyd Williams [1972] Operations Director

**Joseph Camm Farms Limited**
*Incorporated:* 21 March 1962 *Employees:* 18
*Net Worth:* £14,311,667 *Total Assets:* £15,188,856
*Registered Office:* Upper Morton, Babworth, Retford, Notts, DN22 8HG
*Activities:* Growing of cereals (except rice), leguminous crops and oil seeds
*Shareholders:* Ruth Margaret Girdham; Beatrix Mary Easterbrook
*Officers:* Mark Pickard, Secretary; Beatrix Mary Easterbrook [1966] Director/Chartered Accountant; Mark Easterbrook [1966] Director/Brewer; Ruth Margaret Girdham [1959] Director; Margaret Emily Morrell [1931] Director/Farmer

**Cammax Limited**
*Incorporated:* 8 July 1999 *Employees:* 25
*Net Worth:* £1,002,016 *Total Assets:* £3,340,530
*Registered Office:* Unit 2a Willowbridge Way, Whitwood, Castleford, W Yorks, WF10 5NP
*Activities:* Manufacture of other electrical equipment
*Parent:* Cammax Group Limited
*Officers:* Rebecca Rothwell Rooney, Secretary; Julian Paul William Rooney [1964] Managing Director

**Camphill Village Trust Limited (The)**
*Incorporated:* 26 October 1954 *Employees:* 622
*Net Worth:* £104,214,000 *Total Assets:* £106,047,000
*Registered Office:* The Kingfisher Offices, 9 Saville Street, Malton, N Yorks, YO17 7LL
*Activities:* Other residential care activities n.e.c.
*Officers:* Frances Rebecca Anne Wright, Secretary; Timothy John Michael Bishop [1960] Director; Felicity Anne Chadwick-Histed [1963] Director/Partner in Consultancy Publitas Consulting LLP; Christopher Cook [1949] Director/Architect; Stephen George Godwin [1950] Director/Business Development Analyst/Principal; Jean Henderson [1953] Director/Retired; Karen Elizabeth Walker [1955] Director/Education Adviser; Brian Martin Walsh [1960] Executive Director People, Coventry City Council; Lindsey Marie Wishart [1967] Director/Accountant; Jeremy Rupert Young [1960] Director/Research Scientist

**Can-Pack UK Limited**
*Incorporated:* 11 September 2007 *Employees:* 247
*Net Worth:* £54,659,472 *Total Assets:* £91,805,152
*Registered Office:* Plot 18 Skippingdale Industrial Estate, Holyrood Drive, Scunthorpe, N Lincs, DN15 8NN
*Activities:* Manufacture of light metal packaging
*Parent:* Can-Pack Spolka Akcyjna
*Officers:* Philip Fisher, Secretary; Gary Beard [1975] Director; Michael Brooke Burkinshaw [1957] Director; Philip Michael Fisher [1975] Director

**Cancede Limited**
*Incorporated:* 13 November 2009
*Net Worth:* £2,524,000 *Total Assets:* £17,723,000
*Registered Office:* Hilmore House, Gain Lane, Bradford, W Yorks, BD3 7DL
*Activities:* Development of building projects
*Parent:* Optimisation Investments Limited
*Officers:* Jonathan James Burke, Secretary; Jonathan James Burke [1966] Director; Joanna Louise Goff [1978] Finance Director

**Candelisa Limited**
*Incorporated:* 2 April 2008 *Employees:* 18
*Previous:* Candelisa Projects Limited
*Net Worth:* £2,936,816 *Total Assets:* £7,354,347
*Registered Office:* Caroline House, Providence Place, Skipton, N Yorks, BD23 1FB
*Activities:* Construction of domestic buildings
*Shareholders:* Guy Alexander Taylor; Andrew John Phillip; Mirabelle Partners Limited
*Officers:* Dale Walter Chapman [1970] Director; Andrew John Phillip [1963] Director; Guy Alexander Taylor [1973] Director/Property Developer

**The Candlelighters Trust**
*Incorporated:* 10 February 1995 *Employees:* 20
*Net Worth:* £4,299,573 *Total Assets:* £5,343,180
*Registered Office:* 8 Woodhouse Square, Leeds, LS3 1AD
*Activities:* Other human health activities
*Officers:* Lucy Charlotte Fletcher, Secretary; Chiara de Biase [1978] Assistant Director of Patient Services; Yorke Joseph Joan Eaton [1976] Director/Solicitor; Dr Martin Elliott [1967] Director/Doctor; John Robert Goodden [1973] Director/Neurosurgeon; Keith Anthony Hardcastle [1962] Director/Chartered Surveyor & Architect Technicians; David Mayman [1979] Director/Financial Accountant; Susan Mariea Patterson [1963] Director/Business Consultant; Rev Stephen Charles Redman [1959] Director/Christian Minister; Dr Edward Michael Richards [1963] Director/Doctor; Roger John Stocker [1967] Director; Patricia Thompson [1960] Director/Nurse

**Canley Food Packers Ltd**
*Incorporated:* 19 June 2002 *Employees:* 21
*Net Worth:* £2,670,883 *Total Assets:* £3,287,177
*Registered Office:* Food Factory, Canley Food Packers, Wharf Lane, Crowle, N Lincs, DN17 4JW
*Activities:* Packaging activities
*Major Shareholder:* Ian Johnson
*Officers:* Ian Johnson [1960] Director/Food Packer; Mary Anne Johnson [1952] Director

**Canons Garth LLP**
*Incorporated:* 19 June 2015
*Total Assets:* £3,149,078
*Registered Office:* 33 George Street, Wakefield, W Yorks, WF1 1LX

**Cap Hpi Limited**
*Incorporated:* 17 April 2012 *Employees:* 167
*Previous:* CAP Automotive Limited
*Net Worth:* £152,688,992 *Total Assets:* £175,327,008
*Registered Office:* Capitol House, Bond Court, Leeds, LS1 5EZ
*Activities:* Data processing, hosting and related activities
*Parent:* HPI Holding Limited
*Officers:* Anthony Aquila [1964] Director/Chairman [American]; Jason Michael Brady [1968] Director/General Counsel [American]; Renato Carlo Giger [1960] Director [Swiss]; Franciscus Johanes Carolus Overtoom [1966] Director/Regional Finance Officer [Dutch]; Christopher Wright [1971] Director

**The Capernwray Missionary Fellowship of Torchbearers**
*Incorporated:* 2 June 1998 *Employees:* 33
*Net Worth:* £5,617,353 *Total Assets:* £6,319,417
*Registered Office:* Capernwray Hall, Capernwray, Carnforth, Lancs, LA6 1AG
*Activities:* Other accommodation
*Officers:* Philip Charles Burt, Secretary; Peter Maiden [1948] Director/Retired; Rebecca Silver [1958] Director/Teacher; Brian Joseph Sweeney [1957] Director; Michael Thompson [1954] Director/Solicitor; Neil Wrigley [1944] Director/Retired

**Capitol Park Leeds PLC**
*Incorporated:* 24 May 1996
*Net Worth:* £3,958,476 *Total Assets:* £4,509,062
*Registered Office:* 2nd Floor, Victoria Wharf, 4 The Embankment, Sovereign Street, Leeds, LS1 4BA
*Activities:* Development of building projects
*Parent:* Sterling Capitol PLC
*Officers:* James John Robert Murray [1990] Director; Peter Ian Walker [1971] Director

**Car Care Plan (Holdings) Limited**
*Incorporated:* 7 November 1977
*Net Worth:* £29,925,000 *Total Assets:* £30,757,000
*Registered Office:* Jubilee House, 5 Mid Point Business Park, Thornbury, W Yorks, BD3 7AG
*Activities:* Non-life insurance
*Parent:* Amtrust International Limited
*Officers:* Gavin William Work Tinch, Secretary; Jeremy Edward Cadle [1965] Director/Lawyer; Timothy John Heavisides [1959] Director/Chief Executive; John Anthony Levin [1963] Director; Paul Graeme Newton [1959] Director; Benjamin Seamus Russell [1972] Sales Director; Simon Jonathan Wright [1966] Director/Chartered Accountant

**Car Care Plan Limited**
*Incorporated:* 26 May 1965 *Employees:* 307
*Net Worth:* £13,649,000 *Total Assets:* £44,982,000
*Registered Office:* Jubilee House, 5 Mid Point Business Park, Thornbury, W Yorks, BD3 7AG
*Activities:* Non-life insurance
*Parent:* Car Care Plan (Holdings) Limited
*Officers:* Gavin William Work Tinch, Secretary; Jeremy Edward Cadle [1965] Director/Lawyer; Timothy John Heavisides [1959] Director/Chief Executive; John Anthony Levin [1963] Director; Paul Graeme Newton [1959] Finance Director; Benjamin Seamus Russell [1972] Sales Director; Simon Jonathan Wright [1966] Director/Chartered Accountant

**Carafax Limited**
*Incorporated:* 31 December 1984 *Employees:* 26
*Net Worth:* £3,992,958 *Total Assets:* £5,916,370
*Registered Office:* Rotterdam Road, Sutton Fields, Hull, HU7 0XD
*Activities:* Wholesale of hardware, plumbing and heating equipment and supplies
*Major Shareholder:* David Frederick Robinson
*Officers:* Carl Burton, Secretary; Carl Burton [1957] Director; John David Cummings [1949] Director; David Frederick Robinson [1946] Director; Daniel John Sampson [1979] Director

**Caravan Guard Limited**
*Incorporated:* 19 July 2000 *Employees:* 118
*Net Worth:* £5,589,531 *Total Assets:* £10,512,736
*Registered Office:* Caravan Guard Ltd, New Road, Halifax, W Yorks, HX1 2JZ
*Activities:* Activities of insurance agents and brokers
*Shareholders:* Peter Melvyn Wilby; Nora Harriet Margaret Wilby
*Officers:* Graham Lee Dobson, Secretary; Sally Victoria Alexandra Crofts [1974] Director/Insurance; Louise Jane Gabriella Menzies [1976] Director - Insurance Intermediary; Christopher Wayne Nettleton [1971] Director/Insurance Broker; Nora Harriet Margaret Wilby [1949] Director/Administrator; Peter Melvyn Wilby [1947] Director/Insurance Broker; Ryan Alexander James Wilby [1978] Director - Insurance Intermediary

**Carclo Holding Limited**
*Incorporated:* 22 March 2002
*Net Worth:* £33,496,088 *Total Assets:* £33,496,088
*Registered Office:* P O Box 88, 27 Dewsbury Road, Ossett, W Yorks, WF5 9WS
*Activities:* Activities of head offices
*Parent:* Carclo PLC
*Officers:* Richard John Ottaway, Secretary; Christopher John Malley [1967] Director; Richard John Ottaway [1971] Director/Chartered Accountant

**Carclo Overseas Holdings Limited**
*Incorporated:* 15 April 1948
*Net Worth:* £415,756 *Total Assets:* £57,233,328
*Registered Office:* P O Box 88, 27 Dewsbury Road, Ossett, W Yorks, WF5 9WS
*Activities:* Activities of head offices
*Parent:* Carclo PLC
*Officers:* Richard John Ottaway, Secretary; Christopher John Malley [1967] Director; Richard John Ottaway [1971] Director/Chartered Accountant

**Carclo PLC**
*Incorporated:* 8 March 1924 *Employees:* 1,442
*Net Worth:* £52,045,000 *Total Assets:* £160,087,008
*Registered Office:* P O Box 88, 27 Dewsbury Road, Ossett, W Yorks, WF5 9WS
*Activities:* Manufacture of other plastic products
*Officers:* Richard John Ottaway, Secretary; Sarah Louise Matthews-Demers [1975] Director; Jonathan Mark Oatley [1968] Director; Mark Rollins [1962] Director; Peter Charles Slabbert [1962] Director/Chartered Accountant [Irish]; James David Gerard Toohey [1957] Director [Irish]

**Carclo Technical Plastics Limited**
*Incorporated:* 7 August 1995 *Employees:* 206
*Net Worth Deficit:* £847,349 *Total Assets:* £27,493,020
*Registered Office:* P O Box 88, 27 Dewsbury Road, Ossett, W Yorks, WF5 9WS
*Activities:* Manufacture of other plastic products
*Parent:* Carclo PLC
*Officers:* Richard John Ottaway, Secretary; Christopher John Malley [1967] Director; Richard John Ottaway [1971] Director/Chartered Accountant; Patrick Nigel Ward [1963] Director

**Card Factory PLC**
*Incorporated:* 17 April 2014 *Employees:* 9,936
*Net Worth:* £218,400,000 *Total Assets:* £446,500,000
*Registered Office:* Century House, Brunel Road, 41 Industrial Estate, Wakefield, W Yorks, WF2 0XG
*Activities:* Other retail sale in non-specialised stores
*Officers:* Shiv Sibal, Secretary; Karen Rachael Hubbard [1964] Director; Kristian Brian Lee [1974] Director; Paul McCrudden [1978] Director; Paul Stephen Moody [1957] Director/Chairman; Octavia Kate Morley [1968] Director; David Anthony Stead [1958] Director; Roger Mark Whiteside [1958] Director

**Card Protection Plan Limited**
*Incorporated:* 14 April 1980 *Employees:* 143
*Net Worth:* £13,453,865 *Total Assets:* £22,721,984
*Registered Office:* Holgate Park, York, YO26 4GA
*Activities:* Non-life insurance
*Parent:* CPP Holdings Limited
*Officers:* Lorraine Grace Beavis, Secretary; Andrew Kerr Adam Ferguson [1951] Director; David Anthony Ross [1963] Director; Jason Carl Walsh [1971] Director/Chief Executive Officer

**Cardale Asset Management Limited**
*Incorporated:* 11 April 2003 *Employees:* 60
*Net Worth:* £5,586,426 *Total Assets:* £11,074,268
*Registered Office:* 2 Greengate, Cardale Park, Harrogate, N Yorks, HG3 1GY
*Activities:* Fund management activities
*Officers:* Ashley Lawrence Alger [1957] Director/Stockbroker; Peter Richard Heckingbottom [1965] Director; Mark Puleikis [1968] Director; Andrew Mark Tod [1967] Director; Richard Whiteley [1965] Director/Stockbroker

**Cardale Infrastructure Investments Limited**
*Incorporated:* 17 April 2012
*Net Worth Deficit:* £17,587,112 *Total Assets:* £74,881,496
*Registered Office:* 4 Greengate, Cardale Park, Harrogate, N Yorks, HG3 1GY
*Activities:* Activities of head offices
*Parent:* Cardale PFI Investments Limited
*Officers:* Alexander Toby Shedden Parry, Secretary; Robert John Austin [1964] Director; Peter Paul Copley [1956] Director; Alexander Toby Shedden Parry [1976] Director; Christopher Justin Taee [1968] Director; Nigel Duncan Taee [1961] Director

**Cardale Park Properties Ltd**
*Incorporated:* 15 October 2004 *Employees:* 3
*Net Worth:* £1,261,405 *Total Assets:* £5,155,151
*Registered Office:* 1 Cardale Park, Beckwith Head Road, Harrogate, N Yorks, HG3 1RZ
*Activities:* Buying and selling of own real estate
*Major Shareholder:* James Rhodes Beresford
*Officers:* David Andrew Oxley, Secretary; James Rhodes Beresford [1950] Director; Linda Beresford [1951] Director; Chloe Murray [1981] Director; David Andrew Oxley [1969] Director/Accountant

**Cardale PFI Investments Limited**
*Incorporated:* 26 March 2015 *Employees:* 5
*Net Worth Deficit:* £70,411,464 *Total Assets:* £350,339,904
*Registered Office:* 4 Greengate, Cardale Park, Harrogate, N Yorks, HG3 1GY
*Activities:* Activities of head offices
*Shareholder:* Nigel Duncan Taee
*Officers:* Alexander Parry, Secretary; Robert John Austin [1964] Director; Peter Paul Copley [1956] Director; Alexander Toby Shedden Parry [1976] Director; Christopher Justin Taee [1968] Director; Nigel Duncan Taee [1961] Director

**Cardinal Limited**
*Incorporated:* 14 October 2008 *Employees:* 209
*Net Worth:* £10,941,086 *Total Assets:* £23,069,344
*Registered Office:* Fernhill House, Battye Street, Bradford, W Yorks, BD4 8AG
*Activities:* Activities of head offices
*Officers:* Mark Simpson, Secretary; Brian Considine [1938] Director; Timothy Brian Considine [1969] Director

**Cardinal Project Management Limited**
*Incorporated:* 23 January 1998 *Employees:* 44
*Net Worth:* £3,897,261 *Total Assets:* £8,918,508
*Registered Office:* Fernhill House, Battye Street, Bradford, W Yorks, BD4 8AG
*Activities:* Other construction installation
*Parent:* Cardinal Ltd
*Officers:* Mark Simpson, Secretary; Brian Considine [1938] Director; Timothy Brian Considine [1969] Director/Systems

**Cardinal Shopfitting + Systems Limited**
*Incorporated:* 4 September 1989 *Employees:* 155
*Net Worth:* £5,079,883 *Total Assets:* £10,347,988
*Registered Office:* Fernhill House, Battye Street, Bradford, W Yorks, BD4 8AG
*Activities:* Manufacture of other fabricated metal products n.e.c.
*Parent:* Cardinal Ltd
*Officers:* Mark Simpson, Secretary; Brian Considine [1938] Director; Timothy Brian Considine [1969] Director

**Care & Recreation Holdings Limited**
*Incorporated:* 19 September 1996 *Employees:* 646
*Net Worth:* £15,846,389 *Total Assets:* £76,508,272
*Registered Office:* Thorpe Underwood Hall, Great Ouseburn, York, YO5 9SZ
*Activities:* Other business support service activities n.e.c.
*Officers:* Christopher James Hall, Secretary; Christopher James Hall [1969] Director/Chartered Accountant; Amy Katherine Martin [1983] Director; Francis David Martin [1967] Director/Business Executive

**Care Holdings Limited**
*Incorporated:* 12 March 2009 *Employees:* 260
*Net Worth:* £6,608,154 *Total Assets:* £12,543,189
*Registered Office:* Rouse House, 2 Wyther Lane, Kirkstall, Leeds, LS5 3BT
*Activities:* Activities of other holding companies n.e.c.
*Major Shareholder:* Luiz Guilherme
*Officers:* Lynsey Guilherme, Secretary; Luiz Guilherme [1960] Director; Lynsey Guilherme [1974] Director

**Carillion Powerlines Limited**
*Incorporated:* 10 February 2014
*Total Assets:* £15,912,000
*Registered Office:* Unit 4 Potteric Carr Industrial Estate, Potteric Carr Road, Doncaster, S Yorks, DN4 5NP
*Activities:* Other construction installation
*Parent:* SPL Powerlines UK Limited
*Officers:* Berthold Bartsch [1973] Director [Austrian]; Gerhard Ehringer [1965] Director [Austrian]; Martin William Hawley [1963] Director; Guenter Kielmayer [1966] Director [Austrian]

**Caring 4 Croydon Limited**
*Incorporated:* 7 April 2006
*Net Worth Deficit:* £5,116,116 *Total Assets:* £24,892,668
*Registered Office:* 4 Greengate, Cardale Park, Harrogate, N Yorks, HG3 1GY
*Activities:* Other human health activities
*Parent:* Caring 4 Croyon Holdings Limited
*Officers:* Paul William Noake, Secretary; Robert John Austin [1964] Director; Alastair William Hopps [1986] Director/Chartered Accountant; Alexander Toby Shedden Parry [1976] Director/Chartered Accountant; Elizabeth Frances Range [1953] Director/Surveyor

**Carlac Group Limited**
*Incorporated:* 5 July 2004 *Employees:* 89
*Net Worth:* £1,274,241 *Total Assets:* £4,967,024
*Registered Office:* 16-17 Ashfield Way, Whitehall Estate, Leeds, LS12 5JB
*Activities:* Activities of head offices
*Shareholders:* Neil Firth; Melanie Firth
*Officers:* Mark Robert Long, Secretary; Melanie Firth [1963] Director; Neil Firth [1961] Director; Mark Robert Long [1976] Finance Director

**Carlac Limited**
*Incorporated:* 4 June 1969 *Employees:* 89
*Net Worth:* £1,603,642 *Total Assets:* £5,296,316
*Registered Office:* Units 16-17 Ashfield Way, Whitehall Road Industrial Estate, Leeds, LS12 5JB
*Activities:* Wholesale trade of motor vehicle parts and accessories
*Shareholders:* Neil Firth; Melanie Firth
*Officers:* Mark Robert Long, Secretary; Melanie Firth [1963] Director/Sales Executive; Neil Firth [1961] Managing Director; Mark Robert Long [1976] Finance Director

**Carlisle Brass Limited**
*Incorporated:* 27 May 1986 *Employees:* 153
*Net Worth:* £30,777,000 *Total Assets:* £47,148,000
*Registered Office:* c/o Arran Isle Limited, Brindley House, Premier Way, Lowfields Business Park, Elland, W Yorks, HX5 9HF
*Activities:* Non-specialised wholesale trade
*Parent:* Arran Isle Holdings Limited
*Officers:* Rachel Helen Balbi, Secretary; Charlotte Crisp [1971] Finance Director; Angus Grant [1980] Director; Michael James Russell Richards [1964] Director; Mark Wallis [1964] Director; Martin Wardhaugh [1960] Director; Mark Steven Wild [1960] Director/Accountant

**Carlton Court Investments Limited**
*Incorporated:* 23 April 2014 *Employees:* 3
*Net Worth:* £37,768,000 *Total Assets:* £52,106,000
*Registered Office:* Clipper Logistics Group, Gelderd Road, Leeds, LS12 6LT
*Activities:* Activities of venture and development capital companies
*Parent:* Knaresborough Investments Ltd
*Officers:* Marianne Hodgkiss, Secretary; David Arthur Hodkin [1961] Director; Guy Collingwood Jackson [1957] Director/Company Secretary; Steven Nicholas Parkin [1960] Director

**Carmel Education Trust**
*Incorporated:* 13 October 2011 *Employees:* 556
*Net Worth:* £7,146,000 *Total Assets:* £13,294,000
*Registered Office:* Carmel RC College, The Headlands, Darlington, Co Durham, DL3 8RW
*Activities:* General secondary education
*Officers:* Rev John Butters [1948] Director/Catholic Priest; James Matthew Cunningham [1961] Director/Police Officer; Peter Malcolm Frank [1946] Director/Retired Headteacher; Councillor Cynthia Beaver Hughes [1961] Director/Political and Legal Researcher; Maria Matthews [1952] Director/Headteacher (Retired); Patricia Ann McTimoney [1940] Director/Retired Headteacher; Catherine Alison Powell [1967] Director/Civil Servant; Maura Regan [1957] Director/Principal and Chief Executive Officer; Christopher Ronald Wiper [1956] Director/Solicitor

**Carnaby Caravans Group Limited**
*Incorporated:* 10 June 2015 *Employees:* 124
*Net Worth:* £3,339,440 *Total Assets:* £13,002,500
*Registered Office:* Lancaster Road, Carnaby Industrial Estate, Carnaby, Bridlington, E Yorks, YO15 3QY
*Activities:* Activities of head offices
*Major Shareholder:* Nigel Andrew Smailes
*Officers:* Timothy Meadley [1964] Operations Director; Nigel Andrew Smailes [1963] Director

**Carnaby Caravans Limited**
*Incorporated:* 7 January 1976 *Employees:* 124
*Net Worth:* £7,085,509 *Total Assets:* £14,281,634
*Registered Office:* Lancaster Road, Carnaby Industrial Estate, Carnaby, Bridlington, E Yorks, YO15 3QY
*Activities:* Manufacture of caravans
*Parent:* Carnaby Caravans Group Ltd
*Officers:* Timothy Meadley [1964] Director; Nigel Andrew Smailes [1963] Director/Chief Executive; John Stewart Wigglesworth [1965] UK Sales Director

**CarnaudMetalbox Engineering Limited**
*Incorporated:* 10 September 1949 *Employees:* 434
*Net Worth:* £24,528,000 *Total Assets:* £77,520,000
*Registered Office:* Dockfield Road, Shipley, W Yorks, BD17 7AY
*Activities:* Manufacture of machinery for food, beverage and tobacco processing
*Parent:* Crown Packaging Manufacturing UK Limited
*Officers:* Jennifer Patricia Simpson, Secretary; John Patrick Beardsley [1970] Director; Paul William Browett [1961] Director/Vice President/Treasurer; Robert Brown [1962] Director/Head of Finance; Richard Andrew Forti [1953] Director/SVP Business Support [American]; Andrew George Truelove [1973] Director/General Manager

**Carr Mount Estate Limited**
*Incorporated:* 16 April 2008
*Net Worth Deficit:* £568,676 *Total Assets:* £3,312,729
*Registered Office:* Carr Mount, The Carrs, Ruswarp, Whitby, N Yorks, YO21 1RP
*Activities:* Support services to forestry
*Major Shareholder:* Valerie Uppington
*Officers:* Valerie Uppington, Secretary; Valerie Uppington [1960] Director; William John Uppington [1960] Director

**Carrington House Yorkshire Limited**
*Incorporated:* 29 June 2011 *Employees:* 2
*Net Worth:* £1,761,623 *Total Assets:* £4,523,014
*Registered Office:* BCL House, 2 Pavilion Business Park, Royds Hall Road, Leeds, LS12 6AJ
*Activities:* Other letting and operating of own or leased real estate
*Major Shareholder:* Ian Patrick Humphreys
*Officers:* Ian Patrick Humphreys [1964] Director

**Cars 2 Limited**
*Incorporated:* 10 March 2006 *Employees:* 133
*Net Worth:* £5,702,671 *Total Assets:* £17,076,940
*Registered Office:* Waldorf Way, Denby Dale Road, Wakefield, W Yorks, WF2 8DH
*Activities:* Sale of new cars and light motor vehicles
*Major Shareholder:* Allan George Otley
*Officers:* Lindsay Anne Collier, Secretary; Lindsay Anne Collier [1977] Finance Director; Allan George Otley [1961] Director; Callum Thomas Otley [1991] Director; Scott Ledgard Otley [1989] Director

**Richard Carter,Limited**
*Incorporated:* 22 December 1909 *Employees:* 33
*Net Worth:* £4,816,067 *Total Assets:* £5,840,720
*Registered Office:* Neiley Works, 72 New Mill Road, Honley, Huddersfield, W Yorks, HD7 2QQ
*Activities:* Other manufacturing n.e.c.
*Shareholders:* Richard Carter; Charmaine Caroline Carter
*Officers:* Charmaine Caroline Carter [1963] Director; Richard Carter [1961] Director; William Green [1981] Director/Engineer

**Cartonplast (UK) Limited**
*Incorporated:* 18 October 2000 *Employees:* 30
*Net Worth:* £3,558,147 *Total Assets:* £5,600,874
*Registered Office:* Wood Lea, Westoby Lane, Barrow upon Humber, N Lincs, DN19 7DJ
*Activities:* Other food services
*Officers:* Sascha Hans Kripgans, Secretary; Michael Heinrich Heikenfeld [1965] Director [German]; Thomas Edgar Krausch [1964] Director/Manager [German]; Paul Michael Picton [1969] Managing Director

**Carus Green Limited**
*Incorporated:* 21 May 2010 *Employees:* 30
*Net Worth:* £2,554,554 *Total Assets:* £5,998,833
*Registered Office:* Carus Green Golf Club, Burneside Road, Kendal, Cumbria, LA9 6EB
*Activities:* Activities of sport clubs
*Shareholders:* Maurice David Cotter; Graham Charnley Curtin
*Officers:* Maurice David Cotter [1958] Director; Graham Charnley Curtin [1969] Director; Marjorie Yvonne Curtin [1930] Director

**Carver Engineering Holdings Limited**
*Incorporated:* 4 December 2013 *Employees:* 51
*Net Worth:* £7,056,509 *Total Assets:* £9,023,925
*Registered Office:* 11 Brunel Close, Brunel Industrial Estate, Blythe Road, Doncaster, S Yorks, DN11 8QA
*Activities:* Activities of other holding companies n.e.c.
*Shareholders:* Jeff's Management Services; Tim's Management Services Ltd; Phil's Management Services Ltd
*Officers:* Jeffrey Molloy [1958] Director; Philip Molloy [1963] Director; Timothy John Sheppard [1957] Director

**Carver Engineering Services Limited**
*Incorporated:* 29 September 2005 *Employees:* 50
*Net Worth:* £5,343,763 *Total Assets:* £7,671,341
*Registered Office:* 11 Brunel Close, Brunel Industrial Estate, Blyth Road, Harworth, Doncaster, S Yorks, DN11 8QA
*Activities:* Manufacture of metal structures and parts of structures
*Shareholder:* Carver Engineering Holdings Limited
*Officers:* Hayley Stubbs, Secretary; Alan Flint [1958] Director; Peter Paul Lees [1971] Director; Jeffrey Molloy [1958] Works Director; Philip Molloy [1963] Works Director; Timothy John Sheppard [1957] Director; Barry John Simms [1983] Director; Neil Dean Simms [1981] Director

**Cascade Homes Ltd**
*Incorporated:* 19 June 2001
*Net Worth:* £1,052,540 *Total Assets:* £3,089,884
*Registered Office:* 10 Karnac Road, Leeds, LS8 5BL
*Activities:* Management of real estate on a fee or contract basis
*Major Shareholder:* Mumtaz Hussain
*Officers:* Haleem Hussain, Secretary/Director; Haleem Hussain [1980] Director; Mumtaz Hussain [1952] Director

**Cash Converters Yorkshire Limited**
*Incorporated:* 20 August 2007 *Employees:* 213
*Net Worth:* £729,738 *Total Assets:* £4,339,962
*Registered Office:* 28 Prescott Street, Halifax, W Yorks, HX1 2JL
*Activities:* Retail sale of other second-hand goods in stores (not incl. antiques)
*Parent:* JBG Holdings Limited
*Officers:* James Peter Conway Spratley, Secretary/Director; Ben Walter Cox [1986] Director; Gordon Walter Cox [1949] Director; James Peter Conway Spratley [1959] Director

**Cashel Limited**
*Incorporated:* 4 April 2001 *Employees:* 4
*Net Worth Deficit:* £2,350,000 *Total Assets:* £53,765,000
*Registered Office:* Headlands Lane, Knottingley, W Yorks, WF11 0HP
*Activities:* Financial leasing
*Parent:* Ardagh Packaging Holdings Limited
*Officers:* Keith Jeffrey Swindell, Secretary; David John Matthews [1964] Director/Chief Financial Officer; John Passant [1952] Director; Mark Rozmus [1962] Director; Keith Jeffrey Swindell [1959] Director/Accountant

**Cashmere Fibres International Limited**
*Incorporated:* 8 March 1999 *Employees:* 10
*Net Worth:* £33,300 *Total Assets:* £3,604,690
*Registered Office:* Parkview Mills, Raymond Street, Bradford, W Yorks, BD5 8DT
*Activities:* Wholesale of textiles
*Officers:* David Michael Lee [1956] Director; David Kenneth Mallin [1961] Director

**Caspian Group Limited**
*Incorporated:* 15 April 1992 *Employees:* 42
*Previous:* Caspian Access and Plant Hire Limited
*Net Worth:* £2,721,445 *Total Assets:* £7,658,355
*Registered Office:* 115 Cleveland Street, Hull, HU8 7AU
*Activities:* Scaffold erection
*Shareholders:* Victor Neil Garrison; Robert Charles Tyler; Rachel Sarah Garrison; Joan Margaret Tyler
*Officers:* Rachel Sarah Garrison, Secretary; Neil Victor Garrison [1961] Director; Robert Charles Tyler [1945] Director

**Cassellie Limited**
*Incorporated:* 12 June 2009 *Employees:* 77
*Net Worth:* £3,613,396 *Total Assets:* £15,320,947
*Registered Office:* Unit 1-6 Howden Way, Morley, Leeds, LS27 0TF
*Activities:* Wholesale of hardware, plumbing and heating equipment and supplies
*Parent:* Mobility Group Limited
*Officers:* James Christopher Casey [1980] Director; Paul Delaney [1960] Director; Lee Richard Ellis [1972] Director; Annabel Claire Mantel [1978] Director; Lawrence Edward Warriner [1960] Director

**Casterton Leisure Limited**
*Incorporated:* 1 September 1989 *Employees:* 120
*Net Worth:* £6,842,434 *Total Assets:* £9,029,864
*Registered Office:* Priory Close, St Mary's Gate, Lancaster, LA1 1XB
*Activities:* Hotels and similar accommodation
*Major Shareholder:* Eric Wildsmith
*Officers:* Claire Frances Wildsmith, Secretary; Andrew James Wildsmith [1977] Director; Claire Frances Wildsmith [1944] Director; Eric Wildsmith [1945] Director

**Castle 1 Limited**
*Incorporated:* 9 August 2007
*Net Worth:* £437,824,000 *Total Assets:* £527,662,016
*Registered Office:* The Waterfront, Lakeside Boulevard, Doncaster, S Yorks, DN4 5PL
*Activities:* Activities of head offices
*Parent:* K & A Merger Limited
*Officers:* Timothy Mark Beale [1976] Director; Mark Richard Priest [1966] Director; James Michael Douglas Thomson [1966] Director

**Castle Crown Properties Limited**
*Incorporated:* 23 January 2014 *Employees:* 2
*Net Worth:* £8,110,460 *Total Assets:* £33,731,720
*Registered Office:* Rookwith House, Rookwith, Ripon, N Yorks, HG4 4AY
*Activities:* Residents property management
*Shareholders:* Victoria Caroline Jones; Edward James Readdie Page
*Officers:* Victoria Caroline Jones [1979] Director; Edward James Readdie Page [1981] Director

**Castle Hall Academy Trust**
*Incorporated:* 2 August 2011 *Employees:* 117
*Net Worth:* £4,748,000 *Total Assets:* £6,431,000
*Registered Office:* Castle Hall Academy, Richard Thorpe Avenue, Mirfield, W Yorks, WF14 9PH
*Activities:* General secondary education
*Officers:* Debra Neve, Secretary; Kathleen Bronwen Bentall [1944] Director/Retired; Jodie Boyd [1982] Director/Lecturer; Clare Farmer [1964] Director; Anne Patricia Halmshaw [1953] Director/Retired; Nicola Louise Hampshire [1972] Director/Service Development Manager; Zillah Inman [1974] Director/Teacher; Vasant Patel [1962] Governor/Director; Andrew David Pugh [1963] Director/Secondary Headteacher; John Reginald Robinson [1955] Director/Manager; Elizabeth Louise Stephenson [1969] Director/Beauty Salon

**Castle Industrial Supplies Ltd**
*Incorporated:* 30 March 2010 *Employees:* 25
*Net Worth:* £4,098,479 *Total Assets:* £5,993,190
*Registered Office:* Unit 6 Oakwood Way, Carnforth Business Park, Carnforth, Lancs, LA5 9FD
*Activities:* Non-specialised wholesale trade
*Shareholder:* Christopher Lawrence James
*Officers:* Christopher Lawrence James [1972] Director/Sales Manager; Kenneth Ivor James [1944] Director/Business Partner

**Castle Residential Properties Limited**
*Incorporated:* 11 February 2004 *Employees:* 8
*Net Worth:* £579,255 *Total Assets:* £4,814,799
*Registered Office:* 23 Otley Road, Shipley, Bradford, BD17 7DH
*Activities:* Construction of commercial buildings
*Shareholder:* Zamir Ahmed Hussain
*Officers:* Zamir Ahmed Hussain, Secretary/Management Consultant; Shakeel Hussain [1972] Director; Zamir Ahmed Hussain [1961] Director/Management Consultant

**Castlecrafts Limited**
*Incorporated:* 3 July 1954 *Employees:* 203
*Net Worth:* £80,374,000 *Total Assets:* £163,714,000
*Registered Office:* Dewhirst House, Westgate, Driffield, E Yorks, YO25 6TH
*Activities:* Manufacture of other men's outerwear
*Parent:* Dewhirst Group Limited
*Officers:* Christopher John Wilde, Secretary; David Witt [1953] Director; Anthony James Mark Wood [1960] Director

**Castleford Academy Trust**
*Incorporated:* 1 March 2011 *Employees:* 379
*Net Worth:* £15,163,000 *Total Assets:* £20,605,000
*Registered Office:* Castleford Academy, Ferrybridge Road, Castleford, W Yorks, WF10 4JQ
*Activities:* General secondary education
*Officers:* Samantha Lee Stevens, Secretary; Josephine Ann Budby [1965] Finance Director; Adam Neil Fletcher [1979] Director/Solicitor; John Hughes [1953] Director/Trade Union Convenor; Marie Hunter [1957] Director/Retired Headteacher; John Iveson [1966] Director/Retired; Jennifer McNichol [1953] Director/Retired Headteacher; John Morrison [1956] Resources Director; George Paul Panayiotou [1979] Director/Headteacher; Angela Pool [1972] Accounts Director; Sally Wright [1978] Director/Accountant

**Castleford Rugby League Football Club Limited (The)**
*Incorporated:* 15 June 1926 *Employees:* 135
*Net Worth:* £729,657 *Total Assets:* £4,033,585
*Registered Office:* The Jungle, Wheldon Road, Castleford, W Yorks, WF10 2SD
*Activities:* Activities of sport clubs
*Shareholders:* Janet Elaine Fulton; James Ian Fulton
*Officers:* Robert Clarkson, Secretary; John Duff [1969] Director; James Ian Fulton [1961] Director/Farmer; Mark Stuart Grattan [1968] Commercial Director; Dion Lowe [1969] Director/Car Dealer; Steven Vause [1957] Director

**Castlehouse Construction Ltd**
*Incorporated:* 26 February 2009
*Net Worth:* £1,071,662 *Total Assets:* £3,942,378
*Registered Office:* Book End Farm, Timble, Otley, W Yorks, LS21 2NN
*Activities:* Construction of commercial buildings
*Shareholders:* Richard Albert Lumley; Frank Kofler; Alison Julie Bates Lumley
*Officers:* Alison Julie Bates Lumley, Secretary; Andrew Nigel Barrett [1968] Commercial Director; Philip John Dewell [1965] Construction Director; Frank Kofler [1956] Director/Construction Manager; Richard Albert Lumley [1953] Director/Developer

**Castleton Group Limited**
*Incorporated:* 9 April 2008 *Employees:* 68
*Net Worth:* £2,404,999 *Total Assets:* £10,911,922
*Registered Office:* 3 Greengate, Cardale Park, Harrogate, N Yorks, HG3 1GY
*Activities:* Activities of head offices
*Major Shareholder:* Giles Castleton
*Officers:* Sarah Castleton, Secretary; Giles Castleton [1969] Director

**Castlewood Securities Limited**
*Incorporated:* 3 April 1995 *Employees:* 2
*Net Worth:* £3,673,000 *Total Assets:* £5,433,000
*Registered Office:* The Inspire, Hornbeam Square West, Harrogate, N Yorks, HG2 8PA
*Activities:* Activities of head offices
*Parent:* Martins Bidco Limited
*Officers:* James Alexander Burrell [1974] Director; Anthony Gerrard Troy [1962] Director [Irish]

**Caswick Limited**
*Incorporated:* 7 November 1985 *Employees:* 17
*Net Worth:* £2,658,243 *Total Assets:* £3,333,316
*Registered Office:* Sandtoft Road, Belton, Doncaster, S Yorks, DN9 1PN
*Activities:* Manufacture of builders ware of plastic
*Major Shareholder:* Gillian Cawte
*Officers:* Gillian Cawte, Secretary/Director; Christopher John Cawte [1950] Director/Engineer; Gillian Cawte [1958] Director/Secretary; Paul Davies [1955] Director

**Cat Tech (Europe) Limited**
*Incorporated:* 22 February 2002 *Employees:* 34
*Net Worth:* £1,827,931 *Total Assets:* £6,307,947
*Registered Office:* 1 South Park Road, South Park Industrial Estate, Scunthorpe, N Lincs, DN17 2BY
*Activities:* Other specialised construction activities n.e.c.
*Parent:* Cat Tech International Ltd
*Officers:* Karl Barry Thew [1958] Director [New Zealander]; Joe Paul Walker [1974] Director/Accountant

**Cat Tech International Limited**
*Incorporated:* 13 December 2011 *Employees:* 95
*Net Worth:* £46,536 *Total Assets:* £4,877,814
*Registered Office:* 1 South Park Road, Scunthorpe, N Lincs, DN17 2BY
*Activities:* Activities of head offices
*Major Shareholder:* Karl Barry Thew
*Officers:* Andrew Bryant Symmonds [1970] Director/Accountant; Karl Barry Thew [1958] Director [New Zealander]; Joe Paul Walker [1974] Director/Accountant

**Cater-Kwik Group Limited**
*Incorporated:* 8 March 2016
*Net Worth:* £1,729,259 *Total Assets:* £3,562,797
*Registered Office:* The Lakeland Catering Centre, Newlands, Ulverston, Cumbria, LA12 7QQ
*Activities:* Activities of other holding companies n.e.c.
*Major Shareholder:* Matthew Clifford Mayvers
*Officers:* Faye Lisa Mayvers [1972] Director; Matthew Clifford Mayvers [1974] Director

**Cater-Kwik Limited**
*Incorporated:* 7 May 2002 *Employees:* 43
*Net Worth:* £1,823,169 *Total Assets:* £5,177,370
*Registered Office:* The Lakeland Catering Centre, Newlands, Ulverston, Cumbria, LA12 7QQ
*Activities:* Retail of furniture, lighting, and similar (not musical instruments or scores) in specialised store
*Parent:* Cater-Kwik Group Limited
*Officers:* Steven Doyle [1975] Director/IT Marketing; Faye Lisa Mayvers [1972] Director/Sales Person; Matthew Clifford Mayvers [1974] Director/Service Sales Manager

**Caterers Choice Limited**
*Incorporated:* 2 November 1988 *Employees:* 26
*Net Worth:* £6,146,160 *Total Assets:* £33,824,092
*Registered Office:* Parkdale House, 1 Longbow Close, Pennine Business Park, Bradley, Huddersfield, W Yorks, HD2 1GQ
*Activities:* Wholesale of other food, including fish, crustaceans and molluscs
*Shareholders:* Charles Richard Pinder; Sarah Hilary Booth
*Officers:* Sarah Hilary Booth, Secretary; Sarah Hilary Booth [1974] Commercial Director; Charles Richard Pinder [1971] Managing Director

**Caterleisure Services Limited**
*Incorporated:* 17 September 1982 *Employees:* 222
*Net Worth:* £717,329 *Total Assets:* £3,435,542
*Registered Office:* 197-199 Main Street, Wilsden, Bradford, BD15 0HR
*Activities:* Take-away food shops and mobile food stands
*Major Shareholder:* Alan Stuart Peacock
*Officers:* Yvonne Clough, Secretary; Alan Stuart Peacock [1947] Director; Christine Rowbottom [1960] Director

**Catford & Longford Limited**
*Incorporated:* 19 November 1985 *Employees:* 3
*Net Worth:* £1,756,639 *Total Assets:* £9,565,344
*Registered Office:* Abbey Road, Barrow in Furness, Cumbria, LA13 0PA
*Activities:* Hotels and similar accommodation
*Officers:* Brian Gerard Conroy [1971] Director/Hotel Manager; Neil Hopkins-Coman [1962] Director/Chartered Accountant; Timothy Anthony Kilroe [1964] Director [Irish]

**Catfoss Finance Limited**
*Incorporated:* 17 May 2001 *Employees:* 6
*Net Worth:* £3,303,011 *Total Assets:* £22,056,808
*Registered Office:* Elite House, Spellowgate, Driffield, E Yorks, YO25 5UP
*Activities:* Financial leasing
*Parent:* Elite Finance Group Limited
*Officers:* Justin Charles Owen [1970] Director; James Matthew Tate [1972] Managing Director; Gareth Michael Timmins [1979] Director

**Catfoss Renewables Ltd**
*Incorporated:* 14 August 2014 *Employees:* 11
*Net Worth:* £6,215,239 *Total Assets:* £24,056,644
*Registered Office:* Tickton Hall, Tickton, Beverley, E Yorks, HU17 9RX
*Activities:* Activities of head offices
*Shareholders:* Paul Gerald Bentham; Andrew Patrick Foreman
*Officers:* Ian Roundell, Secretary; Andrew Patrick Foreman [1963] Director; Ian Roundell [1965] Director

**The Cathedral Church of England Academy Trust (Wakefield)**
*Incorporated:* 14 November 2011 *Employees:* 122
*Net Worth:* £9,900,000 *Total Assets:* £11,554,000
*Registered Office:* Cathedral Academy, Thornes Road, Wakefield, W Yorks, WF2 8QF
*Activities:* General secondary education
*Officers:* Heather Margaret Mary David [1955] Director/Civil Servant; Mark Andrew Dillon [1965] Director; Richard Jonathan Fox [1977] Director/Manager; John Alwyn Hanson [1948] Director/Education Consultant; Rev June Margaret Lawson [1962] Director of The Mirfield Centre; Robert Howard Marsh [1977] Director/Principal; Ann Louise O'Brien [1957] Director/Education Development Adviser; Adam Daniel Sheard [1981] Director/Teacher; Timothy David Stevens [1980] Director/Minister of Religion; Sarah Hermione Trout [1966] Director/Transition Mentor; Shelagh Anne Wing [1952] Director/Retired Teacher; Claire Louise Young [1978] Director

**Catholic Care (Diocese of Leeds)**
*Incorporated:* 6 May 1982 *Employees:* 139
*Net Worth:* £6,194,500 *Total Assets:* £7,373,479
*Registered Office:* 11 North Grange Road, Headingley, Leeds, LS6 2BR
*Activities:* Residential care activities for learning difficulties, mental health and substance abuse
*Officers:* Carol Ann Hill, Secretary; Vivienne Anne Birch [1961] Director of Quality and Compliance; Joseph Domenic Cortis [1956] Director/Ordained Minister of The Roman Catholic Church [Maltese]; Mark Davison [1983] Director/Composer; Maureen Fletcher [1955] Director/Retired Headteacher; Donal Lucey [1943] Director/RC Priest [Irish]; Timothy Francis Xavier Parr [1961] Director/Chartered Financial Accountant; Susan Mary Chrsitine Rix [1949] Director/Retired Headteacher; Revd Peter Rosser [1945] Director/RC Priest; Bishop Marcus Nigel Ralph Stock [1961] Director/Bishop

**Catterick Caravan & Camping Centre Limited**
*Incorporated:* 21 November 2006 *Employees:* 64
*Net Worth:* £1,950,542 *Total Assets:* £10,158,976
*Registered Office:* Gatherley Road, Catterick Bridge, Richmond, N Yorks, DL10 7JB
*Activities:* Sale of other motor vehicles
*Parent:* Leisure World Group Limited
*Officers:* Christopher Michael Kinsell, Secretary; Christopher Michael Kinsell [1973] Director; Matthew Alexander Kinsell [1979] Sales Director

**Cattle (Holderness) Limited**
*Incorporated:* 3 March 1958 *Employees:* 14
*Net Worth:* £7,490,586 *Total Assets:* £12,681,107
*Registered Office:* West Farm, Sunk Island, Ottringham, Hull, HU12 0AP
*Activities:* Growing of cereals (except rice), leguminous crops and oil seeds
*Shareholders:* Richard Geoffrey Buckle; Richard James Buckle; Robert Paul Buckle
*Officers:* Richard Geoffrey Buckle, Secretary; Richard James Buckle [1971] Director/Farming; Richard Geoffrey Buckle [1947] Director/Farmer; Robert Paul Buckle [1970] Director/Farming

**R.Caudwell (Produce) Limited**
*Incorporated:* 14 January 1964 *Employees:* 18
*Net Worth:* £12,479,800 *Total Assets:* £13,978,393
*Registered Office:* Estate Office, Ludborough, Grimsby, S Humbers, DN36 5SG
*Activities:* Growing of cereals (except rice), leguminous crops and oil seeds
*Officers:* Struan Thomas Caudwell Abbott, Secretary; Rosemary Anne Abbott [1944] Director/Farmer; Struan Thomas Caudwell Abbott [1970] Director/Farmer; Robert Lewis Hartley [1983] Director/Farm Manager; Ralph Michael Pinder [1949] Director/Farm Manager

**Causey Hill Caravan Park Limited**
*Incorporated:* 16 March 2006 *Employees:* 11
*Net Worth:* £1,750,495 *Total Assets:* £3,276,803
*Registered Office:* Medina House, 2 Station Avenue, Bridlington, E Yorks, YO16 4LZ
*Activities:* Recreational vehicle parks, trailer parks and camping grounds
*Shareholder:* Scout Cragg Holiday Park Limited
*Officers:* Mary Teresa Daly, Secretary; Hugh Patrick Daly [1953] Director/Caravan Park Owner; James Joseph Daly [1981] Director/Caravan Park Owner [Irish]; Patrick Martin Daly [1977] Director/Caravan Park Owner [Irish]

**Cavaghan & Gray Group Limited**
*Incorporated:* 15 March 1978
*Net Worth:* £23,498,000 *Total Assets:* £25,709,000
*Registered Office:* Trinity Park House, Fox Way, Wakefield, W Yorks, WF2 8EE
*Activities:* Production of meat and poultry meat products
*Parent:* Convenience Foods Limited
*Officers:* Ranjit Singh Boparan [1966] Director; Ronald Klaas Otto Kers [1969] Director/Group CEO [Dutch]; Craig Ashley Tomkinson [1982] Director/Group CFO

**Cavaghan & Gray Limited**
*Incorporated:* 27 September 1919 *Employees:* 1,102
*Net Worth:* £108,285,000 *Total Assets:* £148,972,000
*Registered Office:* Trinity Park House, Fox Way, Wakefield, W Yorks, WF2 8EE
*Activities:* Growing of vegetables and melons, roots and tubers
*Parent:* Cavaghan & Gray Group Limited
*Officers:* Ranjit Singh Boparan [1966] Director; Ronald Klaas Otto Kers [1969] Director/Group CEO [Dutch]; Keith Richard Packer [1967] Managing Director; Richard Peter Simpson [1965] Finance Director; Craig Ashley Tomkinson [1982] Director/Group CFO

**Caval Limited**
*Incorporated:* 9 January 2008 *Employees:* 313
*Net Worth:* £1,060,106 *Total Assets:* £5,524,719
*Registered Office:* York House, 31 York Place, Leeds, LS1 2ED
*Activities:* Temporary employment agency activities
*Officers:* Jamie Lee Talbot, Secretary; Oliver Joseph Burt [1974] Director/Recruitment Consultant; Matthew James Chapman [1976] Director/Recruitment Consultant; John Graham Hunt [1970] Director/Recruitment; Jamie Lee Talbot [1980] Director/Recruitment Consultant

**Cavalier Marketing Limited**
*Incorporated:* 13 September 1988 *Employees:* 159
*Net Worth:* £13,284,770 *Total Assets:* £26,834,770
*Registered Office:* Cavalier Marketing, North Dean Road, Keighley, W Yorks, BD22 6QY
*Activities:* Manufacture of other furniture
*Parent:* Cavalier Marketing Holdings Limited
*Officers:* John Frazer Harrison [1971] Managing Director; Robert Hudson Harrison [1975] Managing Director

**Cave Developments Limited**
*Incorporated:* 5 February 2004 *Employees:* 1
*Net Worth:* £53,735 *Total Assets:* £3,030,890
*Registered Office:* Northgate, 118 North Street, Leeds, LS2 7PN
*Activities:* Development of building projects
*Parent:* Northern Eye UK Limited
*Officers:* Aimar Lombard-Natheer, Secretary; Jeffrey Barnett [1974] Director; Aimar Lombard-Natheer [1978] Director

**Cawingredients Limited**
*Incorporated:* 20 June 2008 *Employees:* 173
*Net Worth:* £22,491,476 *Total Assets:* £60,866,140
*Registered Office:* Caw House, Conygarth Way, Leeming Bar Business Park, Leeming Bar, Northallerton, N Yorks, DL7 9FD
*Activities:* Manufacture of soft drinks; production of mineral waters and other bottled waters
*Major Shareholder:* Andrew James Cawthray
*Officers:* Mark Kevin Adamson [1984] Director/Chartered Accountant; Elizabeth Burkhardt [1986] Director; Andrew James Cawthray [1957] Director; Susan Cawthray [1958] Director; Hannah Harrison [1983] Director; Peter Richard Harrison [1979] Director; Andrew David Holt [1959] Director/Solicitor

**Caygill Holdings Limited**
*Incorporated:* 27 April 2007 *Employees:* 48
*Net Worth:* £6,493,345 *Total Assets:* £16,830,668
*Registered Office:* LCW House, Chainbar Road, Cleckheaton, W Yorks, BD19 3QF
*Activities:* Sale of new cars and light motor vehicles
*Shareholders:* Andrew Martin Caygill; Susan Caroline Caygill
*Officers:* Susan Caroline Caygill, Secretary; Andrew Martin Caygill [1956] Director; Susan Caroline Caygill [1959] Director

**CB Farms LLP**
*Incorporated:* 5 August 2009
*Net Worth:* £5,295,602 *Total Assets:* £5,338,835
*Registered Office:* The Hall, Newton-le-Willows, Bedale, N Yorks, DL8 1SW
*Officers:* John Kenneth Bell [1974] Member; Leonidas Christophilopoulos [1969] Member; Helen Judith Bell [1973] LLP Member; Sorrel Harriet Katherine Scott Christophilopoulos [1970] LLP Member

**CB Imports Group Limited**
*Incorporated:* 18 October 2007 *Employees:* 307
*Net Worth:* £5,392,000 *Total Assets:* £14,737,000
*Registered Office:* Ardsley Mills, Common Lane, East Ardsley, Wakefield, W Yorks, WF3 2DW
*Activities:* Wholesale of household goods (other than musical instruments) n.e.c
*Officers:* Stephen Wood, Secretary; Frederick William Bacon [1988] Director; Richard John Steele [1955] Director; Sarah Jessica Wragg [1975] Finance Director

**CB Imports Limited**
*Incorporated:* 4 August 1998 *Employees:* 307
*Net Worth:* £8,756,000 *Total Assets:* £18,102,000
*Registered Office:* Ardsley Mills, Common Lane, East Ardsley, Wakefield, W Yorks, WF3 2DW
*Activities:* Wholesale of household goods (other than musical instruments) n.e.c
*Officers:* Sarah Jessica Wragg, Secretary; Frederick William Bacon [1988] Director; Richard John Steele [1955] Director; Sarah Jessica Wragg [1975] Finance Director

**CB Solutions U.K. Ltd**
*Incorporated:* 21 March 2000 *Employees:* 52
*Previous:* Safewood (UK) Limited
*Net Worth:* £1,071,640 *Total Assets:* £4,288,776
*Registered Office:* Halifax Approach, New Cut, Lissett, Driffield, E Yorks, YO25 8PT
*Activities:* Construction of other civil engineering projects n.e.c.
*Major Shareholder:* Christopher John Burrell
*Officers:* Julia Ludolf, Secretary; Matthew Brown [1973] Director; Christopher John Burrell [1957] Director; Jonathan Mark Clark [1974] Director; Kerry-Ann Taylor [1984] Director

**CCL Computers Limited**
*Incorporated:* 15 July 1996 *Employees:* 60
*Net Worth:* £2,787,149 *Total Assets:* £5,736,449
*Registered Office:* Inmoor Road, Cross Lane, Tong, W Yorks, BD11 2PS
*Activities:* Other information technology service activities
*Major Shareholder:* Adrian Clifford Wood
*Officers:* Sarah Joanne Wood, Secretary; Adrian Clifford Wood [1961] Director; Sarah Joanne Wood [1969] Director

**CCL Holdings Limited**
*Incorporated:* 16 March 1993
*Net Worth:* £6,399,000 *Total Assets:* £7,808,000
*Registered Office:* 74 Helsinki Road, Hull, HU7 0YW
*Activities:* Processing and preserving of poultry meat
*Parent:* Cranswick Country Foods PLC
*Officers:* Steven Garrick Glover, Secretary; Nigel Colin Armes [1959] Finance Director; John Armstrong [1979] Finance Director; John Mark Bottomley [1963] Finance Director; Adam Hartley Couch [1968] Director; David Charles Park [1969] Managing Director; Matthew Christopher Ward [1964] Agricultural Director

**CCL Industries (U.K.) Limited**
*Incorporated:* 14 September 1989
*Net Worth:* £387,121,984 *Total Assets:* £483,079,008
*Registered Office:* Pioneer Way, Castleford, W Yorks, WF10 5QU
*Activities:* Other manufacturing n.e.c.
*Officers:* Mark Beckram, Secretary; Richard John Foulsham [1964] Director; Geoffrey Thomas Martin [1954] Director/Executive [American]; Kamel Mormech [1973] Director; Jamie Robinson [1970] Commercial Director

**CCL Label Limited**
*Incorporated:* 25 October 2001 *Employees:* 487
*Net Worth:* £19,408,000 *Total Assets:* £69,546,000
*Registered Office:* Pioneer Way, Castleford, W Yorks, WF10 5QU
*Activities:* Manufacture of printed labels
*Parent:* CCL Industries (UK) Ltd
*Officers:* Mark Beckram, Secretary; Richard John Foulsham [1964] Director; Geoffrey Thomas Martin [1954] Director/Executive [American]; Kamel Mormech [1973] Director; Jamie Robinson [1970] Commercial Director

**CCL Stressing International Limited**
*Incorporated:* 20 November 2003 *Employees:* 15
*Net Worth:* £8,151,898 *Total Assets:* £14,577,359
*Registered Office:* Unit 8 Millennium Drive, Holbeck, Leeds, LS11 5BP
*Activities:* Non-trading company
*Officers:* Matthew Emson, Secretary; Matthew Emson [1971] Director/Accountant; Guy Joseph Naji Tabet [1958] Director/Engineer [French]

**CCL Stressing Systems Limited**
*Incorporated:* 29 March 2000 *Employees:* 25
*Net Worth:* £1,752,607 *Total Assets:* £4,294,300
*Registered Office:* Unit 8 Millennium Drive, Holbeck, Leeds, LS11 5BP
*Activities:* Manufacture of metal structures and parts of structures
*Parent:* CCL Stressing International Limited
*Officers:* Matthew Emson, Secretary; Edward John Birkhead [1988] Director/Engineer; Matthew Emson [1971] Director/Accountant; Jonathan Samuel Machin [1975] Director/Quantity Surveyor; Paul William Stainrod [1965] Director/General Manager; Guy Joseph Naji Tabet [1958] Director/Engineer [French]

**CCL Syrinx (UK Holding) Limited**
*Incorporated:* 21 June 2017
*Net Worth:* £210,373,472 *Total Assets:* £431,160,672
*Registered Office:* Unit 3 Pioneer Way, Castleford, Leeds, WF10 5QU
*Activities:* Dormant company
*Shareholder:* CCL Industries (UK) Limited
*Officers:* Mark Anthony Beckram [1970] Financial Director; Richard John Foulsham [1964] Director; Jamie Robinson [1970] Director

**CCL Syrinx (UK) Limited**
*Incorporated:* 13 December 2016
*Net Worth:* £511,196,544 *Total Assets:* £511,204,416
*Registered Office:* Pioneer Way, Castleford, W Yorks, WF10 5QU
*Activities:* Activities of other holding companies n.e.c.
*Parent:* CCL Syrinx (UK Holding) Ltd
*Officers:* Mark Beckram, Secretary; Mark Anthony Beckram [1970] Director/Accountant; Geoffrey Thomas Martin [1954] Director [American]; Jamie Robinson [1970] Director

**CD (UK) Limited**
*Incorporated:* 7 March 1994 *Employees:* 71
*Net Worth:* £8,377,697 *Total Assets:* £13,375,443
*Registered Office:* Wakefield House, Thistle Way, Gildersome Spur, Gildersome, Morley, Leeds, LS27 7JZ
*Activities:* Non-specialised wholesale trade
*Shareholders:* Geoffrey Brian Baker; Ruth Baker
*Officers:* Gary Mark Baker [1972] Director; Geoffrey Brian Baker [1934] Director; Glynis Toni Hibbert [1945] Director

**CE Holdings Limited**
*Incorporated:* 14 June 2007
*Net Worth:* £673,067 *Total Assets:* £4,000,000
*Registered Office:* Bede House, St Cuthbert's Way, Aycliffe Industrial Park, Newton Aycliffe, Co Durham, DL5 6DX
*Activities:* Activities of head offices
*Shareholders:* Andrew Peter Hinton; Nicholas Andrew Wyatt
*Officers:* Andrew Peter Hinton [1952] Director; Nicholas Andrew Wyatt [1962] Director

**Celdis Limited**
*Incorporated:* 14 March 1977
*Net Worth Deficit:* £399,203,008 *Total Assets:* £43,362,000
*Registered Office:* Farnell House, Forge Lane, Leeds, LS12 2NE
*Activities:* Non-trading company
*Parent:* Premier Farnell Limited
*Officers:* Liam Anthony Heffernan [1972] Director/Accountant [Irish]; Harvey Woodford [1963] Director/VP Corporate Secretary [American]

**Cellhire (Holdings) Limited**
*Incorporated:* 15 September 1994 *Employees:* 97
*Net Worth:* £6,565,753 *Total Assets:* £11,512,957
*Registered Office:* Park House, Clifton Park, York, YO30 5PB
*Activities:* Non-trading company
*Parent:* Cellhire Group Limited
*Officers:* Helen Jane Williams, Secretary; Timothy Rupert Taylor [1970] Finance Director; Helen Jane Williams [1960] Director/Head of HR; Timothy James Williams [1959] Director

**Cellhire Group Limited**
*Incorporated:* 3 May 2007 *Employees:* 97
*Net Worth:* £6,555,753 *Total Assets:* £11,502,957
*Registered Office:* Park House, Clifton Park, York, YO30 5PB
*Activities:* Wireless telecommunications activities
*Major Shareholder:* Timothy James Williams
*Officers:* Helen Jane Williams, Secretary; Timothy Rupert Taylor [1970] Finance Director; Helen Jane Williams [1960] Director/HR Manager; Timothy James Williams [1959] Director

**Cellhire PLC**
*Incorporated:* 1 September 1987 *Employees:* 97
*Net Worth:* £6,555,753 *Total Assets:* £11,502,957
*Registered Office:* Park House, Clifton Park, York, YO30 5PB
*Activities:* Other telecommunications activities
*Parent:* Cellhire (Holdings) Ltd
*Officers:* Helen Jane Williams, Secretary; Matt Bennett [1968] Managing Director; Jonathan William Fitzpatrick [1983] Finance Director; Martyn Stevens [1969] International Business Director; Timothy Rupert Taylor [1970] Financial Director; Peter Whelerton [1970] Technical Director; Timothy James Williams [1959] Director

**Central European Aggregates Limited**
*Incorporated:* 7 June 2004 *Employees:* 23
*Net Worth:* £3,594,520 *Total Assets:* £25,057,604
*Registered Office:* Smithfield House, 92 North Street, Leeds, LS2 7PN
*Activities:* Activities of head offices
*Officers:* Anna Banas [1965] Managing Director [Polish]; Athina Isavella Georgiou [1986] Director/Chartered Accountant [Cypriot]; Keith Michael Mellors [1955] Director; Andreas Pourgouras [1948] Director/Retired; Melina Pyrgou [1968] Director/Advocate [Cypriot]

**Central Insulations Limited**
*Incorporated:* 12 April 1989 *Employees:* 25
*Net Worth:* £2,382,005 *Total Assets:* £5,172,256
*Registered Office:* 19 Wilton Road, Humberston, Grimsby, N E Lincs, DN36 4AW
*Activities:* Other construction installation
*Shareholders:* PW Companies Limited; PW Companies Limited
*Officers:* Paul Andrew Walmsley [1965] Director

**Central Land Holdings Ltd**
*Incorporated:* 17 February 1961 *Employees:* 6
*Net Worth:* £7,583,767 *Total Assets:* £7,986,600
*Registered Office:* Kingswood House, Ashcombe Road, Kingswood, Hull, HU7 3DD
*Activities:* Buying and selling of own real estate
*Shareholder:* Stephanie Elizabeth Fetiveau
*Officers:* John Howard Briggs, Secretary; Vanessa Hilary Chetham [1956] Director; Stephanie Elizabeth Fetiveau [1946] Director/Housewife

**Central North Sea Fibre Telecommunications Company Limited**
*Incorporated:* 12 June 2000
*Net Worth:* £29,087,098 *Total Assets:* £29,087,098
*Registered Office:* 1 Park Row, Leeds, LS1 5AB
*Activities:* Support activities for petroleum and natural gas mining
*Parent:* Tampnet UK Limited
*Officers:* Christian Grinde, Secretary; Christian Grinde [1971] Director/CLO Tampnet AS [Norwegian]; Per Helge Svensson [1961] Director/CEO Tampnet AS [Norwegian]

**Central Properties (Leeds) Limited**
*Incorporated:* 5 October 2001 *Employees:* 2
*Net Worth:* £1,765,490 *Total Assets:* £4,144,391
*Registered Office:* 2 St Annes Parade, Headingley, Leeds, LS6 3NX
*Activities:* Management of real estate on a fee or contract basis
*Shareholders:* John Christopher Heron; Sally Anne Heron
*Officers:* Sally Anne Heron, Secretary/Director; John Christopher Heron [1954] Director; Sally Anne Heron [1956] Director

**Centre at Three Ways**
*Incorporated:* 13 April 2011 *Employees:* 8
*Net Worth:* £8,415,757 *Total Assets:* £8,937,723
*Registered Office:* Centre at Three Ways, Nursery Lane, Ovenden, Halifax, W Yorks, HX3 5SX
*Activities:* Other service activities n.e.c.
*Officers:* Emmajayne Carter, Secretary; Neil Andrew Capper [1969] Director/HMRC Compliance Officer; Emmajayne Carter [1978] Director/Jeweller; Colin Davies [1967] Director/Consultant; Lawrence Howard Fear [1962] Director

**Centrica Offshore UK Limited**
*Incorporated:* 10 July 2001
*Net Worth Deficit:* £7,629,000 *Total Assets:* £366,168,000
*Registered Office:* Woodland House, Woodland Park, Hessle, E Yorks, HU13 0FA
*Activities:* Extraction of natural gas
*Parent:* Centrica Storage Limited
*Officers:* Gregory Craig McKenna [1966] Commercial Director; Darren Oliver [1971] Operated Assets Director; Trine Rath Thomsen [1966] Finance Director [Danish]

**Centrica Storage Holdings Limited**
*Incorporated:* 25 October 2002
*Previous:* Centrica Storage Holdings Limited.
*Net Worth:* £108,855,000 *Total Assets:* £128,684,000
*Registered Office:* Woodland House, Woodland Park, Hessle, E Yorks, HU13 0FA
*Activities:* Activities of other holding companies n.e.c.
*Parent:* GB Gas Holdings Limited
*Officers:* Ian Grant Dawson [1959] Director; Gregory Craig McKenna [1966] Commercial Director

**Centrica Storage Limited**
*Incorporated:* 18 December 1996 *Employees:* 319
*Net Worth:* £157,000,000 *Total Assets:* £233,000,000
*Registered Office:* Woodland House, Woodland Park, Hessle, E Yorks, HU13 0FA
*Activities:* Extraction of natural gas
*Parent:* Centrica Storage Holdings Limited
*Officers:* Ian Grant Dawson [1959] Director; Gregory Craig McKenna [1966] Commercial Director; Darren Oliver [1971] Operated Assets Director; Trine Rath Thomsen [1966] Finance Director [Danish]

**Centurion Europe Holdings Limited**
*Incorporated:* 23 May 2006 *Employees:* 2
*Net Worth:* £4,577,252 *Total Assets:* £4,577,252
*Registered Office:* Centurion House, Hunt Lane, Bentley, Doncaster, S Yorks, DN5 9SH
*Activities:* Non-trading company
*Shareholders:* David Lajos Geczi; Paul Matthew Kantecki
*Officers:* David Lajos Geczi, Secretary/Director; David Lajos Geczi [1968] Director; Paul Matthew Kantecki [1976] Director

**Centurion Europe Limited**
*Incorporated:* 3 July 1984 *Employees:* 113
*Net Worth:* £2,036,207 *Total Assets:* £4,665,562
*Registered Office:* Centurion House, Hunt Lane, Doncaster, S Yorks, DN5 9SH
*Activities:* Wholesale of hardware, plumbing and heating equipment and supplies
*Shareholders:* Paul Matthew Kantecki; David Lajos Geczi
*Officers:* David Lajos Geczi, Secretary; David Lajos Geczi [1968] Director/Buyer; Paul Matthew Kantecki [1976] Director/Sales Accounts Manager

**Century Construction Limited**
*Incorporated:* 16 August 2016 *Employees:* 3
*Net Worth:* £241,626 *Total Assets:* £9,067,115
*Registered Office:* 6 Blenheim Terrace, Leeds, LS2 9HZ
*Activities:* Construction of domestic buildings
*Parent:* YPP Holdings Limited
*Officers:* Zaid Al-Najafi, Secretary; Abdulaziz Mohammad Al-Najafi [1983] Director; Omar Al-Najafi [1987] Director; Zaid Al-Najafi [1991] Director

**Century Health (Nottingham) Limited**
*Incorporated:* 4 February 1999 *Employees:* 6
*Net Worth:* £10,112,849 *Total Assets:* £25,027,772
*Registered Office:* St Vincent House, Normanby Road, Scunthorpe, N Lincs, DN15 8QT
*Activities:* Other business support service activities n.e.c.
*Shareholders:* Clugston PF Limited; Aberdeen Infrastructure (No. 3) Limited
*Officers:* Ian Pattison, Secretary; Michael Andrew Donn [1972] Director; Karen Marie Hill [1977] Director/Investment Manager; Gavin Ingle [1976] Director/Accountant; Stephen John Radcliffe [1955] Director; Philip Robert Taylor [1958] Director/Microbiologist; Robert John Vickers [1956] Director/Chief Executive Officer

**Century Homes Limited**
*Incorporated:* 9 October 1987
*Net Worth:* £4,781,303 *Total Assets:* £6,385,543
*Registered Office:* The East Wing, The Newhall, Newhall Way, Bradford, BD5 8FF
*Activities:* Construction of domestic buildings
*Parent:* Hollin Hall Holdings Limited
*Officers:* James Ernest Marshall, Secretary; Frank Edward Marshall [1978] Director; James Ernest Marshall [1979] Director

**Cephalon (UK) Limited**
*Incorporated:* 5 June 1996 *Employees:* 2
*Net Worth:* £91,222,000 *Total Assets:* £96,363,000
*Registered Office:* Ridings Point, Whistler Drive, Castleford, W Yorks, WF10 5HX
*Activities:* Retail sale of medical and orthopaedic goods in specialised stores (not incl. hearing aids) n.e.c.
*Parent:* Cephalon Limited
*Officers:* Dean Michael Cooper [1972] Director/Chartered Accountant; Kim Innes [1968] Director/General Manager

**Cephalon Limited**
*Incorporated:* 3 September 2003
*Net Worth:* £55,164,000 *Total Assets:* £55,934,000
*Registered Office:* Ridings Point, Whistler Drive, Castleford, W Yorks, WF10 5HX
*Activities:* Activities of head offices
*Parent:* Teva UK Holdings Limited
*Officers:* Dean Michael Cooper [1972] Director/Chartered Accountant; Kim Innes [1968] Director/General Manager

**Ceramica Impex Limited**
*Incorporated:* 14 February 1980 *Employees:* 21
*Net Worth:* £2,816,534 *Total Assets:* £7,787,237
*Registered Office:* Unit 1 Victoria Industrial Park, Victoria Road, Leeds, LS14 2LA
*Activities:* Wholesale of other intermediate products
*Major Shareholder:* Hayrullah Levent Namli
*Officers:* Lucy Fiona Kerrison, Secretary; Hayrullah Levent Namli [1956] Director

**Cerros Properties Limited**
*Incorporated:* 20 February 2004 *Employees:* 4
*Net Worth:* £5,657,604 *Total Assets:* £6,056,470
*Registered Office:* The Barn, 1a Alderstone Rise, Lindley, Huddersfield, W Yorks, HD3 3RL
*Activities:* Other letting and operating of own or leased real estate
*Major Shareholder:* William Michael Cran
*Officers:* Lisel Frances Cran, Secretary; Lisel Frances Cran [1970] Director; William Michael Cran [1949] Director

**Certex Lifting Limited**
*Incorporated:* 6 December 2004 *Employees:* 149
*Net Worth:* £2,453,990 *Total Assets:* £10,067,886
*Registered Office:* Unit C1, Harworth Industrial Estate, Bryans Close, Harworth, Doncaster, S Yorks, DN11 8RY
*Activities:* Manufacture of lifting and handling equipment
*Major Shareholder:* Antonia Margaret Axson Johnson
*Officers:* Adrian Tomkinson, Secretary; Kevin John Smith [1961] Director; Adrian Tomkinson [1963] Finance Director; Ralf Paul Albert Wiberg [1959] Director [Finnish]; Scott Jason Wilcox [1979] Managing Director

**CF Bidco Limited**
*Incorporated:* 31 March 2010
*Net Worth:* £219,379,008 *Total Assets:* £371,140,992
*Registered Office:* Century House, Brunel Road, Wakefield 41 Industrial Estate, Wakefield, W Yorks, WF2 0XG
*Activities:* Activities of head offices
*Parent:* Card Factory PLC
*Officers:* Christopher Robbert Beck [1974] Director; Karen Rachael Hubbard [1964] Director; Kristian Brian Lee [1974] Director

**CG Estates Limited**
*Incorporated:* 21 February 2017 *Employees:* 1
*Net Worth:* £187,246 *Total Assets:* £5,826,814
*Registered Office:* 2 Therm Road, Hull, HU8 7BF
*Activities:* Buying and selling of own real estate
*Parent:* Teddy Clark (Holdings) Limited
*Officers:* William Edward Clark [1967] Director

**CGP Estates Limited**
*Incorporated:* 23 August 1999
*Net Worth:* £1,047 *Total Assets:* £3,961,021
*Registered Office:* Broughton House, Griffin Street, Broughton in Furness, Cumbria, LA20 6HH
*Activities:* Other letting and operating of own or leased real estate
*Parent:* Coordination Group Publications Ltd
*Officers:* Carla Michelle Little, Secretary; Leila Miller [1970] Director; Richard Alan Parsons [1966] Director; Jane Michelle Ross [1968] Director

**Chadwick Lawrence LLP**
*Incorporated:* 19 August 2005 *Employees:* 202
*Net Worth:* £2,207,830 *Total Assets:* £6,533,457
*Registered Office:* 8-16 Dock Street, Leeds, LS10 1LX
*Officers:* Kumer Ali [1968] Member; Steven Charles Bonfield [1954] Member; Paul Jeffrey Campbell [1954] Member; Paul Murray Carvis [1948] Member; Sarah Haller [1971] Member; Daniel James Hirst [1976] Member; Asma Iqbal [1975] Member; Daniel James Krigers [1987] Member; Cheryl Ann Largue [1975] Member; Anthony Martin May [1965] Member; Stuart Lewis Murray [1960] Member; Sarah Louise Power [1979] Member; Howard John Willis [1957] Member; Neil Anthony Wilson [1965] Member; Nicholas Charles Worsnop [1969] Member

**Chalemere Limited**
*Incorporated:* 4 November 1997 *Employees:* 56
*Net Worth:* £6,907,757 *Total Assets:* £7,818,538
*Registered Office:* Westcourt, Gelderd Road, Leeds, LS12 6DB
*Activities:* Residential nursing care facilities
*Parent:* Maria Mallaband Care Group Limited
*Officers:* Christopher Ball [1968] Director; Philip John Burgan [1951] Director; Peter Gervais Fagan [1957] Director; Jason Lock [1972] Director

**Chamber Acorn Fund (Humber) Ltd**
*Incorporated:* 31 March 2004 *Employees:* 6
*Net Worth:* £3,308,443 *Total Assets:* £4,441,418
*Registered Office:* 34-38 Beverley Road, Hull, HU3 1YE
*Activities:* Other business support service activities n.e.c.
*Officers:* Samantha Elise Dennison, Secretary; Samantha Elise Dennison [1973] Director/Company Secretary; Ian Spencer Kelly [1964] Director; Howard O'Neill [1954] Director/Business Consultant (Self Employed); Craig Ross William Simpson [1958] Director

**James Chambers (Timber Merchants) Limited**
*Incorporated:* 17 April 1943 *Employees:* 43
*Net Worth:* £1,942,205 *Total Assets:* £5,986,053
*Registered Office:* Pellon Lane Saw Mills, Pellon Lane, Halifax, W Yorks, HX1 4PX
*Activities:* Agents involved in the sale of timber and building materials
*Parent:* Viewstone Limited
*Officers:* Robert James Moore, Secretary; Sean Anthony Colleran [1958] Director/Timber Merchant; Paul Anthony Fairhurst [1960] Director/Salesman; Karen Lesley Moore [1959] Director; Robert James Moore [1961] Director/Manufacturer

**Tom Chambers Limited**
*Incorporated:* 1 November 1977 *Employees:* 80
*Net Worth:* £783,161 *Total Assets:* £4,935,232
*Registered Office:* AW Nielsen Road, M62 Trading Estate, Goole, E Yorks, DN14 6UE
*Activities:* Manufacture of wooden containers
*Shareholders:* Richard James Medley; Stephen Alan Medley
*Officers:* Stephen Alan Medley, Secretary/Director; Richard James Medley [1967] Engineer-Director; Stephen Alan Medley [1969] Director; Victoria Claire Medley [1971] Marketing Director

**Chambers Parking Limited**
*Incorporated:* 23 November 2005
*Net Worth Deficit:* £529,468 *Total Assets:* £4,558,839
*Registered Office:* Riverside West, Whitehall Road, Leeds, LS1 4AW
*Activities:* Buying and selling of own real estate
*Officers:* Christine Rita Ann Boothroyd, Secretary; Richard Derrick Boothroyd [1955] Director/Chairman; Peter Joseph Rossington [1949] Director

**Chameleon Technology (UK) Limited**
*Incorporated:* 27 September 2010
*Net Worth:* £2,847,435 *Total Assets:* £10,389,502
*Registered Office:* Gardner House, Hornbeam Park Avenue, Hornbeam Park, Harrogate, N Yorks, HG2 8NA
*Activities:* Manufacture of other electrical equipment
*Major Shareholder:* Gary John Martin
*Officers:* Gary John Martin, Secretary; Graeme Allison [1965] Director; Martin Allison [1963] Director; Timothy John Boyle [1959] Director; Gary John Martin [1980] Director/Manager; Michael Eric Woodhall [1967] Director/Manager

**Champagne Warehouse Ltd**
*Incorporated:* 25 October 2000 *Employees:* 9
*Net Worth:* £3,468,115 *Total Assets:* £4,992,298
*Registered Office:* Parkhill Business Centre, Walton Road, Wetherby, W Yorks, LS22 5DZ
*Activities:* Wholesale of wine, beer, spirits and other alcoholic beverages
*Major Shareholder:* Antony Stones
*Officers:* Helen Louise Stones, Secretary/Manager; Teresa Barnard [1969] Marketing Director; Antony Stones [1965] Managing Director; Helen Louise Stones [1967] Director

**Channon and Company Limited**
*Incorporated:* 16 September 1997 *Employees:* 6
*Net Worth:* £5,716,004 *Total Assets:* £7,544,441
*Registered Office:* Midland Buildings, 19a Briggate, Shipley, W Yorks, BD17 7BP
*Activities:* Combined office administrative service activities
*Officers:* Sharon Louise Wooler, Secretary; Gary Andrew Scott Channon [1967] Director/Investment Manager; Simon Channon [1969] Director

**Channon Holdings Limited**
*Incorporated:* 20 March 2013 *Employees:* 14
*Net Worth:* £3,168,368 *Total Assets:* £10,491,141
*Registered Office:* Midland Buildings, 19a Briggate, Shipley, W Yorks, BD17 7BP
*Activities:* Financial management
*Officers:* Sharon Louise Wooler, Secretary; Gary Andrew Scott Channon [1967] Director/Investment Manager; Steven David Tatters [1967] Director/Investment Manager

**YM Chantry Limited**
*Incorporated:* 12 May 2016 *Employees:* 231
*Net Worth:* £942,515 *Total Assets:* £17,957,262
*Registered Office:* Whitehall Park, Whitehall Road, Leeds, LS12 5XX
*Activities:* Printing n.e.c.
*Parent:* York Mailing (Holdings) Limited
*Officers:* Lee David Richardson, Secretary; Stephen Tony Goodman [1970] Director; Peter Greaves [1963] Director; Lee David Richardson [1971] Director

**Chapel Allerton Investments LLP**
*Incorporated:* 8 December 2006 *Employees:* 3
*Net Worth:* £3,036,353 *Total Assets:* £12,931,494
*Registered Office:* 7 Cottage Road, Headingley, Leeds, LS6 4DD
*Officers:* Christopher David Ure [1962] Member; David John Barrass [1964] LLP Member; Gillian Susan Ure [1963] LLP Member

**W.S.Chapman & Sons Limited**
*Incorporated:* 26 March 1957 *Employees:* 4
*Net Worth:* £12,278,359 *Total Assets:* £15,258,661
*Registered Office:* Burgess Hall, Burringham Road, Gunness, Scunthorpe, N Lincs, DN17 3LT
*Activities:* Growing of cereals (except rice), leguminous crops and oil seeds
*Major Shareholder:* James Stanewell Chapman
*Officers:* Josephine Chapman, Secretary; James Stanewell Chapman [1927] Director/Farmer; Josephine Chapman [1939] Director/Secretary; Tina Marie Ogg [1970] Director

**D and K Chapman Limited**
*Incorporated:* 29 August 2012
*Net Worth:* £275,779 *Total Assets:* £3,389,389
*Registered Office:* 5th Floor, Central Square, 29 Wellington Street, Leeds, LS1 4DL
*Activities:* Fund management activities
*Shareholders:* Dale Walter Chapman; Kim Chapman
*Officers:* Dale Walter Chapman, Secretary; Dale Walter Chapman [1970] Director; Kim Chapman [1971] Director

**Chapter of The Order of The Holy Paraclete (The) Unlimited**
*Incorporated:* 20 January 1976 *Employees:* 67
*Net Worth:* £13,063,202 *Total Assets:* £13,378,181
*Registered Office:* St Hildas Priory, Sneaton Castle, Whitby, N Yorks, YO21 3QN
*Activities:* Activities of religious organisations
*Officers:* Sister Jocelyn Mary Carter, Secretary; Sister Karan Rosemary Brewin [1942] Director/Sister in Religion; Sister Jocelyn Mary Carter [1944] Director/Sister in Religion; Sister Carole Clee [1949] Director/Sister in Religion; Sister Heather Francis Crane [1945] Director/Sister in Religion; Sister Janet Elizabeth Davey [1936] Director/Sister in Religion; Sister Dorothy Maureen Dean [1937] Director/Sister in Religion; Sister Hannah Grace Dowler [1955] Director/Sister in Religion

**Charco Ninety-Nine Limited**
*Incorporated:* 17 October 1988
*Net Worth:* £3,130,000 *Total Assets:* £10,815,000
*Registered Office:* Holmfield Industrial Estate, Halifax, W Yorks, HX2 9TN
*Activities:* Activities of production holding companies
*Parent:* Gower Group Limited
*Officers:* Nicola Jane Hardcastle, Secretary; Daniel Arthur Edward Carr [1975] Finance Director; Nicola Jane Hardcastle [1965] Director/Accountant; Anthony George Ryall [1974] Director

**Charlesworth Family Group Limited**
*Incorporated:* 17 August 2015 *Employees:* 6
*Net Worth:* £171,220 *Total Assets:* £9,898,166
*Registered Office:* 250 Deighton Road, Huddersfield, W Yorks, HD2 1JJ
*Activities:* Activities of other holding companies n.e.c.
*Shareholders:* Neil Charlesworth; Judith Ramsden Charlesworth
*Officers:* David Neil Charlesworth [1982] Director; Ian Charlesworth [1969] Director; Judith Ramsden Charlesworth [1944] Director; Leonard Neil Charlesworth [1937] Director; Richard James Charlesworth [1985] Director; Helen Ramsden Thornton [1971] Director

**Charminster Estates Limited**
*Incorporated:* 16 January 1995
*Net Worth:* £1,208,527 *Total Assets:* £5,020,091
*Registered Office:* 120-122 High Northgate, Darlington, Co Durham, DL1 1UR
*Activities:* Buying and selling of own real estate
*Shareholder:* Kenneth Roy Thomason
*Officers:* Richard Thomas Brooke Thomason, Secretary; Julia Ann Brooke Blower [1978] Director/Regeneration Consultant; Emily Sarah Brooke Close [1981] Director/Administrator; Kenneth Roy Thomason [1944] Director/Solicitor; Richard Thomas Brooke Thomason [1972] Managing Director

**Chartford Arthington Limited**
*Incorporated:* 17 November 2009
*Net Worth:* £100 *Total Assets:* £3,307,622
*Registered Office:* C7 Josephs Well, Hanover Walk, Leeds, LS3 1AB
*Activities:* Construction of domestic buildings
*Parent:* J Pullan & Sons Ltd
*Officers:* John Charles Dawson, Secretary; John Charles Dawson [1965] Director; Matthew Fuller [1966] Director; Alistair Mark Pullan [1959] Director; Bruce Scott Strachan [1963] Director/Chartered Surveyor; Christopher Thompson [1960] Director

**Chartford Developments Limited**
*Incorporated:* 7 July 2016 *Employees:* 28
*Net Worth:* £298,338 *Total Assets:* £13,875,027
*Registered Office:* The Tannery, 91 Kirkstall Road, Leeds, LS3 1HS
*Activities:* Construction of domestic buildings
*Shareholder:* Commercial Development Projects Limited
*Officers:* Jonathan Booth [1970] Director; Neil Matthew Clark [1968] Director; Matthew Fuller [1966] Director; Christopher Roy Marshall [1939] Commercial Director; Simon Charles Newton Marshall [1963] Director; Christopher Thompson [1960] Director

**Chase Petroleum Limited**
*Incorporated:* 16 March 2005 *Employees:* 21
*Net Worth:* £2,721,466 *Total Assets:* £4,171,618
*Registered Office:* The Chase, Church Lane, Wentbridge, Pontefract, W Yorks, WF8 3JH
*Activities:* Other letting and operating of own or leased real estate
*Shareholders:* Paul Jervis; Caroline Jervis
*Officers:* David William McRitchie, Secretary; Caroline Jervis [1963] Director/Administrator; Paul Jervis [1956] Director/Management; David William McRitchie [1948] Director/Accountant

**Chatsworth Windows Limited**
*Incorporated:* 8 October 2013
*Net Worth:* £3,758,010 *Total Assets:* £3,758,010
*Registered Office:* Langton House, 124 Acomb Road, York, YO24 4EY
*Activities:* Activities of other holding companies n.e.c.
*Shareholder:* Stuart Anthony Scott
*Officers:* David Ian Costick [1970] Director; Paul Hayton [1970] Director; Stuart Anthony Scott [1970] Managing Director; Jamie Daniel Timothy Smith [1973] Director

**Chaucer Foods Limited**
*Incorporated:* 6 March 1996 *Employees:* 24
*Net Worth:* £26,397,896 *Total Assets:* £41,306,432
*Registered Office:* Unit 26 Brighton Street Industrial Estate, Freightliner Road, Hull, HU3 4EN
*Activities:* Other processing and preserving of fruit and vegetables
*Parent:* Pilgrim Food Holdings Limited
*Officers:* Paul Frampton [1970] Director/Accountant; Tom Malkoski [1956] Director/Chief Executive Officer [American]

**Chaucer Foods UK Limited**
*Incorporated:* 5 March 1982 *Employees:* 137
*Net Worth:* £10,383,000 *Total Assets:* £13,066,000
*Registered Office:* Unit 26 Brighton Street Industrial Estate, Freightliner Road, Hull, HU3 4UN
*Activities:* Manufacture of bread; manufacture of fresh pastry goods and cakes
*Parent:* Pilgrim Food Holdings Limited
*Officers:* Paul Frampton [1970] Director/Accountant; Tom Malkoski [1956] Director [American]

**Checkmate Fire Solutions Limited**
*Incorporated:* 29 July 2003 *Employees:* 29
*Net Worth:* £2,622,852 *Total Assets:* £5,475,015
*Registered Office:* The Second Floor, Rosemount House, Rosemount Estate, Huddersfield Road, Elland, W Yorks, HX5 0EE
*Activities:* Other specialised construction activities n.e.c.
*Parent:* Checkmate Holdings Ltd
*Officers:* Sinead McCullagh, Secretary; Mark Damian Williams [1965] Director/General Manager; Tomasz Wisniewski [1977] Director - Glazing Division [Polish/British]; David Woffendin [1978] Commercial Director

**Checkmate Holdings Ltd**
*Incorporated:* 1 October 2016 *Employees:* 3
*Net Worth:* £1,749,461 *Total Assets:* £3,558,572
*Registered Office:* The Second Floor, Rosemount House, Rosemount Estate, Huddersfield Road, Elland, W Yorks, HX5 0EE
*Activities:* Other specialised construction activities n.e.c.
*Parent:* Checkmate Holdings Group Limited
*Officers:* Simon Richard Moate [1962] Director; Mark Damian Williams [1965] Director/Chief Executive Officer; Alan Wilson [1959] Director; Tomasz Wisniewski [1977] Director [Polish/British]; David Paul Woffendin [1978] Director

**Chemfix Products Limited**
*Incorporated:* 5 December 2001 *Employees:* 67
*Net Worth:* £4,794,752 *Total Assets:* £7,953,865
*Registered Office:* Mill Street East, Dewsbury, W Yorks, WF12 9BQ
*Activities:* Manufacture of other chemical products n.e.c.
*Shareholders:* Briolf Group SL; Jaume Juher; Llorenc Manjarin Juher
*Officers:* Xavier Sague, Secretary; Paul Lionel Evans [1954] Director; Urs Alfred Joos [1961] Managing Director [Swiss]; Jaume Juher [1960] Director [Spanish]; Carles Palomo Reixach [1975] Managing Director [Spanish]; Xavier Sague [1969] Managing Director [Spanish]

**Cheque Exchange Limited**
*Incorporated:* 11 May 1994 *Employees:* 16
*Net Worth:* £1,558,000 *Total Assets:* £6,126,000
*Registered Office:* No 1 Godwin Street, Bradford, W Yorks, BD1 2SU
*Activities:* Financial intermediation not elsewhere classified
*Parent:* N & N Simple Financial Solutions Limited
*Officers:* David George Whincup, Secretary; Christopher Donald Gillespie [1963] Director; Eleanor Thornhill [1974] Director

**Cherry Valley Farms Limited**
*Incorporated:* 19 November 1959 *Employees:* 206
*Net Worth:* £33,085,916 *Total Assets:* £36,448,360
*Registered Office:* Cherry Valley House, Laceby Business Park, Grimsby Road, Laceby, N E Lincs, DN37 7DP
*Activities:* Raising of poultry
*Parent:* Anatis UK Limited
*Officers:* Katharine Mary Butler, Secretary; Katharine Mary Butler [1960] Director/Accountant; Yuqiang Cao [1965] Director/Businessman [Chinese]; Peimin Liang [1974] Director/Businessman [Chinese]; Jiantong Liu [1968] Director/Businessman [Chinese]; Liang Shi [1983] Director/Businessman [Chinese]; John Priestly Vernam [1956] Director; Dr Xinjian Yan [1958] Director/China Operations [Chinese]

**Chesterfield Poultry Limited**
*Incorporated:* 22 August 2002 *Employees:* 67
*Net Worth:* £8,560,189 *Total Assets:* £24,273,272
*Registered Office:* 5 Coulman Street, Thorne, Doncaster, S Yorks, DN8 5JT
*Activities:* Retail sale of meat and meat products in specialised stores
*Shareholders:* Mohamed Fayez Ahmed; Nadeem Iqbal
*Officers:* Mohamed Fayez Ahmed, Secretary; Mohammed Fayez Ahmed [1959] Director; Nadeem Iqbal [1972] Managing Director

**Chicago Bidco Limited**
*Incorporated:* 30 November 2016
*Net Worth:* £21,687,498 *Total Assets:* £73,376,832
*Registered Office:* Cast House, Old Mill Business Park, Leeds, LS10 1RJ
*Activities:* Other activities auxiliary to insurance and pension funding
*Parent:* Chicago Midco Limited
*Officers:* Trevor Charles William Hopkins, Secretary; Jonathan James Cox [1980] Director/Investment Professional; Tim John Hanford [1964] Director/Investment Professional; John William James Spencer [1957] Director

**Chicago Midco Limited**
*Incorporated:* 30 November 2016
*Net Worth:* £10,103,736 *Total Assets:* £83,873,224
*Registered Office:* Cast House, Old Mill Business Park, Gibraltar Island Road, Leeds, LS10 1RJ
*Activities:* Other activities auxiliary to insurance and pension funding
*Officers:* Trevor Charles William Hopkins, Secretary; Jonathan James Cox [1980] Director/Investment Professional; Todd Michael Freebern [1975] Director/Tax Professional [American]; Sally Ann Rocker [1954] Director/Investment and Legal Professional [American]

**Chinnaraja Estates Limited**
*Incorporated:* 8 October 2013 *Employees:* 1
*Net Worth:* £8,197 *Total Assets:* £6,262,404
*Registered Office:* Richard Smedley Chartered Accountants, 2nd Floor, Woodside House, 261 Low Lane, Horsforth, Leeds, LS18 5NY
*Activities:* Other letting and operating of own or leased real estate
*Major Shareholder:* Aravindan Chinnaraja
*Officers:* Aravindan Chinnaraja [1975] Director [Singaporean]

**Chiorino U.K. Limited**
*Incorporated:* 10 January 1975 *Employees:* 48
*Net Worth:* £3,906,026 *Total Assets:* £5,347,593
*Registered Office:* Phoenix Avenue, Green Lane Industrial Park, Featherstone, W Yorks, WF7 6EP
*Activities:* Other manufacturing n.e.c.
*Shareholders:* Matteo Chiorino; Gregorio Chiorino; Elisa Chiorino
*Officers:* Carl Johnson, Secretary; Gregorio Chiorino [1945] Director [Italian]; Carl Johnson [1959] Director/General Manager; Eric Iain Longman [1942] Director/Chartered Accountant

**Chippindale Foods Limited**
*Incorporated:* 17 August 1981 *Employees:* 52
*Net Worth:* £5,937,065 *Total Assets:* £10,942,273
*Registered Office:* Hilmore House, Gain Lane, Bradford, W Yorks, BD3 7DL
*Activities:* Wholesale of dairy products, eggs and edible oils and fats
*Parent:* Wm Morrison Supermarkets P L C
*Officers:* Jonathan Burke, Secretary; Mark Thomas Stitson [1976] Finance Director; Andrew Edward Thornber [1974] Managing Director

**Chippindale Plant Limited**
*Incorporated:* 26 April 1949 *Employees:* 121
*Net Worth:* £8,268,090 *Total Assets:* £34,284,416
*Registered Office:* Prima House, Ring Road, Lower Wortley, Leeds, LS12 5PX
*Activities:* Renting and leasing of construction and civil engineering machinery and equipment
*Shareholders:* Peter Gordon Chippindale; Nigel Paul Chippindale
*Officers:* Antony Charles Atack [1964] Operations Director; Nigel Paul Chippindale [1962] Director

**Chrislind Services Limited**
*Incorporated:* 31 May 1979 *Employees:* 25
*Net Worth:* £4,629,835 *Total Assets:* £5,329,715
*Registered Office:* The Bungalow, Goody Cross Lane, Little Preston, Swillington, Leeds, LS26 8UY
*Activities:* Construction of other civil engineering projects n.e.c.
*Major Shareholder:* Leslie Graham Mills
*Officers:* Ann Mills, Secretary; Ann Mills [1946] Director/Secretary; Leslie Graham Mills [1948] Director/Contracts Manager; Richard James Mills [1977] Director/Engineer; Claire Louise Pilkington [1971] Director

**Christeyns UK Ltd**
*Incorporated:* 6 May 1965 *Employees:* 128
*Net Worth:* £22,950,100 *Total Assets:* £30,519,140
*Registered Office:* Rutland Street, East Bowling, Bradford, W Yorks, BD4 7EA
*Activities:* Manufacture of soap and detergents
*Major Shareholder:* Alain Joseph Andre Bostoen
*Officers:* Julie Susan Roberts, Secretary; David Peter Aveyard [1963] Director; Paul Gerrard Victor Camiel Bostoen [1939] Director [Belgian]; Elisabeth Josepha Margaretha Ghislenus Devos [1941] Director [Belgian]; Nicholas James Garthwaite [1957] Director; Daniel John Kilgallon [1956] Director Sales; Julie Susan Roberts [1969] Director/Chartered Accountant; Scott Alan Grant Wilson [1969] Sales Director; Jozef Maria Jaak Wittouck [1962] Director [Belgian]

**The Christian Trust**
*Incorporated:* 24 December 1993 *Employees:* 91
*Net Worth:* £2,702,878 *Total Assets:* £6,772,846
*Registered Office:* Ellel Grange, Ellel, Lancaster, LA2 0HN
*Activities:* Other education n.e.c.
*Officers:* Robert John Hay, Secretary; David Malcolm Cross [1948] Centre Director; Gillian Fiona Horrobin [1949] Director/Centre Manager; Peter James Horrobin [1943] Director of Ellel Ministries; Roger Pook [1944] Director/Retired; Andrew James Taylor [1971] Director/Minister

**Christians Against Poverty**
*Incorporated:* 3 February 2003 *Employees:* 261
*Net Worth:* £4,901,000 *Total Assets:* £6,721,000
*Registered Office:* Jubilee Mill, North Street, Bradford, W Yorks, BD1 4EW
*Activities:* Non-trading company
*Officers:* Stephen Richard Bonfield, Secretary; Joy Glayla Blundell [1979] Director/Pastor; Matthew Adrian Frost [1965] Director/Charity Chief Executive; Simon Barnaby Gates [1975] Director/Banker; Roger David Hattam [1968] Director; Chine McDonald [1984] Director/Communications; Timothy Michael Morfin [1970] Charity Director; Lisa Annette Pearce [1971] Director/Chief Executive; Jane Kathleen Elizabeth Pleace [1971] Charity Director

**Charles Church Developments Limited**
*Incorporated:* 2 September 1974 *Employees:* 5
*Net Worth:* £507,716,992 *Total Assets:* £1,394,449,024
*Registered Office:* Persimmon House, Fulford, York, YO19 4FE
*Activities:* Construction of domestic buildings
*Parent:* Persimmon Holdings Limited
*Officers:* Tracy Lazelle Davison, Secretary; David Jenkinson [1967] Director; Michael Hugh Killoran [1961] Finance Director; Richard Paul Stenhouse [1971] Director/Accountant

**Church Property Holdings Limited**
*Incorporated:* 10 November 2004 *Employees:* 4
*Net Worth:* £2,253,943 *Total Assets:* £7,774,106
*Registered Office:* 17 Old Leeds Road, Huddersfield, W Yorks, HD1 1SG
*Activities:* Other letting and operating of own or leased real estate
*Shareholders:* Terence Anthony Langley; Graeme Beck
*Officers:* Graeme Beck [1975] Director; Terence Anthony Langley [1975] Director

**CI Estates Limited**
*Incorporated:* 21 February 2017 *Employees:* 1
*Net Worth Deficit:* £93,919 *Total Assets:* £3,938,636
*Registered Office:* 2 Therm Road, Hull, HU8 7BF
*Activities:* Buying and selling of own real estate
*Parent:* Teddy Clark (Holdings) Limited
*Officers:* William Edward Clark [1967] Director

**CID Products LLP**
*Incorporated:* 8 December 2011 *Employees:* 26
*Net Worth:* £770,005 *Total Assets:* £3,034,558
*Registered Office:* CID House, Peckfield Business Park, Phoenix Avenue, Leeds, LS25 4DY
*Officers:* John Soulsby [1957] LLP Member

**Cider of Sweden Ltd**
*Incorporated:* 26 June 2006 *Employees:* 39
*Net Worth:* £12,852,489 *Total Assets:* £48,552,928
*Registered Office:* Albion Court, 5 Albion Place, Leeds, LS1 6JL
*Activities:* Wholesale of wine, beer, spirits and other alcoholic beverages
*Shareholder:* Barry Thomas Connolly
*Officers:* Ciaran Michael Cleland, Secretary; Carl Eric Berg [1946] Director/Consultant [Swedish]; Peter Bronsman [1963] Director [Swedish]; Barry Thomas Connolly [1961] Director [Irish]

**Cielivestock Limited**
*Incorporated:* 18 December 2015
*Net Worth Deficit:* £645 *Total Assets:* £31,567,284
*Registered Office:* Centre for Innovation Excellence in Livestock, York Science Park, IT Centre, Innovation Way, Heslington, York, YO10 5NP
*Activities:* Support activities for animal production (other than farm animal boarding)
*Officers:* Timothy Mark Bennett [1953] Director/FSA Deputy Chair; Fiona Catherine Fell [1962] Director; Charles John Henning [1958] Director/Banker/Farmer; Ursula Lavery [1962] Technical Director [Irish]; Nicholas Charles Major [1961] Director/Agribusiness; Prof Quintin Archibald McKellar [1958] Director/Office of The Vice-Chancellor, University of Hertfordshire; Sophie Florence Throup [1976] Managing Director

**Cilantro Acquisitions Limited**
*Incorporated:* 21 September 2010
*Net Worth:* £25,365,000 *Total Assets:* £57,587,000
*Registered Office:* Denton Hall, Denton, Ilkley, W Yorks, LS29 0HH
*Activities:* Activities of head offices
*Parent:* Cilantro Parent Limited
*Officers:* Rachel Clare Salmon, Secretary; David Stuart Hurcomb [1964] Director/Engineer and Accountant; Michael Porter [1967] Director

**Cilantro Midco Limited**
*Incorporated:* 21 September 2010
*Net Worth:* £33,600,000 *Total Assets:* £47,000,000
*Registered Office:* Denton Hall, Denton, Ilkley, W Yorks, LS29 0HH
*Activities:* Activities of head offices
*Parent:* Schultz Bidco Limited
*Officers:* Rachel Clare Salmon, Secretary; David Stuart Hurcomb [1964] Director/Engineer and Accountant; Michael Porter [1967] Director/Chief Financial Officer

**Cilantro Parent Limited**
*Incorporated:* 21 September 2010
*Net Worth Deficit:* £137,500,000 *Total Assets:* £47,000,000
*Registered Office:* Denton Hall, Denton, Ilkley, W Yorks, LS29 0HH
*Activities:* Activities of head offices
*Parent:* Cilantro Midco Limited
*Officers:* Rachel Clare Salmon, Secretary; David Stuart Hurcomb [1964] Director/Engineer and Accountant; Michael Porter [1967] Director/Chief Financial Officer

**CIP (Mill Road Development) LLP**
*Incorporated:* 22 December 2016
*Net Worth Deficit:* £413,000 *Total Assets:* £7,688,000
*Registered Office:* 1 Park Row, Leeds, LS1 5AB

**Circuit Launderette Services Ltd.**
*Incorporated:* 1 July 1994 *Employees:* 36
*Net Worth:* £20,008,000 *Total Assets:* £33,806,000
*Registered Office:* Meadowcroft Lane, Halifax Lane, Ripponden, W Yorks, HX6 4AJ
*Activities:* Other business support service activities n.e.c.
*Parent:* Vanilla Group Limited
*Officers:* Helen Jane Ashton [1972] Director/Chief Executive Officer; Paul Justin Humphreys [1958] Director

**Cirrus Laminations Limited**
*Incorporated:* 22 August 2005 *Employees:* 3
*Net Worth:* £1,714,952 *Total Assets:* £3,522,401
*Registered Office:* Hunt Street, Whitwood Mere, Castleford, W Yorks, WF10 1NS
*Activities:* Manufacture of other products of wood; manufacture of articles of cork, straw and plaiting materials
*Shareholders:* Glenn Monkman; Vernon Michael Shimwell; Michael Anthony Lundy
*Officers:* Paul George Almond, Secretary; Michael Anthony Lundy [1952] Director/Design Engineer; Glenn Monkman [1957] Director/Manager

**Cirteq Limited**
*Incorporated:* 30 May 1995 *Employees:* 235
*Net Worth:* £6,914,841 *Total Assets:* £10,115,584
*Registered Office:* Hayfield Colne Road, Glusburn, Keighley, W Yorks, BD20 8QP
*Activities:* Manufacture of wire products, chain and springs
*Parent:* Glusburn Holdings Limited
*Officers:* Andrew I'anson Crabtree, Secretary; Andrew I'anson Crabtree [1951] Director/Chartered Accountant; Angus McKay Meikle [1950] Director; Victor Elisabeth Alois Stevens [1957] Director [Belgian]

**Citispace Properties Limited**
*Incorporated:* 9 September 2002
*Net Worth:* £145,468 *Total Assets:* £3,261,657
*Registered Office:* Citispace South, 11 Regent Street, Leeds, LS2 7QN
*Activities:* Other letting and operating of own or leased real estate
*Parent:* Citispace Group Limited
*Officers:* John Robert Kidd [1948] Director; Linda Barbara Plant [1952] Director; David Selwyn Serr [1944] Director

**Citu (Low Fold) LLP**
*Incorporated:* 15 November 2013
*Net Worth Deficit:* £505,986 *Total Assets:* £5,338,028
*Registered Office:* W9 Greenhouse, Beeston Road, Leeds, LS11 6AD

**City & Provincial (Equity Partners 3) Limited**
*Incorporated:* 20 October 2004
*Net Worth Deficit:* £337,759 *Total Assets:* £5,841,187
*Registered Office:* Citispace House, Byron Street, Leeds, LS2 7QJ
*Activities:* Buying and selling of own real estate
*Officers:* Linda Barbara Plant [1952] Director; Stephen Leslie Plant [1960] Director

**City Fusion Limited**
*Incorporated:* 21 November 1978 *Employees:* 2
*Net Worth:* £596,396 *Total Assets:* £10,942,605
*Registered Office:* Kestrel House, 16 Lower Brunswick Street, Leeds, LS2 7PU
*Activities:* Other letting and operating of own or leased real estate
*Parent:* Emco Group Holdings Ltd
*Officers:* Johanna Julia Cohen, Secretary; Henry Selwyn Cohen [1961] Director/Property Developer; Reece Dexter Cohen [1992] Director

**City Health Care Partnership CIC**
*Incorporated:* 8 June 2007 *Employees:* 2,320
*Net Worth:* £9,023,261 *Total Assets:* £37,558,512
*Registered Office:* 5 Beacon Way, Hull, HU3 4AE
*Activities:* Other human health activities
*Officers:* David Taylor, Secretary; Andrew Lawrence Burnell [1966] Director/Chief Executive; Dr Mark Findley [1963] Medical Director; Paul Hillary [1973] Deputy Director; David Adrian Leedham [1967] Development Director; Andrew Charles Lindsey [1947] Director/Retired; Tracy Ann Vickers [1964] Care Group Director; Carol Maria Waudby [1966] Director/Chief Operating Officer

**City of Bradford Y.M.C.A.**
*Incorporated:* 29 November 1994 *Employees:* 18
*Net Worth:* £5,633,574 *Total Assets:* £5,807,779
*Registered Office:* Culture Fusion Building, 125 Thornton Road, Bradford, W Yorks, BD1 2EP
*Activities:* Other accommodation
*Officers:* John Cronin, Secretary; Rev John Oluwagbenga Adereti [1960] Director/Pastor [Nigerian]; Roland Graham Clark [1954] Director/Retired Chartered Accountant; Caroline Jeanne Elizabeth Murie [1955] Director/Retired; Helen Karen Robertshaw [1972] Director/HR Consultant; Kathryn Joyce Smith [1962] Director/Conveyancing Manager

**The City of Leeds YMCA**
*Incorporated:* 21 April 1995 *Employees:* 29
*Net Worth:* £3,177,799 *Total Assets:* £3,660,365
*Registered Office:* The City of Leeds YMCA, Otley Road, Leeds, LS16 6HQ
*Activities:* Other social work activities without accommodation n.e.c.
*Officers:* Maisie Foley, Secretary; Brenda Bray [1939] Director/Retired; Susan Crowther [1956] Director/Bank Clerk; Hamish Ian Elliot [1957] Director/Insurance Brokers; Colin William France [1943] Director/Chartered Quantity Surveyor; Jane Elizabeth Hainsworth [1967] Director/Graphic Designer; John Anthony Leahy [1951] Director/Solicitor; Brian Adrian Newton [1960] Director/Financial Consultant; Christopher Edward Shaw [1948] Director/Company Secretary; John David Spencer [1957] Director

**City Portfolio Limited**
*Incorporated:* 10 July 2007
*Net Worth:* £64,505 *Total Assets:* £3,266,242
*Registered Office:* 21 Castle Hill, Lancaster, LA1 1YN
*Activities:* Construction of domestic buildings
*Parent:* Cityblock Holdings Limited
*Officers:* Alison Jane Bargh, Secretary; Alison Jane Bargh [1961] Operations Director; John Trevor Bargh [1958] Director/Management Consultant

**City Red (Holdings) Limited**
*Incorporated:* 15 December 2003
*Net Worth:* £679,329 *Total Assets:* £3,264,141
*Registered Office:* City Red Properties, City Red House, 35 Cromer Terrace, Leeds, LS2 9JU
*Activities:* Buying and selling of own real estate
*Officers:* Bilal Salameh, Secretary; Ahmed Khalil Al-Ani [1980] Director

**Cityblock Holdings Limited**
*Incorporated:* 29 May 2002
*Net Worth:* £288,056 *Total Assets:* £3,335,509
*Registered Office:* 21 Castle Hill, Lancaster, LA1 1YN
*Activities:* Construction of domestic buildings
*Parent:* Cityblock Limited
*Officers:* Alison Jane Bargh, Secretary/Property Development & Management; Alison Jane Bargh [1961] Director/Property Development & Management; John Trevor Bargh [1958] Director

**Cityblock Lettings Limited**
*Incorporated:* 29 May 2002 *Employees:* 18
*Net Worth:* £3,625,144 *Total Assets:* £3,701,855
*Registered Office:* 21 Castle Hill, Lancaster, LA1 1YN
*Activities:* Management of real estate on a fee or contract basis
*Parent:* Cityblock Holdings Limited
*Officers:* Alison Jane Bargh, Secretary/Property Development & Management; Alison Jane Bargh [1961] Director/Property Development & Management; John Trevor Bargh [1958] Director

**Citygate Developments No.1 Limited**
*Incorporated:* 22 November 2006 *Employees:* 3
*Net Worth:* £11,749,644 *Total Assets:* £24,100,688
*Registered Office:* Millshaw, Leeds, LS11 8EG
*Activities:* Development of building projects
*Parent:* Evans Management Limited
*Officers:* Robert Marshall, Secretary; Roderick Michael Evans [1962] Director; Paul Terence Millington [1962] Director/Accountant; Alan Matthew Syers [1964] Director/Chartered Surveyor

**Citynet Insurance Brokers Limited**
*Incorporated:* 24 February 2000 *Employees:* 76
*Net Worth:* £3,451,307 *Total Assets:* £18,728,236
*Registered Office:* Rossington's Business Park, West Carr Road, Retford, Notts, DN22 7SW
*Activities:* Non-life insurance
*Parent:* Citynet London Holdings Limited
*Officers:* Ryan Christopher Brown [1973] Director; Adrian Colosso [1957] Director; Brendan James McManus [1959] Director; Richard John Scott [1968] Managing Director; David Walland [1968] Director/Chartered Management Accountant; Andrew Mark Walsh [1979] Motor Fleet Director

**Civic PFI Investments Limited**
*Incorporated:* 15 March 2012 *Employees:* 2
*Net Worth Deficit:* £1,692,698 *Total Assets:* £15,092,564
*Registered Office:* 4 Greengate, Cardale Park, Harrogate, N Yorks, HG3 1GY
*Activities:* Activities of head offices
*Parent:* Grosvenor PFI Holdings Limited
*Officers:* Alexander Toby Shedden Parry, Secretary; Alastair William Hopps [1986] Director/Accountant; Alexander Toby Shedden Parry [1976] Director/Company Secretary

**Clariant Oil Services UK Ltd**
*Incorporated:* 16 June 1975 *Employees:* 55
*Net Worth:* £11,482,000 *Total Assets:* £17,972,000
*Registered Office:* Clariant House, Unit 2 Rawdon Park, Yeadon, Leeds, LS19 7BA
*Activities:* Manufacture of other chemical products n.e.c.
*Parent:* Clariant Production UK Ltd
*Officers:* Dean Credland, Secretary; John Walter Jex [1969] Director/General Manager; Andrew Jonathan Lock [1964] Director; Tracyann Otteslev [1973] Director/HR Manager

**Clariant Plastics & Coatings (UK) Ltd**
*Incorporated:* 4 October 2005 *Employees:* 8
*Previous:* Clariant Masterbatches UK Ltd
*Net Worth:* £6,805,000 *Total Assets:* £11,754,000
*Registered Office:* Clariant House, Unit 2 Rawdon Park, Yeadon, Leeds, LS19 7BA
*Activities:* Wholesale of chemical products
*Parent:* Clariant AG
*Officers:* Dean Credland, Secretary; Daniel Hug [1973] Director/Head of Corporate Controlling [Swiss]; Andrew Jonathan Lock [1964] Director; Norbert Merklein [1964] Director [German]; Tracyann Otteslev [1973] Director/HR Manager

**Clariant Production UK Ltd**
*Incorporated:* 29 May 1997 *Employees:* 4
*Net Worth:* £61,516,000 *Total Assets:* £72,015,000
*Registered Office:* Clariant House, Unit 2 Rawdon Park, Yeadon, Leeds, LS19 7BA
*Activities:* Wholesale of chemical products
*Parent:* Clariant Services UK Ltd
*Officers:* Dean Credland, Secretary; Daniel Hug [1973] Director/Head of Corporate Controlling [Swiss]; Oliver Kinkel [1963] Director/General Manager [German]; Andrew Jonathan Lock [1964] Director; Tracyann Otteslev [1973] Director/HR Manager; Adrian Heinz Tillmann [1959] Director [Swiss]

**Clariant Services UK Ltd**
*Incorporated:* 9 March 1995 *Employees:* 16
*Net Worth:* £56,860,000 *Total Assets:* £94,367,000
*Registered Office:* Clariant House, Unit 2 Rawdon Park, Yeadon, Leeds, LS19 7BA
*Activities:* Activities of head offices
*Parent:* Clariant AG
*Officers:* Dean Credland, Secretary; Daniel Hug [1973] Director/Head of Corporate Controlling [Swiss]; Oliver Kinkel [1963] Director/General Manager [German]; Andrew Jonathan Lock [1964] Director; Tracyann Otteslev [1973] Director/HR Manager; Adrian Heinz Tillmann [1959] Director [Swiss]

**Clarion Solicitors Limited**
*Incorporated:* 10 March 2010 *Employees:* 152
*Net Worth:* £4,257,541 *Total Assets:* £10,966,457
*Registered Office:* Elizabeth House, 13-19 Queen Street, Leeds, LS1 2TW
*Activities:* Solicitors
*Officers:* Richard John Moran, Secretary; Martin Robert Grange [1972] Director/Solicitor; Matthew Richard Hattersley [1971] Director/Solicitor; Charles Nicholas Roger Hutton [1966] Director/Solicitor; Ryan Gregory Millmore [1974] Director/Solicitor; Richard John Moran [1969] Director/Solicitor; Justine Marie Osmotherley [1971] Director/Solicitor; Alice Victoria Evelyn Sybil Pratt [1978] Director/Solicitor; Sarah Tahamtani [1977] Director/Solicitor; Simon David Young [1967] Director/Solicitor

**Claritas Solutions Limited**
*Incorporated:* 26 April 1996 *Employees:* 36
*Net Worth:* £916,568 *Total Assets:* £4,886,192
*Registered Office:* 2 Deighton Close, Wetherby, W Yorks, LS22 7GZ
*Activities:* Wired telecommunications activities
*Shareholders:* Glenn Scaife; Angela Jane Sykes-Brown
*Officers:* Kirsty Jayne Sutton, Secretary; Derek George Baker [1969] Director; Jennifer Battersby [1980] Director; Wesley Paul Rowland [1977] Director/Developer; Glenn Scaife [1959] Technical Director; Kirsty Jayne Sutton [1979] Finance Director

**Teddy Clark (Holdings) Limited**
*Incorporated:* 9 November 2007 *Employees:* 1
*Net Worth Deficit:* £1,480,358 *Total Assets:* £7,616,522
*Registered Office:* 2 Therm Road, Hull, HU8 7BF
*Activities:* Activities of head offices
*Parent:* Teddy Clark Group Limited
*Officers:* Mr William Edward Clark [1967] Director

**Clark Care Estates Limited**
*Incorporated:* 21 February 2017 *Employees:* 1
*Net Worth:* £27,477 *Total Assets:* £3,079,726
*Registered Office:* 2 Therm Road, Hull, HU8 7BF
*Activities:* Buying and selling of own real estate
*Parent:* Teddy Clark (Holdings) Limited
*Officers:* William Edward Clark [1967] Director

**S B & A Clark Farming Limited**
*Incorporated:* 16 August 2010
*Net Worth:* £3,174,856 *Total Assets:* £3,213,790
*Registered Office:* Farnleigh Gardens, Stillington Road, Sutton-on-the-Forest, N Yorks, YO61 1EH
*Activities:* Growing of cereals (except rice), leguminous crops and oil seeds
*Parent:* S B and A Clark (York) Ltd
*Officers:* Angela Clark, Secretary; Angela Clark [1956] Director; Stephen Bradley Clark [1954] Director

**Teddy Clark Group Limited**
*Incorporated:* 15 June 2016 *Employees:* 8
*Net Worth:* £1,483,778 *Total Assets:* £23,164,940
*Registered Office:* Unit 2 Therm Road, Hull, HU8 7BF
*Activities:* Activities of head offices
*Major Shareholder:* William Edward Clark
*Officers:* Mr William Edward Clark [1967] Director

**Teddy Clark Limited**
*Incorporated:* 1 October 2001 *Employees:* 6
*Net Worth:* £2,948,658 *Total Assets:* £22,517,372
*Registered Office:* Unit 2 Therm Road, New Cleveland Street, Hull, HU8 7BF
*Activities:* Other letting and operating of own or leased real estate
*Parent:* Teddy Clark (Holdings) Limited
*Officers:* Mr William Edward Clark [1967] Director

**The Clarke Chapman Group Limited**
*Incorporated:* 7 December 2000 *Employees:* 205
*Net Worth:* £4,006,616 *Total Assets:* £8,144,587
*Registered Office:* Enterprise Way, Retford, Notts, DN22 7HH
*Activities:* Manufacture of pumps
*Parent:* Langley Holdings PLC
*Officers:* Alexander Robert Allan [1968] Director; Bernard James Langley [1993] Director; Stephen Douglas Plant [1952] Director

**Clarke Meats Limited**
*Incorporated:* 9 September 1999 *Employees:* 32
*Net Worth:* £2,640,650 *Total Assets:* £3,825,909
*Registered Office:* Unit 1 The Triangle Business Park, Paddock, Huddersfield, W Yorks, HD1 4RR
*Activities:* Wholesale of meat and meat products
*Major Shareholder:* Jonathan Howard Clarke
*Officers:* Jonathan Howard Clarke, Secretary/Poultry Butcher; Jonathan Howard Clarke [1973] Director; Kelly Louise Clarke [1979] Director

**Clarke Telecom Limited**
*Incorporated:* 10 February 2011 *Employees:* 243
*Net Worth:* £5,495,000 *Total Assets:* £20,485,000
*Registered Office:* 3175 Century Way, Thorpe Park, Leeds, LS15 8ZB
*Activities:* Other telecommunications activities
*Parent:* Renew Holdings PLC
*Officers:* Nigel Ernest Newton [1966] Managing Director; Paul Scott [1964] Director/Engineer

**Clarks UK Limited**
*Incorporated:* 25 August 2006 *Employees:* 36
*Net Worth:* £1,366,804 *Total Assets:* £3,945,909
*Registered Office:* 2100 Century Way, Thorpe Park Business Park, Leeds, LS15 8ZB
*Activities:* Manufacture of other food products n.e.c.
*Parent:* Hain Frozen Foods UK Limited
*Officers:* Nicholas John Keen, Secretary; Denise Faltischek [1973] Director/Executive Vice President and General Counsel [American]; James Michael Langrock [1965] Director [American]; Mark Lawrence Schiller [1961] Director [American]; Robin James Skidmore [1968] Director

**Clarks Vehicle Conversions Limited**
*Incorporated:* 29 January 1999 *Employees:* 93
*Net Worth:* £1,055,072 *Total Assets:* £3,292,349
*Registered Office:* Unit 16 Carcroft Enterprise Park, Station Road, Carcroft, Doncaster, S Yorks, DN6 8DD
*Activities:* Manufacture of bodies (coachwork) for motor vehicles (except caravans)
*Officers:* Paul Clark, Secretary/Director; Paul Clark [1970] Director; Brett Harrop [1973] Director; Darren Lord [1970] Director

**Clays of Addingham Limited**
*Incorporated:* 2 June 1971
*Net Worth:* £3,634,242 *Total Assets:* £6,225,383
*Registered Office:* Scale Hill House, Rylstone, Skipton, N Yorks, BD23 6ER
*Activities:* Development of building projects
*Officers:* Ian Michael Clay, Secretary; Joan Clay, Secretary; Sandra Allott [1951] Director; Ian Michael Clay [1970] Director; Joan Clay [1934] Director; Paul John Clay [1965] Director

**Clayton Dewandre Holdings Limited**
*Incorporated:* 28 November 1928
*Net Worth:* £204,166,080 *Total Assets:* £272,478,688
*Registered Office:* Citadel House, 58 High Street, Hull, HU1 1QE
*Activities:* Non-trading company
*Parent:* Wabco Europe Holdings BV
*Officers:* Marcel Zaalberg, Secretary; Lisa Jane Brown [1978] Director/Lawyer; Marcel Zaalberg [1966] Managing Director [Dutch]

**Cleaning and Paper Disposables Limited**
*Incorporated:* 25 April 1988 *Employees:* 53
*Previous:* Cleaning and Paper Disposables PLC
*Net Worth:* £1,986,682 *Total Assets:* £8,135,249
*Registered Office:* Ipark Industrial Estate, Innovation Drive, Hull, HU5 1SG
*Activities:* Non-specialised wholesale trade
*Parent:* CPD Direct Limited
*Officers:* Kirstie Emma Lloyd, Secretary; Antony Bennett [1967] Managing Director; Kirstie Emma Lloyd [1971] Finance Director; Ian Michael Warvill [1964] Operations Director

**Cleckheaton Properties Limited**
*Incorporated:* 3 February 2004 *Employees:* 2
*Net Worth:* £3,038,782 *Total Assets:* £10,957,610
*Registered Office:* c/o Ernest Wilson, Deanhurst Park, Gelderd Road, Leeds, LS27 7LS
*Activities:* Other letting and operating of own or leased real estate
*Shareholders:* Robert Williamson; Eve Williamson
*Officers:* Paul Adam Milton Williamson, Secretary; Tamara Dawn Beckwith [1964] Director; Paul Adam Milton Williamson [1968] Director

**Cleethorpes Properties Limited**
*Incorporated:* 14 November 1977
*Net Worth:* £4,737,018 *Total Assets:* £8,194,487
*Registered Office:* 36 High Street, Cleethorpes, N E Lincs, DN35 8JN
*Activities:* Development of building projects
*Shareholders:* Gillian Lovelle; PLJ Enterprises Ltd
*Officers:* Jonathan Christopher Lovelle, Secretary/Director; John Robert Love [1939] Director/Auctioneer Surveyor; Jonathan Christopher Lovelle [1974] Director

**Cleeve Primary School**
*Incorporated:* 14 November 2013 *Employees:* 74
*Net Worth:* £3,409,086 *Total Assets:* £4,947,934
*Registered Office:* Cleeve Primary School, Wawne Road, Hull, HU7 4JH
*Activities:* Primary education
*Officers:* Anna Jayne Bell [1983] Director/Deputy Headteacher; Janet Mary Brock [1942] Director/Retired; Christine Bushell [1980] Director/Teacher; Michael James Dodd [1974] Director/Headteacher; Terry Dunn [1960] Director/Benefits Specialist; Tanya Grannon [1987] Director/Post Office Clerk; Michelle Kermeen [1980] Director/Deputy Headteacher; Harold Patrick Neilson [1930] Director/Retired

**Clerical Medical Investment Fund Managers Limited**
*Incorporated:* 19 February 1993
*Net Worth:* £4,985,000 *Total Assets:* £5,114,000
*Registered Office:* Trinity Road, Halifax, W Yorks, HX1 2RG
*Activities:* Financial intermediation not elsewhere classified
*Parent:* Halifax Financial Services (Holdings) Limited
*Officers:* Christina Ann Hankin, Secretary; Sean William Lowther [1960] Director; Ian Henry Price [1965] Director

**Cleveland Bridge UK Limited**
*Incorporated:* 9 April 1999 *Employees:* 217
*Net Worth:* £970,000 *Total Assets:* £19,660,000
*Registered Office:* Cleveland House, Yarm Road, Darlington, Co Durham, DL1 4DE
*Activities:* Other specialised construction activities n.e.c.
*Major Shareholder:* Sheikh Abdullah Rushaid Al Rushaid
*Officers:* Rasheed Abdullah Alrushaid [1973] Director/Chairman [Saudi Arabian]; Christopher John Droogan [1958] Director; John Philip Heathcock [1976] Finance Director

**Cleves Cross Learning Trust**
*Incorporated:* 4 October 2013 *Employees:* 68
*Net Worth:* £1,379,711 *Total Assets:* £3,014,084
*Registered Office:* c/o Cleves Cross Primary School, Cleves Cross, Ferryhill, Co Durham, DL17 8QY
*Activities:* Primary education
*Officers:* Helen Andrews [1978] Director/Children's Homes Manager; Sara Jane Clasper [1977] Director/Solicitor; Alison Lazenby [1964] Director/Headteacher; Steven Brian Leigh [1963] Director/Advisor; Leigh Lockey [1958] Director/Retired; John Alexander Bell Muir [1955] Director/Retired; Glenys Joan Newby [1966] Director/Self Employed

**Clicklink Logistics Limited**
*Incorporated:* 18 April 2016
*Net Worth:* £2,727,000 *Total Assets:* £10,690,000
*Registered Office:* Clipper Logistics Group, Gelderd Road, Leeds, LS12 6LT
*Activities:* Freight transport by road
*Shareholders:* Clipper Logistics PLC; John Lewis PLC
*Officers:* Guy Collingwood Jackson, Secretary; Richard Ball [1974] Transport Director; David Arthur Hodkin [1961] Director; Ged Keogh-Peters [1974] Director/Retailer; Antony Gerard Mannix [1963] Director; Berangere Andree Mireille Michel [1973] Finance Director [French]; Dino Rocos [1958] Retail Director

**Cliffe Hill Second Investments Limited**
*Incorporated:* 21 February 1963 *Employees:* 5
*Net Worth:* £13,280,986 *Total Assets:* £14,377,501
*Registered Office:* Carlton House, Bull Close Lane, Halifax, W Yorks, HX1 2EG
*Activities:* Financial intermediation not elsewhere classified
*Shareholder:* Trustees of JH Denham No 2 Settlement
*Officers:* Andrea Bamforth [1976] Director/Chartered Accountant; Linda Valerie Denham [1947] Director; Jonathan Lloyd Algernon Evans [1973] Director; Natalie Claire Howard [1976] Director; Nicola Susan Webb [1974] Director

**The Clifford Street Venture LLP**
*Incorporated:* 5 February 2015
*Net Worth:* £4,803,170 *Total Assets:* £5,025,688
*Registered Office:* Colenso House, Omega 1, Monks Cross Drive, York, YO32 9GZ
*Officers:* Andrew David Hulme [1952] LLP Member; Anne Burnett Hulme [1953] LLP Member; Mark Nelson Richardson [1944] LLP Member; Anna Thorell [1950] LLP Member

**Clifton Properties (Yorkshire) Limited**
*Incorporated:* 17 November 1987
*Net Worth:* £21,746,504 *Total Assets:* £30,976,644
*Registered Office:* 59 Commercial Street, Batley, W Yorks, WF17 5EP
*Activities:* Other letting and operating of own or leased real estate
*Major Shareholder:* Michael Raymond Smith
*Officers:* Robert Charles Thewlis, Secretary; Mathew Paul Smith [1971] Director/Property Manager; Michael Raymond Smith [1946] Director/Carpet Retailer

**Clipper Logistics PLC**
*Incorporated:* 4 April 1995 *Employees:* 4,531
*Net Worth:* £39,318,000 *Total Assets:* £183,248,000
*Registered Office:* Clipper Logistics Group, Gelderd Road, Leeds, LS12 6LT
*Activities:* Freight transport by road
*Officers:* Marianne Hodgkiss, Secretary; David Arthur Hodkin [1961] Director; Antony Gerard Mannix [1963] Director; Steven Nicholas Parkin [1960] Director; Stephen Peter Robertson [1954] Director; Michael John Russell [1951] Director

**J.H. Clissold & Son Ltd.**
*Incorporated:* 4 November 1975 *Employees:* 24
*Net Worth:* £3,644,913 *Total Assets:* £4,512,059
*Registered Office:* Oldgate Mill, North Wing, Otley Road, Bradford, W Yorks, BD3 0DH
*Activities:* Manufacture of other men's outerwear
*Officers:* Franklin Stevens Clare, Secretary; Richard Antony Chambers [1969] Director/Textile Designer; Lisa Joanne Cooper [1969] Director/Accountant; John David Hitt [1964] Director/Vice President of Retail Operations [American]; Frank Xavier O'Reilly [1963] Director/Chartered Accountant [Irish]

**Closepatch Limited**
*Incorporated:* 30 June 1986 *Employees:* 6
*Net Worth:* £3,598,512 *Total Assets:* £4,073,907
*Registered Office:* Rushex House, Lotherton Way, Garforth Industrial Estate, Garforth, Leeds, LS25 2JY
*Activities:* Other letting and operating of own or leased real estate
*Shareholders:* Joanna Rosemary Gilpin; Anthony Craven Gilpin
*Officers:* Anthony Craven Gilpin [1950] Director; Antonia Craven Gilpin [1986] Director/Personal Assistant; Joanna Rosemary Gilpin [1946] Director; Samantha Louise Goodall [1971] Director/Manager

**Cloth Fair Point Capital Limited**
*Incorporated:* 31 January 2014
*Net Worth:* £966,186 *Total Assets:* £3,221,124
*Registered Office:* c/o WPO Limited, Windsor House, Cornwall Road, Harrogate, N Yorks, HG1 2PW
*Activities:* Other professional, scientific and technical activities n.e.c.
*Parent:* Burghmeister Limited
*Officers:* Thomas Michel Ernest Ehret [1952] Director [French]; James Ross Hyett [1988] Director

**Dean Clough Limited**
*Incorporated:* 14 May 1982 *Employees:* 30
*Net Worth:* £11,454,607 *Total Assets:* £58,263,872
*Registered Office:* Office Suite D182, Dean Clough, Halifax, W Yorks, HX3 5AX
*Activities:* Buying and selling of own real estate
*Shareholder:* Jeremy Hall
*Officers:* Anne Moffat, Secretary; Jeremy Hall [1962] Director; Maurice Miller [1947] Director/Chartered Accountant

**CLS Civil Engineering Limited**
*Incorporated:* 26 April 2002 *Employees:* 24
*Net Worth:* £2,301,228 *Total Assets:* £3,744,569
*Registered Office:* Unit 4 Atherton Way, Brigg, N Lincs, DN20 8AR
*Activities:* Construction of commercial buildings
*Major Shareholder:* Charles Llewellyn Salmon
*Officers:* Katharine Margaret Salmon, Secretary; Charles Llewellyn Salmon [1956] Director

**Clugston Construction Limited**
*Incorporated:* 25 January 1961 *Employees:* 441
*Net Worth:* £6,901,099 *Total Assets:* £57,284,892
*Registered Office:* St Vincent House, Normanby Road, Scunthorpe, N Lincs, DN15 8QT
*Activities:* Construction of commercial buildings
*Parent:* Clugston Group Limited
*Officers:* Ian Pattison, Secretary; Andrew Thomas Allingham [1961] Commercial Director; David Westland Antony Clugston [1972] Director; Roderick Malcolm Fry [1959] Director; Ian Pattison [1969] Finance Director; Stephen John Radcliffe [1955] Director; Robert John Vickers [1956] Director/Chief Executive Officer

**Clugston Distribution Services Limited**
*Incorporated:* 25 July 2005 *Employees:* 171
*Net Worth:* £753,882 *Total Assets:* £8,010,413
*Registered Office:* St Vincent House, Normanby Road, Scunthorpe, N Lincs, DN15 8QT
*Activities:* Freight transport by road
*Parent:* Clugston Group Limited
*Officers:* Ian Pattison, Secretary; David Westland Antony Clugston [1972] Director; Timothy Mark Doggett [1973] Director; Ian Pattison [1969] Finance Director; Robert John Vickers [1956] Director/Chief Executive Officer

**Clugston Estates Limited**
*Incorporated:* 12 March 1930
*Net Worth:* £511,442 *Total Assets:* £4,576,244
*Registered Office:* St Vincent House, Normanby Road, Scunthorpe, N Lincs, DN15 8QT
*Activities:* Activities of head offices
*Parent:* Clugston Group Limited
*Officers:* Ian Pattison, Secretary; David Westland Antony Clugston [1972] Director; Ian Pattison [1969] Finance Director; Robert John Vickers [1956] Director/Chief Executive Officer

**Clugston Group Limited**
*Incorporated:* 1 November 1937 *Employees:* 629
*Net Worth:* £14,317,000 *Total Assets:* £86,212,000
*Registered Office:* St Vincent House, Normanby Road, Scunthorpe, N Lincs, DN15 8QT
*Activities:* Activities of head offices
*Shareholder:* John Westland Antony Clugston
*Officers:* Ian Pattison, Secretary; David Westland Antony Clugston [1972] Director; John Westland Antony Clugston [1938] Director/Chairman; John Anthony Brian Kelly [1941] Director; Ian Pattison [1969] Finance Director; Stephen John Radcliffe [1955] Director; Robert John Vickers [1956] Director/Chief Executive Officer; Andrew William Walker [1944] Director/Lawyer

**Clyde Bergemann Materials Handling Limited**
*Incorporated:* 15 April 1994 *Employees:* 80
*Net Worth Deficit:* £5,696,000 *Total Assets:* £13,071,000
*Registered Office:* Lakeside Boulevard, Lakeside, Doncaster, S Yorks, DN4 5PL
*Activities:* Repair of machinery
*Parent:* Clyde Bergemann Investments Limited
*Officers:* Miles Brittain Ratcliffe, Finance Director; Stephen Michael Cragg [1959] Director; Ralph Alexander Ludwig [1963] Director [German]; Miles Brittain Ratcliffe [1965] Finance Director

**Clydesdale Covered Bonds No.2 LLP**
*Incorporated:* 21 May 2010
*Net Worth Deficit:* £3,148,000 *Total Assets:* £1,599,218,944
*Registered Office:* 20 Merrion Way, Leeds, LS2 8NZ

**Clytha Holdings Limited**
*Incorporated:* 26 September 1990 *Employees:* 176
*Net Worth:* £6,686,690 *Total Assets:* £22,035,164
*Registered Office:* Eland Road, Denaby Main, Doncaster, S Yorks, DN12 4HA
*Activities:* Wholesale of metals and metal ores
*Parent:* Endcliffe Holdings Limited
*Officers:* Robert George Anthony Barr [1956] Director [Irish]; Leslie Robert Buxton [1978] Director; James Richard Keeling-Heane [1980] Director; Mark Vincenzo Wadsworth [1973] Director/Systems General Manager; Mark Douglas Wheatley [1979] Director

**CMG Lancaster Limited**
*Incorporated:* 20 November 2015 *Employees:* 37
*Net Worth:* £2,809,208 *Total Assets:* £5,660,518
*Registered Office:* Northgate, White Lund Industrial Estate, Morecambe, Lancs, LA3 3PA
*Activities:* Sale of new cars and light motor vehicles
*Major Shareholder:* David Johnathan Cox
*Officers:* Helen Hayton, Secretary; David Johnathan Cox [1971] Director; Helen Hayton [1970] Director/Group FD

**CNG (Group) Limited**
*Incorporated:* 10 August 2010 *Employees:* 159
*Previous:* HG1 Gas Limited
*Net Worth:* £18,978,228 *Total Assets:* £86,344,368
*Registered Office:* 2 Victoria Avenue, Harrogate, N Yorks, HG1 1EL
*Activities:* Activities of distribution holding companies
*Shareholders:* Jacqueline Louise Hall; Christopher John England; CNG EBT Limited
*Officers:* Christopher John England [1971] Director; Jacqueline Louise Hall [1963] Director; Colin Richard Hollins [1967] Director/Utilities; John Roy Leworthy [1963] Director; James Richard Smith [1986] Director; Michael John Walls [1963] Director

**CNIM Clugston (Avonmouth) Limited**
*Incorporated:* 7 March 2017 *Employees:* 4
*Net Worth Deficit:* £1,141 *Total Assets:* £9,290,450
*Registered Office:* St Vincent House, Normanby Road, Scunthorpe, N Lincs, DN15 8QT
*Activities:* Other specialised construction activities n.e.c.
*Shareholders:* Soluni SA; CNIM SA; Clugston Construction Limited
*Officers:* Andrew Thomas Allingham [1961] Commercial Director; David Richard Alexandre Cinque [1981] Director of Projects [French]; Richard Greenwood [1968] Director/Business Unit Manager; Stephane Richard Scheirich [1969] Project Director [French]

**CO2Sense C.I.C.**
*Incorporated:* 4 March 2005 *Employees:* 2
*Net Worth:* £5,322,862 *Total Assets:* £5,331,176
*Registered Office:* The Tannery, 91 Kirkstall Road, Leeds, LS3 1HS
*Activities:* Other professional, scientific and technical activities n.e.c.
*Officers:* Martin Alderson [1960] Asset Director; Stephen Booth [1959] Director/Renewable Energy Executive; Isobel Mills [1956] Director/Civil Servant; Geoffrey David Sinclair [1972] Director/Corporate Finance

**Coaching Inns (North) Limited**
*Incorporated:* 17 January 2007 *Employees:* 81
*Net Worth:* £134,613 *Total Assets:* £4,309,044
*Registered Office:* Ye Olde Bell, Barnby Moor, Retford, Notts, DN22 8QS
*Activities:* Hotels and similar accommodation
*Parent:* Dukeries Healthcare Ltd
*Officers:* Hilary Jane Levack, Secretary; Catherine Firth [1963] Director/General Manager; Allen Paul Levack [1951] Director; Hilary Jane Levack [1955] Director

**Coachman Caravan Company Limited**
*Incorporated:* 28 April 1986 *Employees:* 188
*Net Worth:* £2,697,307 *Total Assets:* £11,217,928
*Registered Office:* Amsterdam Road, Sutton Fields Industrial Estate, Hull, HU7 0XF
*Activities:* Manufacture of caravans
*Parent:* Coachman Holdings Limited
*Officers:* Elliot James Hibbs [1976] Sales Director; Ian Martin Kershaw [1972] Director; Alan Gerarde Roberts [1952] Production Director; Stephen James Shipley [1957] Director; Jason Thompson [1972] Director

**Coachman Group Limited**
*Incorporated:* 22 September 2016 *Employees:* 188
*Net Worth:* £755,159 *Total Assets:* £13,757,135
*Registered Office:* Coachman Caravans, Amsterdam Road, Sutton Fields Industrial Estate, Hull, HU7 0XF
*Activities:* Activities of production holding companies
*Shareholder:* Elliot James Hibbs
*Officers:* Alf Rikard Ekstrom [1956] Director/CEO KABE AB [Swedish]; Elliot James Hibbs [1976] Managing Director; Ian Martin Kershaw [1972] Director; Stephen James Shipley [1957] Director; Jason Thompson [1972] Director

**Coachman Holdings Limited**
*Incorporated:* 25 October 2001
*Net Worth:* £2,676,127 *Total Assets:* £5,731,257
*Registered Office:* Amsterdam Road, Sutton Fields Industrial Estate, Hull, HU7 0XF
*Activities:* Activities of production holding companies
*Parent:* Coachman Group Limited
*Officers:* Elliot James Hibbs [1976] Managing Director; Ian Martin Kershaw [1972] Director; Stephen James Shipley [1957] Director; Jason Thompson [1972] Director

**Coal Contractors Limited**
*Incorporated:* 29 October 1951 *Employees:* 3
*Net Worth:* £7,689,809 *Total Assets:* £7,834,127
*Registered Office:* Stotforth Hill House, Rushyford, Ferryhill, Co Durham, DL17 0NF
*Activities:* Open cast coal working
*Parent:* Hall Construction Services Limited
*Officers:* Neville John Hall [1956] Director; Stephen Hall [1954] Director; Garry Hutchinson [1955] Director

**Coast and Vale Community Action**
*Incorporated:* 7 March 1997 *Employees:* 27
*Net Worth:* £2,921,055 *Total Assets:* £3,603,644
*Registered Office:* The Street, 12 Lower Clark Street, Scarborough, N Yorks, YO12 7PW
*Activities:* Other information service activities n.e.c.
*Officers:* Melanie Louise Bonney-Kane, Secretary; Lee Barker [1958] Director; Guy Michael Baumann [1970] Director/Entrepreneur; Moira Cunningham [1947] Director/Entrepreneur; Lesley Dixon [1954] Director/Manager; Richard Lincoln Grunwell [1944] Director/Solicitor; Jane Elspeth Mortimer [1948] Director; David Timothy Warner [1947] Director/Consultant

**Cobalt Project Investments (Hull - Sewell) Limited**
*Incorporated:* 25 November 2016
*Net Worth:* £1,001 *Total Assets:* £3,669,589
*Registered Office:* 1 Park Row, Leeds, LS1 5AB
*Activities:* Activities of other holding companies n.e.c.
*Parent:* Sewell Education (Hull BSF) Limited
*Officers:* Jennifer McKay, Secretary; Robert Andrew Cakewell [1969] Director; John Stephen Gordon [1962] Director; David Adrian Leedham [1967] Director/Accountant

**Cobalt Project Investments (Hull) Limited**
*Incorporated:* 3 August 2005 *Employees:* 1
*Net Worth:* £108,130 *Total Assets:* £3,811,053
*Registered Office:* 1 Park Row, Leeds, LS1 5AB
*Activities:* Other business support service activities n.e.c.
*Parent:* PPDI Assetco Limited
*Officers:* Jennifer McKay, Secretary; John Stephen Gordon [1962] Director

**Cobalt Project Investments (Issuer) Limited**
*Incorporated:* 19 July 2013 *Employees:* 3
*Net Worth Deficit:* £637 *Total Assets:* £32,270,988
*Registered Office:* 1 Park Row, Leeds, LS1 5AB
*Activities:* Other business support service activities n.e.c.
*Parent:* Dalmore Capital 12 GP LLP
*Officers:* Jennifer McKay, Secretary; John McDonagh [1969] Director; Alistair Graham Ray [1974] Director

**Cobalt Project Investments (Taycare) Limited**
*Incorporated:* 15 February 2008 *Employees:* 1
*Net Worth:* £158,015 *Total Assets:* £5,057,994
*Registered Office:* 1 Park Row, Leeds, LS1 5AB
*Activities:* Other business support service activities n.e.c.
*Parent:* Cobalt Project Investments Limited
*Officers:* Jennifer McKay, Secretary; John McDonagh [1969] Director

**Cobalt Project Investments Limited**
*Incorporated:* 12 August 2013 *Employees:* 3
*Net Worth Deficit:* £10,905,747 *Total Assets:* £81,794,192
*Registered Office:* 1 Park Row, Leeds, LS1 5AB
*Activities:* Other business support service activities n.e.c.
*Parent:* Dalmore Capital (Para 1) Limited
*Officers:* Jennifer McKay, Secretary; John McDonagh [1969] Director; Alistair Graham Ray [1974] Director

**Cobco 867 Limited**
*Incorporated:* 11 December 2007 *Employees:* 3
*Net Worth Deficit:* £3,370,909 *Total Assets:* £30,822,640
*Registered Office:* Trimble House, Gelderd Road, Gildersome, Morley, Leeds, LS27 7JP
*Activities:* Activities of head offices
*Parent:* Trimble Solutions (UK) Ltd
*Officers:* James Anthony Kirkland, Secretary; James Anthony Kirkland [1959] Director/VP, General Counsel and Assistant Secretary [American]; Algirdas Paul Rimas [1970] Director/Deputy General Counsel [American]; John Peter Schreiber [1959] Director/Vice President Global Tax [American]

**Cockburn Multi Academy Trust**
*Incorporated:* 12 January 2016 *Employees:* 231
*Net Worth:* £35,733,000 *Total Assets:* £38,368,000
*Registered Office:* Cockburn School, Gipsy Lane, Leeds, LS11 5TT
*Activities:* General secondary education
*Officers:* James Daniel Sidgwick, Secretary; Paul Nicholas Brennan [1960] Director/Management & Education Consultant; John Edward Ellis [1940] Director/Retired; Christopher James Graham [1986] Director; David John Gurney [1966] Director/Headmaster; Jonathan Paul Harsine [1962] Director/Education Consultant; Catherine Moore [1975] Director/Solicitor; Kamila Morawiecka-Watkins [1975] Director/HR Business Partner; Peter James Nuttall [1949] Director/Retired; David Arthur Westwell [1943] Director/Retired

**R.S. Cockerill (York) Limited**
*Incorporated:* 29 January 1958 *Employees:* 104
*Net Worth:* £8,560,687 *Total Assets:* £14,150,297
*Registered Office:* Stamford Bridge Road, Dunnington, York, YO19 5AE
*Activities:* Agents specialised in the sale of other particular products
*Shareholders:* Pamela Ann Cockerill; Martin Richard Cockerill
*Officers:* Pamela Ann Cockerill, Secretary/Married Woman; Martin Richard Cockerill [1946] Director/Potato Merchant; Pamela Ann Cockerill [1946] Director/Married Woman; Michael John Dangerfield [1965] Commercial Director; Christopher John Ingle [1963] Finance Director; Rufus John Pilgrim [1970] Commercial Director

**Cod Beck Blenders Limited**
*Incorporated:* 30 August 1988 *Employees:* 112
*Previous:* Gallows Green Services Limited
*Net Worth:* £4,703,321 *Total Assets:* £9,919,414
*Registered Office:* Cod Beck Estate, Dalton, Thirsk, N Yorks, YO7 3HR
*Activities:* Manufacture of other chemical products n.e.c.
*Shareholders:* Keith Boardall; June Mary Boardall; Marcus Keith Boardall; Rowena June Mary Barlow
*Officers:* Marcus Keith Boardall, Secretary/Chartered Accountant; Keith Boardall [1934] Director/Chartered Accountant; Marcus Keith Boardall [1962] Director/Chartered Accountant; Leslie Brown [1949] Director; Steven James Meyer [1979] Director

**Codecrest Limited**
*Incorporated:* 23 February 1987 *Employees:* 58
*Net Worth:* £3,268,692 *Total Assets:* £8,148,503
*Registered Office:* Dalton House, 9 Dalton Square, Lancaster, LA1 1WD
*Activities:* Hotels and similar accommodation
*Parent:* Youngmight Limited
*Officers:* Diane Robinson, Secretary/Hotel Accountant; Geoffrey Goodyear Atkinson [1950] Director

**Cogri Group Limited**
*Incorporated:* 21 September 1989
*Net Worth:* £2,500,344 *Total Assets:* £3,050,348
*Registered Office:* Dene House, North Road, Kirkburton, Huddersfield, W Yorks, HD8 0RW
*Activities:* Floor and wall covering
*Shareholders:* Kevin John Dare; Lynn Ann Dare
*Officers:* Lynn Ann Dare, Secretary; Kevin John Dare [1963] Director; Lynn Ann Dare [1963] Director/Company Secretary

**Cohen & Wilks International (Holdings) Limited**
*Incorporated:* 6 September 2013 *Employees:* 295
*Net Worth Deficit:* £3,293,291 *Total Assets:* £42,264,636
*Registered Office:* Aquatite House, Mabgate, Leeds, LS9 7DR
*Activities:* Manufacture of other wearing apparel and accessories n.e.c.
*Officers:* Zhen Sun [1966] Director/Textile Executive [Canadian]

**Cohen & Wilks International Limited**
*Incorporated:* 23 October 1974 *Employees:* 86
*Net Worth:* £4,491,952 *Total Assets:* £17,741,052
*Registered Office:* Aquatite House, Mabgate, Leeds, LS9 7DR
*Activities:* Agents involved in the sale of textiles, clothing, fur, footwear and leather goods
*Officers:* Jonathan Hayes James Barrow, Secretary; Jonathan Hayes James Barrow [1968] Director/Accountant; Samantha Jane Edwards [1971] Director/Sales Executive; Michelle Foxall [1967] Director/Sales Executive; Zhen Sun [1966] Director/Textile Executive [Canadian]

**Cohen Cramer Limited**
*Incorporated:* 26 September 2013 *Employees:* 51
*Net Worth:* £1,453,392 *Total Assets:* £3,623,129
*Registered Office:* Suite 1B, Joseph's Well, Hanover Walk, Leeds, LS3 1AB
*Activities:* Solicitors
*Shareholders:* Emma Louise Mason; Michael John McDonnell; John Simon Goodwin
*Officers:* Emma Louise Mason, Secretary; John Simon Goodwin [1956] Director/Solicitor; David Stephen Hall [1979] Director/Solicitor; Emma Louise Mason [1976] Director/Solicitor; Mike Massen [1964] Director/Solicitor; Michael John McDonnell [1965] Director/Solicitor

**Collard Cole Limited**
*Incorporated:* 16 October 1992 *Employees:* 2
*Net Worth:* £3,063,548 *Total Assets:* £3,768,471
*Registered Office:* Wood Nook House, Wood Nook Lane, Meltham, Holmfirth, W Yorks, HD9 4DU
*Activities:* Other letting and operating of own or leased real estate
*Major Shareholder:* Peter Collard Cole
*Officers:* Peter Collard Cole, Secretary; Angela Mary Cole [1948] Director/School Teacher; Peter Collard Cole [1936] Director

**Colenso Holdings Limited**
*Incorporated:* 24 July 2017 *Employees:* 4
*Net Worth:* £2,209,586 *Total Assets:* £5,001,160
*Registered Office:* Colenso House, Omega 1, Monks Cross Drive, Huntington, York, YO32 9GZ
*Activities:* Activities of other holding companies n.e.c.
*Shareholders:* Richard James Michael Peak; Maxwell Rowland John Reeves
*Officers:* Susan Ann Jones [1959] Director/Group Financial Controller; Richard James Michael Peak [1970] Director/Chartered Surveyor; Maxwell Rowland John Reeves [1986] Director/Chartered Surveyor; William John Graham Reeves [1956] Director/Chartered Surveyor

**Coletta and Tyson Limited**
*Incorporated:* 7 July 1999 *Employees:* 134
*Net Worth:* £5,574,342 *Total Assets:* £15,400,093
*Registered Office:* 324 Hull Road, Woodmansey, Beverley, N Humbers, HU17 0RU
*Activities:* Growing of other perennial crops
*Officers:* Paul David Tyson, Secretary/Director; Richard John Harling [1972] Director/Accountant; John Tyson [1963] Director; Paul David Tyson [1967] Director

**Coletta Holdings Limited**
*Incorporated:* 14 July 1999 *Employees:* 186
*Net Worth:* £18,416,812 *Total Assets:* £31,140,912
*Registered Office:* 324 Hull Road, Woodmansey, Beverley, N Humbers, HU17 0RU
*Activities:* Activities of head offices
*Shareholders:* Paul David Tyson; John Michael Tyson
*Officers:* Paul David Tyson, Secretary/Director; Richard John Harling [1972] Director/Accountant; John Tyson [1963] Director; Paul David Tyson [1967] Director

**Collaborative Learning Trust**
*Incorporated:* 1 November 2011 *Employees:* 155
*Previous:* Otley Prince Henry's Academy Trust
*Net Worth:* £7,661,000 *Total Assets:* £9,052,000
*Registered Office:* Prince Henry's Grammar School, Farnley Lane, Otley, W Yorks, LS21 2BB
*Activities:* General secondary education
*Officers:* Catherine Owen, Secretary; Ian Benjamin Geoffrey Bond [1973] Director; Rachel Colbourn [1970] Director; Andrew Richard Gilliland [1962] Director/Education; Tony Lenehan [1959] Director; George Petrie [1978] Director; Stella Pollard [1970] Director; Janet Valerie Sheriff [1964] Director/Headteacher; Paul Tranter [1965] Director/Professional Fundraiser; Fiona Wrightson [1961] Director

**College Holdings 2012 Ltd**
*Incorporated:* 19 March 1957 *Employees:* 82
*Net Worth:* £3,299,866 *Total Assets:* £9,530,667
*Registered Office:* Scarborough College, Filey Road, Scarborough, N Yorks, YO11 3BA
*Activities:* Pre-primary education
*Officers:* Alison Jayne Higgins, Secretary; Michael John Baines [1943] Director/Retired; James Andrew Cliffe [1983] Director/Registered Manager Children's Social Care; Jeremy John Cook [1953] Director/Accountant; Simon Nevill Fairbank [1965] Director/Land Agent; Neil Gardner [1951] Director/Retired; Victoria Jane Gillingham [1966] Managing Director - AMDIS; Antony Stephen Green [1952] Director/Owner - A S Green & Company; John Marcus Green [1962] Director/Farmer/Land Owner; Richard Guthrie [1972] Director of Broadland Properties; James Richard Marshall [1960] Managing Director - Lupton Fawcett Dennison Till; John Renshaw [1945] Director/Dentist; Dr Ian Grenville Hugh Renwick [1960] Director/Hospital Consultant; John Stephen Rowlands [1950] Director/Retired; John Francis Watson Swiers [1976] Director/Farmer; Graeme Neville Mansell Young [1973] Director

**The Collegiate Formation Limited**
*Incorporated:* 31 October 1990
*Previous:* Buckedge Limited
*Net Worth:* £3,554,701 *Total Assets:* £3,826,120
*Registered Office:* Thorpe Underwood Hall, Thorpe Underwood, York, YO26 9SZ
*Activities:* Activities of other holding companies n.e.c.
*Parent:* Care & Recreation Holdings Limited
*Officers:* Christopher James Hall, Secretary; Matthew Adshead [1972] Director; Jackie Hales [1950] Director; Christopher James Hall [1969] Director/Accountant; Karen Elizabeth Howells-Lee [1968] Director; Amy Katherine Martin [1985] Director; Laurence McKell [1964] Director

**Collett & Sons Limited**
*Incorporated:* 19 July 2016
*Net Worth:* £239,166 *Total Assets:* £8,199,873
*Registered Office:* Victoria Terminal, Albert Road, Halifax, W Yorks, HX2 0DF
*Activities:* Other transportation support activities
*Officers:* Michael Collett, Secretary; David Collett [1962] Director; Michael Collett [1967] Director; Nigel Andrew Thornton [1962] Director

**Collett Holdings Limited**
*Incorporated:* 11 July 2016 *Employees:* 128
*Net Worth:* £9,165,531 *Total Assets:* £15,135,713
*Registered Office:* Victoria Terminal, Albert Road, Halifax, W Yorks, HX2 0DF
*Activities:* Activities of other holding companies n.e.c.
*Major Shareholder:* David Collett
*Officers:* Michael Collett, Secretary; David Collett [1962] Director; Jack William Collett [1989] Director/Operations Manager; Lincoln Collett [1964] Director; Mark Collett [1965] Director; Michael Collett [1967] Director; Patricia Collett [1942] Director; Richard James Collett [1984] Director/Mechanic; Richard Collett [1942] Director; Richard Collett [1961] Director

**Collett Logistics Limited**
*Incorporated:* 11 December 1975 *Employees:* 128
*Previous:* Collett & Sons Limited
*Net Worth:* £102,625 *Total Assets:* £7,157,548
*Registered Office:* Victoria Terminal, Albert Road, Halifax, W Yorks, HX2 0DF
*Activities:* Freight transport by road
*Parent:* Collett Holdings Ltd
*Officers:* Lincoln Collett [1964] Director; Mark Collett [1965] Director

**Collins (Seafoods) Limited**
*Incorporated:* 26 June 1986 *Employees:* 33
*Net Worth:* £6,000,450 *Total Assets:* £11,950,874
*Registered Office:* Unit 2 Park 2000, Millennium Way, Aycliffe Industrial Park, Newton Aycliffe, Co Durham, DL5 6AR
*Activities:* Wholesale of meat and meat products
*Parent:* Seagold Limited
*Officers:* Claire Elizabeth Carter, Secretary; Gustaf Baldvinsson [1957] Director [Icelander]; Thorsteinn Mar Baldvinsson [1952] Director [Icelander]; Claire Elizabeth Carter [1979] Director; Richard Collins [1954] Director; Kenneth Gary Lethem [1959] Director

**G. Collinson (Construction) Limited**
*Incorporated:* 5 July 1991 *Employees:* 4
*Net Worth:* £70,936 *Total Assets:* £3,635,950
*Registered Office:* 2 West Parade Road, Scarborough, N Yorks, YO12 5ED
*Activities:* Hotels and similar accommodation
*Shareholders:* Graham Alan Collinson; Pamela Gilmore
*Officers:* Graham Collinson, Secretary; Pamela Gilmore [1957] Director/Teacher

**Colne Investments 2 Holdco Limited**
*Incorporated:* 29 December 2014
*Net Worth Deficit:* £1,021,914 *Total Assets:* £22,712,956
*Registered Office:* 1 Park Row, Leeds, LS1 5AB
*Activities:* Other business support service activities n.e.c.
*Parent:* Dalmore Capital 11 GP Limited
*Officers:* Jennifer McKay, Secretary; John McDonagh [1969] Director; Alistair Graham Ray [1974] Director

**Colne Topco Limited**
*Incorporated:* 15 August 2014 *Employees:* 3
*Net Worth Deficit:* £9,721,517 *Total Assets:* £71,750,328
*Registered Office:* 1 Park Row, Leeds, LS1 5AB
*Activities:* Other business support service activities n.e.c.
*Shareholders:* PPDI Assetco Limited; Colne Investments 2 Holdco Limited
*Officers:* Jennifer McKay, Secretary; John McDonagh [1969] Director; Alistair Graham Ray [1974] Director

**Colt Industrial Services Limited**
*Incorporated:* 15 June 1988
*Net Worth:* £2,694,000 *Total Assets:* £4,921,000
*Registered Office:* 4 Rudgate Court, Walton, Wetherby, W Yorks, LS23 7BF
*Activities:* Specialised cleaning services
*Parent:* Augean Property Limited
*Officers:* Mark Rupert Maxwell Fryer [1967] Finance Director; John Hugo Rauch [1970] Director/Group Operating Officer

**The Columbo Group Limited**
*Incorporated:* 16 July 2004 *Employees:* 107
*Net Worth:* £4,296,750 *Total Assets:* £10,746,395
*Registered Office:* BCL House, 2 Pavilion Business Park, Royds Hall Road, Leeds, LS12 6AJ
*Activities:* Public houses and bars
*Shareholders:* Steven Ian Ball; Rizwan Khaleel Shaikh
*Officers:* Steven Ian Ball, Secretary; Steven Ian Ball [1974] Director; Rizwan Khaleel Shaikh [1977] Director

**Combined Selection Group Ltd**
*Incorporated:* 14 July 2009 *Employees:* 130
*Previous:* Combined Selection Ltd
*Net Worth:* £875,944 *Total Assets:* £3,003,851
*Registered Office:* Springwood House, Low Lane, Horsforth, Leeds, LS18 5NU
*Activities:* Activities of head offices
*Shareholders:* Ben Riley; Wayne Underwood
*Officers:* Wayne Underwood, Secretary; Ben Riley [1978] Director/Recruitment Consultant; Wayne Underwood [1972] Director/Recruitment Consultant

**The Comedian's Guide To Survival Limited**
*Incorporated:* 27 January 2014
*Net Worth:* £779,981 *Total Assets:* £4,509,436
*Registered Office:* Highfield Grange, Bubwith, Selby, N Yorks, YO8 6DP
*Activities:* Motion picture production activities
*Officers:* Tobias Angus Giles Mathews, Secretary; Alan Richard Latham [1960] Director/Producer

**Commercial Development Projects Limited**
*Incorporated:* 9 November 1970 *Employees:* 15
*Net Worth:* £75,452,000 *Total Assets:* £156,766,000
*Registered Office:* Huddersfield Road, Elland, W Yorks, HX5 9BW
*Activities:* Development of building projects
*Parent:* Marshall Holdings Limited
*Officers:* Jonathan Booth, Secretary; Jonathan Booth [1970] Director/Accountant; Christopher Roy Marshall [1939] Director/Building Contractor; James Robert Marshall [1965] Director/Surveyor; Simon Charles Newton Marshall [1963] Director/Surveyor

**Commercial Legal Limited**
*Incorporated:* 14 March 2003 *Employees:* 32
*Net Worth:* £4,465,521 *Total Assets:* £17,823,404
*Registered Office:* Unit 1 Carolina Court, Doncaster, S Yorks, DN4 5RA
*Activities:* Other business support service activities n.e.c.
*Major Shareholder:* John Lawrence Radford
*Officers:* Alexandra Maria Sheriff, Secretary; Joshua Charles Barnsdale [1982] Director; Peter Graham Long [1986] Director; John Matthew Parker [1976] Claims Director; John Lawrence Radford [1965] Director/Chief Executive Officer

**Commercial Vehicle Auctions Limited**
*Incorporated:* 30 October 1975 *Employees:* 21
*Net Worth:* £2,768,520 *Total Assets:* £5,251,277
*Registered Office:* Carr Hill, Doncaster, S Yorks, DN4 8DE
*Activities:* Other professional, scientific and technical activities n.e.c.
*Parent:* Ballyvesey Holdings Limited
*Officers:* Harold Hugh Montgomery, Secretary; Ross Dalton [1982] Managing Director; Harold Hugh Montgomery [1948] Director/Haulier

**Communisis BBF Ltd**
*Incorporated:* 20 September 1917
*Net Worth:* £11,453,795 *Total Assets:* £11,453,795
*Registered Office:* Communisis House, Manston Lane, Leeds, LS15 8AH
*Activities:* Dormant company
*Parent:* Robot No. 6 Limited
*Officers:* Sarah Louise Caddy, Secretary; Sarah Louise Caddy [1976] Director/Company Secretary; Jonathan Rowlatt Huber Riddle [1960] Director/Tax Manager

**Communisis Chorleys Ltd**
*Incorporated:* 17 October 1962
*Net Worth:* £4,639,000 *Total Assets:* £4,639,000
*Registered Office:* Communisis House, Manston Lane, Leeds, LS15 8AH
*Activities:* Dormant company
*Parent:* Waddingtons House Limited
*Officers:* Sarah Louise Caddy, Secretary; Sarah Louise Caddy [1976] Director/Company Secretary; Jonathan Rowlatt Huber Riddle [1960] Director/Tax Manager

**Communisis Data Intelligence Limited**
*Incorporated:* 27 June 2014
*Previous:* Psona Group Limited
*Net Worth Deficit:* £1,675,999 *Total Assets:* £7,859,001
*Registered Office:* Communisis House, Manston Lane, Leeds, LS15 8AH
*Activities:* Data processing, hosting and related activities
*Parent:* Communisis Limited
*Officers:* Sarah Caddy, Secretary; Andrew Martin Blundell [1960] Director; Steven Clive Rawlins [1962] Director

**Communisis Limited**
*Incorporated:* 6 April 1994 *Employees:* 2,081
*Previous:* Communisis PLC
*Net Worth:* £139,136,000 *Total Assets:* £327,335,008
*Registered Office:* Communisis House, Manston Lane, Leeds, LS15 8AH
*Activities:* Activities of head offices
*Parent:* OSG Bidco Limited
*Officers:* Sarah Louise Caddy, Secretary; Scott W. Bernstein [1960] Director [American]; Andrew Martin Blundell [1960] Director; Kent Herring [1963] Director [American]; Steven Clive Rawlins [1962] Director

**Communisis One Ltd**
*Incorporated:* 21 March 1978
*Net Worth:* £4,127,000 *Total Assets:* £4,127,000
*Registered Office:* Communisis House, Manston Lane, Leeds, LS15 8AH
*Activities:* Dormant company
*Parent:* Communisis Chorleys Limited
*Officers:* Sarah Louise Caddy, Secretary; Jonathan Rowlatt Huber Riddle [1960] Director/Tax Manager

**Communisis UK Limited**
*Incorporated:* 30 March 1971 *Employees:* 1,680
*Net Worth:* £17,987,000 *Total Assets:* £198,235,008
*Registered Office:* Communisis House, Manston Lane, Leeds, LS15 8AH
*Activities:* Printing n.e.c.
*Parent:* Communisis Limited
*Officers:* Sarah Louise Caddy, Secretary; Andrew Martin Blundell [1960] Director; Steven Clive Rawlins [1962] Director

**Community Foundation for Calderdale**
*Incorporated:* 8 April 1991 *Employees:* 13
*Net Worth:* £11,746,449 *Total Assets:* £11,927,057
*Registered Office:* First Floor, The 1855 Building, Discovery Road, Halifax, W Yorks, HX1 2NG
*Activities:* Other social work activities without accommodation n.e.c.
*Officers:* Nicholas Charles Worsnop, Secretary; Wilhelmus Johannus Maria Batist [1951] Managing Director [Dutch]; Elizabeth Mary Bavidge [1945] Director; Heidi Louise Bingham [1973] Director; Rachel Diane Dilley [1972] Director; Christopher Harris [1958] Director; Alison Sarah Haskins [1963] Director/Charity CEO; Brenda Hodgson [1945] Director/Public Relations Consultant; Shabir Hussain [1970] Director; Lee Martin Kenny [1974] Director; Stuart Vincent Rumney [1961] Director/Chief Operating Officer of a Charity

**Community Foundation for Leeds**
*Incorporated:* 21 May 2002 *Employees:* 15
*Net Worth:* £24,280,000 *Total Assets:* £24,979,000
*Registered Office:* First Floor, 51a St Pauls Street, Leeds, LS1 2TE
*Activities:* Other business support service activities n.e.c.
*Officers:* Sylvie Aurelie Nunn, Secretary; Roohi Sultana Collins [1959] Director/Solicitor; Mark Edward Harvey Emerton [1963] Director/Surgeon; Lorraine Anne Hallam [1957] Director/Local Government Officer; Rachel Louise Hannan [1973] Director/Consultant; Michael Anthony Jackson [1960] Director/Accountant; Nathan Lane [1974] Director/Marketing; George Charles Nicholas Lane Fox [1963] Director; John Patrick McGhee [1955] Director; Craig Suttle-Burton [1965] Director Recruitment; Helen Mary Thomson [1958] Director/Senior Manager

**Community Links (Northern) Ltd**
*Incorporated:* 11 August 1982 *Employees:* 199
*Net Worth:* £2,210,433 *Total Assets:* £5,527,404
*Registered Office:* 3 Limewood Way, Seacroft, Leeds, LS14 1AB
*Activities:* Other human health activities
*Officers:* Ruth Amanda Kettle, Secretary; Cielo Bicol Cartwright [1963] Director/Accountant; Jacqueline Anne Hallam [1961] Director/HR Business Partner; Fawzia Aleema Mir [1968] Director; Cornelle Ruth Parker [1964] Deputy Medical Director; Damian Pocknell [1970] Director/Owner; David Maxwell Strachan [1958] Director/Solicitor; Anne Worrall-Davies [1962] Director/Psychiatrist

**Community of The Resurrection (The)**
*Incorporated:* 1 May 1930 *Employees:* 37
*Net Worth:* £15,514,000 *Total Assets:* £15,969,000
*Registered Office:* House of The Resurrection, Stocksbank Road, Mirfield, W Yorks, WF14 0BN
*Activities:* Activities of religious organisations
*Officers:* The Reverend Oswin Philip Gartside [1960] Director/Clerk in Holy Orders; Father John Gibson Gribben [1944] Director/Clerk in Holy Orders; Father George Paul Alfred Guiver [1945] Director/Clerk in Holy Orders; Philip David John Nichols [1962] Director/Lay Clerk in Religion; Thomas Christopher John Seville [1957] Director/Clerk in Holy Orders

**Community Ventures (Leeds) Limited**
*Incorporated:* 10 June 2004
*Net Worth:* £6,952,861 *Total Assets:* £96,534,992
*Registered Office:* 4340 Park Approach, Thorpe Park, Leeds, LS15 8GB
*Activities:* Construction of commercial buildings
*Shareholders:* Community Health Partnerships Limited; Primaria (Leeds) Limited
*Officers:* Victoria Louise Jagger-Strangeway, Secretary; Bhupinder Singh Chana [1967] Director/Head of Finance; Richard John Coates [1966] Investment Director; David John Harding [1980] Director/Chartered Accountant; Sion Laurence Jones [1974] Fund Management Director; Philip Arthur Would [1971] Director/Asset Management

**Community Ventures Company (No 1) Limited**
*Incorporated:* 10 June 2004 *Employees:* 5
*Net Worth:* £6,668,573 *Total Assets:* £96,138,136
*Registered Office:* 4340 Park Approach, Thorpe Park, Leeds, LS15 8GB
*Activities:* Construction of commercial buildings
*Parent:* Community Ventures Midco (No 1) Limited
*Officers:* Victoria Louise Jagger-Strangeway, Secretary; Bhupinder Singh Chana [1967] Director/Head of Finance; Richard John Coates [1966] Investment Director; David John Harding [1980] Director/Chartered Accountant; Sion Laurence Jones [1974] Fund Management Director; Philip Arthur Would [1971] Director/Asset Management

**Comnet Europe Limited**
*Incorporated:* 8 July 2008 *Employees:* 25
*Net Worth:* £2,019,528 *Total Assets:* £3,490,897
*Registered Office:* 8 Turnberry Park Road, Gildersome, Morley, Leeds, LS27 7LE
*Activities:* Wholesale of electronic and telecommunications equipment and parts
*Officers:* Parke Hess, Secretary; Joseph Grillo [1957] Director [American]

**Compair Holdings Limited**
*Incorporated:* 3 May 2002
*Net Worth:* £5,830,637 *Total Assets:* £5,903,883
*Registered Office:* Springmill Street, Bradford, W Yorks, BD5 7HW
*Activities:* Activities of head offices
*Parent:* GD Holdings Ltd
*Officers:* Mark Elliott Grummett, Secretary; Michael Joseph Scheske [1987] Director/Accountant [American]; Andrew Roger Schiesl [1971] Director/General Council [American]

**Compass Broker Networks Limited**
*Incorporated:* 11 April 2016
*Net Worth:* £1,677,010 *Total Assets:* £3,638,700
*Registered Office:* Hexagon House, Grimbald Crag Close, Knaresborough, N Yorks, HG5 8PJ
*Activities:* Activities of insurance agents and brokers
*Parent:* Compass Broker Holdings Limited
*Officers:* Simon Richard Drew, Secretary; Scott Bennett [1973] Director; Simon Richard Drew [1969] Director/Accountant; John Edward Lincoln [1955] Managing Director; Desmond Joseph O'Connor [1971] Director/Insurance Broker; Dave Truman [1958] Director

**Competition Line (U.K.) Limited**
*Incorporated:* 17 May 1982 *Employees:* 134
*Net Worth:* £10,296,868 *Total Assets:* £18,303,044
*Registered Office:* Competition Line (UK) Ltd, 91 Eastmount Road, Darlington, Co Durham, DL1 1LA
*Activities:* Fitness facilities
*Parent:* Bystad Holdings AB
*Officers:* Timothy John Morant Curtis [1961] Director; Dr Ulla-Britt Gripenstedt [1962] Director [Swedish]; James Leslie Lawrence [1993] Commercial Director; Kathryn Sarah O'Neil [1984] Finance Director; Claes Gunnar Mathias Palme [1954] Director/Consultant [Swedish]; Tomas Richard Folke Thuresson [1963] Director/Chief Executive [Swedish]

**Complete Business Solutions Group Holdings Limited**
*Incorporated:* 29 September 1999 *Employees:* 629
*Previous:* Complete Office (UK) Holdings Limited
*Net Worth Deficit:* £1,777,305 *Total Assets:* £31,663,916
*Registered Office:* Daughters Court, Silkwood Park, Wakefield, W Yorks, WF5 9TQ
*Activities:* Activities of other holding companies n.e.c.
*Shareholders:* Issam Hamid; Richard Coulson
*Officers:* Susan Maria Bennett, Secretary; Richard Coulson [1971] Director; Dylan Glynn Jones [1960] Director; Alexander Guy Rushworth Loudon [1980] Director/Businessman; Chris Newman [1981] Group Operations Director; Darren Roe [1977] Finance Director; Andrew David Woodhouse [1965] Director/Chartered Accountant

**Complete Business Solutions Group Limited**
*Incorporated:* 12 April 1995 *Employees:* 629
*Previous:* Complete Office Solutions (UK) Limited
*Net Worth:* £2,829,017 *Total Assets:* £31,094,758
*Registered Office:* Daughters Court, Silkwood Park, Wakefield, W Yorks, WF5 9TQ
*Activities:* Wholesale of office furniture
*Parent:* Complete Business Solutions Group Holdings Limited
*Officers:* Susan Maria Bennett, Secretary; Susan Maria Bennett [1968] Operations Director; Richard Coulson [1971] Joint Managing Director; Christopher Newman [1981] Commercial Director; Darren Roe [1977] Finance Director; Philip Anthony Sibson [1971] Director; Charles Sebastian Waters [1973] Operations Director

**Complete IT Systems Limited**
*Incorporated:* 24 April 2007 *Employees:* 57
*Net Worth:* £830,158 *Total Assets:* £3,898,793
*Registered Office:* Unit 1 The Courtyard, Mid Point, Thornbury, Bradford, W Yorks, BD3 7AY
*Activities:* Wholesale of computers, computer peripheral equipment and software
*Shareholders:* Paul Denis Spence; Bemjamin Gregg
*Officers:* David William Elson, Secretary; David William Elson [1951] Director; Benjamin John Gregg [1978] Sales Director; Kevin John Roy [1974] Director; Paul Denis Spence [1971] Director

**Computer Services Consultants (U.K.) Limited**
*Incorporated:* 28 March 1988 *Employees:* 3
*Net Worth:* £35,323,960 *Total Assets:* £35,418,812
*Registered Office:* Trimble House, Gelderd Road, Gildersome, Morley, Leeds, LS27 7JP
*Activities:* Business and domestic software development
*Parent:* CSC (Holdings) Limited
*Officers:* James Anthony Kirkland [1959] Director/VP, General Counsel and Assistant Secretary [American]; Algirdas Paul Rimas [1970] Director/Deputy General Counsel [American]; John Peter Schreiber [1959] Director/Vice President Global Tax [American]

**Computype Europe Limited**
*Incorporated:* 20 September 1983 *Employees:* 60
*Net Worth:* £2,998,779 *Total Assets:* £5,036,292
*Registered Office:* Computype, Connaught Road, Kingswood, Hull, HU7 3AP
*Activities:* Manufacture of printed labels
*Parent:* Computype Inc
*Officers:* Sarah Louise Richardson, Secretary; John Newton [1954] Director; Eric Roach [1974] Director/Business Development [American]; Todd Roach [1970] Director/Vice President [American]; Charles Westling [1959] Director [American]

**Con Mech Group Limited**
*Incorporated:* 26 October 1949 *Employees:* 295
*Net Worth:* £16,971,984 *Total Assets:* £26,221,920
*Registered Office:* c/o Henry Williams Group Ltd, Dodsworth Street, Darlington, Co Durham, DL1 2NJ
*Activities:* Manufacture of other fabricated metal products n.e.c.
*Major Shareholder:* Robert Howard Stapleton Dilley
*Officers:* Robert James Dilley, Secretary; Christine Ames [1962] Director; Hazel Margaret Dilley [1946] Director; Dr Jonathan Charles Dilley [1975] Director; Robert James Dilley [1972] Director; Robert Howard Stapleton Dilley [1946] Director; Teresa Lorraine Heathcote [1980] Director; Derek Neil [1964] Director

**Concept Recruitment Group Limited**
*Incorporated:* 27 July 2006 *Employees:* 2,265
*Net Worth:* £4,294,273 *Total Assets:* £9,055,847
*Registered Office:* 4215 Park Approach, Thorpe Park, Leeds, LS15 8GB
*Activities:* Temporary employment agency activities
*Officers:* Elizabeth Sarah Cass, Secretary; Christopher David Cass [1972] Director; Elizabeth Sarah Cass [1972] Director

**Concepta PLC**
*Incorporated:* 22 April 2008 *Employees:* 14
*Previous:* Frontier Resources International PLC
*Net Worth:* £2,939,935 *Total Assets:* £3,481,351
*Registered Office:* 1 Park Row, Leeds, LS1 5AB
*Activities:* Activities of head offices
*Officers:* Barbara Spurrier, Secretary; David John Darrock [1978] Director; Peter Michael Dines [1973] Director; Neil Anthony Mesher [1966] Director; Adam Reynolds [1962] Director; Barbara Joyce Spurrier [1955] Director/Certified Accountant; Matthew Heaton Walls [1964] Director

**Concorde BGW Limited**
*Incorporated:* 11 September 1990 *Employees:* 57
*Net Worth:* £2,129,668 *Total Assets:* £5,439,512
*Registered Office:* Palmer Street, Hyde Park, Doncaster, S Yorks, DN4 5DD
*Activities:* Other specialised construction activities n.e.c.
*Shareholders:* Richard James Wilson; Guy Simon Bostock
*Officers:* Jason Duane Evans, Secretary; Guy Simon Bostock [1973] Director; Richard James Wilson [1966] Managing Director

**Concorde Excel Holdings Limited**
*Incorporated:* 9 May 2008
*Net Worth:* £1,822,145 *Total Assets:* £3,874,174
*Registered Office:* Concorde House, Wakefield Road, Ossett, W Yorks, WF5 9JS
*Activities:* Other information technology service activities
*Major Shareholder:* Barry Arthur Roberts
*Officers:* Neil Christopher Roberts, Secretary; Barry Arthur Roberts [1949] Director; Neil Christopher Roberts [1973] Director; Matthew John Wood [1974] Group Sales Director

**Concorde Technology Group Limited**
*Incorporated:* 2 August 1985 *Employees:* 69
*Previous:* Concorde Informatics Technology Group Limited
*Net Worth:* £1,922,924 *Total Assets:* £3,975,395
*Registered Office:* Concorde House, Wakefield Road, Ossett, W Yorks, WF5 9JS
*Activities:* Information technology consultancy activities
*Major Shareholder:* Barry Arthur Roberts
*Officers:* Neil Roberts, Secretary; Barry Arthur Roberts [1949] Director; Neil Christopher Roberts [1973] Director/Chief Operating Officer; Matthew John Wood [1974] Group Sales Director

**Condor Aviation Limited Liability Partnership**
*Incorporated:* 28 November 2002
*Net Worth:* £12,784,328 *Total Assets:* £12,921,388
*Registered Office:* The Ogden Group of Companies, 30 Victoria Avenue, Harrogate, N Yorks, HG1 5PR
*Officers:* Sir Robert Ogden CBE Lld [1936] Member

**Confection By Design Limited**
*Incorporated:* 30 March 1998 *Employees:* 33
*Net Worth:* £6,096,000 *Total Assets:* £6,842,000
*Registered Office:* Valley House, Hornbeam Park Avenue, Harrogate, N Yorks, HG2 8QT
*Activities:* Manufacture of sugar confectionery
*Officers:* Robert Nicholas Whitehead [1961] Director

**Congregational Memorial Hall Trust (1978) Limited (The)**
*Incorporated:* 15 September 1978 *Employees:* 1
*Net Worth:* £8,153,490 *Total Assets:* £8,180,509
*Registered Office:* 21 North Grove Mount, Wetherby, W Yorks, LS22 7GD
*Activities:* Other social work activities without accommodation n.e.c.
*Officers:* William Duncan, Secretary; Philip Bonnier [1956] Director/Chartered Accountant; Rev Thomas Brand [1986] Ministry Director - EFCC; Revd Barbara Jean Bridges [1955] Director/Minister of Religion; Rev Christopher John Damp [1966] Director/Minister of Religion; John George Ellis [1956] Director/Economist; Revd Gwynne Martin Evans [1948] Director/Minister of Religion; Simon Fairnington [1963] Director/Synod Clerk; Dr Digby Lawson James [1952] Director/Gospel Minister Publisher; Margaret Anne Morris [1943] Director/Retired; Margaret Mary Thompson [1947] Director; Revd Derek Malcolm Wales [1936] Director/Retired; Dr Brian John Woodhall [1938] Director/Retired

**The Coniston Hotel Limited**
*Incorporated:* 3 November 1997 *Employees:* 168
*Net Worth:* £2,094,958 *Total Assets:* £11,673,084
*Registered Office:* Coniston Hall, Coniston Cold, Skipton, N Yorks, BD23 4EB
*Activities:* Hotels and similar accommodation
*Major Shareholder:* Michael John Rennie Bannister
*Officers:* Michael John Rennie Bannister, Secretary; Michael John Rennie Bannister [1933] Director; Nicholas William Ayrton Bannister [1959] Director; Colin Blackett [1961] Director; Louise Bolton [1980] Director/General Manager; Duncan Storey Bowring [1954] Director

**Connection Flooring Limited**
*Incorporated:* 25 January 2012 *Employees:* 108
*Net Worth:* £977,103 *Total Assets:* £9,220,939
*Registered Office:* The Offices & Unit 4-5, The Future Business Park, Shildon, Co Durham, DL4 2RB
*Activities:* Wholesale of furniture, carpets and lighting equipment
*Shareholders:* Jason James Maguire; Daniel Richard Foskett
*Officers:* Kimberley Jane Richardson, Secretary; Daniel Richard Foskett [1988] Managing Director; Jason James Maguire [1973] Director; David Stubbs [1957] Director

**Connection Seating Limited**
*Incorporated:* 19 March 1997 *Employees:* 72
*Net Worth:* £1,897,037 *Total Assets:* £4,871,366
*Registered Office:* Dogley Mills, Penistone Road, Fenay Bridge, Huddersfield, W Yorks, HD8 0LE
*Activities:* Manufacture of office and shop furniture
*Shareholders:* Jonathan David Hill; Annabelle Jane Alexandra Hill
*Officers:* Timothy John O'Sullivan, Secretary; Oliver James Anthony Bond [1972] European Sales Director; Kelvin John Bromley [1955] Sales Director; Andrew James Brook [1977] Operations Director; Annabelle Jane Alexandra Hill [1972] Director; Jonathan David Hill [1968] Director; Timothy John O'Sullivan [1971] Finance Director; Lucy Sarah Storey [1981] Marketing Director

**A.F. Connell Limited**
*Incorporated:* 4 April 1988 *Employees:* 155
*Net Worth:* £1,075,953 *Total Assets:* £5,639,244
*Registered Office:* 1 Alfred Street, West Vale, Greetland, Halifax, W Yorks, HX4 8LT
*Activities:* Construction of other civil engineering projects n.e.c.
*Major Shareholder:* Jonathan Connell
*Officers:* Jonathan Connell, Secretary/Electrician; Jonathan Connell [1969] Director

**Connells Limited**
*Incorporated:* 17 April 1996 *Employees:* 6,995
*Net Worth:* £140,179,008 *Total Assets:* £280,401,984
*Registered Office:* The Bailey, Skipton, N Yorks, BD23 1DN
*Activities:* Activities of financial services holding companies
*Parent:* Skipton Group Holdings Limited
*Officers:* John Joseph Gibson, Secretary; Amanda Jane Burton [1959] Director; David John Cutter [1962] Building Society Director; David Christopher Livesey [1959] Mortgage Services Director; Robert Samuel Duncan Mugenyi Ndawula [1974] Finance Director; David Kerry Plumtree [1969] Director/Chief Executive; Reginald Stephen Shipperley [1958] Director/Estate Agent; Richard John Twigg [1965] Director

**Conquest Bidco Limited**
*Incorporated:* 28 June 2007
*Net Worth:* £11,426,000 *Total Assets:* £166,508,000
*Registered Office:* The Waterfront, Lakeside Boulevard, Doncaster, S Yorks, DN4 5PL
*Activities:* Other business support service activities n.e.c.
*Parent:* Keepmoat Limited
*Officers:* Mark Richard Priest [1966] Director; James Michael Douglas Thomson [1966] Director

**Conroy Brook (Developments) Limited**
*Incorporated:* 1 April 1996 *Employees:* 11
*Net Worth:* £2,149,330 *Total Assets:* £9,414,668
*Registered Office:* Burdwell Works, 172 New Mill Road, Brockholes, Huddersfield, W Yorks, HD9 7AZ
*Activities:* Construction of commercial buildings
*Parent:* Conroy Brook Holdings Limited
*Officers:* Jason Lee Brook, Secretary; Benjamin Jonathan Bailey [1971] Sales Director; Jason Lee Brook [1972] Director/Secretary; Richard Conroy [1972] Director/Builder & Property Developer

**The Conservation Volunteers**
*Incorporated:* 7 April 1970 *Employees:* 244
*Net Worth:* £3,500,000 *Total Assets:* £5,086,000
*Registered Office:* Sedum House, Mallard Way, Doncaster, S Yorks, DN4 8DB
*Activities:* Other professional, scientific and technical activities n.e.c.
*Officers:* Martin Luke Cooper, Secretary; Anthony James Harris Burton [1964] Director/Freelance Consultant; Professor Anthony Derek Howell Crook [1944] Director Deputy Vice Chancellor & Chartered Planner; Michael Charles Kellet [1968] Director; John Anthony Mallalieu [1970] Managing Director; Roger Kitson Perkin [1948] Director; Simon Rennie [1959] Director/Chief Executive; Julie Elizabeth Royce [1957] Associate Director; Richard William Stiff [1958] Director/Local Government Officer

**Conservatory Outlet Group Limited**
*Incorporated:* 22 January 2014 *Employees:* 196
*Previous:* MGK Wakefield Limited
*Net Worth:* £1,971,042 *Total Assets:* £15,094,346
*Registered Office:* The Cutting Room, Thornes Lane Wharf, Thornes Lane, Wakefield, W Yorks, WF1 5RL
*Activities:* Other building completion and finishing
*Shareholders:* Gregory Kane; Michael Alexander Giscombe
*Officers:* Michael Alexander Giscombe [1967] Director; Gregory Kane [1975] Director; Sarah Lyn Van Haazel [1975] Director/Chartered Accountant

**Conservatory Outlet Limited**
*Incorporated:* 13 May 2005 *Employees:* 138
*Net Worth:* £4,410,654 *Total Assets:* £11,177,190
*Registered Office:* The Cutting Room, Thornes Lane Wharf, Wakefield, W Yorks, WF1 5RL
*Activities:* Other building completion and finishing
*Parent:* Conservatory Outlet Group Limited
*Officers:* Michael Alexander Giscombe [1967] Director; Gregory Kane [1975] Director; Andrew John Miller [1966] Business Development Director; Sarah Lyn Van Haazel [1975] Director/Chartered Accountant

**Consort Furniture Limited**
*Incorporated:* 17 March 1988
*Net Worth:* £1,089,942 *Total Assets:* £4,307,978
*Registered Office:* Victoria House, Leads Road, Hull, HU7 0BZ
*Activities:* Manufacture of other furniture
*Major Shareholder:* Michael Alan Sharp
*Officers:* Michael Alan Sharp [1950] Director; Richard Michael Sharp [1973] Managing Director

**The Consortium Academy Trust**
*Incorporated:* 10 June 2011 *Employees:* 609
*Previous:* The Consortium Academy Trust Limited
*Net Worth:* £94,751,584 *Total Assets:* £100,264,216
*Registered Office:* The Consortium Academy Trust, Harland Way, Cottingham, E Yorks, HU16 5PX
*Activities:* Regulation of health care, education, cultural and other social services, not incl. social security
*Officers:* Gillian Stafford, Secretary; Gillian Margaret Barley [1967] Director/Local Government Officer; Ean Blair [1953] Director/Optometry; David Martin Craven [1956] Director/Consultant; Andrew David Crossland [1967] Director/Chief Executive; Richard Sean Firth [1968] Finance Director; Ian Furlong [1958] Director; Peter Alan Hanmer [1967] Director/Accountancy and Audit; Paul Hogan [1960] Director [Irish]; Sharon Wendy Milner [1969] Marketing Director; David John Willoughby [1970] Director

**The Constellation Trust**
*Incorporated:* 26 March 2008 *Employees:* 687
*Previous:* The Constellation Trust Ltd
*Net Worth:* £82,908,000 *Total Assets:* £90,739,000
*Registered Office:* Sirius Academy, 296 Anlaby Park Road South, Hull, HU4 7JB
*Activities:* Pre-primary education
*Officers:* Stephen Malcolm Rogers, Secretary; Lynn Brattan [1954] Director/Retired Business Manager; Kevin Burden [1959] Director/Professor; Rebekah Lorraine Koyuncu [1971] Director/Lecturer; Neil Graham Porteus [1970] Finance Director; Nicola Louise Rhodes [1980] Director/Solicitor; David Swaby [1988] Director/Mortgage and Protection Manager; Michelle Swithenbank [1981] Director; Agostinho Antonio Tombanane [1984] Director/Client Relations Manager [Portuguese/British]; Eddy Wharton [1971] Director/Headteacher; Jacqueline Caron Wright [1956] Director/Hull College Group Assistant Principal HE

**Construction Marine Limited**
*Incorporated:* 7 July 1986 *Employees:* 200
*Net Worth:* £29,841,798 *Total Assets:* £37,419,172
*Registered Office:* The Coach House, Mansion Gate Drive, Chapel Allerton, Leeds, LS7 4SY
*Activities:* Construction of railways and underground railways
*Parent:* CML Group Ltd
*Officers:* Emma Catherine Hawker, Secretary; Maurice Deans [1963] Director; Faye Mortimer Gardner [1978] Director; Nicholas Hensby [1962] Director/Civil Engineer; Charles Mortimer [1980] Director; Geoffrey Generald Mortimer [1953] Director/Civil Engineer; Martin Lee Weston [1956] Director/Civil Engineer

**Consultant Cleaners Limited**
*Incorporated:* 15 May 1978 *Employees:* 876
*Net Worth:* £1,927,502 *Total Assets:* £4,050,103
*Registered Office:* Administration Centre, Station Lane, Heckmondwike, W Yorks, WF16 0NF
*Activities:* General cleaning of buildings
*Parent:* Consultant Services Group Limited
*Officers:* Karl Edward Bell [1962] Director/Cleaning Operations; Carl Fredrik Olof Harrling [1973] Director [Swedish]; Christopher Edward Holder [1973] HR Director; Jonathan Ralph Steen [1968] Director [Swedish]

**Consultant Services Group Limited**
*Incorporated:* 4 November 1969 *Employees:* 1,071
*Net Worth:* £5,850,028 *Total Assets:* £7,797,526
*Registered Office:* Administration Centre, Station Lane, Heckmondwike, W Yorks, WF16 0NF
*Activities:* Activities of head offices
*Parent:* Compuflair Limited
*Officers:* Carl Fredrik Olof Harrling [1973] Director [Swedish]; Jonathan Ralph Steen [1968] Director [Swedish]

**Context World Limited**
*Incorporated:* 11 April 2011 *Employees:* 3
*Net Worth:* £748,249 *Total Assets:* £6,959,775
*Registered Office:* Sanderson House, Station Road, Horsforth, Leeds, LS18 5NT
*Activities:* Market research and public opinion polling
*Shareholders:* Howard Martin Davies; Jeremy Francis Davies
*Officers:* Eleonora Maria Concepcion Betancourt Menendez [1963] Director [Salvadoran]; Howard Martin Davies [1951] Director; Jeremy Alfred Davies [1972] Director; Jeremy Francis Davies [1950] Director; Kenneth Adam Simon [1959] Director

**Continental Sports Limited**
*Incorporated:* 7 December 1964 *Employees:* 115
*Net Worth:* £5,750,626 *Total Assets:* £7,507,731
*Registered Office:* Millgate Mills, Paddock, Huddersfield, W Yorks, HD1 4SD
*Activities:* Manufacture of sports goods
*Shareholders:* Nicholas Booth; Michael Booth; Anthony Booth
*Officers:* Michael Booth, Secretary; Anthony Booth [1974] Director; Diane Jacqueline Booth [1947] Director; Michael Booth [1946] Director; Nicholas Booth [1972] Director/Chartered Accountant

**Continental Wine & Food Limited**
*Incorporated:* 28 December 1960 *Employees:* 214
*Net Worth:* £26,940,560 *Total Assets:* £37,602,080
*Registered Office:* Trafalgar Mills, Leeds Road, Huddersfield, W Yorks, HD2 1YY
*Activities:* Manufacture of wine from grape
*Shareholder:* Alessandro Bevilacqua
*Officers:* Peter John Taylor, Secretary/Accountant; Alessandro Bevilacqua [1955] Director [Italian]; John David Shinwell [1964] Development Director; Peter John Taylor [1957] Financial Director

**Continuity Promotions Limited**
*Incorporated:* 19 September 1988 *Employees:* 2
*Net Worth:* £1,146,945 *Total Assets:* £3,179,899
*Registered Office:* Rockley House, Mill Lane, Rockley, Retford, Notts, DN22 0QP
*Activities:* Other letting and operating of own or leased real estate
*Shareholders:* Davina Janet Rossington; Peter Joseph Rossington
*Officers:* Davina Janet Rossington, Secretary; Davina Janet Rossington [1954] Company Secretary/Director; Peter Joseph Rossington [1949] Director

**The Continuum Group Limited**
*Incorporated:* 5 December 1985 *Employees:* 319
*Net Worth:* £3,923,332 *Total Assets:* £10,816,183
*Registered Office:* Saint Edmunds House, Margaret Street, York, YO10 4UX
*Activities:* Operation of historical sites and buildings and similar visitor attractions
*Parent:* Heritage Projects (Management) Ltd
*Officers:* Andrew Mark Pawson, Secretary; Dr Peter Vincent Addyman [1939] Director/Archaeologist; Juliana Elizabeth Delaney [1955] Director; Susan Garland [1946] Director; Emma Jane Leckie [1966] Director/Researcher; Andrew Mark Pawson [1968] Director/Accountant; Abigail Jane Skipper [1963] Director; Kevin Brian Smith [1970] Group Attractions Director

**Contis Card Solutions Limited**
*Incorporated:* 23 May 2002
*Net Worth Deficit:* £1,783,760 *Total Assets:* £44,930,600
*Registered Office:* Navigation House, Belmont Wharf, Skipton, N Yorks, BD23 1RL
*Activities:* Other business support service activities n.e.c.
*Parent:* Contis Group Limited
*Officers:* Lee Johnstone, Secretary; Flavia Alzetta [1966] Director/Chief Executive [Italian]; Peter John Cox [1945] Director/Company Executive; Lee Johnstone [1975] Finance & Commercial Director

**Contis Financial Services Limited**
*Incorporated:* 6 February 2007
*Net Worth:* £9,863,844 *Total Assets:* £52,986,408
*Registered Office:* Navigation House, Belmont Wharf, Skipton, N Yorks, BD23 1RL
*Activities:* Other business support service activities n.e.c.
*Parent:* Contis Group Limited
*Officers:* Lee Johnstone, Secretary; Flavia Alzetta [1966] Director/Chief Executive [Italian]; Peter John Cox [1945] Chairman/Director; Lee Johnstone [1975] Director/Chartered Accountant

**Contis Group Limited**
*Incorporated:* 11 February 2008 *Employees:* 86
*Net Worth Deficit:* £421,201 *Total Assets:* £64,578,788
*Registered Office:* Navigation House, Belmont Wharf, Skipton, N Yorks, BD23 1RL
*Activities:* Other business support service activities n.e.c.
*Shareholder:* Holger Bagger-Sorensen
*Officers:* Lee Johnstone, Secretary; Flavia Alzetta [1966] Director/Chief Executive [Italian]; Peter John Cox [1945] Director; Joseph Charles Dunne [1949] Director [Irish]; Michael Edward Wilson Jackson [1950] Director; Lee Johnstone [1975] Director/Chief Financial Officer; Fiona Barbara Wilkinson-Huckett [1960] Director

**Contract Experts Limited**
*Incorporated:* 19 October 1989 *Employees:* 3
*Net Worth:* £3,436,977 *Total Assets:* £10,059,955
*Registered Office:* Margaret House, 2 Devonshire Crescent, Leeds, LS8 1EP
*Activities:* Other letting and operating of own or leased real estate
*Shareholder:* Amanda Ann Clare Slevin
*Officers:* Christian David Lax, Secretary; Christian David Lax [1968] Director; Amanda Ann Clare Slevin [1961] Director

**Contract Natural Gas Limited**
*Incorporated:* 11 February 1994 *Employees:* 155
*Net Worth:* £25,894,316 *Total Assets:* £89,012,048
*Registered Office:* 2 Victoria Avenue, Harrogate, N Yorks, HG1 1EL
*Activities:* Distribution of gaseous fuels through mains
*Parent:* CNG (Group) Limited
*Officers:* Christopher John England [1971] Operations Director; Jacqueline Louise Hall [1963] Managing Director; Colin Richard Hollins [1967] Director/Utilities; Antony John Webster [1962] Director

**Contract Vehicles Limited**
*Incorporated:* 29 April 1963 *Employees:* 132
*Net Worth:* £17,031,000 *Total Assets:* £37,597,000
*Registered Office:* Number One Great Exhibition Way, Kirkstall Forge, Leeds, LS5 3BF
*Activities:* Renting and leasing of trucks and other heavy vehicles
*Parent:* Zeus Bidco Limited
*Officers:* Patrick James Rawnsley, Secretary; Timothy Peter Buchan [1963] Director; Eric Ross Burns [1973] Director; Robert Alan Butler [1970] Director; Mark Trevor Phillips [1968] Director; Philip Michael Toft [1964] Director

**Contractsure Limited**
*Incorporated:* 23 November 2001 *Employees:* 20
*Net Worth:* £2,429,531 *Total Assets:* £10,490,174
*Registered Office:* Trueman House, Capitol Boulevard, Tingley, Leeds, LS27 0TS
*Activities:* Financial intermediation not elsewhere classified
*Parent:* Henderson Insurance Brokers Limited
*Officers:* Paul Anthony Deakin [1960] Director; Stephen Farrow [1974] Financial Director; Joseph Edgar Henderson [1951] Director; Jane Elizabeth Kielty- O'Gara [1976] Managing Director

**Control4 EMEA Ltd**
*Incorporated:* 18 March 2008 *Employees:* 32
*Net Worth Deficit:* £188,914 *Total Assets:* £7,566,526
*Registered Office:* Unit 3 Green Park Business Centre, Sutton-on-the-Forest, N Yorks, YO61 1ET
*Activities:* Wholesale of radio, television goods & electrical household appliances (other than records, tapes, CDs)
*Parent:* Control4 Corporation
*Officers:* Joshua David Ellis, Secretary; Joshua David Ellis [1979] Director/General Counsel [American]; Robert Aiden James Fuller [1972] Director/Finance Manager; Mark Stephen Novakovich [1967] Director/Chief Financial Officer [American]

**Controlled Building Measures (Holdings) Limited**
*Incorporated:* 23 October 2009
*Net Worth:* £3,511,946 *Total Assets:* £3,862,796
*Registered Office:* 26 South St Marys Gate, Grimsby, N E Lincs, DN31 1LW
*Activities:* Activities of head offices
*Shareholder:* John Stephen Venney
*Officers:* Karen Venney, Secretary; John Stephen Venney [1964] Director; Karen Chrsitine Venney [1965] Director

**Convenience Foods Limited**
*Incorporated:* 3 March 1988 *Employees:* 2,017
*Net Worth Deficit:* £229,234,000 *Total Assets:* £512,590,016
*Registered Office:* Trinity Park House, Fox Way, Wakefield, W Yorks, WF2 8EE
*Activities:* Production of meat and poultry meat products
*Parent:* Beverley House Investments Limited
*Officers:* Ranjit Singh Boparan [1966] Director; Ronald Klaas Otto Kers [1969] Director/Group CEO [Dutch]; Keith Richard Packer [1967] Managing Director; Richard Peter Simpson [1965] Finance Director; Craig Ashley Tomkinson [1982] Director/Group CFO

**Cook & Lucas Frozen (Holdings) Limited**
*Incorporated:* 22 August 2016 *Employees:* 63
*Net Worth:* £507,518 *Total Assets:* £7,531,154
*Registered Office:* Refrigeration Concepts Building, Humber Steet, Grimsby, N E Lincs, DN31 3HL
*Activities:* Wholesale of other food, including fish, crustaceans and molluscs
*Major Shareholder:* Adam Croft
*Officers:* Deborah Louise Hobson [1971] Director; Antony Mark Lovett [1964] Director

**AE Cook Holdings Limited**
*Incorporated:* 25 April 2016 *Employees:* 4
*Net Worth:* £81,714 *Total Assets:* £3,340,917
*Registered Office:* 1 Greengarth, Yaddlethorpe, Scunthorpe, N Lincs, DN17 2UH
*Activities:* Other letting and operating of own or leased real estate
*Shareholders:* Janet Marilyn Goude; Alan Melvyn Cook
*Officers:* Alan Melvyn Cook, Secretary; Alan Melvyn Cook [1951] Director; Dorothy Betty Cook [1929] Director; Janet Marilyn Goude [1952] Director

**Simon Cook Holdings Limited**
*Incorporated:* 16 August 2016
*Net Worth Deficit:* £16,540 *Total Assets:* £4,719,224
*Registered Office:* 2-3 Humber Dock Street, Hull, HU1 1TB
*Activities:* Buying and selling of own real estate
*Major Shareholder:* Simon Paul, Christopher Cook
*Officers:* Simon Paul Christopher Cook [1967] Director

**Tony Cook Limited**
*Incorporated:* 11 March 1974 *Employees:* 77
*Net Worth:* £1,472,969 *Total Assets:* £3,682,592
*Registered Office:* Skirlaugh Garden and Aquatic Centre, Hull Road, Skirlaugh, Hull, HU11 5AH
*Activities:* Retail sale of hardware, paints and glass in specialised stores
*Shareholders:* Susan Cook; Vanston Anthony Cook
*Officers:* Susan Cook [1949] Director/Secretary; Vanston Anthony Cook [1973] Managing Director

**Coolsilk Limited**
*Incorporated:* 10 December 2013 *Employees:* 295
*Net Worth:* £42,842,360 *Total Assets:* £58,496,148
*Registered Office:* Orchard Villa, Top Pasture Lane, North Wheatley, Retford, Notts, DN22 9BY
*Activities:* Non-trading company
*Shareholders:* Peter Dennis Swann; Karin Louise Swann; Christopher Swann; Barbara Ellison Wilkinson
*Officers:* Karin Louise Swann, Secretary; Karin Louise Swann [1964] Director; Peter Dennis Swann [1963] Director

**Coolsilk Property & Investment Limited**
*Incorporated:* 17 December 2013 *Employees:* 7
*Net Worth:* £60,482,504 *Total Assets:* £74,251,992
*Registered Office:* Orchard Villa, Top Pasture Lane, North Wheatley, Retford, Notts, DN22 9BY
*Activities:* Other professional, scientific and technical activities n.e.c.
*Parent:* Coolsilk Limited
*Officers:* Karin Louise Swann, Secretary; Karin Louise Swann [1964] Director; Peter Dennis Swann [1963] Director

**Ernest Cooper Limited**
*Incorporated:* 2 March 1965 *Employees:* 42
*Net Worth:* £4,534,538 *Total Assets:* £6,631,030
*Registered Office:* Unit 43 Lidgate Crescent, Langthwaite Grange Industrial Estate, South Kirkby, Pontefract, W Yorks, WF9 3NR
*Activities:* Freight transport by road
*Major Shareholder:* Harvey Stuart Cooper
*Officers:* Jason Harvey Cooper, Secretary; Harvey Stuart Cooper [1945] Director/Motor Engineer; Jason Harvey Cooper [1975] Director/Road Haulier; Lee Stuart Cooper [1970] Director/Road Haulier

**J Cooper Properties Limited**
*Incorporated:* 17 March 2016
*Net Worth:* £158,824 *Total Assets:* £3,931,393
*Registered Office:* 7 Carisbrooke Road, Leeds, LS16 5RU
*Activities:* Residents property management
*Major Shareholder:* John Richard Cooper
*Officers:* John Richard Cooper [1979] Director/Property Investor

**Coopland & Son (Scarborough) Limited**
*Incorporated:* 19 March 1949 *Employees:* 1,585
*Net Worth:* £13,489,014 *Total Assets:* £18,574,510
*Registered Office:* Caxton Way, Pindar Business Park, Eastfield, Scarborough, N Yorks, YO11 3YT
*Activities:* Manufacture of bread; manufacture of fresh pastry goods and cakes
*Parent:* CS Food Group Limited
*Officers:* Paul William Coopland, Secretary; Claire Barnes [1968] Director/Sales Manager; Paul William Coopland [1957] Director; Jonathan Paul Stockill [1964] Director/Accountant

**Coordination Group Publications Ltd**
*Incorporated:* 25 August 1999 *Employees:* 212
*Net Worth:* £15,592,023 *Total Assets:* £21,993,424
*Registered Office:* Broughton House, Griffin Street, Broughton in Furness, Cumbria, LA20 6HH
*Activities:* Book publishing
*Major Shareholder:* Richard Alan Parsons
*Officers:* Carla Michelle Little, Secretary; Leila Miller [1970] Director; Richard Alan Parsons [1966] Director; Jane Michelle Ross [1968] Director

**Copernus Limited**
*Incorporated:* 15 January 2010 *Employees:* 176
*Net Worth:* £2,749,036 *Total Assets:* £10,408,615
*Registered Office:* 35 West Dock Street, Hull, HU3 4HH
*Activities:* Wholesale of other food, including fish, crustaceans and molluscs
*Major Shareholder:* Dean Robert Simpson
*Officers:* Dean Robert Simpson [1978] Director

**Copley Motors Limited**
*Incorporated:* 15 September 1976 *Employees:* 10
*Net Worth:* £4,943,427 *Total Assets:* £5,773,797
*Registered Office:* 98 Prospect Avenue, Halifax, W Yorks, HX2 7HP
*Activities:* Sale of new cars and light motor vehicles
*Shareholders:* Luke Stewart Oughton; Ben Edward Oughton
*Officers:* David Normanton [1957] Director/Accountant; Ben Edward Oughton [1989] Director/L4 Master Technician; Luke Stewart Oughton [1992] Director/L3 Diagnostic Technician

**Coral PFI Holdings 2003 Limited**
*Incorporated:* 30 June 2003 *Employees:* 2
*Previous:* Interserve PFI Holdings 2003 Limited
*Net Worth:* £1,607,000 *Total Assets:* £49,410,000
*Registered Office:* 1 Park Row, Leeds, LS1 5AB
*Activities:* Activities of other holding companies n.e.c.
*Parent:* Coral Project Investments (Assetco) Limited
*Officers:* Jennifer McKay, Secretary; John Stephen Gordon [1962] Director

**Coral Project Investments (Assetco) Limited**
*Incorporated:* 13 March 2017
*Net Worth Deficit:* £1,288,928 *Total Assets:* £73,223,288
*Registered Office:* 1 Park Row, Leeds, LS1 5AB
*Activities:* Other business support service activities n.e.c.
*Parent:* Coral Projects Investments (Issuer) Limited
*Officers:* Jennifer McKay, Secretary; John McDonagh [1969] Director; Alistair Graham Ray [1974] Director

**Coral Project Investments (Issuer) Limited**
*Incorporated:* 10 March 2017 *Employees:* 3
*Net Worth Deficit:* £348,389 *Total Assets:* £74,512,208
*Registered Office:* 1 Park Row, Leeds, LS1 5AB
*Activities:* Other business support service activities n.e.c.
*Parent:* Dalmore Capital 18 GP Limited
*Officers:* Jennifer McKay, Secretary; John McDonagh [1969] Director; Alistair Graham Ray [1974] Director

**Core Telecom Limited**
*Incorporated:* 13 January 2005 *Employees:* 15
*Net Worth:* £2,683,953 *Total Assets:* £5,874,960
*Registered Office:* Mazhar House, 48 Bradford Road, Stanningley, Leeds, LS28 6DD
*Activities:* Other business support service activities n.e.c.
*Major Shareholder:* Mahmood Mazhar
*Officers:* Mahmood Mazhar [1966] Director/Accountant; Paul Michael Turner [1964] Director/Accountant

**Coriant UK Limited**
*Incorporated:* 18 December 1978 *Employees:* 23
*Previous:* Tellabs U.K. Limited
*Net Worth:* £7,832,867 *Total Assets:* £9,292,609
*Registered Office:* 1 Park Row, Leeds, LS1 5AB
*Activities:* Other telecommunications activities
*Officers:* Brad David Feller [1973] Director/Chief Financial Officer [American]; Michael MacKinnon [1968] Director/VP International Finance [Canadian]; Kathleen Wood [1969] Director/Senior Legal Services Representative [Irish]

**Corinthian Brands (CBL) Limited**
*Incorporated:* 15 October 2010 *Employees:* 10
*Net Worth:* £2,260,468 *Total Assets:* £4,696,398
*Registered Office:* Conyngham Hall, Bond End, Knaresborough, N Yorks, HG5 9AY
*Activities:* Agents involved in the sale of food, beverages and tobacco
*Officers:* Susan Cottingham, Secretary; Helen Burton [1965] Director; Paul Burton [1957] Director; Susan Claire Cottingham [1959] Director/Accountant; John Hibberd [1962] Director; Sandra Anne Hibberd [1964] Director

**Corkel Holdings Limited**
*Incorporated:* 25 July 2016
*Net Worth:* £4,037,846 *Total Assets:* £4,037,846
*Registered Office:* Pleasureland, Marine Road West, Morecambe, Lancs, LA4 4BU
*Activities:* Dormant company
*Shareholders:* Solomon Luke Reader; Gavin Reader
*Officers:* Gavin Reader [1966] Director; Solomon Luke Reader [1977] Director

**Corkel Limited**
*Incorporated:* 25 August 2004
*Net Worth:* £5,026,974 *Total Assets:* £5,055,635
*Registered Office:* Pleasureland, Marine Road West, Morecambe, Lancs, LA4 4BU
*Activities:* Activities of head offices
*Parent:* Corkel Holdings Limited
*Officers:* Solomon Luke Reader, Secretary; Gavin Reader [1966] Director/Amusement Caterer; Solomon Luke Reader [1977] Director/Amusement Caterer

**Cornbrook Group Ltd**
*Incorporated:* 30 December 2003 *Employees:* 58
*Previous:* Integrated Results Limited
*Net Worth:* £1,765,960 *Total Assets:* £3,454,845
*Registered Office:* International Development Centre, Valley Drive, Ilkley, W Yorks, LS29 8PB
*Activities:* Management consultancy activities other than financial management
*Parent:* Annuity Management AG
*Officers:* Christopher John Hoyle [1974] Major Accounts Director; Matthias Knaur [1975] Director/Chief Executive Officer [Austrian]

**Cornelius Beverage Technologies Limited**
*Incorporated:* 8 August 1947 *Employees:* 64
*Net Worth:* £7,088,000 *Total Assets:* £9,433,000
*Registered Office:* Russell Way, Bradford Road, Brighouse, W Yorks, HD6 4LX
*Activities:* Manufacture of other special-purpose machinery n.e.c.
*Officers:* Lisa Vicky Jane Briggs, Secretary; Lisa Vicky Jane Briggs [1983] Finance Director; Simon Anthony Felton [1967] Director/General Manager

**Cornucopia Investments Limited**
*Incorporated:* 21 August 2013
*Net Worth:* £5,656,961 *Total Assets:* £5,673,495
*Registered Office:* 140 Coniscliffe Road, Darlington, Co Durham, DL3 7RT
*Activities:* Security dealing on own account
*Officers:* Matthew Christopher Bennett [1964] Director/Solicitor; Elizabeth Kate Gardner [1983] Director; Antony William Luckett [1961] Director/Accountant; Janice Rosalind Moyes [1953] Director

**Corporate Document Services Limited**
*Incorporated:* 4 May 1994 *Employees:* 240
*Net Worth:* £5,022,945 *Total Assets:* £11,499,721
*Registered Office:* 7 Eastgate, Leeds, LS2 7LY
*Activities:* Other information technology service activities
*Parent:* The Baird Group
*Officers:* Guy Adrian Van Lopik, Secretary; Fergus Robert Edward Bailie [1979] Director; Robert Ernest Bailie [1943] Director; Mark Lee Gair [1972] Managing Director; Philip Graham Walter [1958] Director

**Corporate Travel Management (North) Limited**
*Incorporated:* 10 November 1950 *Employees:* 123
*Previous:* Redfern Travel Limited
*Net Worth:* £5,914,503 *Total Assets:* £29,248,764
*Registered Office:* Shire House, Humboldt Street, Bradford, W Yorks, BD1 5HQ
*Activities:* Travel agency activities
*Parent:* Alpha-Omega Travel Ltd
*Officers:* Stephen John Fleming, Secretary; Deborah Ann Carling [1963] Director/CEO CTM Travel Europe; Stephen John Fleming [1968] Director/Global CFO [Australian]; Jamie Michael Pherous [1968] Managing Director [Australian]

**Corrboard UK Limited**
*Incorporated:* 23 October 2013 *Employees:* 88
*Net Worth Deficit:* £1,868,930 *Total Assets:* £32,787,916
*Registered Office:* Waldo Way, Normanby Enterprise Park, Scunthorpe, N Lincs, DN15 9GE
*Activities:* Manufacture of corrugated paper and paperboard, sacks and bags
*Shareholder:* VPK Packaging Group NV
*Officers:* John Charles Saynor, Secretary; Paul Barber [1979] Director; Ruth Cook [1968] Managing Director; Richard Coward [1960] Managing Director; Raffan West [1969] Director

**Jimmy Corrigan's Limited**
*Incorporated:* 5 December 2009
*Net Worth:* £6,423,815 *Total Assets:* £6,527,887
*Registered Office:* 2 West Parade Road, Scarborough, N Yorks, YO12 5ED
*Activities:* Activities of other holding companies n.e.c.
*Major Shareholder:* James Lord Corrigan
*Officers:* James Lord Corrigan [1972] Director; Victoria Louisa Corrigan [1975] Director/Manager

**Corrocoat Limited**
*Incorporated:* 17 October 1975 *Employees:* 21
*Net Worth:* £6,792,677 *Total Assets:* £7,755,506
*Registered Office:* Forster Street, Leeds, LS10 1PW
*Activities:* Manufacture of paints, varnishes and similar coatings, mastics and sealants
*Parent:* Corrosioneering Group Limited
*Officers:* Clive Anthony Harper, Secretary; Robert Edward Cole [1970] Sales Director; Graham Dennis Greenwood Sole [1963] Managing Director; Clive Anthony Harper [1957] Director; Nigel Patrick Riley [1957] Director/Engineer; Charles John Watkinson [1946] Director/Chief Executive; Phillip James Watkinson [1967] Director

**Corrosioneering Group Limited**
*Incorporated:* 25 June 1976 *Employees:* 303
*Net Worth:* £8,553,309 *Total Assets:* £16,169,497
*Registered Office:* Forster Street, Leeds, LS10 1PW
*Activities:* Activities of head offices
*Major Shareholder:* Charles John Watkinson
*Officers:* Clive Anthony Harper, Secretary; Clive Anthony Harper [1957] Director; Charles John Watkinson [1946] Director

**Cotterhill Limited**
*Incorporated:* 10 March 2000 *Employees:* 99
*Net Worth:* £12,464,017 *Total Assets:* £31,499,112
*Registered Office:* 43 Russell Street, Darlington, Co Durham, DL1 1PT
*Activities:* Retail sale of textiles in specialised stores
*Shareholders:* Julie Marie Maguire; William Maguire
*Officers:* Julie Maguire, Secretary; Gilbert Maguire [1988] Director; Nathan Maguire [1998] Director; William Maguire [1985] Director; William Maguire [1965] Director/Carpet Retailer; Scott Thomas Mounsey [1978] Finance Director

**John Cotton Group Limited**
*Incorporated:* 1 March 1933 *Employees:* 1,419
*Net Worth:* £73,060,000 *Total Assets:* £120,162,000
*Registered Office:* No 1 Park Row, Leeds, LS1 5AB
*Activities:* Manufacture of non-wovens and articles made from non-wovens, except apparel
*Shareholders:* John Dawson Cotton; Mark Adrian Cotton
*Officers:* Stephen George Swalwell, Secretary; Barbara Cotton [1940] Director [German]; John Dawson Cotton [1940] Director/Chairman; Mark Adrian Cotton [1976] Managing Director; Nicholas John Cotton [1966] Director; David Keith Cruddos [1963] Director; Jonathan Paul Fenton Hurst [1959] Director; Nicholas Hugh Manning [1972] Finance Director

**Country Publications Limited**
*Incorporated:* 12 May 2004 *Employees:* 20
*Net Worth:* £1,713,300 *Total Assets:* £3,184,314
*Registered Office:* Desormais Suite, The Gatehouse, Skipton Castle, Skipton, N Yorks, BD23 1AL
*Activities:* Publishing of consumer and business journals and periodicals
*Officers:* David Proud, Secretary; Christina Grace Benn [1939] Director; Timothy John Benn [1936] Director; David Proud [1963] Director

**Country Style Foods Limited**
*Incorporated:* 31 October 1990 *Employees:* 2,675
*Net Worth:* £43,156,296 *Total Assets:* £86,695,392
*Registered Office:* 50 Pontefract Lane, Leeds, LS9 8HY
*Activities:* Manufacture of bread; manufacture of fresh pastry goods and cakes
*Shareholders:* Joseph Anthony Wood; Christine Elizabeth Wood
*Officers:* Joseph Anthony Wood, Secretary; Stephen John Holding [1966] Director; Charles Joseph Wood [1979] Director; Christine Elizabeth Wood [1943] Director/Baker; Joseph Anthony Wood [1939] Director/Baker

**Countrywide Belmont Limited**
*Incorporated:* 30 April 2013 *Employees:* 124
*Net Worth:* £2,367,488 *Total Assets:* £17,485,080
*Registered Office:* Westcourt, Gelderd Road, Leeds, LS12 6DB
*Activities:* Residential care activities for the elderly and disabled
*Parent:* Countrywide Care Homes Limited
*Officers:* Christopher Ball [1968] Director; Philip John Burgan [1951] Director; Peter Gervais Fagan [1957] Director; Jason Lock [1972] Director

**Countrywide Care Homes (2) Limited**
*Incorporated:* 21 July 2011 *Employees:* 594
*Net Worth:* £9,675,326 *Total Assets:* £12,129,572
*Registered Office:* Westcourt, Gelderd Road, Leeds, LS12 6DB
*Activities:* Residential care activities for the elderly and disabled
*Parent:* Countrywide Care Homes Limited
*Officers:* Christopher Ball [1968] Director; Philip John Burgan [1951] Director; Peter Gervais Fagan [1957] Director; Jason Lock [1972] Director

**Countrywide Care Homes (3) Limited**
*Incorporated:* 13 May 2013 *Employees:* 219
*Net Worth:* £2,287,207 *Total Assets:* £16,138,033
*Registered Office:* Westcourt, Gelderd Road, Leeds, LS12 6DB
*Activities:* Residential nursing care facilities
*Parent:* Countrywide Care Homes Limited
*Officers:* Christopher Ball [1968] Director; Philip John Burgan [1951] Director; Victoria Craddock [1970] Director; Dzenana Delic [1974] Director; Peter Gervais Fagan [1957] Director; Jason Lock [1972] Director

**Countrywide Care Homes Limited**
*Incorporated:* 4 April 2011 *Employees:* 1,861
*Net Worth:* £5,725,000 *Total Assets:* £40,858,000
*Registered Office:* Westcourt, Gelderd Road, Leeds, LS12 6DB
*Activities:* Residential care activities for the elderly and disabled
*Major Shareholder:* Philip John Burgan
*Officers:* Christopher Ball [1968] Director; James Edward Burgan [1979] Commercial Director; Lynne Frances Burgan [1957] Director; Philip John Burgan [1951] Director; Victoria Craddock [1970] Operations Director; Dzenana Delic [1974] HR Director; Peter Gervais Fagan [1957] Director; Jason Lock [1972] Director; Christopher John Womack [1972] Business Development Director; John Charles Wright [1949] Director

**County Properties (Northern) Limited**
*Incorporated:* 23 February 1976 *Employees:* 7
*Net Worth:* £14,057,381 *Total Assets:* £34,685,616
*Registered Office:* 137 Scalby Road, Scarborough, N Yorks, YO12 6TB
*Activities:* Other letting and operating of own or leased real estate
*Parent:* County Properties Group Ltd
*Officers:* Barry Peter Swiers, Company Secretary; John Guthrie [1936] Director; Peter John Guthrie [1971] Director; Richard Guthrie [1972] Director; David Nairn [1963] Director/Surveyor; Martin Robson [1975] Director/Accountant; Ronald Graham Urquhart [1957] Director

**County Turf Limited**
*Incorporated:* 1 October 1999 *Employees:* 27
*Net Worth:* £5,480,116 *Total Assets:* £6,686,297
*Registered Office:* Low Santon Farm, Appleby, Scunthorpe, N Lincs, DN15 0DF
*Activities:* Mixed farming
*Shareholders:* Anna Fraser; Andrew Walker Fraser
*Officers:* Andrew Walker Fraser, Secretary; Alexander Fraser [1933] Director/Farmer; Andrew Walker Fraser [1966] Director/Farmer; Anna Fraser [1968] Director; Christopher David Medley [1974] Operations Director

**Covance Clinical Research Unit Limited**
*Incorporated:* 17 October 1991 *Employees:* 286
*Net Worth:* £9,928,000 *Total Assets:* £36,261,000
*Registered Office:* Springfield House, Hyde Street, Leeds, LS2 9LH
*Activities:* Other professional, scientific and technical activities n.e.c.
*Parent:* Covance Clinical and Periapproval Services Limited
*Officers:* Floyd Samuel Eberts III [1959] Director/Chief Legal Officer [American]; Glenn Andrew Eisenberg [1961] Director [American]; Robert Stewart Pringle [1964] Director

**Covance Laboratories Limited**
*Incorporated:* 28 May 1974 *Employees:* 1,248
*Net Worth:* £50,462,000 *Total Assets:* £129,157,000
*Registered Office:* Otley Road, Harrogate, N Yorks, HG3 1PY
*Activities:* Research and experimental development on biotechnology
*Parent:* Covance Limited
*Officers:* Floyd Samuel Eberts III [1959] Director/Chief Legal Officer [American]; Glenn Andrew Eisenberg [1961] Director/Chief Financial Officer [American]; Robert Stewart Pringle [1964] Director; Stephen Derek Albert Street [1960] Director/General Manager

**Covance Limited**
*Incorporated:* 6 November 1991
*Net Worth:* £26,250,000 *Total Assets:* £26,250,000
*Registered Office:* Otley Road, Harrogate, N Yorks, HG3 1PY
*Activities:* Activities of head offices
*Parent:* Clearstone Holdings (International) Limited
*Officers:* Floyd Samuel Eberts III [1959] Director/Chief Legal Officer [American]; Glenn Andrew Eisenberg [1961] Director/Chief Financial Officer [American]; Robert Stewart Pringle [1964] Director; Stephen Derek Albert Street [1960] Director/General Manager

**Cox 22 Limited**
*Incorporated:* 3 June 1926 *Employees:* 7
*Net Worth:* £8,728,019 *Total Assets:* £8,839,662
*Registered Office:* Woodlands, Gawthorpe Drive, Bingley, Bradford, W Yorks, BD16 4DQ
*Activities:* Buying and selling of own real estate
*Officers:* Ann Louise Leckenby, Secretary; Donald Richard Jaggar [1936] Director; Ann Louise Leckenby [1964] Financial Director

**Cox Automotive Retail Solutions Limited**
*Incorporated:* 22 July 1993 *Employees:* 205
*Previous:* Manheim Retail Services Limited
*Net Worth:* £10,466,000 *Total Assets:* £18,965,000
*Registered Office:* Central House, Leeds Road, Rothwell, Leeds, LS26 0JE
*Activities:* Other service activities n.e.c.
*Parent:* Manheim Europe Limited
*Officers:* Michael Buxton, Secretary; Michael Buxton [1965] Director; Martin Leigh Forbes [1976] Director/Chief Operating Officer; Darren Paul Mornin [1968] Finance Director

**Cox Automotive UK Limited**
*Incorporated:* 9 April 1996
*Previous:* Manheim Europe Limited
*Net Worth:* £77,648,000 *Total Assets:* £95,578,000
*Registered Office:* Central House, Leeds Road, Rothwell, Leeds, LS26 0JE
*Activities:* Other service activities n.e.c.
*Parent:* Manheim Holdings Limited
*Officers:* Michael Buxton, Secretary/Director; Michael Buxton [1965] Director; Martin Leigh Forbes [1976] Director/Chief Operating Officer; Darren Paul Mornin [1968] Finance Director

**D J Cox Limited**
*Incorporated:* 5 June 2000 *Employees:* 238
*Net Worth:* £8,359,794 *Total Assets:* £28,240,468
*Registered Office:* Lancaster Honda, Northgate, White Lund Industrial Estate, Morecambe, Lancs, LA3 3PA
*Activities:* Sale of new cars and light motor vehicles
*Major Shareholder:* David Johnathan Cox
*Officers:* Helen Hayton, Secretary/Group FD; David Johnathan Cox [1971] Director/Motor Retailer; Helen Hayton [1970] Director/Group FD

**Cox Motor Group Limited**
*Incorporated:* 20 November 2015 *Employees:* 238
*Net Worth:* £11,531,012 *Total Assets:* £31,382,536
*Registered Office:* Northgate, White Lund Industrial Estate, Morecambe, Lancs, LA3 3PA
*Activities:* Sale of new cars and light motor vehicles
*Major Shareholder:* David Johnathan Cox
*Officers:* Helen Hayton, Secretary; David Johnathan Cox [1971] Director/Motor Retailer; Helen Hayton [1970] Director/Group FD

**CPD Direct Limited**
*Incorporated:* 8 October 2015 *Employees:* 53
*Net Worth:* £435,644 *Total Assets:* £7,984,005
*Registered Office:* Ipark Industrial Estate, Innovation Drive, Hull, HU5 1SG
*Activities:* Activities of other holding companies n.e.c.
*Shareholders:* Ian Michael Warvill; Antony Bennett; Kirstie Emma Lloyd
*Officers:* Kirstie Emma Lloyd, Secretary; Antony Bennett [1967] Director; Kirstie Emma Lloyd [1971] Finance Director; Ian Michael Warvill [1964] Operations Director

**CPM Group Limited**
*Incorporated:* 18 March 1971 *Employees:* 339
*Net Worth:* £2,012,000 *Total Assets:* £42,393,000
*Registered Office:* Landscape House, Premier Way, Lowfields Business Park, Elland, W Yorks, HX5 9HT
*Activities:* Manufacture of concrete products for construction purposes
*Officers:* Catherine Elizabeth Baxandall, Secretary; Jack Clarke [1965] Director; Martyn Coffey [1962] Director

**CPP European Holdings Limited**
*Incorporated:* 29 January 2002
*Net Worth:* £11,208,000 *Total Assets:* £14,170,000
*Registered Office:* 6 East Parade, Leeds, LS1 2AD
*Activities:* Activities of head offices
*Parent:* CPP Holdings Limited
*Officers:* Lorraine Grace Beavis, Secretary; Oliver Walter Laird [1970] Director/Chief Financial Officer; Jason Carl Walsh [1971] Director/Chief Executive Officer

**CPP Group Limited**
*Incorporated:* 14 March 2008
*Previous:* CPP Group Public Limited Company
*Net Worth:* £8,831,000 *Total Assets:* £38,881,000
*Registered Office:* 6 East Parade, Leeds, LS1 2AD
*Activities:* Activities of head offices
*Parent:* CPPGroup PLC
*Officers:* Lorraine Grace Beavis, Secretary; Emma Justine Shaw [1969] Director/Chief People Officer; Jason Carl Walsh [1971] Director/Chief Executive Officer

**CPP Holdings Limited**
*Incorporated:* 19 August 1982
*Net Worth:* £22,033,000 *Total Assets:* £27,879,000
*Registered Office:* 6 East Parade, Leeds, LS1 2AD
*Activities:* Activities of head offices
*Parent:* CPP Worldwide Holdings Limited
*Officers:* Lorraine Grace Beavis, Secretary; Oliver Walter Laird [1970] Director/Chief Financial Officer; Emma Justine Shaw [1969] Director/Chief People Officer; Jason Carl Walsh [1971] Director/Chief Executive Officer

**CPP International Holdings Limited**
*Incorporated:* 24 September 2002
*Net Worth:* £18,803,000 *Total Assets:* £18,803,000
*Registered Office:* 6 East Parade, Leeds, LS1 2AD
*Activities:* Activities of head offices
*Parent:* CPP Holdings Limited
*Officers:* Lorraine Grace Beavis, Secretary; Oliver Walter Laird [1970] Director/Chief Financial Officer; Jason Carl Walsh [1971] Director/Chief Executive Officer

**CPP Worldwide Holdings Limited**
*Incorporated:* 11 February 2010
*Net Worth Deficit:* £9,109,000 *Total Assets:* £94,434,000
*Registered Office:* 6 East Parade, Leeds, LS1 2AD
*Activities:* Activities of head offices
*Parent:* CPPGroup PLC
*Officers:* Lorraine Grace Beavis, Secretary; Emma Justine Shaw [1969] Director/Chief People Officer; Jason Carl Walsh [1971] Director/Chief Executive Officer

**CPPGroup PLC**
*Incorporated:* 9 February 2010 *Employees:* 593
*Net Worth:* £15,017,000 *Total Assets:* £60,175,000
*Registered Office:* 6 East Parade, Leeds, LS1 2AD
*Activities:* Activities of head offices
*Shareholders:* Phoenix Asset Management Partners Limited; Hamish MacGregor Ogston
*Officers:* Lorraine Grace Beavis, Secretary; Nicholas Ian Cooper [1964] Director & Solicitor; Timothy Roger Elliott [1958] Director; Mark William Hamlin [1954] Director; Oliver Walter Laird [1970] Director/Chief Financial Officer; Sir Richard Douglas Lapthorne [1943] Director; Emma Justine Shaw [1969] Director/Chief People Officer; Jason Carl Walsh [1971] Director/Chief Executive Officer

**CPPGroup Services Limited**
*Incorporated:* 4 August 2014
*Net Worth Deficit:* £2,742,000 *Total Assets:* £4,684,000
*Registered Office:* 6 East Parade, Leeds, LS1 2AD
*Activities:* Other activities auxiliary to insurance and pension funding
*Parent:* CPP Holdings Limited
*Officers:* Lorraine Grace Beavis, Secretary; Gary Douglas Sidle [1966] Director/Finance; Jason Carl Walsh [1971] Director/Chief Executive Officer

**CR Estates Limited**
*Incorporated:* 21 February 2017 *Employees:* 1
*Net Worth Deficit:* £127,722 *Total Assets:* £8,444,143
*Registered Office:* 2 Therm Road, Hull, HU8 7BF
*Activities:* Buying and selling of own real estate
*Parent:* Teddy Clark (Holdings) Limited
*Officers:* William Edward Clark [1967] Director

**Crafter's Companion Limited**
*Incorporated:* 8 March 2006 *Employees:* 138
*Net Worth:* £2,856,718 *Total Assets:* £10,221,818
*Registered Office:* Unit 1 Horndale Avenue, Aycliffe Business Park, Newton Aycliffe, Co Durham, DL5 6DR
*Activities:* Retail sale via mail order houses or via Internet
*Major Shareholder:* Sara Anne Davies
*Officers:* Sara Anne Davies, Secretary/Craft Designer; Sara Anne Davies [1984] Director/Craft Designer; Simon Christopher Davies [1980] Director/Management Accountant; Gerard Scot Downes [1967] Director; Richard David Harpin [1964] Director; Frank Johnson [1950] Director; Kamala Vijayaraghavan [1961] Director

**Craftsman Tools Limited**
*Incorporated:* 1 April 1953 *Employees:* 46
*Net Worth:* £2,705,202 *Total Assets:* £3,099,983
*Registered Office:* Side Copse, Pool Road, Otley, W Yorks, LS21 1JE
*Activities:* Manufacture of other machine tools
*Major Shareholder:* Robert Johnson
*Officers:* Robert Johnson [1955] Director

**The Craggs Country Business Park LLP**
*Incorporated:* 6 May 2011 *Employees:* 2
*Net Worth:* £1,528,422 *Total Assets:* £3,001,132
*Registered Office:* The Craggs Country Business Park, New Road, Cragg Vale, Hebden Bridge, W Yorks, HX7 5TT
*Officers:* Christian Bingham [1971] Member; Heidi Louise Bingham [1973] Member; June Adel Thornber [1946] Member; Ralph Edgar Thornber [1948] Member; Daniel Guy Holmes [1976] LLP Member; Zoe Marie Holmes [1974] LLP Member

**Cragwood International Limited**
*Incorporated:* 5 June 1985 *Employees:* 115
*Net Worth:* £7,986,344 *Total Assets:* £9,766,283
*Registered Office:* Cragwood House, Ecclerigg, Windermere, Cumbria, LA23 1LQ
*Activities:* Other service activities n.e.c.
*Officers:* Robert Bradbury, Secretary; David Hayden Williams [1956] Director/Outdoor Pursuits Manager

**Craig's Motorcycles Limited**
*Incorporated:* 23 April 2008 *Employees:* 27
*Net Worth:* £3,011,725 *Total Assets:* £4,991,389
*Registered Office:* Wesley Place, Dewsbury Ring Road, Dewsbury, W Yorks, WF13 1HX
*Activities:* Sale, maintenance and repair of motorcycles and related parts and accessories
*Major Shareholder:* Craig Bairstow Holmes
*Officers:* Aaron Holmes [1988] Sales Director; Craig Bairstow Holmes [1962] Sales Director; Matthew Holmes [1991] Sales Director; Natasha Holmes [1993] Director/Sales Administration

**Cramscene Limited**
*Incorporated:* 8 December 1976 *Employees:* 28
*Net Worth:* £4,466,718 *Total Assets:* £6,130,488
*Registered Office:* Cramscene House, Scott Lane, Morley, Leeds, LS27 0NQ
*Activities:* Freight transport by road
*Officers:* Charles Phillip Haigh, Secretary/Farmer Haulage Contractor; Charles Phillip Haigh [1938] Director/Farmer Haulage Contractor; John Allen Haigh [1941] Director/Farmer/Haulage Contractor

**Cranage Hall Properties Limited**
*Incorporated:* 19 September 2006 *Employees:* 4
*Net Worth:* £257,000 *Total Assets:* £28,860,000
*Registered Office:* The Inspire, Hornbeam Square West, Harrogate, N Yorks, HG2 8PA
*Activities:* Other letting and operating of own or leased real estate
*Parent:* De Vere 2 Limited
*Officers:* James Alexander Burrell [1974] Director/Accountant; Generaldine Josephine Gallagher [1965] Finance Director [Irish]; Gail Susan Hunter [1963] Human Resources Director; Anthony Gerrard Troy [1962] Director [Irish]

**Cranswick Convenience Foods Limited**
*Incorporated:* 6 April 1988 *Employees:* 1,923
*Net Worth:* £73,507,000 *Total Assets:* £175,806,000
*Registered Office:* Crane Court, Hesslewood Office Park, Ferriby Road, Hessle, E Yorks, HU13 0PA
*Activities:* Production of meat and poultry meat products
*Parent:* Cranswick PLC
*Officers:* Steven Garrick Glover, Secretary; John Mark Bottomley [1963] Director; Adam Hartley Couch [1968] Director; Martin Thomas Peter Davey [1953] Director; Andrew James Jenkins [1963] Sales Director; Samuel Richard Pearl [1983] Director; Stephen Westhead [1972] Director

**Cranswick Country Foods PLC**
*Incorporated:* 27 March 1984 *Employees:* 3,300
*Net Worth:* £266,219,008 *Total Assets:* £401,519,008
*Registered Office:* Crane Court, Hesslewood Office Park, Ferriby Road, Hessle, E Yorks, HU13 0PA
*Activities:* Processing and preserving of meat
*Parent:* Cranswick PLC
*Officers:* Steven Garrick Glover, Secretary; Christopher Aldersley [1972] Director; Darren Andrew [1970] Operations Director; John Mark Bottomley [1963] Director; James Robert Brisby [1974] Director; David Brown [1966] Director; Jacqueline Carter [1967] Director; Neil Edward Clappison [1964] Director; Adam Hartley Couch [1968] Director; Martin Thomas Peter Davey [1953] Director/Chartered Accountant; Rebecca Dearsly [1968] Business Unit Director; John Fletcher [1968] Director; Andrew Gleadow [1980] Director; Marcus Hoggarth [1976] Director; Jason Peter Key [1972] Operations Director; Barry Lock [1969] Site Director; Kate Maxwell [1979] Director; Nicholas George Mitchell [1961] Trading Director; David Charles Park [1969] Managing Director; James Pontone [1977] Director; Simon Ravenscroft [1966] Director; Norman John Smith [1967] Sales Director; Rollo Frederick Thistlethwaite Thompson [1962] Director; Miranda Stephanie Walker [1977] Group HR Director; Graeme Kevin David Watson [1968] Group Engineering Director; Andrew Weir [1956] Director; Neil Willis [1964] Director; Edward Wright [1982] Director

**Cranswick Gourmet Pastry Company Limited**
*Incorporated:* 19 October 2011 *Employees:* 264
*Net Worth:* £700,000 *Total Assets:* £16,481,000
*Registered Office:* Cranes Court, Hesslewood Office Park, Ferriby Road, Hessle, E Yorks, HU13 0PA
*Activities:* Manufacture of other food products n.e.c.
*Parent:* Cranswick Country Foods PLC
*Officers:* Steven Garrick Glover, Secretary; John Mark Bottomley [1963] Director; James Robert Brisby [1974] Director; Adam Hartley Couch [1968] Director; Christopher Andrew Mayer [1979] Director; Andrew William Weir [1956] Director

**Cranswick PLC**
*Incorporated:* 29 September 1972 *Employees:* 6,338
*Net Worth:* £479,900,000 *Total Assets:* £651,299,968
*Registered Office:* Cranes Court, Hesslewood Office Park, Ferriby Road, Hessle, E Yorks, HU13 0PA
*Activities:* Activities of head offices
*Officers:* Steven Garrick Glover, Secretary; Helen Catherine Allum [1965] Director; John Mark Bottomley [1963] Director; James Robert Brisby [1974] Director; Adam Hartley Couch [1968] Director; Martin Thomas Peter Davey [1953] Director; Pamela Powell [1963] Director [American]; Mark James Reckitt [1958] Director; Tim Smith [1955] Director

**Richard Craven (Keighley) Limited**
*Incorporated:* 26 February 1974 *Employees:* 5
*Net Worth:* £4,401,415 *Total Assets:* £5,977,307
*Registered Office:* 3 Gresley Road, Keighley, W Yorks, BD21 5JG
*Activities:* Non-specialised wholesale trade
*Officers:* Deborah Louise Richards, Secretary; Holly Elizabeth Richards [1985] Director

**Craven Cattle Marts Limited**
*Incorporated:* 2 July 1921 *Employees:* 47
*Net Worth:* £10,392,298 *Total Assets:* £13,260,178
*Registered Office:* Auction Mart, Gargrave Road, Skipton, N Yorks, BD23 1UD
*Activities:* Support activities for animal production (other than farm animal boarding)
*Officers:* Jeremy John Eaton, Secretary; Angus Dean [1975] Director/Farmer; Keith Downs [1947] Director/Farmer; John Anthony Hewetson [1960] Director/Farmer; Martyyn Paul Jennings [1979] Director; Generald Ernest Medcalf [1948] Director/Wholesale Meat Processor; Stuart Verity [1948] Director/Farmer; John Kevin Wilson [1959] Director

**Craven Educational Trust**
*Incorporated:* 2 May 2014 *Employees:* 40
*Net Worth:* £3,028,391 *Total Assets:* £4,124,144
*Registered Office:* Craven College, Gargrave Road, Skipton, N Yorks, BD23 1US
*Activities:* General secondary education
*Officers:* Joanne Sherrington, Secretary; Robert Andrew Bellfield [1959] Director/Principal; David John Cutter [1962] Building Society Director; David Alan Halsall [1954] Director/Chairman; David John Mabbitt [1950] Director

**Cravenhurst Properties Limited**
*Incorporated:* 7 March 1961
*Net Worth:* £4,789,000 *Total Assets:* £5,587,000
*Registered Office:* Aquarius House, 6 Mid Point Business Park, Thornbury, Bradford, BD3 7AY
*Activities:* Development of building projects
*Parent:* Univar UK Holdings Limited
*Officers:* Paul Graham Bryant [1973] Director; Jeffrey William Carr [1956] Director/Global Counsel [American]; Sabine Duyfjes [1972] Director/VP & General Counsel EMEA [German]

**Createcity Limited**
*Incorporated:* 3 July 1992 *Employees:* 87
*Net Worth:* £12,680,994 *Total Assets:* £22,212,944
*Registered Office:* The Future Business Park, Darlington Road, Shildon, Co Durham, DL4 2RB
*Activities:* Wholesale of furniture, carpets and lighting equipment
*Parent:* J Maguire Holdings Limited
*Officers:* David Stubbs, Secretary; Alice Victoria Maguire [1975] Strategic Development Director; Jason James Maguire [1973] Director/Carpet Retailer; William Maguire [1944] Director; David Stubbs [1957] Director/Accountant

**The Creative Art House**
*Incorporated:* 4 April 1997 *Employees:* 9
*Net Worth:* £4,017,061 *Total Assets:* £4,070,694
*Registered Office:* Drury Lane, Wakefield, W Yorks, WF1 2TE
*Activities:* Operation of arts facilities
*Officers:* Jeremy Mark Charles Cook [1964] Director/Solicitor; Dr Margaret Lindsay Faull [1946] Director/Retired; Jane Margaret Glaister [1953] Director/Cultural Consultant and Trader; Nina Rogers [1978] Director/Head of Marketing & PR; Steven John Williams [1974] Director/Certified Chartered Accountant; Catherine Anamaria Wills [1948] Director/Arts Practitioner; Nigel Stuart Wilson [1957] Director/Project Manager

**Creativerace Limited**
*Incorporated:* 30 May 1978 *Employees:* 125
*Previous:* Gratterpalm Limited
*Net Worth:* £3,336,358 *Total Assets:* £4,591,329
*Registered Office:* No 1 Leeds, 26 Whitehall Road, Leeds, LS12 1BE
*Activities:* Advertising agencies
*Officers:* Gordon Alex Bethell [1970] Joint Managing Director

**Creditscale Limited**
*Incorporated:* 23 February 1996 *Employees:* 2
*Net Worth:* £1,456,858 *Total Assets:* £4,058,559
*Registered Office:* Whinbank Road, Aycliffe Business Park, Newton Aycliffe, Co Durham, DL5 6AY
*Activities:* Other business support service activities n.e.c.
*Shareholders:* John Finley; Valerie Finley
*Officers:* Julie Raistrick, Secretary; Kelly Jean Vasey, Secretary; John Finley [1952] Director/Manager; Valerie Finley [1952] Director/Manager

**Crerar Hotel Group Limited**
*Incorporated:* 4 December 1902 *Employees:* 576
*Net Worth:* £27,614,252 *Total Assets:* £42,490,916
*Registered Office:* 16 Castle Park, Lancaster, LA1 1YG
*Activities:* Hotels and similar accommodation
*Officers:* Nigel Dearnley, Secretary; John Graham Crerar [1961] Director/Investment Manager; Patrick Lorne Crerar [1968] Director; John Nigel Dearnley [1964] Director/Accountant

**Crescent Estates (Ilkley) Limited**
*Incorporated:* 4 November 1970
*Net Worth:* £3,840,977 *Total Assets:* £4,918,741
*Registered Office:* Lloyds Bank Chambers, Hustlergate, Bradford, W Yorks, BD1 1UQ
*Activities:* Other retail sale of new goods in specialised stores (not commercial art galleries and opticians)
*Shareholders:* Alice Mary Cleoniki Avis; Charles Dionysius Avis
*Officers:* Alice Mary Cleoniki Avis [1962] Director/Manager; Charles Dionysius Avis [1959] Director/Recruitment Consultant

**Crest Brick Slate & Tile Limited**
*Incorporated:* 17 September 1998 *Employees:* 11
*Net Worth:* £3,183,076 *Total Assets:* £5,077,572
*Registered Office:* Howdenshire Way, Knedlington Road, Howden, Goole, E Yorks, DN14 7HZ
*Activities:* Agents involved in the sale of timber and building materials
*Parent:* PVH Holdings Ltd
*Officers:* Frank Langstraat [1952] Director [Dutch]; Simon David Pearson [1962] Director; Alan Jonathan Simpson [1966] Director; Arnold Bernard Gerardus Van Huet [1953] Director [Dutch]; Alan William Virgo [1958] Director

**Crest Roofing Limited**
*Incorporated:* 30 March 1990 *Employees:* 7
*Net Worth:* £5,855,823 *Total Assets:* £8,508,032
*Registered Office:* Howdenshire Way, Knedlington Road, Howden, Goole, E Yorks, DN14 7HZ
*Activities:* Roofing activities
*Parent:* P V H Holdings Ltd
*Officers:* Clive Peter Evans [1959] Director/Roofing Specialist; Frank Langstraat [1952] Director [Dutch]; Simon David Pearson [1962] Director; Alan Jonathan Simpson [1966] Director; Arnold Bernard Gerardus Van Huet [1953] Director [Dutch]; Alan William Virgo [1958] Director

**CRG Holdings Ltd**
*Incorporated:* 10 March 2016
*Net Worth:* £4,756,882 *Total Assets:* £11,518,456
*Registered Office:* 4215 Park Approach, Thorpe Park, Leeds, LS15 8GB
*Activities:* Non-trading company
*Officers:* Christopher David Cass [1972] Director

**CRH Fencing & Security Group (UK) Ltd**
*Incorporated:* 29 July 1993 *Employees:* 305
*Net Worth:* £9,989,000 *Total Assets:* £18,732,000
*Registered Office:* Herons Way, Carr Hill, Balby, Doncaster, S Yorks, DN4 8WA
*Activities:* Other specialised construction activities n.e.c.
*Parent:* CRH (UK) Ltd
*Officers:* Darren Harrison [1975] Service Director; Andrew McMenzie [1967] Director/UK Country Manager; Gilles Rabot [1971] Director [French]; Hans Welting [1956] Managing Director [Dutch]; Michael Wightman [1961] Director

**Crime & Fire Defence Systems Limited**
*Incorporated:* 1 April 1999 *Employees:* 34
*Net Worth:* £1,653,373 *Total Assets:* £4,943,487
*Registered Office:* Unit 1 Crigglestone Industrial Estate, Crigglestone, Wakefield, W Yorks, WF4 3HT
*Activities:* Security systems service activities
*Shareholders:* Christopher Keith Laughton; Amanda Mary Laughton
*Officers:* Amanda Laughton, Secretary; Christopher Keith Laughton [1965] Director; Peter Ian Rushforth [1964] Director; Craig Michael Watts [1970] Director

**Crimson Project Investments (Issuer) Limited**
*Incorporated:* 9 October 2013 *Employees:* 3
*Net Worth:* £2 *Total Assets:* £29,098,004
*Registered Office:* 1 Park Row, Leeds, LS1 5AB
*Activities:* Other business support service activities n.e.c.
*Parent:* Dalmore Capital 13 GP LLP
*Officers:* Jennifer McKay, Secretary; John McDonagh [1969] Director; Alistair Graham Ray [1974] Director

**Crimson Project Investments Limited**
*Incorporated:* 9 October 2013 *Employees:* 3
*Net Worth Deficit:* £4,327,390 *Total Assets:* £25,382,160
*Registered Office:* 1 Park Row, Leeds, LS1 5AB
*Activities:* Other business support service activities n.e.c.
*Parent:* Crimson Project Investments (Issuer) Limited
*Officers:* Jennifer McKay, Secretary; John McDonagh [1969] Director; Alistair Graham Ray [1974] Director

**Cristal Inorganic Chemicals UK Limited**
*Incorporated:* 19 March 2007 *Employees:* 3
*Net Worth:* £305,355,008 *Total Assets:* £305,355,008
*Registered Office:* Laporte Road, Stallingborough, Grimsby, N E Lincs, DN40 2PR
*Activities:* Activities of other holding companies n.e.c.
*Parent:* Cristal Inorganic Chemicals Netherlands B.V.
*Officers:* Maria Jegher, Secretary; Stephen Anthony Box [1959] Director/Financial Controller; Dr Robert McIntyre [1955] European Director of Technology and Innovation; Robert John Sarracini [1976] Site Director [British/Australian]

**Cristal Investments UK Limited**
*Incorporated:* 14 December 2011 *Employees:* 3
*Net Worth:* £60,621,304 *Total Assets:* £60,621,300
*Registered Office:* Laporte Road, Stallingborough, Grimsby, N E Lincs, DN40 2PR
*Activities:* Non-trading company
*Parent:* Millennium Inorganic Chemicals Overseas Holdings
*Officers:* Maria Jegher, Secretary; Stephen Anthony Box [1959] Director/Financial Controller; Dr Robert McIntyre [1955] European Director of Technology and Innovation; Robert John Sarracini [1976] Site Director [British/Australian]

**Cristal Pigment UK Limited**
*Incorporated:* 1 January 1920 *Employees:* 376
*Net Worth:* £311,062,016 *Total Assets:* £528,820,000
*Registered Office:* Laporte Road, Stallingborough, Grimsby, N E Lincs, DN40 2PR
*Activities:* Manufacture of other inorganic basic chemicals
*Parent:* Millennium Inorganic Chemicals Overseas Holdings
*Officers:* Maria Jegher, Secretary; Paul Andrew Hannington Barnett [1978] Director/Accountant; Stephen Anthony Box [1959] Director/Financial Controller; Koen Felix Lodewijk Docx [1974] Director/Finance Manager [Belgian]; Dr Robert McIntyre [1955] Commercial Research Director; Simon Morten [1957] Site Director; Robert John Sarracini [1976] Site Director [British/Australian]; Catherine Jane Simpson [1975] Director/Accountant

**Croda Distillates Limited**
*Incorporated:* 17 April 1916
*Net Worth Deficit:* £425,000 *Total Assets:* £3,208,000
*Registered Office:* Cowick Hall, Snaith, Goole, E Yorks, DN14 9AA
*Activities:* Activities of other holding companies n.e.c.
*Parent:* Croda International PLC
*Officers:* Thomas Michael Brophy, Secretary; Thomas Michael Brophy [1973] Director/Solicitor; Deborah Susan Hill [1971] Director

**Croda Europe Limited**
*Incorporated:* 7 May 1920 *Employees:* 918
*Net Worth:* £323,012,992 *Total Assets:* £513,164,992
*Registered Office:* Cowick Hall, Snaith, Goole, E Yorks, DN14 9AA
*Activities:* Manufacture of pesticides and other agrochemical products
*Parent:* Croda Investments No 3 Limited
*Officers:* Thomas Michael Brophy, Secretary; Stuart Arnott [1966] Director/President - Operations; Sandra Elaine Breene [1968] Managing Director; Thomas Michael Brophy [1973] Director/Group General Counsel and Company Secretary; Martin Conleth Campbell [1968] Finance Director; Anthony Damien Fitzpatrick [1968] Director/President Corporate Development; Stephen Edward Foots [1968] Director/Chief Executive; Maarten Willem Heijbroek [1965] Director/Sector President [Dutch]; Paul Anthony Newton [1967] Director/Management Accountant

**Croda International Public Limited Company**
*Incorporated:* 22 May 1925 *Employees:* 4,270
*Net Worth:* £822,300,032 *Total Assets:* £1,648,700,032
*Registered Office:* Cowick Hall, Snaith, Goole, E Yorks, DN14 9AA
*Activities:* Activities of head offices
*Officers:* Thomas Michael Brophy, Secretary; Roberto Cirillo [1971] Director/General Manager [Swiss]; Alan Murray Ferguson [1958] Director/Chartered Accountant; Jacqueline Patricia Christine Ferguson [1970] Director; Stephen Edward Foots [1968] Director/Chief Executive; Anita Margaret Frew [1957] Director; Doctor Helena Louise Ganczakowski [1962] Director; Dr Keith Layden [1959] Director/Chief Technology Officer; Jeremy Kim Maiden [1961] Director/Accountant; Stephen Geoffrey Williams [1948] Director

**Croda Investments Limited**
*Incorporated:* 27 November 2012 *Employees:* 2
*Net Worth:* £345,567,648 *Total Assets:* £366,340,000
*Registered Office:* Cowick Hall, Snaith, Goole, E Yorks, DN14 9AA
*Activities:* Non-trading company
*Parent:* Croda Overseas Holdings Limited
*Officers:* Jeremy Kim Maiden [1961] Director/Accountant; Graham Lloyd Myers [1963] Director/Group Financial Controller

**Croda Investments No 2 Limited**
*Incorporated:* 27 November 2012 *Employees:* 2
*Net Worth:* £104,165,944 *Total Assets:* £470,505,952
*Registered Office:* Cowick Hall, Snaith, Goole, E Yorks, DN14 9AA
*Activities:* Non-trading company
*Parent:* Croda Investments Inc
*Officers:* Jeremy Kim Maiden [1961] Director/Accountant; Graham Lloyd Myers [1963] Director/Group Financial Controller

**Croda Investments No 3 Limited**
*Incorporated:* 22 December 2015 *Employees:* 2
*Net Worth:* £232,650,000 *Total Assets:* £2,201,199,104
*Registered Office:* Cowick Hall, Snaith, Goole, E Yorks, DN14 9AA
*Activities:* Activities of head offices
*Parent:* Croda International PLC
*Officers:* Jeremy Kim Maiden [1961] Director; Graham Lloyd Myers [1963] Director

**Croda Overseas Holdings Limited**
*Incorporated:* 25 April 1997 *Employees:* 2
*Net Worth:* £373,454,656 *Total Assets:* £536,140,160
*Registered Office:* Cowick Hall, Snaith, Goole, E Yorks, DN14 9AA
*Activities:* Activities of head offices
*Parent:* Croda Investments No 3 Limited
*Officers:* Thomas Michael Brophy, Secretary; Stephen Edward Foots [1968] Director/Chief Executive; Graham Lloyd Myers [1963] Director/Group Financial Controller

**Croft Care Trust**
*Incorporated:* 28 June 1990 *Employees:* 70
*Net Worth:* £4,412,153 *Total Assets:* £4,463,154
*Registered Office:* Croft Care Trust, The Croft, Hawcoat Lane, Barrow in Furness, Cumbria, LA14 4HE
*Activities:* Residential care activities for learning difficulties, mental health and substance abuse
*Officers:* Avis Edmondson [1952] Director/Retired Headmistress; Hayley Lisa Edmondson [1981] Director/Operations Manager; Simon John Edmondson [1980] Director/Principal Cost Engineer; Philip John Heath [1955] Director/Bookseller and Stationer; Brenda Pearce [1939] Director/Retired; Margaret Hilda Pippard [1928] Director/Retired

**Croft Carehomes Limited**
*Incorporated:* 5 February 1998
*Net Worth:* £3,636,599 *Total Assets:* £8,085,563
*Registered Office:* 407 Oakwood Lane, Oakwood, Leeds, LS8 3LF
*Activities:* Residential nursing care facilities
*Officers:* Martin Patrick Creegan, Secretary/Care Home Operator; James Joseph Creegan [1967] Director/Nursing Homes; Martin Patrick Creegan [1964] Director/Care Homes; Matthew Joseph Creegan [1944] Director/Care Homes

**Croft Properties (Harrogate) Limited**
*Incorporated:* 12 January 1960 *Employees:* 3
*Net Worth:* £4,804,906 *Total Assets:* £5,370,855
*Registered Office:* Croft Properties (Harrogate) Ltd, Cold Bath Place, Harrogate, N Yorks, HG2 0PQ
*Activities:* Other letting and operating of own or leased real estate
*Parent:* C K Batchelor Limited
*Officers:* John Albert Bachelor [1940] Director/Retired

**Crofton Academy**
*Incorporated:* 25 May 2011 *Employees:* 129
*Net Worth:* £18,197,492 *Total Assets:* £19,138,986
*Registered Office:* Crofton Academy, High Street, Crofton, Wakefield, W Yorks, WF4 1NF
*Activities:* General secondary education
*Officers:* Sharon Archer [1970] Director; Simon Jeremy Bennett [1948] Director/Retired; Suzanne Gallivan [1973] Director; Sally Kilbride [1971] Director; Stephen Keith Lavell [1952] Director; Susan Jayne Lumsdon [1968] Director/Secretarial Co-ordinator/Legal PA; Timothy Morris [1961] Director/Store Manager; Suzanne Louise Linane Pease [1974] Director/Commercial Manager; Roy Anthony Vaughan [1954] Director/Retired Headteacher; Peter Giles Walker [1973] Director/Headteacher; Stephen Wood [1962] Director/Teacher

**Cromar Building Products Limited**
*Incorporated:* 27 December 1996 *Employees:* 49
*Net Worth:* £4,013,722 *Total Assets:* £9,384,502
*Registered Office:* 3 4 & 5 Northside Industrial Estate, Whitley Bridge, Goole, E Yorks, DN14 0GH
*Activities:* Agents involved in the sale of timber and building materials
*Major Shareholder:* Michael Ernest Marshall
*Officers:* Cheryl Norma Marshall, Secretary; Cheryl Norma Marshall [1958] Director/Company Secretary; Daniel James Marshall [1974] Director; Michael Ernest Marshall [1949] Director

**Crombie Freehold Limited**
*Incorporated:* 6 November 2008 *Employees:* 1
*Net Worth:* £2,844,581 *Total Assets:* £3,405,795
*Registered Office:* Cumberland House, Greenside Lane, Bradford, BD8 9TF
*Activities:* Other letting and operating of own or leased real estate
*Shareholders:* Alan James Lewis; Barnett Waddingham Trustees Limited
*Officers:* Alan James Lewis [1938] Director/Chairman

**Crompton Lamps Limited**
*Incorporated:* 12 October 2005 *Employees:* 50
*Net Worth:* £5,388,514 *Total Assets:* £9,002,155
*Registered Office:* Unit 2 Marrtree Business Park, Bowling Back Lane, Bradford, W Yorks, BD4 8QE
*Activities:* Manufacture of electric lighting equipment
*Parent:* GCH Capital Limited
*Officers:* Andrew Glenn Hiscoe, Secretary; Andrew Glenn Hiscoe [1965] Director; John David Shields [1965] Managing Director

**Cromwell Capital Ventures UK Limited**
*Incorporated:* 26 November 2001
*Previous:* Valad Capital Ventures (UK) Limited
*Net Worth:* £9,269,505 *Total Assets:* £9,269,515
*Registered Office:* 1st Floor, Unit 16 Manor Court Business Park, Scarborough, N Yorks, YO11 3TU
*Activities:* Activities of other holding companies n.e.c.
*Parent:* Cromwell Investment Holdings UK Limited
*Officers:* Robert James Cotterell [1974] Director/Head of Transactions

**Cromwell European Holdings Limited**
*Incorporated:* 9 January 2015 *Employees:* 204
*Net Worth Deficit:* £36,472,468 *Total Assets:* £53,084,368
*Registered Office:* 1st Floor, Unit 16 Manor Court Business Park, Eastfield, Scarborough, N Yorks, YO11 3TU
*Activities:* Activities of other holding companies n.e.c.
*Officers:* Mark Anthony McLaughlin [1974] Managing Director, Europe [Irish]; Paul Louis Weightman [1961] Director/Property Investment & Fund Manager [Australian]

**Cromwell European Management Services Limited**
*Incorporated:* 12 October 1995 *Employees:* 75
*Previous:* Valad Management Services Limited
*Net Worth:* £1,345,869 *Total Assets:* £22,192,710
*Registered Office:* 1st Floor, Unit 16 Manor Court Business Park, Scarborough, N Yorks, YO11 3TU
*Activities:* Management of real estate on a fee or contract basis
*Parent:* Cromwell Holdings Europe Limited
*Officers:* Mark Anthony McLaughlin [1974] Director/Head of Property [Irish]; Timothy William Sewell [1967] Director/European Financial Controller

**Cromwell Holdings Europe Limited**
*Incorporated:* 7 February 2002
*Previous:* Valad Holdings (UK) Limited
*Net Worth:* £728,989 *Total Assets:* £3,747,686
*Registered Office:* 1st Floor, Unit 16, Manor Court Business Park, Scarborough, N Yorks, YO11 3TU
*Activities:* Activities of other holding companies n.e.c.
*Parent:* Cromwell Europe Limited
*Officers:* Timothy William Sewell [1967] Director/European Financial Controller

**Cromwell Investment Management Services Limited**
*Incorporated:* 25 January 1995
*Previous:* Valad Investment Management Services Limited
*Net Worth:* £1,477,552 *Total Assets:* £12,541,688
*Registered Office:* 1st Floor, Unit 16 Manor Court Business Park, Scarborough, N Yorks, YO11 3TU
*Activities:* Dormant company
*Parent:* Cromwell Holdings Europe Limited
*Officers:* Robert James Cotterell [1974] Director/Head of Transactions

**Cromwell Management Holdings Limited**
*Incorporated:* 4 November 1994
*Previous:* Valad Management Holdings Limited
*Net Worth:* £3,161,713 *Total Assets:* £3,721,862
*Registered Office:* 1st Floor, Unit 16 Manor Court Business Park, Scarborough, N Yorks, YO11 3TU
*Activities:* Activities of other holding companies n.e.c.
*Parent:* Cromwell Europe Limited
*Officers:* Timothy William Sewell [1967] Director/European Financial Controller

**Cromwell Poland Retail LLP**
*Incorporated:* 31 January 2013
*Previous:* Valad Poland Retail LLP
*Net Worth:* £722,839 *Total Assets:* £5,729,394
*Registered Office:* 1st Floor, Unit 16 Manor Court Business Park, Scarborough, N Yorks, YO11 3TU

**Cromwell Polythene Limited**
*Incorporated:* 14 March 1988 *Employees:* 33
*Net Worth:* £3,777,285 *Total Assets:* £6,716,504
*Registered Office:* Orion Building, Seafox Court, Sherburn Enterprise Park, Sherburn in Elmet, Leeds, LS25 6PL
*Activities:* Packaging activities
*Shareholders:* Vickers-Lee Holdings Limited; Vickers-Lee Holdings Limited
*Officers:* Debra Jane Lee, Secretary; Paul John Fleetwood [1966] Sales Director; Debra Jane Lee [1962] Director; James Richard Vickers Lee [1963] Director

**Cronkhill Properties Limited**
*Incorporated:* 24 September 1999 *Employees:* 2
*Net Worth:* £664,573 *Total Assets:* £5,573,718
*Registered Office:* c/o Mazars LLP, 3 Wellington Place, Leeds, LS1 3AP
*Activities:* Other letting and operating of own or leased real estate
*Shareholders:* Andrew Richard Cossins; Irene Elizabeth Cossins
*Officers:* Andrew Richard Cossins, Secretary/Hotelier; Andrew Richard Cossins [1955] Director/Hotelier; Irene Elizabeth Cossins [1945] Director/Hotelier

**Crop Health and Protection Limited**
*Incorporated:* 18 December 2015 *Employees:* 5
*Net Worth:* £14,370,064 *Total Assets:* £19,168,354
*Registered Office:* National Agri-Food Innovation Campus, Sand Hutton, York, YO41 1LZ
*Activities:* Support activities for crop production
*Officers:* Fraser Black [1961] Director/Chief Executive Officer; John Michael Bloomer [1965] Director/Consultant; Ian William Campbell [1972] Director; William John Chinn [1952] Director; Caroline Jane Drummond [1963] Director/Leaf CEO; Jonathan David LEA [1958] Director; Hannah Senior [1976] Director; Dr Andrew John Swift [1962] Director; Charles Robert Whitmarsh [1962] Crop Production Director

**James Cropper Converting Limited**
*Incorporated:* 7 March 2003 *Employees:* 59
*Net Worth:* £3,797,000 *Total Assets:* £18,765,000
*Registered Office:* Burneside Mills, Kendal, Cumbria, LA9 6PZ
*Activities:* Manufacture of paper and paperboard
*Parent:* James Cropper PLC
*Officers:* James Francis Aldridge, Secretary; Stephen Anthony Adrian Adams [1964] Managing Director; Isabelle Marguerite Maddock [1968] Director/Financial Controller; Philip Ian Wild [1969] Director

**W. Cropper Limited**
*Incorporated:* 15 April 1977 *Employees:* 41
*Net Worth:* £1,835,926 *Total Assets:* £3,577,196
*Registered Office:* Fourway's Garage, Low Mills, Ghyll Royd, Guiseley, Leeds, LS20 9LU
*Activities:* Other urban, suburban or metropolitan passenger land transport (not underground, metro or similar)
*Shareholders:* David Kellett; Penelope Ann Coaten
*Officers:* Penelope Ann Coaten, Secretary; Penelope Ann Coaten [1947] Director/Coach Hire Operator; David Kellett [1946] Director/Coach Hire Operator

**James Cropper Public Limited Company**
*Incorporated:* 29 November 1889
*Net Worth:* £23,346,000 *Total Assets:* £67,509,000
*Registered Office:* Burneside Mills, Kendal, Cumbria, LA9 6PZ
*Activities:* Manufacture of paper and paperboard
*Officers:* James Francis Aldridge, Secretary; Stephen Anthony Adrian Adams [1964] Director; Mark Alexander James Cropper [1974] Director; Dr Andrew Joseph Hosty [1965] Director; Isabelle Marguerite Maddock [1968] Finance Director; James Edward Sharp [1967] Director/Private Equity Adviser; Martin Thompson [1959] Director; Karl David Watson [1964] Director; Philip Ian Wild [1969] Director; David Robert Wilks [1954] Director/Management Consultant; Patrick John Willink [1964] Director

**James Cropper Speciality Papers Limited**
*Incorporated:* 7 March 2003 *Employees:* 337
*Net Worth:* £5,871,000 *Total Assets:* £48,188,000
*Registered Office:* Burneside Mills, Kendal, Cumbria, LA9 6PZ
*Activities:* Manufacture of paper and paperboard
*Parent:* James Cropper PLC
*Officers:* James Francis Aldridge, Secretary; Stephen Anthony Adrian Adams [1964] Managing Director; Isabelle Marguerite Maddock [1968] Director/Financial Controller; Philip Ian Wild [1969] Director

**Crossco (1317) Limited**
*Incorporated:* 15 April 2013 *Employees:* 2
*Net Worth:* £2,068,306 *Total Assets:* £17,050,328
*Registered Office:* 242 Oxford Road, Gomersal, Cleckheaton, W Yorks, BD19 4RE
*Activities:* Activities of open-ended investment companies
*Shareholders:* Dean Hoyle; Janet Elizabeth Hoyle
*Officers:* Dean Hoyle [1967] Chairman/Director; Janet Elizabeth Hoyle [1967] Director

**Crossco (1318) Limited**
*Incorporated:* 15 April 2013 *Employees:* 2
*Net Worth:* £1,424,147 *Total Assets:* £12,785,712
*Registered Office:* 242 Oxford Road, Gomersal, Cleckheaton, W Yorks, BD19 4RE
*Activities:* Activities of open-ended investment companies
*Shareholders:* Janet Elizabeth Hoyle; Dean Hoyle
*Officers:* Dean Hoyle [1967] Chairman/Director; Janet Elizabeth Hoyle [1967] Director

**Crossgreen Investments Limited**
*Incorporated:* 25 September 2014 *Employees:* 1
*Net Worth:* £770,474 *Total Assets:* £4,717,427
*Registered Office:* Leigh House, 28-32 St Paul's Street, Leeds, LS1 2JT
*Activities:* Other letting and operating of own or leased real estate
*Shareholders:* Thomas Paul Shea; Christopher Thomas Shea; Jonathan Shea
*Officers:* Thomas Paul Shea [1964] Director

**Crosshall Developments (Leeds) Limited**
*Incorporated:* 14 February 2012
*Net Worth:* £1,216,185 *Total Assets:* £3,241,461
*Registered Office:* 25 Melbourne Street, Morley, Leeds, LS27 8BG
*Activities:* Development of building projects
*Shareholders:* Peter Baldwin; John Arthur Baldwin; Aspect Building Solutions Limited
*Officers:* Della Baldwin [1952] Director; John Arthur Baldwin [1952] Director; Peter Baldwin [1948] Director; Susan Patricia Baldwin [1962] Director; Jeremy Coates [1962] Director

**Crosslee Holdings Limited**
*Incorporated:* 18 January 1990 *Employees:* 212
*Net Worth:* £16,705,000 *Total Assets:* £23,576,000
*Registered Office:* Lightcliffe Factory, Hipperholme, Halifax, W Yorks, HX3 8DE
*Activities:* Manufacture of electric domestic appliances
*Shareholders:* David John William Ross; Derek Dudley Clee
*Officers:* David John William Ross, Secretary/Director; David John Clee [1964] Director; Derek Dudley Clee [1942] Director; Jean Phoebe Clee [1940] Director; Peter Derek Clee [1967] Director; David John William Ross [1943] Director; Rosemary Anne Ross [1944] Director

**Crosslee PLC**
*Incorporated:* 8 April 1986 *Employees:* 174
*Net Worth:* £20,462,000 *Total Assets:* £24,261,000
*Registered Office:* Lightcliffe Factory, Hipperholme, Halifax, W Yorks, HX3 8DE
*Activities:* Manufacture of electric domestic appliances
*Parent:* Crosslee Holdings Limited
*Officers:* David Michael Heywood, Secretary; Derek Dudley Clee [1942] Director; David John William Ross [1943] Director

**Crossroads Group Limited**
*Incorporated:* 14 February 2005 *Employees:* 361
*Net Worth:* £5,078,000 *Total Assets:* £44,869,000
*Registered Office:* Pheasant Drive, Birstall, Batley, W Yorks, WF17 9LR
*Activities:* Sale of other motor vehicles
*Major Shareholder:* Martin James Cronin
*Officers:* Jayne Michelle Bulpitt [1970] Finance Director; James Andrew Cowen [1986] Finance Director; Martin James Cronin [1965] Director; Gareth Legg [1979] Director; Keith Ottley [1966] Director

**Crossroads Truck & Bus Limited**
*Incorporated:* 18 October 1956 *Employees:* 318
*Net Worth:* £20,651,000 *Total Assets:* £58,691,000
*Registered Office:* Crossroads Truck & Bus, Pheasant Drive, Birstall, Batley, W Yorks, WF17 9LR
*Activities:* Sale of other motor vehicles
*Parent:* Crossroads Group Limited
*Officers:* Jayne Bulpitt, Secretary; Jayne Michelle Bulpitt [1970] Finance Director; James Andrew Cowen [1986] Finance Director; Martin James Cronin [1965] Director; David Crowley [1966] Director; Ian Paul Middleton [1968] Director

**Crossway Scaffolding (Elland) Limited**
*Incorporated:* 15 December 1995 *Employees:* 100
*Net Worth:* £2,769,350 *Total Assets:* £4,358,293
*Registered Office:* Pennine View, Dewsbury Road, Elland, W Yorks, HX5 9JU
*Activities:* Other specialised construction activities n.e.c.
*Major Shareholder:* Steve Fearnehough
*Officers:* Jill Elizabeth Fearnehough [1965] Director; Stephen Fearnehough [1956] Director

**Crossways Commercial Estates Limited**
*Incorporated:* 27 July 2005
*Net Worth:* £2,000 *Total Assets:* £3,723,000
*Registered Office:* Yorkon House, New Lane, Huntington, York, YO32 9PT
*Activities:* Development of building projects
*Parent:* Shepherd Development Company Limited
*Officers:* Martin Ian Goforth, Secretary; Jonathan Mark Collins [1971] Director/Accountant; Caroline Scott [1961] Director/Accountant

**Crosthwaite Hotels (Westmorland) Limited**
*Incorporated:* 29 March 1947 *Employees:* 185
*Net Worth:* £6,183,792 *Total Assets:* £16,991,574
*Registered Office:* Low Wood, Windermere, Cumbria, LA23 1LP
*Activities:* Hotels and similar accommodation
*Officers:* Timothy Robert James Berry, Secretary/Leisure Director; Benjamin William James Berry [1988] Director; Simon Frederick Michael Berry [1959] Managing Director; Timothy Robert James Berry [1961] Leisure Director; Jonathan Alexander Noel Cook [1963] Director; Douglas Paterson Dale [1952] Director; Jonquil Anna Catherine Doremus Cook [1969] Director; David Huw Neale [1962] Commercial Director; Matthew John Wilkinson [1977] Financial Director

**Crowle Wharf Engineers Limited**
*Incorporated:* 21 February 1966
*Net Worth:* £2,726,154 *Total Assets:* £4,246,109
*Registered Office:* Wharf Road, Ealand, Scunthorpe, N Lincs, DN17 4JW
*Activities:* Manufacture of metal structures and parts of structures
*Parent:* Ryanbridge Limited
*Officers:* Oliver Baker [1959] Director; Dr Christopher Charles Brown [1962] Director; John Seaton Buist [1961] Director/Engineer; Mark Anthony Lifsey [1972] Director/Workshop Manager

**Crown Acquisition Bidco Limited**
*Incorporated:* 3 February 2014
*Net Worth Deficit:* £67,811,000 *Total Assets:* £471,912,992
*Registered Office:* One Park Lane, Leeds, LS3 1EP
*Activities:* Activities of head offices
*Parent:* Crown Acquisition Midco 2 Limited
*Officers:* Colin James Rutter, Secretary; Michael Jon Gordon [1970] Director; Robert Kenneth Campbell Munro [1965] Director/Chief Financial Officer; David Neenan [1965] Director/Executive [American/Irish]; Colin James Rutter [1965] Director; Satrajit Saha [1974] Director [Indian]

**Crown Acquisition Consumer Limited**
*Incorporated:* 29 December 2015
*Net Worth Deficit:* £2,176,000 *Total Assets:* £10,000,000
*Registered Office:* c/o Callcredit Limited, 1 Park Lane, Leeds, LS3 1EP
*Activities:* Non-trading company
*Parent:* Crown Acquisition Topco Limited
*Officers:* Colin James Rutter, Secretary; Michael Jon Gordon [1970] Director/Chief Executive Officer; Robert Kenneth Campbell Munro [1965] Director/Chief Financial Officer; David Neenan [1965] Director/Executive [American/Irish]; Colin James Rutter [1965] Director; Satrajit Saha [1974] Director [Indian]

**Crown Acquisition Midco 2 Limited**
*Incorporated:* 3 February 2014 *Employees:* 1,283
*Net Worth:* £18,687,000 *Total Assets:* £603,542,976
*Registered Office:* One Park Lane, Leeds, LS3 1EP
*Activities:* Activities of head offices
*Parent:* Crown Acquisition Midco Limited
*Officers:* Colin James Rutter, Secretary; Michael Jon Gordon [1970] Director; Robert Kenneth Campbell Munro [1965] Director/Chief Financial Officer; David Neenan [1965] Director/Executive [American/Irish]; Colin James Rutter [1965] Director; Satrajit Saha [1974] Director [Indian]

**Crown Acquisition Midco Limited**
*Incorporated:* 3 February 2014
*Net Worth Deficit:* £142,964,992 *Total Assets:* £291,612,000
*Registered Office:* One Park Lane, Leeds, LS3 1EP
*Activities:* Activities of head offices
*Parent:* Crown Acquisition Topco Ltd
*Officers:* Colin James Rutter, Secretary; Michael Jon Gordon [1970] Director; Robert Kenneth Campbell Munro [1965] Director/Chief Financial Officer; David Neenan [1965] Director/Executive [American/Irish]; Colin James Rutter [1965] Director; Satrajit Saha [1974] Director [Indian]

**Crown Acquisition Topco Limited**
*Incorporated:* 3 February 2014
*Net Worth Deficit:* £202,714,000 *Total Assets:* £611,483,008
*Registered Office:* One Park Lane, Leeds, LS3 1EP
*Activities:* Activities of head offices
*Parent:* Vail Holdings UK Ltd
*Officers:* Gary Friedlander [1959] Director/Executive/Attorney [American]; David Gilbert [1969] Director/Executive [American]; Michael Jon Gordon [1970] Director; David Neenan [1965] Director/Executive [American/Irish]

**Crown Chicken Limited**
*Incorporated:* 12 May 2003 *Employees:* 453
*Net Worth:* £18,417,000 *Total Assets:* £28,061,000
*Registered Office:* Crane Court, Hesslewood Office Park, Ferriby Road, Hessle, E Yorks, HU13 0PA
*Activities:* Raising of poultry
*Parent:* CCL Holdings Ltd
*Officers:* Steven Garrick Glover, Secretary; Nigel Colin Armes [1959] Finance Director; John Armstrong [1979] Finance Director; John Mark Bottomley [1963] Finance Director; Adam Hartley Couch [1968] Director; David Charles Park [1969] Managing Director; Matthew Christopher Ward [1964] Agricultural Director

**The Crown Hotel (Bawtry) Limited**
*Incorporated:* 18 May 2003 *Employees:* 85
*Net Worth:* £870,779 *Total Assets:* £4,327,851
*Registered Office:* The Crown Hotel, High Street, Bawtry, Doncaster, S Yorks, DN10 6JT
*Activities:* Hotels and similar accommodation
*Parent:* Crown Hotel Holdings Limited
*Officers:* Jason Peter Cooper [1968] Director; Craig James Dowie [1964] Director/Hotelier; David Nicholas Pain [1965] Director

**Crown Properties (Scarborough) Limited**
*Incorporated:* 26 October 1999 *Employees:* 4
*Net Worth:* £8,521,135 *Total Assets:* £24,074,540
*Registered Office:* Crown Garage, back Albion Road, Scarborough, N Yorks, YO11 2BT
*Activities:* Other letting and operating of own or leased real estate
*Shareholders:* Tara Ledden; Jenna Ledden
*Officers:* David Andrew Ledden [1967] Director; Joseph Patrick Ledden [1938] Director/Manager [Irish]; Patricia Bernadette Ledden [1937] Director/Retired [Irish]

**Crows Nest Camp Limited**
*Incorporated:* 27 March 1969 *Employees:* 11
*Net Worth:* £3,721,277 *Total Assets:* £6,313,383
*Registered Office:* Crows Nest Farm, Gristhorpe, Filey, N Yorks, YO14 9PS
*Activities:* Recreational vehicle parks, trailer parks and camping grounds
*Major Shareholder:* Ian Richard Palmer
*Officers:* Rebecca Jayne Palmer-Bunting, Secretary; Ian Richard Palmer [1953] Director

**J.W. Crowther & Son Limited**
*Incorporated:* 10 August 1961 *Employees:* 45
*Net Worth:* £7,828,556 *Total Assets:* £8,615,637
*Registered Office:* 11 Bradford Road, Gildersome, Leeds, LS27 7HW
*Activities:* Construction of commercial buildings
*Shareholders:* Paul Richard Crowther; Nigel David Crowther
*Officers:* Paul Richard Crowther, Secretary; Nigel David Crowther [1960] Director/Haulier and Contractor; Paul Richard Crowther [1967] Director/Haulier and Contractor

**John Edward Crowther (Holdings) Public Limited Company**
*Incorporated:* 10 October 1949 *Employees:* 8
*Net Worth:* £7,621,868 *Total Assets:* £8,221,775
*Registered Office:* Bank Bottom Mills, Marsden, Huddersfield, W Yorks, HD7 6HR
*Activities:* Activities of head offices
*Parent:* JEC Investment Company Limited
*Officers:* Edward Rowland Lee, Secretary; Philip Roger Crowther [1969] Director/Farmer; Edward Rowland Lee [1956] Director/Company Secretary

**John Edward Crowther Limited**
*Incorporated:* 27 March 1935
*Net Worth:* £3,474,509 *Total Assets:* £3,617,580
*Registered Office:* Bank Bottom Mills, Marsden, Huddersfield, W Yorks, HD7 6HR
*Activities:* Preparation and spinning of textile fibres
*Officers:* Edward Rowland Lee, Secretary; Philip Roger Crowther [1969] Director/Farmer; Edward Rowland Lee [1956] Director/Company Secretary

**Crystal Investment Holdings Limited**
*Incorporated:* 29 August 2014
*Net Worth:* £200,294 *Total Assets:* £4,491,451
*Registered Office:* Whitby Court, Abbey Road, Shepley, Huddersfield, W Yorks, HD8 8EL
*Activities:* Activities auxiliary to financial intermediation n.e.c.
*Shareholders:* Wayne Brandon Butler; Gavin Bonallie
*Officers:* Gavin Bonallie, Secretary; Gavin Bonallie [1983] Director

**CSC (Holdings) Limited**
*Incorporated:* 7 March 1997 *Employees:* 3
*Net Worth:* £350,335 *Total Assets:* £9,750,335
*Registered Office:* Trimble House, Gelderd Road, Gildersome, Morley, Leeds, LS27 7JP
*Activities:* Activities of head offices
*Parent:* CSC (World) Limited
*Officers:* James Anthony Kirkland [1959] Director/VP, General Counsel and Assistant Secretary [American]; Algirdas Paul Rimas [1970] Director/Deputy General Counsel [American]; John Peter Schreiber [1959] Director/Vice President Global Tax [American]

**CSC (World) Limited**
*Incorporated:* 10 February 2003 *Employees:* 3
*Net Worth:* £2,483,373 *Total Assets:* £11,269,660
*Registered Office:* Trimble House, Gelderd Road, Gildersome, Morley, Leeds, LS27 7JP
*Activities:* Business and domestic software development
*Parent:* Cobco 867 Limited
*Officers:* James Anthony Kirkland [1959] Director/VP, General Counsel and Assistant Secretary [American]; Algirdas Paul Rimas [1970] Director/Deputy General Counsel [American]; John Peter Schreiber [1959] Director/Vice President Global Tax [American]

**Ctrack Europe Holdings Ltd**
*Incorporated:* 23 August 2011 *Employees:* 12
*Net Worth Deficit:* £512,051 *Total Assets:* £11,684,398
*Registered Office:* Stockdale House, Victoria Road, Leeds, LS6 1PF
*Activities:* Other transportation support activities
*Parent:* Inseego Corp
*Officers:* Michelle Elisabeth Leach, Secretary; Ian John Holt [1963] Financial Director; Stephen Michael Smith [1958] Director/Chief Financial Officer [American]; Hilger Wyste Van Dam [1974] Director [Dutch]

**Ctrack Limited**
*Incorporated:* 21 January 2003
*Net Worth:* £3,440,254 *Total Assets:* £5,073,358
*Registered Office:* Stockdale House, Victoria Road, Leeds, LS6 1PF
*Activities:* Other transportation support activities
*Parent:* Inseego Corp
*Officers:* Michelle Elisabeth Leach, Secretary; Ian John Holt [1963] Director/Certified Chartered Accountant; Stephen Clifford Thomas [1966] Sales Director

**Ctrack UK Limited**
*Incorporated:* 29 April 2010 *Employees:* 74
*Net Worth Deficit:* £649,752 *Total Assets:* £5,639,728
*Registered Office:* Stockdale House, Victoria Road, Leeds, LS6 1PF
*Activities:* Other transportation support activities
*Parent:* Inseego Corp
*Officers:* Michelle Elisabeth Leach, Secretary; Ian John Holt [1963] Director/Certified Chartered Accountant; Stephen Clifford Thomas [1966] Sales Director

**CTS (Shopfitting) Limited**
*Incorporated:* 6 January 1998 *Employees:* 88
*Net Worth:* £1,164,118 *Total Assets:* £5,743,038
*Registered Office:* Princes House, Wright Street, Hull, HU2 8HX
*Activities:* Joinery installation
*Shareholders:* Richard Fred Middleton; Wayne Flanagan
*Officers:* Wayne Flanagan, Secretary; Wayne Flanagan [1963] Director; Richard Fred Middleton [1963] Managing Director

**Cube (Yorkshire) Ltd**
*Incorporated:* 8 April 2008 *Employees:* 12
*Net Worth:* £1,065,242 *Total Assets:* £4,465,357
*Registered Office:* 257 Lower Mickletown, Methley, Leeds, LS26 9AN
*Activities:* Remediation activities and other waste management services
*Shareholders:* Nicolas Maurice Clarke; Eva Taylor
*Officers:* Eva Taylor, Secretary; Nicolas Maurice Clarke [1981] Director

**Cubic Holdings Limited**
*Incorporated:* 31 March 1999 *Employees:* 116
*Net Worth:* £3,255,423 *Total Assets:* £18,720,168
*Registered Office:* Eldon House, 201 Penistone Road, Kirkburton, Huddersfield, W Yorks, HD8 0PE
*Activities:* Dormant company
*Shareholders:* Dennis Morgan; Tracey Morgan
*Officers:* Dennis Morgan, Secretary/Sales Director; Dennis Morgan [1961] Sales Director; Tracey Morgan [1962] Director/Administrator

**Cubico (UK) Limited**
*Incorporated:* 17 May 2012 *Employees:* 77
*Net Worth:* £2,193,235 *Total Assets:* £7,524,152
*Registered Office:* Unit 2 Royds Lane, Lower Wortley, Leeds, LS12 6DU
*Activities:* Wholesale of hardware, plumbing and heating equipment and supplies
*Officers:* Laura Kate Green [1978] Director; Craig Alan Waddington [1975] Director

**Cullingworth LLP**
*Incorporated:* 10 November 2010
*Net Worth:* £2,545,760 *Total Assets:* £6,686,769
*Registered Office:* Lumbrook Mills, Westercroft Lane, Northowram, Halifax, W Yorks, HX3 7TY
*Officers:* Roger David Feather [1959] Member; Anthony Langstaff [1971] Member

**Cumbria Wildlife Trust Limited**
*Incorporated:* 16 May 1962 *Employees:* 37
*Net Worth:* £6,875,196 *Total Assets:* £7,107,688
*Registered Office:* Plumgarths, Crook Road, Kendal, Cumbria, LA8 8LX
*Activities:* Botanical and zoological gardens and nature reserves activities
*Officers:* John Handley, Secretary; Julie Anne Barrett [1959] Director/Bursar; Dr. Philip Andrew Frank Byle [1963] Investment Director; Jane Carson [1942] Director/Retired; Emily Sarah Coates [1991] Director/Conservation Support Officer; John Malcolm Farmer [1947] Director/Management Consultant; John Handley [1943] Director/Retired; Professor Graham John Hooley [1951] Director/Retired; Lady Cressida Inglewood [1951] Director/Housewife; David Sharrod [1959] Director; Dr Peter Howard Woodhead [1947] Director/Retired

**Cundall Manor Limited**
*Incorporated:* 3 January 1972 *Employees:* 92
*Net Worth:* £2,436,691 *Total Assets:* £5,843,724
*Registered Office:* Cundall Manor School, Cundall, York, YO61 2RW
*Activities:* Pre-primary education
*Officers:* Christopher Lee Holder, Secretary; Lindsay Elizabeth McPhearson Austin [1977] Director/Retail; Charles Edward Foulds [1955] Director/Teacher; Sir Thomas Colvin William Ingilby [1955] Director/Castle Owner; Simon James Kayll [1963] Finance Director; David John Lister [1958] Director/Farmer; Rachel Powell [1968] Director/School Governor; Dennis Richards [1945] Director/Retired; Joyce Tinkler [1951] Director/Retired; Jonathan Charles Deacon Turner [1966] Managing Director; David Michael Willis [1966] Director; Ralph Alekesio Zoing [1965] Director/Financial Adviser

**Cupa-Burton Group Limited**
*Incorporated:* 19 March 2008
*Net Worth:* £29,487,428 *Total Assets:* £29,487,428
*Registered Office:* Chapman Street, Cleveland Street, Hull, HU8 8AE
*Activities:* Wholesale of wood, construction materials and sanitary equipment
*Parent:* The Carlyle Group, L.P.
*Officers:* Lee Michael George Hustwait, Secretary; Andrew Cowham [1958] Director/Accountant; Antonio Trincado Fernandez [1972] Director [Spanish]; Javier Fernandez Fernandez [1968] Director [Spanish]; Paul Arthur Hattee [1962] Director; Lee Keates [1968] Director/Sales; Eduardo Mera [1971] Managing Director [Spanish]; Javier Quindos [1979] Commercial Director [Spanish]

**Curo Transatlantic Limited**
*Incorporated:* 14 March 2001 *Employees:* 209
*Previous:* Wage Day Advance Limited
*Net Worth:* £11,556,000 *Total Assets:* £21,695,000
*Registered Office:* Wellington Plaza, 31 Wellington Street, Leeds, LS1 4DL
*Activities:* Financial intermediation not elsewhere classified
*Officers:* William Baker [1980] Director/Chief Operating Officer [American]; Julian Miles Graham-Rack [1967] Director/Chief Executive Officer; Duncan Peter Marrison [1981] Director/Chartered Accountant; Eugene Marvin Thomas IV [1976] Director/Chief Legal Officer [American]

**Curtis Wool Direct Holdings Limited**
*Incorporated:* 30 May 2002 *Employees:* 124
*Net Worth:* £17,947,964 *Total Assets:* £38,481,192
*Registered Office:* Lawrence House, Dowley Gap Business Park, Bingley, W Yorks, BD16 1WA
*Activities:* Activities of head offices
*Parent:* Nortura SA
*Officers:* Tim Holgate, Secretary; Knud Peder Daugaard [1950] Director/Vice President [Danish]; David Nigel Gisbourne [1961] Director; Timothy Lloyd Holgate [1966] Director; Erik Steinar Hoeg [1976] Director [Norwegian]; Daniel Andre Isbecque [1964] Director; Kai Linnes [1953] Director [Norwegian]; Kristian Havard Saevik [1973] Director [Norwegian]

**Curtis Wool Direct Limited**
*Incorporated:* 4 January 1980
*Net Worth:* £19,382,892 *Total Assets:* £33,756,576
*Registered Office:* Lawrence House, Dowley Gap Business Park, Bingley, W Yorks, BD16 1WA
*Activities:* Non-specialised wholesale trade
*Parent:* Curtis Wool Direct Holdings Limited
*Officers:* Tim Holgate, Secretary; Knud Peder Daugaard [1950] Managing Director [Danish]; David Nigel Gisbourne [1961] Director; Timothy Lloyd Holgate [1966] Director/Wool Merchant; Erik Steinar Hoeg [1976] Director [Norwegian]; Daniel Andre Isbecque [1964] Sales Director; Kai Linnes [1953] Director [Norwegian]; Kristian Havard Saevik [1973] Director [Norwegian]

**The Manny Cussins Foundation**
*Incorporated:* 23 May 2013
*Net Worth:* £5,456,631 *Total Assets:* £5,574,237
*Registered Office:* 34 Park Cross Street, Leeds, LS1 2QH
*Activities:* Other credit granting n.e.c.
*Officers:* Adrian Cussins [1960] Director/University Professor; Andrew James Cussins [1957] Director; Benjamin Michael Cussins [1975] Director/Head of Operations Retail; Emily Cussins [1984] Director/Photographer; Thomas Cussins [1985] Director/Talent Buyer and Professional Artist Management

**Custom Fittings Limited**
*Incorporated:* 3 June 1981 *Employees:* 71
*Net Worth:* £2,313,448 *Total Assets:* £3,092,957
*Registered Office:* 5th Floor, Central Square, 29 Wellington Street, Leeds, LS1 4DL
*Activities:* Manufacture of wire products, chain and springs
*Parent:* Custom Securities Limited
*Officers:* Andrew Crowther, Secretary; Andrew Crowther [1957] Director/Engineer; Edwin Frederick Crowther [1929] Director/Precision Engineer; Mark Crowther [1960] Director/Engineer

**Cutwel Limited**
*Incorporated:* 23 May 1996 *Employees:* 54
*Net Worth:* £6,027,129 *Total Assets:* £8,172,209
*Registered Office:* Unit A, Riverside Drive, Cleckheaton, W Yorks, BD19 4DH
*Activities:* Wholesale of machine tools
*Parent:* Crossco (1432) Limited
*Officers:* Adam Gillard [1980] Director/General Manager; Alexandra Sharon Moore [1974] Director/Chartered Accountant; Graham James Short [1971] Director/Accountant

**Cyan Bidco Limited**
*Incorporated:* 17 July 2014
*Net Worth Deficit:* £17,746,000 *Total Assets:* £791,876,992
*Registered Office:* 2 Wellington Place, Leeds, LS1 4AP
*Activities:* Activities of other holding companies n.e.c.
*Officers:* Scott Campbell Yelle, Secretary; Rafael Ashkenazi [1974] Director [Israeli]; Johan Fredrik Ekdahl [1965] Director of Corporate Affairs [Swedish]; Trystan Michael Forrest [1970] Director of Legal Affairs; Ian David Fraser Proctor [1965] Finance Director; Guy Nigel Lethbridge Templer [1969] Director

**Cyan Blue Core Limited**
*Incorporated:* 20 April 2016
*Net Worth Deficit:* £100,000 *Total Assets:* £4,000,000
*Registered Office:* 2 Wellington Place, Leeds, LS1 4AP
*Activities:* Activities of other holding companies n.e.c.
*Parent:* Cyan Bidco Limited
*Officers:* Scott Campbell Yelle, Secretary; Richard Flint [1972] Director; Ian David Fraser Proctor [1965] Director

**CYB Intermediaries Limited**
*Incorporated:* 21 August 2000
*Previous:* National Australia Insurance Services Limited
*Net Worth:* £108,416,000 *Total Assets:* £111,651,000
*Registered Office:* 20 Merrion Way, Leeds, LS2 8NZ
*Activities:* Non-life insurance
*Parent:* Clydesdale Bank PLC
*Officers:* Graeme Duncan, Secretary; Stuart Fleming [1969] Director/Head of Enterprise Assurance; Michael James Hart [1967] Director/Bank Executive; Nicholas George Julian Walford [1974] Director/Bank Executive

**CYB Investments Limited**
*Incorporated:* 10 March 1987
*Previous:* National Australia Group Europe Limited
*Net Worth:* £6,000,000 *Total Assets:* £6,000,000
*Registered Office:* 20 Merrion Way, Leeds, LS2 8NZ
*Activities:* Banks
*Parent:* CYBG PLC
*Officers:* Lorna Forsyth McMillan, Secretary; Peter Kelvin Dockar [1979] Director/Bank Executive; Alan Ford Kirkwood [1963] Director/Head of Financial Planning & Performance; Yvonne Easton Sharp [1972] Director/Chartered Accountant

**CYBG PLC**
*Incorporated:* 18 May 2015 *Employees:* 5,769
*Net Worth:* £3,185,999,872 *Total Assets:* £43,456,000,000
*Registered Office:* 20 Merrion Way, Leeds, LS2 8NZ
*Activities:* Activities of head offices
*Officers:* Lorna Forsyth McMillan, Secretary; James Peirson, Secretary; Clive Adamson [1956] Director; David Jonathan Bennett [1962] Director; Paul Jonathan Coby [1955] Director; David Joseph Duffy [1961] Director/Bank Executive [Irish]; Geeta Gopalan [1964] Director; Adrian Thomas Grace [1963] Director; Fiona Anne MacLeod [1967] Director; James Neilson Pettigrew [1958] Director; Darren Scott Pope [1965] Director; Dr Teresa Robson-Capps [1955] Director; Ian Stuart Smith [1966] Director/Bank Executive; Amy Elizabeth Stirling [1969] Director; Timothy Cardwell Wade [1959] Director [Australian]

**Cycene Limited**
*Incorporated:* 18 March 2011 *Employees:* 341
*Net Worth:* £27,779,000 *Total Assets:* £38,569,000
*Registered Office:* Omega Boulevard, Capitol Park, Thorne, Doncaster, S Yorks, DN8 5TX
*Activities:* Manufacture of other furniture
*Parent:* Cycene Investments Limited
*Officers:* Richard Adam, Secretary; Simon Keith Barber [1967] Director; James John Robert Murray [1990] Director

**Cyden Homes Limited**
*Incorporated:* 27 August 1962 *Employees:* 35
*Net Worth:* £41,206,080 *Total Assets:* £50,137,760
*Registered Office:* Manor Farm Offices, Laceby, Grimsby, N E Lincs, DN37 7EA
*Activities:* Other letting and operating of own or leased real estate
*Shareholders:* Geoffrey Frederick Dyson; Jacqueline Diana Dyson
*Officers:* Sarah Powton, Secretary; Andrew Burling [1967] Director; Simon James Capps [1969] Director/Accountant; Geoffrey Frederick Dyson [1949] Director/Chartered Builder; Simon Geoffrey Dyson [1975] Director/Builder; Stuart Hockney [1966] Construction Director

**Cyrus Developments Limited**
*Incorporated:* 28 July 2003 *Employees:* 4
*Net Worth Deficit:* £96,153 *Total Assets:* £3,018,791
*Registered Office:* Lyndhurst, Silver Street, Whitley, Goole, N Humbers, DN14 0JG
*Activities:* Development of building projects
*Officers:* Amanda June Whaley, Secretary/Director; Clare Louise Bennison [1962] Director; Peter James Bennison [1962] Director; Amanda June Whaley [1971] Director; Simon John Whaley [1970] Director

**Czajka Group Holdings Limited**
*Incorporated:* 15 December 2008
*Net Worth:* £10,047,001 *Total Assets:* £11,231,666
*Registered Office:* Victoria House, 66-70 Bingley Road, Saltaire, Shipley, W Yorks, BD18 4DJ
*Activities:* Activities of head offices
*Parent:* Redhall Limited
*Officers:* Janina Czajka, Secretary; Konrad Joseph Czajka [1949] Director

**Czajka Properties Limited**
*Incorporated:* 2 September 1977 *Employees:* 334
*Net Worth:* £11,274,838 *Total Assets:* £15,611,584
*Registered Office:* Victoria House, 66-70 Bingley Road, Saltaire, Shipley, W Yorks, BD18 4DJ
*Activities:* Residential nursing care facilities
*Parent:* Czajka Group Holdings Limited
*Officers:* Janina Czajka, Secretary; Janina Czajka [1951] Director; Konrad Joseph Czajka [1949] Director

**D & J Estate Limited**
*Incorporated:* 20 November 1998 *Employees:* 2
*Net Worth:* £476,109 *Total Assets:* £3,580,721
*Registered Office:* Linton Church, Main Street, Linton, Wetherby, W Yorks, LS22 4HT
*Activities:* Residents property management
*Shareholder:* Jeffrey Paul Newman
*Officers:* Debra Marsha Newman, Secretary; Debra Marsha Newman [1959] Director; Jeffrey Paul Newman [1955] Director/Property

**D & L S Developments Limited**
*Incorporated:* 4 February 2016
*Net Worth:* £222,368 *Total Assets:* £3,372,825
*Registered Office:* Permanent House, 1 Dundas Street, Huddersfield, W Yorks, HD1 2EX
*Activities:* Buying and selling of own real estate
*Shareholders:* David Scacchetti; Luisa Scacchetti
*Officers:* Amanda Jennings [1979] Director; Olivia Robinson [1982] Director; David Scacchetti [1951] Director; Luisa Scacchetti [1951] Director

**D & M Middleton Limited**
*Incorporated:* 11 September 2009 *Employees:* 26
*Net Worth:* £16,492,901 *Total Assets:* £16,753,870
*Registered Office:* Unit 1a Rawfolds Industrial Estate, Bradford Road, Cleckheaton, W Yorks, BD19 5LT
*Activities:* Buying and selling of own real estate
*Shareholders:* Sharon Patricia Matthews; Christopher Thomas Middleton; Donald Middleton
*Officers:* Christopher Thomas Middleton [1966] Director

**D & P Haulage Limited**
*Incorporated:* 15 January 2003 *Employees:* 95
*Net Worth:* £1,331,554 *Total Assets:* £5,260,794
*Registered Office:* Tower House Lane, Saltend, Hull, HU12 8EE
*Activities:* Freight transport by road
*Shareholders:* David Richard Charlton; Paul Graham Charlton
*Officers:* David Richard Charlton, Secretary; David Richard Charlton [1953] Director/Haulage; Paul Graham Charlton [1961] Director/Haulage

**D Sales (U.K.) Limited**
*Incorporated:* 19 August 2005 *Employees:* 17
*Net Worth:* £1,743,164 *Total Assets:* £6,118,134
*Registered Office:* Unit 4 Copley Valley Business Park, Copley Valley Road, Sowerby Bridge, W Yorks, HX6 2WA
*Activities:* Wholesale of other office machinery and equipment
*Shareholders:* Jonathan Peter Whitworth; Zoe Ruth Whitworth
*Officers:* Caroline Morris, Secretary; Jonathan Peter Whitworth [1966] Managing Director; Zoe Ruth Whitworth [1970] Director

**D. S. Estates Limited**
*Incorporated:* 4 March 1950 *Employees:* 5
*Net Worth:* £16,878,968 *Total Assets:* £18,751,736
*Registered Office:* Equitable House, 55 Pellon Lane, Halifax, W Yorks, HX1 5SP
*Activities:* Other letting and operating of own or leased real estate
*Shareholder:* Daniel Charles Simpson
*Officers:* Jacqueline Allison Simpson, Secretary; Dr Christopher Jack Simpson [1956] Director/Medical Practitioner; Daniel Charles Simpson [1959] Director/Property Manager

**D.T. Industries Limited**
*Incorporated:* 15 July 1976
*Net Worth:* £766,122 *Total Assets:* £4,064,433
*Registered Office:* Unit 10 Coulman Road Industrial Estate, Thorne, S Yorks, DN8 5JU
*Activities:* Manufacture of other plastic products
*Shareholders:* Damian Mason; David Mason
*Officers:* Damian Mason, Secretary; Damian Mason [1976] Managing Director; David Mason [1944] Director/Chairman; Jonathan Merchant [1972] Technical Director

**Dacre, Son & Hartley Limited**
*Incorporated:* 14 August 1995 *Employees:* 117
*Net Worth:* £2,264,453 *Total Assets:* £3,603,702
*Registered Office:* 1-5 The Grove, Ilkley, W Yorks, LS29 9HS
*Activities:* Real estate agencies
*Officers:* David John Scarborough, Secretary; Paul David Baxter [1960] Director/Estate Agent; Fiona Rowena Bellamy [1965] Director/Chartered Surveyor; Ian James Bradbury [1964] Director/Estate Agent; Ian Geoffrey Cox [1959] Director/Chartered Surveyor; Jonathan Job Isles [1953] Director/Chartered Surveyor; Peter Frank Leadbeater [1968] Director/Estate Agent; Patrick John McCutcheon [1965] Director/Estate Agent; David William Stuart Ogilvie [1964] Director/Chartered Surveyor; Steven Potts [1975] Director; David John Scarborough [1950] Director; Elisabeth Caren Scull [1962] Director/Chartered Surveyor; Tim Usherwood [1965] Director; James Christopher Wattrus [1958] Director/Chartered Surveyor; Paul Kenneth Wilson [1980] Director

**Dadibhais (Bradford) Limited**
*Incorporated:* 6 September 1990 *Employees:* 26
*Net Worth:* £3,751,440 *Total Assets:* £5,613,929
*Registered Office:* 19-37 Joseph Street, Bradford, W Yorks, BD3 9HR
*Activities:* Wholesale of household goods (other than musical instruments) n.e.c
*Officers:* Ahmed Miya Ismail Dadibhai, Secretary; Ahmed Miya Ismail Dadibhai [1942] Director; Fatima Dadibhai [1949] Director; Muhammad Zakaria [1981] Director/Marketing

**Dadibhais Holdings Limited**
*Incorporated:* 7 May 2008
*Net Worth:* £4,527,693 *Total Assets:* £5,540,435
*Registered Office:* 19-37 Joseph Street, Bradford, BD3 9HR
*Activities:* Activities of other holding companies n.e.c.
*Major Shareholder:* Muhammed Zakariyah Dadibhai
*Officers:* Ahmed Miya Ismail Dadibhai, Secretary; Ahmed Miya Ismail Dadibhai [1942] Director/Secretary; Fatima Dadibhai [1948] Director; Muhammad Zakaria Dadibhai [1981] Director

**Daifuku Logan Ltd**
*Incorporated:* 20 October 1995 *Employees:* 137
*Net Worth:* £2,604,000 *Total Assets:* £27,907,000
*Registered Office:* Sutton Road, Kingston upon Hull, HU7 0DR
*Activities:* Manufacture of other special-purpose machinery n.e.c.
*Parent:* Daifuku Co., Ltd
*Officers:* Christine Boyd, Secretary; Stephen John Fullerton [1967] Director [New Zealander]; Shuichi Honda [1957] Director [Japanese]; Ronald Osborne [1957] Director; Hiroshi Shirako [1957] Director/Material Handling Executive [Japanese]; Patrick William Teo [1964] Director [New Zealander]

**Dakin Industries Limited**
*Incorporated:* 22 March 2013 *Employees:* 2
*Net Worth:* £6,441,854 *Total Assets:* £6,800,247
*Registered Office:* c/o Dakin-Flathers Limited, Boothroyds Way, Featherstone, Pontefract, W Yorks, WF7 6RA
*Activities:* Activities of head offices
*Major Shareholder:* Oliver Graham Garside
*Officers:* Oliver Graham Garside [1966] Director; Margareth Gschnitzer [1965] Director [Italian]

**Dakin-Flathers Limited**
*Incorporated:* 12 November 1931 *Employees:* 48
*Net Worth:* £3,069,436 *Total Assets:* £4,605,679
*Registered Office:* Dakin-Flathers Ltd, Boothroyds Way, Featherstone, Pontefract, W Yorks, WF7 6RA
*Activities:* Manufacture of tools
*Parent:* Dakin Industries Ltd
*Officers:* Margareth Gschnitzer, Secretary [Italian]; Lee James Barker [1972] Operations Director; Oliver Graham Garside [1966] Director; Paul Stefan Greenley [1967] Sales and Marketing Director; Margareth Gschnitzer [1965] Director and Company Secretary [Italian]

**Dakota Pharma Limited**
*Incorporated:* 2 December 2005 *Employees:* 4
*Net Worth:* £1,438,938 *Total Assets:* £4,299,038
*Registered Office:* 8 The Courtyards, Victoria Road, Leeds, LS14 2LB
*Activities:* Wholesale of pharmaceutical goods
*Shareholders:* Marshall Anthony Glynn; Anthony Golombeck
*Officers:* Anthony Golombeck, Secretary; Marshall Anthony Glynn [1962] Director; Anthony Golombeck [1955] Director

**Dalby Offshore Services Limited**
*Incorporated:* 30 August 2007 *Employees:* 43
*Net Worth:* £4,836,160 *Total Assets:* £24,475,796
*Registered Office:* Medina House, 2 Station Avenue, Bridlington, E Yorks, YO16 4LZ
*Activities:* Other professional, scientific and technical activities n.e.c.
*Major Shareholder:* Stuart Hamish McNiven
*Officers:* Kevin Adamson, Secretary; Stuart Hamish McNiven [1959] Managing Director

**Dale Erskine Power Solutions Limited**
*Incorporated:* 10 February 2012 *Employees:* 268
*Net Worth:* £2,377,000 *Total Assets:* £17,713,000
*Registered Office:* Eastfield Industrial Estate, Salter Road, Scarborough, N Yorks, YO11 3DU
*Activities:* Activities of other holding companies n.e.c.
*Parent:* Deps Bidco Limited
*Officers:* James Vaughan Arrowsmith [1968] Director/Investment Manager; Denzil Lee [1948] Director; Timothy John Wilkins [1960] Director/General Manager

**Dale Farm (GB) Limited**
*Incorporated:* 22 April 2003 *Employees:* 175
*Net Worth:* £6,072,000 *Total Assets:* £36,175,000
*Registered Office:* Lakeland Creamery, Shap Road Industrial Estate, Kendal, Cumbria, LA9 6NS
*Activities:* Manufacture of other milk products
*Parent:* Dale Farm Cooperative Ltd
*Officers:* Michael Anthony Dawson, Secretary; John Herbert Scott Dunlop [1956] Director/Farmer; Stephen John Elliott [1957] Finance Director; Nick Whelan [1972] Director/Chief Executive

**Dale Power Solutions Limited**
*Incorporated:* 5 November 1968 *Employees:* 261
*Net Worth:* £9,578,000 *Total Assets:* £21,286,000
*Registered Office:* Salter Road, Eastfield Industrial Estate, Scarborough, N Yorks, YO11 3DU
*Activities:* Manufacture of electric motors, generators and transformers
*Parent:* Dale Erskine Power Solutions Ltd
*Officers:* James Vaughan Arrowsmith [1968] Director/Investment Manager; Mark George Carter [1971] Director; Roger Clay [1957] Director; Denzil Lee [1948] Director; Ralph Letheren [1972] Director; Lance William Lewis [1966] Sales & Marketing Director; Timothy John Wilkins [1960] Director/Chief Executive

**Dalekim Developments Limited**
*Incorporated:* 14 June 2013 *Employees:* 2
*Net Worth:* £763,518 *Total Assets:* £6,346,927
*Registered Office:* 5th Floor, Central Square, 29 Wellington Street, Leeds, LS1 4DL
*Activities:* Buying and selling of own real estate
*Shareholders:* Dale Walter Chapman; Kim Chapman
*Officers:* Dale Walter Chapman [1970] Director; Kim Chapman [1971] Director

**Dalesauna Limited**
*Incorporated:* 8 October 1968 *Employees:* 47
*Net Worth:* £1,994,306 *Total Assets:* £3,751,466
*Registered Office:* Crown Chambers, Princes Street, Harrogate, N Yorks, HG1 1NJ
*Activities:* Other specialised construction activities n.e.c.
*Major Shareholder:* Stephen Roger Hipps
*Officers:* Stephen Roger Hipps, Secretary; Martin Derek Ball [1970] Director; David John Firth [1962] Contracts Director; Jeremy Edward Greenhalgh [1963] Director; Stephen Roger Hipps [1945] Director; Steven Paul Taylor [1959] Finance Director

**Dalestead Limited**
*Incorporated:* 19 May 1995 *Employees:* 6
*Net Worth:* £3,514,411 *Total Assets:* £3,832,406
*Registered Office:* 4 Buttercrambe Road, Stamford Bridge, York, YO41 1AN
*Activities:* Other service activities n.e.c.
*Shareholders:* David Hind; Christine Hind
*Officers:* Christine Hind, Secretary; Christine Hind [1949] Director/Caravan Park Operator; David Anthony Hind [1948] Director/Caravan Park Operator; Kevin Anthony Hind [1975] Director/Manager; Michael Andrew Hind [1978] Director/Manager

**Dalesview Developments Limited**
*Incorporated:* 20 November 2003
*Net Worth:* £464,728 *Total Assets:* £8,615,577
*Registered Office:* Innovation House, Snaygill Industrial Estate, Keighley Road, Skipton, N Yorks, BD23 2QR
*Activities:* Development of building projects
*Officers:* David Stephen Cock [1971] Director

**Dalian Properties Limited**
*Incorporated:* 7 October 1997 *Employees:* 2
*Net Worth:* £5,323,933 *Total Assets:* £13,981,339
*Registered Office:* 57 Micklegate, York, YO1 6LJ
*Activities:* Construction of commercial buildings
*Shareholders:* Ian Craig McManaman; Dale Peter McManaman
*Officers:* Susan Michelle McManaman, Secretary; Dale Peter McManaman [1962] Director/Builder; Ian Craig McManaman [1964] Director/Builder

**Dalkeith Laboratories Limited**
*Incorporated:* 29 January 1999 *Employees:* 14
*Net Worth:* £2,783,491 *Total Assets:* £3,276,042
*Registered Office:* c/o KJA Group, Network House, West 26, Stubs Back Lane, Cleckheaton, W Yorks, BD19 4TT
*Activities:* Manufacture of basic pharmaceutical products
*Shareholders:* Ian John Kirk; Peter Noel Miller Cox
*Officers:* Peter Noel Miller Cox, Secretary/Chemist; Peter Noel Miller Cox [1946] Director/Chemist; Ian John Kirk [1957] Director; Lynne Whiteley [1972] Director/Office Manager

**T L Dallas & Co Limited**
*Incorporated:* 23 December 1959 *Employees:* 75
*Net Worth:* £2,317,075 *Total Assets:* £19,719,796
*Registered Office:* Dallas House, Low Moor, Bradford, W Yorks, BD12 0HF
*Activities:* Non-life insurance
*Parent:* TL Dallas Group Limited
*Officers:* Jonathan William Hollowood, Secretary; Barry Battersby [1948] Director/Insurance Broker; John Derek Butterworth [1958] Director/Insurance Broker; MacKenzie John William Dallas [1976] Director; Jonathan William Hollowood [1979] Director/Chartered Accountant; Simon Darcy Hyde [1959] Credit Broking Director; Michael Peter Martin [1960] Director/Insurance Broker; Polly Eleanor Olivia Staveley [1975] Director/Insurance Broker

**T L Dallas Group Limited**
*Incorporated:* 20 October 1989 *Employees:* 122
*Net Worth:* £6,349,670 *Total Assets:* £25,373,560
*Registered Office:* Dallas House, Low Moor, Bradford, W Yorks, BD12 0HF
*Activities:* Activities of financial services holding companies
*Officers:* Jonathan William Hollowood, Secretary; John Derek Butterworth [1958] Director/Insurance Broker; Michael Peter Martin [1960] Director/Insurance Broker; Graham Hoy Reid [1951] Director/Insurance Broker; Polly Eleanor Olivia Staveley [1975] Director/Insurance Broker

**Dalmore Capital (Carlisle 1) Limited**
*Incorporated:* 11 June 2013 *Employees:* 3
*Net Worth Deficit:* £5,588,739 *Total Assets:* £11,334,521
*Registered Office:* 1 Park Row, Leeds, LS1 5AB
*Activities:* Other business support service activities n.e.c.
*Parent:* Dalmore Capital (Para 1) Limited
*Officers:* Jennifer McKay, Secretary; John McDonagh [1969] Director; Alastair Graham Ray [1974] Director

**Dalmore Capital (Corsham 1) Limited**
*Incorporated:* 30 April 2013 *Employees:* 3
*Net Worth Deficit:* £3,659,235 *Total Assets:* £15,588,716
*Registered Office:* 1 Park Row, Leeds, LS1 5AB
*Activities:* Other business support service activities n.e.c.
*Parent:* Dalmore Capital (Para 1) Limited
*Officers:* Jennifer McKay, Secretary; John McDonagh [1969] Director; Alistair Graham Ray [1974] Director

**Dalmore Capital (Issuer 1) Limited**
*Incorporated:* 19 June 2012 *Employees:* 3
*Net Worth Deficit:* £41,461 *Total Assets:* £255,219,216
*Registered Office:* 1 Park Row, Leeds, LS1 5AB
*Activities:* Other business support service activities n.e.c.
*Parent:* Dalmore Capital 2 GP Limited
*Officers:* Jennifer McKay, Secretary; John McDonagh [1969] Director; Alistair Graham Ray [1974] Director

**Dalmore Capital (Issuer 2) Limited**
*Incorporated:* 19 June 2012
*Net Worth Deficit:* £4,768 *Total Assets:* £33,510,446
*Registered Office:* 1 Park Row, Leeds, LS1 5AB
*Activities:* Other business support service activities n.e.c.
*Parent:* Dalmore Capital 2 GP Limited
*Officers:* Jennifer McKay, Secretary; John McDonagh [1969] Director; Alistair Graham Ray [1974] Director

**Dalmore Capital (Para 1) Limited**
*Incorporated:* 3 May 2012 *Employees:* 3
*Net Worth Deficit:* £5,749,640 *Total Assets:* £249,147,152
*Registered Office:* 1 Park Row, Leeds, LS1 5AB
*Activities:* Other business support service activities n.e.c.
*Parent:* Dalmore Capital (Issuer 1) Limited
*Officers:* Jennifer McKay, Secretary; John McDonagh [1969] Director; Alistair Graham Ray [1974] Director

**Dalmore Capital (Para 2) Limited**
*Incorporated:* 27 September 2012 *Employees:* 3
*Net Worth Deficit:* £4,498,923 *Total Assets:* £28,967,392
*Registered Office:* 1 Park Row, Leeds, LS1 5AB
*Activities:* Other business support service activities n.e.c.
*Parent:* Dalmore Capital (Issuer 2) Limited
*Officers:* Jennifer McKay, Secretary; John McDonagh [1969] Director; Alistair Graham Ray [1974] Director

**Dalmore Capital (Rochdale 2) Limited**
*Incorporated:* 15 August 2014
*Net Worth:* £10 *Total Assets:* £5,901,293
*Registered Office:* 1 Park Row, Leeds, LS1 5AB
*Activities:* Other business support service activities n.e.c.
*Shareholders:* Dalmore Capital (Para 1) Limited; PPDI Assetco Limited
*Officers:* Jennifer McKay, Secretary; John McDonagh [1969] Director; Alistair Graham Ray [1974] Director

**Dalmore Capital (Rochdale) Limited**
*Incorporated:* 15 May 2013 *Employees:* 2
*Net Worth Deficit:* £201,626 *Total Assets:* £4,101,317
*Registered Office:* 1 Park Row, Leeds, LS1 5AB
*Activities:* Other business support service activities n.e.c.
*Parent:* Dalmore Capital (Para 1) Limited
*Officers:* Jennifer McKay, Secretary; John McDonagh [1969] Director; Alistair Graham Ray [1974] Director

**Dalmore Capital Limited**
*Incorporated:* 17 March 2009 *Employees:* 31
*Net Worth:* £6,162,380 *Total Assets:* £10,621,863
*Registered Office:* 1 Park Row, Leeds, LS1 5AB
*Activities:* Security and commodity contracts dealing activities
*Parent:* Dalmore Intermediate Limited
*Officers:* Jennifer McKay, Secretary; John McDonagh [1969] Director; Alistair Graham Ray [1974] Director; Michael Joseph Ryan [1966] Director/Fund Manager [Irish]

**Dalmore Group Limited**
*Incorporated:* 26 January 2016
*Net Worth:* £4,200,100 *Total Assets:* £4,200,100
*Registered Office:* 1 Park Row, Leeds, LS1 5AB
*Activities:* Other business support service activities n.e.c.
*Shareholders:* MM & S JM Limited; Jadin Limited; Aghinagh Limited
*Officers:* Jennifer McKay, Secretary; John McDonagh [1969] Director; Alistair Graham Ray [1974] Director; Michael Joseph Ryan [1966] Director/Fund Manager [Irish]

**Dalmore Highway Investment Holdings Limited**
*Incorporated:* 23 September 2016
*Net Worth:* £6,833,082 *Total Assets:* £53,695,584
*Registered Office:* 1 Park Row, Leeds, LS1 5AB
*Activities:* Activities of construction holding companies
*Parent:* PPDI Assetco Limited
*Officers:* Jennifer McKay, Secretary; John Stephen Gordon [1962] Director; John McDonagh [1969] Director

**Dalmore Intermediate Limited**
*Incorporated:* 11 January 2016
*Net Worth:* £12,000,002 *Total Assets:* £12,000,002
*Registered Office:* 1 Park Row, Leeds, LS1 5AB
*Activities:* Other business support service activities n.e.c.
*Parent:* Dalmore Holdings Limited
*Officers:* Jennifer McKay, Secretary; John McDonagh [1969] Director; Alistair Graham Ray [1974] Director; Michael Joseph Ryan [1966] Director/Fund Manager [Irish]

**Dalquinto Limited**
*Incorporated:* 7 December 1999
*Net Worth:* £3,749,467 *Total Assets:* £4,603,280
*Registered Office:* Bankwood Road, Stapleton, Pontefract, W Yorks, WF8 3DD
*Activities:* Production of meat and poultry meat products
*Shareholders:* David Bosworth Gunner; Edwin John Richard Canvin
*Officers:* David Bosworth Gunner, Secretary/Director; Edwin John Richard Canvin [1950] Director; David Bosworth Gunner [1952] Director; Andrew James McAllister [1965] Managing Director; Amanda Patricia Snowie [1961] Director

**DAM Investments and Properties Limited**
*Incorporated:* 8 October 2010 *Employees:* 3
*Net Worth:* £5,379,282 *Total Assets:* £7,542,690
*Registered Office:* Ramsden Mills, Britannia Road, Huddersfield, W Yorks, HD3 4QG
*Activities:* Other service activities n.e.c.
*Shareholders:* David James Mosley; Adam Paul Mosley; The Hartford Trust
*Officers:* Rebecca Nga-See Mosley, Secretary; Adam Paul Mosley [1975] Director; David James Mosley [1978] Director; James Maurice Vincent Mosley [1929] Director

**Dam Structures Limited**
*Incorporated:* 4 August 2004 *Employees:* 51
*Net Worth:* £5,257,489 *Total Assets:* £11,041,158
*Registered Office:* Heron House, Carnaby Industrial Estate, Lancaster Road, Carnaby, Bridlington, N Humbers, YO15 3QY
*Activities:* Manufacture of metal structures and parts of structures
*Major Shareholder:* Philip Stephen Cook
*Officers:* Geoff Alexander Bissett [1970] Director; Philip Stephen Cook [1975] Director; Joshua Thomas Emerson [1988] Director; Robert Gammon [1958] Director; Richard John Woodhead [1980] Director

**Damac (Transporters) Limited**
*Incorporated:* 6 August 1976 *Employees:* 67
*Net Worth:* £1,195,152 *Total Assets:* £3,725,166
*Registered Office:* Mariner Street, Goole, E Yorks, DN14 5BW
*Activities:* Freight transport by road
*Shareholders:* Catherine Plaskitt; Lee David Mackrill
*Officers:* Catherine Plaskitt, Secretary/Accountant; David Mackrill [1944] Director; Lee David Mackrill [1972] Director; Catherine Plaskitt [1974] Director/Accountant

**Damac Group Limited**
*Incorporated:* 12 May 1999 *Employees:* 78
*Net Worth:* £3,159,301 *Total Assets:* £8,023,029
*Registered Office:* Mariners Street, Goole, N Humbers, DN14 5BW
*Activities:* Activities of head offices
*Shareholders:* Catherine Plaskitt; Lee David Mackrill
*Officers:* Catherine Plaskitt, Secretary/Accountant; David Mackrill [1944] Director; Lee David Mackrill [1972] Director/Teacher; Catherine Plaskitt [1974] Director/Accountant

**Damartex UK Limited**
*Incorporated:* 28 June 1965 *Employees:* 454
*Net Worth:* £17,979,000 *Total Assets:* £46,514,000
*Registered Office:* Bowling Green Mills, Lime Street, Bingley, W Yorks, BD97 1AD
*Activities:* Retail sale via mail order houses or via Internet
*Parent:* Damartex
*Officers:* Stuart Creeley, Secretary; Lynn Cordall [1967] Merchandise Director; Stuart Creeley [1962] Finance Director; Linda Ann Montgomery [1958] HR Director; George Vasili [1960] IT and Logistics Director

**B.Danby & Co,Limited**
*Incorporated:* 29 May 1909 *Employees:* 56
*Net Worth:* £1,626,040 *Total Assets:* £4,477,745
*Registered Office:* English Street, Hull, HU3 2DZ
*Activities:* Wholesale of hardware, plumbing and heating equipment and supplies
*Officers:* Ian Richard Thorp, Secretary; Philip Sidney Dalton [1955] Director/Chairman; Ian Richard Thorp [1965] Managing Director

**Danby Holdings Limited**
*Incorporated:* 15 August 2003 *Employees:* 80
*Net Worth:* £2,620,982 *Total Assets:* £6,512,332
*Registered Office:* English Street, Hull, HU3 2DZ
*Activities:* Activities of head offices
*Shareholders:* Ian Richard Thorp; Philip Sidney Dalton
*Officers:* Ian Richard Thorp, Secretary/Managing Director; Philip Sidney Dalton [1955] Director/Chairman; Ian Richard Thorp [1965] Managing Director

**Danesmoor Holdings Limited**
*Incorporated:* 13 July 2012 *Employees:* 378
*Net Worth:* £52,714,176 *Total Assets:* £63,852,992
*Registered Office:* P O Box 20, Station Road, Aycliffe Business Park, Newton Aycliffe, Co Durham, DL5 6XJ
*Activities:* Activities of head offices
*Major Shareholder:* Mark William Winspear Stephenson
*Officers:* Jonathan Barclay Whisker, Secretary; Mark William Winspear Stephenson [1962] Director; Jonathan Barclay Whisker [1964] Financial Director

**Danesmoor Limited**
*Incorporated:* 8 December 1993 *Employees:* 21
*Net Worth:* £55,195,112 *Total Assets:* £71,081,336
*Registered Office:* P O Box 20, Station Road, Aycliffe Business Park, Newton Aycliffe, Co Durham, DL5 6XJ
*Activities:* Agents involved in the sale of furniture, household goods, hardware and ironmongery
*Officers:* Jonathan Barclay Whisker, Secretary; David Burchnall [1967] Director/Salesman; Marc John Holmes [1965] Director; Mark William Winspear Stephenson [1962] Director; Jonathan Barclay Whisker [1964] Financial Director

**Daniels Chilled Foods Limited**
*Incorporated:* 15 September 1995 *Employees:* 1,094
*Net Worth:* £19,846,000 *Total Assets:* £128,186,000
*Registered Office:* 2100 Century Way, Thorpe Park Business Park, Leeds, LS15 8ZB
*Activities:* Manufacture of other food products n.e.c.
*Parent:* S. Daniels Limited
*Officers:* Nicholas Keen, Secretary; Denise Menikheim Faltischek [1973] Director/Attorney [American]; James Michael Langrock [1965] Director [American]; Mark Lawrence Schiller [1961] Director [American]; Robin James Skidmore [1968] Director

**S.Daniels Limited**
*Incorporated:* 8 December 1944
*Previous:* S.Daniels PLC
*Net Worth:* £40,255,000 *Total Assets:* £40,644,000
*Registered Office:* 2100 Century Way, Thorpe Park Business Park, Leeds, LS15 8ZB
*Activities:* Activities of head offices
*Parent:* Hain Frozen Foods UK Limited
*Officers:* Nicholas Keen, Secretary; Denise Menikheim Faltischek [1973] Director/Attorney [American]; James Michael Langrock [1965] Director [American]; Mark Lawrence Schiller [1961] Director/CEO Hain Celestial [American]; Robin James Skidmore [1968] Director

**Dante Capital Limited**
*Incorporated:* 25 November 2013
*Net Worth:* £770,442 *Total Assets:* £4,315,927
*Registered Office:* Gresham House, 5-7 St Pauls Street, Leeds, LS1 2JG
*Activities:* Other letting and operating of own or leased real estate
*Shareholders:* Simon Edward Chappell; Louise Chappell
*Officers:* Louise Amanda Chappell [1970] Director; Simon Edward Chappell [1970] Director

**Dantex Graphics Limited**
*Incorporated:* 3 March 1967 *Employees:* 49
*Net Worth:* £11,253,383 *Total Assets:* £17,903,000
*Registered Office:* Danon House, 5 Kings Road, Bradford, BD2 1EY
*Activities:* Non-specialised wholesale trade
*Officers:* Torge Steffen, Secretary; Andrew David Abbott [1969] UK Sales Director; Benjamin Danon [1982] Director; Dorit Danon [1948] Director; Richard Danon [1945] Research & Development Director; Richard Hall [1966] R&D Director - Dantex Digital; Torge Steffen [1976] Finance Director [German]

**Dantex Group Limited**
*Incorporated:* 10 August 2006 *Employees:* 115
*Net Worth:* £13,373,000 *Total Assets:* £24,330,000
*Registered Office:* Danon House, 5 Kings Road, Bradford, W Yorks, BD2 1EY
*Activities:* Activities of head offices
*Officers:* Torge Steffen, Secretary; Benjamin Danon [1982] Director; Richard Danon [1945] Research & Development Director

**Daresbury Park Developments Limited**
*Incorporated:* 26 September 2000
*Net Worth:* £6,795,757 *Total Assets:* £6,845,533
*Registered Office:* Huddersfield Road, Elland, W Yorks, HX5 9BW
*Activities:* Other letting and operating of own or leased real estate
*Parent:* Commercial Development Projects Ltd
*Officers:* Jonathan Booth, Secretary/Accountant; Christopher Roy Marshall [1939] Director/Building Contractor; Simon Charles Newton Marshall [1963] Director/Surveyor

**Darley Properties Limited**
*Incorporated:* 20 November 2013
*Net Worth:* £34,064 *Total Assets:* £5,656,353
*Registered Office:* Maple House, Silverdale Close, Darley, Harrogate, N Yorks, HG3 2PQ
*Activities:* Buying and selling of own real estate
*Shareholders:* Paul Stuart James Chapman; Ross William Chapman; Sam Chapman
*Officers:* Paul Stuart James Chapman [1988] Director; Ross William Chapman [1990] Director; Sam Chapman [1992] Director

**Darlington & District Hospice Movement**
*Incorporated:* 4 December 1986 *Employees:* 145
*Net Worth:* £3,816,763 *Total Assets:* £3,986,437
*Registered Office:* The Woodlands, Woodland Road, Darlington, Co Durham, DL3 7UA
*Activities:* Hospital activities
*Officers:* Nicola Jane Myers, Secretary; Dr Harry Byrne [1953] Director/General Practitioner [Irish]; Anne Foster [1946] Director/General Nurse; Mary Lovell [1932] Director/Retired Head of Department Technical; Antony William Luckett [1961] Director/Accountant; Dr Helen McLeish [1970] Director/General Practitioner; Nicholas Charles Tristram Millen [1958] Durham School (Director, International); Steve John Rose [1957] Director/Management Consultant; Sasha Warr [1973] Director/HR Consultant

**Darlington Arena Limited**
*Incorporated:* 9 June 2011
*Net Worth:* £2,347,357 *Total Assets:* £3,310,839
*Registered Office:* Northern Echo Arena, Neasham Road, Darlington, Co Durham, DL2 1DL
*Activities:* Other sports activities
*Parent:* Darlington Mowden Park Rugby Football Club Limited
*Officers:* Michael Birch [1964] Director; Lee Trevor Rust [1980] Director

**The Darlington Farmers Auction Mart Company Limited**
*Incorporated:* 20 March 1926 *Employees:* 38
*Net Worth:* £4,822,652 *Total Assets:* £7,475,696
*Registered Office:* Bank Top Mart, Clifton Road, Darlington, Co Durham, DL1 5DU
*Activities:* Support activities for animal production (other than farm animal boarding)
*Officers:* Andrew Armstrong [1981] Director; James Edward Beadle [1977] Director/Farmer; Eric Blacklock [1964] Director/Farmer; Simon Catterall [1956] Director/Solicitor; Jon Andrew Grieves [1972] Director/Farmer; Richard Heseltine [1972] Director/FCCA; Trevor David Johnson [1953] Director/Farmer; Peter Anthony Guy Monkhouse [1963] Director; John Anthony Ward [1957] Director

**Darlington Homes Limited**
*Incorporated:* 17 September 1992
*Net Worth:* £99,451 *Total Assets:* £5,710,022
*Registered Office:* Sentinel House, Morton Road, Darlington, Co Durham, DL1 4PT
*Activities:* Development of building projects
*Officers:* Michael Cowan, Secretary; John Jack Cullen [1954] Director; Christopher Hunter [1977] Director/Chief Risk Officer; Christopher Ben White [1978] Finance Director

**Darntonb3 Limited**
*Incorporated:* 12 June 2008 *Employees:* 116
*Previous:* Darnton EGS Limited
*Net Worth:* £2,263,824 *Total Assets:* £4,672,629
*Registered Office:* The Coach House, Monk Fryston Hall, Main Street, Monk Fryston, Leeds, LS25 5DU
*Activities:* Other engineering activities
*Major Shareholder:* Alistair William Hamilton
*Officers:* Paul Howard Davies, Secretary; Paul Howard Davies [1970] Director/Chartered Accountant; Alistair Hamilton [1958] Director/Architect; Keith Anthony Hardcastle [1962] Director/Architect; Richard Alexander Lodge [1973] Director/Marketing Manager; Matthew Savory [1959] Director/Architect

**Daropeant Properties Limited**
*Incorporated:* 27 March 1987
*Net Worth:* £2,158,608 *Total Assets:* £3,461,967
*Registered Office:* Daropeant Buildings, Station Road, Bradley, Huddersfield, W Yorks, HD2 1UW
*Activities:* Other letting and operating of own or leased real estate
*Officers:* Janet Anne Antich, Secretary; David Michael Antich [1981] Director/General Manager; Janet Anne Antich [1954] Director/Accountant

**Dart Cubicles LLP**
*Incorporated:* 14 June 2012
*Net Worth:* £540,318 *Total Assets:* £4,017,420
*Registered Office:* Unit 33 Caldervale Business Park, Huddersfield Road, Dewsbury, W Yorks, WF13 3JL
*Officers:* Andrew Thorpe [1963] Member; David Thorpe [1936] Member

**Dart Group PLC**
*Incorporated:* 21 January 1977 *Employees:* 8,411
*Net Worth:* £528,900,000 *Total Assets:* £3,125,600,000
*Registered Office:* Low Fare Finder House, Leeds Bradford Airport, Yeadon, Leeds, LS19 7TU
*Activities:* Activities of head offices
*Shareholder:* Philip Hugh Meeson
*Officers:* Ian Bruce Day, Secretary; Gary James Brown [1966] Finance Director; Rick Green [1962] Director; Stephen Paul Heapy [1969] Director/Chief Executive; Mark Aubrey Seymour Laurence [1968] Director; Philip Hugh Meeson [1947] Director

**Dart Leasing & Finance Limited**
*Incorporated:* 1 March 2017
*Net Worth:* £5,776,168 *Total Assets:* £589,579,136
*Registered Office:* Low Fare Finder House, Leeds Bradford Airport, Yeadon, Leeds, LS19 7TU
*Activities:* Renting and leasing of air passenger transport equipment
*Parent:* Dart Group PLC
*Officers:* Ian Bruce Day, Secretary; Gary James Brown [1966] Director; Philip Hugh Meeson [1947] Director

**Dathan Tool & Gauge Co Limited**
*Incorporated:* 11 August 1964 *Employees:* 48
*Net Worth:* £2,641,987 *Total Assets:* £3,561,795
*Registered Office:* Mean Lane, Meltham, Holmfirth, W Yorks, HD9 5RU
*Activities:* Manufacture of tools
*Shareholder:* Edward Michael Moorhouse
*Officers:* Edward Michael Moorhouse, Company Secretary; Edward Michael Moorhouse [1973] Director/Company Secretary; Richard Andrew Moorhouse [1960] Director/Tool Designer; Robert Charles Moorhouse [1960] Director/Commercial Manager; Simon James Moorhouse [1963] Director/Works Manager

**Paul Davies Limited**
*Incorporated:* 9 February 1979 *Employees:* 4
*Net Worth:* £319,416 *Total Assets:* £5,436,672
*Registered Office:* c/o Mazars LLP, 3 Wellington Place, Leeds, LS1 4AP
*Activities:* Wholesale of metals and metal ores
*Shareholders:* Paul Nicholas Russell Davies; Catherine Louise Davies
*Officers:* Catherine Louise Davies, Secretary; Catherine Louise Davies [1956] Director/Secretary; Paul Nicholas Russell Davies [1951] Director/Coin Dealer

**Davis Tate Ltd**
*Incorporated:* 28 March 2002 *Employees:* 66
*Net Worth:* £5,437,000 *Total Assets:* £7,546,000
*Registered Office:* 2nd Floor, Gateway 2, Station Business Park, Holgate Park Drive, York, YO26 4GB
*Activities:* Real estate agencies
*Parent:* LSLI Ltd
*Officers:* Sapna Bedi FitzGenerald, Secretary; Greig Barker [1969] Finance Director; Matthew John Samuel Bates [1974] Director; Helen Elizabeth Buck [1960] Director; Gregory Winston Young [1966] Director

**The Davy Group Limited**
*Incorporated:* 1 June 1949 *Employees:* 5
*Net Worth:* £4,073,702 *Total Assets:* £4,637,018
*Registered Office:* Suite 3, Aireside House, Royd Ings Avenue, Keighley, W Yorks, BD21 4BZ
*Activities:* Activities of head offices
*Major Shareholder:* Andrew John Davy
*Officers:* Andrew John Davy [1956] Director/Textile Merchant; Barbara Sybilla Maria Davy [1959] Director/Bookkeeper [German]

**Dawn Developments Limited**
*Incorporated:* 14 November 1960 *Employees:* 6
*Net Worth Deficit:* £1,000,694 *Total Assets:* £15,022,132
*Registered Office:* 1 Park Row, Leeds, LS1 5AB
*Activities:* Buying and selling of own real estate
*Parent:* DDEV Holdings Limited
*Officers:* Stewart Harley Rough, Secretary/Director; Alan Gillies MacDonald [1948] Director/Surveyor; Stephen McConnell [1960] Director; Paul O'Donnell [1969] Director; Stewart Harley Rough [1967] Director

**Dawngreen Limited**
*Incorporated:* 4 July 1991 *Employees:* 7
*Net Worth:* £1,248,346 *Total Assets:* £3,128,500
*Registered Office:* Dalton House, 9 Dalton Square, Lancaster, LA1 1WD
*Activities:* Wholesale of grain, unmanufactured tobacco, seeds and animal feeds
*Major Shareholder:* Faith Christine Thompson
*Officers:* Faith Christine Thompson, Secretary/Director; Anne Morris [1971] Director; Faith Christine Thompson [1941] Director

**James Dawson & Son,Limited**
*Incorporated:* 10 March 1896 *Employees:* 344
*Net Worth:* £6,884,000 *Total Assets:* £17,255,000
*Registered Office:* Hesslewood Country Office Park, Ferriby Road, Hessle, E Yorks, HU13 0PW
*Activities:* Machining
*Parent:* Fenner Group Holdings Limited
*Officers:* Debra Bradbury, Secretary; Andrew Maitland Caley [1962] Director/Group Taxation & Treasury Manager; Paul Jeremy Edwards [1967] Director; William John Pratt [1963] Managing Director

**A Dawson and Company (Estates) Limited**
*Incorporated:* 6 October 1943 *Employees:* 8
*Net Worth:* £4,172,226 *Total Assets:* £4,541,688
*Registered Office:* Rudston House, Rudston, Driffield, E Yorks, YO25 4UH
*Activities:* Mixed farming
*Officers:* Angela Mary Wreford Dawson, Secretary; John Nigel Clark [1964] Director/Chartered Surveyor & Valuer; Angela Mary Wreford Dawson [1943] Director/Farmer; Jenny Nicola Mary Dawson [1971] Director/Farmer; Simon Harold Dawson [1943] Director/Farmer

**H. Dawson Sons and Company (Wool) Limited**
*Incorporated:* 27 March 1933 *Employees:* 131
*Net Worth:* £2,858,639 *Total Assets:* £20,891,972
*Registered Office:* Mercury House, Essex Street, Bradford, W Yorks, BD4 7PG
*Activities:* Other service activities incidental to land transportation, n.e.c.
*Shareholders:* Jo Harry Dawson; Andrew Gerrard Dawson
*Officers:* Jo Harry Dawson, Secretary/Director; Andrew Gerrard Dawson [1941] Director/Wool Merchant; Jo Harry Dawson [1972] Director

**DB Cargo (UK) Holdings Limited**
*Incorporated:* 16 October 1995
*Previous:* DB Schenker Rail (UK) Holdings Limited
*Net Worth:* £180,000,000 *Total Assets:* £207,000,000
*Registered Office:* Lakeside Business Park, Carolina Way, Doncaster, S Yorks, DN4 5PN
*Activities:* Freight rail transport
*Parent:* DB (UK) Investments Limited
*Officers:* Helen Louise Young, Secretary; Andrea Rossi [1975] Director/Chief Financial Officer; Hans-Georg Werner [1959] Director/Business Administration [German]

**DB Cargo (UK) Limited**
*Incorporated:* 9 June 1994 *Employees:* 2,109
*Previous:* DB Schenker Rail (UK) Limited
*Net Worth:* £35,000,000 *Total Assets:* £437,000,000
*Registered Office:* Lakeside Business Park, Carolina Way, Doncaster, S Yorks, DN4 5PN
*Activities:* Freight rail transport
*Parent:* DB Cargo (UK) Holdings Limited
*Officers:* Helen Louise Young, Secretary; Andrea Rossi [1975] Director/Chief Financial Officer; Hans-Georg Werner [1959] Director/Business Administration [German]

**DB Cargo Components Limited**
*Incorporated:* 21 April 2005 *Employees:* 3
*Previous:* Axiom Rail Components Limited
*Net Worth:* £8,459,000 *Total Assets:* £12,555,000
*Registered Office:* Lakeside Business Park, Carolina Way, Doncaster, S Yorks, DN4 5PN
*Activities:* Other business support service activities n.e.c.
*Parent:* DB Cargo (UK) Holdings Limited
*Officers:* Helen Louise Young, Secretary; Andrea Rossi [1975] Director/Chief Financial Officer; Hans-Georg Werner [1959] Director/Business Administration [German]

**DB Cargo International Limited**
*Incorporated:* 26 July 1996 *Employees:* 113
*Previous:* DB Schenker Rail International Limited
*Net Worth:* £18,416,000 *Total Assets:* £26,656,000
*Registered Office:* Lakeside Business Park, Carolina Way, Doncaster, S Yorks, DN4 5PN
*Activities:* Freight rail transport
*Parent:* DB Cargo (UK) Holdings Limited
*Officers:* Helen Louise Young, Secretary; Andrea Rossi [1975] Director/Chief Financial Officer; Hans-Georg Werner [1959] Director/Business Administration [German]

**DB Cargo Maintenance Limited**
*Incorporated:* 23 March 1988 *Employees:* 137
*Previous:* Axiom Rail (Stoke) Limited
*Net Worth Deficit:* £972,000 *Total Assets:* £6,127,000
*Registered Office:* Lakeside Business Park, Carolina Way, Doncaster, S Yorks, DN4 5PN
*Activities:* Repair and maintenance of other transport equipment n.e.c.
*Parent:* DB Cargo (UK) Holdings Limited
*Officers:* Helen Louise Young, Secretary; Andrea Rossi [1975] Director/Chief Financial Officer; Hans-Georg Werner [1959] Director/Business Administration [German]

**DB Orthodontics Limited**
*Incorporated:* 28 April 1971 *Employees:* 52
*Net Worth:* £3,351,419 *Total Assets:* £4,378,261
*Registered Office:* Ryefield Way, Silsden, W Yorks, BD20 0EF
*Activities:* Dental practice activities
*Major Shareholder:* David Anthony Burdess
*Officers:* Victoria Ann Coppack, Secretary; Christian Paul Burdess [1974] Marketing Director; David Anthony Burdess [1946] Director/Dental Orthodontic Sales; Victoria Ann Coppack [1982] Sales Director

**DB Systel UK Limited**
*Incorporated:* 4 July 2013 *Employees:* 41
*Net Worth:* £1,805,000 *Total Assets:* £3,713,000
*Registered Office:* Lakeside Business Park, Carolina Way, Doncaster, S Yorks, DN4 5PN
*Activities:* Computer facilities management activities
*Parent:* DB (UK) Investments Limited
*Officers:* Jorg Kiesewalter [1970] Director/HR Manager [German]; Matthias Lorenz [1983] Finance Director [German]; Darren Unwin [1969] Operations Director

**DBS Clothing Limited**
*Incorporated:* 14 January 2013 *Employees:* 51
*Net Worth:* £2,336,236 *Total Assets:* £5,014,169
*Registered Office:* Unit 8a Plaxton Park, Cayton Low Road, Eastfield, Scarborough, N Yorks, YO11 3BQ
*Activities:* Wholesale of clothing and footwear
*Shareholder:* Samuel Harry Joseph Kay
*Officers:* Barry John Gill [1980] Director; Samuel Harry Joseph Kay [1983] Director; David Thompson [1984] Director

**DC Projects (Amber Valley) Limited**
*Incorporated:* 15 May 2003 *Employees:* 3
*Net Worth Deficit:* £5,641,365 *Total Assets:* £24,648,136
*Registered Office:* 4 Greengate, Cardale Park, Harrogate, N Yorks, HG3 1GY
*Activities:* Other amusement and recreation activities n.e.c.
*Parent:* DC Holdings (Amber Valley) Ltd
*Officers:* Alexander Toby Shedden Parry, Secretary; Alastair William Hopps [1986] Director/Accountant; Alexander Toby Shedden Parry [1976] Director/Chartered Accountant

**DC Projects (Rotherham) Limited**
*Incorporated:* 8 November 2006 *Employees:* 3
*Net Worth Deficit:* £8,023,576 *Total Assets:* £33,875,544
*Registered Office:* 4 Greengate, Cardale Park, Harrogate, N Yorks, HG3 1GY
*Activities:* Operation of sports facilities
*Parent:* DC Holdings (Rotherham) Ltd
*Officers:* Alexander Toby Shedden Parry, Secretary; Alastair William Hopps [1986] Director/Accountant; Alexander Toby Shedden Parry [1976] Director/Chartered Accountant

**DC Projects (Wolverhampton) Limited**
*Incorporated:* 25 February 2004 *Employees:* 3
*Net Worth Deficit:* £870,377 *Total Assets:* £10,758,986
*Registered Office:* 4 Greengate, Cardale Park, Harrogate, N Yorks, HG3 1GY
*Activities:* Activities of sport clubs
*Parent:* DC Holdings (Wolverhampton) Ltd
*Officers:* Alexander Toby Shedden Parry, Secretary; Alastair William Hopps [1986] Director/Accountant; Alexander Toby Shedden Parry [1976] Director/Chartered Accountant

**DC3 (Assetco) Limited**
*Incorporated:* 7 April 2017 *Employees:* 3
*Net Worth:* £86,751,000 *Total Assets:* £112,382,664
*Registered Office:* 1 Park Row, Leeds, LS1 5AB
*Activities:* Other business support service activities n.e.c.
*Parent:* DC3 (Issuer) Limited
*Officers:* Jennifer McKay, Secretary; John McDonagh [1969] Director; Alistair Graham Ray [1974] Director

**DC3 (Issuer) Limited**
*Incorporated:* 6 April 2017 *Employees:* 3
*Net Worth:* £86,751,000 *Total Assets:* £112,382,664
*Registered Office:* 1 Park Row, Leeds, LS1 5AB
*Activities:* Other business support service activities n.e.c.
*Parent:* Dalmore Capital 17 General Partner LLP
*Officers:* Jennifer McKay, Secretary; John McDonagh [1969] Director; Alistair Graham Ray [1974] Director

**DCMK Limited**
*Incorporated:* 5 April 2016
*Net Worth:* £2,865,754 *Total Assets:* £3,018,750
*Registered Office:* 133 Marfleet Avenue, Hull, HU9 5SA
*Activities:* Activities of construction holding companies
*Officers:* Desmond Alan Craven [1970] Technical Director; Maarten Jan Kleinhout [1973] Managing Director [Dutch]

**DCSW Ltd**
*Incorporated:* 20 November 2015
*Net Worth:* £2,566,695 *Total Assets:* £5,053,295
*Registered Office:* Meadowcroft Lane, Halifax Road, Ripponden, W Yorks, HX6 4AJ
*Activities:* Activities of head offices
*Parent:* Vanilla Group Limited
*Officers:* Helen Jane Ashton [1972] Director/Chief Executive Officer; Paul Humphreys [1958] Director; Robert McKinlay Wood [1977] Director

**De Smet Rosedowns Limited**
*Incorporated:* 4 December 1893 *Employees:* 90
*Net Worth:* £12,204,000 *Total Assets:* £16,280,000
*Registered Office:* Cannon Street, Hull, HU2 0AD
*Activities:* Manufacture of other special-purpose machinery n.e.c.
*Officers:* Paul Antony Bray, Secretary; Philippe Bayet [1965] Director [French]; Jerome de Bertoult [1967] Finance Director [French]

**De Vere 2 Limited**
*Incorporated:* 4 June 1986 *Employees:* 835
*Previous:* Hayley Conference Centres Ltd
*Net Worth Deficit:* £13,470,000 *Total Assets:* £128,146,000
*Registered Office:* The Inspire, Hornbeam Square West, Harrogate, N Yorks, HG2 8PA
*Activities:* Hotels and similar accommodation
*Parent:* Principal Hayley Group Limited
*Officers:* James Alexander Burrell [1974] Director/Accountant; Generaldine Josephine Gallagher [1965] Finance Director [Irish]; Gail Susan Hunter [1963] Human Resources Director; Anthony Gerrard Troy [1962] Director [Irish]

**De Vere Cotswold Water Park Limited**
*Incorporated:* 8 May 2000 *Employees:* 254
*Previous:* Cotswold Four Pillars Limited
*Net Worth:* £29,752,000 *Total Assets:* £50,655,000
*Registered Office:* The Inspire, Hornbeam Square West, Harrogate, N Yorks, HG2 8PA
*Activities:* Hotels and similar accommodation
*Parent:* Spire Bidco Hotels Limited
*Officers:* John Cody Bradshaw [1978] Director/Hotel Real Estate [American]; James Alexander Burrell [1974] Director/Accountant; Anthony Gerrard Troy [1962] Director/Chief Executive Officer [Irish]

**De Vere Grand Connaught Rooms Limited**
*Incorporated:* 4 February 2009 *Employees:* 139
*Previous:* Troy Management Services (Connaught Rooms) Limited
*Net Worth:* £12,321,000 *Total Assets:* £18,329,000
*Registered Office:* The Inspire, Hornbeam Park, Harrogate, N Yorks, HG2 8PA
*Activities:* Letting and operating of conference and exhibition centres
*Parent:* Principal Hayley Group Limited
*Officers:* James Alexander Burrell [1974] Director/Accountant; Generaldine Josephine Gallagher [1965] Finance Director [Irish]; Gail Susan Hunter [1963] Human Resources Director; Anthony Gerrard Troy [1962] Director [Irish]

**De Vere Limited**
*Incorporated:* 31 October 1978 *Employees:* 1,000
*Previous:* De Vere Venues Limited
*Net Worth:* £10,696,000 *Total Assets:* £181,735,008
*Registered Office:* The Inspire, Hornbeam Square West, Harrogate, N Yorks, HG2 8PA
*Activities:* Hotels and similar accommodation
*Parent:* De Vere Venues Properties Limited
*Officers:* John Cody Bradshaw [1978] Director/Hotel Real Estate [American]; James Alexander Burrell [1974] Director/Accountant; Anthony Gerrard Troy [1962] Director [Irish]

**De Vere Selsdon Estate Limited**
*Incorporated:* 26 November 2003 *Employees:* 140
*Previous:* Troy Management Services (Selsdon Park) Limited
*Net Worth Deficit:* £15,574,000 *Total Assets:* £4,944,000
*Registered Office:* The Inspire, Hornbeam Square West, Harrogate, N Yorks, HG2 8PA
*Activities:* Hotels and similar accommodation
*Parent:* Principal Hayley Group Limited
*Officers:* James Alexander Burrell [1974] Director/Accountant; Generaldine Josephine Gallagher [1965] Finance Director [Irish]; Gail Susan Hunter [1963] Director; Anthony Gerrard Troy [1962] Director [Irish]

**De Vere Tortworth Court Limited**
*Incorporated:* 30 March 1999 *Employees:* 171
*Previous:* De Vere Tortworth Estate Limited
*Net Worth:* £28,967,000 *Total Assets:* £43,208,000
*Registered Office:* The Inspire, Hornbeam Square West, Harrogate, N Yorks, HG2 8PA
*Activities:* Hotels and similar accommodation
*Parent:* Spire Bidco Hotels Limited
*Officers:* John Cody Bradshaw [1978] Director/Hotel Real Estate [American]; James Alexander Burrell [1974] Director/Accountant; Anthony Gerrard Troy [1962] Director/Chief Executive Officer [Irish]

**De Vere Venues Properties Limited**
*Incorporated:* 15 November 2005 *Employees:* 3
*Net Worth:* £71,974,000 *Total Assets:* £140,028,992
*Registered Office:* The Inspire, Hornbeam Square West, Harrogate, N Yorks, HG2 8PA
*Activities:* Other letting and operating of own or leased real estate
*Parent:* De Vere Venues Group Limited
*Officers:* John Cody Bradshaw [1978] Director/Hotel Real Estate [American]; James Alexander Burrell [1974] Director/Accountant; Anthony Gerrard Troy [1962] Director [Irish]

**De Vere Wokefield Estate Limited**
*Incorporated:* 4 November 2010 *Employees:* 239
*Previous:* De Vere Wokefield Trading Limited
*Net Worth:* £34,338,000 *Total Assets:* £37,150,000
*Registered Office:* The Inspire, Hornbeam Square West, Harrogate, N Yorks, HG2 8PA
*Activities:* Hotels and similar accommodation
*Parent:* De Vere Wokefield Property Limited
*Officers:* John Cody Bradshaw [1978] Director/Hotel Real Estate [American]; James Alexander Burrell [1974] Director/Accountant; Anthony Gerrard Troy [1962] Director [Irish]

**De Vere Wokefield Property Limited**
*Incorporated:* 10 December 2007 *Employees:* 3
*Net Worth:* £32,720,000 *Total Assets:* £74,900,000
*Registered Office:* The Inspire, Hornbeam Square West, Harrogate, N Yorks, HG2 8PA
*Activities:* Other letting and operating of own or leased real estate
*Parent:* De Vere Venues Group Limited
*Officers:* John Cody Bradshaw [1978] Director/Hotel Real Estate [American]; James Alexander Burrell [1974] Director/Accountant; Anthony Gerrard Troy [1962] Director [Irish]

**Dean & Wood Limited**
*Incorporated:* 23 April 1949 *Employees:* 170
*Net Worth:* £8,834,000 *Total Assets:* £46,237,000
*Registered Office:* 15 Bruntcliffe Avenue, Leeds 27 Industrial Estate, Morley, Leeds, LS27 0LL
*Activities:* Wholesale of other machinery and equipment
*Officers:* David Patrick Campbell, Secretary; Per Olof Goran Bertland [1957] Director [Swedish]; John David Billson [1960] Director; David Patrick Campbell [1979] Director/Accountant; Simon Karlin [1968] Director [Swedish]

**Deborah Services (Holdings) Limited**
*Incorporated:* 13 January 2003 *Employees:* 1,820
*Net Worth:* £26,491,000 *Total Assets:* £105,279,000
*Registered Office:* Unit C, Cedar Court Office Park, Denby Dale Road, Calder Grove, Wakefield, W Yorks, WF4 3QZ
*Activities:* Installation of industrial machinery and equipment
*Parent:* Actavo Holdings (UK) Limited
*Officers:* Barry O'Donnell, Secretary; Brian Kelly [1977] Director [Irish]; Sean Lucey [1962] Director [Irish]

**Dechra Limited**
*Incorporated:* 16 August 2002 *Employees:* 249
*Net Worth:* £306,510,016 *Total Assets:* £355,960,992
*Registered Office:* Snaygill Industrial Estate, Keighley Road, Skipton, N Yorks, BD23 2RW
*Activities:* Manufacture of basic pharmaceutical products
*Parent:* Dechra Investments Limited
*Officers:* Melanie Jane Hall, Secretary; Richard John Cotton [1961] Director; Anthony Gerard Griffin [1963] Director [Irish]; Ian David Page [1961] Director

**Decidebloom Limited**
*Incorporated:* 21 December 1994 *Employees:* 2,369
*Net Worth:* £71,023,000 *Total Assets:* £224,798,000
*Registered Office:* Stoneacre, Omega Boulevard, Capitol Park, Thorne, Doncaster, S Yorks, DN8 5TX
*Activities:* Sale of new cars and light motor vehicles
*Shareholders:* Richard Stephen Teatum; Christine Patricia Teatum
*Officers:* Nigel Peter Wood, Secretary; Shaun Brookhouse [1967] Operations Director; Kenneth Craig [1950] Director/General Manager; Shaun Foweather [1963] Director/General Manager; Generald Peter George [1959] Operations Director; Richard Stephen Teatum [1957] Director; Paul Vozbutas [1979] Operations Director; Nigel Peter Wood [1964] Director/Accountant

**Decision First Limited**
*Incorporated:* 29 June 2012 *Employees:* 4
*Net Worth:* £1,314,738 *Total Assets:* £3,316,170
*Registered Office:* Cardinal House, 9 Manor Road, Leeds, LS11 9AH
*Activities:* Other business support service activities n.e.c.
*Shareholders:* First Title Ltd; Decision Insight Information Group (UK) Limited
*Officers:* Natalie Andrea Beckham, Secretary; David William Callcott [1959] Finance Director; Justin Samuel Jackson McChesney [1973] Director/Group Chief Accounting Officer; Justin Parkinson [1971] Director; Ian Michael Turner [1961] Director

**Decisionmetrics Limited**
*Incorporated:* 10 August 2004 *Employees:* 101
*Net Worth:* £25,398,000 *Total Assets:* £31,383,000
*Registered Office:* One Park Lane, Leeds, LS3 1EP
*Activities:* Management consultancy activities other than financial management
*Parent:* Callcredit Information Group Limited
*Officers:* Robert Kenneth Campbell Munro, Secretary; Michael Jon Gordon [1970] Director; Robert Kenneth Campbell Munro [1965] Director/Chief Financial Officer

**Deco-Pak Limited**
*Incorporated:* 6 September 2004 *Employees:* 36
*Net Worth:* £1,789,361 *Total Assets:* £3,976,673
*Registered Office:* Leigh House, 28-32 St Paul's Street, Leeds, LS1 2JT
*Activities:* Non-specialised wholesale trade
*Shareholders:* Michael Neuemiah Hall; Gail Colleenay Hall
*Officers:* Gail Ann Coleen Hall, Secretary; Craig Martyn Hall [1984] Director; David Hall [1981] Director; Gail Ann Colleenay Hall [1958] Director; Michael Neuemiah Hall [1957] Director; Rodney John Slater [1959] Director

**Decorative Panels Components Limited**
*Incorporated:* 6 February 2001 *Employees:* 165
*Net Worth:* £4,051,351 *Total Assets:* £14,404,349
*Registered Office:* Century House, Premier Way, Lowfield Business Park, Elland, W Yorks, HX5 9HF
*Activities:* Manufacture of other products of wood; manufacture of articles of cork, straw and plaiting materials
*Shareholder:* Stephen Richard Gaunt
*Officers:* Tania Elizabeth Jones, Secretary/Accountant; Lynn Atkinson [1964] Sales Director; Philip Dalton [1977] Operations Director; Stephen Richard Gaunt [1950] Director/Chairman; Tania Elizabeth Jones [1971] Director/Accountant; Charlotte Louise Metcalfe [1988] Director; John Guy Metcalfe [1963] Managing Director; Julian Tatham [1965] Design Director; Andrew Robert Wortley [1954] Group HR Director

**Decorative Panels Furniture Limited**
*Incorporated:* 15 December 2008 *Employees:* 194
*Net Worth:* £3,297,972 *Total Assets:* £15,174,810
*Registered Office:* Century House, Premier Way, Lowfields Business Park, Elland, W Yorks, HX5 9HF
*Activities:* Manufacture of other furniture
*Shareholder:* Stephen Richard Gaunt
*Officers:* Tania Elizabeth Jones, Secretary/Accountant; Lynn Atkinson [1964] Sales Director; Philip Dalton [1977] Operations Director; Stephen Richard Gaunt [1950] Director/Chairman; Paul Robert Johnson [1961] Operations Director; Tania Elizabeth Jones [1971] Director/Accountant; Charlotte Louise Metcalfe [1988] Director; John Guy Metcalfe [1963] Director; Michael John Sawyer [1968] Operations Director; Julian Tatham [1965] Design Director; Andrew Robert Wortley [1954] Group HR Director

**Decorative Panels Holdings Limited**
*Incorporated:* 24 February 1964 *Employees:* 419
*Net Worth:* £23,434,698 *Total Assets:* £52,168,356
*Registered Office:* Century House, Premier Way, Lowfields Business Park, Elland, W Yorks, HX5 9HF
*Activities:* Manufacture of other furniture
*Shareholder:* Stephen Richard Gaunt
*Officers:* Tania Elizabeth Jones, Secretary/Accountant; Philip Dalton [1977] Group Operations Director; Stephen Richard Gaunt [1950] Director/Chairman; Tania Elizabeth Jones [1971] Financial Director; John Guy Metcalfe [1963] Managing Director

**Decorative Panels Lamination Limited**
*Incorporated:* 6 February 2001 *Employees:* 51
*Net Worth:* £6,240,736 *Total Assets:* £13,370,861
*Registered Office:* Century House, Premier Way, Lowfield Business Park, Elland, W Yorks, HX5 9HF
*Activities:* Manufacture of veneer sheets and wood-based panels
*Shareholder:* Stephen Richard Gaunt
*Officers:* Tania Elizabeth Jones, Secretary/Accountant; Philip Dalton [1977] Operations Director; Stephen Richard Gaunt [1950] Director/Chairman; Tania Elizabeth Jones [1971] Financial Director; Charlotte Louise Metcalfe [1988] Director; John Guy Metcalfe [1963] Managing Director; Michael John Sawyer [1968] Operations Director; Julian Tatham [1965] Design Director; Andrew Robert Wortley [1954] Group HR Director

**Deehurst Limited**
*Incorporated:* 13 February 1981 *Employees:* 66
*Net Worth:* £2,410,542 *Total Assets:* £5,948,578
*Registered Office:* Millshaw, Ring Road, Beeston, Leeds, LS11 8EG
*Activities:* Travel agency activities
*Parent:* Global Travel Solutions Group Ltd
*Officers:* Judi Anne Everatt, Secretary; Roderick Michael Evans [1962] Director; Judi Anne Everatt [1973] Director/Accountant; Elaine Clare Holmes [1959] Director/Travel Agent; Pauline Elizabeth Horsbrough [1939] Director; Gary Derek McLeod [1961] Director/Travel Agent; Paul Terence Millington [1962] Finance Director

**Deep Sea Electronics Limited**
*Incorporated:* 30 June 1977 *Employees:* 173
*Previous:* Deep Sea Electronics PLC
*Net Worth:* £29,986,932 *Total Assets:* £35,025,928
*Registered Office:* Highfield House, Hunmanby Industrial Estate, Hunmanby, N Yorks, YO14 0PH
*Activities:* Manufacture of other electrical equipment
*Parent:* Caledonia Quint Bidco Limited
*Officers:* Craig John Lysons [1972] Director; Michael John Pennock [1982] Director; Scott Andrew Preece [1979] Director; Timothy John South [1960] Director; David Thomson [1973] Director

**Deepocean 1 UK Limited**
*Incorporated:* 12 July 1993 *Employees:* 135
*Net Worth:* £28,897,000 *Total Assets:* £78,220,000
*Registered Office:* Coniscliffe House, Coniscliffe Road, Darlington, Co Durham, DL3 7EE
*Activities:* Other specialised construction activities n.e.c.
*Officers:* Pierre Harry Caine Boyde [1974] Director/Engineer; Frode Garlid [1973] Director/Chief Financial Officer [Norwegian]; Louise Elisabeth Lewin [1981] Director/Solicitor; Ottar Kringen Maeland [1975] Director [Norwegian]; Rhiannon Pamela Carina Piasecki [1980] Finance Director

**Deepsleep Beds UK Ltd**
*Incorporated:* 10 June 2009
*Net Worth:* £937,385 *Total Assets:* £4,038,588
*Registered Office:* Phase 2, Warneford Avenue, Ossett, W Yorks, WF5 9NJ
*Activities:* Manufacture of other textiles n.e.c.
*Parent:* 4DS (Holdings) Ltd
*Officers:* Kamal Aziz [1977] Director; Aftab Hussain Chaudry [1975] Director; Iftikhar Hussain [1980] Director/Manufacturer; Mohammed Tariq Raouf [1982] Director

**Deeside Power (UK) Limited**
*Incorporated:* 11 February 2014 *Employees:* 24
*Net Worth:* £5,641,000 *Total Assets:* £21,852,000
*Registered Office:* Saltend Power Station, Saltend Chemicals Park, Hedon Road, Hull, HU12 8GA
*Activities:* Activities of head offices
*Officers:* Michael Ellis Farr [1964] Director/Power Station Manager; Russell Holland [1976] Director/Finance and Procurement Manager; Scott Jonathan Keen [1974] Director

**Delahope Limited**
*Incorporated:* 10 January 1934 *Employees:* 1
*Net Worth:* £4,362,674 *Total Assets:* £4,716,574
*Registered Office:* Crown Chambers, Princes Street, Harrogate, N Yorks, HG1 1NJ
*Activities:* Financial intermediation not elsewhere classified
*Shareholders:* Heather Lawson; Robert Ian Morgan
*Officers:* Robert Ian Morgan, Secretary; Heather Lawson [1959] Director; Robert Ian Morgan [1959] Director; Dorothy Bainbridge Sayers [1932] Director/Secretary

**Delifresh Limited**
*Incorporated:* 13 May 2002 *Employees:* 220
*Net Worth:* £5,033,623 *Total Assets:* £10,230,132
*Registered Office:* Paul Kershaw House, Essex Street, Bradford, W Yorks, BD4 7PG
*Activities:* Other food services
*Major Shareholder:* Noel Damian John Kershaw
*Officers:* Andrew Peter Nicholls, Secretary/Accountant; Noel Damian John Kershaw [1969] Director/Manager; Gerard Martin Morgan [1969] Operations Director; Andrew Peter Nicholls [1969] Director/Accountant; Reuben Buchanan Sutterby [1966] Sales Director

**Deliver Net Limited**
*Incorporated:* 28 February 2000 *Employees:* 65
*Net Worth:* £1,640,631 *Total Assets:* £7,744,923
*Registered Office:* Healthcare House, Keighley Road, Skipton, N Yorks, BD23 2QR
*Activities:* Non-specialised wholesale trade
*Parent:* Healthcare House Limited
*Officers:* Timothy James Lockett, Secretary; Adele Farquharson [1974] Director; Simon Jeremy Holt [1960] Director; Frances Lockett [1964] Director; Timothy James Lockett [1964] Director

**Dellstrong Limited**
*Incorporated:* 10 March 1999 *Employees:* 4
*Net Worth:* £7,184,820 *Total Assets:* £10,586,897
*Registered Office:* The View, Bridgehead Business Park, Hessle, Hull, HU13 0GD
*Activities:* Non-trading company
*Shareholders:* Timothy Cavill; Edmund Cavill
*Officers:* Edmund Cavill [1948] Director; Timothy Cavill [1952] Director; Timothy Charles Davison [1968] Director; Aeon John Harwood [1971] Director; Kenneth Sturdy [1964] Director

**Delphi Automotive Operations UK Limited**
*Incorporated:* 17 October 2012
*Net Worth:* £587,000,000 *Total Assets:* £702,000,000
*Registered Office:* 1 Park Row, Leeds, LS1 5AB
*Activities:* Other professional, scientific and technical activities n.e.c.
*Shareholders:* Delphi Global Investments LLP; Delphi Luxembourg Limited
*Officers:* William Brenton James Allen [1986] Director/Accountant; Alan Dick [1963] Director/Vice President of Treasury; Olivier Jean Francis Lequeue [1978] Finance Director [Belgian]

**Delta Academies Trust**
*Incorporated:* 23 September 2010 *Employees:* 2,179
*Previous:* School Partnership Trust Academies
*Net Worth:* £156,983,008 *Total Assets:* £215,894,000
*Registered Office:* Education House, Spawd Bone Lane, Knottingley, W Yorks, WF11 0EP
*Activities:* Pre-primary education
*Officers:* Sandra Lesley Bailey [1952] Director/Retired Civil Servant; Sean Peter Cavan [1959] Director/Educationalist; David Haigh [1951] Director/Teacher; Steven Peter Hodsman [1959] Director/Operations Planning Officer; Christopher John Lomas [1969] Director/Head of Private Banking/Wealth; Paul Terence Tarn [1964] Director/Chief Executive; David Stuart White [1947] Director/Retired

**Delta Caravans Holdings Limited**
*Incorporated:* 10 December 2003 *Employees:* 168
*Net Worth:* £11,920,774 *Total Assets:* £15,895,966
*Registered Office:* 240 Leads Road, Hull, HU7 0DF
*Activities:* Manufacture of caravans
*Major Shareholder:* Michael John Isaac
*Officers:* John Isaac, Secretary; John Isaac [1968] Director/Certified Chartered Accountant; Michael John Isaac [1945] Director

**Delta Caravans International Limited**
*Incorporated:* 16 June 2000 *Employees:* 168
*Net Worth:* £4,528,648 *Total Assets:* £8,306,896
*Registered Office:* 240 Leads Road, Hull, HU7 0DF
*Activities:* Manufacture of caravans
*Major Shareholder:* Michael John Isaac
*Officers:* John Isaac, Secretary; John Isaac [1968] Director/Certified Chartered Accountant; Michael John Isaac [1945] Director

**Delta Engineering Group Limited**
*Incorporated:* 6 February 2007 *Employees:* 92
*Net Worth:* £3,336,165 *Total Assets:* £5,569,844
*Registered Office:* Manby Road, South Killingholme, Immingham, N E Lincs, DN40 3DX
*Activities:* Manufacture of metal structures and parts of structures
*Officers:* Karen Anne McNamara, Secretary; Karen Anne McNamara [1963] Director; Michael McNamara [1959] Director

**Delta Salvage Limited**
*Incorporated:* 12 July 2000 *Employees:* 19
*Net Worth:* £720,049 *Total Assets:* £3,982,089
*Registered Office:* Sidings House, Sidings Court, Lakeside, Doncaster, S Yorks, DN4 5NU
*Activities:* Other business support service activities n.e.c.
*Shareholders:* Garry Anthony Hirst; Julie Ann Hirst; Garry Anthony Hirst
*Officers:* Garry Anthony Hirst, Secretary/Director; Garry Anthony Hirst [1966] Director; George Hirst [1935] Director; Julie Ann Hirst [1965] Director

**Deltawaite Limited**
*Incorporated:* 15 April 1997 *Employees:* 27
*Net Worth:* £4,065,043 *Total Assets:* £5,140,750
*Registered Office:* Roose Road, Barrow in Furness, Cumbria, LA13 0EP
*Activities:* Non-specialised wholesale trade
*Shareholders:* Ronald Brocklebank; Ronald Brocklebank Settlement
*Officers:* Jacqueline Brocklebank, Secretary; Guy Anthony Brocklebank [1960] Director; Jacqueline Brocklebank [1962] Director; Karin Marie Brocklebank [1964] Director; Ronald Brocklebank [1930] Director; Neil Harrison [1953] Director; Paul McHugh [1959] Director

**Dempsey Dyer Limited**
*Incorporated:* 21 April 1977 *Employees:* 100
*Net Worth:* £2,310,550 *Total Assets:* £3,906,217
*Registered Office:* Langthwaite Grange Industrial Estate, South Kirkby, Pontefract, W Yorks, WF9 3AP
*Activities:* Other manufacturing n.e.c.
*Shareholder:* Thomas Arthur Frederick
*Officers:* Anne Frances Dyer, Secretary; Peter Frederick Dyer [1982] Director/Manufacturing; Thomas Arthur Frederick Dyer [1947] Director

**Den Hartogh Dry Bulk Logistics Limited**
*Incorporated:* 15 October 1981 *Employees:* 135
*Previous:* Interbulk (UK) Limited
*Net Worth:* £35,409,504 *Total Assets:* £61,055,752
*Registered Office:* 4 Beacon Way, Hull, HU3 4AE
*Activities:* Freight transport by road
*Officers:* Klaas Pieter Den Hartogh [1965] Managing Director [Dutch]; Abraham Cornelius Paape [1959] Finance Director [Dutch]

**Denaro (UK) Limited**
*Incorporated:* 11 July 2011
*Net Worth:* £360 *Total Assets:* £16,208,622
*Registered Office:* 16 Dudley Street, Grimsby, N E Lincs, DN31 2AB
*Activities:* Other service activities n.e.c.
*Officers:* Anthony David Bracken [1961] Director; Colin George Hesketh [1962] Director

**Denaro Partners LLP**
*Incorporated:* 18 April 2012
*Net Worth:* £16,298,346 *Total Assets:* £16,299,361
*Registered Office:* 16 Dudley Street, Grimsby, N E Lincs, DN31 2AB

**J Denham Metals Ltd**
*Incorporated:* 28 July 2009 *Employees:* 26
*Net Worth:* £3,734,349 *Total Assets:* £5,520,155
*Registered Office:* Coppycrooks, West Auckland Road, Shildon, Co Durham, DL14 9PN
*Activities:* Wholesale of waste and scrap
*Officers:* Joseph Denham [1949] Director

**W Denis (Holdings) PLC**
*Incorporated:* 31 July 2003 *Employees:* 72
*Net Worth:* £5,809,131 *Total Assets:* £15,285,091
*Registered Office:* Brigade House, 86 Kirkstall Road, Leeds, LS3 1LQ
*Activities:* Financial management
*Shareholders:* Simon Rupert Thew; Hubert Allan Thew
*Officers:* Ian William Desbottes, Secretary; Ian William Desbottes [1964] Director/Accountant; Hubert Allan Thew [1937] Director/Insurance Broker; Simon Rupert Thew [1966] Director/Insurance Broker; Clive Howard Thurston [1958] Director/Insurance Broker

**W. Denis (Insurance Brokers) PLC**
*Incorporated:* 29 April 1963 *Employees:* 57
*Net Worth:* £1,400,532 *Total Assets:* £10,754,158
*Registered Office:* Brigade House, 86 Kirkstall Road, Leeds, LS3 1LQ
*Activities:* Non-life insurance
*Parent:* W Denis (Holdings) PLC
*Officers:* Ian William Desbottes, Secretary; John Cavanagh [1971] Director/Insurance Broker [Irish]; Ian William Desbottes [1964] Director/Accountant; Mark Jonathan Dutton [1975] Director/Insurance Broker; Paul Johnson [1971] Compliance and Resources Director; Hubert Allan Thew [1937] Director/Insurance Broker; Simon Rupert Thew [1966] Director/Insurance Broker; Clive Howard Thurston [1958] Director; Neil Andrew Tiffin [1969] Director/Insurance Broker

**Dennis Distribution LLP**
*Incorporated:* 1 February 2012 *Employees:* 25
*Net Worth:* £1,849,000 *Total Assets:* £3,734,981
*Registered Office:* Derwent Road, York Road Business Park, Malton, N Yorks, YO17 6YB
*Officers:* John Cedric Dennis [1940] Member; Katie Joanne Dennis [1967] Member

**Denso Marston Ltd**
*Incorporated:* 23 September 1935 *Employees:* 746
*Net Worth:* £38,104,000 *Total Assets:* £57,599,000
*Registered Office:* Marston House, Otley Road, Shipley, W Yorks, BD17 7JR
*Activities:* Manufacture of other fabricated metal products n.e.c.
*Parent:* Denso International Europe B.V.
*Officers:* John Charles White, Secretary; Marco di Rao Marotta [1963] Director [Italian]; David Hanson [1971] Managing Director; Masami Taguchi [1961] Director/Deputy Head of Thermal Systems Business Unit [Japanese]

**Dent Steel Holdings Limited**
*Incorporated:* 4 January 2007
*Net Worth:* £10,070,431 *Total Assets:* £10,167,203
*Registered Office:* Low Moor Steel Works, New Works Road, Low Moor, Bradford, W Yorks, BD12 0QN
*Activities:* Activities of head offices
*Major Shareholder:* Gregory Frederick Hutchings
*Officers:* Grahame Jones [1963] Director; Andrew Peaty [1966] Director/Chief Operating Officer

**Dent Steel Services (Yorkshire) Limited**
*Incorporated:* 22 December 1976 *Employees:* 60
*Net Worth:* £5,932,982 *Total Assets:* £12,449,064
*Registered Office:* Low Moor Steel Works, New Works Road, Low Moor, Bradford, BD12 0QN
*Activities:* Agents involved in the sale of fuels, ores, metals and industrial chemicals
*Major Shareholder:* Gregory Frederick Hutchings
*Officers:* Grahame Jones [1963] Director; Andrew Peaty [1966] Director/Chief Operating Officer

**Depho Estates Limited**
*Incorporated:* 2 June 2004 *Employees:* 68
*Net Worth:* £7,902,616 *Total Assets:* £10,314,646
*Registered Office:* Unit 4 Woodside Court, Clayton Wood Rise, Leeds, LS16 6RF
*Activities:* Other letting and operating of own or leased real estate
*Shareholders:* Deborah Ann Hoban; Peter John Hoban
*Officers:* Deborah Ann Hoban [1959] Director

**Depuy International Limited**
*Incorporated:* 17 February 1997 *Employees:* 446
*Net Worth:* £112,089,000 *Total Assets:* £214,067,008
*Registered Office:* St Anthonys Road, Beeston, Leeds, LS11 8DT
*Activities:* Manufacture of medical and dental instruments and supplies
*Parent:* Johnson & Johnson Medical Limited
*Officers:* Dr Michael Keith Barker [1969] Director/Vice President; Dexter Corbin [1967] Director; Peter O'Sullivan [1957] Finance Director; Alistair John Scholes [1965] Director; Deborah Steane [1966] Director/General Manager

**Derwent Dale Limited**
*Incorporated:* 17 September 2016 *Employees:* 2
*Net Worth:* £19,151 *Total Assets:* £3,409,138
*Registered Office:* 12-13 Alma Square, Scarborough, N Yorks, YO11 1JU
*Activities:* Other letting and operating of own or leased real estate
*Officers:* Anita Georgena Coopland, Secretary; Anita Georgena Coopland [1960] Director; Paul William Coopland [1957] Director

**Desk Top Publishing Micro Systems Limited**
*Incorporated:* 30 April 1992 *Employees:* 101
*Net Worth:* £1,251,279 *Total Assets:* £8,239,714
*Registered Office:* DTP House, Bowcliffe Road, Leeds, LS10 1HB
*Activities:* Other information technology service activities
*Major Shareholder:* Howard James Hall
*Officers:* Catherine Anne Hall, Secretary; Steven John Clegg [1975] Director/Accountant; Catherine Anne Hall [1940] Director/Secretary; David Donald Hall [1937] Director/Agricultural Merchant; Howard James Hall [1964] Director

**DEU Estates Properties Limited**
*Incorporated:* 4 April 2001 *Employees:* 4
*Net Worth:* £9,331,844 *Total Assets:* £11,819,769
*Registered Office:* 138 Cardigan Road, Leeds, LS6 1LU
*Activities:* Renting and operating of Housing Association real estate
*Shareholders:* Surjit Singh; Parminder Jit Kaur
*Officers:* Parminder Jit Kaur, Secretary; Jaskaran Singh Deu [1990] Director/Property Manager; Parandeep Deu [1991] Property Management Director; Parminder Jit Kaur [1966] Director/Property Manager; Surjit Singh [1956] Director/Property Manager

**Jaskaran S Deu Properties Limited**
*Incorporated:* 9 March 2016
*Net Worth:* £262,583 *Total Assets:* £3,000,870
*Registered Office:* 138 Cardigan Road, Leeds, LS6 1LU
*Activities:* Other letting and operating of own or leased real estate
*Major Shareholder:* Jaskaran Singh Deu
*Officers:* Parminder Jit Kaur, Secretary; Jaskaran Singh Deu [1990] Director; Surjit Singh [1956] Director

**Devonshire Club (Holdings) Limited**
*Incorporated:* 6 March 2015 *Employees:* 139
*Net Worth:* £3,317,000 *Total Assets:* £24,948,000
*Registered Office:* 21 Marina Court, Castle Street, Hull, HU1 1TJ
*Activities:* Activities of other holding companies n.e.c.
*Shareholder:* Michael Ashcroft
*Officers:* Mark Robert Carrington [1983] Director/Accountant; Angela Elizabeth Entwistle [1961] Director; Peter Alexander Frederick Harris [1965] Director; Eren Ali Mansur [1991] Director [Turkish]; Metin Necmettin Mansur [1956] Director [Turkish]; Julia Robertson [1958] Director

**Devonshire Square Properties Limited**
*Incorporated:* 11 February 2014
*Net Worth:* £1,915,328 *Total Assets:* £3,620,160
*Registered Office:* The Old Rectory, Sandy Lane, Stockton-on-the-Forest, N Yorks, YO32 9UU
*Activities:* Buying and selling of own real estate
*Shareholders:* Emma Jane Victoria Ashforth; Robert William Ashforth
*Officers:* Robert William Ashforth, Secretary; Emma Jane Victoria Ashforth [1976] Director; Robert William Ashforth [1976] Director

**Dewhirst Group Limited**
*Incorporated:* 1 August 1972
*Net Worth:* £69,976,000 *Total Assets:* £105,796,000
*Registered Office:* Dewhirst House, Westgate, Driffield, E Yorks, YO25 6TH
*Activities:* Activities of head offices
*Parent:* Kirkgate Group Limited
*Officers:* Christopher John Wilde, Secretary; David Witt [1953] Director; Anthony James Mark Wood [1960] Director

**Dewhirst Overseas Limited**
*Incorporated:* 27 February 1995
*Net Worth:* £12,155,585 *Total Assets:* £16,058,204
*Registered Office:* Dewhirst House, Westgate, Driffield, E Yorks, YO25 6TH
*Activities:* Activities of head offices
*Parent:* Dewhirst Group Limited
*Officers:* Christopher John Wilde, Secretary; David Witt [1953] Director; Anthony James Mark Wood [1960] Director

**Dewhirst Properties Limited**
*Incorporated:* 23 November 1990
*Net Worth:* £14,901,689 *Total Assets:* £15,226,755
*Registered Office:* Dewhirst House, Westgate, Driffield, E Yorks, YO25 6TH
*Activities:* Management of real estate on a fee or contract basis
*Parent:* Dewhirst Group Limited
*Officers:* Christopher John Wilde, Secretary; Catherine Mary Witt [1962] Director; David Witt [1953] Director; Anthony James Mark Wood [1960] Director

**Dewhirst Sportswear Limited**
*Incorporated:* 15 September 1947 *Employees:* 18
*Net Worth:* £17,659,288 *Total Assets:* £24,971,532
*Registered Office:* Dewhirst House, Westgate, Driffield, E Yorks, YO25 6TH
*Activities:* Manufacture of other wearing apparel and accessories n.e.c.
*Parent:* Dewhirst Group Limited
*Officers:* Christopher John Wilde, Secretary; David Witt [1953] Director; Anthony James Mark Wood [1960] Director

**The Dewsbury Learning Trust**
*Incorporated:* 26 January 2010
*Net Worth:* £9,660,680 *Total Assets:* £9,660,680
*Registered Office:* Ground Floor, Kirklees Council, Civic Centre 1, Huddersfield, W Yorks, HD1 2NF
*Activities:* Primary education
*Officers:* Jo-Anne Rachael Sanders, Secretary; Derek Graham Cross [1951] Director; Anna Du Quesnay [1982] Director/Assistant Headteacher; Dr Roy Fisher [1953] Director/University Head of Department; Marie Gilluley [1958] Director/College Principal; Carmen Gonzalez-Eslava [1968] Director/Vice Principal [Spanish]; Martin Graham Green [1970] Director/Local Government Officer; Dr Christine Jarvis [1955] Director/Dean; Jennifer Marie Napper [1963] Director/Headteacher

**DFDS Logistics Limited**
*Incorporated:* 25 February 2004 *Employees:* 427
*Previous:* DFDS Logistics Partners Ltd
*Net Worth:* £11,875,085 *Total Assets:* £87,908,800
*Registered Office:* Nordic House, Western Access Road, Immingham Dock, Immingham, N E Lincs, DN40 2LZ
*Activities:* Freight transport by road
*Officers:* Per Lund Jensen, Secretary; Allan James MacIntyre Bell [1978] Director; Edward James Green [1957] Director; Sarah Holloway [1977] Director; Klaus Jonassen [1966] Director; Stephen William MacAulay [1960] Director

**DFDS Logistics Services Limited**
*Incorporated:* 29 November 1982 *Employees:* 444
*Net Worth:* £3,272,670 *Total Assets:* £8,984,952
*Registered Office:* Nordic House, Western Access Road, Immingham Dock, Immingham, N E Lincs, DN40 2LZ
*Activities:* Freight transport by road
*Officers:* Per Lund Jensen, Secretary; Edward James Green [1957] Director; Klaus Jonassen [1966] Director; Matthew O'Dell [1972] Director

**DFDS Pension Limited**
*Incorporated:* 27 December 1963 *Employees:* 4
*Previous:* DFDS Logistics Limited
*Net Worth:* £23,545,000 *Total Assets:* £32,053,000
*Registered Office:* Nordic House, Western Access Road, Immingham Dock, Immingham, N E Lincs, DN40 2LZ
*Activities:* Pension funding
*Officers:* Per Lund Jensen, Secretary; Torben Carlsen [1965] Director/Chief Finance Officer [Danish]; Edward James Green [1957] Director/General Manager; Stephen William MacAulay [1960] Director/General Manager; Niels Smedergaard [1962] Director/Chief Executive Officer [Danish]

**DFDS Seaways Irish Sea Holding Ltd**
*Incorporated:* 17 June 2003 *Employees:* 3
*Net Worth:* £123,123 *Total Assets:* £6,242,159
*Registered Office:* Nordic House, Western Access Road, Immingham Dock, Immingham, S Humbers, DN40 2LZ
*Activities:* Non-trading company
*Officers:* Torben Carlsen [1965] Director [Danish]; Peder Gellert Pedersen [1958] Director [Danish]; Niels Smedegaard [1962] Director [Danish]

**DFDS Seaways Newcastle Limited**
*Incorporated:* 23 November 1970 *Employees:* 76
*Net Worth:* £8,041,481 *Total Assets:* £11,977,824
*Registered Office:* Nordic House, Western Access Road, Immingham Dock, Immingham, N E Lincs, DN40 2LZ
*Activities:* Sea and coastal passenger water transport
*Officers:* Per Lund Jensen, Secretary [Danish]; Niels Smedegaard [1962] Managing Director [Danish]

**DFDS Seaways PLC**
*Incorporated:* 2 April 1981 *Employees:* 582
*Net Worth Deficit:* £4,109,977 *Total Assets:* £55,035,020
*Registered Office:* Nordic House, Western Access Road, Immingham Dock, Immingham, N E Lincs, DN40 2LZ
*Activities:* Operation of warehousing and storage facilities for water transport activities
*Officers:* Per Lund Jensen, Secretary [Danish]; Andrew Geoffrey Byrne [1973] Director; Peder Gellert Pedersen [1958] Director [Danish]; Niels Smedegaard [1962] Managing Director [Danish]

**DFS Furniture Company Limited**
*Incorporated:* 11 February 1970 *Employees:* 7
*Net Worth:* £45,400,000 *Total Assets:* £96,700,000
*Registered Office:* 1 Rockingham Way, Redhouse Interchange, Adwick-le-Street, Doncaster, S Yorks, DN6 7NA
*Activities:* Activities of head offices
*Parent:* DFS Furniture Holdings PLC
*Officers:* Elizabeth McDonald, Secretary; Nicola Jayne Bancroft [1964] Director; Timothy Giles Stacey [1971] Director

**DFS Furniture Holdings PLC**
*Incorporated:* 9 April 2010
*Net Worth:* £97,900,000 *Total Assets:* £703,000,000
*Registered Office:* 1 Rockingham Way, Redhouse Interchange, Adwick-le-Street, Doncaster, S Yorks, DN6 7NA
*Activities:* Activities of head offices
*Parent:* Diamond Holdco 7 Limited
*Officers:* Elizabeth McDonald, Secretary; Nicola Jayne Bancroft [1964] Director; Ian Francis Filby [1959] Director

**DFS Furniture PLC**
*Incorporated:* 27 April 2010 *Employees:* 4,872
*Previous:* DFS Furniture Limited
*Net Worth:* £252,400,000 *Total Assets:* £774,200,000
*Registered Office:* 1 Rockingham Way, Redhouse Interchange, Adwick-le-Street, Doncaster, S Yorks, DN6 7NA
*Activities:* Activities of head offices
*Officers:* Elizabeth McDonald, Secretary; Nicola Jayne Bancroft [1964] Director; Joanna Boydell [1969] Director; Ian Charles Durant [1958] Director; Alison Elizabeth Hutchinson [1967] Director; Stephen Richard Johnson [1963] Director; Christopher Luke Mayhew [1953] Director; Julie Helen Southern [1959] Director; Timothy Giles Stacey [1971] Director

**DFS Trading Limited**
*Incorporated:* 1 July 1983 *Employees:* 3,801
*Net Worth:* £114,200,000 *Total Assets:* £326,100,000
*Registered Office:* 1 Rockingham Way, Redhouse Interchange, Adwick-le-Street, Doncaster, S Yorks, DN6 7NA
*Activities:* Retail of furniture, lighting, and similar (not musical instruments or scores) in specialised store
*Parent:* DFS Furniture Company Ltd
*Officers:* Elizabeth McDonald, Secretary; Nicola Jayne Bancroft [1964] Director of Commercial Finance; Harvey George Ellis [1956] Production Director; Scott Fishburn [1974] Director; Graham Mould [1966] Training Director; Timothy Giles Stacey [1971] Business Development Director; Andrew Stefan Trofimowicz [1962] Marketing Director; Andrew Henry Vaughan-Jones [1953] Buying Director; Toni Wood [1971] Director

**DG Asset Enterprise Ltd**
*Incorporated:* 31 July 2012
*Net Worth:* £432,242 *Total Assets:* £3,327,346
*Registered Office:* Unit 2 Jubilee Way, Grange Moor, Wakefield, W Yorks, WF4 4TD
*Activities:* Other letting and operating of own or leased real estate
*Major Shareholder:* Darren Green
*Officers:* Darren Green [1968] Managing Director

**DGP Intelsius Limited**
*Incorporated:* 25 February 1998 *Employees:* 36
*Net Worth:* £1,931,604 *Total Assets:* £3,693,131
*Registered Office:* 1 Harrier Court, Airfield Business Park, Elvington, York, YO41 4EA
*Activities:* Other business support service activities n.e.c.
*Parent:* DGP Life Science Limited
*Officers:* David Patrick Walsh [1966] Director [Irish]

**Dhoot Transmission (UK) Limited**
*Incorporated:* 23 January 2007 *Employees:* 62
*Net Worth:* £3,280,947 *Total Assets:* £10,371,649
*Registered Office:* Unit 4 Bontoft Avenue, Hull, HU5 4HF
*Activities:* Manufacture of electricity distribution and control apparatus
*Officers:* Dhiren. Vinod Sheth, Secretary [Indian]; Anupama Rahul Dhoot [1975] Director [Indian]; Radhavallabh Ramnath Dhoot [1943] Director [Indian]; Rahul Radhavallabh Dhoot [1973] Director [Indian]; David Michael Earnshaw [1965] Director; Peter Anthony Hesleden [1955] Director

**Diagmed Healthcare Limited**
*Incorporated:* 21 March 2003 *Employees:* 46
*Net Worth:* £10,639,509 *Total Assets:* £13,946,107
*Registered Office:* Lumley Close, Thirsk Industrial Park, Thirsk, N Yorks, YO7 3TD
*Activities:* Hospital activities
*Major Shareholder:* Richard James Edmondson
*Officers:* Denise Jean Edmondson, Secretary; Daniel James Edmondson [1978] Director; Denise Jean Edmondson [1949] Director; Richard James Edmondson [1951] Director

**Diamond Holdco 2 Limited**
*Incorporated:* 27 April 2010
*Net Worth:* £96,600,000 *Total Assets:* £197,300,000
*Registered Office:* 1 Rockingham Way, Redhouse Interchange, Adwick-le-Street, Doncaster, S Yorks, DN6 7NA
*Activities:* Activities of head offices
*Parent:* DFS Furniture PLC
*Officers:* Elizabeth McDonald, Secretary; Nicola Jayne Bancroft [1964] Director; Ian Francis Filby [1959] Director

**Diamond Holdco 7 Limited**
*Incorporated:* 27 April 2010
*Net Worth:* £200,900,000 *Total Assets:* £203,200,000
*Registered Office:* 1 Rockingham Way, Redhouse Interchange, Adwick-le-Street, Doncaster, S Yorks, DN6 7NA
*Activities:* Activities of head offices
*Parent:* Diamond Holdco 2 Limited
*Officers:* Elizabeth McDonald, Secretary; Nicola Jayne Bancroft [1964] Director; Ian Francis Filby [1959] Director

**Diamond Power Specialty Limited**
*Incorporated:* 5 March 1913 *Employees:* 149
*Net Worth:* £23,305,000 *Total Assets:* £28,130,000
*Registered Office:* Unit 5b Heapham Road, Heapham Road Industrial Estate, Gainsborough, Lincs, DN21 1RZ
*Activities:* Machining
*Parent:* Diamond Power International Inc
*Officers:* Christopher James Paul, Secretary; Gary Campbell Cochrane [1977] Managing Director; Mika Jaakko Haikola [1969] Director [Finnish]; Michael Phillip Michael [1964] Director/Engineer [American]

**Diamond Resorts (Europe) Limited**
*Incorporated:* 1 March 1989 *Employees:* 502
*Net Worth Deficit:* £8,737,000 *Total Assets:* £145,904,992
*Registered Office:* Citrus House, Caton Road, Lancaster, LA1 3UA
*Activities:* Other service activities n.e.c.
*Parent:* Diamond Resorts (Group Holdings) PLC
*Officers:* Susan Crook, Secretary/Solicitor; Susan Crook [1961] Director/Solicitor

**Diamond Resorts (Group Holdings) PLC**
*Incorporated:* 15 June 1993
*Net Worth Deficit:* £16,138,000 *Total Assets:* £4,688,000
*Registered Office:* Citrus House, Caton Road, Lancaster, LA1 3UA
*Activities:* Activities of head offices
*Parent:* Diamond Resorts (Holdings) Limited
*Officers:* Susan Crook, Secretary/Solicitor; Charles Alan Bentley [1960] Director/Executive Vice President & Chief Financial Officer [American]; Susan Crook [1961] Director/Solicitor

**Diamond Resorts (Holdings) Limited**
*Incorporated:* 11 March 2004 *Employees:* 511
*Net Worth Deficit:* £38,056,000 *Total Assets:* £129,410,000
*Registered Office:* Citrus House, Caton Road, Lancaster, LA1 3UA
*Activities:* Activities of head offices
*Parent:* Apollo Global Management LLC
*Officers:* Susan Crook, Secretary/Solicitor; Susan Crook [1961] Director/Solicitor

**Diamond Resorts Financial Services Limited**
*Incorporated:* 29 July 1985
*Net Worth:* £5,883,076 *Total Assets:* £22,040,228
*Registered Office:* Citrus House, Caton Road, Lancaster, LA1 3UA
*Activities:* Activities of financial services holding companies
*Parent:* Diamond Resorts (Group Holdings) PLC
*Officers:* Susan Crook, Secretary/Solicitor; Susan Crook [1961] Director/Solicitor

**Diamondcut Limited**
*Incorporated:* 26 June 2000 *Employees:* 1
*Net Worth:* £647,578 *Total Assets:* £3,259,689
*Registered Office:* 8 Springwell Court, Leeds, LS12 1AL
*Activities:* Other letting and operating of own or leased real estate
*Shareholder:* Andrew Mark Stone
*Officers:* Brian Samuel Stone, Secretary; Andrew Mark Stone [1971] Director/Property Developer

**T P Dibdin Limited**
*Incorporated:* 12 April 1995 *Employees:* 5
*Net Worth Deficit:* £747,875 *Total Assets:* £3,045,058
*Registered Office:* The Ice House, Victor Street, Grimsby, N E Lincs, DN32 7QN
*Activities:* Construction of commercial buildings
*Officers:* Ian Harding Davey, Company Secretary; Christine Ruth Barnett [1951] Director; Jonathan Dibdin [1963] Director/Company Accountant; Jonathan Dibdin [1963] Director/Company Accountant

**Alan Dick Communications Limited**
*Incorporated:* 20 September 2011 *Employees:* 159
*Net Worth Deficit:* £9,897,171 *Total Assets:* £5,185,088
*Registered Office:* 11 Billet Lane, Scunthorpe, N Lincs, DN15 9YH
*Activities:* Other telecommunications activities
*Parent:* Panasonic Europe Limited
*Officers:* Michael Geoffrey Irving, Secretary; Josep Betorz Martinez [1969] Finance Director [Spanish]; Yuji Hirota [1962] Director [Japanese]; Carl Lyndon Pocknell [1969] Director

**R.E. Dickie Limited**
*Incorporated:* 2 October 1950
*Net Worth:* £2,300,645 *Total Assets:* £3,332,941
*Registered Office:* West End Works, Parkinson Lane, Halifax, W Yorks, HX1 3UB
*Activities:* Preparation and spinning of textile fibres
*Major Shareholder:* Jamie Robert Dickie
*Officers:* Josephine Tate Dickie, Secretary; Jamie Robert Dickie [1965] Director/Chartered Accountant; Josephine Tate Dickie [1936] Director

**Dickinson Properties UK Limited**
*Incorporated:* 12 May 2005
*Net Worth:* £1,058,809 *Total Assets:* £5,201,517
*Registered Office:* The Old Stables, St Annes in The Grove, Brookfoot Lane, Brighouse, W Yorks, HX3 9SZ
*Activities:* Other letting and operating of own or leased real estate
*Officers:* Sandra Dawn Dickinson, Secretary/Administrator; Timothy Dickinson [1961] Director

**John Dickinson Transport Limited**
*Incorporated:* 31 May 2006 *Employees:* 60
*Net Worth:* £2,149,395 *Total Assets:* £6,952,823
*Registered Office:* The Old Station, Winston, Darlington, Co Durham, DL2 3QQ
*Activities:* Freight transport by road
*Shareholders:* Brenda Dickinson; John Drevor Dickinson
*Officers:* Mrs Brenda Dickinson, Secretary/Director; Mrs Brenda Dickinson [1937] Director; Mr John Drevor Dickinson [1930] Director

**Dickinsons (Plumbing & Heating Contractors) Limited**
*Incorporated:* 28 February 1994 *Employees:* 24
*Net Worth:* £1,999,912 *Total Assets:* £3,715,748
*Registered Office:* Riding House, Cape Industrial Estate, Coal Hill Lane, Farsley, Leeds, LS28 5NA
*Activities:* Other specialised construction activities n.e.c.
*Parent:* Dickinsons Group Services Limited
*Officers:* Michael Dickinson, Secretary/Plumbing & Heating Engineer; Michael Dickinson [1963] Director/Plumbing & Heating Engineer; Robert Dickinson [1971] Director/Plumber; Stephen Dickinson [1960] Director/Plumbing & Heating Engineer

**Dilbag Cloth House Limited**
*Incorporated:* 11 June 1993
*Net Worth:* £11,300,727 *Total Assets:* £13,238,610
*Registered Office:* Dilbag Building, Duncomb Road, Ingleby Road, Bradford, W Yorks, BD8 9AL
*Activities:* Wholesale of textiles
*Officers:* Dilbag Singh, Secretary; Gurmail Kaur [1945] Director; Harpreet Singh Makkar [1975] Marketing Director; Dilbag Singh [1939] Director; Jaswant Singh [1973] Sales Director

**The Dining Club Group Limited**
*Incorporated:* 14 July 2015 *Employees:* 137
*Net Worth Deficit:* £44,312,000 *Total Assets:* £87,564,000
*Registered Office:* Birkby Grange, 85 Birkby Hall Road, Birkby, Huddersfield, W Yorks, HD2 2XB
*Activities:* Activities of other holding companies n.e.c.
*Shareholder:* BDC II (SGP) Limited
*Officers:* Benjamin William Eaton [1979] Director; Allan Farrell [1964] Director; Richard Ian Glynn [1964] Director; Michael Christopher Kalli [1980] Director; Matthew James Legg [1984] Director; Kevin Paul Reynolds [1959] Director; Samantha Shaw [1974] Director; Anwar Sultan [1988] Director; Matthew Joseph Turner [1978] Director

**Dinsdale Farming Limited**
*Incorporated:* 18 April 2012 *Employees:* 7
*Net Worth:* £131,242 *Total Assets:* £3,515,235
*Registered Office:* Manor House Farm, Low Dinsdale, Neasham, Darlington, Co Durham, DL2 1PN
*Activities:* Raising of poultry
*Shareholders:* Harry Trevor Dent; Henry Lloyd Dent; Susan Rachel Dent
*Officers:* Rachel Dent, Secretary; Harry Trevor Dent [1948] Director/Farmer; Henry Lloyd Dent [1985] Director/Farmer; Susan Rachel Dent [1957] Director/Farmer

**Direct Auto Finance Insurance Services Limited**
*Incorporated:* 1 September 1999
*Net Worth:* £3,752,000 *Total Assets:* £3,757,000
*Registered Office:* No 1 Godwin Street, Bradford, W Yorks, BD1 2SU
*Activities:* Non-trading company
*Parent:* Provident Financial PLC
*Officers:* David George Whincup, Secretary; Malcolm John Le May [1958] Director; Simon George Thomas [1964] Director/Chief Finance Officer

**Direct Investments (Yorkshire) Limited**
*Incorporated:* 29 September 1995 *Employees:* 3
*Net Worth:* £3,265,051 *Total Assets:* £4,004,743
*Registered Office:* 15 Westlea Drive, Tingley, Wakefield, W Yorks, WF3 1DH
*Activities:* Development of building projects
*Major Shareholder:* Samantha Ioannou
*Officers:* Samantha Ioannou, Secretary; Samantha Ioannou [1966] Director/Restaurant Owner; Frederick Clive Rodda [1932] Director/Retired Bank Manager

**Direct Trade (Yorkshire) Limited**
*Incorporated:* 22 January 1998 *Employees:* 193
*Net Worth:* £3,615,553 *Total Assets:* £8,143,643
*Registered Office:* Unit 3 Sandall Carr Road, Kirk Sandall, Doncaster, S Yorks, DN3 1QL
*Activities:* Manufacture of other plastic products
*Major Shareholder:* Stephen Paul Green
*Officers:* Stephen Paul Green, Secretary; Danny Paul Colton [1973] Director; Stephen Paul Green [1964] Director

**Dishforth UK Limited**
*Incorporated:* 14 June 2006 *Employees:* 3
*Net Worth:* £4,867,060 *Total Assets:* £4,937,534
*Registered Office:* 8 North Park Road, Harrogate, N Yorks, HG1 5PG
*Activities:* Other letting and operating of own or leased real estate
*Shareholders:* Nicholas James David Hodgson; Timothy Matthew Joseph Hodgson; Judith Helen Hodgson
*Officers:* Judith Helen Hodgson [1950] Director; Nicholas James David Hodgson [1977] Director; Timothy Matthew Joseph Hodgson [1975] Director

**Distribution Cable Jointing Ltd**
*Incorporated:* 6 March 2003 *Employees:* 74
*Net Worth:* £3,848,124 *Total Assets:* £5,001,937
*Registered Office:* Chestnut Farm, Back Lane, Cawood, Selby, N Yorks, YO8 3TB
*Activities:* Electrical installation
*Shareholders:* James John Grayson; Lisa Grayson
*Officers:* Lisa Grayson, Secretary; James John Grayson [1970] Director; Lisa Grayson [1968] Director

**Distrupol Limited**
*Incorporated:* 22 March 1963 *Employees:* 52
*Net Worth:* £34,647,000 *Total Assets:* £40,779,000
*Registered Office:* Aquarius House, 6 Mid Point Business Park, Thornbury, Bradford, W Yorks, BD3 7AY
*Activities:* Manufacture of plastics in primary forms
*Shareholders:* Ellis & Everard (UK Holdings) Limited; Univar UK Limited
*Officers:* Paul Graham Bryant [1973] Director; Jeffrey William Carr [1956] Director/Global Counsel [American]; Sabine Duyfjes [1972] Director/VP & General Counsel EMEA [German]

**J H Dixon & Son LLP**
*Incorporated:* 28 January 2015
*Net Worth:* £3,550,696 *Total Assets:* £4,225,964
*Registered Office:* 20-24 Park Street, Selby, N Yorks, YO8 4PW
*Officers:* Lynne Marie Barnes [1977] Member; Robinson Dixon [1963] Member; Stephen Dixon [1961] Member

**Dixondale Limited**
*Incorporated:* 7 September 1982 *Employees:* 170
*Net Worth:* £126,725,704 *Total Assets:* £132,260,952
*Registered Office:* 7 Robin Lane, High Bentham, Lancaster, LA2 7AB
*Activities:* Management of real estate on a fee or contract basis
*Major Shareholder:* Bernard Rees-Smith
*Officers:* Jenny Louise Barwise, Secretary; Janet Bradbury [1966] Director/Scientist; Dr Shu Chen [1966] Director/Scientist; Dr Jadwiga Furmaniak [1951] Director/Scientist; Dr Michael Powell [1960] Director/Scientist; Dr Bernard Rees Smith [1944] Director/Scientist; Peter Rees-Smith [1950] Director/Solicitor; Dr Jane Sanders [1966] Director/Scientist

**Dixons Academies Charitable Trust Ltd**
*Incorporated:* 6 October 1988 *Employees:* 975
*Net Worth:* £74,152,000 *Total Assets:* £81,480,000
*Registered Office:* Dixons Academies Charitable Trust Ltd, Ripley Street, Bradford, W Yorks, BD5 7RR
*Activities:* General secondary education
*Officers:* Joanne Lynch, Secretary; Professor Grace Alderson [1950] Director/Retired University Professor; Lynn Barrett [1942] Director/Retired; Ruby Khalid Bhatti [1970] Director/Solicitor; John Bowers [1951] Director/Self Employed Consultant; David Hugh Clayton [1957] Director; Bryan Collins [1938] Director/Retired Head/CEO; Brent Fitzpatrick [1949] Director; Martin Joseph Gaskin [1959] Director/Accountant; Susan Richardson [1979] Qualified Accountant/Director

**DKB Crop Protection Limited**
*Incorporated:* 12 February 2002 *Employees:* 11
*Net Worth:* £3,307,768 *Total Assets:* £4,289,687
*Registered Office:* Hill House, Thrintoft, Northallerton, N Yorks, DL7 0PL
*Activities:* Landscape service activities
*Shareholders:* David Barker; Valerie Barker; Vernon John Spinks
*Officers:* Valerie Barker, Secretary; David Barker [1950] Director/Agronomist; Valerie Barker [1956] Director/Secretary; Vernon John Spinks [1962] Director/Agronomist

**DLA Architecture Limited**
*Incorporated:* 31 March 1983 *Employees:* 99
*Net Worth:* £3,716,814 *Total Assets:* £4,839,809
*Registered Office:* 55 St Pauls Street, Leeds, LS1 2TE
*Activities:* Architectural activities
*Officers:* Jonathan Brown [1966] Director/Architect; Mark James Bust [1970] Director/Landscape Architect; Jason Nicholas Clarke [1970] Director/Architect; Mark Corbridge [1964] Director/Architectural Technician; Andrew Peter Hargreaves [1966] Director/Architectural Technician; Jonathan David Knowles [1968] Director/Architect; Christopher Colston Levett [1966] Director/Architect; Richard James Nash [1959] Director/Architect; John Gareth Orrell [1961] Director/Architect; Craig Michael Reed [1973] Director/Architect; Susan Louise Sparling [1974] Director/Architect

**DLA Design Group of Companies Limited**
*Incorporated:* 16 October 1998 *Employees:* 119
*Net Worth:* £3,925,526 *Total Assets:* £5,637,928
*Registered Office:* 55 St Pauls Street, Leeds, LS1 2TE
*Activities:* Architectural activities
*Officers:* Andrew Peter Hargreaves [1966] Director/Architectural Technician; Christopher Colston Levett [1966] Director/Architect; Richard James Nash [1959] Director/Architect; John Gareth Orrell [1961] Director/Architect; Michael Paul Wood [1975] Director/Chartered Accountant

**DLG Legal Services Limited**
*Incorporated:* 21 November 2012
*Net Worth:* £8,257,455 *Total Assets:* £23,490,580
*Registered Office:* 42 The Headrow, Leeds, LS1 8HZ
*Activities:* Activities of patent and copyright agents; other legal activities n.e.c.
*Parent:* DL Insurance Services Limited
*Officers:* Roger Cheston Clifton, Secretary; Tahir Anjam [1964] Director/Chartered Accountant; David Michael Baker [1966] Director; Stuart Robert Forrester [1970] Director of Legal Services and Claims Finance; Steven Maddock [1968] Director/Bank Official; Gail Rutherford [1977] Director; Stuart Nicholas Tait [1971] Director/Solicitor; Humphrey Michael Tomlinson [1962] Director/General Counsel

**John Dobson & Son (Carlton) Limited**
*Incorporated:* 19 April 1952 *Employees:* 54
*Net Worth:* £11,314,280 *Total Assets:* £15,674,872
*Registered Office:* Green End Farm, Carlton, Wakefield, W Yorks, WF3 3QP
*Activities:* Growing of cereals (except rice), leguminous crops and oil seeds
*Major Shareholder:* Simon Howard Dobson
*Officers:* Simon Howard Dobson, Secretary; Simon Howard Dobson [1960] Director/Market Gardener

**P.V. Dobson and Sons (Motors) Limited**
*Incorporated:* 1 February 1979 *Employees:* 35
*Net Worth:* £1,568,649 *Total Assets:* £5,788,301
*Registered Office:* Ivy House Works, Levens, Kendal, Cumbria, LA8 8PG
*Activities:* Sale of new cars and light motor vehicles
*Major Shareholder:* Alan Dobson
*Officers:* Bridget Amanda Hammond, Secretary; Alan Dobson [1938] Director/Garage Proprietor; Andrew Jonathan Dobson [1967] Director; Bridget Amanda Hammond [1963] Financial Director; Christopher Frank Hammond [1962] Director

**Dominion Print Ltd**
*Incorporated:* 3 February 2004 *Employees:* 70
*Previous:* Dominion Screen & Digital Print Ltd
*Net Worth:* £2,237,805 *Total Assets:* £4,256,850
*Registered Office:* Carrwood House, Carrbottom Road, Bradford, W Yorks, BD5 9AG
*Activities:* Printing n.e.c.
*Major Shareholder:* Dominic Clark
*Officers:* Dorothy Elaine Clark, Secretary; Dominic Clark [1957] Director; Thomas Anthony Clark [1986] Director; John Earnshaw [1974] Director; Mark Alexander Byron Ord [1967] Operations Director

**Don Valley Engineering Company Limited**
*Incorporated:* 30 July 1947
*Net Worth:* £1,015,608 *Total Assets:* £3,588,712
*Registered Office:* Sandall Stones Road, Kirk Sandall, Doncaster, S Yorks, DN3 1QR
*Activities:* Manufacture of machinery for mining
*Parent:* Don Valley Engineering Holdings Ltd
*Officers:* Roger Allen [1959] Director/Engineer; Lee Antony Ashurst [1962] Director; Royston Baker [1966] Director/Engineer; Stuart Doleman [1965] Director; Ian Derek Trotter [1969] Director/Engineer

**Don Valley Engineering Holdings Limited**
*Incorporated:* 31 March 2010 *Employees:* 62
*Net Worth:* £3,655,109 *Total Assets:* £5,972,140
*Registered Office:* Sandall Stones Road, Kirk Sandall, Doncaster, S Yorks, DN3 1QR
*Activities:* Activities of other holding companies n.e.c.
*Officers:* Roger Allen [1959] Director/Engineer; Lee Antony Ashurst [1962] Director; Jonathan Lloyd-Davies [1959] Director; Barry Desmond Smith [1950] Director/General Manager

**Donaldson Filter Components Limited**
*Incorporated:* 7 August 1975 *Employees:* 290
*Net Worth:* £31,761,000 *Total Assets:* £42,103,000
*Registered Office:* Citadel House, 58 High Street, Hull, HU1 1QE
*Activities:* Machining
*Parent:* Donaldson UK Holding Limited
*Officers:* Christine Kerry Cook [1975] Director/Accountant; David Ian Jowett [1955] Director/Chartered Accountant; Daniel Jacob King [1972] Director/Accountant [American]; Scott James Robinson [1966] Director/Vice President and Chief Financial Officer [American]; Wim Julien Valere Vermeersch [1966] Director/VP & MD Donaldson EMENA [Belgian]

**Donaldson Filtration (GB) Limited**
*Incorporated:* 24 January 2000 *Employees:* 169
*Net Worth:* £10,384,000 *Total Assets:* £18,457,000
*Registered Office:* Citadel House, 58 High Street, Hull, HU1 1QE
*Activities:* Manufacture of plastics and rubber machinery
*Parent:* Donaldson UK Holding Limited
*Officers:* Christine Kerry Cook [1975] Director/Accountant; Pierre Habran [1963] Director/Employee [Belgian]; David Ian Jowett [1955] Director/Accountant

**C R & C L Donaldson Ltd**
*Incorporated:* 21 October 2008 *Employees:* 11
*Net Worth:* £783,646 *Total Assets:* £5,502,456
*Registered Office:* Hazel House, Tollerton Road, Huby, York, YO61 1JA
*Activities:* Raising of other cattle and buffaloes
*Shareholders:* Carol Lesley Donaldson; Colin Roger Donaldson
*Officers:* Carol Lesley Donaldson [1966] Director/Farmer; Colin Roger Donaldson [1962] Director/Farmer

**Donaldson UK Holding Limited**
*Incorporated:* 30 September 2003
*Net Worth:* £41,559,000 *Total Assets:* £52,894,000
*Registered Office:* Citadel House, 58 High Street, Hull, HU1 1QE
*Activities:* Activities of head offices
*Parent:* Donaldson Europe
*Officers:* David Ian Jowett [1955] Finance Director; Peter Joseph Keller [1969] Director/Corporate Controller [American]; Scott James Robinson [1966] Director/Vice President and Chief Financial Officer [American]; Wim Julien Valere Vermeersch [1966] Director/VP and MD Donaldson EMENA [Belgian]

**Donaldson's Vets Limited**
*Incorporated:* 27 July 2011 *Employees:* 7
*Net Worth:* £4,197,333 *Total Assets:* £5,610,296
*Registered Office:* Maple Street Surgery, off Kings Mill Lane, Aspley, Huddersfield, W Yorks, HD5 9AX
*Activities:* Veterinary activities
*Parent:* Donaldson's Holdings Limited
*Officers:* Andrew Arnold [1977] Director/Veterinary Surgeon; Michael John Hancock [1963] Director/Veterinary Surgeon; Christopher Murphy [1986] Director/Veterinary Surgeon; Martin Ewan Paterson [1972] Director/Veterinary Surgeon; Rhona Margaret Warnock [1974] Director/Veterinary Surgeon; Robert White [1961] Director/Veterinary Surgeon

**Donbac Limited**
*Incorporated:* 24 June 1985 *Employees:* 18
*Net Worth:* £8,730,953 *Total Assets:* £16,169,669
*Registered Office:* 978 Sidings Court, Lakeside, Doncaster, S Yorks, DN4 5NU
*Activities:* Fund management activities
*Officers:* Andrew David Austwick [1979] Director/Fund Manager; James Henry Crowe [1944] Director/Self Employed; Daniel Thomas Fell [1981] Director; Kelvin Fitton [1968] Director/Chartered Accountant; Arthur Ronald Foreman [1953] Operations Director; Susan Harrison [1965] Director/Sector Growth - Key Account Manager Local Authority; Christopher Ian North [1966] Director/Banker; Christopher Luke Scholey [1948] Director/Consultant; Edward Michael Shepherd [1954] Director/Chartered Accountant; Angela Stopforth [1952] Director/Chief Executive; Thomas Wadsworth [1984] Director/Bank Manager

**Doncast Limited**
*Incorporated:* 22 February 1989 *Employees:* 67
*Net Worth:* £947,125 *Total Assets:* £4,446,337
*Registered Office:* Earl of Doncaster, Bennetthorpe, Doncaster, S Yorks, DN2 6AD
*Activities:* Hotels and similar accommodation
*Major Shareholder:* Lynn Rhoden
*Officers:* Lynn Rhoden, Secretary; John Graham Rhoden [1945] Director; Lynn Rhoden [1947] Director

**Doncaster Bus Station Limited**
*Incorporated:* 23 June 2003
*Net Worth Deficit:* £1,824,823 *Total Assets:* £14,642,287
*Registered Office:* Europa House, 20 Esplanade, Scarborough, N Yorks, YO11 2AQ
*Activities:* Management of real estate on a fee or contract basis
*Parent:* Doncaster Bus Station Holdings Limited
*Officers:* David Honeyman [1967] Director/Commercial Manager; Kevin Charles McCabe [1948] Director/Chartered Surveyor; Jeremy John Tutton [1966] Director/Financial Controller

**Doncaster Central Development Trust CIC**
*Incorporated:* 30 January 2008 *Employees:* 3
*Net Worth:* £7,165,699 *Total Assets:* £7,219,111
*Registered Office:* C-View, Church View, Doncaster, S Yorks, DN1 1AF
*Activities:* Other letting and operating of own or leased real estate
*Officers:* Ben McCall, Secretary; Lesley Zoe Cairns [1960] Director/Business Transformation and Improvement Consultant; Imogen Sara Challis [1959] Director/Researcher; Judith Chan [1976] Director/Businesswoman; Linsey Hague [1980] Director/Managing Editor (Publishing); Mohammad Shabir [1955] Director/Shopkeeper

**Doncaster Children's Services Trust Limited**
*Incorporated:* 6 December 2013 *Employees:* 686
*Total Assets:* £12,695,512
*Registered Office:* Colonnades House, Duke Street, Doncaster, S Yorks, DN1 1ER
*Activities:* Other residential care activities n.e.c.
*Officers:* Ben Brown [1968] Director/Administrator; Anthony John Hunter [1954] Director/Chief Executive; Stephen James [1978] Director/Court Liaison Officer; Paul Moffat [1962] Director/Chief Executive Doncaster Children's Services; Malcolm Shaun Morley [1966] Director/Police Officer; Maria Magdalena Nelson [1974] Director/Local Government Officer; Jackie Pederson [1972] Director/Chief Officer - Doncaster CCG; Dr Rupert John Suckling [1968] Director of Public Health; Shelley Thornton [1964] Director/Management Consultant/Accountant; Louise Alexandra Wright [1983] Director/Social Worker; Rukhsana Jabeen Yaqoob [1956] Director/Independent Educational Consultant

**Doncaster Culture and Leisure Trust**
*Incorporated:* 8 April 2002 *Employees:* 652
*Net Worth Deficit:* £3,547,906 *Total Assets:* £5,794,054
*Registered Office:* The Dome, Doncaster Leisure Park, Bawtry Raod, Doncaster, S Yorks, DN4 7PD
*Activities:* Fitness facilities
*Officers:* Terry John Parker, Secretary; Garry John Aylott [1953] Director/Retired; Andrew Russell Burden [1958] Director; Richard Andrew Byrne [1965] Director/Solicitor; Peter John Gleadhall [1960] Director/Self Employed; Marek Janusz Gutowski [1962] Director/Retired; Trevor Jones [1948] Director/Police Officer; Rebecca Sara Leam [1978] Director/Policy & Communications Executive; William Mordue [1963] Director/Councillor; Anne Roberta Roberts [1938] Director/Retired S.R.N

**Doncaster Deaf Trust**
*Incorporated:* 9 November 2000 *Employees:* 248
*Net Worth Deficit:* £309,000 *Total Assets:* £4,476,000
*Registered Office:* Leger Way, Doncaster, S Yorks, DN2 6AY
*Activities:* Primary education
*Officers:* John Douglas Weston, Secretary/Accountant; Marek Janusz Gutowski [1962] Director/Retired; Richard John Hazell [1955] Director/Legal Team Manager; Chris Mangle [1979] Managing Director; Anne Roberta Roberts [1938] Director/Retired; Mark William Antony Warde-Norbury [1962] Director/Banker

**Doncaster Property Trading Limited**
*Incorporated:* 3 February 2016 *Employees:* 4
*Net Worth:* £206,438 *Total Assets:* £4,535,216
*Registered Office:* Unit 12 Merchant Way, Doncaster, S Yorks, DN2 4QR
*Activities:* Development of building projects
*Shareholders:* Nigel Stephen Griffiths; Darran Wayne Griffiths
*Officers:* Darran Wayne Griffiths [1967] Director; Nigel Stephen Griffiths [1966] Director

**Doncaster Rotherham and District Motor Trades Group Training Association Limited**
*Incorporated:* 30 April 1985 *Employees:* 30
*Net Worth:* £5,643,192 *Total Assets:* £5,710,999
*Registered Office:* Rands Lane Industrial Estate, Armthorpe, Doncaster, S Yorks, DN3 3DY
*Activities:* Technical and vocational secondary education
*Officers:* Annette Scott, Secretary; Peter Matthew Coggon [1961] Director/HGV Vehicle and Trailer Servicing; Geoffrey Charles Harmer [1955] Director/Motor Vehicle Repairs; Michael Miller [1949] Director/Engineering Consultant; Annette Scott [1971] Director/Manager; Malcom Frank Stead [1940] Director/Garage Proprietor; Andy Stockham [1964] Director/Fleet Manager; Geoffrey Thompson [1945] Director/Manager; Michael David Wainwright [1948] Director/Garage Partner; Lee Russell Wright [1973] Director/Garage Owner

**Donelec Group Limited**
*Incorporated:* 4 February 2003 *Employees:* 128
*Net Worth:* £3,204,779 *Total Assets:* £6,553,706
*Registered Office:* Donelec Group Ltd, Westfield Industrial Estate, Kirk Lane, Yeadon, W Yorks, LS19 7LX
*Activities:* Activities of head offices
*Shareholder:* Norman Victor Wheat
*Officers:* David Victor Wheat, Secretary; Claire Louise Wheat [1969] Director/Office Manager; David Victor Wheat [1968] Director/Company Secretary; Jessica Elaine Wheat [1977] Director/Office Manager; Jonathan Norman Wheat [1965] Director; Norman Victor Wheat [1945] Director/Engineer; Patricia Margaret Wheat [1943] Director/Office Administration; Richard Henry Wheat [1943] Production Director

**Donisthorpe Hall**
*Incorporated:* 24 September 1999 *Employees:* 183
*Net Worth:* £3,598,859 *Total Assets:* £6,384,996
*Registered Office:* Shadwell Lane, Leeds, LS17 6AW
*Activities:* Medical nursing home activities
*Officers:* Andrew Brown [1946] Director; Susan Elaine Cawthray [1956] Director/CEO Health and Social Care; Ashley David Cohen [1971] Director/Pharmacist; Howard Sidney Cohen [1944] Director/Solicitor; Dr Robert Jeremy Ross [1950] Director/General Practitioner

**Doorstep of Hull**
*Incorporated:* 16 August 1985 *Employees:* 21
*Net Worth:* £3,634,169 *Total Assets:* £3,708,807
*Registered Office:* 151 Fairfax Avenue, Hull, HU5 4QZ
*Activities:* Other accommodation
*Officers:* Gwyneth Anne Sargent, Secretary; David Elliott [1954] Director/Commercial Relationship Manager; William Stevens [1954] Director/Property Services Manager

**Doorway Holdings Limited**
*Incorporated:* 4 February 2014 *Employees:* 530
*Previous:* Fairpoint Legal Services Limited
*Net Worth Deficit:* £15,512,000 *Total Assets:* £36,020,000
*Registered Office:* 21-27 St Pauls Street, Leeds, LS1 2JG
*Activities:* Other business support service activities n.e.c.
*Parent:* Doorway Capital Limited
*Officers:* Gregory Francis Cox, Secretary; Gregory Francis Cox [1971] Director

**Doran Scott Williams & Co Ltd**
*Incorporated:* 8 July 1999 *Employees:* 12
*Net Worth:* £2,820,705 *Total Assets:* £3,610,900
*Registered Office:* 9 Thorne Road, Doncaster, S Yorks, DN1 2HJ
*Activities:* Other business support service activities n.e.c.
*Major Shareholder:* Patrick John Terence Doran
*Officers:* Amanda Dawn Doran [1962] Director; Patrick John Terence Doran [1961] Director

**Dormeuil Manufacturing Limited**
*Incorporated:* 18 January 1979 *Employees:* 53
*Previous:* Minova Limited
*Net Worth:* £4,862,958 *Total Assets:* £12,384,076
*Registered Office:* Flagship Square, Shawcross Business Park, Dewsbury, W Yorks, WF12 7TH
*Activities:* Weaving of textiles
*Officers:* Marcus Nathan Jessop, Secretary; Marcus Nathan Jessop [1972] Director; Benjamin David Jones [1971] Design Director; Janice Lendhill [1955] Director; Christopher Stopford Robinson [1956] Director/Accountant; David John Smith [1960] Director; Gary Lee Whitehead [1973] Director

**Dormot Limited**
*Incorporated:* 9 June 2011 *Employees:* 54
*Previous:* Tomrods Steel Limited
*Net Worth:* £4,132,284 *Total Assets:* £9,525,573
*Registered Office:* Hambleton Steel Works, York Road, Thirsk, N Yorks, YO7 3BT
*Activities:* Activities of head offices
*Officers:* John Darcy Thompson [1950] Director

**Dortech Architectural Systems Limited**
*Incorporated:* 11 September 1990 *Employees:* 55
*Net Worth:* £386,772 *Total Assets:* £3,507,812
*Registered Office:* c/o WGN, 4 Park Place, Leeds, LS1 2RU
*Activities:* Other specialised construction activities n.e.c.
*Parent:* Architectural Systems Limited
*Officers:* Colin Glass [1943] Director; James John Leo Sutherland [1980] Commercial Director; Stephen John Sutherland [1952] Director; Paul Alan Trueman [1978] Contracts Director

**Dortek Limited**
*Incorporated:* 5 May 1989 *Employees:* 56
*Net Worth:* £682,117 *Total Assets:* £5,584,639
*Registered Office:* St Mark Street, Hull, HU8 7ED
*Activities:* Other specialised construction activities n.e.c.
*Parent:* Dortek Limited (Wicklow)
*Officers:* Brenda Fenton, Secretary; Anthony Fenton [1944] Director/Chairman; Michael John Glanville [1968] International Sales Director; Kenneth Raymond Mawer [1952] Operations Director; Alan O'Keane [1965] Managing Director [Irish]; Alphonsus Mary O'Mara [1944] Director [Irish]; Patrick O'Mara [1955] Director/Chartered Accountant [Irish]; James Norval Paul [1942] Director

**Double Two Limited**
*Incorporated:* 2 November 1954 *Employees:* 76
*Net Worth Deficit:* £156,348 *Total Assets:* £4,183,193
*Registered Office:* P O Box 1, Thornes Lane Wharf, Wakefield, W Yorks, WF1 5RQ
*Activities:* Manufacture of other wearing apparel and accessories n.e.c.
*Parent:* The Wakefield Shirt Company Limited
*Officers:* Simon Anthony Balaam, Secretary; Richard John Donner [1967] Director; Richard John Donner [1939] Director

**Double-Ten Limited**
*Incorporated:* 12 June 1992
*Net Worth:* £2,324,368 *Total Assets:* £4,615,297
*Registered Office:* Victoria Spring, Wakefield Road, Heckmondwike, W Yorks, WF15 6BE
*Activities:* Other specialised construction activities n.e.c.
*Major Shareholder:* Carl Nicholas Barnes
*Officers:* Joyce Dolman, Secretary; Carl Nicholas Barnes [1968] Director/Structural Fire Protection

**Dove House Hospice Limited**
*Incorporated:* 28 May 1980 *Employees:* 261
*Previous:* North Humberside Hospice Project Limited
*Net Worth:* £12,636,493 *Total Assets:* £13,038,327
*Registered Office:* Dove House Hospice, Chamberlain Road, Hull, HU8 8DH
*Activities:* Other education n.e.c.
*Officers:* Dr Anna Maria Wolkowski, Secretary; Margaret Butt [1949] Director/Retired; Philip Harry Daniels [1954] Director/Optometrist; James Angus Doyle [1957] Director/Accountant; Francis John Grove Dunning [1946] Director/Barrister; Dr Daniel Robert Harman [1979] Director/Medical Consultant; Helen Marshall [1959] Director/Retired; Anthony Bernard Rowland [1954] Director/Accountant; Dr Rajarshi Roy [1972] Director/Consultant; Penelope Joan Stephenson [1944] Director/Retired; Janet Mary Weatherill [1943] Director/Retired; Dr Emma Louise Wolverson [1984] Director/Clinical Psychologist/Lecturer

**Dovecote Park Limited**
*Incorporated:* 4 March 1996 *Employees:* 686
*Net Worth:* £18,844,000 *Total Assets:* £40,589,000
*Registered Office:* Bankwood Road, Stapleton, Pontefract, W Yorks, WF8 3DD
*Activities:* Processing and preserving of meat
*Officers:* David Bosworth Gunner, Secretary/Director; Edwin John Richard Canvin [1950] Director; David Bosworth Gunner [1952] Director; Andrew James McAllister [1965] Managing Director; Amanda Patricia Snowie [1961] Director

**Dowse Haulage Limited**
*Incorporated:* 5 March 2003 *Employees:* 51
*Net Worth:* £2,959,320 *Total Assets:* £5,033,034
*Registered Office:* The Poplars, Bridge Street, Brigg, N Lincs, DN20 8NQ
*Activities:* Freight transport by road
*Shareholders:* Marc Adrian Dowse; Samantha Jayne Hare
*Officers:* Marc Adrian Dowse [1975] Director/Transport Manager; Samantha Jayne Hare [1973] Director/Accounts Clerk

**DP Publicity Limited**
*Incorporated:* 12 January 2000 *Employees:* 21
*Net Worth:* £6,293,978 *Total Assets:* £11,607,975
*Registered Office:* Westfield House, 7 Westfield Road, Wakefield, W Yorks, WF1 3RB
*Activities:* Media representation services
*Parent:* Pitts Developments Limited
*Officers:* Ian Susans, Secretary; David John Pitts [1961] Director; Ian Susans [1955] Director

**Dr Reddy's Laboratories (UK) Limited**
*Incorporated:* 3 June 1983 *Employees:* 82
*Net Worth:* £27,312,298 *Total Assets:* £36,693,180
*Registered Office:* 6 Riverview Road, Beverley, E Yorks, HU17 0LD
*Activities:* Manufacture of pharmaceutical preparations
*Parent:* Reddys Laboratories (EU) Ltd
*Officers:* Ramanjaneyulu Sane, Secretary; Subir Kohli [1978] Director; Venkata Narsimham Mannam [1968] Director/Vice President - Finance [Indian]; Satish Reddy [1967] Director/Industrialist [Indian]; Clemens Johannes Troche [1965] Director [German]

**Dr. Oetker (UK) Limited**
*Incorporated:* 25 September 2001 *Employees:* 525
*Net Worth:* £70,935,000 *Total Assets:* £112,662,000
*Registered Office:* 4600 Park Approach, Thorpe Park, Leeds, LS15 8GB
*Activities:* Agents involved in the sale of food, beverages and tobacco
*Officers:* Dr Alexander Edelmann [1972] Director [German]; Georg Heerdegen Parsbo [1966] Managing Director [Danish]; Dr Martin Heinrich Theodor Reintjes [1961] Managing Director [German]; Dr. Johannes Rosenthal [1982] Managing Director [German]

**Dr. Reddy's Laboratories (EU) Limited**
*Incorporated:* 13 October 1987 *Employees:* 200
*Net Worth:* £70,178,232 *Total Assets:* £84,630,296
*Registered Office:* Riverview Road, Beverley, E Yorks, HU17 0LD
*Activities:* Manufacture of basic pharmaceutical products
*Officers:* Sumit Kushwaha, Secretary; Subir Kohli [1978] Director; Venkata Narsimham Mannam [1968] Director/VP Finance [Indian]; Clemens Johannes Troche [1965] Managing Director, Betapharm BA [German]

**The Dragonfly Agency Limited**
*Incorporated:* 9 March 2011 *Employees:* 6
*Net Worth:* £1,026,601 *Total Assets:* £3,454,997
*Registered Office:* Sanderson House, Station Road, Horsforth, Leeds, LS18 5NT
*Activities:* Printing n.e.c.
*Shareholders:* Victoria Grant; Anthony Bagshaw
*Officers:* Anthony Wayne Bagshaw [1970] Director; Victoria Grant [1979] Director

**Dransfield Novelty Company Limited**
*Incorporated:* 17 May 1946 *Employees:* 235
*Net Worth:* £14,941,225 *Total Assets:* £17,384,638
*Registered Office:* Dransfield House, Mill Street, Leeds, LS9 8BP
*Activities:* Other amusement and recreation activities n.e.c.
*Officers:* Michael James Smith, Secretary; Robert John Dransfield [1965] Director; Christopher Haley [1968] Director/Certified Accountant; Michael James Smith [1982] Director/Chartered Accountant

**Drax Corporate Limited**
*Incorporated:* 13 September 2005 *Employees:* 147
*Previous:* Drax Finance Limited
*Net Worth:* £1,837,506,944 *Total Assets:* £3,076,291,072
*Registered Office:* Drax Power Station, Selby, N Yorks, YO8 8PH
*Activities:* Production of electricity
*Parent:* Drax Group Holdings Limited
*Officers:* David McCallum, Secretary; Dwight Daniel Willard Gardiner [1964] Director [British/American]; Andrew Robert Koss [1971] Director

**Drax Finco PLC**
*Incorporated:* 10 March 2017
*Net Worth Deficit:* £1,297,000 *Total Assets:* £554,318,016
*Registered Office:* Drax Power Station, Selby, N Yorks, YO8 8PH
*Activities:* Production of electricity
*Parent:* Drax Group Holdings Limited
*Officers:* David McCallum, Secretary; Dwight Daniel William Gardiner [1964] Director [American/British]; Andrew Robert Koss [1971] Director

**Drax Fuel Supply Limited**
*Incorporated:* 29 November 2004 *Employees:* 2
*Net Worth:* £34,855,000 *Total Assets:* £45,458,000
*Registered Office:* Drax Power Station, Selby, N Yorks, YO8 8PH
*Activities:* Production of electricity
*Parent:* Drax Smart Generation Holdco Limited
*Officers:* David McCallum, Secretary; Edward Brian Greensmith [1967] Director; Andrew Robert Koss [1971] Director

**Drax Group Holdings Limited**
*Incorporated:* 24 November 2015 *Employees:* 2
*Net Worth:* £1,773,928,960 *Total Assets:* £1,774,241,024
*Registered Office:* Drax Power Station, Selby, N Yorks, YO8 8PH
*Activities:* Production of electricity
*Parent:* Drax Group PLC
*Officers:* David McCallum, Secretary; Dwight Daniel Willard Gardiner [1964] Director [British/American]; Andrew Robert Koss [1971] Director

**Drax Group PLC**
*Incorporated:* 13 September 2005 *Employees:* 2,507
*Net Worth:* £1,720,099,968 *Total Assets:* £3,517,600,000
*Registered Office:* Drax Power Station, Selby, N Yorks, YO8 8PH
*Activities:* Activities of head offices
*Officers:* Brett Nicholas Gladden, Secretary; Timothy Russell Cobbold [1962] Director; Philip Gotsall Cox [1951] Director; Dwight Daniel Willard Gardiner [1964] Director [British/American]; Nicola Hodson [1966] Director; Andrew Robert Koss [1971] Director; David Clive Lindsell [1947] Director/Chartered Accountant; David Simon Matthew Nussbaum [1958] Director; Vanessa Kate Simms [1975] Director; Andrew Keith Skelton [1971] Director; Anthony David Thorne [1950] Director

**Drax Power Limited**
*Incorporated:* 1 September 2003 *Employees:* 793
*Net Worth:* £1,346,381,056 *Total Assets:* £2,427,275,008
*Registered Office:* Drax Power Station, Selby, N Yorks, YO8 8PH
*Activities:* Production of electricity
*Parent:* Drax Smart Generation Holdco Limited
*Officers:* David McCallum, Secretary; Dwight Daniel Willard Gardiner [1964] Director [British/American]; Edward Brian Greensmith [1967] Director; Andrew Robert Koss [1971] Director; Michael Thomas Patrick [1972] Director; Charlotte Clare Rhodes [1972] Director; John Frederick Watts [1954] Director; Jens Price Wolf [1972] Director [Danish]

**Drax Smart Generation Holdco Limited**
*Incorporated:* 25 October 2011
*Previous:* Drax Group Services Limited
*Net Worth:* £1,633,805,952 *Total Assets:* £1,653,528,960
*Registered Office:* Drax Power Station, Selby, N Yorks, YO8 8PH
*Activities:* Production of electricity
*Parent:* Drax Corporate Limited
*Officers:* David McCallum, Secretary; Dwight Daniel Willard Gardiner [1964] Director [British/American]; Andrew Robert Koss [1971] Director

**Drax Smart Sourcing Holdco Limited**
*Incorporated:* 24 October 2011
*Previous:* Drax (International) Limited
*Net Worth:* £321,616,192 *Total Assets:* £432,537,760
*Registered Office:* Drax Power Station, Selby, N Yorks, YO8 8PH
*Activities:* Production of electricity
*Parent:* Drax Corporate Limited
*Officers:* David McCallum, Secretary; Dwight Daniel Willard Gardiner [1964] Director [British/American]; Andrew Robert Koss [1971] Director

**Drax Smart Supply Holdco Limited**
*Incorporated:* 10 March 2017
*Net Worth:* £441,584,000 *Total Assets:* £449,884,992
*Registered Office:* Drax Power Station, Selby, N Yorks, YO8 8PH
*Activities:* Production of electricity
*Parent:* Drax Corporate Limited
*Officers:* David McCallum, Secretary; Dwight Daniel William Gardiner [1964] Director [American/British]; Andrew Robert Koss [1971] Director

**DRC Contract Services Ltd**
*Incorporated:* 21 March 2011 *Employees:* 108
*Previous:* Deangelo Brothers UK Limited
*Net Worth Deficit:* £1,325,058 *Total Assets:* £7,445,000
*Registered Office:* Bell Wood House, Minskip Road, Boroughbridge, N Yorks, YO51 9HY
*Activities:* Other business support service activities n.e.c.
*Officers:* Clive Freeman [1965] UK Managing Director; Derek Hardy [1961] Director; Robert Whamond [1971] Director

**Dream Property Holdco Limited**
*Incorporated:* 24 February 2017
*Net Worth:* £175,322 *Total Assets:* £4,578,714
*Registered Office:* Barn Cottage, Botany Lane, Lepton, Huddersfield, W Yorks, HD8 0NE
*Activities:* Activities of other holding companies n.e.c.
*Shareholders:* Emma Louise Morris; Russell Paul Morris
*Officers:* Emma Louise Morris [1977] Director; Russell Paul Morris [1969] Director

**Dreamphoto Limited**
*Incorporated:* 11 May 1995
*Net Worth:* £6,657,000 *Total Assets:* £9,242,000
*Registered Office:* Trinity Park House, Fox Way, Wakefield, W Yorks, WF2 8EE
*Activities:* Other service activities n.e.c.
*Parent:* Northern Foods Limited
*Officers:* Ronald Klaas Otto Kers [1969] Director/Group CEO [Dutch]; Craig Ashley Tomkinson [1982] Director/Group CFO

**Dreamplayer Limited**
*Incorporated:* 11 May 1995
*Net Worth:* £6,752,000 *Total Assets:* £9,244,000
*Registered Office:* Trinity Business Park, Fox Way, Wakefield, W Yorks, WF2 8EE
*Activities:* Other service activities n.e.c.
*Parent:* Northern Foods Limited
*Officers:* Ronald Klaas Otto Kers [1969] Director/Group CEO [Dutch]; Craig Ashley Tomkinson [1982] Director/Group CFO

**WJ Drennan Limited**
*Incorporated:* 2 July 2007 *Employees:* 5
*Net Worth:* £87,386 *Total Assets:* £4,729,509
*Registered Office:* High Hedley Hope Farm, Tow Law, Co Durham, DL13 4PR
*Activities:* Production of electricity
*Major Shareholder:* William James Drennan
*Officers:* Stanley David Thomson, Secretary; William James Drennan [1950] Director; Stanley David Thomson [1966] Director

**Dressadmire Limited**
*Incorporated:* 11 May 1995
*Net Worth:* £6,670,000 *Total Assets:* £9,198,000
*Registered Office:* Trinity Park House, Fox Way, Wakefield, W Yorks, WF2 8EE
*Activities:* Other service activities n.e.c.
*Parent:* Northern Foods Limited
*Officers:* Ronald Klaas Otto Kers [1969] Director/Group CEO [Dutch]; Craig Ashley Tomkinson [1982] Director/Group CFO

**Drifford Group Limited**
*Incorporated:* 20 March 2012 *Employees:* 11,059
*Net Worth:* £7,465,000 *Total Assets:* £127,326,000
*Registered Office:* Dewhirst House, Westgate, Driffield, E Yorks, YO25 6TH
*Activities:* Activities of head offices
*Shareholder:* Anthony James Mark Wood
*Officers:* Christopher Wilde, Secretary; David Witt [1953] Director; Anthony James Mark Wood [1960] Director

**Drifford Limited**
*Incorporated:* 19 July 2006
*Net Worth:* £22,205,592 *Total Assets:* £75,502,304
*Registered Office:* Dewhirst House, Westgate, Driffield, E Yorks, YO25 6TH
*Activities:* Activities of head offices
*Parent:* Drifford Group Limited
*Officers:* Christopher John Wilde, Secretary; David Witt [1953] Director; Anthony James Mark Wood [1960] Director

**Drighlington Fibres Limited**
*Incorporated:* 6 June 2001
*Net Worth:* £16,359,000 *Total Assets:* £16,359,000
*Registered Office:* Old Mills, Drighlington, Bradford, W Yorks, BD11 1BY
*Activities:* Non-trading company
*Officers:* Kathryn Anne Davenport, Secretary; Peter Jan Patrik Gyllenhammar [1953] Director [Swedish]; John Olof Hager [1964] Managing Director [Swedish]

**Drinkwater's Mushrooms Limited**
*Incorporated:* 22 January 1981 *Employees:* 240
*Net Worth:* £4,290,724 *Total Assets:* £6,307,143
*Registered Office:* Dalton House, 9 Dalton Square, Lancaster, LA1 1WD
*Activities:* Growing of vegetables and melons, roots and tubers
*Shareholders:* Phyllis Drinkwater; Kenneth Drinkwater
*Officers:* Phyllis Drinkwater, Secretary; Kenneth Stephen Drinkwater [1973] Director/Grower/Manager; Kenneth Drinkwater [1943] Director/Mushroom Farmer; Philip Edward Drinkwater [1967] Director/Grower/Manager; Phyllis Drinkwater [1946] Director/Farmer; Harlan Kemp Sharpe [1960] Director/General Manager

**Drive Devilbiss Healthcare Limited**
*Incorporated:* 8 October 2001 *Employees:* 662
*Previous:* Drive Medical Limited
*Net Worth Deficit:* £24,264,000 *Total Assets:* £99,211,000
*Registered Office:* Drive Devilbiss Healthcare Limited, Heathfield Lane, Birkenshaw, W Yorks, BD11 2HW
*Activities:* Non-specialised wholesale trade
*Parent:* Drive International, LLC
*Officers:* Amy O'Keefe, Secretary; Michael Thomas Waine, Secretary; Grant Abrahams [1979] Retail Director; Harvey Diamond [1953] Director [American]; Gemma Hartley [1978] Service Director; Richard James McGleenan [1970] Director; Timothy Newby [1963] Marketing Director; Jeffrey Schwarz [1960] Director [American]; Mark Thompson [1964] Director; Graham Thomas Turner [1965] Business Support Director; Michael Thomas Waine [1951] Finance Director

**Drive Devilbiss Sidhil Limited**
*Incorporated:* 29 May 1951 *Employees:* 233
*Previous:* Sidhil Limited
*Net Worth:* £9,592,000 *Total Assets:* £15,407,000
*Registered Office:* Drive Devilbiss Healthcare Limited, Heathfield Lane, Birkenshaw, W Yorks, BD11 2HW
*Activities:* Manufacture of other fabricated metal products n.e.c.
*Parent:* Sidhil Group Limited
*Officers:* Gemma Hartley [1978] Service Director; Richard James McGleenan [1970] Managing Director; Graham Thomas Turner [1965] Sales and Marketing Director; Michael Thomas Waine [1951] Finance Director

**Drivecheck Limited**
*Incorporated:* 5 June 1990 *Employees:* 37
*Net Worth:* £5,668,437 *Total Assets:* £12,274,751
*Registered Office:* Cowden Holiday Park, Main Road, Great Cowden, E Yorks, HU11 4UD
*Activities:* Recreational vehicle parks, trailer parks and camping grounds
*Parent:* Larkham Leisure Limited
*Officers:* Rolson William Philip Larkham, Secretary; Rolson Philip William Larkham [1977] Director [Australian]; Tyrone Acer Larkham [1986] Director; William Henry Larkham [1982] Director

**Driver Hire Group Services Limited**
*Incorporated:* 2 February 1988 *Employees:* 65
*Net Worth:* £30,361,536 *Total Assets:* £34,522,716
*Registered Office:* 7 Bradford Business Park, Kings Gate, Bradford, W Yorks, BD1 4SJ
*Activities:* Temporary employment agency activities
*Parent:* Driver Hire Holdings Ltd
*Officers:* Christopher Michael Chidley [1960] Director; Paul Howard McNulty [1970] Finance Director

**Driver Hire Investments Group Limited**
*Incorporated:* 23 July 2007
*Net Worth:* £2,332,082 *Total Assets:* £18,666,760
*Registered Office:* 7 Bradford Business Park, Kings Gate, Bradford, W Yorks, BD1 4SJ
*Activities:* Activities of head offices
*Parent:* Specialist People Services Group Limited
*Officers:* Christopher Michael Chidley [1960] Director; Paul Howard McNulty [1970] Director

**Driver Hire Investments Limited**
*Incorporated:* 10 August 2004
*Net Worth Deficit:* £21,886,846 *Total Assets:* £8,093,015
*Registered Office:* 7 Bradford Business Park, Kings Gate, Bradford, W Yorks, BD1 4SJ
*Activities:* Temporary employment agency activities
*Parent:* Driver Hire Investments Group Limited
*Officers:* Christopher Michael Chidley [1960] Director; Paul Howard McNulty [1970] Director

**Drury Engineering Services Limited**
*Incorporated:* 19 October 2001 *Employees:* 50
*Net Worth:* £3,191,325 *Total Assets:* £3,915,645
*Registered Office:* East Riverside, Immingham Dock, Immingham, N E Lincs, DN40 2LZ
*Activities:* Construction of other civil engineering projects n.e.c.
*Shareholders:* Margaret Ann Drury; Philip John Drury; Margaret Ann Drury; Philip John Drury
*Officers:* Philip John Drury, Secretary/Engineer; Darren Roy Ash [1977] Director/Project Manager; David Philip Drury [1980] Director; Mrs Margaret Ann Drury [1958] Director/Clerical Assistant; Philip John Drury [1957] Director/Engineer; Darren David Summers [1966] Director

**Dryband One Limited**
*Incorporated:* 22 January 1993 *Employees:* 214
*Net Worth:* £4,068,537 *Total Assets:* £6,520,188
*Registered Office:* Cloverdale Care Home, 68 Butt Lane, Laceby, Grimsby, N E Lincs, DN37 7AH
*Activities:* Other business support service activities n.e.c.
*Major Shareholder:* Laxmi Avtar Kaur Khurana
*Officers:* Laxmi Avtar Kaur Khurana, Secretary/Nurse; Laxmi Avtar Kaur Khurana [1947] Director/Nurse; Surinder Pal Singh Khurana [1946] Computer Services Director

**Drydens Limited**
*Incorporated:* 3 December 2008 *Employees:* 165
*Net Worth Deficit:* £2,987,351 *Total Assets:* £5,148,437
*Registered Office:* 4th Floor, Fairfax House, Merrion Street, Leeds, LS2 8BX
*Activities:* Solicitors
*Major Shareholder:* Philip Holden
*Officers:* Steven Robert Heighway [1970] Director of Business Development; Philip Holden [1965] Director/Solicitor; Christopher William Jones [1953] Director; Timothy James Pope [1955] Director/Solicitor

**DSA Chemicals Limited**
*Incorporated:* 28 January 1993 *Employees:* 5
*Net Worth:* £2,950,176 *Total Assets:* £4,021,233
*Registered Office:* Pitman Road, Denaby Industrial Estate, Doncaster, S Yorks, DN12 4LJ
*Activities:* Manufacture of other inorganic basic chemicals
*Parent:* Paleus Group Limited
*Officers:* Mark Wiliam Briscoe [1963] Managing Director; David Hugh Wilson [1971] Director

**DSS Group Limited**
*Incorporated:* 12 March 2016 *Employees:* 83
*Net Worth:* £3,247,190 *Total Assets:* £11,187,691
*Registered Office:* M & D House, Brooklands Road, Adwick-le-Street, Doncaster, S Yorks, DN6 7BA
*Activities:* Activities of other holding companies n.e.c.
*Major Shareholder:* Robert Ian Watson
*Officers:* Steven Roy Edgworth [1959] Director; David Drew Wylie [1963] Director

**Dual Seal Glass Ltd.**
*Incorporated:* 22 March 1995 *Employees:* 125
*Net Worth:* £5,015,124 *Total Assets:* £8,694,570
*Registered Office:* 403 Leeds Road, Huddersfield, W Yorks, HD2 1XU
*Activities:* Shaping and processing of flat glass
*Shareholder:* Nigel David Meredith
*Officers:* Jennifer Mary Meredith, Secretary; David Meredith [1943] Director; Nigel David Meredith [1966] Director; John Michael Pearson [1955] Director; Michael Lindley Thompson [1965] Operations Director; Benjamin Keith Westerby [1980] Director

**Duchy Homes (Holdings) Limited**
*Incorporated:* 20 June 2017 *Employees:* 28
*Net Worth:* £428,127 *Total Assets:* £16,139,335
*Registered Office:* Middleton House, Westland Road, Leeds, LS11 5UH
*Activities:* Activities of other holding companies n.e.c.
*Shareholder:* Stadium Retail (Holdings) Limited
*Officers:* Dominic Michael Lush, Secretary; Jarrod Colin Best [1977] Director; Alexander Martin Clare [1978] Director; Andrew Stuart Fish [1972] Director; Paul Dyson Healey [1970] Director; David James Shann [1973] Director; Paul Whitaker [1968] Director

**Duchy Homes (Humshaugh) Limited**
*Incorporated:* 6 October 2016
*Net Worth:* £100 *Total Assets:* £3,531,879
*Registered Office:* Middleton House, Westland Road, Leeds, LS11 5UH
*Activities:* Buying and selling of own real estate
*Parent:* Duchy Homes Limited
*Officers:* Dominic Michael Lush, Secretary; John Graham Barnes [1977] Director; James Cropper [1954] Director

**Duchy Homes Limited**
*Incorporated:* 18 November 2011 *Employees:* 25
*Net Worth:* £427,782 *Total Assets:* £16,137,645
*Registered Office:* Middleton House, Westland Road, Leeds, LS11 5UH
*Activities:* Construction of domestic buildings
*Parent:* Duchy Homes (Holdings) Limited
*Officers:* Dominic Michael Lush, Secretary; John Graham Barnes [1977] Director; James Cropper [1954] Director; Steven Edward Hird [1972] Director

**R.E. and R. Duffield and Sons Limited**
*Incorporated:* 30 March 1977 *Employees:* 38
*Net Worth:* £4,709,891 *Total Assets:* £6,142,128
*Registered Office:* Green Lane, Melmerby, Ripon, N Yorks, HG4 5JB
*Activities:* Sawmilling and planing of wood
*Major Shareholder:* Howard Robert Duffield
*Officers:* Angela Doris Flinton, Secretary; Nicholas Taylor Collinson [1985] Sales Director; Alison Duffield [1962] Director/Timber Merchant; Howard Robert Duffield [1958] Director/Timber Merchant; Robert Edward Duffield [1932] Director/Timber Merchant; Angela Doris Flinton [1968] Director/Timber Merchant; Duncan Lees [1959] Sales Director

**Peter Duffy Limited**
*Incorporated:* 27 April 1972
*Net Worth:* £14,507,577 *Total Assets:* £17,738,488
*Registered Office:* Connaught House, Park View, Lofthouse Gate, Wakefield, W Yorks, WF3 3HA
*Activities:* Construction of utility projects for fluids
*Parent:* Peter Duffy Holdings Limited
*Officers:* William Mark David Painter, Secretary; Kevin Joseph Duffy [1969] Project Director; Michael Francis Duffy [1965] Contracts Director; Neil Martin Duffy [1972] Plant & Fleet Services Director; Peter Gerard Duffy [1961] Managing Director; Robert John Hudson [1969] Commercial Director

**Dufton Plumbing & Heating Supplies Limited**
*Incorporated:* 15 January 1986 *Employees:* 46
*Net Worth:* £4,200,585 *Total Assets:* £6,674,416
*Registered Office:* Unit 4a, Wellington Road Industrial Estate, Wellington Bridge, Leeds, LS12 2UA
*Activities:* Wholesale of hardware, plumbing and heating equipment and supplies
*Shareholders:* Nigel Peter Fowler; Paul Granville Dufton
*Officers:* Paul Granville Dufton, Secretary/Director; Paul Granville Dufton [1944] Director; Steven Paul Dufton [1968] Director; Nigel Peter Fowler [1965] Director

**Dugdale Compounds Limited**
*Incorporated:* 20 September 2013 *Employees:* 120
*Net Worth:* £1,612,433 *Total Assets:* £14,796,207
*Registered Office:* Valley Mill, Holmes Road, Sowerby Bridge, Halifax, W Yorks, HX6 2AA
*Activities:* Manufacture of plastics in primary forms
*Shareholder:* Darren Rowell
*Officers:* Richard Henry Cheetham Bickerton [1944] Director/Accountant; Thomas Frederick Durkin [1946] Director/Manager; David Anthony Outen [1966] Director/Manager; Darren Rowell [1965] Director; Dr Jeffrey Lewis Ryan [1962] Director/Manager

**Dugdale Limited**
*Incorporated:* 28 November 2000 *Employees:* 120
*Net Worth:* £4,622,173 *Total Assets:* £19,669,692
*Registered Office:* Valley Mill, Sowerby Bridge, W Yorks, HX6 2AA
*Activities:* Manufacture of plastics in primary forms
*Shareholder:* Darren Rowell
*Officers:* Darren Rowell, Secretary; Richard Henry Cheetham Bickerton [1944] Director/Accountant; Thomas Frederick Durkin [1946] Director/Manager; David Anthony Outen [1966] Director/Manager; Darren Rowell [1965] Director/Manager; Dr Jeffrey Lewis Ryan [1962] Director/Manager

**Dukeries Healthcare Limited**
*Incorporated:* 6 October 1997 *Employees:* 373
*Net Worth:* £2,404,556 *Total Assets:* £4,203,954
*Registered Office:* Ye Olde Bell, Barnby Moor, Retford, Notts, DN22 8QS
*Activities:* Other residential care activities n.e.c.
*Parent:* Barnby CH Ltd
*Officers:* Hilary Jane Levack, Secretary; Jacqueline Patricia Brayford [1962] Director/Operations; Allen Paul Levack [1951] Director/Building Contractor; Hilary Jane Levack [1955] Finance Director

**Dukeries Homes Limited**
*Incorporated:* 26 April 2013 *Employees:* 6
*Net Worth:* £1,333,361 *Total Assets:* £5,990,898
*Registered Office:* Suite 2, Chancery Court, 34 West Street, Retford, Notts, DN22 6ES
*Activities:* Development of building projects
*Shareholders:* Stacey Clarke; Stephen Clarke; Andrew David Wilson; Gillian Wilson
*Officers:* Stacey Clarke [1978] Director/Salon Owner; Stephen Clarke [1978] Director; Andrew David Wilson [1963] Director; Gillian Wilson [1972] Director

**Dunelm Optical Co. Limited**
*Incorporated:* 17 July 1973 *Employees:* 72
*Net Worth:* £2,949,077 *Total Assets:* £5,392,817
*Registered Office:* 9 Enterprise Way, Green Lane Industrial Estate, Spennymoor, Co Durham, DL16 6YP
*Activities:* Other manufacturing n.e.c.
*Major Shareholder:* Angela Gillian Beaumont
*Officers:* Anita Deborah Booty, Secretary; Angela Gillian Beaumont [1951] Director; Oliver Peter Julian Beaumont [1983] Director; Anita Deborah Booty [1969] Finance Director

**Dunhills (Pontefract) P L C**
*Incorporated:* 3 November 1919 *Employees:* 739
*Net Worth:* £146,419,776 *Total Assets:* £176,239,808
*Registered Office:* 26 Front Street, Pontefract, W Yorks, WF8 1NJ
*Activities:* Manufacture of sugar confectionery
*Officers:* Christian Cerlienco, Secretary; Christian Cerlienco [1981] Finance Director [Italian]; Jonathon Charles Hughes [1974] Managing Director; Frank Windmann [1966] Works Director [German]

**Dunlop Conveyor Belting Investments Limited**
*Incorporated:* 12 July 2005
*Net Worth:* £2,220,000 *Total Assets:* £3,614,000
*Registered Office:* Hesslewood Country Office Park, Ferriby Road, Hessle, Hull, HU13 0PW
*Activities:* Activities of head offices
*Parent:* Fenner International Limited
*Officers:* Debra Bradbury, Secretary; Andrew Maitland Caley [1962] Director/Group Taxation & Treasury; William John Pratt [1963] Managing Director; Peter Joseph Watson [1956] Director

**Dunlop Oil & Marine Limited**
*Incorporated:* 26 November 1997 *Employees:* 304
*Net Worth:* £12,100,000 *Total Assets:* £44,321,000
*Registered Office:* Moody Lane, Pyewipe, Grimsby, N E Lincs, DN31 2SY
*Activities:* Manufacture of other rubber products
*Parent:* Phoenix Oil & Marine Limited
*Officers:* Dr Ali Reza Kambiez Zandiyeh [1960] Director/General Manager

**Dunns (Long Sutton) Limited**
*Incorporated:* 11 August 2000 *Employees:* 41
*Net Worth:* £6,564,698 *Total Assets:* £11,449,457
*Registered Office:* Lindsey House, Hemswell Cliff, Gainsborough, Lincs, DN21 5TH
*Activities:* Seed processing for propagation
*Officers:* Michael John Thompson, Secretary; Christopher Michael Guest [1986] Director; Stuart James Shand [1962] Director/Agricultural Merchant; David Thomas Sheppard [1961] Director/Grain Trader; Michael John Thompson [1965] Director/Certified Accountant

**Dunsville Primary Academy Trust**
*Incorporated:* 2 October 2012 *Employees:* 483
*Net Worth:* £2,796,739 *Total Assets:* £3,478,569
*Registered Office:* Dunsville Primary School, Broadway, Dunsville, Doncaster, S Yorks, DN7 4HX
*Activities:* Primary education
*Officers:* Teresa Kathleen Ladley, Secretary; Andrew Ian Eastwood [1978] Director/Civil Engineer; Kevin Flint [1958] Director/Headteacher; Colin Peter Hannam [1942] Director/Business Development Consultant; Kenneth Frederick Hulks [1942] Director/Retired; Bryan Peter Jaehrig [1955] Director/Higher Level Teaching Assistant; Jamie Elliott Schofield [1983] Director/Deputy Headteacher; John Roy Stapleton [1950] Director/Retired; Valerie Ann Stapleton [1950] Director/Retired; Frederick George William Tomlinson [1949] Director/Retired Police Officer; Victoria Jane Wilson [1972] Director/Deputy Headteacher

**Dura Beds Ltd**
*Incorporated:* 3 August 2001 *Employees:* 171
*Net Worth:* £2,703,372 *Total Assets:* £4,801,927
*Registered Office:* Kelvin Business Park, Grange Road, Batley, W Yorks, WF17 6PB
*Activities:* Manufacture of mattresses
*Shareholders:* Imran Akhtar; Islam Khan
*Officers:* Imran Akhtar [1971] Operations Director; Mohammed Ishaq [1950] Director/Businessman; Islam Khan [1967] Director/Businessman; Tariq Mahmood [1960] Director/Businessman

**N.L. Durdy & Son Limited**
*Incorporated:* 19 February 1954 *Employees:* 10
*Net Worth:* £1,533,729 *Total Assets:* £3,853,418
*Registered Office:* Well Green, High Street, Barnby Dun, Doncaster, S Yorks, DN3 1DU
*Activities:* Growing of cereals (except rice), leguminous crops and oil seeds
*Major Shareholder:* Nicolas Leslie Durdy
*Officers:* Elizabeth Mary Durdy, Secretary; Elizabeth Mary Durdy [1965] Director; Nicolas Leslie Durdy [1961] Director/Farmer

**Durest Beds Ltd**
*Incorporated:* 4 March 2009
*Net Worth:* £509,566 *Total Assets:* £3,163,497
*Registered Office:* Virginia Mills, Pildacre Lane, Dewsbury, W Yorks, WF12 8NP
*Activities:* Manufacture of mattresses
*Major Shareholder:* Mussrat Iqbal
*Officers:* Imran Ahmed, Secretary; Mussrat Iqbal [1977] Director/Bed Sales

**Durham & Tees Community Ventures Fundco (No.1) Limited**
*Incorporated:* 21 April 2004 *Employees:* 8
*Net Worth Deficit:* £953,113 *Total Assets:* £7,072,157
*Registered Office:* 4340 Park Approach, Thorpe Park, Leeds, LS15 8GB
*Activities:* Development of building projects
*Parent:* Durham & Tees Community Ventures Holdco 1 Limited
*Officers:* Victoria Louise Jagger-Strangeway, Secretary; Richard John Coates [1966] Investment Director; Nigel Michael Fenny [1961] Director; David John Harding [1980] Director/Chartered Accountant; Philip Jonathan Harris [1971] Director; Graeme Niven [1966] Director/Chief Finance Officer; Dean Spencer [1966] Development Director; Philip Arthur Would [1971] Director/Asset Management

**Durham & Tees Community Ventures Fundco (No.2) Limited**
*Incorporated:* 6 June 2005 *Employees:* 8
*Net Worth Deficit:* £713,342 *Total Assets:* £12,648,089
*Registered Office:* 4340 Park Approach, Thorpe Park, Leeds, LS15 8GB
*Activities:* Development of building projects
*Parent:* Durham & Tees Community Ventures Holdco 2 Limited
*Officers:* Victoria Louise Jagger-Strangeway, Secretary; Richard John Coates [1966] Investment Director; Nigel Michael Fenny [1961] Director; David John Harding [1980] Director/Chartered Accountant; Philip Jonathan Harris [1971] Director; Graeme Niven [1966] Director/Chief Finance Officer; Dean Spencer [1966] Development Director; Philip Arthur Would [1971] Director/Asset Management

**Durham & Tees Community Ventures Fundco (No.3) Limited**
*Incorporated:* 13 December 2005 *Employees:* 8
*Net Worth:* £553,877 *Total Assets:* £18,273,004
*Registered Office:* 4340 Park Approach, Thorpe Park, Leeds, LS15 8GB
*Activities:* Development of building projects
*Parent:* Durham & Tees Community Ventures Holdco (No.3) Limited
*Officers:* Victoria Louise Jagger-Strangeway, Secretary; Richard John Coates [1966] Investment Director; Nigel Michael Fenny [1961] Director; David John Harding [1980] Director/Chartered Accountant; Philip Jonathan Harris [1971] Director; Graeme Niven [1966] Director/Chief Finance Officer; Dean Spencer [1966] Development Director; Philip Arthur Would [1971] Director/Asset Management

**Durham & Tees Community Ventures Fundco (No.4) Limited**
*Incorporated:* 1 May 2009 *Employees:* 8
*Net Worth:* £726,800 *Total Assets:* £12,470,140
*Registered Office:* 4340 Park Approach, Thorpe Park, Leeds, LS15 8GB
*Activities:* Development of building projects
*Parent:* Durham & Tees Community Ventures Holdco 4 Limited
*Officers:* Victoria Louise Jagger-Strangeway, Secretary; Richard John Coates [1966] Investment Director; Nigel Michael Fenny [1961] Director; David John Harding [1980] Director/Chartered Accountant; Philip Jonathan Harris [1971] Director; Graeme Niven [1966] Director/Chief Finance Officer; Dean Spencer [1966] Development Director; Philip Arthur Would [1971] Director/Asset Management

**Durham & Tees Community Ventures Limited**
*Incorporated:* 21 April 2004 *Employees:* 8
*Net Worth:* £525,553 *Total Assets:* £54,216,976
*Registered Office:* 4340 Park Approach, Thorpe Park, Leeds, LS15 8GB
*Activities:* Activities of head offices
*Shareholders:* Tees & Durham (Lift) Investments Limited; Community Health Partnerships Limited
*Officers:* Victoria Louise Jagger-Strangeway, Secretary; Richard John Coates [1966] Investment Director; Nigel Michael Fenny [1961] Director; David John Harding [1980] Director/Chartered Accountant; Philip Jonathan Harris [1971] Director; Graeme Niven [1966] Director/Chief Finance Officer; Dean Spencer [1966] Development Director; Philip Arthur Would [1971] Director/Asset Management

**Durham & Tees Community Ventures Primary Care Limited**
*Incorporated:* 21 June 2013 *Employees:* 8
*Net Worth:* £865,419 *Total Assets:* £3,866,079
*Registered Office:* 4340 Park Approach, Leeds, LS15 8GB
*Activities:* Management of real estate on a fee or contract basis
*Parent:* Durham & Tees Community Ventures Holdco (No 5) Limited
*Officers:* Victoria Louise Jagger-Strangeway, Secretary; Richard John Coates [1966] Investment Director; Nigel Michael Fenny [1961] Regional Director; David John Harding [1980] Director/Chartered Accountant; Philip Jonathan Harris [1971] Director; Graeme Niven [1966] Director/Chief Finance Officer; Dean Spencer [1966] Commercial Director; Philip Arthur Would [1971] Director/Asset Management

**Durham Box Company Limited**
*Incorporated:* 20 April 1989 *Employees:* 67
*Net Worth:* £4,157,133 *Total Assets:* £7,850,847
*Registered Office:* Auckland Crescent, St Helen Auckland, Bishop Auckland, Co Durham, DL14 9AD
*Activities:* Manufacture of other paper and paperboard containers
*Officers:* Susan Ann Morris, Secretary; Daniel Christian Morris [1976] Director; Michael John Morris [1950] Sales Director; Susan Ann Morris [1952] Director/Company Secretary

**Dusrolbake Limited**
*Incorporated:* 2 October 1963
*Net Worth:* £283,131 *Total Assets:* £8,685,288
*Registered Office:* 2 West Parade Road, Scarborough, N Yorks, YO12 5ED
*Activities:* Other letting and operating of own or leased real estate
*Parent:* The Goodall Group Limited
*Officers:* Joan Margaret Goodall, Secretary; James Rawling Goodall [1980] Director; Joan Margaret Goodall [1941] Director

**Dutch Imports & Daughters Limited**
*Incorporated:* 4 September 2003
*Net Worth:* £2,590,276 *Total Assets:* £7,495,020
*Registered Office:* Building 104, Baffin Way, Brough, E Yorks, HU15 1YU
*Activities:* Wholesale of household goods (other than musical instruments) n.e.c
*Shareholders:* Charles Kraanen; Karen Michelle Kraanen
*Officers:* Karen Michelle Kraanen, Secretary/Importer Exporter; Charles Kraanen [1962] Director/Importer Exporter [Dutch]; Karen Michelle Kraanen [1962] Director/Importer Exporter

**Duynie Limited**
*Incorporated:* 1 June 2005 *Employees:* 44
*Net Worth:* £1,134,663 *Total Assets:* £7,568,990
*Registered Office:* Unit 10b Thunderhead Ridge, Glasshoughton, Castleford, W Yorks, WF10 4UA
*Activities:* Wholesale of grain, unmanufactured tobacco, seeds and animal feeds
*Parent:* Duynie Holding BV
*Officers:* Johannes Hilbert Muijt, Secretary; Gerardus Christianus Adriana Maria Corsmit [1967] Director [Dutch]; Philip Vincent Sparks [1961] Director

**DVV Holdco Limited**
*Incorporated:* 13 December 2013 *Employees:* 5
*Net Worth Deficit:* £34,806,000 *Total Assets:* £36,534,000
*Registered Office:* The Inspire, Hornbeam Square West, Harrogate, N Yorks, HG2 8PA
*Activities:* Activities of head offices
*Parent:* Principal Hotels Topco 3 Limited
*Officers:* John Cody Bradshaw [1978] Director/Hotel Real Estate [American]; Sarah Broughton [1976] Director; James Alexander Burrell [1974] Director/Accountant; Anthony Gerrard Troy [1962] Director [Irish]

**DVV Investco Limited**
*Incorporated:* 13 December 2013 *Employees:* 1,239
*Net Worth:* £61,327,000 *Total Assets:* £224,646,000
*Registered Office:* The Inspire, Hornbeam Square West, Harrogate, N Yorks, HG2 8PA
*Activities:* Activities of head offices
*Parent:* DVV Holdco Limited
*Officers:* John Cody Bradshaw [1978] Director/Hotel Real Estate [American]; Sarah Broughton [1976] Director; James Alexander Burrell [1974] Director; Anthony Gerrard Troy [1962] Director [Irish]

**DVV Properties 2 Limited**
*Incorporated:* 3 July 2015 *Employees:* 2
*Net Worth:* £10,783,000 *Total Assets:* £85,029,000
*Registered Office:* The Inspire, Hornbeam Square West, Harrogate, N Yorks, HG2 8PA
*Activities:* Other letting and operating of own or leased real estate
*Shareholders:* De Vere Venues Group Limited; De Vere Venues Group Limited
*Officers:* James Alexander Burrell [1974] Director; Anthony Gerrard Troy [1962] Director [Irish]

**Dyneley Holdings Limited**
*Incorporated:* 28 June 2001 *Employees:* 3
*Net Worth:* £29,196,000 *Total Assets:* £29,196,000
*Registered Office:* Alexandra House, Lawnswood Business Park, Redvers Close, Leeds, LS16 6QY
*Activities:* Wholesale of petroleum and petroleum products
*Parent:* Energy Acquisitions UK Limited
*Officers:* Stephen Elliott, Secretary; Stephen Elliott [1962] Director; Benjamin Marcus Jordan [1964] Director; Daire Keating [1978] Director [Irish]; Edward Gerard O'Brien [1970] Director/Accountant [Irish]

**A. Dyson & Son (Patterns) Limited**
*Incorporated:* 3 May 1978 *Employees:* 65
*Net Worth:* £4,949,000 *Total Assets:* £6,826,248
*Registered Office:* Hargreaves Foundry, Water Lane, South Parade, Halifax, W Yorks, HX3 9HG
*Activities:* Activities of other holding companies n.e.c.
*Major Shareholder:* Michael James Hinchliffe
*Officers:* Helen Louise Thornber, Secretary; Michael James Hinchliffe [1959] Director/Foundry Manager; Shirley Hinchliffe [1933] Director; Terence Hinchliffe [1932] Director

**Dyson Properties Limited**
*Incorporated:* 26 November 1959 *Employees:* 4
*Net Worth:* £14,066,556 *Total Assets:* £20,820,920
*Registered Office:* Leigh House, 28-32 St Paul's Street, Leeds, LS1 2JT
*Activities:* Renting and operating of Housing Association real estate
*Shareholders:* John Anthony Dyson; Robert Alan Dyson
*Officers:* Robert Alan Dyson, Secretary; Lady Jacqueline Carmel Dyson [1947] Director; Nicholas Mark Dyson [1974] Director/Solicitor; Robert Alan Dyson [1945] Director/Solicitor

**E & S Environmental Services Limited**
*Incorporated:* 17 November 2004 *Employees:* 92
*Net Worth:* £4,824,000 *Total Assets:* £7,444,000
*Registered Office:* 80 Station Parade, Harrogate, N Yorks, HG1 1HQ
*Activities:* Technical testing and analysis
*Shareholders:* Adler and Allan Limited; E & S Holdings Limited
*Officers:* Andrew Clarke [1974] Director; Robert Leonard Contreras [1962] Director; Michael James Dunn [1965] Director; Nigel Durrant [1969] Director

**E K Holdings Limited**
*Incorporated:* 7 April 1998 *Employees:* 141
*Net Worth:* £3,073,626 *Total Assets:* £6,763,358
*Registered Office:* Lansil Way, Caton Road, Lancaster, LA1 3QY
*Activities:* Activities of head offices
*Shareholders:* Eric Kitchen; Anthony William Kitchen
*Officers:* Anthony William Kitchen, Secretary; Anthony William Kitchen [1958] Director/Secretary; Eric Kitchen [1933] Director/Motor Engineer

**E K Motor Factors Limited**
*Incorporated:* 22 February 1965 *Employees:* 141
*Net Worth:* £2,997,814 *Total Assets:* £6,763,258
*Registered Office:* Lansil Way, Caton Road, Lancaster, LA1 3QY
*Activities:* Wholesale trade of motor vehicle parts and accessories
*Parent:* E K Holdings Limited
*Officers:* Ellen Kitchen, Secretary; Anthony William Kitchen [1958] Director/Secretary; Ellen Kitchen [1936] Director/Company Secretary; Eric Kitchen [1933] Director/Motor Engineer

**E P E International Limited**
*Incorporated:* 12 September 2003 *Employees:* 43
*Net Worth:* £2,170,366 *Total Assets:* £8,517,135
*Registered Office:* Belfry House, Roydsdale Way, Euroway Industrial Estate, Bradford, W Yorks, BD4 6SU
*Activities:* Wholesale of radio, television goods & electrical household appliances (other than records, tapes, CDs)
*Major Shareholder:* Harjinder Singh
*Officers:* Noel Pamment, Secretary; Noel Pamment [1969] Director/Distributor; Harjinder Singh [1970] Director/Distributor

**E-Factor Group Ltd**
*Incorporated:* 24 September 2007 *Employees:* 13
*Previous:* The E-Factor Enterprise (NEL) Limited
*Net Worth:* £487,113 *Total Assets:* £3,594,487
*Registered Office:* The Enterprise Village, Prince Albert Gardens, Grimsby, N E Lincs, DN31 3AT
*Activities:* Other business support service activities n.e.c.
*Officers:* Craig John McKay, Secretary; Gill Margaret Alton [1962] Director/Principal; Andrew James Goudie [1965] Project Director; Pauline Elizabeth Harness [1945] Director; Craig John McKay [1959] Director/Solicitor; Mark Fleetwood Harrison Webb [1964] Director

**E.F.C. Consultancy Limited**
*Incorporated:* 5 July 2002 *Employees:* 3
*Net Worth:* £3,281,559 *Total Assets:* £4,025,118
*Registered Office:* 33 George Street, Wakefield, W Yorks, WF1 1LX
*Activities:* Management consultancy activities other than financial management
*Major Shareholder:* Elizabeth Forbes Burrows
*Officers:* Stephen William Burrows, Secretary; Elizabeth Forbes Burrows [1975] Director/Accountant

**E.W.G.A. Limited**
*Incorporated:* 19 March 2003 *Employees:* 58
*Net Worth:* £360,194 *Total Assets:* £4,036,547
*Registered Office:* EWGA, Hyning Home Farm, Dock Acres, Warton, Lancs, LA6 1HP
*Activities:* Wholesale of wine, beer, spirits and other alcoholic beverages
*Major Shareholder:* Adrian Christopher Moeckell
*Officers:* Janette Alison McLaughlin [1969] Sales Director; Adrian Christopher Moeckell [1960] Director/Wine Importer

**Eagerlux Limited**
*Incorporated:* 19 January 1987
*Net Worth:* £4,403,583 *Total Assets:* £5,265,837
*Registered Office:* Lower Carr Barn, Station Road, Norwood Green, Halifax, W Yorks, HX3 8QD
*Activities:* Other letting and operating of own or leased real estate
*Major Shareholder:* Andrew John Mear
*Officers:* Andrew John Mear [1977] Director/Property Investor

**Eaglesure Limited**
*Incorporated:* 23 June 1992 *Employees:* 8
*Net Worth:* £3,175,640 *Total Assets:* £5,242,539
*Registered Office:* 62 Albion Street, Leeds, LS1 6AD
*Activities:* Other retail sale of new goods in specialised stores (not commercial art galleries and opticians)
*Parent:* Berens & Company Limited
*Officers:* Simon Bennett Walton [1967] Director/Jeweller

**Early Excellence Limited**
*Incorporated:* 19 August 1997 *Employees:* 52
*Net Worth:* £1,764,757 *Total Assets:* £3,246,803
*Registered Office:* The Old School, New Hey Road, Huddersfield, W Yorks, HD3 3YJ
*Activities:* Retail sale of books in specialised stores
*Major Shareholder:* Helen Elizabeth Marsden
*Officers:* Helen Elizabeth Marsden [1963] Director

**Job Earnshaw & Bros.Limited**
*Incorporated:* 11 March 1911 *Employees:* 85
*Net Worth:* £4,027,464 *Total Assets:* £7,944,610
*Registered Office:* Main Offices, Stocksmoor Road, Midgley, Wakefield, W Yorks, WF4 4JG
*Activities:* Silviculture and other forestry activities
*Officers:* Karen Esme Earnshaw, Secretary; Anthony Daniel Earnshaw [1968] Director/Timber Merchant; David Stuart Earnshaw [1935] Director/Timber Merchant; John Stuart Earnshaw [1962] Director/Timber Merchant; Peter Earnshaw [1959] Director/Timber Merchant

**Earthmill Holdings Limited**
*Incorporated:* 7 June 2013 *Employees:* 13
*Net Worth:* £2,601,754 *Total Assets:* £3,597,330
*Registered Office:* Unit 14 Follifoot Ridge Business Park, Pannal Road, Harrogate, N Yorks, HG3 1DP
*Activities:* Other specialised construction activities n.e.c.
*Parent:* Arena Capital Partners Limited
*Officers:* Rosemary Nicholson, Secretary; Barry Vincent Corcoran [1977] Director/Financial Adviser [Irish]; Thomas Alan Costello [1975] Director [Irish]; Ian Greer [1977] Director/Financial Adviser [Irish]; Stephen David Milner [1970] Director

**Earthoil Plantations Limited**
*Incorporated:* 10 April 2003 *Employees:* 5
*Net Worth:* £3,610,000 *Total Assets:* £7,683,000
*Registered Office:* Aquarius House, 6 Mid Point Business Park, Thornbury, Bradford, BD3 7AY
*Activities:* Agents specialised in the sale of other particular products
*Parent:* Univar Limited
*Officers:* Paul Graham Bryant [1973] Director; Sabine Duyfjes [1972] Director/VP & General Counsel EMEA [German]; Matthew John Ottaway [1965] Director/Vice President Focus Industries EMEA

**Easilift Loading Systems Limited**
*Incorporated:* 12 May 1976 *Employees:* 66
*Net Worth:* £1,504,143 *Total Assets:* £4,433,633
*Registered Office:* Pembroke House, Penistone Road, Kirkburton, Huddersfield, W Yorks, HD8 0LF
*Activities:* Manufacture of lifting and handling equipment
*Parent:* Loading Systems Offices BV
*Officers:* Charlotte Jane Lewis, Secretary; Robert John Fay [1968] Director; Ronald Gijsbert Van Wijk [1967] Director [Dutch]

**Easington Caravan Sites Limited**
*Incorporated:* 16 April 1962 *Employees:* 18
*Net Worth:* £1,228,016 *Total Assets:* £3,730,713
*Registered Office:* Long Beach, Easington, Hull, HU12 0TY
*Activities:* Recreational vehicle parks, trailer parks and camping grounds
*Parent:* EHLP Holdings Limited
*Officers:* Ambrose Larkham, Secretary; Ambrose Amos Larkham [1971] Director; Ambrose Larkham [1945] Director; Arron Ainsley Larkham [1983] Director; Christene Margaret Larkham [1951] Director [Australian]; William Henry Larkham [1970] Director [Australian]

**East Coast Construction (N.E.) Ltd**
*Incorporated:* 27 April 2004 *Employees:* 14
*Net Worth:* £8,563,088 *Total Assets:* £13,464,739
*Registered Office:* Ashcourt Group, Foster Street, Hull, HU8 8BT
*Activities:* Development of building projects
*Parent:* Ashcourt Contracts Limited
*Officers:* Leigh Jon Churchill, Secretary; Kurt James Nicholas Bousfield [1983] Managing Director; Nial Christian Bristow [1969] Director; Leigh Jon Churchill [1974] Finance Director; Philip Andrew Reed [1978] Director/Engineer

**East Midlands Instrument Company Limited**
*Incorporated:* 9 May 1996 *Employees:* 122
*Net Worth:* £823,641 *Total Assets:* £4,841,448
*Registered Office:* Laughton Lane, Morton, Gainsborough, Lincs, DN21 3ET
*Activities:* Electrical installation
*Parent:* East Midlands Holdings Ltd
*Officers:* Keven Paul Bingham, Secretary; Keven Paul Bingham [1959] Managing Director; Edward Keith Lovely [1968] Proposals Director

**East Riding Builders & Estate Development Company Limited**
*Incorporated:* 23 January 1947
*Net Worth:* £4,057,514 *Total Assets:* £4,304,615
*Registered Office:* 34-35 Queen Street, Bridlington, N Humbers, YO15 2SP
*Activities:* Construction of other civil engineering projects n.e.c.
*Major Shareholder:* Sally Anne Beswick
*Officers:* Sally Anne Beswick, Secretary/General Manager; Sally Anne Beswick [1950] Director/General Manager

**East Riding Holdings Company**
*Incorporated:* 28 April 1987 *Employees:* 219
*Net Worth:* £7,458,479 *Total Assets:* £34,702,680
*Registered Office:* 62-63 Westborough, Scarborough, N Yorks, YO11 1TS
*Activities:* Activities of other holding companies n.e.c.
*Officers:* Alan Brocklehurst [1964] Director/Chartered Accountant; David Barry Dunn [1956] Director/Production Manager; Paul Anthony Ewen [1963] Director/Media Executive; Mary Irene Mabbett [1951] Director/Secretary; Robert Michael Mabbett [1951] Director; Alan John Richardson [1948] Director/Retired; Paul Nicholas Whitbread [1956] Director

**East Riding Sacks Limited**
*Incorporated:* 23 February 1987 *Employees:* 124
*Net Worth:* £12,214,935 *Total Assets:* £17,122,012
*Registered Office:* 62-63 Westborough, Scarborough, N Yorks, YO11 1TS
*Activities:* manufacture of canvas goods, sacks, etc.
*Parent:* East Riding Holdings Co
*Officers:* Mary Irene Mabbett, Secretary; John Linsley [1974] Operations Director; Mary Irene Mabbett [1951] Director/Secretary; Robert Michael Mabbett [1951] Director

**East Riding Securities Limited**
*Incorporated:* 1 October 1927
*Net Worth:* £3,209,128 *Total Assets:* £3,767,630
*Registered Office:* Citadel House, 58 High Street, Hull, HU1 1QE
*Activities:* Other letting and operating of own or leased real estate
*Officers:* Simon William Watts, Secretary; Christopher Martin Watts [1988] Director/Writer; Martin Roderic Watts [1963] Director; Pamela Maxyne Watts [1941] Director; Simon William Watts [1967] Director/Journalist

**East Transportation Holdings Limited**
*Incorporated:* 21 April 2005 *Employees:* 109
*Net Worth:* £1,643,920 *Total Assets:* £9,231,951
*Registered Office:* Trondheim Way, Stallingborough, Grimsby, N E Lincs, DN41 8FD
*Activities:* Other transportation support activities
*Shareholders:* Paul Anthony Hickling; Danbrit Holdings Limited
*Officers:* Peter Aarosin [1958] Director [Danish]; Paul Anthony Hickling [1967] Director

**East Transportation Limited**
*Incorporated:* 10 May 1995 *Employees:* 109
*Net Worth:* £423,973 *Total Assets:* £5,848,791
*Registered Office:* Trondheim Way, Stallingborough, Grimsby, N E Lincs, DN41 8FD
*Activities:* Freight transport by road
*Parent:* East Transportation Holdings Limited
*Officers:* Peter Aarosin [1958] Director [Danish]; Paul Anthony Hickling [1967] Director

**East Yorkshire Aluminium & Glass Limited**
*Incorporated:* 21 October 1975 *Employees:* 71
*Net Worth:* £2,157,154 *Total Assets:* £4,079,143
*Registered Office:* Wiltshire Road, Dairycoates Industrial Estate, Hull, HU4 6QQ
*Activities:* Manufacture of builders ware of plastic
*Officers:* Roger Nicholas Harrison, Secretary; James Richard Bingham [1946] Director; Christopher George [1948] Director; Roger Nicholas Harrison [1953] Director/Company Accountant; Martin Steven Sutton [1974] Commercial Director; Steven Lee Swallow [1982] Commercial Director; Nicholas Simon Ward [1970] Director

**East Yorkshire Concrete Products Limited**
*Incorporated:* 2 April 2003
*Net Worth:* £4,939,266 *Total Assets:* £5,583,160
*Registered Office:* Happylands Farm, Dringhoe, Beeford, Driffield, E Yorks, YO25 8AG
*Activities:* Other business support service activities n.e.c.
*Shareholders:* Nigel Douglas Robinson; Philippa Jane Robinson; Alexander Douglas Robinson
*Officers:* Philippa Jane Robinson, Secretary/Manufacturer; Alexander Douglas Robinson [1975] Director/Manufacturer; Nigel Douglas Robinson [1947] Director/Manufacturer; Philippa Jane Robinson [1950] Director/Manufacturer

**Eastbay Limited**
*Incorporated:* 29 April 1966
*Net Worth:* £3,281,085 *Total Assets:* £4,423,231
*Registered Office:* Westfield Farm, Thoresby Road, Tetney, Grimsby, N E Lincs, DN36 5JS
*Activities:* Development of building projects
*Shareholder:* John Joseph Ramsden
*Officers:* John Joseph Ramsden [1965] Director

**Eastburn Farms Limited**
*Incorporated:* 8 August 1960 *Employees:* 3
*Net Worth:* £2,386,534 *Total Assets:* £5,244,107
*Registered Office:* Eastburn House, Eastburn, Driffield, E Yorks, YO25 9DP
*Activities:* Growing of cereals (except rice), leguminous crops and oil seeds
*Shareholders:* Patricia Megginson; John Derek Taylor Megginson
*Officers:* John Derek Taylor Megginson, Secretary; Charles Peter Barker [1979] Director/Chartered Accountant; John Derek Taylor Megginson [1944] Director; Patricia Megginson [1942] Director

**Eastman Staples Limited**
*Incorporated:* 3 June 1921 *Employees:* 68
*Net Worth:* £2,941,041 *Total Assets:* £6,183,430
*Registered Office:* 131 Lockwood Road, Huddersfield, W Yorks, HD1 3QW
*Activities:* Wholesale of clothing and footwear
*Major Shareholder:* Andrew Kyprianou
*Officers:* Thomas Philip Houghton, Secretary; Andrew Kyprianou [1961] Director; Petros Soterakis Kyprianou [1986] Director; Colin Ivor Werb [1950] Director

**Eastmist Limited**
*Incorporated:* 19 September 2003 *Employees:* 25
*Net Worth:* £2,421,160 *Total Assets:* £3,910,512
*Registered Office:* Fearnley Farm, Wyke Lane, Wyke, Bradford, W Yorks, BD12 9EQ
*Activities:* Freight transport by road
*Major Shareholder:* Andrew Leadbeater
*Officers:* Mavis Leadbeater, Secretary; Andrew Leabeater [1968] Director/Haulier

**Easypay Services Limited**
*Incorporated:* 2 December 2005 *Employees:* 23
*Net Worth:* £905,277 *Total Assets:* £7,455,299
*Registered Office:* Victoria House, Bradford Road, Guiseley, W Yorks, LS20 8NH
*Activities:* Other business support service activities n.e.c.
*Officers:* Amanda Jane Hobson, Secretary; Amanda Jane Hobson [1973] Director; Sarah Elizabeth Shaw [1970] Director

**Easysoft Limited**
*Incorporated:* 18 January 1993 *Employees:* 20
*Net Worth:* £5,088,242 *Total Assets:* £6,465,506
*Registered Office:* Thorp Arch Grange, Thorp Arch, Wetherby, W Yorks, LS23 7BA
*Activities:* Business and domestic software development
*Major Shareholder:* Stephen John Hill
*Officers:* Mark Morley, Secretary; Jason Stewart Crummack [1970] Director/Manager; Martin John Evans [1966] Director/Software Engineer; Nicholas Gorham [1960] Director/Technical Manager; Stephen John Hill [1963] Director; Mark Morley [1962] Director/Sales and Strategy

**Eaton Smith LLP**
*Incorporated:* 21 February 2007 *Employees:* 67
*Net Worth:* £1,916,619 *Total Assets:* £3,999,898
*Registered Office:* 14 High Street, Huddersfield, W Yorks, HD1 2HA
*Officers:* John Benjamin Cooper [1959] Member; Victoria Louise Heywood [1967] Member; Deborah Anne Melluish [1966] Member; Alison Jane Palmer [1965] Member; Michael Francis Webb [1953] Member; Adele Fiona Whitfield [1972] Member

**Ebac Group Limited**
*Incorporated:* 13 August 1997
*Net Worth:* £9,281,106 *Total Assets:* £19,141,164
*Registered Office:* Ketton Way, Aycliffe Industrial Park, Newton Aycliffe, Co Durham, DL5 6SQ
*Activities:* Other business support service activities n.e.c.
*Parent:* Ebac Holdings Ltd
*Officers:* Amanda Hird, Secretary; Graham Currie [1970] Finance Director; John Malcolm Elliott [1943] Director; Margaret Rose Elliott [1948] Director; Amanda Hird [1969] Operations Director; John Clifford Laverick [1942] Director

**Ebac Holdings Limited**
*Incorporated:* 7 April 2011 *Employees:* 257
*Net Worth:* £7,539,951 *Total Assets:* £23,954,116
*Registered Office:* Ketton Way, Aycliffe Business Park, Newton Aycliffe, Co Durham, DL5 6SR
*Activities:* Other manufacturing n.e.c.
*Parent:* Ebac Foundation
*Officers:* Amanda Hird, Secretary; John Malcolm Elliott [1943] Director; John Clifford Laverick [1942] Director

**Ebac Industrial Products Limited**
*Incorporated:* 12 November 2003 *Employees:* 30
*Net Worth:* £3,817,462 *Total Assets:* £8,636,351
*Registered Office:* St Helen Trading Estate, Bishop Auckland, Co Durham, DL14 9AD
*Activities:* Manufacture of electric domestic appliances
*Parent:* Ebac Group Ltd
*Officers:* Amanda Hird, Secretary; John Malcolm Elliott [1943] Director/Engineer; Stephen Robert Lilly [1959] Director

**Ebac Limited**
*Incorporated:* 5 January 1973 *Employees:* 223
*Net Worth:* £10,344,687 *Total Assets:* £23,696,664
*Registered Office:* Ketton Way, Aycliffe Industrial Park, Newton Aycliffe, Co Durham, DL5 6SR
*Activities:* Other manufacturing n.e.c.
*Parent:* Ebac Group Ltd
*Officers:* Amanda Hird, Secretary; Graham Currie [1970] Finance Director; John Malcolm Elliott [1943] Director/Engineer; Amanda Hird [1969] Operations Director

**Ebco (Holdings) Limited**
*Incorporated:* 18 June 2002 *Employees:* 2
*Net Worth:* £5,090,800 *Total Assets:* £6,190,259
*Registered Office:* Bowlands, Moor Lane, Bilbrough, York, YO23 3PQ
*Activities:* Activities of head offices
*Major Shareholder:* Edward Charles Barker
*Officers:* Lucy Jane Barker, Secretary; Edward Charles Barker [1971] Director

**Ebor Academy Trust**
*Incorporated:* 9 December 2013 *Employees:* 383
*Net Worth:* £13,211,000 *Total Assets:* £19,319,000
*Registered Office:* Ebor Business and Training Centre, The Leyes, Osbaldwick, York, YO10 3PR
*Activities:* Primary education
*Officers:* Andrew Robinson, Secretary; Peter David Acaster [1950] Director; Christopher Chambers [1948] Director/Trustee; Patricia Scott Ellison [1948] Director/Trustee; Duncan Anthony Fraser [1974] Director/Teacher; Susan Lesley Gradwell [1958] Director/Trustee; David Hare [1950] Director/Trustee; Richard Anthony Ludlow [1960] Director; Alan Francis Rowlinson [1943] Director; Alison Smith [1970] Director/Trustee; David Stork [1951] Director/Trustee; Rachel Totten [1951] Director/Trustee; Mark James Williamson [1973] Finance Director

**Ebus Ltd**
*Incorporated:* 29 March 2016
*Net Worth:* £5,000,000 *Total Assets:* £5,000,000
*Registered Office:* 19 Springfield, Scarborough, N Yorks, YO11 1QD
*Activities:* Management consultancy activities other than financial management
*Major Shareholder:* Clive Kevin McNally
*Officers:* Paul Nicholson [1949] Director

**Ebuyer (UK) Limited**
*Incorporated:* 7 March 2000 *Employees:* 228
*Net Worth:* £9,363,905 *Total Assets:* £35,278,404
*Registered Office:* The Nest, Falkland Way, Barton upon Humber, N Lincs, DN18 5RX
*Activities:* Retail sale via mail order houses or via Internet
*Major Shareholder:* Malcolm Stanley Healey
*Officers:* Jane Marie Oldfield, Secretary; Jane Marie Oldfield [1964] Director/Chartered Accountant; Mark Jonathan Pullan [1972] Director/Chartered Accountant; Andrew Allan Roberts [1973] E-Commerce Director; Amber Elizabeth Smith [1983] Sales Director; Lee Robert Weymouth [1981] Commercial Director

**EC Surfacing Ltd**
*Incorporated:* 18 November 2009 *Employees:* 41
*Net Worth:* £1,456,202 *Total Assets:* £3,931,040
*Registered Office:* Europa Way, off Atherton Way, Brigg, N Lincs, DN20 8UN
*Activities:* Construction of roads and motorways
*Shareholders:* Jim Huxford; Ken Drant
*Officers:* James Leslie Huxford, Secretary; Emerson Davis [1980] Director; Kenneth Drant [1956] Director; James Leslie Huxford [1970] Director; Lee Sutton [1974] Director

**Ecco Safety Group (UK) Limited**
*Incorporated:* 19 March 1946 *Employees:* 244
*Previous:* Britax PMG Limited
*Net Worth:* £25,503,252 *Total Assets:* £34,315,408
*Registered Office:* Unit 1 Green Park, Coal Road, Leeds, LS14 1FB
*Activities:* Manufacture of electrical and electronic equipment for motor vehicles and their engines
*Shareholders:* Amy Shapiro Ufberg; Richard Paul Wild; Charles Graham Berwind III; Joanna Berwind Creamer; Jessica Berwind Brummett; James Dwight Berwind
*Officers:* Marco Gunter Betsch [1972] Director [German]; Giovanni Donzelli [1966] Director [Italian]; Daniel Joseph Emmett [1960] Director [American]; Roy McClarty [1974] Director; Douglas Charles Phillips [1970] Director [American]; Enrico Vassallo [1968] Director [Italian]

**ECG Holdings (UK) Limited**
*Incorporated:* 20 April 2000
*Net Worth:* £12,469,527 *Total Assets:* £25,032,388
*Registered Office:* Albion Mills, Albion Road, Bradford, W Yorks, BD10 9TQ
*Activities:* Other business support service activities n.e.c.
*Parent:* Sun Chemical Ltd
*Officers:* Margaret Julia Pearce, Secretary; Paul Richard Bean [1960] Director/Business Manager; Gregory William Hayes [1962] Group Managing Director; Martjin Jan Charles Marie Schoonenberg [1977] Director/General Counsel [Dutch]

**Echem Limited**
*Incorporated:* 23 September 1999 *Employees:* 23
*Net Worth:* £4,666,646 *Total Assets:* £6,066,739
*Registered Office:* Burley House, 147 Kirkstall Road, Leeds, LS3 1JN
*Activities:* Manufacture of other organic basic chemicals
*Parent:* Faci UK Chemicals Limited
*Officers:* Modestino Cavaliere [1941] Managing Director of Faci Group [Italian]; Pauline Macmillan [1958] Director/Operations Manager; Franco Rossi [1951] Director/President of Faci Group [Italian]; William Warnock [1959] Director/Sales Manager

**Eco Modular Buildings Ltd**
*Incorporated:* 3 September 2010 *Employees:* 54
*Net Worth:* £747,752 *Total Assets:* £4,746,178
*Registered Office:* 31 Copenhagen Road, Hull, HU7 0XQ
*Activities:* Other manufacturing n.e.c.
*Parent:* Rawson Brook Group Holdings Limited
*Officers:* Simon Bentley Rawson [1981] Director; John Richard Waldron [1970] Director

**Eco-Power Environmental Limited**
*Incorporated:* 2 July 2013 *Employees:* 42
*Previous:* Attero Recycling Limited
*Net Worth:* £2,732,217 *Total Assets:* £11,108,231
*Registered Office:* Bankwood Lane Industrial Estate, Bankwood Lane, Rossington, Doncaster, S Yorks, DN11 0PS
*Activities:* Treatment and disposal of non-hazardous waste
*Parent:* Attero Waste Group Limited
*Officers:* Louis Calders [1971] Director; Martin James Graves [1970] Director; Lee Jepson [1983] Director; Mark Michael Jepson [1986] Director

**Econ Engineering Limited**
*Incorporated:* 9 December 1959 *Employees:* 201
*Net Worth:* £36,165,472 *Total Assets:* £55,709,648
*Registered Office:* Boroughbridge Road, Ripon, N Yorks, HG4 1UE
*Activities:* Manufacture of other special-purpose machinery n.e.c.
*Shareholders:* Andrew William Lupton; Jonathan Richard Lupton
*Officers:* Andrew William Lupton, Secretary; Andrew William Lupton [1965] Sales Director; Jonathan Richard Lupton [1968] Operations Director; Beverley Jayne Shepherd [1981] Director/Chartered Accountant

**Ecovert Group Limited**
*Incorporated:* 22 August 1996
*Net Worth:* £4,001,000 *Total Assets:* £4,058,000
*Registered Office:* 1 Park Row, Leeds, LS1 5AB
*Activities:* Activities of head offices
*Parent:* Saur (UK) Limited
*Officers:* Stephanie Thomazeau [1971] Director/Group Financial Controller [French]

**ECSC Group PLC**
*Incorporated:* 5 April 2000 *Employees:* 237
*Previous:* ECSC Group Limited
*Net Worth:* £2,385,000 *Total Assets:* £3,841,000
*Registered Office:* 28 Campus Road, Listerhills Science Park, Bradford, W Yorks, BD7 1HR
*Activities:* Information technology consultancy activities
*Officers:* David Carr Mathewson, Secretary; David Carr Mathewson [1947] Director; Elizabeth Ann Gooch [1961] Director; Ian Mann [1967] Director; Lucy Sharp [1980] Director/Consultant

**Eddison & Wanless Limited**
*Incorporated:* 18 October 1989 *Employees:* 48
*Net Worth:* £2,270,835 *Total Assets:* £3,690,601
*Registered Office:* Unit 1 Mallard Industrial Park, Horbury, Wakefield, W Yorks, WF4 5FD
*Activities:* Manufacture of other tanks, reservoirs and containers of metal
*Shareholders:* Janet Wilbraham; Philip Wilbraham
*Officers:* Andrew John Benson, Secretary/Contracts Manager; Andrew John Benson [1971] Commercial Director; Janet Wilbraham [1965] Director/Payroll Supervisor; Kevin Andrew Wilbraham [1989] Director; Philip Wilbraham [1963] Director

**Eddisons Commercial (Holdings) Limited**
*Incorporated:* 8 March 2008 *Employees:* 5
*Net Worth:* £1,468,861 *Total Assets:* £10,489,082
*Registered Office:* Toronto Square, Toronto Street, Leeds, LS1 2HJ
*Activities:* Activities of other holding companies n.e.c.
*Parent:* Begbies Traynor Group PLC
*Officers:* John Ashton Humphrey, Secretary; Richard Keith Roe [1966] Director; David Michael Hicks Rowling [1959] Director; Anthony Lavern Spencer [1969] Director/Chartered Surveyor; Edward Nicholas Taylor [1970] Director/Chartered Accountant; Richard William Traynor [1959] Director

**Eddisons Commercial Limited**
*Incorporated:* 20 November 1996 *Employees:* 159
*Net Worth:* £3,766,885 *Total Assets:* £7,652,497
*Registered Office:* Toronto Square, Toronto Street, Leeds, LS1 2HJ
*Activities:* Management of real estate on a fee or contract basis
*Parent:* Eddisons Commercial (Holdings) Limited
*Officers:* John Ashton Humphrey, Secretary; Richard Keith Roe [1966] Director; Anthony Lavern Spencer [1969] Director/Chartered Accountant

**Eden Holdings (UK) Limited**
*Incorporated:* 27 March 2001 *Employees:* 134
*Net Worth:* £5,335,000 *Total Assets:* £6,937,941
*Registered Office:* 16-20 High Street East, Scunthorpe, N Lincs, DN15 6UH
*Activities:* Other letting and operating of own or leased real estate
*Shareholders:* David Owen Hughes; Karl Adam Howe
*Officers:* David Owen Hughes, Secretary; Karl Adam Howe [1964] Director/Senior Executive; David Owen Hughes [1963] Director/Mobility Salesman

**Eden Rock Estates Limited**
*Incorporated:* 16 November 2006
*Net Worth:* £10,064,976 *Total Assets:* £18,921,228
*Registered Office:* Stanley Harrison House, The Chocolate Works, Bishopthorpe Road, York, YO23 1DE
*Activities:* Development of building projects
*Major Shareholder:* Marytn Robert Harrison
*Officers:* Ann Pearce Scott, Company Secretary; Martyn Robert Harrison [1959] Director; Ann Pearce Scott [1962] Director/Company Secretary

**Edmondsons (Freightliners) Limited**
*Incorporated:* 11 February 1970 *Employees:* 121
*Net Worth:* £1,443,518 *Total Assets:* £3,398,734
*Registered Office:* Southgate, White Lund Industrial Estate, Morecambe, Lancs, LA3 3PB
*Activities:* Freight transport by road
*Shareholders:* Frederick Garry Edmondson; Peter James Edmondson
*Officers:* Frederick Garry Edmondson, Secretary; Frederick Garry Edmondson [1950] Director/Haulier; Jonathan Russell Edmondson [1972] Director/Haulier; Peter James Edmondson [1949] Director/Haulier; Simon Peter Edmondson [1973] Director

**Edmund Optics Ltd.**
*Incorporated:* 6 November 1998 *Employees:* 28
*Net Worth:* £3,980,043 *Total Assets:* £7,113,301
*Registered Office:* 1 Opus Avenue, Nether Poppleton, York, YO26 6BL
*Activities:* Other retail sale not in stores, stalls or markets
*Officers:* Mark Rowlinson, Secretary; Marisa Edmund [1976] Marketing Director [American]; Mark Rowlinson [1971] Director/Management Accountant

**The Education Alliance**
*Incorporated:* 24 February 2011 *Employees:* 634
*Previous:* Hunsley Trust
*Net Worth:* £104,612,000 *Total Assets:* £114,375,000
*Registered Office:* South Hunsley School & Sixth Form College, East Dale Road, Melton, North Ferriby, E Yorks, HU14 3HS
*Activities:* General secondary education
*Officers:* Lisa Andrea Pipes, Secretary; Ann Barker [1939] Director/Retired; Andrew David Bradley [1970] Director/Trustee; Paddy John Creighton Hall [1945] Director/Consultant; Paul Nicholson [1970] IT Director; Shane Nicholson [1968] Director/Trustee; Andrew Mark Steele [1971] Financial Director; Richard Mark Swain [1968] Director/Engineer; Nicola Jane Wicks [1961] Director/Lead Midwife for Education

**Education PFI Investments Limited**
*Incorporated:* 18 November 2011 *Employees:* 2
*Net Worth Deficit:* £1,026,521 *Total Assets:* £10,457,146
*Registered Office:* 4 Greengate, Cardale Park, Harrogate, N Yorks, HG3 1GY
*Activities:* Activities of head offices
*Parent:* Grosvenor PFI Holdings Limited
*Officers:* Alexander Toby Parry, Secretary; Alastair William Hopps [1986] Director/Accountant; Alexander Toby Shedden Parry [1976] Director/Commercial Manager

**The Education Village Academy Trust**
*Incorporated:* 22 August 2011 *Employees:* 319
*Net Worth:* £21,957,000 *Total Assets:* £27,073,000
*Registered Office:* The Education Village, Salters Lane South, Darlington, Co Durham, DL1 2AN
*Activities:* Primary education
*Officers:* Christopher John Ashford [1964] Director/Multi Agency Safeguarding Trainer; Michael Butler [1968] Director; Allan Christopher Dixon [1981] Director/Accountant; Helen Radcliffe [1952] Director/Head of Apprenticeships-Business Development; Ramandeep Singh Sanghera [1987] Director/Chartered Accountant; Heather Irene Scott [1940] Director/Councillor; Shirley Anne Welsh [1966] Director/Headteacher; Deborah Louise Wood [1970] Director/University Administrator

**P.J. Edwards & Co. (UK) Ltd.**
*Incorporated:* 1 June 1987
*Net Worth Deficit:* £685,372 *Total Assets:* £4,167,958
*Registered Office:* Unit 4 Bessemer Way, Sawcliffe Industrial Park, Scunthorpe, N Lincs, DN15 8XE
*Activities:* Construction of other civil engineering projects n.e.c.
*Parent:* Edwards Plant Hire Ltd
*Officers:* Gregory James Edwards, Secretary; Gregory James Edwards [1963] Director/Civil Engineer [Irish]; Joseph Edwards [1927] Director/Contractor [Irish]

**Edwards Excavations Limited**
*Incorporated:* 19 October 1990 *Employees:* 11
*Net Worth:* £3,104,043 *Total Assets:* £3,645,263
*Registered Office:* Woodman Works, South Lane, Elland, W Yorks, HX5 0PA
*Activities:* Site preparation
*Major Shareholder:* Martin Edward Ashworth
*Officers:* Joanne Lesley Ashworth, Secretary; Martin Edward Ashworth [1962] Director/Plant Hire Contractor; Robin Edward Ashworth [1936] Director/Builder & Excavator

**Effective Security Services Limited**
*Incorporated:* 2 February 2005
*Net Worth:* £2,826,019 *Total Assets:* £4,300,405
*Registered Office:* Crown Point House, 110 Hunslet Lane, Leeds, LS10 1ES
*Activities:* Investigation activities
*Parent:* Effective Security Holdings Limited
*Officers:* David John Fullerton [1979] Managing Director

**EFS Chalfont Limited**
*Incorporated:* 18 May 1994
*Net Worth:* £3,396,414 *Total Assets:* £4,169,402
*Registered Office:* Premier House, 2 Jubilee Way, Elland, W Yorks, HX5 9DY
*Activities:* Other letting and operating of own or leased real estate
*Parent:* EFS Group Limited
*Officers:* Richard John Pollard, Secretary; Richard John Pollard [1963] Director/Company Secretary; Emmanuel David Oliver Adrien Sebag [1968] Director; Joel Lawrence Simmonds [1967] Director/Chartered Surveyor

**EFS Group Limited**
*Incorporated:* 8 December 1993 *Employees:* 2
*Net Worth:* £9,664,000 *Total Assets:* £11,070,000
*Registered Office:* Premier House, 2 Jubilee Way, Elland, W Yorks, HX5 9DY
*Activities:* Activities of head offices
*Parent:* EOI European Overseas Investments SARL
*Officers:* Richard John Pollard, Secretary; Jacques Gaston Murray [1920] Director; Jean Jacques Murray [1966] Director; Richard John Pollard [1963] Director/Chartered Accountant; Emmanuel David Oliver Adrien Sebag [1968] Director; Joel Lawrence Simmonds [1967] Director/Chartered Surveyor [American]

**EFS Property Holdings Limited**
*Incorporated:* 5 April 1995 *Employees:* 2
*Net Worth:* £5,087,079 *Total Assets:* £6,542,999
*Registered Office:* Premier House, 2 Jubilee Way, Elland, W Yorks, HX5 9DY
*Activities:* Activities of head offices
*Parent:* EFS Group Limited
*Officers:* Richard John Pollard, Secretary; Jacques Gaston Murray [1920] Director; Jean Jacques Murray [1966] Director; Richard John Pollard [1963] Director/Chartered Accountant; Emmanuel David Oliver Adrien Sebag [1968] Director; Joel Lawrence Simmonds [1967] Director/Chartered Surveyor [American]

**Egg Homes Limited**
*Incorporated:* 17 October 2012
*Previous:* Equity Growth Homes Limited
*Net Worth Deficit:* £229,067 *Total Assets:* £3,620,492
*Registered Office:* 3 Dalton Hall Business Centre, Burton in Kendal, Cumbria, LA6 1BL
*Activities:* Development of building projects
*Major Shareholder:* Christopher John Nelson
*Officers:* Christopher John Nelson [1973] Director/Property Manager

**Eggborough Power Limited**
*Incorporated:* 4 June 1999 *Employees:* 229
*Net Worth Deficit:* £17,000,000 *Total Assets:* £94,000,000
*Registered Office:* Eggborough Power Station, Eggborough, Goole, E Yorks, DN14 0BS
*Activities:* Production of electricity
*Parent:* EP UK Investments Ltd
*Officers:* Tarloke Singh Bains [1968] Director/Chartered Accountant; Adam Charles Booth [1976] Director/Chartered Accountant; Pavel Horsky [1973] Director [Czech]; Daniel Kretinsky [1975] Director [Czech]; Jan Springl [1978] Director [Czech]; Marek Spurny [1974] Director [Czech]

**Egton Medical Information Systems Limited**
*Incorporated:* 31 March 1987 *Employees:* 994
*Net Worth:* £46,155,308 *Total Assets:* £107,616,688
*Registered Office:* Rawdon House, Green Lane, Yeadon, Leeds, LS19 7BY
*Activities:* Business and domestic software development
*Officers:* Christine Benson, Secretary; Dr Shaun O'Hanlon [1964] Director/Chief Medical Officer; Peter John Southby [1973] Director; Ian Taylor [1967] Director; Andrew John Thorburn [1962] Director; Stephen John Wilcock [1967] Director

**EHIF (Denmark) Limited**
*Incorporated:* 22 October 2003
*Net Worth:* £28,117,124 *Total Assets:* £28,147,366
*Registered Office:* 1st Floor, Unit 16 Manor Court Business Park, Scarborough, N Yorks, YO11 3TU
*Activities:* Dormant company
*Parent:* EHIF Limited
*Officers:* Thierry Hubert Francois Leleu [1967] Director/Chief Investment Officer [French]; Paul Christian Roger Weber [1987] Director/Legal Counsel [Luxembourger]

**EHLP Holdings Limited**
*Incorporated:* 19 April 2007
*Net Worth:* £3,017,832 *Total Assets:* £3,017,832
*Registered Office:* Easington Caravan Park, Easington Beach, Easington, E Yorks, HU12 0TY
*Activities:* Non-trading company
*Shareholders:* Ambrose Larkham; Christene Margaret Larkham
*Officers:* Ambrose Larkham, Secretary; Ambrose Larkham [1945] Director; Christene Margaret Larkham [1951] Director [Australian]

**Eido Limited**
*Incorporated:* 29 September 1999 *Employees:* 3
*Net Worth:* £2,848,162 *Total Assets:* £6,295,456
*Registered Office:* Suite 4, Regent House, Hawthorn Road, Leeds, LS7 4PH
*Activities:* Development of building projects
*Shareholders:* Michael Rollins; Paula Ann Tod; Ian James Tod
*Officers:* Ian James Tod, Secretary/Architect; Michael Rollins [1949] Director; Ian James Tod [1945] Director/Designer

**Eimskip UK Limited**
*Incorporated:* 23 January 1912 *Employees:* 40
*Net Worth:* £6,028,712 *Total Assets:* £6,833,338
*Registered Office:* Eimskip, Middleplatt Road, Immingham, N E Lincs, DN40 1AH
*Activities:* Service activities incidental to water transportation
*Parent:* Eimskpafelag Islands Hf
*Officers:* Graham John McRae Walker, Secretary/Chartered Accountant; Michael Peter Lane [1973] Managing Director; Bragi Thor Marinosson [1965] Director [Icelander]; Egill Orn Petersen [1974] Director [Icelander]; Vilhelm Mar Thorsteinsson [1971] Director [Icelander]; Graham John McRae Walker [1963] Director/Chartered Accountant

**Eldercliff Limited**
*Incorporated:* 11 April 2006
*Net Worth:* £1,510,700 *Total Assets:* £6,107,408
*Registered Office:* 37 Otley Road, Leeds, LS6 3AB
*Activities:* Activities of business and employers membership organisations
*Shareholders:* Ann Jennifer Gilman; Irving Simon Lee Gilman
*Officers:* Ann Jennifer Gilman, Secretary/Property; Ann Jennifer Gilman [1948] Director/Property; Irving Simon Lee Gilman [1959] Director/Property

**Eldred (1982) Holdings Limited**
*Incorporated:* 20 May 1982 *Employees:* 5
*Net Worth:* £3,564,790 *Total Assets:* £6,111,096
*Registered Office:* Carrside, Hatfield, Doncaster, S Yorks, DN7 6AZ
*Activities:* Operation of warehousing and storage facilities for land transport activities
*Officers:* Kathleen Jane Eldred, Secretary; Martin Eldred [1959] Director; Tom George Eldred [1990] Director

**Electric Support Limited**
*Incorporated:* 13 April 2006 *Employees:* 3
*Net Worth:* £717,976 *Total Assets:* £3,127,488
*Registered Office:* 5 Hawthorn Park, Coal Road, Leeds, LS14 1PQ
*Activities:* Buying and selling of own real estate
*Parent:* Rushbond PLC
*Officers:* Richard Mark Powell, Secretary; Mark Richard Finch [1967] Director/Chartered Surveyor Chartered Town Planner; Jonathan William Maud [1960] Director; Richard Mark Powell [1967] Director/Chartered Accountant

**Electricity Distribution Services Limited**
*Incorporated:* 26 March 2003 *Employees:* 30
*Net Worth:* £2,626,204 *Total Assets:* £5,493,416
*Registered Office:* P O Box 4, Fisher House, Barrow in Furness, Cumbria, LA14 1HR
*Activities:* Electrical installation
*Officers:* James Henry John Marsh, Secretary; Fergus Hugh Stirling Graham [1973] Marine Support Director; Stuart Charles Kilpatrick [1962] Director; Kenton John Ritson [1963] Director/Electrical Contractor; Simon Timothy Boissier Wyles [1968] Director

**Electrix International Limited**
*Incorporated:* 25 June 1981 *Employees:* 61
*Net Worth:* £4,229,796 *Total Assets:* £8,385,830
*Registered Office:* Dovecot Hill, South Church Enterprise Park, Bishop Auckland, Co Durham, DL14 6XP
*Activities:* Manufacture of other fabricated metal products n.e.c.
*Major Shareholder:* Malcolm Thompson
*Officers:* Dorothy Thompson, Secretary; Christopher Paul Thompson [1982] Operations Director; Malcolm Thompson [1950] Director/Business Manager

**Element 14 Limited**
*Incorporated:* 4 July 1994
*Net Worth:* £38,304,000 *Total Assets:* £40,948,000
*Registered Office:* 150 Armley Road, Leeds, LS12 2QQ
*Activities:* Non-trading company
*Parent:* InOne Holdings Limited
*Officers:* Liam Heffernan [1972] Director/Accountant [American]; Harvey Woodford [1963] Director/VP Corporate Secretary [American]

**Element UK Bidco Limited**
*Incorporated:* 10 March 2017 *Employees:* 4
*Net Worth Deficit:* £9,500,000 *Total Assets:* £149,200,000
*Registered Office:* c/o Karro Food Limited, Norton Grove Industrial Estate, Hugden Way, Norton, Malton, N Yorks, YO17 9NE
*Activities:* Other business support service activities n.e.c.
*Parent:* Element UK Midco Limited
*Officers:* Tim Colson [1985] Investment Director; Stephen Paul Ellis [1971] Director; Seamus Philip Fitzpatrick [1966] Director/Partner [Irish]; Michael Kamiel Jan Alfons Kestemont [1978] Director [Belgian]; Jason Rodrigues [1982] Director

**Element UK Holdco Limited**
*Incorporated:* 10 March 2017
*Total Assets:* £81,900,000
*Registered Office:* c/o Karro Food Limited, Norton Grove Industrial Estate, Hugden Way, Norton, Malton, N Yorks, YO17 9NE
*Activities:* Activities of other holding companies n.e.c.
*Parent:* Element UK Topco Limited
*Officers:* Tim Colson [1985] Investment Director; Seamus Philip Fitzpatrick [1966] Director/Partner [Irish]; Jason Rodrigues [1982] Director

**Element UK Midco Limited**
*Incorporated:* 10 March 2017 *Employees:* 4,065
*Net Worth Deficit:* £4,700,000 *Total Assets:* £279,800,000
*Registered Office:* c/o Karro Food Limited, Norton Grove Industrial Estate, Hugden Way, Norton, Malton, N Yorks, YO17 9NE
*Activities:* Activities of other holding companies n.e.c.
*Parent:* Element UK Holdco Limited
*Officers:* Tim Colson [1985] Investment Director; Seamus Philip Fitzpatrick [1966] Director/Partner [Irish]; Jason Rodrigues [1982] Director

**Element UK Topco Limited**
*Incorporated:* 10 March 2017 *Employees:* 4,065
*Net Worth:* £77,100,000 *Total Assets:* £279,800,000
*Registered Office:* c/o Karro Food Limited, Norton Grove Industrial Estate, Hugden Way, Norton, Malton, N Yorks, YO17 9NE
*Activities:* Activities of other holding companies n.e.c.
*Officers:* Seamus Carr [1960] Director [Irish]; Tim Colson [1985] Investment Director; Stephen Paul Ellis [1971] Director; Seamus Philip Fitzpatrick [1966] Director/Partner [Irish]; Michael Kamiel Jan Alfons Kestemont [1978] Director [Belgian]; Michael Parker [1953] Director; Jason Rodrigues [1982] Director; Diane Susan Walker [1972] Director

**Element14 Finance UK Limited**
*Incorporated:* 2 March 2012
*Net Worth:* £100,706,096 *Total Assets:* £110,437,592
*Registered Office:* 150 Armley Road, Leeds, LS12 2QQ
*Activities:* Activities of distribution holding companies
*Parent:* InOne Holdings Limited
*Officers:* Liam Anthony Heffernan [1972] Director/Accountant [Irish]; Harvey Woodford [1963] Director/VP Corporate Secretary [American]

**Eleonora Sport Limited**
*Incorporated:* 27 January 2014 *Employees:* 2
*Net Worth:* £31,074,836 *Total Assets:* £31,122,922
*Registered Office:* New Court, Abbey Road North, Shepley, Huddersfield, W Yorks, HD8 8BJ
*Activities:* Activities of other holding companies n.e.c.
*Officers:* Daniel Arty [1960] Director/Certified Public Accountant [American]; Massimo Cellino [1956] Director/President [Italian]

**Elevate Multi Academy Trust**
*Incorporated:* 12 June 2017
*Net Worth:* £8,512,535 *Total Assets:* £9,653,428
*Registered Office:* Halfpenny Lane, Knaresborough, N Yorks, HG5 0SL
*Activities:* Primary education
*Officers:* Dianne Mousley, Secretary; Nigel Ashley [1975] Director/Headteacher; David Blanchfield [1975] Director/Civil Servant; John Westwood Brear [1959] Director/Chartered Accountant; Dr Elizabeth June Foster [1948] Director/Education Consultant; Katherine Mary Humpleby [1978] Director/Education Adviser; Graham Richard Shaw [1973] Director/Solicitor; Rev Nigel Craig Sinclair [1965] Director/Clergy; Alison Wilson [1978] Director/Civil Servant

**Eleven Arches**
*Incorporated:* 23 May 2014 *Employees:* 13
*Net Worth:* £26,914,998 *Total Assets:* £33,142,104
*Registered Office:* Flatts Farm, Toronto, Bishop Auckland, Co Durham, DL14 7SF
*Activities:* Performing arts
*Officers:* Louis Stourton Greig [1956] Director/Private Banker; Stefa Janita McManners [1949] Director/Retired Headteacher; Jonathan Garnier Ruffer [1951] Director/Chairman of Auckland Castle Trust; Dennis Tindall [1946] Director/Catholic Priest; Nicholas Timothy Turner [1961] Director/Retired

**Elite Office Furniture (UK) Ltd.**
*Incorporated:* 6 May 1997 *Employees:* 136
*Net Worth:* £22,024,150 *Total Assets:* £24,452,628
*Registered Office:* Britannia Way, Goole, E Yorks, DN14 6ES
*Activities:* Manufacture of office and shop furniture
*Major Shareholder:* John Hull
*Officers:* Robert Clarke [1972] Production Director; Andrew Jason Hull [1972] Seating Director; John Hull [1950] Director; Julian Andrew Jowett [1976] Sales Director

**Elite Systems (GB) Limited**
*Incorporated:* 19 February 1991 *Employees:* 28
*Net Worth:* £4,465,058 *Total Assets:* £5,395,832
*Registered Office:* Elite Systems, Bedford Street, Westgate, Cleckheaton, W Yorks, BD19 5EA
*Activities:* Other manufacturing n.e.c.
*Shareholder:* Anthony Sutcliffe
*Officers:* Lynda Jennifer Sutcliffe, Secretary; Anthony Sutcliffe [1948] Director; Lynda Jennifer Sutcliffe [1950] Director; Marcus Oliver Sutcliffe [1975] Director

**Elitebliss Limited**
*Incorporated:* 24 December 1996
*Net Worth:* £1,642,258 *Total Assets:* £3,954,799
*Registered Office:* Elite Buildings, off Haincliffe Road, Keighley, W Yorks, BD21 5BU
*Activities:* Wholesale of hardware, plumbing and heating equipment and supplies
*Shareholders:* Madan Mohan Abrol; Meena Abrol
*Officers:* Madan Mohan Abrol [1960] Director

**The Elizabethan Academy Trust**
*Incorporated:* 24 February 2012 *Employees:* 140
*Net Worth:* £15,505,561 *Total Assets:* £18,400,954
*Registered Office:* The Elizabethan Academy, Hallcroft Road, Retford, Notts, DN22 7PY
*Activities:* General secondary education
*Officers:* Christopher James Pedrozo D'Albuquerque, Secretary; Dr Derek Cheetham [1947] Director/Retired; Martin Meredith Evans [1965] Managing Director; Richard Colin Green [1955] Director/Retired; Christine Alice Horrocks [1965] Director/Academy Principal; Kathryn Lindsay Jones [1955] Director/Events & Conference Manager; Anthony Neil Leake [1965] Director; Matthew Lister [1990] Director/Teacher; Tony Mason [1966] Director/Teacher; Jacqueline McRory [1972] Director/Office Manager; Shaun Procter-Green [1967] Director/Teacher; Claire Turner [1972] Director/Office Manager; Stephen Walker [1956] Director/Businessman; Terry Robert Wright [1976] Director/Teacher

**Elland Steel Structures (UK) Limited**
*Incorporated:* 21 November 2007 *Employees:* 111
*Net Worth:* £9,214,392 *Total Assets:* £15,173,802
*Registered Office:* Philmar House, Gibbet Street, Halifax, W Yorks, HX2 0AR
*Activities:* Activities of head offices
*Shareholder:* Mark Denham
*Officers:* Antony Denham, Secretary; Antony Denham [1971] Director/Accountant; Daphne Marilyn Denham [1946] Director/Wages Clerk Secretary; Keith Denham [1946] Director/Engineer; Mark Denham [1969] Director/Structural Engineer

**Elland Steel Structures Limited**
*Incorporated:* 6 April 1982 *Employees:* 110
*Net Worth:* £8,921,350 *Total Assets:* £13,462,442
*Registered Office:* Philmar House, Gibbet Street, Halifax, W Yorks, HX2 0AR
*Activities:* Manufacture of metal structures and parts of structures
*Shareholders:* Mark Denham; Elland Steel Structures (UK) Limited
*Officers:* Kelly Denham, Secretary; Daphne Marilyn Denham [1946] Director/Secretary & Wages Clerk; Keith Denham [1946] Director/Engineer; Mark Denham [1969] Director/Design Engineer; Paul Kitching [1968] Director; Jeremy Lees Shorrocks [1965] Director/Contracts Estimator; Andrew Sutcliffe [1973] Director

**Ralph Ellerker (1795) Limited**
*Incorporated:* 8 April 1975 *Employees:* 75
*Net Worth:* £4,967,204 *Total Assets:* £6,852,614
*Registered Office:* Lion Works, Whitehouse Street, Hunslet, Leeds, LS10 1AD
*Activities:* Manufacture of other fabricated metal products n.e.c.
*Officers:* Christine Isobel Schofield, Secretary; Alan Paul Hirst [1968] Sales Director; Andrew Alan Lane [1964] Managing Director; Antony Stuart Metcalfe [1967] Operations Director; Christine Isobel Schofield [1946] Director/Chairman

**Bell Elliot Leisure Limited**
*Incorporated:* 30 June 1969 *Employees:* 18
*Net Worth:* £4,872,318 *Total Assets:* £6,443,571
*Registered Office:* Highfield House, 7 Filey Road, Gristhorpe, Filey, N Yorks, YO14 9PH
*Activities:* Recreational vehicle parks, trailer parks and camping grounds
*Shareholder:* George Dale
*Officers:* Maxine Elson, Secretary; George Dale [1939] Director

**J.T.Ellis and Company Limited**
*Incorporated:* 30 October 1902 *Employees:* 221
*Net Worth:* £8,822,973 *Total Assets:* £13,094,966
*Registered Office:* Silver Street, Huddersfield, W Yorks, HD5 9BA
*Activities:* Manufacture of other furniture
*Parent:* JTE Holdco Ltd
*Officers:* Nicola Nixon, Secretary; Richard Paul Ellis [1968] Director; Thomas George Ellis [1973] Director

**Joshua Ellis and Company,Limited**
*Incorporated:* 13 October 1900 *Employees:* 55
*Net Worth:* £600,582 *Total Assets:* £6,929,004
*Registered Office:* Grange Valley Road, Batley, W Yorks, WF17 6GH
*Activities:* Preparation and spinning of textile fibres
*Parent:* SIL Holdings Limited
*Officers:* Alisa Jayne Edwards-Hinchliffe [1983] Director/Certified Chartered Accountant; Oliver Cameron Platts [1982] Director; Kristie Reeves [1974] Sales and Design Director; Andrew David Seal [1957] Director; Jeremy Charles Seal [1960] Director; Steven Trevor Wilson [1968] Production Director

**Ellis Patents Holdings Limited**
*Incorporated:* 7 February 2012 *Employees:* 67
*Net Worth:* £6,211,456 *Total Assets:* £7,572,219
*Registered Office:* Ellis Patents Holdings Ltd, High Street, Rillington, Malton, N Yorks, YO17 8LA
*Activities:* Manufacture of other plastic products
*Shareholder:* Michael John Saunders
*Officers:* Diane Holmes, Secretary; Christopher John Calvert [1939] Director; Neil Richard Oates Foreman [1946] Director/Chartered Surveyor; Richard Martin Lowish [1952] Director/Retired [American]; Martin Gerard Mullin [1966] Director/Senior VP & GM; Nicholas John Nightingale [1942] Director/Company Secretary; Peter Bertram James Sargent [1932] Director/Chartered Accountant; Richard Armitage Shaw [1957] Director; John Martin Weaving [1959] Director

**Ellis Patents Limited**
*Incorporated:* 13 January 1977 *Employees:* 64
*Net Worth:* £4,469,517 *Total Assets:* £5,879,154
*Registered Office:* High Street, Rillington, Malton, N Yorks, YO17 8LA
*Activities:* Manufacture of other plastic products
*Parent:* Ellis Patents Holdings Ltd
*Officers:* Diane Holmes, Secretary; Christopher John Calvert [1939] Director; Richard Bernard Chambers [1968] Finance Director; Anthony Thomas Conroy [1970] Export Sales Director; Diane Holmes [1970] Purchasing Director; Richard Martin Lowish [1952] Director [American]; Danny MacFarlane [1971] Operations Director; Nicholas John Nightingale [1942] Director/Company Secretary; Richard Armitage Shaw [1957] Director; John Martin Weaving [1959] Director/Accountant

**Elm Bank (Northumberland) Limited**
*Incorporated:* 11 January 2006 *Employees:* 15
*Net Worth:* £3,318,126 *Total Assets:* £8,287,380
*Registered Office:* Marton Hall, Church Lane, Sewerby, Bridlington, E Yorks, YO15 1DS
*Activities:* Recreational vehicle parks, trailer parks and camping grounds
*Shareholders:* Richard John Roberts; KMA Properties Limited
*Officers:* Richard John Roberts, Secretary/Sales Manager; David Robert Allison [1960] Director/Park Owner; Richard John Roberts [1963] Director/Sales Manager; Neil Willson [1960] Managing Director

**Elmet Investments**
*Incorporated:* 15 April 2016 *Employees:* 2
*Net Worth:* £1,499,855 *Total Assets:* £18,146,906
*Registered Office:* Cresswells, Barclays Bank Chambers, Market Street, Hebden Bridge, W Yorks, HX7 6AD
*Activities:* Fund management activities
*Shareholders:* David Stephen Jagger; Anne Suzette Jagger
*Officers:* David Stephen Jagger, Secretary; Anne Suzette Jagger [1951] Director/Retired; David Stephen Jagger [1952] Director/Retired

**Elmwood Design Limited**
*Incorporated:* 13 March 1989 *Employees:* 120
*Net Worth:* £3,739,496 *Total Assets:* £6,811,926
*Registered Office:* 105 Water Lane, Leeds, LS11 5WD
*Activities:* Artistic creation
*Major Shareholder:* Jonathan Peter Sands
*Officers:* Deborah Longbottom, Secretary; Stephen John Gatfield [1958] Director/Chairman; Deborah Longbottom [1968] Director/Accountant; Jonathan Peter Sands [1961] Director/Chairman; Gregory Paul Taylor [1962] Marketing Director; Sarah Louise Wilson [1968] Managing Director

**Elmwood Property Investments Limited**
*Incorporated:* 17 March 1999
*Net Worth:* £3,688,266 *Total Assets:* £7,919,345
*Registered Office:* Dalton House, 9 Dalton Square, Lancaster, LA1 1WD
*Activities:* Development of building projects
*Shareholders:* Philip Andrew Noblett; Paul Francis Noblett; Karl Michael Noblett
*Officers:* Phillip Andrew Noblett, Secretary; Karl Michael Noblett [1963] Director/Builder; Paul Francis Noblett [1960] Director/Builder; Phillip Andrew Noblett [1964] Director/Builder

**Elsham Linc Limited**
*Incorporated:* 2 August 2005 *Employees:* 75
*Net Worth:* £8,458,023 *Total Assets:* £16,355,370
*Registered Office:* Cadas House, Wootton Road, Elsham Top, Brigg, N Lincs, DN20 0NU
*Activities:* Raising of swine and pigs
*Shareholders:* Alexander Godfrey; Samuel Godfrey
*Officers:* Karin Elizabeth Lund, Secretary; Alexander Godfrey [1978] Director/Farmer; James Eric Godfrey [1953] Director; Sam Godfrey [1980] Director/Farmer

**Elsham Wold Estates Limited**
*Incorporated:* 12 June 2007 *Employees:* 106
*Net Worth:* £14,215,336 *Total Assets:* £26,342,422
*Registered Office:* Kahawa House, Elsham Wold Industrial Estate, Elsham, Brigg, N Lincs, DN20 0SP
*Activities:* Activities of other holding companies n.e.c.
*Shareholders:* Simon David Herring; James Timothy Sweeting
*Officers:* Nigel John Bean, Secretary; Simon David Herring [1964] Director; James Timothy Sweeting [1969] Director

**Eltham Properties Limited**
*Incorporated:* 23 April 1958 *Employees:* 2
*Net Worth:* £5,348,535 *Total Assets:* £7,944,296
*Registered Office:* 30-35 Westgate, Huddersfield, W Yorks, HD1 1PA
*Activities:* Development of building projects
*Parent:* Leatham Holdings Limited
*Officers:* Thelma Leatham, Secretary; Joanne Leatham [1974] Director; Mark Andrew Leatham [1962] Director; Richard George Leatham [1959] Director; Thelma Leatham [1935] Director

**Eltherington Group Limited**
*Incorporated:* 2 February 1960 *Employees:* 176
*Net Worth:* £20,247,024 *Total Assets:* £23,686,984
*Registered Office:* Eltherington Business Park, 1305 Hedon Road, Hull, HU9 5QD
*Activities:* Activities of head offices
*Shareholders:* Anthony Graham Eltherington; Patricia Scorgie
*Officers:* Keith James Billinge [1956] Director/Accountant; Craig Anthony Dunn [1970] Director; Anthony Graham Eltherington [1942] Director/Technician; Antony Mark Eltherington [1971] Director; David Anthony Johnson [1965] Director; Patricia Scorgie [1937] Director; Guy Robert Stubbs [1959] Director

**Eltherington Industries Limited**
*Incorporated:* 25 September 2002 *Employees:* 136
*Net Worth:* £9,451,705 *Total Assets:* £12,303,513
*Registered Office:* Eltherington Business Park, 1305 Hedon Road, Hull, HU9 5QD
*Activities:* Manufacture of other plastic products
*Shareholders:* Anthony Graham Eltherington; Patricia Scorgie
*Officers:* Keith James Billinge [1956] Director/Accountant; Anthony Graham Eltherington [1942] Director/Technician; Antony Mark Eltherington [1971] Director; Guy Robert Stubbs [1959] Commercial Director

**Elvaston Investments Limited**
*Incorporated:* 1 October 1982 *Employees:* 3
*Net Worth:* £6,249,009 *Total Assets:* £8,980,586
*Registered Office:* 3 Acorn Business Park, Airedale Business Centre, Skipton, N Yorks, BD23 2UE
*Activities:* Buying and selling of own real estate
*Major Shareholder:* Earl of Charles Henry Leicester Harrington
*Officers:* William Henry Leicester Stanhope, Company Secretary; Martin James Wynne Scriven [1945] Director/Chartered Accountant; William Henry Leicester Stanhope [1967] Director/Company Secretary

**Elvaston Properties Limited**
*Incorporated:* 9 May 1997 *Employees:* 3
*Net Worth:* £3,126,292 *Total Assets:* £4,917,576
*Registered Office:* Holes Beck House, Hartlington, Skipton, N Yorks, BD23 5EE
*Activities:* Other letting and operating of own or leased real estate
*Major Shareholder:* The Earl of Harrington Charles Henry Leicester Stanhope
*Officers:* Martin James Wynne Scriven, Secretary; Martin James Wynne Scriven [1945] Director/Chartered Accountant; William Henry Leicester Stanhope [1967] Director

**Elvington Holdings Limited**
*Incorporated:* 5 February 1974 *Employees:* 36
*Net Worth:* £2,213,666 *Total Assets:* £3,944,619
*Registered Office:* Unit G4, Elvington Industrial Estate, York Road, Elvington, York, YO41 4AR
*Activities:* Other letting and operating of own or leased real estate
*Shareholders:* Susan Elizabeth Garland; Kenneth Garland
*Officers:* Susan Elizabeth Garland, Secretary; Kenneth Garland [1936] Director; Richard Kenneth Garland [1979] Director; Susan Elizabeth Garland [1952] Director; Timothy Nicholas Garland [1983] Business Development Director

**Emacrow Holdings Limited**
*Incorporated:* 3 December 1999 *Employees:* 3
*Net Worth:* £4,743,674 *Total Assets:* £4,743,674
*Registered Office:* 5th Floor, Central Square, 29 Wellington Street, Leeds, LS1 4DL
*Activities:* Non-trading company
*Shareholders:* Andrew Crowther; Mark Crowther
*Officers:* Andrew Crowther, Secretary; Andrew Crowther [1957] Director/Engineer; Edwin Frederick Crowther [1929] Director/Precision Engineer; Mark Crowther [1960] Director/Engineer

**Emacrow Limited**
*Incorporated:* 3 December 1999 *Employees:* 3
*Net Worth:* £6,416,324 *Total Assets:* £9,452,108
*Registered Office:* 5th Floor, Central Square, 29 Wellington Street, Leeds, LS1 4DL
*Activities:* Renting and operating of Housing Association real estate
*Parent:* Emacrow Holdings Limited
*Officers:* Andrew Crowther, Secretary; Andrew Crowther [1957] Director/Engineer; Edwin Frederick Crowther [1929] Director/Precision Engineer; Mark Crowther [1960] Director/Engineer

**Emballator (UK) Limited**
*Incorporated:* 12 October 1998 *Employees:* 126
*Net Worth:* £23,121,002 *Total Assets:* £26,469,628
*Registered Office:* Unit 1 City Link Industrial Park, Phoenix Way, Tyersal, Bradford, W Yorks, BD4 8JP
*Activities:* Manufacture of plastic packing goods
*Major Shareholder:* Agneta Lovisa Carolina Hamrin
*Officers:* Philip George Troop, Secretary; Tomas Bergdahl [1972] Director [Swedish]; Gerard Dibb [1962] Director/Packaging; Carl Johan Simonsson [1960] Director [Swedish]; Philip George Troop [1973] Finance Director

**Emerald Care Holdings Yorkshire Limited**
*Incorporated:* 27 September 2011
*Net Worth:* £452,589 *Total Assets:* £3,158,800
*Registered Office:* Manor Court, Manor Mill Lane, Leeds, LS11 8LQ
*Activities:* Activities of other holding companies n.e.c.
*Major Shareholder:* Patrick Joseph Roche
*Officers:* Steven Graham Hare [1956] Director; Patrick Joseph Roche [1957] Director

**Emerald Group Holdings Limited**
*Incorporated:* 17 July 1998 *Employees:* 374
*Previous:* Emerald Global Publishing Group Limited
*Net Worth:* £13,383,000 *Total Assets:* £48,496,000
*Registered Office:* Howard House, Wagon Lane, Bingley, W Yorks, BD16 1WA
*Activities:* Publishing of learned journals
*Shareholder:* Keith Howard
*Officers:* Emma Jane Tregenza, Secretary; Richard Lloyd Bevan [1960] Director/Group CEO and Deputy Chairman; Peter Brian Casebow [1960] Director; Simon Guy Cox [1976] Director; Melissa Fojt [1991] Director/Social Responsibility Manager; Dr Keith Howard [1931] Director; Peter George Meredith [1942] Director/Company Auditor; John Roger Waterhouse [1945] Director; Victoria Caroline Williams [1976] Director

**Emerald Investments (GB) Limited**
*Incorporated:* 12 January 2012
*Net Worth:* £1,034,605 *Total Assets:* £3,549,150
*Registered Office:* RSM, 5th Floor, Central Square, 29 Wellington Street, Leeds, LS1 4DL
*Activities:* Other letting and operating of own or leased real estate
*Major Shareholder:* Gavin Buckley
*Officers:* Gavin Buckley [1961] Director/Lawyer [Irish]; Nigel Martin Fozard [1947] Director; Stuart Ralph Poppleton [1940] Director/Office Manager

**Emerald Publishing Limited**
*Incorporated:* 17 July 1995 *Employees:* 272
*Previous:* Emerald Group Publishing Limited
*Net Worth:* £9,852,000 *Total Assets:* £31,308,000
*Registered Office:* Howard House, Wagon Lane, Bingley, W Yorks, BD16 1WA
*Activities:* Publishing of learned journals
*Parent:* Emerald Group Holdings Limited
*Officers:* Emma Jane Tregenza, Secretary; Harriet Jane Bell [1973] Marketing Director; Richard Lloyd Bevan [1960] Director/Finance; Simon Guy Cox [1976] Finance Director; Shariq Mumtaz [1976] Director; Tony Roche [1969] Publishing Director; Victoria Caroline Williams [1976] Director

**Emersons Green Limited**
*Incorporated:* 19 February 2007
*Net Worth:* £5,000 *Total Assets:* £4,460,000
*Registered Office:* Yorkon House, New Lane, Huntington, York, YO32 9PT
*Activities:* Development of building projects
*Parent:* Shepherd Development Company Limited
*Officers:* Martin Ian Goforth, Secretary; Jonathan Mark Collins [1971] Director/Accountant; Caroline Scott [1961] Director/Accountant

**EMHEDA Limited**
*Incorporated:* 12 October 2016
*Net Worth:* £149,567 *Total Assets:* £3,191,626
*Registered Office:* New Chartford House, Centurion Way, Cleckheaton, W Yorks, BD19 3QB
*Activities:* Other letting and operating of own or leased real estate
*Shareholders:* John Frederick Swarbrick; Heather Jane Swarbrick
*Officers:* Heather Jane Swarbrick [1959] Director; John Frederick Swarbrick [1958] Director

**Emic Group Limited**
*Incorporated:* 5 May 2015 *Employees:* 122
*Net Worth Deficit:* £28,856 *Total Assets:* £4,949,573
*Registered Office:* Laughton Lane, Morton, Gainsborough, Lincs, DN21 3ET
*Activities:* Activities of head offices
*Shareholder:* Keven Paul Bingham
*Officers:* Keven Paul Bingham [1959] Managing Director; Edward Keith Lovely [1968] Proposals Director

**EMIH Limited**
*Incorporated:* 13 February 1998 *Employees:* 160
*Net Worth:* £32,809,716 *Total Assets:* £33,972,392
*Registered Office:* The Deep, Hull, HU1 4DP
*Activities:* Other letting and operating of own or leased real estate
*Officers:* Neil Graham Porteus, Secretary; Trevor Samuel Eric Boanas [1946] Director/Business Proprietor; Graham Chesters [1944] Director/University Lecturer; David William Gemmell [1940] Director/Retired; Anthony John Hunt [1938] Director/Retired; Alan William Kirkman [1953] Director/Financial Consultant; Philip Alexander Leigh [1959] Director/University Professor; Susan Marialuisa Lockwood [1955] Director/Retired Solicitor; John Alan Parkes [1939] Director/Retired Professional

**Eminox Limited**
*Incorporated:* 20 January 1978 *Employees:* 230
*Net Worth:* £6,830,000 *Total Assets:* £20,876,000
*Registered Office:* The Old Court House, 24 Market Street, Gainsborough, Lincs, DN21 2BE
*Activities:* Manufacture of other fabricated metal products n.e.c.
*Parent:* Hexadex Limited
*Officers:* David John Hodgson, Secretary; Cyril Alexandre Emmanuel Journoux [1981] Sales Director [French]; Nicola Eileen Linsell [1977] Programmes Director; Irfan Harun Ayub Mahomed [1971] Finance Director; Andrew Joseph Meakin [1966] Director/Chartered Accountant; Mark Charles Runciman [1971] Director; Juan Carlos Vicente [1972] Sales Director

**Emis Group PLC**
*Incorporated:* 3 April 2008 *Employees:* 1,906
*Net Worth:* £102,731,000 *Total Assets:* £179,879,008
*Registered Office:* Rawdon House, Green Lane, Yeadon, Leeds, LS19 7BY
*Activities:* Activities of head offices
*Officers:* Christine Benson, Secretary; Kevin James Boyd [1964] Director; Andrew John McKeon [1955] Director; Michael Kevin O'Leary [1952] Director; David William Sides [1970] Director [American]; Peter John Southby [1973] Director; Robin Taylor [1951] Director; Andrew John Thorburn [1962] Director

**Emovis Operations Leeds Ltd**
*Incorporated:* 24 September 2013 *Employees:* 270
*Previous:* Sanef Operations Ltd
*Net Worth:* £10,930,531 *Total Assets:* £18,305,036
*Registered Office:* St John's Offices, Albion Street, Leeds, LS2 8LQ
*Activities:* Other business support service activities n.e.c.
*Parent:* Abertis Infraestructuras SA
*Officers:* Anthony Alicastro [1959] Director [American]; Neil Conway [1967] Managing Director; Bertrand Gorree [1966] Director/Chief Financial Officer [French]; Joanne Aretha Storey [1970] Operations Director

**Employee Pulsecheck Limited**
*Incorporated:* 17 April 2008 *Employees:* 45
*Net Worth:* £2,673,452 *Total Assets:* £5,413,382
*Registered Office:* First Floor, 22 Lendal, York, YO1 8AA
*Activities:* Market research and public opinion polling
*Parent:* Karian Communication Group Limited
*Officers:* Stuart Donald McCletchie, Secretary; Ghassan Karian [1972] Director/PR; Jane Louise Mitchell [1959] Director/Consultant; Nicholas David Michael Smith [1962] Director/Management Consultant

**Empowering Minds Academy Trust**
*Incorporated:* 14 March 2017 *Employees:* 195
*Net Worth:* £18,900,056 *Total Assets:* £22,840,560
*Registered Office:* Southfield Primary School, Tranmoor Lane, Doncaster, S Yorks, DN3 3BN
*Activities:* Primary education
*Officers:* Sarah Cairns [1970] Director/Headteacher; Stephen Michael Coates [1975] Director; Alison England [1978] Director; Kate French [1950] Director; Emma Frost [1972] Director; Kim Kellett [1961] Director; Sarah Lindsay [1966] Director

**Emsley Brothers Limited**
*Incorporated:* 8 August 2003 *Employees:* 72
*Net Worth:* £16,281,857 *Total Assets:* £17,623,108
*Registered Office:* Claro Park, Claro Road, Harrogate, N Yorks, HG1 4BB
*Activities:* Non-trading company
*Shareholders:* John Malcolm Emsley; Peter Henry Emsley
*Officers:* Peter Henry Emsley, Secretary; John Malcolm Emsley [1957] Director; Peter Henry Emsley [1951] Director

**Emsley Crane Hire Limited**
*Incorporated:* 17 October 1979 *Employees:* 72
*Net Worth:* £16,281,041 *Total Assets:* £17,623,108
*Registered Office:* Claro Park, Claro Road, Harrogate, N Yorks, HG1 4BB
*Activities:* Other specialised construction activities n.e.c.
*Parent:* Emsley Brothers Limited
*Officers:* Peter Henry Emsley, Secretary; John Malcolm Emsley [1957] Director/Mechanical Engineer; Peter Henry Emsley [1951] Director/Mechanical Engineer

**Enact Conveyancing Limited**
*Incorporated:* 19 March 2003 *Employees:* 444
*Net Worth:* £3,921,000 *Total Assets:* £6,209,000
*Registered Office:* P O Box HK3, David House, David Street, Leeds, LS11 5QJ
*Activities:* Other professional, scientific and technical activities n.e.c.
*Parent:* Enact Holdings Limited
*Officers:* Amy Allen, Secretary; Amy Jane Allen [1978] Finance Director; Benjamin James Carroll [1976] Managing Director; Alex Allan Clark [1960] Director/Technical Advisor; Charlotte Lesley Local [1980] Director of Conveyancing Operations; Justin Samuel Jackson McChesney [1973] Managing Director; Adam Mark Middlemass [1968] IT Director; Richard Francis Morris [1965] Director/Licensed Conveyancer; Kelly Ann Yates-Cuthbert [1978] Director of Remortgage Operations

**Encon Insulation Limited**
*Incorporated:* 6 July 1978 *Employees:* 547
*Net Worth:* £35,256,000 *Total Assets:* £124,362,000
*Registered Office:* Brunswick House, 1 Deighton Close, Wetherby, W Yorks, LS22 7GZ
*Activities:* Other construction installation
*Parent:* Encon Investments Limited
*Officers:* John Stuart Bedford [1957] Director; Stuart John Moore [1964] Director; John Anthony Osbaldiston [1952] Director/Chartered Accountant

**Encon Investments Limited**
*Incorporated:* 24 October 1997
*Net Worth:* £1,688,000 *Total Assets:* £28,337,000
*Registered Office:* Brunswick House, 1 Deighton Close, Wetherby, W Yorks, LS22 7GZ
*Activities:* Activities of head offices
*Parent:* Encon Limited
*Officers:* John Stuart Bedford [1957] Director; Stuart John Moore [1964] Director

**Encon Limited**
*Incorporated:* 30 July 1997 *Employees:* 629
*Net Worth:* £56,046,000 *Total Assets:* £127,196,000
*Registered Office:* Brunswick House, 1 Deighton Close, Wetherby, W Yorks, LS22 7GZ
*Activities:* Activities of head offices
*Parent:* Liberty2803 Limited
*Officers:* John Stuart Bedford [1957] Director; Stuart John Moore [1964] Director

**Encounter Production Limited**
*Incorporated:* 25 October 2017 *Employees:* 4
*Net Worth:* £761,665 *Total Assets:* £5,888,802
*Registered Office:* Highfield Grange, Bubwith, Selby, N Yorks, YO8 6DP
*Activities:* Motion picture production activities
*Officers:* Alan Richard Latham [1960] Director

**End of Term Limited**
*Incorporated:* 17 February 2016 *Employees:* 1
*Net Worth:* £873,573 *Total Assets:* £5,080,363
*Registered Office:* Highfield Grange, Bubwith, Selby, N Yorks, YO8 6DP
*Activities:* Motion picture production activities
*Officers:* Tobias Angus Giles Mathews, Secretary; Alan Richard Latham [1960] Director/Film Producer

**Endless LLP**
*Incorporated:* 7 December 2005 *Employees:* 36
*Net Worth:* £12,485,000 *Total Assets:* £15,561,000
*Registered Office:* 3 Whitehall Quay, Leeds, LS1 4BF
*Officers:* Darren William Forshaw [1972] Member; Garry Wilson [1967] Member; Mathew William Deering [1977] LLP Member; Tom Andrew Jack [1973] LLP Member; Aidan Paul Robson [1978] LLP Member; Francesco Aurelio Santinon [1966] LLP Member; James Christopher Michael Woolley [1977] LLP Member

**Eneco Burn of Whilk Limited**
*Incorporated:* 8 November 2013
*Net Worth:* £518,354 *Total Assets:* £42,060,384
*Registered Office:* c/o Pinsent Masons LLP, 1 Park Row, Leeds, LS1 5AB
*Activities:* Production of electricity
*Parent:* Eneco UK Limited
*Officers:* Cornelis de Haan [1976] Director [Dutch]

**Eneco Moy Limited**
*Incorporated:* 4 February 2010
*Previous:* Carbon Free Moy Ltd
*Net Worth Deficit:* £1,408,503 *Total Assets:* £68,200,504
*Registered Office:* c/o Pinsent Masons, 1 Park Row, Leeds, LS1 5AB
*Activities:* Production of electricity
*Parent:* Eneco UK Limited
*Officers:* Cornelis de Haan [1976] Director [Dutch]

**Eneco Sevor Limited**
*Incorporated:* 26 January 2011
*Previous:* Eneco UK Solar 01 Limited
*Net Worth Deficit:* £388,188 *Total Assets:* £9,831,945
*Registered Office:* c/o Pinsent Masons LLP, 1 Park Row, Leeds, LS1 5AB
*Activities:* Production of electricity
*Parent:* Eneco UK Limited
*Officers:* Cornelis de Haan [1976] Director [Dutch]

**Eneco UK Limited**
*Incorporated:* 11 June 2008 *Employees:* 17
*Previous:* Eneco Wind UK Limited
*Net Worth:* £205,391,904 *Total Assets:* £298,342,528
*Registered Office:* c/o Pinsent Masons LLP, 1 Park Row, Leeds, LS1 5AB
*Activities:* Other business support service activities n.e.c.
*Shareholder:* City of Rotterdam
*Officers:* Cornelis de Haan [1976] Director [Dutch]

**Energy Containment Concepts Limited**
*Incorporated:* 9 May 2005 *Employees:* 3
*Net Worth:* £2,820,499 *Total Assets:* £3,215,379
*Registered Office:* 19 Peel Street, Marsden, Huddersfield, W Yorks, HD7 6BW
*Activities:* Other specialised construction activities n.e.c.
*Shareholders:* Nicholas Rodney Weir; Mark Ashley Bodenham
*Officers:* Nicholas Rodney Weir, Secretary; Mark Ashley Bodenham [1968] Director; James Douglas Weir [1977] Director; Nicholas Rodney Weir [1941] Director/Manufacturing Agent

**Energy Services (Business Power) Ltd**
*Incorporated:* 4 February 2010 *Employees:* 12
*Net Worth:* £8,603,851 *Total Assets:* £9,019,670
*Registered Office:* Unit 4 Wakefield Office Village, Fryers Way, Silkwood Park, Wakefield, W Yorks, WF5 9TJ
*Activities:* Other business support service activities n.e.c.
*Shareholders:* Brian Makings; Lesley Julie Makings
*Officers:* Brian Makings [1949] Director/Energy Consultant; Lesley Julie Makings [1950] Director/Energy Consultant

**Energy Works (Hull) Limited**
*Incorporated:* 31 October 2011
*Net Worth:* £19,128,000 *Total Assets:* £195,052,000
*Registered Office:* 1 Humber Quays, Wellington Street West, Hull, HU1 2BN
*Activities:* Production of electricity
*Parent:* EWH Finco Limited
*Officers:* Pinchas Cohen [1968] Director/Economist [Israeli]; Robert Hamish McPherson [1976] Director/Chief Executive Officer; Ran Shaul Shelach [1968] Director/Economist [Israeli]; Glenn Smith [1959] Director/Senior Vice President [American]; Charles Spencer [1953] Director; Ben Wright [1972] Director/Chief Financial Officer

**Engie Fabricom UK Limited**
*Incorporated:* 1 November 1974 *Employees:* 274
*Previous:* Fabricom Oil, Gas and Power Limited
*Net Worth:* £3,736,000 *Total Assets:* £30,868,000
*Registered Office:* Origin 3, Origin Way, Europarc, Grimsby, S Humbers, DN37 9TZ
*Activities:* Other specialised construction activities n.e.c.
*Parent:* Engie UK Holding Services Limited
*Officers:* Claire Rachel Bateman, Secretary; Claire Rachel Bateman [1982] Finance Director; Eric de Ribaucourt [1972] Finance Director [Belgian]; Mark Dirckx [1965] Director [Belgian]; Philip Snoeck [1965] Director [Belgian]; Richard Mark Webster [1966] Director/Accountant

**Engie Gas Limited**
*Incorporated:* 27 July 1999
*Previous:* GDF Suez Sales Limited
*Net Worth:* £20,905,000 *Total Assets:* £118,549,000
*Registered Office:* No 1 Leeds, 26 Whitehall Road, Leeds, LS12 1BE
*Activities:* Distribution of gaseous fuels through mains
*Parent:* Engie Supply Holding UK Limited
*Officers:* Sarah Jane Gregory, Secretary; Kevin Adrian Dibble [1968] Director; Nicola Elizabeth Anne Lovett [1969] Director; Robert John Wells [1980] Director/Accountant

**Engie Gas Shipper Limited**
*Incorporated:* 27 July 1999
*Previous:* GDF Suez Solutions Limited
*Net Worth:* £369,000 *Total Assets:* £13,839,000
*Registered Office:* No 1 Leeds, 26 Whitehall Road, Leeds, LS12 1BE
*Activities:* Distribution of gaseous fuels through mains
*Parent:* Engie Supply Holdings UK Limited
*Officers:* Sarah Jane Gregory, Secretary; Kevin Adrian Dibble [1968] Director; Nicola Elizabeth Anne Lovett [1969] Director; Robert John Wells [1980] Director/Accountant

**Engie Power Limited**
*Incorporated:* 18 June 2001 *Employees:* 265
*Previous:* GDF Suez Marketing Limited
*Net Worth:* £20,109,000 *Total Assets:* £406,560,000
*Registered Office:* No 1 Leeds, 26 Whitehall Road, Leeds, LS12 1BE
*Activities:* Agents involved in the sale of fuels, ores, metals and industrial chemicals
*Parent:* Engie Supply Holding UK Limited
*Officers:* Sarah Jane Gregory, Secretary; Kevin Adrian Dibble [1968] Director; Nicola Elizabeth Anne Lovett [1969] Director; Robert John Wells [1980] Director/Accountant

**Engie Supply Holding UK Limited**
*Incorporated:* 13 April 1992
*Previous:* GDF Suez Energy UK Limited
*Net Worth:* £53,404,000 *Total Assets:* £81,534,000
*Registered Office:* No 1 Leeds, 26 Whitehall Road, Leeds, LS12 1BE
*Activities:* Activities of head offices
*Parent:* Stopper Finance B.V.
*Officers:* Sarah Jane Gregory, Secretary; Kevin Adrian Dibble [1968] Director; Nicola Elizabeth Anne Lovett [1969] Director; Wilfrid John Petrie [1965] Director [French]; Simon David Pinnell [1964] Director/Head of Finance

**R.M. English & Son Limited**
*Incorporated:* 15 March 1946 *Employees:* 22
*Net Worth:* £2,342,054 *Total Assets:* £3,285,200
*Registered Office:* Storage and Logistics Centre, Full Sutton Airfield, Full Sutton, York, YO41 1HS
*Activities:* Operation of warehousing and storage facilities for land transport activities
*Shareholder:* Simon Pocklington
*Officers:* Sally Anne Wilkinson, Secretary; Simon Pocklington [1961] Director/Agricultural Merchant; Sally Anne Wilkinson [1962] Director/Sales Representative

**English Lakes Hotels Limited**
*Incorporated:* 16 May 1979
*Net Worth:* £151,586 *Total Assets:* £3,664,076
*Registered Office:* English Lakes Hotels Offices, Low Wood, Ambleside Road, Windermere, Cumbria, LA23 1LP
*Activities:* Activities of head offices
*Officers:* Timothy Robert James Berry, Secretary/Leisure Director; Benjamin William James Berry [1988] Director; Simon Frederick Michael Berry [1959] Managing Director; Timothy Robert James Berry [1961] Leisure Director; Jonathan Alexander Noel Cook [1963] Director; Douglas Paterson Dale [1952] Director; Jonquil Anna Catherine Doremus Cook [1969] Director; David Huw Neale [1962] Commercial Director; Matthew John Wilkinson [1977] Financial Director

**Enhance Academy Trust**
*Incorporated:* 10 January 2012 *Employees:* 396
*Previous:* Wakefield Diocesan Academies Trust
*Net Worth:* £15,180,000 *Total Assets:* £19,751,000
*Registered Office:* Church Bank House, Church Bank, Bradford, W Yorks, BD1 4DY
*Activities:* Primary education
*Officers:* John Patrick Brady [1964] Director; Kevin Glyn Jones [1955] Director/Chief Executive Officer; Linda Margaret Maskill [1951] Director/Retired Headteacher; John Patrick McLeod [1954] Director; Fiona Anne McMahon [1976] Assistant Principal: Director of Sixth Form; Janet Margaret Milne [1957] Director/Teacher; Christopher Ernest Schofield [1962] Director/Solicitor; Kathy Olivia Helen Smith [1974] Director/Chartered Accountant; The Venerable Peter Kenneth Townley [1955] Director/Clerk in Holy Orders

**The Enquire Learning Trust**
*Incorporated:* 3 May 2012 *Employees:* 1,467
*Net Worth:* £61,413,928 *Total Assets:* £80,694,464
*Registered Office:* 18 Appleton Court, Wakefield, W Yorks, WF2 7AR
*Activities:* Other education n.e.c.
*Officers:* Elizabeth Anne Thompson, Secretary; Jim Cassidy [1964] Director; Jill Catherine Foster [1964] Director; Jack Harrison [1950] Director; Richard Michael Hildyard [1971] Director/Chief Executive; Darren Brian Holmes [1965] Director; Ronald Derek Kirk [1945] Director/Councillor; Giles David McCourt [1977] Director/Solicitor; Nigel Woodworth [1967] Director/Accountant

**Enserve Group Limited**
*Incorporated:* 17 September 1996 *Employees:* 3
*Net Worth:* £23,900,000 *Total Assets:* £42,300,000
*Registered Office:* Denton Hall, Denton, Ilkley, W Yorks, LS29 0HH
*Activities:* Activities of head offices
*Parent:* Cilantro Acqusitions Limited
*Officers:* Rachel Clare Salmon, Secretary; David Stuart Hurcomb [1964] Director/Engineer and Accountant; Michael Porter [1967] Director

**Entertainment Alliance (Holdings) Limited**
*Incorporated:* 6 March 2013 *Employees:* 15
*Net Worth:* £961,878 *Total Assets:* £7,882,731
*Registered Office:* Northgate, 118 North Street, Leeds, LS2 7PN
*Activities:* Activities of other holding companies n.e.c.
*Shareholders:* Paul Fitzgerald; Doyle Trading Holdings Limited; Stevens Product Services Limited
*Officers:* Iain Karl Doyle [1970] Director; Paul FitzGenerald [1974] Director; David Valentine Stevens [1976] Director

**Entertainment Alliance (UK) Limited**
*Incorporated:* 20 June 2014 *Employees:* 15
*Net Worth:* £961,978 *Total Assets:* £7,882,731
*Registered Office:* c/o Hentons, Northgate, 118 North Street, Leeds, LS2 7PN
*Activities:* Activities of other holding companies n.e.c.
*Parent:* Entertainment Alliance (Holdings) Limited
*Officers:* Iain Karl Doyle [1970] Director; Paul FitzGenerald [1974] Director; David Valentine Stevens [1976] Director

**Entertainment and Leisure Insurance Services Limited**
*Incorporated:* 7 February 1986 *Employees:* 4
*Net Worth:* £4,562,952 *Total Assets:* £4,935,194
*Registered Office:* Thorpe Underwood Hall, Thorpe Underwood, York, YO26 9SZ
*Activities:* Other activities auxiliary to insurance and pension funding
*Parent:* The Collegiate Formation Ltd
*Officers:* Christopher James Hall, Secretary; Christopher James Hall [1969] Director/Chartered Accountant; Karen Elizabeth Howells-Lee [1968] Director/Executive; Amy Katherine Martin [1983] Director; Francis David Martin [1967] Director/Business Executive

**Envirovent Limited**
*Incorporated:* 29 June 2007 *Employees:* 231
*Net Worth:* £7,448,183 *Total Assets:* £15,519,591
*Registered Office:* Envirovent House, Hornbeam Business Park, Harrogate, N Yorks, HG2 8PA
*Activities:* Manufacture of non-domestic cooling and ventilation equipment
*Shareholder:* Jose Palau Mallol
*Officers:* Samantha Moss, Secretary; Carlos Campderros [1955] Director [Spanish]; Gabriela Nedkova Grigorova [1979] Finance Director [Bulgarian]; Juan Manuel Lecue Yuste [1972] Managing Director [Spanish]; Andrew Makin [1966] Sales Director; Eugene Scotcher [1973] Director; Hilario Tome [1952] Director [Spanish]

**EOF Holdings Limited**
*Incorporated:* 7 March 2012 *Employees:* 136
*Net Worth:* £22,057,984 *Total Assets:* £29,886,888
*Registered Office:* Brittania Way, Goole, E Yorks, DN14 6ES
*Activities:* Non-trading company
*Major Shareholder:* John Hull
*Officers:* John Hull [1950] Director; Julian Andrew Jowett [1976] Sales Director

**EP Realisations Limited**
*Incorporated:* 15 November 1982 *Employees:* 171
*Net Worth:* £7,283,000 *Total Assets:* £25,892,000
*Registered Office:* Benson House, 33 Wellington Street, Leeds, LS1 4JP
*Activities:* Water collection, treatment and supply

**Epax Pharma UK Holdings Unlimited**
*Incorporated:* 20 May 2011
*Net Worth Deficit:* £47,851,000 *Total Assets:* £3,578,000
*Registered Office:* Gilbey Road, Grimsby, S Humbers, DN31 2SL
*Activities:* Activities of production holding companies
*Officers:* Michael McEllone, Secretary; Rolf Andersen [1968] Director [Norwegian]; Egil Magne Haugstad [1957] Director [Norwegian]; Michael McEllone [1974] Finance Director [Irish]

**Epax Pharma UK Ltd**
*Incorporated:* 26 April 2011
*Net Worth:* £3,578,000 *Total Assets:* £3,847,000
*Registered Office:* Gilbey Road, Grimsby, S Humbers, DN31 2SL
*Activities:* Manufacture of basic pharmaceutical products
*Parent:* Epax Pharma UK Holdings Unlimited
*Officers:* Michael McEllone, Secretary; Rolf Andersen [1968] Director [Norwegian]; Egil Magne Haugstad [1957] Director [Norwegian]; Michael McEllone [1974] Director/Scotland [Irish]

**Epil Carlisle Limited**
*Incorporated:* 17 September 2016
*Net Worth:* £9,572,458 *Total Assets:* £9,807,257
*Registered Office:* 10 Sovereign Fold, Knaresborough, N Yorks, HG5 0WJ
*Activities:* Other letting and operating of own or leased real estate
*Major Shareholder:* Darren Broadbent
*Officers:* Darren Broadbent [1967] Director

**EPMS Group Limited**
*Incorporated:* 19 November 2015 *Employees:* 25
*Net Worth:* £1,715,518 *Total Assets:* £6,824,816
*Registered Office:* 1 The Moorings, Waterside Industrial Park, Waterside Road, Stourton, Leeds, LS10 1RW
*Activities:* Activities of other holding companies n.e.c.
*Shareholder:* Donald Stewart Blair
*Officers:* Donald Stewart Blair [1955] Director

**EPMS Supplies Limited**
*Incorporated:* 18 July 2011 *Employees:* 25
*Net Worth:* £2,247,755 *Total Assets:* £5,351,028
*Registered Office:* 1 The Moorings, Waterside Industrial Park, Waterside Road, Stourton, Leeds, LS10 1RW
*Activities:* Wholesale of hardware, plumbing and heating equipment and supplies
*Parent:* EPMS Group Limited
*Officers:* Donald Stewart Blair [1955] Managing Director

**Eppleton Quarry Products Limited**
*Incorporated:* 26 February 2001 *Employees:* 4
*Net Worth:* £6,356,870 *Total Assets:* £8,883,238
*Registered Office:* Stotforth Hill House, Windlestone, Ferryhill, Co Durham, DL17 0NF
*Activities:* Operation of gravel and sand pits; mining of clays and kaolin
*Shareholder:* Hall Construction Services Limited
*Officers:* Neville John Hall [1956] Director; Stephen Hall [1954] Director; Garry Hutchinson [1955] Director

**EPTA George Barker Ltd**
*Incorporated:* 7 June 1962 *Employees:* 373
*Previous:* George Barker & Company (Leeds) Limited
*Net Worth:* £14,666,687 *Total Assets:* £43,515,160
*Registered Office:* Highfield Works, Highfield Road, Idle, Bradford, W Yorks, BD10 8RU
*Activities:* Other manufacturing n.e.c.
*Officers:* Simon James Taylor, Secretary; Massimo Andrea Albertario [1966] Director [Italian]; Luca Lastella [1965] Director/General Manager [Italian]; Geoffrey Charles Mills [1965] Commercial Director; Enzo Santori [1959] Director [Italian]; Simon James Taylor [1968] Director/Accountant

**EPTA Service UK Limited**
*Incorporated:* 11 June 2014 *Employees:* 3
*Net Worth Deficit:* £134,547 *Total Assets:* £3,147,902
*Registered Office:* Highfield Works, Highfield Road, Idle, Bradford, W Yorks, BD10 8RU
*Activities:* Activities of head offices
*Parent:* EPTA S.P.A
*Officers:* Massimo Andrea Albertario [1966] Director [Italian]; Daniele Marongiu [1959] Sales Director [Italian]; Marco NoCivilli [1966] Director/General Manager [Italian]

**Equine and Livestock Insurance Company Limited (The)**
*Incorporated:* 12 December 1934 *Employees:* 47
*Net Worth:* £36,450,000 *Total Assets:* £51,904,000
*Registered Office:* Thorpe Underwood Hall, Thorpe Underwood, Great Ouseburn, York, YO26 9SZ
*Activities:* Other activities auxiliary to insurance and pension funding
*Officers:* Jane Helen Shaw, Secretary; Christopher James Hall [1969] Director/Chartered Accountant; Karen Elizabeth Howells-Lee [1968] Director/Executive; Amy Katherine Martin [1983] Director; Francis David Martin [1967] Director/Business Executive; Peter Edward Myers [1963] Director/Chairman; Elisabeth Mary Walker [1961] Director

**Eridor Investments Limited**
*Incorporated:* 6 November 1972 *Employees:* 2
*Net Worth:* £2,763,038 *Total Assets:* £3,415,185
*Registered Office:* c/o WGN, 4 Park Place, Leeds, LS1 2RU
*Activities:* Renting and operating of Housing Association real estate
*Parent:* Eridor Group Holdings Limited
*Officers:* Jacqueline Rosa Harris, Secretary; Jacqueline Rosa Harris [1948] Director/Representative; Elliot Levey [1973] Director/Executive

**Erivan Holdings Limited**
*Incorporated:* 2 October 1947 *Employees:* 2
*Net Worth:* £3,008,521 *Total Assets:* £3,840,017
*Registered Office:* Inchmarlo, Station Road, Cattal, York, YO26 8DX
*Activities:* Other letting and operating of own or leased real estate
*Major Shareholder:* Simon Nicholas Clark
*Officers:* Georgina Dorcas Clark, Secretary; Nicola Jan Austin [1957] Director; Simon Nicholas Clark [1954] Managing Director

**ERM Regulatory Services Limited**
*Incorporated:* 10 March 2016 *Employees:* 35
*Previous:* JSC International Limited
*Net Worth:* £993,056 *Total Assets:* £13,163,512
*Registered Office:* The Exchange, Station Parade, Harrogate, N Yorks, HG1 1TS
*Activities:* Environmental consulting activities
*Parent:* ERM Emilion Limited
*Officers:* Claudio Bertora [1969] Director [Italian]; Sabine Hoefnagel [1970] Managing Director [Dutch]; David James McArthur [1964] Director

**Ermine Farms Limited**
*Incorporated:* 6 December 1947 *Employees:* 32
*Net Worth:* £4,253,535 *Total Assets:* £5,225,387
*Registered Office:* Grayingham Grange Farm, Grayingham, Gainsborough, Lincs, DN21 4JD
*Activities:* Raising of swine and pigs
*Shareholders:* Stephen Tom Ward; Meryl Suzanne Ward
*Officers:* Susan Cooper, Secretary; Meryl Suzanne Ward [1960] Director; Stephen Tom Ward [1959] Director

**ERS Transition Limited**
*Incorporated:* 22 May 2017 *Employees:* 830
*Net Worth Deficit:* £118,637 *Total Assets:* £6,398,649
*Registered Office:* 2nd Floor, Hetton Court, The Oval, Hunslet, Leeds, LS10 2AT
*Activities:* Other passenger land transport
*Officers:* Alexander John Fraser [1965] Director; Andrew Pooley [1981] Director; John William Smyly [1958] Director

**ESCO (UK) Holdings Limited**
*Incorporated:* 24 April 2003 *Employees:* 3
*Net Worth Deficit:* £377,000 *Total Assets:* £15,135,000
*Registered Office:* Esco (UK) Holdings Limited, Ings Road, Doncaster, S Yorks, DN5 9SN
*Activities:* Activities of head offices
*Parent:* ESCO EMEA Holdings (UK) Limited
*Officers:* Stephen Beresford Robinson, Secretary; Meredith Weisshaar, Secretary; Todd William Abel [1964] Director/VP - Finance & Accounting [American]; Philippe Kaskarian [1963] Director [French]; Jon Owens [1962] Director/Senior Vice President [American]

**ESCO (UK) Limited**
*Incorporated:* 14 July 1982 *Employees:* 1
*Net Worth:* £1,890,000 *Total Assets:* £4,412,000
*Registered Office:* Esco (UK) Limited, Ings Road, Doncaster, S Yorks, DN5 9SN
*Activities:* Casting of steel
*Parent:* ESCO EMEA Holdings (UK) Limited
*Officers:* Stephen Beresford Robinson, Secretary; Meredith Weisshaar, Secretary; Todd William Abel [1964] Director/VP - Finance & Accounting [American]; Philippe Kaskarian [1963] Director [French]; Jon Owens [1962] Director/Senior Vice President [American]

**ESCO EMEA Holdings (UK) Limited**
*Incorporated:* 13 September 2013 *Employees:* 144
*Net Worth:* £2,883,000 *Total Assets:* £31,401,000
*Registered Office:* Esco EMEA Holdings (UK) Limited, Ings Road, Doncaster, S Yorks, DN5 9SN
*Activities:* Activities of head offices
*Officers:* Stephen Beresford Robinson, Secretary; Meredith Weisshaar, Secretary; Todd William Abel [1964] Director/VP - Finance & Accounting [American]; Philippe Kaskarian [1963] Director [French]; Jon Owens [1962] Director/Senior Vice President [American]

**ESCO Hydra (UK) Limited**
*Incorporated:* 6 April 2000 *Employees:* 42
*Net Worth:* £4,720,000 *Total Assets:* £5,411,000
*Registered Office:* Esco Hydra (UK) Limited, Ings Road, Doncaster, S Yorks, DN5 9SN
*Activities:* Manufacture of machinery for mining
*Parent:* ESCO (UK) Holdings Limited
*Officers:* Stephen Beresford Robinson, Secretary; Meredith Weisshaar, Secretary; Philippe Kaskarian [1963] Director [French]; Jon Owens [1962] Director/Executive Vice President [American]; Joseph Theodore Weber [1961] Director [American]

**Eshton Ltd**
*Incorporated:* 12 March 2001 *Employees:* 4
*Net Worth:* £7,789,245 *Total Assets:* £9,288,616
*Registered Office:* First Floor, 15 St Paul's Street, Leeds, LS1 2JG
*Activities:* Buying and selling of own real estate
*Shareholders:* James Harvey Chapman; Jonathan Guy Chapman
*Officers:* Jonathan Guy Chapman, Secretary/Director; James Harvey Chapman [1972] Director; Jonathan Guy Chapman [1976] Director; David Clive Singleton [1974] Director

**Eshton Oakfield Ltd**
*Incorporated:* 15 January 2009
*Previous:* Hamsard 3157 Limited
*Net Worth:* £2,654,096 *Total Assets:* £5,054,957
*Registered Office:* First Floor, 15 St Pauls Street, Leeds, LS1 2JG
*Activities:* Other letting and operating of own or leased real estate
*Shareholders:* Jonathan Guy Chapman; James Harvey Chapman; Adrian Keith Chapman; Elizabeth Sarah Lammas
*Officers:* David Clive Singleton, Secretary; James Harvey Chapman [1972] Director; Jonathan Guy Chapman [1976] Director; David Clive Singleton [1974] Director/Property Developer

**ESP Systex Holdings Limited**
*Incorporated:* 12 January 2010 *Employees:* 421
*Net Worth:* £3,326,281 *Total Assets:* £8,913,763
*Registered Office:* 68-74 Holderness Road, Hull, HU9 1ED
*Activities:* Activities of head offices
*Major Shareholder:* Terence Frederick Dunn
*Officers:* Dr Steven Cassidy [1964] Director; Fiona Dunn [1956] Director; Terence Frederick Dunn [1952] Director; Theresa Frances Slevin [1977] ESP Group COO & Journeycall Managing Director

**Esplanade Group (Scarborough) International Limited**
*Incorporated:* 10 March 2010
*Net Worth:* £17,218,880 *Total Assets:* £43,262,268
*Registered Office:* Europa House, 20 Esplanade, Scarborough, N Yorks, YO11 2AQ
*Activities:* Activities of other holding companies n.e.c.
*Parent:* Scarborough Group International Limited
*Officers:* Kevin Charles McCabe [1948] Director/Chartered Surveyor; Scott Richard McCabe [1975] Managing Director; Simon Charles McCabe [1977] Director; Jeremy John Tutton [1966] Director/Financial Controller

**Esseco UK Limited**
*Incorporated:* 10 April 1985 *Employees:* 77
*Net Worth:* £11,123,654 *Total Assets:* £16,868,916
*Registered Office:* Calder Vale Road, Wakefield, W Yorks, WF1 5PH
*Activities:* Manufacture of other inorganic basic chemicals
*Parent:* Esseco Group SRL
*Officers:* Roger Colin Grant, Secretary; Alberto Cambieri [1965] Director [Italian]; Russel David Etherington [1964] Director; Roger Colin Grant [1968] Director; Andrea Agostino Mangiarotti [1963] Commercial Director [Italian]; Christopher Stuart McKenzie [1965] Director; Fabrizio Zenone [1957] Director/General Manager [Italian]

**Estates U.K. Limited**
*Incorporated:* 20 February 1998 *Employees:* 12
*Net Worth:* £24,466,532 *Total Assets:* £37,416,088
*Registered Office:* 9 Waterside Business Park, Livingstone Road, Hessle, E Yorks, HU13 0EG
*Activities:* Other letting and operating of own or leased real estate
*Major Shareholder:* Andrew Miller
*Officers:* Susan Irene Miller, Secretary; Andrew Miller [1962] Director/Developer; Harry John Miller [1990] Director; James Miller [1988] Director; Sophie Victoria Miller [1987] Director

**Esteem Holdings Limited**
*Incorporated:* 5 October 2004 *Employees:* 247
*Net Worth:* £1,676,000 *Total Assets:* £28,722,000
*Registered Office:* Rofta House, Thorp Arch, Wetherby, Leeds, LS23 7QA
*Activities:* Other information technology service activities
*Parent:* Roc Technologies Limited
*Officers:* Matthew Nicholas Franklin [1970] Director; Duncan Charles Gooding [1971] Director; Paul Hart [1966] Director; Stephen Gary Shirley [1963] Director

**Esteem Systems Limited**
*Incorporated:* 6 April 1984 *Employees:* 241
*Net Worth:* £12,212,000 *Total Assets:* £30,160,000
*Registered Office:* Rofta House, Rudgate, Thorp Arch, Wetherby, W Yorks, LS23 7QA
*Activities:* Information technology consultancy activities
*Parent:* Esteem Holdings Limited
*Officers:* Matthew Nicholas Franklin [1970] Director; Duncan Charles Gooding [1971] Director; Paul Hart [1966] Director; Stephen Gary Shirley [1963] Director

**Esvagt UK Limited**
*Incorporated:* 22 December 2005 *Employees:* 3
*Net Worth:* £642,000 *Total Assets:* £3,320,000
*Registered Office:* Marina Court, Castle Street, Hull, HU1 1TJ
*Activities:* Sea and coastal freight water transport
*Parent:* Esvagt Holdings Limited
*Officers:* Soren Karas [1972] Director/Chief Commercial Officer [Danish]

**Etas Limited**
*Incorporated:* 9 June 1997 *Employees:* 64
*Net Worth:* £6,115,990 *Total Assets:* £7,062,110
*Registered Office:* Bacchus House, Link Business Park, Osbaldwick Link Road, York, YO10 3JB
*Activities:* Other information technology service activities
*Parent:* Robert Bosch UK Holdings Limited
*Officers:* Jonathan David Burton, Secretary; Bernd Alexander Hergert [1961] Director/Executive Vice President [German]; Dr Steffen Tobias Hoffmann [1965] Director [German]; Nicholas John Keeling [1963] Director/Engineering Manager

**Etrickbank Limited**
*Incorporated:* 28 March 1951 *Employees:* 133
*Net Worth:* £3,767,841 *Total Assets:* £9,806,578
*Registered Office:* Cave Castle Hotel, South Cave, Brough, E Yorks, HU15 2EU
*Activities:* Hotels and similar accommodation
*Shareholder:* Melvyn Noel Hogarth
*Officers:* Catherine Mary Hogarth [1957] Director; Stephen Michael Hogarth [1973] Director; Kathryn Elizabeth Nicholson [1976] Director

**Eureka Display Limited**
*Incorporated:* 14 November 2001 *Employees:* 34
*Net Worth:* £1,954,763 *Total Assets:* £3,290,531
*Registered Office:* Don Pedro Avenue, Normanton Industrial Estate, Wakefield, W Yorks, WF6 1TD
*Activities:* Manufacture of office and shop furniture
*Officers:* Patricia Elizabeth Benson, Secretary; Sharon Dawn Skirrow, Secretary; Susanna Teresa Skirrow, Secretary; Alison Catherine Walker, Secretary; Paul Duncan Benson [1946] Director/Chartered Accountant; Anthony Dean Skirrow [1968] Director/Salesman; Martin Skirrow [1964] Director/Engineer; Andrew John Walker [1965] Director/Chartered Accountant

**Eureka! The National Children's Museum.**
*Incorporated:* 19 September 1985 *Employees:* 127
*Net Worth:* £7,246,264 *Total Assets:* £7,620,380
*Registered Office:* Discovery Road, Halifax, W Yorks, HX1 2NE
*Activities:* Museums activities
*Officers:* Teresa Joanne Corbridge, Secretary; Alan John Aubrey [1961] Director; Jin Theng Craven [1968] Director [Singaporean]; Fiona Jane Hesselden [1964] Director; Alison Mary Hope [1957] Director/Accountant; Jane Sheridan Rice-Bowen [1974] Director/Management Consultant; Peter Charles Smart [1950] Director/Solicitor; Leigh Anne Stradeski [1957] Director [Canadian]; Diane Carole Watson [1958] Director; Elizabeth Ann Wood [1955] Director/Professor of Education

**Euro-Pro Europe Limited**
*Incorporated:* 17 April 2013 *Employees:* 67
*Net Worth Deficit:* £8,373,946 *Total Assets:* £53,987,292
*Registered Office:* 15 Mariner Court, Calder Park, Wakefield, W Yorks, WF4 3FL
*Activities:* Retail sale of electrical household appliances in specialised stores
*Shareholders:* Wang Xuning; Mark Rosenzweig
*Officers:* Matthew Edward Broadway [1974] Director; Xuning Wang [1969] Director/Chairman and President of Joyoung Co. Ltd [Chinese]

**Eurocentral Hotels Limited**
*Incorporated:* 8 November 2013 *Employees:* 2
*Net Worth:* £1,943,474 *Total Assets:* £7,130,856
*Registered Office:* Millshaw Ring Road, Beeston, Leeds, LS11 8EG
*Activities:* Other letting and operating of own or leased real estate
*Shareholders:* Michael White Evans; Helga Ingeborg Evans; Sanne Group PLC
*Officers:* Robert Marshall, Secretary; Roderick Michael Evans [1962] Director; Robert Marshall [1979] Director/Chartered Accountant; Paul Terence Millington [1962] Director/Chartered Surveyor

**Europa Caravans Ltd**
*Incorporated:* 21 January 2009 *Employees:* 15
*Net Worth:* £2,116,479 *Total Assets:* £4,730,704
*Registered Office:* Unit 3 Wyke Works, Hedon Road, Hull, HU9 5NL
*Activities:* Other manufacturing n.e.c.
*Shareholders:* Graham Richard Oades; Donald Paul Oades
*Officers:* Graham Richard Oades, Secretary/Director; Donald Paul Oades [1964] Director; Graham Richard Oades [1971] Director

**Europa Crown Limited**
*Incorporated:* 9 May 1990 *Employees:* 37
*Net Worth:* £6,827,000 *Total Assets:* £21,161,000
*Registered Office:* Waterside Park, Livingstone Road, Hessle, E Yorks, HU13 0EG
*Activities:* Management consultancy activities other than financial management
*Parent:* CPM WPS Limited
*Officers:* Philip Blenkiron, Secretary; Philip Blenkiron [1950] Director/Accountant; Paul John Smith [1984] Sales Director; Richard Martin James Young [1955] Director/Engineer

**Europa Wools Limited**
*Incorporated:* 19 September 1988 *Employees:* 23
*Net Worth:* £1,460,723 *Total Assets:* £3,714,700
*Registered Office:* Unit 8 The Old Railway Goods Yard, Scar Lane, Milnsbridge, Huddersfield, W Yorks, HD3 4PE
*Activities:* Wholesale of textiles
*Shareholders:* Lynn Beverley Morsley; Richard David Morsley; Gina Helen Novotny
*Officers:* Lynn Beverley Morsley, Secretary; Lynn Beverley Morsley [1955] Director; Richard David Morsley [1986] Director; Gina Helen Novotny [1989] Director

**European Integrated Carriers Limited**
*Incorporated:* 10 November 1988
*Net Worth:* £1,080,393 *Total Assets:* £5,848,963
*Registered Office:* c/o Global Shipping Services Ltd, Kiln Lane Trading Estate, Stallingborough, Grimsby, N E Lincs, DN41 8DY
*Activities:* Activities of head offices
*Parent:* Global Shipping Services Group Ltd
*Officers:* David Alan Jobes, Secretary/Director; David Alan Jobes [1951] Director

**Europipes (UK) Limited**
*Incorporated:* 15 March 1989 *Employees:* 6
*Net Worth:* £2,991,027 *Total Assets:* £3,337,732
*Registered Office:* Buttfield Road, Howden, E Yorks, DN14 7DY
*Activities:* Other specialised construction activities n.e.c.
*Shareholders:* Robert George Axup; David Andrew Axup
*Officers:* David Andrew Axup, Secretary; David Andrew Axup [1962] Director; Robert George Axup [1955] Director

**Eurotek Foundry Products Limited**
*Incorporated:* 15 November 1991 *Employees:* 18
*Net Worth:* £2,330,610 *Total Assets:* £4,601,235
*Registered Office:* Wistons Lane, Elland, W Yorks, HX5 9DT
*Activities:* Manufacture of other chemical products n.e.c.
*Shareholders:* Dale Cristian Cortney Crystal; Joseph Norman Higgs
*Officers:* Dale Cristian Cortney Crystal, Secretary; Brian Allen [1940] Director; Dale Cristian Cortney Crystal [1961] Managing Director; Raymond Alfred Higgins [1958] Sales Director; Joseph Norman Higgs [1949] Director

**Eurotrail UK Limited**
*Incorporated:* 25 August 1978 *Employees:* 22
*Net Worth:* £1,690,043 *Total Assets:* £12,936,870
*Registered Office:* Eurotrail UK Limited, West End Approach, Morley, W Yorks, LS27 0NB
*Activities:* Renting and leasing of trucks and other heavy vehicles
*Parent:* Steers Group Limited
*Officers:* Sarah Marsden, Secretary/Finance Manager; Adam John Steers [1971] Director; Alan Steers [1950] Director; Jane Carolyn Steers [1950] Director; Mathew Alan Steers [1980] Director

**The Evangelical Fellowship of Congregational Churches Trust Corporation Limited**
*Incorporated:* 5 January 1993
*Net Worth:* £5,170,215 *Total Assets:* £5,584,069
*Registered Office:* Latimer Congregational Church, Grovehill Road, Beverley, E Yorks, HU17 0JD
*Activities:* Activities of religious organisations
*Officers:* Anthony Richard Harrison, Secretary; Reverend John Brown [1950] Director; Reverend William Edward Calder [1953] Director/Minister of Religion; Kevin Ivor Davies [1965] Director/Church Worker; Revd Gwynne Martin Evans [1948] Director/Minister of Religion; Robert William Neilson [1949] Director; Rev Matthew Lloyd Rees [1975] Director/Minister of Religion; Gilbert Frederick Stephenson [1957] Director/Accountant; Philip James Williams [1957] Director/Tax Partner

**Evans (Ashford) Limited**
*Incorporated:* 21 January 2000 *Employees:* 3
*Net Worth:* £5,952,627 *Total Assets:* £10,827,894
*Registered Office:* Millshaw, Leeds, LS11 8EG
*Activities:* Development of building projects
*Parent:* Evans Ashford Investments Limited
*Officers:* Robert Marshall, Secretary; Roderick Michael Evans [1962] Director; Paul Terence Millington [1962] Director/Accountant; Alan Matthew Syers [1964] Director/Chartered Surveyor

**F R Evans (Leeds) Limited**
*Incorporated:* 22 November 2006 *Employees:* 3
*Net Worth:* £2,820,007 *Total Assets:* £29,138,350
*Registered Office:* Millshaw, Leeds, LS11 8EG
*Activities:* Development of building projects
*Parent:* Evans Management Limited
*Officers:* Robert Marshall, Secretary; Roderick Michael Evans [1962] Director; Robert Marshall [1979] Director/Chartered Accountant; Paul Terence Millington [1962] Director/Accountant; Alan Matthew Syers [1964] Director/Chartered Surveyor

**Evans Ashford Investments Limited**
*Incorporated:* 22 November 2006 *Employees:* 2
*Net Worth:* £3,380,942 *Total Assets:* £6,148,712
*Registered Office:* Millshaw, Leeds, LS11 8EG
*Activities:* Development of building projects
*Parent:* Evans Management Limited
*Officers:* Robert Marshall, Secretary; Roderick Michael Evans [1962] Director; Paul Terence Millington [1962] Director/Accountant

**Evans Dakota Hotels Limited**
*Incorporated:* 15 April 2014 *Employees:* 4
*Net Worth:* £251,886 *Total Assets:* £35,645,308
*Registered Office:* Millshaw, Leeds, LS11 8EG
*Activities:* Other letting and operating of own or leased real estate
*Shareholders:* Michael White Evans; Helga Ingeborg Evans; Sanne Group PLC
*Officers:* Robert Marshall, Secretary; Simon David Bottomley [1958] Director/Chartered Surveyor; Roderick Evans [1962] Director; Robert Marshall [1979] Director/Chartered Accountant; Paul Millington [1962] Director; Alan Matthew Syers [1964] Director/Chartered Surveyor

**Evans Easyspace (Chester) Limited**
*Incorporated:* 1 December 2004 *Employees:* 2
*Net Worth:* £2,196,511 *Total Assets:* £3,534,662
*Registered Office:* Millshaw, Ring Road, Beeston, Leeds, LS11 8EG
*Activities:* Other letting and operating of own or leased real estate
*Parent:* Roando Investments Limited
*Officers:* Robert Marshall [1979] Director/Chartered Accountant; Paul Terence Millington [1962] Director/Chartered Accountant; Alan Matthew Syers [1964] Director/Chartered Surveyor

**Evans Homes Limited**
*Incorporated:* 8 December 1999 *Employees:* 3
*Net Worth:* £4,258,249 *Total Assets:* £7,754,500
*Registered Office:* Millshaw, Leeds, LS11 8EG
*Activities:* Development of building projects
*Parent:* Evans Residential Holdings Limited
*Officers:* Robert Marshall, Secretary; Roderick Michael Evans [1962] Director; Paul Terence Millington [1962] Director/Accountant; Alan Matthew Syers [1964] Director/Chartered Surveyor

**Evans Homes No.2 Limited**
*Incorporated:* 22 November 2006 *Employees:* 3
*Net Worth:* £1,948,745 *Total Assets:* £4,610,907
*Registered Office:* Millshaw, Leeds, LS11 8EG
*Activities:* Development of building projects
*Parent:* White Rose Property Investments No.2 Limited
*Officers:* Robert Marshall, Secretary; Roderick Michael Evans [1962] Director; Paul Terence Millington [1962] Director/Accountant; Alan Matthew Syers [1964] Director/Chartered Surveyor

**Evans Management Limited**
*Incorporated:* 25 January 2007 *Employees:* 34
*Net Worth:* £9,850,359 *Total Assets:* £336,796,864
*Registered Office:* Millshaw, Ring Road, Beeston, Leeds, LS11 8EG
*Activities:* Development of building projects
*Shareholders:* Michael White Evans; Helga Ingeborg Evans; Sanne Group PLC
*Officers:* Robert Marshall, Secretary; Roderick Michael Evans [1962] Director; Paul Terence Millington [1962] Director/Accountant; Michael Lewis Prew [1959] Director/Financial Analyst; Alan Matthew Syers [1964] Director/Chartered Surveyor

**Evans Property Holdings Limited**
*Incorporated:* 22 November 2006 *Employees:* 2
*Net Worth:* £52,596,272 *Total Assets:* £133,427,616
*Registered Office:* Millshaw, Leeds, LS11 8EG
*Activities:* Development of building projects
*Shareholders:* Michael White Evans; Sanne Group PLC; Helga Ingeborg Evans
*Officers:* Robert Marshall, Secretary; Roderick Michael Evans [1962] Director; Paul Terence Millington [1962] Director/Accountant

**Evans Regeneration Investments Limited**
*Incorporated:* 22 November 2006 *Employees:* 4
*Net Worth:* £22,720,248 *Total Assets:* £61,051,840
*Registered Office:* Millshaw, Leeds, LS11 8EG
*Activities:* Development of building projects
*Shareholders:* Michael White Evans; Helga Ingeborg Evans; Sanne Group PLC
*Officers:* Robert Marshall, Secretary; Roderick Michael Evans [1962] Director; Paul Terence Millington [1962] Director/Accountant; James Oliver Pitt [1970] Director/Chartered Surveyor; Alan Matthew Syers [1964] Director/Chartered Surveyor

**Evans Residential Holdings Limited**
*Incorporated:* 22 November 2006 *Employees:* 2
*Net Worth:* £6,151,813 *Total Assets:* £7,660,413
*Registered Office:* Millshaw, Leeds, LS11 8EG
*Activities:* Development of building projects
*Parent:* Evans Management Limited
*Officers:* Robert Marshall, Secretary; Roderick Michael Evans [1962] Director; Paul Terence Millington [1962] Director/Accountant

**Evansis Ltd**
*Incorporated:* 6 January 2009
*Net Worth:* £1,369,061 *Total Assets:* £4,777,345
*Registered Office:* 12a Montpellier Parade, Harrogate, N Yorks, HG1 2TJ
*Activities:* Other professional, scientific and technical activities n.e.c.
*Major Shareholder:* Timothy Robert Stuart Gray
*Officers:* Gaynor Gray, Secretary; Gaynor Gray [1966] Director; Timothy Robert Stuart Gray [1963] Director/Engineer

**Ever 2010 Limited**
*Incorporated:* 9 July 1990
*Net Worth:* £400,688,000 *Total Assets:* £450,774,016
*Registered Office:* Asda House, South Bank, Great Wilson Street, Leeds, LS11 5AD
*Activities:* Other retail sale in non-specialised stores
*Parent:* Asda Stores Limited
*Officers:* Alexander Simpson, Secretary; Roger Michael Burnley [1966] Director; Robert Gerard McWilliam [1969] Director; Alexander Simpson [1973] Director

**F.T.Everard & Sons Limited**
*Incorporated:* 1 April 1922
*Net Worth:* £1,105,790 *Total Assets:* £6,777,676
*Registered Office:* P O Box 4, Fisher House, Barrow in Furness, Cumbria, LA14 1HR
*Activities:* Sea and coastal freight water transport
*Parent:* James Fisher and Sons Public Limited Company
*Officers:* James Henry John Marsh, Secretary; Fiona Caroline Everard [1981] Director; Nicholas Paul Henry [1961] Director; Stuart Charles Kilpatrick [1962] Director

**Everard Group Limited**
*Incorporated:* 10 August 2016 *Employees:* 74
*Net Worth:* £2,221,337 *Total Assets:* £7,218,611
*Registered Office:* Unit 1 Technology Close, Green Park Road, Newport, Brough, E Yorks, HU15 2FX
*Activities:* Other service activities n.e.c.
*Shareholders:* James Daniel Everard; Nicolas John Everard
*Officers:* James Daniel Everard [1985] Director/Engineer; Nicolas John Everard [1988] Director/Engineer

**Everik Limited**
*Incorporated:* 7 August 1967 *Employees:* 1
*Net Worth:* £4,024,803 *Total Assets:* £4,233,981
*Registered Office:* 19 Railway Street, Pocklington, York, YO42 2QR
*Activities:* Other letting and operating of own or leased real estate
*Shareholders:* Eric Kimsey; Evelyn Kimsey; Robert Newton Kimsey
*Officers:* Eric George Kimsey [1924] Director/Engineer; Evelyn Pearl Kimsey [1923] Director/Company Secretary [Canadian]; Robert Newton Kimsey [1961] Director/Building Developer

**Everlast (Group) Limited**
*Incorporated:* 7 February 2013 *Employees:* 54
*Net Worth:* £2,546,688 *Total Assets:* £6,277,057
*Registered Office:* The School House, Parkfield Terrace, Pudsey, W Yorks, LS28 6BS
*Activities:* Activities of construction holding companies
*Shareholders:* Michael Douglas Hunter; Jason Lee Cross
*Officers:* Jason Lee Cross [1970] Project Director; Michael Douglas Hunter [1978] Commercial Director

**Everlast Waterproofing Limited**
*Incorporated:* 10 February 2005 *Employees:* 30
*Net Worth:* £2,323,283 *Total Assets:* £5,799,906
*Registered Office:* The School House, Parkfield Terrace, Pudsey, W Yorks, LS28 6BS
*Activities:* Roofing activities
*Parent:* 08394165
*Officers:* Jason Lee Cross [1970] Project Director; Michael Douglas Hunter [1978] Commercial Director

**W Eves & Co (Service Stations) Limited**
*Incorporated:* 9 June 2000 *Employees:* 12
*Net Worth:* £3,925,724 *Total Assets:* £5,034,086
*Registered Office:* First Floor Offices, Four Lane Ends Service Station, Guisborough Road, Whitby, N Yorks, YO21 1LY
*Activities:* Retail sale of automotive fuel in specialised stores
*Officers:* Karen Duke [1978] Director; Pamela Jean Duke [1944] Director

**Eville & Jones (UK) Limited**
*Incorporated:* 15 November 2010 *Employees:* 523
*Net Worth:* £905,606 *Total Assets:* £4,900,053
*Registered Office:* Century House, 1275 Century Way, Thorpe Park, Leeds, LS15 8ZB
*Activities:* Veterinary activities
*Parent:* Eville & Jones (Europe) Limited
*Officers:* Robert David Jones, Secretary; Juan Avila [1966] Director [Spanish]; Peter Charles Eville [1963] Director; Robert David Jones [1964] Director

**Evolution Schools Learning Trust**
*Incorporated:* 7 April 2011 *Employees:* 101
*Net Worth:* £3,865,000 *Total Assets:* £6,884,000
*Registered Office:* Norton College, Langton Road, Norton, Malton, N Yorks, YO17 9PT
*Activities:* General secondary education
*Officers:* Derek MacPhee, Secretary; Robert Charles Slade Hall [1956] Director; Jill Elizabeth Hodges [1957] Director/Retired; John Hudson [1942] Director/Retired Accountant; Philip Loftus [1966] Director/Headteacher; Miranda Stephenson [1955] Director; Karron Young [1969] Director/Schools Advisor

**EWH Holdco Limited**
*Incorporated:* 4 November 2015
*Net Worth:* £8,799,000 *Total Assets:* £196,611,008
*Registered Office:* 1 Humber Quays, Wellington Street West, Hull, HU1 2BN
*Activities:* Production of electricity
*Shareholder:* Bioenergy Infrastructure Holdings
*Officers:* Pinchas Cohen [1968] Director/Economist [Israeli]; Robert Hamish McPherson [1976] Director/Chief Executive Officer; Ran Shaul Shelach [1968] Director/Economist [Israeli]; Glenn Smith [1959] Director/Senior Vice President [American]; Charles Spencer [1953] Director; Ben Wright [1972] Director/Chief Financial Officer

**Exceed Academies Trust**
*Incorporated:* 8 March 2016 *Employees:* 514
*Net Worth:* £56,636,000 *Total Assets:* £61,678,000
*Registered Office:* Horton Park Primary School, Dawnay Road, Bradford, W Yorks, BD5 9LQ
*Activities:* Primary education
*Officers:* Peter James Taylor, Secretary; Victoria Caroline Shelton Eaton [1979] Director/Commercial Delivery Lead, NHS Digital; Jason Edwards [1971] Director/Chief Operating Officer; Trevor Evans [1950] Director/Retired; Elaine Margaret Hughes [1976] Director/Chartered Management Accountant; Nadia Kauser Hussain [1981] Director/Project Manager; Carol Sharon Lambert [1956] Director/Retired; Dr Sandra Georgina Whitson [1938] Director/Retired; Ian Willoughby [1977] Director/Income Officer

**Exceed Learning Partnership**
*Incorporated:* 8 March 2017 *Employees:* 98
*Net Worth:* £3,968,024 *Total Assets:* £5,774,491
*Registered Office:* Hill Top Academy, Edlington Lane, Edlington, Doncaster, S Yorks, DN12 1PL
*Activities:* Primary education
*Officers:* John Blount [1950] Director; Joan Briggs [1949] Director; Richard Brown [1954] Director/Management Consultant; Sarah Louise Creighton [1954] Director/Retired; Diane Lesley Dunn [1956] Director/Management Consultant; Stephen Harry James Edmonds [1977] Director; Melissa Jane Flett [1977] Director/Manager; Leanne Hornsby [1966] Director/Local Government Officer; Carol Ann Swift [1957] Director/Management Consultant; Jill Wood [1977] Managing Director

**Excel Laminating Limited**
*Incorporated:* 2 December 1997
*Net Worth:* £1,253,303 *Total Assets:* £3,568,432
*Registered Office:* Unit 3 Kingston International Business Park, Hedon Road, Hull, HU9 5NX
*Activities:* Other manufacturing n.e.c.
*Parent:* Excel Laminating Holdings Limited
*Officers:* Lesley Diane Thomas, Secretary; Alexander Leslie Thomas [1990] Director; Jeffrey William Thomas [1961] Director/Salesman; Rebecca Diane Thomas [1993] Director

**Exelby Services Limited**
*Incorporated:* 23 December 1976 *Employees:* 82
*Net Worth:* £12,344,597 *Total Assets:* £14,453,305
*Registered Office:* Coneygarth House, Leases Road, Leeming Bar, Northallerton, N Yorks, DL7 9FE
*Activities:* Agents involved in the sale of fuels, ores, metals and industrial chemicals
*Major Shareholder:* Michael Exelby
*Officers:* Shaun Bennington, Secretary; Michael Exelby [1957] Director; Robert Exelby [1986] Operations Director

**Exemplary Group PLC**
*Incorporated:* 6 June 2014 *Employees:* 60
*Net Worth:* £372,256 *Total Assets:* £8,993,956
*Registered Office:* Oracle House, Whitfield Business Park, Manse Lane, Knaresborough, N Yorks, HG5 8BS
*Activities:* Activities of other holding companies n.e.c.
*Major Shareholder:* Peter Lawton Brook
*Officers:* Madeline Esme Mannakee, Secretary; Peter Lawton Brook [1964] Director/Self Employed

**Exlabesa Extrusions (Doncaster) Limited**
*Incorporated:* 20 February 2001 *Employees:* 52
*Previous:* Kaye Aluminium Limited
*Net Worth:* £12,280,915 *Total Assets:* £16,690,285
*Registered Office:* Ogden Road, Wheatley Hills, Doncaster, S Yorks, DN2 4SG
*Activities:* Manufacture of metal structures and parts of structures
*Officers:* Belen Arias Rubiales, Secretary; Felipe Quinta Marino [1979] Director [Spanish]; Fernando Quinta Marino [1970] Director [Spanish]

**Expect Distribution Limited**
*Incorporated:* 25 September 1987 *Employees:* 249
*Net Worth:* £3,390,282 *Total Assets:* £14,897,299
*Registered Office:* Premier Point, Premier Gate, Staithgate Lane, Bradford, W Yorks, BD6 1DW
*Activities:* Freight transport by road
*Shareholders:* Robert Westwell Rushworth; Neil Wayne Rushworth
*Officers:* Robert Westwell Rushworth, Secretary; Elaine Rushworth [1943] Director; Neil Wayne Rushworth [1971] Director; Robert Westwell Rushworth [1944] Director; Andrew David Taylor [1982] Director of Transport; Steven Paul Wood [1955] Director/Consultant

**Explorer (UK) Limited**
*Incorporated:* 10 May 1995 *Employees:* 33
*Net Worth:* £1,847,491 *Total Assets:* £4,102,042
*Registered Office:* Wira Business Park, West Park, Ring Road, Leeds, LS16 6EB
*Activities:* Other information technology service activities
*Parent:* Explorer (UK) Systems Limited
*Officers:* Ian John Thomason, Secretary; Simon Greenwood [1969] Director; Jonathan Lingard [1983] Sales & Marketing Director; Neil Symons [1973] Director; Ian John Thomason [1967] Director

**Explosive Developments Limited**
*Incorporated:* 19 December 1983 *Employees:* 15
*Net Worth:* £1,493,577 *Total Assets:* £3,642,384
*Registered Office:* Halifax Way, Pocklington Industrial Estate, Pocklington, York, YO42 1NP
*Activities:* Manufacture of explosives
*Officers:* John Christopher Hudson, Secretary; John Christopher Hudson [1949] Director/Accountant

**Exponent International Limited**
*Incorporated:* 14 June 2001 *Employees:* 73
*Net Worth:* £10,405,786 *Total Assets:* £14,179,486
*Registered Office:* The Lenz, Hornbeam Business Park, Harrogate, N Yorks, HG2 8RE
*Activities:* Environmental consulting activities
*Parent:* Exponent Inc.
*Officers:* Richard Lee Schlenker, Secretary/Chief Financial Officer [American]; Dr Catherine Ford Corrigan [1968] Director/CEO of Exponent Inc [American]

**Express Bi Folding Doors Limited**
*Incorporated:* 21 March 2007 *Employees:* 190
*Net Worth:* £303,909 *Total Assets:* £7,137,476
*Registered Office:* Unit 23 Millshaw Park Lane, Millshaw Park Industrial Estate, Leeds, LS11 0BL
*Activities:* Manufacture of other furniture
*Shareholders:* Stephen Bromberg; Louise Bromberg
*Officers:* Stephen Bromberg [1958] Director

**Express Group Limited**
*Incorporated:* 29 June 1988 *Employees:* 56
*Net Worth:* £3,541,495 *Total Assets:* £5,699,665
*Registered Office:* College Business Park, Kearsley Road, Ripon, N Yorks, HG4 2RN
*Activities:* Repair of computers and peripheral equipment
*Shareholders:* Linda Mary Whitehouse; David Peter Whitehouse
*Officers:* Rachel Sarah Heath-Smith, Secretary; Darren Brian Ayres [1973] Operations Director; James Simon Blackburn [1971] Commercial Director; Linda Mary Whitehouse [1947] European Director; Peter David Whitehouse [1946] Director/Chairman; Joanna Louise Young [1972] Managing Director

**Extra Detail Limited**
*Incorporated:* 17 March 2010 *Employees:* 686
*Net Worth:* £22,592,000 *Total Assets:* £39,991,000
*Registered Office:* Bankwood Road, Stapleton, Pontefract, W Yorks, WF8 3DD
*Activities:* Processing and preserving of meat
*Shareholders:* David Bosworth Gunner; Edwin John Richard Canvin
*Officers:* David Bosworth Gunner, Secretary; Edwin John Richard Canvin [1950] Director; David Bosworth Gunner [1952] Director; Amanda Patricia Snowie [1961] Director/Retail Butchery Owner

**Extract Technology Limited**
*Incorporated:* 19 June 2006 *Employees:* 75
*Net Worth:* £5,061,955 *Total Assets:* £7,547,920
*Registered Office:* Bradley Junction Industrial Estate, Leeds Road, Huddersfield, W Yorks, HD2 1UR
*Activities:* Manufacture of other special-purpose machinery n.e.c.
*Parent:* Wabash UK Holdings Limited
*Officers:* Melanie Dawn Margolin, Secretary; Kevin Joseph Page [1961] Director/Corporate Officer [American]; Brent L Yeagy [1970] Director/President and Chief Operating Officer for Wabash National Corporation [American]

**Extremis Production Limited**
*Incorporated:* 25 November 2013 *Employees:* 2
*Net Worth:* £849,095 *Total Assets:* £4,683,904
*Registered Office:* Highfield Grange, Bubwith, Selby, N Yorks, YO8 6DP
*Activities:* Motion picture production activities
*Officers:* Alan Richard Latham [1960] Director/Producer

**Extron Electronics UK Limited**
*Incorporated:* 19 May 2005 *Employees:* 47
*Net Worth:* £2,749,000 *Total Assets:* £4,228,000
*Registered Office:* Elizabeth House, 13-19 Queen Street, Leeds, LS1 2TW
*Activities:* Other engineering activities
*Shareholder:* Andrew Carr Edwards
*Officers:* Edward James Ellingwood [1960] Director [American]; Wybe Vellinga [1957] Director [Dutch]

**Extrudakerb (Maltby Engineering) Limited**
*Incorporated:* 15 March 1977 *Employees:* 81
*Net Worth:* £2,289,528 *Total Assets:* £7,108,184
*Registered Office:* Denaby Lane Industrial Estate, Old Denaby, Doncaster, S Yorks, DN12 4JJ
*Activities:* Construction of roads and motorways
*Shareholders:* Willis Arnold Charlesworth; Joan Charlesworth
*Officers:* Joan Charlesworth, Secretary; James Kerber Charlesworth [1968] Director; Joan Charlesworth [1940] Director/Secretary; Willis Arnold Charlesworth [1936] Director/Engineer; Neil Simon Mangham [1979] Financial Director

**EYG Holdings Limited**
*Incorporated:* 14 March 2007 *Employees:* 269
*Net Worth:* £4,245,331 *Total Assets:* £8,615,601
*Registered Office:* Wiltshire Road, Dairycoates Industrial Estate, Hull, HU4 6QQ
*Activities:* Manufacture of builders ware of plastic
*Shareholders:* James Richard Bingham; Nicholas Simon Ward
*Officers:* Roger Nicholas Harrison, Secretary; Lisa Jayne Baxter [1975] Director; James Richard Bingham [1946] Director; Linda Margaret Bingham [1950] Director; Christopher George [1948] Director; Roger Nicholas Harrison [1953] Director/Company Accountant; Louise Amanda Ward [1971] Director; Nicholas Simon Ward [1970] Director

**F & G Commercials (Huddersfield) Ltd**
*Incorporated:* 19 August 1994 *Employees:* 53
*Net Worth:* £3,450,376 *Total Assets:* £16,620,336
*Registered Office:* Bradley Junction Industrial Estate, Leeds Road, Huddersfield, W Yorks, HD2 1UR
*Activities:* Sale of other motor vehicles
*Officers:* Glenn Andrew Stevenson [1969] Director; Frank Woodhead [1965] Director

**F A S 2000 Limited**
*Incorporated:* 5 September 1984 *Employees:* 41
*Net Worth:* £2,713,000 *Total Assets:* £6,409,000
*Registered Office:* Livingstone Road, Hessle, Hull, HU13 0EE
*Activities:* Marine fishing
*Parent:* Fastnet Fish Limited
*Officers:* Paul Morgan Farrar, Secretary; Joy Susan Herd [1962] Financial Director; Roger Eric Johnson [1947] Director; Christian Leslie Marr [1972] Director; Frank Anthony Jamie Osborne [1968] Managing Director; Andrew William Regan [1962] Financial Director; Andrew Keith Weightman [1962] Sales Director

**F and N One Limited**
*Incorporated:* 10 November 2008 *Employees:* 236
*Net Worth:* £60,821,008 *Total Assets:* £66,821,088
*Registered Office:* c/o The Old Court House, Clark Street, Morecambe, Lancs, LA4 5HR
*Activities:* Non-trading company
*Parent:* DWF (Trustee) Limited
*Officers:* Frank Bird [1936] Director

**F M G Support (Ho) Limited**
*Incorporated:* 4 June 1998
*Net Worth:* £990,000 *Total Assets:* £34,444,000
*Registered Office:* Broad Lea House, Dyson Wood Way, Bradley, Huddersfield, W Yorks, HD2 1GZ
*Activities:* Combined office administrative service activities
*Parent:* FMG Support Limited
*Officers:* Mark Francis Chessman [1964] Director; Stephen Edward Oakley [1952] Director; Claire Owens [1983] Finance Director; Paul Harvey Stead [1967] Commercial Director; Martin Ward [1967] Managing Director

**F.S.H. (Group) Limited**
*Incorporated:* 19 February 1996 *Employees:* 215
*Previous:* F.S.H. Maintenance Limited
*Net Worth:* £1,035,891 *Total Assets:* £5,541,053
*Registered Office:* Unit D, Links 31, Willowbridge Way, Whitwood, Castleford, W Yorks, WF10 5NP
*Activities:* Other specialised construction activities n.e.c.
*Major Shareholder:* Ian Michael Wood
*Officers:* Matthew Cappleman [1974] Director; Ian Michael Wood [1958] Director/Builder

**F.T. Construction Group (Holdings) Ltd.**
*Incorporated:* 1 February 1996 *Employees:* 20
*Net Worth:* £4,126,692 *Total Assets:* £6,069,442
*Registered Office:* Construction House, Northallerton, N Yorks, DL7 8ED
*Activities:* Development of building projects
*Parent:* Fordy Thompson (Holdings) Limited
*Officers:* Derek John Greenwell, Secretary; Paul Blades [1963] Director; Keith Edmund Caygill [1953] Director; Derek John Greenwell [1948] Director Company Secretary; Susan Bridget Greenwell [1958] Director; Keith Brian Noddings [1972] Finance Director; Vincent Phillips [1959] Non-Executive Director Chairman; Sarah Louise Anne Wilkinson [1965] Director

**F.T.L. Holdings Limited**
*Incorporated:* 29 March 1984 *Employees:* 3
*Net Worth:* £4,202,000 *Total Assets:* £4,232,000
*Registered Office:* Howley Park Road, Morley, Leeds, LS27 0QS
*Activities:* Activities of head offices
*Officers:* Phoebe Reid [1966] Director; David Keith Runton [1938] Director; Simon James Christopher Runton [1964] Director

**F1rst Actuarial PLC**
*Incorporated:* 7 May 2004 *Employees:* 210
*Net Worth:* £2,048,419 *Total Assets:* £8,577,406
*Registered Office:* Mayesbrook House, Lawnswood Business Park, Redvers Close, Leeds, LS16 6QY
*Activities:* Pension funding
*Officers:* Michael Wilfred Hulme-Vickerstaff, Secretary; Michael Wilfred Hulme-Vickerstaff [1968] Director/Actuary; David Ian Joy [1969] Director/Actuary; Christopher David Martin [1970] Director/Actuary; Mark Steven Riches [1969] Director/Actuary; Hilary Salt [1963] Director/Actuary; Peter Michael Shellswell [1970] Director/Actuary; Alan Edward Smith [1956] Director/Actuary; James Robert Smith [1966] Director/Actuary; Keith John Williams [1959] Director/Actuary

**Fablink Tank Systems Limited**
*Incorporated:* 21 May 2009 *Employees:* 134
*Net Worth:* £296,631 *Total Assets:* £3,372,168
*Registered Office:* Fablink Tank Systems Ltd, Evenwood, Bishop Auckland, Co Durham, DL14 9NJ
*Activities:* Manufacture of other fabricated metal products n.e.c.
*Officers:* Michael Singleton, Secretary; Richard Alan Westley [1974] Director

**Facultatieve Technologies Limited**
*Incorporated:* 22 July 1959 *Employees:* 137
*Net Worth:* £6,044,767 *Total Assets:* £19,797,892
*Registered Office:* Facultatieve Technologies Ltd, Moor Road, Leeds, LS10 2DD
*Activities:* Other manufacturing n.e.c.
*Parent:* Facultatieve Group
*Officers:* John Alan Wood, Secretary; Jacob Andries de Bruijn [1951] Director [Dutch]; Patrick Paul Ghislain de Meyer [1964] Director [Belgian]; Judicus Marinus Henricus Jacobus Keizer [1960] Director/Chief Executive [Dutch]; Jeffrey Stephen Pickard [1959] Operations Director; Paul Antony Thrush [1966] Director/Service & Operations

**Faculty of Queen Ethelburga's Limited**
*Incorporated:* 20 September 1996 *Employees:* 231
*Net Worth:* £1,217,689 *Total Assets:* £11,068,648
*Registered Office:* Thorpe Underwood Hall, Thorpe Underwood, York, YO26 9SZ
*Activities:* Other business support service activities n.e.c.
*Parent:* The Collegiate Formation Ltd
*Officers:* Christopher James Hall, Secretary; Christopher James Hall [1969] Director/Chartered Accountant; Amy Katherine Martin [1983] Director; Francis David Martin [1967] Director/Business Executive

**Fairbriar Developments (Salford) Limited**
*Incorporated:* 23 August 2011
*Net Worth:* £2,094,149 *Total Assets:* £13,838,468
*Registered Office:* Europa House, 20 Esplanade, Scarborough, N Yorks, YO11 2AQ
*Activities:* Development of building projects
*Parent:* Fairbriar Real Estate Developments Limited
*Officers:* Simon Charles McCabe [1977] Director; Jeremy John Tutton [1966] Director/Financial Controller

**Fairbriar Real Estate Developments Limited**
*Incorporated:* 3 March 2014
*Net Worth:* £1,973,395 *Total Assets:* £95,344,480
*Registered Office:* Europa House, 20 Esplanade, Scarborough, N Yorks, YO11 2AQ
*Activities:* Buying and selling of own real estate
*Parent:* Fairbriar Real Estate Limited
*Officers:* Simon Charles McCabe [1977] Director/Development Executive; Jeremy John Tutton [1966] Director/Financial Controller

**Fairbriar Real Estate Limited**
*Incorporated:* 12 February 2014
*Net Worth:* £8,294,132 *Total Assets:* £119,147,808
*Registered Office:* Europa House, 20 Esplanade, Scarborough, N Yorks, YO11 2AQ
*Activities:* Activities of construction holding companies
*Parent:* Fairbriar Residential Developments Limited
*Officers:* Kok Sung Lawrence Chiang [1952] Director [Singaporean]; Simon Charles McCabe [1977] Director; Jeremy John Tutton [1966] Director/Financial Controller; Mi Zaifeng [1985] Director/Businessman [Chinese]

**Fairbriar Residential Developments Limited**
*Incorporated:* 10 March 2010
*Net Worth:* £551,772 *Total Assets:* £11,156,770
*Registered Office:* Europa House, 20 Esplanade, Scarborough, N Yorks, YO11 2AQ
*Activities:* Activities of construction holding companies
*Parent:* Scarborough International Properties Limited
*Officers:* Simon Charles McCabe [1977] Director; Jeremy John Tutton [1966] Director/Financial Controller

**Fairfax Plant Hire Limited**
*Incorporated:* 8 October 1985 *Employees:* 68
*Net Worth:* £6,988,833 *Total Assets:* £21,441,112
*Registered Office:* The Old Brickworks, Hull Road, Hemingbrough, Selby, N Yorks, YO8 6QG
*Activities:* Renting and leasing of construction and civil engineering machinery and equipment
*Shareholders:* Carolyn Love; Kenneth Love
*Officers:* Carolyn Love, Secretary/Director; Carolyn Love [1953] Director; Kenneth Love [1949] Director; Mark Andrew Love [1973] Director; Matthew John Love [1977] Director

**Fairfax Securities Limited**
*Incorporated:* 26 October 1983 *Employees:* 2
*Net Worth:* £5,241,149 *Total Assets:* £12,612,400
*Registered Office:* First Floor, 6 Lisbon Square, Leeds, LS1 4LY
*Activities:* Development of building projects
*Shareholders:* Graham William Forster; Lionel Barry Tyldsley
*Officers:* Elizabeth Anne Tyldsley, Secretary; Graham William Forster [1951] Director/Property Developer; Lionel Barry Tyldsley [1936] Director/Property Developer

**Fairfield Developments (Doncaster) Limited**
*Incorporated:* 11 July 1996
*Net Worth:* £5,773,669 *Total Assets:* £7,650,907
*Registered Office:* The Manor, Bawtry Road, Hatfield Woodhouse, Doncaster, S Yorks, DN7 6PH
*Activities:* Construction of commercial buildings
*Shareholders:* Maureen Holt; John Holt; Richard Alexander Prior
*Officers:* Maureen Holt, Secretary; John Holt [1945] Director/Property Developer; Maureen Holt [1946] Director/Secretary

**Fairhurst Stone Merchants Limited**
*Incorporated:* 1 March 2012 *Employees:* 27
*Net Worth:* £1,016,657 *Total Assets:* £4,798,925
*Registered Office:* Langcliffe Mill, Stainforth Road, Langcliffe, Settle, N Yorks, BD24 9NP
*Activities:* Cutting, shaping and finishing of stone
*Shareholders:* Edward Robert Fairhurst; Keith Fairhurst; Susan Fairhurst
*Officers:* Edward Robert Fairhurst [1981] Director/Stone Merchant Farmer; Susan Fairhurst [1947] Director/Stone Merchant/Farmer

**Falcon Electrical Wholesalers Limited**
*Incorporated:* 13 February 1995 *Employees:* 20
*Net Worth:* £2,273,961 *Total Assets:* £5,118,889
*Registered Office:* Carlton House, Grammar School Street, Bradford, BD1 4NS
*Activities:* Repair of household appliances and home and garden equipment
*Parent:* Treeglade Properties Limited
*Officers:* Jatinder Kaur Bhambra, Secretary; Baljit Singh Bhambra [1959] Director/Electrical Wholesaler

**Falcon Sportswear Limited**
*Incorporated:* 23 October 1974
*Net Worth:* £2,724,643 *Total Assets:* £4,636,836
*Registered Office:* Falcon House, Croft Road, Crossflatts, Bingley, W Yorks, BD16 2DU
*Activities:* Wholesale of clothing and footwear
*Major Shareholder:* Gordon Lionel Brumfitt
*Officers:* Gordon Lionel Brumfitt, Secretary; Gary Frank Brumfitt [1956] Director/Sports Wholesaler; Gordon Lionel Brumfitt [1951] Director; Michael John Brumfitt [1979] Director; Paul Lionel Brumfitt [1977] Director; Simon Kelvin Dooley [1964] Director

**T.W.Falkingham Limited**
*Incorporated:* 28 April 1959 *Employees:* 10
*Net Worth:* £1,496,592 *Total Assets:* £4,226,152
*Registered Office:* Leatham Lodge, Balne Hall Road, Pollington, Goole, N Humbers, DN14 0DY
*Activities:* Growing of cereals (except rice), leguminous crops and oil seeds
*Shareholders:* Matthew Stuart Wood; William Martin Falkingham
*Officers:* Sabira Tall, Secretary; William Martin Falkingham [1950] Director/Farmer; Matthew Stuart Wood [1990] Director/Farmer

**John T. Fall Limited**
*Incorporated:* 4 April 1977 *Employees:* 13
*Net Worth:* £2,549,929 *Total Assets:* £3,569,902
*Registered Office:* Mill Beck, Kirklington, Bedale, N Yorks, DL8 2LX
*Activities:* Growing of cereals (except rice), leguminous crops and oil seeds
*Major Shareholder:* Stephen Charles Fall
*Officers:* Annabel Louise Fall, Secretary; Annabel Louise Fall [1968] Director; Stephen Charles Fall [1963] Director/Farmer

**Fambo UK Limited**
*Incorporated:* 23 February 2005
*Net Worth:* £28,978,000 *Total Assets:* £28,978,000
*Registered Office:* Unit 3 St James Business Park, Grimbald Crag Court, Knaresborough, N Yorks, HG5 8QB
*Activities:* Retail sale of automotive fuel in specialised stores
*Parent:* Fleetcor UK Acquisition Limited
*Officers:* Andrew Robert Blazye [1958] Director/Chief Executive; Eric Richard Dey [1959] Director/Chief Financial Officer [American]; Anita Kravos-Medimorec [1974] Director/Chief Financial Officer; Steven Joseph Pisciotta [1964] Director [American]

**Family Dies Limited**
*Incorporated:* 3 December 2009 *Employees:* 3
*Net Worth:* £1,099,498 *Total Assets:* £5,009,251
*Registered Office:* Highfield Grange, Bubwith, Selby, N Yorks, YO8 6DP
*Activities:* Motion picture production activities
*Parent:* Goldfinch Comedy Limited
*Officers:* Alan Richard Latham [1960] Director

**The Family Fund Trust for Families with Severely Disabled Children**
*Incorporated:* 1 March 1996 *Employees:* 2
*Net Worth:* £3,481,000 *Total Assets:* £14,720,000
*Registered Office:* Unit 4 Alpha Court, Monks Cross Drive, Huntington, York, YO32 9WN
*Activities:* Other human health activities
*Officers:* Paul Barton Smith, Secretary; Mary Ann Bishop [1959] Director/Retired; David Michael Braybrook [1943] Director/Consultant; Kathleen Roseann Fleck [1951] Director; David Peter Lewis [1961] Director/Solicitor; Geoffrey Cyril Linnell [1954] Director; John Grant MacRae [1950] Director/Retired Chartered Accountant; Tara Marie Palmer [1976] Director/Chief Operations Officer; Neil Robert Scott [1966] Director/Chief Finance Officer

**The Family of Learning Trust**
*Incorporated:* 8 August 2011 *Employees:* 164
*Previous:* Beech Hill School
*Net Worth:* £10,454,513 *Total Assets:* £11,917,373
*Registered Office:* Beech Hill School, Mount Pleasant Avenue, Halifax, W Yorks, HX1 5TN
*Activities:* Primary education
*Officers:* Samantha Jayne Bowling [1982] Director/Deputy Headteacher; Christopher Haddock [1950] Director/Solicitor; Shameen Hussain [1973] Director/Headteacher; Sofia Loreen [1979] Director/Nursery Practitioner; Nadim Najib [1973] Director/Banker; Fiona Pether [1982] Director/Headteacher; Meryem Sadiq [1972] Director/Support Assistant; Shazia Sheikh [1975] Director/Local Government Finance Officer; Chris Swallow [1979] Director/Bank Manager

**Farmers Boy Limited**
*Incorporated:* 10 May 1972 *Employees:* 3,031
*Net Worth:* £270,839,008 *Total Assets:* £782,220,992
*Registered Office:* Hilmore House, Gain Lane, Bradford, W Yorks, BD3 7DL
*Activities:* Production of meat and poultry meat products
*Parent:* Wm Morrison Supermarkets Holdings Limited
*Officers:* Jonathan James Burke, Secretary; Andrew James Clappen [1965] Technical Director; Jonathan William Reed [1973] Director; Mark Thomas Stitson [1976] Finance Director; Andrew Edward Thornber [1974] Director

**Farmhouse Fare Limited**
*Incorporated:* 16 October 2001 *Employees:* 197
*Net Worth:* £16,703,000 *Total Assets:* £23,172,000
*Registered Office:* 2100 Century Way, Thorpe Park Business Park, Leeds, LS15 8ZB
*Activities:* Manufacture of other food products n.e.c.
*Parent:* Daniels Chilled Foods Limited
*Officers:* Nicholas Keen, Secretary; Denise Menikheim Faltischek [1973] Director/Executive Vice President and General Counsel [American]; James Michael Langrock [1965] Director [American]; Mark Lawrence Schiller [1961] Director [American]; Robin James Skidmore [1968] Director

**Farmhouse Potato Bakers Limited**
*Incorporated:* 11 March 1985 *Employees:* 223
*Net Worth:* £4,964,725 *Total Assets:* £9,761,861
*Registered Office:* Lancaster Road, Carnaby Industrial Estate, Carnaby, Bridlington, E Yorks, YO15 3QY
*Activities:* Processing and preserving of potatoes
*Parent:* Bannisters Arable Products Limited
*Officers:* Hilary Margaret Bannister, Secretary; Hilary Margaret Bannister [1949] Director; Robert Michael Bannister [1949] Director; Zoe Anne Bannister [1973] Director; Marie Louise Medhurst [1975] Director

**Farmstar Limited**
*Incorporated:* 26 May 1988 *Employees:* 73
*Net Worth:* £3,793,281 *Total Assets:* £16,458,039
*Registered Office:* Grove Farm, Church Lane, Marr, Doncaster, S Yorks, DN5 7AU
*Activities:* Wholesale of agricultural machinery, equipment and supplies
*Shareholders:* Charles Rupert Brown; Daphne Rebecca Moxon
*Officers:* Laura Thomas, Secretary; Brian Maurice Bannister [1960] Branch Director; Charles Rupert Brown [1957] Director/Farmer; Shaun Nigel Husler [1961] Group Service Director; Richard Anthony Lister [1973] Branch Sales Director; Andrew Thomas Waddington [1971] Managing Director

**Farnell Electronic Components Limited**
*Incorporated:* 26 July 1947 *Employees:* 150
*Net Worth:* £16,685,000 *Total Assets:* £17,929,000
*Registered Office:* 150 Armley Road, Leeds, LS12 2QQ
*Activities:* Wholesale of electronic and telecommunications equipment and parts
*Parent:* Farnell Holding Limited
*Officers:* Ralph Lothar Buhler [1968] Director [German]; Liam Anthony Heffernan [1972] Director/Accountant [Irish]; Harvey Woodford [1963] Director/VP Corporate Secretary [American]

**Farnell Holding Limited**
*Incorporated:* 3 June 1969
*Net Worth:* £385,783,008 *Total Assets:* £387,835,008
*Registered Office:* Farnell House, Forge Lane, Leeds, LS12 2NE
*Activities:* Non-trading company
*Parent:* Premier Farnell Limited
*Officers:* Liam Anthony Heffernan [1972] Director/Accountant [Irish]; Harvey Woodford [1963] Director/VP Corporate Secretary [American]

**Farnsworth Investments Limited**
*Incorporated:* 1 March 1990
*Net Worth Deficit:* £2,064,000 *Total Assets:* £8,011,000
*Registered Office:* Trinity Park House, Fox Way, Wakefield, W Yorks, WF2 8EE
*Activities:* Financial intermediation not elsewhere classified
*Parent:* Northern Foods Limited
*Officers:* Ronald Klaas Otto Kers [1969] Director/Group CEO [Dutch]; Craig Ashley Tomkinson [1982] Director/Group CFO

**F.W. Farnsworth Limited**
*Incorporated:* 23 April 1931 *Employees:* 880
*Net Worth Deficit:* £68,270,000 *Total Assets:* £61,223,000
*Registered Office:* Trinity Park House, Fox Way, Wakefield, W Yorks, WF2 8EE
*Activities:* Production of meat and poultry meat products
*Parent:* Beverley House (9000) Limited
*Officers:* Ranjit Singh Boparan [1966] Director; Ronald Klaas Otto Kers [1969] Director/Group CEO [Dutch]; Keith Richard Packer [1967] Managing Director; Richard Peter Simpson [1965] Finance Director; Craig Ashley Tomkinson [1982] Director/Group CFO

**Farsley Transport Limited**
*Incorporated:* 7 October 1996 *Employees:* 90
*Net Worth:* £269,728 *Total Assets:* £3,405,063
*Registered Office:* Unit 4 Leeds West, Gelderd Lane, Leeds, LS12 6AL
*Activities:* Freight transport by road
*Shareholders:* Mandy Chappelow; Neil Chappelow
*Officers:* Joseph Ward, Secretary; Neil Chappelow [1967] Director; Daniel Lee Hardwick [1979] Director; Joseph Ward [1962] Director

**Fast Freeze International Limited**
*Incorporated:* 7 February 1995
*Net Worth:* £7,173,882 *Total Assets:* £12,805,888
*Registered Office:* 22 Longley, Holmfirth, W Yorks, HD9 2JD
*Activities:* Other service activities n.e.c.
*Major Shareholder:* Robert James Dickinson
*Officers:* Patricia Ann Wood, Secretary; Robert James Dickinson [1956] Director; Christopher Kenneth Sharpe [1955] Managing Director [Australian]

**Fast Trade Venture Limited**
*Incorporated:* 8 January 2007 *Employees:* 1
*Net Worth:* £1,317,062 *Total Assets:* £3,251,659
*Registered Office:* Bridge House, 41 Wincolmlee, Kingston upon Hull, HU2 8AG
*Activities:* Wholesale of other food, including fish, crustaceans and molluscs
*Parent:* Gefira Group AG
*Officers:* Denis Zolotarev [1969] Director

**Fastnet Fish Limited**
*Incorporated:* 19 January 1987 *Employees:* 36
*Net Worth:* £8,484,000 *Total Assets:* £36,129,000
*Registered Office:* Livingstone Road, Hessle, Hull, HU13 0EE
*Activities:* Marine fishing
*Parent:* Fastnet Holdings Limited
*Officers:* Paul Morgan Farrar, Secretary; Joy Susan Herd [1962] Financial Director; Roger Eric Johnson [1947] Director; Andrew Leslie Marr [1942] Director; Christian Leslie Marr [1972] Director; Matthew Efford Omley [1969] Director; Andrew William Regan [1962] Financial Director; Andrew Keith Weightman [1962] Director

**Fastnet Holdings Limited**
*Incorporated:* 8 April 1980 *Employees:* 138
*Net Worth:* £14,614,000 *Total Assets:* £51,013,000
*Registered Office:* Livingstone Road, Hessle, Hull, HU13 0EE
*Activities:* Marine fishing
*Parent:* Andrew Marr International Limited
*Officers:* Paul Morgan Farrar, Secretary; Joy Susan Herd [1962] Financial Director; Roger Eric Johnson [1947] Director; Andrew Leslie Marr [1942] Director; Christian Leslie Marr [1972] Director; Andrew William Regan [1962] Financial Director; Andrew Keith Weightman [1962] Director

**Thomas Fattorini Limited**
*Incorporated:* 24 February 1919 *Employees:* 76
*Net Worth:* £4,798,168 *Total Assets:* £5,777,249
*Registered Office:* Skipton Castle, Skipton, N Yorks, BD23 1AQ
*Activities:* Other manufacturing n.e.c.
*Officers:* Gregory Thomas Buhler Fattorini [1962] Director; Sebastian Thomas Buhler Fattorini [1966] Director/Manager; Thomas Robert Buhler Fattorini [1960] Director; Timothy Hugh Thomas Fattorini [1970] Director/Sales Executive; Gary Speakman [1967] Director

**Thomas Fawcett & Sons,Limited**
*Incorporated:* 20 March 1919 *Employees:* 64
*Net Worth:* £9,846,499 *Total Assets:* £12,834,715
*Registered Office:* Eastfield Lane, Castleford, W Yorks, WF10 4LE
*Activities:* Manufacture of other food products n.e.c.
*Shareholder:* James Alastair Geoffrey Fawcett
*Officers:* Joanne Tonks, Secretary; James Alastair Geoffrey Fawcett [1964] Director; Lara Sarah Fawcett [1966] Director/Tennis Coach; Mungo Fawcett [1997] Director/Development; Sara Helen Fawcett [1938] Director; Brian Charles Hickman [1966] Production Director; Julia Mary Pratt [1963] Director

**FC Beamish Bidco Ltd**
*Incorporated:* 6 December 2016
*Net Worth:* £100,710,656 *Total Assets:* £109,660,432
*Registered Office:* Southgate House, Archer Street, Darlington, Co Durham, DL3 6AH
*Activities:* Activities of other holding companies n.e.c.
*Parent:* FC Skyfall Bidco Limited
*Officers:* James Justin Hutchens [1974] Director [American]; David Andrew Smith [1974] Director/Accountant

**Fearnley Rhodes Limited**
*Incorporated:* 9 May 2012
*Net Worth:* £3,297,167 *Total Assets:* £3,309,254
*Registered Office:* Unit 1a Woodvale Workshops, Thornhill Beck Lane, Brighouse, W Yorks, HD6 4AH
*Activities:* Activities of construction holding companies
*Shareholders:* John Fearnley Rhodes; Karen Virginia Rhodes
*Officers:* Jonathan Fearnley Rhodes [1961] Director; Karen Virginia Rhodes [1963] Director

**Febi (UK) Limited**
*Incorporated:* 21 February 1990 *Employees:* 32
*Net Worth:* £2,861,780 *Total Assets:* £11,406,003
*Registered Office:* Bilstein House, Green Lane Industrial Park, Featherstone, Pontefract, W Yorks, WF7 6TA
*Activities:* Wholesale trade of motor vehicle parts and accessories
*Parent:* Bilstein Handels GmbH
*Officers:* Christopher John Dickinson, Secretary; Paul Philip Dodgson [1978] Director; Martin Gorton [1965] Managing Director; Karsten Schussler-Bilstein [1971] Director [German]; Jan Tobias Siekermann [1979] Director [German]

**The Federation of Abbey Schools Academy Trust**
*Incorporated:* 11 July 2011 *Employees:* 98
*Net Worth:* £3,878,000 *Total Assets:* £4,837,000
*Registered Office:* The Federation of Abbey Schools, Infant Building, Cleveland Terrace, Darlington, Co Durham, DL3 8JA
*Activities:* Primary education
*Officers:* David Michael Bailey [1975] Director/Educational Consultant/Regional Network Lead; Peter Alan Bibby [1978] Director/Civil Servant; Jonathan Briggs [1970] Director/Headteacher; Laurence Miles Bryant [1971] Director/IT Manager; Emma Louise de La Motte [1972] Director/Secondary School Teacher (MFL); Vicky Folkes [1973] Director/Teacher; Michael James Fryer [1952] Director; Rita Hall [1953] Director/Retired; Rachel Kershaw [1975] Director/Senior Partner; Nigel Peter Little [1951] Director/Retired; Clare Marley [1979] Director [Irish]; Helen Parkinson [1970] Director; Jodie Scott [1978] Director; Catherine Stow Smith [1975] Director; Peter Malcolm Willson [1941] Director/Retired

**Federation of Mowden Schools Academy Trust**
*Incorporated:* 12 April 2012 *Employees:* 65
*Net Worth:* £5,776,000 *Total Assets:* £6,547,000
*Registered Office:* c/o Mowden Junior School, Conyers Avenue, Darlington, Co Durham, DL3 9DE
*Activities:* Primary education
*Officers:* Angela Taylor, Secretary; Robert Andrew Auty [1985] Director/Accountant; Nicholas Bowerman [1975] Finance Director; Emily Elizabeth Bradshaw [1979] Director/Solicitor; Alison Cockrill [1967] Director/Office Administrator; Michelle Dunwell [1986] Director/Teacher; David Holmes [1968] Director/Regional Sales Manager; Alan Jones [1982] Director/Teacher; Peter Donald King [1969] Director/Headteacher; Tarryn Dimmock Lloyd-Payne [1976] Director/Local Authority Manager; Jacqueline Saint [1954] Director; Christopher Strong [1976] Director of Education; Diane Turner [1955] Director/Childminder; Anthony John Ward [1984] Director/Civil Servant

**The Feel Good Group Limited**
*Incorporated:* 31 July 2006 *Employees:* 268
*Net Worth:* £4,591,457 *Total Assets:* £10,025,705
*Registered Office:* Unit J6, Morton Park Way, Darlington, Co Durham, DL1 4PG
*Activities:* Other retail sale in non-specialised stores
*Parent:* The Feel Good Group (Holdings) Limited
*Officers:* Keith Eliot Smith, Secretary; Matthew John Briggs [1968] Director; Adam Leo Mooney [1964] Managing Director [Irish]; Ciaran John Mooney [1968] Franchise Director [Irish]

**FEL Group Limited**
*Incorporated:* 27 March 1997 *Employees:* 61
*Previous:* Foster Environmental Limited
*Net Worth:* £2,222,011 *Total Assets:* £19,218,502
*Registered Office:* Normanby Gateway, Lysaghts Way, Normanby Road, Scunthorpe, N Lincs, DN15 9YG
*Activities:* Plumbing, heat and air-conditioning installation
*Parent:* Nickle Holdings Limited
*Officers:* Darren Crawford [1972] Director/Service Manager; Gerard Doolan [1962] Director/Chief Executive Officer; John Nigel Higginbottom [1975] Director/Chief Financial Officer; Michelle Wainwright [1973] Operations Director

**H.R. Fell and Sons Limited**
*Incorporated:* 29 December 1978 *Employees:* 4
*Net Worth:* £2,164,348 *Total Assets:* £3,549,643
*Registered Office:* West Grange, Thorganby, York, YO19 6DJ
*Activities:* Raising of sheep and goats
*Officers:* George Frederick Fell [1982] Director; Henry Rudston Fell [1929] Director/Farmer; Louis Michael Rudston Fell [1980] Director; Robert Hugh Fell [1961] Director/Agriculture; Stephen Charles Rudston Fell [1953] Director/Farmer; Anna Mary Morley [1984] Director/Chartered Surveyor

**Felldale Retail Limited**
*Incorporated:* 23 May 2014 *Employees:* 157
*Net Worth:* £1,342,330 *Total Assets:* £3,342,778
*Registered Office:* Rothay Road Industrial Estate, Ambleside, Cumbria, LA22 0HQ
*Activities:* Retail sale of clothing in specialised stores
*Parent:* Lakeland Fashion Limited
*Officers:* Peter Brookes, Secretary; Peter Brookes [1976] Director; Martin Andrew Foster [1966] Director/Chartered Accountant; Robert David Malone [1961] Director; Richard Ellis Standring [1946] Director

**Fellowes Ltd**
*Incorporated:* 30 November 1965 *Employees:* 131
*Net Worth:* £16,476,719 *Total Assets:* £42,890,304
*Registered Office:* Unit 2 Ontario Drive, New Rossington, Doncaster, S Yorks, DN11 0BF
*Activities:* Wholesale of other office machinery and equipment
*Parent:* Fellowes Inc
*Officers:* Andrew John Toon, Secretary; Steven Leroy Carson [1963] Director/VP and General Counsel [American]; James Fellowes [1946] Director [American]; John Everett Fellowes [1978] Director [American]; Andrew John Toon [1958] Director of Finance

**Fellside Property Rentals Limited**
*Incorporated:* 4 September 2012 *Employees:* 3
*Net Worth:* £1,910,849 *Total Assets:* £3,955,431
*Registered Office:* Tarnwater, Milnthorpe Road, Yealand Conyers, Carnforth, Lancs, LA5 9RJ
*Activities:* Other letting and operating of own or leased real estate
*Major Shareholder:* Philip Rogerson
*Officers:* Julie Anne Rogerson [1969] Director; Philip Rogerson [1963] Director

**Fender Care Limited**
*Incorporated:* 14 June 1988 *Employees:* 96
*Net Worth:* £263,799 *Total Assets:* £39,129,128
*Registered Office:* P O Box 4, Fisher House, Barrow in Furness, Cumbria, LA14 1HR
*Activities:* Other business support service activities n.e.c.
*Parent:* Fender Care Marine Solutions Limited
*Officers:* James Henry John Marsh, Secretary; Paul Cansdale [1972] Finance Director; Lara Emma Elteb Griffin-Sparrow [1972] Director; Nicholas Paul Henry [1961] Director; Stuart Charles Kilpatrick [1962] Director; Mark Charles Nicholls [1963] Director

**Fender Care Marine Ltd**
*Incorporated:* 4 July 1995 *Employees:* 15
*Net Worth:* £15,309,649 *Total Assets:* £58,681,588
*Registered Office:* P O Box 4, Fisher House, Barrow in Furness, Cumbria, LA14 1HR
*Activities:* Other business support service activities n.e.c.
*Parent:* Fender Care Marine Solutions Limited
*Officers:* James Henry John Marsh, Secretary; Paul Cansdale [1972] Financial Director; Nicholas Paul Henry [1961] Director; Stuart Charles Kilpatrick [1962] Finance Director; Mark Charles Nicholls [1963] Director; Elizabeth Anne Skinner [1978] Director/Operations Manager

**Fender Care Marine Services Group Limited**
*Incorporated:* 16 August 2004
*Net Worth:* £349,109 *Total Assets:* £12,178,921
*Registered Office:* P O Box 4, Fisher House, Barrow in Furness, Cumbria, LA14 1HR
*Activities:* Activities of head offices
*Parent:* James Fisher Holdings UK Limited
*Officers:* James Henry John Marsh, Secretary; Nicholas Paul Henry [1961] Director; Stuart Charles Kilpatrick [1962] Finance Director; Mark Charles Nicholls [1963] Director

**Fender Steel Limited**
*Incorporated:* 19 January 1981 *Employees:* 23
*Net Worth:* £1,102,465 *Total Assets:* £3,078,503
*Registered Office:* 20 Midland Road, Scunthorpe, N Lincs, DN16 1DQ
*Activities:* Manufacture of metal structures and parts of structures
*Shareholders:* Lee Garry Norris; Colin Norris; Carleen Sheila Norris
*Officers:* Carleen Sheila Norris, Secretary; Carleen Sheila Norris [1939] Director/Company Secretary; Colin Norris [1962] Director/Office Manager; Lee Garry Norris [1971] Director/Office Manager

**J.H. Fenner & Co. (Advanced Engineered Products) Limited**
*Incorporated:* 26 April 1956
*Net Worth:* £6,480,000 *Total Assets:* £9,205,000
*Registered Office:* Hesslewood Country Office Park, Ferriby Road, Hessle, E Yorks, HU13 0PW
*Activities:* Non-trading company
*Parent:* Fenner International Limited
*Officers:* Debra Bradbury, Secretary; Andrew Maitland Caley [1962] Director/Group Taxation & Treasury Manager; William John Pratt [1963] Managing Director

**J.H. Fenner & Co. Limited**
*Incorporated:* 29 December 1953 *Employees:* 106
*Net Worth:* £8,372,000 *Total Assets:* £18,995,000
*Registered Office:* Hesslewood Country Office Park, Ferriby Road, Hessle, E Yorks, HU13 0PW
*Activities:* Machining
*Parent:* Fenner Group Holdings Limited
*Officers:* Debra Bradbury, Secretary; Andrew Maitland Caley [1962] Director/Group Taxation & Treasury Manager; William John Pratt [1963] Managing Director; Peter Joseph Watson [1956] Director

**Fenner Group Holdings Limited**
*Incorporated:* 1 July 1937 *Employees:* 4,189
*Previous:* Fenner Group Holdings PLC
*Net Worth:* £341,900,000 *Total Assets:* £711,100,032
*Registered Office:* Hesslewood Country Office Park, Ferriby Road, Hessle, E Yorks, HU13 0PW
*Activities:* Activities of head offices
*Parent:* Compagnie Generale des Etablissements Michelin SCA
*Officers:* Debra Bradbury, Secretary; Geoffrey James Alderman [1959] Director; Sonia Artinian-Fredou [1966] Director [French]; Benoit Balmary [1967] Director [French]; Marc Henry [1958] Director [French]; Serge Lafon [1962] Director [French]; William John Pratt [1963] Managing Director

**Fenner International Australia Limited**
*Incorporated:* 8 September 2010 *Employees:* 2
*Net Worth:* £8,958,000 *Total Assets:* £93,709,000
*Registered Office:* Hesslewood Country Office Park, Ferriby Road, Hessle, E Yorks, HU13 0PW
*Activities:* Activities of head offices
*Parent:* Fenner International Limited
*Officers:* Debra Bradbury, Secretary; Andrew Maitland Caley [1962] Director/Group Taxation & Treasury Manager; William John Pratt [1963] Managing Director

**Fenner International Limited**
*Incorporated:* 29 December 1953 *Employees:* 4
*Net Worth:* £331,135,008 *Total Assets:* £861,675,008
*Registered Office:* Hesslewood Country Office Park, Ferriby Road, Hessle, E Yorks, HU13 0PW
*Activities:* Activities of head offices
*Parent:* Fenner Group Holdings Limited
*Officers:* Debra Bradbury, Secretary; Andrew Maitland Caley [1962] Director/Group Taxation & Treasury Manager; William John Pratt [1963] Managing Director; Peter Joseph Watson [1956] Director

**Fenton Finance Limited**
*Incorporated:* 21 November 2006 *Employees:* 4
*Net Worth:* £679,104 *Total Assets:* £5,420,254
*Registered Office:* Wesley House, Huddersfield Road, Birstall, Batley, W Yorks, WF17 9EJ
*Activities:* Other credit granting n.e.c.
*Parent:* Continental Cash Collections Limited
*Officers:* Kathryn Ann Sharp, Secretary; Peter O'Hara [1942] Director/Insolvency Practitioner; Sheila Ann Ohara [1947] Director; Kathryn Ann Sharp [1971] Director/Accountant

**Fenton Packaging (Leeds) Limited**
*Incorporated:* 11 August 1945 *Employees:* 2
*Net Worth:* £3,142,741 *Total Assets:* £3,203,371
*Registered Office:* Bridge Street, Morley, Leeds, LS27 0LE
*Activities:* Financial management
*Parent:* Corran Close Ltd
*Officers:* Sharon Lisa Dakin, Secretary; Robert Paul Clarke [1949] Director; Sharon Lisa Dakin [1971] Finance Director

**Fenton Packaging Limited**
*Incorporated:* 22 February 1983 *Employees:* 48
*Net Worth:* £1,889,514 *Total Assets:* £8,333,665
*Registered Office:* Bridge Street, Morley, Leeds, LS27 0LE
*Activities:* Operation of warehousing and storage facilities for land transport activities
*Parent:* Fenton Packaging (Leeds) Ltd
*Officers:* Sharon Lisa Dakin, Secretary; Robert Paul Clarke [1949] Director; Sharon Lisa Dakin [1971] Finance Director; Christopher John Warren [1964] Sales Development Director

**Fenwick Brothers Limited**
*Incorporated:* 27 August 1954 *Employees:* 14
*Net Worth:* £1,983,131 *Total Assets:* £8,669,131
*Registered Office:* Beelsby House, Beelsby, Grimsby, N E Lincs, DN37 0TL
*Activities:* Growing of cereals (except rice), leguminous crops and oil seeds
*Major Shareholder:* Jonathan Hugh Fenwick
*Officers:* Claire Louise Fenwick, Secretary; Jonathan Hugh Fenwick [1957] Director/Farmer

**Ferdinand Properties Limited**
*Incorporated:* 17 January 2007 *Employees:* 4
*Net Worth:* £114,415 *Total Assets:* £3,367,765
*Registered Office:* 7 Mill Dam, Clifford, Wetherby, W Yorks, LS23 6EZ
*Activities:* Renting and leasing of construction and civil engineering machinery and equipment
*Officers:* Stephen John Stocks, Secretary; James Frederick Farrington [1949] Director; Geoffrey Stocks [1945] Director; Jonathan Mark Stocks [1960] Director; Stephen John Stocks [1949] Director

**Fern Hill Holdings Limited**
*Incorporated:* 11 August 1995 *Employees:* 4
*Net Worth:* £7,549,373 *Total Assets:* £7,743,659
*Registered Office:* Fernhill House, Battye Street, Bradford, W Yorks, BD4 8AG
*Activities:* Other letting and operating of own or leased real estate
*Parent:* Reverse Thought Ltd
*Officers:* Mark Simpson, Secretary; Brian Considine [1938] Director; Paul David Benjamin Considine [1965] Director; Timothy Brian Considine [1969] Director

**Ferno (UK) Limited**
*Incorporated:* 8 April 1971 *Employees:* 48
*Net Worth:* £10,203,648 *Total Assets:* £11,357,673
*Registered Office:* Ferno House, Stubs Beck Lane, Cleckheaton, W Yorks, BD19 4TZ
*Activities:* Manufacture of medical and dental instruments and supplies
*Officers:* Elroy Edwin Bourgraf [1931] Director/Management [American]; Joseph George Bourgraf [1960] Director/Company President [American]; Jonathan Stewart Ellis [1968] Managing Director; Gary Hiles [1950] Director/Company Vice President [American]; Malgorzata Anna Nozykowska-Merkle [1969] Finance Director [Polish]; Paul Charles Riordan [1944] Director/Chief Financial Officer [American]

**Festino (Finance) Limited**
*Incorporated:* 28 March 1973 *Employees:* 2
*Net Worth:* £8,832,411 *Total Assets:* £14,596,897
*Registered Office:* The Poplars, Bridge Street, Brigg, S Humbers, DN20 8NQ
*Activities:* Other business support service activities n.e.c.
*Major Shareholder:* David John Hebb
*Officers:* David John Hebb, Secretary; Christopher John Hebb [1984] Director; David John Hebb [1954] Director/Motor Engineer

**Feversham Arms Limited**
*Incorporated:* 8 June 2003 *Employees:* 79
*Net Worth Deficit:* £3,233,856 *Total Assets:* £4,507,774
*Registered Office:* 1-8 High Street, Helmsley, York, YO62 5AG
*Activities:* Hotels and similar accommodation
*Officers:* John Jameson [1955] Director [Zimbabwean]; Wayne Douglas Parham [1963] Director [Zimbabwean]; Roderick Whiteford [1958] Director/Consultant

**Feversham Education Trust**
*Incorporated:* 7 July 2011 *Employees:* 257
*Previous:* Feversham College
*Net Worth:* £26,079,000 *Total Assets:* £28,504,000
*Registered Office:* Feversham Education Trust, Deanstones Lane, Queensbury, Bradford, BD13 2AS
*Activities:* General secondary education
*Officers:* Shakoor Ahmed [1983] Director; Waqas Ahmed [1984] Director/Accountant; John Geoffrey Ashton [1945] Director; Professor Irfan Awan [1967] Director; Ali Jan Haider [1963] Director; Yasmin Hussein [1963] Director/Consultant; Sajjad Khan [1974] Director; Sarfraz Khan [1971] Director; Professor Ihtesham Rehman [1964] Director

**Fibreline Limited**
*Incorporated:* 11 August 1982 *Employees:* 191
*Net Worth:* £1,545,110 *Total Assets:* £5,180,823
*Registered Office:* Victoria Park Mills, Hardings Road, Keighley, W Yorks, BD21 3ND
*Activities:* Other manufacturing n.e.c.
*Parent:* FLD Limited
*Officers:* Shelagh Elisabeth Prudhoe, Secretary; John Jared Nixon Prudhoe [1942] Director/Chairman; Richard Nixon Prudhoe [1968] Managing Director

**Fibrelite Composites Limited**
*Incorporated:* 19 August 1980 *Employees:* 94
*Net Worth:* £9,455,757 *Total Assets:* £11,022,731
*Registered Office:* Unit 2 Snaygill Industrial Estate, Keighley Road, Skipton, N Yorks, BD23 2QR
*Activities:* Manufacture of other plastic products
*Parent:* Dover Energy UK Limited
*Officers:* Ann Jacqueline Preston, Secretary; Kevin Robert Long [1969] Director/President [American]; Ian Peter Thompson [1964] Managing Director

**C.W.Fields & Son Limited**
*Incorporated:* 30 November 1962
*Net Worth:* £4,147,396 *Total Assets:* £5,700,134
*Registered Office:* Station Road Industrial Estate, Station Road, Epworth, Doncaster, S Yorks, DN9 1JZ
*Activities:* Joinery installation
*Parent:* T.D-R. Group Limited
*Officers:* June Dalla Riva, Secretary; John Edward Matthew Cowx [1987] Director/Consultant; June Dalla Riva [1953] Director; Francesca Dalla-Riva [1989] Director; Marc Dalla-Riva [1987] Director; Toni Giacomo Dalla-Riva [1949] Director; Nigel Graham Fields [1963] Director; Robert Readdie [1990] Sales Director

**Filltex Limited**
*Incorporated:* 19 March 2003 *Employees:* 33
*Net Worth:* £1,022,109 *Total Assets:* £3,491,807
*Registered Office:* Unit B, Syke Ing Mills, Syke Lane, Dewsbury, W Yorks, WF12 8HX
*Activities:* Manufacture of other textiles n.e.c.
*Parent:* Hassan (Holdings) Ltd
*Officers:* Saghir Hussain, Secretary; Saghir Hussain [1978] Director/Felt Manufacturer; Zahir Hussain [1979] Director/Employee

**Filtermech Plant Sales Limited**
*Incorporated:* 30 November 1989 *Employees:* 16
*Net Worth:* £5,499,065 *Total Assets:* £8,510,836
*Registered Office:* Unit 6-2 Seckar Wood Industrial Park, Newmillerdam, Wakefield, W Yorks, WF2 6QW
*Activities:* Renting and leasing of trucks and other heavy vehicles
*Parent:* Filtermech Holdings Limited
*Officers:* Benjamin David Hancock [1991] Director; Jon Hewitt [1974] Director; Christopher Michael Maxfield [1953] Director

**Filtronic Broadband Limited**
*Incorporated:* 3 July 1997 *Employees:* 64
*Net Worth Deficit:* £6,632,148 *Total Assets:* £5,738,191
*Registered Office:* Filtronic House, 3 Airport West, Lancaster Way, Yeadon, Leeds, LS19 7ZA
*Activities:* Manufacture of electronic components
*Parent:* Filtronic PLC
*Officers:* Dr Maura Eilis Moynihan, Secretary; Robert Stjohn Smith [1964] Director/Accountant; Michael Tyerman [1978] Director/Accountant; Michael Andrew Weaver [1974] Director/Business Executive

**Filtronic PLC**
*Incorporated:* 25 January 1994 *Employees:* 128
*Net Worth:* £12,161,000 *Total Assets:* £18,600,000
*Registered Office:* Filtronic House, 3 Airport West, Lancaster Way, Yeadon, Leeds, LS19 7ZA
*Activities:* Manufacture of communication equipment other than telegraph, and telephone apparatus and equipment
*Officers:* Dr Maura Eilis Moynihan, Secretary; Reginald Lawrence Gott [1957] Director/Businessman; Peter John Magowan [1967] Director/Businessman; Michael Roy David Roller [1965] Director/Chartered Accountant; Robert Stjohn Smith [1964] Director/Certified Accountant; Michael Tyerman [1978] Director/Accountant

**Filtronic Wireless Ltd**
*Incorporated:* 30 March 1978 *Employees:* 13
*Net Worth:* £6,640,245 *Total Assets:* £16,443,319
*Registered Office:* Filtronic House, 3 Airport West, Lancaster Way, Yeadon, Leeds, LS19 7ZA
*Activities:* Manufacture of telegraph and telephone apparatus and equipment
*Parent:* Isotek (Holdings) Limited
*Officers:* Maura Eilis Moynihan, Secretary; Mark John Black [1967] Director/Engineer; Dr David James Lynch [1966] Director/Electrical Engineer; Robert Stjohn Smith [1964] Director/Accountant; Michael Tyerman [1978] Director/Accountant

**Financial Funding Limited**
*Incorporated:* 28 July 2014
*Net Worth:* £3,644,448 *Total Assets:* £14,594,277
*Registered Office:* 13-15 Netherhall Road, Doncaster, S Yorks, DN1 2PH
*Activities:* Financial intermediation not elsewhere classified
*Shareholders:* Neville Christopher Brown; Diane Glenys Brown
*Officers:* Neville Christopher Brown [1959] Director

**Financial Systems & Consultancy Ltd.**
*Incorporated:* 18 October 1991 *Employees:* 21
*Net Worth:* £602,813 *Total Assets:* £4,479,994
*Registered Office:* Stable Mews, Beechwoods, Elmete Lane, Leeds, LS8 2LQ
*Activities:* Information technology consultancy activities
*Major Shareholder:* Ruth Bentley
*Officers:* Ruth Bentley, Secretary; Edward David Bentley [1992] Director/Consultant; Ruth Bentley [1958] Director/Accountant; Gavin John Dugdale [1986] Director/Account Executive

**Findpath Limited**
*Incorporated:* 27 January 1989 *Employees:* 237
*Net Worth:* £8,282,876 *Total Assets:* £40,093,216
*Registered Office:* Dewsbury Road, Wakefield, W Yorks, WF2 9BE
*Activities:* Activities of head offices
*Major Shareholder:* David Bosomworth
*Officers:* Timothy John Simons, Secretary; David Bosomworth [1954] Director; Timothy John Simons [1966] Director

**Fine Motor Cars Ltd**
*Incorporated:* 12 January 2015
*Net Worth:* £3,236,497 *Total Assets:* £3,260,012
*Registered Office:* 28 North Street, Keighley, W Yorks, BD21 3SE
*Activities:* Non-specialised wholesale trade
*Officers:* Mohamed Avais Khan [1992] Director

**Finespark (Horsham) Limited**
*Incorporated:* 21 January 1992
*Net Worth:* £376,605 *Total Assets:* £5,602,188
*Registered Office:* P O Box 88, 27 Dewsbury Road, Ossett, W Yorks, WF5 9WS
*Activities:* Dormant company
*Parent:* Carclo PLC
*Officers:* Richard John Ottaway, Secretary; Christopher John Malley [1967] Director; Richard John Ottaway [1971] Director/Chartered Accountant

**The Finest Flats Company Limited**
*Incorporated:* 12 February 2001
*Net Worth Deficit:* £5,245 *Total Assets:* £3,260,788
*Registered Office:* Arthington Park, Arthington Lane, Arthington, Otley, W Yorks, LS21 1PH
*Activities:* Buying and selling of own real estate
*Parent:* Quarmby Holdings Limited
*Officers:* John Antony Batty, Secretary; Laura Gabrielle Irene Davies [1977] Director/Interior Designer and Retailer; Hannah Margaret Eames [1980] Director/Retail Project Manager; James Roger Quarmby [1944] Director/Builder; Julia Margaret Quarmby [1950] Director; Oliver Alexander Quarmby [1975] Director/Chartered Surveyor

**Finestline Limited**
*Incorporated:* 10 October 2013
*Net Worth:* £2,102,172 *Total Assets:* £13,480,709
*Registered Office:* c/o WGN, 4 Park Place, Leeds, LS1 2RU
*Activities:* Activities of other holding companies n.e.c.
*Officers:* Robert Neil Fearnley [1979] Director

**Finishchoice Limited**
*Incorporated:* 9 December 1994
*Net Worth:* £2,073,314 *Total Assets:* £4,760,060
*Registered Office:* 5a Craven Mews, Skipton, N Yorks, BD23 2AQ
*Activities:* Development of building projects
*Major Shareholder:* Gregory Wilkinson
*Officers:* Gregory Wilkinson [1957] Director/Builder

**Finlay Beverages Limited**
*Incorporated:* 17 April 1896 *Employees:* 171
*Net Worth:* £1,143,000 *Total Assets:* £32,561,000
*Registered Office:* Elmsall Way, South Elmsall, Pontefract, W Yorks, WF9 2XS
*Activities:* Tea processing
*Parent:* James Finlay Limited
*Officers:* David Charles Morris, Secretary; Ian Peter Fyall Bryson [1967] Managing Director; Guy Rufus Chambers [1970] Managing Director; Darren John Edwards [1967] Director/Accountant; Julian Michael Rutherford [1971] Director/Accountant; Neil Robert Willsher [1962] Director

**Finley Structures Ltd**
*Incorporated:* 28 July 2000 *Employees:* 63
*Net Worth:* £3,017,857 *Total Assets:* £6,042,917
*Registered Office:* Whinbank Road, Aycliffe Industrial Estate, Newton Aycliffe, Co Durham, DL5 6AY
*Activities:* Manufacture of metal structures and parts of structures
*Shareholders:* John Finley; Valerie Finley
*Officers:* Kelly Jean Vasey, Secretary; Gary John Finley [1980] Director; John Finley [1952] Sales Director; Valerie Finley [1952] Director/Fabrication; Julie Raistrick [1975] Director/Office Manager

**Finsbury (Instruments) Limited**
*Incorporated:* 19 October 1978
*Net Worth:* £13,379,000 *Total Assets:* £13,749,000
*Registered Office:* Depuy, St Anthonys Road, Beeston, Leeds, LS11 8DT
*Activities:* Manufacture of medical and dental instruments and supplies
*Parent:* Finsbury Orthopaedics Limited
*Officers:* Alistair John Scholes [1965] Director

**J R Firby Ltd**
*Incorporated:* 8 July 2002 *Employees:* 5
*Net Worth:* £5,648,748 *Total Assets:* £7,047,908
*Registered Office:* Carr House Farm, Slingsby, York, YO62 4AX
*Activities:* Other retail sale in non-specialised stores
*Shareholders:* James Richard Firby; Deborah Firby
*Officers:* Deborah Firby, Secretary/Director; Deborah Firby [1971] Director; James Richard Firby [1967] Director; Robert Richard Firby [2001] Director

**Fire Protection Holdings Limited**
*Incorporated:* 2 December 1999
*Net Worth:* £33,008,000 *Total Assets:* £33,008,000
*Registered Office:* Premier House, 2 Jubilee Way, Elland, W Yorks, HX5 9DY
*Activities:* Other service activities n.e.c.
*Parent:* London Security PLC
*Officers:* Simon Coates, Secretary; Richard John Pollard [1963] Director/Commercial Manager

**Fired Up Corporation Limited**
*Incorporated:* 31 May 1996 *Employees:* 102
*Net Worth:* £2,376,096 *Total Assets:* £5,652,104
*Registered Office:* Fired Up Buildings, St Thomas Road, Longroyd Bridge, Huddersfield, W Yorks, HD1 3LF
*Activities:* Manufacture of electric domestic appliances
*Major Shareholder:* Richard Mark Kaye
*Officers:* Gareth Edward Ackroyd, Secretary; Richard Mark Kaye [1967] Managing Director

**Firsdell Ltd**
*Incorporated:* 3 March 2011
*Net Worth:* £28,900,000 *Total Assets:* £28,900,000
*Registered Office:* Hilmore House, Gain Lane, Bradford, W Yorks, BD3 7DL
*Activities:* Development of building projects
*Parent:* Wm Morrison Supermarkets Holdings Limited
*Officers:* Jonathan James Burke, Secretary; Joanna Louise Goff [1978] Finance Director

**First 4 Lawyers Limited**
*Incorporated:* 2 January 2008 *Employees:* 34
*Net Worth:* £6,655,764 *Total Assets:* £9,482,214
*Registered Office:* Permanent House, Dundas Street, Huddersfield, W Yorks, HD1 2HE
*Activities:* Media representation services
*Parent:* F4L Holdings Limited
*Officers:* Arfan Naveed Anwar, Secretary/Legal; Qamar Zaman Anwar, Secretary/Legal; Arfan Naveed Anwar [1980] Director/Legal; Qamar Zaman Anwar [1982] Director/Legal

**First Actuarial LLP**
*Incorporated:* 24 August 2009 *Employees:* 222
*Net Worth:* £8,732,420 *Total Assets:* £11,129,273
*Registered Office:* Mayesbrook House, Lawnswood Business Park, Redvers Close, Leeds, LS16 6QY
*Officers:* Michael Wilfred Hulme-Vickerstaff [1968] Member; David Ian Joy [1969] Member; Christopher David Martin [1970] Member; Mark Steven Riches [1969] Member; Hilary Salt [1963] Member; Peter Michael Shellswell [1970] Member; Alan Edward Smith [1956] Member; James Robert Smith [1966] Member; Keith John Williams [1959] Member; Colin Roy Freeman [1958] LLP Member; Robert James Hammond [1978] LLP Member; Kate Elizabeth Hulme-Vickerstaff [1977] LLP Member; Timothy Damian Jones [1971] LLP Member; Declan James Keohane [1967] LLP Member; Catherine Jane Lockyer [1968] LLP Member; Richard Mathew Lunt [1977] LLP Member; Andrew John Overend [1975] LLP Member; Mark James Rowlinson [1980] LLP Member; Rohit James Siqueira [1974] LLP Member; David Thomas Thirlwell [1979] LLP Member; Neal Alan Thompson [1969] LLP Member

**First Subsea Limited**
*Incorporated:* 2 February 1994 *Employees:* 24
*Net Worth:* £3,044,678 *Total Assets:* £4,092,604
*Registered Office:* Engineering House, Lune Industrial Estate, Newquay Road, Lancaster, LA1 5QP
*Activities:* Manufacture of lifting and handling equipment
*Major Shareholder:* Ian Alexander Suttie
*Officers:* John Shaw [1965] Managing Director; Ian Alexander Suttie [1947] Director

**First West Yorkshire Limited**
*Incorporated:* 17 February 1986 *Employees:* 2,312
*Net Worth:* £75,695,000 *Total Assets:* £144,775,008
*Registered Office:* Hunslet Park Depot, Donisthorpe Street, Leeds, LS10 1PL
*Activities:* Other urban, suburban or metropolitan passenger land transport (not underground, metro or similar)
*Parent:* Firstbus (North) Limited
*Officers:* Michael Hampson, Secretary; David Brian Alexander [1965] Regional Managing Director; Thomas John Bridge [1976] Operations Director; Simon Paul Carlisle [1968] Engineering Director; Martin Hirst [1974] Commercial Director; Mubarak Hussain Mahmed [1984] Director/Bus Driver; David Paul Matthews [1957] Director

**First York Limited**
*Incorporated:* 24 September 1987 *Employees:* 275
*Net Worth Deficit:* £4,606,000 *Total Assets:* £8,897,000
*Registered Office:* Hunslet Park Depot, Donisthorpe Street, Leeds, LS10 1PL
*Activities:* Other urban, suburban or metropolitan passenger land transport (not underground, metro or similar)
*Parent:* Firstbus (North) Limited
*Officers:* Michael Hampson, Secretary; David Brian Alexander [1965] Regional Managing Director; Marc Bichtemann [1978] Director [German]; Mohammed Imran [1957] Employee Director

**Firsure Limited**
*Incorporated:* 14 February 1980 *Employees:* 4
*Net Worth:* £1,323,315 *Total Assets:* £4,666,987
*Registered Office:* Unit 8 Heather Court, Shaw Wood Way, Doncaster, S Yorks, DN2 5YL
*Activities:* Other letting and operating of own or leased real estate
*Shareholders:* Gail Michelle Parkin; Angela Jane Graves
*Officers:* Christine Fletcher, Secretary; Paul Healand, Secretary; Gail Michelle Parkin [1962] Director; Anthony Phillips [1936] Director

**Ian Firth Hardware Limited**
*Incorporated:* 12 October 1981 *Employees:* 86
*Net Worth:* £2,253,295 *Total Assets:* £5,945,352
*Registered Office:* Lady Ann House, Shaw Cross Business Park, Dewsbury, W Yorks, WF12 7RD
*Activities:* Wholesale of hardware, plumbing and heating equipment and supplies
*Parent:* Ian Firth Holdings Limited
*Officers:* Bernice Bedford Firth, Secretary; Paul Claydon [1985] Director; Beverley Cookson [1963] Finance Director; Bernice Bedford Firth [1949] Director/Company Secretary; Ian Firth [1948] Director; Robin Firth [1953] Sales Director; Amanda Haley [1972] Director

**Ian Firth Holdings Limited**
*Incorporated:* 31 October 2008 *Employees:* 86
*Net Worth:* £4,249,665 *Total Assets:* £7,941,722
*Registered Office:* Lady Ann House, Shaw Cross Business Park, Dewsbury, W Yorks, WF12 7RD
*Activities:* Activities of head offices
*Shareholders:* Bernice Bedford Firth; Ian Firth
*Officers:* Bernice Bedford Firth, Secretary; Bernice Bedford Firth [1949] Director; Ian Firth [1948] Director

**Firth Steels Limited**
*Incorporated:* 18 April 1983 *Employees:* 27
*Net Worth:* £11,941,150 *Total Assets:* £21,548,312
*Registered Office:* Calderbank, River Street, Brighouse, W Yorks, HD6 1LU
*Activities:* Construction of other civil engineering projects n.e.c.
*Major Shareholder:* James Tennant Firth
*Officers:* Susan Patricia Firth, Secretary; Steven Booth [1969] Production Director; James Tennant Firth [1973] Managing Director; Roger Tennant Firth [1943] Director/Steel Merchant; Susan Patricia Firth [1945] Director/Company Secretary

**Fish Administration Limited**
*Incorporated:* 10 May 2001 *Employees:* 53
*Net Worth:* £4,213,968 *Total Assets:* £5,108,011
*Registered Office:* Rossington's Business Park, West Carr Road, Retford, Notts, DN22 7SW
*Activities:* Non-life insurance
*Parent:* PIB Group Limited
*Officers:* Ryan Christopher Brown [1973] Director; Brendan James McManus [1959] Director

**Edward Fisher & Co. Limited**
*Incorporated:* 27 November 1986 *Employees:* 10
*Net Worth:* £4,892,526 *Total Assets:* £5,939,764
*Registered Office:* W M Haigh & Co, Grange Cottage, Womersley, Doncaster, S Yorks, DN6 9BW
*Activities:* Growing of cereals (except rice), leguminous crops and oil seeds
*Major Shareholder:* Edward Hylton Fisher
*Officers:* Catherine Margaret Bradley, Secretary; Edward Hylton Fisher [1954] Director/Farmer; Paul Martyn Fisher [1963] Director/Farmer; William Edward Fisher [1986] Director/Farmer

**James Fisher (Aberdeen) Limited**
*Incorporated:* 16 November 2005
*Net Worth:* £5,636,814 *Total Assets:* £32,731,682
*Registered Office:* P O Box 4, Fisher House, Barrow in Furness, Cumbria, LA14 1HR
*Activities:* Activities of head offices
*Parent:* James Fisher and Sons PLC
*Officers:* James Henry John Marsh, Secretary; Nicholas Paul Henry [1961] Director; Stuart Charles Kilpatrick [1962] Director

**James Fisher and Sons Public Limited Company**
*Incorporated:* 2 February 1926 *Employees:* 2,724
*Net Worth:* £285,000,000 *Total Assets:* £618,600,000
*Registered Office:* P O Box 4, Fisher House, Barrow in Furness, Cumbria, LA14 1HR
*Activities:* Sea and coastal freight water transport
*Officers:* James Henry John Marsh, Secretary; Justin Richard Atkinson [1960] Director; Aedamar Ita Comiskey [1967] Director/Solicitor [Irish]; Fergus Hugh Stirling Graham [1973] Director; Nicholas Paul Henry [1961] Director; Stuart Charles Kilpatrick [1962] Director; David George Moorhouse CBE [1947] Director; Malcolm Stephen Paul [1951] Director/Chartered Accountant; Michael John Lawrence Salter [1947] Director

**James Fisher Everard Limited**
*Incorporated:* 14 March 1956 *Employees:* 16
*Net Worth:* £19,136,050 *Total Assets:* £25,525,968
*Registered Office:* P O Box 4, Fisher House, Barrow in Furness, Cumbria, LA14 1HR
*Activities:* Sea and coastal freight water transport
*Parent:* James Fisher Tankships Holdings Limited
*Officers:* James Henry John Marsh, Secretary; Richard Douglas Burmeister [1956] Director; Neil Burns [1970] Fleet Director; Fiona Caroline Everard [1981] Managing Director; Nicholas Paul Henry [1961] Director; Stuart Charles Kilpatrick [1962] Director

**James Fisher Fender Care Limited**
*Incorporated:* 21 February 2005
*Net Worth:* £538,118 *Total Assets:* £36,385,148
*Registered Office:* P O Box 4, Fisher House, Barrow in Furness, Cumbria, LA14 1HR
*Activities:* Activities of head offices
*Parent:* James Fisher and Sons Public Limited Company
*Officers:* James Henry John Marsh, Secretary; Paul Cansdale [1972] Finance Director; Nicholas Paul Henry [1961] Director; Stuart Charles Kilpatrick [1962] Director

**James Fisher Holdings UK Limited**
*Incorporated:* 12 November 2015
*Net Worth:* £414,697 *Total Assets:* £51,661,944
*Registered Office:* P O Box 4, Fisher House, Barrow in Furness, Cumbria, LA14 1HR
*Activities:* Activities of head offices
*Parent:* James Fisher and Sons PLC
*Officers:* James Henry John Marsh, Secretary; Nicholas Paul Henry [1961] Director; Stuart Charles Kilpatrick [1962] Director

**James Fisher Marine Services Limited**
*Incorporated:* 6 July 2004 *Employees:* 148
*Net Worth:* £26,998,676 *Total Assets:* £78,675,328
*Registered Office:* P O Box 4, Fisher House, Barrow in Furness, Cumbria, LA14 1HR
*Activities:* Other information technology service activities
*Parent:* James Fisher Holdings UK Limited
*Officers:* James Henry John Marsh, Secretary; Richard Douglas Burmeister [1956] Director; Nicholas Paul Henry [1961] Director; Stuart Charles Kilpatrick [1962] Director; Paul Adam Scullion [1979] Finance Director

**James Fisher MFE Limited**
*Incorporated:* 14 May 2014 *Employees:* 22
*Net Worth Deficit:* £2,565,372 *Total Assets:* £19,832,776
*Registered Office:* P O Box 4, Fisher House, Barrow in Furness, Cumbria, LA14 1HR
*Activities:* Other service activities n.e.c.
*Parent:* James Fisher Offshore Limited
*Officers:* James Henry John Marsh, Secretary; Aidan Andrew Douglas [1967] Director; Nicholas Paul Henry [1961] Director; Stuart Charles Kilpatrick [1962] Director; Kenneth Robert Mackie [1961] Director; Graham Ronald James Murdoch [1967] Director

**James Fisher Nuclear Holdings Limited**
*Incorporated:* 29 June 2004
*Net Worth:* £20,572,002 *Total Assets:* £20,624,048
*Registered Office:* P O Box 4, Fisher House, Barrow in Furness, Cumbria, LA14 1HR
*Activities:* Activities of head offices
*Parent:* James Fisher and Sons Public Limited Company
*Officers:* James Henry John Marsh, Secretary; Nicholas Paul Henry [1961] Director; Stuart Charles Kilpatrick [1962] Director; Paul Michael Read [1956] Director; Jason Nicholas Washington [1965] Director/Accountant

**Fisher Outdoor Leisure Holdings Limited**
*Incorporated:* 21 December 2005 *Employees:* 5
*Net Worth:* £5,530,000 *Total Assets:* £10,158,000
*Registered Office:* Roundhouse Road, Faverdale Industrial Estate, Darlington, Co Durham, DL3 0UR
*Activities:* Wholesale of household goods (other than musical instruments) n.e.c
*Parent:* Power Topco Limited
*Officers:* Matthew Barker [1979] Director; James Scott Browning [1966] Managing Director; Ian James Calvesbert [1966] Director; Paul Gibson [1980] Director; Richard Damon Smith [1974] Director

**James Fisher Subtech Group Limited**
*Incorporated:* 25 February 2015
*Previous:* JF (Southern Africa) Ltd
*Net Worth:* £17,179,232 *Total Assets:* £19,753,288
*Registered Office:* P O Box 4, Fisher House, Barrow in Furness, Cumbria, LA14 1HR
*Activities:* Activities of head offices
*Parent:* James Fisher and Sons Public Limited Company
*Officers:* James Henry John Marsh, Secretary; Nicholas Paul Henry [1961] Director; Stuart Charles Kilpatrick [1962] Director

**The Fisherman Limited**
*Incorporated:* 23 June 1960 *Employees:* 25
*Net Worth:* £2,586,109 *Total Assets:* £4,838,050
*Registered Office:* Unit 40 Airedale Business Centre, Keighley Road, Skipton, N Yorks, BD23 2TZ
*Activities:* Sale of new cars and light motor vehicles
*Major Shareholder:* William Marshall Smith Midgley
*Officers:* William Marshall Smith Midgley, Secretary/Director; Edwin John Midgley [1949] Director/Business Manager; Susan Elizabeth Midgley [1951] Director/Assistant; William Marshall Smith Midgley [1975] Director

**Five Star Fish Limited**
*Incorporated:* 30 March 2010 *Employees:* 455
*Net Worth Deficit:* £34,548,000 *Total Assets:* £25,834,000
*Registered Office:* Trinity Park House, Trinity Business Park, Fox Way, Wakefield, W Yorks, WF2 8EE
*Activities:* Processing and preserving of fish, crustaceans and molluscs
*Parent:* Boparan Holdings Limited
*Officers:* Ranjit Singh Boparan [1966] Director; Ronald Klaas Otto Kers [1969] Director/Group CEO [Dutch]; Richard Peter Simpson [1965] Finance Director; Craig Ashley Tomkinson [1982] Director/Group CFO

**Fives Landis Limited**
*Incorporated:* 28 September 2005 *Employees:* 327
*Net Worth:* £25,890,000 *Total Assets:* £53,962,000
*Registered Office:* Eastburn Works, Skipton Road, Cross Hills, Keighley, W Yorks, BD20 7SD
*Activities:* Manufacture of electronic measuring, testing etc. equipment, not for industrial process control
*Parent:* Fives UK Holding Limited
*Officers:* Thalie Benveniste, Secretary; Raphael Constantin [1969] Director [French]; Michael Hall [1961] Managing Director; Denis-Rene Andre Hugelmann [1958] Director/Deputy Chief Executive Officer [French]; Frederic Daniel Sanchez [1960] Director [French]

**Fives UK Holding Limited**
*Incorporated:* 4 November 2002
*Net Worth:* £49,443,024 *Total Assets:* £79,697,720
*Registered Office:* Eastburn Works, Skipton Road, Cross Hills, Keighley, W Yorks, BD20 7SD
*Activities:* Activities of head offices
*Parent:* Fives S.A.S
*Officers:* Thalie Benveniste, Secretary; Suresh Johannes Abye [1979] Director/Group Chief Financial Officer [French]; Frederic Daniel Sanchez [1960] Director [French]

**FJG Property LLP**
*Incorporated:* 3 January 2006
*Net Worth:* £1,067,827 *Total Assets:* £4,126,964
*Registered Office:* Suite 45, Bowcliffe Hall, Bramham, Wetherby, W Yorks, LS23 6LP
*Officers:* Angela May Gallen [1962] Member; Phillip Mark Gallen [1963] Member; David White Watson [1950] LLP Member

**Flamingo Land Resort Limited**
*Incorporated:* 17 December 2009 *Employees:* 388
*Net Worth:* £9,072,313 *Total Assets:* £17,446,090
*Registered Office:* 1 Wheelgate, Malton, N Yorks, YO17 7HT
*Activities:* Activities of amusement parks and theme parks
*Shareholders:* Vicky Samantha Gibb; Gordon Stewart Gibb
*Officers:* Gordon Stewart Gibb [1975] Director; Maureen Ann Gibb [1942] Director/Chairman; Vicky Samantha Gibb [1972] Director; Denise Mary Pullin [1954] Director

**Flannery Civil Engineering Limited**
*Incorporated:* 28 April 1975 *Employees:* 63
*Net Worth:* £548,113 *Total Assets:* £5,374,224
*Registered Office:* Unit 2b Willow Bridge Way, Normanton, Castleford, W Yorks, WF10 5NP
*Activities:* Construction of other civil engineering projects n.e.c.
*Parent:* Flannery Construction Limited
*Officers:* Dominic Anthony Ellis [1982] Director/Quantity Surveyor; Terence Paul Flannery [1956] Managing Director

**Flannery Construction Limited**
*Incorporated:* 24 March 1986 *Employees:* 63
*Net Worth:* £5,848,888 *Total Assets:* £11,389,500
*Registered Office:* Unit 2b Willow Bridge Way, Normanton, Castleford, W Yorks, WF10 5NP
*Activities:* Construction of other civil engineering projects n.e.c.
*Major Shareholder:* Terence Paul Flannery
*Officers:* Dominic Anthony Ellis [1982] Director/Quantity Surveyor; Terence Paul Flannery [1956] Director/Quantity Surveyor

**Flatfish Limited**
*Incorporated:* 16 January 1979 *Employees:* 55
*Net Worth:* £3,573,310 *Total Assets:* £6,579,251
*Registered Office:* Unit 5 Stirling Street, Grimsby, N E Lincs, DN31 3AE
*Activities:* Processing and preserving of fish, crustaceans and molluscs
*Major Shareholder:* Steven David Stansfield
*Officers:* Steven David Stansfield, Secretary; Nigel Colin Clarke [1955] Director/Fish Buyer; Reece James Stansfield [1989] Director/Accounts Manager; Richard John Stansfield [1969] Director/Freezing Manager; Steven David Stansfield [1962] Fish Buyer/Director; Peter Stokes [1950] Director/Company Accountant

**FLD Limited**
*Incorporated:* 30 April 1999 *Employees:* 191
*Net Worth:* £2,787,368 *Total Assets:* £7,429,280
*Registered Office:* Victoria Park Mills, Hardings Road, Keighley, W Yorks, BD21 3ND
*Activities:* Activities of head offices
*Major Shareholder:* John Jared Nixon Prudhoe
*Officers:* Shelagh Elisabeth Prudhoe, Secretary; John Jared Nixon Prudhoe [1942] Director/Chairman; Richard Nixon Prudhoe [1968] Director

**Fleetcor Fuel Cards Europe Limited**
*Incorporated:* 11 November 1986
*Net Worth:* £3,809,000 *Total Assets:* £3,809,000
*Registered Office:* Unit 3 St James Business Park, Grimbald Crag Court, Knaresborough, N Yorks, HG5 8QB
*Activities:* Wholesale of other fuels and related products
*Parent:* Fleetcor Fuel Cards LLC
*Officers:* Andrew Robert Blazye [1958] Director; Eric Richard Dey [1959] Director [American]; Anita Kravos-Medimorec [1974] Director/Chief Financial Officer; Steven Joseph Pisciotta [1964] Director [American]

**Fleetcor UK Acquisition Limited**
*Incorporated:* 27 June 2006 *Employees:* 4
*Net Worth:* £26,024,000 *Total Assets:* £740,777,984
*Registered Office:* Unit 3 St James Business Park, Grimbald Crag Court, Knaresborough, N Yorks, HG5 8QB
*Activities:* Activities of head offices
*Parent:* Fleetcor Luxembourg Holding 2 S.A.R.L
*Officers:* Andrew Robert Blazye [1958] Director/Chief Executive; Eric Richard Dey [1959] Director/Chief Financial Officer [American]; Anita Kravos-Medimorec [1974] Director/Chief Financial Officer; Steven Joseph Pisciotta [1964] Director/Treasurer [American]

**Herbert Fletcher Transport Limited**
*Incorporated:* 13 February 1970 *Employees:* 45
*Net Worth:* £1,792,737 *Total Assets:* £4,788,854
*Registered Office:* M62 Trading Estate, Rawcliffe Road, Goole, E Yorks, DN14 6BZ
*Activities:* Freight transport by road
*Shareholders:* Graham Martin Fletcher; John Paul Fletcher
*Officers:* Graham Martin Fletcher, Secretary; Graham Martin Fletcher [1966] Director; John Paul Fletcher [1969] Director/Transport Manager

**Flexiglobal (UK) Limited**
*Incorporated:* 4 August 2008 *Employees:* 13
*Net Worth:* £573,672 *Total Assets:* £3,263,830
*Registered Office:* 203 Askern Road, Bentley, Doncaster, S Yorks, DN5 0JR
*Activities:* Wholesale of other intermediate products
*Officers:* Mirlene Helen Lorain Taljaard [1964] Director/Consultant [South African]

**Flintbrook Limited**
*Incorporated:* 6 December 1994
*Net Worth:* £5,768,000 *Total Assets:* £37,713,000
*Registered Office:* Lawrence House, Riverside Drive, Cleckheaton, W Yorks, BD19 4DH
*Activities:* Agents involved in the sale of machinery, industrial equipment, ships and aircraft
*Shareholders:* Wesco Aircraft International Holdings Limited; Wesco Aircraft Holdings, Inc
*Officers:* John Holland, Secretary; Jan Alexander Dobrucki [1964] Finance Director; John Generald Holland [1968] Director and Company Secretary [American]; Alexander Murray [1969] Director; Alun Phennah [1968] Supply Chain Director

**Flixborough Wharf Limited**
*Incorporated:* 18 October 1983
*Net Worth:* £3,081,199 *Total Assets:* £4,122,827
*Registered Office:* Boothferry Terminal, Bridge Street, Goole, N Humbers, DN14 5SS
*Activities:* Cargo handling for water transport activities
*Parent:* RMS Europe Group Ltd
*Officers:* Jonathan James Hunter [1972] Director/Chartered Accountant; Ian Dominic Parsons [1949] Director

**Flower of May Holiday Parks Limited**
*Incorporated:* 22 February 1988 *Employees:* 94
*Net Worth:* £26,651,756 *Total Assets:* £31,583,248
*Registered Office:* Medina House, 2 Station Avenue, Bridlington, E Yorks, YO16 4LZ
*Activities:* Other accommodation
*Major Shareholder:* John Graham Atkinson
*Officers:* Helen Joanne Atkinson Pattison, Secretary/Park Operator; John Graham Atkinson [1944] Director/Holiday Park and Farmer; Helen Joanne Atkinson Pattison [1977] Director/Park Operator

**FMG Finance Limited**
*Incorporated:* 9 December 2014
*Net Worth:* £8,619,000 *Total Assets:* £25,840,000
*Registered Office:* Broad Lea House, Dyson Wood Way, Bradley, Huddersfield, W Yorks, HD2 1GZ
*Activities:* Other business support service activities n.e.c.
*Parent:* FMG Group Holdings Limited
*Officers:* Mark Francis Chessman [1964] Director; Stephen Edward Oakley [1952] Director; Claire Owens [1983] Finance Director; Martin Ward [1967] Managing Director

**FMG Group Holdings Limited**
*Incorporated:* 4 December 2014
*Net Worth:* £1,158,000 *Total Assets:* £9,140,000
*Registered Office:* Broad Lea House, Dyson Wood Way, Bradley, Huddersfield, W Yorks, HD2 1GZ
*Activities:* Other business support service activities n.e.c.
*Parent:* Rose Bidco Limited
*Officers:* Mark Francis Chessman [1964] Director; Stephen Edward Oakley [1952] Director; Claire Owens [1983] Finance Director; Martin Ward [1967] Managing Director

**FMG Support (FIM) Ltd**
*Incorporated:* 28 October 1991
*Net Worth:* £8,901,000 *Total Assets:* £53,101,000
*Registered Office:* Broad Lea House, Dyson Wood Way, Bradley, Huddersfield, W Yorks, HD2 1GZ
*Activities:* Activities of call centres
*Parent:* F M G Support (Ho) Limited
*Officers:* Mark Francis Chessman [1964] Director; Stephen Edward Oakley [1952] Director; Claire Owens [1983] Finance Director; Paul Harvey Stead [1967] Commercial Director; Martin Ward [1967] Managing Director

**FMG Support (RRRM) Ltd**
*Incorporated:* 9 November 1992
*Net Worth:* £3,601,000 *Total Assets:* £31,823,000
*Registered Office:* Broad Lea House, Dyson Wood Way, Bradley, Huddersfield, W Yorks, HD2 1GZ
*Activities:* Activities of call centres
*Parent:* F M G Support (Ho) Limited
*Officers:* Mark Francis Chessman [1964] Director; Stephen Edward Oakley [1952] Director; Claire Owens [1981] Finance Director; Paul Harvey Stead [1967] Commercial Director; Martin Ward [1967] Managing Director

**FMG Support Group Limited**
*Incorporated:* 31 January 2008 *Employees:* 364
*Net Worth:* £10,840,000 *Total Assets:* £42,659,000
*Registered Office:* Broad Lea House, Dyson Wood Way, Bradley, Huddersfield, W Yorks, HD2 1GZ
*Activities:* Other business support service activities n.e.c.
*Parent:* FMG Finance Limited
*Officers:* Mark Francis Chessman [1964] Director; Stephen Edward Oakley [1952] Director; Claire Owens [1983] Finance Director; Paul Harvey Stead [1967] Sales Director; Martin Ward [1967] Managing Director

**FMG Support Ltd**
*Incorporated:* 26 July 1999 *Employees:* 361
*Net Worth:* £3,094,000 *Total Assets:* £12,011,000
*Registered Office:* Broad Lea House, Dyson Wood Way, Bradley, Huddersfield, W Yorks, HD2 1GZ
*Activities:* Activities of head offices
*Parent:* FMG Support Group Limited
*Officers:* Mark Francis Chessman [1964] Director; Stephen Edward Oakley [1952] Director; Claire Owens [1983] Finance Director; Paul Harvey Stead [1967] Commercial Director; Martin Ward [1967] Managing Director

**W.E. Foers & Son Limited**
*Incorporated:* 12 January 1983 *Employees:* 4
*Net Worth:* £3,364,769 *Total Assets:* £4,009,069
*Registered Office:* Grange Farm, Carr Lane, Wadworth, Doncaster, S Yorks, DN11 9DP
*Activities:* Growing of cereals (except rice), leguminous crops and oil seeds
*Shareholder:* William Edward Foers
*Officers:* William Edward Foers, Secretary; Vicki Foers [1967] Director; William Edward Foers [1962] Director/Farmer

**Folding Sliding Doors Limited**
*Incorporated:* 9 August 2001 *Employees:* 75
*Net Worth:* £1,655,900 *Total Assets:* £3,867,671
*Registered Office:* FSD Works, Hopbine Avenue, West Bowling, Bradford, BD5 8ER
*Activities:* Other manufacturing n.e.c.
*Shareholders:* Paul Anthony Shearman; Tracey Ann Shearman
*Officers:* Kirstie Wormald, Secretary; Richard Alan Wharfe [1966] Director

**Foot Forward Property Investments Ltd**
*Incorporated:* 18 March 2015
*Net Worth:* £1,262,712 *Total Assets:* £5,306,276
*Registered Office:* The Long Barn, Wakefield Road, Hampole, Doncaster, S Yorks, DN6 7EU
*Activities:* Management of real estate on a fee or contract basis
*Major Shareholder:* Jeffrey Dunnill
*Officers:* Jefferey Dunnill [1963] Director; Izabela Koblenc [1976] Director/Stock Trader [Polish]

**Fope Limited**
*Incorporated:* 14 September 2012
*Net Worth:* £3,885,000 *Total Assets:* £6,663,000
*Registered Office:* Victoria Mills, The Green, Ossett, W Yorks, WF5 0AN
*Activities:* Activities of head offices
*Parent:* Airea PLC
*Officers:* Paul Stevenson, Secretary; Neil Rylance [1956] Director; Paul Stevenson [1978] Director/Accountant

**D. E. Ford Holdings Limited**
*Incorporated:* 20 April 2012
*Net Worth:* £4,690,000 *Total Assets:* £4,690,000
*Registered Office:* Rossington's Business Park, West Carr Road, Retford, Notts, DN22 7SW
*Activities:* Non-life insurance
*Parent:* PIB Group Limited
*Officers:* Ryan Christopher Brown [1973] Director; Brendan James McManus [1959] Director

**George Fordy Properties Limited**
*Incorporated:* 24 October 2001 *Employees:* 3
*Net Worth:* £3,728,361 *Total Assets:* £3,952,424
*Registered Office:* Construction House, High Street, Northallerton, N Yorks, DL7 8ED
*Activities:* Other letting and operating of own or leased real estate
*Major Shareholder:* Susan Bridget Greenwell
*Officers:* Derek John Greenwell, Secretary; Paul Blades [1963] Director; Derek John Greenwell [1948] Director Company Secretary; Keith Brian Noddings [1972] Finance Director

**Foregale Limited**
*Incorporated:* 3 September 1981 *Employees:* 41
*Net Worth:* £2,786,838 *Total Assets:* £4,658,731
*Registered Office:* Union Road, Liversedge, W Yorks, WF15 7JS
*Activities:* Manufacture of other fabricated metal products n.e.c.
*Shareholders:* Nigel Peter Scott; Susan Joan Scott
*Officers:* Nigel Peter Scott, Secretary; Allan Parkinson [1967] Director/Sales Manager; Jamie Christopher Scott [1984] Sales Director; Nigel Peter Scott [1953] Director/Steel Fabricator; Timothy James Scott [1981] Finance Director; Matthew Standring [1974] Director/Sales Manager

**Foremans Properties Limited**
*Incorporated:* 8 April 1999 *Employees:* 7
*Net Worth:* £3,516,690 *Total Assets:* £10,410,496
*Registered Office:* Tickton Hall, Tickton, Beverley, E Yorks, HU17 9RX
*Activities:* Other letting and operating of own or leased real estate
*Parent:* Catfoss Group Holdings Limited
*Officers:* Andrew Patrick Foreman [1963] Director; Benjamin Andrew Foreman [1986] Director

**Foresight North East Lincolnshire Ltd.**
*Incorporated:* 29 August 2001 *Employees:* 37
*Net Worth:* £2,734,231 *Total Assets:* £4,102,212
*Registered Office:* 60 Newmarket Street, Grimsby, N E Lincs, DN32 7SF
*Activities:* Other accommodation
*Officers:* Adrian Alan Wilson, Secretary; Manady Bentham [1964] Director/Supply Teacher; Peter Barry Blendell [1952] Director/Retired; Susan Bluer [1961] Director; Paul Edward Bray [1958] Director; Christopher Stuart Foyster [1974] Director/Insurance Agent; Kevin Arthur Fuller [1959] Director/Retired; Mansoor Gul [1971] Director/Police Constable; Julie Hague [1959] Director; Micheal James Inkson [1949] Director/Retired; Anthony Newton Jewitt [1960] Director/Minister; William John Maynell King [1958] Director/Solicitor; Janet LEA [1955] Director/Tutor; Paul Nicholls [1979] Director; Ronald Shepherd [1959] Director; Paul Ashley Tofton [1988] Director/Accountant

**Forest Homes Limited**
*Incorporated:* 7 January 2016
*Net Worth Deficit:* £87,510 *Total Assets:* £3,876,429
*Registered Office:* Holywood House, Wolsingham, Co Durham, DL13 3HE
*Activities:* Construction of domestic buildings
*Shareholders:* Anne Hill; Robert Angus Hill
*Officers:* Anne Hill, Secretary; Andrea Cassidy [1975] Director; Emma Hill [1979] Director; Robert Angus Hill [1950] Director

**The Forget Me Not Children's Hospice Limited**
*Incorporated:* 15 June 2005 *Employees:* 91
*Net Worth:* £3,691,697 *Total Assets:* £4,034,792
*Registered Office:* Forget Me Not Children's Hospice, Russell House, Fell Greave Road, Huddersfield, W Yorks, HD2 1NH
*Activities:* Other human health activities
*Officers:* Nicola O'Dowd, Secretary; Dr David Birkenhead [1964] Director/Doctor; Rosalind Edwards [1958] Director/Executive Coach/Retired; Sarah Jane Fothergill [1974] Director/Marketing Consultant; Rachael Ann Georgina Heenan [1971] Director/Solicitor; Stacey Louise Hunter [1969] NHS Director; Pritpal Singh Pooni [1984] Director/Chartered Accountant; Dr Gillian Anne Sharpe [1964] Director/Consultant Paediatrician; Kathryn Winterburn [1965] Director/Consultant/Leadership Development

**Formula Films Limited**
*Incorporated:* 27 June 2005
*Net Worth:* £2,460,971 *Total Assets:* £6,552,452
*Registered Office:* Highfield Grange, Bubwith, Selby, N Yorks, YO8 6DP
*Activities:* Motion picture production activities
*Officers:* Alan Richard Latham, Secretary; Alan Richard Latham [1960] Director/Film Financiers

**Forteq (UK) Limited**
*Incorporated:* 12 September 1935 *Employees:* 86
*Net Worth:* £4,145,087 *Total Assets:* £10,260,605
*Registered Office:* Tandem Industrial Estate, Tandem, Huddersfield, W Yorks, HD5 0QR
*Activities:* Manufacture of other plastic products
*Officers:* Paul Michael Wallis, Secretary; Rune Bakke [1960] Director [Norwegian]; Paul Andrew Doggett [1957] Director; Andreas Moser [1962] Director/Chief Financial Officer [Swiss]; Paul Michael Wallis [1959] Managing Director

**Forth Bridges Business Park Developments Limited**
*Incorporated:* 22 November 2006 *Employees:* 2
*Net Worth Deficit:* £2,754,902 *Total Assets:* £14,964,136
*Registered Office:* Millshaw, Leeds, LS11 8EG
*Activities:* Development of building projects
*Parent:* Evans Management Limited
*Officers:* Robert Marshall, Secretary; Roderick Michael Evans [1962] Director; Paul Terence Millington [1962] Director/Accountant

**Fortis Foods Limited**
*Incorporated:* 8 January 2015
*Net Worth:* £30 *Total Assets:* £3,652,139
*Registered Office:* Rakusens House, Clayton Wood Rise, Leeds, LS16 6QN
*Activities:* Manufacture of bread; manufacture of fresh pastry goods and cakes
*Major Shareholder:* Andrew Douglas Simpson
*Officers:* Richard Doyle, Secretary; Andrew Douglas Simpson [1961] Director

**Fortlands Limited**
*Incorporated:* 5 February 1990 *Employees:* 1
*Net Worth:* £19,487,012 *Total Assets:* £28,647,706
*Registered Office:* West House, King Cross Road, Halifax, W Yorks, HX1 1EB
*Activities:* Renting and operating of Housing Association real estate
*Major Shareholder:* Paul Richard Turner
*Officers:* James Peter Banfi, Secretary; John Duncan Turner, Secretary; Paul Martin Walker, Secretary/Solicitor; Paul Richard Turner [1946] Director

**Forward Investment Group LLP**
*Incorporated:* 14 March 2015
*Net Worth:* £6,985,278 *Total Assets:* £23,332,292
*Registered Office:* Mitre House, North Park Road, Harrogate, N Yorks, HG1 5RX
*Officers:* Daniel Ward [1959] Member; Tobias Ward [1957] Member

**Forward Investment LLP**
*Incorporated:* 22 May 2006
*Net Worth:* £5,804,341 *Total Assets:* £7,525,917
*Registered Office:* Mitre House, North Park Road, Harrogate, N Yorks, HG1 5RX
*Officers:* Daniel Ward [1959] Member; Tobias Ward [1957] Member

**Forward Investment Pannal LLP**
*Incorporated:* 17 March 2015
*Net Worth:* £2,375,487 *Total Assets:* £17,801,648
*Registered Office:* Mitre House, North Park Road, Harrogate, N Yorks, HG1 5RX
*Officers:* Daniel Ward [1959] Member; Tobias Ward [1957] Member

**Forza AW Limited**
*Incorporated:* 16 October 2006
*Net Worth:* £11,609,000 *Total Assets:* £12,033,000
*Registered Office:* Unit 1 Foxbridge Way, Normanton Industrial Estate, Normanton, W Yorks, WF6 1TN
*Activities:* Production of meat and poultry meat products
*Parent:* International Procurement and Logistics Limited
*Officers:* Varinder Rehal, Secretary; James Edward Fasey [1973] Finance Director; Max Sandiford Smith Hilliard [1958] Director/Chief Executive; Michael John Bland Snell [1964] Director

**Forza Foods Limited**
*Incorporated:* 15 April 2010 *Employees:* 1,434
*Net Worth:* £56,719,000 *Total Assets:* £85,124,000
*Registered Office:* Unit 1 Foxbridge Way, Normanton Industrial Estate, Normanton, W Yorks, WF6 1TN
*Activities:* Production of meat and poultry meat products
*Parent:* Forza AW Limited
*Officers:* Varinder Rehal, Secretary; James Edward Fasey [1973] Finance Director; Varinder Rehal [1975] Director and Company Secretary; Max Sandiford Smith Hilliard [1958] Director/Chief Executive; Michael John Bland Snell [1964] Director

**Foster Farms Limited**
*Incorporated:* 26 February 2007 *Employees:* 33
*Net Worth:* £1,681,745 *Total Assets:* £4,065,612
*Registered Office:* Willow Croft Farm, Riston Road, Catwick, Beverley, E Yorks, HU17 5PR
*Activities:* Raising of swine and pigs
*Shareholders:* Ashley Nigel Foster; Jane Louise Foster
*Officers:* Jane Louise Foster, Secretary; Ashley Nigel Foster [1972] Director; Jane Louise Foster [1970] Director

**Foundation**
*Incorporated:* 29 June 1984 *Employees:* 188
*Net Worth:* £100,000 *Total Assets:* £3,559,000
*Registered Office:* 3 Limewood Way, Seacroft, Leeds, LS14 1AB
*Activities:* Other social work activities without accommodation n.e.c.
*Officers:* Ruth Amanda Kettle, Secretary; Julia Anne Bates [1978] Director/Head of HR; Richard Brenden Parry [1958] Director/Management Consultant; David Waterman Powell [1946] Director/Interim Manager; Mark Ogilvie Simpson [1974] Director/Vice President - Strategy & Retail Operations; Patricia Anne Taylor [1948] Director/Retired; Philip Turnpenny [1948] Director; Claire Vilarrubi [1973] Director; Christopher John Welch [1963] Director/Housing Professional

**Foundation for Credit Counselling**
*Incorporated:* 19 October 1992 *Employees:* 1,521
*Net Worth:* £21,634,000 *Total Assets:* £26,239,000
*Registered Office:* Wade House, Merrion Centre, Leeds, LS2 8NG
*Activities:* Financial intermediation not elsewhere classified
*Officers:* Joshua Carl Bell [1978] Director/Venture Capitalist; David Raiffe Coates [1951] Director; Barbara Helen Dean [1959] Director/Chief Executive; John Anthony Fingleton [1965] Director/Chief Executive; Timothy James Albert Frost [1965] Director; John Guthrie Griffith-Jones [1954] Charity Director/Retired; Andrew Ratcliffe Hill [1955] Managing Director; Monica Kalia [1972] Director; Susan Tangier Lewis [1953] Director/Self Employed; Christopher John Stern [1957] Managing Director; Lesley Jane Titcomb [1961] Director

**Four Pillars Hotels Limited**
*Incorporated:* 21 March 1977
*Net Worth Deficit:* £391,000 *Total Assets:* £39,966,000
*Registered Office:* The Inspire, Hornbeam Square West, Harrogate, N Yorks, HG2 8PA
*Activities:* Activities of head offices
*Parent:* Spire Bidco Hotels Limited
*Officers:* John Cody Bradshaw [1978] Director/Hotel Real Estate [American]; James Alexander Burrell [1974] Director/Accountant; Anthony Gerrard Troy [1962] Director/Chief Executive Officer [Irish]

**Fourth Argyll Limited**
*Incorporated:* 5 May 1994 *Employees:* 64
*Net Worth:* £1,009,401 *Total Assets:* £10,580,138
*Registered Office:* Beckwith Health Club, Central House, Otley Road, Harrogate, N Yorks, HG3 1UF
*Activities:* Buying and selling of own real estate
*Shareholders:* SG Hambros Limited; SG Hambros Bank Limited
*Officers:* Mark Simon Silver [1960] Director

**Peter Fowler (Electrical) Limited**
*Incorporated:* 3 May 1994 *Employees:* 40
*Net Worth:* £2,882,517 *Total Assets:* £3,730,710
*Registered Office:* 3 Derby Road, Doncaster, S Yorks, DN2 4PQ
*Activities:* Electrical installation
*Shareholders:* Carol Fowler; Peter Fowler; Dean Peter Fowler
*Officers:* Carol Fowler, Secretary; Carol Fowler [1947] Director/Secretary; Dean Peter Fowler [1967] Director/Electrician; Peter Fowler [1946] Director/Electrical Contractor

**Fowler Welch Limited**
*Incorporated:* 28 January 1971 *Employees:* 1,477
*Previous:* Fowler Welch-Coolchain Limited
*Net Worth:* £52,512,000 *Total Assets:* £78,655,000
*Registered Office:* Low Fare Finder House, Leeds Bradford International Airport, Yeadon, Leeds, LS19 7TU
*Activities:* Operation of warehousing and storage facilities for land transport activities
*Parent:* Dart Group PLC
*Officers:* Ian Bruce Day, Secretary; Laurence Norman Black [1964] Technical Director; Gary James Brown [1966] Director/Group Chief Financial Officer; Martin Davies [1968] Operations Director; Matthew Downes [1974] IT Director; Peter Haggerwood [1977] Director/Accountant; Nicholas Daniel Hay [1974] Director; Lynda Kathryn Hulme [1968] HR Director; David Trevor Inglis [1948] Director; John Mark Kerrigan [1979] National Operations Director; Philip Hugh Meeson [1947] Director

**Foxton Farmers Limited**
*Incorporated:* 18 June 1953 *Employees:* 3
*Net Worth:* £2,310,821 *Total Assets:* £4,566,206
*Registered Office:* Manor Farm, Swine Lane, Coniston, Hull, HU11 4JX
*Activities:* Mixed farming
*Shareholders:* Sara Silvani Field; Boarcross Limited
*Officers:* Timothy Charles Field, Secretary; Sara Silvani Field [1965] Director/Secretary; Timothy Charles Field [1958] Director/Farmer; Emily Sara Field-Corrigan [1988] Director

**Fradley Park Developments Limited**
*Incorporated:* 22 November 2006 *Employees:* 3
*Net Worth:* £6,519,134 *Total Assets:* £23,266,396
*Registered Office:* Millshaw, Leeds, LS11 8EG
*Activities:* Development of building projects
*Parent:* Evans Management Limited
*Officers:* Robert Marshall, Secretary; Roderick Michael Evans [1962] Director; Paul Terence Millington [1962] Director/Accountant; Alan Matthew Syers [1964] Director/Chartered Surveyor

**Fradley Properties Ltd**
*Incorporated:* 22 December 1976 *Employees:* 4
*Net Worth:* £6,550,377 *Total Assets:* £6,925,966
*Registered Office:* Millshaw, Leeds, LS11 8EG
*Activities:* Other service activities n.e.c.
*Shareholder:* White Rose Property Investments No.2 Limited
*Officers:* Robert Marshall, Secretary; James Thomas Leavesley [1962] Director; John William Leavesley [1969] Director; Robert Marshall [1979] Director/Chartered Accountant; Alan Matthew Syers [1964] Director

**The Franklyn Group Limited**
*Incorporated:* 14 December 2001 *Employees:* 82
*Net Worth:* £4,409,379 *Total Assets:* £7,226,316
*Registered Office:* 1 Rudgate Court, Walton, Wetherby, W Yorks, LS23 7BF
*Activities:* Activities of head offices
*Parent:* Franklyn Care Ltd
*Officers:* Robert Arthur Fleming [1956] Director; Alisdair Jamie MacArthur [1972] Director; Janet Claire McKenna [1977] Director

**Frazer Estates Limited**
*Incorporated:* 15 March 2002
*Net Worth:* £4,178,222 *Total Assets:* £4,194,749
*Registered Office:* Progression Solicitors, 11 Queen Street, Ulverston, Cumbria, LA12 7AF
*Activities:* Construction of domestic buildings
*Major Shareholder:* Ewan Lindsay Frazer
*Officers:* Ewan Lindsay Frazer, Secretary; Ewan Lindsay Frazer [1958] Director/Company Secretary; Robin Edward Pearson [1978] Director/Builder

**Frear Investments Limited**
*Incorporated:* 15 June 2017
*Net Worth:* £16,302,188 *Total Assets:* £24,756,392
*Registered Office:* 35 Westgate, Huddersfield, W Yorks, HD1 1PA
*Activities:* Activities of head offices
*Shareholders:* Louise Frear; Timothy Craig Frear
*Officers:* Louise Frear [1976] Director; Timothy Craig Frear [1970] Director/Stair Lift Fabricator

**Fredrickson International Limited**
*Incorporated:* 15 January 1992 *Employees:* 281
*Net Worth Deficit:* £17,420,000 *Total Assets:* £4,942,000
*Registered Office:* Ellington House, 9 Savannah Way, Leeds Valley Park, Leeds, LS10 1AB
*Activities:* Other service activities n.e.c.
*Parent:* Interlaken Group Limited
*Officers:* Bill Flynn, Secretary; John Patrick Flaherty [1974] Director/Accountant [Irish]; David Ronald Gagie [1955] Director; Heinz Erwin Friedrich Hilgert [1953] Managing Director [German]; Sara Louise Leckenby [1961] Legal and Compliance Director; John Simon Pears [1973] Director

**Fredshaw & Co Limited**
*Incorporated:* 1 December 1955 *Employees:* 65
*Net Worth:* £3,055,770 *Total Assets:* £4,318,959
*Registered Office:* Victoria Buildings, Albert Street, Lockwood, Huddersfield, W Yorks, HD1 3PR
*Activities:* Manufacture of non-domestic cooling and ventilation equipment
*Officers:* John Howard Rhodes, Secretary; Jayne Rhodes [1966] Director/Secretary; John Howard Rhodes [1963] Managing Director; David Michael Sutton [1968] Director; Gary Tingle [1967] Director

**The Freedom Group of Companies Ltd.**
*Incorporated:* 1 November 1993 *Employees:* 607
*Net Worth:* £39,397,000 *Total Assets:* £70,844,000
*Registered Office:* Denton Hall, Denton, Ilkley, W Yorks, LS29 0HH
*Activities:* Construction of commercial buildings
*Parent:* NGBF Holdings Limited
*Officers:* Rachel Clare Salmon, Secretary; David Stuart Hurcomb [1964] Director/Engineer and Accountant; Michael Porter [1967] Director

**Freedom Refreshments Limited**
*Incorporated:* 10 November 2006 *Employees:* 151
*Net Worth:* £2,553,058 *Total Assets:* £6,419,540
*Registered Office:* Priory House, Gildersome Spur, Gildersome, Morley, Leeds, LS27 7JZ
*Activities:* Activities of head offices
*Parent:* Montagu Group Limited
*Officers:* Paul Martin Allen [1968] Director; Raymond Latimer Hutchinson [1949] Director; Stephen Thomas Alexander Hutchinson [1958] Director; Anne Alexandra Hutchinson-Kane [1947] Director

**Freemans Grattan Holdings Limited**
*Incorporated:* 2 June 1999 *Employees:* 4
*Net Worth:* £48,429,000 *Total Assets:* £109,669,000
*Registered Office:* 66-70 Vicar Lane, Little Germany, Bradford, W Yorks, BD99 2XG
*Activities:* Retail sale via mail order houses or via Internet
*Officers:* Andrew James Lord, Secretary; Markus Fuchshofen [1966] Director/Businessman [German]; John Hinchcliffe [1965] Director/Chief Executive Officer; Neill Lewis McDonald Moore [1966] Director/Chartered Accountant; Marc Erich Bernd Wolfgang Opelt [1962] Director/Businessman [German]

**Freemans Public Limited Company**
*Incorporated:* 8 December 1936 *Employees:* 179
*Net Worth:* £30,256,000 *Total Assets:* £119,725,000
*Registered Office:* 66-70 Vicar Lane, Little Germany, Bradford, W Yorks, BD99 2XG
*Activities:* Retail sale via mail order houses or via Internet
*Parent:* Freemans Grattan Holdings Limited
*Officers:* Andrew James Lord, Secretary; John Hinchcliffe [1965] Director/Chief Executive Officer; Neill Lewis McDonald Moore [1966] Director/Chartered Accountant; Marc Erich Bernd Wolfgang Opelt [1962] Director/Businessman [German]

**T.Freemantle Limited**
*Incorporated:* 17 January 1996 *Employees:* 37
*Net Worth:* £3,662,477 *Total Assets:* £5,476,993
*Registered Office:* 50-54 Oswald Road, Scunthorpe, N Lincs, DN15 7PQ
*Activities:* Manufacture of machinery for paper and paperboard production
*Shareholder:* Tony Freemantle
*Officers:* Lynne Michele Freemantle [1953] Director

**The Fresh Olive Company Ltd.**
*Incorporated:* 24 March 2009 *Employees:* 145
*Net Worth:* £7,442,043 *Total Assets:* £15,261,112
*Registered Office:* The Riverside Building, Livingstone Road, Hessle, E Yorks, HU13 0DZ
*Activities:* Other processing and preserving of fruit and vegetables
*Shareholders:* Adam Wells; George Patrick Bennell; John Charles Hodges
*Officers:* Gary Urmston, Secretary; George Patrick Bennell [1968] Director; John Charles Hodges [1972] Director; Rory Lloyd [1977] Director; Norman Graeme Scott Soutar [1960] Director; Gary Martin Urmston [1967] Director; James Watson [1969] Director; Adam Henry Wells [1967] Director

**Freshwater Biological Association (The)**
*Incorporated:* 3 March 1932 *Employees:* 20
*Net Worth:* £3,803,245 *Total Assets:* £3,878,414
*Registered Office:* The Pearsall Building, The Ferry Landing, Far Sawrey, Ambleside, Cumbria, LA22 0LP
*Activities:* Other letting and operating of own or leased real estate
*Officers:* Dr Steven John Brierley, Secretary; Geoffrey Robert Bateman [1956] Director/Executive Manager; Prof Keith John Beven [1950] Director/Emeritus Professor; Richard Paul Chadd [1964] Director/Freshwater Biologist; Alan Edward Crowden [1952] Director/Publishing Consultant; Prof Ann-Louise Heathwaite [1961] Director/University Lecturer; Ronald Alfred Wilson Middleton [1951] Director/Chief Executive; Dr Guy Woodward [1971] Director/University Lecturer

**Frickley Holdings.Limited**
*Incorporated:* 10 February 1971
*Net Worth:* £9,911,699 *Total Assets:* £10,410,980
*Registered Office:* Woodfield House, New Close Lane, Skelbrooke, Doncaster, S Yorks, DN6 8NA
*Activities:* Growing of cereals (except rice), leguminous crops and oil seeds
*Officers:* Anthony Michael Massarella, Secretary; Charles Michael Scholey [1955] Director/Farmer; Margaret Barbara Scholey [1931] Director/Farmer

**Fridlington Farms Limited**
*Incorporated:* 1 October 1956 *Employees:* 20
*Net Worth:* £2,768,598 *Total Assets:* £6,768,004
*Registered Office:* Bungalow, Well Lane, Sutton-on-the-Forest, N Yorks, YO61 1EF
*Activities:* Mixed farming
*Shareholders:* Stuart Roy Fraser Stark; 1956 Settlement
*Officers:* Jane Fraser Wilson, Secretary; Jean Anne Jackson [1933] Director; Mary Elizabeth Royle [1926] Director; Joan Stark [1932] Director; Stuart Roy Fraser Stark [1958] Director; Jane Fraser Wilson [1955] Director

**Friends of The Lake District**
*Incorporated:* 27 August 2003 *Employees:* 13
*Net Worth:* £4,006,514 *Total Assets:* £4,073,324
*Registered Office:* Friends of The Lake District, Murley Moss, Oxenholme Road, Kendal, Cumbria, LA9 7SS
*Activities:* Activities of other membership organisations n.e.c.
*Officers:* Moira Clare Hucknall, Secretary; Martin John Brimmer [1947] Director/Retired; John Alexander Campbell [1944] Director/Consultant; Judith Helen Cooke [1947] Director/Retired; Philip Alexander Cropper [1946] Director/Retired; David Felton [1977] Director/Businessman; Catherine Grezo [1958] Director/Retired; Sarah Jane Hodgson-Jones [1975] Director/Businesswoman; Anthony Richard Leeming [1950] Director/Retired

**Friends Provident Charitable Foundation**
*Incorporated:* 5 June 2001 *Employees:* 5
*Net Worth:* £33,752,896 *Total Assets:* £37,590,652
*Registered Office:* Blake House, 18 Blake Street, York, YO1 8QG
*Activities:* Other service activities n.e.c.
*Officers:* Joycelin Frances Elizabeth Dawes [1948] Director/Consultant; Paul Tabois Dickinson [1964] Director; Joanna Elson [1965] Director/Charity CEO; Patrick William James Hynes [1964] Director/Operations Manager; Kathleen Mary Joan Kelly [1969] Director/Civil Servant; Robert David Lake [1959] Director/Independent Investment Adviser; Stephen Mark Muers [1977] Director/Civil Servant; Hetan Shah [1975] Director/Charity CEO; Aphra Lilian Marden Sklair [1983] Director/Management Consultant

**Frog Education Limited**
*Incorporated:* 28 February 2000 *Employees:* 54
*Net Worth:* £3,188,686 *Total Assets:* £4,445,981
*Registered Office:* G Mill, Dean Clough Mills, Halifax, W Yorks, HX3 5AX
*Activities:* Other software publishing
*Parent:* Frog Education Group Limited
*Officers:* Martin John Bushnell [1949] Director; Gareth John Davies [1969] Director/IT Consultant; Steven John Holt [1978] Director; Michael Luke Wilkinson [1982] Director; Pei Lou Yeoh [1987] Director [Malaysian]; Dato Seok Hong Yeoh [1959] Director [Malaysian]

**Froneri International Limited**
*Incorporated:* 11 April 2006 *Employees:* 33
*Previous:* Froneri International PLC
*Net Worth Deficit:* £104,741,536 *Total Assets:* £1,859,410,432
*Registered Office:* Richmond House, Leeming Bar, Northallerton, N Yorks, DL7 9UL
*Activities:* Other manufacturing n.e.c.
*Parent:* Froneri Limited
*Officers:* Phil Karl Griffin [1972] Director; Marcello Mattia [1965] Director [Italian]; Ibrahim Mahmood Ibrahim Najafi [1958] Director

**Froneri Limited**
*Incorporated:* 20 April 2016 *Employees:* 12,765
*Net Worth:* £163,001,840 *Total Assets:* £3,390,711,040
*Registered Office:* Richmond House, Leeming Bar, Northallerton, N Yorks, DL7 9UL
*Activities:* Activities of production holding companies
*Officers:* Philip Graham Mellor, Secretary; Sanjay Bahadur [1959] Director/Senior Vice President [Indian]; Patrice Bula [1956] Director/Executive Vice President [Swiss/French]; Luis Cantarell [1952] Director/Executive Vice President [Spanish]; Martin Richard Glenn [1960] Director; Ibrahim Mahmood Ibrahim Najafi [1958] Director; Colm Paul O'Sullivan [1967] Director/Investment Manager [Irish]; Frederic Jacques Maria Paul Stevenin [1966] Director/Investment Manager [French]

**Froneri South Africa Holdings Limited**
*Incorporated:* 16 February 2015
*Previous:* R & R Ice Cream South Africa Holdings Limited
*Net Worth:* £24,744,260 *Total Assets:* £25,641,210
*Registered Office:* Richmond House, Leeming Bar, Northallerton, N Yorks, DL7 9UL
*Activities:* Activities of production holding companies
*Parent:* Froneri International PLC
*Officers:* Phil Karl Griffin [1972] Director; Marcello Mattia [1965] Director [Italian]; Ibrahim Mahmood Ibrahim Najafi [1958] Director

**Frontica Business Solutions Limited**
*Incorporated:* 13 November 2003 *Employees:* 3
*Net Worth:* £3,029,000 *Total Assets:* £6,288,000
*Registered Office:* 1 Park Row, Leeds, LS1 5AB
*Activities:* Activities of head offices
*Parent:* Akastor ASA
*Officers:* Idun Heier [1970] Director/Head of Financial Reporting Akastor [Norwegian]; Oyvind Paaske [1984] Director/Investment Manager [Norwegian]

**David Frost Estate Agents Limited**
*Incorporated:* 10 February 1992 *Employees:* 36
*Net Worth:* £4,556,000 *Total Assets:* £6,114,000
*Registered Office:* 2nd Floor, Gateway 2, Station Business Park, Holgate Park Drive, York, YO26 4GB
*Activities:* Real estate agencies
*Parent:* Vitalhandy Enterprises Ltd
*Officers:* Sapna Bedi FitzGenerald, Secretary; Greig Barker [1969] Finance Director; Helen Elizabeth Buck [1960] Director; Andrew Steven Gilchrist [1966] Managing Director; Gregory Winston Young [1966] Director

**Fruugo.Com Ltd**
*Incorporated:* 3 April 2008 *Employees:* 26
*Net Worth:* £728,296 *Total Assets:* £4,207,140
*Registered Office:* 13 Fountain Street, Ulverston, Cumbria, LA12 7EQ
*Activities:* Other information service activities n.e.c.
*Shareholder:* Dominic William Damien Allonby
*Officers:* Darren John Naylor, Secretary; Dominic William Damien Allonby [1962] Director; Nicholas Michael Carter [1967] Director; Michael John Hancox [1966] Non-Executive Director Chairman; Theodore Thomas Hettich [1982] Director/Chief Sales Officer [American]; Darren John Naylor [1967] Director; Glen Paul Richardson [1982] Director/Chief Marketing Officer; Andrew Thomas [1966] Director; John Walker [1958] Director; Alan White [1955] Director

**FTL Seals Technology Limited**
*Incorporated:* 15 January 1998 *Employees:* 31
*Net Worth:* £14,671,401 *Total Assets:* £16,563,235
*Registered Office:* Leeds Twenty Seven Industrial Estate, Bruntcliffe Avenue, Morley, Leeds, LS27 0TG
*Activities:* Other manufacturing n.e.c.
*Parent:* Idex UK Investment Ltd
*Officers:* Lisa Michelle Anderson, Secretary; Brian Patrick Hanigan, Secretary; Andrew John Hewitt [1964] Director/Business Unit Leader; Eric Shawn McKinley [1984] Director/Business Executive [American]; Neil Thompson [1965] Director/Business Executive; Marc Arthur Uleman [1963] Director/Manager

**The Fuel Card Group Limited**
*Incorporated:* 2 January 1997 *Employees:* 3
*Net Worth:* £35,697,000 *Total Assets:* £36,027,000
*Registered Office:* Alexandra House, Lawnswood Business Park, Redvers Close, Leeds, LS16 6QY
*Activities:* Wholesale of petroleum and petroleum products
*Parent:* Dyneley Holdings Ltd
*Officers:* Stephen Elliott, Secretary; Stephen Elliott [1962] Director; Benjamin Marcus Jordan [1964] Director; Daire Keating [1978] Director [Irish]

**Fuel Card Services Limited**
*Incorporated:* 9 March 1987 *Employees:* 352
*Net Worth:* £30,973,000 *Total Assets:* £150,231,008
*Registered Office:* Alexandra House, Lawnswood Business Park, Redvers Close, Leeds, LS16 6QY
*Activities:* Wholesale of petroleum and petroleum products
*Parent:* The Fuel Card Group Ltd
*Officers:* Stephen Elliott, Secretary/Director; Killian Bane [1986] Finance Director [Irish]; Declan Doorly [1975] Director [Irish]; Stephen Elliott [1962] Director/Accountant; Denise Jane Frost [1967] Commercial Director; Benjamin Marcus Jordan [1964] Director; Daire Keating [1978] Director [Irish]; Edward Gerard O'Brien [1970] Director/Accountant [Irish]

**Fuel Express Limited**
*Incorporated:* 25 September 1997 *Employees:* 5
*Net Worth:* £61,089 *Total Assets:* £3,517,770
*Registered Office:* Suite 2, Belle Vue Business Centre, Elm Tree Street, Wakefield, W Yorks, WF1 5EP
*Activities:* Wholesale of other fuels and related products
*Shareholders:* Alan Davies; G N G Holdings Limited; Bagnalls Group (UK) Ltd
*Officers:* Natalie Ann Lindop, Secretary; Jonathan Phillip Bagnall [1961] Director; Alan Thomas John Davies [1957] Director/Fuel Distributor; Jason Grosvenor [1965] Director

**Fuel Proof Limited**
*Incorporated:* 12 May 2000 *Employees:* 65
*Net Worth:* £2,819,468 *Total Assets:* £4,584,321
*Registered Office:* Middleton Business Park, Middleton Road, Heysham, Lancs, LA3 3FH
*Activities:* Manufacture of other tanks, reservoirs and containers of metal
*Officers:* Julie Ann Turnbull, Secretary; Andrew Richard Hargreaves [1976] Director/Engineer; Treve Robert Henry [1966] Director; Hans Marthinus Meyer [1986] Director [South African]; Roger Arthur Pilkington [1971] Director/Engineer; Julie Ann Turnbull [1964] Director

**The Fuel Trading Company Ltd**
*Incorporated:* 20 April 2009 *Employees:* 11
*Net Worth:* £1,538,546 *Total Assets:* £8,096,272
*Registered Office:* 1 Toft Green, York, YO1 6JT
*Activities:* Wholesale of petroleum and petroleum products
*Major Shareholder:* James Nicholas Lloyd Spencer
*Officers:* Juliette Michelle Spencer, Secretary; Neil Scott Donald [1949] Director; Philip Stephen Hall [1960] Financial Director; Steven Row Irwin [1975] Trading Director; Nicholas James Kenally Smith [1969] Director; James Nicholas Lloyd Spencer [1972] Director; Joe Stephen Tuohy [1984] Commercial Director

**The Fuelcard Company UK Limited**
*Incorporated:* 18 September 2006 *Employees:* 82
*Net Worth:* £71,919,000 *Total Assets:* £107,867,000
*Registered Office:* Unit 3 St James Business Park, Grimbald Crag Court, Knaresborough, N Yorks, HG5 8QB
*Activities:* Wholesale of petroleum and petroleum products
*Parent:* Fambo UK Limited
*Officers:* Eric Richard Dey [1959] Director/Chief Financial Officer [American]; Alan King [1976] Director/Group President UK & Australasia; Anita Kravos-Medimorec [1974] Director/Chief Financial Officer; Steven Joseph Pisciotta [1964] Director [American]

**Fullers Foods Holdings Limited**
*Incorporated:* 22 June 2011 *Employees:* 2
*Previous:* Growers Consortium Limited
*Net Worth:* £17,089,916 *Total Assets:* £17,109,132
*Registered Office:* Leigh House, 28-32 St Pauls Street, Leeds, LS1 2JG
*Activities:* Management consultancy activities other than financial management
*Shareholders:* Jason Victor Fuller; Adam Garvie Fuller
*Officers:* Adam Garvie Fuller [1964] Director; Jason Victor Fuller [1968] Director

**Fullers Foods International PLC**
*Incorporated:* 5 December 1969 *Employees:* 47
*Previous:* Fullers Foods International Limited
*Net Worth:* £5,369,067 *Total Assets:* £37,817,912
*Registered Office:* Leigh House, 28-32 St Pauls Street, Leeds, LS1 2JT
*Activities:* Non-specialised wholesale of food, beverages and tobacco
*Parent:* Growers Consortium Limited
*Officers:* Adam Garvie Fuller, Secretary; Adam Garvie Fuller [1964] Director/Food Wholesaler; Jason Victor Fuller [1968] Director/Food Wholesaler

**Furmanite 1986**
*Incorporated:* 26 March 1986
*Net Worth:* £5,421,000 *Total Assets:* £7,915,000
*Registered Office:* Furman House, Shap Road, Kendal, Cumbria, LA9 6RU
*Activities:* Repair of other equipment
*Parent:* Furmanite Limited
*Officers:* Rachel Dixon, Secretary; Greg Lee Boane [1963] Director/Chief Finance Officer [American]; Andre Charles Bouchard [1965] Director/Senior VP - Legal [American]; Jonathon Anthony Jarvis [1957] Director/Vice President

**Furmanite Limited**
*Incorporated:* 13 August 1990
*Net Worth:* £25,586,000 *Total Assets:* £42,851,000
*Registered Office:* Furman House, Shap Road, Kendal, Cumbria, LA9 6RU
*Activities:* Repair of other equipment
*Parent:* Furmanite Holding B.V.
*Officers:* Rachel Dixon, Secretary; Greg Lee Boane [1963] Director/Chief Finance Officer [American]; Andre Charles Bouchard [1965] Director/Senior VP - Legal [American]; Jonathon Anthony Jarvis [1957] Director/Vice President

**Furness Academies Trust**
*Incorporated:* 5 May 2009 *Employees:* 103
*Previous:* Furness Academy Limited
*Net Worth:* £17,108,000 *Total Assets:* £21,663,000
*Registered Office:* Furness Academy, Park Drive, Barrow in Furness, Cumbria, LA13 9BB
*Activities:* General secondary education
*Officers:* Andrew Robert Judd, Secretary; Gavin Edward Benbow [1978] Director/Head of Finance; Anthony James Hunter Burbridge [1947] Director/Consultant Engineer; Anne Burns [1948] Director/Cumbria County Councillor; Graeme Corkill [1972] Director/Chief Engineer; Edward William Creighton [1967] Director/Head of HR; Jane Dean-Wilcock [1971] Director/Accountant; Hilary Jane Ellam [1960] Director; Adam Mark Hearnden [1962] Safety, Quality & Assurance Director; David Anthony Kelly [1950] Director/Education Consultant; Stuart Mnagg [1974] Director/Operations Area Manager; John Austin Shields [1954] Director/Teacher; Mark Woodham [1961] Director/IT Manager

**Furness Mortgage Services Limited**
*Incorporated:* 13 July 1994
*Net Worth:* £1,735,401 *Total Assets:* £4,281,793
*Registered Office:* 51-55 Duke Street, Barrow in Furness, Cumbria, LA14 1RT
*Activities:* Financial intermediation not elsewhere classified
*Officers:* Philip Nigel Lake, Secretary; Matthew Jon Dobson [1976] Finance Director; Christopher Michael Harrison [1961] Director/Chief Executive; Susan Jane Heron [1963] Marketing and Sales Director; Pamela Adele Mawson [1971] Director/Chief Risk Officer

**Furness Park LLP**
*Incorporated:* 28 February 2007 *Employees:* 22
*Net Worth:* £1,073,616 *Total Assets:* £5,209,486
*Registered Office:* Abbey Road, Barrow in Furness, Cumbria, LA13 9AE
*Officers:* Alan Deric Stoker [1947] Member; Brad Stoker [1972] Member; Glenn Stoker [1974] Member; Helen Stoker [1975] Member; Lynda Stoker [1947] Member; Nicola Stoker [1973] Member

**Furniture Choice Limited**
*Incorporated:* 1 February 2005 *Employees:* 49
*Net Worth:* £1,762,369 *Total Assets:* £3,728,189
*Registered Office:* Unit 22 Bankfield Business Park, Huddersfield Road, Mirfield, W Yorks, WF14 9DD
*Activities:* Retail of furniture, lighting, and similar (not musical instruments or scores) in specialised store
*Shareholders:* Thomas Charles Obbard; Howard James Obbard
*Officers:* Thomas Charles Obbard, Secretary; Howard James Obbard [1974] Director; Thomas Charles Obbard [1975] Director

**Further Instructions Ltd**
*Incorporated:* 15 April 2011
*Net Worth:* £826,352 *Total Assets:* £4,520,987
*Registered Office:* Highfield Grange, Bubwith, Selby, N Yorks, YO8 6DP
*Activities:* Motion picture production activities
*Officers:* Alan Richard Latham [1960] Director/Film Producer; Jack Murray Tarling [1984] Director/Producer

**Fussey Engineering Limited**
*Incorporated:* 12 August 2002 *Employees:* 23
*Net Worth:* £1,927,999 *Total Assets:* £3,559,868
*Registered Office:* Lancaster Approach, North Killingholme, Grimsby, N E Lincs, DN40 3JZ
*Activities:* Construction of other civil engineering projects n.e.c.
*Parent:* Fussey Holding Limited
*Officers:* Janet Eileen Fussey, Secretary/Director; Desmond Generald Fussey [1947] Director; Janet Eileen Fussey [1949] Director; Marcus Andrew Fussey [1969] Director; Michael Des Fussey [1981] Director; David Hamilton [1962] Director; Yvonne Gaye Mager [1957] Director

**Fussey Holdings Limited**
*Incorporated:* 18 March 2010
*Net Worth:* £4,089,902 *Total Assets:* £4,219,902
*Registered Office:* Lancaster Approach, North Killingholme, Grimsby, N E Lincs, DN40 3JZ
*Activities:* Activities of construction holding companies
*Shareholder:* Marcus Andrew Fussey
*Officers:* Desmond Generald Fussey [1947] Director; Janet Eileen Fussey [1949] Director; Marcus Andrew Fussey [1969] Director; Michael Des Fussey [1981] Director; David Hamilton [1962] Director; Yvonne Gaye Mager [1957] Director

**Fussey Piling Ltd**
*Incorporated:* 1 March 1984 *Employees:* 33
*Net Worth:* £3,853,967 *Total Assets:* £5,702,040
*Registered Office:* Lancaster Approach, North Killingholme, Grimsby, N E Lincs, DN40 3JZ
*Activities:* Construction of other civil engineering projects n.e.c.
*Shareholders:* Desmond Fussey; Janet Fussey
*Officers:* Janet Eileen Fussey, Secretary; Desmond Generald Fussey [1947] Director; Janet Eileen Fussey [1949] Director; Marcus Andrew Fussey [1969] Contracts Director; Michael Des Fussey [1981] Director; Graham Robert Hall [1973] Director/Civil Engineer; David Richard Jones [1948] Director/Civil Engineer; Yvonne Gaye Mager [1957] Director/Accountant

**Futurama Limited**
*Incorporated:* 18 May 1998 *Employees:* 35
*Net Worth:* £2,627,589 *Total Assets:* £6,023,623
*Registered Office:* Olympia House, Metro Park 45, Lockwood Court, Leeds, LS11 5TY
*Activities:* Other manufacturing n.e.c.
*Parent:* The Glendower Group Limited
*Officers:* William Jonathan Evans, Secretary; Marc James Edwards [1975] Director; William Jonathan Evans [1962] Director; David Laurence Higgins [1966] Director; David Hurley [1973] Director; Gary John Needham [1967] Director; David Christopher Sharp [1961] Director; Andrew Charles Small [1985] Director

**Futurama Signs Holdings Limited**
*Incorporated:* 4 June 2014 *Employees:* 135
*Net Worth:* £1,994,308 *Total Assets:* £8,478,167
*Registered Office:* Olympia House, Metro Park 45, Lockwood Court, Leeds, LS11 5TY
*Activities:* Activities of head offices
*Officers:* William Jonathan Evans, Secretary; Marc James Edwards [1975] Director; William Jonathan Evans [1962] Director; David Hurley [1973] Director; Steven David Miller [1975] Director/Accountant; David Christopher Sharp [1961] Director

**Futurama Signs Limited**
*Incorporated:* 6 May 1959 *Employees:* 98
*Net Worth:* £1,907,624 *Total Assets:* £5,027,124
*Registered Office:* Olympia House, Metro Park 45, Lockwood Court, Leeds, LS11 5TY
*Activities:* Other manufacturing n.e.c.
*Parent:* Futurama Limited
*Officers:* William Jonathan Evans, Secretary; Gareth Boulton [1981] Business Support Director; Michael Coates [1951] Sales Director; Marc James Edwards [1975] Director; William Jonathan Evans [1962] Director/Certified Chartered Accountant; David Hurley [1973] Director; Linda Jane Myers [1972] Director; David Christopher Sharp [1961] Director

**Future Cleaning Services Limited**
*Incorporated:* 5 March 2004 *Employees:* 2,199
*Net Worth:* £3,350,390 *Total Assets:* £7,383,016
*Registered Office:* 8 Novus Business Park, Opus Avenue, York Business Park, Nether Poppleton, York, YO26 6BL
*Activities:* Specialised cleaning services
*Major Shareholder:* Charles William Chisholm
*Officers:* Jonathan Neil Watts, Secretary; Charles William Chisholm [1970] Director; Joanne Chisholm [1968] Director/Administrator Manager; Stuart James Chisholm [1965] Director; Ringo Daisley Francis [1955] Director; Anthony Nisbet [1957] Director/Manager; Michelle Stephanie Walker [1967] Director/National Contracts Manager; Jonathan Neil Watts [1978] Finance Director

**Future Forwarding (Group) Limited**
*Incorporated:* 14 May 2013 *Employees:* 151
*Net Worth:* £4,230,387 *Total Assets:* £10,603,054
*Registered Office:* Unit 4 Hawthorne House, Dark Lane, Birstall, W Yorks, WF17 9LW
*Activities:* Other transportation support activities
*Parent:* Future Forwarding (Group), Inc.
*Officers:* David John Biggin [1958] Director; Pamela Brown [1965] Director [American]; David William Holland [1957] Director; Colin Geoffrey Smith [1969] Director/Vice President

**Future Forwarding (Holdings) Limited**
*Incorporated:* 26 October 2009
*Net Worth:* £2,010,984 *Total Assets:* £4,028,835
*Registered Office:* Unit 4 Hawthorn House, Dark Lane, Birstall, W Yorks, WF17 9LU
*Activities:* Other transportation support activities
*Parent:* Future Forwarding (Group) Limited
*Officers:* David William Holland, Secretary; David John Biggin [1958] Director; David William Holland [1957] Financial Director; Colin Geoffrey Smith [1969] Director/Vice President

**Future Forwarding Company Limited**
*Incorporated:* 3 July 1978 *Employees:* 39
*Net Worth:* £3,348,832 *Total Assets:* £6,658,975
*Registered Office:* Unit 4 Hawthorne House, Dark Lane, Birstall, W Yorks, WF17 9LW
*Activities:* Other transportation support activities
*Parent:* Future Forwarding (Holdings) Ltd
*Officers:* David William Holland, Secretary; David John Biggin [1958] Director; Pamela Brown [1965] Director [American]; David William Holland [1957] Financial Director; Colin Geoffrey Smith [1969] Director

**G & H Building Services Ltd.**
*Incorporated:* 5 August 1998 *Employees:* 81
*Net Worth:* £1,758,362 *Total Assets:* £8,948,401
*Registered Office:* Firlands Mill, South Parade, Pudsey, W Yorks, LS28 8AD
*Activities:* Electrical installation
*Parent:* G & H Group of Companies Limited
*Officers:* Mark Andrew Greaves, Secretary; Mark Andrew Craven [1978] Director; David Alan Davis [1970] Director; Graham Andrew Kelly [1973] Director/Engineer

**G & R Properties (Yorkshire) Limited**
*Incorporated:* 15 April 2003 *Employees:* 3
*Net Worth:* £41,523 *Total Assets:* £3,700,744
*Registered Office:* 27 Ryedale Way, Tingley, Wakefield, W Yorks, WF3 1AP
*Activities:* Buying and selling of own real estate
*Officers:* Emma Howley, Secretary; Doreen Howley [1956] Director; Gary Howley [1958] Director/Property Development

**G - Tuft Limited**
*Incorporated:* 20 January 2012 *Employees:* 142
*Net Worth:* £2,000,427 *Total Assets:* £10,410,156
*Registered Office:* Thornhill Road Business Park, Tenter Fields, Dewsbury, W Yorks, WF12 9QT
*Activities:* Manufacture of woven or tufted carpets and rugs
*Parent:* G-Tuft (Holdings) Ltd
*Officers:* Peter Sutton, Secretary; John Stewart Graham [1938] Director; Nigel Graham [1951] Production Director; Peter Sutton [1959] Finance Director

**G R Finance Limited**
*Incorporated:* 9 August 2006 *Employees:* 6
*Net Worth:* £1,082,080 *Total Assets:* £3,266,348
*Registered Office:* 15 The Firs, Scarcroft, Leeds, LS14 3JH
*Activities:* Other credit granting n.e.c.
*Shareholders:* Graham Charles Richardson; Steven Wright; Graham Charles Richardson
*Officers:* Steven Wright, Secretary; Graham Charles Richardson [1958] Director; Steven Wright [1978] Director

**G S M Automotive Limited**
*Incorporated:* 18 June 2001 *Employees:* 246
*Net Worth:* £16,827,688 *Total Assets:* £20,025,992
*Registered Office:* Castlegarth Works, Masonic Lane, Thirsk, N Yorks, YO7 1PS
*Activities:* Manufacture of other fabricated metal products n.e.c.
*Officers:* Robert Harvey Ashmeade, Secretary; Robert Harvey Ashmeade [1966] Director; Frances Dodd [1946] Director; Andrew Charles Farthing [1962] Director; Antony John Perry [1947] Director/Accountant; Brian Francis Xavier Reilly [1963] Director

**G S M Group Limited**
*Incorporated:* 9 June 1998
*Net Worth:* £5,441,623 *Total Assets:* £5,697,935
*Registered Office:* Castlegarth Works, Masonic Lane, Thirsk, N Yorks, YO7 1PS
*Activities:* Activities of head offices
*Parent:* GSM Group Holdco Ltd
*Officers:* Gillian Gitsham, Secretary; Frances Dodd [1946] Director; Antony John Perry [1947] Director/Accountant

**G-Tuft (2015) Limited**
*Incorporated:* 18 March 2015 *Employees:* 142
*Net Worth:* £484,500 *Total Assets:* £8,894,229
*Registered Office:* Thornhill Road Business Park, Tenter Fields, Dewsbury, W Yorks, WF12 9QT
*Activities:* Activities of head offices
*Shareholders:* John Stewart Graham; Nigel Graham
*Officers:* John Stewart Graham [1938] Director; Nigel Graham [1951] Director

**G.B. Agencies Limited**
*Incorporated:* 27 October 1983 *Employees:* 45
*Net Worth:* £4,085,500 *Total Assets:* £12,823,125
*Registered Office:* Meridian House, Alexandra Dock North, Grimsby, N E Lincs, DN31 3UA
*Activities:* Other transportation support activities
*Parent:* GBA (Holdings) Limited
*Officers:* John Charles Gunn, Secretary; Maureen Judah [1953] Director; Samson Sassoon Samuel Judah [1953] Director

**G.B. Terminals (Northern) Limited**
*Incorporated:* 22 January 2003 *Employees:* 63
*Net Worth:* £2,550,592 *Total Assets:* £5,838,892
*Registered Office:* Meridian House, Alexandra Dock North, Grimsby, N E Lincs, DN31 3UA
*Activities:* Other transportation support activities
*Shareholders:* Maureen Judah; Samson Sassoon Samuel Judah
*Officers:* John Charles Gunn, Secretary; Maureen Judah [1953] Director; Samson Sassoon Samuel Judah [1953] Director

**G.B. Terminals Limited**
*Incorporated:* 24 June 1991 *Employees:* 291
*Net Worth:* £5,985,986 *Total Assets:* £16,957,776
*Registered Office:* Meridian House, Alexandra Dock North, Grimsby, N E Lincs, DN31 3UA
*Activities:* Operation of warehousing and storage facilities for water transport activities
*Parent:* GBA (Holdings) Limited
*Officers:* John Charles Gunn, Secretary; Maureen Judah [1953] Director; Samson Sassoon Samuel Judah [1953] Director

**G.R. Electrical Services Limited**
*Incorporated:* 3 September 1984 *Employees:* 47
*Net Worth:* £5,134,949 *Total Assets:* £9,073,570
*Registered Office:* Merlin House, Aviation Road, Sherburn Enterprise Park, Sherburn in Elmet, Leeds, LS25 6NB
*Activities:* Electrical installation
*Officers:* Julie Houseman, Secretary; Christopher Houseman [1955] Director; Stephen Shepherd [1960] Director; David Storr [1965] Operations Director

**G2M Capital Limited**
*Incorporated:* 17 March 2016 *Employees:* 9
*Net Worth:* £9,864,427 *Total Assets:* £16,287,647
*Registered Office:* 25 Jetstream Drive, Auckley, Doncaster, S Yorks, DN9 3QS
*Activities:* Activities of other holding companies n.e.c.
*Shareholder:* Paul Darren Morton
*Officers:* Kyle David Gardner [1988] Director; Stephen David Gardner [1958] Director; Paul Darren Morton [1971] Director

**G2M Unilets Limited**
*Incorporated:* 31 July 2001 *Employees:* 2
*Net Worth:* £6,652,235 *Total Assets:* £9,627,463
*Registered Office:* 25 Jetstream Drive, Aukley, Doncaster, S Yorks, DN9 3QS
*Activities:* Other letting and operating of own or leased real estate
*Shareholders:* Paul Darren Morton; Victoria Louise Winchester Morton
*Officers:* Victoria Morton, Secretary; Paul Darren Morton [1971] Director/Accountant

**G3 Remarketing Limited**
*Incorporated:* 10 June 2009 *Employees:* 46
*Net Worth:* £1,821,269 *Total Assets:* £4,897,975
*Registered Office:* Unit 200 Premier Way, Oulton, Leeds, LS26 8ZA
*Activities:* Other service activities n.e.c.
*Shareholder:* Amanda Jane Holtby
*Officers:* Matthew James Dale [1976] Director; Amanda Jane Holtby [1973] Director

**Gablesea Limited**
*Incorporated:* 20 May 1976 *Employees:* 86
*Net Worth:* £3,576,545 *Total Assets:* £11,434,994
*Registered Office:* Howley Park Industrial Estate, Howley Park Road East, Morley, Leeds, LS27 0BN
*Activities:* Manufacture of other fabricated metal products n.e.c.
*Shareholders:* James Harry Chrimes; Graham Patrick Wilson; John Marshall Winn
*Officers:* Graham Patrick Wilson, Secretary; James Harry Chrimes [1931] Director; Philip Anthony Snowden [1953] Sales Director; Graham Patrick Wilson [1947] Director; John Marshall Winn [1947] Director

**Gainsborough Industrial Controls Limited**
*Incorporated:* 7 September 1984 *Employees:* 21
*Net Worth:* £2,267,434 *Total Assets:* £3,624,219
*Registered Office:* Alpha Works, Sandars Road, Heapham Road Industrial Estate, Gainsborough, Lincs, DN21 1RZ
*Activities:* Other manufacturing n.e.c.
*Parent:* Amip Limited
*Officers:* Luke Murphy, Secretary; Andrew Mark Beal [1961] Director/Engineer; Luke Murphy [1966] Director/Chartered Accountant

**Gale and Phillipson Investment Services Ltd**
*Incorporated:* 31 March 2005 *Employees:* 72
*Previous:* Gale and Phillipson Ltd
*Net Worth:* £5,475,042 *Total Assets:* £6,292,617
*Registered Office:* Gallowfields House, Fairfield Way, Richmond, N Yorks, DL10 4TB
*Activities:* Activities auxiliary to financial intermediation n.e.c.
*Parent:* Gale and Phillipson Holdings Ltd
*Officers:* Peter Denis Griffin [1985] Director

**M. Gallagher (Civil Engineering) Limited**
*Incorporated:* 19 November 1996 *Employees:* 10
*Net Worth:* £2,800,995 *Total Assets:* £3,669,975
*Registered Office:* 10 Church Street, Paddock, Huddersfield, W Yorks, HD1 4TR
*Activities:* Construction of other civil engineering projects n.e.c.
*Officers:* Michael James Gallagher [1959] Director [Irish]

**Galtec Solutions Limited**
*Incorporated:* 19 August 2004 *Employees:* 30
*Net Worth:* £1,239,326 *Total Assets:* £4,628,185
*Registered Office:* Bridge End House, Low Lane, Horsforth, Leeds, LS18 4DF
*Activities:* Information technology consultancy activities
*Parent:* Galtec Solutions Holdings Limited
*Officers:* Amy Cooke, Secretary; Mark David Adams [1967] Director; Jamie Roy Bowes [1985] Director; Amy Francesca Cooke [1985] Director; John Steven O'Connell [1980] Director; Tracy Jayne Walker [1967] Central Government Sales Director

**Gamebore Cartridge Co. Limited**
*Incorporated:* 20 August 1974 *Employees:* 39
*Net Worth:* £11,018,321 *Total Assets:* £13,767,753
*Registered Office:* Great Union Street, Kingston upon Hull, HU9 1AR
*Activities:* Hunting, trapping and related service activities
*Major Shareholder:* Donald Murray Rogers
*Officers:* Herold McClure Deason, Secretary; Robert Paul Cove [1949] Director/Company President [Canadian]; Herold McClure Deason [1942] Director/Attorney at Law [American]; Paul David James [1983] Director; Phillip Alan Plowman [1967] Director; Donald Ian Rogers [1972] Director [Canadian]; Donald Murray Rogers [1939] Director/Executive [Canadian]

**Gamston Aviation Limited**
*Incorporated:* 27 October 1977 *Employees:* 20
*Net Worth:* £10,303,195 *Total Assets:* £11,219,322
*Registered Office:* Retford (Gamston) Airport, Gamston Airfield, Gamston, Retford, Notts, DN22 0QL
*Activities:* Service activities incidental to air transportation
*Major Shareholder:* Kevin McDonald
*Officers:* Donna Brigitte McDonald, Secretary; Amie McDonald [1993] Director; Donna Brigitte McDonald [1962] Director; Kevin McDonald [1933] Managing Director

**Gands (U.K.)**
*Incorporated:* 4 February 1993 *Employees:* 540
*Net Worth:* £71,576,000 *Total Assets:* £152,284,992
*Registered Office:* c/o OSI Food Solutions UK Ltd, Luneburg Way, Scunthorpe, N Lincs, DN15 8LP
*Activities:* Activities of head offices
*Shareholders:* Sheldon Lavin; Gerald Arthur Kolschowsky
*Officers:* Martin Howard Back, Secretary; Sherry Anne de Meulenaere, Secretary; Sheldon Lavin [1932] Director/President OSI Industries Inc [American]; David Gerard McDonald [1964] Director [American]

**Ganton School**
*Incorporated:* 10 December 2014 *Employees:* 145
*Net Worth:* £10,062,891 *Total Assets:* £11,985,359
*Registered Office:* Ganton School, 294 Anlaby Park Road South, Hull, HU4 7JB
*Activities:* Primary education
*Officers:* Zoe Alexandra Netherton, Secretary; Annette Burn [1968] Director/Teacher; Sarah Elizabeth Hatley [1975] Director/School Governor; Ian Ibbotson [1973] Director/Education; William Lloyd Jones [1949] Director/Architect; Jane Marie Motherby [1968] Director/School Governor

**Gardner Denver Group Services Limited**
*Incorporated:* 13 November 1987 *Employees:* 500
*Net Worth:* £4,846,706 *Total Assets:* £23,823,616
*Registered Office:* c/o Gardner Denver International Ltd, Springmill Street, Bradford, W Yorks, BD5 7HW
*Activities:* Activities of head offices
*Parent:* Gardner Denver International Ltd
*Officers:* Mark Elliott Grummett, Secretary; Michael Joseph Scheske [1987] Director/Accountant [American]; Andrew Roger Schiesl [1971] Director/General Council [American]

**Gardner Denver Holdings Limited**
*Incorporated:* 25 September 2008
*Net Worth Deficit:* £9,761,434 *Total Assets:* £234,855,392
*Registered Office:* c/o Gardner Denver International Ltd, Springmill Street, Bradford, W Yorks, BD5 7HW
*Activities:* Activities of head offices
*Parent:* GD Global Holdings UK II Ltd
*Officers:* Mark Elliott Grummett, Secretary; Michael Joseph Scheske [1987] Director/Accountant [American]; Andrew Roger Schiesl [1971] Director/General Council [American]

**Gardner Denver Industries Ltd**
*Incorporated:* 10 April 1920
*Net Worth:* £206,976,544 *Total Assets:* £220,029,664
*Registered Office:* Gardner Denver Industries Ltd, Springmill Street, Bradford, W Yorks, BD5 7HW
*Activities:* Activities of head offices
*Parent:* GD Global Holdings UK II Ltd
*Officers:* Mark Elliott Grummett, Secretary; Michael Joseph Scheske [1987] Director/Accountant [American]; Andrew Roger Schiesl [1971] Director/General Council [American]

**Gardner Denver International Ltd**
*Incorporated:* 28 September 1962
*Net Worth:* £74,967,192 *Total Assets:* £116,281,200
*Registered Office:* Gardner Denver International Ltd, Springmill Street, Bradford, W Yorks, BD5 7HW
*Activities:* Activities of head offices
*Parent:* GD Global Holdings UK II Ltd
*Officers:* Mark Elliott Grummett, Secretary; Michael Joseph Scheske [1987] Director/Accountant [American]; Andrew Roger Schiesl [1971] Director/General Council [American]

**Gardner Denver Ltd**
*Incorporated:* 19 April 1995
*Net Worth:* £15,432,000 *Total Assets:* £106,573,000
*Registered Office:* c/o Gardner Denver International Ltd, Springmill Street, Bradford, W Yorks, BD5 7HW
*Activities:* Manufacture of compressors
*Parent:* Gardner Denver International Ltd
*Officers:* Mark Elliott Grummett, Secretary; Michael Joseph Scheske [1987] Director/Accountant [American]; Andrew Roger Schiesl [1971] Director/General Council [American]

**Garlock (Great Britain) Limited**
*Incorporated:* 17 June 1971 *Employees:* 6
*Net Worth:* £6,708,985 *Total Assets:* £15,057,989
*Registered Office:* Ground Floor, Riverside Mills, Elland, W Yorks, HX5 0RY
*Activities:* Manufacture of other chemical products n.e.c.
*Parent:* Enpro Industries, Inc
*Officers:* Julie Fogg, Secretary; Robert Savage McLean, Secretary; Robert George Colton [1963] Director/Business Manager; Christopher Drake [1970] Director/Attorney [American]; Robert McLean [1964] Director/General Counsel [American]; Eric Andre Vaillancourt [1963] Director/VP Global Sales GSP [American]

**Dick Garner & Sons Limited**
*Incorporated:* 6 October 1943 *Employees:* 3
*Net Worth:* £2,964,050 *Total Assets:* £3,327,835
*Registered Office:* Moorhills, Lumley Lane, Kirkby Fleetham, Northallerton, N Yorks, DL7 0SL
*Activities:* Other letting and operating of own or leased real estate
*Officers:* Richard Garner, Secretary; Derek Garner [1954] Director; Richard Garner [1957] Director

**Garrards (Huddersfield) Limited**
*Incorporated:* 11 August 2000 *Employees:* 36
*Net Worth:* £872,121 *Total Assets:* £4,054,810
*Registered Office:* Pellon Lane Sawmills, Pellon Lane, Halifax, W Yorks, HX1 4PX
*Activities:* Sawmilling and planing of wood
*Parent:* Viewstone Limited
*Officers:* Karen Lesley Moore, Secretary; Sean Anthony Colleran [1958] Director/Timber Merchant; Paul Anthony Fairhurst [1960] Director/Sales Manager; Karen Lesley Moore [1959] Director; Robert James Moore [1961] Director/Manufacturer

**Garth Pig Practice Limited**
*Incorporated:* 3 March 2015 *Employees:* 28
*Net Worth:* £101,857 *Total Assets:* £14,541,293
*Registered Office:* Leeman House, Station Business Park, Holgate Park Drive, York, YO26 4GB
*Activities:* Veterinary activities
*Parent:* Origin Group Finance Limited
*Officers:* Joanna Clare Malone [1974] Director; Mark Stanworth [1964] Director

**Garthwest Limited**
*Incorporated:* 17 November 1964 *Employees:* 78
*Net Worth:* £2,430,011 *Total Assets:* £11,755,816
*Registered Office:* Rotterdam Road, Sutton Fields Industrial Estate, Hull, HU7 0XA
*Activities:* Manufacture of other paper and paperboard containers
*Officers:* Elizabeth Cameron West, Secretary/Director; Alexander Raffan West [1969] Joint Managing Director; Angus James West [1965] Director; Elizabeth Cameron West [1942] Director; James Robert West [1932] Director/Chairman; Lindsay Robert West [1967] Joint Managing Director

**Gartland Whalley and Barker Limited**
*Incorporated:* 2 August 1971 *Employees:* 1
*Net Worth:* £22,630,676 *Total Assets:* £52,420,532
*Registered Office:* West House, Kings Cross Road, Halifax, W Yorks, HX1 1EB
*Activities:* Non-trading company
*Officers:* Brian Hersee Heather, Secretary; Kimberley Jane Bond [1968] Director; Anthony Gartland [1941] Director; Daniel Justin Gartland [1971] Director; Deborah Louise Gartland [1973] Director/Finance Manager; Brian Hersee Heather [1953] Director; Kelly Anne Jackson [1967] Director; Jeffrey Whalley [1942] Director

**Gatenbysanderson Holdings Limited**
*Incorporated:* 12 June 2014 *Employees:* 116
*Net Worth Deficit:* £2,610,881 *Total Assets:* £33,596,064
*Registered Office:* 14 King Street, Leeds, LS1 2HL
*Activities:* Other activities of employment placement agencies
*Parent:* Primary IV Group LLP
*Officers:* Alistair Paul Armstrong [1978] Investment Director; Camilla Mary Dyson [1968] Director/Chartered Accountant; Samantha Jayne Ellis [1965] Marketing Director; Jody Goldsworthy [1972] Director/Senior Partner LTC [Australian]; Kevin John Gordon [1966] Director; Oliver Simon Melliss [1981] Investment Director; Wayne Andrew Story [1961] Director; Mark Jonathan Turner [1964] Director/Executive Search Recruiter

**Gatenbysanderson Limited**
*Incorporated:* 30 May 2002 *Employees:* 113
*Net Worth:* £16,179,593 *Total Assets:* £19,690,180
*Registered Office:* 14 King Street, Leeds, LS1 2HL
*Activities:* Other activities of employment placement agencies
*Parent:* Gatenbysanderson Midco Limited
*Officers:* Camilla Mary Dyson [1968] Director/Chartered Accountant; Samantha Jayne Ellis [1965] Marketing Director; Jody Goldsworthy [1972] Director/Senior Partner LTC [Australian]; Kevin John Gordon [1966] Director; Mark Jonathan Turner [1964] Director/Executive Search Recruiter

**Gatenbysanderson Midco Limited**
*Incorporated:* 12 June 2014 *Employees:* 1
*Net Worth Deficit:* £7,111,827 *Total Assets:* £34,396,256
*Registered Office:* 14 King Street, Leeds, LS1 2HL
*Activities:* Other activities of employment placement agencies
*Parent:* Gatenbysanderson Holdings Limited
*Officers:* Camilla Mary Dyson [1968] Director/Chartered Accountant; Samantha Jayne Ellis [1965] Marketing Director; Jody Goldsworthy [1972] Director/Senior Partner LTC [Australian]; Kevin John Gordon [1966] Director; Mark Jonathan Turner [1964] Director/Executive Search Recruiter

**Gateways Educational Trust Limited**
*Incorporated:* 6 September 1961 *Employees:* 70
*Net Worth:* £2,546,848 *Total Assets:* £5,595,886
*Registered Office:* Gateways School, Harewood, Leeds, LS17 9LE
*Activities:* General secondary education
*Officers:* Jeremy David Halliday, Secretary; Louise Jane Atkinson [1968] Director/Headteacher; Robert George Anthony Barr [1956] Director [Irish]; Generaldine Ann Brennan [1957] Director/Retired Teacher; Professor Michael Gerard Brennan [1956] Director/University Professor; Professor David Crossland Hogg [1954] Director/Academic; Stuart Watson [1961] Director/Chartered Accountant; Richard Michael Webster [1960] Director/Chartered Quantity Surveyor; Julie Wrench [1959] Director/Solicitor

**Daniel Gath Homes Limited**
*Incorporated:* 20 February 1997 *Employees:* 14
*Net Worth:* £6,438,994 *Total Assets:* £6,913,615
*Registered Office:* First Floor, 5 Audax Court, Audax Close, York, YO30 4RB
*Activities:* Construction of domestic buildings
*Major Shareholder:* Daniel Joseph Gath
*Officers:* Karen Marie Thomas, Secretary; Daniel Joseph Gath [1966] Director; Andrew Robert Larkin [1965] Construction Director; Daniel James Liddell [1980] Commercial Director

**Gatsby Property Limited**
*Incorporated:* 10 July 2013 *Employees:* 2
*Net Worth Deficit:* £23,453 *Total Assets:* £4,668,372
*Registered Office:* Gresham House, 5-7 St Pauls Street, Leeds, LS1 2JG
*Activities:* Other building completion and finishing
*Major Shareholder:* Jonathan Charles Jackson
*Officers:* Harry Charles Wells Dee [1991] Director/Chartered Surveyor; Jonathan Charles Jackson [1990] Director

**Gaunts Limited**
*Incorporated:* 28 December 1896 *Employees:* 6
*Net Worth:* £14,004,760 *Total Assets:* £17,237,912
*Registered Office:* 52 Springfield, Bagley Lane, Farsley, Leeds, LS28 5LY
*Activities:* Other letting and operating of own or leased real estate
*Shareholder:* Digby Gaunt Chamberlain
*Officers:* Charles Simon Bostock [1965] Director/School Registrar; Digby Gaunt Chamberlain [1951] Director/Chartered Surveyor; Virginia Anne Lowdnes [1960] Director/HR Manager; Christopher Pratt [1961] Director/Chartered Accountant

**Gaynor Sports Limited**
*Incorporated:* 7 January 2010 *Employees:* 53
*Net Worth:* £4,453,397 *Total Assets:* £6,399,801
*Registered Office:* Gaynor Sports Limited, Market Cross, Ambleside, Cumbria, LA22 9BT
*Activities:* Retail sale of clothing in specialised stores
*Officers:* John Montague Gaynor [1945] Director; Margaret Elizabeth Gaynor [1943] Director; Paul Montague Gaynor [1970] Director

**Gazelle Travel Limited**
*Incorporated:* 5 November 1980 *Employees:* 21
*Net Worth:* £1,141,643 *Total Assets:* £6,173,293
*Registered Office:* Gazelle House, 15 North Parade, Bradford, W Yorks, BD1 3JL
*Activities:* Other reservation service activities n.e.c.
*Major Shareholder:* Jamil Mohsin Malik
*Officers:* Jamil Mohsin Malik, Secretary; Jamil Mohsin Malik [1971] Director/Travel Agent; Philip Pritchard [1970] Commercial Director

**GB-Bio Limited**
*Incorporated:* 15 June 2006
*Net Worth Deficit:* £5,929,457 *Total Assets:* £48,060,360
*Registered Office:* Regent's Court, Princess Street, Hull, HU2 8BA
*Activities:* Production of electricity
*Shareholders:* Greenzone Consulting Limited; Solar 21 Renewable Energy Limited
*Officers:* Michael Anthony Bradley [1970] Director [Irish]; Sandra Mary Brennan [1969] Director [Irish]; Jeremy Stuart Saunt [1961] Director; Stuart Saunt [1933] Director

**GBA (Holdings) Limited**
*Incorporated:* 23 February 1990
*Net Worth:* £1,137,991 *Total Assets:* £6,058,541
*Registered Office:* Meridian House, Alexandra Dock North, Grimsby, N E Lincs, DN31 3UA
*Activities:* Other transportation support activities
*Parent:* GBA Group Limited
*Officers:* John Charles Gunn, Secretary; Maureen Judah [1953] Director; Samson Sassoon Samuel Judah [1953] Director

**GBA Group Limited**
*Incorporated:* 13 April 2015 *Employees:* 467
*Net Worth:* £10,515,215 *Total Assets:* £26,581,736
*Registered Office:* Meridian House, Alexandra Dock North, Grimsby, N E Lincs, DN31 3UA
*Activities:* Activities of other holding companies n.e.c.
*Shareholder:* Maureen Judah
*Officers:* John Charles Gunn, Secretary; Maureen Judah [1953] Director; Samson Sassoon Samuel Judah [1953] Managing Director

**GBA Transport Limited**
*Incorporated:* 17 November 2000 *Employees:* 117
*Net Worth:* £1,873,944 *Total Assets:* £5,813,150
*Registered Office:* Meridian House, Alexandra Dock North, Grimsby, N E Lincs, DN31 3UA
*Activities:* Freight transport by road
*Parent:* GBA (Holdings) Limited
*Officers:* John Charles Gunn, Secretary; John Charles Gunn [1966] Director - Corporate Services; Samson Sassoon Samuel Judah [1953] Managing Director; Yaniv Judah [1985] Director

**GBUK Enteral Limited**
*Incorporated:* 11 March 2010 *Employees:* 11
*Net Worth:* £9,688,000 *Total Assets:* £12,149,000
*Registered Office:* Woodland House, Blackwood Hall Business Park, North Duffield, Selby, N Yorks, YO8 5DD
*Activities:* Hospital activities
*Parent:* GBUK Group Limited
*Officers:* Martin Richard Garbett, Secretary; Martin Richard Garbett [1974] Director; Michael John Geering [1972] Director; Peter Vincent John Spiller [1980] Director; Mark Clifton Thompson [1961] Director

**GBUK Group Limited**
*Incorporated:* 25 February 2015 *Employees:* 83
*Net Worth Deficit:* £3,991,000 *Total Assets:* £39,912,000
*Registered Office:* Woodland House, Blackwood Hall Business Park, Selby, N Yorks, YO8 5DD
*Activities:* Activities of head offices
*Parent:* Cooperatief H2 Equity Partners Fund IV Holding W.A.
*Officers:* Martin Richard Garbett, Secretary; Guy Richard Roderick Dew [1980] Director; Martin Richard Garbett [1974] Director; Michael John Geering [1972] Director; Patrick Henricus Lambertus Kalverboer [1972] Director [Dutch]; Guy Rhoderic Mills [1960] Director; Peter Vincent John Spiller [1980] Director; Mark Clifton Thompson [1961] Director

**GBUK Ltd**
*Incorporated:* 24 May 2004 *Employees:* 72
*Net Worth:* £5,179,000 *Total Assets:* £7,339,000
*Registered Office:* Woodland House, Blackwood Hall Business Park, North Duffield, Selby, N Yorks, YO8 5DD
*Activities:* Hospital activities
*Parent:* GBUK Group Limited
*Officers:* Martin Richard Garbett, Secretary; Martin Richard Garbett [1974] Director; Michael John Geering [1972] Director; Peter Vincent John Spiller [1980] Director; Mark Clifton Thompson [1961] Director

**GC Motors Limited**
*Incorporated:* 3 September 2004 *Employees:* 68
*Net Worth:* £2,366,559 *Total Assets:* £9,451,021
*Registered Office:* 3 Greengate, Cardale Park, Harrogate, N Yorks, HG3 1GY
*Activities:* Sale of new cars and light motor vehicles
*Parent:* Castleton Group Limited
*Officers:* Sarah Castleton, Secretary; Giles Castleton [1969] Director

**GCD Limited**
*Incorporated:* 13 December 2002 *Employees:* 2
*Net Worth:* £285,412 *Total Assets:* £4,894,054
*Registered Office:* 12 Alma Square, Scarborough, N Yorks, YO11 1JU
*Activities:* Other letting and operating of own or leased real estate
*Officers:* Anita Georgena Coopland, Secretary; Anita Georgena Coopland [1960] Director; Paul William Coopland [1957] Director

**GD Aria Holdings #2 Limited**
*Incorporated:* 1 June 2012
*Net Worth:* £160,277,872 *Total Assets:* £160,359,152
*Registered Office:* Springmill Street, Bradford, W Yorks, BD5 7HW
*Activities:* Activities of head offices
*Parent:* GD Aria Holdings Ltd
*Officers:* Mark Elliott Grummett, Secretary; Michael Joseph Scheske [1987] Director/Accountant [American]; Andrew Roger Schiesl [1971] Director/General Council [American]

**GD Aria Holdings Limited**
*Incorporated:* 10 November 2011
*Net Worth Deficit:* £6,597,363 *Total Assets:* £130,660,352
*Registered Office:* Springmill Street, Bradford, W Yorks, BD5 7HW
*Activities:* Activities of head offices
*Parent:* U.S. Branch of GD Global Holdings II S.A.R.L.
*Officers:* Mark Elliott Grummett, Secretary; Michael Joseph Scheske [1987] Director/Accountant [American]; Andrew Roger Schiesl [1971] Director/General Council [American]

**GD Global Holdings UK II Limited**
*Incorporated:* 18 November 2014
*Net Worth:* £138,444,368 *Total Assets:* £425,850,304
*Registered Office:* Springmill Street, Bradford, W Yorks, BD5 7HW
*Activities:* Activities of head offices
*Parent:* GD Global Holdings II SARL
*Officers:* Mark Elliott Grummett, Secretary; Michael Joseph Scheske [1987] Director/Accountant [American]; Andrew Roger Schiesl [1971] Director/General Counsel & Secretary [American]

**GDS Holdings Limited**
*Incorporated:* 16 November 2016 *Employees:* 101
*Net Worth:* £11,893 *Total Assets:* £5,177,760
*Registered Office:* Westgate Point, Westgate, Leeds, LS1 2AX
*Activities:* Information technology consultancy activities
*Parent:* GDS Holdings US Inc.
*Officers:* Dexter Hopen, Secretary; Yves Richard Gabriel Duhoux [1974] Director [French]; Lance William Fenton [1980] Director [American]; Paul Greenwood [1972] Director; Dexter Hopen [1989] Director [American]; Lawrence Oliver Huff [1962] Director [American]

**GDS Technologies Limited**
*Incorporated:* 17 March 1998 *Employees:* 37
*Net Worth:* £2,652,046 *Total Assets:* £3,046,197
*Registered Office:* Fusion Point, Ash Lane, Garforth, Leeds, LS25 2GA
*Activities:* Manufacture of other electrical equipment
*Officers:* Angela Utley, Secretary; Steven Arthur Utley [1953] Director

**Gear4music (Holdings) PLC**
*Incorporated:* 26 September 2011 *Employees:* 313
*Previous:* Gear4music (Holdings) Limited
*Net Worth:* £18,947,000 *Total Assets:* £39,731,000
*Registered Office:* Holgate Park Drive, York, YO26 4GN
*Activities:* Activities of head offices
*Shareholder:* Andrew Paul Wass
*Officers:* Christopher David Scott, Secretary; Gareth John Bevan [1978] Commercial Director; Eric Kenelm Ford [1949] Director; Dean Anthony Murray [1962] Director/Chairman; Christopher David Scott [1975] Finance Director; Andrew Paul Wass [1971] Director

**Gear4music Limited**
*Incorporated:* 12 October 1995 *Employees:* 286
*Previous:* Red Submarine Limited
*Net Worth:* £7,254,000 *Total Assets:* £38,425,000
*Registered Office:* Holgate Park Drive, York, YO26 4GN
*Activities:* Retail sale of musical instruments and scores
*Parent:* Gear4music (Holdings) PLC
*Officers:* Christopher David Scott, Secretary; Gareth John Bevan [1978] Commercial Director; Jonathan Richard Meager [1987] Director; Robert John Newport [1978] Director; Christopher David Scott [1975] Finance Director; Thomas Oliver Walder [1979] Director; Andrew Paul Wass [1971] Director

**Gedore U.K. Ltd**
*Incorporated:* 1 March 1983 *Employees:* 19
*Net Worth:* £2,694,634 *Total Assets:* £3,609,554
*Registered Office:* Marton Street, Skipton, N Yorks, BD23 1TF
*Activities:* Agents involved in the sale of furniture, household goods, hardware and ironmongery
*Officers:* Cheryl Louise Hunt, Secretary; Shaun Barry McAllister [1966] Sales Director; Christian Metzler [1960] Director/General Manager [Austrian]; Kieron Leigh Smith [1976] Director; Suzanne Wahab [1965] Director/General Manager [German]

**David Gee Associates Limited**
*Incorporated:* 17 February 1997 *Employees:* 3
*Net Worth:* £4,905,388 *Total Assets:* £5,455,909
*Registered Office:* Unit 4 Monckton Road Industrial Estate, Wakefield, W Yorks, WF2 7AL
*Activities:* Other letting and operating of own or leased real estate
*Officers:* David Malcolm Gee, Secretary; Andrew David Marshall Gee [1966] Director/Haulier; David Malcolm Gee [1938] Director/Haulier; Tracey Gee [1965] Company Secretary/Director; Catherine Shields [1970] Director/Accountant

**Gees Haulage Limited**
*Incorporated:* 3 October 2008 *Employees:* 85
*Net Worth:* £5,372,167 *Total Assets:* £6,619,141
*Registered Office:* Unit 2 Monckton Road Industrial Estate, Wakefield, W Yorks, WF2 7AL
*Activities:* Freight transport by road
*Major Shareholder:* Andrew David Marshall Gee
*Officers:* Catherine Shields, Secretary; Graham Neil Dyson [1965] Director/Transport Manager; Amy Jane Gee [1985] Director/Office Manager; Andrew David Marshall Gee [1966] Director; Steven Martin Andrew Gee [1986] Director/Transport Manager

**Gem Environmental Building Services Limited**
*Incorporated:* 13 December 1999 *Employees:* 68
*Net Worth:* £1,624,246 *Total Assets:* £4,839,994
*Registered Office:* 1 Westleigh Hall, Wakefield Road, Denby Dale, Huddersfield, W Yorks, HD8 8QJ
*Activities:* Other business support service activities n.e.c.
*Parent:* P & S Plumbing (Holdings) Limited
*Officers:* Doug Daldry [1966] Director; Keith Harris [1968] Director; Michael Patrick Neville [1954] Commercial Director

**Gemco Service Limited**
*Incorporated:* 20 February 1998 *Employees:* 118
*Net Worth:* £4,210,875 *Total Assets:* £7,889,650
*Registered Office:* Unit 14c Moderna Business Park, Moderna Way, Mytholmroyd, Hebden Bridge, W Yorks, HX7 5QQ
*Activities:* Repair of machinery
*Parent:* Gemco Corporate Management Limited
*Officers:* Alex Kinley, Secretary; Soren Leon Dyoe Madsen [1964] Director/Chief Executive Officer [Danish]; Wayne Thomas [1960] Director

**Generator Power Limited**
*Incorporated:* 8 October 1997 *Employees:* 199
*Net Worth:* £6,714,725 *Total Assets:* £34,435,704
*Registered Office:* Foxbridge Way, Normanton Industrial Estate, Normanton, W Yorks, WF6 1TW
*Activities:* Renting and leasing of other machinery, equipment and tangible goods n.e.c.
*Major Shareholder:* Stephen Keith Cardwell
*Officers:* Stephen Keith Cardwell [1966] Managing Director

**Genus Pharmaceuticals Holdings Limited**
*Incorporated:* 21 August 1998
*Net Worth:* £10,109,000 *Total Assets:* £44,398,000
*Registered Office:* Manchester Road, Linthwaite, Huddersfield, W Yorks, HD7 5QH
*Activities:* Wholesale of pharmaceutical goods
*Parent:* Stada UK Holdings Ltd
*Officers:* Edwin Charles Blythe, Secretary; Charles Ashley Brierley [1963] Director

**Genus Pharmaceuticals Limited**
*Incorporated:* 6 February 1986
*Net Worth:* £44,653,000 *Total Assets:* £58,685,000
*Registered Office:* Manchester Road, Linthwaite, Huddersfield, W Yorks, HD7 5QH
*Activities:* Manufacture of pharmaceutical preparations
*Parent:* Genus Pharmaceutical Holdings Ltd
*Officers:* Edwin Charles Blythe, Secretary; Charles Ashley Brierley [1963] Director

**Geofabrics Limited**
*Incorporated:* 28 March 1990 *Employees:* 24
*Net Worth:* £2,680,749 *Total Assets:* £4,020,186
*Registered Office:* Skelton Grange Road, Stourton, Leeds, LS10 1RZ
*Activities:* Manufacture of other technical and industrial textiles
*Parent:* Geofabrics Group Limited
*Officers:* Mark Boothroyd, Secretary/Accountant; Mark Boothroyd [1965] Director/Accountant; Gordon Hugh Donald [1956] Managing Director; David Andrew Pass [1966] Director; Mark Anthony Pass [1964] Director/Chartered Accountant; Simon Arthur Pass [1963] Director; Richard Charles Taylor [1949] Director

**Geoplan Spatial Intelligence Limited**
*Incorporated:* 21 July 1986 *Employees:* 18
*Net Worth:* £2,513,601 *Total Assets:* £4,917,325
*Registered Office:* Bilton Court, Wetherby Road, Harrogate, N Yorks, HG3 1GP
*Activities:* Business and domestic software development
*Major Shareholder:* John William Taylor
*Officers:* Sara McCartney [1971] Finance & Operations Director; John William Taylor [1958] Managing Director

**GES Recycling Ltd.**
*Incorporated:* 25 September 2012 *Employees:* 22
*Net Worth:* £1,310,878 *Total Assets:* £6,610,437
*Registered Office:* Tallent Automotive, Aycliffe Business Park, Newton Aycliffe, Co Durham, DL5 6EP
*Activities:* Recovery of sorted materials
*Parent:* Gescrap Desarrollo S.L.
*Officers:* Ignacio Velasco [1964] Director/Entrepreneur [Spanish]

**Gestamp Tallent Limited**
*Incorporated:* 21 April 1948 *Employees:* 2,505
*Net Worth:* £114,296,000 *Total Assets:* £511,540,000
*Registered Office:* 1 Skerne Road, Aycliffe Business Park, Newton Aycliffe, Co Durham, DL5 6EP
*Activities:* Forging, pressing, stamping and roll-forming of metal; powder metallurgy
*Shareholders:* Francisco Jose Riberas Mera; Juan Maria Riberas Mera
*Officers:* David Vazquez Pascual, Secretary; Francisco Lopez Pena [1959] Director/Economist [Spanish]; Francisco Jose Riberas Mera [1968] Director [Spanish]

**Getech Group PLC**
*Incorporated:* 26 January 1994 *Employees:* 95
*Net Worth:* £12,179,000 *Total Assets:* £14,965,000
*Registered Office:* Kitson House, Elmete Hall, Elmete Lane, Leeds, LS8 2LJ
*Activities:* Support activities for petroleum and natural gas mining
*Officers:* Andrew Liam Darbyshire, Secretary; Dr Jonathan Michael Copus [1972] Director; Andrew Liam Darbyshire [1982] Director/Chief Financial Officer; Dr Alison Margaret Fielding [1964] Director; Christopher Hugh Flavell [1957] Director/Geophysicist; Christopher Paul Jepps [1969] Director/Chief Operating Officer; Dr Stuart McNicol Paton [1967] Director; Peter Francis Howard Stephens [1955] Director

**Gettheworldmoving Ltd**
*Incorporated:* 5 September 2007
*Net Worth:* £5,180,730 *Total Assets:* £6,465,605
*Registered Office:* Unit 4 York Road, Leeds, LS15 4TA
*Activities:* Other human health activities
*Officers:* Philip Jeffery Halbish, Secretary; Tim Dudgeon [1983] Director/VP of Finance; Philip Jeffery Halbish [1977] Director/Chief Financial Officer [Australian]; Glenn Lee [1978] Director/Product Manager [Australian]

**GEV Holdings Limited**
*Incorporated:* 19 November 2014 *Employees:* 19
*Net Worth Deficit:* £1,703,390 *Total Assets:* £6,268,332
*Registered Office:* Unit 23 Priory Tec Park, Saxon Way, Priory Park, Hessle, E Yorks, HU13 9PB
*Activities:* Activities of head offices
*Officers:* David Stuart Fletcher, Secretary; David Stuart Fletcher [1971] Director; Alastair Duncan Gadney [1967] Director; Ewan Alisdair Duncan MacKinnon [1976] Investment Director; Andrew Bryant Symmonds [1970] Investment Director

**GFEA Limited**
*Incorporated:* 14 April 2010 *Employees:* 75
*Net Worth:* £2,819,000 *Total Assets:* £4,699,000
*Registered Office:* 2nd Floor, Gateway, 2 Holgate Park Drive, York, YO26 4GB
*Activities:* Real estate agencies
*Parent:* LSLI Ltd
*Officers:* Sapna Bedi FitzGenerald, Secretary; Greig Barker [1969] Finance Director; Helen Elizabeth Buck [1960] Director; Martin John Humphreys [1965] Director; Bernadette Keating [1970] Director; Gregory Winston Young [1966] Director

**GGR Holdings Limited**
*Incorporated:* 15 March 2002 *Employees:* 1
*Net Worth:* £3,974,556 *Total Assets:* £4,020,387
*Registered Office:* No 1 Leeds, 26 Whitehall Road, Leeds, LS12 1BE
*Activities:* Activities of head offices
*Major Shareholder:* Gordon Alex Bethell
*Officers:* Gordon Alex Bethell [1970] Director

**GH Braintree Limited**
*Incorporated:* 20 October 2004 *Employees:* 5
*Net Worth Deficit:* £5,187,591 *Total Assets:* £18,965,940
*Registered Office:* 4 Greengate, Cardale Park, Harrogate, N Yorks, HG3 1GY
*Activities:* Medical nursing home activities
*Parent:* GH Braintree Holdings Limited
*Officers:* Alexander Toby Shedden Parry, Secretary; Alastair William Hopps [1986] Director/Accountant; Alexander Toby Shedden Parry [1976] Director

**GH Brighton Limited**
*Incorporated:* 11 July 2005 *Employees:* 2
*Net Worth:* £29,538,058 *Total Assets:* £95,144,008
*Registered Office:* 4 Greengate, Cardale Park, Harrogate, N Yorks, HG3 1GY
*Activities:* Non-trading company
*Parent:* GH Finance Limited
*Officers:* Alexander Toby Shedden Parry, Secretary; Robert John Austin [1964] Director; Nigel Duncan Taee [1961] Director

**GH Lanchester Road Limited**
*Incorporated:* 11 December 2007 *Employees:* 5
*Net Worth Deficit:* £7,425,368 *Total Assets:* £18,261,228
*Registered Office:* 4 Greengate, Cardale Park, Harrogate, N Yorks, HG3 1GY
*Activities:* Medical nursing home activities
*Parent:* GH Lanchester Road Holdings Limited
*Officers:* Alexander Toby Shedden Parry, Secretary; Alastair William Hopps [1986] Director/Accountant; Alexander Toby Shedden Parry [1976] Director/Company Secretary

**GH Newco 1 Limited**
*Incorporated:* 6 February 2012 *Employees:* 402
*Net Worth:* £8,156,675 *Total Assets:* £12,374,185
*Registered Office:* 4 Greengate, Cardale Park, Harrogate, N Yorks, HG3 1GY
*Activities:* Activities of head offices
*Major Shareholder:* Nigel Duncan Taee
*Officers:* Alexander Toby Shedden Parry, Secretary; Robert John Austin [1964] Director; Peter Paul Copley [1956] Director; Christopher Justin Taee [1968] Director; Nigel Duncan Taee [1961] Director

**GH North Yorkshire Limited**
*Incorporated:* 6 July 2000 *Employees:* 6
*Net Worth:* £537,356 *Total Assets:* £4,651,365
*Registered Office:* 4 Greengate, Cardale Park, Harrogate, N Yorks, HG3 1GY
*Activities:* Construction of commercial buildings
*Parent:* GH North Yorkshire Holdings Ltd
*Officers:* Alexander Toby Shedden Parry, Secretary; Alastair William Hopps [1986] Director/Accountant; Alexander Toby Shedden Parry [1976] Director

**GH Plymouth Grove Limited**
*Incorporated:* 8 December 2005 *Employees:* 4
*Net Worth:* £11,950,334 *Total Assets:* £92,489,056
*Registered Office:* 4 Greengate, Cardale Park, Harrogate, N Yorks, HG3 1GY
*Activities:* Non-trading company
*Parent:* GH Finance Limited
*Officers:* Alexander Toby Shedden Parry, Secretary; Robert John Austin [1964] Director; Peter Paul Copley [1956] Director; Christopher Justin Taee [1968] Director; Nigel Duncan Taee [1961] Director

**GH Runwell Limited**
*Incorporated:* 31 July 2006 *Employees:* 5
*Net Worth Deficit:* £10,204,889 *Total Assets:* £29,948,010
*Registered Office:* 4 Greengate, Cardale Park, Harrogate, N Yorks, HG3 1GY
*Activities:* Medical nursing home activities
*Parent:* GH Runwell Holdings Ltd
*Officers:* Alexander Toby Shedden Parry, Secretary; Alastair William Hopps [1986] Director/Accountant; Alexander Toby Shedden Parry [1976] Director

**GH Stanley Limited**
*Incorporated:* 11 December 2007 *Employees:* 5
*Net Worth Deficit:* £4,744,235 *Total Assets:* £12,385,079
*Registered Office:* 4 Greengate, Cardale Park, Harrogate, N Yorks, HG3 1GY
*Activities:* Medical nursing home activities
*Parent:* GH Stanley Holdings Limited
*Officers:* Alexander Toby Shedden Parry, Secretary; Alastair William Hopps [1986] Director/Accountant; Alexander Toby Shedden Parry [1976] Director

**GHD BondCo PLC**
*Incorporated:* 21 March 2014
*Net Worth:* £8,869,966 *Total Assets:* £213,357,280
*Registered Office:* Bridgewater Place, Water Lane, Leeds, LS11 5BZ
*Activities:* Activities of head offices
*Parent:* Lion/Gloria Bidco Limited
*Officers:* Michael Joseph Hewett, Secretary; Michael Joseph Hewett [1980] Director [American]; Jeroen Franciscus Maria Temmerman [1971] Director/CEO, GHD [Dutch]

**GHD Group Holdings Limited**
*Incorporated:* 4 July 2007
*Net Worth:* £48,563,000 *Total Assets:* £360,796,992
*Registered Office:* Bridgewater Place, Water Lane, Leeds, LS11 5BZ
*Activities:* Activities of head offices
*Parent:* Lion/Gloria Bidco Limited
*Officers:* Michael Joseph Hewett [1980] Director [American]

**GHG-AFCO (Luton) Limited**
*Incorporated:* 11 December 2001 *Employees:* 4
*Net Worth Deficit:* £510,416 *Total Assets:* £5,254,108
*Registered Office:* 4 Greengate, Cardale Park, Harrogate, N Yorks, HG3 1GY
*Activities:* Construction of roads and motorways
*Shareholders:* Afco Luton UK Limited; GH Newco 4 Limited
*Officers:* Alexander Toby Shedden Parry, Secretary; Robert John Austin [1964] Finance Director; Thom Harrow [1952] Director [American]; Charles Stipancic [1961] Director [American]; Christopher Justin Taee [1968] Director/Businessman

**GHSR LLP**
*Incorporated:* 9 December 2011
*Net Worth:* £37,712,664 *Total Assets:* £40,047,832
*Registered Office:* 30 Victoria Avenue, Harrogate, N Yorks, HG1 5PR

**Ghyll Royd Nursing Home Limited**
*Incorporated:* 9 July 2001 *Employees:* 142
*Net Worth:* £3,044,453 *Total Assets:* £4,605,741
*Registered Office:* Paget Hall, Church Street, Gargrave, Skipton, N Yorks, BD23 3NE
*Activities:* Residential care activities for the elderly and disabled
*Major Shareholder:* Michael Anthony Spellman
*Officers:* Marguerita Spellman, Secretary; Joanne Marie Alton [1969] Director; Michael Anthony Spellman [1943] Director; Steven Michael Spellman [1971] Director

**Ghyll Royd Properties Ltd**
*Incorporated:* 3 September 2010 *Employees:* 6
*Net Worth:* £18,321,168 *Total Assets:* £19,857,868
*Registered Office:* Ghyll Croft, 4 Hallcroft Drive, Addingham, Ilkley, W Yorks, LS29 0QN
*Activities:* Other letting and operating of own or leased real estate
*Officers:* Alfred John Feather, Secretary; Adele Catherine Feather [1966] Director/Personal Assistant; Alfred John Feather [1940] Director; Margaret Ann Feather [1940] Director; Alison Margaret King [1964] Director/Occupational Therapist

**Ghyllside School**
*Incorporated:* 13 August 2012 *Employees:* 73
*Net Worth:* £2,738,408 *Total Assets:* £3,579,040
*Registered Office:* Ghyllside School, Gillinggate, Kendal, Cumbria, LA9 4JB
*Activities:* Primary education
*Officers:* Nicola Audin, Secretary; David Anthony Bell [1970] Director/Local Authority; Hilary Brown [1954] Director/Architect; Petrina Charnley-Monk [1975] Director/Governor; Thomas Daniel Charrier [1980] Director/Architect; Martin Robert Curry [1952] Director/Retired; Huw Basil Davies [1971] Director/Headteacher; Philip Thomas Doyle [1970] Operations Director IT Company; Emily Charlotte Garbutt [1975] Director; Diane Wendy Horner [1951] Director; Lucy Johnson [1976] Director/Training Consultant; Mark Jones [1981] Director/Governor; Paul Joseph O'Reilly [1966] Director; Jennifer Ruth Pack [1979] Director/Teacher; Rachel Simpson [1987] Director/Teaching Assistant; Robert Talbot [1948] Director; Marie-Anne Williamson [1962] Director/Deputy Headteacher

**Giacom Holdings Limited**
*Incorporated:* 14 March 2016 *Employees:* 4
*Net Worth:* £13,960,247 *Total Assets:* £18,178,912
*Registered Office:* Bridge Haven, One Saxon Way, Priory Park, Hessle, E Yorks, HU13 9PG
*Activities:* Other information technology service activities
*Parent:* Project Seattle Bidco Limited
*Officers:* Jonathan Francis Connor [1961] Marketing Director; Steven David Law [1967] Director/Chief Technology Officer; David Manning [1963] Operations Director [Irish]; Michael David Wardell [1981] Director

**Gibson Pharmacy Limited**
*Incorporated:* 2 December 2010 *Employees:* 18
*Net Worth Deficit:* £145,310 *Total Assets:* £3,433,925
*Registered Office:* Undercliffe Health Care Centre, Lowther Street, Bradford, W Yorks, BD2 4RA
*Activities:* Dispensing chemist in specialised stores
*Shareholders:* Viran Suresh Patel; Susan Elizabeth Bargh
*Officers:* Susan Elizabeth Bargh, Secretary; Susan Elizabeth Bargh [1964] Director; Viran Suresh Patel [1976] Director/Pharmacist

**Lee Gibson Properties Ltd**
*Incorporated:* 9 April 2013
*Net Worth:* £1,673,197 *Total Assets:* £4,121,361
*Registered Office:* Heathfield Cottage, Whitegate, East Keswick, Leeds, LS17 9HB
*Activities:* Other letting and operating of own or leased real estate
*Major Shareholder:* Lee Paul Gibson
*Officers:* Lee Paul Gibson, Secretary; Lee Paul Gibson [1978] Director

**Simon Gibson Transport Limited**
*Incorporated:* 24 September 2002 *Employees:* 186
*Net Worth:* £4,297,844 *Total Assets:* £20,426,252
*Registered Office:* Unit 1, A W Nielsen Road, Goole, E Yorks, DN14 6UE
*Activities:* Freight transport by road
*Shareholders:* Simon Gibson; GCA Europe S.A.
*Officers:* Delphine Andre [1966] Director [French]; Jacques Duvauchelle [1974] Director [French]; Simon Gibson [1974] Director/Haulage Contractor; Jean-Emmanuel Mongnot [1967] Director [French]

**Gico Limited**
*Incorporated:* 16 February 2007 *Employees:* 3
*Net Worth:* £4,019,164 *Total Assets:* £6,615,675
*Registered Office:* Crimple Manor, Walton Avenue, Pannal, Harrogate, N Yorks, HG3 1EX
*Activities:* Other letting and operating of own or leased real estate
*Parent:* Gico (Holdings) Limited
*Officers:* Claire Helen Gill [1965] Director; Simon Howard Gill [1965] Director

**Giffen Group Limited**
*Incorporated:* 28 November 1930 *Employees:* 95
*Net Worth Deficit:* £2,292,000 *Total Assets:* £11,764,000
*Registered Office:* 3175 Century Way, Thorpe Park, Leeds, LS15 8ZB
*Activities:* Manufacture of other electrical equipment
*Parent:* Giffen Holdings Limited
*Officers:* Andries Petrus Liebenberg [1967] Director [South African]; Mark Peters [1968] Director/Civil Engineer; Paul Scott [1964] Director

**Giggleswick School**
*Incorporated:* 9 May 2005 *Employees:* 236
*Net Worth:* £8,198,661 *Total Assets:* £12,335,618
*Registered Office:* Settle, N Yorks, BD24 0DE
*Activities:* Other letting and operating of own or leased real estate
*Officers:* Matthew Zebedee Hodge, Secretary; Robert Andrew Palles Brocklehurst [1964] Director/Consultant; Ian Michael Cornelius [1969] Commercial Director; Mark Robert Corner [1958] Director/Retired; Thomas Coxon [1990] Art Director; Lee Michael Donner [1979] Director/Architect; John Lambert Ellacott [1963] Director/Chartered Accountant; Heather Jane Hancock [1965] Director/Partner, Accountancy; Gillian Mary Harper [1968] Director/Televison and Video Production; Andrew Miles Jarman [1957] Director/Teacher; Hon William James Kay-Shuttleworth [1979] Director/Teacher; Andrew Richard Mullins [1964] Director/Consultant; Rebekah Helen Taylor [1982] Director/School Principal; Alexander Vincent Thursby [1960] Director/Retired; Sir Gary Keith Verity [1964] Director/Business Consultant; Roderick Richard Waldie [1968] Director/Solicitor; Dr Felix Waldmann [1987] Director/University Lecturer [Australian/Romanian]

**Gilbran (Management) Limited**
*Incorporated:* 30 May 1997
*Net Worth:* £2,021,523 *Total Assets:* £4,037,463
*Registered Office:* Buckle Barton, Sanderson House, Station Road, Horsforth, Leeds, LS18 5NT
*Activities:* Management of real estate on a fee or contract basis
*Major Shareholder:* Nigel Preston Smith
*Officers:* Nigel Preston Smith [1967] Director

**Giles Foods Limited**
*Incorporated:* 7 October 1997 *Employees:* 294
*Net Worth Deficit:* £7,127,000 *Total Assets:* £6,464,000
*Registered Office:* 50 Pontefract Lane, Leeds, LS9 8HY
*Activities:* Manufacture of bread; manufacture of fresh pastry goods and cakes
*Parent:* Country Style Foods Limited
*Officers:* Charles Joseph Wood [1979] Director/Baker; Joseph Anthony Wood [1939] Director/Baker

**Gilbert Gilkes & Gordon Limited**
*Incorporated:* 18 March 1921 *Employees:* 221
*Net Worth:* £16,355,000 *Total Assets:* £29,166,000
*Registered Office:* Canal Head North, Kendal, Cumbria, LA9 7BZ
*Activities:* Manufacture of engines and turbines, except aircraft, vehicle and cycle engines
*Parent:* Gilbert Gilkes & Gordon Holdings Limited
*Officers:* Charles William Nepean Crewdson [1964] Director/Retired Lt Col Armed Services; Victoria Lee Crewdson [1965] Director/Forester; Andrew William Poole [1961] Director; Katherine Louise Rowland [1968] Director

**Gilkes Hydro Investments Limited**
*Incorporated:* 20 June 2015
*Net Worth:* £8,791,757 *Total Assets:* £37,429,784
*Registered Office:* Canal Head North, Kendal, Cumbria, LA9 7BZ
*Activities:* Activities of financial services holding companies
*Parent:* GHI Bidco Limited
*Officers:* Robert Henry Moffett Chaplin [1963] Director; Charles William Nepean Crewdson [1964] Director; Bernd Michael Kussner [1971] Director [Swiss]

**Gill Demolitions Limited**
*Incorporated:* 9 October 1964 *Employees:* 21
*Net Worth:* £3,409,950 *Total Assets:* £4,200,375
*Registered Office:* Progress Works, Hall Lane, Bradford, W Yorks, BD4 7DT
*Activities:* Demolition
*Major Shareholder:* Paul Steven Gill
*Officers:* Jonathan Brian Gill, Secretary; Jonathan Brian Gill [1968] Director/Chartered Accountant; Paul Steven Gill [1962] Director/Demolition Contractor

**Gill Insulation Nottinghamshire Limited**
*Incorporated:* 25 March 1986 *Employees:* 51
*Net Worth:* £2,461,946 *Total Assets:* £4,231,828
*Registered Office:* Brunswick House, 1 Deighton Close, Wetherby, W Yorks, LS22 7GZ
*Activities:* Other construction installation
*Parent:* Encon Investments Limited
*Officers:* John Stuart Bedford [1957] Director; Stuart John Moore [1964] Director

**Gilpin Lodge Country House Hotel Limited**
*Incorporated:* 11 February 1986 *Employees:* 127
*Net Worth:* £4,873,005 *Total Assets:* £11,868,375
*Registered Office:* Gilpin Lodge, Crook Road, Windermere, Cumbria, LA23 3NE
*Activities:* Hotels and similar accommodation
*Shareholders:* Christine Anne Cunliffe; John Anthony Clegg Cunliffe
*Officers:* John Anthony Clegg Cunliffe, Secretary; Zoe Cunliffe, Secretary; Barnaby Cunliffe [1968] Director/Hotel Manager; Benjamin Cunliffe [1971] Director/Architect; Christine Anne Cunliffe [1942] Director; John Anthony Clegg Cunliffe [1944] Hotel Director

**Ginetta Cars Limited**
*Incorporated:* 3 September 1992 *Employees:* 83
*Net Worth Deficit:* £26,714,716 *Total Assets:* £17,868,628
*Registered Office:* Helios, 47 Isabella Road, Garforth, Leeds, LS25 2DY
*Activities:* Manufacture of motor vehicles
*Parent:* LNT Automotive Limited
*Officers:* Philip Miles Raven, Secretary; Matthew Graeme Lowe [1973] Director; Zara Danielle Morris [1986] Finance Director; Philip Miles Raven [1966] Director; Lawrence Neil Tomlinson [1964] Director

**Giroscope Limited**
*Incorporated:* 13 August 1986 *Employees:* 8
*Net Worth:* £3,267,265 *Total Assets:* £5,905,291
*Registered Office:* 69 Coltman Street, Hull, HU3 2SJ
*Activities:* Buying and selling of own real estate
*Officers:* Jonathan Francis Clarke, Secretary/Director; Robert Amesbury [1960] Director; Alan Brocklehurst [1964] Director/Accountant; Jonathan Francis Clarke [1971] Director

**GKF Group Limited**
*Incorporated:* 9 May 1991 *Employees:* 2
*Net Worth:* £1,344,556 *Total Assets:* £5,004,129
*Registered Office:* Ford House, Westfield Mills, Kirk Lane, Yeadon, Leeds, LS19 7LX
*Activities:* Activities of head offices
*Major Shareholder:* Graeme Ford
*Officers:* Carol Amanda Dalton, Secretary; Carol Amanda Dalton [1966] Director; Graeme Ford [1953] Director

**Gladwin Bros. (Farms) Limited**
*Incorporated:* 2 June 1976 *Employees:* 6
*Net Worth:* £4,175,252 *Total Assets:* £4,614,505
*Registered Office:* 38 Horkstow Road, Barton upon Humber, N Lincs, DN18 5DZ
*Activities:* Growing of cereals (except rice), leguminous crops and oil seeds
*Major Shareholder:* Philip Arthur Gladwin
*Officers:* Phillip Arthur Gladwin, Secretary; George William Henry Gladwin [1939] Director/Farmer; James Leonard Gladwin [1944] Director/Farmer; Joanne Gladwin [1965] Director/Product Manager; Phillip Arthur Gladwin [1964] Director/Farmer

**Glassflake Limited**
*Incorporated:* 15 September 1987 *Employees:* 21
*Net Worth:* £4,628,068 *Total Assets:* £5,122,974
*Registered Office:* Forster Street, Leeds, LS10 1PW
*Activities:* Manufacture of flat glass
*Major Shareholder:* Charles John Watkinson
*Officers:* Clive Anthony Harper, Secretary; Simon James Brigham [1976] Director; Clive Anthony Harper [1957] Director; Charles John Watkinson [1946] Director; Dr. Georg Friedrich Leonhard Wiessmeier [1966] Director/Chief Technology and Innovation Officer, Sibelco [German]

**Glasshouses123 Limited**
*Incorporated:* 10 October 2016 *Employees:* 4
*Net Worth Deficit:* £189,106 *Total Assets:* £3,406,748
*Registered Office:* 10 The Stables, Newby Hall, Ripon, N Yorks, HG4 5AE
*Activities:* Buying and selling of own real estate
*Parent:* Silverback Developments Limited
*Officers:* Christopher John Hawkesworth [1946] Director; Simon William Hepden [1971] Director; Nicholas John Moody [1969] Director; Frazer George Roberts [1993] Director

**Glasson Grain Limited**
*Incorporated:* 15 January 1979 *Employees:* 72
*Net Worth:* £16,585,044 *Total Assets:* £27,394,434
*Registered Office:* West Quay, Glasson Dock, Lancaster, LA2 0DB
*Activities:* Wholesale of grain, unmanufactured tobacco, seeds and animal feeds
*Officers:* Charlotte Sarah Elizabeth Sellers, Secretary; David Jonathan Chadwick [1967] Managing Director; Gareth Wynn Davies [1963] Director/Chief Executive; Paul Jefferson Hayton [1971] Trading Director; Robert James Kenyon Ingham [1961] Fertiliser Director; Christopher Paul Leigh [1966] Financial Director; Bryan Paul Roberts [1963] Financial Director

**Gleadell Agriculture Limited**
*Incorporated:* 3 June 1954 *Employees:* 163
*Net Worth:* £16,326,000 *Total Assets:* £68,907,000
*Registered Office:* Lindsey House, Hemswell Cliff, Gainsborough, Lincs, DN21 5TH
*Activities:* Wholesale of grain, unmanufactured tobacco, seeds and animal feeds
*Shareholders:* ADM Arkady Limited; Invivo Grains
*Officers:* Michael John Thompson, Secretary; Stephane Bernhard [1970] Director [French]; Timothy John Cahalin [1964] Director; Jonathan Edward Lane [1976] Director; Gary Thomas McGuigan [1971] Director [Irish]; Stuart James Shand [1962] Director/Agricultural Merchant; David Thomas Sheppard [1961] Director/Grain Trader; Michael John Thompson [1965] Director/Certified Accountant

**Glen Avon Growers Limited**
*Incorporated:* 31 October 1997 *Employees:* 32
*Net Worth:* £2,581,538 *Total Assets:* £3,615,388
*Registered Office:* Glen Avon Growers, Park Lane, Cottingham, E Yorks, HU16 5RX
*Activities:* Growing of vegetables and melons, roots and tubers
*Shareholders:* Suzanne Mary Schellingerhout; David Ian Schellingerhout
*Officers:* Arie Schellingerhout, Secretary; David Ian Schellingerhout [1962] Director/Commercial Grower

**Glen Mhor Estates Limited**
*Incorporated:* 17 March 2016
*Net Worth:* £441,075 *Total Assets:* £13,793,589
*Registered Office:* Myddelton Lodge, Langbar Road, Ilkley, W Yorks, LS29 0EB
*Activities:* Other letting and operating of own or leased real estate
*Shareholders:* Andrew Iain Cope; Wendy Elizabeth Cope
*Officers:* Andrew Iain Cope [1964] Director; Wendy Elizabeth Cope [1969] Director

**Glendon Estates**
*Incorporated:* 9 January 1937 *Employees:* 5
*Net Worth:* £17,839,612 *Total Assets:* £19,246,400
*Registered Office:* Gresham House, 5-7 St Pauls Street, Leeds, LS1 2JG
*Activities:* Financial intermediation not elsewhere classified
*Shareholders:* Katherine Naylor; Fergus Wesley Beadle
*Officers:* Paul David Mitchell, Secretary; Susan Jean Ellison [1938] Director/Retired; Timothy Ellison [1966] Director [Australian]; Christopher John Marshall [1939] Director/Farmer; Clement Marshall [1975] Director [French]; Francois Marshall [1976] Director [French]

**The Glendower Group Limited**
*Incorporated:* 9 November 1989 *Employees:* 135
*Net Worth:* £4,347,285 *Total Assets:* £10,735,516
*Registered Office:* Olympia House, Metro Park 45, Lockwood Court, Leeds, LS11 5TY
*Activities:* Activities of head offices
*Parent:* Futurama Signs Holdings Limited
*Officers:* William Jonathan Evans, Secretary; Gareth Boulton [1981] Director; Marc James Edwards [1975] Director; William Jonathan Evans [1962] Director; Andrew Charles Small [1985] Director

**Glentrool Land and Estates Limited**
*Incorporated:* 30 March 2017
*Net Worth:* £32,403,840 *Total Assets:* £40,509,160
*Registered Office:* 8 Wells Promenade, Ilkley, W Yorks, LS29 9LF
*Activities:* Activities of head offices
*Shareholders:* Paul Richard Nolan; Jeremy John Nolan
*Officers:* Katie Pannu, Secretary; Jeremy John Nolan [1971] Director; Paul Richard Nolan [1968] Director

**Glid Wind Farms Topco Limited**
*Incorporated:* 25 September 2008
*Net Worth Deficit:* £99,034,000 *Total Assets:* £309,873,984
*Registered Office:* Grimsby Renewables, Operations Base, North Quay, Grimsby, N E Lincs, DN31 3SY
*Activities:* Activities of head offices
*Shareholders:* RI Income UK Holdings Limited; UK Green Investment LID Limited
*Officers:* Keith Mangan [1973] Director/Investment Manager [Irish]; Peter George Raftery [1968] Director/Engineer; Karl Ben Smith [1977] Director/Banker; Alexis Eduardo Ulens [1967] Fund Director [Belgian]

**Global Autocare Limited**
*Incorporated:* 3 February 1997 *Employees:* 91
*Net Worth:* £9,848,219 *Total Assets:* £89,336,800
*Registered Office:* Global One, Gelderd Road, Leeds, LS12 6LZ
*Activities:* Maintenance and repair of motor vehicles
*Major Shareholder:* Geoffrey Neil Bloore
*Officers:* Joanne Jean Duncan, Secretary; Geoffrey Neil Bloore [1961] Director; David John Sadler [1974] Finance Director

**Global Components (UK) Ltd**
*Incorporated:* 25 October 2004 *Employees:* 25
*Net Worth:* £2,818,987 *Total Assets:* £5,100,980
*Registered Office:* Greenfield Mills, Warneford Avenue, Ossett, W Yorks, WF5 9NJ
*Activities:* Non-specialised wholesale trade
*Major Shareholder:* Irfan Aslam
*Officers:* Irfan Aslam [1976] Director; Qadir Hussain [1978] Director

**Global George Limited**
*Incorporated:* 19 December 2005
*Net Worth Deficit:* £1,468,000 *Total Assets:* £4,433,000
*Registered Office:* Asda House, South Bank, Great Wilson Street, Leeds, LS11 5AD
*Activities:* Artistic creation
*Parent:* Walmart, Inc
*Officers:* Alexander Simpson, Secretary; Roger Michael Burnley [1966] Director; Robert Gerard McWilliam [1969] Director; Alexander Simpson [1973] Director

**Global Holdings Limited**
*Incorporated:* 11 December 1991
*Net Worth:* £3,750,003 *Total Assets:* £3,750,003
*Registered Office:* The Lodge, Gatherley Moor Farm, Gilling West, Richmond, N Yorks, DL10 5LJ
*Activities:* Activities of head offices
*Officers:* Joe Mulhall [1966] Director/Product Research

**Global Shipping Services Estates Limited**
*Incorporated:* 25 September 1967 *Employees:* 3
*Net Worth:* £5,414,050 *Total Assets:* £8,077,475
*Registered Office:* Kiln Lane Trading Estate, Stallingborough, Grimsby, N E Lincs, DN41 8DY
*Activities:* Other letting and operating of own or leased real estate
*Parent:* European Integrated Carriers Ltd
*Officers:* David Alan Jobes, Secretary/Director; David Alan Jobes [1951] Finance Director; Jharna Jobes [1958] Director/Retired Barrister; Pauline Sandra Leitch [1959] Director/Teacher

**Global Shipping Services Group Limited**
*Incorporated:* 13 May 1997
*Net Worth:* £2,736,370 *Total Assets:* £4,755,545
*Registered Office:* Kiln Lane Trading Estate, Stallingborough, Grimsby, N E Lincs, DN41 8DY
*Activities:* Dormant company
*Parent:* Global Shipping Services Group Holdings Ltd
*Officers:* David Alan Jobes, Secretary/Director; David Alan Jobes [1951] Director

**Global Shipping Services Limited**
*Incorporated:* 15 August 2005 *Employees:* 59
*Net Worth:* £1,436,207 *Total Assets:* £3,049,771
*Registered Office:* Timber Terminal, Normandy Way, Goole, E Yorks, DN14 5SP
*Activities:* Cargo handling for water transport activities
*Parent:* Lupfaw 424 Limited
*Officers:* Peter John Waud [1970] Director

**Globesign Limited**
*Incorporated:* 6 December 2004
*Net Worth:* £9,832,809 *Total Assets:* £14,407,290
*Registered Office:* Castle Mills, Moorend, Cleckheaton, W Yorks, BD19 3PS
*Activities:* Activities of head offices
*Parent:* Victoria Midco Holdings Limited
*Officers:* John Russell Shirt, Secretary; John Russell Shirt [1961] Director/Accountant; Geoffrey Brendon Wilding [1963] Director [New Zealander]

**Glusburn Holdings Limited**
*Incorporated:* 23 January 2002 *Employees:* 238
*Net Worth:* £10,566,879 *Total Assets:* £13,864,061
*Registered Office:* Hayfield, Colne Road, Glusburn, Keighley, W Yorks, BD20 8QP
*Activities:* Manufacture of fasteners and screw machine products
*Shareholders:* Victor Elisabeth Alois Stevens; Andrew I'Anson Crabtree
*Officers:* Andrew I'anson Crabtree, Secretary; Andrew I'anson Crabtree [1951] Director; Victor Elisabeth Alois Stevens [1957] Director [Belgian]

**GM Legato Limited**
*Incorporated:* 16 April 2015 *Employees:* 1
*Net Worth Deficit:* £513,055 *Total Assets:* £7,598,709
*Registered Office:* Airedale House, Albion Street, Leeds, LS1 5AP
*Activities:* Activities of head offices
*Officers:* Marina Berengaria Goodwin, Secretary; Graham David Goodwin [1965] Director

**GM Legato Property Limited**
*Incorporated:* 25 February 2016 *Employees:* 1
*Net Worth:* £362,870 *Total Assets:* £7,057,761
*Registered Office:* Airedale House, Albion Street, Leeds, LS1 5AP
*Activities:* Other letting and operating of own or leased real estate
*Officers:* Marina Berengaria Goodwin, Secretary; Graham David Goodwin [1965] Director

**GMI Construction Group PLC**
*Incorporated:* 12 February 1986 *Employees:* 76
*Net Worth:* £9,778,052 *Total Assets:* £31,016,254
*Registered Office:* Middleton House, Westland Road, Leeds, LS11 5UH
*Activities:* Construction of commercial buildings
*Parent:* Highgrove Group PLC
*Officers:* Dominic Michael Lush, Secretary; Marc Antony Banks [1986] Director; Jarrod Colin Best [1977] Director/Quantity Surveyor; Robert Andrew Bruce [1961] Director; Lee Powell [1975] Director; David James Shann [1973] Director/Chartered Accountant; Martin Peter Watson [1980] Director; Paul Whitaker [1968] Director/Surveyor

**GMI Holdings Limited**
*Incorporated:* 2 May 1997 *Employees:* 6
*Net Worth:* £7,945,485 *Total Assets:* £8,097,364
*Registered Office:* 12th Floor, Basilica, King Charles Street, Leeds, LS1 6LS
*Activities:* Activities of head offices
*Major Shareholder:* Peter John Gilman
*Officers:* Christopher Edward Gilman [1967] Director; Pammi Gilman [1965] Director; Peter John Gilman [1939] Director

**Go Green Limited**
*Incorporated:* 18 September 2000 *Employees:* 96
*Net Worth:* £2,896,580 *Total Assets:* £8,630,826
*Registered Office:* River Torne House, 323 Bawtry Road, Bessacarr, Doncaster, S Yorks, DN4 7PB
*Activities:* Remediation activities and other waste management services
*Officers:* Stephen Paul Bolland, Secretary; Amanda Jayne Bolland [1967] Director; Stephen Paul Bolland [1966] Director/Waste Broker; Carlos Anthony Ferrinho [1967] Director/Manager; Tanya Ferrinho [1970] Director; Jonathan Robert Mimms [1981] Sales Director; Roger Julian Wells [1970] Operations Director

**GO2 Foods Limited**
*Incorporated:* 16 November 2015 *Employees:* 148
*Net Worth:* £2,916,974 *Total Assets:* £8,456,783
*Registered Office:* Coulman Road Industrial Estate, Thorne, Doncaster, S Yorks, DN8 5JS
*Activities:* Manufacture of other food products n.e.c.
*Officers:* Robert Andrew Davies [1954] Director; Paul Stuart Simmonds [1958] Director

**Goball Limited**
*Incorporated:* 14 July 2011 *Employees:* 16
*Net Worth:* £1,857,203 *Total Assets:* £5,440,203
*Registered Office:* 34 Middle Street South, Driffield, E Yorks, YO25 6PS
*Activities:* Sale of other motor vehicles
*Officers:* Graham Botham [1979] Director; Matthew Gallagher [1979] Director

**R.J. & A.E. Godfrey**
*Incorporated:* 13 July 1950 *Employees:* 39
*Net Worth:* £19,740,864 *Total Assets:* £30,923,104
*Registered Office:* Cadas House, Wootton Road, Elsham Top, Brigg, N Lincs, DN20 0NU
*Activities:* Mixed farming
*Shareholders:* Alexander Godfrey; Samuel Godfrey
*Officers:* Karin Elizabeth Lund, Secretary; Alexander Godfrey [1978] Director/Farmer; James Eric Godfrey [1953] Director/Farmer; Sam Godfrey [1980] Director/Farmer

**J.A.Godfrey & Sons,Limited**
*Incorporated:* 9 May 1950 *Employees:* 4
*Net Worth:* £4,868,381 *Total Assets:* £6,024,350
*Registered Office:* Cadas House, Wootton Road, Elsham Top, Brigg, N Lincs, DN20 0NU
*Activities:* Growing of cereals (except rice), leguminous crops and oil seeds
*Parent:* Cadas Limited
*Officers:* Karin Elizabeth Lund, Secretary; Colin George Sanderson [1932] Director/Farmer; Peter Stapleton [1947] Director/Chartered Accountant

**Golam Properties Limited**
*Incorporated:* 22 May 1985
*Net Worth:* £2,065,577 *Total Assets:* £4,425,909
*Registered Office:* 2 Ashleigh Dale, Huddersfield, W Yorks, HD2 2DL
*Activities:* Other accommodation
*Shareholders:* David Dan Goody; Jill Elaine Goody
*Officers:* David Dan Goody, Secretary; Jill Elaine Goody [1949] Director/Pharmacist; Francesca Madeline Pearson [1988] Director/Pharmacy Technician

**Golden Fry Foods Limited**
*Incorporated:* 17 May 1961 *Employees:* 98
*Net Worth:* £7,471,748 *Total Assets:* £15,665,043
*Registered Office:* Goldenfry Foods Ltd, Sandbeck Way, Wetherby, W Yorks, LS22 7DW
*Activities:* Manufacture of condiments and seasonings
*Major Shareholder:* Paul Anthony Herridge
*Officers:* John Paul Herridge, Secretary; Christopher John Hill, Secretary; Elizabeth Herridge [1979] Director; John Paul Herridge [1974] Director/Accountant; Paul Anthony Herridge [1945] Director/Food Products Manufacturer; Peter Anthony Turrill [1955] Director/Food Products Manufacturer

**Goldenfry Limited**
*Incorporated:* 17 July 1989 *Employees:* 98
*Net Worth:* £14,628,701 *Total Assets:* £22,281,904
*Registered Office:* Sandbeck Way, Wetherby, W Yorks, LS22 7DW
*Activities:* Renting and leasing of other machinery, equipment and tangible goods n.e.c.
*Major Shareholder:* Paul Anthony Herridge
*Officers:* John Paul Herridge, Secretary; Christopher John Hill, Secretary; Paul Anthony Herridge [1945] Director/Food Products Manufacturer

**Goldmart Limited**
*Incorporated:* 15 November 1984
*Net Worth:* £3,481,174 *Total Assets:* £3,918,669
*Registered Office:* 2 Houndgate, Darlington, Co Durham, DL1 5RL
*Activities:* Retail sale of watches and jewellery in specialised stores
*Major Shareholder:* Luke Peter Gray Wall-Row
*Officers:* Mark Stansfield, Secretary; Mark Stansfield [1958] Director/Jeweller; Luke Peter Gray Wallrow [1958] Director/Jeweller

**Goliath Footwear Limited**
*Incorporated:* 24 September 2003 *Employees:* 7
*Net Worth:* £2,764,736 *Total Assets:* £10,990,135
*Registered Office:* Goliath House, Chain Bar Road, Cleckheaton, W Yorks, BD19 3QF
*Activities:* Agents involved in the sale of textiles, clothing, fur, footwear and leather goods
*Major Shareholder:* Abdil Vedat Yakupoglu
*Officers:* Levent Gulcan, Secretary; Levent Gulcan [1968] Director [Turkish]; Abdil Vedat Yakupoglu [1961] Director [Turkish]

**John Good & Sons Limited**
*Incorporated:* 9 January 1908 *Employees:* 304
*Previous:* John Good & Sons,Limited
*Net Worth:* £8,281,000 *Total Assets:* £24,148,000
*Registered Office:* Matthew Good House, Bridgehead Business Park, Orchid Road, Hessle, E Yorks, HU13 0DH
*Activities:* Activities of head offices
*Shareholders:* Timothy David Ambrose Good; John Ambrose Good
*Officers:* Jonathan Ramon Garnier [1968] Finance Director; Timothy David Ambrose Good [1980] Director; Kevin John Harrison [1966] Director; James Gerard Jennings [1964] Sales Director; Stewart Oades [1953] Director; Alan Oliver Platt [1969] Director/Company Executive; John David Rutherford [1951] Director

**John Good Shipping Limited**
*Incorporated:* 13 January 1982 *Employees:* 106
*Previous:* John Good Shipping Ltd
*Net Worth:* £1,587,000 *Total Assets:* £11,222,000
*Registered Office:* Matthew Good House, Bridgehead Business Park, Orchid Road, Hessle, Hull, HU13 0DH
*Activities:* Other transportation support activities
*Parent:* John Good & Sons Limited
*Officers:* Paul Scott Ian Ferguson [1978] Commercial Director; Peter James FitzGenerald [1974] Procurement Director; Jonathan Ramon Garnier [1968] Director; Stuart Charles Gosling [1963] Director; James Gerard Jennings [1964] Director; Brian Harold Megran [1953] Director/Shipping Manager; Alan Oliver Platt [1969] Director

**The Goodall Group Limited**
*Incorporated:* 27 March 2001 *Employees:* 3
*Net Worth:* £13,617,770 *Total Assets:* £14,122,672
*Registered Office:* 2 West Parade Road, Scarborough, N Yorks, YO12 5ED
*Activities:* Activities of other holding companies n.e.c.
*Officers:* Joan Margaret Goodall, Secretary; James Rawling Goodall [1980] Director; Joan Margaret Goodall [1941] Director

**Goodprofit Limited**
*Incorporated:* 31 March 2005
*Net Worth:* £395,716 *Total Assets:* £3,578,008
*Registered Office:* Sanderson House, Station Road, Horsforth, Leeds, LS18 5NT
*Activities:* Management consultancy activities other than financial management
*Major Shareholder:* Ronald Harker
*Officers:* Ronald Harker [1941] Director

**M.B. Goodwin (Skipsea) Limited**
*Incorporated:* 21 June 1976 *Employees:* 1
*Net Worth:* £18,556,720 *Total Assets:* £38,195,488
*Registered Office:* Low Skirlington, Skipsea, Driffield, E Yorks, YO25 8SY
*Activities:* Mixed farming
*Major Shareholder:* Michael Ben Goodwin
*Officers:* Michael Ben Goodwin, Secretary; Christine Mary Goodwin [1939] Director; Matthew Richard Goodwin [1968] Director; Michael Ben Goodwin [1933] Director; Simon Michael Goodwin [1964] Director

**Goodwin Development Trust**
*Incorporated:* 5 June 2002 *Employees:* 174
*Net Worth:* £11,531,000 *Total Assets:* £16,475,000
*Registered Office:* The Octagon, Walker Street, Hull, HU3 2RA
*Activities:* Renting and operating of Housing Association real estate
*Officers:* Dianne Julie Hamilton, Secretary; Kellock Ainley [1950] Director/Retired; Natalja Batare [1970] Director/Accountant [Latvian/British]; Ruth Bean [1956] Director/Retired; Altynay Guney [1984] Director/Housing Officer; Anna Frances Heddle [1958] Director/Volunteer; Sharon Elizabeth Igoe [1967] Director/Administrator; Robin Watkin [1963] Director/Volunteer

**M.B. & J. Goodwin Limited**
*Incorporated:* 7 January 1972 *Employees:* 34
*Net Worth:* £5,515,471 *Total Assets:* £8,058,624
*Registered Office:* Low Skirlington, Skipsea, Driffield, E Yorks, YO25 8SY
*Activities:* Mixed farming
*Parent:* M B Goodwin (Skipsea) Limited
*Officers:* Michael Ben Goodwin, Secretary; Christine Mary Goodwin [1939] Director; Christopher Ben Goodwin [1972] Director; Matthew Richard Goodwin [1968] Director; Michael Ben Goodwin [1933] Director; Simon Michael Goodwin [1964] Director; Kevin Peter Obrien [1951] Director

**Gordons LLP**
*Incorporated:* 25 April 2006 *Employees:* 186
*Net Worth:* £6,772,575,232 *Total Assets:* £8,831,439,872
*Registered Office:* 1 New Augustus Street, Bradford, W Yorks, BD1 5LL
*Officers:* Paul Hugh Ayre [1964] Member; Nicholas James Chamberlain [1971] Member; Victoria Louise Davey [1971] Member; John Layfield Holden [1957] Member; Jonathan Asquez [1977] LLP Member; Andrew John Breckenridge [1966] LLP Member; Andrew Brian [1979] LLP Member; Richard Peter Cressall [1986] LLP Member; Graeme Edward Davy [1980] LLP Member; Gregory James Dixon [1986] LLP Member; James Anthony Fawcett [1976] LLP Member; Joanne Marie Fearnley [1969] LLP Member; Michael Andrew Finnett [1978] LLP Member; Duncan Mark Edward Firman [1981] LLP Member; Rachel Hudson [1971] LLP Member; Mark Francois Jones [1982] LLP Member; Anjon Mallik [1973] LLP Member; Stephen Andrew McVey [1979] LLP Member; Simon Terry Mydlowski [1979] LLP Member; John Edward Owen [1974] LLP Member; Phillip John Paget [1965] LLP Member; Wayne Matthew Parker [1959] LLP Member; Richard David Steuart Piper [1969] LLP Member; Sarah Jane Ratcliffe [1978] LLP Member; Diana Mary Smart [1964] LLP Member; Mary Katherine Charlotte Walker [1972] LLP Member; Paul Stephen Young [1970] LLP Member

**The Gorse Academies Trust**
*Incorporated:* 9 December 2010 *Employees:* 220
*Net Worth:* £102,122,000 *Total Assets:* £114,599,000
*Registered Office:* Bruntcliffe Academy, Bruntcliffe Lane, Morley, Leeds, LS27 0LZ
*Activities:* General secondary education
*Officers:* Judith Shore, Secretary; Janice Boucher [1962] Finance Director; Michael Terrence Elliott [1939] Director/Retired; Professor Christopher Andrew Gorse [1968] Director/Professor/Lecturer; Councillor Peter John Gruen [1950] Director/City Councillor; Steve Hall [1960] Director/Retired; Tracy Latham [1964] Director/Nurse; Anne McAvan [1954] Director/Retired Teacher; Susan Ada Slee [1950] Director/Retired; John Arthur Townsley [1965] Director/Executive Headteacher; Richard West [1965] Director/Civil Servant

**Gott Agri Synergy Limited**
*Incorporated:* 19 February 2016 *Employees:* 282
*Net Worth:* £7,545,690 *Total Assets:* £33,995,704
*Registered Office:* Addington Lodge, Addington Road, Nether Kellet, Carnforth, Lancs, LA6 1DZ
*Activities:* Dormant company
*Parent:* Gott Agri Holdings Limited
*Officers:* Adrian David Gott [1981] Director

**Gould Tech Solutions Limited**
*Incorporated:* 26 June 1985 *Employees:* 24
*Net Worth Deficit:* £166,000 *Total Assets:* £7,887,000
*Registered Office:* Link Up House, Ring Road, Lower Wortley, Leeds, LS12 6AB
*Activities:* Business and domestic software development
*Major Shareholder:* Laurence Jeremy Gould
*Officers:* Marcus Lee Mills, Secretary; Ali Nihat Arkan [1965] Director/Chief Executive [Turkish]; Bernadette Judith Byrne [1962] Director; Laurence Jeremy Gould [1952] Director; Michele Gould [1962] Director

**Gradebatch Limited**
*Incorporated:* 5 February 1992
*Net Worth:* £6,352,258 *Total Assets:* £6,356,758
*Registered Office:* Skewkirk Hall, Ness Lane, Tockwith, York, YO26 7QL
*Activities:* Other professional, scientific and technical activities n.e.c.
*Major Shareholder:* John Malcolm Slinger
*Officers:* Jane Rosemary Slinger, Secretary; John Malcolm Slinger [1954] Director

**Peter Gradon Meat and Poultry Marketing Limited**
*Incorporated:* 21 March 2000 *Employees:* 79
*Net Worth:* £6,415,909 *Total Assets:* £8,066,950
*Registered Office:* Marsh Dene Farm, Marsh Lane, Southowram, Halifax, W Yorks, HX3 9NR
*Activities:* Processing and preserving of poultry meat
*Officers:* Peter William Gradon, Secretary; Brenda Gradon [1938] Director (Proposed); Peter William Gradon [1935] Managing Director

**Grafitec Holdings Limited**
*Incorporated:* 9 October 1991
*Net Worth:* £3,317,981 *Total Assets:* £3,749,713
*Registered Office:* Grafic House, Tom Dando Close, Normanton Industrial Estate, Normanton, Wakefield, W Yorks, WF6 1TP
*Activities:* Activities of head offices
*Shareholder:* Christopher John Barrett
*Officers:* Robert Geoffrey Hogg, Secretary; Anthony Claude Barrett [1939] Director; Christopher John Barrett [1964] Director; Robert Geoffrey Hogg [1969] Director

**Graham Developments (Property Holdings) Ltd**
*Incorporated:* 17 September 2004 *Employees:* 2
*Net Worth:* £1,988,067 *Total Assets:* £3,156,885
*Registered Office:* Carlton House, Bull Close Lane, Halifax, W Yorks, HX1 2EG
*Activities:* Development of building projects
*Shareholders:* Tracey Jane Graham; James Spence Graham
*Officers:* Tracey Jane Graham, Secretary; James Spence Graham [1965] Director; Tracey Jane Graham [1970] Director/Administrator

**William S. Graham Limited**
*Incorporated:* 1 April 1897 *Employees:* 3
*Net Worth:* £5,339,318 *Total Assets:* £5,522,348
*Registered Office:* Tenterfields, Thornhill Road Business Park, Dewsbury, W Yorks, WF12 9QF
*Activities:* Preparation and spinning of textile fibres
*Parent:* William S Graham & Sons (Dewsbury) Ltd
*Officers:* Peter Sutton, Secretary; John Stewart Graham [1938] Managing Director; Nigel Graham [1951] Production Director; Peter Sutton [1959] Finance Director

**Grainsby Farms Limited**
*Incorporated:* 18 October 1963 *Employees:* 10
*Net Worth:* £9,978,211 *Total Assets:* £11,215,108
*Registered Office:* The Estate Office, Grainsby, Grimsby, N E Lincs, DN36 5PU
*Activities:* Growing of cereals (except rice), leguminous crops and oil seeds
*Shareholder:* Richard Holland Caton Haigh
*Officers:* Fanny Elizabeth Mary Muldoon, Secretary; Daniel Lewis Caton Haigh [1980] Director/Musician; Hannah Elizabeth Haigh [1981] Director; Richard Holland Caton Haigh [1951] Director/Farmer; Matthew Philip Spence [1978] Director/Farm Manager

**The Grammar School at Leeds**
*Incorporated:* 4 July 1995 *Employees:* 351
*Net Worth:* £9,791,000 *Total Assets:* £22,472,000
*Registered Office:* The Grammar School at Leeds, Alwoodley Gates, Harrogate Road, Leeds, LS17 8GS
*Activities:* General secondary education
*Officers:* Stephen Kingston, Secretary; Elizabeth Enid Bailey [1945] Director/Dental Surgeon; Sir Stephen David Reid Brown Kcvo [1945] Director/Co-Chairman; Jeremy David Cross [1967] Director/Accountant; Mark Richard Curle [1980] Director/Solicitor; Jacqueline Alethea Harper [1962] Director/Lecturer; Professor Abigail Louise Harrison Moore [1972] Director/Senior Academic; Ian Martin Lloyd Jones [1960] Director; Deborah Wendy Kenny [1960] Director/Education Advisor; Dr Almas Latif Khan [1973] Director/Surgeon; Charlene Lyons [1978] Director/Management Consultant; Angus Matthew Martin [1959] Director/Chartered Accountant; Joanne Semple [1969] Design Agency Director; Susan Anne Solyom [1959] Director/Chartered Accountant; Claire Vilarrubi [1973] Director/PhD Student/Graduate Teaching Assistant; Anthony John Walsh [1966] Director/Banker; John Anthony Woodward [1964] Director

**Grand Construction Products Limited**
*Incorporated:* 12 March 2013 *Employees:* 4
*Net Worth:* £1,530,211 *Total Assets:* £3,157,493
*Registered Office:* Ogleforth House, Ogleforth, York, YO1 7JG
*Activities:* Other specialised construction activities n.e.c.
*Shareholders:* John Howard Neal; Christopher Paul Viney
*Officers:* John Howard Neal [1961] Director; Christopher Paul Viney [1975] Sales Director

**Grand Principal Birmingham Limited**
*Incorporated:* 12 December 2016
*Net Worth Deficit:* £190,000 *Total Assets:* £11,593,000
*Registered Office:* The Inspire, Hornbeam Square, West Harrogate, N Yorks, HG2 8PA
*Activities:* Hotels and similar accommodation
*Parent:* Principal Hotels Topco 3 Limited
*Officers:* James Alexander Burrell [1974] Director; Anthony Gerrard Troy [1962] Director [Irish]

**Grand-Riverland & Co. Limited**
*Incorporated:* 8 February 1995
*Net Worth:* £829,959 *Total Assets:* £6,030,480
*Registered Office:* 57 Moorview Way, Skipton, N Yorks, BD23 2JW
*Activities:* Other retail sale not in stores, stalls or markets
*Officers:* Hendrik Dijkstra [1955] Managing Director [Dutch]; Jisk Knijpstra [1974] Director [Dutch]

**Grandlane Limited**
*Incorporated:* 23 January 1996 *Employees:* 18
*Net Worth:* £4,456,024 *Total Assets:* £12,920,167
*Registered Office:* 8 Manor Road, Leeds, LS11 9AH
*Activities:* Other human health activities
*Parent:* Living Care Pharmacy Group Limited
*Officers:* David Andrew Lestner [1962] Director/Pharmacist; Jason Elliot Lestner [1988] Director/Pharmacist

**Samuel Grant (Holdings) Ltd**
*Incorporated:* 15 January 2014 *Employees:* 120
*Net Worth:* £8,025,084 *Total Assets:* £20,389,220
*Registered Office:* Unit 1 Orion Way, Cross Green, Leeds, LS9 0AR
*Activities:* Activities of head offices
*Shareholders:* Andrew David Surrey Grant; Matthew Paul Surrey Grant
*Officers:* Ashley Jon Dean, Secretary; Andrew David Surrey Grant [1970] Director/Packaging Merchant; Matthew Paul Surrey Grant [1974] Director/Packaging Merchant

**Samuel Grant (Leeds) Limited**
*Incorporated:* 22 April 1992 *Employees:* 45
*Net Worth:* £2,780,520 *Total Assets:* £7,189,171
*Registered Office:* Unit 1 Orion Way, Cross Green, Leeds, LS9 0AR
*Activities:* Wholesale of other intermediate products
*Parent:* Samuel Grant (Group) Ltd
*Officers:* Ashley Jon Dean, Secretary; Andrew David Surrey Grant [1970] Director/Packaging Merchant; Matthew Paul Surrey Grant [1974] Director/Packaging Merchant; Martin Harris [1968] Sales Director

**Wm.Grant (Paull) Limited**
*Incorporated:* 26 March 1942 *Employees:* 8
*Net Worth:* £1,172,385 *Total Assets:* £4,793,296
*Registered Office:* Elm Farm, Roos, E Yorks, HU12 0LJ
*Activities:* Mixed farming
*Major Shareholder:* Micheal George Grant
*Officers:* Harry George Willerby Grant [1991] Director; Julie Dawn Grant [1963] Director/Hairdresser; Michael George Grant [1958] Director/Farmer

**Samuel Grant Group Limited**
*Incorporated:* 24 May 1921 *Employees:* 7
*Net Worth:* £6,848,215 *Total Assets:* £9,849,391
*Registered Office:* Unit 1 Orion Way, Cross Green, Leeds, LS9 0AR
*Activities:* Activities of head offices
*Parent:* Samuel Grant (Holdings) Ltd
*Officers:* Ashley Jon Dean, Secretary; Andrew David Surrey Grant [1970] Director/Packaging Merchant; Matthew Paul Surrey Grant [1974] Director/Packaging Merchant; Sheelagh Margaret Grant [1946] Director/Secretary

**Grantley Hall Group Limited**
*Incorporated:* 8 July 2015 *Employees:* 5
*Net Worth Deficit:* £452,392 *Total Assets:* £16,788,204
*Registered Office:* New Court, Abbey Road North, Shepley, Huddersfield, W Yorks, HD8 8BJ
*Activities:* Hotels and similar accommodation
*Major Shareholder:* Valeria Anne Sykes
*Officers:* Richard Anthony Sykes [1964] Director; Valeria Anne Sykes [1943] Director

**Grants Pro-Agri Limited**
*Incorporated:* 29 January 1987 *Employees:* 6
*Net Worth:* £3,236,823 *Total Assets:* £4,922,790
*Registered Office:* Longbridge House Farm, Stillington Road, Easingwold, York, YO61 3ET
*Activities:* Raising of other cattle and buffaloes
*Major Shareholder:* Jane Marie Grant
*Officers:* Jane Marie Grant [1965] Director

**Grantside Limited**
*Incorporated:* 27 May 1993 *Employees:* 5
*Net Worth:* £7,515,436 *Total Assets:* £7,570,232
*Registered Office:* Middlethorpe Manor, Middlethorpe, York, YO23 2QB
*Activities:* Development of building projects
*Major Shareholder:* Steve Davis
*Officers:* Steven Geoffrey Davis, Secretary/Director; Steven Geoffrey Davis [1972] Director/Developer

**Grattan Public Limited Company**
*Incorporated:* 25 June 1930 *Employees:* 442
*Net Worth:* £106,491,000 *Total Assets:* £219,515,008
*Registered Office:* 66-70 Vicar Lane, Little Germany, Bradford, W Yorks, BD99 2XG
*Activities:* Retail sale via mail order houses or via Internet
*Parent:* Freemans Grattan Holdings Limited
*Officers:* Andrew James Lord, Secretary; John Hinchcliffe [1965] Director/Chief Executive Officer; Neill Lewis McDonald Moore [1966] Director/Chartered Accountant; Marc Erich Bernd Wolfgang Opelt [1962] Director/Businessman [German]

**Gravers Care Home Ltd**
*Incorporated:* 23 February 2005 *Employees:* 45
*Net Worth:* £1,856,167 *Total Assets:* £3,420,668
*Registered Office:* 17 Wigginton Road, York, YO31 8HG
*Activities:* Residential care activities for learning difficulties, mental health and substance abuse
*Parent:* Pendale York Ltd
*Officers:* Dale Andrew Graver, Secretary/Care Home Proprietor; Dale Andrew Graver [1958] Director/Care Home Proprietor; Penelope Anne Graver [1953] Director/Care Home Proprietor

**Graycliffe Homes Limited**
*Incorporated:* 15 October 1986 *Employees:* 3
*Net Worth:* £1,720,148 *Total Assets:* £5,174,695
*Registered Office:* 9 Hawthorne Gardens, Leeds, LS16 7TP
*Activities:* Development of building projects
*Shareholders:* Helen Butterfield; Wayne Mark Butterfield; Jean Butterfield
*Officers:* Jean Butterfield, Secretary; Jean Butterfield [1949] Director/Secretary; Wayne Mark Butterfield [1968] Director/Technical Manager

**Graypen Holdings Limited**
*Incorporated:* 16 August 2016
*Net Worth:* £760,002 *Total Assets:* £5,747,106
*Registered Office:* The Bridge, One Graypen Way, Queens Road, Immingham, N E Lincs, DN40 1QN
*Activities:* Activities of head offices
*Shareholders:* Philip Daniel Johnson; Simon John Coghlan
*Officers:* Lee Hutchinson, Secretary; Simon John Coghlan [1969] Group Managing Director; Philip Daniel Johnson [1978] Group Director

**Graypen Limited**
*Incorporated:* 23 October 1969
*Net Worth:* £2,552,811 *Total Assets:* £18,572,252
*Registered Office:* The Bridge, One Graypen Way, Queens Road, Immingham, N E Lincs, DN40 1QN
*Activities:* Sea and coastal freight water transport
*Parent:* Graypen Cymru Limited
*Officers:* Lee Hutchinson, Secretary; Simon John Coghlan [1969] Group Managing Director; Philip Daniel Johnson [1978] Group Director; Daniel Gavin Payne [1973] Director

**Grays Wharf Limited**
*Incorporated:* 12 March 2003 *Employees:* 5
*Net Worth:* £8,362,729 *Total Assets:* £14,220,576
*Registered Office:* Stanley Harrison House, The Chocolate Works, Bishopthorpe Works, York, YO23 1DE
*Activities:* Development of building projects
*Shareholder:* S Harrison Developments Limited
*Officers:* Ann Pearce Scott, Secretary/Accountant; Colin Alfred Foster [1948] Director/Accountant; Richard Gray [1940] Director/Newsagent; Martyn Robert Harrison [1959] Director; Ann Pearce Scott [1962] Director/Accountant

**Great Grimsby Seafood Village Ltd**
*Incorporated:* 13 September 2006 *Employees:* 5
*Net Worth:* £704,588 *Total Assets:* £3,288,822
*Registered Office:* Unit 16 Great Grimsby Seafood Village, Wickham Road, Grimsby, N E Lincs, DN31 3SX
*Activities:* Other letting and operating of own or leased real estate
*Shareholder:* Peter Kevin Dalton
*Officers:* Gary Cadey, Secretary/Director; Toby Oliver James Baxendale [1969] Director; Gary Cadey [1955] Director; Peter Kevin Dalton [1953] Director; LEA Kirwin [1965] Director

**The Great North Air Ambulance Service**
*Incorporated:* 13 May 2002 *Employees:* 81
*Net Worth:* £12,354,860 *Total Assets:* £13,020,887
*Registered Office:* Northumberland Wing, The Imperial Centre, Grange Road, Darlington, Co Durham, DL1 5NQ
*Activities:* Non-scheduled passenger air transport
*Officers:* John Richard Devine [1976] Director/Solicitor; Dawn Catherine Dunn [1962] Director/Marketing Communications Manager; Stephen Groves [1962] Director/National Head of Emergency Preparedness, Resilience; Dr Kyee Han [1951] Clinical Director; James Andrew Harris [1971] Director; Brian Henry Jobling [1968] Director; James Kyle [1976] Director/Wealth Manager; Joan Trench [1954] Director/HR Strategic Lead and Executive Coach; Paul Leonard Turner [1953] Director/International Development Consultant

**Great Rail Journeys Holdings Limited**
*Incorporated:* 24 August 2005
*Net Worth:* £15,646,000 *Total Assets:* £30,205,000
*Registered Office:* c/o Great Rail Journeys Ltd, Saviour House, 9 St Saviourgate, York, YO1 8NL
*Activities:* Activities of head offices
*Parent:* Thomas Bidco Ltd
*Officers:* Julian Appleyard [1971] Director; Peter Richard Liney [1959] Director/Chief Executive Officer; Noeleen Patricia Rita Pritchard [1984] Director; David James Riley [1980] Director; Mark Andrew Taylor [1964] Director

**Great Rail Journeys Limited**
*Incorporated:* 5 June 1996 *Employees:* 156
*Net Worth:* £16,011,000 *Total Assets:* £31,626,000
*Registered Office:* Saviour House, 9 St Saviourgate, York, YO1 8NL
*Activities:* Tour operator activities
*Parent:* Great Rail Journeys Partnership Ltd
*Officers:* Julian Appleyard [1971] Director; Peter Richard Liney [1959] Director/Chief Executive Officer; Noeleen Patricia Rita Pritchard [1984] Director; David James Riley [1980] Director; Mark Andrew Taylor [1964] IT Director

**Great Rail Journeys Partnership Limited**
*Incorporated:* 20 May 2003 *Employees:* 158
*Net Worth:* £18,592,000 *Total Assets:* £34,993,000
*Registered Office:* c/o Great Rail Journeys Limited, Saviour House, 9 St Saviourgate, York, YO1 8NL
*Activities:* Activities of head offices
*Parent:* Great Rail Journeys Holdings Ltd
*Officers:* Julian Appleyard [1971] Director; Peter Richard Liney [1959] Director/Chief Executive Officer; Noeleen Patricia Rita Pritchard [1984] Director; David James Riley [1980] Director; Mark Andrew Taylor [1964] Director

**Jerry Green Dog Rescue**
*Incorporated:* 16 July 2013 *Employees:* 64
*Net Worth:* £12,304,891 *Total Assets:* £12,406,064
*Registered Office:* Jerry Green Dog Rescue, Broughton, Brigg, N Lincs, DN20 0BJ
*Activities:* Other service activities n.e.c.
*Officers:* Ian Arthur Cawsey [1960] Charity Director; Jayne Marie Chudley [1967] Director/Trustee; Lynn Frances Hewison [1984] Director/Trustee; Paul McCartan [1979] Director/Human Resources Manager; Kevin Lawrence Peart [1966] Director/Trustee; Andrew Paul Robinson [1964] Director/Chartered Accountant

**Green Flag Group Limited**
*Incorporated:* 21 June 1991
*Net Worth:* £7,265,877 *Total Assets:* £7,269,389
*Registered Office:* The Wharf, Neville Street, Leeds, LS1 4AZ
*Activities:* Activities of head offices
*Parent:* Green Flag Holdings Limited
*Officers:* Roger Cheston Clifton, Secretary; Roger Cheston Clifton [1964] Director/Secretary; Helen Clare O'Murchu [1967] Director/Head of Financial Reporting; Humphrey Michael Tomlinson [1962] Director/General Counsel & Company Secretary

**Green Flag Limited**
*Incorporated:* 23 February 1971
*Net Worth:* £10,692,000 *Total Assets:* £18,438,000
*Registered Office:* The Wharf, Neville Street, Leeds, LS1 4AZ
*Activities:* Maintenance and repair of motor vehicles
*Parent:* Green Flag Group Limited
*Officers:* Roger Cheston Clifton, Secretary; Roger Cheston Clifton [1964] Director/Secretary; Helen Clare O'Murchu [1967] Director/Head of Financial Reporting; Humphrey Michael Tomlinson [1962] Director/General Counsel & Company Secretary

**Greendown Trust**
*Incorporated:* 7 December 1989 *Employees:* 30
*Net Worth:* £3,462,197 *Total Assets:* £3,498,571
*Registered Office:* Dyneley House, 10 Allerton Hill, Chapel Allerton, Leeds, LS7 3QB
*Activities:* Residential care activities for the elderly and disabled
*Officers:* Simon Timothy Greener, Secretary; Pauline Agnes Beecroft [1944] Director/Christian Science Practitioner; Beverely Ann Jaques [1953] Director; Christopher Norman Jaques [1952] Director/Architect; Rodney Phillips [1944] Director/Retired; David Pickersgill [1939] Director/Retired; Lindsey Patricia Webster [1958] Director/Trust Administrator

**P. W. Greenhalgh Holdings Limited**
*Incorporated:* 29 September 2005
*Net Worth:* £6,073,181 *Total Assets:* £6,076,860
*Registered Office:* Russel Lodge, Skircoat Green Road, Halifax, W Yorks, HX3 0BJ
*Activities:* Other letting and operating of own or leased real estate
*Shareholders:* Andrew Benjamin Greenhalgh; Simon Ross Greenhalgh
*Officers:* Andrew Benjamin Greenhalgh, Secretary; Andrew Benjamin Greenhalgh [1963] Director; Simon Ross Greenhalgh [1964] Director

**Greens Desserts UK Ltd**
*Incorporated:* 3 July 2015 *Employees:* 75
*Net Worth Deficit:* £3,763,374 *Total Assets:* £4,960,122
*Registered Office:* 2 Granary Court, Main Street, Heslington, York, YO10 5JU
*Activities:* Manufacture of bread; manufacture of fresh pastry goods and cakes
*Major Shareholder:* Mahdi Mohamed Hassan Hassani
*Officers:* Mahdi Mohamed Hassan Hassani [1971] Director [Emirati]; Phillip Metcalfe [1958] Director

**Greentech Limited**
*Incorporated:* 24 September 2002 *Employees:* 67
*Net Worth:* £2,031,694 *Total Assets:* £4,955,878
*Registered Office:* Rabbit Hill Business Park, Great North Road, Arkendale, Knaresborough, N Yorks, HG5 0FF
*Activities:* Manufacture of prepared pet foods
*Parent:* Rabbit (Holdings) Limited
*Officers:* Rachel Kay, Secretary/Director; Glenn Alexander Brown [1985] Director/Warehouse Manager; Corin Michael Clifford [1969] Commercial Director; Richard Stephen Gill [1981] Sales Director; Kate Humes [1979] Marketing Director; Rachel Kay [1969] Director; Richard John Kay [1968] Director; Thomas Joseph Parker [1980] Purchasing and Commercial Director; Thomas Richard Wall [1958] Finance and IT Director; Mark John Wood [1978] Brands Director

**Greentek Solutions Ltd**
*Incorporated:* 10 December 2012
*Net Worth:* £686,275 *Total Assets:* £3,440,521
*Registered Office:* Rudgate, Walton, Leeds, LS23 7AU
*Activities:* Wholesale of other intermediate products
*Parent:* The Greentek (Group) Ltd
*Officers:* Garth Anton Christie [1957] Director; David Hugh Michel [1953] Managing Director

**The Greetland Academy Trust**
*Incorporated:* 9 December 2010 *Employees:* 69
*Previous:* The Greetland Academy
*Net Worth:* £3,845,790 *Total Assets:* £4,633,266
*Registered Office:* School Street, Greetland, Halifax, W Yorks, HX4 8JB
*Activities:* Primary education
*Officers:* Amanda Jane Bennett [1967] Director/Headteacher; Dr Angela Birt [1956] Director/Obstetrician; Alexander James Fryer [1967] Director/Business Development Manager; Kenneth Inwood [1947] Director/Educational Consultant; John Edward Berry Midgley [1976] Director; John Carlton Midgley [1945] Director/Education Consultant; Jacqueline Anne Nellis [1963] Director/Self Employed Education Consultant; Peter Graham Newton [1947] Director/Retired Teacher

**Gregory Projects Limited**
*Incorporated:* 12 December 2001 *Employees:* 7
*Net Worth Deficit:* £1,212,595 *Total Assets:* £4,948,035
*Registered Office:* 12 Cardale Court, Cardale Park, Beckwith Head Road, Harrogate, N Yorks, HG3 1RY
*Activities:* Development of building projects
*Parent:* Gregory Property Group Limited
*Officers:* Marjorie Robertson, Secretary; Andrew Mark Foggitt [1965] Director; George Barry Gregory [1940] Director; Trevor Robert Gurney [1948] Director/Chartered Accountant

**Gregory Property Group Limited**
*Incorporated:* 27 November 1984 *Employees:* 7
*Net Worth:* £2,537,944 *Total Assets:* £7,098,403
*Registered Office:* 12 Cardale Court, Cardale Park, Beckwith Head Road, Harrogate, N Yorks, HG3 1RY
*Activities:* Non-trading company
*Shareholder:* George Barry Gregory
*Officers:* Marjorie Robertson, Secretary; Christine Edwina Gregory [1939] Director/Secretary; George Barry Gregory [1940] Director/Property Developer; Trevor Robert Gurney [1948] Director; John Patrick McGhee [1955] Director

**Greif Flexibles UK Limited**
*Incorporated:* 20 October 1999 *Employees:* 91
*Net Worth:* £4,445,694 *Total Assets:* £9,911,659
*Registered Office:* Dalton Airfield, Dalton, Thirsk, N Yorks, YO7 3HE
*Activities:* Other manufacturing n.e.c.
*Parent:* Greif Flexibles Trading Holding BV
*Officers:* Nigel Booth, Secretary; Nigel Booth [1961] Director/Businessman; Christopher David Poole [1965] Director

**Grimsby & Cleethorpes Area Doorstep**
*Incorporated:* 20 April 1990 *Employees:* 20
*Net Worth:* £4,336,211 *Total Assets:* £4,550,084
*Registered Office:* 115 Pasture Street, Grimsby, N E Lincs, DN32 9EE
*Activities:* Other accommodation
*Officers:* Julie Walmsley, Secretary/Manager; Roger David Beard [1947] Director/Retired; Frances Pamela Davey [1934] Director/Retired; Robert Frank Lamb [1951] Director/Retired; James Lockwood [1985] Director/Architect; Christine Ann Peterson [1947] Director/Retired Teacher; Rhieta Kay Prowle [1943] Director/Retired Teacher

**Grimsby Fish Dock Enterprises Limited**
*Incorporated:* 22 April 1991 *Employees:* 33
*Net Worth:* £3,034,383 *Total Assets:* £7,446,493
*Registered Office:* Wharncliffe Road, Fish Docks, Grimsby, N E Lincs, DN31 3QJ
*Activities:* Marine fishing
*Officers:* Martyn Howard Boyers, Secretary/Chief Executive; Andrew John Allard [1960] Director; Petur Bjornsson [1955] Director/Chairman [Icelander]; Martyn Howard Boyers [1955] Director/Chief Executive; Frank Alan Flear [1934] Director; Christopher Mark Goodwin [1956] Director/Businessman; Charles Roger Marr [1960] Director; David Robinson [1965] Director/Investment Manager; Nigel Robin Stinson [1958] Director

**Grimsby Operations Limited**
*Incorporated:* 18 October 1999 *Employees:* 38
*Net Worth:* £3,100,648 *Total Assets:* £3,589,960
*Registered Office:* Integrated Waste Management Facility, South Marsh Road, Stallingborough, N E Lincs, DN41 8BZ
*Activities:* Collection of non-hazardous waste
*Parent:* Cyclerval (UK) Limited
*Officers:* George Richard Guthrie, Secretary; Sharon Julie Hunt [1969] Director/Operations Manager; Albert Henri Yzern [1960] Operations Director [French]

**Grosvenor Facilities Management Limited**
*Incorporated:* 9 August 1995 *Employees:* 393
*Net Worth:* £3,270,691 *Total Assets:* £7,355,590
*Registered Office:* 4 Greengate, Cardale Park, Harrogate, N Yorks, HG3 1GY
*Activities:* Other service activities n.e.c.
*Parent:* Grosvenor House Group Limited
*Officers:* Alastair William Hopps, Secretary; Robert John Austin [1964] Finance Director; Peter Paul Copley [1956] Development/Managing Director; Alexander Toby Shedden Parry [1976] Director/Company Secretary

**Grosvenor Funding Solutions Limited**
*Incorporated:* 18 April 2012
*Net Worth:* £1,191 *Total Assets:* £7,989,280
*Registered Office:* Pavilion 2000, Amy Johnson Way, York, YO30 4XT
*Activities:* Financial intermediation not elsewhere classified
*Shareholders:* Mark Andrew Pepper; Alice Louise Pepper
*Officers:* Mark Andrew Pepper [1965] Director

**Grosvenor House Group Holdings Limited**
*Incorporated:* 11 March 2005 *Employees:* 4
*Net Worth:* £5,882,891 *Total Assets:* £8,041,852
*Registered Office:* 4 Greengate, Cardale Park, Harrogate, N Yorks, HG3 1GY
*Activities:* Activities of head offices
*Parent:* GH Newco 1 Limited
*Officers:* Alexander Toby Shedden Parry, Secretary; Robert John Austin [1964] Finance Director; Peter Paul Copley [1956] Managing Director; Christopher Justin Taee [1968] Director/Retail Manager; Nigel Duncan Taee [1961] Director/Consultant

**Grosvenor House Papers Limited**
*Incorporated:* 24 March 1994 *Employees:* 51
*Net Worth:* £855,666 *Total Assets:* £3,624,968
*Registered Office:* Westmorland Business Park, Kendal, Cumbria, LA9 6NP
*Activities:* Non-specialised wholesale trade
*Shareholders:* Keith Young; Janet Young
*Officers:* Christopher Nicholas Tague, Secretary; Christopher Nicholas Tague [1967] Finance Director; Janet Young [1952] Director/Paper Merchant; Keith Young [1948] Director/Paper Merchant

**Grosvenor PFI Holdings Limited**
*Incorporated:* 12 July 2007 *Employees:* 5
*Net Worth Deficit:* £23,487,572 *Total Assets:* £16,388,580
*Registered Office:* 4 Greengate, Cardale Park, Harrogate, N Yorks, HG3 1GY
*Activities:* Activities of head offices
*Parent:* Cardale PFI Investments Ltd
*Officers:* Alexander Toby Shedden Parry, Secretary; Robert John Austin [1964] Finance Director; Peter Paul Copley [1956] Director; Alexander Toby Shedden Parry [1976] Director/Company Secretary; Christopher Justin Taee [1968] Director; Nigel Duncan Taee [1961] Director

**The Ground Group Limited**
*Incorporated:* 8 February 2002 *Employees:* 7
*Net Worth:* £2,675,000 *Total Assets:* £18,911,886
*Registered Office:* Unit 12 Merchant Way, Doncaster, S Yorks, DN2 4QR
*Activities:* Buying and selling of own real estate
*Shareholders:* Nigel Stephen Griffiths; Darren Wayne Griffiths
*Officers:* Nigel Stephen Griffiths, Secretary/Director; Darren Wayne Griffiths [1967] Director; Nigel Stephen Griffiths [1966] Director

**Ground-Guards Ltd**
*Incorporated:* 10 December 2012
*Net Worth:* £331,448 *Total Assets:* £3,240,552
*Registered Office:* Rudgate, Walton, Leeds, LS23 7AU
*Activities:* Manufacture of other plastic products
*Parent:* The Greentek (Group) Ltd
*Officers:* Garth Anton Christie [1957] Director; David Hugh Michel [1953] Managing Director

**Groundwork North East**
*Incorporated:* 31 March 1992 *Employees:* 174
*Net Worth:* £4,880,364 *Total Assets:* £5,859,213
*Registered Office:* Grosvenor House, 29 Market Place, Bishop Auckland, Co Durham, DL14 7NP
*Activities:* Activities of business and employers membership organisations
*Officers:* Catherine Joanna Culverhouse, Secretary; Ian Brown [1952] Director/Consultant; Thomas Justice [1990] Director/Solicitor; David Martin [1957] Director/Treasurer; Diana Catherine Pearce [1952] Director; John Edward Pritchard [1967] Director of Strategic Planning; Professor Graham Street [1942] Director/Retired; Andrew Roy Thurston [1957] Director/Retired

**Group Auto Union UK and Ireland Limited**
*Incorporated:* 21 February 1979 *Employees:* 73
*Net Worth:* £13,476,045 *Total Assets:* £115,125,920
*Registered Office:* Roydsdale House, Roydsdale Way, Euroway Trading Estate, Bradford, W Yorks, BD4 6SE
*Activities:* Other business support service activities n.e.c.
*Parent:* Alliance Automotive UK Limited
*Officers:* John Frederick Coombes, Secretary; Alistair Stuart Brown [1955] Director [New Zealander]; John Frederick Coombes [1965] Director; Jean-Jacques Mathieu Lafont [1959] Director [Belgian]

**Group-14 Ltd**
*Incorporated:* 10 February 1950
*Net Worth:* £3,571,163 *Total Assets:* £3,694,205
*Registered Office:* Gledco Works, Bankfield Terrace, Leeds, LS4 2JR
*Activities:* Development of building projects
*Shareholders:* Richard Douglas Gledhill; Lorraine Anne Gledhill
*Officers:* Lorraine Anne Gledhill [1953] Director; Richard Douglas Gledhill [1953] Managing Director

**Groupe Samat UK Limited**
*Incorporated:* 20 February 1980 *Employees:* 69
*Net Worth:* £853,398 *Total Assets:* £4,352,138
*Registered Office:* Unit 2 Cliffe Park, Cliffe Park Way, Bruntcliffe Road, Morley, Leeds, LS27 0RY
*Activities:* Freight transport by road
*Officers:* Alphonse Laffont, Secretary [French]; Florence Dupasquier [1973] Director [French]; Alphonse Laffont [1961] Director [French]; Steven James Reid [1967] Director/Manager

**GSD Riverside Limited**
*Incorporated:* 9 January 2015 *Employees:* 2
*Net Worth Deficit:* £3,057,031 *Total Assets:* £4,642,542
*Registered Office:* 14 Southbrook Terrace, Bradford, W Yorks, BD7 1AD
*Activities:* Buying and selling of own real estate
*Major Shareholder:* Shabnam Latif
*Officers:* Shabnam Latif [1981] Director

**GSM Automotive Holdings Limited**
*Incorporated:* 4 March 2014 *Employees:* 249
*Net Worth:* £14,492,283 *Total Assets:* £19,381,160
*Registered Office:* Castlegarth Works, Masonic Lane, Thirsk, N Yorks, YO7 1PS
*Activities:* Non-trading company
*Shareholder:* Barry John Dodd
*Officers:* Robert Harvey Ashmeade, Secretary; Robert Harvey Ashmeade [1966] Director; Frances Dodd [1946] Director; Andrew Charles Farthing [1962] Director; Antony John Perry [1947] Director/Accountant

**GSM Group Holdco Limited**
*Incorporated:* 3 March 2014 *Employees:* 142
*Net Worth:* £11,253,683 *Total Assets:* £13,016,105
*Registered Office:* Castlegarth Works, Masonic Lane, Thirsk, N Yorks, YO7 1PS
*Activities:* Activities of head offices
*Shareholder:* Barry John Dodd
*Officers:* Gillian Gitsham, Secretary; Frances Dodd [1946] Director; Antony John Perry [1947] Director/Accountant

**GSP Distribution Limited**
*Incorporated:* 1 November 2011
*Net Worth:* £50,551 *Total Assets:* £3,963,639
*Registered Office:* Highfield Grange, Bubwith, Selby, N Yorks, YO8 6DP
*Activities:* Motion picture distribution activities
*Officers:* Tobias Angus Giles Mathews, Secretary; Alan Richard Latham [1960] Director/Film Producer

**Guardian Industries U.K. Limited**
*Incorporated:* 11 January 2001 *Employees:* 251
*Net Worth:* £113,111,000 *Total Assets:* £122,736,000
*Registered Office:* Tom Pudding Way, Goole, E Yorks, DN14 8GA
*Activities:* Manufacture of flat glass
*Parent:* Guardian Industries UK Holding Limited
*Officers:* Vincent Pringiers, Secretary; Gustav Boekhoudt [1963] Vice President & Managing Director [Dutch]; Gabor Harakaly [1968] Director/Chief Financial Officer [Hungarian]

**Guardian Industries UK Holding Limited**
*Incorporated:* 9 November 2012
*Net Worth:* £12,093,000 *Total Assets:* £83,650,000
*Registered Office:* Tom Pudding Way, Goole, E Yorks, DN14 8GA
*Activities:* Activities of production holding companies
*Officers:* Ana Martinez de Lecea Noain, Secretary; Gabor Harakaly [1968] Director/Chief Financial Officer [Hungarian]; Vincent Pringiers [1964] Director/Secretary [Belgian]

**Guyson (Holdings) Limited**
*Incorporated:* 2 August 2011 *Employees:* 176
*Net Worth:* £11,125,417 *Total Assets:* £17,016,700
*Registered Office:* Snaygill Industrial Estate, Keighley Road, Skipton, N Yorks, BD23 2QR
*Activities:* Activities of head offices
*Shareholders:* James Robert Farquhar Thomson; Jane Thomson
*Officers:* James Robert Farquhar Thomson [1960] Director

**Guyson International Limited**
*Incorporated:* 9 March 1981 *Employees:* 121
*Net Worth:* £8,303,473 *Total Assets:* £11,385,532
*Registered Office:* Snaygill Industrial Estate, Keighley Road, Skipton, N Yorks, BD23 2QR
*Activities:* Other manufacturing n.e.c.
*Shareholders:* James Robert Farquhar Thomson; Jane Thomson
*Officers:* James Robert Farquhar Thomson [1960] Director

**GVS Filter Technology UK Ltd**
*Incorporated:* 23 September 1991 *Employees:* 339
*Net Worth:* £4,227,440 *Total Assets:* £14,432,078
*Registered Office:* NFC House, Vickers Industrial Estate, Mellishaw Lane, Morecambe, Lancs, LA3 3EN
*Activities:* Other manufacturing n.e.c.
*Parent:* Fenchurch Environmental Group Ltd
*Officers:* Mario Saccone, Secretary; John William Anthony Pike [1962] Director/Operations Manager; Massimo Scagliarini [1965] Director [Italian]

**GW Hire Limited**
*Incorporated:* 24 August 2015 *Employees:* 3
*Net Worth:* £416,547 *Total Assets:* £4,636,280
*Registered Office:* 62-63 Westborough, Scarborough, N Yorks, YO11 1TS
*Activities:* Renting and leasing of construction and civil engineering machinery and equipment
*Major Shareholder:* John Edward Greenwood
*Officers:* John Edward Greenwood [1969] Director

**GWE Biogas Ltd**
*Incorporated:* 22 May 2008 *Employees:* 20
*Net Worth:* £6,565,800 *Total Assets:* £11,058,325
*Registered Office:* Sandhill, Garton Road, Kirkburn, Driffield, E Yorks, YO25 9DR
*Activities:* Production of electricity
*Parent:* GWE Biogas Holdings Limited
*Officers:* Thomas Alan Taylor Megginson, Secretary/Chartered Surveyor; Mathew James Girking [1969] Director/Farmer; Thomas Alan Taylor Megginson [1974] Director

**Gweco 510 Limited**
*Incorporated:* 7 June 2011
*Net Worth:* £851,646 *Total Assets:* £16,644,015
*Registered Office:* 242 Oxford Road, Gomersal, Cleckheaton, W Yorks, BD19 4RE
*Activities:* Buying and selling of own real estate
*Shareholders:* Dean Hoyle; Janet Elizabeth Hoyle
*Officers:* Dean Hoyle [1967] Director; Janet Elizabeth Hoyle [1967] Director

**Gweco 511 Limited**
*Incorporated:* 24 June 2011 *Employees:* 2
*Net Worth:* £11,646,610 *Total Assets:* £46,217,224
*Registered Office:* 242 Oxford Road, Gomersal, Cleckheaton, W Yorks, BD19 4RE
*Activities:* Activities of open-ended investment companies
*Shareholders:* Dean Hoyle; Janet Elizabeth Hoyle
*Officers:* Dean Hoyle [1967] Director; Janet Elizabeth Hoyle [1967] Director

**Gym Bidco Limited**
*Incorporated:* 29 April 2013
*Net Worth:* £65,176,000 *Total Assets:* £172,098,000
*Registered Office:* Town Centre House, Merrion Centre, Leeds, LS2 8LY
*Activities:* Fitness facilities
*Parent:* Gym Midco 2 Limited
*Officers:* Humphrey Michael Cobbold [1964] Director/Chief Executive Officer; Alexander Basil John Wood [1978] Director/Chief Financial Officer

**Gym Midco 2 Limited**
*Incorporated:* 1 May 2013
*Net Worth:* £135,944,992 *Total Assets:* £135,944,992
*Registered Office:* Town Centre House, Merrion Centre, Leeds, LS2 8LY
*Activities:* Fitness facilities
*Parent:* Gym Midco Limited
*Officers:* Humphrey Michael Cobbold [1964] Director/Chief Executive Officer; Alexander Basil John Wood [1978] Director/Chief Financial Officer

**Gym Midco Limited**
*Incorporated:* 29 April 2013
*Net Worth Deficit:* £1,362,000 *Total Assets:* £135,944,992
*Registered Office:* Town Centre House, Merrion Centre, Leeds, LS2 8LY
*Activities:* Fitness facilities
*Parent:* Gym Topco Limited
*Officers:* Humphrey Michael Cobbold [1964] Director/Chief Executive Officer; Alexander Basil John Wood [1978] Director/Chief Financial Officer

**Gym Topco Limited**
*Incorporated:* 29 April 2013 *Employees:* 763
*Net Worth Deficit:* £38,307,000 *Total Assets:* £374,880,992
*Registered Office:* Town Centre House, Merrion Centre, Leeds, LS2 8LY
*Activities:* Fitness facilities
*Parent:* Pinnacle Bidco PLC
*Officers:* Humphrey Michael Cobbold [1964] Director/Chief Executive Officer; Alexander Basil John Wood [1978] Director/Chief Financial Officer

**H & P Freightways Limited**
*Incorporated:* 4 January 1991 *Employees:* 151
*Net Worth:* £5,294,958 *Total Assets:* £12,119,847
*Registered Office:* 1201-1203 Hedon Road, Hull, HU9 5LY
*Activities:* Freight transport by road
*Parent:* H & P Holdings (2016) Limited
*Officers:* Alan Jeffrey Dixon [1954] Director/Transport Manager; John Denis Page [1944] Director; Simon David Page [1972] Director

**H B Tunnelling Limited**
*Incorporated:* 8 August 2009
*Net Worth:* £2,727,851 *Total Assets:* £3,771,455
*Registered Office:* Braemar, Scotland Lane, Horsforth, Leeds, LS18 5SF
*Activities:* Other specialised construction activities n.e.c.
*Shareholders:* Hugh Patrick Boyle; Sheila Boyle
*Officers:* Hugh Patrick Boyle [1967] Director/Manager

**H H Construction (Groundwork Contractors) Limited**
*Incorporated:* 24 April 2008 *Employees:* 16
*Net Worth:* £1,513,169 *Total Assets:* £4,830,673
*Registered Office:* 12 Methley Road, Castleford, W Yorks, WF10 1LX
*Activities:* Other specialised construction activities n.e.c.
*Major Shareholder:* John Anthony Handforth
*Officers:* John Anthony Handforth [1974] Director

**H. B. Projects Limited**
*Incorporated:* 18 December 1998 *Employees:* 204
*Net Worth:* £6,444,841 *Total Assets:* £16,024,207
*Registered Office:* Merrydale House, Roydsdale Way, Euroway Industrial Estate, Bradford, W Yorks, BD4 6SE
*Activities:* Construction of commercial buildings
*Parent:* H. B. Projects Group Limited
*Officers:* Carol Anne Watkinson, Secretary/Accountant; David Monro Baxter [1961] Director; Ed Beck [1970] Operations Director; Michael David Brace [1970] Regional Director; Beverley Peace [1973] Group Compliance Director; Carol Anne Watkinson [1953] Director/Accountant

**H.B. Food Services Ltd**
*Incorporated:* 14 February 2001
*Net Worth:* £1,210,836 *Total Assets:* £5,146,580
*Registered Office:* Vulcun Works, Vulcan Road, Dewsbury, W Yorks, WF13 2NA
*Activities:* Non-specialised wholesale of food, beverages and tobacco
*Shareholder:* Ilyas Bhamji
*Officers:* Abdul Bhamji, Secretary; Abdul Bhamji [1954] Director/Sales; Hassan Bhamji [1977] Director/Sales Representative; Ilyas Bhamji [1983] Director

**H.E.C. Contracting Limited**
*Incorporated:* 8 November 1995 *Employees:* 62
*Net Worth Deficit:* £147,418 *Total Assets:* £4,495,920
*Registered Office:* Electric House, Moderna Way, Mytholmroyd, Hebden Bridge, W Yorks, HX7 5PZ
*Activities:* Electrical installation
*Major Shareholder:* Christopher Horsfall
*Officers:* David Booth [1971] Director; Christopher Horsfall [1961] Director

**H.H Services Limited**
*Incorporated:* 16 July 1982 *Employees:* 6
*Net Worth:* £8,636,325 *Total Assets:* £9,689,649
*Registered Office:* 100 High Ash Drive, Alwoodley, Leeds, LS17 8RE
*Activities:* Other letting and operating of own or leased real estate
*Officers:* Linda Heinz, Secretary/Director; Linda Heinz [1953] Director; Stephen Karl Heinz [1951] Director/Property Developer; Ursula Hobkirk [1969] Director

**H.M. Pigs Limited**
*Incorporated:* 9 April 1996 *Employees:* 10
*Net Worth:* £13,915,707 *Total Assets:* £18,148,660
*Registered Office:* Pond Dale Farm, Gilling West, Richmond, N Yorks, DL10 5LB
*Activities:* Raising of swine and pigs
*Major Shareholder:* Timothy Peter Westgarth
*Officers:* Paul Anthony Hall Westgarth, Secretary; Paul Anthony Hall Westgarth [1967] Director/Manager; Timothy Peter Westgarth [1973] Director/Manager

**H.P.A.S. Limited**
*Incorporated:* 22 December 1992 *Employees:* 705
*Net Worth:* £29,858,000 *Total Assets:* £44,841,000
*Registered Office:* Style House, 14 Eldon Place, Bradford, BD1 3AZ
*Activities:* Other manufacturing n.e.c.
*Parent:* Style Group UK Limited
*Officers:* Richard Kenneth Short, Secretary; Mike Gallacher [1966] Director; Rob James Neale [1978] Director; Giles Richell [1970] Director

**H.S.G. (Packing Cases) Limited**
*Incorporated:* 29 March 1978
*Net Worth:* £2,757,378 *Total Assets:* £4,953,959
*Registered Office:* Long Row, New Works Road, Low Moor, Bradford, BD12 0RT
*Activities:* Other manufacturing n.e.c.
*Officers:* Heather Lesley Ginesi, Secretary; Colin Martin Cutts [1970] Director; Benjamin Neil Ginesi [1976] Director/Computer Advisor; Harold Samuel Ginesi [1948] Director; Heather Lesley Ginesi [1951] Director/Housewife; Simon Andrew Ginesi [1979] Director

**Haas Group International SCM Limited**
*Incorporated:* 21 July 1998 *Employees:* 166
*Net Worth:* £9,021,000 *Total Assets:* £14,203,000
*Registered Office:* Lawrence House, Riverside Drive, Cleckheaton, W Yorks, BD19 4DH
*Activities:* Non-specialised wholesale trade
*Parent:* Wesco Aircraft International Holdings Limited
*Officers:* John Generald Holland, Secretary; John Generald Holland [1968] Director/Senior Vice President & General Counsel [American]; Alexander Murray [1969] Director/Executive VP and COO; Alun Phennah [1968] Supply Chain Director; Thomas Renehan [1962] Director/Executive Officer [American]

**Haas TCM Group of The UK Limited**
*Incorporated:* 14 December 2006
*Net Worth:* £10,365,000 *Total Assets:* £24,733,000
*Registered Office:* Lawrence House, Riverside Drive, Cleckheaton, W Yorks, BD19 4DH
*Activities:* Agents involved in the sale of fuels, ores, metals and industrial chemicals
*Parent:* Haas Group International, LLC
*Officers:* John Generald Holland, Secretary; John Generald Holland [1968] Director/Senior Vice President & General Counsel [American]; Alexander Murray [1969] Director/Executive VP and COO; Alun Phennah [1968] Supply Chain Director; Thomas Renehan [1962] Director/Executive Officer [American]

**Habasit (UK) Limited**
*Incorporated:* 11 February 1999 *Employees:* 141
*Net Worth:* £24,358,000 *Total Assets:* £27,454,000
*Registered Office:* Habegger House, Gannex Park, Dewsbury Road, Elland, W Yorks, HX5 9AF
*Activities:* Other manufacturing n.e.c.
*Parent:* Habasit International AG
*Officers:* Mark Visman, Secretary; Martinus Willebrordus Antonie Maria Aarts [1953] Director [Dutch]; Thomas Carl Maria Gutwald [1962] Director [German]; Stewart Douglas Murdoch [1970] Director; Ivan Julien Luc Salamin [1969] Director [Swiss]; Andrea Volpi [1961] Director [Italian]

**Habico Limited**
*Incorporated:* 17 February 1993
*Net Worth:* £2,867,899 *Total Assets:* £3,321,312
*Registered Office:* Tong Road Industrial Estate, Amberley Road, Leeds, LS12 4BD
*Activities:* Non-specialised wholesale trade
*Major Shareholder:* Andrew Stafford William Boxall
*Officers:* Rachel Victoria Boxall, Secretary; Rachel Victoria Boxall [1973] Director; Dr Sarah Jane Boxall [1972] Director/Patent Attorney; Georgina Marie Matthias [1953] Director/Haberdasher

**HACS Construction Limited**
*Incorporated:* 20 August 1992 *Employees:* 81
*Net Worth:* £473,935 *Total Assets:* £3,888,216
*Registered Office:* Nidderdale House, Station Yard, Ripley, Harrogate, N Yorks, HG3 3BA
*Activities:* Construction of commercial buildings
*Parent:* Hacs Holdings Limited
*Officers:* Adam Jocelyn Houssemayne Du Boulay, Secretary/Director; Edward John Ashworth [1970] Director; Adam Jocelyn Houssemayne Du Boulay [1968] Director; Mark Richard Smith [1959] Managing Director

**Hacs Holdings Limited**
*Incorporated:* 7 April 2005 *Employees:* 86
*Net Worth:* £2,004,242 *Total Assets:* £8,992,585
*Registered Office:* Nidderdale House, Station Yard, Ripley, Harrogate, N Yorks, HG3 3BA
*Activities:* Other letting and operating of own or leased real estate
*Shareholders:* Elizabeth Anne Smith; Mark Richard Smith; Elizabeth Anne Smith; Mark Richard Smith
*Officers:* Elizabeth Anne Smith, Secretary; Mark Richard Smith [1959] Managing Director

**Haddow Group Limited**
*Incorporated:* 15 May 1987 *Employees:* 81
*Previous:* Haddow Group PLC
*Net Worth:* £5,440,764 *Total Assets:* £7,676,344
*Registered Office:* Listers Mill, Heaton Road, Bradford, W Yorks, BD9 4SH
*Activities:* Wholesale of textiles
*Major Shareholder:* Alan Frank Haddow
*Officers:* Nigel John Gould, Secretary; Alan Frank Haddow [1941] Director; Tristan Haigh James Haddow [1978] Director

**Hadrian (Residential) Limited**
*Incorporated:* 8 May 2014
*Net Worth Deficit:* £3,383,712 *Total Assets:* £10,889,535
*Registered Office:* c/o White Rose Accountants, 15a Hallgate, Doncaster, S Yorks, DN1 3NA
*Activities:* Buying and selling of own real estate
*Officers:* Michael Patrick Murray [1969] Director/Property Developer; Glyn Dale Smith [1964] Director/Property Developer

**Hadrian Bidco 2 Limited**
*Incorporated:* 20 April 2007
*Net Worth:* £3,105,000 *Total Assets:* £354,865,984
*Registered Office:* The Inspire, Hornbeam Square West, Harrogate, N Yorks, HG2 8PA
*Activities:* Activities of head offices
*Parent:* Principal Hotels Topco 3 Limited
*Officers:* James Alexander Burrell [1974] Director/Accountant; Generaldine Josephine Gallagher [1965] Finance Director [Irish]; Gail Susan Hunter [1963] Human Resources Director; Anthony Gerrard Troy [1962] Director [Irish]

**Hadrian Bidco Limited**
*Incorporated:* 2 April 2007 *Employees:* 4
*Net Worth:* £16,000 *Total Assets:* £348,416,992
*Registered Office:* The Inspire, Hornbeam Square West, Harrogate, N Yorks, HG2 8PA
*Activities:* Activities of head offices
*Parent:* Venice Hadrian 4 Limited
*Officers:* James Alexander Burrell [1974] Director/Accountant; Generaldine Josephine Gallagher [1965] Finance Director [Irish]; Gail Susan Hunter [1963] Human Resources Director; Anthony Gerrard Troy [1962] Director [Irish]

**J.F. and E. Hadwin Limited**
*Incorporated:* 7 November 1986 *Employees:* 168
*Net Worth:* £11,752,237 *Total Assets:* £35,101,696
*Registered Office:* The Garage, Torver, Coniston, Cumbria, LA21 8BJ
*Activities:* Sale of new cars and light motor vehicles
*Officers:* Anne Doris Hadwin, Secretary; Anne Doris Hadwin [1941] Director; Eric Hadwin [1939] Director/Garage Proprietor; Jason Dean Hadwin [1966] Director

**Rolf C. Hagen (U.K.) Limited**
*Incorporated:* 7 October 1982 *Employees:* 72
*Net Worth:* £6,121,583 *Total Assets:* £11,429,122
*Registered Office:* Rolf C Hagen (UK) Ltd, California Drive, Whitwood Industrial Estate, Castleford, W Yorks, WF10 5QH
*Activities:* Non-specialised wholesale trade
*Shareholders:* Rolf Horst Hagen; Tom Hagen
*Officers:* Tom Hagen, Secretary; Adrian Neil Burgess [1966] Director; Rolf Horst Hagen [1967] Director [Canadian]; Tom Hagen [1961] Director [Canadian]; Philip James Parkinson [1970] Finance Director

**Hague Computer Supplies Limited**
*Incorporated:* 9 June 1980 *Employees:* 49
*Net Worth:* £9,085,318 *Total Assets:* £14,411,105
*Registered Office:* Thomas House, Don Pedro Avenue, Normanton Industrial Estate, Normanton, W Yorks, WF6 1TD
*Activities:* Other retail sale not in stores, stalls or markets
*Officers:* Jane Alison Wain, Secretary; John Sykes [1956] Director; Graham Thomas Wain [1953] Managing Director; Jane Alison Wain [1955] Director

**The Hain Daniels Group Limited**
*Incorporated:* 26 May 2006
*Previous:* Hain Holdings UK Limited
*Net Worth:* £259,484,416 *Total Assets:* £455,222,880
*Registered Office:* 2100 Century Way, Thorpe Park Business Park, Leeds, LS15 8ZB
*Activities:* Activities of head offices
*Parent:* Hain Celestial Jersey Limited
*Officers:* Nicholas Keen, Secretary; Denise Menikheim Faltischek [1973] Director/Attorney [American]; James Michael Langrock [1965] Director [American]; Mark Lawrence Schiller [1961] Director/CEO Hain Celestial [American]; Robin James Skidmore [1968] Director

**Hain Frozen Foods UK Limited**
*Incorporated:* 30 May 2006 *Employees:* 466
*Net Worth:* £414,062,016 *Total Assets:* £518,023,008
*Registered Office:* 2100 Century Way, Thorpe Park Business Park, Leeds, LS15 8ZB
*Activities:* Manufacture of other food products n.e.c.
*Parent:* The Hain Daniels Group Limited
*Officers:* Nicholas Keen, Secretary; Denise Menikheim Faltischek [1973] Director/Attorney [American]; James Michael Langrock [1965] Director [American]; Mark Lawrence Schiller [1961] Director [American]; Robin James Skidmore [1968] Director

**A.W.Hainsworth & Sons Limited**
*Incorporated:* 27 March 1922 *Employees:* 184
*Net Worth:* £8,095,944 *Total Assets:* £11,997,163
*Registered Office:* Spring Valley Mills, Stanningley, Pudsey, W Yorks, LS28 6DW
*Activities:* Preparation and spinning of textile fibres
*Officers:* Adam Wilson Hainsworth [1961] Director; Paul Reuben Hainsworth [1966] Director/Business Development; Thomas Christian Hainsworth [1967] Director

**A.W. Hainsworth Holdings Limited**
*Incorporated:* 2 April 2008 *Employees:* 184
*Net Worth:* £8,099,513 *Total Assets:* £11,997,163
*Registered Office:* Spring Valley Mills, Spring Valley, Stanningley, Pudsey, W Yorks, LS28 6DW
*Activities:* Manufacture of other technical and industrial textiles
*Shareholder:* Thomas Christian Hainsworth
*Officers:* Adam Wilson Hainsworth [1961] Director; Paul Reuben Hainsworth [1966] Director/Business Developer; Thomas Christian Hainsworth [1967] Director; Rachel Clare Taylor [1964] Director

**Hainsworth Sterne & Co. Limited**
*Incorporated:* 25 February 1972 *Employees:* 3
*Net Worth:* £4,157,491 *Total Assets:* £4,704,600
*Registered Office:* 197 High Street, Boston Spa, Wetherby, W Yorks, LS23 6AA
*Activities:* Other letting and operating of own or leased real estate
*Major Shareholder:* Philippa Louise Sterne
*Officers:* Sally Patricia Sterne, Secretary; Philippa Louise Sterne [1966] Director/Artist

**Hair Burst Limited**
*Incorporated:* 17 February 2014
*Net Worth:* £4,036,518 *Total Assets:* £4,469,557
*Registered Office:* Trident House, Shadwell Lane, Leeds, LS17 6DR
*Activities:* Other human health activities
*Officers:* Matthew Cragg [1989] Director/Self Employed; Henry Richard Gwilliam [1988] Director; James Peter Hill [1989] Managing Director

**Hair Tools Limited**
*Incorporated:* 19 October 1995 *Employees:* 18
*Net Worth:* £8,994,562 *Total Assets:* £11,294,763
*Registered Office:* Head Jog House, Netherfield Road, Ravensthorpe, Dewsbury, W Yorks, WF13 3JY
*Activities:* Non-specialised wholesale trade
*Shareholders:* Alison Margaret Brunton; David Neil Brunton
*Officers:* Alison Margaret Brunton, Secretary/Clerk; Alison Margaret Brunton [1962] Director/Clerk; David Brunton [1957] Director/General Manager

**Halbert Limited**
*Incorporated:* 23 May 2016
*Net Worth:* £3,548,386 *Total Assets:* £6,760,236
*Registered Office:* 30 Headingley Lane, Leeds, LS6 2AS
*Activities:* Buying and selling of own real estate
*Major Shareholder:* Simon Jacob Moran
*Officers:* Karen Janine Moran [1969] Director; Simon Jacob Moran [1963] Director

**Halifax Financial Services (Holdings) Limited**
*Incorporated:* 9 March 1989
*Net Worth:* £210,924,000 *Total Assets:* £210,926,000
*Registered Office:* Trinity Road, Halifax, W Yorks, HX1 2RG
*Activities:* Activities of head offices
*Parent:* HBOS Financial Services Limited
*Officers:* Christina Ann Hankin, Secretary; Sean William Lowther [1960] Director; Gregory Miles Norton [1968] Director; Ian Henry Price [1965] Director

**Halifax General Insurance Services Limited**
*Incorporated:* 19 February 1993
*Net Worth:* £41,438,000 *Total Assets:* £260,447,008
*Registered Office:* Trinity Road, Halifax, W Yorks, HX1 2RG
*Activities:* Financial intermediation not elsewhere classified
*Parent:* Lloyds Bank General Insurance Holdings Limited
*Officers:* Natalie Clarice Gracey, Secretary; James Christopher Steuart Hillman [1969] Director; Jacqueline Leiper [1972] Director; Craig James Thornton [1972] Director

**Halifax Investment Services Limited**
*Incorporated:* 18 September 1991
*Net Worth:* £3,388,000 *Total Assets:* £3,388,000
*Registered Office:* Trinity Road, Halifax, W Yorks, HX1 2RG
*Activities:* Other business support service activities n.e.c.
*Parent:* Halifax Financial Services (Holdings) Limited
*Officers:* Christina Ann Hankin, Secretary; Sean William Lowther [1960] Director; Ian Henry Price [1965] Director

**Halifax Loans Limited**
*Incorporated:* 2 November 1988
*Net Worth:* £16,752,000 *Total Assets:* £22,287,000
*Registered Office:* Trinity Road, Halifax, W Yorks, HX1 2RG
*Activities:* Other business support service activities n.e.c.
*Parent:* Bank of Scotland PLC
*Officers:* David Dermot Hennessey, Secretary; Ajey Rajan Agarwal [1975] Director; Jasjyot Singh [1973] Director

**Halifax Rack & Screw Cutting Co. Limited**
*Incorporated:* 10 August 2004 *Employees:* 31
*Net Worth:* £2,984,514 *Total Assets:* £5,447,958
*Registered Office:* Coronation Works, Armytage Road, Brighouse, W Yorks, HD6 1QA
*Activities:* Other manufacturing n.e.c.
*Shareholders:* Colin Richard Jones; Mark Trevor Robinson
*Officers:* Anne Elizabeth Jones [1955] Director; Colin Richard Jones [1957] Finance Director; Adrian Muggleton [1961] Director/Chairman; Alison Jane Robinson [1963] Director; Mark Trevor Robinson [1959] Operations Director

**Halifax Share Dealing Limited**
*Incorporated:* 8 May 1996
*Net Worth:* £57,736,000 *Total Assets:* £98,558,000
*Registered Office:* Trinity Road, Halifax, W Yorks, HX1 2RG
*Activities:* Financial intermediation not elsewhere classified
*Parent:* HBOS PLC
*Officers:* Paul Gittins, Secretary; Carl George Membery [1970] Director; John Patrick O'Dwyer [1967] Director; Manuel Angel Pardavila Gonzalez [1970] Director [Spanish]; Joel Charles Ripley [1974] Director; Karlene Amanda White [1972] Director

**Hall & Associates (Marketing) Ltd**
*Incorporated:* 31 March 1988 *Employees:* 31
*Net Worth:* £3,026,231 *Total Assets:* £4,502,436
*Registered Office:* 2 Tudor Court, York Business Park, York, YO26 6RS
*Activities:* Other manufacturing n.e.c.
*Major Shareholder:* Angela Hall
*Officers:* Paul Lloyd Grewer, Secretary; Paul Lloyd Grewer [1968] Finance Director; Angela Hall [1953] Director/Marketing Consultant; Martin Allen Jenkins [1956] Director/Electrical Power Engineer; Nicola Elizabeth McQuillan [1988] Product Marketing Director

**Kenneth Hall (Builder) Limited**
*Incorporated:* 29 January 1963 *Employees:* 6
*Net Worth:* £4,807,999 *Total Assets:* £4,994,060
*Registered Office:* Stagwood Hill Farm, Coldhill Lane, New Mill, Holmfirth, W Yorks, HD9 7JX
*Activities:* Development of building projects
*Shareholders:* Kenneth Hall; Kenneth Scott Hall; Marcus William Hall
*Officers:* Katie Johnson, Secretary; Audrey Hall [1938] Director; Kenneth Scott Hall [1974] Director; Kenneth Hall [1933] Director; Marcus William Hall [1970] Director

**Hall Construction Services Limited**
*Incorporated:* 21 November 1986 *Employees:* 129
*Net Worth:* £46,951,448 *Total Assets:* £55,951,588
*Registered Office:* Stotforth Hill House, Windlestone, Rushyford, Co Durham, DL17 0NF
*Activities:* Open cast coal working
*Shareholders:* Neville John Hall; Stephen Hall
*Officers:* Neville John Hall [1956] Director/Civil Engineer; Stephen Hall [1954] Director/Civil Engineer; Garry Hutchinson [1955] Director

**Hall Cross Academy Trust**
*Incorporated:* 9 January 2012 *Employees:* 296
*Net Worth:* £11,813,000 *Total Assets:* £16,732,000
*Registered Office:* Hall Cross Academy, Thorne Road, Doncaster, S Yorks, DN1 2HY
*Activities:* General secondary education
*Officers:* Kimberley Ann Sritharan, Secretary; Tausif Abdul [1979] Director/Regional Manager; David Charles Cox [1966] Director/Head of Security; Pippa Dodgshon [1964] Director/Headteacher; Tracy Drabble [1965] Director/Public Sector for The Care Quality Commission; Josephine Foxton [1948] Director/Retired; Thomas Edward Hince [1979] Director/Commercial Manager; Antony King [1973] Director/Year Manager; Beverley John Marshall [1951] Director/Retired; Shaun Masterman [1965] Director/Carer; Lee Parish [1974] Director/Manager; Tony Thorpe [1949] Director/Retired; Andrew Townsend [1978] Director/Certified Chartered Accountant; Ian Trevillion [1975] Director/Primary Teacher; David Antony Westwood [1967] Director/Police Officer; Roger Menai Williams [1945] Director/Solicitor

**Hallborough Properties Limited**
*Incorporated:* 19 February 1985 *Employees:* 4
*Net Worth:* £22,440,108 *Total Assets:* £31,175,850
*Registered Office:* Ilkley Hall, Ilkley Hall Park, Ilkley, W Yorks, LS29 9LD
*Activities:* Other letting and operating of own or leased real estate
*Shareholders:* Nicholas Mark Ogden; Sally Ann Fuller; Amanda Jane Dunn
*Officers:* Sally Ann Fuller, Secretary; Amanda Jane Dunn [1964] Director; Sally Anne Fuller [1969] Director; Joseph Ogden [1937] Director; Nicholas Mark Ogden [1963] Director

**Hallite Seals International Limited**
*Incorporated:* 8 February 1936 *Employees:* 203
*Net Worth:* £2,143,000 *Total Assets:* £9,676,000
*Registered Office:* Hesslewood Country Office Park, Ferriby Road, Hessle, E Yorks, HU13 0PW
*Activities:* Manufacture of plastics in primary forms
*Parent:* Fenner Group Holdings Limited
*Officers:* Debra Bradbury, Secretary; Andrew Maitland Caley [1962] Director/Group Taxation & Treasury; John Mark Curtis [1969] Finance Director; Richard William Hewlett [1960] Director/Manager; Nicholas David Hurt [1970] Director; William John Pratt [1963] Managing Director; Christopher Nigel Wood [1966] Director

**Hallmark Cards (Holdings) Limited**
*Incorporated:* 8 January 1987 *Employees:* 1,310
*Net Worth:* £41,307,000 *Total Assets:* £87,926,000
*Registered Office:* Hallmark Cards (Holdings) Limited, Dawson Lane, Bradford, W Yorks, BD4 6HN
*Activities:* Activities of head offices
*Parent:* HC Crown LLC
*Officers:* Phillipa Jane Dixson, Secretary; Amanda Louise Del Prete [1970] Director [Australian]; Donald Joyce Hall Jr [1955] Director/Business Executive [American]; James Cornelius Shay [1963] Director [American]; Ricky Roop Singh [1977] Director

**Hallmark Cards PLC**
*Incorporated:* 30 July 1997 *Employees:* 1,310
*Net Worth:* £74,777,000 *Total Assets:* £533,958,016
*Registered Office:* Hallmark Cards PLC, Dawson Lane, Bradford, W Yorks, BD4 6HN
*Activities:* Other publishing activities
*Parent:* Hallmark Cards UK
*Officers:* Phillipa Jane Dixson, Secretary; Matthew James Critchlow [1975] Commercial Director; Amanda Louise Del Prete [1970] Director [Australian]; Donald Joyce Hall Jr [1955] Director/Business Executive [American]; Cynthia Lynne Mahoney [1964] Director [American]; James Cornelius Shay [1963] Director [American]; Ricky Roop Singh [1977] Director

**Hallmark Cards Property Company Limited**
*Incorporated:* 22 December 1980
*Net Worth:* £1,967,000 *Total Assets:* £9,833,000
*Registered Office:* Hallmark Cards Property Company Limited, Dawson Lane, Bradford, W Yorks, BD4 6HN
*Activities:* Other letting and operating of own or leased real estate
*Parent:* Hallmark Cards (Holdings) Limited
*Officers:* Phillipa Jane Dixson, Secretary; Amanda Louise Del Prete [1970] Director [Australian]; Ricky Roop Singh [1977] Director

**Hallmark Group Products Limited**
*Incorporated:* 17 January 2001 *Employees:* 19
*Net Worth:* £2,066,083 *Total Assets:* £5,380,724
*Registered Office:* Valletta House, Valletta Street, Hedon Road, Hull, HU9 5NP
*Activities:* Other manufacturing n.e.c.
*Parent:* Hallmark Group Holdings Limited
*Officers:* Scott Chapman [1973] Operations/IT Director; Virginija Petraityte [1984] Director [Lithuanian]; Lorraine Snell [1968] Group Administration Director; Baden Lloyd Sonley [1963] Director; Paul James Spencer [1974] Sales Director

**Hallmark Panels Limited**
*Incorporated:* 22 February 1995 *Employees:* 72
*Net Worth:* £2,386,311 *Total Assets:* £5,352,781
*Registered Office:* Valletta House, Valletta Street, Hedon Road, Hull, HU9 5NP
*Activities:* Other manufacturing n.e.c.
*Parent:* Hallmark Group Products Limited
*Officers:* Scott Chapman [1973] Operations/IT Director; Virginija Petraityte [1984] Director [Lithuanian]; Lorraine Snell [1968] Operations Director; Baden Lloyd Sonley [1963] Director; Paul James Spencer [1974] Sales Director

**Hallriver Holdings Limited**
*Incorporated:* 9 April 2015 *Employees:* 686
*Net Worth:* £10,053,472 *Total Assets:* £25,253,352
*Registered Office:* The Old Maltings, Leeds Road, Tadcaster, N Yorks, LS24 9HB
*Activities:* Non-trading company
*Major Shareholder:* Nicholas Martin Bryan
*Officers:* Nicholas Martin Bryan [1953] Director

**Hambleton Holdings Limited**
*Incorporated:* 27 November 1973 *Employees:* 7
*Net Worth:* £26,484,036 *Total Assets:* £35,550,408
*Registered Office:* Dalton Airfield, Dalton, Thirsk, N Yorks, YO7 3JN
*Activities:* Wholesale of metals and metal ores
*Officers:* Jeanne Martine Elizabeth Bianco, Secretary; Jeanne Martine Elizabeth Bianco [1971] Director; Jennifer Bianco [1984] Director; Matthew Giovanni Bianco [1986] Director/Programmer; Michele Christine Bianco [1973] Director; Robert Jean Francois Bianco [1933] Director; Susan Elizabeth Bianco [1950] Director; Roy Wyatt Fishwick [1968] Director

**Hambleton Steel Group Ltd**
*Incorporated:* 23 February 2017 *Employees:* 78
*Net Worth:* £3,379,898 *Total Assets:* £9,198,661
*Registered Office:* Hambleton Steel, Gatherley Road, Brompton on Swale, N Yorks, DL10 7JH
*Activities:* Construction of commercial buildings
*Shareholders:* James William Grice; Patricia Grice
*Officers:* Patricia Grice, Secretary; James William Grice [1953] Director; Patricia Grice [1955] Director; Martin Hague Jobbings [1951] Director; Colin Richard Watson [1960] Director

**Hambleton Steel Limited**
*Incorporated:* 27 September 1995 *Employees:* 78
*Net Worth:* £3,378,987 *Total Assets:* £7,999,759
*Registered Office:* Gatherley Road, Brompton on Swale, Richmond, N Yorks, DL10 7JH
*Activities:* Construction of commercial buildings
*Shareholders:* James William Grice; Patricia Grice
*Officers:* Patricia Grice, Secretary/Housewife; James William Grice [1953] Director/Manager; Patricia Grice [1955] Director/Housewife; Martin Hague Jobbings [1951] Director/Solicitor; Colin Richard Watson [1960] Director/Steel Fabricator

**Hamilton (Building Contractors) Ltd.**
*Incorporated:* 20 December 1996 *Employees:* 40
*Net Worth:* £1,990,976 *Total Assets:* £4,944,660
*Registered Office:* Unit 56 Challenge Way, Bradford, W Yorks, BD4 8NW
*Activities:* Other specialised construction activities n.e.c.
*Shareholders:* Robert Trevor Storton; Martin Thomas Gibbins
*Officers:* Robert Trevor Storton, Secretary/Surveyor; Martin Thomas Gibbins [1960] Director/Builder; Robert Trevor Storton [1973] Director/Surveyor

**Hamsard 3225 Limited**
*Incorporated:* 18 August 2010 *Employees:* 29
*Net Worth:* £1,298,844 *Total Assets:* £10,140,569
*Registered Office:* Unit 4 Meadowcourt, Millshaw, Leeds, LS11 8LZ
*Activities:* Activities of financial services holding companies
*Officers:* Paul John Castle [1977] Director; Edward Klempka [1951] Director/Accountant; Russell Bradley Mason [1964] Director; Michael David Michaelson [1959] Director; Philip Neville Wilabraham [1958] Director; Dominic Matthew Wilbraham [1987] Director

**Hamsard 3465 Limited**
*Incorporated:* 31 July 2017 *Employees:* 1
*Net Worth Deficit:* £1,179,272 *Total Assets:* £44,824,152
*Registered Office:* Unit 10 Cross Hills Business Park, Cross Hills, Keighley, W Yorks, BD20 7BW
*Activities:* Dormant company
*Parent:* Hamsard 3466 Limited
*Officers:* Marcus Conrad Green, Secretary; James Peter Buckley [1962] Director; Timothy Craig Frear [1970] Director; Marcus Conrad Green [1971] Director; James David Marshall [1987] Director/Investment Manager; Matthew James Marshall [1967] Director; Kevin Alan Still [1970] Director/Chartered Engineer

**Hamsard 3466 Limited**
*Incorporated:* 31 July 2017 *Employees:* 156
*Net Worth Deficit:* £1,168,164 *Total Assets:* £50,445,044
*Registered Office:* Unit 10 Cross Hills Business Park, Cross Hills, Keighley, W Yorks, BD20 7BW
*Activities:* Dormant company
*Shareholders:* Frear Investments Limited; Northedge Capital Nominee Limited
*Officers:* Marcus Conrad Green, Secretary; James Peter Buckley [1962] Director; Timothy Craig Frear [1970] Director; Marcus Conrad Green [1971] Director; James David Marshall [1987] Director/Investment Manager; Matthew James Marshall [1967] Director; Kevin Alan Still [1970] Director/Chartered Engineer

**Hamsard Five Thousand and Eighteen Limited**
*Incorporated:* 9 March 1999 *Employees:* 1
*Net Worth:* £3,762,734 *Total Assets:* £3,784,978
*Registered Office:* Low Moor Hall, Lilly Gate Lane, Brearton, Harrogate, N Yorks, HG3 3BX
*Activities:* Activities of sport clubs
*Shareholders:* Carol Wheeler; Michael John Wheeler
*Officers:* Michael John Wheeler, Secretary; Michael John Wheeler [1955] Director

**Hanbeck Properties Limited**
*Incorporated:* 3 March 2016
*Net Worth:* £322,192 *Total Assets:* £3,769,748
*Registered Office:* 18 Main Street, Ryther, Tadcaster, N Yorks, LS24 9EE
*Activities:* Other letting and operating of own or leased real estate
*Shareholders:* David Smith; Joanne Smith
*Officers:* David Smith [1955] Director/Retired; Joanne Smith [1963] Director/Retired

**E Handcock Limited**
*Incorporated:* 28 January 2002 *Employees:* 25
*Net Worth:* £4,349,510 *Total Assets:* £4,719,172
*Registered Office:* 37 Augusta Street, Grimsby, N E Lincs, DN34 4TH
*Activities:* Freight transport by road
*Major Shareholder:* John Robert Handcock
*Officers:* John Robert Handcock, Secretary; Brian William Handcock [1967] Director/Sustainability Manager; John Robert Handcock [1966] Director/Company Secretary

**Handler Hire Ltd**
*Incorporated:* 20 December 2004 *Employees:* 3
*Previous:* Greenwood Hire Limited
*Net Worth:* £991,912 *Total Assets:* £4,274,199
*Registered Office:* 62-63 Westborough, Scarborough, N Yorks, YO11 1TS
*Activities:* Other specialised construction activities n.e.c.
*Shareholders:* John Edward Greenwood; John Michael Greenwood
*Officers:* Charlotte Elizabeth Bradley, Secretary; John Edward Greenwood [1969] Director

**Hannibal Holdings Limited**
*Incorporated:* 20 August 2015 *Employees:* 1
*Net Worth:* £6,625,000 *Total Assets:* £6,720,000
*Registered Office:* Dakin-Flathers Ltd, Boothroyds Way, Featherstone, Pontefract, W Yorks, WF7 6RA
*Activities:* Activities of head offices
*Major Shareholder:* Oliver Graham Garside
*Officers:* Oliver Graham Garside [1966] Director

**Hanover Developments (Wakefield) Limited**
*Incorporated:* 9 November 1993 *Employees:* 3
*Net Worth:* £1,920,408 *Total Assets:* £5,716,483
*Registered Office:* Unit 11 Mariner Court, Durkar, Wakefield, W Yorks, WF4 3FL
*Activities:* Other building completion and finishing
*Shareholders:* David Lyndon Barraclough; David Henry Rock
*Officers:* David Henry Rock, Secretary/Chartered Surveyor; David Lyndon Barraclough [1950] Director; David Henry Rock [1959] Director/Chartered Surveyor

**Hanover Properties Limited**
*Incorporated:* 12 March 2012
*Net Worth:* £25,561 *Total Assets:* £3,454,798
*Registered Office:* Unit 2 Hanover Street, Keighley, W Yorks, BD21 3QJ
*Activities:* Other letting and operating of own or leased real estate
*Officers:* Asif Karim [1977] Director; Batash Karim [1978] Director

**Karl Hanover Properties Limited**
*Incorporated:* 17 February 2016 *Employees:* 2
*Net Worth:* £5,720,975 *Total Assets:* £11,285,597
*Registered Office:* Knabbs Farm, Skipton Road, Harrogate, N Yorks, HG3 2LT
*Activities:* Other letting and operating of own or leased real estate
*Shareholders:* Karl Brian Hanover; Lucy April Hanover
*Officers:* Karl Brian Hanover [1972] Director; Lucy April Hanover [1980] Director

**Hanson Family Holdings Limited**
*Incorporated:* 16 February 1965 *Employees:* 70
*Net Worth:* £1,730,916 *Total Assets:* £4,950,831
*Registered Office:* 7 Ashgrove Road, Huddersfield, W Yorks, HD2 1FQ
*Activities:* Other business support service activities n.e.c.
*Officers:* Fiona Heather Douglas-Wilkinson, Secretary; The Honourable Robert William Hanson [1960] Director; Evan Richard Charles Lewis [1944] Director

**Hanson Logistics Limited**
*Incorporated:* 18 March 1965 *Employees:* 70
*Net Worth:* £2,069,610 *Total Assets:* £4,869,916
*Registered Office:* 7 Ashgrove Road, Huddersfield, W Yorks, HD2 1FQ
*Activities:* Other transportation support activities
*Officers:* Fiona Heather Douglas-Wilkinson, Secretary; The Honourable Robert William Hanson [1960] Director; William Gilfillan Lamarque [1954] Director; Evan Richard Charles Lewis [1944] Director; Paul Ian Pheasey [1971] Managing Director

**Hanson Plywood (Holdings) Ltd**
*Incorporated:* 22 June 1998 *Employees:* 59
*Net Worth:* £9,950,107 *Total Assets:* £17,334,348
*Registered Office:* Drakes Industrial Estate, Shay Lane, Ovenden, Halifax, W Yorks, HX3 6RL
*Activities:* Activities of head offices
*Major Shareholder:* Gary Malcolm Scott
*Officers:* Gary Malcolm Scott [1961] Director/Plywood Importer; Jack William Scott [1991] Director/Sales Executive; Joseph Michael Scott [1989] Director/Marketing and IT Manager; Maria Scott [1958] Director/Administrator; Thomas George Scott [1993] Director

**Hanson Plywood Limited**
*Incorporated:* 10 February 1938 *Employees:* 54
*Net Worth:* £7,639,517 *Total Assets:* £17,334,192
*Registered Office:* Drakes Industrial Estate, Shay Lane, Ovenden, Halifax, W Yorks, HX3 6RL
*Activities:* Agents involved in the sale of timber and building materials
*Parent:* Hanson Plywood (Holdings) Limited
*Officers:* Adrian Malcolm Alexander Bagott [1942] Director/Timber Merchant; Simon Matthews [1969] Director; Ann Norton [1975] Finance Director; Jonathan Perry [1966] Director; Gary Malcolm Scott [1961] Director/Timber Merchant; Jack William Scott [1991] Director; Thomas George Scott [1993] Director; Stephen Webster [1966] Director/Sales Manager

**Hapimag Resorts & Residences (UK) Limited**
*Incorporated:* 25 January 1984 *Employees:* 35
*Net Worth:* £2,314,000 *Total Assets:* £6,161,000
*Registered Office:* Burnside Park, Kendal Road, Bowness on Windermere, Windermere, Cumbria, LA23 3EW
*Activities:* Hotels and similar accommodation
*Officers:* Evelyn Mary Dugdale, Secretary; Oriano Schubiger [1959] Director/Finance, Area Controller [Swiss]

**Harder Bros (Holdings) Limited**
*Incorporated:* 17 February 2017 *Employees:* 215
*Net Worth:* £5,669,893 *Total Assets:* £9,763,687
*Registered Office:* Valley Mills, Valley Road, Morley, Leeds, LS27 8EX
*Activities:* Activities of other holding companies n.e.c.
*Shareholders:* James Charles Harder; Philip Matthew Sharp
*Officers:* James Charles Harder [1964] Director; Philip Matthew Sharp [1985] Director

**Harder Bros. Limited**
*Incorporated:* 6 April 1961 *Employees:* 168
*Net Worth:* £7,932,334 *Total Assets:* £11,039,431
*Registered Office:* Valley Mills, Valley Road, Morley, Leeds, LS27 8EX
*Activities:* Production of meat and poultry meat products
*Parent:* Harder Bros (Holdings) Limited
*Officers:* Ewa Nosewicz, Secretary; James Charles Harder [1964] Managing Director; Philip Matthew Sharp [1985] Director

**Hardroad Limited**
*Incorporated:* 12 May 2011 *Employees:* 99
*Net Worth:* £10,500,125 *Total Assets:* £16,448,573
*Registered Office:* c/o Border Aggregates, Scotland Road, Carnforth, Lancs, LA5 9JZ
*Activities:* Other letting and operating of own or leased real estate
*Major Shareholder:* Terry Billington
*Officers:* Carolyn Elizabeth Masters, Secretary; Terry Billington [1944] Managing Director; Andrew Hetherington [1969] Finance Director; Stephen Pelter [1957] Director

**James Hare,Limited**
*Incorporated:* 24 March 1902 *Employees:* 26
*Net Worth:* £8,208,438 *Total Assets:* £13,253,238
*Registered Office:* P O Box 72, Monarch House, Queen Street, Leeds, LS1 1LX
*Activities:* Development of building projects
*Officers:* Timothy James Pitt Hare, Secretary; Charles Timothy Pitt Hare [1977] IT Director; Diana Marion Hare [1949] Director; James Arthur Womersley Hare [1932] Director; Saffron Mollie Hare [1973] Sales Director; Timothy James Pitt Hare [1948] Director; Vivien Louise Hare [1940] Director

**Harewood House Trust Limited**
*Incorporated:* 25 March 1986 *Employees:* 43
*Net Worth:* £17,725,346 *Total Assets:* £18,137,920
*Registered Office:* Harewood House, Harewood, Leeds, W Yorks, LS17 9LG
*Activities:* Operation of historical sites and buildings and similar visitor attractions
*Officers:* Damian Francis Clements, Secretary; Iwona Maria Blazwick [1955] Director; Jeremy John Burton [1951] Director; Paul David Broomfield Dolan [1952] Director/Chartered Accountant; David Henry George Lascelles [1950] Director/Film Producer; Diane Jane Lascelles [1956] Director/Designer; Sir Hugh Ashley Roberts [1948] Director/Deputy Surveyor of The Queens; Charles Adam Laurie Sebag-Montefiore [1949] Director; Lady Emily Tsering Shard [1975] Director/Manager

**Hargreaves Enterprises Ltd**
*Incorporated:* 29 July 1947 *Employees:* 22
*Previous:* Laketime Holidays Limited
*Net Worth:* £1,417,219 *Total Assets:* £3,788,370
*Registered Office:* St Andrews, Lake Road, Bowness on Windermere, Cumbria, LA23 3DE
*Activities:* Licenced restaurants
*Major Shareholder:* Stephen David Hargreaves
*Officers:* Graham Hadaway [1988] Director of Brand and Marketing; Stephen David Hargreaves [1974] Director

**Hargreaves Group (GB) Limited**
*Incorporated:* 19 February 2008 *Employees:* 72
*Net Worth:* £2,008,692 *Total Assets:* £13,104,702
*Registered Office:* Thornhill Works, Calder Road, Ravensthorpe, Dewsbury, W Yorks, WF12 9HY
*Activities:* Activities of head offices
*Major Shareholder:* David Michael Beaumont
*Officers:* Tracey Frances Beaumont, Secretary; David Michael Beaumont [1958] Director

**Haricovert Limited**
*Incorporated:* 18 July 2013 *Employees:* 48
*Net Worth:* £1,509,070 *Total Assets:* £3,054,394
*Registered Office:* Ian Walker & Co Chartered Accountants, Heworth House, Melrosegate, Heworth, York, YO31 0RP
*Activities:* Dental practice activities
*Shareholders:* Dirk Schuth; Amita Shahi
*Officers:* Dr Dirk Schuth [1968] Director [German]; Dr Amita Shahi [1969] Director/Dentist

**Harlen Ltd**
*Incorporated:* 16 May 2008 *Employees:* 2
*Net Worth:* £3,695,820 *Total Assets:* £3,789,602
*Registered Office:* c/o Stephen R Allen & Co, 2a Vicarage Lane, Hessle, Hull, HU13 9LQ
*Activities:* Activities of head offices
*Shareholders:* Ross Anthony Harmon; Alison Jane Harmon
*Officers:* Stephen Raymond Allen, Secretary; Stephen Raymond Allen [1959] Finance Director; Ross Anthony Harmon [1970] Sales Director

**Harmony Bridge Limited**
*Incorporated:* 22 February 2017
*Net Worth:* £49,647 *Total Assets:* £9,656,671
*Registered Office:* Estate Office, The Priory Estate, Nun Monkton, York, YO26 8ES
*Activities:* Development of building projects
*Major Shareholder:* Richard David Harpin
*Officers:* Gerard Scot Downes [1967] Director; Richard David Harpin [1964] Director

**Harper & Wilkes Limited**
*Incorporated:* 4 October 2011
*Net Worth:* £4,894,800 *Total Assets:* £4,894,800
*Registered Office:* Crawley Hall, East Crawleyside, Stanhope, Bishop Auckland, Co Durham, DL13 2DX
*Activities:* Activities of head offices
*Major Shareholder:* Shona Wilkes
*Officers:* John Wilkes [1968] Director; Shona Wilkes [1974] Director

**Harpers Environmental Limited**
*Incorporated:* 27 November 1984 *Employees:* 91
*Net Worth:* £1,885,263 *Total Assets:* £6,710,298
*Registered Office:* Cleveland, Carr Lane, Sutton-on-the-Forest, N Yorks, YO61 1EY
*Activities:* Recovery of sorted materials
*Shareholders:* Judith Kathleen Harper; Nicholas Herbert Harper
*Officers:* Mark Bevan Bristow [1960] Health & Safety Director; Nabil El Hindy [1976] Director/Doctor; Nina El Hindy [1977] Director/Credit Controller; Judith Kathleen Harper [1951] Director/Company Secretary; Nicholas Herbert Harper [1954] Director/Chairman; Claire Elizabeth Marlow [1980] Director/Nutritional Therapist

**Harpin Limited**
*Incorporated:* 22 February 1990 *Employees:* 3
*Net Worth:* £9,706,238 *Total Assets:* £26,176,280
*Registered Office:* Estate Office, The Priory Estate, Nun Monkton, York, YO26 8ES
*Activities:* Other letting and operating of own or leased real estate
*Major Shareholder:* Richard David Harpin
*Officers:* Katherine Margaret Harpin, Secretary; Gerard Scot Downes [1967] Director; Richard David Harpin [1964] Director

**Harpin Parkin Aviation Limited**
*Incorporated:* 5 May 2016
*Net Worth Deficit:* £489,039 *Total Assets:* £6,087,185
*Registered Office:* Estate Office, The Priory Estate, Nun Monkton, York, YO26 8ES
*Activities:* Non-scheduled passenger air transport
*Shareholders:* Steven Nicholas Parkin; Richard David Harpin
*Officers:* Danielle Leanne Redfern, Secretary; Richard David Harpin [1964] Director

**The Harratts Group Limited**
*Incorporated:* 1 August 1975 *Employees:* 203
*Net Worth:* £3,545,119 *Total Assets:* £22,443,074
*Registered Office:* Group Head Office, Peel Avenue, Calder Park, off Denby Dale Road, Wakefield, W Yorks, WF2 7UA
*Activities:* Sale of new cars and light motor vehicles
*Shareholders:* Stella Margaret Harratt; Derek Harratt
*Officers:* Stella Margaret Harratt, Secretary; Derek Harratt [1942] Director; Shaun Timothy Harratt [1964] Director; Stella Margaret Harratt [1944] Director

**Harratts Limited**
*Incorporated:* 26 March 1987 *Employees:* 59
*Net Worth:* £1,139,516 *Total Assets:* £4,556,297
*Registered Office:* Group Head Office, Peel Avenue, Calder Park, off Denby Dale Road, Wakefield, W Yorks, WF2 7UA
*Activities:* Sale of new cars and light motor vehicles
*Parent:* The Harratts Group Limited
*Officers:* Stella Margaret Harratt, Secretary; Derek Harratt [1942] Director; Shaun Timothy Harratt [1964] Director; Stella Margaret Harratt [1944] Director

**Harratts of Wakefield Limited**
*Incorporated:* 23 April 1996 *Employees:* 105
*Net Worth Deficit:* £5,392,356 *Total Assets:* £7,398,006
*Registered Office:* Group Head Office, Peel Avenue, Calder Park, off Denby Dale Road, Wakefield, W Yorks, WF2 7UA
*Activities:* Sale of new cars and light motor vehicles
*Parent:* The Harratts Group Limited
*Officers:* Stella Margaret Harratt, Secretary/Director; Derek Harratt [1942] Director; Shaun Timothy Harratt [1964] Director; Stella Margaret Harratt [1944] Director

**Harris CM Limited**
*Incorporated:* 17 December 2008 *Employees:* 28
*Previous:* HCM Projects Limited
*Net Worth:* £1,799,000 *Total Assets:* £11,227,076
*Registered Office:* HCM House, Elmsall Way, South Elmsall, Pontefract, W Yorks, WF9 2XX
*Activities:* Development of building projects
*Parent:* Harris Construction Management Ltd.
*Officers:* Jason Paul Adlam [1971] Director; Jason Kenneth Collins [1970] Director

**Harris Construction Management Limited**
*Incorporated:* 5 July 2003 *Employees:* 43
*Net Worth:* £2,911,611 *Total Assets:* £13,396,922
*Registered Office:* HCM House, Elmsall Way, South Elmsall, Pontefract, W Yorks, WF9 2XX
*Activities:* Activities of head offices
*Shareholders:* Adlam Investments Ltd; Tate Family Office Limited
*Officers:* Andrea Michelle Adlam [1970] Director; Jason Paul Adlam [1971] Director; Claire Lesley Tate [1970] Finance Director; Shane Tate [1972] Director/Engineer MD

**The Harris Group Limited**
*Incorporated:* 31 May 2001 *Employees:* 151
*Net Worth:* £5,705,635 *Total Assets:* £8,047,732
*Registered Office:* 2 St Johns North, Wakefield, W Yorks, WF1 3QA
*Activities:* Management consultancy activities other than financial management
*Parent:* The Harris Partnership (Acquisitions) Limited
*Officers:* Andrew Mark Hamer, Secretary/Chartered Accountant; Nicholas John Charlesworth [1966] Director/Architect; Gary Francis Humphreys [1966] Director/Architect; Paul Stephen Mitchell [1956] Director/Architect; James Michael Richmond [1972] Director/Architect; Michael John Empsall Schorah [1966] Director/Architect

**The Harris Partnership Limited**
*Incorporated:* 22 May 1984 *Employees:* 151
*Net Worth:* £6,145,737 *Total Assets:* £8,125,658
*Registered Office:* 2 St Johns North, Wakefield, W Yorks, WF1 3QA
*Activities:* Architectural activities
*Officers:* Andrew Mark Hamer, Secretary/Chartered Accountant; Carl Antony Braim [1978] Director/Architect; Lee Andrew Brewer [1973] Director/Architect; Nicholas John Charlesworth [1966] Director/Architect; David James Evans [1970] Director/Architectural Technician; Gary Francis Humphreys [1966] Director/Architect; Paul Stephen Mitchell [1956] Director/Architect; James Michael Richmond [1972] Director; Michael John Empsall Schorah [1966] Director/Architect

**Harris Properties (Manchester) Limited**
*Incorporated:* 9 May 1953
*Net Worth:* £3,148,088 *Total Assets:* £3,458,624
*Registered Office:* Doves Rest 4, Harvest View, Bishop Monkton, Harrogate, N Yorks, HG3 3TN
*Activities:* Residents property management
*Major Shareholder:* John Derek Bennett
*Officers:* Susan Bennett, Secretary; John Derek Bennett [1946] Director; Susan Bennett [1947] Director/Company Secretary

**Harrison & Clough,Limited**
*Incorporated:* 8 May 1957 *Employees:* 148
*Net Worth:* £1,863,420 *Total Assets:* £15,851,211
*Registered Office:* P O Box 9, Harclo Road, off Aireworth Road, Keighley, W Yorks, BD21 4EG
*Activities:* Non-specialised wholesale trade
*Parent:* Heathfield Holdings Limited
*Officers:* Stuart James Holloway, Secretary; John Paul Aperghis [1973] Finance Director; Kelvin Ellison [1973] Commercial Director; Joyce Hutchinson [1935] Director/Company Secretary; Neville James Hutchinson [1935] Director/Chairman; Richard Mark Hutchinson [1961] Managing Director; Mark Edward Revak [1962] Operations Director

**L. Harrison (Properties) Limited**
*Incorporated:* 18 May 1993 *Employees:* 6
*Net Worth:* £3,261,420 *Total Assets:* £5,907,462
*Registered Office:* Suite 45, Bowcliffe Hall, Bramham, Wetherby, W Yorks, LS23 6LP
*Activities:* Construction of commercial buildings
*Officers:* Margaret Easton, Secretary; Margaret Easton [1948] Director/Retired; James Edward Harrison [1946] Director/Builder; Georgina Elizabeth Mills [1975] Director/Chartered Accountant

**S. Harrison Developments Limited**
*Incorporated:* 15 October 1998 *Employees:* 13
*Net Worth:* £23,096,000 *Total Assets:* £35,544,000
*Registered Office:* Stanley Harrison House, The Chocolate Works, Bishopthorpe Road, York, YO23 1DE
*Activities:* Other business support service activities n.e.c.
*Parent:* S Harrison Group Limited
*Officers:* Ann Pearce Scott, Secretary; David William Clancy [1962] Director/Property Developer; Martyn Robert Harrison [1959] Director; Ann Pearce Scott [1962] Director/Accountant

**Harrison Electrical Limited**
*Incorporated:* 28 October 1994 *Employees:* 33
*Net Worth:* £2,110,568 *Total Assets:* £3,337,921
*Registered Office:* 1 Wyther Lane, Kirkstall, Leeds, LS5 3BT
*Activities:* Electrical installation
*Officers:* Caroline Mitchell, Secretary/Accounts Manager; Caroline Mitchell [1958] Director/Accounts Manager; James Speight [1970] Director/Electrical Engineer

**Harrison Farms (Kilham) Limited**
*Incorporated:* 10 February 2003
*Net Worth:* £4,508,555 *Total Assets:* £7,549,482
*Registered Office:* West End Farm, Kilham, Driffield, E Yorks, YO25 4RR
*Activities:* Growing of cereals (except rice), leguminous crops and oil seeds
*Officers:* Anita Marcia Harrison, Secretary; Anita Marcia Harrison [1947] Director/Farmer; Jeremy Nicholas Damien Harrison [1972] Director/Farmer; Patrick Richard Maxwell Harrison [1968] Director/Farmer; Richard Priest Harrison [1944] Director/Farmer

**S Harrison Group Limited**
*Incorporated:* 5 December 2001 *Employees:* 16
*Net Worth:* £45,973,000 *Total Assets:* £64,116,000
*Registered Office:* Stanley Harrison House, The Chocolate Works, Bishopthorpe Road, York, YO23 1DE
*Activities:* Activities of head offices
*Major Shareholder:* Martyn Robert Harrison
*Officers:* Ann Pearce Scott, Finance Director; Martyn Robert Harrison [1959] Director; Ann Pearce Scott [1962] Director/Accountant

**D. Harrison Limited**
*Incorporated:* 30 March 1954 *Employees:* 3
*Net Worth:* £2,241,333 *Total Assets:* £3,169,542
*Registered Office:* Sanderson House, Station Road, Horsforth, Leeds, LS18 5NT
*Activities:* Other letting and operating of own or leased real estate
*Major Shareholder:* Lynda Todd
*Officers:* Christopher John Todd [1947] Director; Lynda Todd [1947] Director

**Gordon Harrison Limited**
*Incorporated:* 4 February 1974 *Employees:* 22
*Net Worth:* £3,063,006 *Total Assets:* £3,624,108
*Registered Office:* Monckton Manor, Chevet Lane, Notton, Wakefield, W Yorks, WF4 2PD
*Activities:* Open cast coal working
*Major Shareholder:* Gordon Thomas Harrison
*Officers:* Margaret Slater, Secretary; Gordon Thomas Harrison [1951] Managing Director; Harry Thomas Harrison [1990] Director; Margaret Eleanor Stone [1951] Director

**Harrison Spinks Beds Ltd**
*Incorporated:* 10 July 1933 *Employees:* 425
*Net Worth:* £5,829,564 *Total Assets:* £16,026,563
*Registered Office:* The Innovation Centre, Westland Road, Leeds, LS11 5SB
*Activities:* Manufacture of mattresses
*Officers:* Amanda Jane Shea, Finance Director; Steven Brougham [1957] Sales Director; Amanda Jane Shea [1969] Finance Director; Peter Douglas Spinks [1943] Director/Chairman; Simon Paul Spinks [1969] Managing Director

**Harrison Thompson and Company Limited**
*Incorporated:* 9 December 1991 *Employees:* 67
*Net Worth:* £3,885,864 *Total Assets:* £5,049,391
*Registered Office:* Yeoman House, 121f Whitehall Estate, Whitehall Road, Leeds, LS12 5JB
*Activities:* Other service activities n.e.c.
*Shareholders:* Raymond Harry Saperia; Graeme Clive Brumwell; Anthony Clive Brumwell
*Officers:* Alison Lorraine Starkey, Secretary; Anthony Clive Brumwell [1964] Director; Graeme Clive Brumwell [1962] Contracts Director; Phillip Christopher [1963] Director; Richard Leslie Good [1968] Contracts Director [New Zealander]; Stuart Lindsay Russell [1957] Sales Director

**Harrogate District Hospice Care**
*Incorporated:* 8 April 1987 *Employees:* 103
*Net Worth:* £4,935,107 *Total Assets:* £5,332,411
*Registered Office:* Crimple House, Hornbeam Park Avenue, Harrogate, N Yorks, HG2 8QL
*Activities:* Hospital activities
*Officers:* Rev Anthony James Collins, Secretary/Chief Executive; Victoria Ashley [1977] Director/Consultant; Lesley Rosemary Bers [1957] Director/HR Consultant; John William Charlton [1973] Director/Partner - Deloitte LLP; Jean Rosamund Macquarrie [1960] Director/Journalist; Mark Allan Robinson [1965] Director; Colin James Tweedie [1953] Director/Business Consultant; Karen Jane Wheeldon [1961] Director

**Harrogate Investments Limited**
*Incorporated:* 16 October 1978 *Employees:* 2
*Net Worth:* £2,610,650 *Total Assets:* £3,140,457
*Registered Office:* 2 Mount Parade, Harrogate, N Yorks, HG1 1BX
*Activities:* Buying and selling of own real estate
*Shareholders:* Kenneth Porter; Nancy Lee Porter
*Officers:* Kenneth Porter, Secretary/Retired; Nancy Lee Porter [1937] Director/Retired [American]

**Harrogate Ladies' College Limited**
*Incorporated:* 16 May 1924 *Employees:* 176
*Net Worth:* £7,031,009 *Total Assets:* £10,854,767
*Registered Office:* Harrogate Ladies' College Limited, Clarence Drive, Harrogate, N Yorks, HG1 2QG
*Activities:* Pre-primary education
*Officers:* Michael Beauchamp Mansel Porter, Secretary; Giles Richard Bowring [1955] Director/Retired; Lesley Patricia Byrne [1960] Director/Chartered Accountant; Ann Louise Chesworth [1967] Director/Minister; Susan Elizabeth Clark [1963] Director/Lawyer; Jessica Marjorie Crossley [1962] Director/Headmistress; Mark Piers Kingsley Gardiner [1974] Managing Director; Dame Francine Charlotte Holroyd [1968] Director; Shirley Hooper [1960] Director/Therapist; Susan Brooke Jackson [1950] Director/School Inspector/Education Consultant; Patricia Ann Jones [1941] Director/Community Representative; Nicola Loudon [1987] Director/Investment Manager; Susan Papworth [1966] Director/Investment Manager; Caroline Emma Peasgood [1966] Director/Chartered Surveyor; Julia Mary Roe [1969] Director; John Marshall Edward Skinner [1964] Finance Director

**Harrogate Spring Water Limited**
*Incorporated:* 16 August 2000 *Employees:* 74
*Net Worth:* £4,716,504 *Total Assets:* £19,496,768
*Registered Office:* Harlow Moor Road, Harrogate, N Yorks, HG2 0QB
*Activities:* Manufacture of soft drinks; production of mineral waters and other bottled waters
*Parent:* Harrogate Water Brands Limited
*Officers:* Anthony Joseph Cain [1948] Director; James Anthony Cain [1973] Director; Simon David Knaggs [1966] Operations Director; Robert James Pickering [1964] Director; Damien Michael Wilkinson [1969] Finance Director

**Harrogate Steel Trading Ltd**
*Incorporated:* 11 April 2017 *Employees:* 5
*Net Worth:* £52,334 *Total Assets:* £4,131,983
*Registered Office:* Tattersall House, East Parade, Harrogate, N Yorks, HG1 5LT
*Activities:* Wholesale of metals and metal ores
*Parent:* Harrogate Steel Holdings Ltd
*Officers:* Richard John Searle [1974] Director; Daniel David Worsell [1982] Director

**Harrogate Water Brands Limited**
*Incorporated:* 23 February 2007 *Employees:* 74
*Net Worth:* £479,503 *Total Assets:* £17,489,630
*Registered Office:* Water Brands Limited, Harlow Moor Road, Harrogate, N Yorks, HG2 0QB
*Activities:* Activities of production holding companies
*Shareholders:* Anthony Joseph Cain; Elizabeth Jean Cain
*Officers:* Anthony Joseph Cain [1948] Director; Elizabeth Jean Cain [1947] Director; James Anthony Cain [1973] Director; Robert James Pickering [1964] Director

**Harrogate14 Limited**
*Incorporated:* 31 October 2016 *Employees:* 3
*Net Worth Deficit:* £439,780 *Total Assets:* £6,376,814
*Registered Office:* 10 The Stables, Newby Hall, Ripon, N Yorks, HG4 5AE
*Activities:* Buying and selling of own real estate
*Parent:* Silverback Developments Limited
*Officers:* Simon William Hepden [1971] Director; Nicholas John Moody [1969] Director; Frazer George Roberts [1993] Director

**Harron Group Limited**
*Incorporated:* 19 February 2002 *Employees:* 211
*Net Worth:* £71,970,000 *Total Assets:* £127,229,000
*Registered Office:* Colton House, Temple Point, Bullerthorpe Lane, Leeds, LS15 9JL
*Activities:* Activities of construction holding companies
*Shareholders:* Paul Andrew Harrison; Stephen Thomas Harrison
*Officers:* Richard Miles Wilson, Secretary/Chartered Accountant; Paul Andrew Harrison [1971] Director; Stephen Thomas Harrison [1969] Director

**Harron Homes Limited**
*Incorporated:* 23 January 1995 *Employees:* 211
*Net Worth:* £72,332,000 *Total Assets:* £127,580,000
*Registered Office:* Colton House, Temple Point, Bullerthorpe Lane, Leeds, LS15 9JL
*Activities:* Construction of domestic buildings
*Parent:* Harron Group Limited
*Officers:* Richard Miles Wilson, Secretary/Chartered Accountant; Paul Andrew Harrison [1971] Director; Stephen Thomas Harrison [1969] Director

**Harrowells Limited**
*Incorporated:* 20 August 2014 *Employees:* 127
*Net Worth:* £1,550,264 *Total Assets:* £4,474,978
*Registered Office:* 1 St Saviourgate, York, YO1 8ZQ
*Activities:* Solicitors
*Officers:* James Philip Lewis Ogden, Secretary; Simon Rupert Kay Black [1970] Director/Solicitor; Richard James Hugill [1975] Director/Solicitor; John Kevin Millar [1958] Director/Solicitor; Robert Paul Onyett [1966] Director/Solicitor; Robert Gordon Charles Seaton [1954] Director/Solicitor; Richard Courtney Wood [1973] Director/Solicitor

**Harte Woodworking Limited**
*Incorporated:* 20 December 1973 *Employees:* 111
*Net Worth:* £2,815,534 *Total Assets:* £4,933,464
*Registered Office:* Springfield Mill, Spa Street, Ossett, W Yorks, WF5 0HW
*Activities:* Manufacture of office and shop furniture
*Parent:* Hunter Holdings Limited
*Officers:* Steven Firth, Secretary/Financial Director; Steven Firth [1958] Financial Director; Ian Hunter [1966] Managing Director; Fraser Cameron Thomson [1984] Commercial Director

**Hartford Holdings Limited**
*Incorporated:* 8 October 2010 *Employees:* 169
*Previous:* Hartford Trading Limited
*Net Worth:* £10,103,681 *Total Assets:* £14,385,548
*Registered Office:* Ramsden Mills, Britannia Road, Huddersfield, W Yorks, HD3 4QG
*Activities:* Other business support service activities n.e.c.
*Shareholders:* The Hartford Trust; James Maurice Vincent Mosley
*Officers:* Adam Paul Mosley, Secretary; Adam Paul Mosley [1975] Director; David James Mosley [1978] Director; James Maurice Vincent Mosley [1929] Director

**Hartford Properties Limited**
*Incorporated:* 10 March 2011
*Net Worth:* £708,593 *Total Assets:* £3,345,106
*Registered Office:* Field Farm, Great Gutter Lane, Swanland, E Yorks, HU14 3RA
*Activities:* Other letting and operating of own or leased real estate
*Shareholders:* Keith Ernest Brown; Joan Brown
*Officers:* Joan Brown [1945] Director; Keith Ernest Brown [1944] Director

**Hartford Trading Limited**
*Incorporated:* 29 May 1979 *Employees:* 3
*Previous:* Hartford Holdings Limited
*Net Worth:* £4,283,750 *Total Assets:* £5,093,362
*Registered Office:* Ramsden Mills, Britannia Road, Milnsbridge, Huddersfield, W Yorks, HD3 4QG
*Activities:* Renting and leasing of other machinery, equipment and tangible goods n.e.c.
*Parent:* Hartford Holdings Limited
*Officers:* Adam Paul Mosley, Secretary; Adam Paul Mosley [1975] Director/Chemist; David James Mosley [1978] Director/Sales and Marketing; James Maurice Vincent Mosley [1929] Managing Director

**Hartley Investment Trust Limited**
*Incorporated:* 28 July 1983 *Employees:* 36
*Net Worth:* £40,839,000 *Total Assets:* £55,267,000
*Registered Office:* Cumberland House, Greenside Lane, Bradford, BD8 9TF
*Activities:* Other service activities n.e.c.
*Major Shareholder:* Alan James Lewis
*Officers:* Alan James Lewis [1938] Director/Chairman

**J.E.Hartley Limited**
*Incorporated:* 8 April 1954 *Employees:* 72
*Net Worth:* £18,009,946 *Total Assets:* £31,581,656
*Registered Office:* Roth Hill Lane, Thorganby, York, YO19 6DJ
*Activities:* Growing of cereals (except rice), leguminous crops and oil seeds
*Shareholder:* William Thomas Hartley
*Officers:* Elizabeth Anne Verity, Secretary/Director; William Thomas Hartley [1948] Director; Elizabeth Anne Verity [1943] Director; Tom Edwin Verity [1972] Director

**Hartley Property Trust (1991) Limited**
*Incorporated:* 12 November 1985 *Employees:* 2
*Net Worth:* £3,507,638 *Total Assets:* £6,710,658
*Registered Office:* Cumberland House, Greenside Lane, Bradford, BD8 9TF
*Activities:* Management of real estate on a fee or contract basis
*Shareholders:* Hartley Property Trust Limited; Allan Moreland Murray
*Officers:* Alan James Lewis [1938] Director/Chairman

**Hartley Property Trust Limited**
*Incorporated:* 13 October 1947 *Employees:* 2
*Net Worth:* £20,435,916 *Total Assets:* £25,112,952
*Registered Office:* Cumberland House, Greenside Lane, Bradford, BD8 9TF
*Activities:* Other service activities n.e.c.
*Parent:* Honeytree Trading Co. Limited
*Officers:* Alan James Lewis [1938] Director/Chairman

**Hartshorne Crossroads Group Contracts Limited**
*Incorporated:* 10 October 2012 *Employees:* 1
*Net Worth:* £4,271,000 *Total Assets:* £12,371,000
*Registered Office:* c/o Crossroads Truck & Bus Limited, Pheasant Drive, Birstall, Batley, W Yorks, WF17 9LR
*Activities:* Repair and maintenance of other transport equipment n.e.c.
*Major Shareholder:* Martin James Cronin
*Officers:* Jayne Bulpitt, Secretary; Jayne Michelle Bulpitt [1970] Director; James Cowen [1986] Director; Martin James Cronin [1965] Director

**Hartshorne Group Limited**
*Incorporated:* 26 May 2010 *Employees:* 250
*Net Worth:* £5,211,000 *Total Assets:* £29,690,000
*Registered Office:* Crossroads Group Limited, Pheasant Drive, Birstall, Batley, W Yorks, WF17 9LR
*Activities:* Sale of other motor vehicles
*Major Shareholder:* Martin James Cronin
*Officers:* Phillip David Brookfield [1970] Director; Jayne Michelle Bulpitt [1970] Finance Director; James Andrew Cowen [1986] Finance Director; Brian Cronin [1970] Director; Martin James Cronin [1965] Director

**Hartshorne Motor Services Limited**
*Incorporated:* 22 October 1968 *Employees:* 250
*Net Worth:* £5,518,000 *Total Assets:* £29,713,000
*Registered Office:* Crossroads Truck & Bus Limited, Pheasant Drive, Birstall, Batley, W Yorks, WF17 9LR
*Activities:* Sale of other motor vehicles
*Parent:* Hartshorne Group Limited
*Officers:* Jayne Bulpitt, Secretary; Phillip David Brookfield [1970] Director; Jayne Michelle Bulpitt [1970] Finance Director; James Andrew Cowen [1986] Finance Director; Martin James Cronin [1965] Director

**Hartwell Manufacturing Ltd**
*Incorporated:* 10 April 1973 *Employees:* 71
*Net Worth:* £688,701 *Total Assets:* £3,991,324
*Registered Office:* Milner Way, Ossett, Wakefield, W Yorks, WF5 9AW
*Activities:* Manufacture of other fabricated metal products n.e.c.
*Officers:* Paul Robert Tomlinson, Secretary; Neil Richardson [1959] Director/Engineer; Carl Jacob Tomlinson [1973] Director/Engineer; Paul Robert Tomlinson [1976] Director/Engineer; Robert Leslie Tomlinson [1948] Director/Engineer

**Harvard Group Holdings Limited**
*Incorporated:* 20 July 2015 *Employees:* 465
*Net Worth Deficit:* £24,379,000 *Total Assets:* £18,338,000
*Registered Office:* Unit 1 Tyler Close, Normanton Industrial Estate, Normanton, W Yorks, WF6 1RL
*Activities:* Activities of head offices
*Shareholders:* Roogreen Nominees Limited; ECI Partners LLP
*Officers:* Brian Joseph Davidson [1963] Director; Anthony Hill [1985] Director/Chartered Accountant; Mark Daniel Keeley [1978] Director; Warwick John Ley [1972] Director/Chartered Accountant [Australian/British]

**Hassan (Holdings) Ltd**
*Incorporated:* 5 March 2013 *Employees:* 2
*Net Worth:* £3,447,416 *Total Assets:* £3,977,473
*Registered Office:* Highfield House, Wheelwright Drive, Dewsbury, W Yorks, WF13 4JB
*Activities:* Renting and leasing of other machinery, equipment and tangible goods n.e.c.
*Parent:* Hassan Group Limited
*Officers:* Saghir Hussain [1978] Director; Zahir Hussain [1979] Director

**Hassan Group Limited**
*Incorporated:* 25 March 2016
*Net Worth:* £1,718,046 *Total Assets:* £9,380,766
*Registered Office:* 62 Bradford Road, Dewsbury, W Yorks, WF13 2DU
*Activities:* Activities of other holding companies n.e.c.
*Shareholders:* The Saghir Settlement 2016; The Zahir Settlement 2016
*Officers:* Saghir Hussain [1978] Director; Zahir Hussain [1979] Director

**Hatfields V Limited**
*Incorporated:* 8 March 1983 *Employees:* 41
*Net Worth:* £1,686,207 *Total Assets:* £8,253,861
*Registered Office:* Hatfields, Calder Island Way, Denby Dale Road, Wakefield, W Yorks, WF2 7AW
*Activities:* Sale of new cars and light motor vehicles
*Major Shareholder:* Gareth Sinclair Williams
*Officers:* Justin Sinclair Williams, Secretary; Gareth Sinclair Williams [1964] Director; John Sinclair Williams [1942] Director/Motor Vehicle Dealer

**Hathaway Roofing Limited**
*Incorporated:* 22 April 1997 *Employees:* 82
*Net Worth:* £4,953,523 *Total Assets:* £12,385,601
*Registered Office:* Tindale Crescent, Bishop Auckland, Co Durham, DL14 9TL
*Activities:* Roofing activities
*Major Shareholder:* Simon David Binks
*Officers:* Diane Marie Thompson, Secretary; Simon David Binks [1972] Director; Stephen John Godfrey [1956] Contracts Director; Kevin Hall [1959] Managing Director; Andrew Harrison [1965] Technical Director; Steven Price [1969] Director; Diane Marie Thompson [1965] Finance Director; Mark Watson [1964] Director

**The Haulage (Holdings) Organisation Limited**
*Incorporated:* 17 June 2011 *Employees:* 127
*Net Worth Deficit:* £911,009 *Total Assets:* £5,610,373
*Registered Office:* Swalesmoor Farm, Swalesmoor Road, Halifax, W Yorks, HX3 6UF
*Activities:* Freight transport by road
*Parent:* Leo Group Ltd
*Officers:* James Hutchison [1953] Director

**Havelok Limited**
*Incorporated:* 18 June 2012 *Employees:* 93
*Net Worth Deficit:* £514,354 *Total Assets:* £6,648,812
*Registered Office:* Fiskerton Way, Great Grimsby Business Park, Grimsby, N E Lincs, DN37 9SZ
*Activities:* Processing and preserving of fish, crustaceans and molluscs
*Shareholders:* Daniel Robert Burton; Iceland Seafood Barraclough Limited
*Officers:* Daniel Robert Burton, Secretary; Daniel Robert Burton [1961] Director/Retired; Lee Mark Camfield [1967] Director/Chief Operating Officer; Reynir Jonsson [1978] Director/CFO Icelandic Seafood International HF [Icelander]; Bjarni Armannsson [1968] Director/CEO Iceland Seafood International HF [Icelander]

**Haven Power Limited**
*Incorporated:* 2 August 2006 *Employees:* 431
*Net Worth:* £17,842,000 *Total Assets:* £424,048,992
*Registered Office:* Drax Power Station, Drax, Selby, N Yorks, YO8 8PH
*Activities:* Trade of electricity
*Parent:* Drax Smart Supply Holdco Limited
*Officers:* David McCallum, Secretary; Dwight Daniel Willard Gardiner [1964] Director [British/American]; Carl Goulton [1972] Director; Jonathan Anantha Kini [1979] Director; Andrew Robert Koss [1971] Director/Accountant; Paul Nathan Sheffield [1975] Director

**Havercroft Construction Limited**
*Incorporated:* 28 March 1985
*Net Worth:* £3,652,965 *Total Assets:* £5,952,474
*Registered Office:* Halifax Approach, Elsham Wolds Industrial Estate, Brigg, N Lincs, DN20 0SS
*Activities:* Construction of commercial buildings
*Major Shareholder:* Martyn Kenneth Havercroft
*Officers:* Christine Mary Havercroft, Secretary; Grant Bailey [1965] Director; Christine Mary Havercroft [1953] Director; Martyn Kenneth Havercroft [1950] Director

**Havwoods Australia Limited**
*Incorporated:* 22 April 2010
*Previous:* Select Timbers Limited
*Net Worth:* £959,433 *Total Assets:* £3,605,070
*Registered Office:* Carnforth Business Park, Oakwood Way, Carnforth, Lancs, LA5 9FD
*Activities:* Other business support service activities n.e.c.
*Parent:* Havwoods Global Holdings Limited
*Officers:* Oliver Muckle Whiley [1955] Director; Simon Whiley [1976] Director

**Havwoods Global Holdings Limited**
*Incorporated:* 30 July 2014 *Employees:* 119
*Net Worth:* £15,279,890 *Total Assets:* £25,491,988
*Registered Office:* Carnforth Business Park, Oakwood Way, Carnforth, Lancs, LA5 9FD
*Activities:* Activities of other holding companies n.e.c.
*Shareholder:* Oliver Muckle Whiley
*Officers:* Elizabeth Janette Whiley, Secretary; Elizabeth Janette Whiley [1956] Director; Jonathan Whiley [1984] Director; Nicholas Whiley [1974] Director; Oliver Muckle Whiley [1955] Director; Simon Whiley [1976] Director

**Havwoods Limited**
*Incorporated:* 4 September 1975 *Employees:* 71
*Net Worth:* £16,655,781 *Total Assets:* £22,962,686
*Registered Office:* Carnforth Business Park, Oakwood Way, Carnforth, Lancs, LA5 9FD
*Activities:* Wholesale of wood, construction materials and sanitary equipment
*Parent:* Havwoods Global Holdings Limited
*Officers:* Elizabeth Janette Whiley, Director/Secretary; Elizabeth Janette Whiley [1956] Director; Jonathan Whiley [1984] Director; Nicholas Whiley [1974] Director; Oliver Muckle Whiley [1955] Director; Simon Whiley [1976] Director

**Hawes & Co Limited**
*Incorporated:* 24 September 2013 *Employees:* 40
*Net Worth:* £6,216,000 *Total Assets:* £6,731,000
*Registered Office:* 2nd Floor, Gateway, 2 Holgate Park Drive, York, YO26 4GB
*Activities:* Real estate agencies
*Parent:* LSLI Ltd
*Officers:* Sapna Bedi FitzGenerald, Secretary; Greig Barker [1969] Finance Director; Helen Elizabeth Buck [1960] Director; Richard Martin Gee [1957] Director; Lawson Frederick St John Hewett [1967] Director; Gregory Winston Young [1966] Director

**Hawkesworth Appliance Testing Limited**
*Incorporated:* 23 February 2005 *Employees:* 32
*Net Worth:* £2,398,706 *Total Assets:* £3,690,901
*Registered Office:* Guidance House, York Road, Thirsk, N Yorks, YO7 3BT
*Activities:* Technical testing and analysis
*Shareholders:* Paul Hawkesworth; Jane Hawkesworth
*Officers:* Jane Hawkesworth, Secretary; Timothy George Crowley [1959] Managing Director [Irish]; Stuart Hardcastle [1956] Finance Director; Jane Hawkesworth [1967] Director; Paul Andrew Hawkesworth [1969] Director/Chairman; Michael Hugh Kiddle [1982] Director/Operations Manager; Darren Keith Tonge [1980] Sales Director

**Hawthorn Timber Limited**
*Incorporated:* 22 April 1964 *Employees:* 118
*Net Worth:* £6,274,815 *Total Assets:* £13,361,529
*Registered Office:* Wyke Street, Hedon Road, Hull, HU9 1PA
*Activities:* Other manufacturing n.e.c.
*Shareholders:* Michael Dennis Stone; Trevor Stone
*Officers:* Kirsty Ford, Secretary; Michael Dennis Stone [1955] Director; Trevor Stone [1952] Director; Richard John Thompson [1962] Managing Director

**Hayden Daniel Properties Limited**
*Incorporated:* 21 January 1975 *Employees:* 1
*Net Worth:* £2,787,890 *Total Assets:* £5,130,653
*Registered Office:* 8 Springwell Court, Leeds, LS12 1AL
*Activities:* Other letting and operating of own or leased real estate
*Shareholders:* Martin Nigel Glynn; Doretta B Glynn
*Officers:* Doretta B Glynn, Secretary; Martin Nigel Glynn [1956] Director/Clothing Distributor

**The Hayfield School**
*Incorporated:* 1 March 2011 *Employees:* 130
*Net Worth:* £15,702,000 *Total Assets:* £16,761,000
*Registered Office:* The Hayfield School, Hurst Lane, Auckley, Doncaster, S Yorks, DN9 3HG
*Activities:* General secondary education
*Officers:* Heather Jane Rose, Secretary; Uzma Ahmed [1965] Director/Consultant; Annamarie Alton [1976] Director/Teaching Assistant; Steven Leslie Cross [1964] Director/Market Strategist; Debbie Dickerson [1969] Director/Local Government Officer; Stephen Featherstone [1957] Director/Manager; Nikki Ford [1962] Director/Charity Worker; Lisa Fox [1968] Director/Headteacher; Lesley Esther Gilfedder [1962] Director/Administrator; Graham Hartshorn [1948] Director; Mark Bradley Huby [1978] Director/Financial Adviser; Helen Jackson [1976] Director/Assistant Principal; David Langford [1948] Director/Retired; Lucinda Claire Oldfield [1978] Director/Teacher; Georgina Diane Parkes [1957] Director/Attendance Officer; Angela Scott [1948] Director/Retired; Scott Wilson [1972] Director/Teacher

**Hayley Conference Centres Acquisitions Limited**
*Incorporated:* 28 September 2005
*Net Worth:* £94,673,000 *Total Assets:* £159,500,992
*Registered Office:* The Inspire, Hornbeam Square West, Harrogate, N Yorks, HG2 8PA
*Activities:* Activities of head offices
*Parent:* Hayley Conference Centres Enterprise Limited
*Officers:* James Alexander Burrell [1974] Director/Accountant; Generaldine Josephine Gallagher [1965] Finance Director [Irish]; Gail Susan Hunter [1963] Human Resources Director; Anthony Gerrard Troy [1962] Director [Irish]

**Hayton & Lamb Limited**
*Incorporated:* 20 May 1982 *Employees:* 67
*Net Worth:* £2,196,531 *Total Assets:* £3,576,732
*Registered Office:* Eldon Road, Aycliffe Industrial Estate, Newton Aycliffe, Co Durham, DL5 6UL
*Activities:* Painting
*Major Shareholder:* Paul Gerard Hayton
*Officers:* Susan Lamb, Secretary; Paul Gerard Hayton [1965] Director

**C.T. Hayton Limited**
*Incorporated:* 16 May 1975 *Employees:* 34
*Net Worth:* £1,517,750 *Total Assets:* £4,505,277
*Registered Office:* Sandylands Road, Kendal, Cumbria, LA9 6EX
*Activities:* Agents involved in the sale of machinery, industrial equipment, ships and aircraft
*Major Shareholder:* Geoffrey Croasdale Hayton
*Officers:* Sheila Ann Hayton, Secretary; Geoffrey Croasdale Hayton [1936] Director/Agricultural Engineer; Sheila Ann Hayton [1946] Director

**Hazel Products UK Limited**
*Incorporated:* 10 March 2011 *Employees:* 4
*Net Worth:* £6,378,535 *Total Assets:* £7,059,598
*Registered Office:* Mill House, Troy Road, Horsforth, Leeds, LS18 5TN
*Activities:* Other manufacturing n.e.c.
*Shareholders:* Fiona Hazel Christie; Erika Jane Christie
*Officers:* Garth Anton Christie [1957] Director; Neil Christie [1980] Director

**Hazlewood Holdings Limited**
*Incorporated:* 28 April 2006
*Net Worth:* £1,266,666 *Total Assets:* £5,620,017
*Registered Office:* Dower Hotel & Spa, 48 Bond End, Knaresborough, Harrogate, N Yorks, HG5 9AL
*Activities:* Hotels and similar accommodation
*Parent:* Ashdale UK Limited
*Officers:* Ian Lawrence Hanson, Secretary/Lawyer; Ian Lawrence Hanson [1964] Director/Lawyer; Martin Gregory Michael Wicks [1963] Director/Hotelier

**Haztec International Ltd**
*Incorporated:* 12 February 2001 *Employees:* 37
*Net Worth:* £1,128,272 *Total Assets:* £4,439,099
*Registered Office:* Ford House, Moorfield Estate, Yeadon, Leeds, LS19 7BN
*Activities:* Manufacture of other transport equipment n.e.c.
*Major Shareholder:* Bryn James Tennant
*Officers:* Roderick Bruce MacAulay, Secretary; Peter Edwin Ballard [1950] Director/Equipment Manufacturer; Peter John Cook [1965] Director; Roderick Bruce MacAulay [1958] Director/Chartered Accountant; Bryn James Tennant [1948] Director/Entrepreneur

**HBOS Covered Bonds LLP**
*Incorporated:* 15 May 2003
*Total Assets:* £4,215,993,088
*Registered Office:* Trinity Road, Halifax, W Yorks, HX1 2RG

**HBOS Investment Fund Managers Limited**
*Incorporated:* 24 October 1968
*Net Worth:* £220,111,008 *Total Assets:* £264,628,992
*Registered Office:* Trinity Road, Halifax, W Yorks, HX1 2RG
*Activities:* Financial intermediation not elsewhere classified
*Parent:* Halifax Financial Services (Holdings) Limited
*Officers:* Christina Ann Hankin, Secretary; Catriona Margaret Herd [1965] UK Propositions Director, Longstanding LP&I, Insurance; Sean William Lowther [1960] Director; Gavin MacNeill Stewart [1959] Director

**HC-ONE Beamish Limited**
*Incorporated:* 31 August 2004 *Employees:* 1,295
*Previous:* Helen McArdle Care Limited
*Net Worth:* £1,662,000 *Total Assets:* £10,645,000
*Registered Office:* Southgate House, Archer Street, Darlington, Co Durham, DL3 6AH
*Activities:* Residential nursing care facilities
*Parent:* FC Beamish Bidco Limited
*Officers:* Sir David Behan [1955] Director; James Justin Hutchens [1974] Director [American]; Dr Chaitanya Bhupendra Patel [1954] Director; John Anthony Ransford [1948] Director; David Andrew Smith [1974] Director; Sir William Henry Weston Wells [1940] Director

**HC-ONE Limited**
*Incorporated:* 20 July 2011 *Employees:* 10,957
*Net Worth:* £20,669,000 *Total Assets:* £161,444,000
*Registered Office:* Southgate House, Archer Street, Darlington, Co Durham, DL3 6AH
*Activities:* Residential nursing care facilities
*Parent:* FC Skyfall Bidco Ltd
*Officers:* David Andrew Smith, Secretary; Sir David Behan [1955] Director; James Justin Hutchens [1974] Director [American]; Chaitanya Bhupendra Patel [1954] Director; John Anthony Ransford [1948] Director; David Andrew Smith [1974] Director; Sir William Henry Weston Wells [1940] Director

**HC-ONE Oval Limited**
*Incorporated:* 30 June 2016 *Employees:* 4,477
*Net Worth:* £420,136,000 *Total Assets:* £532,830,016
*Registered Office:* Southgate House, Archer Street, Darlington, Co Durham, DL3 6AH
*Activities:* Activities of other holding companies n.e.c.
*Officers:* David Andrew Smith, Secretary; Sir David Behan [1955] Director; James Justin Hutchens [1974] Director [American]; Dr Chaitanya Bhupendra Patel [1954] Director; John Anthony Ransford [1948] Director; David Andrew Smith [1974] Director; Sir William Henry Weston Wells [1940] Director

**HCF Poultry Limited**
*Incorporated:* 15 January 2004 *Employees:* 132
*Net Worth:* £4,947,123 *Total Assets:* £6,337,507
*Registered Office:* Station Yard, Station Road, Cullingworth, Bradford, W Yorks, BD13 5HP
*Activities:* Processing and preserving of poultry meat
*Shareholders:* Michael Feeley; Kevin Connolly
*Officers:* Michael Feeley, Secretary/Chartered Accountant [Irish]; Kevin Connolly [1967] Director/Chartered Accountant [Irish]; Michael Feeley [1962] Director/Chartered Accountant [Irish]

**HD1 Developments Limited**
*Incorporated:* 19 August 1998 *Employees:* 2
*Net Worth Deficit:* £3,862,214 *Total Assets:* £3,272,814
*Registered Office:* St Georges Quarter, New North Parade, Huddersfield, W Yorks, HD1 5JP
*Activities:* Development of building projects
*Major Shareholder:* Shar Hasan Jan
*Officers:* Mohammad Tayssir Ismail, Secretary; Sher Hasan Jan [1983] Director

**Head Office Interiors Limited**
*Incorporated:* 16 February 2010 *Employees:* 64
*Net Worth:* £1,216,555 *Total Assets:* £6,508,200
*Registered Office:* Cartelli House, 3 Hawthorn Park, Leeds, LS14 1PQ
*Activities:* Other building completion and finishing
*Shareholders:* Adele Harding; Glen Harding
*Officers:* Lee Armstrong [1977] Director; Glen Harding [1978] Director; Scott Harding [1981] Director

**Head UK Ltd**
*Incorporated:* 31 August 2001 *Employees:* 2,484
*Net Worth:* £211,222,032 *Total Assets:* £541,217,600
*Registered Office:* 2 Beezon Road, Kendal, Cumbria, LA9 6BW
*Activities:* Wholesale of other intermediate products
*Officers:* Ralf Bernhart [1951] Director/Chief Financial Officer [Austrian]; Johan Eliasch [1962] Director [Swedish]

**Headland Plant Limited**
*Incorporated:* 1 August 1977 *Employees:* 10
*Net Worth:* £3,417,712 *Total Assets:* £4,607,843
*Registered Office:* 388 Boothferry Road, Hessle, Hull, HU13 0JL
*Activities:* Renting and leasing of construction and civil engineering machinery and equipment
*Shareholders:* Jean Patricia Kolodziej; Bernard Jan Kolodziej
*Officers:* Jean Patricia Kolodziej, Secretary; Bernard Jan Kolodziej [1950] Director/Plant Operator; Jean Patricia Kolodziej [1951] Director/Accountant/Secretary

**James H.Heal and Company Limited**
*Incorporated:* 9 July 1946 *Employees:* 112
*Net Worth:* £11,228,846 *Total Assets:* £13,598,299
*Registered Office:* Richmond Works, Lake View, Halifax, W Yorks, HX3 6EP
*Activities:* Manufacture of electronic measuring, testing etc. equipment, not for industrial process control
*Parent:* Physical Properties Testing Ltd.
*Officers:* Andrew Hemingway [1978] Commercial Director; Jason Malloy [1972] Financial Director; Amanda Louise McLaren [1968] Manufacturing Director; Neil Andrew Pryke [1968] Engineering Director; Donald Edward Templeman [1960] Director [American]

**Healan Ingredients Limited**
*Incorporated:* 18 July 2012 *Employees:* 18
*Net Worth:* £2,049,544 *Total Assets:* £6,801,903
*Registered Office:* Healan Ingredients Limited, Sands Top, North Newbald, E Yorks, YO43 4SW
*Activities:* Non-specialised wholesale trade
*Shareholders:* Stefano Serafino Bruno Camponovo; Muarizio Lapi
*Officers:* Maurizio Lapi [1958] Director [Italian]

**Healing Multi Academy Trust**
*Incorporated:* 13 August 2010 *Employees:* 298
*Net Worth:* £14,140,000 *Total Assets:* £17,398,000
*Registered Office:* Low Road, Healing, Grimsby, N E Lincs, DN41 7QD
*Activities:* Primary education
*Officers:* Hayley Carlberg, Secretary; Karina Marianne Ellis [1973] Director; Jonathan Thornes Goolden [1965] Director/Solicitor; Peter Kipling [1949] Director; Leonora Yvonne Rew Kitchin [1971] Director; Mark Robert Knapton [1973] Director; Debra Peers [1964] Director/Civil Servant; Graham John McRae Walker [1963] Director

**The Health Factor Limited**
*Incorporated:* 28 January 2009
*Net Worth:* £4,177,950 *Total Assets:* £5,100,000
*Registered Office:* 6 Earls Court, Priory Park East, Hull, HU4 7DY
*Activities:* Other business support service activities n.e.c.
*Officers:* Vincent Jamie Gosling, Secretary; Michael Conrad Jackson [1933] Director; Nicholas Adrian Mead [1966] Director; Jaqueline Patricia Robinson [1965] Director; Melvyn Warren Sadofsky [1949] Director/Accountant

**Health Innovations (UK) Limited**
*Incorporated:* 3 April 2007 *Employees:* 63
*Net Worth:* £181,631 *Total Assets:* £4,387,863
*Registered Office:* Airedale Business Centre, Millennium Road, Skipton, N Yorks, BD23 2TZ
*Activities:* Manufacture of basic pharmaceutical products
*Shareholder:* Michael John Davies
*Officers:* Richard Doyle, Secretary; Clare Campbell [1975] Director; Andrew Michael Davies [1982] Director; Michael John Davies [1951] Director; Philip Benjamin Davies [1977] Director

**Health Management (Carlisle) Holdings Limited**
*Incorporated:* 12 May 1998
*Net Worth Deficit:* £19,739,000 *Total Assets:* £71,691,000
*Registered Office:* 1 Park Row, Leeds, LS1 5AB
*Activities:* Activities of other holding companies n.e.c.
*Shareholders:* Dalmore Capital (Carlisle 1) Limited; PFI 2005 Limited
*Officers:* Karen Elizabeth Jarvie-Thomson, Secretary; John Stephen Gordon [1962] Director; Roger Mark Thompson [1954] Director

**Health Management (Carlisle) Limited**
*Incorporated:* 26 March 1993 *Employees:* 2
*Net Worth Deficit:* £19,743,000 *Total Assets:* £71,689,000
*Registered Office:* 1 Park Row, Leeds, LS1 5AB
*Activities:* Other business support service activities n.e.c.
*Parent:* Health Management (Carlisle) Holdings Limited
*Officers:* Karen Elizabeth Jarvie-Thomson, Secretary; John Stephen Gordon [1962] Director; Roger Mark Thompson [1954] Director

**Healthcare House Limited**
*Incorporated:* 6 April 2006 *Employees:* 66
*Net Worth:* £1,919,869 *Total Assets:* £8,932,716
*Registered Office:* c/o Deliver Net Limited, Snaygill Industrial Estate, Keighley Road, Skipton, N Yorks, BD23 2QR
*Activities:* Other service activities n.e.c.
*Shareholders:* Frances Lockett; Timothy James Lockett
*Officers:* Timothy James Lockett, Secretary/Director; Adele Farquharson [1974] Director; Simon Jeremy Holt [1960] Director; Beverley Jane Lockett [1965] Director; Frances Lockett [1964] Director; Timothy James Lockett [1964] Director

**Healthsource (Bromley) Limited**
*Incorporated:* 10 April 2001
*Net Worth:* £2,242,979 *Total Assets:* £8,187,948
*Registered Office:* 4 Greengate, Cardale Park, Harrogate, N Yorks, HG3 1GY
*Activities:* Other human health activities
*Parent:* Healthsource (Bromley) Holdings Limited
*Officers:* Paul William Noake, Secretary; Robert John Austin [1964] Director; Alastair William Hopps [1986] Director/Chartered Accountant; Samuel John Johnston [1949] Director/General Manager; Alexander Toby Shedden Parry [1976] Director

**Healthtrak (UK) Limited**
*Incorporated:* 22 May 2001 *Employees:* 2
*Net Worth:* £2,355,610 *Total Assets:* £6,541,531
*Registered Office:* 50 Brantwood Oval, Bradford, W Yorks, BD9 6QP
*Activities:* Development of building projects
*Shareholder:* Mendhy Hussain Khan
*Officers:* Fatima Jaffar Shahid, Secretary; Dr Mendhy Hussain Khan [1968] Director/Doctor; Fatima Jaffar Shahid [1961] Director/Practice Manager

**Heart Research UK**
*Incorporated:* 27 February 1995 *Employees:* 19
*Net Worth:* £6,194,018 *Total Assets:* £9,454,175
*Registered Office:* Suite 12d, Josephs Well, Hanover Walk, Leeds, LS3 1AB
*Activities:* Other human health activities
*Officers:* Samantha Jane Turner, Secretary; Pierre Bouvet [1953] Director/Judge; Dr Peter Charles Braidley [1963] Director/Hospital Doctor; Richard John Brown [1946] Director/Chartered Accountant; Dr Catherine Jane Dickinson [1963] Director/Physician; Doctor David Frederick Dickinson [1944] Director/Consultant Cardiologist; Julie Fenwick [1957] Director/Cardiac Nurse; Richard Colwyn Hemsley [1945] Director/Chartered Accountant; Anthony Roger Kilner [1948] Director/Solicitor; Anthony David Knight [1943] Director/Paper Manufacturer; Keith Loudon [1933] Director/Stockbroker; Prof Christopher Mark Howard Newman [1959] Director/Cardiologist; Paul Rogerson [1948] Director/Lawyer; Paul Wilson Smith [1955] Director; Kevin Gerard Watterson [1953] Director/Cardiothoracic Surgeon

**Heathfield Holdings Limited**
*Incorporated:* 6 October 2003 *Employees:* 159
*Net Worth:* £8,765,840 *Total Assets:* £20,050,068
*Registered Office:* P O Box 9, Harclo Road, off Aireworth Road, Keighley, W Yorks, BD21 4EG
*Activities:* Other activities auxiliary to insurance and pension funding
*Officers:* Stuart James Holloway, Secretary; John Paul Aperghis [1973] Finance Director; Joyce Hutchinson [1935] Director; Neville James Hutchinson [1935] Director; Phillipa Ann Hutchinson [1963] Director; Richard Mark Hutchinson [1961] Director

**Heathvine Properties Limited**
*Incorporated:* 13 September 2001 *Employees:* 3
*Net Worth:* £1,552,228 *Total Assets:* £3,881,423
*Registered Office:* Livers Farm, Hedon, Hull, HU12 8JU
*Activities:* Development of building projects
*Shareholders:* Sandra Curtis; Howard Curtis
*Officers:* Sandra Rita Curtis, Secretary; Howard Curtis [1954] Director/Property Developer

**Heatseam Limited**
*Incorporated:* 4 July 1996 *Employees:* 55
*Net Worth:* £3,067,608 *Total Assets:* £6,643,113
*Registered Office:* Units 4 & 5 Heatseam Business Park, Ravensthorpe Road, Dewsbury, W Yorks, WF12 9EG
*Activities:* Wholesale of furniture, carpets and lighting equipment
*Major Shareholder:* Glen Andrew Toomes
*Officers:* Glen Andrew Toomes [1969] Director/Carpet Retailer; Samantha Jane Toomes [1969] Director/Sales Manager

**Heavy Duty Parts Limited**
*Incorporated:* 19 December 1994 *Employees:* 21
*Net Worth:* £10,492,581 *Total Assets:* £11,121,196
*Registered Office:* Aurillac Way, Hallcroft Industrial Estate, Retford, Notts, DN22 7PX
*Activities:* Wholesale trade of motor vehicle parts and accessories
*Major Shareholder:* Kevin Booth
*Officers:* Martina Booth, Secretary; Kevin Booth [1968] Director/Sales Engineer

**John Hebb (Motor Engineers) Limited**
*Incorporated:* 11 October 1972
*Net Worth:* £11,717,230 *Total Assets:* £11,739,629
*Registered Office:* 40 Cherry Lane, Wootton, Ulceby, N Lincs, DN39 6RL
*Activities:* Sale of other motor vehicles
*Major Shareholder:* David John Hebb
*Officers:* Catherine Ann Hebb, Secretary; Catherine Ann Hebb [1957] Director/Secretary; Christopher John Hebb [1984] Director; David John Hebb [1954] Director/Motor Engineer; Matthew Richard Hebb [1991] Director

**Hebden Bridge Community Association Ltd**
*Incorporated:* 1 September 2008
*Net Worth:* £2,359,384 *Total Assets:* £4,046,872
*Registered Office:* Hebden Bridge Town Hall, St Georges Street, Hebden Bridge, W Yorks, HX7 7BY
*Activities:* Activities of other membership organisations n.e.c.
*Officers:* Graham Nicholas Mynott, Secretary; Antonio Benitez [1979] Festival Director [Spanish]; Rory Alexander Deighton [1970] Director/Charity Manager; Pat Fraser [1947] Director/Retired; William Lake [1972] Director/Copywriter; Dai Larner [1961] Director/Local Government Officer; Jane Morris [1955] Director/Retired; Richard David Needham [1959] Director/Charity Manager; Amanda Ward [1963] Director/Certified Accountant

**Heck! Food Limited**
*Incorporated:* 2 July 2004 *Employees:* 80
*Previous:* Thirsk Food Logistics Limited
*Net Worth:* £762,886 *Total Assets:* £7,641,158
*Registered Office:* Berry Hills, Kirklington, Bedale, N Yorks, DL8 2NL
*Activities:* Retail sale of meat and meat products in specialised stores
*Shareholders:* Deborah Jane Keeble; Andrew Crispin Keeble; Stephen Alexander Campbell
*Officers:* Deborah Jane Keeble, Secretary/Director; Stephen Alexander Campbell [1965] Director; Andrew Crispin Keeble [1965] Director; Deborah Jane Keeble [1965] Director; William Mark McDavid [1958] Director

**Hector, Lamont, Florence Associates Limited**
*Incorporated:* 19 March 2013 *Employees:* 3
*Net Worth:* £3,453,283 *Total Assets:* £3,746,566
*Registered Office:* York House, Cottingley Business Park, Bradford, W Yorks, BD16 1PE
*Activities:* Other service activities n.e.c.
*Officers:* Graeme Andrew Walker [1955] Director; Susan Margaret Walker [1956] Director

**Hedley Hydraulics Limited**
*Incorporated:* 13 February 1976 *Employees:* 37
*Net Worth:* £960,742 *Total Assets:* £3,244,609
*Registered Office:* 12 Greenhead Road, Huddersfield, W Yorks, HD1 4EN
*Activities:* Manufacture of pumps
*Parent:* Hedley Hydraulics (Holdings) Limited
*Officers:* John David Massey, Secretary; Jeremy Matthew Booker [1967] Director; Stephen Mark Davies [1963] Director/Hydraulic Engineer; John David Massey [1960] Director/Hydraulic Engineer

**Heights (U.K.) Limited**
*Incorporated:* 5 June 1984 *Employees:* 43
*Net Worth:* £3,009,081 *Total Assets:* £4,707,268
*Registered Office:* Wainstalls Mill, Wainstalls, Halifax, W Yorks, HX2 7TJ
*Activities:* Manufacture of other general-purpose machinery n.e.c.
*Officers:* Susan Jones, Secretary/Director; Gary Jones [1947] Director; Morgan Jones [1975] Director; Susan Jones [1947] Director; Elinor Robinson [1973] Director

**Help for Health**
*Incorporated:* 13 February 2002
*Net Worth:* £5,383,978 *Total Assets:* £5,386,331
*Registered Office:* First Floor, Two Humber Quays, Wellington Street West, Hull, HU1 2BN
*Activities:* Other human health activities
*Officers:* Charles Richard Field [1962] Director/Solicitor; Professor Peter William Ray Lee [1944] Director/Consultant Surgeon; Dr Andrew Milner [1951] Director/Assistant Chief Executive; Andrew Mould [1954] Director/Accountant; Stuart Lindley Smith [1951] Director/Consultant Otolaryngologist; Victoria Winterton [1991] Director

**Help-Link UK Limited**
*Incorporated:* 13 March 1998 *Employees:* 250
*Net Worth Deficit:* £27,861,000 *Total Assets:* £3,331,000
*Registered Office:* 3310 Century Way, Thorpe Park, Leeds, LS15 8ZB
*Activities:* Plumbing, heat and air-conditioning installation
*Shareholders:* Homeserve Membership Limited; Homeserve Assistance Limited
*Officers:* Jonathan Mark Godber [1973] Director/Accountant; Paul Nourse [1964] Director; Michael Gregory Reed [1969] Marketing Director

**HEM Holdings Limited**
*Incorporated:* 10 March 2017
*Net Worth:* £1,037,277 *Total Assets:* £4,223,290
*Registered Office:* 15 Wentworth Road, South Park Industrial Estate, Scunthorpe, N Lincs, DN17 2AX
*Activities:* Other business support service activities n.e.c.
*Major Shareholder:* James Lawton
*Officers:* James Lawton, Secretary; James Lawton [1970] Director

**Hemingways (Furnishers) Limited**
*Incorporated:* 22 October 1934 *Employees:* 137
*Net Worth:* £15,728,312 *Total Assets:* £21,237,252
*Registered Office:* Metcalfe House, 23H Kirkgate, Ripon, N Yorks, HG4 1PB
*Activities:* Other business support service activities n.e.c.
*Shareholders:* Michael Robert Johnson; Andrew Robert Johnson
*Officers:* Colm Phelan, Secretary; Andrew Robert Johnson [1967] Director; Michael Robert Johnson [1941] Managing Director

**Hemingways Marketing Services Limited**
*Incorporated:* 26 April 1948 *Employees:* 137
*Net Worth:* £13,255,841 *Total Assets:* £18,481,944
*Registered Office:* Metcalfe House, 23H Kirkgate, Ripon, N Yorks, HG4 1PB
*Activities:* Financial intermediation not elsewhere classified
*Parent:* Hemingways (Furnishers) Limited
*Officers:* Colm Phelan, Secretary; Andrew Robert Johnson [1967] Joint Managing Director; Michael Robert Johnson [1941] Managing Director; Lydia Charmaine Morrison [1969] Confectionery Sales & Marketing Director; Colm Thomas Phelan [1976] Finance Director [Irish]

**Hemplow Limited**
*Incorporated:* 25 February 2003 *Employees:* 4
*Net Worth:* £510,350 *Total Assets:* £5,181,878
*Registered Office:* Bank Bottom Mills, Marsden, Huddersfield, W Yorks, HD7 6HR
*Activities:* Other letting and operating of own or leased real estate
*Officers:* Edward Rowland Lee, Secretary; Anna Carolin Crowther [1939] Director/Farmer; Philip Roger Crowther [1969] Director/Farmer; Gillian Rose Dawson [1944] Director; Edward Rowland Lee [1956] Director/Chartered Accountant

**Henderson Insurance Brokers Limited**
*Incorporated:* 4 February 1986 *Employees:* 417
*Net Worth:* £8,650,391 *Total Assets:* £53,080,428
*Registered Office:* Trueman House, Capitol Park, Tingley, Leeds, LS27 0TS
*Activities:* Non-life insurance
*Parent:* AON UK Limited
*Officers:* Joseph Edgar Henderson [1951] Director; Jane Elizabeth Kielty- O'Gara [1976] Managing Director; Julie Anne Page [1967] Director/Chief Executive; Michael Charles Wright [1967] Director/Insurance Broker

**Hendersons of Selby Limited**
*Incorporated:* 5 August 1996 *Employees:* 35
*Net Worth:* £1,587,486 *Total Assets:* £3,221,085
*Registered Office:* The Old Airfield, Market Weighton Road, Riccall, Selby, N Yorks, YO8 5LD
*Activities:* Freight transport by road
*Shareholders:* Brent Henderson; Neil Henderson
*Officers:* Neil Henderson, Secretary; Brent Henderson [1953] Director/Haulage Contractor; Neil Henderson [1960] Director/Haulage Contractor

**Hensall Group Limited**
*Incorporated:* 22 July 2010 *Employees:* 33
*Previous:* HMS Corp Limited
*Net Worth:* £676,340 *Total Assets:* £6,270,466
*Registered Office:* Roall Hall, Roall Lane, Eggborough, N Yorks, DN14 0NY
*Activities:* Dormant company
*Major Shareholder:* Christopher Lee Bond
*Officers:* Allison Jayne Barlow [1975] Commercial Director; Christopher Lee Bond [1979] Managing Director

**Hensall Mechanical Services Limited**
*Incorporated:* 9 December 1994 *Employees:* 33
*Net Worth:* £3,328,195 *Total Assets:* £8,601,649
*Registered Office:* Roall Hall, Roall Lane, Eggborough, N Yorks, DN14 0NA
*Activities:* Plumbing, heat and air-conditioning installation
*Parent:* Hensall Group Limited
*Officers:* Christopher Lee Bond, Secretary; Allison Jayne Barlow [1975] Commercial Director; Christopher Lee Bond [1979] Director

**Henton & Co LLP**
*Incorporated:* 6 April 2001
*Net Worth:* £2,081,189 *Total Assets:* £4,238,511
*Registered Office:* Northgate, 118 North Street, Leeds, LS2 7PN
*Officers:* Nadeem Ahmed [1967] Member; Pavanjeet Singh Bagri [1981] Member; Simon Gray [1972] Member; Ian Peter Hart [1964] Member; Christopher Michael Howitt [1980] Member

**William Hepworth (Huddersfield) Limited**
*Incorporated:* 5 December 1972 *Employees:* 52
*Net Worth:* £1,286,691 *Total Assets:* £3,427,031
*Registered Office:* 650-652 Leeds Road, Huddersfield, W Yorks, HD2 1UB
*Activities:* Sale of new cars and light motor vehicles
*Parent:* Brighton Holdings Limited
*Officers:* Stephen Brighton, Secretary; Stephen Brighton [1963] Director/Accountant

**Heritage Commercial Finance Limited**
*Incorporated:* 11 May 1972 *Employees:* 6
*Net Worth:* £7,057,843 *Total Assets:* £13,092,778
*Registered Office:* 1 The Old Foundry, Cowgate Welton, Brough, N Humbers, HU15 1NB
*Activities:* Financial leasing
*Shareholders:* Allison Jayne Lee; Margaret Ann Wright; Mark Anthony Wright
*Officers:* Mark Anthony Wright, Secretary; Allison Jayne Lee [1968] Director; Margaret Ann Wright [1944] Director/Company Secretary; Mark Anthony Wright [1971] Managing Director

**Hermes European Logistics Limited**
*Incorporated:* 27 May 2008
*Net Worth:* £8,758,843 *Total Assets:* £9,388,465
*Registered Office:* Capitol House, 1 Capitol Close, Morley, Leeds, LS27 0WH
*Activities:* Freight transport by road
*Parent:* Hermes General Serivce Beteiligungs-Verwaltungsgesellschaft mbH
*Officers:* Hugo William Martin, Secretary; Martijn de Lange [1978] Director [Dutch]; Hugo William Martin [1974] Director of Legal & Public Affairs; Alan Richardson [1977] Finance Director; Carole Maxine Walker [1966] Director/Chief Executive Officer

**Hermes Parcelnet Limited**
*Incorporated:* 22 December 1999 *Employees:* 2,540
*Net Worth:* £88,377,000 *Total Assets:* £218,484,000
*Registered Office:* Capitol House, 1 Capitol Close, Morley, Leeds, LS27 0WH
*Activities:* Freight transport by road
*Parent:* Grattan Public Limited Company
*Officers:* Hugo William Martin, Secretary; Martijn de Lange [1978] Director/Chief Operating Officer [Dutch]; Hugo William Martin [1974] Director of Legal & Public Affairs; Alan Richardson [1977] Financial Director; Carole Maxine Walker [1966] Director/Chief Executive Officer

**Hes Humber Bulk Terminal Limited**
*Incorporated:* 14 October 1981 *Employees:* 27
*Previous:* New Holland Bulk Services Limited
*Net Worth:* £5,739,390 *Total Assets:* £8,467,012
*Registered Office:* Old Ferry Terminal, New Holland, Barrow upon Humber, N Lincs, DN19 7PN
*Activities:* Cargo handling for water transport activities
*Parent:* Hes (UK) Ltd
*Officers:* Michael Graham Hotchkin, Secretary; Barbara Geelen [1974] Director [Dutch]; Robert Allan Grimbleby [1961] Director; Harry Frederik Constantyn Van Rietschoten [1966] Director [Dutch]

**Hesco Bastion Limited**
*Incorporated:* 10 April 1991 *Employees:* 122
*Net Worth:* £42,512,212 *Total Assets:* £47,801,896
*Registered Office:* 41 Knowsthorpe Way, Cross Green Industrial Estate, Leeds, LS9 0SW
*Activities:* Manufacture of other fabricated metal products n.e.c.
*Parent:* Hesco UK Holdings Limited
*Officers:* Mandy Elizabeth Atkinson [1968] Finance Director; Kevin Arthur Lyons [1960] Operations Director; Paul Clifford Skertchly [1962] Director

**Hesco Group Limited**
*Incorporated:* 21 April 2011
*Previous:* Hesco Holdings Limited
*Net Worth:* £105,494,456 *Total Assets:* £114,990,744
*Registered Office:* Unit 41 Knowsthorpe Way, Cross Green Industrial Estate, Leeds, LS9 0SW
*Activities:* Activities of head offices
*Parent:* Praesidiad Limited
*Officers:* Mandy Elizabeth Atkinson [1968] Director

**Heselden Investments Limited**
*Incorporated:* 10 July 2007
*Previous:* PTS Holdings Limited
*Net Worth:* £308,399 *Total Assets:* £4,333,466
*Registered Office:* 7 Lakeland Crescent, Leeds, LS17 7PS
*Activities:* Other business support service activities n.e.c.
*Officers:* Jacqueline Ethel Foster [1950] Director; Linda Louise Gunby [1953] Director; Beverley Heselden [1960] Director; Julie Anne Heselden [1958] Director; Michael Hughes [1960] Director

**Hesley Care & Education Limited**
*Incorporated:* 10 June 2004
*Net Worth:* £5,544,034 *Total Assets:* £20,159,432
*Registered Office:* Central Services, Hesley Hall, Tickhill, Doncaster, S Yorks, DN11 9HH
*Activities:* Other residential care activities n.e.c.
*Parent:* Hesley Holdings Limited
*Officers:* David Bryan Maynard [1973] Sales Director; Susan McLean [1966] Operations Director; Christopher McSharry [1959] Director; Graham Smith [1960] Director/Chairman

**The Hesley Group Limited**
*Incorporated:* 22 November 1991 *Employees:* 1,520
*Net Worth:* £7,894,933 *Total Assets:* £47,874,436
*Registered Office:* Central Services, Hesley Hall, Tickhill, Doncaster, S Yorks, DN11 9HH
*Activities:* Other residential care activities n.e.c.
*Parent:* Hesley Care & Education Limited
*Officers:* David Bryan Maynard [1973] Sales Director; Susan McLean [1966] Operations Director; Christopher McSharry [1959] Director; Graham Smith [1950] Director/Chairman

**Hesley Holdings Limited**
*Incorporated:* 20 March 2008 *Employees:* 1,520
*Net Worth:* £15,764,222 *Total Assets:* £56,175,568
*Registered Office:* Central Services, Hesley Hall, Tickhill, Doncaster, S Yorks, DN11 9HH
*Activities:* Other residential care activities n.e.c.
*Parent:* Honour Project Bidco Limited
*Officers:* David Bryan Maynard [1973] Sales Director; Susan McLean [1966] Operations Director; Christopher McSharry [1959] Director; Graham Smith [1950] Director/Chairman

**Hestview Limited**
*Incorporated:* 8 March 1973 *Employees:* 1,086
*Net Worth:* £56,791,000 *Total Assets:* £139,688,000
*Registered Office:* 2 Wellington Place, Leeds, LS1 4AP
*Activities:* Gambling and betting activities
*Parent:* Cyan Bidco Limited
*Officers:* Scott Campbell Yelle, Secretary; Rafael Ashkenazi [1974] Director [Israeli]; Johan Fredrik Ekdahl [1965] Director of Corporate Affairs [Swedish]; Trystan Michael Forrest [1970] Director of Legal Affairs; Ian David Fraser Proctor [1965] Finance Director; Guy Nigel Lethbridge Templer [1969] Director

**Hever Castle Golf Club Limited**
*Incorporated:* 15 January 1992 *Employees:* 60
*Net Worth:* £180,312 *Total Assets:* £3,660,010
*Registered Office:* 137 Scalby Road, Scarborough, N Yorks, YO12 6TB
*Activities:* Other letting and operating of own or leased real estate
*Parent:* Hever Castle Limited
*Officers:* Barry Peter Swiers, Company Secretary; John Guthrie [1936] Director; Peter John Guthrie [1971] Director; Richard Guthrie [1972] Director; James Maxwell Hill [1974] Director; Duncan Harry Melville Leslie [1969] Director/Chief Executive; Martin Robson [1975] Director/Accountant

**Hever Castle Limited**
*Incorporated:* 15 February 1980 *Employees:* 152
*Net Worth:* £30,131,080 *Total Assets:* £46,064,356
*Registered Office:* 137 Scalby Road, Scarborough, N Yorks, YO12 6TB
*Activities:* Other letting and operating of own or leased real estate
*Parent:* Broadland Properties Limited
*Officers:* Barry Peter Swiers, Company Secretary; John Guthrie [1936] Director; Peter John Guthrie [1971] Director; Richard Guthrie [1972] Director; James Maxwell Hill [1974] Director; Duncan Harry Melville Leslie [1969] Director/Chief Executive; Martin Robson [1975] Director/Accountant; Ronald Graham Urquhart [1957] Director

**Hewitson Limited**
*Incorporated:* 2 November 2004 *Employees:* 55
*Net Worth:* £1,073,834 *Total Assets:* £4,553,179
*Registered Office:* 43 Coniscliffe Road, Darlington, Co Durham, DL3 7EH
*Activities:* Other specialised construction activities n.e.c.
*Parent:* Hewitson Group Ltd
*Officers:* Brian Gibson [1971] Director; Henry Michael Hewitson [1993] Director; Michael Edward Hewitson [1960] Director

**K. Hewitt and Co. Limited**
*Incorporated:* 2 March 1983 *Employees:* 33
*Net Worth:* £5,101,001 *Total Assets:* £6,139,007
*Registered Office:* Clyde House, Gibbon Street, Bishop Auckland, Co Durham, DL14 7DL
*Activities:* Plumbing, heat and air-conditioning installation
*Parent:* K Hewitt Holdings Limited
*Officers:* Raymond Kevin Dobson [1987] Director; David Wade [1982] Director

**K Hewitt Holdings Limited**
*Incorporated:* 8 July 2015
*Net Worth:* £31 *Total Assets:* £6,199,472
*Registered Office:* Clyde House, Gibbon Street, Bishop Auckland, Co Durham, DL14 7DL
*Activities:* Plumbing, heat and air-conditioning installation
*Shareholder:* David Wade
*Officers:* Raymond Kevin Dobson [1987] Director; David Wade [1982] Director

**Hexadex Limited**
*Incorporated:* 31 December 1991 *Employees:* 726
*Net Worth:* £49,858,000 *Total Assets:* £67,620,000
*Registered Office:* The Old Court House, 24 Market Street, Gainsborough, Lincs, DN21 2BE
*Activities:* Activities of head offices
*Officers:* David John Hodgson, Secretary; William James Buchan [1959] Director; Dr Pelham Nigel Hawker [1953] Director; Andrew Joseph Meakin [1966] Director/Chartered Accountant; Barnaby Arthur Jennings Milles [1975] Director [British/Australian]; David Herbert Milles [1942] Director; William David Milles [1970] Director; Dr Robert Joseph Rule [1964] Director

**Hexagon Properties Limited**
*Incorporated:* 27 October 1992
*Net Worth:* £2,482,976 *Total Assets:* £6,102,216
*Registered Office:* The Crescent, Ropergate, Pontefract, W Yorks, WF8 1LY
*Activities:* Construction of domestic buildings
*Shareholders:* Graham Ward; Maureen Ward
*Officers:* Maureen Ward, Secretary; Graham Ward [1954] Director; Maureen Ward [1954] Director Secretary

**Hexon Limited**
*Incorporated:* 7 January 2002 *Employees:* 127
*Net Worth:* £3,064,853 *Total Assets:* £6,268,956
*Registered Office:* 62-63 Westborough, Scarborough, N Yorks, YO11 1TS
*Activities:* Other service activities n.e.c.
*Parent:* Sabrina Health Care Limited
*Officers:* Tamby Seeneevassen [1960] Director/Barrister [Mauritian]

**Heywood Williams Components Limited**
*Incorporated:* 18 July 1990 *Employees:* 151
*Net Worth:* £22,280,000 *Total Assets:* £33,840,000
*Registered Office:* Premier Way, Lowfields Business Park, Elland, W Yorks, HX5 9HF
*Activities:* Activities of head offices
*Parent:* Arran Isle Holdings Limited
*Officers:* Rachel Helen Balbi, Secretary; Oliver Dyson Burgess [1970] Director; Tristan Cooke [1974] Director; Richard Michael Gyde [1964] Director; Samantha Nuckey [1973] Director; Michael James Russell Richards [1964] Director; Martin Wardhaugh [1960] Director; Mark Steven Wild [1960] Director/Accountant; Peter Jonathon Wreford [1962] Director

**HGF Limited**
*Incorporated:* 15 April 2014 *Employees:* 317
*Net Worth:* £11,272,000 *Total Assets:* £21,967,000
*Registered Office:* 1 City Walk, Leeds, LS11 9DX
*Activities:* Activities of patent and copyright agents; other legal activities n.e.c.
*Officers:* Timothy Russell Wright, Secretary; Hsu Min Chung [1975] Director/Patent Attorney; Robert John Harrison [1971] Director; Dr Richard Gavin Jenkins [1967] Director/Patent Attorney; Jason Matthew Lumber [1971] Director/Solicitor; Mark George Francis Lunt [1955] Director/Patent Attorney; Paul Anthony Sanderson [1961] Director/Solicitor; Gary Wilson [1972] Director/Patent Attorney

**Hi Resolution (Production) Limited**
*Incorporated:* 22 December 2000 *Employees:* 8
*Net Worth:* £5,364,311 *Total Assets:* £6,966,081
*Registered Office:* The Inspire, Hornbeam Park, Harrogate, N Yorks, HG2 8PA
*Activities:* Advertising agencies
*Parent:* Airport Media International Limited
*Officers:* Jacqueline Anne Chapple Blease, Secretary/Administrator; Rachael Hird [1967] Director/Accountant; Paul Seymour Shields [1958] Director/Advertising Agent; Stephen Richard Winters [1968] Director/Chartered Accountant

**Hi-Level Enterprises Limited**
*Incorporated:* 4 August 1988 *Employees:* 26
*Net Worth:* £10,921,512 *Total Assets:* £11,438,746
*Registered Office:* Millennium Warehouse, Sandall Lane, Kirk Sandall Industrial Estate, Doncaster, S Yorks, DN3 1QL
*Activities:* Sale, maintenance and repair of motorcycles and related parts and accessories
*Officers:* James Beukelman [1963] Finance Director [American]; Bradley J Roberts [1981] Director [American]; Steve Stubitz [1957] Director [American]; James Wisnoski [1961] Director [American]

**Hi-Wire Limited**
*Incorporated:* 18 February 1998 *Employees:* 32
*Net Worth:* £2,328,303 *Total Assets:* £10,451,624
*Registered Office:* Unit E4, Willowbridge Way, Castleford, W Yorks, WF10 5NP
*Activities:* Manufacture of other electronic and electric wires and cables
*Officers:* Lloyd Frost, Secretary; Darren Goldthorpe [1965] Director/Business Manager; David McLaughlin Gray [1969] Director/Business Executive [American]

**Hiatt Hardware (UK) Limited**
*Incorporated:* 28 January 2009
*Net Worth:* £2,604,669 *Total Assets:* £8,160,066
*Registered Office:* Sidings Court, Lakeside, Doncaster, S Yorks, DN4 5NU
*Activities:* Wholesale of hardware, plumbing and heating equipment and supplies
*Major Shareholder:* Ankesh Agrawal
*Officers:* Ankesh Agrawal, Secretary/Director [Indian]; Ankesh Agrawal [1985] Director; Rajesh Agrawal [1960] Director [Indian]; Rakesh Agrawal [1956] Director [Indian]

**Hickson International Limited**
*Incorporated:* 28 September 1951 *Employees:* 7
*Net Worth Deficit:* £82,710,000 *Total Assets:* £53,776,000
*Registered Office:* Wheldon Road, Castleford, W Yorks, WF10 2JT
*Activities:* Activities of head offices
*Officers:* Nicholas Thomas Carter, Secretary; Nicholas Thomas Carter [1981] Director/Financial Accountant; Alexander Henry Hoy [1966] Director; Anthony William Kelly [1963] Director; Franklin Delano Kicklighter [1958] Director/Business Unit Head of Wood Protection [American]

**Hickson Investments Limited.**
*Incorporated:* 21 August 1985
*Net Worth:* £45,503,000 *Total Assets:* £66,603,000
*Registered Office:* Wheldon Road, Castleford, W Yorks, WF10 2JT
*Activities:* Activities of head offices
*Officers:* Nicholas Thomas Carter, Secretary; Nicholas Thomas Carter [1981] Director/Financial Accountant; Anthony William Kelly [1963] Director

**Hickson Limited**
*Incorporated:* 12 June 1937 *Employees:* 105
*Net Worth:* £3,063,000 *Total Assets:* £37,152,000
*Registered Office:* Wheldon Road, Castleford, W Yorks, WF10 2JT
*Activities:* Manufacture of dyes and pigments
*Officers:* Nicholas Thomas Carter, Secretary; Nicholas Thomas Carter [1981] Director/Financial Accountant; Alexander Henry Hoy [1966] Director; Anthony William Kelly [1963] Director; Franklin Delano Kicklighter [1958] Director/Business Unit Head Wood Protection [American]; Peter Joseph Kitchen [1967] Director/Financial Controller

**Hider Food Imports Limited**
*Incorporated:* 26 March 1965 *Employees:* 103
*Net Worth:* £935,522 *Total Assets:* £11,366,635
*Registered Office:* Wiltshire Road, Hull, HU4 6PA
*Activities:* Non-specialised wholesale trade
*Parent:* Hider Group Holdings Limited
*Officers:* Ian Feller, Secretary; Matthew Bradbury [1980] Director; David Michael Hider [1947] Director/CD & Chairman; Duncan Alexander Hider [1975] Managing Director; Michael Charles Thirkettle [1959] Director; Mark Williams [1962] Director

**Hider Group Holdings Limited**
*Incorporated:* 13 March 2015 *Employees:* 103
*Net Worth:* £937,772 *Total Assets:* £11,366,635
*Registered Office:* c/o Hider Food Imports Limited, Wiltshire Road, Hull, HU4 6PA
*Activities:* Activities of head offices
*Shareholders:* David Michael Hider; Duncan Alexander Hider
*Officers:* David Michael Hider [1947] Director; Duncan Alexander Hider [1975] Director; Michael Charles Thirkettle [1959] Director

**Hidrostal (GB) Limited**
*Incorporated:* 9 November 2006 *Employees:* 69
*Net Worth:* £2,956,162 *Total Assets:* £8,759,691
*Registered Office:* Unit 1 Stadium Park, Altofts Lane, Castleford, W Yorks, WF10 5PZ
*Activities:* Other business support service activities n.e.c.
*Parent:* Hidrostal Holding AG
*Officers:* Annette Boulter, Secretary; Herr Gerd Preissler [1957] Director/General Manager/CEO [German]

**Hidrostal Limited**
*Incorporated:* 14 December 1979 *Employees:* 38
*Net Worth:* £1,420,664 *Total Assets:* £3,636,337
*Registered Office:* Unit 1 Stadium Park, Altofts Lane, Castleford, W Yorks, WF10 5PZ
*Activities:* Manufacture of pumps
*Parent:* Hidrostal (GB) Limited
*Officers:* Annette Boulter [1968] Finance Director; John Davies [1957] Managing Director; Herr Gerd Preissler [1957] Director/General Manager/CEO [German]

**Higgins Agriculture Limited**
*Incorporated:* 9 February 1966 *Employees:* 29
*Net Worth:* £642,521 *Total Assets:* £4,363,908
*Registered Office:* Greenbank House, Finningley, Doncaster, S Yorks, DN9 3BZ
*Activities:* Operation of warehousing and storage facilities for land transport activities
*Officers:* Karen Anne Albone [1964] Director; Iris Higgins [1933] Director; Kevin Paul Higgins [1958] Director

**M. Higgins Limited**
*Incorporated:* 6 June 1979 *Employees:* 44
*Net Worth:* £1,474,719 *Total Assets:* £6,579,923
*Registered Office:* Greenbank House, Finningley, Doncaster, S Yorks, DN9 3BZ
*Activities:* Growing of cereals (except rice), leguminous crops and oil seeds
*Officers:* David Michael Higgins [1956] Managing Director; Iris Higgins [1933] Director; Kevin Paul Higgins [1958] Farms Director

**High Crane Limited**
*Incorporated:* 4 December 1996 *Employees:* 3
*Net Worth:* £8,422,051 *Total Assets:* £8,858,034
*Registered Office:* High Crane Lodge, Hamsterley, Bishop Auckland, Co Durham, DL13 3QS
*Activities:* Mixed farming
*Major Shareholder:* Peter Murray
*Officers:* Jane Hilton, Secretary; Jane Hilton [1964] Director/Education Officer; Peter Murray [1958] Managing Director

**High Croft Care Limited**
*Incorporated:* 10 October 2006
*Net Worth:* £875,926 *Total Assets:* £3,329,588
*Registered Office:* 407 Oakwood Lane, Leeds, LS8 3LF
*Activities:* Residential care activities for the elderly and disabled
*Officers:* Martin Patrick Creegan, Secretary/Director; James Joseph Creegan [1967] Director; Martin Patrick Creegan [1964] Director; Matthew Joseph Creegan [1944] Director

**High Grove Beds Limited**
*Incorporated:* 11 September 2002 *Employees:* 268
*Net Worth:* £11,223,513 *Total Assets:* £15,015,159
*Registered Office:* High Grove Beds Group, Headlands Road, Liversedge, W Yorks, WF15 6QA
*Activities:* Manufacture of mattresses
*Major Shareholder:* Wazarat Ali
*Officers:* Wazarat Ali [1967] Director/Businessman

**High Hedley Hope Farm Limited**
*Incorporated:* 25 January 2013 *Employees:* 5
*Net Worth Deficit:* £283,056 *Total Assets:* £3,806,399
*Registered Office:* High Hedley Hope Farm, Tow Law, Co Durham, DL13 4PR
*Activities:* Raising of dairy cattle
*Shareholders:* Cyrus Armstrong; William James Drennan
*Officers:* Stanley Thomson, Secretary; Cyrus Armstrong [1964] Managing Director

**High Point Estates (Birstall) Limited**
*Incorporated:* 21 August 2001 *Employees:* 1
*Net Worth:* £5,018,583 *Total Assets:* £8,000,337
*Registered Office:* Leigh House, 28-32 St Pauls Street, Leeds, LS1 2JT
*Activities:* Renting and operating of Housing Association real estate
*Major Shareholder:* Dmytro Chervak
*Officers:* Daniel Nicholas Chervak, Secretary; Daniel Nicholas Chervak [1983] Director

**High Point Estates (Bury) Limited**
*Incorporated:* 25 November 1999 *Employees:* 1
*Net Worth:* £2,683,311 *Total Assets:* £5,400,192
*Registered Office:* Leigh House, 28-32 St Pauls Street, Leeds, LS1 2JT
*Activities:* Other letting and operating of own or leased real estate
*Major Shareholder:* Dmytro Chervak
*Officers:* Daniel Nicholas Chervak, Secretary; Daniel Nicholas Chervak [1983] Director

**High Point Estates (Darlington) Limited**
*Incorporated:* 11 May 1999 *Employees:* 1
*Net Worth:* £6,709,110 *Total Assets:* £12,538,468
*Registered Office:* Leigh House, 28-32 St Pauls Street, Leeds, LS1 2JT
*Activities:* Renting and operating of Housing Association real estate
*Major Shareholder:* Dmytro Chervak
*Officers:* Daniel Nicholas Chervak, Secretary; Daniel Nicholas Chervak [1983] Director

**High Point Estates (Gateshead) Limited**
*Incorporated:* 25 November 1999 *Employees:* 1
*Net Worth:* £2,164,657 *Total Assets:* £6,509,340
*Registered Office:* Leigh House, 28-32 St Pauls Street, Leeds, LS1 2JT
*Activities:* Other letting and operating of own or leased real estate
*Major Shareholder:* Dmytro Chervak
*Officers:* Daniel Nichoas Chervak, Secretary; Daniel Nicholas Chervak [1983] Director

**High Point Estates Ltd.**
*Incorporated:* 28 May 1985 *Employees:* 1
*Net Worth:* £71,082,928 *Total Assets:* £154,814,688
*Registered Office:* Leigh House, 28-32 St Pauls Street, Leeds, LS1 2JT
*Activities:* Development of building projects
*Major Shareholder:* Dmytro Chervak
*Officers:* Daniel Nicholas Chervak, Secretary; Daniel Nicholas Chervak [1983] Director

**High Point Residential Limited**
*Incorporated:* 22 October 2001 *Employees:* 1
*Net Worth:* £1,019,919 *Total Assets:* £13,721,190
*Registered Office:* Leigh House, 28-32 St Pauls Street, Leeds, LS1 2JT
*Activities:* Renting and operating of Housing Association real estate
*Parent:* High Point Estates Limited
*Officers:* Daniel Nicholas Chervak, Secretary; Daniel Nicholas Chervak [1983] Director

**High Seat Holdings Limited**
*Incorporated:* 15 September 2009 *Employees:* 474
*Net Worth:* £14,250 *Total Assets:* £12,559,411
*Registered Office:* Units 1-3a Grange Road Business Park, Grange Road, Batley, W Yorks, WF17 6LN
*Activities:* Activities of head offices
*Officers:* Debra Lorraine Burrows [1967] Director; William John Burrows [1963] Director; Guy Charles Critchlow [1970] Director; Paul Richard Roberts [1976] Director; Kevin Michael Wall [1964] Retail Director

**High Seat Limited**
*Incorporated:* 29 September 1967 *Employees:* 370
*Net Worth:* £6,114,976 *Total Assets:* £13,094,334
*Registered Office:* Units 1-3a Grange Road Business Park, Grange Road, Batley, W Yorks, WF17 6LN
*Activities:* Retail of furniture, lighting, and similar (not musical instruments or scores) in specialised store
*Parent:* High Seat Holdings Ltd
*Officers:* William John Burrows, Secretary; Debra Lorraine Burrows [1967] Director; William John Burrows [1963] Director; Guy Charles Critchlow [1970] Director; Paul Richard Roberts [1976] Director; Kevin Michael Wall [1964] Retail Director

**High Street TV (Group) Limited**
*Incorporated:* 28 April 2008 *Employees:* 116
*Net Worth:* £16,591,000 *Total Assets:* £26,878,000
*Registered Office:* Central House, Beckwith Knowle, Otley Road, Harrogate, N Yorks, HG3 1UF
*Activities:* Other retail sale not in stores, stalls or markets
*Parent:* High Street TV Bidco Limited
*Officers:* James Edward Coleman [1968] Director; Andrew Edmund Malcher [1970] Director; Neil Stuart Yewdall [1959] Director/Chief Financial Officer

**High Street TV Bidco Limited**
*Incorporated:* 25 March 2015 *Employees:* 8
*Net Worth:* £6,685,774 *Total Assets:* £25,245,712
*Registered Office:* Central House, Beckwith Knowle, Otley Road, Harrogate, N Yorks, HG3 1UF
*Activities:* Non-trading company
*Parent:* High Street TV Holdings Limited
*Officers:* James Edward Coleman [1968] Director; Indra Klara Harrison [1979] Director; Andrew Edmund Malcher [1970] Director; Garry Wilson [1967] Director; Neil Stuart Yewdall [1959] Director/Chief Financial Officer

**High Street TV Holdings Limited**
*Incorporated:* 25 March 2015 *Employees:* 126
*Net Worth Deficit:* £973,000 *Total Assets:* £28,534,000
*Registered Office:* Central House, Beckwith Knowle, Otley Road, Harrogate, N Yorks, HG3 1LF
*Activities:* Non-trading company
*Shareholders:* Endless IV (GP) LP; Endless LLP
*Officers:* James Edward Coleman [1968] Director; Indra Klara Harrison [1979] Director; Robert Stephen Lister [1956] Director; Andrew Edmund Malcher [1970] Director; Garry Wilson [1967] Director; Neil Stuart Yewdall [1959] Director/Chief Financial Officer

**Highacre Builders Limited**
*Incorporated:* 21 March 1991 *Employees:* 2
*Net Worth:* £24,330 *Total Assets:* £3,926,873
*Registered Office:* Estate Office, North Stainley, Ripon, N Yorks, HG4 3JN
*Activities:* Construction of domestic buildings
*Officers:* Fiona Vivienne Ena Reynard, Secretary; Stephen John Bradley [1970] Director/Certified Chartered Accountant; James Kirk Miles Staveley [1974] Director

**Highbury Homes (Yorkshire) Limited**
*Incorporated:* 21 November 2001 *Employees:* 75
*Net Worth:* £1,921,112 *Total Assets:* £3,035,748
*Registered Office:* Highbury House, Oakhill Road, Brighouse, W Yorks, HD6 1SN
*Activities:* Other construction installation
*Shareholders:* Gareth Clayton Jones; Clifford Thorpe
*Officers:* Gareth Clayton Jones [1981] Operations Director; Andrew James Thorpe [1976] Director/Builder; Clifford Thorpe [1948] Director/Builder

**Highcrest Retail Brands Limited**
*Incorporated:* 23 July 2009 *Employees:* 8
*Net Worth:* £4,748,264 *Total Assets:* £10,745,225
*Registered Office:* Wharfeside, Leather Bank, Burley in Wharfedale, Ilkley, W Yorks, LS29 7HP
*Activities:* Activities of head offices
*Major Shareholder:* George Derek Turner
*Officers:* George Derek Turner [1960] Director

**Highfield Awarding Body for Compliance Limited**
*Incorporated:* 21 January 2008 *Employees:* 161
*Net Worth:* £2,053,591 *Total Assets:* £6,591,566
*Registered Office:* Highfield House, Heavens Walk, Lakeside, Doncaster, S Yorks, DN4 5HZ
*Activities:* Regulation of health care, education, cultural and other social services, not incl. social security
*Shareholders:* Christian Marc Sprenger; Jason Antony Lee Sprenger
*Officers:* Jason Sprenger, Secretary; Christian Marc Sprenger [1976] Director; Jason Antony Lee Sprenger [1973] Director/Chief Executive; Richard Sprenger [1950] Director

**Highfield Caravans Limited**
*Incorporated:* 12 March 1962 *Employees:* 14
*Net Worth:* £6,624,825 *Total Assets:* £9,798,393
*Registered Office:* 331 Queen Street, Withernsea, E Yorks, HU19 2NU
*Activities:* Non-specialised wholesale trade
*Major Shareholder:* Malcolm Squire Kemp
*Officers:* Shaun Malcolm Kemp, Secretary; Malcolm Squire Kemp [1937] Director/Caravan Site Proprietor; Mark John Kemp [1962] Director

**Highgrove Group PLC**
*Incorporated:* 30 November 2004 *Employees:* 80
*Previous:* GMI Construction Holdings PLC
*Net Worth:* £16,981,656 *Total Assets:* £39,043,712
*Registered Office:* Middleton House, Westland Road, Leeds, LS11 5UH
*Activities:* Activities of head offices
*Shareholders:* Jarrod Colin Best; Paul Whitaker
*Officers:* Dominic Michael Lush, Secretary; Jarrod Colin Best [1977] Director; David James Shann [1973] Director/Chartered Accountant; Paul Whitaker [1968] Commercial Director

**Highgrove Property Developments Limited**
*Incorporated:* 22 January 2004 *Employees:* 5
*Net Worth:* £576,346 *Total Assets:* £4,834,297
*Registered Office:* Torevell Dent, Hope Park, Trevor Foster Way, Bradford, BD5 8HH
*Activities:* Buying and selling of own real estate
*Shareholder:* Paul Nicholas Cribb
*Officers:* Paul Nicholas Cribb [1962] Director; Stephanie Ruth Cribb [1965] Director/Counsellor; Elizabeth Clare Kirkby [1967] Director/Teacher; John Dawson Kirkby [1961] Charity Director

**Highstone Estates (Kidderminster) Limited**
*Incorporated:* 12 December 2001
*Net Worth:* £1,512,799 *Total Assets:* £151,183,040
*Registered Office:* Nidderdale View, Darley Road, Birstwith, Harrogate, N Yorks, HG3 2PN
*Activities:* Financial intermediation not elsewhere classified
*Major Shareholder:* Paul Sykes
*Officers:* Peter James Kavanagh, Secretary; Michael Richard Huber [1976] Director; Peter James Kavanagh [1978] Director of Energy Company

**Clare Hill (Huddersfield) LLP**
*Incorporated:* 8 October 2004
*Net Worth:* £2,270,211 *Total Assets:* £3,906,892
*Registered Office:* Loftus Hill, Ferrensby, Knaresborough, N Yorks, HG5 9JT
*Officers:* Charles Richard Jackson [1951] Member; Ian Ross Pullan [1958] Member

**Albert Hill Commercials Limited**
*Incorporated:* 28 January 2000 *Employees:* 7
*Net Worth:* £7,858,439 *Total Assets:* £9,236,276
*Registered Office:* Riverside Industrial Estate, Dodsworth Street, Darlington, Co Durham, DL1 2NG
*Activities:* Sale of other motor vehicles
*Major Shareholder:* Peter William Foster
*Officers:* Diane Roberts, Secretary; Peter William Foster [1971] Director/Vehicle Trader

**Hill Giftware Limited**
*Incorporated:* 12 May 1999 *Employees:* 145
*Net Worth:* £2,115,618 *Total Assets:* £4,463,803
*Registered Office:* Hill House, Oak Tree, Burneston, Bedale, N Yorks, DL8 2JW
*Activities:* Wholesale of household goods (other than musical instruments) n.e.c
*Parent:* Hill House Group Ltd
*Officers:* Benjamin James Hawkins [1987] Director; Nicholas Graham Hill [1972] Director; Paul Andrew Nel [1984] Director; Julian Earle Potter [1975] Director

**Hill House School Limited**
*Incorporated:* 14 June 1967 *Employees:* 130
*Net Worth:* £6,186,090 *Total Assets:* £13,849,135
*Registered Office:* Sixth Avenue, Auckley, Doncaster, S Yorks, DN9 3GG
*Activities:* Primary education
*Officers:* Robert Scott Colbear [1966] Director/Marketing Executive; Dr Antonia Helen Cooper [1970] Director/Clinical Psychologist; Valerie Cusworth [1949] Director/Retired; Richard Anthony de Mulder [1966] Director; Neil Royston Ebden [1973] Director/Banker; Dr Dean Justin Eggitt [1980] Director/GP; Joan Wickes Fearns [1956] Director/Retired; Dr Madeline Jane Fraser [1956] Director/Retired; Maura Jaqueline Jameson [1960] Director/Consultant; Robert Paul Leggott [1970] Director; Jason Antony Lee Sprenger [1973] Director; Michael John Wilson-Maccormack [1970] Director/Architect

**M Hillas (Properties) Limited**
*Incorporated:* 16 November 2000 *Employees:* 3
*Net Worth:* £1,178,577 *Total Assets:* £3,091,541
*Registered Office:* Thorn Tree Farm, Brighouse, Denholme Road, Northowram, Halifax, W Yorks, HX3 7TF
*Activities:* Other letting and operating of own or leased real estate
*Major Shareholder:* Joanne Hillas
*Officers:* Joanne Hillas, Company Secretary; Joanne Hillas [1963] Director/Company Secretary; Mark Stephen Hillas [1961] Director/Commercial Vehicle Dealer

**Hillas Group Limited**
*Incorporated:* 15 February 2016
*Net Worth:* £643,556 *Total Assets:* £3,738,193
*Registered Office:* Otley Mills, Ilkley Road, Otley, W Yorks, LS21 1QS
*Activities:* Activities of other holding companies n.e.c.
*Shareholders:* Charlotte Alice Annie Hillas; James Andrew Hillas; Victoria Elizabeth Hillas
*Officers:* Charlotte Alice Annie Hillas [1988] Director; James Andrew Hillas [1989] Director; Victoria Elizabeth Hillas [1980] Director

**Andrew Hillas Properties Limited**
*Incorporated:* 23 January 1996 *Employees:* 6
*Net Worth:* £7,981,737 *Total Assets:* £12,021,830
*Registered Office:* Otley Mills, Ilkley Road, Otley, W Yorks, LS21 1QS
*Activities:* Other business support service activities n.e.c.
*Parent:* Hillas Group Limited
*Officers:* Charlotte Alice Annie Hillas [1988] Director; James Andrew Hillas [1989] Director; Victoria Elizabeth Hillas [1980] Director

**Hillcrest Garages (Sowerby Bridge) Limited**
*Incorporated:* 23 October 1984 *Employees:* 4
*Net Worth:* £6,413,598 *Total Assets:* £8,434,588
*Registered Office:* Walter Dawson & Son, 9 Kerry Street, Horsforth, Leeds, LS18 4AW
*Activities:* Sale of other motor vehicles
*Officers:* Barbara Anne Roper, Secretary; Barbara Anne Roper [1952] Director; Brian Colin Roper [1956] Director

**Hillcroft Ltd**
*Incorporated:* 2 April 1990 *Employees:* 358
*Net Worth:* £7,584,091 *Total Assets:* £15,501,591
*Registered Office:* Hillcroft Nursing Home, North Road, Carnforth, Lancs, LA5 9LX
*Activities:* Activities of other holding companies n.e.c.
*Shareholders:* John Paul Ayrton; Brian Alan Pinington; David Pinington
*Officers:* Louise Ann Mattinson, Secretary; John Paul Ayrton [1940] Director; Brian Alan Pinington [1946] Director; David Pinington [1949] Director

**Hilldene Holdings Limited**
*Incorporated:* 13 May 2010
*Net Worth:* £1,250,645 *Total Assets:* £4,565,218
*Registered Office:* Heathcliffe, Potterton Lane, Potterton, Leeds, LS15 4NR
*Activities:* Non-trading company
*Major Shareholder:* Barry Barnes
*Officers:* Barry Barnes [1943] Director

**Hillreed Homes Limited**
*Incorporated:* 12 March 1975 *Employees:* 4
*Net Worth:* £79,059,584 *Total Assets:* £99,785,576
*Registered Office:* Persimmon House, Fulford, York, YO19 4FE
*Activities:* Construction of commercial buildings
*Parent:* Hillreed Holdings Limited
*Officers:* Tracy Lazelle Davison, Secretary; David Jenkinson [1967] Director; Michael Hugh Killoran [1961] Finance Director; Richard Paul Stenhouse [1971] Director/Accountant

**Z.Hinchliffe & Sons Limited**
*Incorporated:* 2 October 1903 *Employees:* 127
*Net Worth:* £16,384,667 *Total Assets:* £17,753,418
*Registered Office:* Hartcliffe Mills, Denby Dale, Huddersfield, W Yorks, HD8 8QL
*Activities:* Preparation and spinning of textile fibres
*Parent:* Harold Hinchliffe Limited
*Officers:* John Glennon, Secretary; James Harold Hinchliffe [1960] Director/Spinner; Graham Arthur Wilby [1968] Director/Spinner

**Harold Hinchliffe Limited**
*Incorporated:* 12 October 1962 *Employees:* 127
*Net Worth:* £9,757,259 *Total Assets:* £17,753,664
*Registered Office:* Hartcliffe Mills, Wakefield Road, Denby Dale, Huddersfield, W Yorks, HD8 8QL
*Activities:* Activities of head offices
*Shareholders:* James Harold Hinchliffe; John Robert Hinchliffe
*Officers:* Audrey Marian Kenyon, Secretary; James Harold Hinchliffe [1960] Director/Spinner; Audrey Marian Kenyon [1923] Director/Company Secretary

**Hindle Gears Holdings Limited**
*Incorporated:* 20 November 2015 *Employees:* 51
*Net Worth:* £2,169,097 *Total Assets:* £3,997,931
*Registered Office:* Hapco Works, Caledonia Street, Bradford, W Yorks, BD5 0EL
*Activities:* Manufacture of bearings, gears, gearing and driving elements
*Shareholder:* Richard John Hindle
*Officers:* Peter Roy Bingham [1960] Director; David Hindle [1962] Director/Engineer; Richard John Hindle [1957] Director/Engineer; Steven Richard Widdrington [1951] Director

**Hindle Gears Limited**
*Incorporated:* 3 August 2011 *Employees:* 51
*Net Worth:* £2,619,920 *Total Assets:* £4,419,129
*Registered Office:* Hapco Works, Caledonia Street, Bradford, W Yorks, BD5 0EL
*Activities:* Manufacture of other fabricated metal products n.e.c.
*Parent:* Hindle Gears Holdings Limited
*Officers:* Peter Roy Bingham [1960] Director; David Hindle [1962] Director; Richard John Hindle [1957] Director/Engineer; Steven Widdrington [1951] Director/Company Secretary

**Hindle Group Limited**
*Incorporated:* 9 December 1941 *Employees:* 38
*Net Worth:* £6,628,256 *Total Assets:* £8,165,647
*Registered Office:* Hapco Works, Caledonia Street, Bradford, BD5 0EL
*Activities:* Manufacture of other fabricated metal products n.e.c.
*Shareholders:* Techmotion Limited; Richard John Hindle
*Officers:* Steven Widdrington, Secretary; Peter Roy Bingham [1960] Director; David Hindle [1962] Director/Engineer; Richard John Hindle [1957] Managing Director; Steven Widdrington [1951] Director

**Hindu Cultural Society of Bradford**
*Incorporated:* 11 January 2007 *Employees:* 8
*Net Worth:* £3,780,339 *Total Assets:* £3,780,339
*Registered Office:* 341 Leeds Road, Bradford, W Yorks, BD3 9JY
*Activities:* Other social work activities without accommodation n.e.c.
*Officers:* Dr. Suresh Tailor, Secretary; Samykkurukkal Balakrishnan [1942] Director/Landlord; Mukesh Kumar Chawla [1952] Director; Rajeev Dewedi [1962] Director/Self Employed Accountant; Ravinder Dharni [1962] Director/Businessman; Subhash Dharni [1951] Director/Shopkeeper; Virender Dharni [1962] Director/Businessman; Hridesh Kumar Gupta [1962] Director/Dental Surgeon; Santosh Gupta [1939] Director/Retired [Indian]; Baldev Krishen [1946] Director/Bus Driver; Ashok Kumar Nair [1955] Director/Teacher; Kamaljit Sharma [1960] Director/Civil Servant; Narinder Sharma [1952] Managing Director; Doctor Surinder Pratap Singh [1949] Director/Doctor; Kapel Dev Soni [1930] Director/Retired; Dr Suresh Tailor [1954] Director/Chemist; Natvar Lal Ranchhodji Taylor [1944] Director/Retired; Phoolan Balbev Vig [1949] Director/Shopkeeper

**Hird & Partners LLP**
*Incorporated:* 23 April 2014
*Net Worth:* £3,058,667 *Total Assets:* £3,763,581
*Registered Office:* 2 King Street, Halifax, W Yorks, HX1 1SR
*Officers:* Timothy Adam Keddie Booth [1981] Member; William Edward Richard Burt [1959] Member; Sally Angela Dumbleton [1966] Member; Christopher John Lockett [1968] Member; Peter Edward Scholefield [1962] Member

**Hird (UK) Ltd**
*Incorporated:* 28 November 2011 *Employees:* 1
*Net Worth:* £4,139,523 *Total Assets:* £11,285,611
*Registered Office:* 127-143 English Street, Hull, HU3 2BS
*Activities:* Renting and leasing of construction and civil engineering machinery and equipment
*Shareholders:* Hird Group Holdings Limited; Philip Robert Hird
*Officers:* Robert John Blanchard [1967] Finance Director; Philip Robert Hird [1981] Managing Director; Phillip Stuart Moss [1966] Director; Carl Norfolk [1958] Director; John Mark Wilding [1973] Director

**Hird Limited**
*Incorporated:* 17 November 1982 *Employees:* 89
*Previous:* Peter Hird and Sons Limited
*Net Worth:* £2,538,790 *Total Assets:* £4,947,827
*Registered Office:* 127-143 English Street, Hull, HU3 2BS
*Activities:* Renting and leasing of construction and civil engineering machinery and equipment
*Parent:* Hird Group Holdings Limited
*Officers:* Robert Peter Hird, Secretary; Robert John Blanchard [1967] Finance Director; Christina Hird [1947] Director; Philip Robert Hird [1981] Managing Director; Robert Peter Hird [1939] Director/Chairman; Phillip Stuart Moss [1966] Director/Access Manager; Carl Norfolk [1958] Director; John Mark Wilding [1973] Director

**Hird Rail Services Limited**
*Incorporated:* 30 April 1996 *Employees:* 22
*Net Worth:* £1,744,949 *Total Assets:* £3,328,667
*Registered Office:* Leigh House, 28-32 St Pauls Street, Leeds, LS1 2PX
*Activities:* Other service activities incidental to land transportation, n.e.c.
*Shareholders:* Michael David Hird; Lindsay Dianne Harwood
*Officers:* Lindsay Harwood, Secretary; Gary Michael Elliott [1961] Director; Lindsay Dianne Harwood [1965] Director; Michael David Hird [1964] Director/Railway Manager; John Smith [1968] Director/Manager

**Hire It Plant Limited**
*Incorporated:* 3 April 2014 *Employees:* 2
*Net Worth:* £352,375 *Total Assets:* £3,847,297
*Registered Office:* Sunnybank Farm, Whitehall Road East, Birkenshaw, Bradford, W Yorks, BD11 2LL
*Activities:* Renting and leasing of construction and civil engineering machinery and equipment
*Major Shareholder:* Julie Ann Romani
*Officers:* Jenna Romani [1985] Director; Julie Ann Romani [1964] Director

**Hire Station Limited**
*Incorporated:* 3 September 1997 *Employees:* 1,065
*Net Worth:* £58,656,000 *Total Assets:* £122,384,000
*Registered Office:* c/o VP PLC, Central House, Beckwith Knowle, Otley Road, Harrogate, N Yorks, HG3 1UD
*Activities:* Renting and leasing of other machinery, equipment and tangible goods n.e.c.
*Parent:* VP PLC
*Officers:* Allison Margaret Bainbridge, Secretary; Allison Margaret Bainbridge [1960] Director; Jeremy Frederic George Pilkington [1951] Director; Neil Andrew Stothard [1958] Director

**Hireport Limited**
*Incorporated:* 17 January 1986 *Employees:* 21
*Net Worth:* £3,350,674 *Total Assets:* £4,050,478
*Registered Office:* Waldorf House, Waldorf Way, Wakefield, W Yorks, WF2 8DH
*Activities:* Manufacture of metal structures and parts of structures
*Officers:* Simon Peter Shidlow, Secretary; Christine Batty [1952] Director/Secretary; Mike Batty [1950] Director; Joanne Shidlow [1960] Director/Administrator; Simon Peter Shidlow [1959] Director

**Hisense UK Limited**
*Incorporated:* 28 September 2012 *Employees:* 30
*Net Worth:* £2,643,966 *Total Assets:* £21,817,208
*Registered Office:* Unit 2 Meadow Court, Millshaw, Leeds, LS11 8LZ
*Activities:* Wholesale of radio, television goods & electrical household appliances (other than records, tapes, CDs)
*Parent:* Hisense Luxembourg Holding S.A.R.L.
*Officers:* Hongbo HE [1978] Director [Chinese]; Lu Hou [1972] Director [Chinese]; Dr Lan Lin [1958] Director [American]

**Histon Sweet Spreads Limited**
*Incorporated:* 21 February 2012 *Employees:* 421
*Net Worth:* £268,844,992 *Total Assets:* £311,652,000
*Registered Office:* 2100 Century Way, Thorpe Park Business Park, Leeds, LS15 8ZB
*Activities:* Other processing and preserving of fruit and vegetables
*Parent:* Hain Frozen Foods UK Limited
*Officers:* Nicholas Keen, Secretary; Denise Menikhelm Faltishek [1973] Director/Attorney; James Michael Langrock [1965] Director [American]; Mark Lawrence Schiller [1961] Director/CEO Hain Celestial [American]; Robin James Skidmore [1968] Director

**Hitha Limited**
*Incorporated:* 17 November 2008
*Net Worth:* £3,272,946 *Total Assets:* £3,569,546
*Registered Office:* Northgate, 118 North Street, Leeds, LS2 7PN
*Activities:* Activities of other holding companies n.e.c.
*Major Shareholder:* Alagu Shanmugam Vijaykumar
*Officers:* Dr Alagu Shanmugam Vijaykumar [1965] Director

**HK Timbers Limited**
*Incorporated:* 5 September 2002 *Employees:* 28
*Net Worth:* £2,551,380 *Total Assets:* £3,221,939
*Registered Office:* Laughton Lane, Morton, Gainsborough, Lincs, DN21 3ET
*Activities:* Manufacture of wooden containers
*Parent:* GCH Capital Limited
*Officers:* Richard William Bundock [1970] Managing Director

**HLD (Manchester) Limited**
*Incorporated:* 4 December 2015
*Net Worth Deficit:* £230,151 *Total Assets:* £8,891,788
*Registered Office:* Marshall House, Huddersfield Road, Elland, W Yorks, HX5 9BW
*Activities:* Development of building projects
*Shareholder:* Commercial Development Projects Limited
*Officers:* Jonathan Booth, Secretary; Jonathan Booth [1970] Director; Simon Charles Newton Marshall [1963] Director

**HMCA/S PLC**
*Incorporated:* 10 April 1978 *Employees:* 46
*Net Worth:* £12,957,735 *Total Assets:* £15,311,429
*Registered Office:* Beech Hall, 62 High Street, Knaresborough, N Yorks, HG5 0EA
*Activities:* Activities auxiliary to financial intermediation n.e.c.
*Parent:* Scriven Park Estates Limited
*Officers:* Mark Charles Upton, Secretary; Philip David Allott [1959] Managing Director; Andrew Baker [1970] Director/Compliance Manager; Jane Michelle Blackmore [1968] Director/Association Secretary (Insurance); Terence Allan Briggs [1952] Managing Director; Andrew David Harrop [1964] Finance Director; Barnabas Anthony Richard Skrentny [1964] Director/Pastor; Barnabas Joseph Skrentny [1937] Director/Underwriter [American]

**Hobson and Porter Limited**
*Incorporated:* 12 September 1979 *Employees:* 122
*Net Worth:* £4,341,930 *Total Assets:* £10,670,172
*Registered Office:* Clifford House, Malmo Road, Sutton Fields Industrial Estate, Hull, HU7 0YF
*Activities:* Construction of commercial buildings
*Shareholder:* Peter Leslie Hobson
*Officers:* Jacqueline Louise Blades, Secretary; Michael Andrew Beal [1972] Construction Director; David Malcolm Blades [1961] Director/Contracts Manager; Jacqueline Louise Blades [1968] Director/Office Manager; John Stuart Craven [1965] Director/Quantity Surveyor; Michael David Gibbin [1970] Director/Certified Chartered Accountant; Gillian Hobson [1947] Director; Peter Leslie Hobson [1945] Director; Russell John Horner [1969] Director/Estimator; Richard Hunter [1966] Director/Quantity Surveyor; Julie Annette Smee [1971] Director/Office Administration; Mark Smee [1972] Director

**Hobson Farming Limited**
*Incorporated:* 4 February 1997 *Employees:* 21
*Net Worth:* £4,788,364 *Total Assets:* £8,584,353
*Registered Office:* Naburn Hill Farm, Crockey Hill, York, YO19 4SR
*Activities:* Mixed farming
*Shareholders:* Rodger Timothy Hobson; Victoria Louise Hobson
*Officers:* Vicky Louise Hobson, Secretary; Rodger Timothy Hobson [1964] Director/Farmer; Vicky Louise Hobson [1966] Director

**Jackie Hobson Investments**
*Incorporated:* 23 May 2013
*Previous:* Jackie Hobson Investments Limited
*Net Worth:* £134,890 *Total Assets:* £5,505,791
*Registered Office:* 30 Kings Dale Drive, Menston, Ilkley, W Yorks, LS29 6QN
*Activities:* Fund management activities
*Major Shareholder:* Jacqueline Joan Hobson
*Officers:* Jacqueline Joan Hobson [1948] Director

**T.H.Hobson Limited**
*Incorporated:* 21 August 1951 *Employees:* 23
*Net Worth:* £5,557,587 *Total Assets:* £8,393,925
*Registered Office:* Woodhouse Grange, Sutton on Derwent, York, YO41 4DF
*Activities:* Growing of cereals (except rice), leguminous crops and oil seeds
*Shareholders:* Christopher Thomas Hobson; Nicholas Edward Hobson
*Officers:* Nicholas Edward Hobson, Secretary/Farmer; Christopher Thomas Hobson [1963] Director/Farmer; Nicholas Edward Hobson [1969] Director/Farmer

**Amanda Hobson Limited**
*Incorporated:* 14 February 2013
*Net Worth:* £718,952 *Total Assets:* £4,033,178
*Registered Office:* High Austby Farm, Nesfield, Ilkley, W Yorks, LS29 0BJ
*Activities:* Buying and selling of own real estate
*Parent:* Elsante Estates Group Ltd
*Officers:* Amanda Hobson [1973] Director; Guy Alexander Taylor [1973] Commercial Director

**AC Hobson LLP**
*Incorporated:* 19 September 2011
*Net Worth:* £4,062,108 *Total Assets:* £4,078,145
*Registered Office:* 1 East Park Road, Harrogate, N Yorks, HG1 5QT
*Officers:* Amanda Jane Hobson [1973] Member; Andrew Christopher Hobson [1946] Member; Edward Taylor [2012] Member; Elsa Taylor [2010] Member; Annabelle Taylor [2006] LLP Member

**Hocomm Limited**
*Incorporated:* 14 July 2003 *Employees:* 126
*Net Worth:* £5,501,000 *Total Assets:* £26,200,000
*Registered Office:* East Moor House, Green Park Business Centre, Goose Lane, Sutton on Forest, York, YO61 1ET
*Activities:* Activities of head offices
*Major Shareholder:* Dennis Hoban
*Officers:* Brynmor Roberts, Secretary; Dennis Hoban [1950] Director; Brynmor Roberts [1952] Director

**Anthony Hodges Consulting Limited**
*Incorporated:* 7 May 1998 *Employees:* 77
*Net Worth:* £5,189,436 *Total Assets:* £5,976,207
*Registered Office:* Heath Hall, Heath, Wakefield, W Yorks, WF1 5SL
*Activities:* Management consultancy activities other than financial management
*Shareholders:* Anthony Michael Hodges; Vivienne Hodges
*Officers:* Trevor Ian Posliff, Secretary; Francis Jack Goss [1971] Director; Roger David Hattam [1968] Director/Businessman; Anthony Michael Hodges [1948] Director/Consultant; Vivienne Hodges [1955] Director/Administrator

**Hodgson Sealants (Holdings) Limited**
*Incorporated:* 20 January 2005 *Employees:* 71
*Net Worth:* £3,474,652 *Total Assets:* £6,547,002
*Registered Office:* Belprin Road, Beverley, E Yorks, HU17 0LN
*Activities:* Manufacture of paints, varnishes and similar coatings, mastics and sealants
*Shareholders:* Richard Maxwell Hodgson; Charles Peter Hodgson
*Officers:* Richard Maxwell Hodgson, Secretary/Director; Charles Peter Hodgson [1959] Director; Felicity Hodgson [1933] Director; Jane Caroline Hodgson [1961] Director/Independent Parent Supporter; Karen Elizabeth Hodgson [1960] Director/Counsellor; Richard Maxwell Hodgson [1957] Director

**Hodson Family Investments Limited**
*Incorporated:* 28 October 2014
*Net Worth:* £1,713,281 *Total Assets:* £10,602,043
*Registered Office:* Manor Farm House, 75 George Lane, Notton, Wakefield, W Yorks, WF4 2NQ
*Activities:* Activities of investment trusts
*Shareholders:* Richard Phillip Hodson; Sally Ann Hodson
*Officers:* Stefan Benkov Benev [1963] Director; Richard Phillip Hodson [1951] Director; Sally Ann Hodson [1953] Director

**Hodson Properties Limited**
*Incorporated:* 17 June 1976 *Employees:* 1
*Net Worth:* £2,288,991 *Total Assets:* £3,444,628
*Registered Office:* 33 George Street, Wakefield, W Yorks, WF1 1LX
*Activities:* Development of building projects
*Major Shareholder:* Richard Phillip Hodson
*Officers:* Richard Phillip Hodson, Secretary; Stefan Benkov Benev [1963] Director; Richard Charles Hodson [1977] Director/Insurance Broker; Richard Phillip Hodson [1951] Director/Insurance Broker; Sally Ann Hodson [1953] Director; William Greig Hodson [1982] Director/Student

**Hoerbiger UK Limited**
*Incorporated:* 11 November 1986 *Employees:* 21
*Net Worth:* £7,810,292 *Total Assets:* £21,749,298
*Registered Office:* Unit 2 Maple Park, Lowfields Avenue, Leeds, LS12 6HH
*Activities:* Manufacture of compressors
*Officers:* Rafael Bacher [1975] Director [Austrian]; Richard James Yates [1977] Director/General Manager

**Gawith Hoggarth & Co.,Limited**
*Incorporated:* 10 October 1923 *Employees:* 37
*Net Worth:* £7,293,217 *Total Assets:* £10,106,349
*Registered Office:* Unit 16-22 Lake District Business Park, Mint Bridge Road, Kendal, Cumbria, LA9 6NH
*Activities:* Manufacture of tobacco products
*Major Shareholder:* Irene Mary Gawith
*Officers:* Christopher Steven Gawith [1980] Director; Irene Mary Gawith [1953] Director

**Gawith Hoggarth Tobacco Trading Limited**
*Incorporated:* 18 June 1998 *Employees:* 14
*Net Worth:* £2,994,852 *Total Assets:* £4,386,670
*Registered Office:* Unit 16-22 Lake District Business Park, Mint Bridge Road, Kendal, Cumbria, LA9 6NH
*Activities:* Manufacture of tobacco products
*Shareholders:* Gawith Hoggarth & Co.,Limited; Poschl International GmbH
*Officers:* Irene Mary Gawith, Secretary; Christopher Steven Gawith [1980] Director; Irene Mary Gawith [1953] Director

**Holbeach Buildings LLP**
*Incorporated:* 30 November 2005 *Employees:* 7
*Net Worth:* £1,577,835 *Total Assets:* £3,484,381
*Registered Office:* Dianthus House, Common Lane, North Cave, Brough, N Humbers, HU15 2FT
*Officers:* Henricus Johannes Antonius Maria Brockhoff [1959] Member; Arie Martinus Van Duyn [1951] Member; Hendrik Johannes Gerardus Salome [1954] Member; Arnold Kloostra [1971] LLP Member; Jan Paul Christiaan Rijke [1964] LLP Member

**The Holbeck Charitable Trust**
*Incorporated:* 23 February 2012
*Net Worth:* £2,832,000 *Total Assets:* £3,375,000
*Registered Office:* Rollits LLP, Forsyth House, Alpha Cross, Monks Cross, York, YO32 9WN
*Activities:* Non-trading company
*Officers:* Gerry Morrison, Secretary; Victoria Ann Denman [1979] Director; Francesca Ann Horsfield [1952] Director; Gordon Christopher Horsfield [1946] Director; Joshua Michael John Horsfield [1982] Director/Accountant; John Richard Lane [1963] Director/Solicitor; Camilla Louise Seligman [1984] Director/Teacher

**Holbeck Ghyll Hotel LLP**
*Incorporated:* 25 November 2008
*Net Worth Deficit:* £111,127 *Total Assets:* £8,253,351
*Registered Office:* Holbeck Ghyll Country House Hotel, Holbeck Lane, Windermere, Cumbria, LA23 1LU
*Officers:* Stephen Leahy [1966] Member

**Holbeck Homes Limited**
*Incorporated:* 12 September 1966
*Net Worth:* £4,152,265 *Total Assets:* £4,708,138
*Registered Office:* Cavendish House, Kirkby in Furness, Cumbria, LA17 7UN
*Activities:* Construction of domestic buildings
*Parent:* Holker Holdings Limited
*Officers:* Lucy Georgiana Cavendish [1973] Director; Lord Richard Hugh Baron Cavendish [1941] Director/Landowner; Allen Joseph Gibb [1966] Director; Right Honourable Grania Mary Lady Cavendish [1947] Director

**Holdco 123 Limited**
*Incorporated:* 12 September 2016 *Employees:* 52
*Net Worth:* £12,345,921 *Total Assets:* £24,770,296
*Registered Office:* Leigh House, 28-32 St Pauls Street, Leeds, LS1 2JT
*Activities:* Activities of head offices
*Major Shareholder:* Anthony Stephen Gill
*Officers:* Charlotte Emily Gill, Secretary; Anthony Stephen Gill [1963] Director; Charlotte Emily Gill [1994] Director; Duncan Scott Marrison [1976] Director

**Holden Grange Care Group Limited**
*Incorporated:* 22 February 2016 *Employees:* 6
*Net Worth:* £1,760,537 *Total Assets:* £5,475,938
*Registered Office:* Hillbro Nursing Home, Holden Lane, Shipley, W Yorks, BD17 6RZ
*Activities:* Activities of head offices
*Major Shareholder:* Michael Stephen Berry
*Officers:* Jason Michael Berry [1988] Director/Estates Manager; Leon Carl Berry [1989] Director/Administrative Manager; Michael Stephen Berry [1962] Director/Proprietor

**Holdgrove Limited**
*Incorporated:* 20 November 2001 *Employees:* 2
*Net Worth:* £188,000 *Total Assets:* £10,616,000
*Registered Office:* Second Floor, G Mill, Dean Clough, Halifax, W Yorks, HX3 5AX
*Activities:* Other information technology service activities
*Parent:* SSP Limited
*Officers:* Richard Charles Forrest, Secretary; Stephen Michael Lathrope [1967] Director; Christopher Pennington [1972] Director/Chartered Accountant

**O.& C.Holdsworth Limited**
*Incorporated:* 25 March 1931 *Employees:* 135
*Net Worth:* £448,172 *Total Assets:* £3,181,949
*Registered Office:* 9 Harrison Road, Halifax, W Yorks, HX1 2AF
*Activities:* Tour operator activities
*Officers:* Gillian Shelton, Secretary; Robert Angus Holdsworth [1943] Director; Andrew Kinnaird [1979] Sales Director

**Holetch Holdings Limited**
*Incorporated:* 26 November 1930 *Employees:* 4
*Net Worth:* £12,180,827 *Total Assets:* £12,743,605
*Registered Office:* Gresham House, 5-7 St Pauls Street, Leeds, LS1 2JG
*Activities:* Other service activities n.e.c.
*Shareholders:* Davern Holdings Limited; Ernest Gunner Holdings Limited
*Officers:* David Bosworth Gunner, Secretary/Meat Processor; John Robert Beevers [1968] Director/Chartered Accountant; David Bosworth Gunner [1952] Director/Meat Processor; Susan Linda Siddons [1950] Director/Chartered Accountant; Marilyn Elizabeth Walker [1953] Director

**Holf Investments Limited**
*Incorporated:* 8 April 2002
*Net Worth:* £51,105,532 *Total Assets:* £52,697,452
*Registered Office:* Cardale House, Cardale Court, Beckwith Head Road, Harrogate, N Yorks, HG3 1RY
*Activities:* Development of building projects
*Major Shareholder:* Peter Robert Wilkinson
*Officers:* Timothy Andrew Parkinson, Secretary; Joanne Patricia Wilkinson [1959] Director; Peter Robert Wilkinson [1954] Director

**Holf Technologies Limited**
*Incorporated:* 10 June 1998
*Net Worth:* £8,510,865 *Total Assets:* £8,510,865
*Registered Office:* Cardale House, Cardale Court, Beckwith Head Road, Harrogate, N Yorks, HG3 1RY
*Activities:* Dormant company
*Parent:* Intechnology PLC
*Officers:* Andrew Murdoch Scott Kaberry, Secretary; Andrew Murdoch Scott Kaberry [1946] Director; Peter Robert Wilkinson [1954] Director

**Holgates (Caravan Parks) Limited**
*Incorporated:* 22 August 1956 *Employees:* 120
*Net Worth:* £20,900,164 *Total Assets:* £26,230,654
*Registered Office:* Middlebarrow Plain, Silverdale, Carnforth, Lancs, LA5 0SH
*Activities:* Holiday centres and villages
*Parent:* Blue Brick UK Limited
*Officers:* Judith Margaret Holgate, Secretary; Judith Margaret Holgate [1944] Director/Secretary; Michael William Holgate [1966] Managing Director

**Holgates Holdings Limited**
*Incorporated:* 6 June 2007 *Employees:* 136
*Net Worth:* £16,204,881 *Total Assets:* £27,605,936
*Registered Office:* Middlebarrow Plain, Silverdale, Carnforth, Lancs, LA5 0SH
*Activities:* Activities of head offices
*Major Shareholder:* Michael William Holgate
*Officers:* Judith Margaret Holgate, Secretary; Judith Margaret Holgate [1944] Director; Michael William Holgate [1966] Director

**Holgates Silver Ridge Ltd**
*Incorporated:* 30 September 2010 *Employees:* 2
*Net Worth:* £607,334 *Total Assets:* £4,592,917
*Registered Office:* Middlebarrow Plain, Cove Road, Silverdale, Carnforth, Lancs, LA5 0SH
*Activities:* Recreational vehicle parks, trailer parks and camping grounds
*Shareholders:* Michael William Holgate; Roger Holgate
*Officers:* Michael William Holgate [1966] Director; Roger Holgate [1971] Director

**Holker Estates Co. Limited**
*Incorporated:* 16 February 1968 *Employees:* 79
*Net Worth Deficit:* £132,309 *Total Assets:* £5,605,504
*Registered Office:* Cavendish House, Kirkby in Furness, Cumbria, LA17 7UN
*Activities:* Renting and operating of Housing Association real estate
*Parent:* Holker Holdings Limited
*Officers:* Lucy Georgiana Cavendish [1973] Director/Artist; Lord Richard Hugh Baron Cavendish [1941] Director/Landowner; Allen Joseph Gibb [1966] Director; Right Honourable Grania Mary Lady Cavendish [1947] Director

**Holker Holdings Limited**
*Incorporated:* 1 September 1980 *Employees:* 134
*Net Worth:* £4,678,507 *Total Assets:* £10,308,650
*Registered Office:* Cavendish House, Kirkby in Furness, Cumbria, LA17 7UN
*Activities:* Activities of head offices
*Shareholders:* Richard William James Parry; Charles Edward Vere Cecil
*Officers:* Peter Anthony Bostock [1953] Director/Solicitor; Lucy Georgiana Cavendish [1973] Director; Lord Richard Hugh Baron Cavendish [1941] Director/Landowner; Allen Joseph Gibb [1966] Director; Right Honourable Grania Mary Lady Cavendish [1947] Director; David Neil Sarti [1965] Director

**Holliday International Limited**
*Incorporated:* 8 April 1997
*Net Worth:* £10,440,000 *Total Assets:* £10,561,000
*Registered Office:* P O Box B3, Leeds Road, Huddersfield, W Yorks, HD1 6BU
*Activities:* Activities of other holding companies n.e.c.
*Officers:* Rachael Elizabeth Blakey, Secretary; Saurabh Gurnurkar [1981] Director/Strategy and Corporate Development for The Group [Indian]; Sandeep Varalwar [1968] Director [Indian]; Santosh Varalwar [1962] Director [Indian]

**Hollin Hall Holdings Limited**
*Incorporated:* 13 April 2012
*Net Worth:* £6,395,108 *Total Assets:* £6,400,033
*Registered Office:* The East Wing, The Newhall, Newhall Way, Bradford, BD5 8FF
*Activities:* Buying and selling of own real estate
*Shareholder:* James Ernest Marshall
*Officers:* Frank Edward Marshall [1978] Director; James Ernest Marshall [1979] Director

**J. M. Holling Limited**
*Incorporated:* 12 March 1999 *Employees:* 54
*Net Worth:* £786,602 *Total Assets:* £3,326,978
*Registered Office:* c/o 4L's Packing Ltd, Coulman Street, Thorne, Doncaster, S Yorks, DN8 5JS
*Activities:* Other transportation support activities
*Officers:* Colette Melanie Porter, Secretary/Finance Manager; Peter Holling [1965] Director/Haulage Contractor

**Hollings Limited**
*Incorporated:* 9 February 1996 *Employees:* 62
*Net Worth:* £1,086,552 *Total Assets:* £4,140,444
*Registered Office:* Snaygill Industrial Estate, Keighley Road, Skipton, N Yorks, BD23 2QR
*Activities:* Manufacture of prepared pet foods
*Shareholders:* Jeffrey Alan Hollings; Celia Elizabeth Hollings
*Officers:* Celia Elizabeth Hollings, Secretary; Celia Elizabeth Hollings [1952] Director/Pet Food Manufacturer; Jeffrey Alan Hollings [1952] Director/Pet Food Manufacturer

**Hollingsworth & Vose Air Filtration Limited**
*Incorporated:* 16 February 2000 *Employees:* 53
*Net Worth:* £15,774,000 *Total Assets:* £17,971,000
*Registered Office:* Waterford Bridge, Kentmere, Kendal, Cumbria, LA8 9JJ
*Activities:* Manufacture of other articles of paper and paperboard n.e.c.
*Officers:* Eileen Margaret Swain, Secretary; Jochem Hofstetter [1964] Director [German]; Joseph Kaiser [1962] Director of Operations [German]; John S Madej [1965] Director/Division President - EIF [American]

**Holme Lane Haulage Limited**
*Incorporated:* 8 December 1987 *Employees:* 16
*Net Worth:* £2,926,583 *Total Assets:* £3,158,619
*Registered Office:* Spa Fields Industrial Estate, Slaithwaite, Huddersfield, W Yorks, HD7 5BB
*Activities:* Freight transport by road
*Major Shareholder:* Roger Graham Fell
*Officers:* Christopher Graham Fell, Secretary; Roger Graham Fell [1954] Director/Haulage Contractor

**Holme Styes Holdings Limited**
*Incorporated:* 6 March 1995 *Employees:* 54
*Net Worth:* £13,732,389 *Total Assets:* £18,515,172
*Registered Office:* 22 Longley, Holmfirth, W Yorks, HD9 2JD
*Activities:* Activities of head offices
*Major Shareholder:* Robert James Dickinson
*Officers:* Patricia Ann Wood, Secretary; Robert James Dickinson [1956] Director

**Holmefield Farm Services Limited**
*Incorporated:* 19 April 2002 *Employees:* 17
*Net Worth:* £3,581,192 *Total Assets:* £4,589,170
*Registered Office:* Agriculture House, Murton Lane, Murton, York, YO19 5UF
*Activities:* Veterinary activities
*Major Shareholder:* Francis Patrick Tobin
*Officers:* Francis Patrick Tobin, Secretary; Francis Patrick Tobin [1961] Director [Irish]; Susan Patricia Tobin [1967] Director [Irish]

**K.M. Holmes (Bradford) Limited**
*Incorporated:* 10 February 1978 *Employees:* 7
*Net Worth:* £6,388,768 *Total Assets:* £7,103,112
*Registered Office:* Valley Mills, Valley Road, Bradford, W Yorks, BD1 4RU
*Activities:* Other letting and operating of own or leased real estate
*Officers:* Adam Dale Gallagher, Secretary; Jenny Melissa Holmes [1960] Director; Julian Charles Holmes [1963] Director/Chartered Engineer; Peter Benson Holmes [1944] Director; Sally Kay Holmes [1945] Director; Ann Christine Howarth [1946] Director/Consultant

**Simon Holmes Limited**
*Incorporated:* 27 January 1999
*Net Worth:* £3,052,785 *Total Assets:* £3,075,675
*Registered Office:* Sycamore House, 24 Church Street, Hemswell, Gainsborough, Lincs, DN21 5UQ
*Activities:* Security dealing on own account
*Parent:* Simon Holmes Holdings Limited
*Officers:* Jillian Mary Holmes, Secretary; Jillian Mary Holmes [1944] Director/Dental Nurse; Simon Earl Holmes [1944] Director

**P.Holmes Properties Limited**
*Incorporated:* 17 December 1954
*Net Worth:* £7,751,407 *Total Assets:* £10,937,436
*Registered Office:* Leigh House, St Pauls Street, Leeds, LS1 2JT
*Activities:* Renting and operating of Housing Association real estate
*Parent:* P Holmes Property Holdings Limited
*Officers:* Jennifer Lesser Dyson [1947] Director; Nicholas Mark Dyson [1974] Director; Robert Alan Dyson [1945] Director

**Holmesterne Farm Co. Limited**
*Incorporated:* 25 September 1986 *Employees:* 143
*Net Worth:* £2,215,840 *Total Assets:* £6,213,938
*Registered Office:* Gatherley Road Industrial Estate, Brompton on Swale, Richmond, N Yorks, DL10 7JQ
*Activities:* Processing and preserving of meat
*Shareholders:* Keith Philip Tindell; Martin Lionel Sterne
*Officers:* Richard Pridmore, Secretary; Martin Lionel Sterne [1947] Director; Keith Philip Tindell [1956] Director/Butcher

**Holmfirth Dyers Holdings Limited**
*Incorporated:* 24 August 2016 *Employees:* 70
*Net Worth:* £6,050,003 *Total Assets:* £8,494,353
*Registered Office:* The Watermill, Wheatley Park, Mirfield, W Yorks, WF14 8HE
*Activities:* Activities of other holding companies n.e.c.
*Parent:* Camira Fabrics Limited
*Officers:* Lucy Caroline Bolton [1981] Finance Director; Brian Duckett [1942] Director/Dyer; Martin Douglas Duckett [1967] Director/Dyer; Grant Lindon Russell [1964] Director; Alan Lloyd Williams [1972] Group Operations Director

**Holmfirth Dyers Limited**
*Incorporated:* 19 October 1987 *Employees:* 70
*Net Worth:* £5,744,334 *Total Assets:* £8,208,684
*Registered Office:* The Watermill, Wheatley Park, Mirfield, W Yorks, WF14 8HE
*Activities:* Finishing of textiles
*Parent:* Holmfirth Dyers Holdings Limited
*Officers:* Lucy Caroline Bolton [1981] Finance Director; Brian Duckett [1942] Director/Dyer; Martin Douglas Duckett [1967] Director/Dyer; Grant Lindon Russell [1964] Director; Alan Lloyd Williams [1972] Group Operations Director

**Holmfirth Properties Limited**
*Incorporated:* 8 February 1972
*Net Worth:* £2,946,678 *Total Assets:* £3,538,861
*Registered Office:* Suite 9a, Mercury Quays, Ashley Lane, Shipley, W Yorks, BD17 7DB
*Activities:* Other letting and operating of own or leased real estate
*Parent:* The Harry and Mary Foundation
*Officers:* John Andrew Watson Clough, Secretary; John Andrew Watson Clough [1960] Director/School Master; Mary Clough [1926] Director; David Malcolm Rishworth [1946] Director/Management

**Holt Doctors Limited**
*Incorporated:* 27 February 2009 *Employees:* 78
*Net Worth:* £3,544,300 *Total Assets:* £9,258,548
*Registered Office:* 4th Floor, 1 Belle Vue Square, Broughton Road, Skipton, N Yorks, BD23 1FJ
*Activities:* Temporary employment agency activities
*Shareholders:* Peter Andrew Gregory; Tracy Ward
*Officers:* Kate McAvan, Secretary; Peter Andrew Gregory [1956] Director; Tracy Ward [1973] Director

**Holt Family (Holdings) Limited**
*Incorporated:* 8 August 2011 *Employees:* 109
*Net Worth:* £497,120 *Total Assets:* £8,467,867
*Registered Office:* Carlton House, Grammar School Street, Bradford, W Yorks, BD1 4NS
*Activities:* Dormant company
*Officers:* Damien Michael Holt [1981] Director; Daniel Brendan Holt [1981] Director; Robert Luke Holt [1985] Director; Elizabeth Louise Pix [1986] Director

**Home Marketing Group Ltd**
*Incorporated:* 22 October 2015 *Employees:* 132
*Net Worth:* £4,287,196 *Total Assets:* £11,569,538
*Registered Office:* Beechwood House, The Beechwood Estate, Elmete Lane, Roundhay, Leeds, LS8 2LQ
*Activities:* Advertising agencies
*Major Shareholder:* David Sewards
*Officers:* Danyl Lee Bosomworth [1975] Director; Peter Richard Dudleston [1965] Director; Nicholas Jackson [1972] Director; Richard John Marson [1975] Director; Don Geoffrey McGrath [1973] Director; Samuel Rainey [1972] Director; David Sewards [1967] Director; Christopher Paul Soames [1986] Director

**Home Marketing Limited**
*Incorporated:* 11 July 2000 *Employees:* 132
*Net Worth:* £4,285,724 *Total Assets:* £11,569,537
*Registered Office:* Beechwood House, The Beechwood Estate, Elmete Lane, Roundhay, Leeds, LS8 2LQ
*Activities:* Advertising agencies
*Major Shareholder:* David Sewards
*Officers:* David Sewards, Secretary/Managing Director; Danyl Lee Bosomworth [1975] Director; Ben Cunningham [1976] Director; Richard Dudleston [1965] Director; Nicholas Jackson [1972] Director; Richard John Marson [1975] Director; Don Geoffrey McGrath [1973] Director; Samuel Rainey [1972] Director; David Sewards [1967] Managing Director; Chris Soames [1986] Director

**Home Products Group Limited**
*Incorporated:* 10 December 2013 *Employees:* 4
*Net Worth Deficit:* £5,218 *Total Assets:* £11,646,765
*Registered Office:* Astracast House, Wallis Street, Bradford, BD8 9RR
*Activities:* Activities of other holding companies n.e.c.
*Parent:* Astracast International Holdings Limited
*Officers:* Darren Cooper [1969] Managing Director

**Home Shopping Personal Finance Limited**
*Incorporated:* 8 August 1997
*Net Worth:* £6,982,000 *Total Assets:* £15,134,000
*Registered Office:* Trinity Road, Halifax, W Yorks, HX1 2RG
*Activities:* Financial intermediation not elsewhere classified
*Parent:* Bank of Scotland PLC
*Officers:* Alyson Elizabeth Mulholland, Secretary; Sara Jayne Bayley [1969] Director; Israel Santos Perez [1972] Director [Spanish]

**Homecare (Holdings) Limited**
*Incorporated:* 27 March 1997
*Net Worth:* £8,025,915 *Total Assets:* £9,936,510
*Registered Office:* Holgate Park, Holgate Road, York, YO26 4GA
*Activities:* Activities of head offices
*Parent:* CPP Holdings Limited
*Officers:* Lorraine Grace Beavis, Secretary; David Raymond Jewell [1946] Director/Consultant; Gary Douglas Sidle [1966] Director/Finance

**Homecare Insurance Limited**
*Incorporated:* 24 February 1993 *Employees:* 1
*Net Worth:* £23,372,248 *Total Assets:* £26,177,744
*Registered Office:* Holgate Park, Holgate Road, York, YO26 4GA
*Activities:* Non-life insurance
*Parent:* Homecare (Holdings) Limited
*Officers:* Lorraine Grace Beavis, Secretary; David Raymond Jewell [1946] Director/Consultant; Gary Douglas Sidle [1966] Director/Finance

**Homes for Students Limited**
*Incorporated:* 26 October 2015 *Employees:* 198
*Net Worth:* £1,386,541 *Total Assets:* £3,449,362
*Registered Office:* Hornbeam House, Hornbeam Park, Harrogate, N Yorks, HG2 8QT
*Activities:* Other accommodation
*Shareholder:* Grosvenor Facilities Management Limited
*Officers:* Gavin David Bamberger [1971] Director/Financial Controller, Europe; Elizabeth Corbett [1966] Director [Irish]; Martin Corbett [1960] Director; Alexander Toby Shedden Parry [1976] Director; Graham Rogers [1977] Director

**Hope Learning Trust, York**
*Incorporated:* 10 March 2011 *Employees:* 275
*Previous:* MCE Academy Trust
*Net Worth:* £31,243,000 *Total Assets:* £35,433,000
*Registered Office:* Manor CE Academy, Millfield Lane, Nether Poppleton, York, YO26 6PA
*Activities:* General secondary education
*Officers:* Simon Bryan-Smith, Secretary; Rev Jacqueline Doyle Brett [1962] Director; Michael Ferguson [1974] Director/Deputy Head, St Olave's School [South African]; Philippa Gowland [1972] Director/Solicitor; David John Michael Judson [1951] Director/Retired; David William Kirkham [1955] Director/Retired Lecturer; Dr Julie McGonigle [1974] Director; Charles Anthony Myers [1952] Director; Karen Angela Osborne [1958] Director/Chief Operating Officer; Olivia Seymour [1978] Assistant Director of Education; Andrew Simpkin [1968] Director/Head of Project Delivery; Ian David Thomson [1953] Director/Retired

**Hopkins Properties Limited**
*Incorporated:* 24 July 2003 *Employees:* 4
*Net Worth:* £1,150,045 *Total Assets:* £4,462,459
*Registered Office:* 15 Ropner Gardens, Middleton St George, Darlington, Co Durham, DL2 1FB
*Activities:* Other letting and operating of own or leased real estate
*Shareholders:* Richard Anthony Hopkins; Susan Margaret Hopkins
*Officers:* Susan Margaret Hopkins, Secretary; Richard Anthony Hopkins [1958] Director/Auctioneer; Susan Margaret Hopkins [1956] Director/Retired Dietician

**David Hopkinson Limited**
*Incorporated:* 9 March 1973 *Employees:* 21
*Net Worth:* £778,449 *Total Assets:* £4,497,895
*Registered Office:* Common Farm, Thorpe Audlin, Pontefract, W Yorks, WF8 3HE
*Activities:* Wholesale of mining, construction and civil engineering machinery
*Shareholders:* David Hopkinson; Susan Hopkinson
*Officers:* Susan Hopkinson, Secretary; Christopher John Hopkinson [1967] Director/Sales Manager; David Hopkinson [1942] Director; Richard David Hopkinson [1965] Director/Sales Manager; Susan Hopkinson [1943] Director

**Horbury Bridge (Holdings) Limited**
*Incorporated:* 26 September 2006 *Employees:* 78
*Net Worth:* £5,208,275 *Total Assets:* £8,289,623
*Registered Office:* Machenair House, Wakefield Road, Ossett, Wakefield, W Yorks, WF5 9LB
*Activities:* Other business support service activities n.e.c.
*Shareholders:* Ronald Medley; John Richard Medley
*Officers:* Ronald Medley, Secretary; John Richard Medley [1962] Director; Ronald Medley [1958] Director

**Horizon Academy Trust**
*Incorporated:* 20 February 2013 *Employees:* 348
*Previous:* Biggin Hill Primary Academy
*Net Worth:* £19,591,678 *Total Assets:* £23,183,594
*Registered Office:* Biggin Hill Primary School, Biggin Avenue, Hull, HU7 4RL
*Activities:* Primary education
*Officers:* Kathryn Mary Cutler [1953] Director/Retired; Terry Dunn [1960] Director/Benefits Specialist; Peter Raymond Greef [1953] Director/Retired; Sharon Herrick [1961] Director/HR Schools/Academies Specialist; Michelle Kermeen [1980] Director/Assistant Principal; Richard William Marsden [1945] Director/Retired

**Horizon Platforms Limited**
*Incorporated:* 28 September 2007 *Employees:* 88
*Net Worth:* £2,978,496 *Total Assets:* £11,850,270
*Registered Office:* Unit G1, Rosie Road, Normanton, W Yorks, WF6 1ZB
*Activities:* Renting and leasing of construction and civil engineering machinery and equipment
*Shareholders:* Ben Hirst; Ruairi Sean Michael Duggan
*Officers:* Kevin Appleton [1960] Director/Chairman; Adrian Bleasdale [1973] Operations Director; Ruairi Sean Michael Duggan [1975] Director; Benjamin John Hirst [1978] Director; Bryan James Ian Lawrie [1973] Director; Tanja Willis [1973] Director [South African]

**Hornbeam Park Developments Limited**
*Incorporated:* 18 January 1996 *Employees:* 11
*Net Worth:* £26,049,334 *Total Assets:* £106,295,744
*Registered Office:* The Tower, 4th Avenue, Hornbeam Park, Harrogate, N Yorks, HG2 8QT
*Activities:* Development of building projects
*Major Shareholder:* Christopher John Bentley
*Officers:* Christopher John Bentley [1958] Director

**Horncastle Group PLC**
*Incorporated:* 22 July 1964 *Employees:* 7
*Net Worth:* £25,358,512 *Total Assets:* £40,743,404
*Registered Office:* Unicorn House, 8 Innovation Drive, Newport, Brough, N Humbers, HU15 2FW
*Activities:* Development of building projects
*Major Shareholder:* Andrew Nigel Horncastle
*Officers:* Carole Diane Horncastle, Secretary; Ian Richard Hodges [1962] Director/Surveyor; Andrew Nigel Horncastle [1959] Director; William Anthony Horncastle [1932] Director; David Charles Watson [1957] Director

**Horndean Ltd**
*Incorporated:* 16 April 2004 *Employees:* 60
*Net Worth:* £2,037,854 *Total Assets:* £4,593,790
*Registered Office:* Unit 7, 236 Main Road, Newport, Brough, N Humbers, HU15 2RH
*Activities:* Activities of head offices
*Officers:* Steven Anthony Hinch, Secretary/Director; David Ross Hibbs [1962] Director; Steven Anthony Hinch [1967] Director; John Derrick Holland [1960] Director

**Hornsea Leisure Limited**
*Incorporated:* 9 July 2008 *Employees:* 14
*Net Worth:* £5,420,186 *Total Assets:* £9,212,426
*Registered Office:* Marton Hall, Church Lane, Sewerby, Bridlington, E Yorks, YO15 1DS
*Activities:* Recreational vehicle parks, trailer parks and camping grounds
*Parent:* Shorewood Leisure Group Limited
*Officers:* Neil Willson, Secretary/Managing Director; David Robert Allison [1960] Director; Neil Willson [1960] Managing Director

**Horridge Limited**
*Incorporated:* 3 September 1997 *Employees:* 140
*Previous:* Daniel Footwear Limited
*Net Worth:* £764,636 *Total Assets:* £4,506,226
*Registered Office:* 34 Roundhay Road, Leeds, LS7 1AB
*Activities:* Retail sale of footwear in specialised stores
*Officers:* Geoffrey Sherwood [1957] Director/Accountant

**John Horsfall & Sons (Greetland),Limited**
*Incorporated:* 31 January 1905 *Employees:* 43
*Net Worth:* £12,228,528 *Total Assets:* £16,252,473
*Registered Office:* Birkby Grange, Birkby Hall Road, Huddersfield, W Yorks, HD2 2XB
*Activities:* Other letting and operating of own or leased real estate
*Shareholder:* Peter Horsfall Benson
*Officers:* Robert Stephen Currie, Secretary; Jacqueline Anne Benson [1960] Director/Marketing Assistant; Peter Horsfall Benson [1959] Director/Blanket Manufacturer; David Deakin [1958] Sales Director

**John Horsfall & Sons Limited**
*Incorporated:* 22 October 2004 *Employees:* 12
*Net Worth:* £800,424 *Total Assets:* £3,986,142
*Registered Office:* Birkby Grange, Birkby Hall Road, Huddersfield, W Yorks, HD2 2XB
*Activities:* Wholesale of textiles
*Parent:* John Horsfall & Sons (Greetland) Ltd
*Officers:* Robert Stephen Currie, Secretary; Jacqueline Anne Benson [1960] Director/Marketing Assistant; Peter Horsfall Benson [1959] Director/Blanket Manufacturer; David Deakin [1958] Sales Director

**Horsforth Mill Limited**
*Incorporated:* 10 February 2015
*Net Worth Deficit:* £527,896 *Total Assets:* £12,970,818
*Registered Office:* 20 York Place, Leeds, LS1 2EX
*Activities:* Buying and selling of own real estate
*Shareholders:* Countrylarge Estates Limited; Linda Dangoor
*Officers:* David Frank Khalastchi [1991] Director; Frank Khalastchi [1933] Director/Investor; Michael Robert Khalastchi [1989] Director; Timothy John Smith [1987] Director

**Horsforth School**
*Incorporated:* 16 November 2011 *Employees:* 203
*Net Worth:* £10,086,000 *Total Assets:* £11,451,000
*Registered Office:* Horsforth School, Lee Lane East, Horsforth, Leeds, LS18 5RF
*Activities:* General secondary education
*Officers:* Dr Paul Bell [1974] Director/Headteacher; Dr Keith Bothamley [1960] Director/Education Specialist; Rosemary Edwards [1966] Director/Solicitor; Tessa Freer [1982] Director/Cluster Manager; Katie McFadden [1984] Director/Teacher; Jennifer Ryatt [1969] Director/Head of Systems Administration; Damon Shaw [1973] Director/Commercial Manager; Helen Margaret Shearer [1957] Director/Chartered Physiotherapist; Christopher Townsley [1949] Director/Councillor; Stephen William Wood [1953] Director/Financial Analyst

**Horus Limited**
*Incorporated:* 14 March 1996
*Net Worth:* £2,304,201 *Total Assets:* £4,680,584
*Registered Office:* Gresham House, 5-7 St Pauls Street, Leeds, LS1 2JG
*Activities:* Renting and operating of Housing Association real estate
*Shareholders:* Christopher John Heselton Adams; David William Richardson
*Officers:* Alistair Mark Pullan, Secretary; Christopher John Heselton Adams [1950] Director/Chartered Accountant; Alistair Mark Pullan [1959] Director/Builder; Bruce Scott Strachan [1963] Director/Chartered Surveyor

**Horwood House Properties Limited**
*Incorporated:* 26 September 2006 *Employees:* 4
*Net Worth Deficit:* £2,007,000 *Total Assets:* £24,398,000
*Registered Office:* The Inspire, Hornbeam Square West, Harrogate, N Yorks, HG2 8PA
*Activities:* Other letting and operating of own or leased real estate
*Parent:* De Vere 2 Limited
*Officers:* James Alexander Burrell [1974] Director/Accountant; Generaldine Josephine Gallagher [1965] Finance Director [Irish]; Gail Susan Hunter [1963] Human Resources Director; Anthony Gerrard Troy [1962] Director [Irish]

**Hospice of St. Mary of Furness**
*Incorporated:* 2 May 1986 *Employees:* 92
*Net Worth:* £5,294,762 *Total Assets:* £5,573,820
*Registered Office:* St Marys Hospice, Ford Park, Ulverston, Cumbria, LA12 7JP
*Activities:* Other human health activities
*Officers:* Susan Lake, Secretary; Richard William Bird [1946] Retired Managing Director; Lucy Georgiana Cavendish [1973] Director; Robert Dudley Clark [1946] Director/Trustee; David Corp [1951] Director/Retired; Kay Gilbey [1945] Director/Nursing Officer; Denise Hardy [1960] Director/Clinical Manager; Andrew Phillip James [1965] Director; Graham Arthur Jowett [1952] Retired NHS Director; Dr. Andrew Richard Luksza [1952] Director/Doctor; Graham Paul Servante [1965] Director; Valerie Stangoe [1962] Director/Chief Executive; Kim Wilson [1966] Director/Nurse; Andrew Philip Wren [1970] Director/Chief Executive

**Hospitaller Order of Saint John of God**
*Incorporated:* 31 March 2010 *Employees:* 2
*Net Worth:* £7,075,000 *Total Assets:* £8,411,000
*Registered Office:* St Bedes House, Morton Park, Darlington, Co Durham, DL1 4XZ
*Activities:* Other social work activities without accommodation n.e.c.
*Officers:* Malachy Brannigan, Secretary; Malachy Brannigan [1947] Director/Brother of a Religious Order [Irish]; William Martin Forkan [1942] Director/Brother of a Religious Order [Irish]; Michael Edward Francis [1941] Director/Retired; John Gallagher [1944] Director/Brother of a Religious Order [Irish]; John Lennon [1945] Director/Brother of a Religious Order [Irish]; Robert Moore [1944] Director/Religious; Michael John Nield [1940] Director/Religious Brother

**Geo. Houlton & Sons (Holdings) Limited**
*Incorporated:* 17 May 1935 *Employees:* 129
*Net Worth:* £1,961,237 *Total Assets:* £12,295,495
*Registered Office:* Hyperion Street, Witham, Hull, HU9 1BD
*Activities:* Other letting and operating of own or leased real estate
*Shareholders:* Susan Mary Houlton; Thomas Richard Houlton
*Officers:* Nicolas Bingley Travis, Secretary; Paul Simon Dickerson [1953] Director; Richard Gregory Houlton [1948] Director; Thomas Richard Houlton [1983] Director; Keith William Knights [1954] Director/Chartered Accountant; Simon William Lunt [1952] Director

**Geo Houlton & Sons Limited**
*Incorporated:* 1 May 1982 *Employees:* 127
*Net Worth:* £1,882,822 *Total Assets:* £12,217,081
*Registered Office:* Houlton, Hyperion Street, Hull, HU9 1BD
*Activities:* Construction of commercial buildings
*Parent:* Geo Houlton & Sons (Holdings) Limited
*Officers:* Nicolas Bingley Travis, Secretary; Jamie Ian Craft [1974] Director/Surveyor; Paul Simon Dickerson [1953] Director; Richard Gregory Houlton [1948] Director; Andrew Mark Kingston [1960] Director/Chartered Surveyor; Keith William Knights [1954] Director/Chartered Accountant; David James Padden [1956] Construction Director

**House of Townend Limited**
*Incorporated:* 3 May 1962 *Employees:* 76
*Net Worth:* £1,280,018 *Total Assets:* £6,687,892
*Registered Office:* House of Townend, Wyke Way, Melton, North Ferriby, E Yorks, HU14 3BQ
*Activities:* Wholesale of wine, beer, spirits and other alcoholic beverages
*Parent:* J Townend & Sons (Hull) Ltd
*Officers:* Angus Joseph Whitehead, Secretary; David George Archibald [1972] Director; Neil Robert Goldie [1963] Director; Derek Hill [1945] Director; Alexandra Louise Townend [1967] Director/Hotel General Manager; Jennifer Ann Townend [1940] Director; John Charles Townend [1965] Director; Alan John Whitehead [1951] Director; Angus Joseph Whitehead [1965] Director/Chartered Accountant

**E. Houseman & Son Limited**
*Incorporated:* 29 March 1982 *Employees:* 4
*Net Worth:* £5,066,113 *Total Assets:* £7,225,148
*Registered Office:* Leigh House, 28-32 St Paul's Street, Leeds, LS1 2JT
*Activities:* Freight transport by road
*Major Shareholder:* Kenneth William Houseman
*Officers:* Angela Joy Houseman, Secretary; Andrew William Houseman [1981] Director; Angela Joy Houseman [1954] Director; Kenneth William Houseman [1949] Director/Haulier

**Hoveden Builders Limited**
*Incorporated:* 11 February 1974 *Employees:* 8
*Net Worth:* £3,574,407 *Total Assets:* £3,682,517
*Registered Office:* 51 Hailgate, Howden, Goole, E Yorks, DN14 7ST
*Activities:* Construction of domestic buildings
*Shareholders:* Christopher Charles Longthorp; John Peter Winter
*Officers:* Christopher Charles Longthorp, Secretary; Christopher Charles Longthorp [1956] Director; John Peter Winter [1957] Director/Builder

**Howard Civil Engineering Limited**
*Incorporated:* 4 February 2003 *Employees:* 25
*Net Worth:* £1,379,844 *Total Assets:* £4,958,773
*Registered Office:* Unit 11 Acorn Business Park, Killingbeck Drive, Leeds, LS14 6UF
*Activities:* Construction of other civil engineering projects n.e.c.
*Major Shareholder:* Michael Thomas Howard
*Officers:* Gerard Howard, Secretary; John Stephen Cartwright [1980] Commercial Director; Gerard Declan Howard [1977] Commercial Director [Irish]; Michael Thomas Howard [1975] Director; Peter Howard [1987] Pre-Construction Director

**R.J. Howard Engineers Limited**
*Incorporated:* 27 May 1971 *Employees:* 54
*Net Worth:* £4,145,182 *Total Assets:* £7,151,239
*Registered Office:* Howard House, Lowfields Road, Leeds, LS12 6BS
*Activities:* Construction of other civil engineering projects n.e.c.
*Shareholders:* David William Howard; Richard James Howard; Bridget Howard
*Officers:* Bridget Howard, Secretary; Michael Patrick Gilmartin [1949] Director/Civil Engineer; Steven Anthony Gilmartin [1975] Director; Bridget Howard [1942] Director/Company Secretary; David William Howard [1966] Director/Civil Engineer; Richard James Howard [1939] Director/Civil Engineer

**W.A. Howarth (Aphrodites Lodge) Limited**
*Incorporated:* 27 February 2004
*Net Worth:* £1,162,470 *Total Assets:* £3,344,594
*Registered Office:* Aphrodites Lodge, Longtail Hill, Bowness on Windermere, Cumbria, LA23 3JD
*Activities:* Hotels and similar accommodation
*Major Shareholder:* William Alan Howarth
*Officers:* Robert Alan Moulsdale, Secretary; Matthew Howarth [1991] Director; William Alan Howarth [1956] Director/Hotelier

**B M Howarth Limited**
*Incorporated:* 15 January 2001
*Net Worth:* £4,629,155 *Total Assets:* £5,292,370
*Registered Office:* West House, Kings Cross Road, Halifax, W Yorks, HX1 1EB
*Activities:* Management consultancy activities other than financial management
*Shareholders:* Christopher Bell; Charles Roy Moorby
*Officers:* Christopher Bell, Secretary/Chartered Accountant; Christopher Bell [1957] Director/Chartered Accountant; Charles Roy Moorby [1959] Director/Chartered Accountant

**Howarth Timber & Building Supplies Limited**
*Incorporated:* 24 November 1924 *Employees:* 474
*Net Worth:* £16,544,000 *Total Assets:* £38,387,000
*Registered Office:* Prince Edward Works, Pontefract Lane, Leeds, LS9 0RA
*Activities:* Manufacture of other products of wood; manufacture of articles of cork, straw and plaiting materials
*Officers:* Nicholas David Howarth, Secretary; Andrew Peter Howarth [1955] Director/Timber Merchant; Deborah Jane Howarth [1958] Director; Julie Ann Howarth [1960] Director; Nicholas David Howarth [1957] Director/Timber Merchant; Allister Paul Turner [1973] Director/Chartered Accountant

**Howarth Timber (Windows & Doors) Limited**
*Incorporated:* 1 October 1973 *Employees:* 145
*Net Worth Deficit:* £112,000 *Total Assets:* £4,406,000
*Registered Office:* Prince Edward Works, Pontefract Lane, Leeds, LS9 0RA
*Activities:* Manufacture of other products of wood; manufacture of articles of cork, straw and plaiting materials
*Officers:* Nicholas David Howarth, Secretary; Andrew Peter Howarth [1955] Director/Timber Merchant; Deborah Jane Howarth [1958] Director; Julie Ann Howarth [1960] Director; Nicholas David Howarth [1957] Director/Timber Merchant

**Howarth Timber Engineered Solutions Limited**
*Incorporated:* 13 April 2012 *Employees:* 163
*Net Worth:* £4,859,000 *Total Assets:* £9,133,000
*Registered Office:* Prince Edward Works, Pontefract Lane, Leeds, LS9 0RA
*Activities:* Manufacture of other builders' carpentry and joinery
*Officers:* Andrew Peter Howarth [1955] Director; Nicholas David Howarth [1957] Director; James Leadbetter Provan [1966] Director; Allister Paul Turner [1973] Director/Chartered Accountant

**Howarth Timber Group Limited**
*Incorporated:* 22 August 1900 *Employees:* 1,010
*Net Worth:* £62,071,000 *Total Assets:* £115,232,000
*Registered Office:* Prince Edward Works, Pontefract Lane, Leeds, LS9 0RA
*Activities:* Activities of head offices
*Officers:* Nicholas David Howarth, Secretary; Andrew Peter Howarth [1955] Director/Timber Merchant; Deborah Jane Howarth [1958] Director; Julie Ann Howarth [1960] Director; Nicholas David Howarth [1957] Director/Timber Merchant; Allister Paul Turner [1973] Director/Chartered Accountant

**Hoyer Container Rental UK Limited**
*Incorporated:* 24 March 1992
*Net Worth:* £29,657,452 *Total Assets:* £104,213,136
*Registered Office:* 517 Leeds Road, Huddersfield, W Yorks, HD2 1YJ
*Activities:* Financial leasing
*Parent:* Hoyer UK Ltd
*Officers:* Gregory David McLeen, Secretary; Mark Andrew Binns [1961] Managing Director; Gregory David McLeen [1959] Director/Accountant

**Hoyer Petrolog UK Limited**
*Incorporated:* 22 March 1974 *Employees:* 1,277
*Net Worth:* £30,713,668 *Total Assets:* £53,259,184
*Registered Office:* 517 Leeds Road, Huddersfield, W Yorks, HD2 1YJ
*Activities:* Freight transport by road
*Parent:* Hoyer GmbH Internationale Fachspedition
*Officers:* Gregory David McLeen, Secretary; Mark Andrew Binns [1961] Managing Director; Allan John Davison [1977] Operations Director; Gregory David McLeen [1959] Director/Accountant; Ortwin Paul Nast [1959] Director/Group Chief Executive [German]

**Hoyer UK Limited**
*Incorporated:* 24 March 1992 *Employees:* 89
*Net Worth Deficit:* £4,640,206 *Total Assets:* £4,454,536
*Registered Office:* 517 Leeds Road, Huddersfield, W Yorks, HD2 1YJ
*Activities:* Freight transport by road
*Parent:* Hoyer GmbH Internationale Fachspedition
*Officers:* Gregory David McLeen, Secretary; Hans de Zeeuw [1971] Managing Director [Dutch]; Andreas Theodor Reinhardt [1958] Director [German]

**HPC Laser Holdings Limited**
*Incorporated:* 22 March 2013 *Employees:* 3
*Net Worth:* £4,877,025 *Total Assets:* £5,255,009
*Registered Office:* Castle Mills, Saddleworth Road, Elland, Halifax, W Yorks, HX5 0RY
*Activities:* Combined office administrative service activities
*Parent:* HPC Enterprises Limited
*Officers:* Charlotte Lisa Jacobs, Secretary; Stephen David Cockerham [1971] Sales Director; Charlotte Lisa Jacobs [1971] Director/Company Secretary; Christopher Haldon Jacobs [1968] Director; Neil Anthony Stewardson [1966] Director; Ian Michael Thurley [1966] Director

**HPI Limited**
*Incorporated:* 6 September 2000 *Employees:* 13
*Net Worth:* £102,982,000 *Total Assets:* £168,931,008
*Registered Office:* Capitol House, Bond Court, Leeds, LS1 5EZ
*Activities:* Data processing, hosting and related activities
*Parent:* HPI Holding Limited
*Officers:* Tony Aquila [1964] Director/Chairman [American]; Jason Michael Brady [1968] Director/Attorney [American]; Renato Carlo Giger [1960] Director [Swiss]; Franciscus Johanes Carolus Overtoom [1966] Director/Regional CFO [Dutch]; Christopher Wright [1971] Director

**HRP Holdings Limited**
*Incorporated:* 15 February 1945
*Net Worth:* £4,096,000 *Total Assets:* £4,799,000
*Registered Office:* 15 Bruntcliffe Avenue, Leeds 27 Industrial Estate, Morley, Leeds, LS27 0LL
*Activities:* Activities of head offices
*Parent:* G & L Beijer Ref AB
*Officers:* David Patrick Campbell, Secretary; Per Olof Goran Bertland [1957] Director [Swedish]; John David Billson [1960] Director; David Patrick Campbell [1979] Director; Simon Andrej Karlin [1968] Director [Swedish]

**HRP Limited**
*Incorporated:* 23 December 1964 *Employees:* 85
*Net Worth Deficit:* £533,000 *Total Assets:* £26,911,000
*Registered Office:* 15 Bruntcliffe Avenue, Leeds 27 Industrial Estate, Morley, Leeds, LS27 0LL
*Activities:* Wholesale of other machinery and equipment
*Parent:* G & L Beijer Ref AB
*Officers:* David Patrick Campbell, Secretary; Per Olof Goran Bertland [1957] Director [Swedish]; John David Billson [1960] Director; David Patrick Campbell [1979] Director; Simon Andrej Karlin [1968] Director [Swedish]

**HS Products Ltd**
*Incorporated:* 26 July 2004 *Employees:* 163
*Previous:* Harrison Spinks Components Ltd
*Net Worth:* £15,122,220 *Total Assets:* £18,944,188
*Registered Office:* 6 Millennium Drive, Leeds, LS11 5BP
*Activities:* Manufacture of wire products, chain and springs
*Parent:* Spinko Limited
*Officers:* Amanda Jane Shea, Secretary; Richard Essery [1967] Components Director; Amanda Jane Shea [1969] Director/Chartered Accountant; Peter Douglas Spinks [1943] Director; Simon Paul Spinks [1969] Director

**HSH Cold Stores Limited**
*Incorporated:* 21 August 2003 *Employees:* 87
*Net Worth:* £2,913,980 *Total Assets:* £11,514,369
*Registered Office:* Birchin Way, Grimsby, N E Lincs, DN31 2SG
*Activities:* Operation of warehousing and storage facilities for land transport activities
*Officers:* Christine Anita Howard, Secretary; Anthony John Howard [1972] Director/Cold Store Manager; Christine Anita Howard [1942] Director; Lewis Howard [2000] Director

**HSL Manufacturing Limited**
*Incorporated:* 6 May 1983 *Employees:* 104
*Net Worth:* £895,379 *Total Assets:* £3,022,990
*Registered Office:* Units 1-3a Grange Road Business Park, Grange Road, Batley, W Yorks, WF17 6LN
*Activities:* Manufacture of other furniture
*Parent:* High Seat Holdings Limited
*Officers:* William John Burrows, Secretary; Debra Lorraine Burrows [1967] Director; William John Burrows [1963] Director; Guy Charles Critchlow [1970] Director; Paul Richard Roberts [1976] Director; Kevin Michael Wall [1964] Retail Director

**Huddersfield Fine Worsteds Limited**
*Incorporated:* 27 January 2004 *Employees:* 21
*Net Worth:* £277,576 *Total Assets:* £4,100,423
*Registered Office:* Unit B5, Warhurst Road, Lowfields Business Park, Elland, W Yorks, HX5 9DF
*Activities:* Wholesale of textiles
*Major Shareholder:* Michael Solomon
*Officers:* Zulfikarhusein Zakir, Secretary/Accountant [Canadian]; Michael David Solomon [1938] Director [American]; Zulfikarhusein Zakir [1952] Director/Accountant [Canadian]

**The Huddersfield Town Association Football Club Limited**
*Incorporated:* 21 November 1983 *Employees:* 229
*Net Worth Deficit:* £49,297,328 *Total Assets:* £26,443,560
*Registered Office:* The John Smith's Stadium, Stadium Way, Leeds Road, Huddersfield, W Yorks, HD1 6PX
*Activities:* Activities of sport clubs
*Major Shareholder:* Dean Hoyle
*Officers:* Jennifer Ann Hough, Secretary; Darren Bryant [1968] Finance Director; Roger Michael Burnley [1966] Retail Director; Jennifer Ann Hough [1968] Director/Company Secretary; Dean Hoyle [1967] Director; Sean Michael Jarvis [1966] Commercial Director; Julian Winter [1965] Director/Chief Executive

**Neil Hudgell Limited**
*Incorporated:* 17 November 2009 *Employees:* 137
*Net Worth:* £2,174,009 *Total Assets:* £8,943,898
*Registered Office:* No 2 at The Dock, 46 Humber Street, Hull, HU1 1TU
*Activities:* Solicitors
*Officers:* Neil Michael Hudgell [1966] Director/Solicitor

**Hudson Contract Services Limited**
*Incorporated:* 21 March 1997 *Employees:* 9
*Net Worth:* £1,111,221 *Total Assets:* £60,145,200
*Registered Office:* 1 Mill Lane, Bridlington, E Yorks, YO16 7AP
*Activities:* Other professional, scientific and technical activities n.e.c.
*Shareholders:* David Christopher Jackson; Lesley Ann Jackson
*Officers:* David Christopher Jackson, Secretary; Ian Spencer Anfield [1973] Contracts Director; David George William Bradley [1968] Financial Director; David Christopher Jackson [1955] Director; Lesley Ann Jackson [1953] Director

**John Hudson Trailers Ltd**
*Incorporated:* 30 July 1975 *Employees:* 53
*Net Worth:* £5,170,856 *Total Assets:* £19,632,368
*Registered Office:* Doncaster Road, Bawtry, Doncaster, S Yorks, DN10 6NX
*Activities:* Maintenance and repair of motor vehicles
*Major Shareholder:* Christopher John Hudson
*Officers:* Graham Joseph Robbins, Secretary; Dougal Andrew Cawley [1969] Director/Tyre Dealer; Christopher John Hudson [1946] Director/Commercial Vehicle Dealer; John William Hudson [1971] Director/Trailer Rental & Sales; Graham Joseph Robbins [1973] Director/Company Secretary

**Huggate Church Farm Properties Limited**
*Incorporated:* 14 June 1949 *Employees:* 2
*Net Worth:* £3,098,073 *Total Assets:* £4,083,233
*Registered Office:* Poplars Farm, Ferrensby, Knaresborough, N Yorks, HG5 0RH
*Activities:* Growing of cereals (except rice), leguminous crops and oil seeds
*Shareholder:* Andrew David Cumming
*Officers:* John Graham Cumming, Secretary; Andrew David Cumming [1965] Director/Farmer; Ione Jacqueline Cumming [1974] Director/Farmer; John Graham Cumming [1935] Director/Farmer

**The Hull & East Yorkshire Medical Research Centre**
*Incorporated:* 16 June 2000
*Net Worth:* £8,993,357 *Total Assets:* £9,214,629
*Registered Office:* The Daisy Building, Castle Hill Hospital, Castle Road, Cottingham, E Yorks, HU16 5JQ
*Activities:* General medical practice activities
*Officers:* Professor Nicholas David Stafford, Secretary; Dr Assem Allam [1939] Managing Director Allam Marine Ltd; Michael Colin Auton [1943] Director/Retired; Lisa Bellsey [1956] Director/Retired; Trevor Samuel Eric Boanas [1946] Director/Business Proprietor; Professor John George Franklin Cleland [1955] Director/Medical Practitioner; Peter Edward Dyer [1947] Director/Professor of Physics - Retired; Karen Marie Guest [1964] Director; John Edward Hartley [1966] Director/Surgeon; Victoria Rixon Heuck [1958] Director/Chartered Certified Accountant; Andrew Nigel Horncastle [1959] Director; Sydney Howey [1938] Director/Retired Medical Physicist; Professor Michael John Lind [1957] Director/Medical Practitioner; Dr Christopher Andrew Rowland-Hill [1958] Director/Medical Practitioner; Professor Nicholas David Stafford [1954] Director/Retired Medical Practitioner

**Hull & Humber Chamber of Commerce Industry & Shipping**
*Incorporated:* 16 June 1875 *Employees:* 47
*Net Worth:* £4,536,940 *Total Assets:* £6,171,418
*Registered Office:* 34-38 Beverley Road, Hull, HU3 1YE
*Activities:* Activities of business and employers membership organisations
*Officers:* Samantha Elise Dennison, Secretary; Cetin Kirci Akdemir [1962] Director/Chief Executive Officer; James Phillip Ascough [1959] Director/Media & PR Consultant; Gareth Beese [1972] Strategic Development Director - Construction; Sally Ann Booker [1964] Director/Port Manager; Kathryn Elizabeth Durrant Fillingham [1972] Finance Director; Kevin Stuart Hopper [1979] Director/Accountant; John Philip Jones [1967] Managing Director; Dr Ian Spencer Kelly [1964] Director/Chief Executive; Serena Jayne Walters [1973] Director/Hotel General Manager; Albert Edwin Weatherill [1957] Director/Marine Consultant; Michael Stephen Whitehead [1955] Director; Dafydd Emlyn Williams [1978] Director/Head of Communications

**Hull Cartridge Company Limited**
*Incorporated:* 10 December 1984 *Employees:* 46
*Net Worth:* £6,837,024 *Total Assets:* £8,493,687
*Registered Office:* Bontoft Avenue, National Avenue, Kingston upon Hull, HU5 4HZ
*Activities:* Manufacture of sports goods
*Shareholder:* Susan Jane Claxton
*Officers:* David Howard Bontoft, Secretary/Director; David Howard Bontoft [1958] Director; Susan Jane Claxton [1961] Director

**Hull City Tigers Limited**
*Incorporated:* 12 July 2000 *Employees:* 227
*Net Worth Deficit:* £19,157,488 *Total Assets:* £61,959,872
*Registered Office:* KC Stadium, West Park, Hull, HU3 6HU
*Activities:* Operation of sports facilities
*Parent:* Allamhouse Limited
*Officers:* Dr Assem Allam [1939] Director; Ehab Allam [1971] Director

**Hull Citycare (Fundco 1) Limited**
*Incorporated:* 10 March 2004 *Employees:* 2
*Net Worth Deficit:* £7,972,711 *Total Assets:* £40,124,664
*Registered Office:* c/o Sewell Group PLC, Geneva Way, Leads Road, Hull, HU7 0DG
*Activities:* Other letting and operating of own or leased real estate
*Parent:* Hull Citycare (Intermediate1) Ltd
*Officers:* David Adrian Leedham, Secretary; David Adrian Leedham [1967] Director; Paul Edwin Sewell [1952] Director

**Hull Citycare (Fundco 3) Limited**
*Incorporated:* 7 October 2009 *Employees:* 2
*Net Worth Deficit:* £5,762,880 *Total Assets:* £15,918,468
*Registered Office:* Geneva Way Business Park, Leads Road, Hull, HU7 0DG
*Activities:* Other letting and operating of own or leased real estate
*Parent:* Hull Citycare (Intermediate 3) Limited
*Officers:* David Adrian Leedham, Secretary; David Adrian Leedham [1967] Director/Company Secretary; Paul Edwin Sewell [1952] Director

**Hull Citycare (Fundco 4) Limited**
*Incorporated:* 13 October 2010 *Employees:* 2
*Net Worth Deficit:* £440,387 *Total Assets:* £14,063,685
*Registered Office:* c/o Sewell Group PLC, Geneva Way Business Park, Leads Road, Hull, HU7 0DG
*Activities:* Other letting and operating of own or leased real estate
*Parent:* Hull Citycare (Intermediate 4) Limited
*Officers:* David Adrian Leedham, Secretary; David Adrian Leedham [1967] Director/Company Secretary; Paul Edwin Sewell [1952] Director

**Hull Citycare (Fundco 5) Limited**
*Incorporated:* 7 September 2011 *Employees:* 2
*Net Worth Deficit:* £152,608 *Total Assets:* £9,768,501
*Registered Office:* Geneva Way Business Park, Leads Road, Hull, HU7 0DG
*Activities:* Other letting and operating of own or leased real estate
*Parent:* Hull Citycare (Intermediate 5) Limited
*Officers:* David Adrian Leedham, Secretary; David Adrian Leedham [1967] Director/Company Secretary; Paul Edwin Sewell [1952] Director

**Hull Citycare (Fundco 6) Limited**
*Incorporated:* 29 July 2016
*Net Worth:* £1,000 *Total Assets:* £10,744,770
*Registered Office:* Geneva Way Business Park, Leads Road, Hull, HU7 0DG
*Activities:* Other letting and operating of own or leased real estate
*Parent:* Hull Citycare (Intermediate6) Limted
*Officers:* David Adrian Leedham, Secretary; David Adrian Leedham [1967] Director; Paul Edwin Sewell [1952] Director

**Hull Citycare (Investments) Limited**
*Incorporated:* 10 March 2004 *Employees:* 6
*Net Worth Deficit:* £9,555,330 *Total Assets:* £99,105,784
*Registered Office:* c/o Sewell Group PLC, Geneva Way, Leads Road, Hull, HU7 0DG
*Activities:* Dormant company
*Shareholders:* Cardale Infrastructure Investments Ltd; Sewell Group Ltd
*Officers:* David Adrian Leedham, Company Secretary; Alastair William Hopps [1986] Director/Chartered Accountant; David Adrian Leedham [1967] Director/Company Secretary; Alexander Toby Shedden Parry [1976] Director; Paul Edwin Sewell [1952] Director

**Hull Citycare Limited**
*Incorporated:* 16 October 2003 *Employees:* 6
*Net Worth Deficit:* £15,925,554 *Total Assets:* £92,735,560
*Registered Office:* c/o Sewell Group PLC, Geneva Way, Leads Road, Hull, HU7 0DG
*Activities:* Other letting and operating of own or leased real estate
*Shareholders:* Hull Citycare (Investments) Ltd; Community Health Partnerships Ltd
*Officers:* David Adrian Leedham, Secretary/Accountant; Richard John Coates [1966] Investment Director; Alan Arthur Johnson [1950] Director/Chairman; David Adrian Leedham [1967] Director/Accountant; Alexander Toby Shedden Parry [1976] Director; Emma Louise Sayner [1975] Director/Chief Finance Officer; Paul Edwin Sewell [1952] Director

**Hull Collaborative Academy Trust**
*Incorporated:* 23 May 2013 *Employees:* 756
*Net Worth:* £48,286,700 *Total Assets:* £59,877,336
*Registered Office:* The Marvell College, Barham Road, Hull, HU9 4EE
*Activities:* Primary education
*Officers:* Timothy James Horne, Secretary; Andrew Stephen Barber [1979] Director/Charity CEO; Christopher James Huscroft [1981] Director/Headteacher; Malcolm George Mathias [1952] Director; Michael Henry Whitaker [1953] Director/Education Consultant; Elizabeth Ann Wilson [1952] Director/Retired; Graham David Wilson [1950] Director/Educational Consultant; Pauline Winn [1946] Director/Retired; Cheryl Yates [1973] Director/Human Resource Manager

**Hull Community Church**
*Incorporated:* 16 March 2012 *Employees:* 12
*Net Worth:* £3,107,610 *Total Assets:* £3,135,624
*Registered Office:* Hull Community Church, 310 Newland Avenue, Hull, HU5 2NB
*Activities:* Activities of religious organisations
*Officers:* John David August Bower [1968] Director/Environmental Health Officer; Michael John Bower [1991] Director/Building Surveyor; Anne Fiona Dannerolle [1973] Director/Church Leader; Peter Allen Fearnley [1981] Director/Chartered Accountant; Ralph Nevil Gilbert [1965] Director/Solicitor; Rebekah Sarah Horrigan [1989] Director/Teacher

**Hull Culture and Leisure Limited**
*Incorporated:* 20 February 2015 *Employees:* 480
*Net Worth Deficit:* £1,630,000 *Total Assets:* £5,259,000
*Registered Office:* Dock Office Chambers, New Cross Street, Hull, HU1 3AR
*Activities:* Operation of arts facilities
*Officers:* Peter Allen [1940] Director/Councillor; Marjorie Ann Brabazon [1952] Director; Hester Catherine Bridges [1976] Director/Charity Officer and Local Government Councillor; Councillor John Logan Fareham [1958] Director/Councillor; Nadine Fudge [1944] Director/Councillor; Councillor David McCobb [1980] Director/Councillor; Councillor Rosemary Pantelakis [1954] Director/Councillor; Councillor Denise Thompson [1954] Director/Councillor; Councillor Adam Williams [1982] Director/Councillor

**Hull Super League Limited**
*Incorporated:* 29 April 1998 *Employees:* 70
*Net Worth:* £402,011 *Total Assets:* £3,098,975
*Registered Office:* Hull FC Office, Kingston Communications Stadium, Anlaby Road, Hull, HU3 6JU
*Activities:* Activities of sport clubs
*Officers:* James Samuel Clark [1988] Executive Director; Peter Andrew McCabe [1979] Director; Adam Faulkner Pearson [1964] Director; Sarah Jean Wilkinson [1976] Director

**Hull Trains Company Limited**
*Incorporated:* 18 February 1999 *Employees:* 116
*Net Worth:* £1,591,000 *Total Assets:* £11,179,000
*Registered Office:* 4th Floor, Europa House, 184 Ferensway, Hull, HU1 3UT
*Activities:* Passenger rail transport, interurban
*Parent:* GB Railways Group Limited
*Officers:* Barbara Mary Salter, Secretary; Clive Burrows [1958] Director; Louise Mary Edwards [1961] Managing Director; Andrew Mark James [1966] Director; Stephen Montgomery [1962] Director

**Hull Truck Enterprises Limited**
*Incorporated:* 25 May 2004
*Net Worth:* £117,959 *Total Assets:* £14,026,008
*Registered Office:* Hull Truck Theatre Co Ltd, 50 Ferensway, Hull, HU2 8LB
*Activities:* Operation of arts facilities
*Parent:* Hull Truck Theatre Company Limited
*Officers:* Janthi Rose Mills-Ward, Secretary; David William Gemmell [1940] Director/Councillor; Alan William Kirkman [1953] Director/Accountant; Mark Andrew Willett [1963] Director/Chartered Surveyor

**Hull Truck Theatre Company Limited**
*Incorporated:* 29 April 1975 *Employees:* 61
*Net Worth:* £14,908,533 *Total Assets:* £15,434,528
*Registered Office:* Hull Truck Theatre, 50 Ferensway, Hull, HU2 8LB
*Activities:* Performing arts
*Officers:* Janthi Rose Mills-Ward, Secretary; Sophie Buckley [1975] Director/Employment Judge and Barrister; Professor Peter Glenn Burgess [1961] Director/Deputy Vice-Chancellor; Paul Clay [1966] Director/Arts Consultant; Patricia Anne Coyle [1957] Director of Marketing & Client Relations; Sharon Lesley Darley [1966] Director/Quality of Life Manager; Alan Dix [1948] Director/Arts Consultant; Steve Gallant [1960] Retired Product Director; David William Gemmell [1940] Director/Councillor; Nicola Jane Hallifax [1971] Independent Executive Producer & Creative Director; John Stoakley Hinson [1962] Director/Retired; Alan William Kirkman [1953] Director/Accountant; Councillor Mary Helene O'Mullane [1942] Director/Councillor; Michael Keith Robson [1958] Director/Management Consultant; Everal Antony Walsh [1968] Director/Freelance Performance Artist; Dawn Walton [1963] Artistic Director

**Hull University Union Limited**
*Incorporated:* 5 April 2013 *Employees:* 77
*Net Worth:* £4,954,691 *Total Assets:* £5,412,320
*Registered Office:* Student Central, Cottingham Road, Hull, HU6 7RX
*Activities:* Educational support services
*Officers:* Jane Stafford, Secretary; Alan Bolchover [1973] Director of Fund Raising; Andrew Costigan [1996] Director/Student Officer; Stuart Iain Ferguson [1975] Investment Director; Rebekah Greaves [1996] Director/Student; Isobel Hall [1996] Director/Student Officer; Madeline Holden [1997] Director/Student; Connor Massey [1994] Director/Student; Thomas McNamara [1997] Director/Student Officer; Osaro Otobo [1995] Director/Student; Gaius Jonathan Powell [1965] Director; Kathryn Sharman [1998] Director/Student; Nicholas Wright [1983] Director/Student Officer

**Hultafors Group UK Limited**
*Incorporated:* 4 October 1985 *Employees:* 33
*Net Worth:* £686,705 *Total Assets:* £3,424,593
*Registered Office:* Unit N3, Meltham Mills Industrial Estate, Holmfirth, W Yorks, HD9 4DS
*Activities:* Wholesale of clothing and footwear
*Parent:* Hultafors Group AB
*Officers:* Margaret Gillespie Whitelaw Barnes, Secretary; Bengt Peter Edwinson [1968] Director [Swedish]; Erik Torbjorn Eriksson [1970] Director [Swedish]; Ole Kristian Joedahl [1971] Director [Norwegian]

**Humankind Charity**
*Incorporated:* 30 May 1984 *Employees:* 737
*Previous:* Developing Initiatives for Support in the Community
*Net Worth:* £3,310,632 *Total Assets:* £13,527,386
*Registered Office:* IES Centre, Horndale Avenue, Aycliffe Business Park, Newton Aycliffe, Co Durham, DL5 6DS
*Activities:* Other residential care activities n.e.c.
*Officers:* Camila Horner, Secretary; James Black [1944] Director/Retired; Ian Roberts Dewhirst [1948] Director/Retired; Caroline Gitsham [1967] Director; Vivienne Jane Holmes [1967] Director/Local Government Officer; Christopher Ranulph George Matthews-Maxwell [1944] Director/Land/Property Owner; Sarah Patricia Shepherd [1957] Director; Michael William Treasure [1952] Director

**Humber Education Trust**
*Incorporated:* 9 September 2013 *Employees:* 581
*Previous:* Maybury Primary School
*Net Worth:* £47,739,468 *Total Assets:* £54,871,888
*Registered Office:* Clifton Primary School, Burslem Street, Hull, HU2 9BP
*Activities:* Primary education
*Officers:* John Gavin Barley [1967] Director/Operations Manager; Graeme Brook [1954] Director/Independent Educational Consultant; Paul Joseph Brown [1951] Director/Retired; Gerard Austin Gibbons [1966] Director/Regional Manager; Andrew Jordan [1989] Director/Accountant; Stephen Thomas Kernan [1976] Director/Headteacher; Paul Terrence Stevens [1970] Director/Head of IT and Technology; Brian Ashley Stillings [1980] Director/School Improvement Adviser; Rachel Emma Wilkes [1976] Director; Michael Anthony Wilmot [1956] Finance Director

**Humber Fishing Limited**
*Incorporated:* 19 October 2012
*Net Worth:* £6,626,596 *Total Assets:* £10,582,922
*Registered Office:* c/o Andrew Marr International Limited, Livingstone Road, Hessle, E Yorks, HU13 0EE
*Activities:* Marine fishing
*Parent:* Andrew Marr International Limited
*Officers:* Paul Morgan Farrar, Secretary; Mark James Dougal [1970] Director; Christian Leslie Marr [1972] Director; Andrew William Regan [1962] Director

**Humber Grain Limited**
*Incorporated:* 1 August 2011 *Employees:* 7
*Net Worth:* £323,036 *Total Assets:* £3,282,863
*Registered Office:* 34 Middle Street South, Driffield, E Yorks, YO25 6PS
*Activities:* Support activities for crop production
*Officers:* Edward Peel Mossop, Secretary; Struan Thomas Caudwell Abbott [1970] Director/Farmer; Paul Frank Arden [1962] Director/Farmer; Hannah Elizabeth Haigh [1981] Director; Andrew Charles Jackson [1959] Director/Farmer; Edward Peel Mossop [1955] Director/Farmer; Paul David Field Strawson [1960] Director/Farmer; Philip Graham Wynn [1950] Director/Consultant

**Humber Properties Limited**
*Incorporated:* 4 March 2003
*Net Worth:* £2,170,738 *Total Assets:* £7,213,677
*Registered Office:* Melton Waste Park, Gibson Lane, Melton, E Yorks, HU14 3HH
*Activities:* Management of real estate on a fee or contract basis
*Shareholders:* Derek Michael Taylor; Mark Hornshaw; Paul Anthony Hornshaw
*Officers:* Paul Anthony Hornshaw, Secretary; Mark Hornshaw [1975] Director; Paul Anthony Hornshaw [1972] Director; Derek Michael Taylor [1951] Director

**Humberside Engineering Training Association Limited**
*Incorporated:* 7 April 1971 *Employees:* 70
*Net Worth:* £4,844,598 *Total Assets:* £7,559,012
*Registered Office:* 27-31 Dansom Lane, Hull, HU8 7LA
*Activities:* Other education n.e.c.
*Officers:* Iain Elliott, Secretary; Ashley John Hepton [1989] Director/Chartered Accountant; Dr Malcolm Tony Joslin [1958] Director/Communications Manager; Louise Maloigne [1977] Director/Human Resources Manager; Timothy Mottershead [1964] Director/CES Operations Manager UK & Ireland; Ian Christopher Palmer [1958] Director/Management Consultant; Robert Bryan Charles Ripley [1965] Director/Solicitor; David Paul Sowden [1959] Director/Senior Lecturer; Richard Mark Swain [1968] Director/Engineering Manager

**Humberside Farmers Limited**
*Incorporated:* 22 April 1966 *Employees:* 7
*Net Worth:* £10,920,826 *Total Assets:* £14,111,197
*Registered Office:* The Estate Office, Newbald Lodge Farm, North Newbald, E Yorks, YO43 4TF
*Activities:* Mixed farming
*Shareholders:* Roger David Bramhill; Nicolas Giles Roger Bramhill
*Officers:* Nicholas Giles Roger Bramhill [1971] Director/Journalist; Roger David Bramhill [1940] Farmer/Director

**Humberston Park Special School**
*Incorporated:* 28 June 2011 *Employees:* 116
*Net Worth:* £1,410,943 *Total Assets:* £3,762,086
*Registered Office:* St Thomas Close, Humberston, Grimsby, N E Lincs, DN36 4HS
*Activities:* Other education n.e.c.
*Officers:* Ella Winder, Secretary; Mike Hill [1964] Director/Health and Safety Consultant; Sarah Horrocks [1973] Director; Colin Merriman [1962] Director; Karl Pizzey [1970] Director/Self Employed; Dominic Power [1968] Director/Local Authority; Gemma Rylatt [1972] Director; Jacqueline Saha [1962] Director/Teacher; Roger George Ward [1944] Director/Retired; Andrew Zielinski [1952] Director

**Humdinger Limited**
*Incorporated:* 26 June 2001 *Employees:* 255
*Net Worth Deficit:* £5,787,318 *Total Assets:* £39,320,280
*Registered Office:* Unit 6 Gothenburg Way, Sutton Fields Industrial Estate, Hull, HU7 0YG
*Activities:* Manufacture of other food products n.e.c.
*Parent:* Zetar Limited
*Officers:* Clive Henry Beecham [1953] Director; Lindsey Collier [1974] Director; Stewart Ashley Housecroft [1965] Director/Accountant; Paul Dennis Ramsey [1965] Director; Andreas Romankiewicz [1966] Director [German]; Paul Robert Tripp [1974] Director; Amanda Jayne Wright [1976] Director

**Hummersknott Academy Trust**
*Incorporated:* 9 June 2011 *Employees:* 229
*Net Worth:* £12,651,000 *Total Assets:* £16,601,000
*Registered Office:* Hummersknott Academy, Edinburgh Drive, Darlington, Co Durham, DL3 8AR
*Activities:* General secondary education
*Officers:* Ruth Armer [1980] Director/Teacher; Michael Davidson Dodd [1951] Director/Financial Consultant; Alan James Gowling [1970] Director Business Banking; Stephen Dennis Hunnisett [1958] Director/Vice Principal; Penelope Sarah Ann Jones [1957] Director; James Michael Keating [1972] Director/Executive Principal; David Liddle [1962] Director/Property Developer/Manager; Amanda Allison June Pybus-Coates [1965] Director; Deborah Rachael Sharpe [1988] Director/Solicitor; Naomi Jane Woods [1978] Director/Business Consultant

**Hungate (York) Regeneration Limited**
*Incorporated:* 13 December 2001
*Net Worth:* £8,283,000 *Total Assets:* £29,066,000
*Registered Office:* Millshaw, Leeds, LS11 8EG
*Activities:* Development of building projects
*Shareholders:* Lend Lease Residential (Yorkshire) Limited; White Rose Property Investments No.2 Limited
*Officers:* Robert Marshall, Secretary; John David Clark [1970] Director/Chartered Accountant; Paul Terence Millington [1962] Director/Accountant; James Oliver Pitt [1970] Director/Chartered Surveyor

**Hungerhill Academy Trust**
*Incorporated:* 7 February 2012 *Employees:* 179
*Net Worth:* £13,645,320 *Total Assets:* £17,295,344
*Registered Office:* Hungerhill School, Hungerhill Lane, Edenthorpe, Doncaster, S Yorks, DN3 2JY
*Activities:* General secondary education
*Officers:* Rachel Wilcox, Secretary; Nicholas Burne [1949] Director/Retired; Nicola Crowder [1983] Director/Teacher; Hannah Maria D'Rozario [1989] Director/Teacher; Daniel Thomas Fell [1981] Director/Chief Executive Officer; Kelvin Fitton [1968] Director/Chartered Accountant; Stephen Andrew France [1975] Director/Self Employed; Teresa Kathleen Ladley [1967] Director/School Business Manager; Oliver Marriott [1994] Director/Assistant ICT Technician; David Campbell Munro [1979] Director/Systems and Technology Manager; Dr Stephen John Newman [1956] Director/Lecturer; George William Peacock [1953] Director/Retired; Neil Purvis [1976] Director/Audit Manager; Helen Jean Redford-Hernandez [1964] Director/Headteacher; Andrea Robinson [1961] Director/Local Authority Officer; Paul Martin Senior [1956] Director; Philip Wedell [1956] Director/Kennels Proprietor

**Hunprenco (Precision Engineers) Limited**
*Incorporated:* 26 February 1971 *Employees:* 122
*Net Worth:* £6,665,272 *Total Assets:* £8,977,302
*Registered Office:* Hunmanby Industrial Estate, Bridlington Road, Hunmanby, Filey, N Yorks, YO14 0PH
*Activities:* Other professional, scientific and technical activities n.e.c.
*Shareholders:* Edwin Neesom; Jane Marilyn Neesom
*Officers:* Jane Marilyn Neesom, Secretary; Sarah Ann Ainley [1966] Director; Jane Elizabeth Kinroy [1961] Director; John Alan Lapping [1949] Director; Ivan George McNeill [1959] Director; Edwin Neesom [1931] Director; Jane Marilyn Neesom [1931] Director

**The Hunslet Club**
*Incorporated:* 11 March 2008 *Employees:* 52
*Net Worth:* £3,593,984 *Total Assets:* £3,643,380
*Registered Office:* Hillidge Road, Leeds, LS10 1BP
*Activities:* Technical and vocational secondary education
*Officers:* Rupert Arnold [1960] Director; Andrew Geoffrey Beadnall [1955] Director; David Fell [1948] Director/Retired College Senior Manager; Tom Holliday [1962] Director; Peter Cyril Robert Lewis [1947] Director/Retired Chartered Accountant; Eric Anthony Lumley [1945] Director; Richard Shaw [1972] Director/Project Manager; Clifford Spracklen [1946] Director

**Hunt Group Limited**
*Incorporated:* 15 October 1982 *Employees:* 154
*Net Worth:* £18,475,352 *Total Assets:* £31,947,550
*Registered Office:* 26-30 Midland Road, Scunthorpe, N Lincs, DN16 1DQ
*Activities:* Activities of head offices
*Major Shareholder:* Derrick Thomas Hunt
*Officers:* Gloria Patricia Hunt, Secretary; Brian David Hostad [1967] Finance Director; Darren Robert Hunt [1967] Surfacing Director; Derrick Thomas Hunt [1948] Director/Chairman; Gloria Patricia Hunt [1949] Director/Company Secretary; Shaun Antony Hunt [1970] Director/Vice Chairman

**Huntcliff Academy Trust**
*Incorporated:* 4 January 2012 *Employees:* 68
*Net Worth:* £5,382,991 *Total Assets:* £6,233,588
*Registered Office:* Huntcliff School, Redbourne Mere, Kirton in Lindsey, Gainsborough, Lincs, DN21 4NN
*Activities:* General secondary education
*Officers:* Maxine Sarah Tomlinson, Secretary; Susan Aldridge [1966] Director/Healthcare Manager; Nicholas Alexander Cooke [1980] Director/Health & Safety Professional; Patrick Stephen Daley [1963] Director/Headteacher; Mark Dickinson [1973] Director/Motor Industry Professional; Dr Patricia Frankish [1947] Director/Psychology, Training & Social Care; Edwin Ewart Gibbs [1943] Director/Headteacher; Ian Stewart Haywood [1970] Director/Solicitor; Sally Kelly [1970] Director/Teacher; Angela Naish [1977] Director/Teacher; Rachel Lindsey Whipps [1977] Director; Adam Carl Willey [1984] Director/Education Inclusion Officer

**Hunter Holdings Limited**
*Incorporated:* 21 July 2016 *Employees:* 111
*Net Worth:* £4,172,801 *Total Assets:* £5,278,731
*Registered Office:* Springfield Mill, Spa Street, Ossett, W Yorks, WF5 0HW
*Activities:* Activities of head offices
*Major Shareholder:* Ian Hunter
*Officers:* Steven Firth, Secretary; Steven Firth [1958] Finance Director; Ian Hunter [1966] Managing Director; Fraser Thompson [1984] Commercial Director

**Hunters Franchising Limited**
*Incorporated:* 16 August 2005 *Employees:* 5
*Net Worth:* £552,585 *Total Assets:* £8,272,745
*Registered Office:* Apollo House, Eboracum Way, York, YO31 7RE
*Activities:* Other professional, scientific and technical activities n.e.c.
*Parent:* Hunters Property Group Limited
*Officers:* Edward Anthony Jones, Secretary/Accountant; Glynis Joan Frew [1956] HR Director; Kevin Paul Hollinrake [1963] Director/Estate Agent; Edward Anthony Jones [1970] Director/Accountant; Martin John Robinson [1962] Director/Estate Agent; John Frederick Waterhouse [1946] Director/Estate Agency

**Hunters Property Group Limited**
*Incorporated:* 14 March 2000 *Employees:* 99
*Net Worth:* £1,985,763 *Total Assets:* £14,462,978
*Registered Office:* Apollo House, Eboracum Way, Heworth Green, York, YO31 7RE
*Activities:* Real estate agencies
*Parent:* Hunters Property PLC
*Officers:* Edward Anthony Jones, Secretary; Glynis Joan Frew [1956] HR Director; Harry Douglas Hill [1948] Director; Kevin Paul Hollinrake [1963] Director/Estate Agent; Edward Anthony Jones [1970] Director/Accountant; Martin John Robinson [1962] Director/Estate Agent; John Frederick Waterhouse [1946] Director/Estate Agent

**Hunters Property PLC**
*Incorporated:* 19 February 2015
*Net Worth:* £7,596,000 *Total Assets:* £14,833,000
*Registered Office:* Apollo House, Eboracum Way, Heworth Green, York, YO31 7RE
*Activities:* Real estate agencies
*Officers:* Edward Anthony Jones, Secretary; Dean Andrew Fielding [1965] Director; Glynis Joan Frew [1956] Managing Director; Harry Douglas Hill [1948] Director; Kevin Paul Hollinrake [1963] Director/Estate Agent; Edward Anthony Jones [1970] Director/Accountant

**Huntington Primary Academy**
*Incorporated:* 3 March 2015 *Employees:* 42
*Net Worth:* £2,586,865 *Total Assets:* £3,077,196
*Registered Office:* North Moor Road, Huntington, York, YO32 9QT
*Activities:* Primary education
*Officers:* Patricia Kim Bailey [1959] Director/Headteacher; Garry Binks [1957] Director/Retired Teacher; Stephen Charles Botham [1956] Director/Business Consultant; Eric Brown [1947] Director/Retired; Jessica Kate Crellin Charter [1978] Director/Human Resources; Julie Ann Crampsie [1968] Director/Company Secretary and Accountant; Nicholas Brian Cutt [1967] Director/Royal Mail Manager; Anne Foreman [1976] Director/Teacher; Paul Andrew Gething [1966] Director/Archaeologist; Julie Grainger [1967] Director/Teaching Assistant; Maureen Legge [1964] Director/Head of Human Resources; Stephen Anthony Russell [1968] Director/IT Manager/Software Engineer; Bernadette Mary Smith [1976] Director/Accountant; Charles Philip Welsford Walters [1975] Director/Pastor [British/South African]

**Hurst Group (Northern) Limited**
*Incorporated:* 23 March 1994 *Employees:* 303
*Net Worth:* £4,660,000 *Total Assets:* £12,428,000
*Registered Office:* Aynsley House, Common Road, Low Moor, Bradford, W Yorks, BD12 0UF
*Activities:* Other manufacturing n.e.c.
*Officers:* Leanne Hirst, Secretary; Leanne Jayne Hirst [1970] Director; Gary Stuart Hurst [1967] Director; Jeannie Hurst [1945] Director; Norman Robert Hurst [1938] Director; James Gerard Maye [1954] Director/Accountant

**Hurst Plastics Limited**
*Incorporated:* 17 March 1995 *Employees:* 127
*Net Worth:* £909,000 *Total Assets:* £4,330,000
*Registered Office:* Aynsley House, Common Road, Low Moor, Bradford, W Yorks, BD12 0UF
*Activities:* Other manufacturing n.e.c.
*Officers:* Leanne Hirst, Secretary; Mark John Atkinson [1964] Director/Sales; Gary Stuart Hurst [1967] Director; Jeannie Hurst [1945] Director; Norman Robert Hurst [1938] Director

**Hurst Stores and Interiors Limited**
*Incorporated:* 29 February 1972 *Employees:* 53
*Net Worth:* £3,519,000 *Total Assets:* £5,276,000
*Registered Office:* Aynsley House, Common Road, Low Moor, Bradford, W Yorks, BD12 0UF
*Activities:* Other specialised construction activities n.e.c.
*Officers:* Leanne Hirst, Secretary; James Edward Gilbert [1965] Operations Director; Michael Andrew Hall [1969] Sales and Marketing Director; Gary Stuart Hurst [1967] Director; Jeannie Hurst [1945] Director/Bookkeeper; Norman Robert Hurst [1938] Director/Joiner; Barrie Midgley [1961] Director

**Huskisson Shipping Limited**
*Incorporated:* 20 January 1995
*Net Worth:* £9,061,095 *Total Assets:* £16,800,772
*Registered Office:* 1 Park Row, Leeds, LS1 5AB
*Activities:* Sea and coastal freight water transport
*Parent:* Rever Offshore UK Limited
*Officers:* Mark John Bessell [1964] Director; Neale John Stewart [1963] Director

**Husqvarna UK Limited**
*Incorporated:* 18 March 1970 *Employees:* 353
*Net Worth:* £27,241,000 *Total Assets:* £89,893,000
*Registered Office:* Preston Road, Aycliffe Industrial Park, Newton Aycliffe, Co Durham, DL5 6UP
*Activities:* Manufacture of agricultural and forestry machinery other than tractors
*Officers:* Richard Hall, Secretary; Gunnar Niklas Broberg [1969] Director/Vice President [Swedish]; Terence Burke [1972] Director; Glen Anthony Instone [1977] Director

**Hutton Wandesley Estate LLP**
*Incorporated:* 19 March 2014 *Employees:* 8
*Net Worth:* £12,231,925 *Total Assets:* £12,668,781
*Registered Office:* c/o HPH Accountants LLP, 54 Bootham, York, YO30 7XZ
*Officers:* David Andrew Gray [1963] Member; Christy York [1968] Member; Sasha Annabel York [1972] Member; Brian Turnbull Julius Stevens [1938] LLP Member; Colonel Edward Christopher York [1939] LLP Member

**Hutton Wandesley Farms Company Limited**
*Incorporated:* 30 March 1967 *Employees:* 2
*Net Worth:* £3,011,129 *Total Assets:* £3,065,828
*Registered Office:* 54 Bootham, York, YO30 7XZ
*Activities:* Growing of cereals (except rice), leguminous crops and oil seeds
*Shareholders:* Christopher York; Colonel Edward Christopher York; Brian Turnbull Julius Stevens; David Andrew Gray
*Officers:* Sasha Annabel York, Secretary; Christy York [1968] Director; Colonel Edward Christopher York [1939] Director; Sarah Ann York [1940] Director; Sasha Annabel York [1972] Director

**Hyco Manufacturing Limited**
*Incorporated:* 23 January 1990 *Employees:* 28
*Net Worth:* £3,615,878 *Total Assets:* £4,142,395
*Registered Office:* Normandy Court, Express Way, Castleford, W Yorks, WF10 5NR
*Activities:* Manufacture of other electrical equipment
*Shareholders:* Kirsty Jane McHugh; Michael Francis McHugh
*Officers:* Michael Francis McHugh, Secretary/Director; Kirsty Jane McHugh [1969] Director; Michael Francis McHugh [1961] Director

**Hydram Engineering Limited**
*Incorporated:* 30 March 1994 *Employees:* 226
*Net Worth:* £5,353,537 *Total Assets:* £10,529,852
*Registered Office:* Avenue 1, Chilton Industrial Estate, Ferryhill, Co Durham, DL17 0SG
*Activities:* Manufacture of metal structures and parts of structures
*Parent:* Dynamic Aerospace and Defense Limited
*Officers:* David James Greatorex, Secretary/Managing Director; David James Greatorex [1969] Managing Director; Donald Daniel Nystrom [1970] Director [American]

**Hydramotion Limited**
*Incorporated:* 14 November 1986 *Employees:* 29
*Net Worth:* £2,691,972 *Total Assets:* £3,755,198
*Registered Office:* Seven Street, York Road Business Park, Malton, N Yorks, YO17 6YA
*Activities:* Manufacture of electronic industrial process control equipment
*Major Shareholder:* John Gerrard Gallagher
*Officers:* Julie Gallagher, Secretary; John Gerrard Gallagher [1959] Managing Director

**Hydrastore Limited**
*Incorporated:* 27 September 1989 *Employees:* 37
*Net Worth:* £2,137,263 *Total Assets:* £3,557,458
*Registered Office:* Sandtoft Industrial Estate, Belton, Doncaster, S Yorks, DN9 1PN
*Activities:* Agents specialised in the sale of other particular products
*Parent:* Douglas C Adams & Company Ltd
*Officers:* Steven Brown [1959] Director/Sales Engineer; Julie Alexandra Hoddinott [1958] Director; Allan Stuart Lee [1944] Director; Julian Stuart Lee [1970] Director; Brian McNulty [1951] Director; Stephen James Owen [1964] Director/Hydraulic Engineer

**Hydrema (U.K.) Limited**
*Incorporated:* 12 December 1984 *Employees:* 10
*Net Worth:* £4,050,452 *Total Assets:* £10,793,207
*Registered Office:* Hydrema UK Ltd, Barugh Way, Melmerby Green Road, Barkers Business Park, Melmerby, N Yorks, HG4 5NB
*Activities:* Manufacture of earthmoving equipment
*Major Shareholder:* Jan Werner Jensen
*Officers:* Timothy Wadsworth, Secretary; Timothy Wadsworth [1961] Sales Director; Jan Werner Jensen [1968] Director [Danish]

**Alfred Hymas Limited**
*Incorporated:* 29 February 1956 *Employees:* 110
*Net Worth:* £11,065,285 *Total Assets:* £18,142,768
*Registered Office:* The Lilacs, Burton Leonard, Harrogate, N Yorks, HG3 3SG
*Activities:* Mixed farming
*Shareholder:* Stewart Alan Hymas
*Officers:* Stewart Alan Hymas, Secretary; Dorothy May Hymas [1942] Director/Secretary; Robert Alfred Hymas [1968] Director/Haulage Contractor; Stewart Alan Hymas [1970] Director/Transport Manager; David Frank Whincup [1952] Director/Foreman

**Hymers College Trustee Limited**
*Incorporated:* 30 July 2004 *Employees:* 188
*Net Worth:* £12,210,104 *Total Assets:* £14,094,210
*Registered Office:* 83 Hymers Avenue, Hull, HU3 1LW
*Activities:* Primary education
*Officers:* Kathleen Foster Walker, Secretary; Sameera Anwar West [1975] Director/Lawyer; Michael Peter Astell [1966] Managing Director; Adrian Beecroft [1947] Director/Investment Manager; Peter Glenn Burgess [1961] Director/Pro-Vice Chancellor; Tracey Carruthers [1966] Director/Clinical Educationalist; John Ferdinand Connolly [1977] Director; Dominic Anthony Gibbons [1970] Director/Chartered Surveyor; William Hornby Gore [1944] Director; Glenda Anne Greendale [1959] Director/Teaching Assistant; Martin Charles Sheridan Hall [1957] Director; Jonathan Leafe [1963] Managing Director; Elizabeth Ann Maliakal [1974] Director/Solicitor; Dr Ashok Pathak [1950] Director/Orthopaedic Surgeon; Christopher Martin Read [1969] Director/Company Secretary; John Maybin Vivian Redman [1959] Director; Councillor John Graham Robinson [1961] Director/Councillor; Nicola Shipley [1979] Director/Chartered Accountant; Gemma Victoria Vickerman [1984] Director/Chartered Surveyor; James Robert Wheldon [1967] Director/Property Valuer; Peter John Edward Wildsmith [1950] Director/Judge

**Hystat Systems Limited**
*Incorporated:* 18 February 1976 *Employees:* 69
*Net Worth:* £3,347,858 *Total Assets:* £5,269,435
*Registered Office:* Spa Fields Industrial Estate, New Street, Slaithwaite, Huddersfield, W Yorks, HD7 5BB
*Activities:* Manufacture of pumps
*Shareholder:* Ramon Anthony Wadsworth
*Officers:* Simon James Wadsworth, Secretary; William Iredale [1958] Works Director; Dale Mason [1965] Director; Ramon Anthony Wadsworth [1946] Director/Engineer; Simon James Wadsworth [1975] Director; Christopher Ian Watson [1964] Technical Director

**I & S Properties Limited**
*Incorporated:* 26 June 1997 *Employees:* 4
*Net Worth:* £3,727,839 *Total Assets:* £4,656,348
*Registered Office:* 609a Denby Dale Road, Calder Grove, Wakefield, W Yorks, WF4 3DJ
*Activities:* Other letting and operating of own or leased real estate
*Officers:* Steven Samardzija, Secretary; Graham Ingham [1955] Director/Electrician; Shauna Ingham [1955] Director; Sharon Samardzija [1960] Director; Steven Samardzija [1957] Director

**I A P Investments Ltd**
*Incorporated:* 24 October 2016 *Employees:* 3
*Net Worth:* £57,098 *Total Assets:* £3,836,826
*Registered Office:* c/o Sagars Accountants Ltd, Gresham House, 5-7 St Pauls Street, Leeds, LS1 2JG
*Activities:* Security dealing on own account
*Major Shareholder:* Ian Andrew Proudfoot
*Officers:* Derek Peter Armstrong [1954] Director/Retailer; Ian Andrew Proudfoot [1955] Director; Marcus Alexander Proudfoot [1991] Director

**I'anson Bros Limited**
*Incorporated:* 22 December 1948 *Employees:* 77
*Net Worth:* £16,109,000 *Total Assets:* £18,625,000
*Registered Office:* The Mill, Thorpe Road, Masham, Ripon, N Yorks, HG4 4JB
*Activities:* Manufacture of prepared feeds for farm animals
*Parent:* I'Anson Bros (Holdings) Ltd
*Officers:* Hugh McLeod Clark, Secretary/Accountant; Hugh McLeod Clark [1963] Director/Accountant; Christopher John I'anson [1962] Managing Director; William Edward I'anson [1968] Commercial Director

**I'anson Bros. (Holdings) Limited**
*Incorporated:* 13 May 1996 *Employees:* 77
*Net Worth:* £13,744,000 *Total Assets:* £16,260,000
*Registered Office:* The Mill, Thorpe Road, Masham, Ripon, N Yorks, HG4 4JB
*Activities:* Activities of agricultural holding companies
*Shareholders:* Christopher John I'Anson; William Edward I'Anson
*Officers:* Hugh McLeod Clark, Secretary/Accountant; Hugh McLeod Clark [1963] Director/Management Accountant; Christopher John I'anson [1962] Director; William Edward I'anson [1968] Director

**I-Trust Education**
*Incorporated:* 10 March 2011 *Employees:* 148
*Previous:* Whitehill Community Academy Multi-Academy Trust
*Net Worth:* £7,636,188 *Total Assets:* £8,797,322
*Registered Office:* Whitehill Community Academy, Occupation Lane, Illingworth, Halifax, W Yorks, HX2 9RL
*Activities:* Primary education
*Officers:* Iain Christopher Maris, Secretary; Jonathan Paul Beale [1976] Director/Chartered Financial Planner; Robert James Brownless [1972] Managing Director; John Michael Craven [1976] Director/Postal Worker; Dominic Bryan Furby [1968] Director/Fire Fighter; Iain Christopher Maris [1972] MAT Business Director; Jimmy Richard Sayles [1979] Director/Principal; Shane David Taylor [1982] Director/Teacher; Linda Jane Waugh [1971] Director/Principal

**I.C.S. (UK) Limited**
*Incorporated:* 11 November 1998 *Employees:* 124
*Net Worth:* £3,693,922 *Total Assets:* £9,743,381
*Registered Office:* Neville Road, Bradford, W Yorks, BD4 8TU
*Activities:* Non-specialised wholesale of food, beverages and tobacco
*Parent:* ICS UK (Holdings) Limited
*Officers:* Ismail Bhamji, Secretary; Ismail Bhamji [1966] Director/Salesman; Siddick Bhamji [1961] Director/Salesman

**I.G. Industries Holdings Limited**
*Incorporated:* 15 November 2000 *Employees:* 115
*Net Worth:* £20,655,764 *Total Assets:* £35,140,952
*Registered Office:* The Flarepath, Elsham Wold, Brigg, N Lincs, DN20 0SP
*Activities:* Activities of head offices
*Officers:* Kevan Lari, Secretary; Ahmad Lari [1960] Director [German]; Hossein Lari [1931] Director [British/Iranian]; Kevan Lari [1960] Director; Parvaneh Lari [1940] Director; Mahnaz Larizadeh [1942] Director

**I.G. Industries Public Limited Company**
*Incorporated:* 8 March 1988 *Employees:* 115
*Net Worth:* £20,201,544 *Total Assets:* £34,680,196
*Registered Office:* The Flarepath, Elsham Wold, Brigg, N Lincs, DN20 0SP
*Activities:* Manufacture of other plastic products
*Parent:* I.G. Industries Holdings Limited
*Officers:* Kevan Lari, Secretary; Ahmad Lari [1960] Director [German]; Hossein Lari [1931] Director [British/Iranian]; Kevan Lari [1960] Director; Parvaneh Lari [1940] Director; Mahnaz Larizadeh [1942] Director

**Icando UK Limited**
*Incorporated:* 26 July 2013 *Employees:* 3
*Net Worth:* £11,926,209 *Total Assets:* £12,033,146
*Registered Office:* 8 North Park Road, Harrogate, N Yorks, HG1 5PG
*Activities:* Other service activities n.e.c.
*Shareholders:* Judith Helen Hodgson; Nicholas James David Hodgson; Timothy Matthew Joseph Hodgson
*Officers:* Judith Helen Hodgson [1950] Director; Nicholas James David Hodgson [1977] Director; Timothy Matthew Joseph Hodgson [1975] Director

**The Ice Co Storage & Logistics Limited**
*Incorporated:* 18 June 2009
*Previous:* The Ice Co Storage Preston Limited
*Net Worth:* £2,008,800 *Total Assets:* £7,454,797
*Registered Office:* Joseph Marr House, Units 18-20 Langthwaite Business Park, South Kirkby, W Yorks, WF9 3AP
*Activities:* Processing and preserving of poultry meat
*Parent:* J Marr Limited
*Officers:* David John Lyon [1967] Director; Philip Edward Marr [1984] Director; Paul Andrew Martin [1971] Director; Polly Anna Metcalfe [1986] Director; Annabelle Amy Tyson [1983] Director; Nicholas Giles Wharton [1966] Finance Director

**Ice Fresh Seafood Limited**
*Incorporated:* 15 March 2005 *Employees:* 48
*Net Worth Deficit:* £637,686 *Total Assets:* £6,348,604
*Registered Office:* The Orangery, Hesslewood Country Office Park, Hessle, E Yorks, HU13 0LH
*Activities:* Processing and preserving of fish, crustaceans and molluscs
*Parent:* Seagold Limited
*Officers:* Jonas Baldursson, Secretary; Gustaf Baldvinsson [1957] Director [Icelander]

**Iceco Limited**
*Incorporated:* 25 August 2009
*Net Worth:* £1,226,898 *Total Assets:* £3,384,869
*Registered Office:* Units 18-20 Langthwaite Business Park, South Kirkby, W Yorks, WF9 3AP
*Activities:* Manufacture of other food products n.e.c.
*Parent:* J Marr Limited
*Officers:* Philip Edward Marr [1984] Director; Polly Anna Metcalfe [1986] Director; Annabelle Amy Tyson [1983] Director; Nicholas Giles Wharton [1966] Finance Director

**Iceland Seafood Barraclough Ltd**
*Incorporated:* 10 December 1980 *Employees:* 150
*Net Worth:* £2,750,011 *Total Assets:* £23,803,130
*Registered Office:* 35 Essex Street, Bradford, W Yorks, BD4 7PG
*Activities:* Wholesale of other food, including fish, crustaceans and molluscs
*Officers:* Peter Hawkins, Secretary; Bjarni Armannsson [1968] Director/Chief Executive [Icelander]; Lee Mark Camfield [1967] Director/Chief Operating Officer; Peter Hawkins [1967] Managing Director; Reynir Jonsson [1978] Director/Chief Financial Officer [Icelander]

**Icelolly Bidco Limited**
*Incorporated:* 7 August 2013
*Net Worth:* £987,620 *Total Assets:* £19,288,480
*Registered Office:* Park Row House, 19-20 Park Row, Leeds, LS1 5JF
*Activities:* Activities of other holding companies n.e.c.
*Parent:* Palatine Private Equity LLP
*Officers:* David Clayton [1966] Director; James William Hawksworth [1971] Director/Accountant; Andrew Lees [1964] Director; Richard Singer [1979] Director/Chief Executive

**Icelolly Marketing Limited**
*Incorporated:* 16 December 2005 *Employees:* 61
*Net Worth:* £1,052,874 *Total Assets:* £4,245,141
*Registered Office:* Park Row House, 19-20 Park Row, Leeds, LS1 5JF
*Activities:* Advertising agencies
*Parent:* Palatine Private Equity LLP
*Officers:* David Clinch [1960] Director; James William Hawksworth [1971] Director/Accountant; Antonio Iacobucci [1967] IT Director; Ross Kenneth Matthews [1979] Director; Richard Singer [1979] Director/Chief Executive; Claire Willoughby [1968] Director

**Icelolly Topco Limited**
*Incorporated:* 7 August 2013 *Employees:* 61
*Net Worth Deficit:* £5,732,770 *Total Assets:* £11,246,801
*Registered Office:* Park Row House, 19-20 Park Row, Leeds, LS1 5JF
*Activities:* Activities of other holding companies n.e.c.
*Parent:* Palatine Private Equity LLP
*Officers:* James William Hawksworth [1971] Director/Accountant; Beth Clare Houghton [1974] Director; Andrew Lees [1964] Director; Richard Singer [1979] Director/Chief Executive

**ICH Limited**
*Incorporated:* 9 September 1992 *Employees:* 72
*Net Worth:* £453,054 *Total Assets:* £4,669,889
*Registered Office:* Union Bridge Works, Roker Lane, Pudsey, Leeds, LS28 9LE
*Activities:* Repair of other equipment
*Shareholders:* Stephen Donald Cooper; Danny Robinson
*Officers:* David Atkinson [1982] Director; Neil Edward Blenkin [1964] Director; Robert Stephen Cooper [1984] Director; Stephen Donald Cooper [1951] Director/Chartered Accountant; Carl David Pickard [1988] Director; Graham Pinder [1961] Technical Director; Danny Robinson [1963] Director/Heating/Ventilation Engineer

**ICIEA Limited**
*Incorporated:* 23 July 2003 *Employees:* 91
*Net Worth:* £5,945,000 *Total Assets:* £9,626,000
*Registered Office:* 2nd Floor, Gateway, 2 Holgate Park Drive, York, YO26 4GB
*Activities:* Real estate agencies
*Parent:* LSLI Limited
*Officers:* Sapna Bedi FitzGenerald, Secretary; Greig Barker [1969] Finance Director; Helen Elizabeth Buck [1960] Director; Gregory Winston Young [1966] Director/Estate Agent

**Icon Aerospace Technology Ltd**
*Incorporated:* 14 December 1933 *Employees:* 270
*Previous:* Icon Polymer Limited
*Net Worth:* £6,249,000 *Total Assets:* £15,102,000
*Registered Office:* Victoria Works, Thrumpton Lane, Retford, Notts, DN22 6HH
*Activities:* Manufacture of air and spacecraft and related machinery
*Parent:* Crosslink Technology Holdings Ltd
*Officers:* Craig Andrew Harris [1969] Director/Chief Executive; James Robert Hill [1978] Director/Chief Financial Officer; David James Ring [1962] Director

**The Icon Consultancy Ltd**
*Incorporated:* 25 April 1997 *Employees:* 46
*Previous:* American Crew U.K. Limited
*Net Worth:* £4,362,605 *Total Assets:* £5,290,676
*Registered Office:* Unit 2 Green Park, Coal Road, Leeds, LS14 1FB
*Activities:* Wholesale of perfume and cosmetics
*Parent:* Sweet Squared Limited
*Officers:* James Alan Nordstrom [1957] Director [American]; Samantha Jane Sweet [1969] Director; Samuel Whitney Sweet [1972] Director [American]

**Iconx Holdings Limited**
*Incorporated:* 21 October 2016 *Employees:* 4
*Net Worth:* £1,576 *Total Assets:* £5,440,492
*Registered Office:* Units 2-3 Marrtree Business Park, Ryefield Way, Silsden, Keighley, W Yorks, BD20 0EF
*Activities:* Activities of other holding companies n.e.c.
*Shareholders:* David Anthony Horsfall; Karl Michael Clive Teulon
*Officers:* Jonathan Bradley Cleland [1965] Non-Executive Director Chairman; David Anthony Horsfall [1963] Director; Karl Michael Clive Teulon [1986] Director; Peter Graeme Wear [1978] Director/Chief Financial Officer; Pascal Adrian Wittet [1981] Director

**Iconx Ltd**
*Incorporated:* 19 November 2001 *Employees:* 30
*Net Worth Deficit:* £910,541 *Total Assets:* £5,932,440
*Registered Office:* Units 2-3 Marrtree Business Park, Ryefield Way, Silsden, Keighley, W Yorks, BD20 0EF
*Activities:* Other business support service activities n.e.c.
*Parent:* Iconx Holdings Ltd
*Officers:* David Anthony Horsfall [1963] Director; Karl Teulon [1986] Director; Peter Graeme Wear [1978] Director/Chief Financial Officer

**ICR (Investment 1) Limited**
*Incorporated:* 25 February 2014
*Net Worth:* £727,416 *Total Assets:* £75,326,472
*Registered Office:* Unit 10 Westmorland Business Park, Gilthwaiterigg Lane, Kendal, Cumbria, LA9 6NS
*Activities:* Activities of head offices
*Parent:* ICR Integrity (Holdings) Limited
*Officers:* William John Bayliss [1962] Director; Andrew Bruce [1958] Director; Alan McQuade [1981] Director/Chartered Accountant

**ICR (Investment 2) Limited**
*Incorporated:* 25 February 2014 *Employees:* 2
*Net Worth Deficit:* £11,037 *Total Assets:* £74,709,280
*Registered Office:* Unit 10 Westmorland Business Park, Gilthwaiterigg Lane, Kendal, Cumbria, LA9 6NS
*Activities:* Activities of head offices
*Parent:* ICR (Investment 1) Limited
*Officers:* William John Bayliss [1962] Director; Alan McQuade [1981] Director/Chartered Accountant

**ICR Integrity (Group) Limited**
*Incorporated:* 27 February 2014 *Employees:* 7
*Net Worth Deficit:* £28,991,974 *Total Assets:* £98,230,856
*Registered Office:* Unit 10 Westmorland Business Park, Gilthwaiterigg Lane, Kendal, Cumbria, LA9 6NS
*Activities:* Activities of head offices
*Parent:* ICR (Investment 2) Limited
*Officers:* William John Bayliss [1962] Director; Alan McQuade [1981] Director/Chartered Accountant

**ICR Integrity (Holdings) Limited**
*Incorporated:* 25 February 2014 *Employees:* 165
*Net Worth Deficit:* £52,800,032 *Total Assets:* £62,776,164
*Registered Office:* Unit 10 Westmorland Business Park, Gilthwaiterigg Lane, Kendal, Cumbria, LA9 6NS
*Activities:* Activities of head offices
*Shareholder:* Graphite Capital General Partner VIII LLP
*Officers:* William John Bayliss [1962] Director; Maurice McBride [1954] Director; Alan McQuade [1981] Director/Chartered Accountant; William George Rennie [1966] Director

**ICR Integrity Limited**
*Incorporated:* 13 April 2011 *Employees:* 4
*Net Worth Deficit:* £18,449,452 *Total Assets:* £48,354,312
*Registered Office:* Unit 10 Westmorland Business Park, Gilthwaiterigg Lane, Kendal, Cumbria, LA9 6NS
*Activities:* Activities of head offices
*Parent:* ICR Integrity (Group) Limited
*Officers:* William John Bayliss [1962] Director; Alan McQuade [1981] Director/Chartered Accountant

**Ideal Boilers Limited**
*Incorporated:* 19 December 1936 *Employees:* 755
*Net Worth:* £126,873,000 *Total Assets:* £235,566,000
*Registered Office:* Ideal Boilers Limited, National Avenue, Hull, HU5 4JB
*Activities:* Manufacture of central heating radiators and boilers
*Parent:* ISG Boiler Holdings Limited
*Officers:* Steven Hairsine, Secretary; Shaun Barry Edwards [1968] Director; Pierre-Louis Andre Francois [1956] Director [French]; Steven Hairsine [1975] Director; Yves Lepelletier [1954] Director/General Manager [French]

**Ideal Building Systems Holdings Limited**
*Incorporated:* 19 March 2007 *Employees:* 90
*Net Worth:* £4,354,427 *Total Assets:* £7,430,316
*Registered Office:* Lancaster Road, Carnaby Industrial Estate, Bridlington, E Yorks, YO15 3QY
*Activities:* Activities of head offices
*Shareholders:* Paul Raymond Coates; Malcolm Raymond Laverack
*Officers:* Penelope Eileen Benmasaud, Secretary/Director; Penelope Eileen Benmasaud [1956] Director; Paul Raymond Coates [1969] Director; Malcolm Raymond Laverack [1955] Director

**Ideal Building Systems Limited**
*Incorporated:* 11 December 1992 *Employees:* 70
*Net Worth:* £8,780,202 *Total Assets:* £11,414,167
*Registered Office:* Ideal Building Systems Limited, Lancaster Road, Carnaby Industrial Estate, Bridlington, E Yorks, YO15 3QY
*Activities:* Other specialised construction activities n.e.c.
*Parent:* Ideal Building Systems Holdings Limited
*Officers:* Penelope Eileen Benmasaud, Secretary; Penelope Eileen Benmasaud [1956] Director; Paul Raymond Coates [1969] Managing Director; Malcolm Raymond Laverack [1955] Director

**Ideal Carehomes (Number One) Limited**
*Incorporated:* 18 February 2011 *Employees:* 867
*Net Worth:* £9,434,723 *Total Assets:* £13,229,600
*Registered Office:* Unit 2, Helios 47, Isabella Road, Garforth, Leeds, LS25 2DY
*Activities:* Residential care activities for the elderly and disabled
*Parent:* LNT Group Limited
*Officers:* Philip Miles Raven, Secretary; Matthew Graeme Lowe [1973] Director; Philip Miles Raven [1966] Director

**Ideal Carehomes Limited**
*Incorporated:* 19 December 2016 *Employees:* 39
*Net Worth Deficit:* £715,832 *Total Assets:* £22,937,280
*Registered Office:* Helios 47, Isabella Road, Garforth, Leeds, LS25 2DY
*Activities:* Residential care activities for the elderly and disabled
*Parent:* LNT Group Limited
*Officers:* Phoebe Lucy Tomlinson, Secretary; Matthew Graeme Lowe [1973] Director; Philip Miles Raven [1966] Director; Lawrence Neil Tomlinson [1964] Director

**Ideal Homes Holdings Limited**
*Incorporated:* 15 May 1934
*Net Worth:* £31,203,000 *Total Assets:* £239,766,000
*Registered Office:* Persimmon House, Fulford, York, YO19 4FE
*Activities:* Development of building projects
*Parent:* Persimmon PLC
*Officers:* Tracy Lazelle Davison, Secretary; David Jenkinson [1967] Director; Michael Hugh Killoran [1961] Finance Director; Richard Paul Stenhouse [1971] Director/Accountant

**Ideal Standard (UK) Limited**
*Incorporated:* 31 January 1907 *Employees:* 270
*Net Worth:* £48,475,000 *Total Assets:* £191,520,992
*Registered Office:* The Bathroom Works, National Avenue, Hull, HU5 4HS
*Activities:* Agents involved in the sale of timber and building materials
*Parent:* Ideal Standard Holdings (BC) UK Ltd
*Officers:* Joanne Caroline Elwell, Secretary; David Barber [1965] Finance Director; Jonathan Peter Edge [1971] Director; Joanne Caroline Elwell [1965] Director/Accountant

**Ideal Standard Holdings (BC) UK Ltd**
*Incorporated:* 13 July 2007
*Net Worth Deficit:* £108,383,000 *Total Assets:* £209,936,000
*Registered Office:* The Bathroom Works, National Avenue, Hull, HU5 4JJ
*Activities:* Activities of head offices
*Parent:* Ideal Standard International Holding SARL
*Officers:* Joanne Caroline Elwell, Secretary; David Barber [1965] Finance Director; Maarten Van Hoecke [1979] Tax Director [Belgian]

**Idexx Laboratories Limited**
*Incorporated:* 20 December 1989 *Employees:* 269
*Net Worth:* £8,056,676 *Total Assets:* £18,509,580
*Registered Office:* Grange House, Sandbeck Way, Wetherby, W Yorks, LS22 7DN
*Activities:* Veterinary activities
*Parent:* Idexx Laboratories, Inc.
*Officers:* Lily Joann Lu, Secretary; Willard R Blanche Jr [1974] Director/Vice President, Finance [American]; Jeffery Donn Chadbourne [1975] Senior Director, Finance [American]; Lily Joann Lu [1972] Director/Vice President, Deputy General Counsel [American]; Brian Patrick McKeon [1962] Director/Chief Financial Officer [American]; Paul Tye [1965] Director

**Idexx UK Acquisition Limited**
*Incorporated:* 24 July 2000
*Net Worth:* £6,732,617 *Total Assets:* £12,441,462
*Registered Office:* Grange House, Sandbeck Way, Wetherby, W Yorks, LS22 7DN
*Activities:* Activities of other holding companies n.e.c.
*Parent:* Idexx Laboratories, Inc.
*Officers:* Lily Joann Lu, Secretary; Willard R Blanche Jr [1974] Director/Vice President, Finance [American]; Jeffery Donn Chadbourne [1975] Senior Director, Finance [American]; Lily Joann Lu [1972] Director/Vice President, Deputy General Counsel [American]; Brian Patrick McKeon [1962] Director/Chief Financial Officer [American]; Paul Tye [1965] Director

**Idigital Investments Ltd**
*Incorporated:* 29 September 2014 *Employees:* 5
*Net Worth:* £1,511,786 *Total Assets:* £3,381,763
*Registered Office:* Kidd House, Whitehall Road, Leeds, LS12 1AP
*Activities:* Activities of head offices
*Shareholders:* John Henry Page; Paul Christopher Unsworth
*Officers:* Heather Ellen Page [1962] Director/Human Resources Manager; John Henry Page [1952] Director; Paul Christopher Unsworth [1961] Director; Raj Rani Unsworth [1959] Director/Manager

**IETG Holdings Limited**
*Incorporated:* 6 October 2016 *Employees:* 131
*Net Worth:* £696,867 *Total Assets:* £3,451,281
*Registered Office:* 19 Hornbeam Square South, Hornbeam Park, Harrogate, N Yorks, HG2 8NB
*Activities:* Other business support service activities n.e.c.
*Major Shareholder:* John Nicholas Bentley
*Officers:* Martin Matthew Bentley [1971] Director; Richard Bond [1974] Director/Chartered Accountant; Ian Brian Edwards [1964] Director/Civil Engineer

**IETG Limited**
*Incorporated:* 27 September 2005 *Employees:* 82
*Net Worth:* £3,030,502 *Total Assets:* £4,049,103
*Registered Office:* Hapco House, Cross Green Way, Cross Green Industrial Estate, Leeds, LS9 0SE
*Activities:* Other business support service activities n.e.c.
*Parent:* IETG Holdings Limited
*Officers:* Richard Andrew Bond, Secretary; Martin Matthew Bentley [1971] Director; Richard Bond [1974] Director/Chartered Accountant; Ian Brian Edwards [1964] Director/Business Executive

**IF Cardboard Creations Limited**
*Incorporated:* 16 January 1996 *Employees:* 27
*Net Worth:* £4,965,445 *Total Assets:* £6,328,084
*Registered Office:* Thornton Road Industrial Estate, Thornton Road, Pickering, N Yorks, YO18 7JB
*Activities:* Other manufacturing n.e.c.
*Shareholder:* Anco Far East Limited
*Officers:* Julian David Rhodes, Secretary; John Philip Calvert [1969] Sales and Marketing Director; Terrance Finley [1953] Director [American]; Kim Kraft [1963] Director [American]; Peter Sung-Yan Yu [1959] Director [American]

**IFG Drake Limited**
*Incorporated:* 15 May 1945 *Employees:* 110
*Previous:* Drake Extrusion Limited
*Net Worth:* £13,540,000 *Total Assets:* £18,221,000
*Registered Office:* Old Mills, Drighlington, Bradford, W Yorks, BD11 1BY
*Activities:* Manufacture of man-made fibres
*Officers:* Kathryn Anne Davenport, Secretary; John Olof Hager [1964] Managing Director [Swedish]; Stephen O'Neil [1961] Director

**IFGL Monocon Holdings Limited**
*Incorporated:* 19 August 2005 *Employees:* 3
*Net Worth:* £5,000,000 *Total Assets:* £5,025,000
*Registered Office:* Davy Road, Old Denaby, Doncaster, S Yorks, DN12 4LQ
*Activities:* Activities of head offices
*Parent:* IFGL Worldwide Holdings Limited
*Officers:* Dheeraj Parakh, Secretary; Mihir Prakash Bajoria [1985] Director [Indian]; Dheeraj Parakh [1978] Director/Accountant; Mark Allan Payne [1961] Director

**Igen Trust**
*Incorporated:* 13 February 2008
*Net Worth:* £4,131,406 *Total Assets:* £4,134,763
*Registered Office:* P O Box 330, 15 Newbury Close, Shipley, W Yorks, BD18 9DU
*Activities:* Other education n.e.c.
*Officers:* Claire Elaine Morris, Secretary; Francis James Griffiths [1948] Director; Thomas Murray [1948] Director; Paul Newman [1966] IT Director; William Henry Charles Webster [1961] Director/Consultant

**IHS Lothian Corporate Holdings Limited**
*Incorporated:* 17 December 2014
*Total Assets:* £180,534,000
*Registered Office:* 1 Park Row, Leeds, LS1 5AB
*Activities:* Other business support service activities n.e.c.
*Parent:* UK NPD Investments GP Limited
*Officers:* Jennifer McKay, Secretary; Mark Dening Bradshaw [1975] Director/Banker [Australian]; John McDonagh [1969] Director

**Iles (York) Limited**
*Incorporated:* 8 December 1954 *Employees:* 1
*Net Worth:* £3,923,370 *Total Assets:* £4,091,395
*Registered Office:* Langton House, 124 Acomb Road, Holgate, York, YO24 4EY
*Activities:* Buying and selling of own real estate
*Shareholder:* Paul David Widdicombe
*Officers:* Paul David Widdicombe, Secretary; Avis Aileen Widdicombe [1930] Director/Property Manager; Paul David Widdicombe [1958] Director/Stockbroker

**Illingworth & Gregory Limited**
*Incorporated:* 17 August 1976 *Employees:* 23
*Net Worth:* £2,394,444 *Total Assets:* £4,339,997
*Registered Office:* Geneva Way, Leads Road, Hull, HU7 0DG
*Activities:* Construction of commercial buildings
*Parent:* Illingworth & Gregory (Holdings) Limited
*Officers:* David Adrian Leedham, Secretary; Robert Andrew Cawkwell [1969] Director; Simon John Davison [1974] Director; Jeremy Marcus Illingworth [1977] Purchasing Director; Paul Edwin Sewell [1952] Director

**Illuminating Investments Limited**
*Incorporated:* 18 December 2013 *Employees:* 3
*Net Worth Deficit:* £923,902 *Total Assets:* £13,524,670
*Registered Office:* Beechfield, The Terrace, Boston Spa, Wetherby, W Yorks, LS23 6AH
*Activities:* Development of building projects
*Shareholders:* Matthew David Harding Aspland; John Conrad McDonnell; Michael James McDonnell
*Officers:* Matthew David Harding Aspland [1973] Director/Chartered Surveyor; John Conrad McDonnell [1963] Director; Michael James McDonnell [1970] Director

**Image Colourprint Limited**
*Incorporated:* 8 February 1989 *Employees:* 62
*Net Worth:* £8,675,418 *Total Assets:* £19,749,644
*Registered Office:* Grange Park Lane, Willerby, E Yorks, HU10 6EB
*Activities:* Printing n.e.c.
*Officers:* Stephen William Hadfield, Secretary; Helen Louise Birkin [1971] Director; Roger Edward Birkin [1941] Managing Director

**Image Data Group Limited**
*Incorporated:* 13 December 1989 *Employees:* 238
*Net Worth:* £16,977,234 *Total Assets:* £26,130,586
*Registered Office:* Grange Park Lane, Willerby, E Yorks, HU10 6EB
*Activities:* Printing n.e.c.
*Officers:* Stephen William Hadfield, Secretary; Helen Louise Birkin [1971] Director; Roger Edward Birkin [1941] Managing Director

**Image Digital Print Limited**
*Incorporated:* 9 March 1982 *Employees:* 70
*Net Worth:* £4,495,267 *Total Assets:* £18,137,752
*Registered Office:* Grange Park Lane, Willerby, E Yorks, HU10 6EB
*Activities:* Printing n.e.c.
*Major Shareholder:* Roger Edward Birkin
*Officers:* Stephen William Hadfield, Secretary; Helen Louise Birkin [1971] Director; Roger Edward Birkin [1941] Director

**Imagexps Limited**
*Incorporated:* 6 June 1986 *Employees:* 15
*Net Worth:* £2,602,038 *Total Assets:* £3,842,347
*Registered Office:* Grange Park Lane, Willerby, Hull, HU10 6EB
*Activities:* Printing n.e.c.
*Major Shareholder:* Roger Edward Birkin
*Officers:* Stephen William Hadfield, Secretary; Helen Louise Birkin [1971] Director; Roger Edward Birkin [1941] Director/Chairman; Jason Vivian [1967] Director

**Imbue Property Ltd**
*Incorporated:* 25 March 2014 *Employees:* 2
*Previous:* Andrew James Property Management Ltd
*Net Worth:* £289,099 *Total Assets:* £3,712,231
*Registered Office:* 37-38 Market Street, Ferryhill, Co Durham, DL17 8JH
*Activities:* Buying and selling of own real estate
*Major Shareholder:* Andrew John Tomlinson
*Officers:* Mark Ellison [1965] Director; Andrew John Tomlinson [1973] Director

**Imerys Fused Minerals Hull Limited**
*Incorporated:* 17 November 1992 *Employees:* 61
*Net Worth Deficit:* £1,967,000 *Total Assets:* £7,332,000
*Registered Office:* Hull Road, Salt End, Hull, HU12 8ED
*Activities:* Manufacture of other technical ceramic products
*Parent:* Imerys UK Limited
*Officers:* Henri Simon Trahair-Davies, Secretary; Olivier Berger [1966] Director [French]; Daniel Selkirk [1977] Director

**Imexpart Limited**
*Incorporated:* 3 January 1986 *Employees:* 90
*Net Worth:* £3,307,200 *Total Assets:* £7,574,660
*Registered Office:* Unit E1, Links 31, Willowbridge Way, Whitwood, Castleford, W Yorks, WF10 5NP
*Activities:* Wholesale trade of motor vehicle parts and accessories
*Shareholders:* Arthur Craig Pinkney; Fotoulla Pinkney
*Officers:* Fotoulla Pinkney, Secretary; Natalie Chappell [1968] Director; Martin Lockwood [1966] Director; Arthur Craig Pinkney [1961] Director; Fotoulla Pinkney [1958] Director/Teacher

**Immingham Industrial Estates Limited**
*Incorporated:* 15 August 1973
*Net Worth:* £1,039,355 *Total Assets:* £7,681,638
*Registered Office:* The Ice House, Victor Street, Grimsby, N E Lincs, DN32 7QN
*Activities:* Operation of warehousing and storage facilities for land transport activities
*Officers:* Ian Harding Davey, Secretary; Christine Ruth Barnett [1951] Director; Jonathan Dibdin [1963] Director/Accountant

**Impact (UK) Limited**
*Incorporated:* 6 February 2014 *Employees:* 82
*Net Worth:* £1,719,577 *Total Assets:* £4,638,381
*Registered Office:* Cragwood House, Ecclerigg, Windermere, Cumbria, LA23 1LQ
*Activities:* Other service activities n.e.c.
*Parent:* Impact Development Training Limited
*Officers:* Robert Bradbury, Secretary; David Hayden Williams [1956] Director

**Impact Development Training International Limited**
*Incorporated:* 27 November 2000
*Net Worth:* £6,099,142 *Total Assets:* £17,808,576
*Registered Office:* Cragwood House, Windermere, Cumbria, LA23 1LQ
*Activities:* Other service activities n.e.c.
*Major Shareholder:* David Hayden Williams
*Officers:* Robert Bradbury, Secretary; Adele Esther Blakebrough [1961] Director; Robert Bradbury [1956] Director/Chartered Accountant; Susan Jane Hunt [1959] Director; Derry John Newman [1957] Director; Thomas William Cyril Plimmer [1947] Director; Ann Elizabeth Williams [1957] Director; David Hayden Williams [1956] Director/Outdoor Training Manager

**Impact Development Training Ltd.**
*Incorporated:* 5 March 1990 *Employees:* 142
*Net Worth:* £3,888,965 *Total Assets:* £8,406,503
*Registered Office:* Cragwood House, Windermere, Cumbria, LA23 1LQ
*Activities:* Other service activities n.e.c.
*Parent:* Impact Development Training International Limited
*Officers:* Robert Bradbury, Secretary; Jeremy Benton [1973] Director; David Hayden Williams [1956] Director/Outdoor Training Manager

**Impact Education Multi Academy Trust**
*Incorporated:* 14 May 2013 *Employees:* 15
*Previous:* The Halifax Academy Trust
*Net Worth:* £10,930,000 *Total Assets:* £12,283,000
*Registered Office:* Halifax High, Gibbet Street, Halifax, W Yorks, HX2 0BA
*Activities:* General secondary education
*Officers:* Michael Kay [1977] Director/Headteacher; Patrick Hugh McDermott [1953] Director/Education Consultant; Dr Michael Reddy [1964] Director/Business Architect; Stuart Rees [1979] Director/Education Leadership; Dr Philip Shepherd [1967] Director/Teacher; Philip Anthony Shire [1950] Director/Interim Manager

**Impact Fork Trucks Limited**
*Incorporated:* 19 October 1990 *Employees:* 306
*Net Worth:* £14,423,104 *Total Assets:* £72,072,312
*Registered Office:* Citadel House, 58 High Street, Hull, HU1 1QE
*Activities:* Agents involved in the sale of machinery, industrial equipment, ships and aircraft
*Parent:* ENX Group Limited
*Officers:* Jacqueline Veronica Carr [1968] Director [South African]; Robin Andrew Harris [1965] Finance Director; Terence Kendrew [1959] Managing Director; Gary Derek Neubert [1965] Managing Director [South African]; Lindsy Taylor [1983] Director/Chief Financial Officer [South African]

**Impact Property Services Limited**
*Incorporated:* 20 October 2005 *Employees:* 20
*Net Worth:* £1,026,685 *Total Assets:* £3,773,833
*Registered Office:* Support Office, 71 Greaves Street, Bradford, W Yorks, BD5 7PE
*Activities:* Development of building projects
*Major Shareholder:* Nigel Anthony Delaney
*Officers:* Sharon Julie Brown, Secretary; Nigel Anthony Delaney [1967] Director

**Impala Estates Limited**
*Incorporated:* 14 March 2006 *Employees:* 6
*Net Worth:* £18,409,940 *Total Assets:* £21,522,600
*Registered Office:* 12 Granby Road, Harrogate, N Yorks, HG1 4ST
*Activities:* Other letting and operating of own or leased real estate
*Officers:* Abigail Sophie Louise Hartley, Secretary; James Stewart Anthony Hartley, Secretary; John David Smith Hartley [1956] Director/Accountant; Suzanne Louise Rippon Hartley [1961] Director/Therapist

**Imperial Automotive Limited**
*Incorporated:* 19 September 2001 *Employees:* 106
*Net Worth:* £2,873,997 *Total Assets:* £5,068,302
*Registered Office:* Cross Bank, Balby, Doncaster, S Yorks, DN4 8BE
*Activities:* Retail trade of motor vehicle parts and accessories
*Officers:* Jane Elizabeth Shipton, Secretary; Kevin John Shipton [1955] Director; Thomas Benjamin Maxwell Stanley [1970] Director

**Impex Parts Limited**
*Incorporated:* 23 July 1998 *Employees:* 29
*Net Worth:* £6,795,491 *Total Assets:* £14,392,870
*Registered Office:* Unit 8 United Business Park, Lowfields Road, Leeds, LS12 6UB
*Activities:* Wholesale trade of motor vehicle parts and accessories
*Shareholders:* Stephen William Burrows; E.F.C. Consultancy Limited
*Officers:* Diane Marie Ramsbottom, Secretary; Stephen William Burrows [1970] Director

**Inchem Finance Limited**
*Incorporated:* 9 November 1982 *Employees:* 4
*Net Worth:* £8,315,840 *Total Assets:* £9,140,764
*Registered Office:* 4a Woodbottom, Mirfield, W Yorks, WF14 8HF
*Activities:* Other credit granting n.e.c.
*Major Shareholder:* Richard Thomas Sykes
*Officers:* Elizabeth Mary Sykes, Secretary; Georgina Louise Lucas [1970] Director; Elizabeth Mary Sykes [1946] Director; Julian Shore Sykes [1972] Director; Richard Thomas Sykes [1943] Director

**Inclusion Housing Community Interest Company**
*Incorporated:* 19 March 2007 *Employees:* 51
*Net Worth:* £2,758,186 *Total Assets:* £8,327,506
*Registered Office:* 106 Heworth Green, York, YO31 7TQ
*Activities:* Renting and operating of Housing Association real estate
*Officers:* Sarah Waters, Secretary; Anthony Bell [1960] Director/Vice Principal; Ian Brown [1964] Director; June Grimes [1951] Director/Retired; Kevin John Harwood [1975] Director/Bank Manager; Keith Andrew Lewis [1949] Director/Retired; Guru Dhasaratha Naidoo [1951] Director/Retired; Peter Anthony Ottowell [1955] Director/Retired; Paul William Redfern [1962] Director/Chartered Internal Auditor; Joanna Rubinstein Wild [1968] Director/Self Employed

**Incommunities Group Limited**
*Incorporated:* 22 May 2001 *Employees:* 982
*Net Worth:* £115,769,000 *Total Assets:* £452,579,008
*Registered Office:* The Quays, Victoria Street, Shipley, W Yorks, BD17 7BN
*Activities:* Other accommodation
*Officers:* Robert Terence Ward, Secretary; Kim Hilary Brear [1960] Assistant Director, Homes & Neighbourhoods; Ian Michael Cornelius [1969] Commercial Director; Judith Ann Crowther [1951] Director/Retired; Tansy Jane Hepton [1960] Director/Retired; Generaldine Lesley Howley [1957] Director/Chief Executive; Andrew James Kitchingman [1964] Finance Director; Janet Evelynne Ormondroyd [1954] Director/Retired Chief Executive; Keith Ramsay [1961] Director/Management Consultant; Matthew Alan Walker [1967] Director/Chief Executive; Simon Wilson [1971] Director/Chief Executive

**Indian Queens Power Limited**
*Incorporated:* 6 May 1994 *Employees:* 7
*Net Worth Deficit:* £2,655,000 *Total Assets:* £12,623,000
*Registered Office:* Saltend Power Station, Saltend Chemicals Park, Hedon Road, Hull, HU12 8GA
*Activities:* Production of electricity
*Parent:* IQ Power Holdings Limited
*Officers:* Victor Andrea George Danks [1951] Director/Electricity Generation; Michael Ellis Farr [1964] Director/Power Station Manager; Russell Holland [1976] Director/Finance and Procurement Manager; Scott Jonathan Keen [1974] Director

**Indivior UK Limited**
*Incorporated:* 9 March 2010 *Employees:* 170
*Previous:* RB Pharmaceuticals Limited
*Net Worth:* £747,916,992 *Total Assets:* £848,174,016
*Registered Office:* The Chapleo Building, Henry Boot Way, Priory Park, Hull, HU4 7DY
*Activities:* Manufacture of basic pharmaceutical products
*Parent:* RBP Global Holdings Limited
*Officers:* Kathryn Barbara Hudson, Secretary; Katherine Julie Beard [1979] Director/Chartered Tax Advisor; Massimo D'Angelo [1972] Director [Italian]; Gilles Picard [1962] Director [French]; Ms Amei W Shank [1963] Director [American]; Richard Simkin [1970] Director; Frank Stier [1959] Director [German]; Thomas Weis [1980] Finance Director [German]

**Indomito Properties LLP**
*Incorporated:* 8 October 2004
*Net Worth:* £2,625,826 *Total Assets:* £7,352,491
*Registered Office:* c/o Mazars LLP, 3 Wellington Place, Leeds, LS1 4AP
*Officers:* Andrew Richard Cossins [1955] Member; Irene Elizabeth Cossins [1945] Member

**Industrial Pallet and Transport Services Limited**
*Incorporated:* 18 January 1996 *Employees:* 17
*Net Worth:* £3,140,228 *Total Assets:* £5,019,548
*Registered Office:* The Offices, Glassworks Way, Snape Lane, Harworth, Doncaster, S Yorks, DN11 8SP
*Activities:* Manufacture of other products of wood; manufacture of articles of cork, straw and plaiting materials
*Major Shareholder:* Nicholas Bennett
*Officers:* Nicholas Bennett, Secretary; Lee Bennett [1973] Director/Company Secretary; Nicholas Bennett [1972] Director/Industrial Pallet Sales

**Industrial Textiles & Plastics Ltd**
*Incorporated:* 10 May 1989 *Employees:* 30
*Net Worth:* £1,070,344 *Total Assets:* £3,564,281
*Registered Office:* Stillington Road, Easingwold, York, YO61 3FA
*Activities:* Manufacture of non-wovens and articles made from non-wovens, except apparel
*Parent:* Sarir Holdings Ltd
*Officers:* Alison Kathryn Menage, Secretary; John David Barstow [1954] Director/Stockbroker; David James Dickson [1955] Director/Chartered Accountant; Alison Kathryn Menage [1958] Director/Company Secretary; Richard Keith Arend Menage [1957] Director; Marcus Johnannes Martinus Van Der Voort [1964] Managing Director [Dutch]

**INEOS Compounds Aycliffe Limited**
*Incorporated:* 15 August 2013 *Employees:* 208
*Net Worth:* £4,720,000 *Total Assets:* £47,999,000
*Registered Office:* School Aycliffe Lane, Newton Aycliffe, Co Durham, DL5 6EA
*Activities:* Manufacture of other inorganic basic chemicals
*Parent:* INEOS Compounds Holdings Limited
*Officers:* Steven Jamieson, Secretary; David John Wright Rey, Secretary; Andrew Brown [1981] Director/Chartered Accountant; Alex Hogan [1976] Director; Anthony White [1961] Director/Accountant

**INEOS Compounds Holdings Limited**
*Incorporated:* 14 August 2013 *Employees:* 311
*Net Worth Deficit:* £4,187,455 *Total Assets:* £43,656,452
*Registered Office:* School Aycliffe Lane, Newton Aycliffe, Co Durham, DL5 6EA
*Activities:* Manufacture of other inorganic basic chemicals
*Parent:* INEOS Enterprises Holdings Limited
*Officers:* Steven Jamieson, Secretary; David John Wright Rey, Secretary; Andrew Brown [1981] Director/Chartered Accountant; Alex Hogan [1976] Director; Anthony White [1961] Director/Accountant

**Infact UK Limited**
*Incorporated:* 28 July 2003 *Employees:* 6
*Net Worth:* £2,497,427 *Total Assets:* £3,272,297
*Registered Office:* Natwest Bank Chambers, The Grove, Ilkley, W Yorks, LS29 9LS
*Activities:* Business and domestic software development
*Shareholders:* Chakib Kara-Zaitri; Robert Gerald Hamilton
*Officers:* Robert Generald Hamilton [1956] Director; Chakib Kara-Zaitri [1960] Director/Mechanical Engineer

**Info Supplier Limited**
*Incorporated:* 30 March 2004 *Employees:* 140
*Net Worth Deficit:* £3,633,000 *Total Assets:* £6,431,000
*Registered Office:* 1392 Leeds Road, Bradford, W Yorks, BD3 7AE
*Activities:* Non-trading company
*Shareholders:* James Downs; Nick Vincent Saunders; Nick Hewitt
*Officers:* James Andrew Abbotson Downs, Finance Director; James Andrew Abbotson Downs [1965] Finance Director; Nicholas John Hewitt [1968] Managing Director; Nick Vincent Saunders [1963] Sales Director

**Infra Safety Services Labour Limited**
*Incorporated:* 21 May 2007 *Employees:* 58
*Net Worth Deficit:* £271,745 *Total Assets:* £10,306,807
*Registered Office:* 7 Bradford Business Park, Kings Gate, Bradford, W Yorks, BD1 4SJ
*Activities:* Other construction installation
*Parent:* ISS Labour Group Limited
*Officers:* Gary Beeston [1962] Managing Director; Christopher Michael Chidley [1960] Director; Paul Howard McNulty [1970] Director

**Ingenuity Digital Holdings Limited**
*Incorporated:* 25 February 2011 *Employees:* 134
*Net Worth:* £2,487,058 *Total Assets:* £5,872,834
*Registered Office:* Central House, Otley Road, Harrogate, N Yorks, HG3 1UF
*Activities:* Activities of head offices
*Parent:* Graphene Holdings Limited
*Officers:* Lisa Jayne Higham, Secretary; David Martin Best [1958] Director; Dennis Stephen Engel [1959] Director; Jeremy Mark Fenn [1963] Director; Lisa Jayne Higham [1966] Finance Director

**Inglis and Son (Jewellers) Limited**
*Incorporated:* 29 May 1959 *Employees:* 9
*Net Worth:* £3,061,413 *Total Assets:* £4,916,198
*Registered Office:* 52 Stonegate, York, YO1 2AS
*Activities:* Other retail sale of new goods in specialised stores (not commercial art galleries and opticians)
*Parent:* Berens & Company Limited
*Officers:* Alyson Moss [1970] Director; Markus Elliot Rosenberg [1972] Director; Debra Tomlinson [1964] Finance Director; Simon Bennett Walton [1967] Director/Jeweller

**Inhoco 2082 Limited**
*Incorporated:* 5 June 2000 *Employees:* 56
*Net Worth:* £3,121,090 *Total Assets:* £6,704,825
*Registered Office:* c/o Trupart Limited, Decoy Bank, White Rose Way, Doncaster, S Yorks, DN4 5JD
*Activities:* Activities of head offices
*Parent:* Lupfaw 445 Limited
*Officers:* Jane Farrell [1960] Director; Gareth David Williams [1984] Director

**Inhoco 3498 Limited**
*Incorporated:* 24 October 2008 *Employees:* 2
*Net Worth Deficit:* £31,335,000 *Total Assets:* £78,679,000
*Registered Office:* Meadowcroft Lane, Halifax Road, Ripponden, W Yorks, HX6 4AJ
*Activities:* Activities of other holding companies n.e.c.
*Parent:* JLA Clean Limited
*Officers:* Helen Jane Ashton [1972] Director/Chief Executive Officer; Paul Justin Humphreys [1958] Director

**The Inn at Grasmere Limited**
*Incorporated:* 28 January 2014 *Employees:* 42
*Net Worth:* £939,324 *Total Assets:* £6,251,122
*Registered Office:* Fountains Bent, Darley Road, Birstwith, Harrogate, N Yorks, HG3 2PN
*Activities:* Hotels and similar accommodation
*Parent:* The Inspire Holding Company Ltd
*Officers:* Anthony Troy, Secretary; Anthony Gerrard Troy [1962] Director [Irish]

**Inner Space Stations Limited**
*Incorporated:* 26 July 2004 *Employees:* 48
*Net Worth:* £1,090,938 *Total Assets:* £3,845,064
*Registered Office:* 29a Bishopthorpe Road, York, YO23 1NA
*Activities:* Retail sale of automotive fuel in specialised stores
*Shareholders:* Graham Thomas Kennedy; Deirdre MacDonald Kennedy
*Officers:* Sally Ann Atkinson, Secretary; Deirdre MacDonald Kennedy [1955] Director; Graham Thomas Kennedy [1956] Director

**Innserve Limited**
*Incorporated:* 17 April 2010 *Employees:* 686
*Net Worth:* £3,592,286 *Total Assets:* £16,704,074
*Registered Office:* The Old Maltings, Leeds Road, Tadcaster, N Yorks, LS24 9HB
*Activities:* Other service activities n.e.c.
*Parent:* Hallriver Limited
*Officers:* Nicholas Martin Bryan [1953] Director

**Innserve Technical Solutions Limited**
*Incorporated:* 4 May 2006
*Net Worth:* £1,248,636 *Total Assets:* £4,082,223
*Registered Office:* The Old Maltings, 56 Leeds Road, Tadcaster, N Yorks, LS24 9HB
*Activities:* Other service activities n.e.c.
*Parent:* Innserve Technical Services Group Limited
*Officers:* Nicholas Martin Bryan [1953] Director

**InOne Holdings Limited**
*Incorporated:* 15 January 1996
*Net Worth:* £63,216,000 *Total Assets:* £465,952,000
*Registered Office:* Farnell House, Forge Lane, Leeds, LS12 2NE
*Activities:* Non-trading company
*Parent:* Celdis Limited
*Officers:* Ralf Lothar Buehler [1968] Director/Chief Sales Officer [German]; Liam Anthony Heffernan [1972] Director/Accountant [Irish]; Harvey Woodford [1963] Director/VP Corporate Secretary [American]

**Inoveight Limited**
*Incorporated:* 6 April 2001 *Employees:* 47
*Net Worth:* £7,365,000 *Total Assets:* £37,433,000
*Registered Office:* 12b Beechburn Industrial Estate, Prospect Road, Crook, Co Durham, DL15 8RA
*Activities:* Wholesale of clothing and footwear
*Parent:* Inoveight Holdings Limited
*Officers:* Gary John Mennell, Secretary; Ian Ralph Bailey [1963] Director; Clinton Wayne George Edy [1962] Director; Jonathan Hammond [1975] Finance Director; Hiroaki Kobayashi [1963] Director [Japanese]; Gary John Mennell [1961] Director; Eijiro Nireki [1971] Director [Japanese]; Hitoshi Suyama [1961] Director [Japanese]

**Insituform Technologies Limited**
*Incorporated:* 14 March 1986 *Employees:* 18
*Net Worth:* £6,536,624 *Total Assets:* £8,893,646
*Registered Office:* 3 Roundwood Industrial Estate, Ossett, W Yorks, WF5 9SQ
*Activities:* Remediation activities and other waste management services
*Parent:* Insituform Holdings Ltd
*Officers:* Paul Gibson, Secretary; David Francis Morris, Secretary/General Counsel [American]; Martinus Franciscus Kool [1966] Director [Dutch]; David Francis Morris [1961] Director/General Counsel [American]; Mark Andrew Neal [1968] Director

**Inspire 2 Independence (I2i) Ltd**
*Incorporated:* 16 April 2004 *Employees:* 150
*Net Worth:* £311,593 *Total Assets:* £3,504,633
*Registered Office:* Independence House, Millfield Lane, Nether Poppleton, York, YO26 6PH
*Activities:* Other education n.e.c.
*Shareholders:* Matthew John Gore; James Ian Gore; Kent Andrew Mayall
*Officers:* Jonathan Guy Ballin, Secretary; Jonathan Guy Ballin [1960] Financial Director; James Ian Gore [1976] Director/Chief Operating Officer; Matthew John Gore [1969] Director/Chief Executive Officer; Natalie Mary Keating [1967] Managing Director; Kent Andrew Mayall [1970] Director/Chief Commercial Officer

**The Inspire Holding Company Limited**
*Incorporated:* 28 January 2014 *Employees:* 194
*Net Worth:* £2,635,671 *Total Assets:* £18,613,634
*Registered Office:* Fountains Bent, Birstwith, Harrogate, N Yorks, HG3 2PN
*Activities:* Hotels and similar accommodation
*Parent:* Antony Troy
*Officers:* Anthony Troy, Secretary; Anthony Gerrard Troy [1962] Director [Irish]

**Inspired Learning Multi Academy Trust**
*Incorporated:* 17 July 2015 *Employees:* 110
*Net Worth:* £4,510,214 *Total Assets:* £6,034,157
*Registered Office:* Yarlside Primary School, Red Oak Avenue, Barrow in Furness, Cumbria, LA13 0LH
*Activities:* Pre-primary education
*Officers:* Angela Mary Whittle, Secretary; Stephen Barrett [1969] Director/Combat Systems Design; Jane Buchanan Ridyard [1953] Director of Young Peoples Learning; John Burgess [1982] Director/Nuclear Processes and Procedures Manager BAE; Laura Kendall [1982] Director/Childcare Advisor; Stuart Knagg [1974] Director/Operations Manager; Janine Pierce [1973] Director/Headteacher; Caroline Vernon [1965] Director/Headteacher; Caroline Walker [1975] Director/Headteacher

**Inspired Pet Nutrition Holdings Limited**
*Incorporated:* 19 March 2008
*Previous:* Wagg Foods Holdings Limited
*Net Worth:* £20,985,304 *Total Assets:* £25,455,386
*Registered Office:* c/o Inspired Pet Nutrition Limited, Dalton Airfield, Dalton, Thirsk, N Yorks, YO7 3HE
*Activities:* Activities of head offices
*Parent:* IPN Bidco Limited
*Officers:* Anthony Robert Stones, Secretary; James Scott Lambert [1958] Director; Richard Harrington Page [1966] Director; Thomas Grindrod Page [1968] Director

**Inspired Pet Nutrition Limited**
*Incorporated:* 24 April 1990 *Employees:* 146
*Previous:* Wagg Foods Limited
*Net Worth:* £30,242,604 *Total Assets:* £46,454,408
*Registered Office:* Dalton Airfield, Topcliffe, Thirsk, N Yorks, YO7 3HE
*Activities:* Manufacture of prepared pet foods
*Parent:* Inspired Pet Nutrition Holdings Limited
*Officers:* Anthony Robert Stones, Secretary; Ben Keith Anderson [1971] Director; James Scott Lambert [1958] Director; James Robin Lawson [1975] Director; Richard Harrington Page [1966] Director; Thomas Grindrod Page [1968] Director; Anthony Robert Stones [1988] Finance Director; Graham Derek Wheeler [1963] Managing Director

**Inspiring Futures Academy Trust**
*Incorporated:* 20 March 2017 *Employees:* 137
*Net Worth:* £3,619,725 *Total Assets:* £6,869,202
*Registered Office:* Bentley High Street Primary School, High Street, Bentley, Doncaster, S Yorks, DN5 0AA
*Activities:* Primary education
*Officers:* Beryl Beal [1948] Director; Rev David Berry [1979] Director; Ruth Mary Brook [1955] Director; Paul William Davies [1962] Director; Andrew James Gray [1978] Director; Tracey Elizabeth Rowe [1971] Director

**Instore Limited**
*Incorporated:* 17 December 1938
*Net Worth:* £97,677,952 *Total Assets:* £100,035,008
*Registered Office:* Trident Business Park, Leeds Road, Huddersfield, W Yorks, HD2 1UA
*Activities:* Activities of head offices
*Parent:* Seaham Investments Limited
*Officers:* Hemant Patel, Secretary; Hemant Patel [1961] Finance Director; Abdul Aziz Tayub [1955] Director

**Intechnology PLC**
*Incorporated:* 26 January 2000 *Employees:* 101
*Net Worth Deficit:* £2,898,000 *Total Assets:* £16,785,000
*Registered Office:* Cardale House, Cardale Court, Beckwith Head Road, Harrogate, N Yorks, HG3 1RY
*Activities:* Information technology consultancy activities
*Officers:* Andrew Murdoch Scott Kaberry, Secretary; Andrew Murdoch Scott Kaberry [1946] Finance Director; Bryn Kenneth Sage [1965] Sales Director; Charles Thomas Scott [1949] Director; Peter Robert Wilkinson [1954] Director

**Integra Buildings Limited**
*Incorporated:* 12 June 1997 *Employees:* 85
*Net Worth:* £4,750,736 *Total Assets:* £9,463,415
*Registered Office:* Integra House, Humber Business Park, Hedon Road, Paull, E Yorks, HU12 8AA
*Activities:* Other manufacturing n.e.c.
*Shareholders:* Gary Richard Parker; Paul Tansey
*Officers:* Denise Case, Secretary; Peter Jonathan Drescher [1964] Director/Accountant; Matthew Fortnum [1973] Operations Director; Michael Robert Marriott [1974] Commercial Director; Gary Richard Parker [1968] Director/Electrician; Paul Tansey [1968] Director/Purchasing Manager; Christopher Mark Turner [1980] Director

**Integra Insurance Solutions Limited**
*Incorporated:* 27 November 2008
*Net Worth:* £4,859,000 *Total Assets:* £21,860,000
*Registered Office:* Currer House, Currer Street, Bradford, W Yorks, BD1 5BA
*Activities:* Non-life insurance
*Parent:* Funis GmbH & Co KG
*Officers:* Maria Louise Bell, Secretary; Carlo Cavaliere [1969] Managing Director; Martin William Harry Cox [1971] Managing Director; Anders Larsson [1957] Director [Swedish]; Nicholas James Parr [1957] Director

**Integrated Polymer Systems (U.K.) Limited**
*Incorporated:* 23 July 1991
*Net Worth:* £866,150 *Total Assets:* £3,213,183
*Registered Office:* Thornton Rust Hall, Thornton Rust, Leyburn, N Yorks, DL8 3AW
*Activities:* Other retail sale not in stores, stalls or markets
*Major Shareholder:* Peter Bowers
*Officers:* Gavin Richard Bowers, Secretary; Gavin Richard Bowers [1978] Director; Peter Bowers [1948] Director/Building Manager

**Interaction and Communication Academy Trust Limited**
*Incorporated:* 8 June 2016 *Employees:* 178
*Net Worth:* £10,088,284 *Total Assets:* £12,690,226
*Registered Office:* Castle Hill School, Newsome Road South, Newsome, Huddersfield, W Yorks, HD4 6JL
*Activities:* Other education n.e.c.
*Officers:* John Barry Gledhill [1943] Director/Retired; Joan Haines [1957] Director/Achievement Coach/Education Consultant; Julius Cameron O'Dor [1965] Director/Higher Education Lecturer; Linda Mary O'Neill [1964] Director; Dr Emily Jane Perry [1971] Director/Lecturer; Mark Ian Prior [1958] Project Director; Gillian Robinson [1955] Director/Headteacher; Dr Jonathan Wainwright [1961] Director/Principal Lecturer; Susan Adreienne White [1957] Director/Librarian; Dawn Whiteley [1969] Director; Timothy John Wilkes [1959] Director; David Wilkinson [1963] Local Government Assistant Director

**Interactive Investor Holdings Limited**
*Incorporated:* 27 August 1996
*Previous:* TD Wealth Holdings (UK) Limited
*Net Worth:* £131,677,000 *Total Assets:* £131,677,000
*Registered Office:* Exchange Court, Duncombe Street, Leeds, LS1 4AX
*Activities:* Activities of financial services holding companies
*Parent:* Interactive Investor Limited
*Officers:* Barry Michael Bicknell [1968] Director; Richard Simon Wilson [1966] Director

**Interactive Investor Services Limited**
*Incorporated:* 20 February 1987 *Employees:* 453
*Previous:* TD Direct Investing (Europe) Limited
*Net Worth:* £63,005,000 *Total Assets:* £289,913,984
*Registered Office:* Exchange Court, Duncombe Street, Leeds, LS1 4AX
*Activities:* Financial intermediation not elsewhere classified
*Parent:* Interactive Investor Holdings Limited
*Officers:* Barry Michael Bicknell [1968] Director; Richard Simon Wilson [1966] Director

**Interactive Projects & Design Limited**
*Incorporated:* 7 May 2003 *Employees:* 20
*Net Worth:* £2,756,047 *Total Assets:* £5,989,634
*Registered Office:* Chesnut House, Chesnut Street, Darlington, Co Durham, DL1 1QL
*Activities:* Development of building projects
*Major Shareholder:* James Gerald Tully
*Officers:* Janette Tully, Secretary; Paul George Barber [1967] Director/Manager; James Generald Tully [1958] Director; Janette Tully [1959] Director

**Interbulk (UK) Holdings Limited**
*Incorporated:* 22 May 2000 *Employees:* 2
*Net Worth Deficit:* £72,419,688 *Total Assets:* £12,743,677
*Registered Office:* 4 Beacon Way, Hull, HU3 4AE
*Activities:* Freight transport by road
*Officers:* Klaas Pieter Den Hartogh [1965] Managing Director [Dutch]; Abraham Cornelius Paape [1959] Finance Director [Dutch]

**Interchange and Consort Hotels Limited**
*Incorporated:* 10 February 1971 *Employees:* 206
*Net Worth:* £4,605,012 *Total Assets:* £9,942,964
*Registered Office:* Consort House, Amy Johnson Way, Clifton Moor, York, YO30 4GP
*Activities:* Hotels and similar accommodation
*Officers:* Nicholas Ian Swinscoe, Secretary; Angela Carolyn Burns [1954] Director/CEO Hospitality Industry; Howard James Darking [1953] Director/Hotelier; Russell Hamilton Imrie [1960] Director/Hotelier; Richard James Coopland McIlroy [1961] Director/Hotelier; John Charles Millican [1951] Director/Hotelier; Jeremy Derek Pick [1963] Director/Hotelier; Timothy Mark Brooks Rumney [1965] Director/Hotelier

**Intercontinental Brands (Icb) Limited**
*Incorporated:* 8 February 1990 *Employees:* 97
*Net Worth:* £6,182,484 *Total Assets:* £12,876,102
*Registered Office:* 4 Sceptre House, Hornbeam Square, North Hornbeam Business Park, Harrogate, N Yorks, HG2 8PB
*Activities:* Manufacture of other non-distilled fermented beverages
*Parent:* Intercontinental Brands (Holdings) Limited
*Officers:* Marcus William Black, Secretary; Marcus William Black [1969] Joint Managing Director; Michael John Carthy [1956] Joint Managing Director

**Interface Administration Services Limited**
*Incorporated:* 3 September 2010 *Employees:* 58
*Net Worth:* £2,131,000 *Total Assets:* £13,394,000
*Registered Office:* Shelf Mills, Shelf, Halifax, W Yorks, HX3 7PA
*Activities:* Activities of head offices
*Parent:* Interface Europe Ltd
*Officers:* Simon Carlton, Secretary; Simon Carlton [1962] HR Director; Jan Hasselman [1955] Director/Senior Vice President - Finance [Dutch]

**Interface Europe Ltd.**
*Incorporated:* 27 January 1936 *Employees:* 266
*Net Worth:* £52,958,000 *Total Assets:* £69,083,000
*Registered Office:* Shelf Mills, Shelf, Halifax, W Yorks, HX3 7PA
*Activities:* Manufacture of woven or tufted carpets and rugs
*Parent:* Interface, Inc.
*Officers:* Simon Carlton, Secretary; Simon Carlton [1962] HR Director; Nigel Wilkinson Stansfield [1967] Director/Senior VP; Anton Hendrik Van Keken [1961] Director/Senior VP Operations [Dutch]

**Interface UK Manufacturing Limited**
*Incorporated:* 3 September 2010 *Employees:* 134
*Net Worth:* £9,783,000 *Total Assets:* £23,545,000
*Registered Office:* Shelf Mills, Shelf, Halifax, W Yorks, HX3 7PA
*Activities:* Manufacture of woven or tufted carpets and rugs
*Parent:* Interface Europe Ltd
*Officers:* Simon Carlton, Secretary; Simon Carlton [1962] HR Director; Jan Hasselman [1955] Director/Senior Vice President - Finance [Dutch]

**Interiors UK Limited**
*Incorporated:* 19 July 2004 *Employees:* 81
*Net Worth:* £5,641,406 *Total Assets:* £10,818,129
*Registered Office:* The New Oakes, Wellington Street, Oakes, Huddersfield, W Yorks, HD3 3EP
*Activities:* Other building completion and finishing
*Parent:* IUKH Limited
*Officers:* Angus Austin Gregory [1965] Director; Danny Nolan [1984] Director; Peter Warren Edmond Tyler [1985] Estimating Director

**International Fibres Group (Holdings) Limited**
*Incorporated:* 18 May 1949 *Employees:* 3
*Net Worth:* £43,086,000 *Total Assets:* £48,752,000
*Registered Office:* Old Mills, Drighlington, Bradford, W Yorks, BD11 1BY
*Activities:* Activities of head offices
*Major Shareholder:* Peter Gyllenhammar
*Officers:* Kathryn Anne Davenport, Secretary; Peter Jan Patrik Gyllenhammar [1953] Director [Swedish]; John Olof Hager [1964] Managing Director [Swedish]; Jan Gustaf Lennart Holmstrom [1953] Director [Swedish]

**International Personal Finance Investments Limited**
*Incorporated:* 28 August 1969
*Net Worth:* £128,759,000 *Total Assets:* £533,035,008
*Registered Office:* Number Three, Leeds City Office Park, Meadow Lane, Leeds, LS11 5BD
*Activities:* Activities of head offices
*Parent:* IPF Holdings Limited
*Officers:* Andrew Harvey-Wrate, Secretary; John Nicholas Dahlgreen [1958] Director/Treasurer; Justin Ashley Lockwood [1970] Director; James Alexander Ormrod [1967] Director/Solicitor; Gerard Jude Ryan [1964] Director [Irish]

**International Personal Finance PLC**
*Incorporated:* 5 December 2006 *Employees:* 9,491
*Net Worth:* £496,900,000 *Total Assets:* £1,342,599,936
*Registered Office:* Number Three, Leeds City Office Park, Meadow Lane, Leeds, LS11 5BD
*Activities:* Credit granting by non-deposit taking finance houses and other specialist consumer credit grantors
*Officers:* James Alexander Ormrod, Secretary; Deborah Lee Davis [1963] Director; Antony John Hales [1948] Director; Justin Ashley Lockwood [1970] Director; Johannes Jacobus Mangelaars [1964] Director [Dutch]; Richard Frank Moat [1954] Director; Daniel Noel O'Connor [1959] Director [Irish]; Cathryn Elizabeth Riley [1962] Director; Gerard Jude Ryan [1964] Director [Irish]; Bronwyn Syiek [1964] Director

**International Pipeline Products Limited**
*Incorporated:* 5 October 1984 *Employees:* 81
*Net Worth:* £898,022 *Total Assets:* £3,682,287
*Registered Office:* International Pipeline Products, Gatherley Road, Brompton on Swale, Richmond, N Yorks, DL10 7JH
*Activities:* Manufacture of other plastic products
*Officers:* Darren Mark Williams, Secretary; Keith Appleton [1961] Director; Simon Kim Bell [1957] Director; Surendranath Anjhiah Dhanekula [1978] Director [Indian]; Nikhil Goel [1977] Director [Indian]; Sachin Vijayrao Sanghai [1978] Director [Indian]; Darren Mark Williams [1969] Finance Director

**International Procurement and Logistics Limited**
*Incorporated:* 16 April 2004 *Employees:* 2,137
*Net Worth:* £105,085,000 *Total Assets:* £260,690,000
*Registered Office:* Asda House, South Bank, Great Wilson Street, Leeds, LS11 5AD
*Activities:* Wholesale of fruit and vegetables
*Parent:* Asda Stores Limited
*Officers:* Varinder Rehal, Secretary; John Fallon [1970] Director; James Edward Fasey [1973] Finance Director; Varinder Rehal [1975] Director and Company Secretary; Max Sandiford Smith Hilliard [1958] Director; Michael John Bland Snell [1964] Director

**International Seafoods Limited**
*Incorporated:* 7 November 2011 *Employees:* 537
*Net Worth:* £6,239,000 *Total Assets:* £42,126,000
*Registered Office:* Hilmore House, Gain Lane, Bradford, W Yorks, BD3 7DL
*Activities:* Processing and preserving of fish, crustaceans and molluscs
*Parent:* Wm Morrison Supermarkets Holdings Limited
*Officers:* Jonathan James Burke, Secretary; Andrew James Clappen [1965] Technical Director; Mark Thomas Stitson [1976] Finance Director; Andrew Edward Thornber [1974] Director

**Intouch Advance Limited**
*Incorporated:* 21 May 2001 *Employees:* 28
*Net Worth:* £6,489,628 *Total Assets:* £11,585,966
*Registered Office:* 5th Floor, Central Square, 29 Wellington Street, Leeds, LS1 4DL
*Activities:* Other telecommunications activities
*Major Shareholder:* Simon Pollard
*Officers:* Simon Pollard [1975] Director

**Invalesco Limited**
*Incorporated:* 5 November 2012 *Employees:* 31
*Net Worth:* £56,162 *Total Assets:* £3,076,716
*Registered Office:* Whiteley Garden Centre, Far Common Road, Mirfield, W Yorks, WF14 0DQ
*Activities:* Retail sale of flowers, plants, seeds, fertilizers, pet animals and pet food in specialised stores
*Parent:* GHTC (Holdings) Limited
*Officers:* Martina Ann Allan [1969] Director

**Inventry Limited**
*Incorporated:* 19 October 2010 *Employees:* 62
*Net Worth:* £1,474,607 *Total Assets:* £4,214,776
*Registered Office:* Unit 22-23 Howley Business Village, Morley, Leeds, LS27 0BZ
*Activities:* Business and domestic software development
*Shareholders:* Philip Edward Lawson; Philip Brooke
*Officers:* Philip Brooke, Secretary; Philip Brooke [1983] Director; Philip Edward Lawson [1978] Director; Alain Squitieri [1988] Sales Director

**Investment in Media Limited**
*Incorporated:* 19 June 2009 *Employees:* 3
*Net Worth:* £330,150 *Total Assets:* £3,300,162
*Registered Office:* Loscoe Close, Normanton Industrial Estate, Normanton, W Yorks, WF6 1TW
*Activities:* Publishing of consumer and business journals and periodicals
*Parent:* Aberdeen Industry Investments Limited
*Officers:* Nicholas Robert Alexander [1968] Director; Matthew Robert Carry [1977] Director; Mark Graham Roberts [1970] Director

**Investments in Education Limited**
*Incorporated:* 6 February 2007
*Net Worth:* £14,455 *Total Assets:* £10,751,566
*Registered Office:* 1 Park Row, Leeds, LS1 5AB
*Activities:* Other business support service activities n.e.c.
*Parent:* Dalmore Capital (Para 1) Limited
*Officers:* Jennifer McKay, Secretary; John Stephen Gordon [1962] Director; John McDonagh [1969] Director

**IP Assist Services Limited**
*Incorporated:* 25 September 2002
*Previous:* Techtran Group Limited
*Net Worth:* £33,056,390 *Total Assets:* £33,105,178
*Registered Office:* Leeds Innovation Centre, 103 Clarendon Road, Leeds, LS2 9DF
*Activities:* Other business support service activities n.e.c.
*Parent:* IP Group PLC
*Officers:* Anita Diana Earney, Secretary; Alan John Aubrey [1961] Director; Greg Smith [1978] Director/Accountant

**IPF Development (2003) Limited**
*Incorporated:* 22 December 2003
*Net Worth Deficit:* £22,275,000 *Total Assets:* £10,590,000
*Registered Office:* Number Three, Leeds City Office Park, Meadow Lane, Leeds, LS11 5BD
*Activities:* Other business support service activities n.e.c.
*Parent:* International Personal Finance Investments Limited
*Officers:* Andrew Harvey-Wrate, Secretary; John Nicholas Dahlgreen [1958] Director/Treasurer; John Williams [1968] Director

**IPF Digital Group Limited**
*Incorporated:* 18 December 2006
*Previous:* MCB Finance Group Limited
*Net Worth:* £30,883,732 *Total Assets:* £30,895,244
*Registered Office:* Number Three, Leeds City Office Park, Meadow Lane, Leeds, LS11 5BD
*Activities:* Credit granting by non-deposit taking finance houses and other specialist consumer credit grantors
*Parent:* International Personal Finance PLC
*Officers:* Andrew Harvey-Wrate, Secretary; Justin Ashley Lockwood [1970] Director; James Alexander Ormrod [1967] Director/Solicitor; Gerard Jude Ryan [1964] Director [Irish]; Rami Ryhanen [1967] Director [Finnish]

**IPF Financial Services Limited**
*Incorporated:* 3 December 2002
*Net Worth:* £186,978,944 *Total Assets:* £380,622,848
*Registered Office:* Number Three, Leeds City Office Park, Meadow Lane, Leeds, LS11 5BD
*Activities:* Other business support service activities n.e.c.
*Parent:* IPF Holdings Limited
*Officers:* John Nicholas Dahlgreen [1958] Director/Treasurer; Douglas James Kleppen [1968] Director; John Williams [1968] Director

**IPF Financing Limited**
*Incorporated:* 22 December 2003
*Net Worth:* £76,140,088 *Total Assets:* £691,630,208
*Registered Office:* Number Three, Leeds City Office Park, Meadow Lane, Leeds, LS11 5BD
*Activities:* Other credit granting n.e.c.
*Shareholders:* International Personal Finance Investments Limited; IPF International Limited
*Officers:* Andrew Harvey-Wrate, Secretary; John Nicholas Dahlgreen [1958] Director/Treasurer; John Williams [1968] Director

**IPF Holdings Limited**
*Incorporated:* 29 October 1980
*Net Worth:* £135,952,992 *Total Assets:* £137,332,000
*Registered Office:* Number Three, Leeds City Office Park, Meadow Lane, Leeds, LS11 5BD
*Activities:* Non-trading company
*Parent:* International Personal Finance PLC
*Officers:* Andrew Harvey-Wrate, Secretary; John Nicholas Dahlgreen [1958] Director/Treasurer; Justin Ashley Lockwood [1970] Director; James Alexander Ormrod [1967] Director/Solicitor; Gerard Jude Ryan [1964] Director [Irish]

**IPF International Limited**
*Incorporated:* 14 March 1963 *Employees:* 141
*Net Worth Deficit:* £6,168,000 *Total Assets:* £173,278,000
*Registered Office:* Number Three, Leeds City Office Park, Meadow Lane, Leeds, LS11 5BD
*Activities:* Other business support service activities n.e.c.
*Parent:* International Personal Finance Investments Limited
*Officers:* Andrew Harvey-Wrate, Secretary; John Nicholas Dahlgreen [1958] Director/Treasurer; Justin Ashley Lockwood [1970] Director; James Alexander Ormrod [1967] Director/Solicitor; Gerard Jude Ryan [1964] Director [Irish]

**IPN Bidco Limited**
*Incorporated:* 25 February 2015
*Net Worth Deficit:* £5,318,250 *Total Assets:* £108,688,256
*Registered Office:* c/o Inspired Pet Nutrition Limited, Dalton Airfield, Dalton, Thirsk, N Yorks, YO7 3HE
*Activities:* Manufacture of prepared pet foods
*Parent:* IPN Midco 2 Limited
*Officers:* Scott Arnold Dahnke [1965] Director/Managing Partner [American]; Matthew Zeluck Leeds [1983] Director/Vice President [American]; Andrew Craig Taub [1968] Director/Senior Partner [American]

**IPN Midco 1 Limited**
*Incorporated:* 25 February 2015
*Net Worth:* £3,454,768 *Total Assets:* £94,099,240
*Registered Office:* c/o Inspired Pet Nutrition Limited, Dalton Airfield, Dalton, Thirsk, N Yorks, YO7 3HE
*Activities:* Manufacture of prepared pet foods
*Parent:* IPN Topco Limited
*Officers:* Scott Arnold Dahnke [1965] Director/Managing Partner [American]; Matthew Zeluck Leeds [1983] Director/Vice President [American]; Andrew Craig Taub [1968] Director/Senior Partner [American]

**IPN Midco 2 Limited**
*Incorporated:* 25 February 2015
*Net Worth:* £5,821,560 *Total Assets:* £93,670,928
*Registered Office:* c/o Inspired Pet Nutrition Limited, Dalton Airfield, Dalton, Thirsk, N Yorks, YO7 3HE
*Activities:* Manufacture of prepared pet foods
*Parent:* IPN Midco 1 Limited
*Officers:* Scott Arnold Dahnke [1965] Director/Managing Partner [American]; Matthew Zeluck Leeds [1983] Director/Vice President [American]; Andrew Craig Taub [1968] Director/Senior Partner [American]

**IPN Topco Limited**
*Incorporated:* 25 February 2015 *Employees:* 172
*Net Worth Deficit:* £15,425,768 *Total Assets:* £124,108,288
*Registered Office:* c/o Inspired Pet Nutrition Limited, Dalton Airfield, Dalton, Thirsk, N Yorks, YO7 3HE
*Activities:* Manufacture of prepared pet foods
*Officers:* Scott Arnold Dahnke [1965] Director/Managing Partner [American]; Matthew Zeluck Leeds [1983] Director/Vice President [American]; Richard Harrington Page [1966] Director; Thomas Grindrod Page [1968] Director; Andrew Craig Taub [1968] Director/Senior Partner [American]

**Ipsosolo Limited**
*Incorporated:* 17 July 2009 *Employees:* 11
*Net Worth:* £672,495 *Total Assets:* £3,442,301
*Registered Office:* BCL House, 2 Pavilion Business Park, Royds Hall Road, Leeds, LS12 6AJ
*Activities:* Other service activities n.e.c.
*Shareholders:* Stuart William Ekins; Richard Stanley Herbert; Rolf Hugo Munding
*Officers:* Stuart William Ekins [1968] Marketing Director; Richard Stanley Herbert [1973] Sales Director

**IQ Power Holdings Limited**
*Incorporated:* 27 July 2006
*Previous:* International Power IQ Limited
*Net Worth:* £6,045,000 *Total Assets:* £6,265,000
*Registered Office:* Saltend Power Station, Saltend Chemicals Park, Hedon Road, Hull, HU12 8GA
*Activities:* Activities of head offices
*Officers:* Victor Andrea George Danks [1951] Director/Electricity Generation; Michael Ellis Farr [1964] Director/Power Station Manager; Russell Holland [1976] Director/Finance and Procurement Manager; Scott Jonathan Keen [1974] Director

**IQRA Academy Education Trust**
*Incorporated:* 24 July 2013 *Employees:* 106
*Net Worth:* £7,111,952 *Total Assets:* £7,983,665
*Registered Office:* Iqra Academy, Drummond Road, Bradford, BD8 8DA
*Activities:* Primary education
*Officers:* Asama Javed, Secretary; Shahnaz Anwar-Bleem [1956] Director/Headteacher; Rizwan Aziz [1975] Director; Parwaiz Bashir [1965] Director/Accountant; Peter Anthony Cusack [1960] Director/Assistant Site Manager; Asam Javed [1977] Director/Interpreter; Asama Javed [1974] Director/Solicitor; Alison Jane Lindup [1966] Director/Teacher; Nasar Mohammed [1981] Director/Teacher; Ghazala Nosheen [1990] Director/Customer Registration/Operations; Faqir Rahman [1936] Director/Retired [Pakistani]; Emmerson Wayne Walgrove [1975] Director; Mohammed Younis [1971] Director

**IRISNDT Limited**
*Incorporated:* 3 April 1992 *Employees:* 160
*Net Worth:* £3,938,601 *Total Assets:* £5,021,775
*Registered Office:* Middleplatt Road, Immingham, N E Lincs, DN40 1AH
*Activities:* Technical testing and analysis
*Officers:* Roman Kyrnyckyj, Secretary; Janice May Barbour [1978] Director/Chartered Accountant [Canadian]; Simon Butler [1969] Director; John Dawson [1972] Operations Director; Keith Grimbleby [1960] Director/NDT Manager; Roman Michael Kyrnyckyj [1961] Director/Inspection Engineer; Lee Richardson [1976] Director/NDT Manager; James Richard Sheard [1946] Director/Businessman [Canadian]

**IRISNDT UK Holdings Limited**
*Incorporated:* 1 May 2003 *Employees:* 160
*Net Worth:* £1,962,408 *Total Assets:* £9,754,032
*Registered Office:* Middleplatt Road, Immingham, N E Lincs, DN40 1AH
*Activities:* Activities of other holding companies n.e.c.
*Officers:* Roman Kyrnyckyj, Secretary; Janice May Barbour [1978] Director [Canadian]; Mike Bazzi [1959] Director [American]; Marcel Ronald Blinde [1969] Director [Dutch]; Roman Michael Kyrnyckyj [1961] Director/Inspection Engineer; James Richard Sheard [1946] Director

**The Irongate Group Limited**
*Incorporated:* 10 December 1990 *Employees:* 102
*Net Worth:* £3,841,414 *Total Assets:* £7,051,268
*Registered Office:* Daughters Court, Silkwood Park, Wakefield, W Yorks, WF5 9TQ
*Activities:* Retail sale of books in specialised stores
*Parent:* Complete Business Solutions Group Holdings Limited
*Officers:* Richard Coulson [1971] Director; Adam Joseph Noble [1964] Director; Darren Roe [1977] Director; Sarah Louise Wilson [1980] Human Resources Director

**Isberg Limited**
*Incorporated:* 26 November 1985 *Employees:* 3
*Net Worth:* £2,239,489 *Total Assets:* £3,266,775
*Registered Office:* Room 120, Louis Pearlman Centre, Goulton Street, Hull, HU3 4DL
*Activities:* Combined office administrative service activities
*Major Shareholder:* Petur Bjornsson
*Officers:* Petur Bjornsson [1955] Director [Icelander]

**ISG Boiler Holdings Limited**
*Incorporated:* 8 August 2000
*Net Worth:* £37,618,000 *Total Assets:* £72,959,000
*Registered Office:* National Avenue, Hull, HU5 4JB
*Activities:* Activities of head offices
*Parent:* Bandwood Limited
*Officers:* Steven Hairsine, Secretary; Shaun Barry Edwards [1968] Director; Pierre-Louis Andre Francois [1956] Director [French]; Trevor Terence Harvey [1956] Director

**Island Wharf (100) Limited**
*Incorporated:* 20 September 2002
*Net Worth:* £135,856,992 *Total Assets:* £146,724,000
*Registered Office:* Trinity Park House, Fox Way, Wakefield, W Yorks, WF2 8EE
*Activities:* Other business support service activities n.e.c.
*Parent:* Northern Foods Limited
*Officers:* Ronald Klaas Otto Kers [1969] Director/Group CEO [Dutch]; Craig Ashley Tomkinson [1982] Director/Group CFO

**Island Wharf (300) Limited**
*Incorporated:* 20 September 2002
*Net Worth:* £164,884,000 *Total Assets:* £171,656,992
*Registered Office:* Trinity Park House, Fox Way, Wakefield, W Yorks, WF2 8EE
*Activities:* Other business support service activities n.e.c.
*Parent:* Northern Foods Limited
*Officers:* Ronald Klaas Otto Kers [1969] Director/Group CEO [Dutch]; Craig Ashley Tomkinson [1982] Director/Group CFO

**Isle Education Trust**
*Incorporated:* 18 October 2011 *Employees:* 183
*Net Worth:* £8,253,000 *Total Assets:* £10,576,000
*Registered Office:* South Axholme Academy, Burnham Road, Epworth, Doncaster, S Yorks, DN9 1BY
*Activities:* Primary education
*Officers:* Karen Amanda Wild, Secretary; Paul Barratt [1951] Director/Bookmaker; Trevor Bean [1954] Director/Educationalist; Stuart Carrington [1980] Director/Chief Financial Officer; Aleksandra Flack [1988] Director/Solicitor [Polish]; Steven John Holt [1978] Assistant Managing Director; Sarah Jane Sprack [1972] Director/Principal; James Richard Stables [1978] Director/Senior Audit Manager; Karolina Whilde [1984] Director/Group Property Business Partner, Civil Rolls Royce [Polish]

**Ison Harrison Limited**
*Incorporated:* 24 January 2008 *Employees:* 4
*Net Worth:* £2,794,203 *Total Assets:* £5,097,276
*Registered Office:* Duke House, 54 Wellington Street, Leeds, LS1 2EE
*Activities:* Solicitors
*Shareholders:* Dominic Peter Stewart MacKenzie; Jonathan Leslie Mark Wearing; Richard John Timperley
*Officers:* Jonathan Leslie Mark Wearing, Secretary; Dominic Peter Stewart MacKenzie [1974] Director/Solicitor; Stephen Mark Neale [1965] Director/Solicitor; Richard John Timperley [1968] Director/Solicitor; Jonathan Leslie Mark Wearing [1970] Director/Solicitor

**Isotek (Holdings) Limited**
*Incorporated:* 3 July 1997
*Net Worth:* £3,302,982 *Total Assets:* £3,316,826
*Registered Office:* Filtronic House, 3 Airport West, Lancaster Way, Yeadon, Leeds, LS19 7ZA
*Activities:* Activities of head offices
*Parent:* Filtronic PLC
*Officers:* Maura Eilis Moynihan, Secretary; Dr Maura Eilis Moynihan [1959] Director/Solicitor [Irish]; Robert Stjohn Smith [1964] Director/Accountant

**ISP Holdings (U.K.) Ltd.**
*Incorporated:* 10 August 1999
*Net Worth:* £11,933,000 *Total Assets:* £11,944,000
*Registered Office:* Unit 4b Whinbank Park, Whinbank Road, Aycliffe Business Park, Newton Aycliffe, Co Durham, DL5 6AY
*Activities:* Manufacture of other chemical products n.e.c.
*Officers:* Julie Charlton, Secretary; Frank Jacob Adriaan Jumelet [1960] Director [Dutch]

**ISS Labour Group Limited**
*Incorporated:* 15 October 2013
*Net Worth Deficit:* £2,061,505 *Total Assets:* £10,631,938
*Registered Office:* 7 Bradford Business Park, Kings Gate, Bradford, BD1 4SJ
*Activities:* Activities of head offices
*Parent:* Specialist People Services Group Ltd
*Officers:* Gary Beeston [1962] Director; Christopher Michael Chidley [1960] Director; Paul Howard McNulty [1970] Director

**IT @ Spectrum Limited**
*Incorporated:* 3 January 1985 *Employees:* 48
*Net Worth:* £1,449,121 *Total Assets:* £3,764,226
*Registered Office:* The View, Bridgehead Business Park, Hessle, Hull, HU13 0GD
*Activities:* Information technology consultancy activities
*Parent:* Spectrum Copiers Ltd
*Officers:* Edmund Cavill [1948] Director; Timothy Cavill [1952] Director; Timothy Charles Davison [1968] Director; Aeon John Harwood [1971] Director; Kenneth Sturdy [1964] Director

**Itch Propco Limited**
*Incorporated:* 25 February 2014 *Employees:* 2
*Net Worth:* £10,679,980 *Total Assets:* £11,696,306
*Registered Office:* Silver Street, Huddersfield, W Yorks, HD5 9BA
*Activities:* Other letting and operating of own or leased real estate
*Parent:* Itch Newco Ltd
*Officers:* Nicola Nixon, Secretary; Richard Paul Ellis [1968] Director; Thomas George Ellis [1973] Director

**Ithaca Energy Developments UK Limited**
*Incorporated:* 15 December 2009
*Previous:* Petrofac Energy Developments UK Limited
*Net Worth Deficit:* £9,333,587 *Total Assets:* £7,596,044
*Registered Office:* 1 Park Row, Leeds, LS1 5AB
*Activities:* Other business support service activities n.e.c.
*Parent:* Ithaca Energy (UK) Limited
*Officers:* Graham Andrew Forbes [1970] Director/Chief Financial Officer; Leslie James Thomas [1957] Director/Chief Executive Officer

**Ithaca Epsilon Limited**
*Incorporated:* 26 October 2006
*Net Worth Deficit:* £22,308,520 *Total Assets:* £26,451,092
*Registered Office:* 1 Park Row, Leeds, LS1 5AB
*Activities:* Extraction of crude petroleum
*Parent:* Ithaca Petroleum Limited
*Officers:* Graham Andrew Forbes [1970] Director/Chief Financial Officer; Leslie James Thomas [1957] Director

**Ithaca Gamma Limited**
*Incorporated:* 8 September 2006
*Net Worth Deficit:* £11,245,002 *Total Assets:* £49,386,344
*Registered Office:* 1 Park Row, Leeds, LS1 5AB
*Activities:* Extraction of crude petroleum
*Parent:* Ithaca Petroleum Limited
*Officers:* Graham Andrew Forbes [1970] Director/Chief Financial Officer; Leslie James Thomas [1957] Director

**Ithaca Petroleum Limited**
*Incorporated:* 7 September 2004
*Net Worth:* £295,589,824 *Total Assets:* £295,589,824
*Registered Office:* 1 Park Row, Leeds, LS1 5AB
*Activities:* Extraction of crude petroleum
*Parent:* Ithaca Energy Holdings (UK) Limited
*Officers:* Graham Andrew Forbes [1970] Director/Chief Financial Officer; Leslie James Thomas [1957] Director

**IUKH Limited**
*Incorporated:* 13 June 2014 *Employees:* 81
*Net Worth:* £3,963,877 *Total Assets:* £9,140,600
*Registered Office:* The New Oakes, Wellington Street, Huddersfield, W Yorks, HD3 3EP
*Activities:* Activities of head offices
*Parent:* IUKH GNT Limited
*Officers:* Angus Austin Gregory [1965] Director; Danny Nolan [1984] Director; Peter Warren Edmond Tyler [1985] Director

**Ivy Farm Limited**
*Incorporated:* 13 February 2015 *Employees:* 2
*Net Worth:* £405,790 *Total Assets:* £7,215,347
*Registered Office:* Eastfield House Farm, Station Road, North Thoresby, Grimsby, N E Lincs, DN36 5QU
*Activities:* Other letting and operating of own or leased real estate
*Shareholders:* Mark Robert Casswell; Jonathan Martin
*Officers:* Mark Robert Casswell [1963] Director/Farmer; Jonathan Martin [1971] Director/Farmer

**J & E Importers & Distributors Green Jem Mfg Associates Co Ltd**
*Incorporated:* 2 July 1992 *Employees:* 17
*Net Worth:* £11,471,883 *Total Assets:* £11,941,527
*Registered Office:* Unit 18 Longwood Road, Corringham Road Industrial Estate, Corringham Road, Gainsborough, Lincs, DN21 1QB
*Activities:* Non-specialised wholesale trade
*Shareholders:* Jeremy Hemsley Levick; Ernest Hensley Levick
*Officers:* Janis Palmer Levick, Secretary; Ernest Hemsley Levick [1932] Director; Jeremy Hemsley Levick [1962] Director

**J & L (North East) Limited**
*Incorporated:* 22 July 2003 *Employees:* 3
*Net Worth:* £436,025 *Total Assets:* £3,022,631
*Registered Office:* 16a Durham Road, Spennymoor, Co Durham, DL16 6SH
*Activities:* Buying and selling of own real estate
*Shareholders:* George Ellis; Jeffrey Ellis; Linda Ellis
*Officers:* Jeffrey Ellis, Secretary/Executive; George Ellis [1977] Director/Motor Dealer; Jeffrey Ellis [1953] Director/Executive; Linda Ellis [1949] Director/Executive

**J D Engineering (Northern) Limited**
*Incorporated:* 2 February 2007 *Employees:* 74
*Net Worth:* £2,980,456 *Total Assets:* £7,661,311
*Registered Office:* Unit 1 Technology Close, Green Park Road, Newport, Brough, E Yorks, HU15 2FX
*Activities:* Other service activities n.e.c.
*Parent:* Everard Group Limited
*Officers:* James Daniel Everard [1985] Director/Engineer; Nicolas John Everard [1988] Director/Engineer; Nigel Simon Sparks [1977] Finance Director

**J M Construction (Leeds) Limited**
*Incorporated:* 21 August 1995 *Employees:* 10
*Net Worth:* £2,916,060 *Total Assets:* £7,349,994
*Registered Office:* Suite 1, Peel Mills, Commercial Street, Morley, W Yorks, LS27 8AG
*Activities:* Development of building projects
*Major Shareholder:* John Mulleady
*Officers:* Linda Penny, Secretary; John Mulleady [1952] Managing Director [Irish]; Linda Penny [1962] Director/Supervisor

**J. and H. Property Management Limited**
*Incorporated:* 27 May 1999 *Employees:* 2
*Net Worth:* £674,377 *Total Assets:* £3,732,163
*Registered Office:* Unit 3 Airedale Park, Royd Ings Avenue, Keighley, W Yorks, BD21 4BZ
*Activities:* Other letting and operating of own or leased real estate
*Shareholders:* Robert Andrew Bairstow; Michelle Annette Bairstow
*Officers:* Michelle Annette Bairstow, Secretary; Andrew Robert Bairstow [1965] Director; Michelle Annette Bairstow [1968] Director

**J.B. Components Limited**
*Incorporated:* 2 July 1998 *Employees:* 23
*Net Worth:* £552,149 *Total Assets:* £3,871,059
*Registered Office:* Service Metals, Howley Park Road, Morley, Leeds, LS27 0BN
*Activities:* Manufacture of other fabricated metal products n.e.c.
*Shareholders:* John William Cullen; Graham Patrick Wilson; John Marshall Winn
*Officers:* Graham Patrick Wilson, Secretary; James Harry Chrimes [1931] Director; Graham Patrick Wilson [1947] Director/Aluminium Stock Holder; John Marshall Winn [1947] Director/Aluminium Stockholder

**J.E.C. Investment Company Limited**
*Incorporated:* 22 March 1957 *Employees:* 10
*Net Worth:* £8,224,786 *Total Assets:* £8,405,775
*Registered Office:* Bank Bottom Mills, Marsden, Huddersfield, W Yorks, HD7 6HR
*Activities:* Other letting and operating of own or leased real estate
*Officers:* Edward Rowland Lee, Secretary; Anna Carolin Crowther [1939] Director/Farmer; Philip Roger Crowther [1969] Director/Farmer; Gillian Rose Dawson [1944] Director; Edward Rowland Lee [1956] Director/Chartered Accountant

**J.E.G Hire Limited**
*Incorporated:* 30 November 2009
*Net Worth:* £8,252,024 *Total Assets:* £24,521,016
*Registered Office:* 62-63 Westborough, Scarborough, N Yorks, YO11 1TS
*Activities:* Renting and leasing of other machinery, equipment and tangible goods n.e.c.
*Major Shareholder:* John Edward Greenwood
*Officers:* Charlotte Elizabeth Bradley, Secretary; John Edward Greenwood [1969] Director

**J.P. Distribution Ltd.**
*Incorporated:* 3 October 1980 *Employees:* 75
*Net Worth:* £2,098,927 *Total Assets:* £5,762,155
*Registered Office:* Unit 600 Bretton Park Way, Dewsbury, W Yorks, WF12 9BS
*Activities:* Wholesale of radio, television goods & electrical household appliances (other than records, tapes, CDs)
*Shareholders:* John Anthony Beckingham; Judith Elizabeth Beckingham
*Officers:* Matthew Woolhouse, Secretary; John Anthony Beckingham [1944] Managing Director; Judith Elizabeth Beckingham [1954] Director/Teacher; Graham Neil Bucktrout [1968] Director; Jason Firth [1977] Director/Sale of Kitchen Equipment; Lucy Elizabeth Swinden [1986] Director/Product Development

**J.S.R. Farms Limited**
*Incorporated:* 4 August 1975 *Employees:* 127
*Net Worth:* £40,929,000 *Total Assets:* £65,738,000
*Registered Office:* Southburn Offices, Southburn, Driffield, E Yorks, YO25 9ED
*Activities:* Mixed farming
*Major Shareholder:* Timothy Sykes Rymer
*Officers:* John Richard Maltby, Secretary; Lord Christopher Robin Haskins [1937] Director; Bernard Hoggarth [1952] Director/Manager; John Richard Maltby [1966] Director/Accountant; Charles Edward Parker [1981] Director/Farm Manager; Elizabeth Carol Rymer [1940] Director; Timothy Sykes Rymer [1963] Director/Farm Manager; Stephen John Waite [1987] Director/Commercial Manager

**J.S.R. Genetics Limited**
*Incorporated:* 5 January 2000 *Employees:* 33
*Net Worth Deficit:* £653,000 *Total Assets:* £4,649,000
*Registered Office:* Southburn Office, Southburn, Driffield, E Yorks, YO25 9ED
*Activities:* Raising of swine and pigs
*Officers:* John Richard Maltby, Secretary; Giles Raymond Christie [1971] UK Sales Director; Lord Christopher Robin Haskins [1937] Director/Consultant; Bernard Hoggarth [1952] Director; Caroline Elizabeth Mitchell [1985] Director of Meat Science; Timothy Sykes Rymer [1963] Director/Farmer; Grant Anderson Walling [1973] Director/Geneticist

**J3 Business Park Doncaster LLP**
*Incorporated:* 22 February 2013 *Employees:* 1
*Net Worth:* £6,140,661 *Total Assets:* £9,685,991
*Registered Office:* A E Morris Limited, Bankwood Lane, New Rossington, Doncaster, S Yorks, DN11 0PS
*Officers:* Nichola May Foster [1983] Member; Robert David Patrick Lowe [1971] Member; Alan Edwin Morris [1951] Member; Barbara Ann Morris [1959] Member; Samuel Alan Morris [1980] Member; Thomas Edwin Morris [1982] Member; James Albert Sean Ian Lowe [1982] LLP Member

**JA Hotels Limited**
*Incorporated:* 27 July 2006
*Net Worth Deficit:* £971,335 *Total Assets:* £4,902,313
*Registered Office:* 25-29 Sandy Way, Yeadon, Leeds, LS19 7EW
*Activities:* Hotels and similar accommodation
*Major Shareholder:* Jeremy Peter Leeds
*Officers:* Jeremy Peter Leeds, Secretary; Jeremy Peter Leeds [1956] Director/Hotelier; Louise Karen Leeds [1967] Director/Hotelier

**Jabe Foods Limited**
*Incorporated:* 4 August 2011
*Net Worth:* £490,597 *Total Assets:* £3,990,820
*Registered Office:* Unit 1 Intermezzo Drive, Leeds, LS10 1DF
*Activities:* Other letting and operating of own or leased real estate
*Major Shareholder:* David James Kempley
*Officers:* David James Kempley [1962] Director; Darren Paul Smith [1968] Director/Chartered Accountant

**L Jackson & Co Limited**
*Incorporated:* 17 February 2011 *Employees:* 9
*Net Worth:* £19,947,116 *Total Assets:* £21,661,828
*Registered Office:* Rocket Site Misson, Bawtry, Doncaster, S Yorks, DN10 6ET
*Activities:* Sale of other motor vehicles
*Shareholders:* Andrew Jackson; Matthew David Jackson
*Officers:* Matthew David Jackson [1988] Director/Plant and Machinery Sales Manager

**S Jackson & Sons Holdings Limited**
*Incorporated:* 31 October 2014 *Employees:* 2
*Net Worth:* £2,137,236 *Total Assets:* £3,256,839
*Registered Office:* Holme Hall, Holme Lane, Bottesford, Scunthorpe, N Lincs, DN16 3RE
*Activities:* Growing of cereals (except rice), leguminous crops and oil seeds
*Shareholders:* Andrew Charles Jackson; Robin Arthur Jackson
*Officers:* Andrew Charles Jackson [1959] Director/Farmer; Robin Arthur Jackson [1961] Director

**Norman Jackson (Farmers) Limited**
*Incorporated:* 17 February 1997 *Employees:* 11
*Net Worth:* £2,619,406 *Total Assets:* £7,263,844
*Registered Office:* Low Farm, Somerby, Barnetby, S Humbers, DN38 6BW
*Activities:* Mixed farming
*Parent:* NJF (Lincs Holdings) Limited
*Officers:* James Benjamin Jackson, Secretary; Jonathan Frank Jackson, Secretary/Farmer; James Benjamin Jackson [1982] Director/Manager; Jonathan Frank Jackson [1955] Director/Farmer

**Norman Jackson (Flixborough) Limited**
*Incorporated:* 30 August 1960
*Net Worth:* £853,179 *Total Assets:* £3,089,938
*Registered Office:* Low Farm, Somerby, Barnetby, S Humbers, DN38 6BW
*Activities:* Growing of cereals (except rice), leguminous crops and oil seeds
*Shareholder:* Jonathan Frank Jackson
*Officers:* James Benjamin Jackson, Secretary; James Benjamin Jackson [1982] Director; Jonathan Frank Jackson [1955] Director/Farmer

**William Jackson Food Group Limited**
*Incorporated:* 12 April 2000 *Employees:* 49
*Net Worth:* £139,416,000 *Total Assets:* £170,280,992
*Registered Office:* The Riverside Building, Livingstone Road, Hessle, E Yorks, HU13 0DZ
*Activities:* Activities of head offices
*Parent:* William Jackson & Son Limited
*Officers:* Gary Martin Urmston, Secretary; Katie Amanda Denyer [1978] Risk Assurance Director; John Michael Donovan [1967] Director; Chris Gort [1979] Director/IT Manager; Nicholas Alwyn McLaren Oughtred [1960] Director; Norman Graeme Scott Soutar [1960] Director; Gary Martin Urmston [1967] Director; James Watson [1969] Director

**J.Jackson Limited**
*Incorporated:* 28 September 1956 *Employees:* 6
*Net Worth:* £1,696,016 *Total Assets:* £3,152,644
*Registered Office:* Low Farm, Somerby, Barnetby, S Humbers, DN38 6BW
*Activities:* Growing of cereals (except rice), leguminous crops and oil seeds
*Shareholders:* Jonathan Frank Jackson; William Norman Jackson
*Officers:* James Benjamin Jackson, Secretary; Jonathan Frank Jackson, Secretary; James Benjamin Jackson [1982] Director/Manager; Jonathan Frank Jackson [1955] Director/Farmer

**Andrew Jackson Solicitors LLP**
*Incorporated:* 9 December 2016
*Net Worth:* £2,453,293 *Total Assets:* £4,699,770
*Registered Office:* Marina Court, Castle Street, Hull, HU1 1TJ
*Officers:* Philip Ashworth [1958] Member; Paul Robert Barker [1952] Member; Jonathan Iain Dale [1963] Member; Nicholas Gary Dean [1968] Member; Andrew Stephen Funnell [1973] Member; Richard Jeremy Hoare [1967] Member; Richard Andrew Mays [1960] Member; Andrew Clifton Oliver [1966] Member; Mark Pearson-Kendall [1974] Member; Geoffrey Paul Phillips [1980] Member; Nicholas James Scott [1978] Member; Hugh Edward Smith [1959] Member; Stephen John Temple Unwin [1958] Member; Dominic John Ward [1963] Member

**Jackson's Bakery Limited**
*Incorporated:* 12 April 2000 *Employees:* 416
*Net Worth:* £17,001,000 *Total Assets:* £57,065,000
*Registered Office:* The Riverside Building, Livingstone Road, Hessle, E Yorks, HU13 0DZ
*Activities:* Manufacture of bread; manufacture of fresh pastry goods and cakes
*Parent:* William Jackson Food Group Limited
*Officers:* Gary Martin Urmston, Secretary; Adam Alexander Barraclough [1973] Finance Director; Liam Byrne [1969] Director; Clare Louise Fynney [1977] People Director; Ronald Leary [1968] Director; Jillian Emma Martin [1977] Finance Director; LEA Read [1976] Technical Director; Norman Graeme Scott Soutar [1960] Director; Richard Stables [1973] Director

**Jacksons Building Components Limited**
*Incorporated:* 12 May 2004 *Employees:* 19
*Net Worth:* £5,240,385 *Total Assets:* £6,522,837
*Registered Office:* 103 The Village, Stockton-on-the-Forest, N Yorks, YO32 9UP
*Activities:* Cold forming or folding
*Officers:* Ann Barbara Jackson, Secretary; Ann Barbara Jackson [1944] Director/Building Components Trader; Geoffrey Melvin Jackson [1944] Director/Building Components Trader; Joe Jackson [1971] Director/Building Components Trader; Mark Jackson [1967] Director/Building Components Trader

**Jacksons Transport (West Riding) Limited**
*Incorporated:* 14 July 1993
*Net Worth:* £5,807,115 *Total Assets:* £6,678,589
*Registered Office:* 79 Thornhill Road, Middletown, Wakefield, W Yorks, WF4 4RT
*Activities:* Buying and selling of own real estate
*Major Shareholder:* Beverley Ann Jackson
*Officers:* Beverley Ann Jackson, Secretary; Alan Jackson [1958] Director/Haulage Contractor; Beverley Ann Jackson [1967] Director/Company Secretary

**Jacuzzi Spa and Bath Limited**
*Incorporated:* 15 November 2012 *Employees:* 34
*Net Worth Deficit:* £3,579,153 *Total Assets:* £9,521,383
*Registered Office:* Old Mill Lane, Low Road, Hunslet, Leeds, LS10 1RB
*Activities:* Wholesale of hardware, plumbing and heating equipment and supplies
*Officers:* Fabio Felisi [1966] Director [Italian]; David Michael Hellman [1965] Director/Accountant [American]; Duncan Edwin Simcox [1964] Commercial Director; Kevin Teague [1957] Director/Accountant

**Jaines & Son (Grimsby) Limited**
*Incorporated:* 14 July 1947 *Employees:* 46
*Net Worth:* £889,321 *Total Assets:* £3,085,898
*Registered Office:* Kemp Road, Fish Docks, Grimsby, N E Lincs, DN31 3SY
*Activities:* Wholesale of other food, including fish, crustaceans and molluscs
*Shareholders:* Christopher Paul Sparkes; Christopher Paul Sparkes
*Officers:* Beverley Anne Sparkes, Secretary; Keith Holness [1966] Director; Stephen Michael Little [1966] Director; Glenn Olley [1967] Director; Beverley Anne Sparkes [1958] Director; Christopher Paul Sparkes [1956] Director/Fish Merchant

**Jam Homes Ltd**
*Incorporated:* 23 October 2014 *Employees:* 2
*Net Worth Deficit:* £192,411 *Total Assets:* £3,248,947
*Registered Office:* The Grange, Strensall Road, Earswick, York, YO32 9SW
*Activities:* Other letting and operating of own or leased real estate
*Shareholders:* Jason Peter Gandy; Marie Gandy
*Officers:* Jason Peter Gandy [1970] Director; Marie Gandy [1965] Director

**H. H. James & Son Limited**
*Incorporated:* 24 March 1955 *Employees:* 12
*Net Worth:* £2,502,830 *Total Assets:* £3,125,142
*Registered Office:* Northlands, Winterton, Scunthorpe, S Humbers, DN15 9UP
*Activities:* Growing of cereals (except rice), leguminous crops and oil seeds
*Major Shareholder:* John Hollier James
*Officers:* Moyra Pauline James, Secretary; Anne Elizabeth James [1955] Director/Farmer; John Hollier James [1953] Director/Farmer; Moyra Pauline James [1924] Director/Farmer; William Hollier James [1979] Director

**Douglas James Limited**
*Incorporated:* 3 March 1999 *Employees:* 41
*Net Worth:* £7,482,083 *Total Assets:* £8,828,094
*Registered Office:* Westmoreland House, Westmoreland Street, Hull, HU2 0DJ
*Activities:* Manufacture of ceramic sanitary fixtures
*Major Shareholder:* Malcolm Charles Walker
*Officers:* Lee Davies, Secretary; Lee Davies [1972] Financial Director; Malcolm Charles Walker [1948] Director; Shane Malcolm Walker [1972] Director

**Andrew James UK Ltd**
*Incorporated:* 27 October 2005 *Employees:* 22
*Net Worth:* £4,170,555 *Total Assets:* £11,346,492
*Registered Office:* 37-38 Market Street, Ferryhill, Co Durham, DL17 8JH
*Activities:* Retail sale of electrical household appliances in specialised stores
*Shareholder:* Andrew John Tomlinson
*Officers:* Andrew John Tomlinson, Secretary; Mark Ellison [1965] Director; Alan Richard Neal [1951] Director; Andrew John Tomlinson [1973] Director/Transport Manager

**W.E. Jameson and Son Limited**
*Incorporated:* 7 March 1960 *Employees:* 36
*Net Worth:* £6,359,160 *Total Assets:* £7,898,114
*Registered Office:* Foxholme Lane Mill, Masham, Ripon, N Yorks, HG4 4EL
*Activities:* Manufacture of prepared feeds for farm animals
*Shareholders:* James Malcolm Jameson; Robert Edward Jameson
*Officers:* John Richard Harker, Secretary; John Richard Harker [1955] Director/Accountant; Barbara Jameson [1943] Director; Christopher Robert Jameson [1975] Director/Mill Manager; Graham Edward Jameson [1970] Director/Animal Feed Sales; James Malcolm Jameson [1943] Director; Janet Elizabeth Jameson [1952] Director; Robert Edward Jameson [1952] Director; Jonathan Stansfield [1965] Director/Transport Manager

**JBA Group Limited**
*Incorporated:* 11 October 2007 *Employees:* 534
*Net Worth:* £8,289,727 *Total Assets:* £12,621,534
*Registered Office:* South Barn, Broughton Hall, Skipton, N Yorks, BD23 3AE
*Activities:* Engineering related scientific and technical consulting activities
*Shareholder:* Jeremy Richard Benn
*Officers:* Craig Robson, Secretary; Jeremy Richard Benn [1962] Director/Civil Engineer; William Albert Schlegel [1954] Director/Chartered Civil Engineer; Christopher Ernest Schofield [1962] Director/Solicitor

**JBC Industrial Services Limited**
*Incorporated:* 19 February 1986 *Employees:* 64
*Net Worth:* £1,024,956 *Total Assets:* £3,843,369
*Registered Office:* Head Office, JBC Industrial Services Ltd, Tom Dando Close, Normanton Industrial Estate, Normanton, W Yorks, WF6 1TP
*Activities:* Plumbing, heat and air-conditioning installation
*Parent:* JBC Group Limited
*Officers:* Jamieson John Bashall [1975] Director; Geoffrey Sutcliffe [1959] Director

**JCCO 387 Limited**
*Incorporated:* 2 December 2015 *Employees:* 2
*Net Worth:* £989,000 *Total Assets:* £6,918,258
*Registered Office:* St Mary's Gate, Priory Close, Lancaster, LA1 1XB
*Activities:* Activities of other holding companies n.e.c.
*Shareholders:* Andrew Nigel Appleyard; Christine Doris Appleyard
*Officers:* Andrew Nigel Appleyard [1964] Director; Christine Doris Appleyard [1970] Director

**JCT600 (Properties) Limited**
*Incorporated:* 19 October 1987 *Employees:* 12
*Net Worth:* £45,022,000 *Total Assets:* £122,349,000
*Registered Office:* Tordoff House, Apperley Bridge, Bradford, W Yorks, BD10 0PQ
*Activities:* Development of building projects
*Major Shareholder:* Jack Crossley Tordoff
*Officers:* Nigel Martin Shaw, Secretary; Nigel Martin Shaw [1962] Finance Director; Jack Crossley Tordoff [1935] Director; John Cornel Tordoff [1963] Director/Chief Executive

**JCT600 (Rawdon) Limited**
*Incorporated:* 5 August 1988 *Employees:* 154
*Net Worth:* £34,013,000 *Total Assets:* £60,102,000
*Registered Office:* Tordoff House, Apperley Bridge, Bradford, W Yorks, BD10 0PQ
*Activities:* Sale of new cars and light motor vehicles
*Major Shareholder:* Jack Crossley Tordoff
*Officers:* Nigel Martin Shaw, Secretary; Nigel Martin Shaw [1962] Finance Director; Jack Crossley Tordoff [1935] Director; John Cornel Tordoff [1963] Director/Chief Executive

**JCT600 (South Yorkshire) Limited**
*Incorporated:* 28 January 1983 *Employees:* 245
*Net Worth:* £27,061,000 *Total Assets:* £89,069,000
*Registered Office:* Tordoff House, Apperley Bridge, Bradford, W Yorks, BD10 0PQ
*Activities:* Sale of new cars and light motor vehicles
*Major Shareholder:* Jack Crossley Tordoff
*Officers:* Nigel Martin Shaw, Secretary; Nigel Martin Shaw [1962] Finance Director; Jack Crossley Tordoff [1935] Director; John Cornel Tordoff [1963] Director/Chief Executive

**JCT600 (Yorkshire) Ltd**
*Incorporated:* 22 January 1960 *Employees:* 85
*Net Worth:* £7,847,000 *Total Assets:* £29,522,000
*Registered Office:* Tordoff House, Apperley Bridge, Bradford, W Yorks, BD10 0PQ
*Activities:* Sale of new cars and light motor vehicles
*Major Shareholder:* Jack Crossley Tordoff
*Officers:* Nigel Martin Shaw, Secretary; Nigel Martin Shaw [1962] Finance Director; Jack Crossley Tordoff [1935] Director; John Cornel Tordoff [1963] Director/Chief Executive

**JCT600 Limited**
*Incorporated:* 20 June 1946 *Employees:* 2,185
*Net Worth:* £167,120,000 *Total Assets:* £431,950,016
*Registered Office:* Tordoff House, Apperley Bridge, Bradford, W Yorks, BD10 0PQ
*Activities:* Sale of new cars and light motor vehicles
*Major Shareholder:* Jack Crossley Tordoff
*Officers:* Nigel Martin Shaw, Secretary; Nigel Martin Shaw [1962] Finance Director; Edward Ian Tordoff [1957] Director; Jack Crossley Tordoff [1935] Director; John Cornel Tordoff [1963] Director/Chief Executive

**JCT600 Vehicle Leasing Solutions Limited**
*Incorporated:* 18 July 1968 *Employees:* 43
*Net Worth:* £35,006,000 *Total Assets:* £86,817,000
*Registered Office:* Tordoff House, Apperley Bridge, Bradford, W Yorks, BD10 0PQ
*Activities:* Sale of new cars and light motor vehicles
*Major Shareholder:* Jack Crossley Tordoff
*Officers:* Nigel Martin Shaw, Secretary; Nigel Martin Shaw [1962] Finance Director; Edward Ian Tordoff [1957] Director; Jack Crossley Tordoff [1935] Director; John Cornel Tordoff [1963] Director/Chief Executive

**J. Jeffery (Builder) Limited**
*Incorporated:* 27 March 1963 *Employees:* 20
*Net Worth:* £2,934,103 *Total Assets:* £8,884,784
*Registered Office:* 215 Bradford Road, East Ardsley, Wakefield, W Yorks, WF3 2DN
*Activities:* Agents involved in the sale of timber and building materials
*Shareholders:* William Nigel Jeffery; Richard Andrew Jeffery
*Officers:* Rodney Lamb, Secretary; Richard Andrew Jeffery [1966] Director/Manager; William Nigel Jeffery [1965] Director; William Jeffery [1937] Director

**Jemella Group Limited**
*Incorporated:* 7 May 2003
*Net Worth Deficit:* £631,000 *Total Assets:* £42,189,000
*Registered Office:* Bridgewater Place, Water Lane, Leeds, LS11 5BZ
*Activities:* Activities of head offices
*Parent:* GHD Group Holdings Limited
*Officers:* Philippe Michel Marie Georges, Secretary; Philippe Michel Marie Georges [1971] Director [French]; Michael Joseph Hewett [1980] Director [American]

**Jemella Limited**
*Incorporated:* 28 November 2000 *Employees:* 271
*Net Worth:* £89,752,000 *Total Assets:* £180,370,000
*Registered Office:* Bridgewater Place, Water Lane, Leeds, LS11 5BZ
*Activities:* Wholesale of household goods (other than musical instruments) n.e.c
*Parent:* Jemella Group Limited
*Officers:* Philippe Michel Marie Georges, Secretary; Sebastien Froidefond [1968] Director/HR [French]; Philippe Michel Marie Georges [1971] Director [French]; Michael Joseph Hewett [1980] Director [American]

**Jemmtec Limited**
*Incorporated:* 12 October 2009 *Employees:* 181
*Net Worth:* £11,161,887 *Total Assets:* £16,416,664
*Registered Office:* Magma Ceramics, Low Road, Earlsheaton, Dewsbury, W Yorks, WF12 8BU
*Activities:* Manufacture of refractory products
*Shareholders:* Mark Rodney Stuckey; Thermal Ceramics UK Limited
*Officers:* Ralph Ian Gomarsall [1964] Director; Simon John Rhodes Halliday [1963] Director; Raymond Douglas Hargreaves [1954] Director/Ceramic Manufacturing; Mark Rodney Stuckey [1971] Director/Consultant

**Jenkar Shipping Limited**
*Incorporated:* 13 March 1978 *Employees:* 36
*Net Worth:* £556,136 *Total Assets:* £4,294,948
*Registered Office:* Unit C2, Telford Way, Wakefield 41 Industrial Estate, Wakefield, W Yorks, WF2 0XW
*Activities:* Operation of warehousing and storage facilities for land transport activities
*Parent:* Jenkar (UK) Ltd
*Officers:* Karen Lisa Phillips, Secretary; Jillian Camp [1975] Commercial Director; Martyn David Crookes [1957] Joint Managing Director; Andrew Robert Phillips [1974] Joint Managing Director; Karen Lisa Phillips [1975] Director

**Jennings Roofing Limited**
*Incorporated:* 1 April 1985 *Employees:* 65
*Net Worth:* £5,204,567 *Total Assets:* £10,453,955
*Registered Office:* Unit 4 Emmanuel Trading Estate, Springwell Road, Leeds, LS12 1AT
*Activities:* Roofing activities
*Parent:* Jennings Properties Limited
*Officers:* Wendy Ann Edgell, Secretary; John Martin Briggs [1961] Director/Manager; Eric Holmes [1962] Director/Manager; Graham Roy Jennings [1956] Director/Roofing Contractor; Steven Mark Roberts [1966] Director; Keith Soulsby [1956] Director

**Jessgrove Limited**
*Incorporated:* 11 May 1979 *Employees:* 78
*Net Worth:* £11,767,988 *Total Assets:* £21,343,628
*Registered Office:* Cross Lane Mills, Cross Lane, Bradford, W Yorks, BD7 3JT
*Activities:* Wholesale of textiles
*Officers:* Molly Craven, Secretary; Lee Oliver Craven [1970] Director/General Manager; Molly Craven [1941] Director

**Jet Aire (DC) Limited**
*Incorporated:* 14 November 1997 *Employees:* 97
*Net Worth:* £2,540,685 *Total Assets:* £4,918,243
*Registered Office:* Northways Court, Great North Road, Aberford, Leeds, LS25 3AU
*Activities:* Sewerage
*Major Shareholder:* Charlie Reggie Kirk
*Officers:* Susan Taylor, Secretary; Charles Reggie Kirk [1967] Director; Simon Marcus Lawton [1960] Director; Darren John Pavan [1980] Director [South African]

**Jet2 Transport Services Limited**
*Incorporated:* 13 September 1988
*Net Worth:* £2,000 *Total Assets:* £775,041,984
*Registered Office:* Low Fare Finder House, Leeds Bradford International Airport, Leeds, LS19 7TU
*Activities:* Scheduled passenger air transport
*Parent:* Jet2holidays Limited
*Officers:* Ian Bruce Day, Secretary; Gary James Brown [1966] Director/Accountant; Ian Bruce Day [1972] Legal Director; Stephen Paul Heapy [1969] Director/Chief Executive Officer; Philip Hugh Meeson [1947] Director/Chief Executive

**Jet2.Com Limited**
*Incorporated:* 14 August 1992 *Employees:* 6,889
*Net Worth:* £356,800,000 *Total Assets:* £2,224,199,936
*Registered Office:* Low Fare Finder House, Leeds Bradford Airport, Yeadon, Leeds, LS19 7TU
*Activities:* Scheduled passenger air transport
*Parent:* Dart Group PLC
*Officers:* Ian Bruce Day, Secretary; Sean Lee Ablett [1964] Director; Gary James Brown [1966] Director/Group Chief Financial Officer; John Richard Chambers [1965] Human Resources Director; Ian Bruce Day [1972] Legal Director; Ian Fraser Doubtfire [1954] Director; Gavin John Forth [1965] Marketing Director; Stephen Paul Guy [1958] Procurement Director; Stephen Paul Heapy [1969] Director/Chief Commercial Officer; Christopher Roger Hubbard [1960] Engineering Director; Gary Dennis Isaacs [1962] Director/Chief Information Officer; Stephen Gerard Lee [1963] Director/Commercial Manager; Philip Hugh Meeson [1947] Director; Adam Mulroy [1982] Revenue Director; Philip Ward [1963] Airline Director

**Jet2holidays Limited**
*Incorporated:* 28 June 2002 *Employees:* 886
*Net Worth:* £68,400,000 *Total Assets:* £1,345,900,032
*Registered Office:* Low Fare Finder House, Leeds Bradford Airport, Yeadon, Leeds, LS19 7TU
*Activities:* Tour operator activities
*Parent:* Jet2.Com Limited
*Officers:* Ian Bruce Day, Secretary; Gary James Brown [1966] Director/Group Chief Financial Officer; Ian Bruce Day [1972] Legal Director; Ian Fraser Doubtfire [1954] Director; Gavin John Forth [1965] Marketing Director; Stephen Paul Heapy [1969] Director/Chief Commercial Officer; Stephen Gerard Lee [1963] Commercial Director; Philip Hugh Meeson [1947] Director/Chief Executive Officer; Adam Mulroy [1982] Revenue Director

**J.A.Jewitt**
*Incorporated:* 14 May 1959 *Employees:* 68
*Net Worth:* £9,171,355 *Total Assets:* £11,516,055
*Registered Office:* Low House Farm, Middlestone Moor, Spennymoor, Co Durham, DL16 7QD
*Activities:* Wholesale of meat and meat products
*Shareholders:* Verona Jewitt; The Jewitt Trust
*Officers:* Verona Jewitt, Secretary; Caroline Jane Jewitt [1971] Director/Administrator; Michael David Jewitt [1969] Director/Butcher; Verona Jewitt [1940] Director/Secretary

**J.A. Jewitt (Meat) Limited**
*Incorporated:* 20 February 1979 *Employees:* 68
*Net Worth:* £7,448,914 *Total Assets:* £10,331,672
*Registered Office:* Low House Farm, Middlestone Moor, Spennymoor, Co Durham, DL16 7QD
*Activities:* Wholesale of meat and meat products
*Shareholders:* Michael David Jewitt; Verona Jewitt; J A Jewitt
*Officers:* Verona Jewitt, Secretary; Caroline Jane Jewitt [1971] Director/Administrator; Michael David Jewitt [1969] Director/Butcher; Verona Jewitt [1940] Director/Secretary

**Jito Trading Limited**
*Incorporated:* 16 February 2016
*Net Worth:* £5,011,657 *Total Assets:* £5,019,721
*Registered Office:* Suite 8, Brackenholme Business Park, Selby, N Yorks, YO8 6EL
*Activities:* Other manufacturing n.e.c.
*Shareholders:* Arc Applied Sciences Ltd; Downing One VCT PLC
*Officers:* Jonathan Robin Boss [1969] Director; Michael Kotyk [1964] Director [Austrian]; Michael Braddon Pritchett [1968] Director

**JJC Hire Limited**
*Incorporated:* 12 September 2007 *Employees:* 31
*Net Worth:* £1,913,498 *Total Assets:* £8,236,143
*Registered Office:* Sandscale Park Industrial Estate, Park Road, Barrow in Furness, Cumbria, LA14 4QT
*Activities:* Collection of non-hazardous waste
*Shareholders:* Anne Armer; John Cooper
*Officers:* Robin James Walmsley [1959] Director

**JLA Clean Limited**
*Incorporated:* 18 March 2010
*Net Worth Deficit:* £73,159,000 *Total Assets:* £92,268,000
*Registered Office:* Meadowcroft Lane, Halifax Road, Ripponden, W Yorks, HX6 4AJ
*Activities:* Activities of head offices
*Parent:* JLA Debtco Limited
*Officers:* Helen Jane Ashton [1972] Director/Chief Executive Officer; Paul Justin Humphreys [1958] Director

**JLA Debtco Limited**
*Incorporated:* 18 March 2010 *Employees:* 2
*Net Worth Deficit:* £21,015,000 *Total Assets:* £418,547,008
*Registered Office:* Meadowcroft Lane, Halifax Road, Ripponden, W Yorks, HX6 4AJ
*Activities:* Activities of head offices
*Parent:* JLA Equityco Limited
*Officers:* Helen Jane Ashton [1972] Director/Chief Executive Officer; Paul Justin Humphreys [1958] Director

**JLA Limited**
*Incorporated:* 5 February 1973 *Employees:* 672
*Net Worth:* £9,557,000 *Total Assets:* £101,281,000
*Registered Office:* Meadowcroft Lane, Halifax Road, Ripponden, W Yorks, HX6 4AJ
*Activities:* Wholesale of other machinery and equipment
*Parent:* Vanilla Group Limited
*Officers:* Helen Jane Ashton [1972] Director/Chief Executive Officer; Paul Justin Humphreys [1958] Director

**JLA Total Care Limited**
*Incorporated:* 22 July 1994 *Employees:* 33
*Net Worth:* £47,505,000 *Total Assets:* £89,434,000
*Registered Office:* Meadowcroft Lane, Halifax Road, Ripponden, W Yorks, HX6 4AJ
*Activities:* Renting and leasing of other machinery, equipment and tangible goods n.e.c.
*Parent:* Vanilla Group Limited
*Officers:* Helen Jane Ashton [1972] Director/Chief Executive Officer; Paul Justin Humphreys [1958] Director

**JLM Global Foods Limited**
*Incorporated:* 2 June 2003 *Employees:* 60
*Net Worth:* £2,101,337 *Total Assets:* £3,851,580
*Registered Office:* 37 Allington Way, Yarm Road Business Park, Darlington, Co Durham, DL1 4QB
*Activities:* Manufacture of other food products n.e.c.
*Major Shareholder:* Joyce May Moore
*Officers:* James Alan Moore, Secretary; Anthony Michael Dennett [1945] Director/Accountant; Paul Anthony Huggins [1952] Director; Graeme Alan Moore [1964] Director; James Alan Moore [1940] Director

**JM Developments (Guiseley) Limited**
*Incorporated:* 2 February 2011 *Employees:* 1
*Net Worth:* £1,111,329 *Total Assets:* £4,423,536
*Registered Office:* Suite 1, Peel Mills, Commercial Street, Morley, Leeds, LS27 8AG
*Activities:* Dormant company
*Major Shareholder:* John Mulleady
*Officers:* Linda Penny, Secretary; John Mulleady [1952] Director/Property Developer [Irish]

**JM Packaging Limited**
*Incorporated:* 11 May 1998 *Employees:* 106
*Net Worth:* £4,925,846 *Total Assets:* £10,930,004
*Registered Office:* 5 Malton Enterprise Park, Malton, N Yorks, YO17 6AB
*Activities:* Packaging activities
*Major Shareholder:* Jason Alexander McGill
*Officers:* Jason Alexander McGill [1966] Director

**JMC Developments (Hunslet) Limited**
*Incorporated:* 28 February 2017 *Employees:* 1
*Net Worth:* £62,937 *Total Assets:* £3,687,777
*Registered Office:* Suite 1, Peel Mills, Commercial Street, Morley, Leeds, LS27 8AG
*Activities:* Development of building projects
*Major Shareholder:* John Mulleady
*Officers:* Linda Penny, Secretary; John Mulleady [1952] Director [Irish]

**JMCD Investments Limited**
*Incorporated:* 17 January 2014 *Employees:* 1
*Net Worth:* £3,947,477 *Total Assets:* £20,108,916
*Registered Office:* Beechfield, The Terrace, Boston Spa, Wetherby, W Yorks, LS23 6AH
*Activities:* Fund management activities
*Shareholders:* Rosamund Mary Ives; John Conrad McDonnell
*Officers:* John Conrad McDonnell [1963] Director

**JMS of Doncaster Limited**
*Incorporated:* 29 May 2001 *Employees:* 45
*Net Worth:* £2,087,597 *Total Assets:* £3,969,161
*Registered Office:* JMS of Doncaster Ltd, Brooklands Road, Carcroft, Doncaster, S Yorks, DN6 7BA
*Activities:* Freight transport by road
*Officers:* Amanda Jane Jarvis, Secretary; John Michael Sheard [1971] Director/Haulier

**JNP Estate Agents Limited**
*Incorporated:* 5 May 1999 *Employees:* 47
*Net Worth:* £3,465,000 *Total Assets:* £5,352,000
*Registered Office:* 2nd Floor, Gateway, 2 Holgate Park Drive, York, YO26 4GB
*Activities:* Real estate agencies
*Parent:* LSLI Ltd
*Officers:* Sapna Bedi FitzGenerald, Secretary; Julian Mark Almrott [1971] Director/Estate Agent; Greig Barker [1969] Finance Director; Helen Elizabeth Buck [1960] Director; Gregory Winston Young [1966] Director

**Joda Freight Limited**
*Incorporated:* 28 October 1997 *Employees:* 112
*Net Worth:* £2,707,458 *Total Assets:* £6,221,817
*Registered Office:* Riparian Way, Crosshills, Keighley, W Yorks, BD20 7BW
*Activities:* Freight transport by road
*Parent:* Joda Holdings Ltd
*Officers:* David John Wareing, Secretary/Haulage Contractor; Diane Patricia Collett [1963] Director/Haulage Contractor; John Collett [1960] Director/Haulage Contractor; David John Wareing [1958] Director/Haulage Contractor; Pamela Wareing [1957] Director/Haulage Contractor

**Joda Holdings Limited**
*Incorporated:* 17 March 2005 *Employees:* 112
*Net Worth:* £3,685,672 *Total Assets:* £7,681,555
*Registered Office:* Riparian Way, Cross Hills, Keighley, W Yorks, BD20 7BW
*Activities:* Operation of warehousing and storage facilities for land transport activities
*Shareholders:* David John Wareing; Johnathan Collett
*Officers:* David John Wareing, Secretary/Haulage Contractor; John Collett [1960] Director/Haulage Contractor; David John Wareing [1958] Director/Haulage Contractor

**J. & C. Joel Limited**
*Incorporated:* 4 August 1978 *Employees:* 117
*Net Worth:* £2,735,685 *Total Assets:* £8,797,836
*Registered Office:* Corporation Mill, Corporation Street, Sowerby Bridge, Halifax, W Yorks, HX6 2QQ
*Activities:* Manufacture of other textiles n.e.c.
*Shareholder:* James Thomas Wheelwright
*Officers:* Joseph Levi Wheelwright, Secretary; Matthew James Corbett [1978] Director of Projects and Manufacturing; James Thomas Wheelwright [1978] Director; Nicholas John Worton [1970] Director/Chief Financial Officer

**John Street Developments Limited**
*Incorporated:* 4 May 2006
*Net Worth Deficit:* £391,149 *Total Assets:* £3,066,674
*Registered Office:* Europa House, 20 Esplanade, Scarborough, N Yorks, YO11 2AQ
*Activities:* Buying and selling of own real estate
*Parent:* Sheffield United Limited
*Officers:* Scott Richard McCabe [1975] Director; Jeremy John Tutton [1966] Director/Financial Controller

**Johnny's Entertainments (Tyneside) Limited**
*Incorporated:* 16 January 1973 *Employees:* 68
*Net Worth:* £3,220,821 *Total Assets:* £8,138,466
*Registered Office:* Pleasureland, Marine Road West, Morecambe, Lancs, LA4 4BU
*Activities:* Other amusement and recreation activities n.e.c.
*Parent:* Corkel Limited
*Officers:* Gavin Reader [1966] Director/Amusement Caterer; Solomon Luke Reader [1977] Director/Amusement Caterer; Scott Robson [1981] Director/Accountant

**W.T.Johnson & Sons (Huddersfield) Limited**
*Incorporated:* 26 March 1954 *Employees:* 135
*Net Worth:* £8,015,526 *Total Assets:* £11,385,716
*Registered Office:* Bankfield Mills, Moldgreen, Huddersfield, W Yorks, HD5 9BB
*Activities:* Finishing of textiles
*Shareholders:* Paul Thomas Andrew Johnson; Daniel Peter Johnson
*Officers:* Paul Thomas Andrew Johnson, Secretary; Daniel Peter Johnson [1964] Director/Cloth Finisher; Paul Thomas Andrew Johnson [1962] Director/Cloth Finisher; Peter Thomas Johnson [1936] Director

**Adrian Johnson Limited**
*Incorporated:* 9 November 1999 *Employees:* 8
*Previous:* Post Vintage Engineers Limited
*Net Worth:* £2,372,300 *Total Assets:* £5,759,839
*Registered Office:* 10-12 Pool Business Park, Pool Road, Pool in Wharfedale, Otley, W Yorks, LS21 1FD
*Activities:* Other manufacturing n.e.c.
*Major Shareholder:* Adrian Johnson
*Officers:* Chris Kenneth Johnson, Secretary; Adrian Johnson [1968] Director/Vehicle Restorer

**Johnsons of Whixley Limited**
*Incorporated:* 8 December 1958 *Employees:* 92
*Net Worth:* £4,995,300 *Total Assets:* £8,280,900
*Registered Office:* The Nurseries, Whixley, York, YO26 8AQ
*Activities:* Plant propagation
*Parent:* Johnsons of Whixley Holdings Limited
*Officers:* Graham David Richardson, Secretary/Director; Andrew John Richardson [1963] Director/Nurseryman; Graham David Richardson [1965] Director/Nurseryman; Iain Peter Richardson [1969] Director/Nurseryman; John Michael Richardson [1937] Director/Nurseryman; David Thompson [1951] Director/Management Consultant

**Johnsons Wellfield Ltd**
*Incorporated:* 30 December 1943 *Employees:* 85
*Previous:* Johnsons Wellfield Quarries Limited
*Net Worth:* £3,030,342 *Total Assets:* £6,188,132
*Registered Office:* 5 Barr Street, off Leeds Road, Huddersfield, W Yorks, HD1 6PB
*Activities:* Quarrying of ornamental and building stone, limestone, gypsum, chalk and slate
*Parent:* Myers Group 1959 Limited
*Officers:* John Rodger Myers, Secretary; Anne Jacqueline Myers Berry [1955] Director; James David Myers Berry [1985] Director; Katie Elizabeth Myers Berry [1987] Director; John Rodger Myers [1948] Director/Concrete Technologist

**Johnston and Jeff Limited**
*Incorporated:* 1 January 1964 *Employees:* 37
*Net Worth:* £4,378,014 *Total Assets:* £6,205,282
*Registered Office:* Baltic Buildings, Gateway Business Park, Broad Lane, Gilberdyke, E Yorks, HU15 2TD
*Activities:* Manufacture of prepared pet foods
*Major Shareholder:* Richard Michael Johnston
*Officers:* Richard Michael Johnston, Secretary; Fiona Johnston [1967] Director/Administrator; Richard Michael Johnston [1965] Director/Merchant

**Johnstone's Paints Limited**
*Incorporated:* 4 December 1952
*Net Worth:* £42,339,000 *Total Assets:* £42,605,000
*Registered Office:* Huddersfield Road, Birstall, Batley, W Yorks, WF17 9XA
*Activities:* Activities of head offices
*Parent:* SigmaKalon UK Holding Limited
*Officers:* Jason Paul Metcalf [1973] Marketing Director; Felicity Anne Parry [1967] Finance Director; Steven Pocock [1942] Director/General Manager

**Jones & Egan Estates Limited**
*Incorporated:* 21 August 2015 *Employees:* 3
*Net Worth:* £8,906,592 *Total Assets:* £9,039,471
*Registered Office:* 63 Rusland Park, Kendal, Cumbria, LA9 6AJ
*Activities:* Other letting and operating of own or leased real estate
*Officers:* David Egan [1979] Director; Laura Jean Egan [1982] Director; Susan Jane Jones [1952] Director

**C H Jones Limited**
*Incorporated:* 9 October 1935 *Employees:* 108
*Net Worth:* £59,976,000 *Total Assets:* £159,168,992
*Registered Office:* Unit 3 St James Business Park, Grimbald Crag Court, Knaresborough, N Yorks, HG5 8QB
*Activities:* Wholesale of petroleum and petroleum products
*Parent:* Fleetcor Europe Limited
*Officers:* Eric Richard Dey [1959] Director [American]; Alan King [1976] Director/Group President UK & Australia; Anita Kravos-Medimorec [1974] Director/Chief Financial Officer; Steven Joseph Pisciotta [1964] Director [American]

**Jonro Properties Limited**
*Incorporated:* 17 July 1973 *Employees:* 2
*Net Worth:* £2,931,757 *Total Assets:* £3,258,794
*Registered Office:* Lindum Lodge, Owmby Road, Searby, Barnetby, N Lincs, DN38 6BD
*Activities:* Other letting and operating of own or leased real estate
*Officers:* Caroline Jane Rowbottom [1961] Director/Accounts Manager; John Rowbottom [1935] Director/Engineer

**Jordan & Company (Hull) Limited**
*Incorporated:* 1 September 1965 *Employees:* 50
*Net Worth:* £694,021 *Total Assets:* £3,566,318
*Registered Office:* 45-52 Witham, Kingston upon Hull, HU9 1BS
*Activities:* Sale of new cars and light motor vehicles
*Parent:* J. R. Rix & Sons Limited
*Officers:* Rory Michael Andrew Clarke [1959] Director; James Ian Doyle [1974] Director; David Charles Evans [1953] Director; Peter Jeffrey Hasnip [1953] Director; Duncan John Lambert [1961] Director; Sally Joanna Rix [1965] Director; Timothy John Rix [1963] Director

**John Jordan Limited**
*Incorporated:* 2 July 1996 *Employees:* 35
*Net Worth:* £3,226,008 *Total Assets:* £4,388,892
*Registered Office:* Unit 1a Toll Bar Estate, Sedbergh, Cumbria, LA10 5HA
*Activities:* Retail sale via mail order houses or via Internet
*Shareholders:* Lucy Jane Gray; Martin Robin Gray
*Officers:* Lucy Jane Gray, Secretary; Martin Robin Gray [1961] Director

**T P Jordeson & Company Limited**
*Incorporated:* 11 May 1989 *Employees:* 13
*Net Worth:* £2,752,127 *Total Assets:* £13,142,707
*Registered Office:* 53 The Tannery, Lawrence Street, York, YO10 3WH
*Activities:* Agents involved in the sale of timber and building materials
*Parent:* T P Jordeson (Holdings) Limited
*Officers:* Ben Scarborough [1975] Director; Oliver John Maurice Tompkin [1973] Director

**Jotun Paints (Europe) Limited**
*Incorporated:* 22 December 1967 *Employees:* 220
*Net Worth:* £22,350,000 *Total Assets:* £60,081,000
*Registered Office:* Jotun Paints (Europe) Ltd, Stather Road, Flixborough, Scunthorpe, N Lincs, DN15 8RR
*Activities:* Manufacture of paints, varnishes and similar coatings, mastics and sealants
*Parent:* Jotun A/S
*Officers:* John William West, Secretary; Stian Fjeldskar [1974] Director/Vice President Business Support [Norwegian]; Harald Hvalvik [1956] Director/Regional Vice President [Norwegian]; Michael John Young [1961] Director/General Manager

**JPI (Holdings) Limited**
*Incorporated:* 1 October 2014 *Employees:* 6
*Net Worth:* £341,003 *Total Assets:* £3,998,161
*Registered Office:* Unit C, Nepshaw Lane South, Gildersome, Morley, Leeds, LS27 7JQ
*Activities:* Construction of domestic buildings
*Officers:* James Lloyd Bulmer [1983] Director; Paul Stuart Cooper [1969] Director; Iain Karl Doyle [1970] Director; Paul Michael Frain [1977] Director; Zoe Norcliffe [1983] Director

**JPT Group Limited**
*Incorporated:* 9 March 2017
*Net Worth:* £5,433,000 *Total Assets:* £5,602,600
*Registered Office:* Railway Mill, Lowmoor Road, Cliffe Common, Selby, N Yorks, YO8 6EF
*Activities:* Manufacture of other paper and paperboard containers
*Shareholders:* Stephanie Ann Coates; Kenneth Ronald Coates
*Officers:* George Coates [1992] Director; Harry Coates [1989] Director; Kenneth Ronald Coates [1963] Director; Stephanie Ann Coates [1963] Director

**JRRT (Properties) Limited**
*Incorporated:* 3 May 1977
*Net Worth:* £9,235,586 *Total Assets:* £10,660,518
*Registered Office:* The Garden House, Water End, York, YO30 6WQ
*Activities:* Other letting and operating of own or leased real estate
*Parent:* The Joseph Rowntree Reform Trust Limited
*Officers:* James Keillor Wallace, Secretary; Baroness Sarah Virginia Brinton [1955] Director/Member of The House of Lords; Roger Clarke [1948] Director/Retired; Amy Dalrymple [1977] Director/Head of Policy, Alzheimer Scotland; Alison Rachel Goldsworthy [1983] Director; Dr Julian Leon Huppert [1978] Director/Academic and Politician; Benjamin Morgan Lyons [1990] Director/Communications Consultant; Professor Susan Lesley Mendus [1951] Director/Retired Professor of Political Philosophy; Andrew Colin Neal [1964] Director/Consultant; Lisa Smart [1979] Director/Councillor; Fionna Margaret Ruth Tod [1988] Director/Communications Advisor [British/American]

**JSJ Finance Limited**
*Incorporated:* 12 March 2007
*Net Worth:* £15,838 *Total Assets:* £4,438,561
*Registered Office:* 6 Redcliff Road, Melton Office Village, Melton, E Yorks, HU14 3RS
*Activities:* Credit granting by non-deposit taking finance houses and other specialist consumer credit grantors
*Officers:* James William White, Secretary; Jeremy Sean Blakey [1961] Director; Stephen Hunter [1955] Director; James William White [1978] Director

**JSJ Partnership Limited**
*Incorporated:* 20 August 2008 *Employees:* 173
*Net Worth:* £804,071 *Total Assets:* £9,881,800
*Registered Office:* 6 Redcliff Road, Melton Office Village, Melton, E Yorks, HU14 3RS
*Activities:* Activities of head offices
*Officers:* Jeremy Sean Blakey [1961] Director; Stephen Hunter [1955] Director; James William White [1978] Director

**JT Group (UK) Limited**
*Incorporated:* 3 May 2006
*Net Worth:* £1,763,000 *Total Assets:* £3,700,000
*Registered Office:* 1-4 Whitehall Industrial Estate, Ashfield Way, Farnley, Leeds, LS12 5JB
*Activities:* Activities of other holding companies n.e.c.
*Parent:* JT Holdings (UK) Ltd
*Officers:* Lee Mark Walker, Secretary; Paul Graham Crossley [1966] Director; Lee Mark Walker [1971] Director

**JT Holdings (UK) Limited**
*Incorporated:* 27 February 2014 *Employees:* 76
*Net Worth:* £1,934,000 *Total Assets:* £9,894,000
*Registered Office:* Units 1-4 Whitehall Industrial Estate, Ashfield Way, Farnley, Leeds, LS12 5JB
*Activities:* Activities of other holding companies n.e.c.
*Shareholder:* Paul Graham Crossley
*Officers:* Ryan Scott Bevington [1976] Investment Director; Paul Graham Crossley [1966] Financial Director; Alun Timothy Hall [1961] Director/Chairman; Lee Mark Walker [1971] Director

**JTE Holdco Limited**
*Incorporated:* 25 February 2014 *Employees:* 221
*Net Worth:* £8,832,672 *Total Assets:* £13,105,231
*Registered Office:* Silver Street, Huddersfield, W Yorks, HD5 9BA
*Activities:* Non-trading company
*Shareholders:* Richard Paul Ellis; Thomas George Ellis
*Officers:* Nicola Nixon, Secretary; Richard Paul Ellis [1968] Director; Thomas George Ellis [1973] Director

**JTR and RB Land Developments LLP**
*Incorporated:* 8 October 2007
*Net Worth:* £1,405,975 *Total Assets:* £3,976,540
*Registered Office:* 26 South St Mary's Gate, Grimsby, N E Lincs, DN31 1LW
*Officers:* Roger Peter Burnett [1960] Member; James Michael Toseland [1980] Member

**Jubilee Milling Limited**
*Incorporated:* 1 March 1984 *Employees:* 16
*Net Worth:* £6,249,866 *Total Assets:* £7,705,935
*Registered Office:* Jubilee Milling Limited, Main Street, Amotherby, Malton, N Yorks, YO17 6TA
*Activities:* Support activities for animal production (other than farm animal boarding)
*Parent:* William Thompson Group Holdings Limited
*Officers:* Andrew Mark Richardson, Secretary; Alan Charles Brader [1955] Director; Andrew Mark Richardson [1965] Director; Robert Charles Rook [1952] Director

**Jungle Products Limited**
*Incorporated:* 13 December 1996 *Employees:* 30
*Net Worth:* £1,131,919 *Total Assets:* £3,594,969
*Registered Office:* The Cedar, New York Mills, Summerbridge, Harrogate, N Yorks, HG3 4LA
*Activities:* Retail sale of sports goods, fishing gear, camping goods, boats and bicycles
*Parent:* New York Holdings Limited
*Officers:* Nate Brown [1970] Director/CFO of Santa Cruz Bicycles [American]; Joe Graney [1974] Director/CEO of Santa Cruz Bicycles [American]; George Dickon Hepworth [1975] Director/Manager

**Juratek Limited**
*Incorporated:* 1 June 1982 *Employees:* 47
*Net Worth:* £3,157,123 *Total Assets:* £10,734,957
*Registered Office:* Sidings House, Sidings Court, Lakeside, Doncaster, S Yorks, DN4 5NU
*Activities:* Wholesale trade of motor vehicle parts and accessories
*Officers:* Susan Gaye Hooks, Secretary; Allan Hooks [1957] Director; Matthew Stephen Robinson [1976] Director

**Just Lettings Limited**
*Incorporated:* 3 July 2001 *Employees:* 2
*Net Worth:* £1,747,014 *Total Assets:* £6,414,418
*Registered Office:* 33 Park Place, Leeds, LS1 2RY
*Activities:* Other letting and operating of own or leased real estate
*Shareholders:* Stuart McMartin; Julie McMartin; Caitlin Sarah McMartin
*Officers:* Julie McMartin, Company Secretary; Julie McMartin [1967] Director/Company Secretary; Stuart McMartin [1968] Director

**The Just Partnership Limited**
*Incorporated:* 7 November 2011 *Employees:* 69
*Net Worth:* £1,262,103 *Total Assets:* £6,209,919
*Registered Office:* Kildwick Crossing Garage, Skipton Road, Keighley, W Yorks, BD20 7DS
*Activities:* Sale of new cars and light motor vehicles
*Shareholders:* Maxine Lynda Croft; Paul Brian Wilkinson; Maxine Lynda Croft; Russell Allison; Paul Brian Wilkinson
*Officers:* Russell Allison [1980] Director; Maxine Lynda Croft [1970] Managing Director; Kevin Raymond Tyrrell [1988] Director; Paul Brian Wilkinson [1968] Director

**Just Teachers Limited**
*Incorporated:* 7 February 2005 *Employees:* 85
*Net Worth:* £4,146,645 *Total Assets:* £7,560,216
*Registered Office:* High Corn Mill, Chapel Hill, Skipton, N Yorks, BD23 1NL
*Activities:* Temporary employment agency activities
*Parent:* Just Teachers Holdings Limited
*Officers:* Caroline Marie Cafferty [1981] Director/Recruitment Consultant [Irish]; William John Etchell [1971] Director/Chief Financial Officer; Julian Edward Harley [1957] Director/Chairman; Robyn Julieann Johnstone [1967] Director/Group CEO [British/Australian]; David Mark Jones [1965] Director; Robert Douglas King [1982] Director/Fund Manager

**Just Trays Limited**
*Incorporated:* 27 April 2004 *Employees:* 76
*Net Worth:* £3,595,000 *Total Assets:* £10,259,000
*Registered Office:* Unit 1-4 Whitehall Industrial Estate, Ashfield Way, Farnley, Leeds, LS12 5JB
*Activities:* Other manufacturing n.e.c.
*Parent:* JT Group (UK) Ltd
*Officers:* Lee Mark Walker, Secretary/Financial Director; Paul Graham Crossley [1966] Managing Director; Lee Mark Walker [1971] Financial Director

**Justmerc Limited**
*Incorporated:* 16 December 2014 *Employees:* 3
*Net Worth:* £2,225,994 *Total Assets:* £4,488,915
*Registered Office:* Elite House, Spellowgate, Driffield, E Yorks, YO25 5UP
*Activities:* Activities of other holding companies n.e.c.
*Major Shareholder:* Justin Charles Owen
*Officers:* Justin Charles Owen [1970] Director; James Matthew Tate [1972] Director; Gareth Michael Timmins [1979] Director

**JVL Homewares (UK) Limited**
*Incorporated:* 20 February 2013 *Employees:* 71
*Net Worth:* £624,529 *Total Assets:* £6,732,930
*Registered Office:* Orchard Business Park, Scout Road, Hebden Bridge, W Yorks, HX7 5HZ
*Activities:* Wholesale of household goods (other than musical instruments) n.e.c
*Shareholders:* Mohamed Bouabida; JVL International Ltd
*Officers:* Mohamed Bouabida [1963] Director; Graham Dean Jepson [1977] Finance Director; Philip Julian Pointon [1958] Director

**JZ Flowers International Limited**
*Incorporated:* 3 June 1997 *Employees:* 438
*Net Worth:* £5,929,569 *Total Assets:* £20,573,284
*Registered Office:* Dianthus Business Park, Common Lane, Newport, E Yorks, HU15 2FT
*Activities:* Other manufacturing n.e.c.
*Officers:* Marco Van Zijverden [1962] Director [Dutch]; Jelle Jan Zwemstra [1958] Director [Dutch]; Tessa Louise Hester Zwemstra [1988] Director [Dutch]

**K & A Merger Limited**
*Incorporated:* 11 January 2012
*Net Worth:* £77,418,000 *Total Assets:* £297,492,992
*Registered Office:* The Waterfront, Lakeside Boulevard, Doncaster, S Yorks, DN4 5PL
*Activities:* Activities of head offices
*Parent:* Lakeside 1 Limited
*Officers:* Timothy Mark Beale [1976] Director; Mark Richard Priest [1966] Director; James Michael Douglas Thomson [1966] Director

**K P H (Plant Hire) Limited**
*Incorporated:* 15 May 1972 *Employees:* 18
*Net Worth:* £3,876,577 *Total Assets:* £4,994,515
*Registered Office:* Gelderd Road Industrial Estate, Pennine View, Birstall, Batley, W Yorks, WF17 9NF
*Activities:* Renting and leasing of construction and civil engineering machinery and equipment
*Major Shareholder:* Peter Joseph Newman
*Officers:* Margaret Newman, Secretary; John Newman [1964] Director; Margaret Newman [1942] Director [Irish]; Peter Joseph Newman [1940] Director [Irish]

**K T Hydraulics Limited**
*Incorporated:* 27 September 1985 *Employees:* 22
*Net Worth:* £3,231,449 *Total Assets:* £3,882,359
*Registered Office:* Gannex Park, Dewsbury Road, Elland, W Yorks, HX5 9AF
*Activities:* Manufacture of pumps
*Parent:* KTH Engineering Group Limited
*Officers:* Roger Joseph Fish, Secretary; Richard Andrew Ellis [1967] Director/Engineer; Roger Joseph Fish [1943] Director

**K. Fresh Ltd**
*Incorporated:* 27 September 2000
*Net Worth:* £5,527,652 *Total Assets:* £7,406,139
*Registered Office:* Carr Farm, Rimswell, Withernsea, Hull, HU19 2BZ
*Activities:* Raising of poultry
*Shareholders:* Thomas Christopher Kirkwood; Christopher Derick Kirkwood
*Officers:* Beverley Brookes, Secretary; Christopher Derick Kirkwood [1952] Director; Thomas Christopher Kirkwood [1985] Director/Farmer

**Kadmous Holdings (UK) Limited.**
*Incorporated:* 30 May 1985 *Employees:* 176
*Net Worth:* £1,964,017 *Total Assets:* £6,183,145
*Registered Office:* Horndale Avenue, Aycliffe Industrial Estate, Newton Aycliffe, Co Durham, DL5 6DW
*Activities:* Other manufacturing n.e.c.
*Officers:* Walid El Hage, Secretary; Walid El-Hage [1968] Director/Engineer

**A Kahn Design Limited**
*Incorporated:* 17 August 1998 *Employees:* 30
*Net Worth:* £1,692,687 *Total Assets:* £3,007,146
*Registered Office:* 240 Canal Road, Bradford, BD1 4SX
*Activities:* Wholesale trade of motor vehicle parts and accessories
*Parent:* Kahn Landmark Limited
*Officers:* Jamshed Khan, Secretary; Afzal Kahn [1969] Director/Manufacturing

**Kahn Landmark Limited**
*Incorporated:* 28 February 2000 *Employees:* 3
*Net Worth:* £272,445 *Total Assets:* £4,135,737
*Registered Office:* 240 Canal Road, Bradford, BD1 4SX
*Activities:* Activities of head offices
*Shareholders:* Afzal Kahn; Jamshaid Khan
*Officers:* Jamshaid Khan, Secretary; Afzal Kahn [1969] Director; Jamshaid Kahn [1970] Director/Company Secretary

**Kalon Investment Company Limited**
*Incorporated:* 30 November 1993
*Net Worth:* £11,208,000 *Total Assets:* £160,000,000
*Registered Office:* c/o PPG Architectural Coatings UK Ltd, Huddersfield Road, Birstall, Batley, W Yorks, WF17 9XA
*Activities:* Activities of head offices
*Parent:* SigmaKalon UK Holding Limited
*Officers:* Jason Paul Metcalf [1973] Marketing Director; Felicity Anne Parry [1967] Finance Director; Steven Pocock [1962] Director/General Manager

**Kanika Limited**
*Incorporated:* 20 July 2005
*Net Worth:* £1 *Total Assets:* £5,376,860
*Registered Office:* Swalesmoor Farm, Swalesmoor Road, Halifax, W Yorks, HX3 6UF
*Activities:* Other business support service activities n.e.c.
*Parent:* Leo Group Ltd
*Officers:* Joanne Sawrij, Secretary; Danny Steven Sawrij [1969] Director/Farmer

**Kankku (Holdings) Limited**
*Incorporated:* 7 March 2014
*Net Worth:* £3,120,400 *Total Assets:* £3,587,770
*Registered Office:* Victoria Forge, Victoria Street, Windermere, Cumbria, LA23 1AD
*Activities:* Other letting and operating of own or leased real estate
*Shareholder:* Nicholas Jonathan Fieldhouse
*Officers:* Nicholas Jonathan Fieldhouse [1974] Director/Car Sales

**Kapil Care Homes Limited**
*Incorporated:* 17 January 1985 *Employees:* 118
*Net Worth:* £1,927,706 *Total Assets:* £5,688,672
*Registered Office:* Old Barn, Burringham Road, Scunthorpe, N Lincs, DN17 2AA
*Activities:* Residential care activities for the elderly and disabled
*Shareholder:* Sunil Prakash Kapil
*Officers:* Sunil Prakash Kapil [1966] Director

**Karman Ltd**
*Incorporated:* 9 October 2007 *Employees:* 2
*Net Worth:* £423,961 *Total Assets:* £3,691,680
*Registered Office:* First Floor Offices, County House, Dunswell Road, Cottingham, E Yorks, HU16 4JT
*Activities:* Buying and selling of own real estate
*Shareholder:* Karen Julie Griffin
*Officers:* Nigel Robert Griffin, Secretary/Director; Karen Julie Griffin [1957] Director; Nigel Robert Griffin [1953] Director

**Karro Food Frozen Limited**
*Incorporated:* 24 July 2014 *Employees:* 302
*Net Worth:* £11,913,000 *Total Assets:* £21,787,000
*Registered Office:* c/o Karro Food Frozen Limited, Hugden Way, Norton Grove Industrial Estate, Norton, Malton, N Yorks, YO17 9HG
*Activities:* Processing and preserving of meat
*Parent:* Karro Food Group Limited
*Officers:* Seamus Carr [1960] Managing Director [Irish]; Michael Kamiel Jan Alfons Kestemont [1978] Director [Belgian]; Diane Susan Walker [1972] Director

**Karro Food Group Limited**
*Incorporated:* 29 November 2012 *Employees:* 1
*Net Worth Deficit:* £4,900,000 *Total Assets:* £11,200,000
*Registered Office:* Hugden Way, Norton Grove Industrial Estate, Norton, Malton, N Yorks, YO17 9HG
*Activities:* Activities of production holding companies
*Parent:* Element UK Bidco Limited
*Officers:* Seamus Carr [1960] Director [Irish]; Stephen Paul Ellis [1971] Director; Michael Kamiel Jan Alfons Kestemont [1978] Director [Belgian]; Diane Susan Walker [1972] Director

**Kass Bathroom Products Limited**
*Incorporated:* 24 November 2005
*Net Worth:* £678,826 *Total Assets:* £3,650,768
*Registered Office:* Akroyd House, Akroyd Place, Halifax, W Yorks, HX1 1YH
*Activities:* Other manufacturing n.e.c.
*Shareholder:* James Christopher Casey
*Officers:* Beverley Ann Casey [1977] Director; James Christopher Casey [1980] Director; Katherine Ann Delaney [1962] Director; Paul Delaney [1960] Director/Bathroom Distributor

**Kastronix Limited**
*Incorporated:* 8 December 2005 *Employees:* 9
*Net Worth:* £2,558,750 *Total Assets:* £3,126,226
*Registered Office:* Unit 6 Stoneacres, Grimbald Crag Close, St James Business Park, Knaresborough, N Yorks, HG5 8PJ
*Activities:* Agents involved in the sale of a variety of goods
*Major Shareholder:* Shaun Winstanley
*Officers:* Shaun Winstanley [1969] Managing Director

**Katell Limited**
*Incorporated:* 2 August 2001 *Employees:* 66
*Net Worth:* £1,501,688 *Total Assets:* £3,396,543
*Registered Office:* 478-480 Durham Way North, Aycliffe Industrial Park, Newton Aycliffe, Co Durham, DL5 6HP
*Activities:* Manufacture of other furniture
*Parent:* Charlton & Jenrick Ltd
*Officers:* Andrew John Hurworth, Secretary; Stuart Clark Bailey [1962] Director/Production; Karl Stephen Baines [1973] Sales Director; Barry George Charlton [1946] Director; Andrew John Hurworth [1966] Director/Accountant; William John Jenrick [1940] Director

**Kautex Textron (UK) Limited**
*Incorporated:* 30 March 1988 *Employees:* 179
*Net Worth:* £29,852,000 *Total Assets:* £42,202,000
*Registered Office:* Headlands Road, Liversedge, W Yorks, WF15 6QA
*Activities:* Manufacture of other plastic products
*Parent:* Textron Limited
*Officers:* Natalia Fernanda Rojas-Mera, Secretary; John Michael Ingham [1973] Director/Plant Manager; Javier Perez Pascual [1977] Director/Chief Financial Officer [Spanish]; Jorg Rautenstrauch [1967] Director/President and CEO [German]

**Kaver Limited**
*Incorporated:* 25 March 2011
*Net Worth:* £2,987,800 *Total Assets:* £3,275,567
*Registered Office:* P O Box 55, Eva Lett House, 1 South Crescent, Ripon, N Yorks, HG4 1XW
*Activities:* Activities of other holding companies n.e.c.
*Shareholders:* Graham Mark Pears; Lisa Ann Hunt
*Officers:* Lisa Ann Hunt [1979] Director; Graham Mark Pears [1985] Director

**Kaye Aluminium (Holdings) Limited**
*Incorporated:* 12 May 2004 *Employees:* 234
*Net Worth:* £26,103,040 *Total Assets:* £47,727,748
*Registered Office:* Ogden Road, Wheatley Hills, Doncaster, S Yorks, DN2 4SG
*Activities:* Manufacture of other fabricated metal products n.e.c.
*Officers:* Belen Arias Rubiales, Secretary; Felipe Quinta Marino [1979] Director [Spanish]; Fernando Quinta Marino [1970] Director [Spanish]

**Kaye's Hotels Limited**
*Incorporated:* 10 May 1990 *Employees:* 130
*Net Worth:* £7,381,195 *Total Assets:* £11,197,836
*Registered Office:* Waterton Park Hotel, Walton Hall, Walton, Wakefield, W Yorks, WF2 6PW
*Activities:* Hotels and similar accommodation
*Officers:* Deidre Kaye, Secretary; David Kaye [1942] Director; Deidre Kaye [1947] Director; Tony Stephen Kaye [1964] Director; Debbie Samantha Taylor [1969] Director

**KCA Deutag (Land Rig) Limited**
*Incorporated:* 20 December 2005
*Previous:* Land Rig SPV Limited
*Net Worth:* £3,812,442 *Total Assets:* £3,885,840
*Registered Office:* 1 Park Row, Leeds, LS1 5AB
*Activities:* Extraction of crude petroleum
*Parent:* Abbot Group Limited
*Officers:* Anthony Joseph Byrne [1976] Director/General Counsel; Neil Porteous Gilchrist [1967] Director/Chief Financial Officer; Gary Neil Paver [1967] Director/Senior Vice President Finance

**KCA Deutag Alpha II Limited**
*Incorporated:* 21 February 2008
*Net Worth:* £82,051,680 *Total Assets:* £722,623,808
*Registered Office:* 1 Park Row, Leeds, LS1 5AB
*Activities:* Other business support service activities n.e.c.
*Parent:* KCAD Holdings II Limited
*Officers:* Anthony Joseph Byrne, Secretary; Abdulla Nasser Ahmed Huwaileel Al Mansoori [1949] Director/Chairman [Emirati]; Sheikh Salah Abdelhadi Abdullah Al Qahtani [1969] Director/Vice Chairman [Saudi Arabian]; Robert Keith Ellis [1951] Director; Vahid Farzad [1976] Director/Senior VP; Neil Porteous Gilchrist [1967] Director; John Combothekras Halsted [1964] Director/Investment Manager [American]; Markku Juhani Lonnqvist [1972] Director/Partner [Finnish]; Norrie Andrew McKay [1959] Director; Dean Edward John Merritt [1967] Director; David P. Trucano [1970] Director [American]

**KCA Deutag Alpha Limited**
*Incorporated:* 21 November 2007 *Employees:* 6,117
*Net Worth Deficit:* £40,493,468 *Total Assets:* £1,400,145,152
*Registered Office:* 1 Park Row, Leeds, LS1 5AB
*Activities:* Extraction of crude petroleum
*Parent:* KCA Deutag Alpha II Limited
*Officers:* Anthony Joseph Byrne, Secretary; Abdulla Nasser Ahmed Huwaileel Al Mansoori [1949] Director/Chairman [Emirati]; Sheikh Salah Abdelhadi Abdullah Al Qahtani [1969] Director/Vice Chairman [Saudi Arabian]; Robert Keith Ellis [1951] Director/Management Consultant; Vahid Farzad [1976] Director/Senior VP; Neil Porteous Gilchrist [1967] Director; John Combothekras Halsted [1964] Director/Investment Manager [American]; Markku Juhani Lonnqvist [1972] Director/Partner [Finnish]; Norrie Andrew McKay [1959] Director; Dean Edward John Merritt [1967] Director; David P. Trucano [1970] Director [American]

**KCA Deutag Drilling Group Limited**
*Incorporated:* 29 June 1972
*Net Worth:* £157,212,992 *Total Assets:* £224,063,008
*Registered Office:* 1 Park Row, Leeds, LS1 5AB
*Activities:* Extraction of crude petroleum
*Parent:* Abbot Holdings Limited
*Officers:* Anthony Joseph Byrne [1976] Director/General Counsel; Neil Porteous Gilchrist [1967] Director/Chief Financial Officer; Norrie Andrew McKay [1959] Director/Chief Executive Officer; Gary Neil Paver [1967] Director/SVP - Finance

**KCA Deutag Enterprises Limited**
*Incorporated:* 3 October 2008 *Employees:* 122
*Net Worth Deficit:* £2,993,898 *Total Assets:* £3,749,780
*Registered Office:* 1 Park Row, Leeds, LS1 5AB
*Activities:* Extraction of crude petroleum
*Parent:* Abbot Group Limited
*Officers:* Anthony Joseph Byrne [1976] Director/General Counsel; Gary Neil Paver [1967] Director/Senior Vice President Finance

**KCA Deutag UK Finance PLC**
*Incorporated:* 28 April 2014
*Net Worth:* £5,544,993 *Total Assets:* £673,424,512
*Registered Office:* 1 Park Row, Leeds, LS1 5AB
*Activities:* Other business support service activities n.e.c.
*Parent:* Abbot Group Limited
*Officers:* Anthony Joseph Byrne, Secretary; Anthony Joseph Byrne [1976] Director/Group General Counsel; Neil Porteous Gilchrist [1967] Director/Chief Financial Officer; Gary Neil Paver [1967] Director/SVP - Finance

**KCA European Holdings Limited**
*Incorporated:* 13 September 2001
*Net Worth:* £57,323,000 *Total Assets:* £105,903,000
*Registered Office:* 1 Park Row, Leeds, LS1 5AB
*Activities:* Other business support service activities n.e.c.
*Parent:* KCA Deutag Drilling Group Limited
*Officers:* Anthony Joseph Byrne [1976] Director/General Counsel; Neil Porteous Gilchrist [1967] Director/Chief Financial Officer; Gary Neil Paver [1967] Director/Senior Vice President Finance

**KCAD Holdings I Limited**
*Incorporated:* 8 March 2011 *Employees:* 6,117
*Net Worth Deficit:* £130,335,640 *Total Assets:* £1,129,836,800
*Registered Office:* 1 Park Row, Leeds, LS1 5AB
*Activities:* Other business support service activities n.e.c.
*Shareholder:* Alexander Knaster
*Officers:* Anthony Joseph Byrne, Secretary; Abdulla Nasser Ahmed Huwaileel Al Mansoori [1949] Director/Chairman [Emirati]; Sheikh Salah Abdelhadi Abdullah Al Qahtani [1969] Director/Vice Chairman [Saudi Arabian]; Robert Keith Ellis [1951] Director; Vahid Farzad [1976] Director/Senior VP; John Combothekras Halsted [1964] Director/Investment Manager [American]; Markku Juhani Lonnqvist [1972] Director/Partner [Finnish]; Norrie Andrew McKay [1959] Director; Dean Edward John Merritt [1967] Director; David P. Trucano [1970] Director [American]

**KCAD Holdings II Limited**
*Incorporated:* 8 March 2011
*Net Worth:* £270,975,072 *Total Assets:* £799,920,000
*Registered Office:* 1 Park Row, Leeds, LS1 5AB
*Activities:* Extraction of crude petroleum
*Parent:* KCAD Holdings I Limited
*Officers:* Anthony Joseph Byrne, Secretary; Abdulla Nasser Ahmed Huwaileel Al Mansoori [1949] Director/Chairman [Emirati]; Sheikh Salah Abdelhadi Abdullah Al Qahtani [1969] Director/Vice Chairman [Saudi Arabian]; Robert Keith Ellis [1951] Director; Vahid Farzad [1976] Director/Senior VP; John Combothekras Halsted [1964] Director/Investment Manager [American]; Markku Juhani Lonnqvist [1972] Director/President [Finnish]; Noirman Andrew McKay [1959] Director; Dean Edward John Merritt [1967] Director; David P. Trucano [1970] Director [American]

**KCH (Holdings) Limited**
*Incorporated:* 30 January 2007 *Employees:* 1,574
*Net Worth:* £43,316,000 *Total Assets:* £155,716,992
*Registered Office:* 37 Carr Lane, Hull, HU1 3RE
*Activities:* Activities of head offices
*Parent:* KCOM Group PLC
*Officers:* Sarah Elizabeth Jones, Secretary; Anna Catherine Bielby [1978] Director/Chief Financial Officer; Graham Sutherland [1963] Director/Chief Executive

**KCOM Group Public Limited Company**
*Incorporated:* 21 July 1987
*Net Worth:* £101,193,000 *Total Assets:* £286,041,984
*Registered Office:* 37 Carr Lane, Hull, HU1 3RE
*Activities:* Other telecommunications activities
*Officers:* Sarah Elizabeth Jones, Secretary; Elizabeth Marian Barber [1965] Director/Chartered Accountant; Anna Catherine Bielby [1978] Director/Chartered Accountant; Patrick Jean-Marie de Smedt [1955] Director [Belgian]; Peter Labreque Smith [1958] Director/Consultant; Graham Sutherland [1963] Director/Chief Executive

**KCOM Holdings Limited**
*Incorporated:* 13 February 1997
*Previous:* Kingston Communications Limited
*Net Worth:* £117,366,000 *Total Assets:* £326,521,984
*Registered Office:* 37 Carr Lane, Hull, HU1 3RE
*Activities:* Other telecommunications activities
*Parent:* KCH (Holdings) Limited
*Officers:* Sarah Elizabeth Jones, Secretary; Anna Catherine Bielby [1978] Director/Chief Financial Officer; Graham Sutherland [1963] Director/Chief Executive

**KCOM International Limited**
*Incorporated:* 28 November 1990
*Previous:* Kingston Communications International Limited
*Net Worth:* £15,000,002 *Total Assets:* £15,150,002
*Registered Office:* 37 Carr Lane, Hull, HU1 3RE
*Activities:* Dormant company
*Parent:* KCH (Holdings) Limited
*Officers:* Sarah Elizabeth Jones, Secretary; Anna Catherine Bielby [1978] Director/Chief Financial Officer; Graham Sutherland [1963] Director/Chief Executive

**Keadby Generation Limited**
*Incorporated:* 8 July 1992 *Employees:* 181
*Net Worth Deficit:* £273,500,000 *Total Assets:* £183,900,000
*Registered Office:* Keadby Power Station, Trentside, Keadby, Scunthorpe, N Lincs, DN17 3EF
*Activities:* Production of electricity
*Parent:* SSE Generation Limited
*Officers:* Sally Fairbairn, Secretary; Mark Richard Hayward [1963] Director/Manager; James Isaac Smith [1962] Director/Engineer

**Keelham Farm Shop Limited**
*Incorporated:* 9 September 2008 *Employees:* 323
*Net Worth:* £1,356,771 *Total Assets:* £9,001,236
*Registered Office:* 21 Gargrave Road, Skipton, N Yorks, BD23 1UD
*Activities:* Retail sale in non-specialised stores with food, beverages or tobacco predominating
*Major Shareholder:* Victoria Jane Robertshaw
*Officers:* Gerard Scot Downes [1967] Director; Victoria Jane Robertshaw [1969] Director

**Keep Your Trap Shut Limited**
*Incorporated:* 17 March 2014
*Net Worth:* £756,978 *Total Assets:* £4,568,500
*Registered Office:* Highfield Grange, Bubwith, Selby, N Yorks, YO8 6DP
*Activities:* Motion picture production activities
*Officers:* Alan Richard Latham [1960] Director/Producer

**Keepflying LLP**
*Incorporated:* 27 June 2008 *Employees:* 3
*Net Worth:* £5,922,161 *Total Assets:* £5,972,016
*Registered Office:* Courtfield, St James Drive, Harrogate, N Yorks, HG2 8HT
*Officers:* Elizabeth Bramall [1944] Member; Terence George Bramall [1942] Member

**Keepmoat Homes Limited**
*Incorporated:* 22 December 1987 *Employees:* 968
*Net Worth:* £109,364,000 *Total Assets:* £452,708,000
*Registered Office:* Keepmoat, The Waterfront, Lakeside Boulevard, Doncaster, S Yorks, DN4 5PL
*Activities:* Construction of domestic buildings
*Parent:* Keepmoat Limited
*Officers:* Lyn Michelle Charters, Secretary; Timothy Mark Beale [1976] Director; Mark Richard Priest [1966] Director; James Michael Douglas Thomson [1966] Director

**Keepmoat Limited**
*Incorporated:* 12 March 1986 *Employees:* 1,098
*Net Worth:* £181,755,008 *Total Assets:* £538,776,000
*Registered Office:* Keepmoat, The Waterfront, Lakeside Boulevard, Doncaster, S Yorks, DN4 5PL
*Activities:* Activities of head offices
*Parent:* Castle 1 Limited
*Officers:* Lyn Michelle Charters, Secretary; Timothy Mark Beale [1976] Director; Mark Richard Priest [1966] Director; James Michael Douglas Thomson [1966] Director

**Keigar Homes Limited**
*Incorporated:* 18 January 1979 *Employees:* 57
*Net Worth:* £21,946,888 *Total Assets:* £29,528,278
*Registered Office:* Keigar Lodge, Canberra View, Barton upon Humber, N Lincs, DN18 5GR
*Activities:* Construction of domestic buildings
*Shareholders:* Garry William Whall; Patricia Wendy Whall
*Officers:* Garry William Whall, Secretary; Bradley Warren Whall [1987] Operations Director; Garry William Whall [1960] Director; Nathan William Whall [1984] Sales Director; Patricia Wendy Whall [1960] Director Bookkeeper

**Keighley & District Travel Limited**
*Incorporated:* 20 March 1987 *Employees:* 277
*Net Worth:* £1,422,000 *Total Assets:* £3,375,000
*Registered Office:* Prospect Park, Broughton Way, Starbeck, Harrogate, N Yorks, HG2 7NY
*Activities:* Other passenger land transport
*Parent:* Transdev Blazefield Limited
*Officers:* Alex Lloyd Hornby [1981] Managing Director; Gordon Duncan Irvine [1957] Engineering Director; Seth King [1971] Finance Director

**Keighley and Worth Valley Light Railway Limited**
*Incorporated:* 8 February 1966 *Employees:* 13
*Net Worth:* £385,292 *Total Assets:* £3,633,069
*Registered Office:* The Railway Station, Haworth, Keighley, W Yorks, BD22 8NJ
*Activities:* Passenger rail transport, interurban
*Parent:* Keighley and Worth Valley Railway Preservation Society Ltd
*Officers:* Michael Peter Curtis, Secretary/Computer Analyst; William Nicholas Bennett [1954] Director/Retired Software Engineer; Stuart Bray [1953] Director/Retired; Andy Carter [1967] Director/Railway Driver; Mark Anthony Collinson [1964] Director/Electrical Technician; Peter Eastham [1949] Director/School Teacher; Ross Robert Malcolm Graham [1947] Director/Retired Army Officer; Robert Hustwick [1958] Director/Rail Vehicle Interface Engineer; Christopher Dobson Jowett [1954] Director/Retired; Mark Moorehead [1979] Director/Signalman Examiner; John Reddyhoff [1956] Director/Mechanical Engineer; Philip Shackleton [1948] Director/Retired Teacher; Roger William Wood [1946] Director/Retired

**Keighley and Worth Valley Railway Preservation Society Limited**
*Incorporated:* 26 January 2010 *Employees:* 13
*Net Worth:* £4,790,442 *Total Assets:* £5,042,886
*Registered Office:* The Railway Station, Station Road, Haworth, Keighley, W Yorks, BD22 8NJ
*Activities:* Operation of historical sites and buildings and similar visitor attractions
*Officers:* Michael Peter Curtis, Secretary; Philip Balmforth [1950] Director/Retired Police Officer; William Nicholas Bennett [1954] Director/Retired Software Engineer; William Harper Black [1931] Director/Retired; Peter Eastham [1949] Director/Retired; Matthew Fennell [1982] Director/Railway Operator; Robert Malcolm Ross Graham [1947] Director/Retired; Steven Richard Harris [1952] Director/Retired; Robin Higgins [1944] Director/Retired; John Hoyle [1948] Director/Retired Railway Employee; Robert Hustwick [1958] Director/Engineer; Philip Lawton [1952] Director/Retired Contracts Manager; Tom Ruddock [1992] Director/Teacher; Martin Andrew Shaw [1954] Director/Chartered Accountant; Christopher Graham Smyth [1944] Director/Retired; Dr Matthew John Stroh [1971] Director/Chartered Accountant; Michael Tarran [1942] Director/Retired; Jacqueline Ann Warburton [1959] Director/Retired Nurse

**Keighley Fleece Mills Company Limited**
*Incorporated:* 14 August 1865 *Employees:* 1
*Net Worth:* £4,706,446 *Total Assets:* £6,721,422
*Registered Office:* Old Mills, Moor Top, Drighlington, Bradford, W Yorks, BD11 1BY
*Activities:* Buying and selling of own real estate
*Officers:* Kathryn Davenport, Secretary; Peter Jan Patrik Valentin Gyllenhammar [1953] Director [Swedish]

**Keighley Laboratories,Limited**
*Incorporated:* 4 March 1920 *Employees:* 59
*Net Worth:* £2,442,712 *Total Assets:* £3,154,733
*Registered Office:* Croft House, South Street, Keighley, W Yorks, BD21 1EG
*Activities:* Treatment and coating of metals
*Parent:* Keighley Laboratories Group Ltd
*Officers:* Debbie Jean Mellor, Secretary; Keith Blower [1948] Director; Debbie Jean Mellor [1970] Director; Matthew Robert Mellor [1972] Director/Metallurgist; David Wright [1962] Director/Heat Treatment Specialist

**D.M.Keith Limited**
*Incorporated:* 6 February 1963 *Employees:* 241
*Net Worth:* £7,654,985 *Total Assets:* £27,996,794
*Registered Office:* Stourton Motor Centre, Thwaite Gate, Hunslet, Leeds, LS10 1DY
*Activities:* Sale of new cars and light motor vehicles
*Shareholders:* Dougal MacDonald Keith; Angus MacDonald Keith
*Officers:* Margaret Elisabeth Keith, Secretary; Angus MacDonald Keith [1965] Director; Dougal MacDonald Keith [1963] Director

**The Kej LLP**
*Incorporated:* 7 January 2004
*Net Worth:* £2,221,710 *Total Assets:* £6,713,246
*Registered Office:* Elizabeth House, 13-19 Queen Street, Leeds, LS1 2TW
*Officers:* Karen Elizabeth Commons [1966] Member; Kenneth Ernest Davy [1941] Member; Michelle Jayne Hare [1978] Member

**Kelda Eurobond Co Limited**
*Incorporated:* 21 November 2007 *Employees:* 3,773
*Net Worth:* £157,300,000 *Total Assets:* £9,855,200,256
*Registered Office:* Western House, Halifax Road, Bradford, W Yorks, BD6 2SZ
*Activities:* Financial intermediation not elsewhere classified
*Officers:* Kathy Smith, Secretary; Scott Auty [1978] Director/Fund Manager; Elizabeth Marian Barber [1965] Director/Accountant; Paul Johnstone Barr [1979] Director; Simon Daniel Beer [1980] Director/Asset Manager; Vicky Chan [1983] Director/Financier; Andrew James Dench [1969] Director; Richard David Flint [1968] Director; Mark Edwin Lorkin [1976] Managing Director [British/Australian]; Aparna Narain [1985] Director/Asset Management; Michael Peter Francis Osborne [1980] Director; Anthony Leon Philip Rabin [1955] Director

**Kelda Finance (No.1) Limited**
*Incorporated:* 11 May 2012 *Employees:* 2,681
*Net Worth:* £891,299,968 *Total Assets:* £9,222,899,712
*Registered Office:* Western House, Halifax Road, Bradford, BD6 2SZ
*Activities:* Financial management
*Parent:* Kelda Group Limited
*Officers:* Kathy Smith, Secretary; Elizabeth Marian Barber [1965] Director; Richard David Flint [1968] Director/Chief Executive; Kathy Olivia Helen Smith [1974] Director/Company Secretary

**Kelda Finance (No.2) Limited**
*Incorporated:* 16 May 2012
*Net Worth:* £520,830,016 *Total Assets:* £977,777,024
*Registered Office:* Western House, Halifax Road, Bradford, BD6 2SZ
*Activities:* Financial management
*Parent:* Kelda Finance (No. 1) Limited
*Officers:* Kathy Smith, Secretary; Elizabeth Marian Barber [1965] Director; Richard David Flint [1968] Director/Chief Executive; Kathy Olivia Helen Smith [1974] Director/Company Secretary

**Kelda Finance (No.3) PLC**
*Incorporated:* 26 October 2012
*Net Worth Deficit:* £2,595,000 *Total Assets:* £199,023,008
*Registered Office:* Western House, Halifax Road, Bradford, BD6 2SZ
*Activities:* Financial management
*Parent:* Kelda Finance (No. 2) Limited
*Officers:* Kathy Smith, Secretary; Elizabeth Marian Barber [1965] Director; Richard David Flint [1968] Director/Chief Executive; Raymond O'Toole [1955] Director/Engineer; Anthony Leon Philip Rabin [1955] Director; Kathy Olivia Helen Smith [1974] Director/Company Secretary

**Kelda Group Limited**
*Incorporated:* 1 April 1989 *Employees:* 101
*Net Worth:* £970,902,976 *Total Assets:* £1,011,601,024
*Registered Office:* Western House, Halifax Road, Bradford, W Yorks, BD6 2SZ
*Activities:* Water collection, treatment and supply
*Parent:* Kelda Eurobond Co Limited
*Officers:* Kathy Smith, Secretary; Elizabeth Marian Barber [1965] Director/Accountant; Richard David Flint [1968] Director; Kathy Olivia Helen Smith [1974] Director/Company Secretary

**Kelda Non-Reg Holdco Limited**
*Incorporated:* 21 November 2007
*Net Worth:* £10,038,000 *Total Assets:* £23,010,000
*Registered Office:* Western House, Halifax Road, Bradford, W Yorks, BD6 2SZ
*Activities:* Financial intermediation not elsewhere classified
*Parent:* Kelda Eurobond Co Limited
*Officers:* Kathy Smith, Secretary; Elizabeth Marian Barber [1965] Director/Accountant; Richard David Flint [1968] Director; Kathy Olivia Helen Smith [1974] Director/Company Secretary

**Kelda Water Services Limited**
*Incorporated:* 19 October 1987 *Employees:* 9
*Net Worth:* £9,864,000 *Total Assets:* £22,260,000
*Registered Office:* Western House, Halifax Road, Bradford, W Yorks, BD6 2SZ
*Activities:* Other business support service activities n.e.c.
*Parent:* Kelda Group Limited
*Officers:* Angela Wendy Miriam White, Secretary; Elizabeth Marian Barber [1965] Director/Accountant; Charles Stewart Haysom [1957] Director/Civil Engineer; Benjamin Paul Raistrick [1979] Director/Commercial Manager

**Kelkay Limited**
*Incorporated:* 18 May 2001 *Employees:* 93
*Net Worth:* £10,872,375 *Total Assets:* £15,376,045
*Registered Office:* The Old Airfield, Heck and Pollington Lane, Pollington, E Yorks, DN14 0BA
*Activities:* Non-specialised wholesale trade
*Parent:* Altia Holdings Limited
*Officers:* Anthony Neil Harker [1969] Managing Director; Brian Gerard Harris [1969] Director/SVP, CFO [American]; Robert John Hewitt [1956] Director; Simon Andrew Hupfeld [1976] Director [Australian]; Robert Francis Mehmel [1962] Director/Business Executive [American]; Richard Pyrah [1970] Director/Sales Manager; Jonathan Wilson [1963] Operations Director

**Kelling Midco Limited**
*Incorporated:* 2 June 2014 *Employees:* 108,242
*Previous:* Aghoco 1230 Limited
*Net Worth:* £12,330 *Total Assets:* £25,814,216
*Registered Office:* Unit F, Trident Park, Rosie Road, Normanton, W Yorks, WF6 1ZB
*Activities:* Activities of head offices
*Parent:* Kelling Group Limited
*Officers:* Jonathan Simon Battersby [1964] Director; John Brad Wood [1976] Director

**Kelling Property Limited**
*Incorporated:* 2 June 2014 *Employees:* 76
*Previous:* Kelling Group Limited
*Net Worth:* £3,948,000 *Total Assets:* £55,245,000
*Registered Office:* Unit F, Trident Park, Rosie Road, Normanton, W Yorks, WF6 1ZB
*Activities:* Activities of head offices
*Parent:* Skye Bidco Limited
*Officers:* Jonathan Simon Battersby [1964] Director; John Brad Wood [1976] Director

**Kemira Chemicals (UK) Limited**
*Incorporated:* 7 June 1967 *Employees:* 167
*Net Worth:* £13,320,000 *Total Assets:* £43,831,000
*Registered Office:* Bowling Park Drive, West Bowling, Bradford, W Yorks, BD4 7TT
*Activities:* Manufacture of other chemical products n.e.c.
*Officers:* Linda Christine Crossland, Secretary; David John Normington [1972] Director Product Management; Anders Fredrik Nyren [1969] Director Sales [Swedish]; Elaine Wharton [1964] Director/Senior Manager Human Resources EMEA West

**Rory Kemp Limited**
*Incorporated:* 24 August 1965 *Employees:* 4
*Net Worth:* £1,773,503 *Total Assets:* £4,195,179
*Registered Office:* Glebe Farm, Barton-le-Street, Malton, N Yorks, YO17 0PP
*Activities:* Growing of cereals (except rice), leguminous crops and oil seeds
*Major Shareholder:* Nicholas Rory Kemp
*Officers:* Nicholas Rory Kemp, Secretary; Nicholas Rory Kemp [1962] Director/Farmer

**The Kendal Brewery Arts Centre Trust Limited**
*Incorporated:* 16 February 2000 *Employees:* 51
*Net Worth:* £2,714,950 *Total Assets:* £3,185,556
*Registered Office:* The Brewery, Highgate, Kendal, Cumbria, LA9 4HE
*Activities:* Operation of arts facilities
*Officers:* Michael Paul Jones, Secretary; Terence Richard Clarke [1950] Director/Retired; Michael Paul Jones [1966] Director/Arts Manager; Abigail Lawson [1995] Director/Actor; Susannah Claire Hall Poole [1975] Director/Fashion Designer; Antony John Preedy [1970] Director; David Lee Stevens [1960] Director/Retired; Michael Ransome Sumsion [1968] Director/Lecturer; Claire Elizabeth Welburn [1977] Director/Cultural Manager; Philip Lawrence Whitehurst [1960] Director/Management Consultant; Pauline Yarwood [1947] Director

**Kendal Caravans Limited**
*Incorporated:* 5 May 1988 *Employees:* 38
*Net Worth:* £2,902,904 *Total Assets:* £8,836,437
*Registered Office:* Selside, Kendal, Cumbria, LA8 9LF
*Activities:* Sale of other motor vehicles
*Officers:* Julia Margaret Molyneaux, Secretary; Mark Molyneaux, Secretary; David Stephen Molyneaux [1946] Director/Business Consultant; Julia Margaret Molyneaux [1948] Director/Business Consultant; Mark Molyneaux [1968] Managing Director

**Kendal Nutricare Ltd**
*Incorporated:* 15 January 2015 *Employees:* 113
*Net Worth Deficit:* £1,417,903 *Total Assets:* £5,858,630
*Registered Office:* Mint Bridge Road, Kendal, Cumbria, LA9 6NL
*Activities:* Manufacture of other milk products
*Major Shareholder:* Ross Anthony McMahon
*Officers:* Ross Anthony McMahon [1964] Director/Food Consultant [Irish]

**R. Kendall Limited**
*Incorporated:* 7 September 2016
*Net Worth:* £8,756,969 *Total Assets:* £9,620,688
*Registered Office:* Little Wauldby Farm, Swanland Dale, Swanland, North Ferriby, E Yorks, HU14 3RA
*Activities:* Mixed farming
*Major Shareholder:* Robert Kendall
*Officers:* Robert Kendall [1956] Director/Farmer

**C.G. Kendall Limited**
*Incorporated:* 8 September 2016 *Employees:* 4
*Net Worth:* £8,556,005 *Total Assets:* £8,712,120
*Registered Office:* Arras Farm, Arras, Sancton, York, YO43 4RN
*Activities:* Mixed farming
*Major Shareholder:* Christopher Gordon Kendall

**P & B Kennedy Holdings Limited**
*Incorporated:* 14 June 1995 *Employees:* 214
*Net Worth:* £3,700,883 *Total Assets:* £6,356,910
*Registered Office:* Herncliffe, Spring Gardens Lane, Keighley, W Yorks, BD20 6LH
*Activities:* Residential nursing care facilities
*Officers:* John Kennedy, Secretary; Vivienne Birch [1961] Director of Nursing; John Kennedy [1964] Commercial Director; Simon Kennedy [1962] Director/Medical Doctor/Consultant Anaesthetist; Paul Kennedy Jnr [1965] Director/Police Inspector

**Kennedy Travel (Yorkshire) Limited**
*Incorporated:* 16 August 1977 *Employees:* 57
*Net Worth:* £1,486,665 *Total Assets:* £3,607,680
*Registered Office:* The Kennedy Building, Victoria Road, Leeds, LS11 5AF
*Activities:* Travel agency activities
*Major Shareholder:* Christine Button
*Officers:* Susan Patricia Roberts, Secretary; Ruby May Briggs [1959] Director; Christine Button [1940] Director/Chairman; Jill Christine Button [1960] Director; Susan Patricia Roberts [1956] Director/Financial Controller

**Kentmere Limited**
*Incorporated:* 2 March 1906 *Employees:* 52
*Net Worth:* £6,079,362 *Total Assets:* £7,835,726
*Registered Office:* Staveley, Kendal, Cumbria, LA8 9PB
*Activities:* Manufacture of other paper and paperboard containers
*Officers:* Stephen William Hoyle, Secretary; Robert Holme Barker [1944] Director/Chartered Accountant; Nicholas Bramfitt [1972] Director/Factory Manager; Christopher John Chambers [1947] Director/Chartered Accountant; Penelope Anne Hanks [1952] Director; Stephen William Hoyle [1949] Director/Chartered Accountant; Shaun Patrick Mulvaney [1952] Managing Director

**Kenworth Limited**
*Incorporated:* 9 February 1989 *Employees:* 45
*Net Worth:* £1,070,215 *Total Assets:* £4,398,416
*Registered Office:* Beacon Garage, Catterick Road, Catterick Garrison, N Yorks, DL9 4RZ
*Activities:* Retail sale of automotive fuel in specialised stores
*Major Shareholder:* Barry Stewart Raw
*Officers:* Joan Raw, Secretary/Director Kenworth Ltd; Barry Raw [1954] Director; Joan Raw [1957] Director

**Kepwick Estate Limited**
*Incorporated:* 1 June 2011
*Net Worth:* £11,800,658 *Total Assets:* £12,071,774
*Registered Office:* Kepwick Mill, Kepwick, Thirsk, N Yorks, YO7 4BH
*Activities:* Combined office administrative service activities
*Major Shareholder:* Alexander Digby Guthe
*Officers:* Alexander Digby Guthe [1966] Director

**Kepwick Farms Limited**
*Incorporated:* 1 June 2011
*Net Worth:* £6,345,334 *Total Assets:* £6,358,572
*Registered Office:* Kepwick Mill, Kepwick, Thirsk, N Yorks, YO7 4BH
*Activities:* Other letting and operating of own or leased real estate
*Major Shareholder:* Alexander Digby Guthe
*Officers:* Alexander Digby Guthe [1966] Director

**The Kerfoot Group Limited**
*Incorporated:* 11 June 1980 *Employees:* 120
*Net Worth:* £12,534,682 *Total Assets:* £26,899,852
*Registered Office:* The Olive House, Standard Way Industrial Estate, Darlington Road, Northallerton, N Yorks, DL6 2XA
*Activities:* Manufacture of oils and fats
*Parent:* Avril Pole Vegetal SAS
*Officers:* Alison Rachel Atkins [1971] Director; Sarah Bradley [1974] Director/Chief Executive; Simon Matthew Corner [1979] Commercial Director; Olivier Christophe Marcel Delamea [1969] Director/Chairman [French]; Kim Melanie Newell [1971] Finance Director; Sarah Joanne Stokes [1972] Human Resources Director

**Keston Boilers Limited**
*Incorporated:* 9 April 1998
*Net Worth:* £5,957,000 *Total Assets:* £7,206,000
*Registered Office:* National Avenue, Hull, HU5 4JB
*Activities:* Manufacture of central heating radiators and boilers
*Parent:* ISG Boiler Holdings Ltd
*Officers:* Steven Hairsine, Secretary; Shaun Barry Edwards [1968] Director; Pierre-Louis Andre Francois [1956] Director [French]; Steven Hairsine [1975] Director

**M. Kettlewell (Melmerby) Limited**
*Incorporated:* 3 April 1973 *Employees:* 71
*Net Worth:* £4,980,419 *Total Assets:* £7,295,883
*Registered Office:* Station Depot, Melmerby, Ripon, N Yorks, HG4 5EX
*Activities:* Freight transport by road
*Shareholders:* Paul Robert Kettlewell; Kevin Gordon Kettlewell
*Officers:* Angela Kathleen Kettlewell, Secretary; Angela Kathleen Kettlewell [1957] Director/Company Secretary; Joan Elizabeth Kettlewell [1933] Director/Housewife; Paul Robert Kettlewell [1963] Managing Director; Trevor Malcolm Kettlewell [1961] Sales Director

**Kettlewell Fuels Limited**
*Incorporated:* 26 January 1987 *Employees:* 10
*Net Worth:* £2,071,654 *Total Assets:* £3,466,520
*Registered Office:* Station Depot, Melmerby, Ripon, N Yorks, HG4 5EX
*Activities:* Wholesale of petroleum and petroleum products
*Parent:* M Kettlewell (Melmerby) Ltd
*Officers:* Janet Kettlewell, Secretary; Paul Robert Kettlewell [1963] Director/Haulier; Trevor Malcolm Kettlewell [1961] Director/Oil Distributor

**Kexby Investments Limited**
*Incorporated:* 17 April 2014
*Net Worth:* £6,404,615 *Total Assets:* £6,818,139
*Registered Office:* The Old Vicarage, Kexby, York, YO41 5LA
*Activities:* Activities of venture and development capital companies
*Major Shareholder:* Antony Gerard Mannix
*Officers:* Antony Gerard Mannix [1963] Director; Gina Mannix [1966] Director

**Kexgill (Bradford) Limited**
*Incorporated:* 14 February 2006 *Employees:* 8
*Net Worth:* £3,395,894 *Total Assets:* £11,065,836
*Registered Office:* The Trees, 56 Cottingham Road, Hull, HU6 7RA
*Activities:* Other letting and operating of own or leased real estate
*Officers:* Valerie Fish, Secretary; Michael Hien Sien Lee [1947] Director/Property Manager; Richard Stott [1962] Director/Property Manager

**Kexgill (Construction) Limited**
*Incorporated:* 29 October 2004 *Employees:* 2
*Net Worth Deficit:* £925,604 *Total Assets:* £4,866,866
*Registered Office:* 56 Cottingham Road, Hull, HU6 7RA
*Activities:* Construction of domestic buildings
*Parent:* Kexgill Limited
*Officers:* Valerie Fish, Secretary; Michael Hien Sien Lee [1947] Director/Property Manager; Richard Stott [1962] Managing Director

**Kexgill (Cottingham) 2 Limited**
*Incorporated:* 14 July 2016
*Net Worth:* £2,178,817 *Total Assets:* £16,698,422
*Registered Office:* 56 Cottingham Road, Hull, HU6 7RA
*Activities:* Other letting and operating of own or leased real estate
*Major Shareholder:* Michael Hien Sien Lee
*Officers:* Valerie Fish, Secretary; Michael Lee [1947] Director; Richard Stott [1962] Director

**Kexgill (Durham) Limited**
*Incorporated:* 21 October 2002 *Employees:* 7
*Net Worth:* £2,554,325 *Total Assets:* £7,444,808
*Registered Office:* 56 Cottingham Road, Hull, HU6 7RA
*Activities:* Other letting and operating of own or leased real estate
*Officers:* Valerie Fish, Secretary; Michael Hien Sien Lee [1947] Director; Richard Stott [1962] Director/Chartered Surveyor

**Kexgill (Hull) Limited**
*Incorporated:* 28 April 1995 *Employees:* 2
*Net Worth:* £2,924,143 *Total Assets:* £4,489,505
*Registered Office:* 56 Cottingham Road, Hull, HU6 7RA
*Activities:* Other letting and operating of own or leased real estate
*Officers:* Valerie Fish, Secretary; Michael Hien Sien Lee [1947] Director; Richard Stott [1962] Director/Manager

**Kexgill (Liverpool) Limited**
*Incorporated:* 20 January 1989 *Employees:* 5
*Net Worth:* £9,172,580 *Total Assets:* £14,638,567
*Registered Office:* 56 Cottingham Road, Hull, HU6 7RA
*Activities:* Other letting and operating of own or leased real estate
*Major Shareholder:* Michael Hien Sien Lee
*Officers:* Valerie Fish, Secretary; Michael Hien Sien Lee [1947] Director; Richard Stott [1962] Director/Manager

**Kexgill (Middlesbrough) Limited**
*Incorporated:* 8 June 2001 *Employees:* 9
*Net Worth:* £5,679,582 *Total Assets:* £12,010,203
*Registered Office:* 56 Cottingham Road, Hull, HU6 7RA
*Activities:* Other letting and operating of own or leased real estate
*Officers:* Valerie Fish, Secretary; Michael Hien Sien Lee [1947] Director; Richard Stott [1962] Director/Chartered Surveyor

**Kexgill (Nottingham) Limited**
*Incorporated:* 28 November 2001 *Employees:* 7
*Net Worth:* £4,417,174 *Total Assets:* £10,794,570
*Registered Office:* 56 Cottingham Road, Hull, HU6 7RA
*Activities:* Other letting and operating of own or leased real estate
*Parent:* Kexgill Limited
*Officers:* Valerie Fish, Secretary; Michael Hien Sien Lee [1947] Director; Richard Stott [1962] Director/Chartered Surveyor

**Kexgill (Preston) Limited**
*Incorporated:* 10 December 2001 *Employees:* 8
*Net Worth:* £1,776,793 *Total Assets:* £10,239,568
*Registered Office:* 56 Cottingham Road, Hull, HU6 7RA
*Activities:* Other letting and operating of own or leased real estate
*Parent:* Kexgill Limited
*Officers:* Valerie Fish, Secretary; Michael Hien Sien Lee [1947] Director; Richard Stott [1962] Director/Manager

**Kexgill (Salford) Limited**
*Incorporated:* 13 January 2004 *Employees:* 7
*Net Worth:* £3,248,916 *Total Assets:* £8,434,064
*Registered Office:* 56 Cottingham Road, Hull, HU6 7RA
*Activities:* Other letting and operating of own or leased real estate
*Parent:* Kexgill Limited
*Officers:* Valerie Fish, Secretary; Michael Hien Sien Lee [1947] Director/Property Management; Richard Stott [1962] Director/Manager

**Kexgill (Stockton) Limited**
*Incorporated:* 23 December 2002 *Employees:* 4
*Net Worth:* £1,320,693 *Total Assets:* £7,798,080
*Registered Office:* 56 Cottingham Road, Hull, HU6 7RA
*Activities:* Other letting and operating of own or leased real estate
*Parent:* Kexgill Limited
*Officers:* Valerie Fish, Secretary; Michael Hien Sien Lee [1947] Director; Richard Stott [1962] Director/Manager

**Kexgill Limited**
*Incorporated:* 28 September 1978 *Employees:* 92
*Net Worth:* £45,273,396 *Total Assets:* £131,030,448
*Registered Office:* 56 Cottingham Road, Hull, HU6 7RA
*Activities:* Other letting and operating of own or leased real estate
*Major Shareholder:* Michael Hien Sien Lee
*Officers:* Valerie Fish, Secretary; Michael Hien Sien Lee [1947] Director; Richard Stott [1962] Director/Chartered Surveyor

**Key Electrical Contractors & Storefitters Limited**
*Incorporated:* 29 March 2004 *Employees:* 89
*Net Worth:* £3,503,283 *Total Assets:* £9,025,106
*Registered Office:* First Floor, Rosemount House, Huddersfield Road, Elland, W Yorks, HX5 0EE
*Activities:* Construction of commercial buildings
*Shareholders:* Graham Ingham; Steven Samardzija
*Officers:* Graham Ingham, Secretary; Graham Ingham [1955] Director; Stephen Saddler [1967] Managing Director; Steven Samardzija [1957] Director

**Key Growing Limited**
*Incorporated:* 6 December 1988 *Employees:* 6
*Net Worth:* £3,947,995 *Total Assets:* £9,921,987
*Registered Office:* Kingfisher Court, Plaxton Bridge Road, Woodmansey, Beverley, E Yorks, HU17 0RT
*Activities:* Other letting and operating of own or leased real estate
*Major Shareholder:* Cornelis Jonathan Los
*Officers:* Janet Dale Shaw, Secretary; Cornelis Jonathan Los [1959] Director/Market Gardner

**Keyingham Power Limited**
*Incorporated:* 14 July 2004 *Employees:* 4
*Net Worth:* £5,892,432 *Total Assets:* £13,161,256
*Registered Office:* Mill Nurseries, Ottringham Road, Keyingham, Hull, HU12 9RX
*Activities:* Production of electricity
*Shareholders:* Catharina Audrey Jayne de Lang; David Roy de Lang; Harmanus Gerrit de Lang; Robert Johannes de Lang
*Officers:* Robert Johannes de Lang, Secretary; Catharina Audrey Jayne de Lang [1970] Director/Physiotherapist; David Roy de Lang [1964] Director/Market Gardener; Hermanus Gerrit de Lang [1962] Director/Market Gardener; Robert Johannes de Lang [1968] Director/Market Gardener

**Keyland (Midpoint) Limited**
*Incorporated:* 27 August 1999
*Previous:* Topencounters Limited
*Net Worth Deficit:* £3,000,000 *Total Assets:* £3,592,000
*Registered Office:* Western House, Halifax Road, Bradford, W Yorks, BD6 2SZ
*Activities:* Other business support service activities n.e.c.
*Parent:* Keyland Developments Limited
*Officers:* Angela Wendy Miriam White, Secretary; Charles Edwin Clement [1961] Director/Finance Manager; Peter Garrett [1964] Director/Chartered Surveyor

**Keyland Developments Limited**
*Incorporated:* 19 October 1987 *Employees:* 5
*Net Worth:* £21,566,000 *Total Assets:* £23,295,000
*Registered Office:* Western House, Halifax Road, Bradford, W Yorks, BD6 2SZ
*Activities:* Development of building projects
*Parent:* Kelda Group Limited
*Officers:* Angela Wendy Miriam White, Secretary; Elizabeth Marian Barber [1965] Director/Accountant; Peter Garrett [1964] Director/Chartered Surveyor; Charles Stewart Haysom [1957] Director/Civil Engineer; Nevil George Muncaster [1964] Director/Civil Engineer

**Keyo Agricultural Services Ltd**
*Incorporated:* 19 November 1992 *Employees:* 58
*Net Worth:* £2,392,435 *Total Assets:* £5,305,672
*Registered Office:* Ancholme Business Park, Europa Way, Atherton Way, Brigg, N Lincs, DN20 8AR
*Activities:* Support activities for animal production (other than farm animal boarding)
*Parent:* Keyo Holdings Limited
*Officers:* Gary Baugh, Secretary; Gary Baugh [1965] Director/Contractor to Poultry Industry; Mark Van Den Bos [1956] Technical Director

**Keysterne Limited**
*Incorporated:* 10 April 2002 *Employees:* 2
*Net Worth:* £3,712,256 *Total Assets:* £3,919,797
*Registered Office:* 197 High Street, Boston Spa, W Yorks, LS23 6AA
*Activities:* Other letting and operating of own or leased real estate
*Officers:* Philippa Louise Sterne, Secretary; Philippa Louise Sterne [1966] Director/Landlord; Sally Patricia Sterne [1938] Director/Artist

**Keystone Bidco Limited**
*Incorporated:* 3 June 2014
*Net Worth:* £97,621,000 *Total Assets:* £102,818,000
*Registered Office:* The Waterfront, Lakeside Boulevard, Doncaster, S Yorks, DN4 5PL
*Activities:* Activities of head offices
*Parent:* Keystone Midco Limited
*Officers:* Timothy Mark Beale [1976] Director; Mark Andrew Budd [1975] Director/Investment Professional; Edward Jonathan Cameron Hawkes [1977] Director; Mark Richard Priest [1966] Director; Stephen James Robertson [1960] Director/Investment Manager; James Michael Douglas Thomson [1966] Director

**Keystone Financing PLC**
*Incorporated:* 3 June 2014
*Net Worth Deficit:* £2,832,000 *Total Assets:* £102,332,000
*Registered Office:* The Waterfront, Lakeside Boulevard, Doncaster, S Yorks, DN4 5PL
*Activities:* Activities of head offices
*Parent:* Keystone Bidco Limited
*Officers:* Lyn Charters, Secretary; Timothy Mark Beale [1976] Director; Mark Richard Priest [1966] Director; James Michael Douglas Thomson [1966] Director

**Keystone Healthcare Holdings Limited**
*Incorporated:* 17 July 2014
*Net Worth:* £2,191,176 *Total Assets:* £3,179,007
*Registered Office:* Cooper Bridge Warehouse, Leeds Road, Huddersfield, W Yorks, HD5 0RL
*Activities:* Activities of head offices
*Shareholders:* Richard Ward; Helen Rebecca Ward
*Officers:* Helen Rebecca Ward [1973] Director/Manager; Richard Ward [1967] Director/Medical Services

**Keystone JVCO Limited**
*Incorporated:* 8 April 2014 *Employees:* 1,098
*Net Worth:* £60,360,000 *Total Assets:* £503,755,008
*Registered Office:* Keepmoat, Lakeside Boulevard, Doncaster, S Yorks, DN4 5PL
*Activities:* Activities of head offices
*Officers:* Mark Andrew Budd [1975] Director/Investment Professional; Edward Jonathan Cameron Hawkes [1977] Director; Stephen James Robertson [1960] Director/Investment Manager

**Keystone Midco Limited**
*Incorporated:* 21 May 2014 *Employees:* 1,098
*Net Worth:* £64,057,000 *Total Assets:* £504,443,008
*Registered Office:* The Waterfront, Lakeside Boulevard, Doncaster, S Yorks, DN4 5PL
*Activities:* Activities of head offices
*Parent:* Keystonetopco Limited
*Officers:* Timothy Mark Beale [1976] Director; Mark Andrew Budd [1975] Director/Investment Professional; Edward Jonathan Cameron Hawkes [1977] Director; Mark Richard Priest [1966] Director; Stephen James Robertson [1960] Director/Investment Manager; James Michael Douglas Thomson [1966] Director

**Keystone Topco Limited**
*Incorporated:* 21 May 2014
*Net Worth:* £113,142,000 *Total Assets:* £113,879,000
*Registered Office:* The Waterfront, Lakeside Boulevard, Doncaster, S Yorks, DN4 5PL
*Activities:* Activities of head offices
*Parent:* Keystone JVCO Limited
*Officers:* Timothy Mark Beale [1976] Director; Mark Andrew Budd [1975] Director/Investment Professional; Edward Jonathan Cameron Hawkes [1977] Director; Stephen James Robertson [1960] Director/Investment Manager; David Anthony Sheridan [1962] Director; James Michael Douglas Thomson [1966] Director

**Keystream Limited**
*Incorporated:* 12 February 2007
*Net Worth:* £2,329,080 *Total Assets:* £3,451,256
*Registered Office:* Joseph Marr House, Units 18 Langthwaite Business Park, South Kirkby, W Yorks, WF9 3AP
*Activities:* Manufacture of other food products n.e.c.
*Parent:* J Marr Limited
*Officers:* Philip Edward Marr [1984] Director; Polly Anna Metcalfe [1986] Director; Annabelle Amy Tyson [1983] Director; Nicholas Giles Wharton [1966] Director

**Killgerm Chemicals Limited**
*Incorporated:* 2 March 1993 *Employees:* 53
*Net Worth:* £2,059,270 *Total Assets:* £4,325,529
*Registered Office:* Wakefield Road, Ossett, W Yorks, WF5 9AJ
*Activities:* Manufacture of other chemical products n.e.c.
*Shareholders:* Giles Duncan Ward; Peter Kitson; Gary Arthur Jefferies
*Officers:* Karen Ann Byram, Secretary; Rupert Bartholomew Broome [1967] Managing Director; Philip Dalgliesh [1946] Director/Company Chemist; Sabra Ann Everett [1961] Director/Advertising Marketing; Peter Kitson [1957] Finance Director; Christopher Paul Lawrence [1958] Director/Industrial Chemist

**Killgerm Group Limited**
*Incorporated:* 12 August 1976 *Employees:* 202
*Net Worth:* £10,749,078 *Total Assets:* £20,044,574
*Registered Office:* Killgerm Group Ltd, Wakefield Road, Ossett, W Yorks, WF5 9AJ
*Activities:* Activities of head offices
*Shareholders:* Giles Duncan Ward; Peter Kitson; Gary Arthur Jefferies
*Officers:* Peter Kitson, Finance Director; Rupert Bartholomew Broome [1967] Managing Director; Sabra Ann Everett [1961] Director; Raymond Harrop [1949] Director; Denise Marie Kelly [1965] Director; Peter Kitson [1957] Finance Director; Giles Duncan Ward [1967] Director/Lawyer

**Kinetic Worldwide Limited**
*Incorporated:* 25 June 1984 *Employees:* 164
*Net Worth:* £61,802,536 *Total Assets:* £183,257,792
*Registered Office:* The Inspire, Hornbeam Park, Harrogate, N Yorks, HG2 8PA
*Activities:* Advertising agencies
*Parent:* Poster Publicity Holdings Limited
*Officers:* Jacqueline Anne Chapple Blease, Secretary; Rachael Hird [1967] Director/Accountant; Stuart Michael Taylor [1963] Director

**John H King (Developments) Limited**
*Incorporated:* 6 October 1994 *Employees:* 3
*Net Worth:* £15,758,890 *Total Assets:* £17,186,332
*Registered Office:* Unit 3 Taverner's Walk Industrial Estate, Sheepscar Grove, Leeds, LS7 1AH
*Activities:* Buying and selling of own real estate
*Parent:* John H King (Investments) Limited
*Officers:* Susan Avril King, Secretary/Director; John Henry King [1985] Director/Chartered Surveyor; John Andrew King [1953] Director; Susan Avril King [1959] Director

**John King Chains Limited**
*Incorporated:* 17 March 1988 *Employees:* 59
*Net Worth:* £2,242,727 *Total Assets:* £8,019,393
*Registered Office:* New Climax Works, Lancaster Close, Sherburn in Elmet, Leeds, LS25 6NS
*Activities:* Manufacture of wire products, chain and springs
*Shareholder:* David William Wadsworth
*Officers:* Darren Wood, Secretary; David William Wadsworth [1958] Managing Director; Rosemary Ann Wadsworth [1961] Director/Administration Officer; Darren John Wood [1973] Finance Director

**King Cole Limited**
*Incorporated:* 9 March 1998 *Employees:* 35
*Net Worth:* £4,526,081 *Total Assets:* £5,525,568
*Registered Office:* Merrie Mills, Snaygill Industrial Estate, Keighley Road, Skipton, N Yorks, BD23 2QR
*Activities:* Wholesale of textiles
*Major Shareholder:* Keith Michael Thomas Wilson
*Officers:* Daniel Edmund Burke, Secretary; Keith Michael Thomas Wilson [1959] Director

**King James I Academy, Bishop Auckland Limited**
*Incorporated:* 18 May 2011 *Employees:* 150
*Net Worth:* £12,617,000 *Total Assets:* £14,652,000
*Registered Office:* King James I Academy, South Church Road, Bishop Auckland, Co Durham, DL14 7JZ
*Activities:* General secondary education
*Officers:* Sharon Boughey [1964] Director/Corporate Complaints Officer; George William Campbell [1953] Director/Local Government Officer Accountant; Mrs Rachael Anna Marie Dobinson [1976] Director/Teacher; Alastair L Gardner [1964] Director/International Trade Advisor; Nicholas Grieveson [1966] Director/Headteacher; Mr Peter Hardy [1962] Director; Shane Jeffery John Northgreaves [1965] Director; Keith Philpott [1963] Director/Local Government Officer; Nicole Suzanne Read [1970] Director/Teacher; Ian Robley [1947] Director/Teacher (Academy); Alan Stephen Rodchester [1955] Director/Consultant Headteacher; Gladys Short [1956] Director/Teacher; Debra Smith [1966] Director; Tanya Tucker [1965] Director/Teacher; Elizabeth Varley [1948] Director/Retired Assistant Headteacher; Keith Anthony Wilkinson [1948] Director

**King James's School**
*Incorporated:* 1 August 2012 *Employees:* 106
*Net Worth:* £8,424,000 *Total Assets:* £9,491,000
*Registered Office:* King James's School, St Helen's Gate, Almondbury, Huddersfield, W Yorks, HD4 6SG
*Activities:* General secondary education
*Officers:* Alison Douglas, Secretary; Eleanor Ruth Barraclough [1976] Director/HR Manager/Mediator; Janet Elizabeth Cockroft [1952] Director/Assistant Head; Stephen Dommett [1961] Director/Teacher; Rosalind Arden Farrell [1973] Director/Teacher; Andrew Mark Haigh [1963] Director; David Norman Harling [1963] Director/Management Consultant; Clare Ann Harrower [1969] Director; Jan Jones [1963] Director/Careers Adviser; Matt James Mills [1974] Director/Chief Executive; John Reginald Munro [1957] Director; Patrick O'Brien [1948] Director/Retired; Michelle Louise Oldfield [1974] Director/Education Consultant; Ian Walstan Rimmer [1966] Director/Teacher; Paul Stuart Rushton [1982] Director/Police Officer; Andrea Slater [1965] Director/Supply Teacher; Delia Thorington [1973] Director/Teacher; Michael Edward Wilson [1975] Director/Engineering Manager; Claire Marianne Woodward [1975] Director/Chartered Accountant

**Kingasia Foods Limited**
*Incorporated:* 14 May 1991 *Employees:* 148
*Net Worth:* £4,051,470 *Total Assets:* £5,930,015
*Registered Office:* Middlebank, Doncaster Carr Industrial Estate, Doncaster, S Yorks, DN4 5JJ
*Activities:* Manufacture of prepared meals and dishes
*Major Shareholder:* Kin Him Fong
*Officers:* So Him Fong, Secretary/Director; Kin Him Fong [1955] Director/Manager; So Him Fong [1959] Director

**Kingfisher (Lubrication) Limited**
*Incorporated:* 8 May 1953 *Employees:* 53
*Net Worth:* £3,381,057 *Total Assets:* £3,811,854
*Registered Office:* 136 Meanwood Road, Leeds, LS7 2BT
*Activities:* Manufacture of fasteners and screw machine products
*Major Shareholder:* John Adrian Fisher
*Officers:* John Anthony Dunne, Secretary; John Anthony Dunne [1954] Financial Director; John Adrian Fisher [1951] Managing Director; Richard Holt [1967] Director/Engineer; Lorraine Nugent [1969] Administrative Director

**Kingfisher UPVC Windows & Doors Limited**
*Incorporated:* 11 September 1990 *Employees:* 77
*Net Worth:* £1,112,814 *Total Assets:* £3,209,343
*Registered Office:* Valley Mills, Whitehall Road, Drighlington, Bradford, W Yorks, BD11 1NQ
*Activities:* Manufacture of other plastic products
*Major Shareholder:* Paul Beetham
*Officers:* Lee Beetham [1980] Contracts Director; Paul Beetham [1955] Director/Chairman; Peter Ashley Jackson [1976] Commercial Director; Jonathan Spencer Reynolds [1982] Technical Director; Neil Charles Webster [1953] Director

**Kings Hall Leisure Limited**
*Incorporated:* 15 January 1968 *Employees:* 4
*Net Worth:* £2,585,043 *Total Assets:* £3,270,965
*Registered Office:* 13 Yorkersgate, Malton, N Yorks, YO17 7AA
*Activities:* Activities of other holding companies n.e.c.
*Shareholders:* Janet Wharton; Gilbert Roland Wharton
*Officers:* Janet Wharton, Secretary; Christopher Roland Wharton [1968] Director; Gilbert Roland Wharton [1943] Director; Janet Wharton [1939] Director

**Kings Security Systems Limited**
*Incorporated:* 15 April 1971 *Employees:* 515
*Net Worth:* £57,000 *Total Assets:* £12,329,000
*Registered Office:* 4 St Dunstans Technology Park, Ripley Street, Bradford, W Yorks, BD4 7HH
*Activities:* Security systems service activities
*Parent:* Kings Solutions Group Limited
*Officers:* Gaynor Amanda Kehoe, Secretary; Neil James Cossey [1970] Director; Kerrell Amy Cronly [1986] Director; Kelly Fisher [1982] HR Director; Robin Charles Fisher [1951] Director [South African]; Robert David Forsyth [1969] Director; Darren Scott Gamage [1974] Director/Chief Operating Officer; Tim Goodwill [1979] Director; Emma Jane Shaw [1967] Director; Barry Abraham Stiefel [1949] Director [German]; Rocco Antonio Volpe [1971] Director; Geoffrey Peter Louis Zeidler [1962] Director

**Kings Solutions Group Limited**
*Incorporated:* 15 July 2011 *Employees:* 527
*Net Worth Deficit:* £1,791,000 *Total Assets:* £16,367,000
*Registered Office:* 4 St Dunstans Technology Park, Ripley Street, Bradford, W Yorks, BD4 7HH
*Activities:* Other business support service activities n.e.c.
*Shareholders:* Primekings Holding Limited; James Patrick King
*Officers:* Gaynor Amanda Kehoe, Secretary; Robin Charles Fisher [1951] Director [South African]; Emma Jane Shaw [1967] Director; Barry Abraham Stiefel [1949] Director [German]; Geoffrey Peter Louis Zeidler [1962] Director

**Kingsoak Limited**
*Incorporated:* 16 May 1966
*Net Worth:* £6,569,581 *Total Assets:* £7,094,380
*Registered Office:* Woodlands, Gawthorpe Drive, Bingley, W Yorks, BD16 4DQ
*Activities:* Development of building projects
*Shareholders:* Pamela Susan Jaggar; Paul Richard Jaggar; Ann Louise Leckenby
*Officers:* Donald Richard Jaggar, Secretary; Donald Richard Jaggar [1936] Director; Pamela Susan Jaggar [1961] Director/Admin Manager; Paul Richard Jaggar [1967] Director; Ann Louise Leckenby [1964] Director

**Kingspan Access Floors Limited**
*Incorporated:* 21 January 1903 *Employees:* 154
*Net Worth:* £21,975,098 *Total Assets:* £36,959,488
*Registered Office:* Marfleet, Hull, HU9 5SG
*Activities:* Floor and wall covering
*Parent:* Hewetson Holdings Limited
*Officers:* Paul Christopher Allon [1973] Director; Richard Hewitt Burnley [1965] Managing Director

**Kingspan Hot Water Systems Limited**
*Incorporated:* 22 January 2002
*Net Worth:* £10,092,897 *Total Assets:* £10,295,490
*Registered Office:* Tadman Street, Wakefield, W Yorks, WF1 5QU
*Activities:* Manufacture of other tanks, reservoirs and containers of metal
*Parent:* Kingspan Environmental & Renewables Limited
*Officers:* Barry Keeley [1977] Finance Director

**Kingspan Metl-Con Limited**
*Incorporated:* 15 October 1996
*Net Worth:* £9,210,364 *Total Assets:* £62,542,728
*Registered Office:* St Hildas Street, Sherburn, Malton, N Yorks, YO17 8PQ
*Activities:* Manufacture of other fabricated metal products n.e.c.
*Parent:* Kingspan Limited
*Officers:* Peter Charles Wilson [1956] Director [Irish]

**Kingston Carton Company Limited (The)**
*Incorporated:* 9 March 1917 *Employees:* 65
*Net Worth:* £10,635,891 *Total Assets:* £12,475,833
*Registered Office:* Cumberland Street, Hull, HU2 0PS
*Activities:* Manufacture of other paper and paperboard containers
*Shareholders:* David West Wilson; Peter West Wilson
*Officers:* Richard Wilkinson, Secretary; Arend Buitendam [1951] Managing Director; David West Wilson [1956] Director/Chairman

**Kingston Equity & Finance Limited**
*Incorporated:* 2 December 1985 *Employees:* 14
*Net Worth:* £5,223,693 *Total Assets:* £20,176,028
*Registered Office:* Concord House, Bessemer Way, Scunthorpe, N Lincs, DN15 8XE
*Activities:* Financial intermediation not elsewhere classified
*Shareholder:* John Ralph Williams
*Officers:* Heather Frances Mary Williams, Secretary/Director; Gareth John Williams [1980] Director/Finance Broker; Heather Frances Mary Williams [1954] Director; John Ralph Williams [1952] Director; Stuart Daniel Williams [1983] Director/Finance Broker

**Kingston Research Limited**
*Incorporated:* 1 May 2009 *Employees:* 4
*Net Worth:* £1,037,631 *Total Assets:* £3,337,794
*Registered Office:* c/o Banks Cooper Associates, 21 Marina Court, Hull, HU1 1TJ
*Activities:* Manufacture of other chemical products n.e.c.
*Shareholder:* BP Alternative Energy Investments Limited
*Officers:* David Thomas Anderson [1964] Director/Oil Company Executive; Angela Jean Bond-Blecher [1966] Director/Finance Manager [American]; Andrew Donaghue [1968] Director/Planning and Performance Manager; Jan Koninckx [1961] Business Director, E.I. Du Pont de Nemours & Co., [Belgian/American]

**Kingston Restaurants Limited**
*Incorporated:* 2 September 1997 *Employees:* 1,434
*Net Worth:* £5,635,843 *Total Assets:* £16,441,485
*Registered Office:* 39-41 Jameson Street, Kingston upon Hull, HU1 3JA
*Activities:* Unlicenced restaurants and cafes
*Shareholder:* George Michniewicz
*Officers:* George Vincent Michniewicz, Secretary; Jonathan Peter Betts [1971] Director/VP Franchising; George Vincent Michniewicz [1958] Managing Director; Pamela Ann Michniewicz [1966] Director/Restaurant Operator; Henry William Trickey [1968] Director/Chartered Surveyor

**Kingstown Associates (Holdings) Limited**
*Incorporated:* 27 September 2015 *Employees:* 145
*Net Worth:* £395,386 *Total Assets:* £6,176,275
*Registered Office:* 1 Wadsworth Road, Kellythorpe Industrial Estate, Driffield, E Yorks, YO25 9DJ
*Activities:* Activities of head offices
*Officers:* Wayne Barry [1983] Director; Paul Chambers [1969] Director; Elizabeth Anne Curd [1975] Finance Director; Nigel Mellor [1956] Director; Jody Louise Stephenson [1972] Director; David James Whittle [1955] Director

**Kingstown Associates Limited**
*Incorporated:* 5 November 2008 *Employees:* 145
*Net Worth:* £3,940,594 *Total Assets:* £6,711,871
*Registered Office:* 1 Wadsworth Road, Kelleythorpe Industrial Estate, Driffield, E Yorks, YO25 9DJ
*Activities:* Retail sale via mail order houses or via Internet
*Officers:* Wayne Barry [1983] Director; Paul Chambers [1969] Director; Elizabeth Anne Curd [1975] Finance Director; Nigel Mellor [1956] Director; Jody Louise Stephenson [1972] Director

**Kingstown Furniture Limited**
*Incorporated:* 15 March 1978 *Employees:* 364
*Net Worth:* £1,252,546 *Total Assets:* £7,298,008
*Registered Office:* Victoria House, Leeds Road, Hull, HU7 0BZ
*Activities:* Manufacture of other furniture
*Major Shareholder:* Michael Alan Sharp
*Officers:* Peter Connor [1964] Finance Director; Sean Frost-Palmer [1967] Director/Sales; Michael Alan Sharp [1950] Director/Chairman; Richard Michael Sharp [1973] Director

**Kingstown Holdings Limited**
*Incorporated:* 31 May 1983 *Employees:* 364
*Net Worth:* £8,829,701 *Total Assets:* £14,353,263
*Registered Office:* Victoria House, Leads Road, Hull, HU7 0BZ
*Activities:* Non-trading company
*Major Shareholder:* Michael Alan Sharp
*Officers:* Peter Connor [1964] Finance Director; Michael Alan Sharp [1950] Director/Chairman; Richard Michael Sharp [1973] Managing Director

**Kingstown Works Limited**
*Incorporated:* 5 July 2006 *Employees:* 418
*Net Worth:* £7,517,157 *Total Assets:* £21,234,084
*Registered Office:* Unit 2 Connaught Road, Kingswood, Hull, HU7 3AP
*Activities:* Construction of commercial buildings
*Parent:* Kingston upon Hull City Council
*Officers:* Darren Nicholson, Secretary; Peter Allen [1940] Director/Councillor; Maria Coward [1981] Director/Councillor; Robert Dunstan [1966] Director/Councillor; Councillor John Logan Fareham [1958] Director/Farmer Public Servant; Councillor Daren Russell Hale [1969] Director/Local Government Manager; Diana Anna Hatcher [1946] Director/Councillor; Councillor John Allen Hewitt [1946] Director; Deborah Barbara Matthews [1969] Director/Lawyer; Lynda Mary Petrini [1954] Director/Councillor

**The Kingswood Parks Development Company Limited**
*Incorporated:* 4 January 1995 *Employees:* 2
*Net Worth:* £7,100,139 *Total Assets:* £8,926,311
*Registered Office:* Kingswood House, Ashcombe Road, Kingswood, Hull, HU7 3DD
*Activities:* Buying and selling of own real estate
*Shareholders:* Stephanie Elizabeth Fetiveau; Vanessa Hilary Chetham
*Officers:* John Howard Briggs, Secretary; John Howard Briggs [1947] Director/Chartered Accountant; Norman Harold Broxham [1936] Director/Chartered Accountant; Vanessa Hilary Chetham [1956] Director; Stephanie Elizabeth Fetiveau [1946] Director

**Kino & Co. Limited**
*Incorporated:* 12 August 1913 *Employees:* 8
*Net Worth:* £6,535,008 *Total Assets:* £7,400,904
*Registered Office:* South Mill, White Rose Mills, Holdsworth Road, Holmfield, Halifax, W Yorks, HX3 6SN
*Activities:* Retail sale of textiles in specialised stores
*Officers:* Audrey Julia Fisher, Secretary; John Charles Kino Buckingham [1935] Director; Audrey Julia Fisher [1932] Director

**Kirens International Limited**
*Incorporated:* 19 April 2004 *Employees:* 18
*Net Worth:* £472,422 *Total Assets:* £4,127,790
*Registered Office:* Denim House, 32a Albion Street, Castleford, W Yorks, WF10 1EN
*Activities:* Wholesale of clothing and footwear
*Shareholders:* Jaswinder Singh; Dalwinder Singh
*Officers:* Dalwinder Singh, Secretary; Jaswinder Singh [1974] Director/Manager

**Kirk Sandall Academy Trust**
*Incorporated:* 10 October 2012 *Employees:* 112
*Previous:* Kirk Sandall Infant Academy Trust
*Net Worth:* £7,578,863 *Total Assets:* £9,147,666
*Registered Office:* Kirk Sandall Infant School, Queen Mary Crescent, Kirk Sandall, Doncaster, S Yorks, DN3 1JT
*Activities:* Primary education
*Officers:* Teresa Kathleen Ladley, Secretary; Diane Lesley Dunn [1956] Director/Educational Consultant; Darran Michael Lindley [1979] Director/Regional Business Support Manager - Sainsburys; Berbet Esmilda Lynds [1968] Director; George William Peacock [1953] Director/Retired; Claire Elizabeth Robinson [1973] Director/Headteacher

**Kirkbie Kendal School Academy Trust**
*Incorporated:* 25 February 2011 *Employees:* 137
*Net Worth:* £8,613,259 *Total Assets:* £10,896,320
*Registered Office:* Kirkbie Kendal School, Lound Road, Kendal, Cumbria, LA9 7EQ
*Activities:* General secondary education
*Officers:* Lesley Jean Rudelhoff Scott, Secretary; William Robert Abram [1952] Director/Project Operations Manager; David Armstrong [1967] Director/Building Contractor; Paul Braithwaite [1964] Director/Postal Worker; Dr Naomi Brown [1960] Director/Charity Manager and Consultant; Graham Paul Duckworth [1968] Relationship Director Banking; Michael Duff [1959] Director/Telecommunications Consultant; David Peter Durnford [1968] Director; John Gee [1958] Director/Business Manager; Helen Herbert [1967] Director/Teacher; Philip David Hyman [1964] Director/Headteacher; Sally Parnaby [1957] Director/Retired; Jaki Summerfield [1969] Director/Lecturer; Sarah Vickers Tulley [1971] Director/Research and Compliance Manager Financial Services

**Laurence Kirkby (Farms) Limited**
*Incorporated:* 3 November 1958 *Employees:* 7
*Net Worth:* £5,935,686 *Total Assets:* £6,679,599
*Registered Office:* Beaumontcote, Barton on Humber, N Lincs, DN18 6EN
*Activities:* Growing of cereals (except rice), leguminous crops and oil seeds
*Officers:* Rachel Mary Denton, Secretary; Rachel Mary Denton [1955] Director; William Dickinson Kirkby [1947] Director/Farmer

**Kirkby 2017 Limited**
*Incorporated:* 12 April 2017 *Employees:* 74
*Net Worth Deficit:* £764,062 *Total Assets:* £16,648,575
*Registered Office:* Unit 56 Lidgate Crescent, Langthwaite Grange Industrial Estate, South Kirkby, Pontefract, W Yorks, WF9 3NR
*Activities:* Activities of other holding companies n.e.c.
*Shareholders:* David Edward Lake; Stirling James Oswin
*Officers:* James Alexander Jaffray [1954] Director; David Edward Lake [1980] Director; Stirling James Oswin [1967] Director

**Kirkdale Industrial Training Services Limited**
*Incorporated:* 18 July 1975 *Employees:* 30
*Net Worth:* £3,743,970 *Total Assets:* £4,084,137
*Registered Office:* Kirkdale House, Armytage Road, Brighouse, W Yorks, HD6 1QF
*Activities:* Other education n.e.c.
*Officers:* Malcolm Procter, Secretary; William Dawsom Currie [1943] Director; Andrew Mark Denford [1959] Managing Director; David Edwards [1952] Director/Retired; Ingrid Rona Holdsworth [1948] Director of Personnel; Alan Myers [1946] Director/Professor of Engineering; Malcolm Procter [1946] Director/Engineer; Colin Anthony Somers [1951] Director/Human Resources Manager

**Kirkella Limited**
*Incorporated:* 30 July 1999
*Net Worth:* £3,566,627 *Total Assets:* £44,730,424
*Registered Office:* The Orangery, Hesslewood Country Business Park, Ferriby Road, Hessle, E Yorks, HU13 0LH
*Activities:* Marine fishing
*Parent:* J Marr (Fishing) Ltd
*Officers:* Thorsteinn Mar Baldvinsson [1952] Managing Director [Icelander]; Haraldur Gretarsson [1968] Director [Icelander]; Diederik Parlevliet [1955] Director [Dutch]; Jane Vanessa Sandell [1978] Director; Jan Cornelis Van Der Plas [1954] Director [Dutch]

**Kirkgate Group Limited**
*Incorporated:* 5 March 2001
*Net Worth:* £19,741,000 *Total Assets:* £75,487,000
*Registered Office:* Dewhirst House, Westgate, Driffield, E Yorks, YO25 6TH
*Activities:* Activities of head offices
*Parent:* Winsfield Limited
*Officers:* Christopher John Wilde, Secretary; David Witt [1953] Director; Anthony James Mark Wood [1960] Director

**Kirkleavington Property Company Limited**
*Incorporated:* 12 March 1964
*Net Worth:* £2,807,343 *Total Assets:* £3,953,699
*Registered Office:* 4 Bowcliffe Grange, Bramham, W Yorks, LS23 6UL
*Activities:* Development of building projects
*Parent:* Leonard Jowett (Holdings) Limited
*Officers:* Carolyn June Rippon Jowett, Secretary; Carrie Anne Kirkham, Secretary; Geoffrey Taylor Crute [1943] Director; Linda Joanne Davies [1973] Director/Chartered Surveyor; Nigel David Rippon Jowett [1960] Director

**Kirklees Active Leisure**
*Incorporated:* 29 November 2001 *Employees:* 706
*Net Worth Deficit:* £6,848,404 *Total Assets:* £4,928,029
*Registered Office:* Stadium Business & Leisure Complex, Stadium Way, Huddersfield, W Yorks, HD1 6PG
*Activities:* Sports and recreation education
*Officers:* John Alfred Briggs [1942] Managing Director; Melanie Tina Brooke [1960] Director/Vice Principal - Kirklees College; Adam Neil Fletcher [1979] Director/Solicitor; John Stephen Fletcher [1956] Director/Retired; Satnam Singh Khela [1954] Director/Businessman; David Morby [1954] Director/Lecturer; Cllr Mohan Singh Sokhal [1943] Director/Local Councillor; Sinead Marie Sopala [1972] Director/Marketing Manager [Canadian]; Brian Charles Stahelin [1951] Managing Director; Dawn Stephenson [1960] Director of Corporate Affairs - NHS; Cllr Mark Stephen Thompson [1959] Director/Consultant; Derek Charles Thomson [1956] Director/Project Manager/Accountant

**Kirklees Community Association**
*Incorporated:* 4 March 1993
*Net Worth:* £10,110,280 *Total Assets:* £13,720,258
*Registered Office:* Civic Centre 3, Market Street, Huddersfield, W Yorks, HD1 2EY
*Activities:* Other accommodation
*Officers:* Zoe Stewart, Secretary; Councillor Donald Malcolm Firth [1940] Director/Elected Member; Cllr Eric Archer Firth [1947] Director/Part Time Case Worker; Cllr Nell Cecily Griffiths [1958] Director/Councillor; Tony Hood [1951] Director/Retired; Councillor Robert Christopher Iredale [1948] Director/Elected Member; Musarrat Khan [1970] Director/Councillor; Councillor Carole Pattison [1951] Director/Councillor; Natalie Elaine Pinnock-Hamilton [1954] Director/Authority Development Officer; Peter Wayne Rock [1953] Director/Buyer

**Kirklees Neighbourhood Housing Limited**
*Incorporated:* 14 March 2002 *Employees:* 882
*Net Worth Deficit:* £32,734,000 *Total Assets:* £11,117,000
*Registered Office:* Perseverance House, St Andrews Road, Huddersfield, W Yorks, HD1 6RZ
*Activities:* Management of real estate on a fee or contract basis
*Parent:* The Council of The Borough of Kirklees
*Officers:* Eric Charles Hughes, Secretary; Conroy Gray [1941] Director/Retired; Anthony Hood [1951] Director/Retired; Serena Chantelle Johnson [1984] Director; Aysha Noreen Mansaf [1986] Director/Voluntary Worker; Cllr Andrew Clive Glover Marchington [1967] Director/Local Councillor; Elizabeth Ellen Smaje [1964] Director/Local Councillor; Catherine Mary Smyth [1954] Director/Consultant; Paul Webley [1951] Director/Business Planning; Paul Grenville White [1958] Director

**Kirklees PFI Limited**
*Incorporated:* 13 February 2007 *Employees:* 5
*Net Worth:* £730,073 *Total Assets:* £3,556,793
*Registered Office:* 4 Greengate, Cardale Park, Harrogate, N Yorks, HG3 1GY
*Activities:* Non-trading company
*Parent:* Grosvenor PFI Holdings Limited
*Officers:* Alexander Toby Shedden Parry, Secretary; Alastair William Hopps [1986] Director/Accountant; Alexander Toby Shedden Parry [1976] Director

**Kirklees Stadium Development Limited**
*Incorporated:* 2 March 1992 *Employees:* 216
*Net Worth:* £13,045,812 *Total Assets:* £23,128,936
*Registered Office:* The John Smiths Stadium, Stadium Way, Huddersfield, W Yorks, HD1 6PG
*Activities:* Operation of sports facilities
*Shareholders:* The Huddersfield Town Association Football Club Limited; The Council of The Borough of Kirklees
*Officers:* Paul Kemp, Secretary; Darren Bryant [1968] Finance Director; Gareth Emlyn Davies [1967] Managing Director; Kenneth Ernest Davy [1941] Director/Chairman Simplybiz PLC; Sir John Andrew Harman [1950] Director; Andrew David Harrison [1972] Managing Director - London Stansted Airport; Andrew John Hobson [1971] Managing Director - Fantastic Media UK Ltd; Dean Hoyle [1967] Director/Company Chairman; Councillor Peter Daniel McBride [1939] Director/Retired; Bernard William McGuin [1958] Director/Kirklees Councillor; Kenneth Douglas Sims [1938] Director; Richard Thewlis [1969] Managing Director; Andrew Loyn Watson [1967] Commercial Director; Julian Winter [1965] Director/Chief Executive, Huddersfield Town AFC

**Kirklees Theatre Trust**
*Incorporated:* 26 June 1980 *Employees:* 20
*Net Worth:* £3,247,173 *Total Assets:* £3,715,460
*Registered Office:* c/o Civic Centre III, Second Floor, Legal Services, Huddersfield, W Yorks, HD1 2WZ
*Activities:* Artistic creation
*Officers:* Julie Muscroft, Secretary; Karen Louise Allison [1969] Director/Councillor; Andrew John Bird [1953] Director/Chairman & Education Manager; Kate Elizabeth Edwards [1978] Theatre Company Co-Artistic Director; Valerie Ann Javin [1950] Director/Vice Chairperson, Retired Journalist; Professor Michail Kagioglou [1970] Director/Professor and Dean of Art, Design and Architecture [German]; Carole Ann Pattison [1951] Director/Management Consultant; Marie Anne Peacock [1979] Director/Fundraising Manager; Laura Eve Rawnsley [1954] Director/Business Analyst; Tracy Sharon Sheldon [1962] Managing Director, Brug Consultancy Ltd; David Charles Douglas Thompson [1966] Technical Director, Manchester Festival; Sue Underwood [1962] Director/Comms Manager, University of Leeds; Councillor Gemma Simone Wilson [1980] Director/Councillor

**Kirkminster Engineering Limited**
*Incorporated:* 11 February 2005
*Net Worth:* £463,119 *Total Assets:* £4,301,421
*Registered Office:* Rievaulx House, 1 St Marys Court, Blossom Street, York, YO24 1AH
*Activities:* Other letting and operating of own or leased real estate
*Shareholder:* John David Coidan
*Officers:* Clare Elizabeth Coidan, Secretary; John David Coidan [1960] Director

**Kirkwood Hospice**
*Incorporated:* 23 June 1982 *Employees:* 233
*Net Worth:* £12,451,573 *Total Assets:* £13,277,806
*Registered Office:* 21 Albany Road, Dalton, Huddersfield, W Yorks, HD5 9UY
*Activities:* Other human health activities
*Officers:* Penny Elizabeth Wade, Secretary; Bernard Francis Ainsworth [1947] Director/Civil Engineer; Caroline Black [1962] Director/Head of Marketing; Jane Brady [1957] Assistant Director; Lorraine Annette Chapman [1980] Director/Business Development Manager; Dr Julie Davies [1963] Director/HR Subject Group Leader; David Norman Harling [1963] Director/Management Consultant; Kathryn Susan Hinchliff [1954] Director/Retired; Christina Maria Quinn [1959] Director/Retired; Philip Ronald Sands [1954] Director/Retired; Paul Leslie Scovell [1955] Director/Retired

**Kirncroft Engineering Limited**
*Incorporated:* 4 June 1979 *Employees:* 27
*Net Worth:* £5,538,011 *Total Assets:* £7,674,754
*Registered Office:* Wadworth Hill, Burstwick, Hull, HU12 9EY
*Activities:* Manufacture of doors and windows of metal
*Shareholders:* Robert Pryboda; Martin James Jackson; Barbara Jackson
*Officers:* Martin James Jackson, Secretary; Martin James Jackson [1949] Director/Farmer; Robert Pryboda [1951] Sales Director

**Kirwin Brothers Ltd.**
*Incorporated:* 24 May 1989 *Employees:* 128
*Net Worth:* £2,118,217 *Total Assets:* £6,175,269
*Registered Office:* North Quay, Fish Docks, Grimsby, N E Lincs, DN31 3SY
*Activities:* Wholesale of other food, including fish, crustaceans and molluscs
*Shareholders:* Lea Kirwin; Glen Kirwin
*Officers:* LEA Kirwin, Secretary; Glen Kirwin [1962] Director/Fish Merchant; LEA Kirwin [1965] Director/Fish Merchant

**Alf Kitching Limited**
*Incorporated:* 7 October 1997
*Net Worth:* £3,651,646 *Total Assets:* £4,895,082
*Registered Office:* Double Rivers, Crowle, Scunthorpe, N Lincs, DN17 4DD
*Activities:* Demolition
*Shareholders:* Paul Duncan Kitching; Michael Kitching
*Officers:* Paul Duncan Kitching, Secretary; Michael Kitching [1962] Director/Manager; Paul Duncan Kitching [1969] Director/Manager

**Kitching Plant Hire Ltd**
*Incorporated:* 21 June 2011 *Employees:* 27
*Previous:* D & S Kitching Limited
*Net Worth:* £4,487,327 *Total Assets:* £10,545,089
*Registered Office:* Camwal Road, Starbeck, Harrogate, N Yorks, HG1 4PT
*Activities:* Renting and leasing of other machinery, equipment and tangible goods n.e.c.
*Shareholders:* Shirley Anne Kitching; Jason David Kitching
*Officers:* David Albert Kitching [1943] Director; Jason David Kitching [1975] Director; Matthew John Kitching [1980] Director; Shirley Anne Kitching [1947] Director

**Klinger Holdings Limited**
*Incorporated:* 8 July 1992 *Employees:* 1
*Net Worth:* £4,404,001 *Total Assets:* £4,408,476
*Registered Office:* The Klinger Building, Euroway Trading Estate, Wharfedale Road, Bradford, W Yorks, BD4 6SG
*Activities:* Activities of head offices
*Parent:* Klinger Holdings GmbH (Austria)
*Officers:* Dominic Stephen Henry, Secretary; Michael John Foulds [1968] Director

**Klinger Limited**
*Incorporated:* 23 August 1971 *Employees:* 153
*Net Worth:* £12,374,489 *Total Assets:* £16,253,460
*Registered Office:* The Klinger Building, Wharfedale Road, Euroway Trading Estate, Bradford, W Yorks, BD4 6SG
*Activities:* Machining
*Parent:* Klinger Holdings Limited
*Officers:* Dominic Stephen Henry, Secretary; Oliver James Raymond Bache [1980] Projects Director; Stephen Brackstone [1982] Sales Director; Michael John Foulds [1968] Managing Director; Kevin Adrian Housam [1971] Director; David George Sorrie [1958] Business Development Director

**Kloeckner Metals UK Holdings Limited**
*Incorporated:* 10 December 2004
*Previous:* Klockner UK France Holding Limited
*Net Worth:* £28,304,000 *Total Assets:* £87,190,000
*Registered Office:* Valley Farm Road, Stourton, Leeds, LS10 1SD
*Activities:* Activities of head offices
*Officers:* David Gross [1977] Finance Director [American]; George Clinton Jones [1956] Director

**Kluman and Balter Limited**
*Incorporated:* 28 November 1994 *Employees:* 68
*Net Worth:* £2,507,683 *Total Assets:* £13,826,543
*Registered Office:* Alpha House, Lawnswood Business Park, Redvers Close, Leeds, LS16 6QY
*Activities:* Non-specialised wholesale trade
*Parent:* Brenntag UK Holding Limited
*Officers:* Omer Tahir, Secretary; Russel Argo [1973] Managing Director; Martin Gratton [1969] Finance Director; Danny Kluman [1975] Director; Omer Tahir [1977] Director/Company Secretary; Richard Ward [1972] Director/Chief Operating Officer

**KM School Limited**
*Incorporated:* 3 October 1990 *Employees:* 150
*Net Worth:* £575,563 *Total Assets:* £4,419,731
*Registered Office:* Kings Magna Building, Thorpe Underwood Estate, Great Ouseburn, York, YO26 9SZ
*Activities:* Primary education
*Parent:* The Collegiate Formation Ltd
*Officers:* Christopher James Hall, Secretary; Christopher James Hall [1969] Director/Chartered Accountant; Amy Katherine Martin [1983] Director; Francis David Martin [1967] Director/Business Executive

**KMA Properties Limited**
*Incorporated:* 12 December 2009
*Net Worth:* £2,043,050 *Total Assets:* £4,244,621
*Registered Office:* Marton Hall, Church Lane, Sewerby, Bridlington, E Yorks, YO15 1DS
*Activities:* Other building completion and finishing
*Shareholders:* Megan Rose Allison; Kathryn Isabel Allison-Dean
*Officers:* David Robert Allison [1960] Director; Megan Rose Allison [1996] Director; Kathryn Isabel Allison-Dean [1985] Director

**Knaresborough Investments Limited**
*Incorporated:* 10 January 2001 *Employees:* 3
*Net Worth:* £163,582,000 *Total Assets:* £189,714,000
*Registered Office:* Clipper Logistics Group, Gelderd Road, Leeds, LS12 6LT
*Activities:* Activities of head offices
*Major Shareholder:* Steven Nicholas Parkin
*Officers:* Marianne Hodgkiss, Secretary; David Arthur Hodkin [1961] Director; Guy Collingwood Jackson [1957] Director/Company Secretary; Steven Nicholas Parkin [1960] Director

**Knightsbridge Furniture Productions Limited**
*Incorporated:* 16 January 1958 *Employees:* 134
*Net Worth:* £1,078,272 *Total Assets:* £3,417,668
*Registered Office:* 191 Thornton Road, Bradford, BD1 2JT
*Activities:* Manufacture of other furniture
*Parent:* Townham Limited
*Officers:* Peter Denham [1955] Director; Alan James Towns [1968] Managing Director

**Knightwood Developments Limited**
*Incorporated:* 26 May 2005 *Employees:* 2
*Net Worth:* £1,899,000 *Total Assets:* £3,648,000
*Registered Office:* Rowland Hall, Newsholme, Howden, E Yorks, DN14 7JU
*Activities:* Buying and selling of own real estate
*Parent:* Knightwood Trust Farms Limited
*Officers:* James Watson Eyre Wild, Secretary; Elizabeth Anne Bisson [1963] Director/Land Agent; George David Strawson [1937] Director/Farmer

**Knightwood Holdings (2011) Limited**
*Incorporated:* 27 January 2011 *Employees:* 2
*Net Worth:* £2,768,000 *Total Assets:* £7,325,000
*Registered Office:* Rowland Hall Farm, Rowlandhall Lane, Newsholme, Goole, E Yorks, DN14 7JU
*Activities:* Other letting and operating of own or leased real estate
*Major Shareholder:* George David Strawson
*Officers:* James Watson Eyre Wild, Secretary; Elizabeth Anne Bisson [1963] Director/Land Agent; George David Strawson [1937] Director/Farmer

**Knightwood Trust Farms Limited**
*Incorporated:* 13 May 1996 *Employees:* 3
*Net Worth:* £25,924,000 *Total Assets:* £40,028,000
*Registered Office:* Rowland Hall Farm, Newsholme, Howden, Goole, E Yorks, DN14 7JW
*Activities:* Growing of cereals (except rice), leguminous crops and oil seeds
*Parent:* Knightwood Holdings (2011) Limited
*Officers:* James Watson Eyre Wild, Secretary; Elizabeth Anne Bisson [1963] Director/Land Agent; Colin Garfoot [1952] Director/Farm Manager

**Kober Limited**
*Incorporated:* 18 November 2010 *Employees:* 566
*Net Worth:* £10,562,000 *Total Assets:* £21,515,000
*Registered Office:* Unit 1 Foxbridge Way, Normanton Industrial Estate, Normanton, W Yorks, WF6 1TN
*Activities:* Production of meat and poultry meat products
*Parent:* International Procurement and Logistics Limited
*Officers:* Varinder Rehal, Secretary; James Edward Fasey [1973] Finance Director; Varinder Rehal [1975] Director and Company Secretary; Max Sandiford Smith-Hilliard [1958] Director/Chief Executive; Michael John Bland Snell [1964] Director

**Kokoon Holdings Limited**
*Incorporated:* 17 October 2016
*Net Worth:* £950,010 *Total Assets:* £4,400,010
*Registered Office:* Unit 4 Newhall Business Park, Newhall Way, Bradford, BD5 8FE
*Activities:* Activities of other holding companies n.e.c.
*Shareholders:* James Richard Lister; Jonathan Healey Morris
*Officers:* Richard John Grant [1965] Director [New Zealander]; James Richard Lister [1985] Director; Jonathan Healey Morris [1983] Director; Alan David Taylor [1974] Director

**Kolorcraft Holdings Limited**
*Incorporated:* 20 October 1998 *Employees:* 202
*Net Worth:* £2,989,444 *Total Assets:* £12,842,918
*Registered Office:* Concept House, Milner Way, Ossett, W Yorks, WF5 9JE
*Activities:* Printing n.e.c.
*Officers:* Stephen Stothart, Secretary; Michael Atkinson [1968] Commercial Director; Philip Findley [1956] Managing Director; Stephen Stothart [1963] Finance Director

**Kolorcraft Limited**
*Incorporated:* 11 June 1979 *Employees:* 202
*Net Worth:* £3,863,550 *Total Assets:* £13,469,792
*Registered Office:* Concept House, Mortimer Rise, Milner Way, Ossett, W Yorks, WF5 9JE
*Activities:* Printing n.e.c.
*Parent:* Kolorcraft Holdings Limited
*Officers:* Stephen Stothart, Secretary; Michael Atkinson [1968] Commercial Director; Philip Findley [1956] Managing Director; Stephen Stothart [1963] Finance Director

**Komori U.K. Limited**
*Incorporated:* 15 February 1984 *Employees:* 37
*Net Worth:* £20,598,000 *Total Assets:* £28,190,000
*Registered Office:* Unit 3001 Victoria Road, Seacroft, Leeds, LS14 2LA
*Activities:* Wholesale of other machinery and equipment
*Officers:* Takashi Ikegami [1960] Director [Japanese]; Eiji Kajita [1965] Director [Japanese]; Toshiyasu Kubotera [1962] Director [Japanese]; Ken Sagawa [1969] Director [Japanese]; Neil Edward Sutton [1962] Managing Director; Steven Michael Turner [1963] Managing Director

**Kongsberg Actuation Systems Limited**
*Incorporated:* 4 December 2007 *Employees:* 267
*Net Worth Deficit:* £5,347,000 *Total Assets:* £16,568,000
*Registered Office:* Kongsberg, Foxbridge Way, Normanton Industrial Estate, Normanton, W Yorks, WF6 1TN
*Activities:* Manufacture of other parts and accessories for motor vehicles
*Parent:* Kongsberg Automotive ASA
*Officers:* Thomas Gabrielsen [1975] Director/Vice President Finance [Norwegian]; Michael Shaun Vella [1969] Director/Financial Controller

**Koppers UK Holding Limited**
*Incorporated:* 18 January 1996 *Employees:* 5
*Net Worth:* £2,509,315 *Total Assets:* £24,441,362
*Registered Office:* 1 Park Row, Leeds, LS1 5AB
*Activities:* Other business support service activities n.e.c.
*Parent:* Koppers Holdings Inc
*Officers:* Steven Robert Lacy [1956] Director/Business Manager [American]; Christian Arndal Nielsen [1962] Director/Vice President [Danish]; James Arthur Sullivan [1963] Director/Business Manager [American]; Kent Bo Svendsen [1957] Director/Finance Manager [Danish]; Michael J Zugay [1952] Director/Business Manager [American]

**Koppers UK Limited**
*Incorporated:* 27 January 1928 *Employees:* 3
*Net Worth:* £20,602,864 *Total Assets:* £22,985,516
*Registered Office:* 1 Park Row, Leeds, LS1 5AB
*Activities:* Manufacture of other organic basic chemicals
*Parent:* Koppers UK Holding Limited
*Officers:* Steven Robert Lacy [1956] Director/Business Manager [American]; Christian Arndal Nielsen [1962] Director/Vice President [Danish]; James Arthur Sullivan [1963] Director/Business Manager [American]; Kent Bo Svendsen [1957] Director/Finance Manager [Danish]; Michael J Zugay [1952] Director/Business Manager [American]

**Koso Kent Introl Limited**
*Incorporated:* 25 May 2005 *Employees:* 136
*Net Worth:* £24,821,000 *Total Assets:* £32,175,000
*Registered Office:* Armytage Road, Brighouse, W Yorks, HD6 1QF
*Activities:* Manufacture of taps and valves
*Officers:* Paul Anthony Glew, Secretary; Paul Anthony Glew [1974] Finance Director; Takashi Ikegaya [1930] Director [Japanese]; Yuichi Ikegaya [1973] Director [Japanese]; Lynn Mowbray [1967] Director; Keiko Nakagawa [1964] Director/Attorney [Japanese]

**Koti Industrial & Technical Brushes Limited**
*Incorporated:* 25 May 1990 *Employees:* 3
*Net Worth:* £2,112,265 *Total Assets:* £5,336,888
*Registered Office:* Clayton Wood Rise, West Park, Ring Road, Leeds, LS16 6RH
*Activities:* Non-specialised wholesale trade
*Shareholders:* Nathalie Huybreckx-Van Kouwen; Michel Jozef Rene Lambert Huybreckx
*Officers:* Michel Jozef Huybreckx [1972] Director [Belgian]; John Van Kouwen [1943] Director [Belgian]

**Krimpterm Limited**
*Incorporated:* 29 September 2011 *Employees:* 15
*Net Worth:* £1,763,712 *Total Assets:* £3,749,429
*Registered Office:* Sterling Works, Texas Street, Morley, Leeds, LS27 0HG
*Activities:* Non-specialised wholesale trade
*Shareholders:* Dean Stefan Beal; Automotive & Industrial Consumables Ltd
*Officers:* Sir Dean Stefan Beal [1963] Director; Darshan Patel [1973] Director

**Krone UK Ltd**
*Incorporated:* 23 January 2009 *Employees:* 34
*Net Worth:* £1,146,891 *Total Assets:* £14,104,531
*Registered Office:* Peckfield Business Park, Phoenix Avenue, Micklefield, Leeds, LS25 4DY
*Activities:* Support activities for crop production
*Parent:* Bernard Krone Holding SE & Co KG
*Officers:* Bernard Antonius Klaus Krone [1977] Managing Director [German]; Dr Marcus James Oliver [1976] Managing Director; Alfons Joseph Veer [1954] Managing Director [German]; Wilhelm Voss [1950] Director [German]

**KSDL Land Limited**
*Incorporated:* 4 October 2016
*Net Worth:* £170,064 *Total Assets:* £4,284,844
*Registered Office:* The John Smiths Stadium, Stadium Way, Huddersfield, W Yorks, HD1 6PG
*Activities:* Operation of sports facilities
*Parent:* Kirklees Stadium Development Limited
*Officers:* Steven Charles Bonfield, Secretary; Gareth Emlyn Davies [1967] Director; Sir John Andrew Harman [1950] Director

**KTH Engineering Group Limited**
*Incorporated:* 12 July 2010 *Employees:* 85
*Previous:* Ellis Fish Holdings Limited
*Net Worth:* £5,858,150 *Total Assets:* £7,348,757
*Registered Office:* Gannex Park, Dewsbury Road, Elland, W Yorks, HX5 9AF
*Activities:* Activities of head offices
*Shareholders:* Richard Andrew Ellis; Roger Joseph Fish
*Officers:* Richard Andrew Ellis [1967] Director/Engineer; Roger Joseph Fish [1943] Director

**KTS Wire Limited**
*Incorporated:* 13 November 2008 *Employees:* 57
*Net Worth:* £711,418 *Total Assets:* £4,970,160
*Registered Office:* Howley Park Road, Morley, Leeds, LS27 0BN
*Activities:* Cold drawing of wire
*Parent:* HLW 389 Limited
*Officers:* Lars Gunnarsson [1966] Director [Swedish]; Philip Allan Hobson [1959] Director/Accountant; Toichiro Kumagai [1959] Director [Japanese]; Stephen David Longbottom [1951] Director; Adrianus Willem Raatgeep [1962] Director/Chief Executive [Dutch]; Mark Ian Walker [1970] Operations Director

**Kubler Holdings Limited**
*Incorporated:* 29 March 2016
*Net Worth:* £243,751 *Total Assets:* £3,000,001
*Registered Office:* Helm Bank, Natland, Kendal, Cumbria, LA9 7PS
*Activities:* Activities of head offices
*Major Shareholder:* Claire Elizabeth Kubler
*Officers:* Claire Elizabeth Kubler [1982] Director

**Kudos International Limited**
*Incorporated:* 21 December 2007 *Employees:* 2
*Net Worth Deficit:* £1,434,965 *Total Assets:* £4,014,714
*Registered Office:* Unit 1 Elmsfield Park, Holme, Carnforth, Lancs, LA6 1RJ
*Activities:* Other manufacturing n.e.c.
*Parent:* Peover Eye Investments Limited
*Officers:* Mark Anthony Hill [1973] Finance Director; David Irwin [1966] Director; Bruce Raymond Ledwith [1952] Director

**Kudos Shower Products Limited**
*Incorporated:* 19 May 1999 *Employees:* 116
*Net Worth:* £7,613,588 *Total Assets:* £14,292,851
*Registered Office:* Unit 1 Elmsfield Park, Holme, Carnforth, Lancs, LA6 1RJ
*Activities:* Other manufacturing n.e.c.
*Parent:* Kudos International Limited
*Officers:* Nick Graville [1974] Sales Director; Mark Anthony Hill [1973] Finance Director; David Irwin [1966] Director; Bruce Raymond Ledwith [1952] Director

**Kuwait Petroleum International Lubricants (UK) Limited**
*Incorporated:* 13 November 1986 *Employees:* 30
*Net Worth Deficit:* £1,115,000 *Total Assets:* £10,827,000
*Registered Office:* Second Floor, 3 Colton Mill, Bullerthorpe Lane, Leeds, LS15 9JN
*Activities:* Other treatment of petroleum products (excluding petrochemicals manufacture)
*Parent:* Kuwait Petroleum (U.K. Holdings) Limited
*Officers:* Peter Coules, Secretary; Neil Grieve [1962] Director/Country Manager; Catherine Sheila Macklam [1981] Director/Sales and Operations Manager; David Peter Wright [1976] Supply Chain Director

**KVH Industries UK Limited**
*Incorporated:* 8 May 2013
*Net Worth:* £39,317,616 *Total Assets:* £51,689,388
*Registered Office:* 2a Queen Street, Leeds, LS1 2TW
*Activities:* Activities of head offices
*Parent:* KVH Industries Inc
*Officers:* Felise Feingold, Secretary; Martin Kits Van Heyningen [1959] Director [American]

**KVH Media Group International Limited**
*Incorporated:* 27 April 1953 *Employees:* 9
*Net Worth:* £2,139,000 *Total Assets:* £4,107,000
*Registered Office:* 2a Queen Street, Leeds, LS1 2TW
*Activities:* Motion picture distribution activities
*Parent:* KVH Media Group Limited
*Officers:* Felise Feingold, Secretary; Martin Kits Van Heyningen [1959] Director [American]; Mark Woodhead [1971] Director

**KVH Media Group Limited**
*Incorporated:* 3 January 2008
*Net Worth:* £31,976,000 *Total Assets:* £40,388,000
*Registered Office:* 2a Queen Street, Leeds, LS1 2TW
*Activities:* Activities of head offices
*Parent:* KVH Industries UK Limited
*Officers:* Felise Feingold, Secretary; Mark Woodhead [1971] Director

**KWH (Hull) Limited**
*Incorporated:* 19 February 2016
*Net Worth Deficit:* £187,184 *Total Assets:* £3,052,168
*Registered Office:* Ogleforth House, Ogleforth, York, YO1 7JG
*Activities:* Development of building projects
*Shareholder:* Mandip Singh Nagra
*Officers:* John Howard Neal, Secretary; Paul Winston Kenyon [1955] Director; Shaun Derek Larvin [1976] Director; Mandip Singh Nagra [1968] Director; John Howard Neal [1961] Director

**Kwiktuf Holdings Limited**
*Incorporated:* 7 April 2016 *Employees:* 121
*Net Worth:* £367,465 *Total Assets:* £6,826,050
*Registered Office:* 264 Wincolmlee, Hull, HU2 0PZ
*Activities:* Activities of production holding companies
*Shareholders:* Nigel Charles Thomas; Paul Myers
*Officers:* James Paul Bradley, Secretary; James Paul Bradley [1978] Director/Accountant; Paul Myers [1965] Director; Derek Pinkney [1966] Director; Michelle Saville [1971] Director; Andrew George Thomas [1952] Director; Nigel Charles Thomas [1957] Director

**Kwiktuf Limited**
*Incorporated:* 6 November 2003 *Employees:* 121
*Net Worth:* £2,406,521 *Total Assets:* £5,601,992
*Registered Office:* 264 Wincolmlee, Hull, HU2 0PZ
*Activities:* Shaping and processing of flat glass
*Officers:* James Paul Bradley, Secretary; James Paul Bradley [1978] Director; Paul Myers [1965] Director; Derek Pinkney [1966] Director; Michelle Saville [1971] Director; Andrew George Thomas [1952] Director; Nigel Charles Thomas [1957] Director

**Kysor Europe Limited**
*Incorporated:* 31 October 1966
*Net Worth:* £4,632,085 *Total Assets:* £4,632,085
*Registered Office:* Roydsdale Way, Euroway Industrial Estate, Bradford, W Yorks, BD4 6SE
*Activities:* Dormant company
*Parent:* Borgwarner Inc.
*Officers:* Marlene Fischer [1953] Director/Executive [American]

**L & K Group PLC**
*Incorporated:* 29 June 1900 *Employees:* 73
*Net Worth:* £6,132,995 *Total Assets:* £12,902,260
*Registered Office:* J36 Rural Auction Centre, Crooklands, Milnthorpe, Cumbria, LA7 7FP
*Activities:* Activities of agricultural holding companies
*Officers:* Katie Louise Black, Secretary; Alan John Bargh [1953] Director/Farmer; Jill Marie Bargh [1969] Director/Farmer; David Herbert Barton [1961] Director/Farmer; Stuart Cornthwaite [1953] Director; James Anthony Dixon [1959] Director/Farmer; John Edward Drinkall [1955] Director/Farmer; John Addison Geldard [1951] Director/Farmer; Jonathan Walter Hodgson [1961] Director/Farmer; Professor Monica Mary Lee [1952] Director/Lecturer; Trevor William Wilson [1961] Director/Farmer

**L & O Investments (U.K.)**
*Incorporated:* 20 November 1996
*Net Worth:* £4,706,000 *Total Assets:* £4,710,000
*Registered Office:* OSI Food Solutions UK Ltd, Luneburg Way, Scunthorpe, N Lincs, DN15 8LP
*Activities:* Activities of head offices
*Parent:* OSI International Holding GmbH
*Officers:* Martin Howard Back, Secretary; Sherry Anne de Meulenaere [1958] Director [American]; David Gerard McDonald [1964] Director [American]

**L S S Properties (Leeds) Limited**
*Incorporated:* 9 January 2004
*Net Worth:* £253,420 *Total Assets:* £4,210,357
*Registered Office:* Recycling House, Knowsthorpe Lane, Cross Green Industrial Park, Leeds, LS9 0PF
*Activities:* Other letting and operating of own or leased real estate
*Major Shareholder:* Nigel Charles Woolford
*Officers:* Johanne Louise Woolford, Secretary; Nigel Charles Woolford [1959] Managing Director

**L.F.C. Horkstow Limited**
*Incorporated:* 9 May 1972 *Employees:* 8
*Net Worth:* £620,618 *Total Assets:* £6,041,359
*Registered Office:* The Estate Office, Willoughton Manor, Willoughton, Gainsborough, Lincs, DN21 5SH
*Activities:* Growing of cereals (except rice), leguminous crops and oil seeds
*Shareholders:* John Anthony Shepherdson; James Charles Stewart Reynolds Milligan-Manby; Kevin Simon Webster; Bruce Henry Rowles; Clifford Graham Rowles Nicholson; John William Rowles
*Officers:* Richard Arthur Giles, Secretary; Bruce Henry Rowles [1960] Farmer & Director; Clifford Graham Rowles Nicholson [1955] Farmer & Director

**L.N.T. Construction Limited**
*Incorporated:* 7 November 1994 *Employees:* 147
*Net Worth:* £24,835,014 *Total Assets:* £36,608,320
*Registered Office:* Helios, 47 Isabella Road, Garforth, Leeds, LS25 2DY
*Activities:* Construction of commercial buildings
*Parent:* LNT Group Limited
*Officers:* Philip Miles Raven, Secretary; Matthew Graeme Lowe [1973] Director; Peter Mortimer [1971] Managing Director; Philip Miles Raven [1966] Director; Lawrence Neil Tomlinson [1964] Director

**L.S. Transmission Consultancy Limited**
*Incorporated:* 2 April 2001 *Employees:* 76
*Net Worth:* £2,527,542 *Total Assets:* £5,924,797
*Registered Office:* Yorkshire House, York Road, Little Driffield, Driffield, E Yorks, YO25 5XA
*Activities:* Other professional, scientific and technical activities n.e.c.
*Shareholders:* Nicholas Minns; Martin John Straker; Peter Papanastasiou
*Officers:* Nicholas Minns, Secretary/Land Surveyor; Nicholas Minns [1958] Director/Land Surveyor; Peter Papanastasiou [1955] Director/Civil Engineer; Martin John Straker [1964] Director/Land Surveyor

**L.W. Safety Limited**
*Incorporated:* 23 October 1978 *Employees:* 14
*Net Worth:* £3,719,856 *Total Assets:* £4,164,852
*Registered Office:* Premier House, Jubilee Way, Elland, W Yorks, HX5 9DY
*Activities:* Other service activities n.e.c.
*Parent:* LS UK Fire Group Limited
*Officers:* Gary Robinson, Secretary/Accountant; Richard John Pollard [1963] Director/Chartered Accountant

**LA 2012 Limited**
*Incorporated:* 22 December 2004
*Net Worth:* £87,325,000 *Total Assets:* £162,075,008
*Registered Office:* Linpac, Wakefield Road, Featherstone, Pontefract, W Yorks, WF7 5DE
*Activities:* Manufacture of other plastic products
*Major Shareholder:* Victor Khosla
*Officers:* Robert Burton Lence, Secretary; Michael Philip Nicholls [1960] Finance Director

**The Label Makers Limited**
*Incorporated:* 28 October 1963 *Employees:* 69
*Net Worth:* £6,599,817 *Total Assets:* £9,598,212
*Registered Office:* Prince Street, Bradford, W Yorks, BD4 6HQ
*Activities:* Manufacture of other articles of paper and paperboard n.e.c.
*Shareholders:* David John Nocton Webster; Sarah Elizabeth Fletcher; Jane Katrina Jackson
*Officers:* Zenna Parfaniuk, Secretary; Sarah Elizabeth Fletcher [1959] Director/Counsellor; Jane Katrina Jackson [1964] Director/Learning Support Teacher; Kevin Lyons [1962] Sales Director; Zenna Parfaniuk [1965] Director/Company Secretary; Anthony John Bloye Webster [1932] Director/Chairman; David John Nocton Webster [1962] Managing Director

**Label Worx Limited**
*Incorporated:* 21 October 2008 *Employees:* 13
*Net Worth:* £925,235 *Total Assets:* £3,884,578
*Registered Office:* C4DI @ The Dock, 31-38 Queen Street, Kingston upon Hull, HU1 1UU
*Activities:* Other publishing activities
*Shareholders:* Matthew Abbott; Christopher Patrick Chambers
*Officers:* Matthew Abbott, Secretary; Matthew Abbott [1980] Director; Christopher Patrick Chambers [1979] Director

**Labelon Group Limited**
*Incorporated:* 1 September 2004 *Employees:* 970
*Net Worth:* £11,042,896 *Total Assets:* £94,078,400
*Registered Office:* 1 Park Row, Leeds, LS1 5AB
*Activities:* Manufacture of corrugated paper and paperboard, sacks and bags
*Officers:* Miranda Shui Yau Kong [1955] Director; Wai Yee Lam [1973] Director [Chinese]; Chuk Kwan Wan [1974] Director

**Labelon UK Limited**
*Incorporated:* 18 January 1985 *Employees:* 65
*Net Worth:* £5,710,441 *Total Assets:* £8,381,103
*Registered Office:* 1 Park Row, Leeds, LS1 5AB
*Activities:* Manufacture of other paper and paperboard containers
*Parent:* Labelon Group Limited
*Officers:* Miranda Shui Yau Kong [1955] Director; Sara Nga Kwok [1974] Managing Director; Chuk Kwan Wan [1974] Director

**Lagonda Selsdon Propco Limited**
*Incorporated:* 15 May 2001 *Employees:* 4
*Net Worth Deficit:* £8,540,000 *Total Assets:* £27,487,000
*Registered Office:* The Inspire, Hornbeam Square West, Harrogate, N Yorks, HG2 8PA
*Activities:* Other letting and operating of own or leased real estate
*Parent:* De Vere Selsdon Estate Limited
*Officers:* James Alexander Burrell [1974] Director/Accountant; Generaldine Josephine Gallagher [1965] Finance Director [Irish]; Gail Susan Hunter [1963] Human Resources Director; Anthony Gerrard Troy [1962] Director [Irish]

**John Laithwaite Investments Limited**
*Incorporated:* 23 August 2010
*Net Worth Deficit:* £1,382,899 *Total Assets:* £8,206,637
*Registered Office:* The Howroyd Barn, Barkisland, Halifax, W Yorks, HX4 0AP
*Activities:* Other business support service activities n.e.c.
*Major Shareholder:* John Laithwaite
*Officers:* Danik Lilley Laithwaite [1971] Director; John Laithwaite [1944] Director; Susan Rosemary Laithwaite [1944] Director

**John Laithwaite Partners LLP**
*Incorporated:* 5 October 2011
*Net Worth:* £2,190,461 *Total Assets:* £7,135,912
*Registered Office:* Howroyde Barn, Barkisland, Halifax, W Yorks, HX4 0AP
*Officers:* John Laithwaite [1944] Member; Simon Pilling [1966] LLP Member

**Lake District Estates Company Limited**
*Incorporated:* 6 December 1938 *Employees:* 99
*Net Worth:* £9,242,213 *Total Assets:* £26,777,914
*Registered Office:* Maudlands, Maude Street, Kendal, Cumbria, LA9 4QD
*Activities:* Other retail sale of new goods in specialised stores (not commercial art galleries and opticians)
*Parent:* Lake District Holdings Ltd
*Officers:* Jonathan Ross Winter, Secretary; Ruth Isabel Adorian [1932] Director; Lady Julia Daphne Boyd [1948] Director; Edward James Clarkson Webb [1966] Director/Film Producer; Peter Richard Wavell Hensman [1948] Director/Chartered Accountant; Roger Hensman [1981] Director/Consultant; Lucinda Carolyn Barrett Langton [1978] Director/CRS Manager; Richard Wakefield Raynsford [1945] Director; Thomas Lindsay Wakefield Raynsford [1980] Director/Investment Banker; Carolyn Mary Seel [1958] Director; William Ian Simpson [1951] Director/Farmer; Georgina Anne Townsend [1957] Director; Alexandra Peard Wix [1984] Director/Tour Operator

**Lake District Holdings Limited**
*Incorporated:* 2 September 1987 *Employees:* 166
*Previous:* Battlefields Holdings Limited
*Net Worth:* £13,551,405 *Total Assets:* £28,619,136
*Registered Office:* Maudlands, Maude Street, Kendal, Cumbria, LA9 4QD
*Activities:* Activities of other holding companies n.e.c.
*Officers:* Peter Richard Wavell Hensman, Secretary; Ruth Isabel Adorian [1932] Director; Lady Julia Daphne Boyd [1948] Director; Edward James Clarkson Webb [1966] Director; Peter Richard Wavell Hensman [1948] Director; Roger Hensman [1981] Director/Consultant; Lucinda Carolyn Barrett Langton [1978] Director/CRS Manager; Richard Wakefield Raynsford [1945] Director; Thomas Lindsay Wakefield Raynsford [1980] Director/Investment Banker; Carolyn Mary Seel [1958] Director; William Ian Simpson [1951] Director/Farmer; Georgina Anne Townsend [1957] Director; Alexandra Peard Wix [1984] Director/Tour Operator

**Lake House Investments Limited**
*Incorporated:* 22 January 2009 *Employees:* 1
*Net Worth:* £5,197,646 *Total Assets:* £11,234,444
*Registered Office:* Clifton House, Birkby Lane, Bailiff Bridge, Brighouse, W Yorks, HD6 4JJ
*Activities:* Other letting and operating of own or leased real estate
*Parent:* Blackshaw Holdings (2014) Limited
*Officers:* Susan Brooksbank, Secretary; John Stephen Brooksbank [1956] Director

**Lakehill Estates Limited**
*Incorporated:* 31 January 2003
*Net Worth:* £148,719 *Total Assets:* £5,320,840
*Registered Office:* c/o Dodgson & Co, The Meredith Building, 23-33 Reform Street, Hull, HU2 8EF
*Activities:* Other letting and operating of own or leased real estate
*Shareholders:* Robert David Scott Bousfield; Robert David Scott Bousfield
*Officers:* Robert David Scott Bousfield [1975] Director

**Lakeland Arts**
*Incorporated:* 31 July 2012 *Employees:* 43
*Net Worth:* £14,976,028 *Total Assets:* £16,093,805
*Registered Office:* Abbot Hall Art Gallery, Kirkland, Kendal, Cumbria, LA9 5AL
*Activities:* Museums activities
*Officers:* Martin John Ainscough [1966] Director; Henry Charles Fraser Bowring [1949] Director/Fine Art Consultant; Anthea Fiendley Case [1945] Director/Consultant; Christopher Michael Clarke [1952] Gallery Director; Charles William Nepean Crewdson [1964] Company Chairman & Director; Susan Anne Crewe [1949] Director/Consultant Editor; John Campbell Hudson [1960] Managing Director; Sara Louise Keegan [1946] Director/Retired; Professor Judith Ann Lois Mottram [1960] Director/University Professor; Anthony Rickards Collinson [1949] Director/Solicitor; Bronwen Riley [1967] Director/Trustee; Elizabeth Mary Rink [1948] Director/Retired Scientist; Nicholas William Robert Thompson [1968] Director/Amusement Park

**Lakeland Fashion Limited**
*Incorporated:* 10 March 2015 *Employees:* 157
*Net Worth:* £1,465,588 *Total Assets:* £3,780,324
*Registered Office:* Lakeland, Rothay Road Industrial Estate, Ambleside, Cumbria, LA22 0HQ
*Activities:* Activities of other holding companies n.e.c.
*Shareholders:* Richard Ellis Standring; Martin Andrew Foster
*Officers:* Peter Brookes, Secretary; Martin Andrew Foster [1966] Director; Robert David Malone [1961] Director; Richard Ellis Standring [1946] Director

**Lakeland Leisure Estates Limited**
*Incorporated:* 10 May 1990 *Employees:* 109
*Net Worth:* £15,848,049 *Total Assets:* £34,969,364
*Registered Office:* The Studio, Station Road, Staveley, Kendal, Cumbria, LA8 9NB
*Activities:* Recreational vehicle parks, trailer parks and camping grounds
*Shareholders:* Phillip Trevor Morgan; Carol Morgan
*Officers:* Carol Morgan, Secretary; Carol Morgan [1953] Director/Caravan Park Operator; Claire Zowie Morgan [1988] Director/Business Development Manager; Lorraine Jane Morgan [1996] Director/Office Manager; Louise Emma Morgan [1987] Director/Business Development Manager; Mark Philip Morgan [1990] Managing Director; Phillip Trevor Morgan [1952] Director/Caravan Park Operator

**Lakeland Limited**
*Incorporated:* 19 June 1964 *Employees:* 1,668
*Net Worth:* £60,039,000 *Total Assets:* £83,440,000
*Registered Office:* Alexandra Buildings, Windermere, Cumbria, LA23 1BQ
*Activities:* Retail sale of hardware, paints and glass in specialised stores
*Shareholders:* William Martin Moorhouse Rayner; Samuel Alan Miles Rayner; Julian Anthony Rayner
*Officers:* William Martin Moorhouse Rayner, Secretary; Philip Robert Johnson [1946] Director/Chartered Accountant; Julian Anthony Rayner [1957] Director; Samuel Alan Miles Rayner [1953] Director; William Martin Moorhouse Rayner [1951] Director

**Lakeland Motor Museum Limited**
*Incorporated:* 5 October 2006 *Employees:* 11
*Net Worth:* £2,218,019 *Total Assets:* £4,063,822
*Registered Office:* Winander House, Glebe Road, Bowness on Windermere, Cumbria, LA23 3HE
*Activities:* Museums activities
*Parent:* Winander Leisure Ltd
*Officers:* Andrew James Simon, Secretary; William John Bewley [1945] Director/Boat Proprietor; Edwin Leonard Maher [1954] Director/Attraction Manager; Leslie Micklethwaite [1943] Director/Boat Proprietor; Nigel Wilkinson [1964] Director/Chartered Accountant

**Lakeside 1 Limited**
*Incorporated:* 9 August 2007
*Net Worth:* £21,836,000 *Total Assets:* £35,286,000
*Registered Office:* The Waterfront, Lakeside Boulevard, Doncaster, S Yorks, DN4 5PL
*Activities:* Activities of head offices
*Parent:* Keystone Bidco Limited
*Officers:* Timothy Mark Beale [1976] Director; Mark Andrew Budd [1975] Director/Investment Professional; Edward Jonathan Cameron Hawkes [1977] Director; Mark Richard Priest [1966] Director; Stephen James Robertson [1960] Director/Investment Manager; James Michael Douglas Thomson [1966] Director

**William Lamb (Holdings) Limited**
*Incorporated:* 23 January 1989 *Employees:* 116
*Net Worth:* £8,481,364 *Total Assets:* £15,032,545
*Registered Office:* William Lamb Group Limited, Bottom Boat Road, Stanley, Wakefield, W Yorks, WF3 4AY
*Activities:* Activities of head offices
*Major Shareholder:* Stuart Howard Lamb
*Officers:* Jayne Watson, Secretary; Deborah Jane Baker [1973] Director/PA/Secretary; Dr Ruth Caroline Chataway [1981] Director/Consultant; Jean Lesley Lamb [1950] Director; Stuart Howard Lamb [1948] Director; William Robert Stuart Lamb [1970] Director/Vicar; Jayne Watson [1974] Finance Director; Charlotte Jayne Wheeler [1983] Director/Lawyer

**William Lamb Group Limited**
*Incorporated:* 19 June 1990 *Employees:* 97
*Previous:* William Lamb Footwear Limited
*Net Worth:* £7,724,338 *Total Assets:* £12,731,188
*Registered Office:* Bottomboat Road, Stanley, Wakefield, W Yorks, WF3 4AY
*Activities:* Wholesale of clothing and footwear
*Parent:* William Lamb (Holdings) Limited
*Officers:* Jayne Watson, Secretary; Andrew Nicholas Cook [1958] Design Director; Christopher Hargreaves [1968] Director; Charlotte Jayne Lamb [1983] Director/Lawyer; Stuart Howard Lamb [1948] Director; Jayne Watson [1974] Director

**Lamba Trading Co. Limited**
*Incorporated:* 1 November 1967 *Employees:* 10
*Net Worth:* £11,490,549 *Total Assets:* £14,359,649
*Registered Office:* 3 Park Square, Leeds, LS1 2NE
*Activities:* Wholesale of wine, beer, spirits and other alcoholic beverages
*Shareholder:* Michael Lamba
*Officers:* Michael Lamba, Secretary; Aaron Ishan Lamba [1988] Director; Bimla Lamba [1933] Director; Kabir Raj Lamba [1982] Director; Kamal Lamba [1957] Director [Malaysian]; Michael Lamba [1956] Director/Wholesale Grocer

**H.A. Lambert (Farmers) Limited**
*Incorporated:* 24 September 1953 *Employees:* 4
*Net Worth:* £5,780,538 *Total Assets:* £6,225,982
*Registered Office:* Low Paull Farm, Paull, Hull, HU12 8AX
*Activities:* Growing of cereals (except rice), leguminous crops and oil seeds
*Major Shareholder:* Andrew Alan Lambert
*Officers:* Andrew Alan Lambert, Secretary; Hugh Patrick Burstall [1943] Director/Solicitor; Andrew Alan Lambert [1961] Director/Farmer

**Lambert Automation Limited**
*Incorporated:* 12 December 2006 *Employees:* 173
*Net Worth:* £7,969,664 *Total Assets:* £16,747,762
*Registered Office:* Station Estate, Station Road, Tadcaster, N Yorks, LS24 9SG
*Activities:* Activities of head offices
*Major Shareholder:* Martin Alexander Williams
*Officers:* Dennis McGrath, Secretary; Matthew Maynard Cox [1966] Director; Warren Mark Limbert [1972] Director; Paul Newby [1960] Director; Martin Alexander Williams [1952] Director

**Lambert Engineering Group Limited**
*Incorporated:* 29 October 2001
*Net Worth:* £4,883,898 *Total Assets:* £12,068,040
*Registered Office:* Station Estate, Station Road, Tadcaster, N Yorks, LS24 9SG
*Activities:* Non-trading company
*Parent:* Lambert Automation Limited
*Officers:* Dennis McGrath, Secretary; Matthew Maynard Cox [1966] Director; Warren Mark Limbert [1972] Director; Paul Newby [1960] Director; Martin Alexander Williams [1952] Managing Director

**Lambert Engineering Holdings Limited**
*Incorporated:* 13 May 1996 *Employees:* 4
*Net Worth:* £3,524,298 *Total Assets:* £5,784,532
*Registered Office:* Station Estate, Station Road, Tadcaster, N Yorks, LS24 9SG
*Activities:* Non-trading company
*Parent:* Lambert Automation Ltd
*Officers:* Dennis McGrath, Secretary; Matthew Maynard Cox [1966] Director; Warren Mark Limbert [1972] Director; Paul Newby [1960] Director; Martin Alexander Williams [1952] Director

**Lambert Engineering Limited**
*Incorporated:* 2 January 1973 *Employees:* 173
*Net Worth:* £10,292,308 *Total Assets:* £15,227,867
*Registered Office:* Station Estate, Station Road, Tadcaster, N Yorks, LS24 9SG
*Activities:* Manufacture of other special-purpose machinery n.e.c.
*Parent:* Lambert Automation Ltd
*Officers:* Dennis McGrath, Secretary; Matthew Maynard Cox [1966] Director; Nicholas Green [1980] Production Director; Michael John Lewis [1983] Director; Warren Mark Limbert [1972] Director; Paul Newby [1960] Director; Martin Alexander Williams [1952] Director

**Derek Lambert Polythene Limited**
*Incorporated:* 21 May 1985 *Employees:* 42
*Net Worth:* £1,376,751 *Total Assets:* £4,057,778
*Registered Office:* Keighley Road, Bingley, W Yorks, BD16 2RD
*Activities:* Other manufacturing n.e.c.
*Major Shareholder:* Derek Lambert
*Officers:* Derek Lambert, Secretary; Derek Lambert [1941] Director/Polythene Manufacturer; Gavan Stuart Platts [1950] Works Director

**Lambson Building Products Limited**
*Incorporated:* 2 May 1966 *Employees:* 57
*Net Worth:* £5,822,104 *Total Assets:* £18,868,860
*Registered Office:* Hunt Street, Whitwood Mere, Castleford, W Yorks, WF10 1NS
*Activities:* Manufacture of other products of wood; manufacture of articles of cork, straw and plaiting materials
*Shareholders:* Michael Anthony Lundy; Glenn Monkman
*Officers:* Paul George Almond, Secretary; Michael Anthony Lundy [1952] Director/Design Engineer; Glenn Monkman [1957] Director/Manager

**Lambson Limited**
*Incorporated:* 21 July 1993 *Employees:* 42
*Net Worth:* £8,769,820 *Total Assets:* £14,441,156
*Registered Office:* Clifford House, York Road, Wetherby, W Yorks, LS22 7NS
*Activities:* Wholesale of chemical products
*Shareholders:* Gordon Fraser Hall; Ian Hall
*Officers:* Philip Leslie Calvert, Secretary; Gordon Fraser Hall [1956] Director; Ian Hall [1928] Director/Chairman

**Lambton Clothing Company Partnership LLP**
*Incorporated:* 18 October 2012
*Net Worth:* £385,830 *Total Assets:* £3,217,038
*Registered Office:* Lobley Cottage, Ilton, Ripon, N Yorks, HG4 4JY
*Officers:* Edward Richard Lambert [1962] Member; Gary Miller [1960] Member; Matthew Ian Norton [1963] Member

**Laminated Products Limited**
*Incorporated:* 11 July 1989 *Employees:* 57
*Net Worth:* £429,165 *Total Assets:* £4,130,630
*Registered Office:* Hunt Street, Whitwood Mere, Castleford, W Yorks, WF10 1NS
*Activities:* Manufacture of other products of wood; manufacture of articles of cork, straw and plaiting materials
*Shareholders:* Glenn Monkman; Mike Lundy
*Officers:* Paul George Almond, Secretary; Michael Anthony Lundy [1952] Director/Design Engineer; Glenn Monkman [1957] Director/Manager

**Lancaster Girls' Grammar School**
*Incorporated:* 16 November 2010 *Employees:* 112
*Net Worth:* £12,559,000 *Total Assets:* £13,890,000
*Registered Office:* Lancaster Girls' Grammar School, Regent Street, Lancaster, LA1 1SF
*Activities:* General secondary education
*Officers:* Jane Louise Mason, Secretary; Sarah Katherine Bain [1967] Director of Banking; Jacqueline Shirley Cahalin [1961] Director/Teacher; Anthony James Capper [1971] Director/Trustee; Dr Rachel Dyer [1972] Director/Trustee; Susan Elizabeth Hodgson [1952] Director/Solicitor; Amanda Joan Morgan [1970] Director/Trustee; Allison Jayne Norfolk [1968] Director/Bank Manager; Dr Alison Rachel Palmer [1971] Director/Trustee; Sarah Jane Randall-Paley [1968] Director/Chartered Accountant; Stephen Oliver Sharp [1977] Director/Trustee; Leanne Sharples [1986] Director/School Teacher; Julia Louise Stables [1962] Director/Administrator; Richard Parker Taylor [1962] Director/Chartered Surveyor; Dr Beverley Teresa Wallbank [1977] Director/Trustee; Alison Elaine Whittaker [1961] Director

**Lancaster Royal Grammar School**
*Incorporated:* 14 December 2010 *Employees:* 151
*Net Worth:* £38,379,000 *Total Assets:* £41,996,000
*Registered Office:* Lancaster Royal Grammar School, East Road, Lancaster, LA1 3EF
*Activities:* General secondary education
*Officers:* Richard Charles Gittins, Secretary; Professor Martin Alexander [1955] Director/Professor; Dr John Edward Bentham [1946] Director; Roderick Alexander Drake Burgess [1955] Director; Michael John Burrow [1965] Regional Managing Director; Douglas Howard Cameron [1930] Director; Hugh James Castle [1968] Director/Teacher; Paul Worrall Fitton [1949] Director/Accountant; Ena Margaret Lund [1947] Director; Gillian Ruth Manklow [1958] Director; Richard Thomas Mellon [1971] Director/Teacher; Andrew Colin Neal [1964] Director/Self Employed; Dr Navita Parekh [1972] Managing Director; Wendy Preston [1955] Director/Accountant; Dr Christopher John Pyle [1972] Director/Headmaster; Howard Roberts [1949] Director; Kevin John Roberts [1949] Director; Denise Margaret Sinclair [1952] Director; Phillip Sycamore [1951] Director; Sarah Troughton [1972] Director/Teacher; Andrew Trevor Whipp [1970] Director/Lecturer

**Lancaster University Energy Services Ltd**
*Incorporated:* 9 January 1989
*Net Worth:* £10,136,953 *Total Assets:* £10,163,059
*Registered Office:* University House, Lancaster University, Lancaster, LA1 4YW
*Activities:* Production of electricity
*Officers:* Geoffrey Peter Fielding, Secretary; Nicola Cheryl Banfield [1971] Director/Chief Administrative Officer; Paul Morris [1967] Director; Sarah Jane Randall-Paley [1968] Finance Director

**Land Acquisitions Limited**
*Incorporated:* 12 October 1994
*Net Worth:* £3,777,472 *Total Assets:* £6,306,726
*Registered Office:* 3 Greengate, Cardale Park, Harrogate, N Yorks, HG3 1GY
*Activities:* Development of building projects
*Shareholders:* Paul Douglas Land; Paul Douglas Land
*Officers:* Jacqueline Land, Secretary; Paul Douglas Land [1968] Director/Accountant

**Land Energy Girvan Limited**
*Incorporated:* 9 February 2009 *Employees:* 37
*Net Worth Deficit:* £30,065,776 *Total Assets:* £28,103,104
*Registered Office:* Bisca House, Sawmill Lane, Helmsley, York, YO62 5DQ
*Activities:* Manufacture of other products of wood; manufacture of articles of cork, straw and plaiting materials
*Officers:* John Richard Westmacott, Secretary/Director; Peter James Foley [1969] Director/Financial Analyst [Canadian]; Timothy Stephen Roniger [1961] Director/Chief Financial Officer [Swiss]; John Richard Westmacott [1969] Director

**Landmark Wholesale Limited**
*Incorporated:* 17 May 1960 *Employees:* 39
*Net Worth:* £2,834,511 *Total Assets:* £13,090,641
*Registered Office:* 3 Carolina Court, Wisconsin Drive, Doncaster, S Yorks, DN4 5RA
*Activities:* Agents involved in the sale of food, beverages and tobacco
*Officers:* Andrew Mark Thewlis, Secretary/Director; Shamir Bihal [1974] Director; David Grimes [1965] Director; George Garland Hepburn [1948] Director; Sharmmila Jeganmogan [1979] Director; Manmohan Khurana [1957] Director; Geoffrey Norman John Mills [1958] Managing Director; Amaan Ramzan [1987] Director; James William Oxley Russell [1977] Director; Marcus Singh [1979] Director; Jehangir Suterwalla [1970] Director; Andrew Mark Thewlis [1964] Director; William Christopher Wilcox [1955] Director; Gurdashan Singh Wouhra [1960] Managing Director

**Landown Limited**
*Incorporated:* 16 March 1992 *Employees:* 1
*Net Worth:* £1,724,181 *Total Assets:* £3,492,423
*Registered Office:* The Estate Office, Ashgrove House, Elland, W Yorks, HX5 9JB
*Activities:* Development of building projects
*Major Shareholder:* Paul Ingham Cockcroft
*Officers:* Paul Ingham Cockcroft [1951] Director

**Landplan Properties Limited**
*Incorporated:* 1 December 1993
*Net Worth:* £299,396 *Total Assets:* £4,585,163
*Registered Office:* 302 Harrogate Road, Leeds, LS17 6LY
*Activities:* Buying and selling of own real estate
*Major Shareholder:* Vahid Alam
*Officers:* Gail Louise Alam, Secretary; Gail Louise Alam [1959] Director/Company Secretary; Vahid Alam [1955] Director/Sales Manager

**Landteam Property Investments Limited**
*Incorporated:* 19 July 1999 *Employees:* 1
*Net Worth Deficit:* £412,984 *Total Assets:* £5,195,989
*Registered Office:* Murky Hill Offices, Cow Lane, Middleton Tyas, Richmond, N Yorks, DL10 6RW
*Activities:* Buying and selling of own real estate
*Major Shareholder:* Edward Francis Speir
*Officers:* Edward Francis Speir, Secretary; Edward Francis Speir [1976] Director

**Lane Rental Services Limited**
*Incorporated:* 17 March 1993 *Employees:* 62
*Net Worth:* £3,852,984 *Total Assets:* £9,010,363
*Registered Office:* Hereford Road, Pocklington Industrial Estate, Pocklington, York, YO42 1NR
*Activities:* Construction of roads and motorways
*Major Shareholder:* Michael Alan Reay
*Officers:* Antony James Allison, Secretary; Michael Alan Reay [1962] Director/Civil Engineer

**Lanes Group PLC**
*Incorporated:* 8 June 1999 *Employees:* 2,077
*Net Worth:* £29,957,888 *Total Assets:* £140,026,576
*Registered Office:* 17 Parkside Lane, Parkside Industrial Estate, Leeds, LS11 5TD
*Activities:* Sewerage
*Major Shareholder:* Wayne Trevor Earnshaw
*Officers:* David Richard Nutton, Secretary; Andrew James Brierley [1972] Director; Bruce Yardley Crompton [1956] Director; Wayne Trevor Earnshaw [1963] Director; Richard Elliot Leigh [1975] Director; Kevin Andrew Moon [1960] Director; Scott Thomas Norris [1972] Group Commercial Director; David Richard Nutton [1953] Director/Accountant; Matthew Richard Todd [1971] Director; Alan Wallis [1957] Director

**Langdale Close Properties Limited**
*Incorporated:* 4 November 2004 *Employees:* 3
*Net Worth:* £5,248,720 *Total Assets:* £5,900,451
*Registered Office:* Mazars House, Gelderd Road, Gildersome, Leeds, LS27 7JN
*Activities:* Other letting and operating of own or leased real estate
*Shareholders:* Jane Lesley Twaites; Michael Angus Halliday Bigham
*Officers:* Michael Angus Halliday Bigham, Secretary; Michael Angus Halliday Bigham [1941] Director; Jane Lesley Twaites [1951] Director; Nigel Henry Waller Twaites [1948] Director/Chartered Surveyor

**Langdale Owners PLC**
*Incorporated:* 2 January 1996 *Employees:* 189
*Net Worth:* £4,901,412 *Total Assets:* £13,996,474
*Registered Office:* Langdale Estate, Great Langdale, Ambleside, Cumbria, LA22 9JD
*Activities:* Hotels and similar accommodation
*Officers:* Anne Louise Durnall, Secretary; Don Camilleri [1949] Director [Maltese]; Michael Christopher Coletta [1968] Finance Director; Frederick Osborne Crouch [1938] Director/Lecturer; William Ian Robertson Hamilton [1955] Director/Manager; Nick Owen Lancaster [1963] Managing Director; Joseph Longmuir [1959] Managing Director; Dale Edward Watler [1948] Director/Chartered Accountant

**Langlands Nurseries Limited**
*Incorporated:* 22 June 2004 *Employees:* 155
*Net Worth:* £1,740,997 *Total Assets:* £6,208,712
*Registered Office:* Langlands Nurseries, York Road, Shiptonthorpe, York, YO43 3PN
*Activities:* Retail sale of flowers, plants, seeds, fertilizers, pet animals and pet food in specialised stores
*Parent:* West Vale Holdings Ltd
*Officers:* Janet Ducker, Secretary; James Robert Ducker [1975] Director; Robert Lewis Ducker [1946] Director

**Langley Aviation Limited**
*Incorporated:* 7 January 2000 *Employees:* 3
*Net Worth Deficit:* £9,951,051 *Total Assets:* £27,159,438
*Registered Office:* Enterprise Way, Retford, Notts, DN22 7HH
*Activities:* Non-trading company
*Parent:* Langley Holdings PLC
*Officers:* Anthony John Langley [1954] Director; Bernard James Langley [1993] Director

**Langley Holdings PLC**
*Incorporated:* 15 July 1977 *Employees:* 4,229
*Net Worth:* £567,751,296 *Total Assets:* £791,284,864
*Registered Office:* Enterprise Way, Retford, Notts, DN22 7HH
*Activities:* Activities of head offices
*Major Shareholder:* Anthony John Langley
*Officers:* Bernard Anthony Watson, Secretary; Anthony John Langley [1954] Director; Bernard James Langley [1993] Director; Bernard Anthony Watson [1956] Commercial Director

**Langleys Solicitors LLP**
*Incorporated:* 25 January 2011 *Employees:* 367
*Net Worth:* £5,923,243 *Total Assets:* £11,780,967
*Registered Office:* Queens House, Micklegate, York, YO1 6WG
*Officers:* Sally Marie Cottam [1966] Member; Timothy Dominic Berry Cross [1962] Member; Christopher Mark Day [1971] Member; David Joseph Thompson [1960] Member; Laura Collins [1983] LLP Member; John Patrick Conlon [1969] LLP Member; Andrew Christopher Cragg [1979] LLP Member; Carol Dalton [1974] LLP Member; Huw Morton Edwards [1963] LLP Member; Robin Charles Foyster [1954] LLP Member; Katherine Linda Hindmarch [1970] LLP Member; Peter John Horner [1960] LLP Member; Christian Peter Hunt [1974] LLP Member; Christopher Roderick Simon Price [1960] LLP Member; David William Tonge [1967] LLP Member; David Kenneth Wood [1972] LLP Member

**Lantern Debt Recovery Services Limited**
*Incorporated:* 3 July 2008 *Employees:* 85
*Previous:* Motormile Finance UK Limited
*Net Worth Deficit:* £1,554,161 *Total Assets:* £5,567,328
*Registered Office:* Protection House, 83 Bradford Road, Stanningley, Pudsey, W Yorks, LS28 6AT
*Activities:* Financial intermediation not elsewhere classified
*Parent:* Copper Street One Limited
*Officers:* Wilhelm Peter Klaus Ballmann [1955] Director [German]; Denise Crossley [1961] Director; Trevor Bruce Howe [1958] Director; Gary Antony Jennison [1957] Director/Chairman

**The Lapwing Estate Limited**
*Incorporated:* 30 December 1966 *Employees:* 3
*Previous:* Loveden Estates Limited
*Net Worth:* £16,318,393 *Total Assets:* £16,775,153
*Registered Office:* Everton Carr Farm, Claybank Lane, Everton, Doncaster, S Yorks, DN10 5BZ
*Activities:* Growing of cereals (except rice), leguminous crops and oil seeds
*Parent:* Loveden Estates Limited
*Officers:* James Frederick Spence Brown, Secretary; James Frederick Spence Brown [1982] Director/Accountant; Nigel Denis Spence Brown [1946] Director

**Larchwell Limited**
*Incorporated:* 11 November 1981 *Employees:* 4
*Net Worth:* £3,362,148 *Total Assets:* £6,162,024
*Registered Office:* 19 The Point, Sea View Street, Cleethorpes, N E Lincs, DN35 8EU
*Activities:* Development of building projects
*Shareholders:* Victoria West; David George Christian; Jennifer Anne Christian
*Officers:* Jennifer Anne Christian, Secretary; David George Christian [1938] Director; Jennifer Anne Christian [1942] Director; Richard Pipe [1954] Director; Victoria West [1969] Director

**Larkham Leisure Limited**
*Incorporated:* 19 April 2007 *Employees:* 4
*Net Worth:* £3,227,804 *Total Assets:* £6,181,064
*Registered Office:* Cowden Holiday Park, Main Road, Great Cowden, E Yorks, HU11 4UD
*Activities:* Other retail sale not in stores, stalls or markets
*Shareholder:* Maureen Larkham
*Officers:* Rolson Philip William Larkham, Secretary; Maureen Larkham [1950] Director; Rolson Philip William Larkham [1977] Director [Australian]; Tyrone Acer Larkham [1986] Director; William Henry Larkham [1982] Director

**Larsen Road Limited**
*Incorporated:* 19 September 2008
*Net Worth Deficit:* £3,641,219 *Total Assets:* £4,476,407
*Registered Office:* 5 Larsen Road, Goole, E Yorks, DN14 6XG
*Activities:* Manufacture of other transport equipment n.e.c.
*Parent:* Roubaix Bidco Limited
*Officers:* David Grey [1956] Director

**Las Metals Limited**
*Incorporated:* 15 October 2003 *Employees:* 14
*Net Worth:* £2,272,525 *Total Assets:* £3,043,605
*Registered Office:* 5-7 Banbury Road, Scunthorpe, N Lincs, DN16 1UL
*Activities:* Wholesale of metals and metal ores
*Major Shareholder:* Stephen Dixon
*Officers:* Steven Richard Dixon, Secretary; Steven Richard Dixon [1951] Director/Metal Merchant

**Lashlake Property Limited**
*Incorporated:* 12 June 1947 *Employees:* 7
*Net Worth:* £3,040,251 *Total Assets:* £3,568,852
*Registered Office:* Ravenscliffe Mills, Calverley, Pudsey, W Yorks, LS28 5RY
*Activities:* Other letting and operating of own or leased real estate
*Parent:* Ravenscliffe Property Limited
*Officers:* Steven Knight, Secretary; Charles William Dalrymple Behrens [1965] Director/Chartered Accountant

**Lassic Properties Limited**
*Incorporated:* 8 December 2016 *Employees:* 2
*Net Worth Deficit:* £40,713 *Total Assets:* £3,292,085
*Registered Office:* c/o Home Discount, Dawson Lane, Bradford, W Yorks, BD4 6JD
*Activities:* Other letting and operating of own or leased real estate
*Shareholders:* Rajesh Handa; Suresh Handa
*Officers:* Rajesh Handa [1978] Director; Suresh Handa [1977] Director

**Latitude Digital Marketing Limited**
*Incorporated:* 20 October 2009 *Employees:* 81
*Net Worth Deficit:* £1,260,000 *Total Assets:* £9,214,000
*Registered Office:* One Park Lane, Leeds, LS3 1EP
*Activities:* Data processing, hosting and related activities
*Parent:* Callcredit Information Group Limited
*Officers:* Colin James Rutter, Secretary; Michael Jon Gordon [1970] Director; Robert Kenneth Campbell Munro [1965] Director/Chief Financial Officer; Colin James Rutter [1965] Director

**Laudale Estate LLP**
*Incorporated:* 5 April 2013 *Employees:* 5
*Net Worth:* £9,507,658 *Total Assets:* £10,767,788
*Registered Office:* Bowcliffe Hall, Bramham, Wetherby, W Yorks, LS23 6LP
*Officers:* Jonathan Charles Deacon Turner [1966] Member; Karen Lesley Turner [1969] Member

**Law Distribution Limited**
*Incorporated:* 5 April 1994 *Employees:* 85
*Net Worth:* £2,618,908 *Total Assets:* £3,661,581
*Registered Office:* Pells Yeat Barn, Hop House Lane, Kirkby Lonsdale, Carnforth, Lancs, LA6 2EH
*Activities:* Freight transport by road
*Major Shareholder:* John David Law
*Officers:* Diane Josephine Law, Secretary; Diane Josephine Law [1955] Director/Company Secretary; John David Law [1954] Director/Haulage Contractor; Stanley William Moyser [1954] Commercial Director

**Lawcris Panel Products Limited**
*Incorporated:* 12 March 1982 *Employees:* 214
*Net Worth:* £2,632,183 *Total Assets:* £22,911,604
*Registered Office:* Blue Steel, Knowsthorpe Gate, Cross Green Industrial Estate, Leeds, LS9 0NP
*Activities:* Wholesale of wood, construction materials and sanitary equipment
*Major Shareholder:* Christopher John Hopton
*Officers:* Christopher John Hopton, Secretary; Philip Ian Hall [1970] Sales Director; Simon Philip Hall [1962] Director/Timber Merchant; Christopher John Hopton [1953] Director/Timber Merchant; Ian Matthews [1961] Sales Director; Paul Graham Nuthall [1963] Sales Director

**Stewart Lawton Limited**
*Incorporated:* 2 March 1992
*Net Worth:* £2,319,720 *Total Assets:* £3,495,585
*Registered Office:* York Road, Islington, Tadcaster, N Yorks, LS24 8EA
*Activities:* Sale of other motor vehicles
*Major Shareholder:* Stewart Lawton
*Officers:* Zoe Louise Lister, Secretary; Dean Lawton [1973] Director; Stewart Lawton [1948] Director/Car Dealer

**Lawton Yarns (Holdings) Limited**
*Incorporated:* 20 January 2012
*Net Worth:* £11,012,000 *Total Assets:* £11,012,100
*Registered Office:* Ravens Ing Mills, Ravensthorpe, Dewsbury, W Yorks, WF13 3JF
*Activities:* Activities of other holding companies n.e.c.
*Officers:* Timothy Benson Kay, Secretary; Thomas Karel J. Cappuyns [1970] Director [Belgian]; Timothy Benson Kay [1963] Director; Michael Adrianus Martinus Petrus Smits [1966] Director [Dutch]

**Lawton Yarns Limited**
*Incorporated:* 20 January 2012 *Employees:* 306
*Net Worth:* £12,716,574 *Total Assets:* £29,405,960
*Registered Office:* Ravens Ing Mills, Ravensthorpe, Dewsbury, W Yorks, WF13 3JF
*Activities:* Preparation and spinning of textile fibres
*Parent:* Lawton Yarns (Holdings) Limited
*Officers:* Timothy Benson Kay, Secretary; Thomas Karel Cappunys [1970] Director [Belgian]; Timothy Benson Kay [1963] Director; Michael Adrianus Martinus Petrus Smits [1966] Director [Dutch]

**Henry Lax Limited**
*Incorporated:* 2 October 1979
*Net Worth:* £3,307,604 *Total Assets:* £3,664,009
*Registered Office:* Margaret House, 2 Devonshire Crescent, Leeds, LS8 1EP
*Activities:* Development of building projects
*Shareholders:* Henry Lax Developments Limited; Henry Lax Developments Limited
*Officers:* Joan Mary Lax, Secretary; Susan Nicola Chew [1963] Director; Christian David Lax [1968] Director/Property Developer; Edward Michael Lax [1936] Director; Joan Mary Lax [1938] Director; Nicola Louise Mackaness [1981] Director; Anne Edwina McCullough [1960] Director

**Lazarus Properties Limited**
*Incorporated:* 3 June 1997 *Employees:* 5
*Net Worth:* £23,413,472 *Total Assets:* £38,625,656
*Registered Office:* 3 Bradford Row, Doncaster, S Yorks, DN1 3NF
*Activities:* Other letting and operating of own or leased real estate
*Shareholders:* John Edgar Lloyd Nicholson; Michael Patrick Murray
*Officers:* Michael Patrick Murray [1969] Director; John Edgar Lloyd Nicholson [1962] Director/Farmer

**LBBC Limited**
*Incorporated:* 14 January 2010 *Employees:* 86
*Net Worth:* £8,556,105 *Total Assets:* £12,008,905
*Registered Office:* Beechwood Street, Stanningley, Pudsey, Leeds, LS28 6PT
*Activities:* Manufacture of other special-purpose machinery n.e.c.
*Shareholder:* Iona Pickard
*Officers:* Robert David Pickard, Secretary; Alison Margaret Keag [1964] Director/Housewife; Howard Owen Pickard [1965] Director; Robert David Pickard [1968] Director

**LBIA Holding Limited**
*Incorporated:* 8 December 2006 *Employees:* 360
*Net Worth:* £74,343,000 *Total Assets:* £224,772,992
*Registered Office:* White House, Lane, Leeds, LS19 7TU
*Activities:* Non-trading company
*Parent:* International Airport Bidco Limited
*Officers:* John Andrew Cunliffe [1982] Commercial Director; Paul David French [1980] Director; David Laws [1957] Director/Chief Executive; Christopher Sanders [1957] Aviation Development Director; Simon Whitby [1964] Director

**LDK Investments Ltd**
*Incorporated:* 11 January 2016 *Employees:* 2
*Net Worth:* £43,383 *Total Assets:* £5,002,604
*Registered Office:* 48 Station Road, Holywell Green, Halifax, W Yorks, HX4 9AW
*Activities:* Activities of investment trusts
*Shareholders:* Louise Amanda Banks; Cripps Trust Corporation Limited
*Officers:* Louise Amanda Banks [1970] Director/Businesswoman; Simon David Leney [1952] Director/Solicitor

**Leach Colour Limited**
*Incorporated:* 9 March 1999 *Employees:* 99
*Net Worth:* £4,319,942 *Total Assets:* £6,688,141
*Registered Office:* Bradley Business Park, Dyson Wood Way, Bradley, Huddersfield, W Yorks, HD2 1GN
*Activities:* Printing n.e.c.
*Parent:* A H Leach & Company Limited
*Officers:* Paul Matthew Wadsworth, Secretary; Joelle Fabre-Hoffmeister [1962] Director/Secretary General [French]; Sampiero Lanfranchi [1961] Director [French]; James Adam Lavin [1978] Finance Director; James Michael Parkin [1971] Director

**Leader Limited**
*Incorporated:* 5 June 1997 *Employees:* 2
*Net Worth:* £1,366,747 *Total Assets:* £3,007,682
*Registered Office:* 14-15 Regent Parade, Harrogate, N Yorks, HG1 5AW
*Activities:* Development of building projects
*Major Shareholder:* Barbara Thompson
*Officers:* Barbara Thompson, Secretary; Nancy Hall [1972] Director/Administrator; Edward James Thompson [1974] Director/Racing Driver

**Leading Labels Ltd**
*Incorporated:* 15 January 1993 *Employees:* 193
*Net Worth:* £3,115,740 *Total Assets:* £4,004,716
*Registered Office:* Unit 2 Millfield Lane Trading Estate, Nether Poppleton, York, YO26 6PB
*Activities:* Retail sale of clothing in specialised stores
*Shareholders:* Leading Labels Retail Limited; Leading Labels (Holdings) Limited
*Officers:* Michael John Thornthwaite, Secretary; Andrea Gleed [1972] Group Buying Director; Richard David Gummery [1943] Director/Retailer; Christopher Charles Lockwood [1948] Director/Retailer; Michael John Thornthwaite [1961] Financial Director

**Leading Labels Retail Limited**
*Incorporated:* 30 June 2006 *Employees:* 193
*Previous:* Leading Labels (Holdings) Limited
*Net Worth:* £3,115,742 *Total Assets:* £4,004,717
*Registered Office:* Unit 2 Millfield Lane Trading Estate, Nether Poppleton, York, YO26 6PB
*Activities:* Activities of head offices
*Shareholders:* Leading Labels (Holdings) L Limited; Christopher Charles Lockwood
*Officers:* Christopher Charles Lockwood, Secretary/Retailer; Richard David Gummery [1943] Director/Retailer; Christopher Charles Lockwood [1948] Director/Retailer

**Leading Solvent Supplies Limited**
*Incorporated:* 24 March 1992 *Employees:* 41
*Net Worth:* £1,219,097 *Total Assets:* £3,962,650
*Registered Office:* Marston Business Park, Rudgate, Tockwith, N Yorks, YO26 7QF
*Activities:* Manufacture of other chemical products n.e.c.
*Major Shareholder:* Derek Walker
*Officers:* Derek Neil Walker, Secretary; Robert Heather [1960] Director; Derek Neil Walker [1960] Director

**Learning Accord Multi Academy Trust**
*Incorporated:* 4 July 2016 *Employees:* 87
*Net Worth:* £5,627,918 *Total Assets:* £6,449,308
*Registered Office:* Scissett Church of England Academy, Wakefield Road, Scissett, Huddersfield, W Yorks, HD8 9HR
*Activities:* Primary education
*Officers:* Rev Simone Louise Bennett [1970] Deputy Diocesan Director of Education; Julie Ann Bowdidge [1958] Director/Self Employed Consultant; Antoinette Mary Drinkhill [1962] Director/Executive Headteacher; Theresa Maria France [1954] Director/School Business Manager; Dorothy Gott [1952] Director/Retired Teacher; Gillian Margaret Hamer [1949] Director/Retired Teacher; Steven Horne [1982] Director/Employee Relations Programme Workstream Lead; John William Knox [1965] Director/Head of Finance and Business Support; Janette Skinner [1964] Director/Headteacher

**Leasedrive Limited**
*Incorporated:* 25 August 1983 *Employees:* 167
*Net Worth:* £30,991,000 *Total Assets:* £159,344,992
*Registered Office:* Number One, Great Exhibition Way, Kirkstall Forge, Leeds, LS5 3BF
*Activities:* Sale of new cars and light motor vehicles
*Parent:* Zeus Bidco Limited
*Officers:* Patrick James Rawnsley, Secretary; Timothy Peter Buchan [1963] Director; Robert Alan Butler [1970] Director; Mark Connor [1969] Operations Director; Ian Robert Gibson [1967] Director/Chief Information Officer; Ian Munro Hughes [1968] Commercial Director; Andrew Kirby [1969] Commercial Director; Mark Trevor Phillips [1968] Director

**LEBC Group Limited**
*Incorporated:* 16 May 2000 *Employees:* 208
*Net Worth:* £6,422,213 *Total Assets:* £10,416,084
*Registered Office:* LEBC Group Leeds, 1285 Century Way, Thorpe Park, Leeds, LS15 8ZB
*Activities:* Financial intermediation not elsewhere classified
*Parent:* LEBC Holdings Limted
*Officers:* Oliver Charles James Bogue [1987] Director; Nicholas James Flynn [1974] Director/Financial Adviser; Glynn Ronald Jones [1960] Divisional Director; Sanjiv Karia [1965] Director; Camilla Sarah Kenyon [1973] Investment Director; Jeremy Iain MacKenzie MacLeod [1969] Director/Financial Advisor; John McVicar [1961] Director; Jack McVitie [1962] Director/Financial Services; Derek George Miles [1967] Director/Financial Adviser; Dermid Martin Strain [1962] Finance Director

**LEBC Holdings Limited**
*Incorporated:* 10 May 2000 *Employees:* 190
*Net Worth:* £4,446,198 *Total Assets:* £8,004,615
*Registered Office:* 1285 Century Way, Thorpe Park, Leeds, LS15 8ZB
*Activities:* Non-trading company
*Shareholder:* B.P. Marsh & Company Limited
*Officers:* Oliver Charles James Bogue [1987] Director; Richard Francis [1961] Director; Lillian Kay Forrester Ingram [1957] Director; Sanjiv Karia [1965] Director; Camilla Sarah Kenyon [1973] Investment Director; John McVicar [1961] Director; Jack McVitie [1962] Director/Financial Services; Dermid Martin Strain [1962] Finance Director

**Lebus Furniture Limited**
*Incorporated:* 21 September 2005
*Net Worth:* £410,659 *Total Assets:* £4,566,293
*Registered Office:* Dunlop Way, Queensway Industrial Estate, Scunthorpe, N Lincs, DN16 3RN
*Activities:* Other letting and operating of own or leased real estate
*Parent:* Raket Invest BV
*Officers:* Darrell Peter Thomas Bettany, Secretary/Accountant Company Secretary; Darrell Peter Thomas Bettany [1962] Financial Director; Henk Van Der Veen [1959] Director [Dutch]

**Lebus Upholstery Limited**
*Incorporated:* 14 September 2005 *Employees:* 489
*Net Worth:* £3,181,479 *Total Assets:* £11,432,992
*Registered Office:* Queensway Industrial Estate, Dunlop Way, Scunthorpe, N Lincs, DN16 3RN
*Activities:* Manufacture of other furniture
*Parent:* Tornado Meubelen BV
*Officers:* Darrell Peter Thomas Bettany, Secretary/Financial Director; Darrell Peter Thomas Bettany [1962] Director Finance Accountant; John Brewster [1960] Director; Henk Van Der Veen [1959] Director [Dutch]; Karl Frederick Walker [1958] Director

**Leck Construction Limited**
*Incorporated:* 8 October 1946 *Employees:* 86
*Net Worth:* £281,620 *Total Assets:* £5,617,852
*Registered Office:* Ironworks Road, Barrow in Furness, Cumbria, LA14 2PQ
*Activities:* Development of building projects
*Parent:* Leck Group Limited
*Officers:* Dr David Russell Barker, Secretary; Dr David Russell Barker [1976] Financial Director; Victor Barker [1939] Director; Stephen Neil Croasdale [1979] Director/Quantity Surveyor; Thomas Jackson [1953] Director; Gary Denis Jewell [1966] Director/Surveyor; Andrew Christopher Murphy [1962] Director/Surveyor

**Lectra UK Limited**
*Incorporated:* 9 November 1981 *Employees:* 24
*Net Worth:* £681,299 *Total Assets:* £3,231,251
*Registered Office:* First Floor, Jade Building, Albion Mills, Albion Road, Greengates, Bradford, BD10 9TQ
*Activities:* Other information technology service activities
*Parent:* Lectra SA
*Officers:* Mary Wilcock, Secretary; Jerome Claude Sylvain Viala [1961] Director/Chief Financial Officer [French]

**Ledden Developments Limited**
*Incorporated:* 11 January 2001
*Net Worth:* £7,112,274 *Total Assets:* £12,603,061
*Registered Office:* Crown Garage, Crown Arcade, back Albion Road, Scarborough, N Yorks, YO11 2BT
*Activities:* Other letting and operating of own or leased real estate
*Shareholders:* Tara Ledden; Jenna Ledden; Joseph Patrick Ledden
*Officers:* Douglas James Durrant, Secretary/Financial Consultant; Douglas James Durrant [1954] Director/Business Consultant; David Andrew Ledden [1967] Director; Joseph Patrick Ledden [1938] Director/Property Owner [Irish]

**Leeds and Bradford Boiler Company Limited (The)**
*Incorporated:* 14 November 1892 *Employees:* 85
*Net Worth:* £6,952,065 *Total Assets:* £9,816,651
*Registered Office:* Beechwood Street, Stanningley, Pudsey, W Yorks, LS28 6PT
*Activities:* Manufacture of other special-purpose machinery n.e.c.
*Parent:* LBBC Limited
*Officers:* Robert David Pickard, Secretary/Director; Howard Owen Pickard [1965] Managing Director; Robert David Pickard [1968] Director/Engineer

**Leeds and London Group Ltd**
*Incorporated:* 16 January 2015
*Net Worth:* £7,859,864 *Total Assets:* £8,828,489
*Registered Office:* 44 Spinners Hollow, Ripponden, Sowerby Bridge, W Yorks, HX6 4HY
*Activities:* Activities of head offices
*Shareholders:* KS Company No.1 Limited; KS Company No.2 Limited
*Officers:* Robert Simon Rowell [1958] Director

**Leeds and London Holdings Limited**
*Incorporated:* 10 August 1981
*Net Worth:* £11,338,641 *Total Assets:* £11,502,159
*Registered Office:* 44 Spinners Hollow, Ripponden, Sowerby Bridge, W Yorks, HX6 4HY
*Activities:* Development of building projects
*Parent:* Leeds and London Group Ltd
*Officers:* Robert Simon Rowell, Secretary/Accountant; Robert Simon Rowell [1958] Director/Accountant

**Leeds Bradford Airport Limited**
*Incorporated:* 21 October 1986 *Employees:* 243
*Previous:* Leeds Bradford International Airport Limited
*Net Worth:* £117,633,000 *Total Assets:* £258,012,000
*Registered Office:* Leeds Bradford International Airport, Leeds, LS19 7TU
*Activities:* Scheduled passenger air transport
*Parent:* LBA Midco 2 Limited
*Officers:* Paul David French [1980] Director; David Laws [1957] Director/Chief Executive; Niamh Ann McBreen [1971] Director [Irish]; Simon Whitby [1964] Director

**Leeds Bronze Engineering Limited**
*Incorporated:* 12 January 1998 *Employees:* 89
*Net Worth:* £9,875,000 *Total Assets:* £16,672,000
*Registered Office:* 14 Westland Square, Dewsbury Road, Leeds, LS11 5UB
*Activities:* Manufacture of other fabricated metal products n.e.c.
*Parent:* Calder Group Limited
*Officers:* David James Thompson Trueman, Secretary; Gregory Mark Andrews [1973] Director; Peter James Binnie [1961] Managing Director; Duncan Gornall [1961] Sales and Marketing Director; Richard Benjamin Travers [1955] Director; David James Thompson Trueman [1981] Finance Director

**Leeds Building Society Covered Bonds Limited Liability Partnership**
*Incorporated:* 17 September 2008
*Net Worth Deficit:* £9,429,000 *Total Assets:* £1,761,878,016
*Registered Office:* Holbeck House, 105 Albion Street, Leeds, LS1 5AS

**Leeds Cares**
*Incorporated:* 22 November 2016
*Net Worth:* £37,014,000 *Total Assets:* £53,431,000
*Registered Office:* Ground Floor, Trust Headquarters, Beckett Street, St James's University Hospital, Leeds, LS9 7TF
*Activities:* Other human health activities
*Officers:* Dermot Callinan [1962] Director/Accountant; Roger George Frier [1947] Insurance Director; Caroline Anne Gruen [1955] Director/City Councillor; David Loudon [1960] Director/Stockbrocker; Professor Peter Neil McWilliam [1948] Director/Retired Professor; Linda Pollard [1945] Director; Christopher Ernest Schofield [1962] Director/Solicitor; Edward Max Ziff [1960] Director

**Leeds Church Institute (Incorporated)**
*Incorporated:* 6 June 1919 *Employees:* 7
*Net Worth:* £5,738,838 *Total Assets:* £5,760,635
*Registered Office:* 20 New Market Street, Leeds, LS1 6DG
*Activities:* Other education n.e.c.
*Officers:* Anne Elizabeth Beal [1944] Director/Retired; John Victor Betts [1947] Director/Retired; The Revd Canon Samuel Jon Clint Corley [1976] Director/Clerk in Holy Orders; Joseph Domenic Cortis [1956] Director/Retired [Maltese]; Rev Kathryn Anne Fitzsimons [1957] Director/Anglican Clergy; Rev Simon Anthony Hall [1967] Director/Baptist Minister; Reverend Mark Harwood [1962] Director/Methodist Minister; Canon Ann Dorothea Nicholl [1943] Director/Lay Minister; Patricia Josephine Sandbach [1945] Director/Retired; Revd Shona Margaret Shaw [1975] Director/Minister of Religion

**Leeds City Football Club Limited**
*Incorporated:* 23 May 2003
*Net Worth:* £16,273,257 *Total Assets:* £16,273,257
*Registered Office:* Kirkgate House, Kirkgate, Tadcaster, N Yorks, LS24 9AD
*Activities:* Activities of sport clubs
*Officers:* David Creasey, Secretary; Roy Dixon [1947] Director

**Leeds College of Music**
*Incorporated:* 7 April 2011 *Employees:* 163
*Net Worth:* £8,336,000 *Total Assets:* £14,938,000
*Registered Office:* 3 Quarry Hill, Leeds, LS2 7PD
*Activities:* First-degree level higher education
*Officers:* Colin Booth [1959] Director/College Chief Executive Principal; Cherry Juliette Fricker [1975] Director/Accountant; Gerard Godley [1966] Director/Education [Irish]; Claire Elaine Marsh [1974] Director/Library Manager; Dr. Claire Mera-Nelson [1973] Director; Neal Thomas Parker [1974] Director/Teacher (Deputy Headteacher); Elizabeth Raper [1959] Director; Benjamin Patrick Saunders [1971] Director of Music; Hamish Peter Wilkinson [1997] Director/Students' Union President

**Leeds Commercial Limited**
*Incorporated:* 22 July 1957 *Employees:* 152
*Net Worth:* £16,188,788 *Total Assets:* £54,472,020
*Registered Office:* The Roundhouse, Wellington Road, Leeds, LS12 1DR
*Activities:* Renting and leasing of cars and light motor vehicles
*Major Shareholder:* Christopher John Miller
*Officers:* Paul Bumford [1966] Sales Director; Pat Graham [1958] Operations Director; Christopher John Miller [1962] Director; John Gary Wilson [1962] Finance Director

**Leeds Cricket Football and Athletic Company Limited**
*Incorporated:* 21 February 1889 *Employees:* 183
*Net Worth:* £17,029,816 *Total Assets:* £22,028,116
*Registered Office:* Headingley, St Michael's Lane, Leeds, LS6 3BR
*Activities:* Retail sale of clothing in specialised stores
*Parent:* Leeds Rugby Limited
*Officers:* Peter Graham Hirst, Secretary; Paul Caddick [1950] Director; Gary Hetherington [1954] Director; Peter Graham Hirst [1945] Director; Robert Brian Oates [1970] Commercial Director; Christopher James Anthony Ross [1949] Director/Solicitor; Jeffrey Harold Walton [1942] Director Retail Jewellers

**Leeds Design Innovation Centre Ltd**
*Incorporated:* 18 September 1986 *Employees:* 14
*Net Worth:* £4,946,196 *Total Assets:* £7,179,359
*Registered Office:* 46 The Calls, Leeds, LS2 7EY
*Activities:* Other letting and operating of own or leased real estate
*Shareholders:* Peter John Connolly; Robert Michael Noble
*Officers:* Peter John Connolly, Secretary [Irish]; Peter John Connolly [1948] Director; Paul James Ellison [1974] Director; Robert Michael Noble [1953] Director

**Leeds Diocesan Board of Finance**
*Incorporated:* 20 December 2013 *Employees:* 104
*Net Worth:* £177,124,992 *Total Assets:* £192,356,992
*Registered Office:* 17-19 York Place, Leeds, LS1 2EX
*Activities:* Activities of religious organisations
*Officers:* Deborah Anne Child, Secretary; Matthew John Ambler [1976] Director/Solicitor; Nicholas Baines [1957] Director/Bishop; Simon David Baldwin [1969] Director/Head of Enterprise & Operations; Marilyn Banister [1956] Director/Manager; Kay Elizabeth Brown [1967] Director/Teacher/Chaplain; The Revd Canon Samuel Jon Clint Corley [1976] Director/Clerk in Holy Orders; Dean John Richard Dobson [1964] Director/Dean of Ripon; Jane Catherine Evans [1956] Director; The Right Reverend Dr Jonathan Robert Gibbs [1961] Director/Clerk in Holy Orders; Bishop Helen-Ann MacLeod Hartley [1973] Director/Bishop of Ripon; Rt Revd Dr Toby Matthew Howarth [1962] Director/Clerk in Holy Orders; Andrew John Jolley [1961] Director/Archdeacon; Andrew Alexander Maude [1952] Director/Building Surveyor; Canon Ann Dorothea Nicholl [1943] Director/Retired; Reverend Anthony William Robinson [1956] Director/Clerk in Holy Orders; Paul John Slater [1958] Director/Bishop; Anita Jane Wardman [1958] Director; John Irving Warnett [1953] Director; The Revd Nigel Christopher James Wright [1967] Director/Vicar and Chartered Certified Accountant

**Leeds Golf Leisure LLP**
*Incorporated:* 14 January 2011 *Employees:* 6
*Net Worth:* £6,872 *Total Assets:* £3,805,653
*Registered Office:* Northgate, 118 North Street, Leeds, LS2 7PN
*Officers:* Nadeem Ahmed [1967] Member; Naveen Nazir Ahmed [1962] Member; Nazir Ahmed [1939] Member; Razia Ahmed [1940] Member; Sameer Ahmed [1972] Member

**Leeds Grand Theatre and Opera House Limited**
*Incorporated:* 27 April 1970 *Employees:* 231
*Net Worth Deficit:* £606,228 *Total Assets:* £7,839,015
*Registered Office:* The Grand Theatre, 46 New Briggate, Leeds, LS1 6NZ
*Activities:* Artistic creation
*Parent:* Leeds City Council
*Officers:* Kris Brewster [1980] Director/Head of Products, Proposition & Corporate Communication; Neil Henry Clephan [1957] Director/Teacher; Cllr Jane Alice Dowson [1958] Director/Councillor; Alan Trevor Gay [1957] Director/Retired; Councillor Robert Gettings [1946] Director/Retired; Councillor Generald Thomas Harper [1958] Director/Parliamentary Chief of Staff; Cllr Peter Mervyn Harrand [1944] Director/Councillor; Paul Andrew Scholey [1965] Director; Dr Fiona Elizabeth Spiers [1949] Director/Retired; Rusell Peter Wilkinson [1966] Director/Independent Advisor; Cllr Lucinda Joy Yeadon [1980] Director/Councillor

**Leeds Group PLC**
*Incorporated:* 21 November 1900 *Employees:* 189
*Net Worth:* £18,988,000 *Total Assets:* £26,941,000
*Registered Office:* Old Mills, Whitehall Grove, Drighlington, Bradford, W Yorks, BD11 1BY
*Activities:* Activities of other holding companies n.e.c.
*Officers:* Dawn Henderson, Secretary; Johan Claesson [1951] Managing Director [Swedish]; Jorg Helmut Hemmers [1967] Director [German]; Jan Gustaf Lennart Holmstrom [1953] Director [Swedish]

**The Leeds Jewish Free School**
*Incorporated:* 25 May 2011 *Employees:* 15
*Net Worth:* £2,945,596 *Total Assets:* £3,015,103
*Registered Office:* Leeds Jewish Free School, Henry Cohen Campus, Wentworth Avenue, Leeds, LS17 7TN
*Activities:* General secondary education
*Officers:* Alexander Leonard Abrams [1971] Director; Dr Jason Ian Broch [1972] Director; Daniel Andrew Cohen [1972] Director; Henry Michael Cohen [1947] Director; Reuven Zanvill Cohen [1953] Director; Alan Jeffrey Dunwell [1965] Director; Susan Jayne Jagger [1964] Director/Teacher; Jason Mark Kleiman [1969] Director/Teacher; Lee Lipman [1967] Director/Buyer; Spencer Elliott Weiner [1969] Director

**Leeds Jewish Welfare Board**
*Incorporated:* 27 April 1994 *Employees:* 95
*Net Worth:* £6,612,581 *Total Assets:* £6,919,244
*Registered Office:* 311 Stonegate Road, Leeds, LS17 6AZ
*Activities:* Residential care activities for learning difficulties, mental health and substance abuse
*Officers:* Elizabeth Bradbury, Secretary; Dr Victor Jeffrey Leslie [1944] Director/Retired; Helen Rachel Alice Lewis [1963] Director/NHS Manager; Matthew Basil Lewis [1966] Director/Solicitor; Russell John Manning [1956] Director; Joanne Mornin [1968] Chartered Accountant and Director of Finance & IT; Nicola Joy Ross [1956] Director; Michael Barry Sandpearl [1944] Director/Retired; Simon Bennett Walton [1967] Managing Director

**The Leeds Library**
*Incorporated:* 29 September 2005 *Employees:* 10
*Net Worth:* £7,056,961 *Total Assets:* £7,164,296
*Registered Office:* The Leeds Library, 18 Commercial Street, Leeds, LS1 6AL
*Activities:* Library activities
*Officers:* Carl James Hutton, Secretary; James Alexander Bruce Buchan [1947] Director/Retired; Fiona Ann Gell [1965] Director/Freelance; Richard William Hainsworth [1947] Director/Journalist; Simone Claire Ivatts [1973] Director/PA/Executive Admin Assistant; Michael James Meadowcroft [1942] Director/Consultant; Mary Elizabeth Minkin [1947] Director/Retired; Dr Stuart James Rawnsley [1946] Director/Retired; Dr Martin John Staniforth [1953] Director/Retired; Christine Ann Stead [1945] Director/Retired; Philip Andrew Walker [1964] Director/Project Manager; Ian Christopher Webster [1950] Director/Retired

**Leeds Plywood & Doors Limited**
*Incorporated:* 1 August 1986 *Employees:* 107
*Net Worth:* £10,782,859 *Total Assets:* £20,328,650
*Registered Office:* Midland Road, Hunslet, Leeds, LS10 2RJ
*Activities:* Non-specialised wholesale trade
*Officers:* Louise Anne Curtis, Secretary; Helen Clare Gordon [1973] Director/Buyer; James Douglas Gordon [1943] Director/Door Importer; Lisa Joanne Gordon [1974] Director; Stuart Donald Gordon [1977] Director; Andrew Russell Watson [1971] Operations Director

**Leeds Real Estate Ltd**
*Incorporated:* 24 April 2012 *Employees:* 1
*Previous:* Springwell (Leeds) Limited
*Net Worth:* £1,336,488 *Total Assets:* £4,816,001
*Registered Office:* 32 North Lane, Headingley, Leeds, LS6 3HE
*Activities:* Other letting and operating of own or leased real estate
*Major Shareholder:* Jeremy Peter Chapman
*Officers:* Helen Sarah Batty [1983] Director/Administrator; Jeremy Peter Chapman [1960] Director

**Leeds Rugby Limited**
*Incorporated:* 9 September 1996 *Employees:* 6
*Net Worth:* £2,317,815 *Total Assets:* £5,617,816
*Registered Office:* The Pavilion, St Michaels Lane, Headingley, Leeds, LS6 3BR
*Activities:* Activities of head offices
*Parent:* Caddick Group PLC
*Officers:* Peter Graham Hirst, Secretary; Paul Caddick [1950] Director; Gary Hetherington [1954] Director; Peter Graham Hirst [1945] Director; Robert Brian Oates [1970] Commercial Director; Christopher James Anthony Ross [1949] Director/Solicitor; Jeffrey Harold Walton [1942] Director Retail Jewellers

**Leeds Theatre Trust Limited**
*Incorporated:* 5 February 1968 *Employees:* 176
*Net Worth:* £8,761,018 *Total Assets:* £10,454,614
*Registered Office:* Leeds Playhouse, Playhouse Square, Quarry Hill, Leeds, LS2 7UP
*Activities:* Performing arts
*Officers:* Helen Ruth Nakhwal, Secretary; Neil Adleman [1973] Director/Solicitor; Sir Rodney George Brooke [1939] Director/Solicitor; Alan Dix [1948] Director/Arts Consultant; Michael Henry Ellis [1951] Company/Building Society Director; Kevin Harry Emsley [1953] Director/Solicitor; Sarah Anne Friskney [1978] Director/Chartered Surveyor; David Daniel Jones [1961] Director; Claire Elizabeth Lowson [1968] Director/Brand Consultant; Michael Alan Nabarro [1981] Director/Chief Executive Officer; Ruth Angela Pitt [1952] Director/Media Executive and Consultant; Susan Maria Pitter [1963] Director/Freelance PR & Communications Consultant; Mehboob Ali Rashid [1953] Director/Higher Education; Kenneth Reid [1954] Director/College Management; Keith Ivor Wakefield [1948] Director/Councillor; Simon Richard Walker [1959] Director/Accountant; Sharon Monica Watson [1967] Artistic Director

**Leeds Trinity University**
*Incorporated:* 6 July 2007 *Employees:* 427
*Net Worth:* £25,104,024 *Total Assets:* £47,676,596
*Registered Office:* Brownberrie Lane, Horsforth, Leeds, LS18 5HD
*Activities:* First-degree level higher education
*Officers:* Craig Williams, Secretary; Dr Jason Karl Aldiss [1970] Director/Veterinary Surgeon; Justine Andrew [1970] Director, KPMG; Mark Brockbank [1953] Director/Retired; Roohi Sultana Collins [1959] Director/Solicitor; Andrew Richard Gilliland [1962] Director/Associate Principal Lecturer; Aidan Peter Grills [1971] Director/Chief Executive; Jamie Edmund Hanley [1973] Director/Solicitor; David Roy Haslam [1959] Director/Porter; Martin Anthony Joseph Holden [1962] Director/Accountant; Professor Margaret Ann House [1957] Director/Vice Chancellor; Charles Lee Isherwood [1994] Director/Student Union President (Sabbatical Officer); Professor Vivien Jones [1952] Director/Pro Vice Chancellor; Richard Melvyn Marchant [1954] Director; Andrew Micklethwaite [1959] Director; John James Poskitt [1965] Director & Chartered Surveyor; Elizabeth Anne Richards [1957] Director; Susan Mary Chrsitine Rix [1949] Director; Cameron James Elliot Robson [1970] Director/Senior Civil Servant; Paul Rogerson [1948] Director/Lawyer; Bishop Marcus Nigel Ralph Stock [1961] Director; John Edwin Taylor [1948] Director

**Leeds United Football Club Limited**
*Incorporated:* 1 May 2007 *Employees:* 779
*Net Worth Deficit:* £1,100,032 *Total Assets:* £43,740,748
*Registered Office:* Elland Road Stadium, Elland Road, Leeds, LS11 0ES
*Activities:* Operation of sports facilities
*Shareholder:* Andrea Radrizzani
*Officers:* Ivan Oliver Martin Bravo [1973] Director [Spanish]; Angus Robert Kinnear [1974] Managing Director; Paraag Vijay Marathe [1977] Director [American]; Andrea Radrizzani [1974] Director [Italian]; Andre Tegner [1973] Director [Italian]

**Leeds University Union**
*Incorporated:* 15 June 2010 *Employees:* 517
*Net Worth:* £3,917,637 *Total Assets:* £6,342,411
*Registered Office:* 157 Leeds University Union, Lifton Place, Leeds, LS2 9JZ
*Activities:* Activities of other membership organisations n.e.c.
*Officers:* Asad Ali [1971] Director/Lawyer; Andrew James Digwood [1976] Director/Solicitor; Eyong Ebot-Arrey [1997] Director/Student; Afopefunoluwa Serene Esuruoso [1995] Director/Student; Richard Grindrod [1994] Director/Student; Lauren Rachel Huxley [1994] Director/Student; Colin William Ions [1944] Director/HR Consultant; Roland Dumisani Maposa [1977] Director/Student; Christopher Alfred Morris [1995] Director/Student; Japhet Olatomiwa Oladipo [1990] Director/Student; Matthew Lewis Port [1998] Director/Student; Tamsin Emily Scott [1996] Director/Student; Emily Webb [1993] Director/Student

**Leeds Welding Company Limited (The)**
*Incorporated:* 6 July 1944 *Employees:* 113
*Net Worth:* £992,907 *Total Assets:* £6,369,190
*Registered Office:* Westland Square, Dewsbury Road, Leeds, LS11 5SS
*Activities:* Other manufacturing n.e.c.
*Major Shareholder:* Timothy Paul Archer
*Officers:* Timothy Paul Archer, Secretary/Director; Geoff Scott Almond [1968] Finance Director [Canadian/British]; Timothy Paul Archer [1961] Director; Richard Graham Eaglen [1975] Director; Lee Richard Noyland [1976] Operations Director; Ian Verity [1975] Production Director

**Leger Education Trust**
*Incorporated:* 10 August 2011 *Employees:* 143
*Previous:* Campsmount Community Academy Trust
*Net Worth:* £10,188,000 *Total Assets:* £11,280,000
*Registered Office:* Campsmount Academy, Ryecroft Road, Norton, Doncaster, S Yorks, DN6 9AS
*Activities:* General secondary education
*Officers:* Kirstie Anne Lee, Secretary; Claire Elizabeth Allen [1958] Director/Teacher; Helen Brookes [1976] Director/Teaching Assistant; Melanie Campbell [1966] Director/Housewife; Adam Christopher Dale [1973] Director/Headteacher; Martin Edward Drake [1975] Director/Farmer; Bridget Mary Gill [1958] Director/Administrator; Geoffrey Hall [1941] Director/Retired; Christopher Knight [1953] Director/Accountant; Berbet Esmilda Lynds [1968] Financial Director; David McEwan [1949] Director/Firearms Enquiry Officer/Explosive Liaison Officer; Tracy Julie Millard [1972] Director/Headteacher; Jenny Parkinson [1967] Director/Senior Student Advisor; Lesley Ann Sullivan [1972] Director/Administrative Assistant; Sarah Marie Thompson [1979] Director/Housewife; Rev Mark Wigglesworth [1960] Director/Vicar

**Leigh Holdings Limited**
*Incorporated:* 19 February 2008 *Employees:* 3
*Net Worth:* £31,426,592 *Total Assets:* £32,454,968
*Registered Office:* 35 Westgate, Huddersfield, W Yorks, HD1 1PA
*Activities:* Financial intermediation not elsewhere classified
*Shareholders:* Savesales Limited; Savecastle Limited
*Officers:* Brian Herbert Leigh-Bramwell [1951] Director; Robert Philip Leigh-Bramwell [1986] Director/Property Surveyor; Jennifer Leigh Mitchell [1948] Director

**Leisure Infrastructure Investors Limited**
*Incorporated:* 10 May 2010 *Employees:* 2
*Net Worth:* £1,979,664 *Total Assets:* £11,800,813
*Registered Office:* 4 Greengate, Cardale Park, Harrogate, N Yorks, HG3 1GY
*Activities:* Activities of head offices
*Parent:* Cardale Infrastructure Investments Limited
*Officers:* Alastair William Hopps [1986] Director/Accountant; Alexander Toby Shedden Parry [1976] Director/Company Secretary

**Leisure Park Management Limited**
*Incorporated:* 19 November 1992 *Employees:* 3
*Net Worth:* £4,532,305 *Total Assets:* £4,815,431
*Registered Office:* Owthorne Manor, 2 Hubert Street, Withernsea, E Yorks, HU19 2AT
*Activities:* Recreational vehicle parks, trailer parks and camping grounds
*Major Shareholder:* David Francis Keedy
*Officers:* David Francis Keedy [1944] Director; Jason Brian Keedy [1972] Director/Manager

**Leisure Parks Limited**
*Incorporated:* 5 February 2003 *Employees:* 15
*Net Worth:* £11,407,951 *Total Assets:* £19,558,336
*Registered Office:* Fernbank, Crooklands, Milnthorpe, Cumbria, LA7 7PB
*Activities:* Recreational vehicle parks, trailer parks and camping grounds
*Shareholders:* Craig Ben Ellis; Tracy Louise Stevenson
*Officers:* Tracy Louise Stevenson, Secretary/Caravan Site Operator; Craig Ben Ellis [1961] Director/Civil Engineering Consultant; Tracy Louise Stevenson [1964] Director/Caravan Site Operator

**Leisure Resorts Limited**
*Incorporated:* 15 December 2016 *Employees:* 18
*Net Worth:* £294,676 *Total Assets:* £23,200,224
*Registered Office:* Medina House, 2 Station Avenue, Bridlington, E Yorks, YO16 4LZ
*Activities:* Other holiday and other collective accommodation
*Shareholders:* Claire Molloy; Gary Michael Molloy
*Officers:* Emma Jayne Bristow [1980] Finance Director; Philip Burton [1970] Director; Grant Frederic Gidman [1977] Marketing Director; Gary Michael Molloy [1963] Director

**Leisure World Group Limited**
*Incorporated:* 18 January 2012 *Employees:* 101
*Net Worth:* £2,956,487 *Total Assets:* £16,499,221
*Registered Office:* c/o Catterick Caravan & Camping Centre Limited, Gatherley Road, Brompton on Swale, Richmond, N Yorks, DL10 7JB
*Activities:* Activities of other holding companies n.e.c.
*Shareholders:* Christopher Michael Kinsell; Matthew Alexander Kinsell
*Officers:* Christopher Michael Kinsell, Secretary; Christopher Michael Kinsell [1973] Director; Matthew Alexander Kinsell [1979] Director

**Leman International Transport Limited**
*Incorporated:* 2 July 2009 *Employees:* 65
*Previous:* Aeroship Freightforwarding Ltd
*Net Worth:* £2,388,605 *Total Assets:* £14,544,463
*Registered Office:* Unit 35 Don Pedro Avenue, Normanton Industrial Estate, Normanton, W Yorks, WF6 1TD
*Activities:* Freight transport by road
*Shareholders:* Leman International System Transport A/S; Leman International System Transport A/S
*Officers:* Jesper Renner Autzen [1969] Director [Danish]; Thomas Kroyer [1967] Director [Danish]; Morten Bo Abildokke Rasmussen [1961] Director/Finance & IT Manager [Danish]; Jesper Krupa Thygesen [1978] Director [Danish]

**Lenzing Fibers Grimsby Limited**
*Incorporated:* 14 February 2006 *Employees:* 174
*Net Worth:* £61,890,000 *Total Assets:* £74,945,000
*Registered Office:* Energy Park Way, Grimsby, N E Lincs, DN31 2TT
*Activities:* Manufacture of man-made fibres
*Parent:* Lenzing Aktiengesellschaft
*Officers:* Jemma Louise Turrell, Secretary; Adrian Charles Francis Dodds [1965] Director/Regional HR Manager UK; Philip Munson [1964] Director/Site Manager; Jemma Louise Turrell [1973] Director/Financial Controller

**Leo Group Limited**
*Incorporated:* 8 August 2001 *Employees:* 2
*Net Worth:* £84,301,472 *Total Assets:* £101,921,592
*Registered Office:* Swalesmoor Farm, Swalesmoor Road, Halifax, W Yorks, HX3 6UF
*Activities:* Activities of head offices
*Parent:* Leo Group Holdings Limited
*Officers:* Darren Richard Marr [1970] Director/Accountant; Danny Steven Sawrij [1969] Director/Farmer

**Leodis Academies Trust**
*Incorporated:* 27 July 2011 *Employees:* 437
*Previous:* Woodkirk Academy Trust
*Net Worth:* £15,184,000 *Total Assets:* £18,596,000
*Registered Office:* Woodkirk Academy, Rein Road, Tingley, Wakefield, W Yorks, WF3 1JQ
*Activities:* General secondary education
*Officers:* Wendy Jane Beasley, Secretary; Lawrence John Christensen [1974] Marketing Director; Rebecca Jane Hilde Ganz [1968] Director/Management Consultant; David Thomas Lester [1968] Director; Dr Nicholas Vincent O'Donovan [1971] Director/Dentist; Dr Stephen Antony Rose [1967] Director/Institute Manager; Alan Archibald Simpson [1969] Director/Self Employed; Colin Stribley [1961] Director; Ian West [1958] Director/Instrument Technician

**R H Leonard Limited**
*Incorporated:* 3 February 1967 *Employees:* 6
*Net Worth:* £3,393,173 *Total Assets:* £5,105,254
*Registered Office:* West Hill, Aldbrough, Hull, HU11 4QT
*Activities:* Growing of cereals (except rice), leguminous crops and oil seeds
*Shareholders:* Philippa Elizabeth MacLeod; Guy Thomas Leonard; Mark Benjamin Caley; Kevin Simon Webster
*Officers:* Mark Benjamin Caley, Secretary; Guy Thomas Leonard [1969] Director/Farmer

**The Lerrix Tankship Limited**
*Incorporated:* 13 March 2003
*Net Worth:* £75,835 *Total Assets:* £4,880,827
*Registered Office:* 45 Spyvee Street, Hull, HU8 7JR
*Activities:* Sea and coastal freight water transport
*Parent:* J R Rix & Sons Ltd
*Officers:* Rory Michael Andrew Clarke [1959] Director; James Ian Doyle [1974] Director; David Charles Evans [1953] Director; Duncan John Lambert [1961] Director; Sally Joanna Rix [1965] Director; Timothy John Rix [1963] Director

**Lesjofors Springs (UK) Limited**
*Incorporated:* 22 March 1990 *Employees:* 33
*Net Worth:* £3,668,360 *Total Assets:* £9,578,142
*Registered Office:* Spring Moor, Lindley Moor Road, Huddersfield, W Yorks, HD3 3TD
*Activities:* Wholesale trade of motor vehicle parts and accessories
*Officers:* Robert Simon Glynn, Secretary/Managing Director; Robert Simon Glynn [1967] Managing Director; Kjell-Arne Gunnar Lindback [1952] Group Managing Director [Swedish]; Kurt Hakan Moller [1962] Director [Swedish]

**Lesley, Stephen & Co. Limited**
*Incorporated:* 24 August 2010 *Employees:* 3
*Net Worth:* £18,832 *Total Assets:* £5,132,339
*Registered Office:* The Media Centre, 7 Northumberland Street, Huddersfield, W Yorks, HD1 1RL
*Activities:* Credit granting by non-deposit taking finance houses and other specialist consumer credit grantors
*Shareholder:* Harry Jamieson Cummine
*Officers:* Harry Jamieson Cummine, Secretary; Andrew Gregory Cummine [1984] Director; Harry Jamieson Cummine [1949] Director; Ian Stephen Cummine [1953] Development Director

**The Lettershop Limited**
*Incorporated:* 24 March 1920 *Employees:* 184
*Net Worth:* £10,316,009 *Total Assets:* £21,391,344
*Registered Office:* The Lettershop Group, Whitehall Park, Whitehall Road, Leeds, LS12 5XX
*Activities:* Printing n.e.c.
*Parent:* Hamsard 3302 Limited
*Officers:* Lee David Richardson, Secretary; Simon Timothy Cooper [1971] Director; Stephen Tony Goodman [1970] Director/Accountant; David McGolpin [1961] Director; Lee David Richardson [1971] Director/Accountant

**Letts Properties Limited**
*Incorporated:* 7 March 2017
*Net Worth:* £198,836 *Total Assets:* £3,732,392
*Registered Office:* 650 Barnsley Road, Wakefield, W Yorks, WF2 6QQ
*Activities:* Other letting and operating of own or leased real estate
*Shareholders:* Peter Barrington Letts; Trudi Louise Letts
*Officers:* Peter Barrington Letts [1967] Director; Trudi Louise Letts [1973] Director

**Lewis Civil Engineering Limited**
*Incorporated:* 24 July 1984 *Employees:* 218
*Net Worth:* £5,060,000 *Total Assets:* £15,790,000
*Registered Office:* 3175 Century Way, Thorpe Park, Leeds, LS15 8ZB
*Activities:* Construction of water projects
*Shareholders:* Renew Holdings PLC; Renew Holdings PLC
*Officers:* David Andrew Boden [1961] Director; Nicholas John [1963] Director; Jamie Prichard [1972] Director; Paul Scott [1964] Director

**Derek Lewis Limited**
*Incorporated:* 16 March 1973 *Employees:* 60
*Net Worth:* £423,904 *Total Assets:* £4,751,815
*Registered Office:* Millfield Industrial Estate, Bentley, Doncaster, S Yorks, DN5 0SJ
*Activities:* Other specialised construction activities n.e.c.
*Parent:* Lewis Rhodes Holdings Limited
*Officers:* Louise Morton, Secretary; John Lewis [1956] Director; Thomas Mark Lewis [1985] Director; Darren Baden Rhodes [1969] Director; Dean Robert Whittle [1975] Director

**Lexia Solutions Group Limited**
*Incorporated:* 5 February 2004
*Net Worth:* £5,570,000 *Total Assets:* £19,031,000
*Registered Office:* Unit C, Astra Park, Parkside Lane, Leeds, LS11 5SZ
*Activities:* Activities of head offices
*Major Shareholder:* Jason Martin Davy
*Officers:* Jason Martin Davy [1970] Managing Director; Andrew Mark Finn [1967] Finance Director

**LGK Farms LLP**
*Incorporated:* 10 February 2011 *Employees:* 2
*Net Worth:* £8,942,894 *Total Assets:* £9,245,114
*Registered Office:* Unit 8 Ebor Court, Redhouse Interchange, Adwick-le-Street, Doncaster, S Yorks, DN6 7FE
*Officers:* Lord Graham Kirkham [1944] Member; Lady Pauline Kirkham [1943] Member

**Lhasa Limited**
*Incorporated:* 27 October 1983 *Employees:* 144
*Net Worth:* £9,354,000 *Total Assets:* £16,515,000
*Registered Office:* Granary Wharf House, 2 Canal Wharf, Holbeck, Leeds, LS11 5PS
*Activities:* Other research and experimental development on natural sciences and engineering
*Officers:* Dr Camilla Kay Alexander-White [1971] Director/Programme Manager; Elizabeth Anne Blythe [1966] Director/Chief Internal Auditor; Andrew Thomas Bowie [1979] Director/Management Consultant; Dr Richard John Brennan [1965] Director/Distinguished Scientific Fellow, Preclinical Safety; Samantha Clark [1972] Director/Lawyer; Dr Krista Dobo [1969] Director/Genetic Toxicologist [American]; Professor Valerie Jane Gillet [1962] Director/Professor of Chemoinformatics; Dr Susanne Glowienke [1966] Director/Research Scientist [German]; Dr James Stephen Harvey [1970] Director/Scientist; David Michael Hollins [1957] Director/Banker; Neil Antony Moxon [1960] Director/IT Consultant; Dr Deborah Marion Richardson [1955] Programme Director

**Liberty Guard (U.K.) Limited**
*Incorporated:* 3 October 2002 *Employees:* 43
*Net Worth:* £4,914,204 *Total Assets:* £10,531,724
*Registered Office:* The Old Airfield, Belton Road, Sandtoft, Doncaster, S Yorks, DN8 5SX
*Activities:* Other specialised construction activities n.e.c.
*Major Shareholder:* Gordon Jones
*Officers:* John Bamford, Secretary; Emma Louise Jones Mackie [1977] Director/Manager; Darren Wasilewski [1976] Sales Director

**Liberty Merchant Bar PLC**
*Incorporated:* 1 November 1984 *Employees:* 151
*Previous:* Liberty Merchant Bar Limited
*Net Worth:* £5,585,000 *Total Assets:* £29,232,000
*Registered Office:* Liberty House, Scunthorpe Steel Works, Brigg Road, Scunthorpe, N Lincs, DN16 1XJ
*Activities:* Manufacture of basic iron and steel and of ferro-alloys
*Major Shareholder:* Sanjeev Gupta
*Officers:* Sanjay Tohani, Secretary; Virinder Bahadur Garg [1965] Director; Sanjay Tohani [1971] Director

**Liberty2803 Limited**
*Incorporated:* 25 October 2011 *Employees:* 629
*Net Worth:* £23,866,000 *Total Assets:* £94,697,000
*Registered Office:* Brunswick House, 1 Deighton Close, Wetherby, W Yorks, LS22 7GZ
*Activities:* Activities of head offices
*Major Shareholder:* Stuart John Moore
*Officers:* Stuart John Moore [1964] Director

**Libra Careco CH2 Propco Limited**
*Incorporated:* 7 September 2005
*Net Worth:* £310,822,016 *Total Assets:* £422,870,016
*Registered Office:* Southgate House, Archer Street, Darlington, Co Durham, DL3 6AH
*Activities:* Buying and selling of own real estate
*Parent:* Libra Careco CH2 Propco Holdco Ltd
*Officers:* James Justin Hutchens [1974] Director [American]; David Andrew Smith [1974] Director

**Libra Careco CH3 Propco Limited**
*Incorporated:* 30 September 2005
*Net Worth:* £114,603,000 *Total Assets:* £193,359,008
*Registered Office:* Southgate House, Archer Street, Darlington, Co Durham, DL3 6AH
*Activities:* Buying and selling of own real estate
*Parent:* Libra Careco CH3 Propco Holdco Ltd
*Officers:* James Justin Hutchens [1974] Director [American]; David Andrew Smith [1974] Director

**Libra Careco Investments 1 Limited**
*Incorporated:* 25 November 2004
*Net Worth:* £279,151,520 *Total Assets:* £302,528,736
*Registered Office:* Southgate House, Archer Street, Darlington, Co Durham, DL3 6AH
*Activities:* Other business support service activities n.e.c.
*Parent:* Libra Careco Holdings Ltd
*Officers:* James Justin Hutchens [1974] Director [American]; David Andrew Smith [1974] Director

**Libra Careco Investments 2 Limited**
*Incorporated:* 25 November 2004
*Net Worth:* £83,367,656 *Total Assets:* £98,782,400
*Registered Office:* Southgate House, Archer Street, Darlington, Co Durham, DL3 6AH
*Activities:* Other business support service activities n.e.c.
*Parent:* Libra Careco Investments 1 Ltd
*Officers:* James Justin Hutchens [1974] Director [American]; David Andrew Smith [1974] Director

**Libra Careco Limited**
*Incorporated:* 25 November 2004
*Net Worth Deficit:* £137,949,696 *Total Assets:* £586,443,200
*Registered Office:* Southgate House, Archer Street, Darlington, Co Durham, DL3 6AH
*Activities:* Other business support service activities n.e.c.
*Parent:* Libra Careco Investments 2 Ltd
*Officers:* James Justin Hutchens [1974] Director [American]; David Andrew Smith [1974] Director

**Lidget LLP**
*Incorporated:* 25 September 2008 *Employees:* 80
*Net Worth:* £2,340,017 *Total Assets:* £6,042,062
*Registered Office:* Lindsay House, Brackenbeck Road, Lidget Green, Bradford, W Yorks, BD7 2NF

**Lido Leisure Parks Limited**
*Incorporated:* 19 March 2014 *Employees:* 8
*Net Worth:* £10,128,227 *Total Assets:* £19,417,146
*Registered Office:* Lido Leisure Parks, Wetherby Road, Knaresborough, N Yorks, HG5 8LR
*Activities:* Other holiday and other collective accommodation
*Officers:* Elizabeth Maguire [1972] Director; Frank Maguire Snr [1969] Director

**Lifterz Holdings Limited**
*Incorporated:* 6 June 2016 *Employees:* 86
*Net Worth:* £460,745 *Total Assets:* £16,410,596
*Registered Office:* c/o Lifterz Limited, The Old Fire Station, Dale Street, Ossett, Wakefield, W Yorks, WF5 9HF
*Activities:* Activities of other holding companies n.e.c.
*Shareholder:* Benjamin James Bowers
*Officers:* Benjamin James Bowers [1978] Director; Malcolm Bowers [1949] Director; Patrick Leoni Sceti [1983] Director; Quintin McVinnie Wilson [1969] Director

**Lifterz Limited**
*Incorporated:* 10 November 2006 *Employees:* 85
*Net Worth:* £2,670,790 *Total Assets:* £15,678,441
*Registered Office:* c/o Lifterz Limited, The Old Fire Station, Dale Street, Ossett, Wakefield, W Yorks, WF5 9HF
*Activities:* Renting and leasing of other machinery, equipment and tangible goods n.e.c.
*Parent:* Lifterz Holdings Limited
*Officers:* Benjamin James Bowers [1978] Director/Sales Manager; Malcolm Bowers [1949] Director; Patrick William Elio Leoni Sceti [1983] Director/Corporate Finance Advisor [Italian/British]; Quintin McVinnie Wilson [1969] Director/Training Manager

**Ligentia Group Holdings Limited**
*Incorporated:* 3 March 2017 *Employees:* 356
*Net Worth:* £2,503,000 *Total Assets:* £28,898,000
*Registered Office:* Ligentia House, 6 Butler Way, Stanningley, Leeds, LS28 6EA
*Activities:* Activities of other holding companies n.e.c.
*Shareholders:* Dinder Investments Limited; Richard Nicholas Rostron Jones
*Officers:* Rakesh Kumar Manibhai Patel, Secretary; Daniel John Gill [1980] Director; Richard Nicholas Rostron Jones [1966] Director; Rakesh Kumar Manibhai Patel [1974] Director; Jan Skovgaard [1969] Director/Chief Operating Officer [Danish]

**Ligentia Group Limited**
*Incorporated:* 18 April 2008
*Net Worth:* £349,066 *Total Assets:* £5,240,281
*Registered Office:* Ligentia House, 6 Butler Way, Stanningley, Leeds, LS28 6EA
*Activities:* Other transportation support activities
*Parent:* Ligentia Group Holdings Limited
*Officers:* Rakesh Kumar Manibhai Patel, Secretary; Daniel John Gill [1980] Director; Richard Nicholas Rostron Jones [1966] Director; Rakesh Kumar Manibhai Patel [1974] Director; Jan Skovgaard [1969] Director/Chief Operating Officer [Danish]

**Ligentia UK Limited**
*Incorporated:* 25 June 1996
*Net Worth:* £2,115,000 *Total Assets:* £22,806,000
*Registered Office:* Ligentia House, 6 Butler Way, Stanningley, Leeds, LS28 6EA
*Activities:* Other transportation support activities
*Parent:* Ligentia Holdings Limited
*Officers:* Rakesh Kumar Manibhai Patel, Secretary; Daniel John Gill [1980] Director; Richard Nicholas Rostron Jones [1966] Director; Rakesh Kumar Manibhai Patel [1974] Director

**Lightbrook Limited**
*Incorporated:* 13 October 1992
*Net Worth Deficit:* £455,955 *Total Assets:* £3,315,266
*Registered Office:* 16 Clifton Moor Business Village, James Nicolson Link, Clifton Moor, York, YO30 4XG
*Activities:* Other letting and operating of own or leased real estate
*Parent:* Parkstone Investments Ltd
*Officers:* Emma Jane Gittus [1974] Director; Jill Louise Gittus [1979] Director; John Robert Gittus [1978] Director

**Lighthouse School**
*Incorporated:* 5 April 2011 *Employees:* 55
*Net Worth:* £2,812,131 *Total Assets:* £3,202,463
*Registered Office:* Arthington House, Hospital Lane, Cookridge, Leeds, LS16 6QB
*Activities:* Other education n.e.c.
*Officers:* Darren Ian Cooper [1968] Director/Chartered Accountant; Matthew Charles Cryer [1965] Director; Rada Grkinic [1967] Director; Michelle Francine Hoole [1971] Director/Teacher; Ian Rees Hughes [1965] Director/Solicitor; Deborah Laycock [1961] Director/Independent Trainer/Consultant; Catherine Monica Parlett [1964] Director; Emma Sullivan [1976] Director of 14 -19 Education FE College; Jeremy Robert Tuck [1967] Director/School Principal

**Lighthouse UkCo 6 (Treasury) Limited**
*Incorporated:* 28 December 2001
*Previous:* Findus Treasury Limited
*Net Worth Deficit:* £417,641,984 *Total Assets:* £175,070,000
*Registered Office:* Ross House, Wickham Road, Grimsby, N E Lincs, DN31 3SW
*Activities:* Manufacture of other food products n.e.c.
*Parent:* Lighthouse UKCo 5 (Holdings) Limited
*Officers:* William John Showalter [1963] Director/Chief Financial Officer [American]

**Lights4fun Limited**
*Incorporated:* 30 April 2007
*Net Worth:* £5,362,053 *Total Assets:* £6,162,224
*Registered Office:* The Hamlet, Hornbeam Park, Harrogate, N Yorks, HG2 8RE
*Activities:* Retail sale via mail order houses or via Internet
*Major Shareholder:* Timothy John Naughton
*Officers:* Matthew James Naughton, Secretary; Joanne Naughton [1964] Director; Matthew James Naughton [1987] Director; Timothy John Naughton [1959] Director

**Lightwater Holdings Limited**
*Incorporated:* 6 August 1986
*Net Worth:* £3,396,938 *Total Assets:* £9,558,352
*Registered Office:* North Stainley Estate Office, North Stainley, Ripon, N Yorks, HG4 3JN
*Activities:* Activities of head offices
*Officers:* Fiona Vivienne Ena Reynard, Secretary; Stephen John Bradley [1970] Director/Certified Chartered Accountant; James Kirk Miles Staveley [1974] Director

**Lightwater Leisure Limited**
*Incorporated:* 7 June 1978 *Employees:* 7
*Net Worth:* £4,518,608 *Total Assets:* £5,156,456
*Registered Office:* North Stainley Estate Office, North Stainley, Ripon, N Yorks, HG4 3JN
*Activities:* Other letting and operating of own or leased real estate
*Officers:* Fiona Vivienne Ena Reynard, Secretary; Stephen John Bradley [1970] Director/Certified Chartered Accountant; James Kirk Miles Staveley [1974] Director

**Lightwater Quarries Limited**
*Incorporated:* 7 July 1976 *Employees:* 26
*Net Worth:* £5,500,803 *Total Assets:* £9,082,318
*Registered Office:* North Stainley Estate Office, North Stainley, Ripon, N Yorks, HG4 3JN
*Activities:* Quarrying of ornamental and building stone, limestone, gypsum, chalk and slate
*Officers:* Fiona Vivienne Ena Reynard, Secretary; Stephen John Bradley [1970] Director/Certified Chartered Accountant; Kevin Norman Parker [1958] Quarry Managing Director; James Kirk Miles Staveley [1974] Director

**Walter Lilly & Co. Limited**
*Incorporated:* 28 April 1939 *Employees:* 148
*Net Worth:* £7,719,000 *Total Assets:* £42,538,000
*Registered Office:* 3175 Century Way, Thorpe Park, Leeds, LS15 8ZB
*Activities:* Construction of commercial buildings
*Parent:* YJL Limited
*Officers:* Duncan Michael Beach [1968] Director; Christopher James Cyril Butler [1980] Director; Shaun David Frampton [1971] Director; Andrew James Postlethwaite [1960] Director/Contractor; Paul Scott [1964] Director/Engineer

**Lily Lolo Limited**
*Incorporated:* 4 May 2005
*Net Worth:* £2,866,455 *Total Assets:* £3,182,162
*Registered Office:* 3a Banner Court, Hull, HU4 7DX
*Activities:* Other business support service activities n.e.c.
*Shareholders:* Vikki Jayne Khan; Arfan Ali Khan
*Officers:* Arfan Ali Khan, Secretary; Arfan Ali Khan [1978] Director; Vikki Jayne Khan [1973] Director

**Lilys of London Limited**
*Incorporated:* 28 September 1967
*Net Worth:* £1,295,248 *Total Assets:* £3,755,235
*Registered Office:* 9 Paget Crescent, Huddersfield, W Yorks, HD2 2BZ
*Activities:* Other letting and operating of own or leased real estate
*Shareholders:* Kuldeap Singh Mehat; Gurmit Kaur Dhillon
*Officers:* Amardeep Singh Dhillon, Secretary; Amardeep Singh Dhillon [1972] Director; Bachittar Singh Dhillon [1935] Director/Retired; Joginder Kaur Mehat [1945] Director/Garment Manufacturer

**Limestone Farming Company Limited**
*Incorporated:* 25 July 1936 *Employees:* 57
*Net Worth:* £6,373,466 *Total Assets:* £16,622,000
*Registered Office:* The Estate Office, Willoughton Manor, Willoughton, Gainsborough, Lincs, DN21 5SH
*Activities:* Growing of cereals (except rice), leguminous crops and oil seeds
*Shareholders:* Clifford Graham Rowles Nicholson; John William Rowles
*Officers:* Richard Arthur Giles, Secretary; Bruce Henry Rowles [1960] Farmer & Director; John William Rowles [1929] Farmer & Director; Clifford Graham Rowles Nicholson [1955] Farmer & Director

**Lincoln & York Limited**
*Incorporated:* 28 January 1994 *Employees:* 66
*Net Worth:* £12,089,237 *Total Assets:* £19,566,230
*Registered Office:* Kahawa House, Elsham Wold Industrial Estate, Elsham, Brigg, N Lincs, DN20 0SP
*Activities:* Production of coffee and coffee substitutes
*Parent:* Elsham Wold Estates Limited
*Officers:* Nigel John Bean, Secretary; Simon David Herring [1964] Director; James Timothy Sweeting [1969] Director

**Lincolnshire Employment Accommodation Project Limited**
*Incorporated:* 10 March 1994 *Employees:* 27
*Net Worth:* £1,554,437 *Total Assets:* £3,433,141
*Registered Office:* 22 Market Place, Gainsborough, Lincs, DN21 2BZ
*Activities:* Other accommodation
*Officers:* Lisa Jane Whitelam, Secretary; Angela Jane Allen [1953] Director/Housing Consultant; Graham Bratby [1946] Director; Jill Gabriel Anne Hughes [1950] Director/Retired; Roger Frank Millett [1952] Director/Retired; Mitul Dinesh Shah [1983] Director/Development Surveyor; Debbie Smith [1969] Director/Commercial Banking Manager; Hannah Spencer [1950] Director/Manager of LAGAT; Donna Louise Wakefield [1980] Director/Financial Controller

**Lincolnshire House Association**
*Incorporated:* 26 May 1988 *Employees:* 87
*Net Worth:* £4,619,479 *Total Assets:* £4,674,409
*Registered Office:* Lincolnshire House, Brumby Wood Lane, Scunthorpe, N Lincs, DN17 1AF
*Activities:* Other residential care activities n.e.c.
*Officers:* Susan Kathleen Eynott, Secretary; David John Beverley [1946] Director/Retired; Michael Burnett [1948] Director; Irene Victoria Crowther [1949] Director/Retired; Robert Charles Eynott [1949] Director/Retired; Susan Kathleen Eynott [1950] Director/Hairdresser; Pauline Margaret Fiddler [1947] Director/Retired; Wendy Liles [1949] Director/Retired; Gillian Smith [1960] Director; Nicos Christofolos Sofroniou [1950] Director; Brendan George Taylor [1953] Director; Steven Warne [1964] Director/Solicitor

**Lincs. Electrical Wholesalers Limited**
*Incorporated:* 27 May 1988 *Employees:* 111
*Net Worth:* £5,550,094 *Total Assets:* £12,536,188
*Registered Office:* Unit 16 Primrose Street, Gainsborough, Lincs, DN21 1HU
*Activities:* Non-specialised wholesale trade
*Shareholders:* Andrew Sean Johnson; Brenda Johnson
*Officers:* Andrew Sean Johnson, Secretary/Electrical Contractor; Bruno Hickson [1977] Director; Andrew Sean Johnson [1965] Director

**Lindam Limited**
*Incorporated:* 12 May 1988 *Employees:* 46
*Net Worth:* £10,388,233 *Total Assets:* £14,078,833
*Registered Office:* Central House, Otley Road, Harrogate, N Yorks, HG3 1UF
*Activities:* Wholesale of household goods (other than musical instruments) n.e.c
*Parent:* Munchkin Inc
*Officers:* Steven Dunn [1957] Director [American]; Thomas Emrey [1962] Finance Director [American]; Matthew Toulson [1969] Director

**Lindhurst 2013 Limited**
*Incorporated:* 6 December 2013
*Net Worth:* £4,131,567 *Total Assets:* £4,131,567
*Registered Office:* First Floor, Mayesbrook House, Lawnswood Business Park, Redvers Close, Leeds, LS16 6QY
*Activities:* Dormant company
*Major Shareholder:* Rameshchandra Amritlal Bhogaita
*Officers:* Rameshchandra Amritlal Bhogaita [1952] Director

**Lindley (Holdings) Limited**
*Incorporated:* 26 July 1957 *Employees:* 3
*Net Worth:* £2,620,125 *Total Assets:* £6,186,159
*Registered Office:* Suite One, Peel Mill, Commercial Street, Morley, Leeds, LS27 8AG
*Activities:* Other letting and operating of own or leased real estate
*Major Shareholder:* Thomas Richard Brook Lindley
*Officers:* Jason David Seddon, Secretary; George William Jake Lindley [1995] Director; James Thomas Glen Lindley [1979] Director; Thomas Richard Brook Lindley [1952] Director/Builder; Jason David Seddon [1970] Director/Accountant

**Lindley Church of England Infant School**
*Incorporated:* 27 May 2014 *Employees:* 48
*Net Worth:* £2,637,623 *Total Assets:* £3,228,684
*Registered Office:* Lindley Church of England Infant School, East Street, Lindley, Huddersfield, W Yorks, HD3 3NE
*Activities:* Primary education
*Officers:* Susan Poole, Secretary; Jan Lindsey Balmforth [1967] Director/HLTA; Nicola Dawn Beaumont [1971] Director/Headteacher; Rebecca Black [1958] Director/Retired; Lisa Catherine Burke [1978] Director/Home Maker [Canadian]; Katherine Elizabeth Chamberlain [1970] Director/Solicitor; Claire Louise Coupland [1978] Director/Clerk; Antonia Alexis Firth [1981] Director/Deputy Headteacher; Rev Rachel Naomi Firth [1973] Director/Clerk in Holy Orders; Ian Henry Frank Gibbs [1943] Director/Retired; Andrew James Hamilton [1976] Quality Director; Andrew James Hamilton [1976] Director; Kevin Glyn Jones [1955] Director/Chief Executive; Rachel Jowett [1974] Director/HR Talent Manager; Stephanie Louise Potts [1983] Director/Data Quality Manager; Sarah Smith [1977] Director/Solicitor; Mark Tomlinson [1969] Director/Teacher; Charles Richard Wilson [1963] Director/Manager

**Lindley Junior School**
*Incorporated:* 3 August 2011 *Employees:* 52
*Net Worth:* £3,224,125 *Total Assets:* £3,649,776
*Registered Office:* George Street, Lindley, Huddersfield, W Yorks, HD3 3LY
*Activities:* Primary education
*Officers:* Nicola Armitage [1985] Director/Clinical Coding; Treena Boothby [1971] Director/Accountant; Sharon Adele Farr [1973] Director/Magistrate; Catherine Ruth Green [1980] Director/Teacher; Catherine Marie Jubbs [1961] Director/Headteacher; Jane Alison Large [1958] Director/Learning Support Assistant; Dr Sara Louise Matley [1971] Director/Psychologist; Steve David Noble [1966] Director; Stephanie Louise Potts [1983] Director/Data Quality Manager NHS; Paul Taylforth [1993] Director/Teacher; Geoffrey Trueman [1940] Director/Retired; Noel Watkins [1964] Director/Self Employed

**Lindsey Lodge Limited**
*Incorporated:* 8 November 1989 *Employees:* 143
*Net Worth:* £4,921,762 *Total Assets:* £5,491,938
*Registered Office:* Lindsey Lodge Hospice, Burringham Road, Scunthorpe, N Lincs, DN17 2AA
*Activities:* Other human health activities
*Officers:* Michael Rocke, Secretary; Alan Wilfred Bell [1948] Director/Trustee; Andrew Samuel Horwich [1960] Director/Solicitor; Angela Jane Lidgard [1967] Director/H R Manager; Mark Richard Lowden [1964] Director/Consultant; Dr Patricia Anne Webster [1960] Director/General Medical Practitioner; Pete Wisher [1961] Managing Director

**Linfit Investments Limited**
*Incorporated:* 16 January 1998 *Employees:* 9
*Net Worth:* £1,814,512 *Total Assets:* £11,027,361
*Registered Office:* Unit 1 Linfit Court, Colliers Way, Clayton West, Huddersfield, W Yorks, HD8 9WL
*Activities:* Development of building projects
*Shareholders:* John Vincent Munnelly; Jan Munnelly
*Officers:* Jan Munnelly, Secretary; John Vincent Munnelly [1961] Director

**Lingard Bell Limited**
*Incorporated:* 9 April 2015 *Employees:* 2
*Net Worth:* £3,953,770 *Total Assets:* £5,261,470
*Registered Office:* 21 The Drive, Adel, Leeds, LS16 6BG
*Activities:* Other letting and operating of own or leased real estate
*Major Shareholder:* Carol Rowley
*Officers:* Carol Rowley, Secretary; Carol Rowley [1961] Director; Steven Malcolm Rowley [1964] Director

**Lingfield Education Trust**
*Incorporated:* 12 April 2012 *Employees:* 312
*Previous:* Heathfield Academy Trust
*Net Worth:* £11,724,000 *Total Assets:* £16,401,000
*Registered Office:* Suite J-K, Lingfield House, Lingfield Point, Darlington, Co Durham, DL1 1RW
*Activities:* Primary education
*Officers:* Nicholas John Blackburn [1968] Director/Headteacher; David John Campbell [1951] Director/Semi-Retired Management Consultant; John Stuart Crowther [1945] Director/Retired; Colin William Eglington [1951] Director/Chairman & MD; David William Elliott [1949] Director/Retired Teacher; Graham FitzGenerald [1973] Director/Chartered Accountant; John Martin [1966] Director/Retired; John Richard Steel [1953] Director/Retired; Kathleen Anne Whitmore [1952] Director/Retired

**The Lingholm Estate Limited**
*Incorporated:* 11 July 2013 *Employees:* 49
*Net Worth Deficit:* £831,022 *Total Assets:* £11,620,631
*Registered Office:* c/o Clough Taxation Solutions, New Chartford House, Centurion Way, Cleckheaton, W Yorks, BD19 3QB
*Activities:* Holiday centres and villages
*Officers:* Jennifer Ann Seymour, Secretary; David Terry Seymour [1959] Director; Jane Pamela Seymour [1959] Director; Jennifer Ann Seymour [1985] Director

**Link Distribution (UK) Limited**
*Incorporated:* 22 June 2007 *Employees:* 15
*Net Worth:* £1,680,004 *Total Assets:* £3,122,971
*Registered Office:* Unit 4A Sapper Jordan Rossi Park, Baildon, Shipley, W Yorks, BD17 7AX
*Activities:* Wholesale of computers, computer peripheral equipment and software
*Shareholders:* Craig Donaldson; David Donaldson
*Officers:* Nicol Donaldson, Secretary; Fraser Blakemore [1984] Sales Director; Craig Donaldson [1980] Commercial Director; David Donaldson [1978] Director/Sales; Nicol Danielle Donaldson [1982] Director/Administrator; Stephanie Donaldson [1985] Director/Administrator

**Link Scheme Holdings Ltd**
*Incorporated:* 21 December 2016 *Employees:* 18
*Net Worth:* £1,922,571 *Total Assets:* £4,757,372
*Registered Office:* RSM, 5th Floor, Central Square, 29 Wellington Street, Leeds, LS1 4DL
*Activities:* Other business support service activities n.e.c.
*Officers:* Sir Mark John Boleat [1949] Director; John Easton Gill [1964] Director; Tracey Graham [1965] Director; John Richard Howells [1966] Director/Payments; David James Fletcher Hunt [1942] Director/Solicitor; William Farmer Raynal [1961] Director; Elizabeth Anne Richards [1957] Director; David Rigney [1963] Director

**Link Up Mitaka Limited**
*Incorporated:* 8 February 1984 *Employees:* 256
*Net Worth:* £4,663,000 *Total Assets:* £23,888,000
*Registered Office:* Link-Up House, Wortley Ring Road, Lower Wortley, Leeds, LS12 6AB
*Activities:* Translation and interpretation activities
*Officers:* Marcus Lee Mills, Secretary; Ali Nihat Arkan [1965] Director/Chief Executive [Turkish]; Mark Andrew Daley [1971] Global Operations Director; Laurence Jeremy Gould [1952] Director; Michele Gould [1962] Director; Garry Charles Levitt [1978] Sales Director

**Links Investment Holdings Limited**
*Incorporated:* 6 July 2017
*Net Worth:* £5,577,000 *Total Assets:* £14,129,000
*Registered Office:* Hexagon House, Grimbald Crag Close, St James Business Park, Knaresborough, N Yorks, HG5 8PJ
*Activities:* Activities of financial services holding companies
*Parent:* Broker Network Partner Holdings Limited
*Officers:* Simon Drew, Secretary; Simon Richard Drew [1969] Director/Accountant; Desmond Joseph O'Connor [1971] Director/Insurance Broker; Christopher Travers [1954] Director

**Linkway Distribution Services Limited**
*Incorporated:* 5 September 2002 *Employees:* 10
*Net Worth:* £3,248,061 *Total Assets:* £3,553,048
*Registered Office:* Skelton Grange Road, Stourton, Leeds, LS10 1RZ
*Activities:* Freight transport by road
*Shareholders:* David John Knowles; Sara Elizabeth Knowles
*Officers:* Sara Elizabeth Knowles, Secretary; David John Knowles [1969] Director/Manager

**Linley & Simpson Limited**
*Incorporated:* 11 August 1999 *Employees:* 123
*Net Worth:* £2,807,363 *Total Assets:* £5,042,058
*Registered Office:* 3 Greengate, Cardale Park, Harrogate, N Yorks, HG3 1GY
*Activities:* Management of real estate on a fee or contract basis
*Parent:* Linley & Simpson Group Limited
*Officers:* David William Linley, Secretary; David William Linley [1964] Director/Property Manager; Nicholas David Simpson [1969] Director/Property Manager

**Linpac Finance Limited**
*Incorporated:* 1 October 1975
*Net Worth Deficit:* £246,688,000 *Total Assets:* £286,167,008
*Registered Office:* Linpac, Wakefield Road, Featherstone, Pontefract, W Yorks, WF7 5DE
*Activities:* Activities of head offices
*Major Shareholder:* Victor Khosla
*Officers:* Robert Burton Lence, Secretary; Daniel Alexander Dayan [1964] Director; Michael Philip Nicholls [1960] Director

**Linpac Group Holdings Limited**
*Incorporated:* 12 December 1960
*Net Worth Deficit:* £34,769,000 *Total Assets:* £559,849,024
*Registered Office:* Linpac, Wakefield Road, Featherstone, Pontefract, W Yorks, WF7 5DE
*Activities:* Activities of head offices
*Major Shareholder:* Victor Khosla
*Officers:* Robert Burton Lence, Secretary; Daniel Alexander Dayan [1964] Director; Michael Philip Nicholls [1960] Director

**Linpac Packaging China Holdings Limited**
*Incorporated:* 19 October 2006
*Net Worth Deficit:* £4,333,000 *Total Assets:* £5,538,000
*Registered Office:* Linpac, Wakefield Road, Featherstone, Pontefract, W Yorks, WF7 5DE
*Activities:* Activities of head offices
*Major Shareholder:* Victor Khosla
*Officers:* Robert Burton Lence, Secretary; Michael Philip Nicholls [1960] Director

**Linpac Packaging Limited**
*Incorporated:* 10 March 1969 *Employees:* 378
*Net Worth:* £392,364,000 *Total Assets:* £591,017,984
*Registered Office:* Linpac, Wakefield Road, Featherstone, Pontefract, W Yorks, WF7 5DE
*Activities:* Manufacture of plastic packing goods
*Major Shareholder:* Victor Khosla
*Officers:* Robert Burton Lence, Secretary; Daniel Alexander Dayan [1964] Director; John Alfred Jones [1959] Director/HR & HSHE; Michael Philip Nicholls [1960] Director/Vice President Financial Operations

**Linpac Senior Holdings Limited**
*Incorporated:* 16 July 2009
*Net Worth:* £473,357 *Total Assets:* £161,852,576
*Registered Office:* Linpac, Wakefield Road, Featherstone, Pontefract, W Yorks, WF7 5DE
*Activities:* Activities of head offices
*Major Shareholder:* Victor Khosla
*Officers:* Robert Burton Lence, Secretary; Daniel Alexander Dayan [1964] Director; Michael Philip Nicholls [1960] Finance Director

**Lion Estate and Investment Company Limited**
*Incorporated:* 7 May 1921 *Employees:* 2
*Net Worth:* £3,853,109 *Total Assets:* £4,299,093
*Registered Office:* South Mill, White Rose Mills, Holdsworth Road, Holmfield, Halifax, W Yorks, HX3 6SN
*Activities:* Other letting and operating of own or leased real estate
*Officers:* Audrey Julia Fisher, Secretary; John Charles Kino Buckingham [1935] Director; Audrey Julia Fisher [1932] Director

**Lion/Gloria Bidco Limited**
*Incorporated:* 7 December 2012
*Net Worth:* £134,574,000 *Total Assets:* £353,334,016
*Registered Office:* Bridgewater Place, Water Lane, Leeds, LS11 5BZ
*Activities:* Activities of head offices
*Parent:* Lion/Gloria Holdco Limited
*Officers:* Michael Joseph Hewett [1980] Director [American]

**Lion/Gloria Holdco Limited**
*Incorporated:* 6 December 2012
*Net Worth:* £148,028,992 *Total Assets:* £148,279,008
*Registered Office:* Bridgewater Place, Water Lane, Leeds, LS11 5BZ
*Activities:* Activities of head offices
*Parent:* Lion/Gloria Midco 3 Limited
*Officers:* Michael Joseph Hewett [1980] Director [American]

**Lion/Gloria Midco 2 Limited**
*Incorporated:* 19 December 2012
*Net Worth:* £165,411,008 *Total Assets:* £165,412,992
*Registered Office:* Bridgewater Place, Water Lane, Leeds, LS11 5BZ
*Activities:* Activities of head offices
*Parent:* Lion/Gloria Midco Limited
*Officers:* Michael Joseph Hewett [1980] Director [American]

**Lion/Gloria Midco 3 Limited**
*Incorporated:* 19 December 2012
*Net Worth:* £148,374,000 *Total Assets:* £148,374,000
*Registered Office:* Bridgewater Place, Water Lane, Leeds, LS11 5BZ
*Activities:* Activities of head offices
*Parent:* Lion/Gloria Midco 2 Limited
*Officers:* Michael Joseph Hewett [1980] Director [American]

**Lion/Gloria Midco Limited**
*Incorporated:* 19 December 2012
*Net Worth:* £99,505,000 *Total Assets:* £162,912,000
*Registered Office:* Bridgewater Place, Water Lane, Leeds, LS11 5BZ
*Activities:* Activities of head offices
*Parent:* Lion/Gloria Topco Limited
*Officers:* Michael Joseph Hewett [1980] Director [American]

**Lishman Sidwell Campbell & Price Limited**
*Incorporated:* 19 December 1974 *Employees:* 2
*Net Worth:* £1,711,728 *Total Assets:* £3,405,902
*Registered Office:* Lishman Chambers, 12 Princes Square, Harrogate, N Yorks, HG1 1LY
*Activities:* Management consultancy activities other than financial management
*Shareholders:* Theresa Catherine Lyons; Barrie Price as Nominee for Nicholas Becket Price
*Officers:* Nicholas Becket Price, Secretary; Theresa Catherine Lyons [1966] Director/Bookkeeper; Barrie Price [1937] Director/Accountant; Elizabeth Price [1941] Director/Secretary; Joseph Francis Price [1965] Director/Building Contractor; Nicholas Becket Price [1963] Director/Accountant

**Lissett Residentials Limited**
*Incorporated:* 2 October 1981 *Employees:* 45
*Net Worth:* £2,608,004 *Total Assets:* £3,198,331
*Registered Office:* Pocklington Industrial Estate, Pocklington, York, YO42 1NR
*Activities:* Construction of domestic buildings
*Officers:* Claire Beharrell [1975] Director; Justin Beharrell [1966] Director; Christopher Anthony Close [1964] Director/Architectural Designer

**List Group PLC**
*Incorporated:* 11 February 1976 *Employees:* 512
*Net Worth:* £2,978,835 *Total Assets:* £4,849,657
*Registered Office:* Wintec House, Winterton Road, Scunthorpe, N Lincs, DN15 0AB
*Activities:* Activities of head offices
*Major Shareholder:* Terence Cyril List
*Officers:* Craig Cyril List, Secretary; Craig Cyril List [1969] Director; Dean Terence List [1968] Director/Computer Consultant; Terence Cyril List [1943] Director/Design Engineer

**J.C. Lister Farms Limited**
*Incorporated:* 7 October 1970 *Employees:* 82
*Net Worth:* £3,898,713 *Total Assets:* £12,402,999
*Registered Office:* Ellenthorpe Lodge, Ellenthorpe, Boroughbridge, N Yorks, YO51 9HJ
*Activities:* Raising of swine and pigs
*Shareholders:* Richard William Lister; David John Lister
*Officers:* David John Lister [1958] Director/Farmer; Kathryn Mary Lister [1958] Director; Lilian Julia Lister [1959] Director; Richard William Lister [1963] Director/Farmer

**Lister Horsfall Limited**
*Incorporated:* 22 December 1920 *Employees:* 31
*Net Worth:* £3,483,639 *Total Assets:* £5,096,727
*Registered Office:* Corn Market, Halifax, W Yorks, HX1 1TH
*Activities:* Retail sale of watches and jewellery in specialised stores
*Major Shareholder:* Richard Thomas Lister Horsfall
*Officers:* Maryannig Horsfall, Secretary/Director [French]; Maryannig Horsfall [1959] Director [French]; Nicholas Richard Thomas Lister Horsfall [1983] Director; Richard Thomas Lister Horsfall [1949] Director/Jeweller

**Live Yorkshire Limited**
*Incorporated:* 26 March 2008 *Employees:* 90
*Net Worth:* £2,655,407 *Total Assets:* £3,880,318
*Registered Office:* Crown Chambers, Princes Street, Harrogate, N Yorks, HG1 1NJ
*Activities:* Activities of head offices
*Shareholders:* Marilyn Janet Smith; Martin Phillip Smith
*Officers:* Marilyn Janet Smith, Secretary; Rachael Louise Hirst [1974] Director; Martin Phillip Smith [1947] Director; Robert Charles Smith [1977] Director

**Liveco Limited**
*Incorporated:* 15 November 2004 *Employees:* 41
*Net Worth:* £2,236,608 *Total Assets:* £4,789,303
*Registered Office:* 2 Henson Close, South Church Enterprise Park, Bishop Auckland, Co Durham, DL14 6WA
*Activities:* Development of building projects
*Shareholders:* Gavin Vest; Darren Cooke
*Officers:* Gavin Vest, Secretary/Construction Director; Darren Cooke [1961] Contracts Director; Gavin Vest [1970] Construction Director

**Living Care Group Limited**
*Incorporated:* 17 March 2010
*Net Worth:* £471,006 *Total Assets:* £3,919,208
*Registered Office:* 4215 Park Approach, Leeds, LS15 8GB
*Activities:* Specialists medical practice activities
*Shareholder:* Stephen Mark Feldman
*Officers:* Dr Stephen Mark Feldman [1962] Director

**Living Care Health Limited**
*Incorporated:* 30 April 2013 *Employees:* 1
*Net Worth:* £3,323,677 *Total Assets:* £5,351,610
*Registered Office:* 4215 Park Approach, Leeds, LS15 8GB
*Activities:* Other human health activities
*Parent:* Aghoco 1419 Limited
*Officers:* Dr Stephen Mark Feldman [1962] Director

**Living Care Pharmacy Group Limited**
*Incorporated:* 1 June 2016 *Employees:* 69
*Net Worth:* £2,416,739 *Total Assets:* £10,870,453
*Registered Office:* 8 Manor Road, Leeds, LS11 9AH
*Activities:* Other human health activities
*Major Shareholder:* David Andrew Lestner
*Officers:* David Andrew Lestner [1962] Director/Pharmacist; Jason Elliot Lestner [1988] Director/Pharmacist

**Livwell Limited**
*Incorporated:* 12 March 2008 *Employees:* 110
*Net Worth:* £1,083,000 *Total Assets:* £10,378,000
*Registered Office:* South Park Suite, Unit 1 & 2 North Farm Road, South Park Industrial Estate, Bottesford, Lincs, DN17 2AY
*Activities:* Manufacture of bread; manufacture of fresh pastry goods and cakes
*Parent:* Genius Foods Limited
*Officers:* Jeremy Peter Bradley [1961] Director/Chief Executive Officer; Lucinda Emma Kate Bruce-Gardyne [1971] Director

**LJV Investments Limited**
*Incorporated:* 12 December 2013 *Employees:* 2
*Net Worth Deficit:* £105 *Total Assets:* £4,076,534
*Registered Office:* 6 Rupert Road, Ilkley, W Yorks, LS29 0AQ
*Activities:* Other letting and operating of own or leased real estate
*Officers:* Paul Adrian Campbell [1979] Director; David Terry Seymour [1959] Director; Jane Pamela Seymour [1959] Director

**Llandudno Bay Hotel & Spa Limited**
*Incorporated:* 3 October 2013
*Previous:* MBI Llandudno Bay Hotel & Spa Limited
*Net Worth:* £810,259 *Total Assets:* £7,188,976
*Registered Office:* Unit D2, Elland Riorges Link, Lowfields Business Park, Elland, W Yorks, HX5 9DG
*Activities:* Hotels and similar accommodation
*Parent:* Northern Powerhouse Developments Limited
*Officers:* Gavin Lee Woodhouse [1978] Director/Consultant

**Llandudno Retail Park Limited**
*Incorporated:* 7 March 2006 *Employees:* 4
*Net Worth Deficit:* £50,824,464 *Total Assets:* £47,636,512
*Registered Office:* Welton Grange, Cowgate, Welton, Brough, E Yorks, HU15 1NB
*Activities:* Development of building projects
*Parent:* Stadium Parkgate (Holdings) Ltd
*Officers:* Andrew Stuart Fish, Secretary; Alexander Martin Clare [1978] Director; Andrew Stuart Fish [1972] Director/Accountant; Paul Dyson Healey [1970] Director; Amanda Jayne Standish [1964] Director/PA

**LMB Mechanical Services Limited**
*Incorporated:* 11 December 2006 *Employees:* 63
*Net Worth:* £1,728,101 *Total Assets:* £3,520,634
*Registered Office:* The Old School House, 2 School Street, Cleckheaton, W Yorks, BD19 6AF
*Activities:* Other construction installation
*Parent:* LMB Group (Yorkshire) Ltd
*Officers:* Lindsey Marie Bean, Secretary; Andrew James Bean [1974] Contracts Director; Stephen James Mortimer [1982] Director/Mechanical & Plumbing Services Installations

**LMM Holdings Limited**
*Incorporated:* 25 September 2006 *Employees:* 45
*Net Worth:* £4,502,646 *Total Assets:* £6,827,562
*Registered Office:* Manor Mill Lane, Leeds, LS11 8LQ
*Activities:* Activities of head offices
*Shareholders:* Max William Brasher; Michael Charles Wakelam; Lynsey Jane Silver
*Officers:* Michael Charles Wakelam, Finance Director; Max William Brasher [1967] Director; Laurence Ian Silver [1947] Proposed Director; Lynsey Jane Silver [1979] Director/Purchasing Administrator; Michael Charles Wakelam [1962] Finance Director

**LNT Care Developments Limited**
*Incorporated:* 18 June 2014
*Net Worth Deficit:* £9,883 *Total Assets:* £12,062,556
*Registered Office:* Helios 47, Isabella Road, Garforth, Leeds, LS25 2DY
*Activities:* Buying and selling of own real estate
*Parent:* LNT Group Limited
*Officers:* Nicholas Foster Broadbent [1960] Development Director; Matthew Graeme Lowe [1973] Group Commercial Director; Philip Miles Raven [1966] Director/Lawyer; Lawrence Neil Tomlinson [1964] Director/Chairman

**LNT Group Limited**
*Incorporated:* 13 October 2003 *Employees:* 1,177
*Net Worth:* £4,823,219 *Total Assets:* £61,668,848
*Registered Office:* Helios, 47 Isabella Road, Garforth, Leeds, LS25 2DY
*Activities:* Activities of head offices
*Major Shareholder:* Lawrence Neil Tomlinson
*Officers:* Philip Miles Raven, Secretary; Matthew Graeme Lowe [1973] Group Commercial Director; Philip Miles Raven [1966] Director; Lawrence Neil Tomlinson [1964] Director

**LNT Properties Limited Liability Partnership**
*Incorporated:* 16 March 2004 *Employees:* 8
*Net Worth:* £7,130,566 *Total Assets:* £9,594,800
*Registered Office:* Helios, 47 Isabella Road, Garforth, W Yorks, LS25 2DY
*Officers:* Lawrence Neil Tomlinson [1964] Member; Phoebe Lucy Tomlinson [1969] Member

**Locala Community Partnerships C.I.C.**
*Incorporated:* 30 March 2011 *Employees:* 1,562
*Net Worth:* £3,569,000 *Total Assets:* £10,175,000
*Registered Office:* Beckside Court, Bradford Road, Batley, W Yorks, WF17 5PW
*Activities:* Hospital activities
*Officers:* Christopher Reeve, Secretary; Julie Michelle Bolus [1963] Director; Julie Clennell [1968] Director/Healthcare Manager; Jane Louise Close [1968] Director/Healthcare Manager; Karen Louise Jackson [1966] Director/Healthcare Manager; Diane May McKerracher [1962] Director; Richard Paul Mellor [1970] Director/Healthcare Manager; Adam Patrick Ogilvie [1969] Director; Michael James Russell Richards [1964] Director

**Lockers Trawlers Limited**
*Incorporated:* 8 October 1987 *Employees:* 14
*Net Worth:* £5,601,931 *Total Assets:* £9,104,109
*Registered Office:* Unit 2 Fairfield Way, Stainsacre Industrial Estate, Whitby, N Yorks, YO22 4PU
*Activities:* Marine fishing
*Shareholders:* Arnold Arthur Locker; Sheila Catherine Locker
*Officers:* Sheila Catherine Locker, Secretary; Richard Barker [1960] Director; Rebecca Bennett [1985] Director/Merchandiser; Andrew Robinson Locker [1977] Director; Arnold Arthur Locker [1953] Director; James Arnold Locker [1980] Director; Sheila Catherine Locker [1955] Director

**Lodestone Projects Limited**
*Incorporated:* 20 December 2011 *Employees:* 19
*Net Worth:* £2,541,402 *Total Assets:* £4,457,065
*Registered Office:* 30 Windermere Drive, Alwoodley, Leeds, LS17 7UZ
*Activities:* Development of building projects
*Shareholder:* Richard Anthony Hall
*Officers:* Nicholas Mathew Stott, Secretary; Matthew Stephen Ellis [1974] Director; Richard Anthony Hall [1961] Director; Nicholas Mathew Stott [1971] Director

**Logical Personnel Solutions Limited**
*Incorporated:* 31 July 2006 *Employees:* 287
*Net Worth:* £809,501 *Total Assets:* £12,613,042
*Registered Office:* Arena Point, Merrion Way, Leeds, LS2 8PA
*Activities:* Temporary employment agency activities
*Shareholders:* Benjamin Max Lerner; Stephen John Durant
*Officers:* Benjamin Max Lerner, Secretary/Director; Stephen John Durant [1976] Director; Benjamin Max Lerner [1978] Director

**Logicor (CH) Limited**
*Incorporated:* 6 July 2012 *Employees:* 3
*Net Worth:* £5,075,192 *Total Assets:* £7,666,812
*Registered Office:* Unit 7 Thornes Office Park, Monckton Road, Wakefield, W Yorks, WF2 7AN
*Activities:* Manufacture of electric domestic appliances
*Shareholders:* David Anthony Bowen; Logicor (Group) Limited
*Officers:* Vivien Wishart, Secretary; David Bowen [1963] Director; Neal Howard Whitehall [1956] Director; Vivien Wishart [1968] Director

**Logistik Holdings Limited**
*Incorporated:* 25 March 2014 *Employees:* 101
*Net Worth:* £3,725,489 *Total Assets:* £13,288,749
*Registered Office:* Unit 5 and 6 Carlton Trading Estate, Pickering Street, Armley, Leeds, LS12 2QG
*Activities:* Activities of other holding companies n.e.c.
*Parent:* ICF Consulting Services Limited
*Officers:* Warren Charles Marshall [1974] Director/Vice President, E&A Finance & Accounting [Irish]; Michael Sands [1958] Director/Vice President - Contracts; John Wasson [1961] Director/President & COO [American]

**Logopak International Limited**
*Incorporated:* 9 December 1988 *Employees:* 25
*Net Worth:* £3,652,979 *Total Assets:* £5,277,132
*Registered Office:* Enterprise House, George Cayley Drive, Clifton Moor Industrial Estate, York, YO30 4XE
*Activities:* Manufacture of electronic measuring, testing etc. equipment, not for industrial process control
*Shareholders:* Simon Thackeray; Logopak Systeme GmbH + Co.Kg.
*Officers:* Simon Thackeray, Secretary; Dietrich Barsch [1974] Director [German]; Howard James Jagger [1973] Director; Simon Thackeray [1969] Director

**London Ebor Developments PLC**
*Incorporated:* 16 October 1987 *Employees:* 8
*Previous:* London Ebor Developments Public Limited Company
*Net Worth:* £6,596,227 *Total Assets:* £8,868,088
*Registered Office:* Millfield Lane, Nether Poppleton, York, YO26 6PB
*Activities:* Development of building projects
*Shareholder:* Frederick Hunter Brown
*Officers:* Angus Darcy Brown [1969] Director/Management Services; Duncan Hamilton Brown [1972] Managing Director; Frederick Hunter Brown [1939] Director; Kirstie Isobel Negus [1971] Director/Teacher; Trevor Keith Negus [1968] Director/Business Analyst; Dennis Ryder Reaston [1938] Director/Retired; Paul Stuart Spencer [1957] Director

**The London Oil Refining Co. Limited**
*Incorporated:* 1 March 1991 *Employees:* 72
*Net Worth:* £8,636,911 *Total Assets:* £11,511,164
*Registered Office:* Astonish House, Unit 1 Premier Point, Staithgate Lane, Bradford, W Yorks, BD6 1DW
*Activities:* Manufacture of cleaning and polishing preparations
*Officers:* Alan Stanley Brian Moss, Secretary; Howard William Moss [1974] Managing Director

**London Property Investments Ltd**
*Incorporated:* 2 January 1956 *Employees:* 9
*Net Worth:* £13,351,087 *Total Assets:* £15,061,746
*Registered Office:* 29a Brook Street, Ilkley, W Yorks, LS29 8AA
*Activities:* Development of building projects
*Major Shareholder:* Charles Frederick Denby
*Officers:* Maria Dolores Denby, Secretary; Charles Frederick Denby [1945] Director; Maria Dolores Denby [1948] Director

**London Security PLC.**
*Incorporated:* 21 July 1897 *Employees:* 1,141
*Net Worth:* £103,379,000 *Total Assets:* £140,763,008
*Registered Office:* Premier House, 2 Jubilee Way, Elland, W Yorks, HX5 9DY
*Activities:* Other manufacturing n.e.c.
*Parent:* EOI Fire SARL
*Officers:* Richard John Pollard, Secretary; Marie Claire Leon [1963] Director/Chairman's Assistant [American/French]; Xavier Mignolet [1964] Director/Finance Manager [Belgian]; Jacques Gaston Murray [1920] Director; Jean Jacques Murray [1966] Director; Jean-Pierre Murray [1968] Director [French]; Emmanuel David Oliver Adrien Sebag [1968] Director; Henry Bonner Shouler [1937] Company Chairman Director

**London Wiper Company Limited**
*Incorporated:* 30 September 1987 *Employees:* 52
*Net Worth:* £2,209,134 *Total Assets:* £16,580,775
*Registered Office:* Sidings House, Sidings Court, Lakeside, Doncaster, S Yorks, DN4 5NU
*Activities:* Recovery of sorted materials
*Officers:* Charles Arthur Hughes, Secretary/Director; Charles Arthur Hughes [1929] Director; James Charles Hughes [1988] Director; John Robert Hughes [1958] Production Director

**Londyne Limited**
*Incorporated:* 5 November 2016
*Net Worth:* £248,136 *Total Assets:* £6,530,349
*Registered Office:* c/o H C F Poultry Ltd, Station Road, Cullingsworth, Bradford, BD13 5HP
*Activities:* Activities of other holding companies n.e.c.
*Major Shareholder:* Michael Feeley
*Officers:* Michael Feeley, Secretary; Michael Feeley [1962] Director [Irish]

**Lone Star Estates (1) Limited**
*Incorporated:* 2 December 2016
*Net Worth:* £232,766 *Total Assets:* £4,889,776
*Registered Office:* The Willows, Muddy Lane, Linton, Wetherby, W Yorks, LS22 4HW
*Activities:* Other letting and operating of own or leased real estate
*Major Shareholder:* Anthony Lavern Spencer
*Officers:* Anthony Lavern Spencer [1969] Director/Chartered Surveyor; Simon John Spencer [1970] Director/Construction Manager

**Chas. Long & Son (Aggregates) Limited**
*Incorporated:* 11 March 2003 *Employees:* 72
*Net Worth:* £4,786,523 *Total Assets:* £8,387,234
*Registered Office:* Woodside, North Road, Brompton on Swale, Richmond, N Yorks, DL10 7JL
*Activities:* Wholesale of other intermediate products
*Shareholders:* Charles Barry Long; Charles David Long; Mark Andrew Long
*Officers:* Barbara Anne Horn, Secretary; Charles Barry Long [1943] Director/Haulier; Charles David Long [1969] Director/Haulier; Mark Andrew Long [1973] Director/Mechanic

**J.Long & Sons (Haulage) Limited**
*Incorporated:* 25 September 1961 *Employees:* 168
*Net Worth:* £2,426,162 *Total Assets:* £6,017,895
*Registered Office:* Sandleas Way, Leeds, LS15 8AW
*Activities:* Freight transport by road
*Officers:* David Anthony Long [1955] Director/Haulage Contractor; John Christopher Long [1953] Director/Haulage Contractor; Michael Andrew Long [1965] Director/Haulage Contractor; Stephen Philip Long [1956] Director/Haulage Contractor

**Long Folly Limited**
*Incorporated:* 29 June 2016 *Employees:* 4
*Net Worth:* £251,841 *Total Assets:* £4,052,178
*Registered Office:* Manor House, Main Street, Beeford, E Yorks, YO25 8BD
*Activities:* Non-trading company
*Officers:* David Geoffrey Wharram Curtis [1944] Director/Farmer; Emma Jane Elizabeth Curtis [1967] Director; Lucy Vanessa Mary Curtis [1972] Director; Sarah Rebecca Launders [1968] Director

**Longbeach Leisure Limited**
*Incorporated:* 5 March 1991 *Employees:* 29
*Net Worth:* £1,859,653 *Total Assets:* £4,823,726
*Registered Office:* Beverley Farm, South Cliff, Hornsea, E Yorks, HU18 1TL
*Activities:* Recreational vehicle parks, trailer parks and camping grounds
*Major Shareholder:* Martin Richard Varley
*Officers:* Ian Vincent Appleyard, Secretary; Laura Marie Firth [1975] Director; Martin Richard Varley [1951] Director; Richard James Varley [1979] Director

**Longley Concrete Ltd**
*Incorporated:* 9 August 1947 *Employees:* 117
*Net Worth:* £5,609,071 *Total Assets:* £9,680,275
*Registered Office:* Ravensthorpe Road, Thornhill, Lees, Dewsbury, W Yorks, WF12 9EF
*Activities:* Manufacture of concrete products for construction purposes
*Shareholders:* Roger Longley; Charles Michael Longley; John Arthur Longley
*Officers:* John Arthur Longley, Secretary; Charles Michael Longley [1968] Director/Surveyor; John Arthur Longley [1973] Director/Accountant; Luke James Longley [1987] Director/Project Engineer; Roger Longley [1965] Director/Plant Manager; Michael Edwin Wright [1944] Director/Engineer

**Longley Holdings Limited**
*Incorporated:* 13 June 1986 *Employees:* 117
*Net Worth:* £7,181,324 *Total Assets:* £11,581,313
*Registered Office:* Ravensthorpe Road, Thornhill Lees, Dewsbury, W Yorks, WF12 9EF
*Activities:* Activities of head offices
*Shareholders:* Roger Longley; Charles Michael Longley; John Arthur Longley
*Officers:* John Arthur Longley, Secretary; Charles Michael Longley [1968] Director/Quantity Surveyor; John Arthur Longley [1973] Director/Accountant; Roger Longley [1965] Director/Plant Manager

**Longthorp (Kilpin) Limited**
*Incorporated:* 5 April 1955 *Employees:* 24
*Net Worth:* £3,721,377 *Total Assets:* £8,284,226
*Registered Office:* Burland Holme Road, Howden, Goole, E Yorks, DN14 7LY
*Activities:* Growing of cereals (except rice), leguminous crops and oil seeds
*Major Shareholder:* Richard William Longthorp
*Officers:* Richard William Longthorp, Secretary; Diana Jean Longthorp [1953] Director; Jonathan Marc Longthorp [1979] Director/Farmer; Richard William Longthorp [1953] Director

**Sam Longthorp Limited**
*Incorporated:* 16 October 1964 *Employees:* 5
*Net Worth:* £4,722,288 *Total Assets:* £4,966,755
*Registered Office:* Moorends Farm, Moorends, Doncaster, S Yorks, DN8 4JY
*Activities:* Growing of cereals (except rice), leguminous crops and oil seeds
*Major Shareholder:* Simon Peter Longthorp
*Officers:* Allison Elizabeth Longthorp, Secretary; Simon Peter Longthorp [1962] Director

**The Longwood Engineering Company (Holdings) Limited**
*Incorporated:* 18 December 2003 *Employees:* 91
*Net Worth:* £6,300,951 *Total Assets:* £8,495,572
*Registered Office:* Silver Street, Huddersfield, W Yorks, HD5 9BS
*Activities:* Manufacture of other special-purpose machinery n.e.c.
*Officers:* Laura-Jane Battye, Secretary; Derek Arthur Hayes [1946] Director/Accountant; Catherine Mary Skowron [1952] Director; Alan Geoffrey Taylor [1948] Engineering Director

**Longwood Engineering Company Limited**
*Incorporated:* 5 June 1902 *Employees:* 73
*Net Worth:* £4,132,856 *Total Assets:* £6,187,718
*Registered Office:* Silver Street, Huddersfield, W Yorks, HD5 9BS
*Activities:* Manufacture of other special-purpose machinery n.e.c.
*Shareholder:* Alan Geoffrey Taylor
*Officers:* Laura-Jane Battye, Secretary; Laura-Jane Battye [1965] Director and Company Secretary; Tyrone Littlewood [1964] Production Director; Martin John Alexander Simmons [1963] Finance Director; Alan Geoffrey Taylor [1948] Joint Managing Director; James MacDonald Taylor [1973] Joint Managing Director

**Lookrich Ltd**
*Incorporated:* 16 May 2014 *Employees:* 61
*Net Worth:* £6,059,689 *Total Assets:* £7,098,417
*Registered Office:* Stoneleigh Park, Station Road, Holme, Carnforth, Lancs, LA6 1HR
*Activities:* Manufacture of agricultural and forestry machinery other than tractors
*Shareholders:* Alan Looker; Christopher Richardson
*Officers:* Alan Looker [1960] Director/Manufacturer; Christopher Richardson [1969] Director

**Loop Customer Management Limited**
*Incorporated:* 29 July 1999 *Employees:* 726
*Net Worth:* £3,640,000 *Total Assets:* £8,416,000
*Registered Office:* Western House, Halifax Road, Bradford, W Yorks, BD6 2SZ
*Activities:* Other business support service activities n.e.c.
*Parent:* Kelda Group Limited
*Officers:* Angela Wendy Miriam White, Secretary; Elizabeth Marian Barber [1965] Director/Accountant; Zoe Anne Burns-Shore [1975] Director; Jonathan Harding [1968] Director

**Lorica Insurance Brokers Limited**
*Incorporated:* 27 February 1979 *Employees:* 120
*Net Worth:* £3,948,137 *Total Assets:* £13,358,540
*Registered Office:* Rossington's Business Park, West Carr Road, Retford, Notts, DN22 7SW
*Activities:* Activities of insurance agents and brokers
*Parent:* PIB Group Limited
*Officers:* Ryan Christopher Brown [1973] Director; Carlo Domenico Marelli [1969] Director/Insurance Broker; Brendan James McManus [1959] Director; Stefan Puttnam [1966] Director

**Loscoe Investments Ltd**
*Incorporated:* 16 May 2016 *Employees:* 119
*Net Worth:* £2,491,989 *Total Assets:* £6,132,237
*Registered Office:* c/o Acorn Web Offset Ltd, Loscoe Close, Normanton Industrial Estate, Normanton, W Yorks, WF6 1TW
*Activities:* Activities of other holding companies n.e.c.
*Shareholders:* Matthew Robert Carry; Mark Graham Roberts
*Officers:* Nicholas Robert Alexander [1968] Director; Matthew Robert Carry [1977] Director; Claire Rennison [1978] Director; Mark Graham Roberts [1970] Director

**Lovel Capital Projects Limited**
*Incorporated:* 17 August 2012 *Employees:* 2
*Net Worth:* £1,769,035 *Total Assets:* £5,035,984
*Registered Office:* 22 Molescroft Road, Beverley, E Yorks, HU17 7ED
*Activities:* Buying and selling of own real estate
*Officers:* Philip Foster Lovel, Secretary; Hannah Mary Lovel [1973] Director; Philip Foster Lovel [1972] Director/Chartered Surveyor

**Low Grange Quarry Limited**
*Incorporated:* 24 April 2003
*Net Worth:* £2,638,773 *Total Assets:* £3,735,079
*Registered Office:* Low Grange Quarry, Low Grange, Melsonby, Richmond, N Yorks, DL10 5PN
*Activities:* Other business support service activities n.e.c.
*Shareholder:* David Richardson
*Officers:* David Austen Richardson, Secretary/Farmer; David Austen Richardson [1976] Director/Farmer; David Richardson [1949] Director/Farmer; Fiona Kathleen Richardson [1971] Director

**Low Moor Properties Limited**
*Incorporated:* 20 November 1954 *Employees:* 3
*Net Worth:* £5,847,532 *Total Assets:* £6,108,042
*Registered Office:* Hill Top House, Main Street, Burley in Wharfedale, Ilkley, W Yorks, LS29 7JW
*Activities:* Buying and selling of own real estate
*Shareholders:* Charles Richard Barker; David Maxwell Barker; Alexandra Elizabeth Kassapian
*Officers:* Charles Richard Barker, Secretary; Charles Richard Barker [1951] Director/Chartered Accountant; David Maxwell Barker [1948] Director/Property Manager; Alexandra Elizabeth Kassapian [1965] Director/Secretary

**Low Street Properties Limited**
*Incorporated:* 27 November 2012 *Employees:* 2
*Previous:* LPG Direct Properties Limited
*Net Worth:* £47,764 *Total Assets:* £11,092,812
*Registered Office:* 5 Low Street, North Ferriby, E Yorks, HU14 3DD
*Activities:* Other letting and operating of own or leased real estate
*Shareholders:* Michael John Robinson; Lorraine Anne Robinson
*Officers:* Malcolm Grassam [1950] Director/Solicitor; Lorraine Anne Robinson [1958] Director/Business Manager; Michael John Robinson [1951] Director

**Low Wood Hotel (1958) Limited**
*Incorporated:* 2 September 1958 *Employees:* 142
*Net Worth:* £10,197,897 *Total Assets:* £35,472,832
*Registered Office:* Low Wood, Windermere, Cumbria, LA23 1LP
*Activities:* Hotels and similar accommodation
*Officers:* Timothy Robert James Berry, Secretary/Leisure Director; Benjamin William James Berry [1988] Director; Simon Frederick Michael Berry [1959] Managing Director; Timothy Robert James Berry [1961] Leisure Director; Jonathan Alexander Noel Cook [1963] Director; Douglas Paterson Dale [1952] Director; Jonquil Anna Catherine Doremus Cook [1969] Director; David Huw Neale [1962] Commercial Director; Matthew John Wilkinson [1977] Financial Director

**Lowdham Outdoor Leisure Limited**
*Incorporated:* 8 March 1952 *Employees:* 63
*Net Worth:* £3,049,179 *Total Assets:* £9,090,144
*Registered Office:* Lowdham Leisure Works, Northern Counties, Crosland Hill Road, Huddersfield, W Yorks, HD4 5NU
*Activities:* Retail trade of motor vehicle parts and accessories
*Shareholders:* Wilfred Roger Crafts; Judith Anne Crafts
*Officers:* Wilfred Roger Crafts, Secretary; Ian Edward Brown [1966] Group After Sales Director; Judith Anne Crafts [1947] Director; Wilfred Roger Crafts [1944] Director; Emma Louise Sharpe [1967] Director/Chiropractor; Stephen Richard Sharpe [1963] Group Managing Director

**Lowell Acquisitions Limited**
*Incorporated:* 7 March 2008
*Net Worth:* £7,943,000 *Total Assets:* £109,965,000
*Registered Office:* Ellington House, 9 Savannah Way, Leeds Valley Park, Leeds, LS10 1AB
*Activities:* Other business support service activities n.e.c.
*Parent:* Lowell Funding Limited
*Officers:* Bill Flynn, Secretary; James John Cornell [1973] Director; John Patrick Flaherty [1974] Director/Accountant [Irish]

**Lowell Finance Holdings Limited**
*Incorporated:* 12 March 2012
*Net Worth:* £182,912,992 *Total Assets:* £182,963,008
*Registered Office:* Ellington House, 9 Savannah Way, Leeds Valley Park, Leeds, LS10 1AB
*Activities:* Activities of collection agencies
*Parent:* Metis Bidco Limited
*Officers:* Bill Flynn, Secretary; James John Cornell [1973] Director; John Patrick Flaherty [1974] Director/Accountant [Irish]

**Lowell Financial Ltd**
*Incorporated:* 10 October 2002 *Employees:* 1,171
*Net Worth Deficit:* £6,480,000 *Total Assets:* £16,754,000
*Registered Office:* Ellington House, 9 Savannah Way, Leeds Valley Park, Leeds, LS10 1AB
*Activities:* Activities of collection agencies
*Parent:* Lowell Finance Ltd
*Officers:* Bill Flynn, Secretary; John Patrick Flaherty [1974] Director/Accountant [Irish]; David Ronald Gagie [1955] Director; Heinz Erwin Friedrich Hilgert [1953] Managing Director [German]; Sara Louise Leckenby [1961] Director; John Simon Pears [1973] Director

**Lowell Funding Limited**
*Incorporated:* 7 March 2008
*Net Worth:* £817,000 *Total Assets:* £112,839,000
*Registered Office:* Ellington House, 9 Savannah Way, Leeds Valley Park, Leeds, LS10 1AB
*Activities:* Other business support service activities n.e.c.
*Parent:* Lowell Group Limited
*Officers:* Bill Flynn, Secretary; James John Cornell [1973] Director; John Patrick Flaherty [1974] Director/Accountant [Irish]

**Lowell Group Limited**
*Incorporated:* 7 March 2008
*Net Worth:* £113,017,000 *Total Assets:* £113,017,000
*Registered Office:* Ellington House, 9 Savannah Way, Leeds Valley Park, Leeds, LS10 1AB
*Activities:* Other business support service activities n.e.c.
*Parent:* Lowell Finance Holdings Limited
*Officers:* Bill Flynn, Secretary; James John Cornell [1973] Director; John Patrick Flaherty [1974] Director/Accountant [Irish]

**Lowell Holdings Ltd**
*Incorporated:* 10 March 2004
*Net Worth:* £31,984,000 *Total Assets:* £51,743,000
*Registered Office:* Ellington House, 9 Savannah Way, Leeds Valley Park, Leeds, LS10 1AB
*Activities:* Activities of other holding companies n.e.c.
*Parent:* Lowell Acquisitions Limited
*Officers:* Bill Flynn, Secretary; James John Cornell [1973] Director; John Patrick Flaherty [1974] Director/Accountant [Irish]

**Lowell Portfolio I Ltd**
*Incorporated:* 6 August 2003
*Net Worth:* £130,184,000 *Total Assets:* £825,873,984
*Registered Office:* Ellington House, 9 Savannah Way, Leeds Valley Park, Leeds, LS10 1AB
*Activities:* Activities of other holding companies n.e.c.
*Parent:* Lowell Finance Ltd
*Officers:* Bill Flynn, Secretary; John Patrick Flaherty [1974] Director/Accountant [Irish]; David Ronald Gagie [1955] Director; Heinz Erwin Friedrich Hilgert [1974] Managing Director [German]; Sara Louise Leckenby [1961] Director/Chief Risk Officer; John Simon Pears [1973] Director

**Lowson & Co. Limited**
*Incorporated:* 8 August 1975 *Employees:* 4
*Net Worth:* £1,928,582 *Total Assets:* £3,025,426
*Registered Office:* York Lodge, Seven Corners Lane, Beverley, E Yorks, HU17 7AJ
*Activities:* Buying and selling of own real estate
*Shareholders:* Stephen Thomas Larard; Lawrence Andrew Wride; Mary Wride
*Officers:* David Douglas Grantham, Secretary; Stephen Thomas Larard [1947] Director/Chartered Surveyor; Lawrence Andrew Wride [1952] Director/Builder

**Lowwood Products Company Limited (The)**
*Incorporated:* 26 January 1953 *Employees:* 2
*Net Worth:* £3,286,898 *Total Assets:* £4,072,652
*Registered Office:* 74 Duke Street, Barrow in Furness, Cumbria, LA14 1RX
*Activities:* Production of electricity
*Officers:* Generald Moon, Secretary; James Roger Barratt [1977] Director/Industrial Designer; Oliver William Barratt [1941] Director/Consultant; Elizabeth Helen MacKinnon [1980] Director/Estate Manager; John Patrick Enfield Taylor [1948] Director/Chartered Accountant

**LPD (Holdings) Limited**
*Incorporated:* 11 February 2008 *Employees:* 107
*Net Worth:* £10,489,762 *Total Assets:* £23,032,200
*Registered Office:* Leeds Plywood & Doors Ltd, Midland Road, Leeds, LS10 2RJ
*Activities:* Other letting and operating of own or leased real estate
*Officers:* Louise Anne Curtis, Secretary; Helen Clare Gordon [1973] Director/Buyer; James Douglas Gordon [1943] Director; Lisa Joanne Gordon [1974] Director; Stuart Donald Gordon [1977] Director; Andrew Russell Watson [1971] Operations Director

**LPG Direct Limited**
*Incorporated:* 24 February 2010 *Employees:* 16
*Previous:* LPG Direct (Holdings) Limited
*Net Worth:* £6,840,503 *Total Assets:* £7,693,182
*Registered Office:* 5 Low Street, North Ferriby, N Humbers, HU14 3DD
*Activities:* Other retail sale not in stores, stalls or markets
*Major Shareholder:* Michael John Robinson
*Officers:* Michael David Browne [1988] Director/Office Administrator; Richard Andrew Browne [1985] Director/Project Manager; Malcolm Grassam [1950] Director/Solicitor; Lorraine Anne Robinson [1958] Director; Michael John Robinson [1951] Director

**LPG Homeheat Limited**
*Incorporated:* 1 May 2009 *Employees:* 5
*Net Worth:* £2,116,317 *Total Assets:* £7,874,440
*Registered Office:* Energy House, Hampsthwaite, Harrogate, N Yorks, HG3 2HT
*Activities:* Wholesale of petroleum and petroleum products
*Officers:* Chris Salisbury, Secretary; Edward Illingworth [1992] Director; James Illingworth [1986] Director/Estimator; Laura Illingworth [1984] Director/Event Organiser; Stuart Illingworth [1988] Director/Student; Steven Adrian Walmsley [1957] Director/Sales Executive

**LPT Trading Ltd**
*Incorporated:* 22 January 2013
*Net Worth:* £190 *Total Assets:* £15,070,979
*Registered Office:* Floor 6, Vinovium House, Saddler Street, Bishop Auckland, Co Durham, DL14 7BH
*Activities:* Activities of other holding companies n.e.c.
*Officers:* Peter John Chapman, Secretary; Matthew Charles Arthur Hutton [1953] Director/Farmer; Harriet Cecilia Ruffer [1990] Director/Research Assistant; Dr Jane Mary Ruffer [1956] Director; Jonathan Garnier Ruffer [1951] Director; Nicholas Timothy Turner [1961] Director/Retired; Ashe George Russell Windham [1957] Director (Financial Services)

**LRUK (Holdings) Limited**
*Incorporated:* 28 December 1909 *Employees:* 100
*Previous:* Redcats (UK) Limited
*Net Worth:* £15,932,000 *Total Assets:* £29,838,000
*Registered Office:* 2 Holdsworth Street, Bradford, W Yorks, BD1 4AH
*Activities:* Retail sale via mail order houses or via Internet
*Shareholder:* Ginette Moulin
*Officers:* Craig Roberts, Secretary; Nathalie Catherine Balla [1967] Director/Chief Executive [French]; Richard Burke [1971] Managing Director; Paul Kenworthy [1970] Finance Director; Michael Truluck [1980] Finance Director [South African]

**LRUK (Retail) Limited**
*Incorporated:* 28 June 1910 *Employees:* 75
*Previous:* Redcats (Brands) Limited
*Net Worth:* £47,822,000 *Total Assets:* £66,034,000
*Registered Office:* 2 Holdsworth Street, Bradford, W Yorks, BD1 4AH
*Activities:* Retail sale via mail order houses or via Internet
*Shareholders:* Ginette Moulin; LRUK (Holdings) Limited
*Officers:* Richard Burke [1971] Managing Director; Paul Kenworthy [1970] Finance Director; Michael Truluck [1980] Finance Director [South African]

**LS UK Fire Group Ltd**
*Incorporated:* 26 November 1959
*Net Worth:* £13,221,000 *Total Assets:* £15,036,000
*Registered Office:* Premier House, 2 Jubilee Way, Elland, W Yorks, HX5 9DY
*Activities:* Activities of head offices
*Parent:* Fire Protection Holdings Limited
*Officers:* Simon Coates, Secretary; Jacques Gaston Murray [1920] Director; Jean Jacques Murray [1966] Director; Richard John Pollard [1963] Director/Chartered Accountant; Emmanuel David Oliver Adrien Sebag [1968] Director

**LSS Waste Management Limited**
*Incorporated:* 30 December 1998 *Employees:* 92
*Net Worth:* £1,534,931 *Total Assets:* £6,113,851
*Registered Office:* Recycling House, Knowsthorpe Lane, Cross Green Industrial Park, Leeds, LS9 0PF
*Activities:* Collection of non-hazardous waste
*Major Shareholder:* Nigel Charles Woolford
*Officers:* Johanne Louise Woolford, Secretary; Nigel Charles Woolford [1959] Managing Director

**LTT Vending Ltd**
*Incorporated:* 27 March 1962 *Employees:* 138
*Net Worth:* £2,987,371 *Total Assets:* £7,044,693
*Registered Office:* Priory House, Unit C, Gildersome Spur Industrial Estate, Leeds, LS27 7JZ
*Activities:* Other retail sale not in stores, stalls or markets
*Parent:* Freedom Refreshments Ltd
*Officers:* Raymond Latimer Hutchinson [1949] Director; Stephen Thomas Alexander Hutchinson [1958] Director; Anne Alexandra Hutchinson-Kane [1947] Director

**Lubna Foods Limited**
*Incorporated:* 22 April 1975 *Employees:* 85
*Net Worth:* £1,042,369 *Total Assets:* £7,388,081
*Registered Office:* 164 Garnett Street, Bradford, BD3 9HB
*Activities:* Non-specialised wholesale of food, beverages and tobacco
*Officers:* Ashraf Ali Ebrahim, Secretary; Ashraf Ali Ibn Ebrahim [1962] Director; Abdul Aziz Ebrahim Patel [1967] Director; Ali Ghadafi Patel [1972] Director; Ebrahim Ismail Patel [1933] Director

**Lucas Properties Limited**
*Incorporated:* 6 June 2009
*Net Worth:* £511,461 *Total Assets:* £5,726,689
*Registered Office:* Lower Sowood Farm, Healey Lane, Briestfield, Dewsbury, W Yorks, WF12 0NT
*Activities:* Other letting and operating of own or leased real estate
*Shareholders:* Robert James Lucas; Georgina Louise Lucas
*Officers:* Georgina Louise Lucas [1970] Director; Robert James Lucas [1968] Director/Chartered Surveyor

**A.W.Lumb & Co.Limited**
*Incorporated:* 3 April 1964 *Employees:* 5
*Net Worth:* £5,997,864 *Total Assets:* £15,020,063
*Registered Office:* Dewsbury Depot, A W Lumb & Co Ltd, Mill Street East, Dewsbury, W Yorks, WF12 9BD
*Activities:* Activities of other holding companies n.e.c.
*Officers:* Andrew Christopher Roberts, Secretary; Edward John Cureton [1950] Director/Builders Merchant; Trevor Jones [1952] Director/Builders Merchant; Martin Donald Keay [1964] Director; Gavin Joseph McEntee [1971] Director; Andrew Christopher Roberts [1973] Finance Director; Michael Denis Smith [1955] Director/Building Merchant

**A.W. Lumb (Midlands) Limited**
*Incorporated:* 26 July 1976 *Employees:* 36
*Net Worth:* £10,972,962 *Total Assets:* £15,350,104
*Registered Office:* Dewsbury Depot, A W Lumb & Co Ltd, Mill Street East, Dewsbury, W Yorks, WF12 9BD
*Activities:* Agents involved in the sale of timber and building materials
*Officers:* Andrew Christopher Roberts, Secretary; Edward John Cureton [1950] Director/Builders Merchant; Trevor Jones [1952] Director/Builders Merchant; Martin Donald Keay [1964] Director/Transport Manager; Gavin Joseph McEntee [1971] Director/Builders Merchant; Andrew Christopher Roberts [1973] Finance Director; Michael Denis Smith [1955] Director/Builders Merchant

**A.W. Lumb (Northern) Limited**
*Incorporated:* 24 March 1980 *Employees:* 33
*Net Worth:* £3,360,376 *Total Assets:* £5,752,989
*Registered Office:* Dewsbury Depot, A W Lumb & Co Ltd, Mill Street East, Dewsbury, W Yorks, WF12 9BD
*Activities:* Agents involved in the sale of timber and building materials
*Officers:* Andrew Christopher Roberts, Secretary; Edward John Cureton [1950] Director/Builders Merchant; Trevor Jones [1952] Director; Martin Donald Keay [1964] Director; Gavin Joseph McEntee [1971] Director; Andrew Christopher Roberts [1973] Finance Director; Michael Denis Smith [1955] Director; Darren Andrew Ward [1965] Director

**Luminar Partnership Limited**
*Incorporated:* 17 March 2011
*Net Worth:* £2,747,006 *Total Assets:* £5,872,231
*Registered Office:* Hentons, Northgate, 118 North Street, Leeds, LS2 7PN
*Activities:* Buying and selling of own real estate
*Major Shareholder:* Alagu Shanmugam Vijaykumar
*Officers:* Dr Alagu Shanmugam Vijaykumar [1965] Director

**Andrew Lumley Limited**
*Incorporated:* 30 January 2017 *Employees:* 3
*Net Worth:* £5,429,447 *Total Assets:* £9,274,820
*Registered Office:* 6 Queen Street, Leeds, LS1 2TW
*Activities:* Retail sale of antiques including antique books in stores
*Shareholders:* Andrew Lumley; Juana Celsa Lumley
*Officers:* Andrew Lumley [1953] Director; Juana Celsa Lumley [1948] Director [Spanish]

**Lunchbox Theatrical Productions Limited**
*Incorporated:* 4 August 2004 *Employees:* 45
*Net Worth:* £807,495 *Total Assets:* £4,505,508
*Registered Office:* Unit 5 Welburn Business Park, Greets House Road, Welburn, York, YO60 7EP
*Activities:* Support activities to performing arts
*Shareholders:* James William Thomas Cundall; Rebecca Louise Cundall
*Officers:* James William Thomas Cundall, Secretary/Director; James William Thomas Cundall [1957] Director; Rebecca Louise Cundall [1964] Director

**Lund Court Farm Limited**
*Incorporated:* 30 May 1985 *Employees:* 9
*Net Worth:* £2,469,988 *Total Assets:* £4,612,136
*Registered Office:* 12-13 Alma Square, Scarborough, N Yorks, YO11 1JU
*Activities:* Growing of cereals (except rice), leguminous crops and oil seeds
*Major Shareholder:* Howard Peter Raines
*Officers:* Jane Barton Raines, Secretary; Hannah Caroline Hubb [1977] Director; Sophie MacAuley [1981] Director; Howard Peter Raines [1946] Director/Farmer; Jane Barton Raines [1950] Director/Farmer; Lucy Swan [1980] Director

**Lundie Farming Limited**
*Incorporated:* 17 December 2013 *Employees:* 8
*Net Worth Deficit:* £401,753 *Total Assets:* £6,031,971
*Registered Office:* Little Morton Farm, Little Morton, Retford, Notts, DN22 8BE
*Activities:* Raising of dairy cattle
*Shareholder:* Joseph Frederick Howard
*Officers:* Andrew Robert Howard [1969] Director; Joseph Frederick Howard [1984] Director; Maxwell Edward Howard [1958] Director; Martin Kearney [1984] Director

**Lune Holdings Limited**
*Incorporated:* 9 February 2015
*Net Worth:* £4,376,478 *Total Assets:* £4,943,288
*Registered Office:* The Old Power Station, Lune Industrial Estate, Lancaster, LA1 5QP
*Activities:* Activities of other holding companies n.e.c.
*Shareholders:* Robert Melville Welsh; Margaret Elaine Welsh
*Officers:* Margaret Elaine Welsh [1969] Director; Robert Melville Welsh [1964] Director

**Lunesdale Learning Trust**
*Incorporated:* 12 November 2010 *Employees:* 257
*Previous:* Queen Elizabeth School, Kirkby Lonsdale
*Net Worth:* £12,838,691 *Total Assets:* £17,229,258
*Registered Office:* Queen Elizabeth School, Kirkby Lonsdale, Cumbria, LA6 2HJ
*Activities:* General secondary education
*Officers:* Angela Clare Johnson, Secretary; Dr Sally Elizabeth Chalcraft [1962] Director/Lecturer; Christopher Clarke [1953] Director/Headteacher; Margaret Mary Cunningham [1947] Director; Walter Stewart Lawrenson [1951] Director/Self Employed Builder; Stephen Andrew Nelson [1966] Director/Bank Manager; Fenner James Pearson [1966] Director; Tyrone James Power [1941] Retired Director; Dr Richard Julian Shepherd [1944] Director

**Jack Lunn (Holdings) Limited**
*Incorporated:* 16 January 1980
*Net Worth:* £7,597,960 *Total Assets:* £10,008,020
*Registered Office:* Windsor House, Cornwall Road, Harrogate, N Yorks, HG1 2PW
*Activities:* Activities of head offices
*Shareholders:* Catherine Lunn; Carole Lunn; Roy Lunn
*Officers:* Peter McAteer, Secretary; Richard John Brown [1946] Director; Andrew Lunn [1967] Director; Roy Lunn [1942] Director

**Jack Lunn (Properties) Limited**
*Incorporated:* 24 April 1961 *Employees:* 2
*Net Worth:* £22,486,690 *Total Assets:* £28,038,936
*Registered Office:* Windsor House, Cornwall Road, Harrogate, N Yorks, HG1 2PW
*Activities:* Other letting and operating of own or leased real estate
*Parent:* Jack Lunn (Holdings) Limited
*Officers:* Peter McAteer, Secretary; Richard John Brown [1946] Director; Andrew Lunn [1967] Director; Roy Lunn [1942] Director; Carl Barry Wright [1972] Director

**Lupfaw 365 Limited**
*Incorporated:* 4 March 2013
*Net Worth:* £100 *Total Assets:* £12,934,147
*Registered Office:* The Lettershop Limited, Whitehall Park, Whitehall Road, Leeds, LS12 5XX
*Activities:* Activities of head offices
*Shareholders:* YM Group Limited; York Mailing (Holdings) Limited
*Officers:* Lee David Richardson, Secretary; Simon Timothy Cooper [1971] Director; Stephen Tony Goodman [1970] Director/Accountant; Lee David Richardson [1971] Director/Accountant

**Lupton Fawcett LLP**
*Incorporated:* 21 November 2005 *Employees:* 44
*Net Worth:* £5,502,253 *Total Assets:* £7,764,388
*Registered Office:* Yorkshire House, East Parade, Leeds, LS1 5BD
*Officers:* Robert Neil Cooke [1973] Member; Caroline Frances Mockford [1961] Member; Jonathan Michael Harry Oxley [1961] Member; James David Richardson [1963] Member; Christopher Aubrey Burns [1969] LLP Member; Giles Jonathan Clegg [1966] LLP Member; John David Coleman [1956] LLP Member; Louise Mary Connacher [1969] LLP Member; Jonathan Paul Cripwell [1963] LLP Member; John Christopher Joseph Eaton [1943] LLP Member; Kevin Harry Emsley [1953] LLP Member; Giacomo Angelo Ferraro [1973] LLP Member; Peter William Foskett [1957] LLP Member; Martin Frank Baird Frost [1976] LLP Member; Andrew Ian Gilchrist [1967] LLP Member; Hayden Daniel Glynn [1980] LLP Member; Angela Michelle Gorton [1973] LLP Member; John Robert Harrap [1951] LLP Member; Jeremy Coultas Henderson [1956] LLP Member; Neil Large [1972] LLP Member; Ann Laverty [1968] LLP Member; Clive Sydney Lawrence [1969] LLP Member; Colin Andrew Lindsay [1958] LLP Member; Simon John Lockley [1969] LLP Member; James Richard Marshall [1960] LLP Member; Daniel John McCormack [1976] LLP Member; Jonathan Spencer Moore [1971] LLP Member; Julian Richard Moran [1971] LLP Member; Joan Elizabeth Pettingill [1971] LLP Member; Michele Phillips [1963] LLP Member; Julian Rowden [1958] LLP Member; Howard Arthur Rutter [1954] LLP Member; Jeremy Richard Scott [1966] LLP Member; David Alistair Smyllie [1959] LLP Member; Johanne Clare Spittle [1962] LLP Member; John Randal Herley Sykes [1957] LLP Member; Hugh Carrick Thompson [1963] LLP Member; Jonathan Warner Reed [1975] LLP Member; David Mark Whitaker [1963] LLP Member; Nigel Antony Whitfield [1957] LLP Member; Patricia Whitham [1955] LLP Member

**Luscombe Motors Limited**
*Incorporated:* 19 May 2009 *Employees:* 54
*Net Worth:* £2,825,178 *Total Assets:* £6,620,787
*Registered Office:* Luscombe Suzuki and Mitsubishi, Low Road, Hunslet, Leeds, LS10 1QR
*Activities:* Sale of new cars and light motor vehicles
*Shareholders:* Robin Luscombe; Jennifer Luscombe
*Officers:* Jennifer Luscombe, Secretary; Stuart Andrew Tillotson, Secretary; Robin Luscombe [1961] Director/Landlord; David Francis Taylor [1961] Director/Accountant; Stuart Andrew Tillotson [1953] Director/Accountant

**Luxihomes Limited**
*Incorporated:* 2 December 1986 *Employees:* 27
*Net Worth:* £2,314,093 *Total Assets:* £7,496,106
*Registered Office:* Bessingby Way, Bessingby Industrial Estate, Bridlington, E Yorks, YO16 4SJ
*Activities:* Non-specialised wholesale trade
*Major Shareholder:* John Graham Hesp
*Officers:* Amanda Jayne Hesp, Secretary; Mark Antony Gillett [1961] Director/General Manager; John Graham Hesp [1953] Director/Caravan Sales Executive; Andrew Peter Machin [1970] Director/Works Manager; Karl Robert Smalley [1972] Director/General Sales Manager

**Luxury Fabrics Limited**
*Incorporated:* 20 July 1945 *Employees:* 18
*Net Worth:* £574,243 *Total Assets:* £6,599,472
*Registered Office:* Ladywell Mills, Hall Lane, Bradford, W Yorks, BD4 7DF
*Activities:* Weaving of textiles
*Parent:* SIL Holdings Limited
*Officers:* Simon Laurie Denton [1976] Director; David William Gallimore [1962] Managing Director; Marcia Jennings [1958] Sales Director; Andrew David Seal [1957] Director; Jeremy Charles Seal [1960] Director; Matthew Simpson [1971] Managing Director

**Luxury Fibres Limited**
*Incorporated:* 3 December 2007 *Employees:* 31
*Previous:* Luxury Fibres and Yarns Limited
*Net Worth:* £32 *Total Assets:* £9,774,231
*Registered Office:* Ladywell Mills, Hall Lane, Bradford, W Yorks, BD4 7DF
*Activities:* Other business support service activities n.e.c.
*Parent:* SIL Holdings Limited
*Officers:* Andrew David Seal [1957] Director; Jeremy Charles Seal [1960] Director

**Luxury Yarns International Limited**
*Incorporated:* 18 July 2008 *Employees:* 41
*Previous:* FTS Dyers Limited
*Net Worth:* £15,330 *Total Assets:* £5,865,919
*Registered Office:* Ladywell Mills, Hall Lane, Bradford, W Yorks, BD4 7DF
*Activities:* Other business support service activities n.e.c.
*Parent:* SIL Holdings Ltd
*Officers:* Andrew Wynne Riley [1953] Director; Andrew David Seal [1957] Managing Director; Jeremy Charles Seal [1960] Director; Frank Thornton Steele [1949] Director

**Lymington Holdings Limited**
*Incorporated:* 20 January 2017 *Employees:* 149
*Net Worth:* £5,931,672 *Total Assets:* £13,536,788
*Registered Office:* Hodgson Sealants (Holdings) Limited, Belprin Road, Beverley, E Yorks, HU17 0LN
*Activities:* Activities of production holding companies
*Shareholders:* Charles Peter Hodgson; Richard Maxwell Hodgson
*Officers:* Richard Maxwell Hodgson, Secretary; Charles Peter Hodgson [1959] Director; Jane Caroline Hodgson [1961] Director; Karen Elizabeth Hodgson [1960] Director; Richard Maxwell Hodgson [1957] Director

**Lynn Wind Farm Limited**
*Incorporated:* 7 February 2001
*Net Worth:* £3,466,000 *Total Assets:* £122,575,000
*Registered Office:* Grimsby Renewables, Operations Base, North Quay, Grimsby, N E Lincs, DN31 3SY
*Activities:* Production of electricity
*Parent:* Glid Wind Farms Topco Limited
*Officers:* Keith Mangan [1973] Director/Investment Manager [Irish]; Peter George Raftery [1968] Director/Engineer; Karl Ben Smith [1977] Director/Banker; Alexis Eduardo Ulens [1967] Fund Director [Belgian]

**LZN Limited**
*Incorporated:* 25 July 2003
*Net Worth Deficit:* £827,490 *Total Assets:* £83,167,712
*Registered Office:* c/o Pinsent Masons LLP, 1 Park Row, Leeds, LS1 5AB
*Activities:* Other business support service activities n.e.c.
*Parent:* Eneco UK Limited
*Officers:* Cornelis de Haan [1976] Director [Dutch]

**M & D Foundations & Building Services Limited**
*Incorporated:* 23 February 1999 *Employees:* 76
*Net Worth:* £1,108,215 *Total Assets:* £4,268,973
*Registered Office:* M & D House, Brooklands Road, Adwick-le-Street, Doncaster, S Yorks, DN6 7BA
*Activities:* Construction of other civil engineering projects n.e.c.
*Parent:* Bessacarr Properties Limited
*Officers:* Andrew Robert Wykes, Secretary; Steven Roy Edgworth [1959] Director; Simon Steel [1975] Director; Guy Townsley [1984] Director; David Drew Wylie [1963] Director/Contract Manager; Rikki Wylie [1984] Director; Stephanie Wylie [1987] Director

**M Rugs Limited**
*Incorporated:* 5 March 2014 *Employees:* 2
*Net Worth:* £424,203 *Total Assets:* £3,331,937
*Registered Office:* Unit 3 Maple Way, Aycliffe Business Park, Newton Aycliffe, Co Durham, DL5 6BF
*Activities:* Activities of distribution holding companies
*Shareholders:* PHD Nominees (MR) Limited; Coalfields Growth Fund
*Officers:* Benjamin Daniel Dale [1981] Director/Online Retail; Kyle-Gian Mitchell [1987] Director; Gary Pickering [1989] Director

**M S A Engineering Systems Limited**
*Incorporated:* 8 August 1991
*Net Worth:* £3,019,298 *Total Assets:* £3,900,566
*Registered Office:* Wainstalls Mill, Wainstalls, Halifax, W Yorks, HX2 7TJ
*Activities:* Manufacture of lifting and handling equipment
*Shareholders:* Gary Jones; Susan Jones
*Officers:* Susan Jones, Secretary/Director; Gary Jones [1947] Director; Morgan Jones [1975] Managing Director; Susan Jones [1947] Director; Elinor Robinson [1973] Director

**M. & B. Commercial Properties Limited**
*Incorporated:* 16 June 1977 *Employees:* 3
*Net Worth:* £4,336,701 *Total Assets:* £4,430,949
*Registered Office:* Highlands, Burnley Road, Sowerby Bridge, W Yorks, HX6 2TE
*Activities:* Development of building projects
*Shareholder:* M. & B. Transport Services Limited
*Officers:* Mollie Rushworth, Secretary; John Barry Rushworth [1938] Director; Mollie Rushworth [1943] Director

**M. B. Locking Logistics Group Limited**
*Incorporated:* 24 June 1992 *Employees:* 45
*Net Worth:* £1,487,016 *Total Assets:* £3,090,044
*Registered Office:* Forge House, 42-44 Burley Road, Leeds, LS3 1JX
*Activities:* Security systems service activities
*Major Shareholder:* Michael Leonard Goldberg
*Officers:* Andrew Earnshaw, Secretary; Andrew Michael Earnshaw [1967] Finance Director; Michael Epton [1957] Technical and Operations Director; Michael Leonard Goldberg [1945] Director/Locks and Security Systems; Philip Marshall Goldberg [1973] Director/Solicitor; Ashraf Mohamed [1955] Sales Director

**M. H. Industrial Limited**
*Incorporated:* 8 February 2000 *Employees:* 31
*Net Worth:* £3,980,651 *Total Assets:* £4,913,717
*Registered Office:* M H House, Madeley Street, Hull, HU3 2AH
*Activities:* Manufacture of other fabricated metal products n.e.c.
*Major Shareholder:* Kevin James Mulgrove
*Officers:* Tony Hunt, Secretary; Tony Hunt [1972] Director/Financial Controller; Ragan Michael Leivers [1965] Director/Sales Manager; Kevin James Mulgrove [1956] Sales Director

**M. K. M. Building Supplies Limited**
*Incorporated:* 12 September 1995 *Employees:* 1,167
*Net Worth:* £3,940,000 *Total Assets:* £105,353,000
*Registered Office:* c/o MKM Building Supplies Limited, Stoneferry Road, Hull, HU8 8DE
*Activities:* Agents involved in the sale of timber and building materials
*Parent:* M.K.M. Building Supplies (Holdings) Limited
*Officers:* Keith Thomas, Secretary; Philip William Arthur Johns [1963] Director; David Richard Kilburn [1945] Director; Mark Jonathan Smith [1959] Director

**M.A. Estates Limited**
*Incorporated:* 5 August 1998 *Employees:* 4
*Net Worth:* £2,278,474 *Total Assets:* £3,586,827
*Registered Office:* Victoria Works, Holmfield Industrial Estate, Holmfield, Halifax, W Yorks, HX2 9TN
*Activities:* Other letting and operating of own or leased real estate
*Major Shareholder:* Michael Tyszyk
*Officers:* Michael Tyszyk, Secretary; Andrew Paul Brown [1974] Financial Director; Michael Tyszyk [1959] Director/Office Furniture Manufacturer

**M.B.E. Glazing Systems Limited**
*Incorporated:* 28 October 1992 *Employees:* 82
*Net Worth:* £4,532,967 *Total Assets:* £6,314,125
*Registered Office:* Unit 21 Woodman Works, South Lane, Elland, W Yorks, HX5 0PA
*Activities:* Glazing
*Major Shareholder:* Bhopinder Singh
*Officers:* Graham Pickles, Secretary; Martin Nigel Davison [1965] Director; Eamonn Patrick Devenney [1960] Director; Christopher Hirst [1962] Director; Graham Pickles [1956] Director/Chartered Accountant; Bhopinder Singh [1966] Director; Susan Linda Singh [1964] Director

**M.C.I. Developments Limited**
*Incorporated:* 25 February 2011
*Net Worth:* £19,033,000 *Total Assets:* £28,304,000
*Registered Office:* The Waterfront, Lakeside Boulevard, Doncaster, S Yorks, DN4 5PL
*Activities:* Construction of domestic buildings
*Parent:* Beecham Developments Limited
*Officers:* Timothy Mark Beale [1976] Director; James Andrew Garnett [1983] Director; James Michael Douglas Thomson [1966] Director

**M.K. Consultants (U.K.) Limited**
*Incorporated:* 12 June 1997 *Employees:* 37
*Net Worth:* £3,487,346 *Total Assets:* £4,689,423
*Registered Office:* 190 Hanson Lane, Halifax, W Yorks, HX1 4SD
*Activities:* Manufacture of electronic industrial process control equipment
*Major Shareholder:* Mohammed Khalid Chaudhary
*Officers:* Rehana Kauser Chaudhary, Secretary; Mohammed Khalid Chaudhary [1964] Managing Director; Rehana Kauser Chaudhary [1969] Director

**M.K.M. BS (Holdings) 1 Limited**
*Incorporated:* 27 February 2017 *Employees:* 2
*Net Worth:* £97,570,120 *Total Assets:* £97,570,120
*Registered Office:* c/o MKM Building Supplies, Stoneferry Road, Hull, HU8 8DE
*Activities:* Activities of other holding companies n.e.c.
*Parent:* Mukah (BC) Holdco 1 Limited
*Officers:* David Richard Kilburn [1945] Director; Mark Jonathan Smith [1959] Director

**M.K.M. BS (Holdings) 2 Limited**
*Incorporated:* 28 February 2017
*Net Worth:* £97,465,120 *Total Assets:* £97,465,120
*Registered Office:* c/o MKM Building Supplies, Stoneferry Road, Hull, HU8 8DE
*Activities:* Activities of other holding companies n.e.c.
*Parent:* Mukah (BC) Holdco 2 Limited
*Officers:* David Richard Kilburn [1945] Director; Mark Jonathan Smith [1959] Director

**M.K.M. BS (Holdings) 3 Limited**
*Incorporated:* 3 February 2017
*Net Worth:* £90,560,960 *Total Assets:* £191,589,088
*Registered Office:* c/o MKM Building Supplies, Stoneferry Road, Hull, HU8 8DE
*Activities:* Activities of financial services holding companies
*Parent:* Mukah (BC) Holdco 3 Limited
*Officers:* David Richard Kilburn [1945] Director; Mark Jonathan Smith [1959] Director

**M.K.M. Building Supplies (Durham) Limited**
*Incorporated:* 13 June 2013 *Employees:* 32
*Net Worth:* £1,087,424 *Total Assets:* £5,553,433
*Registered Office:* Stoneferry Road, Hull, HU8 8DE
*Activities:* Agents involved in the sale of timber and building materials
*Parent:* M.K.M. Building Supplies Limited
*Officers:* Keith Thomas, Secretary; David Richard Kilburn [1945] Director; Mark Jonathan Smith [1959] Director

**M.K.M. Building Supplies (Group) Limited**
*Incorporated:* 27 February 2017 *Employees:* 1,167
*Net Worth Deficit:* £4,597,000 *Total Assets:* £299,198,016
*Registered Office:* c/o MKM Building Supplies Limited, Stoneferry Road, Hull, HU8 8DE
*Activities:* Activities of other holding companies n.e.c.
*Officers:* Richard Mark Bishop [1968] Director; Matthias Boyer Chammard [1980] Managing Director [French]; Philip William Arthur Johns [1963] Director; David Richard Kilburn [1945] Director; Linda Ann Kilburn [1951] Director; Robin Marshall [1970] Managing Director; Mark Jonathan Smith [1959] Director

**M.K.M. Building Supplies (Holdings) Limited**
*Incorporated:* 16 December 2005 *Employees:* 1,167
*Net Worth Deficit:* £4,419,000 *Total Assets:* £150,307,008
*Registered Office:* Stoneferry Road, Hull, HU8 8DE
*Activities:* Agents involved in the sale of timber and building materials
*Shareholders:* Mukah (BC) Bidco Limited; David Richard Kilburn
*Officers:* Keith Thomas, Secretary; Philip William Arthur Johns [1963] Director; David Richard Kilburn [1945] Director; Mark Jonathan Smith [1959] Director

**M.K.M. Building Supplies (Hull) Limited**
*Incorporated:* 23 January 1998 *Employees:* 62
*Net Worth:* £3,038,707 *Total Assets:* £8,202,603
*Registered Office:* Stoneferry Road, Hull, HU8 8DE
*Activities:* Agents involved in the sale of timber and building materials
*Parent:* M.K.M. Building Supplies Limited
*Officers:* Keith Thomas, Secretary; David Richard Kilburn [1945] Director; Mark Jonathan Smith [1959] Director

**M.K.M. Leisure Limited**
*Incorporated:* 26 July 2002 *Employees:* 23
*Net Worth:* £1,251,142 *Total Assets:* £4,651,936
*Registered Office:* c/o MKM Building Supplies Limited, Stoneferry Road, Hull, HU8 8DE
*Activities:* Agents involved in the sale of timber and building materials
*Parent:* M.K.M. Building Supplies Limited
*Officers:* Keith Thomas, Secretary; David Richard Kilburn [1945] Director; Mark Jonathan Smith [1959] Director

**M.N.S. Textiles Limited**
*Incorporated:* 27 July 2004 *Employees:* 45
*Net Worth:* £2,996,726 *Total Assets:* £6,850,807
*Registered Office:* MNS Textiles Building, Unit 3-4 Pollard Street South, Milnsbridge, Huddersfield, W Yorks, HD3 4GU
*Activities:* Manufacture of knitted and crocheted fabrics
*Major Shareholder:* Mohammed Akhtar
*Officers:* Mohammed Nadeem Akhtar, Secretary; Mohammed Akhtar [1955] Director/Textile Manager; Shahzad Akhtar [1983] Director/Chief Executive

**M.S. Design International Limited**
*Incorporated:* 18 November 1981 *Employees:* 2
*Net Worth:* £2,579,279 *Total Assets:* £3,276,151
*Registered Office:* Unit 4 South Leeds Trade Centre, 16 Belle Isle Road, Leeds, LS10 2DL
*Activities:* Other letting and operating of own or leased real estate
*Officers:* Hardyal Singh Mehat, Secretary; Hardyal Singh Mehat [1960] Director/Clothing Manufacturer; Surrinder Singh Mehat [1956] Director/Clothing Manufacturer

**M1 Engineering Holdings Limited**
*Incorporated:* 2 September 1997 *Employees:* 60
*Net Worth:* £2,974,447 *Total Assets:* £5,012,289
*Registered Office:* Commondale Way, Euroway Trading Estate, Bradford, W Yorks, BD4 6SQ
*Activities:* Activities of production holding companies
*Major Shareholder:* Peter Kilburn Fox
*Officers:* Peter Kilburn Fox, Secretary/Managing Director; Julie Fox [1956] Director; Peter Kilburn Fox [1956] Director

**M6 Truck Services Limited**
*Incorporated:* 25 June 1976
*Net Worth:* £3,986,756 *Total Assets:* £4,190,038
*Registered Office:* Canal Garage, Preston Patrick, Milnthorpe, Kendal, Cumbria, LA7 7NX
*Activities:* Retail sale of automotive fuel in specialised stores
*Officers:* Clifford Michael Atkinson [1946] Director/Builder; James Dennis Atkinson [1949] Director

**Mabanes Properties Limited**
*Incorporated:* 8 August 1927 *Employees:* 3
*Net Worth:* £4,233,668 *Total Assets:* £4,487,918
*Registered Office:* Gresham House, 5-7 St Pauls Street, Leeds, LS1 2JG
*Activities:* Activities of investment trusts
*Officers:* William Peter Simpson, Secretary; William Peter Simpson [1956] Director; John Raymond Guy Worrall [1959] Director/Barrister; Joseph Raymond Waistell Worrall [1924] Director

**Mabey Hire Limited**
*Incorporated:* 1 July 2009 *Employees:* 450
*Net Worth:* £39,044,924 *Total Assets:* £45,521,832
*Registered Office:* Scout Hill, Ravensthorpe, Dewsbury, W Yorks, WF13 3EJ
*Activities:* Renting and leasing of construction and civil engineering machinery and equipment
*Parent:* Mabey Engineering (Holdings) Limited
*Officers:* Matthew James Eastwood [1972] Director; Ian Thomas Matthews [1975] Director

**Mach Recruitment Limited**
*Incorporated:* 25 October 2007 *Employees:* 2,425
*Net Worth:* £837,280 *Total Assets:* £10,568,476
*Registered Office:* 5 Carlton Court, Leeds, LS12 6LT
*Activities:* Temporary employment agency activities
*Shareholders:* Joanne Zyzak; Tomasz Jozef Zyzak
*Officers:* Tomasz Zyzak, Secretary; Adam Joseph Gee [1984] Operations Director; Joanne Zyzak [1971] Director/Company Secretary; Tomasz Jozef Zyzak [1982] Director [Polish]

**Machenair Limited**
*Incorporated:* 14 October 1987
*Net Worth:* £1,291,978 *Total Assets:* £3,437,308
*Registered Office:* Machenair House, Wakefield Road, Ossett, W Yorks, WF5 9LB
*Activities:* Plumbing, heat and air-conditioning installation
*Shareholder:* Horbury Bridge (Holdings) Limited
*Officers:* Ronald Medley, Secretary; John Richard Medley [1962] Director/Fabricator; Ronald Medley [1958] Director/Fabricator; Michael Paul Rowley [1981] Director

**F. Machin & Sons Limited**
*Incorporated:* 2 December 1977 *Employees:* 3
*Net Worth:* £1,864,975 *Total Assets:* £3,286,054
*Registered Office:* Low Farm, Brandsby, York, YO61 4RW
*Activities:* Mixed farming
*Shareholder:* Richard Edward Machin
*Officers:* Wendy Elizabeth Machin, Secretary; Richard Edward Machin [1939] Director/Farmer; Wendy Machin [1939] Director; William Frank Machin [1981] Director/Chartered Surveyor

**Mack & Lawler Builders Limited**
*Incorporated:* 17 September 1964 *Employees:* 14
*Net Worth:* £15,203,484 *Total Assets:* £16,069,941
*Registered Office:* 57 Micklegate, York, YO1 6LJ
*Activities:* Construction of domestic buildings
*Shareholders:* Ian Craig McManaman; Dale Peter McManaman
*Officers:* Susan Michelle McManaman, Secretary; Dale Peter McManaman [1962] Director/Builder; Fiona Elizabeth McManaman [1962] Director/Company Secretary; Ian Craig McManaman [1964] Director/Builder; Susan Michelle McManaman [1966] Director/Company Secretary

**MacKay Transport & Storage Limited**
*Incorporated:* 12 February 1988 *Employees:* 2
*Net Worth:* £2,562,418 *Total Assets:* £3,290,481
*Registered Office:* 8th Avenue, Flixborough Trading Estate, Scunthorpe, N Lincs, DN15 8SJ
*Activities:* Freight transport by road
*Shareholders:* Michael MacKay; William MacKay
*Officers:* William MacKay, Secretary; Michael MacKay [1949] Director/Haulage Contractor; William MacKay [1951] Director/Haulage Contractor

**Madala Limited**
*Incorporated:* 7 July 2015 *Employees:* 2
*Net Worth:* £3,620,926 *Total Assets:* £3,642,684
*Registered Office:* Springfield, South Stainley, Harrogate, N Yorks, HG3 3LX
*Activities:* Credit granting by non-deposit taking finance houses and other specialist consumer credit grantors
*Shareholders:* David Stafford Fawcus; Mary Winifred Fawcus
*Officers:* David Stafford Fawcus [1933] Director; Mary Winifred Fawcus [1941] Director; Fenella Mary Mountgarret [1965] Director

**Made Television Ltd.**
*Incorporated:* 16 March 2010 *Employees:* 81
*Net Worth:* £2,012,847 *Total Assets:* £6,587,992
*Registered Office:* 21 Savile Mount, Leeds, LS7 3HZ
*Activities:* Television programming and broadcasting activities
*Parent:* Well Made Investments Ltd
*Officers:* James Pearse Conway [1978] Director [Irish]; Jonathan Ralph Flay [1971] Director; Lesley Ann MacKenzie [1966] Director; David John Montgomery [1948] Director; Keith Young [1938] Director

**Madison Hosiery Limited**
*Incorporated:* 2 February 1994 *Employees:* 33
*Net Worth:* £3,077,247 *Total Assets:* £4,849,931
*Registered Office:* Lynda Marilyn House, Mill Green, Leeds, LS12 6HE
*Activities:* Wholesale of clothing and footwear
*Shareholders:* Timothy Newman; Spencer Weiner
*Officers:* Katie Elizebeth Newman [1978] Director; Timothy Newman [1976] Sales Director; Spencer Weiner [1969] Commercial Director

**Magenta Prime Limited**
*Incorporated:* 6 February 2017 *Employees:* 4
*Net Worth Deficit:* £5,041,000 *Total Assets:* £63,914,000
*Registered Office:* New Quay Road, Lancaster, LA1 5QP
*Activities:* Activities of other holding companies n.e.c.
*Parent:* Project Magenta Topco Limited
*Officers:* James Scott Browning [1966] Director/Chairman; Matthew Jonathan Enright [1978] Director/Chartered Accountant; Paul French [1972] Director; Ian Geoffrey Simister [1968] Director; Iain John Wolstenholme [1970] Director

**Mager Homes Limited**
*Incorporated:* 5 February 1980 *Employees:* 3
*Net Worth:* £7,161,494 *Total Assets:* £7,796,762
*Registered Office:* Laburnum Farm, Ludborough, Grimsby, S Humbers, DN36 5SF
*Activities:* Construction of domestic buildings
*Officers:* Stephanie Jane Mager, Secretary; Ian Paul Mager [1955] Director/Builder; Marie Mager [1928] Director/Secretary; Stephanie Jane Mager [1957] Director/Secretary

**Brian Mager Limited**
*Incorporated:* 14 August 1957 *Employees:* 3
*Net Worth:* £5,601,125 *Total Assets:* £6,050,239
*Registered Office:* Laburnum Farm, Livesey Road, Ludborough, Grimsby, N E Lincs, DN36 5SF
*Activities:* Construction of domestic buildings
*Parent:* Mager Homes Limited
*Officers:* Stephanie Jane Mager, Secretary; Ian Paul Mager [1955] Director/Builder; Marie Mager [1928] Director/Secretary; Stephanie Jane Mager [1957] Director/Secretary

**Magneco Metrel U.K. Limited**
*Incorporated:* 14 May 1990 *Employees:* 15
*Net Worth:* £2,403,342 *Total Assets:* £4,127,699
*Registered Office:* Hackworth Industrial Park, Shildon, Co Durham, DL4 1HG
*Activities:* Manufacture of other ceramic products n.e.c.
*Parent:* Charles W Connors Family Fund Limited Partnership
*Officers:* Susan Malloy, Company Secretary [American]; Ann Connors [1937] Director [American]; Charles W Connors [1937] Director/Chief Executive Officer [American]; Colleen Connors [1961] Director/Lawyer [American]; Charles Connors Jr [1962] Director/Manufacturing Vice President [American]; Susan Malloy [1964] Director/Company Secretary [American]

**Magnet Limited**
*Incorporated:* 6 November 1992 *Employees:* 2,028
*Net Worth:* £34,940,000 *Total Assets:* £52,031,000
*Registered Office:* c/o Magnet Limited, 3 Allington Way, Yarm Road Business Park, Darlington, Co Durham, DL1 4XT
*Activities:* Other manufacturing n.e.c.
*Parent:* Nobia Holdings UK Limited
*Officers:* Nicola Jane Hardcastle, Secretary; Anjum Ahmed [1970] Director; Daniel Arthur Edward Carr [1975] Finance Director; Nicola Jane Hardcastle [1965] Director/Company Secretary; Peter Kane [1965] Director; Kristoffer Ljungfelt [1977] Director [Swedish]

**J Maguire Holdings Limited**
*Incorporated:* 29 April 2009 *Employees:* 87
*Net Worth:* £9,110,473 *Total Assets:* £18,642,422
*Registered Office:* The Future Business Park, Darlington Road, Shildon, Co Durham, DL4 2RB
*Activities:* Activities of other holding companies n.e.c.
*Major Shareholder:* Jason James Maguire
*Officers:* David Stubbs, Secretary; Alice Victoria Maguire [1975] Director; Jason James Maguire [1973] Director/Carpet Retailer

**Mailing & Marketing Solutions Ltd**
*Incorporated:* 31 July 2014 *Employees:* 49
*Net Worth:* £527,057 *Total Assets:* £3,020,458
*Registered Office:* Unit 30a, Dudley Hill Business Centre, Knowles Lane, Bradford, W Yorks, BD4 9SW
*Activities:* Other business support service activities n.e.c.
*Shareholders:* Anthony Frances Krajniewski; Mario Krajniewski
*Officers:* Anthony Frances Krajniewski [1985] Director; Mario Krajniewski [1966] Director

**Mailway Packaging Solutions Limited**
*Incorporated:* 18 January 2010 *Employees:* 386
*Net Worth:* £3,986,910 *Total Assets:* £8,035,364
*Registered Office:* 12-16 Pitcliffe Way, West Bowling, Bradford, W Yorks, BD5 7SG
*Activities:* Packaging activities
*Parent:* Mailway Packaging Solutions Group Limited
*Officers:* Elizabeth Alice Astin [1967] Director; Richard Bramma [1967] Director; Peter Anthony Hindle-Marsh [1969] Director; Neil Colin Humphrey [1976] Director

**Main Line Bearing Co. Limited**
*Incorporated:* 16 December 1976 *Employees:* 19
*Net Worth:* £2,031,579 *Total Assets:* £4,444,966
*Registered Office:* First Floor, Mayesbrook House, Lawnswood Business Park, Redvers Close, Leeds, LS16 6QY
*Activities:* Wholesale of other machinery and equipment
*Parent:* Bidco (Impex) Limited
*Officers:* Daksha Bhogaita, Secretary; Rameshchandra Amritlal Bhogaita [1952] Director/Businessman

**Mainport Engineering (1990) Limited**
*Incorporated:* 28 August 1990 *Employees:* 247
*Net Worth:* £1,479,861 *Total Assets:* £4,626,641
*Registered Office:* Central Square, 29 Wellington Street, Leeds, LS1 4DL
*Activities:* Manufacture of metal structures and parts of structures
*Shareholders:* Jeffrey Alan Harries; David Peter Harris; Paul Muxworthy; Leslie Alfred Douglas Alderman
*Officers:* David Peter Adrian Harris, Secretary; Jeffrey Alan Harries [1952] Contracts Director; David Peter Adrian Harris [1953] Director

**Mainprize Offshore Ltd**
*Incorporated:* 9 January 1979 *Employees:* 6
*Net Worth:* £6,068,794 *Total Assets:* £13,539,133
*Registered Office:* 40 Centurion Way, Scarborough, N Yorks, YO12 4LE
*Activities:* Marine fishing
*Major Shareholder:* Robert Rewcroft Mainprize Jnr
*Officers:* Sharon Marie Mainprize, Secretary; Sharon Marie Mainprize [1973] Director; Robert Rewcroft Mainprize Jnr [1974] Director/Master

**Majestic Polymers Limited**
*Incorporated:* 23 February 2004 *Employees:* 9
*Net Worth:* £3,967,938 *Total Assets:* £4,906,682
*Registered Office:* Pitman Road, Denaby Industrial Estate, Doncaster, S Yorks, DN12 4LJ
*Activities:* Manufacture of other inorganic basic chemicals
*Parent:* Paleus Group Limited
*Officers:* Mark Wiliam Briscoe [1963] Managing Director; David Hugh Wilson [1971] Director

**Major Recruitment Limited**
*Incorporated:* 18 April 2008 *Employees:* 948
*Net Worth:* £225,615 *Total Assets:* £4,988,759
*Registered Office:* 16A Market Avenue, Huddersfield, W Yorks, HD1 2BB
*Activities:* Temporary employment agency activities
*Major Shareholder:* Philip Alexander Bottomley
*Officers:* Philip Alexander Michael Bottomley [1962] Director; Lesley Anne Flynn [1963] Director; Elizabeth Ann Harrison [1966] Director; Katie Grace Nebard [1985] Director

**Makin Developments Wakefield Ltd**
*Incorporated:* 16 December 2014 *Employees:* 2
*Net Worth:* £878,632 *Total Assets:* £5,631,460
*Registered Office:* Sturton Grange, Ridge Road, Micklefield, Leeds, LS25 4DZ
*Activities:* Growing of cereals (except rice), leguminous crops and oil seeds
*Major Shareholder:* Christopher William Makin
*Officers:* Gary Proctor, Secretary; Christopher William Makin [1958] Director/Farmer; Jane Patricia Makin [1958] Director/Farmer

**Makins Limited**
*Incorporated:* 5 February 1998 *Employees:* 12
*Net Worth:* £1,498,971 *Total Assets:* £5,984,891
*Registered Office:* Sturton Grange, Berry Lane, Micklefield, Leeds, LS25 4DZ
*Activities:* Non-scheduled passenger air transport
*Major Shareholder:* Christopher William Makin
*Officers:* Gary Proctor, Secretary; Christopher William Makin [1958] Director/Farmer

**Malik Halls 2 Ltd**
*Incorporated:* 27 November 2007 *Employees:* 4
*Net Worth:* £2,886,678 *Total Assets:* £5,567,914
*Registered Office:* 5 Town Hall Buildings, Elland, W Yorks, HX5 9AJ
*Activities:* Other letting and operating of own or leased real estate
*Major Shareholder:* Jarair Malik
*Officers:* Junaid Malik, Secretary; Jarair Imtiaz Malik [1981] Director/Financier

**Malik Halls Limited**
*Incorporated:* 13 July 2007
*Net Worth:* £2,412,943 *Total Assets:* £6,535,921
*Registered Office:* 42 Victoria Road, Elland, Halifax, W Yorks, HX5 0QA
*Activities:* Other letting and operating of own or leased real estate
*Major Shareholder:* Jarair Imtiaz Malik
*Officers:* Osman Malik, Secretary; Jarair Imtiaz Malik [1981] Director/Finance

**Malik Real Estate Limited**
*Incorporated:* 6 March 2006
*Net Worth:* £1,086,212 *Total Assets:* £6,257,083
*Registered Office:* 5 Town Hall Buildings, Elland, W Yorks, HX5 9AJ
*Activities:* Other letting and operating of own or leased real estate
*Major Shareholder:* Afsheen Imtiaz Malik
*Officers:* Jarair Imtiaz Malik, Secretary/Finance Broker; Afsheen Imtiaz Malik [1984] Director/Developer; Junaid Malik [1979] Director

**Maria Mallaband (6) Limited**
*Incorporated:* 29 January 2010 *Employees:* 63
*Net Worth:* £4,847,310 *Total Assets:* £6,931,560
*Registered Office:* Westcourt, Gelderd Road, Leeds, LS12 6DB
*Activities:* Residential care activities for the elderly and disabled
*Parent:* Maria Mallaband Care Group Limited
*Officers:* Christopher Ball [1968] Director; Philip John Burgan [1951] Director; Peter Gervais Fagan [1957] Director; Jason Lock [1972] Director

**Maria Mallaband 16 Limited**
*Incorporated:* 26 February 2014 *Employees:* 225
*Net Worth:* £4,001,680 *Total Assets:* £9,311,598
*Registered Office:* Westcourt, Gelderd Road, Leeds, LS12 6DB
*Activities:* Residential care activities for the elderly and disabled
*Parent:* Maria Mallaband Care Group Limited
*Officers:* Christopher Ball [1968] Director; Philip John Burgan [1951] Director; Peter Gervais Fagan [1957] Director; Jason Lock [1972] Director

**Maria Mallaband 7 Limited**
*Incorporated:* 24 November 2010 *Employees:* 50
*Net Worth:* £5,944,125 *Total Assets:* £7,153,771
*Registered Office:* Westcourt, Gelderd Road, Leeds, LS12 6DB
*Activities:* Residential care activities for the elderly and disabled
*Parent:* Maria Mallaband Care Group Limited
*Officers:* Christopher Ball [1968] Director; Philip John Burgan [1951] Director; Peter Gervais Fagan [1957] Director; Jason Lock [1972] Director

**Maria Mallaband Limited**
*Incorporated:* 24 August 1987 *Employees:* 490
*Net Worth:* £9,975,658 *Total Assets:* £21,589,596
*Registered Office:* Westcourt, Gelderd Road, Leeds, LS12 6DB
*Activities:* Residential care activities for the elderly and disabled
*Parent:* Maria Mallaband Care Group Limited
*Officers:* Christopher Ball [1968] Finance Director; James Edward Burgan [1979] Property Director; Philip John Burgan [1951] Director; Victoria Craddock [1970] Director/Business Manager; Dzenana Delic [1974] HR Director; Peter Gervais Fagan [1957] Director; Jason Lock [1972] Director; Christopher John Womack [1972] Business Development Director

**Maltgrade Limited**
*Incorporated:* 23 July 1993
*Net Worth:* £4,625,711 *Total Assets:* £10,811,841
*Registered Office:* Wootton Grange, Wold Road, Wootton, Ulceby, N Lincs, DN39 6RG
*Activities:* Development of building projects
*Shareholder:* Angela Jane Graves
*Officers:* Mark Arthur Graves, Secretary/Director; Mark Arthur Graves [1957] Director; Jonathan Frank Jackson [1955] Director

**Malton Foods Limited**
*Incorporated:* 11 July 2005 *Employees:* 128
*Net Worth Deficit:* £2,759,595 *Total Assets:* £9,387,252
*Registered Office:* Amotherby, Malton, N Yorks, YO17 6TQ
*Activities:* Other business support service activities n.e.c.
*Officers:* Jonathan Donald Ashmore [1972] Commercial Director; John Charles Goodwin [1951] Director/Investor; Arnoldus Theodorus Maria Van Der Laan [1954] Director [Dutch]

**Malton Road Developments Limited**
*Incorporated:* 11 January 2017
*Net Worth:* £70 *Total Assets:* £3,791,196
*Registered Office:* Ogleforth House, Ogleforth, York, YO1 7JG
*Activities:* Buying and selling of own real estate
*Shareholder:* Neal Investments Limited
*Officers:* Iain Patrick John Leedham [1967] Director; John Howard Neal [1961] Director; Damion Matthew Todd [1977] Director/Property Developer

**Mamas & Papas (Holdings) Limited**
*Incorporated:* 11 December 2003 *Employees:* 921
*Net Worth Deficit:* £2,216,000 *Total Assets:* £65,633,000
*Registered Office:* Colne Bridge Road, Huddersfield, W Yorks, HD5 0RH
*Activities:* Activities of head offices
*Parent:* Stork Beta Limited
*Officers:* Jason Robert Curtis, Secretary; Marco Anatriello [1981] Director/Partner [Italian]; Marco Capello [1960] Director/Partner [Italian]; Riccardo Cincotta [1960] Director [Italian]; Emilio di Spiezio Sardo [1977] Director [Italian]; Jason Greenwood [1971] Director/Chief Operating Officer; David Scacchetti [1951] Director; Sarah Jane Walker [1982] Director

**Mamas & Papas (Retail) Limited**
*Incorporated:* 24 November 1980 *Employees:* 636
*Net Worth Deficit:* £31,276,000 *Total Assets:* £19,428,000
*Registered Office:* Colne Bridge Road, Huddersfield, W Yorks, HD5 0RH
*Activities:* Other retail sale of new goods in specialised stores (not commercial art galleries and opticians)
*Parent:* Mamas & Papas (Holdings) Limited
*Officers:* Jason Robert Curtis, Secretary; Marco Anatriello [1981] Director/Partner [Italian]; Marco Capello [1960] Director/Partner [Italian]; Emilio di Spiezio Sardo [1977] Director [Italian]; Jason Greenwood [1971] Director/Chief Operating Officer; David Scacchetti [1951] Director

**Mamas & Papas Limited**
*Incorporated:* 11 December 2003 *Employees:* 258
*Net Worth Deficit:* £6,444,000 *Total Assets:* £27,253,000
*Registered Office:* Colne Bridge Road, Huddersfield, W Yorks, HD5 0RH
*Activities:* Wholesale of household goods (other than musical instruments) n.e.c
*Parent:* Mamas & Papas (Holdings) Limited
*Officers:* Jason Robert Curtis, Secretary; Marco Anatriello [1981] Director/Partner [Italian]; Marco Capello [1960] Director/Partner [Italian]; Emilio di Spiezio Sardo [1977] Director [Italian]; Jason Greenwood [1971] Director/Chief Operating Officer; David Scacchetti [1951] Director

**Manheim Global Management UK Limited**
*Incorporated:* 16 November 2015 *Employees:* 2,571
*Net Worth:* £94,548,000 *Total Assets:* £416,267,008
*Registered Office:* Central House, Leeds Road, Rothwell, Leeds, LS26 0JE
*Activities:* Non-trading company
*Officers:* Marie Laurene Friedman [1965] Director/Tax and Treasury Services [American]; Sanford H Schwartz [1953] Director/President [American]; Juliette Williams Pryor [1965] Director/Legal Counsel [American]

**Manheim Holdings Limited**
*Incorporated:* 9 January 2014
*Net Worth:* £257,048,000 *Total Assets:* £258,188,000
*Registered Office:* Central House, Leeds Road, Rothwell, Leeds, LS26 0JE
*Activities:* Activities of head offices
*Parent:* Manheim Global Management UK Limited
*Officers:* Michael Buxton, Secretary; Michael Buxton [1965] Director; Martin Leigh Forbes [1976] Director/Chief Operating Officer; Marie Laurene Friedman [1965] Director/Tax and Treasury Services [American]; Darren Paul Mornin [1968] Finance Director

**Manheim Limited**
*Incorporated:* 29 January 1948 *Employees:* 1,819
*Previous:* Manheim Auctions Limited
*Net Worth:* £85,255,000 *Total Assets:* £178,246,000
*Registered Office:* Central House, Leeds Road, Rothwell, Leeds, LS26 0JE
*Activities:* Other service activities n.e.c.
*Parent:* Cox Automotive UK Limited
*Officers:* Michael Buxton [1965] Finance Director; Martin Leigh Forbes [1976] Director/Chief Operating Officer; Darren Paul Mornin [1968] Finance Director

**T.Manners & Sons Limited**
*Incorporated:* 25 February 1916 *Employees:* 68
*Net Worth:* £1,060,036 *Total Assets:* £3,178,039
*Registered Office:* Peel House, 2 Dovecot Hill, South Church Enterprise Park, Bishop Auckland, Co Durham, DL14 6XW
*Activities:* Construction of commercial buildings
*Parent:* Manners Holdings Limited
*Officers:* Robert Bion Manners, Secretary/Engineer; Alan William Crawford [1956] Director; Steven Hodges [1963] Director/Construction; Ian Robert Manners [1981] Director; Kathleen Mary Charlton Manners [1955] Director; Robert Bion Manners [1952] Director/Engineer; Simon Oliver Manners [1983] Director; Martin John Wheelhouse [1957] Director/Works Manager

**Manners Farms Limited**
*Incorporated:* 18 December 1957 *Employees:* 6
*Net Worth:* £2,967,844 *Total Assets:* £4,613,461
*Registered Office:* Thornton Hall, High Coniscliffe, Darlington, Co Durham, DL2 2NB
*Activities:* Mixed farming
*Shareholders:* Michael Preston Manners; Susan Manners
*Officers:* Ralph Manners, Secretary; Michael Preston Manners [1960] Director/Farmer; Ralph Manners [1926] Director/Farmer; Susan Manners [1962] Director

**Manningham Concrete Limited**
*Incorporated:* 24 January 1963 *Employees:* 63
*Net Worth:* £1,443,002 *Total Assets:* £4,359,946
*Registered Office:* Greenside Works, Cemetery Road, Bradford, BD8 9RY
*Activities:* Agents involved in the sale of timber and building materials
*Officers:* Andrew Robert Tomlinson, Secretary/Director; Alan Tomlinson [1962] Director; Andrew Robert Tomlinson [1960] Director

**Manor Coating Systems (Holdings) Limited**
*Incorporated:* 6 November 2013 *Employees:* 77
*Net Worth:* £5,377,350 *Total Assets:* £7,573,066
*Registered Office:* Otley Road, Charlestown, Shipley, W Yorks, BD17 7DP
*Activities:* Activities of production holding companies
*Shareholders:* Dale Smith; Martin Smith; Patrick Dale Smith
*Officers:* Patrick Dale Smith, Secretary; Michael Charles Brannan [1963] Director; Dale Smith [1940] Director; Martin Smith [1948] Director; Patrick Dale Smith [1969] Director

**Manor Coating Systems Limited**
*Incorporated:* 7 January 1938 *Employees:* 77
*Net Worth:* £2,749,743 *Total Assets:* £4,919,538
*Registered Office:* Head Office, Otley Road, Charlestown, Baildon, W Yorks, BD17 7DP
*Activities:* Manufacture of paints, varnishes and similar coatings, mastics and sealants
*Parent:* Manor Coating Systems (Holdings) Limited
*Officers:* Patrick Dale Smith, Secretary/Managing Director; Michael Charles Brannan [1963] Operations Director; Dale Smith [1940] Director/Paint Merchant; Martin Smith [1948] Sales Director; Patrick Dale Smith [1969] Managing Director

**Manor Estate Properties (UK) Limited**
*Incorporated:* 31 October 1997 *Employees:* 7
*Net Worth:* £3,503,649 *Total Assets:* £4,102,503
*Registered Office:* Littlethorpe Manor, Littlethorpe, Ripon, N Yorks, HG4 3LG
*Activities:* Other letting and operating of own or leased real estate
*Shareholders:* May Christin Thackray; Charles Haken Linstad Thackray
*Officers:* May Christin Thackray [1946] Managing Director [Norwegian]

**Manor Farm Feeds Limited**
*Incorporated:* 18 April 1995 *Employees:* 22
*Net Worth:* £2,676,374 *Total Assets:* £4,508,056
*Registered Office:* Medina House, 2 Station Avenue, Bridlington, E Yorks, YO16 4LZ
*Activities:* Manufacture of prepared feeds for farm animals
*Major Shareholder:* Michael Geoffrey Kirkwood
*Officers:* Michael Geoffrey Kirkwood, Secretary/Consultant; Michael Geoffrey Kirkwood [1962] Director/Consultant; Rachel Kirkwood [1966] Director

**Mansfield Pollard (Holdings) Limited**
*Incorporated:* 30 November 2010 *Employees:* 156
*Net Worth:* £3,792,430 *Total Assets:* £7,416,787
*Registered Office:* Edward House, Parry Lane, Bradford, W Yorks, BD4 8TL
*Activities:* Non-trading company
*Major Shareholder:* Richard Alan Pollard
*Officers:* Joanna Zilta Robinson, Secretary; Richard Alan Pollard [1954] Director; Joanna Zilta Robinson [1973] Financial Director

**Mansfield, Pollard & Co. Limited**
*Incorporated:* 6 May 1914 *Employees:* 156
*Net Worth:* £4,251,205 *Total Assets:* £7,875,562
*Registered Office:* Edward House, Parry Lane, Bradford, W Yorks, BD4 8TL
*Activities:* Manufacture of non-domestic cooling and ventilation equipment
*Parent:* Mansfield Pollard (Holdings) Limited
*Officers:* Allison Jayne Howgate, Secretary; Louise Joanne Frankland [1982] Sales Director; Allison Jayne Howgate [1967] Finance Director; Richard Alan Pollard [1954] Director; Gary Mark Roberts [1973] Production Director; Joanna Zilta Robinson [1973] Managing Director

**Manthorpe Building Products Limited**
*Incorporated:* 17 December 1985 *Employees:* 96
*Net Worth:* £9,554,876 *Total Assets:* £15,847,099
*Registered Office:* Broomhouse Lane, Edlington, Doncaster, S Yorks, DN12 1ES
*Activities:* Manufacture of other plastic products
*Parent:* Manthorpe Building Products Holdings Limited
*Officers:* Emma Gayle Versluys, Secretary; Paul Anthony James [1965] Director; Martin Keith Payne [1965] Director

**Mantis Holdings Ltd**
*Incorporated:* 2 October 2015 *Employees:* 64
*Net Worth:* £908,000 *Total Assets:* £10,482,000
*Registered Office:* Birds Royd Lane, Brighouse, W Yorks, HD6 1LT
*Activities:* Activities of head offices
*Shareholders:* Neil Anthony Stewardson; Ian Michael Thurley
*Officers:* Neil Anthony Stewardson [1966] Director; Ian Michael Thurley [1966] Director

**Map Ventilation Limited**
*Incorporated:* 14 August 1986
*Net Worth:* £2,482,871 *Total Assets:* £3,226,428
*Registered Office:* Unit 1 Hanwiz House, Milner Way, Ossett, W Yorks, WF5 9JF
*Activities:* Other non-ferrous metal production
*Parent:* Horbury Bridge (Holdings) Limited
*Officers:* John Richard Medley, Secretary; John Richard Medley [1962] Director/Fabricator; Marilyn Medley [1954] Director; Ronald Medley [1958] Director/Fabricator

**Maramar (Holdings) Limited**
*Incorporated:* 21 March 2007 *Employees:* 12
*Net Worth:* £7,553,309 *Total Assets:* £19,891,792
*Registered Office:* The Gatehouse, The Ridings Business Park, Hopwood Lane, Halifax, W Yorks, HX1 3TT
*Activities:* Other business support service activities n.e.c.
*Major Shareholder:* Martyn Brian Buckley
*Officers:* Patricia Pina Earley, Secretary; Martyn Brian Buckley [1971] Managing Director; Patricia Pina Earley [1970] Operations Director

**Marble 4 Life Ltd**
*Incorporated:* 5 January 2004 *Employees:* 54
*Net Worth:* £2,661,368 *Total Assets:* £3,654,830
*Registered Office:* 56-58 Station Road, Crossgates, Leeds, LS15 7JY
*Activities:* Manufacture of kitchen furniture
*Officers:* Amjad Hussian, Secretary; Amjad Hussain [1977] Director/Manager; Waseem Mahboob [1987] Director/Manager

**Marble Building Products (Yorkshire) Limited**
*Incorporated:* 23 June 1989 *Employees:* 152
*Net Worth:* £4,538,426 *Total Assets:* £7,343,267
*Registered Office:* Full Sutton Industrial Estate, Full Sutton, York, YO41 1HS
*Activities:* Other manufacturing n.e.c.
*Parent:* MBP Holdings Limited
*Officers:* David Bendell [1949] Joint Managing Director; Nicholas Philip Bendell [1961] Joint Managing Director

**Marcrist International Limited**
*Incorporated:* 1 July 1999 *Employees:* 67
*Net Worth:* £4,488,883 *Total Assets:* £9,336,575
*Registered Office:* Marcrist House, Kirk Sandall Industrial Estate, Doncaster, S Yorks, DN3 1QR
*Activities:* Production of abrasive products
*Officers:* Graham Vincent Watson, Secretary; Mario Halbeisen [1952] Director [Swiss]; Mediha Halbeisen [1976] Logistics Director [Swiss]; Graham Vincent Watson [1969] Finance Director

**Mardix Holdings Ltd**
*Incorporated:* 4 May 2006 *Employees:* 467
*Net Worth:* £17,788,768 *Total Assets:* £41,829,688
*Registered Office:* Castle Mills, Units 21 22 & 26 Aynam Road, Kendal, Cumbria, LA9 7DE
*Activities:* Other manufacturing n.e.c.
*Parent:* Anord Mardix Acquisitions Limited
*Officers:* Ingrid Swenson, Secretary; Jeffrey Mark Drazan [1958] Director [American]; Kevin Finegan [1960] Director [Irish]; David Andrew Gardner [1969] Director; Timothy Heston [1979] Director [American]; Shreyas Kataria [1991] Director [Indian]; Alan Nordon [1967] Director [Irish]; Kevin Yamashita [1975] Director [American]

**Mardon Holdings Limited**
*Incorporated:* 6 June 2007 *Employees:* 21
*Net Worth:* £380,922 *Total Assets:* £8,159,258
*Registered Office:* 10 Fenton Street, Lancaster, LA1 1TE
*Activities:* Activities of other holding companies n.e.c.
*Major Shareholder:* Mark John Donoghue
*Officers:* Mark John Donoghue, Secretary; Christine Marie Donoghue [1956] Director/Administrator; Mark John Donoghue [1958] Director

**Mardon Public Limited Company**
*Incorporated:* 8 October 1984 *Employees:* 21
*Net Worth:* £1,507,671 *Total Assets:* £7,780,109
*Registered Office:* Fenton House, 10 Fenton Street, Lancaster, LA1 1TE
*Activities:* Marine fishing
*Major Shareholder:* Mark John Donoghue
*Officers:* Mark John Donoghue, Secretary; Kevin John Bailey [1961] Sales Director; John Joseph Beamer [1964] Director/Manager; Mark John Donoghue [1958] Director; Anthony Turner [1955] Finance Director; Charles Stuart Wilson [1943] Director/Trader

**Marine Services (Grimsby) Limited**
*Incorporated:* 13 March 2000
*Net Worth:* £4,704,396 *Total Assets:* £4,968,947
*Registered Office:* 14 Denby Drive, Cleethorpes, N E Lincs, DN35 9QQ
*Activities:* Sea and coastal freight water transport
*Major Shareholder:* Richard James Harvey
*Officers:* Kathryn Melville, Secretary; Richard James Harvey [1948] Director/Tug Operator

**Maritime Bunkering Limited**
*Incorporated:* 2 February 1996 *Employees:* 5
*Net Worth:* £878,194 *Total Assets:* £5,130,201
*Registered Office:* Wittham House, 45 Spyvee Street, Hull, HU8 7JR
*Activities:* Other transportation support activities
*Parent:* J R Rix & Sons Ltd
*Officers:* Rory Michael Andrew Clarke [1959] Director; James Ian Doyle [1974] Director; David Charles Evans [1953] Director; Nicola Jane Jessop [1970] Director; Duncan John Lambert [1961] Director; Sally Joanna Rix [1965] Director; Timothy John Rix [1963] Director

**Market Town Taverns Limited**
*Incorporated:* 4 August 1998 *Employees:* 260
*Net Worth:* £1,927,043 *Total Assets:* £4,491,026
*Registered Office:* 2nd Floor, Old Bell, 6 Royal Parade, Harrogate, N Yorks, HG1 2SZ
*Activities:* Public houses and bars
*Parent:* Heron and Brearley Limited
*Officers:* Neil Antony Kelly, Secretary; Jonathan David Clague [1948] Director; Charles Stewart Dellborg [1986] Director/Management Accountant [Swiss]; Neil Antony Kelly [1979] Director/Certified Accountant; Ian William Lennox [1956] Director

**Marl International Limited**
*Incorporated:* 25 April 1973 *Employees:* 74
*Net Worth:* £1,644,462 *Total Assets:* £3,213,808
*Registered Office:* Marl Business Park, Ulverston, Cumbria, LA12 9BN
*Activities:* Manufacture of electronic measuring, testing etc. equipment, not for industrial process control
*Parent:* Marl International Holdings Limited
*Officers:* Nathan James Orton [1973] Technical and Procurement Director; Adrian Harold Roderick Rawlinson [1956] Director

**Marpak Extrusions Limited**
*Incorporated:* 12 January 2000 *Employees:* 24
*Net Worth:* £4,037,586 *Total Assets:* £8,719,237
*Registered Office:* 1 Parkview Court, St Pauls Road, Shipley, W Yorks, BD18 3DZ
*Activities:* Manufacture of plastic packing goods
*Shareholders:* Catherine Lynn Gibson; Richard Gary Gibson
*Officers:* James Gary Gibson [1976] Procurement Director; Richard Gary Gibson [1949] Managing Director; Matthew James White [1981] Director of Development; Peter Winterbottom [1964] Managing Director

**J. Marr & Son Limited**
*Incorporated:* 15 March 2010 *Employees:* 312
*Net Worth:* £19,703,798 *Total Assets:* £33,708,872
*Registered Office:* Unit 18 Langthwaite Business Park, South Kirkby, W Yorks, WF9 3AP
*Activities:* Activities of other holding companies n.e.c.
*Officers:* Victor Malcolm Rycroft Dufton [1946] Director; Bridget Stickney Marr [1961] Director; Charles Roger Marr [1960] Director; Philip Edward Marr [1984] Director; Paul Andrew Martin [1971] Director; Polly Anna Metcalfe [1986] Director; Annabelle Amy Tyson [1983] Director; Nicholas Giles Wharton [1966] Director

**J. Marr (Fishing) Limited**
*Incorporated:* 2 October 1897 *Employees:* 5
*Net Worth:* £19,450 *Total Assets:* £12,519,450
*Registered Office:* The Orangery, Hesslewood Country Business Park, Ferriby Road, Hessle, E Yorks, HU13 0LH
*Activities:* Marine fishing
*Parent:* UK Fisheries Ltd
*Officers:* Thorsteinn Mar Baldvinsson [1952] Managing Director [Icelander]; Haraldur Gretarsson [1968] Director [Icelander]; Diederik Parlevliet [1955] Director [Dutch]; Jane Vanessa Sandell [1978] Director; Jan Cornelis Van Der Plas [1954] Director [Dutch]

**J Marr (Property) Limited**
*Incorporated:* 26 March 2002
*Net Worth:* £1,970,480 *Total Assets:* £17,059,528
*Registered Office:* Units 18-20 Langthwaite Business Park, South Kirkby, W Yorks, WF9 3AP
*Activities:* Other letting and operating of own or leased real estate
*Parent:* J Marr & Son Limited
*Officers:* Victor Malcolm Rycroft Dufton [1946] Director; Bridget Stickney Marr [1961] Director; Philip Edward Marr [1984] Director; Polly Anna Metclafe [1986] Director; Annabelle Amy Tyson [1983] Director; Nicholas Giles Wharton [1966] Director

**J. Marr (Seafoods) Limited**
*Incorporated:* 9 July 1924 *Employees:* 43
*Net Worth:* £39,811,000 *Total Assets:* £68,251,000
*Registered Office:* Livingstone Road, Hessle, E Yorks, HU13 0EE
*Activities:* Marine fishing
*Parent:* J Marr Seafoods Holdings Limited
*Officers:* Paul Morgan Farrar, Secretary; Roger Eric Johnson [1947] Director/Company Executive; Alexander George Marr [1970] Director; Michael Ian Arthur Moore [1972] Director; Spencer Morris [1976] Director/Accountant; Andrew William Regan [1962] Director/Company Executive

**Andrew Marr International Limited**
*Incorporated:* 18 April 1986 *Employees:* 310
*Net Worth:* £98,879,000 *Total Assets:* £184,164,992
*Registered Office:* Livingstone Road, Hessle, E Yorks, HU13 0EE
*Activities:* Marine fishing
*Officers:* Paul Morgan Farrar, Secretary; Neil Jenneson [1949] Director; Roger Eric Johnson [1947] Director; Alexander George Marr [1970] Director; Andrew Leslie Marr [1942] Director; Christian Leslie Marr [1972] Director; Sebastian Andrew Marr [1973] Director; Andrew William Regan [1962] Director

**J. Marr Limited**
*Incorporated:* 29 May 1902 *Employees:* 312
*Net Worth:* £18,226,532 *Total Assets:* £24,425,396
*Registered Office:* Joseph Marr House, Unit 18-20 Langthwaite Business Park, South Kirkby, W Yorks, WF9 3AP
*Activities:* Activities of head offices
*Parent:* J Marr & Son Limited
*Officers:* Victor Malcolm Rycroft Dufton [1946] Director; Bridget Stickney Marr [1961] Director; Charles Roger Marr [1960] Director; Philip Edward Marr [1984] Director; Paul Andrew Martin [1971] Director; Polly Anna Metcalfe [1986] Director; Annabelle Amy Tyson [1983] Director; Nicholas Giles Wharton [1966] Director

**Marr Management Limited**
*Incorporated:* 7 December 2005
*Net Worth:* £4,453,992 *Total Assets:* £16,985,716
*Registered Office:* The Orangery, Hesslewood Country Business Park, Ferriby Road, Hessle, E Yorks, HU13 0LH
*Activities:* Marine fishing
*Parent:* J Marr (Fishing) Ltd
*Officers:* Thorsteinn Mar Baldvinsson [1952] Managing Director [Icelander]; Haraldur Gretarsson [1968] Director [Icelander]; Diederik Parlevliet [1955] Director [Dutch]; Jane Vanessa Sandell [1978] Director; Jan Cornelis Van Der Plas [1954] Director [Dutch]

**Marrtree Developments Ltd**
*Incorporated:* 27 August 1937 *Employees:* 5
*Net Worth:* £2,524,885 *Total Assets:* £3,579,177
*Registered Office:* 4a Greengate, Cardale Park, Harrogate, N Yorks, HG3 1GY
*Activities:* Buying and selling of own real estate
*Officers:* William Ross Marshall, Secretary; Frank William Marshall [1938] Director; George Henry Ross Marshall [1978] Director; William Ross Marshall [1975] Director

**Marrtree Investments Limited**
*Incorporated:* 25 May 2012 *Employees:* 3
*Net Worth:* £18,185,228 *Total Assets:* £28,236,368
*Registered Office:* 4a Greengate, Cardale Park, Harrogate, N Yorks, HG3 1GY
*Activities:* Buying and selling of own real estate
*Officers:* George Henry Ross Marshall [1978] Director; William Ross Marshall [1975] Director; Guy Irving Northrop [1958] Director/Certified Chartered Accountant

**Marrtree Residential Ltd**
*Incorporated:* 20 February 2012
*Net Worth:* £573,152 *Total Assets:* £4,302,117
*Registered Office:* 4a Greengate, Cardale Park, Harrogate, N Yorks, HG3 1GY
*Activities:* Other letting and operating of own or leased real estate
*Officers:* George Henry Ross Marshall [1978] Director; William Ross Marshall [1975] Director

**RC Marsden Properties Limited**
*Incorporated:* 14 January 2005 *Employees:* 6
*Net Worth:* £838,765 *Total Assets:* £3,707,617
*Registered Office:* RCM House, Sandbeds Trading Estate, Dewsbury Road, Ossett, W Yorks, WF5 9ND
*Activities:* Other letting and operating of own or leased real estate
*Officers:* Deborah Joy Marsden, Secretary; Richard Charles Marsden [1960] Director/Metals Manufacturer

**Marsh & Parsons (Holdings) Limited**
*Incorporated:* 19 October 2011
*Net Worth:* £52,223,000 *Total Assets:* £54,292,000
*Registered Office:* 2nd Floor, Gateway, 2 Holgate Park Drive, York, YO26 4GB
*Activities:* Activities of other holding companies n.e.c.
*Parent:* LSL Property Services PLC
*Officers:* Sapna Bedi FitzGenerald, Secretary; Helen Elizabeth Buck [1960] Director; Adam Robert Castleton [1964] Director; Ian Denis Crabb [1959] Director; Patrick Humphrey Littlemore [1976] Director

**Frank Marshall & Sons Ltd**
*Incorporated:* 26 April 2013
*Net Worth:* £5,803,921 *Total Assets:* £5,834,777
*Registered Office:* 4a Greengate, Cardale Park, Harrogate, N Yorks, HG3 1GY
*Activities:* Buying and selling of own real estate
*Officers:* George Henry Ross Marshall [1978] Director; William Ross Marshall [1975] Director

**Marshall (Building Contractors) Ltd**
*Incorporated:* 24 March 1969 *Employees:* 34
*Net Worth:* £6,764,156 *Total Assets:* £11,083,207
*Registered Office:* Huddersfield Road, Elland, W Yorks, HX5 9BW
*Activities:* Construction of commercial buildings
*Parent:* Marshall Holdings Limited
*Officers:* Jonathan Booth, Secretary; Jonathan Booth [1970] Director/Accountant; Christopher Roy Marshall [1939] Director/Building Contractor; John Nicholas Marshall [1967] Director/Builder

**Marshall Brothers Finance Co Limited**
*Incorporated:* 26 April 2013 *Employees:* 4
*Net Worth:* £6,111,838 *Total Assets:* £10,042,562
*Registered Office:* 4a Greengate, Cardale Park, Harrogate, N Yorks, HG3 1GY
*Activities:* Buying and selling of own real estate
*Officers:* George Henry Ross Marshall [1978] Director; Margaret Elizabeth Marshall [1949] Director; Rachael Louise Marshall [1975] Director; Rebecca Louise Marshall [1977] Director; William Ross Marshall [1975] Director; Guy Irving Northrop [1958] Director/Certified Chartered Accountant

**Marshall Construction (West Yorkshire) Limited**
*Incorporated:* 31 May 1979 *Employees:* 74
*Net Worth:* £40,367,080 *Total Assets:* £51,951,216
*Registered Office:* Huddersfield Road, Elland, W Yorks, HX5 9BW
*Activities:* Development of building projects
*Parent:* Marshall Holdings Limited
*Officers:* Jonathan Booth, Secretary; Jonathan Booth [1970] Director/Accountant; Christopher Michael Ker [1963] Director/General Manager; Christopher Roy Marshall [1939] Director/Building Contractor; James Robert Marshall [1965] Director; Simon Charles Newton Marshall [1963] Director

**Frank Marshall Estates Limited**
*Incorporated:* 25 May 2012 *Employees:* 5
*Net Worth:* £15,558,644 *Total Assets:* £33,574,296
*Registered Office:* The East Wing, The Newhall, Newhall Way, Bradford, BD5 8FF
*Activities:* Other letting and operating of own or leased real estate
*Shareholders:* Frank Edward Marshall; James Ernest Marshall
*Officers:* Frank Edward Marshall [1978] Director; James Ernest Marshall [1979] Director

**J & E Marshall Finance Limited**
*Incorporated:* 26 April 2013
*Net Worth:* £6,037,638 *Total Assets:* £11,241,074
*Registered Office:* The East Wing, The Newhall, Newhall Way, Bradford, BD5 8FF
*Activities:* Financial management
*Parent:* Schosween 12 Ltd
*Officers:* Frank Edward Marshall [1978] Director; James Ernest Marshall [1979] Director

**Marshall Group Services Limited**
*Incorporated:* 4 August 1976 *Employees:* 26
*Net Worth:* £405,389 *Total Assets:* £25,075,788
*Registered Office:* Huddersfield Road, Elland, W Yorks, HX5 9BW
*Activities:* Combined office administrative service activities
*Parent:* Marshall Holdings Ltd
*Officers:* Jonathan Booth, Secretary; Jonathan Booth [1970] Director/Accountant; Christopher Roy Marshall [1939] Director/Building Contractor

**Marshall Holdings Limited**
*Incorporated:* 11 August 1976 *Employees:* 188
*Net Worth:* £139,208,992 *Total Assets:* £178,856,992
*Registered Office:* Huddersfield Road, Elland, W Yorks, HX5 9BW
*Activities:* Activities of head offices
*Major Shareholder:* Christopher Roy Marshall
*Officers:* Jonathan Booth, Secretary; Jonathan Booth [1970] Director/Accountant; Christopher Roy Marshall [1939] Director/Building Contractor

**Marshall Quarry Products Limited**
*Incorporated:* 7 June 1996 *Employees:* 48
*Net Worth:* £2,873,923 *Total Assets:* £6,028,407
*Registered Office:* 118-122 Scarborough Road, Bridlington, E Yorks, YO16 7NU
*Activities:* Quarrying of ornamental and building stone, limestone, gypsum, chalk and slate
*Officers:* Paul Thompson, Secretary; Adam Carr [1965] Director/Company Manager; Carol Watts [1942] Director/Housewife; David Clifford Watts [1972] Director/General Dealer; Wyndham Richard Watts [1970] Director/Quarry Manager

**Marshall Wooldridge Group Holdings Limited**
*Incorporated:* 21 July 2016
*Net Worth:* £10,000,000 *Total Assets:* £10,000,000
*Registered Office:* 16 Ivegate, Yeadon, Leeds, LS19 7RE
*Activities:* Non-trading company
*Parent:* GRP Retail Holdco Limited
*Officers:* Andrew Hunter, Secretary; Michael Andrew Bruce [1962] Director/Insurance Broker; James Andrew Hall [1970] Director/Insurance Broker

**Marshall Wooldridge Holdings Limited**
*Incorporated:* 13 November 2003
*Net Worth:* £999,399 *Total Assets:* £3,102,582
*Registered Office:* 16 Ivegate, Yeadon, Leeds, LS19 7RE
*Activities:* Non-trading company
*Parent:* Marshall Wooldridge Group Holdings Limited
*Officers:* Andrew Hunter, Secretary; Michael Andrew Bruce [1962] Director/Insurance Broker; James Andrew Hall [1970] Director/Insurance Broker

**Marshall Wooldridge Limited**
*Incorporated:* 30 January 1973 *Employees:* 52
*Net Worth:* £1,633,815 *Total Assets:* £4,489,747
*Registered Office:* 16 Ivegate, Yeadon, Leeds, LS19 7RE
*Activities:* Non-life insurance
*Parent:* Marshall Wooldridge Holdings Limited
*Officers:* Andrew Stewart Hunter, Secretary; Elizabeth Matthewson, Secretary; David Craig Bentley [1962] Director/Insurance Broker; Michael Andrew Bruce [1962] Director/Insurance Broker; James Andrew Hall [1970] Director/Insurance Broker; Andrew Jonathan May [1966] Director; Richard Ian Sykes [1973] Director/Insurance Broker; Neil Thornton [1966] Director/Insurance Broker; Julia Wilding [1975] Director/Insurance Broker

**Marshalls Group Limited**
*Incorporated:* 28 April 1950 *Employees:* 2,129
*Net Worth:* £343,007,008 *Total Assets:* £524,132,000
*Registered Office:* Landscape House, Premier Way, Lowfields Business Park, Elland, W Yorks, HX5 9HT
*Activities:* Activities of head offices
*Parent:* Marshalls PLC
*Officers:* Catherine Elizabeth Baxandall, Secretary; Jack James Clarke [1965] Director; Martyn Coffey [1962] Director

**Marshalls Mono Limited**
*Incorporated:* 7 July 1952 *Employees:* 2,129
*Net Worth:* £347,540,000 *Total Assets:* £436,910,016
*Registered Office:* Landscape House, Premier Way, Lowfields Business Park, Elland, W Yorks, HX5 9HT
*Activities:* Manufacture of concrete products for construction purposes
*Parent:* Marshalls Group Limited
*Officers:* Catherine Elizabeth Baxandall, Secretary; Jack James Clarke [1965] Director; Martyn Coffey [1962] Director

**Marshalls PLC**
*Incorporated:* 13 April 2004 *Employees:* 2,307
*Net Worth:* £236,168,000 *Total Assets:* £415,446,016
*Registered Office:* Landscape House, Premier Way, Lowfields Business Park, Elland, W Yorks, HX5 9HT
*Activities:* Activities of head offices
*Officers:* Catherine Elizabeth Baxandall, Company Secretary; Janet Elizabeth Ashdown [1959] Director; Jack James Clarke [1965] Director; Martyn Coffey [1962] Director; Vanda Murray [1960] Director; Timothy Simon Devereux Pile [1953] Director; Graham Prothero [1961] Finance Director

**Marsylka Manufacturing Co.Limited**
*Incorporated:* 11 December 1946 *Employees:* 835
*Net Worth:* £5,699,445 *Total Assets:* £10,241,097
*Registered Office:* 16 Roydsdale Way, Euroway Industrial Estate, Bradford, W Yorks, BD4 6SE
*Activities:* Manufacture of other women's outerwear
*Shareholders:* John Simon Hainsworth; Andrew Eric Hainsworth; Robert Joseph Hainsworth
*Officers:* Robert Joseph Hainsworth, Secretary; Andrew Eric Hainsworth [1971] Director; John Simon Hainsworth [1969] Director; Robert Joseph Hainsworth [1967] Director; John Hammond Seller [1950] Director

**Martech (UK) Ltd**
*Incorporated:* 12 April 1995 *Employees:* 87
*Net Worth:* £5,168,791 *Total Assets:* £9,339,998
*Registered Office:* Conway House, Tenter Fields, Thornhill Road Business Park, Dewsbury, W Yorks, WF12 9QT
*Activities:* Other manufacturing n.e.c.
*Shareholders:* Craig Andrew Marney; Derek Marney
*Officers:* Liam David Fox [1983] Finance Director; Graham Lewis [1962] Director of OEM Sales; Craig Andrew Marney [1977] Managing Director; Derek Marney [1951] Director/Chairman; Andrew Charles Nixon [1976] Design Director

**The Neil Martin Group Limited**
*Incorporated:* 6 July 2005
*Net Worth:* £710,836 *Total Assets:* £4,684,237
*Registered Office:* Unit 2 Sowerby Woods, Bouthwood Road, Barrow in Furness, Cumbria, LA14 4RD
*Activities:* Development of building projects
*Shareholders:* Julie Kirby; Neil Martin
*Officers:* Neil Martin [1968] Director/Manager

**Martin House**
*Incorporated:* 1 May 1986 *Employees:* 195
*Net Worth:* £22,716,466 *Total Assets:* £24,030,822
*Registered Office:* Martin House, Grove Road, Boston Spa, Wetherby, W Yorks, LS23 6TX
*Activities:* Hospital activities
*Officers:* Martin David Warhurst, Secretary; Martin David Warhurst, Secretary; Dr Anne-Marie Childs [1965] Director/Paediatrician; Zoe Sandra Donaldson [1976] Director/Solicitor; Timothy James Halstead [1958] Director/Solicitor; Rifhat Malik [1967] Director/Health Practitioner; Dr Patricia Ann McKinney [1948] Director/Epidemiological and Health Services Research; Michael Joseph Paul Millington [1966] Director/VP Sales & Marketing; Stephen Plews [1959] Managing Director; Susan Barbara Rumbold [1963] Director/Paediatric Physiotherapist; Jennifer Slee [1955] Director/Solicitor; Tim Straughan [1965] Director/NHS Executive; Jennifer Margaret Wilkinson [1946] Director/Housewife; Professor John Barry Debenham Wright [1960] Director/Professor of Child Psychiatry

**Martindale Group Limited**
*Incorporated:* 18 November 2015 *Employees:* 21
*Net Worth:* £5,514,287 *Total Assets:* £8,144,795
*Registered Office:* 2 Clayton Wood Court, West Park, Leeds, LS16 6QW
*Activities:* Activities of head offices
*Major Shareholder:* Mark Greenwood Robinson
*Officers:* Scott David Owen [1976] Director; Mark Greenwood Robinson [1969] Director

**Martins Bidco Limited**
*Incorporated:* 24 December 2015
*Net Worth Deficit:* £1,000 *Total Assets:* £13,891,000
*Registered Office:* The Inspire, Hornbeam Square, West Harrogate, N Yorks, HG2 8PA
*Activities:* Activities of head offices
*Officers:* James Alexander Burrell [1974] Director; Anthony Gerrard Troy [1962] Director [Irish]

**Marton Mills Company Limited**
*Incorporated:* 10 December 1931 *Employees:* 65
*Net Worth:* £4,205,933 *Total Assets:* £5,752,328
*Registered Office:* Pool Mills, Pool in Wharfedale, Otley, W Yorks, LS21 1TA
*Activities:* Weaving of textiles
*Shareholder:* Richard Lacy Watts
*Officers:* Ben James Fearnley, Secretary; Sarah Kate Rebecca Bainbridge [1979] Design Director; Francis Ian Dodson [1973] Sales Director; Ben James Fearnley [1983] Financial Director; Laura Catherine Fletcher [1976] Managing Director; Jon Gunnell [1972] Weaving Director; Lee Hewitt [1965] Director; Carolyn Mary Watts [1947] Director; Duncan Richard Watts [1941] Director/Chairman; Richard Lacy Watts [1975] Director

**Maru International Limited**
*Incorporated:* 28 August 1985 *Employees:* 98
*Net Worth:* £5,945,650 *Total Assets:* £10,568,979
*Registered Office:* Unit 35 Don Pedro Avenue, Normanton Industrial Estate, Normanton, W Yorks, WF6 1TD
*Activities:* Freight transport by road
*Parent:* Leman International Transport Limited
*Officers:* Jesper Krupa Thygesen [1978] Managing Director [Danish]

**MAS Management Services Ltd**
*Incorporated:* 16 July 2007
*Net Worth:* £1,126,099 *Total Assets:* £9,846,246
*Registered Office:* MNS Textiles Buildings, Pollard Street South, Milnsbridge, Huddersfield, W Yorks, HD3 4GU
*Activities:* Other letting and operating of own or leased real estate
*Shareholder:* Shahzad Akhtar
*Officers:* Mohammed Nadeem Akhtar, Secretary; Majad Akhtar [1981] Director; Mohammed Akhtar [1955] Director; Shahzad Akhtar [1983] Director

**Masco Corporation Limited**
*Incorporated:* 17 January 1985 *Employees:* 1
*Net Worth Deficit:* £9,815,000 *Total Assets:* £277,832,000
*Registered Office:* 1 Park Row, Leeds, LS1 5AB
*Activities:* Activities of head offices
*Parent:* Masco Corporation
*Officers:* Ken Ellis [1965] Director/Accountant; John Palmer Lindow III [1964] Director [American]; Darius Padler [1970] Director [German]

**Masco UK Window Group Limited**
*Incorporated:* 13 May 1991 *Employees:* 1,367
*Net Worth:* £53,954,000 *Total Assets:* £117,109,000
*Registered Office:* 1 Park Row, Leeds, LS1 5AB
*Activities:* Manufacture of builders ware of plastic
*Parent:* Masco Corporation Limited
*Officers:* Darius Padler [1970] Director [German]; Matthew James Mylrea Scoffield [1962] Director/Chief Executive Officer

**Masons Textiles Limited**
*Incorporated:* 11 March 1993 *Employees:* 47
*Net Worth:* £3,148,388 *Total Assets:* £3,386,634
*Registered Office:* Cricketers Close, Carleton New Road, Skipton, N Yorks, BD23 2AZ
*Activities:* Manufacture of man-made fibres
*Major Shareholder:* Andrew Douglas Peden
*Officers:* Michelle Peden, Secretary; Andrew Douglas Peden [1961] Director; Michelle Mary Peden [1975] Director/Administrator

**The Mast Academy Trust**
*Incorporated:* 2 September 2016 *Employees:* 180
*Net Worth:* £13,642,000 *Total Assets:* £15,388,000
*Registered Office:* Scissett Middle School, Wakefield Road, Scissett, Huddersfield, W Yorks, HD8 9JX
*Activities:* Primary education
*Officers:* Baljit Kaur Birring [1962] Director/Educational Adviser; Elizabeth Anne Godman [1951] Director and Educational Consultant; Charles Martyn Jones [1958] Director/Retired; Helen Jones [1970] Director/Academy Principal; Andrea Mills [1969] Finance Director; Rosamond Sophie Roughton [1968] NHS Director; Anthony Raymond Wilkinson [1977] Director/HR Professional; Dr Andrew Williams [1956] Director/Retired; Glen Richard Wilson [1976] Director/Banker

**Masternaut Limited**
*Incorporated:* 15 November 2011 *Employees:* 198
*Net Worth Deficit:* £52,326,000 *Total Assets:* £30,164,000
*Registered Office:* Priory Park, Great North Road, Aberford, Leeds, LS25 3DF
*Activities:* Business and domestic software development
*Officers:* Samantha Gray, Secretary; Djamel Souici, Secretary; Anthony David Johnson [1967] Director; Djamel Souici [1970] Director/General Counsel [German]

**Matisa (U.K.) Limited**
*Incorporated:* 14 December 1964 *Employees:* 13
*Net Worth:* £5,873,728 *Total Assets:* £6,790,409
*Registered Office:* Suite 1, The Limewood Suite, 5 Park Square, Scunthorpe, N Lincs, DN15 6JH
*Activities:* Wholesale of other machinery and equipment
*Parent:* Matisa Materiel Industriel S.A.
*Officers:* Philippe Carrard [1969] Finance Director [Swiss]; Franz Messerli [1964] Director [Swiss]; Kevin Townsend [1963] Managing Director; Rainer Von Schack [1945] Director [German]

**Matrix Chemie Holdings Limited**
*Incorporated:* 14 May 2015 *Employees:* 12
*Previous:* GRI Matrix Limited
*Net Worth:* £1,154,888 *Total Assets:* £7,425,346
*Registered Office:* Leeds Container Base, Valley Farm Way, Wakefield Road, Stourton, Leeds, LS10 1SE
*Activities:* Activities of head offices
*Parent:* Jeto Holdings Limited
*Officers:* David Michael Brooke [1975] Director; Kay Polotnianka [1969] Director

**Matrix Chemie Limited**
*Incorporated:* 23 May 2003 *Employees:* 12
*Net Worth:* £1,649,774 *Total Assets:* £7,425,278
*Registered Office:* Leeds Container Base, Valley Farm Way, Wakefield Road, Stourton, Leeds, LS10 1SE
*Activities:* Wholesale of chemical products
*Parent:* GRI Matrix Limited
*Officers:* David Michael Brooke [1975] Director; David Thomas Kearns [1968] Finance Director; Kay Polotnianka [1969] Director; Graham Royle [1959] Director/Chairman & CEO

**Matrix International Limited**
*Incorporated:* 23 December 1998 *Employees:* 88
*Net Worth:* £5,182,000 *Total Assets:* £7,660,000
*Registered Office:* c/o Bibby Transmissions Limited, Cannon Way, Dewsbury, W Yorks, WF13 1EH
*Activities:* Manufacture of other general-purpose machinery n.e.c.
*Parent:* Altra Industrial Motion UK Limited
*Officers:* Richard Ian Laws, Secretary; Glenn Deegan [1966] Director/VP, Legal & HR, General Counsel [American]; Todd Patriacca [1969] Director/VP Finance/Corporate Controller [American]

**The Matson Ground Estate Company Limited**
*Incorporated:* 27 October 1923 *Employees:* 8
*Net Worth:* £2,725,937 *Total Assets:* £5,129,592
*Registered Office:* 100 Highgate, Kendal, Cumbria, LA9 4HE
*Activities:* Raising of other cattle and buffaloes
*Shareholders:* Francis Alexander Scott; Madeleine Mary Scott; Charlotte Rose Scott; Rebecca Anne Scott; Willliam Lawrence Swan
*Officers:* Charlotte Rose Scott [1954] Director; Francis Alexander Scott [1959] Director; Madeleine Mary Scott [1957] Director; Rebecca Anne Scott [1960] Director/Artist

**Matwest Ltd**
*Incorporated:* 29 September 2006
*Net Worth:* £308,485 *Total Assets:* £4,854,022
*Registered Office:* Manor House, Southside, Scorton, N Yorks, DL10 6DN
*Activities:* Buying and selling of own real estate
*Officers:* Crighton David Mather, Secretary; Aileen Joan Mather [1959] Director/Teacher; Crighton David Mather [1958] Director

**Thomas Mawer Limited**
*Incorporated:* 24 August 1977 *Employees:* 14
*Net Worth:* £9,228,329 *Total Assets:* £19,092,290
*Registered Office:* The Old Coaching House, 3 Union Street, Hull, HU2 8HD
*Activities:* Wholesale of grain, unmanufactured tobacco, seeds and animal feeds
*Parent:* Billhire Limited
*Officers:* Paula Elizabeth Bell [1964] Director/Traders Assistant; Neil Chapman [1960] Director/Sales Manager; Gavin Cowan [1967] Director; Richard William Hitchens [1982] Director; Michael Graham Milton [1957] Director/Senior Trader

**Richard Maxwell Limited**
*Incorporated:* 6 December 2006 *Employees:* 5
*Net Worth:* £88,051 *Total Assets:* £7,065,031
*Registered Office:* Busby Stoop Farm, Skipton Old Airfield, Sandhutton, Thirsk, N Yorks, YO7 4EJ
*Activities:* Production of electricity
*Shareholders:* Stephen Richard Knowlson; Richard Lionel Maxwell
*Officers:* Angela Rose Maxwell, Secretary; Stephen Richard Knowlson [1956] Director; Richard Lionel Maxwell [1947] Director

**Mayfair Curzon Properties Limited**
*Incorporated:* 1 September 2011 *Employees:* 3
*Net Worth:* £159,717 *Total Assets:* £3,831,544
*Registered Office:* 34 Wynmore Avenue, Bramhope, Leeds, LS16 9DE
*Activities:* Other letting and operating of own or leased real estate
*Shareholders:* Shula Lawrence; Jeremy Paul Michael Rider; Emma Charlotte Rider
*Officers:* Shula Lawrence [1973] Managing Director; Jeremy Paul Michael Rider [1982] Director

**Mayflower Specialist School Academy Trust**
*Incorporated:* 27 May 2015 *Employees:* 112
*Net Worth:* £10,596,618 *Total Assets:* £13,236,913
*Registered Office:* Warren Wood - A Specialist Academy, Middlefield Lane, Gainsborough, Lincs, DN21 1PU
*Activities:* Primary education
*Officers:* Anne Collishaw, Secretary; Anne Collishaw [1960] Director/Business Manager; Claire Cumberlidge [1965] Director/Head of School; Jonathan Peter Downes [1965] Director/Operations Manager; Dee Lloyd Freeman [1954] Director/Priest; Penny Holmes [1971] Director/Working Mother and Scientist; Peter Stephen Krick [1960] Director/Solicitor; Michele Lamb [1959] Director/Head of School; Gary Nixon [1965] Director/Executive Principal; Michael John Page [1951] Director/Retired

**Mazuma Mobile Limited**
*Incorporated:* 17 August 2006 *Employees:* 47
*Net Worth:* £4,339,296 *Total Assets:* £5,410,619
*Registered Office:* Fleet House, New Road, Lancaster, LA1 1EZ
*Activities:* Other telecommunications activities
*Parent:* Ecorenew Holdings (UK) Limited
*Officers:* Sarah Fort, Secretary; Kate Elizabeth Child [1978] Commercial Director; Sarah Fort [1983] Finance Director; Craig Richard Smith [1971] Director

**MBI Hawthorn Care Limited**
*Incorporated:* 5 June 2014
*Net Worth Deficit:* £1,652,823 *Total Assets:* £3,460,833
*Registered Office:* Unit D2, Elland Riorges Link, Lowfields Business Park, Elland, W Yorks, HX5 9DG
*Activities:* Residential nursing care facilities
*Major Shareholder:* Gavin Woodhouse
*Officers:* Gavin Lee Woodhouse [1978] Director/Consultant

**MBI Walsden Care Limited**
*Incorporated:* 6 November 2013
*Net Worth Deficit:* £807,839 *Total Assets:* £4,605,765
*Registered Office:* 2nd Floor, No 4 Warehouse, Canal Basin, Sowerby Bridge, W Yorks, HX6 2AG
*Activities:* Residential nursing care facilities
*Major Shareholder:* Gavin Lee Woodhouse
*Officers:* Robin Scott Forster [1981] Director/Consultant

**MBR Acres Limited**
*Incorporated:* 26 April 2017 *Employees:* 41
*Net Worth Deficit:* £188,824 *Total Assets:* £4,425,833
*Registered Office:* The Field Station, Grimston, Aldbrough, Hull, HU11 4QE
*Activities:* Raising of other animals
*Parent:* MFG International Limited
*Officers:* Cyril Desvignes [1969] Director/General Manager, European Operations [French]; Andrew Smith [1972] Director/Chief Operating Officer [American]

**McCain Finance (GB) Limited**
*Incorporated:* 14 February 1995 *Employees:* 5
*Net Worth Deficit:* £1,942,000 *Total Assets:* £36,118,000
*Registered Office:* Havers Hill, Eastfield, Scarborough, N Yorks, YO11 3BS
*Activities:* Activities of financial services holding companies
*Parent:* McCain Foods (G.B.) Limited
*Officers:* Saeeda Naz Amin, Secretary; Saeeda Naz Amin [1969] Finance Director; Alexander George de Freitas [1965] Director/Vice President Finance CE and Lutosa [Australian]; Geoffrey Dent [1957] Finance Director; Andres Zuluaga [1968] Director [Colombian]

**McCain Foods (G.B.) Limited**
*Incorporated:* 22 August 1962 *Employees:* 1,261
*Net Worth:* £120,937,000 *Total Assets:* £246,008,992
*Registered Office:* Havers Hill, Eastfield, Scarborough, N Yorks, YO11 3BS
*Activities:* Other processing and preserving of fruit and vegetables
*Parent:* McCain UK H2 Limited
*Officers:* Saeeda Naz Amin, Secretary; Saeeda Naz Amin [1969] Finance Director; Alan Norton Bridges [1960] Director; Mark Hodge [1973] Marketing Director; Andrew James Hoff [1981] Sales Director; Ross Aleric Hunter [1959] Director; Richard Michael Jones [1967] Director; Allison Douglas McCain [1949] Managing Director [Canadian]; Mark Crocket McCain [1954] Director [Canadian]; Daniel Derrick Metheringham [1979] Agriculture Director; Howard David Snape [1972] Director/Regional President - GB & Ireland; Helen Watts [1967] HR Director

**McCain UK H1 Limited**
*Incorporated:* 14 December 2012
*Net Worth:* £700,876,032 *Total Assets:* £1,301,148,032
*Registered Office:* Havers Hill, Scarborough, N Yorks, YO11 3BS
*Activities:* Activities of production holding companies
*Officers:* Saeeda Naz Amin, Secretary; Saeeda Naz Amin [1969] Finance Director; Alexander George de Freitas [1965] Director/Vice President Finance CE and Lutosa [Australian]; Geoffrey Dent [1957] Finance Director; Andres Zuluaga [1968] Director [Colombian]

**McCain UK H2 Limited**
*Incorporated:* 14 December 2012
*Net Worth:* £1,283,049,984 *Total Assets:* £1,283,360,000
*Registered Office:* Havers Hill, Scarborough, N Yorks, YO11 3BS
*Activities:* Activities of production holding companies
*Parent:* McCain UK H1 Limited
*Officers:* Saeeda Naz Amin, Secretary; Saeeda Naz Amin [1969] Finance Director; Alexander George de Freitas [1965] Director/Vice President Finance CE and Lutosa [Australian]; Geoffrey Dent [1957] Finance Director; Andres Zuluaga [1968] Director [Colombian]

**McCann Limited**
*Incorporated:* 5 December 1978 *Employees:* 32
*Net Worth:* £719,391 *Total Assets:* £3,280,928
*Registered Office:* 31 Abbey Road, Grimsby, N E Lincs, DN32 0HQ
*Activities:* Other transportation support activities
*Shareholders:* Gordon Lamming; John Robert Mager
*Officers:* Alan Frederick Lane, Secretary; Julie Rose Lamming [1959] Director; Jane Elizabeth Mager [1957] Director; John Robert Mager [1948] Director

**M. J. McCarthy (Holdings) Limited**
*Incorporated:* 2 March 1999 *Employees:* 1
*Net Worth:* £4,715,552 *Total Assets:* £9,060,164
*Registered Office:* The Depository, Meanwood Road, Leeds, LS7 2AH
*Activities:* Other letting and operating of own or leased real estate
*Shareholders:* Michael John McCarthy; Margaret McCarthy
*Officers:* Margaret McCarthy [1946] Director; Michael John McCarthy [1973] Director; Michael John McCarthy [1942] Director

**McCarthy Caravans Limited**
*Incorporated:* 10 June 2004 *Employees:* 4
*Net Worth:* £3,709,939 *Total Assets:* £5,504,455
*Registered Office:* Dalton House, 9 Dalton Square, Lancaster, LA1 1WD
*Activities:* Other holiday and other collective accommodation
*Shareholders:* John McCarthy; Helen McCarthy
*Officers:* John McCarthy, Secretary/Caravan Site Operator [Irish]; Helen McCarthy [1966] Director/Caravan Site Operator [Irish]; John McCarthy [1966] Director/Caravan Site Operator [Irish]; Patrick Connor McCarthy [1996] Director

**J.H. McCloy & Co Limited**
*Incorporated:* 12 January 1987 *Employees:* 25
*Net Worth:* £5,015,204 *Total Assets:* £6,288,351
*Registered Office:* Lakeside Byram Park, Byram-Cum-Sutton, Knottingley, W Yorks, WF11 9NG
*Activities:* Growing of cereals (except rice), leguminous crops and oil seeds
*Shareholder:* Andrew David McCloy
*Officers:* Sarah Jane Foster, Secretary; Sarah Jane Foster [1963] Director/Company Secretary; Andrew David McCloy [1960] Director/Farmer; David Peter McCloy [1934] Director/Farmer

**W.McClure Limited**
*Incorporated:* 6 March 1961 *Employees:* 133
*Net Worth:* £4,121,523 *Total Assets:* £6,597,411
*Registered Office:* College Road, Windermere, Cumbria, LA23 1BX
*Activities:* Non-specialised wholesale of food, beverages and tobacco
*Major Shareholder:* William Keith McClure
*Officers:* Matthew Paul McClure, Secretary; Jennie Caroline Foster [1976] Director; Ben Keith McClure [1979] Director; Matthew Paul McClure [1974] Director; William Keith McClure [1944] Director

**McDonald King Limited**
*Incorporated:* 12 August 1991
*Net Worth:* £12,795,573 *Total Assets:* £13,590,029
*Registered Office:* 356 Alwoodley Lane, Leeds, LS17 7DN
*Activities:* Other letting and operating of own or leased real estate
*Major Shareholder:* Margaret McDonald
*Officers:* Margaret McDonald [1938] Director/Property Developer; Simon Richard McDonald [1967] Director/Estate Manager

**R. McDowell Haulage and Distribution Limited**
*Incorporated:* 16 February 1989 *Employees:* 126
*Net Worth:* £2,284,060 *Total Assets:* £8,758,004
*Registered Office:* Thunderbird Depot, Valley Road, Keighley, W Yorks, BD21 4LZ
*Activities:* Freight transport by road
*Parent:* McDowell H & D Limited
*Officers:* Joseph Clayton Balmforth [1963] Director/Transport Manager; Brian Christopher Dent [1962] Director; Nathan Jon Goodridge [1980] Director; Geoffrey David Hirst [1986] Director

**MCE Concept Limited**
*Incorporated:* 12 May 2009
*Net Worth:* £10,998,618 *Total Assets:* £11,001,584
*Registered Office:* 6 Thornes Office Park, Monckton Road, Wakefield, W Yorks, WF2 7AN
*Activities:* Financial management
*Shareholder:* Alexis Daniel Jean Marie Francois
*Officers:* Alexis Daniel Jean Marie Francois [1977] Director [French]; Malika Larbatmi [1965] Director/Businesswoman [Algerian]

**J M McGill Ltd.**
*Incorporated:* 25 June 2002 *Employees:* 138
*Net Worth:* £490,188 *Total Assets:* £4,828,577
*Registered Office:* 106 Warmsworth Road, Doncaster, S Yorks, DN4 0RS
*Activities:* Dispensing chemist in specialised stores
*Major Shareholder:* Jonathan Marcus McGill
*Officers:* Roger William Appleyard, Secretary; Roger William Appleyard [1943] Director; Jonathan Marcus McGill [1965] Director/Pharmacist

**McIlroy Estates Limited**
*Incorporated:* 22 May 1978 *Employees:* 125
*Net Worth:* £3,024,311 *Total Assets:* £4,336,971
*Registered Office:* Mount Pleasant Hotel, Great North Road, Rossington, Doncaster, S Yorks, DN11 0HW
*Activities:* Hotels and similar accommodation
*Shareholders:* Mary Victoria Coubrough; David Robert John McIlroy; Richard James Coopland McIlroy; William Stocks McIlroy
*Officers:* William Stocks McIlroy, Secretary; Mary Victoria Coubrough [1958] Director/Catering Consultant; David Robert John McIlroy [1963] Director/Development Manager; Richard James Coopland McIlroy [1961] Director/Hotel Manager; William Stocks McIlroy [1956] Director/Engineer

**McJunkin Red Man UK Ltd**
*Incorporated:* 5 September 2009 *Employees:* 4
*Net Worth:* £105,649,960 *Total Assets:* £206,370,944
*Registered Office:* Heaton House, Riverside Drive, Cleckheaton, W Yorks, BD19 4DH
*Activities:* Activities of head offices
*Parent:* MRC Global Inc
*Officers:* Grant Richard Bates [1971] Director [Australian]; Elton Ray Bond [1975] Director [American]; Claire Jane Hellmund [1983] Director/Solicitor; Adnan Velic [1980] Director

**McLagan Investments Limited**
*Incorporated:* 30 April 1987 *Employees:* 3
*Net Worth:* £1,474,228,992 *Total Assets:* £4,518,543,872
*Registered Office:* Asda House, Southbank, Great Wilson Street, Leeds, LS11 5AD
*Activities:* Development of building projects
*Parent:* Asda Group Limited
*Officers:* Alexander Simpson, Secretary; Roger Michael Burnley [1966] Director; Robert Gerard McWilliam [1969] Director; Alexander Simpson [1973] Director

**McLean & Appleton (Holdings) Limited**
*Incorporated:* 26 May 1989 *Employees:* 467
*Net Worth:* £25,272,000 *Total Assets:* £96,254,000
*Registered Office:* Hatfields, Calder Island Way, Denby Dale Road, Wakefield, W Yorks, WF2 7AW
*Activities:* Activities of head offices
*Major Shareholder:* Gareth Sinclair Williams
*Officers:* Justin Sinclair Williams, Secretary; Gareth Sinclair Williams [1964] Director; John Sinclair Williams [1942] Director

**McLean & Appleton Limited**
*Incorporated:* 29 March 1924 *Employees:* 19
*Net Worth:* £3,366,069 *Total Assets:* £28,507,228
*Registered Office:* Hatfields, Calder Island Way, Denby Dale Road, Wakefield, W Yorks, WF2 7AW
*Activities:* Activities of head offices
*Shareholder:* Gareth Sinclair Williams
*Officers:* Justin Sinclair Williams, Secretary; Gareth Sinclair Williams [1964] Director; John Sinclair Williams [1942] Director/Motor Vehicle Dealer

**McManus Group Holdings Limited**
*Incorporated:* 30 September 2015 *Employees:* 67
*Net Worth:* £14,283,992 *Total Assets:* £36,173,720
*Registered Office:* Lusteen House, 24 Roydsdale Way, Euroway Industrial Estate, Bradford, W Yorks, BD4 6SE
*Activities:* Activities of head offices
*Major Shareholder:* Aiden Thomas McManus
*Officers:* Graham Hunt [1956] Director/Chartered Accountant; Aiden Thomas McManus [1976] Director; Thomas John McManus [1949] Director

**MCP Environmental Limited**
*Incorporated:* 2 September 2015 *Employees:* 111
*Net Worth Deficit:* £973,330 *Total Assets:* £8,510,657
*Registered Office:* South Bradford Trading Estate, Spartan Road, Low Moor, Bradford, W Yorks, BD12 0RY
*Activities:* Human resources provision and management of human resources functions
*Officers:* Paul Bates [1978] Asbestos Services Director; Catherine Blackshaw [1964] Director/Chartered Accountant; Andrew Stubbs [1971] Managing Director

**Meads Trust.Limited**
*Incorporated:* 21 November 1930 *Employees:* 1
*Net Worth:* £3,210,368 *Total Assets:* £3,485,527
*Registered Office:* 77 North Street, Ripon, N Yorks, HG4 1DS
*Activities:* Other specialised construction activities n.e.c.
*Officers:* Andrew Mark Hutchinson, Secretary; Andrew Mark Hutchinson [1965] Director/Solicitor; Charles Dominic Hanley Hutchinson [1961] Director/Journalist; James Michael Hutchinson [1962] Director/Accountant

**Mech-Tool Engineering Limited**
*Incorporated:* 5 October 2000 *Employees:* 178
*Net Worth:* £8,240,972 *Total Assets:* £15,136,529
*Registered Office:* Mech Tool House, Whessoe Road, Darlington, Co Durham, DL3 0QT
*Activities:* Manufacture of metal structures and parts of structures
*Shareholders:* Veronica Garner; Marshall Kenneth Garner
*Officers:* Kerry Ann Shotton, Secretary; Marshall Kenneth Garner [1951] Director; Veronica Garner [1950] Director

**Mech-Tool Holdings Limited**
*Incorporated:* 6 January 2014 *Employees:* 199
*Net Worth:* £8,897,931 *Total Assets:* £15,303,754
*Registered Office:* Mech-Tool House, Whessoe Road, Darlington, Co Durham, DL3 0QT
*Activities:* Activities of head offices
*Shareholders:* Marshall Kenneth Garner; Veronica Garner
*Officers:* Marshall Kenneth Garner [1951] Director; Veronica Garner [1950] Director

**Mechanical Facilities Services Limited**
*Incorporated:* 25 November 2008 *Employees:* 55
*Net Worth:* £695,537 *Total Assets:* £3,717,567
*Registered Office:* Charity Farm, 10 Bar Road North, Beckingham, Doncaster, S Yorks, DN10 4NN
*Activities:* Electrical installation
*Parent:* NHN Holdings Limited
*Officers:* Natalie Elizabeth Ann Sutherland, Secretary; Paul Manfred Firch [1963] Managing Director; Leanne Clare Franse [1978] Director; Steve John Padley [1968] Director; Natalie Elizabeth Ann Sutherland [1978] Director; Paul Stuart Sutherland [1972] Director/Surveyor

**J. & E. Medcalf Limited**
*Incorporated:* 7 December 1964 *Employees:* 26
*Net Worth:* £1,113,120 *Total Assets:* £3,772,442
*Registered Office:* Bowrake Farm, Addlethorpe Lane, Sicklinghall, Wetherby, W Yorks, LS22 4DD
*Activities:* Raising of dairy cattle
*Shareholder:* Jonathan Edward Medcalf
*Officers:* Claire Medcalf, Secretary; Claire Medcalf [1970] Director/Wholesale Butchers and Farmers; Elizabeth Medcalf [1975] Director/Office Administration; Generald Ernest Medcalf [1948] Director/Farmer; Jonathan Edward Medcalf [1970] Director/Farmer; Robert Medcalf [1981] Director/Butcher-Farmer; Rachael Robinson [1973] Director/Office Administration

**Medetcrown Limited**
*Incorporated:* 30 October 1981 *Employees:* 4
*Net Worth:* £3,122,683 *Total Assets:* £3,156,812
*Registered Office:* Baileys Farm, Lound Low Road, Sutton, Retford, Notts, DN22 8PN
*Activities:* Other letting and operating of own or leased real estate
*Shareholders:* Brian John Perry; Charmaine Diane Perry
*Officers:* Vanessa Jane Goreham, Secretary; Brian John Perry [1946] Managing Director; Charmaine Diane Perry [1947] Director

**Medical Imaging UK Limited**
*Incorporated:* 15 April 2002 *Employees:* 263
*Net Worth:* £2,758,939 *Total Assets:* £8,310,889
*Registered Office:* Rawdon House, Green Lane, Yeadon, Leeds, LS19 7BY
*Activities:* Hospital activities
*Parent:* Emis Group PLC
*Officers:* Christine Benson, Secretary; Peter John Southby [1973] Director; Andrew John Thorburn [1962] Director; Stephen John Wilcock [1967] Director

**Medicare Chemists Limited**
*Incorporated:* 4 March 1991 *Employees:* 36
*Net Worth:* £2,696,481 *Total Assets:* £3,943,095
*Registered Office:* Medicare House, 1 Meltham Road, Lockwood, W Yorks, HD1 3TJ
*Activities:* Dispensing chemist in specialised stores
*Officers:* Naheed Afzal, Secretary; Afzal Mohammed Khan [1959] Director/Pharmacist; Asghar Mohammed Khan [1965] Director/Pre-Registration Pharmacist; Rizwan Hasan Khan [1996] Director

**Megaplant Limited**
*Incorporated:* 24 April 1972 *Employees:* 12
*Net Worth:* £1,518,216 *Total Assets:* £3,102,043
*Registered Office:* Bridge House, 41 Wincolmlee, Kingston upon Hull, HU2 8AG
*Activities:* Renting and leasing of construction and civil engineering machinery and equipment
*Parent:* TWD Yorkshire Limited
*Officers:* Carole Marion Cameron [1963] Director/Administrator; Roger Alan Cameron [1957] Director/Chartered Accountant

**J.K.B.Megginson & Sons Limited**
*Incorporated:* 23 September 1964 *Employees:* 6
*Net Worth:* £2,733,373 *Total Assets:* £7,417,607
*Registered Office:* Kirkburn Grange Farm, Kirkburn, Driffield, E Yorks, YO25 9LP
*Activities:* Mixed farming
*Shareholders:* Simon John Megginson; Andrew Francis Megginson
*Officers:* Simon John Megginson, Secretary; Andrew Francis Megginson [1963] Director/Farmer; Janet Pauline Megginson [1936] Director/Farmer; Simon John Megginson [1961] Director/Farmer

**Melbourne Street Properties Limited**
*Incorporated:* 14 February 1918 *Employees:* 5
*Net Worth:* £5,049,761 *Total Assets:* £6,580,539
*Registered Office:* 23 Grove Crescent South, Boston Spa, Wetherby, W Yorks, LS23 6AY
*Activities:* Other letting and operating of own or leased real estate
*Officers:* Bernard Lynn Marr [1943] Director; Jeremy Norman Marr [1940] Director [Canadian]; Jordan Hugo Marr [1977] Director/IT Consultant [Canadian]; Roderick John Marr [1971] Director/Lighting Manager; Katherine Lynn Wood [1972] Director/Planner

**Meller Flow Trans Limited**
*Incorporated:* 6 October 2000 *Employees:* 26
*Net Worth:* £2,516,382 *Total Assets:* £3,651,184
*Registered Office:* 12 Millersdale Close, Euroway Industrial Estate, Bradford, W Yorks, BD4 6RX
*Activities:* Wholesale trade of motor vehicle parts and accessories
*Officers:* Mark Allcock [1970] Managing Director

**Melrose Pigs Limited**
*Incorporated:* 8 August 2011 *Employees:* 12
*Net Worth:* £3,704,410 *Total Assets:* £5,480,470
*Registered Office:* Melrose Farm, Melbourne, York, YO42 4SS
*Activities:* Raising of swine and pigs
*Shareholders:* John Robert Rowbottom; Eileen Mary Rowbottom
*Officers:* Pamela Fay Dear, Secretary; Pamela Fay Dear [1978] Director; Edward John Rowbottom [1981] Director/Farmer; John Robert Rowbottom [1945] Director/Farmer

**Melrose Textile Co.,Limited**
*Incorporated:* 16 May 1968 *Employees:* 52
*Net Worth:* £3,182,631 *Total Assets:* £5,345,463
*Registered Office:* Allerton Mills, Allerton Road, Bradford, W Yorks, BD15 7QX
*Activities:* Manufacture of other carpets and rugs
*Parent:* Birch Close Trading Ltd
*Officers:* Andrew Peter Murphy [1969] Director

**Mena Commercial Limited**
*Incorporated:* 17 January 2017
*Net Worth Deficit:* £51,887 *Total Assets:* £4,339,879
*Registered Office:* First Floor, 6 Butts Court, Leeds, LS1 5JS
*Activities:* Other letting and operating of own or leased real estate
*Major Shareholder:* Mohammad Alalloush
*Officers:* Mohammed Huque, Secretary; Fahad Alalloush [1981] Director [Kuwaiti]; Mohammad Alalloush [1955] Director [Kuwaiti]; Harry Albazie [1984] Director

**Mena Developments Limted Limited**
*Incorporated:* 17 January 2017
*Net Worth:* £10,000 *Total Assets:* £4,204,611
*Registered Office:* First Floor, 6 Butts Court, Leeds, LS1 5JS
*Activities:* Buying and selling of own real estate
*Major Shareholder:* Mohammad Alalloush
*Officers:* Mohammed Huque, Secretary; Fahad Alalloush [1981] Director [Kuwaiti]; Mohammad Alalloush [1955] Director [Kuwaiti]; Harry Albazie [1984] Director

**Mena Residential Limited**
*Incorporated:* 17 January 2017
*Net Worth:* £3,919 *Total Assets:* £6,000,678
*Registered Office:* First Floor, 6 Butts Court, Leeds, LS1 5JS
*Activities:* Other letting and operating of own or leased real estate
*Major Shareholder:* Mohammad Alalloush
*Officers:* Mohammed Huque, Secretary; Fahad Alalloush [1981] Director [Kuwaiti]; Mohammad Alalloush [1955] Director [Kuwaiti]; Harry Albazie [1984] Director

**Merewood Group Limited**
*Incorporated:* 2 December 1985
*Net Worth:* £9,972,000 *Total Assets:* £19,776,000
*Registered Office:* Persimmon House, Fulford, York, YO19 4FE
*Activities:* Construction of domestic buildings
*Parent:* Persimmon Homes Limited
*Officers:* Tracy Lazelle Davison, Secretary; David Jenkinson [1967] Director; Michael Hugh Killoran [1961] Finance Director; Richard Paul Stenhouse [1971] Director/Accountant

**Meridian Healthcare Limited**
*Incorporated:* 4 October 1985 *Employees:* 1,362
*Net Worth:* £73,537,000 *Total Assets:* £84,519,000
*Registered Office:* Southgate House, Archer Street, Darlington, Co Durham, DL3 6AH
*Activities:* Residential care activities for the elderly and disabled
*Parent:* Meridian Healthcare (Holdings) Limited
*Officers:* Sir David Behan [1955] Director; James Justin Hutchens [1974] Director [American]; Dr Chaitanya Bhupendra Patel [1954] Director; John Anthony Ransford [1948] Director; David Andrew Smith [1974] Director; Sir William Henry Weston Wells [1940] Director

**Meritec Limited**
*Incorporated:* 15 July 1996 *Employees:* 70
*Net Worth:* £1,204,019 *Total Assets:* £4,027,530
*Registered Office:* Meritec House, Acorn Business Park, Keighley Road, Skipton, N Yorks, BD23 2UE
*Activities:* Information technology consultancy activities
*Parent:* Meritec Holdings Limited
*Officers:* Steven Paul Wilkinson, Secretary/Director; Anthony Peter Wild [1954] Director; Rita Wild [1955] Director; Steven Paul Wilkinson [1950] Director; Susan Wilkinson [1950] Director

**Mermaid Panels Limited**
*Incorporated:* 30 November 1987 *Employees:* 13
*Net Worth:* £915,212 *Total Assets:* £3,426,202
*Registered Office:* DBC House, Grimsby Road, Laceby, Grimsby, S Humbers, DN37 7DP
*Activities:* Wholesale of wood, construction materials and sanitary equipment
*Parent:* Wilsonart Limited
*Officers:* William Joseph Thesing, Secretary; David John Campden [1964] Director/Chartered Accountant; Alan Timothy Pearson [1969] Director/Western Europe President; Jeffrey Hugh Robb [1967] Finance Director

**Merrion House Limited Liability Partnership**
*Incorporated:* 6 September 2013
*Net Worth:* £68,954,016 *Total Assets:* £71,154,184
*Registered Office:* Town Centre House, The Merrion Centre, Leeds, LS2 8LY

**Merritt & Fryers Limited**
*Incorporated:* 4 October 1935 *Employees:* 56
*Net Worth:* £3,414,315 *Total Assets:* £6,427,277
*Registered Office:* Firth Street Works, Firth Street, Skipton, N Yorks, BD23 2PX
*Activities:* Manufacture of other builders' carpentry and joinery
*Officers:* Rachel Elizabeth Fryers, Secretary; Rachel Elizabeth Fryers [1973] Director; Robert Paul Fryers [1962] Director; Andrew David Merritt [1972] Director

**Metal Drum Company Limited (The)**
*Incorporated:* 20 September 1961 *Employees:* 70
*Net Worth:* £4,859,727 *Total Assets:* £6,842,350
*Registered Office:* Dene Bridge Road, Chilton, Co Durham, DL17 0NU
*Activities:* Manufacture of steel drums and similar containers
*Major Shareholder:* Jonica Britton
*Officers:* Helen Edwina Britton, Secretary; Jonica Britton [1954] Director; Michael Alan Britton [1951] Director/Engineer; Samuel James Thomas Britton [1984] Director/General Manager

**Metalcraft Europe Limited**
*Incorporated:* 3 September 2008 *Employees:* 33
*Net Worth:* £2,881,790 *Total Assets:* £3,585,118
*Registered Office:* Unit 1b Bowling Park Close, Bradford, W Yorks, BD4 7HG
*Activities:* Manufacture of other fabricated metal products n.e.c.
*Officers:* Patricia Mary Varley, Secretary; Daniel Mark Varley [1978] Director; Nathan James Varley [1976] Director; Patricia Mary Varley [1950] Director

**Metaldyne International (UK) Ltd**
*Incorporated:* 11 June 1997 *Employees:* 104
*Net Worth:* £16,369,194 *Total Assets:* £29,304,598
*Registered Office:* 131 Parkinson Lane, Halifax, W Yorks, HX1 3RD
*Activities:* Manufacture of other parts and accessories for motor vehicles
*Officers:* Keith Alexander Eagle [1964] Managing Director; Yves Jules Robert Andre Gerard [1963] Director/Controller [Belgian]

**Metallink Fluid Power Systems Limited**
*Incorporated:* 8 November 1996 *Employees:* 54
*Net Worth:* £3,880,624 *Total Assets:* £5,127,709
*Registered Office:* Unit BT 35/2 Beechburn Industrial Estate, Crook, Co Durham, DL15 8JL
*Activities:* Manufacture of other fabricated metal products n.e.c.
*Major Shareholder:* Alemanna Bianconcini
*Officers:* Alan Joseph Hook, Secretary; Alemanna Bianconcini [1940] Director/Administration [Italian]; Paolo Borghi [1973] Managing Director [Italian]

**Metamark (UK) Limited**
*Incorporated:* 24 September 1992 *Employees:* 90
*Net Worth:* £12,709,000 *Total Assets:* £18,418,000
*Registered Office:* New Quay Road, Lancaster, LA1 5QP
*Activities:* Other manufacturing n.e.c.
*Officers:* Matthew Jonathan Enright [1978] Director/Chartered Accountant; Paul French [1972] Director/Chief Executive; Ian Geoffrey Simister [1968] Director

**Metamark Group Holdings Limited**
*Incorporated:* 3 February 2017 *Employees:* 94
*Net Worth Deficit:* £4,947,000 *Total Assets:* £68,789,000
*Registered Office:* New Quay Road, Lancaster, LA1 5QP
*Activities:* Activities of other holding companies n.e.c.
*Parent:* Primary Capital IV (Nominees) Limited
*Officers:* James Scott Browning [1966] Director/Chairman; Matthew Jonathan Enright [1978] Director/Chartered Accountant; Paul French [1972] Director; Ian Geoffrey Simister [1968] Director; Iain John Wolstenholme [1970] Director

**Metanoia Film Limited**
*Incorporated:* 11 December 2015 *Employees:* 3
*Net Worth:* £1,316,681 *Total Assets:* £4,052,151
*Registered Office:* Highfield Grange, Bubwith, Selby, N Yorks, YO8 6DP
*Activities:* Motion picture production activities
*Shareholders:* Peter Gerard Dunphy; Phineas Michael Glynn
*Officers:* Alan Richard Latham [1960] Director/Film Producer

**Metcalfe Bros Limited**
*Incorporated:* 8 August 2006
*Net Worth:* £2,222,304 *Total Assets:* £3,421,109
*Registered Office:* Dales Park Works, Cautley, Sedbergh, Cumbria, LA10 5NB
*Activities:* Support services to forestry
*Shareholders:* Stephen George Metcalfe; Richard Thomas Metcalfe
*Officers:* Stephen George Metcalfe, Secretary/Plant Operator; Richard Thomas Metcalfe [1970] Director/Plant Operator; Stephen George Metcalfe [1968] Director/Plant Operator

**Metcalfe Farming Limited**
*Incorporated:* 26 March 2009 *Employees:* 3
*Net Worth:* £1,284,873 *Total Assets:* £4,383,954
*Registered Office:* Horncastle Farm, Nostell, Wakefield, W Yorks, WF4 1QR
*Activities:* Growing of cereals (except rice), leguminous crops and oil seeds
*Shareholders:* Frederick David Metcalfe; Jonathan Frederick Metcalfe; Richard David Metcalfe
*Officers:* Jonathan Frederick Metcalfe, Secretary; Frederick David Metcalfe [1938] Director; Jonathan Frederick Metcalfe [1975] Director; Richard David Metcalfe [1973] Director

**Metcalfe Farms (Haulage) Limited**
*Incorporated:* 27 October 2006 *Employees:* 99
*Net Worth:* £6,995,783 *Total Assets:* £12,141,026
*Registered Office:* Washfold Farm, Leyburn, N Yorks, DL8 5JZ
*Activities:* Freight transport by road
*Officers:* David James Metcalfe, Secretary/Farmer; Andrew Philip Metcalfe [1970] Director/Farmer; Brian John Metcalfe [1966] Director/Farmer; David James Metcalfe [1964] Director/Farmer; John Metcalfe [1942] Director/Farmer; Thora Metcalfe [1944] Director/Farmer

**Methodist Chapel Aid Limited**
*Incorporated:* 2 January 1890 *Employees:* 3
*Net Worth:* £11,998,446 *Total Assets:* £33,576,836
*Registered Office:* 1 Telford Terrace, Albemarle Road, York, YO24 1DQ
*Activities:* Banks
*Officers:* Steven Russell Jones, Secretary; Reverend James Arnold Booth [1949] Director/Minister of Religion; David Jeremy Michael Burchill [1951] Director/Consultant; The Right Reverend Paul John Ferguson [1955] Director/Minister of Religion; Peter John Forward [1947] Director/Retired; Anne Frances Goodman [1963] Director/Chief Executive; Andrew Christopher Jarratt [1975] Director/Chief Executive; Peter Anthony Mills [1949] Director/Accountant; George Alan Pimlott [1947] Director/Retired; Andrew Charles Slim [1952] Director/Consultant

**Methodist Holiday Hotels Limited**
*Incorporated:* 17 June 1940 *Employees:* 59
*Net Worth:* £829,098 *Total Assets:* £3,531,981
*Registered Office:* 12 Alma Square, Scarborough, N Yorks, YO11 1JU
*Activities:* Hotels and similar accommodation
*Officers:* Diane Uhalde, Secretary; Timothy John Boyes [1948] Director; Richard John Kinder [1955] Director/Chartered Accountant; Diane Uhalde [1955] Director

**Metis Bidco Limited**
*Incorporated:* 31 May 2011 *Employees:* 1,643
*Net Worth:* £228,188,000 *Total Assets:* £981,692,992
*Registered Office:* Ellington House, 9 Savannah Way, Leeds Valley Park, Leeds, LS10 1AB
*Activities:* Activities of head offices
*Parent:* Simon Bidco Limited
*Officers:* Bill Flynn, Secretary; James John Cornell [1973] Director; John Patrick Flaherty [1974] Director/Accountant [Irish]; David Ronald Gagie [1955] Director; Heinz Erwin Friedrich Hilgert [1953] Managing Director [German]

**Metroplan Limited**
*Incorporated:* 18 January 1978 *Employees:* 62
*Net Worth:* £992,254 *Total Assets:* £3,541,544
*Registered Office:* Godmund Hall, Burneside, Kendal, Cumbria, LA8 9AD
*Activities:* Non-specialised wholesale trade
*Shareholders:* Geoffrey James Murphy; Sally Clare Murphy
*Officers:* Sally Clare Murphy, Secretary; Daniel Ian Biggs [1977] Technical Director; Geoffrey James Murphy [1944] Managing Director; Jonathan Patrick Murphy [1978] Director; Sally Clare Murphy [1958] Director/Secretary

**J.H. Mewburn Limited**
*Incorporated:* 27 July 1981 *Employees:* 9
*Net Worth:* £750,933 *Total Assets:* £3,999,742
*Registered Office:* Sandsfield Farm, Catwick Lane, Brandesburton, Driffield, E Yorks, YO25 8SB
*Activities:* Growing of cereals (except rice), leguminous crops and oil seeds
*Shareholders:* Sandsfield Limited; James Heppell Mewburn
*Officers:* Dianne Mary Mewburn, Secretary; Dianne Mary Mewburn [1940] Director/Farmer; James Heppell Mewburn [1941] Director/Farmer; Mark Wilson Mewburn [1967] Director/Farmer

**The MFG Academies Trust**
*Incorporated:* 8 February 2011 *Employees:* 377
*Previous:* The Mirfield Free Grammar and Sixth Form Multi-Academy Trust
*Net Worth:* £25,922,000 *Total Assets:* £29,024,000
*Registered Office:* Kitson Hill Road, Mirfield, W Yorks, WF14 9EZ
*Activities:* Primary education
*Officers:* Suzanne Maria Disley, Secretary; Lorraine Barker [1955] Director/Executive Principal; Angela Margaret Dobrucki [1966] MAT Director of Finance; Claire Elcock [1983] Director/Chartered Accountant; John Michael Hardill [1956] Director/Design Consultant; Mark Andrew Pheasey [1969] Operations Director; Jennifer Mary Ryan [1947] Director/Business Consultant; Charles Gerard Thornton [1966] Director/Company Accountant

**MHLL Limited**
*Incorporated:* 25 February 1924 *Employees:* 30
*Previous:* Moxon Huddersfield Limited
*Net Worth:* £2,495,238 *Total Assets:* £7,463,930
*Registered Office:* Yew Tree Mills, Holmbridge, Holmfirth, W Yorks, HD9 2NN
*Activities:* Weaving of textiles
*Officers:* Chaker Mohammad Chamsi-Pasha, Secretary; Chaker Mohammad Chamsi Pasha [1955] Director

**Mibelle Ltd**
*Incorporated:* 4 November 2005 *Employees:* 194
*Net Worth:* £10,323,000 *Total Assets:* £24,631,000
*Registered Office:* Units 3-5 City Link Industrial Park, Phoenix Way, Tyersal, Bradford, W Yorks, BD4 8JP
*Activities:* Manufacture of perfumes and toilet preparations
*Parent:* Mibelle AG
*Officers:* Amanda Frances Louise Caldwell, Secretary; Amanda Frances Louise Caldwell [1971] Director/Chartered Accountant; Gary Brian Clarke [1968] Commercial Director; Massimiliano Costantini [1970] Commercial Director; Gregoire Filiatre [1976] Director/Chartered Accountant [French]; Walter Cornelio Huber [1957] Director [Swiss]; Dr Luigi Pedrocchi [1959] Director [Swiss]; Andrew Martin Sharp [1968] Operations Director

**Microcourt Limited**
*Incorporated:* 23 October 2001 *Employees:* 5
*Net Worth:* £9,767,590 *Total Assets:* £21,245,448
*Registered Office:* UK Greetings, Mill Street East, Dewsbury, W Yorks, WF12 9AW
*Activities:* Retail sale via mail order houses or via Internet
*Major Shareholder:* Donald J. Gogel
*Officers:* Christopher William Haffke [1970] Director/Attorney [American]; Gregory Steinberg [1973] Director/Chief Financial Officer-American Greetings Corp [American]

**Micron Hydraulics Holdings Limited**
*Incorporated:* 20 November 2002
*Net Worth:* £2,245,814 *Total Assets:* £4,035,326
*Registered Office:* 25 Wharfedale Road, Euroway Trading Estate, Bradford, W Yorks, BD4 6SG
*Activities:* Activities of head offices
*Shareholders:* Michael John Plowman; Wendy Janet Plowman
*Officers:* Liah Plowman [1982] Director; Michael John Plowman [1947] Director

**Midas Paper Converters Limited**
*Incorporated:* 26 January 2001 *Employees:* 82
*Net Worth:* £4,156,726 *Total Assets:* £7,408,378
*Registered Office:* Stewart Close, Eccleshill, Bradford, W Yorks, BD2 2EE
*Activities:* Manufacture of paper stationery
*Officers:* Dominic Wilson de Luca, Secretary/Managing Director; John Paul Clemie [1950] Director; Dominic Wilson de Luca [1964] Managing Director; Margaret Ann Deluca [1940] Director; Robert John Kirkham [1946] Director

**Middle Caves Ltd**
*Incorporated:* 24 November 2003 *Employees:* 17
*Net Worth:* £10,831,629 *Total Assets:* £13,399,682
*Registered Office:* Pond Dale, Gilling West, Richmond, N Yorks, DL10 5LB
*Activities:* Raising of swine and pigs
*Major Shareholder:* Paul Anthony Hall Westgarth
*Officers:* Paul Anthony Hall Westgarth, Secretary; Paul Anthony Hall Westgarth [1967] Director/Farmer; Timothy Peter Westgarth [1973] Director/Farmer

**Middlegate (Europe) Limited**
*Incorporated:* 25 June 1990 *Employees:* 75
*Net Worth:* £406,229 *Total Assets:* £4,148,515
*Registered Office:* Marfleet Environmental Technology Park, Westgate Way, Hedon Road, Hull, HU9 5LW
*Activities:* Freight transport by road
*Officers:* David Laws, Secretary; Kim Notman [1974] Director [Belgian]; Laura Jane Notman [1982] Director/Health and Safety Representative

**Middleton Hall Limited**
*Incorporated:* 23 April 1900 *Employees:* 172
*Net Worth:* £4,521,150 *Total Assets:* £8,237,301
*Registered Office:* Middleton Hall, Middleton St George, Darlington, Co Durham, DL2 1HA
*Activities:* Medical nursing home activities
*Major Shareholder:* Jeremy Michael Hutton Walford
*Officers:* Lesley Henderson, Secretary; Lesley Henderson [1960] Director; Pamela Lynne Mooney [1961] Operations Director; Jeremy Michael Hutton Walford [1962] Executive Director; Adrian Walker [1950] Director/Chartered Accountant

**Middleton Lodge Events Limited**
*Incorporated:* 8 December 2006 *Employees:* 81
*Net Worth:* £3,375,857 *Total Assets:* £5,027,341
*Registered Office:* Middleton Lodge, Middleton Tyas, Richmond, N Yorks, DL10 6NJ
*Activities:* Hotels and similar accommodation
*Major Shareholder:* James Jonathon Allison
*Officers:* James Connolly, Secretary; James Jonathon Allison [1978] Director/Engineer

**Middlewood Locks Residential Limited**
*Incorporated:* 4 October 2016
*Net Worth:* £43,655 *Total Assets:* £94,698,736
*Registered Office:* Europa House, 20 Esplanade, Scarborough, N Yorks, YO11 2AQ
*Activities:* Buying and selling of own real estate
*Parent:* Fairbriar Development Holdings Limited
*Officers:* Simon Charles McCabe [1977] Director/Development Executive; Jeremy John Tutton [1966] Director/Financial Controller

**The Miles Partnership Limited**
*Incorporated:* 27 January 2014 *Employees:* 47
*Net Worth Deficit:* £1,974,474 *Total Assets:* £3,010,748
*Registered Office:* Gresham House, 5-7 St Pauls Street, Leeds, LS1 2JG
*Activities:* Other service activities n.e.c.
*Major Shareholder:* Chris Stainton
*Officers:* Christopher Andrew Stainton [1970] Director/Executive Search Consultant

**Roger Miles Plant Sales Ltd.**
*Incorporated:* 23 October 2002 *Employees:* 5
*Net Worth:* £2,241,094 *Total Assets:* £4,255,735
*Registered Office:* Shire House, Gowdall Lane, Pollington, Goole, E Yorks, DN14 0AU
*Activities:* Agents involved in the sale of machinery, industrial equipment, ships and aircraft
*Shareholders:* Roger Miles; Susan Miles
*Officers:* Susan Miles, Secretary; Roger Miles [1949] Director/Plant Dealer; Susan Miles [1949] Director/Secretary; Mathew Luke Stripe [1985] Sales Director

**Mileta Sports Limited**
*Incorporated:* 6 September 1973 *Employees:* 317
*Net Worth:* £9,737,715 *Total Assets:* £13,843,307
*Registered Office:* Spen Vale Mills, Station Lane, Heckmondwike, W Yorks, WF16 0NQ
*Activities:* Retail sale of clothing in specialised stores
*Shareholder:* Ian Ward
*Officers:* Brian George Ward, Secretary; Brian George Ward [1951] Managing Director; Christopher John Ward [1979] Marketing Director; Ian Ward [1953] Sales Director; Mark James Ward [1970] Retail Director

**Milford Limited**
*Incorporated:* 24 April 1974 *Employees:* 44
*Net Worth:* £4,236,144 *Total Assets:* £5,457,512
*Registered Office:* 170 Cardigan Road, Leeds, LS6 1LL
*Activities:* Wholesale of wood, construction materials and sanitary equipment
*Officers:* Kenneth William Coad, Secretary; Kenneth William Coad [1954] Director/Accountant; John David Middleton-Walker [1953] Director

**Mill Garages North East Limited**
*Incorporated:* 18 March 2008 *Employees:* 188
*Net Worth:* £4,363,000 *Total Assets:* £30,837,000
*Registered Office:* Stoneacre, Omega Boulevard, Capitol Park, Thorne, Doncaster, S Yorks, DN8 5TX
*Activities:* Sale of new cars and light motor vehicles
*Parent:* Decidebloom Limited
*Officers:* Shaun Foweather [1963] Director; Richard Stephen Teatum [1957] Director; Nigel Peter Wood [1964] Director

**Mill Mount Properties Limited**
*Incorporated:* 28 May 2015
*Net Worth:* £1,984,000 *Total Assets:* £3,546,000
*Registered Office:* Yorkon House, New Lane, Huntington, York, YO32 9PT
*Activities:* Buying and selling of own real estate
*Parent:* Shepherd Building Group Limited
*Officers:* Martin Ian Goforth, Secretary; Jonathan Mark Collins [1971] Director/Accountant; Janet Rose [1964] Director/Accountant; Caroline Scott [1961] Director/Accountant

**Mill Nurseries Limited**
*Incorporated:* 7 November 1997 *Employees:* 76
*Net Worth:* £9,991,958 *Total Assets:* £25,703,300
*Registered Office:* Mill Nurseries, Ottringham Road, Keyingham, Hull, HU12 9RX
*Activities:* Growing of vegetables and melons, roots and tubers
*Shareholders:* Hermanus Gerrit de Lang; David Roy de Lang; Robert Johannes de Lang; Catharina Audrey Jayne de Lang
*Officers:* Hermanus Gerrit de Lang, Secretary; Catharina Audrey Jayne de Lang [1970] Director/Market Gardener; David Roy de Lang [1964] Director/Market Gardener; Hermanus Gerrit de Lang [1962] Director/Market Gardener; Robert Johannes de Lang [1968] Director/Market Gardener

**Millennium Inorganic Chemicals Overseas Holdings**
*Incorporated:* 16 March 1989 *Employees:* 4
*Net Worth:* £555,143,808 *Total Assets:* £698,991,872
*Registered Office:* Laporte Road, Stallingborough, Grimsby, N E Lincs, DN40 2PR
*Activities:* Activities of other holding companies n.e.c.
*Parent:* Cristal Inorganic Chemicals Netherlands B.V.
*Officers:* Maria Jegher, Secretary; Stephen Anthony Box [1959] Director/Financial Controller; Koen Felix Lodewijk Docx [1974] Director/Finance Manager [Belgian]; Dr Robert McIntyre [1955] Commercial Research Director; Robert John Sarracini [1976] Site Director [British/Australian]

**Millennium Inorganic Chemicals UK Holdings Limited**
*Incorporated:* 25 August 1995 *Employees:* 4
*Net Worth:* £432,966,016 *Total Assets:* £432,994,464
*Registered Office:* Laporte Road, Stallingborough, Grimsby, N E Lincs, DN40 2PR
*Activities:* Activities of other holding companies n.e.c.
*Parent:* Millennium Inorganic Chemicals Overseas Holdings
*Officers:* Maria Jegher, Secretary; Stephen Anthony Box [1959] Director/Financial Controller; Koen Felix Lodewijk Docx [1974] Director/Finance Manager [Belgian]; Dr Robert McIntyre [1955] Commercial Research Director; Robert John Sarracini [1976] Site Director [British/Australian]

**Millennium Insurance Brokers Limited**
*Incorporated:* 26 February 1987
*Net Worth:* £1,313,000 *Total Assets:* £9,300,000
*Registered Office:* Quay Point, Lakeside Boulevard, Doncaster, S Yorks, DN4 5PL
*Activities:* Life insurance
*Parent:* Direct Group Limited
*Officers:* Derek John Coles [1960] Director; Scott William Hough [1971] Director

**J.S. Miller Distribution Limited**
*Incorporated:* 24 November 1999 *Employees:* 14
*Net Worth:* £3,400,705 *Total Assets:* £5,071,590
*Registered Office:* Phoenix Works, 388 Meanwood Road, Leeds, LS7 2JF
*Activities:* Other construction installation
*Parent:* Adam Holdings (Leeds) Limited
*Officers:* Anthony Francis Mulligan, Secretary; Martyn Peter Griffin [1960] Director; Anthony Francis Mulligan [1956] Director; Dewi Emlyn Thomas [1966] Director

**Millers Oils Limited**
*Incorporated:* 14 September 1914 *Employees:* 124
*Net Worth:* £5,699,941 *Total Assets:* £12,280,125
*Registered Office:* Hillside Oil Works, Rastrick Common, Brighouse, W Yorks, HD6 3DP
*Activities:* Other treatment of petroleum products (excluding petrochemicals manufacture)
*Officers:* Steven Cocking [1973] Finance Director; Anthony Richard Lowe [1968] Sales & Marketing Director; Martyn Dennis Mann [1959] Director; Andrew Charles Watson Miller [1950] Director; Janice Elizabeth Ward [1957] Director

**Robin Mills Properties Limited**
*Incorporated:* 24 November 2005 *Employees:* 1
*Net Worth:* £3,994,855 *Total Assets:* £4,934,258
*Registered Office:* Robin Mills, Leeds Road, Idle, Bradford, W Yorks, BD10 9TE
*Activities:* Other letting and operating of own or leased real estate
*Shareholders:* John Currie; Thomas Owen Willets Storey
*Officers:* Dennis Keith Marshall, Secretary; Bruno Chorzelewski [1948] Director; Dennis Keith Marshall [1946] Director; Thomas Owen Willets Storey [1971] Director

**Millwood Investments Limited**
*Incorporated:* 12 August 2005 *Employees:* 763
*Net Worth:* £1,131,550 *Total Assets:* £3,434,627
*Registered Office:* Neptune House, Neptune Street, Hull, HU3 2BP
*Activities:* Activities of head offices
*Major Shareholder:* John Richard Beharrell
*Officers:* John Richard Beharrell, Secretary; Anthony John Beharrell [1946] Director; John Richard Beharrell [1976] Director; Lesley Beharrell [1947] Director; Anthony John Adrian Ford [1944] Director

**Minster Law Limited**
*Incorporated:* 7 February 2003 *Employees:* 606
*Net Worth:* £45,353,000 *Total Assets:* £85,410,000
*Registered Office:* Kingfisher House, Peel Avenue, Wakefield, W Yorks, WF2 7UA
*Activities:* Solicitors
*Parent:* BHL (UK) Holdings Limited
*Officers:* Lucy Sinfield, Secretary; Rachel Helen di Clemente [1977] Director/Solicitor; Martin Jeffrey Hume [1976] Finance Director; Charles Edward Layfield [1973] Director/Solicitor; Ian Robert Leech [1960] Director; Michael Ian Warren [1964] Managing Director; Shirley Louise Woolham [1972] Director/Chief Executive

**Minster Veterinary Practice Ltd**
*Incorporated:* 11 July 2006 *Employees:* 103
*Net Worth:* £1,631,669 *Total Assets:* £4,309,224
*Registered Office:* Leeman House, Station Business Park, Holgate Park Drive, York, YO26 4GB
*Activities:* Veterinary activities
*Parent:* Vetpartners Limited
*Officers:* Joanna Clare Malone [1974] Managing Director and Veterinary Surgeon; Mark Stanworth [1964] Director

**Minstergate Limited**
*Incorporated:* 4 October 2002 *Employees:* 120
*Previous:* Minstergate Hull Limited
*Net Worth:* £666,579 *Total Assets:* £9,219,303
*Registered Office:* Minstergate, Livingstone Road, Hessle, E Yorks, HU13 0AB
*Activities:* Sale of new cars and light motor vehicles
*Officers:* Mark Paul Campey, Secretary; Helen Jane Campey [1974] Director; Mark Paul Campey [1973] Director/Business Manager; James Howard Cuff [1975] Director; Stephen Paul Forster [1972] Director/Dealer Principal

**Minsthorpe Academy Trust**
*Incorporated:* 16 May 2011 *Employees:* 245
*Net Worth:* £20,249,000 *Total Assets:* £23,202,000
*Registered Office:* Minsthorpe Community College, Minsthorpe Lane, South Elmsall, Pontefract, W Yorks, WF9 2UJ
*Activities:* General secondary education
*Officers:* Jayne Marie Germain, Secretary; Terry Boughen [1964] Director; Christine Antoinette Yvonne Britton [1969] Director/Teacher [French]; Terry Michael Cawthorne [1938] Director/Retired; Brian Dickinson [1956] Director/Retired; Wendy Nicola Evans [1967] Director; Raymond Paul Henshaw [1960] Director/Headmaster; Angela Marie Susana Jarratt [1963] Director/Alternative Provision Coordinator; Barry Dean Johnson [1965] Director/Storeman - Street Lighting; Mark Scott [1967] Director; Beverley Lois Semper [1961] Director; William Ian Shaw [1954] Director/Treasurer of The Hairdressing Council for GB

**Mirabelle Partners Limited**
*Incorporated:* 19 September 2002
*Net Worth:* £883,806 *Total Assets:* £4,263,848
*Registered Office:* Suite 3, Aireside House, Aireside Business Centre, Royd Ings Avenue, Keighley, W Yorks, BD21 4BZ
*Activities:* Other letting and operating of own or leased real estate
*Shareholder:* Andrew Christopher Hobson
*Officers:* Dale Walter Chapman, Secretary/Director; Caron April Chapman [1962] Director; Dale Walter Chapman [1970] Director; Kim Chapman [1971] Director; Paul Chapman [1949] Director; Andrew Christopher Hobson [1946] Director

**Mister Capital Holdings Limited**
*Incorporated:* 1 June 2006
*Net Worth:* £1,770,575 *Total Assets:* £4,297,983
*Registered Office:* Empire Suite, 108 St Leonard Gate, Lancaster, LA1 1NN
*Activities:* Buying and selling of own real estate
*Major Shareholder:* Yakub Ahmed Mister
*Officers:* Zubeir Yakub Mister, Secretary; Yakub Ahmed Mister [1948] Commercial Director

**Mitchell Farrar Group LLP**
*Incorporated:* 13 May 2009 *Employees:* 210
*Net Worth:* £749,937 *Total Assets:* £3,272,051
*Registered Office:* Unit 1c Riparian Way, The Crossings Business Park, Cross Hills, Keighley, W Yorks, BD20 7AA
*Officers:* Benjamin George Richard Farrar [1975] Member; Mark James Mitchell [1975] Member; Emily Linda Farrar [1974] LLP Member; Jane Rachel Gibson [1975] LLP Member

**Mitchell's Brewery Limited**
*Incorporated:* 25 August 1989 *Employees:* 278
*Net Worth:* £1,127,000 *Total Assets:* £9,737,000
*Registered Office:* 11 Moor Lane, Lancaster, LA1 1QB
*Activities:* Public houses and bars
*Officers:* Julia Hodge [1969] H R Director

**Mitrefinch Holdings Limited**
*Incorporated:* 22 September 2016 *Employees:* 150
*Net Worth Deficit:* £6,836,314 *Total Assets:* £53,473,184
*Registered Office:* MitreFinch House, Green Lane Trading Estate, Clifton, York, YO30 5YY
*Activities:* Business and domestic software development
*Officers:* Jonathan Scott Bell [1974] Director; Kenneth Cumming Hills [1961] Director; Richard Ibbett [1977] Investment Director; Ian David Jefferson [1970] Director; Matthew Ronald Jenkins [1979] Director/Chief Executive Officer; Ian Francis Kelly [1962] Director

**Mitrefinch Limited**
*Incorporated:* 24 August 1977 *Employees:* 130
*Net Worth:* £5,379,600 *Total Assets:* £11,340,335
*Registered Office:* MitreFinch House, Green Lane Trading Estate, Clifton, York, YO30 5YY
*Activities:* Business and domestic software development
*Parent:* Mitrefinch Holdings Ltd
*Officers:* Ian David Jefferson [1970] Director; Matthew Ronald Jenkins [1979] Director/Chief Executive Officer

**Mitton Aftercare Limited**
*Incorporated:* 30 January 2003 *Employees:* 202
*Net Worth:* £9,284 *Total Assets:* £4,770,649
*Registered Office:* Ronnie Hellewell House, 451 Cleckheaton Road, Bradford, W Yorks, BD12 0HS
*Activities:* Plumbing, heat and air-conditioning installation
*Parent:* H Mitton Limited
*Officers:* Neil Burns [1963] Director; Graham Hawe [1958] Director; Steven Taylor [1976] Director

**H. Mitton Limited**
*Incorporated:* 8 June 2000 *Employees:* 310
*Net Worth:* £384,732 *Total Assets:* £12,295,626
*Registered Office:* MacKenzie House, 451 Cleckheaton Road, Low Moor, Bradford, W Yorks, BD12 0HS
*Activities:* Activities of head offices
*Shareholder:* Steven Taylor
*Officers:* Neil Burns [1963] Director; Graham Hawe [1958] Director; Steven Taylor [1976] Director

**Mitton Mechanical Services Limited**
*Incorporated:* 5 December 1957 *Employees:* 112
*Net Worth:* £2,533,896 *Total Assets:* £9,968,003
*Registered Office:* MacKenzie House, 451 Cleckheaton Road, Bradford, W Yorks, BD12 0HS
*Activities:* Plumbing, heat and air-conditioning installation
*Parent:* H Mitton Limited
*Officers:* Neil Burns [1963] Director; Graham Hawe [1958] Director; Jonathan Stuart Knowles [1982] Director; Steven Taylor [1976] Director

**Mixer Bidco Limited**
*Incorporated:* 29 May 2013
*Net Worth:* £23,000 *Total Assets:* £14,673,000
*Registered Office:* Nutclough Mill, Valley Road, Hebden Bridge, W Yorks, HX7 8EZ
*Activities:* Activities of head offices
*Parent:* Remix Bidco Limited
*Officers:* Nigel Beaumont [1961] Director; Keith Edwards [1965] Director

**MLC Investments Limited**
*Incorporated:* 1 February 1995
*Net Worth:* £491,288 *Total Assets:* £3,540,502
*Registered Office:* Birkby House, Bailiff Bridge, Brighouse, W Yorks, HD6 4JJ
*Activities:* Other letting and operating of own or leased real estate
*Major Shareholder:* David Ross
*Officers:* David John William Ross, Secretary/Director; Susan Loveday [1960] Director/Office Manager; David John William Ross [1943] Director

**MM Band Services Limited**
*Incorporated:* 6 May 2003 *Employees:* 6
*Net Worth:* £1,063,630 *Total Assets:* £3,877,371
*Registered Office:* 6 George Street, Driffield, E Yorks, YO25 6RA
*Activities:* Tour operator activities
*Major Shareholder:* Michael Robert Moulds
*Officers:* Michael Robert Moulds [1968] Director/Second Car Dealer

**MMCD Investments Limited**
*Incorporated:* 20 January 2014 *Employees:* 1
*Net Worth:* £998,434 *Total Assets:* £4,625,559
*Registered Office:* Apperley Grange, Apperley Lane, Rawdon, Leeds, LS19 6LN
*Activities:* Activities of real estate investment trusts
*Shareholders:* Alison Kate McDonnell; Michael James McDonnell
*Officers:* Michael James McDonnell [1970] Director

**MMCG Holdings Limited**
*Incorporated:* 9 May 2014 *Employees:* 2,136
*Net Worth:* £20,442,000 *Total Assets:* £157,572,000
*Registered Office:* Westcourt, Gelderd Road, Leeds, LS12 6DB
*Activities:* Activities of head offices
*Major Shareholder:* Philip John Burgan
*Officers:* Christopher Ball [1968] Director; Lynne Frances Burgan [1957] Director; Philip John Burgan [1951] Director/Pharmacist; Peter Gervais Fagan [1957] Director; Jason Lock [1972] Director; Grace Thomas [1917] Director

**MMCG Limited**
*Incorporated:* 12 March 2010 *Employees:* 72
*Net Worth:* £1,052,272 *Total Assets:* £3,690,782
*Registered Office:* Westcourt, Gelderd Road, Leeds, LS12 6DB
*Activities:* Activities of head offices
*Major Shareholder:* Philip John Burgan
*Officers:* Christopher Ball [1968] Director; Charlotte Burgan [1993] Director; James Edward Burgan [1979] Director; Philip John Burgan [1951] Director; Sarah Burgan [1990] Director; Peter Gervais Fagan [1957] Director; Jason Lock [1972] Director; Grace Thomas [1917] Director; Rachel Womack [1982] Director; John Charles Wright [1949] Director

**MMM Medical Equipment UK Limited**
*Incorporated:* 31 December 1996 *Employees:* 37
*Net Worth:* £2,008,999 *Total Assets:* £3,707,085
*Registered Office:* Units 2 & 3 Gateway Drive Business Park, Gateway Drive, Yeadon, Leeds, W Yorks, LS19 7XY
*Activities:* Other business support service activities n.e.c.
*Major Shareholder:* Michael Koller
*Officers:* Andrew Charles Kaufman, Secretary; Brian Mitchell [1959] Director

**MMS Ship Repair and Dry Dock Co. Ltd**
*Incorporated:* 1 March 1988 *Employees:* 44
*Net Worth:* £4,838,825 *Total Assets:* £5,653,586
*Registered Office:* North East Corner, Alexandra Dock, Hull, HU9 1TA
*Activities:* Repair and maintenance of ships and boats
*Major Shareholder:* Robert Stephen Langton
*Officers:* Lauren Langton, Secretary; Pauline Langton [1928] Director; Robert Stephen Langton [1961] Director

**Mobili Office Design International LLP**
*Incorporated:* 16 September 2010
*Net Worth:* £8,397,722 *Total Assets:* £8,498,451
*Registered Office:* Innovation House, Snaygill Industrial Estate, Keighley Road, Skipton, N Yorks, BD23 2QR
*Officers:* David Stephen Cock [1971] Member

**Mobili Office Limited**
*Incorporated:* 23 August 1996 *Employees:* 57
*Net Worth:* £7,268,957 *Total Assets:* £11,447,704
*Registered Office:* Innovation House, Snaygill Industrial Estate, Keighley Road, Skipton, N Yorks, BD23 2QR
*Activities:* Manufacture of office and shop furniture
*Major Shareholder:* David Stephen Cock
*Officers:* John Nicholas Cock, Secretary; David Stephen Cock [1971] Director

**Mobus Fabrics Limited**
*Incorporated:* 2 August 1994 *Employees:* 23
*Net Worth:* £7,122,524 *Total Assets:* £9,182,448
*Registered Office:* Unit G1, Lacy Way, Lowfields Business Park, Elland, W Yorks, HX5 9DB
*Activities:* Wholesale of textiles
*Parent:* Mobus Fabrics Holdings Limited
*Officers:* Michael Scott Presley, Secretary; David Robert Barnes [1959] Director/Accountant; Ian Bostock [1961] Sales Director; Grant Dean Russell McConnell [1964] Director/Textile Agent; Lee Paxman [1982] Director; Michael Scott Presley [1955] Director

**Moda Living (Angel Gardens) Limited**
*Incorporated:* 8 April 2014 *Employees:* 8
*Net Worth:* £3,449,259 *Total Assets:* £6,289,261
*Registered Office:* Castlegarth Grange, Scott Lane, Wetherby, W Yorks, LS22 6LH
*Activities:* Management of real estate on a fee or contract basis
*Parent:* Moda Living Limited
*Officers:* Paul Andrew Bullers, Secretary; Anthony Brooks [1961] Director; Daniel Reuben Brooks [1984] Director; Oscar Anthony Brooks [1988] Director; Paul Andrew Bullers [1966] Director/Group Accountant; John Paul Caddick [1981] Development Director; Paul Caddick [1950] Director; Myles Edward Hartley [1969] Director; Andrew Stephen Parker [1977] Director; Lee Michael Savage [1970] Director

**Moda Living Limited**
*Incorporated:* 1 July 2014 *Employees:* 8
*Net Worth:* £6,559,509 *Total Assets:* £11,279,698
*Registered Office:* Castlegarth Grange, Scott Lane, Wetherby, W Yorks, LS22 6LH
*Activities:* Buying and selling of own real estate
*Shareholders:* Caddick (JPC Developments) Limited; Caddick Developments Limited
*Officers:* Paul Andrew Bullers, Secretary; Anthony Brooks [1961] Director; Daniel Reuben Brooks [1984] Director; Oscar Anthony Brooks [1988] Director; Paul Andrew Bullers [1966] Director/Group Accountant; John Paul Caddick [1981] Development Director; Paul Caddick [1950] Director; Myles Edward Hartley [1969] Director; Andrew Stephen Parker [1977] Director; Lee Michael Savage [1970] Director

**Modav Limited**
*Incorporated:* 1 March 1996
*Net Worth:* £4,221,571 *Total Assets:* £5,861,486
*Registered Office:* Elizabeth House, 13-19 Queen Street, Leeds, LS1 2TW
*Activities:* Buying and selling of own real estate
*Parent:* Modav UK Limited
*Officers:* Penelope Maureen Ann Grace, Secretary/Director; David Martin Grace [1944] Director; Penelope Maureen Ann Grace [1949] Director; Elizabeth Clare Swap [1976] Director/Housewife

**Modern Market Retailing Limited**
*Incorporated:* 29 April 1999
*Net Worth Deficit:* £122,247,976 *Total Assets:* £98,012,312
*Registered Office:* Trident Business Park, Leeds Road, Huddersfield, W Yorks, HD2 1UA
*Activities:* Dormant company
*Parent:* Instore Limited
*Officers:* Hemant Patel, Secretary; Hemant Patel [1961] Finance Director; Abdul Aziz Tayub [1955] Director

**Modgate Limited**
*Incorporated:* 6 March 1978 *Employees:* 36
*Net Worth:* £2,666,473 *Total Assets:* £3,914,037
*Registered Office:* Parkside Road, Kendal, Cumbria, LA9 7DU
*Activities:* Wholesale of hardware, plumbing and heating equipment and supplies
*Major Shareholder:* Anthony Brian Garnett
*Officers:* Rhys Garnett [1978] Director; Joanna Clare Whiteley [1974] Financial Director

**Modine UK Dollar Limited**
*Incorporated:* 26 April 2005
*Net Worth:* £23,107,040 *Total Assets:* £28,726,482
*Registered Office:* Rawdon Factory, Leeds Road, Rawdon, Leeds, LS19 6JY
*Activities:* Other manufacturing n.e.c.
*Parent:* Modine Manufacturing Company
*Officers:* Simon Andrew Thorburn, Secretary; Samantha Anderegg-Boticki [1984] Finance Director [American]; Anthony Cole [1963] Director; Scott Miller [1964] Director/Company Vice President [American]

**Modular Plantrooms Limited**
*Incorporated:* 13 November 2006 *Employees:* 36
*Net Worth:* £2,125,287 *Total Assets:* £4,243,223
*Registered Office:* 2 Belgrave Crescent, Scarborough, N Yorks, YO11 1UB
*Activities:* Manufacture of metal structures and parts of structures
*Shareholder:* Chris Cade
*Officers:* Christopher Frederick Cade, Secretary; Christopher Frederick Cade [1944] Director; Christopher Lee Cade [1967] Director; Ian Cade [1973] Director; Jill Ruth Cade [1970] Director; Rebekah Elaine Cade [1970] Director; Sandra Cade [1948] Director

**Modus Seabed Intervention Limited**
*Incorporated:* 26 October 1987 *Employees:* 53
*Net Worth:* £3,344,000 *Total Assets:* £17,462,000
*Registered Office:* Beaumont House, Beaumont Street, Darlington, Co Durham, DL1 5RW
*Activities:* Other specialised construction activities n.e.c.
*Officers:* Jason Edward Tompkins, Secretary; Peter Mark Iain Short [1973] Finance Director; Jason Edward Tompkins [1974] Director/Company Executive; Nigel James Ward [1975] Commercial Director

**Mold Systems Limited**
*Incorporated:* 6 May 2009 *Employees:* 69
*Net Worth:* £234,816 *Total Assets:* £3,429,692
*Registered Office:* 1 Millennium Way, Newton Aycliffe Industrial Park, Newton Aycliffe, Co Durham, DL5 6JW
*Activities:* Manufacture of other plastic products
*Major Shareholder:* Ivan Harold Bradbury
*Officers:* David Bradbury [1995] Director; Ivan Harold Bradbury [1946] Director; David McEwan Kinnaird [1959] Director

**Molekula Limited**
*Incorporated:* 17 April 2009 *Employees:* 25
*Net Worth:* £503,423 *Total Assets:* £3,577,469
*Registered Office:* Lingfield Way, Yarm Road Business Park, Darlington, Co Durham, DL1 4XX
*Activities:* Wholesale of chemical products
*Shareholders:* Kalvin Pierre Banks; Kristan Banks; Marina Banks
*Officers:* Kevin Peter Banks [1956] Director/Chemist; Margaret Elizabeth Banks [1962] Director/Farmer; David Bowen [1952] Director; Kathleen Bowen [1956] Director

**Molescroft Farms Limited**
*Incorporated:* 22 March 1965 *Employees:* 8
*Net Worth:* £3,538,456 *Total Assets:* £4,586,125
*Registered Office:* Manor Farm, Manor House, Lane Walkington, Beverley, E Yorks, HU17 8SU
*Activities:* Growing of cereals (except rice), leguminous crops and oil seeds
*Officers:* Tamara Clare Watson Hall, Secretary; Clarissa Diana Hall [1949] Director/Secretary; Jennifer Jane Watson Hall [1933] Director/Teacher; Michael Jonathan Watson Hall [1936] Director/Farmer; Tamara Clare Watson Hall [1974] Director/Farmer; Camilla Rachel Watson Parsonage [1976] Director

**Mondi Scunthorpe Limited**
*Incorporated:* 5 September 1979 *Employees:* 141
*Net Worth Deficit:* £8,482,391 *Total Assets:* £12,075,195
*Registered Office:* Roxburgh House, Clayfield Road, Foxhills Industrial Estate, Scunthorpe, N Lincs, DN15 8QJ
*Activities:* Manufacture of plastic packing goods
*Parent:* Mondi Investments Limited
*Officers:* Alyson Jayne Wiltshire, Secretary; Sandor Kardos [1970] Director [German]; Allan Martin Lock [1970] Director

**Mone Brothers Group Ltd**
*Incorporated:* 31 January 2017 *Employees:* 63
*Net Worth:* £8,057,511 *Total Assets:* £10,327,567
*Registered Office:* Mone Brothers Group Ltd, Albert Road, Morley, Leeds, LS27 8RU
*Activities:* Activities of construction holding companies
*Shareholders:* James Mone; John Mone
*Officers:* Michael Coleman [1971] Director; Siobhan Coleman [1970] Director; Fionnula Hegarty [1973] Director; James Kevin Mone [1964] Director; James Mone [1942] Director; Philip Mone [1966] Director

**Money4yourmotors.Com Limited**
*Incorporated:* 30 January 2015 *Employees:* 103
*Net Worth Deficit:* £3,355,000 *Total Assets:* £4,832,000
*Registered Office:* Central House, Leeds Road, Rothwell, Leeds, LS26 0JE
*Activities:* Other service activities n.e.c.
*Officers:* Michael Buxton, Secretary; Michael Buxton [1965] Director; Patrick Mooney [1957] Director; Darren Paul Mornin [1968] Finance Director

**Monks Cross Property Ltd**
*Incorporated:* 16 June 2014 *Employees:* 2
*Net Worth:* £3,123,404 *Total Assets:* £5,405,451
*Registered Office:* Omega 4, Monks Cross Drive, York, YO32 9GZ
*Activities:* Other letting and operating of own or leased real estate
*Shareholders:* Peter Francis Smith; Maguerita Maria Devenish Smith
*Officers:* Tara Maria Devenish Smith [1982] Director; Maguerita Maria Devenish Smith [1948] Director; Peter Francis Smith [1937] Director

**The Monobuoy Company Ltd.**
*Incorporated:* 15 June 1998 *Employees:* 3
*Net Worth:* £1,771,612 *Total Assets:* £12,727,001
*Registered Office:* 50-54 Oswald Road, Scunthorpe, N Lincs, DN15 7PQ
*Activities:* Manufacture of other special-purpose machinery n.e.c.
*Shareholder:* David John Collard
*Officers:* Jeanette Stephenson, Secretary; John David Collard [1955] Director; Brian Robert Stephenson [1941] Director/Marine Consultant

**Monocon International Refractories Limited**
*Incorporated:* 23 October 1973 *Employees:* 68
*Net Worth:* £12,569,152 *Total Assets:* £22,804,108
*Registered Office:* Denaby Main Industrial Estate, Denaby Lane, Old Denaby, Doncaster, S Yorks, DN12 4LQ
*Activities:* Manufacture of refractory products
*Parent:* IFGL Monocon Holding Limited
*Officers:* Dheeraj Parakh, Secretary; Mihir Prakash Bajoria [1985] Director [Indian]; David Andrew Harris [1955] Director; Dr Paul Myers [1973] Technical Director; Dheeraj Parakh [1978] Director/Accountant; Mark Allan Payne [1961] Sales Director; Manoj Rakhecha [1977] Commercial Director [Indian]

**Monocon Overseas Limited**
*Incorporated:* 15 May 1997 *Employees:* 3
*Net Worth:* £7,008,282 *Total Assets:* £9,008,282
*Registered Office:* Monocon Office, Davy Road, Old Denaby, Doncaster, S Yorks, DN12 4LQ
*Activities:* Non-trading company
*Parent:* Monocon International Refractories Limited
*Officers:* Dheeraj Parakh, Secretary; Mihir Prakash Bajoria [1985] Director [Indian]; Dheeraj Parakh [1978] Director/Chartered Accountant; Manoj Rakhecha [1977] Director [Indian]

**Monread Lodge Nursing Home Limited**
*Incorporated:* 5 June 1995 *Employees:* 59
*Net Worth:* £7,493,660 *Total Assets:* £8,331,274
*Registered Office:* West Court, Gelderd Road, Leeds, LS12 6DB
*Activities:* Residential care activities for the elderly and disabled
*Parent:* Maria Mallaband Care Group Limited
*Officers:* Christopher Ball [1968] Director; Philip John Burgan [1951] Director; Peter Gervais Fagan [1957] Director; Jason Lock [1972] Director

**Monster Group (UK) Limited**
*Incorporated:* 2 March 2007 *Employees:* 25
*Net Worth:* £1,276,992 *Total Assets:* £3,391,308
*Registered Office:* Monster House, Alan Farnaby Way, The Industrial Estate, Sheriff Hutton, York, YO60 6PG
*Activities:* Retail sale via mail order houses or via Internet
*Major Shareholder:* Rana Harvey
*Officers:* Rana Harvey, Secretary; David Harvey [1977] Director; Rana Harvey [1977] Director

**Montpelier Professional Limited**
*Incorporated:* 14 January 2004
*Net Worth Deficit:* £1,154,016 *Total Assets:* £10,701,604
*Registered Office:* Suite 3, 5 Battalion Court, Colburn Business Park, Catterick Garrison, N Yorks, DL9 4QN
*Activities:* Accounting and auditing activities
*Parent:* Montpelier Group (Tax Consultants) Limted
*Officers:* Edward Watkin Gittins [1950] Director/Chartered Accountant

**Montracon Limited**
*Incorporated:* 21 March 1963 *Employees:* 526
*Net Worth:* £4,439,247 *Total Assets:* £53,875,076
*Registered Office:* Carr Hill, Doncaster, S Yorks, DN4 8DE
*Activities:* Manufacture of trailers and semi-trailers
*Parent:* Ballyvesey Holding Limited
*Officers:* Mark David Kidney, Secretary; Philip Ashton [1968] Sales Director; Mark David Kidney [1975] Director/Chartered Management Accountant; Colin John Hugh Montgomery [1976] Director; Harold Hugh Montgomery [1948] Director/Haulier

**Moody Direct Limited**
*Incorporated:* 23 May 2000 *Employees:* 71
*Net Worth:* £1,800,559 *Total Assets:* £5,413,713
*Registered Office:* West Carr Road Industrial Estate, West Carr Road, Retford, Notts, DN22 7SN
*Activities:* Manufacture of machinery for food, beverage and tobacco processing
*Parent:* Moody Direct (Holdings) Ltd
*Officers:* David Tomlinson, Secretary; Paul Gregory [1955] Director; Graham Paul Moody [1948] Director/Chairman; David Tomlinson [1972] Director; Kenneth Wild [1960] Director

**Moolmoor (Waverley) Limited**
*Incorporated:* 6 January 2017 *Employees:* 4
*Net Worth:* £4,559,000 *Total Assets:* £31,842,000
*Registered Office:* Central House, 47 St Paul's Street, Leeds, LS1 2TE
*Activities:* Buying and selling of own real estate
*Shareholders:* Philip Biden; Michael Black; Mandy Dix-Peek; Gerhardus Liebenberg; Christoffel Wiese; Jacob Wiese
*Officers:* Daniel James Smith, Secretary; Pieter Beyers [1977] Director [South African]; David Anthony Harrop [1970] Finance Director; Pieter Andries Lombaard [1969] Director [South African]; Timothy Andrew Vaughan [1965] Managing Director

**Moolmoor Holdings Limited**
*Incorporated:* 16 September 2016 *Employees:* 4
*Net Worth:* £77,000 *Total Assets:* £18,071,000
*Registered Office:* Central House, 47 St Paul's Street, Leeds, LS1 2TE
*Activities:* Buying and selling of own real estate
*Shareholders:* Michael Black; Mandy Dix-Peek; Philip Biden; Gerhardus Liebenberg; Christoffel Wiese; Jacob Wiese
*Officers:* Daniel James Smith, Secretary; Pieter Beyers [1977] Director [South African]; David Anthony Harrop [1970] Finance Director; Pieter Andries Lombaard [1969] Director [South African]; Timothy Andrew Vaughan [1965] Managing Director

**Moolmoor Investments Limited**
*Incorporated:* 16 September 2016
*Net Worth:* £403,000 *Total Assets:* £18,468,000
*Registered Office:* Central House, 47 St Paul's Street, Leeds, LS1 2TE
*Activities:* Buying and selling of own real estate
*Parent:* Moolmoor Holdings Limited
*Officers:* Daniel James Smith, Secretary; Pieter Beyers [1977] Director [South African]; David Anthony Harrop [1970] Finance Director; Pieter Andries Lombaard [1969] Director [South African]; Timothy Andrew Vaughan [1965] Managing Director

**Abraham Moon & Sons Limited**
*Incorporated:* 28 January 1920 *Employees:* 230
*Net Worth:* £17,993,696 *Total Assets:* £25,967,656
*Registered Office:* Netherfield Mills, Guiseley, Leeds, LS20 9PA
*Activities:* Preparation and spinning of textile fibres
*Officers:* Laurence Kevin Brophy, Secretary; Martin Aveyard [1954] Director/Cloth Designer; Laurence Kevin Brophy [1962] Director/Chartered Accountant [Irish]; Judith Lynn Coates [1966] Design Director; John Frederick Robert Pickles [1966] Director/Sales Manager; Jonathan Andrew Sandground [1964] Operations Director; Arthur James Pullar Walsh [1923] Director/Woollen Cloth Manufacturer; John Philip Tempest Walsh [1960] Managing Director

**Abraham Moon Holdings Limited**
*Incorporated:* 26 September 2005 *Employees:* 230
*Net Worth:* £20,990,752 *Total Assets:* £25,967,658
*Registered Office:* Netherfield Mills, Guiseley, Leeds, LS20 9PA
*Activities:* Activities of other holding companies n.e.c.
*Shareholder:* John Philip Tempest Walsh
*Officers:* Laurence Kevin Brophy, Secretary; Laurence Kevin Brophy [1962] Director/Chartered Accountant [Irish]; John Philip Tempest Walsh [1960] Director

**William F.Moore (Warplands) Limited**
*Incorporated:* 30 March 1948 *Employees:* 9
*Net Worth:* £6,865,268 *Total Assets:* £9,540,275
*Registered Office:* Fleet House Farm, West Butterwick, Scunthorpe, N Lincs, DN17 3JZ
*Activities:* Growing of cereals (except rice), leguminous crops and oil seeds
*Shareholders:* David James Moore; Christopher William Moore
*Officers:* Christina Mary Moore, Secretary; Christopher William Moore [1960] Director/Farmer; David James Moore [1962] Director/Farmer

**Moore Building Enterprises Limited**
*Incorporated:* 13 November 1995 *Employees:* 10
*Net Worth:* £4,072,160 *Total Assets:* £7,944,132
*Registered Office:* Unit 12 Clifton Moor Business Village, James Nicolson Link, York, YO30 4XG
*Activities:* Development of building projects
*Officers:* Corrina Eadie, Secretary; Corrina Eadie [1971] Director/Company Secretary; Joseph Robert Moore [1966] Director; William Moore [1947] Director; William Adam Moore [1965] Director

**The George A. Moore Foundation**
*Incorporated:* 14 October 1970 *Employees:* 6
*Net Worth:* £6,876,634 *Total Assets:* £6,943,880
*Registered Office:* 10 South Parade, Leeds, LS1 5QS
*Activities:* General public administration activities
*Officers:* Richard William Dawson [1966] Director; Elizabeth Moore [1933] Director; Jonathan Richard Moore [1958] Director; Paul Daniel Turner [1971] Director/Solicitor

**Moores Furniture Group Limited**
*Incorporated:* 27 November 1972 *Employees:* 511
*Net Worth:* £6,385,000 *Total Assets:* £25,269,000
*Registered Office:* Thorp Arch Estate, Wetherby, W Yorks, LS23 7DD
*Activities:* Manufacture of kitchen furniture
*Parent:* HUK 84 Limited
*Officers:* David Michael Richardson, Secretary; David Amerigo [1964] Director; Michael Brian Barrett [1984] Director; Stephen John Parkin [1961] Director; David Michael Richardson [1969] Director and Company Secretary

**Moorgarth Group Limited**
*Incorporated:* 31 July 2003 *Employees:* 18
*Net Worth:* £2,951,000 *Total Assets:* £49,093,000
*Registered Office:* Central House, 47 St Pauls Street, Leeds, LS1 2TE
*Activities:* Other letting and operating of own or leased real estate
*Shareholders:* Christoffel Wiese; Jacob Wiese; Philip Biden; Gerhardus Liebenberg; Mandy Dix-Peek; Michael Black
*Officers:* Daniel James Smith, Secretary; David Anthony Harrop [1970] Finance Director; Karen Louise Nordier [1967] Finance Director [South African]; Timothy Andrew Vaughan [1965] Managing Director

**Moorgarth Living Limited**
*Incorporated:* 25 July 2016
*Net Worth Deficit:* £11,000 *Total Assets:* £12,148,000
*Registered Office:* Central House, 47 St Paul's Street, Leeds, LS1 2TE
*Activities:* Buying and selling of own real estate
*Parent:* Moorgarth Group Limited
*Officers:* Daniel James Smith, Secretary; David Anthony Harrop [1970] Finance Director; Karen Louise Nordier [1967] Finance Director [South African]; Timothy Andrew Vaughan [1965] Managing Director

**Moorgarth Property Investments Limited**
*Incorporated:* 26 March 2008
*Net Worth:* £308,000 *Total Assets:* £5,648,000
*Registered Office:* Central House, 47 St Pauls Street, Leeds, LS1 2TE
*Activities:* Other letting and operating of own or leased real estate
*Parent:* River Street Properties Ltd
*Officers:* Daniel James Smith, Secretary; David Anthony Harrop [1970] Finance Director; Karen Louise Nordier [1967] Finance Director [South African]; Timothy Andrew Vaughan [1965] Director

**Moorgarth Retail Limited**
*Incorporated:* 15 July 2016 *Employees:* 3
*Net Worth:* £3,232,000 *Total Assets:* £10,794,000
*Registered Office:* Central House, 47 St Paul's Street, Leeds, LS1 2TE
*Activities:* Buying and selling of own real estate
*Shareholders:* Philip Biden; Michael Black; Mandy Dix-Peek; Gerhardus Liebenberg; Christoffel Wiese; Jacob Wiese
*Officers:* Daniel James Smith, Secretary; David Anthony Harrop [1970] Finance Director; Karen Louise Nordier [1967] Finance Director [South African]; Timothy Andrew Vaughan [1965] Managing Director

**Moorhead Excavations Limited**
*Incorporated:* 8 January 1986 *Employees:* 40
*Net Worth:* £1,169,786 *Total Assets:* £4,640,867
*Registered Office:* Westfield Court, Lower Wortley Road, Leeds, LS12 4PX
*Activities:* Site preparation
*Parent:* Willoughby (891) Limited
*Officers:* Colin Fitton [1966] Commercial Director; Philip Horsnall [1961] Director; Jonathan Miles Prutton [1962] Director

**Moorlands Learning Trust**
*Incorporated:* 9 June 2011 *Employees:* 218
*Previous:* Ilkley Grammar School
*Net Worth:* £10,535,000 *Total Assets:* £12,316,000
*Registered Office:* Cowpasture Road, Ilkley, W Yorks, LS29 8TR
*Activities:* General secondary education
*Officers:* Alison Kaye, Secretary; Imogen Clark [1966] Director/Lawyer; Angela Louise Duggan [1962] Director/Chartered Surveyor; Jack Rickard [1969] Director/Project Manager; Lindsey Wharmby [1946] Director/Retired Headteacher; Helen Williams [1975] Director/Headteacher

**Moortown Group Limited**
*Incorporated:* 22 June 2012 *Employees:* 67
*Previous:* Lusteen Holdings Limited
*Net Worth:* £14,375,982 *Total Assets:* £32,377,078
*Registered Office:* Lusteen House, 24 Roydsdale Way, Euroway Industrial Estate, Bradford, W Yorks, BD4 6SE
*Activities:* Construction of other civil engineering projects n.e.c.
*Parent:* McManus Group Holdings Limited
*Officers:* Michael John King [1974] Director/Business Development [Irish]; Aiden Thomas McManus [1976] Director; Thomas John McManus [1949] Director; Dean Jason Moxon [1970] Director/Head of Procurement

**Moortown Plant Limited**
*Incorporated:* 21 November 2000 *Employees:* 5
*Net Worth:* £2,529,871 *Total Assets:* £5,888,806
*Registered Office:* Lusteen House, 24 Roydsdale Way, Euroway Industrial Estate, Bradford, W Yorks, BD4 6SE
*Activities:* Other specialised construction activities n.e.c.
*Parent:* Moortown Group Limited
*Officers:* Aiden Thomas McManus, Secretary; Graham Hunt [1956] Director/Chartered Accountant; Aiden Thomas McManus [1976] Director/Civil Engineer; Generaldine McManus [1949] Director; Thomas John McManus [1949] Director

**Moorview Care Limited**
*Incorporated:* 7 December 2000 *Employees:* 121
*Previous:* Moorview House Limited
*Net Worth:* £1,727,837 *Total Assets:* £3,193,197
*Registered Office:* 107 Cleethorpe Road, Grimsby, N E Lincs, DN31 3ER
*Activities:* Other service activities n.e.c.
*Shareholders:* Stephen Nigel Pycroft; Carol Ann Cook
*Officers:* Carol Ann Cook [1961] Director/Financial Advisor; Neil Philip Franklin [1985] Director

**Morco Products Limited**
*Incorporated:* 21 December 1899 *Employees:* 18
*Net Worth:* £7,817,237 *Total Assets:* £11,196,964
*Registered Office:* Morco House, Riverview Road, Beverley, E Yorks, HU17 0LD
*Activities:* Wholesale of hardware, plumbing and heating equipment and supplies
*Major Shareholder:* Charles Richard Ellison Gillett
*Officers:* Charles Richard Ellison Gillett, Secretary; Charles Richard Ellison Gillett [1961] Managing Director; Charles Anthony Gillett [1931] Director/Chairman; Susan Jane Valda Gillett [1962] Director; William Hildyard [1987] Sales Director; John David Rowley [1965] Commercial Director

**More (UK) Limited**
*Incorporated:* 8 January 2001 *Employees:* 50
*Net Worth:* £3,074,567 *Total Assets:* £5,065,389
*Registered Office:* Tong Road Business Park, Amberley Road, Leeds, LS12 4BF
*Activities:* Wholesale of clothing and footwear
*Officers:* Cheryl Cashmore, Secretary; Cheryl Cashmore [1971] Director; Steven Cashmore [1967] Managing Director

**Morecambe Metals Limited**
*Incorporated:* 12 March 1997 *Employees:* 35
*Net Worth:* £2,347,557 *Total Assets:* £4,660,710
*Registered Office:* Northgate, White Lund Industrial Estate, Morecambe, Lancs, LA3 3AZ
*Activities:* Wholesale of waste and scrap
*Parent:* Morecambe Metals (Holdings) Limited
*Officers:* James Wilson Varley, Secretary; James John Varley [1982] Director/Scrap Metal Merchant; James Varley [1926] Director/Scrap Metal Merchant; James Wilson Varley [1956] Director/Scrap Metal Merchant

**Morgan Travel Limited**
*Incorporated:* 10 May 2001 *Employees:* 28
*Net Worth:* £790,187 *Total Assets:* £4,374,846
*Registered Office:* Ghyll Beck House, Gill Lane, Yeadon, Leeds, LS19 7SE
*Activities:* Travel agency activities
*Parent:* First Event 2008 Limited
*Officers:* Sally Murphy, Secretary; Richard Mark Murphy [1970] Director/Event Organiser

**Morley Glass & Glazing Limited**
*Incorporated:* 18 March 1998 *Employees:* 57
*Net Worth:* £2,192,986 *Total Assets:* £5,557,359
*Registered Office:* Unit 3 Leeds 27 Industrial Estate, Bruntcliffe Way, Morley, Leeds, LS27 0HH
*Activities:* Other manufacturing n.e.c.
*Shareholder:* Ian Andrew Short
*Officers:* Jane Kathryn Short, Secretary; Ian Andrew Short [1964] Managing Director

**Morrey Oils Limited**
*Incorporated:* 20 September 1982 *Employees:* 55
*Net Worth:* £4,905,571 *Total Assets:* £7,673,684
*Registered Office:* c/o Montracon Limited, Carr Hill, Doncaster, S Yorks, DN4 8DE
*Activities:* Freight transport by road
*Parent:* Morrey Oils Holdings Limited
*Officers:* Harold Hugh Montgomery, Secretary; David Matthew Heath [1964] Director; Stephen Patrick Marshall [1974] Managing Director; Harold Hugh Montgomery [1948] Director

**Morris & Co. (Handlers) Limited**
*Incorporated:* 14 January 1976 *Employees:* 32
*Net Worth:* £1,406,277 *Total Assets:* £10,878,698
*Registered Office:* Bankwood Lane, New Rossington, Doncaster, S Yorks, DN11 0PS
*Activities:* Wholesale of waste and scrap
*Shareholders:* Samuel Alan Morris; Thomas Edwin Morris
*Officers:* Barbara Ann Morris, Secretary; Alan Edwin Morris [1951] Director; Samuel Alan Morris [1980] Operations Director; Thomas Edwin Morris [1982] Director/Sales

**Morris & Son (Leeds) Limited**
*Incorporated:* 18 July 1996 *Employees:* 56
*Net Worth:* £4,360,163 *Total Assets:* £6,898,652
*Registered Office:* c/o Mazars LLP, 3 Wellington Place, Leeds, LS1 4AP
*Activities:* Non-specialised wholesale of food, beverages and tobacco
*Officers:* Andrew David Needham, Secretary/Wholesaler; Andrew David Needham [1965] Director/Wholesaler

**Morris and Son (Holdings) Limited**
*Incorporated:* 28 April 2003 *Employees:* 64
*Net Worth:* £1,757,556 *Total Assets:* £5,373,693
*Registered Office:* c/o Mazars LLP, 3 Wellington Place, Leeds, LS1 4AP
*Activities:* Activities of head offices
*Shareholders:* Lindsay Elizabeth Holmes; Andrew David Needham
*Officers:* Andrew David Needham [1965] Director

**Morris Family Investments Ltd**
*Incorporated:* 25 June 2015 *Employees:* 2
*Net Worth:* £430,326 *Total Assets:* £7,000,084
*Registered Office:* Croft House, Farm Manor Road, Farnley Tyas, Huddersfield, W Yorks, HD4 6UL
*Activities:* Financial intermediation not elsewhere classified
*Shareholder:* Philip Morris
*Officers:* Philip Morris [1962] Director; Susan Morris [1963] Director

**A.E. Morris Limited**
*Incorporated:* 24 October 1984
*Net Worth:* £2,211,835 *Total Assets:* £3,911,099
*Registered Office:* Bankwood Lane, New Rossington, Doncaster, S Yorks, DN11 0PS
*Activities:* Other letting and operating of own or leased real estate
*Officers:* Barbara Ann Morris, Secretary; Alan Edwin Morris [1951] Director; Barbara Ann Morris [1959] Director

**Wm Morrison Bananas Limited**
*Incorporated:* 15 July 2013
*Net Worth:* £3,469,000 *Total Assets:* £3,860,000
*Registered Office:* Hilmore House, Gain Lane, Bradford, BD3 7DL
*Activities:* Other processing and preserving of fruit and vegetables
*Parent:* Wm Morrison Produce Limited
*Officers:* Jonathan James Burke, Secretary; Jonathan Paul Hornby [1972] Director; Mark Thomas Stitson [1976] Finance Director; Andrew Edward Thornber [1974] Managing Director

**Wm Morrison Growers Limited**
*Incorporated:* 11 December 2015 *Employees:* 15
*Net Worth:* £1,187,000 *Total Assets:* £9,102,000
*Registered Office:* Stubbings Farm, Otley, W Yorks, LS21 1DN
*Activities:* Other processing and preserving of fruit and vegetables
*Shareholders:* Christopher William Rimmer; Michael John Rimmer
*Officers:* Christopher William Rimmer, Secretary; Jonathan Paul Hornby [1972] Director; Drew James Kirk [1971] Category Director; Christopher William Rimmer [1964] Director; Michael John Rimmer [1967] Director; Andrew Edward Thornber [1974] Manufacturing Managing Director

**Wm Morrison Produce Limited**
*Incorporated:* 4 October 1963
*Net Worth:* £280,356,000 *Total Assets:* £448,190,016
*Registered Office:* Hilmore House, Gain Lane, Bradford, W Yorks, BD3 7DL
*Activities:* Other processing and preserving of fruit and vegetables
*Parent:* Wm Morrison Supermarkets Holdings Limited
*Officers:* Jonathan James Burke, Secretary; Andrew James Clappen [1965] Technical Director; Jonathan Paul Hornby [1972] Director; Mark Thomas Stitson [1976] Finance Director; Andrew Edward Thornber [1974] Director

**Wm Morrison Supermarkets Holdings Limited**
*Incorporated:* 22 June 2017
*Total Assets:* £3,560,000,000
*Registered Office:* Hilmore House, Gain Lane, Bradford, BD3 7DL
*Activities:* Retail sale in non-specialised stores with food, beverages or tobacco predominating
*Parent:* Wm Morrison Supermarkets PLC
*Officers:* Jonathan James Burke, Secretary; Jonathan James Burke [1966] Director; Trevor John Strain [1975] Director

**Wm Morrison Supermarkets P L C**
*Incorporated:* 22 January 1940 *Employees:* 105,487
*Net Worth:* £4,544,999,936 *Total Assets:* £9,667,000,320
*Registered Office:* Hilmore House, Gain Lane, Bradford, W Yorks, BD3 7DL
*Activities:* Retail sale in non-specialised stores with food, beverages or tobacco predominating
*Officers:* Jonathan James Burke, Secretary; Rooney Anand [1964] Director/Chief Executive Officer; Belinda Carew Jones [1958] Director; Richard Colin Neil Davidson [1951] Director; Kevin John Havelock [1957] Director; Andrew Thomas Higginson [1957] Director; Tony Van Kralingen [1958] Director [South African]; David Tom Potts [1957] Director/Chief Executive; Trevor John Strain [1975] Finance Director; The Reverend Paula Anne Vennells [1959] Director/Chief Executive Officer The Post Office

**Morses Club PLC**
*Incorporated:* 16 January 2009 *Employees:* 523
*Previous:* Morses Club Limited
*Net Worth:* £66,520,000 *Total Assets:* £88,911,000
*Registered Office:* Kingston House, Centre 27 Business Park, Woodhead Road, Birstall, Batley, W Yorks, WF17 9TD
*Activities:* Other business support service activities n.e.c.
*Shareholder:* Hay Wain Group Limited
*Officers:* David Gresford Belmont, Secretary; Stephen Ashley Karle [1959] Director; Sir Nigel Graham Knowles [1956] Director; Joanne Carolyn Lake [1963] Director; Paul Mark Smith [1966] Director; Patrick Desmond Storey [1958] Director; Thomas Andrew Thomson [1962] Financial Director; Peter Martin Ward [1960] Director

**The Mortgage Business Public Limited Company**
*Incorporated:* 7 March 1986
*Net Worth:* £242,086,000 *Total Assets:* £9,653,497,856
*Registered Office:* Trinity Road, Halifax, W Yorks, HX1 2RG
*Activities:* Financial intermediation not elsewhere classified
*Parent:* Bank of Scotland PLC
*Officers:* Paul Gittins, Secretary; Robert William Fletcher [1964] Director; Christopher Gowland [1977] Director; Jasjyot Singh [1973] Director; Johan Robin Charles Von Schmidt Auf Altenstadt [1969] Director

**Mortgage Express**
*Incorporated:* 18 July 1989
*Net Worth:* £560,806,976 *Total Assets:* £3,366,981,888
*Registered Office:* P O Box 88, Croft Road, Crossflatts, Bingley, W Yorks, BD16 2UA
*Activities:* Activities of mortgage finance companies
*Parent:* Bradford & Bingley PLC
*Officers:* Claire Louise Craigie, Secretary; Ian John Hares [1958] Director/Banker; Martin Andrew Scott [1962] Finance Director

**James Mortimer,Limited**
*Incorporated:* 21 July 1927 *Employees:* 22
*Net Worth:* £3,879,109 *Total Assets:* £5,543,088
*Registered Office:* Unit 13 Pexton Road, Kelleythorpe Industrial Estate, Driffield, E Yorks, YO25 9DJ
*Activities:* Post-harvest crop activities
*Shareholders:* Maurice Robson; Jill Robson
*Officers:* Christopher Charles Kingsley Atkin, Secretary; Christopher Charles Kingsley Atkin [1962] Director; Simon William Minns [1961] Director/Corn Merchant; Maurice Robson [1944] Director

**Morton Michel Holdings Limited**
*Incorporated:* 7 November 2011
*Net Worth:* £2,112,172 *Total Assets:* £3,135,000
*Registered Office:* Rossington's Business Park, West Carr Road, Retford, Notts, DN22 7SW
*Activities:* Activities of other holding companies n.e.c.
*Parent:* PIB Group Limited
*Officers:* Ryan Christopher Brown [1973] Director; Brendan James McManus [1959] Director

**Mosaic Group Limited**
*Incorporated:* 6 April 2003 *Employees:* 52
*Previous:* Mosaic Print Management Limited
*Net Worth:* £10,415,662 *Total Assets:* £15,431,028
*Registered Office:* Leigh House, 28-32 St Paul's Street, Leeds, LS1 2JT
*Activities:* Pre-press and pre-media services
*Parent:* Mosaic Print Management Holdco Ltd
*Officers:* Anthony Stephen Gill [1963] Director/Chief Executive; Duncan Scott Marrison [1976] Director; Stephen Kenneth Smith [1965] Director; Declan Michael Wadcock [1971] Director

**Mosaic Print Management Holdco Limited**
*Incorporated:* 21 February 2014
*Net Worth:* £2,900,002 *Total Assets:* £5,829,002
*Registered Office:* Leigh House, 28-32 St Paul's Street, Leeds, LS1 2JT
*Activities:* Activities of head offices
*Parent:* Holdco 123 Limited
*Officers:* Anthony Stephen Gill [1963] Director

**The Mosaic Tile Company Limited**
*Incorporated:* 24 May 2001 *Employees:* 38
*Net Worth:* £3,036,728 *Total Assets:* £8,763,970
*Registered Office:* Project House, Armley Road, Leeds, LS12 2DR
*Activities:* Wholesale of wood, construction materials and sanitary equipment
*Shareholders:* BPKT Limited; Adrian Scott Hinchliffe
*Officers:* Adrian Scott Hinchliffe, Secretary/Sales Director; Adrian Scott Hinchliffe [1967] Director; Carol Kavanagh [1962] Group HR Director; Daniel James Lowans [1971] Director; Paul Richard Turner [1970] Director

**Ian Mosey (Feed) Limited**
*Incorporated:* 2 March 2009 *Employees:* 50
*Net Worth:* £8,856,523 *Total Assets:* £14,733,397
*Registered Office:* Village Farm, Gilling East, York, YO62 4JH
*Activities:* Manufacture of prepared feeds for farm animals
*Shareholder:* Brenda Mary Mosey
*Officers:* Brenda Mary Mosey, Secretary; Rebecca Jane Milne [1980] Business Development Director; Basil Ian Mosey [1949] Director; Brenda Mary Mosey [1954] Director; Stephen Charles Mosey [1983] Operations Director; Sarah Elizabeth Stark [1977] Director

**Ian Mosey (Livestock) Limited**
*Incorporated:* 2 March 2009 *Employees:* 33
*Net Worth:* £9,837,735 *Total Assets:* £24,203,228
*Registered Office:* Village Farm, Gilling East, York, YO62 4JH
*Activities:* Raising of swine and pigs
*Shareholder:* Brenda Mary Mosey
*Officers:* Brenda Mary Mosey, Secretary; Charlotte Elizabeth Duggleby [1987] Director; Basil Ian Mosey [1949] Director; Brenda Mary Mosey [1954] Director; Ian John Mosey [1977] Operations Director

**Ian Mosey Limited**
*Incorporated:* 2 August 1979 *Employees:* 89
*Net Worth:* £37,200,628 *Total Assets:* £48,573,188
*Registered Office:* Village Farm, Main Street, Gilling East, York, YO62 4JH
*Activities:* Raising of swine and pigs
*Shareholders:* Basil Ian Mosey; Brenda Mary Mosey
*Officers:* Brenda Mary Mosey, Secretary; Basil Ian Mosey [1949] Director/Farmer; Brenda Mary Mosey [1954] Director

**S.A.Mossop (Farms) Limited**
*Incorporated:* 28 March 1952 *Employees:* 11
*Net Worth:* £1,203,781 *Total Assets:* £4,325,011
*Registered Office:* Middle Farm, Keyholme Lane, Marshchapel, Grimsby, N E Lincs, DN36 5UE
*Activities:* Growing of cereals (except rice), leguminous crops and oil seeds
*Shareholders:* Edward Peel Mossop; Antony John Mossop
*Officers:* Edward Peel Mossop, Secretary; Antony John Mossop [1947] Director/Farmer; Edward Peel Mossop [1955] Director/Company Secretary; Elizabeth Grace Mossop [1957] Director; Helen Margaret Mossop [1949] Director/Housewife

**Motor Depot Limited**
*Incorporated:* 5 November 2001 *Employees:* 208
*Net Worth:* £10,247,949 *Total Assets:* £24,426,590
*Registered Office:* Bridge Haven, One Saxon Way, Priory Park, Hessle, E Yorks, HU13 9PG
*Activities:* Sale of used cars and light motor vehicles
*Shareholders:* Philip John Wilkinson; Raymond John Wilkinson; June Wilkinson
*Officers:* June Wilkinson, Secretary; Matthew Barrick [1985] Director; Graham Botham [1979] Director; Stephen Jon Butterley [1973] Director; Alan Needham [1963] Director; June Wilkinson [1953] Director; Philip John Wilkinson [1975] Director; Raymond John Wilkinson [1948] Director

**Motorhog Holdings Limited**
*Incorporated:* 7 September 2001 *Employees:* 238
*Net Worth:* £13,224,599 *Total Assets:* £28,846,332
*Registered Office:* Bentley Moor Lane, Adwick-le-Street, Doncaster, S Yorks, DN6 7BD
*Activities:* Activities of head offices
*Parent:* Hog Properties Limited
*Officers:* David Martin, Secretary; David Martin [1961] Director; Richard Martin [1965] Director

**Motorhog Limited**
*Incorporated:* 6 November 1962 *Employees:* 236
*Net Worth:* £6,198,485 *Total Assets:* £12,520,971
*Registered Office:* Bentley Moor Lane, Adwick-le-Street, Doncaster, S Yorks, DN6 7BD
*Activities:* Maintenance and repair of motor vehicles
*Parent:* Newhog Holdings Limited
*Officers:* David Martin, Secretary/Motor Engineer; David Martin [1961] Director/Motor Engineer; Richard Martin [1965] Director/Motor Engineer

**Motors Insurance Company Limited**
*Incorporated:* 16 January 1992 *Employees:* 18
*Net Worth:* £90,435,000 *Total Assets:* £246,604,000
*Registered Office:* Jubilee House, 5 Mid Point Business Park, Thornbury, W Yorks, BD3 7AG
*Activities:* Non-life insurance
*Parent:* Car Care Plan (Holdings) Limited
*Officers:* Gavin William Work Tinch, Secretary; Jeremy Edward Cadle [1965] Director/Lawyer; John Anthony Levin [1963] Director; Paul Graeme Newton [1959] Director; Benjamin Seamus Russell [1972] Sales Director; Simon Jonathan Wright [1966] Finance Director

**Motorsure Limited**
*Incorporated:* 8 March 2007 *Employees:* 15
*Net Worth:* £2,062,698 *Total Assets:* £6,373,772
*Registered Office:* Damside, Oakworth Road, Keighley, W Yorks, BD21 1QD
*Activities:* Sale of used cars and light motor vehicles
*Shareholders:* Naveed Balal Bashir; Mohammed Shabir; Mohammed Shakeel
*Officers:* Naveed Balal Bashir, Secretary/Director; Naveed Balal Bashir [1988] Director; Mohammed Shabir [1979] Director; Mohammed Shakeel [1982] Director

**Mott MacDonald Bentley Ltd**
*Incorporated:* 17 August 1999
*Net Worth:* £1,000 *Total Assets:* £27,362,158
*Registered Office:* Keighley Road, Skipton, N Yorks, BD23 2QR
*Activities:* Construction of water projects
*Parent:* J N Bentley Limited
*Officers:* Jonathan David Rhodes, Secretary; David Mark Bentley [1969] Commercial Director; Paul Rogerson Bentley [1967] Contracts Director; Jonathan David Rhodes [1974] Finance and IT Director; Richard Risdon [1974] Operations Director; Paul Smedley [1971] Director/Consultant Engineer; Steven Christopher Tetlow [1966] Director

**Mount School (York) (The)**
*Incorporated:* 13 December 1982 *Employees:* 127
*Net Worth:* £1,300,707 *Total Assets:* £4,270,175
*Registered Office:* Dalton Terrace, York, YO24 4DD
*Activities:* General secondary education
*Officers:* Margaret Bryan [1953] Director/Retired; Linda Clark [1953] Director/Retired; Joan Concannon [1968] Director of External Relations; Janet Dean [1956] University Director; Shoana Morven MacKay [1965] Director/Deputy Head; Joanna Ruth Mahler [1960] Director/Charity Worker; Julian Pattison [1955] Director/Retired; Mike Anthony Porter [1950] Director/Chartered Surveyor (FRICS); Philip Severs [1954] Director/Retired; Nicola Jane Spence [1961] Director/Civil Servant; Paul Rishworth Stansfield [1953] Director/Property Consultant; Alice Louisa Unwin [1985] Director/Trainee Solicitor; Gregory James Willmott [1967] Director/Strategy Consultant; Mary Young [1951] Director/Retired

**Mount St John Equestrian LLP**
*Incorporated:* 27 February 2013 *Employees:* 14
*Net Worth:* £7,787,178 *Total Assets:* £8,013,592
*Registered Office:* Mount St John, Felixkirk, Thirsk, N Yorks, YO7 2DT
*Officers:* Emma Jane Blundell [1986] Member; Jill Blundell [1957] Member

**Mount St John Sporting LLP**
*Incorporated:* 17 August 2011 *Employees:* 13
*Net Worth:* £7,377,780 *Total Assets:* £8,566,312
*Registered Office:* Mount St John, Felixkirk, Thirsk, N Yorks, YO7 2DT
*Officers:* Christopher James Blundell [1955] Member; Mark Robert James Blundell [1990] Member

**Mount Vale Venture LLP**
*Incorporated:* 16 September 2015
*Net Worth:* £3,981,586 *Total Assets:* £3,997,149
*Registered Office:* Colenso House, Omega 1, Monks Cross Drive, Monks Cross, York, YO32 9GZ

**Moventas Gears UK Limited**
*Incorporated:* 25 June 2013 *Employees:* 25
*Previous:* David Brown Wind UK Limited
*Net Worth:* £359,001 *Total Assets:* £10,612,001
*Registered Office:* Moventas Gears UK, Howarth Lane, Huddersfield, W Yorks, HD4 5AZ
*Activities:* Other business support service activities n.e.c.
*Parent:* Moventas Wind UK Limited
*Officers:* Dr Nicholas Dugald Hill [1971] Director; Mika Antero Nieminen [1970] Director [Finnish]

**Moventas Wind UK Limited**
*Incorporated:* 14 June 2013
*Net Worth:* £6,692,001 *Total Assets:* £7,525,001
*Registered Office:* Moventas Gears UK, Howarth Lane, Huddersfield, W Yorks, HD4 5AZ
*Activities:* Other business support service activities n.e.c.
*Shareholder:* Clyde Blowers Capital Fund III LP
*Officers:* Dr Nicholas Dugald Hill [1971] Director; Mika Antero Nieminen [1970] Director [Finnish]

**Mowden Controls Limited**
*Incorporated:* 1 February 1965 *Employees:* 43
*Net Worth:* £4,147,455 *Total Assets:* £4,488,043
*Registered Office:* Mowden Controls Ltd, Mount View, Standard Way Industrial Estate, Northallerton, N Yorks, DL6 2YD
*Activities:* Manufacture of electronic industrial process control equipment
*Shareholders:* Stephen Lewis Williams; Anne Letitia Kirk; Elizabeth Anne Barber
*Officers:* Stephen Lewis Williams, Secretary/Managing Director; Elizabeth Anne Barber [1969] Director; Michael John Green [1945] Director/Retired; Anne Letitia Kirk [1935] Director/Retired; Neil MacLean [1958] Technical Director; Stephen Lewis Williams [1966] Managing Director

**Moxon (Farms) Limited**
*Incorporated:* 22 March 1976 *Employees:* 3
*Net Worth:* £16,809,902 *Total Assets:* £23,582,688
*Registered Office:* Kennels Farm, Barnsley Road, Hemsworth, Pontefract, W Yorks, WF9 4PQ
*Activities:* Growing of cereals (except rice), leguminous crops and oil seeds
*Officers:* Colin Robert Moxon [1982] Director/Farmer; Daphne Moxon [1949] Director; Helen Claire Moxon [1980] Director/Farmer

**MRC Flangefitt Limited**
*Incorporated:* 13 June 1985 *Employees:* 23
*Net Worth:* £4,957,643 *Total Assets:* £14,705,335
*Registered Office:* Heaton House, Riverside Drive, Cleckheaton, W Yorks, BD19 4DH
*Activities:* Wholesale of metals and metal ores
*Parent:* MRC Transmark Limited
*Officers:* Claire Jane Hellmund [1983] Director/Solicitor; Stephen Bradley Smith [1967] Director; Adnan Velic [1980] Director

**MRC Transmark Holdings UK Limited**
*Incorporated:* 26 April 2005 *Employees:* 57
*Net Worth:* £66,087,836 *Total Assets:* £77,447,384
*Registered Office:* Heaton House, Riverside Drive, Cleckheaton, W Yorks, BD19 4DH
*Activities:* Activities of head offices
*Parent:* MRC Transmark Group BV
*Officers:* Grant Richard Bates [1971] Director [Australian]; Elton Ray Bond [1975] Director [American]; Claire Jane Hellmund [1983] Director/Solicitor; Adnan Velic [1980] Director

**MRC Transmark Limited**
*Incorporated:* 25 November 1997 *Employees:* 74
*Net Worth:* £18,170,534 *Total Assets:* £48,901,844
*Registered Office:* Heaton House, Riverside Drive, Cleckheaton, W Yorks, BD19 4DH
*Activities:* Other retail sale not in stores, stalls or markets
*Parent:* MRC Transmark Holdings UK Limited
*Officers:* Sarah Jayne Rawcliffe, Secretary; Claire Jane Hellmund [1983] Director/Solicitor; Stephen Bradley Smith [1967] Managing Director; Adnan Velic [1980] Director

**MS International PLC**
*Incorporated:* 24 March 1960 *Employees:* 431
*Net Worth:* £33,400,000 *Total Assets:* £70,141,000
*Registered Office:* Balby Carr Bank, Balby, Doncaster, S Yorks, DN4 8DH
*Activities:* Activities of head offices
*Shareholder:* Michael James Bell
*Officers:* David Kirkup, Secretary; Michael James Bell [1946] Director/Chairman & Chief Executive; Nicholas Michael Arthur James Bell [1974] Managing Director; David George Hansell [1945] Director; Roger Lane Smith [1945] Director/Solicitor; Michael Patrick Andrew O'Connell [1949] Director; David Pyle [1946] Director

**MSS Developments Limited**
*Incorporated:* 24 May 1966 *Employees:* 2
*Net Worth:* £1,531,646 *Total Assets:* £4,346,895
*Registered Office:* City Mills, Peel Street, Morley, Leeds, LS27 8QL
*Activities:* Development of building projects
*Shareholders:* Alan Senior; Richard Senior
*Officers:* Richard Martin Senior, Secretary; Alan Senior [1947] Managing Director; Richard Martin Senior [1975] Managing Director

**MTS Nationwide Limited**
*Incorporated:* 6 April 1994 *Employees:* 48
*Net Worth:* £2,112,696 *Total Assets:* £8,585,317
*Registered Office:* Unit 2 Silkwood Park, Flanshaw Way, Wakefield, W Yorks, WF2 9LP
*Activities:* Agents involved in the sale of machinery, industrial equipment, ships and aircraft
*Parent:* MTS Nationwide Group Limited
*Officers:* Anthony Charles Miles, Secretary; Iain Shearer Black [1958] Non-Executive Director; Sarah Charlotte Black [1973] Marketing Director; Paul Hunt [1966] MTS Operations Director; Anthony Charles Miles [1960] Finance Director; Anita Jean Tyler [1970] Operations Director; Matthew Ian Watson [1976] Director; Peter Watson [1946] Managing Director; Michael Williamson [1959] Operations Director

**MTW Architectural Limited**
*Incorporated:* 9 March 2005 *Employees:* 21
*Net Worth:* £3,134,073 *Total Assets:* £6,359,153
*Registered Office:* 33 George Street, Wakefield, W Yorks, WF1 1LX
*Activities:* Manufacture of doors and windows of metal
*Shareholders:* Richard Moore; Neville Taylor
*Officers:* Neville Taylor, Secretary/Director; Richard Moore [1972] Managing Director; Neville Taylor [1969] Director

**Mulard Renewables Limited**
*Incorporated:* 4 November 2013
*Net Worth:* £7,165,767 *Total Assets:* £7,395,972
*Registered Office:* Canal Head North, Kendal, Cumbria, LA9 7BZ
*Activities:* Production of electricity
*Parent:* Mulard Renewables Holdings Limited
*Officers:* Charles William Nepean Crewdson [1964] Director; Robert Charles Peter Troughton [1982] Director

**Mulberry Homes Yorkshire Limited**
*Incorporated:* 27 October 2009 *Employees:* 4
*Net Worth Deficit:* £1,270,665 *Total Assets:* £8,294,768
*Registered Office:* Broadacres House, Mount View, Standard Way Industrial Estate, Northallerton, N Yorks, DL6 2YD
*Activities:* Development of building projects
*Parent:* Broadacres Housing Association Ltd
*Officers:* Chris Fawcett, Secretary; Jacqui Bateson [1961] Director/Senior Manager; June Patricia Mulroy [1949] Director/Retired; Peter Anthony Ottowell [1955] Director/Retired; Phil Summers [1960] Director/Retired; Martin Warhurst [1974] Director/Chief Executive; Colin Wilkie [1954] Director/Retired

**Mulgrave Property Group Limited**
*Incorporated:* 13 February 2017 *Employees:* 17
*Net Worth Deficit:* £1,143,944 *Total Assets:* £8,470,761
*Registered Office:* Unit D, Chessingham Park, Common Road, Dunnington, York, YO19 5SE
*Activities:* Construction of domestic buildings
*Major Shareholder:* Marquis of Normanby Constantine Edmund Walter Phipps
*Officers:* Ian Peter Hessay [1965] Director; Mark Robert Hills [1963] Finance Director; Jon Lloyd [1956] Director; Constantine Edmund Walter Phipps [1954] Director

**Multi-Tech Engineering (UK) Limited**
*Incorporated:* 12 April 2006 *Employees:* 29
*Net Worth:* £1,784,798 *Total Assets:* £3,629,821
*Registered Office:* Multi-Tech Engineering (UK) Ltd, Kirkhaw Lane, Ferrybridge, Knottingley, W Yorks, WF11 8RD
*Activities:* Machining
*Shareholders:* Richard Donald Smith; Deborah Ann Smith
*Officers:* Deborah Ann Smith, Secretary; Deborah Ann Smith [1958] Director/Accountant; Richard Donald Smith [1957] Director/Engineer

**Multiflight Charter Services LLP**
*Incorporated:* 18 January 2010
*Net Worth:* £4,791,668 *Total Assets:* £4,961,073
*Registered Office:* South Side Aviation Centre, Leeds Bradford International Airport, Leeds, LS19 7UG
*Officers:* Joanne Haigh [1957] Member; David Richard Hood [1948] Member

**Multiflight Limited**
*Incorporated:* 8 August 1994 *Employees:* 70
*Net Worth:* £11,500,691 *Total Assets:* £14,469,956
*Registered Office:* Southside Aviation Leeds, Bradford Airport, Leeds, LS19 7UG
*Activities:* Non-scheduled passenger air transport
*Major Shareholder:* David Richard Hood
*Officers:* Miles Beecham, Secretary; Miles Beecham [1976] Director/Accountant; Stephen Borrowdale [1963] Managing Director; David Richard Hood [1948] Director/Electronics Engineer

**Multisol Europe Limited**
*Incorporated:* 12 October 2004 *Employees:* 8
*Net Worth:* £10,033,856 *Total Assets:* £23,566,464
*Registered Office:* Alpha House, Lawnswood Business Park, Redvers Close, Leeds, LS16 6QY
*Activities:* Other transportation support activities
*Parent:* Multisol Group Limited
*Officers:* Martin Gratton, Secretary; Martin Gratton [1969] Director; David Garnett Hopkinson [1964] Director; Kevin Eamonn Wright [1964] Managing Director

**Multisol Group Limited**
*Incorporated:* 17 January 2003 *Employees:* 2
*Previous:* Multisol Holdings Limited
*Net Worth:* £46,309,000 *Total Assets:* £46,309,000
*Registered Office:* Alpha House, Lawnswood Business Park, Redvers Close, Leeds, LS16 6QY
*Activities:* Activities of head offices
*Parent:* Multisol Limited
*Officers:* Martin Gratton, Secretary; Martin Gratton [1969] Director; David Garnett Hopkinson [1964] Managing Director

**Multisol Limited**
*Incorporated:* 3 May 1968 *Employees:* 72
*Net Worth:* £5,167,000 *Total Assets:* £53,984,000
*Registered Office:* Alpha House, Lawnswood Business Park, Redvers Close, Leeds, LS16 6QY
*Activities:* Manufacture of other inorganic basic chemicals
*Parent:* Brenntag UK Holding Limited
*Officers:* Martin Gratton, Secretary; Martin Gratton [1969] Director; David Garnett Hopkinson [1964] Managing Director; Kevin Eamonn Wright [1964] Managing Director

**Mumtaz Food Products Limited**
*Incorporated:* 14 May 2008
*Net Worth:* £2,221,701 *Total Assets:* £7,425,491
*Registered Office:* 42 Legrams Lane, Bradford, W Yorks, BD7 1ND
*Activities:* Activities of other holding companies n.e.c.
*Shareholder:* Kauser Gul-Nawaz Akbar
*Officers:* Kauser Gul-Nawaz Akbar, Secretary; Bilal Akbar [1988] Director; Ismail Akbar [1995] Director

**Munchkin UK Trading Company Ltd**
*Incorporated:* 31 December 2009 *Employees:* 46
*Net Worth Deficit:* £2,610,802 *Total Assets:* £21,267,034
*Registered Office:* Central House, Otley Road, Harrogate, N Yorks, HG3 1UF
*Activities:* Dormant company
*Parent:* Munchkin Inc
*Officers:* Steven Dunn [1957] Director [American]; Thomas Emrey [1962] Finance Director [American]

**Munford Haulage Limited**
*Incorporated:* 25 October 2010
*Net Worth:* £3,842,718 *Total Assets:* £6,163,288
*Registered Office:* 0 Stirk House, Cross Lane, York, YO61 1RB
*Activities:* Post-harvest crop activities
*Major Shareholder:* Edna Munford
*Officers:* Peter Andrew Chipp [1983] Director/Accountant; Edna Margaret Munford [1939] Director; Kevin Geoffrey Munford [1961] Director

**Al. Murad D.I.Y. Limited**
*Incorporated:* 5 August 1991 *Employees:* 270
*Net Worth:* £18,411,082 *Total Assets:* £22,633,194
*Registered Office:* Howley Park Road East, Morley, Leeds, LS27 0BN
*Activities:* Retail sale of hardware, paints and glass in specialised stores
*Officers:* Irfan Patel, Secretary; Murad Ali Patel, Secretary; Ismail Murad Ali Patel [1980] Director; Murad Ali Patel [1957] Director

**Murphy (Yorkshire) Ltd**
*Incorporated:* 26 October 2015 *Employees:* 225
*Net Worth:* £1,934,625 *Total Assets:* £6,339,133
*Registered Office:* First Floor, Mayesbrook House, Lawnswood Business Park, Redvers Close, Leeds, LS16 6QY
*Activities:* Other service activities n.e.c.
*Shareholders:* Philip Murphy; David Christopher Mitchell; Janine Elizabeth Murphy
*Officers:* Caroline Nicole Murphy [1974] Director; Janine Elizabeth Murphy [1944] Director; Phillip Edward Murphy [1943] Director; Joanne Catherine Westmoreland [1971] Director

**Murton Feeds Limited**
*Incorporated:* 6 March 2014
*Net Worth:* £100 *Total Assets:* £8,836,661
*Registered Office:* Main Street, Amotherby, Malton, N Yorks, YO17 6TA
*Activities:* Activities of agricultural holding companies
*Parent:* Brandsby Agricultural Trading Association Limited
*Officers:* Alan Charles Brader [1955] Director/Farmer; Robert Charles Rook [1952] Director/Farmer

**Murton Grange Limited**
*Incorporated:* 18 February 1997
*Net Worth:* £3,494,234 *Total Assets:* £5,095,666
*Registered Office:* Myton Hall Farms, Haddocks Lane, Myton on Swale, York, YO61 2RB
*Activities:* Growing of cereals (except rice), leguminous crops and oil seeds
*Major Shareholder:* William James Duncan Morrison
*Officers:* Barbara Jackson, Secretary; William James Duncan Morrison [1976] Director

**Musgrave & Sagar Limited**
*Incorporated:* 29 August 1907 *Employees:* 2
*Net Worth:* £3,871,612 *Total Assets:* £4,021,930
*Registered Office:* Gresham House, 5-7 St Pauls Street, Leeds, LS1 2JG
*Activities:* Other letting and operating of own or leased real estate
*Shareholders:* Rupert Cecil Robin Sagar-Musgrave; Alice Louise Josephine Sagar-Musgrave
*Officers:* Rupert Cecil Robin Sagar-Musgrave, Secretary; Alice Louise Josephine Sagar-Musgrave [1972] Director; Rupert Cecil Robin Sagar-Musgrave [1970] Director

**MV Ingredients Limited**
*Incorporated:* 1 November 2010
*Net Worth:* £9,907,000 *Total Assets:* £16,493,000
*Registered Office:* Arla House, 4 Savannah Way, Leeds Valley Park, Leeds, LS10 1AB
*Activities:* Manufacture of other milk products
*Shareholders:* Volac International Limited; Arla Foods Ingredients UK Limited
*Officers:* Lucy Williams, Secretary; Henrik Andersen [1960] Director [Danish]; Alan Richard Armstrong [1955] Director/Manufacturing; Noah Felix Kalman Franklin [1959] Director; Klaus Kristiansen [1966] Finance Director [Danish]

**MWS Group Ltd**
*Incorporated:* 20 March 2007
*Net Worth Deficit:* £2,349,458 *Total Assets:* £3,536,769
*Registered Office:* 6 Earls Court, Priory Park East, Hull, HU4 7DY
*Activities:* Activities of head offices
*Officers:* Melvyn Warren Sadofsky [1949] Director/Accountant

**My Lockup Limited**
*Incorporated:* 26 July 1983 *Employees:* 7
*Previous:* Lecaflor Limited
*Net Worth:* £2,242,010 *Total Assets:* £5,051,809
*Registered Office:* Unit B, Alanbrooke Industrial Park, Station Road, Topcliffe, Thirsk, N Yorks, YO7 3SE
*Activities:* Other letting and operating of own or leased real estate
*Officers:* Kevin John Doyle [1956] Director

**Myers Building Supplies Ltd**
*Incorporated:* 5 June 1973 *Employees:* 144
*Previous:* Naylor-Myers Limited
*Net Worth:* £9,018,476 *Total Assets:* £16,201,076
*Registered Office:* 5 Barr Street, off Leeds Road, Huddersfield, W Yorks, HD1 6PB
*Activities:* Wholesale of wood, construction materials and sanitary equipment
*Parent:* Myers Group 1959 Limited
*Officers:* John Rodger Myers, Secretary; Anne Jacqueline Myers Berry [1955] Director; James David Myers Berry [1985] Director; Katie Elizabeth Myers Berry [1987] Director; John Rodger Myers [1948] Director/Concrete Technologist

**Myers Group 1959 Ltd**
*Incorporated:* 11 December 1947 *Employees:* 357
*Previous:* Readymix-Huddersfield Limited
*Net Worth:* £14,148,016 *Total Assets:* £29,267,576
*Registered Office:* 5 Barr Street, off Leeds Road, Huddersfield, W Yorks, HD1 6PB
*Activities:* Activities of head offices
*Parent:* Myers Group Holdings Ltd
*Officers:* John Rodger Myers, Secretary; Anne Jacqueline Myers Berry [1955] Director/Clerical; James David Myers Berry [1985] Director; Katie Elizabeth Myers Berry [1987] Director; John Rodger Myers [1948] Director/Concrete Technologist

**Myers Group Holdings Ltd**
*Incorporated:* 15 March 1994 *Employees:* 357
*Previous:* Myers Group (1959) Limited
*Net Worth:* £14,163,017 *Total Assets:* £29,267,572
*Registered Office:* 5 Barr Street, Leeds Road, Huddersfield, W Yorks, HD1 6PB
*Activities:* Dormant company
*Parent:* Isaac Timmins Ltd
*Officers:* John Rodger Myers, Secretary; Anne Jacqueline Myers Berry [1955] Director/Clerical; James David Myers Berry [1985] Director; Katie Elizabeth Myers Berry [1987] Director; John Rodger Myers [1948] Director/Concrete Technologist

**Philip Myers Web (Neston) Limited**
*Incorporated:* 22 June 2004 *Employees:* 127
*Net Worth Deficit:* £658,366 *Total Assets:* £5,642,577
*Registered Office:* Unit 2 Navigation Park, Lockside Road, Leeds, LS10 1EP
*Activities:* Printing n.e.c.
*Officers:* Graham Michael Glynn [1956] Director; Christopher John Howard [1969] Managing Director; Richard James Sandman [1969] Director

**Myrtle Grange Renewables Limited**
*Incorporated:* 24 September 2015
*Net Worth Deficit:* £69,928 *Total Assets:* £3,209,013
*Registered Office:* Myrtle Grange Farm, Main Street, Hensall, Goole, E Yorks, DN14 0RA
*Activities:* Production of electricity
*Major Shareholder:* Christopher Roger Platt
*Officers:* Christopher Roger Platt [1983] Director/Farmer

**Mysing Capital Limited**
*Incorporated:* 2 July 2014
*Previous:* Mysing Properties Limited
*Net Worth:* £1,476,344 *Total Assets:* £16,516,282
*Registered Office:* 9 Fryers Way, Ossett, W Yorks, WF5 9TJ
*Activities:* Other credit granting n.e.c.
*Shareholders:* Steve Turner; Rob Coxon; Matt Ferguson
*Officers:* John Higgins, Secretary; Robert James Coxon [1966] Director; Matthew John Ferguson [1971] Director; John Higgins [1969] Director; Steven Turner [1967] Director

**Mysing Care Limited**
*Incorporated:* 16 July 2015 *Employees:* 187
*Net Worth:* £345,547 *Total Assets:* £13,747,631
*Registered Office:* 9 Fryers Way, Ossett, Wakefield, W Yorks, WF5 9TJ
*Activities:* Residential nursing care facilities
*Officers:* Robert James Coxon [1966] Director; Matthew John Ferguson [1972] Director; John Higgins [1969] Director; Ian Kimberley [1957] Director; Steve Turner [1967] Director

**Mysing Investments 2 Limited**
*Incorporated:* 10 October 2014
*Net Worth:* £260,846 *Total Assets:* £4,833,832
*Registered Office:* 9 Fryers Way, Ossett, Wakefield, W Yorks, WF5 9TJ
*Activities:* Other business support service activities n.e.c.
*Major Shareholder:* Matthew John Ferguson
*Officers:* Matthew John Ferguson [1971] Director

**Mysing Investments 3 Limited**
*Incorporated:* 10 October 2014
*Net Worth:* £289,231 *Total Assets:* £4,957,509
*Registered Office:* 9 Fryers Way, Ossett, Wakefield, W Yorks, WF5 9TJ
*Activities:* Other business support service activities n.e.c.
*Major Shareholder:* Steven Turner
*Officers:* Steven Turner [1967] Director

**Mysing Investments 4 Limited**
*Incorporated:* 10 October 2014
*Net Worth:* £270,007 *Total Assets:* £4,845,257
*Registered Office:* 9 Fryers Way, Ossett, Wakefield, W Yorks, WF5 9TJ
*Activities:* Other business support service activities n.e.c.
*Major Shareholder:* Robert James Coxon
*Officers:* Robert James Coxon [1966] Director

**Mytum & Selby Waste Recycling Limited**
*Incorporated:* 10 January 2002 *Employees:* 31
*Net Worth:* £5,712,471 *Total Assets:* £7,809,105
*Registered Office:* Mill Cross Quarry, Garden Lane, Sherburn in Elmet, N Yorks, LS25 6AT
*Activities:* Collection of non-hazardous waste
*Shareholder:* David Carrie
*Officers:* Christine Carrie, Secretary; Christine Carrie [1960] Director; David Carrie [1957] Director; Rachel Carrie [1984] Director; Steven Carrie [1979] Director

**Naburn Leisure Limited**
*Incorporated:* 12 July 2006 *Employees:* 24
*Net Worth:* £1,034,667 *Total Assets:* £3,459,328
*Registered Office:* Naburn, York, YO19 4RW
*Activities:* Other amusement and recreation activities n.e.c.
*Major Shareholder:* Philip Duncan Bleakley
*Officers:* Pamela Bleakley, Secretary; Philip Duncan Bleakley [1953] Director

**Nafferton Wold Farms Limited**
*Incorporated:* 22 August 1996 *Employees:* 12
*Net Worth:* £4,703,894 *Total Assets:* £8,578,304
*Registered Office:* Field House, Scarborough Road, Driffield, E Yorks, YO25 5UY
*Activities:* Growing of cereals (except rice), leguminous crops and oil seeds
*Shareholders:* Timothy Charles Dewhirst; Catherine Barbara Dewhirst
*Officers:* Catherine Barbara Dewhirst, Secretary; Catherine Barbara Dewhirst [1951] Director/Farmer; Joseph William Dewhirst [1978] Director/Farmer; Richard John Dewhirst [1981] Director/Farmer

**Nagra Properties Limited**
*Incorporated:* 15 October 2002
*Net Worth:* £2,266,313 *Total Assets:* £7,187,409
*Registered Office:* Princes House, Wright Street, Hull, HU2 8HX
*Activities:* Other letting and operating of own or leased real estate
*Major Shareholder:* Mandip Singh Nagra
*Officers:* Mandip Singh Nagra, Secretary/Manager; Mandip Singh Nagra [1968] Director/Manager

**Narang Group Ltd**
*Incorporated:* 21 July 2009 *Employees:* 82
*Net Worth:* £5,480,455 *Total Assets:* £10,552,641
*Registered Office:* Narang House, 121 City Road, Bradford, W Yorks, BD8 8JR
*Activities:* Activities of head offices
*Shareholders:* Jasbir Singh Narang; Ravinder Singh Narang
*Officers:* Jasbir Singh Narang [1966] Director; Ravinder Singh Narang [1969] Director

**Narang Wholesalers Limited**
*Incorporated:* 25 July 1995
*Net Worth:* £5,304,966 *Total Assets:* £10,358,287
*Registered Office:* Narang House, 121 City Road, Bradford, W Yorks, BD8 8JR
*Activities:* Wholesale of wine, beer, spirits and other alcoholic beverages
*Parent:* Narang Group Limited
*Officers:* Jagjeet Singh Kalsi, Secretary; Mohammed Younis Hussain [1971] Director/Wholesalers; Jagjeet Singh Kalsi [1951] Director/Wholesalers; Jasbir Singh Narang [1966] Director

**Narbourne Limited**
*Incorporated:* 7 October 2004 *Employees:* 2
*Net Worth Deficit:* £2,467,772 *Total Assets:* £16,259,516
*Registered Office:* Cumberland House, Greenside Lane, Bradford, BD8 9TF
*Activities:* Development of building projects
*Parent:* Hartley Investment Trust Limited
*Officers:* Alan James Lewis [1938] Director/Chairman

**Nat Flex Group Limited**
*Incorporated:* 5 April 2011 *Employees:* 47
*Net Worth:* £3,387,516 *Total Assets:* £8,320,385
*Registered Office:* 2 Battlefield View, Birkenshaw, Bradford, W Yorks, BD11 2PT
*Activities:* Dormant company
*Officers:* Julia Davys, Secretary; Julia Davys [1966] Finance Director; George Slack [1973] Managing Director; William Barry Twigg [1939] Director

**National Coaching Foundation (The)**
*Incorporated:* 23 January 1987 *Employees:* 98
*Net Worth:* £5,155,714 *Total Assets:* £6,747,385
*Registered Office:* Chelsea Close, off Amberley Road, Armley, Leeds, LS12 4HP
*Activities:* Other sports activities
*Officers:* Wayne Anthony Allison [1968] Director/Coaching Inclusion and Diversity Manager; Elizabeth Jane Broadbent [1970] Director/General Manager; Martha Collins Rolle [1952] Director/Lawyer [American/British]; Alastair Mark Damon Gilmartin Smith [1966] Finance Director; Dr Rosemary Anne Leonard [1956] Director/Medical General Practitioner; Colin Everold Rattigan [1968] Director/Marketing Executive; Richard Thomas James Wheater [1981] Director/Manager; Gillian Caroline Wilmot [1960] Non-Executive Director Chairman

**National Coal Mining Museum for England Trust Ltd**
*Incorporated:* 24 February 1983 *Employees:* 97
*Net Worth:* £5,153,492 *Total Assets:* £7,975,573
*Registered Office:* Caphouse Colliery, New Road, Overton, Wakefield, W Yorks, WF4 4RH
*Activities:* Operation of historical sites and buildings and similar visitor attractions
*Officers:* Julie Elliott, Secretary; Patrick Matthew Carragher [1957] Director/Retired; Tracey Jane Garrett [1969] Director/Media Relations and Communications; Norma Jacqueline Gregory [1969] Director; Councillor Denise Margaret Jeffery [1946] Director/Elected Councillor; Julie Ann Kenny [1957] Director/Chief Executive and Chair; Nigel Pearce [1960] Director/Retired; Trevor Shaw [1951] Director; Baroness Winifred Ann Taylor [1947] Director/Politician; John Philip Whyatt [1957] Director/Retired; David Wilkin [1957] Director/Retired

**National Flexible Limited**
*Incorporated:* 19 December 1997 *Employees:* 47
*Net Worth:* £3,886,617 *Total Assets:* £8,688,595
*Registered Office:* 2 Battlefield View, Birkenshaw, Bradford, BD11 2PT
*Activities:* Packaging activities
*Officers:* Julia Davys, Secretary; Carol Abigail Burdett [1959] Director; David Daniels [1977] Technical Director; Julia Davys [1966] Finance Director; George Slack [1973] Managing Director; Mark Alan Thompson [1973] Sales & Marketing Director; William Barry Twigg [1939] Director

**National Floorcoverings Limited**
*Incorporated:* 3 March 1955 *Employees:* 123
*Net Worth:* £8,847,545 *Total Assets:* £19,545,408
*Registered Office:* Wellington Mills, Huddersfield Road, Liversedge, W Yorks, WF15 7FH
*Activities:* Manufacture of other carpets and rugs
*Parent:* National Floorcoverings Holdings Ltd
*Officers:* John Edward Marriott Walker, Secretary; David Andrew Pass [1966] Director; Mark Anthony Pass [1964] Director; Simon Arthur Pass [1963] Director; David Rhodes [1956] Director; Richard Charles Taylor [1949] Director/Chartered Accountant; John Edward Marriott Walker [1954] Director/Accountant

**National Tube Stockholders Limited**
*Incorporated:* 19 March 1985 *Employees:* 180
*Net Worth:* £36,532,504 *Total Assets:* £55,347,908
*Registered Office:* Dalton Industrial Estate, Dalton, Thirsk, N Yorks, YO7 3HE
*Activities:* Wholesale of metals and metal ores
*Shareholders:* Hambleton NTS Ltd; Sicam SpA
*Officers:* Malcolm John Elders, Secretary; Jeanne Martine Elizabeth Bianco [1971] Director; Paolo Bianco [1969] Director [Italian]

**Nationwide Bearing Company Ltd.**
*Incorporated:* 26 March 1992 *Employees:* 29
*Net Worth:* £4,440,374 *Total Assets:* £5,015,974
*Registered Office:* James Road, Adwick-le-Street, Doncaster, S Yorks, DN6 7HH
*Activities:* Non-specialised wholesale trade
*Shareholders:* Paul Allan Cameron Birley; Lorraine Birley
*Officers:* Lorraine Birley, Secretary; Paul Allan Cameron Birley [1957] Director/Distributor

**Nationwide Structures Limited**
*Incorporated:* 22 May 2000
*Net Worth:* £1,079,392 *Total Assets:* £7,238,779
*Registered Office:* The Picasso Building, Calder Vale Road, Wakefield, W Yorks, WF1 5PF
*Activities:* Manufacture of metal structures and parts of structures
*Shareholder:* Desmond Michael Cullen
*Officers:* Timothy Paul Cullen, Secretary/Accountant; Andrew Beckett [1970] Director; Desmond Michael Cullen [1953] Director; Michael Winship Pollard [1960] Director/Salesman

**Nationwide Window Cleaning Limited**
*Incorporated:* 23 June 2009 *Employees:* 275
*Net Worth:* £3,347,610 *Total Assets:* £8,803,095
*Registered Office:* 3 Colton Mill, Bullerthopre Lane, Leeds, LS15 9JN
*Activities:* Window cleaning services
*Parent:* Tasker Investments Limited
*Officers:* John Thornton Tasker [1966] Director

**Natures Aid Ltd**
*Incorporated:* 25 February 1993 *Employees:* 68
*Net Worth:* £7,932,969 *Total Assets:* £10,550,804
*Registered Office:* c/o Thornton & Ross Ltd, Manchester Road, Linthwaite, Huddersfield, W Yorks, HD7 5QH
*Activities:* Manufacture of other food products n.e.c.
*Parent:* Stada UK Holdings Ltd.
*Officers:* Edwin Charles Blythe, Secretary; Edwin Charles Blythe [1968] Director/Chartered Accountant; Charles Ashley Brierley [1963] Director

**Natures Crops International Limited**
*Incorporated:* 25 February 2004 *Employees:* 19
*Previous:* Technology Crops Limited
*Net Worth Deficit:* £4,668,357 *Total Assets:* £16,466,757
*Registered Office:* Westminster Business Centre, 10 Great North Way, York Business Park, York, YO26 6RB
*Activities:* Growing of cereals (except rice), leguminous crops and oil seeds
*Major Shareholder:* Andrew Bruce Hebard
*Officers:* Andrew Bruce Hebard [1965] Director/President of Business; Simon Meakin [1974] Director/Agronomist

**Naught One Ltd**
*Incorporated:* 12 November 2004 *Employees:* 41
*Net Worth:* £3,428,114 *Total Assets:* £6,758,679
*Registered Office:* Unit D, Knaresborough Technology Park, Manse Lane, Knaresborough, N Yorks, HG5 8LF
*Activities:* Manufacture of other furniture
*Parent:* Naughtone (Holdings) Ltd
*Officers:* David Audis, Secretary; Kieron Jon Bakewell [1978] Director/Designer; Gregory Jay Bylsma [1965] Director/Manufacturing Executive [American]; Kevin David Gingras [1978] Director/Vice President, International Finance [American]; Mark James Hammond [1980] Director/Designer; Richard Scott [1968] Director; Matthew John Welsh [1977] Director/Sales

**Navartis Holdings Limited**
*Incorporated:* 10 April 2014 *Employees:* 53
*Net Worth:* £2,015,569 *Total Assets:* £8,110,066
*Registered Office:* 4 Sidings Court, Doncaster, S Yorks, DN4 5NU
*Activities:* Activities of head offices
*Major Shareholder:* Jim Jonathan Sloan
*Officers:* Keith Heppenstall, Secretary; James Jonathan Sloan [1975] Director

**Navartis Limited**
*Incorporated:* 21 August 2006 *Employees:* 53
*Net Worth:* £3,712,358 *Total Assets:* £9,719,215
*Registered Office:* 4 Sidings Court, Doncaster, S Yorks, DN4 5NU
*Activities:* Temporary employment agency activities
*Parent:* Navartis Holdings Limited
*Officers:* Keith Heppenstall, Secretary; Justyn Faulkner [1977] Director; James Jonathan Sloan [1975] Director

**Navenio Limited**
*Incorporated:* 28 October 2015 *Employees:* 18
*Net Worth:* £5,206,323 *Total Assets:* £5,375,406
*Registered Office:* Leeds Innovation Centre, 103 Clarendon Road, Leeds, LS2 9DF
*Activities:* Satellite telecommunications activities
*Shareholder:* Oxford Sciences Innovation PLC
*Officers:* Matthew Timothy Arnold [1976] Director; Dr Agathoniki Trigoni [1976] Director [Greek]; Timothy Paul Weil [1961] Director

**Navigo Health and Social Care CIC**
*Incorporated:* 2 December 2010
*Net Worth:* £3,269,655 *Total Assets:* £10,013,655
*Registered Office:* Navigo House, 3-7 Brighowgate, Grimsby, N E Lincs, DN32 0QE
*Activities:* Other human health activities
*Officers:* Julie Gray, Secretary; Simon John Beeton [1976] Finance Director; Thomas Henry Hunter [1946] Director/Retired; Kathryn Yvonne Lavery [1951] Director/Business Consultant; Elizabeth Jane Lewington [1958] NHS Director; Richard Andrew Melling [1974] Director/Senior Practitioner (Social Worker); Michael Reeve [1966] Operations Director; Dr Aamer Sajjad [1975] Director/Consultant Psychiatrist; Julie Salt [1965] Director/Council Employee; Andrew Lee Waterhouse [1975] Director

**Naylor Wintersgill Limited**
*Incorporated:* 18 November 2010 *Employees:* 52
*Net Worth:* £1,639,001 *Total Assets:* £3,890,385
*Registered Office:* Carlton House, Grammar School Street, Bradford, W Yorks, BD1 4NS
*Activities:* Accounting and auditing activities
*Officers:* Christopher David Gumbley [1959] Director/Accountant; Vaughan Martyn Houldsworth [1957] Director/Chartered Accountant; Gavin David Lamb [1979] Director/Chartered Accountant; Philippus Lodewyk Venter [1974] Director/Chartered Accountant [South African]; Victoria Wainwright [1974] Director/Chartered Accountant; Alison Marjorie Whalley [1966] Director/Chartered Accountant; Colin David Whitehead [1981] Director/Chartered Accountant; Alan Wintersgill [1950] Director/Chartered Accountant

**Naylors Finance Limited**
*Incorporated:* 2 August 1978 *Employees:* 42
*Net Worth:* £5,492,710 *Total Assets:* £12,038,025
*Registered Office:* 97 Bridge Road, Horbury Bridge, Wakefield, W Yorks, WF4 5NN
*Activities:* Other credit granting n.e.c.
*Major Shareholder:* Roger Joseph Tranter
*Officers:* Claire Lindsey Tranter, Secretary; Roger Joseph Tranter [1945] Director; Stephen Charles Tranter [1963] Director

**NCA Group Limited**
*Incorporated:* 16 September 1994
*Net Worth:* £7,952,000 *Total Assets:* £7,952,000
*Registered Office:* Central House, Leeds Road, Rothwell, Leeds, LS26 0JE
*Activities:* Other service activities n.e.c.
*Parent:* Manheim Limited
*Officers:* Michael Buxton, Secretary/Financial Director; Michael Buxton [1965] Director

**NCI Vehicle Rescue PLC**
*Incorporated:* 23 February 2004 *Employees:* 101
*Net Worth:* £1,314,539 *Total Assets:* £7,056,217
*Registered Office:* 4th Floor, Clarendon House, Victoria Avenue, Harrogate, N Yorks, HG1 1JD
*Activities:* Activities of head offices
*Officers:* Paul Marcus Barrett, Secretary; Craig Astbury [1982] Director; Paul Marcus Barrett [1964] Finance Director; Charles Richard Jackson [1951] Director; Neil Michael Richards-Smith [1969] Director/Insurance Consultant; Richard Philip Sharman [1971] Director

**Neal Investments Limited**
*Incorporated:* 3 December 2014
*Net Worth:* £2,466,135 *Total Assets:* £12,765,337
*Registered Office:* Ogleforth House, Ogleforth, York, YO1 7JG
*Activities:* Other service activities n.e.c.
*Shareholders:* Olivia Claire Neal; Victoria Jade Duckworth
*Officers:* Victoria Jade Duckworth [1992] Director; John Howard Neal [1961] Director; Olivia Claire Neal [1990] Director

**Neargoal Limited**
*Incorporated:* 21 June 1994
*Net Worth:* £5,687,969 *Total Assets:* £12,950,972
*Registered Office:* 21 Dragon Road, Harrogate, N Yorks, HG1 5DB
*Activities:* Renting and operating of Housing Association real estate
*Parent:* Axebell Limited
*Officers:* John Daker Spink, Secretary; David John Spink [1965] Director; John Daker Spink [1940] Director; Kevin Charles Spink [1968] Director

**Neasden Primary School**
*Incorporated:* 9 September 2013 *Employees:* 44
*Net Worth:* £4,400,631 *Total Assets:* £4,869,875
*Registered Office:* Neasden Primary School, Neasden Close, Hull, HU8 0QB
*Activities:* Primary education
*Officers:* Mark Batty [1980] Director/Headteacher; Annabel Cherry Jackson [1980] Director/Assistant Headteacher; Stephen Paul Jones [1957] Director/Foster Carer; Gary Jordan [1959] Director/Registered Mental Health Nurse; Nicola Louise Loten [1969] Director/Headteacher; Pete McGlinchey [1952] Director/Retired; Jamie Pearse [1977] Director/Assistant Headteacher; Colin Ward [1948] Director/Retired

**Needlers Limited**
*Incorporated:* 15 August 2005 *Employees:* 80
*Net Worth:* £3,443,470 *Total Assets:* £12,487,227
*Registered Office:* Reldeen House, Wyke Way, Melton West Business Park, Melton, North Ferriby, N Humbers, HU14 3BQ
*Activities:* Wholesale of clothing and footwear
*Officers:* John Richard Shipley, Secretary; Mark Day [1965] Managing Director; Mark James Keedy [1970] Operations Director; Alistair John Needler [1968] Director; Angela Kate Needler [1969] Director/Cleaning & Hygiene Services; Robert James Russell [1965] Sales Director; John Richard Shipley [1972] Finance Director

**Neerock Limited**
*Incorporated:* 10 January 1991 *Employees:* 1,630
*Net Worth:* £195,292,992 *Total Assets:* £581,259,008
*Registered Office:* Hilmore House, Gain Lane, Bradford, W Yorks, BD3 7DL
*Activities:* Production of meat and poultry meat products
*Parent:* Wm Morrison Supermarkets Holdings Limited
*Officers:* Jonathan James Burke, Secretary; Andrew James Clappen [1965] Technical Director; Jonathan William Reed [1973] Director; Mark Thomas Stitson [1976] Finance Director; Andrew Edward Thornber [1974] Director

**Neill & Brown (Shipping) Limited**
*Incorporated:* 20 June 1979 *Employees:* 60
*Net Worth:* £2,167,951 *Total Assets:* £7,841,667
*Registered Office:* Overseas House, Livingstone Road, Hessle, E Yorks, HU13 0EG
*Activities:* Freight transport by road
*Parent:* Neill & Brown Global Logistics Group Limited
*Officers:* Ian Stanley Halder, Secretary; Carl Andrew [1973] Director; John Charles Brown [1955] Director; Peter Atholl Brown [1949] Director; Ian Stanley Halder [1965] Finance Director; Colin Moody [1960] Director

**Neill & Brown Global Logistics Group Limited**
*Incorporated:* 9 May 1988 *Employees:* 143
*Net Worth:* £7,486,509 *Total Assets:* £15,329,693
*Registered Office:* Overseas House, Livingstone Road, Hessle, E Yorks, HU13 0EG
*Activities:* Activities of head offices
*Officers:* Ian Stanley Halder, Secretary; Carl Andrew [1973] Director; John Charles Brown [1955] Director; Peter Atholl Brown [1949] Director; Ian Stanley Halder [1965] Finance Director; Colin Moody [1960] Director

**Neill & Brown Limited**
*Incorporated:* 7 January 1939 *Employees:* 46
*Net Worth:* £1,355,593 *Total Assets:* £4,346,795
*Registered Office:* Overseas House, Livingstone Road, Hessle, E Yorks, HU13 0EG
*Activities:* Operation of warehousing and storage facilities for land transport activities
*Parent:* Neill & Brown Global Logistics Group Limited
*Officers:* Ian Stanley Halder, Secretary; Carl Andrew [1973] Director; John Charles Brown [1955] Director; Peter Atholl Brown [1949] Director; Ian Stanley Halder [1965] Finance Director; Colin Moody [1960] Director

**Amos Nelson,Limited**
*Incorporated:* 28 June 1921 *Employees:* 7
*Net Worth:* £11,763,048 *Total Assets:* £12,893,315
*Registered Office:* Old Gledstone, Skipton, N Yorks, BD23 3JR
*Activities:* Support services to forestry
*Officers:* Armorel Brandreth Nelson, Secretary; Lucinda Harriet Mullins [1966] Director/Property Manager; Armorel Brandreth Nelson [1941] Director; David George Hargreaves Nelson [1933] Director/Textile Merchant; James Matthew Ryves Nelson [1971] Director/Farmer; Victoria Jane Sandars [1968] Director/P R Consultant; Geoffrey Arnold Shindler [1942] Director/Solicitor

**Neoss Limited**
*Incorporated:* 30 November 2000 *Employees:* 109
*Net Worth:* £6,464,593 *Total Assets:* £9,810,743
*Registered Office:* Floor 3, Windsor House, Cornwall Road, Harrogate, N Yorks, HG1 2PW
*Activities:* Manufacture of medical and dental instruments and supplies
*Officers:* Guy Cameron Leaver, Secretary; Michael John Dormer [1951] Director; Nils Fredrik Engman [1968] Director [Swedish]; James Francis Kenny [1944] Director [Irish]; Guy Cameron Leaver [1964] Finance Director; Denis Knowles Tinsley [1948] Director

**Ness Hall Ltd**
*Incorporated:* 30 July 2003 *Employees:* 38
*Previous:* Homfray Hotels Ltd
*Net Worth:* £5,863,078 *Total Assets:* £9,488,306
*Registered Office:* Ness Hall, East Ness, Nunnington, York, YO62 5XD
*Activities:* Growing of cereals (except rice), leguminous crops and oil seeds
*Major Shareholder:* Richard James Toby Murray Wells
*Officers:* David Murray Wells, Secretary; David Murray Wells [1949] Director/Underwriter; Richard James Toby Murray Wells [1973] Director/Farmer

**L.Nettleton & Son Limited**
*Incorporated:* 27 October 1960 *Employees:* 7
*Net Worth:* £9,994,654 *Total Assets:* £18,787,322
*Registered Office:* Frodingham Hall, Winestead, Hull, HU12 0NR
*Activities:* Growing of cereals (except rice), leguminous crops and oil seeds
*Major Shareholder:* William Guy Nettleton
*Officers:* Sheila Mary Nettleton [1937] Director; William Guy Nettleton [1962] Farmer/Director

**Network Mapping Limited**
*Incorporated:* 20 August 2007 *Employees:* 80
*Net Worth:* £1,733,003 *Total Assets:* £4,223,842
*Registered Office:* Unit 8 Whitfield Business Park, Manse Lane, Knaresborough, N Yorks, HG5 8BS
*Activities:* Other professional, scientific and technical activities n.e.c.
*Parent:* Network Mapping Group Limited
*Officers:* Kevin Paul Jacobs [1963] Director/Electrical Engineer; Timo Juhapekka Keinanen [1960] Director/Chief Financial Officer [Finnish]; David William Langworth [1962] Director International Business; Kai Tapio Lehtinen [1966] Director [Finnish]

**New Century Foods Limited**
*Incorporated:* 10 April 2001 *Employees:* 152
*Net Worth:* £1,595,181 *Total Assets:* £5,890,012
*Registered Office:* 14 Ram Boulevard, Foxhills Industrial Park, Scunthorpe, N Lincs, DN15 8QW
*Activities:* Processing and preserving of meat
*Major Shareholder:* John Walker
*Officers:* John Walker, Secretary; Simon Roderick Mumford [1969] Director/Sales Manager; John Walker [1946] Director/Food Processor

**New Daffodil Limited**
*Incorporated:* 12 August 1986
*Net Worth Deficit:* £54,000 *Total Assets:* £8,696,000
*Registered Office:* 2nd Floor, Gateway, 2 Holgate Park Drive, York, YO26 4GB
*Activities:* Real estate agencies
*Parent:* LSL Property Services PLC
*Officers:* Sapna Bedi Fitzgerlad, Secretary; Helen Elizabeth Buck [1960] Director; Adam Castleton [1964] Director; Paul Hardy [1976] Finance Director

**New Equipment Holdings Limited**
*Incorporated:* 23 February 1984 *Employees:* 75
*Net Worth:* £2,932,196 *Total Assets:* £7,459,879
*Registered Office:* Scrafton Lodge, Leyburn, N Yorks, DL8 4RR
*Activities:* Activities of other holding companies n.e.c.
*Shareholders:* Edward Neil Corner; Nigel Frederick Hartley Corner
*Officers:* Sandra Davies, Secretary; Edward Neil Corner [1937] Director; Kathleen Freda Corner [1941] Director; Nigel Frederick Hartley Corner [1965] Director

**New Kadampa Tradition - International Kadampa Buddhist Union**
*Incorporated:* 22 October 1992 *Employees:* 34
*Net Worth:* £25,356,564 *Total Assets:* £29,285,740
*Registered Office:* Conishead Priory, Priory Road, Ulverston, Cumbria, LA12 9QQ
*Activities:* Activities of religious organisations
*Officers:* Stephen Paul Cowing, Secretary; Jennifer Jane Andrews [1984] Director/Charity Administrator; Paul Anthony Philip Boseley [1955] Director/Charity Administration; Henry Freymueller Shefveland [1969] Director/Minister of Religion [American]; Heather Carolyn Wright [1957] Director/Minister of Religion

**New Month Limited**
*Incorporated:* 25 March 2008 *Employees:* 79
*Net Worth:* £2,882,564 *Total Assets:* £6,219,822
*Registered Office:* Grange Lane North, Scunthorpe, N Lincs, DN16 1BN
*Activities:* Other business support service activities n.e.c.
*Major Shareholder:* Paul Charles Weightman
*Officers:* Keith Richard Hunt, Secretary; Keith Richard Hunt [1955] Director; Marian Weightman [1954] Director; Paul Charles Weightman [1952] Director

**New R & R Ice Cream Limited**
*Incorporated:* 18 October 2010
*Net Worth:* £178,119,472 *Total Assets:* £268,284,784
*Registered Office:* Richmond House, Leeming Bar, Northallerton, N Yorks, DL7 9UL
*Activities:* Activities of production holding companies
*Parent:* R & R PIK PLC
*Officers:* Marcello Mattia, Secretary; Phil Karl Griffin [1972] Director; Marcello Mattia [1965] Director [Italian]; Ibrahim Mahmood Ibrahim Najafi [1958] Director

**Newbegin Holdings Limited**
*Incorporated:* 13 July 2016 *Employees:* 169
*Net Worth:* £4,358,074 *Total Assets:* £27,554,964
*Registered Office:* Newbegin House, 14-16 Newbegin, Beverley, E Yorks, HU17 8EG
*Activities:* Activities of head offices
*Major Shareholder:* Paul Thomas Simpson
*Officers:* Mairi Anne Simpson, Secretary; Paul Thomas Simpson [1963] Director

**Newby Foods Limited**
*Incorporated:* 2 May 2003 *Employees:* 71
*Net Worth:* £7,141,911 *Total Assets:* £8,980,258
*Registered Office:* Marylands, Newby Wiske, Northallerton, N Yorks, DL7 9ER
*Activities:* Production of meat and poultry meat products
*Shareholders:* Phillip Owen Wallace; Colin Richard Dicker
*Officers:* Paul Damian Roe, Secretary; Graham John Bishop [1957] Managing Director; Colin Richard Dicker [1953] Director; Douglas Manning [1946] Operations Director; Phillip Owen Wallace [1949] Director

**Newby Manor Estates Limited**
*Incorporated:* 18 March 1988 *Employees:* 1
*Net Worth:* £963,643 *Total Assets:* £7,140,896
*Registered Office:* 9 Brunswick Drive, Harrogate, N Yorks, HG1 2PZ
*Activities:* Buying and selling of own real estate
*Parent:* Newby Manor Investments Limited
*Officers:* Michael Leslie Madeley, Secretary; Caroline Alison Dawes [1974] Director/Teacher; Stephen John Dawes [1974] Director; Michael Leslie Madeley [1943] Director; Julia Elizabeth Urquhart [1977] Director/Full Time Parent; Shaun Christopher Urquhart [1971] Director/Teaching Assistant

**Newby Manor Investments Limited**
*Incorporated:* 26 February 1990
*Net Worth:* £6,491,520 *Total Assets:* £6,611,178
*Registered Office:* 9 Brunswick Drive, Harrogate, N Yorks, HG1 2PZ
*Activities:* Buying and selling of own real estate
*Shareholders:* Julia Elizabeth Urquhart; Caroline Alison Dawes
*Officers:* Stephen John Dawes, Secretary; Caroline Alison Dawes [1974] Director/Teacher; Stephen John Dawes [1974] Director; Michael Leslie Madeley [1943] Director; Julia Elizabeth Urquhart [1977] Director/Full Time Parent; Shaun Christopher Urquhart [1971] Director/Teacher

**Newclose Properties Limited**
*Incorporated:* 11 December 2002 *Employees:* 1
*Net Worth:* £1,274,845 *Total Assets:* £3,127,167
*Registered Office:* Helm Bank, Natland, Kendal, Cumbria, LA9 7PS
*Activities:* Other letting and operating of own or leased real estate
*Major Shareholder:* Claire Elizabeth Kubler
*Officers:* Claire Elizabeth Kubler [1982] Director

**Newincco 1072 Limited**
*Incorporated:* 7 January 2011
*Net Worth:* £18,336,000 *Total Assets:* £58,600,000
*Registered Office:* Hilmore House, Gain Lane, Bradford, W Yorks, BD3 7DL
*Activities:* Development of building projects
*Parent:* Ascot Road Watford Limited
*Officers:* Jonathan James Burke, Secretary; Jonathan James Burke [1966] Director; Joanna Louise Goff [1978] Finance Director

**Newitt & Co (Properties) Limited**
*Incorporated:* 24 August 2001
*Net Worth:* £8,954,424 *Total Assets:* £9,354,781
*Registered Office:* Rievaulx House, 1 St Marys Court, York, YO24 1AH
*Activities:* Other letting and operating of own or leased real estate
*Officers:* John Arthur Newitt, Secretary/Director; Christine Ann Newitt [1943] Director; John Arthur Newitt [1939] Director

**Newitt & Co Limited**
*Incorporated:* 14 October 2002 *Employees:* 29
*Net Worth:* £1,153,705 *Total Assets:* £3,709,940
*Registered Office:* Claxton Hall, Flaxton, York, YO60 7RE
*Activities:* Retail sale of sports goods, fishing gear, camping goods, boats and bicycles
*Shareholder:* Nicholas John Newitt
*Officers:* Nicholas John Newitt, Secretary; Frank Swiers Newitt [1963] Director; Joanna Mary Newitt [1962] Director; Lisa Joanne Newitt [1970] Director; Nicholas John Newitt [1965] Director

**Newlands Community Association**
*Incorporated:* 20 December 2001
*Net Worth:* £5,955,219 *Total Assets:* £5,958,119
*Registered Office:* Inspire Bradford Business Park, Newlands House, One Newlands Way, Bradford, W Yorks, BD10 0JE
*Activities:* Other service activities n.e.c.
*Officers:* Susan Patricia Hodgson, Secretary; Pauline Jeannette Bland [1961] Director/Marketing & Development Manager; Daniel Fraser Davison [1967] Director/IT Telecoms Consultant; Susan Patricia Hodgson [1958] Director/Project Manager; Maureen Holmes [1960] Director/Centre Manager; Robert Sherry [1955] Director; Iwan Lloyd Williams [1965] Director/Financial Adviser

**Newlands Community Association (Trading) Limited**
*Incorporated:* 7 March 2002 *Employees:* 6
*Net Worth:* £3,147,480 *Total Assets:* £6,015,645
*Registered Office:* Newlands House, One Inspire Bradford Business Park, Newlands Way, Bradford, W Yorks, BD10 0JE
*Activities:* Renting and leasing of other machinery, equipment and tangible goods n.e.c.
*Parent:* Newlands Community Association
*Officers:* Susan Patricia Hodgson, Secretary; Susan Patricia Hodgson [1958] Director/Manager; Robert John Sherry [1955] Director/Volunteer; Iwan Lloyd Williams [1965] Director/Consultant

**Newlay Concrete Limited**
*Incorporated:* 20 March 2008 *Employees:* 65
*Net Worth:* £1,820,986 *Total Assets:* £12,422,077
*Registered Office:* Thornhill Works, Calder Road, Ravensthorpe, Dewsbury, W Yorks, WF12 9HY
*Activities:* Other mining and quarrying n.e.c.
*Officers:* Tracey Frances Beaumont, Secretary; David Michael Beaumont [1958] Director

**Newlincs Development Limited**
*Incorporated:* 4 May 1999 *Employees:* 2
*Net Worth:* £4,304,601 *Total Assets:* £20,158,892
*Registered Office:* Integrated Waste Management Facility, South Marsh Road, Stallingborough, N E Lincs, DN41 8BZ
*Activities:* Other business support service activities n.e.c.
*Officers:* George Richard Guthrie, Secretary; Anne Cecile Eleonore Loussouarn [1971] Director of Finance and Performance [French]; Laurent Magnin [1973] Director [French]

**Newly Weds Foods Acquisition Limited**
*Incorporated:* 6 February 2002 *Employees:* 472
*Net Worth:* £38,997,000 *Total Assets:* £61,465,000
*Registered Office:* Owl Lane, Ossett, W Yorks, WF5 9AX
*Activities:* Other business support service activities n.e.c.
*Major Shareholder:* Charles Angell
*Officers:* John Joseph Seely, Secretary; Charles Angell [1941] Director [American]; John Joseph Seely [1955] Director [American]

**Newly Weds Foods Limited**
*Incorporated:* 20 May 1942 *Employees:* 472
*Net Worth:* £16,838,000 *Total Assets:* £48,375,000
*Registered Office:* Owl Lane, Ossett, W Yorks, WF5 9AX
*Activities:* Manufacture of other food products n.e.c.
*Parent:* Newly Weds Foods Acquisition Limited
*Officers:* John Joseph Seely, Secretary; Charles Angell [1941] Director [American]; Brian Edward Johnson [1955] Director [American]; John Joseph Seely [1955] Director [American]

**Newman Properties Limited**
*Incorporated:* 24 September 1982 *Employees:* 1
*Previous:* Stephen Newman (Properties) Limited
*Net Worth:* £3,323,937 *Total Assets:* £3,447,965
*Registered Office:* 10 The Waterfront, Queens Parade, Cleethorpes, N E Lincs, DN35 0FF
*Activities:* Development of building projects
*Major Shareholder:* Stephen Robert Newman
*Officers:* Christopher Stephen Charles Newman [1987] Director; David Frederick Paul Newman [1989] Director; Peter Kenneth George Newman [1985] Director; Stephen Robert Newman [1949] Director/Builder

**Newport Buildings LLP**
*Incorporated:* 9 January 2007
*Net Worth:* £14,112,796 *Total Assets:* £23,144,372
*Registered Office:* Dianthus House, Common Lane, North Cave, Brough, N Humbers, HU15 2FT
*Officers:* Henricus Johannes Antonius Maria Brockhoff [1959] Member; Pieter Willem de Raadt [1968] LLP Member; Arnold Kloostra [1971] LLP Member; Niels Van Der Plas [1970] LLP Member; Jan Paul Christiaan Rijke [1964] LLP Member; Hendrik Johannes Gerardus Salome [1954] LLP Member; Arie Martinus Van Duyn [1951] LLP Member

**Newquip Limited**
*Incorporated:* 27 May 2005 *Employees:* 27
*Net Worth:* £5,075,797 *Total Assets:* £16,334,907
*Registered Office:* NQ House, Conygarth Way, Leeming Bar Business Park, Northallerton, N Yorks, DL7 9EE
*Activities:* Wholesale of agricultural machinery, equipment and supplies
*Shareholders:* Adam Dye; James Dye
*Officers:* Adam Dye [1980] Director

**Newroc Ltd**
*Incorporated:* 19 November 2003
*Net Worth:* £1,585,795 *Total Assets:* £3,559,408
*Registered Office:* 7 Mercury Road, Gallowfields Trading Estate, Richmond, N Yorks, DL10 4TQ
*Activities:* Activities of construction holding companies
*Major Shareholder:* Graeme Richard Newton
*Officers:* Joanne Katherine Newton, Secretary; Graeme Richard Newton [1968] Director

**Newross Impex Limited**
*Incorporated:* 26 November 1980 *Employees:* 248
*Net Worth:* £4,522,890 *Total Assets:* £11,126,621
*Registered Office:* 2 Cross Green Garth, Cross Green Industrial Estate, Leeds, LS9 0SF
*Activities:* Wholesale of clothing and footwear
*Parent:* General Universal Establishment
*Officers:* Sarah Jane Roy, Secretary/Accountant; Hongmei Chen [1969] Director/Buyer [Chinese]; Jonathon Cope [1986] Director/Student [Israeli]; Simon Cope [1967] Director; Paul Marlow [1963] Retail Director; Kevin Philbin [1959] Director/Solicitor; Robert Charles Siswick [1963] Director

**Newsmith Stainless Limited**
*Incorporated:* 22 December 1969 *Employees:* 108
*Net Worth:* £6,201,279 *Total Assets:* £10,559,840
*Registered Office:* Fountain Works, Child Lane, Roberttown, Liversedge, W Yorks, WF15 7PH
*Activities:* Manufacture of other general-purpose machinery n.e.c.
*Shareholders:* Shelia Newton; Robert John Newton
*Officers:* John Chappell, Secretary; Helen Mandy Newton [1966] Commercial Director; Jonathan Richard Newton [1966] Detergents Director; Robert John Newton [1963] Director; Sheila Newton [1934] Director; Bhupendra Patel [1956] Technical Director

**Harold Newsome Holdings Limited**
*Incorporated:* 28 February 2012
*Net Worth:* £5,779,137 *Total Assets:* £6,379,583
*Registered Office:* Paragon Works, Elder Road, Bramley, Leeds, LS13 4DJ
*Activities:* Activities of head offices
*Major Shareholder:* James Peter Newsome
*Officers:* Clive Peter Newsome [1954] Director/Engineer; James Newsome [1982] Director/Structural Engineer; Paul Newsome [1951] Director/Engineer

**Harold Newsome Limited**
*Incorporated:* 1 May 1937 *Employees:* 41
*Net Worth:* £6,131,797 *Total Assets:* £8,037,933
*Registered Office:* Paragon Works, Elder Road, Bramley, Leeds, LS13 4DJ
*Activities:* Manufacture of metal structures and parts of structures
*Parent:* Harold Newsome Holdings Limited
*Officers:* Gavin Cunningham [1968] Director; Clive Peter Newsome [1954] Director/Engineer; James Peter Newsome [1982] Director/Structural Engineer; Paul Newsome [1951] Director/Engineer; Javinder Singh Suryavansi [1961] Director/Draughtsman

**Nexus Vehicle Holdings Limited**
*Incorporated:* 31 December 2007
*Net Worth Deficit:* £11,945,777 *Total Assets:* £13,119,099
*Registered Office:* Nexus House, Richardshaw Lane, Stanningley, Pudsey, W Yorks, LS28 6AA
*Activities:* Activities of other holding companies n.e.c.
*Parent:* Axis Bidco Limited
*Officers:* Ian Cherry, Secretary; David Martin Brennan [1966] Director/Chief Executive; Ian Cherry [1970] Finance Director; John Christian Ellis [1977] Director

**Nexus Vehicle Management Ltd.**
*Incorporated:* 31 August 1999 *Employees:* 103
*Net Worth:* £24,093,862 *Total Assets:* £37,461,516
*Registered Office:* 141 Richardshaw Lane, Stanningley, Pudsey, W Yorks, LS28 6AA
*Activities:* Renting and leasing of cars and light motor vehicles
*Parent:* Nexus Vehicle Holdings Limited
*Officers:* Ian Cherry, Secretary; David Martin Brennan [1966] Director/Chief Executive; Ian Cherry [1970] Finance Director; John Christian Ellis [1977] Director

**NHP Limited**
*Incorporated:* 11 March 1993
*Net Worth:* £369,454,816 *Total Assets:* £370,082,240
*Registered Office:* Southgate House, Archer Street, Darlington, Co Durham, DL3 6AH
*Activities:* Activities of head offices
*Parent:* Libra Careco Limited
*Officers:* James Justin Hutchens [1974] Director [American]; David Andrew Smith [1974] Director

**NHP Management Limited**
*Incorporated:* 5 December 1996 *Employees:* 2
*Net Worth Deficit:* £5,213,374 *Total Assets:* £14,994,578
*Registered Office:* Southgate House, Archer Street, Darlington, Co Durham, DL3 6AH
*Activities:* Management consultancy activities other than financial management
*Parent:* NHP Limited
*Officers:* James Justin Hutchens [1974] Director [American]; David Andrew Smith [1974] Director

**NHP Operations (York) Limited**
*Incorporated:* 6 December 2002
*Net Worth:* £7,323,799 *Total Assets:* £10,984,877
*Registered Office:* Southgate House, Archer Street, Darlington, Co Durham, DL3 6AH
*Activities:* Other business support service activities n.e.c.
*Parent:* NHP Limited
*Officers:* James Justin Hutchens [1974] Director [American]; David Andrew Smith [1974] Director

**NHP Securities No. 1 Limited**
*Incorporated:* 19 September 1995
*Net Worth:* £154,499,728 *Total Assets:* £179,075,328
*Registered Office:* Southgate House, Archer Street, Darlington, Co Durham, DL3 6AH
*Activities:* Other business support service activities n.e.c.
*Parent:* NHP Limited
*Officers:* James Justin Hutchens [1974] Director [American]; David Andrew Smith [1974] Director

**NHP Securities No. 2 Limited**
*Incorporated:* 5 December 1996
*Net Worth:* £77,649,456 *Total Assets:* £87,624,400
*Registered Office:* Southgate House, Archer Street, Darlington, Co Durham, DL3 6AH
*Activities:* Other business support service activities n.e.c.
*Parent:* NHP Limited
*Officers:* James Justin Hutchens [1974] Director [American]; David Andrew Smith [1974] Director

**NHP Securities No. 3 Limited**
*Incorporated:* 5 December 1996
*Net Worth:* £364,319,808 *Total Assets:* £672,915,008
*Registered Office:* Southgate House, Archer Street, Darlington, Co Durham, DL3 6AH
*Activities:* Other business support service activities n.e.c.
*Parent:* NHP Limited
*Officers:* James Justin Hutchens [1974] Director [American]; David Andrew Smith [1974] Director

**NIC Services Group Limited**
*Incorporated:* 15 March 2004 *Employees:* 4,124
*Net Worth:* £1,019,545 *Total Assets:* £20,897,418
*Registered Office:* Hoyland House, Forge Lane, Armley, Leeds, LS12 2HQ
*Activities:* Combined facilities support activities
*Shareholders:* Gordon Hoyland Spencer; Jacqueline Elsie Spencer
*Officers:* Simon Robert Tidswell, Secretary; Kenneth Henry Atherton [1962] National Operations Director; John Pinnick [1953] Managing Director; Gordon Hoyland Spencer [1932] Director; Jacqueline Elsie Spencer [1938] Director; John David Spencer [1957] Director/Chief Executive Officer; Simon Robert Tidswell [1966] Finance Director

**Michael Nichol-Smith Limited**
*Incorporated:* 16 June 2010
*Net Worth:* £99,768 *Total Assets:* £3,121,033
*Registered Office:* 19 The Square, Retford, Notts, DN22 6DH
*Activities:* Non-trading company
*Major Shareholder:* Michael Nichol-Smith
*Officers:* Michael Nichol-Smith [1954] Director/Civil Engineer

**Nickle Holdings Limited**
*Incorporated:* 15 July 2014 *Employees:* 61
*Net Worth:* £6,422,375 *Total Assets:* £23,754,636
*Registered Office:* Crosby Grange, Ferry Road West, Scunthorpe, N Lincs, DN15 8UH
*Activities:* Activities of head offices
*Major Shareholder:* Carl Richard Foster
*Officers:* Carl Richard Foster [1966] Director/Engineer; Michelle Wainwright [1973] Director

**Nidd Transport Limited**
*Incorporated:* 16 August 1984 *Employees:* 64
*Net Worth:* £2,253,130 *Total Assets:* £4,210,511
*Registered Office:* 2 Mount Parade, Harrogate, N Yorks, HG1 1BX
*Activities:* Freight transport by road
*Major Shareholder:* Antony John White
*Officers:* Heather Jane Glegg, Secretary; Steven James Curtis [1958] Director/Business Development; Heather Jane Glegg [1969] Finance Director; Joanna Lynn Mortimer [1958] Director/Human Resources; Anthony White [1954] Director/Road Haulier

**Nidec SR Drives Ltd.**
*Incorporated:* 12 September 1980 *Employees:* 47
*Net Worth:* £4,297,940 *Total Assets:* £6,723,260
*Registered Office:* East Park House, Otley Road, Harrogate, N Yorks, HG3 1PR
*Activities:* Other professional, scientific and technical activities n.e.c.
*Parent:* Nidec Motor Holdings Corporation
*Officers:* Paul Andrew Rawlins, Secretary; Sidney John Ambort [1960] Director/Divisional President [American]; Geoffrey Thomas Brown [1955] Director; Stephen Paul Cummins [1969] Director/General Manager; Paul Andrew Rawlins [1965] Director/Accountant; Michael Paul Tankard [1970] Sales Director; Dr Michael James Turner [1964] Director; Brian Anthony Weubbels [1972] Director/Chief Financial Officer [American]

**Nightjar Sustainable Power Limited**
*Incorporated:* 14 April 2014
*Net Worth:* £6,123,738 *Total Assets:* £8,106,106
*Registered Office:* Canal Head North, Kendal, Cumbria, LA9 7BZ
*Activities:* Other specialised construction activities n.e.c.
*Parent:* TT Nominees Limited
*Officers:* Charles William Nepean Crewdson [1964] Director; Carl Peter Crompton [1973] Director; David Benjamin Freeder [1981] Investment Director; Matthew Justin Hazell [1971] Director

**Niko (Int) Limited**
*Incorporated:* 26 March 2004 *Employees:* 66
*Net Worth:* £1,501,000 *Total Assets:* £9,616,000
*Registered Office:* Hamnett House, Gibbet Street, Halifax, W Yorks, HX2 0AX
*Activities:* Manufacture of other plastic products
*Officers:* Antony Wood, Secretary/Director; David Ian Cullen [1966] Director; Michael Duggleby [1972] Director; Ruth Louise Jackson [1968] Director/Accountant; Antony Wood [1973] Director

**Niko Extrusions Limited**
*Incorporated:* 4 February 1981 *Employees:* 58
*Net Worth:* £4,024,210 *Total Assets:* £5,690,069
*Registered Office:* Davison Group, Springmill Street, Bradford, W Yorks, BD5 7HF
*Activities:* Other letting and operating of own or leased real estate
*Shareholders:* Michael Terence Davison; Richard Charles Davison
*Officers:* Michael Terence Davison, Secretary/Sales Agent; Christopher Michael Davison [1980] Director; Michael Terence Davison [1956] Director/Sales Agent; Richard Charles Davison [1960] Director/Sales Agent

**Nilerace Limited**
*Incorporated:* 2 August 2004 *Employees:* 2
*Net Worth:* £70,362,496 *Total Assets:* £70,569,888
*Registered Office:* 84 Albion Street, Leeds, LS1 6AG
*Activities:* Other letting and operating of own or leased real estate
*Parent:* Akari Care Group Limited
*Officers:* Oliver James Lightowlers [1972] Director/Chartered Accountant

**Nimbus Building Products Limited**
*Incorporated:* 30 April 2003 *Employees:* 57
*Net Worth:* £3,639,220 *Total Assets:* £16,738,498
*Registered Office:* Hunt Street, Whitwood Mere, Castleford, W Yorks, WF10 1NS
*Activities:* Activities of head offices
*Shareholders:* Glenn Monkman; Mike Lundy
*Officers:* Paul George Almond, Secretary; Michael Anthony Lundy [1952] Director/Design Engineer; Glenn Monkman [1957] Director/Manager

**Ninehundred Communications Group Limited**
*Incorporated:* 26 July 1983 *Employees:* 86
*Previous:* Nine Hundred Communications Group Limited
*Net Worth:* £2,169,746 *Total Assets:* £3,719,733
*Registered Office:* White Rose Way, Doncaster Carr, Doncaster, S Yorks, DN4 5JH
*Activities:* Wholesale of radio, television goods & electrical household appliances (other than records, tapes, CDs)
*Officers:* Glinys Braithwaite, Secretary; Anthony Bellas [1954] Director; Victoria Bellas [1981] Director/Administration Manager; Lucy Bellas-Crookes [1980] Director/Administration Manager; Glinys Braithwaite [1956] Director; Robert Rees [1958] Managing Director; Thomas Stephen Thurlow [1985] Director

**Nippon Gases UK Limited**
*Incorporated:* 6 January 2016 *Employees:* 52
*Previous:* Praxair Gases UK Ltd
*Net Worth:* £32,288,000 *Total Assets:* £44,414,000
*Registered Office:* Gresley Way, Immingham Docks, Immingham, N E Lincs, DN40 2NT
*Activities:* Manufacture of other inorganic basic chemicals
*Officers:* Mathieu Amar [1975] Managing Director France, UK, Ireland [French]; Pedro Mazarrasa Llosa [1983] Director [Spanish]

**Nippon Gohsei UK Ltd.**
*Incorporated:* 16 March 2001 *Employees:* 125
*Net Worth:* £104,661,632 *Total Assets:* £144,577,264
*Registered Office:* Soarnol House, Saltend, Hull, HU12 8DS
*Activities:* Manufacture of plastics in primary forms
*Parent:* Nippon Synthetic Chemical Company Ltd
*Officers:* Peter Michael Des Forges [1965] Director; Gisela Meyer [1954] Director [German]; Yoshiharu Nagao [1959] Director [Japanese]; Takuya Sugimoto [1966] Director [Japanese]; Kazunori Takada [1956] Director [Japanese]; Hiroshi Yamanishi [1963] Director [Japanese]

**Nisa Retail Limited**
*Incorporated:* 29 May 1970 *Employees:* 312
*Net Worth:* £18,832,000 *Total Assets:* £193,080,000
*Registered Office:* Member Support Centre, Waldo Way, Normanby Enterprise Park, Scunthorpe, N Lincs, DN15 9GE
*Activities:* Activities of business and employers membership organisations
*Officers:* Caroline Jane Sellers, Secretary; James Antony Corbett Clark [1968] Director/Accountant; Steven Nuttall [1976] Finance Director; Kenneth Ian Towle [1964] Director/Retail CEO

**Nizh Yug (UK) LLP**
*Incorporated:* 19 December 2011
*Net Worth:* £1,214,120 *Total Assets:* £12,731,267
*Registered Office:* Triune Court, Monks Cross Drive, York, YO32 9GZ
*Officers:* Ramil Mavlyutov [1973] Member

**NK Chemicals Europe Limited**
*Incorporated:* 6 November 1998 *Employees:* 13
*Net Worth:* £3,301,816 *Total Assets:* £4,590,832
*Registered Office:* Jubilee Way, Grange Moor, Wakefield, W Yorks, WF4 4TD
*Activities:* Wholesale of chemical products
*Shareholders:* Ian Johnson; Jeannette Johnson
*Officers:* Jeannette Johnson, Secretary; Ian Johnson [1957] Director; Jeannette Johnson [1953] Director; Wolf Torsten Pieschnick [1965] Director [German]; Hidde Van Der Wal [1960] Director [Dutch]

**NL Commercials Holdings Limited**
*Incorporated:* 20 July 2015
*Net Worth:* £14,644,485 *Total Assets:* £27,305,426
*Registered Office:* Rouse Mill, Rouse Mill Lane, Batley, W Yorks, WF17 5QB
*Activities:* Renting and leasing of trucks and other heavy vehicles
*Major Shareholder:* Nigel Lella
*Officers:* Nigel Lella [1956] Director; Wayne Lella [1979] Director

**NL Commercials Management Ltd**
*Incorporated:* 14 January 2016
*Net Worth:* £56,041 *Total Assets:* £3,295,819
*Registered Office:* Rouse Mill, Rouse Mill Lane, Batley, W Yorks, WF17 5QB
*Activities:* Renting and leasing of cars and light motor vehicles
*Officers:* Nigel Lella [1956] Director; Wayne Lella [1979] Director

**NMT Limited**
*Incorporated:* 15 January 1998 *Employees:* 3
*Net Worth:* £2,307,377 *Total Assets:* £5,563,253
*Registered Office:* Unit 6 Devonshire House, Devonshire Avenue, Leeds, LS8 1AY
*Activities:* Other letting and operating of own or leased real estate
*Officers:* Martin Marshall Mann, Secretary; Nicola Isobelle Fletcher [1973] Director/Housewife

**Nobia Holdings UK Limited**
*Incorporated:* 21 March 2001 *Employees:* 2,338
*Net Worth:* £159,656,992 *Total Assets:* £335,708,992
*Registered Office:* c/o Magnet Limited, 3 Allington Way, Yarm Road Business Park, Darlington, Co Durham, DL1 4XT
*Activities:* Other manufacturing n.e.c.
*Parent:* Nobia AB
*Officers:* Nicola Jane Hardcastle, Secretary; Anjum Ahmed [1970] Director; Daniel Arthur Edward Carr [1975] Finance Director; Nicola Jane Hardcastle [1965] Director/Company Secretary; Peter Kane [1965] Managing Director; Kristoffer Ljungfelt [1977] Director [Swedish]; Paul David Woolston [1963] Director

**Wilf Noble Building Supplies Limited**
*Incorporated:* 18 May 2000 *Employees:* 27
*Net Worth:* £2,048,256 *Total Assets:* £3,171,716
*Registered Office:* Sneaton Lane, Ruswarp, Whitby, N Yorks, YO22 5HL
*Activities:* Wholesale of wood, construction materials and sanitary equipment
*Shareholder:* Wilfred Leslie Noble
*Officers:* Wilfred Leslie Noble, Secretary; Catherine May Noble [1978] Director; James Robert Noble [1981] Director; Wilfred Leslie Noble [1933] Director/Contractor

**D. Noble Limited**
*Incorporated:* 16 March 1966 *Employees:* 55
*Net Worth:* £11,719,299 *Total Assets:* £17,339,764
*Registered Office:* Noble House, Perseverance Street, Castleford, W Yorks, WF10 1LD
*Activities:* Construction of domestic buildings
*Major Shareholder:* Dennis Noble
*Officers:* Barbara Noble, Secretary; Barbara Noble [1937] Director; Christopher David Noble [1962] Managing Director; Dennis Noble [1935] Director (Chairman)

**Nobleoak Limited**
*Incorporated:* 12 June 1992 *Employees:* 51
*Net Worth:* £1,677,364 *Total Assets:* £3,732,759
*Registered Office:* Westmoreland House, Westmoreland Street, Hull, HU2 0DJ
*Activities:* Wholesale of hardware, plumbing and heating equipment and supplies
*Major Shareholder:* Malcolm Charles Walker
*Officers:* Lee Davies, Secretary; Lee Davies [1972] Financial Director; George William Griffin [1956] Production Director; Karen Ann Walker [1961] Director; Malcolm Charles Walker [1948] Director/Company Manager; Patricia May Walker [1948] Director/Company Secretary; Shane Malcolm Walker [1972] Director/Contracts Manager

**Non-Standard Finance PLC**
*Incorporated:* 8 July 2014 *Employees:* 678
*Net Worth:* £232,988,000 *Total Assets:* £447,908,000
*Registered Office:* 7 Turnberry Park Road, Gildersome, Morley, Leeds, LS27 7LE
*Activities:* Activities of financial services holding companies
*Officers:* Sarah Louise Day, Secretary; Niall Booker [1958] Director; Miles Marius Cresswell Turner [1962] Director/Partner; John Philip de Blocq Van Kuffeler [1949] Director [Dutch]; Charles Henry Gregson [1947] Director; Professor Heather Jane McGregor [1962] Director; Nicholas John Teunon [1966] Director/Chief Financial Officer

**Non-Standard Finance Subsidiary II Limited**
*Incorporated:* 25 July 2015
*Net Worth:* £50,931,772 *Total Assets:* £95,067,208
*Registered Office:* 7 Turnberry Park Road, Gildersome, Morley, Leeds, LS27 7LE
*Activities:* Activities of financial services holding companies
*Parent:* NSF Finco Limited
*Officers:* Sarah Louise Day, Secretary; Miles Marius Cresswell-Turner [1962] Director; John Philip de Blocq Van Kuffeler [1949] Director [Dutch]; Nicholas John Teunon [1966] Director

**Non-Standard Finance Subsidiary III Limited**
*Incorporated:* 16 October 2015
*Net Worth:* £161,291,008 *Total Assets:* £176,291,008
*Registered Office:* 7 Turnberry Park Road, Gildersome, Morley, Leeds, LS27 7LE
*Activities:* Activities of financial services holding companies
*Parent:* NSF Finco Limited
*Officers:* Sarah Louise Day, Secretary; Miles Marius Cresswell-Turner [1962] Director; John Philip de Blocq Van Kuffeler [1949] Director [Dutch]; Nicholas John Teunon [1966] Director/Chief Financial Officer

**Nordic Fashions One Limited**
*Incorporated:* 17 May 2012
*Net Worth:* £2,416,971 *Total Assets:* £3,170,169
*Registered Office:* 23 Douglas Towers, Radwell Drive, Bradford, BD5 0QP
*Activities:* Non-specialised wholesale trade
*Officers:* Andrew Guilford [1980] Director/Manager

**Nordika Design Limited**
*Incorporated:* 1 April 1997 *Employees:* 5
*Net Worth:* £4,074,825 *Total Assets:* £4,783,916
*Registered Office:* High Rigg, Panorama Drive, Ilkley, W Yorks, LS29 9RA
*Activities:* Wholesale of furniture, carpets and lighting equipment
*Major Shareholder:* Benjamin Croft Ridgway
*Officers:* Benjamin Croft Ridgway [1969] Director/Manufacturers Agent

**Normanby Estate Company Limited (The)**
*Incorporated:* 22 July 1920 *Employees:* 7
*Net Worth:* £11,973,076 *Total Assets:* £14,659,411
*Registered Office:* Estate Office, Main Street, Normanby, Scunthorpe, N Lincs, DN15 9HS
*Activities:* Other service activities n.e.c.
*Major Shareholder:* Reginald Adrian Berkeley Sheffield
*Officers:* Sir Reginald Adrian Berkeley Sheffield, Secretary; Sir Reginald Adrian Berkeley Sheffield [1946] Director; Robert Charles Berkeley Sheffield [1984] Director; Lady Victoria Penelope Sheffield [1949] Director

**Normanton Golf Club Limited**
*Incorporated:* 16 April 1980 *Employees:* 22
*Net Worth:* £3,029,481 *Total Assets:* £3,297,147
*Registered Office:* Hatfeild Hall, Aberford Road, Stanley, Wakefield, W Yorks, WF3 4JP
*Activities:* Activities of sport clubs
*Officers:* Andrew Steven Booth [1960] Director/Retired; Andrew Hall [1958] Director; Richard Poynton [1954] Director/Retired; John Watson [1946] Director; Michael Edward Francis Withers [1937] Director/Retired

**Normanton Laminating Services Limited**
*Incorporated:* 3 October 1978 *Employees:* 45
*Net Worth:* £3,057,302 *Total Assets:* £6,710,266
*Registered Office:* Lincoln Road, Pocklington Industrial Estate, Pocklington, York, YO42 1NR
*Activities:* Manufacture of other parts and accessories for motor vehicles
*Shareholders:* David Robert Smith; Daniel Nicholas Oates
*Officers:* Carol Mary Chamberlain, Secretary; Daniel Nicholas Oates [1960] Director; David Robert Smith [1965] Managing Director

**K.M. Norris Limited**
*Incorporated:* 24 September 1971
*Net Worth:* £3,590,317 *Total Assets:* £4,267,922
*Registered Office:* West Beck House, West Lane, Askwith, N Yorks, LS21 2JQ
*Activities:* Construction of domestic buildings
*Shareholders:* Adam Walker Norris; Emma Laurena Wilson; Matthew Harold Norris
*Officers:* Matthew Harold Norris, Secretary; Adam Walker Norris [1971] Director/Foreman; Matthew Harold Norris [1973] Director/Builder; Emma Laurena Wilson [1969] Director

**Nortech Foods Limited**
*Incorporated:* 9 December 1982 *Employees:* 75
*Net Worth:* £5,202,345 *Total Assets:* £16,607,925
*Registered Office:* Ings Road, Doncaster, S Yorks, DN5 9TL
*Activities:* Manufacture of oils and fats
*Parent:* Saria Limited
*Officers:* Andrew Richard Smith [1962] Director

**North Bay Leisure Limited**
*Incorporated:* 9 November 2004 *Employees:* 13
*Net Worth:* £3,880,274 *Total Assets:* £8,879,146
*Registered Office:* Marton Hall, Church Lane, Sewerby, Bridlington, E Yorks, YO15 1DS
*Activities:* Other holiday and other collective accommodation
*Parent:* Shorewood Leisure Group Limited
*Officers:* Neil Willson, Secretary; David Robert Allison [1960] Director/Park Operator; Neil Willson [1960] Managing Director

**North Carr Collaborative Academy Trust**
*Incorporated:* 8 February 2013 *Employees:* 201
*Net Worth:* £15,663,062 *Total Assets:* £17,527,096
*Registered Office:* Lothian Way, North Bransholme, Hull, HU7 5DD
*Activities:* Primary education
*Officers:* Janet Drinkall [1958] Director/Headteacher; Katherine Vivienne Rowe [1954] Director/Head of Safeguarding Hull City Football Club; Kenneth Sainty [1951] Director/Retired; Graham John Shaw [1957] Director/Occupational Health & Safety Consultant; Geoffrey David Weston [1947] Director/Retired; Jane Wilson [1956] Director/Retired; Adele Deborah Wrapson [1955] Director/Company Secretary

**The North Halifax Grammar School Academy Trust**
*Incorporated:* 10 May 2011 *Employees:* 129
*Net Worth:* £11,743,000 *Total Assets:* £13,678,000
*Registered Office:* The North Halifax Grammar School, Moorbottom Road, Illingworth, Halifax, W Yorks, HX2 9SU
*Activities:* General secondary education
*Officers:* Emma Sarah Wild Casson, Secretary; Rinat Abdrasilov [1981] Director/Senior Manager [Kyrgyz/British]; Amanda Cade [1974] Director/Accountant; Mary Alice Carrigan [1948] Director/Retired; Kolleen Marie Drury [1970] Director/General Manager; Victoria Harrison-Law [1984] Director/Teacher; Roger Hartley [1947] Director/Retired; Michael Philip Pitts [1964] Director/Businessman; Anand Prathivadi Bhayankaram [1963] Director/Reader in Environmental Economics and Public Policy; Carole Sankey [1961] Director/Teacher; Nicola Sheehan [1971] Director/Head of Therapies; Christopher Walker [1994] Director/Teacher

**North Killingholme Storage Limited**
*Incorporated:* 25 September 1978
*Net Worth:* £5,477,205 *Total Assets:* £7,484,063
*Registered Office:* Lancaster House, Lancaster Approach, North Killingholme, N Lincs, DN40 3JY
*Activities:* Operation of warehousing and storage facilities for land transport activities
*Parent:* Salfina Limited
*Officers:* Jonathan Peter Ranby Nuttall, Secretary; Jonathan Peter Ranby Nuttall [1965] Director

**North Lincs Property Limited**
*Incorporated:* 25 August 1998 *Employees:* 4
*Net Worth:* £11,620,133 *Total Assets:* £20,700,908
*Registered Office:* Sandtoft Industrial Estate, Belton, Doncaster, S Yorks, DN9 1PN
*Activities:* Operation of gravel and sand pits; mining of clays and kaolin
*Shareholder:* Richard John Mills
*Officers:* Karen Mills, Secretary; Richard John Mills [1965] Director

**North Sea Ventilation Limited**
*Incorporated:* 26 July 2012 *Employees:* 74
*Net Worth:* £881,053 *Total Assets:* £3,699,885
*Registered Office:* Charrington Park, West Carr Lane, Hull, HU7 0BW
*Activities:* Manufacture of non-domestic cooling and ventilation equipment
*Parent:* Dynac UK Limited
*Officers:* Paul Hart [1952] Director/Mechanical Engineer; Azmi Nik [1983] Director/Accountant [Malaysian]; Abdul Rahman Bin Mohamed Shariff [1957] Director/Company Executive [Malaysian]; David Paul Young [1959] Director/Engineer

**North York Moors Historical Railway Trust Limited**
*Incorporated:* 31 December 1971 *Employees:* 111
*Net Worth:* £8,763,326 *Total Assets:* £14,445,776
*Registered Office:* Pickering Station, Pickering, N Yorks, YO18 7AJ
*Activities:* Other urban, suburban or metropolitan passenger land transport (not underground, metro or similar)
*Officers:* Dr Simon Brockington, Secretary; John Philip Cureton Bailey [1947] Director/Retired; Andrew Peter Bellwood [1953] Director/Retired; Philip Martin Benham [1949] Director/Retired; Dr Simon Brockington [1971] Director/Civil Servant; Robert Murray Brown [1947] Director/Journalist; Alexander John Bruce [1954] Director/Retired Railway Supervisor; Andrew James Bullivant [1961] Director/HGV Driver; Christopher Cubitt [1946] Director/Train Driver; James Richard Dedicoat [1946] Director/Bank Manager; Christopher James Dickerson [1951] Director/Retired; Ian Christopher Foot [1950] Director/Retired; Colin Graham [1949] Director/Retired; Jennifer Halmshaw [1949] Director/Retired; Andrew John Scott [1949] Museum Director; Bernard Howard Warr [1944] Director/Retired; Alan Whitehouse [1955] Director/Retired

**North Yorkshire Mortgages Limited**
*Incorporated:* 30 March 1988
*Net Worth:* £11,820,000 *Total Assets:* £293,478,016
*Registered Office:* The Bailey, Skipton, N Yorks, BD23 1DN
*Activities:* Activities of mortgage finance companies
*Parent:* Skipton Building Society
*Officers:* John Joseph Gibson, Secretary; Ian Geoffrey Moore [1968] Director of Specialist Lending; Andrew Walter Nelson [1964] Director/Accountant; Henry Varney [1972] Director/General Manager

**North Yorkshire Timber Company Limited**
*Incorporated:* 10 May 1979 *Employees:* 199
*Net Worth:* £4,067,071 *Total Assets:* £11,146,615
*Registered Office:* Standard House, Thurston Road, Northallerton Business Park, Northallerton, N Yorks, DL6 2NA
*Activities:* Wholesale of wood, construction materials and sanitary equipment
*Parent:* NYT (Holdings) Limited
*Officers:* Robert Todd Barclay [1969] Director; Victor Paul Bellas [1964] Director/Timber Salesman; John Alexander George Douglas [1964] Finance Director; Nicholas Peter Kershaw [1972] Managing Director; Neil Andrew McGill [1977] Investment Director; Robert Timmens [1966] Director/Timber Salesman; Stuart Whiteford [1990] Director

**Northallerton Auctions Limited**
*Incorporated:* 9 April 1912 *Employees:* 25
*Net Worth:* £3,067,958 *Total Assets:* £3,463,569
*Registered Office:* Applegarth Mart, Romanby Road, Northallerton, N Yorks, DL7 8LZ
*Activities:* Other business support service activities n.e.c.
*Officers:* Brian Weighell, Secretary; Mark Allen Corner [1971] Director/Farmer; Charles Michael Duffus [1959] Director/Farmer; Martin Jeremy Harland [1965] Director/Farmer; Alan Francis Harrison [1951] Director/Investor; Alan Watson [1954] Director/Farmer; Brian Weighell [1958] Director

**Northamptonshire Leisure Estates Limited**
*Incorporated:* 14 December 2005
*Net Worth Deficit:* £374 *Total Assets:* £23,685,732
*Registered Office:* South Lakeland House, Main A6, Yealand Redmayne, Carnforth, Lancs, LA5 9RN
*Activities:* Activities of amusement parks and theme parks
*Parent:* Pure Leisure Group Limited
*Officers:* Paul Rossiter, Secretary; John Charles Morphet [1954] Managing Director; Paul Rossiter [1964] Director/Chartered Accountant; Gordon Alexander Walker [1964] Operations Director; Trevor James White [1952] Director/Marketing Manager

**Northcoast Seafoods Limited**
*Incorporated:* 25 September 2000 *Employees:* 27
*Net Worth:* £13,198,969 *Total Assets:* £62,163,272
*Registered Office:* Plot 12, Estate Road No 1, South Humberside Industrial Estate, Grimsby, N E Lincs, DN31 2TB
*Activities:* Wholesale of other food, including fish, crustaceans and molluscs
*Shareholders:* Nim Limited; Kangamiut Holding A/S; Fridrik Mar Thorsteinsson
*Officers:* Fridrik Mar Thorsteinsson, Secretary; Ulrik Bjerre Rasmussen [1964] Financial Director [Danish]; Fridrik Mar Thorsteinsson [1971] Director [Icelander]

**Northern Ambition Academies Trust**
*Incorporated:* 8 March 2011 *Employees:* 377
*Previous:* Airedale Academies Trust
*Net Worth:* £22,717,000 *Total Assets:* £26,628,000
*Registered Office:* Airedale Academy, Crewe Road, Airedale, Castleford, W Yorks, WF10 3JU
*Activities:* Pre-primary education
*Officers:* Anastasia Byard, Secretary; Stephen Martin Baker [1955] Trustee Director; Ranjit Das [1965] Director/Training Consultant; Elizabeth Jane Fairhurst [1971] Director/Headteacher; Stephen James Groves [1956] Director/Consultant Engineer; Robert Andrew Hall [1964] Director; Elizabeth Gail Hayden [1981] Director/HR Manager; Alison Latham [1974] Director/Self Employed; Alexander John Nicholson [1987] Director/Lecturer

**Northern Ballet Limited**
*Incorporated:* 31 January 1969 *Employees:* 123
*Net Worth:* £13,832,990 *Total Assets:* £15,609,313
*Registered Office:* 2 St Cecilia Street, Quarry Hill, Leeds, LS2 7PA
*Activities:* Performing arts
*Major Shareholder:* David Hugh Wootton
*Officers:* Judith Hartley, Secretary/Chartered Accountant; Carol Ann Arrowsmith [1954] Director; Councillor Judith Vivienne Blake [1953] Director/Leader of Leeds City Council; Daniel Evans [1973] Artistic Director; Jane Gilbert Boot [1982] Director/Investor; Jolyon Leonard Harrison [1948] Director; Elizabeth Warmington Jackson [1961] Retired Executive Director; Philip Henry Keller [1965] Director; Kevin Patrick O'Hare [1965] Director of The Royal Ballet; Cllr John Michael Procter [1966] Director/Councillor; Anita Rani [1977] Director/Television Presenter/Broadcaster; Paul Graham Smith [1977] Media Director; James William Matthew Taylor [1974] Finance Director; Sir David Hugh Wootton [1950] Director/Solicitor

**Northern Cladding Limited**
*Incorporated:* 26 February 1993 *Employees:* 20
*Net Worth:* £901,668 *Total Assets:* £4,544,325
*Registered Office:* Great North Way, York Business Park, Nether Poppleton, York, YO26 6RB
*Activities:* Construction of commercial buildings
*Officers:* Jacqueline Weston, Secretary; Robert Peter Baines [1967] Commercial Director; Peter Spink [1957] Director; David Andrew Swales [1962] Contracts Director

**Northern Commercials (Mirfield) Limited**
*Incorporated:* 25 March 1971 *Employees:* 353
*Net Worth:* £9,108,000 *Total Assets:* £45,624,000
*Registered Office:* Armytage Road, Wakefield Road Industrial Estate, Brighouse, W Yorks, HD6 1PG
*Activities:* Sale of other motor vehicles
*Parent:* Clipper Logistics PLC
*Officers:* Nigel Scott Charles Morgan, Secretary; David Arthur Hodkin [1961] Director; Steven Nicholas Parkin [1960] Director; Roger Peel [1965] Director/Dealer Principal

**Northern Crop Driers Limited**
*Incorporated:* 8 December 1977 *Employees:* 11
*Net Worth:* £3,330,374 *Total Assets:* £3,705,864
*Registered Office:* Melrose Farm, Melbourne, York, YO42 4SS
*Activities:* Growing of cereals (except rice), leguminous crops and oil seeds
*Shareholders:* John Robert Rowbottom; Eileen Mary Rowbottom; Edward John Rowbottom; Pamela Fay Dear
*Officers:* Pamela Fay Dear, Secretary; Pamela Fay Dear [1978] Director; Edward John Rowbottom [1981] Director/Farmer

**Northern Divers (Holdings) Limited**
*Incorporated:* 12 August 1977
*Net Worth:* £3,084,771 *Total Assets:* £3,417,157
*Registered Office:* Francis House, Humber Place, The Marina, Hull, HU1 1UD
*Activities:* Other letting and operating of own or leased real estate
*Shareholders:* Jane Elizabeth Sparrowe; John Sparrowe
*Officers:* Jane Elizabeth Sparrowe, Secretary; Jane Elizabeth Sparrowe [1942] Director/Company Secretary; John Ashley Sparrowe [1969] Director/Diver

**Northern Energy Supplies Limited**
*Incorporated:* 9 September 1966 *Employees:* 38
*Net Worth:* £2,687,063 *Total Assets:* £6,370,661
*Registered Office:* Energy House, Hampsthwaite, Harrogate, N Yorks, HG3 2HT
*Activities:* Wholesale of petroleum and petroleum products
*Officers:* Christopher Salisbury, Secretary; David Stephen Illingworth [1955] Director/Operations Manager; Howard Seth Illingworth [1958] Director/Chairman; Stuart Illingworth [1988] Operations Director

**Northern Eye UK Limited**
*Incorporated:* 9 September 2005 *Employees:* 1
*Net Worth:* £1,552,302 *Total Assets:* £4,348,676
*Registered Office:* Northgate, 118 North Street, Leeds, LS2 7PN
*Activities:* Other letting and operating of own or leased real estate
*Shareholders:* Avenir Works 1 Limited; Barnett & Daughters Limited
*Officers:* Aimar Lombard-Natheer, Secretary; Jeffrey Barnett [1974] Director/Property Development; Aimar Lombard Natheer [1978] Director/Property Developer

**Northern Foods Finance Limited**
*Incorporated:* 10 March 2000
*Net Worth:* £134,416,000 *Total Assets:* £140,612,000
*Registered Office:* Trinity Park House, Fox Way, Wakefield, W Yorks, WF2 8EE
*Activities:* Financial intermediation not elsewhere classified
*Parent:* Northern Foods Limited
*Officers:* Ronald Klaas Otto Kers [1969] Director/Group CEO [Dutch]; Craig Ashley Tomkinson [1982] Director/Group CFO

**Northern Foods Grocery Group Limited**
*Incorporated:* 4 May 1936 *Employees:* 2,159
*Net Worth:* £116,864,000 *Total Assets:* £254,975,008
*Registered Office:* Trinity Park House, Fox Way, Wakefield, W Yorks, WF2 8EE
*Activities:* Manufacture of rusks and biscuits; manufacture of preserved pastry goods and cakes
*Parent:* Northern Foods Limited
*Officers:* Simon Francis Barriskell [1969] Finance Director; Ranjit Singh Boparan [1966] Director; Ronald Klaas Otto Kers [1969] Director/Group CEO [Dutch]; Craig Ashley Tomkinson [1982] Director/Group CFO

**Northern Foods Limited**
*Incorporated:* 15 August 1949 *Employees:* 337
*Net Worth:* £404,865,984 *Total Assets:* £2,824,233,984
*Registered Office:* Trinity Park House, Fox Way, Wakefield, W Yorks, WF2 8EE
*Activities:* Activities of head offices
*Parent:* BH Acquisitions Limited
*Officers:* Baljinder Kaur Boparan [1968] Director; Ranjit Singh Boparan [1966] Director; Ronald Klaas Otto Kers [1969] Director/Group CEO [Dutch]; Craig Ashley Tomkinson [1982] Director/Group CFO

**Northern Gas Networks Finance PLC**
*Incorporated:* 27 September 2005
*Net Worth:* £50,000 *Total Assets:* £923,840,000
*Registered Office:* 1100 Century Way, Thorpe Park Business Park, Colton, Leeds, LS15 8TU
*Activities:* Transport via pipeline
*Parent:* Northern Gas Networks Limited
*Officers:* Michael Gregory Ashworth, Secretary; Simon Daniel Beer [1980] Director/Head of Asset Management; Loi Shun Chan [1962] Director [Chinese]; Mark John Horsley [1959] Chief Executive Officer of NGN Director; Andrew John Hunter [1958] Director; Hing Lam Kam [1946] Director [Chinese]; Duncan Nicholas MacRae [1970] Director; Neil Douglas McGee [1951] Director [Australian]; Charles Chao Chung Tsai [1957] Director and Chief Executive [Canadian]; Chi Tin Wan [1950] Director [Australian]

**Northern Gas Networks Holdings Limited**
*Incorporated:* 24 August 2004 *Employees:* 1,470
*Net Worth:* £515,600,000 *Total Assets:* £2,949,750,016
*Registered Office:* 1100 Century Way, Thorpe Park Business Park, Colton, Leeds, LS15 8TU
*Activities:* Activities of head offices
*Shareholders:* Beta Central Profits Limited; PG (April) Limited
*Officers:* Michael Gregory Ashworth, Secretary; Simon Daniel Beer [1980] Director/Head of Asset Management; Loi Shun Chan [1962] Director [Chinese]; Mark John Horsley [1959] Chief Executive Officer of NGN Director; Andrew John Hunter [1958] Director; Hing Lam Kam [1946] Director [Chinese]; Duncan Nicholas MacRae [1970] Director; Neil Douglas McGee [1951] Director [Australian]; Charles Chao Chung Tsai [1957] Director and Chief Executive [Canadian]; Chi Tin Wan [1950] Director [Australian]

**Northern Gas Networks Limited**
*Incorporated:* 30 June 2004 *Employees:* 1,470
*Net Worth:* £645,737,984 *Total Assets:* £2,988,598,016
*Registered Office:* 1100 Century Way, Thorpe Park Business Park, Colton, Leeds, LS15 8TU
*Activities:* Transport via pipeline
*Parent:* Northen Gas Networks Holdings Limited
*Officers:* Michael Gregory Ashworth, Secretary; Simon Daniel Beer [1980] Director/Head of Asset Management; John Richard Burnham [1954] Director; Loi Shun Chan [1962] Director [Chinese]; Mark John Horsley [1959] Chief Executive Officer of NGN Director; Andrew John Hunter [1958] Director; Hing Lam Kam [1946] Director [Chinese]; Duncan Nicholas MacRae [1970] Director; Neil Douglas McGee [1951] Director [Australian]; Paul Rogerson [1948] Director; Charles Chao Chung Tsai [1957] Director and Chief Executive [Canadian]; Chi Tin Wan [1950] Director [Australian]

**Northern Gas Networks Operations Limited**
*Incorporated:* 17 March 1998 *Employees:* 1,470
*Net Worth:* £506,000 *Total Assets:* £40,364,000
*Registered Office:* 1100 Century Way, Thorpe Park Business Park, Colton, Leeds, LS15 8TU
*Activities:* Other business support service activities n.e.c.
*Parent:* Northern Gas Networks Limited
*Officers:* Michael Gregory Ashworth, Secretary; Simon Daniel Beer [1980] Director/Head of Asset Management; Loi Shun Chan [1962] Director [Chinese]; Mark John Horsley [1959] Chief Executive Officer of NGN Director; Andrew John Hunter [1958] Director; Hing Lam Kam [1946] Director [Chinese]; Duncan Nicholas MacRae [1970] Director; Neil Douglas McGee [1951] Director [Australian]; Charles Chao Chung Tsai [1957] Director and Chief Executive [Canadian]; Chi Tin Wan [1950] Director [Australian]

**Northern Installations CP LLP**
*Incorporated:* 18 November 2010 *Employees:* 93
*Previous:* Northern Escalator Installations LLP
*Net Worth:* £3,175,076 *Total Assets:* £4,892,649
*Registered Office:* Aireside Business Centre, Royd Ings Avenue, Keighley, W Yorks, BD21 4BZ

**Northern Life Care Limited**
*Incorporated:* 28 November 1984 *Employees:* 1,043
*Net Worth:* £10,064,729 *Total Assets:* £12,343,750
*Registered Office:* 9 Haywra Street, Harrogate, N Yorks, HG1 5BJ
*Activities:* Other human health activities
*Officers:* Clive Patrick Reed, Secretary/Financial Director; Clive Patrick Reed [1957] Financial Director; John Howard Reed [1947] Director/Health Care Administrator

**Northern LPG Supplies Limited**
*Incorporated:* 12 January 1981 *Employees:* 23
*Net Worth:* £3,740,882 *Total Assets:* £4,780,151
*Registered Office:* Energy House, Hampsthwaite, Harrogate, N Yorks, HG3 2HT
*Activities:* Wholesale of petroleum and petroleum products
*Officers:* Christopher Salisbury, Secretary; Laura Harper [1984] Director; David Stephen Illingworth [1955] Director/Operations Manager; Edward Illingworth [1992] Director; Howard Seth Illingworth [1958] Director/Chairman; James Illingworth [1986] Director; Stuart Illingworth [1988] Director; Steven Adrian Walmsley [1957] Director/Manager

**Northern Marquees Limited**
*Incorporated:* 25 November 2002 *Employees:* 2
*Net Worth:* £1,150,296 *Total Assets:* £3,115,892
*Registered Office:* Event House, 45 Coal Pit Lane, Lower Cumberworth, Huddersfield, W Yorks, HD8 8PL
*Activities:* Other service activities n.e.c.
*Major Shareholder:* Andrew Mark Tinker
*Officers:* Nicola Jayne Tinker, Secretary; Andrew Mark Tinker [1967] Director; Nicola Jayne Tinker [1974] Director/Contracts Manager

**Northern Paper Board Limited**
*Incorporated:* 3 February 1998 *Employees:* 27
*Net Worth:* £6,522,283 *Total Assets:* £9,423,499
*Registered Office:* Engine Shed Lane, Skipton, N Yorks, BD23 1TX
*Activities:* Manufacture of paper and paperboard
*Parent:* Aurelius Equity Opportunities SE & Co KGaA
*Officers:* Paul Alistair Curran, Secretary/Director; John Francis Curran [1966] Director; Paul Alistair Curran [1967] Director; Richard Willem Pierre Eugene Houben [1974] Director [Dutch]

**Northern Powerhouse Developments Limited**
*Incorporated:* 7 January 2016 *Employees:* 18
*Net Worth Deficit:* £210,003 *Total Assets:* £19,548,508
*Registered Office:* Unit D2, Elland Riorges Link, Lowfields Business Park, Elland, W Yorks, HX5 9DG
*Activities:* Other letting and operating of own or leased real estate
*Parent:* Northern Powerhouse Developments Hotels Limited
*Officers:* Gavin Lee Woodhouse [1978] Director/Property Developer

**Northern Pump Suppliers Limited**
*Incorporated:* 30 December 1986 *Employees:* 34
*Net Worth:* £1,393,673 *Total Assets:* £3,088,538
*Registered Office:* Upper Castle Street, Bradford, W Yorks, BD5 7RN
*Activities:* Other specialised construction activities n.e.c.
*Parent:* NPS Engineering Group Limited
*Officers:* Rachel Louise Laycock [1978] Sales Director; Andrew James Smith [1976] Managing Director; Barry James Smith [1950] Director/Chairman

**Northern Racing College**
*Incorporated:* 10 June 1988 *Employees:* 38
*Net Worth:* £1,505,635 *Total Assets:* £3,232,424
*Registered Office:* The Stables, Rossington Hall, Great North Road, Doncaster, S Yorks, DN11 0HN
*Activities:* Technical and vocational secondary education
*Officers:* Timothy Lawrence Adams [1945] Director/Retired; Jeffrey Ennis [1952] Director/MP; Nicola Julie Frampton [1966] Director; Susannah Cordelia Gill [1984] Director of External Affairs (ARC); The Honourable Oliver Greenall [1986] Director/Amateur Jockey; James Hetherton [1958] Director/Race Horse Trainer; Sally Iggulden [1976] Director/Chief Executive; Tim Lyle [1946] Director/Retired Trade Union Officer; Christopher Cyril Mallinson [1947] Director; Gerard Sutcliffe [1953] Director; Howard Wright [1945] Director/Journalist

**Northern Star Academies Trust**
*Incorporated:* 7 March 2011 *Employees:* 264
*Previous:* Skipton Girls' High School Academy Trust
*Net Worth:* £17,765,000 *Total Assets:* £22,902,000
*Registered Office:* 77 Gargrave Road, Skipton, N Yorks, BD23 1QN
*Activities:* General secondary education
*Officers:* Cindy Haymes, Secretary; Beverley Dawn Ashby [1958] Director; Ian Andrew Curtis [1950] Director/Retired; Howard Geoffrey Cutler [1943] Director/HR Consultant; Helen Catherine Flynn [1963] Director/Company Secretary; Martin Paul Kelly [1957] Chairman/Director; Jennifer Plews [1972] Director/Headteacher; Steven Scott [1971] Director/Banker

**Northern Touch Limited**
*Incorporated:* 12 June 1997 *Employees:* 59
*Net Worth:* £2,003,183 *Total Assets:* £6,459,714
*Registered Office:* Dower Hotel & Spa, 48 Bond End, Knaresborough, Harrogate, N Yorks, HG5 9AL
*Activities:* Hotels and similar accommodation
*Parent:* Hazlewood Holdings Limited
*Officers:* Ian Lawrence Hanson, Secretary/Lawyer; Ian Lawrence Hanson [1964] Director/Lawyer; Martin Gregory Michael Wicks [1963] Director/Hotelier

**Northgate (CB 2) Limited**
*Incorporated:* 9 March 2012
*Net Worth:* £131,323,000 *Total Assets:* £140,232,992
*Registered Office:* Northgate Centre, Lingfield Way, Darlington, Co Durham, DL1 4PZ
*Activities:* Other service activities n.e.c.
*Parent:* Northgate (Europe) Ltd
*Officers:* Katie Laura Tasker-Wood, Secretary; Richard David Podmore [1979] Director

**Northgate (CB) Limited**
*Incorporated:* 23 April 2010
*Net Worth:* £511,280,992 *Total Assets:* £567,025,024
*Registered Office:* Northgate Centre, Lingfield Way, Darlington, Co Durham, DL1 4PZ
*Activities:* Bookkeeping activities
*Parent:* Northgate (Europe) Limited
*Officers:* Katie Laura Tasker-Wood, Secretary; Richard David Podmore [1979] Director

**Northgate (Europe) Limited**
*Incorporated:* 12 September 2006
*Net Worth:* £74,848,000 *Total Assets:* £1,062,262,016
*Registered Office:* Northgate Centre, Lingfield Way, Darlington, Co Durham, DL1 4PZ
*Activities:* Activities of other holding companies n.e.c.
*Parent:* Northgate PLC
*Officers:* Katie Laura Tasker-Wood, Secretary; Richard David Podmore [1979] Director

**Northgate Lighting Limited**
*Incorporated:* 9 March 2006 *Employees:* 68
*Net Worth:* £1,295,667 *Total Assets:* £7,327,151
*Registered Office:* Regina House, Ring Road, Bramley, Leeds, LS13 4ET
*Activities:* Manufacture of electric lighting equipment
*Major Shareholder:* Adrian Wing Lin Lee
*Officers:* Robert Eastwood, Secretary; Adrian Lee [1968] Director

**Northgate PLC**
*Incorporated:* 2 July 1897 *Employees:* 2,900
*Net Worth:* £539,128,000 *Total Assets:* £1,118,932,992
*Registered Office:* Northgate Centre, Lingfield Way, Darlington, Co Durham, DL1 4PZ
*Activities:* Activities of other holding companies n.e.c.
*Officers:* Katie Laura Tasker-Wood, Secretary; Andrew James Allner [1953] Director; Kevin Michael Bradshaw [1969] Director; Gillian Caseberry [1965] Director; Claire Miles [1972] Director; Andrew Page [1958] Director; William Spencer [1959] Director; Philip James Vincent [1969] Director/Chief Finance Officer

**Northgate Vehicle Hire Limited**
*Incorporated:* 2 July 1979 *Employees:* 1,688
*Net Worth:* £115,170,000 *Total Assets:* £794,702,976
*Registered Office:* Northgate Centre, Lingfield Way, Darlington, Co Durham, DL1 4PZ
*Activities:* Renting and leasing of cars and light motor vehicles
*Parent:* Northgate PLC
*Officers:* Katie Laura Tasker-Wood, Secretary; James Benjamin Feller [1983] Finance Director; Frank Mahon Hayes [1967] Director [Irish]; Katie Laura Tasker-Wood [1981] Director

**Northminster Holdings Limited**
*Incorporated:* 15 April 2011
*Net Worth:* £4,230,865 *Total Assets:* £5,124,340
*Registered Office:* 3 Holly Tree House, Harwood Road, Northminster Business Park, Upper Poppleton, York, YO26 6QU
*Activities:* Activities of head offices
*Major Shareholder:* George Joseph Burgess
*Officers:* George Joseph Burgess [1973] Director

**Northwood Tissue (Lancaster) Limited**
*Incorporated:* 29 October 2012 *Employees:* 41
*Net Worth:* £1,392,401 *Total Assets:* £5,323,686
*Registered Office:* Lansil Way, Caton Road, Lancaster, LA1 3PQ
*Activities:* Manufacture of household and sanitary goods and of toilet requisites
*Parent:* NTIS Investments Ltd
*Officers:* Paul King, Secretary; Christopher John Davies [1965] Director; Adam Scott Fecher [1974] Director; Marc Darren Fecher [1971] Director; Paul Fecher [1946] Director; Paul Edward King [1974] Director/Accountant; David George Thompson [1967] Director

**Norton Healthcare Limited**
*Incorporated:* 13 February 1969 *Employees:* 421
*Net Worth:* £1,411,873,792 *Total Assets:* £1,498,274,944
*Registered Office:* Ridings Point, Whistler Drive, Castleford, W Yorks, WF10 5HX
*Activities:* Manufacture of pharmaceutical preparations
*Parent:* Ivax UK Limited
*Officers:* Dean Michael Cooper [1972] Director/Chartered Accountant; Stephen Llanon Forrester-Coles [1960] Site Director; David Vrhovec [1967] Director [Slovenian]

**Nortonthorpe Industrial Park Limited**
*Incorporated:* 27 June 1995 *Employees:* 3
*Net Worth:* £3,465,162 *Total Assets:* £3,856,785
*Registered Office:* Nortonthorpe Mills, Scissett, Huddersfield, W Yorks, HD8 9LA
*Activities:* Other letting and operating of own or leased real estate
*Major Shareholder:* Eric Arthur Brook
*Officers:* Heather Mary Woodhead, Secretary/Sales Person; Eric Arthur Brook [1942] Director/Property Developer

**Norwich and Peterborough (LBS) Limited**
*Incorporated:* 12 December 1991
*Net Worth:* £2,200,000 *Total Assets:* £94,722,000
*Registered Office:* Yorkshire House, Yorkshire Drive, Bradford, W Yorks, BD5 8LJ
*Activities:* Financial intermediation not elsewhere classified
*Officers:* Helen Clare Nellist, Secretary; Charles Peter Canning [1963] Director; Rob Andrew Purdy [1972] Director/Accountant

**Notman Enterprise Limited**
*Incorporated:* 31 March 2011 *Employees:* 157
*Net Worth:* £3,208,104 *Total Assets:* £15,743,477
*Registered Office:* Marfleet Environmental Technology Park, Westgate Way, Hedon Road, Hull, HU9 5LW
*Activities:* Activities of head offices
*Major Shareholder:* Kim Notman
*Officers:* Kim Notman [1974] Director [Belgian]; Laura Jane Bird Notman [1982] Director/Health and Safety Representative

**Nova Contracting Ltd**
*Incorporated:* 9 January 2008 *Employees:* 75
*Net Worth:* £1,598,402 *Total Assets:* £5,517,528
*Registered Office:* 7 Limewood Way, Leeds, LS14 1AB
*Activities:* Freight transport by road
*Parent:* Ibex Accounting Services Ltd
*Officers:* Jonathan Swale Green [1971] Director/Chartered Surveyor; Marcus Swale Green [1974] Director

**Novaglaze Limited**
*Incorporated:* 23 February 2006 *Employees:* 50
*Net Worth:* £1,642,105 *Total Assets:* £3,101,780
*Registered Office:* NGN House, Queens Mill Road, Lockwood, Huddersfield, W Yorks, HD1 3PG
*Activities:* Shaping and processing of flat glass
*Shareholders:* Kenneth Woodcock; Gillian Anne Woodcock
*Officers:* Gary Smith, Secretary; David Chambers [1954] Director; Tracy Roberts [1965] Director; Gary Smith [1957] Director; Gillian Anne Woodcock [1954] Director; Kenneth Woodcock [1952] Director

**Novus Finance Ltd**
*Incorporated:* 18 March 2008
*Net Worth:* £13,992,119 *Total Assets:* £25,518,256
*Registered Office:* Hunsworth Lane, Cleckheaton, W Yorks, BD19 3UJ
*Activities:* Activities of production holding companies
*Officers:* Michael Boardman, Secretary; Mark Nicholas Horton [1965] Director; Gerardus Christiaan Paulus Jacobus Maters [1967] Director/Global Chief Financial Officer [Dutch]; Jon Stokes [1965] Director [American]

**G. Nowell Limited**
*Incorporated:* 8 January 1992 *Employees:* 2
*Net Worth:* £3,136,354 *Total Assets:* £4,839,493
*Registered Office:* Bridge End Yard, Ribble Terrace, Settle, N Yorks, BD24 9DS
*Activities:* Other letting and operating of own or leased real estate
*Shareholders:* Edward Stuart Nowell; Derek Matthew Nowell
*Officers:* Edward Stuart Nowell, Secretary; Derek Matthew Nowell [1973] Director/Manager Garden Care Equipment; Edward Stuart Nowell [1975] Director

**NSA (Ventures) Limited**
*Incorporated:* 4 October 2001
*Net Worth:* £432,041 *Total Assets:* £4,751,579
*Registered Office:* Unity House, Dudley Road, Darlington, Co Durham, DL1 4GG
*Activities:* Combined office administrative service activities
*Officers:* Darren James Combellack [1985] Director/Car Salvage Dealer; Ian Maurice Hill [1970] Director/Salvage Dealer; Hamish Edward Thomson Irvine [1946] Director; Chris James Morgan [1963] Director/Salvage Dealer; Allen William Frederick Prebble [1961] Director/Vehicle Salvage Owner; Marc John Trent [1966] Managing Director

**NSF Health Sciences Ltd.**
*Incorporated:* 11 September 1997 *Employees:* 26
*Net Worth:* £2,054,925 *Total Assets:* £3,383,283
*Registered Office:* The Georgian House, 22-24 West End, Kirkbymoorside, York, YO62 6AF
*Activities:* Other professional, scientific and technical activities n.e.c.
*Parent:* NSF International UK Ltd
*Officers:* Deborah Jane Cuming, Secretary; Doctor Donna Garren [1967] Director [American]; Marilyn Katz Pek [1945] Director/Biotechnology Business Consultant [American]; Kevan Paul Lawlor [1957] Director/President and Chief Ex Officer [American]; Martin Kevin Lush [1960] Director/Pharmaceutical Consultant; Richard Rabbideau [1938] Director/Attorney (Retired) [American]

**NSS Properties Limited**
*Incorporated:* 7 September 2006 *Employees:* 7
*Net Worth:* £3,421,152 *Total Assets:* £4,185,827
*Registered Office:* 191 Adel Lane, Leeds, LS16 8BY
*Activities:* Buying and selling of own real estate
*Shareholders:* Sandeep Sharma; Sunil Sharma
*Officers:* Nisha Sharma, Secretary; Sandeep Sharma [1969] Director

**NTEX Limited**
*Incorporated:* 26 June 1978 *Employees:* 75
*Net Worth:* £1,131,822 *Total Assets:* £6,641,742
*Registered Office:* Scandinavian Way, Stallingborough, Grimsby, N E Lincs, DN41 8DU
*Activities:* Freight transport by road
*Officers:* Stephen Philip Davis [1969] Director; Thomas Stroem [1954] Director [Swedish]

**Nu-Oval Acquisitions 1 Limited**
*Incorporated:* 10 April 2007
*Net Worth:* £11,157,000 *Total Assets:* £13,598,000
*Registered Office:* Polypipe Ltd, Broomhouse Lane, Edlington, Doncaster, S Yorks, DN12 1ES
*Activities:* Activities of other holding companies n.e.c.
*Parent:* Polypipe Limited
*Officers:* Emma Gayle Versluys, Secretary; Paul Anthony James [1967] Director/Chief Financial Officer; Martin Keith Payne [1965] Director

**Nu-Oval Acquisitions 2 Limited**
*Incorporated:* 10 April 2007
*Net Worth Deficit:* £51,110,000 *Total Assets:* £26,500,000
*Registered Office:* Polypipe Ltd, Broomhouse Lane, Edlington, Doncaster, S Yorks, DN12 1ES
*Activities:* Activities of other holding companies n.e.c.
*Parent:* Nu-Oval Acquisitions 1 Limited
*Officers:* Emma Gayle Versluys, Secretary; Paul Anthony James [1967] Director/Chief Financial Officer; Martin Keith Payne [1965] Director

**Nu-Swift International Limited**
*Incorporated:* 31 May 1933 *Employees:* 54
*Net Worth:* £11,684,957 *Total Assets:* £14,552,840
*Registered Office:* Premier House, 2 Jubilee Way, Elland, W Yorks, HX5 9DY
*Activities:* Other manufacturing n.e.c.
*Parent:* LS UK Fire Group Limited
*Officers:* Richard John Pollard, Secretary; Jean-Jacques Murray [1966] Director; Richard John Pollard [1963] Director/Chartered Accountant

**Nufarm Crop Products UK Limited**
*Incorporated:* 21 June 2004
*Net Worth:* £110,433,000 *Total Assets:* £116,646,000
*Registered Office:* Nufarm, Wyke Lane, Wyke, Bradford, W Yorks, BD12 9EJ
*Activities:* Other research and experimental development on natural sciences and engineering
*Parent:* Nufarm UK Limited
*Officers:* Paul Andrew Binfield [1965] Director [New Zealander]; John Paul Else [1970] Director/Operations Manager; Christopher John Karoly Fazekas [1969] Director/Management [Australian]; Hugo Wilhelm Schweers [1957] Director/Business Executive [German]; Peter Johannes Josef Van Sloun [1959] Director/Financial Controller [German]

**Nufarm UK Limited**
*Incorporated:* 21 December 1993 *Employees:* 335
*Net Worth:* £218,700,992 *Total Assets:* £438,000,992
*Registered Office:* Nufarm, Wyke Lane, Wyke, Bradford, W Yorks, BD12 9EJ
*Activities:* Manufacture of pesticides and other agrochemical products
*Parent:* Medisup Securities Limited
*Officers:* Paul Andrew Binfield [1965] Director [New Zealander]; John Paul Else [1970] Director/Operations Manager; Mark Joseph Joyce [1968] Director/Regional Supply Chain Manager - EUMEA; Elbert Prado [1957] Director/Group Executive Supply Chain Operations [American]; Hugo Wilhelm Schweers [1957] Director/Business Executive [German]; Peter Johannes Josef Van Sloun [1959] Director/Financial Controller [German]

**Numecent Holdings Ltd**
*Incorporated:* 15 July 2008 *Employees:* 5
*Net Worth:* £13,377,876 *Total Assets:* £19,175,376
*Registered Office:* Suite 4, One Sceptre House, Hornbeam Square North, Harrogate, N Yorks, HG2 8PB
*Activities:* Business and domestic software development
*Officers:* Dr Richard Lawrence Hargreaves [1946] Director; Arthur Shingen Hitomi [1972] Director [American]; Mark David Khandjian [1959] Director/Business Executive [American]; Stephen John Maynard [1962] Director; Keh Long NG [1959] Director/Chief Finance Officer [Singaporean]

**Numecent Limited**
*Incorporated:* 11 September 2007 *Employees:* 2
*Net Worth Deficit:* £1,071,205 *Total Assets:* £5,355,629
*Registered Office:* Suite 4, One Sceptre House, Hornbeam Square North, Harrogate, N Yorks, HG2 8PB
*Activities:* Information technology consultancy activities
*Officers:* Peter James Brosnan [1957] Director/IT Consultant; William Rupert Colstream Clunie Cunningham [1969] Director/Finance; Arthur Shingen Hitomi [1972] Director/Software Management/CEO [American]; Osman Kent [1958] Director/Technology Consultant

**Nunns of Grimsby Limited**
*Incorporated:* 6 November 1980 *Employees:* 31
*Net Worth:* £1,159,752 *Total Assets:* £3,545,180
*Registered Office:* Altyre Way, Hewitts Avenue Business Park, Humberston, Grimsby, S Humbers, DN36 4RJ
*Activities:* Sale of new cars and light motor vehicles
*Shareholders:* Steven Austin Nunn; Michael Harris Nunn
*Officers:* Martin David Thompson, Secretary; Jeremy John Hewer Griffiths [1962] Director/Dealer Principal; Michael Harris Nunn [1954] Director

**Nurture Academies Trust**
*Incorporated:* 1 March 2016 *Employees:* 276
*Previous:* The Bradford Birth To 19 Trust
*Net Worth:* £15,226,983 *Total Assets:* £18,768,384
*Registered Office:* Lapage Primary School, Barkerend Road, Bradford, W Yorks, BD3 8QX
*Activities:* Primary education
*Officers:* Paul Bailey [1952] Director/Retired; Gareth Davies [1969] Director; Irwin Robert Freeth [1950] Director/Retired; Diane Jeanette Hadwen [1960] Director/Heritage Education Officer; Louis Harvey [1973] Director/Operations Manager; Yaseen Mohammed [1975] Director/Regeneration Professional; William John Nunes Nabarro [1955] Director/Consultant; Jeremy Leslie Townend [1963] Director/Consultant; Wahid Zaman [1969] Director/Chief Executive Officer

**Nutclough Mill Limited**
*Incorporated:* 23 March 2011 *Employees:* 3
*Net Worth:* £1,331,842 *Total Assets:* £3,032,835
*Registered Office:* 12 Market Street, Hebden Bridge, W Yorks, HX7 6AD
*Activities:* Other letting and operating of own or leased real estate
*Shareholders:* Thomas David Jagger; Rowan Laura Woodward
*Officers:* David Stephen Jagger, Secretary; David Stephen Jagger [1952] Director; Thomas David Jagger [1971] Director; Rowan Laura Woodward [1975] Director

**Nutec Holdings Limited**
*Incorporated:* 25 November 1992
*Net Worth:* £4,188,430 *Total Assets:* £4,217,717
*Registered Office:* Dalton Airfield Industrial Estate, Dalton, Thirsk, N Yorks, YO7 3HE
*Activities:* Non-trading company
*Parent:* Cargill PLC
*Officers:* Dena Michelle L O'Bue, Secretary; Benjamin James Rogers [1970] Director/CPN Europe Supply Chain Lead; Federico Urquidi Negron [1965] Director/UK & Ireland Country Controller [Spanish]

**W. Nutt & Son Limited**
*Incorporated:* 22 March 1954 *Employees:* 11
*Net Worth:* £5,311,426 *Total Assets:* £6,555,392
*Registered Office:* Carr House, East Heslerton, Malton, N Yorks, YO17 8RR
*Activities:* Growing of cereals (except rice), leguminous crops and oil seeds
*Shareholders:* Paul William Nutt; Andrew David Nutt
*Officers:* Paul William Nutt, Secretary; Andrew David Nutt [1960] Director/Farmer; Jill Nutt [1930] Director/Farmer; Paul William Nutt [1958] Director/Farmer

**NVELOPE Rainscreen Systems Limited**
*Incorporated:* 24 January 2002 *Employees:* 24
*Net Worth:* £4,782,447 *Total Assets:* £6,488,198
*Registered Office:* 153 Kirkstall Road, Leeds, LS4 2AT
*Activities:* Other specialised construction activities n.e.c.
*Parent:* Ncase Limited
*Officers:* Thomas Bamberger [1961] Director [German]; Arthur Blank [1959] Director [Swiss]

**Nynet Limited**
*Incorporated:* 26 January 2007 *Employees:* 22
*Net Worth Deficit:* £5,012,099 *Total Assets:* £6,595,646
*Registered Office:* 80 High Street, Starbeck, Harrogate, N Yorks, HG2 7LW
*Activities:* Wired telecommunications activities
*Parent:* North Yorkshire County Council
*Officers:* Scott Walters, Secretary; Richard Alexander Doyle [1956] Director/IT Speciality; Richard Flinton [1965] Director/Local Government Officer; Carl Anthony Les [1949] Director/Hotelier; Don Johannes Josef MacKenzie [1949] Director/County Councillor; Peter Geoffrey Scrope [1955] Director; Scott Walters [1967] Director

**NYOS (York) Limited**
*Incorporated:* 29 September 2009 *Employees:* 56
*Net Worth:* £3,236,793 *Total Assets:* £5,070,907
*Registered Office:* Clifton Park Clinic, Clifton Park Avenue, Clifton, York, YO30 5PB
*Activities:* Specialists medical practice activities
*Officers:* Dr Simon Boyle [1974] Director/Orthopaedic Consultant; Dr Simon Adam Boyce Budgen [1965] Director/Orthopaedic Consultant; Dr Nicholas Charles Carrington [1971] Director/Orthopaedic Consultant; Mark Andrew Fountain [1966] Director/Healthcare Chief Executive; Anthony Joseph Gibbon [1963] Director/Orthopaedic Consultant; Neil Hunt [1966] Director/Orthopaedic Consultant; Dr Anthony Campbell Maury [1970] Director/Orthopaedic Consultant; James Charles Stanley [1974] Director/Orthopaedic Consultant; Ian Alexander Whitaker [1957] Director/Orthopaedic Consultant; Hywel Rhys Williams [1962] Director/Orthopaedic Consultant

**NYT (Holdings) Limited**
*Incorporated:* 31 March 2004 *Employees:* 199
*Net Worth:* £2,712,481 *Total Assets:* £12,042,025
*Registered Office:* c/o North Yorkshire Timber Co Ltd, Standard House, Thurston Road, Northallerton Business Park, Northallerton, N Yorks, DL6 2NA
*Activities:* Activities of other holding companies n.e.c.
*Parent:* Thornbridge Sawmills Limited
*Officers:* Robert Todd Barclay [1969] Director; John Alexander George Douglas [1964] Finance Director; Nicholas Peter Kershaw [1972] Director; Neil Andrew McGill [1977] Investment Director; Stuart Whiteford [1990] Director

**David O'Meara Racing Ltd**
*Incorporated:* 21 March 2009
*Previous:* Helmsley Horse Racing Ltd.
*Net Worth:* £1,738,501 *Total Assets:* £3,451,716
*Registered Office:* Willow Farm, Upper Helmsley, York, YO41 1JX
*Activities:* Raising of other animals
*Shareholders:* David Blaise O'Meara; Steven Nicholas Parkin
*Officers:* David Blaise O'Meara [1977] Director/Racehorse Trainer [Irish]

**Oak Electrical Limited**
*Incorporated:* 14 November 1995 *Employees:* 27
*Net Worth:* £1,773,054 *Total Assets:* £3,798,241
*Registered Office:* Werner Court, Blue Ridge Park, Glasshoughton, Castleford, W Yorks, WF10 4TN
*Activities:* Electrical installation
*Shareholders:* Andrew Paul Cook; Ivan Kavanagh
*Officers:* Andrew Paul Cook, Secretary/Electrician; Andrew Paul Cook [1966] Director/Electrician; Ivan Kavanagh [1968] Director/Electrical Contractor; Brandon Vaughn Pashley [1966] Director/Contracts Manager

**Oakapple Commercial Limited**
*Incorporated:* 16 September 2005 *Employees:* 2
*Net Worth:* £83,878 *Total Assets:* £3,731,493
*Registered Office:* Oakapple House, 1 John Charles Way, Leeds, LS12 6QA
*Activities:* Buying and selling of own real estate
*Parent:* Surcoat Group Limited
*Officers:* David Howard Marsh, Secretary; David Howard Marsh [1955] Director/Accountant; Philip John Taylor [1963] Director/Chairman

**Oakapple Homes (Scarborough) Limited**
*Incorporated:* 10 March 2003 *Employees:* 2
*Net Worth Deficit:* £4,495,747 *Total Assets:* £8,608,046
*Registered Office:* Oakapple House, 1 John Charles Way, Leeds, LS12 6QA
*Activities:* Buying and selling of own real estate
*Major Shareholder:* Philip John Taylor
*Officers:* David Howard Marsh, Secretary; David Howard Marsh [1955] Director/Chartered Accountant; Philip John Taylor [1963] Director/Chairman

**Oakdale Homes Limited**
*Incorporated:* 25 April 1994 *Employees:* 7
*Net Worth Deficit:* £3,124,452 *Total Assets:* £8,445,888
*Registered Office:* Building 2, Enterprise Way, Retford, Notts, DN22 7HH
*Activities:* Construction of commercial buildings
*Parent:* Langley Holdings PLC
*Officers:* Anthony John Langley [1954] Director; Bernard James Langley [1993] Director/General Construction & Civil Engineering; Charlotte Audrey Langley [1991] Director/General Construction & Civil Engineering

**Oakesway Limited**
*Incorporated:* 3 September 2015
*Previous:* MBI Oakesway Limited
*Net Worth Deficit:* £98,819 *Total Assets:* £3,289,298
*Registered Office:* 28 Park Place, Leeds, LS1 2SP
*Activities:* Buying and selling of own real estate
*Shareholders:* Robin Scott Forster; Gavin Lee Woodhouse
*Officers:* Robin Scott Forster [1981] Director

**Oakgate Group Limited**
*Incorporated:* 12 May 1995 *Employees:* 4
*Previous:* Oakgate Group Public Limited Company
*Net Worth:* £1,634,951 *Total Assets:* £3,105,026
*Registered Office:* Castlegarth Grange, Scott Lane, Wetherby, W Yorks, LS22 6LH
*Activities:* Buying and selling of own real estate
*Parent:* Caddick Group PLC
*Officers:* Paul Andrew Bullers, Secretary; Paul Andrew Bullers [1966] Finance Director; Paul Caddick [1950] Director; Richard Edward France [1954] Director

**Oakhurst Court Holdings Limited**
*Incorporated:* 29 April 2010 *Employees:* 109
*Net Worth:* £6,370,423 *Total Assets:* £12,421,883
*Registered Office:* Woodlands of Woolley Residential Home, Woolley Low Moor Lane, Woolley, Wakefield, W Yorks, WF4 2LN
*Activities:* Activities of head offices
*Parent:* Oakhurst Court Holdings (Cayman) Ltd
*Officers:* William Jeremy Davies [1947] Director; Pearl Lorraine Jackson [1958] Director

**Oakland Farms Limited**
*Incorporated:* 4 May 1971 *Employees:* 19
*Net Worth:* £2,377,146 *Total Assets:* £7,089,447
*Registered Office:* Oaklands, Church Lane, Moor Monkton, York, YO26 8LA
*Activities:* Growing of cereals (except rice), leguminous crops and oil seeds
*Shareholders:* Christopher Peter Roach; Peter Dennis Roach
*Officers:* Susanna Margaret Roach, Secretary; Christopher Peter Roach [1964] Director; Susanna Roach [1963] Director

**Oakmere Homes (Lancaster) Limited**
*Incorporated:* 6 June 2014
*Net Worth:* £1,564,712 *Total Assets:* £5,017,910
*Registered Office:* Helm Bank, Natland, Kendal, Cumbria, LA9 7PS
*Activities:* Construction of domestic buildings
*Parent:* Oakmere Homes Northwest Limited
*Officers:* Gary Middlebrook [1954] Managing Director; Mark David Wilkinson [1970] Operations Director

**Oakmere Homes (Longtown) Ltd**
*Incorporated:* 19 July 2007
*Net Worth:* £2,241,661 *Total Assets:* £9,110,162
*Registered Office:* Helm Bank, Natland, Kendal, Cumbria, LA9 7PS
*Activities:* Construction of domestic buildings
*Parent:* Oakmere Homes NW Ltd
*Officers:* Gary Middlebrook [1954] Director; Mark David Wilkinson [1970] Operations Director

**Oakmere Homes (Northwest) Ltd**
*Incorporated:* 3 July 2003 *Employees:* 21
*Net Worth:* £4,158,526 *Total Assets:* £16,467,149
*Registered Office:* Helm Bank, Natland, Kendal, Cumbria, LA9 7PS
*Activities:* Construction of domestic buildings
*Major Shareholder:* Gary Middlebrook
*Officers:* Gary Middlebrook [1954] Director; Mark David Wilkinson [1970] Operations Director

**Oakstone Developments Limited**
*Incorporated:* 12 November 1986 *Employees:* 3
*Net Worth:* £2,785,521 *Total Assets:* £5,537,364
*Registered Office:* The Old Malt Kiln, Bolton Road, Addingham, Ilkley, W Yorks, LS29 0NQ
*Activities:* Other construction installation
*Parent:* Phillips Special Projects Limited
*Officers:* John Grahame Phillips, Secretary; Andrew John Phillips [1981] Director/Projects Manager; John Grahame Phillips [1950] Director/Building Contractor

**Oakvine Limited**
*Incorporated:* 6 January 2015
*Net Worth:* £4,495,975 *Total Assets:* £4,524,440
*Registered Office:* Cannon Street, Hull, HU2 0AB
*Activities:* Residents property management
*Parent:* cbaSadofskys Ltd
*Officers:* Paul Henry Sanderson [1947] Director; Robert Sanderson [1956] Director

**Oakwell Securities Limited**
*Incorporated:* 18 January 1988
*Net Worth:* £2,807,921 *Total Assets:* £4,370,158
*Registered Office:* Oakwell House, 7 Butts Court, Leeds, LS1 5JS
*Activities:* Buying and selling of own real estate
*Shareholder:* Robert-Austin
*Officers:* Robert Austin, Secretary; Mary Margaret Austin [1954] Director/Company Secretary; Matthew Robert Austin [1984] Director/Chartered Surveyor; Robert Austin [1950] Director/Chartered Surveyor

**Oakwood Homeloans Limited**
*Incorporated:* 2 April 2004
*Net Worth:* £3,111,961 *Total Assets:* £3,428,287
*Registered Office:* The Watermill, Broughton, Skipton, N Yorks, BD23 3AG
*Activities:* Activities of mortgage finance companies
*Parent:* Oakwood Homeloans Holdings Limited
*Officers:* Roger Stephen Lansdowne, Secretary; Leonora Veronica Daniel [1962] Director/Banker; David Ashley Jerrard [1972] Director/Banker

**Oakwood Kitchen Design Consultants Limited**
*Incorporated:* 14 July 1983 *Employees:* 39
*Net Worth:* £3,253,300 *Total Assets:* £4,451,192
*Registered Office:* Oakwood House, Jubilee Way, Jubilee Business Park, Grange Moor, Huddersfield, W Yorks, WF4 4TD
*Activities:* Manufacture of other furniture
*Major Shareholder:* Brian Charlton
*Officers:* Brian Charlton, Secretary; Brian Charlton [1951] Director; Michael John Charlton [1975] Director/Sales Administrator; Keith Rowlett Lawson [1953] Director/Buyer

**Oakwood Solicitors Limited**
*Incorporated:* 29 April 2009 *Employees:* 84
*Previous:* Michael Lewin Solicitors Limited
*Net Worth:* £188,378 *Total Assets:* £3,326,741
*Registered Office:* 635 Roundhay Road, Leeds, LS8 4BA
*Activities:* Solicitors
*Parent:* Keech Limited
*Officers:* Abbigail Paige Keech [1977] Director/Solicitor; Jessica Rae Thompson [1987] Director/Solicitor

**Oakwood Veterinary Practice Limited**
*Incorporated:* 10 January 2017 *Employees:* 27
*Net Worth Deficit:* £103,587 *Total Assets:* £4,514,570
*Registered Office:* Leeman House, Station Business Park, Holgate Park Drive, York, YO26 4GB
*Activities:* Veterinary activities
*Parent:* Origin Group Finance Limited
*Officers:* Joanna Clare Malone [1974] Director; Mark Stanworth [1964] Director

**OC317233 LLP**
*Incorporated:* 18 January 2006 *Employees:* 129
*Previous:* Heptonstalls LLP
*Net Worth Deficit:* £3,881,532 *Total Assets:* £6,130,549
*Registered Office:* 7-15 Gladstone Terrace, Goole, E Yorks, DN14 5AH
*Officers:* John Burman [1953] Member; Angele Hart [1968] Member; Shane Steven Hensman [1972] Member; Sarah Jane Johnson [1966] Member; Arthur Shaun Pinchbeck [1962] Member; Clare Pritchard [1973] LLP Member; Nicholas John Lipson Ward-Lowery [1966] LLP Member

**Oceanic Seafoods Limited**
*Incorporated:* 20 August 2009 *Employees:* 5
*Net Worth:* £1,222,713 *Total Assets:* £5,535,861
*Registered Office:* 201 Riverway House, Morecambe Road, Lancaster, LA1 2RX
*Activities:* Processing and preserving of fish, crustaceans and molluscs
*Shareholders:* James Michael Alan Welsh; Three Oceans Fish Company Ltd
*Officers:* James Michael Alan Welsh, Secretary; Jonathan Mark Warburton [1961] Director/Solicitor; James Michael Alan Welsh [1976] Director

**OE Electrics Limited**
*Incorporated:* 16 July 1993 *Employees:* 182
*Net Worth:* £7,085,106 *Total Assets:* £18,108,280
*Registered Office:* OE House, Thomas Maddison Lane, Calder Park, Wakefield, W Yorks, WF4 3GH
*Activities:* Manufacture of other electrical equipment
*Shareholder:* David Richardson Hobbs
*Officers:* Jill Rosemary Hobbs, Secretary/Director; David Richardson Hobbs [1942] Director; Jill Rosemary Hobbs [1943] Director; Sarah Louise Hobbs [1970] Director; Timothy Richard Hobbs [1970] Director; David John Masters [1955] Managing Director

**Office Interiors Wholesale Limited**
*Incorporated:* 12 April 1983 *Employees:* 16
*Net Worth:* £1,972,140 *Total Assets:* £3,807,753
*Registered Office:* The OIW Centre, Airedale Business Park, Royd Ings Avenue, Keighley, W Yorks, BD21 4BT
*Activities:* Wholesale of office furniture
*Major Shareholder:* Michael Wloch
*Officers:* Wendy Ruth Wloch, Secretary; Ben England [1981] Director/Sales; Michael Wloch [1958] Managing Director; Wendy Ruth Wloch [1960] Director/Secretary

**Sir Robert Ogden Estates Ltd**
*Incorporated:* 2 September 1964 *Employees:* 15
*Previous:* Ogden Properties Limited
*Net Worth:* £43,329,768 *Total Assets:* £45,566,088
*Registered Office:* The Ogden Group of Companies, 30 Victoria Avenue, Harrogate, N Yorks, HG1 5PR
*Activities:* Buying and selling of own real estate
*Major Shareholder:* Robert Ogden CBE LLD
*Officers:* Fergus Notman Colvin [1945] Director/Chartered Accountant; Justin Charles Garnett [1972] Director; Timothy John Garnett [1945] Managing Director; Sir Robert Ogden CBE Lld [1936] Director/Company Chairman; Ian Donald Swift [1957] Director/Accountant

**A V Ogden Holdings Limited**
*Incorporated:* 13 May 1963
*Net Worth:* £1,116,552 *Total Assets:* £3,956,171
*Registered Office:* New Chartford House, Centurion Way, Cleckheaton, W Yorks, BD19 3QB
*Activities:* Development of building projects
*Shareholders:* Hazel Ogden; A V Ogden No.1 Settlement
*Officers:* Rachel Jane Adams [1967] Director; Helen Louise Bell [1964] Director; Hazel Ogden [1940] Director; James Patrick Ogden [1969] Director; Richard Gregg Ogden [1965] Director

**OHES Environmental Limited**
*Incorporated:* 9 November 2001 *Employees:* 2
*Net Worth:* £2,004,000 *Total Assets:* £5,539,000
*Registered Office:* 80 Station Parade, Harrogate, N Yorks, HG1 1HQ
*Activities:* Environmental consulting activities
*Parent:* Adler & Allan Limited
*Officers:* Robert Leonard Contreras [1962] Director; Michael James Dunn [1965] Director; Adrian Neal Godwin [1976] Director; Daniel Lewis Jones [1976] Director

**Oilgear European Holdings Limited**
*Incorporated:* 21 February 2007
*Net Worth:* £5,296,126 *Total Assets:* £12,682,128
*Registered Office:* 37 Burley Road, Leeds, LS3 1JT
*Activities:* Manufacture of fluid power equipment
*Officers:* Jodie Baker, Secretary; Frederic Paul Denis Jamet [1962] Director/Oilgear European Vice President [French]; Craig Skylar Lafave [1977] Director/Chief Executive [American]; Francois Masure [1964] Director/Executive [French]

**Oilgear Towler Limited**
*Incorporated:* 10 May 1956 *Employees:* 53
*Net Worth Deficit:* £1,285,642 *Total Assets:* £4,643,851
*Registered Office:* 37 Burley Road, Leeds, LS3 1JT
*Activities:* Manufacture of fluid power equipment
*Parent:* Oilgear European Holdings Ltd
*Officers:* Christopher Howie [1965] Director/Vice President; Frederic Jamet [1962] Director/Vice President [French]

**Olam Food Ingredients UK Limited**
*Incorporated:* 26 January 1994 *Employees:* 43
*Net Worth:* £19,136,000 *Total Assets:* £20,421,000
*Registered Office:* Britannia Way, Goole, E Yorks, DN14 6ES
*Activities:* Manufacture of oils and fats
*Parent:* Olam Europe Limited
*Officers:* Andrew Richard Samuel, Secretary; Gerard Anthony Manley [1958] Director

**Old Clee Primary Academy**
*Incorporated:* 6 February 2013 *Employees:* 89
*Net Worth:* £3,780,970 *Total Assets:* £5,081,918
*Registered Office:* Old Clee Primary School, Colin Avenue, Grimsby, N E Lincs, DN32 8EN
*Activities:* Primary education
*Shareholders:* Richard Claridge; Kevin William Long; Wendy Helena Prestwood
*Officers:* Danielle Barney [1985] Director; Richard Claridge [1985] Director; Victoria Daly [1980] Director; Kevin William Long [1955] Director; Wendy Helena Prestwood [1946] Director; Tracey Anne Roberts [1964] Director; Carolyn Upson [1951] Director

**Old Earth School**
*Incorporated:* 2 August 2011 *Employees:* 75
*Net Worth:* £2,511,507 *Total Assets:* £3,523,845
*Registered Office:* Old Earth School, Lower Edge Road, Elland, W Yorks, HX5 9PL
*Activities:* Primary education
*Officers:* Amanda Clare Aspin [1975] Director/Nursery Manager; Carl Spencer Blakebrough [1969] Director/Technical Author; Joanne Louise Booth [1977] Director/Operations Manager; Janet Mary Day [1951] Director/Teacher; Ruth Margaret Freeman [1971] Director/Teacher; Paul Stephen Reynolds [1964] Director/Headteacher; George Edward Rischardson [1938] Director/Retired; Nicola Elizabeth Spensley [1968] Director/Teaching Assistant; Eric John Stevens [1944] Retired Managing Director; Katrina Thornton [1950] Director/Company Secretary; Malcolm David Wragg [1937] Director/Retired Deputy Headteacher

**Old HK Limited**
*Incorporated:* 27 January 1999
*Net Worth:* £4,318,494 *Total Assets:* £4,318,494
*Registered Office:* H K Timbers Ltd, Laughton Lane, Morton, Gainsborough, Lincs, DN21 3ET
*Activities:* Manufacture of wooden containers
*Officers:* Cassie Olivia Hutchings, Secretary; Cassie Olivia Hutchings [1983] Director/Industrialist; Gregory Frederick Hutchings [1947] Director/Industrialist

**Old Innserve Limited**
*Incorporated:* 10 December 2003 *Employees:* 3
*Net Worth:* £2,320,000 *Total Assets:* £20,957,000
*Registered Office:* The Old Maltings, Leeds Road, Tadcaster, N Yorks, LS24 9HB
*Activities:* Repair of other equipment
*Parent:* Serviced Dispense Equipment (Holdings) Ltd
*Officers:* Thomas Anthony Danaher [1964] Director/On Trade Finance Business Partner; Gerard Lowry [1972] On Trade Development & Operations Director; Radovan Sikorsky [1967] Finance Director [Slovak]

**Olicana Holdings Limited**
*Incorporated:* 1 June 2005 *Employees:* 2
*Net Worth:* £5,761,821 *Total Assets:* £5,880,294
*Registered Office:* Midwood, 65 Curly Hill, Ilkley, W Yorks, LS29 0BA
*Activities:* Activities of head offices
*Shareholders:* Dakin Industries Limited; Rupert George Pearson; Leslie Clare Pearson
*Officers:* Rupert George Pearson, Secretary/Engineer; Lesley Clare Pearson [1965] Director/Company Administrator; Rupert George Pearson [1966] Director/Engineer

**Olicana Properties Limited**
*Incorporated:* 19 May 1967 *Employees:* 1
*Net Worth:* £6,579,507 *Total Assets:* £12,755,480
*Registered Office:* Arthington Park, Arthington, Otley, W Yorks, LS21 1PH
*Activities:* Other letting and operating of own or leased real estate
*Parent:* Quarmby Holdings Limited
*Officers:* John Antony Batty, Secretary; Laura Gabrielle Irene Davies [1977] Director/Interiors Designer and Retailer; Hannah Margaret Eames [1980] Director/Retail Project Manager; James Roger Quarmby [1944] Director; Julia Margaret Quarmby [1950] Director; Oliver Alexander Quarmby [1975] Director/Chartered Surveyor

**Olympus Print Group Limited**
*Incorporated:* 20 August 1993 *Employees:* 78
*Net Worth:* £1,309,954 *Total Assets:* £6,923,480
*Registered Office:* Olympus House, Richardshaw Road, Grangefield Industrial Estate, Pudsey, Leeds, LS28 6QW
*Activities:* Manufacture of printed labels
*Shareholders:* Adrian Ian Brown; Stephen Robert Cartwright
*Officers:* Deborah Jane Thornton, Secretary; Adrian Ian Brown [1963] Director/Sales Manager; Stephen Robert Cartwright [1962] Director/Print Executive; Peter Davies [1966] Director

**Omco UK Limited**
*Incorporated:* 29 September 1995 *Employees:* 86
*Net Worth:* £3,632,304 *Total Assets:* £5,087,586
*Registered Office:* New Street Mills, Carlisle Road, Pudsey, Leeds, LS28 8LW
*Activities:* Manufacture of metal structures and parts of structures
*Parent:* Omco International NV
*Officers:* Mary Patricia Broderick, Secretary; Martyn Timothy Atkinson [1960] Director/General Manager; Willy Wilfried de Four [1959] Director/Financial Controller [Belgian]; Darko Ranogajec [1963] Director/General Manager [Croatian]

**Omega PLC**
*Incorporated:* 24 March 1992 *Employees:* 341
*Net Worth:* £62,785,000 *Total Assets:* £71,615,000
*Registered Office:* Omega Boulevard, Capitol Park, Thorne, Doncaster, S Yorks, DN8 5TX
*Activities:* Manufacture of other furniture
*Parent:* Cycene Limited
*Officers:* Richard Adam, Secretary; Richard David Adam [1971] Finance Director; Simon Keith Barber [1967] Director; John Cahill [1963] Director; Alastair Strang England [1969] Director; Tracey Anne Labbett [1967] Director; James John Robert Murray [1990] Director; Sir Robert Sydney Murray [1946] Director; Richard Harvey Tattersall [1961] Director

**Omega Proteins Limited**
*Incorporated:* 29 October 1999 *Employees:* 221
*Net Worth:* £2,043,599 *Total Assets:* £49,215,280
*Registered Office:* Swalesmoor Farm, Swales Moor Road, Halifax, W Yorks, HX3 6UF
*Activities:* Other manufacturing n.e.c.
*Parent:* Leo Group Ltd
*Officers:* Manjit Singh Powar [1976] Director; Danny Steven Sawrij [1969] Director

**Omega Signs Limited**
*Incorporated:* 31 January 1992 *Employees:* 83
*Net Worth:* £2,093,236 *Total Assets:* £5,029,319
*Registered Office:* Omega Signs, Newmarket Approach, Leeds, LS9 0RJ
*Activities:* Other manufacturing n.e.c.
*Shareholders:* Duncan John Chapman; Anthony Timmermans
*Officers:* Alan Peter Stirling, Finance Director; Duncan John Chapman [1969] Director; Margaret Ann Chapman [1940] Director/Medical Receptionist; Barry Dennehy [1971] Technical & Operations Director; Patrick Gains [1960] Commercial Director; Alan Peter Stirling [1970] Finance Director; Anthony Robert Timmermans [1953] Director Sign Makers; Marc Timmermans [1978] Production Director

**Omnivale Limited**
*Incorporated:* 8 September 1997
*Net Worth:* £5,426,000 *Total Assets:* £16,248,000
*Registered Office:* Manor House Farm, East Drayton, Retford, Notts, DN22 0LG
*Activities:* Buying and selling of own real estate
*Parent:* Strawson Group Developments Limited
*Officers:* James Watson Eyre Wild, Secretary; Elizabeth Anne Bisson [1963] Director; George David Strawson [1937] Director

**Omya UK Limited**
*Incorporated:* 7 June 1947 *Employees:* 231
*Net Worth:* £13,224,000 *Total Assets:* £100,472,000
*Registered Office:* Melton Office, Melton Bottom, Melton, North Ferriby, E Yorks, HU14 3HU
*Activities:* Manufacture of other chemical products n.e.c.
*Officers:* Ryaan Irzaad Abdul [1965] Director/Accountant; William Ian Cardew [1960] Director; Stephane Decraecker [1966] Director/Chief Financial Officer Europe [Belgian]

**On Board Leisure (Holdings) Limited**
*Incorporated:* 20 March 2013
*Net Worth:* £3,500,000 *Total Assets:* £3,500,000
*Registered Office:* Unit 4 Whitehall Court, Whitehall Park, Leeds, LS12 5SN
*Activities:* Non-trading company
*Officers:* Jonathan Philip Dyson, Secretary; Jonathan Philip Dyson [1964] Director; Keith Hamill [1952] Director; Ian Arthur Hendrie [1970] Director; Julian Frederick Nicholls [1951] Director

**On Line Design & Engineering Limited**
*Incorporated:* 11 February 1982 *Employees:* 116
*Previous:* On-Line Design & Engineering Limited
*Net Worth:* £4,252,353 *Total Assets:* £6,530,757
*Registered Office:* On Line House, Pelham Road, Immingham, N E Lincs, DN40 1AB
*Activities:* Manufacture of metal structures and parts of structures
*Parent:* On Line Group Limited
*Officers:* Stephen Anthoney Laird, Secretary; Phillip John Chapman [1966] Director/Civil Engineer; Brendan Patrick Conlan [1968] Director/Engineer; Jeffrey Laird [1946] Director/Chartered Engineer; Stephen Anthoney Laird [1974] Director/Accountant; Andrew James Mitchell [1976] Director/Engineer; Graham Trevor Mumby [1962] Director/Instrument Engineer; Duncan Russell [1964] Director/Chartered Engineer

**On Line Group Limited**
*Incorporated:* 4 October 2012 *Employees:* 411
*Previous:* On Line Design & Engineering Group Limited
*Net Worth:* £7,775,755 *Total Assets:* £11,768,164
*Registered Office:* On Line House, Pelham Road, Immingham, N E Lincs, DN40 1AB
*Activities:* Activities of head offices
*Major Shareholder:* Susan Laird
*Officers:* Louise Jacqueline Arnett [1974] Director/HR Professional; Melanie Jane Dent [1975] Director/Graphic Designer; Jeffrey Laird [1946] Director/Chartered Engineer; Stephen Anthoney Laird [1974] Director/Accountant; Susan Laird [1951] Group Director

**On Line People Limited**
*Incorporated:* 12 March 2012 *Employees:* 209
*Net Worth:* £866,578 *Total Assets:* £6,196,157
*Registered Office:* On Line House, Pelham Road, Immingham, N E Lincs, DN40 1AB
*Activities:* Other activities of employment placement agencies
*Parent:* On Line Group Limited
*Officers:* Jeffrey Laird [1946] Director/Chartered Engineer; Stephen Anthoney Laird [1974] Director/Accountant; Craig Poole [1977] Director

**On-Site Property Solutions Limited**
*Incorporated:* 22 January 2015
*Net Worth:* £281,571 *Total Assets:* £3,097,256
*Registered Office:* 4 Bowcliffe Grange, Bramham, Wetherby, W Yorks, LS23 6UL
*Activities:* Other letting and operating of own or leased real estate
*Officers:* Alexander John Boyle [1985] Director/Property Surveyor; Richard Andrew Crosland [1964] Director/Accountant; Nigel David Rippon Jowett [1960] Director

**One Brewery Wharf Limited**
*Incorporated:* 24 August 2004 *Employees:* 3
*Net Worth:* £1,705,601 *Total Assets:* £3,600,020
*Registered Office:* 5 Hawthorn Park, Coal Road, Leeds, LS14 1PQ
*Activities:* Buying and selling of own real estate
*Parent:* Rushbond PLC
*Officers:* Richard Mark Powell, Secretary; Mark Richard Finch [1967] Director/Chartered Surveyor Chartered Town Planner; Jonathan William Maud [1960] Director; Richard Mark Powell [1967] Director/Chartered Accountant

**One Call Insurance Services Limited**
*Incorporated:* 11 March 2003 *Employees:* 448
*Net Worth:* £17,577,676 *Total Assets:* £41,951,292
*Registered Office:* Saturn Building, First Point, Balby Carr Bank, Doncaster, S Yorks, DN4 5JQ
*Activities:* Activities of insurance agents and brokers
*Major Shareholder:* John Lawrence Radford
*Officers:* Alexandra Maria Sheriff, Secretary; Joshua Charles Barnsdale [1982] Director; William Laurence Broughton [1975] Director/Solicitor; Sarah Louise Chadburn [1978] Compliance Director; John David Goacher [1964] Finance Director; Peter Graham Long [1986] Operations Director; John Matthew Parker [1976] Claims Director; Carolyn Marie Radford [1982] PR Director; John Lawrence Radford [1965] Director/Chief Executive Officer; Oliver Paul Rose [1986] Director; Nicholas Graham Springthorpe [1971] Managing Director; John Steele [1953] Director/Head of Compliance, Risk and Internal Audit

**One Commercial (Claims) Limited**
*Incorporated:* 8 March 2005
*Previous:* UK General (Claims) Limited
*Net Worth Deficit:* £4,523,012 *Total Assets:* £3,040,889
*Registered Office:* Cast House, Old Mill Business Park, Gibraltar Island Road, Leeds, LS10 1RJ
*Activities:* Non-life insurance
*Parent:* PBS Holdings Limited
*Officers:* Elizabeth Brophy, Secretary; Timothy John Smyth [1967] Director

**One Commercial Limited**
*Incorporated:* 28 October 2014 *Employees:* 34
*Net Worth:* £1,512,040 *Total Assets:* £3,067,776
*Registered Office:* Cast House, Gibraltar Island Road, Old Mill Business Park, Leeds, LS10 1RJ
*Activities:* Non-life insurance
*Parent:* PBS Holdings Limited
*Officers:* Elizabeth Brophy, Secretary; Graham Marshall Coates [1956] Director; Allan Crawford Adamson Gribben [1953] Director/Chairman; Timothy John Smyth [1967] Commercial Director

**One Fortress Limited**
*Incorporated:* 6 February 2017 *Employees:* 1
*Net Worth:* £343,701 *Total Assets:* £8,889,610
*Registered Office:* Buy It Direct, Trident Business Park, Huddersfield, W Yorks, HD2 1UA
*Activities:* Buying and selling of own real estate
*Officers:* Nicholas Harvey Glynne, Secretary; Nicholas Harvey Glynne [1966] Director

**One in a Million Free School**
*Incorporated:* 27 March 2012 *Employees:* 52
*Net Worth:* £4,210,332 *Total Assets:* £4,470,556
*Registered Office:* One in A Million Free School, Cliffe Terrace, Bradford, W Yorks, BD8 7DX
*Activities:* General secondary education
*Officers:* Wayne Jacobs, Secretary; Nicholas John Aldridge [1976] Director/Senior Business Manager; David Francis Baldwin [1971] Director/Chief Executive; Susan Margaret Elizabeth Daniells [1957] Director/Business Manager; Stephen Peter Hawthorn-Emmett [1979] Director/Project Manager and Data Protection Officer; Mark Francis Hughes [1975] Director; Rachel Jacobs [1968] Director/Education Consultant; Sharron Ann Mikkelsen [1970] Director/Admin Team Leader; Robert Anthony James Moon [1973] Director Construction; Christopher Ernest Schofield [1962] Director/Solicitor; Richard Graham White [1947] Director/Retired

**One Stop Business Finance Limited**
*Incorporated:* 21 July 2014 *Employees:* 8
*Net Worth:* £46,834 *Total Assets:* £6,297,749
*Registered Office:* The Old Cow Shed, Oak Farm, Laytham, York, YO42 4PP
*Activities:* Financial management
*Shareholders:* Andrew Derek MacKenzie; Amanda Jane MacKenzie
*Officers:* Andrew Derek MacKenzie [1964] Director

**Ontrac Limited**
*Incorporated:* 1 August 2008 *Employees:* 27
*Net Worth:* £8,611,031 *Total Assets:* £10,322,958
*Registered Office:* Leeds Innovation Centre, 103 Clarendon Road, Leeds, LS2 9DF
*Activities:* Information technology consultancy activities
*Parent:* Ontrac Technology Limited
*Officers:* Mark Ian Atkinson [1971] Director; Maxwell James Cawthra [1978] Director; Martyn Stuart Cuthbert [1967] Director; Alex Johnson [1967] Director; Nathan Maxwell [1975] Director/Business Analyst; John Cameron McArthur [1975] Director; Andrew Parry [1961] Projects Director

**Onward Fishing Company Limited**
*Incorporated:* 16 January 1901
*Net Worth:* £18,106,214 *Total Assets:* £20,216,628
*Registered Office:* The Orangery, Hesslewood Country Business Park, Ferriby Road, Hessle, E Yorks, HU13 0LH
*Activities:* Marine fishing
*Officers:* Gustaf Baldvinsson [1957] Managing Director [Icelander]; Thorsteinn Mar Baldvinsson [1952] Director [Icelander]; Haraldur Gretarsson [1968] Managing Director [Icelander]

**Onward Holdings Limited**
*Incorporated:* 31 December 1932 *Employees:* 33
*Net Worth:* £26,707,256 *Total Assets:* £36,181,512
*Registered Office:* Unit 1a Onward Park, Phoenix Avenue, Featherstone, Pontefract, W Yorks, WF7 6EP
*Activities:* Development of building projects
*Officers:* Susan Bacon [1962] Director; Stephen Richard Bloomer [1963] Director/Warehouse Manager; Valerie Bloomer [1941] Director; Robin Lee [1947] Director/Accountant; Carol Rayner [1960] Director/Bookkeeper; Granville Parker Storey [1943] Director; John Mark Storey [1974] Director; Neil Kenneth Storey [1962] Director; Patricia Ann Watson [1957] Director

**Onward Investment Limited**
*Incorporated:* 19 November 2010
*Net Worth:* £21,429,828 *Total Assets:* £45,220,292
*Registered Office:* The Orangery, Hesslewood Country Business Park, Ferriby Road, Hessle, E Yorks, HU13 0LH
*Activities:* Marine fishing
*Officers:* Gustaf Baldvinsson [1957] Managing Director [Icelander]; Thorsteinn Mar Baldvinsson [1952] Chief Executive Director [Icelander]; Ingvar Gudmundur Juliusson [1974] Director/Head of Group Accounting [Icelander]

**Opera North Limited**
*Incorporated:* 13 March 1981 *Employees:* 219
*Net Worth:* £11,489,308 *Total Assets:* £15,910,666
*Registered Office:* Grand Theatre, 46 New Briggate, Leeds, LS1 6NU
*Activities:* Performing arts
*Officers:* Kirsten Jean Bullen, Secretary; Edmund John Seward Anderson [1950] Director; Mark Henry Armour [1954] Finance Director; Nicola Christine Brentnall [1966] Director; Henrietta Jowitt [1959] Deputy Director General; Liza Miranda Ryerson Kellett [1965] Director/Chief Executive; Paul Anthony Lee [1946] Director; Peter Dominic Maniura [1957] Director/Curator; Richard John Mantle [1947] Director; Rosemary Harriet Millard [1965] Director/Deputy CEO; Dr Nima Poovaya-Smith [1953] Director; Jonathan David Pryor [1989] Director/Councillor; John Irving Warnett [1953] Director/Management Consultant

**Opera North Productions Limited**
*Incorporated:* 23 September 2014
*Net Worth:* £1,918 *Total Assets:* £3,450,309
*Registered Office:* Grand Theatre, 46 New Briggate, Leeds, LS1 6NU
*Activities:* Artistic creation
*Parent:* Opera North Limited
*Officers:* Kirsten Jean Bullen, Secretary; Christine Jane Chibnall [1953] Artistic Director; Kieron John Docherty [1969] Technical Director; Clive Roland Lloyd [1959] Managing Director; Richard John Mantle [1947] Director/Chief Executive

**OPH Property Holdings Limited**
*Incorporated:* 19 November 2009 *Employees:* 16
*Net Worth:* £2,746,561 *Total Assets:* £3,056,443
*Registered Office:* 170-172 Roundhay Road, Leeds, LS8 5PL
*Activities:* Hotels and similar accommodation
*Major Shareholder:* Deepak Raju Handa
*Officers:* Gulshan Handa, Secretary; Deepak Raju Handa [1975] Director/Chief Executive Officer

**OPM (Labels & Packaging) Group Limited**
*Incorporated:* 8 March 1972 *Employees:* 75
*Net Worth:* £3,752,856 *Total Assets:* £9,004,478
*Registered Office:* The Colour Box, 55 Gelderd Road, Leeds, LS12 6TG
*Activities:* Manufacture of printed labels
*Major Shareholder:* Christopher John Ellison
*Officers:* Alan Antony Haigh, Secretary; Ian David Michael Bell [1959] Director/Salesman; Arnold Christopher Ellison [1993] Director/Sales Executive; Charlotte Leigh Ellison [1990] Commercial Director; Christopher John Ellison [1965] Director; Susan Jane Ellison [1970] Director/Sales; Alan Antony Haigh [1960] Director/Accountant; Steven Michael Walker [1976] Operations Director

**Optare Group Ltd**
*Incorporated:* 22 May 1984 *Employees:* 316
*Net Worth Deficit:* £50,678,000 *Total Assets:* £50,716,000
*Registered Office:* Unit 3 Hurricane Way South, Sherburn in Elmet, Leeds, LS25 6PT
*Activities:* Manufacture of motor vehicles
*Parent:* Optare PLC
*Officers:* Richard Damian Butler [1968] Director; John Matthew Fickling [1951] Director

**Optare PLC**
*Incorporated:* 23 January 2008 *Employees:* 317
*Net Worth:* £4,897,000 *Total Assets:* £34,286,000
*Registered Office:* Unit 3 Hurricane Way South, Sherburn in Elmet, Leeds, LS25 6PT
*Activities:* Manufacture of motor vehicles
*Shareholder:* Hinduja Automotive Limited
*Officers:* Abhijit Mukhopadhyay, Secretary; Dr. Seshu Bhagavathula [1957] Director [German]; John Matthew Fickling [1951] Director; Gopal Mahadevan [1966] Director/Chief Financial Officer, Ashok Leyland Limited [Indian]; Steven John Norris [1945] Director; Venkat Venkatesan [1956] Director/Corporate Executive

**Optibiotix Health PLC**
*Incorporated:* 19 July 2006
*Net Worth:* £7,045,716 *Total Assets:* £7,669,203
*Registered Office:* Innovation Centre, Innovation Way, Heslington, York, YO10 5DG
*Activities:* Activities of head offices
*Officers:* Gareth Barker [1966] Director; Michael Sean Christie [1957] Director; Richard Colin Neil Davidson [1951] Director; Sofia Kolyda [1973] Director [Greek]; Stephen Patrick Ohara [1960] Director/Scientist; Per Rehne [1970] Director [Danish]; Jan Peter Fredik Wennstrom [1957] Director [Swedish]; Christina Mary Wood [1960] Director

**Optident Limited**
*Incorporated:* 28 January 1985 *Employees:* 48
*Net Worth:* £3,431,294 *Total Assets:* £11,970,613
*Registered Office:* International Development Centre, Valley Drive, Ilkley, W Yorks, LS29 8AL
*Activities:* Non-specialised wholesale trade
*Parent:* Optident Holdings Limited
*Officers:* Patrick Thompson Allen [1966] Director; Timothy Robert Butterfield [1968] Director; Adrian Spencer Martin [1969] Director/Accountant; Robert Nathan Minowitz [1958] Director/Business Executive [American]; Helen Louise Redding [1975] Director/Chief Financial Officer

**Optima International Limited**
*Incorporated:* 22 February 1961
*Net Worth:* £3,662,394 *Total Assets:* £4,665,349
*Registered Office:* Optima House, Askern Road, Toll Bar, Doncaster, S Yorks, DN5 0QY
*Activities:* Manufacture of other special-purpose machinery n.e.c.
*Major Shareholder:* Carol Spiller
*Officers:* Adel Yarnell Spence, Secretary; Tony Mulvey [1975] Director; Carol Spiller [1945] Director; Adel Yarnell Spence [1977] Director/Engineering

**Optima Legal Services Limited**
*Incorporated:* 13 April 2006 *Employees:* 260
*Net Worth:* £6,148,000 *Total Assets:* £8,873,000
*Registered Office:* Hepworth House, Claypit Lane, Leeds, LS2 8AE
*Activities:* Solicitors
*Parent:* Capita Legal Services Limited
*Officers:* Robert David Tolfts [1962] Director; Mark John Tosetti [1977] Director; Craig Daniel Underwood [1973] Director

**Optimisation Developments Limited**
*Incorporated:* 22 July 2008
*Net Worth Deficit:* £157,799,008 *Total Assets:* £123,627,000
*Registered Office:* Hilmore House, Gain Lane, Bradford, W Yorks, BD3 7DL
*Activities:* Other business support service activities n.e.c.
*Parent:* Wm Morrison Supermarkets Holdings Limited
*Officers:* Jonathan James Burke, Secretary; Jonathan James Burke [1966] Director; Joanna Louise Goff [1978] Finance Director

**Optimisation Investments Limited**
*Incorporated:* 22 July 2008
*Net Worth Deficit:* £178,120,992 *Total Assets:* £728,412,992
*Registered Office:* Hilmore House, Gain Lane, Bradford, W Yorks, BD3 7DL
*Activities:* Other business support service activities n.e.c.
*Parent:* Wm Morrison Supermarkets Holdings Limited
*Officers:* Jonathan James Burke, Secretary; Jonathan James Burke [1966] Director; Joanna Louise Goff [1978] Finance Director

**Optimum Medical Solutions Limited**
*Incorporated:* 24 December 2008 *Employees:* 36
*Net Worth:* £1,185,845 *Total Assets:* £3,584,528
*Registered Office:* Tennant Hall, Blenheim Grove, Leeds, LS2 9ET
*Activities:* Manufacture of medical and dental instruments and supplies
*Parent:* Optimum Medical Solutions Leeds Limited
*Officers:* Alexis Adrian Higgins [1980] Director/Sales Manager; Gareth Alexander Rimmington [1980] Director

**Optimum4 Limited**
*Incorporated:* 6 April 1998 *Employees:* 108
*Net Worth:* £11,139,000 *Total Assets:* £15,030,000
*Registered Office:* West One, 100 Wellington Street, Leeds, LS1 4LT
*Activities:* Media representation services
*Parent:* Stickyeyes Limited
*Officers:* Louise Bean, Secretary; Andrew Craig Chalmers [1969] Director/Advertising; Ian Andrew Courts [1975] Director/Accountant; Thomas Malcolm Howard [1971] Director/Accountant; Craig Lister [1971] Director; Timothy James Treleaven [1977] Director/Accountant

**Opus Energy (Corporate) Limited**
*Incorporated:* 6 August 2004 *Employees:* 4
*Net Worth:* £10,542,000 *Total Assets:* £103,078,000
*Registered Office:* Drax Power Station, Selby, N Yorks, YO8 8PH
*Activities:* Trade of electricity
*Parent:* Opus Energy Group Limited
*Officers:* David McCallum, Secretary; Nicola Karen Flanders [1968] Director; Dwight Daniel Willard Gardiner [1964] Director [British/American]; Carl Goulton [1972] Director; Jonathan Anantha Kini [1979] Director

**Opus Energy Group Limited**
*Incorporated:* 4 April 2002 *Employees:* 4
*Net Worth:* £8,556,000 *Total Assets:* £8,751,000
*Registered Office:* Drax Power Station, Selby, N Yorks, YO8 8PH
*Activities:* Activities of head offices
*Parent:* Drax Smart Supply Holdco Limited
*Officers:* David McCallum, Secretary; Nicola Karen Flanders [1968] Director; Dwight Daniel Willard Gardiner [1964] Director [British/American]; Carl Goulton [1972] Director; Jonathan Anantha Kini [1979] Director

**Opus Energy Limited**
*Incorporated:* 26 February 2002 *Employees:* 894
*Net Worth:* £23,981,000 *Total Assets:* £201,091,008
*Registered Office:* Drax Power Station, Selby, N Yorks, YO8 8PH
*Activities:* Trade of electricity
*Parent:* Opus Energy Group Limited
*Officers:* David McCallum, Secretary; Nicola Karen Flanders [1968] Director; Dwight Daniel Willard Gardiner [1964] Director [British/American]; Carl Goulton [1972] Director; Jonathan Anantha Kini [1979] Director

**Opus Gas Supply Limited**
*Incorporated:* 9 April 2009 *Employees:* 4
*Net Worth Deficit:* £1,106,000 *Total Assets:* £44,057,000
*Registered Office:* Drax Power Station, Selby, N Yorks, YO8 8PH
*Activities:* Trade of gas through mains
*Parent:* Opus Energy Group Limited
*Officers:* David McCallum, Secretary; Nicola Karen Flanders [1968] Director; Dwight Daniel Willard Gardiner [1964] Director [British/American]; Carl Goulton [1972] Director; Jonathan Anantha Kini [1979] Director

**Orange Mountain Bikes Limited**
*Incorporated:* 28 July 1988 *Employees:* 18
*Net Worth:* £1,839,336 *Total Assets:* £4,249,007
*Registered Office:* Unit 3 Brookwoods Industrial Estate, Halifax, W Yorks, HX4 9BH
*Activities:* Non-specialised wholesale trade
*Parent:* HLWKH 588 Limited
*Officers:* Ashley Ball [1977] Director

**Orangechart Limited**
*Incorporated:* 9 October 2012
*Net Worth:* £2,829,000 *Total Assets:* £4,018,000
*Registered Office:* Hexagon House, Grimbald Crag Close, Knaresborough, N Yorks, HG5 8PJ
*Activities:* Activities of other holding companies n.e.c.
*Parent:* Links Investment Holdings Limited
*Officers:* Simon Drew, Secretary; Simon Richard Drew [1969] Director/Accountant; Julie Dye [1972] Director; Desmond Joseph O'Connor [1971] Director/Insurance Broker; Danny Parsons [1958] Director/General Insurance; Christopher Travers [1954] Director

**Orcina Limited**
*Incorporated:* 5 March 1986 *Employees:* 17
*Net Worth:* £938,420 *Total Assets:* £3,146,393
*Registered Office:* Daltongate Business Centre, Ulverston, Cumbria, LA12 7AJ
*Activities:* Support activities for petroleum and natural gas mining
*Officers:* Dr Sarah Elizabeth Ellwood [1975] Director/Professional Engineer; David John Heffernan [1970] Director/Software Engineer; Gillian Anne McKinnon [1969] Director/Professional Engineer

**Orean Personal Care Limited**
*Incorporated:* 14 October 2008 *Employees:* 98
*Net Worth:* £2,551,995 *Total Assets:* £6,587,196
*Registered Office:* Unit E1, Stubs Beck Lane, West 26 Industrial Estate, Cleckheaton, W Yorks, BD19 4TT
*Activities:* Manufacture of other chemical products n.e.c.
*Shareholder:* Mark Gary Spence
*Officers:* Sean Michael Spence [1960] Director; Dan Williams [1980] Commercial Director

**Oriel Printing Co. Limited**
*Incorporated:* 30 November 1978 *Employees:* 44
*Net Worth:* £1,512,159 *Total Assets:* £3,091,622
*Registered Office:* Bontoft Avenue, Kingston upon Hull, HU5 4HF
*Activities:* Printing n.e.c.
*Shareholder:* John Wilfred Simms
*Officers:* Jane Simms, Secretary; Christopher John Markwell Holmes [1964] Director/Print Sales; Jane Simms [1954] Director/Company Secretary; Richard Simms [1977] Director/Printer; Robert Simms [1979] Director/Printer

**Oriental Merchant (Europe) Limited**
*Incorporated:* 21 August 2001 *Employees:* 8
*Net Worth:* £965,089 *Total Assets:* £3,888,687
*Registered Office:* 2nd Floor, Woodside House, 261 Low Lane, Horsforth, Leeds, LS18 5NY
*Activities:* Agents involved in the sale of food, beverages and tobacco
*Parent:* Oriental Merchant Pty Limited
*Officers:* Tony Jing-Ying Xie, Secretary; Yun Cai [1968] Director [Chinese]; Jacques Theodore Marie Vaessen [1963] Director [Dutch]; Gordon Guoxiong Wu [1965] Director [Chinese]; Tony Jing-Ying Xie [1964] Director Finance [Australian]; Bernard Tat Kin Yiu [1949] Managing Director [Australian]; Shixin Yu [1962] Director [Chinese]

**Origin Group Finance Limited**
*Incorporated:* 21 November 2013 *Employees:* 2
*Previous:* Westpoint Group Finance Limited
*Net Worth Deficit:* £5,952,141 *Total Assets:* £43,966,280
*Registered Office:* Leeman House, Station Business Park, Holgate Park Drive, York, YO26 4GB
*Activities:* Activities of other holding companies n.e.c.
*Parent:* Origin Group Holdco Limited
*Officers:* Joanna Clare Malone [1974] Director; Mark Stanworth [1964] Director

**Origin Group Holdco Limited**
*Incorporated:* 21 November 2013 *Employees:* 284
*Previous:* Westpoint Group Holdco Limited
*Net Worth Deficit:* £10,693,818 *Total Assets:* £49,017,368
*Registered Office:* Leeman House, Station Business Park, Holgate Park Drive, York, YO26 4GB
*Activities:* Activities of other holding companies n.e.c.
*Parent:* Vetpartners Limited
*Officers:* Joanna Clare Malone [1974] Director; Mark Stanworth [1964] Director

**Origin Packaging Limited**
*Incorporated:* 8 December 2009 *Employees:* 29
*Net Worth:* £2,454,375 *Total Assets:* £6,181,596
*Registered Office:* Melton House, Jackson Way, Melton, North Ferriby, E Yorks, HU14 3HJ
*Activities:* Other manufacturing n.e.c.
*Parent:* Paragon Packaging Company
*Officers:* Joseph William Pocock [1988] Director/Market Research; Timothy James Pocock [1967] Finance Director; Keith Ryan Wade [1982] Managing Director

**Oriium Consulting Ltd**
*Incorporated:* 8 March 2007 *Employees:* 34
*Net Worth:* £649,285 *Total Assets:* £3,147,998
*Registered Office:* Gemini Grange, Sandbeck Way, Wetherby, W Yorks, LS22 7DN
*Activities:* Information technology consultancy activities
*Parent:* Concepta Capital Limited
*Officers:* Katherine Maria Hogg [1976] Director; Christopher Joseph Kiaie [1982] Managing Director; Erica Jane Kiaie [1984] Director/Chartered Accountant; Ryan Matthew McCarry [1976] Director

**Orion Commercial Properties Limited**
*Incorporated:* 19 January 1981
*Net Worth:* £2,152,446 *Total Assets:* £10,578,338
*Registered Office:* 5 Benton Office Park, Bennett Avenue, Benton Hill, Horbury, Wakefield, W Yorks, WF4 5RA
*Activities:* Other letting and operating of own or leased real estate
*Shareholders:* Timothy Lumb; Jean Sandra Lumb
*Officers:* Christine Mary Weston, Secretary; Andrew James Lumb [1972] Construction Director; Jean Sandra Lumb [1945] Director/Secretary; Joanne Sarah Lumb [1970] Commercial Director; Timothy Lumb [1944] Director/Chartered Accountant; Christine Mary Weston [1954] Certified Accountant/Financial Director

**Orion Developments Limited**
*Incorporated:* 9 October 1978 *Employees:* 73
*Net Worth:* £13,300,787 *Total Assets:* £20,479,736
*Registered Office:* 5 Benton Office Park, Bennett Avenue, Benton Hill, Horbury, Wakefield, W Yorks, WF4 5RA
*Activities:* Development of building projects
*Shareholders:* Timothy Lumb; Jean Sandra Lumb
*Officers:* Christine Mary Weston, Secretary; Andrew James Lumb [1972] Construction Director; Joanne Sarah Lumb [1970] Land Director; Simon Timothy Lumb [1972] Director; Timothy Lumb [1944] Director/Chairman; Christine Mary Weston [1954] Managing and Financial Director

**Orion Homes Limited**
*Incorporated:* 13 June 1979 *Employees:* 48
*Net Worth:* £5,856,853 *Total Assets:* £12,947,815
*Registered Office:* 5 Benton Office Park, Bennett Avenue, Benton Hill, Horbury, Wakefield, W Yorks, WF4 5RA
*Activities:* Development of building projects
*Parent:* Orion Developments Limited
*Officers:* Christine Mary Weston, Secretary; Andrew James Lumb [1972] Construction Director; Joanne Sarah Lumb [1970] Land Director; Simon Timothy Lumb [1972] Director; Timothy Lumb [1944] Director/Chartered Accountant Chairman; Christine Mary Weston [1954] Managing Director

**Orkla Foods UK PLC**
*Incorporated:* 10 July 1959 *Employees:* 5
*Net Worth:* £1,227,157 *Total Assets:* £3,709,095
*Registered Office:* 33 George Street, Wakefield, W Yorks, WF1 1LX
*Activities:* Non-specialised wholesale trade
*Officers:* Jan Tore Omarstrand, Secretary; Peter Ditlef Lowzow [1955] Sales Director [Norwegian]; David Woollin [1972] Commercial Director

**Ormsborough Limited**
*Incorporated:* 6 August 2015
*Net Worth:* £8,318,284 *Total Assets:* £8,340,984
*Registered Office:* The Leeming Building, Ludgate Hill, Leeds, LS2 7HZ
*Activities:* Management of real estate on a fee or contract basis
*Officers:* Steven Michael Kenee [1979] Investment Director; John Stewart Leslie [1959] Director; John Brian Peers [1967] Director/Accountant; Jade Renner [1990] Director

**Orphans in Need**
*Incorporated:* 4 October 2011 *Employees:* 27
*Net Worth:* £4,888,656 *Total Assets:* £5,045,423
*Registered Office:* Windsor House, 10 Manchester Road, Bradford, W Yorks, BD5 0QH
*Activities:* Other professional, scientific and technical activities n.e.c.
*Officers:* Shoukat Ali [1960] Director; Ellyot Vincent Doyle [1976] Director; Asif Mohammad [1978] Director; Anish Musa [1978] Director; Valerie Ann Scarll [1957] Director/Bookkeeper; Ismail Vania [1960] Director/Teacher

**Ortho-Care (U.K.) Limited**
*Incorporated:* 26 November 1981 *Employees:* 46
*Net Worth:* £7,233,272 *Total Assets:* £8,244,353
*Registered Office:* 1 Riverside Estate, Saltaire, W Yorks, BD17 7DR
*Activities:* Dental practice activities
*Shareholders:* Richard Garford; Kelvin George Scott
*Officers:* Richard Garford, Secretary; Richard Garford [1957] Director; Kelvin George Scott [1956] Director

**Ortus Secured Finance III Limited**
*Incorporated:* 15 May 2014 *Employees:* 2
*Net Worth:* £2 *Total Assets:* £8,735,002
*Registered Office:* c/o White Rose Accountants, 15a Hallgate, Doncaster, S Yorks, DN1 3NA
*Activities:* Other credit granting n.e.c.
*Shareholder:* Michael Ashley
*Officers:* Michael Patrick Murray [1969] Director/Property Developer; Glyn Dale Smith [1964] Director/Property Developer

**Orvec Holdings Limited**
*Incorporated:* 22 September 2006 *Employees:* 3
*Net Worth:* £394,176 *Total Assets:* £4,111,922
*Registered Office:* Malmo Road, Sutton Fields Industrial Estate, Hull, HU7 0YF
*Activities:* Manufacture of non-wovens and articles made from non-wovens, except apparel
*Parent:* Phipps & Company Limited
*Officers:* Brian John Meddings, Secretary; Brian John Meddings [1951] Director; Ceri Lewis Phipps [1964] Director; Stephen Lawrey Phipps [1957] Director

**Orvec International Limited**
*Incorporated:* 26 April 1974 *Employees:* 39
*Net Worth:* £6,196,478 *Total Assets:* £8,552,193
*Registered Office:* Malmo Road, Sutton Fields Industrial Estate, Hull, HU7 0YF
*Activities:* Manufacture of non-wovens and articles made from non-wovens, except apparel
*Parent:* Phipps & Co Limited
*Officers:* Brian John Meddings, Secretary; Brian John Meddings [1951] Director; William Andrew John Meddings [1982] Finance & Commercial Director; Ceri Lewis Phipps [1964] Director; Stephen Lawrey Phipps [1957] Director; Kevin Richard Stamp [1963] Managing Director

**Orvet UK**
*Incorporated:* 19 April 1996 *Employees:* 3
*Net Worth:* £6,600,633,856 *Total Assets:* £6,602,298,880
*Registered Office:* Ridings Point, Whistler Drive, Castleford, W Yorks, WF10 5HX
*Activities:* Non-trading company
*Parent:* Teva Pharmaceuticals Industries Limited
*Officers:* Dean Michael Cooper [1972] Director/Chartered Accountant; Kim Innes [1968] Director/General Manager; David Vrhovec [1967] Director [Slovenian]

**OSI Food Solutions UK Holdings Limited**
*Incorporated:* 4 April 1990
*Net Worth:* £5,313,000 *Total Assets:* £5,319,000
*Registered Office:* c/o OSI Food Solutions UK Ltd, Luneburg Way, Skippingdale, Scunthorpe, N Lincs, DN15 8LP
*Activities:* Activities of head offices
*Parent:* Gands (U.K.)
*Officers:* Martin Howard Back, Secretary; Martin Howard Back [1952] Director/Accountant; Sherry Anne de Meulenaere [1958] Director [American]; David Gerard McDonald [1964] Director [American]

**OSI Food Solutions UK Limited**
*Incorporated:* 6 June 1978 *Employees:* 172
*Net Worth:* £3,734,000 *Total Assets:* £17,471,000
*Registered Office:* Luneberg Way, Skippingdale, Scunthorpe, N Lincs, DN15 8LP
*Activities:* Production of meat and poultry meat products
*Parent:* Gands (UK)
*Officers:* Martin Howard Back, Secretary; Martin Howard Back [1952] Director/Accountant; Sherry Anne de Meulenaere [1958] Director [American]; David Gerard McDonald [1964] Director [American]

**OSI International Holdings Limited**
*Incorporated:* 18 April 1996
*Net Worth:* £56,687,000 *Total Assets:* £56,770,000
*Registered Office:* Luneburg Way, Scunthorpe, N Lincs, DN15 8LP
*Activities:* Activities of head offices
*Parent:* Gands (UK)
*Officers:* Martin Howard Back, Secretary; Sherry Anne de Meulenaere, Secretary; Sheldon Lavin [1932] Director/President [American]; David Gerard McDonald [1964] Director/VP OSI [American]

**Osprey Green Power Limited**
*Incorporated:* 11 April 2014
*Net Worth:* £5,411,807 *Total Assets:* £5,554,619
*Registered Office:* Canal Head North, Kendal, Cumbria, LA9 7BZ
*Activities:* Other engineering activities
*Parent:* GHI Holdings Limited
*Officers:* Charles William Nepean Crewdson [1964] Director; Carl Peter Crompton [1973] Director

**Osprey Limited**
*Incorporated:* 25 May 1959 *Employees:* 61
*Net Worth:* £5,919,098 *Total Assets:* £6,780,147
*Registered Office:* Osprey Limited, Dunslow Road, Eastfield, Scarborough, N Yorks, YO11 3UT
*Activities:* Manufacture of other plastic products
*Parent:* Electric 'o' Appliances Limited
*Officers:* Anne Elizabeth Smith [1960] Director/Scientist; Jeffrey Gareth Smith [1959] Director/Sales Manager

**Ossett Brewery Group Holdings Limited**
*Incorporated:* 1 August 2016 *Employees:* 349
*Net Worth:* £3,765,738 *Total Assets:* £11,878,732
*Registered Office:* Kings Yard, Low Mill Road, Ossett, W Yorks, WF5 8ND
*Activities:* Activities of other holding companies n.e.c.
*Shareholders:* HU Caret 4 Limited; James Robert Lawson
*Officers:* David Mark Hunter [1962] Director; James Robert Lawson [1972] Director; Sarah Marie Lawson [1985] Director; Jamie Andrew Merrill [1982] Director

**Ossett Brewery Pub Company Limited**
*Incorporated:* 6 January 2004 *Employees:* 205
*Net Worth:* £3,052,557 *Total Assets:* £8,097,317
*Registered Office:* Kings Yard, Low Mill Road, Ossett, W Yorks, WF5 8ND
*Activities:* Licenced restaurants
*Parent:* Ossett Brewery Group Holdings Limited
*Officers:* David Mark Hunter [1962] Director; Paul Andrew Jackson [1970] Operations Director; James Robert Lawson [1972] Director; Sarah Marie Lawson [1985] Director; Jamie Andrew Merrill [1982] Finance Director

**Ossett Holdings Limited**
*Incorporated:* 12 March 2015 *Employees:* 34
*Net Worth:* £4,282,679 *Total Assets:* £10,342,975
*Registered Office:* Zeina House, Milner Way, Ossett, W Yorks, WF5 9JE
*Activities:* Leasing of intellectual property and similar products, except copyright works
*Shareholder:* Safaa Ahmed Mohammed Ali
*Officers:* Safaa Ahmed Mohammed Ali [1956] Director/Food Processor; Abdelamir Daneshyar [1964] Director/Food Processor; Osama Daneshyar [1972] Director/Food Processor

**Oughtred & Harrison (Facilities) Ltd.**
*Incorporated:* 9 June 1988 *Employees:* 178
*Net Worth:* £2,945,107 *Total Assets:* £12,741,410
*Registered Office:* 5 Larsen Road, Goole, E Yorks, DN14 6XG
*Activities:* Other manufacturing n.e.c.
*Shareholders:* Endless LLP; Endless IV (GP) LLP
*Officers:* David Grey [1956] Director; Wesley David Beattie Linton [1977] Director; Kevin Stevens [1967] Operations Director

**Outform EMEA Limited**
*Incorporated:* 6 February 2017 *Employees:* 8
*Net Worth:* £836,263 *Total Assets:* £3,857,686
*Registered Office:* Harden Beck Mill, Harden, Bingley, W Yorks, BD16 1BL
*Activities:* Other business support service activities n.e.c.
*Shareholders:* The Valley Printing Company, Limited; Outform Ltd
*Officers:* Ben Chanoch [1957] Director; James Sinclair Haggas [1966] Director; Jonathan Simon Haggas [1970] Director; Ariel Haroush [1974] Director [Israeli]

**Outwood Grange Academies Trust**
*Incorporated:* 19 August 2009 *Employees:* 3,140
*Net Worth:* £168,666,000 *Total Assets:* £221,362,000
*Registered Office:* Potovens Lane, Outwood, Wakefield, W Yorks, WF1 2PF
*Activities:* General secondary education
*Officers:* Kathryn Ann Bradford, Secretary; Christopher John Dalzell [1957] Business Director; David Robert Earnshaw [1945] Director/Retired; Susan Dawn Hague [1963] Director; Roland David Harden [1953] Director/Retail; Martyn Ellis Oliver [1972] Director/Chief Executive; Ralph Graham Pickles [1946] Director/Consultant

**Outwood Investments Limited**
*Incorporated:* 9 May 2013 *Employees:* 3
*Net Worth:* £414,021 *Total Assets:* £5,827,377
*Registered Office:* 40 Springfield Way, Anlaby, Hull, HU10 6RJ
*Activities:* Other letting and operating of own or leased real estate
*Officers:* Angela Eastwood, Secretary; Nicola Worrell [1966] Director; Robert Worrell [1968] Director

**Ovalhouse Limited**
*Incorporated:* 24 March 1983 *Employees:* 99
*Net Worth:* £960,293 *Total Assets:* £6,979,794
*Registered Office:* c/o Pure Gym Limited, Town Centre House, Merrion Centre, Leeds, LS2 8LY
*Activities:* Fitness facilities
*Parent:* Pure Gym Limited
*Officers:* Humphrey Michael Cobbold [1964] Director/Chief Executive Officer; Alexander Basil John Wood [1978] Director/Chief Financial Officer

**Overdale Trailer Park (Skipton) Limited**
*Incorporated:* 21 April 1960 *Employees:* 7
*Net Worth:* £3,088,974 *Total Assets:* £3,516,148
*Registered Office:* Overdale Trailer Park, Harrogate Road, Skipton, N Yorks, BD23 6AA
*Activities:* Other accommodation
*Shareholder:* Barbara Corfield
*Officers:* Barbara Corfield, Secretary; Barbara Corfield [1942] Director/Secretary; Geoffrey Corfield [1938] Director; Simon Corfield [1965] Director

**Overgate Hospice**
*Incorporated:* 1 August 1980 *Employees:* 120
*Net Worth:* £6,036,902 *Total Assets:* £6,364,767
*Registered Office:* Overgate Hospice, 30 Hullen Edge Road, Elland, Halifax, W Yorks, HX5 0QY
*Activities:* Other human health activities
*Officers:* Paul Barry Andrew [1981] Director/Chartered Surveyor; Steven Peter Brennan [1970] Director/Accountant; Sheila Dent [1950] Director/Retired; Tanya Joyce Jackson [1964] Director/Corporate Affairs Manager; Dr Grahame Peter Smith-Moorhouse [1946] Director/Doctor; Raj Rani Unsworth [1959] Director/Retired HR Professional; Jodie Wielgus [1984] Director/Associate Solicitor; Dr Susan Lesley Wishart [1950] Director/Social Worker

**Overseas Trading Limited**
*Incorporated:* 20 May 2002 *Employees:* 34
*Net Worth:* £703,331 *Total Assets:* £6,927,554
*Registered Office:* OTL House, Methley Road, Castleford, W Yorks, WF10 1PA
*Activities:* Other retail sale in non-specialised stores
*Officers:* John Roger Buitekant, Secretary/Director; John Roger Buitekant [1958] Director; Philip Raymond Jennings [1960] Financial Director; Rupert Benedict Segal [1971] Director; David Revill Wain [1962] Sales & Marketing Director

**Thomas Owen Care Limited**
*Incorporated:* 13 December 1988 *Employees:* 63
*Net Worth:* £3,976,011 *Total Assets:* £8,553,783
*Registered Office:* Thomas Owen House, Lees House Road, Thornhill Lees, Dewsbury, W Yorks, WF12 9BP
*Activities:* Other human health activities
*Major Shareholder:* Kevin Eric Martin
*Officers:* Kevin Eric Martin [1955] Director/Nursing Home Proprietor

**Ray Owen Waste Disposal Limited**
*Incorporated:* 14 May 2001 *Employees:* 19
*Net Worth:* £2,470,250 *Total Assets:* £3,214,959
*Registered Office:* 12 Alma Square, Scarborough, N Yorks, YO11 1JU
*Activities:* Collection of non-hazardous waste
*Shareholder:* Raymond Douglas Owen
*Officers:* Lynda Marie Warburton, Secretary; Neil David Owen [1974] Director; Nickolas Raymond Owen [1979] Director; Raymond Douglas Owen [1950] Director/Waste Disposal Contractor; Lynda Marie Warburton [1979] Director

**Owens Developments Ltd**
*Incorporated:* 9 July 2013
*Net Worth:* £236,805 *Total Assets:* £4,295,975
*Registered Office:* Enterprise House, Field Head Lane, Birstall, W Yorks, WF17 9BN
*Activities:* Buying and selling of own real estate
*Major Shareholder:* Stephen Gregory Owens
*Officers:* Stephen Andrew Owens [1972] Director; Stephen Gregory Owens [1949] Director

**Owens-Corning Britinvest Limited**
*Incorporated:* 26 January 2000 *Employees:* 4
*Net Worth Deficit:* £43,239,000 *Total Assets:* £9,858,000
*Registered Office:* Factory, Hare Park Lane, Liversedge, W Yorks, WF15 8EP
*Activities:* Activities of head offices
*Parent:* Owens Corning
*Officers:* Nicolas Del Monaco [1977] Finance Director [Belgian]; Matthew Raymond Fortunak [1974] Director [American]; Ava Harter [1969] Director/Senior Vice President and General Counsel [American]

**Owens-Corning Veil U.K. Ltd.**
*Incorporated:* 10 December 1951 *Employees:* 87
*Net Worth:* £21,276,000 *Total Assets:* £27,604,000
*Registered Office:* Rayner Mills, Hare Park Lane, Liversedge, W Yorks, WF15 8EP
*Activities:* Manufacture of glass fibres
*Shareholders:* Owens-Corning Britinvest Limited; Owens Corning
*Officers:* Bert Henri Declerck [1972] Director [Belgian]; Nicolas Del Monaco [1977] Finance Director [Belgian]; Emilio Lorenzo Mariani [1966] Director [Italian]; Suman Raha [1966] Director/Business Manager [Indian]; Hans Van Der Steen [1970] Director/Business Leader Structural Composites [Belgian]

**Oxbow Coal Limited**
*Incorporated:* 25 September 1913 *Employees:* 19
*Net Worth:* £16,261,788 *Total Assets:* £40,720,300
*Registered Office:* Southern Way, Immingham Dock, Immingham, N E Lincs, DN40 2NX
*Activities:* Wholesale of other fuels and related products
*Officers:* Matthew Evelyn Goodwin, Secretary; Patrick Sjoerd Bruning [1966] Managing Director [Dutch]; David William Clark [1954] Director/Legal Adviser [American]; Michael John Cusick [1962] Commercial Director; William Douglas Parmelee [1957] Director/Accountant [American]

**Oxbow Sulphur & Fertiliser (UK) Limited**
*Incorporated:* 5 June 1987 *Employees:* 8
*Net Worth Deficit:* £4,742,143 *Total Assets:* £5,158,945
*Registered Office:* Southern Way, Immingham Docks, Immingham, N E Lincs, DN40 2NX
*Activities:* Freight transport by road
*Parent:* Oxbow Sulphur B.V.
*Officers:* Matthew Evelyn Goodwin, Secretary; Patrick Sjoerd Bruning [1966] Director [Dutch]; David William Clark [1954] Director/Legal Adviser [American]; Ewoud Jan Colenbrander [1965] Operations Director [Dutch]; Michael John Cusick [1962] Director; William Douglas Parmelee [1957] Director [American]

**Oxley Developments Company Limited**
*Incorporated:* 12 September 1942 *Employees:* 149
*Net Worth:* £2,044,327 *Total Assets:* £8,761,511
*Registered Office:* Priory Park, Ulverston, Cumbria, LA12 9QG
*Activities:* Manufacture of electronic components
*Parent:* Oxley Group Limited
*Officers:* Darren Mark Cavan [1972] Director; Jacqueline Kelly [1967] Finance Director

**Oxley Group Limited**
*Incorporated:* 27 October 1969 *Employees:* 180
*Net Worth:* £5,558,515 *Total Assets:* £12,609,647
*Registered Office:* Priory Park, Ulverston, Cumbria, LA12 9QG
*Activities:* Activities of head offices
*Major Shareholder:* Ann Shirley Oxley
*Officers:* Peter Graham Wilson Bedwin [1943] Director; Darren Mark Cavan [1972] Director; Jacqueline Kelly [1967] Finance Director; Murielle Thuy-Kieu Madrona [1970] Director/Consultant [French]; Martin Edward Sloan [1955] Director [American]

**Ozziefields Limited**
*Incorporated:* 1 August 2014
*Net Worth:* £5,301,609 *Total Assets:* £5,562,656
*Registered Office:* The Manor House, Fillingham, Gainsborough, Lincs, DN21 5BS
*Activities:* Growing of cereals (except rice), leguminous crops and oil seeds
*Major Shareholder:* Virginia Zara Rose
*Officers:* Alfred Charles Rose [1957] Director/Farmer; Virginia Zara Rose [1963] Director

**P & A Food Management Services Limited**
*Incorporated:* 20 July 1998 *Employees:* 370
*Net Worth:* £780,689 *Total Assets:* £3,995,927
*Registered Office:* Suite 1 & 4 Kingsfield House, Carthorpe, Bedale, N Yorks, DL8 2LL
*Activities:* Other food services
*Parent:* Contract Catering Services (P & A) Holdings Limited
*Officers:* David John Hall, Secretary; David John Hall [1969] Finance Director; Edward Arthur Naylor [1956] Managing Director

**P & J Properties (Yorkshire) Limited**
*Incorporated:* 8 August 2003 *Employees:* 2
*Net Worth:* £4,754,091 *Total Assets:* £5,538,937
*Registered Office:* Claro Park, Claro Road, Harrogate, N Yorks, HG1 4BB
*Activities:* Renting and operating of Housing Association real estate
*Shareholders:* John Malcolm Emsley; Peter Henry Emsley
*Officers:* Peter Henry Emsley, Secretary/Director; John Malcolm Emsley [1957] Director; Peter Henry Emsley [1951] Director

**P and E Yorkshire Ltd**
*Incorporated:* 21 April 2011
*Net Worth:* £781,877 *Total Assets:* £3,100,468
*Registered Office:* 2 Woodside Mews, Clayton Wood Close, West Park, Leeds, LS16 6QE
*Activities:* Wholesale of watches and jewellery
*Major Shareholder:* Patrick Noble
*Officers:* Patrick Noble [1953] Director

**P V H Holdings Limited**
*Incorporated:* 23 March 1990 *Employees:* 29
*Net Worth:* £9,944,454 *Total Assets:* £15,532,225
*Registered Office:* Howdenshire Way, Knedlington Road, Howden, Goole, E Yorks, DN14 7HZ
*Activities:* Activities of construction holding companies
*Shareholders:* Arnold Bernard Gerardus Van Huet; Simon David Pearson
*Officers:* Frank Langstraat [1952] Director [Dutch]; Simon David Pearson [1962] Director; Alan Jonathan Simpson [1966] Director; Arnold Bernard Gerardus Van Huet [1953] Director [Dutch]; Alan William Virgo [1958] Director

**P. & B. (Foods) Limited**
*Incorporated:* 27 August 1970 *Employees:* 120
*Net Worth:* £16,463,970 *Total Assets:* £25,103,768
*Registered Office:* Prologis Park, Newhall Way, Bradford, W Yorks, BD5 8LZ
*Activities:* Non-specialised wholesale of food, beverages and tobacco
*Parent:* P. & B. Foods Holdings Limited
*Officers:* Mohinder Singh Bhatoa, Secretary/Sales Director [Indian]; Mohinder Singh Bhatoa [1950] Sales Director [Indian]; Chandra Patel [1973] Director; Thakorbhai Vitthalbhai Patel [1940] Director

**P. & B. Foods Holdings Limited**
*Incorporated:* 12 November 2010 *Employees:* 120
*Net Worth:* £30,844,464 *Total Assets:* £42,091,252
*Registered Office:* Prologis Park, Newhall Way, Bradford, W Yorks, BD5 8LZ
*Activities:* Non-trading company
*Officers:* Mohinder Singh Bhatoa [1950] Sales Director [Indian]; Chandra Patel [1973] Director; Thakorbhai Vitthalbhai Patel [1940] Director

**P. I. Bioscience Limited**
*Incorporated:* 10 March 2003 *Employees:* 30
*Net Worth Deficit:* £12,274,000 *Total Assets:* £7,030,000
*Registered Office:* Cowick Hall, Snaith, Goole, E Yorks, DN14 9AA
*Activities:* Manufacture of pesticides and other agrochemical products
*Parent:* Plant Impact Limited
*Officers:* Nicholas Ian Challoner [1968] Director/President, Life Sciences; David Timothy Cherry [1969] Managing Director Crop Care and Health Care; Graham Lloyd Myers [1963] Director/Group Financial Controller

**P.D.R. Construction Limited**
*Incorporated:* 9 December 1992 *Employees:* 77
*Net Worth:* £3,416,854 *Total Assets:* £18,647,044
*Registered Office:* Salisbury House, Saxon Way, Priory Park West, Hessle, E Yorks, HU13 9PB
*Activities:* Construction of commercial buildings
*Major Shareholder:* Paul Dransfield
*Officers:* Joanne Dransfield, Secretary; Paul Dransfield [1967] Director; Darren John Kilvington [1975] Director/Estimator; David Harold Maughan [1962] Director/Chartered Surveyor; Lee Richard Newsham [1974] Director/Chartered Accountant; Adam Ernest Thompson [1987] Construction Director; Nigel Weatherall [1965] Director/Quantity Surveyor

**P.K.A. Company Limited**
*Incorporated:* 11 May 1999 *Employees:* 9
*Net Worth:* £3,445,904 *Total Assets:* £3,785,731
*Registered Office:* Sowerby Woods Industrial Estate, Scarth Road, Barrow in Furness, Cumbria, LA14 4QR
*Activities:* Non-specialised wholesale trade
*Major Shareholder:* Jane Armstrong
*Officers:* Jane Armstrong, Secretary/Housewife; Jane Armstrong [1960] Director/Housewife; John James Goodwin [1956] Director/Company Manager

**P.P. Group Holdings Limited**
*Incorporated:* 20 October 2014 *Employees:* 100
*Previous:* The P.P. Group of Companies Limited
*Net Worth:* £9,178,497 *Total Assets:* £16,883,732
*Registered Office:* 100 Henshaw Lane, Yeadon, Leeds, LS19 7RZ
*Activities:* Activities of other holding companies n.e.c.
*Major Shareholder:* Dianne Morley
*Officers:* Peter Daniel McCabe [1968] Director; Dianne Morley [1960] Director

**P.P. Plasma Limited**
*Incorporated:* 8 October 2007 *Employees:* 2
*Previous:* P.P. Group Holdings Limited
*Net Worth:* £1,206,344 *Total Assets:* £9,480,616
*Registered Office:* 100 Henshaw Lane, Yeadon, Leeds, LS19 7RZ
*Activities:* Activities of head offices
*Officers:* Dianne Morley, Finance Director; Ian McAllister [1977] Director; Peter Daniel McCabe [1968] Director; Dianne Morley [1960] Finance Director

**P.P. Profiles (West Yorkshire) Limited**
*Incorporated:* 30 May 1978 *Employees:* 34
*Net Worth:* £3,776,024 *Total Assets:* £5,507,883
*Registered Office:* Springfield Works, Stocks Lane, Batley, W Yorks, WF17 8PA
*Activities:* Other manufacturing n.e.c.
*Officers:* Dianne Morley, Secretary; Peter Daniel McCabe [1968] Director; Daniel Denis Morley [1990] Commercial Director; Dianne Morley [1960] Finance Director

**P.P.S. Electrical Limited**
*Incorporated:* 29 November 1994 *Employees:* 143
*Net Worth:* £2,009,000 *Total Assets:* £5,605,000
*Registered Office:* 3175 Century Way, Thorpe Park, Leeds, LS15 8ZB
*Activities:* Electrical installation
*Parent:* Shepley Engineers Limited
*Officers:* Nicholas Paul Houghton [1960] Director/Chartered Mechanical Engineer; James Paul McBain [1962] Director; Paul Scott [1964] Director/Engineer; Stephen Taylor [1964] Director

**Pace Distribution (Overseas) Limited**
*Incorporated:* 2 August 1996
*Net Worth:* £101,999,384 *Total Assets:* £102,970,624
*Registered Office:* Victoria Road, Saltaire, W Yorks, BD18 3LF
*Activities:* Satellite telecommunications activities
*Shareholders:* Arris Global Ltd; Arris Global Ltd.
*Officers:* David Bernard Potts [1957] Director/Businessman [American]; Anthony Emilien Zuyderhoff [1971] Director [American]

**Pace Overseas Distribution Limited**
*Incorporated:* 9 November 2006
*Net Worth:* £31,677,176 *Total Assets:* £31,677,176
*Registered Office:* Victoria Road, Saltaire, W Yorks, BD18 3LF
*Activities:* Satellite telecommunications activities
*Parent:* Arris Global Ltd.
*Officers:* David Bernard Potts [1957] Director/Businessman [American]; Anthony Emilien Zuyderhoff [1971] Director [American]

**Pacific Lifestyle Limited**
*Incorporated:* 30 March 1982 *Employees:* 57
*Net Worth:* £812,064 *Total Assets:* £7,154,893
*Registered Office:* Stafford Mills, Milnsbridge, Huddersfield, W Yorks, HD3 4JD
*Activities:* Wholesale of furniture, carpets and lighting equipment
*Parent:* Stafford Mills Holdings Limited
*Officers:* Geoffrey Haigh Riley, Secretary; David Geoffrey Headey [1942] Director; Andrew Simon Hutchison [1969] Finance Director; Nigel St John Lawrence [1972] Sales Director; Geoffrey Haigh Riley [1939] Director

**Pacific Shelf 1809 Limited**
*Incorporated:* 26 June 2015 *Employees:* 143
*Net Worth Deficit:* £5,758,000 *Total Assets:* £43,853,000
*Registered Office:* Seabrook House, Duncombe Street, Bradford, BD8 9AJ
*Activities:* Activities of production holding companies
*Parent:* Calbee (UK) Ltd
*Officers:* Jonathan Bye [1963] Director; Makoto Ehara [1958] Director/Executive Vice President [Japanese]; Koichi Kikuchi [1963] Director/Senior Managing Executive Officer [Japanese]; Richard Anthony Robinson [1965] Director; Keiei Sho [1966] Director/Executive Officer [Japanese]; Jonathan Nigel Wood [1976] Commercial Director; Daniel Richard Woodwards [1977] Director

**Packo Inox Limited**
*Incorporated:* 10 December 1938 *Employees:* 1
*Previous:* R J Fullwood and Bland Limited
*Net Worth:* £43,042,836 *Total Assets:* £50,562,288
*Registered Office:* c/o Verder Ltd, Unit 3 California Drive, Castleford, W Yorks, WF10 5QH
*Activities:* Manufacture of agricultural and forestry machinery other than tractors
*Parent:* Verder NV
*Officers:* David Court [1958] Director; Herwig Paul Verhoyen [1960] Finance Director [Belgian]

**Pacy and Wheatley Limited**
*Incorporated:* 10 December 2004 *Employees:* 37
*Net Worth:* £1,286,203 *Total Assets:* £5,658,471
*Registered Office:* Loversall Court, Tickhill Road, Balby, Doncaster, S Yorks, DN4 8QG
*Activities:* Development of building projects
*Shareholders:* Anthony Neil Wheatley; David Wheatley
*Officers:* Lesley Clarke, Secretary; Nigel Chambers [1971] Director; Anthony Neil Wheatley [1970] Director/Manager Civil Engineer; Craig Andrew Wheatley [1973] Director/Site Manager; David Wheatley [1945] Director/Manager

**Padgett Brothers (A To Z) Limited**
*Incorporated:* 4 December 1985 *Employees:* 27
*Net Worth:* £1,803,738 *Total Assets:* £3,030,363
*Registered Office:* 1 Warneford Avenue, Ossett, W Yorks, WF5 9NJ
*Activities:* Agents involved in the sale of furniture, household goods, hardware and ironmongery
*Shareholder:* Terence Graham Padgett
*Officers:* Alison Sarah Padgett, Secretary; Alex Marcus Kenyon [1972] Director; Alison Sarah Padgett [1971] Director; Linda Lin Tai Padgett [1947] Buying Director; Terence Graham Padgett [1945] Managing Director

**Padgetts (Batley) Limited**
*Incorporated:* 24 July 1962 *Employees:* 14
*Net Worth:* £2,957,376 *Total Assets:* £4,032,587
*Registered Office:* 234 Bradford Road, Batley, W Yorks, WF17 6JL
*Activities:* Sale, maintenance and repair of motorcycles and related parts and accessories
*Major Shareholder:* Peter Padgett
*Officers:* Peter Padgett, Secretary; Peter Padgett [1931] Director

**Pagani UK Limited**
*Incorporated:* 23 May 2014
*Net Worth Deficit:* £570,476 *Total Assets:* £6,736,359
*Registered Office:* Sanderson House, Station Road, Horsforth, Leeds, LS18 5NT
*Activities:* Sale of new cars and light motor vehicles
*Major Shareholder:* Li Wang
*Officers:* Timothy Philip Sugden [1964] Director; Li Wang [1983] Director [Chinese]

**Pall Mall Developments Limited**
*Incorporated:* 13 February 2006 *Employees:* 2
*Net Worth:* £2,340,970 *Total Assets:* £3,631,345
*Registered Office:* Suite 1, Aireside House, Royd Ings Avenue, Keighley, W Yorks, BD21 4BZ
*Activities:* Other specialised construction activities n.e.c.
*Shareholders:* Michael Roger Williams; Amer Najeeb Latif; Emma Jane Williams
*Officers:* Amer Najeeb Latif [1966] Director; Michael Roger Williams [1975] Director/Building Consultant

**Pamant Limited**
*Incorporated:* 1 September 1970 *Employees:* 3
*Net Worth:* £6,697,142 *Total Assets:* £7,000,258
*Registered Office:* 510 Scalby Road, Scalby, Scarborough, N Yorks, YO13 0NN
*Activities:* Other letting and operating of own or leased real estate
*Major Shareholder:* Nigel Anthony Taylor
*Officers:* Nigel Anthony Taylor, Secretary; Mark Taylor [1970] Managing Director; Nigel Anthony Taylor [1945] Director

**Panacea Finance Solutions Limited**
*Incorporated:* 28 August 2013
*Previous:* Panacea Property Finance Limited
*Net Worth:* £622,853 *Total Assets:* £3,926,703
*Registered Office:* Concord House, Bessemer Way, Scunthorpe, N Lincs, DN15 8XE
*Activities:* Other credit granting n.e.c.
*Officers:* Steven Carl Fletcher [1962] Director; John Ralph Williams [1952] Director; Stuart Daniel Williams [1983] Director; John Henry Wilson [1963] Director

**Paneltex Limited**
*Incorporated:* 3 May 1991 *Employees:* 350
*Net Worth:* £7,434,622 *Total Assets:* £15,196,796
*Registered Office:* Paneltex House, Somerden Road, Hull, HU9 5PE
*Activities:* Manufacture of bodies (coachwork) for motor vehicles (except caravans)
*Major Shareholder:* Christopher Thomas Berridge
*Officers:* Jane Wesley Berridge, Secretary; Christopher Thomas Berridge [1959] Director/Engineer; Keith Drake [1959] Finance Director; Mark Antony Richardson [1964] Director/IT Manager; Nigel Edward Wilde [1957] Works Director

**Riva Paoletti Limited**
*Incorporated:* 16 January 1987 *Employees:* 32
*Net Worth:* £2,559,506 *Total Assets:* £4,688,811
*Registered Office:* Riva House, Limewood Approach, Leeds, LS14 1NG
*Activities:* Wholesale of textiles
*Major Shareholder:* Andrew Brade Green
*Officers:* Guy Andrew Beswick, Secretary/Director; Guy Andrew Beswick [1963] Director; Andrew Brade Green [1947] Director; Claire Green [1962] Director; Justin Green [1988] Director; Richard Julian Whitworth [1959] Director

**Paragon Creative Limited**
*Incorporated:* 4 April 2002 *Employees:* 128
*Net Worth:* £1,231,551 *Total Assets:* £6,316,103
*Registered Office:* Unit 8 Harrier Court, The Airfield, Elvington, York, YO41 4EA
*Activities:* Other manufacturing n.e.c.
*Officers:* Neil Stewart Jefferies [1977] Director; Mark Colin Pyrah [1972] Sales Director

**Paragon Foodservice Limited**
*Incorporated:* 25 January 2016 *Employees:* 19
*Net Worth:* £2,016,945 *Total Assets:* £6,882,275
*Registered Office:* Unit D, Herons Way, Balby, Doncaster, S Yorks, DN4 8WA
*Activities:* Non-specialised wholesale of food, beverages and tobacco
*Officers:* Metin Pekin [1969] Director

**Paragon Property Investments Limited**
*Incorporated:* 11 February 2009 *Employees:* 120
*Net Worth:* £11,976,695 *Total Assets:* £17,940,832
*Registered Office:* Quadrant 3, Yorkshire Way, Armthorpe, Doncaster, S Yorks, DN3 3FB
*Activities:* Other letting and operating of own or leased real estate
*Major Shareholder:* Metin Pekin
*Officers:* Metin Pekin [1976] Managing Director

**Paragon Quality Foods Ltd**
*Incorporated:* 5 February 1996 *Employees:* 120
*Net Worth:* £7,459,938 *Total Assets:* £13,099,159
*Registered Office:* Paragon Quality Foods Limited, Yorkshire Way, Armthorpe, Doncaster, S Yorks, DN3 3FB
*Activities:* Production of meat and poultry meat products
*Major Shareholder:* Metin Pekin
*Officers:* Metin Pekin [1969] Director

**Paramount Retail Group Holdco Limited**
*Incorporated:* 19 November 2015
*Net Worth:* £536,559 *Total Assets:* £3,048,877
*Registered Office:* Abacus House, Pennine Business Park, Longbow Close, Huddersfield, W Yorks, HD2 1GQ
*Activities:* Activities of other holding companies n.e.c.
*Officers:* Ravi Sharma [1986] Director; Sandeep Sharma [1984] Director

**Paramount Retail Group Holdings Limited**
*Incorporated:* 26 June 1992
*Net Worth:* £2,612,074 *Total Assets:* £3,525,001
*Registered Office:* Abacus House, Pennine Business Park, Longbow Close, Huddersfield, W Yorks, HD2 1GQ
*Activities:* Other letting and operating of own or leased real estate
*Officers:* Ravi Sharma [1986] Director of Finance

**Paramount Wholesale Ltd**
*Incorporated:* 17 September 2015
*Net Worth:* £3,310,983 *Total Assets:* £3,436,105
*Registered Office:* 48 Emperors Wharf, Skeldergate, York, YO1 6DQ
*Activities:* Non-specialised wholesale trade
*Major Shareholder:* Jayson Kelly
*Officers:* Jayson Kelly [1966] Director/Sales

**M H & J Park and Son Limited**
*Incorporated:* 24 April 2006 *Employees:* 62
*Net Worth:* £4,287,186 *Total Assets:* £6,795,207
*Registered Office:* Caton Road, Lancaster, LA1 3PE
*Activities:* Freight transport by road
*Shareholders:* Simon Andrew Park; Martyn Harris Park
*Officers:* Joyce Park, Secretary; David Edmund Park [1970] Director/Solicitor; Joyce Park [1949] Director; Martyn Harris Park [1948] Director; Simon Andrew Park [1977] Director/Manager

**Park Homes (UK) Limited**
*Incorporated:* 10 April 1997 *Employees:* 350
*Net Worth:* £8,635,464 *Total Assets:* £12,422,386
*Registered Office:* 50 Brantwood Oval, Bradford, W Yorks, BD9 6QP
*Activities:* Other business support service activities n.e.c.
*Major Shareholder:* Mendhy Hussain Khan
*Officers:* Fatima Jaffar Shahid, Secretary; Munawar Hussain [1972] Marketing Director; Dr Mendhy Hussain Khan [1968] Director/Doctor; Fatima Jaffar Shahid [1961] Director

**Park Lane Healthcare (Croston Park) Limited**
*Incorporated:* 28 November 1986 *Employees:* 63
*Net Worth:* £4,257,797 *Total Assets:* £9,348,508
*Registered Office:* 46 Hull Road, Cottingham, E Yorks, HU16 4PX
*Activities:* Residential nursing care facilities
*Parent:* Park Lane Healthcare Limited
*Officers:* Christopher Malcolm Lane [1980] Director; Anthony Robert Mitchell [1979] Director; Christopher Robert Mitchell [1958] Director

**Park Lane Healthcare (Magnolia House) Limited**
*Incorporated:* 21 June 2005 *Employees:* 83
*Net Worth:* £1,713,740 *Total Assets:* £7,360,041
*Registered Office:* 46 Hull Road, Cottingham, E Yorks, HU16 4PX
*Activities:* Residential care activities for the elderly and disabled
*Parent:* Park Lane Healthcare Limited
*Officers:* Christopher Malcolm Lane [1980] Director; Anthony Robert Mitchell [1979] Director; Christopher Robert Mitchell [1958] Director/Commercial Finance Broker

**Park Lane Healthcare Limited**
*Incorporated:* 26 April 2005 *Employees:* 186
*Net Worth:* £4,080,291 *Total Assets:* £16,387,404
*Registered Office:* 46 Hull Road, Cottingham, E Yorks, HU16 4PX
*Activities:* Activities of head offices
*Shareholder:* Christopher Robert Mitchell
*Officers:* Christopher Malcolm Lane [1980] Director; Anthony Robert Mitchell [1979] Director; Christopher Robert Mitchell [1958] Director/Commercial Finance Broker

**Park Lane Homes Developments Limited**
*Incorporated:* 27 June 2003 *Employees:* 3
*Net Worth:* £544,069 *Total Assets:* £3,738,700
*Registered Office:* West Hill House, Allerton Hill, Chapel Allerton, Leeds, LS7 3QB
*Activities:* Development of building projects
*Shareholders:* Brian Andrew Clink; James Clink
*Officers:* Brian Andrew Clink [1972] Director; Brian Clink [1952] Director/Property Developer; James Clink [1986] Director

**Park Lane Homes Limited**
*Incorporated:* 7 September 1990 *Employees:* 10
*Net Worth:* £4,323,993 *Total Assets:* £5,550,535
*Registered Office:* Malcolm Jones & Co, Allerton Hill, Chapel Allerton, Leeds, LS7 3QB
*Activities:* Construction of domestic buildings
*Parent:* Park Lane Home Developments Limited
*Officers:* Brian Andrew Clink [1972] Director/Contracts Manager; Brian Clink [1952] Director/Builder; James Clink [1986] Director

**Park Lane Properties (Holdings) Limited**
*Incorporated:* 8 November 2001
*Net Worth:* £922,150 *Total Assets:* £19,017,952
*Registered Office:* Northgate, 118 North Street, Leeds, LS2 7PN
*Activities:* Other business support service activities n.e.c.
*Officers:* Sameer Ahmed, Secretary; Nadeem Ahmed [1967] Director; Naveen Nazir Ahmed [1962] Director; Nazir Ahmed [1939] Director; Razia Ahmed [1940] Director; Sameer Ahmed [1972] Director

**Park Lane Properties (Leeds) Limited**
*Incorporated:* 27 September 1995 *Employees:* 126
*Net Worth:* £42,132,764 *Total Assets:* £130,795,376
*Registered Office:* Northgate, 118 North Street, Leeds, LS2 7PN
*Activities:* Renting and operating of Housing Association real estate
*Officers:* Sameer Ahmed, Secretary/Director; Nadeem Ahmed [1967] Director; Naveen Nazir Ahmed [1962] Director; Nazir Ahmed [1939] Director; Razia Ahmed [1940] Director; Sameer Ahmed [1972] Director

**Park Leisure 2000 (Cornwall) Limited**
*Incorporated:* 18 October 2004 *Employees:* 61
*Net Worth:* £10,366,495 *Total Assets:* £14,655,632
*Registered Office:* Tudor Court, York Business Park, York, YO26 6RS
*Activities:* Holiday centres and villages
*Parent:* Park Leisure 2000 Limited
*Officers:* Andrew Bracey [1967] Director; Aiden Charles Barwick Clegg [1966] Director; Joanne Cowl [1977] Finance Director; Neil Allen Currie [1965] Director; Miles Dewhurst [1972] Director; Robert Charles Stern [1960] Director

**Park Leisure 2000 (Northumberland) Limited**
*Incorporated:* 10 August 2001 *Employees:* 68
*Net Worth:* £20,004,014 *Total Assets:* £24,423,690
*Registered Office:* Tudor Court, York Business Park, York, YO26 6RS
*Activities:* Holiday centres and villages
*Parent:* Park Leisure 2000 Limited
*Officers:* Andrew Bracey [1967] Director; Aiden Charles Barwick Clegg [1966] Director; Joanne Cowl [1977] Finance Director; Neil Allen Currie [1965] Director; Miles Dewhurst [1972] Director; Robert Charles Stern [1960] Director

**Park Leisure 2000 Limited**
*Incorporated:* 14 April 1997 *Employees:* 235
*Net Worth:* £51,051,316 *Total Assets:* £118,243,992
*Registered Office:* Tudor Court, York Business Park, York, YO26 6RS
*Activities:* Holiday centres and villages
*Parent:* Dan at Spyglass Hill-Bid Co Limited
*Officers:* Andrew Bracey [1967] Director; Aiden Charles Barwick Clegg [1966] Director; Joanne Cowl [1977] Finance Director; Neil Curie [1965] Director; Miles Dewhurst [1972] Director; Robert Charles Stern [1960] Director

**Park Leisure Group Limited**
*Incorporated:* 8 February 2017 *Employees:* 364
*Net Worth Deficit:* £1,080,482 *Total Assets:* £142,045,456
*Registered Office:* Unit 1 Tudor Court, York Business Park, York, YO26 6RS
*Activities:* Financial intermediation not elsewhere classified
*Parent:* Ares Management, L.P.
*Officers:* Andrew Bracey [1967] Director; Aiden Charles Barwick Clegg [1966] Director; Joanne Cowl [1977] Director; Neil Allen Currie [1965] Director; Mike Dennis [1976] Director/Investment Professional; Miles Dewhurst [1972] Director; Robert Charles Stern [1960] Director/Retired

**Park Leisure Marketing Limited**
*Incorporated:* 11 January 1999
*Net Worth:* £2,587,840 *Total Assets:* £10,921,698
*Registered Office:* Beverley Farm, South Cliff, Hornsea, E Yorks, HU18 1TL
*Activities:* Recreational vehicle parks, trailer parks and camping grounds
*Major Shareholder:* Martin Richard Varley
*Officers:* Ian Vincent Appleyard, Secretary; Laura Marie Firth [1975] Director; Martin Richard Varley [1951] Director; Richard James Varley [1979] Director

**Park Property (World) Ltd**
*Incorporated:* 17 November 1998
*Net Worth Deficit:* £1,041,582 *Total Assets:* £3,618,756
*Registered Office:* 12 Selborne Grove, Bradford, W Yorks, BD9 4NL
*Activities:* Other letting and operating of own or leased real estate
*Officers:* Kabir Hussain, Secretary/Manager; Kabir Hussain [1969] Director/Manager

**Park Valley Huddersfield Limited**
*Incorporated:* 23 August 2016 *Employees:* 4
*Net Worth:* £9,491,233 *Total Assets:* £9,738,320
*Registered Office:* Suite 5, Park Valley House, Park Valley, Lockwood, Huddersfield, W Yorks, HD4 7BH
*Activities:* Other letting and operating of own or leased real estate
*Major Shareholder:* Martin Douglas Duckett
*Officers:* Pearl Ann Duckett, Secretary; Brian Duckett [1942] Director/Dyer; Martin Douglas Duckett [1967] Director/Dyer; Pearl Ann Duckett [1945] Director/Company Secretary

**Parkacre Enterprises Limited**
*Incorporated:* 16 September 2005 *Employees:* 174
*Net Worth:* £2,559,167 *Total Assets:* £10,942,910
*Registered Office:* Hangar 2, Learoyd Road, Caenby Corner Estate, Hemswell Cliff, Gainsborough, Lincs, DN21 5TJ
*Activities:* Manufacture of basic pharmaceutical products
*Officers:* James Caseley [1976] Sales Director; Charles Stern [1976] Finance Director; John Stern [1979] Director

**Parker & Parker Limited**
*Incorporated:* 16 May 1952 *Employees:* 20
*Net Worth:* £4,145,458 *Total Assets:* £6,917,421
*Registered Office:* Longpool, Kendal, Cumbria, LA9 6BX
*Activities:* Sale of new cars and light motor vehicles
*Shareholders:* Ian Frank Parker; Ian Parker
*Officers:* Christopher Roy Parker, Secretary; Ian Frank Parker [1952] Director/Sales Manager; Simon Parker [1985] Director

**Parkhead Investments Limited**
*Incorporated:* 6 July 2017 *Employees:* 2
*Net Worth Deficit:* £96,142 *Total Assets:* £4,522,850
*Registered Office:* P O Box 505, Brentwood, Newlands Road, Scarborough, N Yorks, YO11 9FZ
*Activities:* Security dealing on own account
*Major Shareholder:* Brian Joseph Davidson
*Officers:* Brian Joseph Davidson [1963] Director; Margaret Davidson [1963] Director

**Parkhouse Lakeland Estate Limited**
*Incorporated:* 25 July 2005
*Net Worth:* £301,205 *Total Assets:* £3,796,162
*Registered Office:* Houghtons Parkhouse Coachworks, Grisleymire Lane, Milnthorpe, Cumbria, LA7 7RF
*Activities:* Other letting and operating of own or leased real estate
*Parent:* Parkhouse Lakeland Investments Ltd
*Officers:* Pamela Audrey Houghton, Secretary; Michael John Houghton [1954] Director/Trailer Manufacturer; Pamela Audrey Houghton [1956] Director

**Parkhouse Lakeland LLP**
*Incorporated:* 25 May 2010 *Employees:* 2
*Net Worth:* £3,911,305 *Total Assets:* £7,300,251
*Registered Office:* Houghtons Parkhouse Coachworks, Grisleymires Lane, Milnthorpe, Cumbria, LA7 7RF
*Officers:* Michael John Houghton [1954] Member; Pamela Audrey Houghton [1956] Member

**Parkin International Engineering Services Limited**
*Incorporated:* 30 March 1976
*Net Worth:* £739,921 *Total Assets:* £7,033,755
*Registered Office:* Sovereign House, Trinity Business Park, Wakefield, W Yorks, WF2 8EF
*Activities:* Other letting and operating of own or leased real estate
*Shareholder:* Richard Neal Parkin
*Officers:* Norma Catherine Parkin, Secretary; Kathryn Ruth Mumby [1974] Director/Financial Management; Francis Neal Parkin [1940] Managing Director; Richard Neal Parkin [1972] Director

**Parkinson - Spencer Refractories Limited**
*Incorporated:* 7 July 1921 *Employees:* 89
*Net Worth:* £2,519,099 *Total Assets:* £4,675,428
*Registered Office:* Holmfield, Halifax, W Yorks, HX3 6SX
*Activities:* Manufacture of refractory products
*Major Shareholder:* David Edwin Parkinson
*Officers:* Joanne Parkinson, Secretary; David Ferguson [1958] Manufacturing Director; Leslie James Robert Gaskell [1957] Technical Director; David Edwin Parkinson [1952] Director; Joanne Parkinson [1987] Director/Company Secretary; Simon Parkinson [1989] Director

**Parkmount Estate Company (Allerton) Limited**
*Incorporated:* 30 October 1968 *Employees:* 2
*Net Worth:* £11,825,065 *Total Assets:* £13,007,789
*Registered Office:* Keighley Business Centre, South Street, Knowle Mill, Keighley, W Yorks, BD21 1SY
*Activities:* Other letting and operating of own or leased real estate
*Parent:* Arthington Estates Limited
*Officers:* Elaine Kunz, Secretary; Elaine Kunz [1950] Director; Karl Antony Kunz [1957] Director/Farmer

**Parkrowe Estates Limited**
*Incorporated:* 11 June 2004
*Net Worth:* £248,630 *Total Assets:* £3,105,474
*Registered Office:* Q4 Building, Rudgate, Tockwith, York, YO26 7DW
*Activities:* Activities of distribution holding companies
*Major Shareholder:* Richard Jonathan Parker
*Officers:* Emma Louise Parker [1967] Director/Marketing Manager; Richard Jonathan Parker [1966] Director

**Parkside Flexibles (Europe) Limited**
*Incorporated:* 6 January 2005 *Employees:* 181
*Net Worth:* £8,242,833 *Total Assets:* £17,008,298
*Registered Office:* Unit H1, Normanton Industrial Estate, Tyler Close, Normanton, W Yorks, WF6 1RL
*Activities:* Printing n.e.c.
*Officers:* Victoria Rayment, Secretary; Mark Nicholas Kennedy Aldridge [1965] Director/Private Equity; Paula Marie Birch [1972] Sales Director; Rosemary Grace [1961] HR Director; Victoria Rayment [1973] Director/Accountant; Nicholas James Smith [1975] Managing Director

**Parkside Property (Yorkshire) Limited**
*Incorporated:* 29 August 2013
*Net Worth:* £695,450 *Total Assets:* £3,635,146
*Registered Office:* Unit H2, Tyler Close, Normanton Industrial Estate, Normanton, W Yorks, WF6 1RL
*Activities:* Buying and selling of own real estate
*Officers:* Victoria Rayment, Secretary; Mark Nicholas Kennedy Aldridge [1965] Director; Victoria Rayment [1973] Director/Accountant; Nicholas James Smith [1975] Managing Director

**Parkway Entertainment Company Limited**
*Incorporated:* 9 November 1983 *Employees:* 84
*Net Worth:* £2,110,414 *Total Assets:* £4,190,562
*Registered Office:* Parkway Cinema, Kings Road, Cleethorpes, N E Lincs, DN35 0AQ
*Activities:* Motion picture distribution activities
*Major Shareholder:* Denise Mary Parkes
*Officers:* Denise Mary Parkes, Secretary; Denise Mary Parkes [1950] Director/Secretary; Gerrard Denis Parkes [1975] Director; Richard James Parkes [1976] Director

**Derek Parnaby Cyclones International Limited**
*Incorporated:* 20 July 1973 *Employees:* 101
*Net Worth:* £11,216,336 *Total Assets:* £12,179,378
*Registered Office:* Chilton Industrial Estate, Chilton, Ferryhill, Co Durham, DL17 0SH
*Activities:* Manufacture of other special-purpose machinery n.e.c.
*Major Shareholder:* Adrian Parnaby
*Officers:* Pauline Isobel Lerigo, Secretary; Thomas Henry Iveson [1950] Director/Commissioning Engineer; Pauline Isobel Lerigo [1960] Director/Secretary; Adrian Parnaby [1958] Director

**Parrs Point Limited**
*Incorporated:* 19 May 1980
*Net Worth:* £5,272,255 *Total Assets:* £6,307,373
*Registered Office:* Trafalgar Mills, Leeds Road, Huddersfield, W Yorks, HD2 1YY
*Activities:* Other letting and operating of own or leased real estate
*Officers:* Andrew William Cowling, Secretary; Alessandro Bevilacqua [1955] Director [Italian]; John David Shinwell [1964] Director/Solicitor

**Partline Limited**
*Incorporated:* 23 January 1995
*Net Worth:* £1,795,563 *Total Assets:* £3,418,526
*Registered Office:* Partline Ltd, Dockfield Road, Shipley, W Yorks, BD17 7AZ
*Activities:* Manufacture of other parts and accessories for motor vehicles
*Shareholders:* William Henry Clark; Joan Clark
*Officers:* William Harvey Clark, Secretary/Engineer; Richard Henry Clark [1973] Director/Engineer; William Henry Clark [1945] Director/Engineer; William Harvey Clark [1970] Director/Engineer

**Partners in Care Limited**
*Incorporated:* 24 July 2001 *Employees:* 92
*Net Worth:* £3,904,603 *Total Assets:* £4,171,081
*Registered Office:* Rouse House, 2 Wyther Lane, Kirkstall, Leeds, LS5 3BT
*Activities:* Other residential care activities n.e.c.
*Officers:* Lynsey Guilherme, Secretary; Luigi Guilherme [1960] Director; Lynsey Guilherme [1974] Director

**The Partnership Investment Fund Limited**
*Incorporated:* 23 March 2004 *Employees:* 1
*Net Worth:* £4,345,357 *Total Assets:* £4,359,853
*Registered Office:* Suite 6.1, Unit 6 Mortec Park, York Road, Leeds, LS15 4TA
*Activities:* Activities of financial services holding companies
*Officers:* Julia Jacquetta Caroline Chapman, Secretary; Mark Richard Hambly [1964] Director; Martin John Hathaway [1966] Director; David Malcolm Horsman [1944] Director/Solicitor; John Grenville Bernard Watson [1943] Director

**PAS Holding Company Ltd**
*Incorporated:* 14 July 2015
*Net Worth:* £100 *Total Assets:* £6,644,989
*Registered Office:* 8 The Courtyards, Victoria Road, Leeds, LS14 2LB
*Activities:* Other information technology service activities
*Officers:* Sheila Ann Thewlis, Secretary; Aidan Dempsey [1960] Director; Marshall Anthony Glynn [1962] Director; Amarpal Singh Randhawa [1976] Director/Pharmacist

**Pasuda (Hire) Limited**
*Incorporated:* 4 November 1992 *Employees:* 7
*Net Worth:* £2,299,881 *Total Assets:* £4,684,255
*Registered Office:* Belton Road, Sandtoft Thorne, Doncaster, S Yorks, DN8 5SY
*Activities:* Renting and leasing of construction and civil engineering machinery and equipment
*Major Shareholder:* Gordon Jones
*Officers:* Susan Jones, Secretary; Benjamin Graham Jones [1974] Director/Sales

**Pasuda Buildings Limited**
*Incorporated:* 10 June 1992 *Employees:* 17
*Net Worth:* £2,575,546 *Total Assets:* £4,699,633
*Registered Office:* Pasuda Buildings Ltd, Belton Road, Sandtoft, Doncaster, S Yorks, DN8 5SX
*Activities:* Other manufacturing n.e.c.
*Major Shareholder:* Gordon Jones
*Officers:* Susan Jones, Secretary

**Patchett Developments Limited**
*Incorporated:* 21 May 1996 *Employees:* 2
*Net Worth:* £2,996,748 *Total Assets:* £3,541,569
*Registered Office:* Ryefield House, 180 Highgate Road, Queensbury, Bradford, W Yorks, BD13 1DS
*Activities:* Development of building projects
*Officers:* Michael John Patchett, Secretary/Builder; Charles Edmund Shepherd Patchett [1948] Director/Builder; Michael John Patchett [1942] Director/Builder

**Ay & Y. Patel (Dewsbury) Limited**
*Incorporated:* 28 January 1987 *Employees:* 87
*Net Worth:* £9,002,125 *Total Assets:* £11,210,200
*Registered Office:* 138 Savile Road, Savile Town, Dewsbury, W Yorks, WF12 9LR
*Activities:* Retail sale of automotive fuel in specialised stores
*Officers:* Ahmed Yusuf Patel, Secretary; Ahmed Yusuf Patel [1942] Director/Motor Fuel Retailer; Ashif Ahmed Patel [1971] Director/Petrol Retailer; Mohmed Hanif Ahmed Patel [1965] Director/Petrol Retailer; Yakub Yusuf Patel [1957] Director/Motor Fuel Retailer; Yunus Yusuf Patel [1948] Director/Motor Fuel Retailer

**Pathfinder Multi Academy Trust**
*Incorporated:* 10 March 2011 *Employees:* 516
*Previous:* Archbishop Holgate's School, A Church of England Academy
*Net Worth:* £35,621,000 *Total Assets:* £40,449,000
*Registered Office:* Archbishop Holgate's School, Hull Road, York, YO10 5ZA
*Activities:* General secondary education
*Officers:* Dr Andrew Clarke [1963] Director; Jacob Adam Drummond [1986] Director/Facilities Manager; John Keith Hattam [1961] Director of Training and Consultant; Sandara Louise Holmes [1973] Director/Quality Specialist; Terry McDermott [1947] Director/Self Employed Education Consultant; Dr Samantha Louise Pugh [1976] Director/University Lecturer; Derek Wilson Scott [1973] Human Resources Director; Christopher John Sharpe [1966] Director/Self-Employed Builder; Alison Smith [1972] Director/Diocesan Adviser; Claire Jacqueline Theyers [1975] Director

**Patrick Construction Group Limited**
*Incorporated:* 20 April 2009
*Net Worth:* £1,987,097 *Total Assets:* £5,233,985
*Registered Office:* 1 Pellon Place, Bradley Business Park, Dyson Wood Way, Huddersfield, W Yorks, HD2 1GT
*Activities:* Activities of head offices
*Shareholder:* Graeme Charles Bird
*Officers:* Beverley Jayne Rockett, Secretary; Simon Bateman [1982] Director; Graeme Charles Bird [1969] Director; Jason Mark McGarvey [1977] Director; Beverley Jayne Rockett [1958] Director; Simon James Taylor [1971] Director

**Patrington Haven Leisure Park Limited**
*Incorporated:* 13 September 1982 *Employees:* 68
*Net Worth:* £1,716,655 *Total Assets:* £6,596,699
*Registered Office:* Patrington Haven Leisure Park, Patrington Haven, Hull, HU12 0PT
*Activities:* Recreational vehicle parks, trailer parks and camping grounds
*Parent:* Ivanhoe Leisure Group Limited
*Officers:* Shaun Willox, Secretary; Graham Howard Sparkes [1947] Director; Mr Guy Howard Sparkes [1980] Director; Shaun Willox [1960] Finance Director

**Pattinson 3 Limited**
*Incorporated:* 5 December 2009 *Employees:* 5
*Net Worth:* £6,040,352 *Total Assets:* £6,754,343
*Registered Office:* Applegarth Middleton, Kirkby Lonsdale, Carnforth, Cumbria, LA6 2LX
*Activities:* Other letting and operating of own or leased real estate
*Major Shareholder:* Christopher Jeth Nicholson
*Officers:* Freya Nicholson, Secretary; Alison Nicholson [1948] Director; Christopher Jeth Nicholson [1958] Director; Freya Christobel Nicholson [1990] Director/Brand Builder; Hebe Calypso Nicholson [1992] Director/Student; Nancy Viola Nicholson [1988] Director/Theatre Set Design

**Pavers Holdings Limited**
*Incorporated:* 12 August 2013 *Employees:* 1,362
*Net Worth:* £63,668,000 *Total Assets:* £73,603,000
*Registered Office:* Catherine House, Harwood Road, Northminster Business Park, Upper Poppleton, York, YO26 6QU
*Activities:* Activities of other holding companies n.e.c.
*Shareholders:* Stuart David Paver; Catherine Kinloch Paver
*Officers:* Stuart David Paver [1961] Director/Retailer

**Pavers Limited**
*Incorporated:* 14 June 1971 *Employees:* 1,362
*Net Worth:* £43,511,000 *Total Assets:* £54,086,000
*Registered Office:* Catherine House, Harwood Road, Northminster Business Park, Upper Poppleton, York, YO26 6QU
*Activities:* Retail sale of footwear in specialised stores
*Parent:* Pavers Holdings Limited
*Officers:* Jason Michael Paver [1986] Director/Retailer; Stuart David Paver [1961] Director/Retailer

**Paw Structures Limited**
*Incorporated:* 21 August 2002 *Employees:* 69
*Net Worth:* £6,251,000 *Total Assets:* £12,039,000
*Registered Office:* Birkbecks, Water Street, Skipton, N Yorks, BD23 1PB
*Activities:* Manufacture of metal structures and parts of structures
*Parent:* Paw Holdings Limited
*Officers:* Matthew Jowett [1979] Director; Paul Smith [1968] Director; James Matthew Walker [1979] Commercial Director; Clive Webberley [1967] Director; Marcus Wood [1972] Director

**Paw Topco Limited**
*Incorporated:* 31 May 2016 *Employees:* 121
*Net Worth:* £319,000 *Total Assets:* £39,269,000
*Registered Office:* Birbecks, Water Street, Skipton, N Yorks, BD23 1PB
*Activities:* Activities of head offices
*Shareholder:* LDC V LP
*Officers:* Robert Edmund Paul Bodnar-Horvath [1956] Director; Matthew Jowett [1979] Director; Daniel Smith [1983] Director; Martyn John Vitty [1975] Director; James Matthew Walker [1979] Director; Marcus Wood [1972] Director

**John Pawson (Holdings) Limited**
*Incorporated:* 6 September 2013
*Net Worth:* £8,646,844 *Total Assets:* £8,996,731
*Registered Office:* 52 St Johns Lane, Halifax, W Yorks, HX1 2BW
*Activities:* Activities of other holding companies n.e.c.
*Major Shareholder:* John Ward Pawson
*Officers:* Catherine Mary Pawson [1956] Director; John Ward Pawson [1949] Director

**D.G. Payne Limited**
*Incorporated:* 24 April 1970 *Employees:* 56
*Net Worth:* £2,482,531 *Total Assets:* £3,223,186
*Registered Office:* 2 Hoylake Road, Moorwell Road Industrial Estate, Scunthorpe, N Lincs, DN17 2AZ
*Activities:* Other food services
*Shareholders:* Donald Gordon Payne; Maureen Payne
*Officers:* Maureen Payne, Secretary; Andrew Geoffrey Binns [1965] Director/Chartered Accountant; Deborah Binns [1962] Director/Administration Manager; Maureen Payne [1936] Director

**Paynes Dairies Limited**
*Incorporated:* 30 April 1998 *Employees:* 122
*Net Worth:* £4,744,255 *Total Assets:* £21,368,500
*Registered Office:* Bar Lane, Boroughbridge, N Yorks, YO51 9LU
*Activities:* Liquid milk and cream production
*Officers:* Charles Anthony Payne, Secretary/Farmer; Kevin Austin Leech [1965] Director; Bryan Payne [1930] Director/Farmer; Charles Anthony Payne [1955] Director/Farmer; Paul Tardoff Williamson [1957] Director/Chartered Accountant

**PBS Construction (North East) Limited**
*Incorporated:* 10 June 1988 *Employees:* 48
*Net Worth:* £1,477,471 *Total Assets:* £3,568,982
*Registered Office:* 1 Trinity Street, Hull, HU3 1JR
*Activities:* Construction of commercial buildings
*Parent:* PBS Construction Group Ltd
*Officers:* Mark David Lee Brooks [1984] Director; Glenn Smurthwaite [1977] Contracts Director; Peter Barry Smurthwaite [1949] Director

**PBS Holdings Limited**
*Incorporated:* 26 November 2004 *Employees:* 2
*Net Worth Deficit:* £4,943,422 *Total Assets:* £8,189,537
*Registered Office:* The Hamlet, Hornbeam Park, Harrogate, N Yorks, HG2 8RE
*Activities:* Activities of financial services holding companies
*Parent:* Rural & Commercial Holdings Limited
*Officers:* Elizabeth Anne Brophy, Secretary; Richard Miles Skingle [1970] Finance Director; Timothy John Smyth [1967] Director

**PC Specialist Limited**
*Incorporated:* 27 May 2003 *Employees:* 86
*Net Worth:* £5,715,043 *Total Assets:* £13,316,483
*Registered Office:* 12 Jubilee Way, Grange Moor, Wakefield, W Yorks, WF4 4TD
*Activities:* Other information technology service activities
*Major Shareholder:* Daniel Martin Williams
*Officers:* Daniel Martin Williams, Secretary; Daniel Martin Williams [1985] Director

**PCS Property Solutions Limited**
*Incorporated:* 31 October 2012 *Employees:* 1
*Net Worth:* £7,853,300 *Total Assets:* £8,500,021
*Registered Office:* 12 Jubilee Way, Grange Moor, Wakefield, W Yorks, WF4 4TD
*Activities:* Other letting and operating of own or leased real estate
*Major Shareholder:* Daniel Martin Williams
*Officers:* Daniel Martin Williams [1985] Director

**PD & MS Holdings Limited**
*Incorporated:* 19 March 2013
*Net Worth Deficit:* £3,324,000 *Total Assets:* £20,147,000
*Registered Office:* 1 Park Row, Leeds, LS1 5AB
*Activities:* Activities of head offices
*Parent:* Project Ires Bidco Limited
*Officers:* Francis Herlihy, Secretary; Francis Herlihy [1966] Director/Accountant; Mark Lunney [1970] Director; Simon Rio [1976] Director/Chief Executive Officer

**PDS Design & Build Limited**
*Incorporated:* 28 July 1998 *Employees:* 31
*Net Worth:* £1,548,823 *Total Assets:* £4,458,734
*Registered Office:* 1 Navigation Court, Calder Park, Wakefield, W Yorks, WF2 7BJ
*Activities:* Joinery installation
*Shareholders:* Andrew Alec Taylor; James Sturgeon
*Officers:* Andrew Alec Taylor, Secretary; Peter Hall [1970] Managing Director; Michael James Ireland [1970] Director; James Sturgeon [1975] Director; Andrew Alec Taylor [1962] Director; Nicholas Edward Taylor [1992] Director

**Peacock & Binnington**
*Incorporated:* 18 June 1937 *Employees:* 117
*Net Worth:* £5,728,634 *Total Assets:* £19,682,708
*Registered Office:* Old Foundry, Bridge Street, Brigg, N Lincs, DN20 8NR
*Activities:* Agents involved in the sale of machinery, industrial equipment, ships and aircraft
*Parent:* Peacock & Binnington Holdings Limited
*Officers:* Mark Peter Farleigh, Secretary; Les Bacon [1957] Challenger Sales Director; Marcus James Bourne [1970] Director; Richard Cross [1972] Director; Mark Peter Farleigh [1981] Finance Director; Graham William Main [1970] Managing Director; Michael Allen Peacock [1933] Director/Chairman; Nicholas Allen Peacock [1969] Director/Barrister; Andrew James Walker [1976] Louth Sales Director

**Peacock & Binnington Holdings Limited**
*Incorporated:* 6 July 1990 *Employees:* 117
*Net Worth:* £5,717,220 *Total Assets:* £19,677,984
*Registered Office:* Old Foundry, Bridge Street, Brigg, N Lincs, DN20 8NR
*Activities:* Activities of head offices
*Shareholder:* Michael Allen Peacock
*Officers:* Mark Peter Farleigh, Secretary; Les Bacon [1957] Director/Salesman; Marcus James Bourne [1970] Director; Richard Cross [1972] Director; Mark Peter Farleigh [1981] Finance Director; Graham William Main [1970] Director; Michael Allen Peacock [1933] Director/Agricultural Engineer; Nicholas Allen Peacock [1969] Director/Barrister; Andrew James Walker [1976] Louth Sales Director

**Peagar Ltd**
*Incorporated:* 14 September 2015
*Net Worth:* £230,939 *Total Assets:* £5,056,063
*Registered Office:* c/o Dakin-Flathers Limited, Boothroyds Way, Green Lane Industrial Estate, Featherstone, Pontefract, W Yorks, WF7 6RA
*Activities:* Other letting and operating of own or leased real estate
*Shareholders:* Rupert George Pearson; Oliver Graham Garside
*Officers:* Oliver Graham Garside [1966] Director; Rupert George Pearson [1966] Director

**Peak Oil Products (Northern) Limited**
*Incorporated:* 30 March 1973 *Employees:* 29
*Net Worth:* £4,523,517 *Total Assets:* £6,785,770
*Registered Office:* Pickering House, 40a York Place, Leeds, LS1 2ED
*Activities:* Agents involved in the sale of fuels, ores, metals and industrial chemicals
*Shareholder:* Thomas Gregory Pearson
*Officers:* Thomas Gregory Pearson, Secretary; Helen Louise Pearson [1967] Director; Neil Alexander Thomas Pearson [1970] Director; Rachel Margaret Pearson [1944] Director; Thomas James Heath Pearson [1978] Director; Thomas Gregory Pearson [1939] Director

**N. Peal (Retail) Limited**
*Incorporated:* 13 December 2006 *Employees:* 55
*Net Worth:* £3,526,126 *Total Assets:* £7,119,010
*Registered Office:* High Barn, Beamsley, Skipton, N Yorks, BD23 6HT
*Activities:* Retail sale of clothing in specialised stores
*Parent:* Water Sprite Limited
*Officers:* Margaret Louise Kleppen, Secretary; Adam Holdsworth [1966] Director

**Pear Tree Projects Limited**
*Incorporated:* 30 October 1992 *Employees:* 73
*Net Worth:* £4,161,935 *Total Assets:* £6,779,746
*Registered Office:* Pear Tree House, Bolam, Darlington, Co Durham, DL2 2UP
*Activities:* Other service activities n.e.c.
*Shareholders:* David Anthony John Bartlett; Andrea Sarah Bartlett
*Officers:* Andrea Sarah Bartlett, Secretary/Property Developer; Andrea Sarah Bartlett [1970] Director/Company Secretary; David Anthony John Bartlett [1966] Director/Property-Care Services Manager

**Peaspring Limited**
*Incorporated:* 8 February 2000 *Employees:* 124
*Net Worth:* £10,274,928 *Total Assets:* £14,056,951
*Registered Office:* c/o Brook Taverner & Co Ltd, Haincliffe Road, Ingrow, Keighley, W Yorks, BD21 5BU
*Activities:* Activities of head offices
*Shareholders:* Jo-Anne Booth; Rebecca Scott; Rachel Jones
*Officers:* Andrew Philip Booth, Secretary/Chartered Accountant; Andrew Philip Booth [1968] Director/Chartered Accountant; Jo-Anne Booth [1969] Director; John Benjamin Jones [1969] Managing Director; Rachel Jones [1970] Director; Jason Edwin Russell Scott [1970] Production Director; Rebecca Scott [1970] Director

**Pebbles Care Limited**
*Incorporated:* 4 August 2003 *Employees:* 158
*Net Worth:* £4,080,204 *Total Assets:* £5,758,576
*Registered Office:* Rouse House, 2 Wyther Lane, Kirkstall, Leeds, LS5 3BT
*Activities:* Other residential care activities n.e.c.
*Major Shareholder:* Luiz Guilherme
*Officers:* Lynsey Guilherme, Secretary; Luigi Guilherme [1960] Director/Property Developer; Lynsey Guilherme [1974] Director

**Pecan Deluxe Candy (Europe) Limited**
*Incorporated:* 8 April 1992 *Employees:* 102
*Net Worth:* £4,621,789 *Total Assets:* £6,265,502
*Registered Office:* F7 First Floor, Lincoln House, Lincoln Way, Ashbrooke Park, Sherburn in Elmet, Leeds, LS25 6PJ
*Activities:* Manufacture of other food products n.e.c.
*Officers:* Robert Ian Cranston, Secretary/Accountant; Bennie Brigham [1944] Director [American]; Jay Brigham [1969] Director/President/CEO [American]; Graham Nicholas Kingston [1968] Managing Director

**H. Peel & Sons Limited**
*Incorporated:* 26 January 1990
*Net Worth:* £2,370,386 *Total Assets:* £3,694,119
*Registered Office:* Dewlon House, Cannon Way, Mill Street West, Dewsbury, W Yorks, WF13 1XL
*Activities:* Joinery installation
*Parent:* H Peel & Sons (Holdings) Limited
*Officers:* Wendy Ann Edgell, Secretary; Dominic James Brogan [1963] Director/Contracts Manager; Russell John Crowther [1968] Contracts Director; Graham Roy Jennings [1956] Director; Andrew Neil Pollock [1955] Director/Contracts Manager; Steven Mark Roberts [1966] Director; Keith Soulsby [1956] Director

**The Peel Entertainment Group Limited**
*Incorporated:* 12 January 1999 *Employees:* 60
*Net Worth:* £2,800,865 *Total Assets:* £5,732,585
*Registered Office:* Pinetum, Broughton Hall, Skipton, N Yorks, BD23 3AE
*Activities:* Performing arts
*Major Shareholder:* Susannah Lee Daley
*Officers:* Kerry Anne Daley, Secretary; Kerry Anne Daley [1968] Director/Entertainment; Susannah Lee Daley [1967] Director/Entertainment Consultant

**Peel Street Developments Limited**
*Incorporated:* 7 August 2007 *Employees:* 1
*Net Worth:* £2,397,997 *Total Assets:* £4,011,677
*Registered Office:* Trinity House, Thurston Road, Northallerton, N Yorks, DL6 2NA
*Activities:* Activities of head offices
*Shareholders:* Jeremy Robin Stephenson; Abigail Louisa Stephenson
*Officers:* Abigail Louisa Stephenson, Secretary; Jeremy Robin Stephenson [1962] Director

**Pegasus World Ltd**
*Incorporated:* 24 April 2006 *Employees:* 5
*Net Worth:* £1,044,635 *Total Assets:* £4,839,671
*Registered Office:* Outgang Lane, Osbaldwick, York, YO19 5UP
*Activities:* Wholesale of clothing and footwear
*Shareholders:* Haizhou Zhou; Liping Hu
*Officers:* Liping Hu [1980] Director; Haizhou Zhou [1983] Director

**Pegler Holdings Limited**
*Incorporated:* 10 October 2003
*Net Worth:* £2,444,000 *Total Assets:* £19,285,000
*Registered Office:* St Catherines Avenue, Doncaster, S Yorks, DN4 8DF
*Activities:* Forging, pressing, stamping and roll-forming of metal; powder metallurgy
*Parent:* Aalberts Industries UK Limited
*Officers:* Kevin Michael Parker, Secretary; Craig Malloy [1970] Finance Director

**Pegler Limited**
*Incorporated:* 20 December 1974 *Employees:* 299
*Net Worth:* £11,527,000 *Total Assets:* £12,466,000
*Registered Office:* Belmont Works, St Catherines Avenue, Doncaster, S Yorks, DN4 8DF
*Activities:* Forging, pressing, stamping and roll-forming of metal; powder metallurgy
*Parent:* Pegler Holdings Limited
*Officers:* Kevin Michael Parker, Secretary; Craig Malloy [1970] Finance Director

**Pegler Yorkshire Group Limited**
*Incorporated:* 5 December 1945 *Employees:* 107
*Net Worth:* £70,696,000 *Total Assets:* £165,936,992
*Registered Office:* Belmont Works, St Catherines Avenue, Doncaster, S Yorks, DN4 8DF
*Activities:* Manufacture of other fabricated metal products n.e.c.
*Parent:* Aalberts Industries France SNC
*Officers:* Kevin Michael Parker, Secretary; Graham Fawcett [1963] Manufacturing Director; Andre in Het Veld [1966] Director [Dutch]; Bryan Liddle [1961] Commercial Director; Craig Malloy [1970] Finance Director; Wiebe Arnold Pelsma [1963] Director [Dutch]

**Pelagia (UK) Limited**
*Incorporated:* 11 September 1992 *Employees:* 60
*Previous:* United Fish Industries (UK) Limited
*Net Worth:* £16,886,000 *Total Assets:* £26,545,000
*Registered Office:* Gilbey Road, Pyewipe, Grimsby, N E Lincs, DN31 2SL
*Activities:* Manufacture of prepared feeds for farm animals
*Officers:* Michael McEllone, Secretary; Arnt-Ove Hoddevik [1965] Director [Norwegian]; Michael McEllone [1974] Director/Company Secretary [Irish]

**Pelican Engineering Co. Limited**
*Incorporated:* 5 March 1926 *Employees:* 145
*Net Worth:* £9,545,885 *Total Assets:* £20,671,300
*Registered Office:* Altofts Lane, Wakefield Europort, Castleford, W Yorks, WF10 5UB
*Activities:* Activities of head offices
*Shareholders:* Richard Basil Crump; Sarah Jane Newton
*Officers:* Amelia Mary Crump [1997] Director; Richard Basil Crump [1964] Director/Engineer; Robert Edward Crump [1930] Director/Engineer; Sarah Jane Newton [1968] Director

**Pelican Engineering Company (Sales), Limited**
*Incorporated:* 6 October 1981 *Employees:* 142
*Net Worth:* £4,072,464 *Total Assets:* £16,256,447
*Registered Office:* Pelican Engineering, Altofts Lane, Wakefield Europort, Castleford, W Yorks, WF10 5UB
*Activities:* Sale of other motor vehicles
*Parent:* Pelican Engineering Co Ltd
*Officers:* Amelia Mary Crump [1997] Director; Gillian Rosemary Crump [1949] Director; Richard Basil Crump [1964] Director; Robert Edward Crump [1930] Director; Sarah Jane Newton [1968] Director

**Pelsis Holding (UK) Limited**
*Incorporated:* 14 September 2009 *Employees:* 266
*Net Worth Deficit:* £9,211,368 *Total Assets:* £67,949,376
*Registered Office:* Sterling House, Grimbald Crag Close, Knaresborough, N Yorks, HG5 8PJ
*Activities:* Activities of head offices
*Parent:* Hamsard 3449 Limited
*Officers:* Paul John Devlin [1966] Director; Peter Anthony Mangion [1961] Director

**Pelsis Limited**
*Incorporated:* 27 July 1981 *Employees:* 105
*Net Worth Deficit:* £4,187,000 *Total Assets:* £12,654,000
*Registered Office:* Sterling House, Grimbald Crag Close, Knaresborough, N Yorks, HG5 8PJ
*Activities:* Other business support service activities n.e.c.
*Parent:* Pelsis Holding (UK) Limited
*Officers:* Paul John Devlin [1966] Director; Peter Anthony Mangion [1961] Managing Director

**Pendle Sportswear Limited**
*Incorporated:* 30 March 2011 *Employees:* 58
*Net Worth:* £2,676,221 *Total Assets:* £4,124,566
*Registered Office:* 1 Little Lane, Ilkley, W Yorks, LS29 8UG
*Activities:* Retail sale of clothing in specialised stores
*Shareholders:* Mary Elizabeth Hall; Philip Hall
*Officers:* Mary Elizabeth Hall [1947] Director [Irish]; Philip Hall [1946] Director/Chartered Accountant; Stephen John Hall [1977] Director

**Pengems Limited**
*Incorporated:* 19 September 1979 *Employees:* 22
*Net Worth:* £4,412,002 *Total Assets:* £6,051,949
*Registered Office:* 34 Park Cross Street, Leeds, LS1 2QH
*Activities:* Retail sale of watches and jewellery in specialised stores
*Major Shareholder:* Michael David Rose
*Officers:* Michael Williams, Secretary; Michael David Rose [1956] Director/Jeweller

**Penman MW Limited**
*Incorporated:* 17 October 2016 *Employees:* 69
*Net Worth Deficit:* £544,334 *Total Assets:* £5,094,460
*Registered Office:* c/o Martin Williams (Hull) Limited, Ellifoot Lane, Burstwick, E Yorks, HU12 9EF
*Activities:* Manufacture of bodies (coachwork) for motor vehicles (except caravans)
*Officers:* Jonathan Brook Cooper [1969] Director; Christopher Martin Williams [1981] Director; Nicholas James Williams [1983] Director

**Penmoor UK Ltd**
*Incorporated:* 23 December 1974 *Employees:* 68
*Net Worth:* £10,414,568 *Total Assets:* £16,559,593
*Registered Office:* Eastfield Mills, The Knowle, Shepley, Huddersfield, W Yorks, HD8 8EA
*Activities:* Renting and leasing of other machinery, equipment and tangible goods n.e.c.
*Parent:* Terrier Holdings Ltd
*Officers:* Andrew Peykoff II [1976] Director/Executive [American]; Kenneth Ratzlaff [1968] Director/Executive [American]; Rali Sanderson [1976] Director/Executive [American]; Charles Alistair Smith [1969] Director; James Maxwell Smith [1971] Director; John Selwyn Smith [1942] Director

**Pennine Camphill Community Limited (The)**
*Incorporated:* 19 January 1977 *Employees:* 23
*Net Worth:* £2,949,208 *Total Assets:* £4,750,787
*Registered Office:* Pennine Camphill Community, Wood Lane, Chapelthorpe, Wakefield, W Yorks, WF4 3JL
*Activities:* Other education n.e.c.
*Officers:* Stephanie McDermott, Secretary; Jane Elizabeth Barry [1953] Director/Retired; Nicholas Henry Dodd [1959] Director; Graham Christopher Franklin [1951] Director/Company Secretary; Dawn Jenkins [1958] Director; Austin McIntyre [1948] Director/Teacher

**Jack Pennington Limited**
*Incorporated:* 29 April 1974 *Employees:* 55
*Net Worth:* £1,989,340 *Total Assets:* £3,628,983
*Registered Office:* Hird Street, Shipley, Bradford, W Yorks, BD17 7ED
*Activities:* Non-specialised wholesale trade
*Parent:* Fingreen Holdings Limited
*Officers:* Andrea Simpson, Secretary; Neil David Hughes [1969] Commercial Director; Simon James Mettrick [1967] Operations Director; Andrea Simpson [1959] Director/Company Secretary; Christopher David Simpson [1952] Managing Director

**Pennock & Ivory Limited**
*Incorporated:* 15 August 2002 *Employees:* 68
*Net Worth:* £2,654,417 *Total Assets:* £4,164,143
*Registered Office:* Athlone Street, Armley, Leeds, LS12 1UB
*Activities:* Taxi operation
*Parent:* Pennock Holdings Limited
*Officers:* Nathan Iestyn Bowles [1976] Director; Andrew Pennock [1966] Director; Paul Robert Ragan [1967] Director; Kevin Richard Thomas [1968] Director

**Pentamon Limited**
*Incorporated:* 5 April 2006 *Employees:* 2
*Net Worth:* £720,991 *Total Assets:* £3,814,085
*Registered Office:* 3 Greengate, Cardale Park, Harrogate, N Yorks, HG3 1GY
*Activities:* Development of building projects
*Parent:* Harwood Developments Limited
*Officers:* Jason David Cherrington [1967] Director

**People Apps Limited**
*Incorporated:* 5 September 2012
*Net Worth:* £1,363,279 *Total Assets:* £3,030,754
*Registered Office:* Unit 2-3 Station Road, Epworth, Doncaster, S Yorks, DN9 1JZ
*Activities:* Business and domestic software development
*Shareholders:* Manjit Sindhar; Satvinder Singh Sindhar; Sukhjinder Singh
*Officers:* Manjit Sindhar [1966] Director; Satvinder Singh Sindhar [1969] Director/IT Consultant; Sukhjinder Singh [1960] Director

**Peover Eye Investments Limited**
*Incorporated:* 28 November 2014 *Employees:* 174
*Net Worth:* £6,368,675 *Total Assets:* £13,407,615
*Registered Office:* Kudos Shower Products Ltd, Elmsfield Park, Holme, Cumbria, LA6 1RJ
*Activities:* Activities of other holding companies n.e.c.
*Major Shareholder:* Bruce Raymond Ledwith
*Officers:* David Irwin [1966] Director; Bruce Raymond Ledwith [1952] Director

**Peppers Marquees Limited**
*Incorporated:* 6 May 1987 *Employees:* 24
*Net Worth:* £2,688,684 *Total Assets:* £3,360,755
*Registered Office:* Crosshill, Snaith, Goole, N Humbers, DN14 9JT
*Activities:* Other service activities n.e.c.
*Major Shareholder:* Thomas Stuart Pepper
*Officers:* Margaret Wendy Pepper, Secretary; Margaret Pepper [1953] Director/Teacher; Thomas Stuart Pepper [1948] Managing Director

**Perago Limited**
*Incorporated:* 29 September 2003 *Employees:* 2
*Net Worth:* £1,856,221 *Total Assets:* £3,030,627
*Registered Office:* 9 Silkwood Business Park, Fryers Way, Ossett, W Yorks, WF5 9TJ
*Activities:* Activities of head offices
*Parent:* Mysing Care Limited
*Officers:* Joanne Elizabeth Scott [1964] Director

**Perio News Limited**
*Incorporated:* 22 February 1988 *Employees:* 3
*Net Worth:* £3,783,916 *Total Assets:* £3,970,407
*Registered Office:* High Beck, Stockton Lane, York, YO32 9UB
*Activities:* Other letting and operating of own or leased real estate
*Officers:* Colin Alfred Foster, Secretary; Richard Gray [1940] Managing Director; Yasmin Delal Gray [1956] Director

**Permoid Industries Limited**
*Incorporated:* 2 January 1991 *Employees:* 176
*Net Worth:* £1,961,217 *Total Assets:* £5,170,345
*Registered Office:* Horndale Avenue, Aycliffe Industrial Estate, Newton Aycliffe, Co Durham, DL5 6DW
*Activities:* Other manufacturing n.e.c.
*Officers:* Brian William Beckett, Secretary; Walid El Hage [1968] Managing Director

**Persimmon Developments (Didcot) Limited**
*Incorporated:* 18 May 2007 *Employees:* 4
*Net Worth:* £11,821,398 *Total Assets:* £15,060,762
*Registered Office:* Persimmon House, Fulford, York, YO19 4FE
*Activities:* Construction of domestic buildings
*Parent:* Persimmon Homes Limited
*Officers:* Tracy Lazelle Davison, Secretary; David Jenkinson [1967] Director; Michael Hugh Killoran [1961] Finance Director; Richard Paul Stenhouse [1971] Director/Accountant

**Persimmon Developments (No 5) Limited**
*Incorporated:* 18 May 2007 *Employees:* 4
*Net Worth:* £52,954,000 *Total Assets:* £158,756,992
*Registered Office:* Persimmon House, Fulford, York, YO19 4FE
*Activities:* Construction of domestic buildings
*Parent:* Persimmon Homes Limited
*Officers:* Tracy Lazelle Davison, Secretary; David Jenkinson [1967] Director; Michael Hugh Killoran [1961] Finance Director; Richard Paul Stenhouse [1971] Director/Accountant

**Persimmon Finance (No.2) Limited**
*Incorporated:* 17 February 2006 *Employees:* 4
*Net Worth:* £85,051,000 *Total Assets:* £85,156,000
*Registered Office:* Persimmon House, Fulford, York, YO19 4FE
*Activities:* Other service activities n.e.c.
*Parent:* Persimmon PLC
*Officers:* Tracy Lazelle Davison, Secretary; David Jenkinson [1967] Director; Michael Hugh Killoran [1961] Finance Director; Richard Paul Stenhouse [1971] Director/Accountant

**Persimmon Finance Limited**
*Incorporated:* 31 October 2000
*Net Worth:* £1,845,303,040 *Total Assets:* £1,847,659,008
*Registered Office:* Persimmon House, Fulford, York, YO19 4FE
*Activities:* Other service activities n.e.c.
*Parent:* Persimmon PLC
*Officers:* Tracy Lazelle Davison, Secretary; David Jenkinson [1967] Director; Michael Hugh Killoran [1961] Finance Director; Richard Paul Stenhouse [1971] Director/Accountant

**Persimmon Harts Limited**
*Incorporated:* 2 August 1989 *Employees:* 4
*Net Worth:* £39,660,000 *Total Assets:* £61,604,000
*Registered Office:* Persimmon House, Fulford, York, YO19 4FE
*Activities:* Other service activities n.e.c.
*Parent:* Persimmon PLC
*Officers:* Tracy Lazelle Davison, Secretary; David Jenkinson [1967] Director; Michael Hugh Killoran [1961] Finance Director; Richard Paul Stenhouse [1971] Director/Accountant

**Persimmon Holdings Limited**
*Incorporated:* 1 November 2000 *Employees:* 5
*Net Worth:* £587,372,032 *Total Assets:* £1,328,592,000
*Registered Office:* Persimmon House, Fulford, York, YO19 4FE
*Activities:* Activities of head offices
*Shareholders:* Persimmon Finance Limited; Persimmon PLC
*Officers:* Tracy Lazelle Davison, Secretary; Duncan Henry Davidson [1941] Director; David Jenkinson [1967] Director; Michael Hugh Killoran [1961] Finance Director; Richard Paul Stenhouse [1971] Director/Accountant

**Persimmon Homes Limited**
*Incorporated:* 16 November 2000 *Employees:* 4,234
*Net Worth:* £853,001,984 *Total Assets:* £4,504,612,864
*Registered Office:* Persimmon House, Fulford, York, YO19 4FE
*Activities:* Development of building projects
*Parent:* Persimmon Holdings Limited
*Officers:* Tracy Lazelle Davison, Secretary; David Jenkinson [1967] Director; Michael Hugh Killoran [1961] Finance Director; Richard Paul Stenhouse [1971] Director/Accountant

**Persimmon Public Limited Company**
*Incorporated:* 22 May 1984 *Employees:* 4,535
*Net Worth:* £3,201,600,000 *Total Assets:* £4,756,800,000
*Registered Office:* Persimmon House, Fulford, York, YO19 4FE
*Activities:* Activities of construction holding companies
*Officers:* Tracy Lazelle Davison, Secretary; Roger William Devlin [1957] Director; David Jenkinson [1967] Director; Rachel Elizabeth Kentleton [1969] Director; Michael Hugh Killoran [1961] Finance Director; Peter Simon Litherland [1964] Director; Marion Jane Sears [1962] Director

**Persimmon Shared Equity Limited**
*Incorporated:* 13 October 1987
*Net Worth:* £22,753,000 *Total Assets:* £160,288,992
*Registered Office:* Persimmon House, Fulford, York, YO19 4FE
*Activities:* Dormant company
*Parent:* Persimmon PLC
*Officers:* Tracy Lazelle Davison, Secretary; David Jenkinson [1967] Director; Michael Hugh Killoran [1961] Finance Director; Richard Paul Stenhouse [1971] Director/Accountant

**Personal Touch Financial Services Limited**
*Incorporated:* 21 July 1997 *Employees:* 124
*Net Worth:* £3,951,876 *Total Assets:* £13,562,463
*Registered Office:* 2nd Floor, Gateway, 2 Holgate Park Drive, York, YO26 4GB
*Activities:* Financial intermediation not elsewhere classified
*Parent:* LSL Property Services PLC
*Officers:* Sapna Bedi FitzGenerald, Secretary; Adam Robert Castleton [1964] Director; Peter Richard Cobley [1967] Finance Director; Richard Stephen Coulson [1960] Director; Mary Jane Cross [1965] Director/Chief Executive Officer; Rajeev Raichura [1979] Director; Jonathan Pearson Round [1964] Director; Toni Smith [1969] Director; Paul Douglas Underwood [1961] Risk & Compliance Director; Maxwell John Wright [1964] Director

**Pet Brands Limited**
*Incorporated:* 13 February 2008 *Employees:* 20
*Net Worth:* £5,591,070 *Total Assets:* £6,702,825
*Registered Office:* Unit 1 Paramount House, Gelderd Road, Birstall, W Yorks, WF17 9QD
*Activities:* Other manufacturing n.e.c.
*Officers:* Poonam Sharma, Secretary; Carl Farraker [1986] Creative Director; Ravi Sharma [1986] Director; Sandeep Sharma [1984] Director/Self Employed

**S.G. Petch Limited**
*Incorporated:* 9 March 1990 *Employees:* 327
*Net Worth:* £7,809,743 *Total Assets:* £46,303,224
*Registered Office:* McMullen Road, Darlington, Co Durham, DL1 1XZ
*Activities:* Sale of new cars and light motor vehicles
*Major Shareholder:* Stephen Guy Petch
*Officers:* Simon David Rees, Secretary; Shaun Burke [1960] Director/General Manager; Andrew Hodgson [1968] Director/Manager; Samantha Marie Petch [1977] Director/Manager; Stephen Guy Petch [1947] Director/Garage Proprietor; Simon David Rees [1956] Director/Accountant

**Pettra Limited**
*Incorporated:* 1 October 2014 *Employees:* 78
*Net Worth:* £831,674 *Total Assets:* £6,614,345
*Registered Office:* 4th Floor, 1 Belle Vue Square, Broughton Road, Skipton, N Yorks, BD23 1FJ
*Activities:* Temporary employment agency activities
*Shareholders:* Peter Andrew Gregory; Tracy Ward
*Officers:* Kate McAvan, Secretary; Peter Andrew Gregory [1956] Director; Tracy Ward [1973] Director

**PFF Packaging (North East) Limited**
*Incorporated:* 27 November 2009 *Employees:* 98
*Previous:* Intelligent Packaging Solutions Limited
*Net Worth Deficit:* £346,786 *Total Assets:* £5,306,425
*Registered Office:* Unit 3 Airedale Park, Royd Ings Avenue, Keighley, W Yorks, BD21 4BZ
*Activities:* Other manufacturing n.e.c.
*Parent:* PFF Packaging Group Limited
*Officers:* Andrew Robert Bairstow [1965] Director; Michelle Annette Bairstow [1968] Director; Nicholas Bairstow [1960] Technical Director; Stephen William Dowe [1951] Finance Director; William James Mapston [1953] Director; Kenton Scott Robbins [1971] Managing Director; Christopher Ian Tate [1964] Finance Director

**PFF Packaging Limited**
*Incorporated:* 25 September 1991 *Employees:* 119
*Net Worth:* £2,223,515 *Total Assets:* £10,488,791
*Registered Office:* Unit 3 Airedale Park, Royd Ings Avenue, Keighley, W Yorks, BD21 4BZ
*Activities:* Manufacture of plastic packing goods
*Parent:* PFF Packaging Group Limited
*Officers:* Michelle Annette Bairstow, Secretary; Andrew Robert Bairstow [1965] Director/Sales Executive; Michelle Annette Bairstow [1968] Company Secretary/Director; Nicholas Hugh Bairstow [1960] Director; Stephen William Dowe [1951] Director; Kenton Scott Robbins [1971] Managing Director; Christopher Ian Tate [1964] Finance Director

**PFI 2005 Limited**
*Incorporated:* 3 October 2005 *Employees:* 4
*Previous:* Interserve PFI 2005 Limited
*Net Worth:* £4,814,000 *Total Assets:* £54,720,000
*Registered Office:* 1 Park Row, Leeds, LS1 5AB
*Activities:* Activities of other holding companies n.e.c.
*Parent:* PFI Para (Holdings) Limited
*Officers:* Jennifer McKay, Secretary; Rory William Christie [1958] Director; John Stephen Gordon [1962] Director; John McDonagh [1969] Director

**PFI Para (Holdings) Limited**
*Incorporated:* 1 October 2012
*Net Worth Deficit:* £24,707,472 *Total Assets:* £127,941,920
*Registered Office:* 1 Park Row, Leeds, LS1 5AB
*Activities:* Activities of other holding companies n.e.c.
*Shareholders:* Dalmore Capital (Para 1) Limited; Coral PFI Holdings 2003 Limited
*Officers:* Jennifer McKay, Secretary; Rory William Christie [1958] Director; John Stephen Gordon [1962] Director; John McDonagh [1969] Director

**PFM Packaging Machinery Limited**
*Incorporated:* 1 July 1987 *Employees:* 27
*Net Worth:* £5,531,122 *Total Assets:* £8,909,439
*Registered Office:* PFM House, 2 Pilgrim Way, Stanningley, Leeds, LS28 6LU
*Activities:* Manufacture of other general-purpose machinery n.e.c.
*Parent:* PFM SpA
*Officers:* Helen Rimmington, Secretary; Andrea Fioravanti [1968] Director/Sales Manager [Italian]; Elizabeth Fioravanti [1934] Director [Italian]; Paolo Fioravanti [1963] Managing Director [Italian]; Sergio Peracchi [1960] Director [Italian]

**Pharmacy2u Limited**
*Incorporated:* 8 July 1999 *Employees:* 218
*Net Worth:* £23,489,000 *Total Assets:* £40,305,000
*Registered Office:* 1 Hawthorn Park, Coal Road, Leeds, LS14 1PQ
*Activities:* Dispensing chemist in specialised stores
*Parent:* P2U Holdings Limited
*Officers:* Scott Lee Fawcett, Secretary; Gary John Dannatt [1971] Director; Daniel Lee [1970] Director/Pharmacist; Mark Jonathan Charles Livingstone [1966] Director

**Phoenix Building Systems Limited**
*Incorporated:* 1 August 2003 *Employees:* 49
*Net Worth:* £1,870,992 *Total Assets:* £4,582,551
*Registered Office:* Princes House, Wright Street, Hull, HU2 8HX
*Activities:* Manufacture of metal structures and parts of structures
*Parent:* Phoenix Building Systems Holdings Ltd
*Officers:* Susan Ann Potter, Secretary; Susan Ann Potter [1959] Finance Director; Martyn Alistair Taylor [1958] Director/Factory Manager; Michael Antony Taylor [1981] Technical Director; Steven Alistair Taylor [1983] Operations Director

**Phoenix Oil & Marine Limited**
*Incorporated:* 12 June 2000 *Employees:* 1
*Net Worth:* £14,509,000 *Total Assets:* £20,066,000
*Registered Office:* Moody Lane, Pyewipe, Grimsby, N E Lincs, DN31 2SY
*Activities:* Activities of head offices
*Parent:* Phoenix Fluid Handling Industry GmbH
*Officers:* Dr Ali Reza Kambiez Zandiyeh [1960] Director/General Manager

**The Phoenix Partnership (Leeds) Ltd**
*Incorporated:* 25 September 2000 *Employees:* 207
*Net Worth:* £60,703,872 *Total Assets:* £69,271,392
*Registered Office:* 129 Low Lane, Horsforth, Leeds, LS18 5PX
*Activities:* Business and domestic software development
*Parent:* TPP Finance Limited
*Officers:* Francis Xavier James Hester [1966] Director

**Phoenix Whirlpools Limited**
*Incorporated:* 5 November 2001 *Employees:* 53
*Net Worth:* £9,779,593 *Total Assets:* £11,287,708
*Registered Office:* Unit 8 Leeds 27 Industrial Estate, Bruntcliffe Avenue, Morley, Leeds, LS27 0LL
*Activities:* Wholesale of household goods (other than musical instruments) n.e.c
*Major Shareholder:* Paul Nicholas Sharp
*Officers:* Paul Nicholas Sharp [1961] Director; Richard Dean Sharp [1985] Director

**Phoenox Textiles Limited**
*Incorporated:* 14 January 1954 *Employees:* 90
*Net Worth:* £11,395,793 *Total Assets:* £14,225,304
*Registered Office:* Spring Grove Mills, Clayton West, Huddersfield, W Yorks, HD8 9HH
*Activities:* Manufacture of other carpets and rugs
*Shareholders:* Charles Edward David Mosley; Adrian Charles Mosley
*Officers:* Adrian Charles Mosley [1971] Operations Director; Brenda Margaret Mosley [1942] Director; Charles Edward David Mosley [1978] Director; Elizabeth Anne Mosley [1968] Sales Director; Nia Elizabeth Mosley [1981] Director/Solicitor

**PIB Group Limited**
*Incorporated:* 3 December 2015 *Employees:* 710
*Net Worth:* £125,827,000 *Total Assets:* £240,946,000
*Registered Office:* Rossington's Business Park, West Carr Road, Retford, Notts, DN22 7SW
*Activities:* Activities of insurance agents and brokers
*Officers:* Ryan Christopher Brown [1973] Director; James Floyd Burr [1966] Director/Investor [American]; Christopher Michael Giles [1964] Director; Brendan James McManus [1959] Director

**PIB Risk Services Limited**
*Incorporated:* 30 January 1992 *Employees:* 209
*Previous:* PIB Risk Services PLC
*Net Worth:* £4,442,755 *Total Assets:* £38,819,148
*Registered Office:* Rossington's Business Park, West Carr Road, Retford, Notts, DN22 7SW
*Activities:* Non-life insurance
*Parent:* PIB Group Limited
*Officers:* Timothy Tracy Brooke [1960] Director; Ryan Christopher Brown [1973] Director; Adrian Colosso [1957] Director; Elisa Marie Griffin [1978] Director/Insurance Brokers; Brendan James McManus [1959] Director/Insurance Broker; Nigel Peter Geoffrey Salisbury [1958] Director/Insurance Broker; Jonathan Paul Stanley [1965] Director/Chief Risk Officer

**Piccadilly Motors Limited**
*Incorporated:* 14 December 1992 *Employees:* 78
*Net Worth:* £9,947,544 *Total Assets:* £12,382,484
*Registered Office:* Piccadilly Motors Ltd, Halfpenny Lane, Knaresborough, N Yorks, HG5 0SL
*Activities:* Sale of new cars and light motor vehicles
*Officers:* Simon Stuart Watts, Secretary; Simon Stuart Watts [1961] Director

**Pick Fisk Limited**
*Incorporated:* 30 May 1997 *Employees:* 40
*Net Worth:* £236,219 *Total Assets:* £8,926,074
*Registered Office:* 537 Tong Road, Leeds, LS12 5AT
*Activities:* Processing and preserving of fish, crustaceans and molluscs
*Shareholders:* Christopher Leonard Pick; Sharon Meredith; Richard Marinass Henricus Oerlemans
*Officers:* Sharon Meredith, Secretary/Fish Processor; Melvyn Haley [1965] Production Director; Sharon Meredith [1950] Director/Fish Processor; Richard Marinass Henricus Oerlemans [1969] Director [Dutch]; Christopher Leonard Pick [1963] Managing Director

**B & B Pickard (Leeds) Limited**
*Incorporated:* 3 August 2012
*Net Worth:* £25,305,568 *Total Assets:* £68,571,768
*Registered Office:* Layton Hall, Layton Road, Rawdon, Leeds, LS19 6QZ
*Activities:* Other letting and operating of own or leased real estate
*Shareholders:* Brian Pickard; Barbara Pickard
*Officers:* Barbara Pickard [1935] Director; Brian Pickard [1935] Director

**Pickards (Commercial) Limited**
*Incorporated:* 1 August 2012
*Net Worth:* £10,061,861 *Total Assets:* £22,219,832
*Registered Office:* Layton Hall, Layton Road, Rawdon, Leeds, LS19 6QZ
*Activities:* Other letting and operating of own or leased real estate
*Shareholders:* Catherine Victoria Coleman; Miles Bryan Pickard; Simon Winston Pickard
*Officers:* Catherine Victoria Coleman, Secretary; Catherine Victoria Coleman [1971] Director/Property Investor; Miles Bryan Pickard [1967] Director/Property Investor; Simon Winston Pickard [1965] Director/Property Investor

**Pickards (Leeds) Limited**
*Incorporated:* 1 August 2012 *Employees:* 17
*Net Worth:* £11,015,443 *Total Assets:* £41,242,272
*Registered Office:* Layton Hall, Layton Road, Rawdon, Leeds, LS19 6QZ
*Activities:* Other letting and operating of own or leased real estate
*Parent:* Pickards Leeds Holdings Limited
*Officers:* Catherine Victoria Coleman, Secretary; Catherine Victoria Coleman [1971] Director/Property Investor; Miles Bryan Pickard [1967] Director/Property Investor; Simon Winston Pickard [1965] Director/Property Investor

**Christopher Pickering Primary School**
*Incorporated:* 10 December 2014 *Employees:* 72
*Net Worth:* £7,310,054 *Total Assets:* £8,784,198
*Registered Office:* Christopher Pickering Primary School, The Compass, 1 Burnham Road, Hull, HU4 7EB
*Activities:* Primary education
*Officers:* Alan Clarke [1972] Director/IT Technician; Kim Clarke [1959] Director/Retired; Kelly Goucher [1983] Director/Teacher; Laura Louise Leeman [1979] Director/Deputy Headteacher; Nicola Louise Loten [1969] Director/Headteacher; Jane Marson [1971] Director/Headteacher

**Pickering Vale (RLH) Limited**
*Incorporated:* 15 April 2009 *Employees:* 1
*Previous:* Ryedale Showground Limited
*Net Worth:* £3,193,974 *Total Assets:* £18,489,496
*Registered Office:* Pickering Showground, Malton Road, Pickering, N Yorks, YO18 8EA
*Activities:* Other letting and operating of own or leased real estate
*Major Shareholder:* Jason Lee Bruton
*Officers:* Jason Lee Bruton, Secretary; Jason Lee Bruton [1968] Director

**J. Pidgeon & Son Limited**
*Incorporated:* 23 September 1944 *Employees:* 22
*Net Worth:* £2,970,564 *Total Assets:* £3,238,835
*Registered Office:* Suite C, Annie Reed Court, Beverley, E Yorks, HU17 0LF
*Activities:* Funeral and related activities
*Parent:* Beverley Funerals Limited
*Officers:* Simon John Barrick [1967] Director; George Anthony David Whittaker [1969] Director

**Pigment Productions Limited**
*Incorporated:* 17 October 2006 *Employees:* 60
*Net Worth:* £2,473,617 *Total Assets:* £5,029,288
*Registered Office:* Chadwick House, off Grange Avenue, Harrogate, N Yorks, HG1 2AN
*Activities:* Manufacture of other articles of paper and paperboard n.e.c.
*Shareholders:* Ian Hamilton O'Brien; Stephen Dennis Baker
*Officers:* Ian Hamilton O'Brien, Secretary/Director; Stephen Dennis Baker [1967] Director; Ian Hamilton O'Brien [1965] Director; Martin Gerard Powderly [1962] Director

**Piksel Limited**
*Incorporated:* 21 April 1995 *Employees:* 500
*Net Worth Deficit:* £4,141,779 *Total Assets:* £38,562,784
*Registered Office:* 1 Innovation Close, Heslington, York, YO10 5ZD
*Activities:* Business and domestic software development
*Officers:* Mark Christie [1970] Director/Chief Technology Officer; Klaus Peter Heiland [1962] Director/Investor/Interim CEO [German]; Ruth Patterson [1987] Director/Solicitor, General Counsel

**Pilgrim Food Holdings Limited**
*Incorporated:* 2 March 2001
*Net Worth:* £35,262,228 *Total Assets:* £35,791,296
*Registered Office:* Unit 26 Brighton Street Industrial Estate, Freightliner Road, Hull, HU3 4EN
*Activities:* Other service activities n.e.c.
*Parent:* Broomco (3555) Limited
*Officers:* Paul Frampton [1970] Director/Accountant; Tom Malkoski [1956] Director/Chief Executive Officer [American]

**Pindar Scarborough Ltd**
*Incorporated:* 8 February 2011 *Employees:* 285
*Net Worth:* £8,973,532 *Total Assets:* £32,081,462
*Registered Office:* The Lettershop Limited, Whitehall Park, Whitehall Road, Leeds, LS12 5XX
*Activities:* Printing n.e.c.
*Officers:* Sarah Belinda Newbould, Secretary; Stephen Tony Goodman [1970] Director/Accountant; Peter Greaves [1962] Managing Director; Lee David Richardson [1971] Director/Accountant

**Ping Europe Limited**
*Incorporated:* 16 August 1973 *Employees:* 252
*Net Worth:* £22,944,544 *Total Assets:* £34,633,984
*Registered Office:* Corringham Road Industrial Estate, Gainsborough, Lincs, DN21 1XZ
*Activities:* Manufacture of sports goods
*Shareholders:* John Andrew Solheim; Allan Dale Solheim
*Officers:* Ian Hamilton Smith, Secretary; John James Clark [1956] Managing Director; Allan Dale Solheim [1940] Director/Manager [American]; John Andrew Solheim [1945] Director/Chairman & Manager [American]; Karsten Louis Solheim [1937] Director [American]

**Pinheiros Corporation Limited**
*Incorporated:* 15 November 2002 *Employees:* 5
*Net Worth:* £445,189 *Total Assets:* £4,774,671
*Registered Office:* 38 Dewsbury Road, Ossett, W Yorks, WF5 9NQ
*Activities:* Printing n.e.c.
*Shareholders:* Jonathan David Pickup; Julian James Brown
*Officers:* Jonathan David Pickup, Secretary; Julian James Brown [1971] Director; Jonathan David Pickup [1967] Director

**Pinion Services Limited**
*Incorporated:* 17 December 2001 *Employees:* 8
*Net Worth:* £2,690,606 *Total Assets:* £7,939,451
*Registered Office:* Novis & Co Chartered Accountants, 1 Victoria Court, Bank Square, Morley, Leeds, LS27 9SE
*Activities:* Information technology consultancy activities
*Parent:* Pinion Solutions Holdings Ltd
*Officers:* Chandra Sekhar Myneni [1971] Director

**Pipe Holdings 1 PLC**
*Incorporated:* 6 June 2005 *Employees:* 2
*Net Worth:* £10,520,000 *Total Assets:* £98,832,000
*Registered Office:* Broomhouse Lane, Edlington, Doncaster, S Yorks, DN12 1ES
*Activities:* Activities of production holding companies
*Officers:* Emma Gayle Versluys, Secretary; Paul Anthony James [1967] Director/Chief Financial Officer; Martin Keith Payne [1965] Director

**Pipe Holdings 2 Limited**
*Incorporated:* 27 June 2005 *Employees:* 2
*Net Worth:* £98,300,000 *Total Assets:* £104,700,000
*Registered Office:* Broomhouse Lane, Edlington, Doncaster, S Yorks, DN12 1ES
*Activities:* Activities of production holding companies
*Parent:* Pipe Holdings 1 PLC
*Officers:* Emma Gayle Versluys, Secretary; Paul Anthony James [1967] Director/Chief Financial Officer; Martin Keith Payne [1965] Director

**Pipe Holdings PLC**
*Incorporated:* 15 June 2004 *Employees:* 2
*Net Worth:* £7,818,000 *Total Assets:* £196,124,992
*Registered Office:* Broomhouse Lane, Edlington, Doncaster, S Yorks, DN12 1ES
*Activities:* Activities of production holding companies
*Parent:* Pipe Holdings 2 Limited
*Officers:* Emma Gayle Versluys, Secretary; Paul Anthony James [1967] Director/Chief Financial Officer; Martin Keith Payne [1965] Director

**Pipeline Engineering & Supply Co. Limited**
*Incorporated:* 27 March 1997 *Employees:* 68
*Net Worth:* £646,000 *Total Assets:* £8,317,000
*Registered Office:* Gatherley Road Industrial Estate, Catterick Bridge, Richmond, N Yorks, DL10 7JG
*Activities:* Manufacture of other plastic products
*Parent:* Circor International
*Officers:* Nicholas Bowerman, Secretary; Rajeev Bhalla [1963] Director [American]; Nicholas Bowerman [1975] Finance Director; Jonathan Gallagher [1969] Director/Operations

**Pipes & Tubes (2010) Limited**
*Incorporated:* 29 March 2010 *Employees:* 47
*Net Worth:* £1,722,765 *Total Assets:* £6,099,530
*Registered Office:* The Tower, Daltongate Business Centre, Ulverston, Cumbria, LA12 7AJ
*Activities:* Other engineering activities
*Major Shareholder:* Kristian Joseph Wilkes
*Officers:* Kristian Joseph Wilkes [1977] Director

**Pipes UK (Holdings) Limited**
*Incorporated:* 21 March 2012 *Employees:* 3
*Net Worth:* £9,568,424 *Total Assets:* £9,568,424
*Registered Office:* c/o Premier Modular Limited, Catfoss Lane, Brandesburton, Driffield, E Yorks, YO25 8EJ
*Activities:* Other manufacturing n.e.c.
*Parent:* Waco International Holdings Limited
*Officers:* Craig Glover, Secretary; Eugenio Pereira Carneiro de SA [1954] Director [Portuguese]; Craig Glover [1963] Director; Stephen John Michael Goodburn [1963] Director [South African]

**Pitcliffe (Holdings) Limited**
*Incorporated:* 25 May 1994
*Net Worth:* £3,900,124 *Total Assets:* £5,207,167
*Registered Office:* 183 Paradise Shopping Precinct, Pasture Lane, Clayton, Bradford, W Yorks, BD7 2SB
*Activities:* Activities of head offices
*Shareholders:* David Blyth; Graham Blyth
*Officers:* David Blyth [1959] Director/CD/Builder; Graham Blyth [1950] Director/CD/Builder

**Pitcliffe Properties Limited**
*Incorporated:* 19 November 1959 *Employees:* 9
*Net Worth:* £13,598,716 *Total Assets:* £14,211,161
*Registered Office:* 183 Paradise Shopping Precinct, Pasture Lane, Clayton, Bradford, W Yorks, BD7 2SB
*Activities:* Development of building projects
*Parent:* Pitcliffe (Holdings) Limited
*Officers:* David Blyth [1959] Director/Builder; Graham Blyth [1950] Director/Builder

**Pitts Wilson Holdings Limited**
*Incorporated:* 22 June 2011 *Employees:* 87
*Net Worth:* £2,176,245 *Total Assets:* £4,489,435
*Registered Office:* Cutler House, Wakefield Road, Bradford, W Yorks, BD4 7LU
*Activities:* Activities of construction holding companies
*Major Shareholder:* Geoffrey Mountain
*Officers:* Paul Martin Baldwin [1968] Managing Director; Geoffrey Mountain [1957] Director

**Pitts Wilson Limited**
*Incorporated:* 4 February 1997 *Employees:* 87
*Net Worth:* £6,712,731 *Total Assets:* £9,049,172
*Registered Office:* Cutler House, Wakefield Road, Bradford, W Yorks, BD4 7LU
*Activities:* Repair of electrical equipment
*Parent:* Pitts Wilson Holdings Limited
*Officers:* Jeremy Harrison, Secretary/Accountant; Paul Martin Baldwin [1968] Managing Director; Paul Nicholas Bottomley [1979] Director; Mark Flude [1960] Director/Electrical Engineer; Jeremy Harrison [1958] Director/Accountant; David Hooley [1959] Director/Electrical Engineer; Geoffrey Mountain [1957] Director; Stuart Sinclair Reid [1970] Director/Mechanical Engineer

**Pittstop (Ripon) Limited**
*Incorporated:* 2 April 1992 *Employees:* 2
*Net Worth:* £4,491,064 *Total Assets:* £4,668,289
*Registered Office:* P O Box 55, Eva Lett House, 1 South Crescent, Ripon, N Yorks, HG4 1XW
*Activities:* Sale of used cars and light motor vehicles
*Shareholders:* David Richard George Pitt; Kathleen Gladys Pitt
*Officers:* Kathleen Gladys Pitt, Secretary; David Richard George Pitt [1953] Director; Kathleen Gladys Pitt [1954] Director

**Place2invest Ltd**
*Incorporated:* 16 January 2012
*Net Worth:* £430,944 *Total Assets:* £6,816,634
*Registered Office:* 50-54 Oswald Road, Scunthorpe, N Lincs, DN15 7PQ
*Activities:* Development of building projects
*Shareholders:* Alexander Hamilton Handy Griffin; Richard William Whittall
*Officers:* Alexander Hamilton Handy Griffin [1960] Director; Christopher Charles Edward Jackson [1963] Director; Richard William Whittall [1965] Director

**Place2live Ltd**
*Incorporated:* 12 March 1999 *Employees:* 5
*Net Worth:* £1,520,841 *Total Assets:* £4,381,720
*Registered Office:* 50-54 Oswald Road, Scunthorpe, N Lincs, DN15 7PQ
*Activities:* Other letting and operating of own or leased real estate
*Major Shareholder:* Christopher Charles Edward Jackson
*Officers:* Louise Geneser Jackson, Secretary; Christopher Charles Edward Jackson [1963] Director

**Planas Properties Limited**
*Incorporated:* 13 February 1997 *Employees:* 5
*Net Worth:* £4,450,102 *Total Assets:* £11,006,546
*Registered Office:* 6 Woodlea Gardens, Meanwood, Leeds, LS6 4SE
*Activities:* Other letting and operating of own or leased real estate
*Officers:* Janet Evelyn Planas, Secretary; Janet Evelyn Planas [1944] Director/Property Management; John Llabres Planas [1941] Director/Property Management

**Pland Stainless Limited**
*Incorporated:* 5 June 2000 *Employees:* 55
*Net Worth:* £3,426,672 *Total Assets:* £4,726,155
*Registered Office:* Ring Road, Lower Wortley, Leeds, LS12 6AA
*Activities:* Manufacture of metal structures and parts of structures
*Parent:* Pland Group Holdings Limited
*Officers:* Ian Hodgson, Secretary; Stephen Duree [1960] Managing Director; Ian Richard Hodgson [1968] Operations Director

**Planet Overseas Holdings Limited**
*Incorporated:* 19 August 1983
*Net Worth:* £9,584,000 *Total Assets:* £9,584,000
*Registered Office:* c/o Arran Isle Limited, Brindley House, Premier Way, Lowfields Business Park, Elland, W Yorks, HX5 9HF
*Activities:* Dormant company
*Parent:* Arran Isle Holdings Limited
*Officers:* Rachel Helen Balbi, Secretary; Michael James Russell Richards [1964] Director; Martin Wardhaugh [1960] Director; Mark Steven Wild [1960] Director/Accountant

**Planet Platforms (Holdings) Limited**
*Incorporated:* 19 February 2007 *Employees:* 33
*Net Worth:* £3,401,224 *Total Assets:* £4,601,497
*Registered Office:* Brunel Close, Century Park, Wakefield 41 Industrial Estate, Wakefield, W Yorks, WF2 0XG
*Activities:* Activities of other holding companies n.e.c.
*Shareholders:* Toby James Pemberton; Peter Pemberton
*Officers:* Gregory John Armitage, Secretary; Mathew Jake Pemberton [1976] Director; Peter Pemberton [1946] Director; Toby James Pemberton [1972] Director

**Plant Impact Limited**
*Incorporated:* 4 May 2005 *Employees:* 56
*Previous:* Plant Impact PLC
*Net Worth:* £10,243,000 *Total Assets:* £13,787,000
*Registered Office:* Cowick Hall, Snaith, Goole, E Yorks, DN14 9AA
*Activities:* Research and experimental development on biotechnology
*Parent:* Croda Europe Limited
*Officers:* Thomas Michael Brophy, Secretary; Nicholas Ian Challoner [1968] Director/President, Life Sciences; David Timothy Cherry [1969] Managing Director Crop Care and Health Care; Graham Lloyd Myers [1963] Director/Group Financial Controller

**Plant Theatre Ltd**
*Incorporated:* 10 September 2008 *Employees:* 2
*Net Worth:* £2,830,901 *Total Assets:* £3,374,575
*Registered Office:* Carlton House, Grammar School Street, Bradford, W Yorks, BD1 4NS
*Activities:* Other manufacturing n.e.c.
*Officers:* Terence Henry Richard Waite, Secretary/Chartered Accountant; Peter Sydney Magee [1954] Director; Terence Henry Richard Waite [1944] Director/Chartered Accountant

**Plasmor (Halton) Limited**
*Incorporated:* 24 July 1981 *Employees:* 44
*Net Worth:* £10,820,330 *Total Assets:* £12,453,471
*Registered Office:* P O Box 44, Womersley Road, Knottingley, W Yorks, WF11 0DN
*Activities:* Manufacture of concrete products for construction purposes
*Parent:* Plasmor Ltd
*Officers:* Neil Marwood, Secretary; James Richard Marshall [1971] Director; Neil Marwood [1972] Finance Director; Julian Antony Slater [1961] Sales Director; John Swain [1959] Group Sales Director

**Plasmor (Sabey Kirby) Limited**
*Incorporated:* 13 March 1947 *Employees:* 19
*Net Worth:* £5,176,233 *Total Assets:* £6,023,699
*Registered Office:* P O Box 44, Womersley Road, Knottingley, W Yorks, WF11 0DN
*Activities:* Manufacture of concrete products for construction purposes
*Parent:* Plasmor Ltd
*Officers:* Neil Marwood, Secretary; James Richard Marshall [1971] Director; Neil Marwood [1972] Finance Director; Julian Antony Slater [1961] Director; John Swain [1959] Group Sales Director

**Plasmor Limited**
*Incorporated:* 17 November 1959 *Employees:* 399
*Net Worth:* £56,434,028 *Total Assets:* £72,021,832
*Registered Office:* P O Box 44, Womersley Road, Knottingley, W Yorks, WF11 0DN
*Activities:* Manufacture of concrete products for construction purposes
*Major Shareholder:* Julian Antony Slater
*Officers:* Neil Marwood, Secretary; James Richard Marshall [1971] Director; Neil Marwood [1972] Finance Director; Julian Antony Slater [1961] Managing Director; Patricia Elizabeth Slater [1933] Director; John Swain [1959] Group Sales Director

**Platinum Print Limited**
*Incorporated:* 18 November 1999
*Net Worth:* £2,318,153 *Total Assets:* £3,134,310
*Registered Office:* Park House, Hookstone Park, Harrogate, N Yorks, HG2 7DB
*Activities:* Printing n.e.c.
*Shareholders:* David Wyvill; Marina Anne Wyvill
*Officers:* Marina Anne Wyvill, Secretary/Administration Manager; David Wyvill [1959] Director/Printer; Marina Anne Wyvill [1961] Director/Administration Manager

**Platinum Stairlifts Limited**
*Incorporated:* 28 March 1996 *Employees:* 123
*Net Worth:* £7,622,412 *Total Assets:* £12,717,056
*Registered Office:* Unit 10 Cross Hills Business Park, Cross Hills, Keighley, W Yorks, BD20 7BW
*Activities:* Manufacture of other fabricated metal products n.e.c.
*Parent:* Hamsard 3465 Limited
*Officers:* Marcus Conrad Green, Secretary; Timothy Craig Frear [1970] Director/Stair Lift Fabricator; Marcus Conrad Green [1971] Director; Matthew James Marshall [1967] Director; Mark Stephen McNulty [1974] Director; Michael Ian Rees [1973] Director; Kevin Alan Still [1970] Director/Chartered Engineer

**Playdale Playgrounds Limited**
*Incorporated:* 11 November 1953 *Employees:* 109
*Net Worth:* £458,172 *Total Assets:* £3,661,032
*Registered Office:* Haverthwaite, Ulverston, Cumbria, LA12 8AE
*Activities:* Manufacture of sports goods
*Shareholders:* John Anthony Croasdale; Gillian Anne Croasdale
*Officers:* Gillian Anne Croasdale, Finance Director; Gillian Anne Croasdale [1959] Director/Accountant; John Anthony Croasdale [1957] Chairman and Director; Barry Leahey [1974] Managing Director

**Plowman Brothers Limited**
*Incorporated:* 31 August 2006
*Net Worth:* £1,715,048 *Total Assets:* £4,208,166
*Registered Office:* Broad Oak Farm, York Road, Sutton-on-the-Forest, N Yorks, YO61 1ER
*Activities:* Manufacture of trailers and semi-trailers
*Shareholders:* Matthew David Plowman; Richard John Plowman
*Officers:* Matthew David Plowman, Secretary/Metal Fabricator; Matthew David Plowman [1972] Director/Metal Fabricator; Richard John Plowman [1964] Director/Metal Fabricator

**PLS Civil Engineering Limited**
*Incorporated:* 14 April 2014 *Employees:* 9
*Net Worth:* £435,716 *Total Assets:* £3,519,202
*Registered Office:* 50-54 Oswald Road, Scunthorpe, N Lincs, DN15 7PQ
*Activities:* Other engineering activities
*Shareholders:* Dennis Cormican; Pipeline Services (UK) Limited
*Officers:* Denis Cormican [1978] Managing Director; David Csehi [1965] Director

**Plum Bidco Limited**
*Incorporated:* 15 May 2015
*Net Worth:* £4,681,752 *Total Assets:* £12,271,020
*Registered Office:* The Hamlet, Hornbeam Park, Harrogate, N Yorks, HG2 8RE
*Activities:* Residential nursing care facilities
*Parent:* Cortina Race LLP
*Officers:* Thomas Allan Brookes [1981] Director; Alex Dupee [1984] Director; Dr Tony Felton [1958] Director; Ian Goulding [1964] Director; Deborah Jane Johnson [1977] Director; Frits Willem Prakke [1966] Director [Dutch]

**Pluss-Staufer Limited**
*Incorporated:* 15 December 1995 *Employees:* 231
*Net Worth:* £5,289,000 *Total Assets:* £89,537,000
*Registered Office:* Melton Office, Melton Bottom, Melton, North Ferriby, E Yorks, HU14 3HU
*Activities:* Manufacture of other inorganic basic chemicals
*Officers:* Ryaan Irzaad Abdul [1965] Director/Head of Finance West Europe; William Ian Cardew [1960] Director

**PMW Quarries Limited**
*Incorporated:* 15 July 2009 *Employees:* 22
*Net Worth:* £421,795 *Total Assets:* £3,439,106
*Registered Office:* Holmfirth Road, Shepley, Huddersfield, W Yorks, HD8 8BB
*Activities:* Quarrying of ornamental and building stone, limestone, gypsum, chalk and slate
*Shareholders:* Anthony Paul Greenleaf; Adele Marie Greenleaf; Daniel Maurice Watson; Marie Joanne Watson; Peter Watson; Marlene Watson
*Officers:* Anthony Paul Greenleaf [1971] Director/Manager; Daniel Maurice Watson [1975] Director/Plant Manager

**Pneumatic & Electrical Holdings Limited**
*Incorporated:* 23 January 2009 *Employees:* 2
*Net Worth:* £2,460,112 *Total Assets:* £3,542,987
*Registered Office:* Unit 4 Trident Business Park, Leeds Road, Huddersfield, W Yorks, HD2 1UA
*Activities:* Other manufacturing n.e.c.
*Shareholder:* Nigel Mark Kitchen
*Officers:* Gareth John Coates [1968] Technical Director; Stephen Leslie Jones [1969] Managing Director; Nigel Mark Kitchen [1963] Director/Executive Chairman; Antoine Sebastien Lanquetin [1975] Sales Director

**Pneumatic & Electrical Systems Limited**
*Incorporated:* 10 September 2002 *Employees:* 27
*Net Worth:* £3,883,750 *Total Assets:* £4,665,656
*Registered Office:* Unit 4 Trident Business Park, Leeds Road, Huddersfield, W Yorks, HD2 1UA
*Activities:* Manufacture of electronic industrial process control equipment
*Shareholder:* Nigel Mark Kitchen
*Officers:* Gareth John Coates [1968] Technical Director; Stephen Leslie Jones [1969] Managing Director; Nigel Mark Kitchen [1963] Director/Executive Chairman; Antoine Sebastien Lanquetin [1975] Sales Director

**Podrigo Ltd**
*Incorporated:* 3 November 2010
*Net Worth:* £2,331,293 *Total Assets:* £3,540,134
*Registered Office:* 20 Cow Green, Halifax, W Yorks, HX1 1HX
*Activities:* Other letting and operating of own or leased real estate
*Major Shareholder:* Patrick James Veitch
*Officers:* Patrick James Veitch [1969] Director

**Pointer Holdings Limited**
*Incorporated:* 9 June 2017 *Employees:* 210
*Net Worth:* £533,479 *Total Assets:* £6,358,180
*Registered Office:* Unit 10-11 Howley Park Business Village, Morley, Leeds, LS27 0BZ
*Activities:* Security systems service activities
*Major Shareholder:* Robert Alexander Rowan
*Officers:* Margaret Laidlaw Rowan [1938] Director/Retired; Robert Alexander Rowan [1961] Director; Robert MacDonald Rowan [1937] Director

**Pollybell Farms Limited**
*Incorporated:* 18 October 1993 *Employees:* 31
*Net Worth:* £1,658,613 *Total Assets:* £3,263,255
*Registered Office:* Little Carr Farm, Carr Road, Gringley on the Hill, Doncaster, S Yorks, DN10 4SN
*Activities:* Growing of vegetables and melons, roots and tubers
*Parent:* Loveden Estates Limited
*Officers:* James Frederick Spence Brown, Secretary; James Frederick Spence Brown [1982] Director/Accountant; Carolyn Coxe [1985] Director; John Cunningham Taylor [1968] Director

**Polyframe Halifax Limited**
*Incorporated:* 20 June 2016 *Employees:* 198
*Net Worth Deficit:* £4,986,000 *Total Assets:* £8,092,000
*Registered Office:* Mile Thorn Works, Gibbet Street, Halifax, W Yorks, HX1 4JR
*Activities:* Manufacture of builders ware of plastic
*Parent:* Customade Group Trading Limited
*Officers:* Dawn Allison Rogers, Secretary; Lance Dominic Gillett [1966] Finance Director; David Brian Leng [1962] Director/Business Executive; Neil Andrew McGill [1977] Director; John Michael Naylor-Leyland [1984] Director

**Polyframe Norwich Ltd**
*Incorporated:* 23 April 2014 *Employees:* 143
*Net Worth:* £2,437,000 *Total Assets:* £6,919,000
*Registered Office:* Mile Thorn Works, Gibbet Street, Halifax, W Yorks, HX1 4JR
*Activities:* Manufacture of builders ware of plastic
*Parent:* Customade Group Trading Limited
*Officers:* Dawn Rogers, Secretary; David Robert Eagle [1967] Managing Director; Lance Dominic Gillett [1966] Finance Director; David Brian Leng [1962] Director/Business Executive; Neil Andrew McGill [1977] Director; John Michael Naylor-Leyland [1984] Director

**Polynt Composites UK Limited**
*Incorporated:* 25 July 1938 *Employees:* 27
*Net Worth:* £8,073,000 *Total Assets:* £19,497,000
*Registered Office:* Laporte Road, Stallingborough, Grimsby, N E Lincs, DN41 8DR
*Activities:* Manufacture of plastics in primary forms
*Officers:* David Peter Betti [1958] Director/Chief Financial Officer [American]; Jeffrey Humberstone [1965] Director/General Manager

**Polypearl Management Ltd**
*Incorporated:* 4 September 2015
*Net Worth:* £5,052,995 *Total Assets:* £15,079,195
*Registered Office:* 54 Oswald Road, Scunthorpe, N Lincs, DN15 7PQ
*Activities:* Activities of head offices
*Shareholder:* Ian Rodney Tebb
*Officers:* Hilary Margaret Tebb, Secretary; Marie Louise Robinson [1973] Director/Finance Manager; Andrew Graham Tebb [1975] Operations Director; Ian Rodney Tebb [1947] Director; Michelle Claire Lorraine Wilson [1981] Director/Office Manager

**Polypipe Group PLC**
*Incorporated:* 19 January 2007
*Net Worth:* £302,000,000 *Total Assets:* £602,800,000
*Registered Office:* Broomhouse Lane, Edlington, Doncaster, S Yorks, DN12 1ES
*Activities:* Activities of production holding companies
*Officers:* Emma Versluys, Secretary; Paul David Dean [1961] Director; Mark William Hammond [1968] Director/Fund Manager; Louise Jane Hardy [1966] Director; Paul Anthony James [1967] Director/Chief Financial Officer; Sheikh Mansurah Tal-At Mannings [1963] Director/Lawyer; Ronald John Edward Marsh [1950] Director; Martin Keith Payne [1965] Director/Chief Executive Officer; Glen Brian Sabin [1958] Director/Chief Operating Officer

**Polypipe Limited**
*Incorporated:* 28 February 1973 *Employees:* 2,747
*Net Worth:* £257,400,000 *Total Assets:* £537,100,032
*Registered Office:* Broomhouse Lane, Edlington, Doncaster, S Yorks, DN12 1ES
*Activities:* Manufacture of plastics in primary forms
*Parent:* Pipe Holdings PLC
*Officers:* Emma Gayle Versluys, Secretary; Paul Anthony James [1967] Director/Chief Financial Officer; Martin Keith Payne [1965] Director; Glen Brian Sabin [1958] Director/Chief Operating Officer

**Polyseam Limited**
*Incorporated:* 26 July 1993 *Employees:* 49
*Net Worth:* £1,934,904 *Total Assets:* £4,520,086
*Registered Office:* 15 St Andrews Road, Huddersfield, W Yorks, HD1 6SB
*Activities:* Manufacture of paints, varnishes and similar coatings, mastics and sealants
*Officers:* Ali Hussain, Secretary; Kjetil Bogstad [1971] Director/Chief Executive Officer [Norwegian]; Wolodymyr Iwan Hluchan [1968] Research & Development Director; Andrew Sutulic [1955] Director

**Pontefract Academies Trust**
*Incorporated:* 14 March 2013 *Employees:* 583
*Net Worth:* £25,877,000 *Total Assets:* £31,935,000
*Registered Office:* The Barracks Business Centre, Wakefield Road, Pontefract, W Yorks, WF8 4HH
*Activities:* Pre-primary education
*Officers:* Debra Samwell, Secretary; Julian Appleyard OBE [1970] Director/Chief Executive Officer; Andrew John Clarke [1969] Banking Risk Director; John Gough [1942] Director/Retired; Dr Philip Antony Jones [1968] Director; Elaine Valerie Shepherd [1959] Director/Retired; David Wilkin [1957] Sales Director/Chair

**Pontefract Park Race Company Limited (The)**
*Incorporated:* 18 October 1919 *Employees:* 13
*Net Worth:* £707,388 *Total Assets:* £3,566,210
*Registered Office:* The Administration Office, Pontefract Racecourse, Pontefract Park, Park Road, Pontefract, W Yorks, WF8 4QD
*Activities:* Operation of sports facilities
*Officers:* James Norman Gundill, Secretary; William Anthony Bethell [1957] Director/Farmer; Peter Box [1947] Director/Leader of Wakefield Council; Anthony Craven Gilpin [1950] Director/Farmer/Consultant; James Norman Gundill [1942] Director/Solicitor; Camilla Anne Halifax [1949] Director; Christopher John Morton [1953] Director/Solicitor; Nicholas Hugh Tremayne Wrigley [1955] Director

**Portakabin (Refurbished) Limited**
*Incorporated:* 24 March 1994 *Employees:* 69
*Previous:* Foremans Relocatable Building Systems Limited
*Net Worth:* £2,428,000 *Total Assets:* £4,883,000
*Registered Office:* Yorkon House, New Lane, Huntington, York, YO32 9PT
*Activities:* Other specialised construction activities n.e.c.
*Parent:* Portakabin Limited
*Officers:* Martin Ian Goforth, Secretary; Derek Paul Carter [1958] Director; Jonathan Mark Collins [1971] Director/Accountant

**Portakabin (Site Accommodation) Limited**
*Incorporated:* 9 August 2006 *Employees:* 95
*Previous:* Konstructa Hire Limited
*Net Worth:* £23,233,000 *Total Assets:* £47,563,000
*Registered Office:* Yorkon House, New Lane, Huntington, York, YO32 9PT
*Activities:* Renting and leasing of other machinery, equipment and tangible goods n.e.c.
*Parent:* Portakabin Limited
*Officers:* Martin Ian Goforth, Secretary; Derek Paul Carter [1958] Director; Jonathan Mark Collins [1971] Director/Accountant; David Anthony Griffiths [1961] Director/General Manager

**Portakabin Limited**
*Incorporated:* 3 March 1961 *Employees:* 1,757
*Net Worth:* £243,852,992 *Total Assets:* £351,055,008
*Registered Office:* Yorkon House, New Lane, Huntington, York, YO32 9PT
*Activities:* Manufacture of metal structures and parts of structures
*Parent:* Shepherd Industries Limited
*Officers:* Martin Ian Goforth, Secretary; Derek Paul Carter [1958] Director; Jonathan Mark Collins [1971] Director/Accountant; Stephen Paul Newell [1965] Director; James Robinson [1967] Director; Dominic Paulo Ruscillo [1962] IT Director; Amanda Clare Stainton [1964] HR Director

**Portbond Limited**
*Incorporated:* 9 March 2009 *Employees:* 52
*Net Worth:* £7,383,547 *Total Assets:* £18,228,068
*Registered Office:* Sidings House, Sidings Court, Doncaster, S Yorks, DN4 5NU
*Activities:* Activities of other holding companies n.e.c.
*Shareholders:* Lisa Mary Pickering; John Robert Hughes
*Officers:* Charles Arthur Hughes, Secretary; Charles Arthur Hughes [1929] Director; James Charles Hughes [1988] Director; John Robert Hughes [1958] Director

**D. D. Porter Limited**
*Incorporated:* 28 March 1963 *Employees:* 77
*Net Worth:* £2,146,668 *Total Assets:* £10,692,574
*Registered Office:* Unit 1 Walnut Business Park, Walnut Street, Halifax, W Yorks, HX1 5JD
*Activities:* Construction of commercial buildings
*Major Shareholder:* Richard Paul Porter
*Officers:* Jeanne Porter, Secretary; Darren Mark Grogan [1970] Director/Quantity Surveyor; Jeanne Porter [1930] Director/Retired Secretary; Richard Paul Porter [1958] Director/Manager; Peter William Priestley [1969] Estimator/Director; Anthony Rogan [1957] Director

**Porth Investments Limited**
*Incorporated:* 14 February 2001 *Employees:* 3
*Net Worth:* £58,540,000 *Total Assets:* £59,397,000
*Registered Office:* Asda House, Southbank, Great Wilson Street, Leeds, LS11 5AD
*Activities:* Development of building projects
*Parent:* Asda Group Limited
*Officers:* Alexander Simpson, Secretary; Roger Michael Burnley [1966] Director; Robert Gerard McWilliam [1969] Director; Alexander Simpson [1973] Director

**Portland of Bawtry Limited**
*Incorporated:* 20 September 1991 *Employees:* 8
*Net Worth:* £4,922,770 *Total Assets:* £5,516,072
*Registered Office:* 9 Thorne Road, Doncaster, S Yorks, DN1 2HJ
*Activities:* Sale of new cars and light motor vehicles
*Major Shareholder:* Clive Robert Watson
*Officers:* Margaret Clair Watson, Secretary; Adam Robert Watson [1990] Director; Clive Robert Watson [1960] Director/Car Dealer; James Robert Watson [1992] Director

**Positive Location Properties Limited**
*Incorporated:* 9 June 1988
*Net Worth Deficit:* £1,850,255 *Total Assets:* £3,799,260
*Registered Office:* 57 Moorview Way, Skipton, N Yorks, BD23 2JW
*Activities:* Development of building projects
*Officers:* Anthony Brent Clowes, Secretary; Anthony Brent Clowes [1943] Director

**Mark H Poskitt Limited**
*Incorporated:* 30 August 1956 *Employees:* 321
*Net Worth:* £17,478,374 *Total Assets:* £25,512,144
*Registered Office:* The Firs, Kellington, Goole, York, DN14 0SB
*Activities:* Mixed farming
*Shareholders:* Stephen Guy Poskitt; Sonia Romayne Poskitt
*Officers:* Stephen Guy Poskitt, Secretary; Judith Clare Poskitt [1963] Director/Account Manager; Sonia Romayne Poskitt [1933] Director/Farmer; Stephen Guy Poskitt [1963] Director/Farmer

**Poster Publicity Group Limited**
*Incorporated:* 8 March 2002
*Net Worth:* £11,292,366 *Total Assets:* £11,381,576
*Registered Office:* The Inspire, Hornbeam Park, Harrogate, N Yorks, HG2 8PA
*Activities:* Advertising agencies
*Parent:* Kinetic Worldwide Group Limited
*Officers:* Jacqueline Anne Chapple Blease, Company Secretary; Rachael Hird [1967] Director/Accountant; Stuart Michael Taylor [1963] Director/Chief Executive

**Poster Publicity Holdings Ltd**
*Incorporated:* 11 March 1996 *Employees:* 2
*Net Worth:* £30,176,492 *Total Assets:* £30,176,492
*Registered Office:* The Inspire, Hornbeam Park, Harrogate, N Yorks, HG2 8PA
*Activities:* Advertising agencies
*Parent:* Poster Publicity Group Limited
*Officers:* Jacqueline Anne Chapple Blease, Secretary; Rachael Hird [1967] Director/Accountant; Stuart Michael Taylor [1963] Director/Chief Executive

**Potato Manufacturing Science Limited**
*Incorporated:* 18 July 1986 *Employees:* 5
*Net Worth:* £2,793,216 *Total Assets:* £4,492,915
*Registered Office:* Whyncrest Farm, Bridlington Road, Hunmanby, Filey, N Yorks, YO14 9RS
*Activities:* Research and experimental development on biotechnology
*Officers:* Elizabeth Maria Swann, Secretary; Alexander Swann [1987] Technical Director; Elizabeth Maria Swann [1958] Director/Secretary [Dutch]; Michael Swann [1946] Director/Food Technologist; Michelle Swann [1989] Director/Account Manager

**Potter Family Holdings Limited**
*Incorporated:* 3 February 2016 *Employees:* 46
*Net Worth:* £6,897,372 *Total Assets:* £12,401,705
*Registered Office:* Village Farm, Catton, Thirsk, N Yorks, YO7 4SQ
*Activities:* Raising of poultry
*Officers:* Adrian Potter [1977] Director; John Roger Potter [1949] Director/Farmer; Oliver James Potter [1975] Director/Manager; Susan Joan Potter [1950] Director/Farmer

**The Potter Group (Holdings) Limited**
*Incorporated:* 24 February 1977
*Previous:* The Potter Group (Holdings) PLC
*Net Worth:* £44,292,648 *Total Assets:* £52,915,188
*Registered Office:* Green Lane, Melmerby, Ripon, N Yorks, HG4 5HP
*Activities:* Activities of other holding companies n.e.c.
*Officers:* Kenneth James Watson, Secretary/Director; Iain James Buntain [1955] Director; Matthew George Lamb [1966] Director; Charles Derrick Potter [1941] Director; Margaret Ann Potter [1940] Director; Kenneth James Watson [1961] Director

**G R Potter Plant Hire Limited**
*Incorporated:* 4 October 2000 *Employees:* 22
*Net Worth:* £5,473,658 *Total Assets:* £12,927,739
*Registered Office:* Village Farm, Catton, Thirsk, N Yorks, YO7 4SQ
*Activities:* Other specialised construction activities n.e.c.
*Major Shareholder:* Giles Roger Potter
*Officers:* Susan Joan Potter, Secretary; Giles Roger Potter [1974] Director/Plant Hire Contractor

**Potters Farm Production LLP**
*Incorporated:* 4 February 2016
*Net Worth:* £379,109 *Total Assets:* £4,315,273
*Registered Office:* Village Farm, Catton, Thirsk, N Yorks, YO7 4SQ
*Officers:* Adrian Potter [1977] Member; John Roger Potter [1949] Member; Oliver James Potter [1975] Member; Susan Joan Potter [1950] Member

**Jonathan Potts Limited**
*Incorporated:* 18 May 1989 *Employees:* 9
*Net Worth:* £2,800,295 *Total Assets:* £3,198,993
*Registered Office:* Estate Road No 1, South Humberside Industrial Estate, Grimsby, N E Lincs, DN31 2TB
*Activities:* Wholesale of waste and scrap
*Major Shareholder:* Norman Leek
*Officers:* Norman Anthony Leek, Secretary/Accountant; Norman Anthony Leek [1943] Director/Accountant

**Poundstretcher Limited**
*Incorporated:* 6 August 1955 *Employees:* 5,725
*Net Worth:* £21,574,962 *Total Assets:* £179,085,936
*Registered Office:* Trident Business Park, Leeds Road, Huddersfield, W Yorks, HD2 1UA
*Activities:* Other retail sale in non-specialised stores
*Officers:* Hemant Patel, Secretary; Martin Crapper [1960] Health & Safety Director; Nadir Lalani [1949] Director/Chairman; Xing Yu Pan [1983] Director/Buyer [Chinese]; Hemant Patel [1961] Finance Director; Somnath Saha [1970] Commercial Director; Abdul Aziz Tayub [1955] Director

**Powar Developments Limited**
*Incorporated:* 14 October 2008 *Employees:* 2
*Net Worth:* £8,550,589 *Total Assets:* £15,710,050
*Registered Office:* Swalesmoor Farm, Swalesmoor Road, Halifax, W Yorks, HX3 6UF
*Activities:* Other letting and operating of own or leased real estate
*Parent:* Leo Group Ltd
*Officers:* Manjit Singh Powar [1976] Director; Danny Steven Sawrij [1969] Director

**Powell (UK) Limited**
*Incorporated:* 26 May 2005 *Employees:* 215
*Net Worth:* £13,842,000 *Total Assets:* £19,313,000
*Registered Office:* Factory Site, Ripley Road, Bradford, W Yorks, BD4 7EH
*Activities:* Manufacture of electricity distribution and control apparatus
*Parent:* Powell International BV
*Officers:* Michael William Metcalf, Secretary; Michael John Galley [1948] Managing Director; Eileen Lynn Howell [1957] Director/Accountant [American]; Michael William Metcalf [1967] Director/Chief Financial Officer [American]

**Powell Engineering UK Limited**
*Incorporated:* 7 October 1999 *Employees:* 86
*Net Worth:* £1,419,848 *Total Assets:* £5,459,230
*Registered Office:* Belton Road, Sandtoft, Doncaster, S Yorks, DN8 5SX
*Activities:* Manufacture of electricity distribution and control apparatus
*Parent:* Vinci Energies UK Holding Limited
*Officers:* Paul James Murray, Secretary; Phillipe Guerin [1967] Director [French]; Simon Innis [1972] Director; Rochdi Ziyat [1960] Director [French]

**Power Body Nutrition Ltd**
*Incorporated:* 19 May 2009 *Employees:* 42
*Net Worth:* £1,733,762 *Total Assets:* £3,695,002
*Registered Office:* 11 Chessingham Park, Common Road, York, YO19 5SE
*Activities:* Non-specialised wholesale trade
*Major Shareholder:* Sebastian Szulczewski
*Officers:* Sebastian Szulczewski [1976] Director/Internet Sales Operator [Polish]

**Power Health Products Limited**
*Incorporated:* 4 February 1972 *Employees:* 71
*Net Worth:* £5,159,673 *Total Assets:* £7,005,117
*Registered Office:* 10 Central Avenue, Airfield Estate, Pocklington, York, YO42 1NR
*Activities:* Non-specialised wholesale trade
*Shareholder:* Michael David McIver
*Officers:* Gail Morgan, Secretary; Amelia Clare McIver [1940] Director; Christine McIver [1962] Director; Michael David McIver [1937] Director; Victoria Clair McIver [1969] Director; Gail Morgan [1965] Director; Helen Elizabeth Whilesmith [1963] Director

**Power Link Machine (UK) Co Limited**
*Incorporated:* 22 February 2010 *Employees:* 23
*Net Worth:* £1,796,093 *Total Assets:* £8,058,320
*Registered Office:* Vickers Building, Hurricane Close, Sherburn in Elmet, Leeds, LS25 6PB
*Activities:* Manufacture of electric motors, generators and transformers
*Major Shareholder:* Han Yan
*Officers:* Anthony Brimble [1963] Director; Han Yan [1981] Director [Chinese]; Yabin Zhang [1976] Director [Chinese]

**Power Plastics Limited**
*Incorporated:* 23 November 2001 *Employees:* 62
*Net Worth:* £2,212,621 *Total Assets:* £4,402,411
*Registered Office:* Station Road, Thirsk, N Yorks, YO7 1PZ
*Activities:* Manufacture of other plastic products
*Shareholder:* Diana Catherine Symington Price
*Officers:* Karen Metcalfe, Secretary/Accountant; Andrew Joseph Beetles [1965] Director/Works Manager; James Alastair Geoffrey Fawcett [1964] Director/Maltster; Karen Metcalfe [1971] Director/Accountant; Simon James Edward Price [1974] Director/Consultant

**Power Topco Limited**
*Incorporated:* 2 March 2016 *Employees:* 212
*Net Worth:* £961,000 *Total Assets:* £46,958,000
*Registered Office:* Roundhouse Road, Faverdale Industrial Estate, Darlington, Co Durham, DL3 0UR
*Activities:* Wholesale of other machinery and equipment
*Parent:* Project Polka Bidco Limited
*Officers:* Matthew Barker [1979] Director; James Scott Browning [1966] Director; Ian James Calvesbert [1966] Director; Paul Gibson [1980] Director; Richard Damon Smith [1974] Director

**Power4all Limited**
*Incorporated:* 23 April 2007
*Net Worth:* £11,654,000 *Total Assets:* £108,909,000
*Registered Office:* Legal Department, Asda House, Southbank, Great Wilson Street, Leeds, LS11 5AD
*Activities:* Distribution of electricity
*Parent:* Asda Group Limited
*Officers:* Alexander Simpson, Secretary; Roger Michael Burnley [1966] Director; Dwayne Mears Milum [1975] Director [American]; Richard James Phillips [1955] Director/Treasurer; Mark Vanderhelm [1972] Director/Vice President, Energy, Walmart Stores Inc [American]

**PPB Ltd**
*Incorporated:* 13 November 1979 *Employees:* 81
*Previous:* Proctor Paper & Board Limited
*Net Worth:* £3,500,758 *Total Assets:* £9,397,063
*Registered Office:* 30 Knowsthorpe Gate, Leeds, LS9 0NP
*Activities:* Wholesale of other intermediate products
*Officers:* Rosemary Lewis Proctor, Secretary; Jason Cooper Buchanan [1964] Director/Paper Merchant; Julie Buchanan [1971] Director; William Graham Cheesebrough [1964] Director/Chartered Accountant; Claire Louise Proctor [1963] Director/Paper Merchant; Elizabeth Frances Proctor [1961] Director/Paper Merchant; John Heriot Proctor [1930] Director/Paper Merchant; Mark Lewis Proctor [1957] Director/Paper Merchant; Richard John Proctor [1964] Director/Paper Merchant; Rosemary Lewis Proctor [1931] Director/Paper Merchant

**PPDI Assetco Limited**
*Incorporated:* 30 December 2013
*Net Worth Deficit:* £14,891,585 *Total Assets:* £359,000,704
*Registered Office:* 1 Park Row, Leeds, LS1 5AB
*Activities:* Other business support service activities n.e.c.
*Parent:* PPDI Finance Limited
*Officers:* Jennifer McKay, Secretary; John McDonagh [1969] Director; Alistair Graham Ray [1974] Director

**PPDI Finance Limited**
*Incorporated:* 30 December 2013 *Employees:* 3
*Net Worth Deficit:* £30,447,472 *Total Assets:* £346,520,192
*Registered Office:* 1 Park Row, Leeds, LS1 5AB
*Activities:* Other business support service activities n.e.c.
*Parent:* PPDI Holdings Limited
*Officers:* Jennifer McKay, Secretary; John McDonagh [1969] Director; Alistair Graham Ray [1974] Director

**PPG Architectural Coatings UK Limited**
*Incorporated:* 2 June 1947 *Employees:* 1,409
*Net Worth:* £130,828,000 *Total Assets:* £193,640,992
*Registered Office:* PPG Architectural Coatings UK Limited, Huddersfield Road, Birstall, Batley, W Yorks, WF17 9XA
*Activities:* Manufacture of paints, varnishes and similar coatings, mastics and sealants
*Parent:* Kalon Investment Company Limited
*Officers:* Matthew Baines [1974] Specification and EWI Director; Paul Richard Dowie [1973] HR Director; Jason Paul Metcalf [1973] Marketing Director; Lee Malcolm Morris [1969] Sales Operations and Logistics Director; Vincent Paul O'Sullivan [1968] Sales Director; Felicity Anne Parry [1967] Finance Director; Steven Pocock [1962] Director/General Manager; Graham Roebuck [1963] Manufacturing Director

**PPG Performance Coatings UK Limited**
*Incorporated:* 5 May 2005 *Employees:* 14
*Net Worth:* £3,103,245 *Total Assets:* £3,297,161
*Registered Office:* PPG Performance Coatings UK Ltd, Huddersfield Road, Birstall, Batley, W Yorks, WF17 9XA
*Activities:* Other business support service activities n.e.c.
*Parent:* SigmaKalon UK Holding Limited
*Officers:* Christopher Paul Ernest Francis, Secretary; Elmer Jon Abraham Bruijnooge [1981] Finance Director [Dutch]; Christopher Paul Ernest Francis [1962] Director

**PR Books Limited**
*Incorporated:* 6 January 2003 *Employees:* 44
*Net Worth:* £1,257,907 *Total Assets:* £3,751,292
*Registered Office:* Unit 2 Mealbank Mill Industrial Estate, Mealbank, Kendal, Cumbria, LA8 9DL
*Activities:* Retail sale of books in specialised stores
*Shareholders:* Paul Farrar; Ruth Lydia Farrar
*Officers:* Mark Farrar [1974] Sales Director; Paul Farrar [1949] Director/Bookseller

**Praesto Consulting UK Ltd**
*Incorporated:* 11 September 2007 *Employees:* 46
*Net Worth:* £1,705,180 *Total Assets:* £4,367,052
*Registered Office:* 9 Ropner Gardens, Middleton St George, Darlington, Co Durham, DL2 1FB
*Activities:* Information technology consultancy activities
*Shareholders:* Jeremy Michael Ranson; Kerrie Ranson
*Officers:* Jeremy Michael Ranson [1977] Director/IT Consultancy Manager

**Prahi Limited**
*Incorporated:* 11 April 2012 *Employees:* 187
*Net Worth:* £2,063,865 *Total Assets:* £14,415,687
*Registered Office:* Sidings House, Sidings Court, Lakeside, Doncaster, S Yorks, DN4 5NU
*Activities:* Wholesale of fruit and vegetables
*Shareholder:* Ashfaq Ahmed
*Officers:* Ashfaq Ahmed [1973] Director

**Prasco UK Limited**
*Incorporated:* 11 May 2005 *Employees:* 60
*Net Worth:* £377,477 *Total Assets:* £3,679,725
*Registered Office:* Unit 4 Alpha Court, Capitol Park, Thorne, Doncaster, S Yorks, DN8 5TZ
*Activities:* Wholesale trade of motor vehicle parts and accessories
*Parent:* Prasco S.P.A
*Officers:* Darren Egan, Secretary; Darren Egan [1978] Director; David John Gibson [1954] Director/Accountant; Stephen David Gray Thompson [1972] Director; Kelvyn David Waugh [1970] Director

**Precious Holdings (Wakefield) Limited**
*Incorporated:* 20 March 1970
*Net Worth:* £9,081,531 *Total Assets:* £9,865,710
*Registered Office:* Sanderson House, Station Road, Horsforth, Leeds, LS18 5NT
*Activities:* Development of building projects
*Major Shareholder:* Barbara Mary Precious
*Officers:* Patrick John Brown, Secretary; David Precious [1991] Director

**Precis (1638) Limited**
*Incorporated:* 2 April 1998
*Net Worth:* £6,137,990 *Total Assets:* £6,139,629
*Registered Office:* 3 Park Square, Leeds, LS1 2NE
*Activities:* Buying and selling of own real estate
*Major Shareholder:* Martin Andrew Joyce
*Officers:* Martin Andrew Joyce [1948] Director

**Prefere Resins UK Limited**
*Incorporated:* 31 July 2013 *Employees:* 43
*Net Worth:* £10,869,000 *Total Assets:* £18,908,000
*Registered Office:* Aycliffe Industrial Park, Heighington Lane, Newton Aycliffe, Co Durham, DL5 6UE
*Activities:* Manufacture of other chemical products n.e.c.
*Officers:* David Green, Secretary; David Green [1963] Director/Vice President of Finance and Controlling; Arno Knebelkamp [1963] Director/Chief Executive Officer [German]; Anja Monika Plugge [1969] Director/Vice President Operations [German]

**Prem Sehmi Holdings Limited**
*Incorporated:* 16 March 2012 *Employees:* 1
*Net Worth:* £3,964,239 *Total Assets:* £4,583,863
*Registered Office:* Barclays Bank Chambers, Market Street, Hebden Bridge, W Yorks, HX7 6AD
*Activities:* Activities of head offices
*Shareholders:* Prem-Pal Singh Sehmi; Rose Sutvant Kaur Sehmi
*Officers:* Dr Prem-Pal Singh Sehmi [1980] Director/Dentist; Dr Rose Sutvant Kaur Sehmi [1979] Director

**Premier Communications Ltd**
*Incorporated:* 27 August 2010 *Employees:* 57
*Net Worth:* £4,423,482 *Total Assets:* £5,962,435
*Registered Office:* Aireville, Sleningford Road, Bingley, W Yorks, BD16 2SF
*Activities:* Retail sale of mobile telephones
*Parent:* Family Connect Limited
*Officers:* Masih Family [1983] Director; Mehrdad Family [1953] Director

**Premier Equine International Limited**
*Incorporated:* 15 April 2002 *Employees:* 26
*Net Worth:* £1,729,791 *Total Assets:* £3,397,804
*Registered Office:* Uplands Lodge, East Marsh Road, Goxhill, N Lincs, DN19 7NQ
*Activities:* Manufacture of other wearing apparel and accessories n.e.c.
*Shareholders:* Clive Howard Davies; Rachel Mary Dent
*Officers:* Irene Davies, Secretary; Clive Howard Davies [1965] Director; Rachel Mary Dent [1968] Director/Company Secretary

**Premier Farnell Limited**
*Incorporated:* 6 April 1966 *Employees:* 77
*Previous:* Premier Farnell PLC
*Net Worth:* £279,060,992 *Total Assets:* £643,708,032
*Registered Office:* Farnell House, Forge Lane, Leeds, LS12 2NE
*Activities:* Activities of distribution holding companies
*Parent:* Avnet Bidco Limited
*Officers:* Liam Anthony Heffernan [1972] Director/Accountant [Irish]; Harvey Woodford [1963] Director/VP Corporate Secretary [American]

**Premier Farnell UK Limited**
*Incorporated:* 28 September 1965 *Employees:* 1,237
*Net Worth:* £256,546,000 *Total Assets:* £439,047,008
*Registered Office:* 150 Armley Road, Leeds, LS12 2QQ
*Activities:* Wholesale of electronic and telecommunications equipment and parts
*Officers:* Ralph Lothar Buhler [1968] Director/VP [German]; Liam Anthony Heffernan [1972] Director/Accountant [Irish]; Harvey Woodford [1963] Director/VP Corporate Secretary [American]

**Premier Housing (Bradford) Ltd**
*Incorporated:* 15 December 2000
*Net Worth:* £1,666,416 *Total Assets:* £8,069,797
*Registered Office:* 2 Princeville Road, Bradford, BD7 2AR
*Activities:* Management of real estate on a fee or contract basis
*Officers:* Benish Akhtar [1989] Director; Gulnaz Khan [1981] Director; Adnan Jawaid Malik [1987] Director; Mohammed Malik [1949] Managing Director; Usman Haroon Malik [1981] Director/Manager; Yasmin Akhtar Malik [1958] Director/Secretary

**Premier Modular Limited**
*Incorporated:* 2 April 1990 *Employees:* 236
*Previous:* Waco UK Limited
*Net Worth:* £22,764,000 *Total Assets:* £47,222,000
*Registered Office:* Catfoss Lane, Brandesburton, Driffield, E Yorks, YO25 8EJ
*Activities:* Other manufacturing n.e.c.
*Parent:* Waco International Holdings Pty
*Officers:* Craig Glover, Secretary; Eugenio Pereira Carneiro de SA [1954] Managing Director [Portuguese]; Craig Glover [1963] Director/Accountant; Stephen John Michael Goodburn [1963] Director [South African]

**Premier People Solutions Limited**
*Incorporated:* 14 November 2006 *Employees:* 68
*Net Worth:* £1,288,907 *Total Assets:* £6,036,372
*Registered Office:* 3 Derwent House, Richmond Business Park, Sidings Court, Doncaster, S Yorks, DN4 5NL
*Activities:* Human resources provision and management of human resources functions
*Shareholders:* Jean Beverley Hasrrison; Alan Woodcock; David John Pearson
*Officers:* Jean Beverley Harrison, Secretary; Jean Beverley Harrison [1953] Director; David John Pearson [1970] Director; Alan Woodcock [1951] Director

**Premier Technical Services Group PLC**
*Incorporated:* 21 November 2006 *Employees:* 457
*Previous:* Premier Technical Services Group Limited
*Net Worth:* £32,435,316 *Total Assets:* £72,842,264
*Registered Office:* 13-14 Flemming Court, Castleford, W Yorks, WF10 5HW
*Activities:* Activities of head offices
*Officers:* Adam John Coates, Secretary; John Robert Foley [1955] Director; Michael James Higgins [1956] Director; Alan Miles Howarth [1948] Director; Paul William Teasdale [1967] Director; Roger Peter Teasdale [1967] Managing Director; Mark Ian Watford [1967] Finance Director

**Premier Traffic Management Limited**
*Incorporated:* 27 November 2000 *Employees:* 129
*Net Worth:* £1,295,274 *Total Assets:* £3,682,012
*Registered Office:* Unit 13 Tudhoe Industrial Estate, Spennymoor, Co Durham, DL16 6TL
*Activities:* Other service activities incidental to land transportation, n.e.c.
*Parent:* PTM Holdings Limited
*Officers:* Jon Beamson [1964] Director; Richard George Elliott [1971] Director; Greig Neil Heywood [1972] Director/Traffic Management; David Thomas Moist [1972] Director; Michael John Rogan [1980] Health and Safety Director

**Premier Vanguard Limited**
*Incorporated:* 28 August 1981 *Employees:* 82
*Net Worth:* £6,019,209 *Total Assets:* £9,270,862
*Registered Office:* 14 Beech Hill, Otley, W Yorks, LS21 3AX
*Activities:* Wholesale of other intermediate products
*Parent:* Midas Paper Converters Limited
*Officers:* Robert John Kirkham, Secretary; John Paul Clemie [1950] Director; Lorraine Vivian Clemie [1955] Director/Speech Therapist; Dominic Wilson Deluca [1964] Director [American]; Margaret Ann Deluca [1940] Director/Company Executive; Rachel Louise Deluca [1966] Director/Company Executive; Jacinta Mary Kirkham [1956] Director/Nursing Sister; Robert John Kirkham [1946] Director

**Premium Leasing Limited**
*Incorporated:* 13 August 2010 *Employees:* 1
*Net Worth:* £1,153,290 *Total Assets:* £12,959,146
*Registered Office:* c/o Thompson Commercials Limited, Salvesen Way, Clive Sullivan Way, Hull, HU3 4UQ
*Activities:* Renting and leasing of other machinery, equipment and tangible goods n.e.c.
*Parent:* Thompson Commercials Group Limited
*Officers:* Paul Thomas Simpson, Secretary; Paul Thomas Simpson [1963] Director

**Premium Motorhomes Limited**
*Incorporated:* 12 July 2012
*Net Worth:* £500,475 *Total Assets:* £4,329,253
*Registered Office:* Plum Tree Trading Estate, Plumtree Farm Industrial Estate, Bawtry Road, Bawtry, Doncaster, S Yorks, DN11 8EW
*Activities:* Manufacture of bodies (coachwork) for motor vehicles (except caravans)
*Shareholders:* Michael Karl Herzberg; Mathew Richard Herzberg
*Officers:* Michael Karl Herzberg, Secretary; Mathew Richard Herzberg [1977] Director; Michael Karl Herzberg [1978] Director

**Premium Restaurants Limited**
*Incorporated:* 10 May 2006 *Employees:* 2,138
*Net Worth:* £6,565,351 *Total Assets:* £21,480,392
*Registered Office:* 6 Carlisle Street, Goole, E Yorks, DN14 5BX
*Activities:* Unlicenced restaurants and cafes
*Shareholders:* Premium Foods Limited; McDonald's Restaurants Limited
*Officers:* Christiane Singh, Secretary [Belgian]; Harriet Jane Kathleen Hounsell [1970] Director/Chief People Officer; John Park [1976] Director/Chartered Accountant; Christiane Singh [1962] Director [Belgian]; Pritpal Grewal Singh [1961] Director

**Premo Fabrications Limited**
*Incorporated:* 30 October 2009 *Employees:* 52
*Net Worth:* £978,090 *Total Assets:* £4,417,726
*Registered Office:* Durham Way South, Aycliffe Business Park, Newton Aycliffe, Co Durham, DL5 6XN
*Activities:* Manufacture of basic iron and steel and of ferro-alloys
*Major Shareholder:* David Andrew Knowles
*Officers:* Beau Damean Stevens, Secretary; David Andrew Knowles [1970] Director; Beau Damean Stevens [1971] Director

**D.J. Prescott (Builders) Limited**
*Incorporated:* 18 January 1984 *Employees:* 4
*Net Worth:* £2,251,346 *Total Assets:* £3,269,550
*Registered Office:* Unit 3 Sidings Court, Old Bridge Road, Hornsea, E Yorks, HU18 1RP
*Activities:* Construction of domestic buildings
*Major Shareholder:* Trevor David Prescott
*Officers:* Georgina Prescott, Secretary; Georgina Prescott [1943] Director/Company Secretary; Trevor David Prescott [1967] Director/Builder

**President Energy Holding UK Limited**
*Incorporated:* 22 August 2011
*Net Worth Deficit:* £2,600,738 *Total Assets:* £51,181,176
*Registered Office:* 1200 Century Way, Thorpe Park Business Park, Leeds, LS15 8ZA
*Activities:* Extraction of crude petroleum
*Parent:* President Energy PLC
*Officers:* Peter Michael Levine [1955] Director/Investor; Robert James Shepherd [1966] Director

**President Energy PLC**
*Incorporated:* 16 April 2004 *Employees:* 42
*Net Worth:* £109,963,840 *Total Assets:* £144,096,416
*Registered Office:* 1200 Century Way, Thorpe Park Business Park, Leeds, LS15 8ZA
*Activities:* Extraction of crude petroleum
*Shareholder:* Peter Michael Levine
*Officers:* Peter Michael Levine, Secretary; Jorge Dario Bongiovanni [1951] Director/Oil and Gas Consultant [Argentinian/Italian]; Peter Michael Levine [1955] Director/Investor; Alexander Charles Moody-Stuart [1966] Director; Robert James Shepherd [1966] Director

**Prestige Recruitment Specialists Limited**
*Incorporated:* 30 October 2000 *Employees:* 2,532
*Net Worth:* £1,821,091 *Total Assets:* £6,193,814
*Registered Office:* Prestige House, 12 Bowlalley Lane, Hull, HU1 1XR
*Activities:* Temporary employment agency activities
*Major Shareholder:* Nigel Darren Stabler
*Officers:* John James Headspith, Secretary; Adam Michael Barnes [1981] Director/Recruitment Consultant; Dawn Louise Benson [1974] Director/Recruitment Consultant; Nigel Darren Stabler [1964] Director

**Prestigious Textiles Limited**
*Incorporated:* 9 February 1988 *Employees:* 120
*Net Worth:* £17,321,262 *Total Assets:* £21,841,024
*Registered Office:* 4 Cross Lane, Westgate Hill Street, Bradford, W Yorks, BD4 0SG
*Activities:* Wholesale of textiles
*Shareholders:* Nicola Brumfitt; Matthew Simon Helliwell; Trevor Allen Helliwell
*Officers:* Nicola Brumfit, Secretary; Graham Richard Bateman [1957] Director; Nicola Brumfit [1977] Director; Andrew David Gautry [1956] Director/Chartered Accountant; Matthew Simon Helliwell [1974] Director; Trevor Allen Helliwell [1947] Textile Director; David Finlay Bateson Walker [1965] Director

**Richard Preston & Son Limited**
*Incorporated:* 28 November 1969 *Employees:* 208
*Net Worth:* £4,439,202 *Total Assets:* £10,394,385
*Registered Office:* Potto, Northallerton, N Yorks, DL6 3HX
*Activities:* Freight transport by road
*Major Shareholder:* Anne Preston MBE
*Officers:* James Richard Godwin [1993] Director; Anne Preston [1937] Director; David Richard Preston [1962] Director/Distribution Manager; Jake David Preston [1995] Director

**Preston Road Neighbourhood Development Company Limited**
*Incorporated:* 12 June 2000
*Net Worth:* £10,375,473 *Total Assets:* £10,550,054
*Registered Office:* The Freedom Centre, 97 Preston Road, Hull, HU9 3QB
*Activities:* Other letting and operating of own or leased real estate
*Officers:* Stephen Peter Garnett, Secretary; Stephen John Alltoft [1951] Director/General Manager; David Bond [1947] Director/Retired; Janet Boyd [1971] Director/Chief Executive; Hester Catherine Bridges [1976] Director/Councillor/Project Lead; Rita Butler [1955] Director/Carer; Kenneth Leighton [1932] Director/Retired; Harold McConnell [1940] Director/Retired; Adele Marie Neale [1984] Director; Rebecca Norman [1982] Director/Company Administration; Revd Richard Paul Phillips [1976] Director/Vicar; Susan Sheppard [1949] Director/Retired; Jean Toker [1933] Director/Retired

**Neil Price Construction Services Limited**
*Incorporated:* 2 March 2007
*Net Worth:* £3,185,755 *Total Assets:* £3,458,963
*Registered Office:* Sowerby Woods Business Park, Bouthwood Road, Barrow in Furness, Cumbria, LA14 4RD
*Activities:* Construction of commercial buildings
*Major Shareholder:* Neil Charles Price
*Officers:* Charles Price, Secretary; Charles Price [1942] Director/Builder; Neil Charles Price [1970] Director

**Price Express Transport Limited**
*Incorporated:* 1 October 1979 *Employees:* 109
*Net Worth:* £2,883,010 *Total Assets:* £4,365,993
*Registered Office:* Carr Hill, Doncaster, S Yorks, DN4 8DE
*Activities:* Freight transport by road
*Officers:* Andrew Bowes Pallister [1970] Director

**Neil Price Limited**
*Incorporated:* 18 March 1996 *Employees:* 18
*Net Worth:* £6,004,533 *Total Assets:* £6,335,094
*Registered Office:* Sowerby Woods Business Park, Bouthwood Road, Barrow in Furness, Cumbria, LA14 4RD
*Activities:* Construction of commercial buildings
*Major Shareholder:* Neil Charles Price
*Officers:* Charles Price, Secretary/Building Consultant; Charles Price [1942] Director; Linsey Crawford Price [1974] Director; Neil Charles Price [1970] Director

**The Priestley Academy Trust**
*Incorporated:* 5 October 2016
*Net Worth:* £16,256,632 *Total Assets:* £20,369,740
*Registered Office:* Green Lane Primary School, Green Lane, Bradford, W Yorks, BD8 8HT
*Activities:* Primary education
*Officers:* Javed Kausar Ahmed [1957] Director/Finance Manager; Ros Garside [1949] Director/Education Consultant; Kevin Paul Holland [1957] Director; Sam Keighley [1967] Director/Chief Executive of a Charity; Ashfaq Ahmed Rahman [1970] Director/Executive Headteacher; Margaret Mercedes Smith [1947] Director/Retired

**Priestley Homes Limited**
*Incorporated:* 5 November 2012
*Net Worth:* £4,162,825 *Total Assets:* £7,361,378
*Registered Office:* Suite K, Priestley House, 170 Elland Road, Leeds, LS11 8BU
*Activities:* Development of building projects
*Major Shareholder:* Nathan Ronald Priestley
*Officers:* Derry Ellen McCulloch [1963] Director; Nathan Ronald Priestley [1987] Director

**Primary Care Commissioning Community Interest Company**
*Incorporated:* 10 July 2009 *Employees:* 28
*Net Worth:* £1,243,882 *Total Assets:* £3,912,403
*Registered Office:* Suite 1a, West One, 114 Wellington Street, Leeds, LS1 1BA
*Activities:* Other professional, scientific and technical activities n.e.c.
*Officers:* Wendie Jane Groves, Secretary; Dr David Geoffrey Colin-Thome [1943] Director; Helen Northall [1968] Director; Francis Julian Paterson [1960] Director

**Primekings Holding Limited**
*Incorporated:* 18 December 2013 *Employees:* 527
*Net Worth Deficit:* £4,835,000 *Total Assets:* £16,538,000
*Registered Office:* 5th Floor, Central Square, 29 Wellington Street, Leeds, LS1 4DL
*Activities:* Non-trading company
*Officers:* Robin Charles Fisher [1951] Director [South African]; Barry Abraham Stiefel [1949] Director [German]

**Primepak Foods Limited**
*Incorporated:* 28 November 2000 *Employees:* 49
*Net Worth:* £4,744,368 *Total Assets:* £5,742,509
*Registered Office:* The Embankment, Kelleythorpe Industrial Estate, Driffield, E Yorks, YO25 9DJ
*Activities:* Wholesale of meat and meat products
*Parent:* Montyredman Holdings Limited
*Officers:* Gillian Johnson, Secretary; Christopher David Johnson [1944] Director/Manager; Gillian Johnson [1944] Director/Manager; Richard David Johnson [1976] Director/Manager

**Primeur Limited**
*Incorporated:* 23 March 1990 *Employees:* 66
*Net Worth:* £912,213 *Total Assets:* £7,130,508
*Registered Office:* Castlefields, Cross Flats, Bingley, W Yorks, BD16 2AF
*Activities:* Non-specialised wholesale trade
*Shareholders:* James Alexander Holcroft Keighley; Stephen Fearnley
*Officers:* Ian Brazier, Secretary; Ian Brazier [1956] Finance Director; Jennifer Douthwaite [1981] Sales Director; Stephen Fearnley [1945] Director; James Alexander Holcroft Keighley [1964] Buying Director

**Primex Plastics Limited**
*Incorporated:* 10 June 1997 *Employees:* 54
*Net Worth:* £3,622,329 *Total Assets:* £5,290,423
*Registered Office:* Beaumont Way, Aycliffe Industrial Park, Newton Aycliffe, Co Durham, DL5 6SN
*Activities:* Manufacture of plastic plates, sheets, tubes and profiles
*Shareholders:* John Farber; Maya Farber
*Officers:* Gia Incardone, Secretary; Michael John Cramer [1955] Director/President [American]; Timothy Robert Schultz [1956] Director/Vice President of Sales and Marketing [American]

**Primus Alliance Nottingham Limited**
*Incorporated:* 22 August 2017
*Net Worth:* £132,018 *Total Assets:* £5,465,345
*Registered Office:* 3 Park Drive, Harrogate, N Yorks, HG2 9AY
*Activities:* Construction of commercial buildings
*Shareholder:* PAG Ventures Ltd
*Officers:* Duncan Stewart Melville [1970] Director; David Russell [1956] Director; Colin Turner [1967] Director

**Principal Hayley Group Limited**
*Incorporated:* 26 November 2003 *Employees:* 4
*Net Worth:* £179,310,000 *Total Assets:* £183,435,008
*Registered Office:* The Inspire, Hornbeam Square West, Harrogate, N Yorks, HG2 8PA
*Activities:* Non-trading company
*Parent:* Principal Hotels Topco 3 Limited
*Officers:* James Alexander Burrell [1974] Director/Accountant; Generaldine Josephine Gallagher [1965] Finance Director [Irish]; Gail Susan Hunter [1963] Director; Anthony Gerrard Troy [1962] Director [Irish]

**Principal Hayley Limited**
*Incorporated:* 5 March 2007 *Employees:* 235
*Net Worth Deficit:* £6,328,000 *Total Assets:* £308,863,008
*Registered Office:* The Inspire, Hornbeam Square West, Harrogate, N Yorks, HG2 8PA
*Activities:* Activities of head offices
*Parent:* Principal Hayley Group Limited
*Officers:* James Alexander Burrell [1974] Director/Accountant; Generaldine Josephine Gallagher [1965] Finance Director [Irish]; Gail Susan Hunter [1963] Human Resources Director; Anthony Gerrard Troy [1962] Director [Irish]

**Principal Hotel Company Limited**
*Incorporated:* 17 December 2014
*Net Worth:* £2,000,000 *Total Assets:* £303,343,008
*Registered Office:* The Inspire, Hornbeam Square West, Harrogate, N Yorks, HG2 8PA
*Activities:* Activities of head offices
*Parent:* Principal Hotels Topco 1 Limited
*Officers:* John Cody Bradshaw [1978] Director/Real Estate [American]; Sarah Broughton [1976] Director/Chartered Accountant; James Alexander Burrell [1974] Director; Anthony Gerrard Troy [1962] Director [Irish]

**Principal Hotels Topco 1 Limited**
*Incorporated:* 16 December 2014 *Employees:* 4,736
*Net Worth:* £44,772,000 *Total Assets:* £1,092,055,040
*Registered Office:* The Inspire, Hornbeam Square West, Harrogate, N Yorks, HG2 8PA
*Activities:* Activities of head offices
*Officers:* John Cody Bradshaw [1978] Director/Real Estate [American]; Sarah Broughton [1976] Director/Chartered Accountant; James Alexander Burrell [1974] Director; Anthony Gerrard Troy [1962] Director [Irish]

**Principal Hotels Topco 3 Limited**
*Incorporated:* 18 December 2014
*Net Worth:* £11,331,000 *Total Assets:* £312,675,008
*Registered Office:* The Inspire, Hornbeam Square West, Harrogate, N Yorks, HG2 8PA
*Activities:* Activities of head offices
*Parent:* Principal Hotel Company Limited
*Officers:* John Cody Bradshaw [1978] Director/Real Estate [American]; Sarah Broughton [1976] Director/Chartered Accountant; James Alexander Burrell [1974] Director; Anthony Gerrard Troy [1962] Director [Irish]

**Principle Global Limited**
*Incorporated:* 31 May 2006 *Employees:* 513
*Previous:* Principle Holdings Limited
*Net Worth:* £27,711,432 *Total Assets:* £89,483,064
*Registered Office:* c/o Principle, Tandem Industrial Estate, Waterloo, Huddersfield, W Yorks, HD5 0AN
*Activities:* Activities of head offices
*Parent:* Principle Global Limited
*Officers:* Simon Paul Blagden [1962] Director; Richard Howard Butterfield [1960] Sales Director; Mark John Deuschle [1959] Director [American]; Victoria Jessica Woodings [1983] Director/Accountant

**Principle Healthcare International Limited**
*Incorporated:* 20 January 2004 *Employees:* 139
*Net Worth:* £4,431,476 *Total Assets:* £9,670,585
*Registered Office:* Principle Healthcare International Ltd, Airedale Business Centre, Millennium Road, Skipton, N Yorks, BD23 2TZ
*Activities:* Manufacture of basic pharmaceutical products
*Major Shareholder:* Michael John Davies
*Officers:* Richard Howard Doyle, Secretary/Chartered Accountant; Andrew Michael Davies [1982] Director; Michael John Davies [1951] Director; Philip Benjamin Davies [1977] Director

**Principle Healthcare Limited**
*Incorporated:* 7 September 2001 *Employees:* 23
*Net Worth:* £1,711,821 *Total Assets:* £4,341,947
*Registered Office:* Airedale Business Centre, Millennium Road, Skipton, N Yorks, BD23 2TZ
*Activities:* Manufacture of basic pharmaceutical products
*Shareholders:* Principle Healthcare International; Principle Healthcare International Ltd
*Officers:* Richard Doyle, Secretary; Clare Campbell [1975] Director; Andrew Michael Davies [1982] Director; Michael John Davies [1951] Director; Philip Benjamin Davies [1977] Director

**Principle Spira Limited**
*Incorporated:* 7 January 1991 *Employees:* 100
*Previous:* Spira Projects Limited
*Net Worth:* £812,215 *Total Assets:* £3,012,591
*Registered Office:* c/o Principle Systems Limited, Tandem Industrial Estate, Waterloo, Huddersfield, W Yorks, HD5 0AN
*Activities:* Manufacture of other builders' carpentry and joinery
*Parent:* Principle Holdings Limited
*Officers:* Richard Howard Butterfield [1960] Director; Victoria Jessica Woodings [1983] Director/Accountant

**Principle Systems Limited**
*Incorporated:* 10 March 1987 *Employees:* 149
*Net Worth:* £11,757,479 *Total Assets:* £22,976,020
*Registered Office:* Tandem Industrial Estate, Waterloo, Huddersfield, W Yorks, HD5 0AL
*Activities:* Other manufacturing n.e.c.
*Parent:* Principle Holdings Limited
*Officers:* Richard Howard Butterfield [1960] Director; Victoria Jessica Woodings [1983] Director/Accountant

**Principles Communications Limited**
*Incorporated:* 29 January 1986 *Employees:* 34
*Net Worth:* £2,345,644 *Total Assets:* £5,959,616
*Registered Office:* White Rose House, Otley Road, Headingley, Leeds, LS6 2AD
*Activities:* Advertising agencies
*Officers:* Christopher Goodwin, Secretary; Mark Curtis [1962] Media Director; Christopher Goodwin [1955] Director; Bernard May [1956] Director

**Print-Leeds Limited**
*Incorporated:* 20 December 2001 *Employees:* 39
*Net Worth:* £1,058,040 *Total Assets:* £5,545,437
*Registered Office:* Tanda Works, Swinnow Lane, Bramley, Leeds, LS13 4TY
*Activities:* Manufacture of printed labels
*Major Shareholder:* Rodney Charles Fisher
*Officers:* Joan Trigg, Secretary; Paul Anthony Fisher [1966] Production Director; Rodney Charles Fisher [1960] Director

**Printcraft Limited**
*Incorporated:* 15 September 2009 *Employees:* 152
*Net Worth:* £11,817,000 *Total Assets:* £14,119,000
*Registered Office:* Century House, Wakefield 41 Industrial Estate, Wakefield, W Yorks, WF2 0XG
*Activities:* Printing n.e.c.
*Parent:* Sportswift Limited
*Officers:* Christopher Robbert Beck [1974] Director; Karen Rachael Hubbard [1964] Director; Kristian Brian Lee [1974] Director

**Priory Primary School**
*Incorporated:* 10 September 2013 *Employees:* 56
*Net Worth:* £3,620,266 *Total Assets:* £4,091,109
*Registered Office:* Priory Primary School, Priory Road, Hull, HU5 5RU
*Activities:* Primary education
*Officers:* Pauline Brown [1951] Director/Retired; Lindsey Michelle Eddom [1981] Director/Health Advisor; Ann Matthews [1959] Director/Higher Level Teaching Assistant; Julia Mitchell [1975] Director/Deputy Headteacher; Megan Lesley Murray [1949] Director/Retired Headteacher; Katherine Patricia O'Hanlon [1967] Director/Headteacher; Tracey Parkinson [1964] Director/Teachers' Aid; Rachel Proctor [1980] Director/Legal Secretary; Jayne Patricia Russell [1966] Director; Stephen John Whaley [1957] Director/Clerk in Holy Orders

**Prious Limited**
*Incorporated:* 19 October 1993 *Employees:* 1
*Net Worth:* £2,103,205 *Total Assets:* £3,366,920
*Registered Office:* c/o Jolliffecork, 33 George Street, Wakefield, W Yorks, WF1 1LX
*Activities:* Activities of other holding companies n.e.c.
*Major Shareholder:* Neil Smillie
*Officers:* Neil Smillie [1954] Director

**Prism Medical Healthcare Limited**
*Incorporated:* 10 January 2014 *Employees:* 485
*Net Worth Deficit:* £24,223,306 *Total Assets:* £26,800,188
*Registered Office:* Unit 4 Jubilee Business Park, Jubilee Way, Grange Moor, W Yorks, WF4 4TD
*Activities:* Activities of head offices
*Parent:* PMH Bidco Limited
*Officers:* Neil Duffy, Secretary; Martim Avillez Caldeira [1977] Director [Portuguese]; Neil Duffy [1966] Director/Chief Financial Officer; Stuart Meldrum [1966] Director; Joao Vicente Goncalves Rosa [1978] Director [Portuguese]

**Prism UK Medical Limited**
*Incorporated:* 11 December 2003 *Employees:* 393
*Net Worth:* £16,907,712 *Total Assets:* £26,944,140
*Registered Office:* Unit 4 Jubilee Business Park, Jubilee Way, Grange Moor, Wakefield, W Yorks, WF4 4TD
*Activities:* Manufacture of lifting and handling equipment
*Parent:* Prism Medical Healthcare Limited
*Officers:* Neil Duffy, Secretary; Neil Duffy [1966] Director/Chief Financial Officer; Stuart Meldrum [1966] Director

**Private Medicare Limited**
*Incorporated:* 4 February 1986 *Employees:* 137
*Net Worth:* £5,215,565 *Total Assets:* £12,527,216
*Registered Office:* Lancaster House, Lancaster Road, Carnaby, Bridlington, N Yorks, YO15 3QY
*Activities:* Residential nursing care facilities
*Parent:* Burlington Care Holdings Limited
*Officers:* Simon John Hill [1965] Director; Andrew Alan Hoggart [1966] Director; Richard Michael Hoggart [1974] Director

**Pro-Pak Foods Limited**
*Incorporated:* 1 May 1998 *Employees:* 378
*Net Worth:* £9,650,394 *Total Assets:* £17,415,384
*Registered Office:* Seven Street, York Road Industrial Park, Malton, N Yorks, YO17 6YA
*Activities:* Manufacture of prepared meals and dishes
*Shareholders:* Clemens Tonnies; Robert Tonnies
*Officers:* Mark Roland Duckworth, Secretary; Justin Mark Appleford [1970] Commercial Director; Mark Roland Duckworth [1967] Financial Director; Jon Andrew Guest [1970] Managing Director; Kevin Watson [1963] Operations Director

**Proactis Holdings PLC**
*Incorporated:* 22 March 2006 *Employees:* 433
*Net Worth:* £93,611,000 *Total Assets:* £185,496,000
*Registered Office:* 2nd Floor, 1 Riverview Court, Castle Gate, Wetherby, W Yorks, LS22 6LE
*Activities:* Activities of head offices
*Officers:* Timothy James Sykes, Secretary/Director; Alan John Aubrey [1961] Director; Sean Anthony McDonough [1960] Director; Rodney Potts [1944] Director; Timothy James Sykes [1969] Director; Sophie Alice Tomkins [1969] Director

**Proactis Limited**
*Incorporated:* 4 April 1996 *Employees:* 108
*Previous:* Proactis Group Limited
*Net Worth:* £2,021,651 *Total Assets:* £16,445,681
*Registered Office:* 2nd Floor, 1 Riverview Court, Castle Gate, Wetherby, W Yorks, LS22 6LE
*Activities:* Information technology consultancy activities
*Parent:* Proactis Holdings PLC
*Officers:* Timothy James Sykes, Secretary/Director; Sean Anthony McDonough [1960] Director; Timothy James Sykes [1969] Director

**Proaktive Ltd**
*Incorporated:* 16 November 2001 *Employees:* 47
*Net Worth:* £858,499 *Total Assets:* £4,428,039
*Registered Office:* Proaktive House, Sidings Court, White Rose Way, Doncaster, S Yorks, DN4 5NU
*Activities:* Activities of insurance agents and brokers
*Parent:* Proaktive Risk Group Ltd
*Officers:* Karen Susan Laycock, Secretary; Joanne Cooling [1972] Risk Services and Claims Director; Ian Laycock [1960] Director/Insurance Broker; Andrew Morley [1970] Director/Insurance Broker

**Procter (Bordley) Limited**
*Incorporated:* 1 March 1977 *Employees:* 4
*Net Worth:* £5,702,870 *Total Assets:* £6,513,314
*Registered Office:* Hathenshaw Farm, Hathenshaw Lane, Denton, Ilkley, W Yorks, LS29 0HR
*Activities:* Other letting and operating of own or leased real estate
*Shareholder:* Alison Procter Brown
*Officers:* Peter Robert Procter Chadwick, Secretary; Alison Procter Brown [1964] Director/University Researcher; Peter Robert Procter Chadwick [1951] Director/Solicitor; Timothy Procter Chadwick [1957] Director; Esme Rosemary Knowles [1949] Director/Housewife

**Procter Bros. Limited**
*Incorporated:* 15 August 1916 *Employees:* 196
*Net Worth Deficit:* £9,963,954 *Total Assets:* £8,224,126
*Registered Office:* 1 Beaconsfield Court, Garforth, Leeds, LS25 1QH
*Activities:* Manufacture of concrete products for construction purposes
*Shareholders:* Jeremy Charles Ashbridge Procter; Anthony Christopher Michael Procter
*Officers:* Keith Michael Kirwin, Secretary/Accountant; Hywel Rhys Davies [1975] Fencing Division Director; Keith Michael Kirwin [1960] Director/Chief Operating Officer; Jeremy Charles Ashbridge Procter [1952] Director/Chairman; John Philip Procter [1982] Director

**Procters Coaches (North Yorkshire No3) Limited**
*Incorporated:* 10 February 2014 *Employees:* 68
*Net Worth:* £3,452,599 *Total Assets:* £5,776,423
*Registered Office:* Tutin Road, Leeming Bar Industrial Estate, Northallerton, N Yorks, DL7 9UJ
*Activities:* Non-trading company
*Major Shareholder:* Kevin John Procter
*Officers:* Claire Elizabeth Alenius, Secretary; Kevin John Procter [1964] Director/Coach Proprietor

**Procters Coaches (North Yorkshire) Limited**
*Incorporated:* 17 April 2000 *Employees:* 71
*Net Worth:* £3,130,629 *Total Assets:* £5,611,037
*Registered Office:* Tutin Road, Leeming Bar Industrial Estate, Northallerton, N Yorks, DL7 9UJ
*Activities:* Other passenger land transport
*Parent:* Procters Coaches (North Yorkshire No3) Limited
*Officers:* Claire Elizabeth Alenius, Secretary; Kevin John Procter [1964] Director/Coach Proprietor

**Production Park Ltd**
*Incorporated:* 24 January 2006 *Employees:* 154
*Previous:* Dark Arches Holdings Limited
*Net Worth:* £6,422,186 *Total Assets:* £16,122,188
*Registered Office:* Unit 5 Lidgate Crescent, Langthwaite Road, Langthwaite Grange Industrial Estate, South Kirkby, Pontefract, W Yorks, WF9 3AP
*Activities:* Activities of other holding companies n.e.c.
*Shareholders:* Adrian Brooks; Adrian Brooks
*Officers:* Adrian Brooks [1957] Director; Ben Hayden Brooks [1987] Director; Lee Robert Brooks [1981] Director; Mansoor Mahmood Hussain [1980] Director; Mark Richard Tucknott [1981] Finance Director

**Produmax Limited**
*Incorporated:* 28 April 1966 *Employees:* 60
*Net Worth:* £5,114,301 *Total Assets:* £8,762,699
*Registered Office:* Unit 2 Sapper Jordan Rossi Park, Baildon, Shipley, W Yorks, BD17 7AX
*Activities:* Manufacture of other fabricated metal products n.e.c.
*Shareholders:* Jeremy Paul Ridyard; Mandy Ridyard
*Officers:* Mandy Ridyard, Secretary; Jeremy Paul Ridyard [1967] Director/Engineer; Mandy Ridyard [1966] Director

**Professional Response Limited**
*Incorporated:* 15 February 1996 *Employees:* 53
*Net Worth:* £2,562,299 *Total Assets:* £3,067,759
*Registered Office:* Howley Park Road East, Morley, Leeds, LS27 0QR
*Activities:* Freight transport by road
*Major Shareholder:* Catherine Helen Dungworth
*Officers:* Veronique Antoinette Collette Jeannine Marot, Secretary; Catherine Helen Dungworth [1967] Director

**Profile Security Group Ltd**
*Incorporated:* 17 April 2000 *Employees:* 1,891
*Net Worth:* £914,412 *Total Assets:* £10,985,373
*Registered Office:* Stable Yard, Walk House Farm, Barrow upon Humber, N Lincs, DN19 7DZ
*Activities:* Dormant company
*Shareholders:* Hon Jonathan Andrew Forbes; Andrew Prendergast
*Officers:* Dharmesh Parekh, Company Secretary; Hon Jonathan Andrew Forbes [1947] Director; Dharmesh Parekh [1970] Director/Accountant; Brigadier Andrew Parker Bowles [1939] Director; Andrew Prendergast [1952] Director

**Profile Security Services Limited**
*Incorporated:* 13 April 1989 *Employees:* 1,890
*Net Worth:* £1,454,589 *Total Assets:* £11,497,011
*Registered Office:* Stable Yard, Walk House Farm, Barrow upon Humber, N Lincs, DN19 7DZ
*Activities:* Other service activities n.e.c.
*Parent:* Profile Security Group Ltd
*Officers:* Dharmesh Parekh, Secretary/Accountant; Hon Jonathan Andrew Forbes [1947] Director; Martin McGowan Scanlon [1958] Managing Director; Dharmesh Parekh [1970] Director/Accountant; Brigadier Andrew Parker Bowles [1939] Director; Andrew Prendergast [1952] Director; Alistair Anthony James Lionel Troughton [1954] Director/Consultant

**Progarm Limited**
*Incorporated:* 3 June 2013 *Employees:* 12
*Net Worth:* £1,667,016 *Total Assets:* £3,045,843
*Registered Office:* Unicorn House, Broad Lane, Gilberdyke, Brough, E Yorks, HU15 2TS
*Activities:* Manufacture of workwear
*Major Shareholder:* Charles Robert Arnett
*Officers:* Anthony Arnett [1977] Director

**Project Aqua Bidco Limited**
*Incorporated:* 17 September 2013 *Employees:* 7
*Net Worth Deficit:* £269,000 *Total Assets:* £166,758,000
*Registered Office:* 69 South Accommodation Road, Leeds, LS10 1NQ
*Activities:* Financial management
*Officers:* Alan Stephen Henderson [1974] Director; Mathew James Edward Hutchinson [1972] Director; Ben Lewis [1984] Director/Private Equity Investor; Neil Anthony Maskrey [1967] Finance Director; Philip Morris [1966] Director; John Steven Naughton [1975] Director; Richard Summers [1971] Director

**Project Aqua Topco Limited**
*Incorporated:* 17 September 2013 *Employees:* 620
*Net Worth Deficit:* £29,045,000 *Total Assets:* £154,470,000
*Registered Office:* 69 South Accommodation Road, Leeds, LS10 1NQ
*Activities:* Activities of head offices
*Officers:* Hamdi Conger [1951] Director; Jonathan Mark Culley [1977] Director; Alan Stephen Henderson [1974] Director; Mathew James Edward Hutchinson [1972] Director; Ben Lewis [1984] Director/Private Equity Investor; Neil Anthony Maskrey [1967] Finance Director; Philip Morris [1966] Director; John Steven Naughton [1975] Director; Richard Summers [1971] Director

**Project Development International Limited**
*Incorporated:* 16 May 2003 *Employees:* 33
*Net Worth:* £2,105,000 *Total Assets:* £3,231,000
*Registered Office:* c/o Pinsent Masons LLP, 1 Park Row, Leeds, LS1 5AB
*Activities:* Support activities for petroleum and natural gas mining
*Major Shareholder:* Narayanaswamy Ramachandran
*Officers:* Ramesh Madhavan [1968] Director/Service [Indian]; Tharmapuram Ramachandran Narayanaswami [1977] Director [Indian]; Michael Noel O'Sullivan [1967] Director/Service [Irish]; Subramanian Rajagopal [1977] Director [Indian]; Narayanaswamy Ramachandran [1948] Director [Indian]

**Project FF & E Limited**
*Incorporated:* 11 January 2010 *Employees:* 62
*Net Worth:* £505,254 *Total Assets:* £4,155,122
*Registered Office:* Dalton House, 17 Harrison Road, Halifax, W Yorks, HX1 2AF
*Activities:* Joinery installation
*Parent:* Project Group UK Limited
*Officers:* Nigel Anthony Barker [1965] Finance Director; Robert Barclay Cole [1978] Bid Director; Martin Corbett [1960] Director/Chairman; Neil Keith Dimmock [1975] Design/Estimating Director; James Anthony Shanks [1967] Business Development Director; James Ronald Watson [1983] Managing Director

**Project Kahn Ltd**
*Incorporated:* 11 November 2003 *Employees:* 16
*Net Worth:* £3,909,866 *Total Assets:* £6,434,416
*Registered Office:* 240 Canal Road, Bradford, BD1 4SX
*Activities:* Sale of used cars and light motor vehicles
*Major Shareholder:* Jamshaid Khan
*Officers:* Jamshed Khan, Secretary; Jamshaid Kahn [1970] Director

**Project Light Bidco Limited**
*Incorporated:* 9 June 2016 *Employees:* 7
*Net Worth:* £45,849,384 *Total Assets:* £45,849,384
*Registered Office:* 84 Albion Street, Leeds, LS1 6AG
*Activities:* Activities of head offices
*Parent:* Project Light Cleanco Limited
*Officers:* Merrill Graham Goulding [1982] Director; Ian Barrie Jackson [1973] Director; Oliver James Lightowlers [1972] Director/Chartered Accountant

**Project Light Cleanco Limited**
*Incorporated:* 9 June 2016
*Net Worth:* £20,461,876 *Total Assets:* £45,624,840
*Registered Office:* 84 Albion Street, Leeds, LS1 6AG
*Activities:* Activities of head offices
*Parent:* Project Light Midco Limited
*Officers:* Merrill Graham Goulding [1982] Director; Ian Barrie Jackson [1973] Director; Oliver James Lightowlers [1972] Director/Chartered Accountant

**Project Light Midco Limited**
*Incorporated:* 9 June 2016
*Net Worth:* £41,899,016 *Total Assets:* £70,127,064
*Registered Office:* 84 Albion Street, Leeds, LS1 6AG
*Activities:* Activities of head offices
*Parent:* Project Light Topco Limited
*Officers:* Merrill Graham Goulding [1982] Director; Ian Barrie Jackson [1973] Director; Oliver James Lightowlers [1972] Director/Chartered Accountant

**Project Light Topco Limited**
*Incorporated:* 9 June 2016 *Employees:* 2,012
*Net Worth:* £10,948,069 *Total Assets:* £94,798,840
*Registered Office:* 84 Albion Street, Leeds, LS1 6AG
*Activities:* Activities of head offices
*Parent:* CSP IV (Cayman 2), L.P.
*Officers:* Dr Clive Edward Bowman [1954] Director; Merrill Graham Goulding [1982] Director; Ian Barrie Jackson [1973] Director; Oliver James Lightowlers [1972] Director/Chartered Accountant

**Project Magnum (Bidco) Limited**
*Incorporated:* 21 July 2010
*Net Worth:* £10,172,000 *Total Assets:* £69,316,000
*Registered Office:* 69 South Accommodation Road, Leeds, LS10 1NQ
*Activities:* Other business support service activities n.e.c.
*Officers:* James Stewart McLean, Secretary; Alan Stephen Henderson [1974] Director; Neil Anthony Maskrey [1967] Finance Director; Philip Morris [1966] Director; John Steven Naughton [1975] Director; Richard Summers [1971] Director

**Project Rock Bidco Limited**
*Incorporated:* 25 January 2016 *Employees:* 5
*Net Worth Deficit:* £8,594,000 *Total Assets:* £55,889,000
*Registered Office:* 10 Mannin Way, Lancaster Business Park, Lancaster, LA1 3SW
*Activities:* Holiday centres and villages
*Parent:* Palatine Private Equity
*Officers:* Beverley Jayne Dixon [1969] Operations Director; Graham Robert Hodgson [1960] Director/Chief Executive Officer; Ronald John Peters [1974] Director/Sales Manager; Andrew Jonathan Wall [1960] Finance Director

**Project Rock Equityco Limited**
*Incorporated:* 25 January 2016 *Employees:* 197
*Net Worth:* £1,011,000 *Total Assets:* £79,369,000
*Registered Office:* 10 Mannin Way, Lancaster Business Park, Lancaster, LA1 3SW
*Activities:* Holiday centres and villages
*Parent:* Palatine Private Equityllp
*Officers:* Beverley Jayne Dixon [1969] Operations Director; Edmund Fazakerley [1969] Director; Graham Robert Hodgson [1960] Director/Chief Executive Officer; George Hope [1962] Director; James Painter [1989] Director/Investment Manager; Ronald John Peters [1974] Director/Sales Manager; Andrew Jonathan Wall [1960] Finance Director

**Project Tulip Topco Limited**
*Incorporated:* 4 May 2016 *Employees:* 196
*Net Worth Deficit:* £13,024,971 *Total Assets:* £30,666,716
*Registered Office:* Olliver, Aske, Richmond, N Yorks, DL10 5HX
*Activities:* Activities of financial services holding companies
*Parent:* Propharma Group MIS Holdings Limited
*Officers:* Dawn Gail Sherman, Secretary; Robert Hugh Chestnut [1961] Director [American]; Jan Johannes Luijendijk [1961] Director/General Manager Europe [Dutch]; Dawn Gail Sherman [1967] Director [American]

**Proma Boatman Limited**
*Incorporated:* 28 July 2016
*Net Worth Deficit:* £4,371 *Total Assets:* £3,284,421
*Registered Office:* 13 Nelson Street, Hull, HU1 1XE
*Activities:* Development of building projects
*Shareholder:* Proma Construction Management Limited
*Officers:* Barrie John Gill [1963] Director; Greg Shannon [1967] Director/Architect

**Proma Construction Management Limited**
*Incorporated:* 14 October 2009 *Employees:* 9
*Net Worth:* £3,198,766 *Total Assets:* £5,155,063
*Registered Office:* 13 Nelson Street, Hull, HU1 1XE
*Activities:* Construction of commercial buildings
*Major Shareholder:* Barrie John Gill
*Officers:* Penny Eleanor Gill, Secretary; Barrie John Gill [1963] Director

**Promenade Car Parks Limited**
*Incorporated:* 19 January 1996
*Previous:* Neptune Car Parks Limited
*Net Worth:* £11,582,906 *Total Assets:* £12,022,440
*Registered Office:* 72 Merrion Street, Leeds, LS2 8LW
*Activities:* Other letting and operating of own or leased real estate
*Parent:* Q-Park Real Estate Holding UK Ltd
*Officers:* Stephen Mark Ellis, Secretary; Adam John Bidder [1970] Managing Director; Stephen Mark Ellis [1965] Director

**Promised Land Developments Limited**
*Incorporated:* 10 February 2004
*Net Worth Deficit:* £3,108,463 *Total Assets:* £13,573,696
*Registered Office:* Cathedral House, St Thomas Road, Huddersfield, W Yorks, HD1 3LG
*Activities:* Development of building projects
*Officers:* James Norman Clarkson, Secretary; Stuart Gladstone [1968] Director/Systems Analyst; Jonathan Skinner [1981] Director

**The Propaganda Agency Limited**
*Incorporated:* 21 May 1996 *Employees:* 32
*Net Worth:* £4,611,465 *Total Assets:* £6,106,919
*Registered Office:* Calls Wharf, 2 The Calls, Leeds, LS2 7JU
*Activities:* Management consultancy activities other than financial management
*Parent:* Access 13 Limited
*Officers:* Bruce Stewart Cameron [1969] Director/Chartered Accountant; Craig William Harrold [1971] Accounts Director; Julian Aaron Horberry [1970] Planning Director; Julian Mark Kynaston [1967] Director; Laura Kynaston [1981] Director; Richard James McMurrough [1968] Accounts Director

**Property Investments (Yorkshire) Limited**
*Incorporated:* 18 September 1998 *Employees:* 3
*Net Worth:* £2,732,326 *Total Assets:* £3,264,421
*Registered Office:* Listers Mills, Heaton Road, Bradford, W Yorks, BD9 4SH
*Activities:* Other letting and operating of own or leased real estate
*Parent:* Haddow Group PLC
*Officers:* Nigel John Gould, Secretary; Alan Frank Haddow [1941] Director

**Property Renaissance Limited**
*Incorporated:* 14 April 1998 *Employees:* 133
*Net Worth:* £4,259,686 *Total Assets:* £7,350,510
*Registered Office:* 28 Kirkgate, Silsden, Keighley, W Yorks, BD20 0AL
*Activities:* Buying and selling of own real estate
*Shareholder:* David Norman Wilkinson
*Officers:* Warrick Robert Burton [1973] Director; Dr David John Oates [1950] Director

**Propharma Group MIS Holdings Limited**
*Incorporated:* 6 November 2013 *Employees:* 323
*Net Worth:* £8,579,610 *Total Assets:* £10,462,714
*Registered Office:* Olliver, Aske, Richmond, N Yorks, DL10 5HX
*Activities:* Other information service activities n.e.c.
*Parent:* Propharma MIS Holdings LLC
*Officers:* Dawn Gail Sherman, Secretary; Robert Hugh Chestnut [1961] Director/Chief Financial Officer [American]; Jan Johannes Luijendijk [1961] Director/GM Europe [Dutch]; Dawn Gail Sherman [1967] Director [American]

**Prorun Limited**
*Incorporated:* 24 June 1996
*Net Worth:* £2,140,004 *Total Assets:* £3,681,824
*Registered Office:* 15a Hall Gate, Doncaster, S Yorks, DN1 3NA
*Activities:* Renting and operating of Housing Association real estate
*Major Shareholder:* Michael Patrick Murray
*Officers:* Michael Patrick Murray [1969] Director

**Prospect Business Centres (Old Jewry) Limited**
*Incorporated:* 17 July 2014
*Net Worth:* £838,750 *Total Assets:* £3,057,513
*Registered Office:* Prospect House, 32 Sovereign Street, Leeds, LS1 4BJ
*Activities:* Combined office administrative service activities
*Major Shareholder:* Warren Christopher Hill
*Officers:* Warren Christopher Hill [1965] Director

**Prospect Business Centres Limited**
*Incorporated:* 5 January 2005 *Employees:* 45
*Net Worth:* £660,382 *Total Assets:* £9,873,365
*Registered Office:* Prospect House, 32 Sovereign Street, Leeds, LS1 4BJ
*Activities:* Other letting and operating of own or leased real estate
*Officers:* Collette Sunderland, Secretary; Charles Cudworth [1973] Director/Surveyor; Warren Christopher Hill [1965] Director

**Prospect Estates Limited**
*Incorporated:* 22 April 1996 *Employees:* 13
*Net Worth:* £30,701,054 *Total Assets:* £48,912,764
*Registered Office:* Prospect Court, 2 Courthouse Street, Otley, W Yorks, LS21 1AQ
*Activities:* Buying and selling of own real estate
*Major Shareholder:* John Ellison Lund
*Officers:* Terri Louise Lund, Company Secretary; John Ellison Lund [1954] Director; Jordan Ellison Lund [1980] Managing Director; Tiffany Louise Lund [1989] Director

**Prospect House (Malpas) Limited**
*Incorporated:* 1 November 1996 *Employees:* 121
*Net Worth:* £3,746,615 *Total Assets:* £4,606,448
*Registered Office:* 9 Silkwood Business Park, Fryers Way, Ossett, W Yorks, WF5 9TJ
*Activities:* Residential nursing care facilities
*Parent:* Mysing Care Limited
*Officers:* Ian Kimberley [1957] Director

**Prospect House Leeds Limited**
*Incorporated:* 19 May 1980 *Employees:* 2
*Net Worth:* £2,700,135 *Total Assets:* £3,504,561
*Registered Office:* Prospect House, 32 Sovereign Street, Leeds, LS1 4BJ
*Activities:* Other letting and operating of own or leased real estate
*Officers:* Warren Christopher Hill [1965] Director

**Prosperity Noor Ltd**
*Incorporated:* 26 July 2016
*Net Worth:* £221,018 *Total Assets:* £13,169,473
*Registered Office:* 9 Broomfield, Leeds, LS16 6AE
*Activities:* Development of building projects
*Officers:* Harith Harry Albazie, Secretary; Zaynab Albazie, Secretary; Dr Ahmed Albazie [1949] Director/Self Employed

**Prospero Growth Limited**
*Incorporated:* 1 July 2014
*Net Worth:* £3,297,208 *Total Assets:* £3,307,131
*Registered Office:* 140 Coniscliffe Road, Darlington, Co Durham, DL3 7RT
*Activities:* Security dealing on own account
*Shareholders:* Isabella Moyes; James Moyes; Amy Moyes-Reader
*Officers:* Matthew Christopher Bennett [1964] Director/Solicitor; Elizabeth Kate Gardner [1983] Director; Antony William Luckett [1961] Director/Accountant; Janice Rosalind Moyes [1953] Director

**Proton (Southern) Limited**
*Incorporated:* 6 April 2004 *Employees:* 17
*Net Worth:* £3,184,355 *Total Assets:* £3,594,407
*Registered Office:* Meadowcroft Lane, Halifax Road, Ripponden, Sowerby Bridge, W Yorks, HX6 4AJ
*Activities:* Wholesale of other machinery and equipment
*Parent:* Vanilla Group Limited
*Officers:* Paul Humphreys, Secretary; Helen Jane Ashton [1972] Director/Chief Executive Officer; Paul Justin Humphreys [1958] Director

**Mark Proudfoot Investments Ltd**
*Incorporated:* 4 November 2016 *Employees:* 3
*Net Worth:* £68,376 *Total Assets:* £5,046,326
*Registered Office:* c/o Sagars Accountants Ltd, Gresham House, 5-7 St Pauls Street, Leeds, LS1 2JG
*Activities:* Security dealing on own account
*Major Shareholder:* Mark Alistair Proudfoot
*Officers:* Luke Alexander Proudfoot [1994] Director; Marcus Alexander Proudfoot [1991] Director; Mark Alistair Proudfoot [1952] Director

**G.W.Proudfoot Limited**
*Incorporated:* 3 January 1952 *Employees:* 175
*Net Worth:* £11,941,257 *Total Assets:* £14,391,309
*Registered Office:* Blinking Sike, Caxton Way, Eastfield Business Park, Eastfield, Scarborough, N Yorks, YO11 3YT
*Activities:* Development of building projects
*Shareholders:* Mark Alistair Proudfoot; Ian Andrew Proudfoot
*Officers:* Derek Peter Armstrong [1954] Director/Retailer; Valerie Aston [1963] Director; Ian Andrew Proudfoot [1955] Director; Marcus Alexander Proudfoot [1991] Director; Mark Alistair Proudfoot [1952] Director

**Provecta Car Plan Limited**
*Incorporated:* 15 August 1995
*Net Worth:* £1,555,000 *Total Assets:* £28,488,000
*Registered Office:* Number One, Great Exhibition Way, Kirkstall Forge, Leeds, LS5 3BF
*Activities:* Renting and leasing of cars and light motor vehicles
*Parent:* Zeus Bidco Limited
*Officers:* Patrick James Rawnsley, Secretary; Timothy Peter Buchan [1963] Director; Robert Alan Butler [1970] Director; Mark Connor [1969] Director; Ian Robert Gibson [1967] Director/Chief Information Officer; Ian Munro Hughes [1968] Director; Andrew Kirby [1969] Commercial Director; Mark Trevor Phillips [1968] Finance Director

**Provenance Hospitality Holdings Limited**
*Incorporated:* 25 April 2014 *Employees:* 225
*Net Worth Deficit:* £3,304,348 *Total Assets:* £17,201,760
*Registered Office:* 4 Wharfe Mews, Cliffe Terrace, Wetherby, W Yorks, LS22 6LX
*Activities:* Public houses and bars
*Major Shareholder:* Christopher Blundell
*Officers:* Christopher James Blundell [1955] Director

**Provenance Hotels Limited**
*Incorporated:* 25 April 2014 *Employees:* 66
*Net Worth Deficit:* £800,525 *Total Assets:* £8,281,924
*Registered Office:* 4 Wharfe Mews, Cliffe Terrace, Wetherby, W Yorks, LS22 6LX
*Activities:* Hotels and similar accommodation
*Parent:* Provenance Hospitality Holdings Ltd
*Officers:* Christopher James Blundell [1955] Director

**Provenance Inns Limited**
*Incorporated:* 27 April 2009 *Employees:* 159
*Net Worth Deficit:* £3,474,314 *Total Assets:* £15,235,845
*Registered Office:* 4 Wharfe Mews, Cliffe Terrace, Wetherby, W Yorks, LS22 6LX
*Activities:* Hotels and similar accommodation
*Parent:* Provenance Hospitality Holdings Ltd
*Officers:* Christopher James Blundell [1955] Director

**Provfin Limited**
*Incorporated:* 22 January 1985
*Net Worth:* £8,827,000 *Total Assets:* £8,834,000
*Registered Office:* No 1 Godwin Street, Bradford, W Yorks, BD1 2SU
*Activities:* Other business support service activities n.e.c.
*Parent:* Yes Car Credit (Holdings) Limited
*Officers:* Kenneth John Mullen [1958] Director/Scottish Solicitor; Simon George Thomas [1964] Director/Chief Finance Officer

**Providence Holdings Limited**
*Incorporated:* 4 August 2004 *Employees:* 110
*Net Worth:* £13,248,866 *Total Assets:* £19,299,356
*Registered Office:* Stamford Bridge Road, Dunnington, York, YO19 5AE
*Activities:* Activities of head offices
*Major Shareholder:* Martin Richard Cockerill
*Officers:* Pamela Ann Cockerill, Secretary; Martin Richard Cockerill [1946] Director; Pamela Ann Cockerill [1946] Director; Samuel Edward Cockerill [1972] Director/Management Consultant

**Provident Financial Management Services Limited**
*Incorporated:* 18 June 1937 *Employees:* 1,046
*Net Worth:* £198,700,000 *Total Assets:* £417,500,000
*Registered Office:* No 1 Godwin Street, Bradford, W Yorks, BD1 2SU
*Activities:* Financial intermediation not elsewhere classified
*Parent:* Provident Financial PLC
*Officers:* David George Whincup, Secretary; Christopher Donald Gillespie [1963] Director; Malcolm John Le May [1958] Director; Simon George Thomas [1964] Director/Chief Finance Officer; Eleanor Thornhill [1974] Director

**Provident Financial PLC**
*Incorporated:* 31 August 1960 *Employees:* 4,684
*Net Worth:* £535,100,000 *Total Assets:* £2,965,900,032
*Registered Office:* No 1 Godwin Street, Bradford, W Yorks, BD1 2SU
*Activities:* Activities of financial services holding companies
*Officers:* Kenneth John Mullen, Secretary; Andrea Margaret Blance [1964] Director; Elizabeth Grace Chambers [1962] Director [American]; Paul William Hewitt [1956] Director; Angela Ann Knight [1950] Director; Malcolm John Le May [1958] Director; Patrick Joseph Robert Snowball [1950] Director; John Coleman Straw [1959] Director; Simon George Thomas [1964] Director/Chief Finance Officer

**Provident Personal Credit Limited**
*Incorporated:* 20 February 1917 *Employees:* 2,056
*Net Worth:* £211,000,000 *Total Assets:* £650,200,000
*Registered Office:* No 1 Godwin Street, Bradford, W Yorks, BD1 2SU
*Activities:* Credit granting by non-deposit taking finance houses and other specialist consumer credit grantors
*Parent:* Provident Financial Management Services Limited
*Officers:* David George Whincup, Secretary; Christopher Donald Gillespie [1963] Director; Malcolm John Le May [1958] Director; Eleanor Thornhill [1974] Director

**Provident Print Limited**
*Incorporated:* 18 January 1988
*Net Worth:* £5,894,000 *Total Assets:* £5,903,000
*Registered Office:* No 1 Godwin Street, Bradford, W Yorks, BD1 2SU
*Activities:* Non-trading company
*Parent:* Provident Financial PLC
*Officers:* Kenneth John Mullen [1958] Director/Scottish Solicitor; Simon George Thomas [1964] Director/Chief Finance Officer

**Provimi Limited**
*Incorporated:* 11 June 1976 *Employees:* 145
*Net Worth Deficit:* £4,079,984 *Total Assets:* £25,682,012
*Registered Office:* Dalton Airfield Industrial Estate, Dalton, Thirsk, N Yorks, YO7 3HE
*Activities:* Manufacture of prepared feeds for farm animals
*Parent:* Cargill PLC
*Officers:* Dena Michelle L O'Bue, Secretary; Benjamin James Rogers [1970] Director/CPN Europe Supply Chain Lead; Federico Urquidi Negron [1965] Director/UK & Ireland Country Controller [Spanish]

**Provu Holdings Limited**
*Incorporated:* 3 April 2017
*Net Worth:* £2,836,764 *Total Assets:* £3,083,614
*Registered Office:* Savile Mill, Savile Street, Milnsbridge, Huddersfield, W Yorks, HD3 4PG
*Activities:* Activities of other holding companies n.e.c.
*Major Shareholder:* Peter John Bryant
*Officers:* Timothy Bray [1979] Technology Director; Peter John Bryant [1942] Director/Consultant and Entrepreneur; Darren Stephen Garland [1967] Managing Director; Andrew Paul Hayes [1980] Director/Product Development Manager; Craig Anthony Herrett [1979] Sales Director

**Pryers Solicitors LLP**
*Incorporated:* 8 March 2008 *Employees:* 65
*Net Worth:* £2,238,768 *Total Assets:* £10,324,270
*Registered Office:* 13 The Stonebow, York, YO1 7NP
*Officers:* Neil Fearn [1969] Member; Philip James Hodgkinson [1972] Member; David John Kirby [1964] Member; Robert John Mares [1967] Member; Robyn Hawxby [1974] LLP Member; Richard Starkie [1975] LLP Member; Carmel Marie Walsh [1967] LLP Member

**Psona Limited**
*Incorporated:* 15 July 1986 *Employees:* 49
*Net Worth Deficit:* £2,042,833 *Total Assets:* £6,308,850
*Registered Office:* Communisis House, Manston Lane, Leeds, LS15 8AH
*Activities:* Data processing, hosting and related activities
*Parent:* Psona Group Limited
*Officers:* Sarah Louise Caddy, Secretary; Andrew Martin Blundell [1960] Director; Steven Clive Rawlins [1962] Director

**PSP Architectural Ltd**
*Incorporated:* 29 November 2007 *Employees:* 67
*Net Worth:* £1,023,333 *Total Assets:* £4,063,337
*Registered Office:* Unit 11 All Saints Industrial Estate, Shildon, Co Durham, DL4 2RD
*Activities:* Architectural activities
*Parent:* Pressed Steel Products (Holdings) Ltd
*Officers:* Kamal Ashraf Abdul Razaq [1946] Director [Omani]; Heath Hindmarch [1967] Managing Director; Tamer Ayoub Qaqish [1977] Director

**PTM Holdings Limited**
*Incorporated:* 18 January 2008
*Net Worth:* £3,148,951 *Total Assets:* £4,316,526
*Registered Office:* 13 Tudhoe Industrial Estate, Spennymoor, Co Durham, DL16 6TL
*Activities:* Non-trading company
*Parent:* Berm Holdings Limited
*Officers:* Jon Beamson [1964] Director; Richard George Elliott [1971] Director; David Thomas Moist [1972] Director; Michael John Rogan [1980] Director

**PTSG Access and Safety Limited**
*Incorporated:* 5 August 1996 *Employees:* 124
*Net Worth:* £9,718,275 *Total Assets:* £18,311,144
*Registered Office:* 13-14 Flemming Court, Castleford, W Yorks, WF10 5HW
*Activities:* Repair of other equipment
*Parent:* Premier Technical Services Group PLC
*Officers:* Sally Ann Bedford, Secretary; Adam John Coates, Secretary; Adam John Coates [1968] Finance Director; John Robert Foley [1955] Director; Paul William Teasdale [1967] Director

**Pugh & Company Limited**
*Incorporated:* 30 March 2000 *Employees:* 23
*Net Worth:* £3,979,551 *Total Assets:* £4,284,749
*Registered Office:* Toronto Square, Toronto Street, Leeds, LS1 2HJ
*Activities:* Real estate agencies
*Parent:* Pugh Holdings Limited
*Officers:* John Ashton Humphrey, Secretary; Richard Keith Roe [1966] Director/Chartered Surveyor; Anthony Lavern Spencer [1969] Director/Chartered Surveyor

**Pugh Holdings Limited**
*Incorporated:* 14 October 2004
*Net Worth:* £62,336 *Total Assets:* £3,341,626
*Registered Office:* Toronto Square, Toronto Street, Leeds, LS1 2HJ
*Activities:* Real estate agencies
*Parent:* Pugh Auction Group Limited
*Officers:* John Ashton Humphrey, Secretary; Richard Keith Roe [1966] Director/Chartered Surveyor; Anthony Lavern Spencer [1969] Director/Chartered Surveyor

**J.Pullan & Sons Limited**
*Incorporated:* 27 November 1923 *Employees:* 41
*Net Worth:* £76,243,360 *Total Assets:* £104,425,352
*Registered Office:* C7 Josephs Well, Hanover Walk, Leeds, LS3 1AB
*Activities:* Development of building projects
*Shareholder:* Alistair Mark Pullan
*Officers:* John Charles Dawson, Secretary; Christopher John Heselton Adams [1950] Director/Chartered Accountant; John Charles Dawson [1965] Director/Co Accountant; Alistair Mark Pullan [1959] Director/Builder; David William Richardson [1944] Director/Chartered Surveyor; Bruce Scott Strachan [1963] Director/Chartered Surveyor

**Abram Pulman & Sons Limited**
*Incorporated:* 17 March 1898 *Employees:* 78
*Net Worth:* £2,863,184 *Total Assets:* £7,765,058
*Registered Office:* Walton Street, Sowerby Bridge, W Yorks, HX6 1AN
*Activities:* Wholesale of metals and metal ores
*Major Shareholder:* David Norbury Shoesmith
*Officers:* John Christopher Horner, Company Secretary; John Christopher Horner [1964] Director/Company Secretary; Margaret Elizabeth McHugh [1961] Director/Teacher; David Norbury Shoesmith [1959] Managing Director; Anne Patricia Wiggins [1958] Director/Self Employed

**Punch Bowl Investments Limited**
*Incorporated:* 29 April 2014
*Net Worth:* £1,353 *Total Assets:* £4,131,045
*Registered Office:* c/o Vale of Mowbray Holdings Ltd, 20 Leases Road, Leeming Bar, Northallerton, N Yorks, DL7 9AW
*Activities:* Other letting and operating of own or leased real estate
*Major Shareholder:* John Gatenby
*Officers:* Mark Gatenby, Secretary; John Gatenby [1946] Director

**Punch Graphix Limited**
*Incorporated:* 24 March 2005
*Net Worth:* £41,945,800 *Total Assets:* £43,236,164
*Registered Office:* Endeavour House, Glaisdale Road, Northminster Business Park, Upper Poppleton, York, YO26 6QT
*Activities:* Other publishing activities
*Officers:* Jayne Evelyn Williams, Secretary; Jeremy Theodore Berenzweig [1972] Director/General Counsel; Marcus Johannes Brussel [1968] Director [Dutch]; Georg Heinrich Johannes Strierath [1976] Director/Senior Counsel [German]

**Pure Collection Limited**
*Incorporated:* 9 July 2002 *Employees:* 280
*Net Worth:* £1,850,055 *Total Assets:* £12,358,425
*Registered Office:* Mowbray House, Mowbray Square, Harrogate, N Yorks, HG1 5AU
*Activities:* Retail sale via mail order houses or via Internet
*Major Shareholder:* Nick Falkingham
*Officers:* Nicholas Bruce Falkingham [1966] Director

**Pure Data Solutions Limited**
*Incorporated:* 8 May 2007 *Employees:* 41
*Net Worth:* £779,462 *Total Assets:* £6,077,301
*Registered Office:* The Mill, Springfield Commercial Centre, Bagley Lane, Farsley, Pudsey, W Yorks, LS28 5LY
*Activities:* Retail sale of computers, peripheral units and software in specialised stores
*Major Shareholder:* Stephen O'Brien
*Officers:* Geoff Botting, Secretary; Cliff Fox [1961] Director; Michelle Lazenby [1975] Director; Stephen Barrie O'Brien [1968] Director

**Pure Gym Limited**
*Incorporated:* 5 September 2008 *Employees:* 763
*Net Worth:* £88,919,000 *Total Assets:* £267,035,008
*Registered Office:* Town Centre House, Merrion Centre, Leeds, LS2 8LY
*Activities:* Fitness facilities
*Parent:* Gym Bidco Limited
*Officers:* Humphrey Michael Cobbold [1964] Director/Chief Executive Officer; Alexander Basil John Wood [1978] Director/Chief Financial Officer

**Pure Leisure Estates Limited**
*Incorporated:* 5 June 2006 *Employees:* 35
*Net Worth Deficit:* £6,440,206 *Total Assets:* £11,205,250
*Registered Office:* South Lakeland House, Main A6, Yealand Redmayne, Carnforth, Cumbria, LA5 9RN
*Activities:* Other amusement and recreation activities n.e.c.
*Parent:* Pure Leisure Group Limited
*Officers:* Paul Rossiter, Secretary; John Charles Morphet [1954] Managing Director; Paul Rossiter [1964] Director/Chartered Accountant; Gordon Alexander Walker [1964] Operations Director; Trevor James White [1952] Director/Marketing Manager

**Pure Leisure Group Limited**
*Incorporated:* 27 April 2004 *Employees:* 346
*Net Worth:* £48,835,000 *Total Assets:* £104,165,000
*Registered Office:* South Lakeland House, Main A6, Yealand Redmayne, Carnforth, Lancs, LA5 9RN
*Activities:* Activities of other membership organisations n.e.c.
*Major Shareholder:* John Charles Morphet
*Officers:* Paul Rossiter, Secretary; John Charles Morphet [1954] Managing Director; Matthew David Morphet [1974] Director/Logistics Manager; Paul Rossiter [1964] Director/Chartered Accountant; Gordon Alexander Walker [1964] Operations Director; Trevor James White [1952] Marketing Director

**Pure Retirement Limited**
*Incorporated:* 30 April 2010 *Employees:* 52
*Net Worth:* £4,813,000 *Total Assets:* £6,701,000
*Registered Office:* 2200 Century Way, Thorpe Park, Leeds, LS15 8ZB
*Activities:* Activities of mortgage finance companies
*Shareholders:* Andrew Robin Thirkill; Timothy John Loy
*Officers:* Jonathan Paul Simpson, Secretary; John Paul Carter [1961] Managing Director; Timothy John Loy [1965] Director/Accountant; Jonathan Paul Simpson [1976] Finance Director; Andrew Robin Thirkill [1959] Director

**Pure Technology Group Limited**
*Incorporated:* 10 April 2015 *Employees:* 88
*Net Worth:* £1,315,914 *Total Assets:* £7,907,969
*Registered Office:* The Mill, Springfield Commercial Centre, Bagley Lane, Farsley, Pudsey, Leeds, LS28 5LY
*Activities:* Activities of head offices
*Major Shareholder:* Stephen Barrie Obrien
*Officers:* Geoffrey Charles Botting, Secretary; Clifford Mark Fox [1961] Director; Michelle Lazenby [1975] Director; Stephen Barrie O'Brien [1968] Director

**Purex International Limited**
*Incorporated:* 25 May 2004 *Employees:* 39
*Net Worth:* £6,985,345 *Total Assets:* £11,668,132
*Registered Office:* QWP House, Capitol Park, Thorne, Doncaster, S Yorks, DN8 5TX
*Activities:* Manufacture of other electrical equipment
*Parent:* QWP Limited
*Officers:* Kenneth Andrew Easey [1961] Director; Trefor Evan Jones [1961] Director

**Purple Bricks Company Limited**
*Incorporated:* 18 October 2005 *Employees:* 5
*Net Worth:* £1,007,199 *Total Assets:* £6,736,512
*Registered Office:* Seven Airport West, Lancaster Way, Yeadon, W Yorks, LS19 7ZA
*Activities:* Other letting and operating of own or leased real estate
*Shareholders:* Clare Bruce Limited; Phil Rushfirth Limited
*Officers:* Carol Rushfirth, Secretary; Clare Elizabeth Bruce [1966] Director/Market Research Consultant; Philip Andrew Rushfirth [1972] Director

**PVM Investments Limited**
*Incorporated:* 16 November 2001
*Net Worth:* £278,450 *Total Assets:* £5,888,400
*Registered Office:* 25 Jetstream Drive, Auckley, Doncaster, S Yorks, DN9 3QS
*Activities:* Other letting and operating of own or leased real estate
*Shareholders:* Paul Darren Morton; Victoria Louise Winchester Morton
*Officers:* Victoria Morton, Secretary; Paul Morton [1971] Director

**PWS Distributors Limited**
*Incorporated:* 27 January 1988 *Employees:* 339
*Net Worth:* £27,086,246 *Total Assets:* £66,023,188
*Registered Office:* P O Box 20, Station Road, Aycliffe Business Park, Newton Aycliffe, Co Durham, DL5 6XJ
*Activities:* Wholesale of household goods (other than musical instruments) n.e.c
*Officers:* Jonathan Barclay Whisker, Secretary; Kevin Francis Gay [1967] IT & Operations Director; Aidan Jackson [1965] Marketing Director; Wesley McKenna [1971] Sales Director; Mark William Winspear Stephenson [1962] Director; Jonathan Barclay Whisker [1964] Financial Director

**Pye Motors,Limited**
*Incorporated:* 23 March 1925 *Employees:* 127
*Net Worth:* £2,780,069 *Total Assets:* £17,435,020
*Registered Office:* Ovangle Road, Morecambe, Lancs, LA3 3PF
*Activities:* Sale of new cars and light motor vehicles
*Shareholder:* Helen Joyce Morley-Pye
*Officers:* Helen Joyce Morley Pye [1962] Director/Motor Trader; Anthony Payne [1936] Director/Motor Trader; Nicholas Payne [1964] Director/Motor Trader; David Lomax Pye [1927] Director/Motor Trader; James Marsland Pye [1931] Director/Motor Trader

**Pyramid Display Materials Limited**
*Incorporated:* 3 June 1986 *Employees:* 117
*Net Worth:* £5,545,607 *Total Assets:* £20,451,652
*Registered Office:* Eldon House, 201 Penistone Road, Kirkburton, Huddersfield, W Yorks, HD8 0PE
*Activities:* Non-specialised wholesale trade
*Parent:* Cubic Holdings Limited
*Officers:* Tracey Morgan, Secretary/Director; Grant Cummings [1963] Director; Colin Doherty [1965] Director; Paul George Edwards [1967] Director; Paul Lee Madsen [1966] Director; Dennis Morgan [1961] Director; Tracey Morgan [1962] Director; Alfred Frank Murphy [1952] Director

**Q Electronics Limited**
*Incorporated:* 25 January 1999 *Employees:* 27
*Net Worth:* £4,257,986 *Total Assets:* £5,377,699
*Registered Office:* Beck House, Hawksworth Road, Horsforth, Leeds, LS18 4JP
*Activities:* Manufacture of communication equipment other than telegraph, and telephone apparatus and equipment
*Shareholders:* Dar Shivtiel; Neil Roughton
*Officers:* Carolyn Shivtiel, Secretary; Neil Roughton [1962] Director/Engineer; Dar Shivtiel [1967] Director/Engineer

**Q Medical Technologies Ltd**
*Incorporated:* 24 January 2005 *Employees:* 24
*Net Worth:* £1,367,017 *Total Assets:* £4,247,232
*Registered Office:* Unit 1a Summerland Trading Estate, Endmoor, Kendal, Cumbria, LA8 0FB
*Activities:* Other human health activities
*Major Shareholder:* Andrew Kemp
*Officers:* Andrew Kemp [1962] Director/Consultant; Charles Melville Pillans [1975] Director/Sales Executive

**Q Underwriting Services Limited**
*Incorporated:* 19 March 2014 *Employees:* 43
*Previous:* TFP Schemes Limited
*Net Worth:* £18,318,458 *Total Assets:* £26,374,618
*Registered Office:* Rossington's Business Park, West Carr Road, Retford, Notts, DN22 7SW
*Activities:* Activities of insurance agents and brokers
*Parent:* PIB Group Limited
*Officers:* Timothy Tracy Brooke [1960] Director; Ryan Christopher Brown [1973] Director/Chief Financial Officer; Adrian Colosso [1957] Director; Bernard Mageean [1956] Director/Insurance; Brendan James McManus [1959] Director; Jonathan Paul Stanley [1965] Director/Chief Risk Officer

**Q-Park (Taunton) Limited**
*Incorporated:* 18 November 2003 *Employees:* 2
*Net Worth:* £14,554,606 *Total Assets:* £14,923,229
*Registered Office:* 72 Merrion Street, Leeds, LS2 8LW
*Activities:* Other letting and operating of own or leased real estate
*Parent:* Universal Parking Ltd
*Officers:* Stephen Mark Ellis, Secretary; Adam John Bidder [1970] Managing Director; Stephen Mark Ellis [1965] Finance Director

**Q-Park Limited**
*Incorporated:* 10 May 1983 *Employees:* 332
*Net Worth:* £7,660,887 *Total Assets:* £134,887,312
*Registered Office:* 72 Merrion Street, Leeds, LS2 8LW
*Activities:* Other letting and operating of own or leased real estate
*Parent:* Universal Parking Ltd
*Officers:* Stephen Mark Ellis, Secretary; Adam John Bidder [1970] Managing Director; Stephen Mark Ellis [1965] Finance Director

**Q-Park Real Estate Holding UK Limited**
*Incorporated:* 26 September 2013 *Employees:* 2
*Net Worth Deficit:* £1,044,889 *Total Assets:* £26,104,000
*Registered Office:* 72 Merrion Street, Leeds, LS2 8LW
*Activities:* Other letting and operating of own or leased real estate
*Officers:* Stephen Mark Ellis, Secretary; Adam John Bidder [1970] Managing Director; Stephen Mark Ellis [1965] Director

**Q-Park Real Estate UK I Limited**
*Incorporated:* 25 September 2013 *Employees:* 2
*Net Worth:* £5,495,438 *Total Assets:* £51,939,968
*Registered Office:* 72 Merrion Street, Leeds, LS2 8LW
*Activities:* Other letting and operating of own or leased real estate
*Parent:* Q-Park Real Estate Holding UK Ltd
*Officers:* Stephen Mark Ellis, Secretary; Adam John Bidder [1970] Managing Director; Stephen Mark Ellis [1965] Director

**Q-Park Real Estate UK II Limited**
*Incorporated:* 25 September 2013 *Employees:* 2
*Net Worth:* £5,011,470 *Total Assets:* £22,553,400
*Registered Office:* 72 Merrion Street, Leeds, LS2 8LW
*Activities:* Other letting and operating of own or leased real estate
*Parent:* Q-Park Real Estate Holding Ltd
*Officers:* Stephen Mark Ellis, Secretary; Adam John Bidder [1970] Managing Director; Stephen Mark Ellis [1965] Director

**Q-Park Real Estate UK III Limited**
*Incorporated:* 25 September 2013 *Employees:* 2
*Net Worth:* £2,057,516 *Total Assets:* £14,955,732
*Registered Office:* 72 Merrion Street, Leeds, LS2 8LW
*Activities:* Other letting and operating of own or leased real estate
*Parent:* Q-Park Real Estate Holding UK Ltd
*Officers:* Stephen Mark Ellis, Secretary; Adam John Bidder [1970] Managing Director; Stephen Mark Ellis [1965] Director

**Q-Park Securities Limited**
*Incorporated:* 13 August 2002 *Employees:* 2
*Net Worth:* £24,537,504 *Total Assets:* £26,951,274
*Registered Office:* 72 Merrion Street, Leeds, LS2 8LW
*Activities:* Other letting and operating of own or leased real estate
*Parent:* Universal Parking Limited
*Officers:* Stephen Mark Ellis, Secretary; Adam John Bidder [1970] Managing Director; Stephen Mark Ellis [1965] Finance Director

**Q-Park UK Limited**
*Incorporated:* 19 March 2001 *Employees:* 2
*Net Worth:* £51,000,000 *Total Assets:* £51,000,000
*Registered Office:* 72 Merrion Street, Leeds, LS2 8LW
*Activities:* Other letting and operating of own or leased real estate
*Officers:* Stephen Mark Ellis, Secretary; Adam John Bidder [1970] Managing Director; Stephen Mark Ellis [1965] Finance Director

**Q. R. I. Ltd**
*Incorporated:* 23 December 1999 *Employees:* 38
*Net Worth:* £5,772,249 *Total Assets:* £6,920,941
*Registered Office:* 40 Stockhill Road, Greengates, Bradford, BD10 9AX
*Activities:* Manufacture of other women's outerwear
*Officers:* Christine Ann Rankin, Secretary; Michael Kelly [1958] Managing Director

**Quad Bidco Limited**
*Incorporated:* 19 December 2013 *Employees:* 635
*Net Worth:* £21,097,000 *Total Assets:* £105,987,000
*Registered Office:* The Inspire, Hornbeam Square West, Harrogate, N Yorks, HG2 8PA
*Activities:* Activities of head offices
*Parent:* Quad Holdco Limited
*Officers:* John Cody Bradshaw [1978] Director/Hotel Real Estate [American]; Sarah Broughton [1976] Director/Chartered Accountant; James Alexander Burrell [1974] Director; Anthony Gerrard Troy [1962] Director [Irish]

**Quality Hydraulic Power Limited**
*Incorporated:* 12 May 1987 *Employees:* 77
*Net Worth:* £10,719,520 *Total Assets:* £13,217,522
*Registered Office:* West House, King Cross Road, Halifax, W Yorks, HX1 1EB
*Activities:* Machining
*Parent:* A & E Holdings Ltd
*Officers:* Royston Bowden [1959] Director; Kevin George Brownlee [1958] Director; Dr Werner Heinz Dieter [1929] Director [German]; Thomas Matthew Leyland [1976] Director

**Quarmby Holdings Limited**
*Incorporated:* 24 April 1972 *Employees:* 3
*Net Worth:* £9,940,465 *Total Assets:* £14,729,808
*Registered Office:* Arthington Park, Arthington, Otley, W Yorks, LS21 1PH
*Activities:* Buying and selling of own real estate
*Officers:* John Antony Batty, Secretary; Laura Gabrielle Irene Davies [1977] Director/Interior Designer and Retailer; Hannah Margaret Eames [1980] Director/Retail Project Manager; James Roger Quarmby [1944] Director; Julia Margaret Quarmby [1950] Director; Oliver Alexander Quarmby [1975] Director/Surveyor

**Quarters Developments Limited**
*Incorporated:* 2 December 2015
*Net Worth:* £89,187 *Total Assets:* £10,485,311
*Registered Office:* 12a Montpellier Parade, Harrogate, N Yorks, HG1 2TJ
*Activities:* Buying and selling of own real estate
*Officers:* Andrew Paul Bartle [1969] Director; Jason Lee Clay [1971] Director

**Quay Propco Limited**
*Incorporated:* 5 March 2014
*Net Worth:* £228,370 *Total Assets:* £7,266,498
*Registered Office:* Fountains Bent, Darley Road, Birstwith, Harrogate, N Yorks, HG3 2PN
*Activities:* Other letting and operating of own or leased real estate
*Parent:* 0864179
*Officers:* Anthony Gerrard Troy [1962] Director [Irish]

**Queen Ethelburga's College Limited**
*Incorporated:* 15 January 1991 *Employees:* 205
*Net Worth:* £2,117,556 *Total Assets:* £24,223,672
*Registered Office:* Thorpe Underwood Hall, Thorpe Underwood, York, YO26 9SZ
*Activities:* Other education n.e.c.
*Parent:* The Collegiate Formation Ltd
*Officers:* Christopher James Hall, Secretary; Christopher James Hall [1969] Director/Chartered Accountant; Amy Katherine Martin [1983] Director; Francis David Martin [1967] Director/Business Executive

**The Queen Katherine School Multi Academy Trust**
*Incorporated:* 17 December 2010 *Employees:* 361
*Net Worth:* £11,043,127 *Total Assets:* £18,388,988
*Registered Office:* The Queen Katherine School, Appleby Road, Kendal, Cumbria, LA9 6PJ
*Activities:* General secondary education
*Officers:* Michael James Walby, Secretary; Beth Curl [1954] Director/Consultant; Anna Catherine Gregg [1991] Director/Trainee Solicitor; Edwin Richards [1948] Director/Retired; Anthony Sinton [1957] Director Headteacher; Stephen Wilkinson [1955] Director/Executive Headteacher

**Queen Margaret's School, York Limited**
*Incorporated:* 15 April 1986 *Employees:* 148
*Net Worth:* £5,586,000 *Total Assets:* £10,384,000
*Registered Office:* Escrick Park, Escrick, York, YO19 6EU
*Activities:* General secondary education
*Officers:* Caroline Jane Bayliss [1954] Director/School Governor; Nigel Frederick Hartley Corner [1965] Director/School Governor; Annabel Lettice Forbes [1973] Director/School Governor; Clare Deborah Granger [1961] Director/School Governor; John Daniel Hoddinott [1963] Director/School Governor; Susan Alison King [1958] Director/School Governor; Catherine Helen Marx [1967] Director/School Governor; Anna Mary Morley [1984] Director/Chartered Surveyor; Robert John Morse [1971] Director/School Governor; Dr Emma Jane Peart [1966] Director/School Governor

**Queens Hotel (Llandudno) Limited**
*Incorporated:* 6 August 2015
*Net Worth Deficit:* £342,725 *Total Assets:* £5,523,962
*Registered Office:* Unit D2, Elland Riorges Link, Lowfields Business Park, Elland, W Yorks, HX5 9DG
*Activities:* Buying and selling of own real estate
*Parent:* Northern Powerhouse Developments Limited
*Officers:* Gavin Lee Woodhouse [1978] Director/Consultant

**Queens Staith Leisure Limited**
*Incorporated:* 25 March 1992 *Employees:* 159
*Net Worth:* £22,047,976 *Total Assets:* £23,884,086
*Registered Office:* Moorside Farm, Lordsmoor Lane, Strensall, York, YO32 5XF
*Activities:* Hotels and similar accommodation
*Major Shareholder:* Philip David Smith
*Officers:* Craig Vincent Smith, Secretary; Craig Vincent Smith [1970] Director; Lee Allen Smith [1975] Director; Philip David Smith [1949] Director

**Queensway Properties Limited**
*Incorporated:* 25 May 1993
*Net Worth Deficit:* £19,255 *Total Assets:* £3,674,828
*Registered Office:* Bridge House, 41 Wincolmlee, Kingston upon Hull, HU2 8AG
*Activities:* Residents property management
*Shareholders:* Nicholas Roy Bishop; Nicholas David Eaton
*Officers:* Nicholas Bishop, Secretary/Director; Nicholas Roy Bishop [1969] Director; Nicholas David Eaton [1970] Director

**Quest 4 Limited**
*Incorporated:* 1 November 1985 *Employees:* 48
*Net Worth:* £4,359,961 *Total Assets:* £6,159,772
*Registered Office:* Q4 Building, Rudgate, Tockwith, York, YO26 7DW
*Activities:* Wholesale of hardware, plumbing and heating equipment and supplies
*Officers:* Paul David Jacobs [1980] Director; Richard Jonathan Parker [1966] Director

**Quest Consumables Limited**
*Incorporated:* 2 April 1973 *Employees:* 89
*Net Worth:* £1,275,708 *Total Assets:* £3,765,156
*Registered Office:* c/o Rema Tip Top Holdings, Westland Square, Leeds, LS11 5XS
*Activities:* Wholesale of machine tools
*Parent:* Firstserve Holdings Limited
*Officers:* Garry Mangham, Secretary; Mark Brian Insley [1959] Director; Geoffrey Simon George MacArthur [1950] Director; Garry Mangham [1963] Director

**Quest Solutions (UK) Ltd**
*Incorporated:* 16 January 2003 *Employees:* 58
*Net Worth:* £1,357,320 *Total Assets:* £5,954,081
*Registered Office:* Unit 1 Euroway Trading Estate, Wharfedale Road, Bradford, W Yorks, BD4 6QB
*Activities:* Glazing
*Shareholders:* Anthony Robert Douglas; Simon Richard Henry
*Officers:* Fiona Jane Douglas, Secretary; Anthony Robert Douglas [1963] Director; Simon Richard Henry [1972] Director

**Quintor (Homes) Limited**
*Incorporated:* 3 November 1992
*Net Worth:* £2,447,700 *Total Assets:* £3,958,950
*Registered Office:* Raywell Hall, Country Lodge Park, Riplingham Road, Raywell, Cottingham, N Humbers, HU16 5YL
*Activities:* Holiday centres and villages
*Shareholders:* Richard William Longthorp; Christopher Charles Longthorp
*Officers:* Richard William Longthorp, Secretary; David Peter Coates [1974] Director; Christopher Charles Longthorp [1956] Director/Accountant; Jonathan Marc Longthorp [1979] Director/Farmer; Richard William Longthorp [1953] Director/Farmer; Philip David MacKay [1969] Director

**Quintor (UK) Limited Liability Partnership**
*Incorporated:* 10 August 2006 *Employees:* 22
*Net Worth:* £4,517,370 *Total Assets:* £7,273,434
*Registered Office:* Raywell Hall, Country Lodge Park, Riplingham Road, Raywell, Cottingham, N Humbers, HU16 5YL

**Quirkco Investments Limited**
*Incorporated:* 6 January 1958 *Employees:* 2
*Net Worth:* £7,619,889 *Total Assets:* £7,982,103
*Registered Office:* The Farmhouse, Upper Bagden Farm, Bagden Lane, Clayton West, Huddersfield, W Yorks, HD8 9LQ
*Activities:* Development of building projects
*Shareholders:* Darrell Jeremy Quirk; Jacqueline Ann Quirk; Rachel Anne Quirk; Robert Nathan Quirk
*Officers:* Darrell Jeremy Quirk, Secretary; Darrell Jeremy Quirk [1958] Director; Jacqueline Ann Quirk [1964] Director

**QWP Limited**
*Incorporated:* 9 October 2014 *Employees:* 46
*Net Worth:* £2,599,514 *Total Assets:* £7,301,590
*Registered Office:* QWP House, Capitol Park, Thorne, Doncaster, S Yorks, DN8 5TX
*Activities:* Activities of head offices
*Shareholders:* Kenneth Andrew Easey; Trefor Evan Jones
*Officers:* Kenneth Andrew Easey [1961] Director; Trefor Evan Jones [1961] Director

**QX Limited**
*Incorporated:* 10 November 2003
*Net Worth:* £1,178,004 *Total Assets:* £3,184,384
*Registered Office:* Castle Chambers, off Mill Bridge, Skipton, N Yorks, BD23 1NJ
*Activities:* Other service activities n.e.c.
*Major Shareholder:* Chrostopher Eric Robinson
*Officers:* Kate Simpson, Secretary; Christopher Eric Robinson [1966] Director

**R & R Ice Cream UK Limited**
*Incorporated:* 21 March 1967 *Employees:* 907
*Net Worth:* £203,268,000 *Total Assets:* £285,327,008
*Registered Office:* Richmond House, Leeming Bar, Northallerton, N Yorks, DL7 9UL
*Activities:* Manufacture of ice cream
*Parent:* Froneri International Limited
*Officers:* Michael John Fraine [1966] Director; Phil Karl Griffin [1972] Marketing Director; Marcello Mattia [1965] Director [Italian]; Ibrahim Mahmood Ibrahim Najafi [1958] Director; Samuel David Wrist [1976] Director

**R & R PIK Limited**
*Incorporated:* 23 April 2013
*Previous:* R & R PIK PLC
*Net Worth Deficit:* £56,074,520 *Total Assets:* £224,768,656
*Registered Office:* Richmond House, Leeming Bar, Northallerton, N Yorks, DL7 9UL
*Activities:* Activities of production holding companies
*Parent:* Riviera Acquisitions Limited
*Officers:* Marcello Mattia, Secretary; Phil Karl Griffin [1972] Director; Marcello Mattia [1965] Director [Italian]; Ibrahim Mahmood Ibrahim Najafi [1958] Director

**R and A Hotels Group Ltd**
*Incorporated:* 3 March 2015 *Employees:* 1
*Net Worth Deficit:* £19,779 *Total Assets:* £6,237,904
*Registered Office:* 170-172 Roundhay Road, Leeds, LS8 5PL
*Activities:* Buying and selling of own real estate
*Major Shareholder:* Raju Handa
*Officers:* Deepak Raju Handa [1975] Director

**R M Solar Limited**
*Incorporated:* 28 June 2006 *Employees:* 135
*Net Worth:* £1,274,991 *Total Assets:* £7,004,510
*Registered Office:* Unit 4 Valencia Park, Gilcar Way, Wakefield Europort, Castleford, W Yorks, WF10 5QS
*Activities:* Wholesale of hardware, plumbing and heating equipment and supplies
*Parent:* Joule Hot Water Systems UK Ltd
*Officers:* Ian Barrett [1981] Director [Irish]; Ronan Philip Ginnell [1982] Director [Irish]

**R Safety Products Holdings Limited**
*Incorporated:* 14 August 2013
*Net Worth:* £430,334 *Total Assets:* £6,583,839
*Registered Office:* Unit B9, Lowfields Close, Lowfields Business Park, Elland, W Yorks, HX5 9DX
*Activities:* Wholesale of other machinery and equipment
*Shareholder:* Robin Neil Womersley
*Officers:* Andrew John Graham [1964] Director; Robin Neil Womersley [1971] Director

**R.P.M. Industrial Services Limited**
*Incorporated:* 17 February 1972 *Employees:* 27
*Net Worth:* £3,774,562 *Total Assets:* £4,143,300
*Registered Office:* Riverside House, Moody Lane, Riverside Industrial Estate, Grimsby, N E Lincs, DN31 2SW
*Activities:* Remediation activities and other waste management services
*Major Shareholder:* Paul Chester
*Officers:* Paul Chester, Secretary; Paul Chester [1965] Director

**R.T. Consultants Limited**
*Incorporated:* 13 March 1991
*Net Worth:* £22,360,996 *Total Assets:* £33,365,464
*Registered Office:* Stoneacre, Omega Boulevard, Capitol Park, Thorne, S Yorks, DN8 5TX
*Activities:* Other letting and operating of own or leased real estate
*Shareholders:* Richard Stephen Teatum; Christine Patricia Teatum
*Officers:* Nigel Peter Wood, Secretary; Christine Patricia Teatum [1951] Director; Richard Stephen Teatum [1957] Director; Nigel Peter Wood [1964] Director

**Rabbit (Holdings) Limited**
*Incorporated:* 23 May 2014 *Employees:* 71
*Net Worth:* £3,612,762 *Total Assets:* £8,346,261
*Registered Office:* Rabbit Hill Business Park, Great North Road, Arkendale, Knaresborough, N Yorks, HG5 0FF
*Activities:* Other letting and operating of own or leased real estate
*Shareholders:* Richard John Kay; Rachel Kay
*Officers:* Rachel Kay, Secretary; Rachel Kay [1969] Director; Richard John Kay [1968] Director

**Rack Systems (Engineering) Ltd.**
*Incorporated:* 29 December 1988 *Employees:* 95
*Net Worth:* £7,269,300 *Total Assets:* £10,485,893
*Registered Office:* 1 Wits End, Kirkby Mills Industrial Estate, Kirkbymoorside, York, YO62 6PG
*Activities:* Manufacture of other fabricated metal products n.e.c.
*Shareholders:* John Richard Lane; Richard James Field; RFB Trustees Five Limited; RFB Trustee Six Limited
*Officers:* Louise Campbell, Secretary; Adam Christian Campbell [1976] Director [Australian]; Christine Winifred Field [1940] Director; Richard James Field [1967] Managing Director; Matthew James Hutchinson [1967] Director/Production Manager

**Rackham Housefloors Limited**
*Incorporated:* 7 January 1980 *Employees:* 80
*Net Worth:* £4,960,651 *Total Assets:* £7,130,419
*Registered Office:* Mill Street, East Dewsbury, W Yorks, WF12 9TA
*Activities:* Other manufacturing n.e.c.
*Shareholders:* Paul Moore; Dawn Moore
*Officers:* Paul Moore [1956] Director; Roger Mark Varley [1964] Director/Technical

**Radical Services Limited**
*Incorporated:* 27 January 1995 *Employees:* 168
*Net Worth:* £3,013,338 *Total Assets:* £3,807,321
*Registered Office:* Rouse House, 2 Wyther Lane, Kirkstall, Leeds, LS5 3BT
*Activities:* Other residential care activities n.e.c.
*Officers:* Lynsey Guilherme, Secretary; Luigi Guilherme [1960] Director; Lynsey Guilherme [1974] Director

**Radicon Transmission UK Limited**
*Incorporated:* 6 October 2010 *Employees:* 57
*Net Worth:* £2,628,142 *Total Assets:* £14,899,201
*Registered Office:* Unit J3, Lowfields Way, Lowfields Business Park, Elland, W Yorks, HX5 9DA
*Activities:* Manufacture of bearings, gears, gearing and driving elements
*Major Shareholder:* Payasvin Bhanubhai Patel
*Officers:* Prashant Amin [1956] Director/Engineer [American]; Chandrakant Babubhai Patel [1939] Director/Business Executive; Dinesh Manubhai Patel [1953] Technical Director [Indian]; Pradip Patel [1947] Director; Prayasvin Patel [1958] Director [Indian]

**Rail Express Systems Limited**
*Incorporated:* 9 June 1994
*Net Worth:* £33,046,000 *Total Assets:* £33,145,000
*Registered Office:* Lakeside Business Park, Carolina Way, Doncaster, S Yorks, DN4 5PN
*Activities:* Freight rail transport
*Parent:* DB Cargo (UK) Holdings Limited
*Officers:* Helen Louise Young, Secretary; Andrea Rossi [1975] Director/Chief Financial Officer; Hans-Georg Werner [1959] Director/Business Administration [German]

**Rainbow Equine Hospital Limited**
*Incorporated:* 24 December 2013
*Net Worth:* £1,728,072 *Total Assets:* £3,064,245
*Registered Office:* Leeman House, Station Business Park, Holgate Park Drive, York, YO26 4GB
*Activities:* Veterinary activities
*Parent:* Vetpartners Limited
*Officers:* Joanna Clare Malone [1974] Director; Mark Stanworth [1964] Director

**Rainbow Schools Trust**
*Incorporated:* 16 December 2010 *Employees:* 53
*Net Worth:* £4,766,423 *Total Assets:* £4,996,443
*Registered Office:* New Chartford House, Centurion Way, Cleckheaton, W Yorks, BD19 3QB
*Activities:* Primary education
*Officers:* Shaukat Ali [1977] Director/IT Trainer; Yassar Ali [1980] Director/NHS Employee; Ruby Khalid Bhatti [1970] Director/Solicitor; Asmi Rashid Darr [1955] Director/Self Employed; Vaneeta Garg [1984] Director/Lecturer; El-Fabeeh Hameed Husein [1947] Director/Consultant; Sadia Kabil Raja [1991] Director/Teacher; Michelle Gizella Khan [1968] Director/Full Time Single Mum; Joseph Lansana Kormoh [1970] Director/Education Consultant [Sierra Leonean]; Taher Nawaz [1950] Director/Chartered Accountant; Amjad Pervez [1958] Director/MD Seafresh

**Rainheath Limited**
*Incorporated:* 28 September 1970 *Employees:* 52
*Net Worth:* £15,733,777 *Total Assets:* £16,679,847
*Registered Office:* Triune Court, Monks Cross Drive, Huntington, York, YO32 9GZ
*Activities:* Growing of cereals (except rice), leguminous crops and oil seeds
*Major Shareholder:* Andrew George Simpson
*Officers:* Andrew George Simpson Snr [1939] Director; Julie Caroline Stephenson [1967] Director

**Raiseprint Limited**
*Incorporated:* 28 April 1997 *Employees:* 44
*Net Worth:* £2,427,961 *Total Assets:* £4,096,926
*Registered Office:* The Innovation Centre, Millennium Road, Airedale Business Centre, Skipton, N Yorks, BD23 2TZ
*Activities:* Printing n.e.c.
*Shareholders:* Louise Elizabeth Bell; David Stephen Bell; Melonie Milsted; Robin Milsted
*Officers:* Louise Elizabeth Bell, Secretary/Administrator; David Stephen Bell [1957] Director/Printer; Louise Elizabeth Bell [1976] Director/Administrator; Melonie Milsted [1970] Director/Printer; Robin Milsted [1965] Director/Printer

**Ral Holdings Limited**
*Incorporated:* 24 May 2017 *Employees:* 1
*Net Worth:* £329,399 *Total Assets:* £3,098,116
*Registered Office:* Unit 4 Healey House, Industrial Estate, Crosland Factory Lane, Huddersfield, W Yorks, HD4 7DQ
*Activities:* Buying and selling of own real estate
*Major Shareholder:* Martin Latham
*Officers:* Martin Latham [1960] Director

**Tony Rampton Trust**
*Incorporated:* 13 February 1974
*Net Worth:* £9,680,746 *Total Assets:* £9,687,264
*Registered Office:* Centre of Excellence, Hope Park, Trevor Foster Way, Bradford, W Yorks, BD5 8HH
*Activities:* Other business support service activities n.e.c.
*Officers:* Sandra Lingwood, Secretary; Debra Ali [1984] Director/Marketing Campaign Manager; Robert Stephen Colledge [1945] Director/Human Resources Manager; Norman Finnigan [1944] Director/Retired; Mary Priestman Johnston [1948] Director/Retired; Angela Kennedy [1968] Director; Andrew John Langridge [1962] Director; Graham Marshall [1948] Director; John Jeremy Pearmund [1953] Director; Phillip Robert Poole [1949] Director/Retired; John Richard Anthony Rampton [1941] Director/Barrister; Dawn Redman [1959] Director/Business Consultant; Christine Noella Southam [1956] Director; Jonathan Stratford Tinning [1969] Director; Dilys Mary Ashton Ward [1940] Director/Retired

**Ramscove Limited**
*Incorporated:* 23 April 1990 *Employees:* 3
*Net Worth:* £11,172,176 *Total Assets:* £13,581,667
*Registered Office:* Sadberge Hall, Sadberge, Darlington, Co Durham, DL2 1RL
*Activities:* Management consultancy activities other than financial management
*Shareholders:* David John Soley; Susan Jane Soley
*Officers:* Susan Jane Soley, Secretary; David John Soley [1949] Director/Management Consultant; Susan Jane Soley [1956] Director/Secretary

**Thomas B. Ramsden & Co. (Bradford) Limited**
*Incorporated:* 9 May 1960 *Employees:* 50
*Net Worth:* £3,341,341 *Total Assets:* £4,365,354
*Registered Office:* Gordon Mills, Netherfield Road, Guiseley, Leeds, LS20 9PD
*Activities:* Finishing of textiles
*Parent:* Thomas Ramsden (Holdings) Limited
*Officers:* Peter Mongomery [1952] Director; Henry Matthew Reynolds Ramsden [1986] Director; Robert Austen Boyd Ramsden [1953] Director; Thomas Piers Austen Ramsden [1983] Director; Thomas Brayshaw Ramsden [1933] Director

**D.B. Ramsden & Company Limited**
*Incorporated:* 31 May 1961 *Employees:* 121
*Net Worth:* £5,891,253 *Total Assets:* £14,676,026
*Registered Office:* Adam Smith Street, Grimsby, S Humbers, DN31 1SJ
*Activities:* Non-specialised wholesale of food, beverages and tobacco
*Parent:* Ramsden Holdings Limited
*Officers:* Louisa Jane Metcalf, Secretary; Dudley Burton Ramsden [1943] Director; Nicholas Ronald Ramsden [1978] Director

**Ramsdens Solicitors LLP**
*Incorporated:* 8 December 2005 *Employees:* 215
*Net Worth:* £4,257,975 *Total Assets:* £6,103,136
*Registered Office:* Oakley House, 1 Hungerford Road, Edgerton, Huddersfield, W Yorks, HD3 3AL
*Officers:* Joanne Louise Coen [1968] Member; Jeremy Mark Charles Cook [1964] Member; Karen Dianne James [1965] Member; Paul Richard Joyce [1963] Member; Steven Gurpal Singh [1961] Member; Helen Elizabeth Thewlis [1972] Member; Paul Sebastien Stefan Booth [1965] LLP Member; David John Bradley [1963] LLP Member; Richard Martin Dean [1976] LLP Member; Gregory John Bernard Dolan [1965] LLP Member; Mark Andrew Hepworth [1961] LLP Member; David Hofton [1961] LLP Member; Julia Dawn Lees [1974] LLP Member; Jill Audra McCurdy [1970] LLP Member; Simon Edward Firth Mills [1964] LLP Member; Stephen Graeme Newman [1961] LLP Member

**Peter Ramsey & Sons (Denholme) Timber Limited**
*Incorporated:* 25 September 1979 *Employees:* 149
*Net Worth:* £2,039,900 *Total Assets:* £5,389,892
*Registered Office:* Wellington Street Sawmills, Sticker Lane, Bradford, W Yorks, BD4 8BW
*Activities:* Manufacture of other products of wood; manufacture of articles of cork, straw and plaiting materials
*Shareholders:* Michael Jonathan Stobbart Ramsey; Patricia Elaine Ramsey
*Officers:* Michael Jonathan Stobbart Ramsey, Secretary; Michael Jonathan Stobbart Ramsey [1962] Director/Timber Merchant; Nicholas Peter Robertshaw Ramsey [1960] Director/Timber Merchant; Patricia Elaine Ramsey [1965] Director/Timber Merchant; Peter Richard Hattersley Ramsey [1935] Director/Timber Merchant

**Peter Ramsey & Sons Limited**
*Incorporated:* 11 November 2002 *Employees:* 153
*Net Worth:* £4,087,872 *Total Assets:* £6,723,840
*Registered Office:* Wellington Street Sawmills, Sticker Lane, Bradford, W Yorks, BD4 8BW
*Activities:* Other letting and operating of own or leased real estate
*Shareholders:* Michael Jonathan Stobbart Ramsey; Patricia Elaine Ramsey
*Officers:* Michael Jonathan Stobbart Ramsey, Secretary/Timber Merchant; Michael Jonathan Stobbart Ramsey [1962] Director/Timber Merchant; Nicholas Peter Robertshaw Ramsey [1960] Director/Timber Merchant; Patricia Elaine Ramsey [1965] Director; Peter Richard Hattersley Ramsey [1935] Director/Timber Merchant

**John Rannoch Limited**
*Incorporated:* 5 July 1933
*Net Worth:* £6,828,000 *Total Assets:* £7,174,000
*Registered Office:* Trinity Park House, Trinity Business Park, Fox Way, Wakefield, W Yorks, WF2 8EE
*Activities:* Production of meat and poultry meat products
*Parent:* 2 Sisters Food Group Limited
*Officers:* Baljinder Kaur Boparan [1968] Director/Manager; Ranjit Singh Boparan [1966] Director; Ronald Klaas Otto Kers [1969] Director/Group CEO [Dutch]; Craig Ashley Tomkinson [1982] Director/Group CFO

**Rapid EPS Limited**
*Incorporated:* 3 November 2009 *Employees:* 31
*Net Worth:* £874,777 *Total Assets:* £3,716,806
*Registered Office:* Unit D, Treefield Industrial Estate, Gelderd Road, Gildersome, Leeds, LS27 7JU
*Activities:* Manufacture of metal structures and parts of structures
*Major Shareholder:* David Michael Brine
*Officers:* David Michael Brine [1959] Director; Jarom Covington [1980] Director; Michael Howard Whittaker [1953] Director

**Rastrick High School Academy Trust**
*Incorporated:* 11 August 2011 *Employees:* 201
*Net Worth:* £12,674,000 *Total Assets:* £15,050,000
*Registered Office:* Rastrick High School, Field Top Road, Rastrick, Brighouse, W Yorks, HD6 3XB
*Activities:* General secondary education
*Officers:* Karen Petrillo, Secretary; Duncan Mackie Brundell [1959] Director/Local Government Officer; Philip Cockcroft [1954] Director/Solicitor; Fiona Cullivan Ward [1966] Director/Headteacher; Geoff Hallas [1934] Director/Retired; Nicholas Midgeley [1961] Director/Architect; Sadhana Patel [1965] Director/Aspirational Learning Mentor; Ian Philp [1942] Director/Retired; Andrea Springthorpe [1978] Director; Andrew Tatham [1942] Director/Retired

**Rathbone Kear Limited**
*Incorporated:* 7 April 2005 *Employees:* 373
*Net Worth:* £40,681,000 *Total Assets:* £76,311,000
*Registered Office:* Hilmore House, Gain Lane, Bradford, W Yorks, BD3 7DL
*Activities:* Manufacture of bread; manufacture of fresh pastry goods and cakes
*Parent:* Wm Morrison Supermarkets Holdings Limited
*Officers:* Jonathan James Burke, Secretary; Andrew James Clappen [1965] Technical Director; Jonathan Paul Hornby [1972] Director; Mark Thomas Stitson [1976] Finance Director; Andrew Edward Thornber [1974] Director

**Ravenheat Manufacturing Limited**
*Incorporated:* 21 January 1987 *Employees:* 18
*Net Worth:* £3,005,534 *Total Assets:* £4,409,816
*Registered Office:* Chartists Way, Morley, Leeds, LS27 9ET
*Activities:* Wholesale of hardware, plumbing and heating equipment and supplies
*Parent:* Ravenheat Holdings Limited
*Officers:* Linda Maude Stephenson, Secretary; Louis Pickersgill [1949] Director; Linda Maude Stephenson [1960] Director/Secretary

**Ravens Ing Properties Limited**
*Incorporated:* 16 January 2015
*Net Worth:* £232,445 *Total Assets:* £3,278,420
*Registered Office:* Ravens Ing Mills, Ravensthorpe, Dewsbury, W Yorks, WF13 3JF
*Activities:* Other letting and operating of own or leased real estate
*Parent:* Lawton Yarns (Holdings) Limited
*Officers:* Timothy Benson Kay, Secretary; Thomas Karel J. Cappuyns [1970] Director [Belgian]; Timothy Benson Kay [1963] Director; Michael Adrianus Martinus Petrus Smits [1966] Director [Dutch]

**Ravensfield Properties Limited**
*Incorporated:* 20 February 2017 *Employees:* 3
*Net Worth:* £2,386,172 *Total Assets:* £7,036,497
*Registered Office:* 4a Woodbottom, Mirfield, W Yorks, WF14 8HF
*Activities:* Buying and selling of own real estate
*Shareholders:* Julian Shore Sykes; Richard Thomas Sykes
*Officers:* Elizabeth Mary Sykes, Secretary; Elizabeth Mary Sykes [1946] Director; Julian Shore Sykes [1972] Director; Richard Thomas Sykes [1943] Director

**Rawdon Asset Finance Limited**
*Incorporated:* 11 May 2009 *Employees:* 6
*Net Worth:* £3,827,567 *Total Assets:* £15,451,812
*Registered Office:* 28 Scotland Way, Horsforth, Leeds, LS18 5SL
*Activities:* Financial leasing
*Officers:* Janet Wainwright, Secretary; Anne Marie Beddis [1953] Director; Terence William Beddis [1949] Director; Richard Dobbins [1941] Director/Accountant; Janet Wainwright [1964] Director/Merchandiser; Liam Francis Wainwright [1962] Director/Finance Consultant

**Rawson Brook Group Holdings Limited**
*Incorporated:* 28 January 2016
*Net Worth:* £1,196,639 *Total Assets:* £3,262,731
*Registered Office:* 31 Copenhagen Road, Hull, HU7 0XQ
*Activities:* Activities of other holding companies n.e.c.
*Shareholders:* Colin Charles Brook; Simon Bentley Rawson
*Officers:* Simon Bentley Rawson [1981] Director; John Richard Waldron [1970] Director

**Rawson Fillings Limited**
*Incorporated:* 10 November 1932
*Net Worth:* £3,077,627 *Total Assets:* £3,077,627
*Registered Office:* Castlebank Mills, Portobello Road, Wakefield, W Yorks, WF1 5PS
*Activities:* Manufacture of non-wovens and articles made from non-wovens, except apparel
*Major Shareholder:* Hector Elsworth Rawson
*Officers:* Andrew Charles Watson, Secretary; Hector Elsworth Rawson [1939] Director; Andrew Charles Watson [1975] Director/Accountant

**W.E.Rawson Limited**
*Incorporated:* 4 June 1930 *Employees:* 196
*Net Worth:* £21,395,982 *Total Assets:* £48,833,896
*Registered Office:* Castle Bank Mills, Portobello Road, Wakefield, W Yorks, WF1 5PS
*Activities:* Manufacture of non-wovens and articles made from non-wovens, except apparel
*Major Shareholder:* Hector Elsworth Rawson
*Officers:* Andrew Charles Watson, Secretary; David John Blades [1966] Operations Director; Alexander Charles Edward Johnson [1962] Managing Director; Nicholas Stephen Penn [1955] Sales Director; Hector Elsworth Rawson [1939] Director; Guy William Beckford Stanton [1973] Sales Director; Andrew Charles Watson [1975] Finance Director

**H B Raylor & Company Limited**
*Incorporated:* 26 January 1946 *Employees:* 9
*Net Worth:* £13,374,565 *Total Assets:* £14,527,726
*Registered Office:* James Street, York, YO10 3DW
*Activities:* Other letting and operating of own or leased real estate
*Shareholder:* Anthony Walter Raylor
*Officers:* Anthony Walter Raylor, Secretary; Angela Louise Anders [1970] Director; Anthony Walter Raylor [1942] Director; Caroline Ann Raylor [1963] Director; Carolyn Clare Raylor [1946] Director; Timothy John Raylor [1961] Director/Professor [British/American]

**Rayner Marketing (Holdings) Limited**
*Incorporated:* 6 August 1980
*Net Worth:* £240,958 *Total Assets:* £3,342,065
*Registered Office:* 8 Navigation Court, Calder Park, Wakefield, W Yorks, WF2 7BJ
*Activities:* Other service activities n.e.c.
*Major Shareholder:* Simon Peter Rayner
*Officers:* Debbie Dawn Rayner, Secretary; Simon Peter Rayner [1968] Director/Marketing Legal Consultant

**Rayrigg Estates Ltd**
*Incorporated:* 6 September 2001 *Employees:* 3
*Net Worth:* £8,932,227 *Total Assets:* £10,113,785
*Registered Office:* Rayrigg Road, Windermere, Cumbria, LA23 1BW
*Activities:* Other letting and operating of own or leased real estate
*Shareholder:* Diana Ruth Matthews
*Officers:* Diana Ruth Matthews, Secretary; Diana Ruth Matthews [1946] Director; Montague Gordon Pattinson Matthews [1977] Director/Social Worker; Rachael Ruth Matthews [1974] Director/Designer

**Raysul Holdings Limited**
*Incorporated:* 18 April 1986 *Employees:* 56
*Net Worth:* £3,878,520 *Total Assets:* £9,573,999
*Registered Office:* Unit 55 Kelleythorpe Industrial Estate, Kelleythorpe, Driffield, E Yorks, YO25 9DJ
*Activities:* Activities of head offices
*Shareholders:* Sulair Holdings Limited; Al-Rawahy Holdings LLC
*Officers:* Nicholas Paul Sullivan, Secretary/Director; Sheikh Aflah Hamed Salim Al-Rawahy [1948] Director [Omani]; Is-Haq Hamed Salim Al-Rawahy [1957] Director; Nicholas Paul Sullivan [1963] Director

**RBM Agricultural Limited**
*Incorporated:* 24 November 1995 *Employees:* 84
*Net Worth:* £4,592,967 *Total Assets:* £14,363,864
*Registered Office:* Holme Road, Market Weighton, York, YO4 3EW
*Activities:* Wholesale of agricultural machinery, equipment and supplies
*Shareholders:* Michael Charles Thompson; Adrian Gerard Denner
*Officers:* Adrian Gerard Denner, Secretary; Adrian Gerard Denner [1953] Director/Engineer; Kay Elizabeth Denner [1954] Director/Housewife

**RCS Limited**
*Incorporated:* 8 November 1982 *Employees:* 33
*Previous:* RCS PLC
*Net Worth:* £1,491,314 *Total Assets:* £3,944,378
*Registered Office:* Randall Park Way, Retford, Notts, DN22 7WF
*Activities:* Printing n.e.c.
*Shareholders:* Michael John Todd; Claire Elizabeth Todd
*Officers:* Michael John Todd, Secretary; Marina Bogatyreva [1983] Financial Director [Russian]; Claire Elizabeth Todd [1959] Director; Michael John Todd [1959] Director

**RDG Midas Holdings (NI) Limited**
*Incorporated:* 15 December 2015
*Net Worth Deficit:* £1,623,000 *Total Assets:* £15,952,000
*Registered Office:* Quay Point, Lakeside Boulevard, Doncaster, S Yorks, DN4 5PL
*Activities:* Activities of financial services holding companies
*Parent:* Direct Group Limited
*Officers:* Scott William Hough [1971] Finance Director

**Read Hyundai Limited**
*Incorporated:* 2 September 2005 *Employees:* 35
*Net Worth:* £1,533,182 *Total Assets:* £5,460,393
*Registered Office:* Read Hyundai Limited, Altyre Way, Grimsby, N E Lincs, DN36 4RJ
*Activities:* Sale of new cars and light motor vehicles
*Parent:* Read Automotive Holdings Limited
*Officers:* Nicola Jane Read, Secretary; Michael David Read [1964] Director; Nicola Jane Read [1963] Director

**Read Hyundai Lincoln Limited**
*Incorporated:* 18 July 2011 *Employees:* 25
*Net Worth:* £1,127,155 *Total Assets:* £4,263,671
*Registered Office:* c/o Read Hyundai, Altyre Way, Hewitts Avenue Business Park, Humberston, Grimsby, S Humbers, DN36 4RJ
*Activities:* Sale of new cars and light motor vehicles
*Parent:* Read Motor Group
*Officers:* Nicola Jane Read, Secretary; Michael David Read [1964] Director/Marketing Manager; Nicola Jane Read [1963] Director/Marketing Manager

**Read Motor Group Limited**
*Incorporated:* 21 December 2009 *Employees:* 100
*Net Worth:* £2,626,936 *Total Assets:* £14,415,330
*Registered Office:* Altyre Way, Hewitts Avenue Business Park, Humberston, Grimsby, S Humbers, DN36 4RJ
*Activities:* Sale of new cars and light motor vehicles
*Major Shareholder:* Michael Read
*Officers:* Nicola Jane Read, Secretary; Michael David Read [1964] Director/Motor Dealer; Nicola Jane Read [1963] Director/Marketing Manager

**Real Life Options**
*Incorporated:* 23 March 1992 *Employees:* 2,044
*Net Worth:* £6,240,000 *Total Assets:* £11,770,000
*Registered Office:* David Wandless House, A1 Business Park, Knottingley Road, Knottingley, W Yorks, WF11 0BU
*Activities:* Residential care activities for the elderly and disabled
*Officers:* Dr Robert Alexander Hendry [1958] Director; Hannah Louise Mounsey [1979] Director; John Roy Swales [1956] Director; David Wilkin [1957] Director/Sales & Marketing

**Real Time Communications Limited**
*Incorporated:* 28 August 2001
*Net Worth:* £4,994,083 *Total Assets:* £5,705,416
*Registered Office:* Central House, Leeds Road, Rothwell, Leeds, LS26 0JE
*Activities:* Other information technology service activities
*Parent:* Cox Automotive UK Limited
*Officers:* Michael Buxton, Secretary/Director; Michael Buxton [1965] Director

**The Real Yorkshire Pudding Co Limited**
*Incorporated:* 18 March 1996 *Employees:* 140
*Net Worth:* £3,069,998 *Total Assets:* £6,142,472
*Registered Office:* Coulman Road Industrial Estate, Thorne, Doncaster, S Yorks, DN8 5JS
*Activities:* Manufacture of other food products n.e.c.
*Parent:* GO2 Foods Limited
*Officers:* Paul Graham Airey [1978] Finance Director; Robert Andrew Davies [1954] Director; Charles Robert Payne [1955] Director; Paul Stuart Simmonds [1958] Director

**Really Useful Products Ltd**
*Incorporated:* 23 December 1999 *Employees:* 372
*Net Worth:* £11,151,045 *Total Assets:* £57,637,776
*Registered Office:* Whistler Drive, Castleford, W Yorks, WF10 5HX
*Activities:* Manufacture of plastic packing goods
*Parent:* Shaman Investments Limited
*Officers:* Marc Anthony Pickles, Secretary; Marc Anthony Pickles [1984] Director; Michael Pickles [1959] Director/Accountant; Julie Helen Walker [1956] Sales Director UK

**Recruitex Limited**
*Incorporated:* 29 July 2010 *Employees:* 2,383
*Net Worth:* £456,576 *Total Assets:* £9,611,688
*Registered Office:* 8 Leodis Court, David Street, Leeds, LS11 5JJ
*Activities:* Activities of head offices
*Major Shareholder:* Andrew Skorupka
*Officers:* Andrew Skorupka, Secretary; Andrew Godfrey [1962] Director; Andrew George Skorupka [1958] Director

**Red Circle Investments Limited**
*Incorporated:* 16 September 2015 *Employees:* 184
*Net Worth:* £287,965 *Total Assets:* £9,715,563
*Registered Office:* Mazars House, Gelderd Road, Gildersome, Leeds, LS27 7JN
*Activities:* Activities of other holding companies n.e.c.
*Major Shareholder:* Rachel Turner
*Officers:* Iain Urquhart McKeand [1963] Director

**Red Embedded Consulting Limited**
*Incorporated:* 3 September 2008 *Employees:* 53
*Net Worth:* £7,041,856 *Total Assets:* £8,682,779
*Registered Office:* The Wave, 1 View Croft Road, Shipley, W Yorks, BD17 7DU
*Activities:* Information technology consultancy activities
*Parent:* Red Embedded Holdings Limited
*Officers:* Dr Stuart James Griffin [1971] Director/Engineer; William Trevredyn Hoath [1960] Director/Chartered Engineer; Darren James Longhorn [1966] Director/Engineer; Shane McCarthy [1973] Director [Irish]; Rahul Mehra [1970] Director/Engineer; Andrew Douglas Stewart [1965] Director/Engineer; David Taylor [1963] Director/Engineer

**Red Hall (Bury) Limited**
*Incorporated:* 25 August 2010
*Net Worth Deficit:* £1,194,506 *Total Assets:* £4,426,807
*Registered Office:* c/o Abbey House Hotel, Abbey Road, Barrow in Furness, Cumbria, LA13 0PA
*Activities:* Hotels and similar accommodation
*Officers:* Brian Gerard Conroy [1971] Director; Neil Hopkins-Coman [1962] Director/Chartered Accountant; Timothy Anthony Kilroe [1964] Director [Irish]

**Red Kite Learning Trust**
*Incorporated:* 9 February 2011 *Employees:* 608
*Previous:* Harrogate Grammar School Academy Trust
*Net Worth:* £36,043,000 *Total Assets:* £45,551,000
*Registered Office:* Harrogate Grammar School, Arthurs Avenue, Harrogate, N Yorks, HG2 0DZ
*Activities:* Primary education
*Officers:* Stephen George Howell, Secretary; Teresa Mary Brooke [1948] Director/Retired; Paul Christopher Brian Cotton [1968] Director/Solicitor; David Stuart Hurcomb [1964] Director/Chief Executive; James Joseph McHugh [1952] Director/School Improvement Partner; Margaret Moyles [1944] Director/Education Consultant; Kevin Paynes [1963] Director/School Improvement Adviser; Richard Edward Sheriff [1964] Director/Headteacher; Jayne Anne Sorrell [1969] Director/Driving Instructor; Dr Patricia Anne Stowell [1955] Director/Medical Practitioner; Christopher Thomas Tulley [1961] Director/Solicitor

**Red Roofs Nursery Limited**
*Incorporated:* 30 January 2003 *Employees:* 42
*Net Worth:* £1,816,735 *Total Assets:* £3,179,791
*Registered Office:* Northmoor Lane, Cottingham, E Yorks, HU16 4JN
*Activities:* Growing of vegetables and melons, roots and tubers
*Shareholders:* Jannan Durnford; Jean Mary Durnford; Christopher John Durnford
*Officers:* Jean Mary Durnford, Secretary/Horticulturist; Christopher John Durnford [1964] Director/Horticulturist; Jean Mary Durnford [1938] Director/Horticulturist

**Redbrick Yorkshire Limited**
*Incorporated:* 1 May 2007 *Employees:* 24
*Previous:* Hit and Miss Limited
*Net Worth:* £208,098 *Total Assets:* £6,879,325
*Registered Office:* Redbrick Mill, 218 Bradford Road, Batley, W Yorks, WF17 6JF
*Activities:* Retail of furniture, lighting, and similar (not musical instruments or scores) in specialised store
*Major Shareholder:* Sara Ann Battye
*Officers:* Alastair Charles Bailey [1967] Director; Joseph Battye [1986] Director; Sara Ann Battye [1950] Director

**Redcentric PLC**
*Incorporated:* 11 February 2013 *Employees:* 501
*Net Worth:* £77,922,000 *Total Assets:* £135,599,008
*Registered Office:* Central House, Beckwith Knowle, Harrogate, N Yorks, HG3 1UG
*Activities:* Activities of head offices
*Officers:* Harneet Jagpal, Secretary; Peter James Brotherton [1967] Director/Chartered Accountant; Christopher Cole [1946] Director; Jonathan Kempster [1963] Director/Accountant; Christian Alexander Rigg [1974] Director; Stephen William Vaughan [1960] Director

**Redcentric Solutions Limited**
*Incorporated:* 7 December 2012 *Employees:* 362
*Net Worth:* £69,091,000 *Total Assets:* £127,581,000
*Registered Office:* Central House, Beckwith Knowle, Harrogate, N Yorks, HG3 1UG
*Activities:* Information technology consultancy activities
*Parent:* Redcentric PLC
*Officers:* Harneet Jagpal, Secretary; Peter James Brotherton [1967] Director/Chartered Accountant

**Redfern Developments and Investments Limited**
*Incorporated:* 14 July 1994
*Net Worth:* £3,424,641 *Total Assets:* £3,570,028
*Registered Office:* 31 St Saviourgate, York, YO1 8NQ
*Activities:* Development of building projects
*Major Shareholder:* Margaret Redfern
*Officers:* Margaret Redfern, Secretary; Margaret Redfern [1948] Director; Ralph Edmund Redfern [1980] Director/Agent Assistant

**Redhall Group PLC**
*Incorporated:* 31 March 1932 *Employees:* 389
*Net Worth:* £29,968,000 *Total Assets:* £41,298,000
*Registered Office:* Unit 3 Calder Close, Wakefield, W Yorks, WF4 3BA
*Activities:* Manufacture of other fabricated metal products n.e.c.
*Officers:* Simon Philip Comer, Secretary; James Dominic Brooke [1971] Director/Fund Manager; Simon Philip Comer [1972] Director; Martyn John Everett [1958] Director; Russell David Haworth [1955] Director; Jonathan Mark Oatley [1968] Director

**Redhall Jex Limited**
*Incorporated:* 4 December 1973 *Employees:* 88
*Net Worth:* £1,423,000 *Total Assets:* £3,230,000
*Registered Office:* Unit 3 Calder Close, Wakefield, W Yorks, WF4 3BA
*Activities:* Manufacture of other fabricated metal products n.e.c.
*Parent:* Redhall Group PLC
*Officers:* Simon Philip Comer, Secretary; Simon Philip Comer [1972] Director; Russell David Haworth [1955] Director

**Redhall Marine Limited**
*Incorporated:* 3 February 1987
*Net Worth:* £5,018,000 *Total Assets:* £5,428,000
*Registered Office:* Unit 3 Calder Close, Wakefield, W Yorks, WF4 3BA
*Activities:* Other specialised construction activities n.e.c.
*Parent:* Redhall Nuclear Limited
*Officers:* Simon Philip Comer, Secretary; Simon Philip Comer [1972] Director; Russell David Haworth [1955] Director

**Redhall Networks Limited**
*Incorporated:* 1 July 1996 *Employees:* 63
*Net Worth:* £3,088,000 *Total Assets:* £4,131,000
*Registered Office:* Unit 3 Calder Close, Wakefield, W Yorks, WF4 3BA
*Activities:* Other business support service activities n.e.c.
*Parent:* Redhall Group PLC
*Officers:* Simon Philip Comer, Secretary; Simon Philip Comer [1972] Director; Russell David Haworth [1955] Director; Gavin James Rabbitt [1964] Managing Director

**Redhead Freight Limited**
*Incorporated:* 3 March 1978 *Employees:* 367
*Net Worth:* £4,499,578 *Total Assets:* £21,135,844
*Registered Office:* Freightspeed House, Woodroyd Industrial Estate, Dealburn Road, Low Moor, Bradford, BD12 0RG
*Activities:* Freight transport by road
*Officers:* Keith Michael Shackleton, Secretary; Philip Andrew Baxter [1967] Operations Director; Robert Michael Cockroft [1961] Sales Director; Mark Spencer Cosgrove [1966] Irish Region Director; Paul Anthony Suggitt [1961] Managing Director

**Redhead Holdings Limited**
*Incorporated:* 26 September 2000
*Net Worth:* £1,233,938 *Total Assets:* £10,350,670
*Registered Office:* Freightspeed House, Woodroyd Industrial Estate, Dealburn Road, Low Moor, Bradford, BD12 0RG
*Activities:* Other letting and operating of own or leased real estate
*Parent:* Schenker Aktiengesellschaft
*Officers:* Keith Michael Shackleton, Secretary; Philip Andrew Baxter [1967] Operations Director; Mark Spencer Cosgrove [1966] Irish Region Director; Paul Anthony Suggitt [1961] Managing Director

**Redhouse Holdings Limited**
*Incorporated:* 4 January 2000
*Net Worth:* £292,672 *Total Assets:* £4,059,024
*Registered Office:* 1st Floor, Unit 16 Manor Court Business Park, Scarborough, N Yorks, YO11 3TU
*Activities:* Activities of other holding companies n.e.c.
*Shareholders:* Cromwell Development Holdings UK Limited; Clugston Estates Limited
*Officers:* Nicholas John Child [1958] Director; Andrew Paul Richardson [1967] Director/Chartered Surveyor; Robert John Vickers [1956] Director

**Redhouse Projects Limited**
*Incorporated:* 5 July 1994
*Net Worth:* £341,292 *Total Assets:* £4,093,192
*Registered Office:* 1st Floor, Unit 16 Manor Court Business Park, Scarborough, N Yorks, YO11 3TU
*Activities:* Development of building projects
*Parent:* Redhouse Holdings Limited
*Officers:* Nicholas John Child [1958] Director; Andrew Paul Richardson [1967] Director/Chartered Surveyor; Robert John Vickers [1956] Director

**Redline Holdings Limited**
*Incorporated:* 16 October 2015 *Employees:* 28
*Net Worth:* £1,391,900 *Total Assets:* £12,463,215
*Registered Office:* Grimbald Crag Road, St James Business Park, Knaresborough, N Yorks, HG5 8PY
*Activities:* Activities of head offices
*Shareholders:* Robert Lee Milner; John Robert Downs Graeme
*Officers:* John Robert Downs Graeme [1967] Director; Robert Lee Milner [1977] Director

**Redline Specialist Cars Limited**
*Incorporated:* 28 February 1997 *Employees:* 28
*Previous:* Red Line Racing Ltd
*Net Worth:* £1,391,900 *Total Assets:* £12,463,215
*Registered Office:* Grimbald Crag Close, St James Business Park, Knaresborough, N Yorks, HG5 8PY
*Activities:* Sale of used cars and light motor vehicles
*Parent:* Redline Holdings Limited
*Officers:* John Robert Downs Graeme, Secretary/Motor Dealer; John Robert Downs Graeme [1967] Director/Motor Dealer; Robert Lee Milner [1977] Director/Motor Dealer

**Redline Worldwide Limited**
*Incorporated:* 26 March 2015 *Employees:* 105
*Net Worth:* £887,847 *Total Assets:* £4,745,741
*Registered Office:* National Security Training Centre, First Avenue, Robin Hood Airport, Doncaster, S Yorks, DN9 3RH
*Activities:* Activities of other holding companies n.e.c.
*Officers:* Sir Gary Robert Coward [1955] Director; Rowan Grobler [1979] Director; Craig Allen Harrison [1968] Director; Paul Mason [1968] Director; Paul Robert Read [1961] Director; Mark Simon Rutherford [1966] Director; Sean Ronald Taylor [1967] Director; James Michael Termini [1967] Director

**Redmayne Capital Limited**
*Incorporated:* 1 September 2000 *Employees:* 5
*Net Worth:* £6,534,000 *Total Assets:* £6,703,000
*Registered Office:* 9 Bond Court, Leeds, LS1 2JZ
*Activities:* Activities of financial services holding companies
*Officers:* Michael Edward John Wheeler, Secretary; Stuart William Davis [1967] Director/Partner; David Loudon [1960] Director/Stockbroker; Keith Loudon [1933] Director/Stockbroker; Kim Louise Rebecchi [1966] Director; Michael Edward John Wheeler [1959] Director/Finance Partner

**Redmayne-Bentley LLP**
*Incorporated:* 26 March 2009 *Employees:* 240
*Net Worth:* £13,695,000 *Total Assets:* £156,738,624
*Registered Office:* 9 Bond Court, Leeds, LS1 2JZ
*Officers:* Stuart William Davis [1967] Member; David Loudon [1960] Member; Keith Loudon [1933] Member; Michael Edward John Wheeler [1959] Member; Nicholas James Bettison [1972] LLP Member; Mark Benjamin Decker [1960] LLP Member; Damien John Duffield [1975] LLP Member

**Redmed Limited**
*Incorporated:* 2 August 2000 *Employees:* 87
*Net Worth:* £1,110,353 *Total Assets:* £3,285,859
*Registered Office:* 1 Butternab Ridge, Huddersfield, W Yorks, HD4 7AW
*Activities:* Public houses and bars
*Major Shareholder:* John James O'Donoghue
*Officers:* John James O'Donoghue, Secretary/Retail Consultant; Peter Jack Marks [1960] Director/Business Consultant; John James O'Donoghue [1960] Director/Retail Consultant

**Redruth Holdings 2 Limited**
*Incorporated:* 13 March 2017 *Employees:* 3
*Net Worth:* £3,196,323 *Total Assets:* £88,805,920
*Registered Office:* 1 Park Row, Leeds, LS1 5AB
*Activities:* Other business support service activities n.e.c.
*Parent:* Dalmore Capital 19 GP Limited
*Officers:* Jennifer McKay, Secretary; John McDonagh [1969] Director; Alistair Graham Ray [1974] Director

**Redruth Holdings Limited**
*Incorporated:* 7 March 2016
*Net Worth:* £6,907,940 *Total Assets:* £191,944,320
*Registered Office:* 1 Park Row, Leeds, LS1 5AB
*Activities:* Other business support service activities n.e.c.
*Parent:* Dalmore Capital 15 GP Limited
*Officers:* Jennifer McKay, Secretary; John McDonagh [1969] Director; Alistair Graham Ray [1974] Director

**Redstart Renewables Limited**
*Incorporated:* 13 March 2014
*Net Worth:* £3,619,046 *Total Assets:* £3,842,365
*Registered Office:* Canal Head North, Kendal, Cumbria, LA9 7BZ
*Activities:* Production of electricity
*Parent:* GHI Holdings Limited
*Officers:* Charles William Nepean Crewdson [1964] Director; Carl Peter Crompton [1973] Director

**Reece Safety Products Ltd**
*Incorporated:* 12 February 2002 *Employees:* 2
*Net Worth:* £4,728,306 *Total Assets:* £5,610,113
*Registered Office:* Unit B9, Lowfields Close, Lowfields Business Park, Elland, W Yorks, HX5 9DX
*Activities:* Other retail sale not in stores, stalls or markets
*Major Shareholder:* Robin Neil Womersley
*Officers:* Andrew John Graham [1964] Director; Robin Neil Womersley [1971] Director

**Reed Boardall Cold Storage Limited**
*Incorporated:* 23 November 1970 *Employees:* 368
*Net Worth:* £35,939,760 *Total Assets:* £45,186,116
*Registered Office:* Bar Lane, Roecliffe, Boroughbridge, N Yorks, YO51 9NN
*Activities:* Freight transport by road
*Parent:* Reed Boardall Holdings Limited
*Officers:* Marcus Keith Boardall, Secretary/Chartered Accountant; Andrew Lyndon Baldwin [1970] Director/Cold Store Manager; Keith Boardall [1934] Director/Chartered Accountant; Marcus Keith Boardall [1962] Director/Chartered Accountant; Graeme Neil Richardson [1968] Director; Sarah Karen Roberts [1982] Finance Director

**The Reed Boardall Group Limited**
*Incorporated:* 20 February 2008 *Employees:* 773
*Net Worth:* £60,184,932 *Total Assets:* £68,733,088
*Registered Office:* Bar Lane, Roecliffe, Boroughbridge, N Yorks, YO51 9NN
*Activities:* Activities of other holding companies n.e.c.
*Shareholders:* Clive Patrick Reed; John Howard Reed; Keith Boardall
*Officers:* Marcus Keith Boardall, Secretary/Accountant; Keith Boardall [1934] Director/Chartered Accountant; Marcus Keith Boardall [1962] Finance Director

**Reed Boardall Transport Limited**
*Incorporated:* 20 March 1985 *Employees:* 374
*Net Worth:* £6,821,150 *Total Assets:* £9,232,017
*Registered Office:* Bar Lane, Roecliffe, Boroughbridge, N Yorks, YO5 9NN
*Activities:* Freight transport by road
*Parent:* Reed Boardall Transport Holdings Limited
*Officers:* Marcus Keith Boardall, Secretary/Chartered Accountant; Andrew Lyndon Baldwin [1970] Director; Keith Boardall [1934] Director; Marcus Keith Boardall [1962] Director/Chartered Accountant; Graeme Neil Richardson [1968] Managing Director; Sarah Karen Roberts [1982] Finance Director

**The Reed Group Ltd**
*Incorporated:* 2 March 2016 *Employees:* 55
*Net Worth:* £1,332,941 *Total Assets:* £5,113,227
*Registered Office:* 43 Coniscliffe Road, Darlington, Co Durham, DL3 7EH
*Activities:* Activities of other holding companies n.e.c.
*Major Shareholder:* Christopher Stephen Reed
*Officers:* Christopher Stephen Reed [1984] Director

**Reeds Rains Limited**
*Incorporated:* 13 December 1990 *Employees:* 918
*Net Worth:* £7,353,000 *Total Assets:* £17,147,000
*Registered Office:* 2nd Floor, Gateway, 2 Holgate Park Drive, York, YO26 4GB
*Activities:* Real estate agencies
*Parent:* LSL Property Services PLC
*Officers:* Sapna Bedi FitzGenerald, Secretary/Solicitor; Oliver Thomas Blake [1971] Managing Director; Helen Elizabeth Buck [1960] Director; Adam Robert Castleton [1964] Director; Paul Hardy [1976] Director; Brian Parker [1954] Director

**Reflecting Roadstuds Limited**
*Incorporated:* 15 March 1935 *Employees:* 7
*Net Worth:* £3,565,697 *Total Assets:* £3,648,784
*Registered Office:* 1 Mill Lane, Boothtown, Halifax, W Yorks, HX3 6TR
*Activities:* Manufacture of other transport equipment n.e.c.
*Officers:* Michael Alan Steele, Secretary/Solicitor; Richard Joseph Brezinski [1962] Director/Motor Engineer; William Martin Dunn [1958] Director/General Manager; Joseph Philip Horton [1967] Director/Office Manager; Robert Andrew Saunderson [1961] Director/Despatch Manager; Jack Stephen Shaw-Dunn [1987] Director/Financial Controller; James Richard Smith [1978] Director; Michael Alan Steele [1947] Director/Retired Solicitor; Robin Shaw Steele [1979] Director/Local Government Officer

**Refood UK Limited**
*Incorporated:* 10 April 2008 *Employees:* 171
*Net Worth:* £5,395,874 *Total Assets:* £67,601,232
*Registered Office:* Ings Road, Bentley, Doncaster, S Yorks, DN5 9TL
*Activities:* Production of electricity
*Parent:* Saria Limited
*Officers:* Phillip Antony Simpson [1966] Director; Andrew Richard Smith [1962] Director/Commercial Manager; Franz-Bernhard Thier [1965] Director [German]

**Refreshment Systems Limited**
*Incorporated:* 20 June 1984 *Employees:* 111
*Net Worth:* £2,327,326 *Total Assets:* £4,521,722
*Registered Office:* 31 Bolling Road, Bradford, W Yorks, BD4 7HN
*Activities:* Other food services
*Shareholders:* Robert Alistair Balmforth; Moira Vivian Balmforth
*Officers:* Noreen Balmforth, Secretary; Moira Vivian Balmforth [1963] Director/Marketing; Noreen Balmforth [1932] Director/Housewife; Robert Alistair Balmforth [1964] Director; William Duncan Balmforth [1939] Director; Steve May [1977] Commercial Director

**Regal Food Products Group PLC**
*Incorporated:* 12 October 2009 *Employees:* 23
*Net Worth:* £2,025,262 *Total Assets:* £6,437,918
*Registered Office:* Regal House, Wallis Street, Bradford, W Yorks, BD8 9RR
*Activities:* Wholesale of other food, including fish, crustaceans and molluscs
*Parent:* RFPG Holdings Limited
*Officers:* Mohammed Younis, Secretary; Mohammed Ali Chaudhry [1974] Director; Absar Younis [1994] Director; Mohammed Younis [1971] Director; Waqar Younis [1990] Director

**Regenco (Winchburgh) Limited**
*Incorporated:* 16 October 2007
*Net Worth:* £214 *Total Assets:* £41,884,600
*Registered Office:* 1 Park Row, Leeds, LS1 5AB
*Activities:* Development of building projects
*Parent:* Regenco Properties LLP
*Officers:* Kirsty Elizabeth Murray, Secretary; Paul Richmond Davidson [1965] Director/Solicitor; James Cairns McMahon [1949] Director

**Regenco Borrower Limited**
*Incorporated:* 3 March 2008
*Net Worth:* £2,382,381 *Total Assets:* £3,190,719
*Registered Office:* 1 Park Row, Leeds, LS1 5AB
*Activities:* Development of building projects
*Parent:* Regenco Properties LLP
*Officers:* Kirsty Elizabeth Murray, Secretary; Paul Richmond Davidson [1965] Director/Solicitor; James Cairns McMahon [1949] Director

**Regenco Properties LLP**
*Incorporated:* 25 March 2008
*Net Worth:* £7,375,900 *Total Assets:* £13,292,072
*Registered Office:* 1 Park Row, Leeds, LS1 5AB

**Regent House Estates Limited**
*Incorporated:* 22 May 1997 *Employees:* 2
*Net Worth:* £1,475,772 *Total Assets:* £3,389,993
*Registered Office:* c/o Roach Bros Curers Limited, Havelock Street, Hessle Road, Hull, HU3 4JH
*Activities:* Other letting and operating of own or leased real estate
*Shareholders:* Adrian Paul Roach; Robert Leslie Roach
*Officers:* Adrian Paul Roach, Secretary/Director; Adrian Paul Roach [1955] Director; Robert Leslie Roach [1957] Director

**Regroup (UK) Limited**
*Incorporated:* 31 May 2002 *Employees:* 43
*Net Worth:* £5,306,368 *Total Assets:* £8,171,819
*Registered Office:* Clipper House, Air Street, Hull, HU5 1RR
*Activities:* Activities of head offices
*Major Shareholder:* John Paul Dixon Waine
*Officers:* Philip Stephen Hall [1960] Director; Anthony George Hurter [1938] Director [South African]; Gregg Anthony Hurter [1962] Director [South African]; John Paul Dixon Waine [1962] Director

**Reliance Garage (Ryedale) Limited**
*Incorporated:* 13 May 1977 *Employees:* 82
*Net Worth:* £4,424,541 *Total Assets:* £12,197,267
*Registered Office:* Medina House, 2 Station Avenue, Bridlington, E Yorks, YO16 4LZ
*Activities:* Sale of new cars and light motor vehicles
*Shareholder:* Raymond Chapman
*Officers:* Felicity Senga Chapman, Secretary; Duncan Raymond Chapman [1971] Director/General Manager; Felicity Senga Chapman [1946] Director; Raymond Chapman [1944] Director

**Reliance Precision Limited**
*Incorporated:* 23 November 1920 *Employees:* 241
*Net Worth:* £17,384,144 *Total Assets:* £20,619,516
*Registered Office:* Rowley Mills, Penistone Road, Lepton, Huddersfield, W Yorks, HD8 0LE
*Activities:* Machining
*Parent:* Reliance RG Limited
*Officers:* Charlotte Mary Brandes [1972] Director/Company Secretary; Ian Laidler [1960] Director; Mark Harry Papworth [1965] Non-Executive Director; Daniel John William Pedley [1966] Non-Executive Director; James David Selka [1966] Director; Ian David Walter [1972] Director/Chartered Accountant; Andrew Edward Blayney Wright [1963] Business Director

**Reliance RG Limited**
*Incorporated:* 21 December 2009 *Employees:* 243
*Net Worth:* £19,515,524 *Total Assets:* £22,761,320
*Registered Office:* Rowley Mills, Penistone Road, Lepton, Huddersfield, W Yorks, HD8 0LE
*Activities:* Activities of production holding companies
*Major Shareholder:* Jennifer Mary Selka
*Officers:* Charlotte Mary Brandes [1972] Director/Engineering Administration; Helen Farmiloe [1962] Director/Executive Coach; Emma Rose Goldsztajn [1964] Director/Housewife; James David Selka [1966] Director/Engineer; William John Selka [1960] Director/Engineer

**Rema Tip Top Automotive UK Limited**
*Incorporated:* 4 April 1963 *Employees:* 47
*Net Worth:* £7,171,033 *Total Assets:* £14,259,143
*Registered Office:* Westland Square, Leeds, LS11 5XS
*Activities:* Wholesale trade of motor vehicle parts and accessories
*Parent:* Rema Tip Top Holdings UK Limited
*Officers:* Garry Mangham, Secretary; Mark Brian Insley [1959] Managing Director; Clifford Bryn Jones [1947] Managing Director; Annerose Schenk [1963] Director/Management of Financial Department [German]

**Rema Tip Top Holdings UK Limited**
*Incorporated:* 17 November 2008 *Employees:* 243
*Net Worth:* £22,705,612 *Total Assets:* £41,746,372
*Registered Office:* Rema Tip Top UK Limited, Westland Square, Leeds, LS11 5XS
*Activities:* Activities of other holding companies n.e.c.
*Officers:* Garry Mangham, Secretary; Mark Brian Insley [1959] Director; Garry Mangham [1963] Finance Director

**Rema Tip Top Industry UK Limited**
*Incorporated:* 9 July 1974 *Employees:* 107
*Net Worth:* £3,937,077 *Total Assets:* £6,395,498
*Registered Office:* West Land Square, Leeds, LS11 5XS
*Activities:* Repair of other equipment
*Parent:* Rema Tip Top Holdings UK Ltd
*Officers:* Garry Mangham, Secretary; Mark Brian Insley [1959] Director; Andrew Paul West [1965] Director

**Renew Holdings PLC.**
*Incorporated:* 24 February 1960 *Employees:* 2,759
*Net Worth:* £75,471,000 *Total Assets:* £284,444,000
*Registered Office:* 3175 Century Way, Thorpe Park, Leeds, LS15 8ZB
*Activities:* Activities of head offices
*Officers:* Sean Christopher Wyndham-Quin, Secretary; David Allen Brown [1960] Director; Shatish Damodar Dasani [1962] Director; David Malcolm Forbes [1960] Director; Andries Petrus Liebenberg [1967] Director [South African]; Paul Scott [1964] Director/Engineer; Sean Christopher Wyndham-Quin [1980] Director

**Renewable Heat Generation Limited**
*Incorporated:* 12 December 2012 *Employees:* 1
*Net Worth:* £354,995 *Total Assets:* £5,557,232
*Registered Office:* Parkside House, 17 East Parade, Harrogate, N Yorks, HG1 5LF
*Activities:* Plumbing, heat and air-conditioning installation
*Shareholders:* Mark Gerald Roberts; Robert Nicholas Jason Schofield
*Officers:* Janet Jean Roberts [1955] Director; Mark Generald Roberts [1962] Director; Pamela Ruth Schofield [1964] Director; Robert Nicholas Jason Schofield [1962] Director

**Keith Rennie Machinery Limited**
*Incorporated:* 29 August 1986 *Employees:* 11
*Net Worth:* £3,801,579 *Total Assets:* £4,160,979
*Registered Office:* Claypit Lane, Bar Lane, Roecliffe, York, YO51 9LS
*Activities:* Wholesale of agricultural machinery, equipment and supplies
*Major Shareholder:* Keith Anthony Rennie
*Officers:* Marilyn Anne Rennie, Secretary; Keith Anthony Rennie [1953] Director; Marilyn Anne Rennie [1952] Director

**Renovotec Investments Limited**
*Incorporated:* 29 January 2013 *Employees:* 4
*Net Worth:* £2,800,699 *Total Assets:* £4,975,395
*Registered Office:* Whitwood Lodge, Whitwood Lane, Castleford, W Yorks, WF10 5QD
*Activities:* Activities of other holding companies n.e.c.
*Officers:* Lance Anthony Bennett [1961] Director; Paula Anne Bennett [1962] Director; Lucy Gilliard [1971] Director; Richard James Gilliard [1972] Director

**Renovotec Ltd**
*Incorporated:* 28 April 1998 *Employees:* 33
*Net Worth:* £1,764,666 *Total Assets:* £5,164,731
*Registered Office:* Whitwood Lodge, Whitwood Lane, Whitwood, Wakefield, W Yorks, WF10 5QD
*Activities:* Other information technology service activities
*Parent:* Renovotec Investments Limited
*Officers:* Lance Anthony Bennett [1961] Director; Paula Anne Bennett [1962] Director; Lucy Gilliard [1971] Director; Richard James Gilliard [1972] Director

**Repchoice Limited**
*Incorporated:* 21 November 1985 *Employees:* 19
*Net Worth:* £5,498,848 *Total Assets:* £6,429,127
*Registered Office:* Unit 1 Chappell Drive, Doncaster, S Yorks, DN1 2RF
*Activities:* Non-specialised wholesale trade
*Major Shareholder:* Munjit Singh
*Officers:* Munjit Singh, Secretary; Satnam Kaur [1959] Director; Munjit Singh [1960] Director

**Replan (U.K.) Limited**
*Incorporated:* 19 January 1983 *Employees:* 39
*Net Worth:* £201,005 *Total Assets:* £3,188,120
*Registered Office:* New Mill Road, Honley, Huddersfield, W Yorks, HD9 6QA
*Activities:* Other specialised construction activities n.e.c.
*Major Shareholder:* Felix Timothy Eaton
*Officers:* Martin James Fleming, Secretary; Felix Timothy Eaton [1957] Director

**Replay Associates Limited**
*Incorporated:* 14 July 2004 *Employees:* 5
*Net Worth:* £7,625,695 *Total Assets:* £20,093,328
*Registered Office:* Old Vicarage, Spennithorne, Leyburn, N Yorks, DL8 5PR
*Activities:* Other letting and operating of own or leased real estate
*Officers:* Pamela Leathley, Secretary; Gordon Ian Leathley [1964] Director; Ian Leathley [1943] Director; John Winston Leathley [1969] Director; Kenneth Andrew Leathley [1967] Director; Pamela Leathley [1943] Director

**Res-Q Outsourcing Solutions Limited**
*Incorporated:* 18 December 2014 *Employees:* 615
*Net Worth Deficit:* £351,873 *Total Assets:* £10,314,955
*Registered Office:* Criterion House, 75-81 George Street, Hull, HU1 3BA
*Activities:* Activities of call centres
*Officers:* Barry Alan Aling [1950] Director; Simon William Lunt [1952] Director/Solicitor; Gillian Clare Marchbank [1972] Operations Director; Nicholas Lee Marshall [1970] Managing Director; Ian Maxwell-Scott [1945] Director/Investment Banker

**Resdev Limited**
*Incorporated:* 4 October 1978 *Employees:* 47
*Net Worth:* £1,632,149 *Total Assets:* £4,292,717
*Registered Office:* Pumaflor House, Ainleys Industrial Estate, Elland, W Yorks, HX5 9JP
*Activities:* Other manufacturing n.e.c.
*Shareholder:* John Clifford Wright
*Officers:* Graham Steven Parratt, Secretary; David Andrew Greenwood [1966] Operations Director; Graham Steven Parratt [1955] Director/Accountant; Mark David Spindley [1961] Commercial Director; Joan Shirley Wright [1944] Director/Businesswoman; John Clifford Wright [1942] Director; Nicholas Michael Wright [1966] Managing Director

**Residue Limited**
*Incorporated:* 8 May 2013
*Net Worth:* £676,586 *Total Assets:* £3,844,579
*Registered Office:* Highfield Grange, Highfield, Bubwith, Selby, N Yorks, YO8 6DP
*Activities:* Motion picture production activities
*Parent:* Matador Pictures Limited
*Officers:* Charlotte Margaret Walls Hardiman [1981] Director

**Resource Management Solutions (North East) Ltd**
*Incorporated:* 9 November 2000 *Employees:* 35
*Net Worth:* £528,319 *Total Assets:* £3,517,428
*Registered Office:* 3 Victoria Road, Darlington, Co Durham, DL1 5SJ
*Activities:* Other activities of employment placement agencies
*Officers:* Leon Thomas Butt, Secretary; Carole Martin [1962] Director/Recruitment

**Responsible Life Limited**
*Incorporated:* 18 February 2010 *Employees:* 42
*Net Worth:* £2,046,605 *Total Assets:* £4,257,952
*Registered Office:* Unit 8 ABC Killinghall Stone Quarry, Ripon Road, Killinghall, Harrogate, N Yorks, HG3 2BA
*Activities:* Activities auxiliary to financial intermediation n.e.c.
*Shareholders:* Paul Edward Starkey; Steven Thomas Wilkie
*Officers:* Paul Starkey, Secretary; Paul Edward Starkey [1956] Director/Entrepreneur; Steven Thomas Wilkie [1986] Director/Entrepreneur

**Retford Wallcoverings Limited**
*Incorporated:* 17 March 1999 *Employees:* 29
*Net Worth:* £2,442,547 *Total Assets:* £4,384,442
*Registered Office:* 28 Corringham Road Industrial Estate, Gainsborough, Lincs, DN21 1QB
*Activities:* Manufacture of paper and paperboard
*Parent:* Erfurt UK Limited
*Officers:* Nicola Campion, Secretary; Christian Hasenclever [1969] Director [German]; Andrew John Simpson [1960] Director/Operations Manager

**The Retreat York**
*Incorporated:* 20 November 2001 *Employees:* 341
*Net Worth:* £43,623,488 *Total Assets:* £44,551,456
*Registered Office:* Heslington Road, York, YO10 5BN
*Activities:* Hospital activities
*Officers:* Ian Holborn, Secretary; Sallie Elizabeth Ashe [1952] Director/Psychotherapist; Jennifer Claire Barraclough [1945] Director/Retired; James Brian Eddington [1958] Director/Retired; Martin Ford [1960] Director; Robert Anthony Griffiths [1956] Director/Management Consultant; Dr John Collingwood Miles [1945] Director/Retired; David John Robson [1944] Director; Michael Gerrard Wash [1954] Director/Management Consultant

**Retsco Limited**
*Incorporated:* 28 January 2003 *Employees:* 3
*Net Worth:* £2,123,158 *Total Assets:* £4,458,163
*Registered Office:* 4 Cheltenham Way, Cleethorpes, N E Lincs, DN35 0UG
*Activities:* Other letting and operating of own or leased real estate
*Shareholders:* Matthew Nathan Ramsden; John Joseph Ramsden
*Officers:* John Joseph Ramsden, Secretary/Developer; Daniel Paul Ramsden [1970] Director/Builder; John Joseph Ramsden [1965] Director/Developer; Matthew Nathan Ramsden [1967] Director/Builder

**Reuse Glass UK Limited**
*Incorporated:* 9 June 1998 *Employees:* 200
*Net Worth:* £13,867,562 *Total Assets:* £49,851,392
*Registered Office:* 49 Lidgate Crescent, Langthwaite Business Park, South Kirkby, Pontefract, W Yorks, WF9 3NR
*Activities:* Treatment and disposal of non-hazardous waste
*Major Shareholder:* Anthony Charles Johnston
*Officers:* Michael James Harris, Secretary; Andrew Stuart, Secretary/Director [Australian]; Mark Henry Richard Iain Wilson, Secretary; Anthony Charles Johnston [1966] Director [Australian]; Andrew John Burleigh Stuart [1967] Director [Australian]

**Rever Offshore International Limited**
*Incorporated:* 12 March 2010 *Employees:* 282
*Previous:* Bibby Offshore Holdings Limited
*Net Worth Deficit:* £122,866,000 *Total Assets:* £95,533,000
*Registered Office:* 1 Park Row, Leeds, LS1 5AB
*Activities:* Support activities for petroleum and natural gas mining
*Officers:* Mark John Bessell [1964] Director; Neale John Stewart [1963] Director

**Rever Offshore North Star Limited**
*Incorporated:* 6 March 2012 *Employees:* 2
*Previous:* Bibby North Star Limited
*Net Worth:* £1,198,264 *Total Assets:* £33,201,140
*Registered Office:* 1 Park Row, Leeds, LS1 5AB
*Activities:* Sea and coastal freight water transport
*Parent:* Rever Offshore UK Limited
*Officers:* Mark John Bessell [1964] Director; Neale John Stewart [1963] Director

**Rever Offshore ROV Limited**
*Incorporated:* 2 September 2011
*Previous:* Bibby Remote Intervention Limited
*Net Worth Deficit:* £20,113,416 *Total Assets:* £11,184,796
*Registered Office:* 1 Park Row, Leeds, LS1 5AB
*Activities:* Support activities for petroleum and natural gas mining
*Parent:* Rever Offshore International Limited
*Officers:* Mark John Bessell [1964] Director; Neale John Stewart [1963] Director

**Rever Offshore UK Limited**
*Incorporated:* 30 July 2003 *Employees:* 253
*Previous:* Bibby Offshore Limited
*Net Worth Deficit:* £33,859,000 *Total Assets:* £26,505,000
*Registered Office:* 1 Park Row, Leeds, LS1 5AB
*Activities:* Support activities for petroleum and natural gas mining
*Parent:* Rever Offshore International Limited
*Officers:* Mark John Bessell [1964] Director; Nichola Etherson [1971] Director; David James Forsyth [1961] Director; Barry John MacLeod [1974] Director; Neale John Stewart [1963] Director; Graeme Wood [1963] Director

**Revis Transport Limited**
*Incorporated:* 16 October 1986 *Employees:* 63
*Net Worth:* £3,193,178 *Total Assets:* £6,257,121
*Registered Office:* Southfield Lane, Tockwith, York, YO26 7QP
*Activities:* Freight transport by road
*Shareholders:* John Henry Revis; John Steven Revis
*Officers:* John Henry Revis, Secretary; John Steven Revis [1979] Director; John Henry Revis [1952] Director/Haulage Contractor

**Reward Capital Limited**
*Incorporated:* 10 February 2015 *Employees:* 7
*Net Worth:* £2,013,000 *Total Assets:* £42,365,000
*Registered Office:* Central House, 47 St Pauls Street, Leeds, LS1 2TE
*Activities:* Other credit granting n.e.c.
*Parent:* Reward Finance Group Ltd
*Officers:* Daniel James Smith, Secretary; Thomas More Flannery [1960] Director; David Anthony Harrop [1970] Finance Director; David Alan Jones [1961] Director; Karen Louise Nordier [1967] Finance Director [South African]; Nicholas Stephen Smith [1975] Sales Director; Timothy Paul Stafford [1968] Risk Director; Gemma Louise Wright [1977] Director

**Reward Finance Group Limited**
*Incorporated:* 23 September 2010 *Employees:* 15
*Previous:* Reward Investments Limited
*Net Worth:* £4,456,000 *Total Assets:* £59,632,000
*Registered Office:* Central House, 47 St Pauls Street, Leeds, LS1 2TE
*Activities:* Activities of financial services holding companies
*Parent:* Reward Investments (No 2) Ltd
*Officers:* Daniel James Smith, Secretary; Thomas More Flannery [1960] Director; David Anthony Harrop [1970] Finance Director; David Alan Jones [1961] Director; Karen Louise Nordier [1967] Finance Director [South African]; Nicholas Stephen Smith [1975] Sales Director; Timothy Paul Stafford [1968] Risk Director; Gemma Louise Wright [1977] Director

**Reward Invoice Finance Limited**
*Incorporated:* 10 February 2015 *Employees:* 15
*Net Worth:* £567,000 *Total Assets:* £12,822,000
*Registered Office:* Central House, 47 St Pauls Street, Leeds, LS1 2TE
*Activities:* Factoring
*Parent:* Reward Finance Group Ltd
*Officers:* Daniel James Smith, Secretary; Thomas More Flannery [1960] Director; David Anthony Harrop [1970] Finance Director; David Alan Jones [1961] Director; Karen Louise Nordier [1967] Finance Director [South African]; Nicholas Stephen Smith [1975] Sales Director; Timothy Paul Stafford [1968] Risk Director; Gemma Louise Wright [1977] Director

**Reynolds 2000 Limited**
*Incorporated:* 9 November 1999 *Employees:* 46
*Net Worth:* £8,326,607 *Total Assets:* £11,799,712
*Registered Office:* Redcliff Court, Redcliff Road, Hessle, E Yorks, HU13 0EY
*Activities:* Construction of commercial buildings
*Major Shareholder:* Christopher Reynolds
*Officers:* Fiona Ruth Reynolds, Secretary; Christopher Robert Reynolds [1958] Director; Fiona Ruth Reynolds [1961] Director; Stephen James Reynolds [1987] Director/Development Manager

**C.R. Reynolds Limited**
*Incorporated:* 23 November 1983 *Employees:* 46
*Net Worth:* £1,111,280 *Total Assets:* £4,589,327
*Registered Office:* Redcliff Court, Redcliff Road, Hessle, E Yorks, HU13 0EY
*Activities:* Construction of roads and motorways
*Officers:* Fiona Ruth Reynolds, Secretary; Neil Ashley Crawford [1973] Director/Certified Accountant; Andrew Gaze [1968] Production Director; Christopher Robert Reynolds [1958] Director/Civil Engineer; Fiona Ruth Reynolds [1961] Director/Company Secretary

**RF Racing Limited**
*Incorporated:* 18 November 2002
*Net Worth:* £3,817,843 *Total Assets:* £6,120,565
*Registered Office:* 2 Belgrave Crescent, Scarborough, N Yorks, YO11 1UB
*Activities:* Activities of sport clubs
*Major Shareholder:* Richard Aidan Fahey
*Officers:* Richard Aidan Fahey [1966] Director/Racehorse Trainer

**RFPG Holdings Limited**
*Incorporated:* 20 February 2012 *Employees:* 17
*Net Worth:* £2,480,636 *Total Assets:* £7,350,758
*Registered Office:* Regal House, Wallis Street, Bradford, BD8 9RR
*Activities:* Activities of other holding companies n.e.c.
*Major Shareholder:* Mohammed Younis
*Officers:* Mohammed Ali Chaudhry [1974] Director; Habib Tariq [1968] Director; Mohammed Younis [1971] Director

**RFS (Ripon) Limited**
*Incorporated:* 5 January 2015 *Employees:* 189
*Net Worth:* £10,450,505 *Total Assets:* £26,941,930
*Registered Office:* Dallamires Lane, Ripon, N Yorks, HG4 1TT
*Activities:* Wholesale of agricultural machinery, equipment and supplies
*Parent:* Ripon Farm Services Limited
*Officers:* Geoffrey Brown [1945] Director; Paul Martin Brown [1975] Director; Stewart Alan Hymas [1970] Director

**Rhal Farms Limited**
*Incorporated:* 24 December 1976
*Net Worth:* £5,257,592 *Total Assets:* £6,331,266
*Registered Office:* Marderby Hall, Felixkirk, Thirsk, N Yorks, YO7 2DR
*Activities:* Other letting and operating of own or leased real estate
*Shareholders:* Robinson Hubert Bosomworth; Doreen Margaret Bosomworth
*Officers:* Robinson Hubert Bosomworth, Secretary; Doreen Margaret Bosomworth [1941] Director/Farmer; Robinson Hubert Bosomworth [1939] Director/Farmer; Trevor Robinson Bosomworth [1970] Director/Pig Enterprise Manager

**Rhino Enterprises Limited**
*Incorporated:* 17 October 1990 *Employees:* 8
*Net Worth:* £5,693,887 *Total Assets:* £11,006,632
*Registered Office:* Regent Buildings, Regent Street, Leeds, LS2 7QA
*Activities:* Other service activities n.e.c.
*Parent:* Rhino Enterprises Holdings Limited
*Officers:* Jack Schofield [1997] Director; James Schofield [1990] Director; Jonathan Marcus William Schofield [1955] Director; Mollie Schofield [1998] Director; Oliver Schofield [1993] Director; Pamela Ruth Schofield [1964] Director/Sales Representative; Robert Nicholas Jason Schofield [1962] Director

**Rhino Enterprises Properties Limited**
*Incorporated:* 23 November 2007 *Employees:* 2
*Net Worth:* £9,202,287 *Total Assets:* £10,246,801
*Registered Office:* Regent Buildings, Regent Street, Leeds, LS2 7QA
*Activities:* Renting and operating of Housing Association real estate
*Parent:* Rhino Enterprises Holdings Limited
*Officers:* Jason Schofield [1962] Director/Businessman; Jonathan Marcus William Schofield [1955] Director

**Rhinox Group Ltd**
*Incorporated:* 7 November 2013 *Employees:* 28
*Previous:* Southern Plant Spares Ltd
*Net Worth:* £935,023 *Total Assets:* £4,480,592
*Registered Office:* Small Wold Farm, North Newbald, E Yorks, YO43 4TW
*Activities:* Repair of machinery
*Major Shareholder:* Rachel Ann Record
*Officers:* Jodie Hooper [1994] Director/Credit Control Manager; William Hooper [1990] Director; Catherine Record [1989] Director; Dale Record [1988] Director/Marketing Manager; Gerard Record [1990] Director/Operations Manager; James Robert Graham Record [1966] Director; Marianne Jane Record [1968] Director; Priscilla Record [1992] Director; Rachel Ann Record [1938] Director

**Rhodar Demolition Limited**
*Incorporated:* 29 May 2001 *Employees:* 63
*Previous:* Bagnall (UK) Limited
*Net Worth:* £912,000 *Total Assets:* £8,489,000
*Registered Office:* Unit C, Astra Park, Parkside Lane, Leeds, LS11 5SZ
*Activities:* Demolition
*Parent:* Lexia Solutions Group Limited
*Officers:* Andrew Mark Finn, Secretary; Jason Martin Davy [1970] Director; Andrew Mark Finn [1967] Director; Andrew Fisk [1962] Director

**Rhodar Limited**
*Incorporated:* 19 July 1976 *Employees:* 393
*Net Worth:* £3,434,000 *Total Assets:* £16,530,000
*Registered Office:* Unit C, Astra Park, Parkside Lane, Leeds, LS11 5SZ
*Activities:* Other specialised construction activities n.e.c.
*Parent:* Lexia Solutions Group Limited
*Officers:* Andrew Mark Finn, Secretary; Anthony Conway [1963] Director; Jason Martin Davy [1970] Director; Jason Ellis [1969] Director; Andrew Mark Finn [1967] Director; David Patrick Hart [1957] Contracts Director; Peter Humphries [1962] Director; Darren Martyn Payne [1968] Director; David Anthony Rhodes [1972] Director; Michael Woods [1965] Director

**A. Rhodes (Haulage) Limited**
*Incorporated:* 26 February 1979 *Employees:* 47
*Net Worth:* £4,455,691 *Total Assets:* £6,441,149
*Registered Office:* Grange Farm, Hazel Bush Lane, Stockton-on-the-Forest, N Yorks, YO32 9TR
*Activities:* Freight transport by road
*Parent:* A Rhodes Group Ltd
*Officers:* Beverley Ann Rhodes, Secretary/Director; Beverley Ann Rhodes [1954] Director; John Rhodes [1953] Director/Haulage Contractor; Martin John Rhodes [1976] Director

**Rhodes Asset Management Limited**
*Incorporated:* 2 June 2006 *Employees:* 3
*Net Worth:* £2,547,036 *Total Assets:* £7,916,497
*Registered Office:* First Floor, 43 Park Place, Leeds, LS1 2RY
*Activities:* Buying and selling of own real estate
*Shareholders:* Tassadaq Javed; Vanessa Javed
*Officers:* Tassadaq Javed, Secretary; Tassadaq Javed [1969] Director/Solicitor; Vanessa Javed [1972] Director/Businesswoman

**Rhomberg Sersa UK Limited**
*Incorporated:* 22 January 1999 *Employees:* 14
*Net Worth:* £1,825,750 *Total Assets:* £10,577,179
*Registered Office:* Moorgate House, Clifton Moor Gate, York, YO30 4WY
*Activities:* Other specialised construction activities n.e.c.
*Parent:* Sersa Holding AG
*Officers:* Richard Cooper, Secretary; Richard Malcolm Cooper [1980] Finance Director; Carl Garrud [1962] Director

**Ribblesdale Motors Limited**
*Incorporated:* 17 December 1947 *Employees:* 41
*Net Worth:* £1,947,828 *Total Assets:* £6,225,803
*Registered Office:* The Garage, Torver, Coniston, Cumbria, LA21 8BJ
*Activities:* Sale of new cars and light motor vehicles
*Parent:* J F & E Hadwin Limited
*Officers:* Anne Doris Hadwin, Secretary; Eric Hadwin [1939] Director/Garage Proprietor; Jason Dean Hadwin [1966] Director

**Riby Grange Farming Company Limited**
*Incorporated:* 31 March 1953 *Employees:* 7
*Net Worth:* £1,791,579 *Total Assets:* £6,900,235
*Registered Office:* Riby Grange, Riby, Grimsby, N E Lincs, DN37 8NT
*Activities:* Growing of cereals (except rice), leguminous crops and oil seeds
*Shareholder:* Mark Needham Burt
*Officers:* Jennifer Barbara Burt, Secretary; Elaine Mary Burt [1936] Director/Housewife; George William Burt [1988] Director/Farmer; Harry Needham Burt [1986] Director/Farmer; Jennifer Barbara Burt [1960] Director; Mark Needham Burt [1962] Director/Farmer

**Hugh Rice (Whitefriargate) Limited**
*Incorporated:* 23 August 2006 *Employees:* 223
*Net Worth:* £4,224,107 *Total Assets:* £6,982,234
*Registered Office:* 48 Queen Street, Hull, HU1 1UU
*Activities:* Retail sale of watches and jewellery in specialised stores
*Parent:* Hugh Rice Holdings Limited
*Officers:* Scott Hynd McIntyre, Secretary; Scott Hynd McIntyre [1968] Director/Certified Chartered Accountant; James Peter Rice [1986] Director/Retail; Michael Rice [1957] Director/Jeweller; Paul John Rice [1977] Director/Jeweller; Danielle Rice-Hewitt [1985] Director

**Hugh Rice Holdings Limited**
*Incorporated:* 1 April 2015 *Employees:* 335
*Net Worth:* £12,188,812 *Total Assets:* £21,837,544
*Registered Office:* 48 Queen Street, Hull, HU1 1UU
*Activities:* Retail sale of watches and jewellery in specialised stores
*Shareholders:* Michael Rice; Paul John Rice
*Officers:* Scott Hynd McIntyre, Secretary; Scott Hynd McIntyre [1968] Finance Director; Diane Tina Rice [1966] Director; James Peter Rice [1986] Director; Michael Rice [1957] Director; Paul John Rice [1977] Director; Sarah Rice [1977] Director; Danielle Rice-Hewitt [1985] Director

**Hugh Rice Limited**
*Incorporated:* 17 October 1986 *Employees:* 99
*Net Worth Deficit:* £63,737 *Total Assets:* £9,960,503
*Registered Office:* 48 Queen Street, Hull, HU1 1UU
*Activities:* Retail sale of watches and jewellery in specialised stores
*Shareholders:* Mike Rice; Paul John Rice
*Officers:* Scott Hynd McIntyre, Secretary; Scott Hynd McIntyre [1968] Director/Certified Chartered Accountant; Diane Tina Rice [1966] Director; James Peter Rice [1986] Director/Retail; Michael Rice [1957] Director/Jeweller; Paul John Rice [1977] Director/Jeweller; Sarah Rice [1977] Director; Danielle Rice-Hewitt [1985] Operations Director

**Jos.Richardson & Son,Limited**
*Incorporated:* 2 June 1945 *Employees:* 133
*Net Worth:* £12,660,664 *Total Assets:* £23,784,202
*Registered Office:* Brackenholme Business Park, Brackenholme, Selby, N Yorks, YO8 6EL
*Activities:* Sale of new cars and light motor vehicles
*Officers:* Karen Patricia Marshall, Secretary; Graham Andrews [1957] Sales Director; Karen Patricia Marshall [1964] Finance Director; Jane Elizabeth Richardson [1975] Director; Joseph William Richardson [1978] Director/Manager

**J.A. Richardson (Electrical) Limited**
*Incorporated:* 20 May 1963 *Employees:* 62
*Net Worth:* £1,806,274 *Total Assets:* £6,821,206
*Registered Office:* 37 St Michaels Lane, Leeds, LS6 3BR
*Activities:* Electrical installation
*Parent:* J.A. Richardson (Holdings) Ltd
*Officers:* Elizabeth Adrienne Richardson, Secretary; Robert Ian Armstrong [1959] Director/Engineer; Elizabeth Adrienne Richardson [1945] Director/Physiotherapist; Lisle Richardson [1945] Director/Engineer; Nicholas Richardson [1972] Director

**Richardsons (Holdings) Limited**
*Incorporated:* 22 October 1997 *Employees:* 51
*Net Worth:* £2,717,416 *Total Assets:* £5,107,250
*Registered Office:* Westgate, Driffield, E Yorks, YO25 6SY
*Activities:* Sale of new cars and light motor vehicles
*Shareholder:* Simon Alec Toby Richardson
*Officers:* Paul Anthony Richardson, Secretary; Paul Anthony Richardson [1937] Director; Simon Alec Toby Richardson [1970] Director

**Richardsons Limited**
*Incorporated:* 20 October 1933 *Employees:* 51
*Net Worth:* £2,717,416 *Total Assets:* £5,108,687
*Registered Office:* Westgate, Driffield, E Yorks, YO25 6SY
*Activities:* Sale of new cars and light motor vehicles
*Parent:* Richardsons (Holdings) Limited
*Officers:* Paul Anthony Richardson, Secretary; Paul Anthony Richardson [1937] Director; Simon Alec Toby Richardson [1970] Director

**Richardsons Westgarth Limited**
*Incorporated:* 29 October 1900
*Net Worth:* £22,688,000 *Total Assets:* £25,226,000
*Registered Office:* Valley Farm Road, Stourton, Leeds, LS10 1SD
*Activities:* Activities of head offices
*Parent:* Kloeckner Metals UK Holdings Limited
*Officers:* David Henry Gross, Secretary; David Gross [1977] Finance Director [American]; George Clinton Jones [1956] Director; Barrie Clive Salter [1970] Director

**Richmond Foods Limited**
*Incorporated:* 11 January 1991 *Employees:* 3
*Net Worth:* £8,061,000 *Total Assets:* £68,350,000
*Registered Office:* Richmond House, Leeming Bar, Northallerton, N Yorks, DL7 9UL
*Activities:* Non-trading company
*Parent:* Ruby Acquisitions Limited
*Officers:* Phil Karl Griffin [1972] Director; Marcello Mattia [1965] Director [Italian]; Ibrahim Mahmood Ibrahim Najafi [1958] Director/Chief Operating Officer

**Richmond Management (Northern) Limited**
*Incorporated:* 14 March 1995 *Employees:* 2
*Net Worth:* £5,307,302 *Total Assets:* £5,530,216
*Registered Office:* 2 Duncombe Way, Duncombe Road, Bradford, BD8 9SY
*Activities:* Other letting and operating of own or leased real estate
*Shareholder:* Mufaddal Shabbir Dudhwala
*Officers:* Mohammed Hussain, Secretary/Director; Azeez Dudhwala [1974] Director; Habib Dudhwala [1978] Director; Mohsin Dudhwala [1950] Director; Mufaddal Shabbir Dudhwala [1974] Director; Mohammed Hussain [1950] Director

**Richmond Properties (UK) Limited**
*Incorporated:* 4 December 2001 *Employees:* 2
*Net Worth:* £2,133,228 *Total Assets:* £3,172,454
*Registered Office:* Field Head, Driffield Road, Molescroft, Beverley, E Yorks, HU17 7LU
*Activities:* Development of building projects
*Major Shareholder:* Wayne Paul Low
*Officers:* Wayne Paul Low [1973] Director/Property Developer

**Riddochhill Developments Limited**
*Incorporated:* 31 March 2006
*Net Worth:* £2,503,389 *Total Assets:* £9,547,524
*Registered Office:* Stotforth Hill House, Windlestone, Rushyford, Co Durham, DL17 0NF
*Activities:* Development of building projects
*Parent:* Hall Construction Services Limited
*Officers:* Neville John Hall [1956] Director; Stephen Hall [1954] Director

**Rider Holdings Limited**
*Incorporated:* 29 June 1988
*Net Worth:* £16,496,000 *Total Assets:* £17,510,000
*Registered Office:* Hunslet Park Depot, Donisthorpe Street, Leeds, LS10 1PL
*Activities:* Activities of head offices
*Parent:* FirstGroup Holdings Limited
*Officers:* Michael Hampson, Secretary; David Brian Alexander [1965] Managing Director; Simon David Pearson [1974] Commercial Director

**Ridge Medical Limited**
*Incorporated:* 10 August 2007 *Employees:* 4
*Net Worth Deficit:* £1,864,090 *Total Assets:* £11,549,248
*Registered Office:* Ridge Medical Centre, Cousen Road, Bradford, W Yorks, BD7 3JX
*Activities:* Other letting and operating of own or leased real estate
*Officers:* Nicholas Nurden, Secretary; Dr Andrew Timothy Hansen [1967] Director/GP; Dr Christopher Paul Harris [1962] Director/GP; Nicholas Stuart Nurden [1967] Director/Business Manager; Dr Susan Marie Towers [1962] Director/Doctor

**Riding Properties Limited**
*Incorporated:* 22 July 1969
*Net Worth:* £6,067,769 *Total Assets:* £7,254,600
*Registered Office:* Cape Industrial Estate, Coal Hill Lane, Farsley, Pudsey, Leeds, LS28 5NA
*Activities:* Other letting and operating of own or leased real estate
*Shareholder:* John Gaunt
*Officers:* John Gaunt, Secretary; Sarah Bunting [1970] Director; Brenda Susan Gaunt [1945] Director; John Gaunt [1938] Director

**The Right Car (UK) Ltd**
*Incorporated:* 4 February 1999 *Employees:* 126
*Net Worth:* £4,820,044 *Total Assets:* £12,748,076
*Registered Office:* Beck View Road, Beverley, E Yorks, HU17 0JT
*Activities:* Sale of new cars and light motor vehicles
*Major Shareholder:* Shaun Anthony Kamis
*Officers:* Mike Jackson, Secretary; Shaun Anthony Kamis [1963] Managing Director

**The Right Fuelcard Company Limited**
*Incorporated:* 1 March 2011 *Employees:* 45
*Net Worth:* £4,634,354 *Total Assets:* £22,248,164
*Registered Office:* Ground Floor, Gibraltar House, Bowcliffe Road, Hunslet, W Yorks, LS10 1HB
*Activities:* Other business support service activities n.e.c.
*Parent:* Edenred S.A.
*Officers:* Paul Simon Althasen [1964] Director; Aurelien Pierre Samuel Briand [1980] Performance Director [French]; Antoine Jacques Alexandre Dumurgier [1973] Director [French]; Jonathan Charles Deacon Turner [1966] Director; Johann Fabrice Martin Vaucanson [1973] Managing Director [French]

**Ring Automotive Limited**
*Incorporated:* 6 December 2004 *Employees:* 155
*Net Worth:* £15,518,000 *Total Assets:* £25,940,000
*Registered Office:* Volvox House, Gelderd Road, Leeds, LS12 6NA
*Activities:* Wholesale trade of motor vehicle parts and accessories
*Parent:* RGI Light Ltd
*Officers:* Joseph Boucher [1983] Director/Chartered Accountant; Andrew Olaf Fischer [1964] Director [German]; Ian Fisher [1950] Director; Jonathan Charles Richardson [1960] Director; Jerzy Franciszek Skalski [1956] Director; Theresa Erica Spencer [1970] Finance Director; Gareth Richard Ware [1976] Trading Director

**Ringways Garages (Leeds) Limited**
*Incorporated:* 14 January 1955 *Employees:* 122
*Net Worth:* £3,183,841 *Total Assets:* £20,519,340
*Registered Office:* Whitehall Road, Leeds, LS12 5NL
*Activities:* Sale of new cars and light motor vehicles
*Parent:* Wortlea Estates (Leeds) Limited
*Officers:* Guy Brian Roberts, Secretary; Michael Joseph Brook [1961] Director/Accountant; Richard Heath Robert Innes [1960] Director; Guy Brian Roberts [1961] Director; Robert Nicholas Roberts [1955] Director; Stephen James Russell [1961] Director

**Ripon Farm Services Limited**
*Incorporated:* 27 September 1982 *Employees:* 189
*Net Worth:* £20,024,560 *Total Assets:* £34,324,872
*Registered Office:* Dallamires Lane, Ripon, N Yorks, HG4 1TT
*Activities:* Activities of head offices
*Officers:* Geoffrey Brown [1945] Managing Director; Paul Martin Brown [1975] Director; Stewart Alan Hymas [1970] Director

**Ripon Race Company Limited (The)**
*Incorporated:* 20 March 1899 *Employees:* 133
*Net Worth:* £1,578,110 *Total Assets:* £3,111,966
*Registered Office:* 77 North Street, Ripon, N Yorks, HG4 1DS
*Activities:* Operation of sports facilities
*Officers:* Andrew Mark Hutchinson, Secretary; Nicholas Robert Armstrong [1976] Sales Director; Charles Nigel Clark [1949] Director/Consultant; Andrew Mark Hutchinson [1965] Director/Solicitor; James Michael Hutchinson [1962] Director; Celia Louise Wallis [1973] Director/Civil Engineer; Andrew Thomas Scott Wells [1957] Director

**Ripon Select Foods Limited**
*Incorporated:* 28 February 1974 *Employees:* 101
*Net Worth:* £12,654,541 *Total Assets:* £21,114,132
*Registered Office:* Dallamires Way North, Ripon, N Yorks, HG4 1TT
*Activities:* Manufacture of other food products n.e.c.
*Shareholders:* Thomas Martin Wood; Sarah Patricia Cooper
*Officers:* Anton Joel Gordon, Secretary; James Mawer Cooper [1962] Operations Director; Sarah Patricia Cooper [1962] Director; Thomas Martin Wood [1964] Director; Thomas Holmes Wood [1937] Director; Brian Young [1952] Director

**Risby Homes Limited**
*Incorporated:* 23 April 1993 *Employees:* 11
*Net Worth:* £2,703,442 *Total Assets:* £3,797,043
*Registered Office:* White House Farm, Little Weighton, E Yorks, HU20 3UT
*Activities:* Construction of domestic buildings
*Shareholder:* Mark Edward Barrett
*Officers:* Simon William Lunt, Secretary; Mark Edward Barrett [1957] Director; Oliver Edward Barrett [1987] Director/Contracts Manager; Sally Margaret Barrett [1957] Director

**Risedale Estates Limited**
*Incorporated:* 30 December 1985 *Employees:* 620
*Net Worth:* £5,289,090 *Total Assets:* £10,270,579
*Registered Office:* Risedale at Abbey Meadow, Duchy Court, Barrow in Furness, Cumbria, LA13 0BF
*Activities:* Residential nursing care facilities
*Shareholders:* Paul Albert Fraser; Charles Threlfall Dent
*Officers:* Barbara Anne Hetherington, Secretary; Charles Threlfall Dent [1961] Director; John George Edmond [1953] Director; Paul Albert Fraser [1951] Director; Barbara Anne Hetherington [1960] Director/Secretary

**Rishworth School**
*Incorporated:* 22 June 2006 *Employees:* 120
*Net Worth:* £4,858,394 *Total Assets:* £6,240,405
*Registered Office:* Rishworth School, Oldham Road, Rishworth, W Yorks, HX6 4QA
*Activities:* Pre-primary education
*Officers:* Joanne Clague, Secretary; Hilary John Barber [1965] Director/Member of The Clergy; Christopher Bell [1957] Director/Chartered Accountant; Fiona Jayne Ellam [1963] Director/University Lecturer; Maxine Garbett [1957] Director/Retired; Philip John Hudson [1960] Director/Retired; Jean Catherine Slim [1944] Director/Retired Teacher; Valerie Isabel Stevens [1945] Director/Retired; Thomas Michael Wheelwright [1946] Director/Retired Surveyor; Dilys Margaret Whitaker [1933] Director

**W.B. Ritchie Farms Limited**
*Incorporated:* 26 September 1997 *Employees:* 5
*Net Worth:* £5,749,503 *Total Assets:* £7,369,583
*Registered Office:* Ings House, Shipton Road, York, YO30 1XJ
*Activities:* Mixed farming
*Shareholders:* William Barr Ritchie; Shelia May Ritchie
*Officers:* Sheila May Ritchie, Secretary/Farmer; David William Ritchie [1978] Director/Farmer; Sheila May Ritchie [1949] Director/Farmer; William Barr Ritchie [1940] Director/Farmer

**River Street Limited**
*Incorporated:* 5 March 2007
*Net Worth:* £2,274,326 *Total Assets:* £3,456,222
*Registered Office:* 50-54 Oswald Road, Scunthorpe, N Lincs, DN15 7PQ
*Activities:* Development of building projects
*Shareholders:* Dome Developments Limited; Paul Stuart Limited
*Officers:* Paul Chrysostomos Tasou, Secretary; Glenn Kinnersley [1962] Director/Design Consultant; Chrysostomos Tasou [1953] Director/Architect

**Riverhead Commercial Services Limited**
*Incorporated:* 29 March 1996 *Employees:* 75
*Net Worth:* £2,135,431 *Total Assets:* £3,774,662
*Registered Office:* Beverley Farm, South Cliff, Hornsea, E Yorks, HU18 1TL
*Activities:* Recreational vehicle parks, trailer parks and camping grounds
*Officers:* Ian Vincent Appleyard, Secretary; Laura Marie Firth [1975] Director; Martin Richard Varley [1951] Director; Richard James Varley [1979] Director

**Riverside Eastern Limited**
*Incorporated:* 7 December 1988 *Employees:* 26
*Net Worth:* £878,895 *Total Assets:* £4,197,234
*Registered Office:* Main Street, Seamer, Scarborough, N Yorks, YO12 4QD
*Activities:* Sale of new cars and light motor vehicles
*Parent:* Riverside Motors Holdings Limited
*Officers:* Christine Vasey, Secretary; Mark Duane Denton [1963] Sales Director; Stephen Wright [1954] Operations Director

**Riverside Healthcare Limited**
*Incorporated:* 28 November 2003 *Employees:* 416
*Net Worth:* £3,020,733 *Total Assets:* £8,214,113
*Registered Office:* c/o Cheswold Park Hospital, Cheswold Lane, Doncaster, S Yorks, DN5 8AR
*Activities:* Residential care activities for learning difficulties, mental health and substance abuse
*Parent:* Denlev Limited
*Officers:* John Graham Rhoden, Secretary/Director; Dr Richard Eaton Pearson [1958] Clinical Director; John Graham Rhoden [1945] Director

**Riverside Hull Limited**
*Incorporated:* 29 September 1999 *Employees:* 31
*Net Worth:* £2,091,266 *Total Assets:* £5,455,122
*Registered Office:* Saxon Way, Priory Park, Hessle, Hull, HU13 9PB
*Activities:* Sale of new cars and light motor vehicles
*Parent:* Riverside Motors Holdings
*Officers:* Michele Denton, Secretary; Mark Duane Denton [1963] Director; Stephen Wright [1954] Director

**Riverside Motors (Doncaster) Limited**
*Incorporated:* 2 July 1982 *Employees:* 70
*Net Worth:* £6,722,390 *Total Assets:* £18,572,256
*Registered Office:* Riverside House, Wheatley Hall Road, Doncaster, S Yorks, DN2 4NL
*Activities:* Sale of new cars and light motor vehicles
*Parent:* Riverside Motors Holdings Limited
*Officers:* Denise Wright, Secretary; Mark Duane Denton [1963] Sales Director; Stephen Wright [1954] Operations Director

**Riviera Acquisitions Limited**
*Incorporated:* 22 March 2013
*Net Worth Deficit:* £37,945,420 *Total Assets:* £269,595,904
*Registered Office:* Richmond House, Leeming Bar, Northallerton, N Yorks, DL7 9UL
*Activities:* Activities of production holding companies
*Parent:* Riviera Topco Limited
*Officers:* Marcello Mattia, Secretary; Phil Griffin [1972] Director; Marcello Mattia [1965] Director [Italian]; Ibrahim Mahmood Ibrahim Najafi [1958] Director

**Riviera Topco Limited**
*Incorporated:* 22 March 2013
*Net Worth:* £10,496 *Total Assets:* £254,074,176
*Registered Office:* Richmond House, Leeming Bar, Northallerton, N Yorks, DL7 9UL
*Activities:* Activities of production holding companies
*Parent:* Froneri Limited
*Officers:* Marcello Mattia, Secretary; Philip Karl Griffin [1972] Director; Marcello Mattia [1965] Director [Italian]; Ibrahim Mahmood Ibrahim Najafi [1958] Director

**J.R. Rix & Sons Limited**
*Incorporated:* 25 January 1957 *Employees:* 587
*Net Worth:* £71,365,304 *Total Assets:* £117,239,224
*Registered Office:* Witham House, 45 Spyvee Street, Hull, HU8 7JR
*Activities:* Wholesale of petroleum and petroleum products
*Shareholders:* Timothy John Rix; Sally Joanna Rix
*Officers:* Rory Michael Andrew Clarke [1959] Director; James Ian Doyle [1974] Director; David Charles Evans [1953] Director; Duncan John Lambert [1961] Director; Sally Joanna Rix [1965] Director; Timothy John Rix [1963] Director

**Rix Petroleum (Hull) Limited**
*Incorporated:* 6 June 1956 *Employees:* 103
*Net Worth:* £875,459 *Total Assets:* £15,674,897
*Registered Office:* Witham House, 45 Spyvee Street, Hull, HU8 7JR
*Activities:* Wholesale of petroleum and petroleum products
*Parent:* J R Rix & Sons Ltd
*Officers:* Rory Michael Andrew Clarke [1959] Director; James Ian Doyle [1974] Director; David Charles Evans [1953] Director; Duncan John Lambert [1961] Director; Sally Joanna Rix [1965] Director; Timothy John Rix [1963] Director; Graham Williamson [1958] Director

**Rixonway Kitchens Limited**
*Incorporated:* 4 August 1978 *Employees:* 427
*Net Worth:* £16,919,166 *Total Assets:* £29,201,846
*Registered Office:* Churwell Vale, Shaw Cross Business Park, Dewsbury, W Yorks, WF12 7RD
*Activities:* Manufacture of kitchen furniture
*Parent:* Rollfold Group Ltd
*Officers:* Nicola Jane Hardcastle, Secretary; Anjum Ahmed [1970] Director; David Balfour [1970] Finance Director; Daniel Arthur Edward Carr [1975] Finance Director; Mark Robert Bates Hughes [1970] Managing Director; Peter Kane [1965] Managing Director; Kristoffer Ljungfelt [1977] Director [Swedish]

**RMS Europe Group Limited**
*Incorporated:* 23 January 2004
*Net Worth:* £4,198,516 *Total Assets:* £10,177,256
*Registered Office:* Boothferry Terminal, Bridge Street, Goole, E Yorks, DN14 5SS
*Activities:* Activities of head offices
*Parent:* RMS Group Holdings Limited
*Officers:* Jonathan James Hunter [1972] Director/Chartered Accountant; Ian Dominic Parsons [1949] Director

**RMS Goole Limited**
*Incorporated:* 26 January 1990 *Employees:* 62
*Net Worth:* £2,255,189 *Total Assets:* £4,764,497
*Registered Office:* Boothferry Terminal, Bridge Street, Goole, N Humbers, DN14 5SS
*Activities:* Freight transport by road
*Parent:* RMS Europe Group Ltd
*Officers:* Craig Robert Hodgson [1986] Director; Jonathan James Hunter [1972] Director/Chartered Accountant; Michael Johnston [1970] Director/General Manager; Ian Dominic Parsons [1949] Director

**RMS Group Holdings Limited**
*Incorporated:* 4 May 2007 *Employees:* 224
*Net Worth:* £4,630,409 *Total Assets:* £20,548,840
*Registered Office:* Boothferry Terminal, Bridge Street, Goole, N Humbers, DN14 5SS
*Activities:* Activities of head offices
*Officers:* Andrew Jonathan Dixon [1968] Managing Director; Stephen Peter Harrison [1977] Director/Investment Professional; Gavin Michael Hindley [1977] Director; Craig Robert Hodgson [1986] Group Commercial Director; Jonathan James Hunter [1972] Finance Director; Ian Dominic Parsons [1949] Director; Jeremy Stuart Saunt [1961] Director/Seed Merchant

**RMS Trent Ports Limited**
*Incorporated:* 17 August 1936 *Employees:* 69
*Previous:* Gunness Wharf Limited
*Net Worth:* £1,114,817 *Total Assets:* £5,666,097
*Registered Office:* Boothferry Terminal, Bridge Street, Goole, N Humbers, DN14 5SS
*Activities:* Cargo handling for water transport activities
*Parent:* RMS Europe Group Ltd
*Officers:* Gavin Michael Hindley [1977] Director; Craig Robert Hodgson [1986] Director; Jonathan James Hunter [1972] Director/Chartered Accountant; Ian Dominic Parsons [1949] Director

**RMSpumptools Limited**
*Incorporated:* 12 August 1983 *Employees:* 76
*Net Worth:* £2,029,007 *Total Assets:* £16,978,528
*Registered Office:* P O Box 4, Fisher House, Barrow in Furness, Cumbria, LA14 1HR
*Activities:* Manufacture of other electrical equipment
*Parent:* James Fisher Holdings UK Limited
*Officers:* James Henry John Marsh, Secretary; Naim Theodore Boueri [1963] Sales Director [Lebanese]; Stanley James Foster Rooke [1954] Director; Douglas Marion Harwell [1975] Director/Engineer [American]; Nicholas Paul Henry [1961] Director; Stuart Charles Kilpatrick [1962] Director; Martin Graham Marsh [1977] Director

**Road Traffic Solutions Limited**
*Incorporated:* 7 January 2004
*Net Worth:* £2,729,626 *Total Assets:* £4,061,396
*Registered Office:* 60-64 Oswald Road, Scunthorpe, N Lincs, DN15 7PQ
*Activities:* Renting and leasing of other machinery, equipment and tangible goods n.e.c.
*Officers:* Ben Thomas Dexter [1988] Managing Director; George Leslie Smith [1949] Director

**Roadridge Limited**
*Incorporated:* 6 July 1982
*Net Worth:* £588,287 *Total Assets:* £4,216,641
*Registered Office:* Whyncrest, Bridlington Road, Hunmanby, N Yorks, YO14 9RS
*Activities:* Other letting and operating of own or leased real estate
*Officers:* Michael Swann, Secretary; Elisabeth Maria Swann [1958] Director/Marketing [Dutch]; Michael Swann [1946] Director/Consultant in Food Science Industry

**Roando Investments Limited**
*Incorporated:* 22 November 2006 *Employees:* 3
*Net Worth:* £1,698,679 *Total Assets:* £17,120,802
*Registered Office:* Millshaw, Leeds, LS11 8EG
*Activities:* Development of building projects
*Parent:* Evans Management Limited
*Officers:* Robert Marshall, Secretary; Roderick Michael Evans [1962] Director; Paul Terence Millington [1962] Director/Accountant; Alan Matthew Syers [1964] Director/Chartered Surveyor

**Roberts Graphics Limited**
*Incorporated:* 18 July 1991 *Employees:* 9
*Net Worth:* £1,202,090 *Total Assets:* £4,036,411
*Registered Office:* Wakefield Europort, Pope Street, Normanton, Wakefield, W Yorks, WF6 2TA
*Activities:* Wholesale of other machinery and equipment
*Shareholder:* Anthony Roberts
*Officers:* Lynn Mary Roberts, Secretary; Philip Henry Michael Hulme [1962] Director/Machinery Salesman; David George Kitson [1978] Director/Machinery Salesman; Anthony Roberts [1953] Director/Sales Manager; James Anthony Roberts [1978] Director/Machinery Salesman; Luke Ralph Daniel Roberts [1987] Director/Salesman; Lynn Mary Roberts [1955] Director/Designer

**John Roberts Holdings Limited**
*Incorporated:* 16 July 1996 *Employees:* 60
*Net Worth:* £6,552,770 *Total Assets:* £11,313,177
*Registered Office:* Christies High Mill, Settle, N Yorks, BD24 9LX
*Activities:* Manufacture of paper and paperboard
*Shareholder:* Paul Adrian Nelson
*Officers:* Jeremy William Smith, Secretary; Claire Louise Beresford [1976] Sales Director; Scott John Littlewood [1979] Operations Director; Paul Adrian Nelson [1959] Managing Director; Timothy Denzil Pryce [1966] Director; Jeremy William Smith [1961] Finance Director

**John Roberts Ventures Limited**
*Incorporated:* 10 August 2012 *Employees:* 60
*Net Worth:* £1,744,406 *Total Assets:* £7,103,004
*Registered Office:* Christies High Mill, Settle, N Yorks, BD24 9LX
*Activities:* Manufacture of corrugated paper and paperboard, sacks and bags
*Officers:* Jeremy William Smith, Secretary; Paul Adrian Nelson [1959] Sales Director; Timothy Denzil Pryce [1966] Director; Jeremy William Smith [1961] Finance Director

**Roberts, Mart (Holdings) Co. Ltd.**
*Incorporated:* 21 January 2005 *Employees:* 195
*Net Worth:* £17,381,418 *Total Assets:* £24,570,988
*Registered Office:* Aire Valley House, Thornes Farm Way, Leeds, LS9 0AN
*Activities:* Activities of head offices
*Major Shareholder:* John Roberts
*Officers:* Craig Worley, Secretary; Benjamin John Roberts [1978] Director; John Roberts [1944] Director; William Peter Roberts [1976] Director

**Roberts, Mart (Properties) Ltd.**
*Incorporated:* 21 January 2005
*Net Worth:* £7,368,941 *Total Assets:* £8,257,779
*Registered Office:* Aire Valley House, Thornes Farm Way, Leeds, LS9 0AN
*Activities:* Other letting and operating of own or leased real estate
*Parent:* Roberts, Mart (Holdings) Limited
*Officers:* Craig Worley, Secretary; Benjamin John Roberts [1978] Director; John Roberts [1944] Director; William Peter Roberts [1976] Director

**Roberts,Mart & Co.Limited**
*Incorporated:* 16 January 1890 *Employees:* 195
*Net Worth:* £12,171,348 *Total Assets:* £19,920,552
*Registered Office:* Aire Valley House, Thornes Farm Way, Leeds, LS9 0AN
*Activities:* Manufacture of plastic packing goods
*Parent:* Roberts, Mart (Holdings) Co. Ltd
*Officers:* Craig Worley, Secretary; Simon Plomer-Roberts [1960] Director; Benjamin John Roberts [1978] Director; John Roberts [1944] Director; William Peter Roberts [1976] Director; Craig Worley [1970] Financial Director

**Robimatic Limited**
*Incorporated:* 16 July 1980 *Employees:* 71
*Net Worth:* £12,607,000 *Total Assets:* £14,201,000
*Registered Office:* Broomhouse Lane, Edlington, Doncaster, S Yorks, DN12 1ES
*Activities:* Manufacture of plastics in primary forms
*Parent:* Polypipe Limited
*Officers:* Emma Gayle Versluys, Secretary; Paul Anthony James [1967] Director/Chief Financial Officer; Martin Keith Payne [1965] Director

**Robinson Contract Services Limited**
*Incorporated:* 16 October 2003 *Employees:* 48
*Net Worth:* £4,624,749 *Total Assets:* £6,686,764
*Registered Office:* Weighbridge Yard, Catfoss Lane, Brandesburton, Driffield, E Yorks, YO25 8EJ
*Activities:* Support activities for crop production
*Officers:* Julia Marie Robinson, Secretary/Director; Neil Terrence Fewlass [1968] Director; Emma Ruth Marsland [1981] Director; Julia Marie Robinson [1967] Director; Craig Rae Stainforth [1971] Director

**James Robinson Fibres Limited**
*Incorporated:* 31 July 1944 *Employees:* 46
*Net Worth:* £14,697,515 *Total Assets:* £19,599,088
*Registered Office:* Millersdale Close, Euroway Industrial Estate, Bradford, W Yorks, BD4 6SG
*Activities:* Preparation and spinning of textile fibres
*Major Shareholder:* Christopher John Frederick Taylor
*Officers:* Nicholas James Batty [1969] Finance Director; Mark Andrew Longley [1961] Director/Sales Executive; Adrian William Tate [1964] Director/Operations; Christopher John Fredrick Taylor [1948] Director/Textile Fibre Manufacturer; Eileen Mary Taylor [1949] Director/Housewife; James Maxwell Taylor [1973] Director/Textile Fibre Manufacturer; Andrew David Thornton [1967] Director/Export Manager

**Robinson Group (Holdings) Limited**
*Incorporated:* 14 November 2000 *Employees:* 41
*Net Worth:* £2,695,497 *Total Assets:* £8,340,191
*Registered Office:* Energy House, Hampsthwaite, Harrogate, N Yorks, HG3 2HT
*Activities:* Non-trading company
*Officers:* Christopher Salisbury, Secretary; David Stephen Illingworth [1955] Director; Howard Seth Illingworth [1958] Director

**Barry Robinson Leisure Limited**
*Incorporated:* 8 August 1979 *Employees:* 90
*Net Worth:* £440,322 *Total Assets:* £3,596,278
*Registered Office:* The Longlands Hotel, Tewitfield, Carnforth, Lancs, LA6 1JH
*Activities:* Hotels and similar accommodation
*Major Shareholder:* Barry Robinson
*Officers:* Fiona Claire Benn, Secretary; Fiona Claire Benn [1974] Director/Hotelier; Barry Robinson [1943] Director

**F. Peter Robinson Limited**
*Incorporated:* 16 July 1957 *Employees:* 8
*Net Worth:* £2,979,554 *Total Assets:* £6,250,694
*Registered Office:* Northumberland Street, Darlington, Co Durham, DL3 7HJ
*Activities:* Other letting and operating of own or leased real estate
*Shareholders:* Frederick Peter Robinson; Stephanie Jane Robinson
*Officers:* Heather Viveca Choules, Secretary; Frederick Peter Robinson [1954] Director/Auctioneer; Stephanie Jane Robinson [1966] Director/Broadcast Journalist

**G.A. Robson and Son Ltd**
*Incorporated:* 24 November 2009
*Net Worth:* £3,425,937 *Total Assets:* £4,589,836
*Registered Office:* New Manor Farm, Carlton Husthwaite, Thirsk, N Yorks, YO7 2BP
*Activities:* Agents involved in the sale of machinery, industrial equipment, ships and aircraft
*Major Shareholder:* Timothy John Robson
*Officers:* Timothy John Robson, Secretary; Elizabeth Ann Robson [1955] Director; Richard George Robson [1972] Director; Timothy John Robson [1952] Director

**Rocal Insulating Panels Ltd.**
*Incorporated:* 21 May 1993 *Employees:* 115
*Net Worth:* £1,053,194 *Total Assets:* £4,992,961
*Registered Office:* Atherton Way, Ancholme Business Park, Brigg, N Lincs, DN20 8AR
*Activities:* Manufacture of veneer sheets and wood-based panels
*Major Shareholder:* James Victor Longley
*Officers:* James Victor Longley, Secretary/Director; Kevin Ashe [1964] Director; James Victor Longley [1948] Director; Sandra Longley [1948] Director/Dress Shop Owner; Stephen John Nadin [1967] Operations Director; Darren Simon Roberts [1965] Director/Sole Proprietor

**Julian Roche Associates Limited**
*Incorporated:* 2 July 1973 *Employees:* 46
*Net Worth:* £4,431,752 *Total Assets:* £7,001,895
*Registered Office:* Ainleys Industrial Estate, Elland, W Yorks, HX5 9JP
*Activities:* Wholesale of radio, television goods & electrical household appliances (other than records, tapes, CDs)
*Shareholders:* Anthony Norman Bate; Elizabeth Bate
*Officers:* Elizabeth Bate, Secretary; Anthony Norman Bate [1963] Director; Elizabeth Bate [1963] Director; Martin Clay [1967] Technical Director; Peter Midgley [1980] Sales Director; Craig Pickard [1985] Director/Project Manager

**Roche Healthcare Limited**
*Incorporated:* 21 November 1994 *Employees:* 416
*Net Worth:* £9,444,461 *Total Assets:* £15,806,044
*Registered Office:* Unit 1 Manor Court, Manor Mill Lane, Leeds, LS11 8LQ
*Activities:* Medical nursing home activities
*Major Shareholder:* Patrick Joseph Roche
*Officers:* Colleen Elizabeth Roche, Secretary; Patrick Joseph Roche [1957] Director/Pharmacist

**Rockar 2 Limited**
*Incorporated:* 25 May 2016 *Employees:* 38
*Net Worth:* £1,045,055 *Total Assets:* £7,253,450
*Registered Office:* 1 Monckton Court, South Newbald Road, North Newbald, E Yorks, YO43 4RW
*Activities:* Sale of new cars and light motor vehicles
*Parent:* Rockar 2016 Limited
*Officers:* Simon Timothy Dixon [1966] Director; Adrian Leonard Pattern [1969] Director

**Rockar 2016 Limited**
*Incorporated:* 26 January 2016 *Employees:* 101
*Net Worth:* £1,510,000 *Total Assets:* £12,854,000
*Registered Office:* 1 Monckton Court, South Newbald Road, Newbald, E Yorks, YO43 4RW
*Activities:* Business and domestic software development
*Shareholder:* Simon Timothy Dixon
*Officers:* Michael Christopher Collis [1965] Director; Simon Timothy Dixon [1966] Director; Richard Edward Manley [1979] Director/Chartered Accountant; Liam May [1985] Director; Andrew David John McEwan [1966] Director; Adrian Leonard Pattern [1969] Director

**Rockliffe Hall Limited**
*Incorporated:* 19 October 2006 *Employees:* 321
*Net Worth:* £27,397,000 *Total Assets:* £71,100,000
*Registered Office:* Rockliffe Hall, Hurworth on Tees, Darlington, Co Durham, DL2 2DU
*Activities:* Hotels and similar accommodation
*Parent:* The Gibson O'Neill Company Limited
*Officers:* Jeremy Robin Bloom, Secretary; Jeremy Robin Bloom [1957] Director; Anthony Warwick Brindle [1950] Director; Stephen Gibson [1958] Director

**Roclad Systems Limited**
*Incorporated:* 26 November 1992 *Employees:* 12
*Net Worth:* £2,410,938 *Total Assets:* £3,251,512
*Registered Office:* 23 Alfred Street, English Street, Hull, HU3 2DD
*Activities:* Construction of commercial buildings
*Parent:* Fedelta Trustees (IOM) Limited
*Officers:* Julie Margaret Oliver, Secretary; Julie Margaret Oliver [1961] Financial Director; Raymond Oliver [1953] Director

**Rodgers Group Limited**
*Incorporated:* 9 May 1989 *Employees:* 3
*Net Worth:* £2,263,311 *Total Assets:* £3,841,600
*Registered Office:* Unit 1 Neiley Industrial Park, New Mill Road, Honley, Holmfirth, W Yorks, HD9 6QE
*Activities:* Activities of other holding companies n.e.c.
*Shareholder:* Donal Vincent O'Meara
*Officers:* Veronica Kearney, Secretary; Veronica Kearney [1956] Director; Carmel O'Meara [1948] Director [Irish]; Donal Vincent O'Meara [1945] Director [Irish]

**Rodgers of York Ltd.**
*Incorporated:* 10 July 1940 *Employees:* 61
*Net Worth:* £2,238,978 *Total Assets:* £4,085,801
*Registered Office:* Monks Cross, Huntington, York, YO32 9JR
*Activities:* Retail sale of carpets, rugs, wall and floor coverings in specialised stores
*Shareholders:* William Francis Browne; James David Browne
*Officers:* Susan Genevieve Browne, Secretary; James David Browne [1973] Director; Susan Genevieve Browne [1944] Director/Company Secretary; William Francis Browne [1970] Director

**Rodgers Plant Hire Ltd.**
*Incorporated:* 24 March 1961 *Employees:* 13
*Net Worth:* £4,398,431 *Total Assets:* £5,509,230
*Registered Office:* Unit 1 Neiley Industrial Park, New Mill Road, Honley, Holmfirth, W Yorks, HD9 6QE
*Activities:* Renting and leasing of construction and civil engineering machinery and equipment
*Officers:* Veronica Kearney, Secretary; Veronica Kearney [1956] Director; Donal Vincent O'Meara [1945] Director [Irish]; John Simon Rodgers [1956] Director

**The Rodillian Multi Academy Trust**
*Incorporated:* 14 March 2012 *Employees:* 486
*Net Worth:* £28,915,000 *Total Assets:* £34,993,000
*Registered Office:* The Rodillian Academy, Longthorpe Lane, Lofthouse, Wakefield, W Yorks, WF3 3PS
*Activities:* General secondary education
*Officers:* Janice Bennett [1952] Director/Retired HMI; Ian Thomas Comfort [1953] Director/Legal Adviser; Christopher David Cooke [1966] Director/HR Consultant; Jennifer May East [1992] Director/Solicitor; Andrew John Goulty [1965] Director/Headteacher; Tracey Joanne Hudson [1977] Director/Financial Executive; Lauren Olivia Hunter [1999] Director/Auditor; Imogen Rhian Sewell [1987] Director/Risk Analyst; Andrew Neil Sorby [1981] Director/Management Accountant

**John Roe (Hull) Limited**
*Incorporated:* 2 July 1999 *Employees:* 26
*Net Worth:* £2,470,513 *Total Assets:* £4,803,830
*Registered Office:* Hanover House, 117-119 Cleethorpe Road, Grimsby, S Humbers, DN31 3ET
*Activities:* Sale of new cars and light motor vehicles
*Shareholders:* Thomas Roe; Thomas Roe
*Officers:* Lorinda Roe, Secretary; Thomas Paul Roe [1991] Director

**Rofin-Sinar UK Ltd.**
*Incorporated:* 2 December 1997 *Employees:* 131
*Net Worth:* £17,984,000 *Total Assets:* £21,237,000
*Registered Office:* Rofin House, Meadow Road, Bridgehead Business Park, Kingston upon Hull, HU13 0DG
*Activities:* Manufacture of other special-purpose machinery n.e.c.
*Parent:* CMR GmbH
*Officers:* Necati Avci [1958] Engineering Director; Andrew John Chambers [1957] Sales Director; Russell Jeynes [1976] Director/Operations Manager; Ralf Kogeler [1960] Director/Entrepreneur [German]; Jason Robert Lee [1975] R&D Director; Klaus Leitner [1970] Director [Austrian]; Christian Zimmer [1965] Director/Entrepreneur [Austrian]

**D L Rogers & Sons Limited**
*Incorporated:* 14 August 2000 *Employees:* 56
*Net Worth:* £2,934,284 *Total Assets:* £5,453,144
*Registered Office:* Chancery Court, 34 West Street, Retford, Notts, DN22 6ES
*Activities:* Freight transport by road
*Shareholders:* Paul Barry Rogers; Neil Lewis Rogers; Jane Rogers; Sharon Dawn Rogers
*Officers:* Sharon Dawn Rogers, Secretary; Jane Rogers [1962] Director/Admin Clerk; Neil Lewis Rogers [1964] Director/Haulage Manager; Paul Barry Rogers [1962] Director/Haulage Manager; Sharon Dawn Rogers [1964] Director/Company Secretary

**Rogerthorpe Manor Hotel Limited**
*Incorporated:* 11 July 2009 *Employees:* 3
*Net Worth:* £1,670,438 *Total Assets:* £4,114,757
*Registered Office:* c/o Ground Floor, St Paul's House, 23 Park Square, Leeds, LS1 2ND
*Activities:* Activities of head offices
*Major Shareholder:* Richard James Metcalfe
*Officers:* Sheila Metcalfe, Secretary; Aimee Victoria Metcalfe [1983] Director; Richard James Metcalfe [1976] Director; Sheila Mary Metcalfe [1949] Director

**ROK Associates Limited**
*Incorporated:* 15 February 1988 *Employees:* 72
*Net Worth:* £3,866,668 *Total Assets:* £5,092,193
*Registered Office:* Unit 1 Peckfield Business Park, Ridge Road, Leeds, LS25 4DY
*Activities:* Activities of head offices
*Shareholders:* Stuart George Reeve; Michael King
*Officers:* Michael King, Secretary; Michael King [1956] Director/Accountant; Stuart George Reeve [1950] Director

**Rolawn Limited**
*Incorporated:* 13 February 2002 *Employees:* 65
*Net Worth:* £4,313,973 *Total Assets:* £8,359,799
*Registered Office:* The Airfield, Seaton Ross, York, YO42 4NF
*Activities:* Growing of other perennial crops
*Shareholders:* Paul Andrew Dawson; Kenneth Eion Dawson
*Officers:* Davina Jane Turner, Secretary; Kenneth Eoin Dawson [1946] Director; Paul Andrew Dawson [1971] Director; Jonathan Mark Hill [1967] Sales and Marketing Director

**Rolco 188 Limited**
*Incorporated:* 20 May 2003
*Net Worth:* £2,655,627 *Total Assets:* £3,194,373
*Registered Office:* Buttfield Road, Howden, E Yorks, DN14 7DY
*Activities:* Activities of head offices
*Shareholder:* David Andrew Axup
*Officers:* David Andrew Axup, Secretary/Director; David Andrew Axup [1962] Director; Robert George Axup [1955] Director

**Rollfields Limited**
*Incorporated:* 2 November 2005 *Employees:* 6
*Net Worth:* £3,613,721 *Total Assets:* £6,038,251
*Registered Office:* Eastfield House, Farm Fen Lane, North Thoresby, Grimsby, N E Lincs, DN36 5QU
*Activities:* Support activities for crop production
*Shareholders:* Frank Roy Casswell; Mark Robert Casswell
*Officers:* Mark Robert Casswell, Secretary/Farmer; Mark Robert Casswell [1963] Director/Farmer

**Rollfold Holdings Limited**
*Incorporated:* 17 May 2006 *Employees:* 2
*Net Worth:* £8,937,000 *Total Assets:* £29,881,000
*Registered Office:* Churwell Vale, Shaw Cross Business Park, Dewsbury, W Yorks, WF12 7RD
*Activities:* Activities of head offices
*Parent:* Nobia Holdings UK Limited
*Officers:* Nicola Jane Hardcastle, Secretary; Anjum Ahmed [1970] Director; David Balfour [1970] Finance Director; Daniel Arthur Edward Carr [1975] Finance Director; Mark Robert Bates Hughes [1970] Managing Director; Peter Kane [1965] Managing Director; Kristoffer Ljungfelt [1977] Director [Swedish]

**Rollings Investments Limited**
*Incorporated:* 13 January 1965 *Employees:* 4
*Net Worth:* £6,657,566 *Total Assets:* £6,954,009
*Registered Office:* 35 Westgate, Huddersfield, W Yorks, HD1 1PA
*Activities:* Buying and selling of own real estate
*Major Shareholder:* Jacqueline Anne Rollings
*Officers:* Jacqueline Anne Rollings, Secretary; Graham Keith Lewis [1947] Director/Solicitor; Jacqueline Anne Rollings [1939] Director; John Rollings [1978] Director; Richard Garsed Warrington [1939] Director/Chartered Accountant

**Rollits Limited Liability Partnership**
*Incorporated:* 25 September 2009
*Net Worth:* £2,163,673 *Total Assets:* £3,439,320
*Registered Office:* Citadel House, 58 High Street, Hull, HU1 1QE
*Officers:* Keith James Benton [1967] Member; George Edward Coyle [1955] Member; Christopher Rex Crystal [1976] Member; Mark Russell Dixon [1972] Member; Christopher John Drinkall [1980] Member; Charles Richard Field [1962] Member; John Paul Flanagan [1980] Member; Neil Richard Franklin [1961] Member; Ralph Nevil Gilbert [1965] Member; Edward Charles Jenneson [1980] Member; John Richard Lane [1963] Member; Douglas Robert Oliver [1958] Member; Sheridan Lesley Ball [1955] LLP Member; Glenn Robert Craft [1955] LLP Member; Andrew James Digwood [1976] LLP Member; Caroline Mary Hardcastle [1974] LLP Member; Edward Peter John Merrick Heppel [1981] LLP Member; David Hextall [1973] LLP Member; Gerry Linda Morrison [1979] LLP Member; David Sam Myers [1982] LLP Member; Jennifer Helen Sewell [1983] LLP Member; Julian Nicholas Wild [1953] LLP Member

**Roman Limited**
*Incorporated:* 27 October 1987 *Employees:* 234
*Net Worth:* £4,243,691 *Total Assets:* £12,695,148
*Registered Office:* Whitworth Avenue, Aycliffe Industrial Park, Newton Aycliffe, Co Durham, DL5 6YN
*Activities:* Other manufacturing n.e.c.
*Officers:* Deborah Louise Green, Company Secretary; Jonathan Malcolm Franks [1961] Finance Director; David Charles Osborne [1970] Sales Director; Generald Charles Osborne [1940] Chairman/Director; Kathryn Isabelle Osborne [1967] Director; Pamela Osborne [1932] Director; Julian Pearson [1968] Commercial Director; Simon Marc Teasdale [1963] Sales Director; John Wright [1956] Operations Director

**Rome Holdco Ltd**
*Incorporated:* 24 January 2013
*Net Worth:* £22,176,000 *Total Assets:* £205,564,000
*Registered Office:* The Inspire, Hornbeam Square West, Harrogate, N Yorks, HG2 8PA
*Activities:* Activities of head offices
*Parent:* Principal Hotels Topco 3 Limited
*Officers:* John Cody Bradshaw [1978] Director/Hotel Real Estate [American]; Sarah Broughton [1976] Director/Chartered Accountant; James Alexander Burrell [1974] Director/Accountant; Anthony Gerrard Troy [1962] Director [Irish]

**Rome Investco Ltd**
*Incorporated:* 24 January 2013 *Employees:* 2,860
*Net Worth Deficit:* £21,097,000 *Total Assets:* £716,057,984
*Registered Office:* The Inspire, Hornbeam Square West, Harrogate, N Yorks, HG2 8PA
*Activities:* Activities of head offices
*Parent:* Rome Holdco Ltd
*Officers:* John Cody Bradshaw [1978] Director/Hotel Real Estate [American]; Sarah Broughton [1976] Director/Chartered Accountant; James Alexander Burrell [1974] Director/Accountant; Anthony Gerrard Troy [1962] Director [Irish]

**Romero Catholic Education Trust**
*Incorporated:* 4 November 2011 *Employees:* 183
*Previous:* St John's Catholic School and Sixth Form College, A Catholic Academy (Bishop Auckland)
*Net Worth:* £620,000 *Total Assets:* £4,078,000
*Registered Office:* St John's Catholic School and Sixth Form College, Woodhouse Lane, Bishop Auckland, Co Durham, DL14 6JT
*Activities:* General secondary education
*Officers:* Jayne Maria Summerbell, Secretary; Dominic Brown [1964] Director/Headteacher; Anthony Patrick Byrne [1955] Director/NHS Manager; Lisa Marie Byron-Ledwith [1969] Director/Headteacher; Joanna Foster [1975] Director/Civil Servant; Alan Gregory [1944] Director/Retired; Bob Hall [1944] Director/Retired; Denise Kirkwood [1958] Director/Teaching Assistant; Geoffrey David O'Hehir [1947] Director/Certified Chartered Accountant; Francis Liam Hugh O'Neill [1960] Director of Operations; Lawrence Albert Petterson [1955] Director/Solicitor; Generald Summerbell [1947] Director/Retired; Dennis Tindall [1946] Director/Catholic Priest; Ann Mary Wake [1953] Director/Retired; Mary Wood [1945] Director/Retired

**Romero Insurance Brokers Limited**
*Incorporated:* 30 April 1997 *Employees:* 102
*Net Worth:* £1,010,885 *Total Assets:* £10,529,661
*Registered Office:* Romero House, 8 Airport West, Lancaster Way, Yeadon, Leeds, LS19 7ZA
*Activities:* Activities of insurance agents and brokers
*Major Shareholder:* Justin Carlos Jose Romero-Trigo
*Officers:* Victoria Anne Romero Trigo, Secretary; Ian Leslie Grasby [1965] Director/Insurance Broking Account Executive; Kieran Kennedy [1971] Director/Insurance Broker; Jonathan Stuart Land [1965] Director; Simon Thomas William Mabb [1976] Director/Manager; Martin Paul Mansley [1974] Director/Insurance Broker; Karl Milner [1962] Director/Insurance Broker; Richard James Nicholson [1976] Director; Victoria Anne Romero Trigo [1979] Financial Director [Spanish]; Justin Carlos Jose Romero-Trigo [1970] Director

**Ronald Coates (Farms) Limited**
*Incorporated:* 9 April 1975
*Net Worth:* £3,206,901 *Total Assets:* £3,207,621
*Registered Office:* 62-63 Westborough, Scarborough, N Yorks, YO11 1TS
*Activities:* Non-trading company
*Shareholders:* Christine Ann Major; Helen Mary Gibbon
*Officers:* Christine Ann Major, Secretary/Director; Helen Mary Gibbon [1954] Director; Christine Ann Major [1952] Director

**Robert Rook Estates Limited**
*Incorporated:* 1 December 1958 *Employees:* 20
*Net Worth:* £3,965,945 *Total Assets:* £6,386,894
*Registered Office:* Weighton Wold Farm, Beverley Road, Market Weighton, E Yorks, YO43 4NE
*Activities:* Mixed farming
*Shareholders:* Robert Charles Rook; John Richard Rook
*Officers:* Robert Charles Rook, Secretary; Charles Robert Rook [1979] Director/Farmer; Edward Webster Rook [1984] Director/Farmer; John Richard Rook [1954] Director/Farmer; Robert Charles Rook [1952] Director/Farmer

**W. & A.C. Rose (Farms) Limited**
*Incorporated:* 8 August 1984 *Employees:* 17
*Net Worth:* £3,932,414 *Total Assets:* £4,613,875
*Registered Office:* Albion House, Manor Farm, Fillingham, Gainsborough, Lincs, DN21 5BS
*Activities:* Growing of cereals (except rice), leguminous crops and oil seeds
*Shareholders:* Alfred Charles Rose; William Rose
*Officers:* Alfred Charles Rose, Secretary; Alfred Charles Rose [1957] Director/Farmer; William Rose [1950] Director/Farmer

**The Rose Learning Trust**
*Incorporated:* 19 December 2013 *Employees:* 301
*Previous:* Richmond Hill Primary Academy Limited
*Net Worth:* £17,021,940 *Total Assets:* £22,075,048
*Registered Office:* Richmond Hill Primary Academy Limited, Melton Road, Sprotbrough, Doncaster, S Yorks, DN5 7SB
*Activities:* Primary education
*Officers:* Philip Crawley [1978] Director/Solicitor; Professor Jonathan Glazzard [1971] Director/Professor of Education; Peter Ian Haynes [1981] Director/Chief Finance Officer; Darren Brian Holmes [1965] Director; Mavis Latham [1945] Director/Governor; Sarah Louise Page [1985] Managing Director; Ellen Walker [1967] Director/Governor

**Rose Roofing Limited**
*Incorporated:* 12 August 1981 *Employees:* 56
*Net Worth:* £3,157,890 *Total Assets:* £7,406,485
*Registered Office:* 1 Flass Lane, Cutsyke, Castleford, W Yorks, WF10 5JW
*Activities:* Other manufacturing n.e.c.
*Parent:* B.R.T. Supplies Limited
*Officers:* Ann Sykes, Company Secretary; Max Abraham [1937] Director; Ann Sykes [1945] Director; Leslie Sykes [1944] Director; Nicholas John Sykes [1975] Director

**Rosehill Polymers Group Limited**
*Incorporated:* 5 July 2007 *Employees:* 95
*Net Worth:* £7,992,593 *Total Assets:* £22,187,772
*Registered Office:* Rose Hill Mill, Beech Road, Sowerby Bridge, W Yorks, HX6 2JT
*Activities:* Activities of other holding companies n.e.c.
*Shareholder:* John Michael Hopkinson
*Officers:* Dr Alexander Hayk Celik [1971] Managing Director; John Michael Hopkinson [1941] Director; Claire Zoe Pinder [1973] Director; Dr Wayne Stevens [1971] Director

**Rosenbauer UK Limited**
*Incorporated:* 2 May 2008 *Employees:* 15
*Previous:* Rosenbauer UK PLC
*Net Worth:* £1,202,475 *Total Assets:* £7,845,870
*Registered Office:* Concept House, Huddersfield Road, Meltham, Holmfirth, W Yorks, HD9 4AN
*Activities:* Fire service activities
*Parent:* Rosenbauer International AG
*Officers:* Hans Detzlhofer [1961] Director/VP Fire and Service Equipment [Austrian]; Oliver North [1981] Director; Christian Traxler [1977] Director/Senior VP [Austrian]; Andreas Zeller [1972] Director [Austrian]

**Roseville Care Homes Limited**
*Incorporated:* 3 July 2003 *Employees:* 230
*Net Worth:* £1,873,148 *Total Assets:* £7,831,545
*Registered Office:* Ash Grove House, Main Street, Upper Poppleton, York, YO26 6DL
*Activities:* Residential care activities for the elderly and disabled
*Major Shareholder:* Dinka Knezevic-Sharp
*Officers:* James Philip Lewis Ogden, Secretary; Dinka Knezevic Sharp [1963] Director

**S.Ross & Co.Limited**
*Incorporated:* 27 May 1933 *Employees:* 45
*Net Worth:* £5,389,201 *Total Assets:* £7,714,117
*Registered Office:* Manor Mill Lane, Leeds, LS11 8LQ
*Activities:* Wholesale of textiles
*Officers:* Michael Charles Wakelam, Secretary/Accountant; Max William Brasher [1967] Sales Director; Laurence Ian Silver [1947] Director; Lynsey Jane Silver [1979] Director/Purchasing; Michael Charles Wakelam [1962] Director/Accountant

**Rossendale Transport Limited**
*Incorporated:* 27 March 1986 *Employees:* 257
*Net Worth:* £2,634,717 *Total Assets:* £6,062,221
*Registered Office:* Prospect Park, Broughton Way, Harrogate, N Yorks, HG2 7NY
*Activities:* Other passenger land transport
*Parent:* Transdev Blazefield Limited
*Officers:* Alex Lloyd Hornby [1981] Director; Gordon Duncan Irvine [1957] Engineering Director; Seth King [1971] Finance Director

**Rossett School**
*Incorporated:* 9 June 2011 *Employees:* 266
*Net Worth:* £12,048,000 *Total Assets:* £14,659,000
*Registered Office:* Rossett School, Green Lane, Harrogate, N Yorks, HG2 9JP
*Activities:* General secondary education
*Officers:* Martin Joseph Joyce, Secretary; Graham Andrew Clark [1953] Director/Chartered Accountant; Hannah Grabham [1978] Deputy Director Sixth Form; Carolyn Heaney [1968] Director; John Hesketh [1951] Director/Freelance Education Consultant; Philip Charles Kilford [1954] Director/Business Manager; Ian John Lewis [1951] Director/Medical Consultant; Catha McAlister-Payne [1970] Director; Anne-Marie Phelps [1975] Director/Teacher; Peter Leonard Snowden [1956] Director; Mark Jonathan Walker [1961] Director; Helen Woodcock [1967] Director/Headteacher; Victoria Young [1985] Director/Teacher

**Rosti Automotive Larkhall Ltd.**
*Incorporated:* 11 May 1990 *Employees:* 340
*Previous:* Rosti UK Ltd
*Net Worth:* £10,403,000 *Total Assets:* £29,650,000
*Registered Office:* Bridge Works, Stamford Bridge, York, YO41 1AL
*Activities:* Manufacture of other plastic products
*Officers:* Sandor Korponai [1969] Director/Business Controller [Swedish]; Joachim Magnusson [1966] Director [Swedish]

**Rosti Automotive Pickering Ltd.**
*Incorporated:* 29 October 2015 *Employees:* 682
*Net Worth Deficit:* £2,435,000 *Total Assets:* £52,551,000
*Registered Office:* Westgate Carr Road, Pickering, N Yorks, YO18 8LX
*Activities:* Manufacture of other plastic products
*Officers:* Sandoor Korpponai [1969] Director/Business Controller [Swedish]; Joachim Magnusson [1966] Director [Swedish]

**Rosti Automotive Stamford Bridge Ltd.**
*Incorporated:* 29 October 2015 *Employees:* 374
*Net Worth:* £7,789,000 *Total Assets:* £25,892,000
*Registered Office:* Bridge Works, Stamford Bridge, York, YO41 1AL
*Activities:* Manufacture of other plastic products
*Officers:* Sandor Korponia [1969] Director/Business Controller [Swedish]; Joachim Magnusson [1966] Director [Swedish]

**Rosti UK Ltd.**
*Incorporated:* 29 October 2015 *Employees:* 27
*Net Worth:* £2,787,000 *Total Assets:* £3,816,000
*Registered Office:* Bridge Works, Stamford Bridge, York, YO41 1AL
*Activities:* Manufacture of other plastic products
*Officers:* Brendan Colgan [1974] Director; Jonas Ewing [1969] Director [Swedish]; Thomas Hansson [1959] Director [Swedish]

**Rothay Garden Hotel Limited**
*Incorporated:* 27 October 1989 *Employees:* 25
*Net Worth:* £3,120,804 *Total Assets:* £7,017,113
*Registered Office:* Rothay Garden Hotel, Broadgate, Grasmere, Cumbria, LA22 9RJ
*Activities:* Hotels and similar accommodation
*Major Shareholder:* Christopher Morton Carss
*Officers:* Christopher Morton Carss [1957] Director/Hotelier; Jillian Wilson [1967] Director/Hotel Front of House Manager

**J Rotherham (Holdings) Limited**
*Incorporated:* 7 September 1995 *Employees:* 283
*Net Worth:* £5,606,939 *Total Assets:* £13,856,126
*Registered Office:* Holme Industrial Estate, Skiff Lane, Holme-on-Spalding-Moor, York, YO43 4BB
*Activities:* Activities of head offices
*Shareholders:* Joseph Rotherham; Mary Rotherham
*Officers:* Joseph Rotherham, Secretary; Elizabeth Louise Kaplan [1977] Finance Director; Frances Mary Rotherham [1949] Director; Joseph Rotherham [1949] Director/Stonemason; Mary Rotherham [1946] Director; Matthew Thomas Rotherham [1982] Managing Director

**Rotherham Group Realisations Limited**
*Incorporated:* 24 July 1995 *Employees:* 350
*Previous:* MTL Group Limited
*Net Worth:* £6,633,000 *Total Assets:* £24,690,000
*Registered Office:* Ernst & Young LLP, 1 Bridgewater Place, Water Lane, Leeds, LS11 5QR
*Activities:* Manufacture of other fabricated metal products n.e.c.
*Officers:* Howard Lyndon Kellett, Secretary/Director; Darren Craig Bradley [1964] Director; Howard Lyndon Kellett [1965] Director; Dr Henry Norman Shirman [1946] Director; Karl Hepworth Stewart [1968] Sales Director

**J Rotherham Masonry Ltd**
*Incorporated:* 1 July 1987 *Employees:* 244
*Net Worth:* £3,442,597 *Total Assets:* £12,172,358
*Registered Office:* Holme Industrial Estate, Skiff Lane, Holme-on-Spalding-Moor, York, YO43 4BB
*Activities:* Cutting, shaping and finishing of stone
*Parent:* J Rotherham (Holdings) Ltd
*Officers:* Joseph Rotherham, Secretary; Anna Jane Buckley [1973] Director/Sales & Marketing; Elizabeth Louise Kaplan [1977] Finance Director; Joseph Rotherham [1949] Director/Stonemason; Mary Rotherham [1946] Director; Matthew Thomas Rotherham [1982] Director

**Rotherham Sand and Gravel Company Limited (The)**
*Incorporated:* 6 November 1930 *Employees:* 15
*Net Worth:* £8,480,449 *Total Assets:* £9,099,646
*Registered Office:* Scrooby Top Quarries, Scrooby, Doncaster, S Yorks, DN10 6AY
*Activities:* Operation of gravel and sand pits; mining of clays and kaolin
*Major Shareholder:* Stephen Paul Scholey
*Officers:* Susan Elizabeth Scholey, Secretary; George Scholey [1987] Director; Nicholas Paul Scholey [1984] Director; Stephen Paul Scholey [1944] Director

**Roubaix Bidco Limited**
*Incorporated:* 29 June 2016 *Employees:* 175
*Net Worth Deficit:* £473,938 *Total Assets:* £11,984,778
*Registered Office:* 5 Larsen Road, Goole, E Yorks, DN14 6XG
*Activities:* Manufacture of other transport equipment n.e.c.
*Shareholders:* Endless IV (GP) LP; Endless LLP
*Officers:* David Grey [1956] Director

**Roundbrand Limited**
*Incorporated:* 4 March 1987 *Employees:* 111
*Net Worth:* £3,701,449 *Total Assets:* £4,950,763
*Registered Office:* Cow House Lane, Armthorpe, Doncaster, S Yorks, DN3 3EE
*Activities:* Manufacture of other plastic products
*Officers:* Mark Williams, Secretary; John Redvers Hilton [1940] Director; Mark Williams [1953] Director

**K Rouse Civil Engineers Limited**
*Incorporated:* 9 December 1996 *Employees:* 112
*Net Worth:* £4,296,428 *Total Assets:* £7,006,178
*Registered Office:* 12a-16 North Street, Wetherby, W Yorks, LS22 6NN
*Activities:* Construction of roads and motorways
*Major Shareholder:* Kevin Patrick Rouse
*Officers:* Jonathan Kingston, Secretary; Mark Antony Bullock [1971] Commercial Director; Jonathan Kingston [1968] Director/Accountant; Kevin Robert Lochhead [1964] Director; Kevin Patrick Rouse [1967] Director; Paul Joseph Rouse [1963] Director

**Rouse Homes Limited**
*Incorporated:* 7 February 2005 *Employees:* 3
*Net Worth:* £1,465,327 *Total Assets:* £15,465,962
*Registered Office:* 12a-16 North Street, Wetherby, W Yorks, LS22 6NN
*Activities:* Construction of domestic buildings
*Major Shareholder:* Kevin Patrick Rouse
*Officers:* Jonathan Kingston, Secretary; Jonathan Kingston [1968] Director/Accountant; Kevin Patrick Rouse [1967] Director; Antony Richard Watling [1964] Director/Management

**Rowanway Limited**
*Incorporated:* 26 September 2001 *Employees:* 3
*Net Worth:* £3,461,896 *Total Assets:* £3,956,956
*Registered Office:* Grange Farm Barn, Kildwick Grange, Kildwick, Keighley, W Yorks, BD20 9AD
*Activities:* Development of building projects
*Shareholder:* Frank Thomas Greenway
*Officers:* Teresa Hazel Greenway, Secretary; Frank Thomas Greenway [1956] Director; Teresa Hazel Greenway [1960] Director/Secretary

**The Joseph Rowntree Reform Trust Limited**
*Incorporated:* 30 November 1939 *Employees:* 3
*Net Worth:* £38,801,536 *Total Assets:* £43,390,568
*Registered Office:* The Garden House, Water End, York, YO30 6WQ
*Activities:* Activities of political organisations
*Officers:* James Keillor Wallace, Secretary; Baroness Sarah Virginia Brinton [1955] Director/Member of The House of Lords; Roger Clarke [1948] Director/Retired; Amy Dalrymple [1977] Director/Head of Policy, Alzheimer Scotland; Alison Rachel Goldsworthy [1983] Director; Dr Julian Leon Huppert [1978] Director/Academic and Politician; Benjamin Morgan Lyons [1990] Director/Communications Consultant; Professor Susan Lesley Mendus [1951] Director/Retired Professor of Political Philosophy; Andrew Colin Neal [1964] Director/Consultant; Lisa Smart [1979] Director/Councillor; Fionna Margaret Ruth Tod [1988] Director/Communications Advisor [British/American]

**Roxor Group Limited**
*Incorporated:* 26 October 2016 *Employees:* 382
*Net Worth:* £1,404,000 *Total Assets:* £41,633,000
*Registered Office:* Hamnett House, Gibbet Street, Halifax, W Yorks, HX2 0AX
*Activities:* Wholesale of hardware, plumbing and heating equipment and supplies
*Shareholder:* Antony Wood
*Officers:* Peter Alan Cowgill [1953] Director/Chairman; David Ian Cullen [1966] Director; Ian Gary Jones [1964] Director; Richard Taylor [1973] Director; Antony Wood [1973] Director

**Royal Armouries (International) Limited**
*Incorporated:* 27 October 1993 *Employees:* 76
*Previous:* Royal Armouries (International) PLC
*Net Worth:* £7,394,000 *Total Assets:* £14,201,000
*Registered Office:* Armouries Drive, Leeds, LS10 1LT
*Activities:* Event catering activities
*Parent:* The Board of Trustees of The Royal Armouries
*Officers:* Dr Edward Alexander Impey [1962] Museum Director; Rodney Phillip Taylor [1966] Director/Museum Professional

**Royd House Investments Limited**
*Incorporated:* 21 April 2017
*Net Worth:* £245,935 *Total Assets:* £5,308,440
*Registered Office:* 14 High Street, Huddersfield, W Yorks, HD1 2HA
*Activities:* Other service activities n.e.c.
*Major Shareholder:* Andrew Mark Schofield
*Officers:* Andrew Mark Schofield [1953] Group Sales and Marketing Director

**Royds Community Association**
*Incorporated:* 12 April 1994 *Employees:* 11
*Net Worth:* £3,330,369 *Total Assets:* £4,006,476
*Registered Office:* Royds Enterprise Park, Future Fields, Buttershaw, Bradford, W Yorks, BD6 3EW
*Activities:* Other business support service activities n.e.c.
*Officers:* Anthony Paul Dylak, Secretary; Helen Aldred [1967] Director/Quantity Surveyor; Mohammed Arif Awan [1956] Director/Retired; Adrian Nicholas Curtis [1965] Executive Director; Laura Hobson [1980] Director/Operations Manager; Bernard Lewis [1949] Director/Church Warden; Rebecca Malin [1975] Associate Director of System Transformation; John Lawrence Marriott [1950] Director; Teresa Maria McDonald [1962] Director/Community Worker; Anthony Martyn Ward [1962] Director/Fire Safety Consultant; Leslie John Webb [1944] Director/Architect; Mark Wilkie [1964] Director

**Royds Estates Limited**
*Incorporated:* 17 June 1991
*Net Worth:* £1,226,638 *Total Assets:* £5,149,735
*Registered Office:* The Estate Office, Gledholt Business Park, Allen Row, Paddock, Huddersfield, W Yorks, HD1 4SB
*Activities:* Other letting and operating of own or leased real estate
*Officers:* Katharine Ann Royds, Secretary; Benjamin Ratcliffe Royds [1991] Director/Property Manager; Maxwell John Royds [1958] Director

**Royds Properties Ltd**
*Incorporated:* 2 November 1987 *Employees:* 5
*Net Worth:* £10,873,274 *Total Assets:* £16,716,515
*Registered Office:* The Estate Office, Gledholt Business Park, Allen Row, Paddock, Huddersfield, W Yorks, HD1 4SB
*Activities:* Other letting and operating of own or leased real estate
*Parent:* George Lumb Holdings Ltd
*Officers:* Benjamin Ratcliffe Royds [1991] Director/Property Management; Katharine Ann Royds [1963] Director/Property Management; Maxwell John Royds [1958] Director/Chartered Accountant

**Mark Royston Contracting Limited**
*Incorporated:* 25 May 2005 *Employees:* 24
*Net Worth:* £3,264,207 *Total Assets:* £4,214,375
*Registered Office:* Manor House Farm, Oxmoor Lane, Biggin, Leeds, LS25 6HJ
*Activities:* Other professional, scientific and technical activities n.e.c.
*Major Shareholder:* Mark Ian Royston
*Officers:* Mark Ian Royston, Secretary; Jayne Ann Lee [1971] Director; Mark Ian Royston [1966] Director

**RP Net Media Ltd**
*Incorporated:* 10 May 2016
*Net Worth:* £5,144,636 *Total Assets:* £5,400,555
*Registered Office:* Northgate, 118 North Street, Leeds, LS2 7PN
*Activities:* Activities of other holding companies n.e.c.
*Major Shareholder:* Robert Parker
*Officers:* Robert Parker [1985] Director

**RPP Group Holdings Limited**
*Incorporated:* 28 February 2012 *Employees:* 115
*Net Worth:* £100,259 *Total Assets:* £5,699,722
*Registered Office:* 5th Floor, Mazars LLP, 3 Wellington Place, Leeds, LS1 4AP
*Activities:* Quantity surveying activities
*Shareholder:* Andrew Cooper
*Officers:* Alex Blenard [1973] Director/Chartered Surveyor; Daren Lee Chessun [1974] Director/Chartered Surveyor; Andrew Cooper [1966] Managing Director; Mark Cooper [1965] Director/Surveyor/Project Manager; Gerard McGeough [1959] Director/Chartered Quantity Surveyor

**RPP Limited**
*Incorporated:* 16 February 2010 *Employees:* 76
*Net Worth:* £335,658 *Total Assets:* £5,547,792
*Registered Office:* 5th Floor, Mazars LLP, 3 Wellington Place, Leeds, LS1 4AP
*Activities:* Architectural activities
*Parent:* RPP Group Holdings Limited
*Officers:* Alex Blenard [1973] Director/Chartered Surveyor; Daren Lee Chessun [1974] Director/Chartered Surveyor; Andrew Cooper [1966] Director; Mark Cooper [1965] Director/Quantity Surveyor Project Manager; Gerard McGeough [1959] Director/Chartered Quantity Surveyor

**Rradar (Holdings) Limited**
*Incorporated:* 19 March 2015 *Employees:* 3
*Net Worth:* £1,806,585 *Total Assets:* £3,307,098
*Registered Office:* 6 Beacon Way, Hull, HU3 4AE
*Activities:* Activities of head offices
*Parent:* Legalosophy Limited
*Officers:* James Richard Butcher [1966] Director/Chartered Accountant; Andrew David Cameron [1973] Director/Solicitor; Gary John Gallen [1968] Director/Solicitor

**RSM Lining Supplies Global Ltd**
*Incorporated:* 29 October 2007 *Employees:* 38
*Net Worth:* £932,636 *Total Assets:* £5,488,917
*Registered Office:* Atkinson Court, Coalpit Road, Denaby Main Industrial Estate, Doncaster, S Yorks, DN12 4LH
*Activities:* Wholesale of chemical products
*Major Shareholder:* Richard Myles Davis
*Officers:* Richard Myles Davis [1979] Director; Daniel Peter Munro [1979] Director

**RSP Investments Limited**
*Incorporated:* 17 December 2015
*Net Worth Deficit:* £123,000 *Total Assets:* £5,886,000
*Registered Office:* Central House, 47 St Pauls Street, Leeds, LS1 2TE
*Activities:* Financial management
*Parent:* River Street Properties Limited
*Officers:* Daniel James Smith, Secretary; David Anthony Harrop [1970] Finance Director; Karen Louise Nordier [1967] Finance Director [South African]; Timothy Andrew Vaughan [1965] Managing Director

**RSR Limited**
*Incorporated:* 7 May 1999 *Employees:* 117
*Net Worth:* £17,973,888 *Total Assets:* £19,709,656
*Registered Office:* 7 Robin Lane, High Bentham, Lancaster, LA2 7AB
*Activities:* Manufacture of basic pharmaceutical products
*Major Shareholder:* Bernard Rees-Smith
*Officers:* Jenny Louise Barwise, Secretary; Janet Bradbury [1966] Director/Scientist; Dr Shu Chen [1966] Director/Scientist; Dr Jadwiga Furmaniak [1951] Director/Scientist; Dr Michael Powell [1960] Director/Scientist; Dr Bernard Rees Smith [1944] Director; Dr Jane Sanders [1966] Director/Scientist

**Ruby Acquisitions Limited**
*Incorporated:* 10 April 2006
*Net Worth:* £88,831,000 *Total Assets:* £187,855,008
*Registered Office:* Richmond House, Leeming Bar, Northallerton, N Yorks, DL7 9UL
*Activities:* Activities of production holding companies
*Parent:* Froneri International PLC
*Officers:* Phil Karl Griffin [1972] Director; Marcello Mattia [1965] Director [Italian]; Ibrahim Mahmood Ibrahim Najafi [1958] Director

**Rudding Park Estate Limited**
*Incorporated:* 26 March 2003 *Employees:* 7
*Net Worth:* £8,410,430 *Total Assets:* £10,945,925
*Registered Office:* Rudding Estate Office, Haggs Farm, Haggs Road, Follifoot, Harrogate, N Yorks, HG3 1EQ
*Activities:* Growing of cereals (except rice), leguminous crops and oil seeds
*Major Shareholder:* Mark Mackaness
*Officers:* Janet Elizabeth Mackaness, Secretary; Mark Mackaness [1952] Director/Chartered Surveyor

**Rudding Park Limited**
*Incorporated:* 20 March 1987 *Employees:* 381
*Net Worth:* £12,604,507 *Total Assets:* £32,252,504
*Registered Office:* Rudding Park, Follifoot, Harrogate, N Yorks, HG3 1JH
*Activities:* Hotels and similar accommodation
*Parent:* Aketon Limited
*Officers:* Graham Molyneux, Secretary; Peter John Banks [1968] Director/Hotel Manager; Judith Mary Mackaness [1946] Director; Nicholas John Mackaness [1984] Director/Management Consultant; Simon Peter Mackaness [1949] Director

**Rufforth Park Limited**
*Incorporated:* 10 November 1987 *Employees:* 67
*Net Worth:* £2,206,537 *Total Assets:* £6,291,053
*Registered Office:* 7 Memorial Avenue, Withernsea, Hull, HU19 2DN
*Activities:* Other service activities n.e.c.
*Major Shareholder:* Roger Martin Ginley
*Officers:* Roger Martin Ginley, Secretary; Roger Martin Ginley [1947] Director

**The Rugby Football League Limited**
*Incorporated:* 21 September 1999 *Employees:* 155
*Net Worth Deficit:* £2,905,551 *Total Assets:* £14,642,323
*Registered Office:* Red Hall, Red Hall Lane, Leeds, LS17 8NB
*Activities:* Other sports activities
*Officers:* Karen Elizabeth Moorhouse, Secretary; Brian Robert Barwick [1954] Director; Christopher Charles Brindley [1964] Director; Christopher John Hurst [1980] Director/Owner C J Hurst Consultancy; Simon Harris Johnson [1966] Director; Karen Elizabeth Moorhouse [1979] Director/Solicitor; Ralph William James Rimmer [1965] Sports Governing Body Director

**Rumford Tankers Limited**
*Incorporated:* 3 October 1991 *Employees:* 2
*Net Worth:* £2,043,255 *Total Assets:* £3,912,882
*Registered Office:* 1 Park Row, Leeds, LS1 5AB
*Activities:* Sea and coastal freight water transport
*Parent:* Rever Offshore UK Limited
*Officers:* Mark John Bessell [1964] Director; Neale John Stewart [1963] Director

**Running Deep Limited**
*Incorporated:* 30 July 1998 *Employees:* 160
*Net Worth:* £1,012,712 *Total Assets:* £4,649,796
*Registered Office:* The Deep Business Centre, Hull, HU1 4BG
*Activities:* Other letting and operating of own or leased real estate
*Parent:* EMIH Limited
*Officers:* Neil Graham Porteus, Secretary; Graham Chesters [1944] Director/University Lecturer; Catherine Clare Duke [1977] Director/Chief Executive; David William Gemmell [1940] Director/Retired; Anthony John Hunt [1938] Director/Retired; Alan William Kirkman [1953] Director/Financial Consultant; Philip Alexander Leigh [1959] Director/University Professor; Susan Marialuisa Lockwood [1955] Director/Retired Solicitor; John Alan Parkes [1939] Director/Retired Professional

**Rural & Commercial Holdings Limited**
*Incorporated:* 3 October 2014 *Employees:* 125
*Net Worth:* £4,204,467 *Total Assets:* £34,431,952
*Registered Office:* The Hamlet, Hornbeam Park, Harrogate, N Yorks, HG2 8RE
*Activities:* Non-life insurance
*Major Shareholder:* Phillip William Henry James
*Officers:* Elizabeth Anne Brophy, Secretary; Allan Crawford Adamson Gribben [1953] Director; Richard Miles Skingle [1970] Finance Director; Malachy Paul Smith [1948] Director [Irish]; Timothy John Smyth [1967] Director/Chief Executive

**Rural Concepts (Libya) Limited**
*Incorporated:* 1 July 2015
*Net Worth:* £100 *Total Assets:* £20,000,000
*Registered Office:* The Estate Office, Broughton Hall, Skipton, N Yorks, BD23 3AE
*Activities:* Dormant company
*Parent:* Rural Concepts Limited
*Officers:* Roger Henry Tempest [1963] Director

**Rural Concepts Construction Limited**
*Incorporated:* 30 June 1998
*Net Worth:* £20,000,002 *Total Assets:* £20,325,900
*Registered Office:* Estate Office, Broughton Hall, Broughton, Skipton, N Yorks, BD23 3AE
*Activities:* Development of building projects
*Parent:* Rural Concepts (Libya) Limited
*Officers:* Roger Henry Tempest [1963] Director/Landowner

**Rural Insurance Group Limited**
*Incorporated:* 21 December 1987 *Employees:* 91
*Net Worth:* £1,844,144 *Total Assets:* £3,622,563
*Registered Office:* The Hamlet, Hornbeam Park, Harrogate, N Yorks, HG2 8RE
*Activities:* Non-life insurance
*Parent:* PBS Holdings Limited
*Officers:* Elizabeth Anne Brophy, Secretary; David Cahoon [1967] Managing Director; Allan Crawford Adamson Gribben [1953] Director/Chairman; Lance Douglas Harvey [1957] Director; Richard Miles Skingle [1970] Finance Director; Malachy Paul Smith [1948] Director [Irish]; Timothy John Smyth [1967] Director

**Rushbond PLC**
*Incorporated:* 8 July 1986 *Employees:* 10
*Net Worth:* £67,855,304 *Total Assets:* £123,159,008
*Registered Office:* 5 Hawthorn Park, Coal Road, Leeds, LS14 1PQ
*Activities:* Buying and selling of own real estate
*Major Shareholder:* Jonathan Maud
*Officers:* Richard Mark Powell, Secretary; Mark Richard Finch [1967] Director/Chartered Surveyors & Chartered Town Planner; Michael John Hartley [1949] Director/Chartered Surveyor; Gina Maud [1966] Director; Jonathan William Maud [1960] Director; Richard Mark Powell [1967] Director/Chartered Accountant; Peter John Stuart Thompson [1946] Solicitor and Director; Nigel Wilkinson [1964] Director/Chartered Accountant

**Rushbond Retail Limited**
*Incorporated:* 22 July 2002 *Employees:* 3
*Net Worth:* £482,003 *Total Assets:* £4,498,241
*Registered Office:* 5 Hawthorn Park, Coal Road, Leeds, LS14 1PQ
*Activities:* Buying and selling of own real estate
*Parent:* Rushbond PLC
*Officers:* Richard Mark Powell, Secretary; Mark Richard Finch [1967] Director/Chartered Surveyor Chartered Town Planner; Jonathan William Maud [1960] Director; Richard Mark Powell [1967] Director/Chartered Accountant

**Russell Armer Group Limited**
*Incorporated:* 14 February 2005 *Employees:* 65
*Net Worth:* £7,227,799 *Total Assets:* £9,707,496
*Registered Office:* Mintsfeet Place, Mintsfeet Road North, Kendal, Cumbria, LA9 6LL
*Activities:* Activities of head offices
*Shareholders:* David Martyn Nicholson; Andrew Christopher Taylor
*Officers:* Karen Patricia Cowgill, Secretary; David Martyn Nicholson [1956] Director; Andrew Christopher Taylor [1960] Director

**Russell Armer Limited**
*Incorporated:* 17 January 1961 *Employees:* 63
*Net Worth:* £6,668,113 *Total Assets:* £9,231,119
*Registered Office:* Mintsfeet Place, Mintsfeet Road North, Kendal, Cumbria, LA9 6LL
*Activities:* Construction of commercial buildings
*Parent:* Russell Armer Group Limited
*Officers:* Karen Patricia Cowgill, Secretary; David Martyn Nicholson [1956] Director/Quantity Surveyor; Andrew Christopher Taylor [1960] Director

**Russell's (Kirbymoorside) Limited**
*Incorporated:* 30 December 1921 *Employees:* 125
*Net Worth:* £7,616,937 *Total Assets:* £22,251,052
*Registered Office:* Eden Works, Eden House Road, Old Malton, Malton, N Yorks, YO17 6RD
*Activities:* Wholesale of agricultural machinery, equipment and supplies
*Officers:* Robert Neil Whitehead, Secretary; John Richard Archer [1943] Director/Solicitor (Retired); Timothy Paul Russell [1967] Managing Director; Henry Edward Shaw [1952] Director; John Shaw [1953] Director/Farmer; William Guy Peter Shaw [1955] Director; Darrell Ward [1969] Finance Director; Robert Neil Whitehead [1956] Director

**RW Refrigeration Wholesale Limited**
*Incorporated:* 22 October 1997 *Employees:* 46
*Net Worth:* £658,000 *Total Assets:* £12,279,000
*Registered Office:* 15 Bruntcliffe Avenue, Leeds 27 Industrial Estate, Morley, Leeds, LS27 0LL
*Activities:* Wholesale of other machinery and equipment
*Officers:* David Patrick Campbell, Secretary; Per Olof Goran Bertland [1957] Director [Swedish]; John David Billson [1960] Director; David Patrick Campbell [1979] Director/Accountant

**RX Systems Limited**
*Incorporated:* 20 March 2003 *Employees:* 149
*Net Worth:* £18,285,620 *Total Assets:* £27,622,706
*Registered Office:* Rawdon House, Green Lane, Yeadon, Leeds, LS19 7BY
*Activities:* Other information technology service activities
*Parent:* Emis Group PLC
*Officers:* Christine Benson, Secretary; Peter John Southby [1973] Director/Chief Financial Officer; Ian Taylor [1967] Managing Director; Andrew John Thorburn [1962] Director

**Ryburn Valley High School**
*Incorporated:* 14 May 2014 *Employees:* 163
*Net Worth:* £14,580,010 *Total Assets:* £16,007,129
*Registered Office:* Ryburn Valley High School, St Peter's Avenue, Sowerby Bridge, W Yorks, HX6 1DF
*Activities:* General secondary education
*Officers:* Melvyn Cross [1949] Director/Justice of The Peace; Michael Craig Robertshaw [1963] Director/Operational Finance Manager; Jeffrey Thomas Tinkler [1953] Director/Retired

**Ryedale Garages (1946) Limited**
*Incorporated:* 21 November 1946 *Employees:* 44
*Net Worth:* £2,136,562 *Total Assets:* £3,413,895
*Registered Office:* Piercy End, Kirkbymoorside, York, YO62 6DG
*Activities:* Sale of new cars and light motor vehicles
*Major Shareholder:* John Stuart Cook
*Officers:* Alexander Stuart Cook, Secretary; Alexander Stuart Cook [1937] Director/Secretary; John Stuart Cook [1969] Director

**Ryedale Printing Works Limited**
*Incorporated:* 20 December 1978 *Employees:* 84
*Net Worth:* £1,027,384 *Total Assets:* £4,157,213
*Registered Office:* Ryedale Group, Kirkdale Road, Kirkbymoorside, York, YO62 6YB
*Activities:* Manufacture of printed labels
*Parent:* Ryedale Group Limited
*Officers:* Stephen Robert Buffoni, Secretary; James John Buffoni [1980] Managing Director; Jill Buffoni [1955] Director; John Peter Buffoni [1950] Director/Master Printer; Karen Jane Buffoni [1959] Director; Stephen Robert Buffoni [1956] Director/Master Printer

**S & A Builders Merchants Limited**
*Incorporated:* 27 November 2015 *Employees:* 27
*Net Worth:* £2,100,445 *Total Assets:* £3,499,354
*Registered Office:* Harmire Enterprise Park, Barnard Castle, Co Durham, DL12 8EH
*Activities:* Agents involved in the sale of timber and building materials
*Shareholder:* Glynis Catterson
*Officers:* Glynis Catterson [1965] Finance Director; Joe Catterson [1994] Director; John Leslie Catterson [1961] Director; Sarah Eve Catterson [1997] Director

**S & J Industries Limited**
*Incorporated:* 9 May 1991 *Employees:* 126
*Net Worth:* £16,933,610 *Total Assets:* £23,298,780
*Registered Office:* Lowfields Road, Leeds, LS12 6ET
*Activities:* Other letting and operating of own or leased real estate
*Officers:* Richard Peter Lumley, Secretary; Robert Christopher Winn Hargreaves [1954] Director; Iain Robertson Manson [1947] Director/Accountant

**S B Homes Ltd.**
*Incorporated:* 29 May 1997 *Employees:* 7
*Net Worth:* £2,418,833 *Total Assets:* £3,116,249
*Registered Office:* 4 Brougham Road, Marsden, Huddersfield, W Yorks, HD7 6BN
*Activities:* Construction of domestic buildings
*Major Shareholder:* Stephen Glen Byram
*Officers:* Rachael Jayne Byram, Secretary; Rachael Jayne Byram [1968] Director/Businesswoman; Sophie Charlotte Byram [1990] Director/Office Manager; Stephen Glen Byram [1966] Director/Builder

**S D C Enterprises Limited**
*Incorporated:* 24 October 2001 *Employees:* 26
*Net Worth:* £2,763,190 *Total Assets:* £4,265,172
*Registered Office:* Pickwick Mills, Huddersfield Road, Thongsbridge, Holmfirth, W Yorks, HD9 3JL
*Activities:* Manufacture of other textiles n.e.c.
*Officers:* Kathryn Hampshire, Secretary; Trevor Lambourne [1958] Director/Research and Innovation Development Manager; John Leslie Morris [1944] Director/Retired; Elizabeth Jane Straughan [1960] Director; Gavin Charles Howe Thatcher [1966] Director; Mark Andrew Yare [1969] Managing Director

**S S Components Limited**
*Incorporated:* 28 January 1997 *Employees:* 22
*Net Worth:* £5,001,905 *Total Assets:* £5,710,000
*Registered Office:* Huddersfield Road, Mirfield, W Yorks, WF14 9DQ
*Activities:* Wholesale trade of motor vehicle parts and accessories
*Shareholders:* John Ashley Smith; Helen Marie Smith
*Officers:* Pauline Dyson, Secretary; Helen Marie Smith [1962] Director; John Ashley Smith [1957] Director/Manager

**S.A.R. Metals Limited**
*Incorporated:* 29 November 2010 *Employees:* 21
*Net Worth:* £1,986,167 *Total Assets:* £4,007,714
*Registered Office:* Unit 1 Pelham Industrial Estate, Manby Road, Immingham, N E Lincs, DN40 2LF
*Activities:* Collection of non-hazardous waste
*Shareholder:* Justas Valentinas
*Officers:* Tomas Sakalys [1986] Director [Lithuanian]; Justas Valentinas [1990] Director [Lithuanian]

**S.A.R. Recycling Ltd**
*Incorporated:* 19 November 2007 *Employees:* 40
*Net Worth:* £2,839,646 *Total Assets:* £4,541,330
*Registered Office:* Unit 1 Pelham Industrial Estate, Manby Road, Immingham, N E Lincs, DN40 2LF
*Activities:* Collection of non-hazardous waste
*Parent:* Serius Group Limited
*Officers:* Sergejus Kavleiskij [1972] Managing Director; Arvydas Pocevicius [1985] Technical Director [Lithuanian]

**S.B.S. (Cumbria) Limited**
*Incorporated:* 27 September 1994
*Net Worth:* £2,950,045 *Total Assets:* £4,984,907
*Registered Office:* Unit 5 Parkside Business Park, Parkside Road, Kendal, Cumbria, LA9 7EN
*Activities:* Agents involved in the sale of timber and building materials
*Major Shareholder:* Nicholas John Uttley
*Officers:* John Stanley Charlton, Secretary; Nicholas John Uttley [1957] Managing Director

**S.M.K. Textiles Limited**
*Incorporated:* 9 July 2002 *Employees:* 15
*Net Worth:* £1,234,001 *Total Assets:* £3,134,391
*Registered Office:* 3 Linefield House, Linefield Road, Batley, W Yorks, WF17 0ES
*Activities:* Manufacture of other furniture
*Officers:* Rifat Shaheen Khan, Secretary; Sultan Mahmood Khan [1971] Director/Textile Merchant

**S.T.L. Trading Company Limited**
*Incorporated:* 14 September 2004 *Employees:* 30
*Previous:* S.T.L. Trading Company
*Net Worth:* £7,250,486 *Total Assets:* £9,109,631
*Registered Office:* Blue Diamond House, Sandall Stones Road, Kirk Sandall Industrial Estate, Doncaster, S Yorks, DN3 1QR
*Activities:* Wholesale of other intermediate products
*Shareholder:* John West
*Officers:* Rachel West, Secretary; John West [1957] Managing Director; Lee West [1982] Director/Sales; Shaun West [1978] Director/Sales; Trevor West [1980] Director/Sales

**S.W. Durham Training Limited**
*Incorporated:* 13 October 1967 *Employees:* 25
*Net Worth:* £3,429,461 *Total Assets:* £3,590,411
*Registered Office:* Durham Way South, Aycliffe Business Park, Newton Aycliffe, Co Durham, DL5 6AT
*Activities:* Technical and vocational secondary education
*Officers:* Judith Eva Layfield, Secretary; Paul Aither [1982] Director/Site Electrical Engineer; Graham Currie [1970] Finance Director; Natalie Davison [1969] Director/College Principal; Andrew Arthur Dunn [1964] Director; Pamela Petty [1968] Managing Director; Stephen John Rose [1957] Director/Plant Manager; Andrew Scott [1963] Director/Engineering Manager

**Sabre Rail Services Limited**
*Incorporated:* 18 June 1987 *Employees:* 89
*Net Worth:* £3,284,052 *Total Assets:* £5,492,826
*Registered Office:* Grindon Way, Heighington Lane Business Park, Newton Aycliffe, Co Durham, DL5 6SH
*Activities:* Manufacture of railway locomotives and rolling stock
*Major Shareholder:* Glenys Thompson
*Officers:* Glenys Thompson, Secretary; Stephen Mark Thompson [1979] Managing Director

**Sabrina Health Care Limited**
*Incorporated:* 10 September 2007 *Employees:* 136
*Net Worth:* £1,979,640 *Total Assets:* £7,129,353
*Registered Office:* 62-63 Westborough, Scarborough, N Yorks, YO11 1TS
*Activities:* Residential nursing care facilities
*Major Shareholder:* Tamby Seeneevassen
*Officers:* Tamby Seeneevassen [1960] Director/Barrister [Mauritian]

**Saferoad UK Ltd**
*Incorporated:* 3 February 2006 *Employees:* 2
*Net Worth:* £2,103,864 *Total Assets:* £6,685,925
*Registered Office:* Concord House, Bessemer Way, Sawcliffe Industrial Park, Scunthorpe, N Lincs, DN15 8XE
*Activities:* Construction of roads and motorways
*Parent:* Saferoad AS
*Officers:* Ian Sheriff, Secretary; Shaun Francis Cummings [1961] Director; Terje Myhre [1965] Director [Norwegian]

**Saferoad VRS Ltd**
*Incorporated:* 3 February 2006 *Employees:* 66
*Net Worth:* £1,265,817 *Total Assets:* £5,996,440
*Registered Office:* Concord House, Bessemer Way, Sawcliffe Industrial Park, Scunthorpe, N Lincs, DN15 8XE
*Activities:* Construction of roads and motorways
*Parent:* Saferoad UK Ltd
*Officers:* Ian Sheriff, Secretary; Shaun Francis Cummings [1961] Managing Director; Terje Myhre [1965] Director [Norwegian]

**Safeway (Overseas) Limited**
*Incorporated:* 3 October 1924 *Employees:* 291
*Net Worth:* £92,548,000 *Total Assets:* £98,877,000
*Registered Office:* Hilmore House, Gain Lane, Bradford, W Yorks, BD3 7DL
*Activities:* Retail sale in non-specialised stores with food, beverages or tobacco predominating
*Parent:* Safeway Stores Limited
*Officers:* Jonathan James Burke, Secretary; Jonathan James Burke [1966] Director/Company Secretary; Joanna Louise Goff [1978] Finance Director

**Safeway Limited**
*Incorporated:* 23 February 1977 *Employees:* 44,819
*Net Worth:* £1,804,999,936 *Total Assets:* £3,827,000,064
*Registered Office:* Hilmore House, Gain Lane, Bradford, W Yorks, BD3 7DL
*Activities:* Retail sale in non-specialised stores with food, beverages or tobacco predominating
*Parent:* Wm Morrison Supermarkets Holdings Limited
*Officers:* Jonathan James Burke, Secretary; Jonathan James Burke [1966] Director; Trevor John Strain [1975] Finance Director

**Safeway Stores Limited**
*Incorporated:* 15 January 1963
*Net Worth:* £859,000,000 *Total Assets:* £4,403,999,744
*Registered Office:* Hilmore House, Gain Lane, Bradford, W Yorks, BD3 7DL
*Activities:* Retail sale in non-specialised stores with food, beverages or tobacco predominating
*Parent:* Stores Group Limited
*Officers:* Jonathan James Burke, Secretary; Jonathan James Burke [1966] Director; Alison Charnock [1969] Director/Solicitor; Gary William Mills [1966] Director; Trevor John Strain [1975] Finance Director

**Saftronics Limited**
*Incorporated:* 2 August 1985 *Employees:* 72
*Net Worth:* £2,398,336 *Total Assets:* £3,756,820
*Registered Office:* Pearson Street, Leeds, W Yorks, LS10 1BQ
*Activities:* Manufacture of other electrical equipment
*Parent:* Saftronics Holdings Limited
*Officers:* Richard John Kinder, Secretary/Chartered Accountant; Mark Christian Godfrey [1969] Director; Andrew Hutchinson [1975] Director/Accountant; Richard John Kinder [1955] Director/Chartered Accountant; Alan Harry Rayner [1962] Director/Sales Manager; Jonathan Paul Andrew Robinson [1966] Director/Operations

**Sagars Accountants Ltd**
*Incorporated:* 2 December 1997 *Employees:* 8
*Net Worth:* £612,964 *Total Assets:* £5,153,313
*Registered Office:* Gresham House, 5-7 St Pauls Street, Leeds, LS1 2JG
*Activities:* Accounting and auditing activities
*Shareholders:* Christopher Winston Jones; John Robert Beevers
*Officers:* John Robert Beevers, Secretary; Fergus Wesley Beadle [1969] Director/Accountant; John Robert Beevers [1968] Director/Chartered Accountant; Kevin Hoult [1975] Director/Chartered Accountant; Alison Margaret Jones [1971] Director/Chartered Accountant; Christopher Winston Jones [1959] Director/Chartered Accountant; Paul Lodder [1978] Director/Accountant; Katharine Naylor [1970] Director/Accountant; Susan Catherine Seaman [1966] Director/Chartered Accountant

**Saint Catherines Hospice Trust**
*Incorporated:* 7 April 1982 *Employees:* 239
*Net Worth:* £8,976,907 *Total Assets:* £9,393,320
*Registered Office:* Saint Catherine's Hospice, Throxenby Lane, Scarborough, N Yorks, YO12 5RE
*Activities:* Specialists medical practice activities
*Officers:* Michael Gary Wilkerson, Secretary; Timothy John Boyes [1948] Managing Director Department Store Group; Malcolm Chell [1955] Director/Retired; Doctor James Francis Philip Garnett [1949] Director/Medical Practitioner; Margaret Middlebrook [1957] Director/HR Manager; Susan Carole Standard-Sheader [1952] Director; John Cyril Stevenson [1946] Director/Retired; Simon Peter Ward [1950] Director/Chartered Surveyor

**Saint Leonard's Property Company Limited**
*Incorporated:* 7 August 2008 *Employees:* 3
*Net Worth:* £4,533,129 *Total Assets:* £10,276,689
*Registered Office:* 5 Hawthorn Park, Coal Road, Leeds, LS14 1PQ
*Activities:* Buying and selling of own real estate
*Parent:* Rushbond PLC
*Officers:* Richard Mark Powell, Secretary; Mark Richard Finch [1967] Director/Chartered Surveyor Chartered Town Planner; Jonathan William Maud [1960] Director; Richard Mark Powell [1967] Director/Chartered Accountant

**Salamander Fabrications Limited**
*Incorporated:* 12 November 1968 *Employees:* 39
*Net Worth:* £2,899,889 *Total Assets:* £4,022,339
*Registered Office:* Commercial Mills, Old Bank, Slaithwaite, Huddersfield, W Yorks, HD7 5HB
*Activities:* Manufacture of other fabricated metal products n.e.c.
*Parent:* Salamander Haskell Holdings Limited
*Officers:* Michael Haskell [1967] Director & Works Manager

**Salendine Nook Academy Trust**
*Incorporated:* 15 December 2011 *Employees:* 165
*Net Worth:* £15,531,000 *Total Assets:* £16,712,000
*Registered Office:* Salendine Nook High School, New Hey Road, Salendine Nook, Huddersfield, W Yorks, HD3 4GN
*Activities:* General secondary education
*Officers:* Virginia Elaine Wood, Secretary; Asifa Ali [1967] Director/NHS Manager; Andrew John Bird [1953] Director/Retired; Stuart Butcher [1944] Director/Retired; Darren Christian [1972] Director/Principal; Nicholas Dodd [1968] Director/6th Form College Teacher; Jacqueline Tracy Field [1961] Director/Social Worker; Aaron Luke Flynn [1987] Director/Teacher; Barbara Ruth Hodgkinson [1950] Director/Retired; Lisa Hogarth [1966] Director/Senior Physiotherapist; Sheena Kitson-Perfitt [1978] Director/Child Protection Officer; Mark Edward Mitchell [1962] Director/Police Sergeant; Dominic Owen [1967] Director/Senior Manager; Andrea Louise Quinlan [1964] Director/Administrator/Clerk; Jonathan Smith [1983] Director/Teacher; James Wood [1968] Director/Commercial Property Management Consultant

**Saltend Cogeneration Company Limited**
*Incorporated:* 1 November 1996
*Net Worth:* £166,016,992 *Total Assets:* £269,847,008
*Registered Office:* Saltend Power Station, Saltend Chemicals Park, Hedon Road, Hull, HU12 8GA
*Activities:* Production of electricity
*Parent:* SCCL Holdings Limited
*Officers:* Michael Ellis Farr [1964] Director/Power Station Manager; Russell Holland [1976] Director/Finance and Procurement Manager; Scott Jonathan Keen [1974] Director

**Salthaugh Grange Farm Limited**
*Incorporated:* 27 January 2005 *Employees:* 4
*Net Worth:* £508,827 *Total Assets:* £3,190,976
*Registered Office:* Mill Nurseries, Ottringham Road, Keyingham, Hull, HU12 9RX
*Activities:* Growing of cereals (except rice), leguminous crops and oil seeds
*Officers:* Catharina Audrey Jayne de Lang, Secretary; Catharina Audrey Jayne de Lang [1970] Director/Physiotherapist; David Roy de Lang [1964] Director/Market Gardener; Hermanus Gerrit de Lang [1962] Director/Market Gardener; Robert Johannes de Lang [1968] Director/Market Gardener

**Salts Estates Limited**
*Incorporated:* 15 April 1987 *Employees:* 104
*Net Worth:* £6,995,294 *Total Assets:* £7,770,405
*Registered Office:* Salts Mill, Victoria Road, Saltaire, Shipley, W Yorks, BD18 3LB
*Activities:* Retail sale of books in specialised stores
*Officers:* Carl David Howarth, Secretary; Maurice Miller [1947] Director; Davina Silver [1979] Director; Margaret Silver [1949] Director; Robin Jeremy Silver [1951] Director; Zoe Silver [1976] Director/Producer

**Salzgitter Mannesmann UK Limited**
*Incorporated:* 13 November 1989 *Employees:* 16
*Previous:* Salzgitter Mannesmann (UK) Limited
*Net Worth:* £2,266,549 *Total Assets:* £16,528,853
*Registered Office:* Simpson House, Windsor Court, Clarence Drive, Harrogate, N Yorks, HG1 2PE
*Activities:* Wholesale of metals and metal ores
*Shareholder:* The State of Lower Saxony
*Officers:* Amanda Mary Mohr, Secretary; Joerg Peter Eugen Grzella [1963] Director [German]; Volker Hans Schult [1958] Director [German]; Julian Thompson [1964] Managing Director

**Samara Properties Limited**
*Incorporated:* 22 April 2016
*Net Worth:* £51,272 *Total Assets:* £15,739,478
*Registered Office:* First Floor, 6 Butts Court, Leeds, LS1 5JS
*Activities:* Hotels and similar accommodation
*Officers:* Harith Albazie, Secretary; Dr Ahmed Albazie [1949] Director; Harith Harry Albazie [1984] Company Secretary/Director; Lena Albazie [1978] Director; Othman Mahmood [1981] Director [Canadian]

**Samsung C & T ECUK Limited**
*Incorporated:* 3 July 2012 *Employees:* 37
*Net Worth Deficit:* £38,012,064 *Total Assets:* £36,701,696
*Registered Office:* Whessoe Technology Centre, Alderman Best Way, Morton Palms, Darlington, Co Durham, DL1 4WB
*Activities:* Engineering design activities for industrial process and production
*Officers:* Yi Heon Hyun [1971] Director/CFO of Whessoe Engineering Ltd [South Korean]

**San Pedro Properties Limited**
*Incorporated:* 31 July 2000 *Employees:* 4
*Net Worth:* £2,789,269 *Total Assets:* £6,881,247
*Registered Office:* St Georges House, Village Street, Norwood Green, Halifax, W Yorks, HX3 8QG
*Activities:* Other letting and operating of own or leased real estate
*Shareholder:* Andrew John Mear
*Officers:* Andrew John Mear [1977] Director/Property Manager; Nicholas James Mear [1979] Director/Property Manager; Simon George Mear [1981] Director/Maintenance Manager

**Sand Le Mere Caravan Park Limited**
*Incorporated:* 2 May 1985 *Employees:* 109
*Net Worth:* £9,873,318 *Total Assets:* £18,399,456
*Registered Office:* Southfield Lane, Tunstall, Hull, HU12 0JF
*Activities:* Holiday centres and villages
*Parent:* Bridge Leisure Parks Limited
*Officers:* Simon Elliott, Secretary; Simon John Elliott [1969] Director; Andrew Stephen Howe [1968] Director; Simon Jamie Williams [1972] Director

**Sandal Motors (Bayern) Limited**
*Incorporated:* 28 July 1978 *Employees:* 132
*Net Worth:* £6,083,282 *Total Assets:* £22,176,564
*Registered Office:* Dewsbury Road, Wakefield, W Yorks, WF2 9BE
*Activities:* Sale of new cars and light motor vehicles
*Parent:* Findpath Limited
*Officers:* Timothy John Simons, Secretary; David Bosomworth [1954] Director; Jason Trevor Carter [1963] Director; Timothy John Simons [1966] Director

**Sandal Motors (Huddersfield) Limited**
*Incorporated:* 21 July 2008 *Employees:* 100
*Net Worth:* £2,386,669 *Total Assets:* £19,528,562
*Registered Office:* Dewsbury Road, Wakefield, W Yorks, WF2 9BE
*Activities:* Sale of new cars and light motor vehicles
*Parent:* Findpath Ltd
*Officers:* Timothy John Simons, Secretary; David Bosomworth [1954] Director; Jason Trevor Carter [1963] Director; Timothy John Simons [1966] Finance Director

**Sandburn York Limited**
*Incorporated:* 17 January 1983 *Employees:* 75
*Net Worth:* £7,151,607 *Total Assets:* £10,959,043
*Registered Office:* 31 St Saviourgate, York, YO1 8NQ
*Activities:* Other holiday and other collective accommodation
*Officers:* James Michael Hogg, Secretary; Hayley Amanda Abdelsatter [1978] Director; Simon Buckley [1972] Director; James Michael Hogg [1973] Director/Estate Manager

**Sanderson Contracts Limited**
*Incorporated:* 10 December 1999 *Employees:* 34
*Net Worth Deficit:* £421,258 *Total Assets:* £7,624,837
*Registered Office:* Sanderson House, 158 Leeds Road, Glasshoughton, W Yorks, WF10 4PD
*Activities:* Other building completion and finishing
*Major Shareholder:* Ian Sanderson
*Officers:* James Martin Mason, Secretary; Andrew Kneeshaw [1970] Commercial Director; James Martin Mason [1959] Finance Director; David Lee Robinson [1979] Director; Ian Sanderson [1965] Director

**Sanderson Weatherall Group Limited**
*Incorporated:* 19 August 2003 *Employees:* 202
*Net Worth Deficit:* £261,809 *Total Assets:* £7,312,636
*Registered Office:* 6th Floor, Central Square, 29 Wellington Street, Leeds, LS1 4DL
*Activities:* Real estate agencies
*Officers:* Martin Walker Archer, Finance Director; Martin Walker Archer [1957] Finance Director; Neil Charles William Bestwick [1976] Director/Chartered Surveyor; Adam Lee Burkinshaw [1977] Director/Chartered Surveyor; Matthew Benedict Clarke [1976] Director/Chartered Surveyor; David Downing [1971] Director/Chartered Surveyor; Richard William Dunn [1969] Director/Partner; Andrew Warwick Ellis [1965] Director/Chartered Surveyor; Richard McIntosh Farr [1959] Director/Chartered Surveyor; Michael Daniel Worsley Hardy [1965] Director; Simon Peter Heather [1968] Director/Chartered Surveyor; Christian Robert Humphreys [1976] Director/Chartered Surveyor; Thomas Anthony Kelly [1959] Director/Chartered Surveyor; Philip Bernard Kenny [1956] Director/Chartered Surveyor; Matthew John Lawrence [1976] Director/Chartered Surveyor; Kevin Michael McGorie [1983] Director/Chartered Surveyor; Elizabeth Tanya McLoughlin [1972] Director/Chartered Surveyor; Matthew Midwinter [1967] Director/Partner; Paul William Moody [1968] Director/Surveyor; David Neilson Murray [1977] Director/Partner; Ian Robert Naylor [1960] Director/Chartered Surveyor; Robert Patterson [1958] Director/Chartered Surveyor; George McLean Penrice [1960] Director/Chartered Surveyor; David Haydn Rastrick [1968] Director/Chartered Surveyor; Mark Sheridan [1986] Director; Neil Simpson [1970] Director/Partner; Ian Charles Vivian [1976] Director/Surveyor; Mark Weston [1966] Director

**Sanderson Weatherall LLP**
*Incorporated:* 7 April 2009 *Employees:* 202
*Net Worth:* £3,440,039 *Total Assets:* £6,891,882
*Registered Office:* 6th Floor, Central Square, 29 Wellington Street, Leeds, LS1 4DL
*Officers:* Martin Walker Archer [1957] Member; Richard McIntosh Farr [1959] Member; Matthew Midwinter [1967] Member; Ian Robert Naylor [1960] Member; David Haydn Rastrick [1968] Member; Neil Simpson [1970] Member; Neil Charles William Bestwick [1976] LLP Member; Adam Lee Burkinshaw [1977] LLP Member; Matthew Benedict Clarke [1976] LLP Member; David Downing [1971] LLP Member; Richard William Dunn [1969] LLP Member; Andrew Warwick Ellis [1965] LLP Member; Michael Daniel Worsley Hardy [1965] LLP Member; Simon Peter Heather [1968] LLP Member; Christian Robert Humphreys [1976] LLP Member; Thomas Anthony Kelly [1959] LLP Member; Philip Bernard Kenny [1956] LLP Member; Matthew John Lawrence [1976] LLP Member; Kevin Michael McGorie [1983] LLP Member; Elizabeth Tanya McLoughlin [1972] LLP Member; Paul William Moody [1968] LLP Member; David Neilson Murray [1977] LLP Member; Robert Patterson [1958] LLP Member; George McLean Penrice [1960] LLP Member; Mark Sheridan [1986] LLP Member; Ian Charles Vivian [1976] LLP Member; Mark Weston [1966] LLP Member

**Sandmoor Properties Limited**
*Incorporated:* 3 February 2012 *Employees:* 1
*Net Worth:* £3,725,907 *Total Assets:* £4,582,230
*Registered Office:* 10 Sandmoor Avenue, Alwoodley, Leeds, LS17 7DW
*Activities:* Other letting and operating of own or leased real estate
*Officers:* Peter John Rider [1947] Director

**Sands Care Holdings Limited**
*Incorporated:* 2 April 2008
*Net Worth:* £563,188 *Total Assets:* £3,404,521
*Registered Office:* 390 Marine Road East, Morecambe, Lancs, LA4 5AU
*Activities:* Renting and operating of Housing Association real estate
*Major Shareholder:* Robert Wilson
*Officers:* Robert Wilson [1955] Director

**Sandsfield Gravel Company Limited**
*Incorporated:* 10 March 1966 *Employees:* 108
*Net Worth:* £4,581,284 *Total Assets:* £14,237,423
*Registered Office:* Sandsfield Farm, Catwick Lane, Brandesburton, Driffield, E Yorks, YO25 8SB
*Activities:* Treatment and disposal of non-hazardous waste
*Parent:* Sandsfield Limited
*Officers:* Dianne Mary Mewburn, Secretary; Dianne Mary Mewburn [1940] Director/Farmer; James Heppell Mewburn [1941] Director/Farmer; Mark Wilson Mewburn [1967] Director/Farmer

**Sandtoft Developments Limited**
*Incorporated:* 10 June 1992
*Net Worth:* £5,347,241 *Total Assets:* £10,004,758
*Registered Office:* Castlegarth Grange, Scott Lane, Wetherby, W Yorks, LS22 6LH
*Activities:* Other letting and operating of own or leased real estate
*Parent:* Caddick Developments Limited
*Officers:* Paul Andrew Bullers, Secretary; Paul Andrew Bullers [1966] Finance Director; Alexandra Esther Caddick [1952] Director; Paul Caddick [1950] Director; Myles Edward Hartley [1969] Director/Chartered Surveyor

**Sangwin Holdings Limited**
*Incorporated:* 2 September 2008 *Employees:* 157
*Net Worth:* £3,499,960 *Total Assets:* £8,648,869
*Registered Office:* Head Office, Dansom Lane South, Hull, HU8 7LN
*Activities:* Other business support service activities n.e.c.
*Major Shareholder:* Ian Douglas Sangwin
*Officers:* David Spurgeon, Secretary; Ian Douglas Sangwin [1940] Director/Civil Engineer; Nicholas John Sangwin [1967] Director; David Spurgeon [1954] Director/Secretary

**Sangwin Plant Hire Limited**
*Incorporated:* 4 February 1969 *Employees:* 36
*Net Worth:* £1,283,880 *Total Assets:* £3,143,003
*Registered Office:* Head Office, Dansom Lane South, Hull, HU8 7LN
*Activities:* Renting and leasing of other machinery, equipment and tangible goods n.e.c.
*Parent:* Sangwin Holdings Limited
*Officers:* David Spurgeon, Chartered Secretary; Andrew Fenton [1962] Operations Director; Ian Douglas Sangwin [1940] Director/Civil Engineer; Nicholas John Sangwin [1967] Director; David Spurgeon [1954] Director/Chartered Secretary

**Sanipex Limited**
*Incorporated:* 9 November 2006 *Employees:* 29
*Net Worth Deficit:* £3,315,343 *Total Assets:* £15,182,837
*Registered Office:* Unit 1 Oakwell Park Trading Estate, Oakwell Way, Birstall, Batley, W Yorks, WF17 9LU
*Activities:* Wholesale of hardware, plumbing and heating equipment and supplies
*Officers:* David Simon Tudor Jones, Secretary; John Adam Lennon [1963] Managing Director; Richard Malcolm Nicholls [1973] Director

**Sanmet Limited**
*Incorporated:* 29 September 1981 *Employees:* 15
*Net Worth:* £2,585,317 *Total Assets:* £3,640,337
*Registered Office:* 110 Sunderland Street, Tickhill, Doncaster, S Yorks, DN11 9ER
*Activities:* Construction of roads and motorways
*Major Shareholder:* Roger Marsden
*Officers:* Zara Marie Marsden, Secretary; Roger Marsden [1965] Director; Zara Marie Marsden [1965] Director; Robert John Skevington [1953] Director

**Sapphire Technologies Limited**
*Incorporated:* 10 April 1996 *Employees:* 47
*Net Worth:* £1,088,000 *Total Assets:* £5,007,000
*Registered Office:* North Point, Faverdale North, Darlington, Co Durham, DL3 0PH
*Activities:* Information technology consultancy activities
*Parent:* Kiplun Ltd
*Officers:* Joseph Andrew Deane, Secretary; Annabel Berry [1976] Director; Joseph Andrew Deane [1968] Director/Chartered Accountant; John Donald Read Fothergill [1961] Director/Group Chairman; David Generald Lannin [1972] Director; Alan Moffat [1961] Director; Mayan Kantilal Shah [1966] Director

**Sargent Electrical Services Limited**
*Incorporated:* 12 February 1997 *Employees:* 158
*Net Worth:* £9,318,479 *Total Assets:* £12,567,135
*Registered Office:* Unit 39 Tokenspire Business Park, Woodmansey, Beverley, E Yorks, HU17 0TB
*Activities:* Manufacture of other electrical equipment
*Shareholders:* Neil Brian Sargent; Ian Leslie Sargent
*Officers:* Neil Brian Sargent, Secretary/Director; Ann Sargent [1969] Director; Ian Leslie Sargent [1964] Director; Leah Joanne Sargent [1967] Director; Neil Brian Sargent [1965] Director

**Sargents Properties Limited**
*Incorporated:* 11 February 2014 *Employees:* 53
*Net Worth:* £2,365,254 *Total Assets:* £7,407,376
*Registered Office:* 1 Ogden Road, Shaw Lane Industrial Estate, Doncaster, S Yorks, DN2 4SE
*Activities:* Other letting and operating of own or leased real estate
*Major Shareholder:* Ian Douglas Allen
*Officers:* Ian Douglas Allen [1953] Director/Manager

**Saria Limited**
*Incorporated:* 7 April 1955 *Employees:* 114
*Net Worth:* £134,111,176 *Total Assets:* £204,424,336
*Registered Office:* Ings Road, Bentley, Doncaster, S Yorks, DN5 9TL
*Activities:* Activities of head offices
*Officers:* Richard Anthony de Mulder [1966] Director/Sales Executive; Robert Vincent Ratcliffe [1958] Director/Senior Operations Manager; Phillip Antony Simpson [1966] Director/Commercial Services Manager; Andrew Richard Smith [1962] Director/Senior Commercial Services Manager; Franz Bernhard Thier [1965] Director [German]

**I.R. Sarjantson Limited**
*Incorporated:* 15 May 1978 *Employees:* 1
*Net Worth:* £3,153,759 *Total Assets:* £3,166,674
*Registered Office:* Woodhouse Lane, Wadworth, Doncaster, S Yorks, DN11 9BN
*Activities:* Retail sale via stalls and markets of other goods
*Major Shareholder:* Pamela Margaret Sarjantson
*Officers:* Pamela Margaret Sarjantson, Secretary; Pamela Margaret Sarjantson [1963] Director

**Sarval (Hartshill) Limited**
*Incorporated:* 21 April 1960 *Employees:* 80
*Net Worth Deficit:* £6,818,701 *Total Assets:* £20,119,218
*Registered Office:* Ings Road, Doncaster, S Yorks, DN5 9TL
*Activities:* Manufacture of oils and fats
*Parent:* Saria Limited
*Officers:* Robert Vincent Ratcliffe [1958] Director; Andrew Richard Smith [1962] Director

**Sarval Limited**
*Incorporated:* 6 April 1954 *Employees:* 110
*Net Worth Deficit:* £10,570,195 *Total Assets:* £17,894,198
*Registered Office:* Ings Road, Doncaster, S Yorks, DN5 9TL
*Activities:* Manufacture of oils and fats
*Parent:* Saria Limited
*Officers:* Robert Vincent Ratcliffe [1958] Director; Phillip Antony Simpson [1966] Director; Andrew Richard Smith [1962] Director/Group Commercial Manager

**Saur (UK) Limited**
*Incorporated:* 19 February 1986
*Net Worth Deficit:* £8,373,000 *Total Assets:* £4,829,000
*Registered Office:* 1 Park Row, Leeds, LS1 5AB
*Activities:* Activities of head offices
*Officers:* Gilles Patrick Jacques Lassartesse [1965] Project and Business Development Director [French]; Stephanie Thomazeau [1971] Director/Group Financial Controller [French]

**Saur Services (Glasgow) Limited**
*Incorporated:* 6 January 1998 *Employees:* 24
*Net Worth Deficit:* £11,234,000 *Total Assets:* £8,585,000
*Registered Office:* 1 Park Row, Leeds, LS1 5AB
*Activities:* Water collection, treatment and supply
*Parent:* Saur (UK) Limited
*Officers:* Frederic Carbonnier [1965] Director [French]; Guillaume Freon [1984] Director/Financial Controller [French]; Gilles Patrick Jacques Lassartesse [1965] Project and Business Development Director [French]

**Savant Limited**
*Incorporated:* 27 November 1986 *Employees:* 36
*Net Worth:* £2,356,086 *Total Assets:* £3,873,696
*Registered Office:* Dalton Hall Business Centre, Dalton Lane, Burton in Kendal, Carnforth, Cumbria, LA6 1BL
*Activities:* Business and domestic software development
*Parent:* Savant Group Limited
*Officers:* Lewis Philip Bambury, Secretary; John Michael Davies [1961] Director/Software Engineer; Peter Bruce Gregg [1961] Director/Project Manager; Stephen David O'Shea [1974] Director/Computer Programmer; Alexandra Rachel Helen Wood [1972] Director/Archive Supervisor

**Savers Wholesale Ltd**
*Incorporated:* 11 April 2016
*Net Worth:* £3,206,501 *Total Assets:* £3,421,983
*Registered Office:* Unit 60 Marston Moor Business Park, York, YO26 7QF
*Activities:* Wholesale trade of motor vehicle parts and accessories
*Major Shareholder:* Terence Paddon
*Officers:* Terence Paddon [1977] Director

**The Saville Group Limited**
*Incorporated:* 30 September 1987 *Employees:* 228
*Net Worth:* £5,885,644 *Total Assets:* £14,998,991
*Registered Office:* Unit 5 Millfield Lane, Nether Poppleton, York, YO26 6PQ
*Activities:* Manufacture of communication equipment other than telegraph, and telephone apparatus and equipment
*Parent:* Sea Holdings Limited
*Officers:* Colin Donald Nixey, Finance Director; Graham Stuart Carling [1963] Director/Central Division Manager; Andrew John Dyson [1969] Director; Colin Etchells [1966] Director/Northern Sales Manager; Colin Donald Nixey [1962] Finance Director; Ann Louise Pickard [1973] Director/Service Division Manager

**Savoy Tyres Limited**
*Incorporated:* 29 March 1974 *Employees:* 90
*Net Worth:* £1,174,733 *Total Assets:* £4,115,287
*Registered Office:* Savoy Road, Kingston upon Hull, HU8 0TY
*Activities:* Retail trade of motor vehicle parts and accessories
*Major Shareholder:* Paul Palmer
*Officers:* Paula Jane Palmer, Secretary; June Palmer [1941] Director; Maurice Palmer [1943] Director; Paul Palmer [1964] Director; Paula Jane Palmer [1964] Accounts Director

**Leo Sawrij Limited**
*Incorporated:* 24 March 1977 *Employees:* 11
*Net Worth:* £13,740,426 *Total Assets:* £33,937,492
*Registered Office:* Swalesmoor Road, Boothtown, Halifax, W Yorks, HX3 6UF
*Activities:* Other letting and operating of own or leased real estate
*Parent:* Leo Group Limited
*Officers:* Manjit Singh Powar [1976] Director; Danny Steven Sawrij [1969] Director/Farmer; Joanne Sawrij [1966] Director

**Say Scaffolding Limited**
*Incorporated:* 15 December 2004 *Employees:* 2
*Net Worth:* £1,940,021 *Total Assets:* £4,703,848
*Registered Office:* Say House, Units 2, 3 & Offices Rudgate Business Centre, Rudgate Lane, Thorp Arch, Wetherby, W Yorks, LS23 7AT
*Activities:* Scaffold erection
*Shareholders:* Say Group Limited; Philip James Wetten
*Officers:* Amanda Jayne Wetten, Secretary/Administrator; Amanda Jayne Wetten [1971] Director/Administrator; Megan Elise Wetten [1998] Director; Philip James Wetten [1968] Director

**Sayers Road Tanker Rentals Limited**
*Incorporated:* 1 November 2001 *Employees:* 6
*Net Worth:* £3,369,209 *Total Assets:* £6,204,066
*Registered Office:* Tutin Road, Leeming Bar Industrial Estate, Northallerton, N Yorks, DL7 9UJ
*Activities:* Maintenance and repair of motor vehicles
*Major Shareholder:* Clifford Sayer
*Officers:* Louise Chambers, Secretary; Clifford Sayer [1965] Director/Tanker Manufacturer

**SB Wakefield Limited**
*Incorporated:* 26 January 2004 *Employees:* 29
*Net Worth:* £626,488 *Total Assets:* £3,012,160
*Registered Office:* Ings Road, Wakefield, W Yorks, WF1 1RF
*Activities:* Sale of new cars and light motor vehicles
*Major Shareholder:* Simon John Bowett
*Officers:* Simon John Bowett, Secretary; John William Bowett [1987] Operations Director; Simon John Bowett [1946] Director

**Scan-Thors (U.K.) Limited**
*Incorporated:* 7 August 1990 *Employees:* 16
*Net Worth:* £3,433,074 *Total Assets:* £6,311,498
*Registered Office:* 35a Keighley Road, Silsden, Keighley, W Yorks, BD20 0EB
*Activities:* Wholesale of furniture, carpets and lighting equipment
*Shareholders:* Martin Kay; Scan-Thor Group ApS
*Officers:* David Patrick Johnson, Secretary/Accountant; David Patrick Johnson [1965] Director/Accountant; Benjamin Oliver Kay [1984] Director; Martin Kay [1947] Managing Director; Knud Thor Larsen [1948] Director [Danish]; Christian Thor Larsen [1975] Director/Manager [Danish]

**Scantech Offshore Limited**
*Incorporated:* 26 October 1998 *Employees:* 61
*Net Worth:* £5,206,494 *Total Assets:* £26,878,544
*Registered Office:* P O Box 4, Fisher House, Barrow in Furness, Cumbria, LA14 1HR
*Activities:* Renting and leasing of other machinery, equipment and tangible goods n.e.c.
*Parent:* James Fisher and Sons PLC
*Officers:* James Henry John Marsh, Secretary; Nicholas Paul Henry [1961] Director; Stuart Charles Kilpatrick [1962] Director; Shaun Colin Ryan [1962] Director

**Scarborough (UK) Limited**
*Incorporated:* 7 October 2009
*Net Worth:* £1 *Total Assets:* £10,995,026
*Registered Office:* Europa House, 20 Esplanade, Scarborough, N Yorks, YO11 2AQ
*Activities:* Activities of other holding companies n.e.c.
*Parent:* Scarborough Holdings (UK) Limited
*Officers:* Simon Charles McCabe [1977] Director/Development Executive

**Scarborough China Holdings Limited**
*Incorporated:* 4 April 2003
*Net Worth Deficit:* £2,878,417 *Total Assets:* £20,171,924
*Registered Office:* Europa House, 20 Esplanade, Scarborough, N Yorks, YO11 2AQ
*Activities:* Activities of other holding companies n.e.c.
*Parent:* Scarborough Overseas Holdings Limited
*Officers:* Simon Charles McCabe [1977] Director/Development Executive

**Scarborough College Limited**
*Incorporated:* 5 December 1896 *Employees:* 82
*Net Worth:* £1,871,030 *Total Assets:* £8,784,149
*Registered Office:* Scarborough College, Filey Road, Scarborough, N Yorks, YO11 3BA
*Activities:* General secondary education
*Parent:* College Holdings 2012 Limited
*Officers:* Alison Jayne Higgins, Secretary; Michael John Baines [1943] Director/Retired; James Andrew Cliffe [1983] Director/Registered Manager Children's Social Care; Jeremy John Cook [1953] Director/Accountant; Simon Nevill Fairbank [1965] Director/Estate Manager; Neil Gardner [1951] Director/Retired; Victoria Jane Gillingham [1966] Managing Director - AMDIS; Antony Stephen Green [1952] Director/Insurance Broker; John Marcus Green [1962] Director/Farmer; Richard Guthrie [1972] Director - Broadland Properties; James Richard Marshall [1960] Director/Solicitor; John Renshaw [1945] Director/Dental Surgeon; Dr Ian Grenville Hugh Renwick [1960] Director/Doctor; John Stephen Rowlands [1950] Director/Retired; John Francis Watson Swiers [1976] Director/Farmer; Graeme Neville Mansell Young [1973] Director

**Scarborough Development Group Limited**
*Incorporated:* 18 January 2010
*Net Worth Deficit:* £17,273,348 *Total Assets:* £36,478,592
*Registered Office:* Europa House, 20 Esplanade, Scarborough, N Yorks, YO11 2AQ
*Activities:* Activities of other holding companies n.e.c.
*Parent:* SDG Newco Limited
*Officers:* Simon Charles McCabe [1977] Director/Development Executive; Jeremy John Tutton [1966] Director/Financial Controller

**Scarborough Enterprises (UK) Limited**
*Incorporated:* 23 August 2011
*Net Worth:* £178,597 *Total Assets:* £4,696,147
*Registered Office:* Europa House, 20 Esplanade, Scarborough, N Yorks, YO11 2AQ
*Activities:* Activities of other holding companies n.e.c.
*Parent:* Seaside Holdings Limited
*Officers:* Simon Charles McCabe [1977] Director; Jeremy John Tutton [1966] Director/Financial Controller

**Scarborough Flower Fund Homes**
*Incorporated:* 21 March 1969 *Employees:* 1
*Net Worth:* £4,790,966 *Total Assets:* £4,839,660
*Registered Office:* 3 Flower Croft, Filey Road, Scarborough, N Yorks, YO11 3AS
*Activities:* Other letting and operating of own or leased real estate
*Officers:* Barry Newton, Secretary; Julie Ann Banks [1960] Director/Charity Manager; David Clarke Chapman [1949] Director/Chartered Surveyor (Retired); Nicholas Rickman Jones [1958] Director/Hotelier; Barry Newton [1941] Director/Solicitor; Brian Charles Pidd [1953] Director/Retired Accountant; William Henry Smith [1937] Director/Retired; Simon Peter Ward [1950] Director/Chartered Surveyor; Geoffrey Frank Winn [1938] Director/Chartered Accountant

**Scarborough Holding Company Limited**
*Incorporated:* 2 March 2011
*Net Worth Deficit:* £964,970 *Total Assets:* £7,495,494
*Registered Office:* Europa House, 20 Esplanade, Scarborough, N Yorks, YO11 2AQ
*Activities:* Activities of other holding companies n.e.c.
*Parent:* Esplanade Group (Scarborough) International Limited
*Officers:* Kevin Charles McCabe [1948] Director/Chartered Surveyor; Scott Richard McCabe [1975] Director; Simon Charles McCabe [1977] Director; Jeremy John Tutton [1966] Director/Financial Controller

**Scarborough Holdings (UK) Limited**
*Incorporated:* 13 November 2009
*Net Worth:* £925,000 *Total Assets:* £16,787,000
*Registered Office:* Europa House, 20 Esplanade, Scarborough, N Yorks, YO11 2AQ
*Activities:* Activities of other holding companies n.e.c.
*Parent:* Esplanade Group (Scarborough) International Limited
*Officers:* Scott Richard McCabe [1975] Managing Director; Simon Charles McCabe [1977] Director/Development Executive; Jeremy John Tutton [1966] Director/Financial Controller

**Scarborough International Properties Limited**
*Incorporated:* 9 September 2014 *Employees:* 29
*Net Worth:* £56,018,000 *Total Assets:* £100,551,000
*Registered Office:* Europa House, 20 Esplanade, Scarborough, N Yorks, YO11 2AQ
*Activities:* Buying and selling of own real estate
*Parent:* Scarborough Group International Limited
*Officers:* John Lewis Burnley [1944] Director/Quantity Surveyor; Paul Michael Kelly [1977] Director/Chartered Surveyor; Simon Andrew Marshall [1974] Director/Senior Executive; Kevin Charles McCabe [1948] Director/Chartered Surveyor; Scott Richard McCabe [1975] Managing Director; Simon Charles McCabe [1977] Director/Development Executive; Jeremy John Tutton [1966] Director/Financial Controller

**Scarborough Management Limited**
*Incorporated:* 7 February 2011 *Employees:* 27
*Net Worth:* £334,088 *Total Assets:* £5,395,960
*Registered Office:* Europa House, 20 Esplanade, Scarborough, N Yorks, YO11 2AQ
*Activities:* Activities of head offices
*Parent:* Scarborough International Properties Limited
*Officers:* Kevin Charles McCabe [1948] Director/Chartered Surveyor; Scott Richard McCabe [1975] Director; Simon Charles McCabe [1977] Director; Jeremy John Tutton [1966] Director/Financial Controller

**Scarborough Overseas Holdings Limited**
*Incorporated:* 2 March 2011
*Net Worth:* £7,773,039 *Total Assets:* £31,460,972
*Registered Office:* Europa House, 20 Esplanade, Scarborough, N Yorks, YO11 2AQ
*Activities:* Activities of other holding companies n.e.c.
*Parent:* Esplanade Group (Scarborough) International Limited
*Officers:* Scott Richard McCabe [1975] Director; Simon Charles McCabe [1977] Director

**Scarborough Partnership Limited**
*Incorporated:* 16 April 2010 *Employees:* 77
*Net Worth:* £41,319,000 *Total Assets:* £42,013,000
*Registered Office:* Europa House, 20 Esplanade, Scarborough, N Yorks, YO11 2AQ
*Activities:* Financial management
*Major Shareholder:* Sandra McCabe
*Officers:* John Lewis Burnley [1944] Director/Quantity Surveyor; Cesidio Martin di Ciacca [1954] Director/Consultant; Evan Richard Charles Lewis [1944] Director; Scott Richard McCabe [1975] Director; Simon Charles McCabe [1977] Director; Jeremy John Tutton [1966] Director/Financial Controller

**Scarborough Partnership Properties Limited**
*Incorporated:* 2 December 2008
*Net Worth Deficit:* £541,436 *Total Assets:* £10,166,303
*Registered Office:* Europa House, 20 Esplanade, Scarborough, N Yorks, YO11 2AQ
*Activities:* Other letting and operating of own or leased real estate
*Parent:* Scarborough Property (UK) Limited
*Officers:* Simon Charles McCabe [1977] Director/Development Executive; Jeremy John Tutton [1966] Director/Financial Controller

**Scarborough Property (UK) Limited**
*Incorporated:* 23 August 2011
*Net Worth:* £66,000 *Total Assets:* £17,229,000
*Registered Office:* Europa House, 20 Esplanade, Scarborough, N Yorks, YO11 2AQ
*Activities:* Activities of other holding companies n.e.c.
*Parent:* Scarborough Enterprises (UK) Limited
*Officers:* Simon Charles McCabe [1977] Director

**Scarborough Property Developments Limited**
*Incorporated:* 7 October 2009
*Net Worth Deficit:* £2,276,182 *Total Assets:* £14,889,419
*Registered Office:* Europa House, 20 Esplanade, Scarborough, N Yorks, YO11 2AQ
*Activities:* Management of real estate on a fee or contract basis
*Parent:* Scarborough (UK) Limited
*Officers:* Kevin Charles McCabe [1948] Director/Chartered Surveyor; Simon Charles McCabe [1977] Director/Development Executive; Jeremy John Tutton [1966] Director/Financial Controller

**Scarborough Rugby Union Football Club Limited**
*Incorporated:* 7 January 2010 *Employees:* 60
*Net Worth:* £3,911,015 *Total Assets:* £4,540,572
*Registered Office:* The J M Guthrie Clubhouse, Silver Royd, Scalby, Scarborough, N Yorks, YO13 0NL
*Activities:* Activities of sport clubs
*Officers:* Colin Trevor Adamson, Secretary; Colin Trevor Adamson [1953] Director/Secretary; Kenneth Anderson [1937] Director/Retired; Timothy John Boyes [1948] Director; Timothy Michael Elliott [1964] Director/General Manager; John Guthrie [1936] Director; Richard Guthrie [1972] Director; Andrew James Hoff [1981] Director; Michael Edwin Holder [1948] Director/Retired; James Hughes [1951] Director; Colin Allen Rennard [1949] Director; John Cyril Stevenson [1946] Director; Graeme Neville Mansell Young [1973] Director

**Scarborough Thorpe Park Holdings Limited**
*Incorporated:* 3 August 2015
*Net Worth:* £22,500,000 *Total Assets:* £22,500,000
*Registered Office:* Europa House, 20 Esplanade, Scarborough, N Yorks, YO11 2AQ
*Activities:* Activities of other holding companies n.e.c.
*Parent:* Scarborough International Properties Limited
*Officers:* Rexiati Aihemaitijiang [1968] Director [Chinese]; Ji Chao [1977] Director [Chinese]; Simon Charles McCabe [1977] Director/Development Executive; Jeremy John Tutton [1966] Director/Financial Controller

**Scattergood & Johnson Limited**
*Incorporated:* 8 August 1924 *Employees:* 115
*Net Worth:* £3,944,220 *Total Assets:* £14,676,210
*Registered Office:* Scattergood & Johnson Ltd, Lowfields Road, Leeds, LS12 6ET
*Activities:* Wholesale of other machinery and equipment
*Parent:* S & J Industries Ltd
*Officers:* Richard Peter Lumley, Secretary; Robert Christopher Winn Hargreaves [1954] Director; Richard Peter Lumley [1966] Director/Chartered Accountant; Iain Robertson Manson [1947] Director/Accountant

**SCD Group Limited**
*Incorporated:* 24 January 1997 *Employees:* 5
*Net Worth:* £1,735,495 *Total Assets:* £3,150,242
*Registered Office:* Norton House, Peckfield Business Park, Phoenix Avenue, Leeds, LS25 4DY
*Activities:* Construction of other civil engineering projects n.e.c.
*Major Shareholder:* Christopher Durkan
*Officers:* Ann Durkan, Secretary; Ann Durkan [1965] Director; Christopher Durkan [1963] Director

**Scheme Underwriting (U.K.) Limited**
*Incorporated:* 29 November 1982
*Net Worth:* £4,112,944 *Total Assets:* £4,447,546
*Registered Office:* The Mill at Scott Hall, 44 Potternewton Mount, Leeds, LS7 2DR
*Activities:* Financial management
*Major Shareholder:* John Bexon
*Officers:* Cynthia Valerie Bexon, Secretary; John Truswell Bexon [1938] Director

**Schenck Process UK Holding Limited**
*Incorporated:* 18 December 2007
*Net Worth Deficit:* £4,172,000 *Total Assets:* £8,609,000
*Registered Office:* Unit 3 Alpha Court, Capitol Park, Thorne, Doncaster, S Yorks, DN8 5TZ
*Activities:* Non-trading company
*Officers:* Nicholas Jones, Secretary; Christoph Haar [1980] Director [German]; Nicholas Paul Jones [1958] Director/Accountant

**Scho62 Investments Limited**
*Incorporated:* 14 March 2016 *Employees:* 1
*Net Worth Deficit:* £3,462 *Total Assets:* £3,143,178
*Registered Office:* Gresham House, 5-7 St Pauls Street, Leeds, LS1 2JG
*Activities:* Other business support service activities n.e.c.
*Major Shareholder:* Robert Nicholas Jason Schofield
*Officers:* Robert Nicholas Jason Schofield [1962] Director

**J.B.Schofield & Sons Limited**
*Incorporated:* 26 February 1964 *Employees:* 8
*Net Worth:* £3,700,421 *Total Assets:* £4,031,223
*Registered Office:* Green Head, Linthwaite, Huddersfield, W Yorks, HD7 5TS
*Activities:* Wholesale of waste and scrap
*Major Shareholder:* Richard Mark Schofield
*Officers:* Richard Mark Schofield, Secretary; Richard Mark Schofield [1959] Director/Scrap Metal Merchant

**A.Schofield (Pontefract) Limited**
*Incorporated:* 2 June 1936
*Net Worth:* £3,144,097 *Total Assets:* £3,208,079
*Registered Office:* Clump Grange Farm, Havercroft Lane, Darrington, Pontefract, W Yorks, WF8 3BP
*Activities:* Other business support service activities n.e.c.
*Major Shareholder:* Charles Edward Schofield
*Officers:* David Archibald Schofield, Secretary; Charles Edward Schofield [1963] Director; David Archibald Schofield [1931] Director; Mary Schofield [1931] Director/Housewife

**Schofield Sweeney LLP**
*Incorporated:* 20 November 2002 *Employees:* 124
*Net Worth:* £4,604,046 *Total Assets:* £5,877,847
*Registered Office:* Church Bank House, Church Bank, Bradford, W Yorks, BD1 4DY
*Officers:* Darren Craig Birkinshaw [1965] Member; Dean Peter Jowett [1979] Member; Alistair Stuart Kennedy [1982] Member; Martin Nicholas Sweeney [1961] Member; Basharat Ali [1962] LLP Member; David John Arundel [1967] LLP Member; Gary Douglas Ashton [1973] LLP Member; Adrian Jon Ballam [1979] LLP Member; Christopher Joseph Blantern [1978] LLP Member; Angela Kathleen Cashin [1974] LLP Member; Alexandra Louise Clements [1970] LLP Member; John David Cowgill [1984] LLP Member; Karen Alison Crutchley [1984] LLP Member; Luisa Margaret D'Alessandro [1974] LLP Member; John Charles Feaster [1980] LLP Member; John Richard Fergusson [1967] LLP Member; Matthew John Fidler [1980] LLP Member; Adam Robert Hastie [1970] LLP Member; Robert John Hayes [1967] LLP Member; Andrew Leonard Turner Hurst [1954] LLP Member; Richard Heath Robert Innes [1960] LLP Member; Ashley Mark Iredale [1964] LLP Member; Leo Francis Philip Jones-Rowe [1984] LLP Member; Robert Daniel Kelly [1961] LLP Member; Steven Millward [1982] LLP Member; Paton Robert Simon Petchey [1960] LLP Member; Amar Rashid [1967] LLP Member; John Robinson [1966] LLP Member; Christopher Ernest Schofield [1962] LLP Member; Simon Paul Shepherd [1973] LLP Member; James Malcolm Staton [1958] LLP Member; Richard Leo Stockdale [1958] LLP Member; David Maxwell Strachan [1958] LLP Member; Manjit Virdee [1976] LLP Member; Diana June Walker [1966] LLP Member; Farooq Mohammed Zar [1978] LLP Member

**C.H. Scholey & Sons Limited**
*Incorporated:* 18 October 1956 *Employees:* 6
*Net Worth:* £2,036,460 *Total Assets:* £3,629,938
*Registered Office:* Lodge Farm, Frickley, Doncaster, S Yorks, DN5 7BX
*Activities:* Growing of cereals (except rice), leguminous crops and oil seeds
*Major Shareholder:* Anthony Howarth Scholey
*Officers:* Sarah Abigail Scholey, Secretary; Anthony Howarth Scholey [1957] Director/Farmer; Sarah Abigail Scholey [1958] Director/Farming

**Schosween 6 Limited**
*Incorporated:* 25 May 2012
*Net Worth:* £8,068,402 *Total Assets:* £8,077,556
*Registered Office:* The East Wing, The Newhall, Newhall Way, Bradford, BD5 8FF
*Activities:* Financial management
*Parent:* Frank Marshall Estates Ltd
*Officers:* Frank Edward Marshall [1978] Director; James Ernest Marshall [1979] Director

**A. Schulman Gainsborough Ltd**
*Incorporated:* 9 October 1996 *Employees:* 75
*Previous:* ICO (UK) Limited
*Net Worth:* £7,013,000 *Total Assets:* £42,659,000
*Registered Office:* Sandars Road, Heapham Road Industrial Estate, Gainsborough, Lincs, DN21 1RZ
*Activities:* Manufacture of other plastic products
*Officers:* Christopher Anthony Bridle, Secretary/Financial Controller; Christopher Anthony Bridle [1964] Director/Management Accountant; Heinrich Benedikt Lingnau-Schneider [1962] Director/Business Executive [German]

**Schultz Bidco Limited**
*Incorporated:* 21 December 2015
*Net Worth Deficit:* £5,147,000 *Total Assets:* £18,554,000
*Registered Office:* Denton Hall, Ilkley, W Yorks, LS29 0HH
*Activities:* Activities of head offices
*Parent:* Schultz Parent Limited
*Officers:* Rachel Clare Salmon, Secretary; David Stuart Hurcomb [1964] Director/Engineer and Accountant; Michael Porter [1967] Director/Chief Financial Officer

**Scientific Games International Holdings Ltd**
*Incorporated:* 24 January 2002
*Net Worth Deficit:* £29,645,000 *Total Assets:* £243,448,992
*Registered Office:* 3 George Mann Road, Leeds, LS10 1DJ
*Activities:* Gambling and betting activities
*Officers:* Terence John McQueen, Secretary; James Edward Bunitsky [1958] Director/Senior Vice President Operations & Finance [American]; Christian Kometer [1967] Director [Austrian]; Mark Wilson Scholey [1957] Director/General Manager

**Scientific Games International Limited**
*Incorporated:* 21 September 1983 *Employees:* 207
*Net Worth:* £117,880,000 *Total Assets:* £160,915,008
*Registered Office:* 3 George Mann Road, Leeds, LS10 1DJ
*Activities:* Printing n.e.c.
*Officers:* Terence John McQueen, Secretary; James Edward Bunitsky [1958] Director/Senior Vice President,Operations & Finance [American]; Christian Kometer [1967] Director Finance and Administration [Austrian]; Mark Wilson Scholey [1957] Director/General Manager

**Scientific Laboratory Supplies Group Ltd**
*Incorporated:* 1 June 2016 *Employees:* 183
*Net Worth:* £16,201,027 *Total Assets:* £28,936,802
*Registered Office:* Orchard House, The Square, Hessle, E Yorks, HU13 0AE
*Activities:* Wholesale of pharmaceutical goods
*Parent:* Dominique Dutscher Distribution SAS
*Officers:* Kristen Jane Chapman, Secretary; Robert Peter Chapman [1955] Managing Director; Dominique Etienne Wencker [1959] Director/General Manager [French]; Younes Zemmouri [1974] Director/Partner [French]

**Scientific Laboratory Supplies Limited**
*Incorporated:* 28 January 1991 *Employees:* 179
*Net Worth:* £5,206,120 *Total Assets:* £15,213,655
*Registered Office:* Orchard House, The Square, Hessle, E Yorks, HU13 0AE
*Activities:* Wholesale of other machinery and equipment
*Parent:* Dominique Dutscher Distribution SAS
*Officers:* Neil Andrew Bewell, Secretary; Neil Andrew Bewell [1974] Director/Chief Financial Officer; Joshua James Robert Chapman [1985] Director/Sales Manager; Robert Peter Chapman [1955] Director; Andrew William Monkman [1960] Director/Buyer; Ian Andrew Roulstone [1968] Sales Director

**Scotfield Group Limited**
*Incorporated:* 14 April 1989 *Employees:* 28
*Net Worth:* £4,642,975 *Total Assets:* £27,355,116
*Registered Office:* Ackworth Lodge, High Ackworth, W Yorks, WF7 7EE
*Activities:* Buying and selling of own real estate
*Major Shareholder:* Martin Rapley
*Officers:* Terence Joseph Padian, Secretary; Stephen Kenneth Holman [1957] Director/Surveyor; Terence Joseph Padian [1950] Director/Accountant; Martin Rapley [1957] Director

**Scothern Construction Limited**
*Incorporated:* 6 March 1989 *Employees:* 11
*Net Worth:* £4,283,473 *Total Assets:* £6,407,802
*Registered Office:* 3 York Road Industrial Park, Rye Close, Malton, N Yorks, YO17 6YD
*Activities:* Construction of commercial buildings
*Major Shareholder:* Paul Andrew Scothern
*Officers:* Jennifer Kay Scothern, Secretary; Ian Henry Scothern [1943] Director; Mark Antony Scothern [1969] Director; Paul Andrew Scothern [1967] Director

**Scout Cragg Holiday Park Limited**
*Incorporated:* 16 April 1959 *Employees:* 11
*Net Worth:* £2,916,527 *Total Assets:* £3,701,204
*Registered Office:* Medina House, 2 Station Avenue, Bridlington, E Yorks, YO16 4LZ
*Activities:* Recreational vehicle parks, trailer parks and camping grounds
*Officers:* Mary Teresa Daly, Secretary/Caravan Site Owner and Dealer; Hugh Patrick Daly [1953] Director/Park Operator; James Joseph Daly [1981] Director/Park Operator [Irish]; Mary Teresa Daly [1956] Director/Caravan Site Owner and Dealer; Patrick Martin Daly [1977] Director [Irish]

**Screen Yorkshire Limited**
*Incorporated:* 19 July 2002 *Employees:* 6
*Net Worth:* £7,552,412 *Total Assets:* £7,964,434
*Registered Office:* Studio 3, 46 The Calls, Leeds, LS2 7EY
*Activities:* Motion picture production activities
*Officers:* George Watts, Secretary; Stephen Abbott [1954] Director/Film Producer; Charles Anthony Cecil [1962] Director/Video Game Developer; Sarah Doole [1961] Creative Director Drama BBC Worldwide; Richard John Gerard [1965] Finance Director; Cameron Robert McCracken [1962] Director/Media Executive; Ian Roe [1963] Director/Finance Consultancy; John Douglas Surtees [1957] Director/General Manager

**Scriven Park Estates Limited**
*Incorporated:* 23 March 2017 *Employees:* 46
*Net Worth:* £13,782,032 *Total Assets:* £16,281,995
*Registered Office:* Beech Hall, 62 High Street, Knaresborough, N Yorks, HG5 0EA
*Activities:* Activities of other holding companies n.e.c.
*Major Shareholder:* Julia Denise Skrentny
*Officers:* Jane Michelle Blackmore [1968] Director; Andrew David Harrop [1964] Director/Chartered Accountant; Barney Joseph Skrentny [1937] Director [American]

**Scroll Bidco Limited**
*Incorporated:* 15 October 2008
*Net Worth:* £1,066,214 *Total Assets:* £55,752,984
*Registered Office:* Rawdon House, Green Lane, Yeadon, Leeds, LS19 7BY
*Activities:* Other information technology service activities
*Parent:* Ascribe Group Limited
*Officers:* Christine Benson, Secretary; Dean Anthony Barber [1977] Director/Group Financial Controller; Peter John Southby [1973] Director/Financial Controller

**Scruton & Co.,(Builders) Limited**
*Incorporated:* 8 July 1942 *Employees:* 14
*Net Worth:* £30,161,268 *Total Assets:* £34,174,472
*Registered Office:* Deck 4 The Riverside Building, Livingstone Road, Hessle, E Yorks, HU13 0DZ
*Activities:* Construction of domestic buildings
*Major Shareholder:* Ian William Scruton
*Officers:* Carol Hutchinson, Secretary; Ian William Scruton [1965] Director/Builder/Joiner; Isobel Julia Scruton [1971] Director

**Wilfred Scruton Limited**
*Incorporated:* 28 June 1951 *Employees:* 52
*Net Worth:* £2,604,193 *Total Assets:* £11,628,653
*Registered Office:* Providence Foundry, Foxholes, Driffield, E Yorks, YO25 3QQ
*Activities:* Repair of machinery
*Shareholders:* Ian John Scruton; Frederick Raymond Marwood
*Officers:* Peter Kenneth Scruton, Secretary; Sally Anne Scruton, Secretary; Laura Rosemary Bell [1989] Director/Accounts Administration; Richard George Bower [1965] Director/Branch Manager; Richard Wayne Gillett [1970] Director/Sales; Ian John Scruton [1956] Managing Director; Julie Marguerite Scruton [1944] Farmer & Director; Peter Kenneth Scruton [1946] Secretary & Director; Sally Anne Scruton [1970] Director/Accounts

**SCS Building Solutions Limited**
*Incorporated:* 1 February 1994 *Employees:* 51
*Net Worth:* £1,782,353 *Total Assets:* £5,772,282
*Registered Office:* Newmarket House, Aberford Road, Stanley, Wakefield, W Yorks, WF3 4AL
*Activities:* Joinery installation
*Parent:* Specialist Ceiling Services Holdings Limited
*Officers:* Andrew Stuart Morson, Secretary; Michelle Chappell Dixon [1981] Financial Director; Paul Flynn [1976] Director; Darren Lee Friend [1983] Director; Rodger McKenzie Lambert [1965] Contracts Director; Andrew Stuart Morson [1964] Commercial Director; Andrew Michael Rippon [1963] Director/Regional Executive; Craig Ian Scott [1985] Director; Nicholas Paul Skill [1966] Estimating Director

**Scunthorpe United Football Club Limited**
*Incorporated:* 6 August 1912 *Employees:* 250
*Net Worth:* £571,275 *Total Assets:* £8,620,104
*Registered Office:* Glanford Park, Jack Brownsword Way, Scunthorpe, N Lincs, DN15 8TD
*Activities:* Operation of sports facilities
*Major Shareholder:* Peter Dennis Swann
*Officers:* James Richard Rodwell [1970] Director Chief Executive; Christopher Swann [1993] Director; Karin Louise Swann [1964] Director; Peter Dennis Swann [1963] Managing Director

**SDG (Boston) Limited**
*Incorporated:* 13 January 2010
*Net Worth:* £164,520 *Total Assets:* £3,596,947
*Registered Office:* Europa House, 20 Esplanade, Scarborough, N Yorks, YO11 2AQ
*Activities:* Development of building projects
*Parent:* Scaborough Development Group Limited
*Officers:* Simon Charles McCabe [1977] Director/Development Executive; Jeremy John Tutton [1966] Director/Financial Controller

**SDG (Newport) Limited**
*Incorporated:* 13 January 2010
*Net Worth Deficit:* £10,383,062 *Total Assets:* £6,199,011
*Registered Office:* Europa House, 20 Esplanade, Scarborough, N Yorks, YO11 2AQ
*Activities:* Development of building projects
*Parent:* Scarborough Development Group Limited
*Officers:* Simon Charles McCabe [1977] Director/Development Executive; Jeremy John Tutton [1966] Director/Financial Controller

**SDG (Preston) Limited**
*Incorporated:* 13 January 2010
*Net Worth Deficit:* £1,763,026 *Total Assets:* £4,322,810
*Registered Office:* Europa House, 20 Esplanade, Scarborough, N Yorks, YO11 2AQ
*Activities:* Development of building projects
*Parent:* Scarborough Development Group Limited
*Officers:* Simon Charles McCabe [1977] Director/Development Executive

**SDG (Rhyl) Limited**
*Incorporated:* 13 January 2010
*Net Worth Deficit:* £2,721,008 *Total Assets:* £19,360,060
*Registered Office:* Europa House, 20 Esplanade, Scarborough, N Yorks, YO11 2AQ
*Activities:* Development of building projects
*Parent:* Scarborough Development Group Limited
*Officers:* Simon Charles McCabe [1977] Director/Development Executive; Jeremy John Tutton [1966] Director/Financial Controller

**SDS International Ltd.**
*Incorporated:* 25 April 1990
*Net Worth:* £3,607,652 *Total Assets:* £3,607,991
*Registered Office:* Craven House, Steeton Grove, Steeton, Keighley, W Yorks, BD20 6TT
*Activities:* Non-trading company
*Shareholders:* Lorraine White; Michael John White
*Officers:* Lorraine White, Secretary; Michael John White [1949] Director/Flexible Ducting Supplier

**SEA Holdings (UK) Limited**
*Incorporated:* 4 January 2017 *Employees:* 261
*Net Worth:* £2,237,001 *Total Assets:* £15,367,506
*Registered Office:* Unit 5 Millfield Lane, Nether Poppleton, York, YO26 6PQ
*Activities:* Other manufacturing n.e.c.
*Officers:* Andrew John Dyson [1969] Director; Mark Nigel Nisbet [1965] Director; Colin Donald Nixey [1962] Director; John Philip Sills [1946] Director

**Sea Holdings Limited**
*Incorporated:* 10 July 1996 *Employees:* 257
*Net Worth:* £2,450,942 *Total Assets:* £14,241,488
*Registered Office:* The Saville Group Ltd, Millfield Lane, Nether Poppleton, York, YO26 6PQ
*Activities:* Other manufacturing n.e.c.
*Parent:* SEA Holdings (UK) Limited
*Officers:* Colin Donald Nixey, Finance Director; Andrew John Dyson [1969] Director; Mark Nigel Nisbet [1965] Director; Colin Donald Nixey [1962] Finance Director

**Seabrook Crisps Holdings Limited**
*Incorporated:* 18 December 2002
*Net Worth:* £20,387,000 *Total Assets:* £23,113,000
*Registered Office:* Seabrook House, Duncombe Street, Bradford, W Yorks, BD8 9AJ
*Activities:* Other business support service activities n.e.c.
*Parent:* Seabrook Group Limited
*Officers:* Daniel Richard Woodwards, Secretary; Jonathan Bye [1963] Director/Chief Executive Officer; Makoto Ehara [1958] Director/Executive Vice President [Japanese]; Koichi Kikuchi [1963] Director/Senior Managing Executive Officer [Japanese]; Richard Anthony Robinson [1965] Director; Keiei Sho [1966] Director/Executive Officer [Japanese]; Jonathan Nigel Wood [1976] Commercial Director; Daniel Richard Woodwards [1977] Finance Director

**Seabrook Crisps Limited**
*Incorporated:* 31 August 1949 *Employees:* 143
*Net Worth:* £17,580,000 *Total Assets:* £22,770,000
*Registered Office:* Seabrook House, Duncombe Street, Bradford, W Yorks, BD8 9AJ
*Activities:* Processing and preserving of potatoes
*Parent:* Seabrook Crisps Holdings Limited
*Officers:* Daniel Richard Woodwards, Secretary; Jonathan Bye [1963] Director/Chief Executive Officer; Makoto Ehara [1958] Director/Executive Vice President [Japanese]; Koichi Kikuchi [1963] Director/Senior Managing Executive Officer [Japanese]; Richard Anthony Robinson [1965] Director; Keiei Sho [1966] Director/Executive Officer [Japanese]; Jonathan Nigel Wood [1976] Commercial Director; Daniel Richard Woodwards [1977] Finance Director

**Seabrook Group Limited**
*Incorporated:* 9 February 2006 *Employees:* 3
*Net Worth Deficit:* £4,995,000 *Total Assets:* £12,284,000
*Registered Office:* Seabrook House, Duncombe Street, Bradford, W Yorks, BD8 9AJ
*Activities:* Manufacture of other food products n.e.c.
*Parent:* Pacific Shelf 1809 Limited
*Officers:* Daniel Richard Woodwards, Secretary; Jonathan Bye [1963] Director/Chief Executive Officer; Makoto Ehara [1958] Director/Executive Vice President [Japanese]; Koichi Kikuchi [1963] Director/Senior Managing Executive Officer [Japanese]; Richard Anthony Robinson [1965] Director; Keiei Sho [1966] Director/Executive Officer [Japanese]; Jonathan Nigel Wood [1976] Commercial Director; Daniel Richard Woodwards [1977] Finance Director

**Seagold Limited**
*Incorporated:* 1 May 1996 *Employees:* 58
*Net Worth:* £7,246,849 *Total Assets:* £27,044,544
*Registered Office:* The Orangery, Hesslewood Country Office Park, Ferriby Road, Hessle, E Yorks, HU13 0LH
*Activities:* Wholesale of other food, including fish, crustaceans and molluscs
*Parent:* Samherji Hf
*Officers:* Gustaf Baldvinsson, Secretary/Sales Director [Icelander]; Gustaf Baldvinsson [1957] Managing Director [Icelander]; Porsteinn Mar Baldvinsson [1952] Director/Chairman [Icelander]

**Seal It Services Limited**
*Incorporated:* 16 July 2002 *Employees:* 101
*Net Worth:* £2,844,306 *Total Assets:* £13,019,669
*Registered Office:* Unit G16 Lowfields Business Park, Lacey Way, Elland, W Yorks, HX5 9DN
*Activities:* Manufacture of glues
*Officers:* Jagruti Sandeep Engineer [1965] Director [Indian]; Sandeep Pravinchandra Engineer [1951] Director [Indian]; Graham Martin Helm [1955] Working Director; David Alan Moore [1958] Managing Director

**Sealord (Europe) Limited**
*Incorporated:* 4 January 1993
*Net Worth:* £11,197,638 *Total Assets:* £11,197,848
*Registered Office:* Cartergate House, 26 Chantry Lane, Grimsby, N E Lincs, DN31 2LJ
*Activities:* Activities of other holding companies n.e.c.
*Officers:* Gary Andrew Neill [1967] Director [New Zealander]; Steven Arnold Yung [1961] Director [Canadian]

**Seamore Court Freehold Limited**
*Incorporated:* 29 March 2007 *Employees:* 2
*Net Worth:* £5,208,132 *Total Assets:* £7,992,165
*Registered Office:* Cumberland House, Greenside Lane, Bradford, BD8 9TF
*Activities:* Management of real estate on a fee or contract basis
*Major Shareholder:* Alan James Lewis
*Officers:* Alan James Lewis [1938] Director/Chairman

**Search Group Holdings Limited**
*Incorporated:* 15 September 2008 *Employees:* 124
*Net Worth:* £5,175,393 *Total Assets:* £10,547,393
*Registered Office:* Market Works, Whitehall Road, Leeds, LS12 6EP
*Activities:* Activities of head offices
*Officers:* Richard Stephen William Search, Secretary; James Charles Search [1966] Director/Group Hire Manager; Richard Stephen William Search [1964] Director/Marketing Manager

**William G. Search Limited**
*Incorporated:* 27 March 1946 *Employees:* 124
*Net Worth:* £4,261,908 *Total Assets:* £8,385,818
*Registered Office:* Market Works, Whitehall Road, Leeds, LS12 6EP
*Activities:* Wholesale of other machinery and equipment
*Parent:* Search Group Holdings Limited
*Officers:* Richard Stephen William Search, Secretary; James Charles Search [1966] Director/Group Hire Manager; Richard Stephen William Search [1964] Director/Marketing Manager

**Seatruck Ferries Holding Ltd**
*Incorporated:* 15 September 2005 *Employees:* 86
*Net Worth:* £11,192,389 *Total Assets:* £97,762,592
*Registered Office:* North Quay, Port of Heysham, Morecambe, Lancs, LA3 2UH
*Activities:* Activities of head offices
*Parent:* Clipper Group A/S
*Officers:* Karen Elizabeth Donaldson, Secretary; Benjamin Simon Coppack [1960] Fleet Director; Karen Elizabeth Donaldson [1960] Director/Accountant; Alistair James Eagles [1970] Director; Jesper Kjaedegaard [1958] Director/Consultant [Danish]; Peter Lybecker [1953] Director/Chairman [Danish]; Peter Norborg [1966] Director/Group CEO [Danish]

**Seatruck Ferries Ltd**
*Incorporated:* 12 December 2005 *Employees:* 68
*Net Worth:* £8,200,573 *Total Assets:* £19,808,392
*Registered Office:* North Quay, Port of Heysham, Morecambe, Lancs, LA3 2UH
*Activities:* Sea and coastal freight water transport
*Parent:* Seatruck Ferries Holding Ltd
*Officers:* Karen Elizabeth Donaldson, Secretary; Benjamin Simon Coppack [1960] Fleet Director; Karen Elizabeth Donaldson [1960] Director/Accountant; Alistair James Eagles [1970] Director

**Seatruck Panorama Ltd**
*Incorporated:* 15 September 2005
*Net Worth:* £1,366,820 *Total Assets:* £22,550,480
*Registered Office:* North Quay, Port of Heysham, Morecambe, Lancs, LA3 2UH
*Activities:* Sea and coastal freight water transport
*Parent:* Clipper Group A/S
*Officers:* Karen Elizabeth Donaldson, Secretary; Benjamin Simon Coppack [1960] Fleet Director; Karen Elizabeth Donaldson [1960] Director; Alistair James Eagles [1970] Director

**Seatruck Pennant Ltd**
*Incorporated:* 15 September 2005
*Net Worth:* £5,359,877 *Total Assets:* £21,841,716
*Registered Office:* North Quay, Port of Heysham, Morecambe, Lancs, LA3 2UH
*Activities:* Sea and coastal freight water transport
*Parent:* Clipper Group A/S
*Officers:* Karen Elizabeth Donaldson, Secretary; Benjamin Simon Coppack [1960] Fleet Director; Karen Elizabeth Donaldson [1960] Director/Accountant; Alistair James Eagles [1970] Director

**Secanim Limited**
*Incorporated:* 4 August 1948 *Employees:* 157
*Net Worth:* £18,218,908 *Total Assets:* £31,335,372
*Registered Office:* Ings Road, Doncaster, S Yorks, DN5 9TL
*Activities:* Manufacture of oils and fats
*Parent:* Saria Limited
*Officers:* Robert Vincent Ratcliffe [1958] Director; Andrew Richard Smith [1962] Director

**Secondtour Limited**
*Incorporated:* 15 March 2012
*Net Worth Deficit:* £601,069 *Total Assets:* £3,247,478
*Registered Office:* Ingerthorpe Grange, Westerns Lane, Markington, Harrogate, N Yorks, HG3 3PD
*Activities:* Other letting and operating of own or leased real estate
*Major Shareholder:* Mark Adrain Cotton
*Officers:* Mark Adrian Cotton [1976] Director

**Securi-Plex Limited**
*Incorporated:* 28 April 1988 *Employees:* 25
*Net Worth:* £1,493,534 *Total Assets:* £3,869,715
*Registered Office:* Avaiation House, Swordfish Way, Sherburn in Elmet, Leeds, LS25 6NG
*Activities:* Security systems service activities
*Parent:* Businesswatch UK Holdings Limited
*Officers:* Nicholas Alexander Petrovic [1982] Finance Director; John Paul Swingewood [1955] Director; Jonathan Edward Wakerley [1977] Director/Group MD

**Security Window Shutters Limited**
*Incorporated:* 24 April 1987 *Employees:* 121
*Net Worth:* £8,346,619 *Total Assets:* £11,836,527
*Registered Office:* Hornby Road, Claughton, Lancaster, LA2 9LA
*Activities:* Manufacture of other fabricated metal products n.e.c.
*Parent:* CRH (UK) Limited
*Officers:* David Edmondson [1966] Director/Management Accountant; Kevin Anthony Russell-Lindeque [1973] Managing Director

**Sedalcol UK Limited**
*Incorporated:* 18 September 2009 *Employees:* 61
*Net Worth:* £44,740,568 *Total Assets:* £105,026,800
*Registered Office:* Denison Road, Selby, N Yorks, YO8 8AN
*Activities:* Manufacture of other non-distilled fermented beverages
*Officers:* Elena Frandino, Secretary; Patrizia Antonacci [1973] Strategic Investments & Development Director [Italian]; Yves Emile Pierre Belegaud [1960] Director [French]; Alexis Francois Eric Duval [1977] Director [French]; Davide Frandino [1969] Director [Italian]; Elena Frandino [1974] Director [Italian]; Luisa Frandino [1972] Director [Italian]; Mario Frandino [1943] Director [Italian]; Christopher Herve [1983] Director [French]

**Sedbergh Hotel Enterprises Limited**
*Incorporated:* 3 February 2017 *Employees:* 4
*Net Worth Deficit:* £18,696 *Total Assets:* £3,211,025
*Registered Office:* Bull Hotel, 44 Main Street, Sedbergh, Cumbria, LA10 5BL
*Activities:* Development of building projects
*Shareholder:* Sedbergh School Developments Limited
*Officers:* Edward Bradwall Barlow [1972] Director; James Edward Ratcliffe [1978] Director/Restaurateur; Anthony William Smith [1956] Director/Consultant; Richard Guy Thomas Stenhouse [1961] Director/Banker

**Sedbergh School**
*Incorporated:* 13 March 2000 *Employees:* 410
*Net Worth:* £17,839,000 *Total Assets:* £27,403,000
*Registered Office:* Sedbergh School, Malim Lodge, Sedbergh, Cumbria, LA10 5RY
*Activities:* Primary education
*Officers:* Peter Stephen Marshall, Secretary; The Venerable Nicholas John Willoughby Barker [1949] Director/Clerk in Holy Orders; Louise Bates [1959] Director/Retired Solicitor; Adrian Jeremy Norville Bedford [1968] Director/Investment Management; Hugh McGill Blair [1954] Director/Management Consultant; John Donington Campbell [1959] Director/Financial Services; Anna Louise Denney [1961] Director/Barrister; Ian Willcox Durrans [1958] Director/Consultant; Sir Michael Roger Gifford [1955] Director/Banker; Richard John Gledhill [1954] Director/Climate Change Consultant; Andrew Richard Gregory [1957] Director/Chief Executive; Claire Theresa Hensman [1948] Non-Executive Director (Voluntary); Richard Noel Papworth [1964] Director/Retired Solicitor; Michael Ronald Piercy [1962] Director/Headmaster; John Henry Bernard Warburton-Lee [1963] Director/Photographer & Farmer; Dr Emma Jane Louise Waring [1977] Director/Academic

**Seismic Image Processing Limited**
*Incorporated:* 30 December 1997 *Employees:* 14
*Net Worth:* £8,843,465 *Total Assets:* £11,113,156
*Registered Office:* 3 West Dene, Allwoodley, Leeds, LS17 8QT
*Activities:* Other business support service activities n.e.c.
*Shareholders:* Jagat Singh Deo; Ranjit Kaur Deo
*Officers:* Ranjit Kaur Deo, Secretary; Jagat Singh Deo [1956] Director/Geophysicist

**Select Alloys & Materials Limited**
*Incorporated:* 18 December 2000
*Net Worth:* £6,076,023 *Total Assets:* £9,519,941
*Registered Office:* Rimswell House, Sandbeck Lane, Tickhill, Doncaster, S Yorks, DN11 9PJ
*Activities:* Precious metals production
*Shareholders:* Terrence Moore; Tracey Moore
*Officers:* Tracey June Moore, Secretary; David Fairchild [1973] Director; Terrence Moore [1958] Director/Broker of Semi Precious Metals; Tracey June Moore [1968] Director

**Select Legal Systems Limited**
*Incorporated:* 27 April 1993 *Employees:* 34
*Net Worth:* £1,182,748 *Total Assets:* £3,561,619
*Registered Office:* Priory Court, Saxon Way, Priory Park, Hessle, E Yorks, HU13 9PB
*Activities:* Business and domestic software development
*Shareholders:* Michael Stuart Craven; Stephen Robert Dixon
*Officers:* Michael Stuart Craven, Secretary/Computer Software; Michael Stuart Craven [1953] Director/Computer Software; Stephen Robert Dixon [1966] Director/Computer Software

**Selkirk Mechanical Handling Limited**
*Incorporated:* 16 September 1996 *Employees:* 15
*Net Worth:* £1,710,289 *Total Assets:* £3,449,140
*Registered Office:* Dairycoates Industrial Estate, Wiltshire Road, Hull, HU4 6PA
*Activities:* Repair of machinery
*Shareholders:* Gary Stephen Selkirk; Simon William Lunt
*Officers:* Simon William Lunt, Secretary; Gary Stephen Selkirk [1954] Director

**W.D.Sellers and Sons Limited**
*Incorporated:* 2 April 1955 *Employees:* 6
*Net Worth:* £12,980,924 *Total Assets:* £21,972,444
*Registered Office:* Enthorpe House Farm, Middleton on the Wolds, Driffield, E Yorks, YO25 9DG
*Activities:* Growing of cereals (except rice), leguminous crops and oil seeds
*Major Shareholder:* James William Morley
*Officers:* James William Morley [1980] Director/Farmer

**Sellers International Limited**
*Incorporated:* 15 November 1978 *Employees:* 5
*Net Worth:* £5,447,506 *Total Assets:* £5,912,552
*Registered Office:* International House, Chapel Hill, Huddersfield, W Yorks, HD1 3EE
*Activities:* Activities of head offices
*Officers:* David Ulrich Armitage, Secretary; Carol Elizabeth Armitage [1948] Director; Charles Edward Armitage [1971] Director/Engineer; David Ulrich Armitage [1943] Director/Chartered Accountant; Joanne Louise Ribeiro [1974] Director/Aromatherapist

**Sellmor Farming Limited**
*Incorporated:* 13 October 2010 *Employees:* 4
*Net Worth Deficit:* £58,845 *Total Assets:* £4,500,691
*Registered Office:* Bridge House, 41 Wincolmlee, Kingston upon Hull, HU2 8AG
*Activities:* Mixed farming
*Major Shareholder:* Richard David Morley
*Officers:* Richard David Morley [1982] Director

**Senator Homes Limited**
*Incorporated:* 20 July 2001 *Employees:* 4
*Net Worth:* £57,024,000 *Total Assets:* £75,256,000
*Registered Office:* Persimmon House, Fulford, York, YO19 4FE
*Activities:* Construction of domestic buildings
*Parent:* Persimmon Homes Limited
*Officers:* Tracy Lazelle Davison, Secretary; David Jenkinson [1967] Director; Michael Hugh Killoran [1961] Finance Director; Richard Paul Stenhouse [1971] Director/Accountant

**Senior Architectural Systems Limited**
*Incorporated:* 18 January 2000 *Employees:* 147
*Net Worth:* £4,590,825 *Total Assets:* £19,397,584
*Registered Office:* Eland Road, Denaby Main, Doncaster, S Yorks, DN12 4HA
*Activities:* Wholesale of metals and metal ores
*Parent:* Clytha Holdings Limited
*Officers:* Leslie Robert Buxton [1978] Director; James Richard Keeling-Heane [1980] Sales Director; Mark Vincenzo Wadsworth [1973] Director/Systems General Manager; Mark Douglas Wheatley [1979] Technical Director

**Sensio Limited**
*Incorporated:* 6 March 2007 *Employees:* 33
*Net Worth:* £1,300,044 *Total Assets:* £3,682,411
*Registered Office:* Unit 7 Speedwell Road, Whitwood, Castleford, W Yorks, WF10 5PY
*Activities:* Agents specialised in the sale of other particular products
*Shareholders:* Michael Paul Linsky; Raymond Linsky
*Officers:* Michael Paul Linsky, Secretary; Michael Paul Linsky [1984] Director; Raymond Linsky [1947] Director

**Sentamu Academy Learning Trust**
*Incorporated:* 26 March 2008 *Employees:* 429
*Previous:* Archbishop Sentamu Academy
*Net Worth:* £32,009,000 *Total Assets:* £35,567,000
*Registered Office:* 1 Bilton Grove, Hull, HU9 5YB
*Activities:* Primary education
*Officers:* Mandy Watson, Secretary; Peter David Duffield [1953] Director/Chartered Accountant; Colin Michael Foster [1958] Director/Accountant; Alison Greaves [1972] Assistant Director of Education; Marjorie Jane Lewis [1967] Director; Professor Carl Wilhelm Irene Pistorius [1958] Director/Engineer

**Serenity Parks Limited**
*Incorporated:* 18 August 2016
*Net Worth:* £81,804 *Total Assets:* £4,315,054
*Registered Office:* 6 Fountain Court, Buccaneer Drive, Finningley, Doncaster, S Yorks, DN9 3GN
*Activities:* Activities of other holding companies n.e.c.
*Officers:* Gary Burns [1981] Director; Gavin Louis Leverett [1970] Director; Andrew Wilson [1972] Director

**Harold Sergeant and Sons Limited**
*Incorporated:* 27 February 1963 *Employees:* 5
*Net Worth:* £2,958,736 *Total Assets:* £3,429,349
*Registered Office:* Weedley Farm, Brough, E Yorks, HU15 1QT
*Activities:* Mixed farming
*Shareholders:* Charles Edwin Sergeant; Geoffrey Neil Sergeant
*Officers:* Geoffrey Neil Sergeant, Secretary; Charles Edwin Sergeant [1940] Director/Farmer; Geoffrey Neil Sergeant [1963] Director/Farmer

**Serius Group Limited**
*Incorporated:* 9 June 2003 *Employees:* 40
*Net Worth:* £2,586,828 *Total Assets:* £4,593,879
*Registered Office:* Lawnswood, Southfields Road, Strensall, York, YO32 5UA
*Activities:* Other service activities n.e.c.
*Parent:* UAB Koncernas Consus
*Officers:* Rasa Poceviciene [1983] Director [Lithuanian]; Joanne Thomas [1967] Director

**Servemet (N.W.) Limited**
*Incorporated:* 27 July 1981 *Employees:* 32
*Net Worth:* £1,377,658 *Total Assets:* £3,011,878
*Registered Office:* Holwey Park Industrial Estate, Howley Park Road East, Morley, Leeds, LS27 0BN
*Activities:* Manufacture of other fabricated metal products n.e.c.
*Shareholder:* John William Cullen
*Officers:* Graham Patrick Wilson, Secretary; Peter Brian Brady [1949] Director; James Harry Chrimes [1931] Director; John William Cullen [1948] Director/Aluminium Stockholder; Howard Anthony Webb [1960] Director; Graham Patrick Wilson [1947] Director/Aluminium Stockholder; John Marshall Winn [1947] Director/Aluminium Stockholder

**Service Metals (Midlands) Limited**
*Incorporated:* 9 March 1987 *Employees:* 56
*Net Worth:* £1,330,822 *Total Assets:* £7,101,123
*Registered Office:* Howley Park Industrial Estate, Howley Park Road East, Morley, Leeds, LS27 0BN
*Activities:* Manufacture of other fabricated metal products n.e.c.
*Shareholders:* Graham Patrick Wilson; James Harry Chrimes; John Marshall Winn
*Officers:* Graham Patrick Wilson, Secretary; James Harry Chrimes [1931] Director; Anthony Philip Walley [1963] Director; Graham Patrick Wilson [1947] Director/Aluminium Stockholder; John Marshall Winn [1947] Director/Aluminium Stockholder

**Service Timber Limited**
*Incorporated:* 7 April 1988 *Employees:* 75
*Net Worth:* £3,418,846 *Total Assets:* £10,107,561
*Registered Office:* Timber Terminal, Breighton Airfield, Bubwith, Selby, N Yorks, YO8 6DJ
*Activities:* Non-specialised wholesale trade
*Major Shareholder:* Martin John Eveson
*Officers:* Claire Louise Eveson, Secretary; Martin John Eveson [1957] Director; Philip Gale Eveson [1957] Director

**Serviced Dispense Equipment (Holdings) Limited**
*Incorporated:* 11 November 2003
*Net Worth:* £11,025,000 *Total Assets:* £133,512,000
*Registered Office:* Maltings Building, Leeds Road, Tadcaster, N Yorks, LS24 9HB
*Activities:* Activities of head offices
*Shareholders:* Carlsberg UK Ltd; Heineken UK Ltd
*Officers:* Richard Anthony Bradbury [1963] Commercial Director; Nicholas Martin Bryan [1953] Director; Thomas Anthony Danaher [1964] Director/On Trade Finance Business Partner; Gerard Lowry [1972] On Trade Development & Operations Director; Radovan Sikorsky [1967] Finance Director [Slovak]

**Serviced Dispense Equipment Limited**
*Incorporated:* 11 November 2003
*Net Worth:* £10,702,000 *Total Assets:* £141,040,992
*Registered Office:* Maltings Building, Leeds Road, Tadcaster, N Yorks, LS24 9HB
*Activities:* Repair of other equipment
*Parent:* Serviced Dispense Equipment (Holdings) Ltd
*Officers:* Richard Anthony Bradbury [1963] Commercial Director; Nicholas Martin Bryan [1953] Director; Thomas Anthony Danaher [1964] Director/On Trade Finance Business Partner; Gerard Lowry [1972] On Trade Development & Operations Director; Radovan Sikorsky [1967] Finance Director [Slovak]

**J L Services & Son Limited**
*Incorporated:* 29 December 2004 *Employees:* 13
*Net Worth:* £1,933,596 *Total Assets:* £3,778,529
*Registered Office:* Network House, Monckton Road Industrial Estate, Wakefield, W Yorks, WF2 7AL
*Activities:* Construction of commercial buildings
*Shareholders:* James Robert Leatham; Andrea Jayne Leatham
*Officers:* Andrea Leatham, Secretary; James Robert Leatham [1974] Director; Robinson Tuck [1985] Director

**Setbray Properties (1997) Limited**
*Incorporated:* 21 March 1997
*Net Worth:* £4,512,982 *Total Assets:* £7,010,128
*Registered Office:* Burlees House, Hanging Royd Lane, Hebden Bridge, W Yorks, HX7 7DD
*Activities:* Residents property management
*Major Shareholder:* Trustees of Derek Parker Settlement
*Officers:* Michael Anthony Parker, Secretary/Textile Agent; Michael Anthony Parker [1960] Director/Textile Agent; Graham Turner [1953] Director

**Seven Technologies Group Limited**
*Incorporated:* 12 June 2003 *Employees:* 103
*Net Worth Deficit:* £1,087,829 *Total Assets:* £14,179,140
*Registered Office:* 1 Low Hall Business Park, Low Hall Road, Horsforth, Leeds, LS18 4EG
*Activities:* Other service activities n.e.c.
*Parent:* Seven Technologies Group Limited
*Officers:* David Anderson [1965] Director; Roland Barzegar [1982] Director/Chief Financial Officer; Michael John Howarth [1967] Director; Adrian William Timberlake [1969] Director/Chief Technical Officer

**Severfield (Design & Build) Limited**
*Incorporated:* 14 November 2000 *Employees:* 189
*Net Worth:* £41,089,000 *Total Assets:* £48,360,000
*Registered Office:* Severs House, Dalton Airfield Industrial Estate, Dalton, Thirsk, N Yorks, YO7 3JN
*Activities:* Manufacture of metal structures and parts of structures
*Parent:* Atlas Ward Holdings Limited
*Officers:* Simon Peter Barnes [1962] Director; Steven Andrew Day [1962] Director; Alan David Dunsmore [1969] Director; Adam Semple [1975] Director/Chartered Accountant; Kate Elizabeth Starkie [1987] Finance Director

**Severfield (UK) Limited**
*Incorporated:* 6 December 1991 *Employees:* 809
*Net Worth:* £23,614,000 *Total Assets:* £128,283,000
*Registered Office:* Severs House, Dalton Airfield Industrial Estate, Dalton, Thirsk, N Yorks, YO7 3JN
*Activities:* Other specialised construction activities n.e.c.
*Parent:* Severfield PLC
*Officers:* Ian Robert Samuel Cochrane [1970] Director; Alan David Dunsmore [1969] Director; Robert William Evans [1972] Surveying Director; Alexander James Harper [1964] Director; Adam Semple [1975] Director/Chartered Accountant; Gary Wintersgill [1971] Director

**Severfield PLC**
*Incorporated:* 6 May 1983 *Employees:* 1,354
*Net Worth:* £168,996,992 *Total Assets:* £253,707,008
*Registered Office:* Severs House, Dalton Airfield Industrial Estate, Dalton, Thirsk, N Yorks, YO7 3JN
*Activities:* Manufacture of metal structures and parts of structures
*Officers:* Mark Sanderson, Secretary; Ian Robert Samuel Cochrane [1970] Director; John Dodds [1945] Director; Alan David Dunsmore [1969] Director; Alun Hughes Griffiths [1954] Director/Management Consultant; John Anthony Osbaldiston [1952] Director/Chartered Accountant; Prof Derek Randall [1961] Executive Director; Adam Semple [1975] Director/Chartered Accountant; Kevin Ian Whiteman [1956] Director

**SEW-Eurodrive Limited**
*Incorporated:* 5 February 1969 *Employees:* 154
*Net Worth:* £31,919,468 *Total Assets:* £41,829,144
*Registered Office:* Sew Eurodrive Limited, Devilliers Way, Trident Park, Normanton, W Yorks, WF6 1GX
*Activities:* Other manufacturing n.e.c.
*Officers:* John Antony Pickup, Secretary; Herr Jurgen Dietmar Blickle [1951] Director/Chief Executive Officer [German]; Mark Holmes [1963] Director/Engineer

**Sewell Construction Limited**
*Incorporated:* 18 November 1953 *Employees:* 85
*Net Worth:* £3,514,843 *Total Assets:* £20,152,884
*Registered Office:* Geneva Way, Leads Road, Hull, HU7 0DG
*Activities:* Construction of commercial buildings
*Parent:* Sewell Group Limited
*Officers:* David Adrian Leedham, Company Secretary; Robert Andrew Cawkwell [1969] Commercial Director; Simon John Davison [1974] Director/Chartered Accountant; Paul Edwin Sewell [1952] Director/Builder

**Sewell Education (Hull) Limited**
*Incorporated:* 21 October 1997 *Employees:* 28
*Net Worth:* £3,596,987 *Total Assets:* £3,838,948
*Registered Office:* Geneva Way, Leads Road, Hull, HU7 0DG
*Activities:* Primary education
*Parent:* Sewell Group Ltd
*Officers:* David Adrian Leedham, Secretary/Director; Simon John Davison [1974] Director/Chartered Accountant; David Adrian Leedham [1967] Director; Paul Edwin Sewell [1952] Director/Builder

**Sewell Education (York) Holdings Limited**
*Incorporated:* 12 August 2004 *Employees:* 2
*Net Worth:* £198,927 *Total Assets:* £7,844,031
*Registered Office:* Geneva Way, Leads Road, Hull, HU7 0DG
*Activities:* Dormant company
*Shareholders:* Sewell Group Limited; PFI Infrastructure Finance Limited
*Officers:* David Adrian Leedham, Secretary; John Ivor Cavill [1972] Director; David Adrian Leedham [1967] Director

**Sewell Education (York) Limited**
*Incorporated:* 26 April 2004 *Employees:* 2
*Net Worth:* £198,927 *Total Assets:* £7,844,031
*Registered Office:* Geneva Way, Leads Road, Hull, HU7 0DG
*Activities:* Other letting and operating of own or leased real estate
*Parent:* Sewell Education (York) Holdings Ltd
*Officers:* David Adrian Leedham, Secretary; John Ivor Cavill [1972] Director; David Adrian Leedham [1967] Director

**Sewell Facilities Management Limited**
*Incorporated:* 1 December 1994 *Employees:* 91
*Net Worth:* £4,151,827 *Total Assets:* £7,629,664
*Registered Office:* Geneva Way, Leads Road, Hull, HU7 0DG
*Activities:* Combined facilities support activities
*Parent:* Sewell Group Ltd
*Officers:* David Adrian Leedham, Secretary; Simon John Davison [1974] Director/Chartered Accountant; Paul Edwin Sewell [1952] Director; Martin James Stead [1976] Director

**Sewell Investments Limited**
*Incorporated:* 2 April 2003 *Employees:* 5
*Net Worth:* £2,563,007 *Total Assets:* £6,967,884
*Registered Office:* Geneva Way, Leads Road, Hull, HU7 0DG
*Activities:* Other letting and operating of own or leased real estate
*Parent:* Sewell Group Limited
*Officers:* David Adrian Leedham, Secretary/Director; Joanne Louise Barnes [1972] Director; Robert Andrew Cawkwell [1969] Director/Chartered Surveyor; Simon John Davison [1974] Director/Chartered Accountant; David Adrian Leedham [1967] Director; Paul Edwin Sewell [1952] Director

**Sewell Retail Limited**
*Incorporated:* 25 October 1989 *Employees:* 230
*Net Worth:* £6,372,000 *Total Assets:* £10,418,000
*Registered Office:* Geneva Way, Leads Road, Hull, HU7 0DG
*Activities:* Retail sale of automotive fuel in specialised stores
*Parent:* Sewell Ventures Limited
*Officers:* David Adrian Leedham, Company Secretary; Katherine Elizabeth Batch [1983] Sales Director; David Craven-Jones [1961] Director; Simon John Davison [1974] Director/Chartered Accountant; Alexandra Sarah Mortimer [1981] Director/Chartered Accountant; Patrick Allan Sewell [1972] Director; Paul Edwin Sewell [1952] Director/Builder; Susan Anne Sewell [1952] Director

**Sewell Ventures Limited**
*Incorporated:* 11 September 2012 *Employees:* 477
*Net Worth:* £9,038,000 *Total Assets:* £34,992,000
*Registered Office:* Geneva Way, Leads Road, Hull, HU7 0DG
*Activities:* Dormant company
*Major Shareholder:* Paul Edwin Sewell
*Officers:* David Adrian Leedham, Secretary; Simon John Davison [1974] Director/Chartered Accountant; Neil Jenneson [1949] Director; David Adrian Leedham [1967] Director/Company Secretary; Patrick Allan Sewell [1972] Director; Paul Edwin Sewell [1952] Director/Builder

**Seymour (Civil Engineering Contractors) Ltd.**
*Incorporated:* 21 June 1978 *Employees:* 226
*Net Worth:* £3,055,000 *Total Assets:* £12,200,000
*Registered Office:* 3175 Century Way, Thorpe Park, Leeds, LS15 8ZB
*Activities:* Construction of commercial buildings
*Parent:* Seymour (C.E.C) Holdings Limited
*Officers:* Kevin James Byrne [1958] Contract Director; Paul Scott [1964] Director/Engineer

**SFS Developments Limited**
*Incorporated:* 14 July 1998 *Employees:* 2
*Net Worth:* £2,048,334 *Total Assets:* £4,141,658
*Registered Office:* Stross House, Scout Hill Mills, Broad Street, Dewsbury, W Yorks, WF13 3SA
*Activities:* Other letting and operating of own or leased real estate
*Major Shareholder:* Tanveer Ali Hussain
*Officers:* Tanveer Ali Hussain, Secretary/Director; Tanveer Ali Hussain [1964] Director

**SFS Group Fastening Technology Limited**
*Incorporated:* 8 July 1983 *Employees:* 70
*Previous:* SFS Intec Holdings Limited
*Net Worth:* £13,623,828 *Total Assets:* £41,601,092
*Registered Office:* 153 Kirkstall Road, Leeds, LS4 2AT
*Activities:* Activities of head offices
*Parent:* SFS Intec Holding AG
*Officers:* Thomas Bamberger, Secretary; Thomas Bamberger [1961] Director [German]; Arthur Blank [1959] Director [Swiss]

**SGS Packaging Europe Holdings Limited**
*Incorporated:* 20 April 2005
*Net Worth:* £3,662,905 *Total Assets:* £22,511,284
*Registered Office:* SGS Bridgehead, Orchid Road, Hull, HU13 0DH
*Activities:* Other manufacturing n.e.c.
*Parent:* SGS International LLC
*Officers:* Richard Russell Jones, Secretary; Richard Russell Jones [1957] Finance Director; Terence Wade Koontz [1963] Director [American]

**SGS Packaging Europe Limited**
*Incorporated:* 30 June 1959 *Employees:* 738
*Net Worth:* £19,110,000 *Total Assets:* £29,994,000
*Registered Office:* SGS Bridgehead, Orchid Road, Bridgehead Business Park, Hessle, E Yorks, HU13 0DH
*Activities:* Pre-press and pre-media services
*Parent:* SGS International LLC
*Officers:* Richard Russell Jones, Secretary; Richard Russell Jones [1957] Finance Director; Terence Wade Koontz [1963] Director [American]; Aidan David Tracey [1968] Director [Canadian]

**Shaks Specialist Cars Ltd**
*Incorporated:* 25 October 2004 *Employees:* 13
*Net Worth:* £912,115 *Total Assets:* £3,280,172
*Registered Office:* Eehad House, Northgate, Huddersfield, W Yorks, HD1 6AP
*Activities:* Sale of other motor vehicles
*Shareholders:* Shakeel Shah; Unaiza Shah
*Officers:* Shakeel Shah, Secretary/Self Employed; Shakeel Shah [1981] Director/Self Employed

**Shallowdale Limited**
*Incorporated:* 20 December 1972 *Employees:* 3
*Net Worth:* £4,432,186 *Total Assets:* £4,902,009
*Registered Office:* 20-22 Bridge End, Leeds, LS1 4DJ
*Activities:* Renting and operating of Housing Association real estate
*Officers:* Nicola Ruth Brackup, Secretary; Suzanne Jane Berson [1962] Director; Nicola Ruth Brackup [1964] Director

**Shaman Investments Limited**
*Incorporated:* 22 October 2009 *Employees:* 381
*Net Worth:* £11,546,153 *Total Assets:* £58,017,644
*Registered Office:* Whistler Drive, Castleford, W Yorks, WF10 5HX
*Activities:* Activities of head offices
*Major Shareholder:* Michael Pickles
*Officers:* Marc Anthony Pickles, Secretary; Marc Anthony Pickles [1984] Director; Michael Pickles [1959] Director/Accountant

**Shand Engineering Limited**
*Incorporated:* 27 November 1972
*Net Worth:* £2,451,834 *Total Assets:* £3,612,644
*Registered Office:* Kiln Lane, Stallingborough, Grimsby, N E Lincs, DN41 8DL
*Activities:* Manufacture of other fabricated metal products n.e.c.
*Parent:* Sturrock and Robson (UK) Ltd
*Officers:* Katie Alice Bellamy, Secretary; Barrie Richard Jarman [1964] Director/Engineer; Dennis Giovanni Mech [1961] Director/Chief Executive; Alan Stuart Merrell [1960] Director/Chief Financial Officer

**Share Multi Academy Trust**
*Incorporated:* 4 August 2011 *Employees:* 247
*Net Worth:* £22,487,000 *Total Assets:* £25,720,000
*Registered Office:* Shelley College, Huddersfield Road, Shelley, Huddersfield, W Yorks, HD8 8NL
*Activities:* General secondary education
*Officers:* Cleo Sylvia Potterton, Secretary; Mark Day [1974] Director/Manager; Michael David Dunkley [1970] Director/Head of ALM (Building Society); Marie Guest [1974] Director; Professor Jeanne Kerrel Keay [1955] Director/University Professor; William Andrew Kent [1953] Director/Retired; John McNally [1968] Director/Principal

**Shared Vision Learning Trust**
*Incorporated:* 6 June 2011 *Employees:* 77
*Previous:* West Park Academy
*Net Worth:* £4,065,000 *Total Assets:* £4,921,000
*Registered Office:* West Park Academy, Alderman Leach Drive, Darlington, Co Durham, DL2 2GF
*Activities:* Primary education
*Officers:* Elizabeth Campbell, Secretary; John Barrie Armstrong [1940] Director/Retired Councillor; John Robert Barrigan [1970] Director/Project Lead with DFE; Dorothy Dodds [1949] Director/Retired; John William Earley [1985] Director/Operations Manager; Jenna-Marie Ford [1985] Director/Deputy Principal; David John Fraser [1984] Director/Teacher; Judith Gainsborough [1959] Director/Consultant - National Autistic Society (Sessional); Lewis Charles Goodwin [1978] Director/Solicitor; Heather Anne Hebden [1969] Director/Nurse; Samantha Ruth Hirst-Caraher [1968] Director/Deputy Headteacher; John McKellar [1951] Director/Retired; Abigail Sarah Rowcroft [1976] Director/Housewife

**Sharma Investments Limited**
*Incorporated:* 10 March 2010
*Net Worth:* £957,510 *Total Assets:* £3,435,021
*Registered Office:* Abacus House, Pennine Business Park, Longbow Close, Huddersfield, W Yorks, HD2 1GQ
*Activities:* Buying and selling of own real estate
*Officers:* Ravi Sharma, Secretary; Ravi Sharma [1986] Director

**Sharp Business Systems UK PLC**
*Incorporated:* 3 June 1987 *Employees:* 366
*Net Worth:* £13,560,000 *Total Assets:* £32,822,000
*Registered Office:* Northern House, Moor Knoll Lane, East Ardsley, Wakefield, W Yorks, WF3 2EE
*Activities:* Renting and leasing of office machinery and equipment (including computers)
*Officers:* David Christopher Cooper, Secretary; Jun Ashida [1966] Director/President [Japanese]; David Christopher Cooper [1958] Finance Director; Russell Adrian Hardiman [1965] Commercial Director; Nomura Seitaro [1976] Director [Japanese]; Stuart Raymond Sykes [1966] Managing Director

**Sharp Holdings Limited**
*Incorporated:* 9 December 2015
*Net Worth:* £854,464 *Total Assets:* £3,992,934
*Registered Office:* Unit 8 Leeds 27 Industrial Estate, Bruntcliffe Avenue, Morley, Leeds, LS27 0LL
*Activities:* Other letting and operating of own or leased real estate
*Major Shareholder:* Richard Dean Sharp
*Officers:* Richard Sharp [1985] Director

**Sharpsmart Limited**
*Incorporated:* 30 July 2001 *Employees:* 52
*Net Worth:* £1,738,351 *Total Assets:* £7,746,783
*Registered Office:* Unit 44 Enterprise City, Meadowfield Avenue, Spennymoor, Co Durham, DL16 6JF
*Activities:* Collection of non-hazardous waste
*Major Shareholder:* Danny Daniels
*Officers:* Dean Justin McPhee, Secretary; Danny Boulas Daniels [1964] Director [Australian]

**Shaw & Rhodes Holdings Limited**
*Incorporated:* 17 February 2004 *Employees:* 65
*Net Worth:* £7,399,306 *Total Assets:* £8,648,749
*Registered Office:* Victoria Buildings, Albert Street, Lockwood, Huddersfield, W Yorks, HD1 3PR
*Activities:* Activities of head offices
*Shareholder:* John Howard Rhodes
*Officers:* Jayne Rhodes, Secretary; John Howard Rhodes [1963] Managing Director

**John Shaw and Son Limited**
*Incorporated:* 1 February 1972 *Employees:* 170
*Net Worth:* £11,031,105 *Total Assets:* £18,144,092
*Registered Office:* The Coach and Travel Centre, Scotland Road, Carnforth, Lancs, LA5 9RQ
*Activities:* Other urban, suburban or metropolitan passenger land transport (not underground, metro or similar)
*Parent:* Zircon Holdings Limited
*Officers:* Pamela Shaw, Secretary; John Paul Shaw [1970] Operations Director; Mark Robert Shaw [1979] Director; Pamela Shaw [1958] Director; Robert Richard Shaw [1948] Director

**Nikolas Shaw Limited**
*Incorporated:* 11 February 1977 *Employees:* 65
*Net Worth Deficit:* £438,772 *Total Assets:* £5,232,817
*Registered Office:* 56-64 St Thomas Street, Scarborough, N Yorks, YO11 1DU
*Activities:* Gambling and betting activities
*Shareholders:* Nikolas Marc Shaw; Rebecca Jane Shaw
*Officers:* Rebecca Jane Shaw, Secretary; Stephen David Mosley [1959] Managing Director; Nikolas Marc Shaw [1957] Director/Amusement Caterer; Rebecca Jane Shaw [1964] Director

**Shaw Moisture Meters (U.K.) Limited**
*Incorporated:* 13 July 1992 *Employees:* 12
*Net Worth:* £3,046,605 *Total Assets:* £3,217,755
*Registered Office:* Len Shaw Building, Bolton Lane, Bradford, W Yorks, BD2 1AF
*Activities:* Manufacture of electronic industrial process control equipment
*Parent:* Amsgro Limited
*Officers:* George Thomas Baker, Secretary; Timothy Peters [1973] Director

**Shaw Pallet Limited**
*Incorporated:* 10 December 1973 *Employees:* 47
*Net Worth:* £2,615,573 *Total Assets:* £3,738,659
*Registered Office:* Shaw Pallet Building, Bridge Street, Slaithwaite, Huddersfield, W Yorks, HD7 5JN
*Activities:* Manufacture of wooden containers
*Parent:* Shaw Pallet (Holdings) Limited
*Officers:* Michael Miodrag Dragicevic, Secretary; John Michael Coupland [1955] Director/Manager; Michael Miodrag Dragicevic [1956] Director/Chartered Accountant; Christopher John Hillaby [1959] Director/Sales & Marketing Executive

**Shaw Timber Limited**
*Incorporated:* 3 August 1976 *Employees:* 62
*Net Worth:* £3,121,313 *Total Assets:* £4,434,503
*Registered Office:* Bridge Street, Slaithwaite, Huddersfield, W Yorks, HD7 5JN
*Activities:* Manufacture of other products of wood, manufacture of articles of cork, straw and plaiting materials
*Parent:* Shaw Timber (Holdings) Limited
*Officers:* Michael Miodrag Dragicevic, Secretary; Stephen John Mullany [1950] Director/Purchasing Executive; Christopher Woodhead [1957] Director/Sales & Marketing Executive

**Shaws (Huddersfield) Limited**
*Incorporated:* 27 March 1902 *Employees:* 29
*Net Worth:* £5,548,155 *Total Assets:* £6,083,441
*Registered Office:* Shaw Park Office Centre, Silver Street, Wakefield Road, Huddersfield, W Yorks, HD5 9AF
*Activities:* Manufacture of condiments and seasonings
*Shareholders:* Terence Peace; Martin Shaw
*Officers:* James Richard Peace, Secretary; Janette Andrea Docker [1964] Director/Accountant; James Richard Peace [1976] Director; Terence Peace [1945] Director; Matthew Shaw [1959] Director/Retired

**S. Sheard & Son Limited**
*Incorporated:* 9 March 1973 *Employees:* 212
*Net Worth:* £12,134,315 *Total Assets:* £18,247,364
*Registered Office:* Solar Works, Calder Street, Greetland, Halifax, W Yorks, HX4 8AQ
*Activities:* Manufacture of other paper and paperboard containers
*Parent:* Sheard Properties Limited
*Officers:* Barbara Whittaker, Secretary; Claire Barbara Greenwood [1978] Director/Waste Paper Manager; Lee Andrew Shackleton [1971] Managing Director; Barbara Whittaker [1946] Director/Waste Paper Merchant; John Stephen Whittaker [1947] Director/Waste Paper Merchant; Roger Jonathan Whittaker [1975] Director/Carton Manufacturer

**Sheard Properties Limited**
*Incorporated:* 15 April 1996 *Employees:* 214
*Net Worth:* £23,101,184 *Total Assets:* £31,255,004
*Registered Office:* Solar Works, Calder Street, Greetland, Halifax, W Yorks, HX4 8AQ
*Activities:* Renting and operating of Housing Association real estate
*Shareholders:* Barbara Whittaker; John Stephen Whittaker
*Officers:* Barbara Whittaker, Secretary/Director; Barbara Whittaker [1946] Director; John Stephen Whittaker [1947] Director

**Shedden Farms Limited**
*Incorporated:* 11 August 1964 *Employees:* 25
*Net Worth:* £1,621,582 *Total Assets:* £6,696,635
*Registered Office:* Shipton Grange, Shipton by Beningbrough, York, YO30 1AP
*Activities:* Growing of cereals (except rice), leguminous crops and oil seeds
*Officers:* Robert Crawford Shedden, Secretary; Ian Campbell Pears [1972] Director; David Farquhar Shedden [1943] Director/Farmer; Hugh Iain Shedden [1975] Director; Margaret Ann Shedden [1947] Director/Farmer; Nicola Ann Shedden [1944] Director/Farmer; Robert Crawford Shedden [1947] Director/Farmer

**Sheds for Logistics Limited**
*Incorporated:* 30 October 2014 *Employees:* 955
*Net Worth:* £27,008,000 *Total Assets:* £37,989,000
*Registered Office:* The Torque Building, Wortley Moor Road, Leeds, LS12 4JH
*Activities:* Activities of other holding companies n.e.c.
*Officers:* Stewart Paul Firth [1970] Director; Timothy Simon Howarth [1958] Director

**Sheetfed Holdings Limited**
*Incorporated:* 31 January 2012
*Net Worth:* £7,596,377 *Total Assets:* £11,822,634
*Registered Office:* Unit 2 Enterprise Park, Enterprise Way, Retford, Notts, DN22 7HH
*Activities:* Wholesale of other machinery and equipment
*Parent:* Langley Holdings PLC
*Officers:* Anthony John Langley [1954] Director; Bernard James Langley [1993] Director

**Sheffield Housing Company Limited**
*Incorporated:* 3 March 2011 *Employees:* 3
*Net Worth Deficit:* £92,462 *Total Assets:* £14,488,862
*Registered Office:* Keepmoat Offices, The Waterfront, Lakeside Boulevard, Doncaster, S Yorks, DN4 5PL
*Activities:* Construction of domestic buildings
*Shareholders:* KGP (SHC) Limited; Sheffield City Council
*Officers:* Elizabeth Buck [1970] Director; Daniel Crew [1986] Director; Philip Howard Elvy [1967] Director; Matthew Francis Harrison [1964] Director/Deputy Chief Executive; Ian Graham Hoad [1980] Operations Director; Stephen John Lapthorne [1971] Director; Sean Michael McClean [1970] Director/Head of Capital Delivery Service; Janet Sharpe [1962] Director; Tim Dion Wray [1970] Finance Director

**Sheffield United (Hotel) Limited**
*Incorporated:* 29 January 2007 *Employees:* 77
*Net Worth Deficit:* £639,654 *Total Assets:* £13,085,297
*Registered Office:* Europa House, 20 Esplanade, Scarborough, N Yorks, YO11 2AQ
*Activities:* Hotels and similar accommodation
*Parent:* Scarborough Partnership Limited
*Officers:* Kevin Charles McCabe [1948] Director/Chartered Surveyor; Scott Richard McCabe [1975] Managing Director; Jeremy John Tutton [1966] Director/Financial Controller

**Sheffield United Group Limited**
*Incorporated:* 2 November 2000
*Previous:* Scarborough United Group Limited
*Net Worth Deficit:* £13,866,827 *Total Assets:* £10,911,900
*Registered Office:* Europa House, 20 Esplanade, Scarborough, N Yorks, YO11 2AQ
*Activities:* Activities of other holding companies n.e.c.
*Parent:* Esplanade Group (Scarborough) International Limited
*Officers:* Scott Richard McCabe [1975] Managing Director; Jeremy John Tutton [1966] Director/Financial Controller

**Shepherd Building Group Limited**
*Incorporated:* 23 March 1960 *Employees:* 1,890
*Net Worth:* £189,300,000 *Total Assets:* £377,500,000
*Registered Office:* Yorkon House, New Lane, Huntington, York, YO32 9PT
*Activities:* Activities of head offices
*Officers:* Martin Ian Goforth, Secretary; Derek Paul Carter [1958] Director; Jonathan Mark Collins [1971] Director; Caroline Johnstone [1960] Director; Henri-Jean Velge [1956] Director [Belgian]; David John Williams [1953] Director

**Shepherd Construction Limited**
*Incorporated:* 21 November 1924 *Employees:* 17
*Net Worth Deficit:* £19,999,000 *Total Assets:* £20,989,000
*Registered Office:* Yorkon House, New Lane, Huntington, York, YO32 9PT
*Activities:* Construction of commercial buildings
*Parent:* Shepherd Building Group Limited
*Officers:* Martin Ian Goforth, Secretary; Philip Andrew Greer [1963] Director

**Shepherd Development Company Limited**
*Incorporated:* 1 January 1965
*Net Worth Deficit:* £4,112,000 *Total Assets:* £8,672,000
*Registered Office:* Yorkon House, New Lane, Huntington, York, YO32 9PT
*Activities:* Development of building projects
*Parent:* Shepherd Building Group Limited
*Officers:* Martin Ian Goforth, Secretary; Caroline Scott [1961] Director/Accountant

**Shepherd Group Built Environment Limited**
*Incorporated:* 7 May 2013
*Net Worth Deficit:* £2,819,000 *Total Assets:* £3,119,000
*Registered Office:* Yorkon House, New Lane, Huntington, York, YO32 9PT
*Activities:* Other business support service activities n.e.c.
*Parent:* Shepherd Building Group Limited
*Officers:* Martin Ian Goforth, Secretary; Caroline Scott [1961] Director/Accountant

**Shepherd Group Properties Limited**
*Incorporated:* 11 October 1961
*Net Worth:* £3,223,000 *Total Assets:* £3,543,000
*Registered Office:* Yorkon House, New Lane, Huntington, York, YO32 9PT
*Activities:* Development of building projects
*Parent:* Shepherd Building Group Limited
*Officers:* Martin Ian Goforth, Secretary; Derek Paul Carter [1958] Director; Jonathan Mark Collins [1971] Director/Accountant; Caroline Scott [1961] Director/Accountant

**Shepherd Homes Limited**
*Incorporated:* 7 November 1945
*Net Worth:* £3,362,000 *Total Assets:* £7,059,000
*Registered Office:* Yorkon House, New Lane, Huntington, York, YO32 9PT
*Activities:* Construction of domestic buildings
*Parent:* Shepherd Building Group Limited
*Officers:* Martin Ian Goforth, Secretary; Jonathan Mark Collins [1971] Director/Accountant; Janet Rose [1964] Director/Accountant; Caroline Scott [1961] Director/Accountant

**Shepherd Industries Limited**
*Incorporated:* 12 June 2009
*Net Worth:* £9,127,000 *Total Assets:* £58,633,000
*Registered Office:* Yorkon House, New Lane, Huntington, York, YO32 9PT
*Activities:* Activities of head offices
*Parent:* Shepherd Building Group Limited
*Officers:* Martin Ian Goforth, Secretary; Derek Paul Carter [1958] Director; Jonathan Mark Collins [1971] Director/Accountant

**Edgar F Shepherd Ltd**
*Incorporated:* 7 May 2010 *Employees:* 31
*Net Worth:* £4,405,382 *Total Assets:* £5,681,888
*Registered Office:* Twinsburn Farm, Heighington, Darlington, Co Durham, DL2 2TU
*Activities:* Treatment and disposal of non-hazardous waste
*Major Shareholder:* Edgar Foster Shepherd
*Officers:* Barbara Shepherd [1937] Director/Traditional Grocer; Edgar Foster Shepherd [1934] Director/Farmer and Wood Shavings Sawdust; Nigel Edgar Charles Herbert Shepherd [1978] Director/Sawdust & Shavings Processor; Simon Edgar Charles Herbert Shepherd [1970] Financial Director

**Shepley Engineers Limited**
*Incorporated:* 9 May 1994 *Employees:* 309
*Net Worth:* £7,466,000 *Total Assets:* £29,014,000
*Registered Office:* 3175 Century Way, Thorpe Park, Leeds, LS15 8ZB
*Activities:* Manufacture of metal structures and parts of structures
*Parent:* Renew Holdings PLC
*Officers:* Nicholas Paul Houghton [1960] Director/Chartered Mechanical Engineer; James Paul McBain [1962] Director; Paul Scott [1964] Director/Engineer

**Shepley Spring Limited**
*Incorporated:* 9 July 1996 *Employees:* 59
*Net Worth:* £7,454,720 *Total Assets:* £11,338,697
*Registered Office:* Eastfield Mills, The Knowle, Shepley, Huddersfield, W Yorks, HD8 8EA
*Activities:* Manufacture of soft drinks; production of mineral waters and other bottled waters
*Parent:* Penmoor UK Ltd
*Officers:* Jason Barlow [1972] Director; Andrew Peykoff II [1976] Director/Executive [American]; Kenneth Ratzlaff [1968] Director/Executive [American]; Rali Sanderon [1976] Director/Executive [American]; Charles Alistair Smith [1969] Director; James Maxwell Smith [1971] Director; John Selwyn Smith [1942] Director

**Sheppee Holdings Ltd**
*Incorporated:* 25 February 2008 *Employees:* 2
*Net Worth:* £581,508 *Total Assets:* £4,390,725
*Registered Office:* Halifax Way, Airfield Business Park, Elvington, York, YO41 4AU
*Activities:* Dormant company
*Parent:* Rise Group SAS
*Officers:* Keith Richard Johnson, Secretary; Simon Philip Holmes [1976] Sales Director; Mark Ashley Johnston [1963] Director

**Sheppee International Limited**
*Incorporated:* 22 February 1993 *Employees:* 40
*Net Worth:* £6,673,168 *Total Assets:* £8,705,707
*Registered Office:* Halifax Way, Airfield Business Park, Elvington, York, YO41 4AU
*Activities:* Manufacture of other special-purpose machinery n.e.c.
*Parent:* Sheppee Holdings Limited
*Officers:* Keith Richard Johnson, Secretary; Simon Philip Holmes [1976] Sales Director; Keith Richard Johnson [1967] Finance Director; Mark Ashley Johnston [1963] Director; Colin Patrick Rice [1965] Technical Director [Irish]

**Sherborne Upholstery Limited**
*Incorporated:* 6 June 1953 *Employees:* 258
*Net Worth:* £13,255,365 *Total Assets:* £15,311,740
*Registered Office:* Pasture Lane, Clayton, Bradford, W Yorks, BD14 6LT
*Activities:* Manufacture of other furniture
*Shareholders:* Christopher David Fort; Kathleen Fort
*Officers:* Daniel Edward Atkinson, Secretary; Daniel Edward Atkinson [1970] Financial Director; Christopher David Fort [1954] Managing Director; Kathleen Fort [1929] Director/Married Woman; Christopher Walker [1967] Production Director

**Sheridan Fabrications Limited**
*Incorporated:* 5 December 1995 *Employees:* 236
*Net Worth:* £1,615,254 *Total Assets:* £11,988,873
*Registered Office:* New Sheridan House, Don Pedro Avenue, Normanton Industrial Estate, Normanton, W Yorks, WF6 1TD
*Activities:* Other manufacturing n.e.c.
*Major Shareholder:* John Nathan Blackburn
*Officers:* Karen Louise Brown, Secretary; John Nathan Blackburn [1967] Managing Director

**Sherwood Restaurants Ltd**
*Incorporated:* 3 November 2008 *Employees:* 544
*Net Worth:* £1,106,748 *Total Assets:* £5,993,591
*Registered Office:* McDonalds Restaurant, The Dome Leisure Park, Bawtry Road, Doncaster, S Yorks, DN4 7PD
*Activities:* Unlicenced restaurants and cafes
*Major Shareholder:* Mark Timothy Clapham
*Officers:* Sally Clapham, Secretary; Mark Timothy Clapham [1963] Director

**SHFT Properties Ltd**
*Incorporated:* 13 November 2014
*Net Worth:* £1,489,208 *Total Assets:* £3,004,954
*Registered Office:* The Dancer, 8 Peterson Road, Wakefield, W Yorks, WF1 4EB
*Activities:* Buying and selling of own real estate
*Parent:* Trustee of Safe Hands Plans Trust
*Officers:* Kyle Bird [1992] Director; Malcolm David Milson [1957] Director

**SHG (Care Villages) Limited**
*Incorporated:* 10 December 2014 *Employees:* 177
*Net Worth Deficit:* £457,508 *Total Assets:* £27,833,068
*Registered Office:* 2 Fusion Court, Aberford Road, Garforth, Leeds, LS25 2GH
*Activities:* Residential care activities for the elderly and disabled
*Shareholders:* Graeme Stuart Lee; Business Growth Fund PLC
*Officers:* Ben Julius Barker [1977] Director/Investment Manager; Timothy Roger Jackson [1977] Director/Chartered Accountant; Graeme Lee [1965] Director; Paul Rodney Phillips [1970] Commercial and Operations Director

**Shine Childcare Limited**
*Incorporated:* 15 April 2004 *Employees:* 101
*Previous:* Shine Property Limited
*Net Worth:* £1,033,626 *Total Assets:* £3,214,316
*Registered Office:* Beck Cottage, Long Causeway, Adel, Leeds, LS16 8EE
*Activities:* Pre-primary education
*Major Shareholder:* Graham Morgan Abbott
*Officers:* Graham Abbott, Secretary; Amika Abbott [1972] Director; Graham Morgan Abbott [1969] Director

**Shine: Support and Help in Education**
*Incorporated:* 16 August 2000 *Employees:* 7
*Net Worth:* £5,009,773 *Total Assets:* £6,592,991
*Registered Office:* Shine, Princes Exchange, 2 Princes Square, Leeds, LS1 4HY
*Activities:* Other education n.e.c.
*Officers:* Fiona Birkett, Secretary; David Wayland Blood [1959] Director/Investment Management [British/American]; Gavin Simon Boyle [1968] Director/Fund Manager; Lorna Fitzsimons [1967] Director/CEO & Co-Founder, The Pipeline; Mark Heffernan [1963] Director/President and CIO of Alwyne Management [British/American]; Sarah Loftus [1968] Director/Head of Strategy & Architecture, Seadrill Management; Ann Dorota Mroz [1959] Director/Editor; Lord Terence James O'Neill [1957] Director/Economist; Cameron Peter James Ogden [1977] Director/Businessman; Raksha Pattni [1969] Director; Stephen Anthony Shields [1960] Director/Retired; Professor Samantha Twiselton [1964] Director of Sheffield Institute of Education

**Shiny Sky Limited**
*Incorporated:* 28 September 2004 *Employees:* 90
*Net Worth:* £1,237,140 *Total Assets:* £6,208,078
*Registered Office:* 107-109 New Road Side, Horsforth, Leeds, LS18 4QD
*Activities:* Taxi operation
*Shareholders:* David Julian Richmond; Belinda Jane Richmond
*Officers:* Hilary Palmer, Secretary; Daniel Graham [1966] Director/Commercial; Belinda Jane Richmond [1961] Director; David Julian Richmond [1964] Director

**Shipton Estates Limited**
*Incorporated:* 22 March 1938 *Employees:* 2
*Net Worth:* £6,789,652 *Total Assets:* £8,815,018
*Registered Office:* Manor Farm, Kirby Grindalythe, Malton, N Yorks, YO17 8DB
*Activities:* Buying and selling of own real estate
*Shareholders:* Antony Willoughby Alexander Outhwaite; Margaret Elizabeth Outhwaite
*Officers:* Margaret Elizabeth Outhwaite, Secretary; Alexander William Antony Outhwaite [1987] Director/Sound Engineer; Antony Willoughby Alexander Outhwaite [1954] Director/Chartered Surveyor; Emily Margret Monica Rose Outhwaite [1989] Director/Window Stylist; Margaret Elizabeth Outhwaite [1955] Director/Teacher; Oliver Alexander Outhwaite [1985] Director/Charity Administrator

**Shirestone Estates Limited**
*Incorporated:* 20 November 2013
*Net Worth:* £25,218,272 *Total Assets:* £25,900,550
*Registered Office:* South View Farm, Low Road, Everthorpe, E Yorks, HU15 2AD
*Activities:* Other letting and operating of own or leased real estate
*Shareholders:* Graham Keith Stonehouse; James Anthony Stonehouse; Julia Alice Stonehouse-Butters; RFB Trustees Five Limited; RFB Trustees Six Limited
*Officers:* Graham Keith Stonehouse [1949] Director; James Anthony Stonehouse [1983] Director/Property Investment; Julia Alice Stonehouse Butters [1987] Director/Property Investment

**Shorewood Leisure Group Limited**
*Incorporated:* 10 May 1990 *Employees:* 122
*Net Worth:* £24,411,356 *Total Assets:* £44,953,364
*Registered Office:* Marton Hall, Church Lane, Sewerby, Bridlington, E Yorks, YO15 1DS
*Activities:* Holiday centres and villages
*Shareholders:* David Robert Allison; David Robert Allison Family 2003 Discretionary Settlement
*Officers:* Neil Willson, Secretary; David Robert Allison [1960] Director; Neil Willson [1960] Managing Director

**Shorewood Parks Limited**
*Incorporated:* 14 June 2005 *Employees:* 31
*Previous:* Percy Wood Leisure Limited
*Net Worth:* £12,209,949 *Total Assets:* £14,052,623
*Registered Office:* Marton Hall, Church Lane, Sewerby, Bridlington, E Yorks, YO15 1DS
*Activities:* Holiday centres and villages
*Parent:* Shorewood Leisure Group Limited
*Officers:* David Robert Allison, Secretary; David Robert Allison [1960] Director/Park Operator; Neil Willson [1960] Managing Director

**Shorts Industries Limited**
*Incorporated:* 8 October 1982 *Employees:* 29
*Net Worth:* £2,033,000 *Total Assets:* £8,306,000
*Registered Office:* 15 Kings Gate, Bradford Business Park, Bradford, W Yorks, BD1 4SJ
*Activities:* Wholesale of other machinery and equipment
*Major Shareholder:* John Donald Read Fothergill
*Officers:* David Philip Cragg, Secretary; David Cragg [1977] Finance Director; John Donald Read Fothergill [1961] Director; Paul Welsby [1959] Managing Director

**J.H.Shouksmith & Sons Limited**
*Incorporated:* 10 September 1919 *Employees:* 65
*Net Worth:* £1,852,157 *Total Assets:* £3,821,416
*Registered Office:* Murton Way, Osbaldwick, York, YO19 5GS
*Activities:* Electrical installation
*Parent:* Shouksmith Holdings Limited
*Officers:* Andrew Timothy Stanley, Secretary; Joanne Elizabeth Durkin [1970] Director; Colin Maxwell Foster [1942] Director; David Ian Shouksmith [1980] Director; Edward Stuart Shouksmith [1982] Commercial Director; Kathleen Elizabeth Shouksmith [1943] Director; Richard Philip Shouksmith [1946] Director/Company Chairman; Andrew Timothy Stanley [1975] Director

**Shouksmith Holdings Limited**
*Incorporated:* 12 October 2007 *Employees:* 65
*Net Worth:* £1,852,157 *Total Assets:* £3,601,372
*Registered Office:* Murton Way, Osbaldwick, York, YO19 5GS
*Activities:* Activities of construction holding companies
*Officers:* Andrew Timothy Stanley, Secretary; Joanne Elizabeth Durkin [1970] Director; Colin Maxwell Foster [1942] Director; David Ian Shouksmith [1980] Director; Edward Stuart Shouksmith [1982] Commercial Director; Kathleen Elizabeth Shouksmith [1943] Director; Richard Philip Shouksmith [1946] Director; Andrew Timothy Stanley [1975] Director

**Shouksmith Properties Limited**
*Incorporated:* 12 October 2007 *Employees:* 6
*Net Worth:* £7,236,598 *Total Assets:* £8,543,958
*Registered Office:* Murton Way, Osbaldwick, York, YO19 5GS
*Activities:* Other letting and operating of own or leased real estate
*Officers:* Andrew Timothy Stanley, Secretary; Joanne Elizabeth Durkin [1970] Director; Colin Maxwell Foster [1942] Director; Mark Howard Foster [1969] Director; David Ian Shouksmith [1980] Director; Edward Stuart Shouksmith [1982] Director; Kathleen Elizabeth Shouksmith [1943] Director; Richard Philip Shouksmith [1946] Director

**Shree Investment PLC**
*Incorporated:* 27 February 2014
*Previous:* Shree Investment Ltd
*Net Worth:* £732,883,968 *Total Assets:* £934,681,024
*Registered Office:* 2 Wellington Place, Leeds, LS1 4AP
*Activities:* Wholesale of computers, computer peripheral equipment and software
*Officers:* Sajid Ali Shah, Secretary; Otemu Daniel Wanogho, Secretary; Mehmet Akgul [1977] Director/Financial Controller [Turkish]; Khalid Hammood Atefi [1959] Director/Financial Consultant [Iraqi]; Christopher Kuar Narain [1975] Finance Director [Canadian]; Sajid Ali Shah [1977] Director; Ali Akbar Sheikh [1986] Commercial Director

**Shulmans LLP**
*Incorporated:* 26 August 2009 *Employees:* 189
*Net Worth:* £5,871,009 *Total Assets:* £8,851,474
*Registered Office:* 10 Wellington Place, Leeds, LS1 4AP
*Officers:* Marcus Daniel Armstrong [1970] Member; Andrew Peter Bradley [1961] Member; Ian Dawson [1969] Member; Rosemary Edwards [1966] Member; Timothy James Halstead [1958] Member; Edwina Sharon Hewson [1974] Member; Simon Michael Jackson [1962] Member; Mark Lumley [1967] Member; Victoria Louise Mortimer [1972] Member; Richard Charles Frederick Wadkin [1959] Member; Councillor Michael Richard Watson [1967] Member; Amanda Beresford [1959] LLP Member; Dawn Hazel Carlisle [1963] LLP Member; Julie-Ann Elizabeth Carr [1969] LLP Member; Lyn Dario [1967] LLP Member; John Matthew Foster [1956] LLP Member; Helen Elizabeth Hill [1977] LLP Member; Christian Peace [1979] LLP Member; Julia Susan Rangecroft [1963] LLP Member; Richard James Robinson [1981] LLP Member; Emma Claire Roe [1976] LLP Member; Thomas Adrian Watkins [1972] LLP Member; Mark Ian Wilkinson [1982] LLP Member; Sarah Rachael Wilson [1969] LLP Member; James Jonathan Wright [1974] LLP Member

**Sia Abrasives (G.B.) Ltd**
*Incorporated:* 26 April 1968 *Employees:* 36
*Net Worth:* £15,000 *Total Assets:* £5,316,000
*Registered Office:* Sia Abrasives (GB) Ltd, Ellistones Lane, Greetland, Halifax, W Yorks, HX4 8NH
*Activities:* Production of abrasive products
*Parent:* Sia Abrasives Holdings Limited
*Officers:* Jonathan David Burton, Secretary; Dr Steffen Tobias Hoffmann [1965] Director [German]; Ute Tanja Lepple [1965] Director/Senior Vice President Finance [German]; Marianne Serre [1964] Managing Director [French]

**Sia Fibral Limited**
*Incorporated:* 28 October 1988 *Employees:* 97
*Net Worth Deficit:* £1,848,000 *Total Assets:* £8,869,000
*Registered Office:* Ellistones Lane, Greetland, Halifax, W Yorks, HX4 8NH
*Activities:* Manufacture of non-wovens and articles made from non-wovens, except apparel
*Shareholders:* Sia Abrasives Holdings Limited; Sia Abrasives Holdings Limited
*Officers:* Jonathan David Burton, Secretary; Dr Steffen Tobias Hoffmann [1965] Director [German]; Uta Tanja Lepple [1965] Director/Senior Vice President [German]; Marianne Serre [1964] Managing Director [French]

**Siccar Point Energy (Holdings) Limited**
*Incorporated:* 25 June 2014 *Employees:* 36
*Net Worth:* £473,909,696 *Total Assets:* £1,665,017,472
*Registered Office:* 1 Park Row, Leeds, LS1 5AB
*Activities:* Other business support service activities n.e.c.
*Officers:* David Sheach, Secretary; Dr Iain Douglas Bartholomew [1958] Director; Dr Nicholas John Cooper [1967] Director/Oil and Gas Executive; Christopher Geoffrey Finlayson [1956] Director; Douglas Weir Fleming [1970] Finance Director; David I. Foley [1967] Director/Private Equity:Energy Investments [American]; Khashayarsha Ali Mohajerani [1987] Director/Private Equity Associate; Jonathan Leslie Roger [1969] Director; Mustafa Mohsin Siddiqui [1979] Director/Finance [American]; Graeme David Sword [1968] Director/Founding Partner Within Private Equity

**Siccar Point Energy E & P Limited**
*Incorporated:* 27 June 1980
*Previous:* OMV (U.K.) Limited
*Net Worth:* £1,189,655,936 *Total Assets:* £1,348,219,392
*Registered Office:* 1 Park Row, Leeds, LS1 5AB
*Activities:* Extraction of crude petroleum
*Officers:* David Sheach, Secretary; Dr Iain Douglas Bartholomew [1958] Director; Douglas Weir Fleming [1970] Director; Jonathan Leslie Roger [1969] Director

**Siccar Point Energy Finance Limited**
*Incorporated:* 25 June 2014
*Net Worth Deficit:* £47,378,048 *Total Assets:* £492,055,744
*Registered Office:* 1 Park Row, Leeds, LS1 5AB
*Activities:* Other business support service activities n.e.c.
*Officers:* David Sheach, Secretary; Dr Iain Douglas Bartholomew [1958] Director; Dr Nicholas John Cooper [1967] Director/Oil and Gas Executive; Christopher Geoffrey Finlayson [1956] Director; Douglas Weir Fleming [1970] Finance Director; David I. Foley [1967] Director/Private Equity Energy Investments [American]; Khashayarsha Ali Mohajerani [1987] Director/Private Equity Associate; Jonathan Leslie Roger [1969] Director; Mustafa Mohsin Siddiqui [1979] Director/Finance [American]; Graeme David Sword [1968] Director/Founding Partner Within Private Equity

**Siccar Point Energy Limited**
*Incorporated:* 26 June 2014 *Employees:* 36
*Net Worth:* £1,016,964,992 *Total Assets:* £1,668,652,672
*Registered Office:* 1 Park Row, Leeds, LS1 5AB
*Activities:* Other business support service activities n.e.c.
*Officers:* David Sheach, Secretary; Dr Iain Douglas Bartholomew [1958] Director; Dr Nicholas John Cooper [1967] Director/Oil and Gas Executive; Christopher Geoffrey Finlayson [1956] Director; Douglas Weir Fleming [1970] Finance Director; David Ignatius Foley [1967] Director/Private Equity:Energy Investments [American]; Khashayarsha Ali Mohajerani [1987] Director/Private Equity Associate; Jonathan Leslie Roger [1969] Director; Mustafa Mohsin Siddiqui [1979] Director/Finance [American]; Graeme David Sword [1968] Director/Founding Partner Within Private Equity

**Siccar Point Energy U.K. Limited**
*Incorporated:* 5 November 2015
*Net Worth:* £41,051,104 *Total Assets:* £239,940,480
*Registered Office:* 1 Park Row, Leeds, LS1 5AB
*Activities:* Other business support service activities n.e.c.
*Parent:* Siccar Point Energy Limited
*Officers:* David Alexander Sheach, Secretary; Dr Iain Douglas Bartholomew [1958] Director; Douglas Weir Fleming [1970] Finance Director; Jonathan Leslie Roger [1969] Director

**Siddall & Hilton Products Limited**
*Incorporated:* 4 November 1997 *Employees:* 64
*Net Worth:* £6,101,000 *Total Assets:* £14,192,000
*Registered Office:* Siddall & Hilton Products Limited, Birds Royd Lane, Brighouse, W Yorks, HD6 1LT
*Activities:* Manufacture of wire products, chain and springs
*Parent:* Siddall Products Ltd
*Officers:* Neil Anthony Stewardson [1966] Managing Director; Ian Michael Thurley [1966] Director

**Sidhil Group Limited**
*Incorporated:* 21 April 2015
*Net Worth:* £27,295,000 *Total Assets:* £34,290,000
*Registered Office:* Drive Devilbiss Healthcare Limited, Heathfield Lane, Birkenshaw, W Yorks, BD11 2HW
*Activities:* Activities of head offices
*Parent:* Drive Devilbiss Healthcare Limited
*Officers:* Richard James McGleenan [1970] Managing Director; Graham Thomas Turner [1965] Director; Michael Thomas Waine [1951] Finance Director

**Siena Bidco Limited**
*Incorporated:* 18 December 2014 *Employees:* 252
*Net Worth:* £1,438,000 *Total Assets:* £34,933,000
*Registered Office:* The Inspire, Hornbeam Square West, Harrogate, N Yorks, HG2 8PA
*Activities:* Activities of head offices
*Parent:* Siena Holdco Limited
*Officers:* John Cody Bradshaw [1978] Director [American]; Sarah Broughton [1976] Director; James Alexander Burrell [1974] Director; Nicholas Mark Chadwick [1981] Director/Hotel Asset Management; Anthony Gerrard Troy [1962] Director [Irish]

**Siena Holdco Limited**
*Incorporated:* 17 December 2014 *Employees:* 252
*Net Worth:* £950,000 *Total Assets:* £34,933,000
*Registered Office:* The Inspire, Hornbeam Square West, Harrogate, N Yorks, HG2 8PA
*Activities:* Activities of head offices
*Officers:* John Cody Bradshaw [1978] Director [American]; Sarah Broughton [1976] Director/Chartered Accountant; James Alexander Burrell [1974] Director; Nicholas Mark Chadwick [1981] Director/Hotel Asset Management; Anthony Gerrard Troy [1962] Director [Irish]

**Sigma GRP Limited**
*Incorporated:* 24 March 2009 *Employees:* 225
*Net Worth:* £5,147,443 *Total Assets:* £14,340,839
*Registered Office:* Unit 9b Alpine Court, Glasshoughton, Castleford, W Yorks, WF10 4TL
*Activities:* Activities of head offices
*Parent:* TH Glasshoughton Bidco Limited
*Officers:* Craig Michael Fairey, Secretary; Craig Anthony Bennett [1978] Director; Craig Michael Fairey [1969] Director

**Sigma Retail Solutions Limited**
*Incorporated:* 12 November 2007 *Employees:* 194
*Net Worth:* £3,180,294 *Total Assets:* £12,064,608
*Registered Office:* Unit 9b Alpine Court, Glasshoughton, Castleford, W Yorks, WF10 4TL
*Activities:* Operation of warehousing and storage facilities for land transport activities
*Parent:* Sigma GRP Limited
*Officers:* Craig Michael Fairey, Secretary; Craig Anthony Bennett [1978] Director; Craig Michael Fairey [1969] Director

**SigmaKalon (BC) UK Limited**
*Incorporated:* 6 December 2002
*Net Worth Deficit:* £13,500,000 *Total Assets:* £233,300,000
*Registered Office:* Huddersfield Road, Birstall, Batley, W Yorks, WF17 9XA
*Activities:* Activities of head offices
*Parent:* PPG Holdings (UK) Limited
*Officers:* Jason Paul Metcalf [1973] Marketing Director; Felicity Anne Parry [1967] Finance Director; Steven Pocock [1962] Director/General Manager

**SigmaKalon UK Holding Limited**
*Incorporated:* 11 October 1922
*Net Worth:* £169,100,000 *Total Assets:* £218,700,000
*Registered Office:* SigmaKalon UK Holding Limited, Huddersfield Road, Birstall, Batley, W Yorks, WF17 9XA
*Activities:* Activities of head offices
*Parent:* SigmaKalon (BC) UK Limited
*Officers:* Jason Paul Metcalf [1973] Marketing Director; Felicity Anne Parry [1967] Finance Director; Steven Pocock [1962] Director/General Manager

**SIL Holdings Limited**
*Incorporated:* 1 October 2001 *Employees:* 221
*Net Worth:* £2,792,000 *Total Assets:* £34,232,000
*Registered Office:* Ladywell Mills, Hall Lane, Bradford, W Yorks, BD4 7DF
*Activities:* Activities of other holding companies n.e.c.
*Parent:* Stonecroft Holdings PLC
*Officers:* Julia Say, Secretary; Meryl Birch [1963] Director; John Andrew Bradley [1967] Finance Director; David William Gallimore [1962] Director; Oliver Cameron Platts [1982] Director; Andrew Wynne Riley [1953] Director; Mark Rooney [1968] Director; Julia Say [1971] Director; Andrew David Seal [1957] Director; Jeremy Charles Seal [1960] Director

**Silentbloc UK Limited**
*Incorporated:* 26 November 1997 *Employees:* 87
*Net Worth:* £2,948,000 *Total Assets:* £5,876,000
*Registered Office:* Victoria Works, Thrumpton Lane, Retford, Notts, DN22 6HH
*Activities:* Manufacture of railway locomotives and rolling stock
*Parent:* Crosslink Technology Holdings Ltd
*Officers:* Craig Andrew Harris [1969] Director/Chief Executive; James Robert Hill [1978] Director/Chief Financial Officer; David James Ring [1962] Director

**Silgan Closures UK Holdings Limited**
*Incorporated:* 18 May 2003 *Employees:* 2
*Previous:* Portola Limited
*Net Worth:* £13,597,000 *Total Assets:* £23,894,000
*Registered Office:* 17-23 Thorne Road, Doncaster, S Yorks, DN1 2RP
*Activities:* Activities of head offices
*Parent:* Silgan Holdings Inc
*Officers:* Philip Crawley, Secretary; Glenn Heighington [1965] Managing Director; Richard Kirkland [1969] Financial Director

**Silgan Closures UK Limited**
*Incorporated:* 2 May 1991 *Employees:* 139
*Previous:* Portola Packaging Limited
*Net Worth:* £14,239,000 *Total Assets:* £29,489,000
*Registered Office:* 17-23 Thorne Road, Doncaster, S Yorks, DN1 2RP
*Activities:* Manufacture of other plastic products
*Parent:* Portola Limited
*Officers:* Philip Crawley, Secretary; Glenn Heighington [1965] Director; Richard Kirkland [1969] Finance Director

**Silver Cross (UK) Limited**
*Incorporated:* 6 December 2002 *Employees:* 59
*Net Worth:* £16,806,000 *Total Assets:* £26,060,000
*Registered Office:* Micklethorn, Broughton, Skipton, N Yorks, BD23 3JA
*Activities:* Wholesale of household goods (other than musical instruments) n.e.c
*Major Shareholder:* Guangchang Guo
*Officers:* William John Lockwood, Secretary; Jonathan David Halsall [1985] Director/Chartered Accountant; Qian Jiabei [1979] Director/Finance [Chinese]; William John Lockwood [1951] Director/Chartered Accountant; Samantha Anne Newton [1962] Sales and Marketing Director; Nicholas John Paxton [1967] Director/Chief Executive; Philip Jeffrey Taylor [1965] Director/Product Designer; Song Xiaoting [1990] Director [Chinese]; Wei Zhang [1978] Director/Finance [Chinese]; Xueqing Zhang [1966] Director [Chinese]

**Silver Cross Nurseries Limited**
*Incorporated:* 23 December 2009
*Net Worth:* £7,045,000 *Total Assets:* £10,777,000
*Registered Office:* Micklethorn, Broughton, Skipton, N Yorks, BD23 3JA
*Activities:* Activities of head offices
*Major Shareholder:* Guangchang Guo
*Officers:* William John Lockwood, Secretary; Jonathan David Halsall [1985] Director/Chartered Accountant; Nicholas John Paxton [1967] Director/Buyer; Wei Zhang [1978] Director/Finance [Chinese]; Xueqing Zhang [1966] Director [Chinese]

**Silver Sands Leisure Park Ltd**
*Incorporated:* 21 September 2011 *Employees:* 38
*Net Worth:* £2,868,428 *Total Assets:* £5,127,095
*Registered Office:* Sand-le-Mere, Southfield Lane, Tunstall, Hull, HU12 0JF
*Activities:* Recreational vehicle parks, trailer parks and camping grounds
*Parent:* Bridge Leisure Parks Limited
*Officers:* Simon John Elliott [1969] Director; Andrew Stephen Howe [1968] Director; Simon Jamie Williams [1972] Director

**Silverback Developments Limited**
*Incorporated:* 13 October 2014 *Employees:* 2
*Net Worth:* £91,227 *Total Assets:* £5,338,422
*Registered Office:* 10 The Stables, Newby Hall, Ripon, N Yorks, HG4 5AE
*Activities:* Development of building projects
*Parent:* Silverback Holdings Limited
*Officers:* Michelle Andrea Hepden [1972] Director; Simon William Hepden [1971] Director; Georgina Alexandra Moody [1976] Director; Nicholas John Moody [1969] Director; Frazer George Roberts [1993] Director

**Simba Smoby Toys (UK) Limited**
*Incorporated:* 27 July 2009 *Employees:* 16
*Net Worth:* £4,017,851 *Total Assets:* £5,821,030
*Registered Office:* Broomfield House, Bolling Road, Bradford, W Yorks, BD4 7BG
*Activities:* Non-specialised wholesale trade
*Shareholders:* Anthony Belford; Simba Toys GmbH & Co KG
*Officers:* Anthony Belford [1947] Director; Richard Adam Belford [1985] Director/Sales Manager; Manfred Duschl [1955] Director/Merchant [German]; Uwe Weiler [1959] Director/Merchant [German]

**Simon Bidco Limited**
*Incorporated:* 29 July 2015 *Employees:* 2
*Net Worth:* £495,696,992 *Total Assets:* £1,285,280,000
*Registered Office:* Ellington House, 9 Savannah Way, Leeds Valley Park, Leeds, LS10 1AB
*Activities:* Activities of financial services holding companies
*Officers:* Bill Flynn, Secretary; James John Cornell [1973] Director; Philip Sebastian Muelder [1974] Director/Partner [German]; Christopher Pell [1978] Director; Colin George Storrar [1971] Director

**Simon Midco Limited**
*Incorporated:* 8 August 2015
*Net Worth:* £198,279,008 *Total Assets:* £640,769,024
*Registered Office:* Ellington House, 9 Savannah Way, Leeds Valley Park, Leeds, LS10 1AB
*Activities:* Activities of financial services holding companies
*Officers:* Bill Flynn, Secretary; David Bruckmann [1989] Director [German]; Cleo Yet-Mann Cheung [1986] Director/Investment Manager [Canadian]; James John Cornell [1973] Director; David Ronald Gagie [1955] Non-Executive Director Chairman; Heinz Hilgert [1953] Managing Director [German]; Philip Sebastian Muelder [1974] Director/Partner [German]; Christopher Pell [1978] Director; Dr Joerg Rockenhauser [1966] Director/Managing Partner [German]; Colin George Storrar [1971] Director; Marvin Teubner [1978] Director

**Simply Biz Limited**
*Incorporated:* 23 August 2002 *Employees:* 305
*Net Worth:* £5,525,267 *Total Assets:* £39,963,884
*Registered Office:* The John Smith's Stadium, Stadium Way, Huddersfield, W Yorks, HD1 6PG
*Activities:* Activities of financial services holding companies
*Parent:* The Simplybiz Group Limited
*Officers:* Sarah Clare Turvey, Secretary; Timothy Paul Clarke [1963] Partner/Director; Kenneth Ernest Davy [1941] Director; David Robert Charles Kershaw [1955] Director; Gary John Kershaw [1970] Compliance Director; Neil Martin Stevens [1978] Director; Matthew Lloyd Timmins [1978] Director; Timothy Hugh Southcombe Trotter [1959] Director/Management Consultant; Sarah Clare Turvey [1970] Director

**Simply Biz Services Limited**
*Incorporated:* 14 November 2002 *Employees:* 10
*Previous:* Simply Biz Services PLC
*Net Worth:* £139,696 *Total Assets:* £7,805,623
*Registered Office:* The John Smith's Stadium, Stadium Way, Huddersfield, W Yorks, HD1 6PG
*Activities:* Activities of financial services holding companies
*Parent:* Simply Biz Ltd
*Officers:* Sarah Clare Turvey, Secretary; Richard Ardron [1974] Director; Kenneth Ernest Davy [1941] Director; David Alan Golder [1958] Director; David Robert Charles Kershaw [1955] Operations Director; Gary John Kershaw [1970] Compliance Director; Janice Louise Laing [1967] Director; Daniel Philip Russell [1978] Director; Neil Martin Stevens [1978] Director; Matthew Lloyd Timmins [1978] Director; Sarah Clare Turvey [1970] Finance Director

**The Simplybiz Group PLC**
*Incorporated:* 2 June 2015 *Employees:* 382
*Previous:* The Simplybiz Group Limited
*Net Worth Deficit:* £5,851,000 *Total Assets:* £37,662,000
*Registered Office:* The John Smith's Stadium, Stadium Way, Huddersfield, W Yorks, HD1 6PG
*Activities:* Activities of head offices
*Shareholder:* Kenneth Ernest Davy
*Officers:* Sarah Clare Turvey, Secretary; Timothy Paul Clarke [1963] Partner/Director; Kenneth Ernest Davy [1941] Director; Gareth Richard Hague [1981] Finance Director; Gary William Hughes [1962] Director; Neil Martin Stevens [1978] Director; Matthew Lloyd Timmins [1978] Director; Timothy Hugh Southcombe Trotter [1959] Director/Management Consultant

**Simpson (York) Holdings Limited**
*Incorporated:* 8 April 1994 *Employees:* 175
*Net Worth:* £9,386,650 *Total Assets:* £24,098,904
*Registered Office:* 10 Hassacarr Close, Chessingham Park, Dunnington, York, YO19 5SN
*Activities:* Other specialised construction activities n.e.c.
*Shareholders:* Ronald Christopher Gatenby; Beryl Gatenby
*Officers:* John Pursehouse, Secretary; Andrew Gatenby [1975] Director; Beryl Gatenby [1949] Director; Ronald Christopher Gatenby [1947] Director/Building Contractor

**Simpson (York) Limited**
*Incorporated:* 5 May 1965 *Employees:* 173
*Net Worth:* £3,493,976 *Total Assets:* £21,269,120
*Registered Office:* 10 Hassacarr Close, Chessingham Park, Dunnington, York, YO19 5SN
*Activities:* Other construction installation
*Shareholders:* Ron Christopher Gatenby; Beryl Gatenby
*Officers:* John Pursehouse, Secretary; Russell Craig Allerton [1967] Director/Quantity Surveyor; Andrew Gatenby [1975] Contracts Director; Beryl Gatenby [1949] Director; Ronald Christopher Gatenby [1947] Director; John Pursehouse [1952] Director/Chartered Accountant; Neil Philip Silcock [1962] Director

**Simpson and Webb Limited**
*Incorporated:* 28 June 1994 *Employees:* 26
*Net Worth:* £1,932,385 *Total Assets:* £5,202,814
*Registered Office:* 129 Beverley Road, Hessle, Hull, HU13 9AN
*Activities:* Licenced restaurants
*Major Shareholder:* Naveed Ahmed Choudry
*Officers:* Yasmin Choudry, Secretary/Accounts Manager; Naveed Ahmed Choudry [1962] Director; Yasmin Choudry [1952] Director/Accounts Manager

**Simpson Millar LLP**
*Incorporated:* 29 June 2005 *Employees:* 481
*Net Worth Deficit:* £12,109,314 *Total Assets:* £30,666,224
*Registered Office:* 21-27 St Pauls Street, Leeds, LS1 2JG
*Officers:* Gregory Francis Cox [1971] Member

**Stephen A. Sims (Cars) Limited**
*Incorporated:* 7 September 1990 *Employees:* 29
*Net Worth:* £914,845 *Total Assets:* £4,159,949
*Registered Office:* Stephen A Sims (Cars) Limited, McMullen Road, Darlington, Co Durham, DL1 1XT
*Activities:* Sale of new cars and light motor vehicles
*Major Shareholder:* Stephen Andrew Sims
*Officers:* Stuart Bromley, Secretary; Stephen Andrew Sims [1955] Director/Motor Dealer

**William Sinclair & Sons (Stationers) Limited**
*Incorporated:* 9 April 1958 *Employees:* 121
*Net Worth:* £15,682,416 *Total Assets:* £17,873,256
*Registered Office:* Silvine Works, North Street, Otley, W Yorks, LS21 1AH
*Activities:* Manufacture of paper stationery
*Shareholders:* Anne Maureen Howard; Susan Margaret Preston
*Officers:* Paul Michael Howard, Secretary; John Clough [1971] Director/Manager; Andrew Howard [1953] Director/Accountant; Paul Michael Howard [1981] Director/Manager

**Sing Kee Group Limited**
*Incorporated:* 20 December 2004 *Employees:* 65
*Net Worth:* £3,948,276 *Total Assets:* £11,057,223
*Registered Office:* 30 Cross Stamford Street, Leeds, LS7 1BA
*Activities:* Renting and operating of Housing Association real estate
*Major Shareholder:* Quoc Thanh Ly
*Officers:* Quoc Thanh Ly, Secretary; Quoc Thanh Ly [1963] Director

**Sing Ko Limited**
*Incorporated:* 10 March 2015 *Employees:* 34
*Net Worth:* £621,017 *Total Assets:* £4,959,659
*Registered Office:* 30 Cross Stamford Street, Leeds, LS7 1BA
*Activities:* Wholesale of meat and meat products
*Parent:* Sing Kee Group Limited
*Officers:* Michael Chuong Han Ly [1986] Director

**Singleton Birch Limited**
*Incorporated:* 23 April 1875 *Employees:* 131
*Net Worth:* £22,402,000 *Total Assets:* £52,426,000
*Registered Office:* Singleton Birch Limited, Melton Ross Quarries, Barnetby, N Lincs, DN38 6AE
*Activities:* Quarrying of ornamental and building stone, limestone, gypsum, chalk and slate
*Officers:* Ellen Patricia Tatterton, Secretary/Accountant; Stuart Robin Counsell [1950] Director/Chartered Accountant; Stephen William Foster [1962] Sales Director; Martyn John Gardiner [1946] Director; Martin David Haworth [1963] Technical Director; Richard Mark Stansfield [1967] Managing Director; Ellen Patricia Tatterton [1961] Director/Accountant

**SIP Properties LLP**
*Incorporated:* 3 April 2013
*Net Worth:* £335,387 *Total Assets:* £5,670,025
*Registered Office:* Thorp Arch Grange, Walton Road, Thorp Arch, Wetherby, W Yorks, LS23 7BA

**Sirdar Group Limited**
*Incorporated:* 13 March 2015
*Net Worth:* £15,000 *Total Assets:* £12,887,000
*Registered Office:* Sirdar Spinning Ltd, Flanshaw Lane, Alverthorpe, Wakefield, W Yorks, WF2 9ND
*Activities:* Activities of head offices
*Parent:* The DMC Group Holding Limited
*Officers:* Jean-Luc Theophile Bikard [1958] Director [French]; Oliver James Lake [1983] Finance Director; Jonathan David Thompson [1975] Managing Director

**Sirdar Holdings Limited**
*Incorporated:* 11 September 2007 *Employees:* 26
*Net Worth:* £1,582,000 *Total Assets:* £22,003,000
*Registered Office:* Sirdar Spinning Ltd, Flanshaw Lane, Alverthorpe, Wakefield, W Yorks, WF2 9ND
*Activities:* Wholesale of textiles
*Parent:* Sirdar Group Limited
*Officers:* Jean-Luc Theophile Bikard [1958] Director [French]; Oliver James Lake [1983] Finance Director; Jonathan David Thompson [1975] Managing Director; Justin Toby Wraight [1970] Director/Chief Executive

**Sirdar Properties Limited**
*Incorporated:* 4 December 2013
*Net Worth:* £381,775 *Total Assets:* £9,354,572
*Registered Office:* Barn Cottage, Botany Lane, Lepton, Huddersfield, W Yorks, HD8 0NE
*Activities:* Other letting and operating of own or leased real estate
*Parent:* Dream Property Holdco Limited
*Officers:* Emma Louise Morris [1977] Director; Russell Paul Morris [1969] Director

**G.W. Sissons and Son Limited**
*Incorporated:* 28 July 1972 *Employees:* 2
*Net Worth:* £9,560,138 *Total Assets:* £9,608,780
*Registered Office:* Sissons House, By-Pass Park Estate, Sherburn in Elmet, Leeds, LS25 6EP
*Activities:* Freight transport by road
*Major Shareholder:* Bryan Leslie Sissons
*Officers:* Bryan Leslie Sissons, Secretary; Bryan Leslie Sissons [1955] Director/Haulage Contractor; Ian Richard Sissons [1950] Director/Haulage Contractor

**Sissons Depot Limited**
*Incorporated:* 3 September 2015 *Employees:* 2
*Net Worth:* £1,304,402 *Total Assets:* £4,075,166
*Registered Office:* Sissons House, Bypass Park Estate, Sherburn in Elmet, Leeds, LS25 6EP
*Activities:* Other letting and operating of own or leased real estate
*Parent:* Sissons Depot Holdings Ltd
*Officers:* Bryan Leslie Sissons [1955] Director; Ian Richard Sissons [1950] Director

**Sissons Limited**
*Incorporated:* 3 September 2015 *Employees:* 6
*Net Worth:* £1,983,187 *Total Assets:* £6,948,688
*Registered Office:* Sissons House, Bypass Park Estate, Sherburn in Elmet, Leeds, LS25 6EP
*Activities:* Other letting and operating of own or leased real estate
*Parent:* Sissons Properties Ltd
*Officers:* Bryan Leslie Sissons [1955] Director; Ian Richard Sissons [1950] Director

**Sissons of Sherburn Holdings Limited**
*Incorporated:* 26 August 2015
*Net Worth:* £9,318,750 *Total Assets:* £9,318,750
*Registered Office:* Sissons House, Bypass Park Estate, Sherburn in Elmet, Leeds, LS25 6EP
*Activities:* Activities of other holding companies n.e.c.
*Major Shareholder:* Bryan Leslie Sissons
*Officers:* Bryan Leslie Sissons [1955] Director; Ian Richard Sissons [1950] Director

**SJS (Norton) Limited**
*Incorporated:* 2 December 2005
*Previous:* SJS (3) Limited
*Net Worth:* £1,676,170 *Total Assets:* £5,025,915
*Registered Office:* 3rd Floor, Airedale House, Albion Street, Leeds, LS1 5AW
*Activities:* Buying and selling of own real estate
*Parent:* St James Securities Group Limited
*Officers:* Paul Richard Piers Morris [1967] Director/Chartered Surveyor; Daniel Nicholas Murray [1976] Project Director; Oliver Alexander Quarmby [1975] Director/Chartered Surveyor

**Skanwear Clothing Company Ltd**
*Incorporated:* 21 June 2010 *Employees:* 32
*Previous:* Skanwear Clothing Company
*Net Worth:* £891,614 *Total Assets:* £3,445,170
*Registered Office:* Sandall Stones Road, Kirk Sandall Industrial Estate, Doncaster, S Yorks, DN3 1QR
*Activities:* Wholesale of clothing and footwear
*Parent:* Vanern Holdings Ltd
*Officers:* Angus Nigel Long [1984] Director/Business Development Manager; Anthony Long [1980] Director/Business Development Manager; Richard Kenneth Long [1958] Director; Russell Long [1978] Director

**SKB2016 Limited**
*Incorporated:* 14 March 2016 *Employees:* 2
*Net Worth:* £348,580 *Total Assets:* £6,301,403
*Registered Office:* Lloyds Bank Chambers, Hustlergate, Bradford, BD1 1UQ
*Activities:* Security dealing on own account
*Shareholders:* Stephen John Brown; Katherine Brown
*Officers:* Katherine Brown [1951] Director; Stephen John Brown [1949] Director

**Skelton Limited**
*Incorporated:* 13 December 2000 *Employees:* 26
*Net Worth:* £4,899,902 *Total Assets:* £6,786,900
*Registered Office:* 46 Knowsthorpe Way, Leeds, LS9 0SW
*Activities:* Collection of non-hazardous waste
*Shareholders:* Dean Jonathan Langton; Dean Jonathan Langton; Rhonda Langton
*Officers:* Rhonda Langton, Secretary/Administrator; Dean Jonathan Langton [1961] Director; Rhonda Langton [1964] Director/Administrator

**John Hornby Skewes and Company Limited**
*Incorporated:* 9 November 1965 *Employees:* 61
*Net Worth:* £4,875,117 *Total Assets:* £5,940,197
*Registered Office:* Salem House, Parkinson Approach, Garforth, Leeds, LS25 2HR
*Activities:* Wholesale of musical instruments
*Officers:* George Anthony Bell, Secretary; George Anthony Bell [1956] Director; Dennis John Drumm [1953] Director; Linda Marion Drumm [1955] Director; Paul Twohey Smith [1964] Director

**Skills for Care Ltd**
*Incorporated:* 27 October 1999 *Employees:* 194
*Net Worth:* £24,965,982 *Total Assets:* £37,581,128
*Registered Office:* West Gate, 6 Grace Street, Leeds, LS1 2RP
*Activities:* Other education n.e.c.
*Officers:* Susan Shaw, Secretary; Suzie Bailey [1968] Director; Louise Elizabeth Bladen [1976] Director; Susan Mary Bott [1956] Director/Charity Manager; Dame Moira Margaret Gibb [1950] Director; Keith Mark Lever [1960] Director/Charity Chief Executive; Dr Mahiben Maruthappu [1988] Director/Chief Executive; Susan Mary McMillan [1956] Director/Retired; Stephen Wayne Scown [1962] Director; Paul Michael Snell [1967] Director/Chief Executive; Neil Barry Taylor [1963] Charity Director; Munira Thobani [1958] Director; Amanda Jillian Thorn [1963] Director; Rachael Wardell [1968] Corporate Director - Local Government

**Jeff Skinner Skip Hire Limited**
*Incorporated:* 6 March 2006 *Employees:* 21
*Net Worth:* £3,108,131 *Total Assets:* £3,619,425
*Registered Office:* The Sidings, Copley Hill, Leeds, LS12 1HY
*Activities:* Recovery of sorted materials
*Major Shareholder:* Rita Dianne Skinner
*Officers:* Laura Jayne Nicholson, Secretary; Terence Ronald Bailey [1958] Director/Transport & Operational Manager; Pamela Dianne Crosby [1967] Director/Equestrian Centre; Rita Dianne Skinner [1945] Director/Waste Removal

**Skipton Business Finance Limited**
*Incorporated:* 2 March 2001 *Employees:* 89
*Net Worth:* £4,747,671 *Total Assets:* £118,995,400
*Registered Office:* The Bailey, Skipton, N Yorks, BD23 1DN
*Activities:* Factoring
*Parent:* Skipton Group Holdings Limited
*Officers:* John Joseph Gibson, Secretary; Gregory Mark Bell [1969] Director; Andrew Paul Grantham [1966] Director; Andrew David Hill [1972] Operations Director; Andrew Walter Nelson [1964] Director/Accountant; Fiona Wlizabeth Nightingale [1970] Director/Chartered Accountant; Alexander Charles Robinson [1969] Director; Ralph Anthony Walker [1946] Director

**Skipton Group Holdings Limited**
*Incorporated:* 20 December 2000
*Net Worth:* £82,868,000 *Total Assets:* £117,420,000
*Registered Office:* The Bailey, Skipton, N Yorks, BD23 1DN
*Activities:* Activities of financial services holding companies
*Parent:* Skipton Building Society
*Officers:* John Joseph Gibson, Secretary; Andrew Paul Bottomley [1965] Director; Amanda Jane Burton [1959] Director; Maria Luisa Cassoni [1951] Director; John Richard Coates [1951] Director; Denise Patricia Cockrem [1962] Director; Ian Michael Cornelius [1969] Commercial Director; David John Cutter [1962] Building Society Director; Robert David East [1960] Director; Denis Arthur Hall [1955] Director; Heather Louise Jackson [1965] Director; Mark Joseph Lund [1957] Director; Robert Samuel Duncan Mugenyi Ndawula [1974] Finance Director; Alexander Charles Robinson [1969] Director; Helen Claire Stevenson [1960] Director

**Skipton Investments Limited**
*Incorporated:* 22 September 2004
*Net Worth Deficit:* £8,017,000 *Total Assets:* £8,571,000
*Registered Office:* The Bailey, Skipton, N Yorks, BD23 1DN
*Activities:* Activities of other holding companies n.e.c.
*Parent:* Skipton Group Holdings Limited
*Officers:* John Joseph Gibson, Secretary; David John Cutter [1962] Director; Alexander Charles Robinson [1969] Director

**Skipton Properties Limited**
*Incorporated:* 27 August 1987 *Employees:* 74
*Net Worth:* £11,550,999 *Total Assets:* £20,746,972
*Registered Office:* Skipton House, Riparian Court, Riparian Way, Crosshills, N Yorks, BD20 7BW
*Activities:* Development of building projects
*Officers:* Linda Mary Verity, Secretary; Sarah Louise Barraclough [1981] Sales Director; Luke Alan Woodrow Davis [1984] Director/Accountant; Brian Verity [1949] Director; Caroline Elizabeth Verity [1984] Director; Linda Mary Verity [1953] Director

**Skirfare Investments Limited**
*Incorporated:* 20 September 2011
*Net Worth:* £10,280,547 *Total Assets:* £127,618,672
*Registered Office:* Throstles Nest, Conistone with Kilnsey, Skipton, N Yorks, BD23 5HT
*Activities:* Fund management activities
*Major Shareholder:* David Richard Hood
*Officers:* David Richard Hood [1948] Director/Entrepreneur

**J.V.Sleightholme Limited**
*Incorporated:* 17 September 1958
*Net Worth:* £3,008,602 *Total Assets:* £3,051,799
*Registered Office:* 2 Belgrave Crescent, Scarborough, N Yorks, YO11 1UB
*Activities:* Mixed farming
*Major Shareholder:* William Owen
*Officers:* Judith Wardlow, Secretary; William Robert Owen [1947] Director/Farmer

**H C Slingsby P L C**
*Incorporated:* 19 April 1948 *Employees:* 105
*Net Worth:* £384,000 *Total Assets:* £14,417,000
*Registered Office:* H C Slingsby PLC, Otley Road, Baildon, Shipley, W Yorks, BD17 7LW
*Activities:* Retail sale via mail order houses or via Internet
*Officers:* Morgan Lawn Morris, Secretary; Morgan Lawn Morris [1971] Financial Director; Dominic Stanley Slingsby [1961] Director

**SLS Group Limited**
*Incorporated:* 30 March 1999 *Employees:* 3
*Net Worth:* £2,569,867 *Total Assets:* £7,132,289
*Registered Office:* Orchard House, The Square, Hessle, E Yorks, HU13 0AE
*Activities:* Activities of head offices
*Parent:* Dominique Dutscher Distribution SAS
*Officers:* Neil Andrew Bewell, Secretary; Neil Andrew Bewell [1974] Director/Chief Financial Officer; Robert Peter Chapman [1955] Director; Dominique Wencker [1959] Director [French]

**F. Smales & Son (Fish Merchants) Limited**
*Incorporated:* 17 August 1973 *Employees:* 217
*Net Worth:* £6,324,604 *Total Assets:* £21,229,200
*Registered Office:* 30 West Dock Street, Hull, HU3 4HL
*Activities:* Processing and preserving of fish, crustaceans and molluscs
*Shareholders:* Lee Smales; Simon Smales
*Officers:* Robin Alistair Orr, Secretary; Nigel John Holt [1959] Director; Robin Alistair Orr [1953] Director/Chartered Accountant; Lee Smales [1960] Managing Director; Simon Smales [1964] Sales Executive & Director

**SmarDTV (UK) Limited**
*Incorporated:* 19 January 1988 *Employees:* 94
*Previous:* Eldon Technology Limited
*Net Worth:* £4,207,793 *Total Assets:* £9,049,656
*Registered Office:* Beckside Design Centre, Millennium Business Park, Station Road, Steeton, Keighley, W Yorks, BD20 6QW
*Activities:* Other research and experimental development on natural sciences and engineering
*Parent:* SmarDTV SA
*Officers:* Mark Beariault [1971] Director/General Counsel [American]; Pascal Lenoir [1960] Director [French]; Wouter Naessens [1978] Director [Belgian]

**Smarts of York Limited**
*Incorporated:* 1 October 2016 *Employees:* 15
*Net Worth:* £2,711,543 *Total Assets:* £3,010,347
*Registered Office:* 61-63 Low Petergate, York, YO1 7HY
*Activities:* Retail sale of clothing in specialised stores
*Shareholders:* Robert Watson Smart; Ashley George Smart; Emma Elizabeth Smart
*Officers:* Ashley George Smart [1976] Director; Emma Elizabeth Smart [1978] Director; Robert Watson Smart [1939] Director

**Smiles for Miles Limited**
*Incorporated:* 28 January 2000 *Employees:* 52
*Net Worth:* £1,926,353 *Total Assets:* £5,917,767
*Registered Office:* 7 Memorial Avenue, Withernsea, E Yorks, HU19 2DN
*Activities:* Gambling and betting activities
*Parent:* Rufforth Park Limited
*Officers:* Roger Martin Ginley, Secretary; Roger Martin Ginley [1947] Director

**G.F.Smith & Son (London),Limited**
*Incorporated:* 25 January 1951 *Employees:* 201
*Net Worth:* £12,575,806 *Total Assets:* £16,438,245
*Registered Office:* Lockwood Street, Hull, HU2 0HL
*Activities:* Manufacture of paper and paperboard
*Officers:* Gareth David Andrew Powell, Secretary; Philip John Alexander [1962] Managing Director; John Stephen Haslam [1964] Managing Director; Glyn Houghton [1963] Director/Paper Merchant; Gareth Geoffrey Sheekey [1973] Finance Director

**R.H. Smith & Sons (Wigmakers) Limited**
*Incorporated:* 6 August 1974 *Employees:* 224
*Net Worth:* £11,223,788 *Total Assets:* £35,659,572
*Registered Office:* Peckett Plaza, Gainsborough Business Park, Gainsborough, Lincs, DN21 1FJ
*Activities:* Non-specialised wholesale trade
*Shareholder:* Raymond Peckett
*Officers:* Generaldine Ann Peckett, Secretary; Dominique Clugston [1974] Director; Elliott Peckett [1977] Director; Generaldine Ann Peckett [1949] Director; Raymond Peckett [1945] Director

**James E. Smith (Northern) Limited**
*Incorporated:* 5 June 2009 *Employees:* 30
*Net Worth:* £1,400,937 *Total Assets:* £4,106,465
*Registered Office:* Helsinki Road, Sutton Fields Industrial Estate, Hull, HU7 0YW
*Activities:* Sawmilling and planing of wood
*Parent:* James E Smith (Timber) Limited
*Officers:* Graham Calam [1965] Director; Graham Frankland [1969] Director; Paul John Hill [1953] Director; Barry Hurst [1943] Director; Bradley Mark Hurst [1971] Director; Charlton Elliot Hurst [1977] Director

**William Smith (Wakefield) Limited**
*Incorporated:* 16 May 1934 *Employees:* 142
*Net Worth:* £5,418,194 *Total Assets:* £9,373,015
*Registered Office:* Red House Farm, Staintondale, Scarborough, N Yorks, YO13 0HA
*Activities:* Growing of cereals (except rice), leguminous crops and oil seeds
*Major Shareholder:* William David Smith
*Officers:* Christine Smith, Secretary; Terence John Pearson [1957] Director; Christine Smith [1949] Director and Farmer; William David Smith [1946] Director and Farmer

**R.Smith (Windermere) Limited**
*Incorporated:* 2 January 1959 *Employees:* 41
*Net Worth:* £2,709,865 *Total Assets:* £7,112,623
*Registered Office:* Rayrigg Showrooms, Rayrigg Road, Bowness on Windermere, Cumbria, LA23 3DN
*Activities:* Sale of new cars and light motor vehicles
*Officers:* Suzanne Williams, Secretary; David Neil Smith [1946] Director; Grant William Smith [1986] Director/Motor Dealer; Robert Neil Smith [1967] Service Director; Ann Margaret Spiby [1935] Director/Retired Hotelier

**T.J.Smith and Nephew,Limited**
*Incorporated:* 2 July 1907 *Employees:* 1,509
*Net Worth:* £334,313,984 *Total Assets:* £770,148,992
*Registered Office:* P O Box 81, 101 Hessle Road, Hull, HU3 2BN
*Activities:* Manufacture of other chemical products n.e.c.
*Parent:* Smith & Nephew Trading Group Limited
*Officers:* John Roderick MacKinnon [1966] Director/Chartered Accountant; Ian Clifford Melling [1978] Director/Accountant; Susan Margaret Swabey [1961] Director/Company Secretary; Simon Charles Clement Tarry [1967] Director

**Smith Bros.(Caerconan) Wholesale Limited**
*Incorporated:* 15 July 1932 *Employees:* 58
*Net Worth:* £11,316,169 *Total Assets:* £12,442,139
*Registered Office:* Greyfriars House, Sidings Court, Doncaster, S Yorks, DN4 5NU
*Activities:* Wholesale of radio, television goods & electrical household appliances (other than records, tapes, CDs)
*Shareholder:* Ryszard Bielenica
*Officers:* Ryszard Bielenica [1951] Director; Mark Peter Jervis [1958] Director; Agnes Sheach [1944] Director

**Smith Brothers (Contracting) Limited**
*Incorporated:* 23 March 1999 *Employees:* 64
*Net Worth:* £4,354,530 *Total Assets:* £11,268,540
*Registered Office:* Unit G8, Navigation Close, Lowfields Business Park, Elland, W Yorks, HX5 9HB
*Activities:* Electrical installation
*Shareholders:* John Smith; Richard Smith
*Officers:* John Smith, Company Secretary/Director; Craig Collinson [1962] Director/Electrical Engineer; Richard Anthony King [1951] Finance Director; David Jon Ogden [1979] Director/Project Manager; John Smith [1957] Company Secretary/Director; Richard Smith [1957] Director

**Darren Smith Builders Limited**
*Incorporated:* 21 July 1986 *Employees:* 12
*Net Worth:* £3,146,906 *Total Assets:* £7,731,458
*Registered Office:* Unit 1 Crossley Woods, Crossley Lane, Mirfield, W Yorks, WF14 0NX
*Activities:* Construction of commercial buildings
*Shareholders:* Darren Smith; Nigel Smith
*Officers:* Nigel Smith, Secretary; Darren Smith [1965] Director/Builder; Nigel Smith [1969] Director/Builder

**William Smith Group 1832 Limited**
*Incorporated:* 5 April 1965 *Employees:* 96
*Previous:* Wm.Smith & Sons (Barnard Castle) Limited
*Net Worth:* £5,308,086 *Total Assets:* £7,326,137
*Registered Office:* Grove Works, Queen Street, Barnard Castle, Co Durham, DL12 8JQ
*Activities:* Manufacture of other fabricated metal products n.e.c.
*Major Shareholder:* Mark Adrian Smith
*Officers:* Lesley Smith, Secretary; Lesley Ann Hennedy [1955] Director; Lesley Smith [1959] Director; Mark Adrian Smith [1958] Director/Technician; Nicola Smith [1985] Director; Norma Lilian Smith [1934] Director/Company Secretary; Robert James Smith [1987] Director

**R.N.Smith Holdings Limited**
*Incorporated:* 4 September 1961 *Employees:* 119
*Net Worth:* £1,580,133 *Total Assets:* £6,777,683
*Registered Office:* Rayrigg Showrooms, Rayrigg Road, Bowness on Windermere, Cumbria, LA23 3DN
*Activities:* Activities of head offices
*Officers:* David Neil Smith [1946] Director; Grant William Smith [1986] Director/Motor Dealer

**Smoothwall Limited**
*Incorporated:* 3 October 2001 *Employees:* 138
*Net Worth Deficit:* £10,325,461 *Total Assets:* £8,108,781
*Registered Office:* Avalon House, 1 Savannah Way, Leeds Valley Park, Leeds, LS10 1AB
*Activities:* Other information technology service activities
*Parent:* Bidco Oasis Limited
*Officers:* Georg Mischa Ell [1981] Director/Chief Executive Officer [German]; Douglas Gerard Hanley [1971] Director/Chief Technology Officer; Richard William Hurd-Wood [1954] Director; James Gavin Logan [1984] Group Sales Director; Manprit Singh Randhawa [1983] Director/Chief Financial Officer; Lisa Jane Stone [1962] Director

**SMS Towage Limited**
*Incorporated:* 5 September 2002 *Employees:* 120
*Net Worth:* £18,167,318 *Total Assets:* £35,185,588
*Registered Office:* Francis House, Humber Place, The Marina, Hull, HU1 1UD
*Activities:* Sea and coastal freight water transport
*Major Shareholder:* Paul Escreet
*Officers:* Gareth Paul Escreet [1980] Director; Paul Escreet [1948] Director/Ship Manager

**Snainton Golf Centre Limited**
*Incorporated:* 22 December 1999 *Employees:* 13
*Net Worth:* £2,048,568 *Total Assets:* £3,262,061
*Registered Office:* Medina House, 2 Station Avenue, Bridlington, E Yorks, YO16 4LZ
*Activities:* Other sports activities
*Shareholders:* Beverley Hinchliffe; John David Hinchliffe
*Officers:* Beverley Hinchliffe, Secretary; Beverley Hinchliffe [1974] Director; John David Hinchliffe [1973] Director/Golf Professional

**The Snaith School Academy Trust**
*Incorporated:* 3 March 2014 *Employees:* 127
*Net Worth:* £20,376,364 *Total Assets:* £21,135,268
*Registered Office:* The Snaith School, Pontefract Road, Snaith, Goole, E Yorks, DN14 9LB
*Activities:* General secondary education
*Officers:* Martin Robert Backhouse [1964] Director/Farmer; Lindsey Annette Bellamy [1959] Director/Staff Nurse; Celia Jane Evans [1954] Director/General and GP Outreach Manager; Graham Wragg [1953] Director/Clerk; Sheena Anne Young [1954] Director/Dentist

**SNF (UK) Limited**
*Incorporated:* 29 May 1986 *Employees:* 51
*Net Worth:* £13,407,430 *Total Assets:* £111,250,928
*Registered Office:* 1 Red Hall Crescent, Paragon Business Village, Wakefield, W Yorks, WF1 2DF
*Activities:* Wholesale of chemical products
*Major Shareholder:* Rene Angelo Pich
*Officers:* Nicola Jayne Bowers, Secretary; Rene Hund [1957] Technical Director [French]; Pascal Andre Louis Remy [1960] Director [French]; Mark Richard Waddington [1970] Director; Ian Andrew Waterhouse [1971] Director/Accountant; Andrew Woollin [1968] Director

**SNF Oil and Gas Ltd**
*Incorporated:* 4 November 1985
*Net Worth:* £6,389,502 *Total Assets:* £94,014,376
*Registered Office:* 1 Red Hall Crescent, Paragon Business Village, Wakefield, W Yorks, WF1 2DF
*Activities:* Manufacture of other organic basic chemicals
*Parent:* S.P.C.M. SA
*Officers:* Nicola Jayne Bowers, Secretary; Andrew Richard Helliwell [1966] Director; Rene Hund [1957] Technical Director [French]; Pascal Andre Louis Remy [1960] Director [French]; Ian Andrew Waterhouse [1971] Director/Accountant; Andrew Woollin [1968] Director

**SNG Commercial (Holdings) Limited**
*Incorporated:* 2 December 2014 *Employees:* 4
*Net Worth:* £2,466,549 *Total Assets:* £4,361,371
*Registered Office:* West 44, 60 Richardshaw Lane, Pudsey, Leeds, LS28 7UR
*Activities:* Wholesale of chemical products
*Parent:* Finance Yorkshire Equity LP
*Officers:* Mark Gunter [1958] Director; Simon Neil Gunter [1983] Director; David James Pugh [1984] Director

**Snugpak Limited**
*Incorporated:* 17 June 1977 *Employees:* 48
*Net Worth:* £4,829,204 *Total Assets:* £6,032,697
*Registered Office:* Waterloo Mills, Howden Road, Silsden, Keighley, W Yorks, BD20 0HA
*Activities:* Manufacture of other textiles n.e.c.
*Officers:* Susan Cheryl Fletcher, Secretary; Darren James Burrell [1969] Sales Director; Michael George Dobson [1965] Joint Managing Director; Susan Cheryl Fletcher [1958] Joint Managing Director

**T Soanes & Son (Potatoes) Ltd**
*Incorporated:* 19 August 2003
*Net Worth:* £6,588,317 *Total Assets:* £7,167,140
*Registered Office:* 33-35 Exchange Street, Driffield, E Yorks, YO25 6LL
*Activities:* Growing of cereals (except rice), leguminous crops and oil seeds
*Major Shareholder:* Andrew Mark Soanes
*Officers:* Sarah Vickers Soanes, Secretary; Andrew Mark Soanes [1965] Director/Farmer

**T Soanes & Son (Poultry) Ltd**
*Incorporated:* 27 August 2004 *Employees:* 80
*Net Worth:* £2,592,122 *Total Assets:* £4,734,096
*Registered Office:* Church Hill Farm, Middleton on the Wolds, Driffield, E Yorks, YO25 9UG
*Activities:* Production of meat and poultry meat products
*Shareholder:* Andrew Mark Soanes
*Officers:* Andrew Mark Soanes [1965] Director

**Clive Soanes (Broilers) Ltd.**
*Incorporated:* 7 November 1986 *Employees:* 7
*Net Worth:* £1,423,731 *Total Assets:* £3,156,680
*Registered Office:* Church Hill Farm, Middleton on the Wolds, Driffield, E Yorks, YO25 9UG
*Activities:* Raising of poultry
*Shareholder:* Margaret Eileen Soanes
*Officers:* Margaret Eileen Soanes, Secretary; Andrew Mark Soanes [1965] Director; Margaret Eileen Soanes [1943] Director/Farmer

**Software Box Limited**
*Incorporated:* 11 March 1987 *Employees:* 126
*Net Worth:* £7,540,000 *Total Assets:* £28,239,000
*Registered Office:* East Moor House, Green Park Business Centre, Goose Lane, Sutton on Forest, York, YO61 1ET
*Activities:* Other information technology service activities
*Parent:* Hocomm Ltd
*Officers:* Brynmor Roberts, Secretary; Dennis Hoban [1950] Director; Brynmor Roberts [1952] Director; Colin John Williams [1964] Director/Sales Executive

**Solina UK Trading Limited**
*Incorporated:* 17 April 1963 *Employees:* 161
*Previous:* New Ivory Limited
*Net Worth:* £7,115,000 *Total Assets:* £14,723,000
*Registered Office:* Ebony House, Ainley Industrial Estate, Elland, W Yorks, HX5 9JP
*Activities:* Manufacture of condiments and seasonings
*Officers:* John Newton, Secretary; Adam Paul Jones [1976] Finance Director; Bertrand Marie Vaz [1960] Director [French]; Laurent Weber [1964] Director [French]

**Solis Film Limited**
*Incorporated:* 29 March 2016 *Employees:* 1
*Net Worth:* £1,089,685 *Total Assets:* £5,788,603
*Registered Office:* Highfield Grange, Bubwith, Selby, N Yorks, YO8 6DP
*Activities:* Motion picture production activities
*Major Shareholder:* Alan Richard Latham
*Officers:* Alan Richard Latham, Secretary; Tobias Angus Giles Mathews, Secretary; Alan Richard Latham [1960] Director/Film Producer

**Solvgrin Limited**
*Incorporated:* 29 January 1973 *Employees:* 4
*Net Worth:* £6,679,543 *Total Assets:* £8,368,349
*Registered Office:* 9 Hawthorne Gardens, Leeds, LS16 7TP
*Activities:* Construction of commercial buildings
*Shareholders:* Wayne Mark Butterfield; Helen Butterfield; Jean Butterfield
*Officers:* Jean Butterfield, Secretary; Jean Butterfield [1949] Director/Secretary; Wayne Mark Butterfield [1968] Director/Technical Manager

**Solway Foods Holdings Limited**
*Incorporated:* 18 May 1994
*Net Worth:* £10,174,000 *Total Assets:* £10,174,000
*Registered Office:* Trinity Park House, Fox Way, Wakefield, W Yorks, WF2 8EE
*Activities:* Activities of head offices
*Parent:* Northern Foods Limited
*Officers:* Ronald Klaas Otto Kers [1969] Director/Group CEO [Dutch]; Craig Ashley Tomkinson [1982] Director/Group CFO

**Solway Foods Limited**
*Incorporated:* 5 November 1987 *Employees:* 2,481
*Net Worth Deficit:* £21,615,000 *Total Assets:* £83,345,000
*Registered Office:* Trinity Park House, Fox Way, Wakefield, W Yorks, WF2 8EE
*Activities:* Other processing and preserving of fruit and vegetables
*Parent:* Solway Foods Holdings Limited
*Officers:* Ranjit Singh Boparan [1966] Director; Ronald Klaas Otto Kers [1969] Director/Group CEO [Dutch]; Keith Richard Packer [1967] Managing Director; Richard Peter Simpson [1965] Finance Director; Craig Ashley Tomkinson [1982] Director/Group CFO

**S.H. Somerscales Limited**
*Incorporated:* 8 December 1975 *Employees:* 32
*Net Worth:* £4,036,651 *Total Assets:* £5,278,844
*Registered Office:* Roxton Lane, Keelby, Grimsby, N E Lincs, DN41 8JB
*Activities:* Sawmilling and planing of wood
*Shareholders:* Stuart Herbert Somerscales; Bessie Mary Somerscales
*Officers:* Bessie Mary Somerscales, Secretary; Bessie Mary Somerscales [1938] Director/Secretary; Daniel Stuart Somerscales [1971] Director; Stuart Andrew Somerscales [1977] Director; Stuart Herbert Somerscales [1938] Director/Timber Merchant

**Somlie Limited**
*Incorporated:* 17 April 2014 *Employees:* 2
*Net Worth:* £35,775,772 *Total Assets:* £38,534,744
*Registered Office:* Park House, Park Lane, Emley, Huddersfield, W Yorks, HD8 9SS
*Activities:* Activities of venture and development capital companies
*Major Shareholder:* Sean Eugene Fahey
*Officers:* Sean Eugene Fahey [1970] Director; Sherlena Marie Fahey [1977] Director

**Sonic Megastore Limited**
*Incorporated:* 29 January 2009 *Employees:* 54
*Net Worth:* £3,408,841 *Total Assets:* £4,970,332
*Registered Office:* Sonic Megastore, Ingleby Road, Bradford, W Yorks, BD8 9AN
*Activities:* Retail sale of electrical household appliances in specialised stores
*Officers:* Parshotam Lal Showan [1977] Director

**Sound Leisure Limited**
*Incorporated:* 7 December 1977 *Employees:* 88
*Net Worth:* £1,700,907 *Total Assets:* £3,387,335
*Registered Office:* Sandleas Way, Leeds, LS15 8AR
*Activities:* Manufacture of consumer electronics
*Parent:* Sound Leisure Holdings Limited
*Officers:* David Malcolm Cross, Secretary; Alan James Black [1945] Director; Christopher John Black [1970] Director; Michael James Black [1974] Director

**South Bank Multi Academy Trust**
*Incorporated:* 16 March 2016 *Employees:* 239
*Net Worth:* £32,628,000 *Total Assets:* £35,510,000
*Registered Office:* Woodthorpe Primary School, Summerfield Road, Woodthorpe, York, YO24 2RU
*Activities:* Primary education
*Officers:* Reuben John Barrett [1972] Director; Patricia Anne Boyle [1957] Director/Retired; Martin Frank Baird Frost [1976] Director; Jill Elizabeth Hodges [1957] Director/Retired; Nicola Catherine Mitchell [1964] Director/Solicitor; Andrea Jayne Preston [1973] HR Director; Helen Jane Priestley [1970] Marketing Director; Edwin Matthew Thomas [1977] Director/Author

**South Coast Catering Limited**
*Incorporated:* 30 May 1991 *Employees:* 121
*Net Worth:* £2,251,000 *Total Assets:* £6,698,000
*Registered Office:* Airedale House, Victoria Road, Eccleshill, Bradford, W Yorks, BD2 2BN
*Activities:* Repair of other equipment
*Officers:* Andrew Wyatt Bristow [1962] Director; Robert Howard Bywell [1973] Director

**South Craven Academy Trust**
*Incorporated:* 5 April 2011 *Employees:* 202
*Net Worth:* £9,659,000 *Total Assets:* £14,636,000
*Registered Office:* South Craven School, Holme Lane, Cross Hills, Keighley, W Yorks, BD20 7RL
*Activities:* General secondary education
*Officers:* Marie Brook, Secretary; Joy Adamson [1972] Director/University Lecturer; Emma Louise Benn [1977] Director/Sales Office Manager; Joan Fleming [1944] Director/Retired; Wendy Caroline Hamilton [1971] Director/Teacher; Stephen Hanson [1958] Director/Policeman; David Harvey [1955] Director; Terry Hawley [1953] Director/Retired; Martyn Paul Hill [1974] Director/Headmaster; Katherine Mary Lloyd [1971] Director/Support Worker; Kika Masters [1965] Director/Premises & Contracts Manager; Paul Morrison [1984] Director/Teacher; Christopher James Pomery [1958] Director/Mature Student

**South Parade Properties Limited**
*Incorporated:* 7 February 1989
*Net Worth:* £9,639,617 *Total Assets:* £14,522,014
*Registered Office:* Oakwell House, 7 Butts Court, Leeds, LS1 5JS
*Activities:* Buying and selling of own real estate
*Shareholders:* Robert-Austin; Andrew Nicholas Carter; Peter Kilmartin
*Officers:* Peter Kilmartin, Secretary; Robert Austin [1950] Director/Surveyor; Andrew Nicholas Carter [1950] Director/Chartered Surveyor; Peter Kilmartin [1948] Director/Architect

**South Westmorland Multi Academy Trust**
*Incorporated:* 25 May 2011 *Employees:* 219
*Previous:* Dallam School
*Net Worth:* £10,649,529 *Total Assets:* £16,987,976
*Registered Office:* Dallam School, Milnthorpe, Cumbria, LA7 7DD
*Activities:* General secondary education
*Officers:* Joanne Hamer, Secretary; Enid Joy Fraser [1948] Director/Retired Headteacher; Roy James Pirie [1947] Director/Retired and Part Time Consultant; Sarah Catherine Swindley [1972] Director; Rupert Timothy Villiers-Smith [1967] Director; Stephen William Wetton [1960] Director/Educational Consultant; Nigel James Whittle [1984] Director/Headteacher; Reverend Susan Elizabeth Wilson [1952] Director/Retired Vicar

**The Southfield Grange Trust**
*Incorporated:* 26 August 2011 *Employees:* 436
*Net Worth Deficit:* £1,183,728 *Total Assets:* £4,592,327
*Registered Office:* The Southfield Grange Campus, Haycliffe Lane, Bradford, W Yorks, BD5 9ET
*Activities:* General secondary education
*Officers:* Sally Birkbeck [1967] Director/Assistant Librarian; Nigel Stuart Redman [1965] Director/ICT Manager; Mohammed Salim [1959] Director/Retail Trader; Peter William Thompson [1958] Director/Bursar; Dominic John Wall [1963] Director/Headteacher

**Southfield Health Care Limited**
*Incorporated:* 26 October 1992
*Net Worth:* £2,621,766 *Total Assets:* £3,711,725
*Registered Office:* Bostocks Boyce Welch, The Counting House, Tower Buildings, Wade House Road, Shelf, W Yorks, HX3 7PB
*Activities:* Other human health activities
*Shareholder:* Naveed Riaz
*Officers:* Iram Riaz, Secretary; Mohammed Riaz [1951] Director; Naveed Riaz [1980] Director/Partner in Two Care Homes

**Southgate - Dan at Spyglass Hill - Bidco Limited**
*Incorporated:* 15 December 2016 *Employees:* 2
*Net Worth Deficit:* £2,852,560 *Total Assets:* £115,435,000
*Registered Office:* Tudor Court, York Business Park, York, YO26 6RS
*Activities:* Financial intermediation not elsewhere classified
*Parent:* Southgate-Dan at Spyglass Hill - Midco Limited
*Officers:* Andrew Bracey [1967] Director; Aiden Charles Barwick Clegg [1966] Director; Joanne Cowl [1977] Director; Neil Allen Currie [1965] Director; Michael Christopher Dennis [1976] Director/Investment Professional; Miles Dewhurst [1972] Director; Robert Charles Stern [1960] Director/Solicitor

**Southgate - Dan at Spyglass Hill - Propco 1 Limited**
*Incorporated:* 8 February 2017
*Net Worth:* £15,603,093 *Total Assets:* £77,815,856
*Registered Office:* Unit 1 Tudor Court, York, YO26 6RS
*Activities:* Buying and selling of own real estate
*Parent:* Southgate-Dan at Spyglass Hill - Bidco Limited
*Officers:* Andrew James Mark Lewis Bracey [1967] Director/Partner at Midlothian Capital Partners; Aiden Charles Barwick Clegg [1966] Director/Partner at Midlothian Capital Partners; Joanne Cowl [1977] Director; Neil Allen Currie [1965] Director/Partner at Midlothian Capital Partners

**Southgate - Dan at Spyglass Hill - Propco 2 Limited**
*Incorporated:* 9 February 2017
*Net Worth Deficit:* £999,275 *Total Assets:* £105,573,624
*Registered Office:* Unit 1 Tudor Court, York Business Park, York, YO26 6RS
*Activities:* Buying and selling of own real estate
*Parent:* Southgate-Dan at Spyglass Hill - Propco 1 Limited
*Officers:* Andrew James Mark Lewis Bracey [1967] Director/Partner at Midlothian Capital Partners; Aiden Charles Barwick Clegg [1966] Director/Partner at Midlothian Capital Partners; Joanne Cowl [1977] Director; Neil Allen Currie [1965] Director/Partner at Midlothian Capital Partners

**Southgate Lighting Limited**
*Incorporated:* 7 February 1992 *Employees:* 37
*Net Worth:* £3,109,482 *Total Assets:* £3,698,735
*Registered Office:* Southgate House, Moorland Road, Drighlington, W Yorks, BD11 1JY
*Activities:* Electrical installation
*Shareholders:* Andrew Stuart; Sharon Stuart
*Officers:* Sharon Stuart, Secretary; Craig Fisher [1977] Sales Director; Andrew Stuart [1962] Director/Contracts Manager; Sharon Stuart [1961] Director

**Southridge Estates Limited**
*Incorporated:* 10 August 2005
*Net Worth:* £650,584 *Total Assets:* £3,498,556
*Registered Office:* 32 Beverley Road, Hull, HU3 1YE
*Activities:* Other letting and operating of own or leased real estate
*Shareholder:* Lee Edward Hatfield
*Officers:* Clare Nicola Whitehead, Secretary; Lee Edward Hatfield [1970] Director; Carl Naylor [1959] Director; Michael Stephen Whitehead [1955] Director

**Sovereign Build Limited**
*Incorporated:* 8 May 2014 *Employees:* 2
*Net Worth:* £4,921,371 *Total Assets:* £5,124,315
*Registered Office:* 15 The Horseshoe, York, YO24 1LY
*Activities:* Development of building projects
*Shareholders:* John Edwin Weatherill; Pauline Elizabeth Weatherill
*Officers:* Pauline Weatherill, Secretary; John Edwin Weatherill [1942] Director/Developer; Pauline Elizabeth Weatherill [1943] Director/Company Secretary

**Sovereign Health Care**
*Incorporated:* 17 August 1905 *Employees:* 48
*Net Worth:* £65,389,776 *Total Assets:* £68,236,264
*Registered Office:* Royal Standard House, 26 Mannningham Lane, Bradford, BD1 3DN
*Activities:* Non-life insurance
*Officers:* Nerissa Jordan Stewart, Secretary; Michael Stuart Bower [1960] Director/Solicitor; Stewart Michael Cummings [1977] Director/HR Business Partner; Simon Rhys Davies [1958] Director; Dr Robert Eddy Dugdale [1949] Director/Retired; Janet Christine Fortune [1958] Director; Christopher Mark Hudson [1957] Retired Financial Director; Russell Steven Piper [1959] Director/Chief Executive

**Sovereign Reserve Limited**
*Incorporated:* 4 January 2010
*Net Worth:* £1,554,811 *Total Assets:* £6,123,735
*Registered Office:* 1265 Century Way, Thorpe Park, Leeds, LS15 8ZB
*Activities:* Financial intermediation not elsewhere classified
*Shareholders:* Janette Mardon; Charles James Mardon
*Officers:* Charles James Mardon [1979] Director/Financial Advisor; Janette Mardon [1979] Director/Office Manager

**SP & PL Holdings Limited**
*Incorporated:* 11 November 2014 *Employees:* 155
*Net Worth:* £631,075 *Total Assets:* £8,442,080
*Registered Office:* Pheasant Drive, Geldard Road Industrial Estate, Birstall, W Yorks, WF17 9LT
*Activities:* Freight transport by road
*Parent:* Bedfords Group Holdings Limited
*Officers:* Lee Michael Nichols [1968] Director; David Ian Storey [1953] Director

**Space4 Limited**
*Incorporated:* 27 January 1999 *Employees:* 88
*Net Worth:* £19,553,000 *Total Assets:* £21,130,000
*Registered Office:* Persimmon House, Fulford, York, YO19 4FE
*Activities:* Construction of domestic buildings
*Parent:* Westbury Limited
*Officers:* Tracy Lazelle Davison, Secretary; David Jenkinson [1967] Director; Michael Hugh Killoran [1961] Finance Director; Richard Paul Stenhouse [1971] Director/Accountant

**Spafield Properties Limited**
*Incorporated:* 1 December 1952 *Employees:* 2
*Net Worth:* £1,285,468 *Total Assets:* £4,326,117
*Registered Office:* 14 Mallard Industrial Estate, Charles Street, Horbury, W Yorks, WF4 5FD
*Activities:* Other letting and operating of own or leased real estate
*Shareholders:* Thomas Simon Beaumont Jackson; Helen Louise May
*Officers:* Thomas Simon Beaumont Jackson, Secretary; Thomas Simon Beaumont Jackson [1956] Director; Helen Louise May [1971] Director

**Specialised Car Covers Limited**
*Incorporated:* 30 June 2010
*Net Worth:* £964,696 *Total Assets:* £3,334,431
*Registered Office:* Riverdale House, Dockfield Road, Shipley, W Yorks, BD17 7AD
*Activities:* Activities of head offices
*Shareholders:* Elliot James Michael Long; Katie Anne Fishwick
*Officers:* Carole Anne Long, Secretary; Katie Anne Fishwick [1977] Director; Carole Anne Long [1947] Director; Douglas Michael Long [1947] Director; Elliot James Michael Long [1981] Director

**Specialised Orthotic Services Limited**
*Incorporated:* 1 December 1994 *Employees:* 83
*Net Worth:* £5,615,349 *Total Assets:* £6,523,001
*Registered Office:* Drive Devilbiss Healthcare Limited, Heathfield Lane, Birkenshaw, Bradford, W Yorks, BD11 2HW
*Activities:* Manufacture of other special-purpose machinery n.e.c.
*Shareholders:* Drive Devilbiss Healthcare Limited; Drive Medical Limited
*Officers:* Michael Thomas Waine, Secretary; Richard James McGleenan [1970] Director; Stuart Pegg [1958] Production Director; Michael Thomas Waine [1951] Director

**Specialist Cars of Malton Limited**
*Incorporated:* 1 April 1999 *Employees:* 19
*Net Worth:* £335,661 *Total Assets:* £7,188,080
*Registered Office:* Unit 22 Seph Way, York Road Business Park, Malton, N Yorks, YO17 6AX
*Activities:* Sale of new cars and light motor vehicles
*Major Shareholder:* John Patrick Hawkins
*Officers:* June Elizabeth Frank, Secretary; John Patrick Hawkins [1959] Director/General Manager

**Specialist Ceiling Services Holdings Limited**
*Incorporated:* 13 March 2002 *Employees:* 51
*Net Worth:* £1,536,139 *Total Assets:* £6,279,840
*Registered Office:* Newmarket House, Aberford Road, Stanley, Wakefield, W Yorks, WF3 4AL
*Activities:* Activities of head offices
*Parent:* SCS Group Holdings Limited
*Officers:* Andrew Stuart Morson, Secretary; Michelle Chappell Dixon [1981] Financial Director; Paul Flynn [1976] Director; Darren Lee Friend [1983] Director; Rodger McKenzie Lambert [1965] Contracts Director; Andrew Stuart Morson [1964] Commercial Director; Craig Ian Scott [1985] Director

**Specialist Coatings Limited**
*Incorporated:* 19 February 1993 *Employees:* 105
*Net Worth:* £4,622,892 *Total Assets:* £11,207,234
*Registered Office:* Faverdale Industrial Estate, Darlington, Co Durham, DL3 0PP
*Activities:* Other business support service activities n.e.c.
*Shareholders:* Irene Mitchell; Allan Mitchell
*Officers:* Irene Mitchell, Secretary; Allan David Mitchell [1970] Director; Dr Allan Mitchell [1941] Director; Irene Mitchell [1941] Director

**Specialist Glass Products Limited**
*Incorporated:* 9 January 2003 *Employees:* 79
*Net Worth:* £1,984,230 *Total Assets:* £3,420,968
*Registered Office:* Unit 2 Milnsbridge Business Centre, Colne Vale Road, Milnsbridge, Huddersfield, W Yorks, HD3 4NY
*Activities:* Manufacture of flat glass
*Shareholders:* John Andrew Taylor; Jonathan Mark Taylor
*Officers:* John Andrew Taylor, Secretary/Director; John Andrew Taylor [1966] Director; Jonathan Mark Taylor [1972] Director

**Specialist People Services Group Limited**
*Incorporated:* 21 April 2011 *Employees:* 208
*Net Worth Deficit:* £1,555,300 *Total Assets:* £35,416,824
*Registered Office:* 7 Bradford Business Park, Kings Gate, Bradford, W Yorks, BD1 4SJ
*Activities:* Activities of head offices
*Parent:* Lloyds Development Capital (Holdings) Ltd
*Officers:* Christopher Michael Chidley [1960] Director; Steven Richard Harrison [1956] Venture Capitalist/Director; Paul Howard McNulty [1970] Finance Director; Anthony William Rieger [1945] Director

**Specialist Power Engineering Contracts Limited**
*Incorporated:* 10 August 2000 *Employees:* 87
*Net Worth:* £6,565,214 *Total Assets:* £8,105,933
*Registered Office:* Unit 5 Eagle Point, Telford Way, Wakefield 41 Industrial Estate, Wakefield, W Yorks, WF2 0XW
*Activities:* Construction of utility projects for electricity and telecommunications
*Parent:* Ipsum Bidco Limited
*Officers:* Greg Nicholas Louden Fernie [1976] Director; Ian Needham [1961] Director/Electrical Engineer; Craig Andrew Wright [1974] Director/Contracts Engineer

**Specialist Surfacing Limited**
*Incorporated:* 10 August 1995 *Employees:* 57
*Net Worth:* £2,937,925 *Total Assets:* £6,689,308
*Registered Office:* 26-30 Midland Road, Scunthorpe, N Lincs, DN16 1DQ
*Activities:* Construction of roads and motorways
*Shareholder:* Derrick Thomas Hunt
*Officers:* Gloria Patricia Hunt, Secretary; Jason Horton [1984] Director/Contracts Manager; Derrick Thomas Hunt [1948] Director/Civil Engineer; Gloria Patricia Hunt [1949] Director/Company Secretary; Shaun Antony Hunt [1970] Director/Vice Chairman; Scott Morse [1972] Director/Contracts Manager; Craig Andrew Tate [1980] Director; Philip Anthony Whitfield [1970] Director

**Specialist Trailer Hire Limited**
*Incorporated:* 14 December 1998
*Net Worth:* £1,616,351 *Total Assets:* £4,799,053
*Registered Office:* Bell Hill, Wood Lane, Rothwell, Leeds, LS26 0RS
*Activities:* Renting and leasing of other machinery, equipment and tangible goods n.e.c.
*Officers:* Paula Marie Murray, Secretary; Carl Alan Liversidge [1969] Director/Trailer Hire; Mark James Liversidge [1969] Director/Trailer Hire; Paula Marie Murray [1966] Director/Accounts Manager

**Specma Samwon Ltd**
*Incorporated:* 28 April 2003 *Employees:* 29
*Previous:* Samwon Tech (Europe) Ltd
*Net Worth:* £3,517,133 *Total Assets:* £4,735,587
*Registered Office:* 20 Welbury Way, Aycliffe Business Park, Newton Aycliffe, Co Durham, DL5 6ZE
*Activities:* Manufacture of other fabricated metal products n.e.c.
*Officers:* Patricia Anne Bake, Secretary; Anders Martin Gunnar Aberg [1967] Director/Accountant [Swedish]; Charl Erasmus [1974] Managing Director; Morten Kjaer Graakjear [1978] Director/Sales Executive [Danish]; Garry Charles Quickfall [1956] Sales Director

**Spectrum Community Health C.I.C.**
*Incorporated:* 30 June 2010 *Employees:* 503
*Net Worth:* £1,846,920 *Total Assets:* £8,265,916
*Registered Office:* 1 Navigation Walk, Wakefield, W Yorks, WF1 5RH
*Activities:* Specialists medical practice activities
*Officers:* Sharon Patricia Hardcastle, Secretary; Julie Fleetwood [1963] Director; Roger Michael Grasby [1948] Director/Board Chair; Alistair Michael Dinham Griggs [1954] Non-Executive Director; Sharon Patricia Hardcastle [1970] Director/Finance and Accountancy; Dr Linda Diane Harris [1965] Director/General Practitioner; Philip Geoffrey Morris [1955] Director/Self Employed; Timothy David Straughan [1965] Director; Debra Jayne Ward [1968] Clinical Operations Director

**Spectrum Yarns Limited**
*Incorporated:* 30 October 1973 *Employees:* 136
*Net Worth:* £4,564,444 *Total Assets:* £10,032,694
*Registered Office:* Spa Mill, New Street, Spa Fields Industrial Estate, Slaithwaite, Huddersfield, W Yorks, HD7 5BB
*Activities:* Preparation and spinning of textile fibres
*Major Shareholder:* Richard Kevin Brown
*Officers:* Ian Porter, Secretary; Danielle Rachael Brown [1985] Director; Richard Kevin Brown [1953] Director/Textile Manager

**Speedboat Acquisitionco Limited**
*Incorporated:* 18 May 2012
*Net Worth Deficit:* £31,336,000 *Total Assets:* £116,901,000
*Registered Office:* Unit 8 South Fork Industrial Estate, Dartmouth Way, Garnet Road, Leeds, LS11 5JL
*Activities:* Manufacture of other food products n.e.c.
*Parent:* Speedboat Midco Limited
*Officers:* Henry Strother Colquhoun Breese [1968] Director/Chartered Accountant; Matthew Lee [1976] Director/Chief Commercial Officer; John Power [1962] Director/Chief Executive Officer

**Speedboat Holdco Limited**
*Incorporated:* 18 May 2012 *Employees:* 768
*Net Worth Deficit:* £86,415,000 *Total Assets:* £117,827,000
*Registered Office:* Unit 8 South Fork Industrial Estate, Dartmouth Way, Garnet Road, Leeds, LS11 5JL
*Activities:* Manufacture of other food products n.e.c.
*Officers:* Henry Strother Colquhoun Breese [1968] Director/Chartered Accountant; Gareth James Knight [1978] Director/Investment Manager; Matthew Lee [1976] Director/Chief Commercial Officer; John Power [1962] Director/Chief Executive Officer; Simon James Edward Roddis [1968] Director/Accountant; Timothy James Whiting [1965] Director/Chairman

**Speedboat LNCO Limited**
*Incorporated:* 18 May 2012 *Employees:* 3
*Net Worth Deficit:* £44,732,000 *Total Assets:* £66,573,000
*Registered Office:* Unit 8 South Fork Industrial Estate, Dartmouth Way, Garnet Road, Leeds, LS11 5JL
*Activities:* Manufacture of other food products n.e.c.
*Parent:* Speedboat Holdco Limited
*Officers:* Henry Strother Colquhoun Breese [1968] Director/Chartered Accountant; Matthew Lee [1976] Director/Chief Commercial Officer; John Power [1962] Director/Chief Executive Officer

**Speedboat Midco Limited**
*Incorporated:* 18 May 2012
*Net Worth:* £64,773,000 *Total Assets:* £65,200,000
*Registered Office:* Unit 8 South Fork Industrial Estate, Dartmouth Way, Garnet Road, Leeds, LS11 5JL
*Activities:* Manufacture of other food products n.e.c.
*Parent:* Speedboat LNCO Limited
*Officers:* Henry Strother Colquhoun Breese [1968] Director/Chartered Accountant; Matthew Lee [1976] Director/Chief Commercial Officer; John Power [1962] Director/Chief Executive Officer

**Speedclad Limited**
*Incorporated:* 4 February 2008 *Employees:* 56
*Net Worth:* £1,590,528 *Total Assets:* £3,897,494
*Registered Office:* Thurston House, Thornfield Business Park, Standard Way, Northallerton, N Yorks, DL6 2XQ
*Activities:* Construction of commercial buildings
*Shareholder:* Anthony Blake
*Officers:* Neil Allen Mercer, Secretary; Anthony Blake [1965] Commercial Director; Fraser Scott Brown [1971] Director; Paul Dingle [1962] Director; Rebecca Elizabeth Forward [1975] Business Services Director; Peter Hurst [1968] Director

**Spellman & Walker Direct Limited**
*Incorporated:* 6 October 2005 *Employees:* 98
*Net Worth:* £5,610,808 *Total Assets:* £7,601,286
*Registered Office:* Graphica House, Chase Way, Bradford, W Yorks, BD5 8SW
*Activities:* Activities of head offices
*Shareholders:* Susan Jane Hirst; Michael Owen Hirst
*Officers:* Nigel Stuart Risby, Secretary; Michael Owen Hirst [1961] Director; Nigel Stuart Risby [1957] Sales Director

**Spellman & Walker Group Limited**
*Incorporated:* 10 October 2005
*Net Worth:* £15,245,666 *Total Assets:* £16,719,959
*Registered Office:* Graphica House, Chase Way, Bradford, W Yorks, BD5 8SW
*Activities:* Printing n.e.c.
*Parent:* Spellman & Walker Direct Limited
*Officers:* Nigel Stuart Risby, Secretary; Michael Owen Hirst [1961] Director; Nigel Stuart Risby [1957] Sales Director

**Spellman & Walker Limited**
*Incorporated:* 13 March 1961 *Employees:* 98
*Net Worth:* £2,344,619 *Total Assets:* £4,127,192
*Registered Office:* Graphica House, Chase Way, Bradford, W Yorks, BD5 8SW
*Activities:* Printing n.e.c.
*Parent:* Spellman & Walker Group Limited
*Officers:* Nigel Stuart Risby, Secretary; Michael Owen Hirst [1961] Director; Nigel Stuart Risby [1957] Sales Director

**Spencer Engineering Group Limited**
*Incorporated:* 30 August 2013 *Employees:* 315
*Net Worth Deficit:* £9,088,000 *Total Assets:* £29,785,000
*Registered Office:* 1 Humber Quays, Wellington Street West, Hull, HU1 2BN
*Activities:* Construction of other civil engineering projects n.e.c.
*Major Shareholder:* Charles Spencer
*Officers:* Gordon Cameron Paul Gratton, Secretary; Gordon Cameron Paul Gratton [1953] Director; Charles Spencer [1953] Director; Noreen Spencer [1957] Director; Gary Thornton [1966] Director

**C Spencer Limited**
*Incorporated:* 11 January 1989 *Employees:* 314
*Net Worth:* £2,284,000 *Total Assets:* £30,131,000
*Registered Office:* 1 Humber Quays, Wellington Street West, Hull, HU1 2BN
*Activities:* Construction of other civil engineering projects n.e.c.
*Major Shareholder:* Charles Spencer
*Officers:* Andrew Beach [1977] Director; Lucy Helen Grierson [1957] Director; Yvonne Moir [1964] HR Director; Michael John Renshaw [1971] Director; Charles Spencer [1953] Managing Director; Noreen Spencer [1957] Finance Director; Gary Thornton [1966] Joint Managing Director

**Spencer Properties (UK) Limited**
*Incorporated:* 21 March 2003 *Employees:* 7
*Net Worth:* £7,196,844 *Total Assets:* £15,287,685
*Registered Office:* 18 Headingley Lane, Leeds, LS6 2AS
*Activities:* Renting and operating of Housing Association real estate
*Shareholders:* Gordon Hoyland Spencer; Jacqueline Elsie Spencer
*Officers:* Simon Robert Tidswell, Secretary; Gordon Hoyland Spencer [1932] Director; Jacqueline Elsie Spencer [1938] Director; John David Spencer [1957] Director

**SPH 2011 Limited**
*Incorporated:* 11 January 2011
*Net Worth:* £389,359,296 *Total Assets:* £503,477,792
*Registered Office:* Welton Grange, Welton, Brough, E Yorks, HU15 1NB
*Activities:* Activities of other holding companies n.e.c.
*Officers:* Andrew Stuart Fish, Secretary; Alexander Martin Clare [1978] Director; Andrew Stuart Fish [1972] Director/Accountant; Paul Dyson Healey [1970] Director; Amanda Jayne Standish [1964] Director/PA

**A.E.Spink Limited**
*Incorporated:* 25 June 1926 *Employees:* 81
*Net Worth:* £9,702,961 *Total Assets:* £13,764,359
*Registered Office:* A E Spink Ltd, Kelham Street, Doncaster, S Yorks, DN1 3RA
*Activities:* Wholesale of wood, construction materials and sanitary equipment
*Shareholders:* Nicholas Martin Harrison; Matthew Ian Harrison
*Officers:* Nicholas Martin Harrison, Secretary; Simon James Biltcliffe [1976] Plumbing Sales Director; Matthew Ian Harrison [1965] Director; Nicholas Martin Harrison [1962] Director; Pamela Harrison [1938] Director; Christopher James Meek [1982] Building Sales Director

**Spinko Limited**
*Incorporated:* 8 June 2001 *Employees:* 588
*Net Worth:* £41,006,904 *Total Assets:* £49,098,048
*Registered Office:* The Innovation Centre, Westland Road, Leeds, LS11 5SB
*Activities:* Manufacture of mattresses
*Officers:* Amanda Jane Shea, Secretary/Chartered Accountant; Peter Douglas Spinks [1943] Director; Simon Paul Spinks [1969] Director

**Spire Bidco Hotels Limited**
*Incorporated:* 4 February 2010
*Net Worth:* £83,084,000 *Total Assets:* £83,090,000
*Registered Office:* The Inspire, Hornbeam Square West, Harrogate, N Yorks, HG2 8PA
*Activities:* Activities of other holding companies n.e.c.
*Parent:* Principal Hotels Topco 3 Limited
*Officers:* John Cody Bradshaw [1978] Director/Hotel Real Estate [American]; James Alexander Burrell [1974] Director/Accountant; Anthony Gerrard Troy [1962] Director [Irish]

**Splicegroup Europe Limited**
*Incorporated:* 20 June 1991 *Employees:* 56
*Net Worth:* £2,179,538 *Total Assets:* £4,210,750
*Registered Office:* The Coach House, Whitehall Road, Drighlington, Bradford, W Yorks, BD11 1LN
*Activities:* Other information technology service activities
*Major Shareholder:* David Woodhead
*Officers:* David Brian Woodhead, Secretary; Andrew Varley [1973] Director; David Brian Woodhead [1958] Director/Company Chairman

**Spooner Industries Limited**
*Incorporated:* 26 November 1959 *Employees:* 149
*Net Worth:* £8,041,000 *Total Assets:* £16,699,000
*Registered Office:* Moorland Engineering Works, Lower Railway Road, Ilkley, W Yorks, LS29 8JB
*Activities:* Manufacture of ovens, furnaces and furnace burners
*Parent:* Aegeus Industries Limited
*Officers:* Michael Jonathan Brook [1961] Managing Director; Brian John Lawrence [1942] Director/Consultant; Dr Andrew David Marson [1972] Technical Director; Paul Morican [1968] Sales Director; Robert Thomas Proctor [1962] Manufacturing Director; Richard Anton Summers [1972] Director; Richard Douglas Michael John Summers [1944] Director

**Sportswift Limited**
*Incorporated:* 16 January 1998 *Employees:* 9,695
*Net Worth:* £50,401,000 *Total Assets:* £128,105,000
*Registered Office:* Century House, Wakefield 41 Industrial Estate, Wakefield, W Yorks, WF2 0XG
*Activities:* Other retail sale in non-specialised stores
*Parent:* CF Bidco Limited
*Officers:* Shiv Sibal, Secretary; Christopher Robbert Beck [1974] Director; Justin Lee Fletcher [1970] Director; Karen Rachael Hubbard [1964] Director; Kristian Brian Lee [1974] Director

**Spring Cottage Academy**
*Incorporated:* 10 September 2013 *Employees:* 67
*Net Worth:* £5,520,347 *Total Assets:* £6,420,685
*Registered Office:* Spring Cottage Primary School, Dressay Grove, Hull, HU8 9JH
*Activities:* Primary education
*Officers:* Terence Dunn [1960] Director/Benefits Manager; Peter Raymond Greef [1953] Director/Business Consultant; Kevin Shaw [1964] Director/Vice Principal

**Springfield Care Services Limited**
*Incorporated:* 10 February 2003 *Employees:* 82
*Net Worth:* £1,788,187 *Total Assets:* £5,017,371
*Registered Office:* 2 Fusion Court, Aberford Road, Garforth, Leeds, LS25 2GH
*Activities:* Residential care activities for the elderly and disabled
*Major Shareholder:* Graeme Stuart Lee
*Officers:* Graeme Stuart Lee [1965] Director

**Springfield Healthcare (Grove House) Limited**
*Incorporated:* 30 March 2017 *Employees:* 4
*Net Worth Deficit:* £133,565 *Total Assets:* £3,904,995
*Registered Office:* 2 Fusion Court, Aberford Road, Garforth, Leeds, LS25 2GH
*Activities:* Residential nursing care facilities
*Parent:* SHG (Care Villages) Limited
*Officers:* Timothy Roger Jackson [1977] Director; Graeme Stuart Lee [1965] Director; Paul Rodney Phillips [1970] Director

**Springfield Healthcare (The Grange) Limited**
*Incorporated:* 17 May 2012 *Employees:* 154
*Net Worth:* £461,985 *Total Assets:* £5,974,054
*Registered Office:* 2 Fusion Court, Aberford Road, Garforth, Leeds, LS25 2GH
*Activities:* Residential care activities for the elderly and disabled
*Parent:* SHG (Care Villages) Limited
*Officers:* Kimberley Joan Malcolm, Secretary; Timothy Roger Jackson [1977] Director/Chartered Accountant; Graeme Stuart Lee [1965] Director; Paul Rodney Phillips [1970] Commercial and Operations Director

**Springfield Solutions Limited**
*Incorporated:* 23 September 1977 *Employees:* 73
*Net Worth:* £3,046,300 *Total Assets:* £6,218,166
*Registered Office:* 1-7 Thomas Street, Hull, HU9 1EH
*Activities:* Printing n.e.c.
*Parent:* Westrhode Limited
*Officers:* Albert William Dass, Secretary/Printer; Albert William Dass [1945] Director/Printer; Matthew Dass [1976] Director; Dennis Ebeltoft [1962] Director [American]; Stephen Geoffrey Forster [1956] Director

**Springfir Estates Limited**
*Incorporated:* 17 October 1969 *Employees:* 4
*Net Worth:* £13,191,844 *Total Assets:* £15,912,141
*Registered Office:* Persimmon House, Fulford, York, YO19 4FE
*Activities:* Development of building projects
*Parent:* Persimmon Homes Limited
*Officers:* Tracy Lazelle Davison, Secretary; David Jenkinson [1967] Director; Michael Hugh Killoran [1961] Finance Director; Richard Paul Stenhouse [1971] Director/Accountant

**SPX Flow Technology Limited**
*Incorporated:* 28 April 1993 *Employees:* 119
*Net Worth:* £7,998,000 *Total Assets:* £15,459,000
*Registered Office:* Eversheds Sutherland (International) LLP, Bridgewater Place, Water Lane, Leeds, LS11 5DR
*Activities:* Manufacture of electronic measuring, testing etc. equipment, not for industrial process control
*Parent:* SPX International Limited
*Officers:* Jaime Manson Easley [1977] Director/Corporate Controller [American]; Stephen Tsoris [1957] Director [American]

**SPX International Limited**
*Incorporated:* 21 March 1953 *Employees:* 245
*Net Worth:* £140,695,008 *Total Assets:* £155,188,000
*Registered Office:* Eversheds LLP, Bridgewater Place, Water Lane, Leeds, LS11 5DR
*Activities:* Other manufacturing n.e.c.
*Parent:* SPX UK Holding Limited
*Officers:* John Martyn Greaves [1962] Director/VP Manufacturing, UK/Europe Operations; Mark Edward Shanahan [1970] Director; Stephen Tsoris [1957] Director [American]

**The Square Chapel Trust**
*Incorporated:* 9 November 1988 *Employees:* 43
*Net Worth:* £10,474,288 *Total Assets:* £11,151,071
*Registered Office:* 10 Square Road, Halifax, W Yorks, HX1 1QG
*Activities:* Operation of arts facilities
*Officers:* David Liam McQuillan, Secretary; Marc Vernon Collett [1959] Director/Management Consultant; Elizabeth Kathleen Dugdale [1952] Director/Retired; Stephen Fearnley [1965] Director/Quality Manager; Britt Harwood [1968] Director/Architect; Jennifer M Lynn [1947] Director/Chief Executive (Urban Regeneration); David Liam McQuillan [1979] Director; Jaqueline Newman [1949] Director/Chief Examiner; Miriam Selma Razaq [1975] Director/PR/Business Manager; Martin Allan West [1954] Director/Retired; Nicholas Charles Worsnop [1969] Director/Solicitor

**Square Peg Properties Limited**
*Incorporated:* 11 December 2015 *Employees:* 1
*Net Worth:* £2,455,002 *Total Assets:* £4,774,451
*Registered Office:* Tutin Road, Leeming Bar Industrial Estate, Northallerton, N Yorks, DL7 9UJ
*Activities:* Other letting and operating of own or leased real estate
*Major Shareholder:* Kevin John Procter
*Officers:* Claire Elizabeth Alenius, Secretary; Kevin John Procter [1964] Director/Coach Proprietor

**SRCL Limited**
*Incorporated:* 18 July 1996 *Employees:* 2,289
*Net Worth Deficit:* £32,073,000 *Total Assets:* £128,540,000
*Registered Office:* Indigo House, Sussex Avenue, Leeds, LS10 2LF
*Activities:* Other business support service activities n.e.c.
*Parent:* Stericycle International Ltd
*Officers:* Charles Anthony Alutto [1965] Director [American]; Daniel Ginnetti [1968] Director/Chief Financial Officer [American]; Robert John Guice [1966] Director/EVP International

**SRH 2011 Limited**
*Incorporated:* 11 January 2011 *Employees:* 4
*Net Worth Deficit:* £17,389,838 *Total Assets:* £72,383,272
*Registered Office:* Welton Grange, Welton, Brough, E Yorks, HU15 1NB
*Activities:* Activities of other holding companies n.e.c.
*Parent:* Stadium Retail Group
*Officers:* Andrew Stuart Fish, Secretary; Alexander Martin Clare [1978] Director; Andrew Stuart Fish [1972] Director/Accountant; Paul Dyson Healey [1970] Director; Amanda Jayne Standish [1964] Director/PA

**SSG Insight Limited**
*Incorporated:* 1 October 2001 *Employees:* 56
*Previous:* Softsols Group Limited
*Net Worth:* £2,743,559 *Total Assets:* £3,286,338
*Registered Office:* 2 Burgage Square, Merchant Gate, Wakefield, W Yorks, WF1 2TS
*Activities:* Dormant company
*Officers:* Martin Howard Thompson, Secretary/Solicitor; Geoffrey Edwards [1943] Director; Michael Ian Edwards [1969] Key Accounts Director; Martin Howard Thompson [1970] Director/Solicitor

**SSL Healthcare Ltd**
*Incorporated:* 28 September 2010 *Employees:* 105
*Net Worth:* £1,156,629 *Total Assets:* £3,548,177
*Registered Office:* Kensington House, 3 Kensington, Bishop Auckland, Co Durham, DL14 6HX
*Activities:* Other service activities n.e.c.
*Shareholders:* Stephen Metcalf; Susan Metcalf; Louise Harvey
*Officers:* Louise Harvey [1973] Director; Stephen Metcalf [1952] Director; Susan Metcalf [1954] Director

**SSP Bidco Limited**
*Incorporated:* 15 July 2008
*Previous:* H & F Sensor Bidco Limited
*Net Worth:* £180,862,000 *Total Assets:* £194,844,000
*Registered Office:* Second Floor, G Mill, Dean Clough, Halifax, W Yorks, HX3 5AX
*Activities:* Other information technology service activities
*Parent:* SSP Midco 1 Limited
*Officers:* Richard Charles Forrest, Secretary; Stephen Michael Lathrope [1967] Director; Christopher Pennington [1972] Director/Chartered Accountant

**SSP Holdings Limited**
*Incorporated:* 1 October 2004
*Net Worth:* £6,637,000 *Total Assets:* £87,847,000
*Registered Office:* Second Floor, G Mill, Dean Clough, Halifax, W Yorks, HX3 5AX
*Activities:* Other software publishing
*Parent:* SSP Bidco Limited
*Officers:* Richard Charles Forrest, Secretary; Stephen Michael Lathrope [1967] Director; Christopher Pennington [1972] Director/Chartered Accountant

**SSP Limited**
*Incorporated:* 14 June 2001 *Employees:* 499
*Net Worth:* £90,384,000 *Total Assets:* £199,524,000
*Registered Office:* Second Floor, G Mill, Dean Clough, Halifax, W Yorks, HX3 5AX
*Activities:* Business and domestic software development
*Parent:* SSP Holdings Limited
*Officers:* Richard Charles Forrest, Secretary; Stephen Michael Lathrope [1967] Director; Christopher Pennington [1972] Director/Chartered Accountant; James Anthony Sadler [1970] Director

**SSP Midco 1 Limited**
*Incorporated:* 15 July 2008
*Previous:* H & F Sensor Holdco Limited
*Net Worth Deficit:* £80,939,000 *Total Assets:* £191,496,992
*Registered Office:* Second Floor, G Mill, Dean Clough, Halifax, W Yorks, HX3 5AX
*Activities:* Other information technology service activities
*Parent:* SSP Midco 2 Limited
*Officers:* Richard Charles Forrest, Secretary; Stephen Michael Lathrope [1967] Director; Christopher Pennington [1972] Director/Chartered Accountant

**SSP Midco 2 Limited**
*Incorporated:* 8 December 2014 *Employees:* 773
*Net Worth Deficit:* £65,673,000 *Total Assets:* £224,683,008
*Registered Office:* Second Floor, G Mill, Dean Clough, Halifax, W Yorks, HX3 5AX
*Activities:* Other information technology service activities
*Parent:* SSP Topco Limited
*Officers:* Richard Charles Forrest, Secretary; Dale Brent Alderson [1979] Director; Andrew Peter Davison [1967] Director/General Counsel; Christopher Richard Hurley [1974] Director/Chief Portfolio Officer; Stephen Michael Lathrope [1967] Director; Christopher Pennington [1972] Director/Chartered Accountant; James Anthony Sadler [1970] Director

**SSP Sirius Solutions Limited**
*Incorporated:* 5 November 1996 *Employees:* 2
*Net Worth:* £12,292,000 *Total Assets:* £34,647,000
*Registered Office:* Second Floor, G Mill, Dean Clough, Halifax, W Yorks, HX3 5AX
*Activities:* Other software publishing
*Parent:* SSP Holdings Limited
*Officers:* Richard Charles Forrest, Secretary; Stephen Michael Lathrope [1967] Director; Christopher Pennington [1972] Director/Chartered Accountant

**SSP Topco Limited**
*Incorporated:* 4 February 2015 *Employees:* 704
*Net Worth Deficit:* £23,606,000 *Total Assets:* £257,456,000
*Registered Office:* Second Floor, G Mill, Dean Clough, Halifax, W Yorks, HX3 5AX
*Activities:* Other information technology service activities
*Officers:* Richard Charles Forrest, Secretary; Dale Brent Alderson [1979] Director; Andrew Peter Davison [1967] Director/General Counsel; Jonathan Halford [1968] Director/Chairman; Christopher Richard Hurley [1974] Director/Chief Portfolio Officer; Stephen Michael Lathrope [1967] Director; Christopher Pennington [1972] Finance Director; James Anthony Sadler [1970] Director

**St Aidan's Church of England Academy Limited**
*Incorporated:* 15 March 2007 *Employees:* 65
*Net Worth:* £9,488,000 *Total Assets:* £11,216,000
*Registered Office:* St Aidan's, Hundens Lane, Darlington, Co Durham, DL1 1LL
*Activities:* General secondary education
*Officers:* Patrick Meirion Baker [1969] Director/Assistant Principal; Anita Susan Blackburn [1952] Director/Vice Principal; Marc Edward Crossland [1967] Director/Self Employed; John Frank de Martino [1944] Director/Accountant; Nicole Gibbon [1970] Director/Principal; Anita Inglis [1970] Director/Group Head of Business Improvement; Christine Anne Large [1961] Director/Teacher; Ruth Lowbridge [1953] Director/Academy Ambassador; Alan James Marshall [1947] Director/Retired; David Barrie Spenceley [1966] Director/Teacher

**St Andrew's Hospice Limited**
*Incorporated:* 30 April 1992 *Employees:* 210
*Net Worth:* £10,490,796 *Total Assets:* £11,055,795
*Registered Office:* St Andrews Hospice, Peaks Lane, Grimsby, N E Lincs, DN32 9RP
*Activities:* Other human health activities
*Officers:* Stephen Alexander Oldridge, Secretary; Ian Jeffrey Hargreaves [1966] Director; David Raymond Hatfield [1945] Director/Chartered Accountant; Geoffrey Enoch Hirst [1939] Director/HR Adviser; Leslie Jones [1944] Director/Business Consultant; Andrew Kenneth North [1958] Director/Management Consultant; Stephen Alexander Oldridge [1975] Director/Solicitor; Steven Terence Parker [1966] Director/Businessman; John Scaife [1952] Director; Dr Anne Elizabeth Spalding [1961] Director/Doctor; Nigel Tranter [1959] Director/Retired

**St Anne's Community Services**
*Incorporated:* 29 December 1972 *Employees:* 1,378
*Net Worth:* £5,822,000 *Total Assets:* £31,932,000
*Registered Office:* 6 St Mark's Avenue, Leeds, LS2 9BN
*Activities:* Renting and operating of Housing Association real estate
*Officers:* Joanna Elizabeth Louise Green, Secretary; Karl Lloyd Beckett [1970] Director/Consultant; Philip Brown [1953] Director/Solicitor; James Dunmore [1971] Director/Commercial Healthcare Executive; Steven Durham [1955] Director; Pauline Garnett [1965] Director/Genetic Counsellor; Ian McIntosh [1959] Director/Retired Solicitor; Terence Moran [1957] Director/Associate Dean Head of School; Gareth Osborne [1970] Director/Management Consultant; Jane Sarah Riley [1966] Director/Independent Management Consultant; Paul Richard Roberts [1976] Director/Chartered Accountant

**St George's Crypt**
*Incorporated:* 20 September 2011 *Employees:* 77
*Net Worth:* £3,245,333 *Total Assets:* £3,458,703
*Registered Office:* St George's Crypt, Great George Street, Leeds, LS1 3BR
*Activities:* Social work activities without accommodation for the elderly and disabled
*Officers:* Paul Nicholas Ayers [1961] Director/Clerk in Holy Orders; Rt Hon John Dominic Battle [1951] Director/Retired Member of Parliament; Dr Nicholas Bishop [1953] Director/General Practitioner; Christopher Stuart Burford [1956] Director/Chartered Accountant; Jane Elizabeth Cooper [1968] Director/Solicitor; Peter Gillions [1953] Director/Teacher; Tracey Anne Greig [1964] Director/Local Authority Manager; Duncan Milwain [1970] Director/Solicitor; Alison Judith Oldfield [1969] Director/Solicitor; Ian Christopher Pickup [1952] Director/Retired Accountant; Revd Elizabeth Louise Woolf [1973] Director/Clerk in Holy Orders

**St Hybald's Academy Trust**
*Incorporated:* 23 March 2012 *Employees:* 60
*Net Worth:* £2,845,164 *Total Assets:* £3,152,142
*Registered Office:* Scawby Academy, West Street, Scawby, Brigg, N Lincs, DN20 9AN
*Activities:* Primary education
*Shareholders:* Stuart Harold Bontoft; John Fenwick Irving; Alan David West
*Officers:* Vanessa Elaine Bowers, Secretary; Sarah Louise Anderson [1980] Director; Nicola Beel [1971] Director/Divisional Support Manager; Zoe Marie Birchall [1974] Director/Executive Headteacher; Stuart Harold Bontoft [1949] Director/Retired; Vanessa Elaine Bowers [1954] Director; Alison Clairhowe [1975] Director; Matthew Charles Clarke [1969] Director; John Fenwick Irving [1947] Director/Retired Education Officer; Neil Reeder [1964] Director; Julie Ann Seaton [1966] Director; Robert Shipman [1967] Director; Jill Swain [1970] Director; Margaret Valentine [1948] Director; Alan David West [1950] Director/Retired Headteacher Self-Employed

**St James Securities Limited**
*Incorporated:* 11 April 2011 *Employees:* 4
*Net Worth:* £4,553,196 *Total Assets:* £4,680,957
*Registered Office:* 3rd Floor, Airedale House, Albion Street, Leeds, LS1 5AW
*Activities:* Buying and selling of own real estate
*Parent:* St James Securities Group Limited
*Officers:* Paul Richard Piers Morris [1967] Director/Chartered Surveyor; Daniel Nicholas Murray [1976] Director/Project Manager; Oliver Alexander Quarmby [1975] Director

**St Leger Homes of Doncaster Limited**
*Incorporated:* 15 September 2005 *Employees:* 721
*Net Worth Deficit:* £31,573,000 *Total Assets:* £4,813,000
*Registered Office:* St Leger Court, White Rose Way, Doncaster, S Yorks, DN4 5ND
*Activities:* Management of real estate on a fee or contract basis
*Parent:* Doncaster Metropolitan Borough Council
*Officers:* Julie Crook, Secretary; Joseph Blackham [1945] Director/Councillor; Anthony French [1959] Director/Designer; Richard Allan Jones [1946] Director/Councillor; Stephen Robert Lyons [1949] Director/Retired; Trevor Franklin Mason [1950] Director/Retired; Robert Dennis Mayo [1965] Director; Councillor Jane Nightingale [1963] Director/Councillor; Dr Ruth Elizabeth Snell [1967] Director/Retired; Paul Francis Tanney [1960] Director/Chief Executive; Maureen Tennison [1948] Director/Retired; Alan Tolhurst [1938] Director/Retired

**St Mary's Academy Trust**
*Incorporated:* 20 January 2012 *Employees:* 196
*Net Worth:* £5,019,387 *Total Assets:* £9,752,173
*Registered Office:* c/o Schofield Sweeney LLP, Springfield House, 76 Wellington Street, Leeds, LS1 2AY
*Activities:* Primary education
*Officers:* Sharon Linda Cook [1952] Director; Tamara Gulliver [1968] Director/Headteacher; Meryl Liddell [1954] Director/Strategic Involvement Manager; Steven Manderson [1960] Director/Retired; Melanie Priestley [1979] Director/Chief Executive Officer; Carl Ramskill [1964] Director/Area Manager; Tracy Rodger [1966] Director/Retired; Susan Williams [1953] Director/Retired Primary Headteacher; Louise Mary Wylie [1965] Director/Solicitor (Non-Practising)

**St Paul's Street (Investments) Limited**
*Incorporated:* 24 July 1986 *Employees:* 5
*Net Worth:* £17,659,124 *Total Assets:* £19,248,686
*Registered Office:* Lodge House, 12 Town Street, Horsforth, Leeds, LS18 4RJ
*Activities:* Development of building projects
*Shareholders:* Peter Kilmartin; Andrew Nicholas Carter; Moira Kilmartin; Louise Mary Carter
*Officers:* Peter Kilmartin, Secretary; Andrew Nicholas Carter [1950] Director/Surveyor; Louise Mary Carter [1959] Director; Moira Kilmartin [1949] Director; Peter Kilmartin [1948] Director/Architect

**St Peter's School, York**
*Incorporated:* 8 June 2009 *Employees:* 271
*Net Worth:* £23,009,050 *Total Assets:* £30,031,820
*Registered Office:* St Peter's School, Clifton, York, YO30 6AB
*Activities:* Other education n.e.c.
*Officers:* Kathryn Valerie Hodges, Secretary; Carol Rosemary Bonita Bailey [1955] Director/Solicitor; Christopher Paul Collingwood [1954] Director/Precentor; Jenny Copley-Farnell [1985] Director/Pharmacist; Dr Nigel Philip Durham [1969] Director/Consultant Cardiologist; Dafydd Huw Enoch [1961] Director/Barrister; Dr Daryl Margaret Hayward [1954] Director/GP; Phillip Hilling [1949] Director & Consultant; Simon Hinchliffe [1973] Director/Headteacher; Ann Rosemary Lees [1952] Diocesan Director of Education; Martin David Matravers [1969] Director/Academic/University Professor; Susan Lesley Palmer OBE [1952] Director/Retired; Adrian John Taylor [1954] Director/Educational Consultant; Paul David Widdicombe [1958] Director/Investment Manager; William Roger Woolley [1951] Director/Retired Local Government Officer

**St. Catherines Developments Limited**
*Incorporated:* 2 November 1967 *Employees:* 1
*Net Worth:* £2,020,030 *Total Assets:* £8,031,653
*Registered Office:* St Catherines Farm, Moorlands Road, Skelton, N Yorks, YO30 1YA
*Activities:* Construction of domestic buildings
*Major Shareholder:* Benjamin Atlay Cleminson
*Officers:* Benjamin Atlay Cleminson [1948] Director/Farmer

**St. Gemma's Hospice**
*Incorporated:* 15 December 1992 *Employees:* 261
*Net Worth:* £11,357,908 *Total Assets:* £12,446,028
*Registered Office:* 329 Harrogate Road, Leeds, LS17 6QD
*Activities:* Hospital activities
*Officers:* Jason Stuart Crowther Kirk, Secretary; Susan May Ansbro [1953] Planning Director; Kuldeep Kaur Bajwa [1960] Director/Consultation and Involvement Officer; Hilary Kathryn Barrett [1958] Managing Director; Dr Peter Winston Belfield [1954] Director/Doctor; Debra Fairley [1965] Director/Nurse; Sr Eileen Fucito [1940] Director/Sister in Religion [American]; Sister Carmel Gorman [1942] Director/Sister in Religion [Irish]; Sister Anne Hammersley [1952] Director/Sister in Religion; Angus Martin [1959] Director/Accountant; Professor Julia Newton-Bishop [1955] Director/Professor of Dermatology; Sister Therese O'Regan [1945] Director/Sister in Religion [Irish]; Christopher Ernest Schofield [1962] Director/Lawyer; Sister Savio Steed [1942] Director/Sister in Religion; June Avis Toovey [1958] Director/Nurse

**St. Laurence Education Trust**
*Incorporated:* 31 July 1997 *Employees:* 304
*Net Worth:* £453,000 *Total Assets:* £5,047,000
*Registered Office:* Ampleforth College, York, YO62 4EY
*Activities:* Primary education
*Officers:* Liam Francis Kelly, Secretary; Christopher John Heselton Adams [1950] Director/Self Employed Chartered Accountant; Elizabeth Catherine Berner [1951] Director; Robin Burdell [1958] Director/Head of Finance and Marketing Appointments; Matthew John Craston [1958] Director/Entrepreneur; Rachel Mary Agnes Fletcher [1950] Director/Retired; James Stephen O'Neill [1945] Director/Retired; Claire Helen Smith [1956] Director/Visiting Professor University of East Anglia; John Randal Herley Sykes [1957] Director/Solicitor

**St. Leonard's Hospice York**
*Incorporated:* 1 October 1979 *Employees:* 138
*Net Worth:* £17,929,508 *Total Assets:* £18,252,448
*Registered Office:* St Leonards Hospice, 185 Tadcaster Road, York, YO24 1GL
*Activities:* Other human health activities
*Officers:* Karen Louise Johnson, Secretary; David John Alexander [1960] Director/Surgeon; David James Dickson [1955] Director/Chartered Accountant; Alistair Mark Mackereth Duncan [1954] Director/Solicitor; Dr Katherine Ann Flemming [1968] Director/University Lecturer; Juliette Ena Cecile Healey [1964] Director/Bank of England Agent [British/Swiss]; Eamonn Mary Patrick Keogh [1961] Director/Town Planning Consultant [Irish]; Dr Christine Anne Kirk [1949] Director/Retired; David James Miller [1946] Director/Retired; Jacqueline Patricia Myers [1971] NHS Director; Dr Lavinia Jane Norton [1954] Director/Retired; Michael Wilson Sturge [1947] Director/Retired

**The St.Quinton LLP**
*Incorporated:* 12 April 2005
*Net Worth:* £3,772,546 *Total Assets:* £3,801,530
*Registered Office:* 6 Newbegin, Beverley, E Yorks, HU17 8EG
*Officers:* Laura Kate Hamzic [1983] Member; Daniel Stephen St. Quinton [1985] Member; Pamela Gaye St. Quinton [1955] Member; Stephen Eric St. Quinton [1956] Member

**Stadium (Bradford) Limited**
*Incorporated:* 27 October 2006 *Employees:* 4
*Net Worth Deficit:* £9,949,806 *Total Assets:* £4,388,861
*Registered Office:* Welton Grange, Welton, Brough, E Yorks, HU15 1NB
*Activities:* Non-trading company
*Parent:* Stadium Parkgate (Holdings) Ltd
*Officers:* Andrew Stuart Fish, Secretary; Alexander Martin Clare [1978] Director; Andrew Stuart Fish [1972] Director/Accountant; Paul Dyson Healey [1970] Director; Amanda Jayne Standish [1964] Director/PA

**Stadium (Newport) Limited**
*Incorporated:* 13 May 1999 *Employees:* 4
*Net Worth:* £103,177,000 *Total Assets:* £105,287,552
*Registered Office:* Welton Grange, Welton, Brough, E Yorks, HU15 1NB
*Activities:* Other letting and operating of own or leased real estate
*Parent:* Stadium Parkgate (Holdings) Ltd
*Officers:* Andrew Stuart Fish, Secretary; Alexander Martin Clare [1978] Director; Andrew Stuart Fish [1972] Director/Chartered Accountant; Paul Dyson Healey [1970] Director; Amanda Jayne Standish [1964] Director/PA

**Stadium Parkgate (Holdings) Limited**
*Incorporated:* 7 May 2004
*Net Worth:* £325,208,352 *Total Assets:* £337,031,200
*Registered Office:* Welton Grange, Welton, Brough, E Yorks, HU15 1NB
*Activities:* Activities of head offices
*Parent:* SPH 2011
*Officers:* Andrew Stuart Fish, Secretary; Alexander Martin Clare [1978] Director; Andrew Stuart Fish [1972] Director/Chartered Accountant; Paul Dyson Healey [1970] Director; Amanda Jayne Standish [1964] Director/PA

**Stadium Retail (Holdings) Limited**
*Incorporated:* 23 July 2004 *Employees:* 4
*Net Worth:* £72,372,936 *Total Assets:* £146,593,472
*Registered Office:* Welton Grange, Welton, Brough, E Yorks, HU15 1NB
*Activities:* Activities of head offices
*Parent:* SRH 2011 Ltd
*Officers:* Andrew Stuart Fish, Secretary; Alexander Martin Clare [1978] Director; Andrew Stuart Fish [1972] Director/Chartered Accountant; Paul Dyson Healey [1970] Director; Amanda Jayne Standish [1964] Director/PA

**Stadium Retail Group Limited**
*Incorporated:* 9 September 2014 *Employees:* 3
*Net Worth Deficit:* £10,881,508 *Total Assets:* £67,777,608
*Registered Office:* Welton Grange, Welton, Brough, E Yorks, HU15 1NB
*Activities:* Activities of head offices
*Major Shareholder:* Paul Dyson Healey
*Officers:* Alexander Martin Clare [1978] Director; Andrew Stuart Fish [1972] Director/Accountant; Paul Dyson Healey [1970] Director

**Stadium Retail Investments (2003) Limited**
*Incorporated:* 15 September 2003 *Employees:* 4
*Net Worth:* £63,514,468 *Total Assets:* £63,514,468
*Registered Office:* Welton Grange, Welton, Brough, E Yorks, HU15 1NB
*Activities:* Non-trading company
*Parent:* Stadium Retail (Holdings) Ltd
*Officers:* Andrew Stuart Fish, Secretary; Alexander Martin Clare [1978] Director; Andrew Stuart Fish [1972] Director/Chartered Accountant; Paul Dyson Healey [1970] Director; Amanda Jayne Standish [1964] Director/PA

**Stadium Retail Investments (2004) Limited**
*Incorporated:* 23 July 2004
*Net Worth:* £865,129 *Total Assets:* £42,654,360
*Registered Office:* Welton Grange, Welton, Brough, E Yorks, HU15 1NB
*Activities:* Development of building projects
*Parent:* Stadium Retail (Holdings) Ltd
*Officers:* Andrew Stuart Fish, Secretary; Alexander Martin Clare [1978] Director; Andrew Stuart Fish [1972] Director/Accountant; Paul Dyson Healey [1970] Director; Amanda Jayne Standish [1964] Director/PA

**Stadium Welton Limited**
*Incorporated:* 26 January 1979 *Employees:* 34
*Net Worth:* £4,982,666 *Total Assets:* £31,995,820
*Registered Office:* Welton Grange, Welton, Brough, E Yorks, HU15 1NB
*Activities:* Development of building projects
*Parent:* SPH 2011
*Officers:* Andrew Stuart Fish, Secretary; Alexander Martin Clare [1978] Director; Andrew Stuart Fish [1972] Director/Chartered Accountant; Paul Dyson Healey [1970] Director; Amanda Jayne Standish [1964] Director/PA

**Staff Finders (Yorkshire) Limited**
*Incorporated:* 28 February 2002 *Employees:* 743
*Net Worth:* £663,725 *Total Assets:* £4,175,663
*Registered Office:* The Old School House, 43 Baker Street, Hull, HU2 8HP
*Activities:* Temporary employment agency activities
*Shareholders:* Andrew Abraham; Lisa Joanne Dale
*Officers:* Lisa Joanne Dale, Secretary; Andrew Abraham [1969] Director; Lisa Joanne Dale [1969] Director

**Stafford Mills Holdings Limited**
*Incorporated:* 19 October 2009 *Employees:* 57
*Net Worth:* £866,369 *Total Assets:* £7,208,849
*Registered Office:* Stafford Mills, Milnsbridge, Huddersfield, W Yorks, HD3 4JD
*Activities:* Wholesale of furniture, carpets and lighting equipment
*Shareholders:* Andrew Simon Hutchison; Nigel St John Lawrence
*Officers:* David Geoffrey Headey [1942] Director; Andrew Simon Hutchison [1969] Finance Director; Nigel St John Lawrence [1972] Sales Director; Geoffrey Haigh Riley [1939] Director

**Stage One Creative Services Limited**
*Incorporated:* 24 January 1996 *Employees:* 170
*Net Worth:* £3,073,297 *Total Assets:* £10,505,640
*Registered Office:* Hangar 88, Marston Business Park, Tockwith, York, YO26 7QF
*Activities:* Other manufacturing n.e.c.
*Shareholder:* Mark Nicholas Johnson
*Officers:* Michael Keith Harrison [1964] Group Financial Director; Mark Nicholas Johnson [1963] Production Director; Timothy Ivan Leigh [1970] Sales & Marketing Director

**Stage One Group Limited**
*Incorporated:* 23 December 2011 *Employees:* 179
*Previous:* Stage One Creative Services Companies Limited
*Net Worth:* £4,620,452 *Total Assets:* £11,837,488
*Registered Office:* Hangar 88, Marston Business Park, Tockwith, York, YO26 7QF
*Activities:* Other manufacturing n.e.c.
*Major Shareholder:* Mark Nicholas Johnson
*Officers:* Elizabeth Anne Johnson, Secretary; Michael Keith Harrison [1964] Director; Mark Nicholas Johnson [1963] Director

**Stainforth Construction LLP**
*Incorporated:* 17 December 2010 *Employees:* 44
*Net Worth:* £3,171,370 *Total Assets:* £8,350,218
*Registered Office:* 1 Butterfield Park, Otley Road, Shipley, W Yorks, BD17 7HE
*Officers:* Lee Terence Barnes [1973] Member; Dean Martyn Slingsby [1964] Member; Christopher Daniel Wilson [1962] Member; Alison Marie Barnes [1972] LLP Member; Michelle Ann Slingsby [1972] LLP Member; Kathleen Wilson [1962] LLP Member

**Stainless Band Limited**
*Incorporated:* 27 February 2007 *Employees:* 52
*Net Worth:* £1,154,434 *Total Assets:* £4,397,619
*Registered Office:* 3 Greengate, Cardale Park, Harrogate, N Yorks, HG3 1GY
*Activities:* Activities of head offices
*Major Shareholder:* Jonathan Patrick Hanson
*Officers:* Jonathan Patrick Hanson [1970] Director

**Stamp Jackson & Procter Limited**
*Incorporated:* 20 February 2017 *Employees:* 49
*Net Worth:* £1,416,427 *Total Assets:* £6,406,011
*Registered Office:* 5 Parliament Street, Hull, HU1 2AZ
*Activities:* Solicitors
*Officers:* Alistair Ian Manson Latham, Secretary; Simon Timothy Burgess [1965] Director/Solicitor; Claire Alexandra Louise Chairman [1977] Director/Solicitor; Simon Richard Thomas Gittings [1960] Director/Solicitor; Neil Robert Holland [1974] Director/Solicitor; Alistair Ian Manson Latham [1971] Director/Solicitor

**Standard Wool (UK) Limited**
*Incorporated:* 29 January 1962 *Employees:* 83
*Net Worth:* £12,487,759 *Total Assets:* £39,450,252
*Registered Office:* Standard House, Trevor Foster Way, Bradford, W Yorks, BD5 8HB
*Activities:* Other manufacturing n.e.c.
*Parent:* Standard Wool UK (Holdings) Limited
*Officers:* Mark Andrews [1963] Production Director; Paul Stuart Hughes [1985] Trading Director; Paul Thomas Hughes [1948] Managing Director; Ian Ralph Marwood [1961] Director

**Standard Wool UK (Holdings) Limited**
*Incorporated:* 1 March 2004 *Employees:* 159
*Net Worth:* £9,416,863 *Total Assets:* £46,660,424
*Registered Office:* Standard House, Trevor Foster Way, Bradford, W Yorks, BD5 8HB
*Activities:* Preparation and spinning of textile fibres
*Major Shareholder:* Paul Thomas Hughes
*Officers:* Kathryn Hughes [1959] Director; Paul Stuart Hughes [1985] Trading Director; Paul Thomas Hughes [1948] Managing Director; Ian Ralph Marwood [1961] Director

**Standeven Builders (Yorkshire) Limited**
*Incorporated:* 8 July 1976
*Net Worth:* £3,934,345 *Total Assets:* £5,742,098
*Registered Office:* 15 Littlethorpe Hill, Hartshead, Liversedge, W Yorks, WF15 8AZ
*Activities:* Other letting and operating of own or leased real estate
*Parent:* Standeven Holdings Limited
*Officers:* Janet Margaret Standeven, Secretary; David Martyn Standeven [1949] Director/Builder; Janet Margaret Standeven [1952] Director

**Standeven Holdings Ltd**
*Incorporated:* 11 August 2014
*Net Worth:* £21,997,734 *Total Assets:* £29,342,384
*Registered Office:* 15 Littlethorpe Hill, Hartshead, Liversedge, W Yorks, WF15 8AZ
*Activities:* Activities of head offices
*Shareholders:* Janet Margaret Standeven; David Martyn Standeven
*Officers:* David Martyn Standeven [1949] Director; Janet Margaret Standeven [1952] Director

**Standeven Properties Limited**
*Incorporated:* 20 June 2001 *Employees:* 6
*Previous:* Kindercare Estates Limited
*Net Worth:* £5,325,353 *Total Assets:* £15,820,355
*Registered Office:* 15 Littlethorpe Hill, Hartshead, Liversedge, W Yorks, WF15 8AZ
*Activities:* Other letting and operating of own or leased real estate
*Officers:* Janet Margaret Standeven, Secretary; David Martyn Standeven [1949] Director; Janet Margaret Standeven [1952] Director

**Stangs Limited**
*Incorporated:* 21 July 1993 *Employees:* 129
*Net Worth:* £5,488,964 *Total Assets:* £10,870,868
*Registered Office:* Russell Chambers, 61a North Street, Keighley, W Yorks, BD21 3DS
*Activities:* Printing n.e.c.
*Shareholder:* Keith Chapman
*Officers:* Ann Wendy Chapman, Secretary; Adrian Keith Chapman [1970] Director/Printer; Ann Wendy Chapman [1948] Director; James Harvey Chapman [1972] Director; Jonathan Guy Chapman [1976] Director; Keith Chapman [1942] Director; Elizabeth Sarah Lammas [1981] Director

**Stanwell Technic Ltd.**
*Incorporated:* 10 October 1990 *Employees:* 35
*Net Worth:* £2,316,810 *Total Assets:* £3,457,458
*Registered Office:* 35 Westgate, Huddersfield, W Yorks, HD1 1PA
*Activities:* Other manufacturing n.e.c.
*Parent:* Stanwell Group Limited
*Officers:* Joanne Thackeray, Secretary; Douglas Mark Gorton [1953] Business Development Director; Joanne Thackeray [1965] Financial Director; Jonathan Whitwam [1973] Commercial Director

**Star Brands (Holdings) Limited**
*Incorporated:* 17 June 2004 *Employees:* 92
*Net Worth:* £1,634,716 *Total Assets:* £8,857,692
*Registered Office:* Unit E, Millshaw Business Living, Global Avenue, Leeds, LS11 8PR
*Activities:* Manufacture of soap and detergents
*Shareholders:* Andrew Micklethwaite; Timothy Robertshaw
*Officers:* Diane Margaret Siddall, Secretary/Manufacturer of Cleaning Products; Andrew Micklethwaite [1959] Director; Philip Graham Siddall [1966] Director/Manufacturer of Cleaning Products

**Star Brands Limited**
*Incorporated:* 19 March 2001 *Employees:* 85
*Net Worth:* £2,506,399 *Total Assets:* £9,633,871
*Registered Office:* Unit E, Millshaw Living, Global Avenue, Leeds, LS11 8PR
*Activities:* Manufacture of soap and detergents
*Parent:* Star Brands Holdings Ltd
*Officers:* Diane Margaret Siddall, Secretary/Manufacturer of Cleaning Products; Philip Graham Siddall [1966] Director/Manufacturer of Cleaning Products

**State Bidco Limited**
*Incorporated:* 7 May 2015 *Employees:* 137
*Net Worth Deficit:* £5,987,000 *Total Assets:* £121,658,000
*Registered Office:* Birkby Grange, 85 Birkby Hall Road, Birkby, Huddersfield, W Yorks, HD2 2XB
*Activities:* Advertising agencies
*Parent:* State Interco Ltd
*Officers:* Benjamin William Eaton [1979] Director; Matthew Joseph Turner [1978] Director

**State Debtco Limited**
*Incorporated:* 14 July 2015
*Net Worth:* £26,944,000 *Total Assets:* £69,906,000
*Registered Office:* Birkby Grange, 85 Birkby Hall Road, Birkby, Huddersfield, W Yorks, HD2 2XB
*Activities:* Activities of other holding companies n.e.c.
*Parent:* The Dining Club Group
*Officers:* Benjamin William Eaton [1979] Director; Matthew Joseph Turner [1978] Director

**State Interco Limited**
*Incorporated:* 14 July 2015
*Net Worth Deficit:* £38,455,000 *Total Assets:* £87,541,000
*Registered Office:* Birkby Grange, 85 Birkby Hall Road, Birkby, Huddersfield, W Yorks, HD2 2XB
*Activities:* Activities of other holding companies n.e.c.
*Parent:* State Debtco Ltd
*Officers:* Benjamin William Eaton [1979] Director; Matthew Joseph Turner [1978] Director

**Status International (UK) Ltd**
*Incorporated:* 22 November 1990 *Employees:* 85
*Net Worth:* £16,122,958 *Total Assets:* £23,357,990
*Registered Office:* Pennine House, Mortimer Street, Cleckheaton, W Yorks, BD19 5AR
*Activities:* Wholesale of household goods (other than musical instruments) n.e.c
*Shareholders:* Peter Barre McVeigh; Nicholas John McVeigh
*Officers:* Nicholas John McVeigh, Secretary; Nicholas John McVeigh [1967] Director; Peter Barre McVeigh [1938] Director; Andrew Myatt [1969] Director; Jonathan Mark Sheard [1971] Director

**Staunch Limited**
*Incorporated:* 22 February 2010 *Employees:* 1
*Net Worth Deficit:* £26,553 *Total Assets:* £5,195,142
*Registered Office:* The Hall, Lairgate, Beverley, E Yorks, HU17 8HL
*Activities:* Development of building projects
*Major Shareholder:* James Robert Healey
*Officers:* Wendy Elizabeth Wrangham, Secretary; Nicholas Anthony Densley [1957] Director; James Robert Healey [1975] Director

**STC Research Foundation**
*Incorporated:* 8 September 2004 *Employees:* 33
*Net Worth:* £2,235,717 *Total Assets:* £4,012,396
*Registered Office:* Stockbridge House, Cawood, Selby, N Yorks, YO8 3TZ
*Activities:* Growing of vegetables and melons, roots and tubers
*Officers:* Graham Philip Ward, Secretary; Prof Janet Mary Bainbridge [1947] Director/Departmental Head; Nigel Derek Bartle [1974] Managing Director; Peter Richard Branfield [1958] Director/Agriculture; Andrew Stanley Burgess [1965] Director; William John Davies [1949] Director/University Professor; Martin Meredith Evans [1965] Director; Colin Malcolm Frampton [1953] Director; Janet Godfrey [1953] Director/Farmer; Julian Hargreaves [1945] Director/Farmer; Carlo Leifert [1960] Director/Professor of Agriculture [German]; Nigel John Patrick [1957] Director; Stephen Guy Poskitt [1963] Director; John Michael Richardson [1937] Director/Exec Chairman

**Charles F.Stead & Company,Limited**
*Incorporated:* 9 April 1904 *Employees:* 69
*Net Worth:* £9,661,906 *Total Assets:* £10,442,861
*Registered Office:* Sheepscar Tannery, Sheepscar, Leeds, LS7 2BY
*Activities:* Tanning and dressing of leather; dressing and dyeing of fur
*Parent:* Charles F. Stead (Holdings) Limited
*Officers:* John Thompson, Secretary; Andrew William Bailey [1980] Director; David William Bailey [1947] Director; Douglas Ernest Crack [1949] Director; Kenneth Douglas Crack [1973] Director; Michael Douglas Crack [1981] Director; Peter John Crack [1945] Director

**Charles F Stead (Holdings) Limited**
*Incorporated:* 13 March 2006 *Employees:* 69
*Net Worth:* £11,289,703 *Total Assets:* £12,313,319
*Registered Office:* Sheepscar Tannery, Sheepscar, Leeds, LS7 2BY
*Activities:* Dormant company
*Shareholder:* David William Bailey
*Officers:* John Thompson, Secretary; David William Bailey [1947] Director; Douglas Ernest Crack [1949] Director; Peter John Crack [1945] Director

**Steadplan Group Limited**
*Incorporated:* 15 July 2015 *Employees:* 64
*Net Worth:* £454,000 *Total Assets:* £6,832,957
*Registered Office:* c/o Steadplan, Whitehall Industrial Estate, Ashfield Way, Leeds, LS12 5JB
*Activities:* Financial management
*Major Shareholder:* James Anthony Smith
*Officers:* James Anthony Smith [1971] Director

**Steamtown Railway Museum Limited**
*Incorporated:* 5 October 1967
*Net Worth:* £1,640,857 *Total Assets:* £3,605,789
*Registered Office:* off Jesson Way, Cragbank, Carnforth, Lancs, LA5 9UR
*Activities:* Passenger rail transport, interurban
*Major Shareholder:* William David Smith
*Officers:* Christine Smith, Secretary; Patricia Marshall [1956] Director; Christine Smith [1949] Director/Farmer; William David Smith [1946] Director/Farmer

**Stearsby Hagg Property Company Limited**
*Incorporated:* 12 December 2016
*Net Worth:* £234,187 *Total Assets:* £5,140,430
*Registered Office:* King Hope, 34 Romanby Road, Northallerton, N Yorks, DL7 8NF
*Activities:* Activities of other holding companies n.e.c.
*Shareholders:* William George Page; Amanda Page
*Officers:* William George Page [1970] Director

**Steel Beams and Columns Limited**
*Incorporated:* 11 February 1982 *Employees:* 4
*Net Worth:* £5,258,337 *Total Assets:* £6,629,005
*Registered Office:* Dalton Airfield, Eldmire Lane, Dalton, Thirsk, N Yorks, YO7 3JN
*Activities:* Wholesale of metals and metal ores
*Officers:* Malcolm John Elders, Secretary; Jeanne Martine Elizabeth Bianco [1971] Director; Matthew Giovanni Bianco [1986] Director; Robert Jean Francois Bianco [1933] Director

**Steel Supplies Limited**
*Incorporated:* 19 May 1999 *Employees:* 36
*Net Worth:* £533,700 *Total Assets:* £3,966,133
*Registered Office:* Bristol Works, Arksey Lane, Doncaster, S Yorks, DN5 0ST
*Activities:* Wholesale of metals and metal ores
*Major Shareholder:* Howard John Todd
*Officers:* Suzanne Jennifer Todd, Secretary; Howard John Todd [1958] Managing Director

**Steeper Group Holdings Limited**
*Incorporated:* 20 January 2017 *Employees:* 442
*Net Worth:* £5,046,309 *Total Assets:* £15,154,591
*Registered Office:* Unit 3 Stourton Link, Intermezzo Drive, Leeds, LS10 1DF
*Activities:* Non-trading company
*Shareholders:* Paul Martin Steeper; John Antony Midgley
*Officers:* John Antony Midgley, Secretary; John Antony Midgley [1965] Director; Paul Martin Steeper [1964] Director

**Hugh Steeper Limited**
*Incorporated:* 23 March 1921 *Employees:* 439
*Net Worth:* £8,166,960 *Total Assets:* £15,346,287
*Registered Office:* Unit 3 Stourton Link, Intermezzo Drive, Leeds, LS10 1DF
*Activities:* Manufacture of medical and dental instruments and supplies
*Parent:* Meditech Group Limited
*Officers:* Emma Claire Harvey-Kitching, Secretary; Carl Chatfield [1964] Director; Mark Leslie Davies [1959] Director; Giles Charles Hodgson [1970] Director; John Antony Midgley [1965] Director; Paul Martin Steeper [1964] Director

**Steers Group Limited**
*Incorporated:* 25 January 1994 *Employees:* 22
*Net Worth:* £2,465,222 *Total Assets:* £12,936,885
*Registered Office:* Steers Group Limited, West End Approach, Morley, W Yorks, LS27 0NB
*Activities:* Activities of head offices
*Major Shareholder:* Alan Steers
*Officers:* Sarah Marsden, Secretary/Finance Manager; Adam John Steers [1971] Director; Alan Steers [1950] Director; Jane Carolyn Steers [1950] Director; Mathew Alan Steers [1980] Director

**Steffco Limited**
*Incorporated:* 5 August 1996 *Employees:* 49
*Net Worth:* £1,856,208 *Total Assets:* £3,652,363
*Registered Office:* 78 Armley Road, Armley, Leeds, LS12 2EJ
*Activities:* Printing n.e.c.
*Parent:* Resource Print Solutions Limited
*Officers:* Joanne Thompson, Secretary; Asif Choudry [1971] Director; Philip George Thompson [1968] Director; Gail Elizabeth Weathers [1966] HR Director; David Woodcock [1972] Technical Director

**J.Stell & Sons,Limited**
*Incorporated:* 11 March 1930 *Employees:* 109
*Net Worth:* £3,070,202 *Total Assets:* £8,343,368
*Registered Office:* Riverside Business Park, Royd Ings Avenue, Keighley, W Yorks, BD21 4AF
*Activities:* Manufacture of other articles of paper and paperboard n.e.c.
*Major Shareholder:* Samuel Vaughan Stell
*Officers:* Samuel Vaughan Stell, Secretary; Richard Ian Guest [1970] Director; Samuel Adrian Stell [1978] Director; Samuel Vaughan Stell [1947] Director/Paper Tube Manufacturer

**Stell Cardboard Tubes Limited**
*Incorporated:* 21 February 2014 *Employees:* 109
*Net Worth:* £2,990,393 *Total Assets:* £8,263,559
*Registered Office:* Riverside Business Park, Royd Ings Avenue, Keighley, W Yorks, BD21 4AF
*Activities:* Manufacture of other articles of paper and paperboard n.e.c.
*Major Shareholder:* Samuel Vaughan Stell
*Officers:* Richard Ian Guest [1970] Director; Samuel Adrian Stell [1978] Director; Samuel Vaughan Stell [1947] Director

**Stem Learning Limited**
*Incorporated:* 23 March 2004 *Employees:* 111
*Previous:* Myscience.Co Limited
*Net Worth Deficit:* £1,306,000 *Total Assets:* £5,703,000
*Registered Office:* National Stem Learning Centre, University of York, York, YO10 5DD
*Activities:* Educational support services
*Officers:* David William James Thorpe-Green, Secretary; Rosemary Elizabeth Bailey [1979] Director/Investment Banker; Professor Judith Merry Bennett [1956] Director/Professor; Simon David John Chaplin [1969] Director; Alison Jane Denholm [1969] Director/Headteacher; Ian Kevin Duffy [1975] Director/Community Development Manager; Julia Elizabeth King [1954] Director/Baroness; Professor Stephen Keith Scott [1958] Director/University Professor; David William James Thorpe-Green [1968] Commercial Director; Professor Gillian Valentine [1965] Director/University Professor; Professor Christopher James Wigginton [1972] Director/University Professor

**GM Stephenson Farm and Commercial LLP**
*Incorporated:* 1 August 2012
*Previous:* Southfield Manor Property LLP
*Net Worth:* £774,092 *Total Assets:* £5,427,241
*Registered Office:* Southfield Farm, Main Street, Flixton, Scarborough, N Yorks, YO11 3UD
*Officers:* Deborah Stephenson [1965] Member; George Martin Stephenson [1969] Member

**Stephenson Group Ltd**
*Incorporated:* 21 December 1900 *Employees:* 84
*Net Worth:* £2,225,355 *Total Assets:* £9,778,523
*Registered Office:* Brookfoot House, Low Lane, Horsforth, Leeds, LS18 5PU
*Activities:* Manufacture of soap and detergents
*Parent:* Thos. Bentley & Son Limited
*Officers:* Thomas James MacAulay Bentley [1971] Director; Thomas Richard Bentley [1943] Director/Chairman; Robert Leo Carr [1973] Operations Director; James Aaron Clews [1988] Sales & Marketing Director; Lisa Flannery [1965] Finance Director; John Michael Story [1963] Managing Director

**G M Stephenson Ltd**
*Incorporated:* 8 September 2006 *Employees:* 15
*Net Worth:* £3,542,801 *Total Assets:* £5,972,901
*Registered Office:* Southfield Farm, Main Street, Flixton, Scarborough, N Yorks, YO11 3UD
*Activities:* Other business support service activities n.e.c.
*Shareholders:* George Martin Stephenson; Deborah Stephenson
*Officers:* George Martin Stephenson, Secretary/Director; Deborah Stephenson [1965] Director; George Martin Stephenson [1969] Director

**Stercap Limited**
*Incorporated:* 28 September 2001 *Employees:* 18
*Net Worth:* £3,520,545 *Total Assets:* £4,509,624
*Registered Office:* Ashley House, 415 Halifax Road, Brighouse, W Yorks, HD6 2PD
*Activities:* Retail sale of carpets, rugs, wall and floor coverings in specialised stores
*Shareholder:* Brian Collin William Wormald
*Officers:* Brian Collin William Wormald, Secretary/Carpet Retailer; Paul Peyton [1964] Sales Director; Brian Collin William Wormald [1956] Director/Carpet Retailer; Craig Ashley Wormald [1980] Director/Carpet Retailer; James Bradley Wormald [1978] Director/Carpet Retailer

**Stericycle International Holdings Canada Limited**
*Incorporated:* 3 October 2011
*Net Worth:* £193,212,992 *Total Assets:* £193,212,992
*Registered Office:* Indigo House, Sussex Avenue, Leeds, LS10 2LF
*Activities:* Non-trading company
*Parent:* Stericycle International Holdings Ltd
*Officers:* Charles Anthony Alutto [1965] Director/Businessman [American]; Daniel Ginnetti [1968] Director/Chief Financial Officer [American]; Robert John Guice [1966] Director/EVP International

**Stericycle International Holdings Limited**
*Incorporated:* 20 June 2011
*Net Worth:* £673,666,048 *Total Assets:* £970,721,152
*Registered Office:* Indigo House, Sussex Avenue, Leeds, LS10 2LF
*Activities:* Activities of head offices
*Parent:* Stericycle Europe S.A.R.L
*Officers:* Charles Anthony Alutto [1965] Director [American]; Daniel Ginnetti [1968] Director/Chief Financial Officer [American]; Robert John Guice [1966] Director/EVP International

**Stericycle International, Ltd.**
*Incorporated:* 1 June 2004 *Employees:* 3
*Net Worth:* £352,176,000 *Total Assets:* £379,075,008
*Registered Office:* Indigo House, Sussex Avenue, Leeds, LS10 2LF
*Activities:* Activities of head offices
*Parent:* Stericycle International Holdings Ltd
*Officers:* Charles Anthony Alutto [1965] Director [American]; Daniel Ginnetti [1968] Director/Chief Financial Officer [American]; Robert John Guice [1966] Director/EVP International

**Sterling Capitol PLC**
*Incorporated:* 2 April 2007 *Employees:* 7
*Net Worth Deficit:* £6,356,303 *Total Assets:* £3,550,808
*Registered Office:* 2nd Floor, Victoria Wharf, 4 The Embankment, Sovereign Street, Leeds, LS1 4BA
*Activities:* Development of building projects
*Major Shareholder:* Robert Sydney Murray
*Officers:* Michael John Heydecke [1956] Director; Nigel Patrick David McClea [1951] Director/Solicitor; James John Robert Murray [1990] Director; Sir Robert Sydney Murray [1946] Director; Peter Ian Walker [1971] Director

**Sterne Properties Limited**
*Incorporated:* 17 October 2003
*Net Worth:* £3,767,703 *Total Assets:* £8,212,129
*Registered Office:* Leigh House, St Paul's Street, Leeds, LS1 2JT
*Activities:* Buying and selling of own real estate
*Shareholders:* Martin Lionel Sterne; Susan Frances Sterne
*Officers:* Susan Frances Sterne, Secretary; Martin Lionel Sterne [1947] Director; Simon James Sterne [1975] Director

**Steve Ltd**
*Incorporated:* 27 June 2000
*Previous:* Forwardthoughts Limited
*Net Worth:* £4,999,685 *Total Assets:* £5,000,104
*Registered Office:* c/o Easysoft Limited, Thorp Arch Grange, Thorp Arch, Wetherby, W Yorks, LS23 7BA
*Activities:* Activities of other holding companies n.e.c.
*Major Shareholder:* Stephen John Hill
*Officers:* Mark Morley, Secretary; Stephen John Hill [1963] Director/Software Consultant

**Peter Stevens Estates Limited**
*Incorporated:* 13 February 2003 *Employees:* 2
*Net Worth:* £19,683,294 *Total Assets:* £33,727,936
*Registered Office:* Leigh House, 28-32 St Paul's Street, Leeds, LS1 2JT
*Activities:* Other letting and operating of own or leased real estate
*Officers:* Alan Rennie Dickson, Secretary; Alan Rennie Dickson [1968] Managing Director; Andrew Stevens [1975] Director; Colin Stevens [1979] Director; Michael Stevens [1977] Director; Richard Ian Stevens [1981] Director/Surveyor

**Stevro (Holdings) Limited**
*Incorporated:* 16 January 2015 *Employees:* 146
*Net Worth:* £3,395,849 *Total Assets:* £7,169,592
*Registered Office:* Dewsbury Mills, Thornhill Road, Dewsbury, W Yorks, WF12 9QE
*Activities:* Activities of head offices
*Shareholders:* Stephen Martin Durrans; Roger Edward Durrans
*Officers:* Roger Edward Durrans [1981] Sales Director; Stephen Martin Durrans [1959] Director

**Stevro Limited**
*Incorporated:* 2 July 2008 *Employees:* 146
*Net Worth:* £1,333,212 *Total Assets:* £4,908,710
*Registered Office:* Dewsbury Mills, Thornhill Road, Dewsbury, W Yorks, WF12 9QE
*Activities:* Manufacture of other furniture
*Parent:* Stevro (Holdings) Limited
*Officers:* Rosemary Elizabeth Durrans, Secretary; Claire Clapham [1973] Finance Director; Roger Edward Durrans [1981] Director/Sales and Marketing; Rosemary Elizabeth Durrans [1959] Director/Justice of The Peace; Stephen Martin Durrans [1959] Director; Liona Claire Ripley [1968] Commercial Director

**Stickyeyes Limited**
*Incorporated:* 10 January 2003
*Net Worth:* £6,937,000 *Total Assets:* £6,937,000
*Registered Office:* West One, 100 Wellington Street, Leeds, LS1 4LT
*Activities:* Other information technology service activities
*Parent:* Mediabrands Limited
*Officers:* Louise Bean, Secretary; Andrew Craig Chalmers [1969] Director; Ian Andrew Courts [1975] Director/Accountant; Thomas Malcolm Howard [1971] Director/Accountant; Craig Lister [1971] Director; Timothy James Treleaven [1977] Director/Accountant

**Stiller Warehousing & Distribution Limited**
*Incorporated:* 27 March 1996 *Employees:* 153
*Net Worth:* £3,454,460 *Total Assets:* £7,204,536
*Registered Office:* Stiller Warehousing, Ridgeway, Aycliffe Business Park, Newton Aycliffe, Co Durham, DL5 6SP
*Activities:* Operation of warehousing and storage facilities for land transport activities
*Major Shareholder:* Paul William Stiller
*Officers:* Andrea Howes, Secretary; Brian Simpson [1968] Operations Director; Gillian Stiller [1959] Director/Accountant; Matthew Paul Stiller [1985] Managing Director; Paul William Stiller [1958] Managing Director

**Stirling Investment Properties LLP**
*Incorporated:* 29 November 2004
*Net Worth Deficit:* £27,095,448 *Total Assets:* £25,892,592
*Registered Office:* Thorp Arch Grange, Walton Road, Thorp Arch, Wetherby, W Yorks, LS23 7BA
*Officers:* David Ian Newett [1959] Member; Jane Elizabeth Newett [1963] Member

**Stirling Properties (Leeds No.2) LLP**
*Incorporated:* 28 June 2005 *Employees:* 3
*Net Worth Deficit:* £10,641,381 *Total Assets:* £3,921,048
*Registered Office:* Thorp Arch Grange, Walton Road, Thorp Arch, Wetherby, W Yorks, LS23 7BA
*Officers:* David Ian Newett [1959] Member; Jane Elizabeth Newett [1963] Member

**Stirling Properties (Leeds No.4) LLP**
*Incorporated:* 16 March 2006
*Net Worth Deficit:* £1,346,258 *Total Assets:* £5,494,491
*Registered Office:* Thorp Arch Grange, Walton Road, Thorp Arch, Wetherby, W Yorks, LS23 7BA
*Officers:* David Ian Newett [1959] Member; Jane Elizabeth Newett [1963] Member

**Stock Redler Limited**
*Incorporated:* 8 October 2003
*Net Worth:* £2,203,000 *Total Assets:* £6,290,000
*Registered Office:* Unit 3 Alpha Court, Capitol Park, Thorne, Doncaster, S Yorks, DN8 5TZ
*Activities:* Manufacture of lifting and handling equipment
*Parent:* Schenck Process UK Holding Limited
*Officers:* Nicholas Jones, Secretary; Richard Geoffrey Ellis [1971] Director; Nicholas Paul Jones [1958] Finance Director

**Stockbridge Technology Centre Limited**
*Incorporated:* 8 March 2001 *Employees:* 33
*Net Worth:* £2,151,036 *Total Assets:* £3,757,252
*Registered Office:* Stockbridge House, Cawood, Selby, N Yorks, YO8 3TZ
*Activities:* Growing of vegetables and melons, roots and tubers
*Parent:* STC Research Foundation Ltd
*Officers:* Graham Philip Ward, Secretary/Manager; Nigel Derek Bartle [1974] Director/General Manager; Michael John Langdale [1961] Operations Director; Graham Philip Ward [1938] Director/Manager

**James Stockdale Limited**
*Incorporated:* 28 February 1955 *Employees:* 51
*Net Worth:* £7,155,360 *Total Assets:* £10,682,791
*Registered Office:* Medina House, 2 Station Avenue, Bridlington, E Yorks, YO16 4LZ
*Activities:* Growing of cereals (except rice), leguminous crops and oil seeds
*Major Shareholder:* James Francis Stockdale
*Officers:* Jason Cockerill, Secretary; Jason Cockerill [1973] Finance Director; James Francis Stockdale [1949] Director/Farm Manager

**Stocks Group Limited**
*Incorporated:* 15 August 2002 *Employees:* 6
*Net Worth:* £2,738,100 *Total Assets:* £3,198,890
*Registered Office:* 18 Woodhouse Road, Scunthorpe, N Lincs, DN16 1BD
*Activities:* Renting and leasing of other machinery, equipment and tangible goods n.e.c.
*Shareholders:* David Stocks; Shirley Margaret Stocks
*Officers:* Anne Margaret Short, Secretary; Christopher James Claypole [1972] Director/Health and Safety Advisor; Anne Margaret Short [1962] Director/Accountant; David Stocks [1951] Director/Engineer; Shirley Margaret Stocks [1950] Director/Admin Manager; Simon David Stocks [1985] Director

**Stockton Drilling Limited**
*Incorporated:* 4 July 2001 *Employees:* 16
*Net Worth:* £250,560 *Total Assets:* £3,844,684
*Registered Office:* Unit 15 Navigation Court, Calder Business Park, Wakefield, W Yorks, WF2 7BJ
*Activities:* Test drilling and boring
*Parent:* Derrynane Holdings Limited
*Officers:* Gearoid O'Connell, Secretary; Fiona Jane O'Connell [1969] Director; Gearoid O'Connell [1970] Director [Irish]

**D. Stoker Group Limited**
*Incorporated:* 31 August 1961 *Employees:* 67
*Net Worth:* £3,477,906 *Total Assets:* £7,775,774
*Registered Office:* 1 Ironworks Road, Barrow in Furness, Cumbria, LA14 2PG
*Activities:* Sale of new cars and light motor vehicles
*Major Shareholder:* Iain Leslie Stoker
*Officers:* Margaret Elizabeth Stoker, Secretary; Iain Leslie Stoker [1954] Managing Director; Margaret Elizabeth Stoker [1955] Director

**Stollers Furniture World Limited**
*Incorporated:* 12 October 1994 *Employees:* 68
*Net Worth:* £3,201,327 *Total Assets:* £5,840,065
*Registered Office:* Walney Road, Barrow in Furness, Cumbria, LA14 5UN
*Activities:* Retail of furniture, lighting, and similar (not musical instruments or scores) in specialised store
*Major Shareholder:* David Stoller
*Officers:* John Robert Crook, Secretary; David Melvyn Stoller [1949] Director/Retail Furnisher; Lee Darrell Stoller [1974] Sales Director

**Stolzle Flaconnage Limited**
*Incorporated:* 30 September 1994 *Employees:* 332
*Net Worth:* £11,207,719 *Total Assets:* £40,760,280
*Registered Office:* Weeland Road, Knottingley, W Yorks, WF11 8AP
*Activities:* Manufacture of hollow glass
*Parent:* Stolzle Oberglas AG
*Officers:* Steven Alan Malpass, Secretary; Thomas Alfons Riss [1970] Director/Chief Executive [German]

**Stoneacre Property Investments Ltd**
*Incorporated:* 21 March 2012 *Employees:* 4
*Net Worth:* £924,501 *Total Assets:* £4,478,092
*Registered Office:* c/o Malcolm Jones & Co LLP, West Hill House, Allerton Hill, Chapel Allerton, Leeds, LS7 3QB
*Activities:* Buying and selling of own real estate
*Shareholders:* Stephen Howard Jacobs; Amanda Louise Jacobs
*Officers:* Stephen Howard Jacobs, Secretary; Amanda Louise Jacobs [1964] Director; Benjamin Louis Jacobs [1988] Director/Property Developer; Joshua Jacobs [1991] Director/Property Developer; Stephen Howard Jacobs [1954] Director/Commodities Dealer

**Stonecroft Holdings Limited**
*Incorporated:* 20 July 2001 *Employees:* 221
*Previous:* Stonecroft Holdings PLC
*Net Worth:* £14,260,000 *Total Assets:* £34,595,000
*Registered Office:* Ladywell Mills, Hall Lane, Bradford, W Yorks, BD4 7DF
*Activities:* Activities of head offices
*Shareholders:* Andrew David Seal; Jeremy Charles Seal
*Officers:* Lucci Dammone [1957] Director/Solicitor; Andrew David Seal [1957] Director; Jeremy Charles Seal [1960] Director; Jayne Stephanie Woodthorpe [1963] Director/Chartered Accountant

**Stoneferry Estates Limited**
*Incorporated:* 15 April 1991
*Net Worth:* £6,934,382 *Total Assets:* £12,629,015
*Registered Office:* 1 Monckton Court, South Newbald Road, North Newbald, E Yorks, YO43 4RW
*Activities:* Other letting and operating of own or leased real estate
*Officers:* Nina Van Beelen, Secretary; Simon Timothy Dixon [1966] Director; Thomas William Healey [1985] Director; Timothy Healey [1958] Director; David Charles Wilbraham [1957] Director

**Stoneferry Limited**
*Incorporated:* 15 August 2011
*Net Worth:* £906,995 *Total Assets:* £8,203,779
*Registered Office:* Witham House, 45 Spyvee Street, Hull, HU8 7JR
*Activities:* Other letting and operating of own or leased real estate
*Officers:* Rory Michael Andrew Clarke [1959] Director; David Charles Evans [1953] Director; Sally Joanna Rix [1965] Director; Timothy John Rix [1963] Director

**Stoneferry Marfleet Limited**
*Incorporated:* 3 December 2007
*Net Worth:* £26,376 *Total Assets:* £5,481,082
*Registered Office:* 1 Monckton Court, South Newbald Road, North Newbald, E Yorks, YO43 4RW
*Activities:* Buying and selling of own real estate
*Officers:* Nina Van Beelen, Secretary; Simon Timothy Dixon [1966] Director; Thomas William Healey [1985] Director; Timothy Healey [1958] Director

**Stonegate Precision Tooling Limited**
*Incorporated:* 8 December 2011 *Employees:* 14
*Net Worth:* £2,139,370 *Total Assets:* £3,128,785
*Registered Office:* Melton House, Wyke Way, Melton, E Yorks, HU14 3HH
*Activities:* Manufacture of tools
*Shareholders:* Graham Hazell; Rebecca Hazell
*Officers:* Carl Hazell [1984] Director/Operational and Sales Manager; Graham Hazell [1963] Director/Business Manager; Damian White [1985] Director

**Stonegrave Aggregates Limited**
*Incorporated:* 27 November 1970 *Employees:* 61
*Net Worth:* £7,202,746 *Total Assets:* £12,979,007
*Registered Office:* Aycliffe Quarry, Aycliffe Village, Co Durham, DL5 6NB
*Activities:* Treatment and disposal of non-hazardous waste
*Major Shareholder:* John Wade
*Officers:* John Wade, Secretary; Paul William Monkhouse [1957] Director/Contracts Manager; John Wade [1943] Director; Bruce David Whitley [1959] Director/Operations Manager

**Stoneledge Plant and Transport Limited**
*Incorporated:* 11 October 1972 *Employees:* 38
*Net Worth:* £1,181,110 *Total Assets:* £4,670,844
*Registered Office:* Station Road, Cottingham, Hull, HU16 4LL
*Activities:* Construction of other civil engineering projects n.e.c.
*Parent:* Stoneledge Holdings Limited
*Officers:* Lee Evans, Secretary; Philip Graham Greenwood [1959] Director; Darren Griffiths [1968] Director

**Stored Value Solutions UK Limited**
*Incorporated:* 25 February 1999 *Employees:* 21
*Net Worth:* £11,653,000 *Total Assets:* £14,857,000
*Registered Office:* Suite 2b, West One, 100 Wellington Street, Leeds, LS1 4LT
*Activities:* Other business support service activities n.e.c.
*Parent:* Stored Value Solutions International, B.V.
*Officers:* Lisa E Peerman [1964] Director/General Counsel [American]; Mark William Vogt [1962] Director/VP, Strategy [American]

**Stores Group Limited**
*Incorporated:* 7 February 1983
*Net Worth:* £264,500,000 *Total Assets:* £1,850,067,968
*Registered Office:* Hilmore House, Gain Lane, Bradford, W Yorks, BD3 7DL
*Activities:* Activities of head offices
*Parent:* Safeway Limited
*Officers:* Jonathan James Burke, Secretary; Jonathan James Burke [1966] Director; Joanna Louise Goff [1978] Finance Director

**The Storey Group Limited**
*Incorporated:* 8 September 1993 *Employees:* 56
*Net Worth:* £599,565 *Total Assets:* £13,510,884
*Registered Office:* 90 Kirkgate, Leeds, LS2 7DJ
*Activities:* Gambling and betting activities
*Major Shareholder:* George Scott Storey
*Officers:* Maureen Ann Hatton, Secretary; Maureen Ann Hatton [1951] Director; George Scott Storey [1964] Commercial Director

**Stork Beta Limited**
*Incorporated:* 3 July 2014 *Employees:* 901
*Net Worth Deficit:* £10,592,000 *Total Assets:* £40,867,000
*Registered Office:* Mamas & Papas, Colne Bridge Road, Huddersfield, W Yorks, HD5 0RH
*Activities:* Other business support service activities n.e.c.
*Parent:* Stork Delta Limited
*Officers:* Jason Robert Curtis, Secretary; Marco Anatriello [1981] Director/Partner [Italian]; Marco Capello [1960] Director/Partner [Italian]; Emilio di Spiezio Sardo [1977] Director [Italian]; Jason Greenwood [1971] Director/Chief Operating Officer; David Scacchetti [1951] Director

**Storth Limited**
*Incorporated:* 16 January 2002 *Employees:* 61
*Net Worth:* £3,922,099 *Total Assets:* £4,828,378
*Registered Office:* Stoneleigh Park, Station Road, Holme, Carnforth, Lancs, LA6 1HR
*Activities:* Manufacture of agricultural and forestry machinery other than tractors
*Shareholders:* Alan Looker; Christopher Richardson
*Officers:* Yvonne Margaret Cooper, Secretary; Alan Looker [1960] Director/Manufacturer; Christopher Richardson [1969] Director/Manufacturer

**Stowe Family Law Finance Limited**
*Incorporated:* 15 December 2016
*Net Worth Deficit:* £2,103,807 *Total Assets:* £27,384,440
*Registered Office:* The Old Court House, Raglan Street, Harrogate, N Yorks, HG1 1LT
*Activities:* Solicitors
*Parent:* Stowe Family Law Holdings Limited
*Officers:* Charles Edward Hartwell [1974] Managing Director; Julian Jack Hawkhead [1975] Director/Solicitor

**Stowe Family Law Holdings Limited**
*Incorporated:* 15 December 2016 *Employees:* 118
*Net Worth Deficit:* £2,399,938 *Total Assets:* £27,304,150
*Registered Office:* The Old Court House, Raglan Street, Harrogate, N Yorks, HG1 1LT
*Activities:* Solicitors
*Shareholders:* Livingbridge 6 LP; Charles Edward Hartwell
*Officers:* Mohammed Akmal Aneese [1985] Director; Charles Edward Hartwell [1974] Managing Director; Julian Jack Hawkhead [1975] Director; Adam Stuart Holloway [1967] Director

**Strachan Furniture Makers Limited**
*Incorporated:* 24 March 1993 *Employees:* 85
*Net Worth:* £1,741,665 *Total Assets:* £3,618,102
*Registered Office:* 2 Dolphin Court, Stanningley Road, Bramley, S Yorks, LS13 4UN
*Activities:* Manufacture of other furniture
*Parent:* Strachan Holdings Limited
*Officers:* Adam James Strachan, Secretary; Adam James Strachan [1968] Managing Director; David George Strachan [1937] Director

**Strachan Holdings Limited**
*Incorporated:* 16 May 2006 *Employees:* 85
*Net Worth:* £5,447,118 *Total Assets:* £7,747,093
*Registered Office:* 2 Dolphin Court, Stanningley Road, Leeds, LS13 4UN
*Activities:* Activities of head offices
*Shareholders:* Adam James Strachan; David George Strachan
*Officers:* Adam James Strachan, Secretary; Adam James Strachan [1968] Managing Director; David George Strachan [1937] Director

**Straight Limited**
*Incorporated:* 26 April 1994 *Employees:* 6
*Net Worth Deficit:* £4,388,000 *Total Assets:* £4,074,000
*Registered Office:* Straight Ltd, Somerden Road, Hull, HU9 5PE
*Activities:* Manufacture of other plastic products
*Officers:* Christian Marcoux, Secretary; Patrick Dalton [1965] Director/Company Executive [Irish]; Alan Walsh [1976] Director/Company Executive [Irish]

**Straight Manufacturing Limited**
*Incorporated:* 1 March 1982 *Employees:* 70
*Net Worth:* £7,190,000 *Total Assets:* £20,969,000
*Registered Office:* Straight Ltd, Somerden Road, Hull, HU9 5PE
*Activities:* Manufacture of other plastic products
*Parent:* Straight Limited
*Officers:* Christian Marcoux, Secretary; Patrick Dalton [1965] Director/Company Executive [Irish]; Alan Walsh [1976] Director/Company Executive [Irish]

**Strainstall Group Limited**
*Incorporated:* 21 July 2000
*Net Worth:* £2,180,883 *Total Assets:* £22,776,506
*Registered Office:* P O Box 4, Fisher House, Barrow in Furness, Cumbria, LA14 1HR
*Activities:* Activities of head offices
*Parent:* James Fisher and Sons Public Limited Company
*Officers:* James Henry John Marsh, Secretary; Nicholas Paul Henry [1961] Director; Stuart Charles Kilpatrick [1962] Director

**Strainstall UK Limited**
*Incorporated:* 28 July 2000 *Employees:* 77
*Net Worth:* £813,284 *Total Assets:* £6,307,703
*Registered Office:* P O Box 4, Fisher House, Barrow in Furness, Cumbria, LA14 1HR
*Activities:* Manufacture of electronic measuring, testing etc. equipment, not for industrial process control
*Parent:* Strainstall Group Limited
*Officers:* James Henry John Marsh, Secretary; Adrian Coventry [1967] Director; Simon Anthony Richard Everett [1977] Director; Nicholas Paul Henry [1961] Director; Stuart Charles Kilpatrick [1962] Finance Director

**Stramongate Properties Limited**
*Incorporated:* 21 June 1984
*Net Worth:* £4,148,733 *Total Assets:* £6,147,928
*Registered Office:* Tanners House, Gulfs Road, Kendal, Cumbria, LA9 4DT
*Activities:* Development of building projects
*Shareholders:* Gillian Rosemary Chesham; Paul Anthony Chesham; Andrew Charles Peill; Maria Anna Amelia Peill
*Officers:* Gillian Rosemary Chesham, Secretary; Gillian Rosemary Chesham [1955] Director; Paul Anthony Chesham [1952] Director/Chartered Surveyor; Andrew Charles Peill [1950] Director/Chartered Surveyor; Maria Anna Amelia Peill [1952] Director

**Strand Paper Northern Limited**
*Incorporated:* 20 March 1989 *Employees:* 10
*Net Worth:* £716,581 *Total Assets:* £3,746,470
*Registered Office:* 12 Westgate, Baildon, Shipley, W Yorks, BD17 5EJ
*Activities:* Wholesale of other intermediate products
*Shareholders:* Charles Julian Platts Jackson; Aina Nelija Jackson
*Officers:* Aina Nelija Jackson, Secretary; Charles Julian Platts Jackson [1956] Director

**Strata Holdings Limited**
*Incorporated:* 1 December 1998 *Employees:* 12
*Net Worth:* £2,408,728 *Total Assets:* £3,849,671
*Registered Office:* Strata House, 300 Hawthorn Avenue, Hull, HU3 5LL
*Activities:* Other manufacturing n.e.c.
*Shareholders:* Graham Edward Fisher; Anthony Richard Schultz
*Officers:* Anthony Richard Schultz, Secretary/Director; Graham Edward Fisher [1963] Director; Ian Michael Jones [1964] Managing Director; Anthony Richard Schultz [1965] Director

**Strata Homes Holdings Limited**
*Incorporated:* 18 July 2014 *Employees:* 191
*Net Worth:* £54,975,000 *Total Assets:* £121,086,000
*Registered Office:* Quay Point, Lakeside Boulevard, Doncaster, S Yorks, DN4 5PL
*Activities:* Activities of head offices
*Shareholders:* Andrew Richard Weaver; Richard Irving Weaver
*Officers:* Julian Nigel Davis, Secretary; Helen Jayne Browne [1975] Director; Julian Nigel Davis [1975] Finance Director; Andrew Richard Weaver [1973] Director; Dorothy Weaver [1950] Director; Richard Irving Weaver [1949] Director/Company Chairman; Simon Daniel Weaver [1977] Director

**Strata Homes Limited**
*Incorporated:* 23 March 1983 *Employees:* 191
*Net Worth:* £54,634,000 *Total Assets:* £121,086,000
*Registered Office:* Quay Point, Lakeside Boulevard, Doncaster, S Yorks, DN4 5PL
*Activities:* Construction of domestic buildings
*Officers:* Julian Nigel Davis, Secretary; Julian Nigel Davis [1975] Finance Director; Andrew Richard Weaver [1973] Director; Richard Irving Weaver [1949] Director

**Strata Homes Midlands Limited**
*Incorporated:* 23 November 2001 *Employees:* 8
*Net Worth:* £5,636,000 *Total Assets:* £6,783,000
*Registered Office:* Quay Point, Lakeside Boulevard, Doncaster, S Yorks, DN4 5PL
*Activities:* Construction of domestic buildings
*Parent:* Strata Homes Limited
*Officers:* Julian Nigel Davis, Secretary; Vernon Joseph Cunningham [1967] Director/Construction; Julian Nigel Davis [1975] Finance Director; Paul Dean Robinson [1964] Director; Nigel Robson [1973] Director; Gemma Smith [1984] Director; Andrew Richard Weaver [1973] Director; Richard Irving Weaver [1949] Director

**Strata Homes Yorkshire Limited**
*Incorporated:* 10 November 1981 *Employees:* 153
*Net Worth:* £46,797,000 *Total Assets:* £132,049,000
*Registered Office:* Quay Point, Lakeside Boulevard, Doncaster, S Yorks, DN4 5PL
*Activities:* Construction of domestic buildings
*Parent:* Strata Homes Limited
*Officers:* Julian Nigel Davis, Secretary; Vernon Joseph Cunningham [1967] Director; Julian Nigel Davis [1975] Finance Director; Paul Dean Robinson [1964] Director; Nigel Robson [1973] Director; Gemma Smith [1984] Director; Andrew Richard Weaver [1973] Director; Richard Irving Weaver [1949] Director

**Strategic Team Group Limited**
*Incorporated:* 26 November 2007 *Employees:* 146
*Net Worth:* £3,249,963 *Total Assets:* £19,079,550
*Registered Office:* Strategic Business Centre, Blue Ridge Park, Thunderhead Ridge, Glasshoughton, Castleford, W Yorks, WF10 4UA
*Activities:* Construction of commercial buildings
*Officers:* Charles Nicholas Tweed, Secretary; Simon Mark Ashton [1960] Director; Andrew Martin Coates [1971] Construction Director; Simon Lazenby [1975] Director/Accountant; Gary Taylor [1968] Director; Andrew Roger Watson [1969] Director

**Strategic Team Maintenance.Co. Limited**
*Incorporated:* 30 December 1999 *Employees:* 141
*Net Worth Deficit:* £1,276,961 *Total Assets:* £14,536,613
*Registered Office:* Strategic Business Centre, Blue Ridge Park, Thunderhead Ridge, Glasshoughton, Castleford, W Yorks, WF10 4UA
*Activities:* Development of building projects
*Parent:* Strategic Team Group Limited
*Officers:* Andrew Charles Poyner, Secretary; Andrew Martin Coates [1971] Director; Andrew Charles Poyner [1978] Director/Lawyer; Gary Taylor [1968] Director; Andrew Roger Watson [1969] Director

**Stratex Warehouse Ltd**
*Incorporated:* 14 December 2016
*Net Worth:* £3,481,597 *Total Assets:* £3,665,653
*Registered Office:* Unit 35a Lake Enterprise Park, Bergen Way, Hull, HU7 0YQ
*Activities:* Non-specialised wholesale trade
*Major Shareholder:* William Dale
*Officers:* William Dale, Secretary; William Dale [1968] Director

**W. H. Strawson (Farms) Limited**
*Incorporated:* 7 March 1968 *Employees:* 10
*Net Worth:* £9,399,402 *Total Assets:* £10,094,875
*Registered Office:* Broughton Grange, Wressle, Brigg, N Lincs, DN20 0BJ
*Activities:* Growing of cereals (except rice), leguminous crops and oil seeds
*Parent:* W.H. Strawson (Farms) Holdings Limited
*Officers:* Andrew Clive Severn [1959] Director/Accountant; William Robert Strawson [1965] Director/Farmer; Winifred Lucy Strawson [1931] Director

**M.F. Strawson (Maidenwell) Limited**
*Incorporated:* 27 November 1990 *Employees:* 7
*Net Worth:* £5,322,700 *Total Assets:* £5,954,116
*Registered Office:* Pyewipe Farm, Aylesby Road, Great Coates, Grimsby, N E Lincs, DN37 9NU
*Activities:* Growing of cereals (except rice), leguminous crops and oil seeds
*Shareholder:* Michael Field Strawson
*Officers:* Paulyn Elizabeth Strawson, Secretary; Michael Field Strawson [1936] Director/Farmer; Niel Andrew Strawson [1964] Director/Chartered Accountant; Paul David Field Strawson [1960] Director/Farmer; Paulyn Elizabeth Strawson [1938] Director; Timothy Michael Strawson [1961] Director

**W. H. Strawson (Notts.) Limited**
*Incorporated:* 7 March 1968 *Employees:* 2
*Net Worth:* £5,592,048 *Total Assets:* £10,272,617
*Registered Office:* The Farm Office, Blyborough Hall, Blyborough, Gainsborough, Lincs, DN21 4HB
*Activities:* Growing of cereals (except rice), leguminous crops and oil seeds
*Parent:* W.H. Strawson (Notts.) Holdings Limited
*Officers:* Andrew Clive Severn [1959] Director/Accountant; Richard Henry Strawson [1966] Director/Farmer; Sophie Strawson [1971] Director

**Strawson Group Developments Limited**
*Incorporated:* 21 February 2008 *Employees:* 14
*Net Worth:* £13,485,780 *Total Assets:* £38,001,176
*Registered Office:* Manor House Farm, East Drayton, Retford, Notts, DN22 0LG
*Activities:* Buying and selling of own real estate
*Major Shareholder:* George David Strawson
*Officers:* James Watson Eyre Wild, Secretary; Elizabeth Anne Bisson [1963] Director/Land Agent; George David Strawson [1937] Director/Farmer

**Strawson Group Investments Limited**
*Incorporated:* 21 February 2008
*Net Worth:* £37,173,000 *Total Assets:* £43,045,000
*Registered Office:* Manor House Farm, East Drayton, Retford, Notts, DN22 0LG
*Activities:* Other letting and operating of own or leased real estate
*Major Shareholder:* George David Strawson
*Officers:* James Watson Eyre Wild, Secretary; Elizabeth Anne Bisson [1963] Director/Land Agent; George David Strawson [1937] Director/Farmer

**Strawson Holdings Limited**
*Incorporated:* 29 September 1981 *Employees:* 16
*Net Worth:* £839,000 *Total Assets:* £22,640,000
*Registered Office:* Manor House Farm, East Drayton, Retford, Notts, DN22 0LG
*Activities:* Buying and selling of own real estate
*Parent:* Strawson Group Developments Limited
*Officers:* James Watson Eyre Wild, Secretary; Elizabeth Anne Bisson [1963] Director/Land Agent; George David Strawson [1937] Director/Farmer

**Strawson Investments Limited**
*Incorporated:* 5 October 2001
*Net Worth:* £5,610,000 *Total Assets:* £10,025,000
*Registered Office:* Manor House Farm, East Drayton, Retford, Notts, DN22 0LG
*Activities:* Other letting and operating of own or leased real estate
*Parent:* Strawson Group Investments Limited
*Officers:* James Watson Eyre Wild, Secretary; Elizabeth Anne Bisson [1963] Director; George David Strawson [1937] Director

**M.F. Strawson Limited**
*Incorporated:* 8 November 1957 *Employees:* 41
*Net Worth:* £17,675,540 *Total Assets:* £23,718,104
*Registered Office:* Pyewipe Farm, Aylesby Road, Great Coates, Grimsby, N E Lincs, DN37 9NU
*Activities:* Growing of cereals (except rice), leguminous crops and oil seeds
*Shareholders:* Niel Andrew Strawson; Paul David Field Strawson
*Officers:* Niel Andrew Strawson, Secretary; Niel Andrew Strawson [1964] Director/Chartered Accountant; Paul David Field Strawson [1960] Director/Farmer

**Peter Strawson Limited**
*Incorporated:* 29 November 1962 *Employees:* 11
*Net Worth:* £1,977,092 *Total Assets:* £4,536,550
*Registered Office:* East Ravendale Farm, East Ravendale, Grimsby, N E Lincs, DN37 0RX
*Activities:* Growing of cereals (except rice), leguminous crops and oil seeds
*Major Shareholder:* George Peter Strawson
*Officers:* Catherine Emma Pearce [1966] Director/Chartered Surveyor; George Peter Strawson [1941] Director/Farmer; Pauline Elizabeth Strawson [1947] Director/Contractor; Roderick Peter Strawson [1973] Director/Ecologist/Forester

**Strawson Management Limited**
*Incorporated:* 2 July 1997 *Employees:* 4
*Net Worth:* £28,790,000 *Total Assets:* £29,667,000
*Registered Office:* Manor House Farm, East Drayton, Retford, Notts, DN22 0LG
*Activities:* Other letting and operating of own or leased real estate
*Parent:* Strawson Group Investments Limited
*Officers:* James Watson Eyre Wild, Secretary; Elizabeth Anne Bisson [1963] Director; George David Strawson [1937] Director

**Streejaane**
*Incorporated:* 17 December 2010
*Previous:* Streejaane Ltd
*Net Worth:* £20,754,384 *Total Assets:* £21,316,900
*Registered Office:* 3365 Century Way, Thorpe Park, Leeds, LS15 8ZB
*Activities:* Activities auxiliary to financial intermediation n.e.c.
*Major Shareholder:* Teresa Jane Grant
*Officers:* Christopher Darwin, Secretary; Christopher James Darwin [1971] Director; Teresa Jane Grant [1960] Director; Timothy William Johnson [1965] Director

**Street Clothes Limited**
*Incorporated:* 23 October 1979 *Employees:* 2
*Net Worth:* £2,847,266 *Total Assets:* £3,270,248
*Registered Office:* Duncan Chambers, 9 Duncan Street, Leeds, LS1 6DQ
*Activities:* Retail sale of clothing in specialised stores
*Shareholders:* Susan Anne Newell; Jeremy Alexander Thompson
*Officers:* Susan Anne Newell, Secretary; Susan Anne Newell [1953] Administrative Director; Jeremy Alexander Thompson [1952] Sales Director

**Stroma Building Control Limited**
*Incorporated:* 16 February 2001 *Employees:* 73
*Previous:* BBS Building Control Limited
*Net Worth:* £2,696,808 *Total Assets:* £5,148,377
*Registered Office:* Unit 4 Pioneer Way, Pioneer Business Park, Castleford, W Yorks, WF10 5QU
*Activities:* Other engineering activities
*Shareholder:* LDC III LP
*Officers:* Steven Lonsdale [1974] Director; Ian O'Connor [1986] Director/Financial Controller

**Stroma Certification Limited**
*Incorporated:* 16 November 2007 *Employees:* 71
*Net Worth:* £4,325,696 *Total Assets:* £5,142,614
*Registered Office:* Unit 4 Pioneer Way, Pioneer Business Park, Castleford, W Yorks, WF10 5QU
*Activities:* Activities of professional membership organisations
*Shareholder:* LDC III LP
*Officers:* Neil James Bleakley [1974] Technical Director; Richard John Dean [1972] Director; Matthew John Ferguson [1971] Director; Martin John Holt [1965] Director; Stephen Horrocks [1983] Director

**Stroma Developments Limited**
*Incorporated:* 12 October 2004 *Employees:* 348
*Net Worth:* £10,929,200 *Total Assets:* £20,115,224
*Registered Office:* Unit 4 Pioneer Way, Pioneer Business Park, Castleford, W Yorks, WF10 5QU
*Activities:* Activities of head offices
*Shareholder:* LDC III LP
*Officers:* Richard John Dean [1972] Director; Martin John Holt [1965] Director

**Stroma Group Limited**
*Incorporated:* 26 March 2014 *Employees:* 353
*Net Worth:* £7,834,498 *Total Assets:* £44,713,036
*Registered Office:* Unit 4 Pioneer Way, Castleford, W Yorks, WF10 5QU
*Activities:* Activities of head offices
*Shareholder:* LDC III LP
*Officers:* Jonathan Scott Bell [1974] Director; Neil Bleakley [1974] Director; Richard John Dean [1972] Director; Martin John Holt [1965] Director; Stephen Horrocks [1983] Director; Andrew David John McEwan [1966] Director

**Stroma Holdings Limited**
*Incorporated:* 18 March 2014
*Net Worth:* £28,999,896 *Total Assets:* £31,600,000
*Registered Office:* Unit 4 Pioneer Way, Castleford, W Yorks, WF10 5QU
*Activities:* Activities of head offices
*Shareholder:* LDC III LP
*Officers:* Richard John Dean [1972] Director; Martin John Holt [1965] Director

**Strong Developments Limited**
*Incorporated:* 6 February 2009
*Net Worth:* £374,273 *Total Assets:* £4,532,970
*Registered Office:* Carnforth Business Park, Oakwood Way, Carnforth, Lancs, LA5 9FD
*Activities:* Other business support service activities n.e.c.
*Shareholders:* Elizabeth Janette Whiley; Oliver Muckle Whiley
*Officers:* Elizabeth Janette Whiley [1956] Director; Oliver Muckle Whiley [1955] Director

**Strong Life Care Limited**
*Incorporated:* 26 January 2010 *Employees:* 165
*Net Worth:* £1,118,049 *Total Assets:* £6,664,062
*Registered Office:* 11 Patch Wood View, Newmillerdam, Wakefield, W Yorks, WF2 6TU
*Activities:* Residential care activities for the elderly and disabled
*Officers:* Harpreet Singh Banwait, Secretary; Harpreet Singh Banwait [1982] Managing Director

**C F Struthers (Holdings) Limited**
*Incorporated:* 3 March 2009 *Employees:* 81
*Net Worth:* £3,078,306 *Total Assets:* £5,902,560
*Registered Office:* Millennium Works, Valletta Street, Hedon Road, Hull, HU9 5NP
*Activities:* Activities of head offices
*Major Shareholder:* Neil Burton
*Officers:* Martin John Graves, Secretary; Neil Burton [1959] Director

**C.F.Struthers Limited**
*Incorporated:* 5 February 1932 *Employees:* 81
*Net Worth:* £6,323,466 *Total Assets:* £9,145,919
*Registered Office:* Millennium Works, Valletta Street, Hull, HU9 5NP
*Activities:* Manufacture of metal structures and parts of structures
*Major Shareholder:* Neil Burton
*Officers:* Martin John Graves, Secretary; Neil Burton [1958] Director

**The John Strutt Conservation Foundation**
*Incorporated:* 18 November 2010 *Employees:* 1
*Net Worth:* £4,853,006 *Total Assets:* £4,910,639
*Registered Office:* John G Hills FRICS, Estate Office, Leyburn, N Yorks, DL8 5EW
*Activities:* Non-trading company
*Officers:* Christine Mary Berry [1959] Director; Sarah Caroline Bradley [1943] Director/Retired; Robert William Dunning [1948] Director; James Simon Radford Elliott [1945] Director/Retired Chartered Surveyor; Edward Anthony Hewetson [1976] Director; Sir Martin Wyatt Holdgate [1931] Director/Retired Civil Servant; Christopher Metcalfe-Gibson [1942] Director; Doctor Stephen David Ward [1943] Director; Peter Welsh [1952] Director/Ecologist

**F.C. Stubbings & Sons Limited**
*Incorporated:* 25 February 1957
*Net Worth:* £6,130,015 *Total Assets:* £8,180,507
*Registered Office:* Northwood Farm, Boynton, Bridlington, E Yorks, YO16 4XN
*Activities:* Growing of cereals (except rice), leguminous crops and oil seeds
*Shareholders:* Richard Nicholas Stubbings; William Anthony Stubbings
*Officers:* Richard Nicholas Stubbings, Secretary; Richard Nicholas Stubbings [1941] Director/Farmer; William Anthony Stubbings [1944] Director/Farmer

**Student Accommodation Provision LLP**
*Incorporated:* 25 June 2010
*Net Worth:* £12,539,741 *Total Assets:* £37,136,236
*Registered Office:* Millshaw, Ring Road, Leeds, LS11 8EG

**Student Accommodation Provision Three LLP**
*Incorporated:* 30 January 2013
*Net Worth:* £16,996,624 *Total Assets:* £46,114,016
*Registered Office:* University of York, Heslington, York, YO10 5DD

**Student Loans Company Limited**
*Incorporated:* 5 July 1989 *Employees:* 181
*Net Worth Deficit:* £28,240,000 *Total Assets:* £144,728,992
*Registered Office:* Memphis Building, Lingfield Point, McMullen Road, Darlington, Co Durham, DL1 1RW
*Activities:* Other credit granting n.e.c.
*Parent:* Secretary of State for Education
*Officers:* Gary Stuart Womersley, Secretary; Christian Norman Brodie [1957] Director/Banker; Antonia Mary Cox [1963] Director/Councillor; Mary Elizabeth Curnock Cook [1958] Director; Simon Peter Devonshire [1967] Director; Natalie Cecilia Elphicke [1970] Director/Chief Executive; David Peter Anthony Gravells [1949] Director; Jacqueline Smillie [1965] Director/Chief Financial Officer; Paula Elizabeth Sussex [1964] Director/Chief Executive; Professor Andrew Brian Wathey [1958] Director/Chief Executive

**Stuncroft Limited**
*Incorporated:* 6 October 2003 *Employees:* 23
*Net Worth:* £2,577,626 *Total Assets:* £5,937,721
*Registered Office:* Unit 2-3 Island Drive, Thorne, Doncaster, S Yorks, DN8 5UE
*Activities:* Wholesale of clothing and footwear
*Major Shareholder:* Cornelia Long
*Officers:* Douglas Mark Bailey [1960] Managing Director

**Sty.Com Limited**
*Incorporated:* 23 October 2000 *Employees:* 48
*Net Worth:* £1,106,317 *Total Assets:* £3,039,501
*Registered Office:* Richmond Court, Morton Road, Darlington, Co Durham, DL1 4PT
*Activities:* Retail sale via mail order houses or via Internet
*Shareholders:* Sabena Al Badr; Haya Al Badr
*Officers:* Kevin Iceton, Secretary; Colin William Eglington [1951] Director/Manager; Margaret Eglington [1953] Purchasing and Operations Director; Kevin Iceton [1973] Director/Accountant; Simon Martin [1966] Director; Michael John Wood [1950] Director/Solicitor

**Style Group Holdings Limited**
*Incorporated:* 5 April 2005
*Net Worth:* £12,250,000 *Total Assets:* £30,555,000
*Registered Office:* Style House, 14 Eldon Place, Bradford, W Yorks, BD1 3AZ
*Activities:* Activities of head offices
*Officers:* Richard Kenneth Short, Secretary; Mike Gallacher [1966] Director; Rob James Neale [1978] Director

**Style Group UK Limited**
*Incorporated:* 25 February 2000 *Employees:* 6
*Net Worth:* £3,058,000 *Total Assets:* £19,416,000
*Registered Office:* Style House, 14 Eldon Place, Bradford, BD1 3AZ
*Activities:* Activities of head offices
*Parent:* Style Group Holdings Ltd
*Officers:* Richard Kenneth Short, Secretary; Mike Gallacher [1966] Director; Rob James Neale [1978] Director

**Styrene Packaging & Insulation Limited**
*Incorporated:* 16 March 1984 *Employees:* 124
*Net Worth:* £5,410,780 *Total Assets:* £18,410,504
*Registered Office:* Morley Carr Road, Low Moor, Bradford, W Yorks, BD12 0RA
*Activities:* Other manufacturing n.e.c.
*Officers:* Maria Edge, Secretary; Joseph William Edge [1981] Director; Maria Edge [1955] Director/Secretary; Michael Edge [1952] Director/Engineer; Paul Edge [1955] Director/Engineer

**Subsea Innovation Limited**
*Incorporated:* 5 October 1995 *Employees:* 24
*Net Worth:* £934,128 *Total Assets:* £4,863,847
*Registered Office:* Innovation House, Centurion Way, Darlington, Co Durham, DL3 0UP
*Activities:* Manufacture of other special-purpose machinery n.e.c.
*Parent:* Tekmar Group PLC
*Officers:* Susan Ann Hurst [1966] Finance Director; Alasdair MacDonald [1965] Director; James Thomas Ritchie-Bland [1990] Director; David Andrew Thompson [1970] Technical Director

**Wm Sugden & Sons Limited**
*Incorporated:* 2 November 1954 *Employees:* 50
*Net Worth:* £186,476 *Total Assets:* £4,235,324
*Registered Office:* P O Box 1, Thornes Lane Wharf, Wakefield, W Yorks, WF1 5RQ
*Activities:* Manufacture of workwear
*Parent:* Wakefield Shirt Company Ltd
*Officers:* Simon Anthony Balaam, Secretary; Richard John Donner [1967] Director; Richard John Donner [1939] Director

**Sukho Limited**
*Incorporated:* 24 March 2003 *Employees:* 263
*Net Worth:* £4,673,384 *Total Assets:* £6,249,959
*Registered Office:* 8 Regent Street, Chapel Allerton, Leeds, LS7 4PE
*Activities:* Licenced restaurants
*Shareholders:* Yupha Kaewkraikhot; Gerrard Michael Marks
*Officers:* Gerrard Michael Marks, Secretary/Restaurateur; Yupha Kaewkraikhot [1968] Director/Restaurateur [British/Thai]; Gerrard Michael Marks [1969] Director/Restaurateur

**Richard Sullivan Consulting Ltd**
*Incorporated:* 16 October 2000
*Net Worth:* £1,590,218 *Total Assets:* £3,394,544
*Registered Office:* 34 Park Cross Street, Leeds, LS1 2QH
*Activities:* Information technology consultancy activities
*Major Shareholder:* Richard John Sullivan
*Officers:* Dr Frederick Donald Sullivan, Secretary; Richard John Sullivan [1968] Director

**Sullivan Homes Limited**
*Incorporated:* 17 March 1997 *Employees:* 2
*Previous:* Sullivan Homes
*Net Worth:* £1,858,373 *Total Assets:* £3,506,058
*Registered Office:* 5th Floor, Central Square, 29 Wellington Street, Leeds, LS1 4DL
*Activities:* Development of building projects
*Major Shareholder:* Andrew Peter Thomas Sullivan
*Officers:* Andrew Peter Thomas Sullivan, Secretary/Director; Andrew Peter Thomas Sullivan [1960] Director; Elizabeth Ivy Maureen Sullivan [1929] Director

**Sullivan Student Properties Limited**
*Incorporated:* 21 January 2011 *Employees:* 2
*Net Worth:* £1,027,149 *Total Assets:* £5,873,082
*Registered Office:* 5th Floor, Central Square, 29 Wellington Street, Leeds, LS1 4DL
*Activities:* Management of real estate on a fee or contract basis
*Shareholders:* Amanda Sullivan; Andrew Peter Thomas Sullivan
*Officers:* Amanda Sullivan [1959] Director/Interior Designer; Andrew Peter Thomas Sullivan [1960] Director

**Sulzer (UK) Holdings Limited**
*Incorporated:* 8 April 1997 *Employees:* 9
*Net Worth Deficit:* £52,008,000 *Total Assets:* £206,959,008
*Registered Office:* Manor Mill Lane, Leeds, LS11 8BR
*Activities:* Other business support service activities n.e.c.
*Parent:* Sulzer AG
*Officers:* Jacqueline Ann Bonas, Secretary; Naveed Hussain [1978] Finance Director; Holger Hans-Jochen Ruckstuhl [1970] Director/Head Group Tax and Holdings [Swiss]; Thomas Dieter Zickler [1966] Director/Head of Group Treasury [German]

**Sulzer Chemtech (UK) Limited**
*Incorporated:* 9 December 1994 *Employees:* 102
*Net Worth Deficit:* £27,800,000 *Total Assets:* £38,804,000
*Registered Office:* Manor Mill Lane, Leeds, LS11 8BR
*Activities:* Installation of industrial machinery and equipment
*Parent:* Sulzer (UK) Holdings Ltd
*Officers:* Jon Glyn Bailey [1971] Director/Senior Vice President Tower Field Service; Naveed Hussain [1978] Finance Director; Jonathan Marley [1972] Director/Head Tower Field Service Division

**Sulzer Pumps (UK) Limited**
*Incorporated:* 4 November 1986 *Employees:* 511
*Net Worth:* £18,282,000 *Total Assets:* £104,992,000
*Registered Office:* Manor Mill Lane, Leeds, LS11 8BR
*Activities:* Manufacture of pumps
*Parent:* Sulzer (UK) Holdings Ltd
*Officers:* Robert John Greenhalf, Secretary; Philippe Andreas Dewitz [1972] Director/Vice President Finance Business Unit EMEA [Swiss]; Naveed Hussain [1978] Finance Director; Andrew James Percy [1971] Director

**Sumo UK Ltd.**
*Incorporated:* 30 October 1996 *Employees:* 35
*Net Worth:* £830,147 *Total Assets:* £5,383,055
*Registered Office:* Redgates, Melbourne, York, YO42 4RG
*Activities:* Manufacture of agricultural and forestry machinery other than tractors
*Parent:* Elsham Wold Estates Limited
*Officers:* Steven English [1961] Director; Simon David Herring [1964] Managing Director; James Timothy Sweeting [1969] Director

**Sun Branding Solutions Ltd**
*Incorporated:* 9 March 1966 *Employees:* 250
*Net Worth:* £11,864,073 *Total Assets:* £18,314,132
*Registered Office:* Albion Mills, Albion Road, Bradford, W Yorks, BD10 9TQ
*Activities:* Other business support service activities n.e.c.
*Parent:* ECG Holdings (UK) Ltd
*Officers:* Margaret Julia Pearce, Secretary; Paul Richard Bean [1960] Director/Business Manager; Charles Allen Heynes [1958] Finance Director; Martjin Jan Charles Marie Schoonenberg [1977] Director/General Counsel [Dutch]

**D & MA Sunderland & Son Limited**
*Incorporated:* 12 November 1998 *Employees:* 3
*Net Worth:* £2,551,246 *Total Assets:* £3,993,593
*Registered Office:* 3 Greengate, Cardale Park, Harrogate, N Yorks, HG3 1GY
*Activities:* Freight transport by road
*Shareholders:* Clare Sunderland; David Sunderland
*Officers:* Clare Sunderland, Secretary/Director; Clare Sunderland [1970] Director; David Sunderland [1964] Director/Property Developer

**Sundown Pets Garden Limited**
*Incorporated:* 2 April 1985 *Employees:* 82
*Net Worth:* £5,394,274 *Total Assets:* £6,651,747
*Registered Office:* Treswell Road, Rampton, Retford, Notts, DN22 0HX
*Activities:* Other amusement and recreation activities n.e.c.
*Major Shareholder:* Audrey Betty Rhodes
*Officers:* Audrey Rhodes, Secretary; Gaynor Susan Corr [1966] Director; Audrey Rhodes [1929] Director

**Sunflower Medical Limited**
*Incorporated:* 19 August 2002
*Net Worth:* £1,114,081 *Total Assets:* £3,135,698
*Registered Office:* Unit 17 Roydsdale Way, Euroway Trading Estate, Bradford, W Yorks, BD4 6SE
*Activities:* Manufacture of other furniture
*Parent:* ESI Process UK Ltd
*Officers:* Marc Darren Byrnes, Secretary/Manufacturing; Kelly Louise Burkitt [1986] Director/Financial Controller; Marc Darren Byrnes [1970] Director/Manufacturing; Ralph Scott Rhodes [1970] Director; Peter Ian Rowlands [1968] Director/Senior Vice President UK

**Sunny Day Capital Limited**
*Incorporated:* 30 March 2010
*Net Worth:* £4,966,000 *Total Assets:* £17,923,000
*Registered Office:* Europa House, 20 Esplanade, Scarborough, N Yorks, YO11 2AQ
*Activities:* Activities of other holding companies n.e.c.
*Shareholder:* Stephen Paul McBride
*Officers:* Stephen Paul McBride [1957] Director; Didier Michel Tandy [1959] Director/Chartered Surveyor

**Sunny Day Property Holdings Limited**
*Incorporated:* 10 December 2008
*Net Worth:* £5,856,497 *Total Assets:* £7,760,491
*Registered Office:* Europa House, 20 Esplanade, Scarborough, N Yorks, YO11 2AQ
*Activities:* Activities of other holding companies n.e.c.
*Major Shareholder:* Didier Michel Tandy
*Officers:* Stephen Paul McBride [1957] Finance Director; Didier Michel Tandy [1959] Director/Chartered Surveyor

**Sunny Day Property Limited**
*Incorporated:* 10 December 2008
*Net Worth:* £167,628 *Total Assets:* £11,299,793
*Registered Office:* Europa House, 20 Esplanade, Scarborough, N Yorks, YO11 2AQ
*Activities:* Activities of other holding companies n.e.c.
*Officers:* Stephen Paul McBride [1957] Finance Director; Didier Michel Tandy [1959] Director/Chartered Surveyor

**Sunny Day Trading**
*Incorporated:* 29 July 1999
*Net Worth:* £4,842,154 *Total Assets:* £17,243,936
*Registered Office:* Europa House, 20 Esplanade, Scarborough, N Yorks, YO11 2AQ
*Activities:* Buying and selling of own real estate
*Officers:* Stephen Paul McBride [1957] Finance Director; Didier Michel Tandy [1959] Director/Chartered Surveyor

**Supagard Limited**
*Incorporated:* 26 October 1987 *Employees:* 35
*Net Worth:* £1,530,465 *Total Assets:* £4,812,167
*Registered Office:* Elizabeth House, 13-19 Queen Street, Leeds, LS1 2TW
*Activities:* Agents specialised in the sale of other particular products
*Major Shareholder:* Jean Quinn
*Officers:* Alison Abbott [1971] Director; David Lawrence Paterson [1979] Director; Pauline Paterson [1978] Director; Jean Quinn [1948] Director; Sandra Quinn [1973] Director; James Patrick Smyth [1969] Director

**Super League (Europe) Limited**
*Incorporated:* 12 August 1996
*Net Worth:* £1,282 *Total Assets:* £7,750,949
*Registered Office:* Red Hall, Red Hall Lane, Leeds, LS17 8NB
*Activities:* Other sports activities
*Officers:* Karen Elizabeth Moorhouse, Secretary; Brian Robert Barwick [1954] Director; Ian Donald Blease [1965] Director; Michael Frank Carter [1968] Director; Kenneth Ernest Davy [1941] Director; Karl Fitzpatrick [1980] Director; James Ian Fulton [1961] Director; Gary Hetherington [1954] Director; Neil Michael Hudgell [1966] Director; David John Hughes [1945] Director/Retired and Club Chairman; Ian Francis Lenagan [1946] Director; Eamonn McManus [1956] Director; Adam Faulkner Pearson [1964] Director; Niel Robert Wood [1958] Director

**Superbreak Mini Holidays Group Limited**
*Incorporated:* 11 May 1990 *Employees:* 6
*Net Worth:* £9,408,000 *Total Assets:* £16,794,000
*Registered Office:* Eboracum Way, Heworth Green, York, YO31 7RE
*Activities:* Activities of head offices
*Parent:* Malvern Travel Limited
*Officers:* Abhishek Goenka [1979] Director/General Manager [Indian]; Ajay Ajit Peter Kerkar [1963] Director [Indian]; Hugo Charles Kimber [1964] Director/Executive Chairman; John Daniel McLaughlin [1978] Director/Group Finance Head

**Superbreak Mini-Holidays Limited**
*Incorporated:* 1 November 1982 *Employees:* 177
*Net Worth:* £17,119,728 *Total Assets:* £34,089,096
*Registered Office:* Eboracum Way, Heworth Green, York, YO31 7RE
*Activities:* Travel agency activities
*Parent:* Superbreak Mini Holidays Group Limited
*Officers:* Abhishek Goenka [1979] Director/General Manager [Indian]; Ajay Ajit Peter Kerkar [1963] Director [Indian]; Hugo Charles Kimber [1964] Director/Executive Chairman; John Daniel McLaughlin [1978] Director/Chief Financial Officer

**Superior Developments Limited**
*Incorporated:* 24 February 1998
*Net Worth:* £3,175,185 *Total Assets:* £3,879,741
*Registered Office:* P O Box 403, 2 Denby Dale Road, Wakefield, W Yorks, WF1 2WT
*Activities:* Buying and selling of own real estate
*Major Shareholder:* Simon James Moy
*Officers:* Simon James Moy, Secretary/Engineer; Sidney Terence Moy [1935] Director/Engineer; Simon James Moy [1967] Director/Engineer

**Support Warehouse Limited**
*Incorporated:* 21 August 2000 *Employees:* 58
*Net Worth:* £1,787,045 *Total Assets:* £3,471,015
*Registered Office:* International Development Centre, Valley Drive, Ilkley, W Yorks, LS29 8PB
*Activities:* Other information technology service activities
*Parent:* Cornbrook Group Ltd
*Officers:* Heather Hardy [1977] Operations Director; Christopher John Hoyle [1974] Major Accounts Director; Lee Paul Moores [1971] Finance Director

**Surcoat Group Limited**
*Incorporated:* 9 March 2009 *Employees:* 14
*Net Worth:* £577,408 *Total Assets:* £3,912,132
*Registered Office:* Oakapple House, 1 John Charles Way, Leeds, LS12 6QA
*Activities:* Buying and selling of own real estate
*Major Shareholder:* Philip John Taylor
*Officers:* David Howard Marsh, Secretary; David Howard Marsh [1955] Director/Accountant; Philip John Taylor [1963] Director

**Surefreight (International) Limited**
*Incorporated:* 18 February 2003 *Employees:* 76
*Net Worth:* £2,283,998 *Total Assets:* £6,638,041
*Registered Office:* 41 Hillam Road Industrial Estate, off Canal Road, Bradford, BD2 1QN
*Activities:* Freight transport by road
*Officers:* Brian Generald McManus, Secretary; Martin Briggs [1962] Director; Anthony Hugh Daly [1959] Director; Brian Generald McManus [1959] Director; Vincent Waddell [1958] Director [Irish]

**Surfachem Group Limited**
*Incorporated:* 28 October 1996
*Net Worth:* £10,597,946 *Total Assets:* £12,830,437
*Registered Office:* 2nd Floor, 2 The Embankment, Sovereign Street, Leeds, LS1 4BA
*Activities:* Activities of head offices
*Major Shareholder:* Mordechai Kessler
*Officers:* Gareth Brewin, Secretary; Mordechai Kessler [1955] Director; Gal Maller [1977] Director; Dr Richard John Alan Smith [1959] Managing Director

**Surfachem Limited**
*Incorporated:* 3 June 1981 *Employees:* 84
*Net Worth:* £28,362,000 *Total Assets:* £48,918,872
*Registered Office:* 2nd Floor, 2 The Embankment, Sovereign Street, Leeds, LS1 4BA
*Activities:* Wholesale of chemical products
*Major Shareholder:* Mordechai Kessler
*Officers:* Gareth Brewin, Secretary; Gregory Charles Barton [1978] Sales and Marketing Director; Fakhara Jones [1967] Director/Technical; Mordechai Kessler [1955] Director; Dr Richard John Alan Smith [1959] Managing Director; William Stevens [1959] Director

**Surgeforward Limited**
*Incorporated:* 12 June 1997
*Net Worth:* £4,901,024 *Total Assets:* £8,375,853
*Registered Office:* Dower Hotel & Spa, 48 Bond End, Knaresborough, Harrogate, N Yorks, HG5 9AL
*Activities:* Activities of head offices
*Parent:* Northern Touch Limited
*Officers:* Ian Lawrence Hanson, Secretary/Lawyer; Ian Lawrence Hanson [1964] Director/Lawyer; Martin Gregory Michael Wicks [1963] Director/Hotelier

**Surgical Innovations Group PLC**
*Incorporated:* 20 September 1988 *Employees:* 70
*Net Worth:* £13,716,000 *Total Assets:* £18,539,000
*Registered Office:* Clayton Wood House, 6, Clayton Wood Bank, Leeds, LS16 6QZ
*Activities:* Manufacture of medical and dental instruments and supplies
*Officers:* Charmaine Roxane Day, Secretary; Paul James Hardy [1960] Director; David John Marsh [1964] Director; Professor Michael John McMahon [1942] Director/Surgeon; Adam Power [1964] Director; Nigel Foster Rogers [1961] Director/Executive Chairman; Melanie Ross [1979] Finance Director; Alistair Henderson Taylor [1941] Director

**Surgical Innovations Limited**
*Incorporated:* 29 January 1992 *Employees:* 57
*Net Worth Deficit:* £1,737,000 *Total Assets:* £7,391,000
*Registered Office:* Clayton Wood House, 6 Clayton Wood Bank, Leeds, LS16 6QZ
*Activities:* Manufacture of medical and dental instruments and supplies
*Parent:* Surgical Innovations Group PLC
*Officers:* Melanie Ross, Secretary; Paul James Hardy [1960] Director; Nigel Foster Rogers [1961] Director; Melanie Ross [1979] Director/Accountant

**SUSD Asset Management (Holdings) Limited**
*Incorporated:* 12 August 2005 *Employees:* 10
*Net Worth:* £4,569,729 *Total Assets:* £4,714,152
*Registered Office:* 21 Marina Court, Castle Street, Hull, HU1 1TJ
*Activities:* Activities of other holding companies n.e.c.
*Major Shareholder:* Michael Ashcroft
*Officers:* Christopher William Lawes, Secretary/Accountant; Peter Alexander Frederick Harris [1965] Director; Michael Ivan Laurie [1949] Director; Ian George Robinson [1947] Director

**Sutcliffe Group Limited**
*Incorporated:* 13 October 1983 *Employees:* 64
*Net Worth:* £2,570,264 *Total Assets:* £4,891,216
*Registered Office:* Waggon Lane, Upton, Pontefract, W Yorks, WF9 1JS
*Activities:* Activities of head offices
*Parent:* Sutcliffe Play Trustees Ltd Employee Benefit Trust
*Officers:* Louise Joanne Siddons, Secretary; Martin Edward Griffin [1958] Managing Director; Andrew Love [1965] Sales Director; Desmond Richard Robin Sutcliffe [1943] Director/Chairman

**Sutcliffe Play Limited**
*Incorporated:* 20 May 1947 *Employees:* 63
*Net Worth:* £1,910,390 *Total Assets:* £3,394,136
*Registered Office:* Waggon Lane, Upton, Pontefract, W Yorks, WF9 1JS
*Activities:* Manufacture of other fabricated metal products n.e.c.
*Parent:* Sutcliffe Group Ltd
*Officers:* Louise Joanne Siddons, Secretary; Martin Edward Griffin [1958] Managing Director; Andrew Love [1965] Sales Director; Timothy Preece [1966] Manufacturing Director; Desmond Richard Robin Sutcliffe [1943] Director/Chairman

**Swaledale Investments Limited**
*Incorporated:* 6 January 2012 *Employees:* 6
*Net Worth:* £6,643,982 *Total Assets:* £38,302,780
*Registered Office:* 4 Wharfe Mews, Cliffe Terrace, Wetherby, W Yorks, LS22 6LX
*Activities:* Security dealing on own account
*Shareholders:* Nigel George Pritchard; Susan Barbara Pritchard
*Officers:* Nigel George Pritchard [1955] Director; Susan Barbara Pritchard [1955] Director

**The Swan Hotel (Newby Bridge) Holdings Limited**
*Incorporated:* 8 February 2006 *Employees:* 110
*Net Worth:* £3,875,137 *Total Assets:* £10,922,865
*Registered Office:* Newby Bridge, Ulverston, Cumbria, LA12 8NB
*Activities:* Hotels and similar accommodation
*Shareholders:* Audrey Campbell Robertson; Sharon Anne Bardsley
*Officers:* Lisa Jayne Gray-Joyce, Secretary; Anne Bardsley [1942] Director; Sharon Anne Bardsley [1969] Director/Chairman; Sarah Gibbs [1981] Managing Director; Audrey Campbell Robertson [1969] Director/Secretary

**The Swan Hotel (Newby Bridge) Limited**
*Incorporated:* 14 May 1996 *Employees:* 110
*Net Worth:* £3,875,137 *Total Assets:* £10,922,865
*Registered Office:* Newby Bridge, Ulverston, Cumbria, LA12 8NB
*Activities:* Hotels and similar accommodation
*Shareholders:* Sharon Anne Bardsley; Audrey Campbell Robertson
*Officers:* Lisa Jayne Gray-Joyce, Secretary; Anne Bardsley [1942] Director; Ottilie India Bardsley [2000] Director; Sharon Anne Bardsley [1969] Director; Claire Anne Dickinson [1977] Director; Sarah Gibbs [1981] Director/General Manager; Craig Jeffrey Hadfield [1977] Food & Beverage Director; Audrey Campbell Robertson [1969] Director

**Swanbridge Veterinary Group Limited**
*Incorporated:* 9 March 2010 *Employees:* 44
*Net Worth:* £2,773,830 *Total Assets:* £3,197,791
*Registered Office:* Suite 1, The Riverside Building, Livingstone Road, Hessle, E Yorks, HU13 0DZ
*Activities:* Veterinary activities
*Officers:* Elizabeth Lucas, Secretary; John Howard Levison [1963] Director

**Swanland Education Trust**
*Incorporated:* 22 June 2011 *Employees:* 161
*Previous:* Swanland Primary School Academy Trust
*Net Worth:* £7,655,694 *Total Assets:* £8,633,242
*Registered Office:* Swanland Primary School, Tranby Lane, Swanland, E Yorks, HU14 3NE
*Activities:* Primary education
*Officers:* Sarah Jane Crawford, Secretary; Sandra Elaine Breene [1968] Director/Business Executive; Neil Ashley Crawford [1973] Director/Accountant; Nathan Ashley Greenfield [1990] Director/Sales Manager; Christopher James Huscroft [1981] Director/Deputy Headteacher; Susan Elizabeth Lyon [1960] Director/Teacher; Estelle Miriam MacDonald [1965] Director/Chief Executive; Katherine Vivienne Rowe [1954] Director/Safeguarding Manager; Michael Henry Whitaker [1953] Director/Education Consultant

**Swarco Traffic Limited**
*Incorporated:* 25 May 1989 *Employees:* 64
*Net Worth:* £1,842,526 *Total Assets:* £5,921,731
*Registered Office:* 7 Mercury Road, Gallowfields Trading Estate, Richmond, N Yorks, DL10 4TQ
*Activities:* Other manufacturing n.e.c.
*Parent:* Swarco Traffic Systems GmbH
*Officers:* Berony Anne Abraham, Secretary; Berony Anne Abraham [1955] Operations Director; Jeremy Peter Cowling [1967] Director; Carl James Dyer [1968] Director/Head of Systems Integration

**SWC Trade Frames Limited**
*Incorporated:* 13 January 2016 *Employees:* 126
*Net Worth:* £459,144 *Total Assets:* £5,527,089
*Registered Office:* Unit 1 The Gateway, Dunslow Road, Eastfield, Scarborough, N Yorks, YO11 3UT
*Activities:* Manufacture of other plastic products
*Shareholder:* Susan Richings
*Officers:* Mark Ralph Catchpole [1970] Director; Matthew Patrick Doherty [1976] Finance Director [Irish]; Ieuan Rhys Thomas Richings [1987] Director; Susan Richings [1957] Director

**Sweco Services UK Limited**
*Incorporated:* 15 April 1992 *Employees:* 778
*Previous:* Grontmij Services Limited
*Net Worth:* £719,000 *Total Assets:* £16,209,000
*Registered Office:* Grove House, Mansion Gate Drive, Leeds, LS7 4DN
*Activities:* Engineering related scientific and technical consulting activities
*Parent:* Sweco UK Holding Limited
*Officers:* Roger Hirons, Secretary; Philip David Bruce [1983] Finance Director; Max Henry Joy [1969] Director/Engineer

**Sweco UK Holding Limited**
*Incorporated:* 30 March 1988 *Employees:* 778
*Previous:* Grontmij Group Limited
*Net Worth:* £18,207,000 *Total Assets:* £31,880,000
*Registered Office:* Grove House, Mansion Gate Drive, Leeds, LS7 4DN
*Activities:* Construction of roads and motorways
*Parent:* Sweco AB
*Officers:* Roger Hirons, Secretary; Philip David Bruce [1983] Finance Director; Anders Bo Carlsson [1956] Director [Swedish]; Max Henry Joy [1969] Director/Engineer

**Sweco UK Limited**
*Incorporated:* 17 January 1994
*Previous:* Grontmij Limited
*Net Worth:* £16,926,000 *Total Assets:* £21,198,000
*Registered Office:* Grove House, Mansion Gate Drive, Leeds, LS7 4DN
*Activities:* Other engineering activities
*Parent:* Sweco UK Holding Limited
*Officers:* Roger Hirons, Secretary; Philip David Bruce [1983] Finance Director; Max Henry Joy [1969] Director/Engineer; Noel Geoffrey Lax [1959] Finance Director

**Sweepcharm Limited**
*Incorporated:* 28 January 1997 *Employees:* 5
*Net Worth:* £3,021,594 *Total Assets:* £3,427,257
*Registered Office:* Medina House, 2 Station Avenue, Bridlington, E Yorks, YO16 4LZ
*Activities:* Recreational vehicle parks, trailer parks and camping grounds
*Shareholders:* James Michael Stainforth; Susan Stainforth
*Officers:* Susan Stainforth, Secretary/Park Operator; Carl James Stainforth [1966] Director/Electrician; Craig Michael Stainforth [1963] Director/Consultant; James Michael Stainforth [1938] Director/Park Operator; Susan Stainforth [1939] Director/Park Operator

**Sweet Squared Limited**
*Incorporated:* 9 August 2006 *Employees:* 69
*Net Worth:* £7,795,607 *Total Assets:* £13,231,162
*Registered Office:* Unit 2 Green Park, Coal Road, Leeds, LS14 1FB
*Activities:* Wholesale of perfume and cosmetics
*Major Shareholder:* Samuel Sweet
*Officers:* Samuel Sweet, Secretary/Director [American]; James Alan Nordstrom [1957] Director/Executive [American]; Samantha Sweet [1969] Director; Samuel Sweet [1972] Director [American]

**Sweeting Brothers (Land Drainage) Limited**
*Incorporated:* 12 October 1971 *Employees:* 22
*Net Worth:* £684,844 *Total Assets:* £3,221,864
*Registered Office:* JWP Creers Chartered Accountant, 20-24 Park Street, Selby, N Yorks, YO8 4PW
*Activities:* Water collection, treatment and supply
*Officers:* Leonard Sweeting, Secretary; Christine Sweeting [1945] Director; Christopher Scruton Sweeting [1959] Director/Farmer; Daniel Leonard Sweeting [1973] Director; John Richard Sweeting [1943] Director/Farmer; Leonard Sweeting [1948] Director/Drainage Contractor

**J.G.Swiers (Helperby) Limited**
*Incorporated:* 3 January 1961 *Employees:* 4
*Net Worth:* £3,290,451 *Total Assets:* £3,625,007
*Registered Office:* Moxby Priory Farm, Marton Cum Moxby, Stillington, York, YO61 1NB
*Activities:* Mixed farming
*Major Shareholder:* Philip James Swiers
*Officers:* Philip James Swiers, Secretary; Jane Mary Swiers [1960] Director; Philip James Swiers [1961] Director/Farmer

**Joseph E.Swiers,Limited**
*Incorporated:* 3 March 1960 *Employees:* 31
*Net Worth:* £4,947,077 *Total Assets:* £9,303,319
*Registered Office:* Norton House, Norton-le-Clay, Helperby, N Yorks, YO61 2RS
*Activities:* Growing of cereals (except rice), leguminous crops and oil seeds
*Major Shareholder:* Timothy James Swiers
*Officers:* Timothy James Swiers, Secretary; Timothy James Swiers [1959] Director/Farmer

**Swift Acquisitions Limited**
*Incorporated:* 27 March 2012 *Employees:* 1,200
*Net Worth:* £81,685,144 *Total Assets:* £127,491,768
*Registered Office:* Dunswell Road, Cottingham, E Yorks, HU16 4JX
*Activities:* Activities of head offices
*Parent:* Swift Leisure Holdings Limited
*Officers:* Richard Paul Smeaton, Secretary; Amy Charlotte Archer [1982] Director; Richard Paul Smeaton [1974] Finance Director; James Stewart Turner [1970] Director

**Swift Group Limited**
*Incorporated:* 1 January 1965 *Employees:* 1,160
*Net Worth:* £35,497,548 *Total Assets:* £80,527,048
*Registered Office:* Dunswell Road, Cottingham, E Yorks, HU16 4JX
*Activities:* Manufacture of caravans
*Parent:* Swift Acquisitions Limited
*Officers:* Richard Paul Smeaton, Secretary; Amy Charlotte Archer [1982] Director; Christopher Milburn [1963] Director; Nicholas John Page [1960] Director; Graham Raper [1960] Director; Richard Paul Smeaton [1974] Finance Director; Andrew Spacey [1968] Director; James Stewart Turner [1970] Director

**Swift Holdings (UK) Limited**
*Incorporated:* 7 November 2003
*Net Worth:* £24,800,454 *Total Assets:* £25,215,926
*Registered Office:* Dunswell Road, Cottingham, E Yorks, HU16 4JX
*Activities:* Other letting and operating of own or leased real estate
*Parent:* Swift Property (East Yorkshire) Limited
*Officers:* Keith Brayshaw, Secretary/Accountant; Keith Brayshaw [1951] Director/Chartered Accountant; Peter Mutlow Smith [1949] Director

**Swift Property (East Yorkshire) Limited**
*Incorporated:* 27 March 2012 *Employees:* 4
*Net Worth:* £26,236,478 *Total Assets:* £27,733,940
*Registered Office:* Dunswell Road, Cottingham, E Yorks, HU16 4JX
*Activities:* Activities of head offices
*Major Shareholder:* Peter Mutlow Smith
*Officers:* Keith Brayshaw, Secretary; Keith Brayshaw [1951] Director/Chartered Accountant; Guy James Mutlow Smith [1974] Director/Racing Driver; Peter Mutlow Smith [1949] Director

**W.Swinbank & Sons Limited**
*Incorporated:* 21 March 1961 *Employees:* 9
*Net Worth:* £1,753,535 *Total Assets:* £3,881,166
*Registered Office:* Greystones, Caldwell, Richmond, N Yorks, DL11 7UB
*Activities:* Growing of cereals (except rice), leguminous crops and oil seeds
*Officers:* Brian Victor Swinbank, Secretary; Brian Victor Swinbank [1945] Director/Farmer; David Andrew Swinbank [1975] Director/Farmer; Ralph Watson Swinbank [1972] Director/Farmer

**Swinton Park Limited**
*Incorporated:* 11 April 2000 *Employees:* 120
*Net Worth:* £7,077,649 *Total Assets:* £15,132,712
*Registered Office:* Swinton Park, Swinton, Ripon, N Yorks, HG4 4JH
*Activities:* Hotels and similar accommodation
*Shareholders:* Mark William Philip Cunliffe-Lister; Felicity Clare Cunliffe-Lister
*Officers:* Felicity Clare Cunliffe-Lister, Secretary/Hotelier; The Honourable Elizabeth Susan Cunliffe-Lister [1944] Director; Felicity Clare Cunliffe-Lister [1970] Director/Hotelier; Mark William Philip Cunliffe-Lister [1970] Director/Hotelier

**Swinton Technology Limited**
*Incorporated:* 18 June 2001 *Employees:* 44
*Net Worth:* £2,762,864 *Total Assets:* £3,482,106
*Registered Office:* Swinton House, Hertford Way, York Road Business Park, Malton, N Yorks, YO17 6YG
*Activities:* Manufacture of other electrical equipment
*Officers:* Christopher Wainwright, Secretary; Jo Belsnes [1966] Director/Senior Software Specialist [Norwegian]; Andrew David Jeffery [1969] Director/Senior Project Engineer; Lynn Katharine Jeffery [1974] Director; Benedict Leach [1965] Managing Director; Jacqui Teresa Leach [1963] Director; Ingrid Jacqueline Sorrell Belsnes [1968] Director [Swedish]; Christopher John Wainwright [1974] Director/Senior Software Specialist

**Switch2 Energy Limited**
*Incorporated:* 31 July 1989 *Employees:* 144
*Previous:* Ener-G Switch2 Limited
*Net Worth:* £6,416,909 *Total Assets:* £9,288,291
*Registered Office:* The Waterfront, Salts Mill Road, Shipley, W Yorks, BD17 7EZ
*Activities:* Plumbing, heat and air-conditioning installation
*Shareholders:* Martin Lothar Ernst Hornig; Thomas Martin Joseph Wilhelm
*Officers:* Christopher John Hull [1966] Director/Chief Financial Officer; Kirsty Jane Lambert [1970] Director; Samantha Jane Scott [1980] Director; Timothy Hays Scott [1950] Director; Anthony Peter Roy Ward [1978] Director

**SWL Holdings Limited**
*Incorporated:* 30 January 2001
*Net Worth:* £1,377,636 *Total Assets:* £6,640,821
*Registered Office:* 19 Cave Road, Brough, Hull, HU15 1HA
*Activities:* Activities of head offices
*Major Shareholder:* Simon William Lunt
*Officers:* Joanne Lunt, Secretary; Joanne Lunt [1968] Director; Simon William Lunt [1952] Director/Solicitor

**Sycamore Lighting Limited**
*Incorporated:* 23 July 1998 *Employees:* 22
*Net Worth:* £3,944,153 *Total Assets:* £4,888,625
*Registered Office:* Unit 6 Astley Lane Industrial Estate, Swillington, Leeds, LS26 8XT
*Activities:* Wholesale of furniture, carpets and lighting equipment
*Parent:* GCH Capital Limited
*Officers:* Gary Wilson [1960] Sales Director

**Sykes House Farm Limited**
*Incorporated:* 6 October 1967 *Employees:* 90
*Net Worth:* £2,202,864 *Total Assets:* £3,880,318
*Registered Office:* Crown Chambers, Princes Street, Harrogate, N Yorks, HG1 1NJ
*Activities:* Wholesale of meat and meat products
*Parent:* Live Yorkshire Limited
*Officers:* Marilyn Janet Smith, Secretary; Rachael Louise Hirst [1974] Director; Martin Phillip Smith [1947] Director; Robert Charles Smith [1977] Director/Manager

**John Sylvester Engineering Company Limited**
*Incorporated:* 13 July 1964 *Employees:* 17
*Net Worth:* £9,931,247 *Total Assets:* £10,716,795
*Registered Office:* Vulcan Street, Dudley Hill, Bradford, W Yorks, BD4 9QU
*Activities:* Wholesale of machine tools
*Officers:* Arthur Sylvester, Secretary; Andrew Charles Sylvester [1975] Director/Company Manager; Arthur Sylvester [1933] Director

**Symington's Limited**
*Incorporated:* 6 August 1990 *Employees:* 766
*Net Worth:* £34,367,000 *Total Assets:* £83,131,000
*Registered Office:* Unit 8 South Fork Industrial Estate, Dartmouth Way, Garnet Road, Leeds, LS11 5JL
*Activities:* Other processing and preserving of fruit and vegetables
*Parent:* Brand Partnership (Holdings) Limited
*Officers:* Henry Strother Colquhoun Breese [1968] Director/Chartered Accountant; Matthew Lee [1976] Director/Chief Commercial Officer; John Power [1962] Director/Chief Executive Officer

**T & G Automotive Ltd**
*Incorporated:* 15 December 1981 *Employees:* 49
*Net Worth:* £3,012,278 *Total Assets:* £5,052,207
*Registered Office:* Unit 12 All Saints Industrial Estate, Darlington Road, Shildon, Co Durham, DL4 2RD
*Activities:* Manufacture of other tanks, reservoirs and containers of metal
*Officers:* Konrad Gehle [1940] Director [German]

**T G L (UK) Limited**
*Incorporated:* 28 February 1997
*Net Worth:* £1,969,300 *Total Assets:* £3,417,897
*Registered Office:* Unit 1 Cross Green Lane, Leeds, LS9 8LJ
*Activities:* Joinery installation
*Shareholders:* Lee Johnson; Adrian Jackson Sunderland
*Officers:* Adrian Jackson Sunderland [1969] Director

**T L B Properties Limited**
*Incorporated:* 22 October 1999
*Net Worth:* £1,750,009 *Total Assets:* £6,458,832
*Registered Office:* 3 Cavendish Court, South Parade, Doncaster, S Yorks, DN1 2DJ
*Activities:* Other letting and operating of own or leased real estate
*Shareholders:* Nadeem Haider Shah; Maureen Shah
*Officers:* Maureen Shah, Secretary/Director; Maureen Shah [1959] Director; Nadeem Shah [1956] Director/Builder; Tariq Navid Shah [1983] Director/Manager

**T M Enterprises Limited**
*Incorporated:* 12 September 1975 *Employees:* 5
*Net Worth:* £3,003,110 *Total Assets:* £5,297,913
*Registered Office:* Estate Office, Eastburn, Driffield, E Yorks, YO25 9DP
*Activities:* Other letting and operating of own or leased real estate
*Parent:* Birch Valley Holdings Limited
*Officers:* John Derek Taylor Megginson, Secretary; Charles Peter Barker [1979] Director/Chartered Accountant; John Derek Taylor Megginson [1944] Director; Patricia Megginson [1942] Director; Thomas Alan Taylor Megginson [1974] Director/Chartered Surveyor

**T R M Marketing Limited**
*Incorporated:* 10 December 1998 *Employees:* 5
*Net Worth:* £2,698,089 *Total Assets:* £5,077,515
*Registered Office:* The Archways, Headlam Hall, Headlam, Darlington, Co Durham, DL2 3HA
*Activities:* Other business support service activities n.e.c.
*Major Shareholder:* Timothy Robert Metcalfe
*Officers:* Timothy Robert Metcalfe, Secretary/Furniture Component Agent; Suzanne Clare Metcalfe [1963] Director; Timothy Robert Metcalfe [1958] Director/Furniture Component Agent

**T W Logistics Limited**
*Incorporated:* 23 January 1996 *Employees:* 57
*Net Worth:* £3,569,196 *Total Assets:* £5,728,179
*Registered Office:* The Old Shipyard, Gainsborough, Lincs, DN21 1NQ
*Activities:* Other manufacturing n.e.c.
*Shareholder:* Michael Jonathan Parker
*Officers:* Patricia Guilliatt Sargent, Secretary; Michael Jonathan Parker [1944] Director; Veronica Ann Parker [1945] Director

**T. Quality Limited**
*Incorporated:* 28 June 1947 *Employees:* 249
*Net Worth:* £8,091,241 *Total Assets:* £16,453,471
*Registered Office:* Ings Road, Doncaster, S Yorks, DN5 9TL
*Activities:* Wholesale of other food, including fish, crustaceans and molluscs
*Parent:* Saria Limited
*Officers:* Darren Creese, Secretary; Richard Graham Brooks [1965] Purchasing Director; Michael John Crees [1972] Sales Director; Darren Creese [1972] Director; Andrew Richard Smith [1962] Director/Group Commercial Manager

**T.L.G. Properties Limited**
*Incorporated:* 24 March 1995 *Employees:* 2
*Net Worth:* £6,129,392 *Total Assets:* £6,853,620
*Registered Office:* Scalebor Park Farm, Moor Lane, Burley in Wharfedale, Ilkley, W Yorks, LS29 7BL
*Activities:* Other letting and operating of own or leased real estate
*Shareholder:* John Cyril Hornby
*Officers:* John Cyril Hornby, Secretary; John Cyril Hornby [1949] Director; Susan Elizabeth Settle [1945] Director

**Tadcaster Pub Company Limited**
*Incorporated:* 13 March 2007 *Employees:* 7
*Net Worth:* £1,200,538 *Total Assets:* £3,244,937
*Registered Office:* Commer House, Station Road, Tadcaster, N Yorks, LS24 9JF
*Activities:* Public houses and bars
*Shareholder:* Jeffrey Alan Anspach
*Officers:* Jeffrey Alan Anspach [1965] Director; James Justin Crawfurd-Porter [1965] Director; Alison Jane Woodfine [1962] Resources Director

**TAG Industries Limited**
*Incorporated:* 18 September 2013
*Net Worth:* £4,164,149 *Total Assets:* £5,638,996
*Registered Office:* Sidings House, Sidings Court, Lakeside, Doncaster, S Yorks, DN4 5NU
*Activities:* Recovery of sorted materials
*Major Shareholder:* Samuel Wightman Cowan
*Officers:* Samuel Wightman Cowan [1959] Director

**Tailormade Design Limited**
*Incorporated:* 26 March 2009 *Employees:* 40
*Net Worth:* £1,883,094 *Total Assets:* £3,200,175
*Registered Office:* Carr Lane, Low Moor, Bradford, W Yorks, BD12 0QY
*Activities:* Printing n.e.c.
*Shareholders:* Stephen McNally; Matthew Simon Sharp
*Officers:* Deborah Antoinette McNally [1956] Director; Stephen McNally [1960] Director; Jacqueline Sharp [1955] Director; Matthew Simon Sharp [1955] Director

**Tajj Limited**
*Incorporated:* 2 January 1986 *Employees:* 4
*Previous:* Jelle Zwemstra Limited
*Net Worth:* £13,751,734 *Total Assets:* £14,319,546
*Registered Office:* Forge Cottage, Kidd Lane, Welton, Brough, N Humbers, HU15 1PH
*Activities:* Other business support service activities n.e.c.
*Shareholders:* Jelle Jan Zwemstra; Astrid Joanne Maria Zwemstra
*Officers:* Astrid Joanne Maria Zwemstra, Secretary [Dutch]; Astrid Joanne Maria Zwemstra [1959] Director/Flower Wholesaler [Dutch]; Jelle Jan Zwemstra [1958] Director/Flower Wholesaler [Dutch]

**Takahe Holdings Ltd**
*Incorporated:* 4 November 2016
*Net Worth:* £3,878,978 *Total Assets:* £6,424,423
*Registered Office:* Suite 3, Aireside House, Aireside Business Centre, Royd Ings Avnue, Keighley, W Yorks, BD21 4BZ
*Activities:* Activities of other holding companies n.e.c.
*Major Shareholder:* James Michael Davis
*Officers:* James Michael Davis [1980] Director

**Talasey Ltd**
*Incorporated:* 21 June 2004 *Employees:* 53
*Previous:* Natural Paving Products (UK) Ltd
*Net Worth:* £5,848,339 *Total Assets:* £15,637,078
*Registered Office:* Belton Road, Sandtoft, Doncaster, S Yorks, DN8 5SX
*Activities:* Non-specialised wholesale trade
*Major Shareholder:* Mark Wall
*Officers:* Duncan Weighill, Secretary; Malcolm Gough [1967] Business Development Director; Mark Wall [1972] Director/Chartered Engineer; Juliette Rose Yeardley [1976] Finance Director

**Talbert Limited**
*Incorporated:* 23 May 2016
*Net Worth:* £5,114,003 *Total Assets:* £9,436,813
*Registered Office:* 30 Headingley Lane, Leeds, LS6 2AS
*Activities:* Buying and selling of own real estate
*Major Shareholder:* Simon Jacob Moran
*Officers:* Karen Janine Moran [1969] Director; Simon Jacob Moran [1963] Director

**Talbot House Limited**
*Incorporated:* 26 October 1999 *Employees:* 1
*Net Worth:* £6,865,037 *Total Assets:* £12,097,344
*Registered Office:* Crown Garage, back Albion Road, Scarborough, N Yorks, YO11 2BT
*Activities:* Other letting and operating of own or leased real estate
*Shareholders:* Tara Ledden; Jenna Ledden
*Officers:* David Andrew Ledden [1967] Director; Joseph Patrick Ledden [1938] Director/Manager [Irish]; Patricia Bernadette Ledden [1937] Director/Retired [Irish]

**Talk Direct (Leeds) Ltd**
*Incorporated:* 2 February 2006 *Employees:* 131
*Net Worth:* £4,380,629 *Total Assets:* £7,075,408
*Registered Office:* Suite 54, Annexe 3, Batley Business Technology Centre, Technology Drive, Grange Road, Batley, W Yorks, WF17 6ER
*Activities:* Other telecommunications activities
*Officers:* Sajid Patel [1987] Director; Zakir Patel [1972] Director

**Tall Oaks Academy Trust Ltd**
*Incorporated:* 8 February 2013 *Employees:* 88
*Net Worth:* £5,690,000 *Total Assets:* £6,570,000
*Registered Office:* White's Wood Academy, Whites Wood Lane, Gainsborough, Lincs, DN21 1TJ
*Activities:* Primary education
*Officers:* Rachel Theresa Maria Ashmore [1970] Director/Education & Volunteering Coordinator; Caroline Joanne Jackson [1973] Director/Local Government Officer; Claire Louise Kirk [1980] Director/Head of Professional Standards; Anna Louise Leng [1980] Director/Headteacher; Brenda Mary Roberts [1953] Director/Specialist Teacher; Susan Wilson [1966] Director/Interim Executive Headteacher

**Talpole Limited**
*Incorporated:* 20 July 1999
*Net Worth:* £3,560 *Total Assets:* £7,187,587
*Registered Office:* Cumberland House, Greenside Lane, Bradford, BD8 9TF
*Activities:* Agents specialised in the sale of other particular products
*Major Shareholder:* Franco Grottoli
*Officers:* Claire Marie Cain [1970] Director/Company Secretary; Christopher Stephen Smith [1972] Director/Trust Manager

**Tamar (Selby) Limited**
*Incorporated:* 25 October 2001
*Net Worth:* £3,759,149 *Total Assets:* £16,411,788
*Registered Office:* Euro Auctions Yard, Roall Lane, Kellington, Goole, N Humbers, DN14 0NY
*Activities:* Other letting and operating of own or leased real estate
*Officers:* Patricia Georgina Keys, Secretary; Derek Irwin Keys [1966] Director

**Tampnet UK Limited**
*Incorporated:* 4 April 2014 *Employees:* 8
*Net Worth Deficit:* £6,618,997 *Total Assets:* £62,346,236
*Registered Office:* 1 Park Row, Leeds, LS1 5AB
*Activities:* Other telecommunications activities
*Officers:* Christian Grinde [1971] Director/CLO Tampnet AS [Norwegian]; Per Helge Svensson [1961] Director/CEO Tampnet AS [Norwegian]

**Tandem 1987 Limited**
*Incorporated:* 27 July 2016 *Employees:* 521
*Previous:* Principle Global Limited
*Net Worth:* £6,488,300 *Total Assets:* £121,148,240
*Registered Office:* Tandem Industrial Estate, Wakefield Road, Huddersfield, W Yorks, HD5 0AL
*Activities:* Activities of other holding companies n.e.c.
*Major Shareholder:* Richard Howard Butterfield
*Officers:* Simon Paul Blagden [1962] Director; Michele Bonello [1968] Director [Italian]; Richard Howard Butterfield [1961] Director; Mark John Deuschle [1959] Director [American]; David Scott Greenwood [1952] Director/Accountant; Victoria Jessica Woodings [1983] Director

**Taniya Properties Ltd**
*Incorporated:* 4 April 2011 *Employees:* 2
*Net Worth:* £3,158,416 *Total Assets:* £6,866,502
*Registered Office:* c/o Hillman & Co, Technology Court, Bradbury Road, Newton Aycliffe, Co Durham, DL5 6DA
*Activities:* Buying and selling of own real estate
*Officers:* Seema Jagota, Secretary; Aminur Choudhury [1971] Director; Taniya Choudhury [1982] Director; Seema Jagota [1973] Director; Javaid Nazir [1969] Director

**Tanks and Vessels Industries Limited**
*Incorporated:* 6 April 1977 *Employees:* 33
*Net Worth:* £6,716,022 *Total Assets:* £9,980,119
*Registered Office:* Bankwood Lane Trading Estate, Bankwood Lane, New Rossington, Doncaster, S Yorks, DN11 0PS
*Activities:* Manufacture of other tanks, reservoirs and containers of metal
*Major Shareholder:* Anthony Derrek Morris
*Officers:* George Arthur Smith, Secretary; Anthony Derrek Morris [1947] Director; George Arthur Smith [1950] Finance Director

**Taodail Hydro Limited**
*Incorporated:* 5 June 2015
*Net Worth:* £1,196,121 *Total Assets:* £4,030,892
*Registered Office:* Canal Head North, Kendal, Cumbria, LA9 7BZ
*Activities:* Production of electricity
*Shareholders:* GHI Taodail Limited; Ben Dronaig Projects Limited
*Officers:* Charles William Nepean Crewdson [1964] Director; Carl Peter Crompton [1973] Director/Finance Executive; Ewen Alan Macpherson [1929] Director/Landowner; Joanne Macpherson [1955] Director/Self-Employed Marketing Consultant

**Taplanes Limited**
*Incorporated:* 6 June 1979 *Employees:* 42
*Net Worth:* £2,868,813 *Total Assets:* £3,558,250
*Registered Office:* Station Court, Nidd, Harrogate, N Yorks, HG3 3BN
*Activities:* Other manufacturing n.e.c.
*Officers:* Jonathan Lee Frewin [1965] Director/Accountant; Rupert Knight Harrison [1960] Director/Finance; Eric Arthur Kolodner [1966] Director/Attorney; Tracey Monica Phillips [1964] Commercial Director

**Target Components Limited**
*Incorporated:* 13 October 1995 *Employees:* 62
*Net Worth:* £3,426,691 *Total Assets:* £5,835,749
*Registered Office:* Unit 5 Pioneer Way, Pioneer Business Park, Castleford, W Yorks, WF10 5QU
*Activities:* Wholesale of computers, computer peripheral equipment and software
*Shareholders:* Paul Cubbage; Ian David Prescott
*Officers:* Paul Cubbage, Secretary; Paul Cubbage [1968] Director/Chartered Accountant; Ian David Prescott [1963] Director

**Tarnhelm Securities Limited**
*Incorporated:* 27 May 1986 *Employees:* 1
*Net Worth:* £3,579,741 *Total Assets:* £4,448,438
*Registered Office:* The Old Mill, Thornton Hill, Easingwold, York, YO6 3QB
*Activities:* Security dealing on own account
*Major Shareholder:* John Alan Cooper
*Officers:* John Alan Cooper [1948] Director/Entrepreneur

**Tasca Tankers Limited**
*Incorporated:* 7 September 1994 *Employees:* 66
*Net Worth:* £302,650 *Total Assets:* £3,594,465
*Registered Office:* Unit 5 Diamond Business Park, Thornes Moor Road, Wakefield, W Yorks, WF2 8PT
*Activities:* Manufacture of other transport equipment n.e.c.
*Shareholders:* Thomas Patrick McDonnell; Alwyn Bowering; Andrew Stokes; Shaun Alexander Harte
*Officers:* Thomas Patrick McDonnell, Secretary/Engineer; Alwyn Bowering [1942] Director; Thomas Patrick McDonnell [1956] Director/Engineer; Andrew Stokes [1965] Director

**Tasker Investments Limited**
*Incorporated:* 24 October 2008
*Net Worth Deficit:* £1,356,751 *Total Assets:* £8,484,931
*Registered Office:* 3 Colton Mill, Bullerthorpe Lane, Leeds, LS15 9JN
*Activities:* Non-trading company
*Parent:* Nationwide Specialist Services Limited
*Officers:* Neil Patrick Inskip [1980] Director; Stuart Lees [1956] Director; John Thornton Tasker [1966] Director

**Taskmaster Resources Limited**
*Incorporated:* 9 December 1996 *Employees:* 2,383
*Net Worth:* £4,051,253 *Total Assets:* £13,193,411
*Registered Office:* 8 Leodis Court, David Street, Leeds, LS11 5JJ
*Activities:* Other activities of employment placement agencies
*Parent:* Recruitmaster Ltd
*Officers:* Andrew George Skorupka, Secretary; Andrew Godfrey [1962] Director/Personnel Manager; Michael Mays [1964] Director/Recruitment Manager; Andrew George Skorupka [1958] Director

**Taste Marketing Ltd**
*Incorporated:* 24 August 2005 *Employees:* 94
*Net Worth:* £3,086,000 *Total Assets:* £11,495,000
*Registered Office:* Birkby Grange, 85 Birkby Hall Road, Birkby, Huddersfield, W Yorks, HD2 2XB
*Activities:* Other business support service activities n.e.c.
*Shareholders:* State Bidco Limited; State Bidco Limited
*Officers:* Benjamin William Eaton [1979] Director; Matthew Joseph Turner [1978] Director

**Tate Fuel Oils Limited**
*Incorporated:* 10 March 1977 *Employees:* 62
*Net Worth:* £4,158,594 *Total Assets:* £11,681,780
*Registered Office:* Steelcroft Works, Gay Lane, Otley, W Yorks, LS21 3BB
*Activities:* Wholesale of petroleum and petroleum products
*Major Shareholder:* George William Tate
*Officers:* George William Tate, Secretary; Andrew George Tate [1972] Director; George William Tate [1939] Director; June Margaret Tate [1942] Director

**Tate of Leeds Limited.**
*Incorporated:* 21 January 1983 *Employees:* 4
*Net Worth:* £1,751,369 *Total Assets:* £3,643,078
*Registered Office:* Balm Road, New Hunslet, Leeds, LS10 2RL
*Activities:* Other professional, scientific and technical activities n.e.c.
*Major Shareholder:* Thomas Patrick Tate
*Officers:* Frances Hazel Tate, Secretary; Frances Hazel Tate [1952] Director; Richard Thomas Anthony Tate [1977] Director/ARC Manager; Thomas Patrick Tate [1948] Director

**Tate Properties Limited**
*Incorporated:* 4 August 1997 *Employees:* 2
*Net Worth:* £1,993,818 *Total Assets:* £4,188,416
*Registered Office:* Balm Road, New Hunslet, Leeds, LS10 2RL
*Activities:* Other letting and operating of own or leased real estate
*Major Shareholder:* Thomas Patrick Tate
*Officers:* Frances Hazel Tate, Secretary; Frances Hazel Tate [1952] Director; Thomas Patrick Tate [1948] Director

**Timothy Taylor & Co.,Limited**
*Incorporated:* 16 November 1929 *Employees:* 123
*Net Worth:* £31,732,548 *Total Assets:* £35,537,816
*Registered Office:* Knowle Spring Brewery, Keighley, W Yorks, BD21 1AW
*Activities:* Manufacture of beer
*Officers:* John Edward Thomas Varley, Secretary; Michael Lloyd Bramley [1951] Director; Timothy Clarke [1957] Director; Benjamin Thomas Dent [1984] Director/Partner; Sarah Louise Dent [1984] Director/Advertising & Sponsorship Manager; Timothy William Dewey [1958] Director/Chief Executive; Claire Hodgson [1985] Director/Marketing Manager; James Clive Orrock Simpson [1965] Director/Wine Shipper; John Edward Thomas Varley [1966] Director/Chartered Accountant; John Philip Tempest Walsh [1960] Director

**F B Taylor (Cable Contractors) Limited**
*Incorporated:* 5 August 1976 *Employees:* 162
*Net Worth:* £1,794,183 *Total Assets:* £6,355,368
*Registered Office:* 5 Camp Hill Close, Ripon, N Yorks, HG4 1QY
*Activities:* Electrical installation
*Parent:* F B Taylor (Holdings) Ltd
*Officers:* Tracey McPherson Baldwin, Secretary; Nigel Baldwin [1964] Director; Colleen Susan Ellerker [1963] Director; Gary Edward John Taylor [1980] Finance Director; John Christopher Taylor [1959] Managing Director; Valerie McPherson Taylor [1938] Director

**F B Taylor (Holdings) Limited**
*Incorporated:* 21 May 2009 *Employees:* 162
*Net Worth:* £6,600,639 *Total Assets:* £10,459,824
*Registered Office:* 5 Camp Hill Close, Ripon, N Yorks, HG4 1QY
*Activities:* Other letting and operating of own or leased real estate
*Shareholders:* Valerie McPherson Taylor; John Christopher Taylor; Colleen Susan Ellerker
*Officers:* Colleen Susan Ellerker [1963] Director; Gary Edward John Taylor [1980] Finance Director; John Christopher Taylor [1959] Director; Valerie McPherson Taylor [1938] Director

**D.G. Taylor Commercial Vehicles Limited**
*Incorporated:* 20 October 1978 *Employees:* 13
*Net Worth:* £14,912,731 *Total Assets:* £16,216,689
*Registered Office:* Hutton Cranswick Industrial Estate, Driffield, E Yorks, YO25 9QE
*Activities:* Sale of other motor vehicles
*Officers:* Yvonne Karen Taylor, Secretary; Yvonne Karen Taylor [1965] Director/Company Secretary

**S.D. Taylor Limited**
*Incorporated:* 1 June 1955 *Employees:* 305
*Net Worth:* £27,630,000 *Total Assets:* £63,347,000
*Registered Office:* 7 Turnberry Park Road, Gildersome, Morley, Leeds, LS27 7LE
*Activities:* Credit granting by non-deposit taking finance houses and other specialist consumer credit grantors
*Parent:* Non-Standard Finance Subsidiary II Limited
*Officers:* Charlotte Norris, Secretary; John Philip de Blocq Van Kuffeler [1949] Director [Dutch]; Paul Gill [1971] Director/Chief Risk Officer; Jonathan Richard Gillespie [1972] Director; Peter Forbes Michael Reynolds [1966] Director, IT & Communications; Nicholas John Teunon [1966] Director; David Reid Thompson [1962] Director

**Tayrol Limited**
*Incorporated:* 22 September 1988 *Employees:* 29
*Net Worth:* £2,035,773 *Total Assets:* £3,326,819
*Registered Office:* Unit Y12 Elvington Industrial Estate, York Road, Elvington, York, YO41 4AR
*Activities:* Manufacture of paper stationery
*Major Shareholder:* Keith Taylor
*Officers:* Keith Taylor, Secretary; Keith Taylor [1953] Director

**TCCP (Clarence Dock) Limited**
*Incorporated:* 19 April 2007 *Employees:* 4
*Net Worth:* £1,893,652 *Total Assets:* £15,597,927
*Registered Office:* Town Centre House, The Merrion Centre, Leeds, LS2 8LY
*Activities:* Other letting and operating of own or leased real estate
*Parent:* Town Centre Car Parks Limited
*Officers:* Mark John Dilley [1972] Finance Director; Lynda Margaret Shillaw [1965] Group Property Director; Charles Benjamin Aaron Ziff [1986] Managing Director; Edward Max Ziff [1960] Director

**TCS (Merrion House JVCO1) Limited**
*Incorporated:* 7 June 2013
*Net Worth:* £11,370,059 *Total Assets:* £23,078,492
*Registered Office:* Town Centre House, The Merrion Centre, Leeds, LS2 8LY
*Activities:* Combined office administrative service activities
*Parent:* TCS Holdings Limited
*Officers:* Mark John Dilley [1972] Finance Director; Lynda Margaret Shillaw [1965] Group Property Director; Edward Max Ziff [1960] Director/Chief Executive

**TCS (Milngavie) Limited**
*Incorporated:* 5 October 2007
*Net Worth:* £5,023,801 *Total Assets:* £23,044,088
*Registered Office:* Town Centre House, The Merrion Centre, Leeds, LS2 8LY
*Activities:* Other letting and operating of own or leased real estate
*Parent:* TCS Freehold Investments Limited
*Officers:* Mark John Dilley [1972] Finance Director; Lynda Margaret Shillaw [1965] Group Property Director; Benjamin Ziff [1986] Managing Director; Edward Max Ziff [1960] Director

**TCS (Whitehall Plaza) Limited**
*Incorporated:* 18 December 2015
*Net Worth:* £1,537,483 *Total Assets:* £14,150,001
*Registered Office:* Town Centre Securities, Town Centre House, Merrion Centre, Leeds, LS2 8LY
*Activities:* Other letting and operating of own or leased real estate
*Parent:* Town Centre Securities PLC
*Officers:* Mark John Dilley [1972] Finance Director; Lynda Margaret Shillaw [1965] Group Property Director; Edward Max Ziff [1960] Director/Chairman & Chief Executive

**TCS Freehold Investments Limited**
*Incorporated:* 16 December 1998
*Net Worth:* £126,671,264 *Total Assets:* £132,934,352
*Registered Office:* Town Centre House, The Merrion Centre, Leeds, LS2 8LY
*Activities:* Buying and selling of own real estate
*Parent:* TCS Properties Limited
*Officers:* Mark John Dilley [1972] Finance Director; Lynda Margaret Shillaw [1965] Group Property Director; Benjamin Ziff [1986] Managing Director; Edward Max Ziff [1960] Director

**TCS Holdings Limited**
*Incorporated:* 27 June 1988 *Employees:* 4
*Net Worth:* £144,150,688 *Total Assets:* £191,937,152
*Registered Office:* Town Centre House, The Merrion Centre, Leeds, LS2 8LY
*Activities:* Buying and selling of own real estate
*Parent:* Town Centre Securities PLC
*Officers:* Mark John Dilley [1972] Finance Director; Lynda Margaret Shillaw [1965] Group Property Director; Benjamin Ziff [1986] Managing Director; Edward Max Ziff [1960] Director

**TCS Leasehold Investments Limited**
*Incorporated:* 16 December 1998
*Net Worth:* £14,193,093 *Total Assets:* £18,371,990
*Registered Office:* Town Centre House, Merrion Centre, Leeds, LS2 8LY
*Activities:* Buying and selling of own real estate
*Parent:* TCS Properties Limited
*Officers:* Mark John Dilley [1972] Finance Director; Lynda Margaret Shillaw [1965] Group Property Director; Benjamin Ziff [1986] Managing Director; Edward Max Ziff [1960] Director

**TCS Properties Limited**
*Incorporated:* 23 June 1993
*Net Worth:* £79,343,112 *Total Assets:* £116,425,048
*Registered Office:* Town Centre House, The Merrion Centre, Leeds, LS2 8LY
*Activities:* Activities of other holding companies n.e.c.
*Parent:* Town Centre Securities PLC
*Officers:* Mark John Dilley [1972] Finance Director; Lynda Margaret Shillan [1965] Group Property Director; Benjamin Ziff [1986] Managing Director; Edward Max Ziff [1960] Director

**TD Holdings Ltd**
*Incorporated:* 25 January 2016 *Employees:* 133
*Net Worth:* £2,955,299 *Total Assets:* £10,644,750
*Registered Office:* Suite 54, Annexe 3, Batley Business & Technology Centre, Technology Drive, Batley, W Yorks, WF17 6ER
*Activities:* Activities of head offices
*Officers:* Sajid Patel [1987] Director; Zakir Patel [1972] Director

**Teal & Mackrill Limited**
*Incorporated:* 22 January 1913 *Employees:* 70
*Net Worth:* £1,197,071 *Total Assets:* £3,475,634
*Registered Office:* 30 Lockwood Street, Hull, HU2 0HN
*Activities:* Manufacture of paints, varnishes and similar coatings, mastics and sealants
*Major Shareholder:* Benjamin Geoffrey Mackrill
*Officers:* Stephen Moore, Secretary; Richard Leigh Burnham [1972] Managing Director; Benjamin Geoffrey Mackrill [1958] Director/Paint Manufacturer

**Team (Impression) Holdings PLC**
*Incorporated:* 27 July 2007 *Employees:* 88
*Net Worth:* £1,327,082 *Total Assets:* £6,890,558
*Registered Office:* Fusion House, 1 Lockwood Close, Leeds, LS11 5UU
*Activities:* Printing n.e.c.
*Major Shareholder:* Peter James Crowson
*Officers:* Simon John Bucktrout [1969] Sales Director; Peter James Crowson [1966] Managing Director

**Team (Impression) Limited**
*Incorporated:* 2 May 2001 *Employees:* 88
*Net Worth:* £1,327,082 *Total Assets:* £6,890,558
*Registered Office:* Fusion House, 1 Lockwood Close, Leeds, LS11 5UU
*Activities:* Printing n.e.c.
*Parent:* Team (Impression) Holdings PLC
*Officers:* Simon John Bucktrout [1969] Sales Director; Peter James Crowson [1966] Managing Director

**Team 17 Digital Limited**
*Incorporated:* 19 June 1991 *Employees:* 112
*Net Worth:* £14,484,013 *Total Assets:* £20,683,972
*Registered Office:* Castleview House, Calder Island Way, Wakefield, W Yorks, WF2 7AW
*Activities:* Ready-made interactive leisure and entertainment software development
*Parent:* Team 17 Holdings Limited
*Officers:* Jonathan Paul Bray, Secretary; Deborah Jayne Bestwick [1970] Director; Jonathan Paul Bray [1962] Finance Director

**Team 17 Holdings Limited**
*Incorporated:* 25 July 2016 *Employees:* 83
*Net Worth:* £7,444,000 *Total Assets:* £60,019,000
*Registered Office:* Castleview House, Calder Island Way, Wakefield, W Yorks, WF2 7AW
*Activities:* Ready-made interactive leisure and entertainment software development
*Shareholder:* Deborah Jayne Bestwick
*Officers:* Deborah Jayne Bestwick [1970] Director; Jonathan Paul Bray [1962] Director

**Team 17 Software Limited**
*Incorporated:* 22 October 2010
*Net Worth:* £4,228,347 *Total Assets:* £4,513,053
*Registered Office:* Castleview House, Calder Island Way, Wakefield, W Yorks, WF2 7AW
*Activities:* Ready-made interactive leisure and entertainment software development
*Parent:* Team 17 Holdings Limited
*Officers:* Deborah Jayne Bestwick, Secretary; Deborah Jayne Bestwick [1970] Director; Joanne Jones [1978] Director/Chief Financial Officer

**Team Industrial Services (UK) Limited**
*Incorporated:* 15 April 1929 *Employees:* 315
*Previous:* Teamfurmanite Limited
*Net Worth:* £24,702,000 *Total Assets:* £47,113,000
*Registered Office:* Furman House, Shap Road, Kendal, Cumbria, LA9 6RU
*Activities:* Repair of other equipment
*Parent:* Furmanite 1986
*Officers:* Rachel Dixon, Secretary; Greg Lee Boane [1963] Director/Chief Finance Officer [American]; Andre Charles Bouchard [1965] Director/Senior VP - Legal [American]; Jonathon Anthony Jarvis [1957] Director/Vice President

**Tebway Limited**
*Incorporated:* 2 March 1983 *Employees:* 8
*Net Worth:* £3,973,468 *Total Assets:* £4,148,219
*Registered Office:* 52-54 Oswald Road, Scunthorpe, N Lincs, DN15 7PQ
*Activities:* Other specialised construction activities n.e.c.
*Parent:* Polypearl Management Ltd
*Officers:* Marie Robinson, Secretary; Andrew Graham Tebb [1975] Operations Director; Hilary Margaret Tebb [1947] Director; Ian Rodney Tebb [1947] Managing Director

**Tech Search Associates Limited**
*Incorporated:* 9 February 2012 *Employees:* 15
*Net Worth:* £877,628 *Total Assets:* £5,791,441
*Registered Office:* Sandford Lodge, Bridge Road, Kirkstall, Leeds, LS5 3BW
*Activities:* Temporary employment agency activities
*Shareholders:* Michael George Warburton; Richard Martin Dobson
*Officers:* Michael George Warburton, Secretary; Richard Martin Dobson [1978] Director/Recruitment Consultant; Michael George Warburton [1974] Director/Recruitment Consultant

**Techbuyer Group Holdings Limited**
*Incorporated:* 16 September 2016 *Employees:* 69
*Net Worth:* £6,434,610 *Total Assets:* £8,492,877
*Registered Office:* Unit C1, Crimple Court, Hornbeam Square North, Harrogate, N Yorks, HG2 8PB
*Activities:* Wholesale of computers, computer peripheral equipment and software
*Major Shareholder:* Kevin Kendal Towers
*Officers:* Andrew Geoffrey Forster, Secretary; Kevin Kendal Towers [1975] Director

**Techbuyer Limited**
*Incorporated:* 27 April 2005 *Employees:* 65
*Previous:* Pinnacle Enterprise Limited
*Net Worth:* £6,468,886 *Total Assets:* £8,512,439
*Registered Office:* Unit C1, Crimple Court, Hornbeam Square North, Harrogate, N Yorks, HG2 8PB
*Activities:* Other information technology service activities
*Major Shareholder:* Kevin Kendal Towers
*Officers:* Andrew Geoffrey Forster, Secretary; Kevin Kendal Towers [1975] Managing Director

**Techmotion Limited**
*Incorporated:* 4 February 2008 *Employees:* 66
*Net Worth:* £3,198,269 *Total Assets:* £6,255,134
*Registered Office:* Hapco Works, Caledonia Street, Bradford, W Yorks, BD5 0EL
*Activities:* Machining
*Shareholder:* Richard John Hindle
*Officers:* Steven Widdrington, Secretary; Peter Roy Bingham [1960] Director; David Hindle [1962] Director; Richard John Hindle [1957] Director/Engineer; Steven Richard Widdrington [1951] Director

**Technical Absorbents Limited**
*Incorporated:* 5 April 1993 *Employees:* 46
*Net Worth:* £17,752,000 *Total Assets:* £19,025,000
*Registered Office:* P O Box 24, 1 Moody Lane, corner of Woad Lane, Great Coates, Grimsby, N E Lincs, DN31 2SS
*Activities:* Preparation and spinning of textile fibres
*Parent:* Bluestar Fibres Investment Company Limited
*Officers:* Michile Ann Riley, Secretary; Dr Zhigang Hao [1978] Director/Chemical Engineer [Chinese]; Michael Koenig [1963] Director/Chief Executive Officer [German]; Michael James Parkington [1969] Director/Engineer

**Technical Arc Ltd**
*Incorporated:* 9 December 2010 *Employees:* 30
*Net Worth:* £3,677,099 *Total Assets:* £4,557,624
*Registered Office:* Technical Arc Ltd, Outgang Lane, Osbaldwick, York, YO19 5UP
*Activities:* Manufacture of other machine tools
*Major Shareholder:* Richard Rycroft
*Officers:* Pamela Maria Rycroft, Secretary; Richard Paul Rycroft [1967] Director/Technician

**Technical Control Systems Limited**
*Incorporated:* 17 March 1969 *Employees:* 56
*Net Worth:* £2,650,251 *Total Assets:* £4,647,000
*Registered Office:* Control Works, Treefield Industrial Estate, Gildersome, Leeds, LS27 7JU
*Activities:* Manufacture of other electrical equipment
*Parent:* North Hill Limited
*Officers:* Nigel Peter Foster [1966] Director; David Alan Jessup [1971] Director; Mark Scally [1969] Director; Jonathan Mark Somers [1968] Director; Neil Capsey Stewart [1966] Director

**Technical Fibre Products Limited**
*Incorporated:* 5 September 1986 *Employees:* 89
*Net Worth:* £10,076,000 *Total Assets:* £28,362,000
*Registered Office:* Burneside, Kendal, Cumbria, LA9 6PZ
*Activities:* Other manufacturing n.e.c.
*Parent:* James Cropper PLC
*Officers:* James Francis Aldridge, Secretary; Isabelle Marguerite Maddock [1968] Director/Financial Controller; Martin Thompson [1959] Director; Philip Ian Wild [1969] Director

**Technikraft Limited**
*Incorporated:* 21 April 1987 *Employees:* 58
*Net Worth:* £2,962,103 *Total Assets:* £3,974,807
*Registered Office:* Brittannia Road, Brittania Road, Goole, E Yorks, DN14 6ET
*Activities:* Wholesale of other fuels and related products
*Parent:* Technikraft Holdings Limited
*Officers:* Malcolm Gibson, Secretary; Philip Mark Fryer [1958] Director; Malcolm Gibson [1956] Director; David Paul Stewart [1969] Director; Graham John Walker [1953] Director/Chemist

**Technimark Limited**
*Incorporated:* 10 September 2009 *Employees:* 65
*Previous:* Classic Industries Europe Limited
*Net Worth:* £7,145,523 *Total Assets:* £8,146,804
*Registered Office:* Kirkcarrion Estate, Gas Lane, Middleton in Teesdale, Barnard Castle, Co Durham, DL12 0TN
*Activities:* Manufacture of other plastic products
*Officers:* Brad Wellington [1968] Director/President [American]

**Technowash Limited**
*Incorporated:* 12 July 2000 *Employees:* 61
*Net Worth:* £207,740 *Total Assets:* £3,227,231
*Registered Office:* 8-10 Standard Way, Standard Way Business Park, Northallerton, N Yorks, DL6 2XE
*Activities:* Manufacture of other special-purpose machinery n.e.c.
*Parent:* Safety-Kleen UK Limited
*Officers:* Andrew Gregory Firth [1964] Director; Andrew Patrick Griffith [1968] Director; Philippe Robert Francis Mauguy [1960] Director [French]; Steven Edward Price [1964] Director

**Techrete (U.K.) Limited**
*Incorporated:* 20 June 1989 *Employees:* 148
*Net Worth:* £8,450,522 *Total Assets:* £17,066,628
*Registered Office:* Station Road, Scawby, Brigg, N Lincs, DN20 9DT
*Activities:* Construction of commercial buildings
*Major Shareholder:* Christopher O'Dea
*Officers:* Denis Farrell, Secretary; Denis Farrell [1966] Director/Chartered Accountant [Irish]; Mark O'Dea [1974] Director/Actuary [Irish]; Marcus Sweeney [1950] Director [Irish]

**Techwax Limited**
*Incorporated:* 24 May 1991 *Employees:* 48
*Net Worth:* £1,989,107 *Total Assets:* £3,251,541
*Registered Office:* Unit 4b Whinbank Park, Whinbank Road, Aycliffe Industrial Park, Newton Aycliffe, Co Durham, DL5 6AY
*Activities:* Manufacture of other chemical products n.e.c.
*Parent:* ISP Holdings (U.K.) Ltd
*Officers:* Julie Charlton, Secretary; Arnoldus Hendrikus Hermanus Bosgoed [1972] Director Finance & Control EMEA [Dutch]; Kevin Higgins [1985] Director/Treasury Manager [American]; Christophe Nicolas Roland Le Louarn [1962] Director/Senior Controller [French]

**Teconnex Limited**
*Incorporated:* 7 September 1979 *Employees:* 390
*Net Worth:* £15,166,000 *Total Assets:* £22,644,000
*Registered Office:* The Old Court House, 24 Market Street, Gainsborough, Lincs, DN21 2BE
*Activities:* Manufacture of other fabricated metal products n.e.c.
*Parent:* Hexadex Limited
*Officers:* Emma Joanne Shakespeare, Secretary; Ian Douglas Brown [1960] Director of Technologies; Kimberley Iverson [1973] HR Director; Michael John Love [1980] Operations Director; Stephen Douglas Evan Lucas [1966] Sales Director; Christopher Paul Marsden [1979] Director of Engineering; Andrew Joseph Meakin [1966] Director/Chartered Accountant; Steven David Pollard [1962] Deputy Managing Director; Paul Sleaford [1961] Managing Director; Darren Jason Spencer [1976] Finance and Commercial Director

**Tees & Durham (Lift) Investments Limited**
*Incorporated:* 10 September 2010 *Employees:* 5
*Net Worth:* £302,093 *Total Assets:* £4,056,162
*Registered Office:* 4340 Park Approach, Thorpe Park, Leeds, LS15 8GB
*Activities:* Non-trading company
*Shareholders:* Community Ventures Investments Limited; Equitix Limited
*Officers:* Victoria Louise Jagger-Strangeway, Secretary; Nigel Michael Fenny [1961] Director; David John Harding [1980] Director/Chartered Accountant; Philip Jonathan Harris [1971] Director; Dean Spencer [1966] Director; Philip Arthur Would [1971] Director/Asset Management

**Teescraft Engineering Limited**
*Incorporated:* 6 April 1981 *Employees:* 107
*Net Worth:* £4,281,884 *Total Assets:* £8,163,295
*Registered Office:* Unit 2 South Church Enterprise Park, Bishop Auckland, Co Durham, DL14 6XB
*Activities:* Machining
*Major Shareholder:* Robert John Yorke
*Officers:* John Clifford Laverick, Secretary/Director; John Clifford Laverick [1942] Director; Robert John Yorke [1971] Director; Stephen Yorke [1963] Director/Logistics Manager

**TEF Transport Limited**
*Incorporated:* 1 November 1973 *Employees:* 100
*Net Worth:* £2,895,119 *Total Assets:* £7,718,015
*Registered Office:* Unit 1 City Link Industrial Park, Phoenix Way, Tyersal, Bradford, W Yorks, BD4 8JP
*Activities:* Freight transport by road
*Shareholders:* Andrew McLaughlin; Linda McLaughlin
*Officers:* Linda McLaughlin, Secretary; Gerard Dibb [1962] Managing Director; Andrew McLaughlin [1967] Director/Transport Manager; Linda McLaughlin [1963] Director/Secretary; Philip George Troop [1973] Finance Director

**TEI Limited**
*Incorporated:* 20 September 2004 *Employees:* 208
*Net Worth:* £1,459,165 *Total Assets:* £9,521,521
*Registered Office:* P O Box 80, Calder Vale Road, Wakefield, W Yorks, WF1 5YS
*Activities:* Other specialised construction activities n.e.c.
*Parent:* TEI Group Ltd
*Officers:* Josephine Ann Budby, Secretary/Accountant; David John Billington [1948] Director; Josephine Ann Budby [1965] Director/Accountant; David Hyland [1966] Commercial Director; Alan James Waddington [1960] Southern Director

**Tekjur Limited**
*Incorporated:* 2 March 2016 *Employees:* 47
*Net Worth:* £747,225 *Total Assets:* £8,325,059
*Registered Office:* Sidings House, Sidings Court, Doncaster, S Yorks, DN4 5NU
*Activities:* Wholesale trade of motor vehicle parts and accessories
*Shareholders:* Allan Hooks; Matthew Stephen Robinson
*Officers:* Susan Gaye, Secretary; Allan Hooks [1957] Director; Matthew Stephen Robinson [1976] Director

**Tekmar Energy Limited**
*Incorporated:* 27 June 2007 *Employees:* 102
*Net Worth:* £13,823,000 *Total Assets:* £19,866,000
*Registered Office:* Unit 1 Park 2000, Millennium Way, Aycliffe Business Park, Newton Aycliffe, Co Durham, DL5 6AR
*Activities:* Other manufacturing n.e.c.
*Parent:* Tekmar Holdings Limited
*Officers:* Russell Edmondson [1978] Operations Director; Sue Hurst [1966] Finance Director; Alasdair MacDonald [1965] Director/Chairman; James Thomas Ritchie-Bland [1990] Director; Terence Henry Sheldrake [1963] Director

**Tekmar Holdings Limited**
*Incorporated:* 1 August 2011 *Employees:* 6
*Net Worth Deficit:* £20,163,000 *Total Assets:* £28,179,000
*Registered Office:* Unit 1 Park 2000, Millennium Way, Aycliffe Business Park, Newton Aycliffe, Co Durham, DL5 6AR
*Activities:* Activities of head offices
*Parent:* Tekmar Limited
*Officers:* Sue Hurst [1966] Finance Director; Alasdair MacDonald [1965] Director/Chairman; James Thomas Ritchie-Bland [1990] Director/Operation Manager

**Tekmar Limited**
*Incorporated:* 19 August 2011 *Employees:* 113
*Previous:* Tekmar Group Limited
*Net Worth Deficit:* £13,205,000 *Total Assets:* £31,411,000
*Registered Office:* Unit 1 Park 2000, Millennium Way, Aycliffe Business Park, Newton Aycliffe, Co Durham, DL5 6AR
*Activities:* Activities of head offices
*Parent:* Tekmar Group PLC
*Officers:* Sue Hurst [1966] Finance Director; Alasdair MacDonald [1965] Director/Chairman; James Thomas Ritchie-Bland [1990] Director/Operations Manager

**Teleware Group PLC**
*Incorporated:* 30 June 2004 *Employees:* 75
*Net Worth:* £601,000 *Total Assets:* £3,863,000
*Registered Office:* Teleware House, York Road, Thirsk, N Yorks, YO7 3BX
*Activities:* Other telecommunications activities
*Major Shareholder:* Geoffrey Richard Haworth
*Officers:* Ged Cooney, Secretary; Helen Kirstie Aston Haworth [1969] Director; Carol Haworth [1943] Director; Geoffrey Richard Haworth [1942] Director; Steven Richard Haworth [1972] Director

**Teleware Public Limited Company**
*Incorporated:* 7 May 2003 *Employees:* 71
*Net Worth:* £4,803,000 *Total Assets:* £7,746,000
*Registered Office:* Teleware House, York Road, Thirsk, N Yorks, YO7 3BX
*Activities:* Other information technology service activities
*Officers:* Ged Cooney, Secretary; Geoffrey Richard Haworth [1942] Director; Paul Stephen Millar [1970] Director/Software Development Manager

**Temeridge Limited**
*Incorporated:* 29 March 2006
*Net Worth Deficit:* £318,816 *Total Assets:* £3,594,795
*Registered Office:* 134 Leeds Road, Shipley, W Yorks, BD18 1BX
*Activities:* Other letting and operating of own or leased real estate
*Shareholders:* John Thomas Lamb; David Darcy Thompson
*Officers:* John Thomas Lamb [1954] Director; John Patrick Thomas Lamb [1982] Director

**Temple Way Properties Limited**
*Incorporated:* 16 June 1972 *Employees:* 5
*Net Worth:* £8,151,642 *Total Assets:* £8,503,374
*Registered Office:* 62 North Lane, Headingley, Leeds, LS6 3HU
*Activities:* Buying and selling of own real estate
*Major Shareholder:* Derek Bethell
*Officers:* Marilyn Bethell, Secretary; Derek Bethell [1941] Director/Property Developer; Marilyn Bethell [1945] Director/Property Developer; Jean Blanchard [1953] Director/Manager

**Templer Management Limited**
*Incorporated:* 26 April 2010
*Net Worth Deficit:* £7,148 *Total Assets:* £4,480,307
*Registered Office:* Sanderson House, Station Road, Horsforth, Leeds, LS18 5NT
*Activities:* Sale of used cars and light motor vehicles
*Major Shareholder:* Jaswant Singh Hare
*Officers:* Jasbir Singh Athwal [1962] Director; Nirvinder Singh Hare [1972] Director; Bryan Metcalfe [1956] Director

**Tenet Business Solutions Limited**
*Incorporated:* 1 December 1997 *Employees:* 7
*Net Worth:* £4,632,505 *Total Assets:* £7,922,442
*Registered Office:* 5 Lister Hill, Horsforth, Leeds, LS18 5AZ
*Activities:* Other business support service activities n.e.c.
*Parent:* Tenet Group Limited
*Officers:* Richard James Fletcher, Secretary; Helen Muriel Ball [1963] Director; Caroline Jane Bradley [1963] Finance Director; Keely Jill Craig [1974] Finance Director; Stephen Mark Jones [1958] Director

**Tenet Group Limited**
*Incorporated:* 19 January 2000 *Employees:* 282
*Net Worth:* £29,886,154 *Total Assets:* £51,504,028
*Registered Office:* 5 Lister Hill, Horsforth, Leeds, LS18 5AZ
*Activities:* Activities of financial services holding companies
*Shareholders:* Standard Life Aberdeen PLC; Aviva PLC
*Officers:* Richard James Fletcher, Secretary; Helen Muriel Ball [1963] Director; Caroline Jane Bradley [1963] Finance Director; Keely Jill Craig [1974] Director; Caroline Anne Dibbs [1969] Director; Jim Ewing [1970] Director; Martin James Greenwood [1954] Director; Phillip Hilling [1949] Director; Alfred Barrington Meeks [1954] Director; Steve Murray [1978] Director

**Tenet Limited**
*Incorporated:* 26 October 1999
*Net Worth:* £17,008,800 *Total Assets:* £17,008,892
*Registered Office:* 5 Lister Hill, Horsforth, Leeds, LS18 5AZ
*Activities:* Activities of financial services holding companies
*Parent:* Tenet Group Limited
*Officers:* Richard James Fletcher, Secretary; Helen Muriel Ball [1963] Director; Karina Bowden [1984] Director; Caroline Jane Bradley [1963] Finance Director; Simon Broadley [1978] Director; Keely Jill Craig [1974] Finance Director; Martin James Greenwood [1954] Executive Director; Stephen Jones [1958] Director; Alfred Barrington Meeks [1954] Director; Ben Wright [1992] Director

**Tenetconnect Limited**
*Incorporated:* 17 October 1991 *Employees:* 107
*Net Worth:* £6,420,120 *Total Assets:* £16,290,184
*Registered Office:* 5 Lister Hill, Horsforth, Leeds, LS18 5AZ
*Activities:* Financial intermediation not elsewhere classified
*Parent:* Tenet Limited
*Officers:* Richard James Fletcher, Secretary; Helen Muriel Ball [1963] Director; Karina Bowden [1984] Director; Caroline Jane Bradley [1963] Finance Director; Simon Broadley [1978] Director; Keely Jill Craig [1974] Finance Director; Martin James Greenwood [1954] Director/Executive Chairman; Stephen Jones [1958] Director; Ben Wright [1982] Director

**Tenetconnect Services Limited**
*Incorporated:* 15 July 1988 *Employees:* 61
*Net Worth:* £4,866,400 *Total Assets:* £7,771,862
*Registered Office:* 5 Lister Hill, Horsforth, Leeds, LS18 5AZ
*Activities:* Financial intermediation not elsewhere classified
*Parent:* Tenet Limited
*Officers:* Richard James Fletcher, Secretary; Helen Muriel Ball [1963] Director; Karina Bowden [1984] Director; Caroline Jane Bradley [1963] Finance Director; Simon Broadley [1978] Director; Keely Jill Craig [1974] Finance Director; Martin James Greenwood [1954] Director/Executive Chairman; Stephen Jones [1958] Director; Ben Wright [1982] Director

**Tenetlime Limited**
*Incorporated:* 3 June 2003 *Employees:* 65
*Net Worth:* £2,070,589 *Total Assets:* £7,109,083
*Registered Office:* 5 Lister Hill, Horsforth, Leeds, LS18 5AZ
*Activities:* Financial intermediation not elsewhere classified
*Parent:* Tenet Limited
*Officers:* Richard James Fletcher, Secretary; Helen Muriel Ball [1963] Director; Karina Bowden [1984] Director; Caroline Jane Bradley [1963] Finance Director; Simon Broadley [1978] Director; Keely Jill Craig [1974] Finance Director; Martin James Greenwood [1954] Director/Executive Chairman; Stephen Jones [1958] Director; Ben Wright [1982] Director

**James H. Tennant Limited**
*Incorporated:* 3 March 1987 *Employees:* 9
*Net Worth:* £1,646,303 *Total Assets:* £4,067,608
*Registered Office:* Manor House Farm, Fraisthorpe, Bridlington, N Humbers, YO15 3QT
*Activities:* Raising of horses and other equines
*Shareholders:* James Herbert Tennant; Susan Mary Tennant
*Officers:* Susan Mary Tennant, Secretary; James Herbert Tennant [1954] Director/Farmer; Susan Mary Tennant [1957] Director/Housewife

**Tennants of Yorkshire Antique and Fine Art Auctioneers Limited**
*Incorporated:* 4 May 1988 *Employees:* 107
*Net Worth:* £5,409,389 *Total Assets:* £11,412,870
*Registered Office:* Harmby Road, Leyburn, N Yorks, DL8 5SG
*Activities:* Other business support service activities n.e.c.
*Shareholders:* Rodney Michael Tennant; Lesley Jane Tennant
*Officers:* Lesley Jean Tennant, Secretary; Audrey Ann Fall [1954] Director/Accounts Manager; Jeremy Michael Pattison [1974] Director/Auctioneer; Alison Clare Tennant [1983] Director/Personal Assistant; Jane Michelle Tennant [1987] Director/Personal Assistant; Lesley Jean Tennant [1954] Director/Company Secretary; Rodney Michael Tennant [1947] Director/Auctioneer and Valuer; Caroline Louise Thomas [1981] Director/Accountant

**Terberg DTS (UK) Limited**
*Incorporated:* 16 June 1998 *Employees:* 125
*Net Worth:* £19,526,494 *Total Assets:* £43,877,000
*Registered Office:* Lowfields Way, Lowfields Business Park, Elland, W Yorks, HX5 9DA
*Activities:* Wholesale of agricultural machinery, equipment and supplies
*Parent:* Terberg Group BV
*Officers:* Nigel Edwin Chubb, Secretary; Alisdair Neill Rae Couper [1966] Managing Director; George Johannes Maria Terberg [1952] Director [Dutch]

**Tereos UK & Ireland Ltd**
*Incorporated:* 8 December 2014 *Employees:* 136
*Net Worth:* £14,287,000 *Total Assets:* £42,158,000
*Registered Office:* Ripley Drive, Normanton Industrial Estate, Normanton, W Yorks, WF6 1RY
*Activities:* Manufacture of sugar
*Officers:* Yves Belegaud [1960] Director [French]; Alexis Duval [1977] Director [French]

**Termrim Construction Limited**
*Incorporated:* 17 June 1976 *Employees:* 31
*Net Worth:* £6,270,985 *Total Assets:* £9,730,742
*Registered Office:* 1 Pellon Place, Dyson Wood Way, Bradley Business Park, Huddersfield, W Yorks, HD2 1GT
*Activities:* Development of building projects
*Parent:* Patrick Construction Group Ltd
*Officers:* Beverley Jayne Rockett, Secretary; Simon Bateman [1982] Director; Graeme Charles Bird [1969] Managing Director; Jason Mark McGarvey [1977] Director; Beverley Jayne Rockett [1958] Director; Simon James Taylor [1971] Development Director

**Tetley's Motor Services Limited**
*Incorporated:* 30 January 1997 *Employees:* 63
*Net Worth:* £2,458,927 *Total Assets:* £3,125,087
*Registered Office:* Hunslet Business Park, 76 Goodman Street, Leeds, LS10 1NY
*Activities:* Other urban, suburban or metropolitan passenger land transport (not underground, metro or similar)
*Shareholders:* Ian Tetley; Angela Elizabeth Tetley
*Officers:* Angela Elizabeth Tetley, Secretary/Director; Angela Elizabeth Tetley [1957] Director/Clerical Officer; Ian Tetley [1963] Director/Chartered Engineer

**TEV Holdings Limited**
*Incorporated:* 22 February 2017 *Employees:* 62
*Net Worth:* £676,745 *Total Assets:* £7,551,275
*Registered Office:* Unit 4 Armytage Road, Brighouse, W Yorks, HD6 1QF
*Activities:* Other manufacturing n.e.c.
*Shareholders:* YFM Equity Partners 2016 (GP) Limited; Anthony Charles Hammersley
*Officers:* Andrew Lee, Secretary; Christopher John Brown [1953] Director; James Lewis Carr-Smith [1978] Director; Christopher Leonard Chisman [1975] Director/Engineer; Anthony Charles Hammersley [1959] Director

**TEV Limited**
*Incorporated:* 13 August 2003 *Employees:* 62
*Net Worth:* £4,643,958 *Total Assets:* £6,080,708
*Registered Office:* Unit 4 Armytage Road, Brighouse, W Yorks, HD6 1QF
*Activities:* Manufacture of non-domestic cooling and ventilation equipment
*Parent:* Thermal Energy Ventures Limited
*Officers:* Andrew Lee, Secretary; Christopher John Brown [1953] Director; James Lewis Carr-Smith [1978] Director; Christopher Leonard Chisman [1975] Director/Engineer; Anthony Charles Hammersley [1959] Director; Andrew Lee [1970] Director

**Teva Acquisition Limited**
*Incorporated:* 25 October 2004 *Employees:* 2
*Previous:* Warner Chilcott Acquisition Limited
*Net Worth:* £123,863,424 *Total Assets:* £2,490,702,080
*Registered Office:* Ridings Point, Whistler Drive, Castleford, W Yorks, WF10 5HX
*Activities:* Activities of head offices
*Parent:* Actavis UK Group Limited
*Officers:* Dean Michael Cooper [1972] Director/Chartered Accountant; Kim Innes [1968] Director/General Manager

**Teva Laboratories UK Limited**
*Incorporated:* 3 May 1954
*Previous:* Forest Laboratories UK Limited
*Net Worth:* £29,107,372 *Total Assets:* £32,736,420
*Registered Office:* Ridings Point, Whistler Drive, Castleford, W Yorks, WF10 5HX
*Activities:* Manufacture of basic pharmaceutical products
*Parent:* Teva Pharma Holdings Limited
*Officers:* Dean Michael Cooper [1972] Director/Chartered Accountant; Kim Innes [1968] Director/General Manager

**Teva UK Holdings Limited**
*Incorporated:* 19 September 2002
*Net Worth:* £70,442,000 *Total Assets:* £170,868,000
*Registered Office:* Ridings Point, Whistler Drive, Castleford, W Yorks, WF10 5HX
*Activities:* Activities of head offices
*Parent:* Orvet UK
*Officers:* Dean Michael Cooper [1972] Director/Chartered Accountant; Kim Innes [1968] Director/General Manager; David Vrhovec [1967] Director [Slovenian]

**Teva UK Limited**
*Incorporated:* 1 July 1935 *Employees:* 792
*Net Worth:* £66,836,000 *Total Assets:* £561,601,984
*Registered Office:* Ridings Point, Whistler Drive, Castleford, W Yorks, WF10 5HX
*Activities:* Manufacture of pharmaceutical preparations
*Parent:* Teva UK Holdings Limited
*Officers:* Dean Michael Cooper [1972] Director/Chartered Accountant; Kim Innes [1968] Director/General Manager; David Vrhovec [1967] Director [Slovenian]

**TFP (Wakefield) Limited**
*Incorporated:* 1 November 2011 *Employees:* 3
*Net Worth:* £3,273,642 *Total Assets:* £7,781,263
*Registered Office:* c/o J & R Naylors of Wakefield Limited, 97 Bridge Road, Horbury Bridge, Wakefield, W Yorks, WF4 5NN
*Activities:* Other letting and operating of own or leased real estate
*Officers:* Lisa Marie Porter [1971] Director; Roger Joseph Tranter [1945] Director; Shaun Andrew Tranter [1967] Director

**TG-F Investments (No. 1) Limited**
*Incorporated:* 26 February 2013
*Net Worth:* £4,620,602 *Total Assets:* £4,623,372
*Registered Office:* Moorside Farm, Moor Lane, East Keswick, Leeds, LS17 9HN
*Activities:* Activities of open-ended investment companies
*Officers:* Anthony Marcus [1946] Director; Jason Robert Marcus [1972] Director

**TG-F Investments (No. 2) Limited**
*Incorporated:* 26 February 2013
*Net Worth:* £369,947 *Total Assets:* £4,610,492
*Registered Office:* Moorside Farm, Moor Lane, East Keswick, Leeds, LS17 9HN
*Activities:* Activities of open-ended investment companies
*Parent:* TG-F Investments (No.1) Limited
*Officers:* Anthony Marcus [1946] Director; Jason Robert Marcus [1972] Director; Simone Isobel Marcus [1947] Director

**TGC (2015) Limited**
*Incorporated:* 28 January 2015 *Employees:* 154
*Net Worth:* £5,174,684 *Total Assets:* £9,489,863
*Registered Office:* Tong Garden Centre, Tong Lane, Bradford, W Yorks, BD4 0RY
*Activities:* Retail sale of flowers, plants, seeds, fertilizers, pet animals and pet food in specialised stores
*Parent:* Birch Valley Holdings Limited
*Officers:* Charles Peter Barker [1979] Director/Chartered Accountant; Mark William Farnsworth [1977] Director/Retailer; Thomas Alan Taylor Megginson [1974] Director

**TGH Acquisitions Limited**
*Incorporated:* 6 February 2008
*Net Worth:* £299,060,992 *Total Assets:* £299,102,016
*Registered Office:* Whitley Lodge, Whitley Bridge, Doncaster, S Yorks, DN14 0HR
*Activities:* Activities of other holding companies n.e.c.
*Parent:* TGH Finance Limited
*Officers:* Jonathan Paul Furniss, Secretary; James Simon Edward Arnell [1969] Director/Investment Manager; Gunter Heinz Otto Dombrowe [1947] Director [German]; Lars Ernst Vilhelm Gatenbeck [1956] Director [Swedish]; Gerard Christopher Loftus [1960] Director; Craig Parsons [1970] Director; Thomas Spencer Patrick [1972] Director

**TGH Capital Limited**
*Incorporated:* 13 January 2014
*Net Worth:* £13,537 *Total Assets:* £6,297,431
*Registered Office:* Bowcliffe Hall, Bramham, Wetherby, W Yorks, LS23 6LP
*Activities:* Financial management
*Major Shareholder:* Timothy James Whitworth
*Officers:* Matthew Edward Bennison [1972] Director; Timothy James Whitworth [1971] Director

**TGH Finance Limited**
*Incorporated:* 6 February 2008 *Employees:* 4
*Net Worth Deficit:* £1,088,786,048 *Total Assets:* £9,628,000
*Registered Office:* Whitley Lodge, Whitley Bridge, Doncaster, S Yorks, DN14 0HR
*Activities:* Activities of other holding companies n.e.c.
*Parent:* TGH Investments Limited
*Officers:* Jonathan Paul Furniss, Secretary; James Simon Edward Arnell [1969] Director/Investment Manager; Craig Parsons [1970] Director; Thomas Spencer Patrick [1972] Director

**TGH Investments Limited**
*Incorporated:* 6 February 2008
*Net Worth Deficit:* £1,024,868,992 *Total Assets:* £298,462,016
*Registered Office:* Whitley Lodge, Whitley Bridge, Doncaster, S Yorks, DN14 0HR
*Activities:* Activities of other holding companies n.e.c.
*Parent:* Tunstall Healthcare Group Limited
*Officers:* Jonathan Paul Furniss, Secretary; James Simon Edward Arnell [1969] Director/Investment Manager; Craig Parsons [1970] Director; Thomas Spencer Patrick [1972] Director/Solicitor

**Thai Leisure Group Limited**
*Incorporated:* 3 July 2012 *Employees:* 872
*Net Worth:* £726,462 *Total Assets:* £20,342,756
*Registered Office:* Apollo House, Eboracum Way, York, YO31 7RE
*Activities:* Licenced restaurants
*Officers:* Atcharaporn Kaewkraikhot [1968] Director; James Ian Leigh [1968] Director of Group Operations; Martin Generald Stead [1966] Director

**Thames Ambulance Service Limited**
*Incorporated:* 8 October 1998 *Employees:* 550
*Net Worth Deficit:* £1,952,494 *Total Assets:* £10,469,663
*Registered Office:* 5 Sidings Court, White Rose Way, Doncaster, S Yorks, DN4 5NU
*Activities:* Hospital activities
*Parent:* The Thames Group (UK) Limited
*Officers:* Luis Gonzaga Higuero Robles [1972] Director [Spanish]; Derek Stevens Laird [1964] Director

**That Company Called If Limited**
*Incorporated:* 27 November 2012 *Employees:* 27
*Net Worth:* £3,724,604 *Total Assets:* £6,405,384
*Registered Office:* Thornton Road Industrial Estate, Thornton Road, Pickering, N Yorks, YO18 7JB
*Activities:* Activities of head offices
*Shareholder:* Anco Far East Limited
*Officers:* Julian Rhodes, Secretary; John Philip Calvert [1969] Director; Terrance Finley [1953] Director [American]; Kim Kraft [1963] Director-Chief Financial Officer [American]; Peter Sung-Yan Yu [1959] Director [American]

**That Good Night Limited**
*Incorporated:* 27 January 2014
*Net Worth:* £711,630 *Total Assets:* £5,444,446
*Registered Office:* Highfield Grange, Bubwith, Selby, N Yorks, YO8 6DP
*Activities:* Motion picture production activities
*Officers:* Alan Richard Latham [1960] Director/Film Producer

**T.& R. Theakston Limited**
*Incorporated:* 6 August 2003 *Employees:* 31
*Net Worth:* £2,422,000 *Total Assets:* £4,944,000
*Registered Office:* The Brewery, Masham, Ripon, N Yorks, HG4 4YD
*Activities:* Manufacture of beer
*Shareholder:* Heineken UK Limited
*Officers:* Simon Francis Owen Theakston, Secretary/Director; Richard Anthony Bradbury [1963] Director; Christopher Michael Jowsey [1965] Director; Edward David Theakston [1962] Director; Nicholas Robert Theakston [1955] Director; Simon Francis Owen Theakston [1957] Director; Timothy James Owen Theakston [1957] Director/Surveyor; William James Collin Wood [1953] Director

**Thebigword Group Limited**
*Incorporated:* 1 September 2005 *Employees:* 548
*Previous:* Thebigword Group PLC
*Net Worth:* £5,077,000 *Total Assets:* £21,526,000
*Registered Office:* Link-Up House, Wortley Ring Road, Lower Wortley, Leeds, LS12 6AB
*Activities:* Translation and interpretation activities
*Major Shareholder:* Laurence Jeremy Gould
*Officers:* Marcus Lee Mills, Secretary; Ali Nihat Arkan [1965] Director/Chief Executive [Turkish]; Joshua Gould [1984] Director; Laurence Jeremy Gould [1952] Director; Michele Gould [1962] Director

**Thebigword Interpreting Services Limited**
*Incorporated:* 1 May 2007 *Employees:* 133
*Net Worth:* £1,505,000 *Total Assets:* £14,014,000
*Registered Office:* Link-Up House, Wortley Ring Road, Lower Wortley, Leeds, LS12 6AB
*Activities:* Translation and interpretation activities
*Major Shareholder:* Laurence Jeremy Gould
*Officers:* Marcus Lee Mills, Secretary; Ali Nihat Arkan [1965] Director/Chief Executive [Turkish]; Mark Andrew Daley [1971] Global Operations Director; Laurence Jeremy Gould [1952] Director/Chairman; Michele Gould [1962] Director; Garry Charles Levitt [1978] Sales Director

**Therapy in Praxis Limited**
*Incorporated:* 14 September 1999 *Employees:* 5
*Net Worth:* £3,304,336 *Total Assets:* £3,487,553
*Registered Office:* 9 Grimbald Crag Court, St James Business Park, Knaresborough, N Yorks, HG5 8QB
*Activities:* General medical practice activities
*Shareholder:* Stephen Walker
*Officers:* Stephen Walker, Secretary; Deborah Jane Walker [1966] Director; Stephen Walker [1963] Director/Practice Manager

**Therma Q Limited**
*Incorporated:* 14 May 2014 *Employees:* 19
*Net Worth:* £664,274 *Total Assets:* £3,295,306
*Registered Office:* Unit 3 Sandbeds Trading Estate, Dewsbury Road, Ossett, W Yorks, WF5 9ND
*Activities:* Manufacture of steam generators, except central heating hot water boilers
*Major Shareholder:* Robert Kwik
*Officers:* Ian Barrett [1981] Director [Irish]; Ronan Philip Ginnell [1982] Director [Irish]; Cameron Holroyd [1960] Director

**Thermac (Hire) Limited**
*Incorporated:* 10 July 1985 *Employees:* 46
*Net Worth Deficit:* £274,000 *Total Assets:* £6,369,000
*Registered Office:* Unit C, Astra Park, Parkside Lane, Leeds, LS11 5SZ
*Activities:* Renting and leasing of other machinery, equipment and tangible goods n.e.c.
*Parent:* Lexia Solutions Group Limited
*Officers:* Andrew Mark Finn, Secretary; Jason Martin Davy [1970] Director; Andrew Mark Finn [1967] Director; Campbell Taylor Rodden [1960] Managing Director

**Thimbleby Farms Limited**
*Incorporated:* 16 February 1996 *Employees:* 22
*Net Worth Deficit:* £785,307 *Total Assets:* £6,072,814
*Registered Office:* York House, Thornfield Business Park, Standard Way Business Park, Northallerton, N Yorks, DL6 2XQ
*Activities:* Mixed farming
*Shareholders:* Andrea Shelley; Andrew Shelley
*Officers:* Andrea Shelley, Secretary; Andrea Shelley [1961] Director; Andrew Edgar Shelley [1960] Director

**Third Energy Services Limited**
*Incorporated:* 24 February 2006
*Net Worth:* £1,378,000 *Total Assets:* £10,075,000
*Registered Office:* Knapton Generating Station, East Knapton, Malton, N Yorks, YO17 8JF
*Activities:* Extraction of crude petroleum
*Shareholder:* Northwharf Nominees Limited
*Officers:* Grant George Emms [1953] Geoscientist/Director [Canadian]; Mr Andrew Mortimer [1963] Director; Rasik Valand [1955] Director

**Third Energy Trading Limited**
*Incorporated:* 24 February 2006
*Net Worth:* £6,000 *Total Assets:* £4,225,000
*Registered Office:* Knapton Generating Station, East Knapton, Malton, N Yorks, YO17 8JF
*Activities:* Extraction of crude petroleum
*Parent:* Third Energy Onshore Limited
*Officers:* Paul Savage, Secretary; Alan Linn [1957] Director; Rasik Valand [1955] Director

**Third Energy UK Gas Limited**
*Incorporated:* 21 May 1979 *Employees:* 15
*Net Worth Deficit:* £37,054,000 *Total Assets:* £50,261,000
*Registered Office:* Knapton Generating Station, East Knapton, Malton, N Yorks, YO17 8JF
*Activities:* Extraction of crude petroleum
*Parent:* Third Energy Onshore Limited
*Officers:* Paul Savage, Secretary; Alan Linn [1957] Director; Rasik Valand [1955] Director

**Thirsk Farmers Auction Mart Company Limited**
*Incorporated:* 25 January 1907 *Employees:* 41
*Net Worth:* £2,044,597 *Total Assets:* £7,472,398
*Registered Office:* Thirsk Rural Business Centre, Blakey Lane, Thirsk, N Yorks, YO7 3AB
*Activities:* Agents selling agricultural raw materials, livestock, textile raw materials and semi-finished goods
*Shareholder:* James Ian Woodhead
*Officers:* Michael Thomas Stephenson, Secretary; Alan Armstrong [1935] Director/Farmer; Rodney Lawrence Cordingley [1964] Director/Chartered Surveyor; John Timothy Garside [1963] Director/Farmer/Livestock Buyer; James Ian Woodhead [1961] Director/Farmer

**Thirsk Investments Limited**
*Incorporated:* 9 April 2014 *Employees:* 3
*Net Worth Deficit:* £186,440 *Total Assets:* £3,652,662
*Registered Office:* 4 Bowcliffe Grange, Bramham, W Yorks, LS23 6UL
*Activities:* Development of building projects
*Shareholders:* Nigel David Rippon Jowett; In-Site Property Solutions Limited
*Officers:* Alexander John Boyle [1985] Director; Richard Andrew Crosland [1964] Director; Nigel David Rippon Jowett [1960] Director

**Thirsk Racecourse Limited**
*Incorporated:* 7 November 1923 *Employees:* 36
*Net Worth:* £3,231,025 *Total Assets:* £6,840,445
*Registered Office:* The Racecourse, Station Road, Thirsk, N Yorks, YO7 1QL
*Activities:* Operation of sports facilities
*Officers:* John Francis Sanderson, Secretary; John Bell [1951] Director/Farmer; Charles Jonathan Dent [1949] Director; Patrick Martin Leicester Hibbert-Foy [1942] Director/Retired; John Francis Sanderson [1941] Director; Charles Andrew Warde-Aldam [1962] Director

**Thistle Insurance Services Limited**
*Incorporated:* 31 March 1938 *Employees:* 229
*Net Worth:* £13,217,000 *Total Assets:* £24,635,000
*Registered Office:* Rossington's Business Park, West Carr Road, Retford, Notts, DN22 7SW
*Activities:* Other business support service activities n.e.c.
*Parent:* PIB Group Limited
*Officers:* Timothy Tracy Brooke [1960] Director; Ryan Christopher Brown [1973] Director; Adrian Colosso [1957] Director; Brendan James McManus [1959] Director; Jonathan Paul Stanley [1965] Director/Chief Risk Officer; Robert Alan Styring [1971] Director

**Thomas Bidco Limited**
*Incorporated:* 13 March 2013 *Employees:* 3
*Net Worth:* £6,999,000 *Total Assets:* £58,475,000
*Registered Office:* Great Rail Journeys Limited, Saviour House, 9 St Saviourgate, York, YO1 8NL
*Activities:* Activities of other holding companies n.e.c.
*Parent:* Thomas Midco Limited
*Officers:* Julian Appleyard [1971] Director; Peter Richard Liney [1959] Director/Chief Executive Officer; Noeleen Patricia Rita Pritchard [1984] Director; David James Riley [1980] Director; Mark Andrew Taylor [1964] IT Director

**Thomas Midco Limited**
*Incorporated:* 13 March 2013
*Net Worth Deficit:* £7,519,000 *Total Assets:* £38,543,000
*Registered Office:* Great Rail Journeys Limited, Saviour House, 9 St Saviourgate, York, YO1 8NL
*Activities:* Activities of other holding companies n.e.c.
*Parent:* Thomas Topco Limited
*Officers:* Julian Appleyard [1971] Director; Peter Richard Liney [1959] Director/Chief Executive Officer; Noeleen Patricia Rita Pritchard [1984] Director; David James Riley [1980] Director; Mark Andrew Taylor [1964] IT Director

**Thomas of York Limited**
*Incorporated:* 11 March 1963 *Employees:* 326
*Net Worth:* £6,015,187 *Total Assets:* £7,593,923
*Registered Office:* St Aelreds, Gilling East, York, YO62 4HR
*Activities:* Manufacture of bread; manufacture of fresh pastry goods and cakes
*Shareholder:* John Thomas
*Officers:* Valerie Christina Louise Thomas, Secretary; Nicola Bale [1969] Director/Chartered Accountant; Stephen Simpson [1959] Director/Bakery Manager; Gareth John Thomas [1963] Director/Builder; John Thomas [1940] Director/Baker; Simon Peter Thomas [1965] Director/Baker; Valerie Christina Louise Thomas [1938] Director/Retired Retail Manager

**Thomas Topco Limited**
*Incorporated:* 13 March 2013 *Employees:* 161
*Net Worth:* £114,000 *Total Assets:* £76,342,000
*Registered Office:* c/o Great Rail Journeys Limited, Saviour House, 9 St Saviourgate, York, YO1 8NL
*Activities:* Activities of other holding companies n.e.c.
*Parent:* Bucharest Bidco Limited
*Officers:* Julian Appleyard [1971] Director; Peter Richard Liney [1959] Director/Chief Executive Officer; Noeleen Patricia Rita Pritchard [1984] Director; David James Riley [1980] Director; Mark Andrew Taylor [1964] IT Director

**Walter Thompson (Contractors) Limited**
*Incorporated:* 3 January 1946 *Employees:* 84
*Net Worth:* £2,536,939 *Total Assets:* £8,218,894
*Registered Office:* Construction House, Northallerton, N Yorks, DL7 8ED
*Activities:* Construction of commercial buildings
*Shareholder:* Susan Bridget Greenwell
*Officers:* Derek John Greenwell, Secretary; Paul Blades [1963] Director; Derek John Greenwell [1948] Director Company Secretary; Paul John Hammerton [1969] Managing Director; Keith Brian Noddings [1972] Finance Director; Richard Andrew Salt [1970] Commercial Director; Graham Michael Shepherd [1974] Director

**Gilbert Thompson (Leeds) Limited**
*Incorporated:* 6 August 1946 *Employees:* 179
*Net Worth:* £3,631,238 *Total Assets:* £11,655,981
*Registered Office:* Yorkshire Produce Centre, Pontefract Lane, Leeds, LS9 0PX
*Activities:* Other letting and operating of own or leased real estate
*Shareholders:* Richard James Thompson; Daniel Charles Thompson
*Officers:* Richard James Thompson, Secretary/Director; Daniel Charles Thompson [1970] Director; Richard James Thompson [1973] Director

**William Thompson (York) Limited**
*Incorporated:* 12 February 1926 *Employees:* 47
*Net Worth:* £2,595,373 *Total Assets:* £11,454,597
*Registered Office:* William Thompson York Limited, Main Street, Amotherby, Malton, N Yorks, YO17 6TA
*Activities:* Support activities for animal production (other than farm animal boarding)
*Parent:* Brandsby Agricultural Trading Association Limited
*Officers:* Andrew Mark Richardson, Secretary; Alan Charles Brader [1955] Director; Andrew Mark Richardson [1965] Director/Buyer; Robert Charles Rook [1952] Director

**Thompson Commercials Limited**
*Incorporated:* 5 May 1954 *Employees:* 166
*Net Worth:* £3,411,264 *Total Assets:* £14,157,114
*Registered Office:* Thompson Commercials Ltd, Salvesen Way, Clive Sullivan Way, Hull, HU3 4UQ
*Activities:* Sale of other motor vehicles
*Parent:* Thompson Commercials Group Limited
*Officers:* Paul Thomas Simpson, Secretary; Paul Thomas Simpson [1963] Director

**Thompson Green & Co. Limited**
*Incorporated:* 30 June 1948
*Net Worth:* £4,415,017 *Total Assets:* £4,531,460
*Registered Office:* 9 Welburn Avenue, West Park, Leeds, LS16 5HJ
*Activities:* Other letting and operating of own or leased real estate
*Officers:* Joan Rosamond Thompson, Secretary; Joan Rosamond Thompson [1945] Director; Judith Anne Thompson [1979] Director

**William Thompson Group Holdings Ltd**
*Incorporated:* 9 January 2007
*Net Worth:* £185,725 *Total Assets:* £3,187,146
*Registered Office:* William Thompson Group Holdings Limited, Main Street, Amotherby, Malton, N Yorks, YO17 6TA
*Activities:* Activities of production holding companies
*Parent:* Murton Feeds Limited
*Officers:* Andrew Mark Richardson, Secretary; Alan Charles Brader [1955] Director; Andrew Mark Richardson [1965] Director; Robert Charles Rook [1952] Director

**Thompson Homes (Yorkshire) Ltd.**
*Incorporated:* 17 September 1999 *Employees:* 4
*Net Worth:* £5,139,386 *Total Assets:* £7,435,295
*Registered Office:* Beacon Works, Beacon Brow Road, Scalby, Scarborough, N Yorks, YO13 0RB
*Activities:* Development of building projects
*Major Shareholder:* Brian Thompson
*Officers:* Nicholas Brazier, Secretary; Samantha Jane Boothby [1979] Director; Brian Thompson [1956] Director/Property Developer

**Thompson Property Ltd**
*Incorporated:* 19 May 2000 *Employees:* 4
*Net Worth:* £7,910,375 *Total Assets:* £13,863,441
*Registered Office:* Beacon Works, Barmoor Lane, Scalby, Scarborough, N Yorks, YO13 0PQ
*Activities:* Other letting and operating of own or leased real estate
*Major Shareholder:* Brian Thompson
*Officers:* Douglas James Durrant, Secretary/Business Consultant; Samantha Jane Boothby [1979] Director; Brian Thompson [1956] Director/Property Developer

**Thomson Limited**
*Incorporated:* 26 February 1974 *Employees:* 35
*Net Worth:* £4,334,922 *Total Assets:* £6,204,113
*Registered Office:* Monk Fryston Park, Betteras Hill Road, South Milford, N Yorks, LS25 5PF
*Activities:* Other engineering activities
*Major Shareholder:* Richard Arthur John Thomson
*Officers:* Trevor Howard Giles, Secretary/Director; Trevor Howard Giles [1948] Director/Accountant; Elizabeth Clare Kaiser [1975] Director; John George Scott [1950] Engineering Director; Richard Arthur John Thomson [1943] Director/Engineer

**Thornber Chicks Limited**
*Incorporated:* 26 November 1959 *Employees:* 3
*Net Worth:* £4,303,311 *Total Assets:* £4,886,439
*Registered Office:* Unit 6 Dean Hey Country Business Park, Cragg Vale, Hebden Bridge, W Yorks, HX7 5RU
*Activities:* Other letting and operating of own or leased real estate
*Officers:* Dina Michelle Ball [1960] Director/Secretary; Heather Gaye Rowntree [1945] Director; Valerie Elizabeth Thornber [1953] Director/Office Manager

**R.E. Thornber Limited**
*Incorporated:* 9 January 1969 *Employees:* 2
*Net Worth:* £2,606,116 *Total Assets:* £4,936,168
*Registered Office:* Dean Hey House, Cragg Vale, Hebden Bridge, W Yorks, HX7 5RU
*Activities:* Other business support service activities n.e.c.
*Shareholders:* Ralph Edgar Thornber; June Adele Thornber
*Officers:* June Adel Thornber, Secretary; June Adel Thornber [1946] Director/Secretarial Assistant; Ralph Edgar Thornber [1948] Director/Poultry Farmer

**Thornhill Community Academy Trust**
*Incorporated:* 17 May 2012 *Employees:* 133
*Net Worth:* £8,864,000 *Total Assets:* £9,660,000
*Registered Office:* Valley Drive, Thornhill, Dewsbury, W Yorks, WF12 0HE
*Activities:* General secondary education
*Officers:* Debra Howard, Secretary; Matthew Craig Burton [1983] Director/Headteacher; Josephine Evans [1961] Director/Housewife; James Griffiths [1977] Director/Police Officer; Wade Hyde [1942] Director/Retired; Ebrahim Jogee [1971] Director/Civil Servant; Marilyn McMahon [1951] Director/Retired; Sahera Patel [1974] Director/Supply Teacher

**Thornsett Vale Limited**
*Incorporated:* 11 January 1995 *Employees:* 110
*Net Worth:* £3,029,729 *Total Assets:* £10,186,243
*Registered Office:* Abbey Road, Barrow in Furness, Cumbria, LA13 0PA
*Activities:* Hotels and similar accommodation
*Officers:* Brian Gerard Conroy [1971] Director/Hotel Manager; Neil Hopkins-Coman [1962] Director/Chartered Accountant; Cassie Marie Kilroe [1967] Director [Irish]; Martin Gerard Kilroe [1970] Sales Director [Irish]; Timothy Anthony Kilroe [1964] Director [Irish]; Andrew Langwallner [1966] Director [Irish]

**Thornton & Ross Limited**
*Incorporated:* 23 November 1922 *Employees:* 590
*Net Worth:* £35,706,000 *Total Assets:* £119,136,000
*Registered Office:* Linthwaite, Huddersfield, W Yorks, HD7 5QH
*Activities:* Manufacture of cleaning and polishing preparations
*Parent:* Stada UK Holdings Ltd
*Officers:* Edwin Charles Blythe, Secretary; Edwin Charles Blythe [1968] Director/Chartered Accountant; Charles Ashley Brierley [1963] Director

**Andy Thornton Limited**
*Incorporated:* 19 September 2005 *Employees:* 101
*Net Worth:* £2,457,759 *Total Assets:* £5,374,938
*Registered Office:* Rosemount, Huddersfield Road, Elland, W Yorks, HX5 0EE
*Activities:* Manufacture of metal structures and parts of structures
*Shareholders:* David Cunningham Hastie; Jonathan Penford; Charles Jonathan Tolley
*Officers:* Jonathan Penford, Secretary; David Cunningham Hastie [1957] Director; Jonathan Penford [1954] Finance Director; Charles Jonathan Tolley [1963] Director; Keith Walker [1960] Director

**Thornton Meat Company Limited**
*Incorporated:* 29 January 2003 *Employees:* 1
*Net Worth:* £7,433,383 *Total Assets:* £18,396,880
*Registered Office:* Swalesmoor Farm, Swales Moor Road, Halifax, W Yorks, HX3 6UF
*Activities:* Other letting and operating of own or leased real estate
*Parent:* Leo Group Ltd
*Officers:* Manjit Singh Powar [1976] Director; Danny Steven Sawrij [1969] Director

**Thorpe Park Developments Limited**
*Incorporated:* 15 January 2001
*Net Worth:* £11,603,595 *Total Assets:* £100,346,288
*Registered Office:* Europa House, 20 Esplanade, Scarborough, N Yorks, YO11 2AQ
*Activities:* Development of building projects
*Parent:* Thorpe Park Holdings Limited
*Officers:* Gordon Clark Aitchison [1964] Director; Rachel Dickie [1984] Director/Investment Manager; Luke Mia Liu Goh [1977] Director [Singaporean]; Laura Mason [1976] Director; Simon Charles McCabe [1977] Director/Development Executive; Jeremy John Tutton [1966] Director/Financial Controller

**Thorpe Park Holdings Limited**
*Incorporated:* 3 August 2015
*Net Worth:* £52,344,000 *Total Assets:* £116,716,000
*Registered Office:* Europa House, 20 Esplanade, Scarborough, N Yorks, YO11 2AQ
*Activities:* Activities of other holding companies n.e.c.
*Shareholders:* Scarborough Thorpe Park Holdings Limited; Legal & General Capital Investments Limited
*Officers:* Gordon Clark Aitchison [1964] Director; Rachel Dickie [1984] Director/Investment Manager; Luke Mia Liu Goh [1977] Director [Singaporean]; Laura Mason [1976] Director; Kevin Charles McCabe [1948] Director/Chartered Surveyor; Simon Charles McCabe [1977] Director/Development Executive; Jeremy John Tutton [1966] Director/Financial Controller

**Thorpe Underwood Services Limited**
*Incorporated:* 22 May 1986 *Employees:* 9
*Net Worth:* £6,771,990 *Total Assets:* £21,104,746
*Registered Office:* Thorpe Underwood Hall, Thorpe Underwood, York, YO26 9SZ
*Activities:* Combined facilities support activities
*Parent:* The Collegiate Formation Ltd
*Officers:* Christopher James Hall, Secretary; Christopher James Hall [1969] Director/Chartered Accountant; Amy Katherine Martin [1983] Director/Executive; Francis David Martin [1967] Director

**Three Oceans Fish Company Limited**
*Incorporated:* 31 July 1991 *Employees:* 69
*Net Worth:* £4,715,965 *Total Assets:* £15,265,449
*Registered Office:* Ocean House, Witty Street, The Boulevard, Hull, HU3 4TT
*Activities:* Processing and preserving of fish, crustaceans and molluscs
*Major Shareholder:* Timothy Duncan Rose
*Officers:* Mark Holmes, Secretary; Geoffrey Duncan Druce [1961] Director/Salesman; Mark Holmes [1976] Financial Director; Martin Hugh Jones [1959] Director; Stephen Christopher Lane [1979] Manufacturing Director; Timothy Duncan Rose [1963] Director; Jonathan Mark Warburton [1961] Director/Chairman

**Three Sixty Water Limited**
*Incorporated:* 16 December 2015 *Employees:* 25
*Net Worth Deficit:* £1,310,000 *Total Assets:* £8,619,000
*Registered Office:* Western House, Halifax Road, Bradford, W Yorks, BD6 2SZ
*Activities:* Activities of other holding companies n.e.c.
*Parent:* Kelda Group Limited
*Officers:* Angela Wendy Miriam White, Secretary; Elizabeth Marian Barber [1965] Director/Accountant; Nicholas Richard Topham [1966] Managing Director

**Three60 Energy Limited**
*Incorporated:* 8 September 2016 *Employees:* 1
*Net Worth:* £11,432,332 *Total Assets:* £11,510,150
*Registered Office:* 1 Park Row, Leeds, LS1 5AB
*Activities:* Activities of other holding companies n.e.c.
*Officers:* Laurent Didier Alessio [1962] Director [French]; Jeffery Neil Joseph Corray [1963] Managing Director [Malaysian]; Kevin Sutherland [1984] Director/Chartered Accountant; Walter Thain [1967] Director

**Thrunscoe Primary and Nursery Academy**
*Incorporated:* 3 April 2012 *Employees:* 51
*Net Worth:* £4,289,313 *Total Assets:* £4,947,708
*Registered Office:* Thrunscoe Primary and Nursery Academy, Trinity Road, Cleethorpes, S Humbers, DN35 8UL
*Activities:* Pre-primary education
*Officers:* Simon Bate [1973] Director/Teacher; Louise Alice Deane [1978] Director; Jill Ashley Goodwin [1963] Director; Alexandra Jade Hanley [1991] Director/Finance Officer at Local Government Office; Gemma Louise Harney [1986] Director; Andrew Steven Pomfret [1964] Director/Ambulance Medic; Rolf Heinz Sperr [1947] Director/Retired [German]; Catherine Standley [1971] Director/Headteacher; Ivan Barry Stead [1943] Director/Independent Funeral Celebrant; Patricia Mary Taylor [1955] Director

**THS Industrial Textiles Limited**
*Incorporated:* 19 June 2009 *Employees:* 17
*Net Worth:* £1,369,976 *Total Assets:* £4,363,876
*Registered Office:* Heathfield Business Park, Heathfield Street, Elland, W Yorks, HX5 9AU
*Activities:* Manufacture of other technical and industrial textiles
*Major Shareholder:* Jonathan Brett Newsome
*Officers:* Carolyn Barnes [1967] Director/Accountant; Adam Jack Charnock [1984] Operations Director; Jonathan Brett Newsome [1963] Director; Colin Alan Stansfield [1979] Sales Director

**G. & A. Thursby Limited**
*Incorporated:* 9 July 1982 *Employees:* 32
*Net Worth:* £4,394,985 *Total Assets:* £4,616,059
*Registered Office:* Warton Road, Carnforth, Lancs, LA5 9EX
*Activities:* Freight transport by road
*Shareholder:* Carol Urban
*Officers:* Carol Urban, Secretary; Brian Urban [1964] Director; Carol Urban [1966] Director

**Thurston Group Limited**
*Incorporated:* 31 December 1970 *Employees:* 221
*Net Worth:* £6,448,013 *Total Assets:* £12,721,272
*Registered Office:* Quarry Hill Industrial Estate, Hawkingcroft Road, Horbury, Wakefield, W Yorks, WF4 6AJ
*Activities:* Manufacture of metal structures and parts of structures
*Shareholders:* Jonathan Leslie Petch; Gordon Burley Thurston; Eric Mould; Thurston Holdings Ltd
*Officers:* Mark Andrew Gibson, Secretary; Mark Andrew Gibson [1963] Finance Director; Eric Mould [1944] Director; Jonathan Leslie Petch [1961] Director/Chief Executive; Gordon Burley Thurston [1950] Director

**Thurston Holdings Limited**
*Incorporated:* 2 July 1998 *Employees:* 221
*Net Worth:* £7,576,297 *Total Assets:* £14,101,056
*Registered Office:* Quarry Hill Industrial Estate, Hawking Croft Road, Horbury, Wakefield, W Yorks, WF4 6AJ
*Activities:* Manufacture of metal structures and parts of structures
*Shareholders:* Jonathan Leslie Petch; Eric Mould; Gordon Burley Thurston
*Officers:* Mark Andrew Gibson, Secretary; Eric Mould [1944] Director; Jonathan Leslie Petch [1961] Director; Gordon Burley Thurston [1950] Director

**Ticket Arena Limited**
*Incorporated:* 3 June 2008 *Employees:* 22
*Net Worth:* £3,856,235 *Total Assets:* £6,773,197
*Registered Office:* 31-32 Park Row, Leeds, LS1 5JD
*Activities:* Other business support service activities n.e.c.
*Major Shareholder:* Reshad Sulleman Hossenally
*Officers:* Jan Victor Dauman [1942] Director/Business Consultant; Reshad Hossenally [1988] Director

**Tickhill Engineering Company Limited**
*Incorporated:* 16 June 1964 *Employees:* 71
*Net Worth:* £9,662,278 *Total Assets:* £12,829,847
*Registered Office:* Cow House Lane, Armthorpe, Doncaster, S Yorks, DN3 3EE
*Activities:* Manufacture of other special-purpose machinery n.e.c.
*Major Shareholder:* George Geoffrey Haith
*Officers:* Jennifer Susan Brindley, Secretary; Jennifer Susan Brindley [1963] Director; Christopher John Haith [1954] Director/Agricultural Engineer; David Ian Haith [1966] Director/Agricultural Engineer; George Geoffrey Haith [1925] Director/Agricultural Engineer; Michael Peter Haith [1959] Director/Agricultural Engineer; Nigel Geoffrey Haith [1956] Director/Agricultural Engineer; Stephen Phillip Haith [1952] Director/Agricultural Engineer

**Jack Tighe Limited**
*Incorporated:* 13 January 1965 *Employees:* 103
*Net Worth:* £3,202,264 *Total Assets:* £5,179,608
*Registered Office:* Redbourne Mere, Kirton Lindsey, Gainsborough, Lincs, DN21 4NW
*Activities:* Painting
*Shareholders:* John Richard Lane; Martin Charles Stamp Tighe; Patricia Anne Catherine Wood
*Officers:* Martin Charles Stamp Tighe, Secretary; Martin Hillyard [1959] Director; Sam John Crashley Panter [1979] Health & Safety Director; Lee Martin Rhodes [1977] Director; David John Welch [1963] Director/Accountant; Paul Wolstencroft [1960] Director/Painting Contractor; Philip Andrew Wood [1959] Director/Engineer

**Til-Ex Limited**
*Incorporated:* 19 July 1984 *Employees:* 37
*Net Worth:* £2,096,965 *Total Assets:* £3,776,357
*Registered Office:* Grove Works, Healey Road, Ossett, W Yorks, WF5 8LN
*Activities:* Other specialised construction activities n.e.c.
*Major Shareholder:* Richard Joseph Elliott
*Officers:* Vicki Ann Elliott, Secretary; Richard Joseph Elliott [1961] Director

**The Tile Company Limited**
*Incorporated:* 23 July 1999 *Employees:* 50
*Net Worth:* £3,810,223 *Total Assets:* £5,869,507
*Registered Office:* The Tile Company Ltd, Malton Road, Monks Cross, York, YO32 9TE
*Activities:* Other retail sale of new goods in specialised stores (not commercial art galleries and opticians)
*Major Shareholder:* Michael Oneill
*Officers:* Diane Marie O'Neill, Secretary/Ladies' Outfitter; Charles Jordan O'Neill [1986] Director; Diane Marie O'Neill [1959] Director/Tile Retailer; James Scott O'Neill [1984] Director; Michael Graham O'Neill [1953] Director/Tile Retailer

**Tillbrook Products UK Ltd**
*Incorporated:* 13 September 2011
*Net Worth:* £1,886,987 *Total Assets:* £3,221,295
*Registered Office:* Unit 5 Flemming Court, Whistler Drive, Castleford, W Yorks, WF10 5HW
*Activities:* Wholesale of coffee, tea, cocoa and spices
*Major Shareholder:* Robert Guy Brandler
*Officers:* Robert Guy Brandler [1966] Director

**Tilsatec Limited**
*Incorporated:* 18 April 2000 *Employees:* 111
*Previous:* Sirdar Spinning Limited
*Net Worth:* £20,058,000 *Total Assets:* £23,887,000
*Registered Office:* Flanshaw Lane, Alverthorpe, Wakefield, W Yorks, WF2 9ND
*Activities:* Wholesale of textiles
*Parent:* Sirdar Group Limited
*Officers:* Jean-Luc Theophile Bikard [1958] Director [French]; Ben Griffiths [1980] Managing Director; Oliver James Lake [1983] Finance Director

**Timec 1444 Limited**
*Incorporated:* 28 November 2013 *Employees:* 49
*Net Worth:* £27,490,372 *Total Assets:* £36,957,308
*Registered Office:* Dalton Airfield, Dalton, Thirsk, N Yorks, YO7 3JN
*Activities:* Wholesale of metals and metal ores
*Officers:* Jeanne Martine Elizabeth Bianco [1971] Director; Jennifer Bianco [1984] Director; Matthew Giovanni Bianco [1986] Director/Programmer; Michele Christine Bianco [1973] Director; Robert Jean Francois Bianco [1933] Director; Roy Wyatt Fishwick [1968] Director

**Isaac Timmins Limited**
*Incorporated:* 30 May 1929 *Employees:* 357
*Net Worth:* £12,684,298 *Total Assets:* £27,926,976
*Registered Office:* 5 Barr Street, off Leeds Road, Huddersfield, W Yorks, HD1 6PB
*Activities:* Activities of head offices
*Shareholders:* John Rodger Myers; Anne Jacqueline Myers Berry
*Officers:* John Rodger Myers, Secretary; Anne Jacqueline Myers Berry [1955] Director/Depot Manager; James David Myers Berry [1985] Director; Katie Elizabeth Myers Berry [1987] Director; John Rodger Myers [1948] Director/Concrete Technologist

**Tissue Regenix Group PLC**
*Incorporated:* 17 October 2006 *Employees:* 79
*Net Worth:* £39,931,000 *Total Assets:* £46,171,000
*Registered Office:* Unit 1 and 2 Astley Way, Astley Lane Industrial Estate, Swillington, Leeds, LS26 8XT
*Activities:* Other business support service activities n.e.c.
*Shareholders:* Invesco Limited; Woodford Investment Management Ltd
*Officers:* Paul Below, Secretary; Gareth Hywel Jones, Secretary; Steven Couldwell [1960] Non-Executive Director; Jonathan Martin Glenn [1968] Director; Randeep Singh Grewal [1967] Director; Professor Shervanthi Homer Vanniasinkam [1958] Director/Doctor; Gareth Hywel Jones [1968] Director; Alan Jonathan Richard Miller [1963] Director/Fund Manager; John Andrew Walter Samuel [1952] Director/Chairman

**Tissue Regenix Limited**
*Incorporated:* 5 May 2006 *Employees:* 39
*Net Worth Deficit:* £7,494,000 *Total Assets:* £31,343,000
*Registered Office:* Unit 1 and 2 Astley Way, Astley Lane Industrial Estate, Swillington, Leeds, LS26 8XT
*Activities:* Other research and experimental development on natural sciences and engineering
*Parent:* Tissue Regenix Group PLC
*Officers:* Gareth Hywel Jones, Secretary; Steven Ashley Couldwell [1960] Director; Gareth Hywel Jones [1968] Director; Alan Jonathan Richard Miller [1963] Director; John Andrew Walter Samuel [1952] Director/Chief Executive

**Titan Cement U.K. Limited**
*Incorporated:* 6 January 1988 *Employees:* 9
*Net Worth:* £5,366,093 *Total Assets:* £6,310,740
*Registered Office:* No 12 Shed, King George Dock, Hull, HU9 5PR
*Activities:* Non-specialised wholesale trade
*Parent:* Titan Cement Company SA
*Officers:* Georgios Damaskinakis [1974] Director/Trading Operations & Administration Manager [Greek]; Constantine Gkikas [1958] Accounting Director [Greek]; Pavlos Paschopoulos [1971] Director/International Trade Manager [Greek]

**Titan Global Finance PLC**
*Incorporated:* 2 April 2007 *Employees:* 4
*Net Worth:* £14,629,012 *Total Assets:* £644,104,512
*Registered Office:* No 12 Shed, King George Dock, Hull, HU9 5PR
*Activities:* Other business support service activities n.e.c.
*Parent:* Titan Cement Company S.A.
*Officers:* Nikolaos Andreadis [1979] Director/Group Treasurer, Titan Cement Co [Greek]; Charles Richard Field [1962] Director/Solicitor; Karen Virginia Fittler [1963] Accountant - Director [American]; Lawrence Hugh Wilt Jnr [1964] Director/Vice President and CFO [American]

**TM Advances Limited**
*Incorporated:* 20 December 2010 *Employees:* 5
*Net Worth:* £373,719 *Total Assets:* £9,973,595
*Registered Office:* Princes Exchange, Princes Square, Leeds, LS1 4HY
*Activities:* Credit granting by non-deposit taking finance houses and other specialist consumer credit grantors
*Officers:* Isobel Leonora Allen [1960] Director; Timothy Mark Allen Jnr [1981] Director

**TMD Friction Holdings (UK) Ltd**
*Incorporated:* 6 December 2012 *Employees:* 4
*Net Worth:* £131,543,432 *Total Assets:* £301,074,112
*Registered Office:* P O Box 18, Centurion House, Centurion Way, Cleckheaton, W Yorks, BD19 3UJ
*Activities:* Activities of head offices
*Parent:* TMD Friction Holdings (Lux) S.A.R.L.
*Officers:* Steven Firbank, Secretary; Takaharu Dannoura [1971] Director/Chief Financial Officer [Japanese]; Steven Firbank [1972] Director/VP Finance IAM; Tetsuya Kumakawa [1968] Director/Chief Executive Officer [Japanese]

**TMD Friction UK Limited**
*Incorporated:* 28 November 2001 *Employees:* 687
*Net Worth:* £131,336,000 *Total Assets:* £150,936,000
*Registered Office:* P O Box 18, Centurion House, Centurion Way, Cleckheaton, W Yorks, BD19 3UJ
*Activities:* Manufacture of other parts and accessories for motor vehicles
*Parent:* TMD Friction Holdings (UK) Limited
*Officers:* Steven Firbank, Secretary; David Edward Baines [1972] Managing Director; Takaharu Dannoura [1971] Director/Chief Financial Officer [Japanese]; Ian Featherstone [1962] R&D Director; Steven Firbank [1972] Director

**TMPC Unlimited**
*Incorporated:* 8 November 2006
*Net Worth:* £562,574 *Total Assets:* £3,247,132
*Registered Office:* The Green, Green Hammerton, York, YO26 8BQ
*Activities:* Manufacture of other furniture
*Shareholder:* Christopher Arthur Charles Main
*Officers:* Karan Michelle Main, Secretary; Alex Thomas Main [1982] Director; Christopher Arthur Charles Main [1954] Director/Furniture Maker; Karan Michelle Main [1956] Director/Furniture Maker; Thomas Sebastian Main [1983] Director

**Tocketts Mill Leisure Limited**
*Incorporated:* 9 July 2008
*Net Worth:* £2,338,443 *Total Assets:* £3,494,093
*Registered Office:* Marton Hall, Church Lane, Sewerby, Bridlington, E Yorks, YO15 1DS
*Activities:* Activities of other holding companies n.e.c.
*Shareholders:* Karen Hague; David Robert Allison
*Officers:* Karen Hague, Secretary; David Robert Allison [1960] Director; Karen Hague [1963] Director/Secretary

**Tocketts Mill Limited**
*Incorporated:* 2 June 1999 *Employees:* 38
*Net Worth:* £3,494,093 *Total Assets:* £6,143,131
*Registered Office:* Marton Hall, Church Lane, Sewerby, Bridlington, E Yorks, YO15 1DS
*Activities:* Recreational vehicle parks, trailer parks and camping grounds
*Parent:* Tocketts Mill Leisure Limited
*Officers:* Karen Hague, Secretary; David Robert Allison [1960] Director/Park Operator; Karen Hague [1963] Director

**Today's Wholesale Services Limited**
*Incorporated:* 3 August 2011 *Employees:* 29
*Net Worth:* £3,118,000 *Total Assets:* £12,075,000
*Registered Office:* 3 Carolina Court, Wisconsin Drive, Doncaster, S Yorks, DN4 5RA
*Activities:* Agents involved in the sale of food, beverages and tobacco
*Officers:* John Schofield, Secretary; John Charles Baines [1956] Trading Director; Darren Paul Goldney [1970] Managing Director; John FitzGenerald Kinney [1963] Retail Director; John Schofield [1954] Finance Director

**Todds Highway Maintenance Limited**
*Incorporated:* 8 November 1996 *Employees:* 29
*Net Worth:* £2,985,513 *Total Assets:* £4,008,790
*Registered Office:* Henson Road, Yarm Road Business Park, Darlington, Co Durham, DL1 4QD
*Activities:* Construction of roads and motorways
*Shareholders:* Graeme Malcolm Todd; Darren James Todd
*Officers:* Malcolm Todd, Secretary/Director; Claire Louise Todd [1976] Director; Darren James Todd [1967] Director; Graeme Malcolm Todd [1971] Director; Malcolm Todd [1947] Director

**TOG 24 Limited**
*Incorporated:* 26 July 2007 *Employees:* 317
*Net Worth:* £8,739,161 *Total Assets:* £12,784,605
*Registered Office:* Spen Vale Mills, Station Lane, Heckmondwike, W Yorks, WF16 0NQ
*Activities:* Retail sale of clothing in specialised stores
*Shareholder:* Ian Ward
*Officers:* Brian George Ward, Secretary/Managing Director; Brian George Ward [1951] Managing Director; Christopher John Ward [1979] Marketing Director; Ian Ward [1953] Sales Director; Mark James Ward [1970] Retail Director

**Togel Contractors Limited**
*Incorporated:* 11 April 1985 *Employees:* 132
*Net Worth:* £945,805 *Total Assets:* £6,214,073
*Registered Office:* 1-3 Hexthorpe Road, Doncaster, S Yorks, DN4 0AD
*Activities:* Other construction installation
*Officers:* Tony Brooke Richardson, Secretary; George Gargett [1949] Director; Paul Leggott [1936] Director; Robert Paul Leggott [1970] Director; Mark Roy Wallace [1969] Director

**Together Housing Finance PLC**
*Incorporated:* 30 October 2012
*Net Worth:* £50,000 *Total Assets:* £258,434,000
*Registered Office:* Bull Green House, Bull Green, Halifax, W Yorks, HX1 2EB
*Activities:* Administration of financial markets
*Parent:* Together Housing Group Limited
*Officers:* Mark Ian Dunford, Secretary; Stephen Roy Close [1958] Director/Group Chief Executive; Mark Ian Dunford [1969] Executive Director Corporate Services; Kevin Ruth [1960] Executive Director Operations & Deputy Group CEO

**Together Roof Energy Limited**
*Incorporated:* 22 March 2011
*Net Worth:* £9,010,008 *Total Assets:* £9,010,120
*Registered Office:* Bull Green House, Bull Green, Halifax, W Yorks, HX1 2EB
*Activities:* Non-trading company
*Parent:* Together Housing Association Limited
*Officers:* Mark Dunford, Secretary; Mark Ian Dunford [1969] Director; Kevin Ruth [1960] Director

**Together Roof Energy SPV Limited**
*Incorporated:* 15 July 2011
*Net Worth:* £702,685 *Total Assets:* £11,927,074
*Registered Office:* Bull Green House, Bull Green, Halifax, W Yorks, HX1 2EB
*Activities:* Electrical installation
*Parent:* Together Roof Energy Limited
*Officers:* Mark Dunford, Secretary; Mark Ian Dunford [1969] Director; Kevin Ruth [1960] Director

**Toiletry Sales Group Limited**
*Incorporated:* 14 November 2012 *Employees:* 63
*Net Worth:* £5,003,987 *Total Assets:* £14,239,072
*Registered Office:* Crigglestone Industrial Estate, High Street, Crigglestone, Wakefield, W Yorks, WF4 3HT
*Activities:* Activities of head offices
*Shareholders:* Sarah Louise Sharp; Richard John Walker
*Officers:* David James Milnes, Secretary; David Lyndon Barraclough [1950] Director; David James Milnes [1950] Director; Sarah Louise Sharp [1975] Director; Richard John Walker [1961] Director

**Toiletry Sales Holdings Limited**
*Incorporated:* 14 February 2005
*Net Worth:* £3,287,486 *Total Assets:* £3,287,486
*Registered Office:* Criggleston Industrial Estate, High Street, Criggleston, Wakefield, W Yorks, WF4 3HT
*Activities:* Activities of head offices
*Officers:* David James Milnes, Secretary; David Lyndon Barraclough [1950] Director

**Toiletry Sales Limited**
*Incorporated:* 4 May 1984 *Employees:* 63
*Net Worth:* £2,781,712 *Total Assets:* £12,016,796
*Registered Office:* Crigglestone Industrial Estate, High Street, Crigglestone, W Yorks, WF4 3HT
*Activities:* Wholesale of pharmaceutical goods
*Officers:* David James Milnes, Secretary; David Lyndon Barraclough [1950] Director; Geoff Carroll [1967] Sales Director; Christopher Stuart Patterson [1971] Director/Chief Executive; Keith Randall [1960] Technical Director; Ian Simons [1965] Operations Director; Richard John Walker [1961] Director

**Tollbar Multi Academy Trust**
*Incorporated:* 28 May 2012 *Employees:* 695
*Net Worth:* £115,345,000 *Total Assets:* £120,580,000
*Registered Office:* Tollbar Multi Academy Trust, Station Road, New Waltham, Grimsby, N E Lincs, DN36 4RZ
*Activities:* Primary education
*Officers:* Gill Margaret Alton [1962] Director/Chief Executive; Jane Cordelia Aukett [1956] Director; Philip Bond [1955] Director; Martyn Douglas Chilvers [1954] Director; Paul Antony Cornford [1959] Director; Michael Leslie Draper [1958] Director; Alec Else [1932] Director; Angela Heather Hampson [1955] Director/Chief Finance Officer; David John Hampson [1950] Director; Andrea Manders [1965] Director/Clerical Assistant; Stephen Geoffrey Woolsey [1956] Director

**Tolsa UK Limited**
*Incorporated:* 22 February 1996 *Employees:* 66
*Net Worth:* £6,302,000 *Total Assets:* £15,134,000
*Registered Office:* Second Avenue, Flixborough Industrial Estate, Scunthorpe, N Lincs, DN15 8SD
*Activities:* Manufacture of other non-metallic mineral products n.e.c.
*Officers:* David Simpson, Secretary; Ciaran Joseph Sullivan [1967] Director/Country Business Manager [Irish]

**Giovanni Tomasso Limited**
*Incorporated:* 4 April 2012
*Net Worth:* £145,865 *Total Assets:* £6,610,512
*Registered Office:* c/o JDS Accounting, 49 Primley Park Road, Leeds, LS17 7HR
*Activities:* Retail sale of antiques including antique books in stores
*Major Shareholder:* Giovanni Francesco Tomasso
*Officers:* Giovanni Francesco Tomasso [1969] Director/Fine Art and Antique Dealer

**Tompkins Investments Limited**
*Incorporated:* 14 December 2010 *Employees:* 1
*Net Worth Deficit:* £8,589,306 *Total Assets:* £5,263,681
*Registered Office:* Beaumont House, Beaumont Street, Darlington, Co Durham, DL1 5RW
*Activities:* Other professional, scientific and technical activities n.e.c.
*Major Shareholder:* Arthur Charles Tompkins
*Officers:* Angela Rosemary Tompkins [1949] Director; Arthur Charles Tompkins [1947] Director; Sophie Jane Tompkins [1988] Director/Legal Counsel

**Tompkins UK Limited**
*Incorporated:* 9 January 2007 *Employees:* 58
*Net Worth:* £6,335,000 *Total Assets:* £19,790,000
*Registered Office:* Beaumont House, Beaumont Street, Darlington, Co Durham, DL1 5RW
*Activities:* Other professional, scientific and technical activities n.e.c.
*Shareholder:* Arthur Charles Tompkins
*Officers:* Angela Rosemary Tompkins [1949] Director; Arthur Charles Tompkins [1947] Director; Jason Edward Tompkins [1974] Managing Director; Nicholas Stewart Charles Tompkins [1972] Director; Sophie Jane Tompkins [1988] Director/Solicitor

**Tomrods Limited**
*Incorporated:* 1 October 1973 *Employees:* 55
*Net Worth:* £4,246,203 *Total Assets:* £11,269,069
*Registered Office:* Hambleton Steel Works, York Road, Thirsk, N Yorks, YO7 3BT
*Activities:* Wholesale of metals and metal ores
*Officers:* Melinda Ann Landure Bruce [1962] Director; Neil Latcham [1974] Sales Director; Jacek Przybyl [1977] Purchasing Director [Polish]; Andrew Keith Shakespeare [1964] Director/Accountant; John Darcy Thompson [1950] Director; Julie Catherine Thompson [1965] Director

**Torne Valley Limited**
*Incorporated:* 7 June 1972 *Employees:* 49
*Net Worth:* £5,296,663 *Total Assets:* £6,419,472
*Registered Office:* Bawtry Road, Tickhill, Doncaster, S Yorks, DN11 9EX
*Activities:* Other retail sale not in stores, stalls or markets
*Major Shareholder:* Kevin McDonald
*Officers:* Donna McDonald, Secretary; Amie McDonald [1993] Director; Donna Brigitte McDonald [1962] Director/Company Secretary; Kevin McDonald [1933] Managing Director

**Torpoint Limited**
*Incorporated:* 25 January 1993 *Employees:* 46
*Net Worth:* £1,986,626 *Total Assets:* £5,566,241
*Registered Office:* Hope Park Business Centre, Hope Park, Trevor Foster Way, Bradford, BD5 8HH
*Activities:* Development of building projects
*Major Shareholder:* Philip Stewart Paterson
*Officers:* Joshua Luke Paterson, Secretary; Joshua Luke Paterson [1989] Director; Philip Stewart Paterson [1965] Director

**Torque Logistics Limited**
*Incorporated:* 28 June 1991 *Employees:* 955
*Net Worth:* £8,455,000 *Total Assets:* £19,717,000
*Registered Office:* The Torque Building, Wortley Moor Road, Wortley, Leeds, LS12 4JH
*Activities:* Operation of warehousing and storage facilities for water transport activities
*Parent:* Sheds for Logistics Limited
*Officers:* Eamonn Patrick Andrew Darcy [1960] Director/Chartered Accountant [Irish]; Stewart Paul Firth [1970] Director/Freight Forwarder; Timothy Simon Howarth [1958] Director

**Torque Retail Services Limited**
*Incorporated:* 9 March 1993 *Employees:* 758
*Net Worth:* £637,000 *Total Assets:* £9,811,000
*Registered Office:* The Torque Building, Wortley Moor Road, Wortley, Leeds, LS12 4JH
*Activities:* Operation of warehousing and storage facilities for water transport activities
*Parent:* Torque Logistics Limited
*Officers:* Stewart Paul Firth [1970] Director/Freight Forwarder; Timothy Simon Howarth [1958] Director

**Torrent Trackside Limited**
*Incorporated:* 6 September 1973 *Employees:* 221
*Net Worth:* £16,492,000 *Total Assets:* £22,689,000
*Registered Office:* c/o VP PLC, Central House, Beckwith Knowle, Otley Road, Harrogate, N Yorks, HG3 1UD
*Activities:* Renting and leasing of other machinery, equipment and tangible goods n.e.c.
*Parent:* VP PLC
*Officers:* Allison Margaret Bainbridge, Secretary; Allison Margaret Bainbridge [1960] Director; Jeremy Frederic George Pilkington [1951] Director/Chairman; Neil Andrew Stothard [1958] Director

**Torsion Group Holdings Limited**
*Incorporated:* 4 April 2017 *Employees:* 54
*Net Worth:* £980,005 *Total Assets:* £6,172,372
*Registered Office:* 2175 Century Way, Thorpe Park, Leeds, LS15 8ZB
*Activities:* Development of building projects
*Major Shareholder:* Daniel Thomas Spencer
*Officers:* Jonathan Michael Carter [1980] Director; Christopher Russell Goodall [1967] Director; Daniel Thomas Spencer [1981] Director

**Total Downstream UK PLC**
*Incorporated:* 8 July 1927
*Net Worth:* £155,378,000 *Total Assets:* £155,406,000
*Registered Office:* Lindsey Oil Refinery, Eastfield Road, North Killingholme, Immingham, N E Lincs, DN40 3LW
*Activities:* Activities of production holding companies
*Parent:* Elf Petroleum UK Limited
*Officers:* Georgina Violet Crowhurst, Secretary; Olivier Jean-Luc Rene Alexandre [1958] Director/Engineer [French]; Jean-Marc Durand [1972] Director/General Manager of Total Lindsey Oil Refinery Limited [French]; Guillaume Eveno [1977] Director/Chemical Engineer [French]

**Total Energy Gas Supplies Limited**
*Incorporated:* 1 November 1999
*Net Worth:* £3,822,673 *Total Assets:* £5,831,533
*Registered Office:* 2 Victoria Avenue, Harrogate, N Yorks, HG1 1EL
*Activities:* Trade of gas through mains
*Parent:* Contract Natural Gas Limited
*Officers:* Christopher John England [1971] Operations Director; Jacqueline Louise Hall [1963] Managing Director; Colin Richard Hollins [1967] Director/Utilities

**Total Foodservice Solutions Limited**
*Incorporated:* 2 March 2004 *Employees:* 115
*Net Worth:* £6,555,083 *Total Assets:* £9,533,898
*Registered Office:* Green Lea Mills, Cross Green Road, Dalton, Huddersfield, W Yorks, HD5 9XX
*Activities:* Non-specialised wholesale of food, beverages and tobacco
*Major Shareholder:* Simon George Howarth
*Officers:* Katie Louise Cuerden [1968] Finance Director; Simon George Howarth [1967] Managing Director; Susan Jane Howarth [1969] Sales and Marketing Director; Jason Roy Sheard [1972] Purchasing Director

**Total Hardware Limited**
*Incorporated:* 19 April 2004 *Employees:* 17
*Net Worth:* £3,937,803 *Total Assets:* £7,425,876
*Registered Office:* Unit B1, Latchmore Park, Latchmore Road, Beeston, Leeds, LS12 6DN
*Activities:* Retail sale of hardware, paints and glass in specialised stores
*Shareholder:* Total Hardware Holdings Limited
*Officers:* Christopher Morris, Secretary; Gary Michael Cox [1972] Director; Christopher Morris [1963] Director

**Total Lindsey Oil Refinery Limited**
*Incorporated:* 12 April 1956 *Employees:* 447
*Net Worth:* £294,468,000 *Total Assets:* £872,945,984
*Registered Office:* Lindsey Oil Refinery, Eastfield Road, North Killingholme, Immingham, N E Lincs, DN40 3LW
*Activities:* Mineral oil refining
*Parent:* Total Downstream UK PLC
*Officers:* Georgina Violet Crowhurst, Secretary; Olivier Jean-Luc Rene Alexandre [1958] Director/Engineer [French]; Jean-Marc Durand [1972] Director/General Manager [French]; Guillaume Eveno [1977] Director/Chemical Engineer [French]; Fabien Mornand [1973] Director/General Manager [French]

**Total Oynx Limited**
*Incorporated:* 25 August 2011 *Employees:* 6
*Net Worth:* £3,167,459 *Total Assets:* £6,421,439
*Registered Office:* Riverview Park, Abbey Lane, Barnard Castle, Co Durham, DL12 9TJ
*Activities:* Holiday centres and villages
*Major Shareholder:* Frank Maguire Snr
*Officers:* Andrew Maguire [1994] Director; Frank Maguire Snr [1969] Director

**Total Recycling Services Limited**
*Incorporated:* 12 August 2009 *Employees:* 92
*Net Worth:* £2,115,000 *Total Assets:* £10,322,000
*Registered Office:* Lingfield Way, Yarm Road Business Park, Darlington, Co Durham, DL1 4PZ
*Activities:* Collection of non-hazardous waste
*Major Shareholder:* Robert Jones
*Officers:* Andrew Mark Dobson [1974] Operations Director; Alex Foreman [1978] Director; Carol Gee [1970] Finance Director; Robert Jones [1975] Director; Mark Rigby [1983] Director/Chartered Accountant; Ross Smith [1966] Director/Chairman; Susan Woodward [1974] Commercial Director

**Total System Services Processing Europe Limited**
*Incorporated:* 31 March 2006 *Employees:* 478
*Net Worth:* £60,981,000 *Total Assets:* £67,058,000
*Registered Office:* Fulford Moor House, Fulford Road, York, YO10 4EY
*Activities:* Other business support service activities n.e.c.
*Parent:* TSYS International Management Limited
*Officers:* David Leonard Chew [1963] Finance Director; Gaylon Murrell Jowers Jnr [1962] Director/Exec Vice President [American]; Dorenda Kay Weaver [1963] Director/Chief Accounting Officer [American]

**Total Value Headhunting LLP**
*Incorporated:* 21 October 2003
*Net Worth:* £3,573,413 *Total Assets:* £3,576,053
*Registered Office:* 5th Floor, Central Square, 29 Wellington Street, Leeds, LS1 4DL
*Officers:* Cary Totman Mills [1972] Member

**The Towel Rail Limited**
*Incorporated:* 14 September 1992 *Employees:* 217
*Net Worth:* £1,749,095 *Total Assets:* £3,148,214
*Registered Office:* Unit I4B Hornbeam Park Oval, Hornbeam Park, Harrogate, N Yorks, HG2 8RB
*Activities:* Retail sale of textiles in specialised stores
*Shareholder:* Linda Shreeve
*Officers:* Stephen Edmundson [1972] Director; Linda Shreeve [1966] Director/Accountant; Julia Wilson [1982] Director; Simon Jeffrey Worrall [1961] Director/Chartered Surveyor

**Tower Centre Hoddesdon Limited**
*Incorporated:* 5 February 2010
*Net Worth:* £12,306,000 *Total Assets:* £41,362,000
*Registered Office:* Hilmore House, Gain Lane, Bradford, W Yorks, BD3 7DL
*Activities:* Development of building projects
*Parent:* Optimisation Developments Limited
*Officers:* Jonathan James Burke, Secretary; Jonathan James Burke [1966] Director; Joanna Louise Goff [1978] Finance Director

**Tower Corporation Limited**
*Incorporated:* 29 March 1996 *Employees:* 6
*Net Worth:* £3,652,659 *Total Assets:* £5,211,001
*Registered Office:* Tower House, Fishergate, York, YO10 4UA
*Activities:* Other letting and operating of own or leased real estate
*Shareholders:* Christopher James Gillam; Fountain Developments Limited
*Officers:* Jane Diana Bell, Secretary/Director; Jane Diana Bell [1955] Director; Christopher James Gillam [1952] Director

**Tower Estates (York) Limited**
*Incorporated:* 11 August 1951 *Employees:* 3
*Net Worth:* £3,222,975 *Total Assets:* £3,640,393
*Registered Office:* 288a Tadcaster Road, York, YO24 1ET
*Activities:* Buying and selling of own real estate
*Officers:* Claire Gorwood, Secretary; Richard Henry Gorwood, Secretary/Director; Michael John Gorwood [1983] Director; Richard Henry Gorwood [1975] Director

**Tower Hill Investments Limited**
*Incorporated:* 28 November 2006 *Employees:* 119
*Net Worth:* £5,569,954 *Total Assets:* £7,861,867
*Registered Office:* Trinity House, Eastfield Road, South Killingholme, Immingham, N E Lincs, DN40 3DQ
*Activities:* Other letting and operating of own or leased real estate
*Parent:* NTEX Limited
*Officers:* Stephen Philip Davis [1969] Director; Thomas Stroem [1956] Director [Swedish]

**Town Centre Car Parks Limited**
*Incorporated:* 29 June 2005 *Employees:* 50
*Net Worth:* £15,212,632 *Total Assets:* £29,039,584
*Registered Office:* Town Centre House, The Merrion Centre, Leeds, LS2 8LY
*Activities:* Other letting and operating of own or leased real estate
*Parent:* Citipark PLC
*Officers:* Mark John Dilley [1972] Group Property Director; Lynda Margaret Shillaw [1965] Group Property Director; Charles Benjamin Aaron Ziff [1986] Managing Director; Edward Max Ziff [1960] Director

**Town Head Farm Products Limited**
*Incorporated:* 24 September 2003 *Employees:* 77
*Net Worth:* £4,549,100 *Total Assets:* £8,098,609
*Registered Office:* Town Head Farm, Grassington, Skipton, N Yorks, BD23 5BL
*Activities:* Raising of dairy cattle
*Major Shareholder:* David Jonathan Oversby
*Officers:* James Paul Mason, Secretary; David Jonathan Oversby [1962] Director/Farmer

**Towndoor Limited**
*Incorporated:* 29 April 1988 *Employees:* 11
*Net Worth:* £13,335,989 *Total Assets:* £20,073,072
*Registered Office:* Estate Office, Gate 7 Meltham Mills Industrial Estate, Meltham, Holmfirth, W Yorks, HD9 4AR
*Activities:* Other letting and operating of own or leased real estate
*Shareholders:* Daniel John Bamforth; Benjamin Shane Bamforth
*Officers:* Benjamin Shane Bamforth [1990] Director/Property Rental; Daniel John Bamforth [1986] Director/Property Rental; Janet Lucy Bamforth [1960] Director

**C.E.A.Towne (Ship Riggers) Limited**
*Incorporated:* 18 December 1951 *Employees:* 59
*Net Worth:* £1,419,828 *Total Assets:* £4,182,719
*Registered Office:* 19 Dairycoates Industrial Estate, Wiltshire Road, Hull, HU4 6PA
*Activities:* Installation of industrial machinery and equipment
*Officers:* Thomas Towne, Secretary; Edmund Cavill [1948] Director/Businessman; Timothy Cavill [1952] Director/Business Executive; Christopher Charles Withers Towne [1949] Director; Thomas Towne [1986] Director/Finance

**J.Townend & Sons (Hull) Limited**
*Incorporated:* 19 June 1923 *Employees:* 196
*Net Worth:* £5,649,689 *Total Assets:* £10,289,166
*Registered Office:* House of Townend, Wyke Way, Melton, North Ferriby, E Yorks, HU14 3BQ
*Activities:* Other letting and operating of own or leased real estate
*Officers:* Angus Joseph Whitehead, Secretary; Alexandra Louise Townend [1967] Hotel Director; Jennifer Ann Townend [1940] Director; John Charles Townend [1965] Director; Angus Joseph Whitehead [1965] Director/Chartered Accountant

**Towngate Estates Limited**
*Incorporated:* 1 April 2004
*Net Worth:* £3,826,000 *Total Assets:* £23,184,000
*Registered Office:* Woodvale House, Woodvale Road, Brighouse, W Yorks, HD6 4AB
*Activities:* Buying and selling of own real estate
*Parent:* Brigdale Limited
*Officers:* Stephen Phillip Forrest, Secretary; Stephen Phillip Forrest [1966] Director/Chartered Accountant; Stephen David Guy [1949] Director/Consultant; Alan David Smith [1967] Director/Chartered Surveyor; David Smith [1940] Director; Robert Brigg Smith [1969] Director/Chartered Surveyor; Valerie Elaine Smith [1942] Director; John Rufus Wignall [1952] Director/Chartered Surveyor

**Towngate PLC**
*Incorporated:* 26 June 1969 *Employees:* 10
*Net Worth:* £17,095,000 *Total Assets:* £30,583,000
*Registered Office:* Woodvale House, Woodvale Road, Brighouse, W Yorks, HD6 4AB
*Activities:* Buying and selling of own real estate
*Officers:* Stephen Phillip Forrest, Secretary; Stephen Phillip Forrest [1966] Director/Chartered Accountant; Stephen David Guy [1949] Director/Consultant; Alan David Smith [1967] Director/Chartered Surveyor; David Smith [1940] Director; Robert Brigg Smith [1969] Director/Chartered Surveyor; Valerie Elaine Smith [1942] Director; John Rufus Wignall [1952] Director/Chartered Surveyor

**Townham Limited**
*Incorporated:* 9 January 2015 *Employees:* 134
*Net Worth:* £1,078,371 *Total Assets:* £3,459,263
*Registered Office:* Permanent House, 1 Dundas Street, Huddersfield, W Yorks, HD1 2EX
*Activities:* Activities of head offices
*Shareholders:* Alan James Towns; Peter Denham
*Officers:* Peter Denham [1955] Director; Alan James Towns [1968] Director

**Townson Tractors Limited**
*Incorporated:* 7 December 1983 *Employees:* 22
*Net Worth:* £3,554,620 *Total Assets:* £4,572,060
*Registered Office:* West End, Hellifield, Skipton, N Yorks, BD23 4HE
*Activities:* Sale of other motor vehicles
*Major Shareholder:* William Townson
*Officers:* William Townson, Secretary/Salesman; William Townson [1948] Director/Salesman

**Towsure Products Limited**
*Incorporated:* 5 November 1976 *Employees:* 60
*Net Worth:* £1,069,333 *Total Assets:* £3,069,355
*Registered Office:* 3365 Century Way, Thorpe Park, Leeds, LS15 8ZB
*Activities:* Wholesale trade of motor vehicle parts and accessories
*Shareholders:* Andrew Stuart Taylor Hogg; Stuart Hogg
*Officers:* Stuart Hogg, Secretary; Andrew Stuart Taylor Hogg [1970] Director; Stuart Hogg [1945] Director

**TPP Finance Limited**
*Incorporated:* 12 February 2014 *Employees:* 1
*Net Worth:* £56,623,236 *Total Assets:* £123,303,680
*Registered Office:* 129 Low Lane, Horsforth, Leeds, LS18 5PX
*Activities:* Activities of other holding companies n.e.c.
*Parent:* TPPH (Leeds) Limited
*Officers:* Francis Xavier James Hester [1966] Director

**TPPH (Leeds) Limited**
*Incorporated:* 3 March 2014 *Employees:* 183
*Net Worth:* £76,976,160 *Total Assets:* £109,793,800
*Registered Office:* 129 Low Lane, Horsforth, Leeds, LS18 5PX
*Activities:* Activities of other holding companies n.e.c.
*Major Shareholder:* Francis Xavier James Hester
*Officers:* Francis Xavier James Hester [1966] Director

**Track Record Holdings Limited**
*Incorporated:* 29 April 2016
*Net Worth:* £3,083,519 *Total Assets:* £3,083,519
*Registered Office:* Merchant House, Piccadilly, York, YO1 9WB
*Activities:* Other information technology service activities
*Officers:* Marguarite Joanna Arnold [1981] Director; Jonathan Paul Cathie [1978] Director; Thomas George John Golding [1970] Director; David Ronald McNair Scott [1973] Director; Matthew Max Edward Royde [1972] Director; Dirk Sinclair Young [1973] Director

**Trackwork Group Limited**
*Incorporated:* 2 April 2008 *Employees:* 450
*Net Worth:* £26,759,000 *Total Assets:* £44,615,000
*Registered Office:* 2 Sandall Lane, Kirk Sandall Industrial Estate, Doncaster, S Yorks, DN3 1LL
*Activities:* Other specialised construction activities n.e.c.
*Major Shareholder:* Mark Jonathan Wilkinson Waind
*Officers:* Mark Jonathan Wilkinson Waind, Secretary; Mark Jonathan Wilkinson Waind [1961] Director

**Trackwork Limited**
*Incorporated:* 29 July 1976 *Employees:* 338
*Net Worth:* £26,924,000 *Total Assets:* £48,096,000
*Registered Office:* P O Box 139, Sandall Lane, Kirk Sandall Industrial Estate, Doncaster, S Yorks, DN3 1LL
*Activities:* Other specialised construction activities n.e.c.
*Parent:* Trackwork Holdings Limited
*Officers:* Gail Marie Rusling, Secretary; Simon Philip Lee [1962] Director/Quantity Surveyor; Mark Jonathan Wilkinson Waind [1961] Managing Director

**Trackwork Moll Limited**
*Incorporated:* 1 June 2011 *Employees:* 88
*Net Worth Deficit:* £8,981,696 *Total Assets:* £5,707,411
*Registered Office:* Sleeper Factory, Ten Pound Walk, Doncaster, S Yorks, DN4 5HX
*Activities:* Manufacture of other fabricated metal products n.e.c.
*Shareholders:* Trackwork Ltd.; Leonhard Moll Betonwerke Beteiligungs-GmbH
*Officers:* Christian Kilger [1965] Director [German]; Mark Jonathan Wilkinson Waind [1961] Director

**Tracsis PLC**
*Incorporated:* 19 January 2004 *Employees:* 667
*Net Worth:* £42,109,000 *Total Assets:* £60,389,000
*Registered Office:* Leeds Innovation Centre, 103 Clarendon Road, Leeds, LS2 9DF
*Activities:* Other software publishing
*Officers:* Maxwell James Cawthra, Secretary; MacDonald Gouveia Andrade [1975] Director; Maxwell James Cawthra [1978] Director/Accountant; Lisa Charles-Jones [1970] Director; Christopher Cole [1946] Director; John Cameron McArthur [1975] Director; Elizabeth Anne Richards [1957] Director

**Tracsis Retail and Operations Limited**
*Incorporated:* 30 May 2001 *Employees:* 25
*Previous:* Datasys Limited
*Net Worth:* £1,799,045 *Total Assets:* £4,264,184
*Registered Office:* Leeds Innovation Centre, 103 Clarendon Road, Leeds, LS2 9DF
*Activities:* Business and domestic software development
*Parent:* Datasys Integration Limited
*Officers:* Maxwell James Cawthra, Secretary; Maxwell James Cawthra [1978] Director/Accountant; Alex Johnson [1967] Finance Director; John Cameron McArthur [1975] Director/Chief Executive; Alexandra Sarginson [1979] Director; David John Thornton [1977] Director

**Tracsis Traffic Data Limited**
*Incorporated:* 17 December 1999 *Employees:* 334
*Previous:* Sky High Technology Limited
*Net Worth:* £3,405,000 *Total Assets:* £6,785,000
*Registered Office:* Templar House, 1 Sandbeck Court, Sandbeck Way, Wetherby, W Yorks, LS22 7BA
*Activities:* Data processing, hosting and related activities
*Parent:* Tracsis PLC
*Officers:* Martyn Peter Woodhouse, Secretary; Peter Agnew [1959] Director; Christopher Jackson [1987] Director; Paul Robert Jackson [1961] Business Development Director; Alex Johnson [1967] Director; Nicholas Mather [1985] Director; Michael Andrew Rodgers [1962] Director/Chairman; Kevin Smith [1966] Director; Grant Wilson [1973] Director; Martyn Peter Woodhouse [1973] Director

**Trade Furniture Company Ltd**
*Incorporated:* 23 December 2004 *Employees:* 19
*Net Worth:* £2,417,644 *Total Assets:* £3,697,477
*Registered Office:* 18 Norquest Industrial Park, Birstall, Batley, W Yorks, WF17 9NE
*Activities:* Wholesale of furniture, carpets and lighting equipment
*Shareholders:* Craig Clark; Tony Clark
*Officers:* Craig Clark, Secretary; Craig Clark [1972] Director; Tony Clark [1976] Director

**Tradepark Limited**
*Incorporated:* 18 December 2012 *Employees:* 5
*Net Worth:* £333,454 *Total Assets:* £6,002,306
*Registered Office:* Floor 2 Reception, Silvester Street Entrance, K2 Tower, Bond Street, Hull, HU1 3EN
*Activities:* Other business support service activities n.e.c.
*Shareholders:* Simon Victor Butters; Mark Robert Butters; Claire Butters
*Officers:* Simon Butters, Secretary; Mark Butters [1976] Director/Property Investor

**Tradeway (Shipping) Limited**
*Incorporated:* 25 January 1980 *Employees:* 18
*Net Worth:* £3,547,106 *Total Assets:* £5,389,989
*Registered Office:* Town End Place, 146 Lowtown, Pudsey, W Yorks, LS28 9AY
*Activities:* Other transportation support activities
*Officers:* Darren Arthur Sexton, Secretary; David Charles Edley [1968] Director [South African]; Glen Henry Gerber [1962] Director [South African]; Jonathan Edward Heald [1971] Director/Shipping Manager; Darren Arthur Sexton [1966] Director/Management Accountant

**Trans-European Port Services (G.B.) Limited**
*Incorporated:* 27 May 1959 *Employees:* 103
*Net Worth:* £3,609,000 *Total Assets:* £6,073,000
*Registered Office:* Freightliner Road, Hessle Road, Hull, HU3 4XL
*Activities:* Freight transport by road
*Parent:* John Good & Sons Limited
*Officers:* David Gladwin, Secretary; Paul Alan Fordon [1970] Managing Director; Jonathan Ramon Garnier [1968] Director/Financial Controller; David Leonard Gladwin [1968] Director/Accountant; Stuart Charles Gosling [1963] Director; Alan Oliver Platt [1969] Managing Director

**Transdek U.K. Limited**
*Incorporated:* 2 April 1997 *Employees:* 47
*Net Worth:* £2,717,043 *Total Assets:* £3,585,193
*Registered Office:* Transdek Ltd, Bryans Close, Harworth, Doncaster, S Yorks, DN11 8RY
*Activities:* Manufacture of other transport equipment n.e.c.
*Major Shareholder:* William Mark Adams
*Officers:* Fiona Mary Adams [1943] Director; Justin Charles MacLennan Adams [1971] Director; William Mark Adams [1942] Managing Director; Dean George Butler [1977] Operations Director; Leon Michael Butler [1971] Sales Director; Philip Gerard Crowe [1962] Director/Chartered Accountant

**Transdev Blazefield Limited**
*Incorporated:* 26 April 1991 *Employees:* 1,044
*Net Worth:* £6,538,000 *Total Assets:* £28,859,000
*Registered Office:* Prospect Park, Broughton Way, Harrogate, N Yorks, HG2 7NY
*Activities:* Other urban, suburban or metropolitan passenger land transport (not underground, metro or similar)
*Parent:* Transdev PLC
*Officers:* Seth King, Secretary; Peter Ian Brogden [1953] Director/Accountant; Alex Lloyd Hornby [1981] Managing Director; Gordon Duncan Irvine [1957] Engineering Director; Ferguson Robertson-Howard [1964] Business Development Director

**Transdev PLC**
*Incorporated:* 22 September 1992 *Employees:* 8
*Net Worth:* £9,878,000 *Total Assets:* £46,053,000
*Registered Office:* Cavendish House, 91-93 Cavendish Street, Keighley, W Yorks, BD21 3DG
*Activities:* Other passenger land transport
*Parent:* Transdev SA
*Officers:* Peter Ian Brogden, Finance Director; Loic Huet [1976] Finance Director [French]; Yann Leriche [1973] Director/Chief Performance Officer [French]; Stefano Marzio [1980] Director/Head of Legal International Business and Risk [Italian]; Ferguson Robertson-Howard [1964] Director; Bartholomeus Cornelis Schmeink [1968] Director [Dutch]

**Transforming Lives for Good (TLG) Ltd**
*Incorporated:* 31 December 1998 *Employees:* 54
*Previous:* TLG Transforming Lives for Good Ltd
*Net Worth:* £1,563,986 *Total Assets:* £6,428,286
*Registered Office:* Centre of Excellence, Hope Park, Bradford, W Yorks, BD5 8HH
*Activities:* General secondary education
*Officers:* Jayne Elizabeth Chenery, Secretary; Andrew Burton [1964] Director; Sheron Delloris Kantor [1971] Director/Educationalist; John Dawson Kirkby [1961] Founder and International Director; Michael Andrew Royal [1968] Director/Social Entrepreneur; Mark Wrangles [1977] Director/Teacher

**Transit 2017 Limited**
*Incorporated:* 15 June 2017
*Net Worth Deficit:* £156,068 *Total Assets:* £11,631,073
*Registered Office:* Administration Building, Brigg Road, Scunthorpe, N Lincs, DN16 1BP
*Activities:* Other business support service activities n.e.c.
*Parent:* British Steel Limited
*Officers:* Damian Paul Hargreaves, Secretary; Roland Junck [1955] Director [Luxembourger]; Generald Reichmann [1976] Director [Austrian]

**Transition Glass Products Limited**
*Incorporated:* 12 March 2003 *Employees:* 6
*Net Worth:* £3,411,316 *Total Assets:* £4,178,820
*Registered Office:* Unit 1 & 2 Globe Court, Coalpit Road, Denaby Industrial Estate, Denaby, Doncaster, S Yorks, DN12 4LH
*Activities:* Manufacture and processing of other glass, including technical glassware
*Parent:* Schott Glaswerke Beteiligungs-Und Export GmbH
*Officers:* Christopher Wanless [1962] Director; Fritz Wolfgang Wintersteller [1962] Director/Manager [Austrian]

**Translift Freight Limited**
*Incorporated:* 23 October 1937 *Employees:* 93
*Net Worth:* £1,915,280 *Total Assets:* £8,482,747
*Registered Office:* Plasmor Ltd, P O Box 44, Womersley Road, Knottingley, W Yorks, WF11 0DN
*Activities:* Freight transport by road
*Parent:* Plasmor Ltd
*Officers:* Neil Marwood, Secretary; James Richard Marshall [1971] Director; Neil Marwood [1972] Finance Director; Julian Antony Slater [1961] Director; John Swain [1959] Group Sales Director

**Transwaste Recycling and Aggregates Limited**
*Incorporated:* 21 October 1999 *Employees:* 43
*Net Worth:* £9,457,734 *Total Assets:* £18,189,920
*Registered Office:* Melton Waste Park, Gibson Lane, Melton, E Yorks, HU14 3HH
*Activities:* Collection of non-hazardous waste
*Shareholders:* Mark Hornshaw; Paul Anthony Hornshaw
*Officers:* Paul Anthony Hornshaw, Secretary; Mark Hornshaw [1975] Director; Paul Anthony Hornshaw [1972] Director; Stuart Mark Wells [1966] Director

**Transwaste Services Limited**
*Incorporated:* 5 March 1999 *Employees:* 25
*Net Worth:* £2,428,131 *Total Assets:* £3,619,830
*Registered Office:* Melton Waste Park, Gibson Lane, Melton, E Yorks, HU14 3HH
*Activities:* Collection of non-hazardous waste
*Officers:* Paul Anthony Hornshaw, Secretary; Mark Hornshaw [1975] Director; Paul Anthony Hornshaw [1972] Director

**Treadwell Developments Limited**
*Incorporated:* 17 October 1968 *Employees:* 4
*Previous:* Treadwell Carpets Limited
*Net Worth:* £3,118,223 *Total Assets:* £4,021,274
*Registered Office:* Unit 9 Hope House, Mabgate, Leeds, LS9 7DR
*Activities:* Development of building projects
*Officers:* Jane Wright, Secretary; Jane Wright [1969] Finance Director; John Gary Wright [1968] Director/Manager

**Trenton (Hull) Limited**
*Incorporated:* 1 March 1984 *Employees:* 95
*Net Worth:* £1,021,000 *Total Assets:* £18,494,908
*Registered Office:* 62-63 Westborough, Scarborough, N Yorks, YO11 1TS
*Activities:* Sale of new cars and light motor vehicles
*Parent:* East Riding Holdings Company
*Officers:* Robert Michael Mabbett [1951] Director; Graham Douglas Pullen [1969] Director/Chartered Accountant; Peter Alan Staveley [1969] Director/General Manager; Andrew Woodhall [1968] Director/General Manager

**Trepko (UK) Limited**
*Incorporated:* 21 June 1990 *Employees:* 47
*Net Worth:* £1,596,565 *Total Assets:* £5,563,531
*Registered Office:* Trepko UK Limited, Marshall Way, Heapham Road Industrial Estate, Gainsborough, Lincs, DN21 1GD
*Activities:* Manufacture of machinery for food, beverage and tobacco processing
*Parent:* H C Holding Investeringsaktieselskab
*Officers:* Mark Leslie Grundy, Secretary; Mark Leslie Grundy [1969] UK Managing Director; Hans Christian Hansen [1949] Director/Economist [Danish]; Jesper Bjoern Hansen [1975] Director/Economist [Danish]; Jacob Ostergaard Knudsen [1977] Director/Electrical Engineer [Danish]

**Trevella Caravan Company Limited**
*Incorporated:* 8 October 1959 *Employees:* 31
*Net Worth:* £3,989,310 *Total Assets:* £5,211,304
*Registered Office:* Sand-le-Mere Caravan Park, Southfield Lane, Tunstall, Hull, HU12 0JN
*Activities:* Holiday centres and villages
*Parent:* Bridge Leisure Parks Limited
*Officers:* Simon Elliot, Secretary; Simon John Elliott [1969] Director; Andrew Stephen Howe [1968] Director; Simon Jamie Williams [1972] Director

**Trevor Iles Limited**
*Incorporated:* 13 August 1973 *Employees:* 124
*Net Worth:* £3,955,893 *Total Assets:* £5,847,279
*Registered Office:* Valley Mills, Valley Road, Bradford, W Yorks, BD1 4RU
*Activities:* Manufacture of other fabricated metal products n.e.c.
*Shareholders:* Sidney Trevor Iles; Kevin Roger Dixon
*Officers:* Graham Scott Iles, Secretary/Director; Daphne Elizabeth Dixon [1948] Director; Kevin Roger Dixon [1948] Director; Anne Lorraine Iles [1938] Director; Claire Iles [1964] Financial Director; Graham Scott Iles [1966] Director; Robert Scott Iles [1963] Director; Sidney Trevor Iles [1938] Director

**Tri-Pack Plastics Limited**
*Incorporated:* 19 November 1973 *Employees:* 29
*Net Worth:* £2,134,923 *Total Assets:* £3,790,524
*Registered Office:* Estate Road No 1, South Humberside Industrial Estate, Pyewipe, Grimsby, N E Lincs, DN31 2TB
*Activities:* Manufacture of plastic packing goods
*Shareholder:* Stephen Woodthorpe Clarke
*Officers:* Wendy Cuene-Grandidier, Secretary; Stephen Woodthorpe Clarke [1947] Director; Johann Oddgeirsson [1961] Managing Director [Icelander]

**Triangle Motor Co. Limited**
*Incorporated:* 15 May 1947 *Employees:* 80
*Net Worth:* £5,701,297 *Total Assets:* £6,271,105
*Registered Office:* Newport, Brough, E Yorks, HU15 2RD
*Activities:* Retail sale of automotive fuel in specialised stores
*Shareholders:* Ailsa Louise Wright; Andrea Claire Bogg
*Officers:* Andrea Claire Bogg [1969] Director; John Neil Hardy [1935] Director; Judith Margaret Hardy [1935] Director; Ailsa Louise Wright [1962] Managing Director

**Tricogen Laboratories Limited**
*Incorporated:* 22 April 1949 *Employees:* 48
*Net Worth:* £1,983,073 *Total Assets:* £3,653,428
*Registered Office:* Whitworth Avenue, Aycliffe Business Park, Newton Aycliffe, Co Durham, DL5 6YN
*Activities:* Other manufacturing n.e.c.
*Major Shareholder:* Paul Anthony Garth Sliufko
*Officers:* Virginia Ann Sliufko, Secretary; Christopher Harry Sliufko [1987] Director; Olivia Mary Sliufko [1982] Director; Paul Anthony Garth Sliufko [1954] Director; Thomas Guy Sliufko [1985] Director/Manager

**Triesse Group Limited**
*Incorporated:* 30 July 2010 *Employees:* 3
*Net Worth:* £124,327 *Total Assets:* £4,852,541
*Registered Office:* Triesse Limited, Lancaster Close, Sherburn Enterprise Park, Sherburn in Elmet, N Yorks, LS25 6NS
*Activities:* Activities of head offices
*Parent:* Consolidated Timber Holdings Limited
*Officers:* David John Colman [1962] Managing Director; Simon David Holdsworth [1956] Director/Chartered Accountant; Andrew Peter Smith [1959] Director

**Triesse Holdings Limited**
*Incorporated:* 20 September 1996 *Employees:* 3
*Net Worth:* £1,837,674 *Total Assets:* £3,980,460
*Registered Office:* Lancaster Close, Sherburn Enterprise Park, Sherburn in Elmet, Leeds, LS25 6NS
*Activities:* Activities of head offices
*Parent:* Consolidated Timber Holdings Limited
*Officers:* David John Colman [1962] Director/Chartered Accountant; Simon David Holdsworth [1956] Director; Andrew Peter Smith [1959] Director

**Triesse Limited**
*Incorporated:* 13 January 1975 *Employees:* 65
*Net Worth:* £7,196,886 *Total Assets:* £11,440,638
*Registered Office:* Lancaster Close, Sherburn Enterprise Park, Sherburn in Elmet, Leeds, LS25 6NS
*Activities:* Other manufacturing n.e.c.
*Officers:* Rachel Louise Stoker, Secretary; David John Colman [1962] Director/Chartered Accountant; Simon David Holdsworth [1956] Director; John Daniel Nield [1966] Director/General Manager; Andrew Peter Smith [1959] Director

**Triline (2014) Limited**
*Incorporated:* 21 March 2014
*Net Worth:* £3,132,082 *Total Assets:* £3,176,688
*Registered Office:* Clayfield Works, London Road, Slaithwaite, Huddersfield, W Yorks, HD7 5BG
*Activities:* Non-trading company
*Shareholders:* Douglas Garry Fearnside; Mark Oldroyd; Michael Walsh
*Officers:* Douglas Garry Fearnside [1962] Production Director; Mark Oldroyd [1973] Operations Director; Michael Walsh [1978] Managing Director

**Trilogy (Leamington Spa) Limited**
*Incorporated:* 6 August 2009
*Net Worth:* £12,802,000 *Total Assets:* £36,630,000
*Registered Office:* Hilmore House, Gain Lane, Bradford, W Yorks, BD3 7DL
*Activities:* Other business support service activities n.e.c.
*Parent:* Optimisation Developments Limited
*Officers:* Jonathan James Burke, Secretary; Jonathan James Burke [1966] Director; Joanna Louise Goff [1978] Finance Director

**Trimble Solutions (UK) Ltd**
*Incorporated:* 13 April 1999 *Employees:* 88
*Previous:* Tekla (UK) Limited
*Net Worth Deficit:* £15,341,729 *Total Assets:* £84,654,480
*Registered Office:* Trimble House, Gelderd Road, Gildersome, Morley, Leeds, LS27 7JP
*Activities:* Information technology consultancy activities
*Shareholders:* Trimble Inc; Trimble Solutions Oy; Trimble Solutions Corporation
*Officers:* Timo Keinanen, Secretary; Richard Charles Fletcher [1973] Director; Timo Keinanen [1960] Director/Chief Financial Officer [Finnish]

**Trinity Developments Leeds Ltd**
*Incorporated:* 11 December 2014
*Net Worth:* £27,430 *Total Assets:* £5,115,757
*Registered Office:* 193 Woodhouse Street, Leeds, LS6 2NY
*Activities:* Development of building projects
*Major Shareholder:* Kissun Parmer
*Officers:* Kissun Parmar [1984] Director

**Trinity Exploration & Production PLC**
*Incorporated:* 21 February 2011 *Employees:* 191
*Net Worth:* £36,597,124 *Total Assets:* £78,960,608
*Registered Office:* c/o Pinsent Masons LLP, 1 Park Row, Leeds, LS1 5AB
*Activities:* Activities of other holding companies n.e.c.
*Officers:* Jeremy Bridglalsingh [1979] Director/Chief Financial Officer [Trinidadian]; Nicholas John Clayton [1963] Director; Bruce Alan Ian Dingwall [1959] Director; James Graeme Menzies [1962] Director; David Alexander Segel [1964] Director [American]; Angus Christian Winther [1967] Director

**Trinity Fire and Security Systems Ltd**
*Incorporated:* 20 January 1997 *Employees:* 326
*Net Worth:* £2,301,134 *Total Assets:* £12,679,837
*Registered Office:* 13 Flemming Court, Whistler Drive, Castleford, W Yorks, WF10 5HW
*Activities:* Security systems service activities
*Parent:* Trinity Ten Limited
*Officers:* Adam Coates, Secretary; Sally Ann Bedford [1968] Director; Paul Andrew Clayton [1968] Finance Director; Adam John Coates [1968] Director; Shaun Rooke Corbett [1972] Contracts Director; Andrew Richard Cotton [1964] Director; Robert Holliday [1966] Regional Director; Paul William Teasdale [1967] Director; Roger Peter Teasdale [1967] Managing Director; Mark Ian Watford [1967] Director/Accountant

**Trinity McQueen Limited**
*Incorporated:* 5 February 2013 *Employees:* 42
*Net Worth:* £1,558,818 *Total Assets:* £4,183,603
*Registered Office:* 3rd Floor, Victoria Wharf, 4 The Embankment, Leeds, LS1 4BA
*Activities:* Market research and public opinion polling
*Parent:* De Rosa (RSL) Ltd
*Officers:* Anna Louise Cliffe [1974] Director; Robin Noel Horsfield [1969] Director

**Trinity Multi Academy Trust**
*Incorporated:* 6 May 2009 *Employees:* 767
*Previous:* Trinity Academy Halifax
*Net Worth:* £44,663,000 *Total Assets:* £49,299,000
*Registered Office:* Trinity Academy Halifax, Shay Lane, Halifax, W Yorks, HX2 9TZ
*Activities:* Primary education
*Officers:* Professor David Michael Baker [1952] Director/Emeritus Professor; Gareth John Davies [1969] Managing Director; Michael Kevin Gosling [1971] Director/Principal/Headteacher; Professor Claire Elizabeth Honess [1967] Director/University Academic; Wayne Keating [1980] Director/Head of Professional Services; Mike Kneafsey [1968] Director; Thomas Michael Miskell [1955] Director; Andrew Woodhead [1966] Director/Credit Manager

**Trinity Ten Limited**
*Incorporated:* 21 May 2010 *Employees:* 326
*Net Worth:* £1,632,099 *Total Assets:* £12,013,802
*Registered Office:* 13 Flemming Court, Whistler Drive, Castleford, W Yorks, WF10 5HW
*Activities:* Activities of head offices
*Parent:* PTSG Electrical Services Limited
*Officers:* Adam Coates, Secretary; Sally Ann Bedford [1968] Director; Adam John Coates [1968] Director; Paul William Teasdale [1967] Director

**Triple A Lets Limited**
*Incorporated:* 13 April 2004 *Employees:* 3
*Net Worth:* £786,719 *Total Assets:* £3,292,363
*Registered Office:* Vesper Lodge, Vesper Lane, Kirkstall, Leeds, LS5 3NR
*Activities:* Other letting and operating of own or leased real estate
*Shareholders:* Anthony Parascandalo; Angela Maria Jobling; Michael Andrew Parascandalo
*Officers:* Angela Maria Jobling, Secretary; Angela Maria Jobling [1967] Director; Anthony Parascandolo [1968] Director/Architect; Michael Andrew Parascandolo [1973] Director/Solicitor

**Triple T Engineering Limited**
*Incorporated:* 6 December 1985 *Employees:* 24
*Net Worth:* £4,218,290 *Total Assets:* £4,503,872
*Registered Office:* Hackworth Industrial Park, Shildon, Co Durham, DL4 1HF
*Activities:* Machining
*Major Shareholder:* Timothy Paul Tarn
*Officers:* Marilyn Tarn, Secretary; Marilyn Tarn [1953] Director; Timothy Paul Tarn [1951] Director/Mechanical Engineer

**Triton Construction Holdings Limited**
*Incorporated:* 10 February 2016 *Employees:* 56
*Net Worth:* £1,643,308 *Total Assets:* £13,598,400
*Registered Office:* Hare Park Mills, Hare Park Lane, Hightown, Liversedge, W Yorks, WF15 8EP
*Activities:* Activities of construction holding companies
*Major Shareholder:* Michael James Parkinson
*Officers:* Ashley Gerard Bickler [1964] Director; Stephen William Bolton [1952] Operations Director; John Paul Duffey [1969] Director; Justin Mark John Goodyear [1971] Director/Estimator; Paul Anthony Halloran [1967] Director; Michael James Parkinson [1965] Director; Jonathan Stephen Rosenberg [1965] Director

**Triton Construction Limited**
*Incorporated:* 4 February 2005 *Employees:* 56
*Net Worth:* £2,025,328 *Total Assets:* £9,560,418
*Registered Office:* Hare Park Mills, Hare Park Lane, Hightown, Liversedge, W Yorks, WF15 8EP
*Activities:* Construction of other civil engineering projects n.e.c.
*Parent:* Triton Construction Group Limited
*Officers:* Ashley Gerard Bickler, Secretary/Director; Ashley Gerard Bickler [1964] Director; Stephen William Bolton [1952] Operations Director NW; Ian David Chapman [1969] Director; John Paul Duffey [1969] Commercial Director; Justin Mark John Goodyear [1971] Director/Estimator; Paul Anthony Halloran [1967] Director; Michael James Parkinson [1965] Director; Jonathan Stephen Rosenberg [1965] Director

**Trojan Plastics Limited**
*Incorporated:* 5 March 1986 *Employees:* 163
*Net Worth:* £5,736,553 *Total Assets:* £9,668,100
*Registered Office:* Ramsden Mills, Britannia Road, Milnsbridge, Huddersfield, W Yorks, HD3 4QG
*Activities:* Manufacture of other plastic products
*Parent:* Hartford Holdings Limited
*Officers:* Adam Paul Mosley, Secretary; Adam Paul Mosley [1975] Director; David James Mosley [1978] Director/Sales and Marketing; James Maurice Vincent Mosley [1929] Managing Director

**Troy Foods Limited**
*Incorporated:* 14 April 2000 *Employees:* 179
*Net Worth:* £1,111,157 *Total Assets:* £9,997,575
*Registered Office:* Unit 1 Intermezzo Drive, Leeds, LS10 1DF
*Activities:* Manufacture of other food products n.e.c.
*Major Shareholder:* David James Kempley
*Officers:* David James Kempley [1962] Director; Tracey Leigh Kempley [1963] Director; Andrew Glyn Murphy [1965] Director

**TRS Tyres Ltd**
*Incorporated:* 2 October 1989 *Employees:* 42
*Net Worth:* £3,063,200 *Total Assets:* £3,705,203
*Registered Office:* Whitegate, White Lund Industrial Estate, Morecambe, Lancs, LA3 3BS
*Activities:* Manufacture of motor vehicles
*Shareholders:* Nicholas Stonier; Luke Stonier
*Officers:* Nicholas Stonier, Secretary; Luke Stonier [1968] Director/Casing Broker; Nicholas Stonier [1970] Director/Casings Broker

**TRU Property Investments Limited**
*Incorporated:* 2 April 1974
*Net Worth:* £859,784 *Total Assets:* £3,282,760
*Registered Office:* Huddersfield Road, Elland, W Yorks, HX5 9BW
*Activities:* Buying and selling of own real estate
*Parent:* Marshall Holdings Limited
*Officers:* Jonathan Booth, Secretary; Jonathan Booth [1970] Director/Accountant; Christopher Roy Marshall [1939] Director/Building Contractor

**Trupart Limited**
*Incorporated:* 28 November 1985 *Employees:* 56
*Net Worth:* £3,121,090 *Total Assets:* £6,704,825
*Registered Office:* Decoy Bank, White Rose Way, Doncaster, S Yorks, DN4 5JD
*Activities:* Wholesale trade of motor vehicle parts and accessories
*Parent:* Inhoco 2082 Limited
*Officers:* Jane Farrell [1960] Director; Gareth David Williams [1984] Director

**Trust Care Ltd**
*Incorporated:* 5 September 2007 *Employees:* 200
*Net Worth:* £1,241,200 *Total Assets:* £8,263,396
*Registered Office:* Lindsfarne, Wadworth Hall Lane, Wadworth, Doncaster, S Yorks, DN11 9BH
*Activities:* Residential nursing care facilities
*Shareholders:* Andrew Savage; Linda Savage
*Officers:* Steven Wilson, Secretary; Andrew Savage [1969] Director/Care Home Owner; Steven Wilson [1975] Director/Care Home Owner

**Trycare Limited**
*Incorporated:* 11 January 1996 *Employees:* 81
*Net Worth:* £3,101,312 *Total Assets:* £5,152,590
*Registered Office:* Rialto Buildings, Station Road, Clayton, Bradford, W Yorks, BD14 6JA
*Activities:* Other business support service activities n.e.c.
*Major Shareholder:* Philip David Mathers
*Officers:* Anita Mathers, Secretary; Craig Peter Cranfield [1967] Director/General Manager; Elaine Langley [1959] Director/Administration Manager; Philip David Mathers [1949] Director

**TSC Engineering Limited**
*Incorporated:* 30 May 2003 *Employees:* 13
*Net Worth:* £8,410,211 *Total Assets:* £20,394,076
*Registered Office:* Unit E, Upper Wharf Street, Shipley, W Yorks, BD17 7DW
*Activities:* Other engineering activities
*Parent:* TSC Offshore (UK) Limited
*Officers:* Man Lai Chung, Secretary; Binghua Jiang [1950] Director/Chairman [American]; Menggui Zhang [1958] Director [American]

**TSP Projects Limited**
*Incorporated:* 9 March 1995 *Employees:* 345
*Previous:* Tata Steel UK Rail Consultancy Limited
*Net Worth:* £26,389,000 *Total Assets:* £53,687,000
*Registered Office:* Meridian House, The Crescent, York, YO24 1AW
*Activities:* Other specialised construction activities n.e.c.
*Parent:* British Steel Limited
*Officers:* Stephen Richard Andrews, Secretary; Stephen Richard Andrews [1971] Director/Chartered Accountant; Daniel Moshe Goldstein [1978] Corporate Director; Samuel Peter Hancock [1980] Director; Niall McCreanor [1965] Director; Marc Joseph Meyohas [1971] Director [French]; Bryan Craig Scott [1959] Managing Director

**TSYS Card Tech Limited**
*Incorporated:* 12 June 2006 *Employees:* 34
*Net Worth:* £11,600,000 *Total Assets:* £31,903,000
*Registered Office:* Fulford Moor House, Fulford Road, York, YO10 4EY
*Activities:* Information technology consultancy activities
*Parent:* TSYS International Management Limited
*Officers:* David Leonard Chew [1963] Finance Director; Gaylon Murrell Jowers Jr [1962] Director/Executive [American]; Rene Kruse [1967] Director [German]; Dorenda Kay Weaver [1963] Director/Chief Accounting Officer [American]

**Tuby Leisure Ltd**
*Incorporated:* 4 May 2016 *Employees:* 28
*Net Worth:* £1,663,558 *Total Assets:* £3,221,076
*Registered Office:* Pleasureland, Pier Road, Whitby, N Yorks, YO21 3PU
*Activities:* Other amusement and recreation activities n.e.c.
*Shareholders:* Julie Tuby; Harry William Tuby
*Officers:* Harry William Tuby [1958] Director; Julie Tuby [1961] Director and Company Secretary; Mitchell Francis Tuby [1988] Director/Arcade Manager

**Neville Tucker (Group) Limited**
*Incorporated:* 24 March 2014 *Employees:* 98
*Net Worth:* £2,620,036 *Total Assets:* £7,952,282
*Registered Office:* Rotterdam Road, Sutton Fields Industrial Estate, Hull, HU7 0XD
*Activities:* Steam and air conditioning supply
*Major Shareholder:* Mark Alan Snape
*Officers:* David Richard Smith [1962] Contracts Director; Mark Alan Snape [1963] Managing Director

**Tucker Mechanical and Electrical Building Services Limited**
*Incorporated:* 15 January 1999 *Employees:* 98
*Previous:* Neville Tucker Heating Limited
*Net Worth:* £4,719,388 *Total Assets:* £7,908,002
*Registered Office:* Rotterdam Road, Sutton Fields Industrial Estate, Hull, HU7 0XD
*Activities:* Installation of industrial machinery and equipment
*Parent:* Neville Tucker (Holdings) Limited
*Officers:* Nicholas Derek Munt [1975] Director; David Richard Smith [1962] Contracts Director; Mark Alan Snape [1963] Senior Contracts Director

**Tudhoe Learning Trust**
*Incorporated:* 26 October 2012 *Employees:* 289
*Net Worth:* £9,559,045 *Total Assets:* £14,660,907
*Registered Office:* Tudhoe Colliery Primary School, Front Street, Tudhoe, Spennymoor, Co Durham, DL16 6TJ
*Activities:* Primary education
*Officers:* Gillian Dixon Pigott, Secretary; Allison Boustead [1983] Director/Deputy Headteacher; David Bowes [1945] Director/Retired; David Collins [1972] Relationship Director Banking; Vivienne Ingleton [1952] Director/Retired; Mike Simpson [1947] Director/Retired; James Hastings Smith [1964] Director/Executive Headteacher; Derek Turner [1942] Director/Retired; Ivan Whitfield [1963] University Employee (Director of Service Function)

**Tudor International Freight Limited**
*Incorporated:* 27 February 1991 *Employees:* 18
*Net Worth:* £1,931,798 *Total Assets:* £3,904,835
*Registered Office:* Low Hall Business Park, Low Hall Road, Horsforth, Leeds, LS18 4EF
*Activities:* Other transportation support activities
*Shareholders:* David Frederick Johnson; Shirley Johnson
*Officers:* Shirley Johnson, Secretary/Director; Adam Johnson [1986] Director/Accountant; David Frederick Johnson [1946] Director/Shipping and Forwarding Executive; Shirley Johnson [1959] Director

**Tudorshore Limited**
*Incorporated:* 19 October 1989
*Net Worth:* £388,821 *Total Assets:* £4,062,978
*Registered Office:* The Mill at Scott Hall, 44 Potternewton Mount, Leeds, LS7 2DR
*Activities:* Development of building projects
*Parent:* Industrial Fibres Limited
*Officers:* Cynthia Valerie Bexon, Secretary; Cynthia Valerie Bexon [1939] Director/Company Secretary; John Truswell Bexon [1938] Director

**Tullo Wind Farm Limited**
*Incorporated:* 4 November 2002
*Net Worth:* £10,434,030 *Total Assets:* £15,216,790
*Registered Office:* c/o Pinsent Masons LLP, 1 Park Row, Leeds, LS1 5AB
*Activities:* Production of electricity
*Parent:* Eneco UK Limited
*Officers:* Cornelis de Haan [1976] Director [Dutch]

**Tunstall Group Acquisition Limited**
*Incorporated:* 24 May 2005
*Net Worth Deficit:* £373,028,000 *Total Assets:* £377,736,992
*Registered Office:* Whitley Lodge, Whitley Bridge, N Yorks, DN14 0HR
*Activities:* Activities of other holding companies n.e.c.
*Parent:* Tunstall Group Finance Limited
*Officers:* Jonathan Paul Furniss, Secretary; Craig Parsons [1970] Director; John Lee Robinson [1958] Director

**Tunstall Group Finance Limited**
*Incorporated:* 23 May 2005 *Employees:* 2
*Net Worth Deficit:* £217,874,000 *Total Assets:* £205,084,992
*Registered Office:* Whitley Lodge, Whitley Bridge, N Yorks, DN14 0HR
*Activities:* Activities of other holding companies n.e.c.
*Parent:* Tunstall Group Holdings Limited
*Officers:* Jonathan Paul Furniss, Secretary; Craig Parsons [1970] Director; John Lee Robinson [1958] Director

**Tunstall Group Holdings Limited**
*Incorporated:* 23 May 2005 *Employees:* 2,940
*Net Worth Deficit:* £360,670,016 *Total Assets:* £378,345,984
*Registered Office:* Whitley Lodge, Whitley Bridge, N Yorks, DN14 0HR
*Activities:* Activities of other holding companies n.e.c.
*Parent:* TGH Acquisitions Limited
*Officers:* Jonathan Paul Furniss, Secretary; Craig Parsons [1970] Director; John Lee Robinson [1958] Director

**Tunstall Group Limited**
*Incorporated:* 20 March 1957 *Employees:* 1,787
*Net Worth:* £200,864,000 *Total Assets:* £399,606,016
*Registered Office:* Whitley Lodge, Whitley Bridge, N Yorks, DN14 0HR
*Activities:* Activities of other holding companies n.e.c.
*Parent:* Blythmore Limited
*Officers:* Jonathan Paul Furniss, Secretary; Craig Parsons [1970] Director; John Lee Robinson [1958] Director

**Tunstall Healthcare (UK) Limited**
*Incorporated:* 30 September 1977 *Employees:* 672
*Net Worth:* £250,740,000 *Total Assets:* £280,566,016
*Registered Office:* Whitley Bridge, N Yorks, DN14 0HR
*Activities:* Manufacture of communication equipment other than telegraph, and telephone apparatus and equipment
*Parent:* Tunstall Group Limited
*Officers:* Jonathan Paul Furniss, Secretary; Gavin Bashar [1963] Director; Katherine Heaton [1976] HR Director; Craig Parsons [1970] Director; Edward James Peck [1971] Finance Director; Elaine Quinn [1963] Director

**Tunstall Healthcare Group Limited**
*Incorporated:* 6 February 2008 *Employees:* 3,081
*Net Worth Deficit:* £1,559,382,016 *Total Assets:* £448,660,992
*Registered Office:* Whitley Lodge, Whitley Bridge, Doncaster, S Yorks, DN14 0HR
*Activities:* Activities of other holding companies n.e.c.
*Officers:* Jonathan Paul Furniss, Secretary; James Simon Edward Arnell [1969] Director; Craig Parsons [1970] Director; Thomas Spencer Patrick [1972] Director/Solicitor

**Tunstall Holdings Limited**
*Incorporated:* 22 September 1999
*Net Worth Deficit:* £74,244,000 *Total Assets:* £216,888,000
*Registered Office:* Whitley Lodge, Whitley Bridge, N Yorks, DN14 0HR
*Activities:* Activities of other holding companies n.e.c.
*Parent:* Tunstall Group Acquisition Limited
*Officers:* Jonathan Paul Furniss, Secretary; Craig Parsons [1970] Director; John Lee Robinson [1958] Director

**Turbine Efficiency Group Limited**
*Incorporated:* 20 December 2011 *Employees:* 3
*Net Worth:* £1,265,394 *Total Assets:* £5,917,165
*Registered Office:* 1 Park Row, Leeds, LS1 5AB
*Activities:* Activities of head offices
*Parent:* Florida Bidco Limited
*Officers:* Trevor James Swales [1963] Director/Chairman; Christopher John Turner [1968] Director/Chief Executive Officer; William James Willows-Chamberlin [1989] Finance Director

**Turkey Mill Investments Limited**
*Incorporated:* 28 May 1997 *Employees:* 8
*Net Worth:* £9,026,133 *Total Assets:* £21,518,080
*Registered Office:* Murky Hill Offices, Cow Lane, Middleton Tyas, Richmond, N Yorks, DL10 6RW
*Activities:* Other letting and operating of own or leased real estate
*Shareholders:* Adrian John Speir; Ralph Congreve
*Officers:* Adrian John Speir, Secretary; Ralph Congreve [1953] Director/Chartered Surveyor; Douglas James Lawson [1958] Director/Chartered Surveyor; Katharine Judith Lawson [1962] Director; Thomas Clifford Sheldon [1952] Director/Chartered Surveyor; Adrian John Speir [1949] Director

**Turnberry Holiday Park Limited**
*Incorporated:* 3 July 2012 *Employees:* 20
*Net Worth:* £1,362,144 *Total Assets:* £6,274,469
*Registered Office:* Sand-le-Mere, Southfield Lane, Tunstall, Hull, HU12 0JN
*Activities:* Holiday centres and villages
*Parent:* Bridge Leisure Parks Ltd
*Officers:* Simon John Elliott [1969] Director; Andrew Stephen Howe [1968] Director; Simon Jamie Williams [1972] Director

**Turnbull (Corn Sales) Limited**
*Incorporated:* 10 August 1973 *Employees:* 2
*Net Worth:* £4,682,825 *Total Assets:* £4,727,308
*Registered Office:* Burghwallis Grange, off Green Lane, Skellow, Doncaster, S Yorks, DN6 8JX
*Activities:* Other letting and operating of own or leased real estate
*Major Shareholder:* William John Turnbull
*Officers:* William John Turnbull, Secretary; Jane Elizabeth Turnbull [1953] Director; William John Turnbull [1951] Director

**Turnbull (Potato Sales) Limited**
*Incorporated:* 30 August 1973 *Employees:* 2
*Net Worth:* £4,298,937 *Total Assets:* £4,335,659
*Registered Office:* Burghwallis Grange, off Green Lane, Skellow, Doncaster, S Yorks, DN6 8JX
*Activities:* Other letting and operating of own or leased real estate
*Major Shareholder:* William John Turnbull
*Officers:* William John Turnbull, Secretary; Jane Elizabeth Turnbull [1953] Director; William John Turnbull [1951] Director

**G.B.Turnbull Limited**
*Incorporated:* 30 June 1958 *Employees:* 5
*Net Worth:* £16,408,705 *Total Assets:* £16,504,861
*Registered Office:* Burghwallis Grange, off Green Lane, Skellow, Doncaster, S Yorks, DN6 8JX
*Activities:* Growing of cereals (except rice), leguminous crops and oil seeds
*Major Shareholder:* William John Turnbull
*Officers:* William John Turnbull, Secretary; Jane Elizabeth Turnbull [1953] Director; William John Turnbull [1951] Director

**A.T.G. Turnbull Limited**
*Incorporated:* 22 March 1965 *Employees:* 8
*Net Worth:* £2,610,300 *Total Assets:* £5,411,669
*Registered Office:* The Farm Office, Prospect Farm, Barnetby, N Lincs, DN38 6EL
*Activities:* Growing of cereals (except rice), leguminous crops and oil seeds
*Shareholders:* Anthony William Henry Turnbull; Anthony William Henry Turnbull
*Officers:* Anthony William Henry Turnbull [1974] Director/Farmer

**Turner & Price Limited**
*Incorporated:* 17 July 1992 *Employees:* 264
*Net Worth:* £8,555,558 *Total Assets:* £19,347,670
*Registered Office:* Wiltshire Road, Dairycoates Industrial Estate, Hull, HU4 6PD
*Activities:* Non-specialised wholesale of food, beverages and tobacco
*Shareholders:* David Pentith Gould; Trevor Charles Harrison; John Robert Gould
*Officers:* Paul Brittain, Secretary; Craig Graham Andrews [1969] Buying Director; Paul Brittain [1969] Finance Director; Richard John Brown [1956] Shipping & Export Director; David Pentith Gould [1938] Director; John Robert Gould [1969] Managing Director; Richard David Gould [1965] Operations Director; Trevor Charles Harrison [1949] Director; Julian Philip Owen [1971] Sales & Marketing Director

**Turner & Townsend Consulting Limited**
*Incorporated:* 2 February 1996 *Employees:* 132
*Previous:* Turner & Townsend Management Solutions Limited
*Net Worth:* £1,539,000 *Total Assets:* £4,532,000
*Registered Office:* Low Hall, Calverley Lane, Horsforth, Leeds, LS18 4GH
*Activities:* Other business support service activities n.e.c.
*Parent:* Turner & Townsend UK Limited
*Officers:* Martin Stephen Jeremy Lathom-Sharp, Secretary; Vincent Patrick Clancy [1964] Director; James Dand [1979] Managing Director Europe [Dutch]; Bill McElroy [1960] Director; Peter Alistair McGettrick [1975] Director; Patricia Moore [1968] Director; Francis Wilkinson [1978] Director/Accountant

**Turner & Townsend Contract Services Limited**
*Incorporated:* 26 July 1990 *Employees:* 58
*Net Worth:* £2,002,000 *Total Assets:* £4,464,000
*Registered Office:* Low Hall, Calverley Lane, Horsforth, Leeds, LS18 4GH
*Activities:* Other business support service activities n.e.c.
*Parent:* Turner & Townsend UK Limited
*Officers:* Martin Stephen Jeremy Lathom-Sharp, Secretary; Vincent Patrick Clancy [1964] Director; James Dand [1979] Managing Director Europe [Dutch]; Peter Alistair McGettrick [1975] Director; Patricia Moore [1968] Director; Timothy John A'court Tapper [1969] Director/Partner; Francis Wilkinson [1978] Director/Accountant

**Turner & Townsend Cost Management Limited**
*Incorporated:* 20 December 2007 *Employees:* 683
*Net Worth:* £10,252,000 *Total Assets:* £30,128,000
*Registered Office:* Low Hall, Calverley Lane, Horsforth, Leeds, LS18 4GH
*Activities:* Other business support service activities n.e.c.
*Parent:* Turner & Townsend UK Limited
*Officers:* Martin Stephen Jeremy Lathom-Sharp, Secretary; Vincent Patrick Clancy [1964] Director; Paul Anthony John Connolly [1970] Director; James Dand [1979] Managing Director Europe [Dutch]; Patricia Moore [1968] Director; Francis Wilkinson [1978] Director/Accountant

**Turner & Townsend Europe Limited**
*Incorporated:* 20 February 1998 *Employees:* 62
*Net Worth:* £1,853,000 *Total Assets:* £4,891,000
*Registered Office:* Low Hall, Calverley Lane, Horsforth, Leeds, LS18 4GH
*Activities:* Other business support service activities n.e.c.
*Parent:* Turner & Townsend International Limited
*Officers:* Martin Stephen Jeremy Lathom-Sharp, Secretary; Vincent Patrick Clancy [1964] Director/Quantity Surveyor; James Dand [1979] Managing Director Europe [Dutch]; Robert Douglas Edwards [1960] Director; Paul Grace [1972] Director [Irish]; Karen Jarman [1960] Finance Director

**Turner & Townsend Group Limited**
*Incorporated:* 2 February 1996 *Employees:* 145
*Net Worth:* £8,191,000 *Total Assets:* £80,440,000
*Registered Office:* Low Hall, Calverley Lane, Horsforth, Leeds, LS18 4GH
*Activities:* Other business support service activities n.e.c.
*Parent:* Turner & Townsend Limited
*Officers:* Martin Stephen Jeremy Lathom-Sharp, Secretary; Vincent Patrick Clancy [1964] Director/Quantity Surveyor; James Dand [1979] Managing Director Europe [Dutch]; Martin Stephen Jeremy Lathom-Sharp [1967] Finance Director; Patricia Moore [1968] Director; Andrew Murray Rowden [1968] Director/Quantity Surveyor

**Turner & Townsend Holdings Limited**
*Incorporated:* 17 September 2015
*Net Worth:* £1,482,000 *Total Assets:* £88,145,000
*Registered Office:* Low Hall, Calverley Lane, Horsforth, Leeds, LS18 4GH
*Activities:* Other business support service activities n.e.c.
*Parent:* Turner & Townsend Partners LLP
*Officers:* Vincent Patrick Clancy [1964] Director; James Dand [1979] Managing Director Europe [Dutch]; Martin Stephen Jeremy Lathom-Sharp [1967] Director; Patricia Moore [1968] Director; Andrew Murray Rowden [1968] Director/Quantity Surveyor

**Turner & Townsend International Limited**
*Incorporated:* 2 January 1980 *Employees:* 249
*Net Worth:* £8,133,000 *Total Assets:* £52,734,000
*Registered Office:* Low Hall, Calverley Lane, Horsforth, Leeds, LS18 4GH
*Activities:* Other business support service activities n.e.c.
*Parent:* Turner & Townsend Group Limited
*Officers:* Martin Stephen Jeremy Lathom-Sharp, Secretary; Vincent Patrick Clancy [1964] Director/Quantity Surveyor; James Dand [1979] Managing Director Europe [Dutch]; Martin Stephen Jeremy Lathom-Sharp [1967] Finance Director; Patricia Moore [1968] Director; Andrew Murray Rowden [1968] Director/Quantity Surveyor; Alan Mariwan Talabani [1974] Director

**Turner & Townsend Limited**
*Incorporated:* 9 January 2008 *Employees:* 4,850
*Previous:* Turner & Townsend PLC
*Net Worth:* £98,186,000 *Total Assets:* £235,692,000
*Registered Office:* Low Hall, Calverley Lane, Horsforth, Leeds, LS18 4GH
*Activities:* Other business support service activities n.e.c.
*Parent:* Turner & Townsend Holdings Limited
*Officers:* Martin Stephen Jeremy Lathom-Sharp, Secretary; Michael Sean Christie [1957] Director; Vincent Patrick Clancy [1964] Director; James Dand [1979] Managing Director Europe [Dutch]; Martin Stephen Jeremy Lathom-Sharp [1967] Director; Patricia Moore [1968] Director; Andrew Murray Rowden [1968] Director/Quantity Surveyor; Jonathan Colin Michael White [1961] Director

**Turner & Townsend Partners LLP**
*Incorporated:* 16 September 2015 *Employees:* 4,763
*Net Worth:* £66,843,000 *Total Assets:* £232,791,008
*Registered Office:* Low Hall, Calverley Lane, Horsforth, Leeds, LS18 4GH
*Officers:* Vincent Patrick Clancy [1964] Member; Martin Stephen Jeremy Lathom-Sharp [1967] Member; Judith Anne Adams [1967] LLP Member; Andrew James Aston [1974] LLP Member; Ian Crawford Ballentine [1970] LLP Member; Julian Courtenay Bartlett [1972] LLP Member; Graeme Richard Baxter [1965] LLP Member; Dave Bell [1969] LLP Member; Matthew John Billingham [1972] LLP Member; John Andrew Lewis Boultwood [1965] LLP Member; Neil Bullen [1969] LLP Member; Kiabi Dara Carson [1973] LLP Member; Michael Stephen Connolly [1970] LLP Member; Paul Anthony John Connolly [1970] LLP Member; James Christopher Corrigan [1983] LLP Member; David Stephen Crewe [1964] LLP Member; Peter Cummings [1971] LLP Member; James Dand [1979] LLP Member; Mark Deakin [1970] LLP Member; Ross Dunkerley [1968] LLP Member; Gary James Easton [1961] LLP Member; Robert Douglas Edwards [1960] LLP Member; David Pettigrew McFarlane Fox [1961] LLP Member; Barry Gater [1977] LLP Member; Suresh Ramchand Gopalani [1961] LLP Member; Michael Grace [1972] LLP Member; Paul James Grace [1972] LLP Member; Ameya Prabhakar Gumaste [1969] LLP Member; David Hancox [1963] LLP Member; Mark Haselau [1969] LLP Member; Gary James Healey [1978] LLP Member; Nicolaas Du Plessis Horn [1970] LLP Member; Aileen Anne Jamieson [1975] LLP Member; Mark Jones [1971] LLP Member; Nicholas Robert Jones [1978] LLP Member; Mark Kelly [1965] LLP Member; Jaime Elizabeth Kerr [1977] LLP Member; Julian Kerwood [1976] LLP Member; Darren Edward Laybourn [1971] LLP Member; Dominic Brian Leadsom [1971] LLP Member; Gael Francois David Lehimas [1973] LLP Member; David Christopher Liddle [1967] LLP Member; Graeme Leslie Vincent Liss [1971] LLP Member; Martin Noel Londra [1971] LLP Member; Mohammed Hanif Loonat [1965] LLP Member; Paul Maitland [1966] LLP Member; Gerard Jude McCabe [1963] LLP Member; Stephen Derek McCartney [1963] LLP Member; Neil Duncan McCowan [1962] LLP Member; James Francis McDade [1966] LLP Member; William John McElroy [1960] LLP Member; Peter Alistair McGettrick [1975] LLP Member; Stephen Augustine McGuckin [1961] LLP Member; Duncan McIndoe [1978] LLP Member; Patricia Moore [1968] LLP Member; Darren Munton [1972] LLP Member; Dennis Nolan [1975] LLP Member; Niall Martin O'Reilly [1971] LLP Member; Anooj Oodit [1976] LLP Member; Richard William Peers [1974] LLP Member; Stephen John Perkins [1973] LLP Member; Gareth Andrew Poole [1979] LLP Member; Ashley Philip Prail [1959] LLP Member; John Charles Price-Stephens [1956] LLP Member; Adam James Ralph [1979] LLP Member; Stefan Reimoser [1972] LLP Member; Mark John Richards [1963] LLP Member; Bradley Richardson [1970] LLP Member; John Robbins [1961] LLP Member; Gail Rogowsky [1972] LLP Member; David Noel Rokesky [1965] LLP Member; Andrew Murray Rowden [1968] LLP Member; Christopher James Sargent [1977] LLP Member; David Mark Savage [1975] LLP Member; Andrew William Scott [1968] LLP Member; Brian Richard Shuptrine [1980] LLP Member; Robert David Stacey [1971] LLP Member; Duncan McIvor Stone [1966] LLP Member; John Stretch [1966] LLP Member; Martin John Sudweeks [1969] LLP Member; Alan Mariwan Talabani [1974] LLP Member; Timothy John A'court Tapper [1969] LLP Member; Brenden Kim Van Rooyen [1972] LLP Member; Christopher Walker [1974] LLP Member; Stephen Walker [1972] LLP Member; Steven William Waltho [1973] LLP Member; Gareth James Whisson [1979] LLP Member; David Scott Whysall [1982] LLP Member; David Alexander Williams [1961] LLP Member; Anthony Wood [1957] LLP Member

**Turner & Townsend Project Management Limited**
*Incorporated:* 16 September 1987 *Employees:* 958
*Net Worth:* £8,824,000 *Total Assets:* £50,771,000
*Registered Office:* Low Hall, Calverley Lane, Horsforth, Leeds, LS18 4GH
*Activities:* Other business support service activities n.e.c.
*Parent:* Turner & Townsend UK Limited
*Officers:* Martin Stephen Jeremy Lathom-Sharp, Secretary; Vincent Patrick Clancy [1964] Director; James Dand [1979] Managing Director Europe [Dutch]; Patricia Moore [1968] Director; Francis Wilkinson [1978] Director/Accountant; David Alexander Williams [1961] Director

**Sam Turner and Sons Limited**
*Incorporated:* 18 December 1945 *Employees:* 187
*Net Worth:* £8,269,175 *Total Assets:* £11,242,189
*Registered Office:* Darlington Road, Northallerton, N Yorks, DL6 2XB
*Activities:* Wholesale of agricultural machinery, equipment and supplies
*Shareholder:* Charles Edward Turner
*Officers:* John Samuel Turner, Secretary; Benjamin Matthew Turner [1980] Director; Charles Edward Turner [1974] Director/Agricultural Merchant; Charles Michael Turner [1948] Director/Agricultural Merchant; John Samuel Turner [1946] Director/Agricultural Merchant; Mark Samuel Turner [1970] Director/Agricultural Merchant

**Turner Commercial Developments Ltd**
*Incorporated:* 1 December 2006 *Employees:* 3
*Previous:* Belton Road Properties Limited
*Net Worth:* £2,551,663 *Total Assets:* £3,278,848
*Registered Office:* Low House, Saw Mill Lane, Addingham, Ilkley, W Yorks, LS29 0ST
*Activities:* Development of building projects
*Shareholders:* Blue Ice Limited; Menston Estates Limited
*Officers:* James Philip Turner, Secretary; James Philip Turner [1965] Director

**Twentyfour28 Limited**
*Incorporated:* 16 August 2017 *Employees:* 2
*Net Worth Deficit:* £275,583 *Total Assets:* £11,757,364
*Registered Office:* 44 Selby Road, Garforth, W Yorks, LS25 1LS
*Activities:* Activities of investment trusts
*Shareholders:* Gillian Hayes; Richard John Hayes
*Officers:* Gillian Hayes [1961] Director; Richard John Hayes [1965] Director

**Twiflex Limited**
*Incorporated:* 14 February 1946 *Employees:* 72
*Net Worth:* £4,071,000 *Total Assets:* £7,295,000
*Registered Office:* Cannon Way, Dewsbury, W Yorks, WF13 1EH
*Activities:* Other manufacturing n.e.c.
*Parent:* Altra Industrial Motion UK Limited
*Officers:* Richard Ian Laws, Secretary; Glenn Deegan [1966] Director/VP, Legal & HR, General Counsel [American]; Todd Patriacca [1969] Director/VP Finance/Corporate Controller [American]

**TWR Developments Limited**
*Incorporated:* 28 July 2008
*Net Worth:* £10,560,040 *Total Assets:* £10,666,259
*Registered Office:* 7 Woodland Road, Ulverston, Cumbria, LA12 0DX
*Activities:* Other business support service activities n.e.c.
*Officers:* Jonathan Lee Hartley, Secretary; Helen Mary Hartley [1957] Director; Jonathan Lee Hartley [1953] Director/Manager; Richard John Hartley [1989] Director; Thomas Murray Hartley [1984] Director; William Jonathon Hartley [1987] Director

**TWS Property Limited**
*Incorporated:* 12 October 2012 *Employees:* 2
*Net Worth:* £2,195,930 *Total Assets:* £9,550,827
*Registered Office:* 33 Thorne Road, Doncaster, S Yorks, DN1 2HD
*Activities:* Other letting and operating of own or leased real estate
*Shareholders:* James Michael Barker; Anthony Ashton Woodhouse
*Officers:* James Michael Barker, Secretary; James Michael Barker [1980] Director; Anthony Ashton Woodhouse [1968] Director

**Tydd St Giles Lodge Developments Limited**
*Incorporated:* 15 April 2005 *Employees:* 1
*Net Worth:* £4,591,019 *Total Assets:* £8,429,567
*Registered Office:* South Lakeland House, Main A6, Yealand Redmayne, Carnforth, Lancs, LA5 9RN
*Activities:* Other sports activities
*Parent:* Pure Leisure Group Limited
*Officers:* Paul Rossiter, Secretary; John Charles Morphet [1954] Managing Director; Paul Rossiter [1964] Director/Chartered Accountant; Gordon Alexander Walker [1964] Operations Director; Trevor James White [1952] Director/Marketing Manager

**TYK Limited**
*Incorporated:* 8 October 1988 *Employees:* 28
*Net Worth:* £871,039 *Total Assets:* £4,296,220
*Registered Office:* Chilton Way, Chilton Industrial Estate, Chilton, Ferryhill, Co Durham, DL17 0SD
*Activities:* Manufacture of refractory products
*Officers:* Jean-Pierre Lefebvre, Secretary; Jean-Pierre Lefebvre [1973] Plant Director [French]; Nobutaka Ushigome [1964] Director [Japanese]

**Tyto Finance Limited**
*Incorporated:* 25 September 2006
*Net Worth:* £700,001 *Total Assets:* £3,946,870
*Registered Office:* Lakeside House, Navigation Court, Calder Park, Wakefield, W Yorks, WF2 7BJ
*Activities:* Activities auxiliary to financial intermediation n.e.c.
*Parent:* Tyto Leasing Limited
*Officers:* Mark Hargreaves, Secretary; Phillip James Bennett [1960] Director; Jonathan Rowland Bourne [1968] Director; Mark Hargreaves [1984] Finance Director; Vineesh Madaan [1971] Managing Director

**U K Insurance Limited**
*Incorporated:* 6 August 1974
*Net Worth:* £1,850,700,032 *Total Assets:* £8,940,399,616
*Registered Office:* The Wharf, Neville Street, Leeds, LS1 4AZ
*Activities:* Non-life insurance
*Parent:* Direct Line Insurance Group PLC
*Officers:* Roger Cheston Clifton, Secretary; Michael Nicholas Biggs [1952] Director/Chartered Accountant; Paul Robert Geddes [1969] Director/Bank Official; Danuta Gray [1958] Director; Mark Julian Gregory [1963] Director; Jane Carolyn Hanson [1967] Director; Michael Anthony Holliday-Williams [1970] Director; Penelope Jane James [1969] Director; Sebastian Richard Edward Cuthbert James [1966] Director/Group CEO; Fiona Catherine McBain [1961] Director; Gregor Ninian Stewart [1964] Director; Clare Eleanor Thompson [1954] Director; Doctor Richard Churchill Ward [1957] Director

**UCLH Investors (Holdings) Limited**
*Incorporated:* 31 May 2012 *Employees:* 6
*Net Worth:* £1,692 *Total Assets:* £80,227,696
*Registered Office:* 1 Park Row, Leeds, LS1 5AB
*Activities:* Activities of other holding companies n.e.c.
*Shareholders:* CFIG Unicorn Holdings SPV, LLC; PFI 2005 Limited
*Officers:* Roger Georges Ammoun [1974] Director/Head of European Energy and Infrastructure; Vikram Bhaskar [1968] Director/Portfolio Manager [Indian]; John Stephen Gordon [1962] Director; Hannah O'Gorman [1971] Director

**UFP (UK) Limited**
*Incorporated:* 12 January 1994 *Employees:* 84
*Net Worth:* £20,147,660 *Total Assets:* £44,503,432
*Registered Office:* Enterprise House, Roydsdale Way, Euroway Trading Estate, Bradford, W Yorks, BD4 6SE
*Activities:* Wholesale of computers, computer peripheral equipment and software
*Parent:* UFP International SA
*Officers:* Nicholas Charles Stokes, Secretary; Sajad Arshad [1970] Director/Computer Supplies Dealer; Charles Zarka [1956] Director/Dealer in Computer Accessories [French]

**UK Ambulances 2 Ltd**
*Incorporated:* 6 December 2012
*Net Worth:* £5,533,585 *Total Assets:* £5,533,585
*Registered Office:* 5 Sidings Court, White Rose Way, Doncaster, S Yorks, DN4 5NU
*Activities:* Non-trading company
*Officers:* Luis Gonzaga Higuero Robles [1972] Director [Spanish]; Derek Stevens Laird [1964] Director

**UK Ambulances Ltd**
*Incorporated:* 6 November 2012 *Employees:* 550
*Net Worth:* £248,918 *Total Assets:* £12,105,635
*Registered Office:* 5 Sidings Court, White Rose Way, Doncaster, S Yorks, DN4 5NU
*Activities:* Non-trading company
*Officers:* Luis Gonzaga Higuero Robles [1972] Director [Spanish]; Derek Stevens Laird [1964] Director

**UK Asset Resolution Limited**
*Incorporated:* 1 July 2010 *Employees:* 175
*Net Worth:* £8,531,800,064 *Total Assets:* £19,812,999,168
*Registered Office:* Croft Road, Crossflatts, Bingley, W Yorks, BD16 2UA
*Activities:* Activities of head offices
*Parent:* Her Majesty's Treasury
*Officers:* John Gornall, Secretary; Ian John Hares [1958] Finance & Investment Director; Susan Carol Langley [1963] Non-Executive Director; Brendan Paul McDonagh [1958] Director [Irish]; Keith Charles William Morgan [1963] Director; Brendan John Russell [1961] Director; John Hartley Tattersall [1952] Director; Holger Randolph Vieten [1969] Director/Head of Banking and Capital Markets [German]

**UK Fisheries Limited**
*Incorporated:* 1 September 2004 *Employees:* 188
*Net Worth:* £76,921,088 *Total Assets:* £174,440,224
*Registered Office:* The Orangery, Hesslewood Country Business Park, Ferriby Road, Hessle, E Yorks, HU13 0LH
*Activities:* Activities of head offices
*Shareholder:* Onward Fishing Company Ltd
*Officers:* Thorsteinn Mar Baldvinsson [1952] Managing Director [Icelander]; Haraldur Gretarsson [1968] Director/Manager [Icelander]; Diederik Parlevliet [1955] Managing Director [Dutch]; Jane Vanessa Sandell [1978] Director; Jan Cornelis Van Der Plas [1954] Managing Director [Dutch]

**UK General Insurance Group Limited**
*Incorporated:* 12 August 2009 *Employees:* 111
*Net Worth Deficit:* £3,188,380 *Total Assets:* £57,652,652
*Registered Office:* Cast House, Old Mill Business Park, Gibraltar Island Road, Leeds, LS10 1RJ
*Activities:* Non-life reinsurance
*Parent:* Chicago Bidco Limited
*Officers:* Trevor Charles William Hopkins, Secretary; Jane Ann Bean [1966] Director/Chief Risk Officer; Jonathan James Cox [1980] Director; Ryan Mark Gill [1983] Finance Director; Timothy John Hanford [1964] Director; Richard Charles William Lewis [1963] Director; Clare Ryder [1970] Director; John William James Spencer [1957] Director

**UK General Insurance Limited**
*Incorporated:* 8 August 2002 *Employees:* 111
*Net Worth:* £7,265,106 *Total Assets:* £21,930,604
*Registered Office:* Cast House, Old Mill Business Park, Gibraltar Island Road, Leeds, LS10 1RJ
*Activities:* Non-life reinsurance
*Parent:* UK General Insurance Group Limited
*Officers:* Trevor Charles William Hopkins, Secretary; Jane Ann Bean [1966] Director/Chief Risk Officer; Jonathan James Cox [1980] Director; Ryan Mark Gill [1983] Finance Director; Timothy John Hanford [1964] Director; Richard Charles William Lewis [1963] Director; Clare Ryder [1970] Director; John William James Spencer [1957] Director

**UK Greetings Limited**
*Incorporated:* 15 December 1997 *Employees:* 2,421
*Net Worth:* £52,361,000 *Total Assets:* £80,218,000
*Registered Office:* Mill Street East, Dewsbury, W Yorks, WF12 9AW
*Activities:* Manufacture of other articles of paper and paperboard n.e.c.
*Major Shareholder:* Donald Gogel
*Officers:* Adrian Smith, Secretary; James Conn [1964] Director; Adrian James Smith [1972] Finance Director; Gregory Michael Steinberg [1973] Director/Chief Financial Officer [American]

**UK Thermos Holdings Limited**
*Incorporated:* 3 March 2010 *Employees:* 25
*Previous:* Brands Home & Leisure Holdings Limited
*Net Worth:* £3,636,011 *Total Assets:* £11,493,671
*Registered Office:* BHL, 1-2 Lockwood Park, Leeds, LS11 5UX
*Activities:* Non-trading company
*Parent:* King Warm Investments Limited
*Officers:* Mark Snape, Secretary; Richard Joseph Dias [1965] Director/President/COO [American]; Yuanfu Alex Huang [1967] Director/Investor [Taiwanese/American]; Seiichi Itoh [1955] Director/Vice President/General Manager [Japanese]; Yuji Katoaka [1962] Executive Director/General Manager [Japanese]; Nicholas John Kime [1966] Managing Director

**UK Thermos Limited**
*Incorporated:* 20 July 2000 *Employees:* 25
*Previous:* Brands Home & Leisure Group Limited
*Net Worth:* £4,148,502 *Total Assets:* £12,006,162
*Registered Office:* BHL, 1-2 Lockwood Park, Leeds, LS11 5UX
*Activities:* Wholesale of household goods (other than musical instruments) n.e.c
*Parent:* UK Thermos Holdings Limited
*Officers:* Mark Snape, Secretary; Richard Joseph Dias [1965] Director/President/COO [American]; Yuanfu Alex Huang [1967] Director/Investor [Taiwanese/American]; Seiichi Itoh [1955] Director/Vice President/General Manager [Japanese]; Yuji Katoaka [1962] Executive Director/General Manager [Japanese]; Nicholas John Kime [1966] Managing Director

**Ukar Corporate Services Limited**
*Incorporated:* 20 June 2013
*Total Assets:* £11,462,000
*Registered Office:* UKAR Corporate Services Limited, Croft Road, Bingley, W Yorks, BD16 2UA
*Activities:* Financial intermediation not elsewhere classified
*Parent:* UK Asset Resolution Limited
*Officers:* Claire Louise Craigie, Secretary; Ian John Hares [1958] Finance & Investment Director; Robert Philip Thackray [1975] Director

**UKDN Waterflow (LG) Limited**
*Incorporated:* 9 May 2007 *Employees:* 218
*Previous:* Lanes Utilities Limited
*Net Worth Deficit:* £999,377 *Total Assets:* £5,705,707
*Registered Office:* 17 Parkside Lane, Parkside Industrial Estate, Leeds, LS11 5TD
*Activities:* Other business support service activities n.e.c.
*Parent:* Lanes Group PLC
*Officers:* David Richard Nutton, Secretary; Andrew James Brierley [1972] Director; Wayne Trevor Earnshaw [1963] Director; Richard Elliot Leigh [1975] Group Sales Director; Kevin Andrew Moon [1960] Director; Scott Thomas Norris [1972] Group Commercial Director; David Richard Nutton [1953] Director/Accountant; Matthew Richard Todd [1971] Rail Director

**UKGlobal Holdings Limited**
*Incorporated:* 10 March 2016 *Employees:* 43
*Net Worth:* £1,640,012 *Total Assets:* £4,242,768
*Registered Office:* 33 George Street, Wakefield, W Yorks, WF1 1LX
*Activities:* Activities of head offices
*Shareholder:* Nicolas Travers Hamblin
*Officers:* Catherine Anne Thornton, Secretary; Matthew David Bray [1968] Director/Chartered Insurance Broker; Nicholas Travers Hamblin [1952] Director/Insurance Broker; Richard Phillip Hodson [1951] Director/Insurance Broker; Richard Charles Hodson [1977] Director/Insurance Broker; James Stephen Proctor [1960] Director/Chartered Accountant; Philip Douglas Truman [1964] Director/Insurance Broker

**UKIOSH Ltd.**
*Incorporated:* 21 October 2011
*Net Worth:* £203,705,456 *Total Assets:* £205,976,640
*Registered Office:* Old Mill Lane, Low Road, Hunslet, Leeds, LS10 1RB
*Activities:* Activities of production holding companies
*Officers:* Fabio Felisi [1966] Director [Italian]; David Michael Hellman [1965] Director/Accountant [American]; Kevin Teague [1957] Director/Accountant

**UKOS Investments Limited**
*Incorporated:* 11 October 2007 *Employees:* 1
*Net Worth:* £58,374,348 *Total Assets:* £59,630,088
*Registered Office:* Old Mill Lane, Low Road, Hunslet, Leeds, LS10 1RB
*Activities:* Other business support service activities n.e.c.
*Officers:* Anthony Lovallo [1961] Director/Attorney [American]

**Ulixes Limited**
*Incorporated:* 14 September 2007
*Net Worth:* £161,467,008 *Total Assets:* £252,112,992
*Registered Office:* Aquarius House, 6 Mid Point Business Park, Thornbury, Bradford, BD3 7AY
*Activities:* Activities of head offices
*Parent:* Univar Inc
*Officers:* Paul Graham Bryant [1973] Director; Jeffrey William Carr [1956] Director/Global Counsel [American]; Sabine Duyfjes [1972] Director/VP & General Counsel EMEA [German]

**Ulrome Seaside Caravan Company Limited**
*Incorporated:* 28 April 1961 *Employees:* 5
*Net Worth:* £4,998,632 *Total Assets:* £5,740,489
*Registered Office:* East Farm, Ulrome, Skipsea, Driffield, E Yorks, YO25 8TT
*Activities:* Other accommodation
*Shareholders:* Jean Catherine Frank; Wilfrid Michael Houghton
*Officers:* Jean Catherine Frank, Secretary; Jean Catherine Frank [1936] Director; Wilfrid Michael Houghton [1945] Director; Edna May Wood [1941] Director

**Ulster Yarns Limited**
*Incorporated:* 14 September 2000 *Employees:* 137
*Net Worth:* £1,481,601 *Total Assets:* £7,488,578
*Registered Office:* Ravensthorpe Mills, Ravensthorpe, Dewsbury, W Yorks, WF13 3NA
*Activities:* Preparation and spinning of textile fibres
*Parent:* Ulster Carpet Mills (Holdings) Limited
*Officers:* John Watkinson, Secretary; Graham Paul Hutton [1969] Operations and Production Director; Raymond Frederick James McKeown [1957] Purchasing and Logistics Director; John Watkinson [1953] Director/Accountant

**Ultima Furniture Systems Limited**
*Incorporated:* 4 June 1985 *Employees:* 328
*Net Worth:* £24,112,116 *Total Assets:* £34,836,156
*Registered Office:* 30 Lidgate Crescent, Langthwaite Grange Industrial Estate, South Kirkby, Pontefract, W Yorks, WF9 3NR
*Activities:* Manufacture of kitchen furniture
*Shareholders:* Clare Joan Ellis; Alfred Wilson Ellis
*Officers:* Clare Joan Ellis, Secretary; Alfred Wilson Ellis [1947] Director; Clare Joan Ellis [1954] Director

**Ultimate (Commercial Interiors) Limited**
*Incorporated:* 28 November 2000 *Employees:* 22
*Net Worth:* £1,611,483 *Total Assets:* £3,546,235
*Registered Office:* No 22 Ryefield Business Park, Belton Road, Silsden, Keighley, W Yorks, BD20 0EE
*Activities:* Other retail sale not in stores, stalls or markets
*Officers:* Mark James Naisbitt, Secretary/Sales Consultant; Mark Anthony Hickey [1973] Director; Mark James Naisbitt [1967] Director; Daniel Platt [1979] Director

**Ultimate Packaging Limited**
*Incorporated:* 30 March 1982 *Employees:* 252
*Net Worth:* £12,993,580 *Total Assets:* £24,737,268
*Registered Office:* Pegasus Way, Europarc, Grimsby, N E Lincs, DN37 9TS
*Activities:* Manufacture of plastic packing goods
*Shareholders:* Nigel Howard Tonge; Christopher Michael Tonge
*Officers:* Michael David Tonge, Secretary; Paul Best [1978] Sales Director; Jeremy Paul Hodson [1965] Director/Accountant; Jonathan Robert McCarthy [1968] Director; Christopher Michael Tonge [1960] Director; Justin Marc Tonge [1979] Director; Michael David Tonge [1962] Director; Nigel Tonge [1955] Director

**Ultra Finishing Limited**
*Incorporated:* 7 December 1984 *Employees:* 97
*Net Worth:* £5,477,000 *Total Assets:* £23,916,000
*Registered Office:* Hamnett House, Gibbet Street, Halifax, W Yorks, HX2 0AX
*Activities:* Manufacture of other fabricated metal products n.e.c.
*Parent:* Shul Co 007 Ltd
*Officers:* David Ian Cullen [1966] Director; Michael Duggleby [1972] Brand Director; Ian Gary Jones [1964] Director; Antony Wood [1973] Director

**Unicolour Limited**
*Incorporated:* 22 March 1984 *Employees:* 7
*Net Worth:* £2,008,000 *Total Assets:* £4,560,577
*Registered Office:* Tandem Works, Wakefield Road, Waterloo, Huddersfield, W Yorks, HD5 0AN
*Activities:* Manufacture of dyes and pigments
*Major Shareholder:* Edward Michael Fair Gleason
*Officers:* Jillian Margaret Gleason, Secretary; Edward Michael Fair Gleason [1949] Director/Chemical Distributor; Jillian Margaret Gleason [1949] Director

**The Union Discount Company of London Limited**
*Incorporated:* 20 February 2002 *Employees:* 1
*Net Worth:* £5,285,396 *Total Assets:* £9,823,346
*Registered Office:* Old Mills, off Whitehall Grove, Drighlington, Bradford, W Yorks, BD11 1BY
*Activities:* Activities of head offices
*Officers:* Kathryn Anne Davenport, Secretary; Peter Jan Patrik Valentin Gyllenhammar [1953] Director [Swedish]

**Unipol Student Homes**
*Incorporated:* 10 July 1997 *Employees:* 51
*Net Worth:* £5,163,810 *Total Assets:* £12,387,303
*Registered Office:* 155-157 Woodhouse Lane, Leeds, LS2 3ED
*Activities:* Other accommodation
*Officers:* Victoria Marlene Tolmie-Loverseed, Secretary; Meri Beth Braziel [1964] Director/Management Consultant [American]; Hannah Louise Brian [1980] Director/Deputy Chief Executive Student Engagement; Jessica Carrier [1996] Director/Sabbatical Officer; David William Arthur Collett [1948] Director/Head Campus and Residential Service; Rachael Lesley Elliott [1968] Director/Manager; Charles Anthony Hind [1996] Director/Sabbatical Officer; Michael Lees [1962] Director/Head of Campus Services; Japhet Olatomiwa Oladipo [1990] Director/Sabbatical Officer; Matthew Lewis Port [1998] Director/Welfare Officer; Priscilla Preston [1965] University Director; Ian Wilson Robertson [1963] Director/Head of Residential Accommodation; Martin Shevill Rushworth [1957] Director/Administrator; David Robert Sladdin [1944] Director/Consultant; Chris James Warrington [1972] Director/University Manager; Andrew William Welsh [1965] Director; Michael Wilkinson [1941] Director/Educational Consultant

**Unison Limited**
*Incorporated:* 3 April 1973 *Employees:* 46
*Net Worth:* £1,730,045 *Total Assets:* £6,534,455
*Registered Office:* Faroe House, Thornburgh Road, Eastfield, Scarborough, N Yorks, YO11 3UY
*Activities:* Manufacture of electronic industrial process control equipment
*Shareholder:* Julian Kidger
*Officers:* Julian Kidger, Secretary; Julian Kidger [1966] Director/Chartered Accountant; Alan Bradley George Pickering [1967] Director/Engineer(Software); Terence John Pickering [1939] Director/Electronics Engineer; Peter James Wilkinson [1944] Marketing Director

**United Anodisers Holdings Limited**
*Incorporated:* 28 December 2006
*Net Worth:* £3,021,263 *Total Assets:* £3,021,263
*Registered Office:* Field Mills, Red Doles Lane, Leeds Road, Huddersfield, W Yorks, HD2 1YG
*Activities:* Activities of head offices
*Officers:* Peter Michael Watts [1962] Director

**United Anodisers Limited**
*Incorporated:* 20 April 2001 *Employees:* 101
*Net Worth:* £3,547,583 *Total Assets:* £6,772,735
*Registered Office:* Field Mills, Red Doles Lane, Leeds Road, Huddersfield, W Yorks, HD2 1YG
*Activities:* Treatment and coating of metals
*Major Shareholder:* James Peter Clarke
*Officers:* James Peter Clarke [1957] Director; Peter Michael Watts [1962] Director

**United Autosports Limited**
*Incorporated:* 20 July 2009 *Employees:* 10
*Net Worth:* £1,444,224 *Total Assets:* £8,462,466
*Registered Office:* Unit 1 Helios 47, 1 Isabella Road, Garforth, Leeds, LS25 2DY
*Activities:* Other sports activities
*Shareholders:* Richard Antony Dean; Zakary Challen Brown
*Officers:* Zakary Challen Brown [1971] Director/Corporation President [American]; Richard Antony Dean [1964] Director

**United Fresh Consortium Limited**
*Incorporated:* 5 July 2007 *Employees:* 4
*Net Worth:* £246,723 *Total Assets:* £4,378,339
*Registered Office:* Paul Kershaw House, Essex Street, Bradford, W Yorks, BD4 7PG
*Activities:* Other food services
*Officers:* Andrew Peter Nicholls, Secretary; Noel Damian John Kershaw [1969] Managing Director; Andrew Peter Nicholls [1969] Director/Accountant; Christian Paynton [1970] Managing Director

**United Healthcare Developments Limited**
*Incorporated:* 26 June 2000 *Employees:* 6
*Net Worth:* £20,134,032 *Total Assets:* £48,652,680
*Registered Office:* Hanover House, 13 Victoria Road, Darlington, Co Durham, DL1 5SF
*Activities:* Other letting and operating of own or leased real estate
*Parent:* United Healthcare Holdings Limited
*Officers:* Katherine Susan Brown, Secretary; David Colin Currer Brown [1965] Director/Surveyor; Katherine Susan Brown [1965] Director

**United Reformed Church (Yorkshire Province) Trust Limited (The)**
*Incorporated:* 19 May 1981 *Employees:* 6
*Net Worth:* £9,837,372 *Total Assets:* £10,248,710
*Registered Office:* Somerset House, St Pauls Street, Morley, Leeds, LS27 9EP
*Activities:* Activities of religious organisations
*Officers:* Sheila Ferguson Duncan, Secretary; Justin Charlesworth [1973] Director/Finance Manager; Reverend Alan Geoffrey Crump [1958] Director/Minister of Religion; William Duncan [1955] Director/Chartered Accountant; Stephen Gooder [1952] Finance Director; Elaine Christine Merlin [1938] Director; John Christopher Reed [1947] Director; Revd Kevin Watson [1953] Director/Minister of Religion

**United Transmission Services Limited**
*Incorporated:* 2 March 1989 *Employees:* 12
*Net Worth:* £2,609,071 *Total Assets:* £3,505,165
*Registered Office:* Russell House, New Brunswick Street, Wakefield, W Yorks, WF1 5QR
*Activities:* Wholesale trade of motor vehicle parts and accessories
*Major Shareholder:* John Spencer
*Officers:* John Spencer [1959] Director

**Univar Europe Limited**
*Incorporated:* 21 August 1973 *Employees:* 182
*Net Worth:* £7,451,000 *Total Assets:* £19,565,000
*Registered Office:* Aquarius House, 6 Mid Point Business Park, Thornbury, Bradford, BD3 7AY
*Activities:* Non-trading company
*Parent:* Univar Limited
*Officers:* Paul Graham Bryant [1973] Director; Jeffrey William Carr [1956] Director/Global Counsel [American]; Sabine Duyfijes [1972] Director/VP & General Counsel EMEA [German]; Richard Nigel Hayes [1969] Director/Regional Vice President - North

**Univar Limited**
*Incorporated:* 6 April 1915 *Employees:* 546
*Net Worth:* £64,959,000 *Total Assets:* £102,042,000
*Registered Office:* Aquarius House, 6 Mid Point Business Park, Thornbury, Bradford, BD3 7AY
*Activities:* Non-specialised wholesale trade
*Parent:* Univar UK Limited
*Officers:* Paul Graham Bryant [1973] Director; Jeffrey William Carr [1956] Director/Global Counsel [American]; Sabine Duyfjes [1972] Director/VP & General Counsel EMEA [German]; Richard Nigel Hayes [1969] Director/Regional Vice President - North

**Univar Specialty Consumables Limited**
*Incorporated:* 12 November 1970 *Employees:* 66
*Net Worth:* £16,272,000 *Total Assets:* £21,154,000
*Registered Office:* Aquarius House, 6 Mid Point Business Park, Thornbury, Bradford, BD3 7AY
*Activities:* Non-specialised wholesale trade
*Parent:* Univar Europe Limited
*Officers:* Paul Graham Bryant [1973] Director; Jeffrey William Carr [1956] Director/Global Counsel [American]; Sabine Duyfjes [1972] Director/VP & General Counsel EMEA [German]

**Univar UK Limited**
*Incorporated:* 7 September 2000
*Net Worth:* £190,382,000 *Total Assets:* £190,382,000
*Registered Office:* Aquarius House, 6 Mid Point Business Park, Thornbury, Bradford, BD3 7AY
*Activities:* Other business support service activities n.e.c.
*Parent:* Ulixes Limited
*Officers:* Paul Graham Bryant [1973] Director; Jeffrey William Carr [1956] Director/Global Counsel [American]; Sabine Duyfjes [1972] Director/VP & General Counsel EMEA [German]

**Univer Manufacturing Company Ltd**
*Incorporated:* 28 December 1987 *Employees:* 46
*Net Worth:* £4,352,988 *Total Assets:* £7,179,782
*Registered Office:* 6 Station Road, Bradford, W Yorks, BD1 4SF
*Activities:* Manufacture of other fabricated metal products n.e.c.
*Shareholders:* Michael Keith Pix; Tecnair Group Limited
*Officers:* Christian Pix, Secretary; Christian Pix [1981] Sales Director; Dominic Pix [1979] Director; Michael Keith Pix [1954] Director

**Universal A.V. Services Limited**
*Incorporated:* 26 April 1990 *Employees:* 37
*Net Worth:* £4,235,048 *Total Assets:* £5,117,309
*Registered Office:* Guy Street, Bradford, W Yorks, BD4 7BB
*Activities:* Activities of conference organisers
*Shareholders:* Jonathan Paul Eden; Nicholas Anthony Fitzpatrick
*Officers:* Nicholas Anthony Fitzpatrick [1968] Director/Audio Visual; Christopher Mark Gardner [1974] Operations Director; Andrew Robinson [1968] Finance Director

**Universal Group Holdings Limited**
*Incorporated:* 12 November 2015 *Employees:* 86
*Net Worth:* £1,064,714 *Total Assets:* £4,349,495
*Registered Office:* c/o Universal Group Holdings Ltd, Guy Street, Bradford, W Yorks, BD4 7BB
*Activities:* Activities of head offices
*Shareholders:* Jonathan Paul Eden; Nicholas Anthony Fitzpatrick
*Officers:* Jonathan Paul Eden [1965] Managing Director; Nicholas Anthony Fitzpatrick [1968] Director; Andrew Robinson [1968] Finance Director; Kirsten Elizabeth Waine [1979] Director

**Universal Parking Limited**
*Incorporated:* 19 March 2001 *Employees:* 2
*Net Worth:* £51,000,000 *Total Assets:* £87,768,552
*Registered Office:* 72 Merrion Street, Leeds, LS2 8LW
*Activities:* Non-trading company
*Parent:* Q-Park UK Limited
*Officers:* Stephen Mark Ellis, Secretary; Adam John Bidder [1970] Managing Director; Stephen Mark Ellis [1965] Finance Director

**The University of Chicago Booth School of Business**
*Incorporated:* 8 February 2005 *Employees:* 23
*Net Worth Deficit:* £19,852,658 *Total Assets:* £13,638,635
*Registered Office:* 1 Park Row, Leeds, LS1 5AB
*Activities:* First-degree level higher education
*Officers:* Daniel Diermeier [1965] Director/Provost, The University of Chicago [American]; Randall Kroszner [1962] Director/Professor [American]; Kimberly Taylor [1967] Director/VP & General Counsel, University of Chicago [American]

**Untha UK Limited**
*Incorporated:* 26 September 2002 *Employees:* 15
*Net Worth:* £507,416 *Total Assets:* £3,430,101
*Registered Office:* Excel House, Becklands Close, Bar Lane, Roecliffe, Boroughbridge, N Yorks, YO51 9NR
*Activities:* Wholesale of waste and scrap
*Major Shareholder:* Anton Unterwurzacher
*Officers:* Marcus Woolhouse Brew [1970] Managing Director; Alois Kitzberger [1973] Director [Austrian]

**UoE Deaconess Limited**
*Incorporated:* 14 September 2011
*Net Worth:* £40,908,956 *Total Assets:* £41,080,680
*Registered Office:* 1 Park Row, Leeds, LS1 5AB
*Activities:* Development of building projects
*Parent:* University of Edinburgh
*Officers:* Terence Lee Fox, Secretary; Richard Michael John Kington [1954] Director of Accommodation Services; Philip Gerard McNaull [1958] Director/Accountant; Elizabeth Welch [1960] Director/Accountant

**Uptownleeds Limited**
*Incorporated:* 11 October 2006 *Employees:* 3
*Net Worth:* £8,184,890 *Total Assets:* £18,066,364
*Registered Office:* 5 Hawthorn Park, Coal Road, Leeds, LS14 1PQ
*Activities:* Development of building projects
*Parent:* Rushbond PLC
*Officers:* Richard Mark Powell, Secretary; Mark Richard Finch [1967] Director/Chartered Surveyor Chartered Town Planner; Jonathan William Maud [1960] Director; Richard Mark Powell [1967] Director/Chartered Accountant

**Urban Development Projects (2) Ltd**
*Incorporated:* 30 November 2011
*Net Worth:* £1,967,809 *Total Assets:* £5,139,914
*Registered Office:* 51 Selby Road, Leeds, LS9 0EW
*Activities:* Other business support service activities n.e.c.
*Major Shareholder:* Shane Patrick Graham
*Officers:* Shane Patrick Graham [1972] Director

**Urban Development Projects Ltd**
*Incorporated:* 20 July 2009 *Employees:* 2
*Net Worth Deficit:* £254,149 *Total Assets:* £4,713,378
*Registered Office:* 51 Selby Road, Leeds, LS9 0EW
*Activities:* Other business support service activities n.e.c.
*Major Shareholder:* Shane Patrick Graham
*Officers:* Shane Patrick Graham [1972] Director/Developer

**Urban I (Blonk Street) Ltd**
*Incorporated:* 28 March 2003 *Employees:* 3
*Net Worth Deficit:* £915,441 *Total Assets:* £4,724,677
*Registered Office:* 3 Bradford Row, Doncaster, S Yorks, DN1 3NF
*Activities:* Construction of domestic buildings
*Major Shareholder:* Stephen Mucklow
*Officers:* Darryl Barker [1972] Director; Stephen Mucklow [1962] Director; Michael Patrick Murray [1969] Director

**Uriah Woodhead & Son Limited**
*Incorporated:* 25 June 1936 *Employees:* 53
*Net Worth:* £7,134,385 *Total Assets:* £7,727,050
*Registered Office:* Canal Works, Canal Road, Bradford, BD1 4SD
*Activities:* Agents involved in the sale of timber and building materials
*Major Shareholder:* Paul Richard Jaggar
*Officers:* Paul Richard Jaggar [1967] Director/Designer

**Uris Central Administration Limited**
*Incorporated:* 22 June 2007 *Employees:* 136
*Previous:* Direct Newco Limited
*Net Worth:* £9,020,000 *Total Assets:* £21,001,000
*Registered Office:* Quay Point, Lakeside Boulevard, Doncaster, S Yorks, DN4 5PL
*Activities:* Activities of financial services holding companies
*Parent:* Ryan Direct Group Limited
*Officers:* Derek John Coles [1960] Director; Scott William Hough [1971] Director

**Uris Group Limited**
*Incorporated:* 22 January 1990 *Employees:* 114
*Previous:* Direct Group Limited
*Net Worth:* £22,646,000 *Total Assets:* £59,545,000
*Registered Office:* Quay Point, Lakeside Boulevard, Doncaster, S Yorks, DN4 5PL
*Activities:* Activities auxiliary to financial intermediation n.e.c.
*Parent:* Ryan Direct Group Limited
*Officers:* Derek John Coles [1960] Director/Chief Executive Officer; Scott William Hough [1971] Director/Chief Finance Officer

**Uris Topco Limited**
*Incorporated:* 17 August 2012
*Previous:* Direct Group Topco Limited
*Net Worth Deficit:* £48,322,000 *Total Assets:* £52,830,000
*Registered Office:* Quay Point, Lakeside Boulevard, Doncaster, S Yorks, DN4 5PL
*Activities:* Activities of financial services holding companies
*Parent:* Nevada Investments 3 Limited
*Officers:* Derek John Coles [1960] Director; Scott William Hough [1971] Director

**URM (UK) Limited**
*Incorporated:* 5 October 2000 *Employees:* 171
*Previous:* Reuse Collections Limited
*Net Worth:* £13,261,691 *Total Assets:* £35,891,136
*Registered Office:* 49 Lidgate Crescent, Langthwaite Business Park, South Kirkby, Pontefract, W Yorks, WF9 3NR
*Activities:* Collection of non-hazardous waste
*Major Shareholder:* Anthony Charles Johnston
*Officers:* Michael James Harris, Secretary; Andrew Stuart, Secretary/Director [Australian]; Mark Henry Richard Iain Wilson, Secretary; Anthony Charles Johnston [1966] Director [Australian]; Andrew John Burleigh Stuart [1967] Director [Australian]

**Urmi Capital Limited**
*Incorporated:* 9 January 2007
*Net Worth:* £100 *Total Assets:* £9,266,426
*Registered Office:* 49 Lidgate Crescent, Langthwaite Business Park, South Kirkby, Pontefract, W Yorks, WF9 3NR
*Activities:* Manufacture and processing of other glass, including technical glassware
*Major Shareholder:* Anthony Charles Johnston
*Officers:* Michael Harris, Secretary; Anthony Charles Johnston [1966] Director [Australian]; Andrew John Burleigh Stuart [1967] Director [Australian]

**Urquhart-Dykes & Lord LLP**
*Incorporated:* 11 March 2004 *Employees:* 69
*Net Worth:* £4,491,393 *Total Assets:* £8,029,631
*Registered Office:* Arena Point, Merrion Way, Leeds, LS2 8PA
*Officers:* Andrew Alton [1969] Member; Gregory Mark Davies [1966] Member; Alan Michael Fiddes [1963] Member; Mark Charles Green [1959] Member; Dr Cerian Elizabeth Jones [1968] Member; Anthony Neil Pawlyn [1966] Member; Gareth Ian Price [1978] Member; Simon Mark Raynor [1959] Member; Alison Elizabeth Frazer Simpson [1966] Member; Garry Philip Stuttard [1967] Member; Rex Martin Vinsome [1963] Member

**USG-Gledco Ltd**
*Incorporated:* 7 December 1995 *Employees:* 99
*Net Worth:* £1,000,847 *Total Assets:* £3,666,937
*Registered Office:* Gledco Works, Bankfield Terrace, Leeds, LS4 2JR
*Activities:* Other manufacturing n.e.c.
*Shareholders:* Richard Douglas Gledhill; Lorraine Anne Gledhill
*Officers:* Richard Douglas Gledhill, Secretary/Managing Director; Lorraine Anne Gledhill [1953] Director/Secretary; Richard Douglas Gledhill [1953] Managing Director; Rodger Francis New [1950] Sales Director

**USI Mayfair Ltd.**
*Incorporated:* 22 September 1997 *Employees:* 2
*Net Worth Deficit:* £18,237,288 *Total Assets:* £73,844,064
*Registered Office:* Old Mill Lane, Low Road, Hunslet, Leeds, LS10 1RB
*Activities:* Other business support service activities n.e.c.
*Officers:* Anthony Lovallo [1961] Director/Attorney [American]; Kevin Teague [1957] Director/Accountant

**V.H.E. Construction PLC**
*Incorporated:* 26 October 1979 *Employees:* 76
*Net Worth:* £2,496,000 *Total Assets:* £19,332,000
*Registered Office:* 3175 Century Way, Thorpe Park, Leeds, LS15 8ZB
*Activities:* Remediation activities and other waste management services
*Parent:* Renew Holdings PLC
*Officers:* Steven Matthew Marshall [1957] Pre Contracts Director; Paul Scott [1964] Director/Engineer; Stephen Stiff [1961] Managing Director; Gordon Ian Wilson [1967] Construction Director

**Vacation Club Partnerships Limited**
*Incorporated:* 16 April 1996
*Net Worth Deficit:* £7,563,511 *Total Assets:* £3,986,417
*Registered Office:* Citrus House, Caton Road, Lancaster, LA1 3UA
*Activities:* Activities of head offices
*Parent:* Diamond Resorts (Group Holdings) PLC
*Officers:* Susan Crook, Secretary/Solicitor; Susan Crook [1961] Director/Solicitor

**Vacform Group (Yorkshire) Limited**
*Incorporated:* 28 April 1967 *Employees:* 42
*Net Worth:* £1,464,847 *Total Assets:* £3,317,902
*Registered Office:* Units 1-3 Felnex Square, Felnex Industrial Estate, Leeds, LS9 0ST
*Activities:* Manufacture of other plastic products
*Parent:* Vacform Group Limited
*Officers:* David Anthony Aarons, Secretary/Director; David Anthony Aarons [1961] Director; Mustafa El-Etriby [1983] Technical Director; Kevin Bernard Quinn [1966] Managing Director

**Valad Diversified LLP**
*Incorporated:* 18 June 2013
*Net Worth:* £312,092,736 *Total Assets:* £660,131,328
*Registered Office:* 1st Floor, Unit 16, Manor Court Business Park, Scarborough, N Yorks, YO11 3TU

**Vale of Mowbray Holdings Limited**
*Incorporated:* 11 June 2004 *Employees:* 247
*Net Worth:* £7,331,876 *Total Assets:* £19,328,004
*Registered Office:* 20 Leases Road, Leeming Bar, Northallerton, N Yorks, DL7 9AW
*Activities:* Production of meat and poultry meat products
*Major Shareholder:* John Gatenby
*Officers:* Mark Jonathon Gatenby [1972] Director/Operations Manager; Giles Francis John Penn [1967] Director/Financial Controller

**Vale of Mowbray Limited**
*Incorporated:* 25 July 1995 *Employees:* 257
*Net Worth:* £9,620,795 *Total Assets:* £20,835,672
*Registered Office:* 20 Leases Road, Leeming Bar, N Yorks, DL7 9AW
*Activities:* Production of meat and poultry meat products
*Parent:* Vale of Mowbray Holdings Limited
*Officers:* Mark Jonathon Gatenby [1972] Director/Operations Manager; Giles Francis John Penn [1967] Director/Financial Controller

**Vallectric (Holdings) Limited**
*Incorporated:* 14 June 2006 *Employees:* 49
*Net Worth:* £817,489 *Total Assets:* £4,345,767
*Registered Office:* 3 Hales Road, Leeds, LS12 4PL
*Activities:* Electrical installation
*Shareholder:* David Antony Allen
*Officers:* David Antony Allen, Secretary; David Antony Allen [1958] Managing Director, Business Services; Gregory Stephen Slater [1968] Managing Director, Operations; Tremayne Shaun Vare [1969] Managing Director, Operations

**Vallectric Limited**
*Incorporated:* 13 October 1959 *Employees:* 38
*Net Worth:* £1,795,441 *Total Assets:* £5,272,812
*Registered Office:* 3 Hales Road, Leeds, LS12 4PL
*Activities:* Electrical installation
*Parent:* Vallectric (Holdings) Limited
*Officers:* David Antony Allen, Secretary; David Antony Allen [1958] Managing Director, Business Services; Gregory Stephen Slater [1968] Managing Director, Operations; Tremayne Shaun Vare [1969] Managing Director, Operations

**The Valley Printing Company, Limited**
*Incorporated:* 2 July 1908 *Employees:* 137
*Net Worth:* £6,250,000 *Total Assets:* £8,330,000
*Registered Office:* Harden Beck Mill, Harden, Bingley, W Yorks, BD16 1BL
*Activities:* Printing n.e.c.
*Shareholder:* John Stansfield Haggas
*Officers:* Jonathan Simon Haggas, Secretary; James Sinclair Haggas [1966] Director; John Stansfield Haggas [1943] Director; Jonathan Simon Haggas [1970] Director

**Valley Vets Ltd.**
*Incorporated:* 20 February 2003 *Employees:* 51
*Net Worth:* £668,419 *Total Assets:* £3,908,383
*Registered Office:* Leeman House, Station Business Park, Holgate Park Drive, York, YO26 4GB
*Activities:* Veterinary activities
*Parent:* Vetpartners Limited
*Officers:* Joanna Clare Malone [1974] Director; Mark Stanworth [1964] Director

**Valli Forecourts Limited**
*Incorporated:* 13 March 2002 *Employees:* 222
*Net Worth:* £15,910,983 *Total Assets:* £27,465,824
*Registered Office:* 44 Warren Street, Savile Town, Dewsbury, W Yorks, WF12 9LX
*Activities:* Retail sale of automotive fuel in specialised stores
*Shareholders:* Dawood Valli; Amina Valli
*Officers:* Samim Valli, Secretary; Farook Valli [1968] Director/Petrol Station Operator; Haroon Valli [1966] Director/Petrol Station Operator; Yunus Valli [1972] Director

**Van Centre (West Yorkshire) Limited**
*Incorporated:* 25 May 2004 *Employees:* 46
*Net Worth:* £3,720,074 *Total Assets:* £13,713,685
*Registered Office:* LCW House, Chain Bar Road, Cleckheaton, W Yorks, BD19 3QF
*Activities:* Sale of new cars and light motor vehicles
*Parent:* Caygill Holdings Ltd
*Officers:* Susan Caroline Caygill, Secretary/Director; Andrew Martin Caygill [1956] Director; Joshua Caygill [1989] Director; Susan Caroline Caygill [1959] Director; Howard John Marshall [1968] Director; Andrew Umpleby [1965] Director; Lucy Walton [1983] Director

**Van-Line Limited**
*Incorporated:* 15 March 2005 *Employees:* 52
*Net Worth:* £2,779,316 *Total Assets:* £4,837,369
*Registered Office:* c/o Rema Tip Top Holdings UK Limited, Westland Square, Leeds, LS11 5XS
*Activities:* Non-specialised wholesale trade
*Parent:* Rema Tip Top Holdings UK Limited
*Officers:* Garry Mangham, Secretary; Mark Brian Insley [1959] Director; Dorothy Rose Thornborrow [1957] Managing Director

**Vanilla Group Limited**
*Incorporated:* 7 December 1990 *Employees:* 2
*Net Worth:* £8,622,000 *Total Assets:* £48,204,000
*Registered Office:* Meadowcroft Lane, Halifax Road, Ripponden, W Yorks, HX6 4AJ
*Activities:* Activities of head offices
*Parent:* Inhoco 3498 Limited
*Officers:* Helen Jane Ashton [1972] Director/Chief Executive Officer; Paul Justin Humphreys [1958] Director

**Vanquis Bank Limited**
*Incorporated:* 15 November 1990 *Employees:* 1,469
*Net Worth:* £289,300,000 *Total Assets:* £1,855,100,032
*Registered Office:* No 1 Godwin Street, Bradford, W Yorks, BD1 2SU
*Activities:* Banks
*Parent:* Provident Financial PLC
*Officers:* Gina Esposito, Secretary; Janet Connor [1964] Director; Andrew Thomas Gosling [1955] Director; Malcolm John Le May [1958] Director; Antoni Feliks Reczek [1953] Director [British/Polish]; Jonathan Caldwell Roe [1955] Director; Oliver White [1968] Finance Director

**Vantage Motor Group Limited**
*Incorporated:* 30 January 2003 *Employees:* 601
*Previous:* Meridian Motor Group Limited
*Net Worth:* £7,322,000 *Total Assets:* £76,638,000
*Registered Office:* Knaresborough Toyota, York Road, Knaresborough, N Yorks, HG5 0SS
*Activities:* Sale of new cars and light motor vehicles
*Shareholders:* Mark Allan Robinson; Philip Michael White
*Officers:* Timothy James Ashley Swindin, Secretary; Andrew Mallory [1969] Sales Operations Director; Mark Allan Robinson [1965] Director; Timothy James Ashley Swindin [1967] Director/Chartered Accountant; Philip Michael White [1949] Director

**Vapour Cloud Limited**
*Incorporated:* 8 November 2013
*Previous:* Everycloud Computing Limited
*Net Worth:* £4,191,757 *Total Assets:* £4,193,161
*Registered Office:* The Gateway, Lowfields Close, Lowfields Business Park, Elland, W Yorks, HX5 9DX
*Activities:* Other information technology service activities
*Officers:* Simon William Thorn, Secretary; David Martin Best [1958] Director/Chartered Accountant; Roy Ernest Davies [1946] Director; Timothy Peter Mercer [1970] Director; Andrew Robert Nash [1972] Director; Jason Philip Sharp [1970] Director/Accountant

**Chris Variava Limited**
*Incorporated:* 1 June 1976 *Employees:* 42
*Net Worth:* £2,268,400 *Total Assets:* £5,085,041
*Registered Office:* Stoneacre, Omega Boulevard, Thorne, Doncaster, S Yorks, DN8 5TX
*Activities:* Sale of new cars and light motor vehicles
*Parent:* Decidebloom Limited
*Officers:* Richard Stephen Teatum [1957] Director; Nigel Peter Wood [1964] Director/Accountant

**Varlink Limited**
*Incorporated:* 5 August 2005 *Employees:* 29
*Net Worth:* £917,943 *Total Assets:* £4,180,519
*Registered Office:* Unit 1 Osbaldwick Industrial Estate, Outgang Lane, York, YO19 5UX
*Activities:* Wholesale of computers, computer peripheral equipment and software
*Shareholder:* Adrian Michael Pullon
*Officers:* Frances Dodd [1946] Director; William James Gordon [1958] Director; Adrian Michael Pullon [1958] Director

**Varnish Bidco Limited**
*Incorporated:* 25 March 2014
*Net Worth Deficit:* £21,897,000 *Total Assets:* £21,158,000
*Registered Office:* Jack Brignall House, Bridgehead Business Park, Hessle, Hull, HU13 0DG
*Activities:* Activities of head offices
*Parent:* Varnish Midco Limited
*Officers:* Antonio Capo [1970] Director/Investment Professional [Italian]; Michael Douglas Comish [1965] Director; Malte Janzarik [1980] Director/Investment Professional [German]; Paul Thomas McClenaghan [1965] Director/C.E.O; Scott Michael Myers [1988] Director/Investment Professional [American]; Shane Malcolm Walker [1972] Director

**Varnish Intermediate Holdco Limited**
*Incorporated:* 8 December 2016
*Net Worth:* £20,701,000 *Total Assets:* £20,725,000
*Registered Office:* Jack Brignall House, Bridgehead Business Park, Hessle, E Yorks, HU13 0DG
*Activities:* Other business support service activities n.e.c.
*Parent:* Varnish Bidco Limited
*Officers:* Antonio Capo [1970] Director/Investment Professional [Italian]; Malte Janzarik [1980] Director/Investment Professional [German]; Scott Michael Myers [1988] Director/Investment Professional [American]; Shane Malcolm Walker [1972] Director

**Varnish Topco Limited**
*Incorporated:* 26 March 2014 *Employees:* 252
*Net Worth Deficit:* £234,680,000 *Total Assets:* £43,533,000
*Registered Office:* Jack Brignall House, Bridgehead Business Park, Hessle, Hull, HU13 0DG
*Activities:* Activities of head offices
*Parent:* TPG Varnish S.A.R.L.
*Officers:* Antonio Capo [1970] Director/Investment Professional [Italian]; Malte Janzarik [1980] Director/Investment Professional [German]; Shane Malcolm Walker [1972] Director

**Vascular Perspectives Limited**
*Incorporated:* 6 August 2003 *Employees:* 12
*Net Worth:* £3,110,881 *Total Assets:* £4,440,302
*Registered Office:* 35 Westgate, Huddersfield, W Yorks, HD1 1PA
*Activities:* Other professional, scientific and technical activities n.e.c.
*Parent:* Vacular Perspectives Holdings Limited
*Officers:* Simon Gerard Carroll, Secretary; Adrian Denis Brown [1969] Director

**VBP Group Limited**
*Incorporated:* 10 August 1995
*Net Worth:* £7,774,855 *Total Assets:* £9,382,823
*Registered Office:* 93-95 Alfred Gelder Street, Hull, HU1 1EP
*Activities:* Construction of commercial buildings
*Major Shareholder:* Andrew Mark Shane Allenby
*Officers:* Simon William Lunt, Secretary; Andrew Mark Shane Allenby [1961] Director/Builder; Phillipa Mary Allenby [1964] Director/Company Secretary

**Vcep Limited**
*Incorporated:* 15 October 2015
*Net Worth:* £2,113,417 *Total Assets:* £17,225,744
*Registered Office:* Peel House, Stocks Lane, Luddenden, Halifax, W Yorks, HX2 6SP
*Activities:* Other letting and operating of own or leased real estate
*Parent:* The C & V Lloyd 2015 Family Settlement
*Officers:* Clive Roland Lloyd [1959] Managing Director; Virginia Annable Lloyd [1959] Sales Director

**Vectair Aviation (1995) Limited**
*Incorporated:* 4 October 1995 *Employees:* 41
*Net Worth:* £5,394,723 *Total Assets:* £12,037,494
*Registered Office:* 7 Lakes Country Park, Wharf Road, Crowle, N Lincs, DN17 4JS
*Activities:* Other retail sale not in stores, stalls or markets
*Major Shareholder:* David Francis Keedy
*Officers:* David Francis Keedy [1944] Director; Jason Brian Keedy [1972] Managing Director; Rhodri John Marlow [1975] Director/Manager

**John Veitch Limited**
*Incorporated:* 28 December 1987 *Employees:* 71
*Net Worth:* £786,424 *Total Assets:* £6,876,713
*Registered Office:* Orchard Business Park, Mytholmroyd, Halifax, W Yorks, HX7 5HZ
*Activities:* Wholesale of household goods (other than musical instruments) n.e.c
*Parent:* JVL Holdings Ltd
*Officers:* Philip Julian Pointon, Secretary; Mohamed Bouabida [1963] Director; Graham Dean Jepson [1977] Director/Accountant; Philip Julian Pointon [1958] Director

**Vellco Limited**
*Incorporated:* 2 February 2001 *Employees:* 55
*Net Worth:* £2,787,617 *Total Assets:* £4,758,357
*Registered Office:* Suite B2, Josephs Well, Hanover Walk, Leeds, LS3 1AB
*Activities:* Recovery of sorted materials
*Shareholder:* Vellco Holdings Limited
*Officers:* Susan Joan Fell, Secretary/Director; Christopher Gerrard Fell [1963] Director; Harry John Fell [1998] Director; Joseph Anthony Fell [1994] Director; Susan Joan Fell [1962] Director

**Venice Bidco 1 Limited**
*Incorporated:* 7 June 2006 *Employees:* 4
*Net Worth:* £14,370,000 *Total Assets:* £19,495,000
*Registered Office:* The Inspire, Hornbeam Square West, Harrogate, N Yorks, HG2 8PA
*Activities:* Activities of head offices
*Parent:* Venice Newco 2 Limited
*Officers:* James Alexander Burrell [1974] Director/Accountant; Generaldine Josephine Gallagher [1965] Finance Director [Irish]; Gail Susan Hunter [1963] Human Resources Director; Anthony Gerrard Troy [1962] Director [Irish]

**Venice Newco 1 Limited**
*Incorporated:* 7 June 2006 *Employees:* 5
*Net Worth:* £4,331,000 *Total Assets:* £4,939,000
*Registered Office:* The Inspire, Hornbeam Square West, Harrogate, N Yorks, HG2 8PA
*Activities:* Activities of head offices
*Parent:* Rome Investco Ltd
*Officers:* John Cody Bradshaw [1978] Director/Hotel Real Estate [American]; James Alexander Burrell [1974] Director/Accountant; Generaldine Josephine Gallagher [1965] Finance Director [Irish]; Gail Susan Hunter [1963] Human Resources Director; Anthony Gerrard Troy [1962] Director [Irish]

**Venn Academy Trust**
*Incorporated:* 29 June 2015 *Employees:* 279
*Net Worth:* £23,543,210 *Total Assets:* £26,482,032
*Registered Office:* c/o Bridgeview Whitehouse, Sullivan Centre, Pickering Road, Hull, HU4 7AD
*Activities:* Primary education
*Officers:* Neil Catterson [1968] Director/Senior Probation Officer; Christopher Summers Fenwick [1943] Director/Retired; Chris Hooper [1977] Director/Education Manager; Terry Johnson [1952] Director/Retired; Mel McAlindon [1965] Director; Christopher Stephen Morris [1980] Project Management Director; Paul Antony Wilson [1966] Director; Simon Witham [1971] Director/Chief Executive

**Ventia Limited**
*Incorporated:* 22 April 2009 *Employees:* 63
*Net Worth:* £171,920 *Total Assets:* £4,497,422
*Registered Office:* Central House, 47 St Pauls Street, Leeds, LS1 2TE
*Activities:* Management of real estate on a fee or contract basis
*Parent:* The Boutique Workplace Company Ltd
*Officers:* Daniel James Smith, Secretary; David Hall [1970] Operations Director; David Anthony Harrop [1970] Finance Director; Karen Louise Nordier [1967] Finance Director [South African]; Timothy Andrew Vaughan [1965] Managing Director; Daniel Reeves Wheble [1976] Director/Property Consultant

**Ventura Telecom Holdings Limited**
*Incorporated:* 10 July 2006 *Employees:* 51
*Net Worth:* £4,340,649 *Total Assets:* £5,329,086
*Registered Office:* Fleet House, New Road, Lancaster, LA1 1EZ
*Activities:* Other telecommunications activities
*Parent:* Ecorenew Holdings (UK) Limited
*Officers:* Sarah Fort, Secretary; Craig Richard Smith [1971] Director

**Venture Business Parks Limited**
*Incorporated:* 15 March 2007
*Net Worth:* £12,485,917 *Total Assets:* £27,460,056
*Registered Office:* 93-95 Alfred Gelder Street, Hull, HU1 1EP
*Activities:* Construction of commercial buildings
*Major Shareholder:* Andrew Mark Shane Allenby
*Officers:* Mark Teal, Secretary; Andrew Mark Shane Allenby [1961] Director

**Venturian Property Development Limited**
*Incorporated:* 1 September 2015
*Net Worth:* £4,525,936 *Total Assets:* £4,583,906
*Registered Office:* 1 Mariner Court, Calder Business Park, Wakefield, W Yorks, WF4 3FL
*Activities:* Construction of domestic buildings
*Parent:* Venturian Group Limited
*Officers:* Gregory Allsopp [1980] Director/Solicitor; Graham Leslie Berks [1954] Director; Paul Richard Halliday [1974] Director; Rachel Jayne Lomax [1965] Director; Stuart Andrew Lomax [1966] Director

**Venturian Property Holdings Limited**
*Incorporated:* 1 September 2015
*Net Worth:* £41,171 *Total Assets:* £4,068,649
*Registered Office:* 1 Mariner Court, Calder Business Park, Wakefield, W Yorks, WF4 3FL
*Activities:* Other letting and operating of own or leased real estate
*Shareholders:* Rachel Jayne Lomax; Stuart Andrew Lomax
*Officers:* Gregory Allsopp [1980] Director/Solicitor; Graham Leslie Berks [1954] Director; Paul Richard Halliday [1974] Director; Rachel Jayne Lomax [1965] Director; Stuart Andrew Lomax [1966] Director

**Verage Limited**
*Incorporated:* 14 July 2003
*Net Worth Deficit:* £528,515 *Total Assets:* £5,134,038
*Registered Office:* 203 Manningham Lane, Bradford, W Yorks, BD8 7HP
*Activities:* Non-specialised wholesale trade
*Officers:* Abid Rehman [1979] Director/Sales Assistant

**Verdant Leisure 2 Limited**
*Incorporated:* 7 July 2011 *Employees:* 96
*Net Worth:* £8,611,000 *Total Assets:* £37,121,000
*Registered Office:* 10 Mannin Way, Lancaster Business Park, Lancaster, LA1 3SW
*Activities:* Holiday centres and villages
*Parent:* Palatine Private Equity LLP
*Officers:* Beverley Jayne Dixon [1969] Director; Graham Robert Hodgson [1960] Director; George Hope [1962] Director; Andrew Jonathan Wall [1960] Director

**Verdant Leisure Limited**
*Incorporated:* 12 October 1990 *Employees:* 96
*Net Worth:* £19,167,000 *Total Assets:* £24,896,000
*Registered Office:* 10 Mannin Way, Lancaster Business Park, Lancaster, LA1 3SW
*Activities:* Holiday centres and villages
*Parent:* Palatine Private Equity LLP
*Officers:* Andrew Wall, Secretary; Beverley Jayne Dixon [1969] Director; Graham Robert Hodgson [1960] Director; George Hope [1962] Director; Andrew Wall [1960] Director

**Verder Limited**
*Incorporated:* 7 February 1996 *Employees:* 70
*Net Worth:* £5,679,601 *Total Assets:* £7,911,800
*Registered Office:* Unit 3 California Drive, Freeway Park, Castleford, W Yorks, WF10 5QH
*Activities:* Manufacture of pumps
*Parent:* Anvast UK Ltd
*Officers:* David Court, Secretary; Kenneth Oliver McCartney [1958] Director [Irish]

**Verulam Holdings Limited**
*Incorporated:* 13 July 2016
*Net Worth:* £4,891,000 *Total Assets:* £11,182,000
*Registered Office:* Hexagon House, Grimbald Crag Close, St James Business Park, Knaresborough, N Yorks, HG5 8PJ
*Activities:* Activities of financial services holding companies
*Shareholders:* Broker Network Partner Holdings Limited; Broker Network Partner Holdings Limited
*Officers:* Simon Drew, Secretary; Simon Richard Drew [1969] Director/Accountant; Vincent Gardner [1967] Director/Insurance Broker; Desmond Joseph O'Connor [1971] Director/Insurance Broker

**Vetpartners Group Finance Limited**
*Incorporated:* 26 August 2015
*Net Worth Deficit:* £690,243 *Total Assets:* £24,834,974
*Registered Office:* Leeman House, Station Business Park, Holgate Park Drive, York, YO26 4GB
*Activities:* Activities of other holding companies n.e.c.
*Parent:* Vetpartners UK Holdings Limited
*Officers:* William David Grout [1984] Director/Investment Manager; Richard Oliver [1982] Director/Investment Manager

**Vetpartners Group Limited**
*Incorporated:* 25 February 2016
*Net Worth:* £18,600,000 *Total Assets:* £20,250,000
*Registered Office:* Leeman House, Station Business Park, Holgate Park Drive, York, YO26 4GB
*Activities:* Activities of other holding companies n.e.c.
*Parent:* Scooby Bidco Limited
*Officers:* Joanna Clare Malone [1974] Director; Mark Stanworth [1964] Director

**Vetpartners Practices Limited**
*Incorporated:* 24 March 2016 *Employees:* 59
*Net Worth:* £13,738 *Total Assets:* £10,890,583
*Registered Office:* Leeman House, Station Business Park, Holgate Park Drive, York, YO26 4GB
*Activities:* Veterinary activities
*Parent:* Vetpartners Limited
*Officers:* Joanna Clare Malone [1974] Director; Mark Stanworth [1964] Director

**Vetpartners UK Holdings Ltd.**
*Incorporated:* 26 August 2015 *Employees:* 1,036
*Net Worth Deficit:* £8,270,667 *Total Assets:* £124,149,576
*Registered Office:* Leeman House, Station Business Park, Holgate Park Drive, York, YO26 4GB
*Activities:* Activities of other holding companies n.e.c.
*Officers:* William David Grout [1984] Director/Investment Manager; Richard John McKillan Oliver [1982] Director/Investment Manager

**Vetuk Limited**
*Incorporated:* 4 November 2015 *Employees:* 29
*Net Worth:* £1,104,021 *Total Assets:* £3,952,552
*Registered Office:* Unit 7-8 Europark, Station Road, Thirsk, N Yorks, YO7 1GQ
*Activities:* Other retail sale not in stores, stalls or markets
*Parent:* Vetuk Holdings Limited
*Officers:* Iain David Booth [1972] Director; Dr Lyane Haywood [1972] Director

**Viamaster Transport Limited**
*Incorporated:* 20 May 1971 *Employees:* 105
*Net Worth:* £4,179,932 *Total Assets:* £11,902,423
*Registered Office:* Europort Distribution Centre, Altofts Lane, Castleford, W Yorks, WF10 5PZ
*Activities:* Freight transport by road
*Shareholders:* Andrew Bernard Warrington; David Kevin Warrington
*Officers:* Andrew Bernard Warrington, Secretary; Andrew Bernard Warrington [1956] Director/Haulage Contractor; David Kevin Warrington [1964] Director/Haulage Contractor

**Vicarage Estate Company,Limited (The)**
*Incorporated:* 8 January 1920 *Employees:* 5
*Net Worth:* £12,342,267 *Total Assets:* £12,843,943
*Registered Office:* Gresham House, 5-7 St Pauls Street, Leeds, LS1 2JG
*Activities:* Other business support service activities n.e.c.
*Parent:* Glendon Estates
*Officers:* Paul David Mitchell, Secretary; Susan Jean Ellison [1938] Director/Housewife; Timothy Ellison [1966] Director [Australian]; Christopher John Marshall [1939] Director/Farmer; Clement Marshall [1975] Director [French]; Francois Marshall [1976] Director [French]

**Mary Randall Vickers & Co Limited**
*Incorporated:* 13 March 2017 *Employees:* 61
*Net Worth:* £30,366,172 *Total Assets:* £34,264,360
*Registered Office:* 6 Clarence Road, Leeds, LS10 1ND
*Activities:* Other manufacturing n.e.c.
*Officers:* Morgan Lawn Morris, Secretary; Morgan Lawn Morris [1971] Financial Director; Nigel Rushworth [1953] Director; Paul Anthony Smailes [1966] Sales & Marketing Director; Peter John Farrar Vickers [1959] Director; William Peter Farrar Vickers [1991] Director; Christopher John Wholley [1960] Technical Director

**Benjn.R.Vickers & Sons,Limited**
*Incorporated:* 9 July 1913 *Employees:* 61
*Net Worth:* £25,152,598 *Total Assets:* £29,050,784
*Registered Office:* Airedale Mills, 6 Clarence Road, Leeds, LS10 1ND
*Activities:* Other manufacturing n.e.c.
*Parent:* Mary Randall Vickers & Co. Limited
*Officers:* Morgan Lawn Morris, Secretary; Morgan Lawn Morris [1971] Finance Director; Nigel Rushworth [1953] Director; Paul Anthony Smailes [1966] Director; Peter John Farrar Vickers [1959] Director; William Peter Farrar Vickers [1991] Director; Christopher John Wholley [1960] Director

**Vickers Laboratories Limited**
*Incorporated:* 2 July 1971 *Employees:* 33
*Net Worth:* £2,824,385 *Total Assets:* £3,616,620
*Registered Office:* Grangefield Industrial Estate, Richardshaw Road, Pudsey, Leeds, LS28 6QW
*Activities:* Manufacture of other chemical products n.e.c.
*Parent:* Vickers Laboratories (Holdings) Limited
*Officers:* Helen Thornley, Secretary; Paul Leroy Bottomley [1965] Commercial Director; Phil Constantine [1965] Operations Director; Stephen Harold Foster [1958] Managing Director

**Victor Investments & Securities Ltd**
*Incorporated:* 4 September 1981 *Employees:* 3
*Net Worth:* £2,403,816 *Total Assets:* £7,844,233
*Registered Office:* 6 Allerton Hill, Chapel Allerton, Leeds, LS7 3QB
*Activities:* Buying and selling of own real estate
*Shareholders:* Raymond Linton; Jennifer Michelle Linton
*Officers:* Raymond Linton, Secretary; Jennifer Michelle Linton [1949] Director; Raymond Linton [1939] Director

**Victor Manufacturing Limited**
*Incorporated:* 28 October 1944 *Employees:* 114
*Net Worth:* £5,841,746 *Total Assets:* £7,312,146
*Registered Office:* Lonsdale Works, Gibson Street, Bradford, W Yorks, BD3 9TF
*Activities:* Manufacture of other fabricated metal products n.e.c.
*Officers:* Steven Robert Jamie Gordon, Secretary; Steven Robert Jamie Gordon [1965] Finance Director; Michael James Inwood [1977] Director; Michael O'Shea [1960] Director; Philip Williams [1962] Operations Director

**Victorguard Care PLC**
*Incorporated:* 17 June 1996 *Employees:* 250
*Net Worth:* £2,255,332 *Total Assets:* £7,893,992
*Registered Office:* 320 Beacon Road, Wibsey, Bradford, W Yorks, BD6 3DP
*Activities:* Residential nursing care facilities
*Shareholders:* Joanne Elizabeth Walkden; Stephen John Walkden
*Officers:* Joanne Elizabeth Walkden, Secretary; Christopher John Eardley [1968] Director/Machinist; Jacqueline Mary Eardley [1941] Director/Retired Teacher; John Barrie Eardley [1940] Director/Retired Headmaster; Joanne Elizabeth Walkden [1966] Director; Stephen John Walkden [1965] Director/Building Contractor

**Victoria Farm Garden Centre Ltd**
*Incorporated:* 1 October 2003 *Employees:* 40
*Net Worth:* £4,712,403 *Total Assets:* £5,169,935
*Registered Office:* 2 Hall Garth, Pickering, N Yorks, YO18 7AW
*Activities:* Other retail sale of new goods in specialised stores (not commercial art galleries and opticians)
*Officers:* Jean Mavis Noble, Secretary; Jean Mavis Noble [1941] Director/Retailer; Mark William Noble [1962] Director/Farmer and Retailer; Paul Robert Noble [1972] Director/Retailer; William Thomas Noble [1933] Director/Farmer and Retailer

**Victoria Plum Limited**
*Incorporated:* 12 March 2001 *Employees:* 231
*Net Worth:* £13,006,000 *Total Assets:* £28,805,000
*Registered Office:* Jack Brignall House, Bridgehead Business Park, Hessle, Hull, HU13 0DG
*Activities:* Other retail sale of new goods in specialised stores (not commercial art galleries and opticians)
*Parent:* Varnish Intermediate Holdco Limited
*Officers:* Antonio Capo [1970] Director/Investment Professional [Italian]; Martin Donald Hargreaves [1966] Director/Chief Financial Officer; Malte Janzarik [1980] Director/Investment Professional [German]; Paul Thomas McClenaghan [1965] Director/Chief Executive; Scott Michael Myers [1988] Director/Investment Professional [American]; Shane Malcolm Walker [1972] Director/Contracts Manager

**Victory Leisure Homes Limited**
*Incorporated:* 23 January 2009 *Employees:* 182
*Net Worth:* £839,093 *Total Assets:* £17,778,096
*Registered Office:* 45 Spyvee Street, Hull, HU8 7JR
*Activities:* Manufacture of caravans
*Parent:* J R Rix & Sons Ltd
*Officers:* Rory Michael Andrew Clarke [1959] Director; James Ian Doyle [1974] Director; David Charles Evans [1953] Director; Duncan John Lambert [1961] Director; Peter Thomas Nevitt [1952] Director; Sally Joanna Rix [1965] Director; Timothy John Rix [1963] Director

**Vida Grange Limited**
*Incorporated:* 30 June 2014 *Employees:* 130
*Previous:* Vida Pannal Limited
*Net Worth Deficit:* £749,615 *Total Assets:* £13,971,124
*Registered Office:* The Power House, 156 Hookstone Drive, Harrogate, N Yorks, HG2 8PF
*Activities:* Other human health activities
*Parent:* Vida Healthcare Limited
*Officers:* Bernadette Mossman [1965] Healthcare Director; Christopher Alan Rycroft [1944] Director; James Adam Rycroft [1972] Director; Mark Adam Rycroft [1969] Director; Jillian Young [1977] Operations Director

**Vida Hall Limited**
*Incorporated:* 20 August 2010 *Employees:* 128
*Previous:* Vida Healthcare Limited
*Net Worth:* £2,294,996 *Total Assets:* £6,491,547
*Registered Office:* The Power House, Hookstone Drive, Harrogate, N Yorks, HG2 8PF
*Activities:* Other human health activities
*Parent:* Vida Healthcare Limited
*Officers:* Bernadette Mossman [1965] Healthcare Director; Christopher Alan Rycroft [1944] Managing Director; James Adam Rycroft [1972] Director/Chairman; Jillian Young [1977] Director/Operations Manager

**Vida Healthcare Limited**
*Incorporated:* 27 June 2014 *Employees:* 249
*Previous:* Rycroft Group (Holdings) Limited
*Net Worth:* £948,387 *Total Assets:* £18,654,348
*Registered Office:* The Power House, 156 Hookstone Drive, Harrogate, N Yorks, HG2 8PF
*Activities:* Development of building projects
*Shareholder:* Christopher Alan Rycroft
*Officers:* Bernadette Mossman [1965] Healthcare Director; Christopher Alan Rycroft [1944] Director; James Adam Rycroft [1972] Director; Mark Adam Rycroft [1969] Director; Jillian Young [1977] Operations Director

**Videcon Holdings Limited**
*Incorporated:* 27 February 2015 *Employees:* 66
*Net Worth:* £7,048,717 *Total Assets:* £18,742,280
*Registered Office:* Unit 1 Concept Business Park, Smithies Lane, Heckmondwike, W Yorks, WF16 0PN
*Activities:* Activities of distribution holding companies
*Officers:* Matthew James Rushall, Secretary; Andrew Croston [1972] Director

**Videcon Ltd**
*Incorporated:* 31 July 1995 *Employees:* 66
*Previous:* Videcon Public Limited Company
*Net Worth:* £5,513,644 *Total Assets:* £15,287,209
*Registered Office:* Unit 1 Concept Business Park, Smithies Lane, Heckmondwike, W Yorks, WF16 0PN
*Activities:* Wholesale of electronic and telecommunications equipment and parts
*Parent:* Videcon Holdings Ltd
*Officers:* Matthew James Rushall, Secretary; Andrew Croston [1972] Sales Director; Ian Stuart Farr [1967] Director; Stephen Andrew Newsome [1972] Director; Matthew James Rushall [1979] Director

**Viewstone Limited**
*Incorporated:* 12 September 1983 *Employees:* 79
*Net Worth:* £5,810,419 *Total Assets:* £14,582,462
*Registered Office:* Pellon Lane Sawmills, Pellon Lane, Halifax, W Yorks, HX1 4PX
*Activities:* Other letting and operating of own or leased real estate
*Shareholders:* Karen Lesley Moore; Robert James Moore
*Officers:* Robert James Moore, Secretary; Karen Lesley Moore [1959] Director/Secretary; Robert James Moore [1961] Director/Packing Case Manufacturer

**Viking Arms Limited**
*Incorporated:* 6 December 1965 *Employees:* 23
*Net Worth:* £2,333,422 *Total Assets:* £3,500,791
*Registered Office:* Summerbridge, Harrogate, N Yorks, HG3 4BW
*Activities:* Wholesale of other intermediate products
*Major Shareholder:* Mavis Hilary Fay Brown
*Officers:* Stephen Michael Day, Secretary; Mavis Hilary Fay Brown [1940] Director; Samantha Emma Ravenhill MacArthur [1972] Director

**Viking Fishing Limited**
*Incorporated:* 19 October 2012
*Net Worth:* £3,033,374 *Total Assets:* £4,168,858
*Registered Office:* c/o Andrew Marr International Limited, Livingstone Road, Hessle, E Yorks, HU13 0EE
*Activities:* Marine fishing
*Parent:* Andrew Marr International Limited
*Officers:* Paul Morgan Farrar, Secretary; Mark James Dougal [1970] Director; Christian Leslie Marr [1972] Director; Andrew William Regan [1962] Director

**Vinewood Limited**
*Incorporated:* 6 October 1983 *Employees:* 3
*Net Worth:* £27,218 *Total Assets:* £24,150,636
*Registered Office:* Thorpe Underwood Hall, Thorpe Underwood, York, YO26 9SZ
*Activities:* Other service activities n.e.c.
*Parent:* Care & Recreation Holdings Ltd
*Officers:* Christopher James Hall, Secretary; Christopher James Hall [1969] Director/Chartered Accountant; Amy Katherine Martin [1983] Director; Francis David Martin [1967] Director/Business Executive

**Vinter Estates Limited**
*Incorporated:* 1 April 2003 *Employees:* 4
*Net Worth:* £15,930,531 *Total Assets:* £59,651,364
*Registered Office:* Leigh House, 28-32 St Pauls Street, Leeds, LS1 2JT
*Activities:* Other letting and operating of own or leased real estate
*Shareholders:* Mark Hunter; Andrew Vincent
*Officers:* Andrew Vincent, Secretary/Director; Mark Hunter [1962] Director; Andrew Vincent [1956] Director

**Virtual College Holdings Limited**
*Incorporated:* 18 May 2016 *Employees:* 156
*Net Worth:* £1,976,090 *Total Assets:* £6,190,192
*Registered Office:* Marsel House, Stephensons Way, Ilkley, W Yorks, LS29 8DD
*Activities:* Activities of head offices
*Shareholders:* Ian Robert Gomersall; Rodney Allen Knox
*Officers:* Neil Thomas Comer, Secretary; Hannah Brindle [1967] Managing Director; Neil Thomas Comer [1959] Director/Chartered Accountant; Dr Ian Robert Gomersall [1950] Director; Rodney Allen Knox [1959] Director

**Virtual College Limited**
*Incorporated:* 2 May 1995 *Employees:* 156
*Net Worth:* £3,136,089 *Total Assets:* £6,425,079
*Registered Office:* Marsel House, Stephensons Way, Ilkley, W Yorks, LS29 8DD
*Activities:* Other education n.e.c.
*Parent:* Virtual College Holdings Limited
*Officers:* Neil Thomas Comer, Secretary; Hannah Brindle [1967] Managing Director; Neil Thomas Comer [1959] Director/Chartered Accountant; Dr Ian Robert Gomersall [1950] Director; Rodney Allen Knox [1959] Director

**Vision Supplies Limited**
*Incorporated:* 18 December 2001 *Employees:* 6
*Net Worth:* £2,754,139 *Total Assets:* £3,134,665
*Registered Office:* Unit 5 Lockwood Close, Lockwood Close Industrial Estate, Leeds, LS11 5UU
*Activities:* Pre-press and pre-media services
*Shareholder:* Paul Waterton
*Officers:* Corrine Waterton, Secretary; Corinne Elaine Waterton [1963] Director; Paul Waterton [1964] Director

**Visit Yorkshire Holdings Ltd**
*Incorporated:* 26 September 2016
*Net Worth:* £4,006,985 *Total Assets:* £11,745,838
*Registered Office:* West House, King Cross Road, Halifax, W Yorks, HX1 1EB
*Activities:* Activities of other holding companies n.e.c.
*Shareholders:* Aimee Louise Barker; Philip Michael Barker; Philip Michael Barker
*Officers:* Aimee Louise Barker [1979] Director; Philip Michael Barker [1967] Director

**Vivimed Labs Europe Ltd**
*Incorporated:* 16 April 1901 *Employees:* 22
*Net Worth:* £9,571,000 *Total Assets:* £13,855,000
*Registered Office:* P O Box B3, Leeds Road, Huddersfield, W Yorks, HD1 6BU
*Activities:* Manufacture of dyes and pigments
*Parent:* Vivimed Labs Ltd
*Officers:* Rachael Elizabeth Blakey, Secretary; Varalwar Manohar Rao [1936] Director [Indian]; Mark Ian Robbins [1957] Director/Chief Executive; Sandeep Varalwar [1968] Director [Indian]; Sanketh Varalwar [1977] Globe Sales & Marketing Director [American]; Santosh Varalwar [1962] Director [Indian]; Subhash Varalwar [1948] Director [Indian]

**Vivimed Labs UK Limited**
*Incorporated:* 7 April 2011
*Net Worth:* £12,610,000 *Total Assets:* £51,978,000
*Registered Office:* P O Box B3, Leeds Road, Huddersfield, W Yorks, HD1 6BU
*Activities:* Activities of other holding companies n.e.c.
*Officers:* Rachael Elizabeth Blakey, Secretary; Saurabh Gurnurkar [1981] Director/Strategy and Corporate Development for The Group [Indian]; Santosh Varalwar [1962] Director [Indian]

**Vodecca Properties Limited**
*Incorporated:* 7 June 1996
*Net Worth:* £4,462,603 *Total Assets:* £5,502,458
*Registered Office:* Windham Farm, Ferry Road, Wawne, Hull, HU7 5XY
*Activities:* Renting and operating of Housing Association real estate
*Major Shareholder:* David Edmunds
*Officers:* Margaret Ann Edmunds, Secretary; David Edmunds [1947] Director/Landlord

**Vogue Leisure Limited**
*Incorporated:* 7 May 1969 *Employees:* 43
*Net Worth:* £1,978,476 *Total Assets:* £3,498,505
*Registered Office:* Fleet House, New Road, Lancaster, LA1 1EZ
*Activities:* Hotels and similar accommodation
*Parent:* Amblewater Ltd
*Officers:* Jason Reid Hewitt, Secretary; Andrew Martin Hewitt [1963] Director; Brian Hewitt [1942] Director/Hotelier; Christine Anne Hewitt [1945] Director/Hotelier; Jason Reid Hewitt [1970] Director/Hotelier

**Von Roll UK Limited**
*Incorporated:* 24 November 1971 *Employees:* 33
*Net Worth:* £4,726,000 *Total Assets:* £5,815,000
*Registered Office:* Wharfedale Road, Euroway Estate, Bierley, Bradford, W Yorks, BD4 6SG
*Activities:* Manufacture of other non-metallic mineral products n.e.c.
*Parent:* Von Roll Insulation & Composites Holding AG
*Officers:* Craig Martin Turner, Secretary; Artur Lust [1982] Director [German]

**Vossloh Cogifer UK Limited**
*Incorporated:* 21 November 2000 *Employees:* 75
*Net Worth:* £5,457,340 *Total Assets:* £8,670,083
*Registered Office:* 80a Scotter Road, Scunthorpe, N Lincs, DN15 8EF
*Activities:* Manufacture of other transport equipment n.e.c.
*Parent:* Vossloh AG
*Officers:* Wendy Anne Preston, Secretary; Nicolas Helary [1972] Director/General Manager [French]; Ian Stuart Lindsay [1959] Director/Engineer; Leif Marten Nordstrom [1969] Regional Director [Swedish]; Jean-Marie Toubeau [1947] Director/Secretary General [Belgian]

**VP PLC**
*Incorporated:* 5 May 1950 *Employees:* 705
*Net Worth:* £154,706,000 *Total Assets:* £440,038,016
*Registered Office:* Central House, Beckwith Knowle, Otley Road, Harrogate, N Yorks, HG3 1UD
*Activities:* Renting and leasing of other machinery, equipment and tangible goods n.e.c.
*Officers:* Allison Margaret Bainbridge, Secretary; Allison Margaret Bainbridge [1960] Director; Jeremy Frederic George Pilkington [1951] Director/Chairman; Stephen Rogers [1951] Director/Accountant; Neil Andrew Stothard [1958] Director; Philip Michael White [1949] Director

**VPG Systems UK Limited**
*Incorporated:* 7 January 2002 *Employees:* 52
*Net Worth:* £25,305,272 *Total Assets:* £28,364,256
*Registered Office:* Airedale House, Canal Road, Bradford, W Yorks, BD2 1AG
*Activities:* Manufacture of electronic measuring, testing etc. equipment, not for industrial process control
*Parent:* Vishay Precision Group
*Officers:* Matthew John Edward Burridge [1957] Director; Robert Anthony Campbell [1958] Director/Accountant; Jonathan Jackson [1969] Director; Steven Charles Klausner [1957] Director/Treasurer [American]

**VTL Group (Holdings) Limited**
*Incorporated:* 11 July 2001 *Employees:* 237
*Net Worth:* £1,921,000 *Total Assets:* £31,666,000
*Registered Office:* St Thomas Road, Huddersfield, W Yorks, HD1 3LG
*Activities:* Activities of head offices
*Shareholders:* Bruno Jouan; Christopher Trevor Elliott
*Officers:* Michael John Baunton [1951] Director; Christopher Trevor Elliott [1972] Director; Barry William Jackson [1981] Director/Investment Manager; Bruno Jouan [1968] Managing Director [French]; Phil White [1958] Finance Director

**VTL Precision (Bradley) Limited**
*Incorporated:* 11 September 1959 *Employees:* 59
*Net Worth Deficit:* £498,000 *Total Assets:* £10,754,000
*Registered Office:* 12 Station Road, Bradley, Huddersfield, W Yorks, HD2 1US
*Activities:* Machining
*Shareholders:* Bruno Jouan; Christopher Trevor Elliott
*Officers:* Christopher Trevor Elliott [1972] Director; Bruno Jouan [1968] Director [French]; Phil White [1958] Finance Director

**VTL Precision (Huddersfield) Limited**
*Incorporated:* 20 October 1997 *Employees:* 130
*Net Worth:* £4,280,000 *Total Assets:* £14,843,000
*Registered Office:* Main Works, St Thomas Road, Huddersfield, W Yorks, HD1 3LG
*Activities:* Machining
*Parent:* VTL Group (Holdings) Ltd
*Officers:* Christopher Trevor Elliott [1972] Director; Bruno Jouan [1968] Managing Director [French]; Phil White [1958] Finance Director

**W F & L Limited**
*Incorporated:* 18 April 2011 *Employees:* 6
*Net Worth:* £2,259,597 *Total Assets:* £4,694,817
*Registered Office:* W H Prior, Railway Court, Doncaster, S Yorks, DN4 5FB
*Activities:* Sale of new cars and light motor vehicles
*Shareholders:* Harry Richard Simpson; Louise Ann Simpson
*Officers:* Louise Ann Simpson, Secretary; Harry Richard Simpson [1961] Director; Louise Ann Simpson [1964] Director

**W W Hotels Limited**
*Incorporated:* 22 September 2004 *Employees:* 85
*Net Worth:* £3,214,766 *Total Assets:* £6,975,428
*Registered Office:* Rendezvous Hotel, Keighley Road, Skipton, N Yorks, BD23 2TA
*Activities:* Hotels and similar accommodation
*Shareholders:* Karen Alison Weaving; Edward Malcolm Weaving
*Officers:* Karen Alison Weaving, Secretary; Edward Malcolm Weaving [1932] Director/Hotelier; Karen Alison Weaving [1951] Director

**W. P. Holdings Limited**
*Incorporated:* 18 December 1984 *Employees:* 1
*Net Worth:* £6,228,066 *Total Assets:* £6,671,719
*Registered Office:* Maserati House, Gelderd Road, Leeds, LS12 1AS
*Activities:* Activities of other holding companies n.e.c.
*Shareholders:* Christine Sands; Peter Ignatius Kirrane
*Officers:* Gary Williams [1966] Director; Olive Williams [1940] Director

**Wabco Automotive U.K. Limited**
*Incorporated:* 6 December 1961 *Employees:* 46
*Net Worth Deficit:* £7,692,000 *Total Assets:* £7,451,000
*Registered Office:* Unit A1, Grange Valley Road, Batley, W Yorks, WF17 6GH
*Activities:* Manufacture of other parts and accessories for motor vehicles
*Parent:* Wabco Europe Holdings BV
*Officers:* Derek Ian Colquhoun, Secretary; Derek Ian Colquhoun [1968] Director/Accountant; David Timothy Rickell [1958] Director/HR Leader

**Waco UK Holdings Limited**
*Incorporated:* 3 November 2005 *Employees:* 3
*Net Worth:* £4,077,000 *Total Assets:* £15,024,000
*Registered Office:* Catfoss Lane, Brandesburton, Driffield, E Yorks, YO25 8EJ
*Activities:* Activities of head offices
*Parent:* Waco International Holdings Limited
*Officers:* Craig Glover, Secretary; Eugenio Pereira Carneiro de SA [1954] Commercial Director [Portuguese]; Craig Glover [1963] Finance Director; Stephen John Michael Goodburn [1963] Director [South African]

**Waddington & Ledger Group Limited**
*Incorporated:* 31 May 2011 *Employees:* 87
*Net Worth:* £7,887,039 *Total Assets:* £10,386,547
*Registered Office:* Lowfields Business Park, Elland, Halifax, W Yorks, HX5 9DA
*Activities:* Activities of head offices
*Major Shareholder:* Bill Cameron
*Officers:* Bill Cameron [1959] Director; Stephen Robert Chambers [1965] Director; Philip Moreland [1948] Director; Gary Mortimer [1966] Director

**Waddington and Ledger Limited**
*Incorporated:* 19 April 1912 *Employees:* 84
*Net Worth:* £3,265,689 *Total Assets:* £5,622,490
*Registered Office:* Lowfields Business Park, Elland, W Yorks, HX5 9DA
*Activities:* Printing n.e.c.
*Parent:* Waddington & Ledger Group Limited
*Officers:* Bill Cameron [1959] Director/Chief Executive; Stephen Robert Chambers [1965] Operations Director; Philip Moreland [1948] Managing Director; Gary Mortimer [1966] Director

**Waddington Limited**
*Incorporated:* 14 March 1921 *Employees:* 2
*Net Worth:* £91,911,000 *Total Assets:* £92,016,000
*Registered Office:* Communisis House, Manston Lane, Leeds, LS15 8AH
*Activities:* Non-trading company
*Parent:* Communisis Limited
*Officers:* Sarah Louise Caddy, Secretary; Sarah Louise Caddy [1976] Director/Company Secretary; Jonathan Rowlatt Huber Riddle [1960] Director/Tax Manager

**P Waddington Limited**
*Incorporated:* 21 February 1947
*Net Worth:* £3,565,460 *Total Assets:* £7,976,666
*Registered Office:* The Refinery, Buck Street, Bradford, W Yorks, BD3 9LP
*Activities:* Activities of other holding companies n.e.c.
*Shareholders:* William Mark Waddington; Sam Nicholas Waddington
*Officers:* Katherine Elizabeth Waddington [1961] Director/Financial Services Training; Sam Nicholas Waddington [1963] Director; William Mark Waddington [1965] Director

**John Wade (Haulage) Limited**
*Incorporated:* 19 February 1980 *Employees:* 51
*Net Worth:* £3,857,394 *Total Assets:* £4,337,429
*Registered Office:* Aycliffe Quarry, Aycliffe Village, Darlington, Co Durham, DL5 6NB
*Activities:* Freight transport by road
*Major Shareholder:* John Wade
*Officers:* John Wade, Secretary; Paul William Monkhouse [1957] Director/Contracts Manager; John Wade [1943] Director; Bruce David Whitley [1959] Director/Operations Manager

**John Wade (Holdings) Limited**
*Incorporated:* 16 April 1997 *Employees:* 124
*Net Worth:* £15,821,090 *Total Assets:* £21,569,942
*Registered Office:* Aycliffe Quarry, Aycliffe Village, Co Durham, DL5 6NB
*Activities:* Activities of other holding companies n.e.c.
*Major Shareholder:* John Wade
*Officers:* John Wade, Secretary; Paul William Monkhouse [1957] Director; John Wade [1943] Director; Bruce David Whitley [1959] Director

**Waiting for Anya Limited**
*Incorporated:* 29 March 2016
*Net Worth:* £673,354 *Total Assets:* £8,349,580
*Registered Office:* Highfield Grange, Bubwith, Selby, N Yorks, YO8 6DP
*Activities:* Motion picture production activities
*Parent:* Goldfinch Family Films Limited
*Officers:* Alan Richard Latham, Secretary; Alan Richard Latham [1960] Director/Film Producer

**Wakefield Acoustics Limited**
*Incorporated:* 21 July 1980 *Employees:* 39
*Net Worth:* £1,660,727 *Total Assets:* £3,421,705
*Registered Office:* Flush Mills, Westgate, Heckmondwike, W Yorks, WF16 0EN
*Activities:* Manufacture of metal structures and parts of structures
*Parent:* Arkanum Management Limited
*Officers:* Paul David Hebden, Secretary; Christopher John Brown [1953] Director; Jane Dawson [1964] Managing Director; Kevin Colin Dawson [1965] Director/Engineer; Paul David Hebden [1965] Director/Accountant; Robert Lomax [1975] Director; Lee Nicholson [1980] Director

**Wakefield and District Health and Community Support Ltd**
*Incorporated:* 6 December 1950 *Employees:* 25
*Net Worth:* £13,336,800 *Total Assets:* £13,404,025
*Registered Office:* 35 Peterson Road, Wakefield, W Yorks, WF1 4DU
*Activities:* Other business support service activities n.e.c.
*Officers:* Kevin John Murray [1954] Director/College Lecturer; Stephen David Storr [1945] Director/Trustee; Elaine Strutt [1952] Director/Trainer; Michael Sykes [1944] Director/Reel Inspection Operator; Margaret Whittaker [1941] Director; David Alfred Wright [1936] Director/Retired

**Wakefield City Academies Trust**
*Incorporated:* 7 December 2010 *Employees:* 1,083
*Net Worth:* £37,552,000 *Total Assets:* £47,336,000
*Registered Office:* The D'Hervart Suite, The Refectory, Doncaster Road, Nostell, W Yorks, WF4 1AB
*Activities:* General secondary education
*Officers:* David John Gurney [1966] Director/Headteacher; Dr John Richard Hargreaves [1960] Director; Terence Neal Mulready [1942] Director/Retired

**Wakefield Grammar School Foundation**
*Incorporated:* 24 July 2001 *Employees:* 478
*Net Worth:* £27,011,166 *Total Assets:* £33,296,932
*Registered Office:* Governors' Office, Green House, 158 Northgate, Wakefield, W Yorks, WF1 3UF
*Activities:* Pre-primary education
*Officers:* Laurence Perry, Secretary; Simon Mark Chamberlain [1970] Director/Solicitor; Jane Emily Claire [1963] Managing Director; Malcolm Golightly [1940] Director/Retired; Caroline Mary Gorton [1979] Director/Banker; Caroline Harrison [1963] Director/Chief Executive; Jonathan David Jeffries [1959] Director/Solicitor; David Gareth Jenkins [1973] Director/University Professor; Helen Janette Massey [1980] Director/Partner; Ian Alistair McKinlay [1972] Director/Solicitor; Dr Mahendra Gulabbhai Patel [1958] Director/University Research Fellow; Elizabeth Claire Peckett [1985] Director/Chartered Surveyor; Penelope Jane Plumpton [1958] Director/Teacher; Martin John Shevill [1955] Director/CEO Consilium Academies; Alison Jane Tetley [1960] Director/Senior Manager; Reverend Leah Beverley Vasey-Saunders [1977] Director/Canon Precentor Wakefield Cathedral; Diane Carole Watson [1958] Director/Financial Advisor; Timothy George Welton [1975] Director/Solicitor

**Wakefield Hospice**
*Incorporated:* 17 July 1986 *Employees:* 131
*Net Worth:* £5,971,390 *Total Assets:* £6,395,988
*Registered Office:* Wakefield Hospice, Aberford Road, Wakefield, W Yorks, WF1 4TS
*Activities:* Other human health activities
*Officers:* Ruth Margaret Hardill, Secretary; Mark David Ashton [1986] Director/Solicitor; David James Barker [1965] Director/Senior Finance Manager; Guy William Cattell [1957] Director/Retail Consultant; Nichola Frances Esmond [1970] Director/Charity Chief Executive; Alistair Paul Howatson [1968] Director/Healthcare Commissioner; Daniel James Lumb [1978] Director/Solicitor; David John Martindale [1963] Sales Director; David Melia [1965] Director of Nursing & Quality, Deputy CEO; Gary Mortimer [1966] Director; Dr Jane Elizabeth Senior [1959] Director/Retired GP

**Wakefield Shirt Company Limited (The)**
*Incorporated:* 4 June 1940 *Employees:* 126
*Net Worth:* £4,016,601 *Total Assets:* £13,469,791
*Registered Office:* P O Box 1, Thornes Lane Wharf, Wakefield, W Yorks, WF1 5RQ
*Activities:* Activities of head offices
*Shareholders:* Richard John Donner; Richard John Donner
*Officers:* Simon Anthony Balaam, Secretary; Richard John Donner [1967] Director; Richard John Donner [1939] Director

**Wakefield88 Limited**
*Incorporated:* 20 February 2014
*Previous:* Jayco88 Management Limited
*Net Worth:* £100 *Total Assets:* £3,342,600
*Registered Office:* 28 Park Square West, Leeds, LS1 2PQ
*Activities:* Non-trading company
*Shareholders:* Adrian Brooks; 500 M Limited
*Officers:* Adrian Brooks [1957] Director; Mansoor Mahmood Hussain [1980] Director

**Wal-Mart Stores (UK) Limited**
*Incorporated:* 26 April 1999
*Net Worth:* £2,495,000,064 *Total Assets:* £8,857,400,320
*Registered Office:* Asda House, Great Wilson Street, Leeds, LS11 5AD
*Activities:* Activities of head offices
*Parent:* Broadstreet Great Wilson Europe Limited
*Officers:* Richard Mayfield [1968] Director; John Caraway McDowell [1964] Director [American]; Chase Nicholas Tacker [1983] Director [American]

**Walk Investments Limited**
*Incorporated:* 4 May 2006 *Employees:* 25
*Net Worth:* £4,667,095 *Total Assets:* £7,851,716
*Registered Office:* Unit C, Nepshaw Lane South, Gildersome, Morley, Leeds, LS27 7JQ
*Activities:* Other retail sale of new goods in specialised stores (not commercial art galleries and opticians)
*Officers:* Iain Karl Doyle [1970] Director; Zoe Norcliffe [1983] Director/Chartered Accountant

**Walker Distribution (Hull) Limited**
*Incorporated:* 4 April 2007 *Employees:* 10
*Net Worth:* £1,797,122 *Total Assets:* £4,667,805
*Registered Office:* Westmoreland House, Westmorland Street, Hull, HU2 0DJ
*Activities:* Wholesale of hardware, plumbing and heating equipment and supplies
*Major Shareholder:* Malcolm Charles Walker
*Officers:* Lee Davies, Secretary; Lee Davies [1972] Director; Malcolm Charles Walker [1948] Director

**Walker Modular Limited**
*Incorporated:* 10 July 2006 *Employees:* 286
*Net Worth:* £32,826,500 *Total Assets:* £48,472,956
*Registered Office:* Westmoreland House, Westmoreland Street, Hull, HU2 0DJ
*Activities:* Other manufacturing n.e.c.
*Major Shareholder:* Malcolm Charles Walker
*Officers:* Lee Davies, Secretary; Lee Davies [1972] Financial Director; Darren Fawcett [1975] Sales Director; George William Griffin [1956] Production Director; Graham Kemp [1965] Production Director; Philip Andrew Trotter [1962] Development Director; Malcolm Charles Walker [1948] Director; Shane Malcolm Walker [1972] Director

**Walker Morris LLP**
*Incorporated:* 25 July 2008 *Employees:* 373
*Net Worth:* £12,592,000 *Total Assets:* £23,690,000
*Registered Office:* Kings Court, 12 King Street, Leeds, LS1 2HL
*Officers:* Jeanette Burgess [1971] Member; Gwendoline Davies [1964] Member; John James Arthur Hamer [1969] Member; Thomas Marc Peel [1973] Member; Malcolm Allan Simpson [1965] Member; David Andrew Smedley [1961] Member; Robert Douglas Aberdein [1979] LLP Member; Ian Alasdair Akitt [1963] LLP Member; Karl Richard Anders [1971] LLP Member; Andrew Beck [1958] LLP Member; Nicholas Barry Canon [1963] LLP Member; Simon Charles Clark [1967] LLP Member; Peter John Considine [1974] LLP Member; William Ellison Cousins [1980] LLP Member; James Andrew Crayton [1979] LLP Member; Trudy Dawn Feaster-Gee [1969] LLP Member; Julian James Harbage [1977] LLP Member; Paul Douglas Hargreaves [1973] LLP Member; David Warwick Hinchliffe [1965] LLP Member; Deborah Anne Jackson [1972] LLP Member; Austin Peter Judson [1971] LLP Member; Jacqueline Louise Judson [1975] LLP Member; David John Kilduff [1957] LLP Member; Nicholas Charles Rushton Lees [1976] LLP Member; Duncan Francis Lole [1975] LLP Member; Daniel Lyon [1982] LLP Member; Martin McKeague [1974] LLP Member; Gawain Douglas Moore [1978] LLP Member; Jeremy David Moore [1961] LLP Member; Richard David Charles Naish [1972] LLP Member; Andrew Charles Northage [1971] LLP Member; Daniel James O'Gorman [1974] LLP Member; Alison Ogley [1980] LLP Member; Judith Mary Pike [1963] LLP Member; Stuart David Ponting [1980] LLP Member; Clare Louise Power [1969] LLP Member; Johanne Susan Ratcliffe [1966] LLP Member; Andrew Stephen Rayment [1971] LLP Member; Richard Mark Sagar [1967] LLP Member; Richard Ian Sandford [1969] LLP Member; Martin Leslie Scott [1959] LLP Member; David Ben Sheppard [1976] LLP Member; Christopher Allen Slater [1966] LLP Member; Michael Frederick Taylor [1962] LLP Member; Sandra Jane Weaver [1969] LLP Member; Christophe Nicholas Woodthorpe [1973] LLP Member

**George Walker Transport Limited**
*Incorporated:* 7 November 1978 *Employees:* 153
*Net Worth:* £2,592,154 *Total Assets:* £8,632,252
*Registered Office:* Howley Park Road, East Howley Park Industrial Estate, Morley, Leeds, LS27 0BN
*Activities:* Freight transport by road
*Shareholders:* George Walker Transport One Limited; George Walker Transport One Limited
*Officers:* David Bywater [1961] Director; Nigel Patrick Jenkinson [1965] Director; Richard Henry Simpson [1965] Managing Director

**George Walker Transport Manchester Limited**
*Incorporated:* 15 July 2009 *Employees:* 82
*Previous:* Palletways Manchester Limited
*Net Worth:* £439,387 *Total Assets:* £3,866,937
*Registered Office:* Howley Park Road, East Howley Park Industrial Estate, Morley, Leeds, LS27 0BN
*Activities:* Freight transport by road
*Parent:* TCP Bidco (California) Limited
*Officers:* David Bywater [1961] Director; Nigel Patrick Jenkinson [1965] Director; Richard Henry Simpson [1965] Managing Director

**Walkers Holdings One Limited**
*Incorporated:* 6 April 2017 *Employees:* 153
*Net Worth:* £2,592,158 *Total Assets:* £8,632,256
*Registered Office:* Howley Park Road, East Howley Park Industrial Estate, Morley, Leeds, LS27 0BN
*Activities:* Activities of other holding companies n.e.c.
*Parent:* TCP Bidco (California) Limited
*Officers:* David Bywater [1961] Director; Nigel Patrick Jenkinson [1965] Director; Richard Henry Simpson [1965] Director

**Herbert Walkers Limited**
*Incorporated:* 1 March 1946 *Employees:* 123
*Net Worth:* £3,972,459 *Total Assets:* £8,889,204
*Registered Office:* 115 Dockfield Road, Shipley, W Yorks, BD17 7AR
*Activities:* Printing n.e.c.
*Major Shareholder:* Keith Chapman
*Officers:* Ann Wendy Chapman, Secretary; Richard Mark Campbell [1960] Director; Ann Wendy Chapman [1948] Director; Keith Chapman [1942] Director; Andrew Christie [1972] Sales Director; Steven Holme [1969] Director; Jonathan Mark Rawlinson [1962] Director; Mark Allan Vanston [1965] Operations Director

**Walkers Nurseries Limited**
*Incorporated:* 24 January 1997 *Employees:* 50
*Net Worth:* £2,148,885 *Total Assets:* £3,287,793
*Registered Office:* Walkers Nurseries, Mosham Road, Blaxton, Doncaster, S Yorks, DN9 3BA
*Activities:* Retail sale of flowers, plants, seeds, fertilizers, pet animals and pet food in specialised stores
*Shareholders:* David Lawrence Walker; Elaine Bodle
*Officers:* Elaine Bodle, Company Secretary; Elaine Bodle [1952] Director/Nurserywoman; David Lawrence Walker [1959] Director

**Ogden Waller Developments LLP**
*Incorporated:* 1 April 2005
*Net Worth Deficit:* £1,661,971 *Total Assets:* £4,088,160
*Registered Office:* New Chartford House, Centurion Way, Cleckheaton, W Yorks, BD19 3QB
*Officers:* Paul John Ogden [1964] Member; Duncan Michael Waller [1962] Member

**Wallum Farms (North) Limited**
*Incorporated:* 25 February 2008 *Employees:* 3
*Net Worth:* £2,479,286 *Total Assets:* £3,087,965
*Registered Office:* Carrside, Hatfield, Doncaster, S Yorks, DN7 6AZ
*Activities:* Mixed farming
*Parent:* Wallum Farms Ltd
*Officers:* Kathleen Jane Eldred, Secretary; Kathleen Jane Eldred [1960] Director/Secretary

**Walney Island South End Caravan Site Limited**
*Incorporated:* 1 October 1973 *Employees:* 40
*Net Worth:* £2,336,994 *Total Assets:* £4,684,419
*Registered Office:* R F Miller & Co, 102 Duke Street, Barrow in Furness, Cumbria, LA14 1RD
*Activities:* Other holiday and other collective accommodation
*Officers:* Michael Mulgrew Jnr, Secretary; Sarah Greig [1969] Director/Secretary; Simon Mulgrew [1965] Director/Farmer; Michael Mulgrew Jnr [1963] Director/Farmer; Michael Mulgrew Snr [1942] Director/Farmer

**The Walshford Inn Limited**
*Incorporated:* 8 December 2000 *Employees:* 40
*Net Worth:* £2,987,183 *Total Assets:* £3,724,859
*Registered Office:* 6 Victoria Avenue, Harrogate, N Yorks, HG1 1ED
*Activities:* Public houses and bars
*Shareholders:* Alicia Jane Roberts; Philip James Roberts
*Officers:* Philip James Roberts, Secretary/Hotelier; Alicia Jane Roberts [1969] Director/Accountant; Philip James Roberts [1964] Director/Hotelier

**Fred Walter & Sons Limited**
*Incorporated:* 27 October 1959 *Employees:* 12
*Net Worth:* £3,905,736 *Total Assets:* £8,104,276
*Registered Office:* Sutton Grange, Sutton Cum Lound, Retford, Notts, DN22 8SB
*Activities:* Raising of sheep and goats
*Parent:* Sutton Grange Farming Limited
*Officers:* Angela Marie Walter, Secretary; Charles Frederick Walter [1964] Director/Farmer; Samuel Frederick Lewis Walter [1990] Director/Farmer

**Jeffrey Walton Jewellery Limited**
*Incorporated:* 22 November 1977 *Employees:* 7
*Net Worth:* £9,091,469 *Total Assets:* £12,903,697
*Registered Office:* 62 Albion Street, Leeds, LS1 6AD
*Activities:* Wholesale of household goods (other than musical instruments) n.e.c
*Parent:* Berens & Company Limited
*Officers:* Alyson Moss [1970] Director; Debra Tomlinson [1964] Finance Director; Simon Bennett Walton [1967] Director/Jeweller

**H Walton Limited**
*Incorporated:* 30 June 2003 *Employees:* 50
*Net Worth:* £4,321,814 *Total Assets:* £9,729,111
*Registered Office:* Old Goole Mill, South Park Road, Goole, E Yorks, DN14 8BD
*Activities:* Wholesale of grain, unmanufactured tobacco, seeds and animal feeds
*Officers:* Anthony James Walton [1968] Director/Feed Merchant; David Hugh Walton [1970] Director/Feed Merchant; Frederick Jason Driffill Walton [1972] Director/Feed Merchant; Hugh Walton [1942] Director/Feed Merchant; Julia Walton [1944] Director/Feed Merchant; Elizabeth Wilburn [1974] Director/Feed Merchant

**Wandahome (Knottingley) Limited**
*Incorporated:* 10 November 1959 *Employees:* 28
*Net Worth:* £1,533,537 *Total Assets:* £4,361,437
*Registered Office:* Great North Road, Knottingley, W Yorks, WF11 0AE
*Activities:* Sale of other motor vehicles
*Major Shareholder:* Reginald Norman Burnley
*Officers:* Nigel Burnley, Secretary; Martin Burnley [1964] Director to Accessory Dept; Nigel Burnley [1965] Sales Director; Reginald Norman Burnley [1936] Director/Caravan Dealer; John Richard Hay [1970] Director/Caravan Dealership

**Wandahome (South Cave) Limited**
*Incorporated:* 17 May 2000 *Employees:* 43
*Net Worth:* £983,987 *Total Assets:* £7,155,596
*Registered Office:* Brough Road, South Cave, Hull, HU15 2DB
*Activities:* Sale of new cars and light motor vehicles
*Major Shareholder:* Steven David Burnley
*Officers:* Steven David Burnley, Secretary; Stephen Mark Bateman [1969] Director; John Burnley [1967] Director; Sophia Anna Burnley [1989] Director; Steven David Burnley [1960] Director

**Wannops Farms Ltd**
*Incorporated:* 19 February 2002 *Employees:* 10
*Previous:* M.E. Wannop & Sons Limited
*Net Worth:* £1,113,107 *Total Assets:* £3,495,135
*Registered Office:* 95 King Street, Lancaster, LA1 1RH
*Activities:* Raising of dairy cattle
*Officers:* Annette Barbara Wannop, Secretary; Annette Barbara Wannop [1962] Director; David George Arthur Wannop [1962] Director

**Ward Bros. (Steel) Limited**
*Incorporated:* 27 July 1976 *Employees:* 76
*Net Worth:* £1,107,472 *Total Assets:* £10,867,774
*Registered Office:* Cleveland House, Cleveland Street, Darlington, Co Durham, DL1 2PE
*Activities:* Recovery of sorted materials
*Officers:* Billy Ward [1978] Director; Nathan Ward [1982] Director

**Peter Ward Homes Limited**
*Incorporated:* 3 October 1983 *Employees:* 36
*Net Worth:* £12,100,675 *Total Assets:* £22,971,718
*Registered Office:* Annie Reed Road, Grovehill, Beverley, E Yorks, HU17 0LF
*Activities:* Other building completion and finishing
*Shareholder:* Peter David Ward
*Officers:* Rosemary Fiona Key, Secretary; Glyn Graham Harrison [1962] Construction Director; Rosemary Fiona Key [1964] Director; Peter David Ward [1954] Director/Builder

**J. & J. Ward Limited**
*Incorporated:* 2 April 2001 *Employees:* 90
*Net Worth:* £1,873,372 *Total Assets:* £18,072,598
*Registered Office:* The Garage, Patrick Brompton, Bedale, N Yorks, DL8 1JP
*Activities:* Freight transport by road
*Parent:* Bulk Logistics Group Limited
*Officers:* Paul William Tolmie [1961] Director; Michael James Ward [1968] Director

**Ward Recycling Limited**
*Incorporated:* 13 February 2002 *Employees:* 128
*Net Worth:* £3,153,162 *Total Assets:* £8,298,018
*Registered Office:* The Bungalow, Warlaby Lane, Ainderby Steeple, Northallerton, N Yorks, DL7 9JX
*Activities:* Collection of non-hazardous waste
*Officers:* Mark Stephen Ward, Secretary; Michael James Ward [1968] Sales Director

**Wardbright Properties Limited**
*Incorporated:* 26 November 1985 *Employees:* 3
*Net Worth:* £4,637,914 *Total Assets:* £11,748,217
*Registered Office:* 103 Princes Avenue, Hull, HU5 3JP
*Activities:* Other letting and operating of own or leased real estate
*Shareholders:* Jennifer Barry; Michael David Barton; Louise Mukerjea
*Officers:* Louise Mukerjea, Secretary/Director; Jennifer Barry [1966] Director/Residential Management Agent; Michael David Barton [1968] Director/Property Developer; Louise Mukerjea [1971] Director

**Warden Farming Company Limited**
*Incorporated:* 30 June 1965 *Employees:* 51
*Net Worth:* £4,973,988 *Total Assets:* £6,267,300
*Registered Office:* Grayingham Grange Farm, Grayingham, Gainsborough, Lincs, DN21 4JD
*Activities:* Growing of cereals (except rice), leguminous crops and oil seeds
*Major Shareholder:* Meryl Ward, Kevin Webster and Stephen Ward
*Officers:* Susan Cooper, Secretary; John Anthony Shepherdson [1954] Director; Meryl Suzanne Ward [1960] Director; Stephen Tom Ward [1959] Director

**A.M. Warkup Limited**
*Incorporated:* 22 January 2002 *Employees:* 41
*Net Worth:* £2,947,546 *Total Assets:* £4,792,934
*Registered Office:* Aerodrome Works, Lissett, Driffield, E Yorks, YO25 8PY
*Activities:* Construction of commercial buildings
*Shareholders:* Arthur Michael Warkup; Susan Mary Warkup
*Officers:* Susan Anne Nicholson, Secretary; Andrew John Hall [1972] Technical Sales Director; Allan Mason [1952] Managing Director; Tracey Ann Middlewood [1965] Director; Norman Oliver Morley [1950] Production Director; Arthur Michael Warkup [1934] Director/Chairman; Sally Young [1962] Director/Administrator

**Warmafloor (GB) Limited**
*Incorporated:* 21 September 1995 *Employees:* 36
*Net Worth:* £3,689,000 *Total Assets:* £4,842,000
*Registered Office:* Wavin, Edlington Lane, Edlington, Doncaster, S Yorks, DN12 1BY
*Activities:* Plumbing, heat and air-conditioning installation
*Parent:* Wavin Limited
*Officers:* Neil Robert John Douglas, Secretary; Neil Robert John Douglas [1964] Director; Paul Maclaurin [1967] Director; Alan Brent Nicholls [1961] Managing Director

**Warmest Welcome Limited**
*Incorporated:* 30 June 2006
*Net Worth:* £861,965 *Total Assets:* £4,400,892
*Registered Office:* New Road, Old Snydale, Pontefract, W Yorks, WF7 6HD
*Activities:* Hotels and similar accommodation
*Shareholder:* Tracey Holroyd
*Officers:* Stephen Michael Holroyd, Secretary; Stephen Michael Holroyd [1963] Director/Nursing Home; Tracey Holroyd [1965] Director/Nursing Home; Sally Ann Sherrie Jennings [1965] Director/Nursing Home

**Warners Fishmerchants Limited**
*Incorporated:* 17 August 1981 *Employees:* 22
*Net Worth:* £2,585,531 *Total Assets:* £6,253,958
*Registered Office:* Unit 5 Decoy Bank North, Lakeside, Doncaster, S Yorks, DN4 5JR
*Activities:* Wholesale of other food, including fish, crustaceans and molluscs
*Officers:* Gary Warner [1966] Director/Fish Merchant

**Warrendale Farms Limited**
*Incorporated:* 31 December 2002 *Employees:* 75
*Net Worth:* £2,198,597 *Total Assets:* £19,096,464
*Registered Office:* High Warrendale Farm, Warter, York, YO42 1XG
*Activities:* Raising of other animals
*Shareholders:* James Cubitt Bloom; Rachel Margaret Bloom
*Officers:* James Cubitt Bloom, Secretary; James Cubitt Bloom [1961] Director/Farmer; Rachel Margaret Bloom [1962] Director/Farmer; James Richard Thornton [1984] Director

**Warrens Emerald Biogas Ltd**
*Incorporated:* 24 April 2009 *Employees:* 11
*Previous:* Emerald Biogas Ltd
*Net Worth:* £3,546,850 *Total Assets:* £14,008,520
*Registered Office:* Emerald Biogas, Preston Road, Aycliffe Business Park, Newton Aycliffe, Co Durham, DL5 6AB
*Activities:* Growing of cereals (except rice), leguminous crops and oil seeds
*Shareholders:* Agricore Ltd; John Warren (Animal By-Products) Limited
*Officers:* Ian Bainbridge, Secretary; Ian Bainbridge [1985] Director/Farmer; Adam Warren [1972] Director/General Manager; Antony Michael Warren [1978] Director/Technical Manager

**Warrens Group Limited**
*Incorporated:* 1 August 1986 *Employees:* 60
*Previous:* John Warren (Animal By-Products) Limited
*Net Worth:* £5,435,391 *Total Assets:* £17,211,688
*Registered Office:* Eden Hall, Hamsterley, Bishop Auckland, Co Durham, DL13 3QG
*Activities:* Treatment and disposal of non-hazardous waste
*Shareholders:* Antony Michael Warren; John Adam Ralph Warren
*Officers:* Elizabeth Elsie Warren, Secretary; Antony Michael Warren [1978] Director/Manager; Elizabeth Elsie Warren [1954] Director/Secretary; John Adam Ralph Warren [1972] Director/Manager; John Neville Ralph Warren [1950] Director/Animal By Products Collector

**Warrington Garages Limited**
*Incorporated:* 29 January 1986 *Employees:* 379
*Net Worth:* £15,470,535 *Total Assets:* £66,355,116
*Registered Office:* Jaguar House, Calder Island Way, Denby Dale Road, Wakefield, W Yorks, WF2 7AW
*Activities:* Sale of new cars and light motor vehicles
*Major Shareholder:* Gareth Sinclair Williams
*Officers:* Justin Sinclair Williams, Secretary; Gareth Sinclair Williams [1964] Director; John Sinclair Williams [1942] Director

**Wartsila Valves Limited**
*Incorporated:* 20 August 1990 *Employees:* 82
*Net Worth:* £6,039,180 *Total Assets:* £15,951,707
*Registered Office:* D Shed, West Building, 72-74 Humber Enterprise Park, Skua Road, Brough, E Yorks, HU15 1EQ
*Activities:* Manufacture of taps and valves
*Parent:* AW Flow Holdings Limited
*Officers:* Mario Zinno, Secretary; Timo Ensio Koponen [1969] Director/Vice President Finance & Control [Finnish]; Arto Juhani Lehtinen [1971] Director [Finnish]; Robert Stewart Moulds [1970] Managing Director; Christopher David Rowlands [1972] Director

**Waste Services Group Limited**
*Incorporated:* 5 July 2001 *Employees:* 80
*Net Worth:* £1,986,864 *Total Assets:* £6,298,529
*Registered Office:* Acumen House, Headlands Lane, Knottingley, W Yorks, WF11 0LA
*Activities:* Collection of hazardous waste
*Parent:* Acumen Group Holdings Limited
*Officers:* Kristian David Sutton, Secretary; Andrew Crossley [1976] Director; Leon Kirk [1965] Managing Director; Kristian David Sutton [1980] Finance Director

**Wastecare Group Limited**
*Incorporated:* 19 November 1996 *Employees:* 431
*Net Worth:* £14,890,403 *Total Assets:* £39,589,716
*Registered Office:* Richmond House, Selby Road, Garforth, Leeds, LS25 1NB
*Activities:* Activities of head offices
*Officers:* Christopher John Gay, Secretary; Peter Timothy Hunt [1955] Director; Rebecca Mary Hunt [1954] Director/Company Secretary; Graeme Michael Parkin [1973] Director; Russell James Scott [1959] Director

**Wastecare Limited**
*Incorporated:* 27 April 1982 *Employees:* 417
*Net Worth:* £5,011,957 *Total Assets:* £17,259,588
*Registered Office:* Richmond House, Selby Road, Garforth, Leeds, LS25 1NB
*Activities:* Precious metals production
*Parent:* Wastecare Group Limted
*Officers:* Christopher John Gay, Secretary; Peter Timothy Hunt [1955] Director; Rebecca Mary Hunt [1954] Director; Graeme Michael Parkin [1973] Director

**Watergate Developments Limited**
*Incorporated:* 14 June 2004
*Net Worth:* £504,305 *Total Assets:* £8,815,089
*Registered Office:* Wykeland House, 47 Queen Street, Hull, HU1 1UU
*Activities:* Development of building projects
*Parent:* Wykeland Limited
*Officers:* Ian Charles Franks, Secretary; David Christopher Donkin [1961] Director/Chartered Surveyor; Dominic Anthony Gibbons [1970] Director; Stephen Peter Hudson [1948] Director; Jonathan David Stubbs [1970] Director/Chartered Surveyor

**Watershed Packaging Limited**
*Incorporated:* 6 December 1993 *Employees:* 89
*Net Worth:* £2,858,326 *Total Assets:* £11,122,858
*Registered Office:* Wigton Heath Farm, Manor House Lane, Leeds, LS17 9JD
*Activities:* Other manufacturing n.e.c.
*Major Shareholder:* John Waters
*Officers:* Anna Wood, Secretary; John Waters [1959] Director [Irish]; Sumbaline Waters [1956] Director/Secretary

**Waterside Colours Limited**
*Incorporated:* 8 September 2016 *Employees:* 34
*Net Worth:* £51,546 *Total Assets:* £7,049,195
*Registered Office:* 21 Marina Court, Castle Street, Hull, HU1 1TJ
*Activities:* Manufacture of dyes and pigments
*Officers:* Simon Andrew Banks-Cooper [1965] Director; William Julian Cortazzi [1961] Director; Siddharth Singhania [1982] Director [Indian]; Vinod Singhania [1957] Director [Indian]

**Waterton Academy Trust**
*Incorporated:* 10 July 2014 *Employees:* 430
*Net Worth:* £17,890,048 *Total Assets:* £21,744,848
*Registered Office:* Walton Primary Academy, The Grove, Walton, Wakefield, W Yorks, WF2 6LD
*Activities:* Primary education
*Officers:* Victoria Lee Collins, Secretary; Paul Charles Beaman [1971] Construction Director; Andrew Russell Buckley [1969] Director/Forensic Assessment Officer; Rebecca Louise Cook [1977] Director/Advisory Teacher; David Dickinson [1965] Director/Headteacher; Andrew Goudie [1963] Director/Equity Release Adviser; Anthony Harpham [1966] Director/Headteacher; Larraine Susan Harrison [1948] Director/Retired; Stephen Johnson [1977] Director/Civil Servant; Helen Mangham [1957] Director/Retired Headteacher

**A.Watkinson Limited**
*Incorporated:* 3 November 1954 *Employees:* 11
*Net Worth:* £3,130,033 *Total Assets:* £3,479,462
*Registered Office:* 53 Goodramgate, York, YO1 7LS
*Activities:* Retail sale of footwear in specialised stores
*Shareholders:* Dorothy Vivian Carrington Preece; Jeffrey William Preece; Diana Margaret Widdicombe
*Officers:* Jeffrey William Preece, Secretary; Dorothy Vivian Carrington Preece [1936] Director; Jeffrey William Preece [1960] Director/Footwear Agent; Diana Margaret Widdicombe [1964] Director/Letting Agent

**Watson Pallets Limited**
*Incorporated:* 2 June 2003 *Employees:* 59
*Net Worth:* £1,415,665 *Total Assets:* £4,140,847
*Registered Office:* Europa Way, Kiln Lane Industrial Estate, Stallingborough, N E Lincs, DN41 8DS
*Activities:* Manufacture of wooden containers
*Parent:* Scott Timber Limited
*Officers:* Alan Gibson [1956] Director; Robert William MacLean [1975] Director; Norman Robert Scott [1968] Director; Tracy Janye Trotter [1975] Director

**Watsons BS (Holdings) Limited**
*Incorporated:* 17 November 2009 *Employees:* 3
*Net Worth:* £3,458,614 *Total Assets:* £3,459,023
*Registered Office:* Watson House, Howden Road, Silsden, Keighley, W Yorks, BD20 0HD
*Activities:* Activities of construction holding companies
*Shareholders:* David Arthur Bottomley; Stuart George Whyte
*Officers:* David Arthur Bottomley [1974] Director/Building Services Engineer; Stuart George Whyte [1968] Director/Engineer; Graeme Paul Wolfenden [1966] Director/Accountant

**W.Clifford Watts Limited**
*Incorporated:* 19 December 1944 *Employees:* 46
*Net Worth:* £5,095,594 *Total Assets:* £10,809,248
*Registered Office:* 118-122 Scarborough Road, Bridlington, E Yorks, YO16 7NU
*Activities:* Operation of gravel and sand pits; mining of clays and kaolin
*Shareholders:* Wyndham Richard Watts; David Clifford Watts; Carol Ann Watts
*Officers:* Paul Thompson, Secretary; Carol Watts [1942] Director/Housewife; David Clifford Watts [1972] Director; Wyndham Richard Watts [1970] Director

**Wauldby Associates Limited**
*Incorporated:* 22 December 2010
*Net Worth:* £5,167,880 *Total Assets:* £6,105,789
*Registered Office:* Old Heritage Garden Centre, Gibson Lane, Melton, North Ferriby, E Yorks, HU14 3HH
*Activities:* Management consultancy activities other than financial management
*Shareholders:* Paul Anthony Hornshaw; Mark Hornshaw
*Officers:* Paul Anthony Hornshaw [1972] Director

**Wavemaster (TGOF) Limited**
*Incorporated:* 22 February 2011
*Net Worth:* £1,923,730 *Total Assets:* £3,983,680
*Registered Office:* Morton House, Morton Lane, Beverley, E Yorks, HU17 9DD
*Activities:* Other professional, scientific and technical activities n.e.c.
*Parent:* Dalby Offshore Services Limited
*Officers:* Kevin Adamson, Secretary; Stuart Hamish McNiven [1959] Director

**Wavin Limited**
*Incorporated:* 8 March 1946 *Employees:* 875
*Net Worth:* £41,817,000 *Total Assets:* £353,940,992
*Registered Office:* Wavin, Edlington Lane, Edlington, Doncaster, S Yorks, DN12 1BY
*Activities:* Manufacture of builders ware of plastic
*Parent:* Wavin Hepworth Limited
*Officers:* Neil Robert John Douglas, Secretary; Neil Robert John Douglas [1964] Director; Paul Maclaurin [1967] Manufacturing Director; Alan Brent Nicholls [1961] Managing Director

**Wavin UK (Holdings) Limited**
*Incorporated:* 3 February 2005
*Net Worth:* £4,457,000 *Total Assets:* £220,024,000
*Registered Office:* Wavin, Edlington Lane, Edlington, Doncaster, S Yorks, DN12 1BY
*Activities:* Activities of head offices
*Officers:* Neil Robert John Douglas, Secretary; Neil Robert John Douglas [1964] Director; Paul Maclaurin [1967] Manufacturing Director; Alan Brent Nicholls [1961] Managing Director; Martinus Petrus Maria Roef [1964] Group Director [Dutch]

**Wax Lyrical Limited**
*Incorporated:* 3 June 1980 *Employees:* 136
*Net Worth:* £8,064,000 *Total Assets:* £10,630,000
*Registered Office:* Lindal Business Park, Lindal in Furness, Ulverston, Cumbria, LA12 0LD
*Activities:* Other manufacturing n.e.c.
*Parent:* Lighthouse Holdings Limited
*Officers:* Moira MacDonald, Secretary; Philip Edward Atherton [1966] Director; Lawrence Frederick Bryan [1960] Director; Jacqueline Mary Gale [1963] Managing Director; Michael Trevor Raybould [1971] Finance Director

**Waxman Ceramics Limited**
*Incorporated:* 21 November 1994 *Employees:* 57
*Net Worth:* £2,411,949 *Total Assets:* £5,809,067
*Registered Office:* Grove Mills, Elland, W Yorks, HX5 9DZ
*Activities:* Non-specialised wholesale trade
*Parent:* Waxman Group Limited
*Officers:* Stephen Mark John, Secretary; David Julian Garlick [1967] Sales Director; Melvyn Joseph Pape [1964] Director; Steven Parker [1972] Contract Sales Director; Jacqueline Waxman [1950] Director; Richard David Waxman [1954] Managing Director; Samuel Marcus Waxman [1985] Director

**Waxman Energy Limited**
*Incorporated:* 8 December 1995 *Employees:* 12
*Net Worth:* £2,895,853 *Total Assets:* £7,637,407
*Registered Office:* Grove Mills, Elland, W Yorks, HX5 9DZ
*Activities:* Non-specialised wholesale trade
*Parent:* Waxman Group Limited
*Officers:* Stephen Mark John, Secretary; Melvyn Joseph Pape [1964] Director; Jacqueline Waxman [1950] Director; Richard David Waxman [1954] Managing Director; Samuel Marcus Waxman [1985] Director

**Waxman Fibres Limited**
*Incorporated:* 21 April 1992 *Employees:* 14
*Net Worth:* £2,398,418 *Total Assets:* £5,268,064
*Registered Office:* Grove Mills, Elland, W Yorks, HX5 9DZ
*Activities:* Wholesale of textiles
*Parent:* Waxman Group Limited
*Officers:* Stephen Mark John, Secretary; Gregory Joseph Cluskey [1964] Sales Director [Irish]; Anthony Riley [1966] Sales Director; Peter Kenneth Seward [1954] Technical Director; Jacqueline Waxman [1950] Director; Richard David Waxman [1954] Managing Director; Samuel Marcus Waxman [1985] Director

**Waxman Group Limited**
*Incorporated:* 9 December 1997 *Employees:* 79
*Net Worth:* £9,440,000 *Total Assets:* £13,167,000
*Registered Office:* Grove Mills, Elland, W Yorks, HX5 9DZ
*Activities:* Other transportation support activities
*Major Shareholder:* Richard David Waxman
*Officers:* Stephen Mark John, Secretary; Gregory Joseph Cluskey [1964] Director [Irish]; Stephen Mark John [1971] Finance Director; Melvyn Joseph Pape [1964] Director; Albert Abraham Waxman [1924] Director; Jacqueline Waxman [1950] Director; Richard David Waxman [1954] Director; Samuel Marcus Waxman [1985] Director

**Waxman Holdings Limited**
*Incorporated:* 7 May 1947 *Employees:* 12
*Net Worth:* £5,893,394 *Total Assets:* £6,221,062
*Registered Office:* Grove Mills, Elland, W Yorks, HX5 9DZ
*Activities:* Renting and operating of Housing Association real estate
*Major Shareholder:* Albert Abraham Waxman
*Officers:* Stephen Mark John, Secretary; Joseph Pape [1964] Director; Alan Paul Waxman [1961] Director; Albert Abraham Waxman [1924] Director; Lily Gertrude Judith Waxman [1929] Director; Richard David Waxman [1954] Director; Susan Diana Waxman [1953] Director

**Waxman International Limited**
*Incorporated:* 1 December 1978 *Employees:* 8
*Net Worth:* £1,269,033 *Total Assets:* £6,112,058
*Registered Office:* Grove Mills, Elland, W Yorks, HX5 9DZ
*Activities:* Wholesale of textiles
*Parent:* Waxman Group Limited
*Officers:* Stephen Mark John, Secretary; Gregory Joseph Cluskey [1964] Sales Director [Irish]; Stephen Mark John [1971] Finance Director; Albert Abraham Waxman [1924] Director; Amber Waxman [1990] Director; Jacqueline Waxman [1950] Director; Joshua Adam Waxman [1987] Director; Richard David Waxman [1954] Director; Samuel Marcus Waxman [1985] Director

**Wayland Farms Limited**
*Incorporated:* 20 October 2008 *Employees:* 93
*Net Worth:* £14,644,000 *Total Assets:* £19,898,000
*Registered Office:* Crane Court, Hesslewood Office Park, Ferriby Road, Hessle, E Yorks, HU13 0PA
*Activities:* Raising of swine and pigs
*Parent:* Cranswick Country Foods PLC
*Officers:* Steven Garrick Glover, Secretary; John Mark Bottomley [1963] Director; Charles Dudley Bowes [1969] Director; Neil Edward Clappison [1964] Director; Adam Hartley Couch [1968] Director; James Pontone [1977] Finance Director

**WDS Component Parts Limited**
*Incorporated:* 16 February 2009 *Employees:* 51
*Net Worth:* £1,528,691 *Total Assets:* £3,899,184
*Registered Office:* Richardshaw Road, Grangefield Industrial Estate, Pudsey, Leeds, LS28 6LE
*Activities:* Machining
*Shareholders:* Simon James Booth; Peter Andrew Crowder
*Officers:* Simon James Booth, Secretary/Accountant; Hazel Dorothy Booth [1966] Director; Simon James Booth [1965] Director/Accountant; Jane Marie Crowder [1965] Director; Peter Andrew Crowder [1965] Director

**We Are Vista Limited**
*Incorporated:* 17 December 1996 *Employees:* 101
*Previous:* Logistik Limited
*Net Worth:* £2,450,952 *Total Assets:* £12,095,238
*Registered Office:* Unit 5 and 6 Carlton Trading Estate, Pickering Street, Armley, Leeds, LS12 2QG
*Activities:* Other professional, scientific and technical activities n.e.c.
*Parent:* Logistik Holdings Ltd
*Officers:* Warren Charles Marshall [1974] Director/Vice President, E&A Finance & Accounting [Irish]; Michael Sands [1958] Director/Vice President - Contracts; John Wasson [1951] Director/President & COO [American]

**Weardale Motor Services Limited**
*Incorporated:* 23 November 1961 *Employees:* 50
*Net Worth:* £3,934,933 *Total Assets:* £5,861,025
*Registered Office:* The Garage, Stanhope, Bishop Auckland, Co Durham, DL13 2YQ
*Activities:* Other passenger land transport
*Shareholder:* Ian Gibson
*Officers:* Allyson Margaret Gibson-Hewison, Secretary; Anthony Maurice Gibson [1966] Director/Mechanic; Ian Gibson [1973] Director/PSV Driver; Roland Stanley Gibson [1939] Director/P S V Operator; Sylvia Gibson [1932] Director/P S V Operator; Allyson Margaret Gibson Hewison [1963] Director/Administrator

**Weavers Properties Limited**
*Incorporated:* 13 May 2004
*Net Worth:* £1,123,893 *Total Assets:* £3,971,355
*Registered Office:* Bridge End Yard, Settle, N Yorks, BD24 9DS
*Activities:* Other letting and operating of own or leased real estate
*Shareholders:* Derek Matthew Nowell; Edward Stuart Nowell
*Officers:* Derek Matthew Nowell [1973] Director/Manager Garden Care Equipment; Edward Stuart Nowell [1975] Company Secretary/Director

**Webasto Thermo & Comfort UK Ltd**
*Incorporated:* 11 November 1987 *Employees:* 38
*Net Worth:* £3,542,000 *Total Assets:* £5,233,000
*Registered Office:* Webasto House, White Rose Way, Doncaster Carr, S Yorks, DN4 5JH
*Activities:* Manufacture of electrical and electronic equipment for motor vehicles and their engines
*Officers:* Patricia Elaine Wraith, Secretary; Heike Andrea Niehues [1970] Director/Senior Business Manager [German]; Steven James Powell [1977] Managing Director

**Webevents Limited**
*Incorporated:* 3 May 2000 *Employees:* 98
*Net Worth:* £4,610,617 *Total Assets:* £5,977,661
*Registered Office:* Central House, Otley Road, Harrogate, N Yorks, HG3 1UF
*Activities:* Advertising agencies
*Parent:* Graphene Holdings Limited
*Officers:* Lisa Higham, Secretary; David Martin Best [1958] Director; Dennis Stephen Engel [1959] Director; Jeremy Mark Fenn [1963] Director; Lisa Jayne Higham [1966] Finance Director

**Robert D. Webster Limited**
*Incorporated:* 8 March 1973 *Employees:* 37
*Net Worth:* £863,436 *Total Assets:* £4,077,063
*Registered Office:* Owstwick Grange, Owstwick, Roos, Hull, HU12 0LH
*Activities:* Agents involved in the sale of machinery, industrial equipment, ships and aircraft
*Shareholders:* Jacqueline Thompson; Robert Ronald Webster
*Officers:* Simon Berry, Secretary; Simon Berry [1957] Finance Director; Emma Louise Cowell [1967] Director; Michael Richard Cowell [1964] Managing Director; John Edward Jackson [1979] After Sales Director; Jacqueline Thompson [1949] Director; Thomas Thompson [1943] Director; James Robert Webster [1984] Operations Director; Pauline Webster [1954] Director; Robert Ronald Webster [1954] Director

**Webster Properties (Skipton) Limited**
*Incorporated:* 5 August 2011
*Net Worth:* £699,536 *Total Assets:* £3,457,989
*Registered Office:* Florence House, Lawkholme Business Park, Lawkholme, Keighley, W Yorks, BD21 3LA
*Activities:* Construction of domestic buildings
*Officers:* Richard Norman Wooler [1954] Director

**Weetwood Hall Limited**
*Incorporated:* 9 May 1991 *Employees:* 127
*Net Worth:* £4,968,700 *Total Assets:* £7,818,058
*Registered Office:* The Company Secretariat, 11-75 E C Stoner Building, University of Leeds, Leeds, LS2 9JT
*Activities:* Hotels and similar accommodation
*Officers:* Helena Mary Smith, Secretary; Professor Julia Bennell [1971] Director/University Professor; Ruth Buller [1965] Director/Head of Human Resources; Martin Leslie Hicks [1953] Managing Director; Dennis Hopper [1957] Director of Residential; Owen Thomas Morton [1951] Director/Chartered Accountant; Professor Alan Clive Roberts [1934] Director/Clinical Scientist; John David Malcolm Stoddart-Scott [1943] Director/Farmer and Estate Manager

**Weidmann Whiteley Limited**
*Incorporated:* 1 December 1980 *Employees:* 117
*Net Worth Deficit:* £447,732 *Total Assets:* £15,068,064
*Registered Office:* Pool Paper Mills, Pool in Wharfedale, Otley, W Yorks, LS21 1RP
*Activities:* Manufacture of paper and paperboard
*Officers:* John Stephen Briggs, Secretary; Jurg Brunner [1961] Director/CEO/President [American]

**Weightlifter Bodies Limited**
*Incorporated:* 21 June 1979 *Employees:* 79
*Net Worth:* £4,992,152 *Total Assets:* £6,760,288
*Registered Office:* Plot 56-57 Grange Lane North, Scunthorpe, N Lincs, DN16 1BN
*Activities:* Manufacture of bodies (coachwork) for motor vehicles (except caravans)
*Parent:* New Month Ltd
*Officers:* Keith Richard Hunt, Secretary; Keith Richard Hunt [1955] Finance Director; Richard Amery Nichols [1955] Group Sales Director; Gary Richard Simons [1960] Director

**Weir Drilling Services Limited**
*Incorporated:* 15 July 1983
*Net Worth:* £15,430,000 *Total Assets:* £15,677,000
*Registered Office:* Britannia House, Huddersfield Road, Elland, W Yorks, HX5 9JR
*Activities:* Non-trading company
*Parent:* Weir Group Investments Limited
*Officers:* Gillian Kyle, Secretary; John Brian Heasley [1974] Director/Chartered Accountant; Graham William Corbett Vanhegan [1964] Director/Chief Legal Officer and Company Secretary

**Weir Valves & Controls UK Limited**
*Incorporated:* 18 January 1966 *Employees:* 167
*Net Worth:* £8,364,000 *Total Assets:* £39,610,000
*Registered Office:* Britannia House, Huddersfield Road, Elland, Halifax, W Yorks, HX5 9JR
*Activities:* Other manufacturing n.e.c.
*Parent:* The Weir Group PLC
*Officers:* Gillian Kyle, Secretary; Jennifer Gillian Magowan [1984] Director/Accountant; Michael Nicholas Mannion [1961] Managing Director; Christopher Joseph Riordan [1960] Commercial Director; Steven David James Wallace [1976] Director/Accountant

**Welcom Digital Limited**
*Incorporated:* 6 July 1999 *Employees:* 60
*Net Worth:* £4,073,213 *Total Assets:* £5,682,894
*Registered Office:* The Exchange, Station Parade, Harrogate, N Yorks, HG1 1TS
*Activities:* Other information technology service activities
*Parent:* Welcom Software Holdings Limited
*Officers:* Christopher John Stones, Secretary; John Barrow [1968] Director; Ian Nigel Corp [1961] Operations Director; Peter Richmond [1958] Director; Nigel Adrian Welch [1960] Director

**Welcom Software Holdings Limited**
*Incorporated:* 12 January 2005 *Employees:* 69
*Net Worth:* £6,263,976 *Total Assets:* £8,026,696
*Registered Office:* The Exchange, Station Parade, Harrogate, N Yorks, HG1 1TS
*Activities:* Activities of other holding companies n.e.c.
*Shareholders:* Nigel Adrian Welch; Karen June Welch
*Officers:* Christopher John Stones, Secretary; Ian Nigel Corp [1961] Director; Karen June Welch [1966] Director; Nigel Adrian Welch [1960] Director/Computer Advisor

**H.I.Weldrick Limited**
*Incorporated:* 18 March 1959 *Employees:* 673
*Net Worth:* £18,624,468 *Total Assets:* £39,377,784
*Registered Office:* Leedale House, Railway Court, Doncaster, S Yorks, DN4 5FB
*Activities:* Dispensing chemist in specialised stores
*Major Shareholder:* Christopher William John Alcock
*Officers:* Paul Appleyard, Secretary; Christopher William John Alcock [1977] Director/Pharmacist; Lynne Hopwood Alcock [1947] Director/Secretary

**Weldtite Products Limited**
*Incorporated:* 15 November 1990 *Employees:* 38
*Net Worth:* £1,396,787 *Total Assets:* £3,495,843
*Registered Office:* Unit 9 Harrier Road, Humber Bridge Industrial Estate, Barton upon Humber, N Lincs, DN18 5RP
*Activities:* Manufacture of bicycles and invalid carriages
*Parent:* CB Baggs Group Ltd
*Officers:* Darren Taylor, Secretary; David Justin Bennett Baggs [1960] Director; Charles Martin Bennett-Baggs [1952] Director; Jonathan Lawrence Anthony Bennett-Baggs [1958] Director; Paul Kay Davis [1968] Managing Director

**Welfare Hire Nationwide Limited**
*Incorporated:* 15 March 2012 *Employees:* 41
*Net Worth:* £3,339,375 *Total Assets:* £15,408,192
*Registered Office:* Unit F, Trident Park, Rosie Road, Normanton, W Yorks, WF6 1ZB
*Activities:* Renting and leasing of construction and civil engineering machinery and equipment
*Parent:* Kelling Midco Limited
*Officers:* Jonathan Simon Battersby [1964] Financial Director; Chris Brown [1965] Director; Danny Cooper [1960] Sales Director; William Brian Kellie [1956] Sales Director; John Brad Wood [1976] Managing Director

**Wellbridge Properties Limited**
*Incorporated:* 22 September 1947
*Net Worth:* £6,517,335 *Total Assets:* £7,161,178
*Registered Office:* 10 Shaftesbury Avenue, Roundhay, Leeds, LS8 1DT
*Activities:* Other letting and operating of own or leased real estate
*Major Shareholder:* Thomas Woodroofe Marshall
*Officers:* Thomas Woodroofe Marshall, Secretary; Thomas Woodroofe Marshall [1947] Director

**Wellesley Holdco Limited**
*Incorporated:* 10 December 2014 *Employees:* 25
*Net Worth:* £20,145,764 *Total Assets:* £87,507,800
*Registered Office:* 1 Park Row, Leeds, LS1 5AB
*Activities:* Extraction of crude petroleum
*Officers:* Christopher James Elliott [1973] Director/Chief Executive; Olivier Patrick Hopkes [1972] Director [Dutch]; Callum Smyth [1967] Director; Graeme David Sword [1968] Director; Richard Tiley [1979] Director

**Richard Wellock & Sons Limited**
*Incorporated:* 1 October 2001 *Employees:* 431
*Net Worth:* £3,794,627 *Total Assets:* £10,084,591
*Registered Office:* The Riverside Building, Livingstone Road, Hessle, E Yorks, HU13 0DZ
*Activities:* Wholesale of fruit and vegetables
*Parent:* Piper Acquisitions Limited
*Officers:* Gary Martin Urmston, Secretary; Michael Beech [1979] Finance Director; Jillian Emma Martin [1977] Director/Chief Operating Officer; Norman Graeme Scott Soutar [1960] Director; Gary Martin Urmston [1967] Director/Chief Financial Officer; Alistair Richard James Wellock [1965] Director/Office/Sales Manager

**Stephen B Wells Limited**
*Incorporated:* 4 August 2004 *Employees:* 14
*Net Worth:* £666,761 *Total Assets:* £4,779,523
*Registered Office:* Manor Farm, Burton Fleming, Driffield, E Yorks, YO25 3PS
*Activities:* Growing of cereals (except rice), leguminous crops and oil seeds
*Major Shareholder:* Stephen Brian Wells
*Officers:* Marie Elaine Wells, Secretary; Stephen Brian Wells [1965] Director/Farming

**Wellvend Limited**
*Incorporated:* 8 November 1982 *Employees:* 35
*Net Worth:* £1,865,131 *Total Assets:* £3,592,303
*Registered Office:* Wellvend House, AW Nielsen Road, Goole, E Yorks, DN14 6UE
*Activities:* Manufacture of electric lighting equipment
*Shareholders:* Kelvin Shone; Anne Bridget Shone
*Officers:* Anne Bridget Shone [1965] Managing Director; Kelvin Shone [1976] Commercial Director

**Wemmergill Moor Limited**
*Incorporated:* 30 April 2003 *Employees:* 31
*Net Worth Deficit:* £7,178,614 *Total Assets:* £6,382,962
*Registered Office:* Kiln Hill, Market Place, Hawes, N Yorks, DL8 3RA
*Activities:* Hunting, trapping and related service activities
*Major Shareholder:* Michael Robin Cannon
*Officers:* Christopher John Mitchell, Secretary/Solicitor; Edward Richard Dawson Johnson [1946] Director/Solicitor; Christopher John Mitchell [1957] Director/Solicitor

**Wensleydale Dairy Products Limited**
*Incorporated:* 29 July 1992 *Employees:* 246
*Net Worth:* £6,062,130 *Total Assets:* £19,702,678
*Registered Office:* The Creamery, Gayle Lane, Hawes, N Yorks, DL8 3RN
*Activities:* Butter and cheese production
*Officers:* Sally Rachel Bowen, Secretary; Sally Rachel Bowen [1973] Finance Director; Lee Coates [1966] Operations Director; Sarah Elizabeth Emmett-Lee [1967] Commercial Director; David Alwyne James Hartley [1962] Director/Production Manager; Philip Keith Jones [1960] Director; David John Salkeld [1956] Director/Chairman

**Wesco Aircraft Europe, Ltd**
*Incorporated:* 19 October 1984 *Employees:* 267
*Net Worth:* £113,651,000 *Total Assets:* £120,411,000
*Registered Office:* Lawrence House, Riverside Drive, Cleckheaton, W Yorks, BD19 4DH
*Activities:* Wholesale of other intermediate products
*Parent:* Wesco Aircraft Holdings, Inc.
*Officers:* John Holland, Secretary; Jan Alexander Dobrucki [1964] Director/Chartered Accountant; John Holland [1968] Director/Lawyer [American]; Alexander Murray [1969] Director; Alun Phennah [1968] Supply Chain Director

**Wescott Homes Limited**
*Incorporated:* 15 December 2003 *Employees:* 4
*Net Worth Deficit:* £1,620,203 *Total Assets:* £31,964,172
*Registered Office:* Persimmon House, Fulford, York, YO19 4FE
*Activities:* Development of building projects
*Parent:* Wescott Holdings Limited
*Officers:* Tracy Lazelle Davison, Secretary; David Jenkinson [1967] Director; Michael Hugh Killoran [1961] Finance Director; Richard Paul Stenhouse [1971] Director/Accountant

**West and North Yorkshire Chamber of Commerce and Industry**
*Incorporated:* 24 November 1897 *Employees:* 81
*Net Worth:* £10,229,561 *Total Assets:* £14,418,096
*Registered Office:* Devere House, Vicar Lane, Little Germany, Bradford, W Yorks, BD1 5AH
*Activities:* Activities of business and employers membership organisations
*Officers:* Julie Alexandra Snook, Secretary; Amanda Beresford [1959] Director/Partner; Michel James Briffett [1971] Director/Chartered Surveyor; Andrew Mark Caton [1963] Building Society Director; Graham Philip Cooper [1958] Director; Bridget Lee Davies [1968] Managing Director; Andrew James Digwood [1976] Director/Solicitor; Paula Marie Dillon [1959] Director/Solicitor; Nicholas James Garthwaite [1957] Managing Director; Generald Robert Jennings [1957] Director/Chartered Surveyor; Sandra Needham [1955] Director; Lee Ramon Underwood [1974] Director; Victoria Wainwright [1974] Director/Chartered Accountant; Suzanne Rachel Watson [1970] Director/PR Consultant; Stephen Thomas Wright [1961] Director

**West Building Supplies Limited**
*Incorporated:* 13 December 2001 *Employees:* 49
*Net Worth:* £828,337 *Total Assets:* £3,037,383
*Registered Office:* Medina House, No 2 Station Avenue, Bridlington, E Yorks, YO16 4LZ
*Activities:* Other retail sale of new goods in specialised stores (not commercial art galleries and opticians)
*Shareholders:* Christopher West; Julie Ann West
*Officers:* Christopher West, Secretary/Building Merchant; Sean Boyd [1970] Director/Manager; Richard Spencer Price [1976] Director; Christopher West [1948] Director/Builders Merchant; Julie Ann West [1962] Director/Marketing Consultant; Oliver Hamilton West [1993] Director

**West Coast Capital Investments Limited**
*Incorporated:* 6 November 1992
*Net Worth:* £30,824,370 *Total Assets:* £38,520,380
*Registered Office:* 1 Park Row, Leeds, LS1 5AB
*Activities:* Non-trading company
*Parent:* West Coast Capital Holdings Limited
*Officers:* Kirsty Elizabeth Murray, Secretary; Sharon Seales, Secretary/Chartered Accountant; Paul Richmond Davidson [1965] Director/Solicitor; James Cairns McMahon [1949] Director; Sharon Seales [1976] Director/Accountant

**West Coast Railway Company Ltd**
*Incorporated:* 9 June 1995
*Net Worth:* £2,155,652 *Total Assets:* £6,100,849
*Registered Office:* off Jesson Way, Cragbank, Carnforth, Lancs, LA5 9UR
*Activities:* Passenger rail transport, interurban
*Officers:* Christine Smith, Secretary; Peter Babbage [1947] Director; Patricia Marshall [1956] Business Services Director; Thomas Richard Smith [1977] Director; William David Smith [1946] Director

**West Ella Estates Limited**
*Incorporated:* 23 February 1976 *Employees:* 5
*Net Worth:* £26,586,372 *Total Assets:* £31,180,200
*Registered Office:* Hall Garth, Goodmanham, York, YO43 3HX
*Activities:* Buying and selling of own real estate
*Major Shareholder:* John Finch Bladon
*Officers:* Alison Morag Bladon, Secretary; Alison Morag Bladon [1955] Director; James Christopher Bladon [1981] Director; John Finch Bladon [1947] Director; Emma Jane Worrall [1983] Director

**West Moor Holdings Limited**
*Incorporated:* 11 May 1999 *Employees:* 80
*Net Worth:* £3,890,448 *Total Assets:* £8,630,989
*Registered Office:* West Moor Farm, West Moor Lane, Armthorpe, Doncaster, S Yorks, DN3 3EA
*Activities:* Growing of cereals (except rice), leguminous crops and oil seeds
*Shareholders:* Catheryne Francis Kelly; John Paul Kelly
*Officers:* Catheryne Francis Kelly, Secretary; Catheryne Francis Kelly [1947] Director/Secretary; John Paul Kelly [1945] Director; Micheal Graham Cliffe Kelly [1977] Director/Pallet Dealer; Simon Frances Cliffe Kelly [1972] Director/Pallet Dealer

**West Park Estates Limited**
*Incorporated:* 23 November 1998 *Employees:* 5
*Net Worth:* £433,162 *Total Assets:* £8,163,670
*Registered Office:* Enterprise House, Thirsk Industrial Park, York Road, Thirsk, N Yorks, YO7 3BX
*Activities:* Buying and selling of own real estate
*Parent:* West Park Group Limited
*Officers:* Richard Anthony Sykes, Secretary; Richard Anthony Sykes [1964] Director

**West Park Group Limited**
*Incorporated:* 12 August 2013 *Employees:* 151
*Net Worth:* £2,200,852 *Total Assets:* £7,607,608
*Registered Office:* Enterprise House, Thirsk Industrial Park, York Road, Thirsk, N Yorks, YO7 3BX
*Activities:* Activities of head offices
*Major Shareholder:* Richard Anthony Sykes
*Officers:* Richard Anthony Sykes [1964] Director

**West Park Inns Limited**
*Incorporated:* 13 July 2012 *Employees:* 3
*Net Worth Deficit:* £125,156 *Total Assets:* £6,600,398
*Registered Office:* Enterprise House, Thirsk Industrial Park, York Road, Thirsk, N Yorks, YO7 3BX
*Activities:* Public houses and bars
*Parent:* West Park Group Limited
*Officers:* Richard Anthony Sykes [1964] Director

**West Park Properties Limited**
*Incorporated:* 20 August 1996
*Net Worth:* £790,002 *Total Assets:* £5,590,729
*Registered Office:* Woodleigh Hall, Knott Lane, Rawdon, Leeds, LS19 6JW
*Activities:* Other letting and operating of own or leased real estate
*Major Shareholder:* Rizwan Haq
*Officers:* Shamim Haq, Secretary; Dr Rizwan Haq [1965] Director/Property Development

**The West Retail Group Limited**
*Incorporated:* 20 February 2004 *Employees:* 4,188
*Net Worth:* £47,644,472 *Total Assets:* £230,448,112
*Registered Office:* The Nest, Falkland Way, Barton upon Humber, N Lincs, DN18 5RL
*Activities:* Activities of head offices
*Major Shareholder:* Malcolm Stanley Healey
*Officers:* Jane Marie Oldfield, Secretary; Malcolm Stanley Healey [1944] Director; William Stanley Healey [1987] Director; Jane Marie Oldfield [1964] Director/Chartered Accountant; Mark Jonathan Pullan [1972] Director/Chartered Accountant

**West Retford Hotel Limited**
*Incorporated:* 22 February 2005 *Employees:* 62
*Net Worth:* £4,504,281 *Total Assets:* £7,079,026
*Registered Office:* 24 North Road, Retford, Notts, DN22 7XG
*Activities:* Hotels and similar accommodation
*Major Shareholder:* Patricia Sara Lavin
*Officers:* Patricia Sara Lavin, Secretary; Andrew John Lavin [1967] Director/Hotel Manager

**West Riding Masonic Charities Limited**
*Incorporated:* 8 October 1945 *Employees:* 2
*Net Worth:* £7,258,849 *Total Assets:* £7,289,974
*Registered Office:* 20 Castle Grove Drive, Leeds, LS6 4BR
*Activities:* Other social work activities without accommodation n.e.c.
*Officers:* Alan Oldfield, Secretary; James Stuart Cadman [1947] Director/Retired; Colin Dent [1941] Director/Retired; Dr Roberto Espindola [1944] Director/Retired; Barry Laurence Hartley [1940] Director/Retired; Jack Pigott [1943] Director/Retired; Howard Frederick Richardson [1944] Director/Retired; Jeremy Philip Turner [1958] Director/Retired; Peter Davis Worth [1958] Managing Director Red Beck Motel Ltd

**West Tower Country House Limited**
*Incorporated:* 25 September 2000 *Employees:* 36
*Net Worth:* £5,229,694 *Total Assets:* £6,655,521
*Registered Office:* 16 Bazil Lane, Overton, Morecambe, Lancs, LA3 3JB
*Activities:* Hotels and similar accommodation
*Parent:* West Tower Property Limited
*Officers:* Laura Bolton, Secretary; David Leathem, Secretary; Paul Charles Bolton [1963] Director; David Stephen Leathem [1969] Director

**West Tower Property Limited**
*Incorporated:* 2 August 2012 *Employees:* 36
*Net Worth:* £1,944,767 *Total Assets:* £6,679,127
*Registered Office:* 16 Bazil Lane, Overton, Morecambe, Lancs, LA3 3JB
*Activities:* Hotels and similar accommodation
*Major Shareholder:* Laura Bolton
*Officers:* Laura Bolton, Secretary; David Leathem, Secretary; Paul Charles Bolton [1963] Director; David Stephen Leathem [1969] Director

**West Yorkshire Fellmongers Limited**
*Incorporated:* 21 January 1983 *Employees:* 3
*Net Worth:* £3,471,416 *Total Assets:* £7,776,726
*Registered Office:* Valley Road, Bradford, W Yorks, BD1 4RU
*Activities:* Tanning and dressing of leather; dressing and dyeing of fur
*Shareholder:* Jacinta Louise Dean
*Officers:* Jacinta Louise Byrne, Secretary; Richard Anthony Brady [1960] Director/Sales Manager; Jacinta Louise Byrne [1973] Director/Finance Manager

**West Yorkshire Spinners Limited**
*Incorporated:* 23 January 1997 *Employees:* 60
*Net Worth:* £4,814,499 *Total Assets:* £7,920,797
*Registered Office:* Unit 2 Airedale Park, Royd Ings Avenue, Keighley, W Yorks, BD21 4DG
*Activities:* Preparation and spinning of textile fibres
*Major Shareholder:* Ernst Magnus Gylfe
*Officers:* Lucille Longbottom, Secretary; Lucille Longbottom [1953] Director/Secretary; Peter Longbottom [1949] Managing Director; Richard Peter Longbottom [1985] Sales & Marketing Director; Michael John Whitaker [1949] Production Director

**West Yorkshire Van Rental Limited**
*Incorporated:* 16 March 1984 *Employees:* 2
*Net Worth:* £3,152,826 *Total Assets:* £5,059,488
*Registered Office:* L C W House, Chainbar Road, Cleckheaton, W Yorks, BD19 3QF
*Activities:* Renting and leasing of cars and light motor vehicles
*Parent:* Caygill Holdings Ltd
*Officers:* Susan Caroline Caygill, Secretary/Director; Andrew Martin Caygill [1956] Director/Sales Manager; Susan Caroline Caygill [1959] Director/Secretary

**Westcourt Group Limited**
*Incorporated:* 28 July 1994 *Employees:* 7
*Net Worth:* £9,316,434 *Total Assets:* £9,457,894
*Registered Office:* 8 North Park Road, Harrogate, N Yorks, HG1 5PG
*Activities:* Development of building projects
*Parent:* Icando UK Limited
*Officers:* Judith Helen Hodgson [1950] Director; Timothy Matthew Joseph Hodgson [1975] Director/Property Manager

**Westcourt Properties Limited**
*Incorporated:* 6 February 1992 *Employees:* 2
*Net Worth:* £5,721,524 *Total Assets:* £18,564,062
*Registered Office:* 8 North Park Road, Harrogate, N Yorks, HG1 5PG
*Activities:* Other letting and operating of own or leased real estate
*Parent:* Westcourt Group Limited
*Officers:* Judith Helen Hodgson [1950] Director; Timothy Matthew Joseph Hodgson [1975] Director/Property Manager

**Westdale Group Limited**
*Incorporated:* 28 September 2016 *Employees:* 66
*Net Worth:* £5,257,352 *Total Assets:* £7,306,822
*Registered Office:* Doncaster Road, Askern, Doncaster, S Yorks, DN6 9JD
*Activities:* Activities of other holding companies n.e.c.
*Major Shareholder:* Malcolm Kitching
*Officers:* Allan Bishop [1956] Director; Lee Bishop [1978] Director; Toni Louise Bishop [1981] Director; Malcolm Kitching [1948] Director; Sandra Jean Kitching [1949] Director

**Westex (Carpets) Limited**
*Incorporated:* 21 February 1980 *Employees:* 197
*Net Worth:* £16,892,000 *Total Assets:* £23,355,000
*Registered Office:* Castle Mills, Moorend, Cleckheaton, W Yorks, BD19 3PS
*Activities:* Manufacture of woven or tufted carpets and rugs
*Parent:* Globesign Limited
*Officers:* John Russell Shirt, Secretary; John Frederick Cooper [1961] Director; John Russell Shirt [1961] Director/Accountant; Geoffrey Brendon Wilding [1963] Director [New Zealander]

**Westfield Farms Limited**
*Incorporated:* 26 April 2000 *Employees:* 40
*Net Worth:* £3,009,630 *Total Assets:* £4,827,856
*Registered Office:* Westfield House, Cropton Lane, Pickering, N Yorks, YO18 8HQ
*Activities:* Support activities for crop production
*Shareholders:* Michael Thomas Wood; Mavis Wood
*Officers:* Mavis Wood, Secretary; Mavis Wood [1946] Director/Farmer; Michael Thomas Wood [1945] Director/Farmer

**Westfield War Memorial Village - Lancaster**
*Incorporated:* 12 August 1919 *Employees:* 1
*Net Worth:* £3,308,222 *Total Assets:* £3,310,989
*Registered Office:* 1 Sir Thomas Storey House, West Road, Lancaster, LA1 5PE
*Activities:* Combined office administrative service activities
*Officers:* Amanda Jane Stretch, Secretary; Thomas Geoffrey Bowring [1949] Director/Land Agent; Revd Robert Arthur Canham [1946] Director/Retired Minister of Religion; Susan Margaret Georgina Charles [1949] Director/County Councillor; Anthony Rickards Collinson [1949] Director/Solicitor; Peter Edward Dew [1934] Director/Retired; Dr David Martin Elliott [1950] Director/Retired Medical Practitioner; Julie Patricia Hardy [1958] Director/Justice of The Peace; Carol Anne Margaret Johnson [1948] Director/Land Owner; Colonel Christopher William Owen [1957] Director/Civil Servant; Christopher John Tomlinson [1969] Director/Commercial Pilot

**G. & M. Westgarth Limited**
*Incorporated:* 3 April 1996 *Employees:* 28
*Net Worth:* £4,234,886 *Total Assets:* £11,462,633
*Registered Office:* Newsham Hall, Newsham, Richmond, N Yorks, DL11 7RA
*Activities:* Raising of swine and pigs
*Major Shareholder:* Mark Andrew William Westgarth
*Officers:* Mark Andrew William Westgarth, Secretary; George William Westgarth [1938] Director/Farmer; Mark Andrew William Westgarth [1970] Director/Farmer

**Westgate Motors Limited**
*Incorporated:* 19 October 1987 *Employees:* 50
*Net Worth:* £3,257,749 *Total Assets:* £5,837,368
*Registered Office:* Moody Lane, Grimsby, N E Lincs, DN31 2SY
*Activities:* Sale of new cars and light motor vehicles
*Parent:* DM Keith Limited
*Officers:* Angus MacDonald Keith [1965] Director; Dougal MacDonald Keith [1963] Director

**W. S. Westin Group Limited**
*Incorporated:* 11 May 1939 *Employees:* 62
*Net Worth:* £3,831,738 *Total Assets:* £7,299,867
*Registered Office:* Phoenix Mill, Leeds Road, Huddersfield, W Yorks, HD1 6NG
*Activities:* Activities of head offices
*Major Shareholder:* John Eastwood
*Officers:* Ian Richard Bostock, Secretary; John Eastwood [1947] Director/Insurance Broker; Ian Gareth Sheppard [1965] Managing Director

**The Westmorland County Agricultural Society Ltd**
*Incorporated:* 15 January 1996 *Employees:* 6
*Net Worth:* £4,500,328 *Total Assets:* £4,812,532
*Registered Office:* Lane Farm, Crooklands, Milnthorpe, Cumbria, LA7 7NH
*Activities:* Support activities for animal production (other than farm animal boarding)
*Officers:* Christine Anne Knipe, Secretary; Charles Henry Bagot [1946] Director/Chartered Surveyor; Karen Lesley Barnes [1968] Director/Banker; James Edgar Barton [1964] Director/Self Employed; Lisa Dawn Bennett [1969] Director/Agricultural Representative; David Crayston [1967] Director/Company Accountant; Christian John Davies [1970] Director/Financial Adviser; James Anthony Dixon [1959] Director/Farmer; Bernard Neil Dowker [1951] Director/Farmer; Paul Anthony Duckett [1965] Director/Builder; David Hall Fell [1952] Director/Chartered Accountant; Charles David Geldard [1975] Director/Farmer; Ian Kenneth Grisedale [1948] Director/Farmer; Peter David Lawrence [1956] Director/Farmer; David Robert Martin [1971] Director/Farmer; Jonathan Charles Mason [1956] Director/Farmer; Stephen Procter [1961] Director/Farmer; Matthew Harold Robinson [1962] Director/Farmer

**Stan Weston LLP**
*Incorporated:* 23 January 2015
*Net Worth:* £1,364 *Total Assets:* £3,115,356
*Registered Office:* Garden Flat, 110 Skipton Road, Ilkley, W Yorks, LS29 9HE
*Officers:* Joanne Bakewell [1969] Member; Andrew Douglas Simpson [1961] Member

**Westpoint Group Trading Limited**
*Incorporated:* 6 January 2014 *Employees:* 137
*Net Worth:* £1,455,711 *Total Assets:* £11,931,653
*Registered Office:* Leeman House, Station Business Park, Holgate Park Drive, York, YO26 4GB
*Activities:* Activities of other holding companies n.e.c.
*Parent:* Origin Group Finance Limited
*Officers:* Joanna Clare Malone [1974] Director; Mark Stanworth [1964] Director

**Westward Care Limited**
*Incorporated:* 19 September 1994 *Employees:* 213
*Net Worth:* £11,830,054 *Total Assets:* £19,425,154
*Registered Office:* Pennington Court, 11 Hunslet Hall Road, Beeston, Leeds, LS11 6TT
*Activities:* Other human health activities
*Shareholders:* David Trevor Spencer; Norman Alan Stubbs
*Officers:* Gail Margaret Lawton, Secretary; Gail Margaret Lawton [1966] Finance Director; David Trevor Spencer [1932] Director/Property Developer; Norman Alan Stubbs [1942] Managing Director

**Westway Veterinary Centres Limited**
*Incorporated:* 4 March 2010 *Employees:* 155
*Net Worth:* £2,802,565 *Total Assets:* £7,757,779
*Registered Office:* Leeman House, Station Business Park, Holgate Park Drive, York, YO26 4GB
*Activities:* Veterinary activities
*Parent:* Vetpartners Limited
*Officers:* Joanna Clare Malone [1974] Managing Director and Veterinary Surgeon; Mark Stanworth [1964] Director

**Wetherby Group of Companies Limited**
*Incorporated:* 21 October 2008 *Employees:* 1
*Net Worth:* £2,372,832 *Total Assets:* £3,010,759
*Registered Office:* Wetherby Stone Products Ltd, Dalton Airfield Industrial Estate, Dalton, Thirsk, N Yorks, YO7 3HE
*Activities:* Other manufacturing n.e.c.
*Shareholders:* John Keith Chalmers; John Keith Chalmers
*Officers:* Alexander John Chalmers, Secretary; Alexander John Chalmers [1980] Director/General Manager; Andrew Sinclair John Chalmers [1977] Director; Iain Robert John Chalmers [1970] Director; John Keith Chalmers [1936] Director/Builder; Deborah Anne Chalmers Groves [1969] Director/Hairdresser

**Wetherby Shade Card Company Limited**
*Incorporated:* 9 July 1959
*Net Worth:* £2,758,261 *Total Assets:* £3,754,946
*Registered Office:* Grangefield Industrial Estate, Pudsey, Leeds, LS28 6QJ
*Activities:* Other manufacturing n.e.c.
*Parent:* Tucker & Oxley Limited
*Officers:* Miranda Claire Oxley Tunbridge, Secretary; M/S Jana Maria Brazill [1959] Director; Bernard Patrick McCulla [1955] Director; Miranda Claire Oxley Tunbridge [1956] Director

**Wetherby Steeplechase Committee,Limited**
*Incorporated:* 30 July 1920 *Employees:* 33
*Net Worth:* £3,808,339 *Total Assets:* £10,453,694
*Registered Office:* The Racecourse, York Road, Wetherby, W Yorks, LS22 5EJ
*Activities:* Operation of sports facilities
*Officers:* John Francis Sanderson, Secretary; Laurence Kirkby [1954] Director/Racecourse Executive; Marc William Nelson [1960] Director; Clifford Graham Rowles Nicholson [1955] Director/Farming; John Francis Sanderson [1941] Director; Charles Andrew Warde-Aldam [1962] Director/Landowner

**Wetherby Stone Products Limited**
*Incorporated:* 9 August 1977 *Employees:* 19
*Net Worth:* £2,410,542 *Total Assets:* £3,478,117
*Registered Office:* Dalton Airfield Industrial Estate, Dalton, Thirsk, N Yorks, YO7 3HE
*Activities:* Other manufacturing n.e.c.
*Shareholders:* Alex John Chalmers; Alexander John Chalmers
*Officers:* Alexander John Chalmers, Secretary; Alexander John Chalmers [1980] Director; Iain Robert John Chalmers [1970] Director; John Keith Chalmers [1936] Director/Builder

**Wetherells Contracts Limited**
*Incorporated:* 10 August 1922 *Employees:* 34
*Net Worth:* £5,211,642 *Total Assets:* £6,314,174
*Registered Office:* 9 The Crescent, Selby, N Yorks, YO8 4PD
*Activities:* Manufacture of beer
*Major Shareholder:* Paul Russell Lucas Wetherell
*Officers:* Paul Russell Lucas Wetherell, Secretary; Gladys Margaret Wetherell [1934] Director/Married Woman; Mark Lucas Wetherell [1965] Director; Paul Russell Lucas Wetherell [1935] Director/Furnishing Contractor

**Weybourne Estates Limited**
*Incorporated:* 9 July 2002 *Employees:* 2
*Net Worth:* £702,595 *Total Assets:* £3,235,418
*Registered Office:* Safari, 14 Cherry Lane, Barrow upon Humber, N Lincs, DN19 7AX
*Activities:* Other letting and operating of own or leased real estate
*Major Shareholder:* Simon Duncan Weightman
*Officers:* Helen Clare Weightman, Secretary; Simon Duncan Weightman [1966] Director

**WFH Propco 1 Limited**
*Incorporated:* 25 September 2012
*Net Worth:* £5,503,563 *Total Assets:* £14,678,707
*Registered Office:* c/o Inspired Pet Nutrition Limited, Dalton Airfield, Dalton, Thirsk, N Yorks, YO7 3HE
*Activities:* Other letting and operating of own or leased real estate
*Parent:* Inspired Pet Nutrition Holdings Limited
*Officers:* Richard Harrington Page [1966] Managing Director; Thomas Grindrod Page [1968] Director

**WGL Bidco Limited**
*Incorporated:* 7 June 2017 *Employees:* 9
*Net Worth Deficit:* £4,000 *Total Assets:* £83,466,000
*Registered Office:* Imperial House, 1251 Hedon Road, Hull, HU9 5NA
*Activities:* Activities of other holding companies n.e.c.
*Officers:* Susan Allan [1971] Finance Director; Peter Munk [1963] Director/C.E.O [Danish]

**WGL Holdco Limited**
*Incorporated:* 7 June 2017 *Employees:* 7
*Net Worth Deficit:* £551,000 *Total Assets:* £49,934,000
*Registered Office:* Imperial House, 1251 Hedon Road, Hull, HU9 5NA
*Activities:* Activities of other holding companies n.e.c.
*Officers:* Susan Allan [1971] Finance Director; Peter Munk [1963] Director/C.E.O [Danish]; Peter Munk [1963] Director/C.E.O [Danish]

**WGL Midco Limited**
*Incorporated:* 7 June 2017 *Employees:* 7
*Net Worth:* £944,000 *Total Assets:* £50,888,000
*Registered Office:* Imperial House, 1251 Hedon Road, Hull, HU9 5NA
*Activities:* Activities of other holding companies n.e.c.
*Officers:* Susan Allan [1971] Finance Director; Peter Munk [1963] Director/C.E.O [Danish]

**Whaleys (Bradford) Limited**
*Incorporated:* 18 December 1930 *Employees:* 43
*Net Worth:* £5,309,238 *Total Assets:* £6,273,664
*Registered Office:* Harris Court, Great Horton, Bradford, W Yorks, BD7 4EQ
*Activities:* Wholesale of textiles
*Major Shareholder:* Peter James McIlvenny
*Officers:* Stephen Martin Baker, Secretary; James Frederick McIlvenny [1928] Director; Peter James McIlvenny [1953] Director; Rosemary Jane McLlvenny [1951] Director

**Wharfedale Homes Limited**
*Incorporated:* 11 June 1993 *Employees:* 8
*Net Worth:* £918,242 *Total Assets:* £4,787,084
*Registered Office:* Unit 5 Whitfield Business Park, Manse Lane, Knaresborough, N Yorks, HG5 8BS
*Activities:* Development of building projects
*Shareholders:* Christopher Allan Patmore; Michael Andrew Brown
*Officers:* Michael Andrew Brown, Secretary/Director; Michael Andrew Brown [1967] Director; Christopher Allan Patmore [1959] Director/Land Buyer

**Michael Wheatley Finance Limited**
*Incorporated:* 23 May 2014
*Net Worth:* £5,899,813 *Total Assets:* £6,730,185
*Registered Office:* Grays Mill House, 2 Beaconsfield Court, Garforth, Leeds, LS25 1QH
*Activities:* Financial intermediation not elsewhere classified
*Parent:* Micahel Wheatley Management Limited
*Officers:* Linda Snowden Wheatley, Secretary; Linda Snowden Wheatley [1951] Director; Michael Wheatley [1947] Director

**Michael Wheatley Management Limited**
*Incorporated:* 20 October 2010 *Employees:* 6
*Net Worth:* £7,157,796 *Total Assets:* £7,322,615
*Registered Office:* Grays Mill House, 2 Beaconsfield Court, Garforth, Leeds, LS25 1QH
*Activities:* Construction of commercial buildings
*Shareholders:* Linda Snowden Wheatley; Frederick Michael Wheatley
*Officers:* Linda Snowden Wheatley, Secretary; Frederick Michael Wheatley [1947] Director; Linda Snowden Wheatley [1951] Director

**Whetley Mills Limited**
*Incorporated:* 6 March 2002 *Employees:* 3
*Net Worth:* £3,043,577 *Total Assets:* £6,159,364
*Registered Office:* Ground Floor, St Paul's House, 23 Park Square South, Leeds, LS1 2ND
*Activities:* Other letting and operating of own or leased real estate
*Shareholder:* Mohammad Salmaan Hussain
*Officers:* Tahir Zeshan Hussain, Secretary; Mohammad Salmaan Hussain [1981] Director; Tahir Zeshan Hussain [1975] Director

**Whinlatter Energy Limited**
*Incorporated:* 15 October 2015
*Net Worth:* £1,839,046 *Total Assets:* £8,379,922
*Registered Office:* Canal Head North, Kendal, Cumbria, LA9 7BZ
*Activities:* Production of electricity
*Parent:* Gilkes Hydro Investments Limited
*Officers:* Charles William Nepean Crewdson [1964] Director; Carl Peter Crompton [1973] Director/Financial Executive

**John H. Whitaker (Holdings) Limited**
*Incorporated:* 2 September 1910 *Employees:* 26
*Net Worth:* £22,240,226 *Total Assets:* £28,863,348
*Registered Office:* Crown Dry Dock, Tower Street, Hull, HU9 1TY
*Activities:* Sea and coastal freight water transport
*Shareholders:* Bernard Michael Shimmin; Francis Henry Perry; William Charles Laughlin
*Officers:* Duncan McGahey, Secretary; Michael Alan Fish [1958] Financial Director; John Mark Whitaker [1960] Managing Director

**John H.Whitaker (Tankers) Limited**
*Incorporated:* 5 February 1927 *Employees:* 13
*Net Worth:* £1,277,397 *Total Assets:* £12,275,578
*Registered Office:* Crown Dry Dock, Tower Street, Hull, HU9 1TY
*Activities:* Sea and coastal freight water transport
*Parent:* John H. Whitaker (Holdings) Limited
*Officers:* Duncan McGahey, Secretary; Michael Alan Fish [1958] Financial Director; Ashley James Jenkins [1965] Director; John William Oaks [1954] Director; John Mark Whitaker [1960] Managing Director

**Whitaker and Leach Limited**
*Incorporated:* 19 February 2008 *Employees:* 55
*Net Worth:* £1,990,281 *Total Assets:* £4,460,693
*Registered Office:* Florence House, Chase Way, Bradford, W Yorks, BD5 8HW
*Activities:* Other construction installation
*Major Shareholder:* Robert Harvey Leach
*Officers:* Robert Harvey Leach, Secretary; Robert Harvey Leach [1965] Director; James Stuart Wood [1975] Director

**Whitaker Fibres Limited**
*Incorporated:* 28 October 1971 *Employees:* 65
*Net Worth:* £3,582,006 *Total Assets:* £9,763,839
*Registered Office:* Cashmere Works, Birksland Street, Bradford, W Yorks, BD3 9SX
*Activities:* Non-specialised wholesale trade
*Parent:* Curtis Wool Direct Limited
*Officers:* Daniel Isbecque, Secretary; Knud Peder Daugaard [1950] Director [Danish]; David Nigel Gisbourne [1961] Managing Director; Timothy Lloyd Holgate [1966] Director; Erik Steinar Hoeg [1976] Director [Norwegian]; Daniel Andre Isbecque [1964] Director; Kai Linnes [1953] Director [Norwegian]; Kristian Havard Saevik [1973] Director [Norwegian]

**Claire Whitaker Limited**
*Incorporated:* 2 November 1989 *Employees:* 1
*Net Worth:* £2,194,288 *Total Assets:* £3,560,849
*Registered Office:* Lingmoor, 16 Rutland Road, Harrogate, N Yorks, HG1 2PY
*Activities:* Other letting and operating of own or leased real estate
*Major Shareholder:* John James Whitaker
*Officers:* Roland John Whitaker, Secretary; John James Whitaker [1962] Director; Katherine Whitaker [1970] Director; Roland John Whitaker [1936] Director

**Whitakers Chocolates Limited**
*Incorporated:* 11 July 1961 *Employees:* 140
*Net Worth:* £3,736,612 *Total Assets:* £6,914,470
*Registered Office:* 85 Keighley Road, Skipton, N Yorks, BD23 2NA
*Activities:* Manufacture of cocoa and chocolate confectionery
*Shareholders:* Roland John Whitaker; William Reginald Whitaker
*Officers:* Sally Clare Thorpe, Secretary; Roland John Whitaker [1936] Director; William Reginald Whitaker [1960] Director

**Whitby Seafoods Limited**
*Incorporated:* 6 December 1984 *Employees:* 377
*Net Worth:* £10,150,195 *Total Assets:* £32,663,260
*Registered Office:* Fairfield Way, Whitby Business Park, Whitby, N Yorks, YO22 4PU
*Activities:* Processing and preserving of fish, crustaceans and molluscs
*Major Shareholder:* John Graham Whittle
*Officers:* Stephen Wormald, Secretary; Patrick William Farnsworth [1947] Director; Russell Scott MacDonald [1972] Supply Chain Director; Michael Murphy [1978] Director; Daniel John Whittle [1981] Managing Director; Edward James Whittle [1978] Operations Director; John Graham Whittle [1951] Director/Chairman; Laura Margaret Whittle [1976] Marketing and Sales Director; Dr David Alan Wormald [1947] Director; Stephen Wormald [1959] Finance Director

**White Cross Rubber Products Limited**
*Incorporated:* 23 March 1983 *Employees:* 19
*Net Worth:* £2,782,633 *Total Assets:* £3,326,903
*Registered Office:* White Cross, Lancaster, LA1 4XS
*Activities:* Manufacture of other rubber products
*Parent:* White Cross Holdings Limited
*Officers:* Irene Harper, Secretary; Karen Louise Bax [1974] Director; Irene Harper [1949] Director/Company Secretary; Philip Andrew Harper [1976] Director/Sales & Marketing Manager; Rodney Harper [1947] Director/Businessman

**WB White Foundry (Holdings) Limited**
*Incorporated:* 9 January 2008
*Net Worth:* £846,659 *Total Assets:* £4,710,018
*Registered Office:* c/o WB White Foundry Limited, Arthur Street, Armytage Road, Brighouse, W Yorks, HD6 1PY
*Activities:* Casting of iron
*Major Shareholder:* Micheal Earnshaw
*Officers:* Peter Fox, Secretary; Michael Earnshaw [1964] Managing Director; Peter Fox [1958] Finance Director; Paul Owens [1966] Commercial Director; Richard Francis Taylor [1962] Works Director

**W B White Foundry Limited**
*Incorporated:* 8 January 1985 *Employees:* 48
*Net Worth:* £4,578,905 *Total Assets:* £5,193,225
*Registered Office:* Arthur Street, Armytage Road, Brighouse, W Yorks, HD6 1PY
*Activities:* Casting of iron
*Major Shareholder:* Micheal Earnshaw
*Officers:* Peter Fox, Secretary; Michael Earnshaw [1964] Managing Director; Peter Fox [1958] Finance Director; Paul Owens [1966] Commercial Director; Richard Francis Taylor [1962] Works Director

**White Horse Machinery Limited**
*Incorporated:* 8 June 1992 *Employees:* 12
*Net Worth:* £3,400,037 *Total Assets:* £11,300,949
*Registered Office:* Unit 3 Fusion Point, Ash Lane, Garforth, Leeds, LS25 2GA
*Activities:* Wholesale of other machinery and equipment
*Major Shareholder:* Robin Anthony Vauvelle
*Officers:* Robin Anthony Vauvelle [1965] Managing Director; David William Watson [1963] Sales Director

**White House Livestock & Energy Limited**
*Incorporated:* 26 April 2012 *Employees:* 4
*Net Worth:* £249,865 *Total Assets:* £3,487,498
*Registered Office:* Thirtleby Grange, Thirtleby, Coniston, E Yorks, HU11 4LL
*Activities:* Other business support service activities n.e.c.
*Shareholders:* Alexandra Mary Wastling; Richard Allen Wastling
*Officers:* Alexandra Mary Wastling [1956] Director; Kathryn Joanne Wastling [1980] Director; Richard Allen Wastling [1954] Director/Farmer; William Richard Wastling [1977] Director/Farmer

**White Rose (Caravan Park) Limited**
*Incorporated:* 14 January 1972 *Employees:* 5
*Net Worth:* £2,628,315 *Total Assets:* £3,570,382
*Registered Office:* White Rose Caravan Park, Hutton Sessay, Thirsk, N Yorks, YO7 3BA
*Activities:* Public houses and bars
*Parent:* Caraluxe Limited
*Officers:* Karen Holden, Secretary; Karen Holden [1961] Director; Martyn Holden [1956] Director/Caravan Park Manager

**White Rose (Leeds) Limited**
*Incorporated:* 8 December 1993 *Employees:* 3
*Net Worth:* £138,027,392 *Total Assets:* £157,780,880
*Registered Office:* Millshaw, Leeds, LS11 8EG
*Activities:* Management of real estate on a fee or contract basis
*Parent:* Evans Property Holdings Limited
*Officers:* Robert Marshall, Secretary; Roderick Michael Evans [1962] Director; Paul Terence Millington [1962] Director/Accountant; James Oliver Pitt [1970] Director/Chartered Surveyor

**White Rose Finance Company Limited**
*Incorporated:* 16 December 1955
*Net Worth:* £5,733,244 *Total Assets:* £5,927,005
*Registered Office:* 137 Scalby Road, Scarborough, N Yorks, YO12 6TB
*Activities:* Financial intermediation not elsewhere classified
*Officers:* Barry Peter Swiers, Company Secretary; John Guthrie [1936] Director; Peter John Guthrie [1971] Director; Richard Guthrie [1972] Director; Martin Robson [1975] Director/Accountant

**White Rose Property Investments No.2 Limited**
*Incorporated:* 22 November 2006 *Employees:* 3
*Net Worth:* £1,631,999 *Total Assets:* £18,602,762
*Registered Office:* Millshaw, Leeds, LS11 8EG
*Activities:* Development of building projects
*Shareholders:* Michael White Evans; Sanne Group PLC; Helga Ingeborg Evans
*Officers:* Robert Marshall, Secretary; Roderick Michael Evans [1962] Director; Rob Marshall [1979] Director/Accountant; Paul Terence Millington [1962] Director/Accountant

**White Rose Residential Sales Limited**
*Incorporated:* 18 August 2014 *Employees:* 1
*Net Worth:* £37,279 *Total Assets:* £17,002,094
*Registered Office:* Equitable House, 55 Pellon Lane, Halifax, W Yorks, HX1 5SP
*Activities:* Development of building projects
*Shareholders:* Patricia Bernadette Brown; Stuart James Brown
*Officers:* Stuart James Brown [1956] Director/Builder

**Whiteghyll Limited**
*Incorporated:* 19 October 1990 *Employees:* 85
*Previous:* Whiteghyll Plastics Limited
*Net Worth:* £1,125,712 *Total Assets:* £3,139,814
*Registered Office:* 3 City Road, Bradford, W Yorks, BD8 8ER
*Activities:* Other manufacturing n.e.c.
*Shareholders:* Ruth Fiona Farmer; Kenneth Alan Wilson
*Officers:* Ruth Fiona Farmer, Secretary; John Dinnewell [1965] Director; Richard Egan [1970] Director; Ruth Fiona Farmer [1961] Director/Accountant; Kenneth Alan Wilson [1960] Managing Director

**H & C Whitehead (Holdings) Limited**
*Incorporated:* 19 December 2005 *Employees:* 1
*Net Worth:* £5,863,744 *Total Assets:* £10,016,459
*Registered Office:* Prospect Works, Bradford Road, Brighouse, W Yorks, HD6 4DJ
*Activities:* Activities of other holding companies n.e.c.
*Major Shareholder:* David Whitehead
*Officers:* David Whitehead [1966] Director

**H. & C. Whitehead Limited**
*Incorporated:* 5 May 1939 *Employees:* 24
*Net Worth:* £3,266,082 *Total Assets:* £4,258,964
*Registered Office:* Prospect Works, Bradford Road, Bailiff Bridge, Brighouse, W Yorks, HD6 4DJ
*Activities:* Finishing of textiles
*Major Shareholder:* David Whitehead
*Officers:* David Whitehead, Secretary/Managing Director; Simon Damian Cooper Pratt [1969] Director/Textile Finisher; David Whitehead [1966] Managing Director

**Whitelock Developments Limited**
*Incorporated:* 22 January 2007 *Employees:* 62
*Net Worth:* £2,092,691 *Total Assets:* £3,373,178
*Registered Office:* Whitelock Developments Ltd, Carleton Road, Skipton, N Yorks, BD23 3BT
*Activities:* Renting and leasing of agricultural machinery and equipment
*Major Shareholder:* John Colin Whitelock
*Officers:* Colin Whitelock, Secretary; John Colin Whitelock [1977] Director/Construction Worker

**Whitston Group Limited**
*Incorporated:* 27 February 2004 *Employees:* 2
*Net Worth:* £4,269,513 *Total Assets:* £4,291,239
*Registered Office:* Unit 5 Festival Building, Ashley Lane, Saltaire, Shipley, W Yorks, BD17 7DB
*Activities:* Activities of head offices
*Major Shareholder:* Justin Patrick Whitston
*Officers:* Patrick Whitston, Secretary; Justin Patrick Whitston [1972] Director

**M.H. Whittaker & Son Limited**
*Incorporated:* 11 October 1978
*Net Worth:* £2,107,909 *Total Assets:* £3,175,060
*Registered Office:* Harewell House, Dacre Banks, Harrogate, N Yorks, HG3 4HQ
*Activities:* Construction of domestic buildings
*Parent:* Toby Whittaker Holdings Limited
*Officers:* Toby Sam Whittaker, Secretary/Managing Director; Jacqueline Ena Jane Hall [1942] Director/Chairman; Toby Sam Whittaker [1967] Managing Director

**Whittaker's Jewellers Limited**
*Incorporated:* 19 January 2004
*Net Worth:* £7,487,648 *Total Assets:* £12,448,789
*Registered Office:* Carlton House, Bull Close Lane, Halifax, W Yorks, HX1 2EG
*Activities:* Other retail sale of new goods in specialised stores (not commercial art galleries and opticians)
*Shareholders:* Jonathan Lloyd Algernon Evans; Natalie Claire Howard
*Officers:* Natalie Claire Howard, Secretary; Jonathan Lloyd Algernon Evans [1973] Director/Sales Representative; Nigel Anthony Evans [1976] Director/Sales Person; Richard James Denham Evans [1974] Director/Sales Person; Natalie Claire Howard [1976] Director/Sales Person

**Whitworth Chemists Limited**
*Incorporated:* 3 August 1999 *Employees:* 298
*Net Worth:* £11,574,893 *Total Assets:* £23,874,412
*Registered Office:* 54a Sunderland Street, Tickhill, Doncaster, S Yorks, DN11 9QJ
*Activities:* Dispensing chemist in specialised stores
*Shareholders:* Dorothy Ann Bradley; Sally Elizabeth Vernon
*Officers:* Dorothy Ann Bradley, Secretary; Jan Barend Badenhorst [1976] Director/Superintendent Pharmacist [British/South African]; Dorothy Ann Bradley [1941] Director; Richard Watson Bradley [1966] Managing Director; Sally Elizabeth Vernon [1973] Director/Fashion Manager

**Whole Crop Marketing Limited**
*Incorporated:* 23 July 2008 *Employees:* 12
*Net Worth:* £1,273,850 *Total Assets:* £3,847,304
*Registered Office:* Manor Farm Office, Main Street, Kirkburn, Driffield, E Yorks, YO25 9DU
*Activities:* Agents selling agricultural raw materials, livestock, textile raw materials and semi-finished goods
*Officers:* David Kenneth Burks [1968] Director/Produce Buyer; Joseph William Dewhirst [1978] Director/Farmer; Ian William Dowson [1948] Director/Farmer; Philip Lachlan Dunn [1965] Director/Business Advisor Farmer; Benjamin Hargreaves [1975] Director/Farmer; Robert Kendall [1956] Director/Farmer; Mark Laurence Robson [1966] Director/Farmer; Andrew Mark Soanes [1965] Director/Farmer; Alan Mark Tomlinson [1962] Director/Trading Manager; Simon Frederick Ullyott [1968] Director/Farmer

**Whymar Limited**
*Incorporated:* 21 March 2002 *Employees:* 1
*Net Worth:* £5,471,753 *Total Assets:* £7,070,277
*Registered Office:* Brake House, 72 Middleton Lane, Middleton St George, Darlington, Co Durham, DL2 1AD
*Activities:* Development of building projects
*Major Shareholder:* John McCardle
*Officers:* Gillian Frances McArdle, Secretary/Accounts Clerk; John McArdle [1953] Director/Solicitor

**Wickframe Limited**
*Incorporated:* 27 April 1984
*Net Worth:* £3,018,078 *Total Assets:* £3,693,858
*Registered Office:* 43 North Park Grove, Leeds, LS8 1EW
*Activities:* Other letting and operating of own or leased real estate
*Officers:* Gregory Charles George Kavazy, Secretary; Helen Claire Hartley [1962] Director; Patra Helenie Heaton [1966] Director; Gregory Charles George Kavazy [1965] Director; Jason Kavazy [1965] Director; Paul Kavazy [1939] Director and Secretary

**H. Wicks (Lindal) Limited**
*Incorporated:* 22 March 1963 *Employees:* 31
*Net Worth:* £4,122,969 *Total Assets:* £7,584,210
*Registered Office:* Sowerby Woods Business Park, Scarth Road, Barrow in Furness, Cumbria, LA14 4QR
*Activities:* Collection of non-hazardous waste
*Parent:* Wicks Group Limited
*Officers:* Jayne Ann Wicks, Secretary; David Robert Wicks [1972] Director; Jayne Ann Wicks [1977] Finance Director

**The Widd Group Limited**
*Incorporated:* 17 August 1998 *Employees:* 62
*Net Worth:* £3,198,748 *Total Assets:* £5,676,439
*Registered Office:* Maserati House, Gelderd Road, Leeds, LS12 1AS
*Activities:* Manufacture of electric lighting equipment
*Parent:* W P Holdings Limited
*Officers:* Simon Fortune, Secretary; Simon John Fortune [1974] Director/Accountant; Gary Williams [1966] Director

**The Wilberforce Trust**
*Incorporated:* 4 June 2001 *Employees:* 93
*Net Worth:* £11,299,631 *Total Assets:* £11,492,402
*Registered Office:* Wilberforce House, 49 North Moor Road, Huntington, York, YO32 9QN
*Activities:* Other accommodation
*Officers:* Philippa Ann Crowther, Secretary; Colin Paul Aspinall [1974] Director/Finance Manager; Stephen James Cluderay [1951] Director/Fire Safety Consultant; Simon Jonathan Cowell [1965] Director/Solicitor; Keith Goodey [1947] Director/Retired Chartered Accountant; Elizabeth Stewart Grierson [1957] Director/Management Consultant; Sue Hawkesworth [1964] Director/Operational Regional Manager; John Patrick Kennedy [1966] Director/Consultant in Care Services; Keith Larcum [1953] Director/Retired

**Wilbraham Securities LLP**
*Incorporated:* 28 March 2008
*Net Worth:* £3,004,776 *Total Assets:* £3,811,011
*Registered Office:* Ferriby Hall, High Street, North Ferriby, E Yorks, HU14 3JP
*Officers:* Rachel Madelaine Glover [1982] Member; Dominic Matthew Wilbraham [1987] Member; Philip Neville Wilbraham [1958] Member; Rosemary Elizabeth Wilbraham [1986] Member; Samuel Benjamin Wilbraham [1984] Member

**Wilby (Group) Limited**
*Incorporated:* 3 November 2011
*Net Worth:* £1,330,023 *Total Assets:* £3,768,314
*Registered Office:* Rossington's Business Park, West Carr Road, Retford, Notts, DN22 7SW
*Activities:* Activities of insurance agents and brokers
*Parent:* PIB Group Limited
*Officers:* Richard Douglas Blackburn [1969] Director/Insurance Broker; Ryan Christopher Brown [1973] Director; Brendan James McManus [1959] Director; Michael Richard Andrew Shaw [1972] Director; Mark Studholme [1962] Director

**Wilby Limited**
*Incorporated:* 15 March 1991
*Net Worth:* £2,472,194 *Total Assets:* £3,744,081
*Registered Office:* Rossington's Business Park, West Carr Road, Retford, Notts, DN22 7SW
*Activities:* Activities of insurance agents and brokers
*Parent:* Wilby Holdings Ltd
*Officers:* Richard Douglas Blackburn [1969] Director/Insurance Broker; Ryan Christopher Brown [1973] Director; Jennifer Burton [1977] Director/Insurance Executive; Brendan James McManus [1959] Director; Michael Richard Andrew Shaw [1972] Director/Insurance Broker; Mark Studholme [1962] Director/Manager

**J.Wild (Confectioners) Limited**
*Incorporated:* 20 July 1939 *Employees:* 226
*Net Worth:* £3,058,044 *Total Assets:* £5,715,947
*Registered Office:* The Bakery, Millennium Business Park, Station Road, Steeton, Keighley, W Yorks, BD20 6RB
*Activities:* Manufacture of bread; manufacture of fresh pastry goods and cakes
*Shareholder:* Sheila Carolyn Bateman
*Officers:* Sheila Carolyn Bateman, Secretary; Sheila Carolyn Bateman [1943] Director/Baker; Elizabeth Marjorie Kassapian [1934] Director/Baker

**Wild Life Group Limited**
*Incorporated:* 11 March 2008 *Employees:* 239
*Previous:* Yorkshire Wildlife Park Limited
*Net Worth:* £12,435,870 *Total Assets:* £20,010,396
*Registered Office:* Brockholes Farm, Brockholes Lane, Branton, Doncaster, S Yorks, DN3 3NH
*Activities:* Botanical and zoological gardens and nature reserves activities
*Shareholder:* Stephen Gregory Minion
*Officers:* Kate Elizabeth Minion, Secretary; John Maurice Minion [1976] Director; Kate Elizabeth Minion [1973] Company Secretary/Director; Stephen Gregory Minion [1946] Director/Engineer; Christopher Rudgard Webster [1957] Director; Cheryl Barbara Williams [1962] Director/Marketing Manager

**J P Wild Limited**
*Incorporated:* 3 August 2005 *Employees:* 36
*Net Worth:* £2,592,316 *Total Assets:* £7,406,808
*Registered Office:* Ingram Road, Holbeck, Leeds, LS11 9RQ
*Activities:* Development of building projects
*Shareholders:* Joanne Kelly; John Paul Doherty
*Officers:* John Paul Doherty, Secretary; Shaun Terence Chadwick [1974] Director; John Paul Doherty [1976] Director; Diarmaid Patrick Kelly [1971] Director [Irish]; Andrew James Shaw [1973] Director

**The Wilf Ward Family Trust**
*Incorporated:* 17 March 2011 *Employees:* 891
*Net Worth:* £21,795,796 *Total Assets:* £22,808,056
*Registered Office:* Westgate House, 5 Westgate, Pickering, N Yorks, YO18 8BA
*Activities:* Residential care activities for learning difficulties, mental health and substance abuse
*Officers:* Catherine Susan Sell, Secretary; James Adamson [1954] Director/Retired; Helen Marie Burke [1960] Director/Consultant; William Linton Denness [1938] Director; Stephanie Yvonne Lacey [1975] Director; Andrew Edwin Marson [1969] Director; Laura Eve Rawnsley [1954] Director/Retired; Christopher George Sellers [1968] Director; Nicholas John Shaw [1957] Director/Non-Practising Solicitor; Malcolm Bruce Smith [1946] Director; Professor Dianne Marie Willcocks [1945] Director/Leadership Consultant

**Wilfreda Luxury Coaches Limited**
*Incorporated:* 28 October 1949 *Employees:* 50
*Net Worth:* £1,647,790 *Total Assets:* £5,430,460
*Registered Office:* The Old Parsonage, North Road, Torworth, Retford, Notts, DN22 8NY
*Activities:* Other passenger land transport
*Shareholder:* Susan Margaret Scholey
*Officers:* Susan Margaret Scholey, Secretary; Nigel Graham Haxby [1968] Director/Engineer; Philip Geoffrey Haxby [1966] Director/Salesman; Peter Antony Scholey [1981] Director; Susan Margaret Scholey [1945] Director

**Wilkes Properties (Wakefield) Limited**
*Incorporated:* 8 February 1960 *Employees:* 1
*Net Worth:* £6,345,090 *Total Assets:* £13,367,784
*Registered Office:* Spa Street, Ossett, Wakefield, W Yorks, WF5 0HP
*Activities:* Other letting and operating of own or leased real estate
*Major Shareholder:* Peter Gerald Wilkes
*Officers:* Nicholas James Marsden Wilkes, Secretary; Nicholas James Marsden Wilkes [1982] Director; Peter Generald Wilkes [1946] Director

**Wilkes Vending Services Limited**
*Incorporated:* 9 November 1961 *Employees:* 80
*Net Worth:* £7,056,573 *Total Assets:* £7,798,800
*Registered Office:* Spa Street, Ossett, Wakefield, W Yorks, WF5 0HP
*Activities:* Non-specialised wholesale trade
*Major Shareholder:* Peter Gerald Wilkes
*Officers:* Peter Generald Wilkes, Secretary; Mark Booth [1962] Director/Service Manager; Peter Generald Wilkes [1946] Director/Vending Machine Proprietor; Stuart Jeffery Worth [1982] Director

**Wilkin Chapman LLP**
*Incorporated:* 12 February 2009 *Employees:* 354
*Net Worth:* £6,689,075 *Total Assets:* £16,247,229
*Registered Office:* Cartergate House, 26 Chantry Lane, Grimsby, N E Lincs, DN31 2LJ
*Officers:* James Mark Carlton [1960] Member; Andrew David Holt [1965] Member; Craig John McKay [1959] Member; Lesley Archer [1969] LLP Member; Edward James Atkin [1979] LLP Member; Flora Mary Bennett [1961] LLP Member; Lisa Michelle Boileau [1969] LLP Member; Paul Bowden [1984] LLP Member; Ruth Brewin [1959] LLP Member; Joshua Lee Briggs [1985] LLP Member; Andrew Peter Burnett [1975] LLP Member; Tean Miles Butcher [1966] LLP Member; Katie Jacqueline Davies [1982] LLP Member; Matthew Thomas George Dix [1977] LLP Member; Jane Eatock [1966] LLP Member; Russell John Eke [1967] LLP Member; Richard John Frogson [1966] LLP Member; Elizabeth Gilliatt [1981] LLP Member; Jonathan Thornes Goolden [1965] LLP Member; Christopher Richard Grocock [1968] LLP Member; Peter Hanson [1967] LLP Member; Catherine Elizabeth Harris [1974] LLP Member; Nikki Ann Hawkins [1984] LLP Member; Steven Paul Hennegan [1973] LLP Member; Imogen Fay Holmes [1974] LLP Member; Richard William Bruno Houltby [1958] LLP Member; Rupert Mark Houltby [1959] LLP Member; Lisa Jane Howes [1971] LLP Member; Jonathan James Judge [1971] LLP Member; James Michael Lloyd [1973] LLP Member; Adam Thomas Marham [1977] LLP Member; James Richard Marsden [1985] LLP Member; Claire Elizabeth Parker [1971] LLP Member; Jonty Sebastian Pearson [1982] LLP Member; Rachael Louise Perry [1981] LLP Member; Sharon Elaine Plumtree [1967] LLP Member; Mark Robinson [1966] LLP Member; Nasim Sharf [1970] LLP Member; Ian Sherburn [1969] LLP Member; Wendy Christina Spalding-Siracusa [1964] LLP Member; Michael James Squirrell [1984] LLP Member; Jonathan Edward Stork [1980] LLP Member; Oliver Richard Tasker [1985] LLP Member; Mark Taylor [1968] LLP Member; Teresa Lynne Thomas [1973] LLP Member; Jonathan Paul West [1972] LLP Member

**V Wilkins & Sons Limited**
*Incorporated:* 27 March 2014 *Employees:* 13
*Net Worth:* £1,761,899 *Total Assets:* £3,508,883
*Registered Office:* Carr Farm, Carr Road, Ulceby, N Lincs, DN39 6TX
*Activities:* Growing of cereals (except rice), leguminous crops and oil seeds
*Major Shareholder:* Richard Paul Wilkins
*Officers:* Richard Paul Wilkins [1971] Director/Farmer; Richard Alan Wilkins [1946] Director/Farmer; Sarah Jane Wilkins [1972] Director/Farmer

**Wilkinson Building Co.(Leeds) Limited**
*Incorporated:* 19 July 1951 *Employees:* 3
*Net Worth:* £34,648,884 *Total Assets:* £36,872,400
*Registered Office:* The Croft, 2 Breary Lane, Bramhope, Leeds, LS16 9AE
*Activities:* Development of building projects
*Shareholders:* Alistair Mark Pullan; J Pullan & Sons Ltd
*Officers:* Margaret Josephine Pullan, Secretary; Alistair Mark Pullan [1959] Director/Builder; Margaret Josephine Pullan [1956] Director [British/Canadian]

**Willerby Group Limited**
*Incorporated:* 27 June 2003
*Previous:* Scaid Investments Limited
*Net Worth:* £88,026,000 *Total Assets:* £103,438,000
*Registered Office:* Imperial House, 1251 Hedon Road, Hull, HU9 5NA
*Activities:* Activities of head offices
*Parent:* WGL Bidco Limited
*Officers:* Susan Allan, Secretary; Susan Allan [1971] Finance Director; Peter Munk [1963] Director [Danish]

**Willerby Group Property Limited**
*Incorporated:* 4 April 1995
*Previous:* Bankside Properties Limited
*Net Worth:* £22,840,000 *Total Assets:* £24,912,000
*Registered Office:* Imperial House, 1251 Hedon Road, Hull, HU9 5NA
*Activities:* Other letting and operating of own or leased real estate
*Parent:* Burndene Investments Limited
*Officers:* Susan Allan, Secretary; Susan Allan [1971] Finance Director; Peter Munk [1963] Director [Danish]

**Willerby Limited**
*Incorporated:* 13 May 1944 *Employees:* 1,007
*Previous:* Willerby Holiday Homes Ltd.
*Net Worth:* £15,812,000 *Total Assets:* £48,543,000
*Registered Office:* Imperial House, 1251 Hedon Road, Hull, HU9 5NA
*Activities:* Manufacture of caravans
*Parent:* Burndene Investments Limited
*Officers:* Susan Allan, Secretary; Susan Allan [1971] Finance Director; Alan Bateman [1961] Technical Director; Clifford Kenneth Beal [1966] Production Director; Kirsten Mary Bolton [1970] Marketing Director; Keith Allan Holland [1959] Sales Director; Peter Munk [1963] Director [Danish]

**Willerby Manor Hotels Limited**
*Incorporated:* 16 September 1965 *Employees:* 125
*Net Worth:* £1,359,235 *Total Assets:* £5,274,239
*Registered Office:* House of Townend, Wyke Way, Melton, North Ferriby, E Yorks, HU14 3BQ
*Activities:* Hotels and similar accommodation
*Parent:* J Townend & Sons (Hull) Ltd
*Officers:* Angus Joseph Whitehead, Secretary; David Henry Roberts [1944] Director; Alexandra Louise Townend [1967] Director/Hotel General Manager; Jennifer Ann Townend [1940] Director; John Charles Townend [1965] Director; Angus Joseph Whitehead [1965] Director/Chartered Accountant

**Willerby Wold Piggeries Limited**
*Incorporated:* 9 December 1964 *Employees:* 34
*Net Worth:* £8,019,373 *Total Assets:* £22,415,580
*Registered Office:* Willerby Pig Farm, Staxton, Scarborough, N Yorks, YO12 4SN
*Activities:* Raising of swine and pigs
*Shareholders:* Michael Bradley; Patricia Lloyd Bradley
*Officers:* Patricia Lloyd Bradley, Secretary; David Howard Bradley [1972] Director; Michael Bradley [1942] Director/Pig Breeder; Patricia Lloyd Bradley [1946] Director/Company Secretary; Richard Andrew Bradley [1969] Director

**William's Den Limited**
*Incorporated:* 9 April 2015 *Employees:* 43
*Net Worth Deficit:* £326,928 *Total Assets:* £4,767,591
*Registered Office:* Castle Farm, Wold Hill, North Cave, Brough, E Yorks, HU15 2LS
*Activities:* Other amusement and recreation activities n.e.c.
*Shareholders:* Christian Henton James Carver; Victoria Margaret Carver
*Officers:* Christian Henton James Carver [1965] Director; Victoria Margaret Carver [1971] Director

**G. Williams & Co. (Grain) Limited**
*Incorporated:* 9 April 1996 *Employees:* 12
*Net Worth:* £2,345,158 *Total Assets:* £5,003,070
*Registered Office:* Beaufort House, Amelia Court, Swanton Close, Retford, Notts, DN22 7HJ
*Activities:* Wholesale of grain, unmanufactured tobacco, seeds and animal feeds
*Shareholders:* Geoffrey Williams; Anthea Margaret Williams
*Officers:* Anthea Margaret Williams, Secretary; David Anthony Cobb [1961] Director/Accountant; Geoffrey Williams [1948] Sales Director

**J.R. Williams & Sons Limited**
*Incorporated:* 8 October 1976 *Employees:* 5
*Net Worth:* £6,137,340 *Total Assets:* £8,860,664
*Registered Office:* Daisy Hill Farm, Burstwick, E Yorks, HU12 9HE
*Activities:* Growing of cereals (except rice), leguminous crops and oil seeds
*Major Shareholder:* Richard Tudor Williams
*Officers:* Richard Tudor Williams, Secretary/Farmer; John Kendall Williams [1987] Director/Farmer; Owen Williams [1992] Director/Farmer; Richard Tudor Williams [1957] Director/Farmer; Thomas Robert Williams [1990] Director/Farmer

**W. & J. Williams (Haulage) Limited**
*Incorporated:* 17 August 1990 *Employees:* 72
*Net Worth:* £978,984 *Total Assets:* £5,538,504
*Registered Office:* 100 Dealburn Road, Low Moor, Bradford, BD12 0RG
*Activities:* Freight transport by road
*Shareholders:* David Clarke; Joan Clarke
*Officers:* David Clarke, Secretary; David Clarke [1964] Director/Haulage Contractor; Joan Clarke [1966] Transport Director

**Martin Williams (Hull) Limited**
*Incorporated:* 8 May 2003 *Employees:* 126
*Net Worth:* £2,147,896 *Total Assets:* £10,197,229
*Registered Office:* Ellifoot Lane, Burstwick, E Yorks, HU12 9EF
*Activities:* Manufacture of other transport equipment n.e.c.
*Major Shareholder:* Martin James Howard Williams
*Officers:* Patricia Mary Williams, Secretary; Christopher Martin Williams [1981] Director/Vehicle Sprayer; Martin James Howard Williams [1948] Director/Motor Body Repairer; Nicholas James Williams [1983] Director/Panel Beater

**Henry Williams Limited**
*Incorporated:* 8 December 1988 *Employees:* 120
*Net Worth:* £4,277,320 *Total Assets:* £6,575,311
*Registered Office:* Henry Williams Group Ltd, Dodsworth Street, Darlington, Co Durham, DL1 2NJ
*Activities:* Forging, pressing, stamping and roll-forming of metal; powder metallurgy
*Officers:* Derek Neil, Secretary; Christine Ames [1962] Director; David Brookes [1977] Director; Steven Adrian Cotton [1964] Sales & Marketing Director; Robert James Dilley [1972] Director; Robert Howard Stapleton Dilley [1946] Director/Chairman; Alan Herron [1964] Director; Andrew John Lazenby [1965] Director; Derek Neil [1964] Financial Director; Micheal Wilson [1962] Director

**Dennis Williams Limited**
*Incorporated:* 22 December 1955 *Employees:* 96
*Net Worth:* £2,445,041 *Total Assets:* £6,319,750
*Registered Office:* 9 Kingsmark Freeway, Euroway Trading Estate, Bradford, W Yorks, BD12 7HW
*Activities:* Wholesale of perfume and cosmetics
*Major Shareholder:* Pamela Briony Lees
*Officers:* Pamela Briony Lees, Secretary; Anthony Richard Lees [1946] Director; Arron Richard Lees [1982] Operations Director; Pamela Briony Lees [1959] Managing Director

**Williamsons Solicitors Limited**
*Incorporated:* 1 December 2009 *Employees:* 131
*Net Worth:* £4,086,960 *Total Assets:* £5,242,581
*Registered Office:* 45 Lowgate, Hull, HU1 1EN
*Activities:* Solicitors
*Shareholders:* Sarah Jane Clubley; William Ogden Waddington
*Officers:* Brian Cook, Secretary; Sarah Jane Clubley [1966] Director/Solicitor; Brian George Cook [1957] Director/Company Secretary; Jane Frances Cousins [1977] Director; Nicholas William Gray [1974] Director; James Edmund Suthers [1966] Director/Solicitors; Willam Ogden Waddington [1954] Director/Solicitor

**Willis of Skipton Limited**
*Incorporated:* 3 March 1986
*Net Worth:* £2,587,893 *Total Assets:* £3,133,318
*Registered Office:* Gargrave Road, Stirton, Skipton, N Yorks, BD23 1UD
*Activities:* Operation of warehousing and storage facilities for land transport activities
*Shareholder:* Daniel Jonathan Willis
*Officers:* Shaun Michael Anson, Secretary/Director; Jane Rachel Anson [1956] Director/Clerk; Shaun Michael Anson [1951] Director; Daniel Jonathan Willis [1978] Director

**Willoughby (891) Limited**
*Incorporated:* 6 May 2016
*Net Worth:* £213,569 *Total Assets:* £3,184,428
*Registered Office:* Westfield Court, Lower Wortley Road, Leeds, LS12 4PX
*Activities:* Activities of head offices
*Shareholders:* Jonathan Miles Prutton; Philip Horsnall
*Officers:* Colin Fitton [1966] Director; Philip Horsnall [1961] Director; Jonathan Miles Prutton [1962] Director

**Tom Willoughby Limited**
*Incorporated:* 25 September 1961 *Employees:* 100
*Net Worth:* £1,530,106 *Total Assets:* £5,250,783
*Registered Office:* Construction House, Northallerton, N Yorks, DL7 8ED
*Activities:* Development of building projects
*Shareholder:* Susan Bridget Greenwell
*Officers:* Derek John Greenwell, Secretary; Paul Blades [1963] Director; Derek John Greenwell [1948] Director Company Secretary; William Darren Johnson [1969] Director; Keith Brian Noddings [1972] Finance Director

**Willow Developments (Howden) Ltd**
*Incorporated:* 4 September 2015 *Employees:* 10
*Net Worth:* £440,426 *Total Assets:* £5,229,335
*Registered Office:* Whitby Court, Abbey Road, Shepley, Huddersfield, W Yorks, HD8 8EL
*Activities:* Construction of domestic buildings
*Shareholders:* Wayne Brandon Butler; Nicholas Lee Palmer
*Officers:* Wayne Brandon Butler [1968] Director; Nicholas Lee Palmer [1978] Director

**Willow Grove Properties Limited**
*Incorporated:* 8 September 1992 *Employees:* 4
*Net Worth:* £2,251,065 *Total Assets:* £3,115,421
*Registered Office:* The Granary, School Lane, Wike, Leeds, LS17 9PD
*Activities:* Other letting and operating of own or leased real estate
*Shareholders:* Anthony Walter Reynolds; Judith Ingrid Reynolds
*Officers:* Judith Ingrid Reynolds, Secretary/Director; Anthony Walter Reynolds [1942] Director; Emma Louise Reynolds [1978] Property Director; Judith Ingrid Reynolds [1944] Director

**Willow Properties (Yorkshire) Limited**
*Incorporated:* 13 February 2015 *Employees:* 5
*Net Worth:* £27,077,822 *Total Assets:* £28,414,364
*Registered Office:* The Business Centre, Deanhurst Park, Gelderd Road, Gildersome, Leeds, LS27 7LG
*Activities:* Other letting and operating of own or leased real estate
*Shareholders:* Eve Williamson; Robert Williamson
*Officers:* Eve Williamson, Secretary; Tamara Dawn Beckwith [1964] Director; Jonathan Stuart Holmes [1975] Director/Property Manager; Eve Williamson [1946] Director/Property Developer; Paul Adam Milton Williamson [1968] Director; Robert Williamson [1945] Director/Property Developer

**Willowbank Holiday Park Limited**
*Incorporated:* 26 June 1998 *Employees:* 11
*Net Worth:* £2,549,427 *Total Assets:* £3,723,613
*Registered Office:* Ash House, Catterick, Richmond, N Yorks, DL10 7PH
*Activities:* Recreational vehicle parks, trailer parks and camping grounds
*Shareholders:* Richard Henry Darling; Judith Anne Darling
*Officers:* Judith Anne Darling, Secretary/Farmer; Judith Anne Darling [1946] Director/Farmer; Richard Henry Darling [1943] Director/Caravan Park Operator; Richard Simon Darling [1971] Director/IT Manager

**Wilson & Co. (Motor Sales) Limited**
*Incorporated:* 28 January 1998 *Employees:* 239
*Net Worth:* £4,925,780 *Total Assets:* £21,434,108
*Registered Office:* Hewitts Avenue, Hewitts Circus, Grimsby, N E Lincs, DN36 4SE
*Activities:* Sale of new cars and light motor vehicles
*Parent:* RJTK Investments Ltd
*Officers:* Marcus Peter McVeigh, Secretary; Marcus Peter McVeigh [1971] Finance Director; Robin Wilson [1957] Managing Director; Thomas Robin Wilson [1987] Director

**L.& W.Wilson (Endmoor) Limited**
*Incorporated:* 16 June 1972 *Employees:* 126
*Net Worth:* £5,066,136 *Total Assets:* £11,448,025
*Registered Office:* Shiralee, Endmoor, Kendal, Cumbria, LA8 0HL
*Activities:* Construction of commercial buildings
*Shareholders:* Betty Hayes; Alan Wilson
*Officers:* Alan Wilson, Secretary; Betty Hayes [1932] Director; Alan Wilson [1957] Director/Haulage Contractor

**Wilson Power Solutions Group Limited**
*Incorporated:* 11 July 2012 *Employees:* 47
*Net Worth:* £7,290,106 *Total Assets:* £12,520,474
*Registered Office:* Westland Works, Westland Square, Leeds, LS11 5SS
*Activities:* Manufacture of electric motors, generators and transformers
*Shareholders:* Erika Milne Hudson; Simon Richard Hudson
*Officers:* Martin Baum [1964] Finance Director; Erika Milne Hudson [1979] Director; Colin Wilson [1948] Director; Dennis Richard Wilson [1947] Director; Simon Richard Wilson [1967] Director

**Wilson Power Solutions Limited**
*Incorporated:* 25 April 1994 *Employees:* 47
*Net Worth:* £6,796,758 *Total Assets:* £10,373,076
*Registered Office:* Westland Works, Westland Square, Leeds, LS11 5SS
*Activities:* Manufacture of electric motors, generators and transformers
*Parent:* Wilson Power Solutions Group Limited
*Officers:* Dennis Richard Wilson, Secretary/CD; Martin Baum [1964] Finance Director; Erika Milne Hudson [1979] Director/Business Development; Colin Wilson [1948] Director; Dennis Richard Wilson [1947] Director/CD/Secretary; Simon Richard Wilson [1967] Director

**Wiltel Limited**
*Incorporated:* 13 July 1966 *Employees:* 67
*Net Worth:* £1,962,504 *Total Assets:* £4,189,114
*Registered Office:* Hyltons Restaurant, Ash Street, Bowness on Windermere, Cumbria, LA23 3EB
*Activities:* Licenced restaurants
*Shareholders:* Ian Parkinson Wilson; Kevin Wilson
*Officers:* Matthew Kevin Moore Wilson, Secretary; David Carl Wilson [1975] Director; Ian Parkinson Wilson [1944] Director/Restaurateur; Kevin Wilson [1943] Director/Restaurateur; Matthew Kevin Moore Wilson [1973] Director/Manager; Richard Ian Wilson [1978] Director; Stephen Terrence Wilson [1970] Director/Manager

**Wilton Cobley (Holdings) Limited**
*Incorporated:* 9 March 2016
*Net Worth:* £550 *Total Assets:* £3,053,056
*Registered Office:* 201a Heneage Road, Grimsby, N E Lincs, DN32 9JW
*Activities:* Activities of construction holding companies
*Shareholders:* Robert Kenneth Ward; Carl Alan Swaby
*Officers:* Carl Alan Swaby [1973] Director; Charlotte Swaby [1975] Director; Emma Ward [1987] Director; Robert Kenneth Ward [1978] Director

**Wilton Cobley Limited**
*Incorporated:* 17 September 1963 *Employees:* 42
*Net Worth:* £3,303,450 *Total Assets:* £4,790,152
*Registered Office:* 201a Heneage Road, Grimsby, N E Lincs, DN32 9JW
*Activities:* Joinery installation
*Shareholders:* Robert Kenneth Ward; Carl Alan Swaby
*Officers:* Carl Alan Swaby [1973] Director; Charlotte Swaby [1975] Director; Emma Ward [1987] Director; Robert Kenneth Ward [1978] Director

**Wilton Developments Limited**
*Incorporated:* 20 September 2005 *Employees:* 5
*Net Worth:* £10,742,992 *Total Assets:* £11,462,232
*Registered Office:* 10 South Parade, Leeds, LS1 5QS
*Activities:* Development of building projects
*Shareholders:* Elizabeth Moore; Jonathan Richard Moore
*Officers:* Richard William Dawson [1966] Director/Chartered Accountant; Angela Louise James [1960] Director; Jason Paul Stowe [1970] Director/Chartered Surveyor; Paul Daniel Turner [1971] Director/Solicitor

**Winander Group Holdings Limited**
*Incorporated:* 19 December 1995 *Employees:* 171
*Net Worth:* £14,473,079 *Total Assets:* £24,012,318
*Registered Office:* Winander House, Glebe Road, Bowness on Windermere, Cumbria, LA23 3HE
*Activities:* Activities of head offices
*Officers:* Andrew James Simon, Secretary; William John Bewley [1945] Director; John Brockbank [1952] Director; Thomas Richard Cowherd [1933] Director; Martin Raymond Dennison [1967] Director/Engineer; Ernest George Fallowfield [1941] Director; Maureen Ann Fleming [1944] Director; Angela Rosemary Kaye Howson [1955] Director; Dawn Margaret Jackson [1987] Director; Leslie Micklethwaite [1943] Director/Business Manager; Antony Jon Rothwell [1948] Director; Sheila Sproat [1930] Director; James Roy Thompson [1947] Director; Evelyn Twaddle [1947] Director/Guest House Proprietor; Nigel Wilkinson [1964] Director/Chartered Accountant; Sharon Gillian Wilkinson [1963] Director/Nurse

**Winander Leisure Limited**
*Incorporated:* 4 October 2006 *Employees:* 22
*Net Worth:* £5,717,409 *Total Assets:* £11,578,051
*Registered Office:* Winander House, Glebe Road, Bowness on Windermere, Cumbria, LA23 3HE
*Activities:* Activities of head offices
*Parent:* Winander Group Holdings Limited
*Officers:* Andrew James Simon, Secretary; William John Bewley [1945] Director/Boat Proprietor; John Brockbank [1952] Director; Thomas Richard Cowherd [1933] Director/Boat Proprietor; Ernest George Fallowfield [1941] Director/Boat Proprietor; Leslie Micklethwaite [1943] Director/Boat Proprietor; Antony Jon Rothwell [1948] Director/Boat Proprietor; Andrew James Simon [1980] Director/Chartered Accountant; James Roy Thompson [1947] Director/Boat Proprietor; Nigel Wilkinson [1964] Director/Chartered Accountant; Keith Robert Wood [1955] Director

**Winder Power Holdings Limited**
*Incorporated:* 4 October 2012 *Employees:* 112
*Net Worth:* £3,030,926 *Total Assets:* £12,482,617
*Registered Office:* Grangefield House, Richardshaw Road, Pudsey, Leeds, LS28 6QS
*Activities:* Activities of production holding companies
*Shareholders:* Enterprise Ventures (General Partner EV Growth) Limited; Enterprise Ventures Limited
*Officers:* Laurence Robert MacKenzie [1961] Director/Chartered Accountant; Paul David Matthews [1968] Director/Manager; Harold McCracken [1949] Director; Andrew Paul Pinkney [1970] Director; Wayne Leslie Thomas [1969] Director/Chartered Accountant

**Winder Power Limited**
*Incorporated:* 9 May 2005 *Employees:* 112
*Net Worth:* £4,933,414 *Total Assets:* £12,564,834
*Registered Office:* Grangefield House, Richardshaw Road, Pudsey, Leeds, LS28 6QS
*Activities:* Manufacture of electric motors, generators and transformers
*Shareholders:* Enterprise Ventures Limited; Enterprise Ventures (General Partner EV Growth) Limited
*Officers:* Laurence Robert MacKenzie [1961] Director; Paul David Matthews [1968] Director; Andrew Paul Pinkney [1970] Director

**Windermere Aquatic Limited**
*Incorporated:* 15 March 1928 *Employees:* 31
*Net Worth:* £6,299,821 *Total Assets:* £12,844,775
*Registered Office:* Glebe Road, Bowness on Windemere, Windermere, Cumbria, LA23 3HE
*Activities:* Other retail sale of new goods in specialised stores (not commercial art galleries and opticians)
*Shareholders:* Grahame Frederick Armer; Jill Caroline Henderson
*Officers:* Grahame Frederick Armer, Secretary; Henry Malcolm Henderson, Secretary; Grahame Frederick Armer [1954] Director; Jill Caroline Henderson [1951] Director

**Windermere Educational Trust Limited**
*Incorporated:* 8 September 1967 *Employees:* 137
*Net Worth:* £20,904,946 *Total Assets:* £26,166,776
*Registered Office:* Brow Head, Windermere, Cumbria, LA23 1NW
*Activities:* Primary education
*Officers:* Susan Ross, Secretary; Carol Julie Burrow [1961] Director; Andrew Paul Chamberlain [1960] Director/Business Consultant; Jason Mark Peter Dearden [1972] Managing Director; Joanne Harris [1972] Director; Alison Claire Hodson [1968] Director

**Windermere Lake Cruises Limited**
*Incorporated:* 22 March 1968 *Employees:* 139
*Net Worth:* £10,763,920 *Total Assets:* £13,335,218
*Registered Office:* Winander House, Glebe Road, Bowness on Windermere, Cumbria, LA23 3HE
*Activities:* Inland passenger water transport
*Parent:* Winander Leisure Ltd
*Officers:* Andrew James Simon, Secretary; William John Bewley [1945] Director/Boat Proprietor; John Brockbank [1952] Director; Jennifer Cormack [1981] Sales & Marketing Director; Thomas Richard Cowherd [1933] Director/Boat Proprietor; Ernest George Fallowfield [1941] Director/Boat Proprietor; Leslie Micklethwaite [1943] Director; Andrew James Simon [1980] Director/Chartered Management Accountant; James Roy Thompson [1947] Director/Boat Proprietor; Nigel Wilkinson [1964] Director/Chartered Accountant; John Woodburn [1956] Director/Boat Operator

**Windsor Engineering (Hull) Limited**
*Incorporated:* 12 April 1989 *Employees:* 183
*Net Worth:* £7,242,407 *Total Assets:* £23,807,120
*Registered Office:* 8 Beacon Way, Hull, HU3 4AE
*Activities:* Renting and leasing of other machinery, equipment and tangible goods n.e.c.
*Major Shareholder:* Gerald Burton
*Officers:* Mark Harrison, Secretary; Generald Burton [1944] Director/Forklift Truck Hire Operator; Jonathan Greg Burton [1974] Director; Stephen Paul Burton [1976] Director; Andrew Lane [1968] Director/Depot Manager

**Windward Phase 2 Limited**
*Incorporated:* 25 October 1946 *Employees:* 30
*Previous:* Windermere Marina Village Limited
*Net Worth:* £6,836,513 *Total Assets:* £13,323,559
*Registered Office:* Windermere Marina Village, Bowness on Windermere, Cumbria, LA23 3JQ
*Activities:* Holiday centres and villages
*Major Shareholder:* Eileen Rebecca Ainscough
*Officers:* Eileen Rebecca Ainscough [1946] Director

**Des Winks Cars Limited**
*Incorporated:* 31 July 1986 *Employees:* 38
*Net Worth:* £2,537,082 *Total Assets:* £5,839,662
*Registered Office:* 62-63 Westborough, Scarborough, N Yorks, YO11 1TS
*Activities:* Sale of used cars and light motor vehicles
*Major Shareholder:* Denise Winks
*Officers:* Martin William Summers, Secretary; Denise Winks [1949] Director/Administrator; Debra Louise Wray [1968] Director; Martin Andrew Wray [1964] Director/Sales Manager

**Winsfield Limited**
*Incorporated:* 15 September 2003
*Net Worth:* £15,235,000 *Total Assets:* £100,829,000
*Registered Office:* Dewhirst House, Westgate, Driffield, E Yorks, YO25 6TH
*Activities:* Activities of head offices
*Parent:* Drifford Limited
*Officers:* Christopher John Wilde, Secretary; David Witt [1953] Director; Anthony James Mark Wood [1960] Director

**Winston (UK) Limited**
*Incorporated:* 22 October 2004 *Employees:* 3
*Net Worth:* £4,195,314 *Total Assets:* £9,158,025
*Registered Office:* The Power House, 156 Hookstone Drive, Harrogate, N Yorks, HG2 8PF
*Activities:* Development of building projects
*Shareholders:* Christopher Alan Rycroft; Barbara Joan Rycroft
*Officers:* James Adam Rycroft, Secretary/Director; Christopher Alan Rycroft [1944] Director; James Adam Rycroft [1972] Director

**John Winter & Company Limited**
*Incorporated:* 30 October 1963 *Employees:* 45
*Net Worth:* £3,906,354 *Total Assets:* £5,428,392
*Registered Office:* P O Box 21, Washer Lane Works, Halifax, W Yorks, HX2 7DP
*Activities:* Wholesale of other intermediate products
*Shareholder:* Roger Haley
*Officers:* Brian Craven, Secretary; Adam Bennett [1971] Sales Director-Foundry Products; Brian Craven [1950] Director/Retired; George Brendan Foster [1956] Sales Director Dental Products; Christopher James Gledhill [1954] Financial Director; Roger Haley [1939] Director/Chairman; Dale Robert Lister [1960] Managing Director

**Dennis Winter (Leven) Limited**
*Incorporated:* 3 March 1965 *Employees:* 7
*Net Worth:* £2,766,943 *Total Assets:* £3,149,011
*Registered Office:* Canal Head Service Station, South Street, Leven, Beverley, N Humbers, HU17 5NY
*Activities:* Sale of other motor vehicles
*Shareholders:* Mark Winter; Kathleen Mavis Winter
*Officers:* Mark Winter, Secretary; Kathleen Mavis Winter [1937] Director/Office Manager; Mark Winter [1963] Director/Mechanic

**Winterquay Limited**
*Incorporated:* 5 November 1996 *Employees:* 12
*Net Worth:* £18,994,764 *Total Assets:* £34,159,640
*Registered Office:* 12 Cardale Court, Cardale Park, Beckwith Head Road, Harrogate, N Yorks, HG3 1RY
*Activities:* Growing of cereals (except rice), leguminous crops and oil seeds
*Major Shareholder:* Douglas Charles Antony Bramall
*Officers:* Alison Rae Lockwood, Secretary; Anna Bramall [1973] Director; Douglas Charles Antony Bramall [1935] Director; Karen Susanah Bramall Ogden [1965] Director; Melanie Jane Foody [1966] Director; Peter Jones [1956] Director; Alison Rae Lockwood [1969] Director/Chartered Accountant

**Winterton Community Academy**
*Incorporated:* 12 July 2012 *Employees:* 58
*Net Worth:* £5,472,262 *Total Assets:* £6,296,931
*Registered Office:* Winterton Community Academy, Newport Drive, Winterton, Scunthorpe, N Lincs, DN15 9QD
*Activities:* General secondary education
*Officers:* Timothy William Bartlett [1959] Director; Abigail Louise Dalowsky [1978] Director/Teacher; Simon Charles Driver [1959] Director; Dr Claire Elizabeth Hunt [1979] Director/Teacher; Timothy Paul Godfrey Johns [1966] Director; Chris Peters [1960] Director; Kevin Rowlands [1973] Director/Headteacher; Joanne Simpson [1968] Director; Amanda Walker [1971] Director

**Wire Estates Limited**
*Incorporated:* 24 October 2014
*Net Worth:* £836,486 *Total Assets:* £3,599,251
*Registered Office:* R M Mason Limited, Suite 4a, 7 Martin Street, Brighouse, W Yorks, HD6 1DA
*Activities:* Other letting and operating of own or leased real estate
*Officers:* Ian Paul Lane [1958] Director; Nigel Michael Lane [1956] Director

**Wirquin Ltd**
*Incorporated:* 3 June 1987 *Employees:* 183
*Net Worth:* £1,285,000 *Total Assets:* £7,686,000
*Registered Office:* Warmsworth Halt Industrial Estate, Warmsworth, Doncaster, S Yorks, DN4 9LS
*Activities:* Manufacture of other plastic products
*Officers:* Gwenhael Le Coent [1974] Group Sales Director [French]

**Wiseton Developments Limited**
*Incorporated:* 6 March 2000 *Employees:* 11
*Previous:* Whitehall Financial Limited
*Net Worth:* £391,820 *Total Assets:* £4,393,150
*Registered Office:* Wiseton Hall, Wiseton, Doncaster, S Yorks, DN10 5AE
*Activities:* Development of building projects
*Shareholders:* Peter William James Birch; Nicola Birch
*Officers:* Peter William James Birch, Secretary; Peter William James Birch [1960] Director; Thomas Phillip Michael Birch [1990] Director

**Withernsea Primary Academy Trust**
*Incorporated:* 6 March 2015 *Employees:* 101
*Net Worth:* £3,449,904 *Total Assets:* £4,889,908
*Registered Office:* Withernsea Primary School, Hull Road, Withernsea, E Yorks, HU19 2EG
*Activities:* Primary education
*Officers:* Susan Boasman [1977] Director/Accountancy Practice Manager; Lyn Good [1950] Director/Retired; Angela Harper [1968] Director/Headteacher; Alison Hoey [1969] Director/Qualified Forensic Auditor; Jane Jackson [1968] Director/Police Officer; Martin Lindgren [1976] Director/Teacher; Joanne Medcalf [1971] Director/Technical Analyst; Victoria Louise Taylor [1971] Director/Police Officer

**Witherslack Group (Holdings) Limited**
*Incorporated:* 24 November 2010 *Employees:* 958
*Net Worth Deficit:* £10,660,568 *Total Assets:* £81,108,952
*Registered Office:* Lupton Tower, Lupton, Carnforth, Lancs, LA6 2PR
*Activities:* Activities of other holding companies n.e.c.
*Parent:* Wordsworth Bidco Limited
*Officers:* Michael Anthony Barrow [1957] Director; Kevin Frederick Dyson [1964] Finance Director; Judith Jones [1965] Commercial Director; Philip David Jones [1962] Managing Director; Howard Charles Tennant [1963] Director

**Witherslack Group Limited**
*Incorporated:* 10 June 1998 *Employees:* 958
*Net Worth:* £39,497,908 *Total Assets:* £66,685,040
*Registered Office:* Lupton Tower, Lupton, Carnforth, Lancs, LA6 2PR
*Activities:* Primary education
*Parent:* Witherslack Group (Holdings) Limited
*Officers:* Kevin Frederick Dyson, Secretary; Michael Anthony Barrow [1957] Director; Kevin Frederick Dyson [1964] Finance Director; Judith Jones [1965] Commercial Director; Philip David Jones [1962] Director; Howard Charles Tennant [1963] Director

**Witt & Son UK Holdings Limited**
*Incorporated:* 4 May 1993 *Employees:* 120
*Net Worth:* £7,680,049 *Total Assets:* £14,443,477
*Registered Office:* Witt House, Wade House Road, Shelf, Halifax, W Yorks, HX3 7BJ
*Activities:* Manufacture of other special-purpose machinery n.e.c.
*Shareholders:* Henrik Torsten Witt; Karsten Christian Witt
*Officers:* John Steven Ashworth, Secretary; Martin Booth [1952] Managing Director; Dr Henrik Torsten Witt [1955] Director [Swedish]; Karsten Christian Witt [1958] Director [Swedish]

**Witton Castle Country Park Limited**
*Incorporated:* 8 November 2007
*Net Worth Deficit:* £6,676,157 *Total Assets:* £13,035,293
*Registered Office:* Marton Hall, Church Lane, Sewerby, Bridlington, E Yorks, YO15 1DS
*Activities:* Other holiday and other collective accommodation
*Parent:* Shorewood Leisure Group Limited
*Officers:* David Robert Allison [1960] Director/Park Owner; Neil Willson [1960] Director

**WJS Properties 2 Limited**
*Incorporated:* 12 October 2007
*Previous:* Abel & Cole Acquisitions Limited
*Net Worth:* £443,000 *Total Assets:* £4,046,000
*Registered Office:* The Riverside Building, Livingstone Road, Hessle, E Yorks, HU13 0DZ
*Activities:* Activities of other holding companies n.e.c.
*Parent:* Wiliam Jackson Food Group Limited
*Officers:* Gary Martin Urmston, Secretary; Norman Graeme Scott Soutar [1960] Director; Gary Martin Urmston [1967] Director

**WMK Securities LLP**
*Incorporated:* 20 August 2010
*Net Worth:* £7,025,258 *Total Assets:* £7,028,678
*Registered Office:* Unit 4 Meadow Court, Millshaw, Leeds, LS11 8LZ
*Officers:* Edward Klempka [1951] Member; Michael David Michaelson [1959] Member; Philip Neville Wilbraham [1958] Member; Caroline Louise Castle [1978] LLP Member; Georgina Lois Faye Coates [1987] LLP Member; Lois Klempka [1948] LLP Member; Victoria Isobel Klempka [1980] LLP Member; Dominic Mathew Wilbraham [1987] LLP Member; Rachel Madelaine Wilbraham [1982] LLP Member; Rosemary Elizabeth Wilbraham [1986] LLP Member; Samuel Benjamin Wilbraham [1984] LLP Member

**WMT Global Holdings LLP**
*Incorporated:* 9 September 2015
*Net Worth:* £39,978,754,048 *Total Assets:* £57,082,150,912
*Registered Office:* Asda House, Southbank, Great Wilson Street, Leeds, LS11 5AD

**WNF Group Limited**
*Incorporated:* 4 February 2000 *Employees:* 368
*Net Worth:* £11,140,618 *Total Assets:* £12,619,406
*Registered Office:* Millennium House, Station Lane, Featherstone, Pontefract, W Yorks, WF7 5BA
*Activities:* Other residential care activities n.e.c.
*Shareholders:* Gerald Clough; Margaret Ann Clough; Maine Road Properties Limited
*Officers:* Steven Clough, Secretary; Generald Clough [1948] Director/Care Home Proprietor; Margaret Ann Clough [1949] Director/Care Home Proprietor; Steven Clough [1978] Director; Stephen Mark Drewitt [1979] Director

**Wold Farms Limited**
*Incorporated:* 20 August 2013 *Employees:* 6
*Net Worth:* £270,000 *Total Assets:* £5,395,000
*Registered Office:* Crane Court, Hesslewood Office Park, Ferriby Road, Hessle, E Yorks, HU13 0PA
*Activities:* Raising of swine and pigs
*Parent:* Cranswick Country Foods PLC
*Officers:* Steven Garrick Glover, Secretary; John Mark Bottomley [1963] Director; Neil Edward Clappison [1964] Director; Adam Hartley Couch [1968] Director; James Pontone [1977] Finance Director

**Wolds Engineering Services Limited**
*Incorporated:* 23 August 1999 *Employees:* 29
*Net Worth:* £2,527,292 *Total Assets:* £3,926,955
*Registered Office:* The Wolds Building, Unit 1 Hampden Road, Pocklington Industrial Estate, Pocklington, York, YO42 1NR
*Activities:* Non-specialised wholesale trade
*Shareholders:* John Oxley; Keeley Oxley
*Officers:* John Kevin Oxley [1968] Director

**Wolds Investments Limited**
*Incorporated:* 17 April 2014
*Net Worth:* £6,391,246 *Total Assets:* £6,823,630
*Registered Office:* c/o Clipper Logistics Group, Gelderd Road, Leeds, LS12 6LT
*Activities:* Activities of venture and development capital companies
*Major Shareholder:* David Arthur Hodkin
*Officers:* Angela Hodkin [1958] Director; David Arthur Hodkin [1961] Director

**Wolds Learning Partnership**
*Incorporated:* 9 December 2016 *Employees:* 213
*Net Worth:* £19,987,952 *Total Assets:* £22,064,938
*Registered Office:* Woldgate School and Sixth Form College, 92 Kilnwick Road, Pocklington, York, YO42 2LL
*Activities:* Other education n.e.c.
*Officers:* Jonathan Britton [1975] Director/Headteacher; Stephen Andrew Burley [1956] Director/Chartered Surveyor; Andrew Graham Cook [1966] Commercial Director; Angela Jane Ekers [1985] Director/Headmistress; John James Sinclair [1964] Director; Karen Julia Taylor [1971] Director/Accountant; Julia Keenan Thomson [1958] Director/Retired

**H.S. Wood (Textiles) Limited**
*Incorporated:* 1 May 1975 *Employees:* 40
*Net Worth:* £2,048,171 *Total Assets:* £5,253,400
*Registered Office:* Park View Mills, Raymond Street, Bradford, W Yorks, BD5 8DT
*Activities:* Wholesale of textiles
*Officers:* Richard Ashley Wood [1963] Director; Stephen Craig Wood [1961] Director/Accountant

**C & K Wood (U.K.) Limited**
*Incorporated:* 16 July 2001 *Employees:* 9
*Net Worth:* £2,699,102 *Total Assets:* £8,581,554
*Registered Office:* Hall Farm, Newton on Derwent, York, YO41 4DB
*Activities:* Raising of poultry
*Major Shareholder:* Timothy Giles Savile Wood
*Officers:* Samantha Binns, Secretary; Tom Longhurst [1985] Director/Accountant; Timothy John Norton [1953] Director; Timothy Giles Savile Wood [1970] Director

**Wood Auto Supplies Limited**
*Incorporated:* 11 June 1965 *Employees:* 51
*Net Worth:* £3,867,425 *Total Assets:* £5,972,761
*Registered Office:* Cromwell Works, Colne Road, Huddersfield, W Yorks, HD1 3ES
*Activities:* Wholesale trade of motor vehicle parts and accessories
*Parent:* Wood Auto (Holdings) Limited
*Officers:* Alan Martin Stead, Secretary; Graham James Heywood [1977] Managing Director; Robert Edward James Heywood [1949] Director/Chairman; Alan Martin Stead [1961] Finance Director

**David Wood Baking Limited**
*Incorporated:* 20 March 2008 *Employees:* 1,391
*Net Worth:* £6,568,318 *Total Assets:* £47,488,092
*Registered Office:* 1 Calverley Road, Oulton, Leeds, LS26 8JD
*Activities:* Production of meat and poultry meat products
*Officers:* Karen Wood, Secretary; David Anthony Wood [1968] Director/Baker; Karen Wood [1972] Director and Manager

**David Wood Baking UK Limited**
*Incorporated:* 6 August 2008 *Employees:* 1,391
*Net Worth:* £6,377,751 *Total Assets:* £47,488,092
*Registered Office:* 1 Calverley Road, Oulton, Leeds, LS26 8JD
*Activities:* Manufacture of bread; manufacture of fresh pastry goods and cakes
*Major Shareholder:* David Anthony Wood
*Officers:* Karen Wood, Secretary; David Anthony Wood [1968] Director/Baker; Karen Wood [1972] Director

**Alan Wood Holdings Limited**
*Incorporated:* 3 September 2015 *Employees:* 8
*Net Worth:* £312,128 *Total Assets:* £3,852,753
*Registered Office:* 341 Beverley Road, Hull, HU5 1LD
*Activities:* Activities of other holding companies n.e.c.
*Officers:* Mark Andrew Barwood [1963] Director/Civil Engineer; Michael Campbell Blake [1957] Director; Mark Geoffrey Coates [1971] Director/Surveyor; Peter Drenon [1956] Director/Civil Engineer; James Andrew Gibson [1975] Director/Civil Engineer; Neil Read [1965] Director; Jonathan Mark Saunders [1966] Director/Geotechnical Engineer

**A & C Wood Limited**
*Incorporated:* 17 May 2011
*Net Worth:* £184,553 *Total Assets:* £3,326,451
*Registered Office:* Hall Farm, Main Street, Newton on Derwent, York, YO41 4DB
*Activities:* Production of electricity
*Officers:* Samantha Louise Savile Binns, Secretary; Timothy Giles Savile Wood [1970] Director/Farmer

**Alan Wood Partnership Limited**
*Incorporated:* 11 February 1986 *Employees:* 87
*Net Worth:* £2,318,471 *Total Assets:* £4,036,357
*Registered Office:* 341 Beverley Road, Hull, HU5 1LD
*Activities:* Other engineering activities
*Parent:* Alan Wood Holdings Limited
*Officers:* Neil Read, Secretary; Mark Andrew Barwood [1963] Director; Michael Campbell Blake [1957] Director/Civil Engineer; Mark Geoffrey Coates [1971] Director/Surveyor; Peter Drenon [1956] Director; James Andrew Gibson [1975] Director; Neil Read [1965] Director/Structural Engineer; Jonathan Mark Saunders [1966] Director

**Woodgreen Construction Holdings Limited**
*Incorporated:* 23 February 2012 *Employees:* 28
*Net Worth:* £2,735,469 *Total Assets:* £6,888,955
*Registered Office:* Unit 3 Oakwell Way, Oakwell Court, Batley, W Yorks, WF17 9LU
*Activities:* Dormant company
*Shareholders:* Jonathan Inman; Karen Inman; Brian Inman
*Officers:* Jonathan Inman [1966] Director

**Woodgreen Construction Limited**
*Incorporated:* 17 October 1991 *Employees:* 28
*Net Worth:* £3,777,726 *Total Assets:* £7,651,792
*Registered Office:* Unit 3 Oakwell Industrial Park, Oakwell Way, Birstall, W Yorks, WF17 9LU
*Activities:* Other specialised construction activities n.e.c.
*Parent:* Woodgreen Construction Holdings Limited
*Officers:* Karen Tracy Inman, Secretary; Jonathan Inman [1966] Director/Construction

**Woodham Academy**
*Incorporated:* 3 August 2012 *Employees:* 117
*Net Worth:* £5,118,000 *Total Assets:* £6,962,000
*Registered Office:* Woodham Academy, Washington Crescent, Newton Aycliffe, Co Durham, DL5 4AX
*Activities:* General secondary education
*Officers:* David Coates, Secretary; Sean Barnett [1964] Managing Director; John Strachan Denham [1946] Director/Retired Primary Headteacher; Richard Charles Eirew [1965] Director/Senior IT Service Manager; Christine Forsyth [1961] Director/Headteacher; Jonathan Jeffery French [1961] Director/Financial Advisor; Robert Michael Gales [1991] Director/Teacher; Richard Paul Heaven [1965] Director/HLTA; Ian Johnson [1981] Director/Telecommunications Worker; David Graham Knight [1957] Director/Financial Adviser; Arthur Marshall [1951] Retired Director; Steven Mark Mendelsohn [1961] Director/Self Employed Consultant; Diane Newton [1964] Director/Administrator; Brian Winwood [1966] Director/Self Employed

**Woodhead Brothers Farms Ltd**
*Incorporated:* 24 May 1983 *Employees:* 11
*Net Worth:* £4,855,446 *Total Assets:* £5,170,012
*Registered Office:* Low Cringles Farm, Bolton Road, Silsden, Keighley, W Yorks, BD20 0NR
*Activities:* Mixed farming
*Officers:* David Woodhead, Secretary; David Woodhead [1950] Director/Farmer/Butcher; John Edward Woodhead [1949] Director/Farmer/Butcher

**Woodhead Investments & Development Services Limited**
*Incorporated:* 21 May 1965 *Employees:* 9
*Net Worth:* £17,348,112 *Total Assets:* £51,137,208
*Registered Office:* 2nd Floor, Woodhead House, 8-10 Providence Street, Wakefield, W Yorks, WF1 3BG
*Activities:* Other letting and operating of own or leased real estate
*Shareholders:* David Melvyn Woodhead; Mark Stephen Woodhead; George Melvyn Walker Woodhead; Susan Woodhead
*Officers:* David Melvyn Woodhead, Secretary/Chartered Surveyor; David Melvyn Woodhead [1976] Director/Chartered Surveyor; George Melvyn Walker Woodhead [1939] Director; Mark Stephen Woodhead [1970] Managing Director; Susan Woodhead [1941] Director

**Edwin Woodhouse & Co. (Investments) Limited**
*Incorporated:* 24 March 1898 *Employees:* 6
*Net Worth:* £18,188,856 *Total Assets:* £20,927,376
*Registered Office:* Sunny Bank Mills, Farsley, Pudsey, W Yorks, LS28 5UJ
*Activities:* Other letting and operating of own or leased real estate
*Officers:* John Michael Andrew Gaunt, Secretary; John Michael Andrew Gaunt [1976] Director/Commercial Property; William John Gaunt [1967] Director/Commercial Property

**Edwin Woodhouse & Co. Limited**
*Incorporated:* 6 April 1961 *Employees:* 6
*Net Worth:* £5,272,239 *Total Assets:* £13,344,132
*Registered Office:* Sunny Bank Mills, Farsley, Pudsey, Leeds, LS28 5UJ
*Activities:* Other letting and operating of own or leased real estate
*Parent:* Edwin Woodhouse & Co (Investments) Ltd
*Officers:* John Michael Andrew Gaunt, Secretary; John Michael Andrew Gaunt [1976] Director/Commercial Property; William John Gaunt [1967] Director/Commercial Property

**Edwin Woodhouse Properties Limited**
*Incorporated:* 11 May 1964
*Net Worth:* £9,736,269 *Total Assets:* £11,176,233
*Registered Office:* Sunny Bank Mills, Farsley, Pudsey, W Yorks, LS28 5UJ
*Activities:* Other letting and operating of own or leased real estate
*Parent:* Edwin Woodhouse & Co (Investments) Ltd
*Officers:* John Michael Andrew Gaunt, Secretary; David John Gaunt [1938] Director/Property Investment; John Michael Andrew Gaunt [1976] Director/Property Investment; Martin Gaunt [1940] Director/Property Investment; William John Gaunt [1967] Director/Property Investment

**M.Woodhouse Transport (Lancaster) Limited**
*Incorporated:* 26 June 1967 *Employees:* 45
*Net Worth:* £3,157,608 *Total Assets:* £4,941,494
*Registered Office:* Pine Garage, Caton Road, Lancaster, LA1 3PE
*Activities:* Freight transport by road
*Major Shareholder:* Malcolm John Woodhouse
*Officers:* Ian Leslie Corbett, Secretary/Accounts Clerk; Ian Leslie Corbett [1947] Director/Accounts Clerk; Janette Christina Woodhouse [1957] Director/Hairdresser; Malcolm John Woodhouse [1956] Director/Transport Manager

**Woodland Healthcare Limited**
*Incorporated:* 25 March 1994 *Employees:* 109
*Net Worth:* £2,878,826 *Total Assets:* £4,327,788
*Registered Office:* Woodlands of Woolley Residential Home, Woolley Low Moor Lane, Woolley, Wakefield, W Yorks, WF4 2LN
*Activities:* Other human health activities
*Parent:* ADL PLC
*Officers:* William Jeremy Davies, Secretary/Surveyor; William Jeremy Davies [1947] Director/Chartered Surveyor; Pearl Lorraine Jackson [1958] Director

**The Woodlands Academy Scarborough**
*Incorporated:* 8 March 2013 *Employees:* 64
*Net Worth:* £1,573,419 *Total Assets:* £3,402,586
*Registered Office:* The Woodlands School, Woodlands Drive, Scarborough, N Yorks, YO12 6QN
*Activities:* Primary education
*Officers:* Rhiann Askew [1975] Director/Carer; Amanda Jill Caton [1972] Director/Accounting Officer; William Chatt [1959] Director; Sarah Louise de Burnham Halliday [1967] Director/Teaching Assistant; Robert Adrian Instone [1970] Director/Teacher; Lisa Ponter [1978] Director/Deputy Headteacher; Louise St Pierre [1973] Director/School Organiser; George Bernard Weekes [1949] Director/Teacher

**Woodlands Home & Garden Group Limited**
*Incorporated:* 10 December 1913 *Employees:* 108
*Previous:* Woodlands Homecare Limited
*Net Worth:* £13,517,222 *Total Assets:* £16,155,704
*Registered Office:* Woodlands, Calverley Lane, Leeds, LS13 1NP
*Activities:* Sawmilling and planing of wood
*Parent:* Woodlands Homecare (Group) Ltd
*Officers:* Ross Peter David Moran, Secretary/Director; Ross Peter David Moran [1984] Director

**Wool Growers (Great Britain) Limited**
*Incorporated:* 28 May 1959 *Employees:* 15
*Net Worth:* £10,851,000 *Total Assets:* £12,594,000
*Registered Office:* Wool House, Sidings Close, Canal Road, Bradford, W Yorks, BD2 1AZ
*Activities:* Other professional, scientific and technical activities n.e.c.
*Parent:* British Wool Marketing Board
*Officers:* Peter Anthony Baren [1960] Director/Accountant; Stephen Gawain Leigh Bradley [1978] Director; Joseph Michael Farren [1971] Director [Irish]; Trevor John Richards [1953] Director/Farmer

**R N Wooler & Co (Developments) Limited**
*Incorporated:* 9 August 2000 *Employees:* 4
*Net Worth:* £2,324,786 *Total Assets:* £15,478,157
*Registered Office:* Florence House, Lawkholme Business Park, Lawkholme Lane, Keighley, W Yorks, BD21 3LA
*Activities:* Development of building projects
*Major Shareholder:* Richard Norman Wooler
*Officers:* Margaret Ann Wooler, Secretary; Andrew Wooler [1978] Director; Gareth David Wooler [1980] Director; Margaret Ann Wooler [1954] Director; Richard Norman Wooler [1954] Director

**R.N. Wooler & Co (Holdings) Limited**
*Incorporated:* 16 July 2002 *Employees:* 288
*Net Worth:* £18,934,576 *Total Assets:* £38,549,788
*Registered Office:* Florence House, Lawkholme Business Park, Lawkholme Lane, Keighley, W Yorks, BD21 3LA
*Activities:* Construction of commercial buildings
*Major Shareholder:* Richard Norman Wooler
*Officers:* Margaret Ann Wooler, Secretary; Andrew Wooler [1978] Director; Gareth David Wooler [1980] Director; Margaret Ann Wooler [1954] Director; Richard Norman Wooler [1954] Director

**R.N. Wooler & Company Limited**
*Incorporated:* 24 July 1985 *Employees:* 288
*Net Worth:* £11,027,373 *Total Assets:* £24,726,868
*Registered Office:* Florence House, Lawkholme Business Park, Lawkholme Lane, Keighley, W Yorks, BD21 3LA
*Activities:* Construction of commercial buildings
*Major Shareholder:* Richard Norman Wooler
*Officers:* Sheila Clarkson, Secretary; Gary Sollitt [1960] Contracts Director; Andrew Wooler [1978] Director; Gareth David Wooler [1980] Director; Margaret Ann Wooler [1954] Director; Richard Norman Wooler [1954] Director

**Woolrow Farm Limited**
*Incorporated:* 15 November 2016 *Employees:* 22
*Net Worth:* £1,940,901 *Total Assets:* £3,433,367
*Registered Office:* Woolrow Farm, Roydhouse, Shelley, Huddersfield, W Yorks, HD8 8LR
*Activities:* Raising of dairy cattle
*Shareholders:* Christopher Hall; Margaret May Hall
*Officers:* Christopher Hall [1959] Director/Farmer; Margaret May Hall [1963] Director/Farmer

**Wooltex U.K. Limited**
*Incorporated:* 4 August 2000 *Employees:* 115
*Net Worth:* £6,122,995 *Total Assets:* £10,794,270
*Registered Office:* Woodland Mill, Dale Street, Huddersfield, W Yorks, HD3 4TG
*Activities:* Manufacture of other textiles n.e.c.
*Shareholders:* Peter Timmins; Kvadrat A/S; Paula Timmins
*Officers:* Carl Winrow, Secretary; Richard David Brook [1971] Director; Sarah Jane Shirley [1961] Director; Peter Timmins [1953] Director/Textile Manufacturing; Carl Winrow [1980] Director

**The Wordsworth Trust**
*Incorporated:* 30 September 1997 *Employees:* 36
*Net Worth:* £14,899,000 *Total Assets:* £15,989,000
*Registered Office:* Dove Cottage, Grasmere, Cumbria, LA22 9SH
*Activities:* Library activities
*Officers:* Amanda Jane Pickup, Secretary; Professor Simon John Julian Bainbridge [1965] Director/Professor; Professor Sir Drummond James Bone [1947] Director/Academic; Gesa Brinkmann [1970] Director/Chartered Accountant [British/German]; Mary Chuck [1943] Director/Retired; John Spencer Collier [1945] Director/Chartered Accountant; Judith Helen Cooke [1947] Director/Public Sector Employee; Dr Anna Mairead Fleming [1989] Director/Projects Manager; Johanna Goode [1967] Director/Headteacher; David Michael Heal [1951] Director/Consultant; Diana Ruth Matthews [1946] Director; Professor David John McKitterick [1948] Director/Retired; Dr Lucy Peltz [1969] Director/Museum Curator; Jennifer Sheila Uglow [1947] Director/Publisher

**Worthington Homes Limited**
*Incorporated:* 16 February 2006 *Employees:* 3
*Previous:* AIW Management Limited
*Net Worth Deficit:* £331,837 *Total Assets:* £4,577,214
*Registered Office:* Lower Goat House, Oldham Road, Rishworth, Halifax, W Yorks, HX6 4QE
*Activities:* Development of building projects
*Major Shareholder:* Rob Erik Worthington
*Officers:* Rob Erik Worthington, Secretary; Rob Erik Worthington [1974] Director

**Wortlea Estates (Leeds) Limited**
*Incorporated:* 25 April 1963 *Employees:* 152
*Net Worth:* £6,267,820 *Total Assets:* £23,860,962
*Registered Office:* Whitehall Road, Lower Wortley, Leeds, LS12 5NL
*Activities:* Activities of head offices
*Officers:* Guy Brian Roberts, Secretary; David Heath Innes [1963] Director; Richard Heath Robert Innes [1960] Director/Solicitor; Guy Brian Roberts [1961] Director; Robert Nicholas Roberts [1955] Director; Joanna Louise Terry [1958] Director

**Wortley Construction Limited**
*Incorporated:* 7 April 1972 *Employees:* 3
*Net Worth:* £2,793,242 *Total Assets:* £3,295,564
*Registered Office:* 78 Marsh Lane, Shepley, Huddersfield, W Yorks, HD8 8AP
*Activities:* Development of building projects
*Major Shareholder:* Nigel Jeremy Addy
*Officers:* Keith Tilsley Addy [1934] Director; Nigel Jeremy Addy [1964] Director/Chartered Surveyor; Yvette Claire Addy [1964] Director

**Wortley Developments Limited**
*Incorporated:* 1 May 1984 *Employees:* 3
*Net Worth:* £4,791,486 *Total Assets:* £5,256,751
*Registered Office:* 78 Marsh Lane, Shepley, Huddersfield, W Yorks, HD8 8AP
*Activities:* Buying and selling of own real estate
*Major Shareholder:* Nigel Jeremy Addy
*Officers:* Keith Tilsley Addy [1934] Director/Builder; Nigel Jeremy Addy [1964] Director/Surveyor; Yvette Claire Addy [1964] Director

**Wot-a-Pullet Limited**
*Incorporated:* 12 August 2004 *Employees:* 63
*Previous:* Wot-An-Egg Co Limited
*Net Worth:* £82,989 *Total Assets:* £5,416,626
*Registered Office:* Quarry House, Cattle Hill, Warter, York, YO42 1XG
*Activities:* Raising of poultry
*Parent:* Warrendale Farms Limited
*Officers:* Maria Jane Pryor, Secretary; James Cubitt Bloom [1961] Director/Farmer; Matthew Richard Green [1962] Director/Farmer; Kevin Morley [1968] Production Director

**Wothersome Limited**
*Incorporated:* 3 December 2013 *Employees:* 3
*Net Worth Deficit:* £784,837 *Total Assets:* £4,863,381
*Registered Office:* The Estate Office, Bramham Park, Wetherby, W Yorks, LS23 6ND
*Activities:* Other business support service activities n.e.c.
*Shareholders:* David Andrew Gray; Patrick Esmond James; Richard Clephane Compton
*Officers:* David Andrew Gray [1963] Director/Chartered Surveyor; George Charles Nicholas Lane Fox [1963] Director; The Honourable Rachel Monica Lane Fox [1967] Director

**Wrapid Group Limited**
*Incorporated:* 24 November 2005
*Net Worth:* £9,329,008 *Total Assets:* £11,443,563
*Registered Office:* 250 Thornton Road, Bradford, BD1 2LB
*Activities:* Activities of head offices
*Parent:* Wrapid Investments Limited
*Officers:* Stephen Patrick York, Secretary; James Richard Clark [1983] Director; Nicole Dillon [1977] Director; Christopher Hudson [1971] Director; Stephen Patrick York [1957] Finance Director

**Wrapid Investments Limited**
*Incorporated:* 17 February 2015 *Employees:* 111
*Net Worth:* £1,433 *Total Assets:* £11,987,472
*Registered Office:* 250 Thornton Road, Bradford, W Yorks, BD1 2LB
*Activities:* Activities of other holding companies n.e.c.
*Officers:* James Richard Clark [1983] Director; Nicole Victoria Dillon [1977] Director; Christopher Hudson [1971] Director; Stephen Patrick York [1957] Director

**Wrapid Manufacturing Limited**
*Incorporated:* 13 May 1998 *Employees:* 111
*Net Worth:* £1,109,531 *Total Assets:* £7,629,174
*Registered Office:* 250 Thornton Road, Bradford, W Yorks, BD1 2LB
*Activities:* Other manufacturing n.e.c.
*Parent:* Wrapid Holdings Limited
*Officers:* Stephen Patrick York, Secretary; William Peter Birkinhead [1945] Director; John Clark [1952] Director; Christopher Hudson [1971] Director; Stephen Patrick York [1957] Director

**Wren Kitchens Limited**
*Incorporated:* 22 January 2009 *Employees:* 3,943
*Previous:* Wren Living Limited
*Net Worth:* £18,628,934 *Total Assets:* £183,475,712
*Registered Office:* The Nest, Falkland Way, Barton on Humber, N Lincs, DN18 5RX
*Activities:* Retail of furniture, lighting, and similar (not musical instruments or scores) in specialised store
*Major Shareholder:* Malcolm Stanley Healey
*Officers:* Jane Marie Oldfield, Secretary; Anthony Gerard Clay [1964] Engineering & Facilities Director; Craig Michael Douglas [1983] IT Director; Alexander David Grant [1971] Finance Director; Malcolm Stanley Healey [1944] Director/Chairman; Jason Anthony Hopper [1969] Southern Sales Director; Gemma Amanda Kerrigan [1981] Customer Service Director; Rafal Ryszard Klimek [1984] Manufacturing & Logistics Director [Polish]; Mohammed Tofiq Malik [1961] Northern Sales Director; Jane Marie Oldfield [1964] Director/Chartered Accountant; Mark Jonathan Pullan [1972] Managing Director; Kevin Selby [1962] Information & Compliance Director; Richard Birnie Durno Walker [1983] Marketing Director; Darren Watts [1971] Showroom Development Director

**Edward P Wright (Holdings) Limited**
*Incorporated:* 13 November 2007 *Employees:* 69
*Net Worth:* £6,478,627 *Total Assets:* £9,432,605
*Registered Office:* Warren Road, Scunthorpe, N Lincs, DN15 6XH
*Activities:* Activities of head offices
*Officers:* Jane Gazi-Wright, Secretary; Jane Gazi-Wright [1966] Director; Paul Edward Wright [1970] Director

**Wright Leisure Limited**
*Incorporated:* 21 March 2011 *Employees:* 661
*Net Worth Deficit:* £18,184,240 *Total Assets:* £36,703,392
*Registered Office:* Unit 1 Kirkstall Industrial Estate, Kirkstall Road, Burley, Leeds, LS4 2AZ
*Activities:* Activities of head offices
*Shareholders:* Jonathan Charles Wright; Paula Elizabeth Wright; Business Growth Fund PLC
*Officers:* Paula Elizabeth Wright, Secretary; Peter Ashley Boddy [1965] Director/Chairman; Helen Louise Gauden [1983] Director/Chief Finance Officer; Stuart James Perrin [1984] Sales Director; Richard David Taylor [1973] Director; Jonathan Charles Wright [1971] Director; Peter William Wright [1967] Director/Chief Executive

**Edward P. Wright Ltd.**
*Incorporated:* 11 September 1989 *Employees:* 69
*Net Worth:* £4,439,943 *Total Assets:* £7,393,920
*Registered Office:* Warren Road, Scunthorpe, N Lincs, DN15 6XH
*Activities:* Sale of used cars and light motor vehicles
*Officers:* Jane Wright, Secretary; Jane Gazi-Wright [1966] Director/Secretary; Paul Edward Wright [1970] Director

**Thomas Wright/Thorite Group Limited**
*Incorporated:* 7 November 1921 *Employees:* 117
*Net Worth:* £2,724,988 *Total Assets:* £7,626,275
*Registered Office:* Thorite House, Laisterdyke, Bradford, W Yorks, BD4 8BZ
*Activities:* Agents involved in the sale of machinery, industrial equipment, ships and aircraft
*Parent:* T Wright Holdings Limited
*Officers:* Stephen Thomas Wright, Secretary; Alan Donkersley [1962] Sales Director; Ross Gowler [1953] Director; Stephen Thomas Wright [1961] Director

**Wrigleys Solicitors LLP**
*Incorporated:* 3 March 2006 *Employees:* 181
*Net Worth:* £5,214,085 *Total Assets:* £8,518,083
*Registered Office:* 19 Cookridge Street, Leeds, LS2 3AG
*Officers:* Leigh Holmes [1970] Member; Paul Stanley Nash [1955] Member; Jonathan Attey [1973] LLP Member; Christopher Mark Billington [1967] LLP Member; Julia Elizabeth Boyes [1964] LLP Member; Lynne Elizabeth Bradey [1978] LLP Member; Marie-Louise Spencer Hamilton [1969] LLP Member; Angus David Alastair Hunter Smart [1978] LLP Member; Malcolm John Lynch [1955] LLP Member; Rachel Meredith [1980] LLP Member; Sylvie Aurelie Nunn [1976] LLP Member; Elizabeth Wilson [1972] LLP Member; Andrew David Wriglesworth [1968] LLP Member

**WSG Property (Holdings) Limited**
*Incorporated:* 20 January 2012 *Employees:* 3
*Net Worth:* £3,840,120 *Total Assets:* £9,044,837
*Registered Office:* Tenterfields, Thornhill Road Business Park, Dewsbury, W Yorks, WF12 0QT
*Activities:* Other letting and operating of own or leased real estate
*Shareholders:* John Stewart Graham; Nigel Graham
*Officers:* Peter Sutton, Secretary; John Stewart Graham [1938] Director; Nigel Graham [1951] Production Director; Peter Sutton [1959] Finance Director

**WTJ Insurance Brokers Limited**
*Incorporated:* 6 August 2001 *Employees:* 32
*Net Worth:* £963,848 *Total Assets:* £3,970,125
*Registered Office:* Landmark House, 556 Leeds Road, Outwood, Wakefield, W Yorks, WF1 2DX
*Activities:* Non-life insurance
*Major Shareholder:* Mark Baines Woodhead
*Officers:* Sharon Marie Fitzpatrick, Secretary; Joseph Bell [1960] Financial Director; Mark Baines Woodhead [1956] Director/Insurance Broker

**WV Associates Limited**
*Incorporated:* 12 March 1984 *Employees:* 40
*Net Worth:* £1,422,234 *Total Assets:* £4,963,336
*Registered Office:* Unit 7 Hatfield Way, South Church Enterprise Park, Bishop Auckland, Co Durham, DL14 6XF
*Activities:* Other manufacturing n.e.c.
*Parent:* Rooster Enterprises Limited
*Officers:* Kim Kong Wong, Secretary; Alexander Joseph Dale [1957] Director; Eric William Deveney [1956] Sales Director; Patrick Anthony Dominick McGonigal [1980] Director; Christopher Arthur Cory Ware [1972] Director; Richard Ivor Wakefield Ware [1939] Director; Kim Kong Wong [1959] Director [Malaysian]

**WYG Engineering Limited**
*Incorporated:* 15 November 1985 *Employees:* 349
*Net Worth:* £19,316,000 *Total Assets:* £27,840,000
*Registered Office:* Arndale Court, Otley Road, Headingley, Leeds, LS6 2UJ
*Activities:* Other engineering activities
*Parent:* WYG Group Limited
*Officers:* Gareth George Arber, Secretary; Benjamin Warwick Whitworth, Secretary; Andrew James Gillespie [1969] Director; Benjamin Warwick Whitworth [1965] Director/Solicitor

**WYG Environment Planning Transport Limited**
*Incorporated:* 26 April 1995 *Employees:* 424
*Net Worth:* £45,145,000 *Total Assets:* £49,606,000
*Registered Office:* Arndale Court, Otley Road, Headingley, Leeds, LS6 2UJ
*Activities:* Urban planning and landscape architectural activities
*Parent:* WYG Group Limited
*Officers:* Gareth George Arber, Secretary; Benjamin Warwick Whitworth, Secretary; Marc Kevan Davies [1974] Director; Andrew James Gillespie [1969] Director

**WYG Group Limited**
*Incorporated:* 16 May 2008 *Employees:* 151
*Net Worth Deficit:* £2,559,000 *Total Assets:* £78,676,000
*Registered Office:* Arndale Court, Otley Road, Headingley, Leeds, LS6 2UJ
*Activities:* Activities of head offices
*Parent:* WYG PLC
*Officers:* Benjamin Warwick Whitworth, Secretary; Iain Geoffrey Clarkson [1967] Director/Chartered Accountant; Douglas Alexander Drysdale McCormick [1962] Director/Chief Executive Officer

**WYG International Projects Limited**
*Incorporated:* 8 May 1996
*Net Worth:* £5,217,000 *Total Assets:* £7,832,000
*Registered Office:* Arndale Court, Otley Road, Headingley, Leeds, LS6 2UJ
*Activities:* Activities of head offices
*Parent:* WYG International Limited
*Officers:* Benjamin Warwick Whitworth, Secretary; Iain Geoffrey Clarkson [1967] Director/Chartered Accountant; Jesper Damgaard [1965] Director [Danish]

**WYG Management Services Limited**
*Incorporated:* 23 June 2003 *Employees:* 163
*Net Worth:* £14,898,000 *Total Assets:* £21,849,000
*Registered Office:* Arndale Court, Otley Road, Headingley, Leeds, LS6 2UJ
*Activities:* Management consultancy activities other than financial management
*Parent:* WYG Group Limited
*Officers:* Gareth George Arber, Secretary; Benjamin Warwick Whitworth, Secretary; Clive Drummond Anderson [1965] Director; Andrew James Gillespie [1969] Director

**WYG PLC**
*Incorporated:* 6 December 1984 *Employees:* 1,560
*Net Worth:* £25,561,000 *Total Assets:* £84,425,000
*Registered Office:* Arndale Court, Otley Road, Headingley, Leeds, LS6 2UJ
*Activities:* Activities of head offices
*Officers:* Benjamin Warwick Whitworth, Secretary; Dr Jeremy John Beeton [1953] Director; Iain Geoffrey Clarkson [1967] Director/Chartered Accountant; Marcia Maria Marini [1967] Director [Italian/Brazilian]; Neil Andrew Masom [1959] Director; Douglas Alexander Drysdale McCormick [1962] Director/Chief Executive Officer

**Wykeland (Humberside) Limited**
*Incorporated:* 5 June 1973
*Net Worth:* £5,043,806 *Total Assets:* £5,527,186
*Registered Office:* Wykeland House, 47 Queen Street, Hull, HU1 1UU
*Activities:* Buying and selling of own real estate
*Parent:* Wykeland Development (Holdings) Limited
*Officers:* Ian Charles Franks, Secretary; Beryl Brignall [1932] Director; David Christopher Donkin [1961] Director/Chartered Surveyor; Dominic Anthony Gibbons [1970] Director/Chartered Surveyor; Stephen Peter Hudson [1948] Director; Jonathan David Stubbs [1970] Director/Chartered Surveyor

**Wykeland Beverley Limited**
*Incorporated:* 28 June 2013
*Net Worth Deficit:* £18,781,664 *Total Assets:* £39,145,688
*Registered Office:* Wykeland House, 47 Queen Street, Hull, HU1 1UU
*Activities:* Other letting and operating of own or leased real estate
*Parent:* Wykeland Beverley Holdings (No.2) Limited
*Officers:* Ian Charles Franks, Secretary; David Christopher Donkin [1961] Director/Chartered Surveyor; Dominic Anthony Gibbons [1970] Director/Chartered Surveyor; Stephen Peter Hudson [1948] Director

**Wykeland Group Limited**
*Incorporated:* 23 October 1989 *Employees:* 23
*Net Worth:* £69,663,904 *Total Assets:* £130,508,288
*Registered Office:* Wykeland House, 47 Queen Street, Hull, HU1 1UU
*Activities:* Activities of head offices
*Shareholders:* Kevin Simon Webster; Stephen Peter Hudson; Jane Bays Allan; David Andrew Dawson
*Officers:* Ian Charles Franks, Secretary; Jane Bays Allan [1957] Director; Beryl Brignall [1932] Director; Sarah Bays Brignall [1958] Director Actress; David Christopher Donkin [1961] Director/Chartered Surveyor; Ian Charles Franks [1965] Director/Chartered Accountant; Dominic Anthony Gibbons [1970] Director; Catherine Bays Hazelwood [1961] Director; Stephen Peter Hudson [1948] Director; Christopher McLaren Oughtred [1952] Director; Neil Andrew Stothard [1958] Director; Jonathan David Stubbs [1970] Director/Chartered Surveyor

**Wykeland Investments Limited**
*Incorporated:* 11 June 1976
*Net Worth:* £6,568,345 *Total Assets:* £7,886,980
*Registered Office:* Wykeland House, 47 Queen Street, Hull, HU1 1UU
*Activities:* Buying and selling of own real estate
*Parent:* Wykeland Properties (Holdings) Limited
*Officers:* Ian Charles Franks, Secretary; Beryl Brignall [1932] Director; David Christopher Donkin [1961] Director/Chartered Surveyor; Dominic Anthony Gibbons [1970] Director/Chartered Surveyor; Stephen Peter Hudson [1948] Director; Jonathan David Stubbs [1970] Director/Chartered Surveyor

**Wykeland Limited**
*Incorporated:* 30 July 1968 *Employees:* 24
*Net Worth:* £3,363,284 *Total Assets:* £26,197,308
*Registered Office:* Wykeland House, 47 Queen Street, Hull, HU1 1UU
*Activities:* Development of building projects
*Parent:* Wykeland Developments (Holdings) Limited
*Officers:* Ian Charles Franks, Secretary; Jane Bays Allan [1957] Director; Beryl Brignall [1932] Director; Sarah Bays Brignall [1958] Director/Actress; David Christopher Donkin [1961] Director/Chartered Surveyor; Dominic Anthony Gibbons [1970] Director/Chartered Surveyor; Catherine Bays Hazelwood [1961] Director & Farmer; Stephen Peter Hudson [1948] Director; Jonathan David Stubbs [1970] Director/Chartered Surveyor

**Wykeland Properties (Holdings) Limited**
*Incorporated:* 10 January 1990
*Net Worth:* £14,268,199 *Total Assets:* £20,498,096
*Registered Office:* Wykeland House, 47 Queen Street, Hull, HU1 1UU
*Activities:* Activities of head offices
*Parent:* Wykeland Group Limited
*Officers:* Ian Charles Franks, Secretary; Beryl Brignall [1932] Director; David Christopher Donkin [1961] Director/Chartered Surveyor; Dominic Anthony Gibbons [1970] Director; Stephen Peter Hudson [1948] Director; Jonathan David Stubbs [1970] Director/Chartered Surveyor

**Wykeland Properties Limited**
*Incorporated:* 16 February 1979
*Net Worth:* £45,446,300 *Total Assets:* £63,119,288
*Registered Office:* Wykeland House, 47 Queen Street, Hull, HU1 1UU
*Activities:* Construction of commercial buildings
*Parent:* Wykeland Properties (Holdings) Limited
*Officers:* Ian Charles Franks, Secretary; Beryl Brignall [1932] Director; David Christopher Donkin [1961] Director/Chartered Surveyor; Dominic Anthony Gibbons [1970] Director/Chartered Surveyor; Stephen Peter Hudson [1948] Director; Jonathan David Stubbs [1970] Director/Chartered Surveyor

**Wykeland Treasury Management Limited**
*Incorporated:* 17 May 2002
*Net Worth:* £3,992,853 *Total Assets:* £15,811,371
*Registered Office:* Wykeland House, 47 Queen Street, Hull, HU1 1UU
*Activities:* Financial intermediation not elsewhere classified
*Parent:* Wykeland Properties (Holdings) Limited
*Officers:* Ian Charles Franks, Secretary; Beryl Brignall [1932] Director; David Christopher Donkin [1961] Director/Chartered Surveyor; Dominic Anthony Gibbons [1970] Director; Stephen Peter Hudson [1948] Director; Jonathan David Stubbs [1970] Director/Chartered Surveyor

**Wynperg Investments Limited**
*Incorporated:* 30 June 1994 *Employees:* 2
*Net Worth:* £3,727,741 *Total Assets:* £7,659,981
*Registered Office:* The Stoneyard, Green Lane, Horbury Junction, Wakefield, W Yorks, WF4 5DY
*Activities:* Buying and selling of own real estate
*Officers:* Trevor Hirst [1938] Director

**Wyreside Leisure Limited**
*Incorporated:* 6 January 2011
*Previous:* VVB Leisure Services Limited
*Net Worth Deficit:* £1,059 *Total Assets:* £3,046,807
*Registered Office:* Wyreside Hall, Wagon Road, Dolphinholme, Lancaster, LA2 9DH
*Activities:* Other amusement and recreation activities n.e.c.
*Major Shareholder:* Rosemary Irene Hudson
*Officers:* Rosemary Hudson, Secretary; Rosemary Irene Hudson [1955] Director

**X-Force UK Ltd**
*Incorporated:* 15 March 2011 *Employees:* 36
*Net Worth:* £858,331 *Total Assets:* £4,369,224
*Registered Office:* 3-1-5 Health Club, Lancaster Business Park, Mannin Way, Caton Road, Lancaster, LA1 3PE
*Activities:* Agents involved in the sale of machinery, industrial equipment, ships and aircraft
*Parent:* X-Force Group Limited
*Officers:* Sean Thornton [1967] Director

**Xander 97 Limited**
*Incorporated:* 17 June 2014 *Employees:* 1
*Net Worth:* £871,479 *Total Assets:* £4,288,115
*Registered Office:* Corries Solicitors, Melroses Yard, Walmgate, York, YO1 9XF
*Activities:* Other service activities n.e.c.
*Major Shareholder:* Bruce Alan Corrie
*Officers:* Bruce Alan Corrie [1963] Director/Solicitor

**Xiros Limited**
*Incorporated:* 17 September 1982 *Employees:* 105
*Net Worth:* £15,212,879 *Total Assets:* £16,471,479
*Registered Office:* Springfield House, Whitehouse Lane, Leeds, LS19 7UE
*Activities:* Manufacture of other textiles n.e.c.
*Major Shareholder:* Bahaa Botros Seedhom
*Officers:* Jonathan Mark Joyce, Secretary; Dr Stewart John Rodney Davies [1960] Director; Peter Duckworth [1948] Director/Barrister; Dr Donald David Haut Junior [1965] Director/Biotech Executive [American]; Jonathan Mark Joyce [1970] Director; Dr Bahaa Botros Seedhom [1941] Director/Reader

**XL Joinery Limited**
*Incorporated:* 27 August 1999 *Employees:* 76
*Net Worth:* £10,925,564 *Total Assets:* £23,120,752
*Registered Office:* Holden Ing Way, Birstall, Batley, W Yorks, WF17 9AD
*Activities:* Wholesale of wood, construction materials and sanitary equipment
*Parent:* Golden Pharos (Europe) Limited
*Officers:* Robert Reah, Secretary; Azura Binti Abdul-Halim [1971] Director [Malaysian]; Jalil Nicholas Kamaruddin [1966] Director [Malaysian]; Ahmad Fadzil Mohamad [1967] Director [Malaysian]; Ungku Safiah Ungku-Ahmad [1971] Managing Director [Malaysian]

**XP School Trust Limited**
*Incorporated:* 2 January 2013 *Employees:* 26
*Previous:* XP School (Doncaster) Limited
*Net Worth:* £5,920,000 *Total Assets:* £6,152,000
*Registered Office:* XP School, Middle Bank, Doncaster, S Yorks, DN4 5NG
*Activities:* General secondary education
*Officers:* Catherine Elizabeth Blair, Secretary; Stephen Cooper Bielby [1974] Director/Prison Governor; Philip Ralph Crawley [1978] Director/Solicitor; Michael Dewsnap [1979] Director/Standards & Assurance Coordinator; Dr Jean Mary Harris-Evans [1967] Director/Lecturer; Richard Paul Pountney [1954] Director/University Lecturer; Rachel Jayne Scott [1975] Director/Auditor; Liam Joseph Scully [1985] Director; Rebecca Varley [1980] Director/Founder

**XTR Holding Limited**
*Incorporated:* 8 December 2015
*Net Worth:* £3,653,211 *Total Assets:* £11,812,812
*Registered Office:* Unit 1 Erivan Park, Wetherby, W Yorks, LS22 7DN
*Activities:* Activities of head offices
*Major Shareholder:* Herr Stephan Koehler
*Officers:* Thomas Jurisch [1962] Managing Director [German]; Stephan Kohler [1967] Director/Businessman [German]; Ian David Worthington [1967] Director

**Y H Residential Limited**
*Incorporated:* 29 November 2002 *Employees:* 34
*Net Worth:* £8,589,000 *Total Assets:* £32,620,000
*Registered Office:* Dysons Chambers, 12-14 Briggate, Leeds, LS1 6ER
*Activities:* Other letting and operating of own or leased real estate
*Officers:* Guy Millichamp, Secretary; Keith Holloway [1953] Director/Housing Consultant; William Lewis Lifford [1951] Director

**Y.E.S. (Your Event Solutions) Limited**
*Incorporated:* 6 February 2002 *Employees:* 20
*Net Worth:* £6,102,930 *Total Assets:* £9,622,847
*Registered Office:* Till Carr Barn, Till Carr Lane, Lightcliffe, Halifax, W Yorks, HX3 8UB
*Activities:* Activities of conference organisers
*Officers:* Mark Richard Gill, Secretary; Mark Richard Gill [1973] Director; Sue Deborah Gill [1971] Managing Director

**Yamato Scale Dataweigh (UK) Ltd.**
*Incorporated:* 11 April 1994 *Employees:* 29
*Net Worth:* £1,577,927 *Total Assets:* £5,545,190
*Registered Office:* Unit 6b Millennium Way, Leeds, LS11 5AL
*Activities:* Manufacture of other special-purpose machinery n.e.c.
*Officers:* Toshihiko Matsuda, Secretary; Chun Ha [1973] Director/General Manager [Chinese]; Stephen Black McCallion [1956] Managing Director; Sadao Nakamura [1944] Director [Japanese]; Hitoshi Tamura [1958] Director/Manager [Japanese]

**Yamuna Renewables Limited**
*Incorporated:* 16 February 2016
*Net Worth:* £4,230,682 *Total Assets:* £4,241,193
*Registered Office:* Suite 8, Brackenholme Business Park, Selby, N Yorks, YO8 6EL
*Activities:* Other manufacturing n.e.c.
*Shareholders:* Arc Applied Sciences Limited; Downing One VCT PLC
*Officers:* Jonathan Robin Boss [1969] Director; Michael Kotyk [1964] Director [Austrian]; Geoffrey Sankey [1951] Director

**Yara UK Limited**
*Incorporated:* 2 August 1999 *Employees:* 225
*Net Worth:* £90,181,000 *Total Assets:* £225,638,000
*Registered Office:* Harvest House, Europarc, Grimsby, N E Lincs, DN37 9TZ
*Activities:* Manufacture of fertilizers and nitrogen compounds
*Shareholder:* Ministry of Trade, Industry and Fisheries, (Norway)
*Officers:* James Henry Domhnull Hancock, Secretary; Anne Grethe Dalane [1960] Director/Chief Financial Officer [Norwegian]; Charles Spenser Grey [1959] Director/Legal Counsel; David John Tomkinson [1965] Operations Director

**Yarborough Academy**
*Incorporated:* 3 April 2012 *Employees:* 62
*Net Worth:* £4,110,200 *Total Assets:* £4,700,732
*Registered Office:* Yarborough Academy, Yarrow Road, Grimsby, N E Lincs, DN34 4JU
*Activities:* Primary education
*Shareholders:* Alan David Nicholson; Elizabeth Cox
*Officers:* Hannah Louise Albery [1985] Director/Headteacher; Carol Anne Bantock [1952] Director/Retired Teacher; Emma Beveridge [1985] Director/Headteacher; Kerry Louise Coulling [1979] Director/Teacher; Elizabeth Cox [1975] Director; Stephanie Christine Hunter [1987] Director; Jennifer Elizabeth Lundy [1956] Director/Teaching Assistant; Alison Wendy Riley [1979] Director/Teacher; Margaret Saville [1947] Director; David Trevor Smith [1957] Director/Retired; Christine Ann Taylor [1948] Director/Retired Teacher; Selina Turner [1982] Director

**Yarm Estates Limited**
*Incorporated:* 10 July 2012
*Net Worth:* £3,525,352 *Total Assets:* £6,726,748
*Registered Office:* Middleton House, Westland Road, Leeds, LS11 5UH
*Activities:* Buying and selling of own real estate
*Officers:* David James Shann, Secretary; Jarrod Colin Best [1977] Director; Martin Trevor Corney [1965] Director/Property Developer; David James Shann [1973] Director/Company Secretary; Ian Jacob Waller [1952] Director/Property Developer

**Yarrows Aggregates Limited**
*Incorporated:* 1 October 2002 *Employees:* 22
*Net Worth:* £2,307,952 *Total Assets:* £6,654,394
*Registered Office:* The Old Hall, Riston Road, Catwick, Beverley, E Yorks, HU17 5PR
*Activities:* Operation of gravel and sand pits; mining of clays and kaolin
*Shareholders:* Paul Adrian Bird; Mark Desmond Bird; John Christopher Bird
*Officers:* Paul Adrian Bird, Secretary/Farmer; John Christopher Bird [1965] Director/Farmer; Mark Desmond Bird [1958] Director/Farmer; Paul Adrian Bird [1956] Director/Farmer

**Yarwood Leather Limited**
*Incorporated:* 27 November 1967 *Employees:* 40
*Net Worth:* £1,137,539 *Total Assets:* £3,719,826
*Registered Office:* Treefield Industrial Estate, Gelderd Road, Gildersome, Morley, Leeds, LS27 7JU
*Activities:* Wholesale of hides, skins and leather
*Officers:* Catherine Lindsay Dixon [1968] Managing Director; John Verity Edward [1969] Operations Director; Mark Hacking [1973] Sales Director; John Lewis Nicholls [1945] Director/Chief Executive Officer

**R.Yates & Sons Limited**
*Incorporated:* 13 January 1936 *Employees:* 42
*Net Worth:* £4,807,562 *Total Assets:* £5,805,021
*Registered Office:* Derwent Foundry, Railway Street, Malton, N Yorks, YO17 7NR
*Activities:* Other retail sale in non-specialised stores
*Parent:* R. Yates & Sons (Holdings) Ltd
*Officers:* Andrew Ross Clark, Secretary; Andrew Ross Clark [1967] Commercial Director; Sarah Jane Mary Clark [1968] Director

**Brian Yates (Interiors) Limited**
*Incorporated:* 3 July 1980 *Employees:* 29
*Net Worth:* £2,603,754 *Total Assets:* £3,169,776
*Registered Office:* 30 Cove Road, Silverdale, Carnforth, Lancs, LA5 0SQ
*Activities:* Wholesale of textiles
*Officers:* Sheila Coombes, Secretary; Brian Yates [1933] Director

**Yates Media Ltd**
*Incorporated:* 26 September 2012 *Employees:* 2
*Net Worth:* £2,827,941 *Total Assets:* £3,505,070
*Registered Office:* 10 Driver Terrace, Silsden, Keighley, W Yorks, BD20 0JR
*Activities:* Other business support service activities n.e.c.
*Major Shareholder:* Lawrence Fairbank Yates
*Officers:* Lawrence Fairbank Yates [1989] Director

**YBS Holdings Limited**
*Incorporated:* 3 April 2006 *Employees:* 79
*Net Worth:* £3,908,054 *Total Assets:* £11,205,948
*Registered Office:* Access Works, Martin Street, Birstall, Batley, W Yorks, WF17 9PJ
*Activities:* Plumbing, heat and air-conditioning installation
*Shareholders:* Andrew David Sutcliffe; Amos Paul Harrison
*Officers:* Amos Paul Harrison, Secretary/Director; Timothy James Anderson [1984] Director; David Howard Broadhurst [1971] Director; Amos Paul Harrison [1965] Director; Darren Ian Hill [1973] Director; Mark Anthony Peat [1971] Director; Andrew David Sutcliffe [1966] Director

**YCE Catering Equipment Limited**
*Incorporated:* 29 July 1986
*Net Worth:* £187,719 *Total Assets:* £3,924,993
*Registered Office:* Unit R1, Gildersome Spur, Gildersome, Morley, Leeds, LS27 7JZ
*Activities:* Other construction installation
*Shareholders:* Richard Ian Isherwood; Lyndon Moorby
*Officers:* Nicholas Mark Anthony Brassett [1971] Director; Richard Ian Isherwood [1964] Director/Partner; Lyndon Moorby [1972] Director

**YCR Distribution Limited**
*Incorporated:* 9 August 1973 *Employees:* 17
*Net Worth:* £2,054,188 *Total Assets:* £3,540,951
*Registered Office:* Horace Waller V C Parade, Shaw Cross Business Park, Dewsbury, W Yorks, WF12 7RF
*Activities:* Wholesale of electronic and telecommunications equipment and parts
*Parent:* Mostyn Limited
*Officers:* Keeley Earnshaw, Secretary; Keeley Earnshaw [1975] Director; Jonathan Thomas Hall [1963] Managing Director; Paula Hall [1964] Director

**Ye Olde Oak Foods Limited**
*Incorporated:* 15 July 1949 *Employees:* 5
*Net Worth Deficit:* £1,673,092 *Total Assets:* £7,676,213
*Registered Office:* No 2 Warehouse, The Wharf, Sowerby Bridge, W Yorks, HX6 2AG
*Activities:* Non-specialised wholesale of food, beverages and tobacco
*Parent:* Struik Foods International B.V.
*Officers:* Peter Alexander Farren [1956] Director

**Yearsleydale LLP**
*Incorporated:* 16 July 2008
*Net Worth:* £14,268,972 *Total Assets:* £14,273,472
*Registered Office:* Citadel House, 58 High Street, Hull, HU1 1QE
*Officers:* Victoria Ann Denman [1979] Member; Francesca Ann Horsfield [1952] Member; Gordon Christopher Horsfield [1946] Member; Joshua Michael John Horsfield [1982] Member; Camilla Louise Seligman [1984] Member

**Yes Car Credit (Holdings) Limited**
*Incorporated:* 5 December 1923
*Net Worth:* £7,039,000 *Total Assets:* £8,847,000
*Registered Office:* No 1 Godwin Street, Bradford, W Yorks, BD1 2SU
*Activities:* Activities of financial services holding companies
*Parent:* Provident Financial PLC
*Officers:* Kenneth John Mullen [1958] Director/Scottish Solicitor; Simon George Thomas [1964] Director/Chief Finance Officer

**Yesss (A) Electrical Ltd**
*Incorporated:* 3 June 2011 *Employees:* 525
*Previous:* Your Electrical Supplies, Service and Solutions (A) Limited
*Net Worth Deficit:* £48,048,000 *Total Assets:* £47,879,000
*Registered Office:* Unit B, Foxbridge Way, Normanton Industrial Estate, Normanton, W Yorks, WF6 1TN
*Activities:* Other professional, scientific and technical activities n.e.c.
*Officers:* Mark Anthony Arthur Abbey [1962] Director/General Manager; Graham Kilner Lockwood [1970] Director/General Manager; Mark Quentin Nolan [1964] Director/General Manager

**Yesss (B) Electrical Ltd**
*Incorporated:* 27 May 2011 *Employees:* 396
*Previous:* Your Electrical Supplies, Service and Solutions (B) Limited
*Net Worth Deficit:* £31,394,000 *Total Assets:* £33,529,000
*Registered Office:* Unit B, Foxbridge Way, Normanton Industrial Estate, Normanton, W Yorks, WF6 1TN
*Activities:* Other professional, scientific and technical activities n.e.c.
*Officers:* Mark Anthony Arthur Abbey [1962] Director/General Manager; Graham Kilner Lockwood [1970] Director/General Manager; Mark Quentin Nolan [1964] Director/General Manager

**Yesss (C) Electrical Ltd**
*Incorporated:* 28 December 2011 *Employees:* 44
*Previous:* Your Electrical Supplies, Service and Solutions (C) Limited
*Net Worth Deficit:* £78,000 *Total Assets:* £3,926,000
*Registered Office:* Unit B, Foxbridge Way, Normanton Industrial Estate, Normanton, W Yorks, WF6 1TN
*Activities:* Wholesale of electronic and telecommunications equipment and parts
*Shareholders:* Ashley Mackie; Adam Mackie
*Officers:* Mark Anthony Arthur Abbey [1962] Director; Graham Lockwood [1970] Director

**YJL Limited**
*Incorporated:* 27 March 1957
*Net Worth:* £2,114,000 *Total Assets:* £27,597,000
*Registered Office:* 3175 Century Way, Thorpe Park, Leeds, LS15 8ZB
*Activities:* Activities of head offices
*Parent:* Renew Holdings PLC
*Officers:* Andries Petrus Liebenberg [1967] Director [South African]; Paul Scott [1964] Director

**YLC Holdings Limited**
*Incorporated:* 17 March 2016 *Employees:* 217
*Net Worth Deficit:* £45,773 *Total Assets:* £3,068,486
*Registered Office:* Unit 14b Hornbeam Park Oval, Hornbeam Park, Harrogate, N Yorks, HG2 8RB
*Activities:* Activities of other holding companies n.e.c.
*Officers:* Kirsteen Elizabeth Leventhal [1965] Director; Ross Louis Leventhal [1958] Director; Linda Shreeve [1966] Director

**YM Group Limited**
*Incorporated:* 14 August 2015 *Employees:* 808
*Net Worth:* £7,407,000 *Total Assets:* £104,400,000
*Registered Office:* Whitehall Park, Whitehall Road, Leeds, LS12 5XX
*Activities:* Printing n.e.c.
*Officers:* Stephen Tony Goodman [1970] Director; Peter Greaves [1963] Director; Christopher William Ivor Lockley Ingram [1965] Director; David McGolpin [1961] Director; Michael Rutherford Newbould [1970] Director; Lee David Richardson [1971] Director

**Yorhold Limited**
*Incorporated:* 4 December 1991
*Net Worth:* £3,750,007 *Total Assets:* £3,750,007
*Registered Office:* The Lodge, Gatherley Moor Farm, Gilling West, Richmond, N Yorks, DL10 5LJ
*Activities:* Activities of head offices
*Major Shareholder:* Joe Mulhall
*Officers:* Joe Mulhall [1966] Director/Product Research

**York & District Investment Company Limited**
*Incorporated:* 9 July 1959 *Employees:* 6
*Net Worth:* £5,706,680 *Total Assets:* £7,250,515
*Registered Office:* 137 Scalby Road, Scarborough, N Yorks, YO12 6TB
*Activities:* Other letting and operating of own or leased real estate
*Parent:* Broadland Properties Limited
*Officers:* Barry Peter Swiers, Company Secretary; John Guthrie [1936] Director; Peter John Guthrie [1971] Director; Richard Guthrie [1972] Director/Surveyor; James Maxwell Hill [1974] Director/Surveyor; Martin Robson [1975] Director/Accountant; Ronald Graham Urquhart [1957] Director

**York Against Cancer**
*Incorporated:* 22 April 2009 *Employees:* 8
*Net Worth:* £4,446,902 *Total Assets:* £5,387,619
*Registered Office:* 31 North Moor Road, Huntington, York, YO32 9QN
*Activities:* Other human health activities
*Officers:* Julie Pamela Russell, Secretary; Doctor Angela Jayne Darby [1969] Director/Doctor; Rachel Elizabeth Goddard [1965] Managing Director; Edward Keith Hayton [1940] Director/Retired Headmaster; Tarnia Jane Hudson [1969] Director; Patricia Anne Kay [1947] Director/Housewife; Prof. Stephen Howard Leveson [1947] Director/Prof of Surgery; Andrew James Proctor [1973] Director/Physician; William Mark Sessions [1944] Director; Patrick Michael Shepherd [1955] Director; Michael John Stower [1952] Director/Surgeon; Gordon Andrew Topping [1946] Director Medhob Ltd; Sarah Barbara Wearing [1977] Director/Accountant; Keith Simpson Wood [1944] Director/Hotelier; John Francis Yeomans [1944] Director/Solicitor; Ian Robert Yeowart [1954] Director

**York Archaeological Trust for Excavation and Research Limited**
*Incorporated:* 19 June 1979 *Employees:* 230
*Net Worth:* £5,676,784 *Total Assets:* £7,535,628
*Registered Office:* 47 Aldwark, York, YO1 7BX
*Activities:* Environmental consulting activities
*Officers:* Gill Gimes, Secretary; Professor Stephen Taffe Driscoll [1958] Director/Archaeologist [Irish]; Elizabeth Margaret Heaps [1950] Director/Retired; Ian Charles Melia [1951] Director/Retired; Richard Keith Morris [1947] Director/Writer; Dr David Richard Joseph Neave [1944] Director/Retired Lecturer; Susan Lesley Palmer [1952] Director/Retired; Professor Anthony William Robards [1940] Director/Retired; Professor Ellen Roberts [1957] Director/Academic; Michael Richard Watson [1958] Director/Solicitor; Peter Michael Wheatcroft [1951] Director/Electronic Engineer

**York Area Quaker Meeting of The Religious Society of Friends (Quakers) in Britain**
*Incorporated:* 27 March 2009 *Employees:* 7
*Net Worth:* £6,175,946 *Total Assets:* £6,352,690
*Registered Office:* Quaker Meeting House, Friargate, York, YO1 9RL
*Activities:* Activities of religious organisations
*Officers:* Dr Keith Stephen Barnes [1945] Director/Retired; Rosalind Mary Bachelor [1948] Director/Retired; Gillian Rosemary Charters [1955] Director/Retired; Alison Mary Clarke [1951] Director/Retired; John Gilham [1947] Director/Retired; Brian Richard Jardine [1948] Director/Retired; Lesley Olwyn O'Neal [1943] Director/Retired; Danielle Jeanine Palmour [1965] Director/Chief Executive [British/American]; Barbara Elizabeth Penny [1947] Director/Retired; Johanna Peronelle Reilly [1955] Director/Retired

**York Bioanalytical (Holdings) Limited**
*Incorporated:* 20 May 2005 *Employees:* 3
*Net Worth Deficit:* £4,561 *Total Assets:* £3,528,036
*Registered Office:* Cedar House, Northminster Business Park, Northfield Lane, Upper Poppleton, York, YO26 6QR
*Activities:* Other research and experimental development on natural sciences and engineering
*Officers:* Lars Linaa Jorgensen [1959] Director/Head of Region North [Danish]; Josephus Wilhelmus Johannes Lamers [1963] Director/Chief Executive Officer [Dutch]

**York Bioanalytical Solutions Limited**
*Incorporated:* 25 May 1999 *Employees:* 60
*Net Worth:* £11,149,401 *Total Assets:* £12,786,844
*Registered Office:* Cedar House, Northminster Business Park, Northfield Lane, Upper Poppleton, York, YO26 6QR
*Activities:* Other research and experimental development on natural sciences and engineering
*Officers:* Lars Linaa Jorgensen [1959] Director/Head of Region North [Danish]; Josephus Wilhelmus Johannes Lamers [1963] Director/Chief Executive Officer [Dutch]

**York City Football Club Limited**
*Incorporated:* 6 March 2003 *Employees:* 89
*Net Worth Deficit:* £4,174,125 *Total Assets:* £4,441,410
*Registered Office:* Bootham Crescent, York, YO30 7AQ
*Activities:* Other sports activities
*Major Shareholder:* Jason Alexander McGill
*Officers:* Richard Adams [1945] Director; Steven John Kilmartin [1954] Director/Chartered Accountant; Ian McAndrew [1950] Director/Chartered Surveyor; Jason Alexander McGill [1966] Director; David Penney [1964] Director

**York Civic Trust**
*Incorporated:* 12 September 1950 *Employees:* 8
*Net Worth:* £7,143,583 *Total Assets:* £7,175,404
*Registered Office:* Fairfax House, Castlegate, York, YO1 9RN
*Activities:* Operation of arts facilities
*Officers:* Dr David Fraser, Secretary; Dr Peter Vincent Addyman [1939] Director/Archaeologist; Verna Elizabeth Ann Campbell [1939] Director/Retired; David John Foster [1938] Director/Retired; Katherine Fleur Giles [1972] Director/University Lecturer; Prof Jane Clare Grenville [1958] Director/Lecturer; Ann Elizabeth Margaret Heaps [1950] Director/Retired; Stephen John Lewis [1959] Director/Chief Feature Writer, The Press; Stephen Eric Lusty [1943] Director/Retired; Andrew John Scott [1949] Director/Retired; Patrick Michael Shepherd [1955] Director/Deputy Chairman of Shepherd Group; Martin John Stancliffe [1944] Director/Surveyor of St Pauls Cathedral; Terence Suthers [1944] Director/Retired Charity CEO; John Frederick Vincent [1952] Director/Retired; Michael Richard Watson [1958] Director/Solicitor

**York Conservation Trust Limited**
*Incorporated:* 6 June 1945 *Employees:* 4
*Net Worth:* £23,508,652 *Total Assets:* £29,086,666
*Registered Office:* 92 Micklegate, York, YO1 6JX
*Activities:* Development of building projects
*Officers:* Jonathan Andrew Bryant, Secretary; Charles Hedley Esdon Butler [1967] Director [Irish]; Patricia Anne Butler [1942] Director [Irish]; Vanessa Rachel Morrell Butler [1970] Director [Irish]; James Robert Morrell [1978] Director; Jeremy Spence Morrell [1976] Director; John Bowes Morrell [1942] Director; Margaret Anne Morrell [1947] Director; Nicholas Cuthbert Morrell [1949] Director; Olivia Holden Morrell [1981] Director; Professor Peter Spence Morrell [1946] Director; Ruth Isobel Morrell [1958] Director

**York Diocesan Board of Finance Limited (The)**
*Incorporated:* 20 October 1927 *Employees:* 67
*Net Worth:* £89,083,000 *Total Assets:* £95,518,000
*Registered Office:* Diocese of York, Amy Johnson Way, York, YO30 4XT
*Activities:* Activities of religious organisations
*Officers:* Canon Peter John Warry, Secretary; Karen Michelle Banks [1978] Director/Teacher; Charles Rodney Barton [1954] Director; Revd Nicholas William Randle Bird [1970] Director/Minister of Religion; Rosalind Patricia Anne Brewer [1947] Director; Daniel Brookes [1959] Director/Health & Safety Officer; The Venerable Andrew Clifford Broom [1965] Director; The Venerable Sarah Ruth Bullock [1964] Director; Dr. Neill Andrew Burgess [1962] Director; Revd Richard Clayton Carew [1972] Director/Minister of Religion; The Right Reverend Paul John Ferguson [1955] Director/Bishop; Rt Revd Dr Jonathan Hugh Frost [1964] Director/Dean; Andrew Michael Hagon [1971] Director; Benedict James Hudson [1966] Director; Dr Nicholas Mark Land [1961] Psychiatrist Executive Medical Director; Canon Richard Liversedge [1946] Director; The Reverend Fiona Ruth Mayer-Jones [1970] Director; Rev Matthew James Porter [1969] Director; Revd Michael John Proctor [1959] Director/Minister of Religion; The Reverend Timothy James Robinson [1959] Director; The Venerable Samantha Jayne Rushton [1965] Director; John Tucker Mugabi Sentamu [1949] Director; Michael Oswald Stallybrass [1952] Director/Railway Operations Consultant; The Right Reverend John Bromilow Thomson [1959] Director; The Right Reverend Alison Mary White [1956] Director

**York Forty-Four Limited**
*Incorporated:* 1 April 1965 *Employees:* 35
*Net Worth:* £5,128,158 *Total Assets:* £9,327,214
*Registered Office:* The Bungalow, Wetherby Road, Boroughbridge, N Yorks, YO51 9HS
*Activities:* Other amusement and recreation activities n.e.c.
*Shareholder:* Philip James Edward Brierley
*Officers:* Phlip James Edward Brierley, Secretary; Philip James Edward Brierley [1968] Director; Timothy Andrew Neil Brierley [1961] Director

**York Heritage (The Hall Thornton Le Dale) Limited**
*Incorporated:* 17 April 1947 *Employees:* 33
*Net Worth:* £3,505,945 *Total Assets:* £6,416,227
*Registered Office:* The Hall, Chestnut Avenue, Thornton Dale, Pickering, N Yorks, YO18 7RR
*Activities:* Residential care activities for the elderly and disabled
*Parent:* York Heritage Ltd
*Officers:* Christopher Malcolm Lane, Secretary; Christopher Malcolm Lane [1980] Director; Anthony Robert Mitchell [1979] Director; Christopher Robert Mitchell [1958] Director

**York Holdings Limited**
*Incorporated:* 25 March 1985 *Employees:* 5
*Net Worth:* £3,279,028 *Total Assets:* £3,479,796
*Registered Office:* Green Lane Trading Estate, Clifton, York, YO30 5PY
*Activities:* Activities of head offices
*Parent:* Yorkshire Sheeting Group Limited
*Officers:* Gillian Michele Jackson, Secretary; Catherine Anne Attwood [1966] Director; Christopher Barry Hall [1936] Director/Retired; Graham Thomas Hall [1969] Director; Vanessa Judith Ray [1968] Director

**York House Investment Company Ltd**
*Incorporated:* 13 January 2014
*Net Worth:* £3,415,251 *Total Assets:* £3,727,366
*Registered Office:* Moore & Smalley, Kendal House, Murley Moss Business Park, Oxenholme Road, Kendal, Cumbria, LA9 7RL
*Activities:* Activities of investment trusts
*Shareholders:* Mark Stephen Hepworth; Paul John Hepworth
*Officers:* John Peter Hepworth [1954] Director; Lynda Christine Hepworth [1954] Director

**York Mailing (Holdings) Ltd**
*Incorporated:* 3 April 2006
*Net Worth:* £4,338,681 *Total Assets:* £24,510,442
*Registered Office:* The Lettershop Limited, Whitehall Park, Whitehall Road, Leeds, LS12 5XX
*Activities:* Printing n.e.c.
*Parent:* York Mailing Group Limited
*Officers:* Lee David Richardson, Secretary; Stephen Tony Goodman [1970] Director/Accountant; Lee David Richardson [1971] Director/Accountant

**York Mailing Group Limited**
*Incorporated:* 26 September 2011
*Net Worth:* £10,583,099 *Total Assets:* £40,232,544
*Registered Office:* The Lettershop Limited, Whitehall Park, Whitehall Road, Leeds, LS12 5XX
*Activities:* Printing n.e.c.
*Parent:* YM Group Limited
*Officers:* Lee David Richardson, Secretary; Stephen Tony Goodman [1970] Director/Accountant; Lee David Richardson [1971] Director/Accountant

**York Mailing Limited**
*Incorporated:* 16 June 1998 *Employees:* 111
*Net Worth:* £9,451,490 *Total Assets:* £24,381,672
*Registered Office:* The Lettershop Limited, Whitehall Park, Whitehall Road, Leeds, LS12 5XX
*Activities:* Printing n.e.c.
*Parent:* York Mailing Holdings Limited
*Officers:* Alison Jane Ingram, Secretary; Stephen Tony Goodman [1970] Director/Accountant; Peter Greaves [1963] Managing Director; Lee David Richardson [1971] Director/Accountant

**York Museums and Gallery Trust**
*Incorporated:* 26 February 2002 *Employees:* 202
*Net Worth:* £7,634,736 *Total Assets:* £11,896,002
*Registered Office:* St Marys Lodge, Marygate, York, YO30 7DR
*Activities:* Museums activities
*Officers:* Paul Lambert, Secretary; David Brian Collingwood Andrews [1963] Director/Consultant [Canadian]; Philip Priestley Ashton [1947] Director/Retired; Julia Michelle Bell [1973] Director; Sita Brand [1962] Director/Chief Executive; Angela Hilda Dean [1956] Non-Executive Director Portfolio; Sarah Jane Drummond [1966] Director/Project Manager; James Roderick Jocelyn Grierson [1960] Director/Chartered Surveyor; Mary Haworth [1973] Director; Zulfiqar Hussain [1961] Director/Entrepreneur; David Richard Jagger [1955] Director; Mark Ellis Powell Jones [1951] Director/Bookseller; Stephen Eric Lusty [1943] Director/Retired; Cllr Ashley Mason [1990] Director/Councillor; Cllr Keith Robert Myers [1954] Director/Councillor; Prof. Dianne Wilcocks [1945] Director/Retired

**York Pullman Bus Company Limited**
*Incorporated:* 10 January 2007 *Employees:* 104
*Net Worth:* £2,351,247 *Total Assets:* £4,614,234
*Registered Office:* 2 Clifton Moor Business Village, James Nicolson Link, York, YO30 4XG
*Activities:* Other passenger land transport
*Parent:* York Pullman Holdings Limited
*Officers:* Maxine Paula James, Secretary; Thomas George James [1966] Director

**York Racecourse Knavesmire LLP**
*Incorporated:* 16 October 2007 *Employees:* 49
*Net Worth:* £44,318,000 *Total Assets:* £54,728,000
*Registered Office:* The Racecourse, Knavesmire Road, York, YO23 1EX
*Officers:* The Lord Grimthorpe [1954] Member; William Anthony Bethell [1957] LLP Member; Alexander Nicholas Cheyne [1960] LLP Member; Christopher Henry Alfred Denny [1972] LLP Member; Bridget Guerin [1961] LLP Member; Nicholas Hugh Tremayne Wrigley [1955] LLP Member

**York Science Park Limited**
*Incorporated:* 15 June 1994
*Net Worth:* £5,672,066 *Total Assets:* £6,774,824
*Registered Office:* Heslington Hall, Heslington, York, YO10 5DD
*Activities:* Other letting and operating of own or leased real estate
*Shareholders:* University of York; University of York
*Officers:* Michael John Slade, Secretary; Philip David Callow [1960] Director/Chartered Surveyor; Jonathan Mark Greenwood [1963] Commercial Director; David Michael Key [1958] Director; Jenny Louise McAleese [1963] Director/Chief Executive; Alan Robert Millard [1962] Director/Consultant; Professor Saul Jonathan Benjamin Tendler [1961] Director/Deputy Vice Chancellor

**York Sports Village LLP**
*Incorporated:* 12 November 2010
*Net Worth:* £19,691,000 *Total Assets:* £20,051,398
*Registered Office:* Heslington, York, YO10 5DD

**York St John University**
*Incorporated:* 30 July 2002 *Employees:* 675
*Net Worth:* £113,247,000 *Total Assets:* £148,270,000
*Registered Office:* Lord Mayors Walk, York, YO31 7EX
*Activities:* First-degree level higher education
*Officers:* Dr Amanda Wilcox, Secretary; Mohammed Ali [1956] Director/Charity Employee; Jonothan Hammond Booth [1958] Director; Thomas Frederick Butler [1940] Director; Catherine Alice Clelland [1959] Finance Director; George Coombs [1995] Director/Students' Union President; Russell Mark Davidson [1958] Director/Lawyer; Dr Robert Charles Edgar [1972] Director/Lecturer; The Right Reverend Paul John Ferguson [1955] Director/Bishop of Whitby; Richard Edward France [1954] Director/Chartered Surveyor; Ann Margaret Green [1951] Director; Professor Graham Henderson [1952] Director/Retired; Stephen Milner [1956] Director/Civil Servant; Margaret Pavlou [1966] Human Resources Director; Professor Karen Ann Stanton [1961] Director/Vice Chancellor; Ian Christopher Wallace [1958] Director/Internal Auditor

**York University Development Company Limited**
*Incorporated:* 18 May 1994 *Employees:* 2
*Net Worth:* £7,109,981 *Total Assets:* £8,654,048
*Registered Office:* Heslington Hall, Heslington, York, YO1 5DD
*Activities:* Other letting and operating of own or leased real estate
*Parent:* University of York
*Officers:* Michael John Slade, Secretary; Jonathan Mark Greenwood [1963] Director; Jeremy Charles Lindley [1964] Finance Director

**York University Energy Supply Company Limited**
*Incorporated:* 10 June 1993 *Employees:* 2
*Net Worth:* £16,752,627 *Total Assets:* £25,546,398
*Registered Office:* Heslington Hall, Heslington, York, YO10 5DD
*Activities:* Trade of electricity
*Parent:* University of York
*Officers:* Michael John Slade, Secretary; Jeremy Charles Lindley [1964] Finance Director; Stephen David Talboys [1970] Director of Estates

**York123 Limited**
*Incorporated:* 15 June 2016 *Employees:* 3
*Net Worth Deficit:* £1,463 *Total Assets:* £6,770,524
*Registered Office:* 10 The Stables, Newby Hall, Ripon, N Yorks, HG4 5AE
*Activities:* Buying and selling of own real estate
*Parent:* Silverback Developments Limited
*Officers:* Simon William Hepden [1971] Director; Nicholas John Moody [1969] Director; Frazer George Roberts [1993] Director

**Yorkare Homes Limited**
*Incorporated:* 7 May 2003 *Employees:* 361
*Net Worth:* £5,111,326 *Total Assets:* £25,719,032
*Registered Office:* Brantingham Thorpe Hall, Brantingham, Brough, N Humbers, HU15 1QG
*Activities:* Residential nursing care facilities
*Shareholders:* John Robert Garton; Evonne Angelina Garton
*Officers:* Evonne Angelina Garton, Secretary; Elizabeth Catherine Garton [1981] Director/Chartered Accountant; Evonne Angelina Garton [1952] Director/Care Home Proprietor; John Robert Garton [1952] Director/Care Home Proprietors; Jonathan James Garton [1986] Operation Director of Care Homes; Laurence Jack Garton [1984] Director/Care Home Developer

**Yorkcare Limited**
*Incorporated:* 28 January 1988 *Employees:* 1
*Net Worth:* £17,204,268 *Total Assets:* £30,700,164
*Registered Office:* 44 Spinners Hollow, Ripponden, Sowerby Bridge, W Yorks, HX6 4HY
*Activities:* Other letting and operating of own or leased real estate
*Parent:* Leeds and London Holdings Limited
*Officers:* Robert Simon Rowell, Secretary/Accountant; Robert Simon Rowell [1958] Director/Accountant

**Yorkcloud Limited**
*Incorporated:* 17 November 1982 *Employees:* 128
*Net Worth:* £2,760,105 *Total Assets:* £5,773,469
*Registered Office:* Rocky Bank, Lakeside, Newby Bridge, Ulverston, Cumbria, LA12 8AS
*Activities:* Hotels and similar accommodation
*Parent:* Lakeside Hotel Windermere Limited
*Officers:* Arthur Geoffrey Bailes, Secretary; Christos Christou [1968] Director; Christopher Jackson Malpas [1948] Director/Baker & Confectioner; David Michael Birkett Snowdon [1936] Director/Baker & Confectioner; Neville Rodney Talbot [1937] Director/Hotelier; Clive Wilson [1964] Director/Hotelier

**Yorkcourt Paragon Limited**
*Incorporated:* 12 December 2001 *Employees:* 1
*Previous:* Yorkcourt (2006) Limited
*Net Worth:* £4,218,562 *Total Assets:* £8,932,128
*Registered Office:* 2 Red Hall Court, Paragon Business Village, Wakefield, W Yorks, WF1 2UN
*Activities:* Buying and selling of own real estate
*Shareholders:* Curtis Jones; Colin Dwight Mackie; Christopher James McClellan
*Officers:* Christopher James McClellan, Secretary; Curtis Jones [1977] Director/Accountant; Colin Dwight Mackie [1954] Director; Christopher James McClellan [1977] Director

**Yorkshare Limited**
*Incorporated:* 11 June 1987
*Net Worth:* £7,700,000 *Total Assets:* £7,700,000
*Registered Office:* Exchange Court, Duncombe Street, Leeds, LS1 4AX
*Activities:* Dormant company
*Parent:* Interactive Investor Holdings Limited
*Officers:* Barry Michael Bicknell [1968] Director; Richard Simon Wilson [1966] Director

**Yorkshire & Lincolnshire Developments Limited**
*Incorporated:* 21 February 2001 *Employees:* 5
*Net Worth:* £2,695,546 *Total Assets:* £10,801,026
*Registered Office:* Holderness House, Bridgehead Business Park, Hessle, Hull, HU13 0DH
*Activities:* Other letting and operating of own or leased real estate
*Officers:* Gemma Caroline Beal [1980] Director; John Luther Beal [1939] Director/Builder; Richard Luther Beal [1970] Director/Builder

**Yorkshire Agricultural Society**
*Incorporated:* 23 September 1982 *Employees:* 119
*Net Worth:* £29,214,966 *Total Assets:* £39,047,912
*Registered Office:* Regional Agricultural Centre, Great Yorkshire Showground, Harrogate, N Yorks, HG2 8NZ
*Activities:* Activities of other membership organisations n.e.c.
*Officers:* Nigel David Pulling, Secretary; Robert Copley [1971] Director; John Steven Andrew Crabtree [1957] Director/Farmer; Charles David Forbes Adam [1957] Director/Landowner; George Charles Nicholas Lane-Fox [1963] Director/Land Owner; Charles Edwin Mills [1955] Director/Farmer; Timothy Paul Russell [1967] Director; Christine Anne Thompson [1961] Director/Farmer

**Yorkshire Air Ambulance Limited**
*Incorporated:* 16 August 2000 *Employees:* 32
*Net Worth:* £25,437,652 *Total Assets:* £25,889,802
*Registered Office:* Cayley House, 10 South Lane, Elland, W Yorks, HX5 0HQ
*Activities:* Other human health activities
*Officers:* Irene Helen Heap, Secretary; Brian Chapman [1959] Director/General Manager; James Eastwood [1964] Group IT Director; Kevin Hynes [1956] Director/Manager; Vivian John Lewis [1959] Director/Retired; Sandra Marson [1965] Director/Business Consultant; Sarah Jane Moore [1963] Director; Dr Judith Alison Parker [1961] Director/General Medical Practitioner; John William Young Strachan Samuel [1956] Finance Director; Amarjit Singh [1961] Director; Dr Peter Howard Smith [1948] Director/Retired; Peter Sunderland [1942] Retired Director

**Yorkshire and Humberside Co-operative Academies Trust**
*Incorporated:* 28 November 2014 *Employees:* 41
*Net Worth:* £4,611,000 *Total Assets:* £5,381,000
*Registered Office:* c/o The John Curwen Co-operative Primary Academy, Leeds Old Road, Heckmondwike, W Yorks, WF16 9BB
*Activities:* Primary education
*Officers:* Kirsty Hacker, Secretary; Margaret Denise Fretwell [1955] Director/Retired; Dr Stuart Julian Harris [1968] Director/Headteacher; Suresh Nadkarni [1977] Director/Solicitor; Colin Wilkes [1951] Director; Melvyn Woodcock [1947] Director/Education Consultant

**Yorkshire and The Humber Co-operative Learning Trust**
*Incorporated:* 14 September 2016 *Employees:* 544
*Net Worth:* £27,629,000 *Total Assets:* £33,312,000
*Registered Office:* Kelvin Hall School, Bricknell Avenue, Hull, HU5 4QH
*Activities:* Primary education
*Officers:* Stuart Carrington, Secretary; Paul Jonathan Britton [1981] Director/Education; Humphrey Forrest [1951] Director/Tribunal Judge; Stephen Paul Jones [1957] Director/Chartered Accountant/Foster Carer; William Edward Maxwell [1955] Director/Retired; James McIntosh [1987] Director/Business Development & Marketing Manager; Christopher Shepherdson [1976] Director/Business Owner/Accounting Student; Andrew Smith [1943] Director/Retired; Peter Thundercliffe [1963] Director; Michael Philip Wood [1963] Director/Health and Safety Consultant; Susan Patricia Claire Wood [1952] Director/Retired

**Yorkshire Bank Home Loans Limited**
*Incorporated:* 12 October 1984
*Net Worth:* £24,197,000 *Total Assets:* £1,080,285,056
*Registered Office:* 20 Merrion Way, Leeds, LS2 8NZ
*Activities:* Activities of mortgage finance companies
*Parent:* Clydesdale Bank PLC
*Officers:* Lorna Forsyth McMillan, Secretary; Michael James Hart [1967] Director/Bank Executive; Ian Stuart Smith [1966] Director/Bank Executive; Nicholas George Julian Walford [1974] Director/Bank Executive

**Yorkshire Baptist Association (Incorporated) (The)**
*Incorporated:* 5 May 1922
*Net Worth:* £2,998,109 *Total Assets:* £3,041,014
*Registered Office:* 1 South Parade, Headingley, Leeds, LS6 3LF
*Activities:* Activities of religious organisations
*Officers:* Elizabeth Frances Allen [1958] Director/NHS Senior Manager; Christopher William Bishop [1947] Director/Retired; Philip David Callow [1960] Director/Commercial Project Manager; John Picton Crosse [1956] Director; Gill Knowles [1958] Director/Deacon; Carol Mavis Moore [1964] Director/Specialist Health Visitor; Kevin Leslie Quinton [1960] Director/Retired IT Manager; Dean Charlton Thorpe [1976] Director/Financial Adviser; Revd Matthew Thomas Wright [1984] Director/Baptist Minister

**Yorkshire Botanicals Limited**
*Incorporated:* 21 April 2015 *Employees:* 49
*Net Worth:* £2,690,714 *Total Assets:* £3,714,776
*Registered Office:* Hesslewood Hall Business Centre, Ferriby Road, Hessle, E Yorks, HU13 0LH
*Activities:* Growing of spices, aromatic, drug and pharmaceutical crops
*Shareholder:* Robert Ian Sayer
*Officers:* Daphne Sansam, Secretary; Nigel Derek Bartle [1974] Director; Robert Ian Sayer [1950] Director/Market Gardener; Thomas Robert Sayer [1983] Director/Program Manager

**Yorkshire Building Services Limited**
*Incorporated:* 18 May 1992 *Employees:* 79
*Net Worth:* £3,772,844 *Total Assets:* £11,068,338
*Registered Office:* Access Works, Martin Street, Birstall, Batley, W Yorks, WF17 9PJ
*Activities:* Electrical installation
*Parent:* YBS Holdings Ltd
*Officers:* Amos Paul Harrison, Secretary/Chartered Accountant; Timothy James Anderson [1984] Director; David Howard Broadhurst [1971] Director; Amos Paul Harrison [1965] Director/Accountant; Darren Ian Hill [1973] Director; Mark Anthony Peat [1971] Director; Andrew David Sutcliffe [1966] Director/Engineer

**Yorkshire Building Society Covered Bonds LLP**
*Incorporated:* 22 September 2006
*Net Worth:* £7,976,000 *Total Assets:* £2,584,763,904
*Registered Office:* Yorkshire House, Yorkshire Drive, Bradford, W Yorks, BD5 8LJ

**Yorkshire Cancer Research**
*Incorporated:* 6 June 1985 *Employees:* 34
*Net Worth:* £46,497,660 *Total Assets:* £47,987,416
*Registered Office:* Jacob Smith House, 7 Grove Park Court, Harrogate, N Yorks, HG1 4DP
*Activities:* Other human health activities
*Officers:* Graham Michael Berville [1956] Director/Strategic Consultant; Rosemary Grace Cook CBE [1959] Director/Chief Executive; Sandra Jane Dodson [1954] Director/Chairman; Margaret Kitching [1957] Director of Nursing & Quality; Janet Mary Myers [1964] Director/Fundraiser; Robert Samuel Duncan Mugenyi Ndawula [1974] Finance Director; Dr Yvette Alison Oade [1959] Director/Doctor; Elizabeth Anne Richards [1957] Director; Catherine Elizabeth Margaret Rustomji [1975] Director/Solicitor; Alan Mark Sidebottom [1968] Director/Chartered Accountant; Christopher John Slater [1963] Associate Director, Leeds Teaching Hospitals; Dr Alan Suggett [1943] Director/Business Consultant

**Yorkshire Caravans of Bawtry Limited**
*Incorporated:* 27 March 1961 *Employees:* 54
*Net Worth:* £683,111 *Total Assets:* £4,661,866
*Registered Office:* Doncaster Road, Bawtry, Doncaster, S Yorks, DN10 6DG
*Activities:* Other retail sale of new goods in specialised stores (not commercial art galleries and opticians)
*Parent:* Y C Leisure Limited
*Officers:* Jonathan Robert Goulden [1973] Director; Andrew Whittaker [1969] Director

**Yorkshire Causeway Schools Trust**
*Incorporated:* 9 June 2011 *Employees:* 317
*Previous:* St Aidan's Church of England Schools Trust
*Net Worth:* £23,703,274 *Total Assets:* £31,047,660
*Registered Office:* St Aidan's Church of England High School, Oatlands Drive, Harrogate, N Yorks, HG2 8JR
*Activities:* Primary education
*Officers:* Christopher Nicholas Burt, Secretary; John Miles Bushell [1938] Director/University Tutor; David John Fisher [1947] Director/Chartered Accountant; Alison Glover [1967] Pastoral Director; Terence Harrison [1943] Director/Retired; Claire Elizabeth Kelley [1956] Director/Office Manager; Seth King [1971] Director/Chartered Accountant; Andrew Edwin Marson [1969] Director/Business Executive; Steven Scarisbrick [1969] Director/Operations Manager; Andrew Symonds [1968] Director/Headteacher; Philip Titchmarsh [1973] Director/Solicitor; Martin Gregory Michael Wicks [1963] Director; John Wood [1954] Director/Headteacher

**Yorkshire Collaborative Academy Trust**
*Incorporated:* 2 July 2015 *Employees:* 104
*Net Worth:* £7,592,000 *Total Assets:* £9,472,000
*Registered Office:* Bilton Grange Primary School, Bilton Lane, Harrogate, N Yorks, HG1 3BA
*Activities:* Primary education
*Officers:* Paul Barrett [1974] Director/Strategic Marketing & Communication Consultant; Jennifer Deborah Baynes [1973] Director/Local Government Officer; Roger Neville Gook [1945] Director/Retired; Ian Paul Moore [1957] Director/Architect; Emma Nicholson [1971] Director/Chartered Project Manager; Donald Parker [1952] Director/Headteacher; Joanne Mary Robinson [1972] Director/Headteacher

**Yorkshire Design Services Limited**
*Incorporated:* 6 April 1987
*Net Worth:* £10,242,331 *Total Assets:* £12,572,297
*Registered Office:* 46 The Calls, Leeds, LS2 7EY
*Activities:* Other letting and operating of own or leased real estate
*Shareholders:* Peter John Connolly; Robert Michael Noble
*Officers:* Peter John Connolly, Secretary; Peter John Connolly [1948] Director; Paul James Ellison [1974] Director; Robert Michael Noble [1953] Director

**Yorkshire Farmhouse Eggs Limited**
*Incorporated:* 30 October 2000 *Employees:* 31
*Net Worth:* £3,775,119 *Total Assets:* £6,621,763
*Registered Office:* Village Farm, Catton, Thirsk, N Yorks, YO7 4SQ
*Activities:* Raising of poultry
*Parent:* Potter Family Holdings Limited
*Officers:* Susan Joan Potter, Secretary; Adrian Potter [1977] Director; John Roger Potter [1949] Director/Farmer; Oliver James Potter [1975] Director/Manager; Susan Joan Potter [1950] Director/Farmer

**Yorkshire Feedstuffs Limited**
*Incorporated:* 21 June 1996
*Net Worth:* £258,420 *Total Assets:* £5,325,380
*Registered Office:* Harvest House, Cottingham Street, Goole, E Yorks, DN14 5RP
*Activities:* Agents selling agricultural raw materials, livestock, textile raw materials and semi-finished goods
*Shareholders:* Gina Louise Brown; Carlo Stanley Urbanowicz; Franco Bernardini
*Officers:* Gina Louise Brown [1972] Trading Director; Carlo Stanley Urbanowicz [1954] Managing Director

**Yorkshire Grain Limited**
*Incorporated:* 15 May 2009 *Employees:* 5
*Net Worth:* £246,216 *Total Assets:* £3,234,188
*Registered Office:* 34 Middle Street South, Driffield, E Yorks, YO25 6PS
*Activities:* Post-harvest crop activities
*Shareholder:* Jonathon Mark Hilton Cox
*Officers:* Christopher Charles Kingsley Atkin, Secretary; Christopher Charles Kingsley Atkin [1962] Director; Jonathan Mark Hilton Cox [1965] Director; Simon William Minns [1961] Director; Maurice Robson [1944] Director; Mark Shaun Storey [1970] Director

**Yorkshire Grown Produce Limited**
*Incorporated:* 20 January 1993 *Employees:* 151
*Net Worth:* £3,597,679 *Total Assets:* £8,498,147
*Registered Office:* Main Road, Newport, Brough, E Yorks, HU15 2PR
*Activities:* Growing of vegetables and melons, roots and tubers
*Shareholders:* Antonio Magistro-Contenta; Vincenzo Magistro-Contenta
*Officers:* Bidar Almozaffar [1953] Director; Sam Almozaffar [1950] Director; Vincent Magistro Contenta [1988] Director

**Yorkshire Halal Meat Supplier Limited**
*Incorporated:* 8 September 2003
*Net Worth:* £5,082,866 *Total Assets:* £8,140,659
*Registered Office:* Shan Buildings, Alice Street, Keighley, W Yorks, BD21 3JD
*Activities:* Production of meat and poultry meat products
*Major Shareholder:* Ali Akbar Shan
*Officers:* Aftab Ali, Secretary/Director; Ali Akbar Shan [1966] Director

**Yorkshire House Development One Limited**
*Incorporated:* 24 July 2015
*Net Worth Deficit:* £5,771 *Total Assets:* £22,661,618
*Registered Office:* Ogleforth House, Ogleforth, York, YO1 7JG
*Activities:* Buying and selling of own real estate
*Shareholders:* Recantos Trust 2015; Neal Investments Ltd
*Officers:* Charles Richard Jackson [1951] Director; John Howard Neal [1961] Director/Businessman

**Yorkshire Housing Finance PLC**
*Incorporated:* 19 September 2014
*Net Worth:* £50,000 *Total Assets:* £140,003,008
*Registered Office:* Dysons Chambers, 12-14 Briggate, Leeds, LS1 6ER
*Activities:* Financial intermediation not elsewhere classified
*Officers:* Guy Millichamp, Secretary; David William Bolton [1968] Director; Guy Christopher Millichamp [1964] Finance Director

**Yorkshire Initiatives Limited**
*Incorporated:* 12 May 2014 *Employees:* 87
*Net Worth:* £867,410 *Total Assets:* £13,516,789
*Registered Office:* Mill Hill, Braegate Lane, Colton, Tadcaster, N Yorks, LS24 8EW
*Activities:* Activities of other holding companies n.e.c.
*Parent:* Braegate Holdings Limited (11535585)
*Officers:* Antony Edwards [1975] Director

**Yorkshire Packaging Systems Limited**
*Incorporated:* 13 June 1977 *Employees:* 22
*Net Worth:* £2,005,409 *Total Assets:* £5,743,710
*Registered Office:* Woodkirk Freight Terminal, Quarry Lane, Woodkirk, Dewsbury, W Yorks, WF12 7JJ
*Activities:* Agents specialised in the sale of other particular products
*Major Shareholder:* David Johnson
*Officers:* Barbara Anne Johnson, Secretary; Johnathan Lewis Braithwaite [1988] Director/Sales Manager; William Raymond Bruce [1959] Director/UK Sales Manager; Barbara Anne Johnson [1948] Director/Secretary; David Johnson [1948] Director/Chairman; Glyn David Johnson [1971] Managing Director; Rachel Diane Johnson [1975] Director/Sales Manager

**Yorkshire Period Hotels Limited**
*Incorporated:* 28 September 2000
*Net Worth:* £94,894 *Total Assets:* £4,147,099
*Registered Office:* Medina House, 2 Station Avenue, Bridlington, E Yorks, YO16 4LZ
*Activities:* Hotels and similar accommodation
*Major Shareholder:* Catherine Mary Hogarth
*Officers:* Catherine Mary Hogarth [1957] Director

**Yorkshire Plywood Limited**
*Incorporated:* 14 January 1986 *Employees:* 39
*Net Worth:* £1,097,594 *Total Assets:* £11,514,519
*Registered Office:* 650 Anlaby Road, Hull, HU3 6UU
*Activities:* Wholesale of wood, construction materials and sanitary equipment
*Shareholders:* Ian Cameron Thomson; John James Aylward
*Officers:* Ian Cameron Thomson, Secretary; John James Aylward [1948] Director/Timber Merchant; Ian Cameron Thomson [1958] Director/Timber Merchant

**Yorkshire Premier Meat Limited**
*Incorporated:* 13 December 2012 *Employees:* 74
*Net Worth:* £1,588,639 *Total Assets:* £10,088,754
*Registered Office:* Unit 56 Lidgate Crescent, Langthwaite Grange Industrial Estate, South Kirkby, Pontefract, W Yorks, WF9 3NR
*Activities:* Wholesale of meat and meat products
*Parent:* ANM Group Limited
*Officers:* James Alexander Jaffray [1954] Director; David Edward Lake [1980] Director; Stirling James Oswin [1967] Director

**Yorkshire Property Finance Ltd**
*Incorporated:* 5 April 2011
*Net Worth:* £276,434 *Total Assets:* £4,289,035
*Registered Office:* 1 The Mews, Little Brunswick Street, Huddersfield, W Yorks, HD1 5JL
*Activities:* Other credit granting n.e.c.
*Shareholders:* Timothy Nicholas Gledhill; Anthony John Newham
*Officers:* Timothy Nicholas Gledhill [1967] Director; Anthony John Newham [1960] Director/Finance Broker

**Yorkshire Prosperity Limited**
*Incorporated:* 13 August 2010 *Employees:* 40
*Net Worth:* £2,019,291 *Total Assets:* £7,125,829
*Registered Office:* 6 Blenheim Terrace, Leeds, LS2 9HZ
*Activities:* Management of real estate on a fee or contract basis
*Parent:* YPP Holdings Limited
*Officers:* Zaid Al-Najafi, Secretary; Omar Al Najafi [1987] Director; Abdulaziz Mohammad Al-Najafi [1983] Director; Zaid Al-Najafi [1991] Director

**The Yorkshire Provender Ltd**
*Incorporated:* 27 February 2007 *Employees:* 27
*Net Worth:* £1,969,000 *Total Assets:* £5,055,000
*Registered Office:* 2100 Century Way, Thorpe Park, Leeds, LS15 8ZB
*Activities:* Manufacture of prepared meals and dishes
*Parent:* Hain Frozen Foods UK Limited
*Officers:* Nicholas John Keen, Secretary; Denise Menikheim Faltischek [1973] Director/Executive Vice President and General Counsel [American]; James Michael Langrock [1965] Director [American]; Mark Lawrence Schiller [1961] Director/CEO Hain Celestial [American]; Robin James Skidmore [1968] Director

**Yorkshire Sculpture Park**
*Incorporated:* 26 January 1998 *Employees:* 223
*Net Worth:* £17,774,160 *Total Assets:* £18,510,892
*Registered Office:* Bretton Hall, West Bretton, Wakefield, W Yorks, WF4 4LG
*Activities:* Operation of arts facilities
*Officers:* Paul Richard Rogers, Secretary; Peter Box [1947] Director/Solicitor Councillor; Peter Alexander Clegg [1950] Director/Architect; Maria de Peverelli [1962] Director/Art Consultant [Italian]; John Edward Foster [1948] Director/Consultant; Rt Hon Alan Milburn [1958] Director/MP; Rupert Generald Nunes Nabarro [1945] Director/Economist; Magnus Von Wistinghausen [1967] Director [German]; Sir Rodney Walker [1943] Director; Greville Thomas Worthington [1963] Director

**Yorkshire Sheeting and Insulation Services Limited**
*Incorporated:* 24 April 1970 *Employees:* 20
*Net Worth:* £1,037,296 *Total Assets:* £5,862,577
*Registered Office:* Green Lane Trading Estate, Clifton, York, YO30 5PY
*Activities:* Other specialised construction activities n.e.c.
*Parent:* York Holdings Limited
*Officers:* Gillian Michele Jackson, Secretary; Graham Thomas Hall [1969] Director; Stephen Marcus Long [1976] Commercial Director; Andrew Thompson [1962] Director

**Yorkshire Sheeting Group Limited**
*Incorporated:* 24 August 2016 *Employees:* 20
*Net Worth:* £4,308,824 *Total Assets:* £9,177,583
*Registered Office:* Green Lane Trading Estate, Clifton, York, YO30 5PY
*Activities:* Activities of other holding companies n.e.c.
*Shareholders:* Catherine Anne Attwood; Graham Thomas Hall; Vanessa Judith Ray
*Officers:* Catherine Anne Attwood [1966] Director; Graham Thomas Hall [1969] Director; Vanessa Judith Ray [1968] Director

**Yorkshire Stone Co. (Bradford) Limited**
*Incorporated:* 29 March 1955 *Employees:* 7
*Net Worth:* £1,576,722 *Total Assets:* £5,224,551
*Registered Office:* Bolton Woods Quarry, Bolton Hall Road, Bradford, W Yorks, BD2 1BQ
*Activities:* Activities of production holding companies
*Officers:* William Ross Marshall, Secretary; Frank Edward Marshall [1978] Director; Frank William Marshall [1938] Director; George Henry Ross Marshall [1978] Director; James Ernest Marshall [1979] Director; William Ross Marshall [1975] Director

**Yorkshire Ventures (Estates) Limited**
*Incorporated:* 3 November 2015 *Employees:* 88
*Net Worth Deficit:* £1,219,883 *Total Assets:* £20,039,540
*Registered Office:* Omega 3, Monks Cross Drive, Huntington, York, YO32 9GZ
*Activities:* Buying and selling of own real estate
*Shareholder:* Charles Richard Jackson
*Officers:* Charles Richard Jackson [1951] Director

**Yorkshire Water Services Finance Limited**
*Incorporated:* 14 January 2003
*Net Worth:* £48,000 *Total Assets:* £1,646,716,032
*Registered Office:* Western House, Halifax Road, Bradford, BD6 2SZ
*Activities:* Banks
*Parent:* Yorkshire Water Services Limited
*Officers:* Kathy Smith, Secretary; Elizabeth Marian Barber [1965] Director/Accountant; Richard David Flint [1968] Director; Kathy Olivia Helen Smith [1974] Director/Company Secretary

**Yorkshire Water Services Holdings Limited**
*Incorporated:* 10 February 2009
*Net Worth:* £778,318,976 *Total Assets:* £778,318,976
*Registered Office:* Western House, Halifax Road, Bradford, BD6 2SZ
*Activities:* Activities of head offices
*Parent:* Kelda Finance (No. 2) Limited
*Officers:* Kathy Smith, Secretary; Elizabeth Marian Barber [1965] Director/Accountant; Richard David Flint [1968] Director; Kathy Olivia Helen Smith [1974] Director/Company Secretary

**Yorkshire Water Services Limited**
*Incorporated:* 1 April 1989 *Employees:* 2,681
*Net Worth:* £1,147,699,968 *Total Assets:* £9,004,600,320
*Registered Office:* Western House, Halifax Road, Bradford, W Yorks, BD6 2SZ
*Activities:* Water collection, treatment and supply
*Parent:* Yorkshire Water Services Holdings Limited
*Officers:* Kathy Smith, Secretary; Scott Auty [1978] Director/Fund Manager; Elizabeth Marian Barber [1965] Director/Accountant; Andrew James Dench [1969] Director; Richard David Flint [1968] Director; Nevil George Muncaster [1964] Director/Civil Engineer; Raymond O'Toole [1955] Director/Engineer; Michael Peter Francis Osborne [1980] Director; Anthony Leon Philip Rabin [1955] Director; Julia Unwin [1956] Director/Consultant; Andrew Wyllie [1962] Director

**Yorkshire Wildlife Trust**
*Incorporated:* 2 May 1946 *Employees:* 127
*Net Worth:* £10,817,228 *Total Assets:* £12,608,122
*Registered Office:* 1 St George's Place, York, YO24 1GN
*Activities:* Botanical and zoological gardens and nature reserves activities
*Officers:* Richard Tripp, Secretary; Mike Cooke [1959] Director/Retired; David Counsel [1944] Director/Retired; Louise Farnell [1969] Director/Fundraising Consultant; Professor Alastair Hugh Fitter [1948] Director/Retired; Paddy John Creighton Hall [1945] Director/Retired Public Sector Consultant; Christine Packer [1960] Director/Local Government Officer; Martin Randle [1954] Director/Retired; Joanna Royle [1966] Director/Head of Marketing; Gurdev Singh [1962] Director; Richard Edward Tripp [1969] Director/Solicitor; Joanna Flower Webb [1961] Director; Hugh Williamson [1951] Director/Retired

**Yorktest Group Limited**
*Incorporated:* 8 June 2017 *Employees:* 38
*Net Worth Deficit:* £1,183,282 *Total Assets:* £8,297,554
*Registered Office:* Units 2-3 Triune Court, Monks Cross Drive, Huntington, York, YO32 9GZ
*Activities:* Activities of other holding companies n.e.c.
*Parent:* Key Capital Partners (Nominees) Limited
*Officers:* Richard David Neil Dawson [1969] Director; Edward William Goold [1948] Director/Chairman; James David Hall [1969] Director

**Yorkwold (Overseas) Limited**
*Incorporated:* 26 October 2004
*Net Worth:* £4,524,155 *Total Assets:* £4,556,288
*Registered Office:* Field House Farm, Scarborough Road, Driffield, E Yorks, YO25 5UY
*Activities:* Growing of cereals (except rice), leguminous crops and oil seeds
*Shareholders:* Kevin John Walker; Yorkwold Pigpro Limited
*Officers:* Kevin John Walker, Secretary; Robert Beckett [1968] Director/Farmer; Joseph William Dewhirst [1978] Director/Farmer; Kevin John Walker [1947] Director/Farmer

**Yorkwold Pigpro Limited**
*Incorporated:* 21 March 1972 *Employees:* 73
*Net Worth:* £21,345,476 *Total Assets:* £27,434,216
*Registered Office:* Field House, Scarborough Road, Driffield, E Yorks, YO25 5UY
*Activities:* Raising of swine and pigs
*Shareholders:* Catherine Barbara Dewhirst; Timothy Charles Dewhirst
*Officers:* Joseph William Dewhirst, Secretary; Robert Beckett [1968] Director/Pig Producer; Joseph William Dewhirst [1978] Director/Pig Producer; Richard John Dewhirst [1981] Director/Farmer; Timothy Charles Dewhirst [1953] Director/Retired

**Yorparks Limited**
*Incorporated:* 20 December 1983 *Employees:* 11
*Net Worth:* £5,303,039 *Total Assets:* £13,209,664
*Registered Office:* 3rd Floor, Goodbard House, 15 Infirmary Street, Leeds, LS1 2JS
*Activities:* Other letting and operating of own or leased real estate
*Shareholder:* Toby James Morton
*Officers:* Kenneth Morton [1942] Director/Project Development Consultant; Richard John Morton [1969] Director/Property Developer; Sally Anne Morton [1971] Director/Developer; Toby James Morton [1973] Director/Car Park Operator

**Yorplace Limited**
*Incorporated:* 26 June 2014 *Employees:* 2
*Net Worth:* £405,632 *Total Assets:* £3,808,853
*Registered Office:* 3rd Floor, Goodbard House, 15 Infirmary Street, Leeds, LS1 2JS
*Activities:* Buying and selling of own real estate
*Major Shareholder:* Toby James Morton
*Officers:* Jane Maragret Morton [1973] Director/Designer; Kenneth Morton [1942] Director; Toby James Morton [1973] Director

**Yorpower Limited**
*Incorporated:* 30 September 2009 *Employees:* 16
*Net Worth:* £1,421,445 *Total Assets:* £3,807,573
*Registered Office:* Electricity Building, Unit 2 Hurricane Close, Sherburn in Elmet, Leeds, LS25 6PB
*Activities:* Agents involved in the sale of machinery, industrial equipment, ships and aircraft
*Shareholders:* Anthony John Brimble; Ian Jeremy Thompson
*Officers:* Anthony John Brimble [1963] Director; Stephen Robert Hammond [1957] Operations Director; Ian Jeremy Thompson [1959] Sales Director

**Yorvik Homes Limited**
*Incorporated:* 21 February 1994 *Employees:* 18
*Net Worth:* £6,453,465 *Total Assets:* £7,978,971
*Registered Office:* First Floor, 4 Audax Court, Audax Close, York, YO30 4RB
*Activities:* Construction of domestic buildings
*Major Shareholder:* Matthew James Gath
*Officers:* Karen Marie Thomas, Secretary; Matthew James Gath [1966] Director; Jean Monroe [1933] Director

**Yorwaste Limited**
*Incorporated:* 25 November 1991 *Employees:* 318
*Net Worth:* £10,613,963 *Total Assets:* £40,264,952
*Registered Office:* Mount View, Standard Way, Northallerton, N Yorks, DL6 2YD
*Activities:* Collection of non-hazardous waste
*Parent:* North Yorkshire County Council
*Officers:* David Raymond Bowe [1962] Director/Local Government Officer; Alexander Boyle [1970] Finance Director; Martin Howard Buckley [1945] Director; Geoffrey Douglas Derham [1962] Director; Neil James Ferris [1969] Director/Local Government Officer; John Phillips [1954] Director; Cllr Andrew Michael Waller [1969] Director/Local Authority Member; John Keith Weighell [1942] Director/Farmer

**Young Herts Limited**
*Incorporated:* 19 January 2007
*Net Worth Deficit:* £4,275,999 *Total Assets:* £16,610,764
*Registered Office:* 4 Greengate, Cardale Park, Harrogate, N Yorks, HG3 1GY
*Activities:* Other human health activities
*Parent:* Young Herts Holdings Limited
*Officers:* Paul William Noake, Secretary; Alastair William Hopps [1986] Director/Chartered Accountant; Alexander Toby Shedden Parry [1976] Director/Chartered Accountant

**Young's Seafood International Holdings Limited**
*Incorporated:* 8 September 1998 *Employees:* 3
*Previous:* Findus UK Group Limited
*Net Worth:* £12,357,000 *Total Assets:* £80,273,000
*Registered Office:* Ross House, Wickham Road, Grimsby, N E Lincs, DN31 3SW
*Activities:* Other business support service activities n.e.c.
*Parent:* Lighthouse UKCo 6 (Treasury) Limited
*Officers:* Timothy Mark Busby [1964] Director; William John Showalter [1963] Director/Chief Financial Officer [American]

**Young's Seafood Limited**
*Incorporated:* 14 April 1999 *Employees:* 2,413
*Net Worth:* £42,920,000 *Total Assets:* £526,859,008
*Registered Office:* Ross House, Wickham Road, Grimsby, N E Lincs, DN31 3SW
*Activities:* Processing and preserving of fish, crustaceans and molluscs
*Parent:* Young's Seafood International Holdings Limited
*Officers:* Timothy Mark Busby [1964] Director; Stuart Ian Caborn [1975] Director; Dominic Eugene Kerrigan [1972] Director; William John Showalter [1963] Director/Group Chief Financial Officer [American]

**Younger Homes (Northern) Limited**
*Incorporated:* 19 July 1985 *Employees:* 2
*Net Worth:* £9,475,226 *Total Assets:* £27,970,892
*Registered Office:* Unit 4 Brookfoot Business Park, Brighouse, W Yorks, HD6 2SD
*Activities:* Construction of commercial buildings
*Shareholders:* Susan Elizabeth Ibberson; William George Ibberson
*Officers:* Susan Elizabeth Ibberson, Secretary; Susan Elizabeth Ibberson [1949] Director/Accountant; William George Ibberson [1949] Director/Builder

**Youngmight Limited**
*Incorporated:* 9 July 1996
*Net Worth:* £3,998,986 *Total Assets:* £3,998,986
*Registered Office:* Dalton House, 9 Dalton Square, Lancaster, LA1 1WD
*Activities:* Activities of other holding companies n.e.c.
*Major Shareholder:* Geoffrey Goodyear Atkinson
*Officers:* Diane Robinson, Secretary/Hotel Accountant; Elysia Ann Atkinson [1947] Director; Geoffrey Goodyear Atkinson [1950] Director/Hotelier

**YP Real Estate Limited**
*Incorporated:* 1 November 2013 *Employees:* 3
*Net Worth Deficit:* £1,581,657 *Total Assets:* £4,325,744
*Registered Office:* Thorpe Arch Grange, Walton Road, Wetherby, W Yorks, LS23 7BA
*Activities:* Buying and selling of own real estate
*Parent:* Stirling Partners Real Estate LLP
*Officers:* George Raymond Iestyn Llewellyn-Smith [1979] Director/Banker; David Ian Newett [1959] Director/Asset Manager; Andrew John Pettit [1968] Director

**YPP Holdings Limited**
*Incorporated:* 29 April 2016 *Employees:* 40
*Net Worth:* £3,483,307 *Total Assets:* £15,885,434
*Registered Office:* 6 Blenheim Terrace, Leeds, LS2 9HZ
*Activities:* Activities of construction holding companies
*Officers:* Zaid Alnajafi, Secretary; Abdulaziz Al-Najafi [1983] Director; Omar Al-Najafi [1987] Director; Zaid Al-Najafi [1991] Director

**YPS Valves Limited**
*Incorporated:* 5 April 1977 *Employees:* 39
*Net Worth:* £4,085,708 *Total Assets:* £5,975,981
*Registered Office:* Grangefield Industrial Estate, Pudsey, W Yorks, LS28 6QW
*Activities:* Manufacture of taps and valves
*Shareholder:* Paulette Ducker
*Officers:* Rachel Wormald, Secretary; Simon Robert Barraclough [1958] Director; Steven Martin Chapman [1950] Director/Engineer; Paulette Ducker [1944] Director; Jonathan Mark Wormald [1973] Director; Rachel Wormald [1974] Director/Accounts

**Ypsomed Limited**
*Incorporated:* 21 January 2010 *Employees:* 30
*Net Worth:* £2,358,372 *Total Assets:* £8,202,953
*Registered Office:* 1 Park Court, Riccall Road, Escrick, N Yorks, YO19 6ED
*Activities:* Wholesale of pharmaceutical goods
*Officers:* Simon Michel [1977] Director/Senior Vice President - Marketing and Sales [Swiss]; Niklaus Ramseier [1963] Director [Swiss]

**YRG Group Limited**
*Incorporated:* 17 February 1997 *Employees:* 75
*Net Worth:* £1,691,005 *Total Assets:* £9,059,953
*Registered Office:* 20 Trinity Lane, Micklegate, York, YO1 6EL
*Activities:* Pre-press and pre-media services
*Major Shareholder:* Mark Charles Gration
*Officers:* Mark Charles Gration, Secretary; David Jonathan Cowley [1971] Director/Graphic Designer; Mark Charles Gration [1961] Director/Reprographics; James Paul Tinker [1974] Director/Graphic Designer; Andrew Mark Woodward [1971] Director/Graphic Designer

**YTC Limited**
*Incorporated:* 12 May 1999 *Employees:* 393
*Net Worth:* £17,759,432 *Total Assets:* £29,499,316
*Registered Office:* Unit 76 Kelleythorpe Industrial Estate, Kellythorpe, Driffield, E Yorks, YO25 9DJ
*Activities:* Other retail sale in non-specialised stores
*Shareholders:* Paul John Nichols; Antony Thomas Nichols; Robert David Nichols
*Officers:* Deborah Jane Bath, Secretary; Antony Thomas Nichols [1965] Director/Retailer; Paul John Nichols [1961] Director/Retailer; Robert David Nichols [1960] Director/Retailer

**YTM Group Limited**
*Incorporated:* 21 December 1981 *Employees:* 137
*Net Worth:* £651,170 *Total Assets:* £5,349,570
*Registered Office:* Innovation House, Willowbridge Way, Castleford, W Yorks, WF10 5NP
*Activities:* Manufacture of other furniture
*Shareholders:* Damien Paul Duffy; Andrew Charles Davies
*Officers:* Andrew Charles Davies [1961] Director/Designer; Damien Paul Duffy [1972] Director; Patrick Duffy [1943] Director

**Z & D Property Investments Limited**
*Incorporated:* 3 August 2015 *Employees:* 2
*Net Worth:* £7,727,222 *Total Assets:* £16,649,207
*Registered Office:* 1 Parkview Court, St Paul's Road, Shipley, W Yorks, BD18 3DZ
*Activities:* Buying and selling of own real estate
*Shareholders:* Zorawer Singh; Daljit Singh
*Officers:* Daljit Singh [1971] Director; Zorawer Singh [1965] Director

**Zaic - A Limited**
*Incorporated:* 26 April 2011 *Employees:* 767
*Net Worth:* £43,752,672 *Total Assets:* £394,169,632
*Registered Office:* 1 Park Row, Leeds, LS1 5AB
*Activities:* Construction of other civil engineering projects n.e.c.
*Officers:* Dmitry Cherskiy [1973] Director/Financial Controller [Russian]; Michael Dedieu [1969] Director [French]; Fernando Echegaray Del Pozo [1959] Director/Chief Operating Officer [Spanish]; Bruno Alfred Erbel [1974] Director [French]; Gustave Gabriel Guillaume Gauquelin [1982] Director/Deputy CEO [French]; Vehbi Serkan Kaptan [1971] Director [Turkish]; Goker Kose [1981] Director/Head of Structured Finance [Turkish]; Christophe Petit [1964] Director [French]; Ahmed Tariq Shaukat [1950] Director/Engineer [American]

**Zain Holdings Limited**
*Incorporated:* 22 June 2016
*Net Worth:* £315,090 *Total Assets:* £5,085,718
*Registered Office:* 69-70 Batley Business & Technology Centre, Technology Drive, Batley, W Yorks, WF17 6ER
*Activities:* Activities of head offices
*Major Shareholder:* Jabir Ali Sheth
*Officers:* Maqsud Dawood Patel [1969] Director; Jabir Ali Sheth [1971] Director

**Zarafa Group Limited**
*Incorporated:* 13 January 2006 *Employees:* 14
*Previous:* Zarafa Holdings Limited
*Net Worth:* £807,242 *Total Assets:* £3,427,392
*Registered Office:* 7 Hungate, Pickering, N Yorks, YO18 7DL
*Activities:* Activities of head offices
*Shareholders:* Robert Douglas Armitage; Andrew Geoffrey Fowles
*Officers:* Robert Douglas Armitage, Secretary; Daniel Robert Armitage [1977] Director; Robert Douglas Armitage [1947] Director/Accountant; Andrew Geoffrey Fowles [1964] Director

**Zarafa Height Solutions Limited**
*Incorporated:* 17 June 1992 *Employees:* 12
*Net Worth:* £3,454,510 *Total Assets:* £4,227,918
*Registered Office:* 7 Hungate, Pickering, N Yorks, YO18 7DL
*Activities:* Other engineering activities
*Parent:* Zarafa Group Limited
*Officers:* Robert Douglas Armitage, Secretary; Daniel Robert Armitage [1977] Director; Robert Douglas Armitage [1947] Director; Andrew Geoffrey Fowles [1964] Director

**Zeffirellis Limited**
*Incorporated:* 5 August 2002 *Employees:* 77
*Net Worth:* £1,140,312 *Total Assets:* £3,111,297
*Registered Office:* c/o Zeffirellis, Compston Road, Ambleside, Cumbria, LA22 9AD
*Activities:* Licenced restaurants
*Major Shareholder:* Derek Abraham Hook
*Officers:* Dorothy Smith, Secretary; Derek Abraham Hook [1948] Director/Restaurateur; Raymond John Hook [1949] Director/Seafarer; Dorothy May Smith [1953] Director/Restaurateur

**Zeina Foods Limited**
*Incorporated:* 7 April 2000 *Employees:* 30
*Net Worth:* £3,543,938 *Total Assets:* £10,196,569
*Registered Office:* Zeina House, Milner Way, Ossett, W Yorks, WF5 9JE
*Activities:* Manufacture of other food products n.e.c.
*Shareholder:* Safaa Ahmed Mohammed Ali
*Officers:* Safaa Ahmed Mohammed Ali, Secretary; Safaa Ahmed Mohammed Ali [1956] Director/Food Processor; Abdelamir Daneshyar [1964] Director/Food Processor; Osama Daneshyar [1972] Director/Food Processor

**Zenith Automotive Holdings Limited**
*Incorporated:* 20 January 2017 *Employees:* 658
*Net Worth:* £197,712,000 *Total Assets:* £1,511,522,944
*Registered Office:* Number One Great Exhibition Way, Kirkstall Forge, Leeds, LS5 3BF
*Activities:* Financial intermediation not elsewhere classified
*Shareholders:* Bridgepoint Advisers Limited; Bev GP LLP
*Officers:* Patrick James Rawnsley, Secretary; Timothy Peter Buchan [1963] Director; Mark Trevor Phillips [1968] Director; Lord Stuart Alan The Lord Rose of Monewden [1949] Non-Executive Director/Chairman; Emma Judith Sophia Watford [1977] Director; Guy Patrick Weldon [1967] Director

**Zenith Ef Limited**
*Incorporated:* 6 May 2010
*Net Worth:* £1,472,000 *Total Assets:* £9,600,000
*Registered Office:* Number One, Great Exhibition Way, Kirkstall Forge, Leeds, LS5 3BF
*Activities:* Renting and leasing of cars and light motor vehicles
*Parent:* Zenith Vehicle Contracts Limited
*Officers:* Patrick James Rawnsley, Secretary; Timothy Peter Buchan [1963] Director; Robert Alan Butler [1970] Director; Mark Trevor Phillips [1968] Finance Director

**Zenith International Freight Holdings Ltd**
*Incorporated:* 24 October 2016 *Employees:* 25
*Net Worth:* £5,821,580 *Total Assets:* £10,986,947
*Registered Office:* Zenith House, Valley Court, Bradford, W Yorks, BD1 4SP
*Activities:* Activities of other holding companies n.e.c.
*Shareholders:* Catherine Anne Usher; Colin Jeffrey Usher
*Officers:* Colin Jeffrey Usher [1959] Director/Freight Forwarder

**Zenith International Freight Limited**
*Incorporated:* 6 July 1999 *Employees:* 25
*Net Worth:* £10,234,175 *Total Assets:* £14,747,042
*Registered Office:* Zenith House, Valley Court, Bradford, W Yorks, BD1 4SP
*Activities:* Operation of warehousing and storage facilities for land transport activities
*Parent:* Zenith International Freight Holdlings Limited
*Officers:* Mark Anthony Wilson, Secretary; Colin Jeffrey Usher [1959] Director/Freight Forwarder

**Zenith Remarketing Limited**
*Incorporated:* 28 March 2011 *Employees:* 13
*Net Worth:* £9,045,000 *Total Assets:* £236,410,000
*Registered Office:* Number One, Great Exhibition Way, Kirkstall Forge, Leeds, LS5 3BF
*Activities:* Renting and leasing of cars and light motor vehicles
*Parent:* Zeus Bidco Limited
*Officers:* Patrick James Rawnsley, Secretary; Timothy Peter Buchan [1963] Director; Robert Alan Butler [1970] Director; Mark Trevor Phillips [1968] Director

**Zenith Vehicle Contracts Limited**
*Incorporated:* 15 June 1988 *Employees:* 415
*Net Worth:* £23,810,000 *Total Assets:* £312,025,984
*Registered Office:* Number One, Great Exhibition Way, Kirkstall Forge, Leeds, LS5 3BF
*Activities:* Renting and leasing of cars and light motor vehicles
*Officers:* Patrick James Rawnsley, Secretary; Timothy Peter Buchan [1963] Director; Robert Alan Butler [1970] Director; Mark Connor [1969] Operations Director; Ian Robert Gibson [1967] Director/Chief Information Officer; Ian Monro Hughes [1968] Director; Andrew Kirby [1969] Commercial Director; Mark Trevor Phillips [1968] Finance Director

**Zetland Estates Limited**
*Incorporated:* 25 March 1999 *Employees:* 2
*Net Worth:* £20,116 *Total Assets:* £11,445,721
*Registered Office:* The Estate Office, Aske Hall, Richmond, N Yorks, DL10 5HJ
*Activities:* Other letting and operating of own or leased real estate
*Major Shareholder:* Hon. Robin Lawrence Dundas
*Officers:* Hon. Robin Lawrence Dundas [1965] Director/Estate Owner; Kathryn Ann Metcalfe [1981] Director/Accounts Manager

**Zeus Bidco Limited**
*Incorporated:* 30 September 2016 *Employees:* 3
*Net Worth Deficit:* £49,373,000 *Total Assets:* £940,974,016
*Registered Office:* Number One Great Exhibition Way, Kirkstall Forge, Leeds, LS5 3BF
*Activities:* Financial intermediation not elsewhere classified
*Parent:* Zeus Midco Limited
*Officers:* Patrick James Rawnsley, Secretary; Timothy Peter Buchan [1963] Director; Robert Alan Butler [1970] Director; Mark Trevor Phillips [1968] Director

**Zeus Finco Limited**
*Incorporated:* 20 January 2017 *Employees:* 3
*Net Worth Deficit:* £4,820,000 *Total Assets:* £516,009,984
*Registered Office:* Number One Great Exhibition Way, Kirkstall Forge, Leeds, LS5 3BF
*Activities:* Financial intermediation not elsewhere classified
*Parent:* Zenith Automotive Holdings Limited
*Officers:* Patrick James Rawnsley, Secretary; Timothy Peter Buchan [1963] Director; Robert Alan Butler [1970] Director; Mark Trevor Phillips [1968] Director

**Zeus Midco Limited**
*Incorporated:* 20 January 2017 *Employees:* 3
*Net Worth:* £2,482,000 *Total Assets:* £507,048,992
*Registered Office:* Number One Great Exhibition Way, Kirkstall Forge, Leeds, LS5 3BF
*Activities:* Financial intermediation not elsewhere classified
*Parent:* Zeus Finco Limited
*Officers:* Patrick James Rawnsley, Secretary; Timothy Peter Buchan [1963] Director; Robert Alan Butler [1970] Director; Mark Trevor Phillips [1968] Director

**Zubrance Limited**
*Incorporated:* 18 August 1995 *Employees:* 60
*Net Worth:* £5,982,000 *Total Assets:* £7,781,000
*Registered Office:* Valley House, Hornbeam Park, Harrogate, N Yorks, HG2 8QT
*Activities:* Manufacture of other food products n.e.c.
*Officers:* Robert Nicholas Whitehead [1961] Managing Director

**Zuka Ltd.**
*Incorporated:* 5 October 1998 *Employees:* 3
*Net Worth:* £1,630,210 *Total Assets:* £3,574,604
*Registered Office:* Armstrong House, First Avenue, Doncaster International Airport, Doncaster, S Yorks, DN9 3GA
*Activities:* Development of building projects
*Major Shareholder:* Ian John Raeburn
*Officers:* Susan Raeburn, Secretary; Ian John Raeburn [1959] Director/Commercial Manager

**The Zurbaran Trust**
*Incorporated:* 14 November 2011
*Net Worth:* £21,217,612 *Total Assets:* £21,224,660
*Registered Office:* Auckland Castle, Market Place, Bishop Auckland, Co Durham, DL14 7NR
*Activities:* Operation of arts facilities
*Officers:* Nicholas John Eldred, Secretary; Dr Jose Luis Colomer [1962] Director/Publisher [Spanish]; Anthony Stewart Worsley Mould [1955] Director/Art Consultant; Jane Mary Ruffer [1956] Director/Medical Practitioner; Jonathan Garnier Ruffer [1951] Director/Investment Manager; Dr Lindsay Raymonde Clifford Stainton [1947] Director/Curator and Author; Sir Stephen John Leadbetter Wright [1946] Director/Retired

**Zyro Limited**
*Incorporated:* 23 May 1995 *Employees:* 212
*Net Worth:* £13,562,000 *Total Assets:* £33,901,000
*Registered Office:* Zyro Limited, Roundhouse Road, Faverdale Industrial Estate, Darlington, Co Durham, DL3 0UR
*Activities:* Non-specialised wholesale trade
*Parent:* Aghoco 1136 Limited
*Officers:* Matthew Barker [1979] Director/Chief Executive; James Scott Browning [1966] Director; Ian James Calvesbert [1966] Director; Paul Gibson [1980] Director; Richard Damon Smith [1974] Director

# Standard Industrial Classification

**01110 Growing of cereals (except rice), leguminous crops and oil seeds** [92]

Aire and Ouse Farms Limited
B.B. Farms Limited
J.H. Bacon Limited
W E Barton Limited
W.S. Bayston & Son Limited
Bishopdyke Enterprises Limited
Bradonwood Limited
Burton Agnes Stud Co Ltd
Joseph Camm Farms Limited
Cattle (Holderness) Limited
R.Caudwell (Produce) Limited
W.S.Chapman & Sons Limited
S B & A Clark Farming Limited
John Dobson & Son (Carlton) Limited
N.L. Durdy & Son Limited
Eastburn Farms Limited
T.W.Falkingham Limited
John T. Fall Limited
Fenwick Brothers Limited
Edward Fisher & Co. Limited
W.E. Foers & Son Limited
Frickley Holdings.Limited
Gladwin Bros. (Farms) Limited
J.A.Godfrey & Sons,Limited
Grainsby Farms Limited
Harrison Farms (Kilham) Limited
J.E.Hartley Limited
M. Higgins Limited
T.H.Hobson Limited
Huggate Church Farm Properties Limited
Hutton Wandesley Farms Co Ltd
S Jackson & Sons Holdings Limited
Norman Jackson (Flixborough) Limited
J.Jackson Limited
H. H. James & Son Limited
Rory Kemp Limited
Laurence Kirkby (Farms) Limited
Knightwood Trust Farms Limited
L.F.C. Horkstow Limited
H.A. Lambert (Farmers) Limited
Lapwing Estate Limited
R H Leonard Limited
Limestone Farming Co Ltd
Longthorp (Kilpin) Limited
Sam Longthorp Limited
Lund Court Farm Limited
Makin Developments Wakefield Ltd
J.H. McCloy & Co Limited
Metcalfe Farming Limited
J.H. Mewburn Limited
Molescroft Farms Limited
William F.Moore (Warplands) Limited
S.A.Mossop (Farms) Limited
Moxon (Farms) Limited
Murton Grange Limited
Nafferton Wold Farms Limited
Natures Crops International Limited
Ness Hall Ltd
L.Nettleton & Son Limited
Northern Crop Driers Limited
W. Nutt & Son Limited
Oakland Farms Limited
Ozziefields Limited
Rainheath Limited
Riby Grange Farming Co Ltd
W. & A.C. Rose (Farms) Limited
Rudding Park Estate Limited
Salthaugh Grange Farm Limited
C.H. Scholey & Sons Limited
W.D.Sellers and Sons Limited
Shedden Farms Limited
William Smith (Wakefield) Limited
T Soanes & Son (Potatoes) Ltd
James Stockdale Limited
W. H. Strawson (Farms) Limited
M.F. Strawson (Maidenwell) Limited
W. H. Strawson (Notts.) Limited
M.F. Strawson Limited
Peter Strawson Limited
F.C. Stubbings & Sons Limited
Joseph E.Swiers,Limited
W.Swinbank & Sons Limited
A.T.G. Turnbull Limited
G.B.Turnbull Limited
Warden Farming Co Ltd
Warrens Emerald Biogas Ltd
Stephen B Wells Limited
West Moor Holdings Limited
V Wilkins & Sons Limited
J.R. Williams & Sons Limited
Winterquay Limited
Yorkwold (Overseas) Limited

**01130 Growing of vegetables and melons, roots and tubers** [17]

Aldby Field Nurseries Limited
W.S. Bayston & Son Limited
Braegate Produce Limited
Joseph Camm Farms Limited
Cavaghan & Gray Limited
John Dobson & Son (Carlton) Limited
Drinkwater's Mushrooms Limited
Glen Avon Growers Limited
Mill Nurseries Limited
S.A.Mossop (Farms) Limited
W. Nutt & Son Limited
Pollybell Farms Limited
Red Roofs Nursery Limited
STC Research Foundation
Stockbridge Technology Centre Limited
James Stockdale Limited
Yorkshire Grown Produce Limited

**01280 Growing of spices, aromatic, drug and pharmaceutical crops**

Yorkshire Botanicals Limited

**01290 Growing of other perennial crops**

Coletta and Tyson Limited
L.F.C. Horkstow Limited
Rolawn Limited

**01300 Plant propagation**

Berrygate Hill Nurseries Limited
Johnsons of Whixley Limited

**01410 Raising of dairy cattle**

J.G. Bellerby (Farms) Limited
High Hedley Hope Farm Limited
T.H.Hobson Limited
Lundie Farming Limited
J. & E. Medcalf Limited
Town Head Farm Products Limited
Wannops Farms Ltd
Woolrow Farm Limited

**01420 Raising of other cattle and buffaloes**

C R & C L Donaldson Ltd
Grants Pro-Agri Limited
High Hedley Hope Farm Limited
Rory Kemp Limited
Limestone Farming Co Ltd
Matson Ground Estate Co Ltd
J.H. Mewburn Limited

**01430 Raising of horses and other equines**

James H. Tennant Limited

**01450 Raising of sheep and goats**

C R & C L Donaldson Ltd
John T. Fall Limited
H.R. Fell and Sons Limited
Matson Ground Estate Co Ltd
J. & E. Medcalf Limited
Fred Walter & Sons Limited

**01460 Raising of swine and pigs** [25]

J S Alton & Son Limited
Brecks Farm Limited
Cattle (Holderness) Limited
C R & C L Donaldson Ltd
Elsham Linc Limited
Ermine Farms Limited
John T. Fall Limited
Foster Farms Limited
J.A.Godfrey & Sons,Limited
H.M. Pigs Limited
J.S.R. Genetics Limited
Limestone Farming Co Ltd
J.C. Lister Farms Limited
Longthorp (Kilpin) Limited
Melrose Pigs Limited
Middle Caves Ltd
Ian Mosey (Livestock) Limited
Ian Mosey Limited
Shedden Farms Limited
Joseph E.Swiers,Limited
Wayland Farms Limited
G. & M. Westgarth Limited
Willerby Wold Piggeries Limited
Wold Farms Limited
Yorkwold Pigpro Limited

**01470 Raising of poultry** [13]

Boarcross Limited
Cherry Valley Farms Limited
Crown Chicken Limited
Dinsdale Farming Limited
Foster Farms Limited
K. Fresh Ltd
Nafferton Wold Farms Limited
Oakland Farms Limited
Potter Family Holdings Limited
Clive Soanes (Broilers) Ltd.
C & K Wood (U.K.) Limited
Wot-a-Pullet Limited
Yorkshire Farmhouse Eggs Limited

**01490 Raising of other animals**

Armthorpe Falconry Limited
Ashton Agricultural and General Limited
B & K Universal Limited
MBR Acres Limited
David O'Meara Racing Ltd
Warrendale Farms Limited

**01500 Mixed farming** [41]

Wm.Allison & Sons Limited
Ashcourt Farms Limited
George W. Barker Limited
Bawtry Farms Limited
Broadland Properties Limited
Cattle (Holderness) Limited
County Turf Limited
A Dawson and Company (Estates) Limited
H.R. Fell and Sons Limited
Foxton Farmers Limited
Fridlington Farms Limited
R.J. & A.E. Godfrey
M.B. Goodwin (Skipsea) Limited
M.B. & J. Goodwin Limited
Wm.Grant (Paull) Limited
Grants Pro-Agri Limited
High Crane Limited
Hobson Farming Limited
Humberside Farmers Limited
Alfred Hymas Limited
J.S.R. Farms Limited
Norman Jackson (Farmers) Limited
C.G. Kendall Limited
R. Kendall Limited
Lund Court Farm Limited
F. Machin & Sons Limited
Manners Farms Limited
J.K.B.Megginson & Sons Limited
Mark H Poskitt Limited
Rainheath Limited
W.B. Ritchie Farms Limited
Robert Rook Estates Limited
Sellmor Farming Limited
Harold Sergeant and Sons Limited
J.V.Sleightholme Limited
F.C. Stubbings & Sons Limited
J.G.Swiers (Helperby) Limited
Thimbleby Farms Limited
Wallum Farms (North) Limited
Fred Walter & Sons Limited
Woodhead Brothers Farms Ltd

**01610 Support activities for crop production**

Crop Health and Protection Limited
Gladwin Bros. (Farms) Limited
Humber Grain Limited
Krone UK Ltd
Moxon (Farms) Limited
Robinson Contract Services Limited
Rollfields Limited
Westfield Farms Limited

**01621 Farm animal boarding and care**

J.H. Mewburn Limited

**01629 Support activities for animal production (other than farm animal boarding)**

Agrimin Limited
Cielivestock Limited
Craven Cattle Marts Limited
Darlington Farmers Auction Mart Co Ltd
Jubilee Milling Limited
Keyo Agricultural Services Ltd
William Thompson (York) Limited
Westfield Farms Limited
Westmorland County Agricultural Society Ltd

**01630 Post-harvest crop activities**

Argrain Holdings Limited
Argrain Limited
Braegate Produce Limited
James Mortimer,Limited
Munford Haulage Limited
W. H. Strawson (Notts.) Limited
Yorkshire Grain Limited

**01640 Seed processing for propagation**

Dunns (Long Sutton) Limited

**01700 Hunting, trapping and related service activities**

Gamebore Cartridge Co. Limited
Wemmergill Moor Limited

**02100 Silviculture and other forestry activities**

Job Earnshaw & Bros.Limited

**02400 Support services to forestry**

Carr Mount Estate Limited
Metcalfe Bros Limited
Amos Nelson,Limited

**03110 Marine fishing** [16]

F A S 2000 Limited
Fastnet Fish Limited
Fastnet Holdings Limited
Grimsby Fish Dock Enterprises Limited
Humber Fishing Limited
Kirkella Limited
Lockers Trawlers Limited
Mainprize Offshore Ltd
Mardon PLC
J. Marr (Fishing) Limited
J. Marr (Seafoods) Limited
Andrew Marr International Limited
Marr Management Limited
Onward Fishing Co Ltd
Onward Investment Limited
Viking Fishing Limited

**05102 Open cast coal working**

Coal Contractors Limited
Hall Construction Services Limited
Gordon Harrison Limited

**06100 Extraction of crude petroleum** [16]

Abbot Group Limited
Ithaca Epsilon Limited
Ithaca Gamma Limited
Ithaca Petroleum Limited
KCA Deutag (Land Rig) Limited
KCA Deutag Alpha Limited
KCA Deutag Drilling Group Limited
KCA Deutag Enterprises Limited
KCAD Holdings II Limited
President Energy Holding UK Limited
President Energy PLC
Siccar Point Energy E & P Limited
Third Energy Services Limited
Third Energy Trading Limited
Third Energy UK Gas Limited
Wellesley Holdco Limited

**06200 Extraction of natural gas**

Centrica Offshore UK Limited
Centrica Storage Limited
President Energy Holding UK Limited
President Energy PLC
Siccar Point Energy E & P Limited
Third Energy UK Gas Limited

**08110 Quarrying of ornamental and building stone, limestone, gypsum, chalk and slate**

Burlington Slate Limited
Johnsons Wellfield Ltd
Lightwater Quarries Limited
Marshall Quarry Products Limited
PMW Quarries Limited
Singleton Birch Limited

**08120 Operation of gravel and sand pits; mining of clays and kaolin**

Eppleton Quarry Products Limited
North Lincs Property Limited
Rotherham Sand and Gravel Co Ltd
W.Clifford Watts Limited
Yarrows Aggregates Limited

**08990 Other mining and quarrying n.e.c.**

Newlay Concrete Limited

**09100 Support activities for petroleum and natural gas mining**

Central North Sea Fibre Telecommunications Co Ltd
Getech Group PLC
Orcina Limited
Project Development International Ltd
Rever Offshore International Limited
Rever Offshore ROV Limited
Rever Offshore UK Limited

**10110 Processing and preserving of meat**

Cranswick Country Foods PLC
Dovecote Park Limited
Extra Detail Limited
Holmesterne Farm Co. Limited
Karro Food Frozen Limited
New Century Foods Limited

**10120 Processing and preserving of poultry meat**

2 Sisters Food Group Limited
CCL Holdings Limited
Crown Chicken Limited
Peter Gradon Meat and Poultry Marketing Ltd
HCF Poultry Limited
Ice Co Storage & Logistics Limited

**10130 Production of meat and poultry meat products** [26]

Mrs. J. C. Altham & Sons (Morecambe) Ltd
Benson Park Limited
T S Bloor & Sons Limited
Boparan Foods Limited
Cavaghan & Gray Group Limited
Convenience Foods Limited
Cranswick Convenience Foods Limited
Dalquinto Limited
Dovecote Park Limited
Farmers Boy Limited
F.W. Farnsworth Limited
Forza AW Limited
Forza Foods Limited
Peter Gradon Meat and Poultry Marketing Ltd
Harder Bros. Limited
Kober Limited
Neerock Limited
Newby Foods Limited
OSI Food Solutions UK Limited
Paragon Quality Foods Ltd
John Rannoch Limited
T Soanes & Son (Poultry) Ltd
Vale of Mowbray Holdings Limited
Vale of Mowbray Limited
David Wood Baking Limited
Yorkshire Halal Meat Supplier Limited

**10200 Processing and preserving of fish, crustaceans and molluscs** [12]

Cavaghan & Gray Limited
Five Star Fish Limited
Flatfish Limited
Havelok Limited
Ice Fresh Seafood Limited
International Seafoods Limited
Oceanic Seafoods Limited
Pick Fisk Limited
F. Smales & Son (Fish Merchants) Ltd
Three Oceans Fish Co Ltd
Whitby Seafoods Limited
Young's Seafood Limited

**10310 Processing and preserving of potatoes**

Arundel Kerr Produce Limited
Bennett Potatoes Limited
Farmhouse Potato Bakers Limited
Seabrook Crisps Limited

**10390 Other processing and preserving of fruit and vegetables** [12]

Cavaghan & Gray Group Limited
Cavaghan & Gray Limited
Chaucer Foods Limited
Farmhouse Potato Bakers Limited
Fresh Olive Co Ltd.
Histon Sweet Spreads Limited
McCain Foods (G.B.) Limited
Wm Morrison Bananas Limited
Wm Morrison Growers Limited
Wm Morrison Produce Limited
Solway Foods Limited
Symington's Limited

**10410 Manufacture of oils and fats** [10]

AAK (UK) Limited
Brocklesby Limited
Dovecote Park Limited
Kerfoot Group Limited
Natures Crops International Limited
Nortech Foods Limited
Olam Food Ingredients UK Limited
Sarval (Hartshill) Limited
Sarval Limited
Secanim Limited

**10511 Liquid milk and cream production**

Arla Foods Limited
Arla Foods UK PLC
Lundie Farming Limited
Paynes Dairies Limited
Town Head Farm Products Limited

**10512 Butter and cheese production**

Wensleydale Dairy Products Limited

**10519 Manufacture of other milk products**

Arla Foods Ingredients UK Limited
Dale Farm (GB) Limited
Kendal Nutricare Ltd
MV Ingredients Limited

**10520 Manufacture of ice cream**

R & R Ice Cream UK Limited

**10611 Grain milling**

E.B.Bradshaw & Sons,Limited

**10612 Manufacture of breakfast cereals and cereals-based food**

Brecks Co Ltd

**10710 Manufacture of bread; manufacture of fresh pastry goods and cakes** [16]

Bettys & Taylors Group Ltd
Bettys & Taylors of Harrogate Ltd
Chaucer Foods UK Limited
Convenience Foods Limited
Coopland & Son (Scarborough) Limited
Country Style Foods Limited
Fortis Foods Limited
Giles Foods Limited
Greens Desserts UK Ltd
Jackson's Bakery Limited
Livwell Limited
Rathbone Kear Limited
Thomas of York Limited
J.Wild (Confectioners) Limited
David Wood Baking Limited
David Wood Baking UK Limited

**10720 Manufacture of rusks and biscuits; manufacture of preserved pastry goods and cakes**

Northern Foods Grocery Group Limited

**10810 Manufacture of sugar**

Tereos UK & Ireland Ltd

**10821 Manufacture of cocoa and chocolate confectionery**

Bettys & Taylors Group Ltd
Bettys & Taylors of Harrogate Ltd
Northern Foods Grocery Group Limited
Whitakers Chocolates Limited

**10822 Manufacture of sugar confectionery**

John Bull (Confectioners) Limited
Confection By Design Limited
Dunhills (Pontefract) P L C

**10831 Tea processing**

Finlay Beverages Limited

**10832 Production of coffee and coffee substitutes**

Bettys & Taylors Group Ltd
Bettys & Taylors of Harrogate Ltd
Bewley's Tea and Coffee UK (Roastery) Ltd
Finlay Beverages Limited
Lincoln & York Limited

**10840 Manufacture of condiments and seasonings**

Golden Fry Foods Limited
Shaws (Huddersfield) Limited
Solina UK Trading Limited

**10850 Manufacture of prepared meals and dishes**

Kingasia Foods Limited
Pro-Pak Foods Limited
Yorkshire Provender Ltd

**10890 Manufacture of other food products n.e.c.** [34]

BPG Acquisitions Limited
BPG Midco Limited
Bee Health Limited
Brand Partnership (Holdings) Limited
Brand Partnership Group Limited
C.K. Foods (Processing) Limited
Chaucer Foods UK Limited
Clarks UK Limited
Convenience Foods Limited
Cranswick Gourmet Pastry Co Ltd
Daniels Chilled Foods Limited
Farmhouse Fare Limited
F.W. Farnsworth Limited
Thomas Fawcett & Sons,Limited
GO2 Foods Limited
Hain Frozen Foods UK Limited
Humdinger Limited
Iceco Limited
JLM Global Foods Limited
Keystream Limited
Lighthouse UkCo 6 (Treasury) Limited
Natures Aid Ltd
Newly Weds Foods Limited
Pecan Deluxe Candy (Europe) Limited
Real Yorkshire Pudding Co Limited
Ripon Select Foods Limited
Seabrook Group Limited
Speedboat Acquisitionco Limited
Speedboat Holdco Limited
Speedboat LNCO Limited
Speedboat Midco Limited
Troy Foods Limited
Zeina Foods Limited
Zubrance Limited

**10910 Manufacture of prepared feeds for farm animals** [16]

A.One Feed Supplements Limited
Adams and Green Limited
CCL Holdings Limited
Crown Chicken Limited
Elsham Linc Limited
I'anson Bros Limited
W.E. Jameson and Son Limited
Manor Farm Feeds Limited
Ian Mosey (Feed) Limited
Ian Mosey Limited
Northern Crop Driers Limited
Pelagia (UK) Limited
Provimi Limited
Sarval (Hartshill) Limited
Sarval Limited
Secanim Limited

**10920 Manufacture of prepared pet foods** [10]

Burgess Group PLC
C & D Foods (Driffield) Unlimited
Greentech Limited
Hollings Limited
IPN Bidco Limited
IPN Midco 1 Limited
IPN Midco 2 Limited
IPN Topco Limited
Inspired Pet Nutrition Limited
Johnston and Jeff Limited

**11020 Manufacture of wine from grape**

Continental Wine & Food Limited

**11040 Manufacture of other non-distilled fermented beverages**

Intercontinental Brands (Icb) Limited
Sedalcol UK Limited

**11050 Manufacture of beer**

Black Sheep Brewery PLC
Joseph Camm Farms Limited
Timothy Taylor & Co.,Limited
T.& R. Theakston Limited
Wetherells Contracts Limited

**11070 Manufacture of soft drinks; production of mineral waters and other bottled waters**

Cawingredients Limited
Harrogate Spring Water Limited
Shepley Spring Limited

**12000 Manufacture of tobacco products**

Gawith Hoggarth & Co.,Limited
Gawith Hoggarth Tobacco Trading Limited

**13100 Preparation and spinning of textile fibres** [17]

Bulmer & Lumb Group Limited
Calder Textiles Limited
Camira Yarns Limited
John Edward Crowther Limited
R.E. Dickie Limited
Joshua Ellis and Co Ltd
William S. Graham Limited
A.W.Hainsworth & Sons Limited
Z.Hinchliffe & Sons Limited
Lawton Yarns Limited
Abraham Moon & Sons Limited
James Robinson Fibres Limited
Spectrum Yarns Limited
Standard Wool UK (Holdings) Limited
Technical Absorbents Limited
Ulster Yarns Limited
West Yorkshire Spinners Limited

**13200 Weaving of textiles** [11]

Arville Textiles Limited
Bower Roebuck & Co.,Limited
Alfred Brown (Worsted Mills) Limited
Camira Fabrics Limited
Camira Transport Fabrics Limited
Dormeuil Manufacturing Limited
A.W.Hainsworth & Sons Limited
Luxury Fabrics Limited
MHLL Limited
Marton Mills Co Ltd
Abraham Moon & Sons Limited

**13300 Finishing of textiles**

Arville Textiles Limited
Camira Fabrics Limited
A.W.Hainsworth & Sons Limited
Holmfirth Dyers Limited
W.T.Johnson & Sons (Huddersfield) Ltd
MHLL Limited
Abraham Moon & Sons Limited
Thomas B. Ramsden & Co. (Bradford) Ltd
H. & C. Whitehead Limited

**13910 Manufacture of knitted and crocheted fabrics**

M.N.S. Textiles Limited

**13922 manufacture of canvas goods, sacks, etc.**

East Riding Sacks Limited

**13931 Manufacture of woven or tufted carpets and rugs**

A.W. (Europe) Limited
Burmatex Limited
G - Tuft Limited
Interface Europe Ltd.
Interface UK Manufacturing Limited
Westex (Carpets) Limited

**13939 Manufacture of other carpets and rugs**

Birch Close Trading Ltd
Burmatex Limited
G - Tuft Limited
Melrose Textile Co.,Limited
National Floorcoverings Limited
Phoenox Textiles Limited

**13950 Manufacture of non-wovens and articles made from non-wovens, except apparel**

Braveshire Limited
John Cotton Group Limited
Industrial Textiles & Plastics Ltd
Orvec Holdings Limited
Orvec International Limited
Rawson Fillings Limited
W.E.Rawson Limited
Sia Fibral Limited

**13960 Manufacture of other technical and industrial textiles**

Arville Textiles Limited
Geofabrics Limited
A.W. Hainsworth Holdings Limited
Industrial Textiles & Plastics Ltd
THS Industrial Textiles Limited

**13990 Manufacture of other textiles n.e.c.**

Deepsleep Beds UK Ltd
Filltex Limited
J. & C. Joel Limited
S D C Enterprises Limited
Snugpak Limited
Wooltex U.K. Limited
Xiros Limited

**14120 Manufacture of workwear**

Ansell Microgard Limited
Progarm Limited
Wm Sugden & Sons Limited

**14131 Manufacture of other men's outerwear**

Castlecrafts Limited
J.H. Clissold & Son Ltd.
Snugpak Limited

**14132 Manufacture of other women's outerwear**

Castlecrafts Limited
Marsylka Manufacturing Co.Limited
Q. R. I. Ltd

**14142 Manufacture of women's underwear**

Marsylka Manufacturing Co.Limited

**14190 Manufacture of other wearing apparel and accessories n.e.c.**

Castlecrafts Limited
Cohen & Wilks International (Holdings) Ltd
Dewhirst Sportswear Limited
Double Two Limited
Premier Equine International Limited
S D C Enterprises Limited

**15110 Tanning and dressing of leather; dressing and dyeing of fur**

Charles F.Stead & Co Ltd
West Yorkshire Fellmongers Limited

**15200 Manufacture of footwear**

Alt Berg Limited

**16100 Sawmilling and planing of wood**
Arbor Forest Products Limited
Bayram Timber Limited
R.E. and R. Duffield and Sons Limited
Garrards (Huddersfield) Limited
James E. Smith (Northern) Limited
S.H. Somerscales Limited
Woodlands Home & Garden Group Limited

**16210 Manufacture of veneer sheets and wood-based panels**
Decorative Panels Lamination Limited
Rocal Insulating Panels Ltd.

**16230 Manufacture of other builders' carpentry and joinery**
Howarth Timber Engineered Solutions Ltd
Merritt & Fryers Limited
Principle Spira Limited

**16240 Manufacture of wooden containers**
Tom Chambers Limited
HK Timbers Limited
Old HK Limited
Shaw Pallet Limited
Watson Pallets Limited

**16290 Manufacture of other products of wood; manufacture of articles of cork, straw and plaiting materials** [12]
Askern UK Limited
British Bung Manufacturing Co Ltd
Cirrus Laminations Limited
Decorative Panels Components Limited
Howarth Timber & Building Supplies Ltd
Howarth Timber (Windows & Doors) Limited
Industrial Pallet and Transport Services Ltd
Lambson Building Products Limited
Laminated Products Limited
Land Energy Girvan Limited
Peter Ramsey & Sons (Denholme) Timber Ltd
Shaw Timber Limited

**17120 Manufacture of paper and paperboard**
James Cropper Converting Limited
James Cropper PLC
James Cropper Speciality Papers Limited
Northern Paper Board Limited
Retford Wallcoverings Limited
John Roberts Holdings Limited
G.F.Smith & Son (London),Limited
Weidmann Whiteley Limited

**17211 Manufacture of corrugated paper and paperboard, sacks and bags**
Corrboard UK Limited
Labelon Group Limited
John Roberts Ventures Limited

**17219 Manufacture of other paper and paperboard containers**
Durham Box Co Ltd
Garthwest Limited
JPT Group Limited
Kentmere Limited
Kingston Carton Co Ltd
Labelon UK Limited
S. Sheard & Son Limited

**17220 Manufacture of household and sanitary goods and of toilet requisites**
Northwood Tissue (Lancaster) Limited

**17230 Manufacture of paper stationery**
Midas Paper Converters Limited
William Sinclair & Sons (Stationers) Ltd
G.F.Smith & Son (London),Limited
Tayrol Limited

**17290 Manufacture of other articles of paper and paperboard n.e.c.**
Bemrose Booth Paragon Limited
Billerudkorsnas Beetham Ltd
Hollingsworth & Vose Air Filtration Ltd
Label Makers Limited
Pigment Productions Limited
J.Stell & Sons,Limited
Stell Cardboard Tubes Limited
UK Greetings Limited

**18121 Manufacture of printed labels**
CCL Label Limited
Computype Europe Limited
OPM (Labels & Packaging) Group Limited
Olympus Print Group Limited
Print-Leeds Limited
Ryedale Printing Works Limited

**18129 Printing n.e.c.** [45]
A B Print Group Limited
Acorn Web Offset Limited
Bahson Colour Print Limited
Bootyman Printers Limited
YM Chantry Limited
Communisis UK Limited
Dominion Print Ltd
Dragonfly Agency Limited
Image Colourprint Limited
Image Data Group Limited
Image Digital Print Limited
Imagexps Limited
Kolorcraft Holdings Limited
Kolorcraft Limited
Labelon UK Limited
Leach Colour Limited
Lettershop Limited
Philip Myers Web (Neston) Limited
OPM (Labels & Packaging) Group Limited
Oriel Printing Co. Limited
Parkside Flexibles (Europe) Limited
Pindar Scarborough Ltd
Pinheiros Corporation Limited
Platinum Print Limited
Print-Leeds Limited
Printcraft Limited
RCS Limited
Raiseprint Limited
Ryedale Printing Works Limited
Scientific Games International Limited
Spellman & Walker Group Limited
Spellman & Walker Limited
Springfield Solutions Limited
Stangs Limited
Steffco Limited
Tailormade Design Limited
Team (Impression) Holdings PLC
Team (Impression) Limited
Valley Printing Company, Limited
Waddington and Ledger Limited
Herbert Walkers Limited
YM Group Limited
York Mailing (Holdings) Ltd
York Mailing Group Limited
York Mailing Limited

**18130 Pre-press and pre-media services**
Mosaic Group Limited
SGS Packaging Europe Limited
Vision Supplies Limited
YRG Group Limited

**19201 Mineral oil refining**
Total Lindsey Oil Refinery Limited

**19209 Other treatment of petroleum products (excluding petrochemicals manufacture)**
Kuwait Petroleum International Lubricants (UK) Ltd
Millers Oils Limited

**20120 Manufacture of dyes and pigments**
Hickson Limited
Unicolour Limited
Vivimed Labs Europe Ltd
Waterside Colours Limited

**20130 Manufacture of other inorganic basic chemicals** [15]
Airedale Chemical Co Ltd
Airedale Chemical Holdings Limited
Arch Chemicals Limited
Bartoline Limited
Cristal Pigment UK Limited
DSA Chemicals Limited
Esseco UK Limited
INEOS Compounds Aycliffe Limited
INEOS Compounds Holdings Limited
Majestic Polymers Limited
Multisol Limited
Nippon Gases UK Limited
Pluss-Staufer Limited
Singleton Birch Limited
Vivimed Labs Europe Ltd

**20140 Manufacture of other organic basic chemicals**
Bartoline Limited
Brenntag UK Limited
Echem Limited
Koppers UK Limited
Multisol Limited
SNF Oil and Gas Ltd

**20150 Manufacture of fertilizers and nitrogen compounds**
Yara UK Limited

**20160 Manufacture of plastics in primary forms** [10]
A-Fax Holdings Limited
A-Fax Limited
Distrupol Limited
Dugdale Compounds Limited
Dugdale Limited
Hallite Seals International Limited
Nippon Gohsei UK Ltd.
Polynt Composites UK Limited
Polypipe Limited
Robimatic Limited

**20200 Manufacture of pesticides and other agrochemical products**

Croda Europe Limited
Nufarm UK Limited
P. I. Bioscience Limited

**20301 Manufacture of paints, varnishes and similar coatings, mastics and sealants**

Belzona International Limited
Corrocoat Limited
Hodgson Sealants (Holdings) Limited
Jotun Paints (Europe) Limited
Manor Coating Systems Limited
PPG Architectural Coatings UK Limited
Polyseam Limited
Teal & Mackrill Limited

**20411 Manufacture of soap and detergents**

Arch UK Biocides Limited
Christeyns UK Ltd
Star Brands (Holdings) Limited
Star Brands Limited
Stephenson Group Ltd

**20412 Manufacture of cleaning and polishing preparations**

Astonish Holdings Limited
London Oil Refining Co. Limited
Star Brands (Holdings) Limited
Star Brands Limited
Thornton & Ross Limited

**20420 Manufacture of perfumes and toilet preparations**

Mibelle Ltd

**20510 Manufacture of explosives**

Explosive Developments Limited

**20520 Manufacture of glues**

Bartoline Limited
Seal It Services Limited

**20590 Manufacture of other chemical products n.e.c.** [24]

Aquaspersions Limited
Bartoline Limited
Belzona Polymerics Limited
Brenntag UK Limited
Chemfix Products Limited
Clariant Oil Services UK Ltd
Cod Beck Blenders Limited
Croda Europe Limited
Esseco UK Limited
Eurotek Foundry Products Limited
Garlock (Great Britain) Limited
ISP Holdings (U.K.) Ltd.
Kemira Chemicals (UK) Limited
Killgerm Chemicals Limited
Kingston Research Limited
Leading Solvent Supplies Limited
Nippon Gases UK Limited
Omya UK Limited
Orean Personal Care Limited
Prefere Resins UK Limited
T.J.Smith and Nephew,Limited
Techwax Limited
Vickers Laboratories Limited
Vivimed Labs Europe Ltd

**20600 Manufacture of man-made fibres**

Blue Star Fibres Co Ltd
IFG Drake Limited
Lenzing Fibers Grimsby Limited
Masons Textiles Limited

**21100 Manufacture of basic pharmaceutical products** [13]

Dalkeith Laboratories Limited
Dechra Limited
Dr. Reddy's Laboratories (EU) Limited
Epax Pharma UK Ltd
Health Innovations (UK) Limited
Indivior UK Limited
Parkacre Enterprises Limited
Principle Healthcare International Ltd
Principle Healthcare Limited
RSR Limited
Teva Laboratories UK Limited
Thornton & Ross Limited
Vivimed Labs Europe Ltd

**21200 Manufacture of pharmaceutical preparations**

Actavis Holdings UK II Limited
Cod Beck Blenders Limited
Dr Reddy's Laboratories (UK) Limited
Genus Pharmaceuticals Limited
Norton Healthcare Limited
Teva UK Limited

**22190 Manufacture of other rubber products**

Dunlop Oil & Marine Limited
White Cross Rubber Products Limited

**22210 Manufacture of plastic plates, sheets, tubes and profiles**

Aflex Hose Limited
Primex Plastics Limited

**22220 Manufacture of plastic packing goods** [11]

Aptar UK Limited
Bericap U.K. Limited.
Emballator (UK) Limited
Linpac Packaging Limited
Marpak Extrusions Limited
Mondi Scunthorpe Limited
PFF Packaging Limited
Really Useful Products Ltd
Roberts,Mart & Co.Limited
Tri-Pack Plastics Limited
Ultimate Packaging Limited

**22230 Manufacture of builders ware of plastic**

Caswick Limited
EYG Holdings Limited
East Yorkshire Aluminium & Glass Limited
Masco UK Window Group Limited
Polyframe Halifax Limited
Polyframe Norwich Ltd
Wavin Limited

**22290 Manufacture of other plastic products** [47]

A-Safe HQ Ltd
A-Safe UK Ltd
Advanced Plastics Limited
Armitage Shanks Ltd
BCA Leisure Ltd
Belgrade Insulations Limited
Bemis Elsham Limited
Bridgewood (UK) Limited
British Bung Manufacturing Co Ltd
Butterfield Signs Limited
Carclo PLC
Carclo Technical Plastics Limited
D.T. Industries Limited
Direct Trade (Yorkshire) Limited
Ellis Patents Holdings Limited
Ellis Patents Limited
Eltherington Industries Limited
Fibrelite Composites Limited
Forteq (UK) Limited
Ground-Guards Ltd
I.G. Industries PLC
International Pipeline Products Limited
Kautex Textron (UK) Limited
Kingfisher UPVC Windows & Doors Limited
LA 2012 Limited
Manthorpe Building Products Limited
Mold Systems Limited
Niko (Int) Limited
Osprey Limited
Pipeline Engineering & Supply Co. Ltd
Polyframe Norwich Ltd
Power Plastics Limited
Rosti Automotive Larkhall Ltd.
Rosti Automotive Pickering Ltd.
Rosti Automotive Stamford Bridge Ltd.
Rosti UK Ltd.
Roundbrand Limited
SWC Trade Frames Limited
A. Schulman Gainsborough Ltd
Silgan Closures UK Limited
Straight Limited
Straight Manufacturing Limited
Technimark Limited
Tri-Pack Plastics Limited
Trojan Plastics Limited
Vacform Group (Yorkshire) Limited
Wirquin Ltd

**23110 Manufacture of flat glass**

Glassflake Limited
Guardian Industries U.K. Limited
Specialist Glass Products Limited

**23120 Shaping and processing of flat glass**

Dual Seal Glass Ltd.
Kwiktuf Limited
Novaglaze Limited
Specialist Glass Products Limited

**23130 Manufacture of hollow glass**

Allied Glass Containers Limited
Allied Glass Group Limited
Ardagh Glass Limited
Stolzle Flaconnage Limited

**23140 Manufacture of glass fibres**

Owens-Corning Veil U.K. Ltd.

**23190 Manufacture and processing of other glass, including technical glassware**
Glassflake Limited
Specialist Glass Products Limited
Transition Glass Products Limited
Urmi Capital Limited

**23200 Manufacture of refractory products**
Jemmtec Limited
Monocon International Refractories Ltd
Parkinson - Spencer Refractories Limited
TYK Limited

**23420 Manufacture of ceramic sanitary fixtures**
Armitage Shanks Ltd
Douglas James Limited

**23440 Manufacture of other technical ceramic products**
Imerys Fused Minerals Hull Limited

**23490 Manufacture of other ceramic products n.e.c.**
Magneco Metrel U.K. Limited

**23610 Manufacture of concrete products for construction purposes**
CPM Group Limited
Longley Concrete Ltd
Marshall Quarry Products Limited
Marshalls Mono Limited
Plasmor (Halton) Limited
Plasmor (Sabey Kirby) Limited
Plasmor Limited
Procter Bros. Limited

**23700 Cutting, shaping and finishing of stone**
Fairhurst Stone Merchants Limited
J Rotherham Masonry Ltd

**23910 Production of abrasive products**
Marcrist International Limited
Sia Abrasives (G.B.) Ltd

**23990 Manufacture of other non-metallic mineral products n.e.c.**
Tolsa UK Limited
Von Roll UK Limited

**24100 Manufacture of basic iron and steel and of ferro-alloys**
Architectural Steel Limited
British Steel Holdings Limited
British Steel Limited
Liberty Merchant Bar PLC
Premo Fabrications Limited

**24310 Cold drawing of bars**
Bekaert Bradford UK Limited
Bright Steels Limited

**24320 Cold rolling of narrow strip**
Bekaert Bradford UK Limited

**24330 Cold forming or folding**
B.W.Industries Ltd
Jacksons Building Components Limited

**24340 Cold drawing of wire**
Anglia Metal Limited
Bekaert Bradford UK Limited
KTS Wire Limited

**24410 Precious metals production**
Select Alloys & Materials Limited
Wastecare Limited

**24450 Other non-ferrous metal production**
Map Ventilation Limited

**24510 Casting of iron**
WB White Foundry (Holdings) Limited
W B White Foundry Limited

**24520 Casting of steel**
Bonds Foundry Co Ltd
ESCO (UK) Limited

**25110 Manufacture of metal structures and parts of structures** [42]
A. & J. Fabtech Limited
AETC Limited
ASD Westok Limited
Richard Alan Engineering Co Ltd
Allerton Steel Limited
Allied Protek Engineering Solutions Ltd
Arlington Automotive NE Limited
B.W.Industries Ltd
Blackrow Engineering Co. Limited
Bonds Foundry Co Ltd
CCL Stressing Systems Limited
Carver Engineering Services Limited
Crowle Wharf Engineers Limited
Dam Structures Limited
Delta Engineering Group Limited
Elland Steel Structures Limited
Eltherington Industries Limited
Exlabesa Extrusions (Doncaster) Limited
Fender Steel Limited
Finley Structures Ltd
Hireport Limited
Hydram Engineering Limited
Mainport Engineering (1990) Limited
Mech-Tool Engineering Limited
Modular Plantrooms Limited
Nationwide Structures Limited
Harold Newsome Limited
Omco UK Limited
On Line Design & Engineering Limited
Paw Structures Limited
Phoenix Building Systems Limited
Pland Stainless Limited
Portakabin Limited
Rapid EPS Limited
Severfield (Design & Build) Limited
Severfield PLC
Shepley Engineers Limited
C.F.Struthers Limited
Andy Thornton Limited
Thurston Group Limited
Thurston Holdings Limited
Wakefield Acoustics Limited

**25120 Manufacture of doors and windows of metal**
Booth Industries Limited
Kirncroft Engineering Limited
MTW Architectural Limited

**25210 Manufacture of central heating radiators and boilers**
Ideal Boilers Limited
Keston Boilers Limited

**25290 Manufacture of other tanks, reservoirs and containers of metal**
M.Brittain (York) Limited
Eddison & Wanless Limited
Fuel Proof Limited
Kingspan Hot Water Systems Limited
T & G Automotive Ltd
Tanks and Vessels Industries Limited
Thurston Group Limited

**25300 Manufacture of steam generators, except central heating hot water boilers**
Therma Q Limited

**25500 Forging, pressing, stamping and roll-forming of metal; powder metallurgy**
Automotive Chassis Products UK Limited
Braime Pressings Limited
Gestamp Tallent Limited
Pegler Holdings Limited
Pegler Limited
Henry Williams Limited

**25610 Treatment and coating of metals**
Agfa Graphics Limited
Keighley Laboratories,Limited
United Anodisers Limited

**25620 Machining** [20]
Richard Alan Engineering Co Ltd
Apex Hydraulics Limited
Arlington Automotive NE Limited
Bibby Transmissions Limited
James Dawson & Son,Limited
Diamond Power Specialty Limited
Donaldson Filter Components Limited
J.H. Fenner & Co. Limited
Garlock (Great Britain) Limited
Klinger Limited
Multi-Tech Engineering (UK) Limited
On Line Design & Engineering Limited
Quality Hydraulic Power Limited
Reliance Precision Limited
Techmotion Limited
Teescraft Engineering Limited
Triple T Engineering Limited
VTL Precision (Bradley) Limited
VTL Precision (Huddersfield) Limited
WDS Component Parts Limited

**25730 Manufacture of tools**
Dakin-Flathers Limited
Dathan Tool & Gauge Co Limited
Mold Systems Limited
Stonegate Precision Tooling Limited

**25910 Manufacture of steel drums and similar containers**
Metal Drum Co Ltd

**25920 Manufacture of light metal packaging**

Ardagh Metal Packaging UK Limited
Bericap U.K. Limited.
Can-Pack UK Limited
Emballator (UK) Limited

**25930 Manufacture of wire products, chain and springs**

Airedale Springs Limited
Bridon International Ltd.
Bruntons Aero Products Limited
Cirteq Limited
Custom Fittings Limited
HS Products Ltd
John King Chains Limited
Siddall & Hilton Products Limited

**25940 Manufacture of fasteners and screw machine products**

Bright Screw Co Ltd
Glusburn Holdings Limited
Kingfisher (Lubrication) Limited

**25990 Manufacture of other fabricated metal products n.e.c.** [65]

ACS Stainless Steel Fixings Limited
Access Panel Co Ltd
Advanced Couplings Limited
Agfa Graphics Limited
Alco Valves Group Limited
B.Allsop Limited
Arkoni Limited
Arlington Automotive NE Limited
B.W.Industries Ltd
Bankside Patterson Limited
Blackhall Engineering Limited
Booth Industries Limited
Bradbury Group Limited
Broady Flow Control Limited
Butterfield Signs Limited
Cardinal Shopfitting + Systems Limited
Con Mech Group Limited
Denso Marston Ltd
Drive Devilbiss Sidhil Limited
Electrix International Limited
Ralph Ellerker (1795) Limited
Eminox Limited
Fablink Tank Systems Limited
Foregale Limited
G S M Automotive Limited
Gablesea Limited
Hartwell Manufacturing Ltd
Hesco Bastion Limited
Hindle Gears Limited
Hindle Group Limited
International Pipeline Products Limited
J.B. Components Limited
Kaye Aluminium (Holdings) Limited
Kingspan Metl-Con Limited
Kirncroft Engineering Limited
Leeds Bronze Engineering Limited
M. H. Industrial Limited
Metalcraft Europe Limited
Metallink Fluid Power Systems Limited
Pegler Yorkshire Group Limited
Pipeline Engineering & Supply Co. Ltd
Pland Stainless Limited
Platinum Stairlifts Limited
Procter Bros. Limited
Produmax Limited
Rack Systems (Engineering) Ltd.
Redhall Group PLC
Redhall Jex Limited
Rotherham Group Realisations Limited
Salamander Fabrications Limited
Security Window Shutters Limited
Servemet (N.W.) Limited
Service Metals (Midlands) Limited
Shand Engineering Limited
William Smith Group 1832 Limited
Specma Samwon Ltd
Sutcliffe Play Limited
Teconnex Limited
Trackwork Moll Limited
Trevor Iles Limited
Triple T Engineering Limited
Ultra Finishing Limited
Univer Manufacturing Co Ltd
Victor Manufacturing Limited
Henry Williams Limited

**26110 Manufacture of electronic components**

BSC Filters Limited
Filtronic Broadband Limited
Oxley Developments Co Ltd

**26200 Manufacture of computers and peripheral equipment**

Adva Optical Networking Limited

**26301 Manufacture of telegraph and telephone apparatus and equipment**

Filtronic Wireless Ltd

**26309 Manufacture of communication equipment other than telegraph, and telephone apparatus and equipment**

Adva Optical Networking Limited
Filtronic PLC
Q Electronics Limited
Saville Group Limited
Tunstall Healthcare (UK) Limited

**26400 Manufacture of consumer electronics**

Sound Leisure Limited

**26511 Manufacture of electronic measuring, testing etc. equipment, not for industrial process control**

Fives Landis Limited
James H.Heal and Co Ltd
Logopak International Limited
Marl International Limited
SPX Flow Technology Limited
Strainstall UK Limited
VPG Systems UK Limited

**26512 Manufacture of electronic industrial process control equipment**

Hydramotion Limited
M.K. Consultants (U.K.) Limited
Mowden Controls Limited
Pneumatic & Electrical Systems Limited
Shaw Moisture Meters (U.K.) Limited
Unison Limited

**26701 Manufacture of optical precision instruments**

Reliance Precision Limited

**27110 Manufacture of electric motors, generators and transformers**

Apelson Appliances UK Ltd
Brook Crompton UK Limited
Dale Power Solutions Limited
Power Link Machine (UK) Co Limited
Wilson Power Solutions Group Limited
Wilson Power Solutions Limited
Winder Power Limited

**27120 Manufacture of electricity distribution and control apparatus**

Acrastyle Limited
Dale Power Solutions Limited
Dhoot Transmission (UK) Limited
Marl International Limited
Powell (UK) Limited
Powell Engineering UK Limited
Winder Power Limited

**27320 Manufacture of other electronic and electric wires and cables**

Amnack Limited
Hi-Wire Limited

**27400 Manufacture of electric lighting equipment**

Crompton Lamps Limited
Northgate Lighting Limited
Wellvend Limited
Widd Group Limited

**27510 Manufacture of electric domestic appliances**

Apelson Appliances UK Ltd
Crosslee Holdings Limited
Crosslee PLC
Ebac Industrial Products Limited
Fired Up Corporation Limited
Logicor (CH) Limited

**27900 Manufacture of other electrical equipment** [18]

Anord Mardix (UK) Limited
Apelson Appliances UK Ltd
Cammax Limited
Chameleon Technology (UK) Limited
Deep Sea Electronics Limited
GDS Technologies Limited
Giffen Group Limited
Hyco Manufacturing Limited
OE Electrics Limited
Purex International Limited
Q Electronics Limited
RMSpumptools Limited
Saftronics Limited
Sargent Electrical Services Limited
Swinton Technology Limited
Technical Control Systems Limited
Victor Manufacturing Limited
Henry Williams Limited

**28110 Manufacture of engines and turbines, except aircraft, vehicle and cycle engines**

ATB Morley Limited
Allam Marine Limited
Gilbert Gilkes & Gordon Limited

**28120 Manufacture of fluid power equipment**

Oilgear European Holdings Limited
Oilgear Towler Limited

**28131 Manufacture of pumps** [11]

Allam Marine Limited
Becker UK Limited
Clarke Chapman Group Limited
Gilbert Gilkes & Gordon Limited
Hedley Hydraulics Limited
Hidrostal Limited
Hystat Systems Limited
K T Hydraulics Limited
SPX Flow Technology Limited
Sulzer Pumps (UK) Limited
Verder Limited

**28132 Manufacture of compressors**

Becker UK Limited
Gardner Denver Ltd
Hedley Hydraulics Limited
Hoerbiger UK Limited

**28140 Manufacture of taps and valves**

Brooksbank Valves Limited
Koso Kent Introl Limited
Wartsila Valves Limited
YPS Valves Limited

**28150 Manufacture of bearings, gears, gearing and driving elements**

David Brown Gear Systems Limited
Hindle Gears Holdings Limited
Radicon Transmission UK Limited
Reliance Precision Limited

**28210 Manufacture of ovens, furnaces and furnace burners**

Apelson Appliances UK Ltd
Spooner Industries Limited

**28220 Manufacture of lifting and handling equipment** [10]

4B Braime Components Limited
4B Elevator Components Limited
Certex Lifting Limited
Clarke Chapman Group Limited
Easilift Loading Systems Limited
First Subsea Limited
M S A Engineering Systems Limited
Prism UK Medical Limited
RMSpumptools Limited
Stock Redler Limited

**28250 Manufacture of non-domestic cooling and ventilation equipment**

Envirovent Limited
Fredshaw & Co Limited
Mansfield, Pollard & Co. Limited
North Sea Ventilation Limited
Spooner Industries Limited
TEV Limited

**28290 Manufacture of other general-purpose machinery n.e.c.**

Aker Offshore Partner Limited
Byworth Boilers Ltd
Heights (U.K.) Limited
Matrix International Limited
Newsmith Stainless Limited
PFM Packaging Machinery Limited
Univer Manufacturing Co Ltd

**28302 Manufacture of agricultural and forestry machinery other than tractors**

Husqvarna UK Limited
Lookrich Ltd
Packo Inox Limited
Storth Limited
Sumo UK Ltd.

**28490 Manufacture of other machine tools**

600 Group PLC
600 UK Limited
Archway Engineering (U.K.) Limited
Boxford Holdings Limited
Craftsman Tools Limited
Fives Landis Limited
Osprey Limited
Technical Arc Ltd

**28921 Manufacture of machinery for mining**

Richard Alan Engineering Co Ltd
Archway Engineering (U.K.) Limited
Carver Engineering Services Limited
Don Valley Engineering Co Ltd
ESCO Hydra (UK) Limited

**28922 Manufacture of earthmoving equipment**

Hydrema (U.K.) Limited

**28930 Manufacture of machinery for food, beverage and tobacco processing**

A.M. Packaging Limited
BW Integrated Systems UK Limited
CarnaudMetalbox Engineering Limited
Moody Direct Limited
Spooner Industries Limited
Trepko (UK) Limited

**28950 Manufacture of machinery for paper and paperboard production**

T.Freemantle Limited
Spooner Industries Limited

**28960 Manufacture of plastics and rubber machinery**

Bradman-Lake Limited
Donaldson Filtration (GB) Limited

**28990 Manufacture of other special-purpose machinery n.e.c.** [27]

Archway Engineering (U.K.) Limited
Thomas Broadbent & Sons,Limited
Calrec Audio Limited
Cornelius Beverage Technologies Limited
Daifuku Logan Ltd
De Smet Rosedowns Limited
Econ Engineering Limited
Extract Technology Limited
Fives Landis Limited
Gilbert Gilkes & Gordon Limited
LBBC Limited
Lambert Engineering Limited
Leeds and Bradford Boiler Co Ltd
Longwood Engineering Company (Holdings) Ltd
Longwood Engineering Co Ltd
Monobuoy Co Ltd.
Multi-Tech Engineering (UK) Limited
Optima International Limited
Derek Parnaby Cyclones International Ltd
Rofin-Sinar UK Ltd.
Sheppee International Limited
Specialised Orthotic Services Limited
Subsea Innovation Limited
Technowash Limited
Tickhill Engineering Co Ltd
Witt & Son UK Holdings Limited
Yamato Scale Dataweigh (UK) Ltd.

**29100 Manufacture of motor vehicles**

Angloco Limited
Ginetta Cars Limited
Optare Group Ltd
Optare PLC
TRS Tyres Ltd

**29201 Manufacture of bodies (coachwork) for motor vehicles (except caravans)**

Clarks Vehicle Conversions Limited
Paneltex Limited
Penman MW Limited
Premium Motorhomes Limited
Weightlifter Bodies Limited

**29202 Manufacture of trailers and semi-trailers**

Montracon Limited
Plowman Brothers Limited

**29203 Manufacture of caravans**

Auto-Trail V.R. Limited
Carnaby Caravans Limited
Coachman Caravan Co Ltd
Delta Caravans Holdings Limited
Delta Caravans International Limited
Swift Group Limited
Victory Leisure Homes Limited
Willerby Limited

**29310 Manufacture of electrical and electronic equipment for motor vehicles and their engines**

Ecco Safety Group (UK) Limited
Webasto Thermo & Comfort UK Ltd

**29320 Manufacture of other parts and accessories for motor vehicles** [11]

Aptiv Services UK Limited
Autoelectro Limited
BBB Services Limited
Borgwarner Limited
Carclo PLC
Kongsberg Actuation Systems Limited
Metaldyne International (UK) Ltd
Normanton Laminating Services Limited
Partline Limited
TMD Friction UK Limited
Wabco Automotive U.K. Limited

**30110 Building of ships and floating structures**

Allam Marine Limited

**30200 Manufacture of railway locomotives and rolling stock**

A1 Steam Locomotive Trust
Sabre Rail Services Limited
Silentbloc UK Limited

**30300 Manufacture of air and spacecraft and related machinery**

Icon Aerospace Technology Ltd

**30920 Manufacture of bicycles and invalid carriages**

Weldtite Products Limited

**30990 Manufacture of other transport equipment n.e.c.**

Haztec International Ltd
Larsen Road Limited
Reflecting Roadstuds Limited
Roubaix Bidco Limited
Tasca Tankers Limited
Transdek U.K. Limited
Vossloh Cogifer UK Limited
Martin Williams (Hull) Limited

**31010 Manufacture of office and shop furniture**

Alliance Office Systems Limited
Cardinal Shopfitting + Systems Limited
Connection Seating Limited
Elite Office Furniture (UK) Ltd.
Eureka Display Limited
Harte Woodworking Limited
Mobili Office Limited

**31020 Manufacture of kitchen furniture**

Marble 4 Life Ltd
Moores Furniture Group Limited
Niko (Int) Limited
Rixonway Kitchens Limited
Ultima Furniture Systems Limited

**31030 Manufacture of mattresses**

AJ Foam Ltd
Dura Beds Ltd
Durest Beds Ltd
Harrison Spinks Beds Ltd
High Grove Beds Limited
Spinko Limited

**31090 Manufacture of other furniture** [28]

Cavalier Marketing Limited
Consort Furniture Limited
Cycene Limited
Decorative Panels Furniture Limited
Decorative Panels Holdings Limited
Dura Beds Ltd
J.T.Ellis and Co Ltd
Express Bi Folding Doors Limited
Fired Up Corporation Limited
HSL Manufacturing Limited
High Grove Beds Limited
Katell Limited
Kingstown Furniture Limited
Knightsbridge Furniture Productions Ltd
Lebus Upholstery Limited
Moores Furniture Group Limited
Naught One Ltd
Oakwood Kitchen Design Consultants Ltd
Omega PLC
Prism UK Medical Limited
S.M.K. Textiles Limited
Sherborne Upholstery Limited
Stevro Limited
Strachan Furniture Makers Limited
Sunflower Medical Limited
TMPC Unlimited
Wetherells Contracts Limited
YTM Group Limited

**32300 Manufacture of sports goods**

Continental Sports Limited
Hull Cartridge Co Ltd
Ping Europe Limited
Playdale Playgrounds Limited

**32500 Manufacture of medical and dental instruments and supplies** [10]

Brandon Medical Co Ltd
Depuy International Limited
Ferno (UK) Limited
Finsbury (Instruments) Limited
Neoss Limited
Optimum Medical Solutions Limited
Hugh Steeper Limited
Surgical Innovations Group PLC
Surgical Innovations Limited
Xiros Limited

**32910 Manufacture of brooms and brushes**

British Bung Manufacturing Co Ltd

**32990 Other manufacturing n.e.c.** [148]

ABI (UK) Limited
ACS Stainless Limited
AKV Cladding Products Ltd
ALM Manufacturing Limited
APC (GB) Limited
Acorn Mobility Services Ltd.
Aegeus Industries Limited
Agrimin Limited
Air Handling Systems Limited
Airedale International Air Conditioning Ltd
Allsigns International Limited
Allsop Holdings Limited
Allure Developments Limited
Alternative Windows (Leeds) Limited
Alton Cars Limited
Amsgro Limited
Applelec Sign Components (UK) Ltd.
Arran Isle Holdings Limited
Ashtree Vision & Safety Limited
Atlas Leisure Homes Limited
BCA Leisure Ltd
Bawtry Carbon International Limited
Blacks Visual Merchandising Limited
Braun & Co. Limited
CCL Industries (U.K.) Limited
Calderys UK Ltd
Caldex Holdings Limited
Caldex Limited
Richard Carter,Limited
Chiorino U.K. Limited
Dempsey Dyer Limited
Dunelm Optical Co. Limited
EPTA George Barker Ltd
Job Earnshaw & Bros.Limited
Ebac Holdings Limited
Ebac Limited
Eco Modular Buildings Ltd
Elite Systems (GB) Limited
Ralph Ellerker (1795) Limited
Eltherington Industries Limited
Europa Caravans Ltd
Excel Laminating Limited
FTL Seals Technology Limited
Facultatieve Technologies Limited
Thomas Fattorini Limited
Fibreline Limited
Folding Sliding Doors Limited
Froneri International Limited
Futurama Limited
Futurama Signs Limited
GVS Filter Technology UK Ltd
Gainsborough Industrial Controls Limited
Greif Flexibles UK Limited
Guyson International Limited
H.P.A.S. Limited
H.S.G. (Packing Cases) Limited
Habasit (UK) Limited
Halifax Rack & Screw Cutting Co. Limited
Hall & Associates (Marketing) Ltd
Hallmark Group Products Limited
Hallmark Panels Limited
Hawthorn Timber Limited
Hazel Products UK Limited
Hurst Group (Northern) Limited
Hurst Plastics Limited
IF Cardboard Creations Limited
Integra Buildings Limited
JZ Flowers International Limited
Jito Trading Limited
Adrian Johnson Limited
Just Trays Limited
Kadmous Holdings (UK) Limited.
Kass Bathroom Products Limited
Kudos International Limited
Kudos Shower Products Limited
Derek Lambert Polythene Limited
Leeds Welding Co Ltd
London Security PLC.
M. H. Industrial Limited
Magnet Limited
Marble Building Products (Yorkshire) Ltd
Mardix Holdings Ltd
Martech (UK) Ltd
Metamark (UK) Limited
Modine UK Dollar Limited
Morley Glass & Glazing Limited
Nobia Holdings UK Limited
Nu-Swift International Limited

Omega Proteins Limited
Omega Signs Limited
Origin Packaging Limited
Oughtred & Harrison (Facilities) Ltd.
P.P. Profiles (West Yorkshire) Limited
PFF Packaging (North East) Limited
Paragon Creative Limited
Pasuda Buildings Limited
Permoid Industries Limited
Pet Brands Limited
Pipes UK (Holdings) Limited
Plant Theatre Ltd
Pneumatic & Electrical Holdings Limited
Portakabin Limited
Premier Modular Limited
Principle Systems Limited
Rackham Housefloors Limited
Reliance Precision Limited
Resdev Limited
Roman Limited
Rose Roofing Limited
SEA Holdings (UK) Limited
SEW-Eurodrive Limited
SGS Packaging Europe Holdings Limited
SPX International Limited
Sea Holdings Limited
Sheridan Fabrications Limited
Stage One Creative Services Limited
Stage One Group Limited
Standard Wool (UK) Limited
Stanwell Technic Ltd.
Strata Holdings Limited
Styrene Packaging & Insulation Limited
Swarco Traffic Limited
T W Logistics Limited
TEV Holdings Limited
Tailormade Design Limited
Taplanes Limited
Technical Fibre Products Limited
Tekmar Energy Limited
Tricogen Laboratories Limited
Triesse Limited
Triple T Engineering Limited
Twiflex Limited
USG-Gledco Ltd
Univer Manufacturing Co Ltd
Vacform Group (Yorkshire) Limited
Mary Randall Vickers & Co Limited
Benjn.R.Vickers & Sons,Limited
WV Associates Limited
Walker Modular Limited
Watershed Packaging Limited
Wax Lyrical Limited
Weir Valves & Controls UK Limited
Wetherby Group of Companies Limited
Wetherby Shade Card Co Ltd
Wetherby Stone Products Limited
Whiteghyll Limited
Wrapid Manufacturing Limited
Yamuna Renewables Limited

**33120 Repair of machinery** [12]

A J Access Platforms Limited
Ace Group (Engineering) Limited
Banner Contracts (Halnaby) Limited
Dennis Barnfield Limited
Becker UK Limited
Boge Compressors Limited
Byworth Boilers Ltd
Clyde Bergemann Materials Handling Ltd
Gemco Service Limited
Rhinox Group Ltd
Wilfred Scruton Limited
Selkirk Mechanical Handling Limited

**33130 Repair of electronic and optical equipment**

Gemco Service Limited

**33140 Repair of electrical equipment**

Allam Marine Limited
Anord Mardix Critical Power Services Ltd
Dale Power Solutions Limited
Pitts Wilson Limited
Powell (UK) Limited

**33150 Repair and maintenance of ships and boats**

Alatas UK Limited
MMS Ship Repair and Dry Dock Co. Ltd

**33170 Repair and maintenance of other transport equipment n.e.c.**

DB Cargo Maintenance Limited
Hartshorne Crossroads Group Contracts Ltd
Swarco Traffic Limited
Martin Williams (Hull) Limited

**33190 Repair of other equipment** [14]

AJH Pump Supply & Repair Limited
Bewley's Tea and Coffee UK (Roastery) Ltd
Clarke Chapman Group Limited
EPTA George Barker Ltd
Furmanite 1986
Furmanite Limited
Gemco Service Limited
ICH Limited
Old Innserve Limited
PTSG Access and Safety Limited
Rema Tip Top Industry UK Limited
Serviced Dispense Equipment Limited
South Coast Catering Limited
Team Industrial Services (UK) Limited

**33200 Installation of industrial machinery and equipment** [17]

AJH Pump Supply & Repair Limited
Actavo (UK) Limited
Airedale Catering Equipment Limited
Richard Alan Engineering Co Ltd
Boge Compressors Limited
Byworth Boilers Ltd
Clyde Bergemann Materials Handling Ltd
Dale Power Solutions Limited
Deborah Services (Holdings) Limited
EPTA George Barker Ltd
Gemco Service Limited
PTSG Access and Safety Limited
Pitts Wilson Limited
Powell (UK) Limited
Sulzer Chemtech (UK) Limited
C.E.A.Towne (Ship Riggers) Limited
Tucker Mechanical and Electrical Building Services Ltd

**35110 Production of electricity** [42]

Arena Capital MP Limited
Blencathra Hydro Limited
Broadland Energy (Donich) Limited
Broadland Energy (Laudale) Limited
Broadland Renewable Energy Limited
Drax Corporate Limited
Drax Finco PLC
Drax Fuel Supply Limited
Drax Group Holdings Limited
Drax Power Limited
Drax Smart Generation Holdco Limited
Drax Smart Sourcing Holdco Limited
Drax Smart Supply Holdco Limited
WJ Drennan Limited
EWH Holdco Limited
Eggborough Power Limited
Eneco Burn of Whilk Limited
Eneco Moy Limited
Eneco Sevor Limited
Energy Works (Hull) Limited
GB-Bio Limited
GWE Biogas Ltd
Indian Queens Power Limited
Keadby Generation Limited
Keyingham Power Limited
Lancaster University Energy Services Ltd
Land Energy Girvan Limited
Lowwood Products Co Ltd
Lynn Wind Farm Limited
Richard Maxwell Limited
Melrose Pigs Limited
Mulard Renewables Limited
Myrtle Grange Renewables Limited
Nafferton Wold Farms Limited
Redstart Renewables Limited
Refood UK Limited
Saltend Cogeneration Co Ltd
Secanim Limited
Taodail Hydro Limited
Tullo Wind Farm Limited
Whinlatter Energy Limited
A & C Wood Limited

**35130 Distribution of electricity**

Lowwood Products Co Ltd
Power4all Limited

**35140 Trade of electricity**

Haven Power Limited
Opus Energy (Corporate) Limited
Opus Energy Limited
York University Energy Supply Co Ltd

**35210 Manufacture of gas**

Refood UK Limited
Warrens Emerald Biogas Ltd

**35220 Distribution of gaseous fuels through mains**

Centrica Storage Limited
Contract Natural Gas Limited
Engie Gas Limited
Engie Gas Shipper Limited
York University Energy Supply Co Ltd

**35230 Trade of gas through mains**

Contract Natural Gas Limited
Opus Gas Supply Limited
Total Energy Gas Supplies Limited

**35300 Steam and air conditioning supply**

Neville Tucker (Group) Limited

**36000 Water collection, treatment and supply**

ACWA Services Limited
G.W. Axup & Co Limited
EP Realisations Limited
Kelda Group Limited
Saur Services (Glasgow) Limited
Sweeting Brothers (Land Drainage) Ltd
York University Energy Supply Co Ltd
Yorkshire Water Services Limited

**37000 Sewerage**

ACWA Services Limited
Jet Aire (DC) Limited
Lanes Group PLC

**38110 Collection of non-hazardous waste** [24]

Acumen Waste Services Limited
Associated Waste Management Limited
Augean North Limited
BW Skip Hire Limited
Blackburns Waste Disposal Limited
Brocklesby Limited
Grimsby Operations Limited
JJC Hire Limited
LSS Waste Management Limited
Lanes Group PLC
Mytum & Selby Waste Recycling Limited
Ray Owen Waste Disposal Limited
Robinson Contract Services Limited
S.A.R. Metals Limited
S.A.R. Recycling Ltd
Sharpsmart Limited
Skelton Limited
Total Recycling Services Limited
Transwaste Recycling and Aggregates Ltd
Transwaste Services Limited
URM (UK) Limited
Ward Recycling Limited
H. Wicks (Lindal) Limited
Yorwaste Limited

**38120 Collection of hazardous waste**

Acumen Waste Services Limited
Sharpsmart Limited
Total Recycling Services Limited
Transwaste Recycling and Aggregates Ltd
Transwaste Services Limited
Waste Services Group Limited

**38210 Treatment and disposal of non-hazardous waste** [17]

Associated Waste Management Limited
Bioganix Ltd
Biowise Limited
Caird Peckfield Limited
Eco-Power Environmental Limited
GWE Biogas Ltd
Mytum & Selby Waste Recycling Limited
Reuse Glass UK Limited
Sandsfield Gravel Co Ltd
Sharpsmart Limited
Edgar F Shepherd Ltd
Singleton Birch Limited
Stonegrave Aggregates Limited
Total Recycling Services Limited
Transwaste Recycling and Aggregates Ltd
Warrens Group Limited
Yorwaste Limited

**38220 Treatment and disposal of hazardous waste**

Sharpsmart Limited
Total Recycling Services Limited

**38320 Recovery of sorted materials** [13]

Advanced Alloy Services Limited
K A Anderson (Metal Recyclers) Limited
GES Recycling Ltd.
Harpers Environmental Limited
London Wiper Co Ltd
Sandsfield Gravel Co Ltd
Jeff Skinner Skip Hire Limited
TAG Industries Limited
Vellco Limited
Ward Bros. (Steel) Limited
Warrens Emerald Biogas Ltd
H. Wicks (Lindal) Limited
Yorwaste Limited

**39000 Remediation activities and other waste management services**

Acumen Waste Services Limited
Biowise Limited
Cube (Yorkshire) Ltd
Go Green Limited
Insituform Technologies Limited
Lanes Group PLC
R.P.M. Industrial Services Limited
Transwaste Recycling and Aggregates Ltd
V.H.E. Construction PLC

**41100 Development of building projects** [212]

4urban (Harrogate) Limited
ACL Estates Limited
Acre Products Limited
Allam Developments Limited
Almara Residential Limited
Argyle Square Properties Limited
Ascot Road Watford Limited
Ashcourt (Durham) Limited
Ashcourt Properties (Newland) Limited
G.P. Atkin Limited
BAA Lynton Limited
BF Propco (No.12) Limited
A.& E.Baines Limited
Barmston Developments Limited
C.K.Batchelor Limited
Beckside Developments Limited
Bennett-Ings (Developments) Limited
Bermar Building Co Ltd
John Betts Quality Used Cars Limited
Bishopdyke Enterprises Limited
Bramall & Ogden Limited
Broadway (SPV) Limited
Brunswick Court Development (Leeds) Ltd
Burgess Group PLC
Burley Developments Group Limited
Burwood House Group Limited
Bussey & Armstrong Projects Limited
Bussey and Armstrong Limited
Cancede Limited
Capitol Park Leeds PLC
Cave Developments Limited
Citygate Developments No.1 Limited
Clays of Addingham Limited
Cleethorpes Properties Limited
Commercial Development Projects Limited
Cravenhurst Properties Limited
Crosshall Developments (Leeds) Limited
Crossways Commercial Estates Limited
Cyrus Developments Limited
Dalesview Developments Limited
Darlington Homes Limited
Direct Investments (Yorkshire) Limited
Doncaster Property Trading Limited
Dukeries Homes Limited
Durham & Tees Community Ventures Fundco (No.1) Ltd
Durham & Tees Community Ventures Fundco (No.2) Ltd
Durham & Tees Community Ventures Fundco (No.3) Ltd
Durham & Tees Community Ventures Fundco (No.4) Ltd
East Coast Construction (N.E.) Ltd
Eastbay Limited
Eden Rock Estates Limited
Egg Homes Limited
Eido Limited
Elmwood Property Investments Limited
Eltham Properties Limited
Emersons Green Limited
Evans (Ashford) Limited
F R Evans (Leeds) Limited
Evans Ashford Investments Limited
Evans Homes Limited
Evans Homes No.2 Limited
Evans Management Limited
Evans Property Holdings Limited
Evans Regeneration Investments Limited
Evans Residential Holdings Limited
F.T. Construction Group (Holdings) Ltd.
Fairbriar Developments (Salford) Limited
Fairfax Securities Limited
Finishchoice Limited
Firsdell Ltd
Forth Bridges Business Park Developments Ltd
Fradley Park Developments Limited
Graham Developments (Property Holdings) Ltd
Grantside Limited
Graycliffe Homes Limited
Grays Wharf Limited
Gregory Projects Limited
Group-14 Ltd
HD1 Developments Limited
HLD (Manchester) Limited
Kenneth Hall (Builder) Limited
Hall Construction Services Limited
James Hare,Limited
Harmony Bridge Limited
Harris CM Limited
Healthtrak (UK) Limited
Heathvine Properties Limited
High Point Estates Ltd.
Hodson Properties Limited
Holf Investments Limited
Hornbeam Park Developments Limited
Horncastle Group PLC
Hungate (York) Regeneration Limited
Ideal Homes Holdings Limited
Illuminating Investments Limited
Impact Property Services Limited
Interactive Projects & Design Limited

J M Construction (Leeds) Limited
JCT600 (Properties) Limited
JMC Developments (Hunslet) Limited
KWH (Hull) Limited
Keyland Developments Limited
Kingsoak Limited
Kirkleavington Property Co Ltd
Land Acquisitions Limited
Landown Limited
Larchwell Limited
Henry Lax Limited
Leader Limited
Leck Construction Limited
Leeds and London Holdings Limited
Linfit Investments Limited
Liveco Limited
Llandudno Retail Park Limited
Lodestone Projects Limited
London Ebor Developments PLC
London Property Investments Ltd
M. & B. Commercial Properties Limited
MSS Developments Limited
Maltgrade Limited
Marshall Construction (West Yorkshire) Ltd
The Neil Martin Group Limited
McLagan Investments Limited
Moore Building Enterprises Limited
Mulberry Homes Yorkshire Limited
Narbourne Limited
Newincco 1072 Limited
Newman Properties Limited
North Lincs Property Limited
A V Ogden Holdings Limited
Onward Holdings Limited
Orion Developments Limited
Orion Homes Limited
Pacy and Wheatley Limited
Park Lane Homes Developments Limited
Patchett Developments Limited
Pentamon Limited
Persimmon Homes Limited
Pitcliffe Properties Limited
Place2invest Ltd
Porth Investments Limited
Positive Location Properties Limited
Precious Holdings (Wakefield) Limited
Priestley Homes Limited
Proma Boatman Limited
Promised Land Developments Limited
Prosperity Noor Ltd
G.W.Proudfoot Limited
J.Pullan & Sons Limited
Quirkco Investments Limited
Redfern Developments and Investments Ltd
Redhouse Projects Limited
Regenco (Winchburgh) Limited
Regenco Borrower Limited
Richmond Properties (UK) Limited
Riddochhill Developments Limited
River Street Limited
Roando Investments Limited
Rowanway Limited
Rural Concepts Construction Limited
SDG (Boston) Limited
SDG (Newport) Limited
SDG (Preston) Limited
SDG (Rhyl) Limited
Sedbergh Hotel Enterprises Limited
Shepherd Development Co Ltd
Shepherd Group Properties Limited
Silverback Developments Limited
Skipton Properties Limited
Sovereign Build Limited
Springfir Estates Limited
St Paul's Street (Investments) Limited
Stadium Retail Investments (2004) Ltd
Stadium Welton Limited
Staunch Limited
Sterling Capitol PLC
Stramongate Properties Limited
Strategic Team Maintenance.Co. Limited
Sullivan Homes Limited
Termrim Construction Limited
Thirsk Investments Limited
Thompson Homes (Yorkshire) Ltd.
Thorpe Park Developments Limited
Torpoint Limited
Torsion Group Holdings Limited
Tower Centre Hoddesdon Limited
Treadwell Developments Limited
Trinity Developments Leeds Ltd
Tudorshore Limited
Turner Commercial Developments Ltd
UoE Deaconess Limited
Uptownleeds Limited
Vida Healthcare Limited
Watergate Developments Limited
Wescott Homes Limited
Westcourt Group Limited
Wharfedale Homes Limited
White Rose Property Investments No.2 Ltd
White Rose Residential Sales Limited
Whymar Limited
J P Wild Limited
Wilkinson Building Co.(Leeds) Limited
Tom Willoughby Limited
Wilton Developments Limited
Winston (UK) Limited
Wiseton Developments Limited
R N Wooler & Co (Developments) Limited
Worthington Homes Limited
Wortley Construction Limited
Wykeland Limited
York Conservation Trust Limited
Zuka Ltd.

**41201 Construction of commercial buildings** [84]

121 Mountco 074 Limited
Alfa Site Services Limited
Bar 24 Limited
Bermar Building Co Ltd
William Birch & Sons Limited
Blue3 (Staffs) Limited
Britannia Construction Limited
Britcon (UK) Limited
CLS Civil Engineering Limited
Caddick Construction Limited
Castle Residential Properties Limited
Castlehouse Construction Ltd
Clugston Construction Limited
Community Ventures (Leeds) Limited
Community Ventures Company (No 1) Ltd
Conroy Brook (Developments) Limited
J.W. Crowther & Son Limited
Dalian Properties Limited
T P Dibdin Limited
East Coast Construction (N.E.) Ltd
Evans (Ashford) Limited
Fairfield Developments (Doncaster) Ltd
Freedom Group of Companies Ltd.
GH North Yorkshire Limited
GMI Construction Group PLC
Graycliffe Homes Limited
H. B. Projects Limited
HACS Construction Limited
Hambleton Steel Group Ltd
Hambleton Steel Limited
L. Harrison (Properties) Limited
Gordon Harrison Limited
Havercroft Construction Limited
Hillreed Homes Limited
Hobson and Porter Limited
Geo Houlton & Sons Limited
Illingworth & Gregory Limited
Key Electrical Contractors & Storefitters Ltd
Kingstown Works Limited
L.N.T. Construction Limited
Leck Construction Limited
Walter Lilly & Co. Limited
T.Manners & Sons Limited
Marshall (Building Contractors) Ltd
Marshall Construction (West Yorkshire) Ltd
Northern Cladding Limited
Oakdale Homes Limited
P.D.R. Construction Limited
PBS Construction (North East) Limited
Pacy and Wheatley Limited
D. D. Porter Limited
Neil Price Construction Services Ltd
Neil Price Limited
Primus Alliance Nottingham Limited
Proma Construction Management Limited
Reynolds 2000 Limited
Roclad Systems Limited
Rural Concepts Construction Limited
Russell Armer Limited
Scothern Construction Limited
J L Services & Son Limited
Sewell Construction Limited
Seymour (Civil Engineering Contractors) Ltd.
Shepherd Construction Limited
Skipton Properties Limited
Darren Smith Builders Limited
Solvgrin Limited
Speedclad Limited
Strategic Team Group Limited
Strategic Team Maintenance.Co. Limited
Techrete (U.K.) Limited
Walter Thompson (Contractors) Limited
VBP Group Limited
Venture Business Parks Limited
A.M. Warkup Limited
Michael Wheatley Management Limited
L.& W.Wilson (Endmoor) Limited
Wilton Developments Limited
R N Wooler & Co (Developments) Limited
R.N. Wooler & Co (Holdings) Limited
R.N. Wooler & Co Ltd
Wykeland Limited
Wykeland Properties Limited
Younger Homes (Northern) Limited

**41202 Construction of domestic buildings** [85]

Adina Developments Ltd
Arncliffe Homes Limited
Bar 24 Limited
Beal Developments Limited
Beaumont Morgan Developments Limited
Berkeley de Veer Limited
Bermar Building Co Ltd
Biker Group Limited
Caddick Construction Limited
Candelisa Limited
Castlehouse Construction Ltd

Century Construction Limited
Century Homes Limited
Chartford Arthington Limited
Chartford Developments Limited
Charles Church Developments Limited
City Portfolio Limited
Cityblock Holdings Limited
Conroy Brook (Developments) Limited
Duchy Homes Limited
East Coast Construction (N.E.) Ltd
Evans (Ashford) Limited
Fairfield Developments (Doncaster) Ltd
Forest Homes Limited
Frazer Estates Limited
Daniel Gath Homes Limited
HACS Construction Limited
Harron Homes Limited
Hexagon Properties Limited
Highacre Builders Limited
Hillreed Homes Limited
Holbeck Homes Limited
Geo Houlton & Sons Limited
Hoveden Builders Limited
JMC Developments (Hunslet) Limited
JPI (Holdings) Limited
Keepmoat Homes Limited
Keigar Homes Limited
Kexgill (Construction) Limited
Kingstown Works Limited
Leck Construction Limited
Lissett Residentials Limited
M.C.I. Developments Limited
Mack & Lawler Builders Limited
Mager Homes Limited
Brian Mager Limited
Marshall (Building Contractors) Ltd
Merewood Group Limited
Mulgrave Property Group Limited
D. Noble Limited
K.M. Norris Limited
Oakmere Homes (Lancaster) Limited
Oakmere Homes (Longtown) Ltd
Oakmere Homes (Northwest) Ltd
P.D.R. Construction Limited
Pacy and Wheatley Limited
Park Lane Homes Limited
Persimmon Developments (Didcot) Limited
Persimmon Developments (No 5) Limited
D.J. Prescott (Builders) Limited
Reynolds 2000 Limited
Risby Homes Limited
Rouse Homes Limited
Russell Armer Limited
S B Homes Ltd.
Scruton & Co.,(Builders) Limited
Senator Homes Limited
J L Services & Son Limited
Sheffield Housing Co Ltd
Shepherd Homes Limited
Skipton Properties Limited
Space4 Limited
St. Catherines Developments Limited
Strata Homes Limited
Strata Homes Midlands Limited
Strata Homes Yorkshire Limited
Strategic Team Maintenance.Co. Limited
Urban I (Blonk Street) Ltd
Venturian Property Development Limited
Webster Properties (Skipton) Limited
M.H. Whittaker & Son Limited
Willow Developments (Howden) Ltd
A & C Wood Limited
Wortley Construction Limited
Yorvik Homes Limited

**42110 Construction of roads and motorways** [15]

EC Surfacing Ltd
Extrudakerb (Maltby Engineering) Limited
GHG-AFCO (Luton) Limited
Hall Construction Services Limited
Lane Rental Services Limited
D. Noble Limited
C.R. Reynolds Limited
K Rouse Civil Engineers Limited
Saferoad UK Ltd
Saferoad VRS Ltd
Sanmet Limited
Specialist Surfacing Limited
Sweco UK Holding Limited
Todds Highway Maintenance Limited
V.H.E. Construction PLC

**42120 Construction of railways and underground railways**

Construction Marine Limited
Giffen Group Limited

**42130 Construction of bridges and tunnels**

Construction Marine Limited
C.R. Reynolds Limited
K Rouse Civil Engineers Limited

**42210 Construction of utility projects for fluids**

AMS No-Dig Limited
J.N. Bentley Limited
Brooke Edgley Specialist Technical Services Ltd
Peter Duffy Limited

**42220 Construction of utility projects for electricity and telecommunications**

AMS No-Dig Limited
Clyde Bergemann Materials Handling Ltd
Hall Construction Services Limited
Specialist Power Engineering Contracts Ltd

**42910 Construction of water projects**

ACWA Services Limited
AMS No-Dig Limited
J.N. Bentley Limited
Construction Marine Limited
Lewis Civil Engineering Limited
Mott MacDonald Bentley Ltd
Sweco UK Holding Limited

**42990 Construction of other civil engineering projects n.e.c.** [38]

Amalgamated Construction Ltd
Ashridge Contractors Limited
Athena Civil Engineering Ltd
Guy Bentley Limited
J.N. Bentley Limited
Bessacarr Properties Limited
CB Solutions U.K. Ltd
Chrislind Services Limited
Coal Contractors Limited
A.F. Connell Limited
Construction Marine Limited
Drury Engineering Services Limited
Peter Duffy Limited
East Riding Builders & Estate Development Co Ltd
P.J. Edwards & Co. (UK) Ltd.
Firth Steels Limited
Flannery Civil Engineering Limited
Flannery Construction Limited
Fussey Engineering Limited
Fussey Piling Ltd
M. Gallagher (Civil Engineering) Ltd
Giffen Group Limited
Howard Civil Engineering Limited
R.J. Howard Engineers Limited
J M Construction (Leeds) Limited
M & D Foundations & Building Services Ltd
Moortown Group Limited
PBS Construction (North East) Limited
C.R. Reynolds Limited
Rowanway Limited
SCD Group Limited
Spencer Engineering Group Limited
C Spencer Limited
Stoneledge Plant and Transport Limited
Sweco UK Holding Limited
Triton Construction Limited
V.H.E. Construction PLC
Zaic - A Limited

**43110 Demolition**

Gill Demolitions Limited
Alf Kitching Limited
Precious Holdings (Wakefield) Limited
Rhodar Demolition Limited
Stonegrave Aggregates Limited

**43120 Site preparation**

J.W. Crowther & Son Limited
Edwards Excavations Limited
Metcalfe Bros Limited
Moorhead Excavations Limited
V.H.E. Construction PLC
L.& W.Wilson (Endmoor) Limited

**43130 Test drilling and boring**

Stockton Drilling Limited

**43210 Electrical installation** [30]

NG Bailey Limited
Baydale Control Systems Limited
Chris Bowker Limited
Broadley (Group) Limited
A.F. Connell Limited
Distribution Cable Jointing Ltd
East Midlands Instrument Co Ltd
Electricity Distribution Services Ltd
Peter Fowler (Electrical) Limited
G & H Building Services Ltd.
G.R. Electrical Services Limited
Giffen Group Limited
H.E.C. Contracting Limited
Harrison Electrical Limited
Key Electrical Contractors & Storefitters Ltd
Mechanical Facilities Services Limited
Moores Furniture Group Limited
Oak Electrical Limited
P.P.S. Electrical Limited
Pitts Wilson Limited
J.A. Richardson (Electrical) Limited
J.H.Shouksmith & Sons Limited

Smith Brothers (Contracting) Limited
Southgate Lighting Limited
Specialist Power Engineering Contracts Ltd
F B Taylor (Cable Contractors) Limited
Together Roof Energy SPV Limited
Vallectric (Holdings) Limited
Vallectric Limited
Yorkshire Building Services Limited

**43220 Plumbing, heat and air-conditioning installation** [23]

Airco Refrigeration and Airconditioning Ltd
Airkool Contracts Limited
Aqua-Therm (Hull) Limited
A.F. Connell Limited
FEL Group Limited
G & H Building Services Ltd.
Help-Link UK Limited
Hensall Mechanical Services Limited
K Hewitt Holdings Limited
K. Hewitt and Co. Limited
JBC Industrial Services Limited
Key Electrical Contractors & Storefitters Ltd
Machenair Limited
Mitton Aftercare Limited
Mitton Mechanical Services Limited
Renewable Heat Generation Limited
J.H.Shouksmith & Sons Limited
Switch2 Energy Limited
Vallectric (Holdings) Limited
Vallectric Limited
Warmafloor (GB) Limited
YBS Holdings Limited
Yorkshire Building Services Limited

**43290 Other construction installation** [25]

AMS No-Dig Limited
Alternative Windows (Leeds) Limited
Armstrong-Priestley Limited
Ashleighsigns Limited
Belgrade Insulations Limited
Cardinal Project Management Limited
Carillion Powerlines Limited
Central Insulations Limited
Encon Insulation Limited
Gill Insulation Nottinghamshire Limited
Hambleton Steel Group Ltd
Hambleton Steel Limited
Highbury Homes (Yorkshire) Limited
Infra Safety Services Labour Limited
Key Electrical Contractors & Storefitters Ltd
Kingstown Works Limited
LMB Mechanical Services Limited
Lodestone Projects Limited
J.S. Miller Distribution Limited
Oakstone Developments Limited
Procter Bros. Limited
Simpson (York) Limited
Togel Contractors Limited
Whitaker and Leach Limited
YCE Catering Equipment Limited

**43310 Plastering**

Highbury Homes (Yorkshire) Limited

**43320 Joinery installation** [12]

B Batch Shopfitters Limited
CTS (Shopfitting) Limited
C.W.Fields & Son Limited
Highbury Homes (Yorkshire) Limited
Lodestone Projects Limited
Moores Furniture Group Limited
PDS Design & Build Limited
H. Peel & Sons Limited
Project FF & E Limited
SCS Building Solutions Limited
T G L (UK) Limited
Wilton Cobley Limited

**43330 Floor and wall covering**

A. Andrews & Sons (Marbles & Tiles) Ltd
Cogri Group Limited
Kingspan Access Floors Limited

**43341 Painting**

Alternative Windows (Leeds) Limited
Alfred Bagnall & Sons (North) Limited
Hayton & Lamb Limited
Jack Tighe Limited

**43342 Glazing**

H.P.A.S. Limited
Highbury Homes (Yorkshire) Limited
M.B.E. Glazing Systems Limited
Quest Solutions (UK) Ltd

**43390 Other building completion and finishing** [13]

Arrow Industrial Group Limited
Butterfield Signs Limited
Conservatory Outlet Group Limited
Conservatory Outlet Limited
Gatsby Property Limited
Hanover Developments (Wakefield) Limited
Head Office Interiors Limited
Interiors UK Limited
KMA Properties Limited
Lodestone Projects Limited
Marshall Construction (West Yorkshire) Ltd
Sanderson Contracts Limited
Peter Ward Homes Limited

**43910 Roofing activities**

Ashford Cladding Systems Limited
B C (Roofing Contractors) Limited
C.K.Batchelor Limited
C.A. Group (Holdings) Limited
C.A. Group Limited
Crest Roofing Limited
Everlast Waterproofing Limited
Hathaway Roofing Limited
Jennings Roofing Limited

**43991 Scaffold erection**

Caspian Group Limited
Say Scaffolding Limited

**43999 Other specialised construction activities n.e.c.** [81]

A.B.G. Limited
Actavo Building Solutions (UK) Limited
Apollo Holdco Limited
Ashcourt Contracts Limited
B & K Systems Limited
BDS (Yorkshire) Limited
NG Bailey Facilities Services Limited
NG Bailey IT Services Limited
NG Bailey Limited
Bee Jay Scaffolding Limited
Booth Industries Limited
Brianplant (Humberside) Limited
CNIM Clugston (Avonmouth) Limited
CRH Fencing & Security Group (UK) Ltd
Cambridge Glasshouse Co Ltd
Cat Tech (Europe) Limited
Checkmate Fire Solutions Limited
Checkmate Holdings Ltd
Cleveland Bridge UK Limited
Concorde BGW Limited
Crossway Scaffolding (Elland) Limited
Dalesauna Limited
Deepocean 1 UK Limited
Dickinsons (Plumbing & Heating Contractors) Ltd
Dortech Architectural Systems Limited
Dortek Limited
Double-Ten Limited
ESCO (UK) Limited
Earthmill Holdings Limited
Elite Systems (GB) Limited
Emsley Crane Hire Limited
Energy Containment Concepts Limited
Engie Fabricom UK Limited
Europipes (UK) Limited
F.S.H. (Group) Limited
Grand Construction Products Limited
H B Tunnelling Limited
H H Construction (Groundwork Contractors) Ltd
Hamilton (Building Contractors) Ltd.
Handler Hire Ltd
Gordon Harrison Limited
Head Office Interiors Limited
Hewitson Limited
Hurst Stores and Interiors Limited
Ideal Building Systems Limited
Interactive Projects & Design Limited
Derek Lewis Limited
Liberty Guard (U.K.) Limited
Machenair Limited
Map Ventilation Limited
Marshall (Building Contractors) Ltd
Meads Trust.Limited
Metcalfe Bros Limited
Modus Seabed Intervention Limited
Moortown Plant Limited
NVELOPE Rainscreen Systems Limited
Nightjar Sustainable Power Limited
Northern Pump Suppliers Limited
Pall Mall Developments Limited
Portakabin (Refurbished) Limited
G R Potter Plant Hire Limited
Redhall Group PLC
Redhall Marine Limited
Replan (U.K.) Limited
Rhodar Limited
Rhomberg Sersa UK Limited
Severfield (UK) Limited
Severfield PLC

Simpson (York) Holdings Limited
Speedclad Limited
Swarco Traffic Limited
TEI Limited
TSP Projects Limited
Tebway Limited
Til-Ex Limited
Trackwork Group Limited
Trackwork Limited
Wetherells Contracts Limited
L.& W.Wilson (Endmoor) Limited
Woodgreen Construction Limited
Yorkshire Sheeting and Insulation Services Ltd

**45111 Sale of new cars and light motor vehicles** [77]

Peter Ambrose (Castleford) Limited
Colin Appleyard Limited
Arrow Commercial Centre (Huddersfield) Ltd
Asset Finance UK Limited
Autobrokers Limited
Simon Bailes Limited
Batchelors of Ripon Limited
Bentley & Bentley Limited
Clive Brook Limited
Burrows Motor Co Ltd
CMG Lancaster Limited
Cars 2 Limited
Caygill Holdings Limited
Copley Motors Limited
D J Cox Limited
Cox Motor Group Limited
Decidebloom Limited
P.V. Dobson and Sons (Motors) Limited
Fisherman Limited
GC Motors Limited
J.F. and E. Hadwin Limited
Harratts Group Limited
Harratts Limited
Harratts of Wakefield Limited
Hatfields V Limited
William Hepworth (Huddersfield) Limited
JCT600 (Rawdon) Limited
JCT600 (South Yorkshire) Limited
JCT600 (Yorkshire) Ltd
JCT600 Limited
JCT600 Vehicle Leasing Solutions Limited
Jordan & Company (Hull) Limited
Just Partnership Limited
D.M.Keith Limited
Leasedrive Limited
Luscombe Motors Limited
Mill Garages North East Limited
Minstergate Limited
Nunns of Grimsby Limited
Pagani UK Limited
Parker & Parker Limited
S.G. Petch Limited
Piccadilly Motors Limited
Portland of Bawtry Limited
Pye Motors,Limited
Read Hyundai Limited
Read Hyundai Lincoln Limited
Read Motor Group Limited
Reliance Garage (Ryedale) Limited
Ribblesdale Motors Limited
Jos.Richardson & Son,Limited
Richardsons (Holdings) Limited
Richardsons Limited
Right Car (UK) Ltd
Ringways Garages (Leeds) Limited
Riverside Eastern Limited
Riverside Hull Limited
Riverside Motors (Doncaster) Limited
Rockar 2 Limited
John Roe (Hull) Limited
Ryedale Garages (1946) Limited
SB Wakefield Limited
Sandal Motors (Bayern) Limited
Sandal Motors (Huddersfield) Limited
Stephen A. Sims (Cars) Limited
R.Smith (Windermere) Limited
Specialist Cars of Malton Limited
D. Stoker Group Limited
Trenton (Hull) Limited
Van Centre (West Yorkshire) Limited
Vantage Motor Group Limited
Chris Variava Limited
W F & L Limited
Wandahome (South Cave) Limited
Warrington Garages Limited
Westgate Motors Limited
Wilson & Co. (Motor Sales) Limited

**45112 Sale of used cars and light motor vehicles** [48]

Affordable Cars (Yorkshire) Limited
Alexanders Prestige Group Limited
Alexanders Prestige Limited
Peter Ambrose (Castleford) Limited
Simon Bailes Limited
Batchelors of Ripon Limited
Bentley & Bentley Limited
John Betts Quality Used Cars Limited
Cars 2 Limited
D J Cox Limited
Decidebloom Limited
Harratts Group Limited
Harratts Limited
Harratts of Wakefield Limited
JCT600 (Rawdon) Limited
JCT600 (South Yorkshire) Limited
JCT600 (Yorkshire) Ltd
JCT600 Limited
JCT600 Vehicle Leasing Solutions Limited
Jordan & Company (Hull) Limited
Luscombe Motors Limited
Minstergate Limited
Motor Depot Limited
Motorsure Limited
Nunns of Grimsby Limited
S.G. Petch Limited
Piccadilly Motors Limited
Pittstop (Ripon) Limited
Portland of Bawtry Limited
Project Kahn Ltd
Pye Motors,Limited
Read Hyundai Lincoln Limited
Redline Specialist Cars Limited
Jos.Richardson & Son,Limited
Richardsons Limited
Right Car (UK) Ltd
Ringways Garages (Leeds) Limited
Riverside Hull Limited
Ryedale Garages (1946) Limited
Sandal Motors (Bayern) Limited
Sandal Motors (Huddersfield) Limited
R.Smith (Windermere) Limited
Templer Management Limited
Trenton (Hull) Limited
Vantage Motor Group Limited
W F & L Limited
Des Winks Cars Limited
Edward P. Wright Ltd.

**45190 Sale of other motor vehicles** [26]

George Allinson (Transport) Limited
Bentley Yorkshire Limited
Britcom International Limited
C.N. Trading Limited
Catterick Caravan & Camping Centre Ltd
Crossroads Group Limited
Crossroads Truck & Bus Limited
F & G Commercials (Huddersfield) Ltd
Goball Limited
Hartshorne Group Limited
Hartshorne Motor Services Limited
John Hebb (Motor Engineers) Limited
Albert Hill Commercials Limited
Hillcrest Garages (Sowerby Bridge) Ltd
L Jackson & Co Limited
Kendal Caravans Limited
Stewart Lawton Limited
Northern Commercials (Mirfield) Limited
Pelican Engineering Company (Sales), Ltd
Selkirk Mechanical Handling Limited
Shaks Specialist Cars Ltd
D.G. Taylor Commercial Vehicles Limited
Thompson Commercials Limited
Townson Tractors Limited
Wandahome (Knottingley) Limited
Dennis Winter (Leven) Limited

**45200 Maintenance and repair of motor vehicles** [50]

C F Abraham Limited
George Allinson (Transport) Limited
Peter Ambrose (Castleford) Limited
Simon Bailes Limited
Batchelors of Ripon Limited
Cars 2 Limited
Copley Motors Limited
D J Cox Limited
Crossroads Group Limited
Crossroads Truck & Bus Limited
Decidebloom Limited
Fisherman Limited
Global Autocare Limited
Green Flag Limited
Harratts Group Limited
Harratts Limited
Harratts of Wakefield Limited
Hartshorne Group Limited
Hartshorne Motor Services Limited
John Hudson Trailers Ltd
JCT600 (Rawdon) Limited
JCT600 (South Yorkshire) Limited
JCT600 (Yorkshire) Ltd
JCT600 Limited
Jordan & Company (Hull) Limited
Luscombe Motors Limited
Minstergate Limited
Motorhog Limited
Northern Commercials (Mirfield) Limited
Nunns of Grimsby Limited
Pelican Engineering Company (Sales), Ltd
S.G. Petch Limited
Piccadilly Motors Limited
Jos.Richardson & Son,Limited
Richardsons Limited
Right Car (UK) Ltd
Ringways Garages (Leeds) Limited
Ryedale Garages (1946) Limited
SB Wakefield Limited

Sandal Motors (Bayern) Limited
Sandal Motors (Huddersfield) Limited
Sayers Road Tanker Rentals Limited
Selkirk Mechanical Handling Limited
R.Smith (Windermere) Limited
D.G. Taylor Commercial Vehicles Limited
Thompson Commercials Limited
Townson Tractors Limited
Vantage Motor Group Limited
Dennis Winter (Leven) Limited
Edward P. Wright Ltd.

**45310 Wholesale trade of motor vehicle parts and accessories** [32]

4x4 Accessories & Tyres Limited
Beal (UK) Limited
Bentley & Bentley Limited
Bremsen Technik (UK) Limited
Bullseye Superfactors Ltd
Business Lines Limited
Carlac Limited
E K Motor Factors Limited
Febi (UK) Limited
Heavy Duty Parts Limited
Imexpart Limited
Impex Parts Limited
Jordan & Company (Hull) Limited
Juratek Limited
A Kahn Design Limited
Lesjofors Springs (UK) Limited
Meller Flow Trans Limited
Northern Commercials (Mirfield) Limited
Prasco UK Limited
Project Kahn Ltd
Rema Tip Top Automotive UK Limited
Richardsons Limited
Ring Automotive Limited
Ringways Garages (Leeds) Limited
S S Components Limited
SB Wakefield Limited
Savers Wholesale Ltd
Tekjur Limited
Towsure Products Limited
Trupart Limited
United Transmission Services Limited
Wood Auto Supplies Limited

**45320 Retail trade of motor vehicle parts and accessories** [28]

Simon Bailes Limited
Batchelors of Ripon Limited
Bullseye Superfactors Ltd
Cars 2 Limited
Crossroads Group Limited
Crossroads Truck & Bus Limited
Decidebloom Limited
Harratts Group Limited
Harratts Limited
Harratts of Wakefield Limited
Hartshorne Group Limited
Hartshorne Motor Services Limited
Imperial Automotive Limited
JCT600 (Rawdon) Limited
JCT600 (South Yorkshire) Limited
JCT600 (Yorkshire) Ltd
JCT600 Limited
A Kahn Design Limited
Lowdham Outdoor Leisure Limited
Northern Commercials (Mirfield) Limited
Pelican Engineering Company (Sales), Ltd
S.G. Petch Limited
Ryedale Garages (1946) Limited
Sandal Motors (Bayern) Limited
Sandal Motors (Huddersfield) Limited
Savoy Tyres Limited
Thompson Commercials Limited
Vantage Motor Group Limited

**45400 Sale, maintenance and repair of motorcycles and related parts and accessories**

D J Cox Limited
Craig's Motorcycles Limited
Hi-Level Enterprises Limited
Padgetts (Batley) Limited
Dennis Winter (Leven) Limited

**46110 Agents selling agricultural raw materials, livestock, textile raw materials and semi-finished goods**

Andrew Atkinson Livestock Limited
Thomas Bell & Sons Limited
I'anson Bros Limited
W.E. Jameson and Son Limited
Thirsk Farmers Auction Mart Co Ltd
Whole Crop Marketing Limited
Yorkshire Feedstuffs Limited

**46120 Agents involved in the sale of fuels, ores, metals and industrial chemicals**

Adler & Allan Limited
Dent Steel Services (Yorkshire) Limited
Engie Gas Limited
Engie Power Limited
Exelby Services Limited
Haas TCM Group of The UK Limited
Peak Oil Products (Northern) Limited
William Smith (Wakefield) Limited

**46130 Agents involved in the sale of timber and building materials** [26]

Arbor Forest Products Limited
Arran Isle Holdings Limited
B & T S Builders Merchants Ltd
G.H.Brooks & Co.(Harrogate) Limited
James Chambers (Timber Merchants) Ltd
Crest Brick Slate & Tile Limited
Cromar Building Products Limited
Hanson Plywood Limited
Howarth Timber & Building Supplies Ltd
Howarth Timber (Windows & Doors) Limited
Ideal Standard (UK) Limited
J. Jeffery (Builder) Limited
T P Jordeson & Co Ltd
A.W. Lumb (Midlands) Limited
A.W. Lumb (Northern) Limited
M. K. M. Building Supplies Limited
M.K.M. Building Supplies (Durham) Ltd
M.K.M. Building Supplies (Holdings) Ltd
M.K.M. Building Supplies (Hull) Limited
M.K.M. Leisure Limited
Manningham Concrete Limited
Merritt & Fryers Limited
S & A Builders Merchants Limited
S.B.S. (Cumbria) Limited
Uriah Woodhead & Son Limited
Woodlands Home & Garden Group Limited

**46140 Agents involved in the sale of machinery, industrial equipment, ships and aircraft** [16]

AMS Bobcat Limited
Big Bale Company (North) Limited
Boge Compressors Limited
Flintbrook Limited
C.T. Hayton Limited
Impact Fork Trucks Limited
MTS Nationwide Limited
Roger Miles Plant Sales Ltd.
OPM (Labels & Packaging) Group Limited
Peacock & Binnington
G.A. Robson and Son Ltd
Wilfred Scruton Limited
Robert D. Webster Limited
Thomas Wright/Thorite Group Limited
X-Force UK Ltd
Yorpower Limited

**46150 Agents involved in the sale of furniture, household goods, hardware and ironmongery**

Danesmoor Limited
Gedore U.K. Ltd
Padgett Brothers (A To Z) Limited
Thirsk Farmers Auction Mart Co Ltd

**46160 Agents involved in the sale of textiles, clothing, fur, footwear and leather goods**

Cohen & Wilks International Limited
Goliath Footwear Limited

**46170 Agents involved in the sale of food, beverages and tobacco**

Boost Drinks Limited
Corinthian Brands (CBL) Limited
Dr. Oetker (UK) Limited
Landmark Wholesale Limited
Oriental Merchant (Europe) Limited
Today's Wholesale Services Limited

**46180 Agents specialised in the sale of other particular products** [11]

Ardent Limited
Audio-Technica Limited
Builders Supply (North West) Limited
R.S. Cockerill (York) Limited
Custom Fittings Limited
Earthoil Plantations Limited
Hydrastore Limited
Sensio Limited
Supagard Limited
Talpole Limited
Yorkshire Packaging Systems Limited

**46190 Agents involved in the sale of a variety of goods**

Kastronix Limited
Padgett Brothers (A To Z) Limited

**46210 Wholesale of grain, unmanufactured tobacco, seeds and animal feeds**

Dawngreen Limited
Duynie Limited
Glasson Grain Limited
Gleadell Agriculture Limited
Thomas Mawer Limited
H Walton Limited
G. Williams & Co. (Grain) Limited

**46240 Wholesale of hides, skins and leather**

Bradford Hide Co Ltd
Yarwood Leather Limited

**46310 Wholesale of fruit and vegetables**

B & F Potatoes Limited
Fresh Olive Co Ltd.
M. Higgins Limited
International Procurement and Logistics Ltd
Prahi Limited
Richard Wellock & Sons Limited

**46320 Wholesale of meat and meat products** [13]

2 Sister Food Services Limited
Clarke Meats Limited
Collins (Seafoods) Limited
Holmesterne Farm Co. Limited
J.A. Jewitt (Meat) Limited
J.A.Jewitt
Landmark Wholesale Limited
J. & E. Medcalf Limited
Primepak Foods Limited
Sing Ko Limited
Sykes House Farm Limited
Today's Wholesale Services Limited
Yorkshire Premier Meat Limited

**46330 Wholesale of dairy products, eggs and edible oils and fats**

Arla Foods (Westbury) Limited
Arla Foods Limited
Chippindale Foods Limited
Dale Farm (GB) Limited
Primepak Foods Limited
Wensleydale Dairy Products Limited
Yorkshire Farmhouse Eggs Limited

**46342 Wholesale of wine, beer, spirits and other alcoholic beverages** [11]

Bon Coeur Fine Wines Limited
Broom House Investments Limited
Champagne Warehouse Ltd
Cider of Sweden Ltd
E.W.G.A. Limited
House of Townend Limited
International Procurement and Logistics Ltd
Lamba Trading Co. Limited
Landmark Wholesale Limited
Narang Wholesalers Limited
Today's Wholesale Services Limited

**46350 Wholesale of tobacco products**

Bull Brand Limited

**46370 Wholesale of coffee, tea, cocoa and spices**

Bewley's Tea and Coffee UK (Roastery) Ltd
Tillbrook Products UK Ltd

**46380 Wholesale of other food, including fish, crustaceans and molluscs** [20]

Arctic Waters Limited
Atlantic Fresh Limited
Caterers Choice Limited
Cook & Lucas Frozen (Holdings) Limited
Copernus Limited
Fast Trade Venture Limited
Flatfish Limited
Iceland Seafood Barraclough Ltd
Jaines & Son (Grimsby) Limited
Kirwin Brothers Ltd.
Mardon PLC
Northcoast Seafoods Limited
Oceanic Seafoods Limited
Oriental Merchant (Europe) Limited
Regal Food Products Group PLC
Seagold Limited
Sing Ko Limited
F. Smales & Son (Fish Merchants) Ltd
T. Quality Limited
Warners Fishmerchants Limited

**46390 Non-specialised wholesale of food, beverages and tobacco** [16]

Dr. Oetker (UK) Limited
Fullers Foods International PLC
H.B. Food Services Ltd
I.C.S. (UK) Limited
Lamba Trading Co. Limited
Lubna Foods Limited
W.McClure Limited
Morris & Son (Leeds) Limited
P. & B. (Foods) Limited
Paragon Foodservice Limited
G.W.Proudfoot Limited
D.B. Ramsden & Co Ltd
T. Quality Limited
Total Foodservice Solutions Limited
Turner & Price Limited
Ye Olde Oak Foods Limited

**46410 Wholesale of textiles** [26]

James C Brett (Yarn Merchants) Ltd
John L. Brierley Limited
J. Brown Fabrics Limited
Cashmere Fibres International Limited
Dilbag Cloth House Limited
Europa Wools Limited
Haddow Group Limited
James Hare,Limited
John Horsfall & Sons Limited
Huddersfield Fine Worsteds Limited
Jessgrove Limited
King Cole Limited
Melrose Textile Co.,Limited
Mobus Fabrics Limited
Narang Wholesalers Limited
Riva Paoletti Limited
Prestigious Textiles Limited
S.Ross & Co.Limited
Sirdar Holdings Limited
Spectrum Yarns Limited
Tilsatec Limited
Waxman Fibres Limited
Waxman International Limited
Whaleys (Bradford) Limited
H.S. Wood (Textiles) Limited
Brian Yates (Interiors) Limited

**46420 Wholesale of clothing and footwear** [25]

A & K Hosiery Limited
Arco Limited
BMB Clothing Limited
Charles Birch Limited
Bosideng UK Limited
Brook Taverner Limited
Joe Browns Ltd
Buxton Pickles Ltd.
DBS Clothing Limited
Double Two Limited
Eastman Staples Limited
Falcon Sportswear Limited
Haddow Group Limited
Hultafors Group UK Limited
Inoveight Limited
Kirens International Limited
William Lamb Group Limited
Madison Hosiery Limited
More (UK) Limited
Needlers Limited
Newross Impex Limited
Pegasus World Ltd
Progarm Limited
Skanwear Clothing Co Ltd
Stuncroft Limited

**46439 Wholesale of radio, television goods & electrical household appliances (other than records, tapes, CDs)**

Bonus Electrical Limited
Control4 EMEA Ltd
E P E International Limited
Hisense UK Limited
J.P. Distribution Ltd.
Ninehundred Communications Group Limited
Julian Roche Associates Limited
Smith Bros.(Caerconan) Wholesale Limited

**46450 Wholesale of perfume and cosmetics**

Icon Consultancy Ltd
Sweet Squared Limited
Dennis Williams Limited

**46460 Wholesale of pharmaceutical goods** [11]

Animalcare Ltd
Apollo Endosurgery UK Ltd
Boston Healthcare Limited
Butt & Hobbs Limited
Dakota Pharma Limited
Genus Pharmaceuticals Holdings Limited
Genus Pharmaceuticals Limited
Principle Healthcare Limited
Scientific Laboratory Supplies Group Ltd
Toiletry Sales Limited
Ypsomed Limited

**46470 Wholesale of furniture, carpets and lighting equipment**

Connection Flooring Limited
Createcity Limited
Heatseam Limited
Nordika Design Limited
Pacific Lifestyle Limited
Scan-Thors (U.K.) Limited
Stafford Mills Holdings Limited
Sycamore Lighting Limited
Trade Furniture Co Ltd

**46480 Wholesale of watches and jewellery**

Buckley Jewellery Limited
P and E Yorkshire Ltd

**46491 Wholesale of musical instruments**

John Hornby Skewes and Co Ltd

**46499 Wholesale of household goods (other than musical instruments) n.e.c** [20]

Charles Birch Limited
Burg-Wachter UK Limited
CB Imports Group Limited
CB Imports Limited
Dadibhais (Bradford) Limited
Dutch Imports & Daughters Limited
Fisher Outdoor Leisure Holdings Limited
Haddow Group Limited
Hill Giftware Limited
JVL Homewares (UK) Limited
Jemella Limited
Lindam Limited
Mamas & Papas Limited
PWS Distributors Limited
Phoenix Whirlpools Limited
Silver Cross (UK) Limited
Status International (UK) Ltd
UK Thermos Limited
John Veitch Limited
Jeffrey Walton Jewellery Limited

**46510 Wholesale of computers, computer peripheral equipment and software**

Complete IT Systems Limited
Link Distribution (UK) Limited
Shree Investment PLC
Target Components Limited
Techbuyer Group Holdings Limited
UFP (UK) Limited
Varlink Limited

**46520 Wholesale of electronic and telecommunications equipment and parts** [10]

Comnet Europe Limited
Farnell Electronic Components Limited
Kastronix Limited
Ninehundred Communications Group Limited
Premier Farnell UK Limited
Julian Roche Associates Limited
Shree Investment PLC
Videcon Ltd
YCR Distribution Limited
Yesss (C) Electrical Ltd

**46610 Wholesale of agricultural machinery, equipment and supplies** [12]

Agriargo UK Limited
Dennis Barnfield Limited
Con Mech Group Limited
Farmstar Limited
Newquip Limited
Osprey Limited
RBM Agricultural Limited
RFS (Ripon) Limited
Keith Rennie Machinery Limited
Russell's (Kirbymoorside) Limited
Terberg DTS (UK) Limited
Sam Turner and Sons Limited

**46620 Wholesale of machine tools**

Cutwel Limited
Marcrist International Limited
Moody Direct Limited
Quest Consumables Limited
John Sylvester Engineering Co Ltd

**46630 Wholesale of mining, construction and civil engineering machinery**

David Hopkinson Limited

**46650 Wholesale of office furniture**

Complete Business Solutions Group Ltd
Office Interiors Wholesale Limited

**46660 Wholesale of other office machinery and equipment**

Complete Business Solutions Group Ltd
D Sales (U.K.) Limited
Fellowes Ltd

**46690 Wholesale of other machinery and equipment** [24]

A J Access Platforms Limited
Amazone Limited
Bidco (Impex) Limited
Dean & Wood Limited
HRP Limited
Husqvarna UK Limited
Impact Fork Trucks Limited
JLA Limited
Komori U.K. Limited
Main Line Bearing Co. Limited
Matisa (U.K.) Limited
Moody Direct Limited
Power Topco Limited
Proton (Southern) Limited
R Safety Products Holdings Limited
RW Refrigeration Wholesale Limited
Roberts Graphics Limited
Scattergood & Johnson Limited
Scientific Laboratory Supplies Limited
William G. Search Limited
Sheetfed Holdings Limited
Shorts Industries Limited
Terberg DTS (UK) Limited
White Horse Machinery Limited

**46711 Wholesale of petroleum and petroleum products** [16]

Ace Gas Limited
Be Fuelcards Ltd
Dyneley Holdings Limited
Fuel Card Group Limited
Fuel Card Services Limited
Fuel Trading Co Ltd
Fuelcard Company UK Limited
C H Jones Limited
Kettlewell Fuels Limited
LPG Homeheat Limited
Northern Energy Supplies Limited
Northern LPG Supplies Limited
J.R. Rix & Sons Limited
Rix Petroleum (Hull) Limited
Tate Fuel Oils Limited
Total Lindsey Oil Refinery Limited

**46719 Wholesale of other fuels and related products** [12]

Ace Gas Limited
Dyneley Holdings Limited
Engie Power Limited
Fleetcor Fuel Cards Europe Limited
Fuel Card Group Limited
Fuel Card Services Limited
Fuel Express Limited
Oxbow Coal Limited
J.R. Rix & Sons Limited
Rix Petroleum (Hull) Limited
Technikraft Limited
Total Lindsey Oil Refinery Limited

**46720 Wholesale of metals and metal ores** [21]

ASD Limited
Advanced Alloy Services Limited
All Steels Trading Limited
Barrett Steel Limited
Michael Barugh Steel Stockholding Ltd
Clytha Holdings Limited
Paul Davies Limited
Firth Steels Limited
Hambleton Holdings Limited
Harrogate Steel Trading Ltd
Las Metals Limited
Leeds Bronze Engineering Limited
MRC Flangefitt Limited
National Tube Stockholders Limited
Abram Pulman & Sons Limited
Salzgitter Mannesmann UK Limited
Senior Architectural Systems Limited
Steel Beams and Columns Limited
Steel Supplies Limited
Timec 1444 Limited
Tomrods Limited

**46730 Wholesale of wood, construction materials and sanitary equipment** [17]

Burton Roofing Merchants Limited
Cupa-Burton Group Limited
Garrards (Huddersfield) Limited
Havwoods Limited
Jacksons Building Components Limited
Lawcris Panel Products Limited
Mermaid Panels Limited
Milford Limited
Mosaic Tile Co Ltd
Myers Building Supplies Ltd
Niko (Int) Limited
Wilf Noble Building Supplies Limited
North Yorkshire Timber Co Ltd
Procter Bros. Limited
A.E.Spink Limited
XL Joinery Limited
Yorkshire Plywood Limited

**46740 Wholesale of hardware, plumbing and heating equipment and supplies** [29]

Abacus Direct Limited
R.O.Arnold,Limited
Barwick of Bradford Limited
Burg-Wachter UK (Holdings) Limited
Carafax Limited
Cassellie Limited
Centurion Europe Limited
Cubico (UK) Limited
B.Danby & Co,Limited
Dufton Plumbing & Heating Supplies Ltd
EPMS Supplies Limited
Elitebliss Limited
Ian Firth Hardware Limited
Hiatt Hardware (UK) Limited
J.P. Distribution Ltd.
Jacuzzi Spa and Bath Limited
Modgate Limited
Morco Products Limited
Myers Building Supplies Ltd
Narang Wholesalers Limited
Nobleoak Limited
Quest 4 Limited
R M Solar Limited
Ravenheat Manufacturing Limited
Roxor Group Limited
Sanipex Limited
A.E.Spink Limited
Ultra Finishing Limited
Walker Distribution (Hull) Limited

**46750 Wholesale of chemical products** [12]

Clariant Plastics & Coatings (UK) Ltd
Clariant Production UK Ltd
Greentech Limited
Lambson Limited
Matrix Chemie Limited
Molekula Limited
Moody Direct Limited
NK Chemicals Europe Limited
RSM Lining Supplies Global Ltd
SNF (UK) Limited
SNG Commercial (Holdings) Limited
Surfachem Limited

**46760 Wholesale of other intermediate products** [23]

Aggregates R Us Ltd
Arco Limited
Automint Limited
Bat 2 Limited
Carafax Limited
Ceramica Impex Limited
Eastman Staples Limited
FTL Seals Technology Limited
Flexiglobal (UK) Limited
Samuel Grant (Leeds) Limited
Greentek Solutions Ltd
Ground-Guards Ltd
Head UK Ltd
Chas. Long & Son (Aggregates) Limited
PPB Ltd
Premier Vanguard Limited
S.T.L. Trading Co Ltd
G.F.Smith & Son (London),Limited
Strand Paper Northern Limited
T. Quality Limited
Viking Arms Limited
Wesco Aircraft Europe, Ltd
John Winter & Co Ltd

**46770 Wholesale of waste and scrap**

Advanced Alloy Services Limited
J Denham Metals Ltd
JJC Hire Limited
Morecambe Metals Limited
Morris & Co. (Handlers) Limited
Jonathan Potts Limited
J.B.Schofield & Sons Limited
Untha UK Limited

**46900 Non-specialised wholesale trade** [78]

Avant Worldwide Ltd
Bender UK Limited
Charles Birch Limited
Bristan Group Limited
CD (UK) Limited
Carlisle Brass Limited
Castle Industrial Supplies Ltd
Cleaning and Paper Disposables Limited
Richard Craven (Keighley) Limited
Curtis Wool Direct Limited
Dantex Graphics Limited
Deco-Pak Limited
Deliver Net Limited
Deltawaite Limited
Depuy International Limited
Drive Devilbiss Healthcare Limited
Engie Power Limited
Fine Motor Cars Ltd
Global Components (UK) Ltd
Greentech Limited
Grosvenor House Papers Limited
Haas Group International SCM Limited
Habico Limited
Rolf C. Hagen (U.K.) Limited
Hair Tools Limited
Harrison & Clough,Limited
Healan Ingredients Limited
Hider Food Imports Limited
Highfield Caravans Limited
J & E Importers & Distributors Green Jem
Mfg Associates Co Ltd
Kelkay Limited
Killgerm Chemicals Limited
Kluman and Balter Limited
Koti Industrial & Technical Brushes Ltd
Krimpterm Limited
Landmark Wholesale Limited
Leeds Plywood & Doors Limited
Lincs. Electrical Wholesalers Limited
Luxihomes Limited
Mardon PLC
Metroplan Limited
Nationwide Bearing Co Ltd.
Nordic Fashions One Limited
Nu-Swift International Limited
Oceanic Seafoods Limited
Optident Limited
Orange Mountain Bikes Limited
Orkla Foods UK PLC
P.K.A. Co Ltd
Paramount Wholesale Ltd
Jack Pennington Limited
Ping Europe Limited
Power Body Nutrition Ltd
Power Health Products Limited
Primeur Limited
Pyramid Display Materials Limited
Repchoice Limited
Service Timber Limited
Shree Investment PLC
Simba Smoby Toys (UK) Limited
R.H. Smith & Sons (Wigmakers) Limited
Stratex Warehouse Ltd
Tailormade Design Limited
Talasey Ltd
Titan Cement U.K. Limited
Today's Wholesale Services Limited
Trevor Iles Limited
Univar Limited
Univar Specialty Consumables Limited
Van-Line Limited
Verage Limited
WDS Component Parts Limited
Waxman Ceramics Limited
Waxman Energy Limited
Whitaker Fibres Limited
Wilkes Vending Services Limited
Wolds Engineering Services Limited
Zyro Limited

**47110 Retail sale in non-specialised stores with food, beverages or tobacco predominating**

Keelham Farm Shop Limited
W.McClure Limited
Wm Morrison Supermarkets Holdings Ltd
Wm Morrison Supermarkets P L C
G.W.Proudfoot Limited
Safeway (Overseas) Limited
Safeway Limited
Safeway Stores Limited

**47190 Other retail sale in non-specialised stores** [17]

Al Halal Supermarket Limited
Asda Stores Limited
Barkers (Northallerton) Limited
W.Boyes & Co.,Limited
W.P.Brown Limited
Card Factory PLC
Con Mech Group Limited
Ever 2010 Limited
Feel Good Group Limited
J R Firby Ltd
Rolf C. Hagen (U.K.) Limited
Overseas Trading Limited
Poundstretcher Limited
Sportswift Limited
Woodlands Home & Garden Group Limited
YTC Limited
R.Yates & Sons Limited

**47210 Retail sale of fruit and vegetables in specialised stores**

Bolster Moor Farm Shop Limited

**47220 Retail sale of meat and meat products in specialised stores**

Bolster Moor Farm Shop Limited
Chesterfield Poultry Limited
Heck! Food Limited
J. & E. Medcalf Limited
Yorkshire Premier Meat Limited

**47230 Retail sale of fish, crustaceans and molluscs in specialised stores**

Warners Fishmerchants Limited

**47240 Retail sale of bread, cakes, flour confectionery and sugar confectionery in specialised stores**

Coopland & Son (Scarborough) Limited

**47250 Retail sale of beverages in specialised stores**

Champagne Warehouse Ltd
House of Townend Limited

**47300 Retail sale of automotive fuel in specialised stores** [13]

Ackworth Service Station Ltd
Brookfield Property (Holdings) Ltd
W Eves & Co (Service Stations) Limited
Exelby Services Limited
Fambo UK Limited
Inner Space Stations Limited
Kenworth Limited
M6 Truck Services Limited
Ay & Y. Patel (Dewsbury) Limited
Jos.Richardson & Son,Limited
Sewell Retail Limited
Triangle Motor Co. Limited
Valli Forecourts Limited

**47410 Retail sale of computers, peripheral units and software in specialised stores**

Pure Data Solutions Limited

**47421 Retail sale of mobile telephones**

Ninehundred Communications Group Limited
Premier Communications Ltd

**47510 Retail sale of textiles in specialised stores**

Cotterhill Limited
Kino & Co. Limited
Towel Rail Limited

**47520 Retail sale of hardware, paints and glass in specialised stores**

Tony Cook Limited
Howarth Timber & Building Supplies Ltd
Lakeland Limited
Merritt & Fryers Limited
Al. Murad D.I.Y. Limited
Total Hardware Limited
Woodlands Home & Garden Group Limited

**47530 Retail sale of carpets, rugs, wall and floor coverings in specialised stores**

Calverts Carpets Limited
Al. Murad D.I.Y. Limited
Rodgers of York Ltd.
Stercap Limited

**47540 Retail sale of electrical household appliances in specialised stores**

Bonus Accessories Limited
Euro-Pro Europe Limited
Andrew James UK Ltd
Jemella Limited
Lakeland Limited
Sonic Megastore Limited

**47591 Retail sale of musical instruments and scores**

Gear4music Limited

**47599 Retail of furniture, lighting, and similar (not musical instruments or scores) in specialised store** [10]

Cater-Kwik Limited
Cubico (UK) Limited
DFS Trading Limited
Furniture Choice Limited
High Seat Limited
Redbrick Yorkshire Limited
Rodgers of York Ltd.
Stollers Furniture World Limited
Andy Thornton Limited
Wren Kitchens Limited

**47610 Retail sale of books in specialised stores**

Early Excellence Limited
Irongate Group Limited
PR Books Limited
Salts Estates Limited

**47640 Retail sale of sports goods, fishing gear, camping goods, boats and bicycles**

Jungle Products Limited
Newitt & Co Limited

**47650 Retail sale of games and toys in specialised stores**

Early Excellence Limited

**47710 Retail sale of clothing in specialised stores** [14]

BMB Clothing Limited
Bonmarche Limited
Joe Browns Ltd
Double Two Limited
Felldale Retail Limited
Gaynor Sports Limited
Leading Labels Ltd
Leeds Cricket Football and Athletic Co Ltd
Mileta Sports Limited
N. Peal (Retail) Limited
Pendle Sportswear Limited
Smarts of York Limited
Street Clothes Limited
TOG 24 Limited

**47721 Retail sale of footwear in specialised stores**

B - Sporting Limited
Charles Birch Limited
Horridge Limited
Pavers Limited
A.Watkinson Limited

**47722 Retail sale of leather goods in specialised stores**

Pavers Limited

**47730 Dispensing chemist in specialised stores**

123 Leeds Limited
Z.A. Akram Limited
Butt & Hobbs Limited
Gibson Pharmacy Limited
J M McGill Ltd.
Medicare Chemists Limited
Pharmacy2u Limited
H.I.Weldrick Limited
Whitworth Chemists Limited

**47749 Retail sale of medical and orthopaedic goods in specialised stores (not incl. hearing aids) n.e.c.**

BSN Medical Limited
Cephalon (UK) Limited

**47760 Retail sale of flowers, plants, seeds, fertilizers, pet animals and pet food in specialised stores**

Bradshaws Driffield (Holdings) Limited
Con Mech Group Limited
Tony Cook Limited
Invalesco Limited
W.E. Jameson and Son Limited
Langlands Nurseries Limited
TGC (2015) Limited
Walkers Nurseries Limited

**47770 Retail sale of watches and jewellery in specialised stores**

Ian Blowers Jewellers Limited
Bradleys Jewellers Limited
Goldmart Limited
Lister Horsfall Limited
Pengems Limited
Hugh Rice (Whitefriargate) Limited
Hugh Rice Holdings Limited
Hugh Rice Limited

**47782 Retail sale by opticians**

Bayfields Z Limited

**47789 Other retail sale of new goods in specialised stores (not commercial art galleries and opticians)** [17]

A.& E.Baines Limited
Berens & Co Ltd
Crescent Estates (Ilkley) Limited
Eaglesure Limited
Job Earnshaw & Bros.Limited
Inglis and Son (Jewellers) Limited
Lake District Estates Co Ltd
Mamas & Papas (Retail) Limited
Tile Co Ltd
Towsure Products Limited
Victoria Farm Garden Centre Ltd
Victoria Plum Limited
Walk Investments Limited
West Building Supplies Limited
Whittaker's Jewellers Limited
Windermere Aquatic Limited
Yorkshire Caravans of Bawtry Limited

**47791 Retail sale of antiques including antique books in stores**

C & H Antiques Limited
Andrew Lumley Limited
Andy Thornton Limited
Giovanni Tomasso Limited

### 47799 Retail sale of other second-hand goods in stores (not incl. antiques)

Cash Converters Yorkshire Limited
Yorkshire Caravans of Bawtry Limited

### 47890 Retail sale via stalls and markets of other goods

I.R. Sarjantson Limited
YTC Limited

### 47910 Retail sale via mail order houses or via Internet [27]

B - Sporting Limited
BMB Clothing Limited
Bonmarche Limited
Brook Taverner Limited
Joe Browns Ltd
Buy It Direct Ltd
Crafter's Companion Limited
Damartex UK Limited
Ebuyer (UK) Limited
Freemans Grattan Holdings Limited
Freemans PLC
Grattan PLC
John Jordan Limited
Kingstown Associates Limited
LRUK (Holdings) Limited
LRUK (Retail) Limited
Lakeland Limited
Lights4fun Limited
Microcourt Limited
Monster Group (UK) Limited
Pavers Limited
Pendle Sportswear Limited
Pure Collection Limited
Ryedale Printing Works Limited
H C Slingsby P L C
Sty.Com Limited
YTC Limited

### 47990 Other retail sale not in stores, stalls or markets [26]

Abel & Cole Limited
Artesian Spas UK Limited
Associated Utility Supplies Limited
BBR Graphic Sales Limited
Banks Lyon Jewellers Limited
Barton Park Homes Limited
Paul Davies Limited
Edmund Optics Ltd.
Engie Power Limited
Furniture Choice Limited
Gear4music Limited
Grand-Riverland & Co. Limited
Hague Computer Supplies Limited
High Street TV (Group) Limited
Integrated Polymer Systems (U.K.) Ltd
LPG Direct Limited
LTT Vending Ltd
Larkham Leisure Limited
Luxihomes Limited
MRC Transmark Limited
Richard Maxwell Limited
Reece Safety Products Ltd
Torne Valley Limited
Ultimate (Commercial Interiors) Limited
Vectair Aviation (1995) Limited
Vetuk Limited

### 49100 Passenger rail transport, interurban

Hull Trains Co Ltd
Keighley and Worth Valley Light Railway Ltd
Steamtown Railway Museum Limited
West Coast Railway Co Ltd

### 49200 Freight rail transport

DB Cargo (UK) Holdings Limited
DB Cargo (UK) Limited
DB Cargo International Limited
Rail Express Systems Limited

### 49319 Other urban, suburban or metropolitan passenger land transport (not underground, metro or similar)

Acklam's Coaches Limited
W. Cropper Limited
First West Yorkshire Limited
First York Limited
North York Moors Historical Railway Trust Ltd
John Shaw and Son Limited
Tetley's Motor Services Limited
Transdev Blazefield Limited

### 49320 Taxi operation

Pennock & Ivory Limited
Shiny Sky Limited

### 49390 Other passenger land transport

Burnley & Pendle Travel Limited
ERS Transition Limited
Keighley & District Travel Limited
Procters Coaches (North Yorkshire) Ltd
Rossendale Transport Limited
Transdev PLC
Weardale Motor Services Limited
Wilfreda Luxury Coaches Limited
York Pullman Bus Co Ltd

### 49410 Freight transport by road [108]

A.D.D. Express Ltd
Acumen Waste Services Limited
Advanced Forwarding Limited
Advanced Processing Limited
Advanced Supply Chain (Logistics) Ltd
George Allinson (Transport) Limited
Arundel Kerr Produce Limited
Autocar Logistics (Irl) Limited
P D Bannister Haulage Limited
S J Bargh Group Limited
S.J.Bargh Limited
R G Bassett & Sons Limited
Bedfords Limited
Bower Green Limited
Brenntag UK Limited
Bring Cargo Limited
G Brocklehurst Transport Limited
Bulk Logistics Group Ltd
Clicklink Logistics Limited
Clipper Logistics PLC
Clugston Distribution Services Limited
Collett Logistics Limited
Ernest Cooper Limited
Cramscene Limited
D & P Haulage Limited
DFDS Logistics Limited
DFDS Logistics Services Limited
Damac (Transporters) Limited
Den Hartogh Dry Bulk Logistics Limited
John Dickinson Transport Limited
Dowse Haulage Limited
East Transportation Limited
Eastmist Limited
Edmondsons (Freightliners) Limited
Expect Distribution Limited
Farsley Transport Limited
Herbert Fletcher Transport Limited
GBA Transport Limited
Gees Haulage Limited
Simon Gibson Transport Limited
Gill Demolitions Limited
R.J. & A.E. Godfrey
M.B. Goodwin (Skipsea) Limited
M.B. & J. Goodwin Limited
Groupe Samat UK Limited
H & P Freightways Limited
E Handcock Limited
Haulage (Holdings) Organisation Limited
Hendersons of Selby Limited
Hermes European Logistics Limited
Hermes Parcelnet Limited
Holme Lane Haulage Limited
E. Houseman & Son Limited
Hoyer Petrolog UK Limited
Hoyer UK Limited
Alfred Hymas Limited
Interbulk (UK) Holdings Limited
JMS of Doncaster Limited
Joda Freight Limited
M. Kettlewell (Melmerby) Limited
Law Distribution Limited
Leman International Transport Limited
Linkway Distribution Services Limited
Chas. Long & Son (Aggregates) Limited
J.Long & Sons (Haulage) Limited
MacKay Transport & Storage Limited
Maru International Limited
R. McDowell Haulage and Distribution Ltd
Metcalfe Farms (Haulage) Limited
Middlegate (Europe) Limited
Moorhead Excavations Limited
Morrey Oils Limited
Multisol Limited
Munford Haulage Limited
NTEX Limited
Neill & Brown (Shipping) Limited
Nidd Transport Limited
Nova Contracting Ltd
Oxbow Sulphur & Fertiliser (UK) Limited
M H & J Park and Son Limited
Richard Preston & Son Limited
Price Express Transport Limited
Professional Response Limited
RMS Goole Limited
Redhead Freight Limited
Reed Boardall Cold Storage Limited
Reed Boardall Transport Limited
Revis Transport Limited
A. Rhodes (Haulage) Limited
Robinson Contract Services Limited
D L Rogers & Sons Limited
SP & PL Holdings Limited
G.W. Sissons and Son Limited
James Stockdale Limited
D & MA Sunderland & Son Limited
Surefreight (International) Limited
T W Logistics Limited
TEF Transport Limited
G. & A. Thursby Limited
Trans-European Port Services (G.B.) Ltd
Translift Freight Limited

Viamaster Transport Limited
John Wade (Haulage) Limited
George Walker Transport Limited
George Walker Transport Manchester Ltd
J. & J. Ward Limited
W. & J. Williams (Haulage) Limited
M.Woodhouse Transport (Lancaster) Ltd

**49500 Transport via pipeline**

Centrica Storage Limited
Northern Gas Networks Finance PLC
Northern Gas Networks Limited

**50100 Sea and coastal passenger water transport**

DFDS Seaways Newcastle Limited

**50200 Sea and coastal freight water transport** [18]

Advanced Forwarding Limited
DFDS Seaways Newcastle Limited
Esvagt UK Limited
F.T.Everard & Sons Limited
James Fisher Everard Limited
James Fisher and Sons PLC
Graypen Limited
Huskisson Shipping Limited
Lerrix Tankship Limited
Marine Services (Grimsby) Limited
Rever Offshore North Star Limited
Rumford Tankers Limited
SMS Towage Limited
Seatruck Ferries Ltd
Seatruck Panorama Ltd
Seatruck Pennant Ltd
John H. Whitaker (Holdings) Limited
John H.Whitaker (Tankers) Limited

**50300 Inland passenger water transport**

Lake District Estates Co Ltd
Windermere Lake Cruises Limited

**50400 Inland freight water transport**

SMS Towage Limited
John H.Whitaker (Tankers) Limited

**51101 Scheduled passenger air transport**

Jet2 Transport Services Limited
Jet2.Com Limited
Leeds Bradford Airport Limited

**51102 Non-scheduled passenger air transport**

Great North Air Ambulance Service
Harpin Parkin Aviation Limited
Jet2.Com Limited
Makins Limited
Multiflight Limited

**51210 Freight air transport**

Advanced Forwarding Limited
Jet2.Com Limited

**52101 Operation of warehousing and storage facilities for water transport activities**

Aztek International Freight Limited
DFDS Seaways PLC
G.B. Terminals Limited
Torque Logistics Limited
Torque Retail Services Limited

**52102 Operation of warehousing and storage facilities for air transport activities**

Aztek International Freight Limited
Torque Logistics Limited
Torque Retail Services Limited

**52103 Operation of warehousing and storage facilities for land transport activities** [40]

4L's Products Limited
Advanced Processing Limited
Aztek International Freight Limited
BSN Medical Distribution Ltd.
F D Bird & Sons Limited
Bower Green Limited
Clicklink Logistics Limited
Clipper Logistics PLC
DFDS Logistics Services Limited
Eldred (1982) Holdings Limited
R.M. English & Son Limited
Fenton Packaging Limited
Fowler Welch Limited
Grants Pro-Agri Limited
HSH Cold Stores Limited
Higgins Agriculture Limited
M. Higgins Limited
E. Houseman & Son Limited
Ice Co Storage & Logistics Limited
Immingham Industrial Estates Limited
JMS of Doncaster Limited
Jenkar Shipping Limited
Joda Holdings Limited
Law Distribution Limited
Makins Limited
Neill & Brown Limited
Nidd Transport Limited
North Killingholme Storage Limited
Onward Holdings Limited
Price Express Transport Limited
RMS Goole Limited
Redhead Freight Limited
Reed Boardall Cold Storage Limited
Sigma Retail Solutions Limited
Stiller Warehousing & Distribution Ltd
T W Logistics Limited
Torque Retail Services Limited
Trans-European Port Services (G.B.) Ltd
Willis of Skipton Limited
Zenith International Freight Limited

**52211 Operation of rail freight terminals**

Aztek International Freight Limited

**52219 Other service activities incidental to land transportation, n.e.c.**

Clipper Logistics PLC
H. Dawson Sons and Company (Wool) Ltd
Hird Rail Services Limited
Premier Traffic Management Limited
D & MA Sunderland & Son Limited
Zenith International Freight Limited

**52220 Service activities incidental to water transportation**

DFDS Seaways PLC
Eimskip UK Limited
Neill & Brown Limited
Rever Offshore International Limited
Rever Offshore ROV Limited
Rever Offshore UK Limited
Torque Logistics Limited

**52230 Service activities incidental to air transportation**

Air Berlin Holding Limited
Gamston Aviation Limited
Neill & Brown Limited
Torque Logistics Limited
Zenith International Freight Limited

**52241 Cargo handling for water transport activities**

Eimskip UK Limited
Flixborough Wharf Limited
G.B. Terminals Limited
Global Shipping Services Limited
Hes Humber Bulk Terminal Limited
Jenkar Shipping Limited
Monobuoy Co Ltd.
RMS Goole Limited
RMS Trent Ports Limited

**52242 Cargo handling for air transport activities**

Jenkar Shipping Limited
Zenith International Freight Limited

**52243 Cargo handling for land transport activities**

Global Shipping Services Limited

**52290 Other transportation support activities** [30]

Bower Green Limited
Collett & Sons Limited
Ctrack Europe Holdings Ltd
Ctrack Limited
Ctrack UK Limited
East Transportation Holdings Limited
Eimskip UK Limited
Future Forwarding (Group) Limited
Future Forwarding (Holdings) Limited
Future Forwarding Co Ltd
G.B. Agencies Limited
G.B. Terminals (Northern) Limited
G.B. Terminals Limited
GBA (Holdings) Limited
Global Shipping Services Limited
John Good Shipping Limited
Hanson Logistics Limited
J. M. Holling Limited
Jenkar Shipping Limited
Ligentia Group Limited
Ligentia UK Limited
M. H. Industrial Limited
Maritime Bunkering Limited
McCann Limited
Monobuoy Co Ltd.
Multisol Europe Limited
Torque Retail Services Limited
Tradeway (Shipping) Limited
Tudor International Freight Limited
Waxman Group Limited

**55100 Hotels and similar accommodation** [72]

Abbey House (Cumbria) Limited
Ashdale UK Limited
Aston Hall Hotel Limited
Bannatyne Hotels Limited
Black Swan (Yorkshire) Limited
Calder Conferences Limited
Casterton Leisure Limited
Catford & Longford Limited
Coaching Inns (North) Limited
Codecrest Limited
G. Collinson (Construction) Limited
Coniston Hotel Limited
Crerar Hotel Group Limited
Crosthwaite Hotels (Westmorland) Limited
Crown Hotel (Bawtry) Limited
De Vere 2 Limited
De Vere Cotswold Water Park Limited
De Vere Limited
De Vere Selsdon Estate Limited
De Vere Tortworth Court Limited
De Vere Wokefield Estate Limited
Doncast Limited
Etrickbank Limited
Feversham Arms Limited
Gilpin Lodge Country House Hotel Limited
Grand Principal Birmingham Limited
Grantley Hall Group Limited
Hapimag Resorts & Residences (UK) Ltd
Hazlewood Holdings Limited
W.A. Howarth (Aphrodites Lodge) Limited
Inn at Grasmere Limited
Inspire Holding Co Ltd
Interchange and Consort Hotels Limited
JA Hotels Limited
Kaye's Hotels Limited
Langdale Owners PLC
Leeds Cricket Football and Athletic Co Ltd
Llandudno Bay Hotel & Spa Limited
Low Wood Hotel (1958) Limited
McIlroy Estates Limited
Meads Trust.Limited
Methodist Holiday Hotels Limited
Middleton Lodge Events Limited
Ness Hall Ltd
Northern Touch Limited
OPH Property Holdings Limited
Provenance Hotels Limited
Provenance Inns Limited
Queens Staith Leisure Limited
Rainheath Limited
Red Hall (Bury) Limited
Barry Robinson Leisure Limited
Rockliffe Hall Limited
Rothay Garden Hotel Limited
Rudding Park Limited
Samara Properties Limited
Sedbergh Hotel Enterprises Limited
Sheffield United (Hotel) Limited
Swan Hotel (Newby Bridge) Holdings Ltd
Swan Hotel (Newby Bridge) Limited
Swinton Park Limited
Thornsett Vale Limited
Vogue Leisure Limited
W W Hotels Limited
Warmest Welcome Limited
Weetwood Hall Limited
West Retford Hotel Limited
West Tower Country House Limited
West Tower Property Limited
Willerby Manor Hotels Limited
Yorkcloud Limited
Yorkshire Period Hotels Limited

**55201 Holiday centres and villages** [22]

Arboretum Devon (RLH) Limited
Bridge Leisure Parks (Finance) Limited
Bridge Leisure Parks (Holdings) Limited
Bridge Leisure Parks Limited
Cotterhill Limited
Holgates (Caravan Parks) Limited
Lingholm Estate Limited
Park Leisure 2000 (Cornwall) Limited
Park Leisure 2000 (Northumberland) Ltd
Park Leisure 2000 Limited
Project Rock Bidco Limited
Project Rock Equityco Limited
Quintor (Homes) Limited
Sand Le Mere Caravan Park Limited
Shorewood Leisure Group Limited
Shorewood Parks Limited
Total Oynx Limited
Trevella Caravan Co Ltd
Turnberry Holiday Park Limited
Verdant Leisure 2 Limited
Verdant Leisure Limited
Windward Phase 2 Limited

**55209 Other holiday and other collective accommodation** [10]

Leisure Resorts Limited
Lido Leisure Parks Limited
Matson Ground Estate Co Ltd
McCarthy Caravans Limited
North Bay Leisure Limited
Rudding Park Limited
Sandburn York Limited
Walney Island South End Caravan Site Ltd
Windward Phase 2 Limited
Witton Castle Country Park Limited

**55300 Recreational vehicle parks, trailer parks and camping grounds** [29]

Akebar Park Leisure Limited
Aureus Leisure Limited
Barton Park Estates Limited
Blue Sky Resorts Limited
Causey Hill Caravan Park Limited
Crows Nest Camp Limited
Drivecheck Limited
Easington Caravan Sites Limited
Bell Elliot Leisure Limited
Elm Bank (Northumberland) Limited
M.B. & J. Goodwin Limited
Holgates Silver Ridge Ltd
Hornsea Leisure Limited
Lake District Estates Co Ltd
Lakeland Leisure Estates Limited
Leisure Park Management Limited
Leisure Parks Limited
Longbeach Leisure Limited
North Bay Leisure Limited
Park Leisure Marketing Limited
Patrington Haven Leisure Park Limited
Riverhead Commercial Services Limited
Scout Cragg Holiday Park Limited
Silver Sands Leisure Park Ltd
Sweepcharm Limited
Tocketts Mill Limited
Vectair Aviation (1995) Limited
Willowbank Holiday Park Limited
Witton Castle Country Park Limited

**55900 Other accommodation** [18]

Boston Mayflower Finance PLC
Capernwray Missionary Fellowship of Torchbearers
City of Bradford Y.M.C.A.
Doorstep of Hull
Flower of May Holiday Parks Limited
Foresight North East Lincolnshire Ltd.
Golam Properties Limited
M.B. Goodwin (Skipsea) Limited
Grimsby & Cleethorpes Area Doorstep
Homes for Students Limited
Incommunities Group Limited
Kirklees Community Association
Lincolnshire Employment Accommodation Project Ltd
Overdale Trailer Park (Skipton) Limited
Ulrome Seaside Caravan Co Ltd
Unipol Student Homes
UoE Deaconess Limited
Wilberforce Trust

**56101 Licenced restaurants** [17]

Better Fish Limited
Bettys & Taylors Group Ltd
Bettys & Taylors of Harrogate Ltd
Bibis Restaurants Limited
Bolster Moor Farm Shop Limited
Continental Wine & Food Limited
Hargreaves Enterprises Ltd
Ossett Brewery Pub Co Ltd
Ray Owen Waste Disposal Limited
Salts Estates Limited
Sandburn York Limited
Simpson and Webb Limited
Sukho Limited
Thai Leisure Group Limited
Willerby Manor Hotels Limited
Wiltel Limited
Zeffirellis Limited

**56102 Unlicenced restaurants and cafes**

Bagel Nash Group Limited
Bradshaws Driffield (Holdings) Limited
Kingston Restaurants Limited
Premium Restaurants Limited
Sherwood Restaurants Ltd
Walkers Nurseries Limited

**56103 Take-away food shops and mobile food stands**

Better Fish Limited
Caterleisure Services Limited

**56210 Event catering activities**

Early Excellence Limited
Royal Armouries (International) Limited
Rudding Park Limited
Sedbergh Hotel Enterprises Limited

**56290 Other food services** [10]

BHJ UK Food Limited
Burbank Produce Limited
C.K. (Fast Food Suppliers) Limited
Cartonplast (UK) Limited
Delifresh Limited
Langlands Nurseries Limited
P & A Food Management Services Limited
D.G. Payne Limited
Refreshment Systems Limited
United Fresh Consortium Limited

**56302 Public houses and bars** [23]

Bar 24 Limited
Blues Kitchen Brixton Limited
C2 Investment Limited
Call Lane Social Leeds Limited
Columbo Group Limited
Flower of May Holiday Parks Limited
M.B. Goodwin (Skipsea) Limited
Hargreaves Enterprises Ltd
Market Town Taverns Limited
Mitchell's Brewery Limited
Ossett Brewery Pub Co Ltd
Ray Owen Waste Disposal Limited
Provenance Hospitality Holdings Limited
Provenance Inns Limited
Redmed Limited
Sedbergh Hotel Enterprises Limited
Tadcaster Pub Co Ltd
Vectair Aviation (1995) Limited
Walshford Inn Limited
West Park Inns Limited
Wetherells Contracts Limited
White Rose (Caravan Park) Limited
Yorkshire Period Hotels Limited

**58110 Book publishing**

Coordination Group Publications Ltd

**58141 Publishing of learned journals**

Emerald Group Holdings Limited
Emerald Publishing Limited

**58142 Publishing of consumer and business journals and periodicals**

Country Publications Limited
Investment in Media Limited

**58190 Other publishing activities**

Hallmark Cards PLC
Label Worx Limited
Punch Graphix Limited
Tailormade Design Limited

**58290 Other software publishing**

Frog Education Limited
Orcina Limited
SSP Holdings Limited
SSP Sirius Solutions Limited
Tracsis PLC

**59111 Motion picture production activities** [15]

Bliss Films Limited
Comedian's Guide To Survival Limited
Encounter Production Limited
End of Term Limited
Extremis Production Limited
Family Dies Limited
Formula Films Limited
Further Instructions Ltd
Keep Your Trap Shut Limited
Metanoia Film Limited
Residue Limited
Screen Yorkshire Limited
Solis Film Limited
That Good Night Limited
Waiting for Anya Limited

**59112 Video production activities**

Screen Yorkshire Limited

**59113 Television programme production activities**

High Street TV (Group) Limited
Screen Yorkshire Limited

**59131 Motion picture distribution activities**

GSP Distribution Limited
KVH Media Group International Limited
Parkway Entertainment Co Ltd

**59140 Motion picture projection activities**

Parkway Entertainment Co Ltd
Zeffirellis Limited

**59200 Sound recording and music publishing activities**

Label Worx Limited

**60200 Television programming and broadcasting activities**

Made Television Ltd.

**61100 Wired telecommunications activities**

Arris International PLC
Claritas Solutions Limited
Nynet Limited

**61200 Wireless telecommunications activities**

8point8 Support Limited
Arris Global Ltd.
Arris International PLC
Cellhire Group Limited
Filtronic PLC

**61300 Satellite telecommunications activities**

Arris Global Ltd.
Arris International PLC
Navenio Limited
Pace Distribution (Overseas) Limited
Pace Overseas Distribution Limited

**61900 Other telecommunications activities** [21]

(Aq) Limited
(Aq) Networks Limited
24 Seven Communications Limited
Abzorb Group Ltd
Arise Virtual Solutions Limited
Arris Global Ltd.
Arris International PLC
NG Bailey IT Services Limited
Cellhire PLC
Central North Sea Fibre Telecommunications Co Ltd
Clarke Telecom Limited
Coriant UK Limited
Alan Dick Communications Limited
Intouch Advance Limited
KCOM Group PLC
KCOM Holdings Limited
Mazuma Mobile Limited
Talk Direct (Leeds) Ltd
Tampnet UK Limited
Teleware Group PLC
Ventura Telecom Holdings Limited

**62011 Ready-made interactive leisure and entertainment software development**

Team 17 Digital Limited
Team 17 Holdings Limited
Team 17 Software Limited

**62012 Business and domestic software development** [24]

Answer Digital Limited
Ascribe Limited
BJSS Limited
CSC (World) Limited
Claritas Solutions Limited
Computer Services Consultants (U.K.) Ltd
Easysoft Limited
Egton Medical Information Systems Ltd
Geoplan Spatial Intelligence Limited
Gould Tech Solutions Limited
Infact UK Limited
Inventry Limited
Masternaut Limited
Mitrefinch Holdings Limited
Mitrefinch Limited
Numecent Holdings Ltd
People Apps Limited
Phoenix Partnership (Leeds) Ltd
Piksel Limited
Rockar 2016 Limited
SSP Limited
Savant Limited
Select Legal Systems Limited
Tracsis Retail and Operations Limited

**62020 Information technology consultancy activities** [28]

NG Bailey IT Services Limited
Concorde Technology Group Limited
ECSC Group PLC
Esteem Systems Limited
Financial Systems & Consultancy Ltd.
GDS Holdings Limited
Galtec Solutions Limited
Hague Computer Supplies Limited
IT @ Spectrum Limited
Intechnology PLC
Meritec Limited
Numecent Limited
Ontrac Limited
Oriium Consulting Ltd
Phoenix Partnership (Leeds) Ltd
Pinion Services Limited
Praesto Consulting UK Ltd
Proactis Limited
Red Embedded Consulting Limited
Redcentric Solutions Limited
SSP Holdings Limited
SSP Limited
Sapphire Technologies Limited
Savant Limited
Richard Sullivan Consulting Ltd
TSYS Card Tech Limited
Tracsis PLC
Trimble Solutions (UK) Ltd

**62030 Computer facilities management activities**

DB Systel UK Limited
Redcentric Solutions Limited
SSP Limited

**62090 Other information technology service activities** [47]

Apttus EMEA Limited
Arrow Enterprise Computing Solutions Ltd
Ascribe Group Limited
Ascribe Holdings Limited
BTL Group Limited
Boxer Properties (Bradford) Limited
CCL Computers Limited
Cammax Limited
Concorde Excel Holdings Limited
Corporate Document Services Limited
Desk Top Publishing Micro Systems Ltd
Esteem Holdings Limited
Etas Limited
Explorer (UK) Limited
James Fisher Marine Services Limited
Giacom Holdings Limited
Holdgrove Limited
Intechnology PLC
KCOM Group PLC
Label Worx Limited
Lectra UK Limited
PAS Holding Co Ltd
PC Specialist Limited
Proactis Limited
RX Systems Limited
Real Time Communications Limited
Redcentric Solutions Limited
Renovotec Ltd
SSP Bidco Limited
SSP Holdings Limited
SSP Limited
SSP Midco 1 Limited
SSP Midco 2 Limited
SSP Topco Limited
Savant Limited
Scroll Bidco Limited
Select Legal Systems Limited
Smoothwall Limited
Software Box Limited
Splicegroup Europe Limited
Stickyeyes Limited
Support Warehouse Limited
Techbuyer Limited
Teleware PLC
Track Record Holdings Limited
Vapour Cloud Limited
Welcom Digital Limited

**63110 Data processing, hosting and related activities** [16]

Callcredit Data Solutions Limited
Callcredit Limited
Callcredit Marketing Limited
Cap Hpi Limited
Claritas Solutions Limited
Communisis Data Intelligence Limited
Corporate Document Services Limited
HPI Limited
Label Worx Limited
Latitude Digital Marketing Limited
Proactis Limited
Psona Limited
Redcentric Solutions Limited
SSP Holdings Limited
TSYS Card Tech Limited
Tracsis Traffic Data Limited

**63120 Web portals**

Corporate Document Services Limited
Proactis Limited

**63990 Other information service activities n.e.c.**

Callcredit Marketing Limited
Coast and Vale Community Action
Communisis UK Limited
Fruugo.Com Ltd
Propharma Group MIS Holdings Limited

**64191 Banks**

CYB Investments Limited
Methodist Chapel Aid Limited
Vanquis Bank Limited
Yorkshire Water Services Finance Limited

**64201 Activities of agricultural holding companies**

I'anson Bros. (Holdings) Limited
L & K Group PLC
Murton Feeds Limited

**64202 Activities of production holding companies** [41]

AKV Group Ltd
Airea Floor Coverings Limited
American Standard (U.K.) Co.
Anatis UK Limited
Angus Holdings Safety Group Limited
Angus International Safety Group Limited
Applied Composites Group Ltd
Arville Holdings Limited
C T Glass Holdings Limited
Charco Ninety-Nine Limited
Coachman Group Limited
Coachman Holdings Limited
Epax Pharma UK Holdings Unlimited
Froneri Limited
Froneri South Africa Holdings Limited
Guardian Industries UK Holding Limited
Harrogate Water Brands Limited
Karro Food Group Limited
Kwiktuf Holdings Limited
Lymington Holdings Limited
M1 Engineering Holdings Limited
Manor Coating Systems (Holdings) Limited
McCain UK H1 Limited
McCain UK H2 Limited
New R & R Ice Cream Limited
Novus Finance Ltd
Pacific Shelf 1809 Limited
Pipe Holdings 1 PLC
Pipe Holdings 2 Limited
Pipe Holdings PLC
Polypipe Group PLC
R & R PIK Limited
Reliance RG Limited
Riviera Acquisitions Limited
Riviera Topco Limited
Ruby Acquisitions Limited
William Thompson Group Holdings Ltd
Total Downstream UK PLC
UKIOSH Ltd.
Winder Power Holdings Limited
Yorkshire Stone Co. (Bradford) Limited

**64203 Activities of construction holding companies** [21]

Beckenreid Limited
Bunton Plant Hire Limited
DCMK Limited
Dalmore Highway Investment Holdings Ltd
Everlast (Group) Limited
Fairbriar Real Estate Limited
Fairbriar Residential Developments Ltd
Fearnley Rhodes Limited
Fussey Holdings Limited
Harron Group Limited
Mone Brothers Group Ltd
Newroc Ltd
P V H Holdings Limited
Persimmon PLC
Pitts Wilson Holdings Limited
Shouksmith Holdings Limited
Triton Construction Holdings Limited
Watsons BS (Holdings) Limited
Wilton Cobley (Holdings) Limited
R.N. Wooler & Co (Holdings) Limited
YPP Holdings Limited

**64204 Activities of distribution holding companies**

Animalcare Group PLC
CNG (Group) Limited
Element14 Finance UK Limited
Hambleton Holdings Limited
M Rugs Limited
Parkrowe Estates Limited
Premier Farnell Limited
Videcon Holdings Limited

**64205 Activities of financial services holding companies** [34]

Advice Champion.co.uk Limited
Ardagh MP Holdings UK Limited
Berry Investment Holdings Limited
Broker Network Partner Holdings Limited
Connells Limited
T L Dallas Group Limited
Diamond Resorts Financial Services Ltd
Gilkes Hydro Investments Limited
Hamsard 3225 Limited
Interactive Investor Holdings Limited
Links Investment Holdings Limited
M.K.M. BS (Holdings) 3 Limited
McCain Finance (GB) Limited
Non-Standard Finance PLC
Non-Standard Finance Subsidiary II Ltd
Non-Standard Finance Subsidiary III Ltd
PBS Holdings Limited
Partnership Investment Fund Limited
Project Tulip Topco Limited
Provident Financial PLC
RDG Midas Holdings (NI) Limited
Redmayne Capital Limited
Reward Finance Group Limited
Simon Bidco Limited
Simon Midco Limited
Simply Biz Limited
Simply Biz Services Limited
Skipton Group Holdings Limited
Tenet Group Limited
Tenet Limited
Uris Central Administration Limited
Uris Topco Limited
Verulam Holdings Limited
Yes Car Credit (Holdings) Limited

**64209 Activities of other holding companies n.e.c.** [251]

ACAD Holdings Limited
AK (SPV) Limited
AMT2 Limited
Abacus Direct Manufacturing Group Ltd
Academic Appointments 2017 Limited
Adare SEC Holdings Limited
Aghoco 1419 Limited
Aketon Limited
Alphamore Corporation Ltd
Alt Berg Holdings Limited
Armstrong Priestley Holdings Limited
Athena PTS Holdings Limited
Atkinson Group (Yorkshire) Limited
Atkinson Holdings Limited
Auden McKenzie Holdings Limited
Axis Bidco Limited
Axis Midco Limited
B.C.A. Group Ltd
BSN Medical UK Holding Limited
Ballards Removals Holdings Limited
Barden Biomass Holdings Limited
Batchelors Motor Group Limited
Birch Valley Holdings Limited
Blackrow Holdings Limited
Brass Agency Group Limited
Brecks Holdings Limited
Bremsen Technik Holdings Ltd
N.R. Burnett (Holdings) Limited
CCL Syrinx (UK) Limited
CNG (Group) Limited
CPD Direct Limited
Caddick (JPC Developments) Limited
Calder Valley Holdings Limited
Care Holdings Limited
Carver Engineering Holdings Limited
Cater-Kwik Group Limited
Centrica Storage Holdings Limited
Charlesworth Family Group Limited
Chatsworth Windows Limited
Cobalt Project Investments (Hull - Sewell) Ltd
Colenso Holdings Limited
Collegiate Formation Limited
Collett Holdings Limited
Complete Business Solutions Group Holdings Ltd
Connells Limited
Coral PFI Holdings 2003 Limited
Jimmy Corrigan's Limited
Cristal Inorganic Chemicals UK Limited
Croda Distillates Limited
Cromwell Capital Ventures UK Limited
Cromwell European Holdings Limited
Cromwell Holdings Europe Limited
Cromwell Management Holdings Limited
Cyan Bidco Limited
Cyan Blue Core Limited
DSS Group Limited
Dadibhais Holdings Limited
Dale Erskine Power Solutions Limited
Devonshire Club (Holdings) Limited
Dining Club Group Limited
Don Valley Engineering Holdings Limited
Dream Property Holdco Limited
Duchy Homes (Holdings) Limited
A. Dyson & Son (Patterns) Limited
EPMS Group Limited
East Riding Holdings Company
Eddisons Commercial (Holdings) Limited
Element UK Holdco Limited
Element UK Midco Limited
Element UK Topco Limited
Eleonora Sport Limited
Elsham Wold Estates Limited
Emerald Care Holdings Yorkshire Limited
Entertainment Alliance (Holdings) Ltd
Entertainment Alliance (UK) Limited
Esplanade Group (Scarborough) International Ltd
Exemplary Group PLC
FC Beamish Bidco Ltd
Finestline Limited
G2M Capital Limited
GBA Group Limited
Goodall Group Limited
HC-ONE Oval Limited
Harder Bros (Holdings) Limited
Hassan Group Limited
Havwoods Global Holdings Limited
Health Management (Carlisle) Holdings Ltd
Hillas Group Limited
Hillcroft Ltd
Hitha Limited
Holliday International Limited
Holmfirth Dyers Holdings Limited
Home Products Group Limited
IRISNDT UK Holdings Limited
Icelolly Bidco Limited
Icelolly Topco Limited
Iconx Holdings Limited
Idexx UK Acquisition Limited
Inhoco 3498 Limited
JCCO 387 Limited
JT Group (UK) Limited
JT Holdings (UK) Limited
Justmerc Limited
Kaver Limited
Kings Hall Leisure Limited
Kirkby 2017 Limited
Kokoon Holdings Limited
LPT Trading Ltd
Lake District Holdings Limited
Lakeland Fashion Limited
Lawton Yarns (Holdings) Limited
Leeds Group PLC
Leisure World Group Limited
Lifterz Holdings Limited
Ligentia Group Holdings Limited
Logistik Holdings Limited
Londyne Limited
Loscoe Investments Ltd
Lowell Holdings Ltd
Lowell Portfolio I Ltd
A.W.Lumb & Co.Limited
Lune Holdings Limited
M.K.M. BS (Holdings) 1 Limited
M.K.M. BS (Holdings) 2 Limited
M.K.M. Building Supplies (Group) Limited
Magenta Prime Limited
J Maguire Holdings Limited
Mardon Holdings Limited
J. Marr & Son Limited
Marsh & Parsons (Holdings) Limited
Metamark Group Holdings Limited
Millennium Inorganic Chemicals Overseas Holdings
Millennium Inorganic Chemicals UK Holdings Ltd
Abraham Moon Holdings Limited
Morton Michel Holdings Limited
Mumtaz Food Products Limited
NYT (Holdings) Limited
New Equipment Holdings Limited
Nexus Vehicle Holdings Limited
Northgate (Europe) Limited
Northgate PLC
Nu-Oval Acquisitions 1 Limited
Nu-Oval Acquisitions 2 Limited
Orangechart Limited
Origin Group Finance Limited
Origin Group Holdco Limited
Ossett Brewery Group Holdings Limited
P.P. Group Holdings Limited
PFI 2005 Limited
PFI Para (Holdings) Limited
Paramount Retail Group Holdco Limited
Pavers Holdings Limited
John Pawson (Holdings) Limited
Peover Eye Investments Limited
Planet Platforms (Holdings) Limited
Portbond Limited
Potter Group (Holdings) Limited
Prahi Limited
Prious Limited
Production Park Ltd
Provu Holdings Limited
RFPG Holdings Limited
RP Net Media Ltd
Rawson Brook Group Holdings Limited
Red Circle Investments Limited
Redhouse Holdings Limited
Redline Worldwide Limited
Reed Boardall Group Limited
Reed Group Ltd
Rema Tip Top Holdings UK Limited
Renovotec Investments Limited
Rodgers Group Limited
Rosehill Polymers Group Limited
SIL Holdings Limited
SPH 2011 Limited
SRH 2011 Limited
SUSD Asset Management (Holdings) Limited
Scarborough (UK) Limited
Scarborough China Holdings Limited
Scarborough Development Group Limited
Scarborough Enterprises (UK) Limited
Scarborough Holding Co Ltd
Scarborough Holdings (UK) Limited
Scarborough Overseas Holdings Limited
Scarborough Property (UK) Limited
Scarborough Thorpe Park Holdings Limited
Scriven Park Estates Limited
Sealord (Europe) Limited
Serenity Parks Limited
Sheds for Logistics Limited
Sheffield United Group Limited
Sissons of Sherburn Holdings Limited
Skipton Investments Limited
Spire Bidco Hotels Limited
State Debtco Limited
State Interco Limited
Stearsby Hagg Property Co Ltd
Steve Ltd
Sunny Day Capital Limited
Sunny Day Property Holdings Limited
Sunny Day Property Limited
TCS Properties Limited
TGH Acquisitions Limited
TGH Finance Limited
TGH Investments Limited
TPP Finance Limited
TPPH (Leeds) Limited
Takahe Holdings Ltd
Tandem 1987 Limited
Thomas Bidco Limited

Thomas Midco Limited
Thomas Topco Limited
Thorpe Park Holdings Limited
Three Sixty Water Limited
Three60 Energy Limited
Tocketts Mill Leisure Limited
Trinity Exploration & Production PLC
Tunstall Group Acquisition Limited
Tunstall Group Finance Limited
Tunstall Group Holdings Limited
Tunstall Group Limited
Tunstall Healthcare Group Limited
Tunstall Holdings Limited
UCLH Investors (Holdings) Limited
Vetpartners Group Finance Limited
Vetpartners Group Limited
Vetpartners UK Holdings Ltd.
Visit Yorkshire Holdings Ltd
Vivimed Labs UK Limited
W. P. Holdings Limited
WGL Bidco Limited
WGL Holdco Limited
WGL Midco Limited
WJS Properties 2 Limited
P Waddington Limited
John Wade (Holdings) Limited
Walkers Holdings One Limited
Welcom Software Holdings Limited
Westdale Group Limited
Westpoint Group Trading Limited
H & C Whitehead (Holdings) Limited
Witherslack Group (Holdings) Limited
Alan Wood Holdings Limited
Wrapid Investments Limited
YLC Holdings Limited
YPP Holdings Limited
Yorkshire Initiatives Limited
Yorkshire Sheeting Group Limited
Yorktest Group Limited
Youngmight Limited
Zenith International Freight Holdings Ltd

**64301 Activities of investment trusts**

Hodson Family Investments Limited
LDK Investments Ltd
Mabanes Properties Limited
Twentyfour28 Limited
York House Investment Co Ltd

**64303 Activities of venture and development capital companies**

British Smaller Companies VCT PLC
British Smaller Companies VCT2 PLC
Carlton Court Investments Limited
Kexby Investments Limited
Somlie Limited
Wolds Investments Limited

**64304 Activities of open-ended investment companies**

Broad Carr Investments Limited
Crossco (1317) Limited
Crossco (1318) Limited
Gweco 511 Limited
TG-F Investments (No. 1) Limited
TG-F Investments (No. 2) Limited

**64305 Activities of property unit trusts**

Beauchamp Real Estate Holdings Limited

**64306 Activities of real estate investment trusts**

MMCD Investments Limited

**64910 Financial leasing**

AMT Vehicle Rental Limited
Bailey Leasing Limited
Cashel Limited
Catfoss Finance Limited
Hartshorne Crossroads Group Contracts Ltd
Heritage Commercial Finance Limited
Hoyer Container Rental UK Limited
Leasedrive Limited
Rawdon Asset Finance Limited

**64921 Credit granting by non-deposit taking finance houses and other specialist consumer credit grantors** [14]

Aberdeen Enterprise Finance Limited
BOS (Shared Appreciation Mortgages) No. 1 PLC
BOS (Shared Appreciation Mortgages) No. 2 PLC
BOS (Shared Appreciation Mortgages) No. 3 PLC
BOS (Shared Appreciation Mortgages) No. 4 PLC
IPF Digital Group Limited
International Personal Finance PLC
JSJ Finance Limited
Lesley, Stephen & Co. Limited
Madala Limited
Provident Personal Credit Limited
Rawdon Asset Finance Limited
TM Advances Limited
S.D. Taylor Limited

**64922 Activities of mortgage finance companies**

Accord Mortgages Limited
Amber Homeloans Limited
Bradford & Bingley PLC
Mortgage Express
North Yorkshire Mortgages Limited
Oakwood Homeloans Limited
Pure Retirement Limited
Yorkshire Bank Home Loans Limited

**64929 Other credit granting n.e.c.** [14]

Access Property Finance Limited
Business & Enterprise Finance Ltd.
The Manny Cussins Foundation
Fenton Finance Limited
G R Finance Limited
IPF Financing Limited
Inchem Finance Limited
Mysing Capital Limited
Naylors Finance Limited
Ortus Secured Finance III Limited
Panacea Finance Solutions Limited
Reward Capital Limited
Student Loans Co Ltd
Yorkshire Property Finance Ltd

**64991 Security dealing on own account** [13]

Acropolis Corporate Limited
Apollo 1 Investments
Apollo 11 Investments
Cornucopia Investments Limited
Finishchoice Limited
Simon Holmes Limited
I A P Investments Ltd
Parkhead Investments Limited
Prospero Growth Limited
Mark Proudfoot Investments Ltd
SKB2016 Limited
Swaledale Investments Limited
Tarnhelm Securities Limited

**64992 Factoring**

Reward Invoice Finance Limited
Skipton Business Finance Limited

**64999 Financial intermediation not elsewhere classified** [60]

2 Plan Wealth Management Limited
Age Partnership Limited
Arch Chemicals UK Finance
Asset Finance UK Limited
Aura DC Limited
Automobile Association Personal Finance Ltd
Aviva Equity Release UK Limited
Aviva Pension Trustees UK Limited
BB Investments
BOS Personal Lending Limited
Ballyvesey Holdings Limited
Beverley House Investments Limited
Cheque Exchange Limited
Clerical Medical Investment Fund Managers Ltd
Cliffe Hill Second Investments Limited
Contractsure Limited
Curo Transatlantic Limited
Delahope Limited
Farnsworth Investments Limited
Financial Funding Limited
Foundation for Credit Counselling
Furness Mortgage Services Limited
Glendon Estates
Grosvenor Funding Solutions Limited
HBOS Investment Fund Managers Limited
Halifax General Insurance Services Ltd
Halifax Share Dealing Limited
Hemingways Marketing Services Limited
Highstone Estates (Kidderminster) Ltd
Home Shopping Personal Finance Limited
Interactive Investor Services Limited
Kelda Eurobond Co Limited
Kelda Non-Reg Holdco Limited
Kingston Equity & Finance Limited
LEBC Group Limited
Lantern Debt Recovery Services Limited
Leigh Holdings Limited
Morris Family Investments Ltd
Mortgage Business PLC
Northern Foods Finance Limited
Norwich and Peterborough (LBS) Limited
Park Leisure Group Limited
Personal Touch Financial Services Ltd
Provident Financial Management Services Ltd
Rawdon Asset Finance Limited
Southgate - Dan at Spyglass Hill - Bidco Ltd
Sovereign Reserve Limited

TCS Properties Limited
Tenetconnect Limited
Tenetconnect Services Limited
Tenetlime Limited
Ukar Corporate Services Limited
Michael Wheatley Finance Limited
White Rose Finance Co Ltd
Wykeland Treasury Management Limited
Yorkshire Housing Finance PLC
Zenith Automotive Holdings Limited
Zeus Bidco Limited
Zeus Finco Limited
Zeus Midco Limited

**65110 Life insurance**

Aviva Life & Pensions UK Limited
Bartlett Group (Holdings) Limited
Millennium Insurance Brokers Limited

**65120 Non-life insurance** [27]

Acumen Credit Insurance Brokers Limited
Bartlett & Co Ltd
Bartlett Group (Holdings) Limited
CYB Intermediaries Limited
Car Care Plan (Holdings) Limited
Car Care Plan Limited
Card Protection Plan Limited
Citynet Insurance Brokers Limited
Contractsure Limited
T L Dallas & Co Limited
W. Denis (Insurance Brokers) PLC
Fish Administration Limited
D. E. Ford Holdings Limited
Henderson Insurance Brokers Limited
Homecare Insurance Limited
Integra Insurance Solutions Limited
Marshall Wooldridge Limited
Millennium Insurance Brokers Limited
Motors Insurance Co Ltd
One Commercial (Claims) Limited
One Commercial Limited
PIB Risk Services Limited
Rural & Commercial Holdings Limited
Rural Insurance Group Limited
Sovereign Health Care
U K Insurance Limited
WTJ Insurance Brokers Limited

**65202 Non-life reinsurance**

Bartlett & Co Ltd
D. E. Ford Holdings Limited
UK General Insurance Group Limited
UK General Insurance Limited

**65300 Pension funding**

DFDS Pension Limited
F1rst Actuarial PLC

**66110 Administration of financial markets**

Together Housing Finance PLC

**66120 Security and commodity contracts dealing activities**

Dalmore Capital Limited
Halifax Share Dealing Limited

**66190 Activities auxiliary to financial intermediation n.e.c.**

Bluestone Leasing Limited
Crystal Investment Holdings Limited
Gale and Phillipson Investment Services Ltd
HMCA/S PLC
Responsible Life Limited
Streejaane
Tyto Finance Limited
Uris Group Limited

**66210 Risk and damage evaluation**

Acorn Assessors Limited

**66220 Activities of insurance agents and brokers** [12]

Benenden Wellbeing Limited
Caravan Guard Limited
Compass Broker Networks Limited
Henderson Insurance Brokers Limited
Lorica Insurance Brokers Limited
One Call Insurance Services Limited
PIB Group Limited
Proaktive Ltd
Q Underwriting Services Limited
Romero Insurance Brokers Limited
Wilby (Group) Limited
Wilby Limited

**66290 Other activities auxiliary to insurance and pension funding**

CPPGroup Services Limited
Chicago Bidco Limited
Chicago Midco Limited
Entertainment and Leisure Insurance Services Ltd
Equine and Livestock Insurance Co Ltd
Heathfield Holdings Limited

**66300 Fund management activities**

Cardale Asset Management Limited
D and K Chapman Limited
Donbac Limited
Elmet Investments
Jackie Hobson Investments
JMCD Investments Limited
Skirfare Investments Limited

**68100 Buying and selling of own real estate** [210]

ADW Enterprises Limited
ATC Properties Limited
C F Abraham Limited
Abstract (Bristol) Limited
Academy Leisure Limited
Aclet Property Management & Services Ltd
Agercon Holdings Limited
Allam Developments Limited
Allied Properties (Hull) Limited
Alta Enterprises Limited
Atlantic Bay Hotel (Woolacombe) Limited
Audley Court Hollins Hall Limited
BPC Yorkshire Limited
Baddow Properties Limited
Bear Leisure Limited
Belle Vue Mills Limited
J.N. Bentley Properties Limited
Binks (Holdings) Limited
Bleu Properties Ltd
Bonus Electrical Group Limited
Bosworth Estates Limited
Bramall Properties Limited
Brewery Wharf (Leeds) Limited
Brigdale Limited
Broadacres Services Limited
Browntree Properties Limited
Buckley Properties (Leeds) Limited
Buy-Investment-Properties Limited
CG Estates Limited
CI Estates Limited
CR Estates Limited
Caddick (City One) Limited
Caddick (Mill Harbour) Limited
Caddick (Rose Wharf) Limited
Caddick (Scarborough) Limited
Caddick Developments Limited
Calverley Reservoir Sales Co Ltd
Cardale Park Properties Ltd
Cave Developments Limited
Central Land Holdings Ltd
Chambers Parking Limited
Charminster Estates Limited
Chartford Arthington Limited
City & Provincial (Equity Partners 3) Ltd
City Red (Holdings) Limited
Clark Care Estates Limited
Dean Clough Limited
Commercial Development Projects Limited
Simon Cook Holdings Limited
Copley Motors Limited
Cox 22 Limited
Crossways Commercial Estates Limited
D & L S Developments Limited
D & M Middleton Limited
Dalekim Developments Limited
Darley Properties Limited
Dawn Developments Limited
Devonshire Square Properties Limited
Duchy Homes (Humshaugh) Limited
Electric Support Limited
Elvaston Investments Limited
Eshton Ltd
Evans Homes Limited
Fairbriar Real Estate Developments Ltd
Fairbriar Real Estate Limited
Finest Flats Co Ltd
Fourth Argyll Limited
Frazer Estates Limited
G & R Properties (Yorkshire) Limited
GSD Riverside Limited
Giroscope Limited
Glasshouses123 Limited
Ground Group Limited
Gweco 510 Limited
HD1 Developments Limited
Hadrian (Residential) Limited
Halbert Limited
Harrogate Investments Limited
Harrogate14 Limited
High Point Estates Ltd.
Highacre Builders Limited
Highgrove Property Developments Limited
Hillcrest Garages (Sowerby Bridge) Ltd
Amanda Hobson Limited
Hollin Hall Holdings Limited
David Hopkinson Limited
Horncastle Group PLC
Horsforth Mill Limited
Iles (York) Limited
Imbue Property Ltd
Impact Property Services Limited

J & L (North East) Limited
JCT600 (Properties) Limited
Jacksons Transport (West Riding) Limited
John Street Developments Limited
Karman Ltd
Keighley Fleece Mills Co Ltd
John H King (Developments) Limited
Kingswood Parks Development Co Ltd
Knightwood Developments Limited
LNT Care Developments Limited
Lamba Trading Co. Limited
Landplan Properties Limited
Landteam Property Investments Limited
Leader Limited
Libra Careco CH2 Propco Limited
Libra Careco CH3 Propco Limited
Lovel Capital Projects Limited
Low Moor Properties Limited
Lowson & Co. Limited
Luminar Partnership Limited
Malton Road Developments Limited
Marrtree Developments Ltd
Marrtree Investments Limited
Frank Marshall & Sons Ltd
Marshall Brothers Finance Co Limited
Matwest Ltd
Mena Developments Limted Limited
Middlewood Locks Residential Limited
Mill Mount Properties Limited
Mister Capital Holdings Limited
Moda Living Limited
Modav Limited
Moolmoor (Waverley) Limited
Moolmoor Holdings Limited
Moolmoor Investments Limited
Moorgarth Living Limited
Moorgarth Retail Limited
Mulberry Homes Yorkshire Limited
NSS Properties Limited
Newby Manor Estates Limited
Newby Manor Investments Limited
Oakapple Commercial Limited
Oakapple Homes (Scarborough) Limited
Oakesway Limited
Oakgate Group Limited
Oakwell Securities Limited
Sir Robert Ogden Estates Ltd
Omnivale Limited
One Brewery Wharf Limited
One Fortress Limited
Owens Developments Ltd
Pall Mall Developments Limited
Parkside Property (Yorkshire) Limited
Precis (1638) Limited
Property Renaissance Limited
Prospect Estates Limited
Prosperity Noor Ltd
J.Pullan & Sons Limited
Quarmby Holdings Limited
Quarters Developments Limited
Queens Hotel (Llandudno) Limited
R and A Hotels Group Ltd
Ral Holdings Limited
Ravensfield Properties Limited
Rhodes Asset Management Limited
Richmond Properties (UK) Limited
Rollings Investments Limited
Rushbond PLC
Rushbond Retail Limited
SHFT Properties Ltd
SJS (Norton) Limited
Saint Leonard's Property Co Ltd
Scarborough International Properties Ltd
Scotfield Group Limited
Sharma Investments Limited
Shipton Estates Limited
South Parade Properties Limited
Southgate - Dan at Spyglass Hill - Propco 1 Ltd
Southgate - Dan at Spyglass Hill - Propco 2 Ltd
St James Securities Limited
Sterne Properties Limited
Stoneacre Property Investments Ltd
Stoneferry Marfleet Limited
Strawson Group Developments Limited
Strawson Holdings Limited
M.F. Strawson Limited
Sunny Day Trading
Superior Developments Limited
Surcoat Group Limited
TCS Freehold Investments Limited
TCS Holdings Limited
TCS Leasehold Investments Limited
TRU Property Investments Limited
Talbert Limited
Taniya Properties Ltd
Temple Way Properties Limited
Tower Estates (York) Limited
Towngate Estates Limited
Towngate PLC
Uptownleeds Limited
Victor Investments & Securities Ltd
Watergate Developments Limited
West Ella Estates Limited
West Park Estates Limited
Wortley Developments Limited
Wykeland (Humberside) Limited
Wykeland Investments Limited
Wykeland Limited
Wykeland Properties Limited
Wynperg Investments Limited
YP Real Estate Limited
Yarm Estates Limited
York123 Limited
Yorkcourt Paragon Limited
Yorkshire House Development One Limited
Yorkshire Ventures (Estates) Limited
Yorplace Limited
Z & D Property Investments Limited
Zuka Ltd.

### 68201 Renting and operating of Housing Association real estate [41]

Abbeyfield Ilkley Society Limited
Acis Group Limited
Airedale House Limited
Argyle Square Properties Limited
Bellutex Limited
Bradford Flower Fund Homes
C. K. Properties (UK) Limited
Carr Mount Estate Limited
Crescent Estates (Ilkley) Limited
DEU Estates Properties Limited
Dyson Properties Limited
Emacrow Limited
Eridor Investments Limited
Fortlands Limited
Goodwin Development Trust
HD1 Developments Limited
High Point Estates (Birstall) Limited
High Point Estates (Darlington) Limited
High Point Residential Limited
Holker Estates Co. Limited
P.Holmes Properties Limited
Horus Limited
Impact Property Services Limited
Inclusion Housing CIC
Kingsoak Limited
Modav Limited
Neargoal Limited
P & J Properties (Yorkshire) Limited
Park Lane Properties (Leeds) Limited
Prorun Limited
Rhino Enterprises Properties Limited
Richmond Properties (UK) Limited
Sands Care Holdings Limited
Shallowdale Limited
Sheard Properties Limited
Sing Kee Group Limited
Spencer Properties (UK) Limited
St Anne's Community Services
Vodecca Properties Limited
Waxman Holdings Limited
H. Wicks (Lindal) Limited

### 68202 Letting and operating of conference and exhibition centres

De Vere Grand Connaught Rooms Limited
Royal Armouries (International) Limited

### 68209 Other letting and operating of own or leased real estate [545]

123 Retail Limited
47A Limited
56 George Street Limited
A-Fax Properties Limited
AJS 22 Ltd
ATC Developments (Leeds) Limited
Abacus Direct Properties Limited
Abirose Limited
C F Abraham Limited
Academy Leisure Limited
Aclet Property Management & Services Ltd
Agercon Limited
Aire Valley Properties Limited
All Property Management Ltd
Allam Developments Limited
Allied Properties (Hull) Limited
Almit Properties Limited
Alta Enterprises Limited
Alvercroft Limited
Amsgro Limited
Mark Anglin Associates Limited
Archbold Holdings Limited
Ashfield (Hull) Limited
Ashton Agricultural and General Limited
Aston Properties (Leeds) Limited
Astorbush Limited
Augean Property Limited
B.C.A. Group Ltd
BBP Group Limited
BBP Investments Limited
Banks Lane Investments Limited
Bannatyne Properties Limited
Bar 24 Limited
M. and B. Barker Limited
P. Barker Properties Limited
Barwick Investments (Leeds) Limited
C.K.Batchelor Limited
Bay Properties Letting Co Ltd
Bayford & Co Ltd
Bayford & Co. (Developments) Limited
W.S. Bayston & Son Limited
Beaumont House Properties Limited

Beech Hill Residential Investments Ltd
Belgrave (North West) Limited
Belle Vue Property Limited
Bellow Properties Limited
Benson Turner Limited
Thos. Bentley & Son Limited
J.N. Bentley Properties Limited
Binks (Holdings) Limited
Birchgrove Estates Limited
Birdsall Estates Co Ltd
Birstall 140 Limited
Blackshaw Holdings Limited
Blenheim House Properties (Bradford) Ltd
Boldarch Limited
Bond House Systems Limited
Bosideng UK Limited
Bossdean Properties Limited
Boston Holdings Limited
Bosworth Estates Limited
Boutique Workplace Co Ltd
Br1dge Estates Limited
Braavos Investments Limited
Bracken Limited
Bradbury Investments Limited
Bradford Trident Limited
Bradonwood Limited
Bramhope Property and Investments Ltd
Bramstone Limited
Bridge Properties & Investments Limited
Brighouse Estate Co (Contractors) Ltd
Britt Broadbent Limited
Broadland Properties Limited
John Brooke & Sons Ltd
Brooklands Business Estates Limited
Brooklands Property Holdings Limited
Browntree Properties Limited
A.E. Burt and Co Ltd
Busysky Limited
C C Properties (Yorkshire) Ltd
C.A. (Evenwood) Limited
CG Estates Limited
CGP Estates Limited
CI Estates Limited
CR Estates Limited
Caddick (City One) Limited
Caddick (Rose Wharf) Limited
Caddick Developments Limited
Calder Properties Limited
Calls' Riverside Property Co Ltd
Calvesten Limited
Cardale Park Properties Ltd
Carrington House Yorkshire Limited
Cerros Properties Limited
Charminster Estates Limited
Chase Petroleum Limited
Chinnaraja Estates Limited
Church Property Holdings Limited
Citispace Properties Limited
City Fusion Limited
Clark Care Estates Limited
Teddy Clark Limited
Cleckheaton Properties Limited
Clifton Properties (Yorkshire) Limited
Closepatch Limited
Collard Cole Limited
Continuity Promotions Limited
Contract Experts Limited
AE Cook Holdings Limited
Copley Motors Limited
Cotterhill Limited
County Properties (Northern) Limited
Cox 22 Limited

Cranage Hall Properties Limited
Croft Properties (Harrogate) Limited
Crombie Freehold Limited
Cronkhill Properties Limited
Crossgreen Investments Limited
Crown Properties (Scarborough) Limited
John Edward Crowther Limited
Cyden Homes Limited
D & M Middleton Limited
D. S. Estates Limited
DG Asset Enterprise Ltd
DVV Properties 2 Limited
Dante Capital Limited
Daresbury Park Developments Limited
Daropeant Properties Limited
De Vere Venues Properties Limited
De Vere Wokefield Property Limited
Depho Estates Limited
Derwent Dale Limited
Jaskaran S Deu Properties Limited
Devonshire Square Properties Limited
Diamondcut Limited
Dickinson Properties UK Limited
Direct Investments (Yorkshire) Limited
Dishforth UK Limited
Doncaster Central Development Trust CIC
Double-Ten Limited
Dusrolbake Limited
EFS Chalfont Limited
EMHEDA Limited
EMIH Limited
Eagerlux Limited
East Riding Securities Limited
Eden Holdings (UK) Limited
Elmwood Property Investments Limited
Elvaston Properties Limited
Elvington Holdings Limited
Emerald Investments (GB) Limited
Epil Carlisle Limited
Erivan Holdings Limited
Eshton Oakfield Ltd
Estates U.K. Limited
Eurocentral Hotels Limited
Evans Dakota Hotels Limited
Evans Easyspace (Chester) Limited
Everik Limited
Fairfield Developments (Doncaster) Ltd
Fellside Property Rentals Limited
Fern Hill Holdings Limited
Finest Flats Co Ltd
Firsure Limited
Fisherman Limited
George Fordy Properties Limited
Foremans Properties Limited
Fourth Argyll Limited
Frazer Estates Limited
Freshwater Biological Association
G2M Unilets Limited
GCD Limited
GM Legato Property Limited
Dick Garner & Sons Limited
Gaunts Limited
David Gee Associates Limited
Ghyll Royd Properties Ltd
Lee Gibson Properties Ltd
Gico Limited
Giggleswick School
Glen Mhor Estates Limited
Global Shipping Services Estates Limited
R.J. & A.E. Godfrey
Graham Developments (Property Holdings) Ltd

Grants Pro-Agri Limited
Great Grimsby Seafood Village Ltd
P. W. Greenhalgh Holdings Limited
Grimsby Fish Dock Enterprises Limited
Ground Group Limited
H.H Services Limited
HD1 Developments Limited
Hacs Holdings Limited
Hainsworth Sterne & Co. Limited
Hallborough Properties Limited
Hallmark Cards Property Co Ltd
Hanbeck Properties Limited
Hanover Properties Limited
Karl Hanover Properties Limited
Hardroad Limited
Hargreaves Enterprises Ltd
Harpin Limited
D. Harrison Limited
Harrogate Investments Limited
Hartford Properties Limited
Hayden Daniel Properties Limited
Hemplow Limited
Hever Castle Golf Club Limited
Hever Castle Limited
High Point Estates (Bury) Limited
High Point Estates (Gateshead) Limited
Highgrove Property Developments Limited
M Hillas (Properties) Limited
Hillcroft Ltd
Amanda Hobson Limited
K.M. Holmes (Bradford) Limited
Holmfirth Properties Limited
Hopkins Properties Limited
David Hopkinson Limited
Horncastle Group PLC
John Horsfall & Sons (Greetland),Limited
Horwood House Properties Limited
Geo. Houlton & Sons (Holdings) Limited
Hull Citycare (Fundco 1) Limited
Hull Citycare (Fundco 3) Limited
Hull Citycare (Fundco 4) Limited
Hull Citycare (Fundco 5) Limited
Hull Citycare (Fundco 6) Limited
Hull Citycare Limited
I & S Properties Limited
Iles (York) Limited
Impala Estates Limited
Itch Propco Limited
Ivy Farm Limited
J. and H. Property Management Limited
J.E.C. Investment Co Ltd
JRRT (Properties) Limited
Jabe Foods Limited
Jam Homes Ltd
Jones & Egan Estates Limited
Jonro Properties Limited
Just Lettings Limited
Kankku (Holdings) Limited
Kepwick Farms Limited
Kexgill (Bradford) Limited
Kexgill (Cottingham) 2 Limited
Kexgill (Durham) Limited
Kexgill (Hull) Limited
Kexgill (Liverpool) Limited
Kexgill (Middlesbrough) Limited
Kexgill (Nottingham) Limited
Kexgill (Preston) Limited
Kexgill (Salford) Limited
Kexgill (Stockton) Limited
Kexgill Limited
Key Growing Limited
Keysterne Limited

John H King (Developments) Limited
Kino & Co. Limited
Kirkleavington Property Co Ltd
Kirkminster Engineering Limited
Knightwood Holdings (2011) Limited
L S S Properties (Leeds) Limited
L.F.C. Horkstow Limited
LJV Investments Limited
LPD (Holdings) Limited
Lagonda Selsdon Propco Limited
Lake District Estates Co Ltd
Lake House Investments Limited
Lakehill Estates Limited
Lamba Trading Co. Limited
Landown Limited
Langdale Close Properties Limited
Lashlake Property Limited
Lassic Properties Limited
Lazarus Properties Limited
Leader Limited
Lebus Furniture Limited
Ledden Developments Limited
Leeds Cricket Football and Athletic Co Ltd
Leeds Design Innovation Centre Ltd
Leeds Real Estate Ltd
Letts Properties Limited
Lightbrook Limited
Lightwater Leisure Limited
Lilys of London Limited
Limestone Farming Co Ltd
Lindley (Holdings) Limited
Lingard Bell Limited
Lion Estate and Investment Co Ltd
Llandudno Retail Park Limited
Lone Star Estates (1) Limited
Lovel Capital Projects Limited
Low Street Properties Limited
Lucas Properties Limited
Jack Lunn (Properties) Limited
M. & B. Commercial Properties Limited
M.A. Estates Limited
M.S. Design International Limited
MAS Management Services Ltd
MLC Investments Limited
Malik Halls 2 Ltd
Malik Halls Limited
Malik Real Estate Limited
Maltgrade Limited
Manor Estate Properties (UK) Limited
J Marr (Property) Limited
Marrtree Investments Limited
Marrtree Residential Ltd
RC Marsden Properties Limited
Frank Marshall Estates Limited
Matson Ground Estate Co Ltd
Matwest Ltd
Richard Maxwell Limited
Mayfair Curzon Properties Limited
M. J. McCarthy (Holdings) Limited
McDonald King Limited
Meads Trust.Limited
Medetcrown Limited
Melbourne Street Properties Limited
Mena Commercial Limited
Mena Residential Limited
Merritt & Fryers Limited
Robin Mills Properties Limited
Mirabelle Partners Limited
Mister Capital Holdings Limited
Monks Cross Property Ltd
Moolmoor (Waverley) Limited
Moolmoor Holdings Limited
Moolmoor Investments Limited
Moore Building Enterprises Limited
Moorgarth Group Limited
Moorgarth Living Limited
Moorgarth Property Investments Limited
Moorgarth Retail Limited
Morris & Co. (Handlers) Limited
A.E. Morris Limited
Musgrave & Sagar Limited
My Lockup Limited
NMT Limited
Nagra Properties Limited
Amos Nelson,Limited
Newclose Properties Limited
Newitt & Co (Properties) Limited
Niko Extrusions Limited
Nilerace Limited
North Lincs Property Limited
Northern Divers (Holdings) Limited
Northern Eye UK Limited
Northern Powerhouse Developments Limited
Nortonthorpe Industrial Park Limited
G. Nowell Limited
Nutclough Mill Limited
Oakapple Commercial Limited
Oakgate Group Limited
Sir Robert Ogden Estates Ltd
A V Ogden Holdings Limited
Olicana Properties Limited
Omnivale Limited
On-Site Property Solutions Limited
Orion Commercial Properties Limited
Outwood Investments Limited
P V H Holdings Limited
PCS Property Solutions Limited
PVM Investments Limited
Pall Mall Developments Limited
Pamant Limited
Paragon Property Investments Limited
Paramount Retail Group Holdings Limited
Park Property (World) Ltd
Park Valley Huddersfield Limited
M H & J Park and Son Limited
Parkhouse Lakeland Estate Limited
Parkin International Engineering Services Ltd
Parkmount Estate Company (Allerton) Ltd
Parrs Point Limited
Pattinson 3 Limited
Peagar Ltd
Perio News Limited
B & B Pickard (Leeds) Limited
Pickards (Commercial) Limited
Pickards (Leeds) Limited
Pickering Vale (RLH) Limited
Place2invest Ltd
Place2live Ltd
Planas Properties Limited
Podrigo Ltd
Potter Group (Holdings) Limited
Powar Developments Limited
Prahi Limited
Precious Holdings (Wakefield) Limited
Preston Road Neighbourhood Development Co Ltd
Procter (Bordley) Limited
Promenade Car Parks Limited
Property Investments (Yorkshire) Limited
Prospect Business Centres Limited
Prospect House Leeds Limited
Prosperity Noor Ltd
J.Pullan & Sons Limited
Punch Bowl Investments Limited
Purple Bricks Co Ltd
Q-Park (Taunton) Limited
Q-Park Limited
Q-Park Real Estate Holding UK Limited
Q-Park Real Estate UK I Limited
Q-Park Real Estate UK II Limited
Q-Park Real Estate UK III Limited
Q-Park Securities Limited
Q-Park UK Limited
Quay Propco Limited
R.T. Consultants Limited
Rabbit (Holdings) Limited
Peter Ramsey & Sons Limited
Ravens Ing Properties Limited
H B Raylor & Co Ltd
Rayrigg Estates Ltd
Redhead Holdings Limited
Regent House Estates Limited
Replay Associates Limited
Retsco Limited
Rhal Farms Limited
Richmond Management (Northern) Limited
Ridge Medical Limited
Riding Properties Limited
Roadridge Limited
Roberts, Mart (Properties) Ltd.
F. Peter Robinson Limited
Royds Estates Limited
Royds Properties Ltd
Rudding Park Estate Limited
Running Deep Limited
S & J Industries Limited
SFS Developments Limited
Salts Estates Limited
San Pedro Properties Limited
Sandmoor Properties Limited
Sandtoft Developments Limited
Sargents Properties Limited
Leo Sawrij Limited
Scarborough Flower Fund Homes
Scarborough Partnership Properties Ltd
Secondtour Limited
Sewell Education (York) Limited
Sewell Investments Limited
Sharma Investments Limited
Sharp Holdings Limited
Shipton Estates Limited
Shirestone Estates Limited
Shouksmith Properties Limited
Sirdar Properties Limited
Sissons Depot Limited
Sissons Limited
Southridge Estates Limited
Spafield Properties Limited
Square Peg Properties Limited
Stadium (Newport) Limited
Standeven Builders (Yorkshire) Limited
Standeven Properties Limited
Peter Stevens Estates Limited
Stoneferry Estates Limited
Stoneferry Limited
Strawson Group Developments Limited
Strawson Group Investments Limited
Strawson Investments Limited
Strawson Management Limited
Street Clothes Limited
Richard Sullivan Consulting Ltd
Swift Holdings (UK) Limited
T L B Properties Limited
T M Enterprises Limited
T.L.G. Properties Limited
TCCP (Clarence Dock) Limited

TCS (Milngavie) Limited
TCS (Whitehall Plaza) Limited
TCS Holdings Limited
TFP (Wakefield) Limited
TWS Property Limited
Talbot House Limited
Tamar (Selby) Limited
Tate Properties Limited
F B Taylor (Holdings) Limited
Temeridge Limited
Gilbert Thompson (Leeds) Limited
Thompson Green & Co. Limited
Thompson Property Ltd
Thornber Chicks Limited
Thornton Meat Co Ltd
Tower Corporation Limited
Tower Hill Investments Limited
Town Centre Car Parks Limited
Towndoor Limited
J.Townend & Sons (Hull) Limited
Treadwell Developments Limited
Triple A Lets Limited
Turkey Mill Investments Limited
Turnbull (Corn Sales) Limited
Turnbull (Potato Sales) Limited
G.B.Turnbull Limited
United Healthcare Developments Limited
Vcep Limited
Venturian Property Holdings Limited
Viewstone Limited
Vinter Estates Limited
WFH Propco 1 Limited
WSG Property (Holdings) Limited
Wardbright Properties Limited
Watergate Developments Limited
Weavers Properties Limited
Wellbridge Properties Limited
West Park Properties Limited
Westcourt Properties Limited
Weybourne Estates Limited
Whetley Mills Limited
Claire Whitaker Limited
White Rose Finance Co Ltd
M.H. Whittaker & Son Limited
Wickframe Limited
Wilkes Properties (Wakefield) Limited
Wilkinson Building Co.(Leeds) Limited
Willerby Group Property Limited
Willow Grove Properties Limited
Willow Properties (Yorkshire) Limited
Wire Estates Limited
Woodhead Investments & Development Services Ltd
Edwin Woodhouse & Co. (Investments) Ltd
Edwin Woodhouse & Co. Limited
Edwin Woodhouse Properties Limited
Wykeland (Humberside) Limited
Wykeland Beverley Limited
Wykeland Investments Limited
Wykeland Properties Limited
Wynperg Investments Limited
Y H Residential Limited
York & District Investment Co Ltd
York Conservation Trust Limited
York House Investment Co Ltd
York Science Park Limited
York University Development Co Ltd
Yorkcare Limited
Yorkshire & Lincolnshire Developments Ltd
Yorkshire Design Services Limited
Yorparks Limited
Z & D Property Investments Limited
Zetland Estates Limited
Zuka Ltd.

**68310 Real estate agencies** [18]

Avenue Lets Limited
Browntree Properties Limited
Dacre, Son & Hartley Limited
Davis Tate Ltd
David Frost Estate Agents Limited
GFEA Limited
Hawes & Co Limited
Hunters Property Group Limited
Hunters Property PLC
ICIEA Limited
JNP Estate Agents Limited
New Daffodil Limited
D. Noble Limited
Pugh & Co Ltd
Pugh Holdings Limited
Reeds Rains Limited
Sanderson Weatherall Group Limited
Thirsk Farmers Auction Mart Co Ltd

**68320 Management of real estate on a fee or contract basis** [52]

Abstract Securities Limited
Ashcourt Properties Limited
Broomgrove Developments Limited
Browntree Properties Limited
Cascade Homes Ltd
Central Properties (Leeds) Limited
Cityblock Lettings Limited
Commercial Development Projects Limited
Community Ventures (Leeds) Limited
Community Ventures Company (No 1) Ltd
Cromwell European Management Services Ltd
DEU Estates Properties Limited
Dewhirst Properties Limited
Dixondale Limited
Doncaster Bus Station Limited
Durham & Tees Community Ventures Primary Care Ltd
Eddisons Commercial Limited
Eido Limited
Foot Forward Property Investments Ltd
Fourth Argyll Limited
Gilbran (Management) Limited
Group-14 Ltd
Hartley Property Trust (1991) Limited
Humber Properties Limited
Impact Property Services Limited
Kirklees Neighbourhood Housing Limited
Linley & Simpson Limited
Marrtree Developments Ltd
Marrtree Investments Limited
Matwest Ltd
Moda Living (Angel Gardens) Limited
Moda Living Limited
Ormsborough Limited
Park Lane Properties (Leeds) Limited
Pickards (Leeds) Limited
Premier Housing (Bradford) Ltd
Prosperity Noor Ltd
J.Pullan & Sons Limited
Quarmby Holdings Limited
Scarborough Property Developments Ltd
Seamore Court Freehold Limited
Sharma Investments Limited
St Leger Homes of Doncaster Limited
Sullivan Student Properties Limited
Thirsk Farmers Auction Mart Co Ltd
Ventia Limited
White Rose (Leeds) Limited
Wilton Developments Limited
Wykeland Limited
Y H Residential Limited
Yorkshire Prosperity Limited
Z & D Property Investments Limited

**69102 Solicitors** [14]

Beaumont ABS Ltd
Clarion Solicitors Limited
Cohen Cramer Limited
Drydens Limited
Harrowells Limited
Neil Hudgell Limited
Ison Harrison Limited
Minster Law Limited
Oakwood Solicitors Limited
Optima Legal Services Limited
Stamp Jackson & Procter Limited
Stowe Family Law Finance Limited
Stowe Family Law Holdings Limited
Williamsons Solicitors Limited

**69109 Activities of patent and copyright agents; other legal activities n.e.c.**

Beaumont ABS Ltd
DLG Legal Services Limited
HGF Limited

**69201 Accounting and auditing activities**

Audit Partnership Limited
Montpelier Professional Limited
Naylor Wintersgill Limited
Sagars Accountants Ltd

**69202 Bookkeeping activities**

Northgate (CB) Limited

**69203 Tax consultancy**

Aventador Consultancy Limited

**70100 Activities of head offices** [669]

2 Plan Group Limited
600 Group (Overseas) Limited
ABI (UK) Group Limited
ABI (UK) Holdings Limited
ABI Alpha Limited
ABI Beta Limited
ABI Bidco Limited
ABI Midco Limited
ADGM Limited
ADL PLC
AFI Bidco Limited
AFI Midco Limited
AFI Topco Limited
AGS Airports Holdings Limited
AGS Airports Investments Limited
AGS Airports Limited
ANB Advanced Solutions Limited
ATC Properties Limited
Aalberts Industries Limited
Aalberts Industries U.K. Ltd.
Abracs 2013 Limited
Abstract Securities Limited
Access 13 Limited
Ackers P Investment Co Ltd
Acropolis Investments Limited
Actavis UK Group Limited
Adler & Allan Group Limited
Adler & Allan Holdings Limited
Advertising Principles Holdings Limited

Airea PLC
Airedale Catering Equipment Group Ltd
Airport Holdings NDH1 Limited
Allamhouse Limited
Almit Group Limited
Altra Industrial Motion UK Holding Ltd
Altra Industrial Motion UK Limited
Aluminium Bronze Valves Limited
Amco Group Holdings Limited
Amco Group Limited
Aptiv (UK) Holdings Limited
Aptiv Financial Investment Services (UK) Ltd
Aptiv Holdings (UK) Limited
Aqmen Holdings Limited
Arch Chemicals UK Holdings Limited
Archbold Holdings Limited
Ardagh Glass (UK) Limited
Ardagh Glass Limited
Arena Group Holdings Limited
Arla Foods UK Holding Limited
Arla Foods UK Property Co Ltd
Arran Isle Limited
Arrow Industrial Holdings Limited
Arville Holdings Limited
Asda Group Limited
Ashlea Landscaping Holdings Limited
Atlantic Acquisition Holdings UK Limited
Audit Partnership Limited
Augean PLC
Avacta Group PLC
Aviva Life Holdings UK Limited
B.R.T. Supplies Limited
B.W. Industries (Group) Limited
B.W. Industries (Holdings) Limited
BBRG (Purchaser) Ltd
BBRG (Subsidiary) Ltd
BBRG Finance (UK) Ltd.
BBRG Holding (UK) Ltd
BBRG Operations (UK) Ltd.
BBRG Production (UK) Ltd.
BH Acquisitions Limited
Alfred Bagnall and Sons Limited
NG Bailey Group Limited
Baird Group (Holdings) Limited
Baird Group Limited
Ballyvesey Holdings Limited
Bandwood Limited
Barnby C H Limited
Barrett Steel Limited
Bartlett Group (Holdings) Limited
L. Batley Holdings Limited
Be Fuelcards Holdings Limited
Beal Securities Limited
Beatty Topco Limited
Beverley House (9000) Limited
Bhullar Limited
Blackrow Corporation Limited
Blacks Industries Limited
Blackshaw Properties (2014) Limited
Bluebird UK Topco Limited
Blythmore Limited
Bondshold Limited
Bonmarche Holdings PLC
Bonus Electrical Group Limited
Boparan Holdings Limited
Boston Holdings Limited
Boulton & Cooper Limited
Bradshaws Driffield (Holdings) Limited
T.F. & J.H. Braime (Holdings) P.L.C.
Brandon Group Limited
Brandon Hire Group Limited
Brenntag Inorganic Chemicals Limited
Brenntag UK Holding Limited
Bridon Holdings Limited
Bridon Limited
Bridon-Bekaert Ropes Group (UK) Ltd
Bridon-Bekaert Ropes Group Ltd
Brighton Holdings Limited
British American Railway Services Ltd
British Mohair Holdings Limited
Broadland Properties Limited
Broker Network Holdings Limited
Broomco (3554) Limited
Broomco (3555) Limited
Browallia Holdings Limited
David Brown Group Limited
Bulmer & Lumb Holdings Limited
C & D Foods (UK) Unlimited
C P Group of Companies Limited
CE Holdings Limited
CF Bidco Limited
CPP European Holdings Limited
CPP Group Limited
CPP Holdings Limited
CPP International Holdings Limited
CPP Worldwide Holdings Limited
CPPGroup PLC
CSC (Holdings) Limited
CYB Investments Limited
CYBG PLC
Caddick Group PLC
Calder Group (Dewsbury) Limited
Callauto Limited
Camira Group Holdings Limited
Carclo Holding Limited
Carclo Overseas Holdings Limited
Cardale Infrastructure Investments Ltd
Cardale PFI Investments Limited
Cardinal Limited
Carlac Group Limited
Carnaby Caravans Group Limited
Castle 1 Limited
Castleton Group Limited
Castlewood Securities Limited
Cat Tech International Limited
Catfoss Renewables Ltd
Central European Aggregates Limited
Centrica Storage Holdings Limited
Cephalon Limited
Cilantro Acquisitions Limited
Cilantro Midco Limited
Cilantro Parent Limited
Civic PFI Investments Limited
Clariant Services UK Ltd
Teddy Clark (Holdings) Limited
Teddy Clark Group Limited
Clugston Estates Limited
Clugston Group Limited
Cobco 867 Limited
Coletta Holdings Limited
Combined Selection Group Ltd
Communisis Limited
Compair Holdings Limited
Concepta PLC
Consultant Services Group Limited
Controlled Building Measures (Holdings) Ltd
Corkel Limited
Corrosioneering Group Limited
Covance Limited
Cranswick PLC
Croda Europe Limited
Croda International PLC
Croda Investments No 3 Limited
Croda Overseas Holdings Limited
Crown Acquisition Bidco Limited
Crown Acquisition Midco 2 Limited
Crown Acquisition Midco Limited
Crown Acquisition Topco Limited
John Edward Crowther (Holdings) PLC
Curtis Wool Direct Holdings Limited
Czajka Group Holdings Limited
DCSW Ltd
DFDS Seaways PLC
DFS Furniture Co Ltd
DFS Furniture Holdings PLC
DFS Furniture PLC
DVV Holdco Limited
DVV Investco Limited
Dakin Industries Limited
Damac Group Limited
Danby Holdings Limited
Danesmoor Holdings Limited
S.Daniels Limited
Dantex Group Limited
Dart Group PLC
Davy Group Limited
Deeside Power (UK) Limited
Dent Steel Holdings Limited
Depuy International Limited
Dewhirst Group Limited
Dewhirst Overseas Limited
Diamond Holdco 2 Limited
Diamond Holdco 7 Limited
Diamond Resorts (Group Holdings) PLC
Diamond Resorts (Holdings) Limited
Donaldson UK Holding Limited
Donelec Group Limited
Dormot Limited
Drax Group PLC
Drifford Group Limited
Drifford Limited
Driver Hire Investments Group Limited
Dunlop Conveyor Belting Investments Ltd
Durham & Tees Community Ventures Limited
E K Holdings Limited
EFS Group Limited
EFS Property Holdings Limited
EPTA Service UK Limited
ESCO (UK) Holdings Limited
ESCO EMEA Holdings (UK) Limited
ESP Systex Holdings Limited
Ebco (Holdings) Limited
Ecovert Group Limited
Education PFI Investments Limited
Elland Steel Structures (UK) Limited
Eltherington Group Limited
Emic Group Limited
Emis Group PLC
Encon Investments Limited
Encon Limited
Engie Supply Holding UK Limited
English Lakes Hotels Limited
Enserve Group Limited
European Integrated Carriers Limited
F.T.Everard & Sons Limited
F.T.L. Holdings Limited
FLD Limited
FMG Support Ltd
Fender Care Marine Services Group Ltd
Fenner Group Holdings Limited
Fenner International Australia Limited
Fenner International Limited
Findpath Limited
Ian Firth Holdings Limited
James Fisher (Aberdeen) Limited
James Fisher Fender Care Limited

James Fisher Holdings UK Limited
James Fisher Nuclear Holdings Limited
James Fisher Subtech Group Limited
James Fisher and Sons PLC
Fives UK Holding Limited
Fleetcor UK Acquisition Limited
Fope Limited
Four Pillars Hotels Limited
Franklyn Group Limited
Frear Investments Limited
Freedom Refreshments Limited
Frontica Business Solutions Limited
Futurama Signs Holdings Limited
G S M Group Limited
G-Tuft (2015) Limited
G.B. Agencies Limited
GBA (Holdings) Limited
GBUK Group Limited
GD Aria Holdings #2 Limited
GD Aria Holdings Limited
GD Global Holdings UK II Limited
GEV Holdings Limited
GGR Holdings Limited
GH Newco 1 Limited
GHD BondCo PLC
GHD Group Holdings Limited
GKF Group Limited
GM Legato Limited
GMI Holdings Limited
GSM Group Holdco Limited
Gands (U.K.)
Gardner Denver Group Services Limited
Gardner Denver Holdings Limited
Gardner Denver Industries Ltd
Gardner Denver International Ltd
Gear4music (Holdings) PLC
Glendower Group Limited
Glentrool Land and Estates Limited
Glid Wind Farms Topco Limited
Global Holdings Limited
Globesign Limited
John Good & Sons Limited
Grafitec Holdings Limited
Samuel Grant (Holdings) Ltd
Samuel Grant Group Limited
Graypen Holdings Limited
Great Rail Journeys Holdings Limited
Great Rail Journeys Partnership Limited
Green Flag Group Limited
Grosvenor House Group Holdings Limited
Grosvenor PFI Holdings Limited
Guyson (Holdings) Limited
HRP Holdings Limited
Hadrian Bidco 2 Limited
Hadrian Bidco Limited
Hain Daniels Group Limited
Halifax Financial Services (Holdings) Ltd
Hallmark Cards (Holdings) Limited
Hannibal Holdings Limited
Hanson Plywood (Holdings) Ltd
Hargreaves Group (GB) Limited
Harlen Ltd
Harper & Wilkes Limited
Harris Construction Management Limited
S Harrison Group Limited
Harvard Group Holdings Limited
Hayley Conference Centres Acquisitions Ltd
Hesco Group Limited
Hexadex Limited
Heywood Williams Components Limited
Hickson International Limited
Hickson Investments Limited.
Hider Group Holdings Limited
M. Higgins Limited
High Seat Holdings Limited
Highcrest Retail Brands Limited
Highgrove Group PLC
Harold Hinchliffe Limited
Hocomm Limited
Holdco 123 Limited
Holden Grange Care Group Limited
Holgates Holdings Limited
Holker Holdings Limited
Holme Styes Holdings Limited
Homecare (Holdings) Limited
Horndean Ltd
Howarth Timber Group Limited
Hunt Group Limited
Hunter Holdings Limited
I.G. Industries Holdings Limited
ICR (Investment 1) Limited
ICR (Investment 2) Limited
ICR Integrity (Group) Limited
ICR Integrity (Holdings) Limited
ICR Integrity Limited
IFGL Monocon Holdings Limited
IQ Power Holdings Limited
ISG Boiler Holdings Limited
ISS Labour Group Limited
IUKH Limited
Ideal Building Systems Holdings Limited
Ideal Homes Holdings Limited
Ideal Standard Holdings (BC) UK Ltd
Idigital Investments Ltd
Ingenuity Digital Holdings Limited
Inhoco 2082 Limited
Inspired Pet Nutrition Holdings Limited
Instore Limited
Interface Administration Services Ltd
International Fibres Group (Holdings) Ltd
International Personal Finance Investments Ltd
Isotek (Holdings) Limited
J.E.C. Investment Co Ltd
JLA Clean Limited
JLA Debtco Limited
JSJ Partnership Limited
William Jackson Food Group Limited
Jemella Group Limited
Johnstone's Paints Limited
K & A Merger Limited
KCH (Holdings) Limited
KCOM Group PLC
KTH Engineering Group Limited
KVH Industries UK Limited
KVH Media Group Limited
Kahn Landmark Limited
Kalon Investment Co Ltd
Keepmoat Limited
Kelling Midco Limited
Kelling Property Limited
Keystone Bidco Limited
Keystone Financing PLC
Keystone Healthcare Holdings Limited
Keystone JVCO Limited
Keystone Midco Limited
Keystone Topco Limited
Killgerm Group Limited
Kingstown Associates (Holdings) Limited
Kirkgate Group Limited
Klinger Holdings Limited
Kloeckner Metals UK Holdings Limited
Knaresborough Investments Limited
Knightwood Holdings (2011) Limited
Kubler Holdings Limited
L & O Investments (U.K.)
LMM Holdings Limited
LNT Group Limited
LS UK Fire Group Ltd
Lakeside 1 Limited
William Lamb (Holdings) Limited
Lambert Automation Limited
Lanes Group PLC
Langley Holdings PLC
Lapwing Estate Limited
Leading Labels Retail Limited
Leeds Rugby Limited
Leeds and London Group Ltd
Leeds and London Holdings Limited
Leigh Holdings Limited
Leisure Infrastructure Investors Limited
Leo Group Limited
Lexia Solutions Group Limited
Liberty2803 Limited
Lightwater Holdings Limited
Linpac Finance Limited
Linpac Group Holdings Limited
Linpac Packaging China Holdings Limited
Linpac Senior Holdings Limited
Lion/Gloria Bidco Limited
Lion/Gloria Holdco Limited
Lion/Gloria Midco 2 Limited
Lion/Gloria Midco 3 Limited
Lion/Gloria Midco Limited
List Group PLC
Live Yorkshire Limited
Longley Holdings Limited
Lookrich Ltd
Jack Lunn (Holdings) Limited
Lupfaw 365 Limited
MMCG Holdings Limited
MMCG Limited
MRC Transmark Holdings UK Limited
MS International PLC
MWS Group Ltd
Mamas & Papas (Holdings) Limited
Manheim Holdings Limited
Mantis Holdings Ltd
J. Marr Limited
Marshall Holdings Limited
Marshalls Group Limited
Marshalls PLC
Martindale Group Limited
Martins Bidco Limited
Masco Corporation Limited
Matrix Chemie Holdings Limited
McJunkin Red Man UK Ltd
McLean & Appleton (Holdings) Limited
McLean & Appleton Limited
McManus Group Holdings Limited
Mech-Tool Holdings Limited
Metis Bidco Limited
Micron Hydraulics Holdings Limited
Millwood Investments Limited
H. Mitton Limited
Mixer Bidco Limited
Morris and Son (Holdings) Limited
Mosaic Print Management Holdco Limited
Motorhog Holdings Limited
Multisol Group Limited
Myers Group 1959 Ltd
NCI Vehicle Rescue PLC
NHP Limited
Narang Group Ltd
Navartis Holdings Limited
Neill & Brown Global Logistics Group Ltd

Newbegin Holdings Limited
Harold Newsome Holdings Limited
Nickle Holdings Limited
Nimbus Building Products Limited
Northern Divers (Holdings) Limited
Northern Foods Limited
Northern Gas Networks Holdings Limited
Northminster Holdings Limited
Notman Enterprise Limited
OSI Food Solutions UK Holdings Limited
OSI International Holdings Limited
Oakgate Group Limited
Oakhurst Court Holdings Limited
Olicana Holdings Limited
On Line Group Limited
Onward Holdings Limited
Optare PLC
Optibiotix Health PLC
Opus Energy Group Limited
Owens-Corning Britinvest Limited
Oxley Group Limited
P V H Holdings Limited
P.P. Plasma Limited
PD & MS Holdings Limited
Park Lane Healthcare Limited
Patrick Construction Group Limited
Paw Topco Limited
Peacock & Binnington Holdings Limited
Peaspring Limited
Peel Street Developments Limited
Pelican Engineering Co. Limited
Pelsis Holding (UK) Limited
Perago Limited
Persimmon Holdings Limited
Persimmon PLC
Phoenix Oil & Marine Limited
Pitcliffe (Holdings) Limited
Polypearl Management Ltd
Prem Sehmi Holdings Limited
Premier Technical Services Group PLC
Principal Hayley Limited
Principal Hotel Co Ltd
Principal Hotels Topco 1 Limited
Principal Hotels Topco 3 Limited
Principle Global Limited
Prism Medical Healthcare Limited
Proactis Holdings PLC
Project Aqua Topco Limited
Project Light Bidco Limited
Project Light Cleanco Limited
Project Light Midco Limited
Project Light Topco Limited
Prospect Business Centres Limited
Providence Holdings Limited
Pure Technology Group Limited
QWP Limited
Quad Bidco Limited
RMS Europe Group Limited
RMS Group Holdings Limited
ROK Associates Limited
Raysul Holdings Limited
Recruitex Limited
Redcentric PLC
Redhall Group PLC
Redhead Holdings Limited
Redline Holdings Limited
Regroup (UK) Limited
Renew Holdings PLC.
Rever Offshore International Limited
Rever Offshore UK Limited
Reynolds 2000 Limited
Richardsons Westgarth Limited
Rider Holdings Limited
Ripon Farm Services Limited
J.R. Rix & Sons Limited
Roberts, Mart (Holdings) Co. Ltd.
Rockar 2016 Limited
Rogerthorpe Manor Hotel Limited
Rolco 188 Limited
Rollfold Holdings Limited
Rome Holdco Ltd
Rome Investco Ltd
J Rotherham (Holdings) Limited
Rradar (Holdings) Limited
Russell Armer Group Limited
SFS Group Fastening Technology Limited
SLS Group Limited
SWL Holdings Limited
Saria Limited
Saur (UK) Limited
Scarborough Management Limited
Schultz Bidco Limited
Search Group Holdings Limited
Seatruck Ferries Holding Ltd
Sellers International Limited
Serviced Dispense Equipment (Holdings) Ltd
Shaman Investments Limited
Shaw & Rhodes Holdings Limited
Shepherd Building Group Limited
Shepherd Industries Limited
Shipton Estates Limited
Sidhil Group Limited
Siena Bidco Limited
Siena Holdco Limited
Sigma GRP Limited
SigmaKalon (BC) UK Limited
SigmaKalon UK Holding Limited
Silgan Closures UK Holdings Limited
Silver Cross Nurseries Limited
Simplybiz Group PLC
Sirdar Group Limited
R.N.Smith Holdings Limited
Solway Foods Holdings Limited
Specialised Car Covers Limited
Specialist Ceiling Services Holdings Ltd
Specialist People Services Group Limited
Spellman & Walker Direct Limited
St James Securities Limited
Stadium Parkgate (Holdings) Limited
Stadium Retail (Holdings) Limited
Stadium Retail Group Limited
Stainless Band Limited
Standeven Holdings Ltd
Steers Group Limited
Stericycle International Holdings Ltd
Stericycle International, Ltd.
Stevro (Holdings) Limited
Stonecroft Holdings Limited
Stores Group Limited
Strachan Holdings Limited
Strainstall Group Limited
Strata Homes Holdings Limited
Strawson Group Developments Limited
Strawson Group Investments Limited
Stroma Developments Limited
Stroma Group Limited
Stroma Holdings Limited
C F Struthers (Holdings) Limited
Style Group Holdings Limited
Style Group UK Limited
Superbreak Mini Holidays Group Limited
Surfachem Group Limited
Surgeforward Limited
Sutcliffe Group Limited
Swift Acquisitions Limited
Swift Property (East Yorkshire) Limited
TD Holdings Ltd
TMD Friction Holdings (UK) Ltd
Tekmar Holdings Limited
Tekmar Limited
Teva Acquisition Limited
Teva UK Holdings Limited
That Company Called If Limited
Isaac Timmins Limited
Toiletry Sales Group Limited
Toiletry Sales Holdings Limited
J.Townend & Sons (Hull) Limited
Townham Limited
Triesse Group Limited
Triesse Holdings Limited
Trinity Ten Limited
Turbine Efficiency Group Limited
UK Asset Resolution Limited
UK Fisheries Limited
UKGlobal Holdings Limited
Ulixes Limited
Union Discount Company of London Limited
United Anodisers Holdings Limited
Universal Group Holdings Limited
VTL Group (Holdings) Limited
Vacation Club Partnerships Limited
Vanilla Group Limited
Varnish Bidco Limited
Varnish Topco Limited
Venice Bidco 1 Limited
Venice Newco 1 Limited
Virtual College Holdings Limited
WYG Group Limited
WYG International Projects Limited
WYG PLC
Waco UK Holdings Limited
Waddington & Ledger Group Limited
Wakefield Shirt Co Ltd
Wal-Mart Stores (UK) Limited
Wastecare Group Limited
Wavin UK (Holdings) Limited
West Moor Holdings Limited
West Park Group Limited
West Retail Group Limited
W. S. Westin Group Limited
Whitston Group Limited
Willerby Group Limited
Willoughby (891) Limited
Winander Group Holdings Limited
Winander Leisure Limited
Winsfield Limited
Wortlea Estates (Leeds) Limited
Wrapid Group Limited
Edward P Wright (Holdings) Limited
Wright Leisure Limited
Wykeland Group Limited
Wykeland Properties (Holdings) Limited
XTR Holding Limited
YJL Limited
Yorhold Limited
York Holdings Limited
Yorkshire Water Services Holdings Ltd
Zain Holdings Limited
Zarafa Group Limited

**70221 Financial management** [19]

Arris International IP Ltd
Bradshaws Driffield (Holdings) Limited
Channon Holdings Limited
W Denis (Holdings) PLC
Fenton Packaging (Leeds) Limited

Isotek (Holdings) Limited
Kelda Finance (No.1) Limited
Kelda Finance (No.2) Limited
Kelda Finance (No.3) PLC
MCE Concept Limited
J & E Marshall Finance Limited
One Stop Business Finance Limited
Project Aqua Bidco Limited
RSP Investments Limited
Scarborough Partnership Limited
Scheme Underwriting (U.K.) Limited
Schosween 6 Limited
Steadplan Group Limited
TGH Capital Limited

**70229 Management consultancy activities other than financial management** [33]

Aghoco 1085 Limited
Amberbeach Ltd.
Ashton Agricultural and General Limited
Batchelors Motor Group Limited
Camira Holdings Limited
Cornbrook Group Ltd
Decisionmetrics Limited
Deepocean 1 UK Limited
E.F.C. Consultancy Limited
Ebus Ltd
Eido Limited
Europa Crown Limited
Fullers Foods Holdings Limited
Goodprofit Limited
Graham Developments (Property Holdings) Ltd
Harris Group Limited
Anthony Hodges Consulting Limited
B M Howarth Limited
Leisure Park Management Limited
Lishman Sidwell Campbell & Price Limited
Meritec Limited
NHP Management Limited
Propaganda Agency Limited
R.T. Consultants Limited
Ramscove Limited
Raysul Holdings Limited
SWL Holdings Limited
Sigma Retail Solutions Limited
Transdev PLC
WYG Management Services Limited
WYG PLC
Wauldby Associates Limited
Winander Group Holdings Limited

**71111 Architectural activities**

DLA Architecture Limited
DLA Design Group of Companies Limited
Ian Firth Hardware Limited
Harris Partnership Limited
PSP Architectural Ltd
RPP Limited

**71112 Urban planning and landscape architectural activities**

WYG Environment Planning Transport Ltd
WYG PLC

**71121 Engineering design activities for industrial process and production**

Clyde Bergemann Materials Handling Ltd
On Line Design & Engineering Limited
Samsung C & T ECUK Limited
Unison Limited

**71122 Engineering related scientific and technical consulting activities**

Jeremy Benn Associates Limited
JBA Group Limited
Red Embedded Consulting Limited
Sweco Services UK Limited
WYG Environment Planning Transport Ltd

**71129 Other engineering activities** [25]

Assent Building Control Limited
Balltec Limited
Brandon Hire Limited
Cameron Integrated Services Limited
Castle Residential Properties Limited
Cat Tech (Europe) Limited
Darntonb3 Limited
Don Valley Engineering Co Ltd
Extron Electronics UK Limited
James Fisher Marine Services Limited
Gilbert Gilkes & Gordon Limited
Orcina Limited
Osprey Green Power Limited
PLS Civil Engineering Limited
Pipes & Tubes (2010) Limited
Stroma Building Control Limited
Sweco UK Limited
TSC Engineering Limited
Thomson Limited
Unison Limited
WYG Engineering Limited
WYG Environment Planning Transport Ltd
WYG PLC
Alan Wood Partnership Limited
Zarafa Height Solutions Limited

**71200 Technical testing and analysis**

ALS Laboratories (UK) Limited
E & S Environmental Services Limited
Hawkesworth Appliance Testing Limited
IRISNDT Limited
PTSG Access and Safety Limited
Strainstall UK Limited

**72110 Research and experimental development on biotechnology**

Avacta Life Sciences Limited
Covance Laboratories Limited
Plant Impact Limited
Potato Manufacturing Science Limited
STC Research Foundation
Stockbridge Technology Centre Limited

**72190 Other research and experimental development on natural sciences and engineering** [10]

4D Pharma PLC
Getech Group PLC
Lhasa Limited
Nufarm Crop Products UK Limited
Red Embedded Consulting Limited
SmarDTV (UK) Limited
Tissue Regenix Limited
Unison Limited
York Bioanalytical (Holdings) Limited
York Bioanalytical Solutions Limited

**73110 Advertising agencies** [15]

Bark and Bite Ltd
Brass Agency Limited
Creativerace Limited
Hi Resolution (Production) Limited
Home Marketing Group Ltd
Home Marketing Limited
Icelolly Marketing Limited
Kinetic Worldwide Limited
Poster Publicity Group Limited
Poster Publicity Holdings Ltd
Principles Communications Limited
Propaganda Agency Limited
Psona Limited
State Bidco Limited
Webevents Limited

**73120 Media representation services**

DP Publicity Limited
First 4 Lawyers Limited
Optimum4 Limited

**73200 Market research and public opinion polling**

Context World Limited
Eido Limited
Employee Pulsecheck Limited
Trinity McQueen Limited

**74100 Specialised design activities**

Superior Developments Limited
Sweco UK Holding Limited
TSP Projects Limited

**74300 Translation and interpretation activities**

Link Up Mitaka Limited
Thebigword Group Limited
Thebigword Interpreting Services Limited

**74901 Environmental consulting activities**

ERM Regulatory Services Limited
Exponent International Limited
OHES Environmental Limited
Sweco UK Limited
York Archaeological Trust for Excavation and Research Ltd

**74902 Quantity surveying activities**

RPP Group Holdings Limited
TSP Projects Limited

**74909 Other professional, scientific and technical activities n.e.c.** [47]

ACM Global Central Laboratory Limited
Abaxis UK Limited
Al-Murad Management Ltd
Alphabet BC Limited
Aptiv European Holdings (UK) Limited
Aptiv Financial Services (UK) Limited
Aptiv Global Holdings (UK) Limited
Aptiv Holdfi (UK) Limited
Aptiv Luxembourg Holdings (UK) Limited
Authentix Limited
Broughton Laboratories Limited
C.S.L. Industrial Limited
CO2Sense C.I.C.
Cloth Fair Point Capital Limited
Commercial Vehicle Auctions Limited
Conservation Volunteers
Coolsilk Property & Investment Limited
Covance Clinical Research Unit Limited
Dalby Offshore Services Limited
Delphi Automotive Operations UK Limited
ERM Regulatory Services Limited
Enact Conveyancing Limited
Evansis Ltd
Freshwater Biological Association
Gradebatch Limited
Hudson Contract Services Limited
Hunprenco (Precision Engineers) Limited
Hunters Franchising Limited
L.S. Transmission Consultancy Limited
NSF Health Sciences Ltd.
Network Mapping Limited
Nidec SR Drives Ltd.
Orphans in Need
Pall Mall Developments Limited
Primary Care Commissioning CIC
Mark Royston Contracting Limited
TSP Projects Limited
Tate of Leeds Limited.
Tompkins Investments Limited
Tompkins UK Limited
Vascular Perspectives Limited
Wavemaster (TGOF) Limited
We Are Vista Limited
Wool Growers (Great Britain) Limited
Yesss (A) Electrical Ltd
Yesss (B) Electrical Ltd
York Archaeological Trust for Excavation and Research Ltd

**74990 Non-trading company** [103]

ACM Global Central Laboratory Operations Ltd
AWLC Limited
Ames Companies UK Ltd.
Areopagus Limited
Asda Financial Services Limited
Asda Holdings UK Limited
Asda Supermarkets Limited
BKS Holdings Limited
Bawtry Investments Limited
Boparan Finance PLC
Borgwarner Holdings Limited
Brecks Holdings Limited
Broadstreet Great Wilson Europe Limited
CB Imports Group Limited
CCL Stressing International Limited
CRG Holdings Ltd
Callcredit Information Group Limited
Celdis Limited
Cellhire (Holdings) Limited
Centurion Europe Holdings Limited
Christians Against Poverty
Clayton Dewandre Holdings Limited
Coolsilk Limited
Cristal Investments UK Limited
Croda Investments Limited
Croda Investments No 2 Limited
Crown Acquisition Consumer Limited
Czajka Group Holdings Limited
DFDS Seaways Irish Sea Holding Ltd
Dellstrong Limited
Direct Auto Finance Insurance Services Ltd
Donelec Group Limited
Drighlington Fibres Limited
Dunlop Conveyor Belting Investments Ltd
EHLP Holdings Limited
EOF Holdings Limited
Element 14 Limited
Emacrow Holdings Limited
Emsley Brothers Limited
F and N One Limited
Farnell Holding Limited
J.H. Fenner & Co. (Advanced Engineered Products) Ltd
GH Brighton Limited
GH Plymouth Grove Limited
GSM Automotive Holdings Limited
Gartland Whalley and Barker Limited
Gregory Property Group Limited
Hallriver Holdings Limited
High Street TV Bidco Limited
High Street TV Holdings Limited
Hilldene Holdings Limited
Holbeck Charitable Trust
IPF Holdings Limited
InOne Holdings Limited
Info Supplier Limited
JTE Holdco Limited
Kingstown Holdings Limited
Kirklees PFI Limited
LBIA Holding Limited
LEBC Holdings Limited
Lambert Engineering Group Limited
Lambert Engineering Holdings Limited
Langley Aviation Limited
Long Folly Limited
Manheim Global Management UK Limited
Mansfield Pollard (Holdings) Limited
Marshall Wooldridge Group Holdings Ltd
Marshall Wooldridge Holdings Limited
Monocon Overseas Limited
Michael Nichol-Smith Limited
Nutec Holdings Limited
On Board Leisure (Holdings) Limited
Orvet UK
P. & B. Foods Holdings Limited
PTM Holdings Limited
Primekings Holding Limited
Principal Hayley Group Limited
Procters Coaches (North Yorkshire No3) Ltd
Provident Print Limited
Richmond Foods Limited
Robinson Group (Holdings) Limited
Ronald Coates (Farms) Limited
SDS International Ltd.
Schenck Process UK Holding Limited
Stadium (Bradford) Limited
Stadium Retail Investments (2003) Ltd
Steeper Group Holdings Limited
Stericycle International Holdings Canada Ltd
The John Strutt Conservation Foundation
TPP Finance Limited
Tasker Investments Limited
Tees & Durham (Lift) Investments Limited
Together Roof Energy Limited
Triline (2014) Limited
UK Ambulances 2 Ltd
UK Ambulances Ltd
UK Thermos Holdings Limited
Univar Europe Limited
Universal Parking Limited
Waddington Limited
Wakefield88 Limited
Weir Drilling Services Limited
West Coast Capital Investments Limited

**75000 Veterinary activities** [14]

Animalcare Ltd
Dechra Limited
Donaldson's Vets Limited
Eville & Jones (UK) Limited
Garth Pig Practice Limited
Holmefield Farm Services Limited
Idexx Laboratories Limited
Minster Veterinary Practice Ltd
Oakwood Veterinary Practice Limited
Rainbow Equine Hospital Limited
Swanbridge Veterinary Group Limited
Valley Vets Ltd.
Vetpartners Practices Limited
Westway Veterinary Centres Limited

**77110 Renting and leasing of cars and light motor vehicles** [18]

Adapted Vehicle Hire Limited
Amvale Limited
Arrow Commercial Centre (Huddersfield) Ltd
Asset Finance UK Limited
Autohorn Fleet Services Limited
Autohorn Group Limited
Leasedrive Limited
Leeds Commercial Limited
NL Commercials Management Ltd
Nexus Vehicle Management Ltd.
Northern Divers (Holdings) Limited
Northgate Vehicle Hire Limited
Provecta Car Plan Limited
Templer Management Limited
West Yorkshire Van Rental Limited
Zenith Ef Limited
Zenith Remarketing Limited
Zenith Vehicle Contracts Limited

**77120 Renting and leasing of trucks and other heavy vehicles** [11]

Access Hire Nationwide Limited
Collett Holdings Limited
Contract Vehicles Limited
Eurotrail UK Limited
Filtermech Plant Sales Limited
Hardroad Limited
Hartshorne Crossroads Group Contracts Ltd
John Hudson Trailers Ltd
Leeds Commercial Limited
NL Commercials Holdings Limited
D.G. Taylor Commercial Vehicles Limited

**77310 Renting and leasing of agricultural machinery and equipment**

Brandon Hire Limited
Whitelock Developments Limited

**77320 Renting and leasing of construction and civil engineering machinery and equipment** [31]

AMS Bobcat Limited
Addplant Limited
Archway Engineering (U.K.) Limited
Brandon Hire Limited
R. Bunton Limited
Bunton Plant Hire Limited
Caspian Group Limited
Chippindale Plant Limited
Elvington Holdings Limited
Fairfax Plant Hire Limited
Ferdinand Properties Limited
Flannery Construction Limited
GW Hire Limited
Gill Demolitions Limited
Headland Plant Limited
Hird (UK) Ltd
Hird Limited
Hire It Plant Limited
David Hopkinson Limited
Horizon Platforms Limited
K P H (Plant Hire) Limited
Alf Kitching Limited
Mabey Hire Limited
Megaplant Limited
Northern Divers (Holdings) Limited
Pasuda (Hire) Limited
Reynolds 2000 Limited
Rodgers Plant Hire Ltd.
F B Taylor (Holdings) Limited
Welfare Hire Nationwide Limited
Whitelock Developments Limited

**77330 Renting and leasing of office machinery and equipment (including computers)**

Sharp Business Systems UK PLC

**77351 Renting and leasing of air passenger transport equipment**

Dart Leasing & Finance Limited

**77390 Renting and leasing of other machinery, equipment and tangible goods n.e.c.** [40]

AFI-Uplift Limited
Actavo (UK) Limited
Bewley's Tea and Coffee UK (Roastery) Ltd
Brandon Hire Limited
Burgess Group PLC
Byworth Boiler Hire Limited
Chase Petroleum Limited
Deborah Services (Holdings) Limited
Generator Power Limited
Goldenfry Limited
Hartford Trading Limited
Hassan (Holdings) Ltd
Hire Station Limited
Impact Fork Trucks Limited
J.E.G Hire Limited
JLA Total Care Limited
Kitching Plant Hire Ltd
Lifterz Limited
MTS Nationwide Limited
Modus Seabed Intervention Limited
Newlands Community Association (Trading) Ltd
Niko Extrusions Limited
Penmoor UK Ltd
Portakabin (Site Accommodation) Limited
Portakabin Limited
Premium Leasing Limited
Road Traffic Solutions Limited
Sangwin Plant Hire Limited
Sayers Road Tanker Rentals Limited
Scantech Offshore Limited
William G. Search Limited
William Smith (Wakefield) Limited
Specialist Trailer Hire Limited
Stocks Group Limited
Thermac (Hire) Limited
Torrent Trackside Limited
VP PLC
Wauldby Associates Limited
M.H. Whittaker & Son Limited
Windsor Engineering (Hull) Limited

**77400 Leasing of intellectual property and similar products, except copyright works**

Ossett Holdings Limited

**78109 Other activities of employment placement agencies**

Combined Selection Group Ltd
Gatenbysanderson Holdings Limited
Gatenbysanderson Limited
Gatenbysanderson Midco Limited
On Line People Limited
Resource Management Solutions (North East) Ltd
Taskmaster Resources Limited

**78200 Temporary employment agency activities** [17]

Bostonair Group Limited
Caval Limited
Concept Recruitment Group Limited
Driver Hire Group Services Limited
Driver Hire Investments Limited
Holt Doctors Limited
Just Teachers Limited
Logical Personnel Solutions Limited
Mach Recruitment Limited
Major Recruitment Limited
Navartis Limited
On Line People Limited
Pettra Limited
Prestige Recruitment Specialists Limited
Resource Management Solutions (North East) Ltd
Staff Finders (Yorkshire) Limited
Tech Search Associates Limited

**78300 Human resources provision and management of human resources functions**

James Fisher Marine Services Limited
MCP Environmental Limited
Niko Extrusions Limited
Premier People Solutions Limited
Resource Management Solutions (North East) Ltd

**79110 Travel agency activities**

Corporate Travel Management (North) Ltd
Deehurst Limited
Icelolly Marketing Limited
Kennedy Travel (Yorkshire) Limited
Morgan Travel Limited
Superbreak Mini-Holidays Limited
York Pullman Bus Co Ltd

**79120 Tour operator activities**

Cairngorm Ski Services Limited
Great Rail Journeys Limited
O.& C.Holdsworth Limited
Jet2holidays Limited
MM Band Services Limited
Morgan Travel Limited

**79909 Other reservation service activities n.e.c.**

Gazelle Travel Limited

**80200 Security systems service activities**

Crime & Fire Defence Systems Limited
Kings Security Systems Limited
M. B. Locking Logistics Group Limited
Pointer Holdings Limited
Securi-Plex Limited
Trinity Fire and Security Systems Ltd

**80300 Investigation activities**

Effective Security Services Limited

**81100 Combined facilities support activities**

Apollo Support Services Group Limited
NIC Services Group Limited
Sewell Facilities Management Limited
Thorpe Underwood Services Limited

**81210 General cleaning of buildings**

Bulloughs Cleaning Services Limited
Consultant Cleaners Limited

**81221 Window cleaning services**

Nationwide Window Cleaning Limited

**81222 Specialised cleaning services**

Colt Industrial Services Limited
Future Cleaning Services Limited
Nationwide Window Cleaning Limited

**81229 Other building and industrial cleaning activities**

Actavo (UK) Limited
Cat Tech (Europe) Limited
Deborah Services (Holdings) Limited

**81300 Landscape service activities**

Tony Cook Limited
DKB Crop Protection Limited
Natures Crops International Limited

**82110 Combined office administrative service activities** [12]

Actavis Holdings UK Ltd.
Channon and Co Ltd
F M G Support (Ho) Limited
R.J. & A.E. Godfrey
HPC Laser Holdings Limited
Isberg Limited
Kepwick Estate Limited
Marshall Group Services Limited
NSA (Ventures) Limited
Prospect Business Centres (Old Jewry) Ltd
TCS (Merrion House JVCO1) Limited
Westfield War Memorial Village - Lancaster

**82190 Photocopying, document preparation and other specialised office support activities**

Arena Group Limited
Corporate Document Services Limited

**82200 Activities of call centres**

Centurion Europe Limited
FMG Support (FIM) Ltd
FMG Support (RRRM) Ltd
Res-Q Outsourcing Solutions Limited

**82301 Activities of exhibition and fair organisers**

Westmorland County Agricultural Society Ltd

**82302 Activities of conference organisers**

Universal A.V. Services Limited
Westmorland County Agricultural Society Ltd
Y.E.S. (Your Event Solutions) Limited

**82911 Activities of collection agencies**

Lowell Finance Holdings Limited
Lowell Financial Ltd

**82920 Packaging activities**

Arrow Film Converters Limited
Canley Food Packers Ltd
Cromwell Polythene Limited
Hazel Products UK Limited
JM Packaging Limited
Mailway Packaging Solutions Limited
National Flexible Limited
Parkacre Enterprises Limited

**82990 Other business support service activities n.e.c.** [276]

A-Safe HQ Ltd
ADP Primary Care Acquisitions Limited
Abbot Group Limited
Abbot Holdings Limited
Abbot Investments (North Africa) Limited
Advanced Diesel Engineering Limited
Agenda Management Services Limited
Ali-A Entertainment Ltd
Allied Glass Holdings Limited
Ambitemp (M & E) Limited
Amvale Medical Transport Limited
Anabas (UK 2) Limited
CV Anderson Ltd
Anglo Indian Exports Limited
Anlaby Office Cleaning Services Limited
Arco Limited
Ardagh Holdings (UK) Limited
Arla Foods Cheese Co Ltd
Asda Foundation
Audasi Holdings Limited
Augean South Limited
Augean Treatment Limited
Aviva Life Services UK Limited
Aviva Wrap UK Limited
B - Sporting Limited
Alfred Bagnall & Sons (Administration) Ltd
NG Bailey Facilities Services Limited
Bates & Co. (Huddersfield) Limited
Batteryback PLC
Be Fuelcards Ltd
Belaris Ltd.
Belem Investments Limited
Bemis Packaging UK Ltd
Birkett Bogmats Limited
Bluestone Leasing Limited
Bond Street Real Estate Holdings Limited
Bootham Crescent Holdings Limited
Bossdean Properties Limited
Broker Network Limited
Brook Group (Holdings) Limited
Brother Bidco Limited
Brother Topco Limited
C L Medicall Aid Limited
Camborne Holdings Limited
Camira Group Ltd
Care & Recreation Holdings Limited
Centrica Offshore UK Limited
Centrica Storage Limited
Century Health (Nottingham) Limited
Cephalon Limited
Chamber Acorn Fund (Humber) Ltd
Circuit Launderette Services Ltd.
Clarks Vehicle Conversions Limited
Cobalt Project Investments (Hull) Ltd
Cobalt Project Investments (Issuer) Ltd
Cobalt Project Investments (Taycare) Ltd
Cobalt Project Investments Limited
Colne Investments 2 Holdco Limited
Colne Topco Limited
Commercial Legal Limited
Community Foundation for Leeds
Conquest Bidco Limited
Contis Card Solutions Limited
Contis Financial Services Limited
Contis Group Limited
Coral Project Investments (Assetco) Ltd
Coral Project Investments (Issuer) Ltd
Core Telecom Limited
Creditscale Limited
Crimson Project Investments (Issuer) Ltd
Crimson Project Investments Limited
DB Cargo Components Limited
DB Cargo Maintenance Limited
DC3 (Assetco) Limited
DC3 (Issuer) Limited
DGP Intelsius Limited
DRC Contract Services Ltd
Dalmore Capital (Carlisle 1) Limited
Dalmore Capital (Corsham 1) Limited
Dalmore Capital (Issuer 1) Limited
Dalmore Capital (Issuer 2) Limited
Dalmore Capital (Para 1) Limited
Dalmore Capital (Para 2) Limited
Dalmore Capital (Rochdale 2) Limited
Dalmore Capital (Rochdale) Limited
Dalmore Group Limited
Dalmore Intermediate Limited
Decision First Limited
Deepocean 1 UK Limited
Delta Salvage Limited
Doorway Holdings Limited
Doran Scott Williams & Co Ltd
Dryband One Limited
E-Factor Group Ltd
ECG Holdings (UK) Limited
East Yorkshire Concrete Products Limited
Easypay Services Limited
Ebac Group Limited
Element UK Bidco Limited
Emacrow Limited
Emovis Operations Leeds Ltd
Eneco UK Limited
Energy Services (Business Power) Ltd
Ever 2010 Limited
Extron Electronics UK Limited
FMG Finance Limited
FMG Group Holdings Limited
FMG Support Group Limited
Faculty of Queen Ethelburga's Limited
Fender Care Limited
Fender Care Marine Ltd
Festino (Finance) Limited
First 4 Lawyers Limited
Frontica Business Solutions Limited
Gem Environmental Building Services Ltd
Global Autocare Limited
Group Auto Union UK and Ireland Limited
HEM Holdings Limited
Hague Computer Supplies Limited
Halifax Investment Services Limited
Halifax Loans Limited
Hanson Family Holdings Limited
S. Harrison Developments Limited
Hartford Holdings Limited
Havwoods Australia Limited
Health Factor Limited
Health Management (Carlisle) Limited
Hemingways (Furnishers) Limited
Heselden Investments Limited
Hidrostal (GB) Limited
Andrew Hillas Properties Limited
Horbury Bridge (Holdings) Limited
IETG Holdings Limited
IETG Limited
IHS Lothian Corporate Holdings Limited
IP Assist Services Limited
IPF Development (2003) Limited
IPF Digital Group Limited
IPF Financial Services Limited
IPF International Limited
Iconx Ltd
Investments in Education Limited
Island Wharf (100) Limited
Island Wharf (300) Limited
Ithaca Energy Developments UK Limited
KCA Deutag (Land Rig) Limited
KCA Deutag Alpha II Limited
KCA Deutag Alpha Limited
KCA Deutag Drilling Group Limited
KCA Deutag Enterprises Limited
KCA Deutag UK Finance PLC
KCA European Holdings Limited
KCAD Holdings I Limited
KCAD Holdings II Limited
Kanika Limited
Kelda Group Limited
Kelda Water Services Limited
Keyland (Midpoint) Limited
Kings Solutions Group Limited
Koppers UK Holding Limited
LZN Limited

John Laithwaite Investments Limited
Libra Careco Investments 1 Limited
Libra Careco Investments 2 Limited
Libra Careco Limited
Lily Lolo Limited
Link Scheme Holdings Ltd
Loop Customer Management Limited
Low Grange Quarry Limited
Lowell Acquisitions Limited
Lowell Funding Limited
Lowell Group Limited
Luxury Fibres Limited
Luxury Yarns International Limited
MMM Medical Equipment UK Limited
Mailing & Marketing Solutions Ltd
Malton Foods Limited
Maramar (Holdings) Limited
Marshall Group Services Limited
Morses Club PLC
Moventas Gears UK Limited
Moventas Wind UK Limited
Mysing Investments 2 Limited
Mysing Investments 3 Limited
Mysing Investments 4 Limited
NHP Operations (York) Limited
NHP Securities No. 1 Limited
NHP Securities No. 2 Limited
NHP Securities No. 3 Limited
New Daffodil Limited
New Month Limited
Newlincs Development Limited
Newly Weds Foods Acquisition Limited
Nilerace Limited
Northallerton Auctions Limited
Northern Gas Networks Operations Limited
Nufarm Crop Products UK Limited
Optimisation Developments Limited
Optimisation Investments Limited
Outform EMEA Limited
Ray Owen Waste Disposal Limited
PPDI Assetco Limited
PPDI Finance Limited
PPG Performance Coatings UK Limited
Park Homes (UK) Limited
Park Lane Properties (Holdings) Limited
Pelsis Limited
Project Magnum (Bidco) Limited
Provfin Limited
Tony Rampton Trust
Redhall Networks Limited
Redruth Holdings 2 Limited
Redruth Holdings Limited
Right Fuelcard Co Ltd
Royds Community Association
SRCL Limited
Sangwin Holdings Limited
Scho62 Investments Limited
A.Schofield (Pontefract) Limited
Seabrook Crisps Holdings Limited
Seismic Image Processing Limited
Shepherd Development Co Ltd
Shepherd Group Built Environment Limited
Siccar Point Energy (Holdings) Limited
Siccar Point Energy Finance Limited
Siccar Point Energy Limited
Siccar Point Energy U.K. Limited
Specialist Coatings Limited
G M Stephenson Ltd
Stored Value Solutions UK Limited
Stork Beta Limited
Strong Developments Limited
Sulzer (UK) Holdings Limited
Sun Branding Solutions Ltd
T R M Marketing Limited
TWR Developments Limited
Tajj Limited
Taste Marketing Ltd
Tenet Business Solutions Limited
Tennants of Yorkshire Antique and Fine Art Auctioneers Ltd
Thistle Insurance Services Limited
R.E. Thornber Limited
Ticket Arena Limited
Tissue Regenix Group PLC
Titan Cement U.K. Limited
Titan Global Finance PLC
Total System Services Processing Europe Ltd
Tradepark Limited
Transit 2017 Limited
Trilogy (Leamington Spa) Limited
Trinity Fire and Security Systems Ltd
Trinity Ten Limited
Trycare Limited
Turner & Townsend Consulting Limited
Turner & Townsend Contract Services Ltd
Turner & Townsend Cost Management Ltd
Turner & Townsend Europe Limited
Turner & Townsend Group Limited
Turner & Townsend Holdings Limited
Turner & Townsend International Limited
Turner & Townsend Limited
Turner & Townsend Project Management Ltd
UKDN Waterflow (LG) Limited
UKOS Investments Limited
USI Mayfair Ltd.
Univar UK Limited
Urban Development Projects (2) Ltd
Urban Development Projects Ltd
Varnish Intermediate Holdco Limited
Vicarage Estate Co Ltd
Wakefield and District Health and Community Support Ltd
White House Livestock & Energy Limited
H. Wicks (Lindal) Limited
Wothersome Limited
Yates Media Ltd
Young's Seafood International Holdings Ltd

**84110 General public administration activities**

GH North Yorkshire Limited
The George A. Moore Foundation

**84120 Regulation of health care, education, cultural and other social services, not incl. social security**

Consortium Academy Trust
Highfield Awarding Body for Compliance Ltd

**84220 Defence activities**

James Fisher Marine Services Limited

**84250 Fire service activities**

Rosenbauer UK Limited

**85100 Pre-primary education** [19]

Aysgarth School Trust Limited
Beckfoot Trust
Bishop Wheeler Catholic Academy Trust
Bradford Academy Trust
Brigshaw Learning Partnership
Cambridge Park Academy Limited
College Holdings 2012 Ltd
Constellation Trust
Cundall Manor Limited
Delta Academies Trust
Giggleswick School
Harrogate Ladies' College Limited
Inspired Learning Multi Academy Trust
Northern Ambition Academies Trust
Pontefract Academies Trust
Rishworth School
Shine Childcare Limited
Thrunscoe Primary and Nursery Academy
Wakefield Grammar School Foundation

**85200 Primary education** [100]

Abbey Multi Academy Trust
Aysgarth School Trust Limited
Batley Academy Trust
Beckfoot Trust
Belmont-Birklands School Trust Limited
Bishop Wheeler Catholic Academy Trust
Bolton Brow Primary Academy
Bradford Academy Trust
Bradford Diocesan Academies Trust
Bright Beginnings Childcare Centre Leeds
Brighter Futures Academy Trust
Brigshaw Learning Partnership
Bronte Academy Trust
Cleeve Primary School
Cleves Cross Learning Trust
College Holdings 2012 Ltd
Consortium Academy Trust
Constellation Trust
Cundall Manor Limited
Delta Academies Trust
Dewsbury Learning Trust
Doncaster Deaf Trust
Dunsville Primary Academy Trust
Ebor Academy Trust
Education Village Academy Trust
Elevate Multi Academy Trust
Empowering Minds Academy Trust
Enhance Academy Trust
Exceed Academies Trust
Exceed Learning Partnership
Family of Learning Trust
Federation of Abbey Schools Academy Trust
Federation of Mowden Schools Academy Trust
Ganton School
Ghyllside School
Giggleswick School
Greetland Academy Trust
Harrogate Ladies' College Limited
Healing Multi Academy Trust
Hill House School Limited
Horizon Academy Trust
Hull Collaborative Academy Trust
Humber Education Trust
Huntington Primary Academy
Hymers College Trustee Limited
I-Trust Education
IQRA Academy Education Trust
Inspired Learning Multi Academy Trust

Inspiring Futures Academy Trust
Isle Education Trust
KM School Limited
Kirk Sandall Academy Trust
Learning Accord Multi Academy Trust
Lindley Church of England Infant School
Lindley Junior School
Lingfield Education Trust
MFG Academies Trust
Mast Academy Trust
Mayflower Specialist School Academy Trust
Neasden Primary School
North Carr Collaborative Academy Trust
Northern Ambition Academies Trust
Nurture Academies Trust
Old Clee Primary Academy
Old Earth School
Christopher Pickering Primary School
Pontefract Academies Trust
Priestley Academy Trust
Priory Primary School
Rainbow Schools Trust
Red Kite Learning Trust
Rishworth School
Rose Learning Trust
Sedbergh School
Sentamu Academy Learning Trust
Sewell Education (Hull) Limited
Shared Vision Learning Trust
South Bank Multi Academy Trust
Spring Cottage Academy
St Hybald's Academy Trust
St Mary's Academy Trust
St. Laurence Education Trust
Swanland Education Trust
Tall Oaks Academy Trust Ltd
Thrunscoe Primary and Nursery Academy
Tollbar Multi Academy Trust
Trinity Multi Academy Trust
Tudhoe Learning Trust
Venn Academy Trust
Wakefield Grammar School Foundation
Waterton Academy Trust
Windermere Educational Trust Limited
Withernsea Primary Academy Trust
Witherslack Group Limited
Woodlands Academy Scarborough
Yarborough Academy
Yorkshire Causeway Schools Trust
Yorkshire Collaborative Academy Trust
Yorkshire and Humberside Co-operative Academies Trust
Yorkshire and The Humber Co-operative Learning Trust

**85310 General secondary education** [127]

Abbey Multi Academy Trust
Academy @ Ridgewood Trust
Accord Multi Academy Trust
Advance Learning Partnership
Armthorpe Academy Trust
Ashwell Academy
Axholme Academy
Aysgarth School Trust Limited
Batley Academy Trust
Batley Multi Academy Trust
Bay Learning Trust
Beckfoot Trust
Belle Vue Girls' School
Beverley Grammar School
Bishop Konstant Catholic Academy Trust
Bishop Wheeler Catholic Academy Trust
Blessed Peter Snow Catholic Academy Trust
Bootham School
Boulevard Academy Trust
Bradford Academy Trust
Bradford College Education Trust
Bradford Girls' Grammar School Trust
Brighouse High School Academy Trust
Brigshaw Learning Partnership
Brooksbank School Sports College
Carmel Education Trust
Castle Hall Academy Trust
Castleford Academy Trust
Cathedral Church of England Academy Trust (Wakefield)
City of Bradford Y.M.C.A.
Cockburn Multi Academy Trust
Collaborative Learning Trust
College Holdings 2012 Ltd
Consortium Academy Trust
Constellation Trust
Craven Educational Trust
Crofton Academy
Cundall Manor Limited
Delta Academies Trust
Dewsbury Learning Trust
Dixons Academies Charitable Trust Ltd
Doncaster Deaf Trust
Education Alliance
Education Village Academy Trust
Elevate Multi Academy Trust
Elizabethan Academy Trust
Enhance Academy Trust
Evolution Schools Learning Trust
Feversham Education Trust
Furness Academies Trust
Gateways Educational Trust Limited
Giggleswick School
Gorse Academies Trust
Grammar School at Leeds
Hall Cross Academy Trust
Harrogate Ladies' College Limited
Hayfield School
Healing Multi Academy Trust
Hill House School Limited
Hope Learning Trust, York
Horsforth School
Hull Collaborative Academy Trust
Hummersknott Academy Trust
Hungerhill Academy Trust
Huntcliff Academy Trust
Hymers College Trustee Limited
Impact Education Multi Academy Trust
Isle Education Trust
KM School Limited
King James I Academy, Bishop Auckland Ltd
King James's School
Kirkbie Kendal School Academy Trust
Lancaster Girls' Grammar School
Lancaster Royal Grammar School
Leeds Jewish Free School
Leger Education Trust
Leodis Academies Trust
Lunesdale Learning Trust
MFG Academies Trust
Mast Academy Trust
Minsthorpe Academy Trust
Moorlands Learning Trust
Mount School (York)
North Halifax Grammar School Academy Trust
Northern Ambition Academies Trust
Northern Star Academies Trust
One in a Million Free School
Outwood Grange Academies Trust
Pathfinder Multi Academy Trust
Pontefract Academies Trust
Queen Katherine School Multi Academy Trust
Queen Margaret's School, York Limited
Rastrick High School Academy Trust
Red Kite Learning Trust
Rishworth School
Rodillian Multi Academy Trust
Romero Catholic Education Trust
Rossett School
Ryburn Valley High School
Salendine Nook Academy Trust
Scarborough College Limited
Sedbergh School
Sentamu Academy Learning Trust
Share Multi Academy Trust
Snaith School Academy Trust
South Bank Multi Academy Trust
South Craven Academy Trust
South Westmorland Multi Academy Trust
Southfield Grange Trust
St Aidan's Church of England Academy Ltd
St. Laurence Education Trust
Thornhill Community Academy Trust
Tollbar Multi Academy Trust
Transforming Lives for Good (TLG) Ltd
Trinity Multi Academy Trust
Venn Academy Trust
Wakefield City Academies Trust
Wakefield Grammar School Foundation
Windermere Educational Trust Limited
Winterton Community Academy
Witherslack Group Limited
Woodham Academy
Woodlands Academy Scarborough
XP School Trust Limited
York Archaeological Trust for Excavation and Research Ltd
Yorkshire Causeway Schools Trust
Yorkshire and The Humber Co-operative Learning Trust

**85320 Technical and vocational secondary education**

Ascentis
Doncaster Deaf Trust
Doncaster Rotherham and District Motor Trades Group Training Association Ltd
Hunslet Club
Northern Racing College
Outwood Grange Academies Trust
S.W. Durham Training Limited

**85410 Post-secondary non-tertiary education**

Consortium Academy Trust
Dewsbury Learning Trust
Moorlands Learning Trust
S.W. Durham Training Limited

**85421 First-degree level higher education**

Ascentis
Leeds College of Music
Leeds Trinity University
St. Laurence Education Trust
University of Chicago Booth School of Business
York St John University

**85422 Post-graduate level higher education**

BFWG Charitable Foundation
York St John University

**85510 Sports and recreation education**

Hungerhill Academy Trust
Kirklees Active Leisure
Sedbergh School

**85520 Cultural education**

Goodwin Development Trust
Leeds College of Music

**85590 Other education n.e.c.** [35]

Aspire-Igen Ltd
Barnard Castle School
Bradford Diocesan Academies Trust
Brathay Trust
Calvary Chapel York
Capernwray Missionary Fellowship of Torchbearers
Christian Trust
Delta Academies Trust
Dove House Hospice Limited
EMIH Limited
Education Village Academy Trust
Enquire Learning Trust
Ganton School
Humberside Engineering Training Association Ltd
Humberston Park Special School
Igen Trust
Inspire 2 Independence (I2i) Ltd
Interaction and Communication Academy Trust Ltd
Kirkdale Industrial Training Services Ltd
Leeds Church Institute (Incorporated)
Lighthouse School
Outwood Grange Academies Trust
Pennine Camphill Community Limited
Premier People Solutions Limited
Queen Ethelburga's College Limited
Running Deep Limited
S.W. Durham Training Limited
STC Research Foundation
Shine: Support and Help in Education
Skills for Care Ltd
St Peter's School, York
Stockbridge Technology Centre Limited
Sweet Squared Limited
Virtual College Limited
Wolds Learning Partnership

**85600 Educational support services** [12]

Advance HE
Aspire-Igen Group Ltd
Brigshaw Learning Partnership
Early Excellence Limited
Education Village Academy Trust
Enhance Academy Trust
Foresight North East Lincolnshire Ltd.
Hull University Union Limited
Pontefract Academies Trust
St Mary's Academy Trust
Stem Learning Limited
Woodlands Academy Scarborough

**86101 Hospital activities** [14]

Cadman Housing Project Ltd
Darlington & District Hospice Movement
Diagmed Healthcare Limited
GBUK Enteral Limited
GBUK Ltd
Harrogate District Hospice Care
Health Management (Carlisle) Holdings Ltd
Health Management (Carlisle) Limited
Locala Community Partnerships C.I.C.
Martin House
Medical Imaging UK Limited
Retreat York
St. Gemma's Hospice
Thames Ambulance Service Limited

**86102 Medical nursing home activities**

Burlington Care Limited
Donisthorpe Hall
GH Braintree Limited
GH Lanchester Road Limited
GH Runwell Limited
GH Stanley Limited
Middleton Hall Limited
Roche Healthcare Limited

**86210 General medical practice activities**

Hull & East Yorkshire Medical Research Centre
Locala Community Partnerships C.I.C.
Therapy in Praxis Limited

**86220 Specialists medical practice activities**

Britto Psychiatry Limited
Dove House Hospice Limited
Great North Air Ambulance Service
Living Care Group Limited
Medical Imaging UK Limited
NYOS (York) Limited
Saint Catherines Hospice Trust
Spectrum Community Health C.I.C.

**86230 Dental practice activities**

ADP Primary Care Services Limited
DB Orthodontics Limited
Haricovert Limited
Locala Community Partnerships C.I.C.
Ortho-Care (U.K.) Limited

**86900 Other human health activities** [49]

Bradford Trident Limited
Candlelighters Trust
Caring 4 Croydon Limited
City Health Care Partnership CIC
Community Links (Northern) Ltd
Darlington & District Hospice Movement
Depuy International Limited
Drive Devilbiss Healthcare Limited
Family Fund Trust for Families with Severely Disabled Children
Foresight North East Lincolnshire Ltd.
Forget Me Not Children's Hospice Limited
Gettheworldmoving Ltd
Grandlane Limited
Hair Burst Limited
Harrogate District Hospice Care
Healthsource (Bromley) Limited
Heart Research UK
Help for Health
Hospice of St. Mary of Furness
Kirkwood Hospice
Leeds Cares
Lindsey Lodge Limited
Living Care Health Limited
Living Care Pharmacy Group Limited
Locala Community Partnerships C.I.C.
Martin House
Medical Imaging UK Limited
Middleton Hall Limited
The George A. Moore Foundation
Navigo Health and Social Care CIC
Northern Life Care Limited
Overgate Hospice
Thomas Owen Care Limited
Q Medical Technologies Ltd
Southfield Health Care Limited
Specialised Orthotic Services Limited
St Andrew's Hospice Limited
St. Leonard's Hospice York
Hugh Steeper Limited
Vida Grange Limited
Vida Hall Limited
Wakefield Hospice
Wakefield and District Health and Community Support Ltd
Westward Care Limited
Woodland Healthcare Limited
York Against Cancer
Yorkshire Air Ambulance Limited
Yorkshire Cancer Research
Young Herts Limited

**87100 Residential nursing care facilities** [25]

Acer Healthcare Operations Limited
Burlington Care Holdings Limited
Chalemere Limited
Countrywide Care Homes (3) Limited
Croft Carehomes Limited
Czajka Properties Limited
HC-ONE Beamish Limited
HC-ONE Limited
P & B Kennedy Holdings Limited
MBI Hawthorn Care Limited
MBI Walsden Care Limited
Middleton Hall Limited
Mysing Care Limited
Park Lane Healthcare (Croston Park) Ltd
Plum Bidco Limited
Private Medicare Limited
Prospect House (Malpas) Limited
Risedale Estates Limited
Sabrina Health Care Limited
Springfield Healthcare (Grove House) Ltd
St Anne's Community Services
Trust Care Ltd
Victorguard Care PLC
Warmest Welcome Limited
Yorkare Homes Limited

**87200 Residential care activities for learning difficulties, mental health and substance abuse** [12]

L'Arche
Avocet Trust
Bridgewood Trust Limited
Catholic Care (Diocese of Leeds)
Croft Care Trust
Czajka Properties Limited

Gravers Care Home Ltd
Leeds Jewish Welfare Board
Risedale Estates Limited
Riverside Healthcare Limited
St Anne's Community Services
Wilf Ward Family Trust

**87300 Residential care activities for the elderly and disabled** [33]

Abbeyfield Ilkley Society Limited
Acer Healthcare Operations Limited
Akari Care Limited
Countrywide Belmont Limited
Countrywide Care Homes (2) Limited
Countrywide Care Homes (3) Limited
Countrywide Care Homes Limited
Czajka Properties Limited
Ghyll Royd Nursing Home Limited
Greendown Trust
HC-ONE Beamish Limited
HC-ONE Limited
High Croft Care Limited
Ideal Carehomes (Number One) Limited
Ideal Carehomes Limited
Kapil Care Homes Limited
Maria Mallaband (6) Limited
Maria Mallaband 16 Limited
Maria Mallaband 7 Limited
Maria Mallaband Limited
Meridian Healthcare Limited
Monread Lodge Nursing Home Limited
Park Lane Healthcare (Magnolia House) Ltd
Project Light Topco Limited
Real Life Options
Risedale Estates Limited
Roseville Care Homes Limited
SHG (Care Villages) Limited
Springfield Care Services Limited
Springfield Healthcare (The Grange) Ltd
Strong Life Care Limited
Victorguard Care PLC
York Heritage (The Hall Thornton Le Dale) Ltd

**87900 Other residential care activities n.e.c.** [18]

Camphill Village Trust Limited
Czajka Properties Limited
Darlington & District Hospice Movement
Doncaster Children's Services Trust Ltd
Dukeries Healthcare Limited
Hesley Care & Education Limited
Hesley Group Limited
Hesley Holdings Limited
Humankind Charity
Lincolnshire House Association
Partners in Care Limited
Pebbles Care Limited
Pennine Camphill Community Limited
Radical Services Limited
Roche Healthcare Limited
WNF Group Limited
Wilf Ward Family Trust
Witherslack Group Limited

**88100 Social work activities without accommodation for the elderly and disabled**

Catholic Care (Diocese of Leeds)
Goodwin Development Trust
Leeds Jewish Welfare Board
Real Life Options
St George's Crypt

**88910 Child day-care activities**

Goodwin Development Trust
Leeds Jewish Welfare Board
Wakefield and District Health and Community Support Ltd

**88990 Other social work activities without accommodation n.e.c.** [21]

Abbeyfield Ilkley Society Limited
L'Arche
Candlelighters Trust
Christian Trust
City of Bradford Y.M.C.A.
City of Leeds YMCA
Community Foundation for Calderdale
Congregational Memorial Hall Trust (1978) Ltd
Darlington & District Hospice Movement
Doncaster Children's Services Trust Ltd
Dove House Hospice Limited
Foundation
Grimsby & Cleethorpes Area Doorstep
Hindu Cultural Society of Bradford
Hospitaller Order of Saint John of God
Humankind Charity
Leeds Jewish Welfare Board
St Anne's Community Services
West Riding Masonic Charities Limited
Wilberforce Trust
Wilf Ward Family Trust

**90010 Performing arts**

Absolutely Cultured Limited
Eleven Arches
Hull Truck Theatre Co Ltd
Leeds Theatre Trust Limited
Northern Ballet Limited
Opera North Limited
Peel Entertainment Group Limited

**90020 Support activities to performing arts**

Absolutely Cultured Limited
Lunchbox Theatrical Productions Limited

**90030 Artistic creation**

Absolutely Cultured Limited
Elmwood Design Limited
Global George Limited
Kirklees Theatre Trust
Leeds Grand Theatre and Opera House Ltd
Leeds Theatre Trust Limited
Opera North Productions Limited

**90040 Operation of arts facilities** [11]

Creative Art House
Hull Culture and Leisure Limited
Hull Truck Enterprises Limited
Kendal Brewery Arts Centre Trust Limited
Kirklees Theatre Trust
Leeds Grand Theatre and Opera House Ltd
Leeds Theatre Trust Limited
Square Chapel Trust
York Civic Trust
Yorkshire Sculpture Park
Zurbaran Trust

**91011 Library activities**

Freshwater Biological Association
Hull Culture and Leisure Limited
Leeds Library
Wordsworth Trust

**91012 Archives activities**

Wordsworth Trust

**91020 Museums activities** [10]

Bowes Museum
Eureka! The National Children's Museum.
Hull Culture and Leisure Limited
Keighley and Worth Valley Light Railway Ltd
Lakeland Arts
Lakeland Motor Museum Limited
North York Moors Historical Railway Trust Ltd
Wordsworth Trust
York Civic Trust
York Museums and Gallery Trust

**91030 Operation of historical sites and buildings and similar visitor attractions**

Auckland Project
Burton Constable Foundation
Continuum Group Limited
Harewood House Trust Limited
Hever Castle Limited
Keighley and Worth Valley Railway Preservation Society Ltd
National Coal Mining Museum for England Trust Ltd
Wordsworth Trust
York Archaeological Trust for Excavation and Research Ltd

**91040 Botanical and zoological gardens and nature reserves activities**

Cumbria Wildlife Trust Limited
EMIH Limited
Harewood House Trust Limited
Running Deep Limited
The John Strutt Conservation Foundation
Wild Life Group Limited
Yorkshire Wildlife Trust

**92000 Gambling and betting activities**

Hestview Limited
Scientific Games International Holdings Ltd
Nikolas Shaw Limited
Smiles for Miles Limited
Storey Group Limited

**93110 Operation of sports facilities** [17]

Bradford Trident Limited
DC Projects (Rotherham) Limited
Etrickbank Limited
Hever Castle Golf Club Limited
Hull City Tigers Limited
Hull Culture and Leisure Limited
KSDL Land Limited
Kirklees Active Leisure
Kirklees Stadium Development Limited
Leeds Cricket Football and Athletic Co Ltd
Leeds United Football Club Limited
Pontefract Park Race Co Ltd
Ripon Race Co Ltd
Rudding Park Limited
Scunthorpe United Football Club Limited
Thirsk Racecourse Limited
Wetherby Steeplechase Committee,Limited

**93120 Activities of sport clubs** [11]

Carus Green Limited
Castleford Rugby League Football Club Ltd
DC Projects (Wolverhampton) Limited
Hamsard Five Thousand and Eighteen Ltd
Huddersfield Town Association Football Club Ltd
Hull City Tigers Limited
Hull Super League Limited
Leeds City Football Club Limited
Normanton Golf Club Limited
RF Racing Limited
Scarborough Rugby Union Football Club Ltd

**93130 Fitness facilities** [13]

Bannatyne Fitness (2) Limited
Bannatyne Fitness Limited
Competition Line (U.K.) Limited
Doncaster Culture and Leisure Trust
Gym Bidco Limited
Gym Midco 2 Limited
Gym Midco Limited
Gym Topco Limited
Kirklees Active Leisure
Ovalhouse Limited
Pure Gym Limited
Wright Leisure Limited
X-Force UK Ltd

**93199 Other sports activities** [13]

BC Bantams Limited
Bradford City Football Club Limited
Darlington Arena Limited
Kirklees Active Leisure
Leeds Rugby Limited
National Coaching Foundation
Rugby Football League Limited
Sandburn York Limited
Snainton Golf Centre Limited
Super League (Europe) Limited
Tydd St Giles Lodge Developments Limited
United Autosports Limited
York City Football Club Limited

**93210 Activities of amusement parks and theme parks**

Flamingo Land Resort Limited
Northamptonshire Leisure Estates Limited
Wild Life Group Limited

**93290 Other amusement and recreation activities n.e.c.** [14]

Bendrigg Trust
Billing Aquadrome Limited
DC Projects (Amber Valley) Limited
Dransfield Novelty Co Ltd
Johnny's Entertainments (Tyneside) Ltd
Leeds Grand Theatre and Opera House Ltd
Naburn Leisure Limited
Pure Leisure Estates Limited
Sundown Pets Garden Limited
Tuby Leisure Ltd
Tydd St Giles Lodge Developments Limited
William's Den Limited
Wyreside Leisure Limited
York Forty-Four Limited

**94110 Activities of business and employers membership organisations**

Eldercliff Limited
Groundwork North East
Hull & Humber Chamber of Commerce Industry & Shipping
Nisa Retail Limited
West and North Yorkshire Chamber of Commerce and Industry
Whymar Limited

**94120 Activities of professional membership organisations**

Stroma Certification Limited

**94910 Activities of religious organisations** [14]

Bridge Street Pentecostal Church
Chapter of The Order of The Holy Paraclete (The) Unlimited
Christian Trust
City of Bradford Y.M.C.A.
Community of The Resurrection
Evangelical Fellowship of Congregational Churches Trust Corporation Ltd
Hindu Cultural Society of Bradford
Hull Community Church
Leeds Diocesan Board of Finance
New Kadampa Tradition - International Kadampa Buddhist Union
United Reformed Church (Yorkshire Province) Trust Ltd
York Area Quaker Meeting of The Religious Society of Friends (Quakers) in Britain
York Diocesan Board of Finance Limited
Yorkshire Baptist Association (Incorporated)

**94920 Activities of political organisations**

The Joseph Rowntree Reform Trust Ltd

**94990 Activities of other membership organisations n.e.c.** [12]

L'Arche
EMIH Limited
Freshwater Biological Association
Friends of The Lake District
Hebden Bridge Community Association Ltd
Leeds University Union
Pure Leisure Group Limited
Scarborough Rugby Union Football Club Ltd
Westmorland County Agricultural Society Ltd
York Civic Trust
Yorkshire Agricultural Society
Yorkshire Wildlife Trust

**95110 Repair of computers and peripheral equipment**

Express Group Limited

**95120 Repair of communication equipment**

Ninehundred Communications Group Limited

**95220 Repair of household appliances and home and garden equipment**

Falcon Electrical Wholesalers Limited

**96010 Washing and (dry-)cleaning of textile and fur products**

Abbey Glen Limited

**96030 Funeral and related activities**

Beverley Funerals Limited
J. Pidgeon & Son Limited

**96040 Physical well-being activities**

Property Renaissance Limited

**96090 Other service activities n.e.c.** [87]

Arizonaco Limited
Asda Southbank Limited
Autohorn Fleet Services Limited
NG Bailey Facilities Services Limited
Bonus Securities Limited
Brent Scaffold Boards Limited
C B T Clinics Limited
Calvadon Limited
Calvary Chapel York
Capernwray Missionary Fellowship of Torchbearers
Centre at Three Ways
Chaucer Foods Limited
Cox Automotive Retail Solutions Limited
Cox Automotive UK Limited
Cragwood International Limited
DAM Investments and Properties Limited
Dalestead Limited
Denaro (UK) Limited
Diamond Resorts (Europe) Limited
Dishforth UK Limited
Dreamphoto Limited
Dreamplayer Limited
Dressadmire Limited
Everard Group Limited
Fast Freeze International Limited
Fire Protection Holdings Limited
James Fisher MFE Limited
Fradley Properties Ltd
Fredrickson International Limited
Freedom Group of Companies Ltd.
Friends Provident Charitable Foundation
G3 Remarketing Limited
Jerry Green Dog Rescue
Grosvenor Facilities Management Limited
Harrison Thompson and Co Ltd
Hartley Investment Trust Limited
Hartley Property Trust Limited
Healthcare House Limited
Hector, Lamont, Florence Associates Ltd
Hestview Limited
Hexon Limited
Holetch Holdings Limited
Icando UK Limited
Impact (UK) Limited
Impact Development Training International Ltd
Impact Development Training Ltd.
Innserve Limited
Innserve Technical Solutions Limited
Ipsosolo Limited
J D Engineering (Northern) Limited
L.W. Safety Limited
Leasedrive Limited
London Security PLC.
Manheim Limited
Miles Partnership Limited
Money4yourmotors.Com Limited

Moorview Care Limited
Murphy (Yorkshire) Ltd
NCA Group Limited
Neal Investments Limited
Newlands Community Association
Normanby Estate Co Ltd
Northern Marquees Limited
Northgate (CB 2) Limited
Nu-Swift International Limited
Pear Tree Projects Limited
Peppers Marquees Limited
Persimmon Finance (No.2) Limited
Persimmon Finance Limited
Persimmon Harts Limited
Pilgrim Food Holdings Limited
Profile Security Services Limited
QX Limited
Rayner Marketing (Holdings) Limited
Rhino Enterprises Limited
Royd House Investments Limited
Rufforth Park Limited
SSL Healthcare Ltd
William G. Search Limited
Serius Group Limited
Seven Technologies Group Limited
Switch2 Energy Limited
Tajj Limited
Vinewood Limited
Wastecare Limited
Wilkes Vending Services Limited
Xander 97 Limited

**98000 Residents property management** [10]

Abbeyfield Ilkley Society Limited
Bhullar Bros.Limited
Blackwood Hall Ltd
Castle Crown Properties Limited
J Cooper Properties Limited
D & J Estate Limited
Harris Properties (Manchester) Limited
Oakvine Limited
Queensway Properties Limited
Setbray Properties (1997) Limited

**99999 Dormant company** [42]

AW Flow Holdings Limited
Anhul Management Limited
Aviva Erfa 15 UK Limited
Axis Topco Limited
Blowers Jewellers Holdings Limited
CCL Syrinx (UK Holding) Limited
Communisis BBF Ltd
Communisis Chorleys Ltd
Communisis One Ltd
Corkel Holdings Limited
Cromwell Investment Management Services Ltd
Cubic Holdings Limited
EHIF (Denmark) Limited
Finespark (Horsham) Limited
Global Shipping Services Group Limited
Gott Agri Synergy Limited
Hamsard 3465 Limited
Hamsard 3466 Limited
Hensall Group Limited
Holf Technologies Limited
Holt Family (Holdings) Limited
Hull Citycare (Investments) Limited
JLA Clean Limited
JM Developments (Guiseley) Limited
KCOM International Limited
Kysor Europe Limited
Lindhurst 2013 Limited
Modern Market Retailing Limited
Munchkin UK Trading Co Ltd
Myers Group Holdings Ltd
Nat Flex Group Limited
Persimmon Shared Equity Limited
Planet Overseas Holdings Limited
Profile Security Group Ltd
Rural Concepts (Libya) Limited
SSG Insight Limited
Sewell Education (York) Holdings Limited
Sewell Ventures Limited
Sheppee Holdings Ltd
Charles F Stead (Holdings) Limited
Woodgreen Construction Holdings Limited
Yorkshare Limited

*This page is intentionally left blank*

Printed in 8pt Nimbus Sans L

Designed by URW++ Design and Development GmbH

Dellam Publishing Limited

2 Heath Drive, Sutton, Surrey, SM2 5RP

Fax: 020 8770 7478 email: enquiries@dellam.com

SAN: 0177881 EAN/GLN: 5030670177882

www.ingramcontent.com/pod-product-compliance
Lightning Source LLC
La Vergne TN
LVHW082004200926
848481LV00010B/2800